Chicago Daily News National Almanac For

GEO. H. MORRILL CO.

MANUFACTURERS

PRINTING

AND

LITHOGRAPHIC

INKS

OFFICES

BOSTON	NEW YORK
CHICAGO	SAN FRANCISCO
LONDON	LOS ANGELES

[THIRTIETH YEAR]

THE CHICAGO DAILY NEWS

ALMANAC

AND YEAR-BOOK

FOR

1914

COMPILED BY JAMES LANGLAND, M. A.

ISSUED BY

THE CHICAGO DAILY NEWS COMPANY

PREFACE.

Nothing will give a better idea of the general scope of this volume than an examination of the index which begins on the next page. From this it will be seen that the subjects comprised are varied and numerous and that all the information given is intended primarily for reference purposes. The book, in other words, is a compact encyclopedia which endeavors to answer the questions that are most commonly asked by seekers after present-day knowledge not readily obtained elsewhere.

To summarize adequately the contents of a publication of this kind is impracticable and in view of the comprehensive index furnished unnecessary. Mention may be made, however, of a few of the important historical events of 1913 with which it deals. These include:

The practical completion of the Panama canal, one of the great engineering feats of modern times.

Final ratification and proclamation of the sixteenth and seventeenth amendments to the federal constitution, one giving congress power to pass an income tax law and the other providing for the direct election of United States senators.

Inauguration of President Woodrow Wilson and beginning of first democratic national administration since 1897.

Passage by the 63d congress in extra session of a tariff act largely reducing customs duties, placing many articles on the free list and providing for the imposition of a federal income tax; also, passage by the house at the same session of a bill for the establishment of federal reserve banks and an elastic currency. The text of the income tax law is given in full.

Revolutions and disorder in Mexico, resulting in a serious conflict with the United States.

Impeachment of William Sulzer, governor of New York.

Floods in Ohio and Indiana and tornadoes in the west and south, causing heavy loss of life and property.

End of war against Turkey by Balkan states and armed conflict between the allies themselves, resulting in establishment of new frontiers.

INDEX—1914.

NOTE—Table of contents of previous issues of The Daily News Almanac and Year-Book will be found on page 648.

INDEX TO ADVERTISEMENTS.

ALMANAC AND YEAR-BOOK

FOR 1914

Astronomical calculations prepared by Berlin H. Wright, Lake Helen,
Fla., and expressed in mean local time unless otherwise indicated.

BEGINNING AND LENGTH OF SEASONS.

Sun enters Sign.	Con-stel-lation.	Long.	Date.	Eastern time.	Central time.			D. H. M.
♉	270°	♐	Dec. 22..	5:35 a. m.	4:35 a. m. 1913	Winter begins and lasts....	89 0 36	south of equator
♈	0°	✕	Mar. 21..	6:11 a. m.	5:11 a. m. 1914	Spring begins and lasts.....	92 19 44	north of equator
♋	90°	✕	June 22..	1:55 a. m.	0:55 a. m. 1914	Summer begins and lasts..	93 14 39	north of equator
♎	180°	♍	Sept. 23..	4:34 p. m.	3:34 p. m. 1914	Autumn begins and lasts...	89 18 49	south of equator
♉	270°	♐	Dec. 22..	11:23 a. m.	10:23 a. m. 1914	Winter begins. Tropical yr..	565 5 48	

ERAS OF TIME.

The Gregorian year 1914 corresponds to the following eras:
The latter part of the 138th and the beginning of
the 139th year of the Independence of the United
States.
The year 1332-33 of the Mohammedan era; the year
1333 beginning Nov. 19.
The year 4611 (nearly) of the Chinese era, beginning now, Jan. 1.

The year 8023 of the Greek church, beginning Jan. 14.
The year 5674-75 of the Jewish era; year 5675 be-
gins Sept. 21, or at sunset Sept. 20.
The year 7422-23 of the Byzantine era, beginning
Sept. 1.
The year 2574 of the Japanese era.
The first day of January is the 2,420,134th day
since the commencement of the Julian period.

CHRONOLOGICAL CYCLES.

Dionysian period................ 243	Jewish Lunar cycle............ 12	Julian period.......,..........6627
Solar cycle...................... 19	Epact (moon's age Jan. 1)..... 3	Dominical letter................ D
Roman Indiction................ 12	Lunar cycle (golden number).. 15	

EXPLANATORY NOTE—The Dominical letter or
letters (two for leap year), or Sunday letters,
indicate the day of the year on which the first
Sunday occurs, the first seven letters of the alphabet being used. Thus, for 1914, the Dominical
letter is D, the fourth letter of the alphabet, and
hence the fourth day of the year will be the first
Sunday of the year. In leap years two letters are
used, the first being for January and February,
and the latter, being the preceding letter, answers for the last ten months, in order to maintain the cycle. The rule for obtaining the Dominical letter for any year is somewhat complicated and for that reason is omitted here. The
Golden Number is that number of a cycle of nineteen years which shows how many years have
elapsed since the new moon fell on Jan. 1, for in
nearly nineteen years the solar and lunar years
nearly come together. The chief use of this cycle
is in fixing the date of Easter, and in this same
connection is used the Epact. The Solar Cycle
is the number of years that have elapsed since
the days of the week fell on the same days of
the year, or when there will, therefore, be a recur-
rence of the Dominical or Sunday Letter. This
would be the case every seven years but for leap
year, hence four times seven is the cycle, or
twenty-eight years. It is the remainder found by
adding nine to the year and dividing the sum by
twenty-eight. The Roman Indiction is a cycle of
fifteen years and is of no utility except to chronologers. It is the remainder found by adding
three to the year and dividing by fifteen. The
Julian Period is a cycle of 7,980 years and is the
product of the three cycles, Golden Number (19),
Solar Cycle (28) and Roman Indiction (15), and
hence shows the time when these cycles will coincide, or begin at the same time. The first of
this cycle will be completed in the year 2267; it
is the year + 4713. The Dionysian Period is a
cycle of 532 years and is called the great Paschal
cycle, being the product of a completed solar and
lunar cycle (28×19). It is the remainder found
by adding 457 to the year and dividing by 532,
and with the Julian Period is chiefly used by
chronologers. The Jewish Lunar Cycle is always
three less than the Golden Number and is used
by the Jews in fixing the time of their festivals.

JEWISH OR HEBREW CALENDAR YEAR 5674-75 A. M.

The year 5674 is the 12th and 5675 the 13th of the 299th cycle of 19 years.

Year.	Number.	Name.	Day.	Feast, festival or fast.	Gregorian date.
5674	4	Tebet	10	Fast of Tebet	Thursday, January 8, 1914
5674	5	Sh'vat	1	Rosh-Chodesh	Wednesday, January 28, 1914
5674	6	Adar	1	Rosh-Chodesh	Thursday-Friday, February 26-27, 1914
5674	6	Adar	13	Fast of Esther	Wednesday, March 11, 1914
5674	6	Adar	14 and 15	Purim	Thursday-Friday, March 12-13, 1914
5674	7	Nissan	1	Rosh-Chodesh	Saturday, March 28, 1914
5674	7	Nissan	15	First day of Passover	Saturday, April 11, 1914
5674	8	Iyar	1	Rosh-Chodesh	Sunday-Monday, April 26-27, 1914
5674	8	Iyar	18	Lag B'Omer (33d day of Omer)	Thursday, May 14, 1914
5674	9	Sivan	1	Rosh-Chodesh	Tuesday, May 26, 1914
5674	9	Sivan	6	First day of Pentecost	Sunday, May 31, 1914
5674	10	Tammuz	1	Rosh-Chodesh	Wednesday-Thursday, June 24-25, 1914
5674	10	Tammuz	17	Fast of Tammuz	Saturday, July 11, 1914
5674	11	Av or Ab	1	Rosh-Chodesh	Friday, July 24, 1914
5674	11	Av or Ab	9	Fast of Av	Saturday*, August 1, 1914
5674	12	Elul	1	Rosh-Chodesh	Saturday-Sunday, August 22-23, 1914
5675	1	Tishri	1	1st day of New Year	Monday, September 21, 1914
5675	1	Tishri	3	Fast of Gedaliah	Wednesday, September 23, 1914
5675	1	Tishri	10	Yom Kippoor	Wednesday, September 30, 1914
5675	1	Tishri	15	First Day of Tabernacles	Monday, October 5, 1914
5675	1	Tishri	21	Hoshanna-Rabbah	Sunday, October 11, 1914
5675	1	Tishri	22	Sh'mini-Atseres	Monday, October 12, 1914
5675	1	Tishri	23	Simchas-Torah	Tuesday, October 13, 1914
5675	2	Chesvan	1	Rosh-Chodesh	Tuesday-Wednesday, October 20-21, 1914
5675	3	Kislev	1	Rosh-Chodesh	Thursday, November 19, 1914
5675	3	Kislev	25	First day of Chanukah	Sunday, December 13, 1914
5675	4	Tebet	1	Rosh-Chodesh	Friday, December 18, 1914
5675	4	Tebet	10	Fast of Tebet	Sunday, December 27, 1914
5675	5	Sh'vat	1	Rosh-Chodesh	Saturday, January 16, 1915

*Observed the day following.

GREEK CHURCH AND RUSSIAN CALENDAR—A. D. 1914. A. M. 8023.

New style.	Old style.	HOLY DAYS.	New style.	Old style.	HOLY DAYS.
Jan. 14	Jan. 1	Circumcision.	July 12	June 29	Peter and Paul, Chief Apostles.
Jan. 19	Jan. 6	Theophany (Epiphany).	Aug. 14	Aug. 1	First Day of Theotokos.
Feb. 15	Feb. 2	Hypopante (Purification)	Aug. 19	Aug. 6	Transfiguration.
Feb. 21	Feb. 8	Septuagesima.	Aug. 28	Aug. 15	Repose of Theotokos.
Feb. 28	Feb. 15	Carnival Sunday.	Sept. 12	Aug. 30	St. Alexander Nevsky.*
Mch. 14	Mch. 1	First Sunday in Lent.	Sept. 21	Sept. 8	Nativity of Theotokos.
Apl. 18	Apl. 5	Palm Sunday.	Sept. 27	Sept. 14	Exaltation of Cross.
Apl. 23	Apl. 10	Good Friday.	Oct. 1	Oct. 1	Patronage of Theotokos.
Apl. 25	Apl. 12	Easter (Holy Pasche).	Nov. 28	Nov. 15	First Day of Nativity.
May 6	Apl. 23	St. George.	Dec. 4	Nov. 21	Entrance of Theotokos.
May 22	May 9	St. Nicholas.	Dec. 21	Dec. 8	Conception of Theotokos.
May 27	May 14	Coronation of Emperor*.	1915.		
June 3	May 21	Ascension.	Jan. 7	Dec. 25	Nativity (Christmas).
June 13	May 31	Pentecost.			

*Peculiar to Russia.

MOHAMMEDAN CALENDAR YEAR 1332-33.

The year 1332 is the 12th and 1333 is the 13th of the 45th cycle of 30 years.

Year.	No.	Name.	Begins.	Lasts, days.	Year.	No.	Name.	Begins.	Lasts, days.
1332	3	Rabia I	January 28	30	1332	10	Schawall	August 23	29
1332	4	Rabia II	February 27	29	1332	11	Dulkaeda	September 21	30
1332	5	Jomhadi I	March 28	30	1333	12	Dulhegzla	October 21	29
1332	6	Jomhadi II	April 27	29	1333	1	Muharrem	November 19	30
1332	7	Rajeb	May 26	30	1333	2	Saphar	December 19	29
1332	8	Sheban	June 25	29	1333	3	Rabia I	January 17, 1915	30
1332	9	Ramadan (Fasting)	July 24	30					

AVERAGE DEPTH OF OCEANS AND SEAS.

	Feet.		Feet.		Feet.		Feet.
Antarctic	10,860	Pacific	12,960	China	492	Mexico, Gulf of	4,622
Arctic	5,160	Baltic	122	Japan	7,320	North	300
Atlantic	12,200	Bering	900	Mediterranean	4,560	Okhotsk	5,040
Indian	11,136	Caribbean	7,614				

The mean depth of all the oceans and seas is estimated to be from 2 to 2½ miles. The greatest depth reported is 31,614 feet, or nearly 6 miles, near the island of Guam in the Pacific. The greatest known depth in the Atlantic is 27,366 feet, off the coast of Porto Rico.

ORDER OF PRESIDENTIAL SUCCESSION.

In case of the removal, death, resignation or inability of both the president and vice-president, then the secretary of state shall act as president until the disability of the president or vice-president is removed or a president is elected. The rest of the order of succession is: Secretary of the treasury, secretary of war, attorney-general, postmaster-general, secretary of the navy, secretary of the interior, secretary of agriculture and secretary of commerce and labor. The acting president, in case congress is not in session, must call a special session, giving twenty days' notice.

☽ First Quar., 4th.　☾ Full Moon, 11th.　1st MONTH.　JANUARY, 1914.　31 DAYS.　☽ Last Quar., 18th.　☾ New Moon, 26th.

DAY OF YEAR	DAYS IN YEAR	DAY OF MONTH	DAY OF WEEK	MOON'S PLACE (Con.D)	SUN AT NOON MARK (H.M.S.)	MOON IN MERIDIAN (H.M.)	NY etc. Sun rises	NY etc. Sun sets	NY etc. Moon sets and rises	St. Louis Sun rises	St. Louis Sun sets	St. Louis Moon sets and rises	St. Paul Sun rises	St. Paul Sun sets	St. Paul Moon sets and rises
1	365	1	Thursday	≈ 13	12 3 33	4 13	7 28	4 39	10 4	7 16	4 51	10 6	7 39	4 29	10 2
2	364	2	Friday	≈ 25	12 4 2	4 53	7 28	4 40	11 4	7 16	4 52	11 4	7 39	4 30	11 4
3	363	3	Saturday	✕ 7	12 4 30	5 31	7 28	4 42	morn	7 16	4 53	morn	7 38	4 31	morn
4	362	4	SUNDAY	✕ 19	12 4 57	6 11	7 28	4 43	1	7 16	4 53	1	7 38	4 32	1
5	361	5	Monday	♈ 1	12 5 25	6 52	7 28	4 44	56	7 16	4 54	51	7 38	4 33	1
6	360	6	Tuesday	♈ 13	12 5 51	7 36	7 28	4 45	2 7	7 16	4 55	2 0	7 38	4 34	2 15
7	359	7	Wednesday	♈ 25	12 6 18	8 25	7 27	4 47	3 12	7 16	4 56	3 3	7 37	4 35	3 22
8	358	8	Thursday	♉ 8	12 6 43	9 17	7 27	4 47	4 14	7 16	4 57	4 2	7 37	4 36	4 26
9	357	9	Friday	♉ 21	12 7 9	10 14	7 27	4 48	5 25	7 16	4 58	5 11	7 37	4 37	5 39
10	356	10	Saturday	♊ 4	12 7 33	11 14	7 27	4 49	6 29	7 16	4 59	6 16	7 37	4 38	6 44
11	355	11	SUNDAY	♊ 18	12 7 57	morn	7 27	4 50	rises	7 16	5 1	rises	7 36	4 39	rises
12	354	12	Monday	♋ 2	12 8 21	14	7 27	4 51	5 24	7 15	5 2	5 36	7 36	4 40	5 13
13	353	13	Tuesday	♋ 16	12 8 44	1 11	7 27	4 52	6 45	7 15	5 3	6 50	7 36	4 41	6 34
14	352	14	Wednesday	♌ 1	12 9 6	2 6	7 27	4 52	7 58	7 15	5 4	8 0	7 36	4 42	7 55
15	351	15	Thursday	♌ 15	12 9 28	2 57	7 27	4 54	9 15	7 15	5 6	9 17	7 35	4 44	9 13
16	350	16	Friday	♍ 29	12 9 49	3 47	7 25	4 55	10 30	7 14	5 6	10 29	7 34	4 46	10 31
17	349	17	Saturday	♍ 14	12 10 9	4 35	7 25	4 56	11 42	7 14	5 7	11 39	7 34	4 47	11 47
18	348	18	SUNDAY	♍ 28	12 10 29	5 23	7 24	4 58	morn	7 13	5 8	morn	7 33	4 48	morn
19	347	19	Monday	♎ 12	12 10 48	6 13	7 23	4 59	59	7 13	5 9	53	7 32	4 49	1 6
20	346	20	Tuesday	♎ 26	12 11 7	7 2	7 22	5 0	2 14	7 12	5 10	2 4	7 31	4 50	2 24
21	345	21	Wednesday	♏ 9	12 11 23	7 49	7 21	5 2	3 31	7 12	5 12	3 19	7 30	4 52	3 43
22	344	22	Thursday	♏ 23	12 11 40	9 0	7 20	5 3	4 43	7 11	5 13	4 28	7 29	4 54	4 56
23	343	23	Friday	♐ 6	12 11 56	9 59	7 19	5 4	5 47	7 11	5 14	5 32	7 29	4 55	6 2
24	342	24	Saturday	♐ 19	12 12 11	10 57	7 20	5 4	6 39	7 10	5 15	6 25	7 28	4 56	6 54
25	341	25	SUNDAY	♑ 2	12 12 26	11 50	7 19	5 5	7 20	7 10	5 16	7 8	7 27	4 57	7 33
26	340	26	Monday	♑ 15	12 12 39	ev. 40	7 19	5 6	sets	7 9	5 17	sets	7 26	4 58	sets
27	339	27	Tuesday	♒ 27	12 12 52	1 26	7 18	5 7	6 46	7 8	5 18	6 52	7 25	4 59	6 39
28	338	28	Wednesday	♒ 12	12 13 4	2 9	7 17	5 8	7 49	7 8	5 18	7 52	7 24	5 1	7 46
29	337	29	Thursday	♓ 21	12 13 16	2 49	7 16	5 10	8 55	7 7	5 19	9 52	7 23	5 2	8 52
30	336	30	Friday	✕ 3	12 13 26	3 28	7 15	5 11	10 0	7 6	5 20	9 59	7 23	5 3	9 56
31	335	31	Saturday	✕ 15	12 13 35	4 7	7 15	5 12	10 53	7 6	5 21	10 49	7 22	5 5	10 57

☽ First Quar., 3d.　☾ Full Moon, 10th.　2d MONTH.　FEBRUARY, 1914.　28 DAYS.　☽ Last Quar., 17th.　☾ New Moon, 24th.

DAY OF YEAR	DAYS IN YEAR	DAY OF MONTH	DAY OF WEEK	MOON'S PLACE (Con.D)	SUN AT NOON MARK (H.M.S.)	MOON IN MERIDIAN (H.M.)	NY etc. Sun rises	NY etc. Sun sets	NY etc. Moon rises and sets	St. Louis Sun rises	St. Louis Sun sets	St. Louis Moon sets and rises	St. Paul Sun rises	St. Paul Sun sets	St. Paul Moon rises and sets
32	334	1	SUNDAY	✕ 27	12 13 44	4 47	7 14	5 13	11 55	7 5	5 22	11 49	7 21	5 7	morn
33	333	2	Monday	♈ 8	12 13 52	5 29	7 12	5 14	morn	7 4	5 23	morn	7 20	5 8	1
34	332	3	Tuesday	♈ 21	12 13 59	6 15	7 11	5 15	59	7 3	5 25	50	7 19	5 10	1 8
35	331	4	Wednesday	♉ 3	12 14 5	7 4	7 10	5 17	2 7	7 2	5 26	1 52	7 17	5 11	2 14
36	330	5	Thursday	♉ 16	12 14 10	7 56	7 9	5 18	3 9	7 1	5 27	2 55	7 16	5 12	3 22
37	329	6	Friday	♊ 29	12 14 14	8 56	7 8	5 20	4 11	7 0	5 28	3 57	7 15	5 13	4 26
38	328	7	Saturday	♊ 12	12 14 19	9 55	7 6	5 21	5 11	6 59	5 29	4 56	7 13	5 15	5 26
39	327	8	SUNDAY	♋ 26	12 14 24	10 54	7 5	5 23	6 0	6 58	5 30	5 46	7 12	5 16	6 11
40	326	9	Monday	♋ 10	12 14 24	11 51	7 4	5 24	6 41	6 57	5 31	6 30	7 10	5 18	6 52
41	325	10	Tuesday	♋ 25	12 14 25	morn	7 3	5 25	rises	6 56	5 33	rises	7 9	5 20	rises
42	324	11	Wednesday	♌ 10	12 14 25	46	7 2	5 26	6 53	6 55	5 34	6 58	7 7	5 21	6 50
43	323	12	Thursday	♌ 25	12 14 24	1 37	7 0	5 28	8 8	6 54	5 35	8 12	7 5	5 23	8 12
44	322	13	Friday	♍ 9	12 14 23	2 24	7 0	5 29	9 24	6 53	5 36	9 28	7 4	5 24	9 32
45	321	14	Saturday	♍ 24	12 14 22	3 18	6 59	5 30	10 46	6 51	5 38	10 40	7 2	5 25	10 51
46	320	15	SUNDAY	♎ 8	12 14 20	4 9	6 58	5 32	morn	6 50	5 39	11 58	7 1	5 27	morn
47	319	16	Monday	♎ 22	12 14 17	5 2	6 56	5 33	7	6 49	5 40	morn	7 1	5 27	
48	318	17	Tuesday	♏ 6	12 14 13	5 57	6 54	5 34	1 22	6 48	5 41	1 11	6 59	5 31	1 34
49	317	18	Wednesday	♏ 20	12 14 8	6 55	6 52	5 36	2 35	6 46	5 42	2 22	6 57	5 32	2 50
50	316	19	Thursday	♐ 3	12 14 3	7 53	6 50	5 38	3 41	6 45	5 44	3 26	6 55	5 34	3 56
51	315	20	Friday	♐ 16	12 13 57	8 51	6 49	5 39	4 39	6 44	5 44	4 22	6 54	5 35	4 52
52	314	21	Saturday	♐ 29	12 13 50	9 45	6 47	5 40	5 26	6 43	5 45	5 8	6 52	5 36	5 34
53	313	22	SUNDAY	♑ 11	12 13 43	10 35	6 46	5 41	5 54	6 41	5 47	5 43	6 50	5 38	5
54	312	23	Monday	♑ 23	12 13 35	11 22	6 45	5 43	6 20	6 40	5 48	6 12	6 48	5 39	6 29
55	311	24	Tuesday	♒ 5	12 13 27	ev. 5	6 44	5 44	sets	6 39	5 49	sets	6 47	5 40	sets
56	310	25	Wednesday	♒ 18	12 13 18	46	6 43	5 45	6 42	6 38	5 50	6 44	6 46	5 42	6 40
57	309	26	Thursday	♓ 29	12 13 8	1 25	6 41	5 46	7 41	6 36	5 51	7 41	6 44	5 43	7 42
58	308	27	Friday	✕ 11	12 12 58	2 4	6 39	5 47	8 42	6 35	5 51	8 39	6 43	5 45	8 45
59	307	28	Saturday	✕ 23	12 12 47	2 44	6 38	5 48	9 44	6 34	5 52	9 44	6 41	5 46	9 44

For far western points within any of the above zones of latitude add 2 min. for each hour of longitude to the moon's rising, setting and southing.　For far eastern points subtract 2 min. for each hour of longitude from the moon's rising, setting and southing.

☽ First Quar., 4th. / ⊕ Full Moon, 11th.   **3d MONTH.**   # MARCH, 1914.   **31 DAYS.**   **☾ Last Quar., 18th. / ⊗ New Moon, 26th.**

DAY OF YEAR	DAYS IN YEAR	DAY OF MONTH	DAY OF WEEK.	MOON'S PLACE	SUN AT NOON MARK.	MOON IN MERIDIAN.	New York, Chicago, Iowa, Neb., Pa., S. Wis., S. Mich., N. Ill., Ind., O. — Sun rises	Sun sets	Moon sets and rises	St. Louis, S. Ill., Va., Ky., Mo., Kas., Col., Cal., Ind., Ohio. — Sun rises	Sun sets	Moon sets and rises	St. Paul, N. H. Wis. and Mich., N. E. New York, Minn., Ore. — Sun rises	Sun sets	Moon sets and rises
				Con.D	H. M. S.	H. M.	H. M.	H. M.	H. M.	H. M.	H. M.	H. M.	H. M.	H. M.	H. M.
60	306	1	SUNDAY	♈ 5	12 12 36	3 25	6 36	5 50	10 46	6 32	5 54	10 38	6 39	5 48	10 54
61	305	2	Monday	♈ 17	12 12 24	4 9	6 35	5 51	11 50	6 31	5 55	11 40	6 38	5 49	morn
62	304	3	Tuesday	♈ 29	12 12 12	4 56	6 34	5 53	morn	6 30	5 56	morn	6 36	5 50	1
63	303	4	Wednesday	♉ 11	12 11 59	5 47	6 32	5 54	54	6 28	5 57	41	6 34	5 52	1 7
64	302	5	Thursday	♉ 24	12 11 46	6 42	6 30	5 56	1 58	6 26	5 58	1 44	6 32	5 53	2 13
65	301	6	Friday	♊ 7	12 11 32	7 39	6 28	5 57	2 50	6 24	5 59	2 41	6 30	5 55	3 11
66	300	7	Saturday	♊ 20	12 11 18	8 37	6 26	5 58	3 50	6 23	6 0	3 36	6 28	5 56	4 5
67	299	8	SUNDAY	♋ 4	12 11 3	9 34	6 24	5 59	4 35	6 21	6 1	4 22	6 27	5 57	4 45
68	298	9	Monday	♋ 18	12 10 48	10 29	6 22	6 0	5 11	6 19	6 2	5 1	6 25	5 58	5 21
69	297	10	Tuesday	♌ 3	12 10 33	11 22	6 20	6 1	5 41	6 18	6 3	5 35	6 23	6 0	5 48
70	296	11	Wednesday	♌ 18	12 10 17	morn	6 18	6 3	rises	6 17	6 4	rises	6 21	6 2	rises
71	295	12	Thursday	♍ 3	12 10 1	13	6 17	6 4	7 2	6 16	6 5	7 2	6 19	6 3	7 4
72	294	13	Friday	♍ 18	12 9 44	1 5	6 15	6 6	8 22	6 14	6 6	8 18	6 17	6 4	8 26
73	293	14	Saturday	♎ 3	12 9 28	1 57	6 13	6 7	9 43	6 13	6 7	9 35	6 15	6 5	9 50
74	292	15	SUNDAY	♎ 18	12 9 11	2 51	6 11	6 7	11 5	6 12	6 7	10 54	6 13	6 6	11 16
75	291	16	Monday	♏ 3	12 8 54	3 48	6 10	6 8	morn	6 10	6 8	morn	6 11	6 7	morn
76	290	17	Tuesday	♏ 16	12 8 36	4 47	6 9	6 9	24	6 8	6 9	11	6 9	6 8	38
77	289	18	Wednesday	♐ 30	12 8 19	5 47	6 7	6 10	1 33	6 6	6 10	1 19	6 7	6 9	1 48
78	288	19	Thursday	♐ 13	12 8 11	6 46	6 5	6 11	2 34	6 4	6 11	2 19	6 5	6 10	2 49
79	287	20	Friday	♑ 26	12 7 43	7 41	6 4	6 12	3 20	6 3	6 12	3 6	6 3	6 11	3 34
80	286	21	Saturday	♒ 8	12 7 25	8 33	6 2	6 13	3 57	6 2	6 13	3 45	6 1	6 13	4 0
81	285	22	SUNDAY	♒ 20	12 7 7	9 20	6 0	6 14	4 25	6 1	6 14	4 16	6 0	6 15	4 34
82	284	23	Monday	♓ 2	12 6 49	10 4	5 58	6 15	4 48	5 59	6 15	4 41	5 58	6 16	4 54
83	283	24	Tuesday	♓ 14	12 6 30	10 45	5 56	6 16	5 7	5 59	6 16	5 3	5 56	6 17	5 11
84	282	25	Wednesday	♈ 26	12 6 13	11 25	5 54	6 17	5 26	5 57	6 17	5 24	5 54	6 19	5 28
85	281	26	Thursday	♈ 8	12 5 54	ev. 5	5 53	6 19	sets	5 55	6 18	sets	5 52	6 20	sets
86	280	27	Friday	♉ 20	12 5 36	43	5 52	6 20	7 35	5 52	6 19	7 31	5 50	6 21	7 40
87	279	28	Saturday	♊ 2	12 5 18	1 23	5 51	6 21	8 37	5 50	6 20	8 30	5 48	6 22	8 44
88	278	29	SUNDAY	♊ 14	12 5 0	2 6	5 50	6 22	9 39	5 49	6 21	9 30	5 46	6 24	9 49
89	277	30	Monday	♋ 26	12 4 41	2 52	5 48	6 24	10 45	5 48	6 22	10 33	5 44	6 26	10 57
90	276	31	Tuesday	♋ 8	12 4 23	3 41	5 46	6 25	11 47	5 46	6 23	11 34	5 43	6 27	morn

☽ First Quar., 3d. / ⊕ Full Moon, 10th.   **4th MONTH.**   # APRIL, 1914.   **30 DAYS.**   **☾ Last Quar., 17th. / ⊗ New Moon, 25th.**

DAY OF YEAR	DAYS IN YEAR	DAY OF MONTH	DAY OF WEEK.	MOON'S PLACE	SUN AT NOON MARK.	MOON IN MERIDIAN.	New York, Chicago, Iowa, Neb., Pa., S. Wis., S. Mich., N. Ill., Ind., O. — Sun rises	Sun sets	Moon sets and rises	St. Louis, S. Ill., Va., Ky., Mo., Kas., Col., Cal., Ind., Ohio. — Sun rises	Sun sets	Moon sets and rises	St. Paul, N. E. Wis. and Mich., N. E. New York, Minn., Ore. — Sun rises	Sun sets	Moon sets and rises
				Con.D	H. M. S.	H. M.	H. M.	H. M.	H. M.	H. M.	H. M.	H. M.	H. M.	H. M.	H. M.
91	275	1	Wednesday	♋ 20	12 4 5	4 34	5 44	6 26	morn	5 45	6 24	morn	5 42	6 28	6
92	274	2	Thursday	♌ 3	12 3 47	5 29	5 43	6 27	49	5 43	6 25	34	5 40	6 29	1 4
93	273	3	Friday	♌ 16	12 3 29	6 25	5 41	6 28	1 42	5 42	6 26	1 28	5 38	6 30	1 57
94	272	4	Saturday	♍ 29	12 3 11	7 20	5 39	6 29	2 29	5 40	6 26	2 16	5 36	6 31	2 43
95	271	5	SUNDAY	♎ 13	12 2 53	8 14	5 37	6 30	3 0	5 39	6 27	2 55	5 34	6 32	3 18
96	270	6	Monday	♎ 27	12 2 36	9 7	5 35	6 31	3 38	5 37	6 28	3 30	5 32	6 34	3 46
97	269	7	Tuesday	♏ 11	12 2 19	9 58	5 33	6 32	4 6	5 36	6 29	4 0	5 30	6 35	4 11
98	268	8	Wednesday	♏ 26	12 2 1	10 48	5 31	6 33	4 30	5 34	6 30	4 28	5 28	6 36	4 32
99	267	9	Thursday	♐ 11	12 1 45	11 40	5 29	6 34	4 53	5 33	6 31	4 54	5 26	6 37	4 52
100	266	10	Friday	♐ 27	12 1 28	morn	5 27	6 35	rises	5 31	6 32	rises	5 24	6 39	rises
101	265	11	Saturday	♑ 12	12 1 11	34	5 26	6 36	8 36	5 29	6 33	8 27	5 23	6 40	8 45
102	264	12	SUNDAY	♑ 27	12 0 54	1 32	5 24	6 37	9 59	5 28	6 34	9 47	5 21	6 41	10 12
103	263	13	Monday	♒ 11	12 0 40	2 32	5 23	6 38	11 16	5 26	6 35	11 2	5 19	6 42	11 31
104	262	14	Tuesday	♒ 25	12 0 24	3 34	5 21	6 39	morn	5 24	6 36	morn	5 18	6 43	n.o'n
105	261	15	Wednesday	♓ 9	12 0 9	4 36	5 20	6 40	37	5 23	6 36	9	5 17	6 46	30
106	260	16	Thursday	♓ 22	11 59 54	5 34	5 19	6 42	1 16	5 22	6 37	1 2	5 15	6 46	1 31
107	259	17	Friday	♈ 5	11 59 40	6 28	5 17	6 43	1 59	5 21	6 38	1 47	5 13	6 47	2 12
108	258	18	Saturday	♈ 17	11 59 25	7 18	5 16	6 44	2 29	5 19	6 39	2 19	5 11	6 48	2 39
109	257	19	SUNDAY	♉ 30	11 59 12	8 3	5 14	6 45	2 53	5 18	6 40	2 46	5 9	6 49	3 1
110	256	20	Monday	♉ 12	11 58 50	8 45	5 12	6 46	3 14	5 17	6 41	3 10	5 7	6 51	3 19
111	255	21	Tuesday	♊ 24	11 58 46	9 25	5 10	6 47	3 33	5 16	6 42	3 30	5 6	6 53	3 35
112	254	22	Wednesday	♊ 5	11 58 34	10 3	5 9	6 48	3 50	5 15	6 42	3 50	5 2	6 54	3 50
113	253	23	Thursday	♋ 17	11 58 17	10 42	5 7	6 49	4 7	5 14	6 44	9	5 0	6 56	4 21
114	252	24	Friday	♋ 29	11 58 11	11 22	5 6	6 50	4 29	5 13	6 44	4 31	4 59	6 57	4 21
115	251	25	Saturday	♌ 11	11 58 0	ev. 5	5 4	6 52	sets	5 11	6 45	sets	4 58	6 58	sets
116	250	26	SUNDAY	♌ 23	11 57 49	50	5 3	6 53	8 36	5 9	6 46	8 25	4 57	6 59	8 48
117	249	27	Monday	♍ 5	11 57 30	1 38	5 2	6 54	9 39	5 7	6 46	9 26	4 56	7 0	9 53
118	248	28	Tuesday	♍ 17	11 57 30	2 30	5 0	6 55	10 42	5 5	6 47	10 27	4 54	7 1	10 57
119	247	29	Wednesday	♎ 30	11 57 21	3 24	4 59	6 56	11 37	5 4	6 49	11 23	4 52	7 3	11 52
120	246	30	Thursday	♎ 12	11 57 13	4 19	4 57	6 57	morn	5 3	6 50	morn	4 50	7 4	morn

First Quar., 3d.
Full Moon, 9th. 5th MONTH. **MAY, 1914.** 31 DAYS. **Last Quar., 16th.**
New Moon, 24th.

DAY OF YEAR.	DAYS IN YEAR.	DAY OF MONTH	DAY OF WEEK.	MOON'S PLACE	SUN AT NOON MARK.	MOON IN MERIDIAN.	New York, Chicago, Iowa, Neb., Pa., S. Wis., S. Mich., N. Ill., Ind., O.			St. Louis, S. Ill., Va., Ky., Mo., Kas., Col., Cal., Ind., Ohio.			St. Paul, N. E. Wis. and Mich., N. E. New York, Minn., Ore.		
							Sun rises.	Sun sets.	Moon sets and rises.	Sun rises.	Sun sets.	Moon sets and rises.	Sun rises.	Sun sets.	Moon sets and rises.
				Con. D.	H. M. S.	H. M.	H. M.	H. M.	H. M.	H. M.	H. M.	H. M.	H. M.	H. M.	H. M.
121	245	1	Friday.....	♓ 25	11 57 5	5 14	4 56	6 58	29	5 2	6 51	12	4 49	7 5	40
122	244	2	Saturday...	♈ 8	11 56 57	6 7	4 55	6 59	1 27	5 1	6 52	55	4 48	7 6	1 19
123	243	3	SUNDAY..	♈ 22	11 56 50	6 58	4 54	7 0	1 40	5 0	6 53	1 31	4 48	7 7	1 49
124	242	4	Monday....	♉ 6	11 56 44	7 47	4 53	7 2	2 6	4 59	6 54	2 0	4 44	7 8	2 13
125	241	5	Tuesday....	♉ 20	11 56 38	8 36	4 52	7 3	2 31	4 58	6 55	2 28	4 43	7 9	2 34
126	240	6	Wednesday	♊ 5	11 56 33	9 26	4 50	7 4	2 54	4 57	6 56	2 53	4 42	7 11	2 54
127	239	7	Thursday..	♊ 20	11 56 28	10 17	4 49	7 5	3 17	4 56	6 57	3 19	4 40	7 12	3 15
128	238	8	Friday.....	♋ 5	11 56 24	11 13	4 48	7 6	3 41	4 55	6 58	3 46	4 39	7 13	3 35
129	237	9	Saturday...	♋ 20	11 56 20	morn	4 46	7 7	rises	4 54	6 59	rises	4 38	7 14	rises
130	236	10	SUNDAY..	♌ 5	11 56 17	12	4 45	7 8	8 49	4 53	7 0	8 36	4 37	7 16	9 3
131	235	11	Monday....	♌ 20	11 56 15	1 14	4 44	7 9	10 4	4 52	7 0	9 49	4 36	7 17	10 19
132	234	12	Tuesday....	♍ 4	11 56 13	2 18	4 42	7 10	11 6	4 51	7 1	10 51	4 35	7 18	11 21
133	233	13	Wednesday	♍ 14	11 56 12	3 20	4 41	7 11	11 53	4 50	7 2	11 40	4 34	7 19	morn
134	232	14	Thursday..	♎ 1	11 56 11	4 18	4 40	7 12	morn	4 49	7 3	morn	4 32	7 20	7
135	231	15	Friday.....	♎ 14	11 56 11	5 11	4 39	7 13	28	4 48	7 3	18	4 31	7 21	39
136	230	16	Saturday...	♏ 26	11 56 11	5 59	4 38	7 14	57	4 48	7 4	49	4 30	7 23	1 5
137	229	17	SUNDAY..	♐ 8	11 56 12	6 42	4 37	7 15	1 18	4 47	7 5	1·12	4 29	7 24	1 23
138	228	18	Monday....	♐ 20	11 56 14	7 23	4 36	7 16	1 37	4 46	7 6	1 34	4 28	7 25	1 40
139	227	19	Tuesday....	♑ 2	11 56 16	8 2	4 35	7 17	1 54	4 45	7 7	1 53	4 27	7 26	1 55
140	226	20	Wednesday	♑ 14	11 56 19	8 41	4 34	7 18	2 12	4 44	7 8	2 14	4 26	7 27	2 11
141	225	21	Thursday..	♑ 26	11 56 22	9 21	4 34	7 19	2 32	4 44	7 9	2 36	4 25	7 28	2 27
142	224	22	Friday.....	♒ 8	11 56 26	10 2	4 33	7 20	2 51	4 43	7 10	2 58	4 24	7 29	2 44
143	223	23	Saturday...	♒ 20	11 56 31	10 47	4 32	7 21	3 14	4 43	7 11	3 23	4 23	7 30	3 5
144	222	24	SUNDAY..	♓ 2	11 56 36	11 34	4 31	7 22	3 46	4 42	7 12	3 57	4 22	7 31	3 34
145	221	25	Monday....	♓ 14	11 56 41	ev. 26	4 30	7 23	sets	4 42	7 13	sets	4 21	7 32	sets
146	220	26	Tuesday....	♈ 27	11 56 47	1 19	4 29	7 24	9 32	4 41	7 13	9 17	4 20	7 34	9 47
147	219	27	Wednesday	♈ 9	11 56 53	2 15	4 28	7 25	10 24	4 41	7 14	10 7	4 19	7 35	10 39
148	218	28	Thursday..	♉ 22	11 57 0	3 10	4 27	7 26	11 6	4 40	7 15	10 54	4 18	7 36	11 19
149	217	29	Friday.....	♊ 5	11 57 8	4 3	4 26	7 27	11 41	4 39	7 16	11 31	4 17	7 37	11 52
150	216	30	Saturday...	♊ 19	11 57 16	4 54	4 26	7 28	morn	4 39	7 17	morn	4 16	7 38	morn
151	215	31	SUNDAY..	♋ 3	11 57 24	5 43	4 26	7 29	10	4 38	7 17	3	4 16	7 39	17

First Quar., 1st. 30th.
Full Moon, 7th. 6th MONTH. **JUNE, 1914.** 30 DAYS. **Last Quar., 15th.**
New Moon, 23d.

DAY OF YEAR.	DAYS IN YEAR	DAY OF MONTH	DAY OF WEEK.	MOON'S PLACE	SUN AT NOON MARK.	MOON IN MERIDIAN.	New York, Chicago, Iowa, Neb., Pa., S. Wis., S. Mich., N. Ill., Ind., O.			St. Louis, S. Ill., Va., Ky., Mo., Kas., Col., Cal., Ind., Ohio.			St. Paul, N. E. Wis. and Mich., N. E. New York, Minn., Ore.		
							Sun rises.	Sun sets.	Moon sets and rises.	Sun rises.	Sun sets.	Moon sets and rises.	Sun rises.	Sun sets.	Moon sets and rises.
				Con. D.	H. M. S.	H. M.	H. M.	H. M.	H. M.	H. M.	H. M.	H. M.	H. M.	H. M.	H. M.
152	214	1	Monday....	♋ 16	11 57 32	6 30	4 25	7 29	35	4 38	7 18	31	4 15	7 40	39
153	213	2	Tuesday....	♌ 0	11 57 41	7 18	4 25	7 30	59	4 38	7 19	54	4 15	7 41	1 7
154	212	3	Wednesday	♌ 14	11 57 51	8 8	4 25	7 30	1 19	4 38	7 19	1 21	4 14	7 41	1 18
155	211	4	Thursday..	♍ 29	11 58 1	8 59	4 25	7 31	1 41	4 37	7 20	1 45	4 14	7 42	1 37
156	210	5	Friday.....	♍ 14	11 58 11	9 55	4 24	7 31	2 7	4 37	7 20	2 15	4 14	7 42	2 0
157	209	6	Saturday...	♎ 29	11 58 21	10 55	4 24	7 32	2 39	4 37	7 21	2 50	4 13	7 43	2 29
158	208	7	SUNDAY..	♏ 13	11 58 32	11 56	4 24	7 33	3 20	4 37	7 21	3 33	4 13	7 43	3 6
159	207	8	Monday....	♏ 28	11 58 43	morn	4 24	7 33	rises	4 36	7 22	rises	4 13	7 44	rises
160	206	9	Tuesday....	♐ 12	11 58 54	1 1	4 23	7 34	9 43	4 36	7 22	9 30	4 13	7 44	9 58
161	205	10	Wednesday	♐ 26	11 59 6	2 3	4 23	7 34	10 25	4 36	7 23	10 13	4 12	7 45	10 37
162	204	11	Thursday..	♑ 9	11 59 17	2 59	4 23	7 35	10 59	4 36	7 24	10 47	4 12	7 46	11 4
163	203	12	Friday.....	♑ 22	11 59 30	3 50	4 23	7 36	11 27	4 36	7 24	11 14	4 12	7 47	11 28
164	202	13	Saturday...	♒ 4	11 59 42	4 36	4 23	7 37	11 41	4 36	7 24	11 37	4 12	7 47	11 45
165	201	14	SUNDAY..	♒ 16	11 59 54	5 19	4 23	7 37	11 59	4 36	7 25	11 57	4 12	7 48	12 0
166	200	15	Monday....	♒ 28	12 0 7	5 59	4 23	7 38	morn	4 36	7 25	morn	4 12	7 49	morn
167	199	16	Tuesday....	♓ 10	12 0 20	6 38	4 23	7 38	17	4 36	7 26	18	4 12	7 50	16
168	198	17	Wednesday	♓ 22	12 0 32	7 18	4 23	7 39	35	4 36	7 26	39	4 12	7 50	32
169	197	18	Thursday..	♈ 4	12 0 45	7 59	4 23	7 39	55	4 36	7 26	1 0	4 12	7 51	49
170	196	19	Friday.....	♈ 16	12 0 59	8 42	4 23	7 39	1 17	4 36	7 27	1 25	4 12	7 51	1 8
171	195	20	Saturday...	♉ 28	12 1 12	9 28	4 23	7 39	1 44	4 36	7 27	1 54	4 13	7 51	1 33
172	194	21	SUNDAY..	♉ 10	12 1 25	10 19	4 24	7 40	2 14	4 36	7 27	2 28	4 13	7 51	2 0
173	193	22	Monday....	♊ 23	12 1 38	11 12	4 24	7 40	3 1	4 37	7 27	3 15	4 13	7 51	2 46
174	192	23	Tuesday....	♋ 6	12 1 51	ev. 8	4 24	7 40	sets	4 37	7 27	sets	4 13	7 51	sets
175	191	24	Wednesday	♋ 19	12 2 4	1 4	4 24	7 40	9 5	4 37	7 27	8 50	4 13	7 51	9 19
176	190	25	Thursday..	♌ 2	12 2 17	1 59	4 24	7 40	9 43	4 37	7 27	9 33	4 13	7 51	9 54
177	189	26	Friday.....	♌ 14	12 2 30	2 51	4 25	7 40	10 13	4 38	7 27	10 5	4 13	7 51	10 21
178	188	27	Saturday...	♍ 29	12 2 42	3 41	4 25	7 40	10 40	4 38	7 27	10 35	4 14	7 51	10 46
179	187	28	SUNDAY..	♍ 13	12 2 55	4 29	4 25	7 40	11 1	4 38	7 27	10 59	4 14	7 51	11 3
180	186	29	Monday....	♎ 27	12 3 7	5 15	4 26	7 40	11 23	4 39	7 27	11 24	4 14	7 51	11 22
181	185	30	Tuesday....	♍ 11	12 3 19	6 3	4 26	7 40	11 46	4 40	7 27	11 50	4 15	7 51	11 43

☉ Full Moon, 7th.
☾ Last Quar., 15th.   **7th MONTH.**   # JULY, 1914.   **31 DAYS.**   ☉ New Moon, 22d.
☽ First Quar., 29th.

DAY OF YEAR.	DAYS IN YEAR.	DAY OF MONTH	DAY OF WEEK.	MOON'S PLACE	SUN AT NOON MARK.	MOON IN MERIDIAN.	New York, Chicago, Iowa, Neb., Pa., S. Wis., S. Mich., N. Ill., Ind., O.			St. Louis, S. Ill., Va., Ky., Mo., Kas., Col., Cal., Ind., Ohio.			St. Paul, N. E. Wis. and Mich., N. E. New York, Minn., Ore.		
							Sun rises.	Sun sets.	Moon sets and rises.	Sun rises.	Sun sets.	Moon sets and rises.	Sun rises.	Sun sets.	Moon sets and rises.
				Con. D.	H. M. S.	H. M.	H. M.	H. M.	H. M.	H. M.	H. M.	H. M.	H. M.	H. M.	H. M.
182	184	1	Wednesday	♍ 25	12 3 31	6 52	4 27	7 40	morn	4 40	7 27	morn	4 16	7 51	morn
183	183	2	Thursday	♎ 9	12 3 43	7 45	4 28	7 40	10	4 40	7 27	16	4 17	7 51	3
184	182	3	Friday	♎ 24	12 3 54	8 42	4 29	7 40	38	4 41	7 27	45	4 18	7 51	1 26
185	181	4	Saturday	♏ 8	12 4 6	9 42	4 30	7 40	1 13	4 41	7 27	1 25	4 18	7 51	1 1
186	180	5	SUNDAY	♏ 22	12 4 15	10 45	4 30	7 40	2 0	4 42	7 27	2 14	4 19	7 51	1 45
187	179	6	Monday	♐ 6	12 4 26	11 47	4 31	7 39	2 58	4 43	7 26	3 12	4 20	7 50	2 43
188	178	7	Tuesday	♐ 20	12 4 38	morn	4 32	7 39	rises	4 44	7 26	rises	4 21	7 50	rises
189	177	8	Wednesday	♑ 4	12 4 45	45	4 32	7 39	8 55	4 44	7 26	8 44	4 21	7 50	9 5
190	176	9	Thursday	♑ 17	12 4 55	1 39	4 33	7 39	9 21	4 45	7 25	9 13	4 22	7 49	9 29
191	175	10	Friday	♑ 30	12 5 3	2 28	4 33	7 38	9 44	4 46	7 25	9 39	4 22	7 48	9 49
192	174	11	Saturday	♒ 12	12 5 12	3 13	4 34	7 37	10 3	4 46	7 24	10 1	4 23	7 48	10 5
193	173	12	SUNDAY	♒ 24	12 5 20	3 54	4 35	7 37	10 21	4 47	7 24	10 21	4 24	7 47	10 21
194	172	13	Monday	♓ 6	12 5 27	4 34	4 35	7 36	10 39	4 47	7 24	10 41	4 24	7 46	10 37
195	171	14	Tuesday	♓ 18	12 5 34	5 14	4 36	7 36	10 59	4 48	7 23	11 2	4 25	7 46	10 54
196	170	15	Wednesday	♈ 30	12 5 41	5 54	4 36	7 35	11 19	4 49	7 23	11 26	4 26	7 45	11 11
197	169	16	Thursday	♈ 12	12 5 47	6 36	4 37	7 34	11 44	4 50	7 22	11 53	4 27	7 44	11 34
198	168	17	Friday	♈ 24	12 5 53	7 21	4 38	7 34	morn	4 51	7 21	morn	4 28	7 43	morn
199	167	18	Saturday	♉ 6	12 5 58	8 10	4 39	7 33	17	4 51	7 21	29	4 29	7 42	4
200	166	19	SUNDAY	♉ 19	12 6 3	9 2	4 39	7 33	56	4 52	7 20	1 9	4 30	7 41	41
201	165	20	Monday	♊ 2	12 6 7	9 57	4 40	7 32	1 44	4 53	7 20	1 58	4 31	7 40	1 29
202	164	21	Tuesday	♊ 15	12 6 10	10 53	4 41	7 31	2 42	4 54	7 19	2 56	4 32	7 39	2 27
203	163	22	Wednesday	♋ 28	12 6 13	11 50	4 42	7 30	3 51	4 54	7 19	4 3	4 33	7 38	3 38
204	162	23	Thursday	♋ 12	12 6 16	ev. 44	4 43	7 29	sets	4 55	7 18	sets	4 34	7 37	sets
205	161	24	Friday	♋ 25	12 6 18	1 36	4 44	7 28	8 42	4 56	7 17	8 36	4 35	7 36	8 46
206	160	25	Saturday	♌ 9	12 6 19	2 25	4 45	7 27	9 5	4 57	7 16	9 2	4 36	7 35	9 8
207	159	26	SUNDAY	♌ 23	12 6 20	3 13	4 46	7 26	9 28	4 58	7 15	9 28	4 37	7 34	9 28
208	158	27	Monday	♍ 8	12 6 20	4 1	4 47	7 25	9 51	4 59	7 14	9 53	4 38	7 33	9 48
209	157	28	Tuesday	♍ 22	12 6 19	4 50	4 48	7 24	10 13	4 59	7 13	10 19	4 39	7 32	10 7
210	156	29	Wednesday	♎ 6	12 6 18	5 41	4 49	7 23	10 40	5 0	7 12	10 49	4 40	7 31	10 31
211	155	30	Thursday	♎ 20	12 6 16	6 36	4 50	7 22	11 16	5 0	7 12	11 26	4 41	7 30	11 5
212	154	31	Friday	♏ 4	12 6 14	7 34	4 51	7 21	11 55	5 1	7 11	morn	4 42	7 30	11 41

☉ Full Moon, 5th.
☾ Last Quar., 13th.   **8th MONTH.**   # AUGUST, 1914.   **31 DAYS.**   ☉ New Moon, 21st.
☽ First Quar., 27th.

DAY OF YEAR.	DAYS IN YEAR.	DAY OF MONTH	DAY OF WEEK.	MOON'S PLACE	SUN AT NOON MARK.	MOON IN MERIDIAN.	New York, Chicago, Iowa, Neb., Pa., S. Wis., S. Mich., N. Ill., Ind., O.			St. Louis, S. Ill., Va., Ky., Mo., Kas., Col., Cal., Ind., Ohio.			St. Paul, N. E. Wis. and Mich., N. E. New York, Minn., Ore.		
							Sun rises.	Sun sets.	Moon sets and rises.	Sun rises.	Sun sets.	Moon sets and rises.	Sun rises.	Sun sets.	Moon sets and rises.
				Con. D.	H. M. S.	H. M.	H. M.	H. M.	H. M.	H. M.	H. M.	H. M.	H. M.	H. M.	H. M.
213	153	1	Saturday	♏ 18	12 6 11	8 34	4 52	7 19	morn	5 2	7 10	9	4 44	7 29	morn
214	152	2	SUNDAY	♐ 2	12 6 7	9 35	4 53	7 18	47	5 2	7 9	1 1	4 44	7 27	32
215	151	3	Monday	♐ 16	12 6 3	10 34	4 54	7 17	1 53	5 3	7 8	4	4 45	7 25	1 38
216	150	4	Tuesday	♐ 29	12 5 58	11 29	4 54	7 16	3 0	5 4	7 7	3 12	4 46	7 24	2 47
217	149	5	Wednesday	♑ 12	12 5 53	morn	4 55	7 15	rises	5 5	7 6	rises	4 47	7 22	rises
218	148	6	Thursday	♑ 25	12 5 47	20	4 56	7 14	7 46	5 7	7 5	7 40	4 49	7 19	7 53
219	147	7	Friday	♒ 8	12 5 40	1 6	4 57	7 13	8 7	5 7	7 4	8 4	4 50	7 19	8 10
220	146	8	Saturday	♒ 20	12 5 33	1 48	4 59	7 12	8 25	5 8	7 3	8 24	4 51	7 18	8 26
221	145	9	SUNDAY	♓ 2	12 5 25	2 30	5 0	7 10	8 44	5 8	7 2	8 46	4 53	7 17	8 43
222	144	10	Monday	♓ 14	12 5 16	3 10	5 1	7 9	9 2	5 9	7 1	9 6	4 54	7 15	8 58
223	143	11	Tuesday	♓ 26	12 5 7	3 50	5 2	7 7	9 22	5 10	7 0	9 28	4 55	7 14	9 15
224	142	12	Wednesday	♈ 8	12 4 58	4 31	5 3	7 6	9 44	5 11	6 59	9 53	4 56	7 13	9 35
225	141	13	Thursday	♈ 20	12 4 48	5 14	5 4	7 5	10 13	5 12	6 57	10 24	4 58	7 12	10 2
226	140	14	Friday	♉ 2	12 4 37	6 1	5 5	7 4	10 48	5 13	6 56	11 2	4 59	7 10	10 34
227	139	15	Saturday	♉ 14	12 4 26	6 51	5 7	7 3	11 31	5 14	6 54	11 46	5 0	7 9	11 16
228	138	16	SUNDAY	♉ 27	12 4 14	7 44	5 8	7 2	morn	5 15	6 53	morn	5 2	7 8	morn
229	137	17	Monday	♊ 10	12 4 2	8 40	5 8	7 1	27	5 16	6 51	41	5 3	7 6	12
230	136	18	Tuesday	♊ 23	12 3 50	9 36	5 9	6 59	1 31	5 18	6 50	1 45	5 4	7 4	1 17
231	135	19	Wednesday	♋ 6	12 3 37	10 32	5 10	6 57	2 42	5 17	6 49	2 54	5 6	7 2	2 30
232	134	20	Thursday	♋ 20	12 3 23	11 25	5 11	6 55	3 57	5 18	6 48	4 5	5 7	7 1	3 48
233	133	21	Friday	♌ 4	12 3 9	ev. 16	5 12	6 53	sets	5 19	6 46	sets	5 7	7 0	sets
234	132	22	Saturday	♌ 19	12 2 54	1 6	5 13	6 51	7 32	5 20	6 44	7 30	5 8	6 58	7 33
235	131	23	SUNDAY	♍ 3	12 2 39	1 55	5 14	6 49	7 55	5 22	6 42	7 57	5 10	6 56	7 53
236	130	24	Monday	♍ 18	12 2 24	2 45	5 16	6 48	8 17	5 23	6 40	8 22	5 11	6 55	8 13
237	129	25	Tuesday	♎ 3	12 2 8	3 37	5 16	6 47	8 44	5 23	6 40	8 52	5 11	6 52	8 36
238	128	26	Wednesday	♎ 17	12 1 51	4 31	5 17	6 45	9 14	5 24	6 39	9 24	5 12	6 50	9 3
239	127	27	Thursday	♏ 1	12 1 35	5 29	5 18	6 44	9 54	5 25	6 37	10 7	5 14	6 48	9 40
240	126	28	Friday	♏ 15	12 1 17	6 28	5 20	6 43	10 42	5 26	6 36	10 57	5 16	6 46	10 27
241	125	29	Saturday	♏ 29	12 1 0	7 29	5 21	6 41	11 43	5 27	6 35	11 58	5 17	6 45	11 28
242	124	30	SUNDAY	♐ 12	12 0 42	8 28	5 22	6 39	morn	5 28	6 34	morn	5 18	6 43	morn
243	123	31	Monday	♐ 26	12 0 24	9 23	5 23	6 38	51	5 28	6 33	1 4	5 19	6 41	37

Full Moon, 4th.
Last Quar., 12th.   **9th MONTH. SEPTEMBER, 1914. 30 DAYS**   New Moon, 19th.
First Quar., 26th.

Day of Year	Days in Year	Day of Month	Day of Week	Moon's Place	Sun at Noon Mark	Moon in Meridian	New York, Chicago, Iowa, Neb., Pa., S. Wis., S. Mich., N. Ill., Ind., O.			St. Louis, S. Ill., Va., Ky., Mo., Kas., Col., Cal., Ind., Ohio.			St. Paul, N. E. Wis. and Mich., N. E. New York, Minn., Ore.		
							Sun rises.	Sun sets.	Moon sets and rises.	Sun rises.	Sun sets.	Moon sets and rises.	Sun rises.	Sun sets.	Moon sets and rises.
				Con.D.	H. M. S.	H. M.	H. M.	H. M.	H. M.	H. M.	H. M.	H. M.	H. M.	H. M.	H. M.
244	122	1	Tuesday....	♉9	12 0 5	10 14	5 24	6 36	2 3	5 29	6 32	2 14	5 20	6 39	1 51
245	121	2	Wednesday	♉21	11 59 46	11 1	5 25	6 34	3 13	5 29	6 30	3 22	5 21	6 38	3 4
246	120	3	Thursday..	♊4	11 59 27	11 45	5 26	6 32	4 22	5 30	6 29	4 28	5 23	6 36	4 16
247	119	4	Friday......	♊16	11 59 7	morn	5 27	6 30	rises	5 31	6 27	rises	5 24	6 34	rises
248	118	5	Saturday...	♊28	11 58 48	26	5 28	6 29	6 46	5 32	6 25	6 49	5 25	6 32	6 48
249	117	6	SUNDAY..	♋11	11 58 28	1 6	5 29	6 27	7 7	5 33	6 23	7 10	5 26	6 30	7 4
250	116	7	Monday....	♋22	11 58 7	1 46	5 30	6 25	7 25	5 34	6 22	7 31	5 28	6 28	7 20
251	115	8	Tuesday...	♌4	11 57 47	2 27	5 31	6 24	7 47	5 35	6 21	7 55	5 29	6 26	7 39
252	114	9	Wednesday	♌16	11 57 27	3 10	5 32	6 22	8 14	5 36	6 19	8 24	5 30	6 24	8 3
253	113	10	Thursday..	♍28	11 57 6	3 55	5 33	6 20	8 45	5 37	6 17	8 58	5 31	6 22	8 32
254	112	11	Friday......	♍10	11 56 45	4 43	5 34	6 18	9 25	5 37	6 15	9 39	5 32	6 20	9 10
255	111	12	Saturday...	♎22	11 56 24	5 34	5 35	6 16	10 15	5 38	6 14	10 29	5 33	6 18	10 0
256	110	13	SUNDAY..	♎5	11 56 3	6 28	5 36	6 15	11 14	5 39	6 13	11 28	5 34	6 17	10 59
257	109	14	Monday....	♏18	11 55 42	7 23	5 37	6 13	morn	5 40	6 12	morn	5 35	6 15	morn
258	108	15	Tuesday...	♏1	11 55 21	8 17	5 38	6 11	19	5 41	6 10	32	5 36	6 13	6
259	107	16	Wednesday	♐14	11 55 0	9 11	5 39	6 9	1 31	5 42	6 8	1 41	5 37	6 11	1 21
260	106	17	Thursday..	♐28	11 54 38	10 3	5 41	6 7	2 47	5 43	6 6	2 54	5 39	6 9	2 40
261	105	18	Friday......	♑13	11 54 17	10 53	5 42	6 6	4	5 44	6 4	7	5 41	6 7	3 55
262	104	19	Saturday...	♑28	11 53 56	11 44	5 43	6 4	5 20	5 45	6 3	5 21	5 42	6 5	5 19
263	103	20	SUNDAY..	♒13	11 53 35	ev.34	5 44	6 2	sets	5 46	6 1	sets	5 43	6 3	sets
264	102	21	Monday....	♒28	11 53 13	1 26	5 45	6 0	6 44	5 47	6 0	6 50	5 44	6 1	6 37
265	101	22	Tuesday...	♓13	11 52 52	2 22	5 46	5 59	7 14	5 47	5 59	7 24	5 46	6 0	7 4
266	100	23	Wednesday	♓27	11 52 33	3 20	5 47	5 58	7 50	5 48	5 57	8 2	5 47	5 58	7 37
267	99	24	Thursday..	♈12	11 52 11	4 21	5 48	5 56	8 39	5 49	5 55	8 53	5 48	5 56	8 25
268	98	25	Friday......	♈26	11 51 51	5 23	5 49	5 54	9 36	5 50	5 53	9 50	5 49	5 54	9 21
269	97	26	Saturday...	♉9	11 51 30	6 23	5 50	5 52	10 43	5 51	5 51	10 56	5 50	5 52	10 28
270	96	27	SUNDAY..	♉23	11 51 10	7 19	5 51	5 50	11 53	5 52	5 50	morn	5 52	5 50	11 40
271	95	28	Monday....	♊6	11 50 49	8 12	5 52	5 49	morn	5 53	5 49	5	5 53	5 48	morn
272	94	29	Tuesday...	♊18	11 50 29	8 59	5 53	5 47	1 5	5 54	5 47	1 14	5 54	5 46	55
273	93	30	Wednesday	♋1	11 50 10	9 43	5 54	5 45	2 13	5 55	5 45	2 19	5 55	5 44	2 6

Full Moon, 3d.
Last Quar., 12th.   **10th MONTH. OCTOBER, 1914. 31 DAYS**   New Moon, 19th.
First Quar., 25th.

Day of Year	Days in Year	Day of Month	Day of Week	Moon's Place	Sun at Noon Mark	Moon in Meridian	New York, Chicago, Iowa, Neb., Pa., S. Wis., S. Mich., N. Ill., Ind., O.			St. Louis, S. Ill., Va., Ky., Mo., Kas., Col., Cal., Ind., Ohio.			St. Paul, N. E. Wis. and Mich., N. E. New York, Minn., Ore.		
							Sun rises.	Sun sets.	Moon sets and rises.	Sun rises.	Sun sets.	Moon sets and rises.	Sun rises.	Sun sets.	Moon sets and rises.
				Con.D.	H. M. S.	H. M.	H. M.	H. M.	H. M.	H. M.	H. M.	H. M.	H. M.	H. M.	H. M.
274	92	1	Thursday...	♋13	11 49 50	10 25	5 56	5 44	3 21	5 56	5 43	3 25	5 57	5 43	3 17
275	91	2	Friday......	♋25	11 49 31	11 5	5 57	5 42	4 24	5 56	5 42	4 26	5 58	5 40	4 29
276	90	3	Saturday...	♌7	11 49 12	11 45	5 58	5 40	5 26	5 57	5 41	5 25	5 59	5 39	5 27
277	89	4	SUNDAY...	♌19	11 48 53	morn	5 59	5 38	rises	5 58	5 40	rises	6 0	5 38	rises
278	88	5	Monday....	♍1	11 48 35	25	6 0	5 37	5 51	5 59	5 38	5 58	6 1	5 36	5 44
279	87	6	Tuesday...	♍13	11 48 17	1 5	6 1	5 35	6 18	6 0	5 36	6 27	6 2	5 34	6 8
280	86	7	Wednesday	♍25	11 48 0	1 51	6 2	5 33	6 47	6 1	5 34	6 58	6 3	5 32	6 35
281	85	8	Thursday...	♎7	11 47 42	2 38	6 3	5 32	7 23	6 2	5 33	7 37	6 5	5 30	7 9
282	84	9	Friday......	♎19	11 47 26	3 28	6 4	5 30	8 9	6 3	5 31	8 24	6 6	5 28	7 54
283	83	10	Saturday...	♏1	11 47 10	4 20	6 5	5 29	9 9	6 4	5 29	9 16	6 7	5 26	8 46
284	82	11	SUNDAY...	♏13	11 46 54	5 13	6 7	5 26	10 7	6 5	5 28	10 11	6 8	5 24	9 42
285	81	12	Monday....	♏26	11 46 39	6 5	6 8	5 25	11 11	6 6	5 27	11 12	6 10	5 22	11 0
286	80	13	Tuesday...	♐9	11 46 24	6 59	6 9	5 23	morn	6 7	5 26	morn	6 12	5 20	morn
287	79	14	Wednesday	♐22	11 46 10	7 50	6 10	5 21	23	6 8	5 24	30	6 13	5 19	13
288	78	15	Thursday...	♑6	11 45 56	8 40	6 11	5 19	1 36	6 9	5 23	1 41	6 14	5 17	1 30
289	77	16	Friday......	♑21	11 45 43	9 29	6 12	5 18	2 51	6 10	5 22	2 54	6 16	5 16	2 48
290	76	17	Saturday...	♒6	11 45 30	10 10	6 13	5 17	4 7	6 11	5 20	4 7	6 17	5 14	4 7
291	75	18	SUNDAY...	♒21	11 45 18	11 10	6 14	5 16	5 24	6 12	5 19	5 21	6 18	5 12	5 27
292	74	19	Monday....	♓6	11 45 7	ev.5	6 16	5 15	sets	6 13	5 18	sets	6 19	5 10	sets
293	73	20	Tuesday...	♓21	11 44 56	1 4	6 17	5 13	5 48	6 14	5 17	5 56	6 21	5 8	5 34
294	72	21	Wednesday	♈6	11 44 46	2 1	6 18	5 11	6 18	6 15	5 16	6 42	6 22	5 6	6 15
295	71	22	Thursday...	♈21	11 44 37	3 10	6 19	5 9	7 24	6 16	5 14	7 39	6 24	5 5	7 9
296	70	23	Friday......	♉5	11 44 28	4 13	6 21	5 7	8 31	6 17	5 12	8 42	6 25	5 3	8 16
297	69	24	Saturday...	♉19	11 44 20	5 13	6 22	5 4	9 41	6 17	5 11	9 54	6 27	5 2	9 22
298	68	25	SUNDAY...	♊2	11 44 13	6 8	6 24	5 4	10 55	6 18	5 10	11 5	6 28	5 1	10 45
299	67	26	Monday....	♊15	11 44 6	6 57	6 25	5 2	morn	6 19	5 8	morn	6 30	4 59	11 58
300	66	27	Tuesday...	♊28	11 44 0	7 42	6 26	5 1	6	6 20	5 7	12	6 31	4 57	morn
301	65	28	Wednesday	♋11	11 43 55	8 24	6 27	5 0	1 12	6 21	5 6	1 17	6 32	4 55	1 8
302	64	29	Thursday...	♋23	11 43 50	9 5	6 28	4 59	2 16	6 22	5 5	2 19	6 33	4 54	2 14
303	63	30	Friday......	♌6	11 43 46	9 44	6 29	4 58	3 18	6 23	5 3	3 18	6 34	4 52	3 18
304	62	31	Saturday...	♌18	11 43 43	10 24	6 30	4 57	4 19	6 24	5 3	4 17	6 35	4 51	4 21

⊕ Full Moon, 2d.
☾ Last Quar., 10th.   **11th MONTH. NOVEMBER, 1914. 30 DAYS.**   ● New Moon, 17th.
☽ First Quar., 24th.

Day of Year	Days in Year	Day of Month	Day of Week	Moon's Place	Sun at Noon Mark.	Moon in Me-rid-ian.	New York, Chicago, Iowa, Neb., Pa., S. Wis., S. Mich., N. Ill., Ind., O.			St. Louis, S. Ill., Va., Ky., Mo., Kas., Col., Cal., Ind., Ohio.			St. Paul, N. E. Wis. and Mich., N. E. New York, Minn., Ore.		
							Sun rises.	Sun sets.	Moon sets and rises.	Sun rises.	Sun sets.	Moon sets and rises.	Sun rises.	Sun sets.	Moon sets and rises.
				Con. D.	H. M. S.	H. M.	H. M.	H. M.	H. M.	H. M.	H. M.	H. M.	H. M.	H. M.	H. M.
305	61	1	SUNDAY.	♓ 28	11 43 41	11 5	6 31	4 55	5 21	6 26	5 1	5 16	6 38	4 49	5 26
306	60	2	Monday....	♈ 9	11 43 40	11 49	6 33	4 54	6 32	6 27	5 0	6 15	6 39	4 48	6 30
307	59	3	Tuesday...	♈ 22	11 43 39	morn	6 34	4 53	rises	6 28	4 59	rises	6 40	4 47	rises
308	58	4	Wednesday	♉ 4	11 43 39	35	6 35	4 52	5 24	6 29	4 58	5 37	6 41	4 46	5 11
309	57	5	Thursday..	♉ 16	11 43 40	1 24	6 36	4 50	6 6	6 30	4 57	6 20	6 42	4 43	5 51
310	56	6	Friday.....	♉ 28	11 43 42	2 15	6 37	4 49	6 56	6 31	4 56	7 11	6 44	4 42	6 41
311	55	7	Saturday..	♊ 10	11 43 44	3 8	6 38	4 48	7 55	6 32	4 55	8 9	6 45	4 41	7 41
312	54	8	SUNDAY..	♊ 22	11 43 48	4 0	6 39	4 47	8 59	6 33	4 54	9 11	6 46	4 40	8 47
313	53	9	Monday....	♋ 5	11 43 52	4 52	6 40	4 46	10 7	6 34	4 53	10 17	6 47	4 39	9 57
314	52	10	Tuesday...	♋ 18	11 43 57	5 42	6 41	4 45	11 17	6 35	4 53	11 24	6 48	4 38	11 10
315	51	11	Wednesday	♌ 1	11 44 3	6 31	6 43	4 44	morn	6 37	4 52	morn	6 50	4 36	morn
316	50	12	Thursday..	♌ 15	11 44 10	7 18	6 44	4 43	29	6 38	4 51	33	6 52	4 35	25
317	49	13	Friday.....	♍ 29	11 44 18	8 6	6 45	4 42	1 42	6 39	4 50	1 43	6 53	4 34	1 41
318	48	14	Saturday..	♍ 14	11 44 27	8 55	6 46	4 41	2 57	6 40	4 50	2 56	6 55	4 33	2 59
319	47	15	SUNDAY..	♍ 29	11 44 36	9 47	6 48	4 40	4 16	6 41	4 49	4 11	6 56	4 32	4 21
320	46	16	Monday....	♎ 14	11 44 47	10 43	6 49	4 39	5 37	6 42	4 49	5 30	6 58	4 31	5 45
321	45	17	Tuesday...	♎ 30	11 44 58	11 44	6 51	4 38	7 3	6 43	4 48	6 52	6 59	4 30	7 14
322	44	18	Wednesday	♏ 15	11 45 10	ev.48	6 52	4 38	sets	6 44	4 47	sets	7 0	4 30	sets
323	43	19	Thursday..	♏ 30	11 45 23	1 54	6 54	4 37	6 10	6 45	4 47	6 24	7 2	4 29	5 55
324	42	20	Friday.....	♐ 14	11 45 37	2 58	6 55	4 37	7 21	6 46	4 46	7 34	7 3	4 28	7 7
325	41	21	Saturday..	♐ 28	11 45 51	3 57	6 56	4 36	8 38	6 47	4 45	8 49	7 5	4 27	8 22
326	40	22	SUNDAY..	♑ 11	11 46 7	4 50	6 57	4 35	9 52	6 48	4 45	10 0	7 6	4 26	9 43
327	39	23	Monday....	♑ 24	11 46 23	5 38	6 58	4 34	11 1	6 49	4 44	11 7	7 7	4 26	10 55
328	38	24	Tuesday...	♒ 7	11 46 40	6 22	6 59	4 33	morn	6 50	4 44	morn	7 9	4 25	morn
329	37	25	Wednesday	♒ 19	11 46 57	7 3	7 0	4 33	8	6 51	4 43	11	7 10	4 24	5
330	36	26	Thursday..	♓ 1	11 47 16	7 43	7 1	4 32	1 10	6 52	4 43	1 11	7 11	4 23	1 9
331	35	27	Friday.....	♓ 13	11 47 35	8 23	7 3	4 31	2 12	6 53	4 42	2 10	7 12	4 22	2 13
332	34	28	Saturday..	♓ 25	11 47 56	9 4	7 4	4 31	3 14	6 54	4 42	3 9	7 13	4 22	3 18
333	33	29	SUNDAY..	♈ 7	11 48 15	9 46	7 5	4 31	4 15	6 55	4 42	4 10	7 14	4 21	4 22
334	32	30	Monday....	♈ 19	11 48 36	10 32	7 6	4 31	5 16	6 56	4 42	5 7	7 15	4 21	5 25

⊕ Full Moon, 2d.
☾ Last Quar., 10th.   **12th MONTH. DECEMBER, 1914. 31 DAYS.**   ● New Moon, 16th.
☽ First Quar., 24th.

Day of Year	Days in Year	Day of Month	Day of Week	Moon's Place	Sun at Noon Mark.	Moon in Me-rid-ian.	New York, Chicago, Iowa, Neb., Pa., S. Wis., S. Mich., N. Ill., Ind., O.			St. Louis, S. Ill., Va., Ky., Mo., Kas., Col., Cal., Ind., Ohio.			St. Paul, N. E. Wis. and Mich., N. E. New York, Minn., Ore.		
							Sun rises.	Sun sets.	Moon sets and rises.	Sun rises.	Sun sets.	Moon sets and rises.	Sun rises.	Sun sets.	Moon sets and rises.
				Con. D.	H. M. S.	H. M.	H. M.	H. M.	H. M.	H. M.	H. M.	H. M.	H. M.	H. M.	H. M.
335	31	1	Tuesday....	♉ 1	11 48 58	11 20	7 7	4 31	6 20	6 57	4 41	6 9	7 16	4 21	6 32
336	30	2	Wednesday	♉ 13	11 49 21	morn	7 8	4 30	rises	6 58	4 41	rises	7 17	4 20	rises
337	29	3	Thursday..	♉ 25	11 49 44	11	7 9	4 30	4 53	6 59	4 41	5 7	7 18	4 20	4 38
338	28	4	Friday.....	♊ 7	11 50 8	1 4	7 10	4 30	5 49	7 0	4 41	6 3	7 19	4 19	5 33
339	27	5	Saturday ..	♊ 19	11 50 32	1 57	7 11	4 29	6 53	7 1	4 41	7 5	7 20	4 19	6 40
340	26	6	SUNDAY..	♋ 2	11 50 57	2 49	7 12	4 29	7 58	7 2	4 41	8 8	7 22	4 19	7 47
341	25	7	Monday....	♋ 15	11 51 22	3 39	7 13	4 29	9 7	7 3	4 41	9 15	7 23	4 19	8 59
342	24	8	Tuesday....	♋ 28	11 51 48	4 27	7 14	4 29	10 17	7 4	4 41	10 22	7 24	4 19	10 12
343	23	9	Wednesday	♌ 11	11 52 15	5 14	7 15	4 29	11 28	7 5	4 41	11 30	7 25	4 19	11 26
344	22	10	Thursday...	♌ 25	11 52 42	6 0	7 16	4 29	morn	7 6	4 41	morn	7 26	4 19	morn
345	21	11	Friday.....	♍ 9	11 53 9	6 46	7 17	4 29	39	7 7	4 41	39	7 27	4 19	40
346	20	12	Saturday ..	♍ 23	11 53 37	7 35	7 18	4 29	53	7 8	4 41	1 50	7 28	4 19	1 56
347	19	13	SUNDAY..	♎ 8	11 54 5	8 27	7 19	4 29	3 9	7 9	4 42	3 3	7 29	4 19	3 16
348	18	14	Monday....	♎ 23	11 54 34	9 23	7 20	4 29	4 31	7 9	4 42	4 21	7 30	4 20	4 41
349	17	15	Tuesday....	♏ 8	11 55 3	10 25	7 21	4 30	5 55	7 10	4 42	5 42	7 31	4 20	6 6
350	16	16	Wednesday	♏ 23	11 55 32	11 31	7 21	4 30	7 13	7 10	4 43	6 59	7 32	4 20	7 27
351	15	17	Thursday..	♐ 8	11 56 1	ex.36	7 21	4 30	sets	7 10	4 43	sets	7 32	4 20	sets
352	14	18	Friday.....	♐ 22	11 56 37	1 39	7 22	4 31	6 12	7 11	4 43	6 24	7 33	4 21	5 59
353	13	19	Saturday ..	♑ 6	11 57 0	2 37	7 23	4 31	7 29	7 12	4 44	7 39	7 34	4 21	7 19
354	12	20	SUNDAY..	♑ 19	11 57 30	3 30	7 23	4 32	8 43	7 13	4 44	8 51	7 35	4 22	8 36
355	11	21	Monday....	♒ 2	11 58 0	4 18	7 24	4 32	9 53	7 13	4 44	9 57	7 35	4 22	9 49
356	10	22	Tuesday....	♒ 15	11 58 30	4 59	7 24	4 34	10 59	7 13	4 45	11 1	7 35	4 22	10 58
357	9	23	Wednesday	♒ 27	11 59 0	5 40	7 25	4 34	morn	7 14	4 45	morn	7 36	4 23	morn
358	8	24	Thursday..	♓ 10	11 59 30	6 20	7 25	4 35	3	7 14	4 46	1	7 36	4 24	3
359	7	25	Friday.....	♓ 21	11 59 59	7 1	7 26	4 35	1 3	7 15	4 46	59	7 37	4 25	1 6
360	6	26	Saturday ..	♈ 3	12 0 30	7 43	7 26	4 36	2 6	7 15	4 47	2 0	7 37	4 26	2 12
361	5	27	SUNDAY..	♈ 15	12 0 59	8 27	7 26	4 36	3 8	7 15	4 48	3 0	7 38	4 26	3 17
362	4	28	Monday....	♈ 27	12 1 29	9 14	7 27	4 37	4 10	7 16	4 49	3 59	7 38	4 26	4 21
363	3	29	Tuesday....	♉ 9	12 1 58	10 4	7 27	4 38	5 12	7 16	4 50	4 57	7 38	4 28	5 26
364	2	30	Wednesday	♉ 21	12 2 27	10 57	7 28	4 38	6 12	7 16	4 51	5 58	7 39	4 29	6 26
365	1	31	Thursday..	♊ 4	12 2 56		7 28	4 39	7 10	7 16	4 51	6 54	7 39	4 29	7 23

A READY-REFERENCE CALENDAR.

For ascertaining any day of the week for any given time within two hundred years from the introduction of the New Style, *1753 to 1952 inclusive.

YEARS 1753 TO 1952.											Jan.	Feb.	Mar.	Apr.	May	June	July	Aug.	Sept.	Oct.	Nov.	Dec.
1761 1801	1767 1807	1778 1818	1789 1829	1795 1835	1846	1857 1903	1863 1914	1874 1925	1885 1931	1891 1942	4	7	7	3	5	1	3	6	2	4	7	2
1762 1802	1773 1813	1779 1819	1790 1830		1841	1847	1858 1909	1869 1915	1875 1926	1886 1937	1897 1943	5	1	1	4	6	2	4	7	3	5	1	3
1757 1803	1763 1814	1774 1825	1785 1831	1791 1842	1853	1859 1910	1870 1921	1881 1927	1887 1938	1898 1949	6	2	2	5	7	3	5	1	4	6	2	4
1754 1805	1765 1811	1771 1822	1782 1833	1793 1839	1799 1850 1901	1861 1907	1867 1918	1878 1929	1889 1935	1895 1946	2	5	5	1	3	6	1	4	7	2	5	7
1755 1806	1766 1817	1777 1823	1783 1834	1794 1845	1800 1851 1902	1862 1913	1873 1919	1879 1930	1890 1941	1947	3	6	6	2	4	7	2	5	1	3	6	1
1758 1809	1769 1815	1775 1826	1786 1837	1797 1843	1854 1905	1865 1911	1871 1922	1882 1933	1893 1939	1899 1950	7	3	3	6	1	4	6	2	5	7	3	5
1753 1810	1759 1821	1770 1827	1781 1838	1787 1849	1798 1855	1866 1906	1877 1917	1883 1923	1894 1934	1900 1945 1951	1	4	4	7	2	5	7	3	6	1	4	6

LEAP YEARS.								..	29	..	..	..	..	..	..	..	..	..
1764	1792	1804	1832	1860	1888	1928	......	7	3	4	7	2	5	7	3	6	1	4	6
1768	1796	1808	1836	1864	1892	1904	1932	5	1	2	5	7	3	5	1	4	6	2	4
1772	....	1812	1840	1868	1896	1908	1936	3	6	7	3	5	1	3	6	2	4	7	2
1776	....	1816	1844	1872	....	1912	1940	1	4	5	1	3	6	1	4	7	2	5	7
1780	....	1820	1848	1876	....	1916	1944	6	2	3	6	1	4	6	2	5	7	3	5
1756	1784	1824	1852	1880	....	1920	1948	4	7	1	4	6	2	4	7	3	5	1	3
1760	1788	1828	1856	1884	....	1924	1952	2	5	6	2	4	7	2	5	1	3	6	1

1	2	3	4	5	6	7
Monday 1	Tuesday..... 1	Wednesday. 1	Thursday ... 1	Friday....... 1	Saturday.... 1	SUNDAY... 1
Tuesday..... 2	Wednesday. 2	Thursday... 2	Friday 2	Saturday.... 2	SUNDAY... 2	Monday...... 2
Wednesday. 3	Thursday... 3	Friday 3	Saturday.... 3	SUNDAY... 3	Monday...... 3	Tuesday..... 3
Thursday... 4	Friday 4	Saturday.... 4	SUNDAY ... 4	Monday...... 4	Tuesday..... 4	Wednesday. 4
Friday 5	Saturday.... 5	SUNDAY... 5	Monday...... 5	Tuesday..... 5	Wednesday. 5	Thursday... 5
Saturday.... 6	SUNDAY... 6	Monday...... 6	Tuesday..... 6	Wednesday. 6	Thursday... 6	Friday 6
SUNDAY... 7	Monday...... 7	Tuesday..... 7	Wednesday. 7	Thursday... 7	Friday 7	Saturday.... 7
Monday...... 8	Tuesday..... 8	Wednesday. 8	Thursday... 8	Friday 8	Saturday.... 8	SUNDAY... 8
Tuesday..... 9	Wednesday. 9	Thursday... 9	Friday 9	Saturday.... 9	SUNDAY... 9	Monday...... 9
Wednesday.10	Thursday...10	Friday 10	Saturday....10	SUNDAY...10	Monday......10	Tuesday.....10
Thursday...11	Friday 11	Saturday....11	SUNDAY...11	Monday......11	Tuesday.....11	Wednesday.11
Friday 12	Saturday....12	SUNDAY...12	Monday......12	Tuesday.....12	Wednesday.12	Thursday...12
Saturday....13	SUNDAY...13	Monday......13	Tuesday.....13	Wednesday.13	Thursday...13	Friday 13
SUNDAY...14	Monday......14	Tuesday.....14	Wednesday.14	Thursday...14	Friday 14	Saturday....14
Monday......15	Tuesday.....15	Wednesday.15	Thursday...15	Friday 15	Saturday....15	SUNDAY...15
Tuesday.....16	Wednesday.16	Thursday...16	Friday 16	Saturday....16	SUNDAY...16	Monday......16
Wednesday.17	Thursday...17	Friday 17	Saturday....17	SUNDAY...17	Monday......17	Tuesday.....17
Thursday. 18	Friday 18	Saturday....18	SUNDAY...18	Monday......18	Tuesday.....18	Wednesday.18
Friday 19	Saturday....19	SUNDAY...19	Monday......19	Tuesday.....19	Wednesday.19	Thursday...19
Saturday....20	SUNDAY...20	Monday......20	Tuesday.....20	Wednesday.20	Thursday...20	Friday 20
SUNDAY...21	Monday......21	Tuesday.....21	Wednesday.21	Thursday...21	Friday 21	Saturday....21
Monday......22	Tuesday.....22	Wednesday.22	Thursday...22	Friday 22	Saturday....22	SUNDAY...22
Tuesday.....23	Wednesday.23	Thursday...23	Friday 23	Saturday....23	SUNDAY...23	Monday......23
Wednesday.24	Thursday...24	Friday 24	Saturday....24	SUNDAY...24	Monday......24	Tuesday.....24
Thursday...25	Friday 25	Saturday....25	SUNDAY...25	Monday......25	Tuesday.....25	Wednesday.25
Friday 26	Saturday....26	SUNDAY...26	Monday......26	Tuesday.....26	Wednesday.26	Thursday...26
Saturday....27	SUNDAY...27	Monday......27	Tuesday.....27	Wednesday.27	Thursday...27	Friday 27
SUNDAY...28	Monday......28	Tuesday.....28	Wednesday.28	Thursday...28	Friday 28	Saturday....28
Monday......29	Tuesday.....29	Wednesday.29	Thursday...29	Friday 29	Saturday....29	SUNDAY...29
Tuesday.....30	Wednesday.30	Thursday...30	Friday 30	Saturday....30	SUNDAY...30	Monday......30
Wednesday.31	Thursday...31	Friday 31	Saturday....31	SUNDAY...31	Monday......31	Tuesday.....31

NOTE—To ascertain any day of the week first look in the table for the year required and under the months are figures which refer to the corresponding figures at the head of the columns of days below. For example: To know on what day of the week July 4 was in the year 1895, in the table of years look for 1895, and in a parallel line, under July, is figure 1, which directs to column 1, in which it will be seen that July 4 falls on Thursday.

*1752 same as 1773 from Jan. 1 to Sept. 2. From Sept. 14 to Dec. 31 same as 1780 (Sept. 3-13 were omitted).—This Calendar is from Whitaker's London Almanack, with some revisions.

CHART OF THE HEAVENS.

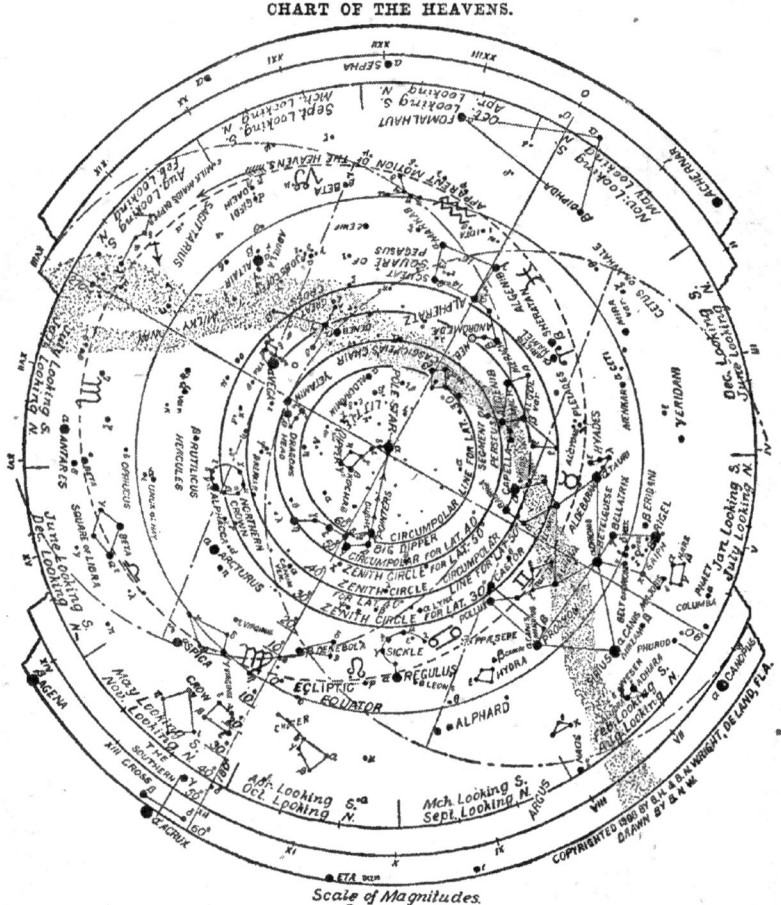

Scale of Magnitudes.

EXPLANATION—The chart of the heavens shows all the bright stars and groups visible in the United States, Canada, Mexico, Cuba and Hawaii. Stars of the third magnitude are sometimes shown in order to complete a figure.

If a bright uncharted body be seen near the "ecliptic circle" it must be a planet. To locate the planets or moon refer to the tables "Position of Planets" and "Moon's Place" in the almanac pages, find the proper signs on the chart on the "ecliptic circle" and an inspection of that part of the heavens, comparing with the chart, will serve to identify the planet and all the surrounding objects. Of course there must be somewhat of distortion south of the equator, but not sufficient to be confusing or to prevent the use of the pointer system. For instance, an extension of the west side of the square of Pegasus three times as far south will come close to Fomalhaut.

Because of the earth's motion from west to east (opposite to the direction of the arrow in the chart), the stars rise 4m. earlier each day or 30m. per week, or 2h. a month. The chart shows the position at 9 p. m. Then if the position for any other hour be desired, as for 7 p. m., count ahead one month, or back one month for 11 p. m., and so on for any hour of the night.

A circle described from the zenith on the "zenith circle" for the desired latitude with a radius of 90° (see graduated meridian) will show about what stars are above the horizon. Thus Capella is near the overhead (zenith) point on latitude 40° north Jan. 15, 9 p. m., as will be the Big Dipper at 3 a. m. Then from these stars all the surrounding visible groups can be identified. The "pointers" being 5° apart and always in sight, may be used as a convenient unit of measure; also when visible the Belt of Orion, 3°, or the sides of the square of Pegasus.

The observer is always supposed to stand under the overhead point and to face south and north alter-nately, bearing in mind that to the right is west when facing south and east when looking north.

STORY OF OUR WORLD FAMILY FOR 1914.

THE SUN—This great head and center of our celestial family, of something like 800 known members, will be affected with his greatest number of spots in 1914-1915. At intervals of about eleven years spots can always be seen on his face and weather conditions are correspondingly affected. These spots vary greatly in size from a diameter of 800 to 50,000 miles. The earth could be rolled into the largest and would be like a marble in a teacup. Some of these spots are holes in the bright photosphere which envelops the dark, solid interior of the sun. This is proven by their change in outline as they apparently move across his face. This class of spots proves that the sun revolves upon his axis in 25.35 days, or apparently, to us, in 27.25 days. There are other spots that do not uniformly change in outline with their change in apparent position. Such are believed to be dense floating cloud masses. The largest spots can easily be seen with the unaided eye protected by smoked or colored glass, which precaution should always be taken to prevent serious injury to the eye.

Twice this year he causes our dark shadow to nearly envelop the moon and twice he causes the moon's shadow to fall upon the earth, thus causing two solar and two lunar eclipses (see Eclipses). These eclipses prove and show the rotundity of the earth, those of the moon enabling us to see the round outline of the earth's shadow on the moon's bright face, and those of the sun by the difference in the rate of motion of the shadow of the moon on the earth, which motion is greatest when it strikes near our horizon.

MERCURY—Very few people have seen this coy planet to know it, yet he is easily seen and distinguishable from a star when one knows just when and where to seek him. He is that member of our planet group nearest the sun, so far as known. Some astronomers claim to have seen one nearer, and to it the name Vulcan has been given. Mercury is so close to the sun that his orbital motion is about double that of the earth, and being only about one-third as distant from the sun it follows he can only be seen during an eclipse of the sun, or for a brief time when he is at or near his greatest angular distance from the sun. As this distance is about 18° and as our morning twilight begins when the sun is 18° directly below the horizon and our evening twilight lasts until the sun is a like distance below the horizon, it follows that Mercury can be best seen at the beginning of the morning and end of the evening twilight when brightest (see "Planets, Brightest"), and always near that point of the horizon cut by the sun. At intervals of 7, 13, 33 and 46 years Mercury passes directly between the earth and sun, when he may be seen on the sun's face—a transit (see under "Eclipses"). These must occur in May or November. This year, Nov. 7, and the next in May, 1924, and again in 1927 (November), again in May, 1937, and November, 1940. The first wholly visible in this country will be in 1953 and 1960. The May transits take place at the descending node at intervals of 13 and 33 years, while those of November occur at the planet's ascending node at 7 and 13 year intervals, three of the latter to one of the former.

VENUS—The most beautiful of our world family and whose very appropriate sign, as the goddess of beauty, is a handled mirror, will be too near the sun for the first three months of the year to attract much attention (see under "Planets, Brightest"). In the course of one revolution about the sun in 225 days she presents to our vision all the phases of the moon and for the same reason, viz., our inability to see all of her illuminated hemisphere except when at her "full" or when she is at superior conjunction, setting at sunrise, being on the opposite side of the earth from the sun (see chart "Visibility of the Planets"). These phases are visible with slight optical aid such as a $15 telescope, good opera or field glass, affording much satisfaction and such pleasure as Galileo experienced when he first saw them by the aid of his homemade telescope. These phases are shown in the annexed cut, which explains why the concave side is always on the side away from the sun as in the case of our moon.

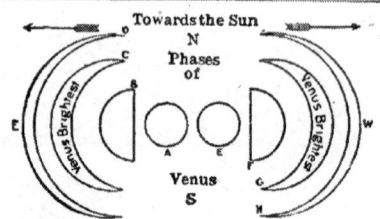

Towards the Sun

Phases of Venus

As seen in the morning west of sun.

As seen in the evening east of sun.

Explanation:
A—Fifteen days before superior conjunction, or Jan. 27, 1914.
B—At greatest elongation west—Feb. 6, 1915.
C—When brightest as a morning star—from Dec. 25, 1914, to Jan. 3, 1915.
D—Just after inferior conjunction, or Dec. 1-10, 1914.
E—Fifteen days after superior conjunction—Feb. 25, 1914.
F—At greatest elongation east—Sept. 18, 1914.
G—When brightest as an evening star—Oct. 18-28, 1914.
H—Just before inferior conjunction—Nov. 21-27, 1914.

VENUS' COURSE AMONG THE STARS, CONJUNCTIONS WITH THE MOON, STARS AND OTHER PLANETS.

April 1, in Aquarius and 20° south of the west side of the great square of Pegasus.
April 27, 5° south of the moon and midway between the Hyades and Pleiades, or seven stars.
May 15, 2° north of Saturn in the most interesting part of the heavens with Aldebaran and the Pleiades below, the glorious Orion south and Auriga to the north (see Chart of the Heavens).
May 27, 3° south of moon in Gemini, forming nearly an equilateral triangle with Procyon to the southeast and Castor and Pollux to the northeast.
June 15, between Procyon and Castor.
June 26, 46' south of the moon in Cancer (the moon's mean apparent diameter is about 30', which will serve as a measure of short distances near the moon). When the distance apart in the conjunctions with the moon is 45' or less there is liable to be an occultation or eclipse of the planet by the moon. The distance apart is given between centers and as seen from the earth's center.
July 13, in Leo 1° north of Regulus in the handle of the Sickle, Venus being the brighter.
July 26, 2° north of moon.
Aug. 5, 10' south of Mars nearly occulting him, making a most striking and beautiful sight when about midway between Regulus and Spica Virginis.
Aug. 24, 3° north of moon.
Aug. 31, 30' north of Spica Virginis.
Sept. 15-30, in square of Libra.
Sept. 18, at greatest elongation east of the sun. 46° 27'.
Sept. 23, 1° north of moon.
Oct. 21, 24' south of moon—an occultation, a comparison of the similar phases of the moon and Venus at this time will be interesting.
Nov. 6 to Dec. 16, retrogrades or moves backward past the stars or from east to west, after which she advances eastward the remainder of the year.
Nov. 18, 1° north of moon; Nov. 21, 2° 45' south of Mars.
Nov. 27, at inferior conjunction with the sun or between the earth and sun, and she will be invisible

for some days before and after this date, and when next visible will be on the other, west, side of the sun as a morning star.

Dec. 15, 7° north of moon and nearly at her brightest again at the close of the year, the bright star Beta Scorpii just south of her.

MARS—The god of war, the ruddy or red planet, will be a very conspicuous object the first part of the year, faint in October and November and invisible in December. His itinerary and aspects will be as follows:

Jan. 1, nearest to the earth or 62,000,000 miles distant, being in Gemini about 3° southwest of Pollux, forming a right angle with Castor. His apparent motion will be backward or from east to west until Feb. 12, and then from west to east.

Jan. 5, at opposition or 180° from the sun, rising at sunset and brightest.

Jan. 11, 34' south of moon and an occultation or eclipse of Mars by the moon.

Feb. 7, 1° 9' south of moon; March 6, 1° 49' south of moon; April 3, 2° south of moon.

April 10, 90° east of sun, passing the meridian at 6 eve—eastern quadrature.

April 21, 2° 34' north of Neptune while yet in Gemini in line with Castor and Pollux and 7° from the latter; May 2, 1° 36' south of moon.

May 30, 42' south of moon and an occultation.

June 23, less than 1° north of Regulus in the end of the handle of the Sickle.

June 27, 36' north of moon, an occultation: July 26, 2° north of moon; Aug. 24, 3½° south.

Sept. 15, 2° 30' south of Spica Virginis; Sept. 21 and Oct. 20, about 5° north of moon.

Nov. 13, 4° 36' north of moon; Nov. 20, 2° north of Beta Scorpii and 7° northwest of Antares.

Nov. 21, 2° 45' south of Venus; Nov. 22, 4° north of Antares.

ASTEROIDS OR PLANETOIDS—About 700 of these "pocket planets" have their orbits between those of Mars and Jupiter. They are believed to be fragments of a broken-up world or planet or planetary ring. The largest of these is less than 500 miles in diameter and most of them less than 100 and the smallest not over ten or fifteen. Only one, Vesta, is ever visible to the naked eye. Because of the smallness in size and density of these bodies a stone dropped from an elevation on one of them would only fall 8½ inches the first second, a bullet shot from one would never return and a stone thrown into space would continue on until under the controlling influence (power of gravitation) of some other body, as our sun or one of the major planets. It would eventually become a meteorite and upon entering the atmospheric envelope of such planet, as our earth, become so rapidly heated by the friction generated as to burst with a loud report, sending its brilliant fragments to earth as aerolites.

JUPITER—The giant planet and partial sun will be too near the sun early in the year for good seeing, being in conjunction with the sun Jan. 20. Inasmuch as his year is equal to thirty of ours he will traverse but one sign or 30° of the zodiac in one year. Throughout most of the year he will be in Capricornus. He will pass his opposition to the sun Aug. 11, rising at sunset and brightest. His conjunctions with the moon will be as follows: April 18, 1° 50' north; May 16, 1° 13' north; June 12, 28' north; an occultation. July 10, 17' north; Aug. 6 and Sept. 12, all occultations in southern latitude; Sept. 29 and Oct. 26, 1° north. Again he will be occulted by the moon Nov. 3 and Dec. 20.

SATURN—The ringed planet will be most conspicuous near the beginning and end of the year, being in conjunction with the sun June 19 and practically invisible for weeks before and after that date. He will be found in Taurus most of the time, only in September, October and November he strays a little over the line into Gemini, and in one of the most interesting parts of the heavens (see mention under Venus at the time of her conjunction with Saturn May 16). His conjunctions with the moon will be as follows: Jan. 9, Feb. 5, March 4 and April 1, in all of which he will be about 6° south of the moon; also Aug. 16, Sept. 13, Oct. 10, Nov. 7 and Dec. 4, in all of which he will be 5° south.

The wonderful ring system of Saturn may be seen to a better advantage in 1914-1915 than will

be the case until 1928-1929. These rings are inclined about 28° to the earth's orbit and about every fifteen years they are presented edgewise to us and are then invisible to the very best of telescopes for several days; again when their dark or unilluminated side is toward us they disappear for several months. (See the annexed illustration, which shows their appearance in 1907 and in 1914.) From this year on they will gradually grow dimmer until 1922, when they will disappear, being edgewise to us, and as they are only about fifty miles thick and 1,000,000,000 of miles distant no telescope can bring them out. There are at least three rings, the outermost having a diameter of 173,000 miles. The astronomer Herschel declared it his belief that the Almighty left mankind this inheritance of unfinished work of world making as a hint, throwing light upon his methods. For the belief was and still is that in time these rings will break up and become transformed into additional satellites or

SATURN AND HIS RINGS.
Upper figure shows him as seen in 1907 with comparative size of the earth to the left. Lower figure shows him as he will appear in June, 1914.

moons, of which Saturn has ten. Always moonlight nights there and their day only ten hours long and a year consists of 25,000 days.

URANUS—May be most certainly seen early in March. March 4 he will be 9' south of Jupiter in Capricornus. He will be brightest in August and can just be detected by the naked eye and a perfect knowledge of his position previously located on a good chart of the heavens, using the pointer system, picking out certain well known stars whose line of direction is toward him.

NEPTUNE—The most distant of our planet family known will be best seen in January and with telescopic aid only. He will, however, be 2° 34' south of Mars April 21. (See mention under Mars.)

COMETS—Besides the previously named members there are about 500 known comets which belong to this family. These are divided into groups according to the particular planet under whose control they are. In this affiliation they are not constant, however, occasionally exchanging to another as influences are brought to bear upon them by the worlds near which they pass in their vast journeyings through space. We know of no important comet due this year, though new ones are liable to appear at any time, possibly visiting us for the first time.

All these, with our sun, earth and planets are together moving through space at the rate of 600 miles per minute toward a point in the heavens near the great sun Vega Lyra, which point is known as the "apex of the sun's way."

THE BRIGHTEST STARS.

NAME.	Constellation or group.	Magnitude. (v.; variable.)	Right ascension. Sidereal time.	Declination.	For upper meridian passage. Mn. time.	For rising, subtract For setting, add.† For lat. 30° N.	For lat. 40° N.	For lat. 50° N.
			H. M.	Deg. Min.	H. M.	H. M.	H. M.	H. M.
Alpheratz	Andromeda	2.1	0 4	+28 36	0 3	7 18	7 52	8 39
Caph	Cassiopeia	2.4	0 4	+58 40	0 4			
Algenib	Pegasus	2.8	0 9	+14 41	0 8	6 39	6 51	7 18
Alpha	Phoenix	3.0	0 21	−43 19	0 21	3 51*	2 25*	
Schedir	Cassiopeia	2.3 v	0 35	+56 30	0 35	9 56		
Diphda	Cetus (whale)	2.2	0 39	−18 39	0 38	5 20	4 53	4 36
Gamma	Cassiopeia	2.3	0 51	+60 14	0 50			
Mirach	Andromeda	2.2	1 5	+35 9	1 4	7 37	8 29	9 48
Delta	Cassiopeia	2.4	1 20	+59 46	1 19			
Polaris	Ursa Minor	2.2	1 27	+88 50	1 24			
Achernar	Eridanus	0.4	1 34	−57 41	1 34	1 37*		
Sheratan	Aries (ram) ♈	2.8	1 50	+20 22	1 49	6 54	7 14	7 52
Almaach	Andromeda	2.2	1 58	+41 54	1 57	8 0	9 21	
Hamel	Aries ♈	2.1	2 2	+23 3	2 1	7 1	7 26	8 6
Mira	Cetus	2.1 v	2 14	− 3 26	2 13	5 54	5 51	5 46
Menkar	Cetus	2.6	2 58	+ 3 44	2 56	6 12	6 13	6 20
Algol	Perseus	2.6 v	3 2	+40 37	3 0	8 0	9 10	
Marfak	Perseus	1.9	3 18	+49 33	3 18	8 52		
Alcyone	Taurus (bull) ♉	3.1	3 41	+23 50	3 41	7 3	7 29	8 13
Aldebaran	Taurus ♉	1.0	4 31	+16 20	4 29	6 39	6 58	7 26
Capella	Auriga	0.1	5 10	+45 55	5 9	8 28	10 14	
Rigel	Orion	0.3	5 10	− 8 18	5 9	5 45	5 31	5 27
El Nath	Taurus ♉	1.8	5 21	+28 32	5 19	7 18	7 52	8 49
Mintaka	Orion	2.3	5 27	− 0 22	5 26	6 2	6 2	6 2
Al Nilam	Orion	1.8	5 32	− 1 15	5 30	6 1	6 1	6 1
Phact	Colomba (dove)	2.7	5 36	−34 8	5 35	4 30	3 37*	2 33*
Saiph	Orion	2.3	5 43	− 9 42	5 42	5 42	5 26	5 17
Betelgeuse	Orion	0.9	5 50	+ 7 24	5 49	6 22	6 26	6 42
Menkalina	Auriga	2.0	5 53	+44 56	5 51	8 22	9 53	
Canopus	Argus	0.8	6 22	−52 39	6 21	2 46*		
Alhena	Gemini (twins) ♊	2.0	6 33	+16 29	6 31	6 44	6 59	7 24
Sirius	Canis Major	−1.4	6 41	−16 36	6 40	5 25	5 1	4 45
Adhara	Canis Major	1.6	6 55	−28 51	6 54	4 51	4 7	3 20
Castor	Gemini ♊	1.9	7 29	−32 5	7 27	7 30	8 11	9 19
Procyon	Canis Minor	0.5	7 35	+ 5 27	7 33	6 17	6 19	6 30
Pollux	Gemini ♊	1.2	7 40	+28 15	7 38	7 17	7 50	8 42
Beta	Cancer (crab) ♋	3.8	8 12	+ 9 28	8 10	6 27	6 33	6 50
Alphard	Hydra	2.1	9 23	− 8 16	9 21	5 45	5 37	5 24
Regulus	Leo (lion) ♌	1.3	10 4	+12 25	10 1	6 34	6 44	7 4
Eta	Argus	1.6 v	10 42	−59 13	10 39	1 3*		
Dubhe	Ursa Major	2.0	10 58	+62 14	10 56			
Denebola	Leo ρ	2.2	11 44	+15 4	11 42	6 41	6 54	7 18
Acrux	Southern Cross	1.6	12 22	−62 36	12 19	1 0*		
Beta	Corvus (crow)	2.8	12 30	−22 54	12 27	5 9	4 35	4 13
Mizar	Ursa Major	2.4	13 20	+55 22	13 18			
Spica	Virgo (virgin) ♍	1.1	13 20	−10 42	13 18	5 40	5 23	5 12
Agena	Centaurus	0.7	13 57	−59 56	13 54	1 9*		
Arcturus	Bootes	0.2	14 12	+19 39	14 9	6 42	7 12	7 45
Bengula	Centaurus	0.2	14 33	−60 28	14 30	0 53*		
Alpha	Libra (scales) ♎	2.9	14 46	−15 40	14 43	5 27	5 4	4 47
Kochab	Ursa Minor	2.2	14 51	+74 31	14 48			
Alpha	Northern Crown	2.3	15 31	+27 1	15 29	7 13	7 41	8 34
Unuk	Serpent Bearer	2.7	15 40	+ 6 42	15 37	6 20	6 23	6 35*
Beta	Scorpion ♏	2.9	16 0	−19 34	15 57	5 16	4 54	4 24
Antares	Scorpion ♏	1.2	16 24	−26 14	16 20	4 58	4 20	3 42
Rutilicus	Hercules	2.8	16 26	+21 41	16 23	6 58	7 20	7 57
Etamin	Dragon	2.5	17 54	+51 30	17 51	9 8		
Vega	Lyra	0.1	18 34	+38 42	18 30	7 52	8 51	10 52
Delta	Sagittarius ♐	2.1	18 50	−26 25	18 46	4 58	4 19	3 38*
Altair	Eagle	0.9	19 46	+ 8 38	19 43	6 24	6 30	6 45
Alpha	Capricorn ♑	3.7	20 13	−12 49	20 9	5 29	5 19	4 56
Deneb	Cygnus (swan)	1.4	20 38	+44 58	20 35	9 22	9 56	
Alderamin	Cepheus	2.6	21 16	+62 13	21 12			
Beta	Aquarius ♒	2.9	21 27	− 5 58	21 23	5 41	5 43	5 35
Enif	Pegasus	2.4	21 40	+ 9 28	21 36	6 26	6 33	6 50
Alpha	The Crane	1.9	22 33	−47 24	21 58	3 26*	1 21*	
Fomalhaut	Pisces Australis	1.3	22 53	−30 6	22 48	4 46	4 0	3 11
Markab	Pegasus	2.5	23 0	+14 44	22 56	6 39	6 52	7 16
Iota	Pisces ♓	4.8	23 35	+ 5 9	23 31	6 16	6 17	6 25

†Explanation: By the absolute scale of magnitudes stars brighter than Aldebaran and Altair are indicated by fractional or negative quantities; thus Vega 0.2 and Sirius —1.4. As the magnitudes increase the brilliancy decreases, each increase of a unit being equal to a decrease of about two and one-half in brightness.

To ascertain when any star or constellation will be on the upper meridian add the number opposite in the column "For Meridian Passage" to the figures in the table on the following page "Sidereal Noon," taking note whether such figures be "Morn." or "Eve." If "Morn." and the sum is more than 12h. the result will be Eve. of same day; if "Eve." and the sum is more than 12h. the result will be Morn. of the next day. Having found the time of meridian passage, for the rising subtract and for the setting add the numbers opposite the star in the column headed "For Rising and Setting" and observe the directions as to Morn. and Eve. given for the meridian passage. Those marked (.....) in the last columns are circumpolar. Stars having an asterisk (*) in the last columns are only to be seen in the far south and then when near the meridian, as the vapors of the horizon will prevent seeing them when they rise or set. To tell how high up from the nearest point of the horizon a star will be at its meridian passage subtract the star's declination from 90° and if the result is less than the latitude of the place

of the observer that star will neither rise nor set, but is circumpolar, and the difference between that result and the latitude shows the star's altitude above the north point of the horizon or below the southern horizon. Or (90°—Dec.) —lat. =alt. or elevation of the star above the nearest point of the horizon at meridian passage for stars of a southern declination. Examples:

```
Sidereal noon, Oct. 30,            9:28 p. m.
Fomalhaut "in Merid." col,        22:48
                                  ------
                                  32:16
             Subtract,            24:00
                                  ------
                                  8:16 p. m. of the 31st,
                                       time of merid-
                                       ian passage.
Fomalhaut ris. and set. col. add 4:00 for lat. 40° N.
                                  ------
                                  12:16 = 0:16 a. m. of
                                       Nov. 1, the time
                                       of setting.
```

Fomalhaut Dec., 30° S, 90° – 30° = 60°, – 40° = 20°, altitude of Fomalhaut in latitude 40° at its meridian passage. To measure celestial distances with the eye keep in mind that one-third of the distance from the zenith to the horizon is 30°. For smaller measurements use the belt of Orion, 3° long, or the sides of the Square of Pegasus; the "pointers" in the "big dipper," which are nearly 5° apart—a convenient celestial yardstick because always to be seen. In the case of a star whose dec. is such as to bring it nearer to the zenith than to a horizon at meridian passage, it will be more convenient to use its zenith distance as a means of locating it. The difference between the latitude and dec. is this zenith distance. If the dec. is greater than the latitude then such distance is to be counted northward, otherwise southward from the zenith.

SIDEREAL NOON OR MERIDIAN PASSAGE OF THE VERNAL EQUINOX.
(For use in connection with star table. See note under same.)

	Jan.	Feb.	March.	April.	May.	June	July.	Aug.	Sept.	Oct.	Nov.	Dec
	H. M.	H. M.	H. M.	H. M.	H. M.	H. M.	H. M.	H. M.	H. M.	H. M.	H. M.	H. M.
1	5 19	3 17	1 27	11 25	9 27	7 25	5 27	3 26	1 24	11 22	9 20	7 22
2	5 15	3 13	1 23	11 21	9 23	7 21	5 24	3 22	1 20	11 18	9 16	7 18
3	5 11	3 9	1 19	11 17	9 19	7 18	5 20	3 18	1 16	11 14	9 12	7 14
4	5 7	3 5	1 15	11 13	9 16	7 14	5 16	3 14	1 12	11 10	9 8	7 10
5	5 3	3 2	1 11	11 10	9 12	7 10	5 12	3 10	1 8	11 7	9 4	7 6
6	4 59	2 58	1 7	11 6	9 8	7 6	5 8	3 6	1 4	11 3	9 0	7 2
7	4 56	2 54	1 4	11 2	9 4	7 2	5 4	3 2	1 0	10 58	8 56	6 58
8	4 52	2 50	1 0	10 58	9 0	6 58	5 0	2 58	0 56	10 54	8 52	6 54
9	4 48	2 46	0 56	10 54	8 56	6 54	4 56	2 54	0 52	10 50	8 48	6 51
10	4 44	2 42	0 52	10 50	8 52	6 50	4 52	2 50	0 48	10 46	8 45	6 47
11	4 40	2 38	0 48	10 46	8 48	6 46	4 48	2 46	0 44	10 42	8 41	6 43
12	4 36	2 34	0 44	10 42	8 44	6 42	4 44	2 42	0 40	10 39	8 37	6 39
13	4 32	2 30	0 40	10 38	8 40	6 38	4 40	2 38	0 37	10 35	8 33	6 35
14	4 28	2 26	0 36	10 34	8 36	6 34	4 36	2 34	0 33	10 31	8 29	6 31
15	4 24	2 22	0 32	10 30	8 32	6 30	4 32	2 31	0 29	10 28	8 25	6 27
16	4 20	2 18	0 28	10 26	8 28	6 26	4 28	2 27	0 25	10 23	8 21	6 23
17	4 16	2 14	0 24	10 22	8 24	6 23	4 25	2 23	0 21	10 19	8 17	6 19
18	4 12	2 10	0 20	10 18	8 20	6 19	4 21	2 19	0 17	10 15	8 13	6 15
19	4 8	2 6	0 16	10 14	8 17	6 15	4 17	2 15	0 13	10 11	8 9	6 11
20	4 4	2 3	0 12	10 11	8 13	6 11	4 13	2 11	0 9	10 7	8 5	6 8
21	4 0	1 59	0 8	10 7	8 9	6 7	4 9	2 7	0 5	10 3	8 1	6 4
22	3 57	1 55	0 5	10 3	8 5	6 3	4 5	2 3	11 57	9 59	7 57	6 0
23	3 53	1 51	0 1	9 59	8 1	5 59	4 1	1 59	11 53	9 55	7 53	5 56
24	3 49	1 47	11 57	9 55	7 57	5 55	3 57	1 55	11 49	9 51	7 49	5 52
25	3 45	1 43	11 53	9 51	7 53	5 51	3 53	1 51	11 45	9 47	7 46	5 48
26	3 41	1 39	11 49	9 47	7 49	5 47	3 49	1 47	11 41	9 43	7 42	5 44
27	3 37	1 35	11 45	9 43	7 45	5 43	3 45	1 43	11 38	9 40	7 38	5 40
28	3 33	1 31	11 41	9 39	7 41	5 39	3 41	1 39	11 34	9 36	7 34	5 36
29	3 29		11 37	9 35	7 37	5 35	3 37	1 35	11 30	9 32	7 30	5 32
30	3 25		11 33	9 31	7 33	5 31	3 33	1 32	11 26	9 28	7 26	5 28
31	3 21		11 29		7 29		3 30	1 28		9 24		5 24

NOTE—Black figures are p. m.; all others a. m.

THE SIGNS AND CONSTELLATIONS OF THE ZODIAC

Until recently it was taken for granted that the present relationship between signs and constellations of the zodiac was generally understood, as all astronomical textbooks mention their disagreement and explain the cause. The numerous letters of inquiry concerning differences between the data in this almanac and certain others show the necessity for this note of explanation.

Thousands of years ago when the zodiac, that belt of the heavens about 16° in width within which move the moon and planets, was formed and divided into twelve parts or seasons called signs, each containing certain star groups called constellations, each was given the name of an object or animal which never did bear any relationship to the configuration of the stars in that group or division, but which did or is supposed to have reference to certain astronomical or other facts. Thus Libra, ♎, the scales or balance, comes at the autumnal equinox when there is an equilibrium or balance between the length of day and night the world over. Aquarius, ♒, the water-bearer, and whose sign is the Egyptian sign for running water, comes at the season of greatest rains in Egypt, and so on.

Since the time when these divisions were made and named, owing to the precession of the equinoxes, resulting from the differing polar and equatorial diameters of the earth, the signs have moved back west nearly a whole division or constellation and where ♈ was the first, ♓ now is. Hence, though the sun now enters the sign ♈ March 20, it is a month later when he enters the constellation ♈. It must be apparent, therefore, that any supposed influence or relationship which early astrologers attributed to the position of the sun, moon or planets when in certain of these divisions can no longer exist, as the sign now only represents that space or division of the zodiac where the controlling constellation was 2,000 or more years ago, but is not now. Nevertheless some almanacs still give the signs for the moon's place, which is very misleading to those who attempt to follow her in her course among the stars. Hence, this almanac gives the constellations and discards the ancient picture of the disemboweled man as relics of the age of superstition. The sign is retained for sun's place in connection with the seasons and sun's path through the zodiac each month because of its relationship to the equinoxes and solstices.

EPHEMERIS OF THE PRINCIPAL PLANETS FOR 1914.

Central standard time.

DATE.	VENUS. Right ascension.	VENUS. Northern states.	VENUS. Southern states.	MARS. Right ascension.	MARS. Northern states.	MARS. Southern states.	JUPITER. Right ascension.	JUPITER. Northern states.	JUPITER. Southern states.	SATURN. Right ascension.	SATURN. Northern states.	SATURN. Southern states.
	Hour	Rises. Morn. H. M.	Rises. Morn. H. M.	Hour.	Sets. Morn. H. M.	Sets. Morn. H. M.	Hour.	Rises. Morn. H. M.	Rises. Morn. H. M.	Hours.	Morn. Sets. H. M.	Morn. Sets. H. M.
Jan. 1	XVIII¼	6 50	6 27	VII¼	8 12	7 47	XIX¾	....Invisible...		IV¾	5 17	4 58
11	XIX	7 3	6 40	VII	7 10	6 43	XX	....Invisible...		IV¾	4 35	4 16
21	XIX¾	7 17	6 56	VI¾	6 24	5 45	XX	....Invisible...		IV½	3 54	3 35
Feb. 1	XX¾	Sets.	Sets.	VI½	5 30	5 1	XX¼	6 49	6 30	IV½	3 9	2 50
11	XXI¾	Eve.	Eve.	VI½	4 44	4 17	XX½	6 17	5 59	IV½	2 29	2 10
21	XXII½	5 46	5 56	VI½	4 6	3 39	XX¾	5 40	5 27	IV¾	1 51	1 32
Mch. 1	XXIII	6 5	6 11	VI½	3 39	3 12	XX¾	5 19	5 2	IV¾	1 21	1 2
11	XXIII¾	6 30	6 32	VI¾	3 8	2 42	XX¾	4 50	4 30	IV¾	0 43	0 24
21	XXIV½	6 53	6 51	VII	2 39	2 14	XXI	4 10	3 58	IV¾	Eve.	Eve.
April 1	I½	7 18	7 11	VII¼	2 10	1 45	XXI¼	3 36	3 21	IV¾	11 29	11 10
11	II¼	7 43	7 31	VII½	1 45	1 21	XXI¼	3 3	2 46	IV¾	10 53	10 34
21	III	8 8	7 52	VII¾	1 21	0 58	XXI½	2 27	2 12	V	10 19	9 59
May 1	III¾	8 31	8 12	VIII¼	1 3	0 36	XXI½	1 51	1 37	V	9 44	9 24
11	IV¾	8 55	8 33	VIII½	0 31	0 11	XXI½	1 15	1 1	V¼	9 10	8 50
21	V½	9 14	8 50	VIII¾	Eve.	Eve.	XXI½	Eve.	Eve.	V¼	8 38	8 17
June 1	VI½	9 29	9 5	IX¼	11 42	11 25	XXI½	11 53	11 39	V¼	....Invisible...	
11	VII½	9 38	9 15	IX¾	11 19	11 2	XXI½	11 17	11 3	V½	....Invisible...	
21	VIII¼	9 41	9 21	X	11 0	10 44	XXI½	10 37	10 23	V½	....Invisible...	
July 1	IX	9 38	9 21	X¼	10 26	10 16	XXI½	9 58	9 44	V½	Rises Morn.	Rises Morn.
11	X	9 29	9 16	X¾	10 2	9 53	XXI½	9 16	9 2	V¾	2 28	2 49
21	X¾	9 18	9 9	XI	9 34	9 29	XXI½	8 35	8 20	V¾		
Aug. 1	XI½	9 2	8 58	XI½	9 6	9 3	XXI½	....Invisible...		VI	1 51	2 11
11	XII	8 46	8 46	XII	8 41	8 40	XXI½	Sets.	Sets.	VI	1 16	1 36
21	XII¾	8 28	8 33	XII¼	8 14	8 16	XXI¼	Morn.	Morn.	VI	0 41	1 1
Sept. 1	XIII½	8 6	8 18	XII¾	7 47	7 51	XXI¼	3 29	3 45	VI	Eve.	0 18
11	XIV	7 50	8 4	XIII	7 23	7 29	XXI¼	2 45	2 59	VI	11 25	Eve.
21	XIV¾	7 34	7 52	XIII½	7 0	7 9	XXI¼	1 59	2 16	VI¼	10 45	11 8
Oct. 1	XV¼	7 15	7 37	XIV	6 37	6 48	XXI¼	1 20	1 37	VI¼	10 11	10 30
11	XV¾	6 57	7 22	XIV½	6 15	6 28	XXI¼	0 41	0 58	VI¼	9 31	9 51
21	XVI¼	6 39	7 5	XIV¾	5 55	6 10	XXI¼	Eve.	Eve.	VI¼	8 52	9 12
Nov. 1	XVI½	6 11	6 39	XV¼	5 20	5 42	XXI¼	11 19	11 35	VI¼	8 8	8 28
11	XVI¾	5 34	6 3	XV¾	5 16	5 35	XXI¼	10 45	11 1	VI¼	7 27	7 47
21	XVI¼	Rises.	Rises.	XVI¼	5 1	5 22	XXI¼	10 11	10 27	VI¼	6 45	7 5
Dec. 1	XVI½	Morn.	Morn.	XVII	4 47	5 10	XXI½	9 40	9 55	VI¼	Sets.	Sets.
11	XV¾	5 32	5 15	XVII½	4 38	5 2	XXI½	9 8	9 23	VI¼	Morn.	Morn.
21	XVI	4 45	4 30	XVIII	...Invisible...		XXI½	8 44	8 54	V¾	7 17	6 57

NOTE—Inasmuch as the meridian passage of the major planets is an invisible event for one-half of the year, and that of Venus always so, we have substituted the right ascensions. This is of greater utility, inasmuch as by it, in connection with the chart of the heavens, the paths of these planets may be followed as they pass through the constellations or signs of the zodiac, as they may always be found near the ecliptic circle. On the chart the right ascension (corresponding to longitude on the earth) is marked in Roman characters around the margin and the hour spaces can readily be divided into the fractions given in the table. Then connect the point of right ascension (R. A.) indicated with the pole star by any straight edge, as the margin of an envelope, and where such line cuts the ecliptic circle will be the approximate location of the planet.

EXAMPLE—The right ascension of Venus, as shown by the table, on May 11 is IV¾ and that point in the right ascension circle connected with Polaris intersects the ecliptic circle just east of the Pleiades or seven stars, where Venus will be located at that time.

The time of rising and setting is expressed in mean or sun time. If the standard time is desired see table for converting the one into the other. But unless the observer has a water horizon and desires to know the exact time of the rising and setting the figures are quite near enough for purposes of identification.

DIFFERENCE IN TIME.

When it is 12 o'clock noon in New York, N. Y., or other places having eastern time, the corresponding time in the cities named below is:

Aden, Arabia	8:00 p. m.,	Monday
Amsterdam, Holland	5:20 p. m.,	Monday
Apia, Samoa	5:33 a. m.,	Tuesday
Berlin, Germany	5:53 p. m.,	Monday
Bern, Switzerland	5:29 p. m.,	Monday
Bombay, India	9:51 p. m.,	Monday
Bremen, Germany	5:33 p. m.,	Monday
Brussels, Belgium	5:17 p. m.,	Monday
Calcutta, India	10:53 p. m.,	Monday
Chicago, Ill.	*11:00 a. m.,	Monday
Christiania, Norway	5:42 p. m.,	Monday
City of Mexico, Mexico	10:24 a. m.,	Monday
Colon, Panama	11:40 a. m.,	Monday
Constantinople, Turkey	6:56 p. m.,	Monday
Copenhagen, Denmark	5:40 p. m.,	Monday
Denver, Colorado	†10:00 a. m.,	Monday
Dublin, Ireland	4:34 p. m.,	Monday
Edinburgh, Scotland	4:47 p. m.,	Monday
Hamburg, Germany	5:10 p. m.,	Monday
Havana, Cuba	11:30 a. m.,	Monday
Havre, France	5:00 p. m.,	Monday
Hongkong, China	12:37 a. m.,	Tuesday
Honolulu, Hawaii	6:29 a. m.,	Monday
Lisbon, Portugal	5:00 p. m.,	Monday
Liverpool, England	4:48 p. m.,	Monday
London, England	5:00 p. m.,	Monday
Madrid, Spain	4:45 p. m.,	Monday
Manila, Philippines	1:03 a. m.,	Tuesday
Melbourne, Australia	2:39 a. m.,	Tuesday
Paris, France	5:09 p. m.,	Monday
Pekin, China	12:45 a. m.,	Tuesday
Pretoria, South Africa	6:55 p. m.,	Monday
Rome, Italy	5:49 p. m.,	Monday
Rio de Janeiro, Brazil	2:07 p. m.,	Monday
St. Petersburg, Russia	7:01 p. m.,	Monday
San Francisco, Cal.	‡9:00 a. m.,	Monday
San Juan, Porto Rico	12:35 p. m.,	Monday
Sitka, Alaska	7:58 a. m.,	Monday
Stockholm, Sweden	6:12 p. m.,	Monday
Sydney, New South Wales	3:04 a. m.,	Tuesday
The Hague, Holland	5:17 p. m.,	Monday
Tokyo, Japan	2:18 a. m.,	Tuesday
Valparaiso, Chile	12:13 p. m.,	Monday
Vienna, Austria	6:05 p. m.,	Monday
Yokohama, Japan	2:19 a. m.,	Tuesday

*Same in all places having central time. †In all places having mountain time. ‡In all places having Pacific time.

VISIBILITY OF THE PRINCIPAL PLANETS, 1914.

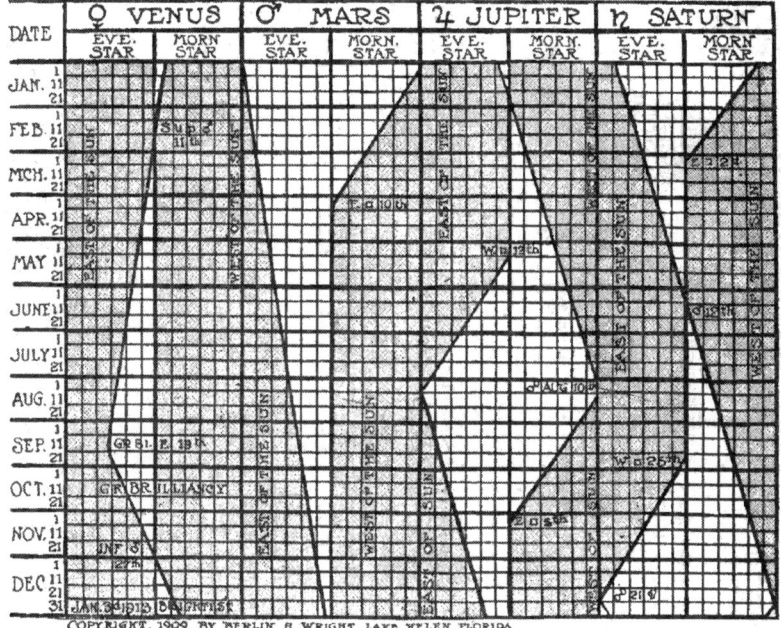

COPYRIGHT, 1909, BY BERLIN H WRIGHT LAKE HELEN, FLORIDA

EXPLANATORY NOTE—The figure shows at a glance when all of the major planets are brightest and whether east of the sun (evening star) or west of him and morning stars, at the time. It also shows the relative duration of visibility and brightness as to the superior planets, Mars, Jupiter and Saturn. With Venus, the light shaded portion simply is the approximate measure of duration and place of visibility and not of brilliancy, while of the others it (the light portion) shows both the duration and brilliancy. Thus Jupiter will be brightest the 10th of August and then will shine equally in the morning and evening; the last of December he will decrease almost to invisibility. Venus, being an inferior planet between the earth and sun, can never be seen opposite the sun, as in the case of the others on the chart, nor is she at her greatest

brilliancy when farthest (in angular distance) from the sun, as shown.

From this it will be seen that the light portions represent the comparative angular distance of the planets from the sun. Then each of the twelve spaces will be one hour spaces of 15° each, when the day and night are equal, and more when the night is more than twelve hours' duration.

Of course the chart can only show an approximation as to the boundaries of the light portion. It will, however, prove a valuable aid to the average person who is not an astronomer in understanding the movements of the planets and definitely settling the question of what constitutes evening and morning stars. In this connection see "Planets, Brightest," "Evening and Morning Stars" and the table of "Rising, Setting and Meridian Passage of the Planets."

PLANETS BRIGHTEST OR BEST SEEN, INVISIBLE, EVENING AND MORNING STARS, ETC.

Mercury will be brightest as an evening star Feb. 15-20 and Oct. 18-22, setting about 1 hour and 15 minutes after the sun; also April 5-10 and Nov. 17-27 as a morning star, rising about 1 hour and 15 minutes before the sun. Invisible at all other times. Venus will be brightest as an evening star Oct. 20-26 and again as a morning star Dec. 27 to Jan. 3, 1915. Mars will be an all night star and brightest in January and invisible in December. Jupiter will be invisible in January and brightest the latter part of July and first part of August. Saturn will be very bright and almost an all night star at the

beginning of the year and invisible in the month of June. Venus will be a morning star until Feb. 11 and after Nov. 27 and an evening star the balance of the year. Mars will be an evening star as long as visible, or until December. Jupiter will be a morning star from Jan. 20 to May 12 and an evening star the remainder of the year. Saturn will be a morning star from June 13 to Sept. 25 and an evening star the remainder of the year.

In this almanac a planet is called a morning star when rising after midnight and an evening star when it rises before midnight.

NUMBER OF THE STARS.

According to the best astronomers the number of stars that can be seen by a person of average eyesight is only about 7,000. The number visible

through the telescope has been estimated by J. E. Gore at 70,000,000 and by Profs. Newcomb and Young at 100,000,000.

CHART SHOWING LIGHT AND DARK MOON FOR 1914.

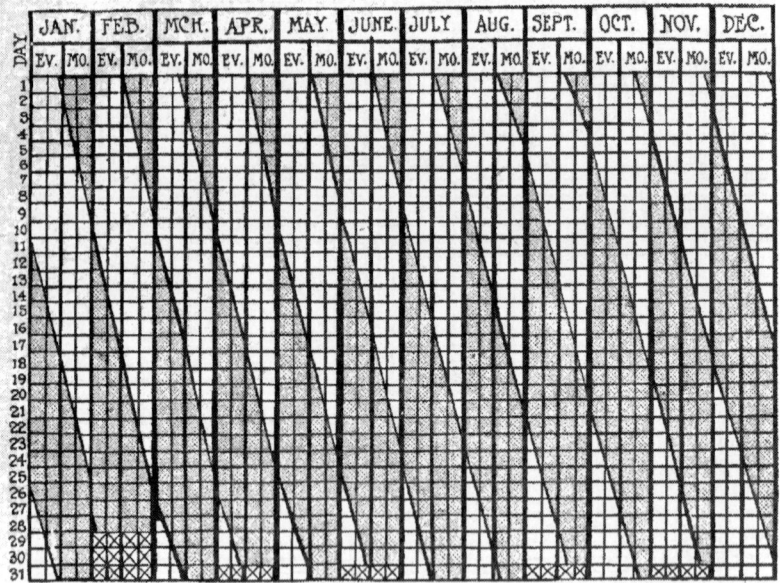

EXPLANATION—The small spaces represent 3 hours of time, or 6 hours in the morning and 6 hours in the evening, and the middle division the midnight line. The light portions show approximately the number of hours of moonlight or the reverse for each night of the year. Thus in April the moon will set at midnight on the 1st, at 3 a. m. on the 5th and at 6 a. m. on the 10th, shining all night, and will rise at 3 a. m. on the 26th, when the last three hours of the night will be daylight, and there will be no moonlight from the 24th to the 26th and at the last of the month there will be moonlight for the first half of the night.

FACTS ABOUT THE SUN AND PLANETS.

Name.	Diameter, Miles.	Distance from sun. Miles.	Period or rev.Days.
Sun	866,400	....	....
Mercury	3,030	36,000,000	88
Venus	7,700	67,200,000	225
Earth	7,918	92,900,000	365
Mars	4,230	141,500,000	687
Jupiter	86,500	483,300,000	4,333
Saturn	73,000	886,000,000	10,759
Uranus	31,900	1,781,900,000	30,687
Neptune	34,800	2,791,600,000	60,181

The sun's surface is 12,000 and its volume 1,300,000 times that of the earth, but the mass is only 332,000 times as great and its density about one-quarter that of the earth. The force of gravity at the surface of the sun is twenty-seven times greater than that at the surface of the earth. The sun rotates on its axis once in 25.3 days at the equator, but the time is longer in the higher latitudes, from which fact it is presumed that the sun is not solid, at least as to its surface.

THE EARTH AND THE MOON.

Earth—The equatorial diameter of the earth is 7,926.5 miles and the polar diameter 7,899.5 miles; equatorial circumference, 25,000. The linear velocity of the rotation of the earth on its axis at the equator is 24,840 miles a day, or 1,440 feet a second; its velocity in its orbit around the sun is approximately nineteen miles per second, the length of the orbit being about 560,000,000 miles. The superficial area of the earth, according to Encke, the astronomer, is 197,108,580 square miles, of which two-thirds is water and one-third land. The planetary mass is about 256,000,000 cubic miles.

Moon—The moon has a diameter of 2,163 miles, a circumference of about 6,800 miles and a surface area of 14,685,000 square miles. Her mean distance from the earth is 238,840 miles. The volume of the moon is about 1-49th that of the earth and the density about 3⅗ that of water. The time from new moon to new moon is 29 days 12 hours 44.05 minutes. The moon has no atmosphere and no water and is a dead world.

Light travels at the rate of 186,300 miles per second. It requires 8 minutes and 8 seconds for light to come from the sun to the earth.

ROMAN AND GREEK GODS AND GODDESSES.

Roman.	Greek.	Divinity of.
Apollo	Apollon	The sun.
Aurora	Eos	The dawn.
Eolus	Eolus	The winds.
Bacchus	Dyonysus	Wine.
Bellona	Enyo	War.
Ceres	Demeter	Harvest.
Cupid	Eros	Love.
Cybele	Rhea	Nature.
Diana	Artemis	The chase.
Juno	Hera	Heaven.
Jupiter	Zeus	Heaven.
Mars	Ares	War.
Mercury	Hermes	Commerce.
Minerva	Athena	Wisdom.
Neptune	Poseidon	Sea.
Pluto	Hades	Lower world.
Saturn	Kronos	Agriculture.
Venus	Aphrodite	Love.
Vesta	Hestia	Purity.
Vulcan	Hephestus	Fire.

ECLIPSES FOR THE YEAR 1914.

There will be four eclipses this year, two of the sun and two of the moon, and a transit of Mercury, as follows:

I. Annular of the sun Feb. 24, invisible in North America; visible in the southern Pacific ocean, antarctic region and extreme southern end of South America.

II. Partial of the moon on the evening of March 11 and morning of the 12th. The size of the eclipse will be about 11 digits, as shown in the annexed figure when at (b) or the middle. The first contact of the limbs of the shadow and the moon will

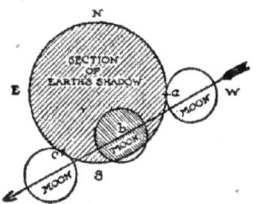

Lunar eclipse of March 11.

take place at (a) on the eastern limb of the moon, from which point she will pass in the direction of the arrow through the great block shadow of the earth, whose presence and boundary is only made visible by the immersion of the full moon's bright face therein—one of the visible proofs of the rotundity of the earth, as only a round body can cast a round shadow. The following is the standard time of the different phases:

ville, thence northerly to Indianapolis, Des Moines, Fargo and Winnipeg roughly marks the southern and western boundary of the area of visibility and west and south of this line no part of the eclipse will be visible.

IV. Partial of the moon Sept. 4. The beginning only will be visible in the United States and that only on the Pacific coast, as far east as Colorado and New Mexico, where the moon will be setting as the eclipse begins and to the west of which the moon will set more or less eclipsed on her southern limb, as shown in the annexed cut. The Pa-

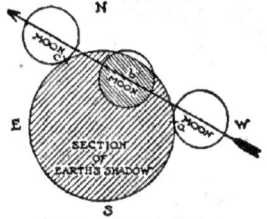

Lunar eclipse of Sept. 4.

cific standard time of the visible phases is: Beginning at (a) 4:16 a. m., middle at (b) 5:55 a. m. It will be seen by the cuts that at the time of the eclipse II. the moon will be moving southward, being at her descending node, while in this one she will be at her ascending node and moving northward.

V. A transit of the planet Mercury across the disk of the sun Nov. 7. The sun will rise with

	Inter.-Col.	Eastern.	Central.	Mountain.	Pacific.
	H.M.	H.M.	H.M.	H.M.	H.M.
Begins at (a)	10:42 p. m.	9:42 p. m.	8:42 p. m.	7:42 p. m.	6:42 p. m.
Middle at (b)	0:13 a. m.	11:13 p. m.	10:13 p. m.	9:13 p. m.	8:13 p. m.
Ends at (c)	1:44 a. m.	0:44 a. m.	11:44 p. m.	10:44 p. m.	9:44 p. m.

III. Total of the sun Aug. 21, visible as a small partial eclipse on the sun's northern limb in northeastern North America. Throughout the great lakes region the sun will rise with the eclipse on. A line from Newport, R. I., through New York city to Washington, D. C., thence westerly to Louis-

the planet on its face. This event can only be seen with the aid of a small telescope, opera or field glass, and smoked or stained glass should always be used between the eye and instrument, as otherwise the eye will suffer seriously from the concentrated rays of the sun.

CHURCH CALENDAR FOR 1914.

Jan. 1—New Year's day (circum.).
Jan. 6—Epiphany—12th day.
Jan. 25—St. Paul.
Feb. 2—Purification B. V. M.
Feb. 8—Septuagesima Sunday.
Feb. 14—St. Valentine's day.
Feb. 15—Sexigesima Sunday.
Feb. 22—Quinquagesima Sunday.
Feb. 24—St. Matthias.
Feb. 25—Ash Wednesday (Lent begins).
March 1—Quadragesima Sunday.
March 4, 6, 7—Ember days.
March 22—Mid-Lent Sunday.
March 25—Annunciation.
April 5—Palm Sunday.
April 10—Good Friday.
April 12—Easter Sunday.

April 19—Low Sunday.
April 23—St. George.
April 25—St. Mark.
May 1—Philip and James.
May 17—Rogation Sunday.
May 21—Ascension (Holy Thursday).
May 31—Pentecost (Whitsunday).
June 3, 5, 6—Ember days.
June 7—Trinity Sunday.
June 11—St. Barnabas.
June 11—Corpus Christi.
June 24—Nativity John the Baptist.
June 29—St. Peter.
July 22—Mary Magdalen.
July 25—St. James.
Aug. 6—Transfiguration.
Aug. 24—St. Bartholomew.

Sept. 14—Exaltation Holy Cross.
Sept. 16, 18, 19—Ember days.
Sept. 21—St. Matthew.
Sept. 29—Michaelmas.
Oct. 18—St. Luke.
Oct. 28—Sts. Simon and Jude.
Oct. 31—Halloween.
Nov. 1—All Saints' day.
Nov. 2—All Souls' day.
Nov. 26—Thanksgiving.
Nov. 29—First Sunday in Advent.
Nov. 30—St. Andrew.
Dec. 16, 18, 19—Ember days.
Dec. 21—St. Thomas.
Dec. 25—Christmas.
Dec. 26—St. Stephen.
Dec. 27—St. John the Evangelist.

LOSS OF THE LINER TITANIC.

Date—April 15, 1912.
Place—Atlantic ocean, lat. 41:16 north, long. 50:14 west.
Persons aboard—2,223.

Lives lost—1,517.
Persons saved—706.
Cause of disaster—Collision with iceberg.

EMBER DAYS.

Wednesday, Friday and Saturday	after	1st Sunday in Lent	March 4, 6 and 7
		Pentecost	June 3, 5 and 6
		September 14	September 16, 18 and 19
		December 13	December 16, 18 and 19

TIME AND STANDARDS OF TIME.

Various kinds of time are in use in this country:

1. Astronomical Time or Mean Solar Time—This is reckoned from noon through the twenty-four hours of the day and is used mainly by astronomical observatories and in official astronomical publications. It is the legal time of the dominion of Canada, though "standard" and "mean" time are in general use there as in this country.

2. Mean Local Time—This is the kind that was in almost universal use prior to the introduction of standard time. This time was based upon the time when the mean sun* crosses the meridian and the day begins at midnight. When divided into civil divisions—years, months, weeks, days, etc.—it is sometimes called civil time.

3. Standard Time—For the convenience of the railroads and business in general a standard of time was established by mutual agreement in 1883 and by this calculation trains are now run and local time is regulated. By this system the United States, extending from 65° to 125° west longitude, is divided into four time sections, each of 15° of longitude, exactly equivalent to one hour (7½° or 30m. on each side of a meridian), commencing with the 75th meridian. The first or eastern section includes all territory between the Atlantic coast and an irregular line drawn from Buffalo to Charleston, S. C., the latter city being its southernmost point.

The second or central section includes all the territory between this eastern line and another irregular line extending from Bismarck, N. D., to the mouth of the Rio Grande. The third or mountain section includes all the territory between the last named line and nearly the western borders of Idaho, Nevada and Arizona. The fourth or Pacific section includes all the territory of the United States between the boundary of the mountain section and the Pacific coast. Inside of each of these sections standard time is uniform and the time of each section differs from that next to it by exactly one hour, as shown on the map.

*Owing to the eccentricity of the earth's orbit and the inclination of the equator to the ecliptic, the apparent motion of the sun is retarded or accelerated according to the earth's place in its orbit. Hence, to take the actual sun as a guide would necessitate years, days and their subdivisions of unequal length. Therefore an imaginary or "mean sun" was invented. The difference between apparent and mean time is called the "equation of time" and may amount to a quarter of an hour in twenty-four hours. It is the difference between the figures in "Sun at noon mark" column in calendar and twelve hours. The figures on a correct sun dial give the apparent time.

STANDARDS OF TIME.

The following is the table of times, based upon the meridians used by the United States and Canada:

NAME OF TIME.	Degrees.	Central meridian from Greenwich.	Nearest place.
Intercolonial or Atlantic	60	4 hours west	About 3½ degrees east of Halifax, N.S.
Eastern	75	5 hours west	Between New York and Philadelphia
Central	90	6 hours west	St. Louis and New Orleans.
Mountain	105	7 hours west	Denver, Col.
Pacific	120	8 hours west	1½ degrees east of Sacramento, Cal.
Sitka	135	9 hours west	¼ degree east of Sitka, Alaska.
Tahiti	150	10 hours west	¼ degree west of the island of Tahiti
Hawaiian	157½	10 hrs. 31 min. west	Near center of Molokai.

It is obvious that to express the time of rising and setting of the sun and moon in standard time would limit the usefulness of such data to the single point or place for which it was computed, while in mean time it is practically correct for places as widely separated as the width of the continent (see note at bottom of February calendar), and persons having obtained the mean time by the rising or setting of the sun or moon may easily ascertain the correct standard time of any event by making use of the following table and map:

STANDARD TIME TABLE.

To obtain standard time, add or subtract the figures given to local time.

City.	Standard division.	Correction. Min.
Albany, N. Y.—Eastern	Sub.	5
Austin, Texas—Central	Add	31
Baltimore, Md.—Eastern	Add	6
Baton Rouge, La.—Central	Add	4
Bismarck, N. D.—Cent	Add	43
Boston, Mass.—Eastern	Sub.	16
Buffalo, N. Y.—Eastern	Add	16
Burlington, Iowa—Cent	Add	5
Cairo, Ill.—Central	Sub.	3
Charleston, S. C.—East	Add	20
Chicago, Ill.—Central	Sub.	10
Cincinnati, O.—Central	Sub.	22
Cleveland, O.—Central	Sub.	33
Columbia, S. C.—Eastern	Add	24
Columbus, O.—Central	Sub.	28
Dayton, O.—Central	Sub.	23
Denver, Col.—Mountain	Add	0
Des Moines, Ia.—Central	Add	14
Detroit, Mich.—Central	Sub.	28
Dubuque, Iowa—Central	Add	3
Duluth, Minn.—Central	Add	9
Erie, Pa.—Central	Sub.	39
Evansville, Ind.—Central	Sub.	10
Ft. Gibson, Ok. N.—Cent	Add	21
Fort Smith, Ark.—Cent	Add	19
Fort Wayne, Ind.—Cent	Sub.	20
Galena, Ill.—Central	Add	2
Galveston, Tex.—Central	Add	19
Gr. Haven, Mich.—Cent	Sub.	13
Harrisburg, Pa.—Eastern	Add	7
Houston, Tex.—Central	Add	21
Huntsville, Ala.—Cent	Sub.	12
Indianapolis, Ind.—Cent	Sub.	16
Jackson, Miss.—Central	Add	1
Jacksonville, Fla.—Cent	Sub.	33
Janesville, Wis.—Cent	Sub.	4
Jefferson City, Mo.—Cent	Add	9
Kansas City, Mo.—Cent	Add	19
Keokuk, Iowa—Central	Add	6
Knoxville, Tenn.—Cent	Sub.	24
LaCrosse, Wis.—Central	Add	5
Lawrence, Kas.—Central	Add	21
Lexington, Ky.—Central	Sub.	23
Little Rock, Ark.—Cent	Add	9
Louisville, Ky.—Central	Sub.	18
Lynchburg, Va.—Eastern	Add	17
Memphis, Tenn.—Cent	Sub.	0
Milwaukee, Wis.—Cent	Sub.	8
Mobile, Ala.—Central	Sub.	8
Montgomery, Ala.—Cent	Sub.	15
Nashville, Tenn.—Cent	Sub.	13
N. Haven, Conn.—East	Sub.	8
New Orleans, La.—Cent	Add	0
New York, N. Y.—East	Sub.	4
Norfolk, Va.—Eastern	Add	5
Ogdensburg, N. Y.—East	Add	2
Omaha, Neb.—Central	Add	24
Pensacola, Fla.—Central	Sub.	11
Philadelphia, Pa.—East	Add	1
Pittsburgh, Pa.—Eastern	Add	20
Portland, Me.—Eastern	Sub.	19
Providence, R. I.—East	Sub.	14
Quincy, Ill.—Central	Add	6
Raleigh, N. C.—Eastern	Add	15
Richmond, Va.—Eastern	Add	10
Rochester, N. Y.—East	Add	11
Rock Island, Ill.—Cent	Add	3
S. Francisco, Cal.—Pac	Add	10
Santa Fe, N.M.—Mountain	Add	4
Savannah, Ga.—Central	Sub.	36
Shreveport, La.—Central	Add	15
Springfield, Ill.—Central	Sub.	2
St. Joseph, Mo.—Cent	Add	19
St. Louis, Mo.—Central	Add	1
St. Paul, Minn.—Cent	Add	12
Superior City, Wis.—Cent	Add	8
Syracuse, N. Y.—East	Add	5
Toledo, O.—Central	Sub.	26
Trenton, N. J.—Eastern	Sub.	1
Utica, N. Y.—Eastern	Add	1
Washington, D. C.—East	Add	8
Wheeling, W. Va.—East	Add	23
Wilmington, Del.—East	Add	2
Wilmington, N. C.—East	Add	13
Yankton, S. D.—Central	Add	29

All the calculations in this Almanac and Year-Book are based upon mean or clock time unless otherwise stated. The sun's rising and setting are for the upper limb, corrected for parallax and refraction. In the case of the moon no correction is needed, as in the sun, for "parallax and refraction"; with her they are of an opposite nature and just balance each other. The figures given, therefore, are for the moon's center on a true horizon such as the ocean affords.

The calculations in each of the geographical divisions of each calendar page will apply with sufficient accuracy to all places in the contiguous North American zones indicated by the headings of the divisions.

The heavy dotted lines show the arbitrary (standard) divisions of time in the United States. The plus and minus marks on either side of the meridian lines show whether it is necessary to add to or subtract from the mean time of points east or west of these lines to arrive at actual standard time. Example: Chicago is 2½° east of the 90th meridian; therefore Chicago local time = 2½ + 4 = 10 to be subtracted from mean time to = standard time, and for Boston standard (eastern) time, 16m. must be subtracted from mean time.

FOREIGN STANDARDS OF TIME.

	Central meridian.	Fast or slow on Greenwich.		Central meridian.	Fast or slow on Greenwich.
	Degrees.	H.M.S.		Degrees.	H. M.
Japan..................	135 east	9 00 00 fast	West Australia...............	120 east	8 00 fast
Spain*.................	0	0 00 00	South Australia.............	142½ east	9 30 fast
Argentina.............	64+ west	3 51 38.8 slow	New Zealand..............	172½ east	11 30 fast
Ecuador..............	81+ west	5 24 15 slow	Victoria.................		
Natal.................	30 east	2 00 00 fast	New South Wales........	150 east	10 00 fast
Cape Colony..........	22½ east	1 30 00 fast	Queensland.............		
Mid-Europe...........	15 east	1 00 00 fast	Tasmania..............		
Egypt.................	30 east	2 00 00 fast	Eastern Europe..........	30 east	2 00 fast

*In Spain the hours are counted from 0 to 21, avoiding the use of a. m. and p. m.

CALENDAR FOR 1915.

	S	M	T	W	T	F	S		S	M	T	W	T	F	S		S	M	T	W	T	F	S		S	M	T	W	T	F	S
JAN..	..	..	..	..	..	1	2	APRIL..	..	..	..	..	1	2	3	JULY..	..	..	..	..	1	2	3	OCT..	..	..	..	..	..	1	2
	3	4	5	6	7	8	9		4	5	6	7	8	9	10		4	5	6	7	8	9	10		3	4	5	6	7	8	9
	10	11	12	13	14	15	16		11	12	13	14	15	16	17		11	12	13	14	15	16	17		10	11	12	13	14	15	16
	17	18	19	20	21	22	23		18	19	20	21	22	23	24		18	19	20	21	22	23	24		17	18	19	20	21	22	23
	24	25	26	27	28	29	30		25	26	27	28	29	30	..		25	26	27	28	29	30	31		24	25	26	27	28	29	30
	31	..	..	..	..	..	..																		31	..	..	..	..	..	..
FEB..	..	1	2	3	4	5	6	MAY...	..	..	..	..	..	..	1	AUG..	1	2	3	4	5	6	7	NOV..	..	1	2	3	4	5	6
	7	8	9	10	11	12	13		2	3	4	5	6	7	8		8	9	10	11	12	13	14		7	8	9	10	11	12	13
	14	15	16	17	18	19	20		9	10	11	12	13	14	15		15	16	17	18	19	20	21		14	15	16	17	18	19	20
	21	22	23	24	25	26	27		16	17	18	19	20	21	22		22	23	24	25	26	27	28		21	22	23	24	25	26	27
	28	..	..	..	..	..	..		23	24	25	26	27	28	29		29	30	31	..	..	..	..		28	29	30	..	..	..	..
									30	31	..	..	..	..	..																
MAR..	..	1	2	3	4	5	6	JUNE..	..	..	1	2	3	4	5	SEPT..	..	..	1	2	3	4		DEC..	..	..	1	2	3	4
	7	8	9	10	11	12	13		6	7	8	9	10	11	12		5	6	7	8	9	10	11		5	6	7	8	9	10	11
	14	15	16	17	18	19	20		13	14	15	16	17	18	19		12	13	14	15	16	17	18		12	13	14	15	16	17	18
	21	22	23	24	25	26	27		20	21	22	23	24	25	26		19	20	21	22	23	24	25		19	20	21	22	23	24	25
	28	29	30	31	..	..	..		27	28	29	30	..	..	..		26	27	28	29	30	..	..		26	27	28	29	30	31	..

EASTER SUNDAY DATES.

Year	Date	Year	Date	Year	Date	Year	Date
1850	March 31	1884	April 13	1918	March 31	1935	April 21
1851	April 20	1885	April 5	1919	April 20	1936	April 12
1852	April 11	1886	April 25	1920	April 4	1937	March 28
1853	March 27	1887	April 10	1921	March 27	1938	April 17
1854	April 16	1888	April 1	1922	April 16	1939	April 9
1855	April 8	1889	April 21	1923	April 1	1940	March 24
1856	March 23	1890	April 6	1924	April 20	1941	April 13
1857	April 12	1891	March 29	1925	April 12	1942	April 5
1858	April 4	1892	April 17	1926	April 4	1943	April 25
1859	April 24	1893	April 2	1927	April 17	1944	April 9
1860	April 8	1894	March 25	1928	April 8	1945	April 1
1861	March 31	1895	April 14	1929	March 31	1946	April 21
1862	April 20	1896	April 5	1930	April 20	1947	April 6
1863	April 5	1897	April 18	1931	April 5	1948	March 28
1864	March 27	1898	April 10	1932	March 27	1949	April 17
1865	April 16	1899	April 2	1933	April 16	1950	April 9
1866	April 1	1900	April 15	1934	April 1		
1867	April 21	1901	April 7				
1868	April 12	1902	March 30				
1869	March 28	1903	April 12				
1870	April 17	1904	April 3				
1871	April 9	1905	April 23				
1872	March 31	1906	April 15				
1873	April 13	1907	March 31				
1874	April 5	1908	April 19				
1875	March 28	1909	April 11				
1876	April 16	1910	March 27				
1877	April 1	1911	April 16				
1878	April 21	1912	April 7				
1879	April 13	1913	March 23				
1880	March 28	1914	April 12				
1881	April 17	1915	April 4				
1882	April 9	1916	April 23				
1883	March 25	1917	April 8				

The earliest date on which Easter Sunday has fallen within a century was March 22, 1818. As will be seen from the above table it fell on March 23 in 1856 and 1913. The time of the celebration of the principal church days which depend upon Easter is as follows:

Days.	Before Easter.
Septuagesima Sunday	9 weeks
First Sunday in Lent	6 weeks
Ash Wednesday (beginning of Lent)	46 days
Palm Sunday	8 days
	After Easter.
Rogation Sunday	5 weeks
Ascension Day (Holy Thursday)	40 days
Pentecost (Whitsunday)	7 weeks
Trinity Sunday	8 weeks

STATE NICKNAMES AND STATE FLOWERS.

State.	Nickname.	Flower.
Alabama	Cotton state	Goldenrod
Arizona		Sequoia cactus
Arkansas	Bear state	Apple blossom
California	Golden state	Poppy
Colorado	Centennial state	Columbine
Delaware	Blue Hen state	Peach blossom
Florida	Peninsula state	
Georgia	Cracker state	Cherokee rose
Idaho*		Syringa
Illinois*	Sucker state	Violet
Indiana†	Hoosier state	Carnation
Iowa	Hawkeye state	Wild rose
Kansas	Sunflower state	Sunflower
Kentucky	Blue Grass state	Blue grass
Louisiana	Pelican state	Magnolia
Maine	Pine Tree state	Pine cone
Maryland	Old Line state	
Massachusetts	Bay state	
Michigan	Wolverine state	Apple blossom
Minnesota	Gopher state	Moccasin
Mississippi	Bayou state	Magnolia
Montana	Stub Toe state	Bitter root
Missouri		Goldenrod
Nebraska		Goldenrod
Nevada	Silver state	

State.	Nickname	Flower.
New Hampshire	Granite state	
New Jersey	Jersey Blue state	Sugar maple (tree)
New York	Empire state	Rose
North Carolina	Old North state	
North Dakota	Flickertail state	Goldenrod
Ohio	Buckeye state	
Oklahoma		Mistletoe
Oregon	Beaver state	Oregon grape
Pennsylvania	Keystone state	
Rhode Island	Little Rhody	Violet
South Carolina	Palmetto state	
South Dakota	Swinge Cat state	
Tennessee	Big Bend state	
Texas	Lone Star state	Bluebonnet
Utah		Sego lily
Vermont	Green Mountain state	Red clover
Virginia	The Old Dominion	
Washington	Chinook state	Rhododendron
West Virginia	The Panhandle.	
Wisconsin	Badger state	

Note—Only nicknames that are well known and "state flowers" officially adopted or commonly accepted are given in the foregoing list.
*Native state tree, the native oak. †Official state song, "On the Banks of the Wabash."

BURIAL PLACES OF AMERICAN PRESIDENTS.

George Washington—Mount Vernon, Va.
John Adams—Quincy, Mass.
Thomas Jefferson—Monticello, Va.
James Madison—Montpelier, Va.
James Monroe—Richmond, Va.
John Quincy Adams—Quincy, Mass.
Andrew Jackson—Hermitage, Nashville, Tenn.
Martin Van Buren—Kinderhook, N. Y.
William Henry Harrison—North Bend, O.
John Tyler—Richmond, Va.
James Knox Polk—Nashville, Tenn.
Zachary Taylor—Springfield, Ky.

Millard Fillmore—Buffalo, N. Y.
Franklin Pierce—Concord, N. H.
James Buchanan—Lancaster, Pa.
Abraham Lincoln—Springfield, Ill.
Ulysses S. Grant—New York, N. Y.
Rutherford B. Hayes—Fremont, O.
James A. Garfield—Cleveland, O.
Chester A. Arthur—Albany, N. Y.
Benjamin Harrison—Indianapolis, Ind.
William McKinley—Canton, O.
Grover Cleveland—Princeton, N. J.

STATES AND TERRITORIES IN THE UNION.

There are forty-eight states in the union and three territories, the latter including Hawaii, the District of Columbia and Alaska. The District of Columbia is governed by three commissioners, appointed by the president of the United States under laws passed directly by congress. Alaska has a governor, appointed by the president, and a legislature. (See "Alaska" in this volume.) Porto Rico, the Philippines and other island possessions of the United States are not technically territories, each having a special form of government.

Wallinger Photo, Chicago.
WILLIAM J. BRYAN,
Secretary of State.

Copyright, Harris & Ewing, Washington.
JOSEPHUS DANIELS,
Secretary of the Navy.

Copyright, Harris & Ewing, Washington.
L. M. GARRISON,
Secretary of War.

Copyright, Harris & Ewing, Washington.
WILLIAM G. M'ADOO,
Secretary of the Treasury.

Copyright, Harris & Ewing, Washington, D. C.
WOODROW WILSON,
President.

Copyright, Clinedinst, Washington, D. C.
DAVID S. HOUSTON,
Secretary of Agriculture.

Copyright, Harris & Ewing, Washington, D. C.
JAMES C. M'REYNOLDS,
Attorney-General.

Copyright, Harris & Ewing, Washington.
WILLIAM B. WILSON,
Secretary of Labor.

Copyright, Harris & Ewing, Washington.
A. S. BURLESON,
Postmaster-General.

Moffett Photo, Chicago.
FRANKLIN K. LANE,
Secretary of the Interior.

Copyright, Clinedinst, Washington, D.C.
W. C. REDFIELD,
Secretary of Commerce.

Copyright, Harris & Ewing, Washington, D. C.
THOMAS R. MARSHALL,
Vice-President.

THE PRESIDENT AND HIS CABINET.

THE PRESIDENT, VICE-PRESIDENT AND CABINET.

Woodrow Wilson, president of the United States—Born in Staunton, Va., Dec. 28, 1856; educated in private schools, Princeton university, University of Virginia and Johns Hopkins university; practiced law in Atlanta, Ga., 1882-1883; professor of history and political economy, Bryn Mawr college, 1885-1888, and Wesleyan university, 1888-1890; professor of jurisprudence and politics, Princeton university, 1890-1910; president of same, 1902-1910; author of various books on government, history and literature; democrat; governor of New Jersey, 1911-1913; elected president of the United States, 1912; inaugurated March 4, 1913. Mr. Wilson is of Scotch-Irish parentage and is a presbyterian; married in 1885 to Ellen Louise Axson, Savannah, Ga.; has three daughters, Margaret, Eleanor and Jessie.

Thomas Riley Marshall, vice-president of the United States—Born in Manchester, Ind., March 14, 1854; educated in Wabash college; admitted to the bar, 1875; practiced in Columbia City, Ind., as senior member of the firm of Marshall & McNagny and Marshall, McNagny & Clugston, 1892-1909; democrat; governor of Indiana, 1909-1913; elected vice-president of the United States, 1912; sworn in March 4, 1913. Mr. Marshall's ancestors settled in America in prerevolutionary days; married in 1895 to Lois I. Kimsey of Angola, Ind.; belongs to presbyterian church.

William Jennings Bryan, secretary of state—Born at Salem, Ill., March 19, 1860; educated in Illinois college, Jacksonville, Ill., and Union College of Law, Chicago; admitted to bar, 1883, practicing in Jacksonville, Ill., and later in Lincoln, Neb.; member of congress, 1891-1895; editor Omaha World-Herald, 1894-1896; nominated for president of the United States at democratic conventions of 1896, 1900 and 1908, but defeated on each occasion; established the Commoner at Lincoln, Neb., in 1900; took leading part in democratic national convention of 1912; appointed secretary of state by President Wilson, March 5, 1913.

William Gibbs McAdoo, secretary of the treasury—Born near Marietta, Ga., Oct. 31, 1863; educated in the University of Tennessee; studied law and was admitted to the bar in 1885; practiced in Chattanooga, Tenn.; counsel for Central Railroad and Banking company, and Richmond & Danville Railroad company; removed to New York, N. Y., in 1892, becoming law partner of William McAdoo; president and director of the Hudson & Manhattan Railroad company, operating Hudson river tunnel system; independent in politics; appointed secretary of the treasury March 5, 1913.

Lindley M. Garrison, secretary of war—Born in Camden, N. J., Nov. 28, 1864; educated in public schools and University of Pennsylvania; admitted to the bar in 1886 and practiced two years in Philadelphia, Pa.; admitted to New Jersey bar in 1888 and practiced until June 15, 1904; then became vice-chancellor of New Jersey, serving until March, 1913; appointed secretary of war by President Wilson and took the oath of office March 5, 1913.

James Clark McReynolds, attorney-general—Born in Elkton, Ky., Feb. 3, 1862; graduated from Vanderbilt university, 1882, and from law department of University of Virginia, 1884; engaged in private practice; professor of law in Vanderbilt university, 1900-1903; assistant attorney-general of the United States, 1903-1907; moved to New York and was specially retained by the government in litigation against the tobacco trust, the coal railroad combination and other corporations; gold democrat; appointed attorney-general of the United States March 5, 1913.

Albert Sidney Burleson, postmaster-general—Born in San Marcos, Tex., June 7, 1863; educated at Texas Agricultural and Mechanical college, Baylor university and University of Texas, graduating from last named institution in 1884; admitted to bar, 1885; assistant city attorney of Austin, Tex., 1885-1890; attorney of 26th Texas judicial district, 1891-1896; democrat; member of 56th, 57th, 58th, 59th, 60th, 61st and 62d congresses; elected to 63d congress, but resigned on being appointed postmaster-general March 5, 1913.

Josephus Daniels, secretary of the navy—Born in Washington, N. C., May 18, 1862; educated in Wilson (N. C.) Collegiate institute; editor of Advance in same place at age of 18; studied law and was admitted to the bar, but never practiced; became editor of the Raleigh State Chronicle, 1885; state printer of North Carolina, 1887-1893; chief clerk department of the interior, 1893-1895; democrat and active in politics; editor of Raleigh News and Observer, 1895-1913; appointed secretary of the navy March 5, 1913.

Franklin Knight Lane, secretary of the interior—Born in Prince Edward island, Canada, July 15, 1864; educated in University of California, and began practice of law in San Francisco in 1889; corporation counsel of that city, 1897-1902; democratic candidate for governor of California, 1902; received party vote for United States senator in legislature, 1903; appointed a member of the interstate commerce commission in December, 1905; appointed secretary of the interior March 5, 1913.

David Franklin Houston, secretary of agriculture—Born in Monroe, N. C., Feb. 17, 1866; graduated from South Carolina college, 1887, and from Harvard university, 1892; professor of political science in University of Texas, 1900-1902; president Agricultural and Mechanical college of Texas, 1902-1905, and of University of Texas, 1905-1908; chancellor of Washington university, St. Louis, Mo., 1908-1913; trustee John F. Slater fund and member of Rockefeller sanitary commission; appointed secretary of agriculture March 5, 1913.

William Cox Redfield, secretary of commerce—Born in Albany, N. Y., June 18, 1858; educated in Pittsfield (Mass.) high school; treasurer of J. H. Williams & Co., Brooklyn, 1887-1901; vice-president Warp Twisting-In Machine company, 1904; president Sirocco Engineering company, 1907-1911; director Equitable Life Assurance society; commissioner of public works, Brooklyn borough, 1902-1903; democrat; member 62d congress; appointed secretary of commerce March 5, 1913.

William Bauchop Wilson, secretary of labor—Born in Blantyre, Scotland, April 2, 1862; came to United States in 1870; educated in common schools of Pennsylvania; worked as miner from 1871 to 1898; president of district miners' union, 1888-1890; assisted in organization of United Mine Workers of America in 1890; secretary and treasurer of National Union of Miners, 1900-1908; democrat; member of 60th, 61st and 62d congresses; appointed secretary of the newly created department of labor March 5, 1913.

SHORTHAND CHAMPIONSHIP.

In a shorthand speed contest held at the annual meeting of the National Shorthand Reporters' association in Chicago, Aug. 20-21, 1913, Nathan Behrin of New York was the victor. He wrote at the rate of 200 words a minute for five minutes with only eight errors. At 240 words a minute he made fourteen errors and at 280 words a minute forty-four errors. His accuracy average was 98.3 per cent. J. D. Carson of Chicago had an accuracy average of 93.8 per cent. Miss Paula Werning of New York had an accuracy average of 96.5 per cent in the 240 words a minute contest.

SPEED ON TYPEWRITER.

Miss Bessie Friedman of New York, N. Y., won the all professional typewriting contest at the national business exposition in Chicago, Sept. 9, 1913, with a record of 116 words a minute. The championship in 1912 was won by Miss Florence E. Wilson of New York, N. Y., with the same record—116 words a minute.

INAUGURATION OF PRESIDENT WILSON.

Woodrow Wilson of New Jersey was sworn in as president and Thomas Riley Marshall of Indiana as vice-president of the United States in Washington, D. C., at noon March 4, 1913. The day was partly cloudy, but otherwise pleasant, contrasting sharply with the stormy weather that prevailed at the inauguration of Taft and Sherman in 1909. The customary procedure was followed, Mr. Marshall first taking the oath of office, administered by Senator Jacob H. Gallinger, the president pro tempore, in the senate chamber. After the new vice-president had delivered his inaugural address and the members of the new senate had been sworn in, a procession was formed for the march to the east front of the capitol, where the oath was administered to Mr. Wilson by Edward D. White, chief justice of the United States Supreme court. Placing his hand on the bible, the new chief executive said:

"I do solemnly swear that I will faithfully execute the office of president of the United States and will, to the best of my ability, preserve, protect and defend the constitution of the United States."

After kissing the open bible President Wilson delivered his inaugural address, the full text of which is as follows:

"There has been a change of government. It began two years ago, when the house of representatives became democratic by a decisive majority. It has now been completed. The senate about to assemble will also be democratic. The offices of president and vice-president have been put into the hands of democrats. What does the change mean? That is the question that is uppermost in our minds to-day. That is the question I am going to try to answer, in order, if I may, to interpret the occasion.

"It means much more than the mere success of a party. The success of a party means little except when the nation is using that party for a large and definite purpose. No one can mistake the purpose for which the nation now seeks to use the democratic party. It seeks to use it to interpret a change in its own plans and point of view. Some old things with which we had grown familiar, and which had begun to creep into the very habit of our thought and of our lives, have altered their aspect as we have latterly looked critically upon them, with fresh awakened eyes; have dropped their disguises and shown themselves alien and sinister. Some new things, as we look frankly upon them, willing to comprehend their real character, have come to assume the aspect of things long believed in and familiar, stuff of our own convictions.

"We have been refreshed by a new insight into our own life. We see that in many things that life is very great. It is incomparably great in its material aspects, in its body of wealth, in the diversity and sweep of its energy, in the industries which have been conceived and built up by the genius of individual men and the limitless enterprise of groups of men. It is great, also, very great, in its moral force. Nowhere else in the world have noble men and women exhibited in more striking forms the beauty and the energy of sympathy and helpfulness and counsel in their efforts to rectify wrong, alleviate suffering and set the weak in the way of strength and hope. We have built up, moreover, a great system of government, which has stood through a long age as in many respects a model for those who seek to set liberty upon foundations that will endure against fortuitous change, against storm and accident. Our life contains every great thing, and contains it in rich abundance.

"But the evil has come with the good, and much fine gold has been corroded. With riches has come inexcusable waste. We have squandered a great part of what we might have used, and have not stopped to conserve the exceeding bounty of nature, without which our genius for enterprise would have been worthless and impotent, scorning to be careful, shamefully prodigal as well as admirably efficient. We have been proud of our industrial achievements, but we have not hitherto stopped thoughtfully enough to count the human cost, the cost of lives snuffed out, of energies overtaxed and broken, the fearful physical and spiritual cost to the men and women and children upon whom the dead weight and burden of it all has fallen pitilessly the years through. The groans and agony of it all had not yet reached our ears, the solemn, moving undertone of our life, coming up out of the mines and factories and out of every home where the struggle had its intimate and familiar seat. With the great government went many deep, secret things which we too long delayed to look into and scrutinize with candid, fearless eyes. The great government we loved has too often been made use of for private and selfish purposes, and those who used it had forgotten the people.

"At last a vision has been vouchsafed us of our life as a whole. We see the bad with the good, the debased and decadent with the sound and vital. With this vision we approach new affairs. Our duty is to cleanse, to reconsider, to restore, to correct the evil without impairing the good, to purify and humanize every process of our common life without weakening or sentimentalizing it. There has been something crude and heartless and unfeeling in our haste to succeed and be great. Our thought has been 'Let every man look out for himself, let every generation look out for itself,' while we reared giant machinery which made it impossible that any but those who stood at the levers of control should have a chance to look out for themselves. We had not forgotten our morals. We remembered well enough that we had set up a policy which was meant to serve the humblest as well as the most powerful, with an eye single to the standards of justice and fair play, and remembered it with pride. But we were very heedless and in a hurry to be great.

"We have come now to the sober second thought. The scales of heedlessness have fallen from our eyes. We have made up our minds to square every process of our national life again with the standards we so proudly set up at the beginning and have always carried at our hearts. Our work is a work of restoration.

"We have itemized with some degree of particularity the things that ought to be altered and here are some of the chief items: A tariff which cuts us off from our proper part in the commerce of the world, violates the just principles of taxation and makes the government a facile instrument in the hands of private interests; a banking and currency system based upon the necessity of the government to sell its bonds fifty years ago and perfectly adapted to concentrating cash and restricting credits; an industrial system which, take it on all its sides, financial as well as administrative, holds capital in leading strings, restricts the liberties and limits the opportunities of labor, and exploits, without renewing or conserving, the natural resources of the country; a body of agricultural activities never yet given the efficiency of great business undertakings or served as it should be through the instrumentality of science taken directly to the farm, or afforded the facilities of credit best suited to its practical needs; water courses undeveloped, waste places unreclaimed, forests untended, fast disappearing without plan or prospect of renewal, unregarded waste heap at every mine.

"We have studied as perhaps no other nation has the most effective means of production, but we have not studied cost or economy as we should, either as organizers of industry, as statesmen or as individuals. Nor have we studied and perfected the means by which government may be put at the service of humanity, in safeguarding the health of the nation, the health of its men and its women and its children, as well as their rights in the struggle for existence.

"This is no sentimental duty. The firm basis of government is justice, not pity. These are matters of justice. There can be no equality of opportunity, the first essential of justice in the body politic, if men and women and children be not shielded in their lives, their very vitality, from the consequences of great industrial and social processes which they cannot alter, control or singly cope

with. Society must see to it that it does not itself crush or weaken or damage its own constituent parts. The first duty of law is to keep sound the society it serves. Sanitary laws, pure food laws and laws determining conditions of labor which individuals are powerless to determine for themselves are intimate parts of the very business of justice and legal efficiency.

"These are some of the things we ought to do, and not leave the others undone, the old fashioned, never to be neglected, fundamental safeguarding of property and of individual right. This is the high enterprise of the new day; to lift everything that concerns our life as a nation to the light that shines from the hearthfire of every man's conscience and vision of the right. It is inconceivable that we should do this as partisans; it is inconceivable we should do this in ignorance of the facts as they are or in blind haste.

"We shall restore, not destroy. We shall deal with our economic system as it is and as it may be modified, not as it might be if we had a clean sheet of paper to write upon, and step by step we shall make it what it should be, in the spirit of those who question their own wisdom and seek counsel and knowledge, not shallow self-satisfaction or the excitement of excursions whither they cannot tell. Justice, and only justice, shall always be our motto.

"And yet it will be no cool process of mere science. The nation has been deeply stirred—stirred by a solemn passion, stirred by the knowledge of wrong, of ideals lost, of government too often debauched and made an instrument of evil. The feelings with which we face this new age of right and opportunity sweep across our heartstrings like some air out of God's own presence, where justice and mercy are reconciled and the judge and the brother are one. We know our task to be no mere task of politics, but a task which shall search us through and through, whether we be able to understand our time and the need of our people, whether we be indeed their spokesmen and interpreters, whether we have the pure heart to comprehend and the rectified will to choose our high course of action.

"This is not a day of triumph; it is a day of dedication. Here muster, not the forces of party, but the forces of humanity. Men's hearts wait upon us; men's lives hang in the balance; men's hopes call upon us to say what we will do. Who shall live up to the great trust? Who dares fail to try? I summon all honest men, all patriotic, all forward looking men, to my side. God helping me, I will not fail them, if they will but counsel and sustain me!"

Mr. Wilson was accompanied to and from the capitol by his predecessor in office, President Taft, who at the close of the address said:

"Mr. President, I wish you a successful administration and the carrying out of your aims. We will all be behind you."

The new president was also congratulated by Vice-President Marshall, William J. Bryan, prospective secretary of state, and a host of other distinguished men who witnessed the inauguration. The crowd of spectators in front of the stand where the exercises took place was declared by competent judges to be the largest that was ever present on such an occasion. In the afternoon President Wilson reviewed a parade lasting four hours and at night the city was brightly illuminated.

LEADING ART GALLERIES OF THE WORLD.

The following list includes only the principal collections of paintings and sculptures readily accessible to the public in Europe and America.

EUROPE.

AUSTRIA-HUNGARY.
Academy of Art, Vienna.
Albertina, Vienna.
Imperial art gallery, Vienna.
Liechtenstein gallery, Vienna.
National gallery, Budapest.

BELGIUM.
Museum, Antwerp.
Palace of Fine Arts, Brussels.
Musee Wiertz, Brussels.

DENMARK.
Thorvaldsen museum, Copenhagen.
Ny-Carlsberg Glyptothek, Copenhagen.
National art gallery, Copenhagen.

FRANCE.
Louvre,* Paris.
Luxembourg, Paris.
Museum, Versailles.

GERMANY.
National gallery, Berlin.
Old and New museums, Berlin.
Pergamon museum, Berlin.
Emperor Frederick museum, Berlin.
Dresden gallery,* Dresden.
Old and New Pinakothek,* Munich.
Glyptothek, Munich.

HOLLAND.

Ryk's museum, Amsterdam.
Fodor museum, Amsterdam.
Six Collection, Amsterdam.
Townhall, Haarlem.
Lakenhal, Leyden.
Boymans museum, Rotterdam.
Mauritshuis, The Hague.

ITALY.
Vatican,* Rome.
Uffizi gallery,* Florence.
Pitti gallery,* Florence.
Brera gallery, Milan.
Poldi museum, Milan.
National museum, Naples.
Academy of Fine Arts, Venice.

NORWAY.
National gallery, Christiania.

RUSSIA.
Hermitage, St. Petersburg.

SPAIN.
Museo del Prado,* Madrid.
Museo Provincial, Seville.

SWEDEN.
National gallery, Stockholm.

UNITED KINGDOM.
British museum, London.
National gallery,* London.
Dore gallery, London.
Walker art gallery, Liverpool.
Art galleries, Glasgow.

AMERICA.

CANADA.
Fraser institute, Montreal.
The Basilica, Quebec.

MEXICO.
National museum, City of Mexico.

UNITED STATES.
Art institute, Chicago, Ill.
Art museum, Cincinnati, O.
Art museum, Worcester, Mass.
Carnegie institute, Pittsburgh, Pa.
Corcoran art gallery, Washington, D. C.
Layton art gallery, Milwaukee, Wis.
Lenox collection, public library, New York, N. Y.
Metropolitan Museum of Art,* New York, N. Y.
Museum of Art, Toledo, O.
Museum of Fine Arts, Boston, Mass.
Museum of Fine Arts, St. Louis, Mo.
New York Historical society, New York, N. Y.
Pennsylvania Academy of Fine Arts, Philadelphia, Pa.
*Of first rank.

FIRE HORROR IN BINGHAMTON, N. Y.

Through the burning of the Freeman Overall factory at 7 Wall street, Binghamton, N. Y., July 22, 1913, sixty-five woman employes lost their lives, while thirty were seriously injured. The building was a four story brick structure, the whole of which was occupied by the Freeman Overall company for manufacturing purposes. The fire was discovered at 2:30 o'clock in the afternoon and an alarm was sounded at once. Several alarms had been given within the previous three months for fire drill purposes in accordance with a recent law, this led the employes to think that the last alarm was of a similar nature, and they took their time about getting ready to leave, with the result that those on the third and fourth floors were trapped by the flames, which spread with great rapidity. Escape by the stairway was cut off and few were able to make use of the single fire escape in the rear. Many threw themselves from the windows and were dashed to death or badly injured on the ground below.

ABRAHAM LINCOLN MEMORIAL IN WASHINGTON, D. C.

EAST ELEVATION OF THE LINCOLN MEMORIAL IN WASHINGTON, D. C.

By an act approved Feb. 9, 1911, congress created a commission to be known as the Lincoln memorial commission to procure and determine upon a location, plan and design for a monument or memorial in the city of Washington, D. C., to the memory of Abraham Lincoln, subject to the approval of congress. The commission named consisted of William H. Taft, Shelby M. Cullom, Joseph G. Cannon, George Peabody Wetmore, Samuel Walker McCall, Hernando D. Money and Champ Clark. Senator Money died Sept. 18, 1912, and his place was taken by Senator Thomas S. Martin of Virginia. The commission was authorized to employ the services of architects, artists and sculptors and to avail itself of the services or advice of the commission of fine arts, created by the act of May 17, 1910. It was further provided that as soon as might be practicable after the adoption of a design and its approval by congress its construction should be entered upon and carried to completion under the direction of the memorial commission and the supervision of the secretary of war, under a contract or contracts entered into by the secretary of war in a total sum not exceeding $2,000,000.

Sixteen meetings were held by the memorial commission and March 4, 1911, the commission of fine arts was required to make suggestions as to the locations, plans and designs for a monument or memorial to Lincoln and to give advice as to certain specified locations. The commission of fine arts, by D. H. Burnham, its chairman, reported July 17, 1911, that it was unanimous in its approval of a site in Potomac park for the location of the memorial, the general form of which had been decided upon in accordance with designs submitted by Henry Bacon, architect, of New York city. The main reason for selecting the park site was that for a long distance in every direction the surroundings were absolutely free for such treatment as would best enhance the effect of the memorial. It would also be the place of honor on the main east and west axis of the city, in line with the capitol and the Washington monument. John Hay, one of Lincoln's secretaries and biographers, had often expressed his preference for the location in words like these:

"Lincoln, of all Americans next to Washington, deserves this place of honor. He was of the immortals. You must not approach too close to the immortals. His monument should stand alone, remote from the common habitations of man, apart from the business and turmoil of the city—isolated, distinguished, serene."

Mr. Bacon, the architect, in describing his design for the memorial, said:

"On the great axis, planned over a century ago, we have at one end the capitol, which is the monument of the government, and to the west, over a mile distant from the capitol, is the monument to Washington, one of the founders of the government. If the Lincoln memorial is built on this same axis still farther to the west, by the shore of the Potomac, we will there have the monument of the man who saved the government, thus completing an unparalleled composition which cannot fail to impart to each of its monuments a value in addition to that which each standing alone would possess."

The memorial commission reported to congress Dec. 4, 1912, that after a careful examination and discussion of the design presented by Mr. Bacon it had adopted it unanimously and recommended that congress approve the construction of the memorial on the selected site in Potomac park in accordance with the plans and designs of Mr. Bacon.

The following joint resolution was passed by the senate Jan. 24, by the house Jan. 29, and approved by President Taft Feb. 1, 1913:

"That the plan, design and location for a Lincoln memorial, determined upon and recommended to congress Dec. 4, 1912, by the commission created by the act entitled 'An act to provide a commission to secure plans and designs for a monument or memorial to the memory of Abraham Lincoln,' approved Feb. 9, 1911, be, and the same are hereby approved."

DESCRIPTION OF MEMORIAL.

The following details of the Lincoln memorial are from the architect's description as reported by the memorial commission:

The memorial is to be composed of four features—a statue of Abraham Lincoln, a memorial of his Gettysburg speech, a memorial of his second inaugural address and a symbol of the union of the United States, which he saved. The most important object is the statue of Lincoln, which is placed in the center of the memorial, and by virtue of its imposing position in the place of honor, the gentleness, power and intelligence of the man, expressed as far as possible by the sculptor's art, will predominate." The part of the edifice where the statue is to be placed will not be occupied by any other object. The smaller halls at each side of the

central space will be devoted to the Gettysburg address and the second inaugural address shown by bronze letters arranged on monumental tablets. While these memorials can be seen from any part of the hall, they are to be partially screened from the central portion, where the statue is placed, by means of a row of Ionic columns.

Surrounding the walls inclosing these memorials of the man is to be a colonnade forming a symbol of the union, each column representing one of the thirty-six states existing at the time of Lincoln's death, and on the walls appearing above the colonnade and supported at intervals by eagles are forty-eight memorial festoons, one for each state existing at the present time.

By means of terraces the ground at the site of the Lincoln memorial will be raised until the floor of the memorial itself will be 45 feet higher than the present grade. First a circular terrace, 1,000 feet in diameter, is raised 11 feet above the present grade and on its outer edge will be planted four concentric rows of trees, leaving a plateau in the center 755 feet in diameter. In the center of this plateau, surrounded by a wide roadway and walks, will rise an eminence supporting a rectangular stone terrace wall 14 feet high, 256 feet long and 186 feet wide. On this rectangular terrace will rise the marble memorial. All the foundations will be built on concrete piling extending down to the solid rock. Three steps 8 feet high will form a platform under the columns. The platform at its base will be 204 feet long and 134 feet wide.

The colonnade will be 188 feet long and 118 feet wide, the columns being 44 feet high and 7 feet 5 inches in diameter at their base. The total height of the structure above the finished grade at the base of the terrace will be 99 feet. The finished grade being 23 feet above the present grade, the total height of the building above the present grade will be 122 feet. The outside of the memorial hall will be 84 feet wide and 156 feet long. The colonnaded entrance will be 45 feet wide and 44 feet high, and will be equipped with sliding bronze grilles, filled with plate glass, so that the hall may be closed at night and on other occasions as required. The central hall, where the statue is to stand, will be 60 feet wide, 70 feet long and 60 feet high. The halls where the memorials of the speeches are to be placed will be 27 feet wide, 57 feet long and 60 feet high. The inferior columns will be of the Ionic order and will be 50 feet high.

GETTYSBURG ADDRESS.
Nov. 19, 1863.

"Four score and seven years ago our fathers brought forth on this continent a new nation, conceived in liberty and dedicated to the proposition that all men are created equal. Now we are engaged in a great civil war, testing whether that nation or any nation so conceived and so dedicated can long endure. We are met on a great battle field of that war. We have come to dedicate a portion of that field as a final resting place for those who here gave their lives that that nation might live. It is altogether fitting and proper that we should do this. But in a larger sense we cannot dedicate, we cannot consecrate, we cannot hallow this ground. The brave men, living and dead, who struggled here have consecrated it far above our power to add or detract. The world will little note, nor long remember, what we say here, but it can never forget what they did here. It is for us, the living, rather to be dedicated here to the unfinished work which they who fought here have thus far so nobly advanced. It is rather for us to be here dedicated to the great task remaining before us, that from these honored dead we take increased devotion to that cause for which they gave the last full measure of devotion; that we here highly resolve that these dead shall not have died in vain; that this nation, under God, shall have a new birth of freedom, and that government of the people, by the people and for the people shall not perish from the earth."

CULLOM, RESIDENT COMMISSIONER.

The following bill was unanimously passed by the senate and house March 2 and approved by the president March 4, 1913:

"Be it enacted, etc., That in the exercise of its control and direction for the construction of the Lincoln memorial, authorized by the act of congress approved Feb. 9, 1911, the commission created by said act shall designate to perform the duty of resident commissioner to represent the commission in the oversight of the work the Hon. Shelby M. Cullom, who, at the time of the adoption of this act, is the senior member of the commission in continuous service of the United States, and for the special service of the member so designated he shall be entitled to receive compensation at the rate of $5,000 a year out of the appropriations for the construction of such memorial."

SECOND INAUGURAL ADDRESS.
March 4, 1865.

The closing paragraphs of the second inaugural address follow:

"Fondly do we hope, fervently do we pray, that this mighty scourage of war may speedily pass away. Yet, if God wills that it continue until all the wealth piled by the bondman's 250 years of unrequited toil shall be sunk, and until every drop of blood drawn with the lash shall be paid with another drawn with the sword, as was said 3,000 years ago, so still it must be said that the judgments of the Lord are true and righteous altogether.

"With malice toward none, with charity for all, with firmness in the right as God gives us to see the right, let us finish the work we are in, to bind up the nation's wounds, to care for him who shall have borne the battle, and for his widow and his orphans, to do all which may achieve and cherish a just and lasting peace among ourselves and with all nations."

FATAL THEATER FIRES AND PANICS SINCE 1811.

Theater or hall and date.	Lives lost.
Banquet theater, Oporto, March 21, 1888	200
Barnsley, England (hall), Jan. 11, 1908	16
Barraque theater, Belgium, Dec. 22, 1912	12
Bologne, Russia, March 6, 1911	120
Cannonsburg, Pa., opera house, Aug. 26, 1911	26
Carlsruhe theater, St. Petersburg, 1847	200
Central theater, Philadelphia, April 28, 1892	6
Conway's theater, Brooklyn, Dec. 5, 1876	295
Exeter theater, England, Sept. 5, 1887	200
Flores theater, Acapulco, Mex., Feb. 14, 1909	250
Front Street theater, Baltimore, Dec. 8, 1895	23

Theater or hall and date.	Lives lost.
Houston Street theater, New York, N. Y., Feb. 2, 1913	2
Iroquois, Chicago, Dec. 30, 1903	575
Lehman's theater, St. Petersburg, 1836	700
Opera Comique, Paris, May 25, 1887	75
Rhonde's opera house, Boyertown, Pa., Jan. 13, 1908	170
Richmond (Va.) theater, Dec. 26, 1811	70
Ring theater, Vienna, Dec. 8, 1881	640
Verins, France, March 9, 1913	10
Villareal theater, Spain, May 27, 1912	80

THE WORLD'S MOST FAMOUS DIAMONDS.

Name.	Carats.	Name.	Carats.	Name.	Carats.
Cullinan	3,025	Imperatrice Eugenie	51	Pacha d'Egypt	40
D'Angleterre (blue)	44¼	Kohinoor (1st cutting)	279	Regent	136¾
Etoile Polaire	40	Kohinoor (2d cutting)	106 1-16	Sancy	53½
Etoile du Sud	124	Loterie d'Angleterre	49	Shah	86
Grand Duc de Toscane	133.16	Nassak	78⅝	Tiffany	969
Great Mogul	279 3-16	Orloff	194¾	Tiffany (yellow)	125

NATIONAL PARKS IN THE UNITED STATES.

(Under supervision of the secretary of the interior.)

NAME.	Location.	Created.	Acres.
Antietam	Maryland	Aug. 20, 1890	43
Casa Grande Ruin	Arizona	June 22, 1892	480
Chickamauga and Chattanooga	Georgia and Tennessee	Aug. 18, 1890	6,195
Crater Lake	Oregon	May 22, 1902	159,360
General Grant	California	Oct. 1, 1890	2,560
Gettysburg	Pennsylvania	Feb. 11, 1895	877
Glacier	Montana	May 11, 1910	981,681
Hot Springs Reservation	Arkansas	June 16, 1880	912
Mesa Verde	Colorado	June 29, 1906	42,376
Mount Rainier	Washington	May 22, 1899	207,360
Platt	Oklahoma	June 29, 1906	848
Rock Creek	District of Columbia	Sept. 27, 1890	1,606
Sequoia	California	Oct. 1, 1890	160,000
Shiloh	Tennessee	Dec. 27, 1894	3,000
Sully's Hill	North Dakota	June 4, 1904	960
Vicksburg	Mississippi	Feb. 21, 1899	1,233
Wind Cave	South Dakota	Jan. 9, 1903	10,522
Yellowstone	Montana and Wyoming	March 1, 1872	2,142,720
Yosemite	California	Oct. 1, 1890	967,680
Zoological	District of Columbia	March 2, 1889	170

NOTES ON NATIONAL PARKS.

Antietam—Battle field of the civil war in Washington county, Maryland.

Casa Grande Ruin—Remains of a large prehistoric building near Florence, Ariz.

Chickamauga and Chattanooga—Battle fields of the civil war in the vicinity of Chattanooga, Tenn.

Crater Lake—Park contains remarkable mountain lake and fine scenery in the Cascade range, Klamath county, Oregon; may be reached from Klamath Falls or from Medford on the Southern Pacific road.

General Grant—In Fresno and Tulare counties, California; forest and mountain scenery; reached from Sanger on the Southern Pacific line.

Gettysburg—Battle field of the civil war in southeastern Pennsylvania.

Glacier—Tract of mountainous country in northern Montana with glaciers, lakes, forests and peaks.

Hot Springs Reservation—Tract of land in Garland county, Arkansas, noted for its springs of warm mineral-waters.

Mesa Verde—In the extreme southwestern part of Colorado; contains pueblo and other ruins; reached from Mancos on the Rio Grande Southern road.

Mount Rainier—Mountain district in southern Washington; reached from Ashford on the Tacoma Eastern railroad and from Fairfax on the Northern Pacific road.

Platt—Tract of land containing sulphur springs in Murray county, Oklahoma; reached by Santa Fe and St. Louis & San Francisco railroads.

Rock Creek—Park in outskirts of Washington, D. C.

Sequoia—Mountain tract in Tulare county, California, containing forest of big trees; reached from Visalia.

Shiloh—Battle field of civil war in Hardin county, southern Tennessee.

Sully's Hill—On the shore of Devil's lake, North Dakota; contains elevation on which Gen. Alfred Sully with a few men withstood a band of Indians for several days in 1863; reached from Devil's Lake, Narrows and Tokio stations on the Great Northern railroad.

Vicksburg—Battle field of civil war near city of same name in Mississippi.

Wind Cave—Canyon and extensive cave in Custer county, South Dakota, twelve miles from Hot Springs, on the Northwestern and Burlington roads; in Black Hills region.

Yellowstone—Famous park in Wyoming, Montana and Idaho, containing geysers and many other natural phenomena as well as beautiful mountain, lake and river scenery; reached from stations on the Northern Pacific, Burlington and Oregon Short Line roads.

Yosemite—Splendid valley in the Sierras in Mariposa county, California; reached from Merced on the Sante Fe and Southern Pacific roads by way of the Yosemite Valley railroad.

Zoological—Park in Washington, D. C., devoted to the zoological collection of the government; adjoins Rock Creek park.

PRESERVATION OF AMERICAN ANTIQUITIES.

By law approved June 8, 1906, entitled "An act for the preservation of American antiquities," the president of the United States is authorized, in his discretion, to declare by proclamation historic landmarks, historic and prehistoric structures and other objects of historic or scientific interest that are situated upon lands owned or controlled by the United States to be national monuments. Under such authority the following monuments have been created:

Name and state.	Year.	Acres.
Big Hole battle field, Mont	1910	8
Chaco canyon, N. M	1907	20,629
Cinder cone,* Cal	1907	5,120
Colorado, Col	1911	13,883
Devil's tower,* Wyo	1906	1,152
Devil postpile,* Cal	1911	800
El Morro, N. M	1906	160
Gila cliff dwellings,* N. M	1907	160
Gran Quivira, N. M	1909	160
Grand canyon,* Ariz	1908	806,400
Jewel cave,* S. D	1908	1,280
Lassen peak,* Cal	1907	1,280
Lewis and Clark cavern, Mont	1908	160
Montezuma castle, Ariz	1906	160
Mount Olympus,* Wash	1909	608,640
Muir Woods, Cal	1908	295
Mukuntuweap, Utah	1909	15,840
Natural bridges, Utah	1909	2,740
Navajo, Ariz	1909	600
Oregon caves,* Ore	1909	480
Petrified forest, Ariz	1906	25,625
Pinnacles,* Cal	1908	2,080
Rainbow bridge, Utah	1910	160
Shoshone cavern, Wyo	1909	210
Sitka, Alaska	1910	57
Tonto,* Ariz	1907	640
Tumacacori, Ariz	1908	10
Wheeler,* Col	1908	300

*Administered by department of agriculture; others by interior department, except the Big Hole battle field, which is under the war department.

NOTES ON NATIONAL MONUMENTS.

Big Hole battle field—Scene of fight at Big Hole pass on Big Hole or Wisdom river, Aug. 9, 1877, between Nez Perce Indians under Chief Joseph and a small force of soldiers commanded by Col. John Gibbon; in Silver Bow county, Montana; reached from Melrose.

Chaco canyon—Located in San Juan and McKinley counties, New Mexico; contains extensive prehistoric communal or pueblo ruins.

Cinder cone—An elevation in Lassen county in northern California; is of importance as illustrating volcanic activity in the vicinity 200 years ago.

Colorado—Extraordinary examples of erosion in Mesa county, western Colorado; reached from Grand Junction.

Devil postpile—Natural formations, including Rainbow waterfalls, within the Sierra national forest

in California; area set aside is on middle fork of San Joaquin river.

Devil's tower—A lofty and isolated rock in Crook county, Wyoming; is an extraordinary example of the effect of erosion in the higher mountains.

El Morro—An elevation near Wingate station on the Santa Fe railroad in New Mexico; contains prehistoric ruins and interesting rock inscriptions.

Gila cliff dwellings—In the Mogollon mountains, New Mexico; known also as the Gila Hot Springs cliff houses; are among the best preserved remains of the cliff dwellers of the southwest.

Gran Quivira—Ruined town not far from Manzano in the central part of New Mexico; remains of large cathedral and chapel and of many houses thought to date from prehistoric times.

Grand canyon—In northwestern Arizona; greatest eroded canyon within the United States.

Jewel cave—A natural formation of scientific interest within the Black Hills national forest in Custer county, South Dakota.

Lassen peak—In national forest of same name in Shasta county, northern California; marks the southern terminus of the long line of extinct volcanoes in the Cascade range, from which one of the greatest volcanic fields in the world extends.

Lewis and Clark cavern—An extraordinary limestone cavern near Limespur, Jefferson county, Montana.

Montezuma castle—Large prehistoric ruin or cliff dwelling on Beaver creek, Arizona.

Mount Olympus—Mountain in the state of Washington; has extensive glaciers and on its slopes are the breeding grounds of the Olympic elk.

Muir woods—In Marin county, California; an extensive growth of redwood trees of great age and size; land presented to the government by William Kent of Chicago.

Mukuntuweap—Canyon in southwestern Utah through which flows the north fork of the Rio Virgin or Zion river; an extraordinary example of canyon erosion.

Natural bridges—Rock formations in southeastern Utah extending over streams or chasms; have loftier heights and greater spans than any other similar formations known; reserved as extraordinary examples of stream erosion.

Navajo—Within the Navajo Indian reservation in Arizona; includes a number of prehistoric cliff dwellings and pueblo ruins new to science.

Oregon caves—Within the Siskiyou national forest in Oregon; caves are of natural formation and of unusual scientific interest and importance.

Petrified forest—Deposits of fossilized or mineralized wood in Gila and Apache counties, Arizona.

Pinnacles—A series of natural formations of rock with a number of caves underlying them; located within Pinnacles national forest in California.

Rainbow bridge—An extraordinary natural bridge in southeastern Utah, having an arch which in form and appearance is much like a rainbow; is 309 feet high and 278 feet span; of scientific interest as an example of eccentric stream erosion.

Shoshone cavern—A cave in Big Horn county, Wyoming, of unknown extent, but of many windings and ramifications and containing vaulted chambers of large size, magnificently decorated with sparkling crystals and beautiful stalactites, and containing pits of unknown depth.

Sitka—Tract of about fifty-seven acres within public park, near Sitka, Alaska; battle ground of Russian conquest of Alaska in 1804; site of former village of Kiki-Siti tribe, the most warlike of Alaska Indians; contains numerous totem poles constructed by the Indians, recording the genealogical history of their several clans.

Tonto—Comprises two prehistoric ruins of ancient cliff dwellings in Gila county, Arizona.

Tumacacori—Ruin of an ancient Spanish mission of brick, cement and mortar in Santa Cruz county, Arizona.

Wheeler—Volcanic formations illustrating erratic erosion; in Rio Grande and Cochetopa national forests in southwestern Colorado.

RESERVATIONS FOR THE PROTECTION OF WILD LIFE.

[From a report by T. S. Palmer, assistant chief biological survey.]

In the last forty years many reservations have been created which directly or incidentally protect wild life. The largest is Yellowstone National park, established in 1872. Some of the lighthouse reservations, which in recent years have become important refuges, are even older. Since 1872 other national parks have been set aside, military parks have been established on battle fields, national monuments have been created for the protection of objects of scientific interest and reservations have been set aside for the protection of the breeding grounds of waterfowl and other birds. Of the national reservations sixty-six are under the department of agriculture, twelve under the interior department, nine under the commerce and labor department, five under the war department and one each under the navy department, the Smithsonian institution and the District of Columbia. Of the sixteen national parks, ten may properly be considered game refuges. These are the Yellowstone in Wyoming, the National Zoological and Rock Creek parks in the District of Columbia, the Sequoia, Yosemite and General Grant parks in California, Mount Rainier in Washington, Crater Lake in Oregon, Wind Cave park in South Dakota and Glacier park in Montana. The National Zoological park is under the Smithsonian institution and the Rock Creek is in charge of a board of control, consisting of the commissioners of the District of Columbia and the chief engineers of the army. The others are under the jurisdiction of the department of the interior.

In 1912 Yellowstone National park contained 35,000 elk, 550 moose, 520 antelope, 210 mountain sheep, 49 wild buffalo and about 150 captive buffalo. There are also many deer, bears and beaver. The National Zoological park contains one of the largest collections of living mammals and birds in the United States. Deer, bears and mountain sheep are found in the Yosemite and Sequoia parks and

also in Crater Lake and Mount Rainier parks. Glacier park has beaver, deer, elk, moose, wild sheep and many goats and bears. There is but little large game in General Grant, Rock Creek and Wind Cave parks, but they are utilized as refuges. Wind Cave park is to be a game preserve for buffalo, elk and other species. The national military parks are important as refuges because they furnish protection at all seasons to small mammals and birds under comprehensive law for the protection of wild life, enacted in 1897. They also form with other military reservations a chain of refuges for migratory land birds in line with their northward flight. These military reservations are Chickamauga, Chattanooga and Shiloh, Tenn.; Vicksburg, Miss.; Antietam, Md., and Gettysburg, Pa. Some of the soldiers' homes have extensive grounds in which birds and small game are protected.

NATIONAL GAME PRESERVES.

There are nine national game preserves or reservations chiefly for big game. They comprise two national game preserves in Arizona and Oklahoma; the national bison range in Montana, the Mount Olympus national monument in the state of Washington, the small Fire island moose reservation in Cook inlet, Alaska; the Muir Woods and Pinnacles national monuments in California, and the Colorado national monument and the Mukuntuweap national monument in Utah. The department of agriculture has jurisdiction over the two game preserves and the Mount Olympus national monument, which are under the immediate charge of the forest service, and the bison and moose reservations, which are in charge of the biological survey. The department of the interior has charge of the other four national monuments. The wild life on the game preserves and national monuments is protected by the acts under which these reservations were created, while the buffalo on the bison range, the elk on the Mount Olympus monument and the moose on Fire

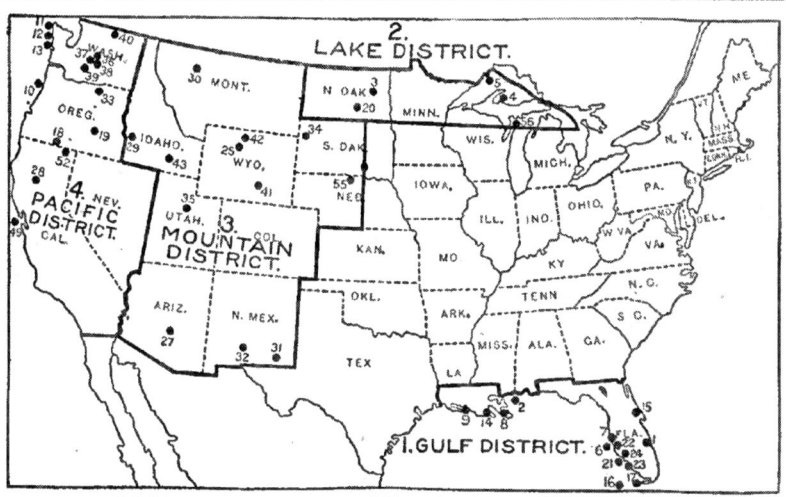

LOCATION OF NATIONAL BIRD RESERVATIONS AND ADMINISTRATIVE DISTRICTS.

island are protected under the laws of Montana, Washington and Alaska.

The Wichita game preserve in Oklahoma was established in 1905 and contains 57,120 acres. It shelters a herd of buffalo which in July, 1912, numbered forty animals. The national bison range in Montana, created in 1908, has an area of 18,521 acres and contains a herd of buffalo numbering eighty-one July 1, 1912. There are also small herds of elk and antelope and some deer on these preserves. The Grand Canyon game preserve in Arizona contains a good many deer and a few sheep. The Mount Olympus national monument in Washington has an area of 608,640 acres and is the home of the Roosevelt elk, supposed to number about 2,000. There are also many deer.

BIRD RESERVATIONS.

For the purpose of preserving the native wild birds of the country from destruction, the United States in 1903 inaugurated the plan of setting aside regions that contain important colonies of breeding birds as bird reservations or "refuges." The first reserve created was that including Pelican Island, Florida, containing a colony of brown pelicans. Since then many other reserves have been established by executive order in various parts of the union. The localities set aside are under the supervision of the secretary of agriculture, who appoints the inspectors and wardens. The reservations are grouped in six administrative districts, each in charge of an inspector, who supervises the work of the wardens stationed on the reservations. Under a federal law, approved June 28, 1906 (criminal code, section 84), it is unlawful for any person to hunt, trap, capture, willfully disturb or kill any bird of any kind or take the eggs of such birds on any lands of the United States which have been set apart or reserved as breeding grounds for birds by any law, proclamation or executive order, except under such rules as the secretary of agriculture may prescribe. Violations of the law are punishable by fines up to $500, or imprisonment for six months, or both.

With few exceptions the bird reservations are small rocky islands or tracts of marsh land of no agricultural value, or comprise the smallest legal subdivisions of land immediately adjoining the reservoirs on reclamation projects in the west. Among the small reservations may be mentioned Green Bay, Wis., less than two acres in extent; Pelican Island, Florida, less than six, and Stump Lake, a little over twenty-seven acres. On the other hand, the Niobrara reservation in Nebraska includes 10,000 to 12,000 acres. The Klamath lake and Malheur lake reservations in Oregon each comprise extensive strips of marsh lands. Following is a list alphabetically arranged of the bird reservations in the United States, with numbers corresponding to those on the accompanying map:

Belle Fourche, S. D..	34	Klamath Lake, Ore..	18
Bering Sea, Alaska..	44	Loch-Katrine, Wyo..	25
Bogoslof, Alaska..	51	Malheur Lake, Ore..	19
Breton Island, La..	2	Matlacha Pass, Fla..	23
Bumping Lake. Wash..	39	Minidoka, Idaho..	43
Carlsbad, N. M..	31	Mosquito Inlet, Fla..	15
Chase Lake, N. D..	20	Niobrara, Neb..	55
Clealum, Wash..	38	Palma Sola, Fla..	22
Clear Lake, Cal..	52	Passage Key, Fla..	6
Cold Springs, Ore..	33	Pathfinder, Wyo..	41
Conconully, Wash..	40	Pelican Island, Fla..	1
Copalis Rock, Wash..	13	Pine Island, Fla..	21
Culebra, P. R..	48	Pribilof, Alaska..	50
Deer Flat, Idaho..	29	Quillayute Needles,	
East Park, Cal..	28	Alaska	12
East Timbalier, La..	14	Rio Grande, N. M..	32
Farallon, Cal..	49	St. Lazaria, Alaska..	46
Flattery Rocks, Wash..	11	Salt River, Ariz..	27
Forrester Isl.. Alaska..	53	Shell Keys, La..	9
Green Bay. Wis..	56	Shoshone, Wyo..	42
Hawaiian Islands, Ha-		Siskiwit, Mich..	5
waii	26	Strawberry Vall'y, Utah..	35
Hazy Islands, Alaska..	54	Stump Lake, N. D..	3
Huron Islands, Mich..	4	Tern Islands, La..	8
Indian Key, Fla..	7	Three Arch Rocks, Ore..	10
Island Bay, Fla..	24	Tortugas Keys, Fla..	16
Kachess, Wash..	37	Tuxedni, Alaska..	45
Keechelus, Wash..	36	Willow Creek, Mont..	30
Key West, Fla..	17	Yukon Delta, Alaska..	47

The most important birds protected on the reservations in the Gulf district are brown pelicans, gulls, terns, herons and ducks. The principal birds in the lake district are gulls, ducks and white pelicans. The two Michigan reservations contain the largest known breeding colonies of the herring gull on inland waters. The Green Bay (Wis.) reservation also has a colony of these birds. The reservation at Stump lake, North Dakota, is the breeding place of several kinds of ducks, and is the only

point at which the white winged scoter is known to breed in the United States. At Chase lake are colonies of white pelicans and ring-billed gulls.

The reservations in the mountain district are chiefly valuable as refuges for water fowl and shore birds during the spring and autumn migrations. The Niobrara reservation is important chiefly as a breeding ground for sharp-tailed grouse and prairie chickens. The coast refuges in the Pacific district contain great rookeries of California guillemots, pigeon guillemots, tufted puffins, auklets, cormorants, ashy petrels and other sea birds. At the Klamath and Malheur reservations are found large colonies of Canada geese, gulls, Caspian terns, grebes, white pelicans and ducks. On the Alaska reservations are found auklets, puffins, cormorants, guillemots and petrels. The Yukon delta reservation embraces nesting grounds of ducks and geese, including the emperor goose. The birds on the Hawaiian reservation are chiefly albatrosses, petrels, terns, teal and rail.

OTHER RESERVATIONS.

Under the heading of fur seal, fishery, lighthouse and naval reservations are included ten refuges for aquatic mammals and birds and for fish. These reservations comprise the fur seal reservation on the Pribilof islands, three fishery reservations and five lighthouse reservations, all under the jurisdiction of the department of commerce and labor and in immediate charge of the bureau of fisheries and the bureau of lighthouses, and the Midway islands naval reservation. On the Pribilof islands are fur seals and sea lions, on the lighthouse reservations at Ano Nuevo island, Farallon island and Point Reyes, Cal., are rookeries of sea lions; on all the lighthouse reservations are breeding colonies of sea-birds, while at Afognak and Yes Bay, Alaska, and Baird, Cal., are fish cultural stations, established chiefly for the propagation of salmon. The Midway islands, which were set aside as a government reservation in 1903, are the home of various kinds of sea birds, including albatrosses. The canary, Laysan finch and Laysan rail have been successfully introduced. The reservation is in charge of the navy department.

STATE GAME PRESERVES.

Several national reservations have become game preserves through subsequent state legislation. Among these are the Teton and Big Horn in Wyoming, the Pinnacles in California, the Payette river in Idaho, the Yellowstone and Pryor Mountain in Montana and the Superior in Minnesota. The Superior national forest, which was made a state game preserve in 1909, contains 1,420,000 acres. In each case the game is protected primarily by state laws and the reservation patrolled and maintained by co-operation between the state and the general government.

SUMMARY OF RESERVATIONS.

Following is a summary by states and territories of all the national reservations for the protection of wild life:

Alaska—Two fishery reservations, 1 fur seal reservation, 1 moose reservation, 8 bird reservations; total, 12.

Arizona—One national game preserve, 1 bird reservation; total, 2.

California—Three national parks; 2 national monuments, 1 fish cultural station, 3 lighthouse reservations; total, 12.

Colorado—One national monument.

District of Columbia—Two national parks.

Florida—Ten bird reservations.

Hawaii—One naval reservation, 1 bird reservation; total, 2.

Idaho—One national forest containing a state game preserve; 2 bird reservations; total, 3.

Louisiana—Four bird reservations, 1 lighthouse reservation; total, 5.

Maryland—One military national park.

Michigan—Two bird reservations.

Minnesota—One national forest containing a state game preserve.

Mississippi—One military national park.

Montana—One national park, 1 bird reservation, 2 national forests containing state game preserves; total, 4.

New Mexico—Two bird reservations.

Nebraska—One bird reservation.

North Dakota—Two bird reservations.

Oklahoma—One game preserve.

Oregon—One national park, 4 bird reservations; total, 5.

Pennsylvania—One military national park.

Porto Rico—One bird reservation.

South Dakota—One national park, 1 bird reservation.

Tennessee—Two military national parks.

Utah—One national monument, 1 bird reservation; total, 2.

Washington—One national park, 1 national monument, 8 bird reservations, 1 lighthouse reservation; total, 11.

Wisconsin—One bird reservation.

Wyoming—One national park, 2 national forests containing state game preserves, 3 bird reservations; total, 6.

Grand total, 95.

AMERICAN HALL OF FAME.

"The Hall of Fame for Great Americans" is the name of a building on University Heights in New York city, in which are inscribed on bronze tablets the names of famous American men and women. Nominations for the honor are made by the public and are submitted to a committee of 100 eminent citizens. In the case of men fifty-one votes are required and in the case of women forty-seven. The first balloting took place in October, 1900, when the following were chosen:

George Washington.
Abraham Lincoln.
Daniel Webster.
Benjamin Franklin.
Ulysses S. Grant.
John Marshall.
Thomas Jefferson.
Ralph W. Emerson.

H. W. Longfellow.
Robert Fulton.
Horace Mann.
Henry W. Beecher.
James Kent.
Joseph Story.
John Adams.
Washington Irving.

Jonathan Edwards.
Samuel F. B. Morse.
David G. Farragut.
Henry Clay.
Nathaniel Hawthorne.
George Peabody.
Robert E. Lee.
Peter Cooper.
Eli Whitney.
John J. Audubon.
William E. Channing.
Gilbert Stuart.
Asa Gray.

CHOSEN IN 1905.
John Quincy Adams.
James Russell Lowell.
William T. Sherman.
James Madison.
John G. Whittier.

Alexander Hamilton.
Louis Agassiz.
John Paul Jones.
Mary Lyon.
Emma Willard.
Maria Mitchell.

CHOSEN IN 1910.
Harriet Beecher Stowe.
Oliver Wendell Holmes.
Edgar Allan Poe.
Roger Williams.
James Fenimore Cooper.
Phillips Brooks.
William Cullen Bryant.
Frances E. Willard.
Andrew Jackson.
George Bancroft.
John Lothrop Motley.

THE CAPITOL AT WASHINGTON.

The corner stone of the original capitol building was laid by President Washington Sept. 18, 1793. The north wing was finished in 1810 and the south wing in 1811, a wooden passageway connecting them. The original designs of the structure were made by Dr. William Thornton. The two wings were burned by the British in 1814, but were immediately restored. In 1827 the original building was completed at a cost of $2,433,844.13. Extensions of the wings were begun in 1851 and completed in 1859. The dome, which is 287 feet 5 inches in height, was completed in 1865. The capitol stands in latitude 38 degrees 53 minutes 20.4 seconds north and longitude 77 degrees 00 minutes 35.7 seconds west from Greenwich. The area covered by the building is 153,112 square feet.

CONSTITUTION OF THE UNITED STATES.

September 17, 1787.

PREAMBLE. We, the people of the United States, in order to form a more perfect union, establish justice, insure domestic tranquillity, provide for the common defense, promote the general welfare and secure the blessings of liberty to ourselves and our posterity, do ordain and establish this constitution for the United States of America:

ARTICLE I.

Section I. All legislative powers herein granted shall be vested in a congress of the United States, which shall consist of a senate and house of representatives.

Section II. 1. The house of representatives shall be composed of members chosen every second year by the people of the several states, and the electors in each state shall have the qualifications requisite for electors of the most numerous branch of the state legislature.

2. No person shall be a representative who shall not have attained to the age of 25 years and been seven years a citizen of the United States, and who shall not, when elected, be an inhabitant of that state in which he shall be chosen.

3. Representatives and direct taxes shall be apportioned among the several states which may be included within this union, according to their respective numbers, which shall be determined by adding to the whole number of free persons, including those bound to service for a term of years, and excluding Indians not taxed, three-fifths of all other persons. The actual enumeration shall be made within three years after the first meeting of the congress of the United States, and within every subsequent term of ten years, in such manner as they shall by law direct. The number of representatives shall not exceed one for every 30,000, but each state shall have at least one representative, and until such enumeration shall be made the state of New Hampshire shall be entitled to choose three; Massachusetts, eight; Rhode Island and Providence Plantations, one; Connecticut, five; New York, six; New Jersey, four; Pennsylvania, eight; Delaware, one; Maryland, six; Virginia, ten; North Carolina, five; South Carolina, five, and Georgia, three.

4. When vacancies happen in the representation from any state the executive authority thereof shall issue writs of election to fill such vacancies.

5. The house of representatives shall choose their speaker and other officers and shall have the sole power of impeachment.

Section III. 1. The senate of the United States shall be composed of two senators from each state, chosen by the legislature thereof, for six years, and each senator shall have one vote.

2. Immediately after they shall be assembled in consequence of the first election they shall be divided, as equally as may be, into three classes. The seats of the senators of the first class shall be vacated at the expiration of the second year; of the second class, at the expiration of the fourth year, and of the third class at the expiration of the sixth year, so that one-third may be chosen every second year, and if vacancies happen by resignation or otherwise, during the recess of the legislature of any state, the executive thereof may make temporary appointments until the next meeting of the legislature, which shall then fill such vacancies.

3. No person shall be a senator who shall not have attained the age of 30 years and been nine years a citizen of the United States, and who shall not, when elected, be an inhabitant of that state for which he shall be chosen.

4. The vice-president of the United States shall be president of the senate, but shall have no vote unless they be equally divided.

5. The senate shall choose their other officers and also a president pro tempore in the absence of the vice-president or when he shall exercise the office of president of the United States.

6. The senate shall have the sole power to try all impeachments. When sitting for that purpose they shall be on oath or affirmation. When the president of the United States is tried the chief justice shall preside, and no person shall be convicted without the concurrence of two-thirds of the members present.

7. Judgment, in cases of impeachment, shall not extend further than to removal from office and disqualification to hold and enjoy any office of honor, trust or profit under the United States, but the party convicted shall, nevertheless, be liable and subject to indictment, trial, judgment and punishment according to law.

Section IV. 1. The times, places and manner of holding elections for senators and representatives shall be prescribed in each state by the legislature thereof, but the congress may at any time, by law, make or alter such regulations, except as to the places of choosing senators.

2. The congress shall assemble at least once in every year, and such meeting shall be on the first Monday in December, unless they shall, by law, appoint a different day.

Section V. 1. Each house shall be the judge of the elections, returns and qualifications of its own members, and a majority of each shall constitute a quorum to do business, but a smaller number may adjourn from day to day, and may be authorized to compel the attendance of absent members, in such manner and under such penalties as each house may provide.

2. Each house may determine the rules of its proceedings, punish its members for disorderly behavior, and, with the concurrence of two-thirds, expel a member.

3. Each house shall keep a journal of its proceedings, and from time to time publish the same, excepting such parts as may, in their judgment, require secrecy; and the yeas and nays of the members of either house, on any question, shall, at the desire of one-fifth of those present, be entered on the journal.

4. Neither house, during the session of congress, shall, without the consent of the other, adjourn for more than three days, nor to any other place than that in which the two houses shall be sitting.

Section VI. 1. The senators and representatives shall receive a compensation for their services, to be ascertained by law, and paid out of the treasury of the United States. They shall, in all cases, except treason, felony and breach of the peace, be privileged from arrest during their attendance at the session of their respective houses and in going to or returning from the same, and for any speech or debate in either house they shall not be questioned in any other place.

2. No senator or representative shall, during the time for which he was elected, be appointed to any civil office under the authority of the United States which shall have been created, or the emoluments whereof shall have been increased, during such time, and no person holding any office under the United States shall be a member of either house during his continuance in office.

Section VII. 1. All bills for raising a revenue shall originate in the house of representatives, but the senate may propose or concur with amendments, as on other bills.

2. Every bill which shall have passed the house of representatives and the senate shall, before it becomes a law, be presented to the president of the United States; if he approve, he shall sign it, but if not, he shall return it, with his objections, to that house in which it shall have originated, who shall enter the objections at large on their journal and proceed to reconsider it. If, after such reconsideration, two-thirds of that house shall agree to pass the bill, it shall be sent, together with the objections, to the other house, by which it shall likewise be reconsidered, and if approved by two-thirds of that house it shall become a law. But in all such cases the votes of both houses shall be determined by yeas and nays, and the names of the persons voting for and against the bill shall be entered on the journal of each house respectively. If any bill shall not be returned by the president within ten days (Sundays excepted) after it shall have been presented to him, the same shall be a law, in like manner as if he had signed it, unless the congress, by their adjourn-

ment, prevent its return, in which case it shall not be a law.

3. Every order, resolution or vote to which the concurrence of the senate and house of representatives may be necessary (except on a question of adjournment) shall be presented to the president of the United States, and before the same shall take effect shall be approved by him, or, being disapproved by him, shall be repassed by two-thirds of the senate and house of representatives, according to the rules and limitations prescribed in case of a bill.

Section VIII. The congress shall have power—

1. To lay and collect taxes, duties, imposts and excises, to pay the debts and provide for the common defense and general welfare of the United States, but all duties, imposts and excises shall be uniform throughout the United States.

2. To borrow money on the credit of the United States.

3. To regulate commerce with foreign nations and among the several states and with the Indian tribes.

4. To establish an uniform rule of naturalization and uniform laws on the subject of bankruptcies throughout the United States.

5. To coin money, regulate the value thereof and of foreign coin, and fix the standard of weights and measures.

6. To provide for the punishment of counterfeiting the securities and current coin of the United States.

7. To establish postoffices and postroads.

8. To promote the progress of science and useful arts by securing, for limited times, to authors and inventors, the exclusive right to their respective writings and discoveries.

9. To constitute tribunals inferior to the Supreme court. To define and punish piracies and felonies committed on the high seas and offenses against the law of nations.

10. To declare war, grant letters of marque and reprisal and make rules concerning captures on land and water.

11. To raise and support armies, but no appropriation of money to that use shall be for a longer term than two years.

12. To provide and maintain a navy.

13. To make rules for the government and regulation of the land and naval forces.

14. To provide for calling forth the militia to execute the laws of the union, suppress insurrections and repel invasions.

15. To provide for organizing, arming and disciplining the militia and for governing such part of them as may be employed in the service of the United States, reserving to the states respectively the appointment of the officers and the authority of training the militia according to the discipline prescribed by congress.

16. To exercise exclusive legislation in all cases whatsoever over such district (not exceeding ten miles square) as may, by cession of particular states and the acceptance of congress, become the seat of government of the United States, and to exercise like authority over all places purchased, by the consent of the legislature of the state in which the same shall be, for the erection of forts, magazines, arsenals, dockyards and all other needful buildings; and.

17. To make all laws which shall be necessary and proper for carrying into execution the foregoing powers and all other powers vested by this constitution in the government of the United States or in any department or officer thereof.

Section IX. 1. The migration or importation of such persons as any of the states now existing shall think proper to admit shall not be prohibited by the congress prior to the year one thousand eight hundred and eight, but a tax or duty may be imposed on such importation, not exceeding $10 for each person.

2. The privilege of the writ of habeas corpus shall not be suspended, unless when, in cases of rebellion or invasion, the public safety may require it.

3. No bill of attainder or ex post facto law shall be passed.

4. No capitation or other direct tax shall be laid, unless in proportion to the census or enumeration hereinbefore directed to be taken.

5. No tax or duty shall be laid on articles exported from any state. No preference shall be given, by any regulation of commerce or revenue, to the ports of one state over those of another; nor shall vessels bound to or from one state be obliged to enter, clear or pay duties in another.

6. No money shall be drawn from the treasury but in consequence of appropriations made by law, and a regular statement and account of receipts and expenditures of all public money shall be published from time to time.

7. No title of nobility shall be granted by the United States, and no person holding any office of profit or trust under them shall, without the consent of congress, accept of any present, emolument, office or title of any kind whatever, from any king, prince or foreign state.

Section X. 1. No state shall enter into any treaty, alliance or confederation; grant letters of marque and reprisal; coin money; emit bills of credit; make anything but gold and silver coin a tender in payment of debts; pass any bill of attainder, ex post facto law, or law impairing the obligation of contracts, or grant any title of nobility.

2. No state shall, without the consent of the congress, lay any imposts or duties on imports or exports except what may be absolutely necessary for executing its inspection laws, and the net produce of all duties and imposts laid by any state on imports or exports shall be for the use of the treasury of the United States, and all such laws shall be subject to the revision and control of the congress. No state shall, without the consent of congress, lay any duty of tonnage, keep troops or ships of war in time of peace, enter into any agreement or compact with another state or with a foreign power or engage in war, unless actually invaded or in such imminent danger as will not admit of delay.

ARTICLE II.

Section I. 1. The executive power shall be vested in a president of the United States of America. He shall hold his office during the term of four years, and together with the vice-president, chosen for the same term, be elected as follows:

2. Each state shall appoint, in such manner as the legislature thereof may direct, a number of electors, equal to the whole number of senators and representatives to which the state may be entitled in the congress, but no senator or representative or person holding an office of trust or profit under the United States shall be appointed an elector.

3. The electors shall meet in their respective states and vote by ballot for two persons, of whom one at least shall not be an inhabitant of the same state with themselves. And they shall make a list of all the persons voted for and of the number of votes for each, which list they shall sign and certify and transmit sealed to the seat of government of the United States, directed to the president of the senate. The president of the senate shall, in the presence of the senate and house of representatives, open all the certificates and the votes shall then be counted. The person having the greatest number of votes shall be the president, if such number be a majority of the whole number of electors appointed, and if there be more than one who have such majority and have an equal number of votes, then the house of representatives shall immediately choose, by ballot, one of them for president; and if no person have a majority, then from the five highest on the list the said house shall, in like manner, choose the president. But in choosing the president the votes shall be taken by states, the representation from each state having one vote; a quorum for this purpose shall consist of a member or members from two-thirds of the states, and a majority of all the states shall be necessary to a choice. In every case after the choice of the president the person having the greatest number of votes of the electors shall be the vice-president. But if there should remain two or more who have equal votes the senate shall choose from them, by

ballot, the vice-president. [The foregoing provisions were changed by the 12th amendment.]

4. The congress may determine the time of choosing the electors and the day on which they shall give their votes, which day shall be the same throughout the United States.

5. No person except a natural-born citizen or a citizen of the United States at the time of the adoption of this constitution shall be eligible to the office of president; neither shall any person be eligible to that office who shall not have attained to the age of 35 years and been fourteen years a resident within the United States.

6. In case of the removal of the president from office or of his death, resignation or inability to discharge the powers and duties of the said office, the same shall devolve on the vice-president; and the congress may, by law, provide for the case of removal, death, resignation or inability both of the president and vice-president, declaring what officer shall then act as president, and such officer shall act accordingly, until the disability be removed or a president shall be elected.

7. The president shall, at stated times, receive for his services a compensation, which shall neither be increased nor diminished during the period for which he shall have been elected, and he shall not receive within that period any other emolument from the United States or any of them.

8. Before he enters on the execution of his office he shall take the following oath or affirmation:

I do solemnly swear (or affirm) that I will faithfully execute the office of president of the United States, and will, to the best of my ability, preserve, protect and defend the constitution of the United States.

Section II. 1. The president shall be commander in chief of the army and navy of the United States and of the militia of the several states when called into the actual service of the United States. He may require the opinion, in writing, of the principal officer in each of the executive departments upon any subject relating to the duties of their respective offices, and he shall have the power to grant reprieves and pardons for offenses against the United States except in cases of impeachment.

2. He shall have power, by and with the advice and consent of the senate, to make treaties, provided two-thirds of the senators present concur, and he shall nominate, and, by and with the advice and consent of the senate, shall appoint ambassadors, other public ministers and consuls, judges of the Supreme court and all other officers of the United States whose appointments are not herein otherwise provided for and which shall be established by law. But the congress may, by law, vest the appointment of such inferior officers as they think proper in the president alone, in the courts of law or in the heads of departments.

3. The president shall have power to fill up all vacancies that may happen during the recess of the senate by granting commissions, which shall expire at the end of their next session.

Section III. He shall, from time to time, give to the congress information of the state of the union and recommend to their consideration such measures as he shall judge necessary and expedient. He may, on extraordinary occasions, convene both houses or either of them, and in case of disagreement between them, with respect to the time of adjournment, he may adjourn them to such time as he shall think proper. He shall receive ambassadors and other public ministers. He shall take care that the laws be faithfully executed, and shall commission all officers of the United States.

Section IV. The president, vice-president and all civil officers of the United States shall be removed from office on impeachment for and conviction of treason, bribery or other high crimes and misdemeanors.

ARTICLE III.

Section I. The judicial power of the United States shall be vested in one Supreme court and in such inferior courts as the congress may, from time to time, ordain and establish. The judges, both of the Supreme and inferior courts, shall hold their offices during good behavior, and shall, at stated times, receive for their services a compensation, which shall not be diminished during their continuance in office.

Section II. 1. The judicial power shall extend to all cases, in law and equity, arising under this constitution, the laws of the United States and treaties made or which shall be made, under their authority; to all cases affecting ambassadors, other public ministers and consuls; to all cases of admiralty and maritime jurisdiction; to controversies to which the United States shall be a party; to controversies between two or more states; between a state and citizens of another state; between citizens of different states; between citizens of the same state, claiming lands under grants of different states, and between a state or the citizens thereof and foreign states, citizens or subjects.

2. In all cases affecting ambassadors, other public ministers and consuls and those in which a state shall be a party the Supreme court shall have original jurisdiction. In all the other cases before mentioned the Supreme court shall have appellate jurisdiction, both as to law and fact, with such exceptions and under such regulations as the congress shall make.

3. The trial of all crimes, except in cases of impeachment, shall be by jury, and such trials shall be held in the state where the said crimes shall have been committed, but when not committed within any state the trial shall be at such place or places as the congress may by law have directed.

Section III. 1. Treason against the United States shall consist only in levying war against them or in adhering to their enemies, giving them aid and comfort. No person shall be convicted of treason unless on the testimony of two witnesses to the same overt act or on confession in open court.

2. The congress shall have power to declare the punishment of treason, but no attainder of treason shall work corruption of blood or forfeiture except during the life of the person attainted.

ARTICLE IV.

Section I. Full faith and credit shall be given in each state to the public acts, records and judicial proceedings of every other state. And the congress may, by general laws, prescribe the manner in which such acts, records and proceedings shall be proved and the effect thereof.

Section II. 1. The citizens of each state shall be entitled to all privileges and immunities of citizens in the several states.

2. A person charged in any state with treason, felony or other crime, who shall flee from justice and be found in another state, shall, on demand of the executive authority of the state from which he fled, be delivered up, to be removed to the state having jurisdiction of the crime.

3. No person held to service or labor in one state under the laws thereof, escaping into another, shall, in consequence of any law or regulation therein, be discharged from such service or labor, but shall be delivered up on claim of the party to whom such service or labor may be due.

Section III. 1. New states may be admitted by the congress into this union, but no new state shall be formed or erected within the jurisdiction of any other state, nor any state be formed by the junction of two or more states or parts of states, without the consent of the legislatures of the states concerned as well as of the congress.

2. The congress shall have power to dispose of and make all needful rules and regulations respecting the territory or other property belonging to the United States, and nothing in this constitution shall be so construed as to prejudice any claims of the United States or of any particular state.

Section IV. The United States shall guarantee to every state in this union a republican form of government, and shall protect each of them against invasion, and on application of the legislature or of the executive (when the legislature cannot be convened) against domestic violence.

ARTICLE V.

The congress, whenever two-thirds of both houses shall deem it necessary, shall propose amendments to this constitution, or, on the application of the legislatures of two-thirds of the several states, shall call a convention for proposing amendments, which, in either case, shall be valid to all intents and purposes as part of this constitution, when ratified by the legislatures of three-fourths of the several states or by conventions in three-fourths thereof, as the one or the other mode of ratification may be proposed by the congress; provided, that no amendment which may be made prior to the year one thousand eight hundred and eight shall in any manner affect the first and fourth clauses in the ninth section of the first article, and that no state, without its consent, shall be deprived of its equal suffrage in the senate.

ARTICLE VI.

Section I. 1. All debts contracted and engagements entered into before the adoption of this constitution shall be as valid against the United States under this constitution as under the confederation.

2. This constitution and the laws of the United States which shall be made in pursuance thereof, and all treaties made or which shall be made under authority of the United States, shall be the supreme law of the land, and the judges in every state shall be bound thereby, anything in the constitution or laws of any state to the contrary notwithstanding.

3. The senators and representatives before mentioned and the members of the several state legislatures and all executive and judicial officers, both of the United States and of the several states, shall be bound, by oath or affirmation, to support this constitution, but no religious test shall ever be required as a qualification to any office or public trust under the United States.

ARTICLE VII.

The ratification of the conventions of nine states shall be sufficient for the establishment of this constitution between the states so ratifying the same.

Done in convention, by the unanimous consent of the states present, the seventeenth day of September, in the year of our Lord one thousand seven hundred and eighty-seven, and of the independence of the United States of America the twelfth.

AMENDMENTS TO THE CONSTITUTION.

Proposed by congress and ratified by the legislatures of the several states, pursuant to article V. of the original constitution.

I. Congress shall make no law respecting an establishment of religion or prohibiting the free exercise thereof, or abridging the freedom of speech or of the press, or the right of the people peaceably to assemble and to petition the government for a redress of grievances.

II. A well-regulated militia being necessary to the security of a free state, the right of the people to keep and bear arms shall not be infringed.

III. No soldier shall, in time of peace, be quartered in any house without the consent of the owner; nor in wartime but in a manner to be prescribed by law.

IV. The right of the people to be secure in their persons, houses, papers and effects against unreasonable searches and seizures shall not be violated, and no warrants shall issue but upon probable cause, supported by oath or affirmation, and particularly describing the place to be searched and the persons or things to be seized.

V. No person shall be held to answer for a capital or otherwise infamous crime unless on a presentment or indictment of a grand jury except in cases arising in the land or naval forces or in the militia, when in actual service, in time of war or public danger; nor shall any person be subject for the same offense to be twice put in jeopardy of life or limb; nor shall he be compelled in any criminal case to be a witness against himself, nor be deprived of life, liberty or property without due process of law; nor shall private property be taken for public use without just compensation.

VI. In all criminal prosecutions the accused shall enjoy the right to a speedy and public trial by an impartial jury of the state and district wherein the crime shall have been committed, which district shall have been previously ascertained by law, and to be informed of the nature and cause of the accusation; to be confronted with the witnesses against him; to have compulsory process for obtaining witnesses in his favor, and to have the assistance of counsel for his defense.

VII. In suits at common law, where the value in controversy shall exceed $20, the right of trial by jury shall be preserved, and no fact tried by a jury shall be otherwise re-examined in any court of the United States than according to the rules of the common law.

VIII. Excessive bail shall not be required, nor excessive fines imposed, nor cruel and unusual punishments inflicted.

IX. The enumeration in the constitution of certain rights shall not be construed to deny or disparage others retained by the people.

X. The powers not delegated to the United States by the constitution nor prohibited by it to the states are preserved to the states respectively or to the people.

XI. The judicial power of the United States shall not be construed to extend to any suit in law or equity commenced or prosecuted against one of the United States by citizens of another state or by citizens or subjects of any foreign state.

XII. Section 1. The electors shall meet in their respective states and vote by ballot for president and vice-president, one of whom at least shall not be an inhabitant of the same state with themselves; they shall name in their ballots the person voted for as president, and in distinct ballots the person voted for as vice-president, and they shall make distinct lists of all persons voted for as president and of all persons voted for as vice-president, and of the number of votes for each, which list they shall sign and certify and transmit sealed to the seat of the government of the United States, directed to the president of the senate; the president of the senate shall, in the presence of the senate and house of representatives, open all the certificates and the votes shall then be counted; the person having the greatest number of votes for president shall be the president, if such number be a majority of the whole number of electors appointed, and if no person have such majority, then from the persons having the highest numbers, not exceeding three, on the list of those voted for as president, the house of representatives shall choose immediately, by ballot, for president. But in choosing the president the votes shall be taken by states, the representation from each state having one vote; a quorum for this purpose shall consist of a member or members from two-thirds of the states, and a majority of all the states shall be necessary to a choice. And if the house of representatives shall not choose a president whenever the right of choice shall devolve upon them before the fourth day of March next following, then the vice-president shall act as president, as in the case of the death or other constitutional disability of the president.

Section 2. The person having the greatest number of votes as vice-president shall be the vice-president, if such number be a majority of the whole number of electors appointed, and if no person have a majority, then from the two highest numbers on the list the senate shall choose a vice-president. A quorum for the purpose shall consist of two-thirds of the whole number of senators and a majority of the whole number shall be necessary to a choice.

Section 3. But no person constitutionally ineligible to the office of president shall be eligible to that of vice-president of the United States.

XIII. Section 1. Neither slavery nor involuntary servitude, except as a punishment for crime whereof the party shall have been duly convicted, shall exist within the United States or any place subject to their jurisdiction.

Section 2. Congress shall have the power to enforce this article by appropriate legislation.

XIV. Section 1. All persons born or naturalized in the United States and subject to the jurisdic-

tion thereof are citizens of the United States and of the state wherein they reside. No state shall make or enforce any law which shall abridge the privileges or immunities of citizens of the United States, nor shall any state deprive any person of life, liberty or property without due process of law, nor deny to any person within its jurisdiction the equal protection of the laws.

Section 2. Representatives shall be apportioned among the several states according to their respective numbers, counting the whole number of persons in each state, excluding Indians not taxed. But when the right to vote at any election for the choice of electors for president and vice-president of the United States, representatives in congress, the executive and judicial officers of a state or the members of the legislature thereof is denied to any of the male inhabitants of such state, being 21 years of age and citizens of the United States, or in any way abridged, except for participation in rebellion or other crime, the basis of representation therein shall be reduced in the proportion which the number of such male citizens shall bear to the whole number of male citizens 21 years of age in such state.

Section 3. No person shall be a senator or representative in congress or elector of president and vice-president, or hold any office, civil or military, under the United States, or under any state, who, having previously taken the oath as a member of congress or as an officer of the United States, or as a member of any state legislature, or as an executive or judicial officer of any state, to support the constitution of the United States, shall have engaged in insurrection or rebellion against the same or given aid or comfort to the enemies thereof. But congress may, by a vote of two-thirds of each house, remove such disability.

Section 4. The validity of the public debt of the United States, authorized by law, including debts incurred for payment of pensions and bounties for services in suppressing insurrection or rebellion, shall not be questioned. But neither the United States nor any state shall assume or pay any debt or obligation incurred in aid of insurrection or rebellion against the United States or any claim for the loss or emancipation of any slave, but all such debts, obligations and claims shall be held illegal and void.

Section 5. The congress shall have the power to enforce by appropriate legislation the provisions of this article.

XV. Section 1. The right of citizens of the United States to vote shall not be denied or abridged by the United States or any state on account of race, color or previous condition of servitude.

Section 2. The congress shall have power to enforce this article by appropriate legislation.

XVI. The congress shall have power to lay and collect taxes on incomes, from whatever sources derived, without apportionment among the several states and without regard to any census or enumeration.

XVII. The senate of the United States shall be composed of two senators from each state, elected by the people thereof, for six years, and each senator shall have one vote. The electors in each state shall have the qualifications requisite for electors of the most numerous branch of the state legislatures. When vacancies happen in the representation of any state in the senate, the executive authority of such state shall issue writs of election to fill such vacancies: Provided, That the legislature of any state may empower the executive thereof to make temporary appointment until the people fill the vacancies by election as the legislature may direct.

INCOME TAX LAW PROCLAIMED.

Feb. 25, 1913, Secretary of State Philander C. Knox signed a proclamation announcing the adoption of the income tax amendment as a part of the constitution. The proclamation was as follows:

To All to Whom These Presents May Come, Greeting:

Know ye that the congress of the United States at the first session, 61st congress, in the year 1909 passed a resolution in the words and figures following, to wit:

"Joint resolution proposing an amendment to the constitution of the United States:

"Resolved, by the senate and house of representatives of the United States of America in congress assembled (two-thirds of each house concurring therein), That the following article is proposed as an amendment to the constitution of the United States, which, when ratified by the legislatures of three-fourths of the several states, shall be valid, to all intents and purposes, as a part of the constitution:

" 'Article 6. The congress shall have power to lay and collect taxes on incomes from whatever source derived without apportionment among the several states and without regard to any census or enumeration.' "

And further, that it appears from official documents on file in this department that the amendment to the constitution of the United States proposed, as aforesaid, has been ratified by the legislatures of the states of Alabama, Kentucky, South Carolina, Illinois, Mississippi, Oklahoma, Maryland, Georgia, Texas, Ohio, Idaho, Oregon, Washington, California, Montana, Indiana, Nevada, North Carolina, Nebraska, Kansas, Colorado, North Dakota, Michigan, Iowa, Missouri, Maine, Tennessee, Arkansas, Wisconsin, New York, South Dakota, Arizona, Minnesota, Louisiana, Delaware and Wyoming, in all thirty-six.

And further, that the states whose legislatures have so ratified the said proposed amendment constitute three-fourths of the whole number of states of the United States.

And further, that it appears from official documents on file in this department that the legislatures of New Jersey and New Mexico have passed resolutions ratifying the said proposed amendments.

Now, therefore, let it be known that I, Philander C. Knox, secretary of state for the United States, by virtue and in pursuance of section 205 of the revised statutes of the United States, do hereby certify that the amendment aforesaid has become valid to all intents and purposes as a part of the constitution of the United States.

In testimony whereof I have hereunto set my hand and caused the seal of the department of state to be affixed.

(Signed)   PHILANDER C. KNOX.

DIRECT ELECTION OF UNITED STATES SENATORS.

May 31, 1913, Secretary of State William Jennings Bryan signed a proclamation announcing the adoption of the constitutional amendment providing for the direct election of United States senators by the people of the several states. The proclamation was as follows:

To All to Whom These Presents May Come, Greeting:

Know ye that the congress of the United States at the second session, 62d congress, in the year 1912, passed a resolution in the words and figures following, to-wit:

"Joint resolution proposing an amendment to the constitution providing that senators shall be elected by the people of the several states.

"Resolved, by the senate and house of representatives of the United States of America in congress assembled (two-thirds of each house concurring therein), That in lieu of the first paragraph of section 3 of article I. of the constitution of the United States, and in lieu of so much of paragraph 2 of the same section as relates to the filling of vacancies, the following be proposed as an amendment to the constitution, which shall be valid to all intents and purposes as part of the constitution when ratified by the legislatures of three-fourths of the states:

" 'The senate of the United States shall be composed of two senators from each state, elected by the people thereof, for six years, and each senator shall have one vote. The electors in each state shall have the qualifications requisite for electors of the most numerous branch of the state legislatures.

" 'When vacancies happen in the representation of any state in the senate, the executive authority

of such state shall issue writs of election to fill such vacancies: Provided, That the legislature of any state may empower the executive thereof to make temporary appointment until the people fill the vacancies by election as the legislature may direct.

"This amendment shall not be so construed as to affect the election or term of any senator chosen before it becomes valid as part of the constitution."

And, further, that it appears from official documents on file in this department that the amendment to the constitution of the United States proposed as aforesaid has been ratified by the legislatures of the states of Massachusetts, Arizona, Minnesota, New York, Kansas, Oregon, North Carolina, California, Michigan, Idaho, West Virginia, Nebraska, Iowa, Montana, Texas, Washington, Wyoming, Colorado, Illinois, North Dakota, Nevada, Vermont, Maine, New Hampshire, Oklahoma, Ohio, South Dakota, Indiana, Missouri, New Mex-

ico, New Jersey, Tennessee, Arkansas, Connecticut, Pennsylvania and Wisconsin.

And, further, that the states whose legislatures have so ratified the said proposed amendment constitute three-fourths of the whole number of states in the United States.

Now, therefore, be it known that I, William Jennings Bryan, secretary of state of the United States, by virtue and in pursuance of section 205 of the revised statutes of the United States, do hereby certify that the amendment aforesaid has become valid to all intents and purposes as a part of the constitution of the United States.

In testimony whereof, I have hereunto set my hand and caused the seal of the department of state to be affixed.

Done at the city of Washington, this thirty-first day of May, in the year of our Lord one thousand nine hundred and thirteen and of the independence of the United States of America the one hundred and thirty-seventh.

[Seal]   WILLIAM JENNINGS BRYAN.

SABOTAGE, SYNDICALISM AND DIRECT ACTION.

SABOTAGE.

The word sabotage is derived from the French "sabot," meaning wooden shoe. Originally the term "sabotage" was used as a slang expression for working clumsily, but since 1897 it has been employed to describe a principle or method of labor warfare. It has been variously defined as being equivalent to "bad work for bad wages," to the old Scotch "go canny" ("go slow") and to "soldiering." As generally understood it means the substitution of secretly inefficient, unprofitable or even destructive work for the open strike by employes who are dissatisfied with their wages or conditions of labor; in the more extreme cases it means secret violence, such as tampering with machinery or spoiling the products of industry.

"It is," says John Spargo in his book on "Syndialism, Industrial Unionism and Socialism," "the principle of action capable of an almost infinite variety of applications. It may involve violence or it may be peaceful. It may involve destruction of property or it may not. It may be based on illegal acts or it may not. It may consist of telling lies or of telling the simple truth. It is, therefore, exceedingly difficult to formulate a satisfactory definition of it clearly, though we may understand its meaning. It is essentially a furtive and stealthy policy, practiced by individual workers, having for its aim the obstruction of industry and business to such an extent that employers will suffer a loss of profits so great as to be compelled to grant the workers' demand."

Arturo M. Giovanetti, a defender and advocate of sabotage, gives two definitions as follows:

"A. Any conscious and willful act on the part of one or more workers intended to slacken and reduce the output of production in the industrial field, or to restrict trade and reduce profits in the commercial field, in order to secure from their employers better conditions or to enforce those promised or maintain those already prevailing, when no other way of redress is open.

"B. Any skillful operation on the machinery of production intended not to destroy it or permanently render it defective, but only temporarily to disable it and put it out of running condition in order to make impossible the work of scabs and thus secure the complete and real stoppage of work during a strike."

SYNDICALISM.

Syndicalism, as commonly understood in America, is that type of radical trade unionism which aims to destroy the state as at present constituted and make labor supreme. It had its origin in the

French Confederation Generale du Travail (General Confederation of Labor), an organization of workers known for their advocacy of violence in the settlement of differences between capital and labor. "Briefly stated," says Samuel P. Orth in "Socialism and Democracy in Europe," "it is class war in its most violent form without the aid of parliaments and politics; with the enginery of the general strike, and the spirit of universal upheaval and anarchy."

"Syndicalism," says John Spargo, "is a form of labor unionism which aims at the abolition of the capitalist system based upon the exploitation of the workers and its replacement by a new social order free from class domination and exploitation. Its distinctive principle as a practical movement is that these ends are to be attained by the direct actions of the unions, without parliamentary action or the intervention of the state. The distinctive feature of its ideal is that in the new social order the political state will not exist, the only form of government being the administration of industry directly by the workers themselves."

In America the syndicalist movement is led by the Industrial Workers of the World, of which William D. Haywood is the best known representative.

DIRECT ACTION.

"Direct action" in industrial disputes is any action taken by the workers without the intervention of the state. It includes sabotage, strikes, boycotts, assaults on the person, destruction of property and violence of all kinds. It is defined by its advocates as any method which drives the employer, either by interest or fear, to yield to labor's demand.

THE GENERAL STRIKE.

The "general strike" may be defined as the cessation of labor by workers of many kinds for some economic or political purpose. As the term is now employed, such a strike is usually national in scope and the benefit sought is of wide application. Thus the Swedish general strike of 1909 was for more wages and shorter hours for working people in general. This was an economic strike, but proved a failure. The general strike in Belgium in 1913 was for the reform of the electoral system and was a success in that the government was obliged to take the matter up for consideration, which was all that the strikers asked. There have been a considerable number of these strikes in recent years with varying results. The general strike advocated by the syndicalists is the cessation of all work for the purpose of destroying capitalism and establishing a new social and industrial order.

JUDICIAL RECALL IN CALIFORNIA.

Charles Weller, a police judge in San Francisco, Cal., was "recalled" April 22, 1913, by a vote of 30,784 to 29,934, Wiley F. Crist being elected in his place. The charge against Judge Weller was that he had permitted the assailant of a young girl to escape by reducing his bail to such an extent that

he forfeited it and escaped. It was found that he had in many similar cases fixed bail at an unduly small amount. The recall election was held under the constitutional provision adopted by California in 1911 and was the first of its kind in the United States.

HOLIDAYS IN THE UNITED STATES.

GENERALLY OR LOCALLY OBSERVED.

Arbor Day—Usually fixed by governor.
Bennington Battle Day—Aug. 16.
Christmas Day—Dec. 25.
Columbus Day—Oct. 12.
Confederate Memorial Day—See Decoration day.
Davis, Jefferson, Birthday—June 3.
Decoration Day—Federal, May 30; confederate, April 26 (Alabama, Georgia, Florida, Mississippi) and May 10 (North and South Carolina).
Election Days—See Election Calendar.
Flag Day—June 14; designated by governor.
Georgia Day—Feb. 12.
Independence Day—July 4.
Jefferson's Birthday—April 13.
Labor Day—First Monday in September.
Landing Day—July 25 (Porto Rico).
Lee's Birthday—Jan. 19.
Lincoln's Birthday—Feb. 12.
Maine (Battle Ship) Day—Feb. 15.
Mardi Gras—February (New Orleans).
McKinley Day—Jan. 29.
Mecklenburg Independence Declaration—May 20.
Memorial Day—See Decoration day.
Mothers' Day—Second Sunday in May.
New Orleans, Battle of—Jan. 8.
New Year's Day—Jan. 1.
Patriots' Day—April 19 (Maine, Massachusetts).
Pioneers' Day—July 15 (Idaho), July 24 (Utah).
Texas Independence Day—March 2.
Thanksgiving Day—Last Thursday in November.
Washington's Birthday—Feb. 22.

HOLIDAYS IN THE VARIOUS STATES.

Alabama—Jan. 1; Jan. 19 (Lee's birthday); Feb. 22; Mardi Gras (the day before Ash Wednesday, first day of Lent); Good Friday (the Friday before Easter); April 26 (Confederate Memorial day); June 3 (Jefferson Davis' birthday); July 4; Labor day (first Monday in September); Thanksgiving day (last Thursday in November); Dec. 25.

Alaska—Jan. 1; Feb. 22; May 30 (Memorial day); July 4; Thanksgiving day; Dec. 25.

Arizona—Jan. 1; Arbor day (first Monday in February); Feb. 22; May 30; July 4; general election day; Thanksgiving day; Dec. 25.

Arkansas—Jan. 1; Feb. 22; July 4; Thanksgiving day; Oct. 12 (Columbus day); Dec. 25.

California—Jan. 1; Feb. 22; May 30; July 4; Sept. 9 (Admission day); Labor day (first Monday in September); Oct. 12; general election day in November; Thanksgiving day; Dec. 25.

Colorado—Jan. 1; Feb. 22; Arbor and School day (third Friday in April); May 30; July 4; first Monday in September; general election day; Oct. 12; Thanksgiving day; Dec. 25; every Saturday afternoon from June 1 to Aug. 31 in the city of Denver.

Connecticut—Jan. 1; Feb. 12 (Lincoln's birthday); Feb. 22; Good Friday; May 30; July 4; Labor day (first Monday in September); Thanksgiving day; Dec. 25.

Delaware—Jan. 1; Feb. 22; May 30; July 4; first Monday in September; Oct. 12; Thanksgiving day; Dec. 25.

District of Columbia—Jan. 1; Feb. 22; March 4 (Inauguration day); May 30; July 4; first Monday in September; Thanksgiving day; Dec. 25.

Florida—Jan. 1; Jan. 19 (Lee's birthday); Arbor day (first Friday in February); Feb. 22; April 26 (Confederate Memorial day); June 3 (Jefferson Davis' birthday); July 4; first Monday in September; Thanksgiving day; general election day; Dec. 25.

Georgia—Jan. 1; Jan. 19 (Lee's birthday); Feb. 22; April 26 (Confederate Memorial day); June 3 (Jefferson Davis' birthday); July 4; first Monday in September; Thanksgiving day; Arbor day (first Friday in December); Dec. 25.

Idaho—Jan. 1; Feb. 22; Arbor day (first Friday after May 1); July 4; first Monday in September; Oct. 12; general election day; Thanksgiving day; Dec. 25.

Illinois—Jan. 1; Feb. 12 (Lincoln's birthday); Feb. 22; May 30; July 4; Labor day (first Monday in September); Oct. 12 (Columbus day);

---

general, state, county and city election days; Saturday afternoons; Thanksgiving day; Dec. 25; Arbor, Bird, Flag and Mothers' days are appointed by the governor, but are not legal holidays. Like McKinley day (Jan. 29), "Remember the Maine" day (Feb. 15), Douglas day (April 23), they are observed by special exercises, flag displays, etc.; banks are not closed. Arbor and Bird days usually come on the third Friday of April in the northern part of the state and the fourth Friday of October in the southern part. Flag day is June 14 and Mothers' day the second Sunday in May.

Indiana—Jan. 1; Feb. 22; May 30; July 4; first Monday in September; Oct. 12; general election day; Thanksgiving day; Dec. 25.

Indian Territory—July 4; Dec. 25.

Iowa—Jan. 1; Feb. 22; May 30; July 4; first Monday in September; general election day; Thanksgiving day; Dec. 25.

Kansas—The only holidays by statute are Feb. 12; Feb. 22; May 30; Labor day (first Monday in September) and Arbor day; Oct. 12; but the days commonly observed in other states are holidays by general consent.

Kentucky—Jan. 1; Feb. 22; May 30; first Monday in September; Oct. 12; Thanksgiving day; general election day; Dec. 25.

Louisiana—Jan. 1; Jan. 8 (anniversary of the battle of New Orleans); Feb. 22; Mardi Gras (day before Ash Wednesday); Good Friday (Friday before Easter); April 26 (Confederate Memorial day); July 4; Nov. 1 (All Saints' day); general election day; fourth Saturday in November (Labor day, in the parish of New Orleans only); Dec. 25; every Saturday afternoon in New Orleans.

Maine—Jan. 1; Feb. 22; Good Friday; May 30; July 4; Labor day; Thanksgiving day; Dec. 25.

Maryland—Jan. 1; Feb. 22; May 30; July 4; first Monday in September; Sept. 12 (Defenders' day); Oct. 12; general election day; Dec. 25; every Saturday afternoon.

Massachusetts—Feb. 22; April 19 (Patriots' day); May 30; July 4; first Monday in September; Thanksgiving day; Dec. 25.

Michigan—Jan. 1; Feb. 22; Oct. 12; general election day; May 30; July 4; first Monday in September; Thanksgiving day; Dec. 25.

Minnesota—Jan. 1; Feb. 12; Feb. 22; Good Friday (Friday before Easter); May 30; July 4; first Monday in September; Thanksgiving day; general election day; Dec. 25; Arbor day (as appointed by the governor).

Mississippi—First Monday in September; by common consent July 4, Thanksgiving day and Dec. 25 are observed as holidays.

Missouri—Jan. 1; Feb. 22; May 30; July 4; Labor day; Oct. 12; general election day; Thanksgiving day; Dec. 25; every Saturday afternoon in cities of 100,000 or more inhabitants.

Montana—Jan. 1; Feb. 22; Arbor day (third Tuesday in April); May 30; July 4; first Monday in September; Oct. 12; general election day; Thanksgiving day; Dec. 25; any day appointed by the governor as a fast day.

Nebraska—Jan. 1; Feb. 22; Arbor day (April 22); May 30; July 4; first Monday in September; Thanksgiving day; Dec. 25.

Nevada—Jan. 1; Feb. 22; July 4; Thanksgiving day; Dec. 25.

New Hampshire—Feb. 22; fast day appointed by the governor; May 30; July 4; first Monday in September; Thanksgiving day; general election day; Dec. 25.

New Jersey—Jan. 1; Feb. 22; May 30; July 4; first Monday in September; Oct. 12; general election day; Thanksgiving and fast days, and every Saturday afternoon.

New Mexico—Jan. 1; July 4; Thanksgiving and fast days; Dec. 25; Decoration, Labor and Arbor days appointed by the governor.

New York—Jan. 1; Feb. 12; Feb. 22; May 30; July 4; first Monday in September; Oct. 12; general election day; Thanksgiving and fast days; Dec. 25; every Saturday afternoon.

North Carolina—Jan. 1; Jan. 19 (Lee's birthday); May 10 (Confederate Memorial day); May 20

(anniversary of the signing of the Mecklenburg declaration of independence) ; July 4; state election day in August; first Thursday in September (Labor day); Thanksgiving day; Dec. 25; every Saturday afternoon.

North Dakota—Jan. 1; Feb. 12; Feb. 22; May 30; July 4; Arbor day (when appointed by the governor); general election day; Thanksgiving day; Dec. 25.

Ohio—Jan. 1; Feb. 22; May 30; July 4; first Monday in September; Oct. 12; general election day; Thanksgiving day; Dec. 25; every Saturday afternoon in cities of 50,000 or more inhabitants.

Oklahoma—Jan. 1; Feb. 22; May 30; July 4; Oct. 12; general election day; Thanksgiving day; Dec. 25.

Oregon—Jan. 1; Feb. 22; May 30; first Saturday in June; July 4; first Monday in September; general election day; Thanksgiving day; public fast day; Dec. 25.

Pennsylvania—Jan. 1; Feb. 12; Feb. 22; May 30; Good Friday; July 4; first Monday in September; Oct. 12; general election day; Thanksgiving day; Dec. 25; every Saturday afternoon.

Philippines—Jan. 1; Feb. 22; Thursday and Friday of Holy week; July 4; Aug. 13; Thanksgiving day; Dec. 25; Dec. 30.

Porto Rico—Jan. 1; Feb. 22; Good Friday; May 30; July 4; July 25 (Landing day); Thanksgiving day; Dec. 25.

Rhode Island—Jan. 1; Feb. 22; second Friday in May (Arbor day); May 30; July 4; first Monday in September; Oct. 12; general election day; Thanksgiving day; Dec. 25.

South Carolina—Jan. 1; Jan. 19 (Lee's birthday); Feb. 22; May 10 (Confederate Memorial day); June 3 (Jefferson Davis' birthday); general election day; Thanksgiving day; Dec. 25, 26, 27.

South Dakota—Same as in North Dakota.

Tennessee—Jan. 1; Good Friday; May 30; July 4; first Monday in September; general election day;

Thanksgiving day; Dec. 25; every Saturday afternoon.

Texas—Jan. 1; Feb. 22 (Arbor day); March 2 (anniversary of Texas independence); April 21 (anniversary of battle of San Jacinto); July 4; first Monday in September; Oct. 12; general election day; appointed fast days; Thanksgiving day; Dec. 25.

Utah—Jan. 1; Feb. 22; April 15 (Arbor day); May 30; July 4; July 24 (Pioneer day); first Monday in September; Thanksgiving day and appointed fast days; Dec. 25.

Vermont—Jan. 1; Feb. 22; May 30; July 4; Aug. 16 (Bennington Battle day); Labor day; Oct. 12; Thanksgiving day; Dec. 25.

Virginia—Jan. 1; Jan. 19 (Lee's birthday); Feb. 22; July 4; first Monday in September; Thanksgiving and appointed fast days; Dec. 25; every Saturday afternoon.

Washington—Jan. 1; Feb. 12 (Lincoln's birthday); Feb. 22; May 30; July 4; first Monday in September; Oct. 12; general election day; Thanksgiving day; Dec. 25.

West Virginia—Jan. 1; Feb. 12; Feb. 22; May 30; July 4; Labor day; general election day; Thanksgiving day; Dec. 25.

Wisconsin—Jan. 1; Feb. 22; May 30; July 4; first Monday in September; general election day; Thanksgiving day; Dec. 25.

Wyoming—Jan. 1; Feb. 12; Feb. 22; May 30; July 4; first Monday in September; general election day; Dec. 25.

The national holidays, such as July 4, New Year's, etc., are such by general custom and observance and not because of congressional legislation. Congress has passed no laws establishing holidays for the whole country. It has made Labor day a holiday in the District of Columbia, but the law is of no effect elsewhere.

GREAT EARTHQUAKES IN MODERN TIMES.

SAN FRANCISCO, CAL.

Date—April 18, 1906.
Lives lost—452.
Persons injured—1,500.
Persons made homeless—265,000.
Property loss—$350,000,000 (estimated).
Loss of insurance companies—$132,823,067.21.
Buildings destroyed—60,000.
Blocks or squares burned—453.
Area of burned district—3.96 square miles.
Relief appropriation by congress—$2,500,000.
Relief subscription—$11,000,000.

VALPARAISO, CHILE.

Date—Aug. 16, 1906.
Lives lost—1,500.
Property loss—$100,000,000.

KINGSTON, JAMAICA.

Date—Jan. 14, 1907.
Lives lost—1,100.
Persons injured—2,000.
Property loss—$25,000,000.
Buildings destroyed—6,000.
Area of ruined district—50 acres.
Area affected by earthquake—300 acres.
Duration of first shock—35 seconds.
Duration of fire after earthquake—40 hours.

SICILY AND CALABRIA.

Date—Dec. 28, 1908.
Day of week—Monday.
Hour—5:23 a. m.
Duration of shock—35 seconds.
Lives lost—76,483.
Persons injured—95,470.
Persons made homeless—1,100,000.
Property destroyed—(No estimate attempted).
Region affected—Northeastern Sicily and southwestern Calabria.
Chief cities and towns destroyed or damaged—In Sicily: Messina, Faro, Santa Teresa, Scaileta. In Calabria: Reggio, Gallico, San Giovanni, San Eufemia, Pellaro, Palmi, Canniteilo.

CARTAGO, COSTA RICA.

Date—May 5, 1910.
Hour—7 p. m.
Lives lost—1,500.

TURKEY.

Date—Aug. 9, 1912.
Lives lost—3,000.
Persons injured—6,000.
Persons homeless—40,000.

PRESIDENTIAL ELECTION IN FRANCE.

Raymond Poincare, lawyer, member of the French academy and statesman, was elected president of France at Versailles, Jan. 17, 1913, for the seven year term ending February, 1920. His closest competitor for the honor was Jules Pams, minister of agriculture. The vote on the first ballot was indecisive, as no candidate received a majority, but on the second M. Poincare received 483 votes to 296 for M. Pams and 69 for Marie Edouard Valliant. Presidential elections in France take place in Versailles, the choice being made by the national assembly, composed of both chambers of parliament. The people of the country have no direct voice in the matter. Following is a list of the presidents of France since the establishment of the third republic and the dates of their election:

M. Thiers, Aug. 31, 1871.
Marshal MacMahon, May 24, 1873.
Jules Grevy, Jan. 30, 1879.
Marie F. S. Carnot, Dec. 3, 1887.
Jean Casimir Perier, June 27, 1894.
Francois Felix Faure, Jan. 17, 1895.
Emile Loubet, Feb. 18, 1899.
Armand Fallieres, Jan. 18, 1906.
Raymond Poincare, Jan. 17, 1913.

UNITED STATES REVENUE CUTTER SERVICE.

In a general way the duties which the revenue cutter service is called upon to perform may be classified as follows:

1. Assistance of vessels in distress.
2. Co-operation with the navy in times of war.
3. Destruction of derelicts and other menaces to navigation.
4. Protection of the customs revenue.
5. Enforcement of the navigation and other laws governing merchant vessels and motor boats.
6. Regulation and policing of regattas and marine parades.
7. Enforcement of laws relating to anchorage of vessels.
8. Enforcement of the neutrality laws.
9. Enforcement of quarantine and immigration laws.
10. Suppression of mutinies on board merchant vessels.
11. Protection of game and the seal and other fisheries in Alaska; suppression of illegal traffic in firearms, ammunition and spirits in Alaska.
12. Co-operation with the life-saving service by the instruction, drilling and inspection of its crews.

The revenue cutter service, which is organized on a military basis, is under control of the secretary of the treasury, the assistant secretary having supervision. The administration is in charge of a captain commandant, whose office is in Washington, D. C. The authorized commissioned personnel consists of 159 line officers, 81 engineer officers and 2 constructors, a total of 242. The total authorized complement of warrant officers, petty officers and men is 1,576. Commissioned officers are appointed from cadets at the School of Instruction, New London, Conn. The school course extends over three years and embraces instruction in professional and academic subjects. Admission is by competitive examination and candidates must not be less than 18 nor more than 24 years of age. Candidates for the engineer corps must be not less than 21 nor more than 26 years of age.

Warrant officers are appointed by the secretary of the navy and hold their appointments during good behavior. Petty officers and other men are enlisted for periods of one year. After three successive enlistments an increase in pay is allowed; the law also provides an annual sum for uniforms. Efficiency in the enlisted ranks is rewarded by promotion to the several grades of petty officers and the warrant officers are selected from the petty officers as vacancies occur. The pay of the commissioned personnel is fixed by congress to correspond with the pay and allowances of like rank in the army.

By law the officers of the revenue cutter service rank as follows:

Captain commandant, with colonel in army and captain in navy.

Senior captain and engineer in chief, with lieutenant-colonel in army and commander in the navy.

Captain and captain of engineers, with major in army and lieutenant-commander in navy.

First lieutenant and first lieutenant of engineers, with captain in army and senior lieutenant in navy.

Second lieutenant and second lieutenant of engineers, with first lieutenant in army and junior lieutenant in navy.

Third lieutenant and third lieutenant of engineers, with second lieutenant in army and ensign in navy.

Following are the names, dates of construction (in parentheses), chief dimensions, tonnage, armament, speed and headquarters of the vessels of the revenue cutter service:

FIRST CLASS VESSELS.

Acushnet (1908)—Length, 152 feet; beam, 29 feet; draft, 13 feet 9 inches; displacement, 800 tons; two one-pounder guns; speed, 12½ knots; Woods Hole, Mass.

Algonquin (1898)—Length 205 feet 6 inches; beam, 32 feet; draft, 13½ feet; displacement, 1,181 tons; four six-pounder guns; speed, 16 knots; San Juan, P. R.

Androscoggin (1908)—Length, 210 feet; beam, 35 feet 2 inches; draft, 17½ feet; displacement, 1,600 tons; four six-pounder guns; Portland, Me.

Apache (1891)—Length, 188 feet; beam, 29 feet; draft, 9 feet 3 inches; displacement, 700 tons; three three-pounder guns; Baltimore, Md.

Bear (1874)—Length, 198 feet; beam 28½ feet; draft, 18 feet 2 inches; displacement 1,700 tons; speed, 8 knots; three six-pounder guns; San Diego, Cal.

Gresham (1897)—Length, 205½ feet; beam, 32 feet; draft, 12½ feet; displacement, 1,090 tons; speed, 17 knots; four six-pounder guns; Boston, Mass.

Itasca (1893)—Length, 189½ feet; beam, 32 feet; draft, 13 feet 10 inches; displacement, 980 tons; speed, 14½ knots; four six-pounder guns; practice ship.

McCulloch (1897)—Length, 219 feet; beam, 32 feet 6 inches; draft, 15 feet 11 inches; displacement, 1,400 tons; four six-pounder guns; San Francisco, Cal.

Manning (1897)—Length, 205 feet; beam, 32 feet; draft, 13 feet 9 inches; displacement, 1,150 tons; speed, 17 knots; four six-pounder guns; Astoria, Ore.

Miami (1912)—Length, 190 feet; beam, 32½ feet; draft, 14 feet 1 inch; displacement, 1,300 tons; three six-pounder guns; speed, 12½ knots; Key West, Fla.

Mohawk (1902)—Length, 205½ feet; beam, 32 feet; draft, 12 feet 7 inches; displacement, 1,150 tons; four six-pounder guns; New York, N. Y.

Onondaga (1898)—Length, 205½ feet; beam, 32 feet; draft, 13 feet 2 inches; displacement, 1,190 tons; four six-pounder guns; Norfolk, Va.

Seminole (1900)—Length, 188 feet; beam, 29½ feet; draft, 11 feet 8 inches; displacement, 845 tons; nominal speed, 16½ knots; four six-pounder guns; Wilmington, N. C.

Seneca (1908)—Length, 204 feet; beam, 34 feet; draft, 17 feet 3 inches; displacement, 1,445 tons; speed, 12½ knots; four six-pounder guns; used exclusively as a derelict destroyer; New York, N. Y.

Snohomish (1907)—Length, 152 feet; beam, 29 feet; draft, 15 feet 5 inches; displacement, 880 tons; two one-pounder guns; used chiefly for life saving purposes on north Pacific coast; Port Angeles, Wash.

Tahoma (1909)—Length, 191 feet 8 inches; beam, 32½ feet; draft, 14½ feet; displacement, 1,215 tons; four six-pounder guns; Port Townsend, Wash.

Thetis (1881)—Length, 188¼ feet; beam, 29 feet; draft, 17 feet 10 inches; displacement, 1,250 tons; three three-pounders; Honolulu, H. I.

Tuscarora (1902)—Length, 178 feet; beam, 30 feet; draft, 10 feet 11 inches; displacement, 740 tons; one three-pounder gun; Milwaukee, Wis.

Unalga (1912)—Length, 190 feet; beam, 32½ feet; draft, 14 feet 1 inch; displacement, 1,180 tons; speed, 12½ knots; three six-pounder guns; Juneau, Alaska.

Yamacraw (1909)—Length, 191 feet 8 inches; beam, 32½ feet; draft, 13 feet; displacement, 1,080 tons; four six-pounders; Savannah, Ga.

SECOND CLASS VESSELS.

Colfax—Length, 179 feet 5 inches; beam 25 feet; draft, 10 feet; displacement, 496 tons; used as station ship at service depot, Arundel Cove, Md.

Morrill (1889)—Length 145 feet 3 inches; beam 24 feet; draft, 9½ feet; displacement, 420 tons; one three-pounder gun; Detroit, Mich.

Pamlico (1907)—Length, 158 feet; beam, 30 feet; draft, 5 feet 8 inches; displacement, 450 tons; two three-pounder guns; Newbern, N. C.

Windom (1896)—Length, 170 feet 8 inches; beam, 27 feet; draft, 9½ feet; displacement, 670 tons; three three-pounder guns; Galveston, Tex.

Winona (1890)—Length, 148½ feet; beam, 26 feet 3 inches; draft, 6 feet 10 inches; displacement, 400 tons; one three-pounder gun; Mobile, Ala.

Woodbury (1864)—Length, 146½ feet; beam, 28½ feet; draft, 11 feet 7 inches; displacement, 500 tons; one three-pounder gun; Eastport, Me.

THIRD CLASS VESSELS AND LAUNCHES.

Alert (1907)—Launch; length, 61½ feet; Mobile, Ala.
Arcata (1903)—Tug, length, 85 feet; displacement, 140 tons; Port Townsend, Wash.
Calumet (1894)—Harbor boat; length, 94½ feet; displacement, 170 tons; New York, N. Y.
Davey (1908)—Harbor vessel; length, 92½ feet; displacement, 180 tons; New Orleans, La.
Golden Gate (1896)—Harbor vessel; length, 110 feet; displacement, 240 tons; San Francisco, Cal.
Guide (1907)—Motor boat; length, 70 feet; New York, N. Y.
Guthrie (1895)—Harbor vessel; length, 88 feet; displacement, 150 tons; Baltimore, Md.
Hartley (1875)—Harbor vessel; length, 64½ feet; displacement, 65 tons; San Francisco, Cal.
Hudson (1893)—Harbor vessel; length, 96½ feet; displacement, 180 tons; New York, N. Y.
Mackinack (1903)—Harbor vessel; length, 110 feet; displacement, 240 tons; Sault Ste. Marie, Mich.
Manhattan (1873)—Harbor vessel; length, 102 feet; displacement, 145 tons; New York, N. Y.
Patrol (1899)—Motor launch; length, 36 feet 2 inches; Chicago, Ill.
Penrose (1883)—Launch; length, 67 feet; Pensacola, Fla.
Scout (1896)—Steam launch; length, 65 feet; Port Townsend, Wash.
Tybee (1895)—Steam launch; length, 63 feet; Savannah, Ga.
Vigilant (1910)—Motor launch; length, 45 feet; Sault Ste. Marie, Mich.
Winnisimmet (1903)—Harbor vessel; length, 96½ feet; displacement, 180 tons; Boston, Mass.

Wissahickon (1904)—Harbor vessel; length, 96½ feet; displacement, 195 tons; Philadelphia, Pa.

OPERATIONS IN 1912.*

Lives saved from drowning	106
Persons on board vessels assisted	2,212
Persons in distress cared for	275
Vessels boarded and papers examined	24,918
Vessels seized or reported for violation of law	1,208
Fines and penalties incurred by vessels reported	$224,210.00
Regattas and marine parades patrolled	31
Derelicts removed or destroyed	45
Vessels to which assistance was given	260
Value of vessels assisted	$10,545,573.00
Value of derelicts recovered	$166,175.00
Appropriation for 1912	$2,463,000.00
Expended for maintenance and repairs	$2,458,246.56

*Fiscal year ended June 30.

ADMINISTRATION, 1912-1913.

Chief of Division—Captain Commandant Ellsworth P. Bertholf.
Assistant Chief of Division—Henry S. Merrill.
Superintendent Construction and Repairs—Senior Captain Howard Emery.
Engineer in Chief—Charles McAllister.
Personnel and Operations—Capt. Preston H. Uberroth.
Equipment Officer—First Lieutenant Leonard T. Cutter.
Ordnance Officer—First Lieutenant Bernard H. Camden.

FREE PUBLIC EMPLOYMENT OFFICES.

Free employment bureaus have been established in a number of states, chiefly for two reasons: First, the necessity of curbing the evils of private agencies through competition, and, second, the belief that it is the duty of the state to make some provision for its unemployed. According to a bulletin of the United States bureau of labor issued in March, 1913, employment agencies maintained by the state and designated as either free employment bureaus or free employment offices, now exist in fifteen states. Following is a list of these states, with the year of the passage of the law creating such bureaus and the number and location of such offices:

Colorado, 1907, 3 offices; Colorado Springs, Denver, Pueblo.
Connecticut, 1905, 5 offices; Bridgeport, Hartford, New Haven, Norwich, Waterbury.
Illinois, 1899, 6 offices; 3 in Chicago, 1 each in Peoria, East St. Louis, Springfield.
Indiana, 1909, 1 office; Indianapolis.
Kansas, 1901, 1 office; Topeka.
Maryland, 1902, 1 office; Baltimore.
Massachusetts, 1906, 3 offices; Boston, Fall River, Springfield.
Michigan, 1905, 5 offices; Detroit, Grand Rapids, Jackson, Kalamazoo, Saginaw. Three other offices had been authorized for Bay City, Battle Creek and Muskegon, but were not established at the time of the report.
Minnesota, 1905, 3 offices; Duluth, Minneapolis, St. Paul.
Missouri, 1899, 3 offices; Kansas City, St. Joseph, St. Louis.

Ohio, 1890, 5 offices; Cleveland, Columbus, Cincinnati, Dayton, Toledo.
Oklahoma, 1908, 3 offices; Oklahoma, Muskogee, Enid.
Rhode Island, 1908, 1 office; Providence.
West Virginia, 1901, 1 office; Wheeling.
Wisconsin, 1901, 4 offices; LaCrosse, Milwaukee, Oshkosh, Superior.

Free municipal employment bureaus are also maintained in Los Angeles and Sacramento, Cal.; Butte and Great Falls, Mont.; Newark, N. J.; Seattle, Tacoma, Spokane and Everett, Wash. Various philanthropic and semiphilanthropic agencies are engaged in the distribution of labor in all large cities. Among these may be mentioned immigrant societies, municipal lodging houses, public and private charity associations, the Salvation Army, Volunteers of America and the Young Men's and Young Women's Christian associations. The Y. M. C. A. branches secured positions for 31,539 unemployed persons in 1910 and for 30,525 in 1911. The results accomplished at the state free employment agencies are shown by the following statistics of positions secured for unemployed persons:

State and year.	Pos.	State and year.	Pos.
Colorado, 1910	18,865	Minnesota, 1910	51,713
Connecticut, 1910	8,126	Missouri, 1911	6,827
Indiana, 1911	2,846	Ohio, 1911	47,963
Illinois, 1911	59,827	Oklahoma, 1911	14,942
Kansas, 1911	3,290	Rhode Island, 1911	1,728
Maryland, 1911	1,271	W. Virginia, 1912	1,926
Massachusetts, 1911	56,463	Wisconsin, 1910	23,852
Michigan, 1911	46,757		

FLOWER AND GEM SYMBOLS OF MONTHS.

Month.	Flower.	Gem.
January	Snowdrop	Garnet.
February	Primrose	Amethyst.
March	Violet	Bloodstone.
April	Daisy	Diamond.
May	Hawthorn	Emerald.
June	Honeysuckle	Chalcedony.
July	Water lily	Ruby.
August	Poppy	Sardonyx.
September	Morning glory	Sardoryx.
October	Hops	Aquamarine.

Month.	Flower.	Gem.
November	Chrysanthemum	Topaz.
December	Holly	Turquoise.

The above gem symbols are those of Polish tradition. The Jewish gem symbols of the months are: January, garnet; February, amethyst; March jasper; April, sapphire; May, chalcedony, carnelian or agate; June, emerald; July, onyx; August, carnelian; September, chrysolite; October, aquamarine or beryl; November, topaz; December, ruby.

UNITED STATES MILITARY ACADEMY.

West Point, N. Y.

The United States military academy is a school for the practical and theoretical training of cadets for the military service of the United States. When any cadet has completed the course of four years satisfactorily he is eligible for promotion and commission as a second lieutenant in any arm or corps in the army in which there may be a vacancy, the duties of which he may have been judged competent to perform.

Appointments — Each congressional district and territory, including the District of Columbia and Porto Rico, is entitled to have one cadet at the academy. Each state is also entitled to have two cadets from the state at large and forty are allowed from the United States at large. The law provides that for six years from July 1, 1916, whenever any cadet shall have finished three years of his course at the academy his successor may be admitted. The appointment from a congressional district is made upon the recommendation of the representative in congress from that district and those from the state at large upon the recommendations of the senators of the state. The appointments for the United States at large are made by the president upon his own selection. The appointment from the District of Columbia is made on the recommendation of the district commissioners and that from Porto Rico on the recommendation of the resident commissioner. Appointments are made one year in advance of admission. For each candidate appointed two alternates should be nominated. Four cadets from the Philippines are admitted.

Examinations—On the second Tuesday in January of each year the candidate selected for appointment must appear for mental and physical examination before boards of army officers at such places as the war department may designate. Candidates who pass will be admitted to the academy on March 1 following.

Mental Requirements—Each candidate must show that he is well versed in algebra, to include quadratic equations and progressions, plane geometry, English grammar, composition and literature, descriptive and physical geography and general and United States history.

Physical Requirements—No candidate will be admitted who is under 17 or over 22 years of age, or less than five feet four inches in height at the age of 17, or five feet five inches at the age of 18 and upward, or who is deformed or afflicted with any disease or infirmity which would render him unfit for military service. Candidates must be unmarried.

Pay—The pay of a cadet is $600 a year and one ration a day, or commutation therefor at 30 cents a day. The total is $709.50, to begin with his admission to the academy. No cadet is allowed to receive money or other supplies from his parents or from any other person without the sanction of the superintendent.

Enlistment—Before receiving his warrant of appointment a candidate for admission is required to sign an agreement to serve in the army of the United States eight years from the time of his admission to the academy.

UNITED STATES NAVAL ACADEMY.

Annapolis, Md.

The United States naval academy is a school for the practical and theoretical training of young men for the naval service of the United States. The students are styled midshipmen. The course of study is six years—four years at the academy and two years at sea—at the expiration of which time the examination for final graduation takes place. Midshipmen who pass are appointed to fill vacancies in the lower grade of the line of the navy, and occasionally to fill vacancies in the marine corps and in certain of the staff corps of the navy.

Appointments — Two midshipmen are allowed for each senator, representative and delegate in congress, two for the District of Columbia and five each year from the United States at large. The appointments from the District of Columbia and five each year at large are made by the president. One midshipman is allowed from Porto Rico, who must be a native of that island. The appointment is made by the president on the recommendation of the governor of Porto Rico. Candidates must be actual residents of the districts from which they are nominated.

Examinations—Two examinations for the admission of midshipmen are held each year. The first is held on the third Tuesday in April under the supervision of the civil service commission at certain specified points in each state and territory. All those qualifying mentally, who are entitled to appointment in order of nomination, will be notified by the superintendent of the naval academy when to report at the academy for physical examination, and if physically qualified will be appointed. The second and last examination is held on the third Tuesday in June at Annapolis, Md. Alternates are given the privilege of reporting for mental examination at the same time as the principals. Examination papers are all prepared at the academy and the examinations of candidates are finally passed upon by the academic board. Certificates from colleges and high schools will not be accepted in lieu of the entrance examinations at the naval academy.

Mental Requirements—Candidates will be examined in punctuation, spelling, arithmetic, geography, English grammar, United States history, world's history, algebra through quadratic equations and plane geometry (five books of Chauvenet's geometry or an equivalent).

Physical Requirements—All candidates must, at the time of their examination for admission, be between the ages of 16 and 20 years. A candidate is eligible for appointment the day he becomes 16 and is ineligible on the day he becomes 20 years of age. Candidates are required to be of good moral character, physically sound, well formed and of robust constitution. The height of candidates for admission must not be less than five feet two inches between the ages of 16 and 18 years, and not less than five feet four inches between the ages of 18 and 20 years. The minimum weight at 16 years is 105 pounds with an increase of five pounds for each additional year or fraction of a year over one-half. Candidates must be unmarried.

Pay—The pay of a midshipman is $600 a year, beginning at the date of his admission. Midshipmen must supply themselves with clothing, books, etc., the total expense of which amounts to $280.64. Traveling expenses to the academy are paid by the government.

Enlistment—Each midshipman on admission is required to sign articles by which he binds himself to serve in the United States navy eight years (including his time of probation at the naval academy).

UNITED STATES CIVIL SERVICE.

Civil service act approved Jan. 16, 1883.

Officers—Three commissioners are appointed by the president to assist him in classifying the government offices and positions, formulating rules and enforcing the law. Their office is in Washington, D. C. The chief examiner is appointed by the commissioners to secure accuracy, uniformity and justice in the proceedings of the examining boards. The secretary to the commission is appointed by the president.

General Rules—The fundamental rules governing appointments to government positions are found in the civil service act itself. Based upon these are many other regulations formulated by the commission and promulgated by the president from time to time as new contingencies arise. The present rules were approved March 20, 1903, and went into effect April 15, 1903. In a general way they require that there must be free, open examinations of applicants for positions in the public service; that appointments shall be made from those graded highest in the examinations; that appointments to the service in Washington shall be apportioned among the states and territories according to population; that there shall be a period (six months) of probation before any absolute appointment is made; that no person in the public service is for that reason obliged to contribute to any political fund or is subject to dismissal for refusing to so contribute; that no person in the public service has any right to use his official authority or influence to coerce the political action of any person. Applicants for positions shall not be questioned as to their political or religious beliefs and no discrimination shall be exercised against or in favor of any applicant or employe on account of his religion or politics. The classified civil service shall include all officers and employes in the executive civil service of the United States except laborers and persons whose appointments are subject to confirmation by the senate.

Examinations—These are conducted by boards of examiners chosen from among persons in government employ and are held twice a year in all the states and territories at convenient places. In Illinois, for example, they are usually held at Cairo, Chicago and Peoria. The dates are announced through the newspapers or by other means. They can always be learned by applying to the commission or to the nearest postoffice or custom house. Those who desire to take examinations are advised to write to the commission in Washington for the "Manual of Examinations," which is sent free to all applicants. It is revised semiannually to Jan. 1 and July 1. The January edition contains a schedule of the spring examinations and the July edition contains a schedule of the fall examinations. Full information is given as to the methods and rules governing examinations, manner of making application, qualifications required, regulations for rating examination papers, certification for and chances of appointment, and as far as possible it outlines the scope of the different subjects of general and technical examinations. These are practical in character and are designed to test the relative capacity and fitness to discharge the duties to be performed. It is necessary to obtain an average percentage of 70 to be eligible for appointment, except that applicants entitled to preference because of honorable discharge from the military or naval service for disability resulting from wounds or sickness incurred in the line of duty need obtain but 65 per cent. The period of eligibility is one year.

Qualifications of Applicants—No person will be examined who is not a citizen of the United States; who is not within the age limitations prescribed; who is physically disqualified for the service which he seeks; who has been guilty of criminal, infamous, dishonest or disgraceful conduct; who has been dismissed from the public service for delinquency and misconduct or has failed to receive absolute appointment after probation; who is addicted to the habitual use of intoxicating liquors to excess, or who has made a false statement in his application. The age limitations in the more important branches of the public service are: Postoffice, 18 to 45 years; rural letter carriers, 17 to 55; internal revenue, 21 years and over; railway mail,

18 to 35; lighthouse, 18 to 50; life saving, 18 to 45; general departmental, 20 and over. These age limitations are subject to change by the commission. They do not apply to applicants of the preferred class. Applicants for the position of railway mail clerk must be at least 5 feet 6 inches in height, exclusive of boots or shoes, and weigh not less than 135 pounds in ordinary clothing and have no physical defects. Applicants for certain other positions have to come up to similar physical requirements.

Method of Appointment—Whenever a vacancy exists the appointing officer makes requisition upon the civil service commission for a certification of names to fill the vacancy, specifying the kind of position vacant, the sex desired and the salary. The commission thereupon takes from the proper register of eligibles the names of three persons standing highest of the sex called for and certifies them to the appointing officer, who is required to make the selection. He may choose any one of the three names, returning the other two to the register to await further certification. The time of examination is not considered, as the highest in average percentage on the register must be certified first. If after a probationary period of six months the name of the appointee is continued on the roll of the department in which he serves the appointment is considered absolute.

Removals—No person can be removed from a competitive position except for such cause as will promote the efficiency of the public service and for reasons given in writing. No examination of witnesses nor any trial shall be required except in the discretion of the officer making the removal.

Salaries—Entrance to the department service is usually in the lowest grades, the higher grades being generally filled by promotion. The usual entrance grade is about $900, but the applicant may be appointed at $840, $760 or even $600.

EMPLOYES IN THE FEDERAL CIVIL SERVICE.

June 30, 1912.

IN WASHINGTON.

White house	27
State department	252
Treasury department	7,572
War department	2,309
Navy department	1,136
Postoffice department	1,852
Interior department	5,928
Department of justice	1,371
Department of agriculture	3,404
Department of commerce and labor	2,590
Interstate commerce commission	709
Civil service commission	174
Smithsonian institution	695
State, war and navy department building	235
Isthmian canal commission	162
Government printing office	3,942
Total	**32,368**

OUTSIDE WASHINGTON.

Treasury department—	
Supervising architect	4,263
Mints and assay offices	855
Subtreasury service	398
Public health service	3,335
Life saving service	2,239
Customs service	7,631
Internal revenue service	3,918
Miscellaneous	668
War department—	
Quartermaster's department	8,404
Ordnance department	4,692
Engineer department	13,385
Miscellaneous	2,209
Navy department—	
Trade and labor positions	25,000
Exclusive of trade and labor positions	2,880
Postoffice department—	
Postoffice service	101,463
Fourth class postmasters	50,501
Rural free delivery service	43,007
Railway mail service	17,532

Interior department—		Steamboat inspection service	309
Land service	1,320	Miscellaneous	2,767
Pension agency service	4,994	Interstate commerce commission	64
Indian service	7,303	Civil service commission	31
Reclamation service	2,067	Isthmian canal service	1,206
Miscellaneous	596		
Department of justice	2,278	Total	334,901
Department of agriculture	10,887	Grand total*	395,460
Department of commerce and labor—			
Lighthouse service	6,544	*Includes unclassified employes of isthmian canal
Immigration service	1,739	commission.

THE PRESIDENTIAL ELECTION OF 1916.

The next president and vice-president of the United States will be chosen Nov. 7, 1916. As is well known, these officials are not elected directly by the people, but by electors, who are voted for on the party tickets on the date named. The electors chosen meet on the second Monday in January following their election in their respective states and vote by ballot for president and vice-president of the United States. The result is transmitted to the president of the senate in Washington. On the second Wednesday in February succeeding the meeting of the electors the electoral votes are opened and counted in the presence of both houses of congress and the result announced by the president of the senate.

While the president and vice-president are thus formally elected in 1917, the actual choice is made in 1916. In the spring and summer of that year national party conventions will be held for the nomination of candidates for president and vice-president of the United States for the term beginning March 4, 1917. These conventions are not provided for by the constitution, but it has become the invariable rule that the candidates presented by them are voted for by the presidential electors. The latter are nominated at the state party conventions or primaries and are elected on the first Tuesday after the first Monday in November of every fourth year, preceding the end of the presidential term. Each state is entitled to as many electors as it has senators and representatives. No senator or representative or person holding an office of trust or honor under the United States may be an elector. The twelfth amendment to the constitution prescribes how the electors shall meet and cast their ballots and how congress shall count the votes. The article is as follows:

"The electors shall meet in their respective states and vote by ballot for president and vice-president, one of whom at least shall not be an inhabitant of the same state with themselves; they shall name in their ballots the person voted for as president, and in distinct ballots the person voted for as vice-president, and they shall make distinct lists of all persons voted for as president and of all persons voted for as vice-president, and of the number of votes for each, which list they shall sign and certify and transmit, sealed, to the seat of the government of the United States, directed to the president of the senate.

"The president of the senate shall, in the presence of the senate and house of representatives, open all the certificates and the votes shall then be counted: the person having the greatest number of votes for president shall be the president, if such number be a majority of the whole number of electors appointed; and if no person have such majority, then from the persons having the highest numbers, not exceeding three, on the list of those voted for as president, the house of representatives shall choose immediately by ballot the president. But in choosing the president the votes shall be taken by states, the representation from each state having one vote; a quorum for this purpose shall consist of a member or members from two-thirds of the states, and a majority of all the states shall be necessary to a choice. And if the house of representatives shall not choose a president, whenever the right of choice shall devolve upon them, before the 4th day of March next following, then the vice-president shall act as president, as in the case of the death or other constitutional disability of the president.

"The person having the greatest number of votes as vice-president shall be the vice-president, if such number be a majority of the whole number of electors appointed, and if no person have a majority, then from the two highest numbers on the list the senate shall choose the vice-president; a quorum for the purpose shall consist of two-thirds of the whole number of senators, and a majority of the whole number shall be necessary to a choice. But no person constitutionally ineligible to the office of president shall be eligible to that of vice-president of the United States."

Section 5, article II., of the constitution prescribes the qualifications of the president as follows:

"No person except a natural born citizen or a citizen of the United States at the time of the adoption of the constitution shall be eligible to the office of president; neither shall any person be eligible to that office who shall not have attained to the age of 35 years and been fourteen years a resident within the United States."

The qualifications of the vice-president are the same as those of the president.

HARVEST MOON AND HUNTER'S MOON.

The full moon in September that falls near the autumnal equinox (Sept. 23) is called the harvest moon. Because at that time it is in that part of its orbit where it makes the smallest angle with the horizon, it appears to rise at nearly the same hour for several nights in succession, thus giving an unusual number of moonlight evenings. The same thing occurs to a slightly less degree at the time of the first full moon after the equinox, when it is called the hunter's moon. "It is true," says Prof. George C. Comstock in his "Text-Book of Astronomy," "that on the average the moon rises and sets fifty-one minutes later each day than on the day before. But there is a good deal of irregularity in the retardation of the time of moonrise and moonset, since the time of rising depends largely upon the particular point of the horizon at which the moon appears, and between two days this point may change so much as to make the retardation considerably greater or less than its average value. In northern latitudes this effect is particularly marked in the month of September, when the eastern horizon is nearly parallel with the moon's apparent path in the sky, and near the time of full moon in that month the moon rises on several successive nights at nearly the same hour, and in a less degree the same is true for October. This highly convenient arrangement of moonlight has caused the full moons of these two months to be christened respectively the harvest moon and the hunter's moon."

UNITED STATES COINAGE MINTS AND ASSAY OFFICES.

Coinage mints of the United States are located in Philadelphia, Pa.; San Francisco, Cal., and Denver, Col. The government assay offices are in New York, N. Y.; Carson, Nev.; Denver, Col.; Boise, Idaho; Helena, Mont.; Charlotte, N. C.; St. Louis, Mo.; Deadwood, S. D.; Seattle, Wash.; New Orleans, La., and Salt Lake City, Utah. The mint in Philadelphia was established in 1792 and the others as follows: San Francisco, 1852, and Denver, 1904.

APPLICATIONS FOR PATENTS.

[Condensed from Rules of Practice in the United States patent office.]

A patent may be obtained by any person who has invented or discovered any new and useful art, machine, manufacture or composition of matter, or any new and useful improvement thereof not previously patented or described in this or any other country, for more than two years prior to his application, unless the same is proved to have been abandoned. A patent may also be obtained for any new design for a manufacture, bust, statue, alto-relievo or bas-relief; for the printing of woolen, silk or other fabrics; for any new impression, ornament, pattern, print or picture to be placed on or woven into any article of manufacture; and for any new, useful and original shape or configuration of any article of manufacture, upon payment of fees and taking the other necessary steps.

Applications for patents must be in writing, in the English language and signed by the inventor if alive. The application must include the first fee of $15, petition, specification and oath, and drawings, model or specimen when required. The petition must be addressed to the commissioner of patents and must give the name and full address of the applicant, must designate by title the invention sought to be patented, must contain a reference to the specification for a full disclosure of such invention and must be signed by the applicant.

The specification must contain the following in the order named: Name and residence of the applicant with title of invention; a general statement of the object and nature of the invention; a brief description of the several views of the drawings (if the invention admits of such illustration); a detailed description; claim or claims; signature of inventor and signatures of two witnesses. Claims for a machine and its product and claims for a machine and the process in the performance of which the machine is used must be presented in separate applications, but claims for a process and its product may be presented in the same application.

The applicant, if the inventor, must make oath or affirmation that he believes himself to be the first inventor or discoverer of that which he seeks to have patented. The oath or affirmation must also state of what country he is a citizen and where he resides. In every original application the applicant must swear or affirm that the invention has not been patented to himself or to others with his knowledge or consent in this or any foreign country more than two years prior to his application, or on an application for a patent filed in any foreign country by himself or his legal representatives or assigns more than seven months prior to his application. If application has been made in any foreign country, full and explicit details must be given. The oath or affirmation may be made before any one who is authorized by the laws of his country to administer oaths.

Drawings must be on white paper with india ink and the sheets must be exactly 10x15 inches in size, with a margin of one inch. They must show all details clearly and without the use of superfluous lines.

Applications for reissues must state why the original patent is believed to be defective and tell precisely how the errors were made. These applications must be accompanied by the original patent and an offer to surrender the same; or, if the original be lost, by an affidavit to that effect and certified copy of the patent. Every applicant whose claims have been twice rejected for the same reasons may appeal from the primary examiners to the examiners in chief upon the payment of a fee of $10.

The duration of patents is for seventeen years except in the case of design patents, which may be for three and a half, seven or fourteen years, as the inventor may elect.

Caveats or notices given to the patent office of claims to inventions to prevent the issue of patents to other persons upon the same invention, without notice to caveators, may be filed upon the payment of a fee of $10. Caveats must contain the same information as applications for patents.

Schedule of fees and prices:

Original application	$15.00
On issue of patent	20.00
Design patent (3½ years)	10.00
Design patent (7 years)	15.00
Design patent (14 years)	30.00
Caveat	10.00
Reissue	30.00
First appeal	10.00
Second appeal	20.00

For certified copies of printed patents:

Specifications and drawing, per copy	$0.05
Certificate	.25
Grant	.50
For manuscript copies of records, per 100 words	.10
If certified, for certificate	.25
Blue prints of drawings, 10x15, per copy	.25
Blue prints of drawings, 7x11, per copy	.15
Blue prints of drawings, 5x8, per copy	.05
For searching records or titles, per hour	.50
For the Official Gazette, per year, in United States	5.00

PATENT OFFICE STATISTICS.

Yr.	Applications.	Issues.	Yr.	Applications.	Issues.
1902	46,641	27,886	1908	60,142	33,642
1903	50,213	31,699	1909	64,408	37,421
1904	52,143	30,934	1910	63,293	35,930
1905	54,971	30,399	1911	67,370	34,084
1906	56,482	31,965	1912	70,976	37,731
1907	57,679	36,620	1913	67,988	38,754

REGISTRATION OF TRADE MARKS.

Under the law passed by congress Feb. 20, 1905, and effective April 1, 1905, citizens of the United States, or foreigners living in countries affording similar privileges to citizens of the United States, may obtain registration of trade-marks used in commerce with foreign nations, or among the several states, or with Indian tribes, by complying with the following requirements: First, by filing in the patent office an application therefor in writing, addressed to the commissioner of patents, signed by the applicant, specifying his name, domicile, location and citizenship; the class of merchandise and the particular description of goods comprised in such class to which the trade-mark is appropriated; a statement of the mode in which the same is applied and affixed to goods, and the length of time during which the trade-mark has been used. With this statement shall be filed a drawing of the trade-mark, signed by the applicant or his attorney, and such number of specimens of the trade-mark as may be required by the commissioner of patents. Second, by paying into the treasury of the United States the sum of $10 and otherwise complying with the requirements of the law and such regulations as may be prescribed by the commissioner of patents.

The application must be accompanied by a written declaration to the effect that the applicant believes himself to be the owner of the trade-mark sought to be registered and that no other person or corporation has the right to use it; that such trade-mark is in use and that the description and drawing presented are correct. Trade-marks consisting of or comprising immoral or scandalous matter, the coat of arms, flag or other insignia of the United States or of any state or foreign nation cannot be registered. Fees for renewal of trade-marks and for filing opposition to registration are $10 each; for appeals from examiners to the commissioner of patents, $15 each.

Further information may be had by applying to the commissioner of patents, Washington, D. C.

COPYRIGHT LAWS OF THE UNITED STATES.

The act to amend and consolidate the acts respecting copyright, in force July 1, 1909, as amended by the act approved Aug. 24, 1912, provides that any person entitled thereto, upon complying with the provisions of the law, shall have the exclusive right (a) to print, reprint, publish, copy and vend the copyrighted work; (b) to translate the copyrighted work or make any other version of it if it be a literary work; to dramatize it if it be a nondramatic work; to convert it into a novel or other nondramatic work if it be a drama; to arrange or adapt it if it be a musical work; to finish it if it be a model or design for a work of art; (c) to deliver or authorize the delivery of the copyrighted work if it be a lecture, sermon, address or similar production; (d) to perform the copyrighted work publicly if it be a drama or, if it be a dramatic work and not reproduced in copies for sale, to vend the manuscript or any record thereof; to make or to procure the making of any transcription or record thereof by which it may in any manner be exhibited, performed or produced, and to exhibit, perform or produce it in any manner whatsoever; (e) to perform the copyrighted work publicly for profit if it be a musical composition and for the purpose of public performance for profit and to make any arrangement or setting of it in any system of notation or any form of record in which the thought of an author may be read or reproduced.

So far as it secures copyright controlling the parts of instruments serving to reproduce mechanically the musical work the law includes only compositions published after the act went into effect; it does not include the works of a foreign author or composer unless the country of which he is a citizen or subject grants similar rights to American citizens. Whenever the owner of a musical copyright has used or permitted the use of the copyrighted work upon the part of instruments serving to reproduce mechanically the musical work, any other person may make a similar use of the work upon the payment to the owner of a royalty of 2 cents on each such part manufactured. The reproduction or rendition of a musical composition by or upon coin-operated machines shall not be deemed a public performance for profit unless a fee is charged for admission to the place where the reproduction occurs.

The works for which copyright may be secured include all the writings of an author.

The application for registration shall specify to which of the following classes the work in which copyright is claimed belongs:

(a) Books, including composite and cyclopedic works, directories, gazetteers and other compilations.

(b) Periodicals, including newspapers.

(c) Lectures, sermons, addresses, prepared for oral delivery.

(d) Dramatic or dramatic-musical compositions.

(e) Musical compositions.

(f) Maps.

(g) Works of art; models or designs for works of art.

(h) Reproductions of a work of art.

(i) Drawings or plastic works of a scientific or technical character.

(j) Photographs.

(k) Prints and pictorial illustrations.

(l) Motion picture photo plays.

(m) Motion pictures other than photo plays.

These specifications do not, however, limit the subject matter of copyright as defined in the law nor does any error in classification invalidate the copyright protection secured.

Copyright extends to the work of a foreign author or proprietor only in case he is domiciled in the United States at the time of the first publication of his work or if the country of which he is a citizen grants similar copyright protection to citizens of the United States.

Any person entitled thereto by the law may secure copyright for his work by publication thereof with the notice of copyright required by the act, and such notice shall be affixed to each copy published or offered for sale in the United States. Such person may obtain registration of his claim to copyright by complying with the provisions of the act, including the deposit of copies, whereupon the register of copyrights shall issue to him a certificate as provided for in the law. Copyright may also be had of the works of an author of which copies are not reproduced for sale by the deposit with claim of copyright of one complete copy, if it be a lecture or similar production, or a dramatic or musical composition; of a title and description, with one print taken from each scene or act, if the work be a motion picture photo play; of a photographic print if it be a photograph; of a title and description, with not less than two prints taken from different sections of a complete motion picture, if the work be a motion picture other than a photo play, or of a photograph or other identifying reproduction thereof if it be a work of art or a plastic work or drawing.

After copyright has been secured there must be deposited in the copyright office in Washington, D. C., two complete copies of the best edition thereof, which copies, if the work be a book or periodical, shall have been produced in accordance with the manufacturing provisions of the act, or if such work be a contribution to a periodical for which contribution special registration is requested one copy of the issue or issues containing such contribution. Failure to deposit the copies within a given time after notice from the register of copyrights makes the proprietor of the copyright liable to a fine of $100 and twice the retail price of the work, and the copyright becomes void.

The text of all books and periodicals specified in paragraphs (a) and (b) above, except the original text of a book of foreign origin in a language other than English, must in order to secure protection be printed from type set within the limits of the United States, either by hand, machinery or other process, and the printing of the text and the binding of the books must also be done within the United States. An affidavit of such manufacture is required.

The notice of copyright required consists either of the word "copyright" or the abbreviation "copr.," accompanied by the name of the copyright proprietor, and if the work be a printed literary, musical or dramatic work, the notice must also include the year in which the copyright was secured by publication. In the case, however, of copies of works specified in paragraphs (f) to (k) inclusive (given above) the notice may consist of the letter C inclosed within a circle, accompanied by the initials, monogram, mark or symbol of the copyright proprietor, provided his name appears elsewhere on the copies. In the case of a book or other printed publication the notice shall be applied on the title page or on the page immediately following, or if a periodical either upon the title page or upon the first page of text of each separate number or under the title heading; or if a musical work upon its title page or the first page of music.

Where the copyright proprietor has sought to comply with the law with respect to notice, the omission of such notice by mistake from a particular copy or copies shall not invalidate the copyright or prevent recovery for infringement against any person who, after actual notice of the copyright, begins an undertaking to infringe it, but shall prevent the recovery of damages against an innocent infringer who has been misled by the omission of the notice.

In the case of a book in English published abroad before publication in this country, the deposit in the copyright office within thirty days of one copy of the foreign edition, with a request for the reservation of the copyright, secures for the author or owner an ad interim copyright for thirty days after such deposit is made.

The copyright secured by the act endures for twenty-eight years from the date of the first publication. In the case of any posthumous work, periodical, encyclopedic or other composite work upon which the copyright was originally secured by the proprietor thereof, or of any work copyrighted by a corporate body, or by an employer for whom such work is made for hire, the proprietor of such copyright shall be entitled to a renewal of the copyright in such work for the further term of twenty-

eight years when application for such renewal shall have been made within one year prior to the expiration of the original term. In the case of any other copyrighted work, including a contribution by an individual author to a periodical or to a cyclopedic or other composite work when such contribution has been separately copyrighted, the author of such work, if living, or the heirs, executors or next of kin, if the author be dead, shall be entitled to a renewal of the copyright for a further term of twenty-eight years. In default of such application for renewal the copyright in any work shall end at the expiration of twenty-eight years.

If any person shall infringe the copyright in any work protected under the copyright laws of the United States, such person shall be liable:

(a) To an injunction restraining such infringement.

(b) To pay to the copyright proprietor such damages as the copyright proprietor may have suffered due to the infringement, as well as all the profits which the infringer shall have made from such infringement, and in proving profits the plaintiff shall be required to prove sales only and the defendant shall be required to prove every element of cost which he claims, or in lieu of actual damages or profits such damages as to the court shall appear to be just, and in assessing such damages the court may, in its discretion, allow the amounts as hereinafter stated (in numbered paragraphs), but in the case of a newspaper reproduction of a copyrighted photograph such damages shall not exceed the sum of $200 nor be less than $50, and such damages shall in no other case exceed the sum of $250 and shall not be regarded as a penalty. In the case of the infringement of an undramatized or nondramatic work by means of motion pictures, where the infringer shows that he was not aware that he was infringing, the damages shall not exceed $100; in the case of the infringement under like circumstances of a copyrighted dramatic or dramatico-musical work the entire sum recoverable shall not exceed $5,000 nor be less than $250.

1. In the case of a painting, statue or sculpture, $10 for every infringing copy made or sold by or found in the possession of the infringer or his agents or employes;

2. In the case of any work enumerated in the list (given above) of works for which copyright may be asked, except a painting, statue or sculpture, $1 for every infringing copy.

3. In the case of a lecture, sermon or address, $50 for every infringing delivery.

4. In the case of dramatic or dramatico-musical or a choral or orchestral composition, $100 for the first and $50 for every subsequent infringing performance; in the case of other musical compositions, $10 for every infringing performance.

(c) To deliver up on oath all articles alleged to infringe a copyright.

(d) To deliver up on oath for destruction all the infringing copies or devices, as well as all plates, molds, matrices or other means for making such infringing copies, as the court may order.

(e) Whenever the owner of a musical copyright has used or permitted the use of the copyrighted work upon the parts of musical instruments serving to reproduce mechanically the musical work, then in case of infringement by the unauthorized manufacture, use or sale of interchangeable parts, such as disks, rolls, bands or cylinders for use in mechanical music-producing machines, no criminal action shall be brought, but in a civil action an injunction may be granted upon such terms as the court may impose and the plaintiff shall be entitled to recover in lieu of profits and damages a royalty as provided in the act.

Any person who shall willfully and for profit infringe any copyright, or willfully aid or abet such infringement, shall be deemed guilty of a misdemeanor, and upon conviction thereof shall be punished by imprisonment for not exceeding one year or by a fine of not less than $100 nor more than $1,000, or both, in the discretion of the court. It is provided, however, that nothing in the act shall prevent the performance of religious or secular works, such as oratorios, cantatas, masses or octavo choruses by public schools, church choirs or vocal societies, provided the performance is for charitable or educational purposes and not for profit.

Any person who shall fraudulently place a copyright notice upon any uncopyrighted article, or shall fraudulently remove or alter the notice upon any copyrighted article, shall be deemed guilty of a misdemeanor and shall be subject to a fine of not less than $100 nor more than $1,000. Any person who shall knowingly sell or issue any article bearing a notice of United States copyright which has not been copyrighted in this country, or who shall knowingly import any article bearing such notice, shall be liable to a fine of $100.

During the existence of the American copyright in any book the importation of any piratical copies thereof or of any copies not produced in accordance with the manufacturing provisions of the copyright law, or of any plates of the same not made from type set in this country, or any copies produced by lithographic or photo-engraving process not performed within the United States, is prohibited. Except as to piratical copies this does not apply:

(a) To works in raised characters for the blind;

(b) To a foreign newspaper or magazine, although containing matter copyrighted in the United States printed or reprinted by authority of the copyright owner, unless such newspaper or magazine contains also copyright matter printed without such authorization;

(c) To the authorized edition of a book in a foreign language of which only a translation into English has been copyrighted in this country;

(d) To any book published abroad with the authorization of the author or copyright proprietor under the following circumstances:

1. When imported, not more than one copy at a time, for individual use and not for sale, but such privilege of importation shall not extend to a foreign reprint of a book by an American author copyrighted in the United States;

2. When imported by or for the use of the United States;

3. When imported, for use and not for sale, not more than one copy of any such book in any one invoice, in good faith, by or for any society or institution incorporated for educational, literary, philosophical, scientific or religious purposes, or for the encouragement of the fine arts, or for any college, academy, school or seminary of learning, or for any state school, college, university or free public library in the United States;

4. When such books form parts of libraries or collections purchased en bloc for the use of societies, institutions or libraries, or form parts of the library or personal baggage belonging to persons or families arriving from foreign countries and are not intended for sale.

No criminal actions shall be maintained under the copyright law unless the same be begun within three years after the cause of action arose.

Copyright may be assigned, mortgaged or bequeathed by will.

There shall be appointed by the librarian of congress a register of copyrights at a salary of $4,000 a year and an assistant register at $3,000 a year. These with their subordinate assistants shall perform all the duties relating to the registration of copyrights. The register of copyrights shall keep such record books in the copyright office as are required to carry out the provisions of the law, and whenever deposit has been made in the copyright office of a copy of any work under the provisions of the act he shall make entry thereof.

In the case of each entry the person recorded as the claimant of the copyright shall be entitled to a certificate of registration under seal of the copyright office.

The register of copyrights shall receive and the persons to whom the services designated are rendered shall pay the following fees: For the registration of any work subject to copyright, $1, which sum is to include a certificate of registration under seal: Provided, that in the case of photographs the fee shall be 50 cents where a certificate is not demanded. For every additional certificate of registration made, 50 cents. For recording and certifying any instrument of writing for the assignment of copyright or license, or for any copy of such certificate or license, duly certified, if not over 300 words in length, $1; if more than 300 and less than 1,000, $2; if more than 1,000 words in length, $1

additional for each 1,000 words or fraction thereof over 300 words. For recording the notice of user or acquiescence specified in the act, 25 cents for each notice of not over fifty words and an additional 25 cents for each additional 100 words. For comparing any copy of an assignment with the record of such document in the copyright office and certifying the same under seal, $1. For recording the extension or renewal of copyright, 50 cents. For recording the transfer of the proprietorship of copyrighted articles, 10 cents for each title of a book or other article in addition to the fee for recording the instrument of assignment. For any requested search of copyright office records, indexes or deposits, 50 cents for each full hour consumed in making such search. Only one registration at one fee shall be required in the case of several volumes of the same book deposited at the same time.

For copyright blanks and additional information as to copyright regulations address the register of copyrights, library of congress, Washington, D. C.

ROOSEVELT-NEWETT LIBEL CASE.

Oct. 12, 1912, George E. Newett, proprietor and editor of Iron Age, a weekly paper issued in Ishpeming, Mich., wrote and published an article in which he charged that Theodore Roosevelt, then a candidate for president of the United States, was addicted to the excessive use of liquor—that he "got drunk." Oct. 25, the same year, Mr. Roosevelt began suit for libel against Mr. Newett, claiming damages in the sum of $10,000. The case came up for trial in the County court at Marquette, Mich., May 26, 1913, before Judge Richard C. Flannigan of Norwich, Mich. The plaintiff was represented by James H. Pound and W. S. Hill and the defendant by William P. Belden and Horace Andrews. A jury consisting mainly of miners, teamsters and farmers was secured on the opening day and then testimony on behalf of the plaintiff was introduced.

Col. Roosevelt, who took the stand first, testified that he was not an abstainer, but that he had never been drunk in his life. He would occasionally take a little champagne at public dinners or light wines with his meals. He rarely drank mint juleps and whisky, and brandy only when prescribed by his physicians. The only liquor he drank on his African trip was seven ounces of brandy when he had an attack of fever. Among the witnesses called to prove that Col. Roosevelt was a man of strictly sober habits were James R. Garfield, Gifford Pinchot, Truman H. Newberry, Maj.-Gen. Leonard Wood, Dr. Lyman Abbott, George B. Cortelyou, Dr. Albert Shaw, William Loeb, Jr., Jacob A. Riis, Admiral George Dewey and a number of physicians and newspaper men. All testified orally or by deposition that the plaintiff did not "get drunk" as charged in the Iron Age article.

Saturday afternoon, May 31, Mr. Newett took the stand and read a statement in which he recounted his reasons for making the statement that Col. Roosevelt was an intemperate man. He had relied chiefly upon rumors he had heard and allegations he had read in the newspapers that the former president was a drinking man. In the face of the unqualified testimony of so many distinguished men who had been in a position for years to know the truth he was forced to the conclusion that he had been mistaken. "I am unwilling to continue to assert," added the defendant, "that Mr. Roosevelt actually and in fact drank to excess." Mr. Newett closed by saying that in publishing the article complained of he acted in good faith.

At the conclusion of the statement Mr. Roosevelt asked the court to instruct the jury that he desired only nominal damages. "I did not go into this case for money," he said. "I did not go into it for any vindictive purpose. I went into it, and, as the court said, I made my reputation an issue because I wished once for all during my lifetime thoroughly and comprehensively to deal with these slanders so that never again will it be possible for any man in good faith to repeat them. I have achieved my purpose and I am content."

Judge Flannigan reviewed briefly the circumstances and the law in the case and then directed the jury to give a verdict in the plaintiff's favor for nominal damages, which, under the law of Michigan, was 6 cents. This was done and the case ended. Each of the parties to the suit paid his own expenses.

HIGHEST POINT IN EACH STATE.
[Compiled by N. H. Darton of the United States geological survey.]

State and place.	Elevation.	State and place.	Elevation.
Alabama, Che-aw-ha mountain	2,407	Montana, Granite peak	12,834
Alaska, Mount McKinley	20,300	Nebraska, plains in southwestern corner	5,300
Arizona, San Francisco peak	12,611	Nevada, Wheeler peak	13,058
Arkansas, Magazine mountain	2,800	New Hampshire, Mount Washington	6,290
California, Mount Whitney	14,501	New Jersey, High Point	1,809
Colorado, Mount Elbert	14,436	New Mexico, peak near Truchas peak	13,306
Connecticut, Bear mountain	2,355	New York, Mount Marcy	5,344
Delaware, near Brandywine	440	North Carolina, Mount Mitchell	6,711
District of Columbia, Fort Reno	421	North Dakota, south part of Bowman county	3,500
Florida, near Mount Pleasant station	301	Ohio, 1½ miles east of Bellefontaine	1,540
Georgia, Brasstown Bald mountain	4,768	Oklahoma, near Kenton	4,700
Idaho, Hyndman peak	12,078	Oregon, Mount Hood	11,225
Illinois, Charles mound, Jo Daviess county	1,257	Pennsylvania, Blue Knob	3,136
Indiana, near summit Randolph county	1,285	Rhode Island, Durfee hill	805
Iowa, five miles southeast of Sibley	1,670	South Carolina, Sassafras mountain	3,548
Kansas, west boundary no. of Arkansas river	4,135	South Dakota, Harney peak	7,240
Kentucky, The Double, Harlem county	4,100	Tennessee, Mount Guyot	6,636
Louisiana, summits in western parishes	400	Texas, El Capitan, Guadaloupe mountain	8,690
Maine, Mount Katahdin (west)	5,269	Utah, Mount Emmons	13,428
Maryland, Backbone mountain	3,400	Vermont, Mount Mansfield	4,406
Massachusetts, Mount Greylock	3,505	Virginia, Mount Rogers	5,719
Michigan, Porcupine mountain	2,023	Washington, Mount Rainier	14,363
Minnesota, Misquah hills, Cook county	2,230	West Virginia, Spruce Knob	4,860
Mississippi, near Holly Springs	602	Wisconsin, Rib hill, Marathon county	1,940
Missouri, Tom Sauk mountain	1,800	Wyoming, Mount Gannett	13,785

FIRE IN HOT SPRINGS, ARK.

More than fifty city blocks were swept by fire in Hot Springs, Ark., Sept. 5, 1913. The conflagration started in a negro's cabin at the foot of West mountain at 3:30 p. m., and continued until midnight, laying in ruins every building on an area more than a mile long and from seven to ten blocks wide. Some 2,500 persons were made homeless and property to an estimated value of $6,000,000 was destroyed. Among the buildings destroyed were the city's light, water and power plants, county courthouse, high school building, Park, Moody and Princess hotels and the Arkansas sanitarium. The business center of the city narrowly escaped destruction.

NATIONAL RAILWAY, TELEGRAPH AND POSTAL STATISTICS.

[From report compiled by bureau of statistics, Washington, D. C.]

Country.	Year.	Rail-ways.	Tele-graphs.	Post-offices.	Postal routes.	Postal service performed.	Val. domestic money and postal orders sent.	Value for eign money orders sent.
		Miles.	Miles.	No.	Miles.	Miles.		
Argentina..................	1911	19,620	37,905	2,095	45,372	17,867,2'9	$5,264,986	$391,822
Australian Commonwealth........	1911	18,012	44,100	7,834	132,242	35,900,962	37,843,386	22,705,610
New Zealand..............	1912	2,827	11,316	2,312			9,639,057	2,313,363
Austria-Hungary...........	1911	28,658						
Austria...................	1910	......	31,723	10,273	144,201	83,938,587	308,653,218	93,946,960
Hungary................	1910	......	15,576	6,152	69,974	51,939,383	227,828,281	68,071,269
Belgium.................	1912	5,303	4,855	1,658	5,614	68,319,201	79,451,574	10,317,820
Belgian Kongo...........	1912	770	1,387	66	13,919	887,572	26,002	146,810
Bolivia.................	1911	635	3,111	200				
Brazil.................	1911	13,750	36,199	3,246				
Bulgaria..............	1911	1,198	4,052	2,220	15,434	5,160,831	6,694,180	3,808,025
Canada................	1911	25,400	42,312	13,859		52,065,274	52,568,483	31,497,459
Costa Rica.............	1911	427	1,514*	199				
Guatemala............	1911	422	3,823	311				
Honduras.............	1910	106	3,220	204				
Nicaragua	1910	171	3,457*	135				
Panama..............	1912	202		96				
Salvador.............	1910	97	2,573*	93	1,848	36,601		2,838
Chile.................	1911	3,606	24,051*	1,104	28,752	7,464,518	5,991,526	850,248
China................	1911	5,104	20,327	6,201			2,501,195	
Colombia.............	1911	621	10,076	500				
Cuba.................	1910	2,123	5,065	487	5,324	2,545,828		
Denmark.............	1911	2,294	2,265	1,574	6,437	9,715,803	48,003,083	3,159,968
Ecuador.............	1910	350	3,318	81				
Egypt...............	1911	3,639	8,694	1,701	6,399	6,055,257	21,844,073	3,154,038
France..............	1911	37,323	113,583	14,014	308,691	333,830,358	519,107,524	20,537,962
Algeria............	1911	2,142	9,414	661	3,228	8,104,012	75,825,364	547,751
Tunis.............	1911	1,080	2,931	419	5,182	2,761,489	4,847,007	2,779,647
Indo-China........	1911	1,196	8,738	315	20,840	6,865,698	4,005,374	2,051,350
Colonies, other.....	1912	1,371	10,506	617	37,717	6,845,886	3,931,044	2,125,914
German empire.......	1912	38,654	142,020	50,503	90,594		2,316,212,526	60,457,843
Colonies..........	1911	2,862	4,973	188			22,107,195	
Greece............	1911	1,000	5,052	1,083			3,236,816	453,198
Haiti.............	1911	64	124	90	2,371	102,944		
India, British....	1911	32,839	74,828	19,667	155,544	116,626,009	124,084,470	2,601,702
Italy.............	1912	10,871	34,655	11,124	42,783	62,578,017	496,230,303	7,174,475
Japan.............	1911	5,355	26,395	7,717	70,889	77,087,161	116,641,935	328,714
Formosa..........	1911	291	1,613	135				
Chosen (Korea)....	1912	767	3,451	445	21,037	4,809,780	9,467,742	25,785
Luxemburg........	1911	326	426	124	785	1,105,754	5,892,428	8,162,059
Mexico...........	1912	16,103	22,452	2,858	55,247	22,933,529	26,172,628	3,460,950
Netherlands......	1911	2,010	4,728	1,511	9,906	21,071,382	35,210,679	5,978,049
East Indies......	1910	1,895	9,430	1,703	1,621,345	7,112,676	6,712,849	843,403
West Indies, etc..	1910	11*		12			89,176	253,753
Norway...........	1911	1,917	6,843	3,496	65,171	12,618,315	12,466,373	2,312,693
Paraguay.........	1911	222	2,485	485				
Persia...........	1910	34	6,630	109	7,456	1,565,552		850
Peru.............	1911	1,656	7,950	714			966,487	94,574
Portugal.........	1911	1,798	5,705	4,044	20,358	12,307,175	10,850,517	499,068
Colonies........	1910	1,002	5,841	773	24,842	2,879,607	268,428	408,068
Roumania........	1912	2,283	4,519	2,979	64,697	17,255,010	13,013,575	4,258,608
Russia...........	1911	46,058	126,559	15,701	204,891	92,208,403	1,077,529,693	10,886,214
Finland.........	1911	2,328		2,138				
Santo Domingo....	1911	175	1,281	81				
Servia...........	1911	590	2,703	1,620	2,107	835,350	7,080,257	741,913
Siam.............	1911	677	4,527	179	4,954	474,688	810,986	29,487
Spain............	1911	9,199	26,441	5,074	37,001			
Sweden...........	1911	8,682	6,983	4,056	40,463	7,304,614	67,758,990	3,562,004
Switzerland......	1911	3,176	2,221	4,280	7,653	20,466,402	119,134,901	15,696,730
Turkey..........	1910	4,138	28,251	929	29,938	5,592,951	15,931,695	156,433
Crete...........	1909	......	229	28			587,371	162,500
Union of South Africa...	1911	8,092	14,920	2,587				12,981,797
United kingdom...	1911	23,417	61,396	24,243			438,506,870	14,786,088
British colonies...	1911	6,828	27,883	2,392				
United States.....	1911	254,732	220,978	58,729	435,470	578,165,212	583,337,604	97,090,025
Philippines.......	1912	643	4,500	587			5,592,201	1,832,973
Porto Rico.......	1912	340	500					
Uruguay..........	1911	1,561	4,849	1,031				
Venezuela........	1911	575	4,721	284				
Total...........		663,964	1,355,694	313,776	3,367,998	1,785,289,441	6,958,562,505	470,005,59

*Miles of wire. Other figures are for miles of line.

GERMAN TORPEDO BOAT DESTROYER SUNK.

The German torpedo boat destroyer S178 was rammed and sunk by the cruiser Yorck in the North sea off Helgoland on the night of March 4-5, 1913. Of the crew two officers and sixty-nine men lost their lives. Some were killed in the collision, others were drowned, but the greater number froze to death while clinging to spars from the wreckage. The S178 was returning during the night from maneuvers in which it had participated with the battle ship fleet, the cruiser squadron and sixty-four other torpedo boat destroyers. A heavy sea was running and when the S178 tried to cross the bows of the Yorck it became unmanageable and was cut in two by the cruiser, which was going at full speed. The storm made the rescue of the men almost impossible and many of the corpses were not picked up until the morning of March 6.

STATISTICS OF POPULATION.
POPULATION OF THE UNITED STATES (1910).

The thirteenth census of the United States was taken by the bureau of the census as of April 15, 1910. It included continental United States, the territories of Alaska and Hawaii and Porto Rico; also persons in the military and naval service who were stationed abroad. The population according to this division, compared with that in 1900, was:

	1910.	1900.
Alaska	64,356	63,592
Hawaii	191,909	154,001

	1910.	1900.
Porto Rico	1,118,012	*953,243
Soldiers and sailors abroad	55,608	91,219
Noncontiguous territory	1,429,885	1,262,055
Continental United States	91,972,266	75,994,575
United States (area of enumeration)	93,402,151	†77,256,630

*Census of 1899. †Includes 953,243 persons enumerated in Porto Rico in 1899.

POPULATION OF THE UNITED STATES AT EACH CENSUS (1850-1910).
[From the reports of the superintendents of the census.]

STATE OR TERRITORY.	1910.		1900.		1890.		1880.		1870.		1860.		1850.	
Alabama	2,138,093	18	1,828,697	17	1,513,017	17	1,262,505	16	996,992	18	964,201	12	771,623
Arkansas	1,574,449	25	1,311,564	24	1,128,179	25	802,625	26	484,471	25	435,450	26	209,897
California	2,377,549	12	1,485,053	22	1,208,130	24	864,694	24	560,247	26	379,994	29	92,597
Colorado	799,024	31	539,700	31	412,198	35	194,327		39,864		34,277		
Connecticut	1,114,756	29	908,420	29	746,258	28	622,700	25	537,454	24	460,147	21	370,792
Delaware	202,322	42	184,735	41	168,493	37	146,608	34	125,015	32	112,216	30	91,532
Florida	752,619	32	528,542	32	391,422	34	269,493	33	187,748	31	140,424	31	87,445
Georgia	2,609,121	11	2,216,331	12	1,837,353	13	1,542,180	12	1,184,109	11	1,057,286	9	906,185
Idaho	325,594	43	161,772	43	84,385								
Illinois	5,638,591	3	4,821,550	3	3,826,351	4	3,077,871	4	2,539,891	4	1,711,951	11	851,470
Indiana	2,700,876	8	2,516,462	8	2,192,404	6	1,978,301	6	1,680,637	6	1,350,428	7	988,416
Iowa	2,224,771	10	2,231,853	10	1,911,896	10	1,624,615	11	1,194,020	20	674,913	27	192,214
Kansas	1,690,949	22	1,470,495	19	1,427,096	20	996,096	29	364,399	33	107,206		
Kentucky	2,289,905	14	2,147,174	11	1,858,635	8	1,648,690	8	1,321,011	9	1,155,684	8	982,405
Louisiana	1,656,388	23	1,381,625	25	1,118,587	22	939,946	21	726,915	17	708,002	18	517,762
Maine	742,371	30	694,466	30	661,086	27	648,936	23	626,915	22	628,279	16	583,169
Maryland	1,295,346	26	1,188,044	27	1,042,390	23	934,943	20	780,894	19	687,049	17	583,034
Massachusetts	3,366,416	7	2,805,346	6	2,238,943	7	1,783,085	7	1,457,351	7	1,231,066	6	994,514
Michigan	2,810,173	9	2,420,982	9	2,093,889	9	1,636,937	13	1,184,059	16	749,113	20	397,654
Minnesota	2,075,708	19	1,751,394	20	1,301,826	28	780,773	28	439,706	30	172,023	33	6,077
Mississippi	1,797,114	20	1,551,270	23	1,289,600	18	1,131,597	18	827,922	13	791,305	15	606,526
Missouri	3,293,335	5	3,106,665	5	2,679,184	5	2,168,380	5	1,721,295	8	1,182,012	13	682,044
Montana	376,053	41	243,329	42	132,159								
Nebraska	1,192,214	27	1,066,300	26	1,058,910	30	452,402	35	122,993	35	28,841		
Nevada	81,875	45	42,335	45	45,761	38	62,266	37	42,491	36	6,857		
New Hampshire	430,572	36	411,588	33	376,530	31	346,991	31	318,300	27	326,073	22	517,976
New Jersey	2,537,167	16	1,883,669	18	1,444,933	19	1,131,116	17	906,096	21	672,035	19	489,555
New York	9,113,614	1	7,268,894	1	5,997,853	1	5,082,871	1	4,382,759	1	3,880,735	1	3,097,394
North Carolina	2,206,287	15	1,893,810	15	1,617,947	15	1,399,750	14	1,071,361	12	992,622	10	869,039
North Dakota	577,056	39	319,146	39	182,719								
Ohio	4,767,121	4	4,157,545	4	3,672,316	3	3,198,062	3	2,665,260	3	2,339,511	3	1,980,329
Oklahoma	1,657,155	23											
Oregon	672,765	35	413,536	38	313,767	36	174,768	36	90,923	34	52,465	32	13,294
Pennsylvania	7,665,111	2	6,302,115	2	5,258,014	2	4,282,891	2	3,521,951	2	2,906,215	2	2,311,786
Rhode Island	542,610	34	428,556	35	345,506	33	276,531	32	217,353	29	174,620	28	147,545
South Carolina	1,515,400	24	1,340,316	23	1,151,149	21	995,577	22	705,606	18	703,708	14	668,507
South Dakota	583,888	37	401,570	37	328,808								
Tennessee	2,184,789	13	2,020,616	13	1,767,518	12	1,542,359	9	1,258,520	10	1,109,801	5	1,002,717
Texas	3,896,542	6	3,048,710	7	2,235,523	11	1,591,749	19	818,579	23	604,215	25	212,592
Utah	373,351	40	276,749	40	207,905								
Vermont	355,956	38	343,641	36	332,422	32	332,286	30	330,551	26	315,098	23	314,120
Virginia	2,061,612	17	1,854,184	15	1,655,980	14	1,512,565	10	1,225,163	5	1,596,318	4	1,421,661
Washington	1,141,990	33	518,103	34	349,390								
West Virginia	1,221,119	28	958,800	28	762,794	29	618,457	27	442,014				
Wisconsin	2,333,860	14	2,069,042	14	1,686,880	16	1,315,497	15	1,054,670	15	775,881	24	305,391
Wyoming	145,965	44	92,531	44	60,705								
The states	91,100,542		74,610,523		62,116,811		49,371,340		38,155,505		31,218,021		23,067,262
Alaska	64,356	7	63,592										
Arizona	204,354	6	122,931	4	59,620	5	40,440	8	9,658				
Dakota						3	135,177	7	14,181	5	4,837		
District of Columbia	331,069	3	218,718	1	230,392	1	177,624	1	131,700	2	75,080	2	51,687
Hawaii	191,909	5	154,001										
Idaho							32,610						
Indian Territory			2	332,050			8						
Montana							8	39,159					
New Mexico	327,301	2	195,310	2	153,593	4	119,565	5	20,595	1	93,516	1	61,547
Oklahoma		1	398,331	3	61,834				91,874				
In service of U. S. stationed abroad	55,608		91,219										
Utah						2	143,963	3	86,786	3	40,273	3	11,380
Washington						5	75,116	4	23,955	4	11,594		
Wyoming						9	20,789	9	9,118				
Porto Rico	1,118,012												
The territories	2,292,609		1,604,943		505,439		784,443		402,866		225,300		124,674
United States	93,402,151		76,303,387		62,622,250		50,155,783		38,588,371		31,443,321		23,191,876
Per cent of gain	20.9		21		24.9		30.08		22.65		35.58		35.86

NOTE—The narrow column under each census year shows the order of the states and territories when arranged according to magnitude of population.

DISTRIBUTION BY GEOGRAPHIC DIVISIONS.

Per cent of total population of continental United States in each of the nine geographic divisions:

Division.	1910.	1909.	1890.	1850.
New England	7.4	7.4	7.5	11.8
Middle Atlantic	21.0	20.3	20.2	25.4
East North Central	19.8	21.0	21.4	19.5
West North Central	12.7	13.6	14.2	3.8
South Atlantic	13.3	13.7	14.1	20.2
East South Central	9.1	9.9	10.2	14.5
West South Central	9.6	8.6	7.5	4.1
Mountain	2.9	2.2	1.9	0.3
Pacific	4.6	3.2	3.0	0.5
United States	100.0	100.0	100.0	100.0

Including the population of the Philippines and other possessions, the population living under the American flag in 1910 was as follows:

United States	93,402,151
Philippines (1903)	7,635,426
Guam, estimated	9,000
Samoa, estimated	6,100
Panama canal zone, estimated	50,000
Total	101,102,677

POPULATION OF THE UNITED STATES AT EACH CENSUS (1790-1840).
[From the reports of the superintendents of the census.]

STATE OR TERRITORY.		1840.		1830.		1820.		1810.		1800.		1790.
Alabama	12	590,756	15	309,527	19	127,901						
Arkansas	25	97,574	27	30,398	25	14,273						
California												
Colorado												
Connecticut	20	309,978	16	297,675	14	275,248	9	261,942	8	251,002	8	237,964
Delaware	26	78,085	24	76,748	22	72,749	19	72,674	17	64,273	16	59,096
Florida	27	54,477	25	34,730								
Georgia	9	691,392	10	516,823	11	340,989	11	252,433	12	162,686	13	82,548
Idaho												
Illinois	14	476,183	20	157,445	24	55,211	23	12,282				
Indiana	10	685,866	13	343,031	18	147,178	21	24,520	20	5,641		
Iowa	28	43,112										
Kansas												
Kentucky	6	779,828	8	687,917	6	564,317	7	406,511	9	220,955	14	73,677
Louisiana	19	352,411	19	215,739	17	153,407	18	76,556				
Maine	13	501,793	12	399,455	12	298,335	14	228,705	14	151,719	11	96,540
Maryland	15	470,019	11	447,040	10	407,350	8	380,546	7	341,548	6	319,728
Massachusetts	8	737,699	8	610,408	7	523,287	5	472,040	5	422,845	4	378,787
Michigan	23	212,267	26	31,639	26	8,765	24	4,762				
Minnesota												
Mississippi	17	375,651	22	136,621	21	75,448	20	40,352	19	8,850		
Missouri	16	383,702	21	140,455	23	66,586	22	20,845				
Montana												
Nebraska												
Nevada												
New Hampshire	22	284,574	18	269,328	15	244,161	16	214,460	11	183,858	10	141,885
New Jersey	18	373,306	14	320,823	13	277,575	12	245,562	10	211,149	9	184,139
New York	1	2,428,921	1	1,918,608	1	1,372,812	2	959,049	3	589,051	5	340,120
North Carolina	7	753,419	5	737,987	4	638,829	4	555,500	4	478,103	3	393,751
North Dakota												
Ohio	3	1,519,467	4	937,903	5	581,434	13	230,760	18	45,365		
Oregon												
Pennsylvania	2	1,724,033	2	1,348,233	3	1,049,458	3	810,091	3	602,365	2	434,373
Rhode Island	24	108,830	23	97,199	20	83,059	17	76,931	16	69,122	15	68,825
South Carolina	11	594,398	9	581,185	8	502,741	6	415,115	6	346,591	7	249,073
South Dakota												
Tennessee	5	829,210	7	681,904	9	422,823	10	261,727	15	105,602	17	35,691
Texas												
Vermont	21	291,948	17	280,652	16	235,966	15	235,981	13	154,465	12	85,425
Virginia	4	1,239,797	3	1,211,405	2	1,065,366	1	974,600	1	880,200	1	747,610
Washington												
West Virginia	29	80,945										
Wisconsin												
Wyoming												
The states		17,019,641		12,820,868		9,600,783		7,215,858		5,294,390		
Alaska												
Arizona												
Dakota												
District of Columbia	1	43,712	1	39,834	1	33,039	1	24,023	1	14,093		
Idaho												
Indian Territory												
Montana												
New Mexico												
Oklahoma												
Utah												
Washington												
Wyoming												
The territories		43,712		39,834		33,039		24,023		14,093		
On public ships in service of United States		6,100		5,318								
United States		17,069,453		12,866,020		9,638,453		7,239,881		5,308,483		3,929,214
Per cent of gain		32.67		33.55		33.06		36.38		35.10		

NOTE—The narrow column under each census year shows the order of the states and territories when arranged according to magnitude of population.

GROWTH OF POPULATION OF THE UNITED STATES.

States and territories.	1910.	1900.	1890.	Increase 1900 to 1910— Number.	Per ct.	Increase 1890 to 1900— Number.	Per ct.	Rank 1910.	Rank 1900.
Alabama	2,138,093	1,828,697	1,513,401	309,396	16.9	315,296	20.8	18	18
Arizona	204,354	122,931	88,243	81,423	66.2	34,688	39.8	46	47
Arkansas	1,574,449	1,311,564	1,128,211	262,885	20.0	183,353	16.3	25	25
California	2,377,549	1,485,053	1,213,393	892,496	60.1	271,655	22.4	12	21
Colorado	793,024	539,700	412,249	259,324	48.0	126,451	30.6	32	32
Connecticut	1,114,756	908,420	746,254	206,336	22.7	162,162	21.7	31	29
Delaware	202,322	184,735	168,493	17,587	9.5	16,242	9.6	47	45
District of Columbia	331,069	278,718	230,392	52,351	18.8	48,326	21.0	43	41
Florida	752,619	528,542	391,422	224,077	42.4	137,120	35.0	33	33
Georgia	2,609,121	2,216,331	1,837,353	392,790	17.7	378,978	20.6	10	11
Idaho	325,594	161,772	88,548	163,822	101.3	73,224	82.7	45	46
Illinois	5,638,591	4,821,550	2,826,352	817,041	16.9	995,198	26.0	3	3
Indiana	2,700,876	2,516,462	2,192,404	184,414	7.3	324,058	14.8	9	8
Iowa	2,224,771	2,231,853	1,912,297	*7,082	*0.3	319,556	16.7	15	10
Kansas	1,690,949	1,470,495	1,428,108	220,454	15.0	42,387	3.0	22	22
Kentucky	2,289,905	2,147,174	1,858,635	142,731	6.6	288,539	15.5	14	12
Louisiana	1,656,388	1,381,625	1,118,588	274,763	19.9	263,037	23.5	24	23
Maine	742,371	694,466	661,086	47,905	6.9	33,380	5.0	34	31
Maryland	1,295,346	1,188,044	1,042,390	107,302	9.0	145,654	14.0	27	26
Massachusetts	3,366,416	2,805,346	2,238,947	561,070	20.0	566,399	25.3	6	7
Michigan	2,810,173	2,420,982	2,093,890	389,191	16.1	327,092	15.6	8	9
Minnesota	2,075,708	1,751,394	1,310,283	324,314	18.5	441,111	33.7	19	19
Mississippi	1,797,114	1,551,270	1,289,600	245,844	15.8	261,670	20.3	21	20
Missouri	3,293,335	3,106,665	2,679,185	186,670	6.0	427,480	16.0	7	5
Montana	376,053	243,329	142,924	132,724	54.5	100,405	70.3	40	43
Nebraska	1,192,214	1,066,300	1,062,656	125,914	11.8	3,644	0.3	29	27
Nevada	81,875	42,335	47,355	39,540	93.4	†5,020	†10.6	49	49
New Hampshire	430,572	411,588	376,530	18,984	4.6	35,058	9.3	39	37
New Jersey	2,537,167	1,883,669	1,144,933	653,498	34.7	478,736	39.4	11	15
New Mexico	327,301	195,310	160,282	131,991	67.6	35,028	21.9	44	44
New York	9,113,614	7,268,894	6,003,174	1,844,720	25.4	1,265,720	21.1	1	1
North Carolina	2,206,287	1,893,810	1,617,949	312,477	16.5	275,861	17.1	16	15
North Dakota	577,056	319,146	190,983	257,910	80.8	128,163	67.1	37	40
Ohio	4,767,121	4,157,545	3,672,329	609,576	14.7	485,216	13.2	4	4
Oklahoma	1,657,155	790,391	258,657	866,764	109.7	531,734	205.6	23	30
Oregon	672,765	413,536	317,704	259,229	62.7	95,832	30.2	35	36
Pennsylvania	7,665,111	6,302,115	5,258,113	1,362,996	21.6	1,044,002	19.9	2	2
Rhode Island	542,610	428,556	345,506	114,054	26.6	83,050	24.0	38	35
South Carolina	1,515,400	1,340,316	1,151,149	175,084	13.1	183,167	16.4	26	24
South Dakota	583,888	461,570	348,600	182,318	45.4	52,979	15.2	36	34
Tennessee	2,184,789	2,020,616	1,767,518	164,172	8.1	253,098	14.3	17	14
Texas	3,896,542	3,048,710	2,235,527	847,832	27.8	813,183	36.4	5	6
Utah	373,351	276,749	210,779	96,602	34.9	65,970	31.3	41	42
Vermont	355,956	343,641	332,422	12,315	3.6	11,219	3.4	42	39
Virginia	2,061,612	1,854,184	1,655,980	207,428	11.2	198,204	12.0	20	17
Washington	1,141,990	518,103	357,232	623,887	120.4	160,871	45.0	30	34
West Virginia	1,221,119	958,800	762,794	262,319	27.4	196,006	25.7	28	28
Wisconsin	2,333,860	2,069,042	1,693,330	264,818	12.8	375,712	22.2	13	13
Wyoming	145,965	92,531	62,555	53,434	57.7	29,976	47.9	48	48
Continental United States	91,972,266	75,994,575	62,947,714	15,947,691	21.0	13,046,861	20.7	..	..
Alaska	64,356	63,592	*32,052	764	1.2	31,540	98.4	..	..
Hawaii	191,909	154,001	89,990	37,908	24.6	64,011	71.1	..	..
Porto Rico	1,118,012	†953,799	....	164,709	17.3	....	....	..	..
‡Total United States	93,346,543	77,165,957	63,069,756	16,151,132	20.9	13,142,412	22.7	..	..

*Decrease. †In 1899. ‡Does not include soldiers and sailors stationed abroad.

DECENNIAL INCREASE OF POPULATION.
Continental United States.

Census.	Population.	Increase.	Per cent.
1910	91,972,266	15,977,691	21.0
1900	75,994,575	13,046,861	20.7
1890	62,947,714	12,791,931	25.5
1880	50,155,783	11,597,412	30.1
1870	38,558,371	7,115,050	22.6
1860	31,443,321	8,251,445	35.6
1850	23,191,876	6,122,423	35.9
1840	17,069,453	4,203,433	32.7
1830	12,866,020	3,227,567	33.5
1820	9,638,453	2,398,572	33.1
1810	7,239,881	1,931,395	36.4

Census.	Population.	Increase.	Per cent.
1800	5,308,483	1,379,269	35.1
1790	3,929,214	....	....

Division.	INCREASE (1900-1910). No.	Per ct.
New England	960,664	17.2
Middle Atlantic	3,861,214	25.0
East North Central	2,265,049	14.2
West North Central	1,290,498	12.5
South Atlantic	1,751,415	16.8
East South Central	862,144	11.4
West South Central	2,252,244	34.5
Mountain	958,860	57.2
Pacific	1,775,612	73.5

CENTER OF POPULATION AND MEDIAN LINES.

The center of population, according to the bureau of the census, may be said to represent the center of the gravity of the population. If the surface of the United States be considered as a rigid plane without weight, capable of sustaining the population distributed thereon, individuals being assumed to be of equal weight, and each, therefore, to exert a pressure on any supporting pivotal point directly proportional to his distance from the point, the pivotal point on which the plane balances would, of course, be its center of gravity, and this is the point referred to by the term "center of population" as used by the census bureau in its reports.

The median point, which may be described as the numerical center of population, is in no sense a center of gravity. In determining the median point distance is not taken into account, and the location of the units of population is considered only in

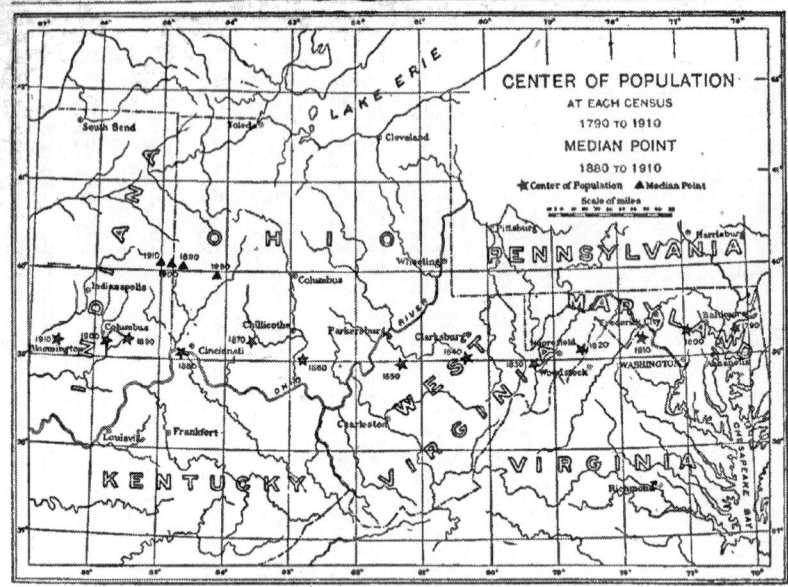

CENTER OF POPULATION
AT EACH CENSUS
1790 TO 1910
MEDIAN POINT
1880 TO 1910
★ Center of Population   ▲ Median Point
Scale of miles

relation to the intersecting median lines—as being north or south of the median parallel and east and west of the meridian.

The position of the center of population and its movement during each decade since 1790 is shown in the following table:

Census year.	North latitude.			West longitude.			Approximate location by important towns.	Movement in miles during preceding decade.			
	D.	M.	S.	D.	M.	S.		Direct line.	West-ward.	North-ward.	South ward.
1790....	39	16	30	76	11	12	....23 miles east of Baltimore, Md.................	....	....	....	....
1800....	39	16	6	76	56	30	....18 miles west of Baltimore, Md.................	40.6	40.6	....	0.5
1810....	39	11	30	77	37	12	....40 miles northwest by west of Washington, D. C.	36.9	36.5	....	5.3
1820....	39	5	42	78	33	0	....16 miles north of Woodstock, Va..............	50.5	50.1	....	6.7
1830....	38	57	54	79	16	54	....19 miles west-southwest of Moorefield, W. Va.*.	40.4	39.4	....	9.0
1840....	39	2	0	80	18	0	....16 miles south of Clarksburg, W. Va.*........	55.0	54.8	4.7	....
1850....	38	59	0	81	19	0	....23 miles southeast of Parkersburg, W. Va.*....	54.8	54.7	....	3.5
1860....	39	0	24	82	48	48	....20 miles south of Chillicothe, O.............	80.6	80.6	1.6	....
1870....	39	12	0	83	35	42	....48 miles east by north of Cincinnati, O.......	44.1	42.1	13.3	....
1880....	39	4	8	84	39	40	....8 miles west by south of Cincinnati, O.........	58.1	57.4	....	9.1
1890....	39	11	56	85	32	53	....20 miles east of Columbus, Ind..............	48.6	47.7	9.0	....
1900....	39	9	36	85	48	54	....6 miles southeast of Columbus, Ind...........	14.6	14.4	....	2.8
1910.....	39	10	12	86	32	20	....In the city of Bloomington, Ind.............	39.0	38.9	0.8	....

*West Virginia formed part of Virginia until 1869.

MEDIAN LINES.

In connection with the definition of the median point another method of presenting facts with regard to the geographical distribution of the population has been noted, involving the location of median lines. A parallel of latitude is determined which evenly divides the population so that the population north of that parallel is the same as that south. Similarly, a meridian of longitude is determined which divides the population evenly as between east and west. In calculating these median lines it is necessary, in the case of the square degrees of latitude and longitude which are traversed by the lines themselves, to assume that the population is evenly distributed through these square degrees or to make an estimated adjustment where this is obviously not the case.

The eastern terminus of the median parallel, according to the census of 1910, is on the New Jersey coast near Seagirt. In its course west this line passes through central New Jersey, leaving the state near Burlington and entering Pennsylvania a few miles north of Philadelphia, thence passing through Norristown and continuing through southern Pennsylvania and across the northern extremity of West Virginia, leaving the latter state at a point a few miles north of Wheeling. It nearly bisects Ohio, Indiana and Illinois, crossing about ten miles north of Columbus, O.; twenty-five miles north of Indianapolis, Ind., and about twenty miles north of Springfield, Ill. Through Missouri it runs about thirty miles south of the Iowa and Missouri line, thence passing through Nebraska about ten miles north of its southern boundary, and across the northern part of Colorado, passing about five miles north of Boulder City. Its location in Utah is about forty-five miles south of Salt Lake City. There are no large towns near its course across the northern part of Nevada and California. The western terminus of the median parallel is on the Pacific coast, in Humboldt county, California, about five miles north of Point Delgada and twenty miles south of Cape Mendocino, the point of continental United States extending farthest west.

The median meridian starts at Whitefish point, on the northern peninsula of Michigan, near the eastern

end of Lake Superior, thence passing south about twenty-five miles west of Lansing and through Indiana about ten miles west of the Indiana-Ohio boundary and twenty-five miles west of Cincinnati. South of the Ohio river it bisects Kentucky, crosses eastern Tennessee and leaves that state twenty miles east of Chattanooga. Through Georgia it passes close to the Georgia-Alabama line, about two miles west of Columbus, Ga., leaving the state near the intersection of the Alabama, Georgia and Florida boundary lines. It then crosses the northwestern part of Florida and terminates in the Gulf of Mexico at the city of Apalachicola. The following table shows the movement of the median lines from 1880 to 1910, inclusive:

Census year.	Median parallel. north latitude.			Median meridian. west longitude.			Movement in miles. Median northward.	Median westward
	D.	M.	S.	D.	M.	S		
1880.....	39	57	00	84	7	12	....	....
1890.....	40	2	51	84	40	1	6.6	27.0
1900.....	40	4	22	84	51	29	2.4	10.8
1910.....	40	6	24	84	59	50	2.3	7.5

MEDIAN POINT.

The exact location of the median point is indicated by the median lines already shown; in the following table its approximate location with reference to certain towns is described:

APPROXIMATE LOCATION BY IMPORTANT TOWNS.

1880......16 miles nearly due west of Springfield, O.
1890......5 miles southwest of Greenville, O.
1900......In Spartanburg, Ind.
1910......3 miles south of Winchester, Ind.

POPULATION BY COLOR OR RACE.

GENERAL SUMMARY.

Color or race.	1910.	1900.
White	81,731,957	66,809,196
Negro	9,827,763	8,833,994
Indian	265,683	237,196
Chinese	71,531	89,863
Japanese	72,157	24,326
All other	3,175	
Total	91,972,266	75,994,575

BY STATES (1910).

State.	White.	Negro.	Indian.
Alabama	1,228,832	908,282	909
Arizona	171,468	2,009	29,201
Arkansas	1,131,026	442,891	460
California	2,259,672	21,645	16,371
Colorado	783,415	11,453	1,482
Connecticut	1,098,597	15,174	152
Delaware	171,102	31,181	5
District of Columbia	236,128	94,446	68
Florida	443,634	308,669	74
Georgia	1,431,802	1,176,987	95
Idaho	319,221	651	3,488
Illinois	5,526,962	109,049	188
Indiana	2,639,961	60,320	279
Iowa	2,209,191	14,973	471
Kansas	1,634,352	54,030	2,444
Kentucky	2,027,951	261,656	234
Louisiana	941,086	713,874	780
Maine	739,995	1,363	892
Maryland	1,062,639	232,250	55
Massachusetts	3,324,926	38,055	688
Michigan	2,785,247	17,115	7,519
Minnesota	2,059,227	7,084	9,053
Mississippi	786,111	1,009,487	1,253
Missouri	3,134,932	157,452	313
Montana	360,580	1,834	10,745
Nebraska	1,180,293	7,689	3,502
Nevada	74,276	513	5,240
New Hampshire	429,906	564	34
New Jersey	2,445,894	89,760	168
New Mexico	304,594	1,628	20,573
New York	8,966,845	134,191	6,046
North Carolina	1,500,511	697,843	7,851
North Dakota	569,855	617	6,346
Ohio	4,654,897	111,452	127
Oklahoma	1,444,531	137,612	74,825
Oregon	655,090	1,492	5,090

State.	White.	Negro.	Indian.
Pennsylvania	7,467,713	193,919	1,503
Rhode Island	532,492	9,529	284
South Carolina	679,161	835,843	331
South Dakota	563,771	817	19,137
Tennessee	1,711,432	473,088	216
Texas	3,204,848	690,049	702
Utah	366,583	1,144	3,123
Vermont	354,298	1,621	26
Virginia	1,389,809	671,096	539
Washington	1,109,111	6,058	10,997
West Virginia	1,156,817	64,173	36
Wisconsin	2,320,555	2,900	10,142
Wyoming	140,318	2,235	1,486
Total	81,731,957	9,827,763	265,683

BY STATES—CONTINUED.

State.	Chinese.	Japanese.	Other.
Alabama	62	4	4
Arizona	1,305	371	....
Arkansas	62	9	1
California	36,248	41,356	2,257
Colorado	373	2,300	1
Connecticut	462	71	....
Delaware	30	4	....
District of Columbia	369	47	11
Florida	191	50	1
Georgia	233	4	....
Idaho	859	1,363	12
Illinois	2,103	285	4
Indiana	276	38	2
Iowa	97	36	3
Kansas	16	107	....
Kentucky	52	12	....
Louisiana	507	31	110
Maine	108	13	....
Maryland	378	24	....
Massachusetts	2,582	151	14
Michigan	241	49	2
Minnesota	275	67	2
Mississippi	257	2	4
Missouri	535	99	4
Montana	1,285	1,585	24
Nebraska	112	590	28
Nevada	927	864	55
New Hampshire	67	1	....
New Jersey	1,139	206	....
New Mexico	248	258	19
New York	5,266	1,247	19
North Carolina	80	2	....
North Dakota	39	59	....
Ohio	569	76	....
Oklahoma	139	48	....
Oregon	7,363	3,418	312
Pennsylvania	1,784	190	2
Rhode Island	272	33	....
South Carolina	57	8	....
South Dakota	121	42	....
Tennessee	43	8	2
Texas	595	340	8
Utah	371	2,110	20
Vermont	8	3	....
Virginia	154	14	....
Washington	2,709	12,929	186
West Virginia	90	3	....
Wisconsin	226	34	3
Wyoming	246	1,596	84
Total	71,531	72,157	3,175

NEGROES IN LARGE CITIES.

City.	1910.	1900.	Pct. 1910.
Albany, N. Y.	1,037	1,178	1.0
Atlanta, Ga.	51,902	35,727	33.5
Baltimore, Md.	84,749	79,258	15.2
Birmingham, Ala.	52,305	16,575	39.4
Boston, Mass.	13,564	11,691	2.0
Bridgeport, Conn.	1,332	1,149	1.3
Buffalo, N. Y.	1,773	1,698	0.4
Cambridge, Mass.	4,707	3,888	4.5
Chicago, Ill.	44,103	30,150	2.0
Cincinnati, O.	19,639	14,482	5.4
Cleveland, O.	8,448	5,988	1.5
Columbus, O.	12,739	8,201	7.0
Dayton, O.	4,842	3,387	4.2
Denver, Col.	5,426	3,923	2.5

City.	1910.	1900.	Pct. 1910.
Detroit, Mich.	5,741	4,111	1.2
Fall River, Mass.	355	324	0.3
Grand Rapids, Mich.	665	604	0.6
Indianapolis, Ind.	21,816	15,931	9.3
Jersey City, N. J.	5,960	3,704	2.2
Kansas City, Mo.	23,566	17,567	9.5
Los Angeles, Cal.	7,599	2,131	2.4
Louisville, Ky.	40,522	39,139	18.1
Lowell, Mass.	133	136	0.1
Memphis, Tenn.	52,441	49,910	40.0
Milwaukee, Wis.	980	862	0.3
Minneapolis, Minn.	2,592	1,548	0.9
Nashville, Tenn.	36,523	30,044	33.1
New Haven, Conn.	3,561	2,887	2.7
New Orleans, La.	89,262	77,714	26.3
New York, N. Y.	91,709	60,666	1.9
Newark, N. J.	9,475	6,694	2.7
Oakland, Cal.	3,055	1,026	2.0
Omaha, Neb.	4,426	3,443	3.6
Paterson, N. J.	1,529	1,182	1.2
Philadelphia, Pa.	84,459	62,613	5.5
Pittsburgh, Pa.	25,623	20,355	4.8
Portland, Ore.	1,045	775	0.5
Providence, R. I.	5,316	4,817	2.4
Richmond, Va.	46,733	32,230	36.6
Rochester, N. Y.	879	601	0.4
St. Louis, Mo.	43,960	35,516	6.4
St. Paul, Minn.	3,144	2,263	1.5
San Francisco, Cal.	1,642	1,654	0.4
Scranton, Pa.	567	521	0.4
Seattle, Wash.	2,296	406	1.0
Spokane, Wash.	723	376	0.7

City.	1910.	1900.	Pct. 1910.
Syracuse, N. Y.	1,124	1,034	0.8
Toledo, O.	1,877	1,710	1.1
Washington, D. C.	94,446	86,702	28.5
Worcester, Mass.	1,241	1,104	0.9

NEGRO POPULATION BY CENSUS YEARS.

1910.	9,828,294	1840	2,873,648
1900.	8,840,789	1830	2,328,642
1890.	7,488,788	1820	1,771,656
1880.	6,580,793	1810	1,377,808
1870.	4,880,009	1800	1,002,037
1860.	4,441,830	1790	757,206
1850.	3,638,808		

PER CENT INCREASE BY COLOR OR RACE
(1900-1910).

Division.	White.	Negro.	*Other.
New England	17.3	12.2	†—9.5
Middle Atlantic	24.9	28.2	—1.8
East North Central	14.1	16.7	25.3
West North Central	12.8	2.0	—0.1
South Atlantic	20.4	10.3	28.5
East South Central	14.1	6.1	1.3
West South Central	40.9	17.1	17.1
Mountain	59.5	37.7	15.6
Pacific	75.4	39.1	28.4
United States	22.3	11.2	17.4

*Includes Indian, Chinese, Japanese and all other. †Minus sign (—) denotes decrease.

CLASSIFICATION OF POPULATION BY SEX.

GENERAL SUMMARY 1910.

Class.	Male.	Female.	*Ratio.
White	42,178,245	39,553,712	106.6
Negro	4,885,881	4,941,882	98.9
Indian	135,133	130,550	103.5
Chinese	66,856	4,675	1,420.1
Japanese	63,070	9,087	694.1
All other	2,092	83	—
Native white	34,654,457	33,731,955	102.7
Native parentage	25,229.218	24,259,357	104.0
Foreign parentage	6,456,793	6,459,518	100.0
Mixed parentage	2,968,446	3,013,080	98.5
Foreign born	7,523,788	5,821,767	129.2
Total population	47,332,277	44,639,989	106.0

BY CENSUS YEARS.

Year.	Male.	Female.	*Ratio.
1910.	47,332,277	44,639,989	106.0
1900.	38,816,448	37,178,127	104.4
1890.	32,237,101	30,710,613	105.0
1880.	25,518,820	24,636,963	103.6
1870.	19,493,565	19,064,806	102.2
1860.	16,085,204	15,358,117	104.7
1850.	11,837,660	11,354,216	104.3
1840.	8,688,532	8,380,921	103.7
1830.	6,532,489	6,333,531	103.1
1820.	4,896,605	4,741,848	103.2

*Males to 100 females.

BY STATES (1910).

State.	Male.	Female.
Alabama	1,074,209	1,063,884
Arizona	118,582	85,772
Arkansas	810,025	764,424
California	1,322,973	1,054,576
Colorado	430,697	368,327
Connecticut	563,641	551,115
Delaware	103,435	98,887
Dist. Columbia.	158,050	172,019
Florida	394,166	358,452
Georgia	1,305,019	1,304,102
Idaho	185,546	140,048
Illinois	2,911,652	2,726,938
Indiana	1,383,299	1,317,577
Iowa	1,148,171	1,076,600
Kansas	885,912	805,037
Kentucky	1,161,709	1,128,196
Louisiana	835,275	821,113
Maine	377,053	365,319
Maryland	644,225	651,121
Massachusetts.	1,655,226	1,711,190
Michigan	1,454,534	1,355,639

State.	Male.	Female.
Minnesota	1,108,511	967,197
Mississippi	905,761	891,353
Missouri	1,687,838	1,605,497
Montana	226,866	149,187
Nebraska	627,782	564,432
Nevada	52,551	29,324
New Hampshire	216,290	214,282
New Jersey	1,286,463	1,250,704
New Mexico	175,245	152,056
New York	4,584,581	4,529,023
North Carolina	1,098,471	1,107,816
North Dakota.	317,554	259,502
Ohio	2,434,765	2,332,356
Oklahoma	881,573	775,582
Oregon	384,255	288,510
Pennsylvania.	3,942,137	3,722,974
Rhode Island	270,251	272,251
South Carolina	751,842	763,558
South Dakota.	317,101	266,787
Tennessee	1,103,491	1,081,298
Texas	2,017,612	1,878,930

State.	Male.	Female.
Utah	196,857	176,494
Vermont	182,568	173,388
Virginia	1,035,348	1,026,264
Washington	658,650	483,340
West Virginia	644,044	577,075
Wisconsin	1,208,541	1,125,319
Wyoming	91,666	54,299
Total	47,332,122	44,640,144

BY GEOGRAPHIC DIVISIONS.

	Male.	Female.
New England	3,265,137	3,287,544
Middle Atlantic	9,813,181	9,502,711
East North Cent.	9,393,792	8,857,829
West North Cent.	6,692,869	5,545,052
South Atlantic	6,134,600	6,060,295
East South Cent.	4,245,170	4,164,731
West South Cent.	4,544,485	4,240,049
Mountain	1,478,010	1,155,507
Pacific	2,365,878	1,826,426

BY PRINCIPAL CITIES (1910).

City.	Male.	Female.
Albany, N. Y.	48,270	51,983
Atlanta, Ga.	74,501	80,338
Baltimore, Md.	268,195	290,290
Birmingham, Ala.	67,268	65,417
Boston, Mass.	329,703	340,852
Bridgeport, Conn.	52,549	49,505
Buffalo, N. Y.	212,502	211,213
Cambridge, Mass.	50,161	54,678
Chicago, Ill.	1,125,764	1,059,619
Cincinnati, O.	177,511	186,080

City.	Male.	Female.
Cleveland, O.	289,262	271,401
Columbus, O.	91,452	90,059
Dayton, O.	58,848	57,729
Denver, Col.	107,395	105,986
Detroit, Mich.	240,354	225,412
Fall River, Mass.	57,627	61,668
Gr. Rapids, Mich.	55,539	57,032
Indianapolis, Ind.	116,069	117,581
Jersey City, N. J.	137,457	130,322
Kansas City, Mo.	126,414	121,967

City.	Male.	Female.
Los Angeles, Cal.	162,569	156,539
Louisville, Ky.	108,549	115,380
Lowell, Mass.	51,525	54,769
Memphis, Tenn.	66,270	64,835
Milwaukee, Wis.	189,488	184,369
Minneapolis, Minn.	157,345	144,063
Nashville, Tenn.	52,155	59,209
New Haven, Conn.	66,695	66,910
New Orleans, La.	163,239	175,836
New York, N. Y.	2,382,482	2,384,401

City.	Male.	Female.	City.	Male.	Female.	City.	Male.	Female.
Newark, N. J....	173,389	174,089	Providence, R. I.	110,288	114,038	Seattle, Wash....	136,773	100,421
Oakland, Cal.....	78,222	71,952	Richmond, Va...	60,905	66,723	Spokane, Wash...	57,513	46,889
Omaha, Neb......	64,802	59,294	Rochester, N. Y..	108,352	109,797	Syracuse, N. Y...	68,806	68,443
Paterson, N. J...	62,439	63,161	St. Louis, Mo....	346,068	340,961	Toledo, O.........	84,691	83,806
Philadelphia, Pa.	760,463	788,545	St. Paul, Minn...	111,809	102,935	Washington, D. C.	158,050	173,019
Pittsburgh, Pa...	273,589	260,315	San Francisco,Cal.	236,901	180,011	Worcester, Mass.	73,424	72,562
Portland, Ore....	118,868	88,346	Scranton, Pa....	65,591	64,276			

MEN OF VOTING AGE—21 YEARS AND OVER.

BY STATES.

State.	*Total.	White.	Negro.
Alabama	513,111	298,943	213,923
Arizona	74,051	65,097	764
Arkansas	395,824	284,301	111,365
California	920,397	846,207	8,143
Colorado	271,648	264,603	4,283
Connecticut	347,692	342,392	4,765
Delaware	61,887	52,804	9,050
District of Columbia..	103,761	75,765	27,621
Florida	214,195	124,311	89,659
Georgia	620,616	353,569	266,814
Idaho	110,863	107,469	328
Illinois	1,743,182	1,701,042	39,983
Indiana	822,434	801,431	20,651
Iowa	663,672	657,914	5,443
Kansas	508,529	490,225	17,588
Kentucky	603,454	527,661	75,694
Louisiana	414,919	240,001	174,211
Maine	235,727	234,855	476
Maryland	367,908	303,561	63,963
Massachusetts	1,021,669	1,008,431	12,591
Michigan	870,876	862,222	6,296
Minnesota	642,669	636,903	3,390
Mississippi	426,953	192,741	233,701
Missouri	973,062	919,480	52,921
Montana	155,017	148,733	851
Nebraska	353,626	348,915	3,225
Nevada	40,026	36,632	229
New Hampshire........	136,668	136,393	200
New Jersey...........	774,702	744,843	28,601
New Mexico..........	94,637	88,733	644
New York............	2,836,773	2,783,371	45,877
North Carolina.......	506,134	357,611	146,752
North Dakota........	173,890	171,941	311
Ohio	1,484,265	1,444,477	39,188
Oklahoma	447,266	395,377	36,841
Oregon	257,188	245,343	766
Pennsylvania	2,309,026	2,242,597	64,272
Rhode Island........	163,834	160,412	3,067
South Carolina......	335,046	165,769	169,155
South Dakota........	178,189	172,722	341
Tennessee	552,668	433,431	119,142
Texas	1,003,357	835,962	166,398
Utah	104,115	100,436	568
Vermont	113,506	112,513	975
Virginia	523,532	363,659	159,593
Washington	441,294	422,679	3,170
West Virginia........	338,349	315,498	22,757
Wisconsin	683,743	679,841	1,692
Wyoming	63,201	59,698	1,225

United States........26,999,151 24,357,514 2,458,873

*Includes 62,967 Indians, 60,421 Chinese and 56,638 Japanese.

BY PRINCIPAL CITIES.

City.	*Total.	White.	Negro.
Albany, N. Y..............	32,000	31,596	379
Atlanta, Ga..............	44,510	30,577	13,865
Baltimore, Md..........	163,654	137,025	26,214
Birmingham, Ala.........	40,699	24,248	16,441
Boston, Mass............	208,321	202,105	5,670
Bridgeport, Conn.......	32,991	32,461	471
Buffalo, N. Y...........	128,133	127,300	740
Cambridge, Mass........	30,262	28,777	1,384
Chicago, Ill............	700,590	680,950	17,845
Cincinnati, O...........	113,919	106,508	7,397
Cleveland, O............	177,386	173,847	3,298
Columbus, O............	60,892	55,821	5,023
Dayton, O..............	38,236	36,432	1,781
Denver, Col............	71,990	69,256	1,199
Detroit, Mich..........	150,017	147,737	2,224
Fall River, Mass........	31,647	31,441	133
Grand Rapids, Mich......	34,295	34,008	264
Indianapolis, Ind.......	76,743	69,141	7,586
Jersey City, N. J........	80,866	78,617	2,104
Kansas City, Mo..........	87,457	78,269	9,101

City.	*Total.	White.	Negro.
Los Angeles, Cal.........	114,889	107,633	2,571
Louisville, Ky..........	67,676	53,980	13,687
Lowell, Mass...........	31,300	31,206	44
Memphis, Tenn.........	44,309	27,031	17,238
Milwaukee, Wis........	113,106	112,651	396
Minneapolis, Minn......	105,305	103,961	1,227
Nashville, Tenn........	30,774	28,023	2,713
New Haven, Conn.......	40,510	39,233	1,191
New Orleans, La.......	96,997	71,387	25,269
New York, N. Y........	1,433,749	1,397,766	30,855
Newark, N. J..........	103,234	99,998	3,015
Oakland, Cal...........	53,967	49,163	1,238
Omaha, Neb...........	43,216	41,263	1,885
Paterson, N. J.........	36,873	36,343	453
Philadelphia, Pa.......	468,813	439,654	28,120
Pittsburgh, Pa.........	166,424	156,818	9,362
Portland, Ore..........	88,908	81,921	525
Providence, R. I.......	68,983	66,948	1,765
Richmond, Va..........	37,204	23,911	13,279
Rochester, N. Y.......	69,564	69,217	305
St. Louis, Mo..........	221,913	205,085	16,381
St. Paul, Minn........	72,073	70,439	1,673
San Francisco, Cal.....	175,961	164,127	831
Scranton, Pa..........	37,059	36,837	216
Seattle, Wash.........	101,685	85,052	1,204
Spokane, Wash........	40,254	39,439	305
Syracuse, N. Y........	44,713	44,261	437
Toledo, O.............	52,748	51,990	719
Washington, D. C......	103,761	75,765	27,621
Worcester, Mass.......	45,601	45,147	384

*Includes Indian, Chinese, etc.

NOTE—Of the native white males 21 years of age and over in 1910, 13,211,731, or 48.9 per cent, were of native parentage, and 4,498,966, or 16.7 per cent, were of foreign or mixed parentage. The foreign born whites 21 years of age and over numbered 6,646,817, or 24.6 per cent.

CITIZENSHIP OF FOREIGN BORN WHITE MALES (1910).

(21 years of age and over.)

BY STATES.

State.	Naturalized.	1st papers.	Alien.
Alabama	4,841	684	2,793
Arizona	5,912	1,113	14,574
Arkansas	5,284	595	1,388
California	137,274	27,708	99,940
Colorado	35,245	6,536	19,615
Connecticut	60,608	9,100	69,431
Delaware	2,707	658	3,189
District of Columbia....	6,474	1,058	2,304
Florida	5,959	782	7,411
Georgia	4,023	625	1,846
Idaho	12,817	2,478	6,215
Illinois	317,339	43,482	174,581
Indiana	42,523	13,320	18,354
Iowa	90,573	6,654	20,275
Kansas	39,145	6,173	12,247
Kentucky	13,225	815	2,754
Louisiana	10,024	1,166	9,151
Maine	14,994	1,490	23,672
Maryland	24,256	3,278	13,573
Massachusetts	189,125	30,016	212,033
Michigan	167,304	26,235	76,550
Minnesota	179,187	26,222	58,132
Mississippi	2,445	257	1,233
Missouri	65,612	10,117	25,835
Montana	27,635	6,749	16,937
Nebraska	57,270	9,924	12,347
Nevada	5,606	1,282	4,479
New Hampshire...........	16,415	1,421	19,377
New Jersey..............	128,438	24,511	122,076
New Mexico.............	4,267	709	6,048
New York...............	502,033	131,095	475,259
North Carolina..........	1,439	194	827
North Dakota...........	46,636	9,824	10,965

State.	Naturalized.	1st papers.	Alien.
Ohio	142,465	17,509	113,856
Oklahoma	12,074	1,477	4,449
Oregon	29,675	7,591	17,430
Pennsylvania	248,827	46,416	367,766
Rhode Island	32,040	5,314	31,996
South Carolina	1,602	184	739
South Dakota	32,495	8,020	4,376
Tennessee	5,444	464	1,867
Texas	43,383	6,833	37,865
Utah	15,251	2,415	9,626
Vermont	10,811	1,164	9,652
Virginia	6,411	859	4,693
Washington	68,895	15,258	43,203
West Virginia	7,263	1,353	22,545
Wisconsin	142,848	47,708	42,937
Wyoming	6,837	1,937	8,125
Total	3,034,117	570,772	2,266,535
Per cent	45.6	8.6	34.1

NOTE—The citizenship of 775,393, or 11.7 per cent of the foreign born males 21 years of age and over, was not reported.

BY PRINCIPAL CITIES.

	Naturalized.	1st papers.	Alien.
Albany, N. Y.	4,827	462	1,661
Atlanta, Ga.	1,011	193	565
Baltimore, Md.	16,643	2,664	9,559
Birmingham, Ala.	1,179	186	839
Boston, Mass.	47,791	10,438	40,516
Bridgeport, Conn.	6,563	1,028	8,136
Buffalo, N. Y.	29,409	4,413	16,255
Cambridge, Mass.	7,162	1,189	5,866
Chicago, Ill.	190,693	31,585	124,553
Cincinnati, O.	17,253	1,733	6,259
Cleveland, O.	40,482	7,826	40,221
Columbus, O.	4,453	414	2,349
Dayton, O.	3,451	296	2,964
Denver, Col.	10,959	2,102	3,801
Detroit, Mich.	32,891	7,271	28,733
Fall River, Mass.	8,268	732	10,594
Grand Rapids, Mich.	7,758	1,016	3,301
Indianapolis, Ind.	6,088	1,189	1,795
Jersey City, N. J.	16,556	3,067	14,404
Kansas City, Mo.	6,953	890	2,564
Los Angeles, Cal.	14,097	2,730	8,662
Louisville, Ky.	5,704	380	1,152
Lowell, Mass.	7,928	427	9,397
Memphis, Tenn.	1,964	197	808
Milwaukee, Wis.	24,755	9,887	14,435
Minneapolis, Minn.	23,462	5,427	10,305
Nashville, Tenn.	951	80	170
New Haven, Conn.	8,628	1,426	7,693
New Orleans, La.	6,133	595	3,703
New York, N. Y.	318,091	106,525	339,473

City.	Naturalized.	1st papers.	Alien.
Newark, N. J.	21,427	4,982	19,204
Oakland, Cal.	16,237	2,864	5,968
Omaha, Neb.	7,079	2,103	2,868
Paterson, N. J.	9,817	1,387	6,029
Philadelphia, Pa.	69,415	15,533	63,156
Pittsburgh, Pa.	28,797	5,355	28,439
Portland, Ore.	11,251	3,058	7,097
Providence, R. I.	12,988	2,815	14,910
Richmond, Va.	943	123	563
Rochester, N. Y.	13,003	2,947	8,361
St. Louis, Mo.	33,681	7,049	15,918
St. Paul, Minn.	17,671	2,586	5,576
San Francisco, Cal.	36,375	10,681	21,872
Scranton, Pa.	7,930	964	6,801
Seattle, Wash.	16,438	3,058	11,474
Spokane, Wash.	5,495	1,374	3,451
Syracuse, N. Y.	7,036	862	4,715
Toledo, O.	8,752	724	4,308
Washington, D. C.	6,474	1,058	2,304
Worcester, Mass.	9,126	1,514	11,184

WOMEN 21 YEARS OF AGE AND OVER (1910).

State.	Number.	State.	Number.
Alabama	501,959	New York	2,757,521
Arizona	43,891	North Carolina	519,575
Arkansas	351,994	North Dakota	122,466
California	671,386	Ohio	1,398,341
Colorado	213,425	Oklahoma	356,194
Connecticut	335,131	Oregon	168,322
Delaware	58,442	Pennsylvania	2,114,008
Dist. Columbia	116,148	Rhode Island	166,391
Florida	178,685	South Carolina	343,968
Georgia	613,149	South Dakota	134,187
Idaho	69,818	Tennessee	542,408
Illinois	1,567,491	Texas	884,218
Indiana	770,658	Utah	85,729
Iowa	603,644	Vermont	106,883
Kansas	438,934	Virginia	518,473
Kentucky	579,756	Washington	277,727
Louisiana	395,354	West Virginia	284,969
Maine	225,736	Wisconsin	611,157
Maryland	373,819	Wyoming	28,840
Massachusetts	1,074,485		
Michigan	786,033	United States.	24,555,754
Minnesota	512,411	White	22,059,236
Mississippi	412,941	Native parent-	
Missouri	896,152	age	12,484,481
Montana	81,741	Foreign parent-	
Nebraska	298,049	age*	4,567,647
Nevada	18,140	Foreign born	5,007,108
New Hampshire	135,372	Negro	2,427,742
New Jersey	736,659	Indian	60,169
New Mexico	73,152	Other	8,607

*Foreign or mixed parentage.

MALES OF MILITIA AGE—18 TO 44 YEARS (1910).

State.	Number.	State.	Number.	State.	Number.	State.	Number.
Alabama	401,145	Kansas	370,227	New Jersey	597,513	Texas	804,980
Arizona	58,962	Kentucky	457,493	New Mexico	73,097	Utah	84,449
Arkansas	311,792	Louisiana	388,343	New York	2,156,361	Vermont	73,685
California	665,522	Maine	151,325	North Carolina	392,193	Virginia	398,728
Colorado	203,982	Maryland	271,373	North Dakota	145,628	Washington	349,872
Connecticut	257,996	Massachusetts	760,324	Ohio	1,076,928	West Virginia	275,048
Delaware	44,634	Michigan	616,729	Oklahoma	357,933	Wisconsin	497,922
Dist. Columbia	78,349	Minnesota	491,113	Oregon	190,553	Wyoming	54,654
Florida	171,688	Mississippi	345,745	Pennsylvania	1,788,619		
Georgia	497,095	Missouri	721,166	Rhode Island	125,213	United States.	20,473,684
Idaho	86,384	Montana	123,232	South Carolina	276,788	Total in 1900.	16,182,702
Illinois	1,330,556	Nebraska	267,497	South Dakota	146,635	Per cent 1910*	22.3
Indiana	580,557	Nevada	29,383	Tennessee	423,088	Per cent 1900*	21.3
Iowa	475,839	New Hampshire	90,357				

*Per cent of total population.

POPULATION BY AGE PERIODS.

Age period.	Total.	Male.	Female.	Age period.	Total.	Male.	Female.
Under 5 years	10,631,364	5,380,596	5,250,768	60 to 64 years	2,267,150	1,185,966	1,081,184
Under 1 year	2,217,342	1,123,409	1,093,933	65 to 69 years	1,679,503	863,994	815,509
5 to 9 years	9,760,632	4,924,123	4,836,509	70 to 74 years	1,113,728	561,644	552,084
10 to 14 years	9,107,140	4,601,753	4,505,387	75 to 79 years	667,362	331,280	336,022
15 to 19 years	9,063,603	4,527,282	4,536,321	80 to 84 years	321,754	153,745	168,009
20 to 24 years	9,056,984	4,580,290	4,476,694	85 to 89 years	122,818	56,335	66,483
25 to 29 years	8,180,003	4,244,348	3,935,655	90 to 94 years	33,473	14,553	18,920
30 to 34 years	6,972,185	3,656,768	3,315,417	95 to 99 years	7,391	3,045	4,346
35 to 39 years	6,396,100	3,367,016	3,029,084	100 years and over	3,555	1,380	2,175
40 to 44 years	5,261,587	2,786,350	2,475,237	Age unknown	169,055	114,443	54,612
45 to 49 years	4,469,197	2,378,916	2,090,281				
50 to 54 years	3,900,791	2,110,013	1,790,778	All ages	91,972,266	47,332,277	44,639,989
55 to 59 years	2,786,951	1,488,437	1,298,514				

DISTRIBUTION BY AGE PERIODS OF TOTAL POPULATION IN 1910.

Age period.	White.	Negro.	Indian.
90 to 94 years..........	27,161	5,850	458
95 to 99 years..........	4,757	2,447	187
100 years and over....	764	2,675	116
Age unknown...........	134,224	31,040	949
All ages..............	81,731,957	9,827,763	265,683

CLASSIFIED BY BROADER AGE PERIODS (1910).

Class and age period.	Total.	Male.	Female.
Total population......	91,972,266	47,332,277	44,639,989
Under 5 years........	10,631,364	5,380,596	5,250,768
5 to 14 years........	18,867,772	9,525,876	9,341,896
15 to 24 years........	18,120,587	9,107,572	9,013,015
25 to 44 years........	26,809,875	14,054,482	12,755,393
45 to 64 years........	13,424,089	7,163,332	6,260,757
65 years and over....	3,949,524	1,985,976	1,963,548
Native white — Native			
parentage	49,488,575	25,229,218	24,259,357
Under 5 years........	6,546,282	3,326,237	3,220,045
5 to 14 years........	11,185,298	5,669,886	5,515,412
15 to 24 years........	9,771,977	4,886,442	4,886,535
25 to 44 years........	12,946,441	6,642,210	6,304,231
45 to 64 years........	6,740,000	3,547,325	3,192,675
65 years and over....	2,201,068	1,089,349	1,111,719
Native white—Foreign			
or mixed parentage.18,897,837		9,425,239	9,472,598
Under 5 years........	2,674,125	1,350,473	1,323,652
5 to 14 years........	4,551,444	2,289,629	2,261,815
15 to 24 years........	4,078,683	2,008,982	2,069,701
25 to 44 years........	5,210,109	2,565,634	2,644,475
45 to 64 years........	2,117,386	1,076,222	1,041,164
65 years and over....	255,586	128,662	126,924
Foreign born—White..13,345,545		7,523,788	5,821,757
Under 5 years........	102,507	51,940	50,567
5 to 14 years........	656,839	331,955	324,984
15 to 24 years........	2,104,142	1,175,674	928,468
25 to 44 years........	5,879,979	3,442,770	2,437,209
45 to 64 years........	3,392,518	1,894,735	1,497,783
65 years and over....	1,183,349	607,008	576,341
Negro	9,827,763	4,885,881	4,941,882
Under 5 years........	1,263,288	629,320	633,968
5 to 14 years........	2,401,819	1,197,249	1,204,570
15 to 24 years........	2,091,211	990,102	1,101,109
25 to 44 years........	2,638,178	1,304,098	1,324,080
45 to 64 years........	1,108,103	595,554	512,549
65 years and over....	294,124	152,482	141,642
Indian	265,683	135,133	130,550
Under 5 years........	40,384	20,202	20,182
5 to 14 years........	67,934	34,548	33,386
15 to 24 years........	50,330	25,887	24,453
25 to 44 years........	60,175	30,840	29,335
45 to 64 years........	32,925	17,055	15,870
65 years and over....	12,986	6,130	6,856
Chinese, Japanese and			
other	146,863	133,018	13,845
Under 5 years........	4,778	2,424	2,354
5 to 14 years........	4,438	2,609	1,829
15 to 24 years........	24,244	21,495	2,749
25 to 44 years........	74,993	68,930	6,063
45 to 64 years........	33,157	32,441	716
65 years and over....	2,411	2,345	66

NOTE—The years under 5 may be designated as early childhood; those from 5 to 14 as the school period; those from 15 to 24 as the period of youth; those from 25 to 44 as the prime of life; those from 45 to 64 as middle or late middle life, and those of 65 and over as old age.

URBAN AND RURAL POPULATION BY AGE (1910).

	Population.		Pct. of total.	
Age period.	Urban.	Rural.	Urban.	Rural.
Under 5 years.....	4,200,291	6,431,073	9.9	13.0
5 to 9 years.......	3,773,917	5,986,715	8.9	12.1
10 to 14 years.....	3,627,408	5,479,732	8.5	11.1
15 to 19 years.....	4,003,271	5,660,332	9.4	10.3
20 to 24 years.....	4,670,558	4,486,426	10.7	9.1
25 to 29 years.....	4,338,392	3,841,611	10.2	7.8
30 to 34 years.....	3,697,202	3,274,993	8.7	6.6
35 to 44 years.....	6,133,259	5,524,428	14.4	11.2
45 to 54 years.....	4,195,722	4,184,266	9.8	8.5
55 to 64 years.....	2,302,142	2,751,959	5.4	5.6
65 years and over	1,693,010	2,256,514	4.0	4.6
5 to 14 years......	7,401,325	11,466,447	17.4	23.2
15 to 24 years.....	8,573,829	9,546,758	20.1	19.3
25 to 44 years.....14,168,853		12,641,022	33.2	25.6
45 to 64 years.....	6,497,864	6,936,225	15.2	14.1
All ages.........42,623,383		49,348,883	46.3	53.7

AGE PERIODS BY COLOR (1910).

Age period.	White.	Negro.	Indian.
Under 6 years..........	9,322,914	1,262,288	40,384
Under 1 year..........	1,955,605	252,386	8,216
*5 to 9 years..........	8,475,173	1,246,553	36,541
10 to 14 years........	7,918,408	1,155,266	31,393
15 to 19 years.......	7,968,391	1,060,416	28,486
20 to 24 years........	7,986,411	1,030,795	21,844
25 to 29 years........	7,257,136	881,227	18,137
30 to 34 years........	6,267,276	668,089	15,243
35 to 39 years........	5,731,845	633,449	14,834
40 to 44 years........	4,780,272	455,413	11,961
45 to 49 years........	4,061,062	386,909	9,887
50 to 54 years........	3,555,313	326,070	9,343
55 to 59 years........	2,564,206	209,622	7,171
60 to 64 years........	2,069,323	186,502	6,524
65 to 69 years........	1,549,954	123,550	4,482
70 to 74 years........	1,030,884	78,839	3,382
75 to 79 years........	620,992	44,018	2,105
80 to 84 years........	294,555	25,579	1,565
85 to 89 years........	110,936	11,166	691

POPULATION OF STATES BY AGE PERIODS (1910).

	Under 5.	5-14.	15-24.	25-44.	45-64.	65-*.
State.	Pct.	Pct.	Pct.	Pct.	Pct.	Pct.
Alabama 14.6		25.2	20.6	24.5	11.9	3.1
Arizona 12.1		19.6	18.7	33.6	12.8	2.8
Arkansas 14.7		24.7	20.7	25.1	11.8	2.9
California 8.1		14.7	18.1	35.6	17.8	5.3
Colorado 10.3		18.2	18.8	33.1	15.9	3.3
Connecticut 10.1		17.7	18.8	31.7	16.3	5.3
Delaware 9.9		18.0	19.1	29.4	17.2	5.2
Dist. of Columbia. 8.1		15.1	18.9	36.1	16.4	5.1
Florida 12.9		22.8	20.6	28.5	12.0	2.9
Georgia 14.4		25.4	20.7	24.7	11.5	3.1
Idaho 12.4		20.9	19.1	31.0	13.5	2.7
Illinois 10.6		18.9	18.9	31.0	15.0	4.3
Indiana 10.2		19.3	18.9	29.0	17.0	5.5
Iowa 10.6		20.3	19.6	27.9	15.8	5.6

State.	Under 5. Pct.	5-14. Pct.	15-24. Pct.	25-44. Pct.	45-64. Pct.	65-*. Pct.
Kansas	11.3	20.5	20.0	27.7	15.1	5.2
Kentucky	12.9	23.0	19.9	26.3	13.6	4.1
Louisiana	13.5	24.9	20.5	26.6	11.2	3.0
Maine	9.7	17.7	17.1	28.2	18.9	8.2
Maryland	10.6	20.3	18.4	29.1	15.8	4.7
Massachusetts	9.8	17.2	18.5	32.5	16.7	5.2
Michigan	10.6	19.0	18.9	28.9	16.9	5.6
Minnesota	10.9	20.9	20.8	28.6	14.3	4.1
Mississippi	14.4	25.8	20.7	25.0	10.7	3.0
Missouri	10.9	20.1	19.9	29.2	15.1	4.6
Montana	10.2	17.0	19.4	36.5	13.8	2.4
Nebraska	11.8	21.0	20.8	27.7	14.4	4.3
New Hampshire	9.2	17.0	17.4	29.2	19.2	7.9
New Jersey	10.5	18.6	19.2	32.1	15.2	4.2
New Mexico	13.8	23.0	19.4	27.5	13.1	3.0
New York	9.9	17.4	19.5	32.5	16.0	4.6
North Carolina	15.1	25.4	20.5	23.1	12.2	3.5
North Dakota	14.3	22.4	20.5	29.0	11.3	2.2
Ohio	10.1	18.1	18.9	30.5	16.8	5.5
Oklahoma	14.6	24.4	20.1	26.6	11.7	2.5
Oregon	8.9	16.8	19.5	33.7	16.7	4.2
Pennsylvania	11.5	19.4	19.2	30.7	14.8	4.3
Rhode Island	10.0	17.6	19.5	32.0	16.2	4.6
South Carolina	15.1	26.5	21.4	23.4	10.6	2.9
Tennessee	13.5	23.5	20.5	25.5	13.0	3.8
Texas	13.8	24.8	20.9	25.9	11.6	2.8
Utah	14.1	25.0	19.9	27.5	11.8	3.3
Vermont	9.6	18.0	16.8	28.5	18.8	8.2
Virginia	13.0	24.0	20.0	25.5	13.2	4.1
Washington	9.5	16.9	19.4	35.1	15.3	3.2
West Virginia	13.8	22.9	20.2	27.5	12.0	3.5
Wisconsin	11.0	21.2	19.9	27.3	15.4	5.1
Wyoming	10.5	16.4	21.1	37.8	12.1	1.9
United States		20.5	19.7	29.1	14.6	4.3

*65 years and over.

City.	Under 5. Pct.	5-14. Pct.	15-24. Pct.	25-44. Pct.	45-64. Pct.	65-*. Pct.
Buffalo, N. Y.	10.0	18.3	20.6	32.3	15.5	3.4
Cambridge, Mass.	10.3	17.5	18.4	33.3	16.0	4.4
Chicago, Ill.	10.2	17.3	21.0	34.3	14.1	2.8
Cincinnati, O.	8.9	15.4	20.4	34.3	17.4	4.4
Cleveland, O.	11.1	17.4	20.5	34.4	13.4	3.0
Columbus, O.	7.9	14.8	20.3	36.1	16.8	4.0
Dayton, O.	8.1	15.4	19.5	34.6	17.0	4.4
Denver, Col.	7.9	15.2	18.9	36.4	17.5	3.6
Detroit, Mich.	10.5	16.7	21.3	34.1	14.0	3.3
Fall River, Mass.	11.7	20.4	20.2	30.2	14.2	3.4
Grand Rapids, Mich.	10.0	17.0	19.9	31.9	16.4	4.6
Indianapolis, Ind.	8.0	15.3	19.4	35.9	17.0	4.3
Jersey City, N. J.	11.0	19.6	20.0	32.9	13.6	2.9
Kansas City, Mo.	7.5	13.7	20.3	37.8	16.0	3.5
Los Angeles, Cal.	7.1	13.0	18.1	38.2	18.7	4.8
Louisville, Ky.	8.4	16.7	20.7	32.7	16.4	4.0
Lowell, Mass.	9.8	17.0	20.1	33.0	15.9	4.1
Memphis, Tenn.	8.2	14.9	21.8	38.2	13.4	2.9
Milwaukee, Wis.	10.1	18.5	21.7	31.8	14.4	3.4
Minneapolis, Minn.	8.6	14.8	22.4	35.4	14.9	3.3
Nashville, Tenn.	9.2	17.8	21.9	32.2	15.1	3.8
New Haven, Conn.	10.3	18.1	18.9	32.5	15.8	4.3
New Orleans, La.	9.5	18.9	20.5	32.6	14.2	3.8
New York, N. Y.	10.6	18.1	20.8	33.9	13.7	2.8
Newark, N. J.	11.1	18.5	19.8	33.0	14.2	3.3
Oakland, Cal.	8.4	14.1	18.3	36.7	17.6	4.9
Omaha, Neb.	8.4	15.3	21.7	36.0	15.1	3.3
Paterson, N. J.	10.0	19.1	20.0	32.2	14.8	3.8
Philadelphia, Pa.	9.9	17.2	19.3	33.4	16.0	4.0
Pittsburgh, Pa.	10.8	17.8	20.3	34.3	13.7	2.9
Portland, Ore.	6.8	12.0	20.2	41.1	16.7	3.2
Providence, R. I.	9.7	16.5	19.0	34.2	16.2	4.2
Richmond, Va.	9.1	17.1	22.3	33.4	14.3	3.6
Rochester, N. Y.	8.7	15.5	20.2	34.3	16.8	4.3
St. Louis, Mo.	8.7	16.1	20.9	35.2	15.2	3.6
St. Paul, Minn.	8.6	16.3	23.4	34.3	14.4	2.9
San Francisco, Cal.	7.0	11.9	18.9	40.9	16.5	3.8
Scranton, Pa.	11.8	20.2	20.8	31.5	12.8	2.8
Seattle, Wash.	7.2	12.5	19.5	42.1	15.1	2.6
Spokane, Wash.	8.7	14.5	19.8	38.9	15.1	2.6
Syracuse, N. Y.	8.7	15.6	19.7	34.3	17.1	4.6
Toledo, O.	9.4	17.2	19.7	33.6	16.1	4.0
Washington, D. C.	8.1	15.1	18.9	36.1	16.4	5.1
Worcester, Mass.	9.9	17.1	19.1	33.7	15.8	4.3

*65 years and over.

POPULATION OF CITIES BY AGE PERIODS (1910).

City.	Under 5. Pct.	5-14. Pct.	15-24. Pct.	25-44. Pct.	45-64. Pct.	65-*. Pct.
Albany, N. Y.	7.6	14.9	18.6	35.5	18.5	5.4
Atlanta, Ga.	10.1	17.4	22.3	34.1	13.0	2.9
Baltimore, Md.	10.7	18.3	21.5	35.4	11.7	2.1
Boston, Mass.	9.5	16.7	18.3	35.1	16.2	4.0
Bridgeport, Conn.	10.4	16.8	20.4	34.8	14.2	3.3

POPULATION BY MARITAL CONDITION (1910).

UNITED STATES AS A WHOLE—ALL AGES.

Condition.	Male Number.	Pct.	Female Number.	Pct.
Total	47,332,277	100.0	44,639,989	100.0
Single	27,455,607	58.0	23,522,121	52.7
Married	18,093,498	38.2	17,688,169	39.6
Widowed	1,471,472	3.1	3,176,426	7.1
Divorced	156,176	0.3	185,101	0.4
Not reported	155,524	0.3	68,172	0.2

POPULATION 15 YEARS OF AGE AND OVER.

Condition.	Male Number.	Pct.	Female Number.	Pct.
Single	12,550,129	38.7	8,933,170	29.7
Married	18,092,600	55.8	17,684,687	58.9
Widowed	1,471,390	4.5	3,176,228	10.6
Divorced	156,162	0.5	185,068	0.6
Not reported	155,524	0.5	68,172	0.2

MARITAL CONDITION BY AGE PERIODS.

Age period.	Single.	Married.	Widowed.	Divorced.
15 to 19—Male	4,448,967	51,877	1,110	347
Female	3,985,764	513,239	10,261	3,650
20 to 24—Male	3,432,161	1,100,093	18,815	6,732
Female	2,163,683	3,225,362	55,354	20,370
25 to 34—Male	2,767,957	4,964,769	110,431	34,571
Female	1,516,726	5,443,894	224,327	57,262
35 to 44—Male	1,026,502	4,873,153	198,791	42,688
Female	628,516	4,410,310	411,896	49,289
45 to 64—Male	722,701	5,771,639	593,642	58,177
Female	499,564	4,383,497	1,324,838	47,134
65 and over—Male	123,322	1,305,768	539,058	13,075
Female	124,223	687,335	1,140,558	6,903

MARITAL CONDITION BY NATIVITY AND COLOR.

POPULATION 15 YEARS OF AGE AND OVER.

	Single.	Married.	Widowed.	Divorced.
Native white—Nat. parentage—Male	6,185,324	9,144,099	728,883	87,456
Female	4,644,122	9,219,385	1,523,560	100,053
Native white—Foreign or mixed parentage—Male	2,906,042	2,677,706	160,779	24,688
Female	2,453,017	3,008,623	382,318	30,206
Foreign born white Male	2,268,916	4,432,135	384,726	23,059
Female	994,110	3,624,003	800,112	20,542
Negro—Male	1,083,472	1,749,228	189,970	20,146
Female	823,996	1,775,949	459,831	33,286
Indian—Male	27,391	46,154	5,319	679
Female	16,324	49,095	10,071	959
Chinese—Male	34,330	26,449	1,139	45
Female	680	2,016	229	5
Japanese—Male	42,688	15,918	495	86
Female	908	5,581	96	17

MARITAL CONDITION BY STATES.

POPULATION 15 YEARS AND OVER.

State and sex.	Single.	Married.	Widowed.	Divorced.
Alabama—Male	222,125	386,415	31,463	2,828
Female	169,126	388,191	80,137	5,313
Arizona—Male	39,106	40,708	3,723	661
Female	12,035	35,601	5,668	533
Arkansas—Male	170,709	292,715	29,093	2,653
Female	108,141	292,600	51,628	3,504
California—Male	480,292	495,538	46,423	10,784
Female	219,546	459,167	95,949	10,499

State and sex.	Single.	Married.	Wid-owed.	Di-vorced.
Colorado—Male	129,826	167,799	13,457	2,782
Female	65,931	160,545	25,752	3,043
Delaware—Male	28,027	41,451	3,752	184
Female	20,576	40,915	7,970	205
Georgia—Male	266,405	479,746	37,164	2,209
Female	269,231	475,941	98,502	4,250
Idaho—Male	59,751	64,043	4,497	943
Female	21,475	58,904	5,599	467
Illinois—Male	813,770	1,143,793	86,077	11,008
Female	577,197	1,113,982	191,345	13,172
Indiana—Male	333,109	585,360	49,604	7,865
Female	242,128	576,524	96,210	8,478
Iowa—Male	308,673	447,132	35,574	4,891
Female	219,845	442,599	67,423	5,285
Kansas—Male	229,894	348,915	27,585	3,943
Female	143,352	343,529	47,021	3,868
Kentucky—Male	285,864	435,835	38,207	4,020
Female	291,589	436,478	78,648	5,656
Maine—Male	95,261	158,941	17,531	2,636
Female	72,543	156,535	32,444	2,490
Maryland—Male	171,625	246,717	22,100	1,498
Female	149,842	247,837	51,842	1,791
Massachusetts—Male	479,048	655,740	56,800	4,331
Female	465,040	644,531	143,519	5,968
Michigan—Male	373,079	602,102	47,409	7,479
Female	256,062	587,253	92,424	7,504
Minnesota—Male	362,119	373,701	29,355	2,835
Female	224,076	369,196	51,175	2,996
Mississippi—Male	135,076	321,009	27,979	2,874
Female	136,722	323,929	66,661	4,666
Missouri—Male	435,219	685,938	56,518	7,020
Female	308,184	680,819	118,472	8,558
Montana—Male	91,760	74,423	5,338	1,175
Female	25,961	64,185	7,380	834
Nebraska—Male	176,975	233,273	16,353	2,396
Female	109,278	230,441	28,980	2,417
Nevada—Male	22,508	18,160	2,023	608
Female	4,411	14,109	2,124	275
New Jersey—Male	346,544	524,166	39,812	1,552
Female	279,432	506,985	94,289	1,984
New Mexico—Male	43,684	61,948	5,987	759
Female	21,461	61,048	9,845	867
New York—Male	1,327,597	1,840,960	145,844	7,436
Female	1,109,671	1,793,358	373,190	10,227
North Carolina—Male	234,954	382,288	26,543	999
Female	207,677	386,872	68,302	1,698
North Dakota—Male	98,659	102,080	6,091	664
Female	46,828	98,370	8,133	657
Ohio—Male	634,137	1,022,124	83,738	10,594
Female	481,784	991,870	178,798	12,386
Oklahoma—Male	197,510	321,850	26,662	3,151
Female	100,265	317,430	36,128	2,863
Oregon—Male	140,653	137,984	12,660	3,412
Female	55,242	128,182	17,540	2,225
Pennsylvania—Male	1,056,327	1,560,397	117,728	7,138
Female	800,392	1,473,465	259,641	8,604
South Carolina—Male	154,312	259,205	18,986	401
Female	130,808	263,611	54,714	832
South Dakota—Male	96,007	108,368	7,686	1,189
Female	49,274	105,949	11,137	1,026
Tennessee—Male	242,482	409,478	35,783	3,074
Female	186,773	411,118	79,932	5,177
Texas—Male	466,562	717,027	57,862	6,278
Female	296,498	713,569	118,712	9,283
Utah—Male	51,890	68,608	3,686	730
Female	30,083	66,255	9,949	914
Vermont—Male	45,567	77,671	8,281	1,281
Female	32,963	75,681	15,215	990
Virginia—Male	250,218	364,751	31,628	1,760
Female	205,232	366,488	73,120	2,614
Washington—Male	245,634	231,139	18,207	4,666
Female	88,669	214,653	26,560	5,932
West Virginia—Male	161,746	236,044	15,211	1,431
Female	99,881	225,691	28,276	1,863
Wisconsin—Male	343,440	444,704	34,570	3,875
Female	246,039	435,336	67,563	4,289
Wyoming—Male	40,383	28,498	2,042	500
Female	8,225	24,199	2,164	340

MARITAL CONDITION BY LARGE CITIES.*

POPULATION 15 YEARS AND OVER.

City and sex.	Single.	Married.	Widowed.	Divorced.
Baltimore, Md.—Male	76,598	106,466	9,318	922
Female	76,947	108,520	27,605	1,198
Boston, Mass.—Male	106,277	122,810	10,802	914
Female	101,490	120,215	30,110	1,516
Buffalo, N. Y.—Male	63,152	83,284	5,684	396
Female	52,939	81,424	16,112	456
Chicago, Ill.—Male	343,206	412,081	27,586	3,949
Female	251,715	423,839	76,813	5,890
Cincinnati, O.—Male	56,365	70,868	6,427	904
Female	51,293	70,435	20,416	1,409
Cleveland, O.—Male	58,160	113,234	18,835	1,247
Female	70,667	98,741	6,336	992
Detroit, Mich.—Male	52,074	92,488	15,996	1,598
Female	29,830	49,634	10,113	129
Jersey City, N. J.—Male	40,102	51,147	4,358	113
Female	29,830	49,634	10,113	129
Los Angeles, Cal.—Male	51,501	71,807	5,559	1,433
Female	35,307	70,635	16,544	1,728
Milwaukee, Wis.—Male	55,852	74,449	4,394	724
Female	46,515	71,129	12,127	1,123
Minneapolis, Minn.—Male	66,540	58,384	4,193	596
Female	40,647	56,684	9,643	869
New Orleans, La.—Male	47,705	59,532	5,934	382
Female	42,644	69,852	22,449	698
New York, N. Y.—Male	711,954	912,366	62,451	3,079
Female	617,885	892,969	183,897	5,213
Newark, N. J.—Male	46,760	76,082	4,697	223
Female	40,009	68,914	13,210	289
Philadelphia, Pa.—Male	216,401	304,450	26,818	1,440
Female	204,179	300,629	71,509	1,904
Pittsburgh, Pa.—Male	83,849	104,125	7,303	555
Female	64,722	98,734	19,760	814
St. Louis, Mo.—Male	109,565	136,793	11,474	1,712
Female	83,462	134,797	33,702	2,605
San Francisco, Cal.—Male	96,430	81,243	7,451	2,532
Female	44,858	74,790	18,260	2,694
Washington, D. C.—Male	48,164	64,432	6,253	535
Female	46,474	65,688	21,152	849

*Cities of 250,000 or more population in 1900.

FOREIGN BORN POPULATION OF THE UNITED STATES.

TOTAL FOREIGN BORN.

Country of birth.	1910.	1900.	*Pct. increase.
Northwestern Europe	6,740,400	7,016,311	—3.9
Great Britain	1,221,283	1,167,623	4.6
England	877,719	840,513	4.4
Scotland	261,076	233,524	11.8
Wales	82,488	93,586	—11.9
Ireland	1,352,251	1,615,459	—16.3
Germany	2,501,333	2,813,628	—11.1
Scandinavian countries	1,250,732	1,072,092	16.7
Norway	403,877	336,388	20.1
Sweden	665,207	582,614	14.3
Denmark	181,649	153,690	18.2
Netherlands	120,063	94,931	26.5
Belgium	49,400	29,757	66.0
Luxemburg	3,071	3,031	1.3
France	117,418	104,197	12.7
Switzerland	124,848	115,593	8.0
Southern and Eastern Europe	5,048,583	1,832,394	175.4
Portugal	59,360	30,608	93.9
Spain	22,108	7,050	213.6
Italy	1,343,125	484,027	177.5
Russia and Finland	1,732,462	640,743	170.4
Russia	1,602,782	578,102	177.2
Finland	129,680	67,039	107.0
Austria-Hungary	1,670,582	637,009	162.3
Austria	1,174,973	491,295	139.2
Hungary	495,609	145,714	240.1
Balkan peninsula	220,946	....	....
Roumania	65,929	15,032	338.6
Bulgaria	11,498	....	....
Servia	4,639	....	....
Montenegro	5,374	....	....
Greece	101,282	8,515	1089.5
Turkey and Europe	32,280	9,910	......
Europe	11,791,841	8,871,786	32.9
China	56,756	81,534	—30.4
Japan	67,744	24,788	173.3
India	4,664	2,031	129.6
Turkey in Asia	59,729	....	....
Other Asiatic	2,581	11,896	—78.2
Asia	191,484	120,248	59.2

Country of birth.	1910.	1900.	*Pct. in-crease.
Canada—Newfoundland	... 1,209,717	1,179,922	2.5
Canada—French	385,083	395,126	—2.5
Canada—Other	819,554	784,795	4.4
West Indies	47,635	25,435	87.3
Cuba	15,133	11,081	26.6
Other West Indies	32,502	14,354	126.4
Mexico	221,915	103,393	114.6
Central America	1,736	3,897	—55.5
South America	8,228	4,733	73.3
America	1,489,231	1,317,380	13.0
Africa	3,992	2,538	57.3
Australia	9,035	6,807	32.7
Atlantic Islands	18,274	9,768	87.1
Pacific Islands	2,415	2,013	20.0
Country not specified	2,687	2,546	5.5
Born at sea	6,927	8,196	—15.5
Total foreign born	13,515,886	10,341,276	30.7

*Minus sign (—) denotes decrease.

NOTE—The figures for Europe include 2,858 from countries not specified in 1910 and 22,575 in 1900. Bulgaria, Servia and Montenegro were included under "country not specified" in 1900. Turkey in Europe and Turkey in Asia were combined in the 1900 census. Newfoundland was included with Canada in 1900 census.

POPULATION OF FOREIGN BIRTH OR PARENTAGE (1910).

Country of origin.	Foreign born.	Both parents foreign.	One parent foreign.
Austria	1,174,924	709,070	117,585
Belgium	49,397	26,448	13,419
Bulgaria*	21,451	948	286
Canada—French	385,083	230,976	216,179
Canada—Other	810,987	859,204	704,099
Denmark	181,621	147,648	76,795
England	876,455	592,285	653,702
France	117,236	78,937	96,216
Germany	2,501,181	3,911,847	1,869,590
Greece	101,264	5,524	2,877
Hungary	495,600	191,059	13,568
Ireland	1,352,155	2,141,577	1,010,628
Italy	1,343,070	635,187	60,103
Mexico	219,802	107,866	54,333
Netherlands	120,053	116,331	57,190
Norway	403,858	410,951	164,290
Portugal	57,623	41,680	11,819
Roumania	65,920	20,707	1,094
Russia—Finland	1,732,421	949,316	70,938
Scotland	261,034	175,391	223,238
Spain	21,977	4,387	6,770
Sweden	665,183	546,788	152,244
Switzerland	124,834	90,669	86,147
Turkey in Asia	59,702	17,480	1,449
Turkey in Europe	32,221	2,560	533
Wales	82,479	84,934	81,534
Other foreign countries	88,014	31,362	40,919
Mixed foreign parentage†		1,177,092	
Total	13,345,545	12,916,311	5,981,526

*Includes Servia and Montenegro. †Parents born in different foreign countries.

NOTE—The above table includes white residents of the United States born abroad (foreign born), those having both parents born in the country specified (both parents foreign) and those having one parent born in the country specified and the other in the United States (one parent foreign).

POPULATION OF FOREIGN BIRTH OR PARENTAGE BY STATES (1910).

State.	Foreign born.	—Parentage.— *Foreign.	†Mixed foreign.
Alabama	19,286	32,417	2,829
Arizona	48,765	42,176	2,206
Arkansas	17,046	26,698	2,414
California	586,432	635,889	61,244
Colorado	129,587	181,428	14,683
Connecticut	329,574	374,489	20,720
Delaware	17,492	25,873	1,686
District of Columbia	24,902	45,086	3,031
Florida	40,633	35,825	2,863
Georgia	15,477	25,672	1,698
Idaho	42,578	75,195	6,834
Illinois	1,205,314	1,723,847	99,650
Indiana	159,663	359,551	14,293
Iowa	273,765	632,181	30,159
Kansas	135,450	292,105	17,433
Kentucky	40,162	124,704	5,597
Louisiana	52,766	112,717	8,146
Maine	110,562	134,955	6,101
Maryland	104,944	191,838	7,994
Massachusetts	1,059,245	1,176,447	80,901
Michigan	597,550	964,882	69,997
Minnesota	543,595	941,136	56,828
Missouri	229,799	518,201	27,483
Montana	94,713	166,809	9,137
Nebraska	176,662	362,353	19,177
Nevada	19,691	20,961	2,266
New Hampshire	96,667	103,117	4,328
New Jersey	660,788	777,797	52,982
New Mexico	23,146	26,321	1,351
New York	2,748,011	3,007,248	204,767
North Carolina	6,092	8,851	416
North Dakota	156,654	251,236	16,429
Ohio	598,374	1,024,393	53,139
Oklahoma	40,442	94,044	5,293
Oregon	113,136	135,238	12,323
Pennsylvania	1,442,374	1,896,267	104,223
Rhode Island	179,141	194,646	12,688
South Carolina	6,179	11,137	592
South Dakota	100,790	217,491	12,577
Tennessee	18,607	38,367	2,456
Texas	241,938	361,914	13,143
Utah	65,822	131,527	16,675
Vermont	49,921	75,085	3,235
Virginia	27,057	37,943	2,262
Washington	256,241	282,528	26,223
West Virginia	57,218	57,638	2,646
Wisconsin	512,865	1,044,761	59,297
Wyoming	29,020	32,504	2,949
Total	13,515,886	18,897,837	1,177,092

*Native white persons having both parents born in same country, or one parent born in foreign country and the other in the United States. †Native whites whose parents were born in different foreign countries.

MOTHER TONGUE OF FOREIGN BORN POPULATION (1910).

White persons born in Germany, Austria, Hungary and Russia classified by mother tongue.

GERMANY.

Mother tongue.	Number.	Pct.
German	2,260,256	90.4
Polish	190,096	7.6
Yiddish and Hebrew	7,910	0.3
Dutch and Frisian	6,510	0.3
Bohemian and Moravian	6,263	0.3
Danish	5,232	0.2
French	3,131	0.1
Lithuanian and Lettish	1,486	0.1
Slavic (not specified)	698	*
Magyar	564	*
Russian	552	*
All other	18,483	0.7
Total Germany	2,501,181	100.0

AUSTRIA.

Mother tongue.	Number.	Pct.
Polish	329,418	28.0
Bohemian and Moravian	219,214	18.7
German	157,917	13.4
Yiddish and Hebrew	124,588	10.6
Slovenian	117,749	10.0
Croatian	68,602	5.8
Slovak	55,766	4.7
Ruthenian	17,169	1.5
Russian	13,781	1.2
Servian	11,693	1.0
Slavic (not specified)	11,196	1.0
Italian	10,724	0.9
Roumanian	3,399	0.3
Lithuanian and Lettish	1,399	0.1

Mother tongue.	Number.	Pct.
Greek	839	0.1
All other	31,429	2.7
Total Austria	1,174,924	100.0

HUNGARY.

	Number	Pct
Magyar	227,742	46.0
Slovak	107,954	21.8
German	73,338	14.8
Yiddish and Hebrew	19,896	4.0
Roumanian	15,679	3.2
Croatian	9,060	1.8
Slovenian	5,510	1.1
Slavic (not specified)	6,837	1.4
Servian	5,018	1.0
Ruthenian	4,465	0.9
Polish	2,637	0.5

Mother tongue	Number.	Pct.
Bohemian and Moravian	1,755	0.4
Russian	1,400	0.3
Bulgarian	1,352	0.3
All other	12,967	2 6
Total Hungary	495,600	100.0

RUSSIA.

	Number.	Pct.
Yiddish and Hebrew	838,193	52 3
Polish	418,370	26 1
Lithuanian and Lettish	137,046	8 6
German	121,638	7 6
Russian	40,542	2 5
Finnish	5,865	0.4
Ruthenian	3,402	0.2
Slovak	1,709	0 1
Slavic (not specified)	1,658	0 1
Greek	1,230	0 1
Armenian	945	0.1
Bohemian and Moravian	898	0.1

Mother tongue.	Number.	Pct.
Swedish	592	*
All other	30,664	1 9
Total Russia	1,602,752	100 0

*Less than one-tenth of 1 per cent.

TOTAL FOREIGN WHITE STOCK BY COUNTRY OF ORIGIN (1910)

Country of origin.	Number.	Pct.
Austria	2,001,559	6 2
Belgium	59,264	0 3
Bulgaria, Servia, Montenegro	22,685	0.1
Canada—French	932,238	2 9
Canada—Other	1,832,377	5.7
Denmark	400,064	1 2
England	2,322,442	7.2
France	292,389	0 9
Germany	8,282,618	25.7
Greece	109,665	0 3
Hungary	700,227	2 2
Ireland	4,504,360	14 0
Italy	2,098,360	6 5

Mother tongue.	Number.	Pct.
Mexico	382,002	1.2
Netherlands (Holland)	293,574	0.9
Norway	979,099	3 0
Portugal	111,122	0 3
Roumania	87,721	0 3
Russia and Finland	2,752,675	8.5
Scotland	659,663	2 0
Spain	33,134	0 1
Sweden	1,364,215	4 3
Switzerland	301,650	0 9
Turkey in Asia	78,631	0.2
Turkey in Europe	35,314	0.1
Wales	248,947	0.8
All other countries	160,295	0.5
Of mixed foreign parentage*	1,177,092	3 7
All for'n countries	32,243,382	100.0

*Native whites whose parents were born in different foreign countries.

FOREIGN BORN POPULATION BY STATES (1910).

CLASSIFIED BY COUNTRY OF ORIGIN.

State.	Austria	Belgium	*Bulgaria	Canada French	Canada Other	China	†Cuba	Denm'rk	Engl'nd	Finl'nd.
Alabama	904	45	196	96	737	44	230	197	2,365	38
Arizona	1,483	50	371	177	1,650	1,016	37	884	3,500	560
Arkansas	1,268	111	17	119	955	44	27	178	1,519	15
California	17,165	1,464	880	3,109	41,568	27,764	654	14,209	48,703	6,159
Colorado	13,043	375	609	789	8,792	320	99	2,756	12,928	1,239
Connecticut	23,642	330	59	18,889	7,868	385	341	2,724	22,463	776
Delaware	992	8	1	63	441	29	34	52	1,558	9
District Columbia	459	41	10	109	1,052	270	243	176	2,638	21
Florida	228	50	14	151	1,577	156	17,050	295	3,078	89
Georgia	349	27	6	70	731	174	226	112	1,671	49
Idaho	1,561	94	576	796	4,545	773	13	2,254	4,983	652
Illinois	163,025	9,399	1,875	7,440	33,311	1,560	551	17,369	60,363	2,390
Indiana	11,831	2,298	576	789	5,049	196	82	900	9,783	215
Iowa	15,967	929	635	944	10,675	76	76	17,961	16,789	140
Kansas	12,094	1,703	118	1,087	6,101	16	74	2,760	11,262	49
Kentucky	1,032	73	77	98	972	34	42	75	2,819	18
Louisiana	1,597	292	25	250	941	346	630	239	2,086	118
Maine	831	30	32	35,013	41,210	65	80	929	5,551	831
Maryland	8,254	59	31	110	1,320	299	453	237	5,211	47
Massachusetts	35,455	1,745	169	134,659	162,710	1,873	2,287	3,406	92,658	10,744
Michigan	31,034	5,683	375	28,083	144,780	187	150	6,315	42,737	31,144
Minnesota	37,121	1,557	2,421	11,062	30,059	249	112	16,137	12,139	26,637
Missouri	16,222	1,000	451	779	7,290	452	272	1,729	13,760	120
Montana	8,350	235	2,155	2,874	10,968	1,098	39	1,943	8,981	4,111
Nebraska	24,362	491	183	674	6,661	89	47	13,674	8,009	79
Nevada	822	26	178	272	1,575	760	16	616	1,793	174
New Hampshire	2,438	175	21	40,865	17,013	53	40	131	4,862	1,198
New Jersey	56,779	1,867	122	1,203	7,932	932	1,917	5,059	50,375	1,640
New Mexico	1,233	44	167	111	912	202	25	116	1,101	26
New York	245,094	3,484	1,033	24,563	98,988	4,482	17,483	12,544	146,870	8,760
North Carolina	139	5	2	29	514	61	43	36	940	18
North Dakota	5,149	229	264	2,376	19,131	30	9	5,355	3,070	1,186
Ohio	72,857	1,525	1,697	2,310	21,382	398	245	1,837	43,347	3,988
Oklahoma	3,389	191	115	320	2,551	127	65	650	2,981	18
Oregon	5,241	573	1,095	1,146	11,263	6,468	68	3,215	7,998	4,734
Pennsylvania	251,774	5,250	1,407	1,246	14,737	1,468	2,105	3,034	109,115	2,413
Rhode Island	6,130	959	50	34,087	7,867	215	316	328	27,834	297
South Carolina	222	97	1	39	243	46	59	51	517	42
South Dakota	5,372	237	501	998	5,012	98	17	6,294	4,024	1,331
Tennessee	637	27	11	91	1,065	40	71	163	2,045	21
Texas	20,570	328	240	356	3,178	492	359	1,289	8,498	160
Utah	1,870	74	346	114	1,676	311	9	8,300	18,083	1,012
Vermont	1,087	25	2	14,643	11,415	7	37	172	2,464	293
Virginia	1,281	48	10	104	1,256	126	233	240	3,687	50
Washington	12,745	1,223	1,647	3,711	35,771	2,301	175	7,804	19,430	8,709
West Virginia	8,360	800	100	88	784	62	46	67	3,511	127
Wisconsin	38,692	4,020	393	7,992	17,004	163	54	16,454	13,959	5,705
Wyoming	3,966	82	331	143	1,288	204	38	962	2,985	1,380

*Including Servia and Montenegro. †And other West Indies.

State.	France	Germany	Greece	Hungary	Ireland	Italy	Japan	Mexico	Netherlands	Norway.
Alabama	592	3,603	633	585	1,167	2,696	5	81	127	266
Arizona	323	1,846	10	22	1,150	699	284	14,172	23	123
Arkansas	387	6,815	179	285	1,079	1,699	9	132	145	76
California	17,407	76,307	372	799	44,476	22,777	10,264	8,086	1,015	5,060
Colorado	1,374	17,071	2,272	1,632	8,710	14,375	2,245	2,602	710	1,787
Connecticut	2,619	31,127	1,074	13,855	58,954	56,954	65	19	304	1,265
Delaware	170	2,573	34	247	3,985	2,893	4	2	20	38
District Columbia	511	5,179	342	155	5,347	2,761	44	26	64	149
Florida	285	2,446	836	79	1,069	4,538	46	145	85	304
Georgia	224	3,029	941	230	1,655	545	5	25	52	145

State.	France	Germany.	Greece.	Hungary,	Ireland.	Italy	Japan	Mexico	Netherlands.	Norway
Idaho	332	5,049	1,843	202	1,782	2,067	1,330	133	261	2,566
Illinois	7,972	319,199	10,031	39,859	93,455	72,163	274	672	14,402	32,913
Indiana	2,388	62,179	1,370	14,370	11,266	6,911	41	47	2,131	531
Iowa	1,618	98,759	3,356	1,178	17,756	5,843	33	620	11,337	21,924
Kansas . ..	2,657	34,508	1,410	1,078	8,100	3,520	111	8,429	906	1,294
Kentucky	645	19,351	273	725	5,914	1,316	11	28	140	53
Louisiana ...	5,345	8,926	237	397	3,757	20,333	30	1,025	113	295
Maine	290	1,252	579	157	7,890	3,468	12	28	27	580
Maryland .	552	36,657	463	2,089	9,705	6,969	23	10	203	363
Massachusetts	5,926	30,555	11,413	1,996	222,367	85,056	150	71	1,597	5,432
Michigan .	2,421	131,586	1,196	11,597	20,434	16,861	56	86	33,471	7,638
Minnesota .	1,460	109,628	1,660	5,682	15,859	9,669	67	52	3,542	105,303
Missouri .	2,794	88,226	2,790	11,533	23,297	12,984	100	1,413	988	660
Montana	639	8,669	1,905	1,486	9,469	6,592	1,566	67	1,054	7,170
Nebraska	639	57,302	3,459	1,453	8,124	3,799	583	290	872	2,750
Nevada . .	653	1,916	1,051	44	1,702	2,831	855	732	44	255
New Hampshire	169	2,046	2,634	66	10,613	2,071	1	6	48	491
New Jersey .	6,240	122,880	1,575	47,610	82,758	115,446	193	97	12,698	5,351
New Mexico	326	1,746	167	209	644	1,959	254	11,918	86	151
New York . .	23,472	436,911	10,097	96,843	367,889	472,201	1,163	555	12,652	23,013
North Carolina	114	1,074	174	37	306	521	2	10	28	39
North Dakota	265	16,572	1,083	2,855	2,498	1,262	58	8	709	45,937
Ohio ..	4,838	175,095	2,555	85,881	40,062	41,620	70	85	2,278	1,110
Oklahoma ..	749	10,090	590	348	1,801	2,564	47	2,744	230	351
Oregon ..	1,159	17,958	3,555	1,160	4,995	5,532	3,277	199	618	6,543
Pennsylvania	10,093	195,202	4,221	123,495	165,109	196,122	181	153	1,231	2,290
Rhode Island..	1,711	4,459	951	294	29,713	27,287	30	8	143	578
South Carolina..	70	1,744	282	40	676	316	7	2	19	82
South Dakota	252	21,544	231	594	2,930	1,158	38	15	2,656	20,918
Tennessee . .	305	3,903	374	376	2,296	2,034	8	45	78	89
Texas	1,821	44,929	756	926	5,357	7,190	316	125,016	424	1,785
Utah	303	3,963	4,039	171	1,657	3,117	2,050	166	1,392	2,305
Vermont	219	798	113	539	4,940	4,594	3	6	25	102
Virginia	300	4,228	721	1,784	2,450	2,449	14	12	99	311
Washington	2,340	29,388	4,187	1,160	10,180	13,121	12,177	145	2,157	12,177
West Virginia. .	535	6,327	787	5,939	2,292	17,292	4	10	60	38
Wisconsin .	1,396	233,384	2,764	10,554	14,049	9,273	34	39	7,379	57,000
Wyoming	316	2,638	1,915	437	1,359	1,961	1,575	188	79	623

State.	Portugal.	Roumania	Russia	Scotland	Spain.	Sweden	Switzerland	Turkey (Asia)	Turkey (Europe).	Wales
Alabama .	4	108	1,531	1,120	74	753	213	389	128	230
Arizona ..	29	16	311	576	857	845	314	128	44	210
Arkansas	1	38	760	442	9	385	804	169	45	148
California ..	22,539	1,120	18,610	13,695	4,229	26,212	14,521	3,709	812	2,416
Colorado .	43	324	13,618	4,269	177	12,446	1,467	333	217	1,989
Connecticut .	707	718	54,121	6,750	92	18,208	1,806	1,739	696	656
Delaware ...	1	39	3,429	344	5	232	78	10	9	34
District Columbia .	2	41	3,393	705	51	359	281	139	41	87
Florida	30	323	547	606	4,199	729	146	291	744	63
Georgia . . .	23	85	3,224	527	91	289	169	376	99	89
Idaho	49	19	743	1,282	1,047	4,985	1,319	73	129	722
Illinois	291	4,306	149,016	20,755	364	115,424	8,661	2,690	2,453	4,091
Indiana	6	709	9,599	3,419	40	5,081	2,765	809	2,274	1,498
Iowa	8	384	6,310	5,162	40	26,763	3,675	600	479	2,434
Kansas	9	67	15,311	3,591	282	13,309	2,853	237	287	1,615
Kentucky	3	100	3,222	641	24	190	1,653	369	55	222
Louisiana .	73	111	1,805	455	719	344	421	949	196	82
Maine	82	20	4,752	2,389	111	2,203	56	744	721	204
Maryland ...	37	229	27,537	1,955	84	421	452	80	44	583
Massachusetts .	26,437	858	117,261	28,416	549	39,562	1,341	12,546	3,592	1,513
Michigan	20	610	37,978	9,953	53	26,374	2,780	1,567	342	786
Minnesota	16	2,008	17,541	4,373	53	122,428	2,992	698	523	1,623
Missouri	44	1,522	21,402	8,651	266	6,554	6,141	1,084	1,000	1,219
Montana	31	266	2,228	3,373	49	6,412	988	301	42	884
Nebraska ...	7	295	13,020	2,242	21	23,219	2,150	572	247	824
Nevada ..	305	8	135	469	778	708	468	25	15	168
New Hampshire...	110	26	4,345	1,979	17	2,068	78	891	1,965	68
New Jersey	145	2,208	93,567	17,513	495	10,547	7,549	2,396	389	1,203
New Mexico	10	6	228	509	100	365	172	123	17	93
New York....	660	34,443	558,956	39,437	3,766	53,705	16,315	9,478	5,004	7,464
North Carolina... .	29	7	711	435	8	112	68	402	107	35
North Dakota	3	1,070	31,910	1,696	13	12,160	560	392	270	222
Ohio .. .	182	3,974	48,756	10,705	123	5,522	10,988	2,031	1,935	9,377
Oklahoma	19	27	5,807	1,218	47	1,028	770	376	135	365
Oregon	174	258	5,321	3,387	462	10,099	3,853	197	553	585
Pennsylvania ..	225	7,752	240,935	32,046	354	23,467	7,484	4,486	2,754	29,255
Rhode Island ...	6,501	415	9,765	6,272	40	7,405	221	3,132	658	268
South Carolina	3	9	786	239	14	95	36	263	43	11
South Dakota	2	65	13,189	1,102	5	9,998	800	246	233	503
Tennessee	2	77	2,484	681	26	363	800	159	20	232
Texas	89	259	5,739	2,038	848	4,706	1,773	1,125	227	301
Utah	8	18	566	2,853	24	7,227	1,691	215	146	1,672
Vermont	79	17	2,455	2,615	351	1,331	214	189	31	1,043
Virginia	85	72	4,379	1,246	69	368	246	484	144	225
Washington	179	211	10,961	7,101	385	32,199	3,447	423	728	1,976
West Virginia ...	3	259	5,143	1,088	464	279	500	726	420	880
Wisconsin .. .	9	446	29,664	3,885	34	25,739	8,036	791	397	2,607
Wyoming	50	57	763	1,812	120	2,497	251	151	262	419

POPULATION OF FOREIGN PARENTAGE BY STATES (1910).

Native white persons having both parents born in the country specified, or one parent so born and the other native

State.	Austria	Belgium	*Bulgaria	Canada. French	Canada. Other	†Cuba	Denmark	England	Finland	France
Alabama	758	31	22	165	1,044	60	233	4,619	37	1,148
Arizona	451	35	18	233	1,868	14	413	3,774	139	3,810
Arkansas	1,269	72	21	308	1,652	20	270	4,195	15	1,003
California	8,415	770	96	4,957	47,474	424	12,287	66,821	2,836	15,223
Colorado	8,292	279	41	1,742	12,797	69	2,955	23,722	618	2,280
Connecticut	14,523	189	22	24,476	8,344	176	2,263	30,004	455	2,616
Delaware	407	....	....	61	371	19	36	3,025	...	262
District Columbia	351	33	4	184	1,388	95	149	5,061	6	558
Florida	190	45	6	178	1,653	9,742	271	4,497	48	505
Georgia	309	40	1	124	954	122	105	3,216	16	583
Idaho	714	65	4	1,221	6,891	10	5,212	16,073	202	626
Illinois	117,324	5,459	90	16,137	48,299	264	16,151	108,063	792	13,791
Indiana	6,005	1,907	21	2,214	8,552	45	1,274	24,886	100	6,699
Iowa	23,919	857	17	3,192	25,660	88	23,780	46,639	51	4,500
Kansas	12,763	1,343	23	3,838	14,832	35	4,457	30,840	15	4,230
Kentucky	685	115	16	209	1,530	21	136	7,229	14	2,154
Louisiana	1,287	439	10	455	1,553	638	517	5,681	69	14,609
Maine	389	20	19	40,494	49,884	52	,1,055	6,927	383	321
Maryland	8,005	44	2	167	1,630	168	246	10,644	8	1 139
Massachusetts	18,256	417	17	160,623	147,515	514	2,669	91,882	5,426	3,993
Michigan	19,488	4,822	21	54,826	193,985	100	8,486	77,599	24,404	6,249
Minnesota	38,958	1,604	63	24,145	45,270	52	21,387	24,370	17,826	3,022
Missouri	13,567	911	16	2,175	13,269	190	2,527	34,662	64	8,202
Montana	4,471	159	26	3,730	12,430	16	1,998	11,756	2,512	746
Nebraska	38,449	364	6	2,117	15,135	39	13,889	22,585	46	1,748
Nevada	219	17	6	349	1,891	6	700	3,245	59	371
New Hampshire	990	34	.....	40,489	19,966	28	124	6,478	636	199
New Jersey	31,429	1,001	45	1,572	8,813	693	4,611	71,744	619	6,799
New Mexico	474	26	3	293	1,330	10	166	2 294	..	437
New York	137,163	1,534	81	45,132	100,727	3,245	8,173	194,961	2,746	22,509
North Carolina	85	5	..	66	601	21	41	1,706	20	179
North Dakota	6,051	260	2	4,760	25,747	4	6,848	6,253	1,424	629
Ohio	52,713	1,171	165	5,051	26,009	139	1,958	84,777	3,313	14,026
Oklahoma	4,948	161	34	1,016	6,133	39	1,095	10,516	14	1,701
Oregon	2,332	508	25	1,917	15,366	39	3,558	14,717	2,977	1,566
Pennsylvania	151,329	3,291	165	2,430	18,230	859	2,917	180,409	1,275	13,353
Rhode Island	2,950	213	3	39,127	7,638	156	261	25,309	165	669
South Carolina	194	11	.	32	313	27	77	1,031	5	219
South Dakota	7,384	347	6	2,900	11,204	30	8,669	10,851	1,694	851
Tennessee	504	25	12	224	1,455	22	206	4,453	14	786
Texas	32 534	215	8	718	5,430	140	1,786	17,797	58	3,994
Utah	758	19	25	349	3,026	4	18,311	49,934	523	480
Vermont	436	22	2	25,876	16,037	10	142	3,959	174	270
Virginia	1,012	38	5	200	1,431	42	235	6,751	28	510
Washington	6,186	577	25	5,667	39,003	60	7,274	27,065	4,539	2,704
West Virginia	2,495	348	4	188	1,187	7	99	6,804	37	785
Wisconsin	43,035	9,939	40	20,413	33,367	47	21,861	38 529	3,991	3,661
Wyoming	1,524	54	5	316	2,110	5	1,387	5,881	774	352

*Including Servia and Montenegro. †And other West Indies.

State.	Germany.	Greece	Hungary	Ireland	Italy	Mexico.	Netherlands.	Norway	Portugal	Roumania
Alabama	8,528	126	300	4,892	1,981	51	107	282	10	58
Arizona	3,810	11	63	3,351	658	21,650	71	270	9	9
Arkansas	14,780	36	270	4,491	953	83	235	126	2	*14
California	130,077	480	1 351	107,204	39,017	17,593	2,113	7 194	29,192	388
Colorado	38,811	48	998	24,387	9,815	787	1,024	2,247	46	120
Connecticut	47,106	103	7,612	123,505	32,820	14	268	703	760	328
Delaware	4,993	16	129	10,054	1,636	2	22	27	3	12
District Columbia	13,119	73	699	7,037	1,620	11	168	386	33	55
Florida	5,046	91	45	2,596	2,875	62	95	461	46	185
Georgia	6 838	145	184	5,889	428	16	90	141	16	41
Idaho	12,174	27	67	6,537	560	41	378	3,510	33	1
Illinois	695,226	1,148	12,207	236,983	44,525	119	18,002	35,525	646	1 076
Indiana	202,021	108	4,252	41,942	2,229	44	3,240	662	22	76
Iowa	261 247	154	849	74 259	1,714	44	17,411	44,978	12	77
Kansas	99,028	61	1,009	30,732	2,113	312	1,761	2,402	28	7
Kentucky	72,909	30	133	23,773	1,229	24	324	79	7	42
Louisiana	32,369	142	304	15,105	22,678	645	195	344	171	23
Maine	2 004	53	70	17 059	1,120	3	45	506	114	6
Maryland	98 673	161	700	29,998	4,200	18	295	308	43	74
Massachusetts	47,174	1,003	1,133	410,160	45,621	37	1,289	2,938	15,986	252
Michigan	293,170	148	2,601	60,981	7,893	43	54,560	9,136	29	159
Minnesota	287 232	180	2,978	56,915	3,339	39	5,892	174,304	18	673
Missouri	279,287	161	3,043	75,346	8,134	161	1,944	1 080	18	397
Montana	17,999	29	656	18,962	1,409	36	962	6,773	10	25
Nebraska	144,412	55	689	29 538	1,041	29	2,219	4,957	25	57
Nevada	3,418	9	10	4 300	1,131	139	47	199	115	2
New Hampshire	2,487	88	42	19,976	871	2	35	361	43	8
New Jersey	210,756	307	21,089	177,743	76,405	74	14,805	3,001	81	1,029
New Mexico	4,397	3	72	2 079	868	10,030	121	180	8	..
New York	797,706	1,180	44,486	723 263	266,867	239	15,531	12,392	511	12,662
North Carolina	2,274	29	20	1,095	249	7	34	41	13	17
North Dakota	43,195	20	1,313	9 203	103	3	1,202	77,347	7	383

State.	Germany.	Greece.	Hungary.	Ireland.	Italy.	Mexico.	Netherlands.	Norway	Portugal.	Roumania
Ohio	498,704	399	80,254	126,791	20,712	80	3,592	922	189	534
Oklahoma	31,696	44	352	10,191	1,505	489	527	857	11	8
Oregon	35,402	116	378	11,948	1,284	97	1,069	6,592	155	52
Pennsylvania	453,499	629	56,214	405,376	102,432	97	1,448	1,646	274	2,399
Rhode Island	6,564	102	155	58,490	15,578	6	99	339	4,325	172
South Carolina	3,955	49	31	2,646	232	4	15	59	7	5
South Dakota	61,250	11	468	14,419	445	12	4,022	39,828	6	17
Tennessee	10,629	66	359	8,848	1,725	30	148	153	8	21
Texas	126,859	208	572	17,559	6,822	108,682	566	2,661	99	94
Utah	5,965	23	70	4,333	1,111	39	861	3,205	16	9
Vermont	1,349	18	93	14,687	2,023	3	35	73	40	1
Virginia	9,564	71	699	7,037	1,620	11	168	386	33	55
Washington	58,096	139	547	25,378	2,462	83	2,648	24,361	247	64
West Virginia	18,584	30	1,852	10,848	3,897	1	71	41	2	21
Wisconsin	561,559	226	2,612	60,786	3,967	22	14,441	100,701	40	104
Wyoming	5,496	22	170	3,877	528	148	92	626	8	12

State.	Russia.	Scotland.	Spain	Sweden.	Switzerland	Turkey (Asia).	Turkey (Europe).	Wales	Other countries	*Mxd parentage.
Alabama	1,103	2,401	170	755	376	185	31	456	198	2,289
Arizona	149	946	61	729	318	55	5	351	129	2,206
Arkansas	654	1,255	28	550	1,151	51	13	405	232	2,414
California	10,579	18,464	2,225	20,261	13,498	1,662	149	4,520	9,375	61,244
Colorado	8,809	7,419	128	12,968	2,217	170	26	3,428	502	14,683
Connecticut	29,432	8,303	89	16,296	1,445	496	52	848	521	20,720
Delaware	1,999	553	21	293	64	10	3	116	73	1,666
District Co'umbia	2,340	1,312	62	303	324	84	7	248	171	3,031
Florida	368	1,092	1,345	799	192	88	9	109	323	2,863
Georgia	2,254	1,217	105	349	256	173	14	143	205	1,698
Idaho	769	3,173	134	6,000	2,039	37	1	2,434	328	6,834
Illinois	78,944	32,857	245	114,709	12,998	592	119	7,546	3,151	99,659
Indiana	4,986	7,098	51	6,720	7,460	294	32	2,592	716	14,293
Iowa	12,861	8,786	151	7,873	11,066	423	38	3,258	1,108	27,483
Kansas	23,184	9,278	78	22,322	6,662	87	21	3,608	617	17,433
Kentucky	2,395	1,807	41	322	2,924	131	18	616	264	5,597
Louisiana	1,389	1,365	1,693	592	905	467	66	191	678	8,146
Maine	2,415	2,712	66	2,105	62	293	52	347	278	8,101
Maryland	19,433	4,889	93	470	493	30	20	1,439	564	7,594
Massachusetts	59,239	27,071	326	28,908	1,067	3,259	351	1,715	10,805	80,901
Michigan	22,045	15,525	50	30,563	4,411	514	81	1,573	1,424	69,997
Minnesota	12,736	8,282	49	145,591	5,589	261	41	2,909	1,992	56,828
Missouri	12,861	8,786	151	7,873	11,066	423	38	3,258	1,108	27,483
Montana	1,215	3,538	22	5,392	1,036	84	3	1,436	241	9,137
Nebraska	11,865	6,288	43	35,267	4,217	292	34	2,258	512	19,177
New Hampshire	1,546	2,329	19	1,488	85	249	38	67	110	4,328
New Jersey	53,117	20,587	231	7,801	6,211	756	77	3,082	1,337	52,982
New Mexico	158	910	51	384	266	92	9	186	84	1,351
New York	289,372	51,249	1,817	36,532	13,241	2,361	556	13,264	4,261	204,767
North Carolina	628	762	16	106	115	127	13	66	99	413
North Dakota	30,276	2,422	9	14,640	1,157	249	16	559	225	16,429
Ohio	27,393	19,429	105	6,533	22,959	609	219	22,139	1,388	53,139
Oklahoma	8,778	3,563	33	2,001	1,720	198	54	940	337	5,297
Oregon	3,472	5,068	118	8,099	4,320	43	21	1,057	619	12,363
Pennsylvania	146,506	50,426	280	26,218	10,347	1,507	362	57,048	2,578	104,222
Rhode Island	5,123	6,154	32	5,810	148	760	48	387	672	12,688
South Carolina	661	555	32	88	51	116	14	18	102	592
South Dakota	19,824	3,080	4	13,294	1,650	96	18	1,560	474	12,577
Tennessee	1,757	1,352	42	518	1,597	75	10	599	183	2,546
Texas	4,879	4,799	215	6,895	2,843	466	73	665	1,133	13,143
Utah	312	7,623	25	9,836	2,548	35	1	4,695	716	16,675
Vermont	1,166	2,758	77	1,090	98	83	46	1,159	93	3,235
Virginia	3,228	1,933	45	353	309	300	46	317	235	2,262
Washington	7,025	9,139	138	23,884	3,759	112	41	3,252	839	26,223
West Virginia	2,151	2,236	91	320	1,503	289	69	1,329	102	2,646
Wisconsin	15,763	9,122	36	29,647	12,840	283	74	6,250	1,108	50,297
Wyoming	334	2,418	14	2,053	403	11	12	810	113	2,949

*Mixed foreign parentage

FOREIGN BORN IN CITIES OF 250,000 OR MORE INHABITANTS (1910)

Country of birth	Baltimore	Boston.	Buffalo.	Chicago.	Cincinnati.	Cleveland.	Detroit.	Jersey City.	Los Angeles.	Milwaukee. &c.
Austria	6,540	2,413	9,284	132,063	1,638	42,059	14,160	4,978	2,510	11,553
Belgium	28	682	27	2,665	24	90	2,237	173	213	86
Bulgaria*	14	36	10	515	134	46	65	7	116	64
Canada—French	45	3,098	566	4,633	73	571	4,166	107	592	218
Canada—Other	752	47,802	16,868	26,688	887	8,794	38,648	1,010	7,686	1,671
China	243	819	57	1,335	16	155	24	132	1,481	39
Cuba†	357	1,070	45	393	40	71	58	212	119	31
Denmark	133	1,031	200	11,484	79	448	411	346	1,096	619
England	2,698	13,671	7,070	27,912	1,872	11,420	9,038	4,633	7,581	2,080
Finland	36	455	58	1,191	10	499	59	681	261	110
France	357	1,081	684	3,036	665	494	636	596	1,916	251
Germany	26,024	8,701	43,815	182,289	28,426	41,408	44,675	16,131	9,684	64,816
Greece	347	1,497	220	6,564	180	275	585	179	361	1,104
Hungary	1,358	426	2,742	28,938	6,344	31,503	5,935	1,084	820	5,571
Ireland	6,806	66,041	9,423	65,965	6,224	11,316	5,584	16,124	3,878	1,966
Italy	5,043	31,380	11,399	45,169	2,245	10,836	5,724	12,060	3,802	3,374
Japan	12	61	12	220	6	15	28	5	3,931	......

Country of birth.	Balti-more.	Boston.	Buffalo.	Chicago.	Cin-cinnati.	Cleve-land.	Detroit.	Jersey City.	Los Angeles.	Milwau-kee.
Mexico	6	24	20	188	15	18	27	14	5,632	12
Netherlands	106	486	314	9,632	322	1,076	584	243	408	615
Norway	199	1,914	253	24,186	37	512	235	1,360	1,003	2,144
Portugal	26	1,296	12	50	8	3	5	25	128	1
Roumania	216	373	106	3,344	454	761	313	196	297	267
Russia	24,803	41,892	11,349	121,786	4,999	25,477	16,644	13,667	4,758	11,992
Scotland	518	5,062	1,978	10,305	458	2,880	3,320	1,668	1,589	647
Spain	49	268	24	243	20	28	18	72	384	21
Sweden	237	7,123	1,021	63,035	114	1,657	601	1,280	3,414	787
Switzerland	228	415	639	3,494	696	1,373	595	553	828	833
Turkey (Asia)	50	2,088	207	1,175	245	497	561	103	385	78
Turkey (Europe)	24	623	97	711	280	351	125	28	120	147
Wales	99	315	217	1,818	177	1,298	170	139	414	231
All other	309	1,222	262	2,400	121	339	311	172	726	195
Total	77,662	243,365	118,689	783,428	56,859	196,170	157,534	77,987	66,133	111,529

Country of birth.	Minne-apolis.	New Orleans.	New York.	Newark.	Phila-delphia.	Pitts-burgh.	St. Louis.	S. Fran-cisco.	Wash., D. C.
Austria	6,075	645	190,246	12,963	19,860	21,400	11,171	9,641	469
Belgium	63	91	2,260	70	478	100	353	448	41
Bulgaria*	235	5	540	10	100	71	165	160	10
Canada—French	1,637	101	2,844	199	301	86	260	474	109
Canada—Other	5,905	387	23,476	1,126	3,735	1,741	2,256	5,701	1,052
China	92	219	3,936	194	866	197	351	6,914	270
Cuba†	24	468	16,415	183	1,529	124	141	291	243
Denmark	2,030	117	7,997	360	1,119	110	441	3,119	176
England	2,799	1,356	78,483	6,698	36,564	9,528	5,226	9,821	2,638
Finland	875	34	7,410	69	226	70	46	1,846	21
France	293	3,671	18,293	697	2,659	885	1,218	6,252	511
Germany	8,650	6,122	278,137	22,177	61,480	29,438	47,766	24,137	5,179
Greece	463	175	8,038	297	589	773	1,312	2,275	242
Hungary	1,176	90	76,627	6,029	12,495	6,576	8,759	1,347	155
Ireland	2,867	2,996	252,672	11,225	83,196	18,873	14,272	23,153	5,347
Italy	653	8,066	340,770	20,494	45,308	14,120	7,594	16,919	2,761
Japan	33	20	957	10	87	27	43	4,191	44
Mexico	14	289	426	10	59	17	180	1,792	26
Netherlands	209	43	4,193	202	349	109	422	500	64
Norway	16,402	181	22,281	190	1,144	117	204	3,769	149
Portugal	....	36	431	8	54	2	14	593	2
Roumania	1,412	93	33,586	1,160	4,413	1,521	1,055	583	41
Russia	5,654	1,254	484,193	21,912	90,697	26,391	15,481	4,643	3,393
Scotland	1,060	257	23,123	2,547	9,177	3,283	1,313	3,689	705
Spain	21	453	3,359	54	200	23	227	1,177	51
Sweden	26,478	160	34,952	782	2,429	1,355	1,129	6,970	359
Switzerland	299	247	10,452	779	2,013	1,007	2,653	2,587	281
Turkey (Asia)	219	192	6,160	127	973	453	730	320	139
Turkey (Europe)	61	46	3,695	48	525	79	938	402	41
Wales	213	20	1,779	106	1,033	2,159	197	403	87
All other	187	499	6,626	281	1,049	290	406	3,302	206
Total	86,099	28,333	1,944,357	111,007	384,707	140,924	126,223	142,298	24,902

*Including Servia and Montenegro. †And other West Indies.

FOREIGN BORN IN CITIES OF 100,000 TO 250,000 INHABITANTS (1910).

City.	Total.	Austria.	Canada.	*England.	Germany.	Hungary.	Ireland.	Italy.	†Scandi-navia.	‡Russia.
Albany, N. Y.	18,218	586	959	1,682	4,620	67	4,545	2,205	188	2,460
Atlanta, Ga.	4,501	113	256	595	729	92	302	95	102	1,342
Birmingham, Ala.	5,730	134	239	1,343	706	78	309	1,360	183	592
Bridgeport, Conn.	36,264	3,858	1,277	3,901	2,811	6,975	5,685	5,022	2,200	4,142
Cambridge, Mass.	35,328	156	10,172	2,851	728	102	10,637	1,545	2,131	3,735
Columbus, O.	16,363	818	696	1,935	5,722	970	1,809	1,619	168	1,534
Dayton, O.	13,892	660	407	620	5,817	2,761	976	356	80	1,527
Denver, Col.	39,749	1,698	3,492	5,920	6,636	465	3,965	2,664	6,029	5,627
Fall River, Mass.	50,958	2,614	16,260	11,964	234	3	5,194	1,025	189	2,182
Grand Rapids, Mich.	28,387	549	3,221	1,148	4,546	209	871	319	1,366	3,622
Indianapolis, Ind.	19,842	1,227	848	1,628	7,518	852	3,255	658	436	1,255
Kansas City, Mo.	25,466	571	1,760	2,927	5,456	332	3,267	2,579	2,666	3,431
Louisville, Ky.	17,473	316	371	938	8,471	441	2,700	654	137	2,014
Lowell, Mass.	43,494	1,948	16,342	5,751	255	24	9,983	259	772	1,886
Memphis, Tenn.	6,520	361	337	691	1,429	71	803	1,140	205	956
Nashville, Tenn.	3,017	81	185	246	554	177	572	91	46	596
New Haven, Conn.	42,989	1,109	1,335	2,663	4,115	473	9,004	13,159	1,919	8,049
Oakland, Cal.	40,546	1,267	3,150	5,304	5,546	248	4,160	3,800	4,794	1,118
Omaha, Neb.	27,179	3,414	1,218	1,989	4,861	654	1,849	2,361	6,860	2,614
Paterson, N. J.	45,485	883	487	7,791	6,741	483	4,971	9,317	243	6,867
Portland, Ore.	50,312	2,548	5,211	5,363	7,490	584	2,267	2,557	8,723	4,892
Providence, R. I.	76,999	1,574	8,835	12,676	6,076	126	15,801	17,306	4,058	7,518
Richmond, Va.	4,136	118	122	652	892	36	405	511	67	829
Rochester, N. Y.	59,076	1,688	9,718	5,979	14,624	415	5,230	10,638	607	7,187
St. Paul, Minn.	56,657	3,909	4,435	2,879	14,025	1,989	4,184	1,995	16,810	4,432
Scranton, Pa.	35,122	3,184	301	7,716	4,325	1,214	5,302	3,549	142	8,571
Seattle, Wash.	67,456	2,025	10,708	8,553	6,176	345	3,177	3,547	17,749	3,877
Spokane, Wash.	21,820	712	4,450	2,898	2,755	126	1,021	1,545	5,786	877
Syracuse, N. Y.	30,848	1,265	3,257	2,942	6,903	212	4,877	4,756	200	5,278
Toledo, O.	32,144	879	3,180	2,052	15,308	2,927	1,971	270	323	3,345
Worcester, Mass.	48,597	362	8,415	4,012	580	20	10,535	2,889	8,599	10,219

*Includes Scotland and Wales. ?Comprises Norway, Sweden and Denmark. ‡Includes Finland.

NATIVE AND FOREIGN BORN BY STATES (1910).

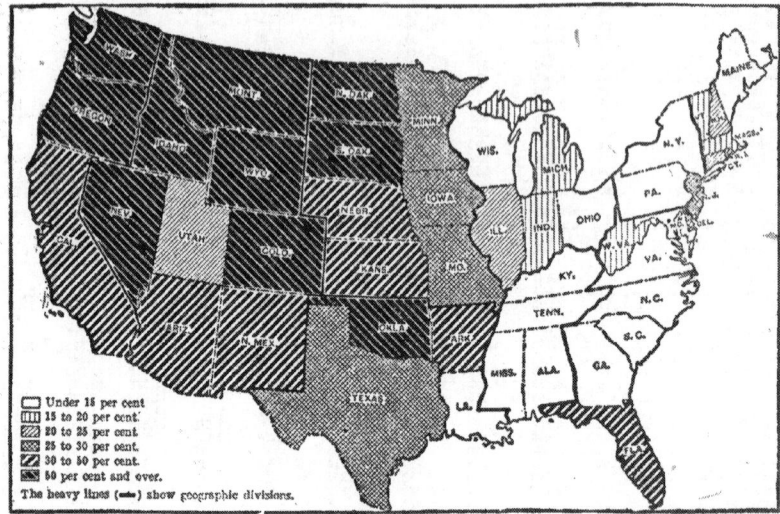

Under 15 per cent
15 to 20 per cent.
20 to 25 per cent.
25 to 30 per cent.
30 to 50 per cent.
50 per cent and over.

The heavy lines (━) show geographic divisions.

PERCENTAGE OF NATIVE POPULATION LIVING IN EACH STATE BORN IN OTHER STATES.

State.	Born in state.*	Born in other states.	Foreign born.
Alabama	1,857,916	257,031	19,286
Arizona	78,949	74,699	48,765
Arkansas	1,055,940	494,075	17,046
California	902,396	862,263	586,432
Colorado	233,516	480,264	129,587
Connecticut	607,074	174,680	329,574
Delaware	137,181	47,285	17,492
District of Columbia	139,251	154,622	24,902
Florida	463,003	244,836	40,633
Georgia	2,364,349	221,545	15,477
Idaho	90,225	190,063	42,578
Illinois	3,406,628	997,189	1,205,314
Indiana	2,031,245	501,420	159,663
Iowa	1,416,584	524,774	273,765
Kansas	823,628	732,968	135,450
Kentucky	2,021,385	215,517	40,162
Louisiana	1,405,926	190,309	52,766
Maine	578,739	50,009	110,562
Maryland	1,026,355	161,783	104,944
Massachusetts	1,861,820	434,104	1,059,245
Michigan	1,761,685	426,226	597,550
Minnesota	1,121,376	402,137	543,595
Missouri	2,322,925	825,738	229,799
Montana	99,214	177,783	94,713
Nebraska	595,551	414,056	176,662
Nevada	21,640	39,790	19,691
New Hampshire	248,629	82,562	96,667
New Jersey	1,344,164	525,075	660,788
New Mexico	184,749	117,954	23,146
New York	5,647,063	686,616	2,748,611
North Carolina	2,089,728	108,605	6,092
North Dakota	197,847	216,996	156,654
Ohio	3,546,991	607,352	598,374
Oklahoma	515,212	1,092,844	40,442
Oregon	325,102	329,538	113,136
Pennsylvania	5,638,263	589,204	1,442,371
Rhode Island	267,116	94,710	179,141
South Carolina	1,431,028	76,996	6,179
South Dakota	225,125	254,762	100,790
Tennessee	1,873,327	286,419	18,607
Texas	2,730,757	907,908	241,938
Utah	243,054	60,655	65,822
Vermont	250,480	52,165	49,921
Virginia	1,843,152	188,886	27,057
Washington	262,694	608,226	256,241
West Virginia	931,077	229,925	57,213
Wisconsin	1,558,455	256,529	512,865
Wyoming	31,782	84,269	29,020
	61,185,305	16,910,114	13,515,886

*State of residence.

PERCENTAGES OF NATIVE AND FOREIGN BORN (1910).

State.	Total population.	Born in state.*	Born in other states.	Foreign born.
Alabama	2,138,093	86.9	12.0	0.9
Arizona	204,354	38.6	36.6	23.9
Arkansas	1,574,449	67.1	31.4	1.1
California	2,377,549	38.0	36.3	24.7
Colorado	799,024	29.2	53.8	16.2
Connecticut	1,114,756	54.5	15.7	29.6
Delaware	202,322	67.8	23.4	8.6
District of Columbia	331,069	42.1	49.7	7.5
Florida	752,619	61.5	32.5	5.4
Georgia	2,609,121	90.6	8.5	0.6
Idaho	325,594	27.7	58.4	13.1
Illinois	5,638,591	60.4	17.7	21.4
Indiana	2,700,876	75.2	18.6	5.9
Iowa	2,224,771	63.7	23.6	12.3
Kansas	1,690,949	48.7	42.8	8.0
Kentucky	2,289,905	88.7	9.4	1.8
Maine	742,371	78.0	6.7	14.9
Maryland	1,295,346	79.2	12.5	8.1
Massachusetts	3,366,416	55.3	12.9	31.5
Michigan	2,810,173	62.7	15.5	21.2
Minnesota	2,075,708	54.0	19.4	26.2
Mississippi	1,797,114	87.0	12.2	0.8
Missouri	3,293,335	67.5	25.0	7.0
Montana	376,053	26.4	47.2	25.2
Nebraska	1,192,214	50.0	34.7	14.8
Nevada	81,875	26.4	48.5	24.1
New Hampshire	430,572	57.7	19.2	22.5
New Jersey	2,537,167	53.0	20.7	26.0
New Mexico	327,301	56.4	36.0	7.1
New York	9,113,614	62.0	7.5	30.2

State.	Total population.	Born in state.	Born in other states.	For-eign born.
North Carolina........	2,206,287	94.7	4.9	0.3
North Dakota.........	577,056	34.3	37.6	27.1
Ohio	4,767,121	74.4	12.7	12.6
Oklahoma	1,657,155	31.1	65.9	2.4
Oregon	672,765	33.5	49.0	16.8
Pennsylvania	7,665,111	73.6	7.4	18.8
Rhode Island........	542,610	48.2	17.5	33.0
South Carolina......	1,515,400	94.4	5.1	0.4
South Dakota........	583,888	38.6	43.6	17.3
Tennessee	2,184,789	85.7	13.1	0.9
Texas	3,896,542	70.1	23.3	6.2
Utah	373,351	65.1	16.2	17.6
Vermont	355,956	70.4	14.7	14.0
Virginia	2,061,612	89.4	9.2	1.3
Washington	1,141,990	23.0	53.3	23.4
West Virginia........	1,221,119	76.2	18.8	4.7
Wisconsin	2,333,860	66.8	11.0	22.0
Wyoming	145,965	21.8	57.7	19.9
United States........	91,972,266	66.5	18.4	14.7

NOTE—The total population includes persons born in the United States, state of birth not reported, persons born in outlying possessions, or at sea under the United States flag, and American citizens born abroad. Their combined number was only 360,961, or 0.4 per cent of the total population.

URBAN AND RURAL POPULATION.

The census bureau classifies as urban population that residing in cities and other incorporated places of 2,500 inhabitants or more. The proportion of the total population of continental United States living in urban and rural territory at the censuses of 1910 and 1900 was as follows:

	1910.		1900.	
	Population.	Pr.ct.	Population.	Pr.ct.
Urban	42,623,383	46.3	30,797,185	40.5
Rural	49,348,883	53.7	45,197,390	59.5
Total	91,972,266	100.0	75,994,575	100.0

In 1890 the per cent of urban population was 36.1 and of the rural, 63.9; in 1880 the urban was 29.5 and the rural, 70.5.

By geographic divisions the per cent of urban and rural population in 1910 was as follows:

Division.	Total.	Urban.	Rural
New England......................	7.1	12.8	2.2
Middle Atlantic....................	21.0	32.2	11.3
East North Central................	19.8	22.6	17.5
West North Central...............	12.7	9.1	15.7
South Atlantic....................	13.3	7.3	18.4
East South Central...............	9.1	3.7	12.9
West South Central...............	9.6	4.6	13.8
Mountain	2.9	2.2	3.4
Pacific	4.6	5.6	3.7
Total	100.0	100.0	100.0

By states the urban and rural population in 1910 was as follows:

State.	Urban.	Rural.	Per cent. Urban.	Rural.
Maine	381,443	360,928	51.4	48.6
New Hampshire.....	255,099	175,473	59.2	40.8
Vermont	168,943	187,013	47.5	52.5
Massachusetts	3,125,367	241,049	92.8	7.2
Rhode Island......	524,654	17,956	96.7	3.3
Connecticut	999,839	114,917	89.7	10.3
New York.........	7,185,494	1,928,129	78.8	21.2
New Jersey.......	1,907,210	629,957	75.2	24.8
Pennsylvania	4,630,669	3,034,442	60.4	39.6
Ohio	2,665,143	2,101,978	55.9	44.1
Indiana	1,143,835	1,557,041	42.4	57.6
Illinois	3,476,929	2,161,662	61.7	38.3
Michigan	1,327,044	1,483,129	47.2	52.8
Wisconsin	1,004,320	1,329,540	43.0	57.0
Minnesota	850,294	1,225,414	41.0	59.0
Iowa	680,054	1,544,717	30.6	69.4
Missouri	1,398,817	1,894,518	42.5	57.5
North Dakota......	63,236	513,820	11.0	89.0
South Dakota......	76,673	507,215	13.1	86.9
Nebraska	310,852	881,362	26.1	73.9
Kansas	493,790	1,197,159	29.2	70.8
Delaware	97,085	105,237	48.0	52.0
Maryland	658,192	637,154	50.8	49.2
District of Columbia	331,069	....	100.0	....

State.	Urban.	Rural.	Per cent. Urban.	Rural.
Virginia	476,529	1,585,083	23.1	76.9
West Virginia.......	228,242	992,877	18.7	81.3
North Carolina......	318,474	1,887,813	14.4	85.6
South Carolina.....	224,832	1,296,568	14.8	85.2
Georgia	538,650	2,070,471	20.6	79.4
Florida	219,080	533,539	29.1	70.9
Kentucky	555,442	1,734,463	24.3	75.7
Tennessee	441,045	1,743,744	20.2	79.8
Alabama	370,431	1,767,662	17.3	82.7
Mississippi	207,311	1,589,803	11.5	88.5
Arkansas	202,681	1,371,768	12.9	87.1
Louisiana	96,516	1,159,872	30.0	70.0
Oklahoma	320,155	1,327,000	19.3	80.7
Texas	938,104	2,958,438	24.1	75.9
Montana	133,420	242,633	35.5	64.5
Idaho	69,898	255,696	21.5	78.5
Wyoming	43,221	102,744	29.6	70.4
Colorado	408,840	394,184	50.7	49.3
New Mexico........	46,571	280,730	14.2	85.8
Arizona	63,260	141,094	31.0	69.0
Utah	172,934	200,417	46.3	53.7
Nevada	13,367	68,508	16.3	83.7
Washington	605,530	536,460	53.0	47.0
Oregon	307,060	365,705	45.6	54.4
California	1,469,739	907,810	61.8	38.2
United States.......	42,623,383	49,348,883	46.3	53.7

INCREASE IN URBAN AND RURAL POPULATION.

Comparing the rate of growth in urban and rural communities, it is shown by the census bureau that during the period between the census of 1900 and that of 1910 the increase in urban population in continental United States was 11,013,738, or 34.8 per cent, while the increase in rural population was 4,963,953, or 11.2 per cent. There had been an increase in urban population in every state, while in six states there had been an actual decrease in rural population. These states were: New Hampshire, 5.4 per cent; Vermont, 4.2 per cent; Ohio, 1.3 per cent; Indiana, 5.1 per cent; Iowa, 7.2 per cent; Missouri, 5.1 per cent.

POPULATION OF ALASKA (1910).

BY RECORDER'S DISTRICTS.

District.	Population.	District.	Population.
Aleutian islands....	1,083	Kuskokwim	2,711
Bristol bay.........	4,502	Koyukuk	455
Cape Nome.........	3,924	Mount McKinley...	232
Chandalar	368	Nabesna	103
Circle	799	Noatak-Kobuk	2,262
Cook Inlet.........	677	Nulato	785
Copper Center.....	563	Ophir	562
Cordova	1,779	Otter	1,234
Council City.......	686	Port Clarence.....	1,001
Eagle	543	Prince William	
Fairbanks	7,675	sound	210
Fairhaven	543	Rampart	370
Fort Gibbon.......	858	Sitka	2,210
Fortymile	341	Skagway	1,980
Hot Springs.......	372	St. Lawrence island	293
Iliamna	271	St. Michael.......	2,255
Juneau	5,854	Tanana	430
Kantishna	68	Unga peninsula...	1,303
Kayak	622	Valdez	4,815
Kenai	1,692	Wrangell	1,652
Ketchikan	3,520		
Kodiak	2,448	Total, 1910.......	64,356
Kougarok	998	Total, 1900.......	63,592

BY TOWNS.

District.	Population.	District.	Population.
Cordova	1,152	Nome	2,600
Douglas	1,722	Treadwell	1,222
Fairbanks	3,541	Valdez	810
Juneau	1,644	Wrangell	743
Ketchikan	1,613		

POPULATION OF PORTO RICO.

	1910.	1899.
Territory of Porto Rico..............	1,118,012	953,423
San Juan city......................	48,716	32,048
Ponce city.........................	35,027	27,952
Mayaguez city......................	16,591	15,187
Caguas city........................	10,354	5,450
Arecibo city........................	9,612	8,008
Guayama city.......................	8,321	5,334

POPULATION OF HAWAII (1910).

County.	Population.
Hawaii	55,382
Honolulu	82,028
Kalawao	785
Kauai	23,952
Maui	28,762
Total, 1910	191,909

Total, 1900	154,001
Per cent increase	24.6

CITIES.

Hilo	6,745
Honolulu	52,183

AREA OF THE UNITED STATES IN SQUARE MILES (1910).

Arranged according to rank in gross area.

State.	Rank.	Gross.	Land.	Water.*
Texas	1	265,896	262,398	3,498
California	2	158,297	155,652	2,645
Montana	3	146,997	146,201	796
New Mexico	4	122,634	122,503	131
Arizona	5	113,956	113,810	146
Nevada	6	110,690	109,821	869
Colorado	7	103,948	103,658	290
Wyoming	8	97,914	97,594	320
Oregon	9	96,699	95,607	1,092
Utah	10	84,990	82,184	2,806
Minnesota	11	84,682	80,858	3,824
Idaho	12	83,888	83,354	534
Kansas	13	82,158	81,774	384
South Dakota	14	77,615	76,868	747
Nebraska	15	77,520	76,808	712
North Dakota	16	70,837	70,183	654
Oklahoma	17	70,057	69,414	643
Missouri	18	69,420	68,727	693
Washington	19	69,127	66,836	2,291
Georgia	20	59,265	58,725	540
Florida	21	58,666	54,861	3,805
Michigan	22	57,980	57,480	500
Illinois	23	56,665	56,043	622
Iowa	24	56,147	55,586	561
Wisconsin	25	56,066	55,256	810
Arkansas	26	53,335	52,525	810
North Carolina	27	52,426	48,740	3,686
Alabama	28	51,998	51,279	719
New York	29	49,204	47,654	1,550
Louisiana	30	48,506	45,409	3,097
Mississippi	31	46,965	46,362	503
Pennsylvania	32	45,126	44,832	294
Virginia	33	42,627	40,262	2,365
Tennessee	34	42,022	41,687	335
Ohio	35	41,040	40,740	300
Kentucky	36	40,598	40,181	417
Indiana	37	36,354	36,045	309
Maine	38	33,040	29,895	3,145
South Carolina	39	30,989	30,495	494
West Virginia	40	24,170	24,022	148
Maryland	41	12,327	9,941	2,386
Vermont	42	9,564	9,124	440
New Hampshire	43	9,341	9,031	310
Massachusetts	44	8,266	8,039	227
New Jersey	45	8,224	7,514	710
Connecticut	46	4,965	4,820	145
Delaware	47	2,370	1,965	405
Rhode Island	48	1,248	1,067	180
District of Columbia	49	70	60	10
Total		3,026,789	2,973,890	52,899

*Does not include water surface of oceans, the Gulf of Mexico or the great lakes lying within the jurisdiction of the United States.

AREA (SQUARE MILES) BY CENSUS YEARS.

Continental United States.

Year.	Gross.	Land.	Water.
1910	3,026,789	2,973,890	52,899
1900	3,026,789	2,974,159	52,630
1890	3,026,789	2,973,965	52,824
1880	3,026,789	2,973,965	52,824
1870	3,026,789	2,973,965	52,824
1860	3,026,789	2,973,865	52,824
1850	2,997,119	2,944,337	52,782
1840	1,792,223	1,753,598	38,635
1830	1,792,223	1,753,588	38,635
1820	1,792,223	1,753,588	38,635
1810	1,720,122	1,685,865	34,257
1800	892,135	867,980	24,155
1790	892,135	867,980	24,155

The water area does not include the surface of the oceans, the Gulf of Mexico or the great lakes lying within the jurisdiction of the United States.

INCREASE IN AREA OF THE UNITED STATES.

Accession.	Gross area in square miles.	Area.
Area in 1790		892,135
Louisiana purchase, 1803		827,987
Florida, 1819		58,666
Treaty with Spain, 1819		13,435
Texas, 1845		389,166
Oregon, 1846		286,541
Mexican cession, 1848		529,189
Gadsden purchase, 1853		29,670
Total continental		3,026,789
Alaska, 1867		590,884
Hawaii, 1898		6,449
Philippines, 1899		115,026
Porto Rico, 1899		3,435
Guam, 1899		210
Samoa, 1900		77
Panama canal zone, 1904		436
Total outlying		716,517
Grand total United States		3,743,306

POPULATION PER SQUARE MILE BY STATES.

State.	1910.	1900.	1890.	1880.
Alabama	41.7	35.7	29.5	24.6
Arizona	1.8	1.1	0.8	0.4
Arkansas	30.0	25.0	21.5	15.3
California	15.3	9.5	7.8	5.5
Colorado	7.7	5.2	4.0	1.9
Connecticut	231.3	188.5	154.8	129.2
Delaware	103.0	94.0	85.7	74.6
District of Columbia	5517.8	4645.3	3972.3	3062.5
Florida	13.7	9.6	7.1	4.9
Georgia	44.4	37.7	31.3	26.3
Idaho	3.9	1.9	1.1	0.4
Illinois	100.6	86.1	68.3	55.0
Indiana	74.9	70.1	61.1	55.1
Iowa	40.0	40.2	34.4	29.2
Kansas	20.7	18.0	17.5	12.2
Kentucky	57.0	53.4	46.3	41.0
Louisiana	36.5	30.4	24.6	20.7
Maine	24.8	23.2	22.1	21.7
Maryland	130.3	119.5	104.9	94.0
Massachusetts	418.8	349.0	278.5	221.8
Michigan	48.9	42.1	36.4	28.5
Minnesota	25.7	21.7	16.2	9.7
Mississippi	38.8	33.5	27.8	24.4
Missouri	47.9	45.2	39.0	31.6
Montana	2.6	1.7	1.0	0.3
Nebraska	15.5	13.9	13.8	5.9
Nevada	0.7	0.4	0.4	0.6
New Hampshire	47.7	45.6	41.7	38.4
New Jersey	337.7	250.7	192.3	150.5
New Mexico	2.7	1.6	1.3	1.0
New York	191.2	152.5	126.0	106.7
North Carolina	45.3	38.9	32.2	28.7
North Dakota	8.2	4.5	2.7	*
Ohio	117.0	102.1	90.1	78.5
Oklahoma	23.9	†11.4	‡3.7	‡
Oregon	7.0	4.3	3.3	1.8
Pennsylvania	171.0	140.6	117.2	95.5
Rhode Island	508.5	401.6	328.8	259.2
South Carolina	49.7	44.0	37.7	32.6
South Dakota	7.6	5.2	4.5	*
Tennessee	52.4	48.5	42.4	37.0
Texas	14.8	11.6	8.5	6.1
Utah	4.5	3.4	2.6	1.8

*North Dakota territory, 0.9. †Oklahoma and Indian territory combined. ‡Less than one-tenth. Alaska with a gross area of 590,884 square miles has a population of 0.1 per square mile; Hawaii, 6,449 square miles, 29.8 per square mile, and Porto Rico, 3,435 square miles, 325.5 per square mile.

State.	1910.	1900.	1890.	1880.
Vermont	39.0	37.7	36.4	36.4
Virginia	51.2	46.1	41.1	37.6
Washington	17.1	7.8	5.3	1.1
West Virginia	50.8	39.9	31.8	25.7
Wisconsin	42.2	37.4	30.6	23.8
Wyoming	1.5	0.9	0.6	0.2
United States	30.9	25.6	21.2	16.9

NOTE—The density of population is obtained by dividing the population of each state and of continental United States by its total land area in square miles at each census.

POPULATION PER SQUARE MILE LAND AREA.

Census year.	Continental United States. Population.	Land area.	Per sq. mile.
1910	91,972,266	*2,973,890	30.9
1900	75,994,575	2,974,159	25.6
1890	62,947,714	2,973,965	21.2
1880	50,155,783	2,973,965	16.9
1870	38,558,371	2,973,965	13.0
1860	31,443,321	2,973,965	10.6
1850	23,191,876	2,944,337	7.9
1840	17,069,453	1,753,588	9.7
1830	12,866,020	1,753,588	7.3
1820	9,638,453	1,753,588	5.5
1810	7,239,881	1,685,865	4.3
1800	5,308,483	867,980	6.1
1790	3,929,214	867,980	4.5

*Net reduction of 269 square miles of land due to drainage of lakes and swamps in Illinois and Indiana (201 square miles of land), the building of the Roosevelt and Laguna reservoirs and the overflow of the Colorado river into the Salton sea in California (470 square miles of water surface).

ACRES PER INHABITANT.

Census year.	Continental United States. Population.	Acres land.	Per inhab- itant.
1910	91,972,266	1,903,289,600	20.7
1900	75,994,575	1,903,461,760	25.0
1890	62,947,714	1,903,337,600	30.2

BY STATES AND DIVISIONS (1910).

State and div.	Acres.	State and div.	Acres.
Maine	25.8	North Carolina	14.1
New Hampshire	13.4	South Carolina	12.9
Vermont	16.4	Georgia	14.4
Massachusetts	1.5	Florida	46.7
Rhode island	1.3	**South Atlantic**	14.1
Connecticut	2.8		
New England	6.1	Kentucky	11.2
New York	3.3	Tennessee	12.2
New Jersey	1.9	Alabama	15.3
Pennsylvania	3.7	Mississippi	16.5
Middle Atlantic	3.3	**East South Central**	13.7
Ohio	5.5	Arkansas	21.4
Indiana	8.5	Louisiana	17.5
Illinois	6.4	Oklahoma	26.8
Michigan	13.1	Texas	43.1
Wisconsin	15.2	**West South Central**	31.3
East North Central	8.6	Montana	248.8
Minnesota	24.9	Idaho	163.8
Iowa	16.0	Wyoming	427.9
Missouri	13.4	Colorado	83.0
North Dakota	77.8	New Mexico	239.5
South Dakota	84.3	Arizona	356.4
Nebraska	41.2	Utah	140.9
Kansas	31.0	Nevada	858.4
West North Central	28.1	**Mountain**	208.8
Delaware	6.2	Washington	37.5
Maryland	4.9	Oregon	91.0
District of Columbia	0.1	California	41.9
Virginia	12.5	**Pacific**	48.6
West Virginia	12.6	**Continental U. S.**	20.7

IRRIGATION IN THE UNITED STATES.

[From census bureau report.]

State.	Farms.	Acres.	Cost.
Arizona	4,841	320,051	$17,677,966
California	39,352	2,664,104	72,580,030
Colorado	25,857	2,792,032	56,636,443
Idaho	16,439	1,430,848	40,977,688
Kansas	1,066	37,479	1,365,563
Montana	8,970	1,679,084	22,970,958
Nebraska	1,852	255,950	7,798,310
Nevada	2,406	701,833	6,721,924
New Mexico	12,795	461,718	9,154,897
North Dakota	69	10,248	836,482
Oklahoma	137	4,388	47,200
Oregon	6,669	686,129	12,760,214
South Dakota	500	63,248	3,043,140
Texas	4,150	164,283	7,346,708
Utah	19,709	999,410	14,028,717
Washington	7,664	334,378	16,219,149
Wyoming	6,297	1,133,302	17,700,980
Total	158,713	13,708,485	307,866,369

Note—The above figures are for arid land alone and do not include rice land. The statistics of number of farms and the acreage irrigated are for 1909; the cost is to July 1, 1910.

The total length of ditches used for irrigation in 1910 was 125,591 miles and there were 6,812 reservoirs having a combined capacity of 12,581,129 acre-feet. The number of pumping plants reported was 13,996 and the acreage supplied by them 477,625. The relative importance of the several classes of irrigation enterprises is shown by the following percentages of acreage irrigated in 1909:

Class.	Per cent.
United States reclamation service	2.9
United States Indian service	1.3
Carey act enterprises	2.1
Irrigation districts	3.8
Co-operative enterprises	33.8
Individual and partnership enterprises	45.5
Commercial enterprises	10.6

Classified by source of water supply, the acreage irrigated was as follows: From streams, by gravity, 12,763,797; by pumping, 157,775; from wells, by flowing, 144,400; by pumping, 307,496; from reser-voirs, 98,193; from lakes, by gravity, 58,284; by pumping, 12,354; from springs, 196,186.

CROPS ON IRRIGATED LAND (1909).

State.	Acreage.	Value.	Val. per acre.
Arizona	171,362	$4,718,100	$27.54
California	1,196,767	52,057,007	43.50
Colorado	1,650,356	39,478,994	23.92
Idaho	772,684	16,582,213	21.46
Kansas	23,118	477,025	21.57
Montana	909,342	14,535,960	15.99
Nebraska	137,211	1,973,860	14.39
Nevada	356,079	5,339,475	15.00
New Mexico	230,034	5,705,923	24.80
North Dakota	3,273	56,215	17.18
Oklahoma	2,806	51,995	18.53
Oregon	368,911	7,489,255	20.30
South Dakota	38,438	505,684	13.16
Texas	58,227	2,645,385	45.43
Utah	579,744	14,642,792	25.26
Washington	169,483	7,994,531	49.82
Wyoming	583,786	7,362,983	12.61
Total	7,241,561	181,617,396	25.08

The percentages of the total acreage devoted to important crops on irrigated lands were: Alfalfa, 30.6; wild grasses, 21.1; oats, 10.2; wheat, 7.6; barley, 3.3; orchard fruits, 3.3; other tame or cultivated grasses, 3; grains cut green, 2.9; timothy alone, 2.8; sugar beets, 2.5; timothy and clover mixed, 2.5; potatoes, 2.3; corn, 1.8; tropical and subtropical fruits, 1.4. Crops grown on irrigated land show an excess yield of 28.6 per cent over those grown on unirrigated land.

IRRIGATION FOR RICE GROWING.

The total acreage irrigated for rice growing in Louisiana, Texas and Arkansas in 1909 was 694,306, of which 54.7 per cent was in Louisiana, 41.3 per cent in Texas and 4 per cent in Arkansas. The enterprises which were completed or under way in 1910 were reported as capable of irrigating 950,706 acres in that year and of serving ultimately a total of 1,134,322 acres. The total cost of rice irrigation enterprises to July 1, 1910, was $13,587,639.

PERSONS OF SCHOOL AGE AND SCHOOL ATTENDANCE (1910).

6 to 20 years inclusive. [From census bureau report.]

BY STATES AND DIVISIONS.

	Total	Attend'g school. Number.	Pct.
New England—			
Maine	195,197	132,082	67.7
New Hampshire	111,634	73,487	65.8
Vermont	94,701	66,845	70.6
Massachusetts	881,024	588,029	66.7
Rhode Island	148,102	90,328	61.0
Connecticut	298,454	192,497	64.5
Middle Atlantic—			
New York	2,454,428	1,563,374	63.7
New Jersey	708,525	440,903	62.2
Pennsylvania	2,194,363	1,366,542	62.3
East North Central—			
Ohio	1,313,809	868,578	66.1
Indiana	777,889	513,623	66.0
Illinois	1,615,914	1,025,053	63.4
Michigan	796,887	539,739	67.7
Wisconsin	732,544	484,629	66.2
West North Central—			
Minnesota	648,775	443,761	68.4
Iowa	675,222	469,778	69.6
Missouri	993,998	646,866	65.1
North Dakota	183,336	117,453	64.1
South Dakota	183,979	122,640	66.7
Nebraska	373,868	261,219	69.9
Kansas	515,156	363,695	70.6
South Atlantic—			
Delaware	57,932	35,304	60.9
Maryland	388,486	227,024	58.4
District of Columbia	79,249	50,859	64.2
Virginia	697,643	392,498	56.3
West Virginia	396,813	259,971	65.5
North Carolina	785,583	481,450	61.3
South Carolina	564,260	291,307	51.6
Georgia	925,865	480,378	51.9
Florida	243,917	128,659	52.7
East South Central—			
Kentucky	755,709	461,195	61.0
Tennessee	738,478	438,547	59.4
Alabama	750,357	385,449	51.4
Mississippi	644,805	388,072	60.2
West South Central—			
Arkansas	551,672	324,035	58.7
Louisiana	575,866	248,420	43.1
Oklahoma	566,323	383,816	67.8
Texas	1,363,713	790,736	58.0
Mountain—			
Montana	93,771	60,678	64.7
Idaho	96,819	66,779	69.0
Wyoming	35,776	23,920	64.3
Colorado	215,940	147,626	68.4
New Mexico	105,403	64,342	61.0
Arizona	56,897	30,355	53.4
Utah	121,016	85,006	70.2
Nevada	16,132	10,141	62.9
Pacific—			
Washington	293,478	195,259	66.5
Oregon	175,386	117,078	66.8
California	555,554	361,077	65.0
Geographic Divisions—			
New England	1,729,112	1,143,268	66.1
Middle Atlantic	5,357,256	3,370,819	62.9
East North Central	5,237,043	3,431,622	65.5
West North Central	3,574,334	2,425,412	67.9
South Atlantic	4,139,789	2,347,450	56.7
East South Central	2,889,349	1,673,263	57.9
West South Central	3,057,574	1,747,007	57.1
Mountain	741,754	487,947	65.8
Pacific	1,024,418	673,414	65.7
Total United States	27,750,599	17,300,202	62.3

BY PRINCIPAL CITIES.

City.	Total	Attend'g school. Number.	Pct.
Albany, N. Y.	23,794	14,816	62.3
Atlanta, Ga.	43,981	23,881	54.3
Baltimore, Md.	153,586	79,933	52.0
Birmingham, Ala	36,939	20,135	54.5
Boston, Mass	169,116	115,210	68.1
Bridgeport, Conn	26,938	16,262	60.4
Buffalo, N. Y.	120,366	73,412	61.0
Cambridge, Mass	27,426	19,152	69.8
Chicago, Ill	594,012	349,037	58.8
Cincinnati, O	93,618	55,474	59.3
Cleveland, O.	150,887	92,094	61.0
Columbus, O.	44,354	27,631	62.3
Dayton, O.	28,726	17,624	61.4
Denver, Col.	51,958	34,537	66.5
Detroit, Mich	122,979	69,808	56.8
Fall River, Mass.	36,235	22,839	63.0
Grand Rapids, Mich.	30,138	19,141	63.5
Indianapolis, Ind.	56,997	35,014	61.4
Jersey City, N. J.	78,300	47,198	60.3
Kansas City, Mo.	57,467	34,220	59.5
Los Angeles, Cal.	69,036	44,995	65.2
Louisville, Ky.	60,690	35,762	58.9
Lowell, Mass.	28,570	17,603	61.6
Memphis, Tenn.	32,462	17,169	52.9
Milwaukee, Wis.	109,078	63,228	58.0
Minneapolis, Minn.	75,611	48,655	64.3
Nashville, Tenn.	31,803	18,191	57.2
New Haven, Conn.	36,263	24,252	66.9
New Orleans, La.	98,468	52,799	53.6
New York, N. Y.	1,334,357	828,720	62.1
Newark, N. J.	97,544	61,916	63.5
Oakland, Cal.	34,153	22,253	65.2
Omaha, Neb.	31,381	20,685	64.2
Paterson, N. J.	36,457	21,779	59.7
Philadelphia, Pa.	470,342	271,332	57.9
Pittsburgh, Pa.	146,609	85,777	58.5
Portland, Ore.	43,272	26,146	60.4
Providence, R. I.	57,559	35,309	61.3
Richmond, Va.	35,271	17,986	51.0
Rochester, N. Y.	54,998	33,752	61.1
St. Louis, Mo.	181,402	101,320	55.9
St. Paul, Minn.	58,946	37,187	63.1
San Francisco, Cal.	85,368	50,128	58.7
Scranton, Pa.	39,397	22,964	58.3
Seattle, Wash.	49,294	31,099	63.1
Spokane, Wash.	24,150	15,259	63.2
Syracuse, N. Y.	34,171	21,131	61.8
Toledo, O.	45,314	28,198	62.2
Washington, D. C.	79,249	50,859	64.2
Worcester, Mass.	38,277	24,928	65.1

CHILDREN 6 TO 14 YEARS OF AGE.

For the combined group 6 to 14 years, inclusive—the most common years of school attendance—there was a total of 16,832,374 persons reported in 1910 and of this number 13,706,980, or 81.4 per cent, attended school. Following are the figures for this group by geographical divisions:

Division.	Total	Attend'g school. Number.	Pct.
New England	1,020,848	938,171	91.9
Middle Atlantic	3,165,516	2,797,524	88.4
East North Central	3,113,033	2,774,423	89.1
West North Central	2,147,108	1,878,360	87.5
South Atlantic	2,601,537	1,829,989	70.3
East South Central	1,813,364	1,273,522	70.2
West South Central	1,939,183	1,336,748	69.3
Mountain	455,409	372,092	81.7
Pacific	586,371	506,153	86.3
United States	16,832,374	13,706,982	81.4

TOTAL SCHOOL ATTENDANCE 1910.

Classified by sex, color, race, nativity, parentage and age.

Male	9,037,655	Male	783,869
Female	8,972,236	Female	886,781
		Indian	53,488
Total	18,009,891	Chinese	3,887
		Japanese	2,512
White	16,279,292	All other	92
Male	8,220,847	Native white	15,627,786
Female	8,058,445	Male	7,882,607
Negro	1,670,650	Female	7,745,179

Native par'nt'ge.	11,110,583	Male	338,240
Male	5,611,901	Female	313,266
Female	5,498,682	Age—Under 6 yrs.	396,431
		6 to 9 years...	5,678,320
Foreign or mixed		10 to 14 years.	8,028,662
parentage ...	4,517,203	15 to 20 years.	3,593,222
Male	2,270,706	15 to 17 years.	2,748,386
Female	2,246,497	18 to 20 years.	844,836
		21 years and	
Foreign born		over	313,256
white	651,506		

URBAN AND RURAL ATTENDANCE.

	Urban.		Rural.	
Age period.	Number.	Pct.	Number.	Pct.
Under 6 years........	212,994	2.8	183,437	1.7
6 to 9 years........	2,442,305	32.7	3,236,015	30.7
10 to 14 years........	3,326,340	44.5	4,702,322	44.7
15 to 20 years........	1,330,324	17.8	2,262,898	21.5
21 and over........	168,057	2.2	145,199	1.4
Total	7,480,020	100.0	10,529,871	100.0

DWELLINGS AND FAMILIES (1910).

In census usage a "dwelling" is any building in which one or more persons reside. A mere cabin, or room in a warehouse, occupied by a single person, is a census dwelling, while on the other hand an apartment house containing many families constitutes only one dwelling. Only occupied dwellings are included in the following tables. The term "family" as used in census reports means a household or group of persons, whether related by blood or not, who share a common abode, usually also sharing the same table. If one person lives alone he constitutes a family, while on the other hand those who dwell in a hotel or institution in which many people live are also treated as forming a single family. There is, however, no considerable difference between the average size of all families under the census usage and the average size of what are commonly termed families or households in popular speech. In 1900 the difference for the United States as a whole was only 0.1 per cent.

At each census from 1850 to 1910 a decrease was shown in the average number of persons per dwelling and the average number per family. The decrease in the average number per dwelling has been due to the decrease in the average per family, the influence of which has been partly offset by the increased construction of tenements and other dwellings containing more than one family.

In 1910 there were 7,254,242 dwellings and 9,499,765 families in urban communities, while there were 10,551,603 dwellings and 10,755,790 families in rural communities. For urban communities the number of persons to a dwelling averaged 5.9 and to a family 4.5; for rural communities the number of persons to a dwelling averaged 4.7 and to a family 4.6.

BY STATES.

State.	Dwell- ings.	*Per- sons.	Fam- ilies.	†Per- sons.
Alabama	441,249	5.0	454,787	4.7
Arizona	45,286	4.5	47,927	4.3
Arkansas	227,625	4.8	333,368	4.7
California	513,481	4.6	563,636	4.2
Colorado	183,874	4.3	194,467	4.1
Connecticut	181,911	6.1	246,659	4.5
Delaware	43,183	4.7	44,951	4.5
District of Columbia..	58,513	5.7	71,339	4.6
Florida	165,818	4.5	171,422	4.4
Georgia	530,631	4.9	553,264	4.7
Idaho	71,830	4.5	73,669	4.4
Illinois	1,006,848	5.6	1,254,717	4.5
Indiana	631,554	4.3	654,891	4.1
Iowa	498,943	4.5	512,515	4.3
Kansas	385,672	4.4	395,771	4.3
Kentucky	469,669	4.9	494,788	4.6
Louisiana	331,220	5.0	344,144	4.8
Maine	159,437	4.7	177,960	4.2
Maryland	253,805	5.1	274,824	4.7
Massachusetts	511,926	6.6	734,013	4.6
Michigan	618,222	4.5	657,418	4.3
Minnesota	380,809	5.5	416,452	5.0
Mississippi	376,420	4.8	384,724	4.7
Missouri	677,196	4.9	749,812	4.4
Montana	82,811	4.5	86,602	4.3
Nebraska	258,967	4.6	265,549	4.5
Nevada	23,044	3.6	23,677	3.5
New Hampshire........	88,871	4.8	103,156	4.2
New Jersey...........	497,295	6.2	558,202	4.5
New Mexico...........	75,888	4.3	79,883	4.1
New York.............	1,178,686	7.7	2,046,845	4.5
North Carolina........	430,570	5.1	440,334	5.0
North Dakota.........	118,757	4.9	120,910	4.8
Ohio	1,024,800	4.7	1,138,165	4.2
Oklahoma	342,488	4.8	351,167	4.7

State.	Dwell- ings.	*Per- sons.	Fam- ilies.	†Per- sons.
Oregon	144,832	4.6	151,868	4.4
Pennsylvania	1,507,483	5.1	1,636,628	4.7
Rhode Island.........	79,725	6.8	117,976	4.6
South Carolina........	302,842	5.0	315,204	4.8
South Dakota.........	127,739	4.6	131,060	4.5
Tennessee	444,814	4.9	462,553	4.7
Texas	779,177	5.0	798,426	4.9
Utah	72,649	5.1	77,339	4.8
Vermont	77,466	4.6	85,178	4.2
Virginia	400,445	5.1	419,452	4.5
Washington	238,822	4.8	254,692	4.5
West Virginia........	239,123	5.1	248,840	4.9
Wisconsin	462,355	5.0	499,639	4.7
Wyoming	30,969	4.7	32,092	4.5
United States........	17,805,842	5.2	20,255,555	4.5
In 1900.............	14,430,145	5.3	16,187,715	4.7
In 1890.............	11,483,318	5.5	12,690,152	4.9

*Persons to a dwelling. †Persons to a family.

BY PRINCIPAL CITIES.

City.	Dwell- ings.	*Per- sons.	Fam- ilies.	†Per- sons.
Albany, N. Y.........	15,437	6.5	24,069	4.2
Atlanta, Ga..........	30,308	5.1	35,813	4.3
Baltimore, Md........	101,905	5.5	118,851	4.7
Birmingham, Ala......	26,989	4.9	31,050	4.3
Boston, Mass.........	73,919	9.1	139,700	4.8
Bridgeport, Conn.....	14,924	6.8	21,689	4.7
Buffalo, N. Y........	62,335	6.8	91,328	4.6
Cambridge, Mass......	14,577	7.2	22,765	4.6
Chicago, Ill.........	246,744	8.9	473,141	4.6
Cincinnati, O........	49,525	7.3	87,541	4.2
Cleveland, O.........	90,465	6.2	124,822	4.5
Columbus, O..........	39,580	4.6	42,646	4.3
Dayton, O............	26,692	4.4	28,370	4.1
Denver, Col..........	44,736	4.8	51,339	4.2
Detroit, Mich........	83,124	5.6	100,356	4.6
Fall River, Mass.....	10,962	10.9	24,378	4.9
Grand Rapids, Mich...	23,432	4.8	26,925	4.2
Indianapolis, Ind....	53,359	4.3	58,645	4.0
Jersey City, N. J....	27,805	9.6	56,790	4.7
Los Angeles, Cal.....	69,061	4.6	78,678	4.1
Louisville, Ky.......	41,686	5.4	52,155	4.3
Lowell, Mass.........	15,956	7.1	21,932	4.8
Memphis, Tenn........	26,710	4.9	31,154	4.2
Milwaukee, Wis.......	60,724	6.2	80,566	4.6
Minneapolis, Minn....	46,903	6.4	63,241	4.8
Nashville, Tenn......	22,118	5.0	26,077	4.2
New Haven, Conn......	17,466	7.6	29,271	4.6
New Orleans, La......	67,192	5.0	73,277	4.6
New York, N. Y.......	305,698	15.6	1,020,827	4.7
Newark, N. J.........	38,693	9.0	77,039	4.5
Oakland, Cal.........	31,740	4.7	36,723	4.1
Omaha, Neb...........	23,657	5.2	26,359	4.7
Paterson, N. J.......	15,812	7.9	27,978	4.5
Philadelphia, Pa.....	295,220	5.2	327,263	4.7
Pittsburgh, Pa.......	86,942	6.1	110,451	4.8
Portland, Ore........	37,436	5.5	43,029	4.9
Providence, R. I.....	28,765	7.8	49,129	4.6
Richmond, Va.........	22,205	5.7	26,914	4.7
Rochester, N. Y......	38,860	5.6	46,787	4.7
St. Louis, Mo........	105,650	6.5	155,555	4.4
St. Paul, Minn.......	32,616	6.6	41,548	5.2
San Francisco, Cal...	65,025	6.4	86,414	4.8
Scranton, Pa.........	22,143	5.9	26,312	4.9
Seattle, Wash........	43,559	5.4	51,042	4.6
Spokane, Wash........	20,282	5.1	22,676	4.6
Syracuse, N. Y.......	23,300	5.9	31,551	4.4
Toledo, O............	35,888	4.7	39,677	4.2
Washington, D. C.....	58,513	5.7	71,339	4.6
Worcester, Mass......	15,199	9.7	30,743	4.7

*Persons to a dwelling. †Persons to a family.

ILLITERACY IN THE UNITED STATES (1910).

The following statistics, except where otherwise specified, relate only to persons 10 years of age or over. The bureau of the census classifies as illiterate all persons 10 years of age or over who are unable to write, regardless of their ability to read.

PERCENTAGE OF ILLITERACY.

The following table shows the total population 10 years of age and over and the number and percentage of illiterate by color or race, nativity and parentage:

Class.	Population.	Illiterate.	Pct.
White	63,933,870	3,184,633	5.0
Native	50,989,341	1,534,272	3.0
Native parentage	37,081,278	1,378,884	3.7
Foreign or mixed parentage	13,908,063	155,388	1.1
Foreign born	12,944,529	1,650,361	12.7
Negro	7,317,922	2,227,731	30.4
Indian	188,758	85,445	45.3
Chinese	68,924	10,891	15.8
Japanese	67,661	6,213	9.2
All other	3,155	1,250	39.9
United States	71,580,270	5,516,163	7.7

The corresponding percentages of illiterates at three previous censuses were: 1880, 17.0; 1890, 13.3; 1900, 10.7.

ILLITERACY BY SEX.

	Male.		Female.	
Class.	Illiterate.	Pct.	Illiterate.	Pct.
White	1,662,505	5.0	1,522,128	4.9
Native	796,055	3.1	738,217	2.9
Native parentage	715,926	3.8	662,958	3.7
Foreign or mixed parentage	80,129	1.2	75,259	1.1
Foreign born	866,450	11.8	783,911	13.3
Negro	1,096,000	30.1	1,131,731	30.7
Indian	40,104	41.5	45,341	49.2
Chinese	9,849	15.0	1,042	30.2
Japanese	5,247	8.6	966	14.1
All other	1,245	40.5	5	....
United States	2,814,950	7.6	2,701,213	7.8

URBAN AND RURAL ILLITERACY (PER CENT).

Class.	Total.	Urban.	Rural.
White	5.0	4.2	5.8
Native	3.0	0.8	4.8
Native parentage	3.7	0.9	5.4
Foreign or mixed parentage	1.1	0.7	1.9
Foreign born	12.7	12.6	13.2
Negro	30.4	17.6	36.1
All other	31.6	11.0	40.1

PERCENTAGE ILLITERATES BY SECTIONS.

Section.	1910.	1900.
New England	5.3	6.0
Middle Atlantic	5.7	5.8
East North Central	2.4	4.3
West North Central	2.9	4.1
South Atlantic	16.0	23.9
East South Central	17.4	24.9
West South Central	13.2	20.5
Mountain	6.9	9.6
Pacific	3.0	4.2
Northern states	4.3	5.0
Southern states	15.6	23.3
Western states	4.4	6.3
United States	7.7	10.7

ILLITERATES BY STATES.

	1910.		1900.	
State.	Number.	Pct.	Number.	Pct.
Alabama	352,710	22.9	443,590	34.0
Arizona	32,953	20.9	27,304	29.0
Arkansas	142,954	12.6	190,665	20.4
California	74,902	3.7	58,959	4.8
Colorado	23,780	3.7	17,779	4.2
Connecticut	53,685	6.0	42,973	5.9
Delaware	13,240	8.1	17,531	12.0
District of Columbia	13,812	4.9	20,028	8.6
Florida	77,818	13.8	84,285	21.9
Georgia	389,775	20.7	480,420	30.5
Idaho	5,453	2.2	5,505	4.6

	1910.		1900.	
State.	Number.	Pct.	Number.	Pct.
Illinois	168,294	3.7	157,958	4.2
Indiana	66,213	3.1	90,539	4.6
Iowa	29,889	1.7	40,172	2.3
Kansas	28,968	2.2	32,513	2.9
Kentucky	208,084	12.1	262,954	16.5
Louisiana	352,179	29.0	381,145	38.5
Maine	24,554	4.1	29,060	5.1
Maryland	73,397	7.2	101,947	11.1
Massachusetts	141,541	5.2	134,043	5.9
Michigan	74,800	3.3	80,482	4.2
Minnesota	49,235	3.0	52,946	4.1
Mississippi	290,235	22.4	351,461	32.0
Missouri	111,116	4.3	152,844	6.4
Montana	14,457	4.8	11,675	6.1
Nebraska	18,009	1.9	17,997	2.3
Nevada	4,702	6.7	4,645	13.3
New Hampshire	16,386	4.6	21,075	6.2
New Jersey	113,502	5.6	86,658	5.9
New Mexico	48,697	20.2	46,971	33.2
New York	406,020	5.5	318,100	5.5
North Carolina	291,497	18.5	386,251	28.7
North Dakota	13,070	3.1	12,719	5.6
Ohio	124,774	3.2	131,541	4.0
Oklahoma	67,567	5.6	67,826	12.1
Oregon	10,504	1.9	10,686	3.3
Pennsylvania	354,290	5.9	299,376	6.1
Rhode Island	33,854	7.7	29,004	8.4
South Carolina	276,980	25.7	338,659	35.9
South Dakota	12,750	2.9	14,832	5.0
Tennessee	221,071	13.6	306,930	20.7
Texas	282,904	9.9	314,018	14.5
Utah	6,821	2.5	6,141	3.1
Vermont	10,806	3.7	16,247	5.8
Virginia	232,911	15.2	312,120	22.9
Washington	18,416	2.0	12,740	3.1
West Virginia	74,866	8.3	80,105	11.4
Wisconsin	57,769	3.2	73,779	4.7
Wyoming	3,874	3.3	2,878	4.0
United States	5,516,163	7.7	6,180,069	10.7

ILLITERATES BY CITIES.

(Cities of 100,000 or more population in 1910.)

	1910.		1900.	
City.	Number.	Pct.	Number.	Pct.
Albany, N. Y.	2,762	3.2	2,181	2.8
Atlanta, Ga.	10,813	8.6	11,406	15.8
Baltimore, Md.	20,325	4.4	29,148	7.2
Birmingham, Ala.	11,025	10.4	5,986	19.1
Boston, Mass.	24,468	4.4	23,320	5.1
Bridgeport, Conn.	4,440	5.4	2,999	5.3
Buffalo, N. Y.	12,745	3.7	13,152	4.8
Cambridge, Mass.	2,540	2.0	3,388	4.6
Chicago, Ill.	79,911	4.5	51,142	3.9
Cincinnati, O.	9,576	3.1	8,843	3.4
Cleveland, O.	20,675	4.6	14,091	4.7
Columbus, O.	4,442	2.9	3,290	3.2
Dayton, O.	2,224	2.3	1,797	2.6
Denver, Col.	3,841	2.1	1,979	1.9
Detroit, Mich.	18,731	5.0	9,062	4.1
Fall River, Mass.	12,276	13.2	12,110	14.9
Grand Rapids, Mich.	2,271	2.2	2,136	3.1
Indianapolis, Ind.	5,874	3.0	6,004	4.3
Jersey City, N. J.	11,797	5.6	7,171	4.5
Kansas City, Mo.	4,937	2.3	5,258	3.9
Los Angeles, Cal.	5,258	1.9	1,956	2.3
Louisville, Ky.	9,866	5.3	14,567	8.9
Lowell, Mass.	5,172	6.0	6,843	8.8
Memphis, Tenn.	8,855	8.0	14,989	18.7
Milwaukee, Wis.	10,765	3.6	8,243	3.8
Minneapolis, Minn.	6,139	2.4	2,977	1.8
Nashville, Tenn.	7,947	9.8	9,460	14.4
New Haven, Conn.	7,502	7.0	4,875	5.6
New Orleans, La.	18,987	6.9	30,820	13.6
New York, N. Y.	254,208	6.7	181,835	6.8
Newark, N. J.	16,553	6.0	11,715	6.1
Oakland, Cal.	3,863	3.0	1,614	2.9
Omaha, Neb.	2,798	2.7	1,662	2.0
Paterson, N. J.	6,927	6.9	5,191	6.3
Philadelphia, Pa.	57,700	4.6	45,546	4.4
Pittsburgh, Pa.	26,627	6.2	20,402	5.8
Portland, Ore.	2,145	1.2	3,925	5.1
Providence, R. I.	14,236	7.7	10,029	7.0
Richmond, Va.	8,641	8.3	9,501	13.7

City.	1910 Number.	Pct.	1900 Number.	Pct.
Rochester, N. Y.......	6,916	3.8	3,499	2.7
St. Louis, Mo.........	21,123	3.7	20,359	4.4
St. Paul, Minn........	3,751	2.1	3,956	3.1
San Francisco, Cal....	7,697	2.1	8,960	3.1
Scranton, Pa.........	8,933	8.9	6,814	8.8
Seattle, Wash........	2,217	1.1	901	1.3
Spokane, Wash........	1,123	1.3	554	1.8
Syracuse, N. Y........	5,629	2.8	2,800	3.2
Toledo, O............	3,809	2.8	3,865	3.7
Washington, D. C.....	13,812	4.9	20,028	8.6
Worcester, Mass......	5,977	5.0	4,580	4.9

ILLITERATES OF VOTING AGE.
(Males 21 years of age and over.)
BY STATES.

State.	1910 Number.	Pct.	1900 Number.	Pct.
Alabama	124,494	24.3	139,649	33.7
Arizona	14,463	19.5	11,215	25.4
Arkansas	53,440	13.5	62,615	20.0
California	42,727	4.6	33,485	6.2
Colorado	11,343	4.2	7,689	4.1
Connecticut	23,562	6.8	18,984	6.8
Delaware	6,272	10.1	7,538	14.0
District of Columbia..	5,082	4.9	7,052	8.4
Florida	29,886	14.0	30,949	22.1
Georgia	141,541	22.8	158,247	31.6
Idaho	3,416	3.1	2,326	5.4
Illinois	79,433	4.6	67,481	4.8
Indiana	33,583	4.1	40,016	5.6
Iowa	14,204	2.1	17,061	2.7
Kansas	14,716	2.9	14,216	3.4
Kentucky	87,516	14.5	102,528	18.8
Louisiana	119,716	28.6	122,638	37.6
Maine	13,070	6.5	13,952	6.4
Maryland	31,228	8.5	40,952	12.5
Massachusetts	61,909	6.1	53,694	6.4
Michigan	38,703	4.4	39,230	5.5
Minnesota	23,603	3.7	20,856	4.1
Mississippi	107,843	25.2	118,067	33.8
Missouri	51,284	5.3	60,327	7.0
Montana	8,812	5.7	6,209	6.1
Nebraska	8,545	2.4	7,388	2.5
Nevada	2,399	6.0	2,271	12.8
New Hampshire........	8,413	6.2	10,295	7.9
New Jersey...........	51,086	6.6	38,305	6.9
New Mexico...........	16,634	17.6	15,585	28.3
New York............	170,030	6.0	130,004	5.9
North Carolina.......	107,663	21.3	122,658	29.4
North Dakota.........	5,464	3.1	6,187	5.1
Ohio	62,998	4.2	58,698	4.8
Oklahoma	28,707	6.4	21,950	10.6
Oregon	6,460	2.5	6,938	4.8
Pennsylvania	179,982	7.8	139,982	7.7
Rhode Island.........	14,456	8.8	11,675	9.2
South Carolina.........	90,707	27.1	99,516	35.1
South Dakota.........	5,550	3.1	5,628	5.0
Tennessee	86,677	15.7	105,851	21.7
Texas	109,328	10.9	113,783	16.4

State.	1910 Number.	Pct.	1900 Number.	Pct.
Utah	3,477	3.3	2,470	3.7
Vermont	6,039	5.3	8,544	7.9
Virginia	92,917	17.7	113,353	25.3
Washington	10,580	2.4	6,635	3.4
West Virginia........	35,040	10.4	32,066	12.9
Wisconsin	27,038	4.0	31,136	5.5
Wyoming	2,594	4.1	1,636	4.3
United States........	2,273,603	8.4	2,288,470	10.8

BY PRINCIPAL CITIES.

City	1910 Number.	Pct.	1900 Number.	Pct.
Albany, N. Y..........	1,219	3.8	762	2.7
Atlanta, Ga..........	3,806	8.1	3,396	14.6
Baltimore, Md........	7,701	4.7	10,152	7.2
Birmingham, Ala......	4,348	10.7	2,051	16.7
Boston, Mass.........	9,335	4.5	8,111	4.6
Bridgeport, Conn.....	1,815	5.5	1,203	5.5
Buffalo, N. Y.........	5,664	4.4	5,168	5.3
Cambridge, Mass......	978	3.2	1,097	4.1
Chicago, Ill..........	35,636	5.1	20,572	4.0
Cincinnati, O........	3,962	3.5	3,114	3.4
Cleveland, O.........	9,418	5.3	5,786	5.2
Columbus, O.........	2,063	3.4	1,406	3.5
Dayton, O...........	1,069	2.8	679	2.6
Denver, Col..........	1,580	2.2	716	1.7
Detroit, Mich........	9,709	6.5	3,587	4.5
Fall River, Mass......	4,942	15.6	4,158	15.5
Grand Rapids, Mich...	933	2.7	823	3.3
Indianapolis, Ind....	2,712	3.5	2,526	4.8
Jersey City, N. J.....	5,519	6.8	3,094	5.1
Kansas City, Mo......	2,634	2.3	2,096	2.9
Los Angeles, Cal.....	2,270	2.0	886	2.7
Louisville, Ky........	4,024	5.9	5,836	9.8
Lowell, Mass.........	2,266	7.2	2,592	9.6
Memphis, Tenn.......	3,163	7.1	5,745	18.3
Milwaukee, Wis......	5,147	4.6	3,059	4.1
Minneapolis, Minn....	2,770	2.6	1,205	1.9
Nashville, Tenn.......	2,901	9.4	3,169	14.3
New Haven, Conn.....	3,037	7.5	1,866	5.7
New Orleans, La......	6,301	6.5	10,078	13.4
New York, N. Y......	91,815	6.4	65,556	6.5
Newark, N. J........	6,227	6.0	4,598	6.5
Oakland, Cal........	1,877	3.5	741	3.6
Omaha, Neb.........	1,429	3.3	612	1.8
Paterson, N. J........	2,584	7.0	1,876	6.3
Philadelphia, Pa......	22,222	4.7	17,588	4.5
Pittsburgh, Pa.......	14,165	8.5	10,588	7.8
Portland, Ore........	1,187	1.3	2,261	8.5
Providence, R. I......	5,738	8.3	3,830	7.2
Richmond, Va........	3,147	8.6	3,369	14.4
Rochester, N. Y......	3,158	4.5	1,327	2.9
St. Louis, Mo........	9,106	4.1	7,026	4.1
St. Paul, Minn.......	1,676	2.2	1,251	2.6
San Francisco, Cal...	3,521	2.0	3,596	2.8
Scranton, Pa.........	4,515	12.2	2,985	10.6
Seattle, Wash........	1,373	1.4	698	1.5
Spokane, Wash.......	709	1.8	304	2.0
Syracuse, N. Y.......	2,821	6.3	1,071	3.3
Toledo, O...........	1,802	3.4	1,592	4.2
Washington, D. C.....	5,082	4.9	7,052	8.4
Worcester, Mass......	2,732	6.0	1,788	5.0

GREAT MINING DISASTERS IN RECENT YEARS.
(In which 100 or more lives were lost.)

Birmingham, Ala., May 5, 1910; 175 dead.
Bolton, England, Dec. 21, 1910; 300 dead.
Briceville, Tenn., Dec. 9, 1911; 100 dead.
Cherry, Ill., Nov. 13, 1909; 289 dead.
Cheswick, Pa., Jan. 25, 1904; 182 dead.
Coahuila, Mex., Feb. 1, 1902; 102 dead.
Coal Creek, Tenn., May 19, 1902; 227 dead.
Courriere, France, March 10, 1906; 1,060 dead.
Ennis, W. Va., Dec. 30, 1908; 100 dead.
Finleyville, Pa., April 23, 1912; 115 dead.
Gerthe, Germany, Aug. 8, 1912; 103 dead.
Hamm, Germany, Nov. 12, 1908; 300 dead.
Hanna, Wyo., June 30, 1903; 235 dead.
Jacob's Creek, Pa., Dec. 19, 1907; 230 dead.
Johnstown, Pa., July 10, 1902; 113 dead.

Khartsisk, Russia, June 18, 1905; 500 dead.
La Esperanza, Mex., Feb. 19, 1907; 123 dead.
Littleton, Ala., April 8, 1911; 128 dead.
Mariauna, Pa., Nov. 28, 1909; 154 dead.
Mononagh, Pa., Dec. 6, 1907; 360 dead.
Newcastle, England, Feb. 16, 1909; 100 dead.
Telluride, Col., Nov. 20, 1901; 100 dead.
Toyooka, Japan, July 20, 1907; 400 dead.
Virginia City, Ala., Feb. 20, 1905; 100 dead.
Watertown, Wales, July 11, 1905; 144 dead.
Welongong, Australia, July 31, 1902; 120 dead.
Whitehaven, England, May 12, 1910; 137 dead.
Senghenydd, Wales, Oct. 14, 1913; 423 dead.
Dawson, N. M., Oct. 22; 261 dead.

COAL MINERS KILLED IN THE UNITED STATES.

1893..................	965	1898..................	1,064	1903..................	1,752	1908..................	2,449
1894..................	957	1899..................	1,216	1904..................	2,004	1909..................	2,668
1895..................	1,057	1900..................	1,492	1905..................	2,232	1910..................	2,840
1896..................	1,120	1901..................	1,549	1906..................	2,116	1911..................	2,719
1897..................	947	1902..................	1,895	1907..................	3,197	1912..................	2,360

POPULATION OF THE WORLD.

[Based upon the Statesman's Year-Book for 1913 and publications of the bureau of the census.]

BY GRAND DIVISIONS.

Africa	127,387,297
Asia	917,761,686
Europe	451,975,668
North America	133,008,023
Oceania	53,109,317
South America	50,141,890
Total	1,733,383,881

AFRICA.

Abyssinia (est. 1913)	8,000,000
Anglo-Egyptian Sudan (1913)	3,000,000
British colonies,etc.(1913)	35,980,913
Egypt (1907)	11,287,359
French Africa (1907)	24,576,850
German Africa (est. 1913)	13,419,500
Italian Africa (est. 1913)	523,176
Belgian Kongo (est. 1913)	15,000,000
Liberia (1913)	2,120,000
Morocco (1913)	5,000,000
Portuguese Africa (1913)	8,243,655
Spanish Africa (1913)	235,844
Total	127,387,297

ASIA.

Afghanistan (est. 1913)	5,900,000
Bhutan (1913)	250,000
Ceylon (1911)	4,106,535
Cyprus (1911)	274,108
China (1911)	433,553,030
French Indo-China* (1911)	16,598,442
Hongkong (1911)	366,145
India, British (1911)	315,132,537
Japan (1912)	69,148,930
Kiauchau (1913)	168,900
Labuan (1911)	6,546
Malay states (1911)	1,965,947
Nepal (1911)	5,000,000
Oman (1911)	500,000
Persia (1913)	9,500,000
Portuguese Asia (1901)	895,789
Russia in Asia (1911)	25,664,500
Samos (1907)	53,424
Siam (1910)	8,117,953
Straits Settlements(1911)	707,523
Turkey in Asia (1911)	19,705,200
Weihaiwei (1911)	147,177
Total	917,761,686

*Including French India.

EUROPE.

Andorra (1913)	5,231
Austria-Hungary (1910)	49,458,721
Belgium (1911)	7,490,411
Bulgaria (1910)	4,337,516
Crete (1904)	310,200
Denmark (1911)	2,775,076
France (1911)	39,601,509
Germany (1910)	64,925,993
Great Britain (1911)	45,369,090
Greece (1909)	2,666,000
Iceland (1911)	125,791
Italy (1911)	34,671,377
Luxemburg (1910)	259,891
Monaco (1909)	19,121
Montenegro (1910)	250,000
Netherlands (1911)	6,022,452
Norway (1910)	2,391,782
Portugal (1911)	5,957,985
Roumania (1912)	7,248,061
Russia (1911)	138,274,500
San Marino (1912)	10,791
Servia (1910)	2,911,701
Spain (1910)	19,588,688
Sweden (1911)	5,561,799
Switzerland (1910)	3,741,971
Turkey (1912)	8,000,000
Total	451,975,668

NORTH AMERICA.

Bahamas (1911)	56,439
Bermuda (1911)	18,994
Canada (1911)	7,206,643
Costa Rica (1911)	388,266
Cuba (1910)	2,220,278
Curacao (1910)	54,469
Danish West Indies (1911)	27,086
French islands (1907)	397,000
Greenland (1911)	13,517
Guatemala (1910)	1,992,600
Haiti (1909)	2,029,700
Honduras (1910)	553,446
Honduras, British (1911)	40,809
Jamaica (1911)	831,383
Leeward islands (1911)	127,789
Mexico (1910)	15,063,207
Newfoundland* (1911)	242,619
Nicaragua (1910)	600,000
Panama (1912)	426,928
Porto Rico (1910)	1,118,012
Salvador (1912)	1,161,426

Santo Domingo (1911)	708,000
United States† (1913)	97,401,366
Windward islands (1911)	323,246
Total	133,008,023

*Including Labrador. †Including Alaska.

OCEANIA.

Australian Federation (1911)	4,568,707
Borneo and Sarawak, British (1911)	708,000
Dutch East Indies (1905)	38,000,000
Fiji islands (1911)	139,541
Gilbert islands (1911)	26,863
Guam (1910)	11,973
Hawaii (1910)	191,909
New Caledonia* (1907)	85,800
New Guinea, British (1911)	272,057
New Guinea, German† (1905)	357,800
New Zealand (1911)	1,038,000
Philippine islands (1903)	7,635,426
Solomon islands (1905)	150,500
Tonga islands (1911)	23,737
Total	53,109,317

*Including other French dependencies. †Including Samoan and other German islands in the Pacific.

SOUTH AMERICA.

Argentine Republic (est. 1911)	7,171,910
Bolivia (1910)	2,267,935
Brazil (est. 1911)	23,070,969
Chile (1910)	3,415,060
Colombia (1912)	5,475,961
Ecuador (1910)	1,500,000
Falkland islands (1911)	3,239
Guiana, British (1911)	295,784
Guiana, French (1907)	27,000
Guiana, Dutch (1911)	86,233
Paraguay (1911)	700,000
Peru (1896)	4,609,999
Trinidad (1911)	340,300
Uruguay (1911)	1,172,500
Venezuela (1912)	2,743,841
Total	50,141,890

INDIAN RESERVATIONS AND POPULATION (1912).

State.	Acres.	Population.	State.	Acres.	Population.	State.	Acres.	Population.
Arizona	19,457,745	40,754	Nebraska	5,140	3,832	Utah	179,194	1,309
California	364,743	17,517	Nevada	686,706	5,262	Washington	2,368,060	11,833
Colorado	483,910	860	New Mexico	1,866,849	21,374	Wisconsin	304,309	9,816
Florida	23,542	446	New York	87,677	5,426	Wyoming	95,307	1,697
Idaho	481,518	3,823	North Carolina	63,211	2,078	Miscellaneous		8,362
Iowa	3,251	364	North Dakota	810,389	8,289			
Kansas	1,364	1,317	Oklahoma	2,628,334	117,444	Total, 1912	38,903,388	319,216
Michigan	923	7,519	Oregon	1,212,705	6,401	Total, 1900	77,865,373	270,544
Minnesota	582,671	11,116	South Dakota	1,639,947	20,333	Total, 1890	104,314,349	243,524
Montana	5,555,902	11,242	Texas		702	Total, 1880	154,741,554	256,127

LARGEST CITIES IN THE WORLD.

Population according to latest census reports or official estimates.

City.	Year.	Population.	City.	Year.	Population.	City.	Year.	Population.
Aachen	1910	156,143	Antung†	1911	161,000	Barmen	1910	169,214
Aberdeen	1911	153,503	Antwerp	1911	308,618	Basel	1910	131,914
Adelaide*	1911	192,429	Astrakhan	1910	144,231	Batavia	1905	138,551
Agra	1911	185,449	Athens	1907	167,479	Beirut†	1912	150,000
Ahmedabad	1911	215,835	Atlanta	1910	154,839	Belem†	1912	200,000
Albany	1910	100,253	Augsburg	1910	102,487	Belfast	1911	386,449
Aleppo†	1912	210,000	Bagdad	1912	235,000	Benares	1911	203,804
Alexandria	1907	332,246	Bahia†	1911	230,000	Berlin	1910	2,071,257
Alger	1911	172,397	Baltimore	1910	558,485	Birmingham, Eng.	1911	525,833
Allahabad	1911	171,697	Bangalore	1911	189,485	Birmingham, Ala.	1910	132,683
Altona	1910	172,628	Bangkok	1910	628,675	Bochum	1910	136,931
Amoy†	1911	114,000	Barcelona	1910	560,000	Bogota	1912	121,257
Amritsar	1911	152,756	Bareilly	1911	129,462	Bologna	1911	160,719
Amsterdam	1911	580,960	Bari	1911	103,670	Bolton	1911	180,851

City.	Year.	Population.
Boston	1910	670,585
Bombay	1911	979,445
Bordeaux	1911	261,678
Bradford	1811	248,454
Bremen	1910	247,437
Breslau	1910	512,105
Bridgeport, Ct.	1910	102,054
Brighton, England	1911	131,227
Brisbane*	1911	143,514
Bristol, England	1911	357,048
Brunn	1910	125,727
Brunswick	1910	143,552
Brussa†	1912	110,060
Brussels*	1910	646,400
Bucharest	1912	338,169
Budapest	1910	880,371
Buenos Aires	1913	1,434,820
Buffalo	1910	423,715
Cairo, Egypt	1907	654,476
Calcutta*	1911	1,122,313
Cambridge, Mass.	1910	104,839
Canton†	1911	900,000
Cardiff	1911	182,259
Carlsruhe	1910	134,313
Cassel	1910	153,196
Catania	1911	210,703
Cawnpore	1911	178,557
Changsha†	1911	250,000
Charlottenburg	1910	305,978
Chemnitz	1910	287,807
Chicago	1910	2,185,283
Chinkiang†	1911	184,000
Christiania	1910	241,834
Chungking†	1911	598,000
Cincinnati	1910	362,591
Cleveland	1910	560,663
Cologne	1910	516,527
Colombo	1911	213,396
Columbus	1910	181,511
Constantinople†	1912	1,200,000
Copenhagen*	1910	559,398
Cordoba, Arg. Rep.†	1912	100,000
Coventry	1911	106,349
Cracow	1910	151,886
Crefeld	1910	129,406
Croydon	1911	169,551
Dacca	1910	108,551
Damascus†	1912	350,000
Danzig	1910	170,337
Dayton	1910	116,577
Delhi	1911	232,837
Denver	1910	213,381
Derby, England	1911	123,410
Detroit	1910	465,766
Dortmund	1910	214,226
Dresden	1910	548,308
Dublin	1911	402,030
Duisburg	1910	229,483
Dundee	1911	165,004
Dusseldorf	1910	358,728
Dvinsk	1910	110,912
Edinburgh	1911	320,318
Elberfeld	1910	170,195
Erfurt	1910	111,463
Essen	1910	294,653
Fall River	1910	119,295
Florence	1911	232,860
Frankfurt	1910	414,576
Fuchow†	1911	624,000
Gelsenkirchen	1910	169,513
Geneva	1910	125,520
Genoa	1911	272,221
Ghent	1911	166,719
Glasgow	1911	784,496
Goteborg	1911	170,606
Grand Rapids	1910	112,571
Graz	1910	151,781
Guadalajara	1910	118,799
Halifax, England	1911	101,552
Halle	1910	180,843
Hamborn, Germany	1910	101,703
Hamburg	1910	931,035
Hangchow†	1911	350,000
Hankow†	1911	826,000
Hanover	1910	302,375
Havana	1910	319,884
Havre	1911	136,159
Helsingfors	1910	147,218
Hiroshima	1908	142,763
Hongkong	1911	366,145
Huddersfield	1911	107,821
Hull	1911	277,991
Hyderabad	1911	500,623
Indianapolis	1910	233,650
Ivanovo	1910	108,023
Jaipur	1911	137,008
Jersey City	1910	267,779
Johannesburg	1911	237,226
Jubbulpore	1911	100,651
Kanzawa	1908	110,994
Kansas City	1910	248,381
Karachi	1911	151,903
Kazan	1911	188,100
Kharkov	1910	236,042
Kiel	1910	211,627
Kiev	1811	505,060
Kishinev	1911	123,100
Kobe	1908	378,197
Konigsberg	1910	245,994
Kure	1908	100,679
Kyoto	1908	442,462
Lahore	1911	228,687
Leeds	1911	445,550
Leicester	1911	227,222
Leipsic	1910	589,250
Lemberg	1910	206,113
Liege	1910	167,676
Lille	1911	217,807
Lima	1908	140,884
Lisbon	1911	356,009
Liverpool	1911	746,421
Livorno	1911	105,315
London, Greater.	1911	7,251,358
Los Angeles	1910	319,198
Louisville	1910	223,928
Lowell	1910	106,294
Lucknow	1911	259,798
Lyons	1911	523,796
Madras	1911	518,660
Madrid	1910	571,539
Madura	1911	134,130
Magdeburg	1910	279,629
Mainz	1910	110,634
Malaga	1910	133,043
Manchester, Eng.	1911	714,333
Mandalay	1911	138,299
Manila	1903	219,298
Mannheim	1910	193,902
Marseilles	1911	550,619
Meerut	1911	116,227
Melbourne	1911	600,169
Memphis	1910	131,105
Messina	1910	126,557
Mexico City	1910	470,659
Milan	1911	599,200
Milwaukee	1910	373,857
Minneapolis	1910	301,408
Minsk	1910	101,166
Montevideo	1912	352,487
Montreal	1911	470,480
Moscow	1911	1,533,400
Mukden	1911	158,132
Mulheim	1910	112,580
Munich	1910	596,467
Murcia	1910	124,985
Nagasaki	1908	176,480
Nagoya	1908	378,231
Nagpur	1911	101,415
Nancy	1911	119,949
Nanking†	1911	267,000
Nantes	1911	170,535
Naples	1911	678,031
Nashville	1910	110,364
Neukolln	1910	237,282
Nice	1911	142,940
Ningpo†	1911	350,000
Nishni-Novgorod	1911	108,809
Newark, N. J.	1910	347,469
Newcastle	1911	266,603
New Haven	1910	133,605
New Orleans	1910	339,075
New York	1910	4,766,883
Norwich, England	1911	121,478
Nottingham	1911	259,904
Richmond	1910	127,628
Nurnberg	1910	333,142
Oakland	1910	150,174
Oldham	1911	147,483
Omaha	1910	124,096
Oporto	1911	167,955
Oran	1910	123,086
Osaka	1908	1,226,590
Palermo	1911	341,088
Paris	1811	2,888,110
Paterson	1910	125,600
Patna	1911	136,153
Pernambuco†	1911	150,000
Philadelphia	1910	1,549,008
Pingyang†	1912	146,000
Pittsburgh	1910	533,905
Plauen	1910	121,272
Plymouth, England	1911	112,030
Poona	1911	158,856
Porto Alegre†	1911	100,000
Posen	1910	156,691
Portland, Ore.	1910	207,214
Portsmouth, England	1911	231,141
Prague	1910	223,741
Preston	1911	117,088
Providence	1910	224,326
Puebla	1910	101,214
Rangoon	1911	293,316
Rheims	1911	116,178
Riga	1911	232,300
Rio de Janeiro	1911	1,128,637
Rochester, N. Y.	1910	218,149
Rome	1911	542,123
Rosario†	1910	180,000
Rostov-on-Don	1909	121,300
Rotterdam	1911	436,018
Roubaix	1911	122,723
Rouen	1911	124,987
Saarbrucken	1910	105,089
St. Etienne	1911	148,656
St. Louis	1910	687,029
St. Paul	1910	214,744
St. Petersburg	1910	1,962,400
Salford	1911	231,357
Saloniki†	1912	174,000
San Francisco	1910	416,912
Santiago, Chile	1910	332,724
Sao Paulo†	1910	450,000
Saratov	1910	206,300
Schoeneberg	1910	172,823
Scranton	1910	129,867
Seattle	1910	237,194
Seoul	1912	278,958
Seville	1910	155,366
Shanghai†	1911	651,000
Sheffield	1911	454,632
Singapore	1911	302,321
Smyrna†	1912	375,000
Soerabaya	1905	150,198
Soerakarta	1905	118,378
Sofia	1910	102,812
Southampton	1911	119,012
South Shields	1911	108,647
Spokane	1910	104,402
Srinagar	1911	126,344
Stettin	1910	236,113
Stockholm	1911	346,599
Stockport	1911	108,682
Stoke-on-Trent	1911	234,534
Strassburg	1910	178,891
Stuttgart	1911	286,218
Suchow†	1911	500,000
Sunderland	1911	151,159
Surat	1911	114,863
Swansea	1911	114,663
Sydney, N. S. W.*	1911	636,353
Syracuse	1910	137,249
Szeged	1910	118,328
Tabriz†	1913	200,000
Teheran†	1913	280,000
The Hague	1911	288,577
Tientsin†	1911	800,000
Tokyo	1908	2,186,079
Toledo	1910	168,497

City.	Year.	Popu-lation.	City.	Year.	Popu-lation.
Toronto	1911	376,538	Vitebsk	1911	103,340
Toulon	1911	104,582	Washington	1910	331,069
Toulouse	1911	149,576	Wenchow†	1911	100,000
Trichinopoly	1911	122,028	West Ham	1911	289,030
Trieste	1910	229,510	Wiesbaden	1910	109,002
Tula	1911	136,530	Wilmersdorf	1910	109,716
Tunis†	1907	250,000	Winnipeg	1911	136,035
Turin	1911	427,106	Worcester, Mass.	1910	145,986
Ufa	1910	103,485	Wuhu†	1911	122,000
Utrecht	1911	121,217	Yaroslav	1910	111,876
Valencia	1910	233,348	Yekaterinoslav	1909	195,870
Valparaiso	1910	179,815	Yokohama	1908	294,303
Vancouver	1911	100,401	Zaragoza	1910	105,788
Venice	1911	160,719	Zurich	1910	189,088
Vienna	1910	2,031,498			
Vilna	1911	190,210	*With suburbs. †Estimated.		

RANK OF FIFTEEN LARGEST CITIES.

City.	Rank.	Population.
London	1	7,251,358
New York	2	4,766,883
Paris	3	2,888,110
Tokyo	4	2,186,079
Chicago	5	2,185,283
Berlin	6	2,071,257
Vienna	7	2,031,498
St. Petersburg	8	1,962,400
Philadelphia	9	1,549,008
Moscow	10	1,533,400
Buenos Aires	11	1,434,820
Osaka	12	1,226,590
Constantinople	13	1,200,000
Rio de Janeiro	14	1,128,637
Calcutta	15	1,122,313

METROPOLITAN DISTRICTS (1910).

Statistics have been compiled by the bureau of the census showing the population of the chief cities of the United States together with their suburbs, comprising what may be termed "metropolitan districts." A district of this character is defined as consisting of the city together with the urban portion of the territory lying within ten miles of the city limits. The following table shows the metropolitan districts of cities having a population of 200,000 or more in 1910:

City.	Metropolitan district.	City proper.	Outside.
New York	6,474,568	4,766,883	1,707,685
Chicago	2,446,921	2,185,283	261,638
Philadelphia	1,972,342	1,549,008	423,334
Boston	1,520,470	670,585	849,885
Pittsburgh	1,042,855	533,905	508,950
St. Louis	828,733	687,029	141,704
San Francisco-Oakland.	686,873	416,912	119,787
Oakland		150,174	
Baltimore	658,715	558,485	100,230
Cleveland	613,270	560,663	52,607
Cincinnati	563,804	363,591	200,213
Minneapolis-St. Paul...	526,256	501,408	10,194
St. Paul		214,744	
Detroit	500,982	465,766	35,216
Buffalo	488,661	423,715	64,946
Los Angeles	438,226	319,198	119,028
Milwaukee	427,175	373,857	53,318
Providence	395,972	224,326	171,646
Washington	367,869	331,069	36,800
New Orleans	348,109	339,075	9,034
Kansas City (Mo. and Kas.)	340,446	248,381	9,374
Kansas City, Kas.		82,331	
Louisville	286,358	223,928	62,230
Rochester	248,512	218,149	30,363
Seattle	239,269	237,194	2,075
Indianapolis	237,783	233,650	4,133
Denver	219,034	213,381	5,933
Portland, Ore.	215,048	207,214	7,834

NOTE—The following statement gives the name and population of each municipality of 5,000 inhabitants or more falling within the territory adjacent to each of the above cities:

New York District—New York: Yonkers city, 79,803; Mount Vernon city, 30,919; New Rochelle city, 28,867; Mamaroneck village, 5,699. New Jersey: Newark city, 347,469; Jersey City, 267,779; Paterson city, 125,600; Elizabeth city, 73,409; Hoboken city, 70,324; Bayonne city, 55,545; Passaic city, 54,773; West Hoboken town, 35,403; East Orange city, 34,271; Perth Amboy city, 32,121; Orange city, 29,630; Montclair town, 21,550; Union town, 21,023; Kearny town, 18,659; Bloomfield town, 15,070; Harrison town, 14,498; Hackensack town, 14,050; West New York town, 13,560; Irvington town, 11,877; Englewood city, 9,924; Rahway city, 9,337; Rutherford borough, 7,045; South Orange village, 6,014; Nutley town, 6,009; Roosevelt borough, 5,786; Guttenberg town, 5,647.

Chicago District—Illinois: Evanston city, 24,978; Oak Park village, 19,444; Cicero town, 14,557; Chicago Heights city, 14,525; Blue Island village, 8,043; Maywood village, 8,033; Harvey city, 7,227; Forest Park village, 6,594; Berwyn city, 5,841; LaGrange village, 5,282. Indiana: Hammond city, 20,925;

East Chicago city, 19,098; Gary city, 16,802; Whiting city, 6,587.

Philadelphia District—Pennsylvania: Chester city, 38,537; Norristown borough, 27,875; Bristol borough, 9,256; Conshohocken borough, 7,480; Darby borough, 6,305. New Jersey: Camden city, 94,538; Gloucester city, 9,462; Burlington city, 8,336.

Boston District—Cambridge city, 104,839; Lynn city, 89,336; Somerville city, 77,236; Malden city, 44,404; Salem city, 43,697; Newton city, 39,806; Everett city, 33,484; Quincy city, 32,642; Chelsea city, 32,452; Waltham city, 27,834; Brookline town, 27,792; Medford city, 23,150; Revere town, 18,219; Peabody town, 15,721; Melrose city, 15,715; Hyde Park town, 15,507; Woburn city, 15,308; Framingham town, 12,948; Weymouth town, 12,835; Watertown town, 12,875; Wakefield town, 11,404; Arlington town, 11,187; Winthrop town, 10,132; Natick town, 9,866; Winchester town, 9,309; Dedham town, 9,284; Braintree town, 8,066; Saugus town, 8,047; Norwood town, 8,014; Milton town, 7,924; Marblehead town, 7,338; Stoneham town, 7,090; Swampscott town, 6,204; Belmont town, 5,542; Wellesley town, 5,413; Needham town, 5,026.

Pittsburgh District—McKeesport city, 42,694; Braddock borough, 19,357; Wilkinsburg borough, 18,924; Homestead borough, 18,713; Duquesne borough, 15,727; McKees Rocks borough, 14,702; North Braddock borough, 11,824; Carnegie borough, 10,009; Sharpsburg borough, 8,153; Jeanette borough, 8,077; Millvale borough, 7,861; New Kensington borough, 7,707; Tarentum borough, 7,414; Swissvale borough, 7,381; Bellevue borough, 6,323; Wilmerding borough, 6,133; Carrick borough, 6,117; Rankin borough, 6,042; Etna borough, 5,830; Knoxville borough, 5,651; St. Clair borough, 5,646; East Pittsburgh borough, 5,615; Glassport borough, 5,540; Coraopolis borough, 5,252; Munhall borough, 5,185.

St. Louis District—Missouri: Wellston city, 7,312; Webster Groves city, 7,080. Illinois: East St. Louis city, 58,547; Granite city, 9,903; Madison village, 5,046.

San Francisco-Oakland District—Berkeley city, 40,434; Alameda city, 23,383; Richmond city, 6,802; San Rafael city, 5,934.

Cleveland District—Lakewood city, 15,181; East Cleveland city, 9,179; Newburgh city, 5,813.

Cincinnati District—Ohio: Norwood city, 16,185; Madisonville city, 5,193; St. Bernard city, 5,002. Kentucky: Covington city, 53,270; Newport city, 30,309; Dayton city, 6,979; Bellevue city, 6,683.

Detroit District—Wyandotte city, 8,287.

Buffalo District—Lackawanna city, 14,549; North Tonawanda city, 11,955; Tonawanda city, 8,290.

Los Angeles District—Pasadena city, 30,291; Long Beach city, 17,809; Santa Monica city, 7,847; Alhambra city, 5,021.

Milwaukee District—West Allis city, 6,645; South Milwaukee city, 6,092.

Providence District—Pawtucket city, 51,622; Warwick town, 26,629; Central Falls city, 22,754; Cranston city, 21,107; East Providence town, 15,808; Cumberland town, 10,107; Lincoln town 9,825; Johnston town, 5,935; North Providence town, 5,407.

Washington District—Alexandria city (Va.), 15,329. Kansas City (Mo. and Kas.) District—Rosedale city (Kas.), 5,960.

Louisville District—Indiana: New Albany city, 20,629; Jeffersonville city, 10,412.

POPULATION OF CHIEF AMERICAN CITIES (1910).

PLACES WITH MORE THAN 100,000 INHABITANTS IN 1910.

City	1910	1900	1899	1880.	1870	1860	1850.
New York, N. Y.	4,766,883	3,437,202	1,515,301	1,206,299	942,292	805,651	515,547
Chicago, Ill	2,185,283	1,698,575	1,099,850	503,298	298,977	108,206	29,963
Philadelphia. Pa	1,549,008	1,293,697	1,046,964	847,170	674,022	565,529	121,376
St. Louis, Mo	687,029	575,238	451,770	350,518	310,864	160,773	77,860
Boston, Mass..	670,585	560,892	448,477	362,839	250,526	177,812	136,881
Cleveland, O	560,663	381,768	261,353	160,146	92,829	43,417	17,034
Baltimore, Md.	558,485	508,957	434,439	332,313	267,354	212,418	169,054
Pittsburgh, Pa	533,905	451,512	343,904	156,389	86,076	49,217	46,601
Detroit, Mich....	465,766	285,704	205,876	116,340	79,577	45,619	21,019
Buffalo, N. Y.	423,715	352,387	255,664	155,134	117,714	81,129	42,261
San Francisco, Cal	416,912	342,782	298,997	233,959	149,473	56,802	34,776
Milwaukee, Wis..	373,857	285,315	204,463	115,587	71,440	45,246	20,061
Cincinnati, O	363,591	325,902	296,908	255,139	216,239	161,044	115,435
Newark, N. J.	347,469	246,070	181,830	136,508	105,059	71,914	38,894
New Orleans, La	339,075	287,104	242,039	216,090	191,418	168,675	116,375
Washington, D C...	331,669	278,718	230,393	147,293	109,199	61,120	40,001
Los Angeles, Cal..	319,198	102,479	50,395	—11,183	5,728	4,385	1,610
Minneapolis, Minn	301,408	202,718	164,738	46,887	13,066	2,564	...
Jersey City, N J.	267,779	206,433	163,003	120,722	82,546	29,226	6,856
Kansas City, Mo	248,381	163,752	132,716	55,735	32,260	4,418	...
Seattle, Wash	237,194	50,671	42,837	3,533	1,107	...	...
Indianapolis, Ind	233,650	169,164	105,436	75,056	48,244	18,611	8,091
Providence, R I	224,326	175,597	132,146	104,857	68,904	50,666	41,513
Louisville, Ky	223,928	204,731	161,129	123,758	100,753	68,033	43,194
Rochester, N. Y	218,149	162,608	133,896	89,366	62,386	48,204	36,403
St Paul, Minn	214,744	163,065	133,155	41,473	20,030	10,401	1,112
Denver, Col	213,581	133,859	106,713	35,639	4,759	4,759	...
Portland, Ore	207,214	90,426	46,385	17,577	8,293	2,874	821
Columbus, O	181,511	125,560	88,150	51,647	31,274	18,554	17,882
Toledo, O......	168,497	131,822	81,434	50,137	30,972	13,768	3,829
Atlanta, Ga	154,839	89,672	66,533	37,409	21,789	9,554	2,572
Oakland, Cal	150,174	66,960	48,682	34,555	10,500	1,543	...
Worcester, Mass	145,986	118,421	84,655	58,291	41,105	24,960	17,049
Syracuse, N. Y	137,249	108,374	83,143	51,792	43,051	28,119	22,271
New Haven, Conn	133,605	108,027	81,293	62,382	50,840	39,267	20,345
Birmingham, Ala	132,683	38,415	26,178	3,086	...	...	...
Memphis, Tenn	131,105	102,320	64,495	33,592	40,226	22,623	8,841
Scranton, Pa	129,867	102,026	75,215	45,850	35,092	9,223	...
Richmond, Va	127,628	85,050	81,388	63,600	51,038	37,910	27,570
Paterson, N J	125,600	105,171	78,347	51,031	33,579	19,586	11,334
Omaha, Neb	124,096	102,555	140,452	30,518	16,083	1,883	...
Fall River, Mass	119,295	104,863	74,398	48,961	26,766	14,026	11,524
Dayton, O.	116,577	85,333	61,220	38,678	30,473	20,081	10,977
Grand Rapids, Mich	112,571	87,565	60,278	32,016	16,507	8,085	2,686
Nashville, Tenn	110,364	80,865	76,163	43,350	25,865	16,948	10,165
Lowell, Mass	106,294	94,969	77,696	59,475	40,298	36,827	33,383
Cambridge, Mass	164,839	91,886	70,028	52,669	18,547	26,060	15,215
Spokane, Wash	104,402	36,848	19,922	350	...	...	...
Bridgeport, Conn..	102,054	70,996	48,866	27,643	18,969	13,299	7,560
Albany, N. Y	100,253	94,151	94,923	90,758	69,658	62,367	50,763

POPULATION OF NEW YORK CITY BY BOROUGHS

	1910	1900.	1890		1910	1900	1890
Manhattan borough	2,331,542	1,850,093	1,441,216	Richmond borough	85,969	67,021	51,693
Bronx borough	430,980	200,507	88,908	Queens borough	284,041	152,999	87,050
Brooklyn borough	1,634,351	1,166,582	838,547	Total New York city	4,766,883	3,437,202	2,507,414

DECENNIAL INCREASE OF CITIES WITH MORE THAN 100,000 IN 1910.

City.	1900 to 1910 Number	Pr ct.	1890 to 1900 Number.	Pr ct	1880 to 1890 Number	Pr ct
New York, N Y	1,329,681	38 7	1,921,901	126 8	309,002	25.6
Chicago, Ill.	486,708	28 7	598,725	54.4	596,665	118.6
Philadelphia, Pa	255,311	19 7	246,733	23 6	199,794	23 6
St. Louis, Mo.	111,791	19 4	123,468	27.3	101,252	28 9
Boston, Mass	109,693	19 6	112,415	25.1	85,638	23 6
Cleveland, O	178,895	46 9	120,415	46.1	101,207	63.2
Baltimore, Md	49,528	9 7	74,518	17 2	102,126	30 7
Pittsburgh, Pa	82,393	18 2	82,999	34 8	82,228	52 6
Detroit, Mich	180,062	63 0	79,828	38 8	89,536	77 0
Buffalo, N Y	71,328	20 2	96,723	37 8	100,530	64.8
San Francisco, Cal	74,130	21 6	43,785	14 6	65,038	27.8
Milwaukee, Wis..	88 542	31 0	80,847	39.5	88,881	76 9
Cincinnati, O	37,689	11 8	28,994	9 8	41,769	16 4
Newark, N J	101,399	41 2	64,240	35 3	45,322	33 2
New Orleans, La	51,971	18 1	45,065	18 6	25,949	12 0
Washington, D C	53,351	18 8	48,326	21 0	52,768	29 7
Los Angeles, Cal	216,719	211 5	52,084	103 4	39,212	350 6
Minneapolis, Minn	98,690	48 6	37,980	23 1	117,851	251 4
Jersey City, N. J	61,346	29 7	43,430	26 6	42,281	35.0
Kansas City, Mo	84,752	51 7	31,036	23 4	76,931	137 9
Seattle, Wash	156,523	194 0	37,834	88 3	39,304	1112 5
Indianapolis, Ind....	64,486	38.1	63,728	60 4	30,380	40.5

City.	1900 to 1910		1890 to 1900		1880 to 1890	
	Number.	Pr.ct.	Number.	Pr.ct.	Number.	Pr.ct.
Providence, R. I...............	48,729	27.8	43,451	39.9	27,289	26.0
Louisville, Ky.................	19,197	9.4	43,602	27.1	37,371	30.2
Rochester, N. Y...............	55,541	34.2	28,712	21.4	44,530	49.8
St. Paul, Minn................	51,679	31.7	29,909	22.5	91,683	221.1
Denver, Col...................	79,522	59.4	27,146	25.4	71,084	199.5
Portland, Ore.................	116,788	140.2	44,041	94.9	28,808	162.9
Columbus, O..................	55,951	44.6	37,410	42.4	36,503	70.7
Toledo, O....................	26,675	27.8	50,388	61.9	31,287	62.4
Atlanta, Ga..................	64,967	72.3	24,339	37.1	28,124	75.2
Oakland, Cal.................	83,214	124.3	18,278	37.5	14,127	40.9
Worcester, Mass...............	27,565	23.3	33,766-	39.9	26,364	45.2
Syracuse, N. Y..............	28,875	26.8	20,231	23.0	36,351	70.2
New Haven, Conn..............	25,578	23.6	26,729	32.9	18,416	29.3
Birmingham, Ala..............	94,270	245.4	12,237	46.7	23,092	748.3
Memphis, Tenn................	28,785	28.1	37,825	58.6	30,903	92.0
Scranton, Pa.................	27,841	27.2	26,811	35.6	29,365	64.0
Richmond, Va.................	85,050	50.1	3,662	4.5	17,788	28.0
Paterson, N. J...............	20,429	19.4	26,824	34.2	27,316	53.5
Omaha, Neb...................	21,541	21.0	37,897	27.0	109,934	360.2
Fall River, Mass.............	14,432	13.8	26,824	34.2	27,316	53.5
Dayton, O....................	31,244	36.6	24,113	39.4	22,542	58.3
Grand Rapids, Mich...........	25,006	28.5	27,287	45.3	28,262	88.3
Nashville, Tenn..............	29,489	36.6	4,697	6.2	32,813	75.7
Lowell, Mass.................	11,225	11.9	17,273	22.2	18,221	30.6
Cambridge, Mass..............	12,953	14.1	21,858	31.2	17,359	33.0
Spokane, Wash................	67,654	183.3	19,672	530.6	....	....
Bridgeport, Conn.............	31,058	43.7	22,130	45.3	21,223	76.3
Albany, N. Y.................	6,102	6.5	*772	*0.8	4,165	4.6

*Decrease.

AMERICAN CITIES WITH POPULATION OF 25,000 TO 100,000 IN 1910.

City.	Population.			Pr. ct. inc.		City.	Population.			Pr. ct. inc.	
	1910.	1900.	1890.	1900-1910.	1890-1900.		1910.	1900.	1890.	1900-1910.	1890-1900.
Akron, O...........	69,067	42,728	27,601	61.6	54.8	Galveston, Tex......	36,981	37,789	29,084	*2.1	29.9
Allentown, Pa......	51,913	35,416	25,228	46.6	40.4	Green Bay, Wis......	25,236	18,684	9,069	35.1	106.0
Altoona, Pa........	52,127	38,973	30,337	33.8	28.5	Hamilton, O.........	35,279	23,914	17,566	47.5	36.1
Amsterdam, N. Y....	31,267	20,929	17,336	49.4	20.7	Harrisburg, Pa......	64,186	50,167	39,385	27.9	27.4
Atlantic City, N. J..	46,150	27,838	13,055	65.8	113.2	Hartford, Conn......	98,915	79,350	63,230	23.9	50.0
Auburn, N. Y.......	34,668	30,345	25,858	14.2	17.4	Haverhill, Mass.....	44,115	37,175	27,412	18.7	35.6
Augusta, Ga........	41,040	39,441	33,300	4.1	18.4	Hazleton, Pa........	25,452	14,230	11,872	78.9	19.9
Aurora, Ill........	29,807	24,147	19,688	23.4	22.6	Hoboken, N. J.......	70,324	59,364	43,648	18.5	36.0
Austin, Tex........	29,860	22,258	14,575	34.2	52.7	Holyoke, Mass.......	57,730	45,712	35,637	26.3	28.3
Battle Creek, Mich..	25,267	18,563	13,197	36.1	40.7	Houston, Tex........	78,800	44,633	27,557	76.6	62.0
Bay City, Mich.....	45,166	27,628	27,939	63.5	*0.8	Huntington, W. Va...	31,161	11,923	10,108	161.4	18.0
Bayonne, N. J......	55,545	32,722	19,033	69.7	71.9	Jackson, Mich.......	31,433	25,180	20,798	24.8	21.1
Berkeley, Cal......	40,434	13,214	5,101	206.0	159.0	Jacksonville, Fla....	57,699	28,429	17,201	103.0	65.3
Binghamton, N. Y...	48,443	39,647	35,005	22.2	13.3	Jamestown, N. Y.....	31,297	22,892	16,038	36.7	42.7
Bloomington, Ill....	25,768	23,286	20,484	10.7	13.7	Johnstown, Pa.......	55,482	35,936	21,805	54.4	64.8
Brockton, Mass.....	56,878	40,063	27,294	42.0	46.8	Joliet, O...........	34,670	29,353	23,264	18.1	26.2
Brookline, Mass....	27,792	19,935	12,103	39.4	64.7	Joplin, Mo..........	32,073	26,023	9,943	23.2	161.7
Butte, Mont........	39,165	30,470	10,722	28.5	184.2	Kalamazoo, Mich.....	39,437	24,404	17,853	61.6	36.7
Camden, N. J.......	94,538	75,935	58,313	24.5	30.2	Kansas City, Kas....	82,331	51,418	38,316	60.1	34.2
Canton, O..........	50,217	30,667	26,189	63.7	17.1	Kingston, N. Y......	25,908	24,535	21,261	5.6	15.4
Cedar Rapids, Iowa..	32,811	25,656	18,020	27.9	42.4	Knoxville, Tenn.....	36,346	32,637	22,535	11.4	44.8
Charleston, S. C....	58,533	55,807	54,955	5.4	1.6	LaCrosse, Wis.......	30,417	28,895	25,090	5.3	15.2
Charlotte, N. C.....	34,014	18,091	11,557	88.0	56.5	Lancaster, Pa.......	47,227	41,459	32,011	13.9	29.5
Chattanooga, Tenn...	44,604	30,154	29,100	47.9	3.6	Lansing, Mich.......	31,229	16,485	13,102	89.4	25.8
Chelsea, Mass......	32,452	34,072	27,909	*4.8	22.1	Lawrence, Mass......	85,892	62,559	44,654	37.3	40.1
Chester, Pa........	38,537	33,988	20,226	13.4	68.0	Lewiston, Me........	26,247	23,761	21,701	10.5	9.5
Chicopee, Mass.....	25,401	19,167	14,050	32.5	36.4	Lexington, Ky.......	35,099	26,369	21,567	33.1	22.3
Clinton, Iowa......	25,577	22,698	13,619	12.7	66.7	Lima, O.............	20,508	21,723	15,981	40.4	35.9
Colorado Sprgs., Col.	29,078	21,085	11,140	37.9	89.3	Lincoln, Neb........	43,973	40,169	55,154	9.6	*27.2
Columbia, S. C.....	26,319	21,108	15,353	24.7	37.6	Little Rock, Ark....	45,941	38,307	25,874	19.9	48.1
Council Bluffs, Iowa.	29,292	25,802	21,474	13.5	20.2	Lorain, O...........	28,883	16,028	4,863	80.2	229.6
Covington, Ky......	53,270	42,938	37,371	24.1	14.9	Lynchburg, Va.......	29,494	18,891	19,709	56.1	*4.2
Dallas, Tex........	92,104	42,638	38,067	116.0	12.0	Lynn, Mass..........	89,336	68,513	55,727	30.4	22.9
Danville, Ill.......	27,871	16,354	11,491	70.4	42.3	Macon, Ga...........	40,665	23,272	22,746	74.7	2.3
Davenport, Iowa....	43,028	35,254	26,872	22.1	31.2	McKeesport, Pa......	42,694	34,227	20,741	24.7	65.0
Decatur, Ill.......	31,140	20,754	16,841	50.0	23.2	Madison, Wis........	25,531	19,164	13,426	33.2	42.7
Des Moines, Iowa....	86,368	62,139	60,093	39.0	24.0	Malden, Mass........	44,404	33,664	23,031	31.9	46.2
Dubuque, Iowa......	38,494	36,297	30,311	6.1	19.7	Manchester, N. H....	70,063	56,987	44,126	22.9	29.1
Duluth, Minn.......	78,466	52,969	33,115	48.1	60.0	Mansfield, O........	27,265	24,296	21,652	12.2	12.2
Easton, Pa.........	28,523	25,238	14,481	13.0	74.3	Marion, Ind.........	38,136	30,346	21,883	25.7	38.7
East Orange, N. J..	34,371	21,506	13,282	53.8	61.9	Mobile, Ala.........	51,521	38,469	31,076	33.9	23.8
East St. Louis, Ill..	58,547	29,655	15,169	97.4	95.5	Montgomery, Ala.....	38,136	30,346	21,883	25.7	38.7
El Paso, Tex.......	39,279	15,906	10,338	146.9	53.9	Mount Vernon, N. Y..	30,919	21,228	10,830	45.7	96.0
Elgin, Ill.........	25,976	22,433	17,823	15.8	25.9	Muskogee, Okla......	25,278	4,254	†	494.2	....
Elizabeth, N. J.....	73,409	52,130	37,764	40.8	38.0	Nashua, N. H........	26,005	23,598	19,311	8.8	23.8
Elmira, N. Y.......	37,176	35,672	30,893	4.2	15.5	Newark, O...........	25,404	18,157	14,270	39.9	27.3
Erie, Pa...........	66,525	52,733	40,634	26.2	29.8	New Bedford, Mass...	96,652	62,442	40,733	54.8	53.3
Evansville, Ind.....	69,647	59,007	50,756	18.0	16.3	New Britain, Conn...	43,916	25,998	16,519	68.9	57.4
Everett, Mass......	33,484	24,336	11,068	37.6	119.9	Newburgh, N. Y......	27,805	24,943	23,087	11.5	8.9
Fitchburg, Mass.....	37,826	31,531	22,037	20.0	43.1	Newcastle, Pa.......	36,280	28,339	11,600	28.0	144.3
Flint, Mich........	38,550	13,103	9,903	194.2	33.7	Newport, Ky.........	30,309	28,301	24,918	7.1	13.6
Fort Wayne, Ind....	63,933	45,115	35,393	41.7	27.5	Newport, R. I.......	27,149	22,441	19,457	21.0	15.3
Fort Worth, Tex....	73,312	26,688	23,076	174.7	15.7	New Rochelle, N. Y..	28,867	14,720	9,057	96.1	62.5
						Newton, Mass........	39,806	33,587	24,379	18.5	37.8

City.	Population. 1910.	1900.	1890.	Pr. ct. inc. 1900-1910.	1890-1900.
Niagara Falls, N. Y..	30,445	19,457	†	56.5	....
Norfolk, Va..........	67,452	46,624	34,871	44.7	33.7
Norristown, Pa......	27,875	22,265	19,791	25.2	12.5
Ogden, Utah.........	25,580	16,313	14,889	56.8	9.6
Oklahoma City, Okla.	64,205	10,037	4,151	539.7	141.8
Orange, N. J........	29,630	24,141	18,844	22.7	28.1
Oshkosh, Wis........	33,062	28,284	22,836	16.9	23.9
Pasadena, Cal.......	30,291	9,117	4,882	232.2	86.7
Passaic, N. J.......	54,773	27,777	13,028	97.2	113.2
Pawtucket, R. I.....	51,622	39,231	27,633	31.5	42.0
Peoria, Ill.........	66,950	56,100	41,024	19.3	36.7
Perth Amboy, N. J...	32,121	17,699	9,512	81.5	86.1
Pittsfield, Mass....	32,121	21,766	17,281	47.6	26.0
Portland, Me........	58,571	50,145	36,425	16.8	37.7
Portsmouth, Va......	33,190	17,427	13,268	90.5	31.3
Poughkeepsie, N. Y..	27,936	24,029	22,206	16.3	8.2
Pueblo, Col.........	44,395	28,157	24,558	57.7	14.7
Quincy, Ill.........	36,587	36,252	31,494	0.9	15.1
Quincy, Mass........	32,642	23,899	16,723	36.6	42.9
Racine, Wis.........	38,002	29,102	21,014	30.6	38.5
Reading, Pa.........	96,071	78,961	58,661	21.7	34.6
Roanoke, Va.........	34,874	21,495	16,159	62.2	33.0
Rockford, Ill.......	45,401	31,051	23,584	46.2	31.7
Sacramento, Cal.....	44,696	29,282	26,386	52.6	11.0
Saginaw, Mich.......	50,510	42,345	46,322	19.3	*8.6
St. Joseph, Mo......	77,403	102,979	52,324	*24.8	96.8
Salem, Mass.........	43,697	35,956	30,801	21.5	16.7
Salt Lake City, Utah.	92,777	53,531	44,843	73.3	19.4
San Antonio, Tex ..	96,614	53,321	37,673	81.2	41.5
San Diego, Cal......	39,578	17,700	16,159	123.6	9.5
San Jose, Cal.......	28,946	21,500	18,060	34.6	19.0
Savannah, Ga........	65,064	54,244	43,189	19.9	25.6
Schenectady, N. Y...	72,826	31,682	19,902	129.9	59.2
Sheboygan, Wis......	26,398	22,962	16,359	15.0	40.4
Shenandoah, Pa......	25,774	20,321	15,944	26.8	27.5
Shreveport, La......	28,015	16,013	11,979	75.0	33.7
Sioux City, Iowa....	47,828	33,111	37,806	44.4	*12.4
Somerville, Mass....	77,236	61,643	40,152	25.3	53.5
South Bend, Ind.....	53,684	35,999	21,819	49.1	65.0
South Omaha, Neb....	26,259	26,001	9,662	1.0	222.5
Springfield, Ill....	51,678	34,159	24,963	51.3	36.8
Springfield, Mass...	88,926	62,059	44,179	43.3	40.5
Springfield, Mo.....	35,201	23,267	21,850	51.3	6.5
Springfield, O......	46,521	38,253	31,895	22.7	19.9
Stamford, Conn......	25,138	15,997	†	57.1	....
Superior, Wis.......	40,384	31,091	11,983	29.9	159.5
Tacoma, Wash........	83,743	37,714	36,006	122.0	4.7
Tampa, Fla..........	37,782	15,839	5,532	138.6	186.3
Taunton, Mass.......	34,259	31,036	25,448	10.4	22.0
Terre Haute, Ind....	58,157	36,673	30,217	52.6	21.4

City.	Population. 1910.	1900.	1890.	Pr. ct. inc. 1900-1910.	1890-1900.
Topeka, Kas.........	43,684	33,608	31,007	30.0	8.4
Trenton, N. J.......	96,815	73,307	57,458	32.1	27.6
Troy, N. Y..........	76,813	60,651	60,956	26.6	*0.5
Utica, N. Y.........	74,419	56,383	44,007	32.0	28.1
Waco, Tex...........	26,425	20,686	14,445	27.7	43.2
Waltham, Mass.......	27,834	23,481	18,707	18.5	25.5
Warwick, R. I.......	26,629	21,316	17,761	24.9	20.0
Waterbury, Conn.....	73,141	45,859	28,646	59.5	60.1
Waterloo, Iowa......	26,693	12,580	6,674	112.2	88.5
Watertown, N. Y.....	26,730	21,696	14,725	23.2	47.3
West Hoboken, N. J..	35,403	23,094	11,665	53.3	98.0
Wheeling, W. Va.....	41,641	38,878	34,522	7.1	12.4
Wichita, Kas........	52,450	24,671	23,853	112.6	3.6
Wilkes-Barre, Pa....	67,105	51,721	37,718	29.7	37.1
Williamsport, Pa....	31,860	28,757	27,132	10.8	6.0
Wilmington, Del.....	87,411	76,508	61,431	14.3	24.5
Wilmington, N. C....	25,748	20,976	20,056	22.7	4.6
Woonsocket, R. I....	38,125	28,204	20,830	38.7	35.4
Yonkers, N. Y.......	79,803	47,921	32,033	66.5	49.6
York, Pa............	44,750	33,708	20,793	32.8	62.1
Youngstown, O.......	79,066	44,885	33,220	76.2	35.1
Zanesville, O.......	28,026	22,238	21,009	19.1	12.6

*Decrease. †Incorporated since 1890.

CITIES OF FASTEST GROWTH, 1900 TO 1910.

Rank.	City.	Population. 1910.	Pr.ct.inc. 1900-1910.
1.	Oklahoma City, Okla....	64,205	539.7
2.	Muskogee, Okla.........	25,278	494.2
3.	Birmingham, Ala........	132,685	245.4
4.	Pasadena, Cal..........	30,291	232.2
5.	Los Angeles, Cal.......	319,198	211.5
6.	Berkeley, Cal..........	40,434	206.0
7.	Flint, Mich............	38,550	194.3
8.	Seattle, Wash..........	237,194	194.0
9.	Spokane, Wash..........	104,402	183.3
10.	Fort Worth, Tex.......	73,312	174.7
11.	Huntington, W. Va.....	31,161	161.4
12.	El Paso, Tex..........	39,279	146.9
13.	Tampa, Fla............	37,782	138.5
14.	Schenectady, N. Y.....	72,826	129.9
15.	Portland, Ore.........	207,214	129.2
16.	Oakland, Cal..........	150,174	124.3
17.	San Diego, Cal........	39,578	123.6
18.	Tacoma, Wash..........	83,743	122.0
19.	Dallas, Tex...........	92,104	116.0
20.	Wichita, Kas..........	52,450	112.6
21.	Waterloo, Iowa........	26,693	112.2
22.	Jacksonville, Fla.....	57,699	103.0

POPULATION OF INCORPORATED PLACES IN 1910.

Includes, with some exceptions,* only towns and cities having more than 3,000 inhabitants in 1910.
[From reports of federal census bureau.]

ALABAMA.
Alabama City....... 4,313
Anniston........... 12,794
Bessemer........... 10,864
Birmingham.........132,685
Decatur............ 4,228
Dothan............. 7,016
Eufaula............ 4,259
Florence........... 6,689
Gadsden............ 10,557
Girard............. 4,214
Greenville......... 3,377
Huntsville......... 7,611
Lanett............. 3,820
Mobile............. 51,521
Montgomery......... 38,136
New Decatur........ 6,118
Opelika............ 4,734
Phenix............. 4,555
Selma.............. 13,649
Sheffield.......... 4,865
Talladega.......... 5,854
Troy............... 4,961
Tuscaloosa......... 8,407
Tuscumbia.......... 3,324
Union Springs..... 4,055

ALASKA.
Cordova............ 1,152
Douglas............ 1,722
Fairbanks.......... 3,541
Juneau............. 1,644
Ketchikan.......... 1,613
Nome............... 2,600
Treadwell.......... 1,222
Valdez............. 810
Wrangell........... 743

ARIZONA.
Bisbee............. 9,019
Clifton............ 4,874
Douglas............ 6,437
Flagstaff.......... 1,633
Globe.............. 7,083
Jerome............. 2,393
Mesa............... 1,692
Nogales............ 3,514
Phoenix............ 11,134
Prescott........... 5,092
Tempe.............. 1,473
Tombstone.......... 1,582
Tucson............. 13,193
Williams........... 1,267
Winslow............ 2,381
Yuma............... 2,914

ARKANSAS.
Argenta............ 11,138
Batesville......... 3,399
Blytheville........ 3,849
Camden............. 3,995
Eldorado........... 4,202
Eureka Springs..... 3,228
Fayetteville....... 4,471
Fort Smith........ 23,975
Helena............. 8,772
Hope............... 3,639
Hot Springs........ 14,434
Jonesboro.......... 7,123
Little Rock........ 45,941
Marianna........... 4,810
Mena............... 3,953
Newport............ 3,557
Paragould.......... 5,248
Pine Bluff......... 15,102
Texarkana.......... 5,655
Van Buren.......... 3,878

CALIFORNIA.
Alameda............ 23,383
Alhambra........... 5,021
Bakersfield........ 12,727
Berkeley........... 40,434
Chico.............. 3,750
Coalinga........... 4,199
Colton............. 3,980
Corona............. 3,540
Eureka............. 11,845
Fresno............. 24,892
Grass Valley....... 4,520
Hanford............ 4,829
Long Beach......... 17,809
Los Angeles........319,198
Marysville......... 5,430
Merced............. 3,102
Modesto............ 4,034
Monrovia........... 3,576
Monterey........... 4,923
Napa............... 5,791
Oakland............150,174
Ocean Park......... 3,119
Ontario............ 4,274
Oroville........... 3,859
Palo Alto.......... 4,486
Pasadena........... 30,291
Petaluma........... 5,880
Pomona............. 10,207
Red Bluff.......... 3,530
Redding............ 3,572
Redlands........... 10,449
Richmond........... 6,802
Riverside.......... 15,212
Sacramento......... 44,696
Salinas............ 3,736
San Bernardino..... 12,779
San Diego.......... 39,578
San Francisco......416,912
San Jose........... 28,946
San Leandro........ 3,471
San Luis Obispo.... 5,157
San Mateo.......... 4,384
San Rafael......... 5,934
Santa Ana.......... 8,429
Santa Barbara...... 11,659
Santa Clara........ 4,348
Santa Cruz......... 11,146
Santa Monica....... 7,847
Santa Rosa......... 7,817
South Pasadena..... 4,649
Stockton........... 23,253

Vallejo 11,340
Visalia 4,550
Watsonville 4,446
Whittier 4,550
Woodland 3,187

COLORADO.

Alamosa 3,013
Boulder 9,539
Canon City 5,162
Colorado City 4,823
Colorado Springs 29,078
Cripple Creek 6,206
Denver 213,381
Durango 4,686
Fort Collins 8,210
Grand Junction 7,754
Greeley 8,179
La Junta 4,154
Leadville 7,508
Longmont 4,256
Loveland 3,651
Montrose 3,254
Pueblo 44,395
Rocky Ford 3,230
Salida 4,425
Sterling 3,044
Trinidad 10,204
Victor 3,162

CONNECTICUT.

Ansonia 15,152
Berlin 2,728
Bethel 3,792
Branford 6,047
Bridgeport 102,054
Bristol 13,502
Danbury 20,234
Darien 3,943
Derby 8,991
East Hartford 8,138
East Windsor 3,362
Enfield 9,719
Fairfield 6,134
Farmington 3,478
Glastonbury 4,796
Greenwich 16,463
Griswold 4,233
Groton 6,495
Guilford 3,001
Hamden 5,850
Hartford 98,915
Huntington 6,545
Killingly 6,564
Litchfield 3,005
Manchester 13,641
Meriden 27,265
Middletown 11,851
Milford 4,366
Naugatuck 12,722
New Britain 43,916
New Canaan 3,667
New Haven 133,605
New London 19,659
New Milford 5,010
Newtown 3,012
Norwalk 6,954
Norwich 20,367
Orange 11,272
Plainfield 6,719
Plymouth 5,021
Portland 3,425
Putnam 6,637
Ridgefield 3,118
Rockville 7,977
Salisbury 3,522
Seymour 4,786
South Norwalk 8,968
Southington 6,516
Stafford 5,233
Stamford 25,138
Stonington 9,154
Stratford 5,712
Suffield 3,841
Thomaston 3,533
Thompson 4,804
Torrington 16,840
Wallingford 11,155
Waterbury 73,141
Waterford 3,097
Watertown 3,850

West Hartford 4,808
Westport 4,259
Wethersfield 3,148
Willimantic 11,230
Winchester 8,679
Windsor 4,178
Windsor Locks 3,715

DELAWARE.

Dover 3,720
New Castle 3,351
Wilmington 87,411

DIST. OF COLUMBIA.

Washington 331,069

FLORIDA.

Apalachicola 3,065
Daytona 3,082
Fernandina 3,482
Gainesville 6,183
Jacksonville 57,699
Key West 19,945
Lake City 5,032
Lakeland 3,719
Live Oak 3,460
Miami 5,471
Ocala 4,370
Orlando 3,894
Palatka 3,779
Pensacola 22,982
Quincy 3,204
St. Augustine 5,494
St. Petersburg 4,127
Sanford 3,570
Tallahassee 5,018
Tampa 37,782
West Tampa 8,258

GEORGIA.

Albany 8,190
Americus 8,063
Athens 14,913
Atlanta 154,839
Augusta 41,040
Bainbridge 4,217
Barnesville 3,068
Brunswick 10,182
Carrollton 3,297
Cartersville 4,067
Cedartown 3,551
Columbus 20,554
Cordele 5,883
Cuthbert 3,210
Dalton 5,324
Dawson 3,827
Douglas 3,550
Dublin 5,795
East Point 3,682
Elberton 6,483
Fitzgerald 5,795
Gainesville 5,925
Griffin 7,478
Hawkinsville 3,420
LaGrange 5,587
Macon 40,665
Marietta 5,949
Milledgeville 4,385
Monroe 3,029
Moultrie 3,349
Newnan 5,548
Quitman 3,915
Rome 12,099
Savannah 65,064
Summerville 4,361
Thomasville 6,727
Toccoa 3,120
Valdosta 7,656
Washington 3,065
Waycross 14,485

HAWAII.

Hilo 6,745
Honolulu 52,183

IDAHO.

Blackfoot 2,202
Boise 17,358
Caldwell 3,543
Coeur d'Alene 7,291
Idaho Falls 4,827
Lewiston 6,043

Nampa 1,295
Pocatello 9,110
Moscow 3,670
Preston 2,110
Sandpoint 2,993
Twin Falls 5,258
Wallace 3,090
Weiser 2,600

ILLINOIS.

(Places of 2,000 or more inhabitants.)

Abingdon 2,464
Aledo 2,144
Alton 17,528
Anna 2,809
Arcola 2,100
Aurora 29,807
Averyville 2,668
Batavia 4,436
Beardstown 6,107
Belleville 21,122
Belvidere 7,253
Benton 2,675
Berwyn 5,841
Bloomington 25,768
Blue Island 8,043
Breese 2,128
Bridgeport 2,703
Brookfield 2,186
Bushnell 2,619
Cairo 14,548
Canton 10,453
Carbondale 5,411
Carlinville 3,616
Carmi 2,833
Carrollton 2,323
Carterville 2,971
Carthage 2,373
Casey 2,157
Centralia 9,680
Champaign 12,421
Charleston 5,884
Chester 2,747
Chicago 2,185,283
Chicago Heights 14,525
Cicero (town) 14,557
Clinton 5,165
Coal City 2,667
Collinsville 7,478
Columbia 2,076
Cuba 2,019
Danville 27,871
Decatur 31,140
DeKalb 8,102
Des Plaines 2,348
Dixon 7,216
Downers Grove 2,601
Duquoin 5,454
Dwight 2,156
East Moline 2,665
East St. Louis 58,547
Edwardsville 5,014
Effingham 3,898
Eldorado 3,366
Elgin 25,976
Elmhurst 2,360
Evanston 24,978
Fairbury 2,505
Fairfield 2,479
Farmington 2,421
Flora 2,704
Forest Park 6,594
Freeport 17,567
Fulton 2,174
Galena 4,835
Galesburg 22,089
Galva 2,498
Geneseo 3,199
Geneva 2,451
Georgetown 2,207
Gibson 2,086
Gillespie 2,241
Granite 9,903
Greenville 3,178
Harrisburg 5,309
Harvard 3,008
Harvey 7,227
Havana 3,525
Herrin 6,861
Highland 2,675

Highland Park 4,209
Hillsboro 3,424
Hinsdale 2,451
Hoopeston 4,698
Jacksonville 15,326
Jerseyville 4,113
Johnston 3,248
Joliet 34,670
Kankakee 13,986
Kewanee 9,307
LaGrange 5,282
Lake Forest 3,349
LaSalle 11,537
Lawrenceville 3,235
Lemont 2,284
Lewistown 2,312
Lincoln 10,892
Litchfield 5,971
Lockport 2,555
Macomb 5,774
Madison 5,046
Marion 7,093
Marissa 2,904
Marseilles 3,291
Marshall 2,569
Mascoutah 2,081
Mattoon 11,456
Maywood 8,032
Melrose Park 4,806
Mendota 3,806
Metropolis 4,655
Minonk 2,070
Moline 24,199
Momence 2,201
Monmouth 9,128
Morgan Park 3,694
Morris 4,563
Morrison 2,410
Mound City 2,837
Mount Carmel 6,934
Mount Olive 3,501
Mount Vernon 8,007
Murphysboro 7,485
Naperville 3,449
Nashville 2,135
Newton 2,106
Normal 4,024
North Chicago 3,306
Oak Park 19,444
O'Fallon 2,018
Olney 6,011
Oregon 2,180
Ottawa 9,535
Pana 6,055
Paris 7,664
Park Ridge 2,009
Paxton 2,912
Pekin 9,897
Peoria 66,950
Peru 7,984
Petersburg 2,587
Pinckneyville 2,722
Pittsfield 2,095
Pontiac 6,090
Portland 3,194
Princeton 4,131
Quincy 36,587
River Forest 2,456
Robinson 3,863
Rochelle 2,732
Rock Falls 2,657
Rock Island 24,335
Rockford 45,401
Roodhouse 2,171
Rushville 2,422
St. Charles 4,046
Salem 2,669
Sandwich 2,557
Savanna 3,691
Shelbyville 3,590
South Wilmington 2,403
Sparta 3,081
Spring Valley 7,035
Springfield 51,678
Staunton 5,049
Steger 2,161
Sterling 7,467
Streator 14,253
Sullivan 2,621

Sycamore	3,926
Taylorville	5,446
Toluca	2,407
Tuscola	2,453
Upper Alton	2,918
Urbana	8,245
Vandalia	2,974
Venice	3,718
Virden	4,000
Warsaw	2,254
Waterloo	2,091
Watseka	2,476
Waukegan	16,069
West Chicago	2,378
West Frankfort	2,111
West Hammond	4,948
Westville	2,607
Wheaton	3,423
Whitehall	2,854
Wilmette	4,943
Winnetka	3,168
Witt	2,170
Woodstock	4,331
Zion City	4,789

INDIANA.

Alexandria	5,096
Anderson	22,476
Attica	3,335
Auburn	3,919
Aurora	4,410
Bedford	8,716
Bloomington	8,838
Bluffton	4,987
Boonville	3,934
Brazil	9,340
Clinton	6,229
Columbia City	3,448
Columbus	8,813
Connersville	7,738
Crawfordsville	9,371
Decatur	4,471
Dunkirk	3,031
East Chicago	19,098
Elkhart	19,282
Elwood	11,028
Evansville	69,647
Fort Wayne	63,933
Frankfort	8,634
Franklin	4,502
Garrett	4,149
Gary	16,802
Gas City	3,224
Goshen	8,514
Greencastle	3,790
Greenfield	4,448
Greensburg	5,420
Hammond	20,925
Hartford	6,187
Huntington	10,272
Indianapolis	233,650
Jasonville	3,295
Jeffersonville	10,412
Kendallville	4,981
Kokomo	17,010
Lafayette	20,081
Laporte	10,525
Lawrenceburg	3,930
Lebanon	5,474
Linton	5,906
Logansport	19,050
Madison	6,934
Marion	19,359
Martinsville	4,529
Michigan City	19,027
Mishawaka	11,886
Mitchell	3,438
Mount Vernon	5,563
Muncie	24,005
New Albany	20,629
New Castle	9,446
Noblesville	5,073
Peru	10,910
Plymouth	3,838
Portland	5,130
Princeton	6,448
Richmond	22,324
Rochester	3,364
Rushville	4,925
Seymour	6,305
Shelbyville	9,500
South Bend	53,684
Sullivan	4,115
Tell City	3,369
Terre Haute	58,157
Tipton	4,075
Union	3,209
Valparaiso	6,987
Vincennes	14,895
Wabash	8,687
Warsaw	4,430
Washington	7,854
West Lafayette	3,867
West Terre Haute	3,083
Whiting	6,587
Winchester	4,266

IOWA.

Albia	4,969
Ames	4,223
Atlantic	4,560
Belle Plaine	3,121
Boone	10,347
Burlington	24,324
Carroll	3,546
Cedar Falls	5,012
Cedar Rapids	32,811
Centerville	6,936
Charlton	3,794
Charles City	5,892
Cherokee	4,884
Clarinda	3,832
Clinton	25,577
Council Bluffs	29,292
Creston	6,924
Davenport	43,028
Decorah	3,592
Denison	3,133
Des Moines	86,368
Dubuque	38,494
Eaglegrove	3,387
Estherville	3,404
Fairfield	4,970
Fort Dodge	15,543
Fort Madison	8,900
Glenwood	4,052
Grinnell	5,036
Independence	3,517
Indianola	3,283
Iowa City	10,091
Keokuk	14,008
Knoxville	3,190
Le Mars	4,157
Maquoketa	3,570
Marion	4,400
Marshalltown	13,374
Mason City	11,230
Missouri Valley	3,187
Mount Pleasant	3,874
Muscatine	16,178
Newton	4,616
Oelwein	6,028
Oskaloosa	9,466
Ottumwa	22,012
Pella	3,021
Perry	4,630
Red Oak	4,830
Shenandoah	4,976
Sioux City	47,828
Spencer	3,005
Vinton	3,336
Washington	4,390
Waterloo	26,693
Waverly	3,205
Webster City	5,208

KANSAS.

Abilene	4,118
Arkansas City	7,508
Atchison	16,429
Beloit	3,082
Caney	3,597
Chanute	9,272
Cherryvale	4,304
Clay Center	3,438
Coffeyville	12,687
Columbus	3,064
Concordia	4,415
Dodge City	3,214
Eldorado	3,129
Emporia	9,058
Fort Scott	10,463
Fredonia	3,040
Frontenac	3,396
Galena	6,096
Garden	3,171
Great Bend	4,622
Herington	3,273
Horton	3,600
Hutchinson	16,364
Independence	10,480
Iola	9,032
Junction	5,598
Kansas City	82,331
Lawrence	12,374
Leavenworth	19,363
McPherson	3,546
Manhattan	5,722
Newton	7,862
Olathe	2,272
Osawatomie	4,046
Ottawa	7,650
Paola	3,207
Parsons	12,463
Pittsburg	14,755
Pratt	3,302
Rosedale	5,960
Salina	9,688
Topeka	43,684
Wellington	7,034
Wichita	52,450
Winfield	6,700

KENTUCKY.

Ashland	8,688
Bellevue	6,683
Bowling Green	9,173
Catlettsburg	3,520
Covington	53,270
Cynthiana	3,603
Danville	5,420
Dayton	6,979
Earlington	3,931
Frankfort	10,465
Franklin	3,063
Georgetown	4,533
Harrodsburg	3,147
Henderson	11,452
Hopkinsville	9,419
Lebanon	3,077
Lexington	35,099
Louisville	223,928
Ludlow	4,163
Madisonville	4,966
Mayfield	5,916
Maysville	6,141
Middlesboro	7,305
Mount Sterling	3,932
Newport	30,309
Owensboro	16,011
Paducah	22,760
Paris	5,859
Princeton	3,015
Richmond	5,340
Russellville	3,111
Shelbyville	3,412
Somerset	4,491
Winchester	7,156

LOUISIANA.

Alexandria	11,213
Baton Rouge	14,897
Crowley	5,099
Donaldsonville	4,090
Franklin	3,867
Houma	5,024
Jennings	3,925
Kentwood	3,609
Lafayette	6,392
Lake Charles	11,449
Minden	3,662
Monroe	10,209
Morgan City	5,477
New Iberia	7,499
New Orleans	339,075
Opelousas	4,623
Plaquemine	4,955
Ruston	3,377
Shreveport	28,015
Thibodaux	3,824

MAINE.

Auburn	15,064
Augusta	13,211
Bangor	24,803
Bath	9,396
Belfast	4,618
Biddeford	17,079
Brewer	5,667
Brunswick	6,621
Calais	6,116
Camden	3,015
Caribou	5,377
Chelsea	3,216
Dexter	3,539
Eastport	4,961
Eden	4,441
Ellsworth	3,549
Fairfield (town)	4,435
Farmington (town)	3,210
Fort Fairfield (t'n)	4,381
Fort Kent	3,710
Gardiner	5,311
Houlton	5,845
Kennebunk	3,099
Kittery	3,533
Lewiston	26,247
Lisbon	4,116
Lubec	3,363
Madison (town)	3,379
Millinocket	3,368
Norway (town)	3,002
Old Town	6,317
Orono	3,555
Paris (town)	3,436
Portland	58,571
Presque Isle (t'n)	5,179
Rockland	8,174
Rumford (town)	6,777
Sanford	9,049
Skowhegan	5,341
South Portland	7,471
Van Buren	3,065
Waterville	11,458
Westbrook	8,281

MARYLAND.

Annapolis	8,609
Baltimore	558,485
Brunswick	2,721
Cambridge	6,407
Crisfield	3,468
Cumberland	21,839
Easton	3,083
Frederick	10,411
Frostburg	6,028
Hagerstown	16,507
Havre de Grace	4,212
Salisbury	6,690
Westminster	3,295

MASSACHUSETTS.

Abington	5,455
Adams	13,026
Agawam	3,501
Amesbury	9,894
Amherst	5,112
Andover	7,301
Arlington	11,187
Athol	8,533
Attleborough	16,215
Barnstable	4,676
Belmont	5,542
Beverly	18,650
Blackstone	5,648
Boston	670,585
Braintree	8,066
Bridgewater	7,684
Brockton	56,878
Brookline	27,792
Cambridge	104,839
Canton	4,797
Chelmsford	5,010
Chelsea	32,452
Chicopee	25,401

Clinton	13,075	Sutton	3,075	Saginaw	50,510
Concord	6,421	Swampscott	6,204	St. Johns	3,154
Dalton	3,568	Taunton	34,259	St. Joseph	5,936
Danvers	9,407	Templeton	3,756	Sault Ste. Marie..	12,615
Dartmouth	4,378	Tewksbury	3,750	South Haven	3,577
Dedham	9,284	Uxbridge	4,671	Sturgis	3,635
Dracut	3,461	Wakefield	11,404	Three Rivers	5,072
Dudley	4,267	Walpole	4,892	Traverse City	12,115
East Bridgewater.	3,363	Waltham	27,831	Wyandotte	8,287
Easthampton	8,524	Ware	8,774	Ypsilanti	6,230
Easton	5,139	Wareham	4,102		
Everett	33,484	Warren	4,188	**MINNESOTA.**	
Fairhaven	5,122	Watertown	12,875	Albert Lea	6,192
Fall River	119,295	Webster	11,509	Alexandria	3,001
Falmouth	3,144	Wellesley	5,413	Anoka	3,972
Fitchburg	37,826	West Springfield..	9,224	Austin	6,960
Foxborough	3,863	Westborough	5,446	Bemidji	5,099
Framingham	12,948	Westfield	16,044	Brainerd	8,526
Franklin	5,641	Weymouth	12,895	Chisholm	7,684
Gardner	14,699	Whitman	7,292	Cloquet	7,031
Gloucester	24,398	Williamstown	3,708	Crookston	7,559
Grafton	5,705	Winchendon	5,678	Duluth	78,466
Great Barrington.	5,926	Winchester	9,309	Ely	3,572
Greenfield	10,427	Winthrop	10,132	Eveleth	7,036
Hardwick	3,524	Woburn	15,308	Faribault	9,001
Haverhill	44,115	Worcester	145,986	Fergus Falls	6,887
Hingham	4,965			Hastings	3,983
Holyoke	57,730	**MICHIGAN.**		Hibbing	8,832
Hudson	6,743	Adrian	10,763	Lake City	2,142
Hyde Park	15,507	Albion	5,833	Little Falls	6,078
Ipswich	5,777	Allegan	3,419	Mankato	10,365
Lawrence	85,892	Alpena	12,706	Minneapolis	301,408
Lee	4,103	Ann Arbor	14,817	Montevideo	3,056
Leicester	3,237	Battle Creek	25,267	Moorhead	4,840
Lenox	3,060	Bay City	45,166	New Ulm	5,648
Leominster	17,580	Belding	4,119	Northfield	3,265
Lexington	4,918	Benton Harbor	9,185	Owatonna	5,658
Lowell	106,294	Bessemer	4,583	Red Wing	9,048
Ludlow	4,948	Big Rapids	4,519	Rochester	7,844
Lynn	89,336	Boyne City	5,218	St. Cloud	10,600
Malden	44,404	Cadillac	8,375	St. Paul	214,744
Mansfield	5,183	Charlotte	4,886	St. Peter	4,176
Marblehead	7,338	Cheboygan	6,859	South St. Paul	4,510
Marlborough	14,579	Coldwater	5,945	Stillwater	10,198
Maynard	6,390	Crystal Falls	3,775	Thief River Falls.	3,714
Medfield	3,466	Detroit	465,766	Two Harbors	4,990
Medford	23,150	Dowagiac	5,088	Virginia	10,473
Melrose	15,715	Escanaba	13,194	Waseca	3,054
Methuen	11,448	Flint	38,550	West Minneapolis.	3,022
Middleborough	8,214	Gladstone	4,211	Willmar	4,135
Milford	13,055	Grand Haven	5,856	Winona	18,583
Millbury	4,740	Grand Rapids	112,571		
Milton	7,924	Greenville	4,045	**MISSISSIPPI.**	
Monson	4,758	Hamtramck	3,559	Aberdeen	3,708
Montague	8,856	Hancock	8,981	Bay St. Louis	3,388
Natick	9,866	Hastings	4,383	Biloxi	5,049
Needham	5,026	Highland Park	4,120	Brookhaven	5,293
New Bedford	96,652	Hillsdale	5,001	Canton	3,929
Newburyport	14,949	Holland	10,490	Clarksdale	4,079
Newton	39,806	Houghton	5,113	Columbus	8,988
North Adams	22,019	Ionia	5,030	Corinth	5,020
North Andover	5,529	Iron Mountain	9,216	Greenville	9,610
N. Attleborough	9,562	Ironwood	12,821	Greenwood	5,836
North Brookfield.	3,075	Ishpeming	12,448	Gulfport	6,386
Northampton	19,431	Jackson	31,433	Hattiesburg	11,733
Northbridge	8,807	Kalamazoo	39,437	Jackson	21,262
Norwood	8,014	Lansing	31,229	Laurel	8,465
Orange	5,282	Lapeer	3,946	McComb	6,237
Oxford	3,361	Laurium	8,537	Meridian	23,285
Palmer	8,610	Ludington	9,132	Moss Point	3,054
Peabody	15,721	Manistee	12,381	Natchez	11,791
Pittsfield	32,121	Manistique	4,722	Pascagoula	3,379
Plymouth	12,141	Marine City	3,770	Tupelo	3,881
Provincetown	4,369	Marquette	11,503	Vicksburg	20,814
Quincy	32,642	Marshall	4,236	Water Valley	4,275
Randolph	4,301	Menominee	10,507	West Point	4,864
Reading	5,818	Monroe	6,893	Yazoo	6,796
Revere	18,219	Mount Clemens	7,707		
Rockland	6,928	Mount Pleasant.	3,972	**MISSOURI.**	
Rockport	4,211	Muskegon	24,062	Aurora	4,148
Salem	43,697	Negaunee	8,460	Boonville	4,252
Saugus	8,047	Niles	5,156	Brookfield	5,749
Somerville	77,236	Norway	4,974	Cape Girardeau	8,475
Southbridge	12,592	Owosso	9,639	Carrollton	3,452
South Hadley	4,894	Petoskey	4,778	Carterville	4,539
Spencer	6,740	Pontiac	14,532	Carthage	9,483
Springfield	88,926	Port Huron	18,863	Caruthersville	3,655
Stoneham	7,090	Red Jacket	4,211	Charleston	3,144
Stoughton	6,316	River Rouge	4,163	Chillicothe	6,265

Clinton	4,992
Columbia	9,662
De Soto	4,721
Excelsior Springs.	3,909
Flat River	5,112
Fulton	5,228
Hannibal	18,341
Independence	9,859
Jefferson	11,850
Joplin	32,073
Kansas City	248,381
Kennett	3,033
Kirksville	6,347
Kirkwood	4,171
Lexington	5,242
Louisiana	4,454
Macon	3,584
Maplewood	4,976
Marceline	3,920
Marshall	4,869
Maryville	4,762
Mexico	5,939
Moberly	10,923
Monette	4,177
Neosho	3,661
Nevada	7,176
Poplar Bluffs	6,916
Richmond	3,664
St. Charles	9,437
St. Joseph	77,403
St. Louis	687,029
Sedalia	17,822
Sikeston	3,327
Slater	3,258
Springfield	35,201
Trenton	5,656
Warrensburg	4,689
Washington	3,670
Webb	11,817
Webster Groves	7,080
Wellston	7,312

MONTANA.

Anaconda	10,151
Billings	10,031
Bozeman	5,107
Butte	39,165
Deer Lodge	2,570
Glendive	2,428
Great Falls	13,948
Hamilton	3,240
Havre	3,624
Helena	12,515
Kalispell	5,549
Lewiston	2,992
Livingston	5,359
Miles City	4,697
Missoula	12,369
Red Lodge	4,860
Walkerville	2,491

NEBRASKA.

Alliance	3,105
Beatrice	9,356
Benson	3,170
Columbus	5,014
Fairbury	5,294
Falls City	3,255
Fremont	8,718
Grand Island	10,326
Hastings	9,338
Holdredge	3,059
Kearney	6,202
Lincoln	43,973
McCook	3,765
Nebraska City	5,488
Norfolk	6,025
North Platte	4,793
Omaha	124,096
Plattsmouth	4,287
South Omaha	26,259
University Place	3,200
York	6,235

NEVADA.

Carson City	2,466
Ely	2,055
Reno	10,867
Sparks	2,500
Virginia City	2,244

NEW HAMPSHIRE.

Berlin	11,780
Claremont	7,529
Concord	21,497
Conway	3,413
Derry	5,123
Dover	13,247
Exeter	4,897
Franklin	6,132
Haverhill	3,498
Keene	10,068
Laconia	19,183
Lancaster	3,054
Lebanon	5,718
Littleton	3,053
Manchester	70,063
Milford	2,932
Nashua	26,005
Newmarket	3,348
Newport	3,765
Pembroke	3,062
Portsmouth	11,269
Rochester	8,868
Somersworth	6,704

NEW JERSEY.

Asbury Park	10,150
Atlantic City	46,150
Bayonne	55,545
Bloomfield	15,070
Boonton	4,930
Bordentown	4,250
Bound Brook	3,970
Bridgeton	14,209
Burlington	8,336
Camden	94,538
Carlstadt	3,807
Cliffside Park	3,334
Collingswood	4,795
Dover	7,468
East Newark	3,163
East Orange	34,371
East Rutherford	4,275
Elizabeth	73,409
Englewood	9,924
Fort Lee	4,472
Freehold	3,233
Garfield	10,213
Glen Ridge	3,260
Gloucester	9,462
Guttenberg	5,647
Hackensack	14,050
Haddonfield	4,142
Hammonton	5,088
Harrison	14,498
Hawthorne	3,400
Hoboken	70,324
Irvington	11,877
Jersey City	267,779
Kearny	18,659
Keyport	3,554
Lambertville	4,657
Lodi	4,138
Long Branch	13,298
Madison	4,658
Millville	12,461
Montclair	21,550
Morristown	12,507
Newark	347,469
New Brunswick	23,388
Newton	4,467
North Plainfield	6,117
Nutley	6,009
Orange	29,630
Passaic	54,773
Paterson	125,600
Perth Amboy	32,121
Phillipsburg	13,903
Plainfield	20,550
Pleasantville	4,390
Princeton	5,136
Rahway	9,337
Raritan	3,672
Red Bank	7,398
Ridgewood	5,416
Roosevelt	5,786
Roselle Park	3,138
Rutherford	7,045
Salem	6,614
Secaucus	4,740
Somerville	5,060
South Amboy	7,007
South Orange	6,014
South River	4,772
Summit	7,500
Trenton	96,815
Union	21,023
Vineland	5,282
Wallington	3,448
Washington	3,567
Westfield	6,420
West Hoboken	35,403
West New York	13,560
West Orange	10,980
Woodbury	4,642

NEW MEXICO.

Albuquerque	11,020
Artesia	1,883
Carlsbad	1,736
Clovis	3,255
Deming	1,864
Gallup	2,204
Las Cruces	3,836
Las Vegas (city)	3,755
Las Vegas (town)	3,179
Portales	1,292
Raton	4,539
Roswell	6,172
Santa Fe	5,072
Silver City	3,217
Socorro	1,560
Tucumcari	2,526

NEW YORK.

Albany	100,253
Albion	5,016
Amsterdam	31,267
Auburn	34,668
Baldwinsville	3,099
Ballston Spa	4,139
Batavia	11,613
Bath	3,884
Binghamton	48,443
Brockport	3,579
Buffalo	423,715
Canandaigua	7,217
Canastota	3,247
Carthage	3,563
Catskill	5,296
Cohoes	24,709
Corning	13,730
Cortland	11,504
Dansville	3,938
Depew	3,921
Dobbs Ferry	3,455
Dunkirk	17,221
East Syracuse	3,274
Ellenville	3,114
Elmira	37,176
Fairport	3,112
Fishkill Landing	3,902
Fort Edward	3,762
Frankfort	3,303
Fredonia	5,285
Freeport	4,836
Fulton	10,480
Geneva	12,446
Glens Falls	15,243
Gloversville	20,642
Goshen	3,081
Gouverneur	4,123
Granville	3,920
Green Island	4,737
Greenport	3,089
Hastings-Upon-Hudson	4,552
Haverstraw	5,669
Hempstead	4,964
Herkimer	7,520
Hoosick Falls	5,532
Hornell	13,617
Hudson	11,417
Hudson Falls	5,189
Ilion	6,588
Ithaca	14,802
Jamestown	31,297
Johnstown	10,447
Kingston	25,908
Lackawanna	14,549
Lancaster	4,364
Leroy	3,771
Lestershire	3,776
Little Falls	12,273
Lockport	17,970
Lyons	4,460
Malone	6,467
Mamaroneck	5,699
Matteawan	6,727
Mechanicsville	6,634
Medina	5,683
Middletown	15,313
Mount Vernon	30,919
New Rochelle	28,867
New York	4,766,883
Newark	6,227
Newburgh	27,805
Niagara Falls	30,445
North Tarrytown	5,421
North Tonawanda	11,955
Norwich	7,422
Nyack	4,619
Ogdensburg	15,933
Olean	14,743
Oneida	8,317
Oneonta	9,491
Ossining	11,480
Oswego	23,368
Owego	4,633
Patchogue	3,824
Peekskill	15,245
Penn Yan	4,597
Perry	4,388
Plattsburg	11,138
Port Chester	12,809
Port Jervis	9,564
Potsdam	4,036
Poughkeepsie	27,936
Rensselaer	10,711
Rochester	218,149
Rockville Center	3,667
Rome	20,497
Rye	3,964
Sag Harbor	3,408
Salamanca	5,792
Saranac Lake	4,983
Saratoga Springs	12,693
Saugerties	3,929
Schenectady	72,826
Seneca Falls	6,588
Solvay	5,139
Syracuse	137,249
Tarrytown	5,600
Tonawanda	8,290
Troy	76,813
Tupper Lake	3,067
Utica	74,419
Walden	4,004
Walton	3,103
Wappingers Falls	3,195
Warsaw	3,206
Waterford	3,245
Waterloo	3,931
Watertown	26,730
Watervliet	15,074
Waverly	4,855
Wellsville	4,382
White Plains	15,949
Whitehall	4,917
Yonkers	79,803

NORTH CAROLINA.

Asheville	18,762
Burlington	4,808
Charlotte	34,014
Concord	8,715
Durham	18,241
Elizabeth City	8,412
Fayetteville	7,045
Gastonia	5,759
Goldsboro	6,107
Greensboro	15,896
Greenville	4,101
Henderson	4,503
Hickory	3,716
High Point	9,525
Kinston	6,995
Lenoir	3,364
Lexington	4,163
Monroe	4,082
Mooresville	3,400
Mount Airy	3,844
Newbern	9,961
Oxford	3,019
Raleigh	19,218
Reidsville	4,829
Rocky Mount	8,051
Salem	5,533
Salisbury	7,153
Shelby	3,127
Statesville	4,599
Tarboro	4,129
Thomasville	3,877
Washington	6,211
Wilmington	25,748
Wilson	6,717
Winston	17,167

NORTH DAKOTA.

Bismarck	5,443
Devils Lake	5,157
Dickinson	3,678
Fargo	14,331
Grand Forks	12,478
Jamestown	4,358
Mandan	2,873
Minot	6,188
Valley City	4,606
Williston	3,124

OHIO.

Akron	69,067
Alliance	15,083
Ashland	6,795
Ashtabula	18,266
Athens	5,463
Barberton	9,410
Barnesville	4,233
Bellaire	12,946
Bellefontaine	8,238
Bellevue	5,209
Bowling Green	5,222
Bridgeport	2,974
Bryan	3,641
Bucyrus	8,122
Byesville	3,156
Cambridge	11,327
Canal Dover	6,621
Canton	50,217
Carthage	3,618
Celina	3,493
Chillicothe	14,508
Cincinnati	363,591
Circleville	6,744
Cleveland	560,663
Columbus	181,511
Conneaut	8,319
Coshocton	9,603
Crestline	3,807
Crooksville	3,028
Cuyahoga Falls	4,020
Dayton	116,577
Defiance	7,327
Delaware	9,076
Delphos	5,038
Dennison	4,008
East Cleveland	9,179
East Liverpool	20,387
East Palestine	3,537
East Youngstown	4,972
Eaton	3,187
Elmwood Place	3,423
Elyria	14,825
Findlay	14,858
Fostoria	9,597
Fremont	9,939
Galion	7,214
Gallipolis	5,560
Girard	3,736
Greenfield	4,228
Greenville	6,237
Hamilton	35,279
Hillsboro	4,296
Ironton	13,147
Jackson	5,468
Kent	4,488
Kenton	7,185
Lakewood	15,181

Lancaster	13,093	Norman	3,724
Lima	30,508	Nowata	3,672
Lisbon	3,084	Oklahoma City	64,205
Lockland	3,439	Okmulgee	4,176
Logan	4,850	Perry	3,133
Loudon	3,530	Sapulpa	8,283
Lorain	28,883	Shawnee	12,474
Madisonville	5,193	Stillwater	3,444
Mansfield	20,768	Sulphur	3,684
Marietta	12,923	Tulsa	18,182
Marion	18,232	Vinita	4,082
Martins Ferry	9,133	Wagoner	4,018
Marysville	3,576		
Massillon	13,879	**OREGON.**	
Miamisburg	4,271		
Middleport	3,194	Albany	4,275
Middletown	13,152	Ashland	5,020
Mingo Junction	4,049	Astoria	9,599
Mount Vernon	9,087	Baker City	6,742
Napoleon	4,007	Corvallis	4,552
Nelsonville	6,082	Eugene	9,009
New Philadelphia	8,542	Grants Pass	3,897
Newark	25,404	LaGrande	4,843
Newburgh	5,813	Medford	8,840
Niles	8,361	Oregon City	4,287
Norwalk	7,858	Pendleton	4,460
Norwood	16,185	Portland	207,214
Oberlin	4,365	Roseburg	4,738
Orrville	3,191	St. Johns	4,872
Painesville	5,501	Salem	14,094
Piqua	13,388	The Dalles	4,880
Pomeroy	4,023		
Port Clinton	2,007	**PENNSYLVANIA.**	
Portsmouth	23,481		
Ravenna	5,310	Allentown	51,913
Reading	3,985	Altoona	52,127
Rockport	2,179	Ambridge	5,205
St. Bernard	5,002	Apollo	3,006
St. Marys	5,732	Archbald	7,194
Salem	8,943	Ashland	6,855
Sandusky	19,989	Ashley	5,601
Shelby	4,903	Athens	3,796
Sidney	6,607	Avalon	4,317
Springfield	46,921	Avoca	4,634
Steubenville	22,391	Bangor	5,369
Struthers	3,370	Barnesboro	3,535
Tiffin	11,894	Beaver	3,456
Toledo	168,497	Beaver Falls	12,191
Toronto	4,271	Bellefonte	4,145
Troy	6,122	Bellevue	6,322
Uhrichsville	4,761	Berwick	5,357
Upper Sandusky	3,779	Bethlehem	12,837
Urbana	7,739	Blairsville	3,572
Van Wert	7,157	Blakely	5,345
Wadsworth	8,073	Bloomsburg	7,413
Wapakoneta	5,349	Brackenridge	2,134
Warren	11,081	Braddock	19,357
Washington Court House	7,277	Bradford	14,544
Wellston	6,875	Bridgeport	3,860
Wellsville	7,769	Bristol	3,256
Wilmington	4,491	Brookville	3,003
Wooster	6,136	Butler	20,728
Xenia	8,706	Canonsburg	3,891
Youngstown	79,066	Carbondale	17,040
Zanesville	28,026	Carlisle	10,303
		Carnegie	10,009
OKLAHOMA.		Carrick	6,117
		Catasauqua	5,250
Ada	4,349	Chambersburg	11,800
Altus	4,821	Charleroi	9,615
Alva	2,688	Chester	38,537
Anadarko	3,439	Clairton	2,326
Ardmore	8,618	Clearfield	6,851
Bartlesville	6,181	Clifton Heights	3,155
Blackwell	3,266	Coaldale	5,154
Chickasha	10,320	Coatesville	11,084
Coalgate	3,255	Columbia	11,454
Durant	5,330	Connellsville	12,845
El Reno	7,872	Conshohocken	7,480
Elk	3,165	Coraopolis	5,252
Enid	13,799	Corry	5,991
Frederick	3,027	Coudersport	3,100
Guthrie	11,654	Crafton	4,583
Hobart	3,845	Danville	7,517
Hugo	4,582	Darby	6,305
Lawton	7,788	Dickson City	9,331
McAlester	12,954	Penora	8,174
Mangum	3,667	Dorranceton	4,046
Muskogee	25,278	Downington	3,326
		Doylestown	3,304
		Dubois	12,623

Dunmore	17,615	New Castle	36,280
Duquesne	15,727	New Kensington	7,707
Duryea	7,487	Norristown	27,875
East Conemaugh	5,046	North Braddock	11,824
East Mauch Chunk	3,548	Northampton	8,729
East Pittsburgh	5,615	Northumberland	3,517
East Stroudsburg	3,330	Oakmont	2,436
Easton	28,523	Oil City	15,657
Edwardsville	8,407	Old Forge	11,324
Ellwood City	3,902	Olyphant	8,505
Emaus	3,501	Parsons	4,338
Ephrata	3,192	Patton	3,907
Erie	66,525	Pen Argyl	3,967
Etna	5,830	Philadelphia	1,549,008
Exeter	3,537	Phillipsburg	3,585
Ford City	4,850	Phoenixville	10,743
Forest City	5,749	Pitcairn	4,975
Frackville	5,118	Pittsburgh	533,905
Franklin	9,767	Pittston	16,267
Freedom	3,069	Plymouth	16,996
Freeland	6,197	Pottstown	15,599
Galeton	4,027	Pottsville	20,236
Gallitzin	2,504	Quakertown	3,801
Gettysburg	4,030	Rankin	6,342
Gilberton	5,401	Reading	96,071
Girardville	4,396	Renovo	4,621
Glassport	5,540	Reynoldsville	3,189
Greater Punxsutawney	9,058	Ridgway	5,408
Greensburg	13,012	Rochester	5,903
Greenville	5,909	Royersford	3,073
Grove City	2,674	St. Clair (Allegheny)	5,640
Hanover	7,057	St. Clair (Schuylkill)	6,455
Harrisburg	64,186	St. Marys	6,436
Hazleton	25,452	Sayre	6,426
Hollidaysburg	3,734	Schuylkill Haven	4,747
Homestead	18,713	Scottdale	5,456
Huntingdon	6,861	Scranton	129,867
Indiana	5,749	Sewickley	4,479
Jeannette	8,077	Shamokin	19,588
Jermyn	3,158	Sharon	15,270
Jersey Shore	5,381	Sharpsburg	8,153
Johnsonburg	4,334	Sharpsville	3,634
Johnstown	55,482	Shenandoah	25,774
Juniata	5,285	Shippensburg	3,457
Kane	6,626	Slatington	4,454
Kingston	6,449	South Bethlehem	19,973
Kittanning	4,311	South Brownsville	3,943
Knoxville	5,651	South Fork	4,592
Lancaster	47,227	South Sharon	10,190
Lansford	8,321	South Williamsport	3,734
Lansdale	3,551	Steelton	14,246
Lansdowne	4,066	Stroudsburg	4,379
Larksville	9,288	Summit Hill	4,209
Latrobe	8,777	Sunbury	13,770
Lebanon	19,240	Susquehanna	3,478
Leechburg	3,624	Swissvale	7,381
Lehighton	5,316	Swoyersville	5,396
Lewisburg	3,081	Tamaqua	9,462
Lewistown	8,166	Tarentum	7,414
Lockhaven	7,772	Taylor	9,060
Luzerne	5,426	Throop	5,133
McAdoo	3,389	Titusville	8,533
McKees Rocks	14,702	Towanda	4,281
McKeesport	42,694	Turtle Creek	4,095
Mahanoy City	15,936	Tyrone	7,176
Mauch Chunk	2,952	Union City	3,684
Mayfield	3,662	Uniontown	13,344
Meadville	12,780	Vandergrift	3,876
Mechanicsburg	4,469	Vandergrift Hgts.	3,438
Media	3,562	Warren	11,080
Meyersdale	3,741	Washington	18,779
Middletown	5,374	Waynesboro	7,199
Millvale	7,861	Waynesburg	3,545
Milton	7,460	Wellsboro	3,183
Miners Mills	3,159	West Berwick	5,512
Minersville	7,240	West Chester	11,767
Monaca	3,376	West Hazleton	4,715
Monessen	11,775	West Homestead	3,009
Monongahela	7,598	West Pittston	6,848
Moosic	3,964	Wilkes-Barre	67,105
Mount Carmel	17,532	Wilkinsburg	18,924
Mount Oliver	4,241	Williamsport	31,860
Mount Pleasant	5,812	Wilmerding	6,133
Mount Union	3,338	Windber	8,013
Munhall	5,185	Winton	5,280
Nanticoke	18,877	Wyoming	3,010
Nazareth	3,978	York	44,750
New Brighton	8,329		

RHODE ISLAND.

Bristol	8,565
Burrillville	7,878
Central Falls	22,754
Coventry	5,848
Cranston	21,107
Cumberland	10,107
East Greenwich	3,420
East Providence	15,808
Johnston	5,935
Lincoln	9,825
Newport	27,149
North Kingstown	4,048
North Providence	5,407
Pawtucket	51,622
Providence	224,326
Scituate	3,493
South Kingstown	5,176
Tiverton	4,632
Warren	6,585
Warwick	26,629
Westerly	8,696
Woonsocket	38,125

SOUTH CAROLINA.

Abbeville	4,459
Aiken	3,911
Anderson	9,654
Camden	3,569
Charleston	58,833
Chester	4,754
Clinton	3,272
Columbia	26,319
Darlington	3,789
Florence	7,057
Gaffney	4,767
Georgetown	5,530
Greenville	15,741
Greenwood	6,614
Laurens	4,818
Marion	3,844
Newberry	5,028
Orangeburg	5,906
Rock Hill	7,216
Spartanburg	17,517
Sumter	8,109
Union	5,623

SOUTH DAKOTA.

Aberdeen	10,753
Deadwood	3,653
Huron	5,791
Lead	8,392
Madison	3,137
Mitchell	6,515
Pierre	3,656
Rapid City	3,854
Redfield	3,060
Sioux Falls	14,094
Watertown	7,010
Yankton	3,787

TENNESSEE.

Bristol	7,148
Chattanooga	44,604
Clarksville	8,548
Cleveland	5,549
Columbia	5,754
Dyersburg	4,149
Fayetteville	3,439
Harriman	3,061
Humboldt	3,446
Jackson	15,779
Johnson City	8,502
Knoxville	36,346
Lebanon	3,659
LeNoir City	3,392
Memphis	131,105
Morristown	4,007
Murfreesboro	4,679
Nashville	110,364
Paris	3,881
Park City	5,126
Rockwood	3,660
Tullahoma	3,049
Union City	4,389

UTAH.

Brigham	8,685
Eureka	3,416
Logan	7,522
Murray	4,057
Ogden	25,580
Park City	3,439
Provo City	8,925
Salt Lake City	92,777
Spanish Fork	3,464
Springville	3,356

TEXAS.

Abilene	9,204
Amarillo	9,957
Austin	29,860
Ballinger	3,536
Bay City	3,156
Beaumont	20,640
Beeville	3,269
Belton	4,164
Big Spring	4,102
Bonham	4,844
Brenham	4,718
Brownsville	10,517
Brownwood	6,697
Bryan	4,132
Cameron	3,263
Childress	3,818
Cleburne	10,364
Coleman	3,046
Corpus Christi	8,222
Corsicana	9,749
Crockett	3,947
Cuero	3,109
Dallas	92,104
Denison	13,632
Denton	4,732
Eagle Pass	3,536
El Paso	39,279
Ennis	5,669
Fort Worth	73,312
Gainesville	7,624
Galveston	36,981
Georgetown	3,096
Gonzales	3,139
Greenville	8,850
Hillsboro	6,115
Houston	78,800
Houston Heights	6,984
Laredo	14,855
Longview	5,155
McKinney	4,714
Marlin	3,878
Marshall	11,452
Mineral Wells	3,950
Mount Pleasant	3,137
Nacogdoches	3,369
Navasota	3,284
New Braunfels	3,165
Orange	5,527
Palestine	10,482
Paris	11,269
Port Arthur	7,663
Quanah	3,127
San Angelo	10,321
San Antonio	96,614
San Marcos	4,071
Seguin	3,116
Sherman	12,412
Smithville	3,167
Stamford	3,902
Sulphur Springs	5,151
Sweetwater	4,176
Taylor	5,314
Teague	3,288
Temple	10,993
Terrell	7,050
Texarkana	9,790
Tyler	10,400
Uvalde	3,998
Vernon	3,195
Victoria	3,673
Waco	26,425
Waxahachie	6,205
Weatherford	5,074
Wichita Falls	8,200
Yoakum	4,657

VERMONT.

Barre	10,734
Barton (town)	3,346
Bennington	6,211
Fellows Falls	4,883
Brattleboro	6,517
Burlington	20,468
Derby (town)	3,639
Fair Haven (town)	3,095
Hardwick (town)	3,201
Hartford	4,179
Lyndon (town)	3,204
Montpelier	7,856
Newport (town)	3,684
Northfield (town)	2,226
Poultney (town)	2,644
Randolph (town)	3,191
Rutland	13,546
St. Albans	6,381
St. Johnsbury	6,693
Springfield	3,250
Swanton (town)	3,628
Waterbury (town)	3,373
West Rutland	3,427
Winooski	4,520

VIRGINIA.

Alexandria	15,329
Bristol	6,247
Buena Vista	3,245
Charlottesville	6,765
Clifton Forge	5,748
Covington	4,234
Danville	19,020
Fredericksburg	5,874
Hampton	5,505
Harrisonburg	4,879
Lynchburg	29,494
Martinsville	3,368
Newport News	20,205
Norfolk	67,452
Petersburg	24,127
Portsmouth	33,190
Pulaski	4,807
Radford	4,202
Richmond	127,628
Roanoke	34,874
Salem	3,849
South Boston	3,516
Staunton	10,604
Suffolk	7,008
Winchester	5,864
Wytheville	3,054

WASHINGTON.

Aberdeen	13,660
Anacortes	4,168
Bellingham	24,298
Centralia	7,311
Chehalis	4,507
Ellensburg	4,209
Everett	24,814
Hillyard	3,276
Hoquiam	8,171
North Yakima	14,082
Olympia	6,996
Port Townsend	4,181
Puyallup	4,544
Roslyn	3,126
Seattle	237,194
Snohomish	3,244
South Bend	3,023
Spokane	104,402
Tacoma	83,743
Vancouver	9,300
Walla Walla	19,364
Wenatchee	4,050

WEST VIRGINIA.

Benwood	4,976
Bluefield	11,188
Charleston	22,996
Chester	3,184
Clarksburg	9,201
Elkins	5,260
Fairmont	9,711
Grafton	7,563
Hinton	3,656
Huntington	31,161
Keyser	3,705
Martinsburg	10,698
Morgantown	9,150
Moundsville	8,918
Parkersburg	17,842
Princeton	3,027
Richwood	3,061
Wellsburg	4,189
Wheeling	41,641
Williamson	3,561

WISCONSIN.

Antigo	7,196
Appleton	16,773
Ashland	11,594
Baraboo	6,324
Beaver Dam	6,758
Beloit	15,125
Berlin	4,636
Burlington	3,212
Chippewa Falls	8,893
Cudahy	3,691
Depere	4,477
Eau Claire	18,310
Fond du Lac	18,797
Fort Atkinson	3,877
Grand Rapids	6,521
Green Bay	25,236
Janesville	13,894
Kaukauna	4,717
Kenosha	21,371
LaCrosse	30,417
Lake Geneva	3,079
Madison	25,531
Manitowoc	13,027
Marinette	14,610
Marshfield	5,783
Menasha	6,081
Menominee	5,036
Merrill	8,659
Milwaukee	373,857
Monroe	4,410
Neenah	5,734
New London	3,383
Oconomowoc	3,054
Oconto	5,629
Oshkosh	33,062
Platteville	4,452
Plymouth	3,094
Port Washington	3,792
Portage	5,440
Prairie du Chien	3,149
Racine	38,002
Rhinelander	5,637
Rice Lake	3,968
Ripon	3,739
Sheboygan	26,398
South Milwaukee	6,092
Sparta	3,973
Stevens Point	8,692
Stoughton	4,761
Sturgeon Bay	4,262
Superior	40,384
Tomah	3,419
Two Rivers	4,850
Washburn	3,830
Watertown	8,829
Waukesha	8,740
Waupun	3,362
Wausau	16,560
Wauwatosa	3,346
West Allis	6,645
Whitewater	3,224

WYOMING.

Casper	2,639
Cheyenne	11,320
Douglas	2,246
Evanston	2,583
Laramie	8,237
Rawlins	4,256
Rock Springs	5,778
Sheridan	8,408

STATISTICS OF CHIEF AMERICAN CITIES.

[From reports of the census bureau.]

INCORPORATION AND AREA.

City.	*Incorp.	†Area.	City.	*Incorp.	†Area.	City.	*Incorp.	†Area.
New York, N. Y.	1653	183,555	Kansas City, Mo.	1853	37,443	Richmond, Va.	1782	6,388
Chicago, Ill.	1837	117,793	Seattle, Wash.	1869	36,162	Paterson, N. J.	1851	5,157
Philadelphia, Pa.	1701	83,349	Indianapolis, Ind.	1831	21,130	Omaha, Neb.	1857	15,400
St. Louis, Mo.	1822	39,277	Providence, R. I.	1832	11,352	Fall River, Mass.	1854	21,723
Boston, Mass.	1822	24,743	Louisville, Ky.	1824	13,230	Dayton, O.	1841	10,061
Cleveland, O.	1836	29,209	Rochester, N. Y.	1834	12,876	Grand Rapids, Mich.	1850	10,731
Baltimore, Md.	1796	19,290	St. Paul, Minn.	1854	33,383	Nashville, Tenn.	1806	10,932
Pittsburgh, Pa.	1816	26,510	Denver, Col.	1859	37,028	Lowell, Mass.	1836	8,308
Detroit, Mich.	1824	26,103	Portland, Ore.	1851	30,975	Cambridge, Mass.	1846	4,014
Buffalo, N. Y.	1832	24,791	Columbus, O.	1816	13,018	Spokane, Wash.	1883	23,539
San Francisco, Cal.	1850	29,760	Toledo, O.	1837	16,025	Bridgeport, Conn.	1836	7,906
Milwaukee, Wis.	1847	14,586	Atlanta, Ga.	1847	16,423	Albany, N. Y.	1686	6,914
Cincinnati, O.	1819	31,893	Oakland, Cal.	1854	29,248	New Bedford, Mass.	1847	12,173
Newark, N. J.	1836	14,826	Worcester, Mass.	1848	23,683	San Antonio, Tex.	1837	22,905
New Orleans, La.	1805	125,440	Syracuse, N. Y.	1848	11,083	Hartford, Conn.	1784	10,956
Washington, D. C.	1802	38,408	New Haven, Conn.	1784	11,460			
Los Angeles, Cal.	1851	63,480	Birmingham, Ala.	1871	30,881	*First incorporation. †Land area		
Minneapolis, Minn.	1867	32,069	Memphis, Tenn.	1849	11,759	in acres in 1910.		
Jersey City, N. J.	1827	8,320	Scranton, Pa.	1866	12,362			

RECEIPTS, PAYMENTS AND DEBTS (1911).

City.	*Receipts.	†Payments.	‡Debt.
New York, N. Y.	$198,194,320	$250,859,736	$1,096,860,999
Chicago, Ill.	66,190,212	62,352,468	93,478,047
Philadelphia, Pa.	39,378,126	44,077,953	114,202,637
St. Louis, Mo.	20,237,211	22,595,123	28,534,587
Boston, Mass.	34,318,967	29,868,708	117,042,089
Cleveland, O.	14,933,821	16,512,506	45,119,760
Baltimore, Md.	13,843,058	15,268,568	64,800,883
Pittsburgh, Pa.	18,498,178	19,650,447	58,413,165
Detroit, Mich.	12,040,388	12,304,523	14,622,630
Buffalo, N. Y.	11,934,794	13,126,381	28,782,418
S. Francisco, Cal.	12,520,600	17,444,202	19,479,350
Milwaukee, Wis.	9,324,290	9,459,677	12,614,543
Cincinnati, O.	13,343,765	15,842,599	63,540,707
Newark, N. J.	12,112,540	13,335,307	39,760,474
Los Angeles, Cal.	13,065,796	16,743,273	25,283,078
New Orleans, La.	8,106,988	8,290,169	42,474,293
Washington, D.C.	13,441,394	12,291,507	11,717,978
Minneapolis, Minn.	8,679,953	9,945,941	20,460,033
Jersey City, N. J.	6,945,666	13,398,808	29,077,984
Seattle, Wash.	13,373,049	17,006,326	33,703,251
Kansas City, Mo.	7,505,002	7,619,958	10,133,261
Indianapolis, Ind.	4,677,126	4,956,152	4,796,523
Providence, R. I.	5,761,132	5,158,206	19,676,651
Louisville, Ky.	6,062,813	6,079,990	13,602,456
Rochester, N. Y.	5,696,488	7,336,647	16,095,546
Denver, Col.	6,571,228	6,661,750	6,910,465
Portland, Ore.	9,019,240	14,872,353	24,951,261
St. Paul, Minn.	4,511,913	4,623,810	12,304,327
Columbus, O.	4,395,941	4,963,387	16,122,714
Toledo, O.	3,738,087	4,002,015	11,366,057
Atlanta, Ga.	3,272,527	4,328,753	6,229,569
Oakland, Cal.	4,317,738	5,246,266	4,952,973
Worcester, Mass.	3,768,219	4,223,734	11,283,378
Birmingham, Ala.	2,003,333	3,152,134	7,760,960
Syracuse, N. Y.	3,415,550	3,591,979	10,272,437
N. Haven, Conn.	2,537,368	2,538,489	4,014,858
Memphis, Tenn.	2,959,793	4,324,884	11,234,640
Scranton, Pa.	1,712,963	1,843,041	3,560,746
Richmond, Va.	3,540,147	3,737,364	11,315,759
Paterson, N. J.	1,993,966	1,959,871	4,474,134
Omaha, Neb.	2,996,489	3,881,714	9,725,843
Fall River, Mass.	2,315,410	2,315,344	7,388,919
Dayton, O.	2,428,946	2,466,727	5,385,588
Gr. Rapids, Mich.	2,434,718	3,005,476	4,101,653
Spokane, Wash.	3,860,779	6,600,352	12,165,266
Nashville, Tenn.	1,952,701	2,308,948	5,979,065
Lowell, Mass.	2,048,212	2,162,689	4,182,276
Cambridge, Mass.	3,208,276	2,683,313	11,457,650
Bridgeport, Conn.	1,715,786	1,685,336	2,145,051
N. Bedford, Mass.	2,457,820	3,274,923	8,440,286
S. Antonio, Tex.	1,406,009	1,419,458	2,941,530
Hartford, Conn.	2,711,951	2,969,785	7,964,361
Albany, N. Y.	2,262,018	2,276,120	5,560,797

*Receipts from revenue. †For cost of government.
‡Outstanding at close of year.

RECEIPTS FROM SPECIAL SOURCES (1910).

City.	*Taxes.	†Licenses.	‡Water.
New York, N. Y.	$141,679,985	$7,163,721	$13,379,677
Chicago, Ill.	35,798,371	9,015,639	5,620,688
Philadelphia, Pa.	21,062,486	3,240,144	4,577,781
St. Louis, Mo.	12,052,177	1,519,396	2,049,810
Boston, Mass.	23,268,661	1,186,862	2,826,467
Cleveland, O.	8,920,779	1,329,587	1,175,469
Baltimore, Md.	8,570,699	1,295,236	1,057,392
Pittsburgh, Pa.	12,610,788	915,187	1,826,787
Detroit, Mich.	6,841,409	869,900	856,620
Buffalo, N. Y.	5,832,916	711,489	969,882
San Francisco, Cal.	8,020,052	1,344,663	1,920
Milwaukee, Wis.	5,428,588	777,940	693,741
Cincinnati, O.	7,984,008	1,120,345	1,138,456
Newark, N. J.	6,276,068	650,985	1,192,996
New Orleans, La.	5,342,826	938,121	892,497
Washington, D. C.	5,339,676	668,935	550,589
Los Angeles, Cal.	6,190,389	781,105	1,140,300
Minneapolis, Minn.	6,038,034	472,131	474,670
Jersey City, N. J.	2,160,471	552,800	1,215,732
Kansas City, Mo.	3,215,128	542,253	989,762
Seattle, Wash.	3,685,087	403,142	763,773
Indianapolis, Ind.	2,685,945	298,947	3,772
Providence, R. I.	3,549,982	318,288	762,970
Louisville, Ky.	3,284,204	547,814	762,550
Rochester, N. Y.	3,373,956	233,361	595,509
St. Paul, Minn.	2,689,333	423,530	483,541
Denver, Col.	4,069,574	425,861	8,892
Portland, Ore.	2,966,303	484,363	644,590
Columbus, O.	2,493,825	269,486	424,921
Toledo, O.	1,884,449	307,275	297,918
Atlanta, Ga.	1,538,473	251,998	349,108
Oakland, Cal.	1,653,352	288,388	....
Worcester, Mass.	2,378,771	177,120	421,827
Syracuse, N. Y.	2,143,705	174,395	348,887
New Haven, Conn.	1,959,325	185,897	....
Birmingham, Ala.	436,118	333,176	6,042
Memphis, Tenn.	1,632,213	93,369	397,324
Scranton, Pa.	1,060,658	273,717	....
Richmond, Va.	1,746,583	176,263	233,367
Paterson, N. J.	1,281,781	197,276	....
Omaha, Neb.	1,938,601	284,868	....
Fall River, Mass.	1,639,624	154,334	220,631
Dayton, O.	1,393,209	161,986	152,276
Grand Rapids, Mich.	975,873	71,778	193,322
Nashville, Tenn.	1,055,182	55,200	260,940
Lowell, Mass.	1,540,874	137,610	220,736
Cambridge, Mass.	2,173,511	4,695	380,253
Spokane, Wash.	1,235,899	242,029	472,646
Bridgeport, Conn.	1,221,916	154,854	....
Albany, N. Y.	1,318,670	134,133	357,568

*General and special property taxes, business taxes and poll taxes. †Including permits. ‡Water supply systems.

LICENSE RECEIPTS SPECIFIED (1910).

City.	Liquor.	Business.	Dog.	Gen'l.	Permits.
New York.	$5,864,744	$854,044	....	$53,099	$591,834
Chicago	7,253,076	849,118	$122,970	602,220	188,255
Philadelphia.	1,953,440	117,449	....	14,748	154,507
St. Louis.	1,126,750	218,908	23,945	121,454	28,339
Boston	1,088,809	60,475	29,091	8,847	....
Cleveland	1,301,127	14,558	4,700	3,410	5,792
Baltimore	1,144,821	71,442	23,601	38,296	1,076
Pittsburgh	766,181	65,623	6,390	76,993	....

City.	Liquor.	Business.	Dog.	Gen'l.P'rmits.
Detroit	791,745	36,576	16,944	2,805	21,830
Buffalo	609,954	71,368	11,339	15,481	12,347
S. Francisco.	1,078,955	209,795	9,018	9,556	37,339
Milwaukee	429,450	290,423	24,588	2,180	31,299
Cincinnati	968,716	84,484	4,758	49,553	13,034
Newark	575,340	49,555	2,363	......	23,727
New Orleans.	654,519	251,865	2,904	7,743	11,090
Washington.	452,092	143,818	21,922	6,124	44,979
Los Angeles.	406,614	278,260	18,305	12,627	65,300
Minneapolis.	407,680	24,628	5,895	7,344	16,494
Jersey City.	507,344	20,011	2,322	......	23,122
Kansas City.	310,250	173,970	15,868	28,182	13,983
Seattle	320,218	53,874	8,315	......	20,736
Indianapolis..	196,084	27,580	14,360	44,579	16,314
Providence	266,800	35,629	11,103	2,584	2,172
Louisville	353,574	151,989	8,872	33,379	......
Rochester	209,934	12,963	7,985	2,479	......
St. Paul	397,920	24,584	654	......	6,072
Denver	295,655	101,367	8,076	7,402	13,361
Portland, Ore.	349,288	103,292	16,872	4,663	10,248
Columbus	225,970	11,100	2,198	20,669	9,549
Toledo	299,442	6,560	......	......	1,273
Atlanta	......	248,303	1,233	2,462	......
Oakland	193,155	60,485	9,904	2,676	22,168
Worcester	160,463	11,828	3,242	1,587	......
Syracuse	150,124	15,344	4,456	1,469	3,002
New Haven.	166,621	5,189	2,631	1,598	9,859
Birmingham..	......	318,551	1,462	8,949	9,214
Memphis	......	86,148	......	......	7,221
Scranton	250,779	13,103	3,673	331	5,831
Richmond	75,000	93,680	7,344	244	......
Paterson	169,000	14,213	6,040	......	8,023
Omaha	260,170	16,363	3,691	......	4,644
Fall River..	144,188	8,761	......	1,385	......
Dayton	144,587	5,167	801	8,591	2,840
Gr. Rapids..	48,475	16,433	4,478	......	2,392
Nashville	1,500	55,045	......	......	1,655
Lowell	128,292	7,990	......	1,057	271
Cambridge	50	3,490	......	1,155	......
Spokane	214,074	21,460	2,128	3,069	1,298
Bridgeport	144,687	2,160	2,152	1,194	4,631
Albany	124,775	5,075	3,352	884	67

PAYMENTS FOR SPECIFIED PURPOSES (1910).

City.	Courts.	Police.	Fire prot'n.
New York, N. Y.	$6,181,837	$16,396,347	$9,383,601
Chicago, Ill.	1,857,454	6,457,631	3,091,610
Philadelphia, Pa.	1,141,120	4,556,004	1,489,241
St. Louis, Mo.	634,316	2,011,826	1,331,267
Boston, Mass.	816,318	2,224,177	1,570,665
Cleveland, O.	340,024	829,735	763,714
Baltimore, Md.	225,149	1,290,619	894,398
Pittsburgh, Pa.	464,485	1,102,443	999,988
Detroit, Mich.	312,882	814,917	821,917
Buffalo, N. Y.	295,734	1,000,518	960,471
San Francisco, Cal.	495,352	1,481,894	1,438,964
Milwaukee, Wis.	298,684	592,026	740,141
Cincinnati, O.	308,030	850,502	846,341
Newark, N. J.	199,242	820,370	618,345
New Orleans, La.	241,751	415,584	486,593
Washington, D. C.	313,736	1,116,445	649,534
Los Angeles, Cal.	249,736	482,489	362,088
Minneapolis, Minn.	185,219	373,455	544,882
Jersey City, N. J.	29,203	631,640	358,759
Kansas City, Mo.	13,106	499,302	385,946
Seattle, Wash.	8,973	416,933	403,010
Indianapolis, Ind.	4,027	384,239	406,239
Providence, R. I.	10,796	455,113	464,799
Louisville, Ky.	26,631	429,285	355,452
Rochester, N. Y.	25,514	387,733	451,165
St. Paul, Minn.	19,901	281,796	371,181
Denver, Col.	238,419	273,494	363,142
Portland, Ore.	2,989	259,359	346,681
Columbus, O.	25,622	255,346	311,738
Toledo, O.	15,580	204,594	261,049
Atlanta, Ga.	4,358	240,232	200,340
Oakland, Cal.	12,690	186,192	205,330
Worcester, Mass.	......	205,315	253,072
Syracuse, N. Y.	20,990	195,958	225,483
New Haven, Conn.	34,909	263,524	247,521
Birmingham, Ala.	6,879	124,378	160,541
Memphis, Tenn.	10,726	201,184	184,164
Scranton, Pa.	2,000	106,016	98,869
Richmond, Va.	38,333	154,172	161,807
Paterson, N. J.	8,814	177,403	220,905
Omaha, Neb.	4,868	157,635	442,714

City.	Courts.	Police.	Fire prot'n.
Fall River, Mass.	......	169,480	164,482
Dayton, O.	11,883	178,439	183,244
Grand Rapids, Mich.	12,389	117,256	175,366
Nashville, Tenn.	3,590	120,236	143,176
Lowell, Mass.	......	153,921	175,162
Cambridge, Mass.	......	168,948	128,483
Spokane, Wash.	5,125	102,602	169,560
Bridgeport, Conn.	12,361	134,922	179,173
Albany, N. Y.	16,160	194,162	185,203

City.	Health.	Street cleaning.	Highways.
New York, N. Y.	$2,879,773	$8,224,192	$15,678,136
Chicago, Ill.	475,074	957,225	2,484,797
Philadelphia, Pa.	523,374	1,227,795	2,692,385
St. Louis, Mo.	177,816	748,396	1,654,804
Boston, Mass.	457,861	505,459	2,262,505
Cleveland, O.	159,336	223,665	914,074
Baltimore, Md.	161,334	383,951	1,122,498
Pittsburgh, Pa.	251,062	424,614	1,361,550
Detroit, Mich.	116,767	378,159	1,091,298
Buffalo, N. Y.	114,562	218,065	1,032,164
San Francisco, Cal.	116,148	255,529	834,724
Milwaukee, Wis.	76,299	208,344	556,176
Cincinnati, O.	78,019	225,981	1,052,338
Newark, N. J.	204,886	222,363	586,424
New Orleans, La.	173,700	203,419	486,968
Washington, D. C.	151,229	294,867	1,191,301
Los Angeles, Cal.	76,473	114,428	778,399
Minneapolis, Minn.	52,973	121,876	738,163
Jersey City, N. J.	35,006	143,486	297,187
Kansas City, Mo.	49,479	220,350	260,677
Seattle, Wash.	119,723	147,199	300,215
Indianapolis, Ind.	46,661	109,899	338,119
Providence, R. I.	77,144	84,893	521,965
Louisville, Ky.	56,942	121,055	335,979
Rochester, N. Y.	56,449	145,438	484,431
St. Paul, Minn.	36,726	97,013	478,785
Denver, Col.	83,900	120,417	532,661
Portland, Ore.	21,483	145,313	260,018
Columbus, O.	29,870	98,837	93,285
Toledo, O.	24,854	56,478	252,076
Atlanta, Ga.	53,887	52,828	232,495
Oakland, Cal.	21,690	71,141	340,322
Worcester, Mass.	53,349	93,643	341,982
Syracuse, N. Y.	78,498	101,127	242,953
New Haven, Conn.	27,027	67,382	235,431
Birmingham, Ala.	32,611	15,573	123,331
Memphis Tenn.	52,876	61,246	296,890
Scranton, Pa.	9,102	34,000	156,487
Richmond, Va.	36,101	36,808	157,471
Paterson, N. J.	19,488	29,988	108,876
Omaha, Neb.	27,661	59,921	196,292
Dayton, O.	15,296	51,955	159,080
Fall River, Mass.	60,649	43,913	232,191
Grand Rapids, Mich.	64,519	25,460	98,552
Nashville, Tenn.	23,709	51,781	150,467
Lowell, Mass.	24,543	42,656	197,927
Cambridge, Mass.	59,889	35,986	232,423
Spokane, Wash.	36,482	64,181	170,048
Bridgeport, Conn.	9,565	48,500	222,838
Albany, N. Y.	20,447	64,598	120,283

City.	*Charities.	†Education.	‡Recrea'n.
New York, N. Y.	$9,944,789	$32,490,598	$3,424,223
Chicago, Ill.	1,823,710	9,942,737	2,734,427
Philadelphia, Pa.	2,640,154	6,443,482	808,192
St. Louis, Mo.	856,451	3,130,227	314,606
Boston, Mass.	1,607,430	4,800,344	1,141,481
Cleveland, O.	597,654	2,976,764	262,489
Baltimore, Md.	664,813	1,937,416	344,640
Pittsburgh, Pa.	516,678	3,141,249	410,612
Detroit, Mich.	354,295	1,877,578	352,519
Buffalo, N. Y.	526,562	1,843,228	271,763
San Francisco, Cal.	699,071	1,771,884	398,596
Milwaukee, Wis.	457,930	1,787,908	169,444
Cincinnati, O.	608,309	1,953,487	160,373
Newark, N. J.	636,728	2,122,343	247,007
New Orleans, La.	209,602	1,015,587	85,251
Washington, D. C.	301,701	2,141,889	291,501
Los Angeles, Cal.	256,488	1,397,453	187,530
Minneapolis, Minn.	152,378	1,725,597	209,920
Jersey City, N. J.	94,690	1,154,742	77,119
Kansas City, Mo.	183,790	1,121,131	200,071
Seattle, Wash.	26,232	1,387,043	142,037
Indianapolis, Ind.	509,990	1,085,178	77,236
Providence, R. I.	129,243	1,042,467	86,509
Louisville, Ky.	234,133	822,008	84,850

City	*Charities.	†Education	‡Recrea'n
Rochester, N Y..	209,470	938,440	179,194
St. Paul, Minn	93,633	928,169	132,127
Denver, Col	267,279	1,223,543	218,270
Portland, Ore	4,863	920,898	76,033
Columbus, O	43,821	789,859	22,552
Toledo, O	33,471	777,671	95,889
Atlanta, Ga	139,765	382,253	53,158
Oakland, Cal.	2,870	686,276	55,098
Worcester, Mass	222,976	842,432	45,882
Syracuse, N Y	155,426	671,164	45,395
New Haven, Conn	114,328	712,476	46,149
Birmingham, Ala	29,910	280,865	11,083
Memphis, Tenn	53,655	394,102	115,853
Scranton, Pa		577,063	16,471
Richmond, Va	76,048	299,452	54,331
Paterson, N J	55,789	538,602	21,253
Omaha, Neb	59	617,866	47,742
Fall River, Mass	158,561	590,946	24,051
Dayton, O .	76,038	527,761	13,077
Grand Rapids, Mich	33,980	552,121	30,069
Nashville, Tenn.	46,761	306,533	39,296
Lowell, Mass ...	132,319	436,065	24,060
Cambridge, Mass ..	87,674	554,609	69,351
Spokane, Wash.	19,291	595,194	38,331
Bridgeport, Conn	112,480	324,818	28,743
Albany, N Y .	49,410	413,168	96,893

*Including hospitals and corrections †Including libraries, art galleries and museums ‡Including parks, playgrounds, baths and public entertainments.

VALUE OF PUBLIC PROPERTIES AND ASSESSED VALUATION (1910).

City	*Property	†Valuation
New York, N. Y.	$1,131,900,028	$8,322,958,952
Chicago, Ill	177,661,753	848,994,536
Philadelphia, Pa	194,173,725	1,458,851,890
St. Louis, Mo .	68,556,028	614,993,752
Boston, Mass	156,062,201	1,409,479,723
Cleveland, O	63,072,831	274,970,605
Baltimore, Md.	50,973,824	682,633,316
Pittsburgh, Pa	90,578,482	755,818,383
Detroit, Mich	45,450,151	372,070,980
Buffalo, N Y	33,816,013	339,801,975
San Francisco, Cal	39,471,922	515,420,989
Milwaukee, Wis	25,980,177	247,573,150
Cincinnati, O ▸	48,194,890	256,253,260
Newark, N J .	50,831,149	345,969,576
New Orleans, La .	32,748,985	230,931,347
Washington, D C	35,048,415	310,346,131
Los Angeles, Cal	37,374,400	290,905,664
Minneapolis, Minn	24,276,754	213,143,434
Jersey City, N J	13,552,716	241,561,118
Kansas City, Mo	25,218,481	149,632,785
Seattle, Wash	27,311,776	205,262,448
Indianapolis, Ind.......	8,236,383	185,714,765
Providence, R I .	16,317,012	259,145,060
Louisville, Ky .	18,299,095	173,780,853
Rochester, N Y	16,063,821	177,864,240
St. Paul, Minn .	17,100,000	133,608,888
Denver, Col	14,088,828	135,467,050
Portland, Ore	17,953,336	231,161,600
Columbus, O .	11,967,632	101,588,930
Toledo, O. .	9,185,462	83,002,390
Atlanta, Ga . ..	10,513,513	120,480,498
Oakland, Cal	12,824,430	107,157,050
Worcester, Mass	13,391,772	141,896,607
Syracuse, N Y .	11,912,277	113,847,973
New Haven, Conn ...	5,630,589	126,825,548
Birmingham, Ala	3,607,543	65,815,026
Memphis, Tenn	12,381,821	92,984,254
Scranton, Pa	2,657,168	72,509,180
Richmond, Va	14,295,258	120,010,973
Paterson, N J	3,786,075	95,243,369
Omaha, Neb	6,847,175	29,155,775
Fall River, Mass .	8,219,851	92,626,570
Dayton, O . .	6,123,129	62,621,280
Grand Rapids, Mich.	5,639,176	83,528,700
Nashville, Tenn	9,954,450	75,896,248
Lowell, Mass	8,916,810	80,094,801
Cambridge, Mass	16,189,886	106,958,135
Spokane, Wash	8,468,594	85,619,405
Bridgeport, Conn	3,675,238	84,724,478
Albany, N Y	8,434,889	93,495,318

*Value of land, buildings and equipment owned by city †Assessed valuation of all real, personal and other property in city.

BASIS OF ASSESSMENT (PER CENT TRUE VALUE), 1910.

City	Real property.	Personal property.
New York, N Y	100	100
Chicago, Ill	33	25
Philadelphia, Pa	100	100
St Louis, Mo	60	40
Boston, Mass	100	100
Cleveland, O	60	60
Baltimore, Md	100	100
Pittsburgh, Pa .	80	80
Detroit, Mich	100	100
Buffalo, N Y	75	75
San Francisco, Cal	50	20
Milwaukee, Wis	60	60
Cincinnati, O .	60	60
Newark, N J	100	100
New Orleans, La	75	75
Washington, D C	67	100
Los Angeles, Cal	50	25
Minneapolis, Minn	50	33
Jersey City, N J	100	100
Kansas City, Mo	50	50
Seattle, Wash	45	45
Indianapolis, Ind	60	60
Providence, R I	100	100
Louisville, Ky.	70	70
Rochester, N Y. .	80	80
St Paul, Minn	69	30
Denver, Col....	50	50
Portland, Ore . .	57	57
Columbus, O. .	60	60
Toledo, O..	60	60
Atlanta, Ga	50	60
Oakland, Cal . .	50	50
Worcester, Mass	100	100
Syracuse, N Y .	88	100
New Haven, Conn	100	100
Birmingham, Ala .	50	50
Memphis, Tenn . . .	60	40
Richmond, Va .	75	75
Paterson, N J	100	100
Omaha, Neb .	15	15
Dayton, O	60	60
Fall River, Mass	100	100
Grand Rapids, Mich	80	80
Nashville, Tenn	75	75
Lowell, Mass .	100	100
Cambridge, Mass	100	100
Spokane, Wash	41	41
Bridgeport, Conn .	100	100
Albany, N Y	100	100

TAX LEVIES AND TAX RATES (1910).

City	Levy	*Rate per $1,000.	†Per capita
New York, N Y	$136,327,740	$17 73	$28 60
Chicago, Ill	37,279,539	13 53	17 06
Philadelphia, Pa	21,465,806	14 66	13 81
St Louis, Mo	11,618,303	11 41	16 91
Boston, Mass	21,627,003	15 05	31 67
Cleveland, O	9,228,210	20 14	16 46
Baltimore, Md .	8,980 284	18 89	16 08
Pittsburgh, Pa	12,291,933	12 93	22.83
Detroit, Mich.	7,390,684	19 86	15 87
Buffalo, N Y	7,920,223	18 67	18 69
San Francisco, Cal	8,488,984	6 65	20 36
Milwaukee, Wis.... ..	6,066,640	14 70	16 23
Cincinnati, O .	7,348,115	17 21	20 21
Newark, N J .	5,862,905	16 72	16 65
New Orleans, La ..	5,353,938	17 25	15 66
Washington, D C	4,655,192	10 28	14 06
Los Angeles, Cal	6,292 631	9 42	19 71
Minneapolis, Minn	5,193,095	11 50	17 23
Jersey City, N J	3,048,766	12 60	11 37
Kansas City, Mo	3,412,748	11 30	13 74
Seattle, Wash .	4,542 073	9 96	19 15
Indianapolis, Ind .	2,881,593	9 24	12 24
Providence, R I	3,843,468	14 70	16 98
Louisville, Ky	3 214,946	12 95	14 36
Rochester, N Y..........	3,410,800	16.06	15.44
St Paul, Minn .	2,786,384	10 68	12 98
Denver, Col	4,505 033	16 63	21 11
Portland, Ore	2,722,663	6 71	13 14
Columbus, O	2,554,807	'15 09	14 08
Toledo, O	2,309,820	16.70	13.71

City.	Levy.	*Rate per $1,000.	†Per capita.
Atlanta, Ga	1,521,764	7.50	9.73
Oakland, Cal	1,648,168	7.69	10.98
Worcester, Mass	2,073,456	14.01	13.63
Syracuse, N. Y	2,159,904	17.58	15.74
New Haven, Conn	2,080,101	16.00	15.19
Birmingham, Ala	658,150	5.99	4.96
Memphis, Tenn	1,627,224	9.71	12.41
Scranton, Pa	1,081,773	11.34	7.92
Richmond, Va	1,696,013	10.50	13.16
Paterson, N. J	1,102,742	11.33	8.59
Omaha, Neb	1,812,268	9.32	14.60
Fall River, Mass	1,539,928	15.84	12.33
Dayton, O	1,495,009	14.32	12.82
Grand Rapids, Mich	1,181,971	11.31	10.49
Nashville, Tenn	1,118,956	11.06	10.14
Lowell, Mass	1,419,796	17.02	12.85
Cambridge, Mass	2,041,587	18.61	18.98
Spokane, Wash	1,499,134	7.18	14.36
Bridgeport, Conn	1,388,842	15.71	13.04
Albany, N. Y	1,403,471	15.39	14.09

*Rate of general property taxes per $1,000 of reported true value. †Per capita of property taxes.

PER CAPITA RECEIPTS, PAYMENTS AND DEBT (1910).

City.	*Receipts.	†Paymts.	‡Debt.
New York, N. Y	$41.49	$50.85	$214.96
Chicago, Ill	29.04	27.58	43.75
Philadelphia, Pa	24.57	27.27	64.73
St. Louis, Mo	28.47	28.04	42.16
Boston, Mass	48.62	44.10	172.13
Cleveland, O	26.05	28.03	76.12
Baltimore, Md	24.43	27.63	111.04
Pittsburgh, Pa	35.25	35.01	105.71
Detroit, Mich	24.39	23.39	29.64
Buffalo, N. Y	25.55	33.29	64.27
San Francisco, Cal	29.37	42.43	41.79
Milwaukee, Wis	22.05	25.21	35.09
Cincinnati, O	37.36	41.39	173.11
Newark, N. J	33.04	31.88	110.18
New Orleans, La	22.36	25.62	108.82
Washington, D. C	34.99	35.04	40.07
Los Angeles, Cal	32.69	49.71	69.34
Minneapolis, Minn	25.83	29.66	58.44
Jersey City, N. J	20.06	21.55	81.99
Kansas City, Mo	28.21	28.93	33.83
Seattle, Wash	48.92	65.06	122.66
Indianapolis, Ind	18.67	19.72	20.94
Providence, R. I	24.61	22.39	87.75
Louisville, Ky	24.22	29.11	59.24
Rochester, N. Y	25.71	27.60	65.84
St. Paul, Minn	20.94	24.36	57.84
Denver, Col	33.95	31.06	29.51
Portland, Ore	32.63	51.86	78.41
Columbus, O	23.17	23.03	87.05
Toledo, O	20.50	20.59	65.51
Atlanta, Ga	18.23	20.20	35.07
Oakland, Cal	26.40	26.02	31.07
Worcester, Mass	24.35	26.66	71.22
Syracuse, N. Y	24.16	26.99	72.70
New Haven, Conn	18.00	19.40	30.56
Birmingham, Ala	9.26	15.60	47.84
Memphis, Tenn	20.64	32.85	78.62
Scranton, Pa	13.25	15.23	26.40
Richmond, Va	22.89	24.70	87.95
Paterson, N. J	15.40	15.94	36.18
Omaha, Neb	25.52	26.22	72.53
Fall River, Mass	18.53	23.89	63.84
Dayton, O	17.74	18.47	44.62
Grand Rapids, Mich	17.03	23.96	32.48
Nashville, Tenn	16.48	16.44	50.55
Lowell, Mass	19.47	18.34	39.45
Cambridge, Mass	27.20	24.17	112.48
Spokane, Wash	23.98	58.72	85.69
Bridgeport, Conn	15.58	16.54	21.55
Albany, N. Y	21.22	22.51	50.87

*Revenue receipts. †Governmental cost payments. ‡Gross debt in 1910.

PER CAPITA PAYMENTS FOR SPECIFIED PURPOSES (1910).

City.	Gvmt.	Police.	Fire.	Health.	Sanitation.
New York, N. Y	$3.14	$3.44	$1.97	$0.60	$2.01
Chicago, Ill	2.55	2.96	1.41	0.22	1.37
Philadelphia, Pa	2.93	2.94	0.96	0.34	1.20
St. Louis, Mo	2.09	2.93	1.65	0.26	1.54
Boston, Mass	3.03	3.32	2.34	0.68	2.44

City.	Gvmt.	Police.	Fire.	Health.	Sanitation.
Cleveland, O	2.16	1.50	1.26	0.28	1.18
Baltimore, Md	1.72	2.31	1.60	0.29	1.32
Pittsburgh, Pa	3.92	2.05	1.87	0.47	1.38
Detroit, Mich	1.80	1.75	1.76	0.25	1.11
Buffalo, N. Y	2.07	2.36	2.27	0.27	1.19
San Francisco, Cal	3.32	3.55	3.45	0.28	1.23
Milwaukee, Wis	1.98	1.58	1.98	0.30	1.84
Cincinnati, O	3.15	2.34	2.33	0.21	1.40
Newark, N. J	2.06	2.36	1.78	0.59	1.53
New Orleans, La	1.76	1.23	1.44	0.51	1.80
Washington, D. Q	2.06	3.37	1.96	9.46	1.95
Los Angeles, Cal	2.84	1.51	1.13	0.24	0.62
Minneapolis, Minn	1.84	1.24	1.81	0.18	0.88
Jersey City, N. J	1.99	2.36	1.34	0.13	0.82
Kansas City, Mo	1.92	2.01	1.55	0.30	1.11
Seattle, Wash	1.83	1.76	1.70	0.50	0.57
Indianapolis, Ind	0.54	1.64	2.00	0.20	1.66
Providence, R. I	1.65	2.03	2.07	0.34	1.10
Louisville, Ky	1.20	1.92	1.59	0.25	1.13
Rochester, N. Y	1.44	1.86	2.17	0.27	1.79
St. Paul, Minn	1.13	1.31	1.73	0.17	0.80
Denver, Col	3.77	1.28	1.70	0.39	0.72
Portland, Ore	0.84	1.25	1.67	0.10	0.86
Columbus, O	0.90	1.41	1.72	0.22	1.11
Toledo, O	0.97	1.21	1.55	0.15	0.59
Atlanta, Ga	0.78	1.55	1.30	0.35	1.55
Oakland, Cal	1.24	1.24	1.37	0.14	0.90
Worcester, Mass	0.92	1.41	1.73	0.37	1.50
Syracuse, N. Y	1.67	1.43	1.61	0.57	1.38
New Haven Conn	1.05	1.97	1.85	0.20	0.75
Birmingham, Ala	0.57	0.94	1.21	0.24	0.63
Memphis, Tenn	0.86	1.53	1.40	0.40	1.12
Scranton, Pa	0.70	0.82	0.76	0.07	0.96
Richmond, Va	1.27	1.21	1.27	0.28	1.05
Paterson, N. J	0.68	1.41	1.76	0.16	0.69
Omaha, Neb	1.17	1.27	3.57	0.22	0.78
Fall River, Mass	0.76	1.42	1.38	0.51	0.89
Dayton, O	0.99	1.53	1.57	0.13	1.02
Grand Rapids, Mich	0.99	1.04	1.56	0.57	0.66
Nashville, Tenn	0.58	1.06	1.30	0.21	0.81
Lowell, Mass	0.92	1.43	1.65	0.23	0.94
Cambridge, Mass	1.08	1.61	1.23	0.57	1.62
Spokane, Wash	1.43	0.98	1.62	0.35	1.41
Bridgeport, Conn	0.80	1.32	1.76	0.09	0.88
Albany, N. Y	1.71	1.94	1.85	0.20	0.74

City.	Highways.	*Charities.	Schools.	†Libraries.	‡Recreation.
New York, N. Y	$3.29	$2.09	$6.45	$0.56	$0.72
Chicago, Ill	1.14	0.83	4.36	0.19	1.26
Philadelphia, Pa	1.74	1.70	3.92	0.24	0.52
St. Louis, Mo	2.41	1.25	4.23	0.23	0.46
Boston, Mass	3.37	2.40	6.59	0.57	1.70
Cleveland, O	1.63	1.07	4.79	0.51	0.47
Baltimore, Md	2.01	1.19	3.34	0.13	0.62
Pittsburgh, Pa	2.55	0.97	5.16	0.73	0.77
Detroit, Mich	2.34	0.76	3.78	0.25	0.76
Buffalo, N. Y	2.44	1.24	3.97	0.38	0.64
San Francisco, Cal	2.00	1.68	4.03	0.22	0.96
Milwaukee, Wis	1.49	1.22	4.41	0.32	9.45
Cincinnati, O	2.89	1.67	5.01	0.36	0.44
Newark, N. J	1.69	1.83	5.79	0.32	0.71
New Orleans, La	1.40	0.62	2.89	0.11	0.25
Washington, D. C	3.60	2.97	6.27	0.29	0.88
Los Angeles, Cal	2.44	0.80	3.77	0.33	0.59
Minneapolis, Minn	2.45	0.51	5.35	0.37	0.70
Jersey City, N. J	1.11	0.35	4.14	0.17	0.29
Kansas City, Mo	1.05	0.74	4.31	0.29	0.81
Seattle, Wash	1.27	0.11	5.29	0.48	0.60
Indianapolis, Ind	1.45	0.47	4.30	0.25	0.33
Providence, R. I	2.33	0.58	4.51	0.14	0.39
Louisville, Ky	1.50	1.05	3.38	0.29	0.38
Rochester, N. Y	2.93	1.01	4.54	...	0.86
St. Paul, Minn	2.23	0.44	4.04	0.28	0.62
Denver, Col	3.40	1.25	5.49	0.25	1.02
Portland, Ore	1.25	0.02	4.29	0.15	0.37
Columbus, O	0.51	0.24	4.21	0.14	0.12
Toledo, O	1.50	0.26	4.45	0.15	6.57
Atlanta, Ga	1.50	0.90	2.92	0.14	0.34
Oakland, Cal	2.27	0.03	4.03	0.34	0.37
Worcester, Mass	2.34	1.53	5.39	0.38	0.31
Syracuse, N. Y	1.77	1.13	4.56	0.33	0.33
New Haven, Conn	1.76	0.86	5.12	0.22	0.33
Birmingham, Ala	0.93	0.23	2.07	0.04	0.08
Memphis, Tenn	2.26	0.41	2.88	0.13	0.88
Scranton, Pa	1.20	...	4.27	0.17	0.13
Richmond, Va	1.23	0.60	2.34	0.01	0.42

City.	High-ways.	*Chari-ties.	†Libra-Schools.	‡Recre-ries.	ation.	City.	High-ways.	*Chari-ties.	†Libra-Schools.	‡Recre-ries.	ation.
Paterson, N. J.	0.87	0.44	4.09	0.20	0.17	Spokane, Wash.	1.63	0.18	5.46	0.25	0.37
Omaha, Neb.	1.58	¶	4.74	0.24	0.58	Bridgeport, Conn.	2.18	1.10	3.01	0.17	0.28
Fall River, Mass.	1.95	1.33	3.95	0.25	0.29	Albany, N. Y.	1.20	0.49	3.98	0.14	0.97
Dayton, O.	1.36	0.65	4.32	0.21	0.11						
Grand Rapids, Mich.	0.88	0.30	4.48	0.43	0.27	*Charities include hospitals and corrections. †In-cluding art galleries and museums. ‡Including parks, playgrounds, baths and public entertain-ments. ¶Less than one-half of 1 cent.					
Nashville, Tenn.	1.36	0.42	2.62	0.16	0.036						
Lowell, Mass.	1.86	1.25	3.89	0.21	0.23						
Cambridge, Mass.	2.22	0.84	5.01	0.28	0.66						

DISTANCES BETWEEN AMERICAN CITIES.

By the shortest usually traveled railroad routes. Compiled from the war department's official table of distances.

FROM 🖙 To	New York.	Chicago.	Phila-elphia.	St. Louis.	Boston.	Baltimore	Cleveland	Buffalo.	San Fran-cisco.	Pitts-burgh.	Cincin-nati.	Milwau-kee.	New Or-leans.	Washing-ton.	Minneap-olis.
	Mls.	Mls.	Mls.	Mls.	Mls.	Mls.	Mls.	Mls.	Mls.	Mls.	Mls.	Mls.	Mls.	Mls.	Mls.
Albany	145	832	236	1,028	202	333	480	297	3,106	567	724	917	1,517	1,142	1,252
Atlanta	876	733	785	611	1,106	688	736	919	2,805	805	492	818	496	648	1,153
Baltimore	188	802	97	934	418	...	474	398	3,076	334	533	887	1,184	40	1,223
Boston	217	1,034	321	1,230	...	418	682	499	3,306	674	926	1,119	1,602	458	1,454
Buffalo	412	525	416	731	499	398	183	...	2,799	270	427	610	1,256	438	915
Chicago	912	...	821	284	1,034	802	357	525	2,274	468	298	85	912	790	430
Cincinnati	757	298	666	341	926	593	244	427	2,572	313	...	383	829	553	718
Cleveland	584	357	403	548	682	474	...	183	2,631	135	244	442	1,073	437	777
Columbus, O.	637	314	546	428	820	511	138	321	2,588	196	116	389	935	471	734
Denver	1,934	1,022	1,843	916	2,056	1,850	1,379	1,557	1,371	1,490	1,257	1,107	1,347	1,810	884
Detroit	686	272	669	488	750	649	173	251	2,546	321	263	357	1,092	655	692
Duluth	1,391	479	1,300	728	1,513	1,281	701	1,004	2,258	947	777	422	1,447	1,269	162
El Paso	2,310	1,465	2,219	1,245	2,414	2,179	1,703	1,915	1,287	1,808	1,586	1,550	1,195	2,139	1,521
Galveston	1,792	1,144	1,691	850	2,012	1,604	1,408	1,501	2,157	1,481	1,157	1,229	410	1,554	1,340
Grand Rapids, Mich.	821	178	815	462	878	795	582	579	2,452	...	508	263	1,050	764	569
Helena	2,452	1,546	2,361	1,549	2,574	2,342	1,607	2,065	1,250	2,008	1,538	1,455	2,152	2,320	1,119
Indianapolis	823	183	754	240	935	704	283	466	2,457	381	111	268	888	664	603
Jacksonville, Fla.	983	1,097	892	975	1,213	795	1,045	1,193	3,098	1,057	841	1,182	616	755	1,517
Kansas City	1,342	458	1,251	277	1,466	1,211	755	907	1,881	898	618	543	880	1,171	573
Los Angeles	3,149	2,265	3,058	2,084	3,018	2,562	2,774	...	475	2,705	2,425	2,350	2,007	2,978	2,301
Louisville	871	304	780	274	1,040	703	358	541	2,468	427	114	389	778	663	724
Memphis	1,157	527	1,099	311	1,387	969	738	921	2,430	807	494	612	396	929	897
Milwaukee	997	85	906	369	1,119	887	442	610	2,359	553	383	...	997	875	335
Minneapolis	1,382	420	1,291	598	1,461	1,229	777	945	2,096	888	718	335	1,283	1,316	...
Mobile	1,231	929	1,140	647	1,461	1,043	1,029	1,212	2,623	1,088	785	1,014	141	1,003	1,233
Montreal	386	841	477	1,051	330	574	623	434	3,115	704	829	926	1,655	814	1,135
Newark, N. J.	9	903	82	1,059	226	179	575	405	3,177	435	748	988	1,363	219	1,323
New Haven	76	980	167	1,141	140	264	628	445	3,254	520	833	1,065	1,448	304	1,400
New Orleans	1,372	912	1,281	699	1,602	1,184	1,073	1,256	2,482	1,142	829	997	...	1,144	1,285
New York	...	912	91	1,065	217	188	584	442	3,186	444	757	997	1,372	228	1,332
Ogden	2,436	1,494	2,315	1,414	2,528	2,296	1,851	2,019	780	1,962	1,792	1,579	1,801	2,284	1,316
Omaha	1,405	493	1,314	413	1,527	1,295	1,750	1,018	1,781	961	791	578	1,080	1,288	381
Philadelphia	91	821	...	974	321	97	493	416	3,095	353	666	905	1,281	137	1,241
Pittsburgh	444	466	353	621	674	334	135	270	...	318	553	742	1,142	802	989
Portland, Me.	332	1,149	436	1,345	115	533	797	614	3,325	789	1,041	1,234	1,717	573	1,569
Portland, Ore.	3,204	2,292	3,113	2,212	3,326	3,094	2,649	2,817	772	2,760	2,590	2,378	2,746	3,082	2,042
Providence	190	1,034	281	1,230	45	378	682	499	3,308	634	926	1,119	1,602	418	1,454
Quebec	530	1,013	621	1,343	402	718	795	612	3,287	876	1,039	1,837	1,837	789	1,433
Richmond, Va.	348	879	252	918	573	155	553	553	3,153	417	581	964	1,046	115	1,299
Rochester, N. Y.	373	603	361	799	430	354	251	68	2,877	338	495	688	1,324	394	1,023
St. Joseph, Mo.	1,362	470	1,301	327	1,474	1,261	875	1,058	1,867	948	668	555	941	1,221	485
St. Louis	1,035	284	974	...	1,230	934	548	731	2,194	621	341	369	699	894	586
St. Paul	1,322	410	1,231	526	1,444	1,212	767	935	2,086	878	708	325	1,275	1,309	10
San Antonio	1,945	1,204	1,852	929	2,150	1,755	1,468	1,651	1,911	1,541	1,217	1,280	571	1,715	1,320
San Francisco	3,186	2,274	3,095	2,194	3,308	3,076	2,631	2,799	...	2,742	2,572	2,350	2,482	3,064	2,096
Seattle	3,151	2,239	3,000	2,352	3,273	2,941	2,596	2,764	957	2,707	2,537	2,154	2,931	3,029	1,818
Spokane	2,812	1,900	2,721	1,932	2,934	2,702	2,357	2,425	1,205	2,368	2,198	1,815	2,535	2,690	1,479
Springfield, Mass.	139	956	230	1,131	99	327	583	400	3,209	583	327	1,090	1,511	367	1,355
Tampa, Fla.	1,195	1,309	1,104	1,187	1,425	1,007	1,297	1,405	3,310	1,269	1,053	1,394	829	967	1,729
Toledo	705	244	615	487	795	595	113	296	2,518	261	203	329	1,092	595	604
Washington	228	790	137	894	458	40	437	438	3,064	302	553	875	1,141	...	1,210

DISTANCES BETWEEN GREAT SEAPORTS.

TO PRINCIPAL EUROPEAN PORTS.

Distances in nautical miles traversed by full powered steamships in traveling from Boston, New York, Philadelphia and Baltimore to London, Liverpool, Glasgow, Antwerp, Hamburg and Havre by northern and southern routes. Computed by United States hydrographic office.

From— Boston (Boston lightship) to—	North-ern.	South-ern.
London	3,139	3,258
Liverpool	2,896	3,053
Glasgow	2,815	2,987
Antwerp	3,184	3,303
Hamburg	3,446	3,565
Havre	2,990	3,109

From— New York (the Battery) to—	North-ern.	South-ern.
London	3,313	3,423
Liverpool	3,070	3,198
Glasgow	2,989	3,152
Antwerp	3,358	3,469
Hamburg	3,620	3,730
Havre	3,164	3,274

Philadelphia (Market street wharf) to—	North-ern.	South-ern.
London	3,456	3,566
Liverpool	3,213	3,341
Glasgow	3,132	3,295
Antwerp	3,501	3,611
Hamburg	3,763	3,873
Havre	3,307	3,417

From— Baltimore (the basin) to—	North- ern.	South- ern.
London	3,606	3,716
Liverpool	3,363	3,491
Glasgow	3,282	3,445
Antwerp	3,651	3,761
Hamburg	3,913	4,023
Havre	3,457	3,567

FROM OTHER EUROPEAN PORTS.

From— Glasgow (Greenock) to—	Aug.15- Jan. 14	Jan.15- Aug. 14
Montreal by south of Cape Race	2,864	2,864
St. John, New Brunswick	2,673	2,930
Boston (navy yard)	2,776	2,934
New York (the Battery)	2,951	3,099
Philadelphia	3,104	3,252
Baltimore	3,258	3,406
Newport News	3,135	3,283
New Orleans	4,486	4,632
Galveston	4,662	4,708

Southampton to—		
Montreal	3,059	3,059
St. John, New Brunswick	2,817	2,923
Boston (navy yard)	2,920	3,027
New York (the Battery)	3,095	3,192
Philadelphia	3,248	3,345
Baltimore	3,402	3,499
Newport News	3,279	3,376
New Orleans	4,620	4,625
Galveston	4,796	4,801

Bremen to—		
Montreal	3,534	3,534
St. John, New Brunswick	3,292	3,398
Boston (navy yard)	3,395	3,502
New York (the Battery)	3,570	3,667
Philadelphia	3,723	3,820
Baltimore	3,877	3,974
Newport News	3,754	3,851
New Orleans	5,095	5,100
Galveston	5,271	5,276

Rotterdam to—		
Montreal	3,293	3,293
St. John, New Brunswick	3,051	3,157
Boston (navy yard)	3,154	3,261
New York (the Battery)	3,329	3,426
Philadelphia	3,482	3,579
Baltimore	3,636	3,733
Newport News	3,513	3,610
New Orleans	4,854	4,859
Galveston	5,030	5,035

Copenhagen (via English channel) to—		
Montreal	3,834	3,834
St. John, New Brunswick	3,592	3,698
Boston (navy yard)	3,695	3,802
New York (the Battery)	3,870	3,967
Philadelphia	4,023	4,120
Baltimore	4,177	4,274
Newport News	4,054	4,151
New Orleans	5,395	5,400
Galveston	5,571	5,576

From— Marseilles to—	Aug.15- Jan. 14	Jan.15- Aug. 14
Montreal	3,873	3,873
St. John, New Brunswick	3,605	3,620
Boston (navy yard)	3,708	3,724
New York (the Battery)	3,883	3,889
Philadelphia	4,036	4,042

Genoa to—		
Montreal	4,040	4,040
St. John, New Brunswick	3,772	3,787
Boston (navy yard)	3,875	3,891
New York (the Battery)	4,050	4,056

GENERAL TABLE.

Nautical miles from New York, New Orleans, San Francisco and Port Townsend by shortest all-water routes. [From "Transportation Routes and Systems of the World," by O. P. Austin of the bureau of statistics, Washington, D. C.]

Port.	New York.	New Orleans.	San Francisco.	Pt.Town- send.
Aden	6,532	7,870	11,508	11,390
Antwerp	3,358	4,853	13,671	14,446
Batavia	10,182	11,598	7,800	7,600
Bombay	8,120	9,536	9,780	9,580
Brest	2,954	4,458	13,209	13,984
Buenos Aires	5,868	6,318	7,511	8,286
Calcutta	9,830	11,239	8,990	8,896
Callao	9,603	10,142	4,012	4,769
Cape Town	6,815	7,374	10,454	11,229
Colombo	8,618	10,146	8,900	8,700
Colon	1,981	1,380	*3,324	*4,990
Gibraltar	3,207	4,576	12,734	13,509
Hamburg	3,620	5,243	13,998	14,773
Havana	1,227	597	12,900	13,675
Havre	3,164	4,760	13,307	14,082
Hongkong	11,610	12,892	6,086	6,886
Honolulu	13,209	13,719	2,097	2,370
Liverpool	3,070	4,553	13,503	14,278
Manila	11,556	12,946	6,289	6,985
Marseilles	3,876	5,266	13,324	14,099
Melbourne	12,670	12,933	7,040	7,311
Naples	4,172	5,562	13,699	14,474
New Orleans	1,741	......	13,559	14,298
New York	......	1,741	13,089	13,848
Nome	15,840	16,249	2,705	2,358
Odessa	5,370	6,760	14,897	15,672
Pernambuco	3,696	3,969	9,439	10,214
Port Said	5,122	6,509	12,810	12,610
Port Townsend	13,849	14,298	775	......
Punta Arenas	6,890	7,346	6,199	6,958
Panama	*2,028	*1,427	3,277	4,052
Rio de Janeiro	4,778	5,218	8,339	9,114
San Francisco	13,089	13,559	......	775
St. Petersburg	4,632	6,223	†14,960	†15,730
San Juan, P. R.	1,428	1,539	12,199	12,974
Singapore	10,170	11,560	7,502	7,206
Sitka	14,391	14,841	1,302	732
Shanghai	12,360	13,750	5,550	5,290
Tehuantepec	‡2,036	†812	¶2,189	¶2,964
Valparaiso	8,460	8,733	5,140	5,902
Vladivostok	17,036	17,445	4,706	4,357
Wellington	11,500	11,773	5,909	6,415
Yokohama	13,040	14,471	4,536	4,240

*Via Panama canal. †Approximately. ‡Eastern end railroad. ¶Western end.

PRINCIPAL SEAPORTS OF THE WORLD.

Vessel tonnage movement in the foreign trade at the principal ports of the world. [From reports compiled by the bureau of statistics, department of commerce and labor, Washington, D. C.]

Port.	Year.	Entered.	Cleared.
Aden, Arabia	1912	3,594,888	3,592,154
Alexandria, Egypt	1911	3,443,705	3,414,966
Antwerp, Belgium	1911	13,330,639	13,325,781
Baltimore, Md.	1912	1,192,037	1,489,406
Barcelona, Spain	1910	2,464,111	1,645,045
Bilbao, Spain	1910	2,148,286	1,609,378
Bombay, India	1911	1,829,997	1,652,871
Bordeaux, France	1910	2,062,188	2,194,755
Boston, Mass.	1912	2,948,244	1,872,493
Boulogne, France	1910	2,523,146	2,510,454
Bremen, Germany	1911	1,495,487	1,437,371
Bremerhaven, Germany	1911	1,696,538	1,608,388
Buenos Aires, Argentina	1908	5,981,477	5,079,863
Calcutta, India	1911	2,059,652	1,741,638
Cape Town, U. of S. A.	1911	2,195,902	1,952,023
Cardiff, Wales	1911	5,526,426	8,328,647

Port.	Year.	Entered.	Cleared.
Colombo, Ceylon	1911	7,674,152	7,623,170
Constantinople, Turkey	1912	*20,171,065	......
Copenhagen, Denmark	1910	3,135,096	3,239,621
Fremantle, Australia	1911	802,960	607,843
Galveston, Tex.	1912	1,025,257	1,349,347
Genoa, Italy	1910	4,562,082	4,025,097
Gibraltar	1911	5,963,529	5,800,634
Glasgow, Scotland	1911	2,146,512	3,418,771
Hamburg, Germany	1911	11,830,949	11,945,239
Havana, Cuba	1911	3,117,313	3,121,372
Havre, France	1910	4,028,057	4,138,173
Hongkong (Victoria)	1911	4,562,082	4,025,097
Hull, England	1911	3,534,964	3,185,290
Kobe, Japan	1911	5,640,946	5,539,847
Liverpool, England	1911	7,887,719	6,880,273
London, England	1911	11,973,249	9,004,974
Marseilles, France	1910	8,161,344	8,186,315
Melbourne, Australia	1911	550,259	372,216
Moji, Japan	1911	4,026,421	4,113,479
Montreal, Canada	1912	1,702,690	1,683,261

Port.	Year.	Entered.	Cleared.	Port.	Year.	Entered.	Cleared.
Nagasaki, Japan	1911	2,418,310	2,382,144	Santos, Brazil	1911	3,440,880	3,310,414
Naples, Italy	1910	3,303,898	3,296,825	Shanghai, China	1911	9,176,309	9,429,996
New Orleans, La	1912	2,214,681	2,360,043	Singapore, Straits Sts	1911	7,737,785	7,717,691
New York, N. Y	1912	13,673,765	13,549,128	Sydney, Australia	1911	991,706	944,972
Odessa, Russia	1910	1,413,157	1,354,952	Tampico, Mexico	1911	551,693	762,195
Philadelphia, Pa	1912	2,700,193	2,187,408	Tyne ports, England	1911	5,954,493	6,842,199
Port Natal, U. of S. A	1911	3,078,745	3,133,359	Trieste, Austria	1911	2,031,995	2,021,034
Puget Sound, Wash	1912	2,498,150	2,857,818	Valette, Malta	1912	4,119,221	4,121,599
Riga, Russia	1910	1,683,826	1,744,846	Vancouver, Canada	1912	1,884,846	1,874,263
Rio de Janeiro, Brazil	1911	4,541,820	3,696,907	Vera Cruz, Mexico	1911	995,086	788,024
Rotterdam, Holland	1911	11,052,186	10,800,490	Victoria, Canada	1912	1,874,102	1,748,749
St. Petersburg, Russia	1910	1,897,547	1,894,816	Vladivostok, Russia	1910	895,417	826,250
San Francisco, Cal	1912	928,289	1,154,942	Yokohama, Japan	1911	3,645,162	3,448,773

WINES AND LIQUORS CONSUMED IN THE UNITED STATES.

YEAR.	WINES.		MALT LIQUORS.		DISTILLED SPIRITS.		Total wines and liquors.	Per capita of all wines and liquors.
	Consumption	Per capita	Consumption	Per capita	Consumption	Per capita.		
	Gallons.	Gals.	Gallons.	Gals.	Pf. gallons.	Pf. gls.	Gallons.	Gallons.
1840	4,873,096	.29	23,310,843	1.36	43,060,884	2.52	71,244,823	4.17
1850	6,315,871	.27	36,563,009	1.58	51,833,473	2.23	94,712,353	4.08
1860	11,059,141	.35	101,346,669	3.22	89,968,651	2.86	202,374,461	6.43
1870	12,225,007	.32	204,756,156	5.31	79,895,768	2.07	296,876,931	7.70
1880	28,098,179	.56	414,220,195	8.26	63,526,694	1.27	505,076,400	10.09
1890	28,945,933	.46	855,792,355	13.67	87,829,562	1.40	972,578,878	15.53
1900	29,988,467	.39	1,221,500,160	16.01	97,248,382	1.27	1,319,176,033	17.76
1905	35,059,717	.41	1,538,150,770	18.02	120,870,278	1.42	1,694,692,765	19.85
1906	46,485,223	.53	1,699,985,642	19.54	127,754,544	1.47	1,874,225,409	21.55
1907	57,738,848	.65	1,821,987,627	20.56	140,064,436	1.58	2,019,690,911	22.79
1908	52,121,646	.58	1,828,732,448	20.26	125,379,314	1.39	2,006,233,408	22.22
1909	61,779,589	.67	1,752,634,428	19.07	121,130,094	1.32	1,935,544,011	21.06
1910	60,548,078	.65	1,851,840,256	19.79	133,538,684	1.42	2,045,427,018	21.86
1911	69,859,232	.67	1,966,911,744	20.65	138,585,980	1.46	2,160,356,935	22.79
1912	56,424,711	.58	1,932,531,184	19.96	139,496,331	1.44	2,128,452,226	21.98

COFFEE AND TEA CONSUMED IN THE UNITED STATES.

YEAR ENDED JUNE 30.	COFFEE.				TEA.			
	Imports.	Value.	Price*	Per capita†	Imports.	Value.	Price*	Per capita†
	Pounds.		Cents.	Lbs.	Pounds.		Cents.	Lbs.
1830	51,488,248	$4,227,021	8.3	2.98	8,609,415	$2,425,018	23.3	.53
1840	94,996,095	8,546,222	8.8	5.06	20,000,595	5,427,010	24.1	.99
1850	145,272,687	11,234,835	7.6	5.60	29,872,654	4,719,232	14.1	1.22
1860	202,144,733	21,385,797	10.8	6.79	31,696,657	8,315,327	26.3	.84
1870	235,256,574	24,234,879	10.3	6.00	47,408,481	13,863,273	29.4	1.10
1880	446,850,727	60,360,769	13.5	8.78	72,162,956	19,782,931	27.4	1.39
1890	499,159,120	78,297,432	16.0	7.83	83,896,829	12,317,493	15.0	1.33
1900	787,991,911	52,467,943	7.5	9.81	84,845,197	10,558,110	12.4	1.09
1905	1,046,028,441	84,710,383	8.1	12.00	102,706,599	16,230,808	15.8	1.19
1906	853,799,615	73,514,444	8.6	9.74	93,621,750	14,580,878	15.6	1.06
1907	986,595,923	78,382,823	7.9	11.17	86,368,490	13,915,544	16.1	.96
1908	892,692,410	67,863,830	7.6	9.84	94,149,564	16,309,870	17.3	1.03
1909	1,031,749,705	79,341,076	11.45	9.53	114,016,530	18,562,676	16.2	1.25
1910	873,988,689	69,504,946	7.9	9.53	85,626,370	13,671,946	16.0	.89
1911	878,322,468	90,949,965	10.3	9.27	102,655,942	17,613,569	17.2	1.04
1912	887,747,747	118,233,958	13.3	9.28	101,406,816	18,207,141	18.0	1.05

*Average import price per pound. †Consumption per capita based on net imports.

PORK PACKING STATISTICS.
Season from Nov. 1 to March 1.

CITY.	1911-12	1910-11	1909-10	1908-09	1907-08	1906-07	1905-06	1904-05	1903-04
	No. hogs	No. hogs	No. hogs	No. hogs	No. hogs	No. hogs	No. hogs	No. hogs	No. hogs
Chicago	2,638,044	2,067,995	2,063,544	2,640,765	2,570,475	2,493,739	2,592,866	2,312,588	2,925,900
Cincinnati	262,249	205,562	196,471	245,323	297,472	226,988	255,167	293,209	247,947
Indianapolis	629,308	418,743	469,081	703,205	747,074	540,486	600,423	516,230	479,380
Kansas City	1,593,875	919,982	985,118	1,520,481	1,365,221	1,135,931	1,202,736	1,231,408	881,674
Louisville	70,100	58,190	69,853	96,608	83,647	69,581	154,767	184,446	126,251
*Milwaukee	551,619	415,191	365,829	583,338	684,069	453,463	467,407	384,425	423,024
Omaha	949,232	674,619	531,049	700,772	742,794	687,274	800,470	738,131	746,696
St. Louis	1,021,198	720,696	705,368	884,937	706,029	656,696	650,132	761,982	627,550

*Includes Cudahy.

PRODUCTION OF IRON AND STEEL RAILS IN THE UNITED STATES.

Year.	Iron.	Steel.	Total.	Year.	Iron.	Steel.	Total.
1900	1,592	2,271,108	2,272,700	1911	230	2,635,801	2,636,031
1905	871	2,283,840	2,284,711	1912	234	2,822,556	2,822,790
1910		3,023,845	3,023,845				

UNITED STATES MORTALITY STATISTICS.

[Bureau of the census report.]

DEATHS PER 1,000 OF POPULATION IN THE REGISTRATION AREA.

Annual av.

	1906-1910.	1907.	1908.	1909.	1910.	1911.
The registration area..	15.1	16.0	14.8	14.4	15.0	14.2
Registration cities.....	16.2	17.1	15.7	15.4	16.1	15.3
Registration states....	15.0	15.9	14.7	14.2	14.7	13.9
Cities in registration states	16.3	17.5	15.9	15.4	15.9	15.1
Rural part of registration states............	13.4	14.0	13.2	13.0	13.4	12.7
Registration cities in other states..........	15.9	16.3	15.4	15.6	16.9	16.9

The registration area includes twenty-three states, the District of Columbia and thirty-eight cities in nonregistration states, containing 57.9 per cent of the total estimated population of continental United States. The total number of deaths reported in this area in 1911 was 839,284. The estimated population of the area was 59,275,977 and the death rate was consequently 14.2 per 1,000 of population.

IN REGISTRATION STATES.

Death rates per 1,000 population.

State.	1906.	1907.	1908.	1909.	1910.	1911.
California	14.1	14.6	14.1	13.4	13.5	13.7
Colorado	14.0	15.3	14.5	14.2	13.8	12.9
Connecticut	16.2	16.5	14.8	15.0	15.6	15.4
Indiana	12.8	13.0	12.8	12.9	13.5	12.9
Kentucky	....	....	....	....	....	13.2
Maine	16.0	16.4	15.7	15.6	17.1	16.1
Maryland	16.0	16.4	15.8	15.5	16.0	15.8
Massachusetts	16.3	17.0	15.9	15.4	16.1	15.3
Michigan	14.0	13.6	13.4	13.1	14.1	13.2
Minnesota	....	....	....	....	10.9	10.5
Missouri	....	....	....	....	....	13.1
Montana	....	....	....	....	10.6	10.2
New Hampshire.......	17.7	17.6	16.8	16.9	17.3	17.1
New Jersey...........	15.9	16.1	14.8	14.7	15.5	14.7
New York............	16.9	17.3	15.9	15.7	16.1	15.5
North Carolina.......	....	....	....	....	15.7	14.3
Ohio	....	....	....	12.9	13.7	13.1
Pennsylvania	16.0	15.9	15.1	14.7	15.6	14.2
Rhode Island.........	17.4	17.8	15.9	15.6	17.1	15.5
Utah	....	....	....	....	10.8	10.3
Vermont	16.7	16.2	15.9	15.7	16.0	15.8
Washington	....	....	9.3	9.8	10.9	8.9
Wisconsin	....	....	11.7	11.8	12.0	11.5
Total	15.7	15.9	14.7	14.2	14.7	13.9

Total includes District of Columbia. Blanks indicate that the states concerned were not registration states in the years specified.

DEATH RATES IN AMERICAN CITIES.

Per 1,000 of population.

City.	Annual-av. 1906-1910.	1907.	1908.	1909.	1910.	1911.
Albany, N. Y..........	18.6	19.2	18.6	17.6	19.4	20.4
Atlanta, Ga...........	19.4	21.4	18.1	17.2	18.9	19.8
Baltimore, Md........	19.5	20.5	19.0	18.7	19.2	18.4
Birmingham, Ala......	*	*	17.8	18.2	19.5	18.2
Boston, Mass..........	17.9	18.6	18.3	16.8	17.2	17.1
Bridgeport, Conn......	15.5	17.2	14.5	14.4	15.2	13.9
Buffalo, N. Y.........	16.0	16.7	15.3	15.2	16.3	14.5
Cambridge, Mass......	15.1	15.1	16.0	14.7	15.0	15.2
Chicago, Ill..........	14.9	15.7	14.5	14.6	15.1	14.5
Cincinnati, O.........	18.1	18.1	18.0	16.5	17.4	16.5
Cleveland, O..........	14.1	15.2	13.3	12.9	14.3	13.8
Columbus, O..........	15.1	15.5	15.2	14.0	15.4	14.3
Dayton, O............	15.5	17.1	14.8	15.4	14.8	13.7
Denver, Col..........	17.5	18.7	18.3	17.0	16.4	15.5
Detroit, Mich.........	14.8	14.9	13.7	14.0	15.9	14.4
Fall River, Mass......	19.7	21.3	20.5	19.1	18.4	17.4
Grand Rapids, Mich...	13.3	13.1	12.7	11.9	14.6	13.6
Indianapolis, Ind.....	15.2	15.8	14.2	14.3	16.3	14.7

Annual av.

City.	1906-1910.	1907.	1908.	1909.	1910.	1911.
Jersey City, N. J......	17.7	19.1	17.4	16.8	16.3	15.8
Kansas City, Mo......	14.6	15.3	14.1	14.4	15.9	15.4
Los Angeles, Cal......	14.8	16.5	13.8	13.7	14.0	14.5
Louisville, Ky........	17.4	19.0	17.0	15.5	16.7	16.1
Lowell, Mass.........	19.4	20.6	19.2	18.9	19.7	17.7
Memphis, Tenn.......	20.6	21.5	20.1	20.1	21.4	21.3
Milwaukee, Wis.......	13.7	13.8	12.7	13.7	13.8	11.9
Minneapolis, Minn....	11.0	10.6	10.7	10.7	12.3	11.5
Nashville, Tenn.......	19.3	19.6	19.4	18.1	18.7	20.5
Newark, N. J.........	17.2	18.5	16.2	16.5	16.5	14.8
New Haven, Conn.....	17.3	18.1	16.4	16.9	16.5	16.7
New Orleans, La......	21.7	23.5	22.3	20.2	21.3	20.4
New York, N. Y.......	16.9	18.3	16.3	16.0	16.0	15.2
Oakland, Cal.........	15.4	18.6	14.9	14.2	12.7	13.7
Omaha, Neb..........	13.8	12.5	13.2	14.7	15.1	14.3
Paterson, N. J........	15.7	15.6	15.5	15.3	14.7	14.6
Philadelphia, Pa......	17.7	18.6	17.3	16.4	17.4	16.6
Pittsburgh, Pa........	18.0	19.3	17.3	15.8	17.9	14.9
Portland, Ore.........	10.3	11.0	9.9	9.8	11.0	10.9
Providence, R. I......	17.6	19.1	16.6	16.1	17.7	15.6
Richmond, Va........	22.5	23.4	21.7	20.7	22.6	21.0
Rochester, N. Y......	14.7	15.5	13.7	14.4	14.6	14.4
St. Louis, Mo........	15.6	15.9	14.7	15.8	15.8	15.4
St. Paul, Minn.......	11.0	10.9	10.5	11.4	11.9	10.9
San Francisco, Cal....	16.1	16.6	15.5	15.0	15.1	15.2
Scranton, Pa.........	16.3	15.7	16.4	16.3	16.4	14.8
Seattle, Wash........	9.8	10.8	9.3	10.0	10.1	8.8
Spokane, Wash.......	12.8	13.3	13.4	12.6	13.0	11.6
Syracuse, N. Y.......	15.2	15.2	15.7	14.5	15.4	14.3
Toledo, O............	14.9	15.3	14.6	14.6	14.6	14.9
Washington, D. C.....	19.6	20.1	19.1	19.0	19.6	18.7
Worcester, Mass......	17.1	19.1	16.7	15.5	16.9	15.7

*Nonregistration city.

DEATH RATES IN FOREIGN COUNTRIES.

Per 1,000 persons living.

Country.	1906 to 1910.	1910.	Country.	1906 to 1910.	1910.
Australia	10.4	10.7	Japan	*22.0	†20.9
Austria	21.2	22.3	Netherlands ..	13.6	14.3
Belgium	*15.8	†17.0	New Zealand..	9.7	9.7
Bulgaria	*26.6	†22.5	Norway	13.5	13.8
Ceylon	27.3	30.8	Ontario (prov.)	14.0	14.0
Chile	32.5	31.3	Prussia	16.0	17.3
Denmark	12.9	13.7	Roumania	25.2	26.0
England, Wales	13.5	14.7	Russia(Europ'n) †		730.9
Finland	16.6	17.4	Scotland	15.3	16.1
France	17.9	19.2	Servia	*29.3	†22.4
Germany	*17.2	†19.9	Spain	23.3	24.3
Hungary	23.6	25.0	Sweden	14.0	14.3
Ireland	17.1	17.3	Switzerland ..	*16.1	†17.5
Italy	19.6	21.0	*1909. †1901 to 1905. ‡No		
Jamaica	23.1	24.4	figures available.		

DEATH RATES IN FOREIGN CITIES.

Per 1,000 persons living.

City.	1910.	1911.	City.	1910.	1911.
Amsterdam	12.2	12.4	Montreal	22.4	*
Belfast	18.6	17.2	Moscow	26.9	27.2
Berlin	14.7	15.6	Munich	15.9	15.8
Breslau	19.1	19.5	Paris	16.7	17.2
Brussels	13.6	13.9	Prague	18.4	16.3
Budapest	19.3	19.4	Rio de Janeiro..	20.6	20.4
Bucharest	25.6	26.1	Rotterdam	12.2	12.1
Christiania	11.9	13.5	St. Petersburg..	24.1	20.8
Copenhagen	14.2	14.8	Stockholm	14.6	12.7
Dresden	19.1	14.6	Sydney	10.4	10.9
Dublin	19.9	21.4	The Hague......	12.5	12.7
Edinburgh	14.6	16.0	Toronto	21.3	*
Glasgow	15.1	17.7	Trieste	22.9	24.0
Hamburg	14.2	14.7	Turin	14.9	*
London	12.7	15.0	Venice	19.0	22.8
Melbourne	12.7	12.8	Vienna	15.8	16.4
Milan	17.1	20.1			

*Figures not available.

DEATHS FROM CERTAIN CAUSES (1911).

Number in registration area and rate per 100,000 of population.

Cause.	Number.	Rate.	Cause.	Number.	Rate.	Cause.	Number.	Rate.
All causes............	839,284	1,415.9	Smallpox	130	0.2	Whooping cough.......	6,692	11.3
Typhoid fever........	12,451	21.0	Measles	5,922	10.0	Diphtheria, croup.....	11,174	18.9
Malaria	1,802	3.0	Scarlet fever.........	5,243	8.8	Influenza	9,294	15.7

Cause.	Number.	Rate.	Cause.	Number.	Rate.	Cause.	Number.	Rate.
Tuberculosis of lungs	81,796	138.0	Bronchitis, chronic..	5,077	8.6	Cirrhosis of liver.....	8,310	14.0
Tuberc. meningitis...	5,237	8.8	Pneumonia	52,868	89.2	Bright's disease......	57,803	97.5
Other tuberculosis...	7,172	12.1	Other respiratory dis.	35,223	59.4	Puerperal fever......	4,376	7.4
Cancer	44,024	74.3	Stomach diseases....	10,917	18.4	Congenital debility...	46,899	79.1
Meningitis	7,285	12.5	Diarrhea, enteritis...	45,868	77.4	Senility	13,974	23.6
Cerebral hemorrhage.	45,309	76.1	Appendicitis	6,896	11.6	Violence	*54,028	91.1
Heart disease (org.).	83,525	140.9	Hernia	7,061	11.9	Suicide	9,622	16.2
Bronchitis, acute....	6,482	10.9				*Exclusive of suicides.		

DEATHS FROM EXTERNAL CAUSES (1911).

Number in registration area and rate per 100,000 of population.

Cause.	No.	Rate.	Cause.	No.	Rate.	Cause.	No.	Rate.
Suicide	9,622	16.2	In mines and quarries	2,372	4.0	Excessive cold.........	188	0.3
Food poisoning..........	481	0.8	By machines	1,239	2.1	Effects of heat........	3,165	5.3
Other poisoning........	1,399	2.4	Other crushing.......	13,572	22.9	Lightning	240	0.4
Conflagration	869	1.5	Railroad accidents...	7,696	13.0	Electricity	513	0.9
Burns (except conflag.).	4,567	7.7	Street car accidents...	1,883	3.2	Fractures	363	0.6
Absorption of gas.......	2,143	3.6	Automobile accidents.	1,291	2.2	Other violence.........	2,471	4.2
Drowning (accidental)..	5,571	9.4	By other vehicles.....	2,237	3.8	Homicide (total).......	3,907	6.6
Traumatism by firearms	1,327	2.2	Landslide	465	0.8	By firearms...........	2,347	4.0
By cutting, etc........	122	0.2	Injuries by animals.....	520	0.9	By cutting, piercing...	638	1.1
By fall................	8,905	15.0	Starvation	94	0.2	By other means.......	922	1.6

DEATH RATES BY AGE AND SEX (1911).

Per 1,000 of population.

Age groups.	Both sexes.	Males.	Fe-males.	Age groups.	Both sexes.	Males.	Fe-males.	Age groups.	Both sexes.	Males.	Fe-males.
All ages.........	14.9	15.8	14.0	10 to 14 years.....	2.2	2.4	2.1	45 to 54 years....	14.5	16.1	12.9
Under 5 years...	36.6	39.8	33.3	15 to 19 years.....	3.5	3.7	3.3	55 to 64 years....	28.4	30.9	26.0
Under 1 year....	125.5	138.6	112.1	20 to 24 years....	5.0	5.3	4.7	65 to 74 years....	58.3	61.6	55.1
1 to 4 years......	12.8	13.3	12.2	25 to 34 years....	6.3	6.7	6.0	75 years and over.143.0	147.4	139.2	
5 to 9 years......	3.2	3.4	3.1	35 to 44 years.....	9.4	10.4	8.3				

DEATH RATES BY COLOR (1911).

Per 100,000 of population.

Cause.	White.	Colored.	Cause.	White.	Colored.	Cause.	White.	Colored.
All causes...........1,373.7	2,180.1		Cancer	75.0	57.0	Bright's disease.....	94.3	170.4
Typhoid	19.9	44.9	Heart disease.......	137.8	211.8	Violence	88.7	146.0
Influenza	15.3	23.9	Bronchitis	18.9	33.6	Suicide	16.5	10.3
Tuberculosis (lungs).	126.2	405.3	Pneumonia	128.4	252.2			

DEATHS FROM TUBERCULOSIS.

The total number of deaths from all forms of tuberculosis in the registration area during 1911 was 94,205, the death rate being 158.9 per 100,000—slightly lower than the rates for the preceding years (160.3 and 160.8 for 1910 and 1909, respectively). The rates for these three years were considerably lower than the annual averages for the quinquennial periods 1901 to 1905 (192.6) and 1906 to 1910 (168.7). There would consequently appear to be a marked reduction in the death rate from this disease, though the rate for 1909, 1910 and 1911 remained practically unchanged.

The death rate of the colored population from tuberculosis of the lungs was more than three times the death rate of the white population in 1911. The rate for the former was 405.3 and for the latter 126.2.

The highest death rates from tuberculosis shown for the states in the registration area were those of Kentucky (229.9), Colorado (218), California (206.8), Maryland (203.3), and the lowest rates were those of Utah (46.7), Michigan (96.1), Wisconsin (103.8), Washington (106.7) and Montana (107.1).

The cities of 100,000 population or over in 1910 having the highest death rates from tuberculosis in 1911 were Denver (292.7), Los Angeles (277.5), Albany (269.4), Cincinnati (265.3) and New Orleans (260.5). Those with the lowest rates were Milwaukee (106.4), Portland, Ore. (106.9), Spokane (109.4), Grand Rapids (110.3) and Scranton (112.7).

It must be remembered that in such states as Colorado and California and such cities as Denver and Los Angeles the high death rates from tuberculosis are in large part due to the fact that many nonresidents suffering from the disease go there in the hope of being benefited by the climate. The returns include the deaths of such nonresidents.

DEATHS FROM CANCER.

Cancer caused 44,024 deaths in the registration area in 1911. The death rate (74.3 per 100,000) was slightly lower than that for 1910 (76.2), but higher than that for any earlier year for which records are available. Employing corrected rates based upon a standard distribution of population by sex and age, cancer increased just one-fourth (25 per cent) from 1901 to 1911. The increase for males (30 per cent) was somewhat greater than the increase for females (22 per cent). Deaths from cancer are comparatively rare among persons under 25 years of age. In 1911 the rates per 100,000 population over the age of 25 were as follows: 25 to 34 years, 13.9; 35 to 44 years, 61.0; 45 to 54 years, 166.3; 55 to 64 years, 352.4; 65 to 74 years, 566.7; 75 years and over, 794.7.

The highest death rates from cancer in the registration states were in Vermont (191). Maine (98.6), New Hampshire (96.8), Massachusetts (94.4) and Rhode Island (88). The lowest rates were shown for Montana (40), Kentucky (42.7), Washington (46.1) and Utah (51.9). The cities having the highest death rates from cancer in 1911 were Albany (122.8), Boston (111.2), San Francisco (110.6), Oakland (105.3) and Cambridge (104.1). Cities with the lowest rates were Memphis (51.9), Seattle (57.4), Atlanta (61.2), Detroit (65.1) and Jersey City (65.5).

INFANT MORTALITY.

There has been a marked reduction in the infant death rate in recent years. The per cent of decrease in the death rate per 1,000 of population under 1 year of age from 1900 to 1911 was 19. Only four of the large cities of the country showed an increase. These were Minneapolis (4), St. Paul (19), Syracuse (11) and Portland, Ore. (10).

MARRIAGE AND DIVORCE IN THE UNITED STATES.
[From report of federal census bureau.]
MARRIAGE AND DIVORCE STATISTICS BY STATES.

STATE OR TERRITORY	MARRIAGES					DIVORCES				
	Number, 1887-1906.	Annual average 1898 to 1902.		Annual average 1888 to 1892.		Number 1887 to 1906.	Annual average† per 100,000 population.			
		Number	Per 10,000 Pop.	Number	Per 10,000 Pop.		1900.	1890.	1880.	1870.
Alabama	372,525	20,227	111	15,727	104	22,807	49	54	27	10
Arkansas	310,767	16,902	129	13,217	117	29,541	136	90	53	24
California	189,539	9,561	64	7,167	59	25,170	108	84	84	52
Colorado	98,877	5,457	101	4,361	103	15,844	158	197	138	60
Connecticut	136,984	7,034	77	6,216	83	9,224	50	66	61	84
Delaware	25,374	1,322	72	963	58	887	16	18	10	7
District of Columbia	50,244	3,114	112	1,513	66	2,325	58	34	31	30
Florida	114,486	6,176	117	4,314	110	7,686	79	57	53	23
Georgia	401,206	21,640	98	16,541	90	10,401	26	24	14	10
Idaho	25,390	1,359	84	705	80	3,205	120	93	58	67
Illinois	841,717	44,858	93	38,421	100	82,209	100	75	68	51
Indiana	493,990	26,451	105	22,453	102	60,721	142	104	70	69
Indian Territory	67,412	4,847	124	736	41	6,751	113	53		
Iowa	366,350	19,298	86	16,474	86	34,874	93	67	60	49
Kansas	275,062	14,112	96	12,795	90	28,904	109	84	44	51
Kentucky	359,783	19,526	91	15,399	83	30,641	84	58	35	28
Louisiana	243,881	13,421	97	10,150	91	9,785	41	29	10	5
Maine	86,532	5,519	79	5,726	87	14,194	117	88	78	61
Maryland	195,875	10,740	90	7,916	76	7,920	40	24	12	12
Massachusetts	468,267	24,117	86	21,031	94	22,940	47	32	30	25
Michigan	424,096	23,008	95	18,726	89	42,371	104	72	72	47
Minnesota	242,147	13,118	75	10,275	78	15,646	55	41	27	21
Mississippi	343,500	17,574	113	11,778	91	19,963	74	48	30	12
Missouri	579,807	30,340	98	25,700	96	54,766	103	71	40	29
Montana	36,362	2,188	90	1,294	91	6,454	167	139	125	73
Nebraska	170,820	8,825	85	8,357	78	16,711	82	71	43	29
Nevada	7,075	527	124	238	59	1,045	111	97	106	99
New Hampshire	77,764	3,916	95	3,720	99	8,617	112	106	85	53
New Jersey	335,809	15,042	80	15,740	109	7,441	23	18	13	9
New Mexico	25,625	1,307	67	1,018	64	2,437	73	46	12	1
New York	1,205,655	63,082	87	49,584	83	29,125	23	17	16	16
North Carolina	313,725	17,142	91	13,074	81	7,047	24	12	6	3
North Dakota	44,022	2,454	77	1,339	70	4,617	88	47	46	
Ohio	727,408	37,979	91	32,984	90	63,982	91	64	48	37
Oklahoma	45,415	3,326	85	347	44	7,969	129	46		
Oregon	67,475	3,429	85	2,801	88	10,145	134	108	92	80
Pennsylvania	896,533	48,088	76	39,059	74	29,686	33	21	13	8
Rhode Island	72,836	3,726	87	3,214	93	6,953	47	32	30	25
South Carolina*									1	
South Dakota	54,782	3,094	77	2,128	61	7,108	95	65	48	25
Tennessee	395,990	20,975	104	17,432	99	30,447	89	62	38	24
Texas	620,445	34,905	115	23,894	107	62,855	131	82	49	21
Utah	51,250	2,789	101	2,127	101	4,670	92	74	114	62
Vermont	58,472	2,977	87	2,807	84	4,740	75	49	47	50
Virginia	295,377	16,886	88	12,818	77	12,129	39	22	11	6
Washington	87,182	7,747	92	2,975	83	16,219	184	109	73	84
West Virginia	170,810	9,532	99	6,692	88	10,308	64	41	25	18
Wisconsin	337,583	16,802	81	16,009	95	22,867	65	51	41	38
Wyoming	13,500	839	91	426	68	1,772	118	86	711	99
Total	12,832,044					945,625				

*No record kept.   †For the five years of which the year stated is the median year.

MARRIAGE LAWS.

Marriage may be contracted without the consent of parents by males who are 21 years of age or more. This is the rule in about all the states having laws on the subject. In Arizona the age is 18. For females the age is 21 in Connecticut, Florida, Kentucky, Louisiana, Ohio, Pennsylvania, Rhode Island, South Dakota, Virginia, West Virginia and Wyoming; 16 is the age in Arizona, Maryland and Nebraska and 18 in the other states. Marriages contracted before the age of consent are illegal in nearly all the states.

Marriage licenses are required in practically all the states.

Marriages between whites and negroes are prohibited by law in Alabama, Arizona, Arkansas, California, Colorado, Delaware, District of Columbia, Florida, Georgia, Idaho, Indiana, Kentucky, Maryland, Mississippi, Missouri, Nebraska, Nevada, North Carolina, Oklahoma, Oregon, South Carolina, Tennessee, Texas, Utah, Virginia and West Virginia. Michigan specifically declares such marriages valid.

Marriages between first cousins are prohibited in Arizona, Arkansas, Illinois, Indiana, Kansas, Louisiana, Missouri, Montana, Nevada, New Hampshire, North Dakota, Ohio, Oklahoma, Oregon, Pennsylvania, South Dakota and Wyoming. Step-relatives are not permitted to intermarry except in California, Colorado, Florida, Georgia, Idaho, Minnesota, New Mexico, New York, North Carolina, Oregon, Utah and Wisconsin.

MARRIAGE RATES.

For the year 1900 the marriage rate based on the total population of continental United States and including the total number of marriages reported was 90 per 10,000 population. The rate in 1890 the rate was 87 per 10,000 population. The rate in 1900 per 10,000 unmarried population 15 years of age and over was 312; in 1890 it was 304. (See also Population by Marital Condition.)

DIVORCE RATES.

The percentage of increase of divorces as compared with the percentage of increase in population is shown by the following figures:

Year.	Divorces.	Increase.	Population.	Increase.
1900	55,751	66.6	75,994,575	20.
1890	33,461	70.2	62,947,714	25.5
1880	19,663	79.4	50,155,783	30.1

CAUSES FOR DIVORCE.
Summary of the laws in effect in various states and territories.

STATE OR TERRITORY.	Cruelty.	Desertion.	Fraud or force.	Imprisonment.	Incompetency.	Intemperance.	Neglect.	Male.	Female.	Residence required.	Remarriage permitted.	Alimony.
Alabama	Yes.	2 yrs.	Yes.	2 yrs.	Yes.	Yes.		17	14	1 to 5 y.	Yes.	Yes
Alaska	Yes.	2 yrs.			Yes.	Hab'l.				3 yrs.		
Arizona	Yes.	1 yr.	Yes.	Felony.	Yes.	Yes.	1 yr.	18	16	1 yr.	Yes.	Yes
Arkansas	Yes.	1 yr.	Yes.	Felony.	Yes.	1 yr.		17	14	1 yr.	Yes.	Yes
California	Yes.	1 yr.	Yes.	Felony.		1 yr.	1 yr.	18	15	1 yr.	Yes.	Yes
Colorado	Yes.	1 yr.		Felony.	Yes.	1 yr.	1 yr.			1 yr.	Yes.	Yes
Connecticut	Yes.	3 yrs.	Yes.	Felony.		Hab'l.				3 yrs.	Yes.	Yes
Delaware	Yes.	2 yrs.	Fraud.	Felony.	Yes.	Hab'l.	3 yrs.	18	16	2 yrs.	Yes.	Yes
District of Columbia	Yes.	2 yrs.	No.	Felony.	Yes.	No.		16	14	2 yrs.	Yes*.	Yes
Florida	Yes.	1 yr.			Yes.	Yes.	1 yr.			2 yrs.	Yes.	Yes
Georgia	Yes.	3 yrs.	Yes.	Felony.	Yes.	Hab'l.		17	14	None.	No.	Yes
Idaho	Yes.	1 yr.	Yes.	Felony.		1 yr.	1 yr.	18	18	6 mos.	Yes.	Yes
Illinois	Yes.	2 yrs.	Felony.	Yes.		2 yrs.		18	16	1 yr.	Yes.	Yes
Indiana	Yes.	2 yrs.	Yes.	Felony†.	Yes.	Hab'l.	2 yrs.	18	16	2 yrs.	Yes.	Yes
Iowa	Yes.	2 yrs.	Yes.	Felony†.	Yes.	Hab'l.		16	14	1 yr.	Yes.	Yes
Kansas	Yes.	1 yr.	Yes.	Felony†.	Yes.	Hab'l.	Yes.	15	12	1 yr.	Yes.	Yes
Kentucky	Yes.	1 yr.	Yes.	Felony.	Yes.	1 yr.	1 yr.	14	12	1 yr.	Yes.	Yes
Louisiana	Yes.	Yes.	Yes.	Felony.	Yes.	Hab'l.		16	14		Yes.	Yes
Maine	Yes.	3 yrs.			Yes.	Hab'l.	Yes.			1 yr.	Yes.	Yes
Maryland		3 yrs.			Yes.					2 yrs.	Yes.	Yes
Massachusetts	Yes.	3 yrs.	Fraud.	5 yrs.	Yes.	Hab'l.	Yes.			3 to 5 y.	Yes.	Yes
Michigan	Yes.	2 yrs.	Yes.	3 yrs.	Yes.	Hab'l.	Yes.	18	16	1 to 2 y.	Yes.	Yes
Minnesota	Yes.	1 yr.	Yes.	Yes†.	Yes.	1 yr.		18	15	1 yr.	Yes.	Yes
Mississippi	Yes.	2 yrs.		Felony.	Yes.	Hab'l.				1 to 2 y.	Yes.	Yes
Missouri	Yes.	1 yr.	Yes.	Felony.	Yes.	1 yr.		15	12	1 yr.	Yes.	Yes
Montana	Yes.	1 yr.	Yes.	Felony.	Yes.	1 yr.		18	16	1 yr.	Yes.	Yes
Nebraska	Yes.	2 yrs.	Yes.	3 yrs.	Yes.	Hab'l.	Yes.	18	16	1 yr.	Yes.	Yes
Nevada	Yes.	1 yr.	Yes.	Felony.	Yes.	Hab'l.	1 yr.	18	16	6 mos.	Yes.	Yes
New Hampshire	Yes.	3 yrs.	Yes.	1 yr.	Yes.	3 yrs.	3 yrs.	14	13	1 yr.	Yes.	Yes
New Jersey	Yes.	2 yrs.	Yes.		Yes.					2 yrs.	Yes.	Yes
New Mexico	Yes.	1 yr.		Felony.	Yes.	Hab'l.	Yes.	18	15	1 yr.	Yes.	Yes
New York	Yes.		Force.		Yes.			18	16	Actual	Yes.	Yes
North Carolina	Yes.	2 yrs.	Yes.	Felony.	Yes.			16	14		Yes.	Yes
North Dakota	Yes.	1 yr.	Yes.	Felony.	Yes.	1 yr.	1 yr.	18	15	1 yr.	Yes.	Yes
Ohio	Yes.	3 yrs.	Yes.	Felony.	Yes.	3 yrs.	Yes.	18	16	1 yr.	Yes.	Yes
Oklahoma	Yes.	1 yr.	Yes.	Felony.	Yes.	Hab'l.	Yes.	18	15	1 yr.	Yes.	Yes
Oregon	Yes.	1 yr.	Yes.	Felony.	Yes.	1 yr.		18	15	1 yr.	Yes.	Yes
Pennsylvania	Yes.	2 yrs.	Yes.	2 yrs.	Yes.					1 yr.	Yes.	Yes
Rhode Island	Yes.	5 yrs.		Felony.	Yes.	Hab'l.	Yes.			2 yrs.	Yes.	Yes
South Carolina‡			Yes.									
South Dakota	Yes.	1 yr.		Felony.	Yes.	1 yr.	1 yr.	18	15	1 yr.	Yes.	Yes
Tennessee	Yes.	2 yrs.	Yes.	Felony.	Yes.	Hab'l†	Yes.			2 yrs.	Yes.	Yes
Texas	Yes.	3 yrs.	Fraud.	Felony.	Yes.	Hab'l.		16	14	6 mos.	Yes.	Yes
Utah	Yes.	1 yr.	Yes.	Felony.	Yes.	Hab'l.	Yes.	16	14	1 yr.	Yes.	Yes
Vermont	Yes.	3 yrs.	Yes.	3 yrs.	Yes.		Yes.			1 yr.	Yes.	Yes
Virginia		3 yrs.	Yes.	Yes.	Yes.			14	12	1 yr.	Yes.	Yes
Washington	Yes.	1 yr.	Yes.	Yes.	Yes.	Hab'l.	Yes.			1 yr.	Yes.	Yes
West Virginia	Yes.	3 yrs.	Yes.	Yes.	Yes.			18	16	1 yr.	Yes.	Yes
Wisconsin	Yes.	1 yr.	Yes.	3 yrs.	Yes.	1 yr.	Yes.	18	15	1 yr.	Yes.	Yes
Wyoming	Yes.	1 yr.	Yes.	Yes.	Yes.	Hab'l.	1 yr.	18	16	1 yr.	Yes.	Yes

*Innocent party only. †Subsequent to marriage. ‡South Carolina has no divorce law, but marriages may be annulled.

NOTE—Consanguinity, infidelity and bigamy are causes for divorce in all states having divorce laws. Permanent insanity is cause for divorce in Idaho, Maine, Virginia, Utah and Washington under certain conditions.

HEIGHTS AND WEIGHTS OF ADULTS.

Height.	Weight.	Height.	Weight.	Height.	Weight.	Height.	Weight.
5 ft. 1 in	128 pounds	5 ft. 4 in	149 pounds	5 ft. 7 in	158 pounds	5 ft. 10 in	181 pounds
5 ft. 2 in	135 pounds	5 ft. 5 in	152 pounds	5 ft. 8 in	166 pounds	5 ft. 11 in	186 pounds
5 ft. 3 in	142 pounds	5 ft. 6 in	155 pounds	5 ft. 9 in	173 pounds	6 ft. 0 in	190 pounds

HEIGHTS AND WEIGHTS OF CHILDREN.

Height.	Weight. lbs.	Height.	Weight. lbs.	Height.	Weight. lbs.	Height.	Weight. lbs.
At birth.1 ft. 8 in.	8	2 years..3 ft. 0 in.	32	6 years..3 ft. 10 in.	49	10 years.4 ft. 6 in.	68
6 months 2 ft. 0½ in.	16	3 years..3 ft. 4 in.	36½	7 years..4 ft. 0 in.	52½	11 years.4 ft. 8 in.	74
1 year...2 ft. 5 in.	24	4 years..3 ft. 6 in.	41	8 years..4 ft. 2 in.	56½	12 years.4 ft. 10 in.	80
1½ years.2 ft. 8½ in.	28	5 years..3 ft. 8 in.	45	9 years..4 ft. 4 in.	62		

PULSE AT DIFFERENT AGES.

Newborn infants, per minute	130 to 140	Seventh to fourteenth year, per minute	80 to 90
First year, per minute	115 to 130	In adult age, per minute	70 to 75
Second year, per minute	95 to 110	In old age, per minute	60 to 75
Third year, per minute	85 to 95		

LARGEST LAKES IN THE UNITED STATES.

Lake Michigan is the largest lake entirely within the United States. It has an area of 22,450 square miles. Lake Okeechobee, in Florida, has an area of 1,250 square miles. Lake Champlain has an area of 600 square miles and extends six miles into Canada. Great Salt Lake varies as to its area. It was 2,360 square miles in 1870, but has receded since then. Lake Winnebago, in Wisconsin, has an area of approximately 200 square miles. Yellowstone lake has an area of 140 square miles.

DAYS OF GRACE, INTEREST AND STATUTE OF LIMITATIONS.

STATE.	Days of grace.	INTEREST. Legal rate.	INTEREST. By contract.	LIMITATIONS. Judgments.	LIMITATIONS. Notes.	LIMITATIONS. Accounts.	STATE.	Days of grace.	INTEREST. Legal rate.	INTEREST. By contract.	LIMITATIONS. Judgments.	LIMITATIONS. Notes.	LIMITATIONS. Accounts.
		P. ct.	P. ct.	Yrs.	Yrs.	Yrs.			P. ct.	P. ct.	Yrs.	Yrs.	Yrs.
Alabama.............	Yes	8	8	20	†6	3	Montana.............	No	8	Any	10	8	5
Alaska.............	Yes	8	12	10	6	1	Nebraska.............	No	7	10	5	5	4
Arkansas.............	Yes	6	10	10	5	3	Nevada.............	No	7	Any	6	4	4
Arizona.............	No	6	12	5	4	3	New Hampshire...	No*	6	6	20	6	6
California.............	No	7	Any	5	4	4	New Jersey.............	No	6	6	20	6	6
Colorado.............	No	8	Any	20	6	6	New Mexico.............	Yes	6	12	7	6	4
Connecticut	No	6	6	...†...	..5..	6	New York.............	No	6	6	20	6	6
Delaware	No	6	6	10	6	3	North Carolina...	Yes*	6	6	10	3	3
Dist. of Columbia...	No	6	10	12	3	3	North Dakota......	No	7	12	10	6	6
Florida.............	No	8	10	20	5	2	Ohio	No	6	8	15	15	6
Georgia.............	No	7	8	7	6	4	Oklahoma.............	Yes	6	10	5	5	3
Idaho.............	No	7	12	6	5	4	Oregon.............	Yes	6	10	10	6	6
Illinois.............	No	5	7	20	10	5	Pennsylvania...	No	6	6	5	6	6
Indiana.............	No	6	8	20	10	6	Rhode Island......	Yes*	6	Any	20	6	6
Iowa.............	No	6	8	20	10	5	South Carolina...	Yes*	7	8	10	6	6
Kansas.............	No	6	10	5	5	3	South Dakota......	Yes	7	12	20	6	6
Kentucky.............	No	6	6	15	15	5	Tennessee.............	No	6	6	10	6	6
Louisiana.............	No	5	8	10	5	3	Texas.............	Yes*	6	10	10	4	2
Maine.............	Yes*	6	Any	20	6	6	Utah.............	No	8	12	8	6	4
Maryland.............	No	6	6	12	3	3	Vermont.............	No	6	6	8	6	6
Massachusetts...	Yes*	6	Any	20	6	6	Virginia.............	No	6	6	20	5	2
Michigan.............	No	5	7	10	6	6	Washington......	No	6	12	6	6	3
Minnesota.............	No	7	10	10	6	6	West Virginia......	No	6	6	10	10	5
Mississippi.............	Yes	6	8	7	6	3	Wisconsin.............	No	6	10	20	6	6
Missouri.............	No	6	8	10	10	5	Wyoming.............	No	8	12	21	5	8

*Sight, yes; demand, no. †Under seal 10. ‡No law. §Negotiable notes 6, nonnegotiable 17.

TABLE OF MONTHLY WAGES.

DAYS.	$10	$11	$12	$13	$14	$15	$16	$17	$18	$19	$20	$21	$22	$23	$24	$25
1....	.38	.42	.46	.50	.54	.58	.62	.65	.69	.73	.77	.81	.85	.88	.92	.96
2..................	.77	.85	.92	1.00	1.08	1.15	1.23	1.31	1.38	1.46	1.54	1.62	1.69	1.77	1.85	1.92
3..................	1.15	1.27	1.38	1.50	1.62	1.73	1.85	1.96	2.08	2.19	2.31	2.42	2.54	2.65	2.77	2.88
4..................	1.54	1.69	1.85	2.00	2.15	2.31	2.46	2.62	2.77	2.92	3.08	3.23	3.38	3.54	3.69	3.85
5..................	1.92	2.12	2.31	2.50	2.69	2.88	3.08	3.27	3.46	3.65	3.85	4.04	4.23	4.42	4.62	4.81
6..................	2.31	2.54	2.77	3.00	3.23	3.46	3.69	3.92	4.15	4.38	4.62	4.85	5.08	5.31	5.54	5.77
7..................	2.69	2.96	3.23	3.50	3.77	4.04	4.31	4.58	4.85	5.12	5.38	5.65	5.92	6.19	6.46	6.73
8..................	3.08	3.38	3.69	4.00	4.31	4.62	4.92	5.23	5.54	5.85	6.15	6.46	6.77	7.08	7.38	7.69
9..................	3.46	3.81	4.15	4.50	4.85	5.19	5.54	5.88	6.23	6.58	6.92	7.27	7.62	7.96	8.31	8.65
10..................	3.85	4.23	4.62	5.00	5.38	5.77	6.15	6.54	6.92	7.31	7.69	8.08	8.46	8.85	9.23	9.62
11..................	4.23	4.65	5.08	5.50	5.92	6.35	6.77	7.19	7.62	8.04	8.46	8.88	9.31	9.73	10.15	10.58
12..................	4.62	5.08	5.44	6.00	6.46	6.92	7.38	7.85	8.31	8.77	9.23	9.69	10.15	10.62	11.08	11.54
13..................	5.00	5.50	6.00	6.50	7.00	7.50	8.00	8.50	9.00	9.50	10.00	10.50	11.00	11.50	12.00	12.50
14..................	5.38	5.92	6.46	7.00	7.54	8.08	8.62	9.15	9.69	10.23	10.77	11.31	11.85	12.38	12.92	13.46
15..................	5.77	6.35	6.92	7.50	8.08	8.65	9.23	9.81	10.38	10.96	11.54	12.12	12.69	13.27	13.85	14.42
16..................	6.15	6.77	7.38	8.00	8.62	9.23	9.85	10.46	11.08	11.69	12.31	12.92	13.54	14.15	14.77	15.38
17..................	6.54	7.19	7.85	8.50	9.15	9.81	10.46	11.12	11.77	12.42	13.08	13.73	14.38	15.04	15.69	16.35
18..................	6.92	7.62	8.31	9.00	9.69	10.38	11.08	11.77	12.46	13.15	13.85	14.54	15.23	15.92	16.62	17.31
19..................	7.31	8.04	8.77	9.50	10.23	10.96	11.69	12.42	13.15	13.88	14.62	15.35	16.08	16.81	17.54	18.27
20..................	7.69	8.46	9.23	10.00	10.77	11.54	12.31	13.08	13.85	14.62	15.38	16.15	16.92	17.69	18.46	19.23
21..................	8.08	8.88	9.69	10.50	11.31	12.12	12.92	13.73	14.54	15.35	16.15	16.96	17.77	18.58	19.38	20.19
22..................	8.46	9.31	10.15	11.00	11.85	12.69	13.54	14.38	15.23	16.08	16.94	17.77	18.62	19.46	20.31	21.15
23..................	8.85	9.73	10.62	11.50	12.38	13.27	14.15	15.04	15.92	16.81	17.69	18.58	19.46	20.35	21.23	22.12
24..................	9.23	10.15	11.08	12.00	12.92	13.85	14.77	15.69	16.62	17.54	18.46	19.38	20.31	21.23	22.15	23.08
25..................	9.62	10.58	11.54	12.50	13.46	14.42	15.38	16.35	17.31	18.27	19.23	20.19	21.15	22.12	23.08	24.04

TABLE OF YEARLY WAGES.

Per year.	Per month.	Per week.	Per day.	Per year.	Per month.	Per week.	Per day.	Per year.	Per month.	Per week.	Per day.
$20 is	$1.67	$0.38	$0.05	$100 is	$8.33	$1.92	$0.27	$180 is	$15.00	$3.45	$0.49
25	2.08	.48	.07	105	8.75	2.01	.29	185	15.42	3.55	.51
30	2.50	.58	.08	110	9.17	2.11	.30	190	15.83	3.64	.52
35	2.92	.67	.10	115	9.58	2.21	.32	195	16.25	3.74	.53
40	3.33	.77	.11	120	10.00	2.30	.33	200	16.67	3.84	.55
45	3.75	.86	.12	125	10.42	2.40	.34	205	17.08	3.93	.56
50	4.17	.96	.14	130	10.83	2.49	.34	210	17.50	4.03	.58
55	4.58	1.06	.15	135	11.25	2.59	.37	215	17.92	4.12	.59
60	5.00	1.15	.16	140	11.67	2.69	.38	220	18.33	4.22	.60
65	5.42	1.25	.18	145	12.08	2.78	.40	225	18.75	4.31	.62
70	5.83	1.34	.19	150	12.50	2.88	.41	230	19.17	4.41	.63
75	6.25	1.44	.21	155	12.92	2.97	.42	235	19.58	4.51	.64
80	6.67	1.53	.22	160	13.33	3.07	.44	240	20.00	4.60	.66
85	7.08	1.63	.23	165	13.75	3.16	.45	245	20.42	4.70	.67
90	7.50	1.73	.25	170	14.17	3.26	.47	250	20.83	4.79	.69
95	7.92	1.82	.26	175	14.58	3.36	.48				

SIMPLE INTEREST TABLE.

NOTE—To find the amount of interest at 2½ per cent on any given sum, divide the amount given for the same sum in the table at 5 per cent by 2; at 3½ per cent divide the amount at 7 per cent by 2, etc.

Amt.	Interest.	1 day.	2 days.	3 days.	4 days.	5 days.	6 days.	7 days.	8 days.	9 days.	10 days.	20 days.	1 month.	2 mos.	3 mos.	4 mos.	5 mos.	6 mos.	1 year.
$1	3															1	1	1	3
	4														1	1	2	2	4
	5											1		1	2	2	2	3	5
	6											1	1	1	2	2	2	3	6
	7											1	1	1	2	2	3	4	7
$2	3									1		1	1	1	2	2	2	3	6
	4									1		1	1	2	2	2	3	4	8
	5								1	1		1	2	2	3	3	4	5	10
	6								1	1		1	2	3	4	5	6	12
	7							1	1	1		2	2	4	5	6	7	14
$3	3									1		1	2	3	3	4	5	9
	4								1	1		1	2	3	4	5	6	12
	5							1	1	1		1	2	3	5	6	8	15
	6							1	1	1		2	3	5	6	8	9	18
	7					1	1	1	1		2	4	5	7	9	11	21
$4	3									1		1	2	3	4	5	6	12
	4									1		1	2	4	5	6	8	16
	5							1	1	1		2	3	5	7	8	10	20
	6					1	1	1	1		2	4	6	8	10	12	24
	7					1	1	1	2		2	5	7	9	12	14	28
$5	3								1		1	2	4	5	7	8	15
	4							1	1		1	3	5	6	8	10	20
	5					1	1	1	1		2	4	6	8	10	13	25
	6				1	1	1	1		2	3	5	8	10	13	15	30
	7				1	1	1	1		2	3	6	9	12	15	18	35
$10	3					1	1	1	1		2	5	7	10	12	15	30
	4				1	1	1	1	1		2	3	6	10	13	16	20	40
	5			1	1	1	1	1		2	3	6	13	17	21	25	50
	6		1	1	1	1	1	2	2	2	3	5	10	15	20	25	30	60
	7		1	1	1	1	1	2	2	2	4	6	12	18	23	29	35	70
$25	3		1	1	2	2	2	2	1	2	4	6	12	19	25	31	38	75
	4	1	1	2	2	2	3	3	5	8	16	25	33	41	50	1.00
	5	1	1	2	2	3	3	3	7	10	21	31	42	52	63	1.25
	6	1	2	2	3	3	4	4	8	13	25	38	50	63	75	1.50
	7	1	2	2	3	3	4	4	5	10	15	29	44	58	73	88	1.75
$50	3	1	1	2	2	3	4	4	5	6	11	12	25	37	50	62	75	1.50
	4	1	1	2	3	3	4	4	5	6	11	16	33	50	67	85	1.00	2.00
	5	1	2	3	3	4	6	7	7	14	21	42	63	83	1.04	1.25	2.50
	6	1	2	3	4	5	6	7	8	8	17	25	50	75	1.00	1.25	1.50	3.00
	7	1	2	3	4	5	6	7	9	19	29	58	88	1.17	1.46	1.75	3.50
$100	3	1	1	2	3	4	5	6	6	7	8	16	25	50	75	1.00	1.25	1.50	3.00
	4	1	2	3	4	6	6	8	10	11	22	33	66	1.00	1.33	1.67	2.00	4.00
	5	1	3	4	6	7	8	10	11	13	14	28	42	83	1.25	1.67	2.08	2.50	5.00
	6	2	3	5	7	8	10	12	13	15	17	33	50	1.00	1.50	2.00	2.50	3.00	6.00
	7	2	4	6	8	10	12	14	16	18	19	39	58	1.17	1.75	2.33	2.92	3.50	7.00

COMPOUND INTEREST ON ONE DOLLAR.

Years.	3%.	4%.	5%.	6%.	7%.	Years.	3%.	4%.	5%.	6%.	7%.
1	1.03	1.04	1.05	1.06	1.07	9	1.30	1.42	1.55	1.70	1.83
1½	1.04	1.06	1.07	1.09	1.10	9½	1.32	1.45	1.59	1.75	1.92
2	1.06	1.08	1.10	1.12	1.14	10	1.34	1.48	1.63	1.80	1.98
2½	1.07	1.10	1.13	1.15	1.18	100	19.25	50.50	131.50	340.00	868.00
3	1.09	1.12	1.15	1.19	1.22						
3½	1.10	1.14	1.18	1.22	1.27						
4	1.12	1.17	1.21	1.26	1.31						
4½	1.14	1.19	1.24	1.30	1.36						
5	1.16	1.21	1.28	1.34	1.41						
5½	1.17	1.24	1.31	1.38	1.45						
6	1.19	1.26	1.34	1.42	1.51						
6½	1.21	1.29	1.37	1.46	1.56						
7	1.23	1.31	1.41	1.51	1.61						
7½	1.24	1.34	1.44	1.55	1.67						
8	1.26	1.37	1.48	1.60	1.73						
8½	1.28	1.39	1.52	1.65	1.79						

WHEN MONEY DOUBLES AT INTEREST.

	Interest.			Interest.	
	Simple.	Comp'd.		Simple.	Comp'd.
Rate.	Years.	Years.	Rate.	Years.	Years.
1	100.80	69.66	4½	22.22	15.75
1¼	66.66	46.56	5	20.00	14.21
2	50.00	35.00	5½	18.18	12.94
2½	40.00	28.07	6	16.67	11.90
3	33.33	23.45	6½	15.38	11.00
3½	28.57	20.15	7	14.29	10.24
4	25.00	17.67	7½	13.33	9.58

LIBRARY OF CONGRESS.

The library of congress was established in 1800 in the city of Washington, D. C. It was burned in 1814, and in 1851 lost 35,000 volumes by fire. The present library building, which cost $6,347,000, was opened to the public in November, 1897. It is located a short distance east of the capitol and is the largest and finest building of its kind in the world.

June 30, 1912, the library contained 2,012,393 books and pamphlets, 129,123 maps, 591,632 pieces of music and 349,745 photographs, prints, engravings and lithographs. The copyright office is a distinct division of the library with its own force of employes. The total number of employes in the library is 494 and the annual cost of maintenance is now about $788,000, including $200,000 for printing and binding.

The librarian of congress is Herbert Putnam, salary, $6,500; chief assistant librarian, Appleton P. C. Griffin, $4,000.

WEIGHTS AND MEASURES USED IN THE UNITED STATES.

LONG MEASURE.

12 inches	= 1 foot.	
3 feet	= 1 yard	= 36 inches.
5½ yards	= 1 rod	= 16½ feet.
40 rods	= 1 furlong	= 660 feet.
8 furlongs	= 1 mile	= 5,280 feet.

MARINERS' MEASURE.

6 feet	= 1 fathom.	
120 fathoms	= 1 cable length.	
7½ cable lengths	= 1 mile.	
6250 feet	= 1 statute mile.	
6085 feet	= 1 nautical mile.	
3 marine miles	= 1 marine league.	

LIQUID MEASURE.

4 gills	= 1 pint.	
2 pints	= 1 quart.	
4 quarts	= 1 gallon.	
31½ gallons	= 1 barrel.	
2 barrels	= 1 hogshead.	

SQUARE MEASURE.

144 square inches	= 1 square foot.	
9 square feet	= 1 square yard.	
10¼ square yards	= 1 square rod.	
160 square rods	= 1 acre.	
640 acres	= 1 square mile.	
36 square miles	= 1 township.	

CUBIC MEASURE.

1,728 cubic inches	= 1 cubic foot.
27 cubic feet	= 1 cubic yard.
128 cubic feet	= 1 cord of wood or stone.
1 gallon contains 231 cubic inches.	
1 bushel contains 2,150.4 cubic inches.	
A cord of wood is 8 ft. long, 4 ft. wide & 4 ft. high.	

DRY MEASURE.

2 pints	= 1 quart.
8 quarts	= 1 peck.
4 pecks	= 1 bushel.

CIRCULAR MEASURE.

60 seconds	= 1 minute.
60 minutes	= 1 degree.
360 degrees	= 1 circle.
1 degree	= 60 geographic miles.
1 geographic mile	= 1.1527 statute miles.
1 degree of the equator	= 69.124 statute miles.

APOTHECARIES' WEIGHT.

20 grains	= 1 scruple
3 scruples	= 1 dram.
8 drams	= 1 ounce.
12 ounces	= 1 pound.

AVOIRDUPOIS WEIGHT.

27 11-32 grains	= 1 dram.
16 drams	= 1 ounce.
16 ounces	= 1 pound.
2,000 lbs.	= 1 short ton.
2,240 lbs.	= 1 long ton.

TROY WEIGHT.

24 grains	= 1 pennyweight.
20 pennyw's	= 1 ounce.
12 ounces	= 1 pound

TIME MEASURE.

60 seconds	= 1 minute.
60 minutes	= 1 hour.
24 hours	= 1 day.
365 days	= 1 year.
100 years	= 1 century.

STATIONERS' TABLE.

24 sheets	= 1 quire.
20 quires	= 1 ream.
2 reams	= 1 bundle.
5 bundles	= 1 bale.

COUNTING.

12 things	= 1 dozen.
12 dozen	= 1 gross.
12 gross	= 1 great gross
20 things	= 1 score.

CLOTH MEASURE.

2¼ inches	= 1 nail.
4 nails	= 1 quarter
4 quarters	= 1 yard.

MISCELLANEOUS.

3 inches	= 1 palm.
4 inches	= 1 hand.
6 inches	= 1 span.
18 inches	= 1 cubit.
21.8 inches	= 1 bible cubit.
2½ feet	= 1 military pace.

SURVEYORS' MEASURE.

7.92 inches	= 1 link.
25 links	= 1 rod.
4 rods	= 1 chain.
10 chains	= 1 furlong.
8 furlongs	= 1 mile.

THE METRIC SYSTEM.

The metric system is in general use in all the principal nations of Europe and America with the exception of Great Britain, Russia and the United States, where it is authorized but not compulsory. Its use for scientific purposes is common throughout the world.

WEIGHTS.

Milligram (.001 gram)	=	.0154 grain.
Centigram (.01 gram)	=	.1543 grain.
Decigram (.1 gram)	=	1.5432 grains.
Gram	=	15.432 grains.
Decagram (10 grams)	=	.3527 ounce.
Hectogram (100 grams)	=	3.5274 ounces.
Kilogram (1,000 grams)	=	2.2046 pounds.
Myriagram (10,000 grams)	=	22.046 pounds.
Quintal (100,000 grams)	=	220.46 pounds.
Millier or tonneau—ton(1,000,000 grams)	=	2,204.6 pounds.

DRY.

Milliliter (.001 liter)	=	.061 cubic inch.
Centiliter (.01 liter)	=	.6102 cubic inch.
Deciliter (.1 liter)	=	6.1022 cubic inches.
Liter	=	.908 quart.
Decaliter (10 liters)	=	9.08 quarts.
Hectoliter (100 liters)	=	2.838 bushels.
Kiloliter (1,000 liters)	=	1.308 cubic yards.

LIQUID.

Milliliter (.001 liter)	=	.0338 fluid ounce.
Centiliter (.01 liter)	=	.338 fluid ounce
Deciliter (.1 liter)	=	.845 gill.
Liter	=	1.0567 quarts.
Decaliter (10 liters)	=	2.6418 gallons.
Hectoliter (100 liters)	=	26.417 gallons.
Kiloliter (1,000 liters)	=	264.18 gallons.

LENGTH.

Millimeter (.001 meter)	=	.0394 inch.
Centimeter (.01 meter)	=	.3937 inch.
Decimeter (.1 meter)	=	3.937 inches.
Meter	=	39.37 inches.
Decameter (10 meters)	=	393.7 inches.
Hectometer (100 meters)	=	328 feet 1 inch.
Kilometer (1,000 meters)	=	.62137 mile (3,280 feet 10 inches).
Myriameter(10,000 meters)	=	6.2137 miles.

SURFACE.

Centare (1 square meter)	=	1,550 sq. inches.
Are (100 square meters)	=	119.6 sq. yards.
Hectare (10,000 sq. meters)	=	2.471 acres.

METRIC EQUIVALENTS.

1 grain	=	0.06480 gram.
1 ounce	=	28.3495 grams.
1 pound	=	0.45359 kilogram.
1 dram (apoth.)	=	3.6967 grams.
1 scruple (apoth.)	=	1.2322 grams.
1 quart (dry)	=	1.1012 liters.
1 peck (dry)	=	8.8098 liters.
1 bushel	=	0.35239 hectoliter.
1 quart (liq.)	=	0.94636 liter.
1 gallon	=	3.78543 liters.
1 inch	=	25.4001 millimeters.
1 inch	=	2.54001 centimeters.
1 inch	=	0.0254 meter.
1 foot	=	0.3048 meter.
1 yard	=	0.9144 meter.
1 mile	=	1.6093 kilometers.
1 sq. inch	=	645.16 sq. millimeters.
1 sq. foot	=	0.0929 sq. meter.
1 sq. yard	=	0.8361 sq. meter.
1 sq. mile	=	2.5900 sq. kilometers.
1 acre	=	0.4017 hectare.
1 cubic inch	=	16.387 cubic millimeters.
1 cubic foot	=	0.02832 cubic meter.
1 cubic yard	=	0.7645 cubic meter.

ELECTRICAL UNITS DEFINED.

Ohm—Unit of resistance; represents resistance offered to an unvarying electric current by a column of mercury at the temperature of ice, 14.4421 grams in mass, of a cross-sectional area of 1.00093 square millimeters and of the length of 106.3 centimeters.

Ampere—Unit of current; decomposes .0009324 of a gram of water in one second or deposits silver at the rate of .001118 of a gram per second, when passed through a solution of nitrate of silver in water.

Volt—Unit of electro motive force; one volt equals one ampere of current passing through a substance having one ohm of resistance.

Coulomb—Unit of quantity; amount of electricity transferred by a current of one ampere in one second.

Farad—Unit of capacity; capacity of a condenser charged to a potential of one volt by one coulomb. A microfarad is one-millionth of a farad.

Joule—Unit of work; equivalent to energy expended in one second by one ampere current in one ohm resistance.

Watt—Unit of power; equivalent to work done at the rate of one joule per second. A kilowatt is 1,000 watts.

STATUTORY WEIGHTS OF THE BUSHEL.

STATE OR TERRITORY.	Wheat.	Rye.	Oats.	Barley.	Buckwheat.	Shelled corn.	Corn on cob.	Cornmeal.	Bran.	Potatoes, Irish.	Potatoes, sweet.	Carrots.	Onions.	Turnips.	Beets.	Beans.	Peas.	Apples.	Dried apples.	Dried peaches.	Castor beans.	Flax seed.	Hemp seed.	Millet.	Timothy seed.	Blue grass seed.	Hungarian gr. seed.	Clover seed.
United States	60	56	32	48	42	..	..	48	..	60	..	..	..	..	..	60	60	..	24	..	50	56	..	..	..	..	..	..
Alabama	60	56	32	47	..	56	70	46	..	60	55	..	..	55	..	60	60	..	24	38	..	..	..	..	..	..	..	..
Arizona	60	56	32	45	..	54	..	..	..	60	..	..	..	60	..	..	..	..	..	..	..	..	..	..	..	..	..	..
Arkansas	60	56	32	48	52	56	70	48	20	60	56	..	57	57	..	60	60	50	24	33	..	56	..	50	60	14	..	60
California	60	54	32	50	40	52	..	..	..	60	..	..	..	..	..	..	..	..	..	..	..	..	..	..	..	..	..	..
Colorado	60	56	32	48	52	56	70	50	..	60	..	..	57	..	..	60	..	..	..	..	..	44	..	45	14	..	..	60
Connecticut	60	56	32	48	48	56	..	..	20	60	54	50	52	50	50	60	60	60	48	25	33	..	55	..	45	..	..	60
Delaware	60	..	..	..	..	56	..	..	..	60	..	..	..	..	..	..	..	..	..	..	..	..	..	..	..	..	..	..
District of Columbia	..	..	32	..	..	56	..	..	..	60	..	..	..	..	..	..	..	..	..	..	..	..	..	..	..	..	..	..
Florida	60	56	32	48	..	56	70	48	20	60	60	..	56	54	..	60	..	..	48	24	33	48	..	..	50	..	..	..
Georgia	60	56	32	47	52	56	70	48	20	60	55	..	57	55	..	60	60	..	24	33	..	56	44	..	45	14	..	60
Hawaii	60	56	32	48	..	56	..	..	..	60	..	..	..	..	..	..	..	..	..	..	..	..	..	..	..	..	..	..
Idaho	60	50	32	48	42	56	..	..	..	60	..	..	..	..	..	..	..	..	45	28	25	..	54	..	..	..	..	60
Illinois	60	56	32	48	52	56	70	48	20	60	50	..	57	55	..	60	..	..	24	33	46	56	44	..	45	14	..	60
Indiana	60	56	32	48	50	56	68	50	..	60	55	..	48	55	..	60	..	..	25	33	46	..	44	50	45	14	..	60
Iowa	60	56	32	48	52	56	70	..	20	60	40	..	57	..	..	60	..	48	24	33	46	56	44	50	45	14	50	60
Kansas	60	56	32	48	50	56	70	50	20	60	50	..	57	55	..	60	..	48	24	33	50	56	44	50	45	14	50	60
Kentucky	60	56	32	47	56	56	70	50	20	60	55	..	57	60	..	60	60	..	24	33	45	56	44	50	45	14	50	60
Louisiana	60	56	32	48	..	56	..	..	..	60	..	..	..	..	..	..	..	..	..	..	..	..	..	..	..	..	..	..
Maine	60	50	32	48	48	56	..	..	50	..	60	..	50	52	50	60	60	60	44	..	..	..	..	..	45	..	..	..
Maryland	..	..	..	26	..	..	..	..	..	..	56	..	..	..	..	..	..	..	..	..	..	..	..	..	..	..	..	..
Massachusetts	60	56	32	48	48	56	..	50	20	60	54	50	53	..	..	60	60	48	25	33	..	55	..	..	45	..	..	60
Michigan	60	56	32	48	48	56	70	50	..	60	56	..	54	58	..	60	60	48	22	28	46	56	44	50	45	14	50	60
Minnesota	60	56	32	48	50	56	70	..	..	60	55	45	52	..	50	60	60	60	50	28	28	..	50	48	45	14	48	60
Mississippi	60	56	32	48	48	56	72	48	20	60	60	..	57	55	..	60	60	..	26	33	46	56	44	50	45	14	50	60
Missouri	60	56	32	48	52	56	70	50	20	60	56	50	57	42	..	60	60	48	24	33	46	56	44	50	45	14	48	60
Montana	60	56	32	48	52	56	70	50	20	60	..	50	57	55	50	60	60	45	..	..	..	56	44	..	45	14	..	60
Nebraska	60	56	32	48	52	56	70	50	20	60	50	..	57	55	..	60	60	..	24	33	46	56	44	50	45	14	50	60
New Hampshire	60	56	32	48	50	56	..	50	..	60	..	..	..	..	..	..	..	..	..	..	..	..	..	..	..	..	..	..
New Jersey	60	56	32	48	50	56	..	..	..	60	54	..	57	..	..	60	60	50	25	33	..	55	..	..	..	..	..	64
New York	60	56	32	48	48	56	..	50	20	60	54	50	57	..	..	60	60	48	25	33	..	55	..	..	45	..	..	60
North Carolina	60	56	32	48	50	56	..	..	..	60	..	..	..	60	..	..	..	..	..	..	..	55	..	..	..	..	..	60
North Dakota	60	56	32	48	42	56	70	..	20	60	46	..	52	60	60	60	60	..	..	..	..	56	..	50	45	..	..	60
Ohio	60	56	32	48	50	56	68	..	20	60	50	50	55	60	60	56	60	60	50	24	33	..	56	44	50	..	50	60
Oklahoma	60	56	32	48	42	56	70	..	20	60	46	..	52	60	60	60	60	..	..	..	..	56	..	42	..	..	..	60
Oregon	60	56	32	46	42	56	..	..	..	60	..	..	..	..	..	..	..	..	45	28	28	..	..	..	..	..	..	60
Pennsylvania	60	56	32	47	48	56	..	..	..	56	..	..	50	..	..	..	..	..	..	..	..	..	..	..	..	..	..	60
Rhode Island	60	56	32	48	48	56	70	50	20	60	54	50	50	50	50	60	60	48	25	33	46	54	44	50	45	..	50	60
South Carolina	..	..	..	..	..	..	..	48	..	..	..	..	..	..	..	..	..	..	..	..	..	..	..	..	..	..	..	..
South Dakota	60	56	32	48	42	56	70	..	20	60	46	..	52	60	60	60	60	..	24	24	46	56	44	50	45	14	48	60
Tennessee	60	56	32	48	50	56	70	..	20	60	56	50	57	50	60	60	60	..	45	28	28	..	56	44	50	45	..	60
Texas	60	56	32	48	42	56	70	..	20	60	55	..	57	60	..	60	60	..	45	28	28	..	56	44	50	45	..	60
Vermont	60	56	32	48	48	56	..	..	..	60	..	50	52	60	60	62	60	46	..	..	..	..	..	..	45	..	..	60
Virginia	60	56	30	48	52	56	70	50	..	56	56	..	57	55	..	60	60	..	24	33	40	..	56	44	50	45	14	48	60
Washington	60	56	32	48	42	56	..	..	..	60	..	..	..	..	..	..	..	..	45	28	28	..	56	..	..	45	..	..	60
West Virginia	60	56	32	48	52	56	..	..	..	60	..	..	..	60	..	60	60	50	25	33	..	56	44	50	45	..	48	60
Wisconsin	60	56	32	48	50	56	70	50	20	60	54	50	57	42	50	60	60	50	25	33	..	56	44	50	45	..	48	60

NOTE—Rye meal takes 48 pounds to the bushel in the District of Columbia and 50 in Maine, Massachusetts, New York, Rhode Island and Wisconsin. The metric system is used in the Philippines and Porto Rico.

TABLE OF SPECIFIC GRAVITY.

Compared with water.

Water, distilled	100	Iron, cast	721
Water, sea	103	Ivory	183
Alcohol	84	Lead	1,135
Aluminum	256	Mahogany	106
Ash	84	Maple	75
Beech	85	Marble	270
Beer	102	Milk, cow's	102
Brass	840	Milk, goat's	101
Butter	94	Oak	117
Cedar	61	Oil, olive	92
Chalk	279	Opium	134
Cider	102	Platina	2,136
Coal	136	Porcelain	226
Copper	895	Silver	1,047
Cork	21	Steel	783
Diamond	353	Sulphur	203
Ebony	133	Tin	729
Fir	65	Turpentine	99
Glass	389	Walnut	67
Gold	1,926	Wine	100
Ice	92	Zinc	691
Indigo	77		

THERMOMETERS COMPARED.

There are three kinds of thermometers, with varying scales, in general use throughout the world —the Fahrenheit, Reaumur and centigrade. The freezing and boiling points on their scales compare as follows:

Thermometer.	Freezing pt.	Boiling pt.
Fahrenheit	32 degrees	212 degrees
Reaumur	zero	80 degrees
Centigrade	zero	100 degrees

The degrees on one scale are reduced to their equivalents on another by these formulas:

Fahrenheit to Reaumur—Subtract 32, multiply by four-ninths.

Fahrenheit to Centigrade—Subtract 32, multiply by five-ninths.

Reaumur to Fahrenheit—Multiply by nine-fourths, add 32.

Reaumur to Centigrade—Multiply by five-fourths.

Centigrade to Fahrenheit—Multiply by nine-fifths, add 32.

Centigrade to Reaumur—Multiply by four-fifths.

BANKING STATISTICS.

[From reports of the comptroller of the currency.]

NATIONAL BANKS OF THE UNITED STATES.

YEAR ENDED MARCH 1—	Banks.	Capital.	Surplus.	Total dividends.	Net earnings.	RATIOS.		
						Dividends to capital.	Dividends to capital and surplus.	Earnings to capit'l and surpl's
1870	1,526	$409,008,886	$84,112,020	$43,246,925	$58,218,118	10.5	8.8	11.8
1880	2,045	454,606,073	116,187,926	35,526,140	38,035,984	7.8	6.2	6.7
1890	3,244	607,428,365	200,837,659	49,575,355	63,756,914	8.1	6.1	8.6
1900	3,571	603,396,550	250,543,068	47,433,357	69,984,810	7.9	5.6	3.2
1901	3,765	622,396,094	257,948,290	50,219,115	87,674,175	8.1	5.7	10.0
1902	4,131	659,608,169	285,623,449	64,802,442	99,103,168	9.8	6.8	10.5
1903	4,451	688,817,835	324,462,477	60,123,622	102,743,721	8.7	5.9	10.1
1904	4,914	746,385,438	372,551,716	73,640,123	116,475,135	9.9	6.6	10.4
1905	5,356	768,114,231	402,330,800	70,996,522	105,196,154	9.2	6.1	9.0
1906	5,685	779,544,247	414,799,562	80,831,561	113,662,521	10.4	6.8	9.5
1907*	6,017	837,002,528	501,774,458	144,376,245	219,195,804	17.2	10.8	16.4
1908	6,562	901,384,244	552,562,178	98,149,236	132,254,329	10.89	6.75	9.1
1909	5,788	919,143,822	585,407,483	92,993,450	131,185,750	10.12	6.18	8.72
1910	6,984	963,457,540	630,150,719	105,898,622	154,167,489	10.99	6.65	9.67
1911	7,165	1,008,180,225	693,951,760	114,695,112	156,985,513	11.38	6.83	9.35
1912	7,397	1,031,383,425	704,346,706	120,300,872	149,056,603	11.96	6.96	8.59
Average, 43 years		623,397,709	254,330,436	57,142,245	75,726,559	9.17	6.51	8.63
Aggregate, 43 years				2,457,116,551	3,256,242,044			

*March 1, 1906, to June 30, 1907.

NATIONAL BANK NOTES.

Issued since 1864 and outstanding Oct. 31, 1912, by denominations and amount.

Denomination.	Issued.	Outstanding.	Denomination.	Issued.	Outstanding.
Ones	$23,169,677	$343,587	One hundreds	$351,445,359	$35,076,250
Twos	15,495,038	164,312	Five hundreds	11,947,000	87,500
Fives	1,587,187,420	139,997,046	One thousands	7,379,000	23,000
Tens	2,321,483,180	330,089,730			
Twenties	1,401,708,060	227,332,780	Total	5,922,574,825	750,472,349
Fifties	202,812,100	17,358,150	NOTE—Gold notes and fractions not included.		

NATIONAL BANKS CLASSIFIED BY CAPITAL.

Class.	Number.	Per ct.
$25,000	2,004	27.09
Over $25,000 and less than $50,000	381	5.15
$50,000 and less than $100,000	2,321	31.38
$100,000 and less than $250,000	2,006	27.12
$250,000 and less than $1,000,000	498	6.73
$1,000,000 and less than $5,000,000	169	2.29
$5,000,000 and over	18	.24

The national banks having $5,000,000 or more capital in 1913 were:

Bank of Commerce, New York, N. Y., $25,000,000.
National City, New York, N. Y., $25,000,000.
Continental and Com'ercial, Chicago, Ill., $21,500,000.
First National, New York, N. Y., $10,000,000.

First National, Chicago, Ill., $10,000,000.
National Bank of Com'rce, St. Louis, Mo., $10,000,000.
Shawmut, Boston, Mass., $10,000,000.
Bank of California, San Francisco, Cal., $8,500,000.
Mechanics' and Metals, New York, N. Y., $6,000,000.
Farmers' Deposit, Pittsburgh, Pa., $6,000,000.
Mellon National, Pittsburgh, Pa., $6,000,000.
Wells Fargo-Nevada, San Francisco, Cal., $6,000,000.
First National, Cincinnati, O., $6,000,000.
Fourth National, New York, N. Y., $5,000,000.
American Exchange, New York, N. Y., $5,000,000.
Chase, New York, N. Y., $5,000,000.
National Park, New York, N. Y., $5,000,000.
First National, Boston, Mass., $5,000,000.

SAVINGS-BANK STATISTICS OF UNITED STATES FROM 1820.

YEAR.	Number of banks.	Number of depositors.	Deposits.	Average to each depositor.	Average per capita in U. S.	YEAR.	Number of banks.	Number of depositors.	Deposits.	Average to each depositor.	Average per capita in U. S.
1820	10	8,635	$1,138,576	$131.86	$0.12	1903	1,078	7,035,228	$2,935,204,845	$417.21	$36.52
1830	36	38,085	6,973,504	183.09	.54	1904	1,157	7,305,443	3,060,178,611	418.89	37.43
1840	61	78,701	14,051,520	178.54	.82	1905	1,237	7,696,229	3,261,236,119	423.74	39.17
1850	108	251,354	43,431,130	172.78	1.87	1906	1,319	8,027,192	3,482,137,198	433.79	41.13
1860	278	693,870	149,277,504	215.13	4.75	1907	1,415	8,588,811	3,690,078,945	429.64	42.87
1870	517	1,630,846	549,874,358	337.17	14.26	1908	1,453	8,705,848	3,660,553,945	420.47	41.84
1880	629	2,335,582	819,106,973	350.71	16.33	1909	1,703	8,831,863	3,713,405,710	420.45	41.75
1890	921	4,258,895	1,524,844,506	358.03	24.55	1910	1,759	9,142,908	4,070,486,246	445.20	45.05
1900	1,002	6,107,083	2,449,547,885	401.10	31.75	1911	1,884	9,794,647	4,212,583,598	430.09	44.82
1902	1,036	6,666,672	2,750,177,290	412.53	34.81	1912	1,922	10,010,304	4,451,818,522	444.72	46.58

BANKING POWER OF THE UNITED STATES (1912).

CLASSIFICATION.	No.	Capital.	Surplus, etc.	Deposits.	Circulation.	Total.
National banks	7,372	$1,033,570,075	$950,827,515	$5,884,407,144	$708,690,593	$8,577,495,927
State, etc. banks	17,823	977,272,830	1,215,331,634	11,198,606,444		13,391,210,908
Non-reporting banks	3,800	70,000,000	40,000,000	470,000,000		580,000,000
Total	28,995	2,080,843,505	2,206,159,149	17,553,013,588	708,690,593	22,548,706,835

DEPOSITS IN ALL BANKS JUNE 14, 1912.

Banks.	No.	Savings deposits.	Total deposits.
State	15,381	$657,477,220.31	$2,919,977,897.99
Mutual savings	630	3,592,530,070.33	3,608,657,828.11
Stock savings	1,292	574,822,459.57	842,897,859.61
Loan and trust	1,410	910,850,167.60	3,674,578,238.92
Private	1,110	26,868,853.68	152,494,618.90
National	7,372	733,643,936.11	5,825,461,163.56
Total	25,195	6,496,192,707.60	17,024,067,606.89

BANKS OF ALL KINDS IN THE UNITED STATES (JUNE 14, 1912).

(Includes national, savings, state and private banks and loan and trust companies.) †Per

State.	Banks.	*Deposits.	capita.
Alabama	324	$81,427,137.88	$7.32
Alaska	17	2,805,247.04	.84
Arizona	51	22,014,683.71	9.76
Arkansas	376	48,846,407.18	2.57
California	746	795,604,872.36	148.84
Colorado	322	119,707,138.45	20.89
Connecticut	207	413,640,023.77	251.32
District of Columbia	29	67,486,072.05	31.43
Florida	204	61,125,603.20	20.93
Georgia	760	121,461,915.77	9.97
Hawaii	12	17,068,921.15	25.14
Idaho	184	33,296,898.22	5.67
Illinois	1,290	1,087,896,164.02	55.77
Indiana	892	318,602,887.51	24.07
Iowa	1,457	406,964,427.86	57.83
Kansas	1,110	160,267,644.06	3.69
Kentucky	614	137,044,129.86	8.45
Louisiana	243	114,312,484.62	17.39
Maine	163	179,671,075.55	187.03
Maryland	234	251,180,967.91	104.48
Massachusetts	441	1,426,854,037.75	246.42
Michigan	607	441,981,179.60	75.28
Minnesota	1,031	323,141,780.94	27.52
Mississippi	263	63,677,169.30	5.11
Missouri	1,364	449,693,434.42	12.23
Montana	212	66,716,429.93	19.31
Nebraska	926	190,164,262.38	14.95
Nevada	32	15,576,303.51	41.61
New Hampshire	120	118,101,849.10	228.52
New Jersey	353	512,710,708.36	99.46
New Mexico	85	17,582,547.70	6.55
New York	939	4,653,357,925.68	190.89
North Carolina	429	79,198,806.18	7.52
North Dakota	715	66,037,571.88	8.55
Ohio	1,025	764,396,988.11	63.83
Oklahoma	913	85,829,974.35	.80
Oregon	250	195,274,123.89	22.64
Pennsylvania	1,306	1,578,026,687.29	75.00
Philippines	12	16,257,764.21	....
Porto Rico	11	8,956,362.82	1.60
Rhode Island	56	219,051,702.94	233.52
South Carolina	346	59,958,286.48	16.02
South Dakota	623	72,142,341.53	7.87
Tennessee	476	122,945,642.87	8.12
Texas	1,237	235,751,823.24	3.27
Utah	99	52,665,961.66	52.66
Vermont	96	91,121,084.92	219.77
Virginia	336	137,825,336.52	19.77
Washington	242	164,615,594.50	34.07
West Virginia	297	110,634,105.30	20.78
Wisconsin	717	295,165,033.12	29.76
Wyoming	87	18,155,612.87	17.61
Total	25,195	17,024,067,606.89	.....

*Individual. †Savings deposits per capita.

STATE BANKS IN THE UNITED STATES (JUNE 14, 1912).

State.	Banks.	*Individual.	Savings.
Alabama	214	$25,299,672.00	$6,541,489.22
Alaska	15	2,221,382.32	....
Arizona	25	7,798,469.79	1,121,456.18
Arkansas	310	23,316,299.09	1,950,314.23
California	375	84,721,027.89	39,887,529.51
Colorado	156	7,615,265.77	1,171,509.27
Connecticut	7	10,466,079.59	....
Delaware	4	1,514,083.42	625,345.64

State.	Banks.	*Individual.	Savings.
Florida	143	17,297,867.82	5,699,130.64
Georgia	582	30,959,982.06	9,076,725.97
Hawaii	8	8,664,761.02	4,707,123.10
Idaho	115	9,208,737.66	698,589.85
Illinois	538	72,523,660.70	56,956,587.66
Indiana	319	37,001,156.11	7,322,087.43
Iowa	273	27,048,677.00	25,256,022.97
Kansas	877	64,065,406.08	3,329,255.24
Kentucky	411	33,509,160.70	8,037,235.33
Louisiana	177	18,268,506.37	3,345,219.21
Maryland	57	9,636,812.57	11,018,389.67
Michigan	393	64,413,457.38	133,533,009.02
Minnesota	745	36,415,929.25	13,784,341.39
Mississippi	289	26,778,966.43	5,751,973.10
Missouri	1,147	126,403,345.41	4,579,027.63
Montana	116	10,435,979.93	2,068,301.53
Nebraska	662	39,614,552.73	10,539,026.02
Nevada	19	5,445,153.59	1,771,615.58
New Hampshire	10	1,324,582.64	5,867,055.69
New Jersey	22	10,363,151.74	5,591,680.03
New Mexico	33	2,161,301.81	26,289.69
New York	191	385,078,269.74	59,263,334.62
North Carolina	309	17,660,668.25	4,930,849.14
North Dakota	564	16,347,744.24	3,783,455.57
Ohio	362	39,238,795.72	30,275,179.19
Oklahoma	695	26,449,699.18	505,785.85
Oregon	126	24,484,793.45	5,521,199.60
Pennsylvania	157	37,173,951.37	99,911,481.37
Philippines	12	10,481,572.19	1,157,163.65
Porto Rico	11	6,654,416.01	1,832,814.19
Rhode Island	4	2,374,986.42	126,673.01
South Carolina	255	15,747,348.02	7,330,179.73
South Dakota	504	17,674,156.25	1,741,786.54
Tennessee	344	28,274,889.16	....
Texas	630	33,854,801.52	979,900.16
Utah	64	12,775,676.80	5,507,506.48
Virginia	226	20,272,424.83	10,875,599.14
Washington	216	27,266,099.05	17,328,125.63
West Virginia	159	20,783,768.26	9,172,875.53
Wisconsin	557	42,030,684.46	26,476,729.22
Wyoming	49	3,078,983.07	500,283.43
Total	13,381	1,609,117,069.91	657,477,220.31

*Subject to check without notice.

PRIVATE BANKS IN THE UNITED STATES (JUNE 14, 1912).

State.	Banks.	*Individual.	Savings.
Alabama	8	$1,075,351.52	$336,698.29
Arizona	1	121,329.43	....
California	5	696,690.70	134,812.82
Colorado	29	1,852,660.58	147,573.40
Florida	7	237,126.92	164,349.89
Georgia	17	393,859.61	54,749.17
Idaho	6	459,125.51	68,372.86
Indiana	194	14,185,424.32	1,549,298.71
Illinois	259	17,921,860.39	8,594,190.73
Iowa	107	6,606,533.37	2,285,440.24
Kansas	4	312,027.37	....
Maryland	1	19,093.20	46,353.82
Michigan	80	2,246,370.01	1,594,280.59
Mississippi	4	469,252.68	....
Missouri	31	2,259,215.31	....
Montana	28	4,654,713.64	477,431.47
New Jersey	12	804,393.62	253,562.70
New York	50	4,011,665.01	4,498,338.00
Ohio	149	11,142,656.02	3,111,773.27
Oregon	5	462,729.85	13,919.29
Pennsylvania	20	3,393,175.50	3,148,306.65
South Carolina	3	337,883.23	....
South Dakota	14	....	....
Texas	53	2,905,265.80	341,974.36
Utah	1	249,876.52	....
Washington	9	555,877.10	42,496.51
Wyoming	3	292,030.66	....
Total	1,110	78,339,600.91	26,868,853.68

*Subject to check without notice.

NOTE—It is estimated that there are more than 4,000 private banking concerns in the United States, but less than one-third of this number furnish reports for statistical purposes.

SAVINGS BANKS OF THE UNITED STATES.

STATE.		1911.				1 12.		
	Banks.	De-positors.	Deposits.	Aver-age.*	Banks.	De-positors.	Deposits.	Aver-age.*
Alabama	2	4,000	$504,067.91	$126.01	11	24,925	$2,652,784.50	$106.43
Arizona	1	700	389,905.92	557.14	1	798	429,789.14	538.58
Arkansas	3	3,713	928,018.13	249.99	5	2,015	331,063.13	164.29
California	123	688,168	362,965,096.41	527.44	122	597,519	407,006,665.52	681.16
Colorado	9	17,196	3,812,389.91	194.93	8	14,955	2,816,670.85	188.30
Connecticut	87	587,175	284,807,814.03	485.04	85	595,360	295,517,758.45	496.30
Delaware	2	83,396	10,273,475.68	308.18	2	33,575	10,800,113.45	321.67
District of Columbia	15	70,746	12,205,693.81	172.53	12	61,165	8,911,160.62	145.69
Florida	4	7,654	1,269,268.62	108.88	3	5,311	1,244,731.89	234.36
Georgia	29	49,789	11,187,058.46	224.68	24	42,184	10,608,118.56	252.82
Idaho	3	1,765	226,349.84	128.24	4	1,489	355,565.80	238.79
Indiana	5	33,873	12,356,715.57	365.18	5	33,583	12,677,454.80	377.49
Iowa	697	497,260	168,068,098.53	337.99	728	539,763	187,363,040.37	347.12
Kansas	11	20,863	3,709,286.29	177.79	13	19,668	4,137,242.16	210.35
Kentucky	15	35,174	5,575,907.16	152.82	13	83,416	5,786,782.57	173.17
Louisiana	9	59,754	16,825,931.64	281.58	11	72,464	19,059,912.57	263.13
Maine	49	224,406	88,680,336.41	395.22	49	224,665	92,209,826.61	410.43
Maryland	46	214,888	99,428,408.68	402.69	51	269,311	103,679,889.94	384.98
Massachusetts	192	2,138,838	790,931,542.57	370.26	93	2,179,973	824,778,925.86	378.33
Michigan	23	119,733	44,612,277.50	372.60	25	156,635	55,879,088.22	356.70
Minnesota	9	103,115	25,506,294.51	247.36	11	109,739	27,985,860.13	254.11
Mississippi	20	11,623	2,631,555.77	225.05	20	15,117	4,283,195.51	283.33
Montana	2	3,468	2,300,772.58	663.42	2	4,826	2,410,181.04	499.41
Nebraska	19	14,040	2,356,273.36	160.40	19	17,730	2,849,551.12	160.71
Nevada	1	1,301	914,398.98	702.70	1	1,493	1,162,799.26	759.17
New Hampshire	55	190,669	87,383,225.61	458.29	54	197,724	92,123,970.88	465.92
New Jersey	27	317,925	111,403,370.26	350.41	27	334,748	117,278,834.49	361.13
New Mexico	9	2,877	558,487.08	194.12	10	3,406	658,296.47	193.27
New York	141	2,810,188	1561,168,449.10	555.54	140	3,024,746	1633,495,812.16	540.04
North Carolina	25	32,159	7,328,005.28	228.01	26	41,149	7,269,464.78	176.66
North Dakota					2	4,197	651,073.36	155.12
Ohio	66	253,646	89,260,972.17	351.91	63	302,350	105,907,535.41	350.28
Oklahoma	2	1,399	231,936.83	165.78	2	1,345	299,340.88	170.51
Oregon	12	36,603	11,997,744.12	326.09	13	32,984	13,545,007.66	410.65
Pennsylvania	11	474,709	186,535,650.91	392.94	12	450,112	196,140,892.80	406.53
Rhode Island	17	143,145	55,459,963.11	597.15	17	141,619	76,791,462.05	542.23
South Carolina	27	38,588	11,341,101.52	293.09	25	36,340	10,473,691.22	288.21
Tennessee	20	38,000	11,226,854.95	295.44	13	31,028	8,621,000.67	277.84
Utah	5	33,890	8,711,020.65	257.04	11	52,100	12,951,603.83	248.30
Vermont	21	110,644	44,610,453.82	403.18	19	124,742	45,383,859.12	363.82
Virginia	35	62,030	19,956,340.10	321.67	20	31,213	9,484,506.68	503.86
Washington	9	24,189	8,689,447.52	359.28	10	25,451	9,578,696.09	376.35
West Virginia	8	25,241	4,411,150.17	175.94	8	31,065	4,666,786.48	150.22
Wisconsin	16	57,149	18,895,298.32	330.68	20	64,877	21,065,419.84	324.69
Wyoming	2	1,347	599,140.26	444.79	2	1,465	626,723.06	427.79
Total	1,864	9,597,185	4212,583,598.53	438.93	1,922	10,010,304	4451,818,522.88	444.72

NOTE—The statistics for Illinois, Missouri and South Dakota are included in reports on state banks with savings departments. June 14, 1912, there were 538 such banks in Illinois with $56,956,- 557.66 savings deposits. In Missouri there were 1,147 banks with $4,579,027.68 savings deposits. In South Dakota there were 504 banks with $1,741,786.54 in savings deposits.   *To each depositor.

SAVINGS DEPOSITS IN NATIONAL BANKS (JUNE 4, 1913).

State.	Banks.	With savings deposits	Savings deposits.	State.	Banks.	With savings deposits	Savings deposits.
Maine	69	43	$24,120,447.31	Ohio	380	167	42,656,146.38
New Hampshire	56	15	1,925,537.66	Indiana	264	71	9,617,374.55
Vermont	49	31	9,011,843.60	Illinois	457	240	44,713,566.04
Massachusetts	180	35	15,910,306.46	Michigan	99	88	45,215,105.75
Rhode Island	20	5	5,220,718.71	Wisconsin	129	110	35,418,313.93
Connecticut	79	14	3,497,610.78	Minnesota	271	154	18,877,599.59
				Iowa	340	132	10,403,195.75
New England states	453	143	59,686,464.52	Missouri	133	30	3,428,705.39
New York	474	240	84,851,995.17	Middle states	2,063	992	210,329,997.38
New Jersey	200	152	60,029,284.94	North Dakota	144	47	1,149,111.28
Pennsylvania	836	624	201,406,779.21	South Dakota	103	50	1,457,928.30
Delaware	26	15	2,055,525.60	Nebraska	242	47	3,891,978.05
Maryland	105	80	22,090,404.93	Kansas	213	54	1,905,777.18
District of Columbia	12	4	1,298,971.49	Montana	57	21	1,924,239.75
				Wyoming	30	12	587,548.42
Eastern states	1,653	1,115	371,832,961.39	Colorado	126	39	8,008,174.28
Virginia	183	90	28,653,611.42	New Mexico	40	8	207,661.67
West Virginia	116	70	9,756,259.37	Oklahoma	325	57	1,373,050.27
North Carolina	73	42	5,837,634.71	Western states	1,280	335	20,475,459.20
South Carolina	48	39	8,844,239.58	Washington	77	69	17,159,427.25
Georgia	118	48	8,729,484.06	Oregon	83	35	3,716,929.06
Florida	52	42	11,141,955.83	California	252	106	23,051,411.53
Alabama	87	41	7,860,936.63	Idaho	54	30	1,395,799.92
Mississippi	33	11	1,252,132.90	Utah	23	17	3,480,969.16
Louisiana	31	15	1,978,255.16	Nevada	11	4	614,240.56
Texas	514	63	8,728,699.08	Arizona	13	3	44,752.47
Arkansas	49	15	983,235.96	Alaska	2	1	81,674.33
Kentucky	144	27	4,156,304.70	Pacific states	515	254	49,525,224.28
Tennessee	107	41	9,144,145.66	Hawaii	4	3	354,964.73
Southern states	1,505	543	106,864,895.06	United States	7,473	3,385	829,070,166.56

FOREIGN POSTAL SAVINGS BANKS.

Country.	Year.	Depositors.	Deposits.	Av. de-posits.
Austria	1911	2,261,658	$46,317,745	$20.48
Belgium	1910	2,384,511	157,150,474	65.90
Bulgaria	1910	280,775	9,129,433	32.52
Finland	1910	59,723	1,396,856	23.39
France	1910	5,786,035	329,974,979	57.03
Hungary	1910	775,970	21,894,118	28.22
Italy	1910	5,160,008	324,279,617	62.84
Netherlands	1910	1,510,033	66,039,592	43.73
Russia	1912	2,691,361	192,456,580	70.09
Sweden	1911	565,759	12,645,957	22.35
United kingdom	1911	12,370,646	859,027,319	69.44
Bahama	1910	2,186	132,602	60.66
Canada	1912	146,310	42,682,232	291.73
British Guiana	1910	18,004	738,175	41.00
Dutch Guiana	1910	9,478	337,925	35.65
British India	1910	1,378,916	51,478,416	37.33
Ceylon	1910	85,954	932,236	10.85
Straits Settlements	1910	4,312	382,667	88.74
Fed. Malay States	1910	5,312	330,431	62.20
Dutch East Indies	1911	91,898	3,616,685	39.36
Japan	1912	11,950,158	91,896,942	7.69
Formosa	1911	100,819	955,592	9.48
Cape of Good Hope	1910	105,369	10,411,974	98.81
Gold Coast	1911	3,137	169,262	52.96
Orange Free State	1910	7,646	868,291	113.56
Rhodesia	1910	3,396	435,299	131.67
Sierra Leone	1911	6,002	485,735	80.93
Transvaal	1910	71,185	8,769,798	123.20
Egypt	1910	104,095	2,255,664	21.67
Tunis	1910	5,701	1,288,268	225.97
New South Wales	1910	368,306	73,926,126	200.72
Victoria	1911	595,424	84,065,980	141.19
Queensland	1911	127,219	31,033,520	243.94
Tasmania	1910	24,403	3,401,304	139.40
Western Australia	1911	99,017	19,916,371	201.14
New Zealand	1910	380,714	68,641,934	180.30
Philippines	1912	35,802	1,177,435	32.89
United States	1912	300,000	28,000,000	93.33

SAVINGS BANKS OF PRINCIPAL COUNTRIES.
(Including postal savings banks.)

Country.	Year.	Deposits.	Average.*
Austria	1910	$1,287,455,592	$45.06
Belgium	1911	206,212,879	27.49
Bulgaria	1910	9,129,423	2.13
Chile	1910	10,543,275	3.09
Denmark	1910	174,182,302	63.18
Egypt	1910	2,255,664	.19
France	1911	1,084,230,303	27.35
Germany	1910	3,993,775,184	61.98
Hungary	1910	41,970,006	2.01
Italy	1911	797,159,527	22.98
Japan	1912	165,003,616	3.20
Netherlands	1910	107,758,077	18.13
Norway	1910	135,886,457	56.78
Roumania	1910	11,616,820	1.69
Russia	1912	784,117,885	4.79
Spain	1910	46,931,094	2.40
Sweden	1911	229,491,283	41.54
Switzerland	1908	303,196,216	93.14
United kingdom	1911	1,117,110,447	24.67
Canada	1912	56,855,198	7.99
Total†		11,096,223,947	12.91
United States		4,479,818,523	46.66

*Per inhabitant. †Includes minor countries and colonies not named in table.

APPROPRIATIONS BY 62D CONGRESS—THIRD SESSION.

Title.	Reported to house.	Passed house.	Reported to senate.	Passed senate.	Law, 1913-14.	Law, 1912-13.
Agriculture	$17,563,275.00	$17,503,325.00	$18,566,580.00	$18,553,202.00	$17,986,945.00	$16,651,496.00
Army	93,990,177.56	93,905,177.56	94,585,728.51	94,585,728.51	94,266,145.51	90,958,712.98
Diplomatic and consular	3,764,642.66	3,707,642.66	3,745,642.66	3,783,642.66	3,730,642.66	3,638,047.41
District of Columbia	11,221,964.00	10,720,534.00	11,702,899.00	11,751,999.00	11,375,639.00	10,670,733.00
Fortification	5,218,250.00	5,218,250.00	5,218,250.00	5,218,250.00	5,218,250.00	4,096,285.00
Indian	7,674,658.28	7,776,853.28	13,127,747.23	13,229,447.23	9,411,129.98	8,920,970.66
Legislative	34,897,505.50	84,809,583.50	35,385,714.62	35,403,040.62	35,183,864.50	34,216,463.38
Military academy	1,069,870.87	1,069,870.87	1,124,596.87	1,134,500.87	1,099,734.57	1,094,928.26
Navy	146,617,824.53	138,079,460.53	138,824,016.02	140,794,120.02	140,809,645.55	123,225,007.76
Pension	180,300,000.00	180,300,000.00	180,300,000.00	180,300,000.00	180,300,000.00	165,146,145.84
Postoffice	283,721,481.00	284,164,181.00	285,689,542.00	285,809,542.00	285,876,271.00	271,429,599.00
Rivers and harbors	37,112,958.00	37,112,958.00	41,195,945.00	42,034,945.00	41,073,034.00	31,039,970.50
Sundry civil	113,271,614.66	113,163,620.66	118,525,736.91	119,523,000.91	114,718,396.91	112,039,184.40
Total	936,454,217.06	927,711,457.06	947,892,392.82	958,121,508.82	942,540,746.96	873,056,634.19
Deficiency, 1913, and prior years	24,235,740.17	24,224,110.17	28,048,624.53	28,604,672.38	28,081,549.18	9,700,939.67
Total	960,689,957.23	951,935,567.23	975,911,007.15	986,726,181.20	970,622,296.09	882,757,573.86
Miscellaneous					500,000.00	3,448,712.93
Total regular					971,122,296.09	886,206,286.79
Permanent annual					127,525,664.12	133,208,424.12
Grand total, regular and permanent annual appropriations					1,098,647,960.21	1,019,412,710.91

TOTALS FOR PREVIOUS SIX CONGRESSES.

Congress.	Years.	Amount.	Congress.	Years.	Amount.	Congress.	Years.	Amount.
56th	1901-1902	$1,440,489,438.87	58th	1905-1906	1,600,053,544.80	60th	1909-1910	$2,052,411,841.79
57th	1903-1904	1,553,683,002.57	59th	1907-1908	1,799,537,864.70	61st	1911-1912	2,053,891,290.72

CRUDE PETROLEUM PRODUCED IN THE UNITED STATES.

Year.	Gallons.	Year.	Gallons.	Year.	Gallons.	Year.	Gallons.
1900	2,661,233,568	1903	4,219,376,154	1906	6,312,746,312	1909	7,649,639,508
1901	2,914,346,148	1904	4,916,663,682	1907	6,976,004,070	1910	8,801,354,016
1902	3,729,210,472	1905	5,658,138,360	1908	7,498,148,910	1911	9,258,874,422

PRODUCTION BY STATES IN 1911.

State.	*Barrels.	State.	*Barrels.	State.	*Barrels.	State.	*Barrels.
California	81,134,391	Kentucky	472,458	Oklahoma	56,069,637	Wyoming	186,695
Colorado	226,926	Louisiana	10,841,395	Pennsylvania	8,248,126		
Illinois	31,317,028	Missouri	7,995	Texas	9,526,474	Total	220,449,391
Indiana	1,695,289	New York	952,515	West Virginia	9,795,464	Total value, $134,044,752	
Kansas	1,278,819	Ohio	8,817,112			*Barrels of 42 gallons.	

MONEY AND FINANCE.

WORLD'S PRODUCTION OF GOLD AND SILVER IN 1911.

[From report of the director of the mint. Figures are for calendar year.]

Country.	Gold.	Silver.	Country.	Gold.	Silver.	Country.	Gold.	Silver.
Untd. States.	$96,890,000	$32,615,700	Russia	32,151,600	257,700	Guiana, Dutch	523,400	....
Canada	9,762,100	17,689,900	Servia	265,300	20,300	Guiana, Fr...	2,229,100	....
Mexico	24,880,100	42,677,500	Spain	....	2,242,300	Cent. Amer..	3,360,400	654,300
Cuba	20,000	....	Sweden	2,000	10,700	British India	11,054,100	56,300
Africa	191,538,400	574,600	Turkey	500	927,700	China	3,314,600	....
Australasia..	60,184,200	8,952,300	Argentina	289,000	109,700	Br. E. Indies	1,339,400	....
Aus.-Hungary	2,185,100	830,900	Bolivia-Chile.	238,100	2,420,000	Dutch E. Ind.	3,387,100	251,600
France	1,707,100	385,000	Brazil	3,834,500	25,500	Indo-China ..	55,000	....
Germany	62,900	3,022,400	Colombia	3,167,800	441,400	Japan	4,007,500	2,383,800
Great Britain	39,600	73,600	Ecuador	276,800	12,200	Korea	2,889,400	5,100
Greece	....	476,700	Peru	455,900	3,578,500	Siam	56,500	....
Italy	44,800	539,200	Uruguay	70,600	....			
Norway	....	157,700	Venezuela	364,800	235,900	Total	461,542,100	121,682,300
Portugal	2,400	63,700	Guiana, Brit.	892,000	....			

COINAGE OF GOLD AND SILVER BY NATIONS IN 1911.

[Reported by the director of the mint.]

Country.	Gold.	Silver.	Country.	Gold.	Silver.	Country.	Gold.	Silver.
Untd. States.	$56,176,823	$6,457,302	Bulgaria	....	....	Montenegro...	....	....
Philippines...	....	463,270	Chile	124,368	136,464	Morocco	....	3,078,667
Abyssinia	....	401,440	China	....	36,349,759	Netherlands..	3,113,667	1,125,600
Aus.-Hungary	9,547,469	9,547,071	Colombia	....	847,600	Dutch E. Ind.	....	562,800
Lichtenstein.	....	....	Costa Rica...	....	....	Norway	....	111,220
Belgium	....	2,445,889	Denmark	986,396	150,534	Persia	....	474,641
Bolivia	....	....	Egypt	....	1,630,709	Peru	266,340	45,253
Brazil	93,266	3,645,727	Finland	621,460	59,444	Portugal	....	....
Australias.	48,347,716	1,707,105	France	24,846,092	1,197,903	Russia	515,085	2,585,811
Canada	1,250,428	985,679	Indo-China	....	699,054	Roumania	....	979,152
Br. E. Africa	....	75,000	Germany	249	9,672,003	San Salvador	....	1,522,101
Ceylon	....	200,000	Germany	25,485,309	528,805	Siam	....	....
Newfoundland	....	100,000	East Africa..	....	528,805	Spain	....	55,361
Grt. Britain.	161,062,453	11,021,247	Greece	....	942,191	Sweden	....	16,683
Guiana, Brit.	....	2,433	Honduras	....	45	Switzerland..	1,544,000	386,000
Honduras	....	9,500	Italy	193,000	650,336	Travancore...	....	40,555
Hongkong	....	31,446,858	Italian So-			Turkey	22,724,870	862,275
India	....	6,538,830	maliland	....	....	Venezuela	424,090	1,798,541
Straits Set-			Japan	14,820,480	4,446,568			
tlements	....	40,007	Chosen(Korea)	....	....	Total	372,143,555	148,156,282
Sarawak	....	15,000	Mexico	....	1,712,000			

PRODUCT OF GOLD AND SILVER IN THE UNITED STATES (1792-1911).

[For 1792-1873 is by R. W. Raymond, commissioner, and since by the director of the mint.]

PERIOD.	Gold.	Silver.	Total.	PERIOD.	Gold.	Silver.	Total.
April 2, 1792-July 31, 1834	$14,000,000	Insignificant	$14,000,000	1899	$71,053,000	$70,806,000	$141,859,000
July 31, 1834-Dec. 31, 1844	7,500,000	$250,000	7,750,000	1900	79,171,000	74,533,000	153,704,000
1845-1850	103,036,769	300,000	103,336,769	1901	78,667,000	71,388,000	150,055,000
1851-1860	551,000,000	1,100,000	552,100,000	1902	80,000,000	71,758,000	151,758,000
1861-1870	474,250,000	100,750,000	575,000,000	1903	73,591,700	70,206,000	143,797,700
1871-1880	395,300,000	360,300,000	755,600,000	1904	80,464,700	57,682,800	138,147,500
1881-1890	326,620,000	535,056,000	861,676,000	1905	88,180,700	34,222,000	122,402,700
1891	33,175,000	75,417,000	108,592,000	1906	94,373,800	38,256,400	132,630,200
1892	53,000,000	82,101,000	115,101,000	1907	90,435,700	37,299,700	127,735,400
1893	35,955,000	77,576,000	113,531,000	1908	94,560,000	28,050,600	122,610,600
1894	39,500,000	64,000,000	103,500,000	1909	99,673,400	28,455,200	128,128,600
1895	46,610,000	72,051,000	118,661,000	1910	96,269,100	30,854,500	127,123,600
1896	53,088,000	76,069,000	129,157,000	1911	96,890,000	32,615,700	129,505,700
1897	57,363,000	69,637,000	127,000,000				
1898	64,463,000	70,384,000	134,847,000	Total	3,358,463,500	1,629,972,000	4,988,435,000

WORLD'S PRODUCTION OF GOLD AND SILVER SINCE 1492.

[From report of the director of the mint, 1912.]

CALENDAR YEARS.	Gold.	Silver (coining value).	Per cent gold.	Per cent silver.	CALENDAR YEARS.	Gold.	Silver (coining value).	Per cent gold.	Per ct. silver.
1492—1520	$107,931,000	$54,703,000	66.4	33.6	1841—1850	$363,928,000	$324,400,000	52.9	47.7
1521—1544	114,205,000	98,988,000	55.9	44.1	1851—1855	662,596,000	184,169,000	78.3	21.9
1545—1560	90,492,000	207,240,000	30.4	69.6	1856—1860	670,415,000	188,092,000	78.1	21.1
1561—1580	90,917,000	248,990,000	26.7	73.3	1861—1865	614,944,000	228,861,000	72.9	27.0
1581—1600	98,095,000	348,254,000	22.0	78.0	1866—1870	643,071,000	278,313,000	70.0	30.5
1601—1620	113,248,000	351,579,000	24.4	75.6	1871—1875	577,883,000	409,532,000	58.5	41.0
1621—1640	110,324,000	337,221,000	25.2	74.8	1876—1880	572,931,000	509,256,000	53.0	47.5
1641—1660	116,571,000	304,525,000	27.7	72.3	1881—1885	495,582,000	594,773,000	45.5	54.5
1661—1680	123,048,000	280,766,000	30.5	69.5	1886—1890	564,474,000	704,074,000	44.5	55.6
1681—1700	142,088,000	284,240,000	33.5	66.5	1891—1895	814,736,000	1,018,708,000	44.4	55.4
1701—1720	170,403,000	295,629,000	36.6	63.4	1896—1900	1,296,505,400	1,071,148,400	54.6	45.8
1721—1740	253,611,000	358,480,000	41.4	58.6	1901—1905	1,610,309,700	1,066,848,300	60.2	39.9
1741—1760	327,161,000	443,232,000	42.5	57.5	1906	402,503,000	213,403,600	65.3	34.7
1761—1780	275,211,000	542,658,000	33.7	66.3	1907	412,906,000	238,166,600	63.4	36.6
1781—1800	236,464,000	730,810,000	24.4	75.6	1908	448,006,200	262,634,500	62.8	37.2
1801—1810	118,152,000	371,677,000	24.1	75.9	1909	454,059,100	274,233,700	62.3	37.7
1811—1820	76,063,000	224,786,000	25.3	74.0	1910	455,259,800	296,652,300	61.4	38.6
1821—1830	94,479,000	191,444,000	33.0	67.8	1911	461,542,100	291,546,400	61.3	38.7
1831—1840	134,841,000	247,930,000	35.2	64.1					

STOCK OF GOLD AND SILVER IN THE UNITED STATES.

FISCAL YEAR ENDED JUNE 30.	POPULA-TION.	TOTAL COIN AND BULLION.		PER CAPITA.		
		Gold.	Silver.	Gold.	Silver	Total metallic
1873	41,677,000	$135,000,000	$6,149,305	$3.23	$0.15	$3.38
1880	50,155,783	351,841,206	148,522,678	7.01	2.96	9.97
1890	62,622,250	1,695,563,029	463,211,919	11.10	7.39	18.49
1900	76,891,000	1,034,439,264	647,371,030	13.45	8.42	21.87
1905	83,259,000	1,357,881,186	686,401,168	16.31	8.24	24.55
1906	84,692,000	1,472,995,209	687,958,920	17.40	8.12	25.52
1907	86,074,000	1,466,056,632	705,380,224	17.03	8 20	25.23
1908	87,493,000	1,615,140,575	723,594,595	18.46	8.27	26.73
1909	88,926,000	1,649,567,131	725,550,073	18.45	8.16	26.61
1910	90,363,000	1,635,424,513	727,078,304	18.10	8.05	26.15
1911	93,983,000	1,753,184,114	732,002,448	18.65	7.79	26.44
1912	95,656,000	1,812,856,241	741,184,095	18.95	7.75	26.70

PRICE OF BAR SILVER IN LONDON.

Highest, lowest and average price of bar silver per ounce British standard (.925) since 1872 and the equivalent in United States gold coin of an ounce 1.000 fine, taken at the average price.

CALENDAR YEAR.	Lowest quotation	Highest quotation	Average quotation.	Value of a fine oz. at av. quotat'n	CALENDAR YEAR.	Lowest quotation.	Highest quotation.	Average quotation.	Value of a fine oz. at av. quotat'n
	d	d	d			d.	d.	d.	
1872	59¼	61⅛	60 5-16	$1.322	1893	30½	38⅞	35 9-16	$0.78081
1873	57½	59 13-16	59¼	1.298	1894	27	31⅞	28 7-16	.63479
1874	57¼	59½	58 5-16	1.278	1895	27 3-16	31⅜	29⅜	.65406
1875	55½	57⅞	56¾	1.246	1896	29⅜	31 15-16	30¾	.67437
1876	46¾	58⅝	52¾	1.156	1897	23½	29 13-16	27 9-16	.60492
1877	53½	58½	54 13-16	1.201	1898	25	28⅝	26 15-16	.59010
1878	49¼	55¼	52 9-16	1.152	1899	26⅝	29	27 7-16	.60154
1879	48¾	53¾	51¼	1.123	1900	27	30¼	28 5-16	.62007
1880	51⅞	52¾	52¼	1.145	1901	24 15-16	29 9-16	27 3-16	.59565
1881	50⅞	52¼	51 15-16	1 138	1902	21 11-16	26 1-16	24 1-16	.52795
1882	50	52¾	51 13-16	1.136	1903	21 11-16	28½	24⅞	.54257
1883	50	51 3-16	50⅝	1.110	1904	24 7-16	28 9-16	26 13-32	.57876
1884	49½	51¾	50¾	1.112	1905	25 7-16	30 5-16	27 27-32	.61087
1885	46⅜	50	48 9-16	1.0645	1906	29	33⅝	30⅞	.67629
1886	42	47	45⅜	.9946	1907	24¼	32 7-16	30 9-16	.66152
1887	43¼	47⅛	44⅝	.97823	1908	22	27	24 11-32	.53490
1888	41⅞	44 9-16	42⅞	.93897	1909	22	24 13-16	23.7024	.52010
1889	42	44⅜	41 11-16	.93512	1910	23 3-16	26	24 21-32	.5405.7
1890	43⅝	54⅝	47¾	1.04633	1911	23 11-16	26½	24 19-32	.53928
1891	43⅝	48¼	45 1-16	.98782	1912	25¼	29 11-16	28 3-64	.61470
1892	37⅜	43¾	39¾	.87106					

PRODUCT OF GOLD AND SILVER BY STATES AND TERRITORIES.

Approximate distribution, by producing states and territories, for the calendar years 1910 and 1911 as estimated by the director of the mint.

STATE OR TERRITORY	GOLD.				SILVER.			
	1910.		1911.		1910.		1911.	
	Fine ounces.	Value.	Fine ounces.	Value.	Fine ounces.	Commercial value.	Fine ounces.	Commercial value.
Alabama	1,593	$32,900	890	$18,400	300	$200	200	$100
Alaska	787,148	16,271,800	806,179	16,665,200	153,900	83,100	3,228,900	252,900
Arizona	165,113	3,413,200	170,348	3,521,400	2,655,700	1,434,100	3,228,900	1,771,400
California	988,854	20,441,400	964,041	19,928,600	1,791,600	967,400	1,270,800	686,300
Colorado	992,967	20,526,500	925,839	19,138,800	8,523,600	4,602,400	7,334,200	3,958,800
Georgia	1,161	24,000	1,548	32,000	300	200	600	300
Idaho	50,113	1,035,900	65,688	1,357,900	7,027,000	3,794,600	8,184,900	4,419,800
Illinois					2,000	1,100	4,000	2,200
Kentucky					100	100		
Maryland			5	100			100	100
Michigan					262,200	141,600	507,700	274,100
Missouri					32,200	17,400	49,100	26,500
Montana	179,974	3,720,400	176,554	3,649,700	12,282,900	6,632,800	12,165,900	6,568,500
Nevada	913,015	18,873,700	875,438	18,095,900	12,366,000	6,677,800	13,185,900	7,120,400
New Hampshire	283	59,900			700	400		
New Mexico	23,084	477,300	36,847	761,700	779,000	420,600	1,341,400	724,300
North Carolina	3,122	64,500	3,478	71,900	8,300	4,500	1,000	500
Oregon	32,900	681,400	30,679	634,400	43,800	23,600	44,800	24,200
Philippines	7,471	154,400	9,448	195,300	1,800	1,000	3,100	1,700
Porto Rico	50	1,000	97	2,000			100	100
South Carolina	1,827	37,800	972	20,100				
South Dakota	260,206	5,380,200	359,402	7,429,500	120,600	65,100	200,300	108,200
Tennessee	136	2,800	576	11,900	69,800	37,700	107,000	57,800
Texas	18	400	189	3,900	364,400	196,800	444,200	239,900
Utah	208,627	4,312,700	217,020	4,488,300	10,445,900	5,640,800	11,650,600	6,290,500
Virginia	44	900	150	3,100	200	100	200	100
Washington	38,962	805,600	40,635	840,000	204,900	110,600	230,300	124,400
Wyoming	199	4,100	1,030	21,300	1,300	700	700	400

MONEY OF THE WORLD (JAN. 1, 1912).

Monetary systems and approximate stocks of money in the principal countries of the world as reported by the director of the mint.

COUNTRY.	Monetary standard.	Monetary unit.	Gold in thousands of dollars.	Silver in thousands of dollars.	Uncovered paper in thousands of dollars.	Per Capita. Gold.	Per Capita. Silver.	Per Capita. Paper.	Per Capita. Total.
United States............	Gold..	Dollar...............	$1,799,600	$735,900	$764,500	$18.98	$7.76	$8.07	$34.81
Austria-Hungary........	Gold..	Crown...............	356,500	122,900	197,800	7.21	2.49	4.00	13.70
Belgium	Gold..	Franc...............	....	11,100	139,000	5.00	1.52	19.04	25.56
Australasia.............	Gold..	Pound sterling......	222,400	10,000	....	50.54	2.27	.....	52.81
Canada	Gold..	Dollar...............	....	7,700	79,100	22.29	1.74	12.76	36.29
United kingdom........	Gold..	Pound sterling......	710,500	116,800	115,200	15.80	2.59	2.56	20.95
India...................	Gold..	Pound sterling and rupee.............	....	142,400	45,400	.14	.48	.16	.78
South Africa............	Gold..	Pound sterling......	65,400	20,000	....	8.38	2.56	.....	10.94
Straits Settlements*.....	Gold..	Dollar...............	....	19,000	7,500	4.25	11.88	4.68	20.81
Bulgaria	Gold..	Lev.................	....	4,800	9,900	1.93	1.20	2.47	5.60
Cuba....................	Gold..	Peseta..............	42,000	5,000	....	20.00	2.38	.....	22.38
Denmark................	Gold..	Crown...............	38,500	7,900	17,300	14.19	2.92	6.41	23.62
Egypt	Gold..	Piaster.............	182,700	14,300	6,600	16.17	1.26	.58	18.01
Finland.................	Gold..	Markkaa............	10,600	500	14,900	3.66	.17	5.13	8.96
France..................	Gold..	Franc...............	1,200,000	411,100	245,900	30.53	10.46	6.26	47.25
Germany................	Gold..	Mark................	233,600	276,100	3.16	3.90	4.24	11.30
Greece..................	Gold..	Drachma............	4,400	3,000	27,600	1.69	1.15	10.62	13.46
Haiti...................	Gold..	Gourde.............	3,400	2,500	8,200	2.20	1.67	5.47	9.40
Italy...................	Gold..	Lira................	....	24,100	182,500	8.51	.71	5.38	14.60
Japan...................	Gold..	Yen.................	183,900	61,200	101,700	2.57	1.23	1.95	5.55
Mexico.................	Gold..	Peso................	....	56,000	51,200	2.08	3.73	3.41	9.22
Netherlands.............	Gold..	Florin..............	75,800	23,000	64,700	12.81	4.92	10.95	28.70
Norway.................	Gold..	Crown...............	20,800	3,700	8,700	8.67	1.54	3.62	13.83
Portugal................	Gold..	Milreis.............	14,500	33,100	69,900	2.69	6.13	12.94	21.76
Roumania...............	Gold..	Lei.................	32,700	12,900	43,200	4.81	1.86	6.35	13.01
Russia..................	Gold..	Ruble...............	946,500	78,800	....	5.91	.49	.....	6.40
Servia..................	Gold..	Dinar...............	1,300	....	4,900	2.32	.46	1.75	4.53
Siam....................	Gold..	Tical...............	52,200	2,100	....	.01	7.46	.30	7.77
Argentina...............	Gold..	Peso................	9,400	692,200	35.47	1.34	98.89	135.70
Bolivia.................	Gold..	Boliviano...........	700	2,000	3.39	.80	.87	4.56
Brazil..................	Gold..	Milreis.............	25,000	77,900	5.68	1.22	3.80	10.70
Chile...................	Gold..	Peso................	....	8,500	19,000	.14	2.43	5.43	8.00
Colombia...............	Gold..	Dollar...............	....	10,000	2.33	2.33
Ecuador................	Gold..	Sucre...............	5,400	1,300	1,700	3.69	.87	1.19	5.70
Guiana (British)........	Gold..	Pound sterling......	....	400	100	.33	1.34	.33	2.00
Guiana (Dutch).........	Gold..	Florin..............	....	300	300	2.00	3.00	3.00	8.00
Guiana (French)........	Gold..	Franc...............	....	100	600	1.00	1.00	6.00	8.00
Paraguay...............	Gold..	Peso................	....	42,900	19.00	.....	53.63	72.63
Peru....................	Gold..	Sol.................	12,200	2,400	....	2.71	.53	.....	3.24
Uruguay................	Gold..	Peso................	....	4,500	8,000	13.82	3.90	7.28	25.00
Venezuela..............	Gold..	Bolivar.............	8,100	10,800	900	1.19	4.15	.31	5.65
Spain...................	Gold..	Peseta..............	213,100	258,800	76,000	10.82	19.04	3.85	27.71
Sweden.................	Gold..	Crown...............	26,000	8,000	34,700	4.81	1.59	6.43	12.83
Switzerland.............	Gold..	Franc...............	65,700	13,500	27,900	19.91	4.09	8.45	32.45
Turkey.................	Gold..	Piaster.............	142,400	26,400	....	5.93	1.10	.....	7.03
Central American states..	Silver†	Peso................	1,400	9,200	89,900	.26	1.74	16.96	18.96
Total.................			2,621,200	3,567,500					

*Includes the Malay states, Ceylon and Johore. †Except Costa Rica and British Honduras, gold standard countries. Blank spaces indicate that no satisfactory information is available.

COINAGE OF GOLD AND SILVER OF THE WORLD (1900-1911).

CALENDAR YEAR.	GOLD. Fine ounces.	GOLD. Value.	SILVER. Fine ounces.	SILVER. Coining value.	CALENDAR YEAR.	GOLD. Fine ounces.	GOLD. Value.	SILVER. Fine ounces.	SILVER. Coining value.
1900........	17,170,053	$354,936,497	136,907,648	$177,011,902	1906........	17,721,058	$366,330,450	120,339,501	$155,590,466
1901........	12,001,557	248,093,787	107,439,696	138,911,891	1907........	19,921,014	411,803,902	171,561,490	221,816,876
1902........	10,662,098	220,405,125	149,826,725	193,715,362	1908........	15,828,573	327,205,649	151,352,824	195,688,499
1903........	11,634,007	240,496,274	161,159,508	208,867,849	1909........	15,153,116	313,242,714	87,729,951	113,427,331
1904........	22,031,285	455,427,085	145,352,335	172,270,379	1910........	23,004,542	454,874,248	78,786,842	108,915,627
1905........	11,898,037	245,954,257	73,371,385	103,880,205	1911........	18,002,444	372,143,555	117,297,898	148,156,282

GOLD AND SILVER COINAGE OF THE UNITED STATES.
By calendar years.

YEAR.	Gold.	Silver.	YEAR.	Gold.	Silver.	YEAR.	Gold.	Silver.	YEAR.	Gold.	Silver.
1877....	$43,999,864	$28,393,045	1886.	$28,945,542	$32,086,709	1895...	$59,616,358	$5,698,010	1904....	$234,402,428	$15,695,610
1878....	49,786,052	28,518,850	1887.	23,972,383	35,191,081	1896...	47,653,000	23,089,899	1905....	49,698,441	6,332,247
1879....	39,080,080	27,569,776	1888.	31,380,808	33,025,606	1897...	76,028,485	18,487,297	1906....	77,593,045	10,651,087
1880....	62,308,279	27,411,694	1889.	21,413,931	35,496,683	1898...	77,985,757	23,034,033	1907....	131,907,490	13,178,435
1881....	96,850,080	27,940,164	1890.	20,467,182	39,202,908	1899...	111,344,220	26,061,520	1908....	131,658,632	12,391,775
1882....	65,887,685	27,973,132	1891.	29,222,005	27,518,858	1900...	99,272,942	36,295,321	1909....	58,776,907	8,567,852
1883....	29,241,990	29,246,968	1892.	34,787,222	12,641,078	1901...	101,735,188	30,838,461	1910....	104,723,733	3,740,468
1884....	23,991,756	28,534,866	1893.	56,997,020	8,802,797	1902...	47,184,932	30,028,107	1911....	56,176,822	6,455,701
1885....	27,773,012	28,962,176	1894.	79,546,160	9,200,351	1903...	43,683,970	19,874,440	1912....	17,484,522	7,340,995

BULLION VALUE OF 371¼ GRAINS OF PURE SILVER AT THE ANNUAL AVERAGE PRICE OF SILVER.

Year.	Value.	Year.	Value.	Year.	Value.	Year.	Value.	Year.	Value.	Year.	Value
1890	$1.045	1878	$0.892	1885	$0.823	1892	$0.674	1899	$0.465	1906	$0.593
1870	1.027	1879	.869	1886	.769	1893	.603	1900	.479	1907	.511
1873	1.003	1880	.885	1887	.757	1894	.490	1901	.460	1908	.414
1874	.989	1881	.875	1888	.726	1895	.505	1902	.408	1909	.402
1875	.980	1882	.878	1889	.723	1896	.522	1903	.419	1910	.418
1876	.900	1883	.857	1890	.809	1897	.467	1904	.447	1911	.417
1877	.929	1884	.859	1891	.764	1898	.456	1905	.472	1912	.475

COMMERCIAL RATIO OF SILVER TO GOLD.

Year.	Ratio.	Year.	Ratio.	Year.	Ratio.	Year.	Ratio.	Year.	Ratio.	Year.	Ratio.
1700	14.81	1830	15.82	1869	15.60	1880	18.05	1891	20.92	1902	39.15
1720	15.04	1850	15.70	1870	15.57	1881	18.16	1892	23.72	1903	38.10
1740	14.94	1860	15.29	1871	15.57	1882	18.19	1893	26.49	1904	35.70
1750	14.55	1861	15.50	1872	15.63	1883	18.64	1894	32.56	1905	33.87
1760	14.14	1862	15.35	1873	15.92	1884	18.57	1895	31.60	1906	30.54
1770	14.62	1863	15.37	1874	16.17	1885	19.41	1896	30.59	1907	31.24
1780	14.72	1864	15.37	1875	16.59	1886	20.78	1897	34.20	1908	38.64
1790	15.04	1865	15.44	1876	17.88	1887	21.13	1898	35.03	1909	39.74
1800	15.68	1866	15.43	1877	17.22	1888	21.99	1899	34.36	1910	38.22
1810	15.77	1867	15.57	1878	17.94	1889	22.10	1900	33.33	1911	38.33
1820	15.62	1868	15.59	1879	18.40	1890	19.76	1901	34.68	1912	33.62

FINANCIAL AND COMMERCIAL STATISTICS OF THE UNITED STATES (1880-1912).

(Upon a per capita basis.)

YEAR.	Population, June 1.	GOVERNMENT FINANCE PER CAPITA.							GOLD AND SILVER.			
		Amount of money in the United States.	Money in circulation.	Debt, less cash in treasury.	Interest paid.	Net ordinary receipts.	Net ordinary expenditures.	Disbursements for pensions.	Coin value of paper money, July 1.	Commercial ratio of silver to gold.	Annual average price of silver in London, per oz.	Bullion Value of United States silver dollar.
1880	50,155,783	$24.04	$19.41	$38.27	$1.50	$6 65	$5.34	$1.14	$1.00	$18.05	$1.145	$.895
1890	62,622,250	34.24	22.82	14.22	.47	6.44	4.75	1.71	1.00	19.76	1.046	.809
1900	76,905,387	30.66	26.93	14.62	.44	7.43	6.39	1.89	1.00	33.33	.620	.47958
1902	79,003,000	32.45	28.47	12.27	.35	7.11	5.96	1.75	1.00	39.15	.528	.40885
1903	80,372,000	33.40	29.42	11.51	.32	6.93	6.23	1.72	1.00	38.10	.543	.41980
1904	81,752,000	34.29	30.77	11.85	.30	6.80	7.11	1.74	1.00	35.70	.579	.44763
1905	83,148,000	34.68	31.08	11.91	.30	6.54	6.81	1.71	1.00	33.87	.610	.47200
1906	84,154,000	36.45	32.32	11.46	.28	7.02	6.72	1.68	1.00	30.54	.677	.52355
1907	85,817,239	36.80	32.22	10.22	.25	7.70	6.73	1.62	1.00	31.24	.662	.51161
1908	87,189,332	38.76	34.72	10.76	.24	6.87	7.58	1.77	1.00	39.64	.535	.41371
1909	88,666,034	38.45	34.93	11.56	.24	6.79	7.45	1.82	1.00	39.74	.520	.40281
1910	92,174,515	37.84	34.33	11.35	.23	7.48	7.30	1.77	1.00	38.22	.540	.41825
1911	93,792,505	37.91	34.20	10.83	.23	7.46	6.96	1.68	1.00	38.33	.530	.41700
1912	95,410,503	38.14	34.54	10.77	.24	7.23	6.84	1.61	1.00	33.62	.614	.47543

YEAR.	COINAGE PER CAPITA OF—		PRODUCTION PER CAPITA OF—		INTERNAL REVENUE.		Merchandise imported for consumption per capita.	CUSTOMS REVENUE.			
	Gold.	Silver.	Gold.	Silver.	Collected per capita.	Expenses of collecting. Per cent.		Duty collected per capita.	Average ad valorem rate of duty. On dutiable. Per cent.	On free and dutiable. Per cent.	Expenses of collecting. Per cent.
1880	$1.24	$0.55	$0.72	$0.69	$2.47	2.95	$12.51	$3.64	43.48	29.07	3.23
1890	.53	.63	.52	.91	2.28	2.65	12.16	3.60	44.41	29.12	2.98
1900	1.50	.48	1.04	.47	3.87	1.51	10.93	3.02	49.46	27.62	3.70
1903	.54	.25	.92	.36	2.87	1.94	12.28	3.42	49.08	27.85	2.98
1904	2.95	.19	.98	.41	2.85	1.94	11.73	3.04	48.78	26.80	3.32
1905	.60	.08	1.06	.41	2.82	1.85	12.74	3.03	45.24	23.77	3.48
1906	.92	.13	1.14	.45	2.96	1.76	13.05	3.38	44.16	24.22	3.00
1907	1.54	.15	1.04	.44	3.14	1.72	15.97	3.72	42.55	23.28	2.55
1908	1.51	.14	1.10	.31	2.88	1.85	13.11	3.13	42.94	23.88	3.35
1909	1.00	.09	1.12	.32	2.78	1.85	13.91	3.21	43.15	22.99	3.41
1910	1.13	.04	1.40	.33	3.14	1.73	16.54	3.50	41.52	21.41	3.20
1911	.59	.07	1.02	.34	3.44	1.55	16.05	3.25	41.22	20.29	3.50
1912	.18	.07	.96	.35	3.36	1.57	16.94	3.15	40.12	18.58	3.47

FINANCIAL AND COMMERCIAL STATISTICS OF THE U. S.—Continued.

YEAR.	EXPORTS.						CONSUMPTION PER CAPITA.							
	Domestic merchandise.		Per cent of domestic products exported.											
	Exports per capita.	Manuf'r'd products. Total exports.	Cotton.	Wheat.	Corn.	Bituminous coal.	Raw cotton.	Wheat.	Corn.	Sugar.	Coffee.	Tea.	Distilled spirits.	Malt liquors.	Wines.
		Per ct.	P. ct.	P. ct.	P. ct.	P. ct.	Lbs.	Bu.	Bu.	Lbs.	Lbs.	Lbs.	Pf.gl	Gal.	Gal.
1880	$16.43	14.78	65.73	40.18	6.43	.66	19.94	5.35	28.88	42.90	8.78	1.89	1.27	8.26	.56
1890	13.50	21.18	68.15	22.31	4.85	1.33	18.50	6.09	32.09	52.80	7.83	1.33	1.40	13.67	.46
1900	17.96	35.30	65.18	34.00	10.30	3.14	22.57	4.74	24.44	65.20	9.81	1.09	1.27	16.01	.39
1902	17.16	33.48	64.47	31.37	1.84	2.68	25.65	6.50	18.92	72.80	13.37	.94	1.56	17.49	.61
1903	17.32	33.81	65.01	30.28	3.04	2.24	24.64	5.81	30.45	71.10	10.79	1.30	1.46	18.04	.47
1904	17.87	36.47	60.27	16.92	2.59	2.55	25.29	6.35	26.74	75.30	11.75	1.34	1.48	18.22	.52
1905	17.94	40.96	61.55	7.99	3.66	2.69	33.07	6.13	28.59	70.00	12.11	1.23	1.45	18.50	.41
1906	21.41	30.93	62.69	14.09	4.43	2.54	26.51	7.08	30.55	76.10	9.15	1.10	1.51	20.20	.53
1907	21.60	30.92	64.93	19.95	2.95	2.88	29.53	6.86	33.11	77.50	11.36	.99	1.63	21.23	.65
1908	21.04	40.91	66.18	25.71	2.12	2.80	29.23	5.40	29.10	75.42	10.40	1.07	1.44	20.97	.58
1909	17.82	40.98	62.93	17.19	1.41	3.04	25.13	6.22	29.71	82.24	11.74	1.29	1.57	19.07	.67
1910	18.28	44.85	65.85	12.73	1.49	3.07	28.67	7.05	29.44	79.90	9.53	.89	1.43	19.79	.65
1911	21.15	45.07	62.70	10.91	2.27	3.18	.....	6.03	30.07	77.15	9.28	1.04	1.46	20.66	.67
1912	22.41	47.02	.....	12.88	1.65	4.06	.....	5.71	25.99	82.48	9.23	1.05	1.44	19.98	.58

YEAR.	CONSUMPTION OF RAW WOOL.		Tonnage of vessels, annual increase or (+ or −).	Imports and exports of merchandise carried in American vessels.	POSTOFFICE DEPARTMENT.		PUBLIC SCHOOLS.	
	Total per capita.	Per cent foreign.			Revenue per capita.	Expenditure per capita.	Population 5 to 18 years of age.	Expenditures per capita of population 5 to 18 years of age.
	Lbs.		Per cent	Per cent			Millions	
1880	6.11	34.9	— 2.48	17.4	$0.66	$0.73	15.1	$5.17
1890	6.08	27.0	+ 2.71	12.9	.97	1.11	18.5	7.60
1900	5.73	34.4	+ 6.18	9.3	1.34	1.46	21.4	10.04
1901	5.18	34.9	+ 6.96	8.2	1.44	1.49	22.0	10.85
1902	6.07	34.1	+ 4.95	8.8	1.54	1.59	22.3	10.57
1903	5.74	37.8	+ 4.99	9.1	1.67	1.73	22.7	11.10
1904	5.66	37.0	+ 3.35	10.3	1.76	1.86	23.0	11.86
1905	6.52	45.5	+ 2.62	12.1	1.84	2.05	23.4	12.46
1906	5.88	39.6	+ 3.38	12.0	2.00	2.17	23.8	12.94
1907	5.81	40.0	+ 3.95	10.6	2.13	2.25	24.3	13.63
1908	4.95	27.9	+ 6.15	9.08	2.19	2.36	24.6	15.10
1909	6.67	44.5	+ .82	9.5	2.30	2.53	24.2	16.56
1910	6.89	44.7	+ 1.61	8.7	2.43	2.49	25.0	17.03
1911	4.77	28.89	+ 1.74	8.7	2.54	2.53	24.8	17.09
1912	5.19	3.87	+ .99	9.4	2.58	2.60	.....	.....

PRESIDENT TAFT'S BUDGET PLAN.

In a special message to congress Feb. 26, 1913, President William H. Taft recommended the adoption of a budget system of making proposed expenditures conform to expected revenue, pointing out that the United States was the only important nation not having such a system. He advised the organization of a budget committee of congress to act as a final clearing house through which all the recommendations of committees having to do with revenues and expenditures should pass before taking the form of bills. Some of the advantages of the budget system pointed out by Mr. Taft were:

It would be a means of locating responsibility for estimates in keeping with revenues.

It would be a means of allowing congress to see how much gross it will have to spend before it begins appropriating for each department or detail of government machinery.

It would furnish congress and the public with ready reference to reports and detailed records of account.

It would produce an adequate organization for assembling and classifying information to be used in telling the country what has been done and of the government's future needs.

It would aid many bureaus hitherto organized but directed under an inconsistent and ill defined programme to work with a well defined purpose.

To carry out the budget plan, to reduce the deficit and the fixed charges against the government the president proposed to create a sinking fund commission to consist of the chairman of the finance committee of the senate, the chairman of the house ways and means committee, the attorney-general and secretary of the treasury, with the comptroller of the treasury as annual auditor of the sinking fund account.

AMERICAN AND EUROPEAN ZOOLOGICAL GARDENS.

American.
Detroit—In Belle Isle park.
Chicago—In Lincoln park.
Cincinnati—Zoological park.
Milwaukee—In West park.
New York—In Bronx park.
New York—In Central park.
Philadelphia—Zoological park.

Pittsburgh—In Schenley park.
San Francisco—In Golden Gate park.
Washington—National Zoological park.

European.
Amsterdam—"Artis."
Antwerp—Dierentuin.

Berlin—Thiergarten.
Cologne—Zoologisch garten.
Copenhagen—Dyrehave.
Dublin—In Phoenix park.
Hamburg—Zoologisch garten.
Hamburg—Hagenbeck collection.
Hanover—Zoologisch garten.
London—In Regent's park.

NATIONAL DEBTS, REVENUES AND EXPENDITURES.

[From report of bureau of statistics, Washington, D. C.]

COUNTRY.	Year.	Total debt in United States currency.	Rates of interest. Per ct.	Interest and other annual charges (budget estimate).	Revenue.	Expenditure.	PER CAPITA OF— Debt.	Interest.	Revenue	Expenditure.
Argentina	1912	$670,428,000	4 -6	$32,528,000	$140,825,000	$134,488,000	$93.48	$4.54	$19.64	$18.75
Australian Commonwealth	1911	48,901,000	......	......	66,200,000	64,036,000	10.63	......	14.39	13.91
States	1911	1,209,975,000	3 -4	50,489,000	181,840,000	181,274,000	......	......	......	......
New Zealand	1911	394,567,000	3 -4	11,964,000	68,345,000	63,603,000	371.27	11.26	89.48	59.85
Austria-Hungary	1911	1,051,346,000	3 -5	42,695,000	92,954,000	92,954,000	20.57	.84	1.82	1.82
Austria	1912	1,433,511,000	3 -5	53,145,000	592,149,000	592,087,000	50.62	1.88	20.91	20.91
Hungary	1912	1,224,677,000	3 -5	60,423,000	376,108,000	376,097,000	58.64	2.89	18.01	18.01
Belgium	1912	741,044,000	2½-3	29,567,000	136,751,000	136,751,000	98.58	3.93	18.19	18.19
Kongo, Belgian	1912	54,741,000	3 -4	1,490,000	8,756,000	13,309,000	2.74	.07	.44	.66
Bolivia	1912	13,311,000	3 -10	1,348,000	6,711,000	6,757,000	5.87	.59	2.96	2.98
Brazil	1912	663,667,000	4 -5	29,637,000	167,320,000	177,592,000	31.43	1.40	7.92	8.41
Bulgaria	1912	135,300,000	4½-6	7,749,000	36,723,000	36,463,000	31.25	1.79	8.48	8.42
Canada	1911	474,941,000	2½-4	14,116,000	117,780,000	87,774,000	67.06	1.99	16.63	12.39
Central America—Costa Rica	1913	14,624,000	4 -5	706,000	4,138,000	4,127,000	37.69	1.82	10.67	10.64
Guatemala	1911	17,846,000	4 -8	1,761,000	3,723,000	4,150,000	8.79	.87	1.83	2.04
Honduras	1913	118,301,000	5 -10	282,000	2,126,000	2,126,000	209.01	.50	3.76	3.76
Nicaragua	1910	9,641,000	6	394,000	1,518,000	1,205,000	16.07	.66	2.53	2.01
Panama	1911	51,000	7	4,000	3,366,000	3,360,000	.13	.01	8.70	8.68
Salvador	1911	13,149,000	2 -6	1,454,000	5,391,000	5,177,000	7.70	.85	3.16	3.03
Chile	1911	210,136,000	4½-5	8,212,000	72,227,000	72,675,000	51.53	2.40	21.08	21.24
China	1912	636,822,000	4 -5	33,696,000	193,261,000	375,147,000	1.90	.10	.58	1.12
Colombia	1912	23,465,000	3 -6	2,544,000	11,115,000	11,115,000	4.66	.51	2.21	2.21
Cuba	1912	61,319,000	4½-6	4,628,000	44,116,000	44,001,000	27.62	2.08	19.87	19.82
Denmark	1912	90,010,000	3 -3½	3,000,000	25,592,000	31,329,000	32.65	1.11	9.28	11.86
Ecuador	1913	20,593,000	4 -10	1,100,000	9,921,000	9,921,000	13.79	.73	4.40	7.15
Egypt	1912	460,476,000	3 -4	22,682,000	78,594,000	76,122,000	40.80	2.01	6.96	6.74
France	1912	6,283,675,000	2¾-3	185,775,000	868,178,000	868,107,000	158.67	4.69	21.92	21.92
Algeria	1912	10,289,000	3½	3,291,000	28,017,000	28,015,000	1.85	.59	5.04	5.04
Tunis	1912	68,936,000	3 -3½	2,989,000	10,519,000	10,518,000	35.74	1.55	5.45	5.45
Indo-China	1911	47,461,000	2½-3½	2,153,000	25,454,000	25,454,000	2.79	.13	1.50	1.50
Colonies (n. e. s.)	1911	50,533,000	3 -4	2,335,000	26,413,000	25,313,000	2.37	.09	1.05	1.01
German empire	1913	1,219,430,000	3 -4	57,128,000	686,900,000	686,900,000	18.78	.88	10.58	10.58
States	1911	3,705,754,000	3 -4	158,726,000	1,426,309,000	1,400,553,000	57.08	2.44	21.99	21.57
Colonies	1913	20,130,000	......	1,464,000	15,002,000	30,204,000	1.44	.10	1.08	2.16
Greece	1912	177,910,000	2½-5	7,069,000	27,815,000	27,662,000	66.73	2.65	10.43	10.38
Haiti	1913	42,863,000	2½-5	2,984,000	6,244,000	6,244,000	17.15	1.19	2.50	2.50
India—British	1912	1,348,992,000	3 -3½	47,576,000	396,666,000	382,983,000	4.28	.15	1.26	1.22
Italy	1913	2,669,748,000	3 -5	97,074,000	510,677,000	507,623,000	76.97	2.80	14.72	14.64
Japan	1913	1,271,745,000	4 -5	70,877,000	286,837,000	286,837,000	25.06	1.40	5.65	5.65
Formosa	1913	......	......	......	22,572,000	22,572,000	......	......	6.65	6.65
Chosen (Korea)	1913	14,569,000	6 -6½	1,189,000	26,340,000	26,340,000	1.04	.08	1.87	1.87
Liberia	1911	1,700,000	5	85,000	490,000	490,000	1.13	.06	.33	.33
Luxemburg	1912	2,091,000	3½	261,000	3,608,000	3,982,000	8.04	1.00	13.88	15.32
Mexico	1911	219,213,000	3 -5	14,418,000	55,349,000	60,812,000	15.50	.95	3.66	4.02
Netherlands	1912	467,709,000	2½-3	15,213,000	81,231,000	89,251,000	77.67	2.53	13.49	14.82
East Indies	1912	......	......	......	94,053,000	106,877,000	......	......	2.48	2.82
Possessions in America	1912	......	......	......	2,732,000	3,256,000	......	......	18.46	22.00
Norway	1911	98,531,000	3 -3½	4,120,000	33,073,000	32,403,000	41.19	1.72	13.83	13.55
Paraguay	1912	7,643,000	3 -7	835,000	3,564,000	4,075,000	9.55	1.04	4.45	5.09
Peru	1912	26,253,000	1 -5½	542,000	16,826,000	16,826,000	5.70	.12	3.65	3.65
Portugal	1913	968,324,000	3 -5	37,999,000	81,663,000	85,802,000	178.56	7.00	14.64	14.10
Colonies	1911	......	......	......	12,345,000	12,600,000	......	......	1.44	1.47
Roumania	1913	294,061,000	4 -5	17,582,000	97,590,000	96,606,000	41.49	2.48	13.77	13.63
Russia	1913	4,604,945,000	3 -6	207,497,000	1,637,259,000	1,652,830,000	27.72	1.25	9.86	9.95
Finland	1910	34,360,000	3 -4½	1,635,000	32,911,000	33,543,000	11.03	.52	10.57	10.77
Santo Domingo	1911	14,646,000	5	1,844,000	4,800,000	4,806,000	20.69	2.60	6.86	6.79
Servia	1912	128,078,000	2 -5	6,209,000	25,238,000	25,238,000	43.31	2.12	8.54	8.54
Siam	1912	10,135,000	4½	456,000	23,180,000	23,149,000	......	......	3.71	3.71
Spain	1911	1,815,691,000	4 -5	73,074,000	202,531,000	187,210,000	92.59	3.73	10.33	9.55
Sweden	1913	144,030,000	3 -4	8,130,000	70,491,000	70,491,000	25.90	1.46	12.67	12.67
Switzerland	1912	23,614,000	3 -3½	1,384,000	17,903,000	18,640,000	6.29	.37	4.77	4.97
Turkey	1913	554,441,000	3½-4	64,271,000	134,262,000	152,198,000	22.30	2.58	5.40	6.12
Union of South Africa	1913	566,129,000	3 -5	15,862,000	78,409,000	81,670,000	94.78	2.66	13.13	13.67
United kingdom	1912	3,527,270,000	2½-2¾	119,229,000	900,742,000	868,890,000	77.75	2.63	19.86	19.15
Colonies (n. e. s.)	1911	186,190,000	3 -4	6,556,000	106,603,000	92,417,000	4.49	.16	2.43	2.23
United States	1912	1,027,575,000	2 -4	22,616,000	992,249,000	965,274,000	10.61	.23	10.25	9.97
Philippines	1912	16,125,000	4	713,000	14,893,000	15,104,000	1.96	.11	1.54	1.65
Uruguay	1912	136,341,000	3½-5	8,593,000	34,702,000	34,076,000	115.74	7.29	29.46	29.44
Venezuela	1913	37,729,000	3	1,275,000	10,133,000	10,133,000	18.75	.46	3.69	3.69
Total	....	41,736,701,000	......	1,686,763,000	11574,143,000	11687,714,000	......	......	......	......

NOTE—The years for which the revenues and expenditures are given are approximately, but not in all cases, the same as those for the debts.

BIRTH STONES.

[Authorized by American Jewelers' association.]

January .... Garnet
February ..... Amethyst
March....Aqua marine, ...bloodstone
April ....Diamond
May .... Emerald
June....Pearl, moonstone
July ....Ruby
Aug...Moonstone, peridot
September .... Sapphire
Oct.....Opal, tourmaline
November .... Topaz
December ...Turquoise, ...lapis lazuli

STATEMENT OF THE PUBLIC DEBT (JUNE 30, 1913).

INTEREST-BEARING DEBT.

TITLE OF LOAN.	Authorizing act.	Rate.	Issued.	Amount issued.	Total outstanding June 30. 1913.
Consols of 1930	March 14. 1900	2 per cent	1900	$646,250,150	$646,250,150
Loan of 1908-1918	June 13, 1898	3 per cent	1898	198,792,660	63,945,460
Loan of 1925	Jan. 14, 1875	4 per cent	1895-1896	162,815,400	118,489,900
Panama canal loan:					
Series 1906	June 28, 1902, & Dec.21.1905	2 per cent	1906	54,631,980	54,631,980
Series 1908	June 28, 1902, & Dec.21.1905	2 per cent	1908	30,000,000	30,000,000
Series 1911	Aug. 5, 1909, Feb. 4, 1910,				
Postal savings bonds:	and March 2, 1911	3 per cent	1911	50,000,000	50,000,000
(1st, 2d and 3d series)	June 25, 1910	2½ per cent	1911-12	1,314,140	1,314,140
1913-53 (fourth series)	June 25, 1910	2½ per cent	1913	1,074,980	1,074,980
Aggregate int.-bearing debt				1,144,879,310	965,706,610

DEBT ON WHICH INTEREST HAS CEASED SINCE MATURITY.

Funded loan of 1891, continued at 2 per cent. called for redemption May 18, 1900; interest ceased Aug. 18, 1900	$5,000.00
Funded loan of 1891, matured Sept. 2, 1891	23,650.00
Loan of 1904, matured Feb. 2, 1904	13,250.00
Funded loan of 1907, matured July 2, 1907	700,400.00
Refunding certificates, matured July 1, 1907	13,570.00
Old debt matured at various dates prior to Jan. 1, 1861, and other items of debt matured at various dates subsequent to Jan. 1, 1861	903,680.25
Aggregate of debt on which interest has ceased since maturity	1,659,550.25

DEBT BEARING NO INTEREST.

United States notes—Feb. 25, 1862; July 11, 1862; March 3, 1863	$346,681,016.00
Old demand notes—July 17, 1861; Feb. 12, 1862	53,152.50
National bank notes—Redemption fund*—July 14, 1890	22,092,806.00
Fractional currency—July 17, 1862; March 3, 1863; June 30, 1864, less $8,375,934 estimated as lost or destroyed, act of June 21, 1879	6,854,609.90
Aggregate of debt bearing no interest	375,681,584.40

CERTIFICATES AND NOTES ISSUED ON DEPOSITS OF COIN AND SILVER BULLION.

CLASSIFICATION.	In circulation.	In the treasury.	Outstanding.
Gold certificates—March 3, 1863; July 12, 1882; March 14, 1900	$1008,532,749	$78,194,420	$1,086,727,169
Silver certificates—Feb. 28, 1878; Aug. 4, 1886; March 3, 1887; March 14, 1900	470,189,192	13,360,808	483,550,000
Treasury notes of 1890—July 14, 1890; March 14, 1900	2,656,781	3,219	2,660,000
Aggregate of certificates and treasury notes offset by cash in the treasury	1,481,378,722	91,558,447	1,572,937,169

RECAPITULATION OF PUBLIC DEBT.

Classification.	June 30. 1913	May 31, 1913
Interest-bearing debt	$965,706,610.00	$965,706,610.00
Debt on which interest has ceased since maturity	1,659,550.26	1,660,900.26
Debt bearing no interest	375,681,584.40	375,127,979.40
Aggregate of interest and noninterest bearing debt	1,343,047,744.66	1,342,495,489.60
Certificates and treasury notes offset by an equal amount of cash in treasury	1,572,937,169.00	1,565,162,169.06

CASH IN THE TREASURY AND CURRENT LIABILITES—GENERAL FUND.

ASSETS.		LIABILITIES.	
Cash in treasury offices—Gold coin	$23,084,092.92	Current liabilities in treasury offices—	
Gold certificates	78 194,420.00	Outstanding warrants and checks	$14,750,825.00
Standard silver dollars	9,191,059.00	Balances to the credit of disbursing officers	77,059,610.15
Silver certificates	13,360,808.00	Postoffice department balances	10,883,411.02
United States notes	8,757,310.00	Miscellaneous items (assets of banks in liquidation, etc.)	4,564,519.53
Treasury notes of 1890	3,219.00	Coupons and interest matured	142,353.48
Certified checks on banks	62,200.77	National bank notes: redemption fund	22,092,806.00
National bank notes	42,895,985.20	National bank 5 per cent fund	26,593,969.00
	†176,349,691.89		156,001,514.23
In national bank depositaries—			
To credit of treasurer of United States	74,160,472.33		
To credit of postmasters, judical officers, etc.	5,588,827.18	In national bank depositories—	
In transit or checks not cleared	23,000,000.00	Balances to credit of postmasters, judical officers. etc.	5,588,827.18
Available cash in treasury and banks	279,048,924.40	Outstanding warrants	494,915.46
Free and available balance in treasury and banks—		Current liabilities in treasury and banks	162,145,156.87
Available cash as above ..$279,008,924 40			
Current liabilities.contra.. 162,145,156.87		In treasury Philippines—	
Free balance	116,953,837.53	Balances to credit of disbursing officers	3,186,102.50
In treasury Philippines—		Outstanding warrants	421,261.69
To credit of treasurer United States	1,667,510.48		
To credit of disbursing officers	3,189,102.50	Balances in treasury offices, limited tender or unavailable—Silver bullion	2,054,492.54
Balances in treasury offices, limited tender or unavailable—Silver bullion	2,054,492.54	Total liabilities against cash	165,752,521.06
Subsidiary silver coin	20,785,510.86		
Fractional currency	276.37	Net balance in general fund	142,396,835.47
Minor coin	2,006,469.38		
Total cash assets in general fund	308,149,356.53	Total liabilites and net balance	308,149,356.53

THE CURRENCY TRUST FUNDS, THE GENERAL FUND, AND THE GOLD RESERVE FUND.

Assets.		Liabilities.	
Currency trust funds—Gold coin......	$887,471,847.00	Outstanding certificates — Gold certifi-	
Gold bullion...........................	199,255,322.00	cates outstanding....................	$1,086,727,169.00
Total gold........................	1,086,727,169.00	Silver certificates outstanding...........	483,550,000.00
Silver dollars......................	483,550,000.00	Treasury notes outstanding............	2,660,000.00
Silver dollars of 1890...............	2,660,000.00	Total outstanding certificates........	1,572,937,169.00
Total currency trust funds...........	1,572,937,169.00	General fund liabilities and balance—	
General fund—		Total liabilities against cash, as above	165,752,521.06
Total cash assets, as above...........	308,149,356.53	Balance in general fund,	
Gold reserve fund—Gold coin..........	100,000,000.00	as above............... $142,396,835.47	
Gold bullion......................	50,00,000.00	Gold reserve............... 150,000,000.00	
Grand total cash assets in treasury.....	2,031,086,525.53	Total net balances......	292,396,835.47
			2,031,086,525.53

CIRCULATION STATEMENT (JULY 1, 1913).

CLASSIFICATION.	General stock of money in the U S. June 2, 1913.	General stock of money in the U S. July 1, 1913.	**Held in treasury as assets of the government July 1, 1913.	MONEY IN CIRCULATION.		
				July 1, 1913.	July 1, 1912.	Jan. 1, 1879.
Gold coin(including bullion in treas.)	$1,801,369,895	$1,868,790,890	$173,084,093	$808,979,598	$807,445,193	$96,262,850
Gold certificates††	....	....	78,194,420	1,008,582,749	842,622,184	21,189,280
Standard silver dollars..............	565,590,020	565,618,020	9,991,659	72,076,861	70,330,728	5,790,721
Silver certificates†‡	....	....	13,283,808	470,189,192	469,049,230	413,360
Subsidiary silver................	175,299,876	175,471,210	20,765,511	154,705,699	141,351,758	67,982,601
Treasury notes of 1890............	2,688,000	2,660,000	3,219	2,656,781	2,919,625	....
United States notes.................	346,681,016	346,681,016	8,757,310	337,923,706	337,922,128	‡‡310,288,511
National bank notes................	755,294,066	759,157,906	42,895,885	716,261,921	705,196,304	314,339,398
Total.....................	3,706,922,873	3,718,379,012	347,055,005	3,371,326,007	4,276,786,615	816,206,721

Population of continental United States July 1, 1913, estimated at 97,337,000; circulation per capita, $34.64.

*The "National Bank Notes: Redemption Fund" was established under requirement of the act of July 14, 1890, which states: Deposits made by national banks to redeem circulating notes shall be covered into the treasury as miscellaneous receipts and the treasury shall redeem from the general cash the circulating notes which come into its possession subject to redemption. The balance of deposits shall, at the close of each month, be reported on the monthly public debt statement as a debt of the United States bearing no interest.

†This includes $38,398,248.20 which the treasury has redeemed and for which it will receive payment from national banks.

‡The balances in national banks are considerably in excess of authorized deposits on account of large payments of corporation taxes and other revenue at the end of the fiscal year.

§The act of July 14, 1890, provides that deposits made by national banks to redeem circulating notes shall be covered into the treasury as miscellaneous receipts, and that the treasury shall redeem from the general cash the circulating notes which come into its possession subject to redemption.

‖Reserved against $346,681,016 of United States notes and $2,660,000 of treasury notes of 1890.

**This statement of money held in the treasury as assets of the government does not include deposits of public money in national bank depositories to the credit of the treasurer of the United States, amounting to $74,160,472.33. For a full statement of assets see public debt statement.

††For redemption of outstanding certificates an exact equivalent in amount of the appropriate kinds of money is held in the treasury, and is not included in the account of money held as assets of the government.

‡‡Includes $33,190,000 currency certificates, act June 8, 1872.

ANALYSIS OF THE PUBLIC DEBT.

JULY 1.	Debt on which interest has ceased.	Debt bearing no interest.*	Outstanding principal.	Cash in the treasury.	Principal of debt less cash in treasury.	Population of the United States.	Debt per capita.	Interest per capita.
1890..................	$1,815,805.26	$825,011,289.47	$1,552,140,204.73	$661,355,834.20	$924,465,218.53	62,947,714	$14.22	$0.47
1891..................	1,614,705.26	933,852,766.35	1,545,996,591.61	694,083,839.83	851,912,751.78	63,844,000	13.34	.37
1892..................	2,785,875.26	1,000,648,939.57	1,558,464,144.53	746,931,681.03	841,526,463.60	65,086,000	12.93	.35
1893..................	2,094,060.26	958,854,525.87	1,545,985,686.13	707,016,210.89	838,969,475.75	66,349,000	12.64	.35
1894..................	1,851,240.26	995,300,506.42	1,632,253,636.68	792,940,256.13	899,313,380.55	67,632,000	13.30	.38
1895..................	1,721,590.26	958,197,731.99	1,675,120,983.25	811,081,686.46	864,039,314.75	68,934,000	13.08	.42
1896..................	1,600,890.26	920,839,543.14	1,769,840,323.40	853,905,635.51	915,934,687.89	70,254,000	13.60	.49
1897..................	1,346,880.26	968,900,855.64	1,817,672,665.90	925,649,765.87	992,022,900.03	71,502,900	13.78	.48
1898..................	1,262,680.00	947,901,845.64	1,796,531,995.90	769,446,504.76	1,027,085,492.14	72,947,000	14.08	.47
1899..................	1,218,300.26	944,610,256.66	1,991,927,306.92	836,607,071.73	1,155,320,235.19	74,318,000	15.55	.54
1900..................	1,176,320.26	1,312,305,911.41	2,136,961,491.67	1,029,249,838.78	1,107,711,257.89	75,994,575	14.58	.44
1901..................	1,415,620.26	1,154,770,273.63	2,143,326,933.89	1,098,587,845.92	1,044,739,119.97	77,612,569	13.46	.38
1902..................	1,280,860.26	1,226,259,345.63	2,158,610,445.80	1,189,153,204.85	969,457,241.04	79,230,563	12.24	.35
1903..................	1,205,090.26	1,286,718,281.63	2,202,464,781.89	1,277,453,144.58	925,011,637.31	80,848,557	11.44	.32
1904..................	1,970,920.26	1,366,875,224.88	2,264,003,585.14	1,296,771,811.39	967,231,773.75	82,466,551	11.73	.29
1905..................	1,370,245.26	1,378,006,478.68	2,274,615,063.84	1,365,467,439.06	909,147,624.78	84,084,645	11.77	.29
1906..................	1,128,135.26	1,440,874,563.78	2,337,161,889.04	1,372,726,162.26	964,435,696.79	85,702,589	11.25	.27
1907..................	1,086,815.26	1,561,206,968.00	2,457,188,061.54	1,578,501,306.51	878,686,755.03	87,320,553	10.06	.25
1908..................	4,130,015.26	1,726,172,266.28	2,636,806,271.54	1,688,673,862.16	938,132,409.08	88,938,527	10.55	.24
1909..................	2,883,855.26	1,723,344,898.78	2,639,546,241.04	1,615,684,710.35	1,023,861,530.70	90,656,621	11.31	.25
1910..................	2,124,895.26	1,737,223,452.78	2,652,665,838.04	1,606,216,652.79	1,046,449,185.25	92,174,515	11.35	.23
1911..................	1,879,830.26	1,848,367,586.43	2,765,600,606.69	1,749,816,268.23	1,015,884,338.46	93,792,569	10.83	.23
1912..................	1,760,450.26	1,902,896,653.90	2,868,373,874.16	1,840,799,176.88	1,027,574,697.28	95,410,503	10.77	.24
1913..................	1,659,550.26	1,948,618,753.40	2,915,984,913.66	2,031,086,525.53	881,898,388.13	97,337,000	....	....

*Includes certificates issued against gold, silver and currency deposited in the treasury.

OUTSTANDING PRINCIPAL OF PUBLIC DEBT.

On Jan. 1 of each year from 1791 to 1843, inclusive, and on July 1 of each year since.

Year.	Amount.	Year.	Amount.	Year.	Amount.	Year.	Amount.	Year.	Amount.
1791	$75,463,476.52	1816	$127,334,933.74	1841	$5,250,875.54	1865	$2,680,647,869.74	1890	1,552,140,204.73
1792	77,227,924.66	1817	123,591,965.16	1842	13,594,480.73	1866	2,773,236,173.69	1891	1,545,996,591.61
1793	80,358,634.04	1818	103,466,633.83	1843	20,201,226.27	1867	2,678,126,103.87	1892	1,588,464,144.63
1794	78,427,404.77	1819	95,529,648.28	1843	32,742,922.00	1868	2,611,687,851.19	1893	1,545,985,686.13
1795	80,747,587.39	1820	91,015,566.15	1844	23,461,652.50	1869	2,588,452,213.94	1894	1,632,253,636.68
1796	83,762,172.07	1821	89,987,427.66	1845	15,925,303.01	1870	2,480,672,427.81	1895	1,676,120,983.25
1797	82,064,479.33	1822	93,546,676.98	1846	15,550,202.97	1871	2,353,211,332.32	1896	1,769,840,323.40
1798	79,228,529.12	1823	90,875,877.28	1847	38,826,534.77	1872	2,253,251,328.78	1897	1,817,672,665.90
1799	78,408,669.77	1824	90,269,777.77	1848	47,044,862.23	1873	2,234,482,993.20	1898	1,796,531,995.90
1800	82,976,294.35	1825	83,788,332.71	1849	63,061,858.69	1874	2,251,690,468.43	1899	1,991,927,306.92
1801	83,038,050.80	1826	81,955,059.99	1850	63,452,773.55	1875	2,232,284,531.95	1900	2,136,961,091.67
1802	80,712,632.25	1827	73,987,357.20	1851	68,304,796.02	1876	2,180,395,067.15	1901	2,143,326,933.89
1803	77,054,686.40	1828	67,475,043.87	1852	66,199,341.71	1877	2,205,301,392.10	1902	2,158,610,445.39
1804	86,427,120.88	1829	58,421,413.67	1853	59,803,117.70	1878	2,256,205,892.53	1903	2,202,464,781.89
1805	82,312,150.50	1830	48,565,406.50	1854	42,242,222.42	1879	2,340,567,232.04	1904	2,261,003,585.14
1806	75,723,270.66	1831	39,123,191.68	1855	35,586,956.56	1880	2,120,415,370.63	1905	2,274,615,063.84
1807	69,218,398.64	1832	24,322,235.18	1856	31,932,537.90	1881	2,069,013,569.58	1906	2,337,161,839.04
1808	65,196,317.97	1833	7,001,698.83	1857	28,699,831.85	1882	1,918,312,994.03	1907	2,457,188,061.54
1809	57,023,192.09	1834	4,760,082.08	1858	44,911,881.03	1883	1,884,171,728.07	1908	2,626,806,271.54
1810	53,173,217.52	1835	33,733.05	1859	58,496,837.88	1884	1,830,528,923.57	1909	2,639,546,241.04
1811	48,005,587.76	1836	37,513.05	1860	64,842,287.88	1885	1,863,964,873.14	1910	2,652,665,838.04
1812	45,209,737.90	1837	336,957.83	1861	90,580,873.72	1886	1,775,063,013.78	1911	2,765,600,606.69
1813	55,962,827.57	1838	3,308,124.07	1862	524,176,412.13	1887	1,657,602,592.63	1912	2,868,373,874.16
1814	81,487,846.24	1839	10,434,221.14	1863	1,119,772,138.63	1888	1,692,858,984.58	1913	2,915,984,913.66
1815	99,833,660.15	1840	3,573,343.32	1864	1,815,784,370.57	1889	1,619,052,922.23		

GOVERNMENT RECEIPTS AND DISBURSEMENTS BY FISCAL YEARS.

	1913.	1912.	1911.	1910.	1909.	1908.
1. Ordinary receipts	$723,782,921.16	$691,778,465.37	$701,372,374.99	$675,511,715.02	$603,589,489.84	$601,060,723.27
Ordinary disbursements	683,699,692.10	654,553,963.47	654,137,997.89	659,705,391.08	662,324,444.77	621,102,390.64
Excess of receipts (+) or disbursements (—)	+40,083,229.06	+37,224,501.90	+47,234,377.10	+15,806,323.94	—58,734,954.93	—20,041,667.37
2. Panama canal receipts	....	33,189,104.15	18,102,170.04	....	30,731,008.21	25,367,768.67
Panama canal disbursements	41,741,258.03	35,327,370.66	37,063,515.33	33,911,673.37	31,419,442.41	38,093,929.04
Excess of receipts (+) or disbursements (—)	—41,741,258.03	—2,138,266.51	—18,961,345.29	—33,911,673.37	—688,434.20	—12,726,160.37
3. Public debt receipts	23,400,850.00	20,537,645.00	40,232,555.00	31,674,292.50	45,624,239.50	79,789,636.50
Public debt disbursements	24,191,610.50	28,648,327.53	35,223,336.35	33,049,695.50	104,996,770.00	73,891,906.50
Excess of receipts (+) or disbursements (—)	—790,760.50	—8,110,682.53	+5,009,218.65	—1,375,403.00	—59,372,530.50	—5,877,730.00
Excess of all receipts (+) or all disbursements (—)	—2,448,789.47	+26,975,552.86	+33,282,250.46	—19,480,752.42	—118,795,919.63	—26,890,097.74
Balance in general fund at close of year	164,703,689.52	167,152,478.99	140,176,926.13	106,894,675.67	126,375,428.10	245,171,347.73

COINS OF THE UNITED STATES (1792-1912).

GOLD COINS.

Double Eagles—Authorized to be coined, act of March 3, 1849; weight, 516 grains; fineness, .900. Total amount coined to June 30, 1912, $2,352,587,300. Full legal tender.

Eagles—Authorized to be coined, act of April 2, 1792; weight, 270 grains; fineness, .916⅔; weight changed, act of June 28, 1834, to 258 grains; fineness changed, act of June 28, 1834, to .899225; fineness changed, act of Jan. 18, 1837, to .900. Total amount coined to June 30, 1912, $406,112,890. Full legal tender.

Half-Eagles—Authorized to be coined, act of April 2, 1792; weight, 135 grains; fineness, .916⅔; weight changed, act of June 28, 1834, to 129 grains; fineness changed, act of June 28, 1834, to .899225; fineness changed, act of Jan. 18, 1837, to .900. Total amount coined to June 30, 1912, $371,802,850. Full legal tender.

Quarter-Eagles—Authorized to be coined, act of April 2, 1792; weight, 67.5 grains; fineness, .916⅔; weight changed, act of June 28, 1834, to 64.5 grains; fineness changed, act of June 28, 1834, to .899225; fineness changed, act of Jan. 18, 1837, to .900. Total amount coined to June 30, 1912, $38,950,520. Full legal tender.

Three-Dollar Piece—Authorized to be coined, act of Feb. 21, 1853; weight, 77.4 grains; fineness, .900; coinage discontinued, act of Sept. 26, 1890. Total amount coined, $1,619,376. Full legal tender.

One Dollar—Authorized to be coined, act of March 3, 1849; weight, 25.8 grains; fineness, .900; coinage discontinued, act of Sept. 26, 1890. Total amount coined, $19,499,337. Full legal tender.

One Dollar, Louisiana Purchase Exposition—Authorized June 28, 1902; weight, 25.8 grains; fineness, .900. Total amount coined, $250,000.

One Dollar, Lewis and Clark Exposition—Authorized April 13, 1904; weight, 25.8 grains; fineness, .900. Total amount coined, $60,000.

SILVER COINS.

Dollar—Authorized to be coined, act of April 2, 1792; weight, 416 grains; fineness, .8924; weight changed, act of Jan. 18, 1837, to 412½ grains; fineness changed, act of Jan. 18, 1837, to .900; coinage discontinued, act of Feb. 12, 1873. Total amount coined to Feb. 12, 1873, $8,031,238. Coinage reauthorized, act of Feb. 28, 1878; coinage discontinued after July 1, 1891, except for certain purposes, act of July 14, 1890. Amount coined to June 30, 1912, $578,303,848. Full legal tender except when otherwise provided in the contract.

Trade Dollar—Authorized to be coined, act of Feb. 12, 1873; weight, 420 grains; fineness, .900; legal tender limited to $5, act of June 22, 1874 (rev. stat.); coinage limited to export demand and legal tender quality repealed, joint resolution, July 22, 1876; coinage discontinued, act of Feb. 19, 1887. Total amount coined, $35,965,924.

Lafayette Souvenir Dollar—Authorized by act of March 3, 1899; weight, 412½ grains; fineness, .900. Total amount coined, $50,000.

Half-Dollar—Authorized to be coined, act of April 2, 1792; weight, 208 grains; fineness, .8924; weight changed, act of Jan. 18, 1837, to 206¼ grains; fineness changed, act of Jan. 18, 1837, to .900; weight changed, act of Feb. 21, 1853, to 192 grains; weight changed, act of Feb. 12, 1873, to 12½ grams, or 192.9 grains. Total amount coined to June 30, 1912, $186,668,075. Legal tender, $10.

Columbian Half-Dollar—Authorized to be coined, act of Aug. 5, 1892; weight, 192.9 grains; fineness, .900. Total amount coined, $2,500,000. Legal tender, $10.

Quarter-Dollar—Authorized to be coined, act of April 2, 1792; weight, 104 grains; fineness, .8924; weight changed, act of Jan. 18, 1837, to 103⅛ grains; fineness changed, act of Jan. 18, 1837, to .900; weight changed, act of Feb. 21, 1853, to 96 grains; weight changed, act of Feb. 12, 1873, to 6¼ grams, or 96.45

grains. Total amount coined to June 30, 1912, $98,617,202.50. Legal tender, $10.

Columbian Quarter-Dollar—Authorized to be coined, act of March 3, 1893; weight, 96.45 grains; fineness, .900. Total amount coined, $10,000. Legal tender, $10.

Twenty-Cent Piece—Authorized to be coined, act of March 3, 1875; weight, 5 grains, or 77.16 grains; fineness, .900; coinage prohibited, act of May 2, 1878. Total amount coined, $271,000.

Dime—Authorized to be coined, act of April 2, 1792; weight, 41.6 grains; fineness, .8924; weight changed, act of Jan. 18, 1837, to 41½ grains; fineness changed, act of Jan. 18, 1837, to .900; weight changed, act of Feb. 21, 1853, to 38.4 grains; weight changed, act of Feb. 12, 1873, to 2½ grams, or 38.58 grains. Total amount coined to June 30, 1912, $67,708,802.50. Legal tender, $10.

Half-Dime—Authorized to be coined, act of April 2, 1792; weight, 20.8 grains; fineness, .8924; weight changed, act of Jan. 18, 1837, to 20% grains; fineness changed, act of Jan. 18, 1837, to .900; weight changed, act of Feb. 21, 1853, to 19.2 grains; coinage discontinued, act of Feb. 12, 1873. Total amount coined, $4,880,219.40.

Three-Cent Piece—Authorized to be coined, act of March 3, 1851; weight, 12⅜ grains; fineness, .750; weight changed, act of March 3, 1853, to 11.52 grains; fineness changed, act of March 3, 1853, to .900; coinage discontinued, act of Feb. 12, 1873. Total amount coined, $1,282,087.20.

MINOR COINS.

Five-Cent (nickel)—Authorized to be coined, act of May 16, 1866; weight, 77.16 grains; composed of 75 per cent copper and 25 per cent nickel. Total amount coined to June 30, 1912, $36,149,156.05. Legal tender for $1, but reduced to 25 cents by act of Feb. 12, 1873.

Three-Cent (nickel)—Authorized to be coined, act of March 3, 1865; weight, 30 grains; composed of 75 per cent copper and 25 per cent nickel. Total amount coined, $941,349.48. Legal tender for 60 cents, but reduced to 25 cents by act of Feb. 12, 1873. Coinage discontinued, act of Sept. 26, 1890.

Two-Cent (bronze)—Authorized to be coined, act of April 22, 1864; weight, 96 grains, composed of 95 per cent copper and 5 per cent tin and zinc. Coinage discontinued, act of Feb. 12, 1873. Total amount coined, $912,020.

Cent (copper)—Authorized to be coined, act of April 2, 1792; weight, 264 grains; weight changed, act of Jan. 14, 1793, to 208 grains; weight changed by proclamation of the president, Jan. 26, 1796, in conformity with act of March 3, 1795, to 168 grains; coinage discontinued, act of Feb. 21, 1857. Total amount coined, $1,562,887.44.

Cent (nickel)—Authorized to be coined, act of Feb. 21, 1857; weight, 72 grains; composed of 88 per cent copper and 12 per cent nickel. Coinage discontinued, act of April 22, 1864. Total amount coined, $2,007,720.

Cent (bronze)—Authorized, act of April 22, 1864; weight, 48 grains; composed of 95 per cent copper and 5 per cent tin and zinc. Total amount coined to June 30, 1912, $20,684,521.83. Legal tender, 25 cents.

Half-Cent (copper)—Authorized to be coined, act of April 2, 1792; weight, 132 grains; weight changed, act of Jan. 14, 1793, to 104 grains; weight changed by proclamation of the president, Jan. 26, 1796, in conformity with act of March 3, 1795, to 84 grains; coinage discontinued, act of Feb. 21, 1857. Total amount coined, $39,926.11.

*TOTAL COINAGE.		COINAGE, 1912.	
Gold	$3,280,882,273.00	Gold	$12,749,090.00
Silver	976,257,159.60	Silver	9,655,405.25
Minor	62,297,580.91	Minor	2,163,340.15
Total	4,319,437,013.51	Total	24,567,835.40

*To end of fiscal year, June 30, 1912.

APPROXIMATE VALUE OF FOREIGN COINS.

(c, copper; g, gold; s, silver.)

COIN.	COUNTRY.	U. S. equivalent.	COIN.	COUNTRY.	U. S. equivalent.
Argentina, g	Argentine Republic.	$4.82	Leu, s	Roumania	$0.193
Balboa, g	Panama	1.00	Libra, g	Peru	4.866
Bolivar, s	Venezuela	.193	Lira, s	Italy	.193
Boliviano, s	Bolivia	.389	Lira, g	Turkey	4.40
Cash, c	China	.006	Mark, s	Germany	.238
Cent	China	.005	Mark, g	Finland	.193
Cent	Mexico	.005	Medjidie, g	Turkey	.88
Centime, c	France	.002	Milreis, s	Brazil	.546
Colon, g	Costa Rica	.465	Milreis, g	Portugal	1.08
Condor, g	Colombia	10.00	Napoleon, g	France	3.86
Condor, g	Chile	7.30	Onlik, s	Turkey	.40
Condor, g	Ecuador	4.90	Ore, c	Scandinavia	.0025
Crown, s	Austria	.203	Para, s	Turkey	.001
Crown, s	Denmark	.268	Penny, c	Great Britain	.02
Crown, s	Great Britain	1.22	Perper, g	Montenegro	.203
Crown, s	Norway	.268	Peseta, s	Spain	.193
Crown, s	Sweden	.268	Peso, g	Argentine Republic	.96
Dinar, g	Servia	.193	Peso, s	Central America	.436
Dinero, s	Peru	.05	Peso, g	Chile	.365
Dollar, g	British Honduras	1.00	Peso, g	Colombia	1.00
Dollar, g	Newfoundland	1.014	Peso, g	Cuba	.91
Dollar, g	British possessions	1.00	Peso, s	Mexico	.498
Dollar, g	Colombia	1.00	Peso, s	Paraguay	.436
Dollar, g	Liberia	1.00	Peso, g	Philippines	.50
Dollar, g	Straits Settlements	.57	Peso, g	Uruguay	1.034
Dollar, s	China	.48	Pfennig, c	Germany	.0025
Dollar, g	Santo Domingo	1.00	Piaster, c	Cochin China	.55
Doubloon, g	Chile	3.65	Piaster, s	Cyprus	.05
Drachma, s	Greece	.193	Piaster, s	Turkey	.044
Escudo, g	Chile	1.82	Pound, g	Egypt	4.94
Farthing, c	Great Britain	.005	Pound, g	Great Britain	4.866
Florin, s	Austria	.49	Ruble, g	Russia	.515
Florin, s	Great Britain	.49	Rupee, s	India	.324
Florin, g	Netherlands	.402	Scudo, g, s	Italy	.95
Franc, s	France	.193	Sen, c	Japan	.005
Franc, g	Belgium	.193	Shilling, s	Great Britain	.24
Franc, g	Switzerland	.193	Sixpence, s	Great Britain	.12
Gourde, s	Haiti	.965	Sol, s	Peru	.49
Guilder, s	Netherlands	.40	Soldo, c	Italy	.01
Guinea, g	Great Britain	5.04	Sovereign, g	Great Britain	4.866
Gulden, s	Austria	.49	Sucre, g	Ecuador	.487
Heller, s	Austria	.004	Tael (customs), s	China	.727
Kopeck, c	Russia	.005	Tical, s	Siam	.370
Kran, s	Persia	.17	Yen, s	Japan	.498
Krone (see crown)					

LIFE INSURANCE IN THE UNITED STATES.

YEAR.	ORDINARY.		INDUSTRIAL.		TOTAL.	
	Policies.	Amount.	Policies.	Amount.	Policies.	Amount.
1850	20,407	$68,614,189				
1860	60,000	180,000,000				
1870	830,226	2,262,847,000				
1880	679,690	1,564,183,552	236,674	$20,533,469	916,364	$1,584,717,001
1890	1,319,561	3,620,057,439	3,883,529	429,521,128	5,203,090	4,049,578,567
1900	3,176,051	7,093,152,380	11,219,296	1,468,986,306	14,395,347	8,562,138,746
1910	6,954,119	13,227,218,168	23,034,463	3,177,047,874	29,988,582	16,404,261,042
1911	7,633,263	14,578,989,906	24,708,499	3,423,790,536	32,401,762	18,002,780,439

	Total income.	Payments to policyholders.	Assets.	Liabilities.	Surplus.
1890	$196,938,069	$90,007,820	$770,972,061	$678,681,309	$92,290,752
1900	400,257,606	168,687,601	1,742,414,173	1,493,378,709	249,035,464
1910	781,011,249	387,302,073	5,875,877,059	3,325,878,393	519,998,693
1911	836,160,804	414,208,448	4,164,491,698	3,645,906,554	518,585,144

AMERICAN TABLE OF MORTALITY.
Used by insurance companies in computing expectation of life.

Age.	No. living.	No. dying.	Exp't'n of life.	Age.	No. living.	No. dying.	Exp't'n of life.	Age.	No. living.	No. dying.	Exp't'n of life.
10	100,000	749	48.72	39	78,862	756	28.90	68	43,133	2,243	9.47
11	99,251	746	48.09	40	78,106	765	28.18	69	40,890	2,321	8.91
12	98,505	743	47.45	41	77,341	774	27.45	70	38,569	2,391	8.48
13	97,762	740	46.80	42	76,567	785	26.72	71	36,178	2,448	8.00
14	97,022	737	46.16	43	75,782	797	26.00	72	33,730	2,487	7.55
15	96,285	735	45.50	44	74,985	812	25.27	73	31,243	2,505	7.11
16	95,550	732	44.85	45	74,173	828	24.54	74	28,738	2,501	6.68
17	94,818	729	44.19	46	73,345	848	23.81	75	26,237	2,476	6.27
18	94,089	727	43.53	47	72,497	870	23.08	76	23,761	2,431	5.88
19	93,362	725	42.87	48	71,627	896	22.36	77	21,330	2,369	5.49
20	92,637	723	42.20	49	70,731	927	21.63	78	18,961	2,291	5.11
21	91,914	722	41.53	50	69,804	962	20.91	79	16,670	2,196	4.74
22	91,192	721	40.85	51	68,842	1,001	20.20	80	14,474	2,091	4.39
23	90,471	720	40.17	52	67,841	1,044	19.49	81	12,383	1,964	4.05
24	89,751	719	39.49	53	66,797	1,091	18.79	82	10,419	1,816	3.71
25	89,032	718	38.81	54	65,706	1,143	18.09	83	8,603	1,648	3.39
26	88,314	718	38.12	55	64,563	1,199	17.40	84	6,955	1,470	3.08
27	87,596	718	37.43	56	63,364	1,200	16.72	85	5,485	1,292	2.77
28	86,878	718	36.73	57	62,104	1,325	16.05	86	4,193	1,114	2.47
29	86,160	719	36.03	58	60,779	1,394	15.39	87	3,079	933	2.18
30	85,441	720	35.33	59	59,385	1,468	14.74	88	2,146	744	1.91
31	84,721	721	34.63	60	57,917	1,546	14.10	89	1,402	555	1.66
32	84,000	723	33.92	61	56,371	1,628	13.47	90	847	385	1.42
33	83,277	726	33.21	62	54,743	1,713	12.86	91	462	246	1.19
34	82,551	729	32.50	63	53,030	1,800	12.26	92	216	137	.98
35	81,822	732	31.78	64	51,230	1,889	11.67	93	79	58	.80
36	81,090	737	31.07	65	49,341	1,980	11.10	94	21	18	.64
37	80,353	742	30.35	66	47,361	2,070	10.54	95	3	3	.50
38	79,611	749	29.62	67	45,291	2,158	10.00				

FIRE AND MARINE INSURANCE.

YEAR.	Companies.	Income.	PAYMENTS TO POLICYHOLDERS		
			Losses.	Dividends	Total.
1890	580	$157,857,983	$75,334,517	$5,334,495	$80,768,012
1900	439	198,312,577	108,307,171	8,446,110	116,753,281
1910	597	381,545,814	166,780,763	20,709,261	187,490,024
1911	593	388,462,193	183,476,741	18,771,959	202,248,700

CASUALTY AND MISCELLANEOUS INSURANCE.

YEAR.	Companies.	Income.	Payments to policyholders.
1890	34	$9,758,413	$2,033,306
1900	62	32,309,619	10,166,796
1910	177	111,041,748	41,455,472
1911	196	118,981,773	47,968,648

UNITED STATES TELEGRAPH STATISTICS (WESTERN UNION).

YEAR.	Miles of wires.	Offices.	Messages.	Receipts.	Expenses.	Profits.	*Toll. Cents.	*Cost. Cents.
1900	933,153	22,900	63,167,783	$24,758,570	$18,593,2.6	$6,165,394	30.8	25.1
1901	972,766	24,238	65,657,049	25,354,151	19,668,903	6,685,248	30.9	25.1
1902	1,029,984	23,567	69,374,883	28,073,095	20,780,766	7,292,329	31.0	25.7
1903	1,089,212	23,120	69,790,896	29,167,687	20,953,215	8,214,472	31.4	25.6
1904	1,135,465	23,458	67,903,973	29,249,390	21,361,915	7,887,475	31.7	24.1
1905	1,184,557	23,814	67,477,339	29,033,635	21,845,570	7,188,065	31.6	27.3
1906	1,256,847	24,323	71,487,082	30,675,655	23,605,072	7,070,583	31.6	37.6
1907	1,321,199	24,780	74,804,551	32,856,406	26,532,196	6,324,210	33.7	30.2
1908	1,359,430	23,853	62,371,287	28,582,212	25,179,215	3,402,997	33.7	34.3
1909	1,382,500	24,321	68,053,439	30,541,073	23,193,966	7,347,107	34.1	28.5
1910	1,429,049	24,425	75,135,405	33,889,202	26,614,502	7,274,900	33.7	30.2
1911	1,487,345	24,926	77,780,782	37,158,929	30,058,632	7,105,357	33.8	33.1
1912	1,517,317	25,392	90,000,000	42,987,807	36,065,826	6,923,971		

*Average per message.

CHRONOLOGICAL SURVEY OF PEACE MOVEMENTS.

Compiled by Charles E. Beals, secretary of the Chicago Peace society.

New York Peace society, organized 1815, first in the world.

Many state societies organized in quick succession.

A national organization, the American Peace society, formed in 1828, in which the state societies merged themselves.

Peace movement spread rapidly until the time of the Crimean war, American civil war, etc.

Great peace jubilees held throughout the country in 1871.

International Law association organized, 1873.

Interparliamentary union formed, 1889.

International peace bureau established in Bern, 1891.

First Lake Mohonk arbitration conference, 1895.

American Society of International Law organized. 1906.

Intercollegiate Peace association, 1905.

Association for International Conciliation, 1907.

Peace day, 18th of May (Hague day).

Peace Sunday, the Sunday before Christmas.

American Society for the Judicial Settlement of International Disputes, 1910.

Carnegie endowment for international peace, 1910.

INTERNATIONAL PEACE CONGRESSES.

First series: 1, London, 1843; 2, Brussels, 1848; 3, Paris, 1849; 4, Frankfort, 1850; 5, London, 1851; 6, Edinburgh, 1853.

Second series: 1, Geneva, 1867; 2, Paris, 1878; 3, Brussels, 1882; 4, Bern, 1884.

Present series: 1, Paris, 1889; 2, London, 1890; 3, Rome, 1891; 4, Bern, 1892; 5, Chicago, 1893; 6, Antwerp, 1894; 7, Budapest, 1896; 8, Hamburg, 1897; 9, Paris, 1900; 10, Glasgow, 1901; 11, Monaco, 1902; 12, Rouen, 1903; 13, Boston, 1904; 14, Lucerne, 1905; 15, Milan, 1906; 16, Munich, 1907; 17, London, 1908; 18, Stockholm, 1910; 19, Geneva, 1912; 20, The Hague, 1913.

NATIONAL PEACE CONGRESSES IN THE UNITED STATES.

First: New York in 1907.

Second: Chicago in 1909.

Third: Baltimore in 1911.

Fourth: St. Louis in 1913.

INTERGOVERNMENTAL PEACEMAKING.

Joint disarmament by Great Britain and United States along Canadian border, 1817 to present time.

Central American High Court of Nations established.

Pan-American congress, 1889, led to establishment of International Bureau of American Republics, 1890.

Pacific settlement of over 600 international disputes.

The statue of The Christ of the Andes, commemorating joint disarmament of Chile and Argentina, erected, 1904.

Nearly fifty public international unions (e. g. the Universal Postal union) already in operation.

HAGUE PEACE CONFERENCES.

First Hague conference, May 18, 1899, of twenty-six nations.

Second Hague conference, June 15, 1907, of forty-four nations.

Third Hague conference, to be held about 1915.

THE HAGUE COURT OF ARBITRATION.

The permanent court of arbitration at The Hague, instituted July 29, 1899, consists of from one to four representatives of the governments participating in The Hague peace conference of 1899 or signing the convention providing for the court. The members of the court from the greater powers are as follows:

France—Leon Bourgeois, A. Decrais, Baron d'Estournelles de Constant, Louis Renault.

Germany—Herr Kriege, Herr von Martitz, Herr von Staff, Herr von Bar.

Great Britain—Sir Edward Fry, Earl de Desart, Sir E. Satow, Sir Charles Fitzpatrick.

Italy—Jean B. P. Guarnaschelli, Guido Fusinato, Victor E. Orlando, Tommaso Tittoni.

Japan—Itchiro Motono, Henry Willard Denison.

United States—Elihu Root, John W. Griggs, George Gray, Oscar S. Straus.

Secretary—Gen. Baron Michiels von Derduynen.

RECORD OF HAGUE DECISIONS.

1. The Pius fund case, Mexico vs. United States, Oct. 14, 1902.

2. The Venezuela case, Great Britain, Germany and Italy vs. Venezuela, Feb. 22, 1904.

3. The Japanese house tax case, Great Britain, France and Germany vs. Japan, May 22, 1905.

4. The Muscat dhows case, Great Britain vs. France, Aug. 8, 1905.

5. The Casa Blanca case, France vs. Germany, May 22, 1909.

6. The boundary case, Norway vs. Sweden, Oct. 23, 1909.

7. The North Atlantic fisheries case, United States vs. Great Britain, Sept. 7, 1910.

8. The Orinoco Steamship company claims case, United States vs. Venezuela, Oct. 25, 1910.

9. The Savarkar case, France vs. Great Britain, Feb. 24, 1911.

10. Arrears of indemnity case, Russia vs. Turkey, Feb. 24, 1911.

11. Canevaro claim, France vs. Italy, Feb. 24, 1911.

12. Seizure of French ships, France vs. Italy.

PALACE OF PEACE DEDICATED.

The Palace of Peace at The Hague, Holland, was dedicated Aug. 28, 1913. The ceremony of handing the edifice over to the Dutch foreign minister was carried out in the great court in the presence of Queen Wilhelmina and a gathering of distinguished diplomats, representatives of peace societies and persons prominent in the arts and sciences. Abraham van Karnebeek, president of the Carnegie

PALACE OF PEACE AT THE HAGUE.

Foundation, made a brief speech in turning the building over to its new custodians, and Jonkheer Reneke van Swindern, Dutch minister for foreign affairs, accepted it on behalf of the diplomatic corps at The Hague, in which its custody is vested under the presidency of the Dutch foreign ministry.

The structure was the gift of Andrew Carnegie, who in 1903 placed at the disposal of the Dutch government the sum of $1,500,000 for the purpose, as expressed in his offer, "of erecting and maintaining at The Hague a courthouse and library for the permanent court of arbitration established by the treaty of July 29, 1899." The Dutch government appropriated $275,000 for a site in the wooded park stretching from The Hague to Scheveningen. The corner stone was laid July 30, 1907.

FOURTH AMERICAN PEACE CONGRESS.

The fourth American peace congress was held in St. Louis, Mo., May 1-3, 1913. Among the leading speakers were Andrew Carnegie, Former Vice-President Charles W. Fairbanks, Congressman Richard Bartholdt, John Wesley Hill, Mrs. Lucia Ames Mead and Prof. William J. Hull. Resolutions were

passed urging the repeal of the toll exemption on the Panama canal, approving the Taft peace treaties, opposing the effort to extend military training in the schools and asking the president to open negotiations for a reduction of armaments.

ORGANIZATIONS FOR THE PROMOTION OF PEACE.

AMERICAN PEACE SOCIETY.
President—Senator Theodore E. Burton, Washington, D. C.
Secretary—Benjamin F. Trueblood, LL. D., 313 Colorado building, Washington, D. C.
Executive Director—Arthur D. Call, Washington, D. C.
Treasurer—George W. White, Washington, D. C.
Director Central-West Department—Charles E. Beals, 30 North LaSalle street, Chicago, Ill.

AMERICAN SOCIETY FOR THE JUDICIAL SETTLEMENT OF INTERNATIONAL DISPUTES.
Honorary President—William H. Taft.
President—Joseph H. Choate, New York, N. Y.
Vice-President—Charles W. Eliot, Cambridge, Mass.
Secretary—James Brown Scott, Washington, D C.,
Treasurer—J. G. Schmidlapp, Cincinnati, O.

AMERICAN ASSOCIATION FOR INTERNATIONAL CONCILIATION.
Secretary—Frederick P. Keppel, postoffice substation 84, New York, N. Y.
CARNEGIE ENDOWMENT FOR INTERNATIONAL PEACE.
2 Jackson place, Washington, D. C.
President—Elihu Root.
Secretary—James Brown Scott.
WORLD PEACE FOUNDATION.
40 Mount Vernon street, Boston, Mass.
Founder—Edwin Ginn.
President—David Starr Jordan.
Secretary—Edwin D. Mead.

THE INTERCOLLEGIATE PEACE ASSOCIATION.
President—President Charles F. Thwing, Western Reserve university, Cleveland, O.
Secretary—Dean S. F. Weston, Antioch college, Yellow Springs, O.

THE AMERICAN SCHOOL PEACE LEAGUE.
Secretary—Mrs. Fanny Fern Andrews, 405 Marlborough street, Boston, Mass.
THE MOHONK CONFERENCE ON INTERNATIONAL ARBITRATION.
Host—Daniel Smiley, Mohonk Lake, N Y.
Secretary—H. C. Phillips, Mohonk Lake, N. Y.

CHRONOLOGY OF RECENT WARS.

SPANISH-AMERICAN WAR, 1898.
Maine blown up	Feb. 15
Diplomatic relations broken	April 21
Cuban blockade declared	April 22
War declared by Spain	April 24
War declared by United States	April 25
Dewey's victory at Manila	May 1
Hobson's Merrimac exploit	June 3
U. S. army corps lands in Cuba	June 21
Battle at El Caney and San Juan	July 1
Cervera's fleet destroyed	July 3
Santiago de Cuba surrenders	July 17
Peace protocol signed	Aug. 12
Surrender of Manila	Aug. 13
Peace treaty signed in Paris	Dec. 12

PHILIPPINE WAR, 1899-1902.
Hostilities begun	Feb. 4, 1899
Battles around Manila	Feb. 4-7, 1899
Battle at Pasig	March 13, 1899
Santa Cruz captured	April 25, 1899
San Fernando captured	May 5, 1899
Battle of Bacoor	June 13, 1899
Battle of Imus	June 16, 1899
Battle of Colamba	July 26, 1899
Battle of Calulut	Aug. 9, 1899
Battle at Angeles	Aug. 16, 1899
Maj. John A. Logan killed	Nov. 11, 1899
Gen. Gregorio del Pilar killed	Dec. 10, 1899
Gen. Lawton killed	Dec. 19, 1899
Taft commission appointed	Feb. 25, 1900
Aguinaldo captured	March 23, 1901
End of the war	April 30, 1902
Military governorship ended	July 4, 1902

ANGLO-BOER WAR, 1899-1902.
Boers declare war	Oct. 10, 1899
Boers invade Natal	Oct. 12, 1899
Battle of Glencoe	Oct. 20, 1899
Battle of Magersfontein	Dec. 10, 1899
Battle of Coleshurg	Dec. 31, 1899
Spion Kop battles	Jan. 23-25, 1900
Kimberley relieved	Feb. 15, 1900
Gen. Cronje surrenders	Feb. 27, 1900
Ladysmith relieved	March 1, 1900
Mafeking relieved	May 17, 1900
Johannesburg captured	May 30, 1900
Orange Free State annexed	May 30, 1900
Pretoria captured	June 4, 1900
South African Republic annexed	Sept. 1, 1900
Gen. Methuen captured	March 7, 1902
Treaty of peace signed	May 31, 1902

RUSSO-JAPANESE WAR, 1904-1905.
Hostilities begun by Japan	Feb. 8, 1904
War declared	Feb. 10, 1904
Petropavlovsk sunk	April 13, 1904
Battle of the Yalu	May 1, 1904
Battle ship Hatsuse sunk	May 15, 1904
Cruiser Yoshino sunk	May 15, 1904
Nanshan hill battles	May 21-27, 1904

Dalny captured	May 30, 1904
Vafangow battle	June 14, 1904
Kaiping captured	July 8, 1904
Port Arthur invested	July 26-31, 1904
Newchwang evacuated	July 25, 1904
Haicheng evacuated	Aug. 3, 1904
Port Arthur naval battle	Aug. 10, 1904
Battle of Liaoyang	Aug. 26-Sept. 4, 1904
Battle of Sha river	Oct. 12-18, 1904
Dogger bank affair	Oct. 22, 1904
203-Meter hill captured	Nov. 30, 1904
North Keekwan captured	Dec. 18, 1904
Ehrlungshan captured	Dec. 25, 1904
Sungshushan captured	Dec. 31, 1904
Port Arthur surrendered	Jan. 1-2, 1905
Battle of Heikoutal	Jan. 27-Feb. 4, 1905
Battle of Mukden	Feb. 24-March 12, 1905
Battle of Sea of Japan	May 27-28, 1905
Roosevelt peace proposal	June 7, 1905
Sakhalin captured	July 31, 1905
Portsmouth peace conference	Aug. 9-29, 1905
Peace treaty signed	Sept 5, 1905

ITALIAN-TURKISH WAR, 1911-1912.
War declared by Italy	Sept. 29, 1911
Tripoli bombarded	Oct. 3, 1911
Tripoli captured	Oct. 5, 1911
Turks repulsed by Italians	Oct. 30, 1911
Seven Turkish gunboats sunk	Jan. 7, 1912
Beirot bombarded	Feb. 24, 1912
Tripoli annexed	Feb. 25, 1912
Island of Rhodes seized	May 4, 1912
Battle at Zanzur oasis	June 9, 1912
Town of Sidi Ali captured	July 14, 1912
Peace treaty signed	Oct 18, 1912

BALKAN-TURKISH WAR.
Balkan-Turkish war began	Oct. 9, 1912
War formally declared	Oct. 18, 1912
Battle of Kirk Kilesseh	Oct. 24, 1912
Battle of Lule Burgas	Oct. 29-31, 1912
Saloniki captured	Nov. 8, 1912
Monastir captured	Nov. 18, 1912
London peace conference	Dec. 16, 1912
Peace conference ended	Jan. 29, 1913
War resumed	Feb. 8, 1913
Janina captured	March 6, 1913
Adrianople captured	March 27, 1913
Scutari captured	April 23, 1913
Powers occupy Scutari	May 14, 1913
Peace treaty signed	May 30, 1913

BALKAN-BULGARIAN WAR.
Fighting is begun	May 23, 1913
Battle of Makres	June 10, 1913
Kilkish is captured	July 4, 1913
Seres and Kavala are captured	July 9, 1913
Roumania wars on Bulgaria	July 12, 1913
Turks attack Bulgaria	July 12, 1913
Turks reoccupy Adrianople	July 21, 1913
Peace treaty signed	Aug. 10, 1913

IMPORTS OF MERCHANDISE.

Fiscal years ended June 30.

ARTICLES IMPORTED.	1911.		1912.		1913.	
	Quant's.	Values.	Quant's.	Values.	Quant's.	Values.
Aluminum, crude..............lbs	....	....	14,803,196	$1,830,276	26,958,354	$4,315,293
Manufactures of..................	....	....	....	238,711	....	739,777
Animals..........................	....	$6,850,964	....	7,580,555	....	9,585,791
Antimony—Ore, regulus, metal..........lbs	10,036,491	541,568	13,919,164	698,218	19,684,624	1,134,467
Art works.........................	....	22,495,842	....	36,092,536	....	52,875,637
Asbestos, unmanufactured.............tons	57,124	1,318,583	60,541	1,378,521	74,367	1,760,874
Asphaltum and bitumen.............tons	152,568	707,746	193,578	885,304	211,873	952,080
Automobiles....................No.	888	1,898,843	963	2,134,181	748	1,759,380
Parts of........................	....	351,916	....	304,144	....	263,827
Beads and bead ornaments...........	....	1,163,752	....	1,905,209	....	1,878,731
Bones, etc., unmanufactured..........	....	1,168,924	....	1,068,653	....	885,808
Brass, for remanufacture..........lbs	3,954,423	518,562	4,203,955	437,940	8,888,902	894,133
Breadstuffs.......................	....	13,455,732	....	18,529,794	....	16,521,666
Bristles......................lbs	3,542,913	2,976,481	3,461,975	5,047,027	3,578,584	5,504,663
Bronze, manufactures of............	....	765,974	....	796,974	....	778,869
Brushes, etc.,....................	....	2,241,008	....	2,067,149	....	2,049,303
Buttons..........................	....	762,888	....	1,130,353	....	4,855,843
Cement.....................lbs	932,977	324,949	451,979	168,802	309,085	722,821
Chemicals, drugs and dyes..........	....	86,311,537	....	82,785,610	....	98,520,155
Clays or earths.................tons	305,473	1,946,712	324,328	2,036,261	372,049	2,304,399
Clocks and parts of................	....	369,292	....	681,972	....	809,715
Watches and parts of............	....	2,368,679	....	2,813,671	....	2,615,744
Coal, bituminous................tons	1,761,210	4,975,914	1,300,242	3,711,479	1,578,264	4,968,556
Cocoa or cacao (crude)..............lbs	138,058,841	14,552,879	145,968,845	15,931,556	140,639,172	17,383,042
Prepared....................lbs	2,912,081	708,007	2,816,885	658,836	3,469,686	787,678
Coffee..........................lbs	875,366,797	90,567,788	885,201,247	117,816,545	863,130,757	118,963,209
Copper—Ore...................tons	370,834	5,796,066	433,277	6,631,378	469,767	9,444,108
Matte and regulus.............tons	30,616	1,868,476	29,294	2,731,804	31,112	4,225,385
Pigs, ingots, bars, etc..............lbs	268,183,621	31,966,223	282,851,320	35,791,011	299,754,769	45,812,551
Cork, unmanufactured..............	....	4,274,810	....	3,242,319	....	3,152,070
Manufactures of................	....	2,435,008	....	2,346,415	....	2,350,684
Cotton—Unmanufactured..........lbs	113,768,313	24,776,530	109,780,071	20,217,581	121,552,016	22,367,318
Manufactures of................	....	66,906,551	....	65,152,755	....	66,065,857
Diamonds, uncut.................	....	9,280,943	....	9,853,519	....	12,339,553
Cut but not set................	....	24,407,235	....	24,537,150	....	27,213,047
Total diamonds, precious stones, etc....	....	40,633,157	....	41,297,759	....	49,529,845
Earthen, stone and china ware........	....	11,411,685	....	9,907,608	....	10,172,763
Feathers, natural and artificial.......	....	9,845,344	....	8,480,029	....	12,661,783
Fertilizers.......................	....	18,109,282	....	19,109,282	....	19,928,097
Fibers—Unmanufactured..........tons	290,434	30,752,250	326,479	34,402,806	407,098	49,075,659
Manufactures of................	....	54,715,990	....	59,659,849	....	76,972,416
Fish............................	....	14,939,311	....	14,553,347	....	15,430,280
Fruits and nuts...................	....	41,615,067	....	45,577,202	....	42,628,653
Furs—Undressed..................	....	15,351,001	....	17,399,198	....	16,717,208
Manufactures of................	....	8,267,947	....	8,583,029	....	8,147,535
Glass and glassware...............	....	6,881,891	....	6,210,025	....	6,537,296
Grease and oils...................	....	1,335,392	....	1,490,325	....	1,312,900
Hair, unmanufactured.............lbs	19,297,601	4,755,131	17,177,299	4,994,726	18,025,862	5,853,578
Hats, bonnets, etc., and materials for....	....	7,518,261	....	9,686,464	....	10,907,145
Hay...........................tons	....	....	690,004	6,473,230	155,763	1,514,311
Hides and skins.................lbs	374,891,395	70,504,980	537,768,098	102,476,321	573,346,507	117,386,174
Hide cuttings, raw................	....	1,625,042	....	1,707,171	....	1,767,189
Hops..........................lbs	8,557,531	2,706,890	8,991,125	2,231,348	8,494,144	2,852,965
Household goods, etc..............	....	4,975,955	....	4,702,955	....	5,085,022
India rubber—Unmanufactured.......	....	92,910,513	....	105,037,506	....	101,333,158
Manufactures of................	....	936,408	....	915,534	....	1,294,536
Iron—Ore.....................tons	2,133,633	6,691,711	2,004,240	6,119,875	2,246,353	7,035,185
Iron and steel, manufactures of.......	....	34,205,968	....	26,551,040	....	33,536,358
Ivory—Animal..................lbs	534,200	1,343,556	518,914	1,341,079	722,187	1,821,358
Vegetable....................lbs	20,851,466	772,066	23,076,847	789,602	29,656,278	977,525
Lead and manufactures of..........lbs	208,709,726	4,196,760	189,064,460	3,937,560	145,100,196	3,409,060
Leather and manufactures of.........	....	14,636,720	....	16,196,790	....	18,116,800
Manganese, ore and oxide..........tons	269,211	1,453,172	197,959	1,292,425	387,166	2,196,661
Matting and mats..............sq yds	26,229,252	1,947,601	25,870,411	1,819,224	21,555,120	1,651,813
Meat and dairy products...........	....	13,904,345	....	13,774,560	....	14,596,017
Metals and manufactures of.........	....	9,007,015	....	5,908,067	....	6,853,712
Musical instruments..............	....	1,623,100	....	1,614,415	....	1,787,298
Nickel ore and matte..............	....	3,946,293	....	4,565,818	....	6,398,228
Oilcloths.....................sq yds	5,321,964	2,102,612	4,450,400	1,917,998	4,202,786	1,840,578
Oils of all kinds..................	....	33,023,687	....	31,348,692	....	34,112,583
Paints, pigments and colors.........	....	2,045,548	....	1,905,491	....	2,144,074
Paper stock, crude................	....	5,481,680	....	5,918,358	....	7,271,405
Paper and manufactures of..........	....	18,626,880	....	17,900,949	....	21,538,845
Printing paper................lbs	114,413,231	2,507,670	119,578,074	2,482,968	301,297,305	6,054,023
Photographic films and plates........	....	1,356,086	....	1,208,057	....	1,693,836
Pipes and smokers' articles..........	....	1,445,002	....	1,478,060	....	1,332,094
Plants, trees, shrubs, etc...........	....	2,729,440	....	2,905,029	....	3,206,584
Platinum and manufactures of,.......	....	3,768,203	....	5,018,832	....	5,213,998
Plumbago.....................tons	20,156	1,678,625	18,591	1,428,386	26,222	1,972,127
Salt..........................lbs	291,339,057	401,324	263,681,516	364,164	275,369,540	377,654
Seeds...........................	....	29,757,958	....	25,641,172	....	17,423,553
Shells, unmanufactured............	....	1,884,714	....	2,219,135	....	1,887,409
Silk—Unmanufactured.............	....	74,924,004	....	69,541,672	....	84,914,717
Manufactured.................	....	28,620,495	....	24,556,871	....	27,590,000
Artificial, manufactures of......	....	3,279,559	....	2,647,499	....	3,278,262

IMPORTS OF MERCHANDISE—Continued.

ARTICLES IMPORTED.	1911. Quant's.	Values.	1912. Quant's.	Values.	1913. Quant's.	Values.
Soap...................................		$830,744		$797,836		$789,437
Spices.............................lbs	58,222,912	4,946,200	63,116,548	5,974,170	65,225,401	6,187,136
Spirits—Malted liquors...............gals	7,293,892	3,336,966	7,175,505	3,279,926	7,696,650	3,290,265
Wines...............................		8,551,613		9,591,451		10,078,707
Mineral waters.......................		903,709		1,012,647		1,008,127
Stone—Marble and manufactures of,......		1,477,304		1,384,012		1,393,940
Sugar..............................lbs	3,997,978,265	96,691,096	4,104,618,393	115,515,079	4,740,041,488	103,633,823
Sulphur ore.........................tons	894,281	3,108,089	985,296	3,919,450	964,559	4,111,636
Tanning materials, crude..............		1,683,514		1,735,056		2,036,318
Tea................................lbs	102,653,942	17,613,569	101,406,816	18,267,141	94,812,800	17,433,688
Tin................................lbs	103,439,058	37,935,978	111,204,452	46,214,198	114,716,069	53,112,594
Tobacco—Leaf.......................lbs	45,927,280	27,855,996	53,006,779	31,918,670	67,454,745	35,919,079
Manufactures of......................		5,416,466		5,470,706		6,577,403
Toys................................		7,964,835		7,893,582		7,935,555
Vegetables..........................		9,293,855		18,544,373		11,358,761
Wood and manufactures of.............		52,931,863		52,502,131		61,824,088
Wool—Unmanufactured...............lbs	137,647,641	23,228,005	193,400,713	33,078,342	195,293,255	35,579,823
Manufactures of......................		18,569,791		14,012,819		16,318,141
Zinc and manufactures of..............		1,319,679		1,446,239		2,742,370
Total value merchandise* { free { dut.		776,972,509 750,253,596		881,670,830 771,594,104		987,494,162 825,484,072
Total value imports*.................		1,527,226,105		1,653,264,934		1,812,978,234

*Including articles not specified in above table.

EXPORTS OF DOMESTIC MERCHANDISE.
Fiscal years ended June 30.

ARTICLES EXPORTED.	1911. Quant's.	Values.	1912. Quant's.	Values.	1913. Quant's.	Values.
Abrasives............................		$1,347,225		$1,654,718		$2,311,382
Agricultural implements..............		35,973,398		35,640,005		40,572,852
Animals—Cattle......................No.	150,100	18,163,920	105,506	8,870,075	24,714	1,177,199
Hogs..............................No.	8,451	74,032	19,038	159,370	15,832	151,747
Horses.............................No.	25,145	3,845,255	34,828	4,764,815	28,707	3,990,102
Mules.............................No.	6,585	1,070,051	4,901	732,095	4,744	733,796
Sheep.............................No.	121,491	696,372	157,263	626,985	187,182	605,725
Total animals, including fowls.......		19,048,653		15,447,987		7,080,122
Art works...........................		680,506		943,427		818,604
Brass...............................		6,230,092		8,880,942		8,854,636
Breadstuffs—Barley..................bu	9,599,346	5,581,900	1,585,242	1,267,999	17,538,703	11,411,819
Bread and biscuit...................lbs	14,022,002	840,608	12,978,048	757,280	12,582,480	730,097
Corn..............................bu	63,781,458	35,961,479	40,038,795	28,957,450	49,054,967	28,800,544
Cornmeal..........................brls	463,266	1,456,683	439,624	1,519,792	428,794	1,444,559
Oatmeal...........................lbs	32,416,892	1,043,867	9,112,433	376,188	48,553,349	1,514,848
Oats..............................bu	2,044,912	882,718	2,171,503	1,135,635	33,759,177	13,206,247
Wheat.............................bu	23,729,802	22,040,273	30,160,212	28,477,584	91,602,574	89,095,428
Wheat flour........................brls	10,129,435	49,366,948	11,006,487	50,999,707	11,304,805	53,171,537
Total breadstuffs (all kinds)........		124,913,537		123,970,715		211,098,339
Cars, carriages, etc.................		30,534,836		42,633,303		54,585,888
Automobiles........................No.	11,803	12,995,049	21,757	21,550,139	25,286	26,012,934
Celluloid and manufactures of........		1,494,214		2,034,371		1,639,046
Cement, hydraulic..................brls	2,971,274	4,349,290	3,423,747	5,085,046	3,999,715	5,822,107
Chemicals, drugs and medicines.......		23,007,434		25,117,217		26,574,519
Clocks and watches..................		3,126,771		3,542,145		3,606,257
Coal...............................tons	14,985,487	45,013,436	17,688,949	52,648,750	20,708,582	65,037,221
Coke..............................tons	946,474	3,309,994	805,819	2,938,191	900,672	3,318,437
Coffee—Green......................lbs	84,853,601	5,107,949	40,779,638	6,864,468	50,721,758	8,679,422
Roasted...........................lbs	1,434,290	272,532	1,468,767	306,090	1,469,043	331,370
Confectionery.......................		990,125		1,046,144		1,282,198
Copper—Ore........................tons	41,862	1,935,296	65,625	3,123,805	64,341	2,958,790
Manufactures of......................		103,813,110		113,958,919		140,164,913
Cotton—Unmanufactured.............bales	7,829,036	585,318,869	10,675,445	565,849,271	8,724,572	547,357,125
Manufactures of......................		40,851,918		50,763,511		53,743,977
Dental goods........................		2,453,231		2,656,917		2,847,898
Earthen, stone and china ware........		3,138,188		4,481,382		4,967,019
Eggs...............................doz	8,558,712	1,787,019	15,405,800	3,335,952	20,409,300	4,891,653
Electrical machinery.................		18,727,455		20,169,362		26,772,816
Explosives..........................		4,763,242		5,050,858		5,267,566
Fertilizers........................tons	1,282,591	10,721,132	1,276,520	10,573,908	1,347,726	11,400,088
Fibers, manufactures of..............		8,565,900		9,898,528		10,963,946
Fish...............................		24,438,435		8,640,838		9,711,932
Fruits and nuts......................		10,475,517		50,963,638		37,079,102
Furs and fur skins...................		3,246,891		14,975,449		18,389,586
Glass and glassware.................		3,494,153		3,494,153		4,195,642
Glucose and grape sugar............lbs	181,993,046	3,595,383	171,156,259	3,916,897	260,149,246	4,652,396
Gold and silver, manufactures of.....		520,196		453,773		425,175
Jewelry............................		1,302,502		1,397,044		1,467,942
Grease—Lubricating.................		} 5,177,581		2,193,963		2,339,015
Soap stock and other................				4,486,329		4,844,342

EXPORTS OF DOMESTIC MERCHANDISE—CONTINUED.

ARTICLES EXPORTED.	1911.		1912.		1913.	
	Quant's.	Values.	Quant's.	Values.	Quant's.	Values.
Hair and manufactures of...............		$1,274,845		$1,426,111		$1,672,192
Hay...........................tons	55,031	1,032,040	59,730	1,039,040	60,720	961,429
Hides and skins other than furs.........lbs	44,504,235	4,802,637	25,246,800	3,158,495	26,140,278	3,448,924
Hops...........................lbs	13,104,774	2,130,972	13,190,663	4,648,505	17,591,195	4,764,713
Household and personal effects,.........		7,094,366		8,230,470		10,272,892
India rubber, manufactures of............		12,452,502		12,822,918		14,324,894
Instruments, scientific, etc.............		1,718,685		1,802,903		1,856,998
Iron ore........................tons	787,568	2,496,291	831,872	2,806,636	1,221,387	3,684,443
Iron and steel and manufactures of,,......		222,700,724		259,709,399		304,606,797
Lamps, chandeliers, etc.............		2,961,762		2,822,032		3,170,233
Leather and manufactures of............		53,673,056		60,756,372		63,886,551
Meat and dairy products—Beef, canned...lbs	10,824,504	1,254,979	11,026,431	1,363,404	6,840,348	837,826
Beef, fresh........................lbs	42,510,731	4,478,401	15,264,320	1,596,319	7,362,388	902,149
Beef, cured........................lbs	40,283,749	3,501,179	38,087,907	2,832,160	25,856,919	2,489,965
Oleo oil........................lbs	138,696,906	13,658,762	126,467,124	13,434,018	92,849,757	10,868,258
Oleomargarine........................lbs	3,794,989	408,459	3,027,425	372,567	2,987,582	311,485
Tallow........................lbs	29,813,154	1,933,681	39,451,419	2,588,046	30,388,046	1,910,439
Bacon........................lbs	156,675,310	21,211,605	208,574,208	24,907,197	200,996,584	25,647,167
Hams, cured........................lbs	157,709,316	20,708,882	204,044,491	24,983,376	159,544,687	21,641,586
Lard........................lbs	476,107,587	52,509,217	532,255,865	52,090,441	497,925,484	55,860,102
Neutral lard........................lbs	37,886,812	4,184,234	62,317,909	6,655,029	44,777,692	5,129,899
Pork, canned........................lbs	4,010,862	483,189	5,390,902	681,127	4,148,343	565,039
Pork, fresh........................lbs	1,355,378	159,654	2,597,880	297,198	2,457,997	310,574
Pork, pickled........................lbs	45,729,471	4,944,448	56,321,409	5,348,594	53,749,023	5,699,136
Lard compounds........................lbs	73,754,400	7,070,967	62,522,888	5,183,699	93,165,409	8,242,993
Mutton........................lbs	2,160,259	219,517	3,595,543	349,875	5,206,019	591,960
Poultry and game..................		981,805		907,955		1,308,379
Sausage and sausage meats..............lbs	4,716,610	601,596	8,036,591	1,045,834	8,011,318	1,085,745
Other meat products—Canned........		1,180,123		1,298,152		1,086,463
Butter........................lbs	4,877,797	1,059,482	6,092,235	1,408,482	3,585,600	872,804
Cheese........................lbs	10,366,605	1,288,379	6,337,559	898,055	2,599,058	441,186
Milk, condensed................. lbs	12,180,445	996,105	20,642,738	1,651,879	16,525,922	1,432,848
Total meat and dairy products.....		149,329,737		156,290,876		158,883,526
Motor boats........................No.	663	381,940	596	684,339	516	768,523
Musical Instruments..................		3,471,401		3,606,936		3,799,731
Naval stores (rosin, tar, etc.).........		25,422,720		26,754,987		20,471,992
Nickel, oxide and matte.............lbs	18,947,810	6,004,414	26,561,990	8,749,675	27,881,277	9,275,714
Oil cake and meal...............lbs	1,477,656,478	19,581,127	1,962,394,695	28,096,171	2,049,361,136	29,444,252
Oils—Animal........................gals	1,181,630	788,860	2,425,584	1,263,246	3,660,361	1,585,600
Mineral........................gals	1,616,540,746	98,115,516	1,793,665,038	112,472,100	1,989,772,713	137,237,762
Vegetable..................		19,805,232		26,908,931		24,044,401
Paints, pigments and colors..............		6,204,746		7,072,617		7,681,938
Paper stock, except wood pulp...........lbs	85,290,314	2,597,539	54,634,617	1,830,077	32,021,038	635,095
Paper and manufactures of..............		10,219,499		19,458,050		21,779,503
Paraffin and paraffin wax.............lbs	218,592,330	7,378,756	249,502,699	8,128,480	290,678,861	9,619,273
Perfumeries, cosmetics, etc............		1,009,959		1,147,630		1,441,982
Phonographs, etc..................		2,983,688		2,520,292		2,806,978
Photographic goods..................		7,142,603		9,445,446		9,137,287
Salt........................lbs			111,008,966	383,062	128,035,915	441,673
Seeds..................		2,475,098		2,898,802		3,564,837
Silk, manufactures of..................		1,538,548		1,992,745		2,380,828
Soap..................		4,046,081		4,536,028		4,629,567
Spirits—Malt liquors..................		1,075,559		1,161,319		1,371,463
Distilled........................gals	1,308,964	1,885,401	1,634,580	2,974,520	1,886,150	2,218,159
Wines........................gals	1,304,994	518,536	957,120	396,262	1,075,151	418,898
Starch........................lbs	158,239,178	3,137,552	83,644,749	1,965,401	110,897,591	2,609,716
Stone, including marble..............		1,690,180		1,898,555		2,256,822
Sugar and molasses—Molasses...........gals	3,386,811	854,108	9,513,441	984,636	2,145,613	255,973
Sirup........................gals	12,001,799	1,752,119	19,146,986	2,539,055	14,309,029	1,937,648
Sugar, refined........................lbs	54,947,444	2,244,579	79,594,034	3,681,012	43,944,761	1,681,302
Tin, manufactures of..................		999,796		1,234,029		1,458,790
Tobacco—Unmanufactured...............lbs	355,327,072	39,255,320	379,845,320	43,251,857	418,796,906	49,353,595
Manufactures of..................		4,583,584		5,603,183		5,814,973
Toys..................		1,013,194		645,287		829,518
Vegetables..................		5,545,691		6,541,118		7,358,697
Wood and manufactures of..............		92,255,951		96,782,186		115,704,777
Wool and manufactures of..............		2,266,478		2,535,901		4,483,506
Zinc and manufactures of..............		1,779,599		2,305,611		1,754,840
Total value exports of domestic mdse*		2,013,549,025		2,170,319,828		2,428,506,358
Total value exports of foreign mdse.		35,771,174		34,002,581		37,377,791
Total value exports except gold and silver...		2,049,320,199		2,204,322,409		2,465,884,149

*Including articles not specified in above table.

FAMOUS STREETS OF THE WORLD.

Berlin—Unter den Linden.
Buenos Aires—Avenida de Mayo.
Chicago—State street and Michigan avenue.
City of Mexico—Paseo de la Reforma.
Cleveland—Euclid avenue.
Dublin—Sackville street.

Edinburgh—Princes street.
London—Fleet street and the Strand.
Madrid—Paseo del Prado.
Munich—Ludwigstrasse.
New Orleans—Canal street.
New York—Broadway.
Paris—Avenue des Champs Elysees,

Philadelphia—Chestnut street.
Rio de Janeiro—Avenida Central.
Rome—The Corso.
San Francisco—Market street.
St. Petersburg—Nevski Prospect.
Vienna—Ringstrasse.
Washington—Pennsylvania avenue,

SUMMARY OF IMPORTS AND EXPORTS OF MERCHANDISE.

Fiscal years ended June 30.

GROUPS.	1911.		1912.		1913.	
IMPORTS.	Dollars.	Per ct.	Dollars.	Per ct.	Dollars.	Per ct.
Free of duty—Foodstuffs in crude condition and food animals...	147,262,425	18.95	180,127,316	20.43	179,548,290	18.21
Foodstuffs partly or wholly manufactured...	12,388,851	1.59	16,629,253	1.89	11,131,619	1.13
Crude materials for use in manufacturing...	490,521,730	51.55	441,309,448	50.05	608,872,245	61.63
Manufactures for further use in manufacturing...	142,772,647	18.37	154,257,659	17.38	179,389,755	18.17
Manufactures ready for consumption...	64,927,575	8.36	77,724,778	8.82	97,346,671	9.92
Miscellaneous...	9,149,281	1.18	12,622,396	1.43	9,305,582	.94
Total free of duty...	776,972,509	100.00	881,670,830	100.00	987,494,162	100.00
Dutiable—Foodstuffs in crude condition, and food animals...	33,932,438	4.52	50,280,914	6.51	31,009,819	3.83
Foodstuffs partly or wholly manufactured...	159,667,650	21.28	179,471,375	23.26	183,548,923	22.24
Crude materials for use in manufacturing...	110,840,410	14.77	114,676,598	14.86	123,352,198	14.94
Manufactures for further use in manufacturing...	145,013,005	19.33	140,481,475	18.21	169,496,498	20.53
Manufactures ready for consumption...	296,494,605	39.52	282,294,185	36.59	312,631,365	37.88
Miscellaneous...	4,305,488	.58	4,739,562	.57	4,815,269	.58
Total dutiable...	750,253,596	100.00	771,594,104	100.00	825,484,072	100.00
Free and dutiable—Foodstuffs in crude condition, and food animals...	181,194,863	11.87	230,358,230	13.93	211,458,109	11.66
Foodstuffs partly or wholly manufactured...	172,006,501	11.26	196,100,608	11.86	194,680,542	10.74
Crude materials for use in manufacturing...	511,362,140	33.48	555,986,041	33.63	653,224,443	34.93
Manufactures for further use in manufacturing...	287,785,652	18.84	293,739,134	17.77	348,886,253	19.24
Manufactures ready for consumption...	361,422,180	23.67	360,018,963	21.78	410,608,036	22.65
Miscellaneous...	13,454,769	.88	17,061,958	1.03	14,120,831	.78
Total imports of merchandise...	1,527,226,105	100.00	1,653,264,934	100.00	1,812,978,234	100.00
Per cent of free...		50.87		53.3		54.47
Duties collected from customs...	314,497,071		311,257,348		318,142,344	
Remaining in warehouse at the end of the month...						
EXPORTS.						
Domestic—Foodstuffs in crude condition, and food animals...	103,401,553	5.13	99,809,270	4.60	181,693,263	7.48
Foodstuffs partly or wholly manufactured...	282,916,883	14.00	318,838,433	14.68	320,401,482	13.19
Crude materials for use in manufacturing...	715,019,206	35.42	723,008,839	33.31	730,983,704	30.10
Manufactures for further use in manufacturing...	309,151,989	15.35	348,149,521	16.04	408,962,311	16.84
Manufactures ready for consumption...	598,367,852	29.57	672,268,163	30.98	778,008,849	32.04
Miscellaneous...	7,592,542	.38	8,155,560	.38	8,447,449	.35
Total domestic...	2,013,549,025	100.00	2,170,319,828	100.00	2,428,506,358	100.00
Foreign—Free of duty...	20,201,089	56.48	20,451,423	60.15	22,051,706	59.00
Dutiable...	15,570,085	43.52	13,551,158	39.85	15,826,085	41.00
Total foreign...	35,771,174	100.00	34,002,581	100.00	37,877,791	100.00
Total exports...	2,049,320,199		2,204,322,409		2,465,884,149	
Excess of exports...	522,094,094		551,057,475		652,905,915	
Total imports and exports...	3,576,546,304		3,857,587,343		4,278,862,383	

GOLD AND SILVER.				TONNAGE.		
METAL.	1912.	1913.		VESSELS.	1912.	1913.
Gold—Imports...	$48,936,500	$69,194,025		Entered—Sailing...	2,388,124	2,690,065
Exports...	57,328,348	77,762,622		Steam...	43,760,947	47,949,108
Silver—Imports...	47,059,219	41,368,516		Cleared—Sailing...	2,475,445	2,810,477
Exports...	64,890,665	71,614,311		Steam...	43,940,467	48,340,489

IMPORTS AND EXPORTS OF DOMESTIC AND FOREIGN MERCHANDISE BY CONTINENTS (1906-1913)

Fiscal years ended June 30.

CONTINENT.	1906.	1907.	1908.	1909.	1910.	1911.	1912.	1913.
Imports—Europe...	$653,282,184	$747,291,255	$608,014,147	$654,622,918	$806,271,380	$768,367,760	$819,585,328	$892,865,384
North America...	235,364,719	263,576,349	238,815,898	263,999,920	306,767,496	305,406,798	334,072,039	361,943,659
South America...	140,422,816	160,165,557	124,966,590	163,578,724	196,164,786	182,629,750	215,069,310	217,747,058
Asia and Oceania	204,865,329	242,260,820	209,222,482	224,610,035	231,126,597	243,724,182	262,022,265	313,995,809
Africa...	12,628,755	21,127,464	16,236,675	15,108,627	17,489,739	27,213,620	22,585,888	26,425,344
Total...	1,226,563,843	1,434,421,425	1,194,341,792	1,311,920,224	1,557,819,968	1,527,226,105	1,653,354,934	1,812,978,234
Exports—Europe...	1,200,179,235	1,298,452,380	1,283,600,155	1,148,756,321	1,135,914,551	1,306,275,778	1,341,732,789	1,479,076,009
North America...	308,381,909	349,840,641	324,674,000	309,475,694	385,520,069	457,059,179	516,837,671	617,411,765
South America...	75,159,781	82,157,174	83,583,919	76,561,691	93,246,829	108,894,894	132,310,451	146,147,995
Asia and Oceania..	140,581,154	133,889,857	144,574,047	148,182,075	111,751,906	151,489,741	189,398,074	194,159,465
Africa...	19,562,361	16,511,026	20,340,505	17,065,434	18,851,389	25,600,607	24,043,424	29,088,917
Total...	1,743,864,500	1,880,851,078	1,856,773,346	1,683,011,104	1,744,984,726	2,049,320,199	2,204,322,409	2,465,884,149

VALUE OF IMPORTS AND EXPORTS OF MERCHANDISE BY COUNTRIES.
Fiscal years ended June 30.

COUNTRY.	IMPORTS.			EXPORTS.		
	1911.	1912.	1913.	1911.	1912.	1913.
Europe—Austria-Hungary	$16,968,090	$16,713,794	$19,192,414	$19,514,787	$22,388,930	$23,320,696
Azores and Madeira Islands	188,904	196,558	323,569	174,943	230,787	238,302
Belgium	37,084,743	41,677,438	41,941,014	45,016,622	51,587,618	66,845,462
Bulgaria	284,254	462,436	440,537	89,763	171,708	163,749
Denmark	1,712,800	2,832,072	3,974,570	13,196,950	15,767,348	18,687,794
Finland	190,055	179,947	124,189	2,216,482	2,390,654	3,615,485
France	115,414,784	124,548,436	136,877,990	135,271,648	135,388,851	146,100,201
Germany	163,242,560	171,380,580	188,069,071	287,405,814	306,959,021	331,684,212
Gibraltar	6,824	17,289	7,917	428,909	565,448	467,544
Greece	3,133,049	3,623,306	3,179,816	627,830	968,641	1,216,195
Iceland and Faroe Islands	53	30,077	90,125	5,599	18,968	83,977
Italy	47,334,809	48,028,522	54,307,364	60,580,766	65,261,398	76,285,278
Malta, Gozo, etc	14,427	15,699	34,174	230,704	549,648	449,616
Netherlands	32,926,492	35,568,436	38,186,967	96,103,769	103,762,659	125,909,862
Norway	8,000,490	9,251,716	8,419,359	7,356,405	8,391,725	8,391,458
Portugal	7,015,359	6,200,190	6,870,228	2,689,910	2,755,654	4,187,158
Roumania	275,597	91,773	348,483	964,898	906,819	2,417,591
Russia in Europe	11,004,164	20,646,925	26,958,690	23,534,267	21,515,600	25,361,795
Servia and Montenegro	574,143	695,050	694,393	13,058	26,990	7,616
Spain	19,784,998	21,931,434	23,220,012	25,064,916	25,057,490	31,471,723
Sweden	8,532,422	9,521,755	11,174,419	7,973,820	9,451,011	12,104,366
Switzerland	25,652,299	23,958,697	23,260,180	704,808	855,855	826,549
Turkey in Europe	7,540,440	9,852,709	9,917,890	2,536,141	2,597,299	2,217,073
United Kingdom—England	220,502,139	229,611,084	252,469,237	536,591,730	522,618,028	546,909,159
Scotland	23,877,402	23,590,411	24,470,119	27,373,395	30,826,638	36,400,492
Ireland	16,909,565	19,739,205	18,825,584	12,648,649	10,932,522	13,750,656
Total United Kingdom	291,289,106	272,940,700	295,564,940	576,613,974	564,372,186	597,150,307
Total Europe	768,167,700	819,585,326	892,806,884	1,508,275,778	1,341,732,789	1,479,076,009
North America—Bermuda	599,516	622,687	483,236	1,357,631	1,466,720	1,466,412
British Honduras	1,184,373	1,260,573	1,563,209	1,562,583	1,468,666	1,439,360
Canada	100,863,418	108,813,308	120,571,180	269,806,013	329,257,194	415,200,049
Central American States—Costa Rica	4,838,416	3,817,851	3,098,735	3,473,376	3,647,197	3,514,908
Guatemala	2,562,488	2,644,037	3,105,981	2,431,769	2,519,052	3,658,587
Honduras	2,657,009	2,780,972	3,200,591	2,126,014	2,461,969	3,195,627
Nicaragua	1,442,299	1,505,147	1,437,909	2,475,792	2,486,878	2,925,807
Panama	3,506,735	4,425,044	4,234,010	20,867,919	23,547,869	24,562,247
Salvador	1,463,792	1,519,964	1,371,598	2,100,713	2,421,294	2,389,971
Total Central American States	16,470,739	16,693,015	16,449,824	33,475,583	37,083,539	40,247,147
Greenland	12,890	36,810	40,120		1,551	
Mexico	57,450,111	65,915,313	77,543,842	61,281,715	52,847,129	54,571,564
Miquelon, Langley, etc	6,987	13,755	1,211	67,200	54,498	65,688
Newfoundland and Labrador	1,380,935	1,281,222	1,151,875	4,604,382	4,586,622	4,889,618
British West Indies—Barbados	310,913	325,435	335,549	1,451,628	1,518,646	1,484,684
Jamaica	6,242,700	6,325,906	5,391,988	4,375,585	4,973,295	5,287,219
Trinidad and Tobago	4,965,110	5,027,219	5,393,550	3,375,159	3,354,681	3,119,389
Other British	1,039,857	1,356,141	1,624,075	2,667,049	2,970,481	2,939,664
Total British West Indies	12,558,580	13,034,801	12,044,263	11,873,400	12,817,073	12,811,156
Cuba	110,309,468	120,154,396	126,088,173	60,709,062	62,203,661	70,581,554
Danish West Indies	155,117	489,689	48,051	810,537	924,730	894,087
Dutch West Indies	858,256	482,644	675,362	768,862	999,007	1,020,504
French West Indies	25,257	58,470	79,726	1,578,181	1,465,696	1,723,124
Haiti	813,713	800,178	874,731	5,358,761	7,271,909	6,640,265
Santo Domingo	3,532,453	4,385,070	3,723,774	3,805,329	4,425,482	5,802,767
Total West Indies	127,527,814	139,435,128	144,139,169	84,904,072	90,071,878	99,473,057
Total North America	305,496,793	334,672,039	361,943,059	457,059,179	516,831,597	611,411,765
South America—Argentina	29,090,732	29,847,016	26,863,732	43,918,511	53,158,179	52,894,834
Bolivia	527	9,884	330	891,624	991,525	940,744
Brazil	100,967,184	123,881,644	120,155,855	27,240,146	34,678,081	42,638,467
Chile	19,941,000	20,161,848	27,655,420	12,044,578	15,491,846	16,076,763
Colombia	8,994,680	11,219,381	15,992,321	4,905,934	5,748,859	7,397,896
Ecuador	3,628,805	3,728,963	3,037,689	2,238,539	2,143,605	2,553,785
Falkland Islands				1,368	584	725
Guiana—British	478,050	1,214,540	105,933	1,850,867	1,788,935	1,813,745
Dutch	999,221	948,682	821,460	723,855	792,213	704,487
French	81,438	50,811	85,586	237,034	248,824	337,714
Paraguay	34,518	9,413	58,285	86,386	161,981	187,867
Peru	9,314,080	10,124,069	9,666,579	5,567,125	5,522,469	7,341,903
Uruguay	1,613,796	3,231,676	2,450,097	5,317,711	6,580,395	7,523,145
Venezuela	7,635,256	10,657,969	10,952,351	3,791,620	4,705,605	5,737,118
Total South America	182,623,750	215,089,316	217,747,038	108,804,894	132,310,451	146,147,993
Asia—Aden	1,620,631	1,764,096	1,829,401	1,126,942	2,134,422	1,658,349
China	34,227,503	29,573,782	39,010,800	19,287,836	24,361,199	21,326,834
China (leased territory)—British		7,801	277		1,259	2,600
French				189,711	716	13,000
German	914,830	856,288	722,745	357,988	251,162	488,900
Japanese	137,751	21,879	21,935	388,542	672,274	608,110
Total China	35,280,084	30,459,700	39,755,757	20,223,077	25,286,640	22,439,604
Chosen (Korea)	245,551	193,729	5,153	1,144,583	1,123,159	1,570,926
British East Indies—British India	43,052,047	50,948,901	67,936,830	9,414,203	15,628,059	11,040,039
Straits Settlements	19,958,513	23,403,645	35,582,185	2,143,242	2,735,746	3,606,901
Other British	8,723,264	9,809,977	12,559,147	380,351	433,787	462,016
Total British	72,633,824	85,252,523	116,178,182	11,937,796	18,797,592	15,108,956

VALUE OF IMPORTS AND EXPORTS BY COUNTRIES.—CONTINUED.

COUNTRY.	IMPORTS.			EXPORTS.		
	1911.	1912.	1913.	1911.	1912.	1913.
Dutch East Indies..	$9,994,163	$13,825,506	$6,221,954	$3,213,598	$3,209,097	$3,151,693
French East Indies.	87	4,589		255,944	140,180	484,881
Portuguese East Indies.						4,012
Hongkong.	2,718,315	3,114,601	4,019,552	7,756,138	10,335,543	10,431,049
Japan.	78,527,496	80,607,469	91,653,240	36,721,409	53,478,046	57,741,815
Persia.	1,055,603	1,226,093	1,970,474	21,899	123,050	2,120
Russia in Asia.	1,199,298	1,445,677	2,356,537	1,179,782	1,208,828	1,101,419
Siam.	75,306	85,169	116,565	372,368	428,035	485,058
Turkey in Asia.	10,150,372	9,354,217	12,341,385	1,403,912	1,200,929	1,096,748
Other Asia.		135,395	124,208		144	
Total Asia.	213,449,730	225,468,250	276,462,368	85,422,428	117,461,635	115,056,620
Oceania—British Oceania:						
Australia and Tasmania.	9,102,868	9,606,423	10,956,200	37,524,586	39,380,508	43,351,855
New Zealand.	2,676,870	2,436,361	4,385,162	7,555,962	7,791,236	9,079,497
Other British.	14,766	94,515	109,080	506,342	314,128	276,876
Total British.	11,794,504	12,137,299	15,450,442	45,586,890	47,365,807	52,708,168
French Oceania.	1,017,478	1,055,747	1,011,774	637,264	694,000	833,543
German Oceania.	62,072	13,870	76,977	113,546	138,423	176,341
Philippine Islands.	17,400,308	23,257,199	21,010,248	19,723,113	23,736,133	25,384,793
Total Oceania.	30,274,452	36,464,115	37,543,441	66,060,813	71,368,513	79,102,845
Africa—Abyssinia.			3,211			
Belgian Kongo.				6,740	16,713	14,905
British Africa—West.	212,155	190,060	361,546	2,041,898	2,795,141	3,311,870
South.	2,160,342	2,203,329	3,305,562	12,842,442	12,771,229	14,488,501
East.	1,184,191	1,200,744	667,241	639,517	731,233	1,052,138
Total British Africa.	3,556,688	3,534,123	4,334,339	15,523,852	16,297,603	18,852,009
Canary Islands.	95,121	141,052	154,366	683,526	792,976	1,267,785
French Africa.	672,851	687,305	732,869	1,460,955	2,150,822	4,142,512
German Africa.	598,274	397,814	678,312	234,456	345,467	563,902
Italian Africa.		245	12,877	2,161	1,600	3,253
Liberia.	745	864	2,319	103,761	84,386	96,900
Madagascar.	61,575	42,866	41,812	14,294	36,779	3,804
Morocco.	206,229	136,954	100,426	42,207	35,137	30,200
Portuguese Africa.	250,036	92,426	376,646	3,595,737	2,450,787	2,248,071
Spanish Africa.				20,422	12,816	23,702
Turkey in Africa—Egypt.	21,674,653	17,364,414	19,907,528	2,314,596	1,751,203	1,691,833
Tripoli.	69,448	188,585	80,849		39,045	181,041
Total Africa.	27,213,620	22,585,888	26,425,344	23,607,107	24,043,424	29,088,917
Grand total.	1,597,226,105	1,653,264,934	1,812,978,234	2,049,320,199	2,204,322,409	2,465,884,149

DUTIES COLLECTED ON IMPORTS, 1910, 1911, 1912.

On principal articles or groups of articles imported into the United States for consumption.

Articles.	1910.	1911.	1912.	Articles.	1910.	1911.	1912.
Animals	$1,036,098	$906,275	$1,367,634	Spirits, distilled	$9,115,898	$9,093,027	$8,942,120
Breadstuffs	2,410,461	3,701,843	4,993,694	Wines	6,462,235	5,495,390	5,809,014
Chemicals	7,236,631	7,198,403	7,033,225	Oils	2,433,309	3,402,783	3,120,374
Cotton*	38,077,844	35,806,582	35,253,110	Paints	587,992	630,975	612,706
Earthenware	6,547,378	6,669,292	5,876,725	Paper*	4,040,841	4,439,113	2,699,026
Fibers†	481,014	358,255	447,706	Rice	1,458,307		
Fibers‡	21,942,092	20,471,331	22,250,338	Silk*	17,665,994	16,792,244	14,096,458
Fish	2,223,323	2,479,659	2,192,545	Sugar	53,098,071	52,804,189	50,945,310
Fruits and nuts.	8,428,437	8,017,396	8,407,965	Tobacco*	24,124,239	26,159,615	25,871,508
Furs*	2,641,112	2,114,521	2,130,915	Toys	2,320,039	2,855,521	2,758,383
Glass*	3,343,248	3,659,215	3,630,824	Vegetables	2,550,843	2,906,384	6,642,322
Iron and steel.	12,375,286	10,160,992	8,837,875	Wool*	4,349,911	4,192,573	4,257,662
Jewelry	5,026,570	4,678,975	4,101,904	Wool†	21,128,729	12,482,855	14,454,234
Leather*	5,345,755	4,831,143	4,805,429	Wool‡	20,771,964	16,483,662	12,599,246
Malt liquors.	2,027,254	2,075,029	2,014,344	*Including manufactures of. †Unmanufactured.			
Meat, dairy products	2,800,397	3,167,494	3,157,219	‡Manufactured. §Included with breadstuffs.			

UNITED STATES LIFE SAVING SERVICE.

The life saving establishment of the United States at the close of the fiscal year ended June 30, 1912, comprised 284 stations, of which 203 were on the Atlantic and gulf coasts, 61 on the coasts of the great lakes, 19 on the Pacific coast and 1 on the Ohio river. The keepers and crews numbered in all about 700 men. Statistics of the service for the year ended June 30, 1912, and from Nov. 1, 1871, when the system was established, to June 30, 1912, follow:

	1912.	1871-1912.
Disasters	1,730	24,441
Persons involved	7,193	159,332
Lives lost	16	1,330

	1912.	1871-1912.
Persons succored	444	24,201
Days' succor given	814	54,516
Value of vessels	$16,710,900	$231,360,845
Value of cargoes	2,537,405	86,909,229
Property involved	13,248,305	318,270,074
Property saved	11,155,170	256,228,037
Property lost	2,093,135	62,042,037

The total number of disasters on the lake coasts in the course of the year ended June 30, 1912, was 592; persons succored at stations, 85; days' succor afforded, 181; value of property involved, $4,182,115; property saved, $3,851,980; property lost, $280,135; lives lost, 2; persons on board 2,059.

TOTAL VALUE OF IMPORTS AND EXPORTS INTO AND FROM THE UNITED STATES.

From Oct. 1, 1790, to June 30, 1913.

FISCAL YEAR.*	MERCHANDISE.			SPECIE.		MDSE. AND SPECIE COMBINED.		
	Imports.	Exports.	Excess of imports (roan.) or exports (Italics).	Imports, gold and silver.	Exports, gold and silver.	Total imports.	Total exports.	Excess of imports (roman) or exports (Italics).
1790..........	$23,000,000	$20,205,156	$2,794,844			$23,000,000	$20,205,156	$2,794,814
1791..........	29,200,000	19,012,041	10,187,959			29,200,000	19,012,041	10,187,959
1792..........	31,500,000	20,753,098	10,746,902			31,500,000	20,753,098	10,746,902
1793..........	31,100,000	26,109,572	4,990,428			31,100,000	26,109,572	4,990,428
1794..........	34,600,000	33,043,725	1,556,275			34,000,000	33,043,725	1,556,275
1795..........	69,756,268	47,989,872	21,766,396			69,756,268	47,989,872	21,766,396
1796..........	81,436,164	68,574,625	22,861,539			81,436,164	58,574,625	22,961,539
1797..........	75,379,406	51,294,710	24,084,696			75,379,406	51,294,710	24,084,696
1798..........	68,551,700	61,327,411	7,924,289			68,551,700	61,327,411	7,224,289
1799..........	79,069,148	78,665,522	403,626			79,069,148	78,665,522	403,626
1800..........	91,252,768	70,971,780	20,280,988			91,252,768	70,971,780	20,280,988
1801..........	111,363,511	93,020,513	18,342,998			111,363,511	93,020,513	18,342,998
1802..........	76,333,333	71,957,144	4,376,189			76,333,333	71,957,144	4,376,189
1803..........	64,666,666	55,800,033	8,866,633	Specie included with		64,666,666	55,800,033	8,806,633
1804..........	85,000,000	77,699,074	7,300,926	merchandise prior		85,000,000	77,699,074	7,300,926
1805..........	120,600,000	95,566,021	25,033,979	to 1821.		120,600,000	95,566,021	25,033,979
1806..........	129,410,000	101,536,963	27,873,037			129,410,000	101,536,963	27,873,037
1807..........	138,500,000	108,343,150	30,156,850			138,500,000	108,343,150	30,156,850
1808..........	56,990,000	22,430,960	34,559,040			56,990,000	22,430,960	34,559,040
1809..........	59,400,000	52,203,233	7,193,767			59,400,000	52,203,233	7,196,767
1810..........	85,400,000	66,757,970	18,642,030			85,400,000	66,757,970	18,642,030
1811..........	53,400,000	61,316,832	7,916,832			53,400,000	61,316,832	7,916,832
1812..........	77,030,000	38,527,236	38,502,764			77,030,000	38,527,236	38,502,764
1813..........	22,005,000	27,856,017	5,851,017			22,005,000	27,856,017	5,851,017
1814..........	12,965,000	6,927,441	6,037,559			12,965,000	6,927,441	6,037,559
1815..........	113,041,274	52,557,753	60,483,521			113,041,274	52,557,753	60,483,521
1816..........	147,103,000	81,920,052	65,182,948			147,103,000	81,920,052	65,182,948
1817..........	99,250,000	87,671,569	11,578,431			99,250,000	87,671,569	11,578,431
1818..........	121,750,000	93,281,138	28,468,867			121,750,000	93,281,138	28,468,867
1819..........	87,125,000	70,142,521	16,982,479			87,125,000	70,142,521	16,982,479
1820..........	74,450,000	69,691,692	4,758,331			74,450,000	69,691,692	4,758,331
1821..........	64,520,894	54,596,823	75,459	$8,064,890	$10,478,050	62,585,724	65,074,382	2,488,658
1822..........	79,871,695	61,350,101	18,521,594	3,369,846	10,810,180	83,241,541	72,160,281	11,081,260
1823..........	72,481,371	68,323,043	4,155,328	5,097,896	6,372,987	77,579,267	74,699,030	2,880,237
1824..........	72,169,172	68,972,105	3,197,067	8,378,970	7,014,552	80,548,142	75,986,657	4,561,485
1825..........	90,189,310	90,738,333	549,023	6,150,765	8,797,065	96,340,075	99,535,388	3,195,313
1826..........	78,033,511	72,890,789	5,203,722	6,880,966	4,704,563	84,974,477	77,595,352	7,379,125
1827..........	71,332,598	74,309,947	2,977,009	8,151,130	8,014,880	79,484,003	87,324,526	2,840,759
1828..........	81,020,085	64,021,210	16,998,875	7,489,741	8,243,476	88,509,824	72,264,686	16,245,138
1829..........	67,088,915	67,434,651	345,736	7,403,612	4,924,020	74,492,527	72,358,671	2,133,856
1830..........	62,720,956	71,670,785	8,849,779	8,155,964	2,178,773	70,876,920	73,849,508	2,972,588
1831..........	95,885,179	72,296,632	23,589,527	7,305,945	9,014,981	103,191,124	81,310,583	21,880,541
1832..........	95,121,762	81,520,603	13,601,159	5,907,504	5,656,840	101,029,266	87,176,943	13,852,323
1833..........	101,047,946	87,528,732	13,519,211	7,070,368	2,611,701	108,118,311	90,140,438	17,977,878
1834..........	108,609,700	102,290,215	6,349,485	17,911,632	2,076,758	126,521,332	104,366,973	22,181,359
1835..........	136,764,206	115,215,802	21,548,493	13,131,447	6,477,775	149,895,742	121,693,577	28,202,165
1836..........	176,579,154	124,338,704	52,240,450	13,400,881	4,324,336	189,980,035	128,663,040	61,316,995
1837..........	130,372,503	111,443,127	19,023,676	10,516,414	5,976,249	140,889,317	117,419,376	23,569,841
1838..........	95,970,288	104,978,570	9,008,282	17,747,116	3,508,946	113,717,404	108,488,616	5,293,788
1839..........	156,490,056	112,251,673	44,245,285	5,595,176	8,776,743	162,092,132	121,028,416	41,053,716
1840..........	98,258,706	123,668,932	25,410,226	8,882,813	8,417,014	107,141,519	132,085,946	24,944,427
1841..........	122,957,544	111,817,471	11,140,073	4,988,633	10,034,332	127,916,177	121,851,803	6,094,374
1842..........	96,075,071	99,877,995	3,802,924	4,818,589	4,818,589	100,162,067	104,691,534	4,529,447
1843..........	42,433,464	82,825,689	40,392,225	22,820,265	1,520,791	64,753,799	84,346,480	19,592,681
1844..........	102,604,606	105,745,832	3,141,226	5,830,429	5,454,214	108,435,035	111,200,046	2,765,011
1845..........	113,184,322	106,040,111	7,144,211	4,201,382	8,606,495	117,354,564	114,646,606	2,607,958
1846..........	117,914,065	109,583,248	8,330,817	3,777,732	3,905,268	121,691,797	113,488,516	8,203,281
1847..........	122,424,349	156,741,598	34,317,249	24,121,289	1,907,024	146,545,638	158,648,622	12,102,984
1848..........	148,638,644	138,190,515	10,448,129	6,360,284	15,841,616	154,998,928	154,032,131	966,797
1849..........	141,206,199	140,351,172	855,027	6,651,240	5,404,648	147,857,439	145,755,820	2,101,619
1850..........	173,509,526	144,375,726	29,133,800	4,628,792	7,522,994	178,138,318	151,898,720	26,239,598
1851..........	210,771,429	188,915,259	21,856,170	5,453,503	29,472,752	216,224,932	218,388,011	2,163,079
1852..........	207,440,398	166,984,231	40,456,167	5,505,044	42,674,135	212,945,442	209,658,366	3,287,076
1853..........	263,777,265	203,489,282	60,287,983	4,201,382	27,486,875	267,978,647	230,976,157	37,002,490
1854..........	297,803,794	237,043,764	60,760,030	6,758,587	41,281,504	304,562,381	278,325,268	26,237,113
1855..........	257,808,708	218,909,503	38,899,205	3,659,812	56,247,343	261,468,520	275,156,846	13,688,326
1856..........	310,432,310	281,219,423	29,212,887	4,207,632	45,745,485	314,639,942	326,984,908	12,324,966
1857..........	348,428,342	293,823,760	54,604,582	12,461,799	69,136,922	360,890,141	362,960,682	2,070,541
1858..........	263,338,654	272,011,374	8,672,620	19,274,496	52,633,147	282,613,150	324,644,421	42,031,271
1859..........	331,333,341	292,902,051	38,431,290	7,434,789	63,887,411	338,768,130	356,789,462	18,021,332
1860..........	353,616,119	333,576,057	20,040,062	8,550,135	66,546,239	362,166,254	400,122,296	37,956,042
1861..........	289,310,542	219,553,833	69,756,709	46,339,611	29,791,080	355,650,153	249,344,913	96,305,240
1862..........	189,356,677	190,670,501	1,313,284	16,415,052	38,587,640	205,771,729	227,258,141	21,786,412
1863..........	243,335,815	203,964,447	39,371,368	9,584,105	64,156,611	252,919,920	268,121,058	15,201,138
1864..........	316,447,283	158,837,988	157,609,295	13,115,612	105,896,541	329,562,895	264,234,529	65,328,366
1865..........	238,745,580	166,029,303	72,716,277	9,810,072	67,643,726	248,555,652	233,672,529	14,883,123
1866..........	434,812,066	548,860,522	85,962,544	10,700,092	86,044,071	445,512,158	634,903,593	10,608,565
1867..........	395,761,096	294,506,141	101,254,955	22,070,475	60,808,372	417,831,571	355,374,513	62,457,058
1868..........	357,436,440	281,952,899	75,483,541	14,188,368	93,784,102	371,624,808	375,737,001	4,112,193
1869..........	417,506,379	286,117,697	131,388,652	19,807,876	57,138,590	437,314,255	343,256,077	94,058,178
1870..........	435,958,408	392,771,768	43,186,640	26,419,179	58,155,608	462,377,587	450,927,434	11,450,153
1871..........	520,223,684	442,820,178	77,408,506	21,270,024	98,441,988	541,493,708	541,262,166	231,542
1872..........	626,595,077	444,177,586	182,417,491	13,743,689	79,877,534	640,338,766	524,055,120	116,283,646

TOTAL VALUE OF IMPORTS AND EXPORTS—CONTINUED.

FISCAL YEAR.	MERCHANDISE.			SPECIE.		MDSE. AND SPECIE COMBINED.		
	Imports.	Exports.	Excess of imports (rom.) or exports (italics).	Imports, gold and silver.	Exports, gold and silver.	Total imports.	Total exports.	Excess of imports (roman) or exports (italics).
1873	$642,136,210	$522,479,922	$119,656,288	$21,480,937	$84,608,574	$663,617,147	$607,088,496	$56,528,651
1874	567,406,342	586,283,040	18,876,698	28,454,906	66,630,405	595,861,248	652,913,445	57,052,197
1875	533,005,436	513,442,711	19,562,725	20,900,717	92,132,142	553,906,153	605,574,853	51,668,700
1876	460,741,190	540,384,671	79,643,481	15,996,681	56,506,362	476,677,871	596,890,973	120,213,102
1877	451,323,126	602,475,220	151,152,094	40,774,414	56,162,237	492,097,540	658,637,457	166,539,917
1878	437,051,532	694,865,766	257,814,234	29,821,314	33,740,125	466,872,846	728,605,891	261,733,045
1879	445,777,775	710,439,441	264,661,666	20,296,000	24,997,441	466,073,775	735,436,882	269,363,107
1880	607,954,746	835,638,658	267,683,912	93,034,310	17,142,919	780,989,056	852,781,577	91,792,521
1881	642,664,628	902,377,346	259,712,718	110,575,497	19,406,847	753,240,125	921,784,193	168,544,068
1882	724,639,574	750,542,257	25,902,683	42,472,390	49,417,479	767,111,964	799,956,736	32,847,772
1883	723,180,914	823,839,402	100,658,488	28,489,391	81,820,333	751,670,305	855,659,735	103,989,430
1884	667,697,693	740,513,609	72,815,916	37,426,262	67,133,383	705,123,955	807,646,992	102,523,037
1885	577,527,329	742,189,755	164,662,426	43,242,323	42,231,525	620,769,652	784,421,290	163,651,628
1886	635,436,136	679,524,830	44,088,694	38,593,656	72,463,410	674,029,792	751,988,240	77,958,448
1887	692,319,768	716,183,211	23,863,443	60,170,792	35,997,691	752,490,560	752,180,902	309,658
1888	723,957,114	695,954,507	28,002,607	59,337,986	46,414,183	783,295,100	742,368,690	40,926,410
1889	745,131,652	742,401,375	2,730,277	25,965,673	96,641,533	774,094,725	839,942,908	64,948,183
1890	789,310,409	857,828,684	68,518,275	33,976,326	52,148,420	823,286,735	909,977,104	86,690,369
1891	844,916,196	884,480,810	39,564,614	36,259,447	108,953,842	881,175,643	993,434,452	112,258,809
1892	827,402,462	1,030,278,148	202,875,686	69,654,540	83,005,886	897,057,002	1,113,284,034	216,227,032
1893	866,400,922	847,665,194	18,735,728	44,567,633	149,418,163	910,768,555	997,083,357	86,314,802
1894	654,994,622	892,140,572	237,145,950	85,785,071	54,595,933	740,730,293	1,019,509,898	278,839,605
1895	731,969,965	807,538,165	75,568,200	56,595,933	113,763,767	788,565,904	921,301,932	132,736,028
1896	779,724,674	882,606,938	102,882,264	62,302,251	172,951,617	842,026,925	1,055,558,555	213,531,630
1897	764,730,412	1,050,993,556	286,263,144	115,548,007	102,306,218	880,278,419	1,153,301,774	273,023,355
1898	616,049,654	1,231,482,330	615,432,676	151,319,455	70,511,630	767,369,109	1,301,993,960	534,624,851
1899	697,148,489	1,227,023,302	529,874,813	119,629,659	96,841,141	816,778,148	1,320,864,443	504,086,295
1900	849,941,184	1,394,483,082	544,541,898	79,829,488	104,079,034	929,770,672	1,499,462,116	569,691,446
1901	823,172,165	1,487,764,991	664,592,826	102,437,708	117,470,357	925,609,873	1,605,235,848	679,625,475
1902	903,320,948	1,341,719,401	478,398,453	80,253,508	98,301,340	983,574,456	1,480,020,741	496,436,285
1903	1,025,719,237	1,420,141,679	394,422,442	69,145,518	91,340,551	1,094,864,756	1,520,482,533	425,617,778
1904	991,087,371	1,460,827,271	469,739,900	226,824,182	130,932,688	1,117,911,553	1,591,759,959	473,848,406
1905	1,117,513,071	1,518,561,603	401,048,595	81,133,826	141,442,826	1,198,646,897	1,660,004,502	461,357,605
1906	1,226,563,843	1,743,864,500	517,300,657	140,664,270	103,442,654	1,367,228,113	1,847,307,154	520,079,041
1907	1,434,421,425	1,880,853,078	446,420,653	157,456,873	108,138,249	1,591,878,298	1,988,989,327	397,111,029
1908	1,194,341,792	1,860,773,346	666,431,554	192,995,419	130,354,126	1,387,337,210	1,991,127,472	603,790,662
1909	1,311,920,224	1,663,011,104	351,090,880	87,968,799	147,214,619	1,399,879,023	1,810,225,714	410,346,691
1910	1,556,947,430	1,744,984,720	188,037,290	88,557,899	173,850,076	1,645,504,529	1,918,734,796	273,230,267
1911	1,527,226,105	2,049,520,199	522,094,094	119,544,262	87,259,611	1,646,770,367	2,136,579,810	489,809,443
1912	1,653,354,934	2,204,332,409	550,967,475	95,998,771	122,219,014	1,749,341,653	2,326,541,422	577,199,769
1913	1,812,978,234	2,495,884,149	632,905,915	110,462,541	149,376,933	1,923,440,775	2,615,261,062	691,820,307

*Fiscal year ended Sept. 30 prior to 1843; since that date ended June 30.

NOTE—Merchandise and specie are combined in the columns at right of table for the purpose of showing the total inward and outward movement of values by years.

ASSASSINATION OF KING GEORGE OF GREECE.

King George I. of Greece was assassinated in the city of Saloniki, Macedonia, March 18, 1913. He was taking an afternoon walk in the streets, accompanied by an aid de camp, Lieut.-Col. Francoudis, and two Cretan military policemen as an escort, when a man rushed up behind him and shot him in the back with a revolver. The bullet, which was fired at a distance of two paces, entered below the left shoulder blade, passed through the heart and came out below the stomach. The king did not die instantly, but passed away before he reached the hospital to which he was hurried.

The assassin, who was a Greek, was immediately seized by the king's escort and taken to a police station, where he gave the name of Aleko Schinas. His answers to the questions put to him gave the impression that he was irresponsible, but later it developed that he was an anarchist who held a grudge against the king because the government had closed his school at Volo, Thessaly, for spreading anarchistic doctrines.

Prince Nicholas, the king's third son, was the only other member of the royal family present in Saloniki at the time of the tragedy. He announced the death of his father to the officers of the army and invited them to swear fidelity to their new sovereign, King Constantine. The latter was at Janina,

but hurried to Saloniki on receiving the news of his father's assassination. King George had been in Saloniki since Nov. 12, 1912, arriving there a few days after its capture from the Turks by the Greek army. He had been one of the most active of the sovereigns engaged in the Turkish-Balkan war and the success of the Greek forces had won for him great popularity at home. His long stay in Saloniki was for the purpose of demonstrating Greece's title to retain permanent possession of the city with its fine harbor. Schinas committed suicide May 6 by throwing himself from the window of a police station in Athens. King George was born Dec. 24, 1845. He was the second son of King Christian of Denmark and was given the name of Prince William. March 18, 1863, he was elected king of the Hellenes and began his reign Nov. 2 the same year, taking the title of George I. He was the brother of the dowager queen of England and the dowager empress of Russia, and was related to most of the royal families of Europe by blood or marriage.

Prince Constantine, who succeeded him on the throne of Greece, was born Aug. 2, 1868. He was married Oct. 27, 1889, to Princess Sophia of Prussia, sister of Emperor William II. His son, Prince George, born July 19, 1890, is the new heir-apparent.

LONGEST RIVERS OF THE WORLD.

River.	Miles.	River.	Miles.	River.	Miles.	River.	Miles.
Mississippi-Mo.	4,194	LaPlata	2,950	Mekong	2,600	Hwangho	2,300
Nile	3,670	Lena	2,860	Niger	2,600	Yukon	2,050
Amazon	3,300	Kongo	2,900	Yenisei	2,500	Colorado	2,000
Ob	3,235	Amur	2,700	Volga	2,325	Indus	2,000
Yangtsekiang	3,000						

UNION SCALE OF WAGES AND HOURS OF LABOR.

In a bulletin issued by the United States bureau of labor statistics Aug. 15, 1913, the union scale of wages and hours of labor for more than forty trades in thirty-nine important cities of the United States are shown. The wage scales are all for time rates. The following table shows the per cent of change in hours per week and in rates of wages per hour between 1907 and 1912. The hours of labor and rate of wages in the particular trade in 1907 have been considered equal to 100.0. Thus a trade for which the scale of wages was 25 cents an hour in 1907 and 35 cents an hour in 1912 shows an advance of 40 per cent, while a trade for which the scale of wages was 50 cents an hour in 1907 and 60 cents an hour in 1912 shows an advance of 20 per cent. The advance per hour was 10 cents in both instances, but by reason of the different level of wages in 1907 the advance was in the first case 40 per cent and in the second case 20 per cent.

BAKERY TRADES.	*Pct.	†Pct.
Bakers, first hands.	17.7	22.5
Bakers, second hands.	8.6	26.6
Bakers, third hands.	10.1	40.7
BUILDING TRADES.		
Bricklayers	2.1	5.5
Building laborers	2.5	6.5
Carpenters	1.2	11.1
Cement workers (finishers)	1.8	5.7
Cement workers' helpers.	.7	16.2
Cement workers' laborers.	1.4	17.5
Gasfitters	.1	9.1
Hodcarriers	3.0	5.9
Inside wiremen.	1.3	15.4
Inside wiremen's helpers.	2.6	11.7
Marble setters.	1.5	5.1
Painters	1.9	12.6
Plasterers	.9	5.0
Plasterers' laborers.	1.0	8.2
Plumbers	1.2	10.7
Sheet metal workers.	1.7	12.9
Steamfitters	2.0	13.1
Steamfitters' helpers.	1.7	15.1
Stonemasons	1.8	5.8
Structural iron workers.	2.7	11.1
MARBLE AND STONE TRADES.		
Granite cutters.	2.0	5.3
Stonecutters	.5	1.6
METAL TRADES.		
Blacksmiths	2.1	10.3
Blacksmiths' helpers.	2.2	16.4
Boilermakers	1.6	15.6
Boilermakers' helpers.	2.4	16.9
Coremakers	2.3	13.8
Machinists	2.2	9.6
Molders, iron.	1.3	7.4
Patternmakers, wood.	2.8	8.3
PRINTING TRADES, BOOK AND JOB.		
Bookbinders	11.1	16.8
Compositors, book and job.	No change.	10.0
Electrotypers:		
Battery men and builders	4.2	17.5
Finishers	5.3	12.8
Molders	5.1	12.7
Linotype operators	.2	7.0
Press feeders	9.8	22.6
Pressmen, cylinder presses.	6.0	21.0
Pressmen, platen presses.	5.1	14.8
PRINTING TRADES, NEWSPAPER.		
Compositors, daywork	.5	10.4
Compositors, nightwork	.1	6.1
Linotype operators, daywork	.4	8.6
Linotype operators, nightwork	.3	5.9
Pressmen, web presses, daywork	1.5	12.1

	*Pct.	†Pct.
Pressmen, web presses, nightwork	1.5	9.1
Stereotypers, daywork	1.7	9.1
Stereotypers, nightwork	1.6	9.5

*Per cent of decrease in hours per week in 1912 compared with 1907.   †Per cent of increase in wages per week May 15, 1912, compared with May 15, 1907.

NOTE—The figures of the above table are based on a comparison of the rates of wages on May 15 each year, and the hours prevailing during the whole year, any change in hours, if for more than three months during the year, being taken into consideration. The per cent of change for each city was given a weight equal to the approximate number of union employes in the trade in that city.

UNION WAGES PER HOUR IN 1912.

BAKERY TRADES.	New York.	Chicago.	San Francisco.
Occupations.	Cents.	Cents.	Cents.
Bakers, first hands	33.71	37.04	46.30
Bakers, second hands	28.57	35.13	38.89
Bakers, third hands	21.48	29.63	37.04
BUILDING TRADES.			
Bricklayers	70.00	72.50	87.50
Carpenters	62.50	65.00	62.50
Cement workers	62.50	62.50	75.00
Cement workers' helpers	37.50	47.50	62.50
Gasfitters	68.75	68.75	75.00
Hodcarriers	37.50	45.00	50.00
Inside wiremen	56.25	75.00	62.50
Inside wiremen's helpers	27.50		18.75
Laborers	32.50	37.50	27.78
Marble setters	62.50		62.50
Painters	50.00	60.00	56.25
Plasterers	68.75	75.00	87.50
Plasterers' laborers	40.63		62.50
Plumbers	68.75	68.75	75.00
Sheet metal workers	59.38	62.50	68.75
Steamfitters	68.75	72.00	75.00
Stonemasons	57.50	72.50	
Structural iron workers	62.50	68.00	62.50
GRANITE AND STONE TRADES.			
Granite cutters, inside men	50.00	40.63	62.50
Granite cutters, outside men	56.25	56.25	68.75
Stonecutters	62.50	62.50	62.50
METAL TRADES.			
Blacksmiths, shopmen	45.28	40.00	50.00
Blacksmiths' helpers	28.08	30.00	37.50
Boilermakers, shopmen	41.67	40.00	50.00
Boilermakers' helpers	43.13	32.50	31.25
Coremakers	38.89	38.89	50.00
Machinists	38.24	39.00	43.75
Molders, iron	38.89	38.89	50.00
Patternmakers, wood	53.13	47.50	62.50
PRINTING TRADES, BOOK AND JOB.			
Bookbinders, finishers	47.92	40.63	50.00
Compositors, English	47.88	46.88	50.00
Electrotypers, battery men	50.00	37.50	56.25
Finishers	62.50	45.83	56.25
Molders	62.50	52.08	56.25
Linotype operators, English	52.13	50.00	64.44
Press feeders, cylinder	38.54	38.48	38.38
PRINTING TRADES, NEWSPAPER.			
Compositors, English, daywork	64.44	62.00	64.44
Compositors, English, nightwork	71.11	67.00	71.11
Linotypers, English, daywork	64.44	*50.00	64.44
Linotypers, English, nightwork	71.11	*55.00	71.11
Pressmen, journeymen, daywork	53.33	50.00	68.89
Pressmen, journeymen, nightwork	65.79	57.14	68.89
Stereotypers, daywork	56.25	58.06	60.00
Stereotypers, nightwork	72.37	58.06	60.00

*Minimum sliding scale.

WORKMEN'S COMPENSATION AND INSURANCE LAWS.

[From federal bureau of labor report.]

Up to the close of 1912 the following states had enacted laws providing for compensation and insurance of workmen in cases of accident: Arizona, California, Illinois, Kansas, Maryland, Massachusetts, Michigan, Nevada, New Hampshire, New Jersey, New York, Ohio, Rhode Island, Washington and Wisconsin. The elective or compulsory compensation system is provided in all these states with the exception of Maryland, Massachusetts, Ohio and Washington, where insurance systems are in force. The industries covered include all (except casual employes) in California, Michigan, New Jer-

sey, Wisconsin, Maryland, Massachusetts, Ohio and Rhode Island; all but railroad employes, in New York; all engaged in especially dangerous occupations, in Illinois, Kansas, New Hampshire, Arizona, Nevada and Washington. The burden of cost is on the employer in all the states having compensation or insurance laws, except that in Maryland 50 per cent and in Ohio 10 per cent is borne by the employe. To be compensated disability must continue more than one week in California, Wisconsin, Maryland and Ohio; more than six working days in Illinois; more than two weeks in Kansas, Michigan, New Hampshire, New Jersey, New York, Rhode Island, Arizona and Massachusetts; more than ten days in Nevada; "loss of earning power shall exceed 5 per cent" in Washington.

Following is the rate of compensation for death, for total disability and for partial disability:

DEATH.

Arizona—2,400 times one-half the daily wages; $4,000 maximum; no dependents, medical and burial expenses.

California—3 years' earnings; $1,000 minimum, $5,000 maximum; no dependents, $100.

Illinois—4 years' earnings; $1,500 minimum, $3,500 maximum; no dependents, $150.

Kansas—3 years' earnings; $1,200 minimum, $3,600 maximum; no dependents, $100.

Maryland—3 years' earnings; $1,000 minimum; no dependents, $75 minimum, $100 maximum.

Massachusetts—50 per cent of weekly wage for 300 weeks; $4 minimum, $10 maximum; no dependents, $200.

Michigan—50 per cent of weekly wages for 300 weeks; $4 minimum, $10 maximum; no dependents, $200.

Nevada—3 years' earnings; $2,000 minimum, $3,000 maximum; no dependents, $300; deduction for contributory negligence.

New Hampshire—150 times weekly earnings; not more than $3,000; no dependents, $100.

New Jersey—25 to 60 per cent of wages for 300 weeks; $5 minimum, $10 maximum; no dependents, $200.

New York—1,200 times daily earnings; $3,000 maximum; no dependents, $100.

Ohio—$150 funeral expenses; 66⅔ per cent of wages for six years; $1,500 minimum, $3,400 maximum.

Rhode Island—50 per cent of weekly wages for 300 weeks; $4 minimum, $10 maximum; no dependents, $200.

Washington—$75 funeral expenses; spouse receives $20 monthly; each child up to 3, $5 per month; maximum, $4,000.

Wisconsin—4 years' earnings; $1,500 minimum, $3,000 maximum; no dependents, $100.

TOTAL DISABILITY.

Arizona—50 per cent of average semimonthly earnings, during disability, not to exceed $4,000.

California—65 per cent of weekly wages for not more than 15 years, total not to exceed 3 years' earnings; if nurse is required, 100 per cent; minimum wages per annum, $333.33; maximum, $1,666.66.

Illinois—50 per cent of weekly earnings for 8 years; $5 minimum, $12 maximum, up to $3,500.

Kansas—50 per cent of weekly earnings; $6 minimum, $15 maximum, for not more than 10 years.

Maryland—50 per cent of average weekly wages during previous 12 months, if so long in employers' service; if not, then a weekly benefit for such shorter period as he may have been in such service.

Massachusetts—50 per cent of weekly wages for not over 500 weeks; $4 minimum, $10 maximum, total not to exceed $3,000.

Michigan—50 per cent of weekly wages for not over 500 weeks; $4 minimum, $10 maximum; total not to exceed $4,000.

Nevada—60 per cent of weekly earnings; specified increases for specified maimings, total not to exceed $3,000; deduction for contributory negligence.

New Hampshire—50 per cent of average weekly earnings; maximum, $10 for not more than 300 weeks.

New Jersey—50 per cent of wages for 400 weeks; $5 minimum, $10 maximum.

New York—50 per cent of wages (not more than $10 weekly) for not more than 8 years.

Ohio—66⅔ per cent of wages until death, if permanently disabled; $5 minimum, $12 maximum.

Rhode Island—50 per cent of weekly earnings for not over 500 weeks; $4 minimum, $10 maximum.

Washington—$20 per month if single, $25 if married; for each child under 16 years, $5 per month, not over $35 in all; deduction for removal of safeguard by employe.

Wisconsin—65 per cent of wages; if nurse is required, 100 per cent after 90 days; no total to exceed 4 years' earnings.

PARTIAL DISABILITY.

Arizona—50 per cent of wage decrease until recovery, not to exceed $4,000.

California—65 per cent of wage decrease; wages considered and total payments same as for total disability.

Illinos—50 per cent of wage decrease; $12 maximum for not more than 8 years.

Kansas—25 to 50 per cent of weekly earnings; $3 minimum, $12 maximum, for not more than 10 years.

Maryland—Difference between amount for total disability and amount workman is able to earn after the injury; fixed proportions for specified injuries.

Massachusetts—50 per cent of weekly wage loss; $10 maximum, for not more than 300 weeks; fixed rates for specified injuries.

Michigan—50 per cent of wage decrease; $10 maximum, for not over 300 weeks; fixed rates for specified injuries.

Nevada—Such proportion of 60 per cent of earnings as loss of capacity bears to total loss; maimings as in case of total disability.

New Hampshire—50 per cent of wage loss; maximum, $10 per week; not more than 300 weeks.

New Jersey—Proportionate, fixed scale.

New York—50 per cent of wage decrease; same limits as for total disability.

Ohio—66⅔ per cent of wage decrease for 6 years; $5 per week minimum, $12 maximum; not over $3,400 in all.

Rhode Island—50 per cent of wage decrease; $10 maximum, for not more than 300 weeks; fixed rates for specified injuries.

Washington—Proportionate; not over $1,500.

Wisconsin—65 per cent of wage decrease; no total to exceed four years' earnings.

OTHER PROVISIONS.

The maximum allowed for medical or surgical aid in any state is $200. In some states it is allowed only in case the employe dies leaving no dependents. In other cases the cost of medical attendance for two or three weeks is allowed.

Disputes are settled in California by the industrial accident board with limited appeal to courts; in Illinois by arbitrators for each case with appeal to courts; in Kansas by local committees or arbitrators with court review allowed; in Michigan by industrial accident board, arbitration and appeals to Supreme court; in New Hampshire by proceedings in equity; in New Jersey by judges of Court of Common Pleas; in New York by courts; in Rhode Island by courts; in Wisconsin by industrial commission with appeal to courts; in Arizona by arbitration, reference to attorney-general or appeal to courts; in Nevada by arbitrators for each and appeal to courts if decision is not unanimous; in Maryland by arbitration if so provided in contract; in Massachusetts by arbitrators for each case, industrial accident board and appeal to courts on points of law; in Ohio by state liability board of awards and limited appeal to courts; in Washington by industrial insurance department with appeal to courts.

LARGEST CAR FERRY IN THE WORLD.

The largest car ferry in the world is the Contra Costa, built in 1913 for the Southern Pacific railroad at Oakland, Cal. It operates across the Carquinez straits, between Porta Costa, Cal., and Benicia. It is 433 feet long and 116 feet wide and has a tonnage of 3,800. It has four tracks on which two locomotives and thirty-six freight cars or twenty-four passenger cars can be carried at one time.

WHOLESALE PRICES (1890 AND 1913).

[From bulletin of the bureau of labor, Washington, D. C.]

Wholesale prices in 1912 advanced sharply during the first five months and a strong upward tendency was maintained to the end of the year. The most important feature in the movement of prices during the year was the marked increase in the great groups of farm products, food, fuel and lighting, and metals and implements.

The average of wholesale prices in 1912, as measured by the prices of 255 commodities, was 3.4 per cent higher than the average for 1911, and with this advance the level was 1.5 per cent above the high average of 1910 prices. Wholesale prices during 1912 were 18.3 per cent higher than in 1890; 20.9 per cent higher than in 1900; 48.9 per cent higher than in 1897, the year of lowest prices in the twenty-three year period from 1890 to 1912, and 33.6 per cent higher than the average price for the ten years 1890 to 1899.

The upward movement of prices which began July, 1905, reached its highest point in 1907 in October, from which month there was a general decline until August, 1908. Beginning with September, 1908, wholesale prices increased without a break in any month up to March, 1910; from this time to December, 1910, prices declined slightly. Prices in January, 1911, showed a slight decline from those of December, 1910, but through the year 1911 the fluctuation from month to month was small. During the first months of 1912 prices rose rapidly until May, when slight recessions occurred during June and August. In September and October prices were again higher, reaching the level of May in November, with a loss in December, 1912, of less than one-fourth of 1 per cent.

Wholesale prices in May and November, 1912, were higher than at any other time in the twenty-three year period from 1890 to 1912, being 18.5 per cent higher than in July, 1905; 3.4 per cent higher than in October, 1907; 11.5 per cent higher than in August, 1908, and 1.2 per-cent higher than in March, 1910. Wholesale prices in December, 1912, were 12.8 per cent higher than in December, 1905; 3.6 per cent higher than in December, 1910, and 4.6 per cent higher than in December, 1911.

Wholesale prices for 1912, as stated above, were higher than for any other year of the twenty-three year period, 1890 to 1912, covered by the bureau of labor statistics price reports, and they were also higher than for any year since 1883.

Comparing 1912 with 1911, the group of commodities showing the greatest increase in prices was fuel and lighting, the increase in the group as a whole being 9.4 per cent. The only group showing a decrease was that comprising lumber and building materials, which declined 2.1 per cent in 1912.

The following table shows the average wholesale prices of certain commodities in the calendar years 1911 and 1912:

FARM PRODUCTS.

Commodity.	1911.	1912.
Barley, choice to fancy, bu	$1.10	$1.02
Cattle, steers, choice, 100 lbs	7.23	9.36
Cattle, steers, good, 100 lbs	6.73	8.40
Corn, cash, bu	.59	.69
Cotton, upland, middling, lb	.13	.12
Flaxseed, No. 1, bu	2.39	1.87
Hay, timothy, No. 1, ton	19.66	20.41
Hides, green, salted, lb	.15	.18
Hogs, heavy, 100 lbs	6.75	7.60
Hogs, light, 100 lbs	6.73	7.55
Hops, New York state, choice, lb	.36	.41
Horses, draft, good, per head	259.75	220.50
Mules, 16 hands, per head	214.62	192.03
Oats, cash, bu	.38	.44
Poultry, live, fowls, lb	.14	.15
Rye, No. 2 cash, bu	.90	.80
Sheep, wethers, good, 100 lbs	4.28	4.93
Sheep, wethers, plain, 100 lbs	3.94	4.90
Tobacco, burley, good leaf, 100 lbs	11.35	11.43
Wheat, cash	.98	1.05

FOOD, ETC.

Commodity	1911	1912
Beans, medium, choice, bu	2.29	4.66
Bread, crackers, oyster, lb	.07	.06
Bread, crackers, soda, lb	.07	.06
Bread, loaf (New York market), lb	.04	.04
Butter, creamery, Elgin, lb	.26	.30

Commodity.	1911.	1912.
Canned corn, No. 2, dozen cans	1.07	.95
Canned peas, No. 2, dozen cans	1.50	1.62
Canned tomatoes, No. 3, dozen cans	1.11	1.42
Cheese, New York state, cream, lb	.14	.15
Coffee, Rio, No. 7, lb	.13	.15
Eggs, fresh, fancy, dozen	.30	.33
Fish, cod, dry, quintal	7.96	8.10
Fish, herring, split, brl	6.86	7.50
Fish, mackerel, salt, brl	16.00	13.21
Fish, salmon, canned, 12 cans	2.10	2.18
Flour, buckwheat, 100 lbs	2.44	2.45
Flour, rye, brl	4.69	4.52
Flour, wheat, spring, brl	5.08	5.27
Flour, wheat, winter, brl	3.98	4.69
Fruit, apples, evaporated, lb	.12	.08
Fruit, currants, in barrels, lb	.08	.07
Fruit, prunes, in boxes, lb	.12	.07
Fruit, raisins, California, box	1.41	1.42
Glucose, 100 lbs	1.86	2.31
Lard, prime, lb	.09	.10
Meal, corn, fine white, 100 lbs	1.29	1.65
Meal, corn, fine yellow, 100 lbs	1.29	1.65
Meat, bacon, short clear sides, lb	.09	.11
Meat, bacon, short rib sides, lb	.09	.11
Meat, beef, fresh, lb	.11	.13
Meat, beef, salt, extra mess, brl	12.91	15.79
Meat, beef, salt, hams, brl	28.60	29.88
Meat, hams, smoked, lb	.14	.14
Meat, mutton, dressed, lb	.08	.08
Meat, pork, salt, mess, brl	19.16	19.29
Milk, fresh, quart	.03	.04
Molasses, New Orleans, gal	.41	.44
Poultry, dressed, fowl, lb	.15	.16
Rice, domestic, lb	.05	.05
Salt, American, brl	.83	.99
Soda, bicarbonate of, lb	.01	.01
Spices, pepper, lb	.10	.11
Starch, pure corn, lb	.06	.06
Sugar, granulated, lb	.05	.05
Tallow, lb	.06	.06
Tea, Formosa, fine, lb	.24	.24
Vegetables, cabbage, ton	10.00	8.94
Vegetables, onions, brl	3.10	2.12
Vegetables, potatoes, bu	.77	.91
Vinegar, cider, gal	.20	.16

CLOTHS AND CLOTHING.

Commodity	1911	1912
Bags, 2 bushel, Amoskeag, each	.20	.18
Blankets, all wool, 5 lbs. to pair, lb	1.00	1.02
Blankets, cotton, 2 lbs. to pair, lb	.57	.57
Boots and shoes, men's brogans, pair	1.06	1.23
Boots and shoes, men's calf shoes, pair	3.00	3.06
Boots and shoes, women's solid grain, pr.	1.02	1.09
Broadcloths, first quality, yard	2.02	2.08
Calico, American, prints, yard	.05	.05
Carpets, Brussels, yard	1.20	1.24
Carpets, ingrain, yard	.53	.58
Carpets, Wilton, yard	2.23	2.31
Cotton flannels, 3½ yards to lb., yard	.08	.10
Cotton thread, 6 card, 200 yd. spls., spool	.04	.04
Cotton yarns, cones, 22-1, lb	.21	.20
Denims, Amoskeag, yard	.14	.14
Drillings, brown, yard	.08	.08
Flannels, white, yard	.43	.45
Ginghams, Amoskeag, yard	.07	.06
Horse blankets, wool, lb	.75	.77
Hosiery, men's cotton ½ hose, 12 pairs	.80	.83
Hosiery, women's cotton hose, 12 pairs	1.84	1.85
Leather, harness, oak, lb	.37	.38
Leather, sole, hemlock, lb	.24	.26
Overcoatings, covert cloth, yard	1.80	1.91
Overcoatings, twill, yard	1.75	1.35
Print cloths, yard	.03	.04
Sheetings, bleached, Atlantic, yard	.21	.21
Sheetings, bleached, Pepperell, yard	.24	.23
Sheetings, brown, Indian Head, yard	.08	.08
Shirtings, bleached, Fruit of Loom, yd	.09	.08
Shirtings, bleached, Wamsutta, yard	.11	.10
Silk, raw, Italian, lb	3.89	3.81
Silk, raw, Japan, lb	3.47	4.45
Suitings, clay worsted, 12 ounce, yard	1.09	1.21
Suitings, indigo blue, wool, yard	1.49	1.52
Suitings, serge, yard	1.13	1.14
Tickings, Amoskeag, yard	.13	.13
Trouserings, worsted, yard	2.38	2.36
Underwear, shirts, drawers, wool, doz.	27.00	27.00

Commodity.	1911.	1912.
Women's dress goods, poplar cloth, yard	.20	.19
Wool, Ohio, fine fleece, scoured, lb......	.65	.65
Worsted yarns, lb....................	1.21	1.22

FUEL AND LIGHTING.

Candles, 14 ounce, lb.................	.07	.07
Coal, anthracite, broken, ton...........	4.20	4.35
Coal, anthracite, chestnut, ton.........	5.00	5.28
Coal, anthracite, egg, ton..............	4.81	5.03
Coal, anthracite, stove, ton............	4.81	5.03
Coal, bituminous, ton.................	3.02	3.13
Coke, Connellsville, ton...............	1.64	2.40
Matches, parlor, 144 boxes............	1.50	1.50
Petroleum, crude, brl.................	1.39	1.57
Petroleum, refined, gal...............	.07	.08

METALS AND IMPLEMENTS.

Augers, extra, 1 inch, each...........	.34	.35
Axes, M. C. O., Yankee, each.........	.65	.70
Bar iron, common, lb.................	.01	.01
Barb wire, galvanized, 100 lbs........	2.18	2.13
Chisels, 1 inch, each.................	.25	.25
Copper, ingot, lb....................	.12	.16
Copper, sheet, hot rolled, lb..........	.17	.21
Copper, wire, bare, lb................	.14	.17
Doorknobs, steel, pair...............	.25	.27
Files, 8 inch, dozen..................	.93	.93
Hammers, Maydole, No. 1½, each.....	.44	.44
Lead, pig, lb........................	.04	.04
Lead pipe, 100 lbs...................	5.02	5.20
Locks, common mortise, each..........	.10	.12
Nails, 8 penny, fence, 100 lbs.........	1.71	1.71
Pig iron, Bessemer, ton...............	15.71	15.94
Pig iron, foundry, No. 1, ton..........	15.71	16.56
Planes, Bailey, No. 5, each...........	1.54	1.54
Saws, crosscut, Disston, No. 2, each...	1.78	1.78
Shovels, Ames, No. 2, dozen..........	7.45	7.45
Silver, bar, fine, ounce..............	.54	.61
Spelter, western, lb.................	.06	.07
Steel billets, ton....................	21.46	22.38
Steel rails, ton.....................	28.00	28.00
Tin, pig, lb........................	.43	.46
Tinplates, domestic, 100 lbs..........	3.86	3.55
Trowels, M. C. O., brick, each........	.35	.35
Vises, solid boxes, 50 lbs. each.......	4.37	4.14
Wood screws, 1 inch, gross...........	.10	.12
Zinc, sheet, 100 lbs.................	7.05	7.92

LUMBER AND BUILDING MATERIALS.

Brick, common, M....................	5.89	6.76
Carbonate of lead, lb................	.07	.07
Cement, Portland, brl................	1.46	1.31
Doors, white pine, each..............	1.60	1.51
Hemlock, M feet....................	20.68	21.45
Lime, common, brl..................	1.11	1.08
Linseed oil, raw, gal.................	.88	.67

Commodity.	1911.	1912.
Maple, hard, M feet..................	34.32	36.45
Oak, white, M feet...................	54.68	56.23
Oak, white, quartered, M feet.........	87.18	86.50
Oxide of zinc, lb....................	.05	.05
Pine, white, boards, M feet...........	38.35	37.23
Pine, yellow, flooring, M feet.........	46.55	44.53
Pine, yellow, siding, M feet..........	30.59	33.14
Plate glass, polished, sq. ft..........	.32	.30
Poplar, M feet......................	61.59	61.50
Putty, lb...........................	.01	.01
Rosin, good, strained, lb.............	6.72	6.64
Shingles, cypress, M.................	3.61	3.48
Spruce, M feet......................	24.27	26.95
Tar, brl............................	2.12	2.00
Turpentine, spirits of, gal............	.68	.47
Window glass, firsts, 50 sq. ft........	2.25	2.24

DRUGS AND CHEMICALS.

Alcohol, grain, gal..................	2.53	2.57
Alcohol, wood, gal..................	.50	.50
Alum, lump, lb.....................	.02	.02
Brimstone, crude, ton...............	22.00	22.00
Glycerin, refined, lb.................	.23	.18
Muriatic acid, lb....................	.01	.01
Opium, natural, lb..................	6.43	7.12
Quinine, American, ounce............	.14	.18
Sulphuric acid, lb...................	.01	.01

HOUSEFURNISHING GOODS.

Earthenware, plates, white, doz.......	.46	.43
Earthenware, cups and saucers, gross..	3.41	3.41
Furniture, bedroom sets, each........	13.75	15.25
Furniture, chairs, maple, doz.........	9.00	9.50
Furniture, chairs, kitchen, doz........	5.75	6.00
Furniture, tables, kitchen, doz........	21.00	22.80
Glassware, nappies, doz.............	.11	.11
Glassware, pitchers, doz.............	.80	.80
Glassware, tumblers, common, doz....	.11	.11
Table cutlery, knives, forks, gross....	5.00	5.29
Woodenware, pails, doz..............	1.75	1.75
Woodenware, tubs, nest of 3.........	1.65	1.65

MISCELLANEOUS.

Cottonseed meal, ton................	29.77	31.46
Cottonseed oil, lb...................	.05	.06
Jute, raw, lb.......................	.05	.05
Malt, western, bu..................	1.28	1.11
Paper, news, lb.....................	.02	.02
Paper, manila wrapping, lb...........	.05	.05
Proof spirits, gal...................	1.34	1.36
Rope, manila, lb....................	.09	.10
Rubber, lb.........................	1.11	1.05
Soap, castile, lb....................	.08	.07
Starch, laundry, lb..................	.03	.04
Tobacco, plug, lb...................	.44	.44
Tobacco, smoking, granulated, lb......	.63	.63

ATTEMPT TO ASSASSINATE KING ALFONSO.

Rafael Sanchez Allegro, an anarchist from Barcelona, fired three shots at King Alfonso of Spain in Madrid Sunday afternoon April 13, 1913, but none of the bullets reached the mark. Accompanied by his staff, the king was riding along the Calle de Acala on his return from the ceremony of swearing in the recruits. He had reached a point opposite the Bank of Spain when a man rushed out from the sidewalk and seized the bridle of the king's horse with one hand and presented a revolver with the other. The royal rider, realizing the situation, instantly dug his spurs into his horse, which reared violently. The man fired, but the bullet, instead of entering Alfonso's breast, buried itself in the neck of the horse. The weapon was fired at such close range that the king's left hand glove was blackened by the powder. Only quickness of thought and action saved his life.

The assailant was thrown to the ground by a secret service man, but managed to free his right arm and fired two more shots at the king. Both went wild and, policemen coming up, he was overpowered after a fierce struggle, handcuffed and conveyed to prison. It was there learned that the assassination of the king was planned by anarchists and that Allegro had been appointed to carry out the plot.

King Alfonso was shot at in January, 1904, and on May 30, 1905, a bomb was thrown at him as he and President Loubet were leaving the opera in Paris. May 31, 1906, on the day of his marriage, a bomb was thrown at the vehicle in which he and his bride were seated receiving the plaudits of the people of Madrid. Seventeen persons were killed on that occasion, but the royal couple escaped unhurt.

FASTEST TRIPS AROUND THE WORLD.

John Henry Mears bettered the record for the fastest trip around the world by 3 days 22 hours 7 minutes and 37 seconds when he arrived in New York, N. Y., Aug. 6, 1913. His time was 35 days 21 hours 35 minutes and ½ second. The best previous record was that made by Andre Jaeger-Schmidt of Paris in 1911—39 days 19 hours 42 minutes and 37½ seconds. Mears' mileage was 21,066, while that of Jaeger-Schmidt was 19,309. Both took a northern route by way of Russia. The Frenchman started from Paris and passed through Vladivostok, Japan, Vancouver, Montreal, New York and Cherbourg. Mears started from New York and passed through London, Paris, Berlin, St. Petersburg, Korea, Yokohama, Victoria, Seattle and Chicago. In 1889 Mrs. Nellie Seaman, better known as Nellie Bly, girdled the globe in 72 days 6 hours and 11 minutes. In 1903 Henry Frederick made the trip in 54 days 7 hours and 20 minutes.

RELATIVE WHOLESALE PRICES OF COMMODITIES.

In this table, prepared by the bureau of labor in Washington, the average wholesale price in New York and other primary markets of each article for the years 1890-1899, inclusive, is taken as the base price and is represented by 100. The relative price is the average wholesale price for each year from 1900 to 1912, inclusive, compared with the base price.

FARM PRODUCTS.

YEAR.	Barley	Cattle.	Corn.	Cotton	Flax-seed.	Hay (timo-thy).	Hides.	Hogs.	Hops.	Oats.	Sheep.	Wheat
1890	111.6	87.4	103.8	142.9	125.5	95.8	99.6	89.6	148.0	115.6	118.0	118.9
1900	106.2	173.9	100.2	123.8	145.7	110.9	127.4	115.2	53.7	84.5	114.3	93.7
1905	107.0	110.2	131.7	123.1	107.6	107.9	152.6	119.9	150.9	111.2	128.5	134.6
1906	112.8	113.1	121.8	142.0	99.1	124.3	164.7	141.3	92.0	122.1	133.5	105.6
1907	169.0	122.8	138.8	153.0	106.1	162.4	155.3	137.8	98.1	167.4	123.5	120.8
1908	161.8	126.7	179.9	134.8	108.0	118.3	142.6	131.4	67.1	189.5	109.6	131.8
1909	148.7	136.3	175.5	156.0	140.6	129.0	175.8	171.6	113.4	178.9	120.1	159.7
1910	151.7	148.2	152.7	194.8	208.7	165.6	165.0	202.7	146.1	143.5	122.9	146.1
1911	243.1	142.1	155.1	168.0	214.8	188.5	157.6	152.9	206.1	143.2	89.8	131.1
1912	224.7	177.5	180.2	148.2	167.6	195.7	187.8	172.1	231.5	162.9	111.7	139.7

FOOD, ETC.

YEAR.	Beans.	Crack-ers.	Bread.	Butter	Cheese	Coffee.	Eggs.	Fish, cod.	Flour, wheat.	Dried apples.	Glu-cose.	Lard.
1890	121.5	111.4	100.6	103.1	97.1	136.6	99.1	101.7	120.7	134.1	....	96.8
1900	125.8	94.0	100.6	100.4	114.3	62.6	100.7	94.9	89.4	72.6	104.9	105.6
1905	128.8	95.1	100.6	111.9	122.8	63.4	138.2	132.4	126.2	82.5	125.1	113.9
1906	113.8	90.5	100.6	113.3	133.0	61.8	133.2	136.2	99.5	115.5	142.9	135.6
1907	105.4	90.5	100.6	127.2	143.3	50.1	141.2	138.6	113.5	99.5	159.4	140.7
1908	135.9	90.5	100.6	124.1	138.2	47.8	142.0	130.7	126.1	101.9	186.2	138.8
1909	146.7	91.1	106.5	133.8	150.5	59.6	160.8	125.7	134.0	90.8	174.4	178.7
1910	143.7	97.5	109.8	137.2	159.3	72.5	165.0	124.2	127.9	98.7	136.9	191.6
1911	137.0	90.5	109.6	121.8	141.9	102.1	151.7	142.5	118.2	142.0	131.0	138.8
1912	167.4	90.5	109.6	136.8	166.7	111.3	168.9	145.1	122.7	97.6	163.1	160.4

YEAR.	Meal, corn.	Bacon	Fresh beef.	Sm'k'd hams.	Mut-ton.	Salt pork.	Milk.	Mo-lasses.	Rice.	Salt.	Sugar.	Tea.
1890	100.3	89.3	89.2	101.1	123.7	104.5	103.1	112.4	107.8	112.5	130.5	96.3
1900	97.4	111.4	104.3	104.2	98.4	107.5	107.5	151.5	97.7	142.1	112.8	104.0
1905	130.8	118.5	104.0	106.3	113.9	123.9	113.3	102.5	74.3	102.7	111.2	94.2
1906	124.2	139.6	101.2	125.6	120.7	150.5	118.0	107.9	84.5	101.4	95.5	82.8
1907	133.5	141.3	114.7	132.4	116.0	151.0	131.4	109.7	95.2	112.6	98.4	81.0
1908	158.8	133.5	121.1	114.8	114.5	187.3	129.0	112.7	111.2	111.5	104.5	75.1
1909	158.4	173.8	123.1	133.1	119.2	183.5	122.5	111.1	110.3	116.1	100.7	82.0
1910	145.5	197.3	133.2	167.1	133.3	204.1	144.3	117.5	97.5	107.1	104.9	84.5
1911	127.0	140.6	127.4	142.2	99.7	164.7	131.8	128.9	89.3	117.5	112.8	85.3
1912	162.5	164.0	157.3	145.2	111.3	165.8	144.3	138.2	97.5	140.2	106.7	86.8

CLOTHS AND CLOTHING.

YEAR.	Bags, 2-bush. Amoskeag.	Blan-kets, wool.	Boots and shoes, men's.	Calico. Ameri-can.	Broad-cloths.	Car-pets, in-grain.	Cotton flan-nels.	Cotton thread.	Cotton yarns.	Den-ims.	Drill-ings.	Ging-hams.
1890	113.9	108.3	101.0	117.5	113.7	108.6	103.1	101.6	111.3	112.5	119.4	117.3
1900	112.6	107.1	94.3	94.1	108.0	103.5	104.5	120.1	115.0	102.8	105.9	96.6
1905	109.6	119.0	100.0	93.5	115.2	116.2	121.0	120.1	107.8	103.7	126.0	96.6
1906	129.1	122.0	108.0	99.5	116.6	116.2	130.7	120.1	124.6	118.1	135.5	106.0
1907	138.5	119.0	109.0	99.6	116.6	121.2	139.9	134.8	137.1	132.3	144.2	123.5
1908	134.3	113.1	109.0	121.0	115.6	116.6	117.4	131.7	110.5	111.1	123.4	102.8
1909	134.6	119.0	114.8	104.3	116.6	111.1	116.8	126.4	123.5	119.9	123.0	110.3
1910	146.0	125.5	117.4	97.1	117.8	111.1	127.5	126.4	133.9	138.9	144.2	131.8
1911	146.0	119.0	116.7	105.8	116.6	111.1	141.6	126.4	130.6	131.9	143.9	127.8
1912	152.2	122.0	119.0	100.4	120.0	122.1	142.2	125.4	125.0	129.9	140.2	117.8

YEAR.	Ho-siery, cotton	Leath-er, sole heml'k	Print cloths.	Sheet-ings.	Shirt-ings.	Silk, raw.	Suit-ings, serge.	Tick-ings.	Under-wear, wool.	Wom-en's dress goods.	Wool, Ohio.	Wor-sted yarns.
1890	133.3	99.1	117.7	122.1	116.1	122.7	....	113.1	106.2	119.8	134.6	120.4
1900	82.1	128.4	108.6	111.3	103.4	106.0	107.6	102.1	100.4	119.1	118.0	118.3
1905	82.1	118.1	110.0	110.2	102.7	95.5	121.1	102.1	100.4	128.4	117.2	123.0
1906	85.3	130.9	127.7	121.5	112.3	101.6	136.8	119.0	115.8	134.9	112.3	127.0
1907	94.8	136.4	167.4	134.3	153.4	131.1	139.5	129.4	115.8	134.9	113.0	127.3
1908	88.9	129.3	118.0	138.7	125.4	98.2	132.0	106.0	115.8	127.1	107.3	120.8
1909	96.1	131.5	126.5	129.3	124.7	102.9	142.0	111.3	115.8	137.8	119.0	129.3
1910	95.4	127.2	134.8	130.8	126.0	94.1	138.9	121.1	115.8	146.6	107.0	123.0
1911	94.9	122.5	122.8	121.1	118.8	91.3	123.7	125.6	115.8	141.1	98.4	113.5
1912	98.4	133.0	134.5	120.9	113.9	89.6	125.3	121.4	115.8	138.0	105.0	119.8

RELATIVE PRICES OF COMMODITIES.—CONTINUED.

YEAR.	FUEL AND LIGHTING			METALS AND IMPLEMENTS.								
	Coal, Anth.	Petroleum, crude.	Petroleum, refined.	Barb wire.	Hammers.	Lead, pig.	Nails.	Pig iron.	Planes.	Saws.	Shovels.	Steel rails.
1890	103.5	95.4	112.9	141.2	96.9	115.5	125.2	137.0	107.4	112.7	100.1	121.9
1900	97.1	148.5	131.6	134.4	115.9	116.8	123.1	141.5	107.0	98.6	115.9	123.9
1905	125.1	152.1	111.2	94.3	129.0	125.7	99.9	118.7	115.7	98.6	96.9	107.4
1906	134.8	175.5	117.4	96.1	129.0	154.8	105.7	141.8	129.3	101.3	96.9	107.4
1907	121.9	190.5	127.0	104.3	129.0	144.9	113.3	165.8	115.7	101.3	99.7	107.4
1908	124.3	195.6	133.9	103.8	129.0	110.8	108.7	123.9	115.7	101.3	93.4	107.4
1909	124.8	182.7	128.7	93.4	129.0	112.6	102.5	126.3	115.7	101.3	96.9	107.4
1910	124.7	147.7	118.6	84.4	129.8	117.6	100.9	124.8	125.4	101.3	98.4	107.4
1911	124.7	142.8	112.9	86.3	121.8	116.8	93.5	114.0	116.5	101.3	94.7	107.4
1912	129.3	173.0	127.9	84.5	121.8	116.3	93.5	115.7	116.5	101.3	94.7	107.4

YEAR.	METALS AND IMPLEMENTS.				LUMBER AND BUILDING MATERIALS.							
	Tin, pig.	Trowels.	Vises.	Zinc, sheet.	Brick.	Cement.	Doors.	Lime.	Linseed oil.	Maple.	Oak, white.	Pine, yellow.
1890	115.5	100.0	106.1	114.0	118.0	......	125.8	117.5	135.8	100.0	101.2	112.4
1900	163.7	100.0	109.4	114.8	94.4	106.1	145.5	82.0	135.7	103.8	109.1	112.2
1905	170.3	100.0	106.1	128.5	143.7	71.5	163.2	106.9	161.1	115.1	126.5	134.9
1906	213.6	100.0	115.9	135.0	153.7	78.9	153.5	113.7	89.5	117.0	134.7	158.9
1907	211.1	100.0	147.4	140.9	110.7	82.4	157.5	113.9	95.7	121.7	147.5	165.2
1908	160.2	100.0	147.4	123.1	91.8	73.1	161.3	125.4	96.5	119.3	131.7	165.2
1909	161.1	100.0	155.2	125.1	114.8	70.7	164.2	125.4	127.9	117.0	129.4	178.9
1910	186.3	100.0	151.3	132.2	102.8	72.5	154.8	125.4	186.7	120.0	144.9	166.8
1911	232.8	102.9	147.4	132.7	105.9	73.2	148.3	133.0	193.9	129.5	146.1	165.7
1912	252.0	102.9	139.6	149.2	121.5	65.9	189.9	130.2	148.3	137.5	150.2	179.5

YEAR.	LUMBER AND BUILDING MATERIALS.							DRUGS AND CHEMICALS.				
	Poplar.	Putty.	Shingles.	Spruce.	Tar.	Turpentine.	Window glass.	Alcohol, grain.	Alum.	Glycerin.	Quinine.	Sulphuric acid.
1890	97.2	110.8	118.7	113.5	122.4	122.0	103.6	92.5	109.0	126.3	133.1	98.9
1900	120.3	120.3	101.0	121.1	118.1	142.7	125.5	106.5	104.8	108.3	135.2	134.8
1905	153.7	69.0	96.6	149.3	145.9	187.7	128.5	108.3	104.8	88.5	85.4	139.3
1906	162.5	75.3	114.9	178.0	162.5	138.9	115.7	110.0	104.8	80.7	67.4	112.4
1907	185.2	75.9	149.8	167.3	193.3	189.8	130.8	112.6	104.8	98.9	72.2	112.4
1908	185.8	75.9	125.4	144.9	132.8	135.6	99.7	117.7	104.8	106.6	63.7	114.6
1909	183.7	75.9	115.8	176.0	135.9	146.8	107.8	116.8	104.8	121.5	57.2	112.4
1910	196.1	72.8	123.8	171.4	187.1	204.3	136.2	113.9	104.8	153.1	56.9	112.4
1911	196.4	72.8	127.9	169.2	176.4	203.1	104.7	113.1	104.8	162.2	56.9	112.4
1912	196.1	72.8	123.5	187.9	166.0	140.7	104.1	114.7	104.8	131.7	71.8	112.4

YEAR.	HOUSEFURNISHING GOODS.						MISCELLANEOUS.					
	Earthenw're plates.	Chairs.	Tables.	Tumblers.	Kniv's and forks.	Wooden enware.	Cott'n-seed oil.	Malt.	Rope.	Soap.	Starch.	Tobacco, plug.
1890	108.0	113.0	103.9	101.4	127.9	122.5	113.2	106.7	120.0	104.4	106.6	102.2
1900	106.6	129.1	108.1	101.4	94.9	107.0	116.8	98.0	141.3	107.7	97.7	111.9
1905	105.6	129.1	108.1	84.5	110.4	107.6	88.6	87.5	127.9	114.2	94.5	123.7
1906	106.6	148.3	114.3	84.5	99.8	107.6	118.7	92.1	134.0	114.2	105.5	122.0
1907	106.6	161.4	124.7	84.5	107.0	118.8	160.0	147.2	138.1	117.9	116.1	118.6
1908	104.0	152.0	124.7	74.6	89.4	122.5	134.4	132.7	108.7	123.0	124.4	118.6
1909	104.1	145.3	124.7	75.6	82.5	122.5	144.5	111.9	90.0	183.1	123.3	118.6
1910	104.8	145.3	138.6	67.6	82.5	119.7	196.1	126.1	94.1	171.4	113.1	118.6
1911	104.8	145.3	145.5	62.0	82.5	122.5	153.0	152.5	93.3	148.7	93.4	111.1
1912	104.8	153.3	157.9	62.0	87.3	118.8	151.3	108.9	95.3	131.5	107.8	111.1

SUMMARY OF RELATIVE PRICES OF COMMODITIES, 1900 TO 1912, BY GROUPS.
Average price for 1890–1899—100.

YEAR.	Farm prod'cts.	Food, etc.	Cloths and clothing	Fuel and lighting	Metals and implements.	Lumber and building material	Drugs and chemicals.	Housefurnishing goods.	Miscellaneous.	All commodities.
1900	109.5	104.2	101.0	120.9	120.5	105.7	115.7	106.1	108.3	110.5
1901	116.9	105.9	102.0	119.5	111.9	116.7	115.2	110.9	107.4	108.5
1902	130.5	111.3	107.1	134.3	117.2	118.8	114.2	112.2	114.1	112.9
1903	118.8	107.1	106.6	149.3	117.6	121.4	112.2	113.0	113.6	113.6
1904	126.2	107.2	109.8	132.6	109.6	122.7	110.0	111.7	111.7	113.0
1905	124.9	108.7	112.0	128.8	122.6	127.8	109.1	109.1	112.8	115.9
1906	123.6	112.6	120.0	129.5	135.2	140.1	101.2	111.0	121.1	122.4
1907	137.1	117.8	126.7	135.0	143.4	146.9	109.6	118.5	127.1	129.5
1908	133.1	120.6	116.9	150.8	125.4	133.1	110.4	114.0	119.9	122.8
1909	153.1	124.7	110.6	129.3	124.8	134.4	112.4	111.7	125.9	126.5
1910	164.6	128.7	124.7	125.4	128.5	153.2	117.0	111.6	133.1	131.6
1911	162.0	131.3	119.6	122.4	119.4	151.9	120.3	111.1	131.2	129.3
1912	171.3	139.5	120.7	133.9	126.1	148.2	122.9	118.7	133.2	133.6

RETAIL PRICES OF FOOD, COAL AND GAS.

Investigation by the federal bureau of labor showed that the cost of living in the United States in June, 1913, was approximately 60 per cent higher than the average between 1890 and 1900; more than 3 per cent higher than it was in 1912 and nearly 15 per cent higher than it was in 1911. Fifteen articles of food, which represent approximately two-thirds of the expenditure for food by the average workingman's family, showed the following percentages of increase in price June 15, 1913, as compared with the average price for the ten year period 1890-1899:

Article.	Pct. incr.	Article.	Pct. incr.
Bacon, smoked	128.5	Cornmeal	67.3
Pork chops	111.0	Potatoes, Irish	44.4
Round steak	102.5	Butter, creamery	41.8
Ham, smoked	84.0	Eggs, fresh	40.8
Hens	76.8	Milk, fresh	38.4
Rib roast	75.0	Flour, wheat	28.6
Sirloin steak	75.2	Sugar, granulated	*8.0
Lard, pure	66.5	*Decrease.	

The following table shows the percentage of increase in the prices of certain articles of food June 15, 1913, as compared with the prices June 15, 1912:

Article.	Pct. incr.	Article.	Pct. incr.
Bacon, smoked	16.2	Eggs, fresh	11.7
Ham, smoked	14.1	Round steak	10.1
Pork chops	13.4	Sirloin steak	9.8
Hens	11.8	Lard, pure	7.2

Article.	Pct. incr.	Article.	Pct. incr.
Rib roast	6.8	Sugar, granulated	*15.2
Butter, creamery	5.8	Flour, wheat	*7.7
Milk, fresh	4.1	Cornmeal	*3.9
Potatoes, Irish	*31.9	*Decrease.	

RELATIVE RETAIL PRICES OF FOOD.

The relative price, or index number, as it is technically called, of any article is the per cent which the price of that article at any certain date is of the price of the same article at a date or period which has been selected as the base or standard. The base selected for the compilation of retail prices of food is the average price for the ten year period 1890 to 1899. The average price for a number of years more nearly represents normal conditions than does the price for a single year, because of unusual conditions which may prevail in any one year. In the first section of the following table is shown for each of the five geographical divisions and for the United States as a whole the simple average of the relative prices of the fifteen articles of food specified in the foregoing tables. In computing the relative prices shown in the second section of the table the relative price of each of the fifteen articles was weighted according to the average consumption in workingmen's families in the particular geographical division or in the United States as a whole. The divisions are indicated by letters: N. A., North Atlantic; S. A., South Atlantic; N. C., North Central; S. C., South Central; W., Western; U. S., United States. The average price for 1890-1899 equals 100.

Year. or month.	Simple average of relative prices.						Relative prices, weighted according to the average consumption.					
	N. A.	S. A.	N. C.	S. C.	W.	U. S.	N. A.	S. A.	N. C.	S. C.	W.	U. S.
1890	101.7	100.4	102.0	100.6	105.0	102.0	101.9	100.6	101.7	100.9	105.2	101.9
1891	102.7	101.8	104.5	102.3	107.6	103.6	102.1	101.6	104.4	102.8	106.9	103.4
1892	101.7	101.3	101.8	99.9	104.0	101.7	101.8	101.2	101.9	100.1	103.4	101.6
1893	104.8	102.5	106.4	104.2	103.0	104.6	104.4	102.7	106.2	104.2	102.1	104.1
1894	99.4	99.6	100.0	100.3	98.1	99.5	99.2	99.6	99.6	100.4	98.0	99.2
1895	97.2	98.2	97.0	97.8	96.0	97.2	97.2	97.8	97.1	97.9	96.6	97.1
1896	95.7	97.1	93.9	95.4	94.1	94.9	95.9	97.3	94.0	95.7	94.2	95.2
1897	97.3	97.3	95.8	96.6	94.6	96.4	97.4	97.4	96.1	96.9	94.9	96.7
1898	100.3	99.7	99.3	100.4	96.7	99.4	100.2	99.7	99.5	99.9	98.0	99.7
1899	99.7	102.3	99.4	101.8	100.2	100.5	100.0	102.0	99.6	101.3	101.8	100.8
1900	103.0	104.7	102.5	102.2	100.7	102.9	103.0	104.4	102.5	102.1	102.2	103.0
1901	108.9	110.3	110.6	110.5	104.6	109.5	108.0	109.7	109.5	109.7	104.2	108.5
1902	116.3	116.7	117.4	119.3	111.9	116.5	114.0	115.6	115.4	118.7	110.1	114.6
1903	116.3	115.6	117.3	121.4	112.4	116.9	113.7	114.6	115.5	120.3	109.9	114.7
1904	117.6	115.8	118.1	122.2	114.8	118.3	115.5	114.9	116.2	121.1	111.1	115.2
1905	116.8	116.3	118.1	122.4	115.4	118.3	115.0	115.7	116.3	121.3	111.8	116.4
1906	121.4	120.8	122.3	125.8	118.9	122.4	119.1	120.0	120.6	125.0	116.0	120.3
1907	126.4	126.4	127.3	131.7	126.5	128.0	123.9	125.9	126.0	130.9	121.8	125.9
1908	129.2	131.0	133.1	138.8	128.4	132.5	126.5	129.8	131.5	137.5	123.9	130.1
1909	134.7	139.2	141.4	148.3	137.4	140.3	131.2	137.8	139.1	147.1	131.2	137.2
1910	140.3	149.8	149.7	157.8	146.3	148.5	135.2	148.4	147.0	158.7	138.8	144.1
1911	139.3	145.2	146.9	153.6	145.9	146.9	134.0	142.9	144.4	157.0	139.1	143.0
1912	151.4	155.4	159.8	166.9	151.0	157.9	148.7	163.3	157.6	165.3	145.9	154.3
1913—January	153.6	157.3	160.4	169.1	154.3	159.5	151.9	156.9	159.9	168.8	151.1	157.9
February	152.2	156.0	160.2	166.7	151.6	157.8	150.0	154.4	159.4	166.2	148.0	155.8
March	153.3	156.2	163.3	168.0	151.0	159.4	150.4	155.2	162.2	167.5	147.8	158.7
April	156.1	160.2	165.9	171.5	151.6	161.2	152.8	159.0	164.2	170.8	146.2	158.9
May	156.1	158.6	164.6	171.7	152.8	161.7	151.1	156.8	161.2	170.3	146.3	157.2
June	158.8	162.0	165.9	173.9	155.5	164.2	153.4	158.9	162.2	. 148.7	159.2	

Considering prices in the United States as a whole, the simple average of the relative prices for fifteen principal articles of food shows the following per cent advance:
Jan. 15, 1913, compared with Jan. 15, 1912........3.8
Feb. 15, 1913, compared with Feb. 15, 1912........3.3
March 15, 1913, compared with March 15, 1912....6.0
April 15, 1913, compared with April 15, 1912.....2.9

When the relative prices are weighted according to the average consumption of the various articles of food in workingmen's families the changes in prices within the year were as follows: Pct. adv.
Jan. 15, 1913, compared with Jan. 15, 1912.........2.9
Feb. 15, 1913, compared with Feb. 15, 1912.........3.2
March 15, 1913, compared with March 15, 1912....6.2
April 15, 1913, compared with April 15, 1912......4.1

RELATIVE PRICE OF FOOD BY ARTICLES.
(Average price for 1890-1900=100.)

Year or month.	Sirloin steak.	Round steak.	Rib roast.	Pork chops.	Bacon, smkd.	Ham, smkd.	Lard, pure.	Hens.	Wheat flour.	Corn meal.	Eggs, str.fr.	Butter, cr'mry.	Pota- toes.	Sugar, gran.	Milk, fresh.
1890	99.3	97.6	98.7	96.5	96.5	98.3	98.5	102.8	110.2	101.3	100.3	99.2	109.0	120.8	100.4
1891	98.7	98.0	99.6	98.8	97.2	99.5	100.0	104.8	112.4	111.5	105.6	105.7	117.1	103.1	100.5
1892	99.5	98.0	99.6	101.1	99.9	101.5	104.4	104.2	104.0	107.7	105.3	106.8	95.4	96.9	100.5
1893	99.4	98.5	98.4	105.0	108.9	107.1	119.2	104.3	95.1	104.0	105.5	106.6	111.8	102.6	100.5
1894	98.1	97.4	97.9	100.9	102.6	101.7	106.4	98.2	85.3	104.4	97.4	102.0	101.8	95.2	100.3
1895	98.7	98.2	97.9	99.7	98.7	98.9	89.8	97.3	89.6	101.0	98.8	97.4	90.6	91.8	100.4
1896	99.8	100.5	99.4	97.8	96.3	96.5	92.1	96.1	94.2	92.8	90.3	93.1	73.8	96.2	100.1
1897	99.6	101.8	100.1	97.5	97.0	98.5	89.0	92.3	104.7	91.3	94.0	93.7	92.6	94.3	100.0
1898	102.1	102.8	102.2	99.7	100.2	97.2	93.5	96.8	106.9	92.9	97.9	95.3	103.9	99.7	99.8

Year or month.	Sirloin steak.	Round steak.	Rib roast.	Pork chops.	Bacon, smkd.	Ham, smkd.	Lard, pure	Hens.	Wheat flour.	Corn meal.	Eggs, str.fr.	Butter, cr'm'y.	Pota- toes.	Sugar, gran.	Milk, fresh.
1899	104.4	107.0	106.1	103.2	102.9	100.5	97.1	103.4	94.8	92.9	101.6	97.6	98.8	99.6	98.8
1900	107.1	109.8	109.3	108.9	110.3	106.9	104.9	98.6	94.6	95.6	89.1	101.2	92.8	103.9	100.0
1901	109.4	114.0	112.7	119.0	121.3	111.1	119.6	105.0	94.9	107.6	107.7	103.0	114.0	102.1	101.4
1902	114.6	122.3	118.6	127.8	135.9	120.6	135.6	113.6	95.6	123.9	119.4	109.8	116.7	92.8	104.1
1903	110.6	116.8	117.0	126.1	140.4	122.1	126.0	119.3	102.1	122.1	110.2	114.7	93.7	107.4
1904	111.0	120.8	117.0	123.1	138.5	119.4	116.3	120.6	118.3	122.9	131.1	108.1	119.0	100.4	107.4
1905	110.6	120.0	116.2	125.0	139.3	119.4	115.8	123.6	118.6	123.5	131.3	111.4	109.3	101.8	108.1
1906	114.2	124.4	120.5	135.9	150.5	127.8	127.3	128.0	108.3	124.5	134.2	118.3	114.6	97.2	110.0
1907	116.7	128.4	123.0	140.9	157.7	131.0	133.5	131.3	118.2	133.5	138.2	127.3	122.2	98.7	118.9
1908	119.9	135.5	126.7	144.6	163.2	133.8	134.3	134.9	127.1	142.6	142.8	127.9	129.8	101.3	123.2
1909	126.1	140.6	132.2	158.7	176.4	142.1	150.5	145.7	138.1	145.7	154.7	134.3	133.4	100.0	126.2
1910	134.0	149.9	137.7	178.3	204.4	159.4	172.9	155.9	135.9	147.9	158.2	139.9	119.5	102.5	131.6
1911	134.9	152.6	138.6	170.3	197.2	155.9	145.3	151.6	127.9	147.2	150.2	131.3	157.0	111.1	132.7
1912	153.0	174.3	155.5	187.8	199.0	160.4	154.3	158.3	132.9	160.3	162.5	147.4	168.2	108.8	135.6
1913—January	160.8	183.1	161.6	189.0	210.8	167.4	161.7	162.4	126.9	156.0	184.8	162.7	124.8	100.7	140.5
February	160.8	184.5	162.7	189.4	211.6	169.1	162.3	166.6	127.4	156.0	163.5	123.6	95.1	140.2
March	166.2	191.2	168.1	203.6	217.2	174.0	164.5	172.8	127.2	155.2	131.3	165.2	120.5	93.9	139.5
April	172.7	199.1	173.4	218.0	222.9	178.1	166.8	179.7	127.2	155.7	126.4	161.3	119.2	92.7	139.3
May	173.6	199.7	173.5	211.9	224.5	179.8	166.7	179.3	127.8	156.0	132.5	144.0	125.8	92.3	138.6
June	175.2	202.5	175.0	211.0	228.5	184.0	166.5	176.8	128.6	157.3	140.8	141.3	144.4	82.0	138.4

COAL.

Relative retail prices of coal in ton lots, for household use, on April 15, 1907 to 1913, by geographical divisions. (Price on April 15, 1907=100.):

PENNSYLVANIA ANTHRACITE, WHITE ASH, STOVE.						
Geographical division.	Ap.15, 1908.	Ap.15, 1909.	Ap.15, 1910.	Ap.15, 1911.	Ap.15, 1912.	Ap.15, 1913.
North Atlantic	100.7	101.0	98.3	99.8	110.8	104.9
South Atlantic	102.4	102.8	101.4	103.3	110.2	113.1
North Central	99.6	100.2	100.5	101.2	105.6	106.5
South Central	101.3	101.7	101.7	102.0	103.9	112.2
Western	95.0	95.0	95.0	95.0	95.0	90.0
PENNSYLVANIA ANTHRACITE, WHITE ASH, CHESTNUT.						
North Atlantic	100.7	101.0	98.3	101.6	113.5	107.4
South Atlantic	102.5	102.8	101.9	105.7	112.6	115.4
North Central	99.7	100.0	100.3	102.6	107.5	109.0
South Central	101.0	99.0	100.3	101.5	103.9	113.0
BITUMINOUS.						
North Atlantic	100.0	100.0	100.0	100.0	101.5	102.9
South Atlantic	103.3	96.7	96.7	110.0	110.0	110.0
North Central	100.9	98.9	104.8	104.4	107.0	107.1
South Central	99.8	94.3	98.6	100.7	100.9	110.6
Western	107.2	105.1	105.1	107.2	104.7	104.6

The actual prices of coal per ton in some of the principal cities of the United States on April 15, 1913, were as follows:

Pennsylvania anthracite, stove size—Boston, $7.25; Buffalo, $6 to $6.30; Chicago, $7.50; Cincinnati, $7.50 to $8; Cleveland, $7.25 to $7.50; Detroit, $7.25 to $8; Indianapolis, $8 to $9; Kansas City, Mo., $11 to $11.50; Louisville, $9; Milwaukee, $7.25 to $7.50; Minneapolis, $8.75; New Orleans, $10; New York, $6.25 to $6.75; Omaha, Neb., $11 to $12; Philadelphia, $6.50 to $6.75; Pittsburgh, $7.25 to $8.25; St. Louis, $7.25 to $7.50; San Francisco, $9.50; Washington, D. C., $7.

Pennsylvania anthracite, chestnut—Boston, $7.50; Buffalo, $6.25 to $6.55; Chicago, $7.75; Cincinnati, $7.75 to $8; Cleveland, $7.50 to $7.75; Detroit, $7.50 to $8.25; Indianapolis, $8.25 to $9.25; Kansas City, Mo., $9; Louisville, $9; Milwaukee, $7.50 to $7.75; Minneapolis, $9; New Orleans, $10.50; New York, $6.25 to $7; Omaha, $11 to $12; Philadelphia, $6.75 to $7; Pittsburgh, $7.25 to $8.25; St. Louis, $7.50 to $8; San Francisco (Colorado or New Mexico anthracite), $16 to $17; Washington, D. C., $7.15.

Bituminous—Chicago, $4.50 to $5.25; Cincinnati, $3.50 to $3.75; Cleveland, $3.75 to $4.75; Detroit, $4.50 to $4.75; Indianapolis, $2.50 to $6; Kansas City, Mo., $4 to $4.75; Louisville, $4.15 to $4.25; Milwaukee, $4.25 to $6; Minneapolis, $5.25 to $5.80; New Orleans (per barrel of 200 pounds), $5.50 to $7; New York, $6.25 to $7; Omaha, $4.75 to $7; Pittsburgh (1,900 pounds), $2 to $3.25; St. Louis, $2.50 to $3.75; San Francisco, $12.

Note—The tons referred to in the foregoing are of 2,000 pounds except as to Philadelphia, Pittsburgh and Washington, where the tons are of 2,240 pounds.

GAS.

Three companies reported a change of price in gas between Oct. 15, 1912, and April 15, 1913. In New Haven, Conn., the price was reduced from 95 cents to 90 cents; Company C in New York reduced its price from 85 cents to 80 cents and in Washington, D. C., Company A increased its price from 85 cents to $1.

PRICE PER 1,000 FEET MANUFACTURED GAS.

	Oct. 15. 1912.	Apr. 15. 1913.
North Atlantic division:		
Boston, Mass.—Company A	$0.80	$0.80
Company C	.80	*
Buffalo, N. Y	1.00	1.00
Fall River, Mass	.80	.80
Manchester, N. H	1.10	1.10
Newark, N. J	1.00	1.00
New Haven, Conn	.95	.90
New York. N. Y.—Company A	.80	.80
Company B	.80	.80
Company C	.85	.80
Company D	1.00	1.00
Company E	.80	.80
Company F	.80	.80
Company G	.80	.80
Company H	.80	.80
Company I	.80	.80
Company J	.80	.80
Philadelphia, Pa.—Company A	1.00	1.00
Company B	1.00	1.00
Pittsburgh, Pa.—Company A	1.00	1.00
Company B	1.00	1.00
Providence, R. I	.85	.85
Scranton, Pa.—Company A	.95	.95
Company B	1.20	1.20
South Atlantic division:		
Atlanta, Ga	1.00	1.00
Baltimore, Md	.90	.90
Charleston, S. C	1.00	*
Jacksonville, Fla	1.20	1.20
Richmond, Va	.90	.90
Washington, D. C.—Company A	.85	1.00
Company B	.85	.85
North central division:		
Chicago, Ill	.80	.80
Cleveland, O	.80	.80
Detroit, Mich.—Company A	.75	.75
Company B	†.75	†.75
Indianapolis, Ind.—Company A	.60	.60
Company B	.60	.60
Milwaukee, Wis	.75	.75
Minneapolis, Minn.—Company A	.85	.85
Company B	1.19	1.19
Omaha, Neb	1.15	1.15
St. Louis, Mo	.80	.80
South central division:		
Birmingham, Ala	1.00	1.00
Louisville, Ky.:		
For illuminating purposes	1.00	1.00
For cooking and heating purposes	.75	.75
Memphis, Tenn	1.00	1.00
New Orleans, La	1.10	1.10
Western division:		
Denver, Col	.85	.85
Los Angeles, Cal.—Company A	.75	.75
Company B	.75	.75
Company C	.75	.75
Portland, Ore	.95	.95

	Oct. 15.	Apr. 15.
Salt Lake City, Utah:‡	1912.	1913.
For illuminating purposes.........	§1.30	$1.30
For cooking and heating purposes..	¶.90	¶.90
San Francisco, Cal.....................	.75	.75
Seattle, Wash.........................	1.00	1.00

NATURAL GAS.

North Atlantic division:

Buffalo, N. Y.....................	**.30	**.30
Pittsburgh, Pa.—Company C.........	.27½	.27½
Company D...........................	.30	.30
Company E...........................	.27½	.27½
Company F...........................	.27½	.27½
Company G...........................	.27½	.27½
Company H...........................	.27½	.27½

	Oct. 15.	Apr. 15.
North central division:	1912.	1913.
Cincinnati, O........................	.30	.30
Cleveland, O.........................	.30	.30
Kansas City, Mo.....................	.27	.27
South central division:		
Dallas, Tex..........................	.45	.45
Little Rock, Ark....................	.40	.40

*No quotation. †Rate for one section of Detroit served by this company, 80 cents. ‡Combination light and fuel rate, April, 1913, 94½ cents. §Rate entered is for first 2,000 cubic feet; all over 2,000 cubic feet, $1.20. ¶Rate entered is for first 2,000 cubic feet; next 20,000 cubic feet, 80 cents; all over 22,000 cubic feet, 70 cents. **For cooking and heating purposes only.

AMERICAN INHERITANCE TAX LAWS.

	Collateral. Rates.		Direct. Rates,Exemp-	
State.	Per cent.	Exemption.	Per cent.	tion.
Arkansas	5	....	...	......
California	1½-15	$500-$2,000	1-3	¹$4,000
Colorado	3-6	500	2	10,000
Connecticut	3	10,000	1-2	10,000
Delaware²	5	500	...	......
Idaho	1½-15	500-2,000	1-3	4,000
Illinois	2-6	500-2,000	1	20,000
Indiana	1-15	100-500	1-15	10,000
Iowa	5	1,000	...	......
Kentucky	5	500	...	......
Louisiana³	5	....	2	10,000
Maine	4	500	...	......
Maryland	2½	500	...	......
Massachusetts	3-5	1,000	1-2	10,000
Michigan	5	100	¹1	2,000
Minnesota	1½-5	10,000	1½-5	10,000
Missouri	5	....	...	......
Montana	5	500	¹1	7,500
Nebraska	2-6	500-2,000	1	10,000
New Hampshire..	5	....	...	......
New Jersey........	5	500	...	......
New York..........	5	500	1	10,000
North Carolina....1½-15		2,000	2-4	2,000
North Dakota......	2	25,000	...	......
Ohio	5	200	...	......
Oklahoma	1-5	100-500	1	⁴5,000
Oregon	2-6	500-2,000	1	⁵5,000
Pennsylvania	5	250	...	......
South Dakota......	2-10	100-500	1	5,000
Tennessee	5	250	...	......
Texas	2-12	500-2,000	...	......
Utah	5	10,000	5	10,000
Vermont	6	....	...	......
Virginia	5	....	...	......
Washington	3-12	....	¹1	10,000
West Virginia......	3-7½	....	1	20,000
Wisconsin 1½-15		100-500	1-3	¹2,000
Wyoming	5	500	2	⁶10,000

¹Widows and (except in Wisconsin) minor children taxable only on the excess above $10,000 received by each. ²Tax payable only by strangers in blood. ³Tax not payable when the property bore its just proportion of taxes prior to the owner's death. ⁴Applies to personal property only. ⁵Decedents' estates of less than $10,000 are also exempt. ⁶For the surviving husband or wife and children, if residents of Wyoming, $25,000. ⁷For widows, $10,000.

Note—The Oklahoma rates are subject to increase when the inheritance exceeds a certain amount in the various classes.

INHERITANCE TAX IN INDIANA.

Under the inheritance tax law passed by the legislature of Indiana in 1913 rates are imposed on all sums not in excess of $25,000, ranging from 1 per cent in the case of direct or lineal descendants to 5 per cent in the case of remote relatives, strangers or corporations. When the amount is more than $25,000 and less than $50,000 the rate varies from 1½ per cent to 7½ per cent; when more than $50,000 and less than $100,000, from 2 per cent to 10 per cent; when more than $100,000 and less than $500,000, from 2½ per cent to 12½ per cent; on all sums of $500,000 or more the rate varies from 3 per cent to 15 per cent. An exemption of $10,000 is allowed to a widow and $2,000 to each

other direct or lineal descendant or ancestor. Exemptions in the case of relatives more remote or strangers range from $100 to $500.

INHERITANCE TAXES COLLECTED.

State.	1911.	1912.	Per capita.
Arizona*	....	$1,212.13	$ .0059
Arkansas	$18,284.30	23,664.40	.0150
California	1,506,993.33	1,115,713.78	.4690
Colorado	206,573.96	206,573.96	.2585
Connecticut	1,125,951.17	1,080,482.20	.9693
Delaware	11,023.23	8,351.66	.0414
Georgia†	....	....	......
Idaho	4,224.62	4,224.62	.0130
Illinois	1,984,116.06	1,984,116.06	.3519
Indiana†	....	....	......
Iowa	240,964.26	249,845.20	.1123
Kansas	121,566.54	265,404.06	.1570
Kentucky	106,291.35	101,577.28	.0443
Louisiana	95,099.59	195,068.97	.1177
Maine	147,263.95	276,052.02	.3719
Maryland	310,943.21	289,605.89	.2236
Massachusetts	2,213,835.21	2,210,960.20	.6563
Michigan	504,978.84	366,437.57	.1304
Minnesota	487,681.96	678,512.99	.3269
Missouri	480,783.06	479,517.35	.1456
Montana	14,009.12	8,959.40	.0233
Nebraska‡	....	....	......
Nevada†	....	....	......
New Hampshire......	114,685.11	175,249.66	.4070
New Jersey..........	745,777.16	903,190.89	.3560
New York............	8,157,343.66	12,163,188.84	1.3335
North Carolina......	9,822.32	5,264.65	.0024
North Dakota........	303.85	12,486.98	.0216
Ohio	30,743.39	80,881.59	.0170
Oklahoma	6,079.53	12,528.31	.0076
Oregon	67,508.23	67,508.23	.1003
Pennsylvania	1,587,665.83	2,064,598.65	.2694
South Dakota........	2,242.53	16,152.97	.0277
Tennessee	134,525.80	164,961.79	.0755
Texas	27,007.54	47,579.03	.0122
Utah	242,800.31	1,047,569.96	2.8059
Vermont	71,982.95	92,716.71	.2605
Virginia	22,331.47	43,763.13	.0212
Washington	120,920.83	186,230.98	.1631
West Virginia.......	107,510.69	168,233.37	.1378
Wisconsin	848,033.78	783,528.90	.3357
Wyoming	....	316.45	.0022
Total 21,886,971.74		27,572,250.83	

*Law enacted in 1912. †Law enacted in 1913. ‡The inheritance tax law of Nebraska is not a source of state revenue. The revenue inures to the various counties and is used exclusively to improve the public highways in the county where decedent had resided or where the property was located.

There are only seven states now without inheritance tax laws, namely, Alabama, Florida, Kansas, Mississippi, New Mexico, Rhode Island and South Carolina. The latest states to adopt this progressive method of collecting revenue were Arizona in 1912 and Nevada, Georgia and Indiana in 1913.

In their message to the legislatures in 1913 the governors of Alabama, Florida and New Mexico advised the enactment of the inheritance tax in these states.

Pursuant to the recommendation of Gov. Hodges the inheritance law was repealed in Kansas in April, 1913.

MERCHANT MARINE OF THE UNITED STATES.

[From the reports of the bureau of navigation.]

YEAR.	IN FOREIGN TRADE.		IN COASTWISE TRADE.		WHALE FISHERIES.		COD AND MACK-EREL FISH-ERIES.	Total.	Annual inc. (+) or dec.(−)
	Steam.	Total.	Steam.	Total.	Steam.	Total.			
	Tons.	Tons.	Tons.	Tons.	Tons.	Tons.	Tons.	Tons.	Per cent.
1860	97,296	2,379,396	770,641	2,644,867	......	166,841	162,764	5,353,868	+ 4.06
1870	192,544	1,448,846	862,551	2,638,247	......	67,954	91,460	4,246,507	+ 2.41
1880	146,604	1,314,402	1,064,954	2,637,686	......	38,408	77,538	4,068,034	− 2.43
1890	192,705	928,062	1,661,458	3,409,435	4,925	18,635	68,967	4,424,497	+ 2.71
1900	337,356	816,795	2,289,825	4,286,516	3,986	9,899	51,629	5,164,855	+ 6.18
1904	549,958	888,628	3,041,262	5,355,164	4,218	10,140	57,603	6,291,535	+ 3.25
1905	596,594	913,750	3,140,314	5,441,688	4,626	10,763	60,342	6,456,543	+ 2.62
1906	586,749	928,466	3,384,002	5,674,044	4,596	11,020	61,439	6,674,969	+ 3.38
1907	598,155	861,466	3,664,210	6,010,001	3,970	9,680	57,047	6,938,784	+ 3.96
1908	595,147	930,413	4,099,045	6,371,862	3,560	9,655	53,515	7,365,445	+ 6.15
1909	575,226	878,523	4,157,557	6,451,642	3,300	8,952	50,308	7,388,755	+ 0.32
1910	533,468	782,517	4,330,896	6,668,966	3,599	9,308	47,291	7,508,082	+ 1.61
1911	582,186	863,485	4,505,567	6,720,313	3,544	9,176	45,806	7,638,790	+ 1.74
1912	616,053	923,225	4,543,276	6,737,046	3,653	8,876	45,036	7,714,183	+ 0.99

VESSELS BUILT IN THE UNITED STATES.

[From the reports of the bureau of navigation.]

YEAR.	New England coast.		On entire seaboard.		Mississippi and tribu-taries.		On great lakes.		Total.		Sail.		Steam.	
	No.	Tons.	No.	Tons.	No.	Tons.	No.	Tons.	No.	Tons.	No.	Tons.	No.	Tons.
1890	208	78,577	756	169,091	104	16,506	191	108,526	1,051	294,123	505	102,873	410	159,045
1900	199	72,179	1,107	249,006	215	14,173	125	130,611	1,447	393,790	504	116,460	422	202,528
1904	170	51,417	878	208,288	187	10,821	119	159,433	1,184	378,542	330	64,908	613	255,744
1905	192	119,377	823	230,716	178	6,477	101	93,123	1,102	330,316	310	79,418	640	197,702
1906	146	132,311	850	146,883	167	6,591	204	265,271	1,221	418,745	229	55,209	650	315,707
1907	106	44,428	815	219,753	165	7,284	177	244,291	1,157	471,352	147	24,907	674	365,405
1908	151	70,938	1,034	296,937	207	6,114	216	341,165	1,457	614,216	184	31,981	925	481,624
1909	130	27,337	866	181,748	207	5,940	174	100,402	1,247	238,000	141	28,950	821	148,208
1910	111	23,442	887	167,829	198	5,488	281	168,751	1,361	342,098	127	19,358	936	257,993
1911	94	23,653	1,004	190,612	202	6,398	216	94,157	1,422	291,162	82	10,092	969	227,231
1912	95	23,052	1,076	136,485	205	5,286	224	90,898	1,505	232,669	95	21,221	1,051	153,496

DISASTERS TO SHIPPING.

On and near the coasts and on the rivers of the United States and American vessels at sea and on the coasts of foreign countries.

YEAR.	Wrecks*	Lives lost.	Loss on vessels.	Loss on cargoes.	YEAR.	Wrecks*	Lives lost.	Loss on vessels.	Loss on cargoes.
1890	1,470	556	$7,653,490	$2,172,595	1902	1,359	581	$8,824,820	$2,309,355
1891	1,475	448	6,034,605	2,593,010	1903	1,172	351	6,820,790	1,601,520
1892	1,556	646	7,386,675	2,577,870	1904	1,182	1,454	7,011,775	1,722,210
1893	1,481	401	7,763,996	2,003,855	1905	1,209	267	8,187,500	2,263,795
1894	1,653	803	8,576,885	2,158,655	1906	1,328	499	10,089,610	2,245,305
1895	1,496	704	7,590,540	1,944,810	1907	1,670	624	13,709,915	3,052,110
1896	1,592	859	6,485,595	2,018,140	1908	1,841	374	9,555,825	2,152,155
1897	1,206	299	6,442,175	1,731,765	1909	1,317	403	9,491,635	3,830,825
1898	1,191	743	10,728,250	1,740,515	1910	1,493	463	11,058,840	2,565,580
1899	1,574	742	8,932,835	2,431,905	1911	1,227	262	9,505,905	1,694,630
1900	1,254	252	7,186,990	3,350,500	1912	1,447	195	8,213,375	1,941,010

*Total or partial.

WORLD'S SHIPS, RAILWAYS, TELEGRAPHS AND CABLES.

[Report of the bureau of statistics, Washington, D. C.]

Development by decades of carrying power, commerce and means of communication from 1800 to 1911.

YEAR.	Popu-lation.	COMMERCE.		VESSEL TONNAGE.			Rail-ways.	Tele-graphs	Cables
		Total.	Per capita.	Sail.	Steam.	Total.			
	Mil-lions.	Mil-lions of dollars	Dol-lars.	Thou-sand tons.	Thou-sand tons.	Thou-sand tons.	Thou-sand miles.	Thou-sand miles.	Thou-sand miles.
1800	640	1,479	2.31	4,026	......	4,026	......	......	......
1820	780	1,659	2.13	5,814	20	5,834	......	......	......
1830	847	1,981	2.34	7,100	111	7,211	0.2	......	......
1840	950	2,789	2.93	9,012	368	9,380	5.4	......	......
1850	1,075	4,049	3.76	11,470	864	12,334	24.0	5	1-40
1860	1,205	7,246	6.01	14,890	1,710	16,600	67.4	100	1½
1870	1,310	10,663	8.14	12,900	3,040	15,940	139.9	281	15
1880	1,439	14,761	10.26	14,400	5,880	20,280	224.9	440	49
1890	1,488	17,519	11.80	12,640	8,295	20,935	390.0	768	132
1900	1,500	20,105	13.33	8,119	13,856	21,975	500.0	1,180	200
1910	1,616	33,654	20.81	4,366	23,392	28,298	637.0	1,507	291
1911	1,680	35,389	21.71	4,083	24,978	29,061	666.0	1,556	318

AGRICULTURAL STATISTICS.
WHEAT CROP OF COUNTRIES NAMED (1906-1912).

COUNTRY.	1906.	1907.	1908.	1909.	1910.	1911.	1912.
	Bushels.	Bushels.	Bushels.	Bushels.	Bushels.	Bushels.	Bushels.
United States......................	735,261,000	634,087,000	664,602,000	683,350,000	635,121,000	621,338,000	730,267,000
Canada:							
New Brunswick..............	407,000	411,000	349,000	396,000	371,000	270,000	225,000
Ontario	22,109,000	18,019,000	18,057,000	16,262,000	17,805,000	19,232,000	13,538,000
Manitoba	61,250,000	39,688,000	50,269,000	52,705,000	41,159,000	60,275,000	58,359,000
Saskatchewan..............	37,040,000	27,692,000	34,742,000	85,197,000	81,139,000	97,655,000	93,849,000
Alberta........................	3,966,000	4,194,000	6,842,000	9,579,000	6,563,000	36,143,000	30,574,000
Other..........................	3,000,000	2,687,000	2,175,000	2,605,000	2,923,000	2,246,000	2,051,000
Total Canada..............	127,772,000	92,691,000	112,434,000	166,744,000	149,990,000	215,851,000	199,236,000
Mexico......	8,000,000	9,000,000	8,000,000	10,000,000	11,976,000	12,000,000	12,000,000
Total North America..........	871,033,000	735,778,000	785,836,000	860,094,000	797,087,000	849,189,000	941,503,000
Argentina.....................	134,981,000	155,993,000	192,489,000	136,162 000	131,010,000	145,981,000	166,190,000
Chile..........................	12,157,000	15,776,000	18,915,000	17,743,000	19,743,000	18,000,000	20,000,000
Uruguay.......................	4,606,000	6,867,000	7,430,000	8,595,000	7,750,000	6,009,000	8,757,000
Total South America	151,694,000	178,636,000	218,834,000	182,500,000	158,503,000	169,990,000	194,947,000
Austria-Hungary:							
Austria........................	58,255,000	52,369,000	62,129,000	58,468,000	57,589,000	58,890,000	69,712,000
Hungary proper..........	197,409,000	120,509,000	152,205,000	118,352,000	169,700,000	175,039,000	73,328,000
Croatia-Slavonia..........	10,351,000	10,179,000	13,220,000	11,662,000	11,434,000	15,210,000	11,314,000
Bosnia-Herzegovina..............	2,693,000	2,169,000	3,023,000	2,594,000	2,671,000	2,941,000	2,993,000
Total Austria-Hungary......	268,708,000	185,217,000	230,577,000	186,076,000	241,394,000	252,051,000	257,347,000
Belgium.......................	12,964,000	15,835,000	13,963,000	14,603,000	12,449,000	14,616,000	15,000,000
Bulgaria	89,109,000	23,545,000	36,486,000	32,671,000	42,217,000	48,000,000	45,000,000
Denmark......................	4,161,000	4,343,000	4,318,000	3,529,000	4,647,000	4,469,000	5,500,000
Finland........................	150,000	135,000	135,000	134,000	128,000	125,000	130,000
France.........................	324,919,000	376,999,000	317,765,000	356,193,000	257,667,000	315,444,000	334,871,000
Germany......................	144,754,000	127,843,000	138,442,000	138,000,000	141,884,000	149,411,000	160,224,000
Greece.........................	8,000,000	8,000,000	8,000,000	7,000,000	7,000,000	8,000,000	7,000,000
Italy...........................	176,464,000	177,543,000	152,236,000	189,959,000	153,168,000	192,335,000	165,720,000
Montenegro...................	200,000	200,000	200,000	200,000	200,000	200,000	200,000
Netherlands...................	4,942,000	5,325,000	5,121,000	4,158,000	4,371,000	5,648,000	4,500,000
Norway	303,000	230,000	353,000	312,000	294,000	271,000	332,000
Portugal.......................	9,000,000	6,000,000	5,000,000	8,000,000	9,000,000	11,850,000	7,500,000
Roumania.....................	113,867,000	42,257,000	54,813,000	56,751,000	110,761,000	90,886,000	88,924,000
Russia:							
Russia proper.............	344,765,000	340,416,000	383,016,000	586,819,000	552,067,000	346,372,000	....
Poland........................	21,152,000	18,175,000	21,182,000	21,194,000	22,757,000	24,129,000	....
Northern Caucasia.........	85,046,000	79,184,000	84,964,000	103,465,000	124,589,000	76,537,000	....
Total Russia (European).....	450,963,000	437,775,000	489,162,000	711,478,000	699,413,000	447,038,000	623,728,000
Servia.........................	13,211,000	8,375,000	11,495,000	13,392,000	12,000,000	13,000,000	14,000,000
Spain..........................	140,656,000	100,331,000	119,970,000	144,105,000	137,448,000	148,485,000	109,783,000
Sweden........................	6,650,000	5,953,000	6,754,000	6,978,000	7,450,000	7,915,000	7,852,000
Switzerland...................	4,000,000	4,000,000	3,527,000	3,568,000	2,756,000	3,524,000	3,000,000
Turkey (European)........	25,000,000	18,000,000	25,000,000	20,000,000	19,462,000	20,000,000	18,000,000
United kingdom: Great Britain—							
England......................	57,583,000	53,855,000	51,371,000	60,121,000	53,464,000	60,729,000	54,249,000
Scotland.....................	2,063,000	1,953,000	1,854,000	2,111,000	2,620,000	2,786,000	2,124,000
Wales........................	1,308,000	1,138,000	966,000	1,147,000	1,122,000	1,118,000	2,472,000
Ireland.......................	1,527,000	1,367,000	1,428,000	1,809,000	1,716,000	1,656,000	1,564,000
Total united kingdom........	62,481,000	58,313,000	55,629,000	65,188,000	58,322,000	66,289,000	59,409,000
Total Europe................	1,810,550,000	1,606,603,000	1,678,968,000	1,962,566,000	1,927,106,000	1,804,705,000	1,926,100,000
British India................	319,962,000	317,023,000	227,983,000	284,361,000	358,049,000	369,630,000	366,370,000
Cyprus........................	2,410,000	2,636,000	2,601,000	1,912,000	2,238,000	1,983,000	2,000,000
Japanese empire:							
Japan........................	20,282,000	22,795,000	22,587,000	22,966,000	24,487,000	25,645,000	26,514,000
Formosa.....................	178,000	200,000	200,000	200,000	200,000	200,000	200,000
Total Japanese empire.......	20,460,000	22,995,000	22,787,000	23,165,000	24,687,000	25,845,000	26,714,000
Persia.........................	16,000,000	16,000,000	16,000,000	16,000,000	16,000,000	16,000,000	16,000,000
Russia:							
Central Asia..............	11,486,000	27,085,000	21,416,000	26,429,000	24,003,000	20,579,000	....
Siberia	45,833,000	45,771,000	55,755,000	45,269,000	52,140,000	50,116,000	....
Transcaucasia	108,000	63,000	66,000	94,000	133,000	102,000	....
Total Russia (Asiatic)........	57,427,000	72,919,000	77,237,000	71,792,000	76,282,000	70,797,000	103,253,000
Turkey (Asiatic),...............	35,000,000	35,000,000	35,000,000	35,000,000	35,000,000	35,000,000	35,000,000
Total Asia....................	451,249,000	466,573,000	381,608,000	432,231,000	513,792,000	524,881,000	549,357,000
Algeria........................	34,323,000	31,261,000	30,000,000	34,769,000	35,722,000	35,874,000	27,507,000
Cape of Good Hope..........	2,000,000	2,000,000	1,916,000	....	....	....	....
Egypt..........................	25,000,000	25,000,000	25,000,000	30,000,000	32,623,000	38,046,000	32,000,000
Natal..........................	8,000	3,000	3,000	....	....	....	....
Anglo-Egyptian Sudan...........	542,000	500,000	500,000	....	....	....	....
Tunis..........................	4,906,000	6,314,000	2,838,000	6,430,000	5,512,000	8,635,000	4,225,000
Union of South Africa...........	....	....	....	2,500,000	2,500,000	2,500,000	2,500,000
Total Africa..................	66,779,000	65,078,000	60,257,000	73,699,000	76,357,000	85,055,000	66,232,000

WHEAT CROP OF COUNTRIES NAMED (1906-1912)—CONTINUED.

COUNTRY.	1906.	1907.	1908.	1909.	1910.	1911.	1912.
	Bushels.	Bushels.	Bushels.	Bushels.	Bushels.	Bushels.	Bushels.
Australia:							
Queensland....................	1,173.000	1,144.000	715.000	1,241.000	1,621.000	1,057,000	294,000
New South Wales............	21,391,000	22,506,000	9,444,000	15,971,000	29,431,000	28,793,000	25,879,000
Victoria........................	24,156,000	23,331,000	12,482,000	24,081,000	29,687,000	35,910,000	21,550,000
South Australia..............	20,778,000	18,917,000	19,739,000	20,009,000	25,936,000	25,112,000	20,994,000
Western Australia..........	2,381,000	2,845,000	3,918,000	2,538,000	5,779,000	6,083,000	4,496,000
Tasmania......................	801,000	672,000	665,000	723,000	819,000	1,156,000	681,000
Total commonwealth.........	70,680,000	68,515,000	46,063,000	64,563,000	93,263,000	98,109,000	73,894,000
New Zealand..................	7,013,000	5,782,000	5,743,000	9,049,000	9,008,000	8,535,000	7,490,000
Total Australasia............	77,693,000	74,297,000	51,806,000	73,612,000	102,271,000	106,644,000	81,384,000
Grand total...................	3,428,998,000	3,136,965,000	3,176,479,000	3,581,519,000	3,575,055,000	3,540,717,000	3,759,523,000

CORN CROP OF COUNTRIES NAMED (1906-1912).

COUNTRY.	1906.	1907.	1908.	1909.	1910.	1911.	1912.
	Bushels.	Bushels.	Bushels.	Bushels.	Bushels.	Bushels.	Bushels.
United States..................	2,927,416,000	2,592,320,000	2,668,651,000	2,552,190,000	2,886,260,000	2,531,488,000	3,124,746,000
Canada..........................	24,745,000	23,276,000	22,868,000	19,258,000	18,913,000	18,773,000	16,570,000
Mexico..........................	70,000,000	70,000,000	150,000,000	170,000,000	190,766,000	190,000,000	
Total North America.......	3,022,161,000	2,685,596,000	2,841,519,000	2,741,448,000	3,095,739,000	2,740,261,000	
Argentina.......................	194,912,000	71,768,000	136,055,000	177,155,000	175,187,000	27,675,000	295,849,000
Chile.............................	840,000	1,500,000	1,211,000	1,178,000	1,878,000	1,221,000	
Uruguay........................	3,236,000	5,359,000	6,000,000	6,671,000	6,509,000	3,643,000	
Total South America........	198,988,000	78,627,000	143,273,000	185,004,000	183,565,000	32,539,000	
Austria-Hungary:							
Austria.......................	18,177,000	16,599,000	15,170,000	16,102,000	17,388,000	11,856,000	15,053,000
Hungary proper.............	162,973,000	155,619,000	146,124,000	161,858,000	187,733,000	137,421,000	181,826,000
Croatia-Slavonia............	25,589,000	17,934,000	20,536,000	21,752,000	25,589,000	24,005,000	14,166,000
Bosnia-Herzegovina.........	8,936,000	6,468,000	8,821,000	10,972,000	10,051,000	8,416,000	8,555,000
Total Austria-Hungary.......	215,675,000	196,620,000	190,651,000	210,684,000	240,761,000	181,698,000	220,600,000
Bulgaria.........................	27,780,000	14,080,000	20,717,000	20,472,000	28,360,000	30,500,000	
France...........................	14,581,000	24,027,000	26,247,000	26,075,000	23,399,000	16,860,000	
Italy..............................	93,008,000	88,513,000	95,953,000	99,289,000	101,722,000	93,680,000	98,668,000
Portugal.........................	11,023,000	15,000,000	15,000,000	15,000,000	15,000,000	15,000,000	
Roumania.......................	130,546,000	57,576,000	78,892,000	70,138,000	103,695,000	110,712,000	104,612,000
Russia:							
Russia proper................	59,320,000	41,903,000	49,663,000	29,223,000	63,089,000	67,842,000	
Poland........................		1,000					
Northern Caucasia..........	11,181,000	8,860,000	11,449,000	10,375,000	14,093,000	14,087,000	
Total Russia (European)...	70,501,000	50,764,000	61,112,000	39,598,000	77,182,000	81,919,000	79,964,000
Servia...........................	27,786,000	17,691,000	21,010,000	34,453,000	33,204,000	26,531,000	
Spain............................	18,714,000	25,372,000	20,115,000	26,483,000	27,366,000	28,730,000	25,069,000
Total Europe..................	609,614,000	489,643,000	529,697,000	541,699,000	650,094,000	585,630,000	
Algeria..........................	544,000	402,000	426,000	807,000	556,000	554,000	374,000
Cape of Good Hope..........	3,200,000	3,550,000					
Egypt............................	30,000,000	35,000,000	65,000,000	65,000,000	70,294,000	67,903,000	69,913,000
Natal............................	3,845,000	2,984,000					
Anglo-Egyptian Sudan......	300,000	300,000					
Union of South Africa......			20,000,000	20,000,000	20,000,000	20,000,000	
Total Africa...................	37,889,000	42,236,000	85,426,000	85,807,000	90,850,000	88,457,000	
Australian commonwealth....	8,608,000	10,493,000	8,388,000	8,908,000	11,113,000	13,455,000	9,186,000
New Zealand..................	653,000	419,000	519,000	736,000	750,000	478,000	287,000
Total Australasia............	9,261,000	10,912,000	8,907,000	9,644,000	11,863,000	13,933,000	9,473,000
Grand total...................	3,877,913,000	3,307,014,000	3,508,822,000	3,557,150,000	4,026,967,000	3,460,820,000	

OTHER CROPS BY COUNTRIES.

OATS (1912).	Bushels.	Country.	Bushels.	Country.	Bushels.	Country.	Bushels.
United States,1,418,337,000		Roumania	20,775,000	Austria-Hung.	149,120,000	Japanese emp.	90,669,000
Canada	361,733,000	Russia (Eu.)..	972,111,000	Belgium	4,000,000	Russia (Asia)	104,872,000
Mexico	17,000	Servia	4,750,000	Bulgaria	15,000,000	Africa	40,710,000
Argentina	69,169,000	Spain	23,035,000	Denmark	22,900,000	Australasia ..	3,080,000
Chile	2,000,000	Sweden	75,900,000	Finland	6,754,000		
Uruguay	1,825,000	Untd. kingdom	180,215,000	France	50,646,000	Total 1,437,807,000	
Austria-Hung.	231,217,000	Cyprus	590,000	Germany	159,924,000		
Belgium	38,000,000	Russia (Asia)	95,473,000	Italy	8,403,000	RYE (1912).	
Bulgaria	11,500,000	Africa	17,854,000	Netherlands...	4,000,000	United States	35,664,000
Denmark	42,400,000	Australasia ..	20,301,000	Norway	3,086,000	Canada	2,584,000
Finland	26,618,000			Roumania ...	21,295,000	Mexico	70,000
France	328,601,000	Total 4,485,231,000		Russia (Eu.)..	451,861,000	Austria-Hung.	176,742,000
Germany	586,987,000			Servia	4,600,000	Belgium	23,500,000
Italy	28,306,000	BARLEY (1912).		Spain	59,994,000	Bulgaria	10,000,000
Netherlands..	36,000,000	United States	223,824,000	Sweden	13,660,000	Denmark	18,500,000
Norway	11,607,000	Canada	44,014,000	Untd. kingdom	60,164,000	Finland	12,344,000
		Mexico	6,500,000	Cyprus	2,000,000	France	50,936,000

Country.	Bushels.
Germany	456,800,000
Italy	5,285,000
Netherlands...	16,000,000
Norway	1,042,000
Roumania ..	3,583,000
Russia (Eu.)..	1,011,029,000
Servia	1,500,000
Spain	18,867,000
Sweden	23,323,000
Untd.kingdom	1,500,000
Russia (Asia)	32,953,000
Australasia ..	148,000
Total	**1,901,181,000**

POTATOES (1911).

United States	292,737,000
Canada	66,023,000
Mexico	924,000
Newfoundland	1,533,000
Argentina	18,923,000
Chile	7,440,000
Austria-Hung.	620,263,000
Belgium	104,718,000
Bulgaria	430,000
Denmark	29,523,000
Finland	22,691,000
France	423,573,000
Germany ...	1,263,024,000
Greece	331,000
Italy	62,140,000
Luxemburg ..	4,461,000
Malta	834,000
Netherlands...	103,468,000
Norway	22,617,000
Roumania ..	5,669,000
Russia (Eu.)..	1,143,124,000
Servia	2,154,000
Spain	93,089,000
Sweden	52,669,000
Switzerland..	46,712,000
Untd.kingdom	280,753,000
Japan	24,719,000
Russia (Asia)	32,931,000
Africa	3,960,000
Australasia ..	17,878,000
Total	**4,478,711,000**

TOBACCO (1911).

	Pounds.
United States	905,109,000
Porto Rico....	10,000,000
Canada	16,513,000
Cuba	66,930,000
Guatemala ..	1,300,000
Jamaica	495,000
Mexico	34,711,000
SantoDomingo	42,000,000
Argentina ...	15,178,000
Bolivia	3,000,000
Brazil	40,761,000
Chile	150,000
Ecuador	165,000
Paraguay ...	13,000,000
Peru	1,500,000
Austria-Hung.	183,372,000
Belgium	22,046,000
Bulgaria	23,473,000
Denmark	258,000
France	40,423,000
Germany	64,385,000
Greece	16,534,000
Italy	24,783,000
Netherlands..	1,700,000
Roumania ...	20,509,000
Russia (Eu.)..	160,130,000
Servia	3,698,000
Sweden	1,712,000
Switzerland..	1,232,000
Turkey (Eu.).	49,177,000
British India.	450,000,000

Country.	Pounds.
Brit.N.Borneo	2,663,000
China	18,016,000
Java	116,000,000
Sumatra	51,395,000
Formosa	1,726,000
Japan	93,787,000
Philippines ..	56,257,000
Russia (Asia)	34,872,000
Africa	36,023,000
Oceania	1,992,000
Total	**2,626,985,000**

FLAXSEED (1911).

	Bushels.
United States..	19,370,000
Canada	7,867,000
Mexico	150,000
Argentina	23,424,000
Uruguay	660,000
Austria-Hungary	901,000
Belgium	300,000
Bulgaria	10,000
France	496,000
Italy	341,000
Netherlands	374,000
Roumania	603,000
Russia (Eu.)..	20,544,000
Sweden	17,000
British India..	22,544,000
Russia (Asia)..	1,105,000
Algeria	16,000
Total	**98,622,000**

RICE (1911).

	Pounds.
Untd. States	637,056,000
Hawaii	25,820,000
Guatemala..	1,300,000
Honduras ..	8,100,000
Mexico	124,900,000
Argentina...	19,000,000
Brazil	184,704,000
Brit. Guiana	91,000,000
Dut. Guiana	4,376,000
Peru	114,313,000
Bulgaria ...	6,606,000
France	1,437,000
Greece	2,900,000
Italy	652,153,000
Spain	287,303,000
Turkey(Eu.)	1,387,000
Brit. India.	81,298,000,000
Ceylon	320,000,000
China	47,204,000,000
Chosen(Kor.)	3,200,000,000
Formosa ...	1,329,000,000
Fr.Ind.China	5,000,000,000
Japan	16,240,000,000
Java-Madura	7,566,000,000
Philippines..	1,201,000,000
Russia(Asia)	363,000,000
Siam	6,824,000,000
Straits Set's	77,000,000
Turk'y(Asia)	137,230,000
Africa	1,478,328,000
Fiji	5,000,000
Total	**174,404,983,000**

HOPS (1912).

United States..	50,000,000
Austria-Hung'y	47,632,000
Belgium	7,000,000
France	6,820,000
Germany ...	45,334,000
Netherlands...	158,000
Russia	8,800,000
England	41,825,000
Australasia ...	2,589,000
Total	**210,158,000**

BEANS (1911).*

Country.	Bushels.
Un. States (1909)..	11,145,000
Canada	1,156,000
Chile	1,360,000
Austria	8,932,000
Denmark	525,000
France	8,187,000
Italy	18,990,000
Luxemburg ..	51,000
Netherlands ..	1,664,000
Roumania ..	4,602,000
Russia (Eu.)..	2,588,000
Servia	1,453,000
Spain	14,372,000
Sweden	171,000
United kingdom.	7,984,000
Algeria	1,101,000
Australasia ..	1,032,000

PEAS (1911).*

Un. States (1909)	7,110,000
Canada	4,502,000
Chile	44,000
France	1,137,000
Luxemburg	31,000
Netherlands ..	1,838,000
Roumania	598,000
Russia (Eu.)..	33,943,000
Servia	13,050
Spain	4,684,000
Sweden	1,277,000
United kingdom.	3,824,000
Algeria	294,000
New Zealand...	523,000

*Incomplete returns.

SUGAR (1911-12).

Cane.	*Tons.
United States..	304,000
Hawaii	531,000
Porto Rico....	331,300
Mexico	152,600
Central America.	20,700
British W. Indies	303,800
Cuba	1,866,000
Danish W. Indies	11,600
French W. Indies	177,900
South America..	681,500
Spain	21,000
British India..	2,390,400
Malay states...	12,000
Formosa	202,500
Japan	64,700
Java	1,413,000
Philippines	183,000
Africa	380,400
Oceania	262,900
Total cane....	**9,138,300**

Beet.	
United States..	535,000
Canada	9,900
Austria-Hungary	1,124,900
Belgium	231,000
Bulgaria	6,000
Denmark	51,900
France	448,000
Germany ...	1,474,100
Greece	1,000
Italy	165,000
Netherlands ...	270,000
Roumania ...	27,000
Russia	1,808,800
Servia	7,300
Spain	85,000
Sweden	121,000
Switzerland ...	3,600
Total beet....	**6,369,500**
Total sugar...	**15,507,800**

*Long tons.

COTTON (1911).

Country.	*Bales.
United States...	15,893,113
Mexico	200,455
West Indies.....	14,542
Brazil	270,000
Peru	76,369
Greece	32,285
British India..	3,284,519
China	1,200,000
Persia	123,277
Russia (Asia)..	690,553
Turkey (Asia)..	131,000
British Africa...	32,616
Egypt	1,514,730
Sudan	13,222
Total	**†23,421,055**

*Bales of 500 pounds gross or 478 pounds net.
†Includes crops of countries not specified in table.

COFFEE (1911).

	Pounds.
Porto Rico....	49,146,000
Hawaii	2,632,000
Guatemala ...	90,000,000
Costa Rica....	27,869,000
Nicaragua	26,943,000
Salvador	62,764,000
Honduras	5,000,000
Mexico	70,000,000
Haiti	53,100,000
Santo Domingo	4,550,000
Trinidad	2,000
Jamaica	6,726,000
Guadeloupe ...	2,115,000
Leeward Isls...	9,000
Brazil	1,489,137,000
Venezuela ...	97,659,000
Colombia ...	85,000,000
Bolivia	1,500,000
Ecuador	8,000,000
Peru	978,000
Dutch Guiana	357,000
British Guiana	136,000
Dutch E.Indies	48,190,000
Malay states..	1,443,000
British India.	27,002,000
Ceylon	38,000
North Borneo.	1,000
Sarawak	14,000
Arabia	15,374,000
Africa	21,893,000
New Caledonia	1,431,000
Queensland ...	81,000
Total	**2,189,944,000**

RAW SILK (1911).

Italy	886,000
France	7,694,000
Spain	194,000
Austria-Hungary	772,000
Anatolia ...	1,290,000
Syria-Cyprus ..	1,157,000
Turkey (other)..	353,000
Saloniki	827,000
Balkan states..	275,000
Greece	137,000
Caucasus	1,058,000
Persia	1,329,000
China	12,909,000
Japan	20,657,000
British India..	529,000
Total	**54,167,000**

CROPS OF 1912 BY STATES.
CORN.

State.	Acres.	Yield,bu.	Bushels.	Value.	State.	Acres.	Yield,bu.	Bushels.	Value.
Alabama	3,150,000	17.2	54,180,000	$53,862,000	Arkansas	2,475,000	20.4	50,490,000	33,828,000
Arizona	16,000	33.0	528,000	528,000	California ...	52,000	37.0	1,924,000	1,635,000

State.	Acres.	Yield,bu.	Bushels.	Value.
Colorado	420,000	20.8	8,736,000	4,368,000
Connecticut...	60,000	50.0	3,000,000	2,310,000
Delaware	195,000	34.0	6,630,000	3,381,000
Florida	655,000	13.0	8,515,000	6,727,000
Georgia	3,910,000	13.8	53,072,000	45,864,000
Idaho	12,000	32.8	394,000	276,000
Illinois	10,658,000	40.0	426,320,000	174,791,000
Indiana	4,947,000	40.3	199,364,000	83,733,000
Iowa	10,047,000	43.0	432,021,000	151,207,000
Kansas	7,575,000	23.0	174,225,000	69,690,000
Kentucky	3,600,000	30.4	109,440,000	60,192,000
Louisiana	1,805,000	18.0	34,490,000	22,093,000
Maine	16,000	40.0	640,000	480,000
Maryland	670,000	36.5	24,455,000	13,450,000
Massachusetts	47,000	45.0	2,115,000	1,716,000
Michigan	1,625,000	34.0	55,250,000	31,492,000
Minnesota ...	2,266,000	34.5	78,177,000	28,925,000
Mississippi ..	3,106,000	18.3	56,840,000	40,356,000
Missouri	7,622,000	32.0	243,904,000	112,196,000
Montana	24,000	25.5	612,000	428,000
Nebraska	7,609,000	24.0	182,616,000	67,568,000
Nevada	1,000	30.0	30,000	29,000
N. Hampshire	23,000	46.0	1,058,000	794,000
New Jersey..	273,000	38.0	10,374,000	13,884,000
New Mexico..	93,000	22.4	2,082,000	1,562,000
New York....	512,000	38.6	19,763,000	13,834,000
N. Carolina..	2,808,000	18.2	51,106,000	42,418,000
North Dakota	328,000	26.7	8,758,000	3,766,000
Ohio	4,075,000	42.8	174,410,000	78,484,000
Oklahoma ..	5,448,000	18.7	101,878,000	41,770,000
Oregon	20,000	31.5	630,000	651,000
Pennsylvania.	1,149,000	42.5	61,582,000	38,797,000
Rhode Island.	11,000	41.5	456,000	401,000
S. Carolina...	1,915,000	17.9	34,728,000	29,136,000
South Dakota	2,495,000	30.6	76,347,000	28,248,000
Tennessee ..	3,332,000	26.5	88,298,000	53,862,000
Texas	7,300,000	21.0	153,300,000	98,112,000
Utah	9,000	30.0	280,000	202,000
Vermont	45,000	40.0	1,800,000	1,296,000
Virginia	1,980,000	24.0	47,520,000	33,739,000
Washington..	31,000	27.3	846,000	651,000
West Virginia	725,000	33.8	24,505,000	15,928,000
Wisconsin ..	1,632,000	35.7	58,262,000	29,714,000
Wyoming ...	16,000	23.0	368,000	236,000
Un. States..	107,083,000	29.2	3,124,746,000	1,520,454,000

WHEAT (WINTER AND SPRING).

State.	Acres.	Yield,bu.	Bushels.	Value.
Alabama	30,000	10.6	318,000	$359,000
Arizona	23,000	30.7	707,000	778,000
Arkansas	94,000	10.0	940,000	884,000
California ...	370,000	17.0	6,290,000	5,850,000
Colorado	452,000	24.2	10,968,000	8,006,000
Delaware	111,000	17.5	1,942,000	1,864,000
Georgia	132,000	9.3	1,228,000	1,498,000
Idaho	510,000	28.6	10,658,000	9,013,000
Illinois	1,182,000	8.3	9,810,000	8,641,000
Indiana	1,260,000	8.0	10,080,000	9,374,000
Iowa	650,000	19.8	12,850,000	10,023,000
Kansas	5,956,000	15.5	92,290,000	68,295,000
Kentucky	686,000	10.0	8,860,000	6,791,000
Maine	3,000	23.5	70,000	72,000
Maryland	599,000	15.0	8,985,000	8,682,000
Michigan	700,000	10.0	7,000,000	6,720,000
Minnesota ...	4,325,000	15.5	67,038,000	48,933,000
Mississippi ..	8,000	12.0	96,000	93,000
Missouri	1,900,000	12.5	23,750,000	21,375,000
Montana	803,000	24.1	19,346,000	12,381,000
Nebraska	3,123,000	17.6	55,052,000	37,985,000
Nevada	39,000	29.2	1,137,000	1,137,000
New Jersey...	79,000	18.5	1,462,000	1,433,000
New Mexico..	59,000	20.9	1,232,000	1,109,000
New York....	335,000	16.0	5,360,000	3,306,000
N. Carolina..	598,000	8.9	5,322,000	5,907,000
North Dakota	7,990,000	18.0	143,820,000	99,236,000
Ohio	1,220,000	8.0	9,760,000	9,565,000
Oklahoma ..	1,570,000	12.8	20,096,000	15,072,000
Oregon	842,000	25.0	21,018,000	15,132,000
Pennsylvania.	1,240,000	18.0	22,320,000	21,204,000
S. Carolina...	79,000	9.2	727,000	865,000
South Dakota	3,675,000	14.2	52,185,000	36,008,000
Tennessee ..	674,000	10.5	7,077,000	7,077,000
Texas	735,000	15.0	11,025,000	10,253,000
Utah	236,000	25.7	6,059,000	4,544,000
Vermont	1,000	25.0	25,000	24,000
Virginia	741,000	11.6	8,596,000	8,682,000
Washington...	2,285,000	23.5	53,728,000	36,535,000

State.	Acres.	Yield,bu.	Bushels.	Value.
West Virginia	233,000	14.5	3,378,000	3,412,000
Wisconsin ...	188,000	19.0	3,564,000	2,958,000
Wyoming	76,000	28.7	2,181,000	1,745,000
Un. States..	45,814,000	15.9	730,267,000	555,280,000

OATS.

State.	Acres.	Yield,bu.	Bushels.	Value.
Alabama	260,000	20.0	5,200,000	$3,224,000
Arizona	6,000	44.7	268,000	188,000
Arkansas	175,000	19.9	3,482,000	1,741,000
California ...	200,000	39.0	7,800,000	4,290,000
Colorado	290,000	42.8	12,412,000	4,717,000
Connecticut...	11,000	30.7	338,000	166,000
Delaware	4,000	30.5	122,000	55,000
Florida	43,000	17.2	740,000	518,000
Georgia	364,000	20.8	7,571,000	4,921,000
Idaho	348,000	48.9	17,017,000	5,956,000
Illinois	4,220,000	43.3	182,726,000	54,818,000
Indiana	1,990,000	40.1	79,799,000	23,940,000
Iowa	4,928,000	44.2	217,818,000	58,811,000
Kansas	1,729,000	32.0	55,040,000	19,264,000
Kentucky	150,000	26.9	4,035,000	1,775,000
Louisiana	34,000	20.8	707,000	546,000
Maine	133,000	34.6	4,602,000	2,347,000
Maryland	45,000	30.0	1,350,000	608,000
Massachusetts	8,000	34.0	272,000	128,000
Michigan	1,485,000	34.9	51,826,000	17,103,000
Minnesota ...	2,948,000	41.7	122,932,000	31,962,000
Mississippi ..	113,000	17.4	1,966,000	1,180,000
Missouri	1,125,000	33.0	37,125,000	58,811,000
Montana	476,000	48.0	22,848,000	7997,000
Nebraska	2,275,000	24.4	55,510,000	16,653,000
Nevada	10,000	40.0	400,000	208,000
N. Hampshire	12,000	39.0	468,000	225,000
New Jersey...	67,000	27.6	1,849,000	814,000
New Mexico..	53,000	34.7	1,839,000	828,000
New York....	1,192,000	30.3	36,714,000	15,420,000
N. Carolina..	204,000	18.6	3,794,000	2,352,000
North Dakota	2,300,000	41.4	95,220,000	20,948,000
Ohio	2,120,000	44.0	93,280,000	20,782,000
Oklahoma ..	936,000	25.1	23,494,000	3,927,000
Oregon	359,000	38.2	13,714,000	5,623,000
Pennsylvania.	1,099,000	33.1	36,377,000	14,915,000
Rhode Island.	2,000	28.6	57,000	26,000
S. Carolina...	324,000	21.5	6,966,000	4,598,000
South Dakota	1,550,000	33.8	52,390,000	13,098,000
Tennessee ...	258,000	21.7	5,599,000	2,632,000
Texas	865,000	25.1	31,140,000	9,989,000
Utah	91,000	46.4	4,222,000	2,069,000
Vermont	77,000	35.0	3,311,000	1,589,000
Virginia	175,000	22.2	3,885,000	2,020,000
Washington..	284,000	48.2	13,689,000	5,476,000
West Virginia	111,000	28.0	3,108,000	1,461,000
Wisconsin ...	2,272,000	37.3	67,050,000	27,119,000
Wyoming ...	205,000	41.8	8,569,000	3,171,000
Un. States..	37,917,000	37.4	1,418,337,000	452,469,000

RYE.

State.	Acres.	Yield,bu.	Bushels.	Value.
Alabama	1,000	11.5	12,000	$16,000
Arkansas	1,000	10.5	10,000	10,000
California ...	8,000	17.6	141,000	127,000
Colorado	25,000	19.5	488,000	268,000
Connecticut...	7,000	17.5	122,000	112,000
Delaware	1,000	14.0	14,000	11,000
Georgia	11,000	9.2	101,000	141,000
Idaho	3,000	22.0	66,000	40,000
Illinois	48,000	16.0	768,000	532,000
Indiana	64,000	14.5	928,000	631,000
Iowa	35,000	19.0	665,000	412,000
Kansas	30,000	15.9	477,000	324,000
Kentucky	21,000	13.0	273,000	240,000
Maryland	27,000	15.5	418,000	334,000
Massachusetts	3,000	18.5	56,000	56,000
Michigan	370,000	13.3	4,921,000	3,199,000
Minnesota ...	262,000	23.0	6,026,000	2,013,000
Missouri	15,000	14.8	222,000	178,000
Montana	10,000	23.5	235,000	141,000
Nebraska	55,000	16.0	880,000	493,000
New Jersey...	72,000	17.5	1,260,000	995,000
New York....	128,000	16.5	2,112,000	1,605,000
N. Carolina..	44,000	9.3	409,000	429,000
North Dakota	48,000	18.0	864,000	406,000
Ohio	57,000	15.5	884,000	663,000
Oklahoma ..	4,000	12.0	48,000	42,000
Oregon	22,000	16.0	352,000	246,000
Pennsylvania.	232,000	17.5	4,935,000	3,800,000

State.	Acres.	Yield,bu.	Bushels.	Value.
S. Carolina...	3,000	9.5	28,000	41,000
South Dakota	16,000	19.5	312,000	162,000
Tennessee ...	17,000	11.5	196,000	192,000
Texas	2,000	16.6	33,000	36,000
Utah	6,000	15.0	90,000	61,000
Vermont	1,000	20.0		18,000
Virginia	48,000	15.5	418,000	334,000
Washington...	9,000	20.0	180,000	117,000
West Virginia	17,000	13.0	221,000	186,000
Wisconsin ...	341,000	18.3	6,240,000	3,806,000
Wyoming	3,000	19.0	57,000	37,000
Un. States..	2,117,000	16.8	35,664,000	23,636,000

BARLEY.

State.	Acres.	Yield,bu.	Bushels.	Value.
Arizona	25,000	40.0	1,440,000	$664,000
California ...	1,392,000	30.0	41,760,000	29,232,000
Colorado	76,000	29.0	2,964,000	1,482,000
Idaho	159,000	43.5	6,916,000	3,527,000
Illinois	57,000	31.5	1,796,000	952,000
Indiana	9,000	29.5	266,000	160,000
Iowa	470,000	31.0	10,950,000	7,576,000
Kansas	176,000	23.5	4,136,000	1,654,000
Kentucky ...	3,000	26.0	78,000	58,000
Maine	4,000	26.2	105,000	81,000
Maryland ...	4,000	27.0	108,000	73,000
Michigan ...	87,000	26.0	2,262,000	1,470,000
Minnesota ...	1,490,000	28.2	42,018,000	17,227,000
Missouri	6,000	24.8	149,000	93,000
Montana	39,000	36.5	1,424,000	755,000
Nebraska ...	113,000	22.0	2,486,000	1,044,000
Nevada	12,000	41.0	492,000	428,000
N. Hampshire	1,000	28.0	28,000	24,000
New Mexico..	2,000	35.0	70,000	50,000
New York....	82,000	26.0	2,132,000	1,450,000
North Dakota	1,176,000	29.9	35,162,000	12,307,000
Ohio	20,000	31.0	620,000	341,000
Oklahoma	8,000	20.0	160,000	80,000
Oregon	119,000	36.0	4,284,000	2,356,000
Pennsylvania.	7,000	27.5	192,000	131,000
South Dakota	887,000	26.0	23,062,000	9,686,000
Tennessee ...	2,000	26.0	52,000	42,000
Texas	6,000	29.3	176,000	137,000
Utah	25,000	45.0	1,125,000	664,000
Vermont	13,000	35.0	455,000	364,000
Virginia	10,000	25.0	250,000	188,000
Washington...	183,000	43.0	7,869,000	4,428,000
Wisconsin ...	845,000	29.4	24,910,000	13,664,000
Wyoming	11,000	34.0	374,000	232,000
Un. States..	7,530,000	29.7	223,824,000	112,957,000

BUCKWHEAT.

State.	Acres.	Yield,bu.	Bushels.	Value.
Connecticut...	3,000	20.5	62,000	$55,000
Delaware	4,000	16.0	64,000	42,000
Illinois	4,000	22.0	88,000	70,000
Indiana	5,000	19.0	95,000	69,000
Iowa	7,000	19.0	133,000	100,000
Kansas	1,000	16.0	16,000	12,000
Maine	14,000	20.4	412,000	288,000
Massachusetts	2,000	21.0	42,000	36,000
Michigan ...	64,000	17.0	1,088,000	707,000
Minnesota ...	6,000	21.0	126,000	82,000
Missouri	2,000	15.0	30,000	28,000
Nebraska ...	1,000	18.0	18,000	16,000
N. Hampshire	1,000	31.0	31,000	22,000
New Jersey...	12,000	22.0	264,000	190,000
New York....	277,000	23.8	6,593,000	4,220,000
N. Carolina..	10,000	17.5	175,000	149,000
Ohio	21,000	19.5	410,000	287,000
Pennsylvania.	306,000	24.2	7,405,000	4,739,000
Tennessee ...	3,000	18.0	54,000	42,000
Vermont	8,000	30.0	240,000	173,000
Virginia	24,000	21.5	516,000	387,000
West Virginia	37,000	24.0	888,000	666,000
Wisconsin ...	17,000	17.0	289,000	191,000
Un. States..	841,000	22.9	19,249,000	12,720,000

FLAXSEED.

State.	Acres.	Yield,bu.	Bushels.	Value.
Colorado	12,000	8.0	96,000	$120,000
Iowa	35,000	11.5	402,000	498,000
Kansas	50,000	6.0	300,000	390,000
Minnesota ...	404,000	10.2	4,121,000	4,945,000
Missouri	12,000	6.0	72,000	79,000
Montana	460,000	12.0	5,520,000	6,182,000
Nebraska	2,000	9.5	300,000	390,000
North Dakota	1,246,000	9.7	12,086,000	13,778,000

State.	Acres.	Yield,bu.	Bushels.	Value.
Oklahoma ...	1,000	9.0	9,000	12,000
South Dakota	619,000	8.6	5,323,000	6,015,000
Wisconsin ...	10,000	12.5	125,000	155,000
Un. States..	2,851,000	9.8	28,073,000	32,202,000

POTATOES.

State.	Acres.	Yield,bu.	Bushels.	Value.
Alabama	15,000	81	1,215,000	$1,094,000
Arizona	1,000	125	125,000	156,000
Arkansas ...	25,000	70	1,750,000	1,610,000
California ...	78,000	130	10,140,000	6,591,000
Colorado ...	85,000	95	8,075,000	3,811,000
Connecticut...	23,000	107	2,461,000	1,920,000
Delaware ...	11,000	100	1,100,000	770,000
Florida	11,000	93	1,023,000	1,125,000
Georgia	12,000	78	936,000	814,000
Idaho	35,000	185	6,475,000	1,878,000
Illinois	137,000	101	6,900,000	8,302,000
Indiana	87,000	114	9,918,000	4,959,000
Iowa	174,000	109	18,966,000	8,724,000
Kansas	70,000	82	5,740,000	4,190,000
Kentucky ...	51,000	101	5,151,000	3,451,000
Louisiana ...	20,000	73	1,518,000	1,212,000
Maine	117,000	198	21,240,000	12,741,000
Maryland ...	37,000	112	1,755,000	2,404,000
Massachusetts	26,000	130	3,380,000	2,535,000
Michigan ...	350,000	105	36,750,000	15,068,000
Minnesota ...	245,000	135	33,075,000	9,261,000
Mississippi ..	10,000	89	890,000	801,000
Missouri	95,000	84	7,980,000	6,506,000
Montana	37,000	165	6,105,000	2,442,000
Nebraska ...	118,000	80	9,440,000	4,814,000
Nevada	12,000	178	2,136,000	1,282,000
N. Hampshire	17,000	140	2,380,000	1,452,000
New Jersey...	92,000	108	6,132,000	6,558,000
New Mexico..	9,000	100	900,000	585,000
New York....	360,000	106	38,160,000	22,133,000
N. Carolina..	30,000	85	2,550,000	1,938,000
North Dakota	52,000	128	6,656,000	1,864,000
Ohio	186,000	112	20,832,000	11,041,000
Oklahoma ...	29,000	60	1,740,000	1,618,000
Oregon	65,000	155	10,075,000	3,123,000
Pennsylvania.	265,000	109	28,851,000	16,464,000
Rhode Island.	5,000	113	565,000	435,000
S. Carolina...	10,000	90	900,000	1,008,000
Tennessee ...	38,000	88	3,344,000	2,341,000
Texas	52,000	63	3,276,000	3,440,000
Utah	19,000	185	3,515,000	1,722,000
Vermont	26,000	140	3,640,000	2,002,000
Virginia	95,000	87	8,265,000	5,372,000
Washington...	68,000	167	11,356,000	4,088,000
West Virginia	47,000	112	5,264,000	3,264,000
Wisconsin ...	291,000	120	34,920,000	11,873,000
Wyoming	11,000	140	1,540,000	924,000
Un. States..	3,711,000	113.4	420,647,000	212,550,000

HAY.

State.	Acres.	Yield.	Tons.	Value.
Alabama	209,000	1.25	261,000	$3,811,000
Arizona	113,000	3.40	384,000	4,608,000
Arkansas ...	286,000	1.23	352,000	4,224,000
California ...	2,500,000	1.53	3,825,000	52,402,000
Colorado ...	870,000	2.19	1,905,000	16,574,000
Connecticut...	379,000	1.15	436,000	9,810,000
Delaware ...	72,000	1.33	96,000	1,440,000
Florida	43,000	1.25	54,000	977,000
Georgia	234,000	1.35	316,000	5,372,000
Idaho	692,000	2.80	1,938,000	12,209,000
Illinois	2,516,000	1.30	3,266,000	41,152,000
Indiana	1,885,000	1.37	2,582,000	29,435,000
Iowa	3,537,000	1.40	4,952,000	47,044,000
Kansas	1,627,000	1.50	2,440,000	18,544,000
Kentucky ...	815,000	1.23	1,002,000	13,727,000
Louisiana ...	142,000	1.65	234,000	2,972,000
Maine	1,231,000	1.16	1,428,000	19,564,000
Maryland ...	381,000	1.51	575,000	8,280,000
Massachusetts	477,000	1.25	596,000	12,814,000
Michigan ...	2,395,000	1.33	3,185,000	40,456,000
Minnesota ...	1,661,000	1.53	2,541,000	16,282,000
Mississippi ..	201,000	1.48	297,000	3,712,000
Missouri	3,187,000	1.30	4,143,000	40,601,000
Montana	640,000	1.90	1,216,000	10,693,000
Nebraska	1,150,000	1.35	1,552,000	13,037,000
Nevada	227,000	3.00	681,000	5,925,000
N. Hampshire	501,000	1.25	626,000	9,390,000
New Jersey..	362,000	1.44	521,000	10,430,000

State.	Acres.	Yield.	Tons.	Value.
New Mexico..	187,000	2.33	436,000	3,706,000
New York....	4,720,000	1.25	5,900,000	87,910,000
N. Carolina..	293,000	1.30	381,000	6,363,000
North Dakota	364,000	1.40	510,000	2,805,000
Ohio	2,960,000	1.36	4,026,000	52,328,000
Oklahoma ...	385,000	1.25	481,000	3,559,000
Oregon	790,000	2.20	1,738,000	14,425,000
Pennsylvania.	3,173,000	1.43	4,537,000	70,777,000
Rhode Island.	58,000	1.13	66,000	1,465,000
S. Carolina..	194,000	1.15	223,000	4,034,000
South Dakota	460,000	1.46	672,000	4,099,000
Tennessee ...	888,000	1.30	1,154,000	18,233,000
Texas	387,000	1.40	542,000	5,637,000
Utah	368,000	2.78	1,023,000	8,184,000
Vermont	1,010,000	1.50	1,515,000	21,210,000
Virginia	741,000	1.20	889,000	13,513,000
Washington...	776,000	2.20	1,707,000	17,241,000
West Virginia	745,000	1.38	1,028,000	15,420,000
Wisconsin ...	2,250,000	1.60	3,600,000	43,560,000
Wyoming ...	452,000	1.90	859,000	7,387,000
Un. States..	49,530,000	1.47	72,691,000	856,695,000

TOBACCO.

State.	Acres.	Yield.	Pounds.	Value.
Alabama	300	750	225,000	$79,000
Arkansas	800	650	520,000	94,000
Connecticut...	17,500	1,700	29,750,000	7,170,000
Florida	3,100	840	2,604,000	781,000
Georgia	1,400	830	1,162,000	349,000
Illinois	900	760	684,000	62,000
Indiana	18,700	800	14,960,000	1,346,000
Kentucky	441,780	780	343,980,000	29,926,000
Louisiana ...	500	300	150,000	45,000
Maryland	26,000	660	17,160,000	1,373,000
Massachusetts	5,800	1,700	9,860,000	2,357,000
Missouri	6,000	1,000	6,000,000	720,000
N. Hampshire	100	1,700	170,000	31,000
New York	4,000	1,300	5,200,000	655,000
N. Carolina..	179,000	620	110,980,000	17,757,000
Ohio	86,200	920	79,304,000	7,217,000
Pennsylvania.	44,200	1,450	64,320,000	4,448,000
S. Carolina..	35,000	700	24,500,000	2,670,000
Tennessee ...	110,000	660	72,600,000	5,155,000
Texas	200	700	140,000	24,000
Vermont	100	1,700	170,000	31,000
Virginia	187,000	600	112,200,000	13,464,000
West Virginia	15,800	760	12,008,000	1,321,000
Wisconsin ...	42,200	1,290	54,438,000	5,988,000
Un. States..	1,225,800	785.5	962,855,000	104,063,000

RICE.

State.	Acres.	Yield.	Bushels.	Value.
Alabama	300	30.0	9,000	$8,000
Arkansas ...	90,800	37.5	3,405,000	3,201,000
California ...	1,400	50.0	70,000	64,000
Florida	600	25.0	15,000	14,000
Georgia	900	30.0	27,000	24,000
Louisiana ...	352,600	33.5	11,812,000	10,985,000
Mississippi ...	2,200	35.0	77,000	69,000
N. Carolina...	400	25.0	10,000	9,000
S. Carolina...	8,000	25.0	200,000	186,000
Texas	265,600	35.5	9,429,000	8,863,000
Un. States..	722,800	34.7	25,054,000	23,423,000

COTTON.

State.	Bales.*	State.	Bales.*
Alabama	1,381,436	South Carolina..	1,216,259
Arkansas	827,154	Tennessee	299,793
Florida	54,043	Texas	5,126,848
Georgia	1,851,455	Virginia	24,398
Louisiana	394,484	Other states....	15,927
Mississippi	1,049,299		
Missouri	58,220	Total 14,313,015	
North Carolina..	892,582	*Equivalent 500 pound	
Oklahoma	1,076,107	bales.	

SHEEP AND WOOL (1912).

State.	Sheep, April 1.	Wool, washed and unwashed, pounds.	Wool, scoured, pounds.
Alabama	115,000	373,750	231,725
Arizona	850,000	5,695,000	1,936,300
Arkansas	100,000	400,000	240,000
California	1,700,000	11,900,000	3,927,000
Colorado	1,200,000	8,040,000	2,653,200
Connecticut	15,000	85,500	49,590
Delaware	5,000	26,500	14,840
Florida	95,000	308,750	191,425
Georgia	175,000	656,250	374,063
Idaho	2,100,000	15,540,000	5,594,400
Illinois	675,000	4,556,250	2,414,813
Indiana	825,000	5,280,000	2,904,000
Iowa	850,000	5,737,500	2,983,500
Kansas	225,000	1,575,000	551,250
Kentucky	775,000	3,565,000	2,245,950
Louisiana	140,000	525,000	320,250
Maine	150,000	937,500	543,750
Maryland	128,000	729,600	408,576
Massachusetts	23,000	143,750	83,375
Michigan	1,500,000	10,125,000	5,265,000
Minnesota	450,000	3,037,500	1,609,875
Mississippi	150,000	562,500	243,125
Missouri	1,100,000	7,425,000	4,083,750
Montana	4,300,000	31,175,000	11,846,500
Nebraska	275,000	1,760,000	668,800
Nevada	825,000	5,775,000	1,905,750
New Hampshire.......	33,000	214,500	111,540
New Jersey	17,000	91,800	50,490
New Mexico..........	2,900,000	18,850,000	6,597,500
New York............	625,000	3,750,000	1,950,000
North Carolina.......	150,000	562,500	326,250
North Dakota........	250,000	1,750,000	700,000
Ohio	2,700,000	16,875,000	8,606,250
Pennsylvania	650,000	4,095,000	2,170,350
Rhode Island........	5,000	30,900	17,400
South Carolina.......	30,000	108,000	62,640
South Dakota........	475,000	3,206,250	1,218,375
Tennessee	475,000	1,900,000	1,140,000
Texas	1,400,000	9,100,000	3,094,000
Utah	1,750,000	11,550,000	4,042,500
Vermont	90,000	607,500	303,750
Virginia	450,000	2,025,000	1,296,000
Washington .....\....	400,000	3,600,000	1,116,000
West Virginia	575,000	3,162,500	1,644,500
Wisconsin	650,000	4,290,000	2,316,600
Wyoming	3,900,000	32,175,000	10,617,750
United States......38,481,000		304,043,400	136,866,652
In 1911.............39,761,000		318,547,900	139,896,195

PRINCIPAL FARM CROPS OF THE UNITED STATES BY YEARS.

[From tables prepared by the department of agriculture.]

YEAR.	CORN.			WHEAT.		
	Acres.	Bushels.	Value.	Acres.	Bushels.	Value.
1902.................................	94,043,613	2,523,648,312	$1,017,017,349	46,202,424	670,063,008	$422,224,117
1903.................................	88,091,193	2,244,176,925	952,968,801	49,454,967	637,821,835	443,024,826
1904.................................	92,231,581	2,467,480,934	1,087,461,440	44,074,875	552,399,517	510,489,874
1905.................................	94,011,369	2,707,993,540	1,116,696,738	47,854,079	692,979,489	518,372,727
1906.................................	96,737,581	2,927,416,091	1,166,626,472	47,305,829	735,260,970	490,332,760
1907.................................	99,931,000	2,592,320,000	1,336,901,000	45,211,000	634,087,000	554,437,000
1908.................................	101,788,000	2,668,651,000	1,616,145,000	47,557,000	664,602,000	616,826,000
1909.................................	98,383,000	2,552,190,000		44,261,000	683,350,000	
1910.................................	104,035,000	2,886,260,000	1,384,817,000	45,681,000	635,121,000	561,051,000
1911.................................	105,825,000	2,531,488,000	1,565,258,000	49,543,000	621,338,000	543,068,000
1912.................................	107,083,000	3,124,746,000	1,520,454,000	45,814,000	730,267,000	555,280,000

PRINCIPAL FARM CROPS OF THE UNITED STATES—Continued.

Year.	Oats.			Rye.		
	Acres.	Bushels.	Value.	Acres.	Bushels.	Value.
1902	28,653,144	987,842,712	$303,584,852	1,978,548	33,630,592	$17,080,793
1903	27,638,126	784,094,199	297,661,665	1,906,894	29,363,416	15,993,871
1904	27,842,669	894,596,552	279,900,013	1,792,673	27,234,565	18,745,543
1905	28,046,746	953,216,197	277,047,537	1,662,508	27,616,045	16,754,657
1906	30,958,768	964,904,522	306,292,978	2,001,904	33,374,833	19,671,243
1907	31,837,000	754,443,000	384,568,000	1,926,000	31,566,000	23,058,000
1908	32,344,000	807,156,000	381,171,000	1,948,000	31,851,000	23,455,000
1909	35,157,000	1,007,129,000	....	2,195,000	29,520,000	....
1910	37,548,000	1,186,341,000	408,388,000	2,185,000	34,897,000	24,953,000
1911	37,763,000	922,298,000	414,663,000	2,127,000	33,119,000	27,557,000
1912	37,917,000	1,418,337,000	452,469,000	2,117,000	35,664,000	28,636,000

Year.	Barley.			Buckwheat.		
	Acres.	Bushels.	Value.	Acres.	Bushels.	Value.
1902	4,661,063	134,954,023	$61,898,634	804,889	14,529,770	$8,954,704
1903	4,993,137	131,861,391	60,166,313	804,393	14,243,644	8,650,733
1904	5,145,878	139,748,954	58,651,807	798,625	15,008,396	9,390,768
1905	5,095,528	136,651,029	55,047,196	760,118	14,585,082	8,565,499
1906	6,323,757	178,916,484	74,235,997	789,208	14,641,937	8,727,443
1907	6,448,000	153,597,000	102,290,000	800,000	14,290,000	9,975,000
1908	6,646,000	166,756,000	92,442,000	805,000	15,874,000	12,004,000
1909	7,698,000	173,321,000	....	878,000	14,849,000	....
1910	7,743,000	173,832,000	100,426,000	860,000	17,598,000	11,636,000
1911	7,627,000	160,240,000	139,182,000	833,000	17,549,000	12,735,000
1912	7,530,000	223,824,000	112,957,000	841,000	19,249,000	12,720,000

Year.	Potatoes.			Hay.		
	Acres.	Bushels.	Value.	Acres.	Tons.	Value.
1902	2,965,587	284,632,789	$134,111,436	39,825,227	50,857,576	$342,086,364
1903	2,916,855	247,127,880	151,638,094	39,953,759	61,305,940	556,376,880
1904	3,015,675	332,830,300	150,673,392	39,998,802	60,696,028	529,107,625
1905	2,996,757	260,741,294	160,821,080	39,361,960	60,531,611	519,959,784
1906	3,013,150	308,038,382	157,547,392	42,476,224	57,145,959	592,539,671
1907	3,124,000	297,942,000	183,880,000	44,028,000	63,677,000	743,507,000
1908	3,257,000	278,985,000	197,039,000	46,486,000	70,798,000	655,423,000
1909	3,669,000	389,195,000	....	45,744,000	64,938,000	689,345,000
1910	3,720,000	349,032,000	194,508,000	45,691,000	60,978,000	747,769,000
1911	3,619,000	292,737,000	233,778,000	45,017,000	47,444,000	694,570,000
1912	3,711,000	420,647,000	212,550,000	49,530,000	72,691,000	856,695,000

Year.	Tobacco.			Cotton.		
	Acres.	Pounds.	Value.	Acres.	Bales.	Value.
1902	1,039,734	821,823,963	$57,563,510	25,758,139	10,725,422	$458,051,005
1903	1,037,735	815,972,425	55,514,627	27,114,103	10,050,953	599,694,724
1904	808,409	660,460,720	53,392,959	28,016,893	9,851,129	576,499,824
1905	776,112	633,033,719	48,674,118	30,053,739	13,438,012	561,100,346
1906	795,059	682,428,530	68,292,647	32,049,000	13,273,809	640,311,538
1907	820,800	698,126,000	71,411,000	31,311,000	11,107,179	613,630,436
1908	875,425	718,061,980	74,130,185	32,444,000	13,241,799	588,814,828
1909	1,285,000	1,055,765,000	....	30,938,000	10,004,949	688,350,000
1910	1,366,000	1,103,415,000	102,142,000	32,403,000	11,608,616	850,320,000
1911	1,013,000	905,109,000	85,210,000	36,045,000	16,250,276	850,840,000
1912	1,226,000	962,855,000	104,063,000	34,283,000	14,313,015	920,630,000

AVERAGE FARM VALUE OF CROPS.

Dec. 1.	Wheat.	Oats.	Corn.	Rye.	Barley.	Buckwheat.	Potatoes.	Hay, per ton
	Cents.	Cents.	Cents.	Cents.	Cents.	Cents.	Cents.	Doll'rs
1902	63.0	30.7	40.3	50.8	45.9	59.6	47.1	9.06
1903	69.5	34.1	42.5	54.5	45.6	60.7	61.4	9.08
1904	92.4	31.3	44.1	68.8	42.0	62.2	45.3	8.72
1905	74.8	29.1	41.2	61.1	40.3	58.7	61.7	8.52
1906	66.7	31.7	39.9	58.9	41.5	59.6	51.1	10.37
1907	87.4	44.3	51.6	73.1	66.6	69.8	61.7	11.08
1908	92.4	47.2	60.6	73.6	55.4	75.6	70.6	8.98
1909	99.0	40.5	59.6	76.9	55.2	69.9	54.9	10.62
1910	88.3	34.1	48.0	72.2	57.8	65.7	55.7	12.26
1911	87.4	45.0	61.8	83.2	86.9	72.6	79.9	14.64
1912	76.0	31.9	48.7	66.3	50.4	66.1	50.5	11.79

SUGAR PRODUCTION IN THE UNITED STATES BY YEARS.
In long tons.

Year.	Beet sugar.	Cane Sugar.					Total.
		Louisiana.	Other southern states.	Porto Rico.	Hawaii.	Philippines.	
1903–4	214,825	228,477	19,800	130,000	328,103	84,000	1,005,205
1904–5	215,173	335,000	15,000	145,000	380,576	108,875	1,198,624
1905–6	279,303	330,000	12,000	213,000	383,225	145,525	1,363,143
1906–7	481,796	230,000	13,000	255,000	390,000	150,500	1,470,296
1907–8	413,954	345,000	12,000	209,000	465,288	15,000	1,376,242
1908–9	380,254	350,000	15,000	215,000	465,000	150,000	1,575,254
1909–10	457,562	325,000	10,000	308,000	462,000	120,000	1,683,175
1910–11	455,511	300,000	11,000	261,000	506,096	147,016	1,711,523
1911–12	535,298	297,000	7,143	332,318	551,480	188,077	1,985,286
1912–13	618,354		8,036				

BEET SUGAR IN THE UNITED STATES.

STATE AND YEAR.	Factories in operation.	Area harvested.	Average yield of beets per acre.	Beets worked.	Sugar manufactured.	Estimat'd average extraction of sugar.	Average sugar in beets.	Average purity co-efficient of beets.	Av. length of campaign.
1912.	No.	Acres.	Short tons.	Short tons.	Pounds.	Per cent.	Per cent.	Per cent.	Days
California	11	111,416	9.01	1,004,328	138,994,000	15.82	18.79	83.99	90
Colorado	17	144,999	11.32	1,641,861	216,010,000	13.16	16.19	84.81	91
Michigan	18	124,211	6.75	838,784	96,049,000	11.83	14.72	84.75	74
Utah and Idaho	10	56,962	10.81	615,749	84,532,000	13.70	16.45	86.83	87
Wisconsin*	11	53,986	9.90	534,438	57,921,000	10.84	14.43	82.30	87
Other states	8	63,706	9.25	589,217	80,340,000	13.64	16.61	84.13	88
Totals and averages	73	555,300	9.41	5,224,377	692,556,000	13.26	16.39	84.49	86
1911	66	473,877	10.68	5,062,335	599,500,000	11.84	15.89	......	94
1910	61	398,029	10.17	4,027,292	1,020,344,000	12.61	16.35	84.35	83
1909	65	420,262	9.71	4,081,382	1,024,938,000	12.56	16.1	84.11	83
1908	62	364,913	9.36	3,414,891	851,768,000	12.47	15.74	83.5	74
1907	63	370,804	10.16	3,767,871	927,366,490	12.30	15.8	83.6	89
1906	63	378,074	11.36	4,236,112	967,224,000	11.42	14.0	82.2	105
1905	52	307,364	8.67	2,665,913	~25,841,228	11.74	15.3	83.0	77
1904	48	197,784	10.47	2,071,539	484,226,430	11.69	15.3	83.1	78
1903	49	242,576	8.56	2,076,494	481,209,087	11.59	15.1	......	75
1902	41	218,400	8.76	1,886,812	436,811,685	11.52	14.6	83.3	94
1901	36	175,083	9.63	1,685,689	369,211,733	10.95	14.8	82.2	88

*Includes Ohio, Indiana and Illinois.

SUGAR BEET PRODUCTION IN EUROPE.

[From report of the International Institute of Agriculture.]

Country.	1912. Acres.	1911. Acres.	1912. Tons (2,000 lbs).	1911. Tons (2,000 lbs).	Country.	1912. Acres.	1911. Acres.	1912. Tons (2,000 lbs).	1911. Tons (2,000 lbs).
Prussia	1,053,454	865,559	14,289,352	6,609,550	Croatia and Slavonia	7,413	7,413	99,207	66,138
Belgium	163,086	150,237	2,094,370	1,826,995	Italy	130,963	131,260	1,818,795	1,587,753
Bulgaria	7,413	7,331	49,604	68,342	Roumania	35,491	33,613	352,736	289,962
Denmark	74,871	61,528	885,729	805,208	Russia	1,860,196	1,923,758	14,523,444	14,343,901
Spain	106,438	82,121	1,189,353	964,463	Sweden	......	......	1,091,480	905,124
France	696,346	600,280	7,037,204	4,669,082					

GRAIN CROPS OF THE CANADIAN NORTHWEST.

Bushels produced in 1910 and 1911.

PROVINCE.	WHEAT. 1911.	WHEAT. 1912.	OATS. 1911.	OATS. 1912.	BARLEY. 1911.	BARLEY. 1912.
Manitoba	60,275,000	58,899,000	57,593,000	53,806,000	14,447,000	14,965,000
Saskatchewan	97,665,000	93,849,000	97,962,000	105,115,000	5,445,000	6,926,000
Alberta	36,143,000	30,574,000	56,964,000	62,936,000	4,151,000	5,780,000
Total	194,083,000	183,322,000	212,819,000	231,857,000	24,043,000	26,671,000

VALUE IN 1912 OF CROPS REPORTED QUANTITATIVELY.

Crops represented are: Corn, wheat, oats, barley, rye, buckwheat, flaxseed, rice, potatoes, hay, tobacco and lint cotton.

State.	Value.	Rank.	State.	Value.	Rank.
Texas	$407,166,000	1	Virginia	79,248,000	26
Illinois	289,326,000	2	Wash'gton	68,279,000	27
Iowa	284,395,000	3	Louisiana	61,600,000	28
Missouri	196,968,000	4	W.Virginia	41,658,000	29
Ohio	190,718,000	5	Oregon	41,377,000	30
Kansas	182,363,000	6	Montana	40,419,000	31
Pennsylv'a	176,275,000	7	Colorado	38,846,000	32
Minnesota	160,615,000	8	Maine	35,573,000	33
Georgia	159,762,000	9	Maryland.	35,207,000	34
N. Dakota	155,110,000	10	Idaho	33,499,000	35
Indiana	153,647,000	11	N. Jersey.	27,464,000	36
New York.	152,533,000	12	Vermont	26,707,000	37
Nebraska..	141,634,000	13	Con'ectic't	21,543,000	38
Wisconsin.	139,032,000	14	Mass'us'ts	19,555,000	39
N.Carolina	128,395,000	15	Utah	17,446,000	40
Alabama..	128,350,000	16	Florida	15,280,000	41
Oklahoma.	126,332,000	17	Wyoming..	13,732,000	42
Michigan..	116,209,000	18	N. Hamp.	11,938,000	43
Kentucky..	116,160,000	19	Nevada ...	9,009,000	44
S. Carolina	112,593,000	20	N. Mexico.	7,840,000	45
Mississippi	111,482,000	21	Delaware..	7,563,000	46
Tennessee.	106,200,000	22	Arizona ...	7,511,000	47
California .	100,729,000	23	Rhode Isl.	2,327,000	48
S. Dakota.	99,680,000	24			
Arkansas..	95,886,000	25	U. S.	4,695,161,000	

NUMBER AND VALUE OF LIVE STOCK (1913).

Farm animals.	Number.	Av. price.	Total value.
Horses	20,567,000	$110.77	$2,278,222,000
Mules	4,386,000	124.31	545,245,000
Milch cows	20,497,000	45.02	922,783,000
Other cattle	36,030,000	26.36	949,645,000
Sheep	51,482,000	3.94	202,779,000
Swine	61,178,000	9.86	603,109,000

The states having the largest number of farm animals of each of the above kinds Jan. 1, 1913, were:

Horses—Iowa, 1,568,000; Illinois, 1,482,000; Texas, 1,181,000; Kansas, 1,099,000; Missouri, 1,084,000; Nebraska, 1,027,000; Ohio, 892,000; Indiana, 846,000; Minnesota, 822,000; Oklahoma, 758,000; North Dakota, 712,000; South Dakota, 702,000; Wisconsin, 665,000; Michigan, 640,000; New York, 609,000.

Mules—Texas, 724,000; Missouri, 326,000; Georgia, 310,000; Mississippi, 280,000; Tennessee, 276,000; Alabama, 270,000; Oklahoma, 269,000; Arkansas, 233,000; Kentucky, 229,000; Kansas, 222,000.

Milch Cows—Wisconsin, 1,504,000; New York, 1,485,000; Iowa, 1,337,000; Minnesota, 1,129,000; Texas, 1,034,000; Illinois, 1,007,000; Pennsylvania, 943,000; Ohio, 869,000; Michigan, 798,000; Missouri, 789,000; Indiana, 634,000.

Cattle (other than milch cows)—Texas, 5,022,000; Iowa, 2,607,000; Nebraska, 1,902,000; Kansas, 1,778,000; California, 1,454,000; Missouri, 1,440,000; Illinois, 1,228,000; Oklahoma, 1,155,000; Minnesota, 1,139,000;

Wisconsin, 1,135,000; Colorado, 921,000; South Dakota, 894,000; New York, 876,000; Ohio, 814,000; Arizona, 778,000; Montana, 717,000.

Sheep—Montana, 5,111,000; Wyoming, 4,472,000; Ohio, 3,435,000; New Mexico, 3,300,000; Idaho, 2,-951,000; Oregon, 2,644,000; California, 2,603,000; Michigan, 2,139,000; Texas, 2,073,000; Utah, 1,990,000; Colorado, 1,737,000; Missouri, 1,650,000; Arizona, 1,570,000; Nevada, 1,487,000; Kentucky, 1,320,000; Indiana, 1,-317,000; Iowa, 1,249,000; Illinois, 1,036,000.

Swine—Iowa, 8,720,000; Illinois, 4,315,000; Missouri, 4,087,000; Nebraska, 3,798,000; Indiana, 3,709,000; Ohio, 3,399,000; Kansas, 2,611,000; Texas, 2,493,000; Wisconsin, 2,030,000; Georgia, 1,888,000; Kentucky, 1,-638,000.

AVERAGE AGE OF MARKETED HOGS.

The average age at which swine are usually marketed in the United States is 11 months. The lowest average for any state is 9 months in Maine, New Hampshire, Vermont, New York and Michigan, while the highest average is in Lousiana, which is 15 months. In the north Atlantic states and also in the north central states east of the Mississippi river the average is 9.6 months; in the north central states, west of the Mississippi river, 10.7 months; in the south Atlantic states, 11.8 months; in the south central states, 12.7 months, and in the Rocky mountain and far western states, 12 months.

AVERAGE VALUE PER HEAD OF FARM ANIMALS.

On Jan. 1 of years indicated.

Animals.	1913.	1912.	1911.	1910.	1909.	1900-1909.	1890-1899.	1880-1889.	1870-1879.
Horses	$110.77	$105.94	$111.67	$108.19	$95.64	$71.99	$48.24	$67.78	$62.07
Mules	124.31	120.51	125.62	119.84	107.84	84.98	58.79	76.63	75.65
Milch cows	45.02	39.39	40.49	35.79	32.36	30.12	23.35	26.65	27.27
Other cattle	26.36	21.20	20.85	19.41	17.49	18.09	16.53	19.77	17.54
Sheep	3.94	3.46	3.73	4.08	3.43	3.13	2.23	2.21	2.32
Swine	9.86	8.00	9.35	9.14	6.55	6.46	4.81	5.18	4.76

WHEAT HARVEST CALENDAR.

January—Australia, New Zealand, Chile, Argentine Republic.

February and March—Upper Egypt, India.

April—Lower Egypt, India, Syria, Cyprus, Persia, Asia Minor, Mexico, Cuba.

May—Texas, Algeria, Central Asia, China, Japan, Morocco.

June—California, Oregon, Mississippi, Alabama, Georgia, North Carolina, South Carolina, Tennessee, Virginia, Kentucky, Kansas, Arkansas, Utah, Colorado, Missouri, Turkey, Greece, Italy, Spain, Portugal, south of France.

July—New England, New York, Pennsylvania, Ohio, Indiana, Michigan, Illinois, Iowa, Wisconsin, southern Minnesota, Nebraska, upper Canada, Roumania, Bulgaria, Austria, Hungary, south of Russia, Germany, Switzerland, south of England.

August—Central and northern Minnesota, Dakotas, Manitoba, lower Canada, British Columbia, Belgium, Holland, Great Britain, Denmark, Poland, central Russia.

September and October—Scotland, Sweden, Norway, north of Russia.

November—Peru, South Africa.

December—Burma, New South Wales.

CROP ESTIMATES FOR 1913.

[From Farmers' Bulletin for Nov. 11, 1913.]

Crops.	Yield per acre.	Production.
Corn	23	2,463,017,000 bushels
Buckwheat	17	14,455,000 bushels
Potatoes	89	328,550,000 bushels
Sweet potatoes	95	55,760,000 bushels
Flaxseed	8	19,234,000 bushels
Tobacco	790	903,875,000 pounds
Wheat	15	730,267,000 bushels
Oats	29	1,122,139,000 bushels
Barley	24	223,824,000 bushels
Rye	16	35,664,000 bushels
Hay	1.31	63,460,000 tons

COTTON STATISTICS OF UNITED STATES.

Year.	Production. Bales.*	Consumption. Bales.*	Exports. Bales.*
1790	3,138	11,000	379
1800	73,222	18,829	41,822
1810	177,824	35,565	124,116
1820	334,728	100,000	249,787
1830	732,218	129,938	553,960
1840	1,347,640	245,045	1,060,408
1850	2,136,083	422,626	1,854,474
1860	3,841,416	841,975	615,082
1870	4,024,527	1,026,583	2,922,757
1880	6,356,998	1,865,922	4,453,495
1890	8,562,089	2,604,491	5,850,219
1900	10,266,527	3,603,516	8,806,572
1910	12,005,688	4,516,779	8,808,195

Year.	Production. Bales.*	Consumption. Bales.*	Exports. Bales.*
1911	16,250,276	5,181,826	10,681,332
1912	14,313,015	....	....

*Equivalent 500 pound bales.

WORLD'S COTTON SPINDLES AND MILL CONSUMPTION OF RAW COTTON IN 1912.

[From report of United States census bureau.]

	Spindles.	Bales.*
United States—		
Cotton growing states	11,583,000	2,712,000
Other states	18,996,000	2,655,000
Europe—		
United kingdom	55,317,000	4,250,000
Germany	10,726,000	1,795,000
Russia	8,800,000	1,650,000
France	7,400,000	1,014,000
Austria-Hungary	4,798,000	830,000
Italy	4,580,000	920,000
Spain	2,200,000	330,000
Switzerland	1,408,000	110,000
Belgium	1,388,000	222,000
Sweden	530,000	100,000
Portugal	480,000	70,000
Netherlands	454,000	83,000
Denmark	84,000	25,000
Norway	74,000	11,000
Other European countries	200,000	60,000
British India	6,195,000	1,705,000
Japan	2,192,000	1,190,000
China	831,000	350,000
Brazil	1,000,000	180,000
Canada	855,000	125,000
Mexico	630,000	115,000
All other countries	275,000	75,000
Total in 1912	140,996,000	20,587,000
Total in 1911	137,792,000	19,013,000

*Bales of 500 pounds each.

RELATIVE IMPORTANCE OF LEADING CROPS.

[From the Crop Reporter.]

The relative importance of value in the different agricultural products does not change materially from year to year; even in a lapse of ten years, from one census to another, there is not much change in the relative standing of the leading crops.

Corn is by far the leading crop; from the census of 1900 to the census of 1910 its value had increased more than 73 per cent; nevertheless it represented 27.6 per cent of the value of all crops in 1900 and 26.2 per cent in 1910. Hay and forage represented 18.1 per cent of the value of all crops in 1900 and 15 per cent in 1910. Cotton (including cotton seed) represented 12.4 per cent in 1900 and 15 per cent in 1910. Wheat represented 12.3 per cent in 1900 and 12 per cent in 1910, oats 7.2 per cent in 1900 and 7.6 per cent in 1910. The increased relative im-

portance of cotton is due largely to the great increase in the use and value of cotton seed.

The five articles mentioned, corn, hay, cotton, wheat and oats, represented 75.6 per cent of the value of all crops in 1909 and 75.8 per cent in 1910. In other words, all the numerous minor crops, including fruits, vegetables, nuts and cereals not mentioned, represent less than one-fourth of the value of all products of the soil. It is partly for this reason that these five articles receive so much prominence in crop reporting.

PER CAPITA CONSUMPTION OF WHEAT IN PAST DECADE.

[From the Crop Reporter of the department of agriculture.] Seed is excluded and flour is reduced to wheat equivalent.

Country.	Bushels.	Country.	Bushels.
Canada	9.5	Netherlands	4.2
Belgium	8.3	Roumania	4.0
France	7.9	Denmark	3.5
Spain	6.1	Chile	3.4
United kingdom	6.0	Germany	3.2
Switzerland	6.0	Russia	2.7
Australia	5.5	Servia	2.5
Italy	5.4	Sweden	2.5
United States	5.3	Egypt	2.5
Uruguay	5.3	Portugal	1.8
Argentina	5.2	British India	.8
Bulgaria	5.0	Mexico	.8
Austria-Hungary	4.3	Japan	.5

DAIRY INDUSTRIES OF CANADA.

According to the census of dairy industries of Canada, taken in June, 1911, for the calendar year 1910, there were then 1,035 butter making factories in the dominion with 2,044 employes and an output of 57,328,191 pounds of butter, valued at $13,726,546. The patrons of the factories numbered 76,579 and they received as their share of the value $11,832,705. Cheese factories numbered 2,154, with 70,778 patrons and 3,189 employes. The combined product was 162,450,802 pounds of cheese, valued at $17,524,021, of which the patrons received $15,209,855. There were 436 factories making both butter and cheese, with 22,766 patrons and 914 employes. The quantity of butter made was 7,690,189 pounds, valued at $1,870,861, and of cheese 37,453,403 pounds, with a value of $4,063,103. Patrons were paid $1,625,644 for butter and $3,540,566 for cheese. There were 11 factories making condensed milk, the amount produced in 1910 being 27,831,596 pounds, with a value of $1,813,971.

VINEYARDS AND WINE PRODUCTION OF CERTAIN COUNTRIES.

[From report of the International Institute of Agriculture.]

	1912.	1911.	1912.	1911.
	Acres.	Acres.	Gallons.	Gallons.
Spain	3,123,356	3,187,533	369,836,000	389,572,846
France	4,148,663	4,156,501	1,567,559,288	1,185,740,254
Italy	11,008,305	11,063,161	1,162,348,000	1,126,793,360
Lux'mb'rg	2,830	2,618	1,074,379	3,614,797
Roumania	174,030	176,523	33,021,250	26,243,625
Switz'land	58,563	58,563	23,854,55▶	22,580,459

NATIONAL HOME FOR DISABLED VOLUNTEER SOLDIERS.
Established by act of Congress March 21, 1866.

Names and Location of Branches—Central, Dayton, O.; Northwestern, Milwaukee, Wis.; Southern, Hampton. Va.; Eastern, Togus. Me.; Western, Leavenworth, Kas.; Marion, Marion. Ind.; Pacific, Santa Monica, Cal.; Danville, Danville, Ill.; Mountain, Johnson City, Tenn.; Battle Mountain Sanitarium, Hot Springs, S. D.

Board of Managers—The president of the United States, the chief justice of the Supreme court, the secretary of war ex officis, Washington, D. C.; president, Maj. James W. Wadsworth, 346 Broadway, New York, N. Y.; secretary, John M. Holley, LaCrosse, Wis.; Maj. William Warner, Kansas City, Mo.; Col. Henry H. Markham, Pasadena, Cal.; Lieut. Franklin Murphy, Newark, N. J.; Col. Edwin P. Hammond, Lafayette, Ind.; Gen. Joseph S. Smith, Bangor, Me.; Lieut. Oscar M. Gottschalk, Dayton, O.; Z. D. Massey, Sevierville, Tenn.; Capt. Lucien S. Lambert, Galesburg, Ill.; Gen. P. H. Barry, Greeley, Neb. General treasurer—Maj. Moses Harris.

REQUIREMENTS FOR ADMISSION.
1. Honorable discharge from the United States service.
2. Disability which prevents the applicant from earning a living by labor.
3. Applicants for admission will be required to abide by all the rules and regulations made by the board of managers, perform all the duties required of them and obey all the lawful orders of the officers of the home.
4. A soldier or sailor to be admitted must forward with his application his discharge paper, his pension certificate if he is a pensioner, and his discharge from a state home if he has been an inmate of such home. These papers are retained at the branch to which he is admitted to prevent their loss or fraud, but are returned to him when he is discharged. Soldiers or sailors whose pensions exceed $16 a month are not admitted to the home except for special reasons.

The National Home for Disabled Volunteer Soldiers is supported by the United States government. The annual appropriation for that purpose is about $4,000,000.

STATE SOLDIERS' HOMES.
There are a number of state homes for disabled volunteer soldiers, who, for various reasons, are unable to obtain admission to the national homes. The federal government contributes toward the support of the state homes the sum of $100 for each soldier, based upon the average attendance for the year; the remainder of the expenses is paid by the states themselves. Some of the homes are on the cottage plan. Following is a list of the state homes:

California—Yountville.	New Hampshire—Tilton.
Colorado—Monte Vista.	New Jersey—Kearny and Vineland.
Connecticut — Noroton Heights.	New York—Bath and Oxford.
Idaho—Boise.	North Dakota—Lisbon.
Illinois—Quincy.	Ohio—Sandusky.
Indiana—Lafayette.	Oregon—Roseburg.
Iowa—Marshalltown.	Pennsylvania—Erie.
Kansas—Fort Dodge.	Rhode Island—Bristol.
Massachusetts—Chelsea.	S. Dakota—Hot Springs.
Michigan—Grand Rapids.	Vermont—Bennington.
Minnesota—Minnehaha.	Washington—Orting and Port Orchard.
Missouri—St. James.	Wisconsin—Waupaca.
Montana—Columbus Falls.	Wyoming—Cheyenne.
Nebraska—Grand Island and Milford.	

HOME FOR REGULAR ARMY SOLDIERS.
The United States maintains a home for disabled and discharged soldiers of the regular army at Washington, D. C. All soldiers who have served twenty years in the army and all soldiers who have incurred such disability, by wounds, disease or injuries in the line of duty while in the regular army as unfits them for further service are entitled to admission to the home. The home is in charge of a board of commissioners, consisting of the governor of the home, the adjutant-general of the army, the judge-advocate, the commissary-general, the quartermaster-general, the chief of engineers and the surgeon-general. The present governor is Lieut.-Gen. S. B. M. Young (retired).

CONFEDERATE SOLDIERS' HOMES.
Confederate veterans of the civil war have a home at Beauvoir, near Biloxi, Miss. The residence there of Jefferson Davis in his last years was secured in 1902 as a refuge for helpless old southern soldiers by the United Sons of Confederate Veterans. It is supported by that society and the United Daughters of the Confederacy. Another home for confederate veterans was opened in Washington, D. C., May 24, 1913, by the women of the Southern Relief association.

FARMS AND FARM PROPERTY IN THE UNITED STATES.

[From census bureau report.]

SUMMARY FOR 1910 AND 1900.

	1910 (Apr. 15).	1900 (June 1).	Increase.* Amount.	Pr. ct.
Population	91,972,266	75,994,575	15,977,691	21.0
Urban population†	42,623,383	21,609,645	11,013,738	34.8
Rural population‡	49,348,883	44,384,930	4,963,953	11.2
Number of all farms...........................	6,361,502	5,737,372	624,130	10.9
Land area of the country, acres...............	1,903,289,600	1,903,461,760	—172,160	.....
Land in farms, acres..........................	878,798,325	838,591,774	40,206,551	4.8
Improved land in farms, acres.................	478,451,750	414,498,487	63,953,263	15.4
Average acreage per farm......................	138.1	146.2	—8.1	—5.5
Average improved acreage per farm.............	75.2	72.2	3.0	4.2
Per cent of total land area in farms..........	46.2	44.1	....	.....
Per cent of land in farms improved............	54.4	49.4	....	.....
Per cent of total land area improved..........	25.1	21.8	....	.....
Value of farm property, total.................	$40,991,449,090	$20,439,901,164	$20,551,547,926	100.5
Land	28,475,674,169	13,058,007,995	15,417,666,174	118.1
Buildings	6,325,451,528	3,556,639,496	2,768,812,032	77.8
Implements and machinery.................	1,265,149,783	749,775,970	515,373,813	68.7
Domestic animals, poultry and bees.......	4,925,173,610	3,075,477,703	1,849,695,907	60.1
Average value of all property per farm.......	6,444	3,563	2,881	80.9
Avge. value of all property per acre of land in farms	46.64	24.37	22.27	91.4
Average value of land per acre...............	32.40	15.57	16.83	108.1

*A minus sign (—) denotes decrease. †Population of incorporated places having, in 1910, 2,500 or more inhabitants. The figure for 1900 does not represent the urban population according to that census, but is the population in that year of the territory classified as urban in 1910. ‡Total, exclusive of urban.

FARMS, FARM LAND AND FARM PROPERTY: 1870 TO 1900.

	1910.	1900.	1890.	1880.	1870.
Population	91,972,266	75,994,575	62,947,714	50,155,783	38,558,371
Number of all farms...............	6,361,502	5,737,372	4,564,641	4,008,907	2,659,985
Land area of the country, acres........	1,903,289,600	1,903,461,760	1,903,337,600	1,903,337,600	1,903,337,600
Land in farms, acres.............	878,798,325	838,591,774	623,218,619	536,081,835	407,735,041
Improved land in farms, acres........	478,451,750	414,498,487	357,616,755	284,771,042	188,921,099
Average acreage per farm..............	138.1	146.2	136.5	133.7	153.3
Average improved acreage per farm..	75.2	72.2	78.3	71.0	71.0
Per cent of total land area in farms..	46.2	44.1	32.7	28.2	21.4
Per cent of land in farms improved..	54.4	49.4	57.4	53.1	46.3
Per cent of total land area improved..	25.1	21.8	18.8	15.0	9.9
Value of farm property, total.........	$40,991,449,090	$20,439,901,164	$16,082,267,689	$12,180,501,538	$8,944,857,749
Land and buildings.................	34,801,125,697	16,614,647,491	13,279,252,649	10,157,096,776	7,444,054,462
Implements and machinery..........	1,265,149,783	749,775,970	494,247,467	406,526,055	270,913,676
Domestic animals, poultry and bees.	4,925,173,610	3,075,477,703	2,308,767,573	1,576,884,707	1,229,889,605
Average value of all property per farm.	6,444	3,563	3,523	3,038	3,363
Average value of all property per acre of land in farms.	46.64	24.37	25.81	22.72	21.94
Average value of land and buildings per acre.....................	39.60	19.81	21.31	19.02	18.26

AGRICULTURAL INCREASE SINCE 1850.

Period.	Population.	Farms.	Acres.*	Improved.†	Value.‡
1900–1910..........................	15,977,691	624,130	40,206,551	63,953,263	$20,551,547,926
1890–1900..........................	13,046,861	1,172,731	215,373,155	56,881,732	4,357,633,475
1880–1890..........................	12,791,931	555,734	87,136,784	72,845,713	3,901,766,151
1870–1880..........................	11,597,412	1,348,922	128,346,794	95,849,943	3,235,642,789
1860–1870..........................	7,115,050	615,908	522,503	25,810,379	964,364,686
1850–1860..........................	8,251,445	595,004	113,651,924	50,078,106	4,013,149,483
1880–1910—Amount	41,816,483	2,352,595	342,716,490	193,680,708	28,810,947,552
Per cent.........................	83.4	58.7	63.9	68.0	236.5
1850–1880—Amount	26,963,907	2,559,834	242,521,221	171,738,428	8,213,157,958
Per cent.........................	116.3	176.6	82.6	151.9	207.0
1850–1910—Amount	68,780,390	4,912,429	585,237,711	365,419,136	37,024,105,510
Per cent.........................	296.6	339.0	193.4	323.3	933.2

*In farms. †Improved land in farms. ‡Of farm property.

AVERAGE ACRES AND VALUE PER FARM (1910).

State.	Acres.	Property.*	Land.†	Per acre.‡	State.	Acres.	Property.*	Land.†	Per acre.‡
Alabama	78.9	$1,408	$825	$10.46	Louisiana	86.6	2,499	1,558	17.99
Arizona	135.1	8,142	4,590	33.97	Maine	104.9	3,320	1,441	13.73
Arkansas	81.1	1,864	1,146	14.13	Maryland	103.4	5,849	3,241	32.32
California	316.7	18,308	14,395	47.16	Massachusetts	77.9	6,135	2,859	36.69
Colorado	293.1	10,645	7,853	26.81	Michigan	91.5	5,261	2,973	32.48
Connecticut	81.5	5,344	2,693	33.03	Minnesota	177.3	9,456	6,527	36.82
Delaware	95.9	5,830	3,224	33.63	Mississippi	67.6	1,554	926	13.69
District Columbia..	27.9	39,062	33,152	1,186.53	Missouri	124.8	7,405	5,216	41.80
Florida	105.0	2,863	1,874	17.84	Montana	516.7	13,269	8,651	16.74
Georgia	92.6	1,995	1,273	13.74	Nebraska	297.8	16,038	12,450	41.80
Idaho	171.5	9,911	7,140	41.63	Nevada 1,009.6	22,462	13,119	12.99
Illinois	129.1	15,595	12,270	95.02	New Hampshire....	120.1	3,833	1,646	13.70
Indiana	98.8	8,396	6,164	62.36	New Jersey........	76.9	7,600	3,707	48.23
Iowa	156.3	17,259	12,910	82.68	New Mexico.......	315.9	4,469	2,770	8.77
Kansas	244.0	11,467	8,648	35.45	New York..........	102.2	6,732	3,283	32.13
Kentucky	85.6	2,986	1,869	21.83	North Carolina....	88.4	2,119	1,352	15.29

State.	Acrea.	Property.*	Land.†	Per acre.‡
North Dakota	382.3	13,109	9,822	25.69
Ohio	88.6	6,994	4,727	53.34
Oklahoma	151.7	4,828	2,413	22.49
Oregon	256.8	11,609	9,048	35.23
Pennsylvania	84.8	6,715	2,875	33.92
Rhode Island	83.8	6,234	2,836	33.86
South Carolina	76.5	2,223	1,523	19.89
South Dakota	335.1	15,018	11,625	34.69
Tennessee	81.5	2,490	1,510	18.53
Texas	269.1	5,311	3,909	14.53
Utah	156.7	6,957	4,590	29.28
Vermont	142.6	4,445	1,785	12.53

State.	Acres.	Property.*	Land.†	Per acre.‡
Virginia	105.9	3,397	2,145	20.24
Washington	268.4	11,346	9,208	44.18
West Virginia	103.7	3,255	2,142	20.65
Wisconsin	118.9	7,978	5,148	43.39
Wyoming	777.6	15,217	8,092	10.41
United States	138.1	6,444	4,476	32.40
United States 1900	146.2	3,563	2,276	15.57

*Average value of all farm property. †Average value of land per farm only. ‡Average value per acre of farm land.

CROPS OF THE UNITED STATES IN 1909.

[Officially reported by the bureau of the census.]

Later and detailed figures on the principal crops are given elsewhere in this volume.

Crop.	Production.	Value.
Cereals, bu	4,512,564,465	$2,665,539,714
Corn, bu	2,552,189,630	1,438,553,919
Oats, bu	1,007,142,980	414,697,422
Wheat, bu	683,379,259	657,656,801
Barley, bu	173,344,212	92,458,571
Buckwheat, bu	14,849,332	9,330,592
Rye, bu	29,520,457	20,421,812
Kafir corn, bu	17,597,305	10,816,940
Emmer, spelt, bu	12,702,710	5,684,050
Rough rice, bu	21,838,580	16,019,607
Other grains, seeds	....	97,536,085
Dry edible beans, bu	11,251,160	21,771,482
Other beans, bu	179,733	241,060
Dry peas, bu	7,129,294	10,963,739
Peanuts, bu	19,415,816	18,271,515
Flaxseed, bu	19,512,765	28,970,554
Miscellaneous seeds	....	768,625
Grass seed, bu	6,671,348	15,137,683
Flower, vegetable seeds	....	1,411,013
Hay and forage, tons	97,453,735	$24,004,877
Tobacco, lbs	1,055,764,806	104,302,856
Cotton bales	10,649,268	703,619,308
Cotton seed, tons	5,324,634	121,076,984
Sugar crops	....	61,648,942
Sugar beets, tons	3,392,857	19,880,724
Sorghum cane, tons	1,647,262	10,174,457
Sugar cane, tons	6,240,260	26,415,952
Maple sugar and sirup	....	5,177,809
Minor crops	....	18,068,658
Broom corn, lbs	78,959,958	5,134,434
Hemp, lbs	7,483,295	412,699
Hops, lbs	40,718,748	7,844,745
All other	....	4,676,780
Vegetables	....	418,110,154
Potatoes, bu	388,194,965	166,423,910
Sweet potatoes, bu	59,232,070	35,429,176
Other vegetables	....	216,257,068
Fruits and nuts	....	222,024,316
Small fruits, qts	426,565,863	29,974,481
Strawberries, qts	255,702,035	17,913,926
Blackberries, qts	55,343,570	3,909,831
Raspberries, qts	60,918,196	6,132,277
Cranberries, qts	38,243,069	1,755,613
All other, qts	16,359,002	1,262,834
Orchard fruits, bu	216,083,695	140,867,347
Apples, bu	147,522,318	83,231,492
Peaches, bu	35,470,276	28,781,075
Pears, bu	8,840,733	7,916,600
Plums, prunes, bu	15,480,170	10,299,495
Cherries, bu	4,126,099	7,231,160
Apricots, bu	4,150,263	2,884,119
All other, bu	493,836	529,403
Grapes, lbs	2,571,065,205	22,027,961
Tropical fruits	....	24,706,753
Oranges, boxes	19,487,481	17,566,464
Lemons, boxes	2,770,313	2,993,738
Grapefruit, boxes	1,189,259	2,060,610
Figs, lbs	35,060,395	803,810
Pineapples, crates	778,651	734,090
Olives, lbs	16,405,483	404,574
All other	....	143,467
Nuts, lbs	62,328,010	4,447,674
Almonds, lbs	6,673,539	711,970
Pecans, lbs	9,890,769	971,596
Walnuts, lbs	22,026,524	2,297,336
All other, lbs	23,617,178	466,772

Crop.	Production.	Value.
Flowers, plants	....	24,872,329
Nursery products	....	21,050,522
Forest farm products	....	195,396,283
Total all crops	....	5,487,161,223
Total, 1899	....	2,998,704,412

KAFIR CORN AND MILO MAIZE.*

State.	Acres.	Bushels.	Value.
Arkansas	1,294	15,284	$12,074
California	44,308	938,049	725,704
Colorado	11,971	139,234	94,486
Kansas	388,495	5,115,415	3,046,799
Missouri	15,543	228,386	152,248
Nebraska	2,016	20,212	15,712
New Mexico	63,570	543,350	392,393
Oklahoma	532,515	4,658,752	2,591,036
Texas	573,384	5,860,444	3,785,453
United States	1,635,153	17,597,305	10,816,940
Total, 1899	266,513	5,169,113	1,367,040

*Kafir corn and milo maize are cereals belonging to the millet family and used in this country mainly as feed for live stock. They are making headway as dry farming crops in sections of light rainfall.

VALUE OF ALL CROPS BY STATES.

[From report of the bureau of the census.] Figures in parentheses show rank of each state in agriculture in 1909.

State.	Value of crops.	State.	Value of crops.
Illinois (1)	$372,270,470	Virginia (26)	$100,631,157
Iowa (2)	314,666,298	Washington(27)	78,927,053
Texas (3)	298,133,466	Louisiana (28)	77,336,143
Ohio (4)	230,337,981	Colorado (29)	50,974,953
Georgia (5)	226,595,436	Oregon (30)	49,040,725
Missouri (6)	220,663,724	Maryland (31)	43,920,149
Kansas (7)	214,859,597	W.Virginia (32)	40,374,776
New York (8)	209,168,236	N. Jersey (33)	40,340,491
Indiana (9)	204,209,812	Maine (34)	39,317,647
Nebraska (10)	196,125,632	Florida (35)	36,141,894
Minnesota (11)	193,451,474	Idaho (36)	34,357,851
N. Dakota (12)	180,635,520	Mass'us'ts (37)	31,948,095
Pennsylva. (13)	166,735,898	Montana (38)	29,714,563
Michigan (14)	162,004,681	Vermont (39)	27,444,836
California (15)	153,111,013	Connecticut(40)	22,487,999
Wisconsin (16)	148,359,216	Utah (41)	18,484,615
Mississippi (17)	147,315,621	N. Hamp. (42)	15,976,175
Alabama (18)	144,287,947	Wyoming (43)	10,022,961
N. Carolina (19)	142,890,192	Delaware (44)	9,121,809
S. Carolina (20)	141,890,192	N. Mexico (45)	8,922,397
Kentucky (21)	138,973,107	Nevada (46)	5,923,536
Oklahoma (22)	133,454,405	Arizona (47)	5,496,872
S. Dakota (23)	125,507,249	Rhode Isl'd(48)	~3,937,077
Tennessee (24)	120,706,211	Dist. Col. (49)	546,479
Arkansas (25)	119,419,025		

MINOR FARM CROPS IN 1909.

EMMER AND SPELT.*

State.	Acres.	Bushels.	Value.
Colorado	15,522	324,713	$153,065
Illinois	1,633	41,999	20,574
Iowa	7,256	139,839	65,436
Kansas	49,969	786,362	342,846
Michigan	6,472	154,103	97,414
Minnesota	30,891	757,339	338,841
Missouri	7,935	194,540	47,543

State.	Acres.	Bushels.	Value.
Montana	1,308	39,830	24,643
Nebraska	65,681	1,221,975	484,791
New York	1,582	33,890	22,110
North Dakota	101,144	2,564,732	1,102,782
Oklahoma	8,659	94,580	54,690
South Dakota	259,611	6,098,982	2,627,533
Texas	4,624	44,316	27,118
Wisconsin	6,090	166,301	89,118
Wyoming	1,521	35,677	22,918
United States	573,622	12,702,710	5,584,050

*Grains used chiefly for fodder. Nearly all is emmer, spelt being cultivated in only a few scattered localities. No report of production made in 1899.

DRY EDIBLE BEANS.

State.	Acres.	Bushels.	Value.
Alabama	1,157	15,212	$19,887
Arizona	2,301	18,457	44,997
Arkansas	819	4,090	6,588
California	157,987	3,328,218	6,295,457
Colorado	5,040	53,926	128,701
Connecticut	208	2,845	7,045
Delaware	55	648	1,387
Florida	2,641	21,835	43,919
Georgia	2,947	16,546	30,018
Idaho	1,915	33,816	76,314
Illinois	1,153	6,866	12,842
Indiana	1,721	15,228	30,929
Iowa	615	5,699	12,428
Kansas	70	636	1,321
Kentucky	12,434	70,557	105,309
Louisiana	311	5,557	6,982
Maine	10,341	87,565	275,334
Maryland	196	1,833	3,342
Massachusetts	446	4,979	12,382
Michigan	403,669	5,282,511	9,716,315
Minnesota	4,697	62,822	124,996
Mississippi	1,092	8,727	23,647
Missouri	1,281	9,385	20,354
Montana	342	2,958	
Nebraska	1,173	5,941	
Nevada	14	222	
New Hampshire	3,180	22,546	62,783
New Jersey	403	2,941	6,150
New Mexico	20,756	85,795	282,023
New York	115,698	1,681,506	3,689,064
North Carolina	5,531	35,937	57,528
North Dakota	544	5,073	12,862
Ohio	1,139	13,665	30,082
Oklahoma	575	2,520	5,942
Oregon	562	8,032	23,242
Pennsylvania	1,269	12,021	28,136
Rhode Island	54	817	2,084
South Carolina	1,528	6,825	12,778
South Dakota	809	5,285	12,575
Tennessee	3,398	19,526	40,966
Texas	1,846	12,895	26,205
Utah	196	3,352	10,006
Vermont	2,390	26,359	72,873
Virginia	4,777	29,435	61,864
Washington	353	3,311	9,656
West Virginia	8,111	29,794	81,049
Wisconsin	14,574	154,570	263,911
Wyoming	273	1,876	5,018
United States	802,991	11,251,160	21,771,482
Total, 1899	453,841	5,064,490	7,633,636

DRY PEAS.

State.	Acres.	Bushels.	Value.
Alabama	85,034	418,007	$660,270
Arizona	13	92	293
Arkansas	52,730	229,444	376,076
California	2,959	57,468	101,016
Colorado	24,230	258,281	397,540
Connecticut	4	72	121
Delaware	1,615	4,650	25,278
Florida	7,144	56,713	98,383
Georgia	210,315	736,009	1,204,783
Idaho	234	4,875	9,160
Illinois	41,076	185,020	275,373
Indiana	13,082	98,254	133,996
Iowa	731	9,007	11,669
Kansas	825	5,235	10,739
Kentucky	8,465	44,772	84,511
Louisiana	33,150	161,659	252,362

State.	Acres.	Bushels.	Value.
Maine	537	4,963	10,134
Maryland	742	5,603	11,143
Massachusetts	30	480	944
Michigan	94,932	1,162,403	1,337,420
Minnesota	835	14,964	18,384
Mississippi	73,090	285,768	570,508
Missouri	23,036	169,357	180,391
Montana	1,184	21,670	37,757
Nebraska	26	169	308
New Hampshire	122	934	1,965
New Jersey	91	863	1,711
New Mexico	2,485	30,829	35,077
New York	4,007	71,486	117,558
North Carolina	169,934	651,567	1,024,228
North Dakota	399	5,543	8,368
Ohio	323	3,041	5,298
Oklahoma	6,245	33,282	63,857
Oregon	436	9,344	16,035
Pennsylvania	87	989	2,100
Rhode Island	4	73	102
South Carolina	265,632	711,863	1,311,454
South Dakota	1,783	10,598	11,223
Tennessee	36,640	133,924	245,434
Texas	46,777	254,361	402,854
Utah	126	3,222	5,753
Vermont	127	1,262	2,092
Virginia	12,091	66,488	127,211
Washington	3,196	91,032	116,065
West Virginia	232	1,490	3,312
Wisconsin	78,017	1,165,055	1,654,928
Wyoming	326	9,231	9,552
United States	1,305,099	7,129,294	10,963,739
Total, 1899	968,370	9,449,210	7,908,966

GRASS SEED.

Class.	Bushels.	Value.
Clover	1,025,816	$6,925,122
Timothy	2,878,790	4,018,951
Alfalfa	263,328	2,051,840
Millet	588,270	491,566
Other	1,915,144	1,650,204
Total, 1909	6,671,348	15,137,683
Total, 1899	4,865,078	8,228,417

Leading states in the production of grass seed in 1909:

State.	Bushels.	Value.
Iowa	1,118,044	$1,721,289
Illinois	1,289,966	1,719,420
Wisconsin	262,301	1,499,401
Minnesota	945,666	1,496,438
Ohio	288,605	1,352,136
Indiana	165,488	785,041

MINOR SEEDS (1909).

Sorghum cane seed—	Acres.	Bushels.	Value.
Colorado	704	9,147	$5,799
Illinois	155	3,122	1,884
Kansas	53,706	656,522	404,329
Missouri	456	6,054	4,775
Nebraska	7,209	83,134	46,899
New Mexico	193	1,021	1,248
Oklahoma	4,250	30,435	23,079
Texas	5,483	38,683	50,255
Other states	341	5,589	6,054
Total	72,497	833,707	544,322
Mustard—			
California	1,964	*3,168,270	100,731
Sunflower—			
California	257	6,855	6,264
Illinois	3,969	49,004	44,539
Indiana	430	6,330	5,894
Other states	75	1,488	1,621
Total	4,731	63,677	58,318
Hemp seed—			
Kentucky	563	5,416	20,007
Chufas seed—			
Georgia	481	12,531	28,194
Broom corn seed—			
Illinois	30	1,011	5,050
New Mexico	184	583	1,627
Texas	702	1,216	3,404

	Acres.	Bushels.	Value.
Other states........	155	4,023	4,671
Total	1,071	6,833	14,752
Tobacco seed—			
Pennsylvania	.....	200	1,400
Other states........	1	189	389
Total	1	389	1,789

*Pounds.

FLOWER AND VEGETABLE SEEDS.

The total value of flower and vegetable seeds raised in 1909 was $1,411,013. The leading states in the production of such seeds were: California, $594,724; Illinois, $194,626; New York, $72,991; New Jersey, $53,300.

BROOM CORN.

State.	Acres.	Pounds.	Value.
Arkansas	332	106,576	$8,198
California	1,023	614,250	32,509
Colorado	5,631	1,187,791	71,717
Illinois	32,452	19,309,425	1,457,172
Indiana	323	153,259	13,461
Iowa	156	75,370	6,670
Kansas	41,064	8,768,853	593,947
Kentucky	342	157,286	13,641
Missouri	5,339	1,774,536	115,243
Nebraska	458	157,146	11,116
New Mexico	4,470	644,892	33,492
Ohio	170	92,292	9,116
Oklahoma	216,350	42,741,725	2,559,235
Tennessee	1,348	347,064	27,733
Texas	9,448	2,368,490	140,533
Virginia	107	46,016	3,586
All other states	1,089	414,987	37,065
Total, 1909	326,102	78,959,958	5,134,434
Total, 1899	178,584	90,947,370	3,588,414

HEMP.

	Acres.		
California	300	600,000	$39,000
Illinois	...	50	5
Indiana	335	395,467	21,755
Kentucky	6,855	6,420,232	348,386
All other states	157	67,546	3,553
Total, 1909	7,647	7,483,295	412,699
Total, 1899	16,042	11,750,630	456,338

HOPS.

California	8,391	11,994,953	$1,731,110
New York	12,023	8,677,138	2,597,981
Oregon	21,779	16,582,562	2,838,860
Washington	2,433	3,432,504	665,493
Wisconsin	30	13,290	9,041
All other states	46	18,301	2,260
Total, 1909	44,693	40,718,748	7,844,745
Total, 1899	55,613	49,209,704	4,081,929

CHICORY.*

Michigan	5,584	19,204,000	$70,020
All other states	5	80,000	440
Total, 1909	5,589	19,284,000	70,460
Total, 1899	3,069	21,495,870	73,627

*Roasted and pulverized root of herb of aster family; used as adulterant of coffee or substitute for it.

CHUFAS.*

State.	Acres.	Bushels.	Value.
Florida	1,072	21,500	$43,470
North Carolina	376	6,880	10,529
All other states	264	3,881	8,392
Total, 1909	1,712	32,261	62,391
Total, 1899			16,734

*A sedge, the tuberous roots of which are edible.

GINSENG.*

State.	Acres.	Value.
Michigan	†	$13,794
Missouri	†	21,868
New York	†	27,138
Ohio	†	16,639
Pennsylvania	†	15,291
Wisconsin	16	25,977
All other states	7	31,181
Total	23	151,888

*A herb of the genus aralia with a root having aromatic and stimulant qualities; exported to China. †Reported in small fractions.

MINT.

State.	Acres.	Pounds.	Value.
Indiana	1,814	36,621	$58,110
Michigan	6,360	121,169	194,391
All other states	21	301	499
Total, 1909	8,195	158,091	253,000
Total, 1899	8,591	187,427	143,618

TEASELS.*

State.	Acres.	Tons.	Value.
New York	110	61	$10,760
All other states	52	17	3,000
Total, 1909	162	78	12,760

Not reported separately in 1899.
*Teasels or teazels are the burs or heads of a plant of the genus dipsacus; used in dressing cloth.

WILLOWS.

State.	Acres.	Tons.	Value.
Maryland	159	112	$16,800
New York	405	667	19,038
All other states	97	78	8,337
Total, 1909	661	857	44,175
Total, 1899	521	...	36,523

PEANUTS.

State.	Acres.	Bushels.	Value.
Alabama	100,609	1,573,796	$1,490,654
Arkansas	10,192	168,608	183,364
California	99	2,991	2,883
Florida	126,150	2,315,089	2,146,862
Georgia	160,317	2,569,787	2,440,926
Kansas	48	2,047	2,669
Louisiana	25,020	412,037	422,232
Mississippi	13,997	284,791	317,236
Missouri	130	3,220	4,040
New Mexico	126	1,375	2,177
North Carolina	195,134	5,980,919	5,368,826
Oklahoma	1,564	31,880	34,984
South Carolina	7,596	154,822	144,211
Tennessee	18,952	547,240	386,765
Texas	64,327	1,074,998	1,075,110
Virginia	145,213	4,284,340	4,239,832
All other states	413	7,876	9,152
Total	869,887	19,415,816	18,271,929
Total, 1899	516,654	11,964,109	7,270,515

ORCHARD FRUITS.

APPLES.

State.	Trees.	Bushels.	Value.
Alabama	1,468,436	888,396	$820,745
Arizona	62,027	72,814	109,395
Arkansas	7,650,103	2,296,043	1,322,785
California	2,482,762	6,335,073	2,901,662
Colorado	1,688,425	3,559,094	3,405,442
Connecticut	798,734	1,540,996	833,168
Delaware	429,733	183,094	115,371
District of Columbia	1,654	2,952	2,162
Florida	8,180	3,405	3,849
Georgia	1,878,209	895,613	555,744
Idaho	1,005,668	659,959	610,504
Illinois	9,900,627	3,093,321	2,111,866
Indiana	5,764,821	2,759,134	1,720,811
Iowa	5,847,034	6,746,668	3,550,729
Kansas	6,929,673	1,356,438	807,865
Kentucky	5,538,267	7,368,499	3,066,776
Louisiana	93,304	33,875	28,744
Maine	3,476,616	3,636,181	2,121,818
Maryland	1,288,482	1,822,824	902,077
Massachusetts	1,367,379	2,550,259	1,780,290
Michigan	7,534,343	12,332,296	5,969,080
Minnesota	1,380,396	1,044,156	769,114
Mississippi	427,652	265,841	213,714
Missouri	14,359,673	9,968,977	4,885,544
Montana	696,753	567,054	566,938
Nebraska	2,937,178	3,321,073	1,612,765
Nevada	74,454	74,449	66,097
New Hampshire	1,240,885	1,108,424	637,990
New Jersey	1,063,626	1,406,778	956,108
New Mexico	542,528	417,143	420,536
New York	11,248,203	25,499,324	13,343,028
North Carolina	4,910,171	4,775,693	2,014,670
North Dakota	15,941	4,374	7,270
Ohio	8,504,886	4,663,752	2,970,851
Oklahoma	2,955,810	742,182	573,076
Oregon	2,029,913	1,930,926	1,656,944

State.	Trees.	Bushels.	Value.
Pennsylvania	8,000,456	11,048,430	5,557,616
Rhode Island	182,009	212,908	147,125
South Carolina	581,767	362,800	276,410
South Dakota	274,862	191,784	158,729
Tennessee	4,838,922	4,640,444	2,172,475
Texas	1,138,852	168,008	160,655
Utah	517,039	350,023	319,691
Vermont	1,183,529	1,459,689	752,237
Virginia	7,004,548	6,103,941	3,129,833
Washington	3,009,337	2,672,100	2,925,761
West Virginia	4,570,948	4,225,163	2,461,074
Wisconsin	2,430,232	2,232,112	1,896,681
Wyoming	27,773	17,836	37,580
United States	151,322,840	147,522,318	83,231,493
Production, 1899		175,397,600	
Trees not of bearing age in 1910, 42,266,243.			

PEACHES AND NECTARINES.

State	Trees	Bushels	Value
Alabama	3,177,331	1,416,584	$1,055,971
Arizona	51,415	50,102	80,325
Arkansas	6,859,962	1,901,647	1,502,996
California	7,829,011	9,267,118	4,573,118
Colorado	793,372	692,258	764,561
Connecticut	461,711	269,990	417,598
Delaware	1,177,402	16,722	21,402
Florida	290,850	114,998	128,029
Georgia	10,609,119	2,655,499	2,182,813
Idaho	73,990	18,734	28,149
Illinois	2,860,120	1,122,570	999,516
Indiana	2,130,298	1,174,389	1,123,248
Iowa	1,090,749	23,180	24,950
Kansas	4,394,894	24,567	28,418
Kentucky	2,245,402	1,623,379	1,062,138
Louisiana	903,352	290,623	228,084
Maine	5,102	2,014	3,205
Maryland	1,497,724	324,609	361,617
Massachusetts	154,592	91,756	138,716
Michigan	2,907,170	1,686,586	1,700,330
Minnesota	1,571	599	659
Missouri	6,588,034	1,484,548	1,110,550
Mississippi	1,726,298	1,156,817	925,288
Montana	538	128	235
Nebraska	1,188,373	110,180	91,129
Nevada	6,329	3,171	4,500
New Hampshire	57,571	23,218	37,884
New Jersey	1,216,476	441,440	652,771
New Mexico	136,191	32,533	37,195
New York	2,457,187	1,736,483	2,014,088
North Carolina	2,661,791	1,344,410	1,041,767
North Dakota	90	35	71
Ohio	3,133,268	1,036,340	1,349,311
Oklahoma	4,783,825	357,644	326,315
Oregon	273,162	179,030	194,314
Pennsylvania	2,383,027	1,023,570	1,351,175
Rhode Island	39,342	17,704	30,609
South Carolina	1,336,142	643,040	557,303
South Dakota	1,315	148	167
Tennessee	3,163,737	1,579,019	1,055,379
Texas	9,737,827	729,631	703,649
Utah	544,314	143,237	156,451
Vermont	5,492	2,221	4,399
Virginia	1,585,505	242,446	227,141
Washington	536,875	84,494	118,918
West Virginia	1,424,582	328,901	368,584
Wisconsin	4,163	956	552
Wyoming	46	5	30
United States	94,506,657	35,470,276	28,781,078
Total in 1899	99,919,000	15,432,603	
Trees not of bearing age in 1910, 8,803,885.			

GRAPES.

	Vines.	Pounds.	Value.
Alabama	287,431	1,723,490	$81,986
Arizona	131,579	837,842	25,371
Arkansas	805,921	2,693,797	97,985
California	144,097,670	1,979,686,525	10,846,812
Colorado	254,292	1,037,614	28,026
Connecticut	107,054	1,317,682	43,523
Delaware	260,963	1,938,267	43,967
District of Columbia	5,196	28,530	1,059
Florida	20,962	1,086,344	38,357
Georgia	277,658	2,767,366	90,216
Idaho	68,269	604,227	18,814
Illinois	2,170,340	16,582,785	426,468
Indiana	1,049,232	12,517,353	287,707

State.	Vines.	Pounds.	Value.
Iowa	1,983,465	11,708,336	330,078
Kansas	2,889,845	6,317,684	184,673
Kentucky	605,002	3,680,182	137,326
Louisiana	31,041	106,595	6,099
Maine	9,731	231,529	6,954
Maryland	138,801	2,152,382	53,282
Massachusetts	58,277	1,132,938	30,858
Michigan	11,013,576	120,635,997	1,531,057
Minnesota	61,916	293,805	11,021
Mississippi	77,012	760,563	44,262
Missouri	3,026,626	17,871,816	488,755
Montana	986	370	17
Nebraska	1,221,736	4,752,217	137,295
Nevada	26,607	376,205	12,045
New Hampshire	15,862	375,164	10,926
New Jersey	1,603,280	6,501,221	132,957
New Mexico	250,076	425,415	16,101
New York	31,802,097	253,006,361	3,961,677
North Carolina	411,278	15,116,920	336,083
North Dakota	379	360	14
Ohio	8,326,800	43,933,207	858,594
Oklahoma	2,388,213	3,762,727	122,045
Oregon	381,302	3,206,874	98,776
Pennsylvania	5,271,264	34,020,198	850,708
Rhode Island	7,662	152,937	9,759
South Carolina	79,708	2,016,506	88,620
South Dakota	38,647	144,634	4,789
Tennessee	338,758	1,979,480	85,423
Texas	712,261	1,502,618	78,325
Utah	204,445	1,576,363	28,126
Vermont	9,318	203,011	6,328
Virginia	424,701	4,108,694	156,266
Washington	322,007	1,704,005	51,412
West Virginia	284,074	3,224,751	92,884
Wisconsin	148,348	701,329	25,537
Wyoming	74	159	32
United States	223,701,522	2,571,065,295	22,027,961
Total, 1899		1,300,984,097	14,090,234
Vines not of bearing age in 1909, 59,928,644.			

APRICOTS.

	Trees.	Bushels.	Value.
Arizona	6,665	6,849	310,053
California	2,992,453	4,066,823	2,768,921
Colorado	16,841	11,403	15,658
Kansas	187,381	374	512
New York	16,050	9,805	14,490
Oklahoma	173,515	1,123	1,270
Oregon	10,656	4,616	7,727
Pennsylvania	10,363	2,502	4,437
Texas	66,533	1,839	2,364
Utah	28,978	12,047	12,097
Washington	36,088	10,789	17,280
All other states	124,191	22,093	29,310
United States	3,669,714	4,150,263	2,642,128
Production, 1899		2,642,128	

QUINCES.

	Vines.	Pounds.	Value.
California	76,979	32,638	$26,266
Connecticut	9,826	4,627	7,027
Illinois	30,804	6,723	8,037
Indiana	56,827	17,973	22,431
Kentucky	29,893	11,537	11,757
Maryland	20,936	6,359	8,383
Massachusetts	7,484	2,863	5,754
Michigan	35,461	13,484	16,858
New Jersey	14,777	6,442	10,583
New York	169,031	132,461	135,345
Ohio	245,040	81,101	101,369
Oregon	8,102	5,354	5,140
Pennsylvania	176,849	62,350	102,431
West Virginia	50,708	13,163	18,676
All other states	221,682	31,707	37,186
United States	1,154,393	428,672	517,243
Production not reported separately in 1899.			

CHERRIES.

	Vines.	Pounds.	Value.
Alabama	25,566	3,588	$4,783
Arizona	812	476	849
Arkansas	60,046	5,993	8,424
California	522,304	501,013	951,624
Colorado	203,806	88,937	173,895
Connecticut	12,119	3,617	8,164
Delaware	16,143	2,634	4,850
District of Columbia	435	235	568

State.	Trees.	Bushels.	Value.
Florida	666	374	448
Georgia	50,723	4,979	7,199
Idaho	61,881	22,609	41,766
Illinois	843,283	287,376	453,474
Indiana	815,742	363,993	508,516
Iowa	908,764	260,432	455,022
Kansas	661,267	34,409	76,734
Kentucky	212,118	52,163	74,340
Louisiana	975	527	921
Maine	14,288	2,403	7,164
Maryland	82,305	42,315	60,121
Massachusetts	13,396	4,761	10,843
Michigan	760,183	338,945	590,820
Minnesota	25,189	1,526	2,973
Mississippi	13,748	2,819	3,749
Missouri	622,832	123,314	222,510
Montana	19,938	7,497	17,985
Nebraska	494,468	89,873	164,872
Nevada	1,588	431	894
New Hampshire	9,463	1,408	4,133
New Jersey	102,124	44,636	87,225
New Mexico	21,925	6,384	10,684
New York	673,989	271,397	544,508
North Carolina	168,065	53,788	60,453
North Dakota	5,076	209	445
Ohio	1,144,271	338,644	657,406
Oklahoma	295,042	2,372	4,393
Oregon	223,456	181,089	269,934
Pennsylvania	1,025,031	475,093	909,975
South Carolina	60,274	10,987	15,880
South Dakota	51,613	5,924	12,981
Tennessee	201,830	36,803	60,294
Texas	29,439	1,062	663
Utah	79,775	21,492	54,170
Vermont	18,006	2,506	7,651
Virginia	352,783	132,871	134,428
Washington	241,038	131,392	278,547
West Virginia	332,429	79,723	111,043
Wisconsin	290,495	81,340	152,119
Wyoming	919	68	251
United States	11,822,044	4,126,099	7,231,160
Production in 1899		2,873,499	
Trees not of bearing age in 1910, 5,621,660.			

PLUMS AND PRUNES.

Alabama	211,991	61,712	$45,039
Arizona	12,196	8,240	16,261
Arkansas	731,276	194,649	137,734
California	7,168,705	9,317,979	5,473,539
Colorado	143,921	81,339	81,854
Connecticut	30,209	13,663	19,419
Delaware	27,115	657	540
District of Columbia	104	10	24
Florida	39,921	16,250	18,976
Georgia	357,323	60,845	46,368
Idaho	302,855	179,027	132,801
Illinois	600,087	78,566	80,384
Indiana	566,988	77,065	89,073
Iowa	1,155,041	158,036	192,421
Kansas	624,648	12,250	14,001
Kentucky	355,858	139,346	102,446
Louisiana	149,929	31,473	24,641
Maine	43,576	14,637	31,954
Maryland	69,996	13,526	16,192
Massachusetts	41,345	17,814	28,253
Michigan	464,917	181,188	205,765
Minnesota	233,736	19,920	27,808
Mississippi	257,140	101,974	79,971
Missouri	917,851	234,872	211,472
Montana	21,140	8,777	11,642
Nebraska	351,321	41,910	50,934
Nevada	6,716	3,857	4,654
New Hampshire	23,152	7,542	14,039
New Jersey	46,547	9,594	13,476
New Mexico	51,257	15,528	17,054
New York	919,017	553,522	519,192
North Carolina	168,883	61,496	45,274
North Dakota	19,147	1,048	1,866
Ohio	1,001,734	215,657	278,506
Oklahoma	436,421	25,916	28,134
Oregon	1,764,896	1,747,587	838,783
Pennsylvania	744,148	295,158	396,061
Rhode Island	4,836	1,872	3,586
South Carolina	82,212	48,754	37,555
South Dakota	268,268	31,748	36,872
Tennessee	499,627	139,093	86,743

State.	Trees.	Bushels.	Value.
Texas	1,020,339	75,222	77,925
Utah	135,619	68,249	54,040
Vermont	32,920	7,205	12,927
Virginia	171,667	22,597	22,772
Washington	823,082	1,032,077	600,503
West Virginia	234,859	32,948	48,522
Wisconsin	105,909	15,907	20,944
Wyoming	4,564	659	1,842
United States	23,445,009	15,480,170	10,299,495
Production in 1899		8,764,032	
Trees not of bearing age in 1910, 6,923,581.			

PEARS.

Alabama	142,300	100,041	$86,866
Arizona	16,351	13,289	21,331
Arkansas	221,764	87,547	38,140
California	1,410,905	1,928,097	1,660,963
Colorado	99,982	132,536	210,685
Connecticut	56,758	41,322	41,652
Delaware	449,692	105,357	52,022
District of Columbia	1,045	455	412
Florida	110,709	98,223	80,119
Georgia	262,982	149,667	134,604
Idaho	65,113	42,649	48,045
Illinois	786,349	249,365	202,965
Indiana	708,729	319,925	243,698
Iowa	191,125	44,449	58,777
Kansas	292,383	19,412	21,543
Kentucky	337,355	251,536	187,951
Louisiana	57,630	35,554	31,069
Maine	46,688	38,964	43,524
Maryland	540,583	367,359	168,561
Massachusetts	113,385	96,071	110,069
Michigan	1,136,151	666,923	535,771
Minnesota	2,792	400	465
Mississippi	118,556	101,288	96,777
Missouri	606,973	142,547	148,789
Montana	10,297	7,542	12,008
Nebraska	59,285	6,700	9,802
Nevada	3,946	4,083	5,119
New Hampshire	36,816	24,224	25,206
New Jersey	731,616	463,290	254,582
New Mexico	37,220	29,435	29,688
New York	2,141,596	1,348,089	1,418,218
North Carolina	243,367	84,019	81,347
North Dakota	24	8	15
Ohio	899,019	374,871	332,727
Oklahoma	207,271	7,450	9,248
Oregon	273,542	374,622	386,977
Pennsylvania	796,882	378,825	356,340
Rhode Island	16,907	12,501	14,577
South Carolina	105,251	65,680	67,685
South Dakota	1,844	162	447
Tennessee	233,407	83,557	78,448
Texas	558,478	110,967	114,279
Utah	79,355	38,654	44,365
Vermont	26,315	20,763	23,788
Virginia	457,177	74,486	63,424
Washington	290,876	319,804	328,895
West Virginia	154,908	29,916	32,101
Wisconsin	29,841	12,992	16,551
Wyoming	178	16	65
United States	15,171,524	8,840,733	7,910,600
Production in 1899		6,625,417	
Trees not of bearing age in 1910, 8,803,885.			

CITRUS FRUIT.

ORANGES.

	Trees.	Boxes.	Value.
Arizona	33,373	32,247	$52,341
California	6,615,895	14,436,180	12,951,505
Florida	2,766,618	4,852,967	4,304,987
Louisiana	266,116	149,979	222,330
Mississippi	10,452	3,779	3,648
Texas	42,384	10,694	22,090
Total	9,737,927	19,487,481	17,566,464
Production, 1899		6,167,891	

LEMONS.

California	941,293	2,756,221	2,976,571
Florida	11,740	12,367	13,253
Total	956,920	2,770,313	2,993,738
Production, 1899		876,876	

GRAPEFRUIT (POMELOES).

California	43,424	122,515	143,180
Florida	656,213	1,061,537	1,907,816
Total	710,640	1,189,250	2,060,610
Production in 1899		30,790	

LIMES.

State.	Trees.	Boxes.	Value.
Florida	45,369	11,302	12,457
Total	45,387	11,318	12,478
Production, 1899	......	22,839	......

TANGERINES.

	Trees.	Boxes.	Value.
California	3,637	3,581	4,188
Florida	23,234	34,871	64,082
Total	27,271	38,752	68,776

MANDARINS.

	Trees.	Boxes.	Value.
Louisiana	6,875	3,340	5,945
Total	7,227	3,896	6,553

KUMQUATS.

	Trees.	Boxes.	Value.
Florida	1,955	1,091	2,768
Total	1,988	1,112	2,826

NOTE—The totals in above tables are for the United States. Production of tangerines, mandarins and kumquats in 1899 not reported.

NONCITRUS TROPICAL AND SUBTROPICAL FRUITS.

FIGS.

	Trees.	Pounds.	Value.
Alabama	52,731	1,773,126	$80,960
Arkansas	4,174	80,707	5,953
California	269,001	22,990,353	260,153
Florida	12,784	474,287	20,866
Georgia	49,424	1,183,494	50,326
Louisiana	71,464	2,025,303	87,009
Mississippi	65,397	1,949,301	107,609
North Carolina	21,054	660,624	22,632
South Carolina	24,807	975,136	49,169
Texas	230,171	2,411,876	97,078
Virginia	10,136	234,057	9,652
All other states	10,497	302,126	12,383
Total	821,640	35,060,395	803,810
Production, 1899	......	12,994,834	......

Trees not of bearing age in 1910, 1,028,717.

PINEAPPLES.

	Plants.	Crates.	Value.
Florida	36,190,758	778,644	$734,069
Total (U. S.)	36,191,389	778,651	734,090
Production, 1899	......	95,456	......

Plants not of bearing age in 1910, 2,602,813.

OLIVES.

	Trees.	Pounds.	Value.
Arizona	9,353	264,895	$3,073
California	836,347	16,132,412	401,277
Total	846,175	16,405,493	404,574
Production, 1899	......	5,053,637	......

Trees not of bearing age in 1910, 123,784.

BANANAS.

	Trees.	Bunches.	Value.
Florida	22,032	10,048	$5,638
Total	23,114	10,060	5,661

Trees not of bearing age in 1910, 7,515.

AVOCADO PEARS.

	Trees.	Crates.	Value.
Florida	12,054	4,920	$10,100

Trees not of bearing age in 1910, 23,072.

GUAVAS.

	Trees.	Pounds.	Value.
California	7,031	95,053	$4,018
Florida	8,293	258,709	7,604
Total	15,347	344,062	11,628
Production, 1899	......	1,677,165	......

Trees not of bearing age in 1910, 3,807.

MANGOES.

	Trees.	Boxes.	Value.
Florida	4,904	5,278	$5,739

Trees not bearing in 1910, 7,775.

PERSIMMONS (JAPANESE).

	Trees.	Bushels.	Value.
California	3,274	2,696	$3,344
Florida	4,987	1,615	2,066
Texas	4,449	1,175	2,136
Total	16,491	6,793	9,087
Production in 1899	......	2,721	......

Trees not of bearing age in 1910, 17,176.

LOQUATS.

State.	Trees.	Boxes.	Value.
California	3,711	4,516	$5,830
Total	3,791	4,541	5,880

Trees not of bearing age in 1910, 1,011.

POMEGRANATES.

	Trees.	Pounds.	Value.
Alabama	1,672	19,090	$617
Arizona	776	23,360	477
Calif. rnia	1,771	30,075	968
Georgia	1,308	27,365	920
Nevada	2,887	45,550	915
Total	8,933	152,825	4,203

Trees not of bearing age in 1910, 9,275.

DATES.

	Trees.	Pounds.	Value.
Total	4,551	9,947	$533

Trees not of bearing age in 1910, 22,269.

SMALL FRUITS.

ACREAGE, PRODUCTION AND VALUE.

	Acres.	Quarts.	Value.
Alabama	1,232	1,907,193	$165,386
Arizona	76	112,190	12,987
Arkansas	8,032	8,965,572	601,722
California	9,687	26,824,120	1,789,214
Colorado	2,829	4,294,988	398,836
Connecticut	1,597	3,823,522	316,752
Delaware	8,687	14,425,209	649,732
District of Columbia	12	24,109	1,875
Florida	1,356	2,396,673	302,383
Georgia	988	1,262,155	111,754
Idaho	1,673	2,072,141	201,525
Illinois	11,723	13,602,676	1,109,147
Indiana	5,919	7,424,681	612,725
Iowa	7,211	10,344,052	966,894
Kansas	5,400	5,477,274	454,200
Kentucky	4,387	4,972,702	357,597
Louisiana	3,587	6,420,207	486,988
Maine	1,260	2,285,413	233,124
Maryland	16,595	26,277,054	1,227,548
Massachusetts	9,552	29,260,143	1,676,790
Michigan	21,419	27,214,659	2,028,865
Minnesota	3,738	4,476,575	493,406
Mississippi	836	1,407,301	107,171
Missouri	17,009	23,696,221	1,761,409
Montana	562	766,791	85,586
Nebraska	1,411	1,594,421	159,169
Nevada	37	50,287	5,683
New Hampshire	618	998,244	107,365
New Jersey	24,069	38,822,987	1,954,125
New Mexico	66	76,532	9,335
New York	22,496	37,857,829	2,875,495
North Carolina	6,701	12,827,427	853,076
North Dakota	399	285,696	39,641
Ohio	11,591	15,721,023	1,296,343
Oklahoma	2,745	2,310,367	202,291
Oregon	5,122	9,348,490	641,194
Pennsylvania	8,678	13,620,047	1,175,016
Rhode Island	281	437,560	43,033
South Carolina	856	1,408,099	113,254
South Dakota	419	401,295	47,263
Tennessee	12,539	13,895,493	923,613
Texas	5,053	6,182,742	480,331
Utah	1,416	3,118,395	217,327
Vermont	469	826,122	92,030
Virginia	7,295	11,342,980	671,843
Washington	5,568	13,490,930	941,415
West Virginia	2,913	2,336,562	191,002
Wisconsin	6,305	9,782,779	765,437
Wyoming	106	96,883	13,984
United States	272,460	426,565,863	29,974,481
Total, 1899	309,770	463,218,612	25,029,757

SMALL FRUITS BY CLASSES.

	Acres.	Quarts.	Value.
Strawberries	143,045	254,702,035	$17,913,926
Blackberries, dewberries	49,004	55,343,570	3,909,831
Raspberries, loganberri's	48,668	60,918,196	5,132,277
Currants	7,862	10,448,532	790,431
Gooseberries	4,765	5,282,843	417,034
Cranberries	18,431	38,243,060	1,755,613
All other	685	627,627	55,369
Total	272,460	426,565,863	29,974,481

SMALL FRUIT ACREAGE BY STATES (1909).

The states having the largest acreage devoted to the principal classes of small fruits are as follows:

State.	Acres.	State.	Acres.
Strawberries—		Michigan	8,786
Maryland	14,292	Ohio	3,869
Tennessee	10,761	Pennsylvania	2,594
Missouri	9,048		
New Jersey	8,684	Currants—	
Michigan	8,051	New York	2,557
Arkansas	7,361	Michigan	609
Delaware	7,194	Pennsylvania	558
Virginia	6,606	California	407
New York	6,382	Ohio	359
North Carolina	5,420	Wisconsin	298
Illinois	5,410	Iowa	253
Blackberries and		Illinois	252
dewberries —			
Missouri	5,975	Gooseberries—	
New Jersey	4,232	Illinois	603
Illinois	3,503	Missouri	555
Michigan	2,973	Indiana	274
Texas	2,773	New York	259
Kansas	2,682	Ohio	226
California	2,576		
Ohio	2,425	Cranberries—	
Iowa	2,279	New Jersey	9,030
Raspberries and		Massachusetts	6,577
loganberries—		Wisconsin	1,689
New York	11,067	New York	277
		Michigan	201

NUTS—PRODUCTION AND VALUE.

TOTAL BY STATES.

State.	Pounds.	Value.
Alabama	439,282	$37,986
Arizona	35,834	4,485
Arkansas	787,854	27,513
California	28,378,115	2,959,845
Connecticut	137,987	5,102
Florida	382,535	47,456
Georgia	845,553	61,106
Illinois	714,478	20,550
Indiana	439,644	7,344
Iowa	1,721,265	36,922
Kansas	402,714	7,625
Kentucky	946,428	17,231
Louisiana	796,925	73,169
Maryland	318,148	5,687
Massachusetts	134,920	3,671
Michigan	961,137	18,956
Mississippi	866,504	99,855
Missouri	2,823,368	39,746
Nebraska	384,325	8,906
New Hampshire	254,521	3,684
New Jersey	249,626	7,116
New York	2,773,858	74,420
North Carolina	1,244,629	28,535
Ohio	559,093	11,691
Oklahoma	1,019,238	62,168
Oregon	177,632	13,208
Pennsylvania	3,795,804	90,447
South Carolina	376,013	26,888
Tennessee	783,570	14,041
Texas	5,945,932	562,542
Virginia	841,572	22,161
West Virginia	974,312	16,049
Wisconsin	609,428	18,196
All other states	1,205,666	22,373
Total, 1909	62,328,010	4,447,674
Total, 1899	40,028,825	1,949,931

ALMONDS.

	Trees.	Pounds.	Value.
Arizona	6,639	33,759	$4,193
California	1,166,730	6,692,513	700,304
All other states	14,593	67,267	7,473
Total	1,187,962	6,793,539	711,970
Production, 1899		7,142,710	

Trees not of bearing age in 1910, 389,575.

WALNUTS (PERSIAN OR ENGLISH).

	Trees	Pounds.	Value.
California	853,237	21,432,266	$2,247,193
Mississippi	2,765	66,492	6,949
Oregon	9,526	79,060	8,288

State.	Trees.	Pounds.	Value.
All other states	48,802	448,706	34,906
Total	914,270	22,026,524	2,297,336
Production, 1899		10,668,065	

Trees not of bearing age in 1910, 806,413.

PECANS.

Alabama	44,683	228,341	$60,670
Arkansas	13,958	249,956	88,060
Florida	42,512	307,632	46,800
Georgia	75,519	354,046	47,845
Illinois	28,330	107,069	10,301
Louisiana	36,527	723,578	70,635
Mississippi	60,524	637,293	79,936
Missouri	48,822	147,420	10,467
North Carolina	6,876	74,861	8,194
Oklahoma	96,766	894,172	59,481
South Carolina	33,366	159,823	20,442
Texas	1,087,619	5,832,367	556,203
All other states	44,019	174,212	15,987
Total	1,619,521	9,890,769	971,596
Production in 1899		3,206,850	

Trees not of bearing age in 1910, 1,685,066.

VEGETABLES.

POTATOES.

(See crops of 1912.)

SWEET POTATOES AND YAMS.

	Acres.	Bushels.	Value.
Alabama	66,613	3,457,386	$3,578,710
Arkansas	22,388	1,685,308	1,359,669
California	5,111	572,814	355,624
Delaware	5,229	733,746	276,679
Florida	21,905	2,083,665	1,231,238
Georgia	84,038	7,426,131	4,349,806
Illinois	10,568	1,050,932	506,780
Indiana	1,561	178,300	139,886
Iowa	2,274	232,413	125,981
Kansas	4,883	358,021	373,432
Kentucky	11,882	1,326,245	839,454
Louisiana	56,953	4,251,086	2,357,729
Maryland	7,956	1,065,956	488,751
Mississippi	56,045	4,427,988	3,073,290
Missouri	7,938	876,234	567,413
Nebraska	279	28,500	28,121
New Jersey	22,504	3,186,499	1,527,074
North Carolina	84,740	8,493,283	4,333,297
Ohio	1,143	133,798	104,181
Oklahoma	5,056	359,451	350,553
Pennsylvania	1,306	128,770	104,484
South Carolina	48,878	4,319,926	2,606,606
Tennessee	26,216	2,504,490	1,625,056
Texas	42,010	2,730,083	2,197,799
Virginia	40,838	5,270,202	2,681,472
West Virginia	2,079	215,582	170,086
United States	641,255	59,232,070	35,429,176
Total, 1899	537,312	42,517,412	19,863,840

OTHER VEGETABLES.

(Excluding potatoes and sweet potatoes and yams.)

	Acres.	Value.
Alabama	69,468	$5,379,577
Arizona	4,302	379,293
Arkansas	60,251	4,843,442
California	79,163	6,886,885
Colorado	32,422	2,349,634
Connecticut	16,250	1,965,695
Delaware	22,939	1,102,620
District of Columbia	964	167,376
Florida	57,600	6,314,313
Georgia	91,413	5,580,368
Idaho	10,929	1,007,667
Illinois	120,291	9,392,296
Indiana	114,262	7,498,024
Iowa	80,402	5,266,411
Kansas	48,757	2,963,733
Kentucky	115,007	8,287,497
Louisiana	38,221	3,000,864
Maine	25,288	2,153,003
Maryland	108,084	5,729,400
Massachusetts	37,220	6,189,857
Michigan	90,861	6,286,645
Minnesota	46,021	3,359,052

State.	Acres.	Value.
Mississippi	61,223	5,868,275
Missouri	129,570	8,268,281
Montana	7,300	928,906
Nebraska	36,164	2,118,393
Nevada	1,952	264,122
New Hampshire	8,855	1,071,551
New Jersey	86,227	7,566,493
New Mexico	8,219	567,154
New York	175,402	15,963,384
North Carolina	95,980	6,496,308
North Dakota	13,383	1,069,125
Ohio	123,461	11,393,791
Oklahoma	51,011	2,610,239
Oregon	23,129	2,448,917
Pennsylvania	94,111	10,013,920
Rhode Island	5,275	636,656
South Carolina	51,994	3,705,991
South Dakota	15,150	1,033,163
Tennessee	100,055	7,015,686
Texas	124,690	8,099,306
Utah	7,006	717,776
Vermont	8,548	872,183
Virginia	124,354	8,989,467
Washington	24,410	2,988,510
West Virginia	43,524	4,519,894
Wisconsin	70,123	4,593,865
Wyoming	2,933	332,120
United States	2,763,269	216,257,068
Total, 1899	2,162,130	120,281,811

SUGAR CROPS.

SUGAR CANE.

	Acres.	Tons.	Value.
Alabama	27,211	226,634	$1,157,166
Arkansas	3,330	19,868	152,298
Florida	12,928	142,517	1,089,698
Georgia	37,046	317,460	2,268,110
Louisiana	329,684	4,941,996	17,752,537
Mississippi	24,861	222,000	804,876
North Carolina	294	1,494	10,697
South Carolina	7,053	59,865	434,634
Texas	34,315	207,502	1,669,683
Other states	127	324	2,242
United States	476,849	6,240,260	26,415,952
Total, 1899	4,202,203	20,541,636	

SORGHUM CANE.

Alabama	17,819	72,388	$450,263
Arizona	586	1,451	13,886
Arkansas	33,071	93,123	658,075
California	647	3,021	14,826
Colorado	3,169	7,161	43,520
Florida	379	2,173	10,113
Georgia	35,612	64,336	419,561
Illinois	15,039	90,287	496,114
Indiana	12,253	79,672	465,618
Iowa	6,225	29,957	173,259
Kansas	15,406	60,821	251,762
Kentucky	62,327	226,393	1,416,565
Louisiana	1,690	6,073	34,277
Michigan	416	2,765	18,599
Minnesota	1,709	13,253	83,966
Mississippi	17,851	55,359	343,417
Missouri	45,088	201,206	1,036,363
Nebraska	4,034	10,477	61,025
New Mexico	2,371	2,819	26,877
North Carolina	21,227	86,462	541,294
Ohio	4,709	28,644	180,543
Oklahoma	25,546	64,599	489,112
South Carolina	8,445	27,612	185,358
Tennessee	52,907	205,901	1,145,933
Texas	55,027	101,691	955,769
Utah	340	1,654	12,873
Virginia	8,288	41,449	223,224
West Virginia	8,607	48,094	300,218
Wisconsin	2,281	13,735	84,626
Other states	1,020	5,776	37,297
United States	444,089	1,647,262	10,174,457
Total, 1899	293,152	1,910,046	6,103,102

SUGAR BEETS.

Arizona	4,443	49,630	$236,997
California	78,957	845,191	4,320,532
Colorado	108,082	1,231,712	6,061,152

State.	Acres.	Tons.	Value.
Idaho	15,601	179,661	813,604
Illinois	1,181	14,981	77,732
Indiana	756	7,194	40,861
Iowa	1,051	7,117	35,024
Kansas	5,851	50,736	256,262
Michigan	78,779	707,639	4,014,123
Minnesota	2,238	24,140	118,625
Montana	8,804	109,434	546,832
Nebraska	4,191	39,874	180,247
New Mexico	55	239	1,492
New York	1,313	10,990	59,200
Ohio	7,036	63,696	319,667
Oregon	1,176	15,606	74,902
Utah	27,472	413,946	1,858,600
Washington	1,820	13,794	85,954
Wisconsin	12,379	127,526	667,185
Wyoming	1,207	13,418	61,398
Other states	1,791	6,333	50,335
United States	364,093	3,932,857	19,880,724
Total, 1899	110,170	793,353	3,323,240

MAPLE SUGAR AND SIRUP.
(Made in 1909.)

	Sugar, lbs.	Sirup, gals.	Value.
Connecticut	10,207	4,236	$6,988
Illinois	5,366	18,492	23,502
Indiana	33,419	273,728	300,755
Iowa	6,173	8,596	11,495
Kentucky	10,697	3,547	6,681
Maine	15,388	43,971	52,137
Maryland	351,908	12,172	34,386
Massachusetts	156,952	53,091	77,559
Michigan	233,301	269,093	333,791
Minnesota	11,399	17,808	23,362
Missouri	11,638	9,389	12,950
New Hampshire	558,811	111,500	182,341
New York	3,160,300	993,242	1,240,684
Ohio	257,592	1,323,431	1,099,948
Pennsylvania	1,188,049	391,242	471,213
Vermont	7,726,817	409,953	1,086,923
Virginia	44,976	6,046	12,233
West Virginia	140,060	31,176	46,568
Wisconsin	27,199	124,117	150,038
All other states	49,954	1,588	4,945
Total, 1909	14,060,206	4,106,418	5,177,809
Total, 1899	11,928,770	2,056,611	2,636,711

FLOWERS AND PLANTS, NURSERY PRODUCTS AND FARM FOREST PRODUCTS.

The following table shows the value of flowers and plants and nursery products raised on farms and in florists' and nursery establishments and forest products on farms, including firewood, fencing material, logs, railroad ties, telegraph and telephone poles, etc.:

	Flowers and plants.	Nursery products.	Forest products.
Alabama	$168,239	$259,057	$6,308,151
Arizona	11,177	4,535	45,312
Arkansas	153,421	198,579	6,914,262
California	1,388,513	2,212,788	2,949,732
Colorado	468,685	72,090	305,719
Connecticut	1,047,431	261,506	1,861,853
Delaware	71,429	39,057	346,062
District of Columbia	303,599	150	50
Florida	69,106	478,174	2,375,882
Georgia	271,427	366,432	8,928,390
Idaho	43,314	143,234	1,280,512
Illinois	3,694,801	822,284	3,325,259
Indiana	1,212,891	411,357	5,603,322
Iowa	657,393	845,912	3,649,032
Kansas	273,715	948,493	1,366,950
Kentucky	392,409	115,963	7,843,142
Louisiana	126,212	87,643	3,584,340
Maine	301,005	23,244	5,573,763
Maryland	597,601	456,900	2,349,045
Massachusetts	2,455,467	605,875	2,658,410
Michigan	1,143,764	642,774	7,911,901
Minnesota	603,935	863,014	5,181,508
Mississippi	100,321	74,946	6,602,942
Missouri	653,903	529,294	8,406,823
Montana	104,601	174,427	541,800
Nebraska	356,168	553,053	795,053
Nevada	1,620	493	42,748

State.	Flowers and plants.	Nursery products.	Forest products.	State.	Flowers and plants.	Nursery products.	Forest products.
New Hampshire....	236,144	11,897	3,610,178	Tennessee	344,579	697,703	8,510,710
New Jersey.........	2,857,709	681,814	758,515	Texas	474,360	1,253,110	8,925,662
New Mexico.......	31,121	9,182	253,822	Utah	81,116	188,648	6,730
New York.........	5,148,949	2,750,957	10,365,651	Vermont	78,726	11,014	3,638,537
North Carolina....	126,995	266,968	11,364,134	Virginia	362,488	159,992	10,118,851
North Dakota.....	47,221	30,997	235,386	Washington	518,226	526,681	3,754,293
Ohio	2,384,830	890,350	5,761,941	West Virginia......	78,377	79,268	4,604,484
Oklahoma	92,016	171,952	1,602,720	Wisconsin	592,839	301,027	9,550,428
Oregon	268,833	783,020	2,889,991	Wyoming	12,289	1,680	104,259
Pennsylvania	3,803,418	922,569	7,986,599				
Rhode Island......	558,543	75,544	312,022	United States....	34,872,329	21,050,822	195,306,283
South Carolina....	52,094	4,409	4,513,092	Total, 1899........	18,758,864	10,123,873	109,864,774

INTERNATIONAL TRADE IN AGRICULTURAL PRODUCTS (1911).

WHEAT.

Exports—	Bushels.
Argentina	83,993,460
Australia	55,147,840
Austria-Hung'y	15,160
Belgium	22,723,350
British India...	52,803,245
Bulgaria	11,121,995
Canada	60,474,020
Chile	509,261
Germany	11,390,400
Netherlands ...	46,170,743
Roumania	67,658,882
Russia	144,795,697
Servia	3,366,243
United States..	32,668,615
Other countries	16,801,727
Total	609,440,638

Imports—	
Austria-Hung'y	4,901,024
Belgium	82,191,689
Brazil	9,527,692
Brit. S. Africa	2,918,816
Denmark	3,059,944
France	78,755,778
Germany	91,429,660
Greece	7,934,138
Italy	43,300,144
Japan	2,019,164
Mexico	3,988,730
Netherlands ...	58,569,927
Portugal	3,024,080
Spain	6,764,525
Sweden	6,333,068
Switzerland ...	16,142,122
Unit'd kingdom..	182,352,177
Other countries.	9,056,977
Total	612,269,655

WHEAT FLOUR.

Exports—	Barrels.
Argentina	1,332,726
Australia	1,794,805
Austria-Hung'y	122,422
Belgium	750,100
British India..	581,064
Bulgaria	755,907
Canada	3,542,124
Chile	*69,215
France	192,539
Germany	1,820,238
Netherlands ..	190,584
Roumania	455,452
Russia	1,354,580
Servia	80,184
United kingdom	802,259
United States..	11,258,030
Other countries.	1,794,535
Total	26,896,764

Imports—	
Belgium	47,400
Brazil	1,645,630
British Guiana.	176,319
Brit. S. Africa	722,421
Canary islands.	106,968
China	1,485,063
Cuba	852,876
Denmark	599,172

Imports—	Barrels.
Dutch E. Indies	800,000
Egypt	1,813,225
Finland	1,123,140
France	155,405
Germany	172,035
Greece	14,490
Jamaica	243,053
Japan	200,301
Martinique	55,329
Netherlands ...	2,241,574
Newfoundland..	384,928
Norway	645,282
Philippines	381,534
Singapore	230,401
Spain	668
Sweden	79,102
Switzerland ...	515,082
Trinidad-T'bago	269,501
United kingdom	5,681,535
Other countries	2,502,102
Total	23,144,553

CORN.

Exports—	Bushels.
Argentina	4,928,265
Austria-Hung'y	156,216
Belgium	8,846,390
Brit. S. Africa	3,892,164
Bulgaria	13,980,152
Netherlands ...	5,939,283
Roumania	23,419,157
Russia	52,759,472
Servia	4,627,040
United States..	63,533,483
Uruguay	192,359
Other countries	5,465,000
Total	187,738,981

Imports—	
Austria-Hung'y	7,885,811
Belgium	24,814,463
Brit. S. Africa	29,459
Canada	16,440,351
Cuba	3,002,432
Denmark	11,085,021
Egypt	227,370
France	19,742,322
Germany	29,366,872
Italy	15,117,655
Mexico	8,907,181
Netherlands ...	25,743,031
Norway	1,019,181
Portugal	518,042
Russia	338,870
Spain	5,684,772
Sweden	459,755
Switzerland ...	4,059,590
United kingdom	77,449,105
Other countries	2,162,000
Total	253,953,274

COTTON.

Exports—	*Bales.
Belgium	255,114
Brazil	67,554
British India...	1,738,922
China	244,828
Egypt	1,372,654
France	320,974

Exports—	*Bales.
Germany	186,465
Netherlands ...	136,976
Persia	128,031
Peru	65,059
United States..	8,919,524
Other countries	145,000
Total	13,581,111

Imports—	
Austria-Hung'y	907,223
Belgium	582,567
Canada	156,911
France	1,469,108
Germany	2,179,585
Italy	875,714
Japan	1,124,703
Mexico	10,750
Netherlands ...	270,358
Russia	935,248
Spain	417,014
Sweden	92,297
Switzerland ...	112,749
United kingdom	4,008,175
United States..	211,716
Other countries	296,000
Total	13,650,118

*500 pounds gross.

COTTON SEED OIL.

Exports—	Gallons.
Belgium	1,041,514
Egypt	488,139
France	186,215
Netherlands ...	43,367
United kingdom	6,781,525
United States..	43,003,606
Other countries	51,000
Total	51,595,366

Imports—	
Algeria	128,128
Australia	118,973
Austria-Hung'y	15,285
Belgium	2,336,776
Brazil	669,888
Canada	1,829,949
Egypt	185,820
France	2,728,942
Germany	6,391,018
Italy	3,598,760
Malta	234,289
Martinique	324,217
Mexico	3,692,532
Netherlands ...	3,543,667
Norway	1,491,788
Roumania	301,594
Senegal	402,247
Servia	396,413
Sweden	680,306
United kingdom	7,360,939
Uruguay	383,332
Other countries	3,530,000
Total	40,344,863

OIL CAKE AND MEAL.

Exports—	Pounds.
Argentina	44,594,296
Austria-Hung.	158,739,137
Belgium	174,256,679

Exports—	Pounds.
British India.	159,808,765
Canada	36,945,700
China	147,064,800
Denmark	16,212,849
Egypt	187,772,396
France	465,864,608
Germany	514,189,220
Italy	89,839,434
Mexico	41,310,271
Netherlands..	210,956,236
Russia	1,452,290,914
Un. kingdom.	46,336,640
Un. States...	1,638,536,925
Other count's	60,243,000
Total	5,444,961,873

Imports—	
Austria-Hung.	48,057,855
Belgium	529,596,468
Canada	6,662,000
Denmark	948,132,542
Dut. E. Indies	2,229,624
Finland	25,587,518
France	314,795,275
Germany	1,668,379,551
Italy	11,872,432
Japan	195,154,267
Netherlands..	643,155,253
Norway	63,452,511
Sweden	357,198,203
Switzerland ..	88,450,757
Un. kingdom.	754,779,200
Other count's	30,021,000
Total	5,687,524,456

UNMANUFACTURED TOBACCO.

Exports—	
Aden	5,939,803
Algeria	13,426,455
Austria-Hung'y	24,672,689
Brazil	40,761,118
British India..	34,560,174
Bulgaria	4,812,382
Ceylon	4,097,520
Cuba	34,822,228
Dut. E. Indies..	170,226,297
Greece	18,629,114
Mexico	1,231,928
Netherlands ..	3,713,177
Paraguay	11,282,772
Persia	4,555,765
Philippines ...	27,656,358
Russia	22,950,226
Santo Domingo.	30,441,476
Turkey	77,800,000
United States..	370,283,512
Other countries	26,833,000
Total	928,095,994

Imports—	
Aden	8,988,786
Argentina	14,046,649
Australia	14,900,520
Austria-Hung'y	50,428,902
Belgium	20,694,712
British India..	5,196,389
Canada	17,814,612
China	13,026,400

Imports—	Pounds.
Denmark	10,674,012
Egypt	19,007,722
Finland	9,376,830
France	61,189,114
Germany	162,019,581
Italy	43,459,941
Netherlands	57,265,903
Norway	3,730,800
Portugal	5,701,360
South'n Nigeria	5,060,750
Spain	48,931,123
Sweden	10,054,186
Switzerland	18,154,229
United kingdom	91,236,859
United States	52,901,433
Other countries	42,504,000
Total	**786,364,795**

RICE.

Exports—	
Belgium	100,314,577
British India	5,783,915,236
Dut. E. Ind.	133,178,832
France	66,625,432
Fr. In.-China	2,603,117,237
Germany	456,659,086
Netherlands	476,776,051
Penang	334,457,652
Siam	1,365,349,405
Singapore	808,021,088
Other count's	825,394,000
Total	**12,953,808,596**

Imports—	
Austria-Hun.	201,771,360
Belgium	177,040,647
Brazil	23,813,514
British India	344,818,143
Ceylon	820,868,266
China	707,040,667
Cuba	255,748,276
Dut. E. Ind..	1,346,967,283
Egypt	84,841,328
France	539,668,144
Germany	923,694,301
Japan	573,188,667
Mauritius	151,761,344
Netherlands..	738,228,176
Penang	422,610,271
Perak	167,793,146
Philippines	404,929,261
Russia	258,371,629
Selangor	137,780,822
Singapore	987,531,558
Un. kingdom.	682,871,840
Un. States..	185,846,041
Other count's	1,152,471,000
Total	**11,289,455,684**

HOPS.

Exports—	
Austria-Hung'y	11,765,950
Belgium	8,958,288
France	398,812
Germany	16,744,378
Netherlands	1,153,967
New Zealand	205,296
Russia	2,224,296
United kingdom	5,478,816
United States	14,104,004
Other countries	60,000
Total	**61,093,747**

Imports—	
Australia	906,902
Austria-Hung'y.	2,180,129
Belgium	8,822,752
British India..	284,704
Brit. S. Africa.	541,184
Canada	1,271,365
Denmark	1,006,841
France	7,443,171
Germany	6,099,908
Netherlands	2,910,685
Russia	1,045,213

Imports—	Pounds.
Sweden	842,159
Switzerland	1,255,520
United kingdom	16,921,520
United States	5,567,477
Other countries	3,821,000
Total	**60,920,530**

SUGAR.

Exports—	
Argentina	149,792
Austria-Hun.	1,334,957,831
Barbados	61,570,656
Belgium	360,159,071
Brazil	79,824,820
Brit. Guiana.	222,584,992
British India	44,184,224
China	23,585,867
Cuba	3,865,742,384
Dut. E. Ind.	2,952,301,805
Egypt	23,818,750
Fiji islands.	163,147,376
France	293,646,106
Germany	1,890,045,688
Guadeloupe	94,505,201
Martinique	88,086,424
Mauritius	522,816,784
Netherlands.	432,358,890
Peru	270,848,265
Philippines...	460,078,408
Reunion	73,854,810
Russia	1,000,127,492
S. Domingo..	193,498,948
Trinidad, Tobago	84,978,544
Un. kingdom.	64,010,688
Other count's	496,199,000
Total	**15,107,080,816**

Imports—	
Argentina	114,596,100
Australia	74,537,344
Brit. India...	1,271,138,184
Br. S. Africa	74,706,959
Canada	599,766,858
Chile	190,970,283
China	575,434,133
Denmark	25,478,121
Egypt	100,896,189
Finland	98,181,156
France	379,321,271
Italy	20,836,116
Japan	175,271,067
Netherlands..	204,365,296
New Zealand	123,957,569
Norway	106,228,453
Persia	201,246,499
Portugal	72,565,350
Singapore	113,436,667
Switzerland..	230,862,405
Turkey	302,618,943
Un. kingdom.	3,718,859,760
Un. States...	4,134,206,342
Other count's	631,221,000
Uruguay	57,086,651
Total	**13,597,789,716**

TEA.

Exports—	
British India	265,022,376
Ceylon	186,594,055
China	194,552,890
Dutch E. Indies	38,468,956
Formosa	22,211,721
Japan	37,096,253
Singapore	2,116,533
Other countries	6,834,000
Total	**752,896,694**

Imports—	
Argentina	3,672,050
Australia	34,759,385
Austria-Hung'y	3,550,508
British India..	10,748,451
Brit. S. Africa.	5,534,164
Canada	33,424,715

Imports—	Pounds.
Chile	3,625,403
China	16,630,000
Dut. E. Indies.	6,276,269
France	2,962,101
Fr. Indo-China.	2,859,227
Germany	8,404,817
Netherlands	11,466,387
New Zealand..	8,071,471
Persia	8,127,241
Russia	153,288,472
Singapore	5,244,533
Un. kingdom...	293,502,178
United States..	104,165,654
Other countries	37,448,000
Total	**753,761,026**

COFFEE.

Exports—	
Belgium	28,112,984
Brazil	1,489,137,017
British India.	24,593,408
Colombia	90,090,000
Costa Rica.	27,868,693
Dut. E. Indies	52,517,307
Guatemala	90,000,000
Haiti	53,100,000
Jamaica	6,725,712
Mexico	48,265,376
Netherlands..	195,902,019
Nicaragua	26,942,720
Salvador	62,764,000
Singapore	3,964,533
United States	36,383,953
Venezuela	97,658,703
Other count's.	36,380,000
Total	**2,370,316,425**

Imports—	
Argentina	24,481,677
Austria-Hung.	127,196,161
Belgium	93,176,925
Br. S. Africa.	24,954,103
Cuba	26,598,543
Denmark	32,207,663
Egypt	15,147,710
Finland	28,255,397
France	244,829,648
Germany	404,034,617
Italy	58,391,256
Netherlands	289,272,720
Norway	29,431,108
Russia	25,219,302
Singapore	4,740,667
Spain	28,325,699
Sweden	71,844,764
Switzerland	23,707,387
United States	800,208,533
Other count's.	78,545,000
Total	**2,458,597,536**

ROSIN.

Exports—	
Austria-Hung'y	1,988,108
Belgium	46,345,864
Germany	52,353,738
Greece	17,201,969
Netherlands	62,976,231
Russia	47,317,266
Spain	19,508,814
United States	676,323,200
Other countries	327,000
Total	**924,342,190**

Imports—	
Argentina	30,674,099
Australia	15,064,336
Austria-Hung'y	80,856,130
Belgium	79,432,311
Brazil	53,919,843
British India..	5,516,672
Canada	25,797,400
Chile	7,744,919
Cuba	3,199,188
Denmark	3,170,215

Imports—	Pounds.
Dut. E. Indies.	8,727,582
Finland	7,194,610
Germany	246,054,083
Italy	36,950,860
Japan	10,235,131
Netherlands	78,441,824
Norway	6,537,212
Roumania	4,649,049
Russia	73,782,206
Servia	586,298
Spain	1,959,537
Switzerland	4,988,569
Un. kingdom	158,346,384
Uruguay	5,526,727
Other countries	13,206,000
Total	**943,471,195**

TURPENTINE.

Exports—	Gallons.
Belgium	2,156,527
France	3,126,215
Germany	419,701
Netherlands	2,288,251
Russia	2,697,621
Spain	1,125,831
United States..	18,197,659
Other countries	714,000
Total	**30,725,805**

Imports—	
Argentina	617,398
Australia	858,757
Austria-Hung'y	2,517,868
Belgium	3,611,852
Canada	1,123,050
Chile	260,825
Germany	8,367,039
Italy	965,870
Netherlands	3,475,256
New Zealand...	240,994
Russia	274,773
Sweden	130,928
Switzerland	440,644
United kingdom	7,154,047
Other countries	1,131,000
Total	**31,171,301**

RUBBER.

Exports—	Pounds.
Angola	5,200,000
Belgian Kongo.	7,494,461
Belgium	20,209,013
Bolivia	8,036,982
Brazil	78,371,605
Dut. E. Indies.	6,832,891
Ecuador	1,218,253
France	26,142,808
French Guinea.	4,226,236
French Kongo..	3,978,860
Gold Coast....	2,668,667
Ivory Coast....	3,023,878
Kamerun	15,571,122
Mexico	19,445,463
Netherlands	7,045,533
Peru	5,842,014
Senegal	1,526,624
Singapore	3,756,000
South'n Nigeria	2,164,286
Venezuela	897,411
Other countries	16,772,000
Total	**250,546,187**

Imports.	
Austria-Hung'y	6,762,831
Belgium	24,657,300
Canada	3,790,061
France	39,711,019
Germany	44,002,493
Italy	5,334,912
Netherlands	10,279,767
Russia	14,894,472
United kingdom	37,487,632
United States..	82,851,725
Other countries	10,474,000
Total	**280,156,202**

WOOD PULP. Exports—	Pounds.
Austria-Hung.	218,780,756
Belgium	95,275,940
Canada	519,027,600
Finland	251,911,906
Germany	378,484,185
Norway 1,	369,248,047
Russia	55,260,132
Sweden 1,	868,461,199
Switzerland ..	13,407,716
United States	18,988,131
Other count's	8,458,000
Total 4,	797,303,612
Imports—	
Argentina ...	53,447,039
Austria-Hung.	16,710,207
Belgium	301,781,340
Denmark	104,576,524
France	801,927,439
Germany	137,682,561
Italy	175,641,805
Japan	71,020,549
Portugal	17,389,931
Russia	59,452,105
Spain	89,508,197
Sweden	11,568,127
Switzerland ..	17,893,195
Un. kingdom..1,	716,158,080
Un. States...1,	124,650,568
Other count's	65,864,000
Total 4,	765,281,667
BUTTER. Exports—	
Argentina	3,076,813
Australia 101,	722,136
Austria-Hung'y	4,512,816
Belgium	3,345,134
Canada	9,712,206
Denmark 197,	481,675
Finland	27,229,718

Exports—	Pounds.
France	31,517,623
Germany	554,898
Italy	8,147,320
Netherlands ..	66,512,901
New Zealand...	33,867,344
Norway	3,679,125
Russia 168,	704,448
Sweden	48,888,522
United States..	6,374,989
Other countries	4,299,000
Total 719,	626,665
Imports—	
Belgium	15,161,411
Brazil	4,944,999
Brit. S. Africa.	4,155,799
Denmark	6,026,935
Dut. E. Indies.	4,278,796
Egypt	2,181,403
Finland	1,315,394
France	19,938,182
Germany 123,	619,418
Netherlands ...	6,038,929
Russia	1,808,023
Sweden	343,029
Switzerland ...	12,097,742
Un. kingdom...466,	719,680
Other countries	29,508,000
Total 698,	137,740
CHEESE. Exports—	
Bulgaria	7,549,046
Canada 169,	179,147
France	28,620,779
Germany	2,178,806
Italy	61,403,181
Netherlands ...113,	607,416
New Zealand...	49,187,488
Russia	8,945,249
Switzerland ...	66,593,470
United States..	13,781,176

Exports—	Pounds.
Other countries	10,369,000
Total 531,	414,758
Imports—	
Algeria	6,182,360
Argentina	10,845,391
Australia	318,891
Austria-Hung'y	12,473,406
Belgium	29,641,555
Brazil	3,241,214
Brit. S. Africa.	5,039,086
Cuba	4,807,741
Denmark	1,203,491
Egypt	8,927,997
France	49,422,723
Germany	45,954,446
Italy	11,915,422
Russia	4,008,810
Spain	4,929,248
Switzerland ...	7,643,789
United kingdom.257,	133,744
United States..	45,447,329
Other countries.	18,550,000
Total 527,	686,523
WOOL. Exports—	
Algeria	15,314,254
Argentina 291,	086,566
Australia 710,	674,149
Belgium 235,	209,810
British India..	62,143,913
Br. S. Africa..153,	289,110
Chile	23,904,822
China	47,275,467
France	81,886,560
Germany	35,581,362
Netherlands ..	21,432,125
New Zealand..175,	981,629
Persia	10,323,935
Peru	10,426,027
Russia	30,871,677

Exports—	Pounds.
Spain	24,757,321
Turkey	40,156,183
United kingdom.	31,373,218
Uruguay 103,	595,404
Other countries.	42,046,000
Total 2,	147,329,532
Imports—	
Austria-Hung'y	65,148,135
Belgium 340,	039,704
British India..	22,468,689
Canada	6,876,934
France	24,730,592
Germany 468,	711,629
Japan	8,323,399
Netherlands ...	29,376,348
Russia 104,	325,654
Sweden	5,791,041
Switzerland ...	11,634,556
United kingdom.568,	230,493
United States..155,	922,510
Other countries.	53,914,000
Total 2,	444,493,684

*AGRICULTURAL EXPORTS BY YEARS.	
1898...........	$859,018,946
1899...........	792,811,783
1900...........	844,616,530
1901...........	951,628,331
1902...........	857,113,533
1903...........	878,480,557
1904...........	859,160,264
1905...........	826,904,777
1906...........	976,647,104
1907...........	1,054,405,416
1908...........	1,017,396,404
1909...........	903,238,122
1910...........	871,158,425
1911...........	1,030,794,402
1912...........	1,048,433,768
*From United States.	

STATE PRISONS IN THE UNITED STATES.

Alabama—Wetumpka.
Alaska—Sitka (U. S. jail).
Arizona—Florence.
Arkansas—Little Rock.
California—Folsom.
  San Quentin.
Colorado—Canon City.
Connecticut—Weathersfield.
Delaware—Wilmington (workhouse).
District of Columbia—U. S. jail.
Florida—Tallahassee (commission).
Georgia—Atlanta (commission).
Illinois—Joliet, Chester.
Idaho—Boise.
Indiana—Michigan City.
  Indianapolis (women).
Iowa—Fort Madison, Anamosa.
Kansas—Lansing.
Kentucky—Frankfort.
  Eddyville (branch).
Louisiana—Baton Rouge.
Maine—Thomaston.
Maryland—Baltimore.

Massachusetts—Charlestown.
  Bridgewater.
  South Framingham (women).
Michigan—Jackson.
  Marquette (branch).
Minnesota—Stillwater.
Mississippi—Jackson (commission).
Missouri—Jefferson City.
Montana—Deer Lodge.
Nebraska—Lincoln.
Nevada—Carson City.
New Hampshire—Concord.
New Mexico—Santa Fe.
New Jersey—Trenton.
New York—Auburn.
  Dannemora (Clinton).
  Sing Sing (Ossining).
North Carolina—Raleigh.
North Dakota—Bismarck.
Ohio—Columbus.
Oklahoma—McAlester.
Oregon—Salem.
Pennsylvania—Philadelphia.
  Allegheny (Pittsburgh).

Rhode Island—Howard.
South Carolina—Columbia.
South Dakota—Sioux Falls.
Tennessee—Nashville.
  Petros (branch).
Texas—Huntsville.
  Rusk.
Utah—Salt Lake City.
Vermont—Windsor.
Virginia—Richmond.
Washington—Walla Walla.
West Virginia—Moundsville.
Wisconsin—Waupun.
Wyoming—Rawlins.

UNITED STATES PRISONS.

Atlanta, Ga.—Penitentiary.
Fort Leavenworth, Kas.—Penitentiary.
McNeil's Island, Wash.—Penitentiary.
Mare Island, Cal.—Naval prison.
Boston, Mass.—Naval prison.
Portsmouth, N. H.—Naval prison.

DISTANCE OF VISIBILITY OF OBJECTS ON THE LAKES.

[From "List of Lights and Fog Signals" issued by the United States lighthouse board.]

Height, feet.	Dist., miles.	Height, feet.	Dist., miles.	Height, feet.	Dist., miles.	Height, feet.	Dist., miles.	Height, feet.	Dist., miles.	Height, feet.	Dist., miles.
5	2.96	55	9.81	110	13.87	450	28.06	600	32.40	800	37.42
10	4.18	60	10.25	120	14.49	590	29.58	650	33.73	900	39.69
15	5.12	65	10.67	130	15.08	550	31.02	700	35.00	1,000	41.33
20	5.92	70	11.07	140	15.65						
25	6.61	75	11.46	150	16.20						
30	7.25	80	11.83	200	18.71						
35	7.83	85	12.20	250	20.92						
40	8.37	90	12.55	300	22.91						
45	8.87	95	12.89	350	24.75						
50	9.35	100	13.23	400	26.46						

The distances of visibility given in the above table are those from which an object may be seen by an observer whose eye is at the lake level; in practice, therefore, it is necessary to add to these a distance of visibility corresponding to the height of the observer's eye above lake level.

MANUFACTURES IN THE UNITED STATES.

[Bureau of census report, 1912.]

COMPARATIVE SUMMARY, 1860-1910.

	1910.	1900.	1890.	1880.	1870.	1860.
Establishments........................	268,491	207,562	355,415	253,852	252,148	140,433
Capital................................	$18,428,270,000	$9,978,825,200	$6,525,156,486	$2,790,272,606	$2,118,208,769	$1,009,855,715
Salaried persons......................	790,267	364,202	461,009			
Salaries..............................	$938,575,000	$380,889,091	$391,908,208			
Wage earners*.........................	6,615,046	4,715,023	4,251,613	2,732,595	2,053,996	1,311,246
Wages.................................	$3,427,038,000	$2,009,735,799	$1,891,228,321	$947,953,795	$775,584,343	$378,878,966
General expenses......................	$18,453,080,000	$905,600,225	$631,225,035			
Cost of materials.....................	$12,141,791,000	$6,577,614,074	$5,162,044,076	$3,396,823,549	$2,488,427,242	$1,031,605,092
Value of products†....................	$20,672,052,000	$11,411,121,122	$9,372,437,283	$5,369,579,191	$4,232,325,442	$1,885,861,676

*Average number. †Gross value at factory.

NOTE—The years are census years. The statistics are for the preceding calendar year in each case.

PER CENT INCREASE BY DECADES.

Decade.	Establishments.	Capital.	Wage earners.	Wages.	Materials.	Products.	Value added.
1849-1859	14.1	89.4	37.0	60.0	85.8	85.0	84.1
1859-1869	79.6	67.8	56.6	63.8	93.0	79.5	63.3
1869-1879	0.7	64.7	33.0	62.8	90.6	74.5	41.4
1879-1889	40.0	133.8	55.6	99.5	52.0	74.5	113.4
1889-1899	44.1	50.4	24.8	22.7	42.3	38.7	34.3
1899-1909	29.4	105.3	40.4	70.6	84.6	81.2	76.6

RANK OF LEADING INDUSTRIES IN 1909.

According to value of products.

Industry.	Rank.	Product.	Per cent increase.
Slaughtering, packing......	1	$1,370,568,000	48.6
Foundries, machine shops.....	2	1,228,475,000	39.5
Lumber and timber............	3	1,156,129,000	30.7
Iron and steel...............	4	985,723,000	46.3
Flour and grist mills........	5	883,584,000	23.9
Printing and publishing......	6	737,876,000	63.6
Cotton goods.................	7	628,392,000	39.5
Clothing, men's..............	8	568,077,000	39.7
Boots and shoes..............	9	512,798,000	43.4
Wool, worsteds, felt.........	10	435,979,000	36.5
Tobacco manufactures.........	11	416,695,000	25.8
Cars, etc., by steam roads*...	12	405,601,000	30.9
Bread, bakery goods..........	13	396,865,000	47.2
Blast furnaces...............	14	391,429,000	68.8
Clothing, women's............	15	384,752,000	55.4
Copper, smelting, refining...	16	378,806,000	57.3
Malt liquors.................	17	374,730,000	25.6
Leather, tanning, etc........	18	327,874,000	29.8
Sugar and molasses†..........	19	279,249,000	0.7
Butter, cheese, condensed milk	20	274,558,000	63.2
Paper and wood pulp..........	21	267,657,000	41.8
Automobiles	22	249,202,000	729.7
Furniture and refrigerators..	23	239,887,000	34.9
Petroleum, refining..........	24	236,998,000	35.4
Electrical machinery.........	25	221,369,000	57.2
Liquors, distilled...........	26	204,699,000	55.9
Hosiery and knit goods.......	27	200,144,000	46.0
Copper, tin, sheet iron......	28	199,824,000	66.6
Silk, silk goods.............	29	196,912,000	47.7
Lead, smelting, refining.....	30	167,406,000	9.9
Gas, illuminating, heating...	31	166,814,000	33.3
Carriages, wagons............	32	159,893,000	2.6
Canning, preserving..........	33	157,101,000	20.4
Brass, bronze products.......	34	149,989,000	46.5
Oil, cotton seed, cake.......	35	147,868,000	53.4
Agricultural implements......	36	146,329,000	30.6
Medicines, drugs, etc........	37	141,942,000	20.9
Confectionery	38	134,796,000	54.8
Paint and varnish............	39	124,889,000	37.5
Cars for steam roads†........	40	123,730,000	11.3
Chemicals	41	117,689,000	56.5
Marble and stone work........	42	113,093,000	33.3
Leather goods................	43	104,719,000	27.5

*Includes general shop construction and repairs by steam railroad companies. †Not including beet sugar. ‡Not including operations of railroad companies. §From 1904 to 1909.

NOTE—The increase in all industries combined from 1904 to 1909 was 39.7 per cent; that of all the minor industries not included in the foregoing table was 41.8 per cent in the same period. This is presumed to indicate a tendency toward diversification in manufacturing.

MANUFACTURES BY SPECIFIED INDUSTRIES (1909).

Industry.	Persons.*	Value products.
Agricultural implements.........	60,229	$146,329,000
Artificial flowers, plumes......	11,583	23,981,000
Artificial stone................	15,202	18,596,000
Artists' materials..............	865	2,340,000
Automobiles	85,359	249,202,000
Awnings, tents, sails...........	5,747	14,499,000
Axle grease.....................	334	1,481,000
Babbitt metal, solder...........	1,491	19,768,000
Bags, not paper.................	8,838	54,882,000
Bags, paper.....................	3,683	15,698,000
Baking powders, yeast...........	3,531	20,775,000
Baskets, willow ware............	5,419	5,695,000
Beet sugar......................	8,359	48,122,000
Belting, hose, leather..........	4,370	23,632,000
Belting, hose, rubber...........	7,304	24,709,000
Bicycles, motorcycles...........	5,017	10,699,000
Billiard tables.................	1,776	5,878,000
Blacking, polishing.............	4,407	14,679,000
Bluing	545	1,074,000
Bone, carbon, lampblack.........	302	1,093,000
Boots and shoes.................	215,923	512,798,000
Boots, shoes, rubber............	18,899	49,721,000
Boxes, cigar....................	6,852	8,491,000
Boxes, fancy, paper.............	43,568	54,450,000
Brass and bronze................	45,441	149,989,000
Bread, bakery products..........	144,322	396,865,000
Brick and tile..................	85,764	92,776,000
Brooms, brushes.................	15,143	29,126,000
Butter, cheese, condensed milk..	31,506	274,558,000
Butter, reworking...............	418	8,200,000
Buttons	18,004	22,708,000
Candles	649	3,130,000
Canning, preserving.............	71,372	157,101,000
Card cutting, designing.........	702	1,031,000
Carpets, not rag................	34,706	71,188,000
Carpets, rag....................	2,688	2,568,000
Carriages, sleds, children's....	5,769	8,805,000
Carriages, wagons...............	82,944	159,893,000
Cars, repairs, by R. R. Cos.....	301,273	405,601,000
Cars, etc., by street railways..	23,699	31,963,000
Cars for steam railways.........	47,094	123,730,000
Cars for street railways........	4,005	7,810,000
Cash registers, calculators.....	9,249	23,708,000
Cement	29,511	63,205,000
Charcoal	731	872,000
Chemicals	27,791	117,689,000
China decorating................	436	786,000
Chocolate, cocoa................	3,404	22,390,000
Clocks, watches.................	25,439	35,197,000
Cloth, sponging, finishing......	1,167	1,544,000
Clothing, horse.................	1,830	4,135,000
Clothing, men's.................	271,437	568,077,000
Clothing, men's button holes....	1,031	781,000
Clothing, women's...............	179,021	384,752,000
Coffee, spice...................	13,516	110,533,000
Coffins, etc....................	11,448	24,526,000
Coke	31,226	95,697,000
Confectionery	54,854	134,796,000
Cooperage, etc..................	29,717	60,348,000
Copper, tin, sheet iron.........	86,934	199,824,000
Cordage, twine, etc.............	27,214	61,020,000
Cordials, sirups................	1,638	9,662,000
Cork, cutting...................	3,376	5,940,000

Industry.	Persons.*	Value products.
Corsets	19,611	33,257,000
Cotton goods	387,771	628,392,000
Crucibles	398	1,849,000
Cutlery, tools	37,161	53,266,000
Dairymen's supplies, etc.	6,431	15,463,000
Dentists' materials	1,982	10,836,000
Drug grinding	1,152	6,007,000
Dyeing textiles	47,393	83,556,000
Dyestuffs, extracts	3,015	15,955,000
Electrical machinery	105,600	221,309,000
Electroplating	3,558	4,510,000
Emery, abrasive wheels	2,446	6,711,000
Enameling, japanning	2,418	3,316,000
Engravers' materials	189	921,000
Engraving, die sinking	1,782	2,250,000
Engraving, wood	480	711,000
Explosives	7,058	40,140,000
Fancy articles	14,194	22,632,000
Fertilizers	21,950	103,960,000
Files	4,521	5,691,000
Firearms, ammunition	16,042	34,112,000
Fire extinguishers, chemical	300	754,000
Fireworks	1,567	2,269,000
Flags, regalia, etc	4,522	8,114,000
Flavoring extracts	2,634	8,828,000
Flax, hemp, dressed	216	467,000
Flour, gristmill products	66,054	883,584,000
Food preparations	20,965	125,331,000
Foundry, shop products	615,485	1,228,475,000
Foundry supplies	710	2,298,000
Fuel, manufactured	112	311,000
Fur goods	16,152	55,938,000
Furnishing goods, men's	43,935	87,710,000
Furniture, refrigerators	144,140	239,886,000
Furs, dressed	1,473	2,391,000
Galvanizing	1,689	7,338,000
Gas, electric fixtures	22,906	45,057,000
Gas, illuminating, heating	51,007	166,814,000
Glass	72,573	92,095,000
Glass, ornamenting	11,090	16,101,000
Gloves, leather	12,950	23,631,000
Glucose and starch	5,827	48,799,000
Glue	2,840	12,718,000
Gold, silver foil	1,553	2,636,000
Gold, silver, refining	690	23,612,000
Graphite, refining	262	1,140,000
Grease and tallow	5,504	22,419,000
Grindstones	1,485	1,688,000
Haircloth	621	2,230,000
Hair work	4,383	11,216,000
Hammocks	325	578,000
Hand stamps, stencils	2,539	3,673,000
Hat and cap materials	2,618	8,236,000
Hats, caps, unspecified	7,609	13,689,000
Hats, fur, felt	27,091	47,865,000
Hats, straw	8,704	21,424,000
Hones, whetstones	173	268,000
Horseshoes	360	1,015,000
Hosiery, knit goods	136,130	200,143,000
Housefurnishing goods	5,916	18,509,000
Ice, manufactured	21,107	49,953,000
Ink, printing	1,864	8,865,000
Ink, writing	824	2,505,000
Instruments, scientific	6,175	10,504,000
Iron, steel, blast furnaces	43,061	391,429,000
Iron, steel, rolling mills	260,762	985,723,000
Iron, steel, bolts, nuts, etc	12,395	24,485,000
Iron, steel, doors, shutters	1,816	3,006,000
Iron, steel forgings	9,193	20,293,000
Iron, steel, nails, spikes	3,229	8,192,000
Iron, steel pipe, wrought	7,309	30,886,000
Jewelry	36,992	80,350,000
Jewelry cases	2,441	3,116,000
Kaolin, ground earths	2,351	4,681,000
Labels, tags	2,880	4,670,000
Lapidary work	886	9,173,000
Lard, refined, not packers'	515	10,326,000
Lasts	2,029	4,158,000
Lead, bar, etc	1,044	9,145,000
Leather goods	43,525	104,719,000
Leather, tanned, etc	67,100	327,874,000
Lime	15,659	17,952,000
Liquors, distilled	8,328	204,699,000
Liquors, malt	66,725	374,730,000
Liquors, vinous	2,726	13,121,000
Locomotives, not made by railroad companies	16,945	31,582,000
Looking glass frames	7,470	13,475,000
Lumber products	784,989	1,156,129,000
Malt	2,237	28,252,000
Marble and stone work	77,275	113,093,000
Matches	4,220	11,353,000
Mats and matting	1,040	2,442,000
Mattresses	14,109	35,733,000
Millinery goods	46,301	85,894,000
Mineral, soda waters	22,060	43,508,000
Mirrors	3,509	9,571,000
Models, patterns, not paper	5,450	8,868,000
Moving pictures	718	4,206,000
Mucilage, paste	901	4,918,000
Musical instruments	2,269	3,228,000
Musical inst., pianos, organs	41,882	89,790,000
Needles, pins, hooks, eyes	4,978	6,694,000
Oakum	129	338,000
Oil, castor	70	905,000
Oil, essential	408	1,737,000
Oil, linseed	1,753	36,739,000
Oil, not specified	3,144	30,865,000
Oilcloth, linoleum	5,557	23,339,000
Oleomargarine	773	8,148,000
Optical goods	7,809	11,735,000
Paint and varnish	21,896	124,859,000
Paper, wood pulp	81,473	267,657,000
Paper goods	22,385	55,171,000
Paper patterns	1,755	2,611,000
Patent medicines, etc	41,101	141,942,000
Paving materials	1,731	6,229,000
Peanuts, roasting, etc	2,177	9,737,000
Pencils, lead	4,513	7,379,000
Pens, fountain, gold	1,820	4,738,000
Pens, steel	755	577,000
Petroleum, refining	16,640	236,998,000
Phonographs, graphophones	5,928	11,726,000
Photographic goods	6,596	22,561,000
Photo engraving	7,277	11,624,000
Pipes, tobacco	3,090	5,312,000
Pottery, terra cotta	61,022	76,119,000
Printing, publishing	398,466	737,876,000
Pulp goods	882	1,770,000
Pumps, not steam	2,623	5,583,000
Rice, cleaning	1,777	22,371,000
Roofing materials	3,530	19,204,000
Rubber goods	31,284	128,436,000
Rules, ivory, wood	127	144,000
Safes, vaults	4,060	8,491,000
Salt	5,580	11,328,000
Sand, emery paper	779	4,358,000
Saws	5,757	11,536,000
Scales, balances	4,275	8,786,000
Screws, machine	1,863	3,014,000
Screws, wood	3,758	6,199,000
Sewing machines	20,556	28,262,000
Shipbuilding	44,949	73,360,000
Shoddy	2,320	7,446,000
Show cases	3,943	7,167,000
Signs, advertising	7,277	13,546,000
Silks, silk goods	105,238	196,912,000
Silver and plated ware	18,774	42,229,000
Slaughtering, packing	108,716	1,370,568,000
Smelting, refining, copper	16,832	378,806,000
Smelting, refining, lead	8,059	167,406,000
Smelting, refining, zinc	7,156	34,206,000
Smelting, refining, not from ore	2,596	28,072,000
Soap	18,393	111,358,000
Soda water apparatus	2,399	6,556,000
Sporting goods	5,993	11,052,000
Springs, steel, car	3,573	9,005,000
Stationery goods	7,938	16,547,000
Statuary, art goods	2,172	3,442,000
Steam packing	4,498	12,160,000
Stereotyping, electrotyping	3,061	6,384,000
Stoves, furnaces	42,921	78,853,000
Sugar, molasses (no beet)	15,658	279,249,000
Sulphuric, nitric, acids	2,582	9,884,000
Surgical appliances	5,805	12,399,000
Tin plate, terneplate	5,846	47,970,000
Tinfoil	762	3,419,000
Tobacco manufactures	197,637	416,695,000
Toys and games	6,072	8,264,000
Turpentine, rosin	44,524	25,285,000
Typefounding, printing materials	2,597	4,704,000
Typewriters, supplies	12,101	19,719,000
Umbrellas, canes	6,505	15,864,000
Upholstering materials	4,777	13,054,000

Industry	Persons.*	Value products.	Industry	Persons *	Value products.
Vault lights, ventilators	453	957,000	Wirework, rope, cable.	14,994	41,933,000
Vinegar and cider	3,073	8,448,000	Wood distillation	3,095	9,737,000
Wall paper	4,746	14,449,000	Wood carpet	221	490,000
Wall plaster	5,624	12,804,000	Wood preserving	2,875	14,099,000
Washing machines	2,294	5,825,000	Wood, turned, carved	16,243	22,199,000
Waste	2,122	11,398,000	Wool pulling	759	5,181,000
Wheelbarrows	775	1,625,000	Wool scouring	1,262	3,289,000
Whips	1,946	3,949,000	Woolen goods	175,176	435,979,000
Windmills	2,742	6,677,000	All other industries	132	390,000
Window shades	4,770	18,571,000	*Includes proprietors, salaried officials, clerks and
Wire	19,945	84,486,000	wage earners

PERSONS ENGAGED IN MANUFACTURING (1909).

Summary prepared by census bureau, 1912, showing distribution by class, sex and age

Class	Total	Male	Female
Proprietors and firm members	273,265	263,265	9,592
Salaried officers of corporations	80,735	78,937	1,798
Superintendents and managers	133,173	130,304	2,869
Total proprietors and officials	487,173	472,914	14,259
Clerks	576,359	437,056	139,303
Wage earners (average number)	6,615,046	5,252,293	1,362,753
Total all classes	7,678,578	6,162,263	1,516,315
Sixteen years of age and over	6,452,800	5,162,547	1,290,253
Under 16 years of age	162,246	89,746	72,500

OCCUPATIONAL STATUS BY LEADING INDUSTRIES (1909)

Industry.	Total.	Owners.*	Clerks	Wage earners.
Agricultural implements	60,229	2,489	7,189	59,551
Automobiles	85,359	2,564	7,074	75,721
Boots and shoes	215,923	5,752	11,874	198,297
Brass and bronze products	45,441	2,160	2,663	40,618
Bread, bakery products	144,322	29,136	14,970	100,216
Butter, cheese, condensed milk	31,506	10,480	2,595	18,431
Canning and preserving	71,972	6,920	5,084	59,968
Carriages and wagons	82,944	8,844	4,172	69,928
Cars, shop construction, etc	301,273	6,974	12,125	282,174
Cars, steam railroad	47,094	1,041	2,967	43,086
Chemicals	27,791	1,086	2,991	23,714
Clothing, men's	271,437	12,041	19,700	239,696
Clothing, women's.	179,021	9,281	15,997	153,743
Confectionery	54 854	3,362	6,854	44,638
Copper, tin, sheet iron	86,934	7,269	6,050	73,615
Cotton goods.	387,771	4,461	4,430	378,880
Electrical machinery.	105,600	4,121	14,223	87,256
Flour and grist mill products	66,054	18,763	7,838	39,453
Foundry, machine shop products	615,485	31,605	52,869	531,011
Furniture, refrigerators	144,140	7,281	8,407	128,452
Gas, illuminating, heating	51,007	2,986	10,806	37,215
Hosiery, knit goods	136,130	3,308	3,547	129,275
Iron and steel, blast furnaces	43,061	1,119	3,513	38,429
Steel works and rolling mills	260,762	4,286	16,400	240,076
Leather goods	43,525	4,209	4,409	34,907
Leather, tanned, curried, etc	67,100	2,331	2,567	62,202
Liquors, distilled.	8,328	1,111	787	6,430
Liquors, malt	66,725	4,362	7,784	54,579
Lumber, timber.	784,989	68,165	21,805	695,019
Marble and stone	77,275	8,453	3,219	65,603
Oil, cotton seed, cake	21,273	2,167	2,035	17,071
Paint and varnish	21,896	2,016	5,640	14,240
Paper and wood pulp	81,473	2,298	3,197	75,978
Patent medicines, etc	41,101	5,647	12,559	22,895
Petroleum, refining	16,640	671	2,040	13,929
Printing, publishing	388,466	49,332	80,700	258,434
Silk and silk goods	105,238	2,236	3,965	99,037
Slaughtering, packing	108,716	3,514	15,474	89,728
Smelting, refining, copper	16,832	275	929	15 628
Smelting, refining, lead	8,059	132	503	7,424
Sugar, molasses	15,658	789	1,343	13,526
Tobacco manufactures.	197,637	21,012	9,815	166,810
Woolen, worsted, felt goods	175,176	3,192	3,262	168,722
All other industries	1,916,361	117,932	149,988	1,648,441
Total	7,678,578	487,173	576,359	6,615,046

*Includes salaried officers of corporations, superintendents and managers

MANUFACTURES BY STATES (1909).

State	Capital invested	Gross value of product	State.	Capital invested	Gross value of product
Alabama	$173,180 000	$145,962,000	Delaware	$60,906,000	$52,840,000
Arizona	32,873,000	50,257,000	District of Columbia	30,553,000	25,288,000
Arkansas	70,174,000	74,916,000	Florida	65,291,000	72,890,000
California	537,134,000	529,761,000	Georgia	202,778,000	202,863,000
Colorado	162,668,000	130,044,000	Idaho	32,477,000	22,400,000
Connecticut	517,546,000	490,272,000	Illinois	1,548,171,000	1,919,277,000

State.	Capital invested.	Gross value of product.
Indiana	508,717,000	579,075,000
Iowa	171,219,000	259,238,000
Kansas	156,090,000	325,104,000
Kentucky	172,779,000	223,754,000
Louisiana	221,816,000	223,949,000
Maine	202,260,000	176,029,000
Maryland	251,227,000	315,669,000
Massachusetts	1,279,687,000	1,490,529,000
Michigan	583,947,000	685,109,000
Minnesota	275,416,000	409,420,000
Mississippi	72,393,000	80,555,000
Missouri	444,343,000	574,111,000
Montana	44,588,000	73,272,000
Nebraska	99,901,000	199,019,000
Nevada	9,806,000	11,887,000
New Hampshire	139,390,000	164,581,000
New Jersey	977,172,000	1,145,529,000
New Mexico	7,743,000	7,898,000
New York	2,779,497,000	3,369,490,000
North Carolina	217,185,000	216,656,000
North Dakota	11,585,000	19,137,000
Ohio	1,300,733,000	1,437,936,000
Oklahoma	38,373,000	53,682,000
Oregon	89,082,000	93,005,000
Pennsylvania	2,749,006,000	2,626,742,000
Rhode Island	290,901,000	280,344,000
South Carolina	173,221,000	113,236,000
South Dakota	13,018,000	17,870,000
Tennessee	167,924,000	180,217,000
Texas	216,876,000	272,896,000
Utah	52,627,000	61,989,000
Vermont	73,470,000	68,310,000
Virginia	216,392,000	219,794,000
Washington	222,261,000	220,746,000
West Virginia	150,922,000	161,949,000
Wisconsin	605,657,000	590,305,000
Wyoming	6,195,000	6,249,000
Total 1909	18,428,270,000	20,672,052,000
Total 1899	8,975,256,000	11,406,927,000
Per cent increase	105.3	81.2

MANUFACTURES IN FIFTY LEADING CITIES (1909).

City.	Value of product.	Rank in product.	Wage earners.
New York, N. Y.	$2,029,693,000	1	554,002
Chicago, Ill.	1,281,171,000	2	293,977
Philadelphia, Pa	746,076,000	3	251,884
St. Louis, Mo	328,495,000	4	87,371
Cleveland, O	271,461,000	5	84,728
Detroit, Mich	252,992,000	6	81,011
Pittsburgh, Pa	243,454,000	7	67,474
Boston, Mass	237,457,000	8	69,637
Buffalo, N. Y	218,804,000	9	51,412
Milwaukee, Wis	208,324,000	10	59,502
Newark, N. J	202,511,000	11	59,955
Cincinnati, O	194,516,000	12	60,192
Baltimore, Md	186,978,000	13	71,444
Minneapolis, Minn	165,405,000	14	26,962
Kansas City, Kas	164,081,000	15	12,294
San Francisco, Cal	133,041,000	16	28,244
Jersey City, N. J	128,775,000	17	25,454
Indianapolis, Ind	126,522,000	18	31,815
Providence, R. I	120,241,000	19	46,381
Rochester, N. Y	112,676,000	20	39,108
Louisville, Ky	101,284,000	21	27,023
South Omaha, Neb	92,436,000	22	6,806
Youngstown, O	81,271,000	23	10,498
Lawrence, Mass	79,993,000	24	30,542
New Orleans, La	78,794,000	25	17,188
Worcester, Mass	77,148,000	26	28,321
Bayonne, N. J	73,641,000	27	7,519
Akron, O	73,158,000	28	15,831
Perth Amboy, N. J	73,093,000	29	5,866
Lynn, Mass	71,503,000	30	27,368
Paterson, N. J	69,584,000	31	32,004
Los Angeles, Cal	68,586,000	32	17,327
Bridgeport, Conn	65,609,000	33	25,775
Fall River, Mass	64,146,000	34	37,139
Peoria, Ill	63,061,000	35	5,981
Toledo, O	61,230,000	36	18,878
Omaha, Neb	60,854,000	37	8,023
Dayton, O	60,378,000	38	21,549
Lowell, Mass	60,271,000	39	32,575
Yonkers, N. Y	59,234,000	40	12,711
St. Paul, Minn	58,990,000	41	19,389
Kansas City, Mo	54,704,000	42	14,643
New Bedford, Mass	53,238,000	43	26,566
Denver, Col	51,538,000	44	12,058
Reading, Pa	51,135,000	45	24,145
New Haven, Conn	51,071,000	46	23,547
Seattle, Wash	50,569,000	47	11,331
Waterbury, Conn	50,350,000	48	20,120
Syracuse, N. Y	49,435,000	49	18,148
Camden, N. J	49,138,000	50	16,527

MANUFACTURES IN CITIES OF 10,000 OR MORE INHABITANTS

State and city.	Value of product.
Alabama—Anniston	$4,333,000
Bessemer	6,106,000
Birmingham	24,128,000
Mobile	5,429,000
Montgomery	5,443,000
Arizona—Phœnix	1,467,000
Tucson	2,037,000
Arkansas—Argenta	4,842,000
Fort Smith	3,739,000
Little Rock	4,690,000
California—Berkeley	4,435,000
Fresno	11,090,000
Oakland	22,345,000
Sacramento	13,977,000
San Diego	4,741,000
San Jose	5,611,000
Stockton	11,849,000
Colorado—Pueblo	3,345,000
Connecticut—Ansonia	20,088,000
Danbury	10,318,000
Hartford	40,690,000
Meriden	16,317,000
New Britain	22,021,000
New London	4,483,000
Norwich	9,389,000
Stamford	8,739,000
Willimantic	6,733,000
Delaware—Wilmington	38,069,000
District of Columbia	25,289,000
Florida—Jacksonville	6,722,000
Key West	3,965,000
Tampa	17,653,000
Georgia—Atlanta	33,038,000
Augusta	10,456,000
Columbus	8,552,000
Macon	10,703,000
Savannah	6,734,000
Idaho—Boise	1,661,000
Illinois—Alton	10,096,000
Aurora	10,954,000
Belleville	4,615,000
Bloomington	4,868,000
Cairo	4,440,000
Canton	2,942,000
Champaign	846,000
Chicago Heights	10,839,000
Cicero	1,461,000
Danville	3,351,000
Decatur	9,768,000
East St. Louis	18,228,000
Elgin	11,120,000
Evanston	3,778,000
Freeport	7,811,000
Galesburg	2,913,000
Jacksonville	2,299,000
Joliet	38,817,000
Kankakee	2,723,000
LaSalle	5,308,000
Lincoln	570,000
Mattoon	1,434,000
Moline	20,892,000
Oak Park	1,118,000
Peoria	63,061,000
Quincy	11,436,000
Rock Island	5,387,000
Rockford	22,266,000
Springfield	8,497,000
Streator	2,137,000
Waukegan	19,984,000
Indiana—Anderson	13,765,000
East Chicago	5,483,000
Elkhart	6,932,000
Ellwood	8,498,000
Evansville	22,929,000
Fort Wayne	23,687,000
Hammond	15,589,000
Kokomo	5,451,000
Lafayette	5,542,000
Laporte	3,972,000
Logansport	4,201,000
Marion	4,442,000
Michigan City	8,290,000
Mishawaka	10,883,000
Muncie	9,684,000
New Albany	3,493,000
Richmond	10,374,000
South Bend	27,854,000
Terre Haute	21,792,000
Vincennes	4,234,000
Iowa—Burlington	8,443,000
Cedar Rapids	24,824,000
Clinton	7,490,000
Council Bluffs	3,769,000
Davenport	18,802,000
Des Moines	23,585,000
Dubuque	15,376,000
Keokuk	7,389,000
Marshalltown	4,822,000
Muscatine	6,166,000
Ottumwa	14,838,000
Sioux City	37,425,000
Waterloo	8,999,000
Kansas—Atchison	4,405,000
Coffeyville	4,752,000

State and city.	Value of product.	State and city.	Value of product.	State and city.	Value of product.
Hutchinson	3,614,000	Mississippi—Jackson	3,113,000	Canton	28,583,000
Leavenworth	4,875,000	Meridian	4,238,000	Chillicothe	4,345,000
Topeka	17,821,000	Vicksburg	2,229,000	Columbus	49,032,000
Wichita	22,564,000	Missouri—Hannibal	6,195,000	East Liverpool	6,829,000
Kentucky—Covington	8,712,000	Jefferson City	5,446,000	Elyria	8,065,000
Frankfort	3,083,000	Joplin	4,136,000	Hamilton	18,184,000
Henderson	2,932,000	St. Joseph	17,626,000	Ironton	7,118,000
Lexington	2,851,000	Sedalia	2,333,000	Lancaster	4,074,000
Newport	6,491,000	Springfield	5,382,000	Lima	7,254,000
Owensboro	3,505,000	Montana—Billings	1,243,000	Lorain	38,987,000
Paducah	4,907,000	Butte	2,464,000	Mansfield	8,183,000
Louisiana—Alexandria	1,279,000	Helena	1,803,000	Marion	5,667,000
Lake Charles	2,251,000	Missoula	1,171,000	Massillon	4,788,000
Monroe	1,255,000	Nebraska—Grand Island.	1,837,000	Middletown	16,517,000
Shreveport	3,643,000	Lincoln	7,010,000	Newark	7,851,000
Maine—Auburn	8,843,000	Nevada—Reno	1,862,000	Norwood	9,584,000
Augusta	4,662,000	New Hampshire—Berlin.	5,985,000	Piqua	6,931,000
Bangor	3,346,000	Concord	6,477,000	Portsmouth	7,277,000
Biddeford	9,012,000	Dover	6,370,000	Sandusky	5,947,000
Lewiston	10,475,000	Keene	3,483,000	Springfield	19,246,000
Portland	11,950,000	Laconia	3,818,000	Steubenville	21,187,000
Waterville	3,179,000	Manchester	46,812,000	Warren	5,988,000
Maryland—Cumberland.	4,595,000	Nashua	17,326,000	Youngstown	81,271,000
Frederick	2,911,000	New Jersey—Bloomfield.	5,895,000	Zanesville	9,145,000
Hagerstown	3,197,000	Bridgetown	2,469,000	Oklahoma—Enid	2,453,000
Massachusetts—Adams..	6,410,000	East Orange	3,725,000	Guthrie	1,443,000
Attleborough	15,160,000	Elizabeth	29,147,000	Muskogee	2,279,000
Beverly	8,653,000	Harrison	13,142,000	Oklahoma City	7,868,000
Brockton	45,972,000	Hoboken	20,413,000	Shawnee	2,081,000
Cambridge	44,227,000	Millville	4,182,000	Oregon—Portland	46,861,000
Chelsea	17,003,000	New Brunswick	10,005,000	Salem	2,208,000
Chicopee	19,219,000	Orange	9,176,000	Pennsylvania—	
Clinton	7,845,000	Passaic	9,176,000	Allentown	26,263,000
Everett	8,747,000	Phillipsburg	9,150,000	Altoona	16,763,000
Fitchburg	23,252,000	Plainfield	3,649,000	Beaver Falls	6,400,000
Framingham	6,917,000	Trenton	49,009,000	Braddock	5,094,000
Gardner	6,485,000	Union	7,941,000	Butler	11,058,000
Gloucester	7,753,000	West Hoboken	5,577,000	Chester	19,373,000
Haverhill	35,377,000	West New York	9,274,000	Columbia	4,807,000
Holyoke	40,097,000	New Mexico—Albuquer-		Easton	6,915,000
Leominster	10,531,000	que	1,288,000	Erie	24,226,000
Malden	8,206,000	New York—Albany	22,826,000	Harrisburg	22,725,000
Marlboro	10,382,000	Amsterdam	22,449,000	Hazleton	4,707,000
Milford	4,442,000	Auburn	15,961,000	Johnstown	48,106,000
Newburyport	6,931,000	Batavia	4,401,000	Lancaster	15,979,000
Newton	6,279,000	Binghamton	17,114,000	Lebanon	11,429,000
North Adams	10,315,000	Cohoes	14,831,000	McKeesport	42,495,000
Northampton	6,999,000	Cortland	6,395,000	McKees Rocks	9,787,000
Peabody	15,549,000	Dunkirk	6,576,000	New Castle	38,038,000
Pittsfield	15,215,000	Elmira	8,067,000	Norristown	7,413,000
Plymouth	11,618,000	Fulton	7,867,000	Oil City	4,122,000
Quincy	10,505,000	Geneva	5,154,000	Phoenixville	5,876,000
Salem	14,576,000	Glens Falls	4,877,000	Pottstown	12,505,000
Somerville	38,687,000	Gloversville	14,171,000	Pottsville	9,138,000
Springfield	31,773,000	Hornell	3,648,000	Reading	51,135,000
Taunton	15,380,000	Hudson	3,506,000	Scranton	26,385,000
Wakefield	5,527,000	Jamestown	14,720,000	Sharon	9,581,000
Waltham	7,814,000	Johnstown	6,574,000	South Bethlehem	26,417,000
Watertown	11,546,000	Kingston	5,986,000	Sunbury	4,450,000
Webster	11,296,000	Little Falls	8,460,000	Warren	5,744,000
Westfield	7,362,000	Lockport	8,168,000	Washington	4,337,000
Weymouth	6,627,000	Middletown	4,658,000	Wilkesbarre	13,526,000
Woburn	5,408,000	Newburgh	9,928,000	Williamsport	13,348,000
Michigan—Adrian	6,085,000	Niagara Falls	28,652,000	York	18,622,000
Alpena	3,964,000	North Tonawanda	9,600,000	Rhode Island—	
Battle Creek	20,174,000	Ogdensburg	4,948,000	Central Falls	5,471,000
Bay City	10,294,000	Olean	10,005,000	Cranston	5,525,000
Flint	24,118,000	Oswego	10,413,000	Cumberland	9,827,000
Grand Rapids	42,231,000	Peekskill	7,888,000	East Providence	7,146,000
Holland	4,622,000	Port Chester	6,243,000	Pawtucket	37,696,000
Jackson	14,006,000	Poughkeepsie	9,151,000	Warwick	10,589,000
Kalamazoo	17,904,000	Rome	14,423,000	Woonsocket	28,218,000
Lansing	16,567,000	Schenectady	38,165,000	S. Carolina—Charleston.	6,951,000
Manistee	3,344,000	Troy	37,980,000	Columbia	5,872,000
Marquette	1,254,000	Utica	31,199,000	Spartanburg	4,338,000
Menominee	3,728,000	Watertown	8,527,000	South Dakota—Aberdeen	1,575,000
Muskegon	9,648,000	N. Carolina—Asheville..	3,250,000	Sioux Falls	4,667,000
Pontiac	5,894,000	Charlotte	10,460,000	Tennessee—Chattanooga.	16,036,000
Port Huron	3,585,000	Durham	23,271,000	Jackson	2,710,000
Saginaw	18,833,000	Wilmington	5,005,000	Knoxville	8,149,000
Sault Ste. Marie	4,619,000	Winston	16,778,000	Memphis	30,043,000
Traverse City	2,289,000	North Dakota—Fargo	2,477,000	Nashville	29,650,000
Minnesota—Duluth	17,180,000	Grand Forks	1,910,000	Texas—Austin	2,845,000
Mankato	3,723,000	Ohio—Alliance	6,135,000	Beaumont	4,831,000
St. Cloud	2,299,000	Ashtabula	3,459,000	Dallas	26,959,000
Stillwater	2,586,000	Bellaire	10,091,000	El Paso	3,637,000
Winona	11,199,000	Cambridge	4,291,000	Fort Worth	8,651,000

State and city.	Value of product.	State and city.	Value of product.	State and city.	Value of product.
Galveston	6,308,000	Roanoke	7,261,000	Fond du Lac	8,227,000
Houston	23,015,000	Washington—Aberdeen	3,590,000	Green Bay	6,235,000
San Antonio	13,435,000	Bellingham	4,690,000	Janesville	5,156,000
Sherman	4,676,000	Everett	7,423,000	Kenosha	23,182,000
Utah—Ogden	3,713,000	North Yakima	2,175,000	LaCrosse	14,102,000
Salt Lake City	13,351,000	Spokane	18,880,000	Madison	5,467,000
Vermont—Barre	3,852,000	W. Virginia—Charleston	3,235,000	Manitowoc	5,939,000
Burlington	6,800,000	Huntington	6,511,000	Marinette	3,309,000
Rutland	2,680,000	Martinsburg	2,516,000	Oshkosh	14,739,000
Virginia—Alexandria	4,420,000	Parkersburg	5,499,000	Racine	24,673,000
Danville	5,389,000	Wheeling	27,077,000	Sheboygan	11,299,000
Lynchburg	10,188,000	Wisconsin—Appleton	6,673,000	Superior	6,574,000
Norfolk	10,341,000	Ashland	2,748,000	Wausau	6,287,000
Petersburg	8,896,000	Beloit	5,886,000	Wyoming—Cheyenne	1,577,000
Richmond	47,358,000	Eau Claire	5,855,000		

SPECIFIED INDUSTRIES IN DETAIL.

AGRICULTURAL IMPLEMENTS.

Establishments, 640; capital, $256,281,086; persons employed, 60,229; wage earners, 50,551; wages, $28,-608,615; salaries, $10,129,938; total expenses, $117,-940,357; cost of materials, $60,306,519; value of products, $146,329,268. Leading states in industry, according to value of products: Illinois, $57,268,000; New York, $14,971,000; Ohio, $14,440,000; Indiana, $13,670,000; Wisconsin, $11,411,000; Michigan, $9,-273,000.

AUTOMOBILES AND PARTS.

Establishments, 743; persons engaged in industry, 85,359; wage earners, 75,721; capital, $173,837,000; salaries, $9,479,000; wages, $48,694,000; cost of materials, $131,646,000; value of products, $249,202,000; automobiles turned out in 1909, 126,593. Michigan led in number and value of motor vehicles manufactured; Indiana was second and Ohio third in number of automobiles produced, but in value of output Ohio was second and Indiana third. Ohio led in manufacture of electric and steam automobiles.

BICYCLES AND MOTORCYCLES.

Establishments, 95; persons employed, 5,017; wage earners, 4,437; capital, $9,780,000; wages, $2,908,000; cost of materials, $5,083,000; value of products, $10,699,000. The number of bicycles made decreased from 1,182,691 in 1899 to 233,707 in 1909. The output of motorcycles increased from 160 in 1899 to 18,628 in 1909 with a total value of $3,015,988 as compared with $33,674 in 1899.

CARRIAGES AND WAGONS.

Establishments, 5,492; persons engaged in industry, 82,944; wage earners, 69,928; capital, $175,474,-000; salaries, $7,960,000; wages, $37,596,000; cost of materials, $81,951,000; value of products, $159,893,000. In 1904 the number of establishments was 5,588 and persons engaged in the industry, 90,751. The advent of the automobile and motor truck has had a retarding influence on the industry. The value of the products increased only 2.6 per cent from 1904 to 1909. Ohio ranks first in the industry, with Indiana second and Illinois third.

DYESTUFFS AND EXTRACTS.

Establishments, 107; persons engaged in industry, 3,015; wage earners, 2,397; capital, $17,935,000; wages, $1,291,000; cost of materials, $9,684,000; value of products, $15,955,000. Leading states in industry and value of products: New York, $4,505,310; New Jersey, $3,130,214; Pennsylvania, $2,345,251; Tennessee, $1,313,020; Virginia, $1,199,706. Important products and value:

Products.	Pounds.	Value.
Oak and chestnut extracts	287,908,285	$6,061,162
Logwood extract	32,317,248	991,974
Hemlock extract	12,588,678	280,487
Artificial dyestuffs	12,267,399	3,462,436

ESSENTIAL OILS.

Establishments, 68; persons engaged in industry, 408; capital, $1,365,438; expenses, $1,522,171; value of products, $1,737,234. Five leading states in industry: Michigan, New Jersey, Connecticut, New York, Pennsylvania. Connecticut is the chief producer of oil of black birch and witch-hazel ex-

tract; Michigan of oil of peppermint, spearmint, tansy and wormwood; New Jersey of oil of wintergreen, and Virginia of oil of sassafras.

EXPLOSIVES.

Establishments, 86; persons engaged in industry, 7,058; capital, $50,167,976; value of products, $40,129,-661. New Jersey is the leading state in the industry. The total production of smokeless powder in 1909 was 6,315,167 pounds valued at $4,292,984; guncotton, 257,212 pounds valued at $124,660; nitroglycerin, 20,977,317 pounds valued at $1,542,317; dynamite and "permissible explosives" (for use in coal mines), 204,763,299 pounds valued at $19,562,955; gunpowder and blasting powder, 246,339,875 pounds valued at $11,344,692.

FERTILIZERS.

Establishments, 550; capital, $121,537,451; persons engaged in industry, 21,960; fertilizers made, 5,240,-164 tons valued at $92,369,631. Georgia was the leading state in the industry, Maryland second and Florida third. Important materials used: Animal and vegetable ammoniates, phosphate rock, potash salts, nitrate of soda, ammonium sulphates, sulphuric acid, fish and pyrites.

FLOUR AND GRISTMILL PRODUCTS.

Establishments, 11,691; persons engaged in industry, 66,054; wage earners, 39,453; capital, $349,-152,000; wages, $21,517,000; salaries, $12,517,000; cost of materials, $767,576,000; value of products, $883,-584,000. Minnesota is the most important state in the industry. In 1909, 104,042,999 bushels of wheat and 12,340,167 bushels of other grains were used in the merchant mills of that state, and 22,737,404 barrels of flour were produced. New York in 1909 used 30,073,407 bushels of wheat and 40,271,986 bushels of other grains. More corn, buckwheat and oats were ground in New York than in any other state. The value of breakfast foods manufactured in 1909 was nearly $37,000,000.

FUR-FELT HATS.

Establishments, 273; persons in industry, 27,091; wage earners, 25,064; capital, $35,734,000; wages, $14,223,000; cost of materials, $22,109,000; value of products, $47,865,000. Leading states in the fur-felt hat industry are Pennsylvania, Connecticut, New York, New Jersey and Massachusetts in the order named.

LEATHER GLOVES AND MITTENS.

Establishments, 377; persons in industry, 12,950; salaries and wages, $6,019,872; cost of materials, $13,208,001; value of products, $23,630,598; rank of leading states in industry: New York, first; Wisconsin, second; Illinois, third; California, fourth; center of industry, Fulton county, New York.

MUSICAL INSTRUMENTS.

Pianos and organs and piano and organ parts and materials—Establishments, 507; persons in industry, 41,882; wage earners, 38,020; capital, $103,-234,000; wages, $22,762,000; cost of materials, $43,765,-000; value of products, $89,790,000; pianos produced in 1909, 374,154, valued at $59,601,225. New York and Illinois were leading states in the manufacture of upright pianos, the number for the two states aggregating 244,994. In the manufacture of grand

pianos, New York and Massachusetts led, reporting 6,831 in 1909. Illinois led in manufacture of reed organs, while in the value of pipe organs manufactured Massachusetts, New York and Illinois reported about equal amounts.

Phonographs and graphophones—Total value of products, $11,725,996, of which $5,406,684 represented complete instruments and the remainder records and blanks, horns, needles and other supplies. New Jersey is the leading state in the industry.

PAINT AND VARNISH.

Establishments, 791; wage earners, 14,240; persons employed, 21,896; salaries and wages, $18,649,074; cost of materials, $79,015,555; value of products, $124,889,422. In 1909 New York was the leading state in the industry and Pennsylvania came next.

PAPER AND WOOD PULP.

Establishments, 777; persons employed, 81,473; wage earners, 75,978; wages and salaries, $50,314,-643; capital, $409,348,000; cost of materials, $165,-442,341; value of products, $267,656,964. Of the 777 establishments 538 made paper exclusively, 81 made pulp exclusively and 158 made both paper and pulp. In 1909 New York ranked first in the industry in value of products but was second to Massachusetts in number of wage earners and value added by manufacture. Maine ranked third. In 1909 the quantity of wood pulp used in the paper mills was 2,826,591 tons, compared with 1,653,711 tons in 1899. Of the 4,216,708 tons of paper of all kinds made in 1909, 1,175,554 tons, or 27.9 per cent, was news paper.

SHIPBUILDING.

Establishments, 1,353; persons employed, 44,949; wage earners, 40,506; wages, $25,267,886; cost of materials, $31,214,358; value of products, $73,360,315. Of the total number of vessels of more than five tons launched in 1909 New York built 19.5 per cent and Pennsylvania 12.9 per cent. Ohio led in aggregate tonnage with New York, New Jersey and

Virginia following in order. Maine was first in tonnage of sailing vessels constructed. The number of sail vessels launched decreased from 648 in 1899 to 119 in 1909 and the gross tonnage from 80,294 to 17,459. The number of motor boats of more than five tons increased 189.9 per cent in gross tonnage from 1904 to 1909. The number of small power boats of less than five tons launched by private establishments was 8,577 in 1909 as against 1,687 in 1899.

STEEL WORKS AND ROLLING MILLS.

Establishments, 446; persons employed, 260,762; wage earners, 240,076; wages, $163,200,758; value of products, $985,722,534. Of the total number of establishments in 1909, 362, or 81.2 per cent, were located in New York, New Jersey, Pennsylvania, West Virginia, Ohio, Indiana and Illinois. These states furnished 91 per cent of the output.

TIN-PLATE AND TERNEPLATE.

Establishments, 31; persons employed, 5,846; capital, $10,995,000; cost of materials, $41,889,000; value of products, $47,970,000. Pennsylvania produced 57.7 per cent of the total tin-plate product of the country in 1909; West Virginia, 16.8 per cent, and Ohio 14 per cent. Of the total terneplate product Pennsylvania produced 24.5 per cent, West Virginia 35.8 per cent and Ohio 28.8 per cent. The number of establishments decreased from 1899 to 1909 but the value of products increased 50.4 per cent.

WIRE.

Establishments, 56; persons employed, 19,945; wage earners, 18,064; capital, $60,157,000; cost of materials, $60,543,000; value of products, $84,486,000. In the production of steel and iron wire Pennsylvania led in 1909 with 851,448 tons, or 35.6 per cent of the total amount drawn. In copper wire New Jersey led with 63,452 tons or 43.1 per cent of the total; in wire made from brass and other metals or alloys Connecticut produced 32,304,963 pounds, or 92.8 per cent of the total output.

MANUFACTURES IN ALASKA, HAWAII AND PORTO RICO (1909).

	Alaska.	Hawaii.	Porto Rico.		Alaska.	Hawaii.	Porto Rico.
Establishments	152	509	939	Expenses	$9,454,000	$31,753,000	$31,139,000
Persons engaged in				Services	2,328,000	2,795,000	4,898,000
manufactures ...	3,479	7,572	18,122	Salaries	380,000	686,000	1,259,000
Proprietors	135	1,074	1,478	Wages	1,948,000	2,109,000	3,639,000
Salaried employes	245	594	1,062	Materials	5,120,000	25,629,000	21,473,000
Wage earners.....	3,099	5,904	15,582	Miscellaneous	2,006,000	3,329,000	4,762,000
Primary horsepower	3,975	41,930	34,005	Value of products..	11,340,000	47,404,000	36,750,000
Capital $13,060,000	$23,975,000	$25,544,000		Value added by mfr.	6,220,000	21,775,000	15,271,000

MOTHERS' PENSION LEGISLATION.

Laws providing for what are variously termed "mothers' pensions," "widows' pensions" and "parents' pensions" have been passed by a number of states in the union within the last five years. While the acts themselves differ in details their general purpose is the same, namely, to enable mothers or parents in poor financial circumstances to care for their young children by means of pensions paid by the county. A resume of a few of these laws will serve to give an idea of their scope.

Ohio—The act (1913) provides that juvenile courts may pay to destitute widows and women whose husbands are completely disabled, have deserted them or are serving prison sentences $15 a month for a child under 14 years of age and $7 a month for each additional child under that age.

Utah—The mothers' pension law, effective March 21, 1913, provides that mothers who are compelled to work for a living are to receive $10 a month to support one child and $5 for every other child. The law's aim is to permit mothers to remain at home with their young children in order to rear them properly.

Washington—The mothers' pension act provides that mothers not supported by husbands are to receive

$15 a month for the first child and $5 for each additional child.

Illinois—The act approved June 5, 1911, amending the act relating to dependent and delinquent children, provides that if the parent or parents of a dependent or delinquent child are poor and unable properly to care for such child, but are otherwise proper guardians and it is for the welfare of such child to remain at home, the juvenile court may enter an order finding such facts and fixing the amount of money necessary to enable the parent or parents to care for such child properly. No fixed sum is named in the act, the amount being left to the discretion of the court. The county provides the money. The amount appropriated by Cook county for this purpose in 1913 was $165,000.

Missouri—In Jackson county (Kansas City) widows are given allowances ranging from $8 to $22 a month to enable them to remain at home and look after their children.

Included among the states having mothers' pension laws are California, Colorado, Idaho, Illinois, Iowa, Massachusetts, Michigan, Minnesota, Missouri, Nebraska, New Jersey, Ohio, Oregon, Pennsylvania, South Dakota, Utah, Washington and Wisconsin.

MINERAL PRODUCTS OF THE UNITED STATES.

[Prepared by the United States geological survey.]

MINERALS.	Unit of measure.	1909 Quantity.	1909 Value.	1910 Quantity.	1910 Value.	1911 Quantity.	1911 Value.
Aluminum	Pounds	34,210,000	$6,575,000	47,734,000	$8,955,700	46,125,000	$8,084,000
Asbestos	Short tons	3,085	62,603	3,683	68,357	7,604	119,865
Asphaltum	Short tons	208,655	1,938,273	260,680	3,680,067	360,004	3,828,751
Barytes (crude)	Long tons	58,377	198,561	42,975	121,746	38,445	122,792
Bauxite	Long tons	129,101	679,447	148,232	716,258	155,618	750,649
Borax	Pounds	41,484	1,524,365	42,357	1,201,842	53,330	1,569,151
Cement	Barrels	65,399,889	52,797,973	77,785,141	68,752,082	79,547,958	66,705,186
Clay products	Short tons		166,321,213		170,115,464		162,236,181
Coal, anthracite	Long tons	72,374,249	149,415,847	75,433,246	160,275,902	80,771,488	175,189,392
Coal, bituminous	Short tons	379,744,257	405,486,777	417,114,142	469,281,719	405,757,101	451,177,484
Copper	Pounds	1,092,951,624	142,083,711	1,080,153,543	137,180,257	1,097,232,749	137,154,692
Corundum, emery	Short tons	1,850	18,185	1,028	15,077	659	6,778
Feldspar	Short tons	76,539	401,788	81,102	502,452	92,700	579,008
Fluorspar	Short tons	50,702	291,747	69,247	430,196	87,048	611,447
Fuller's earth	Short tons	33,486	301,604	32,922	293,709	40,837	383,124
Garnet (abrasive)	Short tons	2,972	102,315	3,814	113,874	4,076	121,748
Gold (coining value)	Troy ounces	4,821,701	99,673,400	4,657,018	96,269,100	4,687,053	96,890,000
Graphite	Pounds	6,294,400	313,271	5,590,692	235,783	4,790,000	256,050
Grindstones			804,051		706,294		907,316
Gypsum	Short tons	2,253,785	5,906,738	2,379,657	6,523,029	2,326,970	6,462,035
Infusorial earth	Short tons		122,548		130,006		147,402
Iron (pig)	Long tons	25,795,471	415,175,000	27,308,567	425,115,215	23,257,288	327,334,624
Lead	Short tons	354,188	30,469,108	372,227	32,755,976	406,148	36,553,350
Manganese ore	Long tons	1,544	19,675	2,258	22,892	2,457	24,586
Mica, sheet	Pounds	1,809,532	234,482	2,476,190	283,832	1,887,201	310,254
Mica, scrap	Short tons	4,090	46,047	4,065	53,205	3,512	45,550
Mineral paints	Short tons	79,888	2,419,710	85,685	2,174,739	143,850	7,842,588
Mineral waters	Gals. sold	64,674,486	6,994,134	62,080,125	6,857,586	63,923,119	6,837,888
Natural gas			63,206,941		70,756,158		74,127,584
Oilstones			274,019		228,694		214,991
Petroleum	Barrels	182,134,274	128,348,783	209,556,048	127,896,878	220,449,391	134,044,752
Phosphate rock	Long tons	2,330,152	10,772,120	2,654,988	10,917,000	3,043,279	11,900,293
Platinum	Troy ounces	658	15,950	773	25,277	940	40,890
Precious stones			534,890		295,797		342,692
Pyrite	Long tons	217,070	1,028,157	238,154	958,608	301,458	1,164,871
Quartz	Short tons	135,409	249,466	63,577	193,757	87,943	155,122
Quicksilver	Flasks	21,075	888,710	20,601	958,153	21,256	977,969
Salt	Barrels	30,117,646	8,343,831	30,306,656	7,900,344	31,183,968	8,345,892
Silver (commercial value)	Troy ounces	54,721,500	28,455,200	57,187,900	30,851,500	60,399,400	32,615,700
Sulphur	Short tons	238,312	4,412,068	255,554	4,605,112	265,664	4,787,047
Talc, soapstone	Short tons	81,862	862,002	79,008	84,213	81,621	1,062,732
Zinc	Short tons	230,225	24,364,300	252,479	27,267,732	271,621	30,964,794
Total*			1,885,925,186		2,063,714,805		1,918,326,253

*Includes also minerals not mentioned in list.

COAL PRODUCTION BY STATES (1911).

In tons of 2,240 pounds.

ANTHRACITE.			
Pennsylvania	80,771,488	Montana	2,657,463
Colorado-New		New Mexico	2,780,345
Mexico	88,001	North Carolina	107
		North Dakota	448,775
BITUMINOUS.		Ohio	27,464,273
Alabama	13,411,983	Oklahoma	2,744,859
Arkansas	1,881,062	Oregon	41,662
California	10,399	Pennsylvania	129,244,788
Colorado	9,011,602	Tennessee	5,743,889
Georgia	147,509	Texas	1,763,029
Idaho	1,826	Utah	2,243,906
Illinois	47,927,784	Virginia	6,129,187
Indiana	12,679,781	Washington	3,190,013
Iowa	6,546,114	West Virginia	53,421,054
Kansas	5,584,132	Wyoming	6,022,200
Kentucky	12,238,249		
Maryland	4,183,746	Total bitumi-	
Michigan	1,317,923	nous	362,195,125
Missouri	3,357,685	Grand total	443,054,614

COAL PRODUCTION BY YEARS.

Tons of 2,240 pounds.

Year.	Anthracite.	Bituminous.
1889	25,580,189	38,242,641
1890	41,489,858	99,377,073
1900	51,309,214	189,480,097
1901	51,231,353	189,567,957

Year.	Anthracite.	Bituminous.
1902	60,242,560	201,632,276
1903	66,678,392	252,389,837
1904	65,382,842	248,738,941
1905	69,405,958	281,239,252
1906	63,698,803	306,084,481
1907	76,487,860	352,408,054
1908	74,384,297	296,903,826
1909	72,443,624	338,987,997
1910	75,514,296	372,239,703
1911	80,859,489	362,195,125

PIG IRON PRODUCTION IN THE UNITED STATES.

In tons of 2,240 pounds. Calendar year, 1912.

State.	Tons.	State.	Tons.
Alabama	1,862,909	Ohio	6,802,637
Colorado	297,731	Pennsylvania	12,551,959
Connecticut	17,366	Tennessee	338,238
Illinois	2,887,359	Virginia	256,167
Kentucky	68,760	West Virginia	274,360
Maryland	219,546	Wisconsin	303,370
Michigan	1,770,628		
New Jersey	26,876	Total	29,727,137
New York	1,939,231	Total, 1911	23,649,547

NOTE—In the foregoing table Colorado includes Missouri, Washington, California and Oregon; Connecticut includes Massachusetts; Georgia includes Texas; Michigan includes Indiana, and Wisconsin includes Minnesota.

WEDDING ANNIVERSARIES.

First—Cotton.
Second—Paper.
Third—Leather.
Fifth—Wooden.

Seventh—Woolen.
Tenth—Tin.
Twelfth—Silk and fine linen.

Fifteenth—Crystal.
Twentieth—China.
Twenty-fifth—Silver.
Thirtieth—Pearl.

Fortieth—Ruby.
Fiftieth—Golden.
Seventy-fifth—Diamond.

MINES AND QUARRIES IN THE UNITED STATES.

[From reports of census bureau, 1912 and 1913.]

In 1909 in the United States, exclusive of Alaska, Hawaii, Porto Rico and other outlying noncontiguous territory, 23,682 operators conducted 27,240 mines and quarries and 166,448 petroleum and natural gas wells. Of the operators 3,749 were engaged solely in development work upon which, in 1909, the sum of $31,548,736 was expended. In Alaska in 1909 there were 673 operators, who employed 8,025 persons, in the mining industry. The total expenses of these operators amounted to $13,229,200, while the capital invested was reported as $47,749,164. The total value of products was $16,333,427, of which amount $16,327,752 consisted of gold and silver. In Hawaii and Porto Rico the total value of product for the eighteen operators reported was only $26,414.

The total number of persons engaged in connection with producing mines, quarries and wells, as reported on Dec. 15, 1909, or nearest representative day, was 1,139,332, of whom wage earners numbered 1,065,283, proprietors and firm members 29,922 and salaried employes 44,127. In mines, quarries and wells for which development work only was carried on there were a total of 27,616 persons, of whom 21,499 were wage earners. Of the total number of persons, 1,166,948, employed in productive and nonproductive mines, 1,158,775 were men 16 years of age and over, and 8,173 were boys under 16 years of age. Distributed by sex, 1,162,840 were male and 4,108 female, the latter being employed in supervisory and clerical capacities.

The total capital invested in all mining enterprises on Dec. 31, 1909, as reported, was $3,662,527,064, of which $3,380,525,841 was invested in productive enterprises and $282,001,223 in those in which development work only was carried on.

SUMMARY BY INDUSTRIES.

Industry. Fuels—	Mines, etc.	Expenses.	Value products.	Persons engaged.
Coal, anth...	423	$139,524,467	$149,180,471	178,094
Coal, bitum..	6,013	$95,907,026	427,962,464	592,677
Petroleum and natural gas..	166,320	135,638,644	185,416,684	62,172
Peat	10	96,034	109,047	203
Metals—				
Iron	483	74,071,830	106,947,082	55,176
Copper	368	107,673,212	134,616,987	55,258
Precious metals—				
Deep mines...	2,843	68,764,692	83,885,928	37,755
Placer mines.	880	6,810,482	10,237,252	5,436
Lead and zinc	1,142	24,458,299	31,363,094	24,397
Quicksilver...	12	718,861	868,458	640
Manganese....	8	21,725	20,435	65
Building stone—				
Limestone ...	1,916	23,875,507	29,832,492	41,029
Granite	826	16,192,138	18,997,976	22,211
Sandstone ...	677	6,526,438	7,702,422	11,025
Marble	108	4,842,935	6,239,120	6,649
Slate	219	5,831,256	6,054,174	10,121
Traprock	220	5,090,538	5,578,317	6,748
Bluestone	637	1,182,873	1,588,406	3,020
Miscellaneous—				
Asbestos	20	72,747	65,140	88
Asph'lt'm and bitum. rock	19	301,673	466,461	241
Barytes	42	176,967	224,766	372
Bauxite	10	316,221	670,829	726
Buhr and mill stones	14	18,354	34,441	79
Clay	336	2,289,198	2,945,948	4,351
Corundum and emery	6	7,459	18,185	19
Feldspar	28	238,896	271,437	363
Fluorspar ...	15	319,426	288,509	376
Fuller's earth	21	274,776	315,762	380
Garnet '......	4	98,206	101,920	120
Graphite	20	328,690	344,130	436
Grindstones...	25	339,261	413,296	436
Gypsum	223	4,905,662	5,812,810	4,215
Infusorial earth	16	61,083	75,503	99
Magnesite ...	13	62,444	68,463	84
Marl	3	17,812	13,307	28
Mica	78	182,828	206,794	698
Mineral pigments	26	115,860	151,015	246
Monazite and zircon	4	50,909	64,472	34

Industry.	Mines, etc.	Expenses.	Value products.	Persons engaged.
Oil,scythe and whet stones	45	99,259	206,028	232
Phosphate rock	153	7,421,430	10,781,192	8,573
Prec'us stones	27	195,908	315,464	115
Pumice	4	6,087	30,097	25
Pyrite	12	734,355	676,984	1,160
Quartz	14	155,418	231,025	208
Sulphur	4	4,538,389	4,432,066	460
Talc and soapstone	46	1,036,371	1,174,516	1,452
Tripoli	7	42,493	66,557	73
Tungsten	116	365,780	563,457	227
All other industries* ..	27	740,874	778,938	560
Total		1,042,642,693	1,238,410,322	1,139,332

*Includes enterprises as follows: Antimony, 1; bismuth, 1; borax, 2; chromite, 2; manganiferous iron, 2; nickel and cobalt, 1; tin, 1.

SUMMARY BY STATES.

State.	Mines.	Wells.	Expenses.	Value product.
Maine	102	.....	$1,876,341	$2,056,063
New Hampshire	53	.....	1,204,966	1,308,597
Vermont	182	.....	6,795,268	8,221,323
Massachusetts..	147	.....	2,987,175	3,467,888
Rhode Island...	27	.....	673,877	897,606
Connecticut ..	75	.....	1,158,491	1,375,765
New York.....	752	11,342	9,987,768	13,334,975
New Jersey...	151	.....	4,507,940	8,347,501
Pennsylvania ..	3,060	59,750	300,977,955	349,959,786
Ohio	964	35,067	53,852,530	63,787,112
Indiana	480	10,373	20,312,752	23,934,201
Illinois	759	10,918	68,718,121	78,658,974
Michigan	173	21	61,819,838	67,714,479
Wisconsin	286	.....	5,508,751	7,459,404
Minnesota	250	.....	38,574,180	58,684,852
Iowa	431	.....	13,694,714	13,877,781
Missouri	1,224	39	27,515,101	31,667,525
North Dakota...	53	6	570,140	564,812
South Dakota...	43	3	5,154,263	6,452,417
Nebraska	20	.....	260,049	322,517
Kansas	582	3,402	15,831,787	18,722,634
Delaware	9	.....	508,937	516,213
Maryland	173	.....	5,006,157	5,782,045
Virginia	244	.....	8,863,954	8,795,646
West Virginia..	718	15,146	71,347,631	76,287,589
North Carolina.	130	.....	1,416,075	1,358,617
South Carolina.	32	.....	1,034,823	1,252,792
Georgia	109	.....	2,064,236	2,874,595
Florida	96	.....	5,999,532	8,846,665
Kentucky	442	1,109	11,721,722	12,100,075
Tennessee	365	1	11,969,267	12,602,547
Alabama	302	.....	22,442,278	24,350,667
Arkansas	146	62	4,309,211	4,603,845
Louisiana	2	246	6,641,585	6,547,050
Oklahoma	212	12,113	21,071,609	25,637,892
Texas	92	2,279	8,177,783	10,742,150
Montana	543	.....	46,520,645	54,951,961
Idaho	370	.....	7,198,763	8,649,342
Wyoming	95	21	9,053,467	10,572,188
Colorado	1,575	76	38,630,288	45,680,135
New Mexico....	285	.....	5,563,423	5,587,744
Arizona	251	.....	28,606,216	34,217,651
Utah	235	.....	16,606,628	22,083,282
Nevada	374	.....	14,415,728	23,271,597
Washington ...	170	.....	7,800,722	10,537,556
Oregon	161	.....	1,222,468	1,191,512
California	1,279	4,316	52,565,278	63,282,454
Geographic divisions—				
New England..	596	.....	14,696,118	17,227,242
Middle Atlantic	3,903	71,122	315,473,663	370,742,262
East N. Central	2,662	56,379	200,211,992	237,534,170
West N. Central	2,603	3,450	101,690,234	130,252,638
South Atlantic	1,652	15,146	98,151,245	105,714,462
East S. Central	1,109	1,110	46,133,257	49,143,239
West S. Central	452	14,700	40,200,158	47,530,937
Mountain	3,728	97	166,596,458	205,953,900
Pacific	1,610	4,316	61,589,468	75,111,522
Total U. S...	18,164	166,320	1,042,642,693	1,283,410,322

The states leading in the number of persons engaged in mining, quarrying, etc., were: Pennsylvania, 405,685; Illinois, 86,389; West Virginia, 82,808; Ohio, 62,874; Michigan, 42,133; Alabama, 32,643; Missouri, 32,462; Indiana, 31,292.

DISTRIBUTION OF MINING INDUSTRIES.

Figures, by leading states, for each of the nine leading mineral industries in 1909:

ANTHRACITE COAL.

State.	Operators.	Employes.	Product.	Per cent.
Pennsylvania ...	189	173,263	$148,957,824	98.9

BITUMINOUS COAL.

State.	Operators.	Employes.	Product.	Per cent.
Pennsylvania ...	689	184,408	147,466,417	34.5
Illinois	470	74,445	53,030,545	12.4
West Virginia...	307	69,668	46,929,592	11.0
Ohio	441	44,405	27,353,663	6.4
Alabama	112	23,479	18,459,433	4.3
Colorado	86	15,461	15,782,197	3.7
Indiana	223	22,357	15,918,123	3.5
Iowa	258	17,623	12,682,106	3.0
Kentucky	240	19,655	10,003,481	2.3
Kansas	118	12,791	9,835,614	2.3
Wyoming	35	7,829	9,721,134	2.3
Washington	32	6,155	9,226,793	2.2
Tennessee	85	11,154	6,688,454	1.6
Oklahoma	56	8,814	6,185,078	1.4
Missouri	173	9,526	5,881,034	1.4
Montana	48	4,612	5,117,444	1.2

PETROLEUM AND NATURAL GAS.

State.	Operators.	Employes.	Product.	Per cent.
Pennsylvania ...	3,030	7,397	39,197,475	21.1
Ohio	1,188	5,897	29,620,959	16.0
California	339	7,007	29,310,335	15.8
West Virginia..	412	7,093	28,188,087	15.2
Illinois	323	4,059	18,855,815	10.2
Oklahoma	711	3,066	17,685,092	9.5
Kansas	217	1,302	6,681,780	3.6
Texas	163	1,405	6,391,313	3.4

COPPER.

State.	Operators.	Employes.	Product.	Per cent.
Montana	35	13,697	45,960,517	34.1
Arizona	43	11,394	31,614,116	23.5
Michigan	7	13,022	30,165,443	22.4
California	9	2,510	10,104,373	7.5
Utah	22	3,304	8,432,099	6.3

IRON.

State.	Operators.	Employes.	Product.	Per cent.
Minnesota	20	16,218	57,076,135	53.4
Michigan	24	16,125	32,168,133	30.1
Alabama	25	5,666	4,939,149	4.6
New York	14	2,542	3,095,023	2.9
Wisconsin	6	1,455	2,972,584	2.8

PRECIOUS METALS—DEEP MINES.

State.	Operators.	Employes.	Product.	Per cent.
Colorado	439	7,586	27,147,937	32.4
Nevada	218	3,818	17,807,945	21.2
California	395	6,622	9,690,956	11.6
Utah	108	3,905	8,541,522	10.2
Idaho	69	3,077	7,926,602	9.4
South Dakota...	13	3,456	6,120,970	7.3

PRECIOUS METALS—PLACER MINES.

State.	Operators.	Employes.	Product.	Per cent.
California	392	3,073	8,751,032	85.5

LEAD AND ZINC.

State.	Operators.	Employes.	Product.	Per cent.
Missouri	617	16,319	22,565,528	71.9
Wisconsin	88	1,753	1,983,907	6.3
Kansas	189	848	1,059,540	3.4
Oklahoma	47	724	695,235	2.2

LIMESTONE.

State.	Operators.	Employes.	Product.	Per cent.
Pennsylvania ...	311	7,179	4,733,819	15.9
Illinois	81	3,276	3,977,359	13.3
Indiana	126	3,724	3,616,696	12.1
Ohio	144	3,746	3,363,149	11.3
New York	127	3,104	2,656,142	8.9
Missouri	144	2,427	2,027,902	6.8

GRANITE.

State.	Operators.	Employes.	Product.	Per cent.
Vermont	51	2,035	2,829,522	14.9
Massachusetts ..	82	2,278	2,185,986	11.5
Maine	85	2,132	1,761,801	9.3
California	62	1,318	1,518,916	8.0
Wisconsin	21	1,448	1,433,105	7.5
New Hampshire	40	1,305	1,205,811	6.3

PHOSPHATE ROCK.

State.	Operators.	Employes.	Product.	Per cent.
Florida	26	5,105	8,488,801	78.7
Tennessee	23	1,725	1,395,942	12.9
South Carolina..	5	1,307	862,409	8.0

NEWSPAPERS OF THE UNITED STATES (1913).

[From Ayer's American Newspaper Annual.]

State or ter.	Daily.	Wkly.	Total*	State or ter.	Daily.	Wkly.	Total*	State or ter.	Daily.	Wkly.	Total*
Alabama	27	191	248	Maryland	17	112	163	Porto Rico....	11	6	21
Alaska	10	14	24	Massachusetts..	85	391	661	Rhode Island..	14	26	56
Arizona	15	46	65	Michigan	82	530	731	South Carolina.	15	113	166
Arkansas	32	255	312	Minnesota	39	637	748	Tennessee	16	122	298
California	163	540	863	Mississippi	17	201	246	Texas	100	816	1,021
Colorado	47	323	417	Missouri	81	733	966	Vermont	9	82	101
Connecticut ...	36	95	158	Montana	19	160	193	Virginia	34	173	262
Delaware	3	28	37	Nebraska	30	543	629	Washington ...	37	301	393
Dist. Columbia.	7	22	79	Nevada	11	31	46	Utah	6	73	98
Florida	21	137	173	New Hampshire	16	82	114	West Virginia..	30	174	222
Georgia	27	257	358	New Jersey.....	50	275	369	Wisconsin	65	538	679
Hawaii	7	17	28	New Mexico....	6	106	119	Wyoming	5	66	80
Idaho	9	134	157	New York......	207	1,031	1,994				
Illinois.........	175	1,056	1,779	North Carolina.	29	203	304	Total in 1913..2,476		16,322	22,855
Indiana	152	525	774	North Dakota...	13	334	353	Total in 1912..2,459		16,229	22,837
Iowa	65	778	959	Ohio	173	720	1,163				
Kansas	70	632	747	Oklahoma	48	567	646	Canada (1913).	157	1,053	1,508
Kentucky	28	216	306	Oregon	25	205	285				
Louisiana	21	170	227	Pennsylvania ..	215	839	1,299	*Includes newspapers and peri-			
Maine	13	94	135	Philippines	13	4	29	odicals of all issues.			

THE ASSOCIATED PRESS (1913-1914).

President—Frank B. Noyes, Washington, D. C.
First vice-president—Chas. H. Taylor, Boston, Mass.
Second vice-president—Crawford Hill, Denver. Col.
Secretary and general manager—Melville E. Stone, New York, N. Y.
Assistant to general manager—Frederick R. Martin, New York, N. Y.
Treasurer—J. R. Youatt, New York, N. Y.
Directors—Thomas G. Rapier, New Orleans Picayune; Herman Ridder, New York Staats Zeitung; Victor F. Lawson, Chicago Daily News; Charles A. Rook, Pittsburgh Dispatch; Clark Howell, Atlanta Constitution; Charles W. Knapp, St. Louis Republic; Frank B. Noyes, Washington Star; Adolph S. Ochs, New York Times; W. L. McLean, Philadelphia Bulletin; W. R. Nelson, Kansas City

Star; V. S. McClatchy, Sacramento Bee; A. C. Weiss, Duluth Herald; Charles H. Clark, Hartford Courant; W. H. Cowles, Spokane Spokesman-Review; Samuel Bowles, Springfield Republican.
Executive committee—Frank B. Noyes, Washington; Victor F. Lawson, Chicago; Charles W. Knapp, St. Louis; Charles A. Rook, Pittsburgh; Charles H. Clark, Hartford; Adolph S. Ochs, New York; W. L. McLean, Philadelphia.

AMERICAN NEWSPAPER PUBLISHERS' ASSOCIATION.
President—Elbert H. Baker, Cleveland, O.
Vice-president—Herbert L. Bridgman, Brooklyn, N. Y.
Secretary—John S. Bryant. Richmond, Va.
Treasurer—William J. Pattison, New York, N. Y.

ARCTIC AND ANTARCTIC EXPLORATION.

DISASTER TO SCOTT EXPEDITION.

Capt. Robert F. Scott, leader of the British antarctic expedition, which sailed from London on the Terra Nova June 1, 1910, met a tragic death in March, 1912, after he had succeeded in reaching the south pole. Four of his companions, Dr. E. A. Wilson, Lieut. H. R. Bowers, Capt. L. E. G. Oates and Petty Officer E. Evans shared his fate. The last named died Feb. 17, partly from concussion of the brain, caused by a fall. Capt. Oates, with hands and feet badly frostbitten, felt that he was a burden to the others, and on March 17 walked

out into the teeth of a blizzard and was not seen again. "We knew that Oates was walking to his death," read a paragraph in Capt. Scott's diary, which was found later, "but though we tried to dissuade we knew it was the act of a brave man and an Englishman."

Scott, Wilson and Bowers pushed on toward the north whenever the weather, which was abnormally bad, permitted them to travel. March 21 they were forced to camp in latitude 79 degrees 40 minutes south, longitude 169 degrees 23 minutes east. This was 155 miles south of the expedition's base at

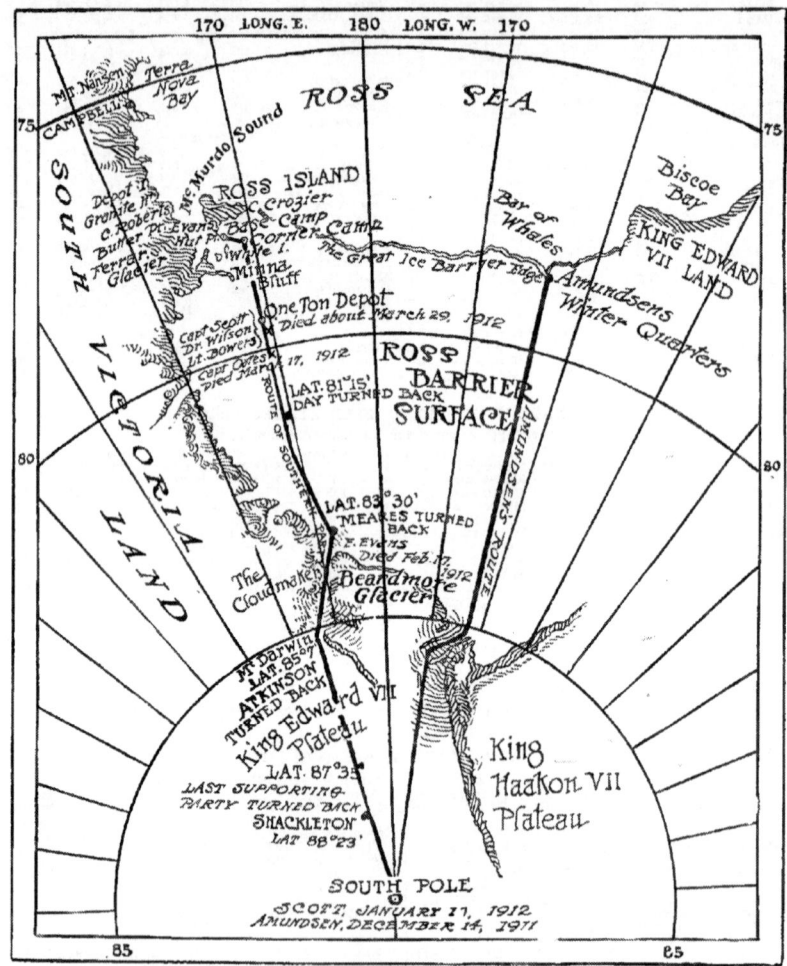

MAP SHOWING WHERE CAPT. SCOTT AND COMPANIONS DIED.

Cape Evans on McMurdo bay and only eleven miles from a depot of supplies known as One Ton camp. Had they been able to reach this depot they would have been saved, as it contained plenty of food and fuel. But they were not able to reach it. An unusually severe blizzard lasting nine days set in and they could not leave their tent. Their scanty provisions and fuel gave out and they died from starvation and exposure. Their bodies were found by a search party on the 12th of the following November.

This, in brief, is the story brought by the Terra Nova to Oamaru, New Zealand, Feb. 10, 1913, of the tragic ending of the British antarctic expedition.

As noted above, the Terra Nova sailed from London June 1, 1910, and from Cardiff, where Capt. Scott joined the ship, June 15. It left Christchurch, New Zealand, Nov. 29 and arrived on the shores of McMurdo bay early in January, 1911. Headquarters were established at Cape Evans, eight miles north of Discovery station. Provisions for three years, twenty ponies, seven mules, sledges, scientific instruments and other articles to be used by the explorers were landed. Work was begun at once to carry out the plans of the expedition, which included the exploration of King Edward land by an eastern party and of the coast range of Victoria land by a western party, and an attempt to reach the pole by a southern party. The eastern party was unable to land on King Edward land and went instead to Cape Adare. The Terra Nova, which conveyed this party, arrived at the Bay of Whales in Ross sea in time to communicate with the Fram, which had reached there with the Amundsen expedition. The British ship then went back to New Zealand, arriving there March 27, 1911. It went south again in the fall of that year and returned to Akaroa, New Zealand, April 1, 1912, with the news that Capt. Scott was remaining in the south for another year to complete his work. He announced that he was at 87 degrees 32 minutes south, or within about 150 miles of the pole. This was Jan. 3, 1912, and was the last word received from him until the Terra Nova, which again sailed for Cape Evans Dec. 13, 1912, returned to New Zealand in February, 1913, with the news of his death.

Much valuable work was done by the eastern and western parties in the way of surveying and in collecting biological and geological specimens. They experienced hardships from the severity of the weather and some of them had narrow escapes from starvation, but all eventually found their way back to headquarters or were picked up by the Terra Nova.

The greatest importance, of course, was attached to the work of the southern party, which was under the personal command of Capt. Scott. After the headquarters had been established in January, 1911, the work of preparing supply depots for the journey to the pole was begun. A base camp was established on the ice barrier seven miles southeast of Hut point, the old Discovery headquarters, which was fifteen miles south of the new headquarters and connected with it by telephone. Another depot was established at what was called Corner camp on the barrier ice, twenty-seven miles southeast of Base camp. By Feb. 16, 1911, Capt. Scott and his men had conveyed a ton of stores to One Ton camp at 79 degrees 30 minutes south. In this work many of the ponies were lost and by April only eight were left. Motor sledges were also used in conveying stores to the southern depots, but the engines soon broke down owing to overheating and the machines were abandoned.

Nov. 2, 1911, Capt. Scott, with Lieut. L. E. G. Oates as second in command, left Hut point on the final effort to reach the pole. The party marched at the rate of about fifteen miles a day and as each degree of latitude was reached a depot with a week's supply of food was established. As the loads grew lighter the ponies were killed to furnish food for the dogs. The weather for a time was good, but when latitude 83 degrees 24 minutes south was reached the temperature rose above the freezing point and the going became bad. The surviving ponies were killed before the barrier surface was left. Dec. 10 the Beardmore glacier was reached and here the dog teams were sent back, the men dragging the loaded sledges themselves thereafter. Dec. 21 they were on a plateau 8,600 feet above sea level and about thirty miles west of Mount Darwin.

On the last day of 1911 the party was in latitude 86 degrees 56 minutes south and Jan. 4 it had advanced to latitude 87 degrees 35 minutes. Here the last supporting party, consisting of Lieut. Evans, W. Lashley and Petty Officer Crean, left Capt. Scott and returned to Hut point. The advance party now was made up of five men—Capt. Scott, Dr. E. A. Wilson, Lieut. H. R. Bowers, Capt. L. E. G. Oates and Petty Officer Edgar Evans. They were about 156 statute miles from the pole and had a month's supply of food. They proceeded at the rate of twelve miles a day and finally reached the south pole Jan. 17, or a month after Capt. Roald Amundsen had arrived at the same point. The Norwegian explorer's hut and the records left by him were found intact, the tracks of his dogs being easily followed except in some places where they had been obliterated by snow drifts. Jan. 17 was cloudy and satisfactory observations could not be taken, but on the following day the sun shone and sights were taken with a four-inch theodolite. The result arrived at was practically the same as that figured out by Capt. Amundsen, who used a sextant with an artificial horizon, the difference in the location of the pole amounting only to about half a mile. The thermometer registered 20 degrees below zero at the pole. Photographs of Capt. Scott and his party and also of the Amundsen tent as found were taken.

After spending two days at the pole the party started back toward the north. At first all went well. The temperature was from 20 to 30 degrees below zero, but the men were able on some days to make as much as eighteen miles. Both the depots on the plateau were found and the supplies secured. When the top of Beardmore glacier was reached Dr. Wilson and Lieut. Bowers visited Buckley island and made a collection of fossil bearing sandstones and coal specimens. Another halt for geological investigation was made at Cloudmaker mountain, on the side of which valuable specimens were secured. The marching from this point became very difficult and in descending the glacier rough ice was encountered. Here Petty Officer Edgar Evans fell and suffered a concussion of the brain, which partly incapacitated him from walking. Feb. 17 he fell behind and when the others returned to find him he was in a state of collapse and died before they could bring him into camp.

The delay caused by this fatal accident left the party in a shaken and weakened condition. When they reached the barrier ice they encountered low temperatures, strong head winds and sandlike snow, which made progress difficult. The marches became shorter and shorter owing to the causes mentioned and also to the giving out of Capt. Oates. The latter suffered severely from frostbitten hands and feet, but struggled on as best he could until March 16. On the evening of that day when they went into camp he expressed the wish that he might go to sleep and not awake. He slept, but awoke in the morning and then, feeling that he was imperiling the lives of his comrades, he said: "I am just going outside and may be gone for some time." Then he walked out into the blizzard which was blowing at the time and he was not seen again.

Capt. Scott, Dr. Wilson and Lieut. Bowers pushed on northward whenever the weather, which was extremely unfavorable, permitted, and finally, as related above, reached a point eleven miles south of One Ton camp. Here they were overtaken by a blizzard lasting nine days and here at some time between March 21 and 29 they died from starvation and exposure.

Three expeditions for the relief of the southern party were sent out by Surgeon Atkinson. The first consisted of A. Cherry Gerrard, assistant geologist, and Demetri, with two dog teams. They reached

One Ton camp March 3 and remained there until March 10, when they were compelled to return to Hut point because the dog food was running short and both Gerrard and Demetri were ill. Two other men were sent out and they got as far as Corner camp, where they were compelled to turn back by severe weather. The third and last search party, headed by Surgeon Atkinson and provided with seven mules, dog teams and provisions for three months, left Cape Evans Oct. 30. They reached One Ton camp, where all was found in order, and then on Nov. 12 they sighted the southern party's tent. Entering it, they found Capt. Scott sitting with his back against the tent pole and his two companions lying in their sleeping bags. Beside them were the records they had brought with them from the south, including photographic films, which, on being developed later in New Zealand, gave a dozen excellent negatives of the members at the south pole and of the Amundsen tent. The geologic and other specimens they had gathered on the way were also intact and were brought back to civilization.

The bodies having been identified, the inner tent was placed over them and a large cairn of snow erected with a cross on top bearing the following record:

"Left this cross and cairn erected over the remains of Capt R. F. Scott, C. V. O. R. N.; Dr. E. A. Wilson and Lieut. H. R. Bowers, S. R. N., as a slight token to perpetuate their gallant and successful attempt to reach the pole. This they did on the 17th of January, 1912, after the Norwegians had already done so on the 1st day of December, 1911.

"Also to commemorate their two gallant comrades, Capt. L. E. G. Oates of Inniskillen dragoons, who walked to his death in a blizzard willingly about twenty miles south of this place to try and save his comrades beset by hardship, and Petty Officer Edgar Evans, who died at the foot of the Beardmore glacier.

CAPT. ROBERT F. SCOTT.

"The Lord gave and the Lord hath taken away. Blessed be the name of the Lord'."

The record was signed by the members of the search party. They then went twenty-three miles farther south in an attempt to find the body of Capt. Oates, but failed. A cairn and cross were erected to his memory near the spot where he had left his comrades to go to his death. The searchers then returned to Cape Evans.

Capt. Scott's diary was found between his head and the tent pole against which he was resting. The last entry was dated March 25, 1912, and concluded as follows:

"For my own sake I do not regret this journey, which has shown that Englishmen can endure hardships, help one another and meet death with as great a fortitude as ever in the past.

"We took risks. We knew we took them. Things have come out against us and therefore we have no cause for complaint, but bow to the will of Providence, determined still to do our best to the last.

"But if we have been willing to give our lives to this enterprise, which is for the honor of our country, I appeal to our countrymen to see that those who depend on us are properly cared for.

"Had we lived I should have had a tale to tell of the hardihood, endurance and courage of my companions which would have stirred the heart of every Englishman.

"These rough notes and our dead bodies must tell the tale, but surely, surely a great rich country like ours will see that those who are dependent on us are properly provided for."

The eastern, or northern, party, as it came to be known, under command of Lieut. V. L. A. Campbell, also had a narrow escape from starvation. It had been picked up at Cape Adare and landed for a short sledge journey in January, 1912. It returned to Terra Nova bay Feb. 17 expecting to be picked up by the Terra Nova. The ship, however, was prevented from reaching them by insuperable ice conditions and had to leave the party to make its own way back to Cape Evans, some 200 miles away. Winter set in, and for six and a half months they were compelled to live in a small igloo or ice hut. Their diet was seal meat and blubber eked out with a few biscuits and a very small quantity of cocoa and sugar. They suffered from enteritis and Petty Officer Browning came near collapsing. They started for Cape Evans Sept. 30, 1912, and on the way were fortunate enough to find a small food depot left by Griffith Taylor. They arrived at Cape Evans early in November and there learned for the first time that the southern party was missing, and a little later when the search party under Surgeon Atkinson returned from the south their worst fears were realized.

Feb. 14, 1913, a great memorial service for Capt. Scott and his heroic companions was held in St. Paul's cathedral in London. It was attended by people of every walk in life, from King George down to men and women of the humblest occupations. Later subscriptions were made to a fund for the relief of dependent relatives of the dead explorers. Capt. Scott's wife, who was on her way to Australia to meet her husband at the time the news of his death was made known to the world, was given the title which she would have had if he had lived and became Lady Scott.

DISASTER TO GERMAN SPITZBERGEN EXPEDITION.

Early in 1912 Lieut. Schroeder-Stranz began the organization in Germany of an elaborate expedition for the circumnavigation of northern Europe and Asia by means of a northeast passage, hoping to repeat the achievement of Nordenskjold in 1878-1879. To prepare himself for arctic work he led a preliminary expedition to Spitzbergen, sailing from Tromso, Norway, in August in the small steamer Herzog Ernst. The party numbered fifteen, of whom ten were Germans and five Norwegians. Ice was encountered on both the east and west coasts of Spitzbergen. Lieut. Schroeder-Stranz and three companions were set ashore in August to make a practice trip across Northeast land and were not heard of afterward. In September the ice conditions were such that to save the ship its commander, Capt. Alfred Ritscher, was compelled to beach it in Treurenburg bay; here it was soon frozen in. Not having planned to spend a winter in the arctics, the expedition was in danger of running short of food. It was decided to make an attempt to reach Wijde bay on foot, as it was understood that more provisions were to be had there. The party left the steamer Sept. 21 and first went to Mosel bay, nine miles distant. After the first day's march the Norwegian sailors turned back to the steamer. The others proceeded, but it took them five days to cover the nine miles. At Mosel bay Dr. Detmers and Herr Moeser, taking provisions and one dog with them, started for Advent bay. As nothing was seen or heard of them afterward, they undoubtedly perished.

Capt. Ritscher, Artist Herr Rave and Dr. Rudinger reached Wijde bay Oct. 4, but provisions were scarce and while Rave and Rudinger returned to the ship the captain set out alone for Advent bay, where he arrived Dec. 27 in a pitiable condition. Norwegian and German relief expeditions were organized by Capt. Staxrud and Capt. Lerner. The former reached the Herzog Ernst April 21, 1913, and rescued Herr Rave and Dr. Rudinger and four Norwegians. Herr Eberhardt had disappeared Dec. 24, leaving no trace, and one of the Norwegians had died from exposure and starvation. Capt. Lerner's relief ship, the Levenskjold, was sunk, but he and his crew of eight sailors and five explorers managed to escape. Of the fifteen men forming the Schroeder-Stranz expedition only seven were saved. The disaster was attributed to complete lack of experience in arctic work.

AUSTRALIAN ANTARCTIC EXPEDITION.

Word was received Feb. 25, 1913, from the Australian antarctic expedition commanded by Dr. Douglas Mawson that Lieut. B. F. S. Ninnis of the City of London regiment of royal fusiliers and Dr. Xavier Merz of Switzerland were dead. The first reports, which were received by wireless from the Aurora, the expedition's ship, did not give any details. In a message to Lord Dawson, governor-general of Australia, Dr. Mawson said:
"Our sledging season has been very successful. We have opened up a large area of new land both east and west of Commonwealth bay. We have obtained important new data from numbers of stations in close proximity to the magnetic pole."
Later it was learned that Lieut. Ninnis died Dec. 4, 1911, while he, Dr. Mawson, and Dr. Merz were exploring a new coast line 300 miles southeast of the winter quarters. The lieutenant and a dog team, with almost the party's whole food supply, fell into an unfathomable crevasse. Dr. Merz died Jan. 17, 1912, from malnutrition. Dr. Mawson himself arrived at the base Feb. 7 after a narrow escape from death in the heavily crevassed areas.
The expedition headed by Dr. Mawson consisted of nearly fifty men, most of them graduates of Australian and New Zealand universities. It was financed by popular subscriptions and its purpose was to make a complete geographical and magnetic survey of the antarctic region between Cape Adare and Baussburg. The expedition landed on Adelie (Wilkes) land in the fall of 1911. March 12, 1912, the Aurora reached Hobart, Tasmania, with news that everybody was well and that the party had made numerous valuable discoveries. It was then expected that all the members of the expedition would return to Australia in the spring of 1913, but Dr. Mawson and six companions missed connections with the Aurora and it was announced by wireless that they would probably winter on Adelie land.

EXPEDITION TO CROCKER LAND.

Dr. Donald B. MacMillan, at the head of a party of scientists, sailed in the Newfoundland sealing steamship Diana, a wooden vessel of 473 tons, from Boston, Mass., July 5, 1913, on an expedition to Crocker land, which was first sighted by Peary in 1906. It is supposed to be the most northerly land on the globe. After a stop at Sydney, N. S., the Diana sailed north July 11 and six days later word was received by wireless that the vessel had stranded on Barge point, forty miles west of Battle Harbor, in the Straits of Belle Isle. It was floated without serious difficulty and proceeded on its way north. The expedition was sent out by the American Geographical society and the American Museum of Natural History. Among the scientists engaged were Ensign Fitzhugh Green, U. S. N., expert in mapmaking, seismology and terrestrial magnetism; W. E. Ekblaw, geologist, botanist and ornithologist, and Dr. M. C. Tanquary, zoologist. Besides exploring Crocker land the expedition hoped to investigate the region west and southwest of Cape Thomas Hubbard and north of the Parry islands to determine the location of the edge of the continental shelf and to delineate the coast line along parts of Grant land and Axel Heiberg land.

STEFANSSON EXPEDITION.

Vilhjalmar Stefansson entered upon a second exploring expedition in arctic waters to the north of Alaska and British Columbia in 1913. He had three vessels, the Karluk, a steam whaler of 320 tons; the gasoline schooner Mary Sachs of thirty-three tons, and the power boat Alaska. Capt. Robert Bartlett, sailing master of Peary's ship, the Roosevelt, was second in command. A scientific staff of eleven persons, in addition to Mr. Stefansson and Dr. R. M. Anderson, made up a party, which, together with the captain and crews, was one of the largest ever sent out for exploring work in that part of the world. Among the men in the expedition were George Malloch, specialist in stratigraphy; J. J. O'Neill, mining geologist; Kenneth Chipman, topographer; J. R. Cox, topographer; James Murray, biologist and oceanographical stu-

dent; Fritz Johanson, ichthyologist; Henry Beauchamp and Dr. D. Jennes, anthropologists; A. Forbes Mackay, surgeon; W. T. McKinlay, physicist, and Dr. R. M. Anderson, ethnologist. The expedition, which is financed by the Canadian government and is to stay in the arctics three years, left Port Clarence, Alaska, July 28.

EXPLORATION IN GREENLAND.

Knud Rasmussen, the Danish explorer, who started out July 10, 1910, on an expedition to northern Greenland, returned to Denmark in May, 1913. He confirmed Myllus Ericksen's discovery that the so-called Peary channel did not exist and that Peary land was not an island, but was united to Greenland. He discovered new land which he named Christian X. land. The expedition was mainly a scientific one, and besides mapping the region connecting Greenland with Peary land, it devoted much time to ethnographical and ethnological investigation.
Koch Expedition—Capt. Koch, a Danish explorer, with three companions, crossed the inland ice of Greenland from Cape Bismarck to Upernivik, a distance of about 750 miles, between April 20 and July 15, 1913. The party encountered many hardships and came near starving.

EXPEDITION TO KING EDWARD VII. LAND.

Arrangements were made in 1913 for an expedition to King Edward VII. land to start in August, 1914, under command of J. Foster Stackhouse, who was associated with Capt. Scott in organizing the voyage of the Terra Nova. The party will use the steam yacht Polaris, which was built especially for ice navigation. King Edward VII. land stretches from the great ice barrier in the antarctic ocean and has not been explored except near the sea.

AMUNDSEN'S NORTH POLAR EXPEDITION.

Capt. Roald Amundsen made preparations in 1913 for his voyage toward the north pole by way of the Bering sea. His plan was to use the Fram and let it drift with the current across the polar regions. He estimated that the voyage would take from four to five years, but his ship would carry provisions for seven years. The Fram was to be equipped with wireless apparatus.

THE POLAR RECORD.

Year.	Explorer.	ARCTIC.	Deg.	Min.
1871	—Capt. Hall		82	16
1876	—Capt. Nares		83	10
1879	—Lieut. De Long		77	15
1882	—Lieut. Greely		83	24
1890	—Lieut. Peary		83	50
1891	—Lieut. Peary		83	24
1895	—Fridtjof Nansen		86	14
1900	—Duke d'Abruzzi		86	33
1902	—Lieut. Peary		84	17
1904	—Anthony Fiala		83	13
1906	—Commander Peary		87	6
1909	—Commander Peary		90	(Pole)
		ANTARCTIC.		
1774	—Capt. Cook		71	15
1823	—Capt. Weddell		74	15
1842	—Capt. Ross		77	49
1895	—Borchgrevink		74	10
1898	—De Gerlache		71	36
1900	—Borchgrevink		78	50
1902	—Capt. Scott		82	17
1909	—Lieut. Shackleton		88	23
1911	—Roald Amundsen		90	(Pole)
1912	—Robert F. Scott		90	(Pole)

NEW POLAR LAND DISCOVERED.

Commander Wilkitzky of the Russian navy, in charge of an expedition sent out by the St. Petersburg authorities to explore arctic waters north of Siberia, with a view to promoting navigation between Bering sea and the Lena and the Kolyma rivers, reported on his arrival at St. Michaels, Alaska, Oct. 11, 1913, that he had discovered a considerable body of new land. He said it was in latitude 81 north and longitude 102 east and that

it extended from about sixty miles north of Cape Chelyuskin for a distance of some 200 nautical miles. With his ships, the ice breakers Taimyr and Valgatz, he cruised in a northwesterly direction along the coast of the new land to latitude 81 north, longitude 96 east. Here he was forced to turn away from the land by solid ice. He then followed the shore in a southeasterly direction to longitude 104 east, latitude 79 north, where the coast turned toward the northeast. This voyage was made in July and August, 1913. Prior to making

this discovery the expedition, which left Vladivostok early in July, had surveyed the coast from the mouth of the Kolyma river to Cape Chelyuskin. It was the commander's intention to proceed west to the Yenesei river on the other side of the Taimyr peninsula, but ice was encountered, and in trying to get beyond it on the north the new land was discovered. This was described by Commander Wilkitzky as mountainous and as covered with snow almost to the sea. He named it Nicholas II. land in honor of the czar.

CIVIL SERVICE IN AMERICAN CITIES.

The federal census bureau in Washington, D. C., made an inquiry early in 1913 relating to civil service examinations in the cities of the United States having a population of 30,000 or more. In response to letters sent out by the bureau 77 cities reported that such examinations were required for appointments in all departments; 32 that they were required in some but not all departments, while 76 reported that no examinations were required. Following are the cities which require civil service examinations for practically all departments:

Cities of 300,000 or more population:

New York, N. Y.	San Francisco, Cal.
Chicago, Ill.	Milwaukee, Wis.
Philadelphia, Pa.	Cincinnati, O.
Boston, Mass.	Newark, N. J.
Cleveland, O.	Los Angeles, Cal.
Pittsburgh, Pa.	New Orleans, La.
Buffalo, N. Y.	Washington, D. C.

Cities of 200,000 to 300,000 population:

Jersey City, N. J.	New Haven, Conn.
Seattle, Wash.	Scranton, Pa.
Kansas City, Mo.	Paterson, N. J.
Indianapolis, Ind.	Fall River, Mass.
Rochester, N. Y.	Dayton, O.
Portland, Ore.	Spokane, Wash.
Columbus, O.	Lowell, Mass.
Toledo, O.	Cambridge, Mass.
Oakland, Cal.	New Bedford, Mass.
Worcester, Mass.	Albany, N. Y.
Syracuse, N. Y.	

Cities of 50,000 to 200,000 population:

Trenton, N. J.	Springfield, Mass.
Lynn, Mass.	Duluth, Minn.
Lawrence, Mass.	Somerville, Mass.
Tacoma, Wash.	Troy, N. Y.
Des Moines, Iowa.	Oklahoma City, Okla.
Kansas City, Kas.	Holyoke, Mass.
Yonkers, N. Y.	Brockton, Mass.
Youngstown, O.	Springfield, Ill.

Cities of 30,000 to 50,000 population:

Binghamton, N. Y.	Auburn, N. Y.
Springfield, O.	Taunton, Mass.
Sacramento, Cal.	Everett, Mass.
Chattanooga, Tenn.	Pittsfield, Mass.
Malden, Mass.	Quincy, Mass.
Haverhill, Mass.	Amsterdam, N. Y.
Salem, Mass.	Jamestown, N. Y.
Topeka, Kas.	Mt. Vernon, N. Y.
Newton, Mass.	Niagara Falls, N. Y.
Fitchburg, Mass.	Muskogee, Okla.
Elmira, N. Y.	Chelsea, Mass.
Hamilton, O.	New Rochelle, N. Y.
East Orange, N. Y.	Lorain, O.

Among the larger cities requiring examination for appointment in one or more departments, principally fire and police, are Baltimore, Md.; Detroit, Mich.; Denver, Col.; Birmingham, Ala.; Memphis, Tenn.; Richmond; Va.; Nashville, Tenn., and Hartford, Conn.

Among the cities which do not require examination for any branch of the civil service are St. Louis, Mo.; Minneapolis and St. Paul, Minn.; Providence, R. I.; Louisville, Ky.; Omaha, Neb.; Grand Rapids, Mich.; Bridgeport, Conn., and San Antonio, Tex.

BENEVOLENT INSTITUTIONS IN THE UNITED STATES.

[From report of bureau of the census.]

The total number of benevolent institutions reported in 1910 is 5,397, classified as follows: institutions for the care of children, 1,152; societies for the protection and care of children, 212; institutions for the care of adults or adults and children, 1,442; institutions for the education and care of the blind and deaf, 119; hospitals, classed as benevolent, 1,896, and dispensaries, classed as benevolent, 576.

In these institutions, or under their care, there were at the close of the year 380,337 persons, apportioned as follows: Institutions for children, 107,401; societies for the protection and care of children, 35,279; institutions for adults or adults and children, 121,876; institutions for the blind and deaf, 851; hospitals, 28,869. The movement of inmates during the year is indicated by the fact that 82,011 children were received into institutions, while 37,825 were placed in families or institutions, mostly in families and chiefly by societies for their care; 788,691 persons were received into institutions for adults or adults and children, and 2,554 into institutions for the blind and deaf; 1,975,838 patients were treated in hospitals and 2,439,059 in dispensaries.

As compared with the previous report, that for 1904, the number of institutions reported shows an increase of 1,346 (day nurseries, of which 166 were reported in 1904, were not included in 1910); inmates of institutions at close of year, an increase of 95,975; children received into institutions during the year, an increase of 11,186; patients treated in hospitals, an increase of 911,326, and in dispensaries of 827,408. There was a decrease of 109,319 in

the number of persons received into institutions for adults or adults and children, and of 4,471 in the number received into institutions for the blind and deaf.

Two items are of special interest: The collection for the first time of data in regard to the placing out of children in families, and the notably increased interest manifested in the treatment of tuberculosis, which accounts for a very considerable degree for the increase in the number of dispensaries and to some degree of hospitals and sanitariums. Thus the net number of dispensaries added to the list is 420, and of these nearly 200 are county dispensaries established in the state of Pennsylvania by the department of health for the treatment of tuberculosis. The decrease of 109,319 in the number of persons received into institutions for the care of adults or adults and children is chiefly confined to institutions for the temporary care of men who are destitute.

Noting the distribution of institutions in the states, it appears that New York leads with 797, an increase of 209 over the figures in 1904; Pennsylvania has 692, an increase of 301; Massachusetts 359, an increase of 104; Illinois 324, an increase of 39; Ohio, 211, an increase of 52, and New Jersey 207, an increase of 58. Almost all the states show an increase (generally in about the same proportion), which would indicate that the interest in the problem of caring for those who may be called "wards of the state" is by no means limited to the centers of population, but extends throughout the entire country.

Foreign Governments.

Rulers and cabinets of the leading countries, with the latest statistics of their area, population, exports and imports.

GREAT BRITAIN.

GOVERNMENT—King, George V.; heir-apparent, Edward Albert, prince of Wales.

Prime Minister and First Lord of the Treasury—*H. H. Asquith.

Lord Chancellor—*Viscount R. B. Haldane.
Lord President of the Council—Viscount Morley.
Chancellor of Exchequer—*David Lloyd-George.
Home Secretary—*Reginald McKenna.
Foreign Secretary—*Sir Edward Grey.
Colonial Secretary—*L. V. Harcourt.
Secretary for War—*Col. John E. B. Seely.
Secretary for India and Lord Privy Seal—*Marquis of Crewe.
First Lord of Admiralty—*W. L. Spencer Churchill.
Secretary for Ireland—*Augustine Birrell.
Secretary for Scotland—*T. McKinnon Wood.
President of the Board of Trade—*Sydney C. Buxton.
President of the Local Government Board—*John Burns.
President of the Board of Agriculture—*Walter Runciman.
President of the Board of Education—*Joseph Albert Pease.
Postmaster-General—*Herbert Louis Samuel.
Chancellor of Duchy—*Charles E. Hobhouse.
First Commissioner of Works—*Earl Beauchamp.
Attorney-General—*Sir R. D. Isaacs.
Lord Lieutenant of Ireland—Earl of Aberdeen.
Lord Advocate—A. Ure.
Solicitor-General—Sir J. A. Simon.
Solicitor-General for Scotland—A. M. Anderson.
Attorney-General for Ireland—Ignatius O'Brien.
Solicitor-General for Ireland—Thomas F. Molony.
  *Members of the cabinet.

The British parliament, in which the highest legislative authority is vested, consists of the house of lords and the house of commons. The former in 1913 had 636 members and the latter 670. The sessions usually last from February to August.

AREA AND POPULATION—The total area of England, Scotland, Ireland, Wales, the Isle of Man and the Channel islands is 121,391 square miles; the total for the British empire is 11,498,825 square miles. The total population of the empire in 1911 was 421,178,965. The population of the united kingdom April 3, 1911, when the last census was taken, was: England, 34,045,290; Wales, 2,025,202; Scotland, 4,759,445; Ireland, 4,390,219; Isle of Man, 52,034; Channel islands, 96,900. Total, 45,369,090.

The cities of England and Wales having more than 100,000 population each were in 1911:

London	4,522,961	Sunderland	151,162
Liverpool	746,566	Oldham	147,495
Manchester	714,427	Blackburn	133,064
Birmingham	525,960	Brighton	131,250
Leeds	445,568	Gateshead	116,925
Sheffield	454,653	Derby	123,433
Bristol	357,059	Southampton	119,039
West Ham	289,102	Plymouth	112,042
Bradford	288,505	Norwich	121,493
Newcastle	266,671	Birkenhead	130,832
Kingston-upon-Hull	278,024	Preston	117,113
Nottingham	259,942	Halifax	101,556
Leicester	227,242	Burnley	106,337
Salford	231,380	Middlesbrough	104,787
Portsmouth	231,165	Stockport	108,693
Stoke-on-Trent	234,553	South Shields	108,649
Cardiff	182,280	Coventry	106,377
Bolton	180,885	Huddersfield	107,825
Croydon	169,559	Swansea	114,673

The figures given in the above table for London are for the inner or registration district alone. Including the outer belt of suburban towns, which are within the metropolitan police district, the population of "Greater London" April 3, 1911, was 7,251,358.

Population of the chief cities in Scotland in 1911:

Glasgow	784,455	Dundee	165,006
Edinburgh	320,315	Paisley	84,477
Aberdeen	133,084	Leith	80,489

Greenock	68,911	Govan	89,725
Perth	36,995	Partick	66,848
Kilmarnock	34,729	Coatbridge	43,287

The total population of Ireland in 1911 was 4,390,219, against a total of 4,458,775 in 1901.

Population of the chief cities of Ireland in 1911:

Dublin	309,272	Lurgan	12,135
Belfast	385,492	Lisburn	12,172
Cork	76,632	Wexford	11,455
Limerick	38,402	Sligo	11,163
Londonderry	40,799	Kilkenny	13,112
Waterford	27,450	Kingstown	17,227
Galway	15,936	Portadown	11,727
Dundalk	13,128	Ballymena	11,376
Drogheda	12,425	Clonmel	10,277
Newry	13,450		

EXPORTS AND IMPORTS—The total exports of the British empire in 1912 were $5,745,642,500; of the united kingdom, $2,936,339,000; total imports of the empire, $6,528,065,000; of the united kingdom, $3,724,482,000.

The total exports of the united kingdom to the United States in 1913 were $295,564,940; imports, $597,150,307.

INDIA.

GOVERNMENT—Governor-general, Sir Charles Hardinge. Legislative authority vested in a council of sixty-eight members, thirty-six being official and thirty-two nonofficial.

AREA AND POPULATION—The total area of British India is 1,773,088 square miles. The total population according to the census of March 10, 1911, is 315,132,527, divided among the provinces as follows:

Ajmer-Marwara	501,395	Madras	41,405,404
Assam	34,018,527	Northwest provinces	2,196,933
Bengal	52,668,269	United provinces	47,182,044
Bombay presidency	19,672,642	Punjab	19,974,956
Burma	12,115,217	Baluchistan	414,412
Central provinces	13,916,308	Andamans	26,459
Coorg	174,976		

Population of the large cities in 1911:

Calcutta	1,222,313	Delhi	232,837
Bombay	979,445	Lahore	228,687
Madras	518,660	Cawnpore	178,557
Haidarabad	500,623	Agra	185,449
Lucknow	259,798	Ahmedabad	215,835
Rangoon	293,316	Allahabad	171,697
Benares	203,804	Poona	158,856

DOMINION OF CANADA.

GOVERNMENT—The Canadian parliament consists of eighty-seven life senators and a house of commons of 221 members, there being one representative for every 25,367 of population, based upon the census of 1911. The governor-general is the duke of Connaught, appointed in 1911, and the council is made up of the following. Premier, Robert L. Borden; minister of agriculture, Martin Burrell; customs, Dr. D. J. Reid; finance, W. T. White; inland revenue, W. B. Nantel; interior, R. Rogers; justice, C. J. Doherty; labor, T. W. Crothers; marine and fisheries, J. D. Hazen; militia, S. Hughes; postmaster-general, L. P. Pelletier; public works, Louis Coderre; railways and canals, Francis Cochrane; secretary of state, Dr. W. J. Roche; trade and commerce, George E. Foster; ministers without portfolio, A. E. Kemp, J. A. Lougheed, George H. Perley. The governor-general gets a salary of $50,000 a year, the premier $12,000 and the other ministers $7,000 each.

AREA AND POPULATION—The total area of Canada is 3,729,665 square miles, of which 3,603,919 is land area. Area of provinces:

Province	Sq. miles.	Province	Sq. miles.
Alberta	255,285.00	Manitoba	73,731.72
Brit. Columbia	355,855.00	New Brunswick	27,985.11
Nova Scotia	21,427.77	Saskatchewan	251,700.00
Ontario	260,862.00	Yukon	207,076.00
Prince Edward island	2,184.36	Northwest territories	1,921,685.00
Quebec	351,873.00	Total	3,729,664.56

*Area increased in 1912 to 251,832 square miles.
†Increased in 1912 to 407,262 square miles. ‡Increased in 1912 to 706,834 square miles. §Decreased in 1912 to 1,242,224 square miles.

The census taken June 1, 1911, showed the following population by provinces:

Province.	1911.	1901.	Increase.	Pr. ct. incr.
Alberta	374,663	73,022	301,641	413.08
British Columbia	392,480	178,657	213,822	119.68
Manitoba	455,614	255,211	200,403	78.52
New Brunswick	351,889	331,120	20,769	6.27
Nova Scotia	492,338	459,574	32,764	7.13
Ontario	2,523,274	2,182,947	340,281	15.5º
Prince Edward Isl.	93,728	103,259	*9,531	*9.23
Quebec	2,003,232	1,648,898	354,434	21.46
Saskatchewan	492,432	91,279	401,153	439.48
Yukon	8,512	27,219	*18,707	*68.73
Northwest territ's	18,481	20,129	*1,648	*8.19
Total	7,206,643	5,371,315	1,833,212	34.13

*Decrease.

Population by sex and per square mile in 1911:

Province.	Male.	Female.	Total.	Per sq. mile.
Alberta	223,989	150,674	374,663	1.47
British Columbia.	251,619	140,861	392,480	1.09
Manitoba	250,056	205,558	455,614	6.18
New Brunswick..	179,867	172,022	351,889	12.61
Nova Scotia	251,019	241,319	492,358	22.94
Ontario	1,299,290	1,223,984	2,523,274	9.67
Prince Edward Isl.	47,069	46,659	93,728	42.91
Quebec	1,011,247	991,465	2,002,712	5.69
Saskatchewan	291,730	200,702	492,432	1.95
Yukon	6,508	2,004	8,512	......
Northwest territ's	8,530	8,421	16,951	......
Total Canada...	3,820,887	3,383,640	7,204,527	1.92

The rural population in 1911 was 3,924,063 and the urban population 3,280,444. In 1901 the rural population was 3,369,018 and the urban population 2,002,297. The increase of rural population in the ten years was therefore 556,065 and of the urban 1,278,147, or 16.48 per cent for the rural and 63.83 per cent for the urban.

The population of the principal cities and towns in 1911 was:

Amherst, N. S....	8,973	Regina, Sas........	30,213
Arnprior, Ont......	4,405	Revelstoke, B. C...	3,017
Barrie, Ont........	6,420	St. Boniface, Man.	7,483
Belleville, Ont....	9,876	St. Catherines, Ont.	12,484
Berlin, Ont........	15,196	St. Hyacinthe, Que.	9,797
Brandon, Man.....	13,839	St. Jean, Que.....	5,903
Brantford, Ont....	23,132	St. John, N. B.....	42,511
Brockville, Ont...	9,374	St. Thomas, Ont..	14,054
Calgary, Alb......	43,704	Sarnia, Ont.......	9,947
Charlottetown,		Saskatoon, Sas.....	12,004
P. E. I.	11,198	Sault Ste. Marie,	
Chatham, N. B..	4,666	Ont..............	10,984
Chatham, Ont....	10,770	Shawinigan Falls,	
Chicoutimi, Que..	5,880	Ont..............	4,265
Cobalt, Ont.......	5,638	Sherbrooke, Que..	16,405
Coborg, Ont......	5,074	Smith'a Falls, Ont.	6,370
Collingwood, Ont.	7,090	Sorel, Que........	8,420
Cornwall, Ont....	6,598	Ingersoll, Ont.....	4,763
Dartmouth, N. S..	5,058	Joliette, Qne.....	6,346
Dawson, Yukon...	3,013	Kamloops, B. C....	3,772
Dundas, Ont......	4,299	Kaslo, B. C.......	3,146
Edmonton, Alb...	24,990	Kenora, Ont......	6,158
Fernie, B. C......	3,146	Kingston, Ont.....	18,874
Fort William, Ont.	16,499	Lachine, Que......	10,699
Fraserville, Que...	6,774	Leathbridge, Alb..	8,050
Fredericton, N. B.	7,208	Levis, Que........	7,452
Galt, Ont........	10,299	Lindsay, Ont......	6,964
Glace Bay, N. S..	12,562	London, Ont......	46,300
Goderich, Ont....	4,552	Maisonneuve, Que.	18,684
Granby, Que......	4,750	Medicine Hat, Alb.	5,608
Grand Mere, Que..	4,783	Midland, Ont.....	4,663
Guelph, Ont......	15,175	Moncton, N. B....	11,345
Halifax, N. S.....	46,619	Montreal, Que.....	470,480
Hamilton, Ont....	81,969	Moosejaw, Sas.....	13,823
Hawkesbury, Ont.	4,400	Nanaimo, B. C....	8,306
Hull, Que........	18,222	Nelson, B. C......	4,476
Portage La Prairie,		New Glasgow, N. S.	6,383
Man............	5,892	New Westminster,	
Port Arthur, Ont.	11,220	B. C...........	13,199
Port Hope, Ont...	5,092	Niagara Falls, Ont.	9,248
Prince Albert, Sas.	6,254	North Bay, Ont...	7,737
Prince Rupert, B.C.	4,184	North Toronto, Ont.	5,362
Quebec, Que.......	78,190	North Sydney, N. S.	5,418

North Vancouver,		Thetford Mines, Que.	7,261
B. C...........	8,306	Toronto, Ont......	376,538
Orillia, Ont......	6,828	Trois-Rivieres, Que.	13,691
Oshawa, Ont......	7,436	Truro, N. S.......	6,107
Ottawa, Ont......	87,062	Valley Field, Que.	9,449
Outremont, Que...	4,820	Vancouver, B. C...	100,401
Owen Sound, Ont.	12,558	Verdun, Que......	11,629
Paris, Ont........	4,098	Victoria, B. C.....	31,660
Pembroke, Ont....	5,626	Waterloo, Ont.....	4,359
Peterborough, Ont.	18,360	Welland, Ont......	5,318
Springhill, N. S...	6,713	Westmount, Que...	14,579
Stratford, Ont...	12,946	Westville, N. B....	4,417
Strathcona, Alb...	5,579	Windsor, Ont......	17,829
Sudbury, Ont......	4,150	Winnipeg, Man.....	136,035
Sydney, N. S.....	17,723	Woodstock, Ont...	9,320
Sydney Mines, N. S.	7,470	Yarmouth, N. S...	6,600

Population by origin (1911):

British total....	3,896,985	Finnish	15,497
English	1,823,150	Grecian	3,594
Irish	1,050,384	Hindu	2,342
Scotch	997,880	Indian	105,492
Welsh	24,848	Italian	45,411
Other	723	Japanese	9,021
French	2,054,890	Jewish	75,681
German	393,320	Negro	16,877
Austro-Hungarian	129,103	Polish	33,365
Austrian	42,535	Russian	43,142
Bukovinian	9,960	Scandinavian	107,535
Galician	35,158	Swiss	6,625
Hungarian	11,605	Turkish	3,880
Ruthenian	29,845	Various	18,310
Belgian	9,593	Unspecified	147,345
Bulgar'n-Ruman'n	5,875		
Chinese	27,774	Total populat'n.	7,206,643
Dutch	54,986		

MANUFACTURES—[From census taken in June, 1911, for year 1910.]

	1900.	1910.
Establishments	14,650	19,218
Capital	$446,916,487	$1,247,583,609
Employes on salaries	30,691	44,077
Salaries	$23,876,146	$43,779,715
Employes on wages	208,482	471,126
Wages	$89,573,204	$197,228,701
Raw materials	$266,527,858	$601,509,018
Value products	$481,053,375	$1,165,975,639

Industries by principal groups (1910):

Groups	Establishments.	Capital.	Wage earners.	Value products.
Food products.	6,985	$123,044,523	52,730	$245,669,321
Textiles	1,444	108,787,407	72,672	135,902,441
Iron and steel.	824	123,561,319	48,558	113,640,610
Timber, lumber	4,999	259,889,715	110,049	184,630,376
Leather prod'ts	399	48,788,803	22,742	62,850,413
Paper, printing	773	62,677,612	22,894	46,458,053
Liquors	260	43,237,757	4,688	28,936,782
Chemicals	178	26,926,124	5,274	27,798,833
Clay, glass, stone products	771	45,859,507	17,699	25,781,860
Metals o t h e r than steel...	341	67,133,540	17,502	73,241,796
Tobacco	173	21,659,935	8,763	25,329,322
Vehicles	465	49,397,096	33,778	69,712,114
Vessels	172	10,351,765	4,414	6,575,417
Miscellaneous..	1,011	235,148,103	28,537	104,618,560
Hand trades...	423	11,120,403	8,826	14,829,741
Total	19,218	1,247,583,609	471,126	1,165,975,639

Religions of Canada in 1911. Figures here given are only for denominations having more than 10,000 members:

Adventists	10,406	Greek church.....	$8,507
Anglicans	1,043,017	Jews	74,564
Baptists	382,666	Lutherans	230,864
Buddhists	10,012	Mennonites	44,611
Christians	16,773	Methodists	1,079,892
Confucians	14,562	Mormons	15,971
Congregat'nalists	34,054	Presbyterians ...	1,115,324
Disciples	11,329	Protestants	30,265
Doukhobors	10,493	Roman catholics ..	2,833,041
Evangelicals	10,595	Salvation Army..	18,834

IMPORTS AND EXPORTS—The total value of the imports for the year ended March 31, 1912, was $559,220,936; exports, $315,317,250. Imports from the United States (1913), $415,260,049; exports to the United States, $120,571,180.

COMMONWEALTH OF AUSTRALIA.

July 9, 1900, the British parliament passed an act empowering the six provinces of Australia to form a federal union and Jan. 1, 1901, the new commonwealth was proclaimed at Sydney, N. S. W. Its first parliament was opened May 9, 1901, by the prince of Wales (now George V.), heir-apparent to the British throne, acting for his father, King Edward VII. The capital at present is in Melbourne.

GOVERNMENT—The federal parliament is made up of a senate of thirty-six members, six from each original state, and a house of representatives of seventy-five members, apportioned as follows: New South Wales, 27; Victoria, 21; Queensland, 10; South Australia, 7; Western Australia, 5; Tasmania, 5. The king is represented by the governor-general. He and the council of seven ministers exercise the executive power. The governor-general is paid a salary of $50,000 a year. The governor-general is Baron Denman. The ministers are: Joseph H. Cook, home affairs and prime minister; W. H. Irvine, attorney-general; L. E. Groom, trade and customs; E. D. Millen, defense; A. Wynne, postmaster-general; P. M. Glynn, external affairs; Sir J. Forrest, treasurer.

AREA AND POPULATION—The commonwealth has a total area of 2,974,581 square miles, divided among the states as follows:

New South Wales.310,372	Northern Territory.523,620
Victoria 87,884	Western Australia.975,920
Queensland 670,500	Tasmania 26,215
South Australia...380,070	

The total population of the commonwealth as enumerated April 2, 1911, was 4,455,005, divided among the states as follows:

New South Wales.1,648,448	West'n Australia 282,114
Victoria 1,315,551	Tasmania 191,211
Queensland 605,813	
South Australia.. 408,558	Total 4,455,005
Northern Territ'y 3,310	

The population of Melbourne in 1911 was 600,160; Sydney (1911), 636,353; Adelaide (1911), 192,429; Wellington (1911), 70,729; Brisbane (1911), 143,514.

EXPORTS AND IMPORTS—The total exports of the states in the commonwealth in 1912 were $394,185,000; total imports, $390,490,000. Australia in 1913 exported merchandise valued at $10,956,200 to the United States and imported merchandise worth $43,-351,855.

UNION OF SOUTH AFRICA.

Sept. 29, 1909, the British parliament passed an act empowering the four self governing colonies of South Africa—Cape of Good Hope, Natal, Transvaal and Orange Free State—to form a federal government to be known as the Union of South Africa. This was proclaimed May 31, 1910, at Pretoria, the seat of government, other services taking place at Cape Town, the seat of the legislature.

The executive government is vested in the king, represented by a governor-general, and an executive council and in ten ministers of state. Legislative power is vested in a parliament consisting of a senate and a house of assembly. The senate contains forty members, eight of whom are nominated by the governor-general in council and thirty-two elected by the four provinces, each of which is entitled to eight senators. The assembly consists of 121 members, chosen in electoral divisions as follows: The Cape of Good Hope, 51; Natal, 17; Transvaal, 36; Orange Free State, 17. Senators are elected for ten years and assemblymen for five. The English and Dutch languages are both official.

Governor-General—Lord Herbert John Gladstone. Cabinet: Premier and minister of agriculture, Gen. Louis Botha; finance and defense, J. C. Smuts; railways, Henry Burton; justice and native affairs, J. W. Sauer; education and mines, F. S. Malan; interior and lands, A. Fischer; posts and telegraphs and public works, Sir T. Watt.

Area in square miles and population in 1911:

Province.	Area.	Population.
Cape of Good Hope.................276,995		2,563,024
Natal 35,290		1,191,958
Transvaal 110,426		1,676,611
Orange Free State................50,389		528,906
Total 473,100		5,958,499

IMPORTS AND EXPORTS—The total imports of the four states in 1911 were valued at $182,117,590 and the exports at $283,120,000. Exports to the United States in 1913, $3,305,552; imports, $14,488,501.

ALBANIA.

Albania is an autonomous country, formerly a part of Turkey in Europe, but lost to the Ottomans as a result of the Balkan war. Its precise limits have not yet (October, 1913) been determined precisely by the powers, in the hands of which it was left by the treaty of London of May 30, 1913. It has a population of approximately 950,000 and an area of about 20,000 square miles.

AUSTRIA-HUNGARY.

GOVERNMENT—Emperor of Austria and king of Hungary, Francis Joseph I.; heir-presumptive (his nephew, son of the late Archduke Charles Louis), the Archduke Francis Ferdinand of Este.

Joint or common ministry:
Foreign Affairs—Count Leopold Berchtold.
War—Gen. Krobatkin.
Finance—Dr. de Bilinski.
Cabinet for Austria:
Premier—Count F. M. G. Stuergkh.
Interior—Dr. Karl Baron Heinold.
Commerce—Dr. Rudolph S. von Bonnot.
Finance—Wenzel von Zaleski.
Railways—Dr. von Forster.
Instruction—Dr. Max von Hussarek.
Agriculture—Franz Zenker.
Justice—Dr. Hochenburger.
National Defense—Marshal von Georgi.
Labor—Herr Ottokar Trnka.
Cabinet for Hungary:
Premier—Count Stephan Tisza.
Interior—Johann Sandor.
Finance—Johann Teleszky.
Defense—Samuel Hazay.
Justice—Dr. Francis Z. Szekely.
Commerce—Ladislas Beathy.
Agriculture—Baron Stephan B. von Rajecz.
Education—Count Johann Zichy.

The empire of Austria and the kingdom of Hungary are sovereign states, each with its own constitution, legislative bodies and system of administration, co-ordinate in rank and mutually independent within the domain of home affairs. Foreign representation (embassies and consulates), the army and navy, customs (import and export duties), and the administration of the annexed provinces (Bosnia and Herzegovina) are, however, conducted in common. Legislation on matters affecting the interests of the dual monarchy as a whole is intrusted to the delegations—two bodies of sixty members each, chosen from among members of the two legislative chambers of Austria and Hungary respectively.

AREA AND POPULATION—Area of Austria, 115,903 square miles; of Hungary, 125,395 square miles. The population of Austria in 1910 was 28,324,940. The population of Hungary in 1910 was 20,886,787. Total population for both countries in 1910 was 49,211,727.

Largest cities of Austria in 1910:

Vienna 2,031,498		Brunn	125,737
Trieste 229,475		Czernowitz	87,128
Prague 223,741		Pilsen	80,343
Lemberg 206,113		Linz	67,817
Cracow (1909)... 151,886		Pola	58,081
Gratz 151,781			

Largest cities of Hungary in 1910:

Budapest 880,371		Poszony	78,223
Szeged 118,328		Temesvar	72,555
Szabadka 94,610		Kecskemet	66,834
Debreczen 92,729		Arad	63,166
Zagrab 79,038		Hodmezo Vasarholy	62,445

IMPORTS AND EXPORTS—The value of the imports into the Austro-Hungarian customs territory in 1912 was $722,030,000; exports, $554,973,000. Chief imports are cotton, coal, wool, maize, tobacco, coffee and wines; principal exports, lumber and wool manufactures, sugar, eggs, barley, lignite, malt, leather, gloves and shoes. Imports from the United States in 1913, $23,320,690; exports to United States, $19,192,414.

BELGIUM.

GOVERNMENT—King, Albert I. Cabinet: Premier and Minister of Railways—Ch. de Broqueville.
War—Gen. Hellebaut.
Foreign Affairs—M. J. Davignon.
Interior—Paul Berryer.
Finance—M. Levie.
Justice—H. Carton de Wiart.
Agriculture and Public Works—G. Helleputte.
Industry and Labor—M. A. Hubert.
Science and Arts—P. Poulet.
Colonies—J. Renkin.
Railways—A. Van de Vyvere.
Marine, Posts and Telegraphs—P. Segers.

The legislative power is vested in the king, senate and chamber of representatives. The senate has 120 members and the chamber 186, or one for every 40,000 inhabitants.

AREA AND POPULATION—Total area, 11,373 square miles. Total population, 1910, 7,423,784; estimated population, 1911, 7,490,411. Population of the largest cities Dec. 31, 1911:

Antwerp ....308,618 | Liege 167,676
Brussels (capital)..646,400 | Ghent 166,719

IMPORTS AND EXPORTS—The imports in 1912 amounted to $899,722,000 and the exports to $753,-001,000. The trade with the United States in 1913 was: Imports, $66,845,462; exports, $41,941,614. Chief imports are cereals, textiles and metal goods; chief exports, cereals, raw textiles, tissues, iron, glass, hides, chemicals and machinery.

BULGARIA.

GOVERNMENT—King, Ferdinand. Legislation is enacted by the sobranje, a single chamber of 209 members elected for five years. Bulgaria in 1908 declared itself independent of Turkey, under the suzerainty of which country it had been an autonomous principality.

AREA AND POPULATION—Area, about 36,900 square miles. Population Dec. 31, 1910, 4,329,108; now about 5,000,000; population of Sofia, the capital, 102,769.

IMPORTS AND EXPORTS—Exports in 1911, $35,634,000; imports, $38,087,000. Exports to the United States in 1913, $440,537; imports, $103,749. The exports are mainly cereals and the imports textiles.

DENMARK.

GOVERNMENT—King, Christian X.; heir apparent, Prince Christian Frederick. Cabinet:
Premier and Minister of Justice—M. Zahle.
Finance and Foreign Affairs—Eduard Brandes.
Home Affairs—Ove Rode.
Agriculture—M. Pederson.
Instruction—Rev. K. Nielsen.
Commerce—O. H. V. Muus.
Finance—H. Juergensen.
Defense—M. Munch.

Legislative authority is vested in the landsthing and folkething. The former, which is the upper house, has 66 members, twelve of whom are appointed for life, the remainder being elected for terms of eight years. The folkething, or lower house, has 114 members, each elected for three years.

AREA AND POPULATION—Denmark's area is 15,582 square miles and total population in 1911, 2,775,076. Copenhagen, the capital, has a population of 462,161; with suburbs, 559,398.

IMPORTS AND EXPORTS—Total exports in 1911, $172,585,000; imports, $192,525,000. The imports from the United States in 1913 were $18,687,794; exports, $2,974,670. Leading articles of export are butter, pork, eggs and lard; of import, textiles, cereals, wood, iron manufactures and coal.

FRANCE.

GOVERNMENT—President, Raymond Poincare; term expires 1920.
Premier and Minister of Public Instruction—Jean Barthou.
Justice—M. Ratier.
Foreign Affairs—Stephen Pichon.
Colonies—Jean Morel.
Finance—M. Dumont.

War—Eugene Etienne.
Marine—Pierre Baudin.
Public Works—M. Thierry.
Agriculture—M. Clementel.
Labor—M. Cheron.
Interior—L. Klotz.

Legislative authority is vested in the chamber of deputies and the senate. The former has 597 members, each of whom is elected for four years. The senate has 300 members elected for nine years. The presidential term is seven years.

AREA AND POPULATION—France has a total area of 207,054 square miles. The area of the French colonies and dependencies throughout the world is 4,367,746 square miles. Total population (1911) of France proper, 39,601,509. Population of the principal cities in 1911:

Paris ....2,888,110 | Nantes 170,535
Marseilles .... 550,619 | Toulouse 149,576
Lyons .... 523,796 | St. Etienne...... 148,656
Bordeaux .... 261,678 | Nice 142,940
Lille .... 217,807 | Havre 136,159

IMPORTS AND EXPORTS—The total imports in 1912 amounted to $1,534,515,000; exports, $1,280,818,000. Exports to the United States in 1913, $136,877,990; imports from, $146,100,201. The chief exports are textiles, wine, raw silk, wool, small wares and leather; imports, wine, raw wool, raw silk, timber and wood, leather, skins and linen.

GERMANY.

GOVERNMENT—Emperor and king of Prussia, Wilhelm II.; heir-apparent, Prince Friedrich Wilhelm. Cabinet officers:
Imperial Chancellor—Dr. Theobald von Bethmann-Hollweg.
Foreign Affairs—Herr Gottlieb von Jagow.
Interior—Herr Klemens Delbruck.
Navy—Admiral Alfred von Tirpitz.
Justice—Herr Dr. Lisco.
Colonies—Herr Dr. Solf.
Treasury—Herr Kuehn.
Postal Affairs—Dr. Reinhold Kraetke.
Commerce—Herr Reinhold Sydow.
President of Imperial Railway Administration—Herr von Breitenbach.
Railways—Herr Wackerzapp.
Imperial Exchequer—Herr von Magdeburg.
Imperial Bank—Herr Havenstein.
Imperial Debt Commission—Herr Kuhn.

The Prussian minister of war, Gen. Josias O. O. von Heeringen, while nominally having jurisdiction over Prussian army affairs only, represents the imperial government in the reichstag in military matters and is, for all practical purposes, German secretary for war. Of the various independent states of Germany only the kingdoms of Prussia, Saxony, Bavaria and Wurttemberg have their own ministers of war.

Legislative authority is vested in a bundesrath, or senate, of 61 members, and a reichstag, or house, of 397 members. The latter are elected for five year terms on a popular franchise and the senators are appointed from the state governments for each session.

AREA AND POPULATION—The area of the states in the empire is 208,780 square miles; area of dependencies about 1,027,820 square miles; grand total, 1,236,600 square miles.

The last federal census was taken Dec. 1, 1910. According to this the population of the empire was 64,905,993. The estimated population of the foreign dependencies is 13,946,200. State population in 1910:

Prussia	40,165,219	Saxe-Meiningen.	278,762
Bavaria	6,887,291	Anhalt	331,128
Wurttemberg	2,437,574	Saxe-Coburg-	
Baden	2,142,833	Gotha	257,177
Saxony	4,806,661	Saxe-Altenburg..	216,128
Hesse	1,282,219	Lippe	150,937
Mecklenburg-		Schwarzburg-Rud	100,702
Schwerin	639,958	Schwarzburg-	
Oldenburg	483,042	Sond	89,917
Brunswick	494,339	Reuss, junior	
Saxony	417,149	branch	152,752
Mecklenburg-		Schaumburg-	
Strelitz	106,442	Lippe	46,652

Hamburg	1,014,664	Waldeck	61,707
Reuss, cider		Alsace-Lorraine.	1,874,014
branch	72,769		
Lubeck	116,599	Total	64,925,293
Bremen	295,715		

German cities having more than 150,000 inhabitants in 1910 included the following:

Berlin	2,071,257	Bremen	247,437
Hamburg	931,035	Duisburg	229,483
Munich	596,467	Dortmund	214,226
Dresden	548,308	Halle-on-Saale	180,843
Leipzig	589,850	Altona	172,628
Breslau	512,105	Strassburg	178,891
Cologne	516,527	Kiel	211,627
Frankfort a. M.	414,576	Elberfeld	170,195
Nurnberg	333,142	Mannheim	193,902
Dusseldorf	358,728	Danzig	170,337
Hanover	302,375	Barmen	169,214
Stuttgart	286,218	Rixdorf	237,289
Chemnitz	287,807	Gelsenkirchen	169,513
Magdeburg	279,629	Aachen	156,143
Charlottenburg	305,978	Schoeneberg	172,823
Essen	294,653	Posen	156,691
Stettin	236,113	Cassel	153,196
Konigsberg	245,994		

EXPORTS AND IMPORTS—Total exports (1912), $2,-115,482,090; total imports, $2,449,517,000.
During the fiscal year ended June 30, 1913, Germany exported $188,963,071 worth of merchandise to the United States and imported merchandise valued at $331,684,212.

SOVEREIGNS OF STATES.

Anhalt—Duke, Friedrich.
Baden—Grand duke, Friedrich II.
Bavaria—King, Ludwig III.
Brunswick—Duke, Ernst August.
Hesse—Grand duke, Ernst Ludwig.
Lippe—Count, Leopold IV.
Mecklenburg-Schwerin—Grand duke, Friedrich Franz IV.
Mecklenburg-Strelitz—Grand duke, Adolph Friedrich.
Oldenburg—Grand duke, Friedrich August.
Prussia—King, Wilhelm II.
Reuss, Elder Branch—Prince, Heinrich XXIV.
Reuss, Younger Branch—Prince, Heinrich XXVII.
Saxe-Altenburg—Duke, Ernst.
Saxe-Coburg and Gotha—Duke, Charles Edward.
Saxe-Meiningen—Duke, Georg II.
Saxony (grand duchy)—Grand duke, Wilhelm Ernst.
Saxony—King, Friedrich August III.
Schaumburg-Lippe—Prince, Adolf.
Schwarzburg-Rudolstadt—Prince, Gunther.
Waldeck—Prince, Friedrich.
Wurttemberg—King, Wilhelm II.

GREECE.

GOVERNMENT—King, Constantine I.; heir-apparent, Prince George, duke of Sparta. Cabinet:
President of the Council and Minister of War—M. Venezelos.
Marine—M. Stratos.
Foreign—M. Coromilas.
Worship and Instruction—M. Tsirimakos.
Interior—M. Repoulis.
Finance—M. Alexandre Diomidis.
Commerce and Agriculture—M. Michalakopoulis.
Justice—M. Raktivan.
Legislative authority is vested in one chamber, the boule, consisting of 235 members, each of whom is elected for four years.
AREA AND POPULATION——Total area, about 45,000 square miles. Population in 1913, 4,500,000 (estimated). Athens in 1907 had 167,479 inhabitants; Piræus, 73,579, and Patras, 37,724.
EXPORTS AND IMPORTS—The total exports in 1911 amounted in value to $28,180,500; imports, $36,697,485. Exports to the United States in 1913, $3,179,816; imports from the United States, $1,216,195. The leading exports are currants, ores, olive oil and figs; imports, foodstuffs, textiles, coal and timber.

ITALY.

GOVERNMENT—King, Victor Emmanuel III.; heir to the crown, his son Humbert, prince of Piedmont, born Sept. 16, 1904.

President of Council and Minister of the Interior—Sig. Giolitti.
Foreign Affairs—Marquis A. di San Giuliano.
Grace and Justice—Sig. Finocebiario Aprile.
Treasury—Sig. Tedesco.
Finance—Sig. Facta.
War—Gen. Paolo Spingardi.
Marine—Admiral Leonardi Cattolica.
Public Instruction—Sig. Credaro.
Public Works—Sig. Sacchi.
Agriculture, Industry and Commerce—Sig. Nitti.
Posts and Telegraph—Sig. Calissano.
Colonies—Sig. Bertolini.
Legislative authority rests in the king and parliament. The latter consists of a senate of 369 members (in 1912) and a chamber of deputies of 508 members.
AREA AND POPULATION—The area of Italy is 110,659 square miles. According to the census of June 19, 1911, the total population was 34,671,377. Population of the principal cities:

Naples	678,031	Florence	232,860
Milan	599,200	Catania	210,703
Rome	542,123	Bologna	172,628
Turin	427,106	Venice	160,719
Palermo	331,088	Messina	126,557
Genoa	272,221	Livorno	105,315

IMPORTS AND EXPORTS—The value of merchandise exported in 1912 was $462,456,000; imported, $695,-592,000. The total value of exports to the United States in 1913 was $54,107,364; imports from the United States, $76,285,278. Chief imports are coal, cotton, grain, silk, wool, timber, machinery, sugar and oil; chief exports, silk, wine, oil, coral, sulphur, hemp and flax.

MONTENEGRO.

King, Nicholas I. Area 7,500 square miles; population, 650,000; of the capital, Cettinje, 4,500. Total exports in 1910, $498,200; imports, $1,761,300. Montenegro has practically no trade with the United States. Chief exports are sumach, smoked sardines, cattle, sheep, goats, cheese, olive oil, wine and tobacco. Imports include petroleum, salt, maize, cottons, hardware, sugar, coffee and rice.

NORWAY.

GOVERNMENT—King, Haakon VII.; crown prince, Olaf.
President of Council and Minister of Agriculture—Gunnar Knudsen.
Foreign Affairs—M. Ihlen.
Justice—Lars Abrahamsen.
Commerce—Johan Castberg.
Labor—M. Urbye.
Finance—A. Omholt.
Education and Worship—A. O. Bryggesaa.
Defense—Gen. Keilhan.
Legislative authority is vested in the storthing, consisting of 123 members elected for three years through universal suffrage by men and women. The storthing consists of two houses, the odelsthing and the lagthing. The former is made up of three-fourths of the members of the storthing and the latter of one-fourth.
AREA AND POPULATION—The total area of Norway is 124,130 square miles. Total population in December, 1910, 2,391,782. Christiania in 1910 had a population of 241,834 and Bergen 76,867.
IMPORTS AND EXPORTS—The value of the imports in 1912 was $135,671,000; exports, $87,084,000. Exports to the United States in 1913, $8,418,359; imports, $8,391,458. The chief exports are timber and wood manufactures, wood pulp, malty food, paper and minerals; imports, breadstuffs, groceries, yarn, textiles, vessels and machinery.

PORTUGAL.

GOVERNMENT—President, Manoel de Arriaga. Cabinet:
Premier and Minister of Finance—Dr. Affonso Costa.
Foreign Affairs—Senhor Antonio Maceira.
Interior—Senhor Rodrigo Rodrigues.
Justice—Senhor Alvaro de Castro.
Public Works—Senhor Antonio Maria da Silva.
War—Maj. Pereira Bastos.

Marine—Senhor Freitas Ribeiro.

Colonies—Senhor Almeida Ribeiro.

Legislative authority is vested in a national council of 164 members and an upper house of seventy-one members. The first elections were held May 28, 1911, and the assembly opened June 19. On the same day the republic was officially recognized by the United States.

AREA AND POPULATION—Total area, including Azores and Madeira, 35,490 square miles. Area of possessions in Africa and Asia, 801,050 square miles. The population of the home country with the Azores and Madeira in 1911 was 5,957,985; of the colonies in Africa and Asia, 9,139,444. In 1910 Lisbon had a population of 356,009 and Oporto 167,955.

IMPORTS AND EXPORTS—Total imports in 1911, $122,627,314; total exports, $61,417,450. Imports from the United States in 1913, $4,167,158; exports to the United States, $6,870,223. The chief imports are foodstuffs, cotton, sugar, fish, wool, leather, coal and coffee; chief exports, wine, sardines, copper ore, olives and figs.

ROUMANIA.

GOVERNMENT—King, Carol I.; heir-apparent, Ferdinand, prince of Roumania.

Legislative authority is vested in a senate of 120 members elected for eight years and a chamber of deputies of 183 members elected for four years.

AREA AND POPULATION—The total area is about 55,000 square miles. The population in 1899 was 5,956,690; estimated in 1913, 7,111,000. Population of the principal towns (in 1912): Bucharest, 338,109; Jassy, 75,882; Galatz, 71,719; Braila, 64,730.

EXPORTS AND IMPORTS—The value of the exports in 1910 was $79,075,000; of the imports, $118,985,000. The chief exports are cereals and the leading imports are textiles. Exports to the United States in 1913, $348,481; imports from, $2,417,591.

RUSSIA.

GOVERNMENT—Czar, Nicholas II.; heir-apparent, Grand Duke Alexis.

Premier and Minister of Finance—F. Kokovtseff.

Foreign Affairs—M. Sazonoff.

Interior—M. Maklakoff.

Instruction—M. Casso.

Imperial House and Domains—Gen. Baron de Fredericks.

Justice—M. Scheglovitoff.

Agriculture—M. Krivoshein.

Commerce—M. Timasheff.

Railways—M. Rukhloff.

Controller—M. Kharitonoff.

Procurator of the Holy Synod—M. Sabler.

War—Gen. Sukhomlinoff.

Navy—Vice-Admiral Grigorowich.

Legislative authority is vested in the czar, duma and council of the empire.

AREA AND POPULATION—Area, 8,764,586 square miles. Total population in 1911, 167,003,400. Population of the principal cities:

St. Petersburg	1,962,400	Riga	331,300
Moscow	1,533,400	Kiev	595,060
Warsaw	872,478	Kharkov	226,042
Odessa	505,600	Saratov	206,300
Lodz	408,330	Vilna	190,210

IMPORTS AND EXPORTS—The total value of the imports in 1911 was $598,266,000; of the exports, $819,577,000. The exports to the United States in 1913 amounted in value to $26,958,690; imports from the United States, $25,363,795. The chief exports are foodstuffs, timber, oil, furs and flax; imports, raw cotton, wool, metals, leather, hides, skins and machinery.

FINLAND.

Grand Duke—The emperor of Russia.

Governor-General—Gen. Seyn.

The grand duchy of Finland, though nominally autonomous, is now practically a province of Russia. It has a parliament of 200 members chosen by direct election. The right to vote is possessed by men and women alike after they reach their 24th year. The area of Finland is 125,689 square miles and the population Jan. 1, 1911, was 3,084,000.

SERVIA.

GOVERNMENT—King, Peter I. (Karageorgevitch); heir-apparent, Prince Alexander (second son). Legislative authority is vested in a single chamber, called "skupshtina," of 160 elected members.

AREA AND POPULATION—Area, about 37,600 square miles. Population in 1910, 2,911,701; now about 4,550,000. The capital, Belgrade, has 90,890 inhabitants.

EXPORTS AND IMPORTS—Total value of exports in 1911, $22,565,000; imports, $22,277,000. Exports to the United States in 1913, $694,395; imports, $7,616. The exports are mainly agricultural products and animals and the imports cotton and woolen goods and metals.

SPAIN.

GOVERNMENT—King, Alfonso XIII.; heir-apparent, Prince Alfonso. Cabinet:

Premier—Edouardo Dato.

Foreign Affairs—Marquis Lima.

Interior—Senor Sanchez Guerra.

Finance—Count Bugalial.

War—Gen. Echaque.

Marine—Admiral Miranda.

Public Works and Agriculture—Marquis Vadillo.

Public Instruction—Senor Bergamin.

Justice—Senor Ugarte.

AREA AND POPULATION—Total area, 194,733 square miles. Total population of Spain, census of 1910, 19,588,688. Population of large cities:

Madrid	571,539	Carthagena	96,983
Barcelona	560,000	Saragossa	105,788
Valencia	233,348	Bilbao	92,514
Seville	155,366	Granada	77,425
Malaga	133,045	Cadiz	67,174
Murcia	124,985	Valladolid	67,742

IMPORTS AND EXPORTS—The exports of Spain in 1912 amounted to $188,966,000; imports, $189,029,000. Total exports to the United States in 1913, $23,220,012; imports, $25,067,490. Chief exports are wine, sugar, timber, animals, glassware and pottery; imports, cotton and cotton manufactures, machinery, drugs and chemical products.

SWEDEN.

GOVERNMENT—King, Gustaf V.; crown prince, Gustaf Adolf.

Minister of State—Karl Staaf.

Foreign Affairs—Count Albert Ahrensvard.

War—D. K. Bergstrom.

Finance—Baron A. T. Adelswaerd.

Marine—Jacob Larsson.

Education—Dr. F. Berg.

Interior—P. A. V. Schotte.

Agriculture—Alfred Petersson.

Justice—Gustaf Sandstrom.

Legislative authority is vested in a parliament of two chambers, the first of which has a membership of 150 and the second 230. Members of the upper house are elected for nine years and those of the lower for three years. The first chamber is elected by municipal representatives. To be eligible one must own real estate worth at least $0,000 crowns or pay taxes on an income of at least 4,000 crowns. The second chamber constituents must have an income of at least 800 crowns or own real estate worth at least 1,000 crowns.

AREA AND POPULATION—The total area of Sweden is 172,876 square miles. The population Dec. 31, 1911, was 5,561,799. The population of the principal cities at the same time was:

Stockholm	346,599	Norrkoping	46,629
Gothenburg	170,606	Helsingborg	33,225
Malmo	89,719		

IMPORTS AND EXPORTS—The total exports in 1912 were valued at $192,960,000; imports, $198,320,000. Exports to the United States in 1913, $11,174,419; imports, $12,104,366. The leading articles of export are timber and machinery; of import, textile goods and foodstuffs.

SWITZERLAND.

GOVERNMENT—President of Federal Council (1913), M. Edouard Muller.

Vice-President—Arthur Hoffman.

Legislative authority is vested in a state and a national council, the former having forty-four and

the latter 167 members. The national councilors are elected directly by the people; the state councilors are elected in some cantons by the people and in others by the cantonal legislature. The chief executive authority is vested in the bundesrath, or federal council, one member of which is the chief of one of the federal departments. Its decrees are enacted as a body. Its members are elected president in rotation.

Switzerland owns its main railroads, its telegraph and telephone system and monopolizes the manufacture and sale of alcohol.

AREA AND POPULATION—Total area, 15,976 square miles. The population, according to the census of Dec. 1, 1910, was 3,741,971. Population of the largest cities:

Zurich	189,088	Bern	85,264
Basel	131,914	Lausanne	63,926
Geneva	125,520	St. Gallen	37,657

EXPORTS AND IMPORTS—Total exports in 1912, $262,020,000; imports, $381,966,000. Exports to the United States in 1913, $23,260,180; imports, $26,549. The articles chiefly exported are cottons, silks, clocks and watches; imported, foodstuffs, silk, minerals and metals, clothing and animals.

THE NETHERLANDS.

GOVERNMENT—Queen, Wilhelmina; prince consort, Henry of Mecklenburg-Schwerin; heir, Princess Juliana. Cabinet:

Prime Minister and Minister of the Interior—Mr. P. W. A. Cort vander Linden.
Foreign Affairs—Jonkheer Dr. J. Loudon.
Agriculture, Commerce, Industry and Labor—Mr. W. F. Treub.
War—Maj.-Gen. N. Bosboom.
Navy—Capt. S. S. Rambonnet.
Justice—Mr. B. Ort.
Finance—Mr. A. E. J. Bertling.
Colonies—Mr. Th. B. Pleyte.
Waterways—Dr. C. Lely.

Legislative authority is vested in the states-general, composed of two chambers, the first having fifty members and the second 100. The latter are elected directly and the former by the provincial states.

AREA AND POPULATION—The area of Holland, or the Netherlands, is 12,648 square miles. The total population Dec. 31, 1911, was 6,022,452. That of the chief cities Dec. 31, 1911, was:

Amsterdam	580,930	Groningen	77,221
Rotterdam	436,018	Haarlem	69,988
The Hague	288,577	Arnhem	64,634
Utrecht	121,317	Leiden	59,133

IMPORTS AND EXPORTS—In 1911 Holland imported $1,332,874,000 worth of merchandise and exported $1,090,848,000. In 1913 the exports to the United States amounted to $38,180,967 and the imports from the same country at $125,909,862. Chief imports are iron and steel and their manufactures, textiles, coal, cereals and flour; exports, butter, sugar and cheese.

TURKEY.

GOVERNMENT—Sultan, Mehmed V. Cabinet:
Grand Vizier and Minister for Foreign Affairs—Prince Said Halim.
President Council of State—Halil Bey.
Sheik-ul-Islam—Mehmed Essad Pasha.
Minister of the Interior—Talaat Bey.
Marine—Mahmud Pasha.
Finance—Rifaat Bey.
Public Instruction—Shukri Bey.
Religions Foundation and Justice—Irahim Bey.
Public Works—Osman Nizami Pasha.
War—Gen. Izzet Pasha.
Posts and Telegraphs—Oskian Effendi.
Commerce—Suleiman el Bustani.

A constitutional form of government was adopted July 24, 1908, with legislative authority vested in a parliament.

AREA AND POPULATION—The area of that part of Turkey under control of the sultan is 1,590,000 square miles. The total population of all parts of the empire is about 23,000,000. Constantinople has about 1,203,000 inhabitants.

EXPORTS AND IMPORTS—The total exports in 1912 amounted in value to $172,871,605 and the imports to

$129,967,759. The exports to the United States in 1913 amounted to $9,917,890 in value and the imports to $2,597,239. The principal articles imported are cloth and clothing, sugar, coffee, flour, rice and manufactures of iron; exports, grapes, silk, grain, cocoons, wool, cotton, carpets, hides and skins.

ASIA.

AFGHANISTAN.

Ameer, Habibullah Khan; population, about 5,900,000; area, 250,000 square miles. No statistics as to imports and exports of Afghanistan are available. The chief productions are preserved fruits, spices, wool, silk, cattle and tobacco.

BOKHARA.

Ameer, Sayid Mir Alim Khan; heir, Sayid Mir Ibrahim. The area of Bokhara is about 83,000 square miles and the population 1,250,000. The products are corn, tobacco, fruit, silk and hemp. Since 1873 Bokhara has been a dependency of Russia.

CHINA.

GOVERNMENT—President, Yuan Shih-kai; vice-president, Li Yuan Hung. The president and vice-president are each elected for a term of five years. Legislative power is vested in a national assembly or parliament of two houses. The senate has 274 members and the house of representatives 596.

AREA AND POPULATION—Total area of China, with dependencies, 4,277,170 square miles; estimated population, 433,553,030.

EXPORTS AND IMPORTS—The total exports in 1912 amounted to $274,822,000 and the imports to $350,906,000. During the fiscal year 1913 goods to the value of $21,326,834 were imported from the United States. The total exports in the same period to the United States amounted to $39,010,800. The articles imported from America consist mainly of flour, kerosene, sago, india rubber, shoes, ginseng, quicksilver, white shirting, drills and broadcloth. Among the leading exports are tea, furs, wool, mats, fans, essential oils, straw braid, silks, hair, hides, hemp.

JAPAN.

GOVERNMENT—Emperor, Yoshihito; crown prince, Hirohito. Cabinet:
Premier—Count Gombei Yamamoto.
Foreign Affairs—Baron Nobuakis Makino.
Finance—Baron Korekiyo Takahashi.
War—Lieut.-Gen. Baron Kikoshi.
Navy—Admiral Saito.
Justice—Masahisa Matsuda.
Education—Sajima Motoda.
Agriculture and Commerce—Tatsuo Yamamoto.
Interior—Kei Hara.
Communications—Girin Okuda.

Legislative authority is vested in the emperor and the imperial diet. This consists of the house of peers and the house of representatives, the former having 369 and the latter 379 members.

AREA AND POPULATION—The total area of Japan is 175,540 square miles. The population according to the census of Dec. 31. 1912, was 52,200,679, exclusive of Formosa, the Pescadores and the south half of Sakhalin. The total population, including Korea, Formosa and Sakhalin, was 69,147,930 in 1912. Cities having more than 100,000 inhabitants are:

Tokyo (1908)	2,186,079	Kobe	378,197
Osaka	1,226,590	Nagasaki	176,480
Kyoto	442,462	Hiroshima	142,763
Yokohama	394,303	Kanafawa	110,994
Nagoya	378,231	Kure	100,679

IMPORTS AND EXPORTS—The total imports in 1912 amounted in value to $307,844,000; exports, $261,258,000. In 1913 the imports from the United States were valued at $57,741,815, and the exports to the same country at $91,633,240. The chief exports are raw silk, cotton, yarn, copper, coal and tea; imports, sugar, cotton, iron and steel, machinery, petroleum and wool.

CHOSEN (KOREA).

Formerly an empire, but now a Japanese colony. Estimated area, 86,000 square miles. Population in 1912, 13,461,299. Seoul, the capital, has 278,958 inhabitants.

KHIVA.

Khan, Seyid Asfendiar Khan; heir-apparent, Nasyr Tycuara; area, 24,000 square miles; population 800,000. Products are cotton and silk. Khiva is a Russian vassal state.

PERSIA.

Shah or emperor, Sultan Ahmad Shah; regent, Abu'l Kassim Khau. Under the constitution granted in 1906 legislative authority was vested in a national council of 156 members and a senate of 60 members. The area of Persia is about 628,000 square miles and the population 9,500,000. Imports in 1911-1912, $57,020,845; exports, $42,978,400. Imports from the United States in 1913, $2,120; exports to $1,970,-474. Teheran, the capital, has a population of about 280,000. Chief among the products are silk, fruits, wheat, barley and rice.

SIAM.

King, Chowfa Maha Vajirvudh. Area, 195,000 square miles; population (1910), 8,117,953. Bangkok, the capital, has 628,675 inhabitants. The imports in 1911-1912 were $27,712,800, and the exports $32,068,205. Imports from the United States in 1913, $485,958; exports to, $116,565. Chief among the exports are rice, teak and marine products; imports, cotton goods and opium.

AFRICA.

ABYSSINIA.

Emperor, Lidj Eyassu. Total area of Abyssinia 432,432 square miles; population, 10,000,000. The exports are coffee, hides and skins, gum, wax, gold and ivory.

ALGERIA.

Algeria is a colony of France. Governor-General —M. Lutaud. Area, 343,500 square miles; population in 1911, 5,492,569. Chief imports are cotton, skins and furs and wood work; exports, wine, sheep, and cereals.

EGYPT.

Khedive, Abbas Hilmi; heir-apparent, Mohammed Abdul Mouneim. Total area of Egypt, 400,000 square miles; area of the Anglo-Egyptian Sudan, 984,520 square miles. The population of Egypt proper in 1907 was 11,189,978; of the Anglo-Egyptian Sudan, 3,000,000. Population of Cairo, 654,476; Alexandria, 332,246. Great Britain controls the state finances and is represented at Cairo by a "financial adviser," who sits in the council of ministers. The present adviser is Field Marshal Viscount Kitchener. The total exports in 1912 were valued at $172,-871,500, and the imports at $129,538,795. Imports from the United States in 1913, $1,660;833; exports to, $19,907,828. The exports consist chiefly of cereals, raw cotton and provisions; imports, wool, coal, textiles and metal manufactures.

BELGIAN KONGO.

Congo was made a Belgian colony in 1908. The estimated area is 909,654 square miles and the negro population about 15,000,000. Europeans numbered 4,003 in January, 1911. Among the leading articles of export are ivory, rubber, cocoa, palm nuts, palm oil, copal gum and coffee. Total imports in 1911, $23,399,500; exports, $26,669,500.

LIBERIA.

President—Daniel E. Howard. Legislative power is vested in a senate of nine members and a house of representatives of fourteen members. The total area of the republic is about 40,000 square miles and the population 2,120,000. The exports in 1909 were valued at $970,500 and the imports at $1,065,200. Imports from the United States in 1913, $96,900; exports to, $2,319. The chief exports are rubber, palm oil, cocoa, ivory, ginger and camwood. Imports are cottons, provisions, wood and iron manufactures and gin.

MOROCCO.

Sultan, Mulai Youssef. Morocco is a French protectorate. Area about 219,000 square miles; population, 5,000,000. Total imports in 1911, $26,547,580; exports, $17,049,100. Imports from the United States in 1913, $30,200; exports to, $100,426. The chief imports are cotton, sugar and tea; exports, eggs, almonds, goatskins, beans, peas, linseed, wool, wax and cattle.

TUNIS.

Bey, Sidi Mohammed; heir-presumptive, Sidi Mohammed Ben Mamoun Bey. Tunis is under the protectorate of France and that country is represented by a resident-general. Total area, 50,000 square miles; population in 1910, 1,923,217; foreigners, 148,-476 (1911). Imports in 1911, $24,036,600; exports, $28,-720,000. Chief exports are wheat, barley, olives and palms.

MEXICO.

GOVERNMENT—The republic of Mexico is divided into twenty-seven states, three territories and one federal district, each with a local government, but all subject to the federal constitution. Representatives are elected for two years each and are apportioned at the rate of one for each 40,000 inhabitants; the senators, of whom there are fifty-six, are elected by the people in the same manner as representatives. The president holds office four years and may be elected for several consecutive terms.

See "Revolutions in Mexico" in this volume.

AREA AND POPULATION—The total area, including islands, is 767,005 square miles. The population, according to the federal census of 1910, is 15,063,207. The population of leading cities of the republic follows: City of Mexico (capital), 470,659; Guadalajara, 118,789; Puebla, 101,214; Monterey, 81,006; San Luis Potosi, 82,946; Pachuca, 38,620; Aguas Calientes, 44,800; Zacatecas, 25,905; Durango, 34,085; Toluca, 31,247; Leon, 63,263; Merida, 61,999; Queretaro, 35,011; Morelia, 39,116; Oaxaca, 37,469; Orizaba, 32,-894; Chihuahua, 39,061; Vera Cruz, 29,164.

COMMERCE—The chief exports of Mexico are precious metals, coffee, tobacco, hemp, sisal, sugar, dyewoods and cabinet woods, cattle and hides and skins. In 1912 the total exports amounted to $149,-007,000; total imports for the same year were $71,-330,000. The trade of Mexico is chiefly with the United States, Great Britain, France, Germany and Spain. In 1913 the imports from the United States were $54,571,584; exports to, $77,543,842.

SOUTH AMERICAN REPUBLICS.

ARGENTINE REPUBLIC.

President, Dr. Roque Saenz Pena; capital, Buenos Aires. Area, 1,153,119 square miles. Population (1911), 7,171,910; Buenos Aires, 1,383,663 (in 1912). Total exports in 1912, $463,578,000; imports, $371,-384,000. Exports to the United States in 1913, $26,-863,732; imports, $52,894,834. Chief exports, sheep, wool, cattle, hides, frozen meats and wheat; imports, machinery, agricultural implements, railway cars, engines and supplies and manufactures of iron and steel.

BOLIVIA.

President, Gen. Ismael Montes; capital, Sucre. Area, 708,195 square miles. Population (1910), 2,267,-935; LaPaz, 78,856; Chocachamba, 24,512; Sucre, 23,416. Total exports in 1911, $33,052,400; imports, $23,348,500. Exports to the United States in 1913, $350; imports, $940,744. Chief exports, silver, tin, copper, coffee, rubber; imports, provisions, clothing, hardware, spirits, silks and woolens.

BRAZIL.

President, Marshal Hermes da Fonseca; capital, Rio de Janeiro. Area, 3,218,991 square miles. Population (est. 1911), 23,070,969; Rio de Janeiro (1911), 1,128,637; Sao Paulo (1911), 450,000; Bahia, 290,000; Pernambuco, 160,000. Exports (1912), $363,274,000; imports, $308,409,000. Exports to the United States in 1913, $120,155,855; imports, $42,638,467. Chief exports, coffee, sugar, tobacco, cotton and rubber; imports, cotton goods, manufactures of iron and steel, furniture, mineral oils, breadstuffs and provisions.

CHILE.

President, Ramon Barros Luco; capital, Santiago. Area, 292,580 square miles. Population in 1910, 3,415,060; Santiago, 332,724; Valparaiso, 179,815; Concepcion, 55,554. Total exports in 1911, $123,884,000; imports, $127,281,000. Exports to the United States in 1913, $27,655,420; imports, $16,076,763. Chief exports, nitrate, wool, hides and leather; imports, sugar, coal, cotton goods, cashmeres, oil, galvanized iron.

COLOMBIA.

President, Carlos E. Restrepo; capital, Bogota. Area, 461,606 square miles. Population in 1912, 5,475,961; Bogota, 121,257. Total exports (1911), $22,-375,899; total imports, $18,108,863. Exports to the United States in 1913, $15,992.321; imports, $7,397,696. Chief exports, gold, silver and other minerals, coffee, cocoa, cattle, sugar, tobacco and rubber; imports, manufactures of iron and steel, cotton goods.

ECUADOR.

President, Gen. Leonidas Plaza; capital, Quito. Area, 116,000 square miles. Population, 1,500,000; Quito, 70,000; Guayaquil, 80,600. Total exports in 1911, $14,035,230; imports (1910), $8,024,105. Exports to the United States in 1913, $3,037,689; imports, $2,553,785. Chief exports, coffee, cocoa, rice, sugar, rubber, cabinet woods, chemicals and minerals; imports, cotton, provisions, manufactures of iron and steel, clothing and mineral oils.

PARAGUAY.

President, Edouardo Schaerer; capital, Asuncion. Area, 171,770 square miles. Population (est. 1911), 800,000; Asuncion (1911), 80,000. Total exports in 1911, $4,828,890; imports, $6,478,495. Exports to the United States in 1913, $58,285; imports, $187,807. Chief exports, mate (or Paraguay tea), tobacco, hides, timber, oranges; imports, cotton goods, machinery and provisions.

PERU.

President, Guillermo Billinghurst; capital, Lima. Area, 695,733 square miles. Population estimated (1912) at 4,000,000; Lima, 140,884; Callao, 31,000. Total exports in 1911, $37,110,000; imports, $31,856,500. Exports to the United States in 1913, $9,666,579; imports, $7,341,903. Chief exports, cotton, coffee, sugar, cinchona, india rubber, dyes and medicinal plants; imports, woolens, cotton, machinery and manufactures of iron.

URUGUAY.

President, Senor Don Jose Battle y Ordonyez; capital, Montevideo. Area, 72,210 square miles. Population (1911), 1,177,560; Montevideo (1912), 352,487. Total exports in 1912, $48,455,000; imports, $49,380,000. Exports to the United States in 1913, $2,450,697; imports, $7,522,145. Chief exports, animal and agricultural products; imports, manufactured articles.

VENEZUELA.

President, Juan Vicente Gomez; capital, Caracas. Area 393,976 square miles. Population (1912), 2,743,-841; Caracas, 75,000. Total exports in 1912, $25,-261,000; imports, $20,569,000. Exports to the United States in 1913, $10,852,331; imports, $5,737,118. Chief exports, coffee, hides, cabinet woods, rubber and chemicals; imports, machinery, manufactures of iron and steel, provisions, furniture and mineral wools.

CENTRAL AMERICAN STATES.

COSTA RICA.

President, Don Ricardo Jiminez; capital, San Jose. Area, 23,000 square miles. Population (1911), 389,266; San Jose, 31,668. Total exports (1911), $9,182,500; imports, $9,129,000. Exports to the United States in 1913, $3,098,735; imports, $3,514,908. Chief exports, coffee and bananas; imports, cotton, machinery, iron and steel manufactures, woolens and worsteds.

GUATEMALA.

President, Manuel E. Cabrera; capital, Guatemala de Nueva. Area, 48,290 square miles. Population (1910), 1,992,000; of the capital, 96,000. Total exports (1911), $10,981,724; imports, $6,514,421. Exports to the United States in 1913, $3,106,981; imports, $3,653,587. Chief exports, coffee and bananas; imports, cotton and cereals.

HONDURAS.

President, Dr. Francisco Bertrand; capital, Tegucigalpa. Area, 46,250 square miles. Population (1910), 553,446; Tegucigalpa, 23,137. Total exports (1912), $3,159,700; imports, $3,264,700. Exports to the United States in 1913, $3,200,591; imports, $3,195,627. Chief exports, bananas, coffee, cattle, cocoanuts and wood; chief import, cotton.

NICARAGUA.

President, Senor Adolfo Diaz; capital, Managua. Area, 49,200 square miles. Population, 600,000; Managua, 34,872; Leon, 62,569. Total exports (1910), $4,545,076; imports, $2,850,305. Exports to the United States in 1913, $1,437,939; imports, $2,925,807. Chief exports, cattle and coffee; imports, flour, wine, beer, barbed wire, cotton goods, sewing machines, kerosene, calico and tallow.

PANAMA.

President, Dr. Belisario Parras; term expires Sept. 30, 1916. Independence of Panama declared Nov. 3, 1903; constitution adopted Feb. 13, 1904. Legislative power is vested in a national assembly composed of deputies elected by the people. The ratio of representation is one deputy for each 10,000 inhabitants. The term of office is four years. The area of the republic is 31,571 square miles and the population (1912), 426,928; city of Panama (1912), 37,505; Colon, 17,748. The exports to the United States in the fiscal year ended June 30, 1913, amounted to $4,234,010, and the imports to $23,547,869. The chief articles of export are bananas, rubber, coffee and pearls.

SALVADOR.

President, Carlos Melendez; capital, San Salvador. Area, 7,225 square miles. Population (1912), 1,161,426; San Salvador, 59,540. Total exports (1911), $8,883,351; imports, $5,113,118. Exports to the United States in 1913, $1,371,568; imports, $2,389,971. Chief exports, coffee, indigo, sugar, tobacco and balsams; imports, cotton, spirits, flour, iron goods, silk and yarn.

CUBA.

GOVERNMENT—President, Gen. Mario Menocal; vice-president, Enrique Jose Varona; terms expire May 20, 1917. Cabinet officers in 1913:

Secretary of State—Cosme de la Torriente.
Secretary of Justice—Cristobal de la Guardia.
Secretary of the Interior—Col. Aurelio Hevia.
Secretary of the Treasury—Leopoldo Cancio.
Secretary of Public Works—Jose Ramon Villalon.
Secretary of Agriculture—Gen. Emilio Nunez.
Secretary of Public Instruction—Ezequael Garcia.

Under the constitution the legislative power is exercised by two elective bodies—the house of representatives and the senate, conjointly called congress. The senate is composed of four senators from each of the six provinces, elected for eight years by the provincial councilmen, and by a double number of electors, constituting together an electoral board.

The house of representatives is composed of one representative for each 25,000 inhabitants or fraction thereof over 12,500, elected for four years by direct vote. One-half of the members of the house are elected every two years. The salary of members of congress is $3,600 a year.

ORGANIZATION OF THE REPUBLIC—The organization of the republic of Cuba, begun in 1900, was practically completed on the 20th of May, 1902, when the military occupation of the island by the United States came to an end and Gen. Tomas Estrada Palma was inaugurated as the first president.

AREA AND POPULATION—The total area of Cuba is 44,164 square miles. The population in 1910, when the last census was taken, was 2,220,278.

Population of provinces (1910):

Havana	575,266	Matanzas	260,060
Santa Clara	514,325	Pinar del Rio	254,620
Oriente	480,667	Camaguey	135,340

Population of principal cities in 1910:

Havana	319,884	Colon	52,006
Cienfuegos	70,416	Holquin	50,224
Camaguey	66,460	Pinar del Rio	50,071
Matanzas	64,385	Santa Clara	46,626
Manzanillo	54,900	Guantanamo	43,300
Santiago	53,614	Gibara	39,343

About 70 per cent of the population is white.

IMPORTS AND EXPORTS—The total imports in 1912 (calendar year) amounted to $118,937,000 and the exports to $146,676,000. The imports from the United States in 1913 were valued at $70,581,154 and the exports at $126,088,173. The principal articles of export are sugar, tobacco and cigars, iron and manganese ore, fruit, coffee, cocoa, molasses and sponges; of import, animals, breadstuffs, coal and

coke, iron and steel, wood, liquor, cotton, chemicals and vegetables.

HAITI.

President, Michel Oreste. The area of Haiti is 10,204 square miles and the population about 2,029,700. Coffee, cocoa and logwood are the leading articles sold. Total exports (1911), $7,682,000; imports, $7,948,117. Exports to the United States in 1913, $874,731; imports, $6,640,265.

SANTO DOMINGO.

President, Jose Borda Valdez. The republic has an area of 19,325 square miles and a population (1911) of 708,000. Santo Domingo, the capital, has 22,000 inhabitants. In 1911 the exports amounted to $11,032,366 and the chief articles shipped were coffee, cocoa and mahogany; imports, $7,126,877. Exports to the United States in 1913, $3,728,774; imports, $5,802,767.

UNITED STATES AND THE LATIN-AMERICAN REPUBLICS.

President Woodrow Wilson issued a formal statement of the policy which the administration proposed to follow with respect to the republics of Central and South America. The statement follows:

"One of the chief objects of my administration will be to cultivate the friendship and deserve the confidence of our sister republics of Central and South America and to promote in every proper and honorable way the interests which are common to the peoples of the two continents. I earnestly desire the most cordial understanding and co-operation between the peoples and leaders of America and therefore deem it my duty to make this brief statement.

"Co-operation is possible only when supported at every turn by the orderly processes of just government based on law, not upon arbitrary or irregular force. We hold, as I am sure all thoughtful leaders of republican government everywhere hold, that just government rests always upon the consent of the governed and that there can be no freedom without order based upon law and upon the public conscience and approval.

"We shall look to make these principles the basis of mutual intercourse, respect and helpfulness between our sister republics and ourselves. We shall lend our influence of every kind to the realization of these principles in fact and practice, knowing that disorder, personal intrigue and defiance of constitutional rights weaken and discredit government and injure none so much as the people who are unfortunate enough to have their common life and common affairs tainted and disturbed. We can have no sympathy with those who seek to seize the power of government to advance their own personal interests or ambition. We are the friends of peace, but we know that there can be no lasting or stable peace in such circumstances. As friends, therefore, we shall prefer those who act in the interest of peace and honor, who protect private rights and respect the restraints of constitutional provision. Mutual respect seems to us the indispensable foundation of friendship between states, as between individuals.

"The United States has nothing to seek in Central and South America except the lasting interests of the peoples of the two continents, the security of governments intended for the people and for no special group or interest, and the development of personal and trade relationships between the two continents which shall redound to the profit and advantage of both and interfere with the rights and liberties of neither.

"From these principles may be read so much of the future policy of this government as it is necessary now to forecast, and in the spirit of these principles I may, I hope, be permitted with as much confidence as earnestness to extend to the governments of all the republics of America the hand of genuine disinterested friendship and to pledge my own honor and the honor of my colleagues to every enterprise of peace and amity that a fortunate future may disclose."

THE MONROE AND DRAGO DOCTRINES.

The "Monroe doctrine" was enunciated by President Monroe in his message to congress Dec. 2, 1823. Referring to steps taken to arrange the respective rights of Russia, Great Britain and the United States on the northwest coast of this continent, the president went on to say:

"In the discussions to which this interest has given rise, and in the arrangements by which they may terminate, the occasion has been deemed proper for asserting, as a principle in which the rights and interests of the United States are involved, that the American continents, by the free and independent condition which they have assumed and maintain, are henceforth not to be considered as subjects for future colonization by any European power. * * * We owe it, therefore, to candor and to the amicable relations existing between the United States and those powers to declare that we should consider any attempt on their part to extend their system to any portion of this hemisphere as dangerous to our peace and safety. With the existing colonies or dependencies of any European power we have not interfered and shall not interfere. But with the governments who have declared their independence and maintain it, and whose independence we have, on great consideration and on just principles, acknowledged, we could not view any interposition for the purpose of oppressing them or controlling in any other manner their destiny by any European power in any other light than as the manifestation of an unfriendly disposition toward the United States."

DRAGO DOCTRINE.

When in the winter of 1902-03 Germany, Britain and Italy blockaded the ports of Venezuela in attempt to make the latter country settle up its debts Dr. L. F. Drago, a noted jurist of Argentina, maintained that force cannot be used by one power to collect money owing to its citizens by another power. Prominence was given to the contention by the fact that it was officially upheld by Argentina and favored by other South American republics. The principle embodied has become generally known as the "Drago doctrine."

LODGE RESOLUTION.

In connection with the reported attempt of Japan to obtain land for the establishment of a naval base in Magdalena bay, on the western coast of Mexico, the senate of the United States adopted the following resolution Aug. 2, 1912:

"Resolved, That when any harbor or other place in the American continents is so situated that the occupation thereof for naval or military purposes might threaten the communications or the safety of the United States, the government of the United States could not see without grave concern the possession of such harbor or other place by any corporation or association which has such relation to another government, not American, as to give that government practical power of control for national purposes."

COAST LINE OF THE UNITED STATES.

In nautical miles.

Atlantic coast	1,773	Hawaiian islands	628	Western rivers	4,344
Gulf coast	1,607	Guam	80	Total	17,539
Porto Rico	269	Midway	20	Philippines	11,444
Pacific coast	1,571	Samoan islands	83	Grand total	28,983
Alaska	4,123	Northern lakes and rivers	3,041		

COLONIES AND DEPENDENCIES OF NATIONS.

AUSTRIA-HUNGARY.

	Sq. miles.	Population.
Bosnia and Herzegovina	19,768	1,928,883

BELGIUM.

	Sq. miles.	Population.
Belgian Kongo	909,654	15,000,000

CHINA.

	Sq. miles.	Population.
Chinese Turkestan	550,330	1,200,000
Manchuria	363,610	16,000,000
Mongolia	1,367,600	2,600,000
Tibet	463,200	6,500,000

DENMARK.

	Sq. miles.	Population.
Greenland	46,740	11,893
Iceland	39,756	85,089
West Indies	138	27,086

FRANCE.

	Sq. miles.	Population.
Algeria	343,500	5,231,850
Annam	52,100	6,128,000
Cambodia	45,000	1,800,000
Cochin China	20,000	2,968,600
Comoro isles	620	86,000
Guadeloupe	689	182,110
Guiana	34,060	39,349
India, French	196	277,000
Kongo, French	669,280	5,000,000
Laos	98,400	650,000
Madagascar	228,015	2,701,000
Martinique	378	182,000
Mayotte	140	11,610
Morocco*	200,000	5,000,000
New Caledonia	7,200	55,800
Reunion	970	201,000
Sahara	1,544,000	800,000
St. Pierre and Miquelon	96	6,000
Somali coast	5,790	180,900
Tahiti, etc	1,544	30,000
Tonquin	46,400	10,000,000
Tunis	45,779	1,500,000
West Africa,* French:		
Dahomey		749,000
Guinea		1,498,000
Ivory coast	1,585,810	896,000
Mauretania		400,000
Senegal		915,000
Upper Senegal-Niger		4,415,000
*Protectorate.		

GREAT BRITAIN.

	Sq. miles.	Population.
Aden, Perim, Socotra	10,387	57,859
Ascension	34	400
Australia	3,065,120	4,727,005
Bahamas	4,404	55,944
Barbados	166	171,982
Basutoland	10,293	405,832
Bechuanaland	275,000	125,350
Bermuda	19	18,994
Borneo and Sarawak	73,106	700,000
British Guiana	90,500	296,041
British Honduras	8,598	40,510
British New Guinea	90,540	272,057
Canada	3,729,665	7,204,527
Cape of Good Hope	276,995	2,563,024
Ceylon	25,330	4,109,054
Cyprus	3,584	273,857
East Africa protectorate	202,000	2,295,336
Falkland islands	6,500	2,272
Federated Malay States	27,700	1,035,933
Fiji	7,740	139,541
Gambia	3,619	160,807
Gibraltar	2	19,596
Gold Coast	80,000	1,502,898
Hongkong	405	366,145
India	1,773,088	314,955,240
Jamaica	4,207	831,383
Leeward islands	701	127,189
Malta	117	228,442
Mauritius	850	374,625
Natal	35,371	1,191,958
Newfoundland-Labrador	162,734	242,966
New Zealand	104,751	1,071,428
Northern Nigeria	256,400	8,069,071
Nyasaland	39,801	970,199
Orange Free State	50,392	526,392
Rhodesia	439,575	1,770,871

	Sq. miles.	Population.
St. Helena	47	3,477
Seychelles	156	22,620
Sierra Leone	30,000	1,400,000
Solomon and Tonga islands	12,556	210,000
Somaliland	68,000	302,859
Southern Nigeria	77,260	7,836,189
Straits Settlements	1,630	707,523
Swaziland	6,536	99,959
Transvaal	110,426	1,676,611
Trinidad and Tobago	1,868	330,074
Turks and Caicos islands	166	5,615
Uganda	223,500	3,508,564
Weihaiwei	285	147,133
Windward islands	672	329,246
Zanzibar	1,020	197,199

GERMANY.

	Sq. miles.	Population.
Bismarck archipelago	20,000	189,000
Caroline islands	560	55,446
German East Africa	384,180	10,032,000
German New Guinea	95,160	322,300
German Southwest Africa	322,450	83,900
Kamerun	191,130	2,303,200
Kiauchau	200	33,000
Samoan islands	1,000	33,500
Togoland	33,700	1,000,000

GREECE.

	Sq. miles.	Population.
Crete	3,400	310,200

ITALY.

	Sq. miles.	Population.
Eritrea	45,800	450,000
Somaliland	139,430	400,000
Tripoli*	406,000	1,300,000
*Annexed in 1912.		

JAPAN.

	Sq. miles.	Population.
Chosen (Korea)	13,458	14,055,869
Formosa	13,458	3,392,063
Kwantung	1,256	462,399
Pescadores	50	65,410
Sakhalin	12,500	35,823

NETHERLANDS.

	Sq. miles.	Population.
Bali and Lombok	4,065	523,535
Banca	4,446	115,189
Billiton	1,863	36,858
Borneo	212,737	1,233,655
Celebes	72,010	851,905
Curacao	403	52,758
Dutch Guiana	46,060	78,124
Java and Madura	50,554	30,098,008
Molucca islands	43,864	407,906
New Guinea	151,789	200,000
Riau-Lingga archipelago	16,301	112,216
Sumatra	161,812	4,029,503
Timor	17,698	308,600

PORTUGAL.

	Sq. miles.	Population.
Angola	484,800	4,119,000
Cape Verde islands	1,480	147,424
Damao, Diu	169	56,285
East Africa	293,400	3,120,000
Goa	1,469	475,513
Guinea	13,940	820,000
Macao, etc	4	63,991
Prince's and St. Thomas	360	43,103
Timor	7,330	300,000

RUSSIA.

	Sq. miles.	Population.
Bokhara	83,000	1,250,000
Khiva	24,000	800,000

SPAIN.

	Sq. miles.	Population.
Fernando Po, etc	814	23,844
Rio de Oro and Adrar	73,000	12,000
Spanish Guinea	12,000	200,000

TURKEY.

	Sq. miles.	Population.
Samos	193	53,424
Egypt	400,000	11,139,978

UNITED STATES.

	Sq. miles.	Population.
Alaska	590,884	64,356
Guam	210	9,000
Hawaii	6,449	191,909
Panama canal zone	474	50,000
Porto Rico	3,435	1,118,012
Philippines	115,026	7,635,426
Samoan islands	77	6,100

NONCONTIGUOUS POSSESSIONS OF THE UNITED STATES.

THE PHILIPPINE ISLANDS.

The Philippine islands were ceded to the United States by Spain Dec. 10, 1898. Maj.-Gen. Merritt was the first military governor. He was succeeded in August, 1899, by Maj.-Gen. E. S. Otis, who in turn was followed in May, 1900, by Maj.-Gen. Arthur MacArthur. The last named remained in office until July 4, 1901, when the military author.ity was transferred to Gen. A. R. Chaffee. By order of the president Gen. Chaffee was relieved of his duties as military governor July 4, 1902, and the office terminated. The Philippine commission was at the same time made the superior authority. Sept. 2 the islands were divided into three military departments, to be known as the department of Luzon, the department of Visayas and the department of Mindanao.

July 1, 1902, congress passed an act providing temporarily for the government of the Philippines, providing for the election by popular vote, two years after a census of the islands had been taken and published, of delegates to an assembly, consisting of not more than 100 members nor less than fifty, apportioned among the provinces as nearly as possible according to population. This assembly should, together with the Philippine commission appointed by the president of the United States, exercise the legislative power heretofore exercised by the commission alone, the members of the commission acting as an upper house and the elected assemblymen as a lower house. The members of the assembly were to hold office two years and annual sessions of the legislature not exceeding ninety days in length were to be held.

The first election was held July 30, 1907, when eighty members of the legislature were chosen, the total vote being 97,803. The first session was formally opened Oct. 16 by William H. Taft, United States secretary of war, the first civil governor of the islands after they came into American possession. Sergio Osmena was elected president.

OFFICIALS AND SALARIES—The Philippine commission consisted in October, 1913, of Francis B. Harrison of New York, Henderson S. Martin of Kansas, Clinton L. Riggs of Maryland, Winfred T. Denison of New York, Rafael Palma, Victorino Mafa, Jaime C. de Veyra, Vicente Ilustre and Vicente Singson of the Philippines. The officers in 1913 were:

Governor-General—Francis Burton Harrison.
Vice-Governor—Henderson S. Martin.
Secretary Interior Department—Winfred T. Denison.
Secretary Finance and Justice—Victorino Mafa.
Secretary Public Instruction—Henderson S. Martin.
Secretary of Commerce and Police—Clinton L. Riggs.
Executive Secretary—Frank W. Carpenter.
Auditor—Clifford H. French.
Treasurer—Jeremiah L. Manning.
Director of Education—Frank L. Crone.
Director of Posts—C. M. Cotterman.
Attorney-General—Ignacio Villamor.
Chief Justice Supreme Court—Cayetano S. Arellano.

The governor receives $20,000 a year ($15,000 as governor-general) and the other American commissioners receive $15,500 each ($10,500 being for their services as heads of departments). The commissioners not heads of departments get $7,500 each. The salaries of other leading officials are: Executive secretary, $9,000; assistant executive secretary, $6,000; auditor, $6,000; collector of customs, $6,000; attorney-general, $6,000; chief justice Supreme court, $10,000; associate justices, $10,000; superintendent of public education, $6,000; director-general of posts, $6,000; treasurer, $6,000.

AREA AND POPULATION—The total land and water area of the Philippine archipelago is 832,968 square miles; land area, 115,026; population (est. 1912), 8,460,052. The population of Manila in 1910 was 234,409. The population of the principal islands in 1903 was: Bohol, 243,148; Cebu, 592,247; Jolo, 44,718; Leyte, 357,641; Luzon, 3,798,507; Marinduque, 50,601; Mindanao, 499,634, of whom 252,940 are uncivilized; Negros, 460,776 (21,217 uncivilized); Panay, 743,646 (14,933 uncivilized); Samar, 222,690.

PRODUCTS AND CLIMATE—The chief products are hemp, sugar, coffee, tobacco leaf, copra, cigars and indigo. Between 800,000 and 700,000 bales of hemp are exported annually.

The climate of the Philippine islands is considered excellent for the tropics. The mean temperature in Manila ranges from 77 in January to 83 in May. June, July, August and September are the rainy months, March, April and May the hot and dry, and October, November, December, January and February the temperate and dry.

TRADE WITH THE UNITED STATES—The shipments of merchandise from the United States to the Philippines in the fiscal year ended June 30, 1913, amounted in value to $25,360,646, as compared with $23,793,935 in 1912. The principal articles sent were: Breadstuffs, $1,726,839; cotton manufactures, $7,077,165; iron and steel manufactures, $5,475,840; mineral oils, $1,611,089. The imports into the United States amounted in value to $21,010,248, as compared with $23,257,199 in 1912. The principal articles imported were: Unmanufactured manila, $12,989,174; sugar, $4,549,199; tobacco, $2,326,264.

IMPORTS AND EXPORTS—The total imports of the Philippine islands in the fiscal year 1912 amounted to $54,549,980; total exports, $59,319,836.

ISLAND OF PORTO RICO.

Porto Rico, according to the decision of the United States Supreme court in the insular cases May 27, 1901, is a territory appurtenant and belonging to the United States, but not a part of the United States within the revenue clause of the constitution. The island was ceded to the United States by Spain Dec. 10, 1898, and was under military rule until the Foraker law went into effect May 1, 1900. In accordance with the third section of that act, the legislative assembly of Porto Rico having put into operation a system of local taxation to meet the necessities of government, President McKinley on the 25th of July, 1901—the anniversary of the landing of American troops on the island in 1898—proclaimed free trade between the United States and Porto Rico.

GOVERNMENT—Civil government, under the provisions of the Foraker act, was established May 1, 1900. The upper house consists of eleven members, six of whom are "cabinet" officers appointed by the president; the lower house is made up of thirty-five delegates elected by the people every two years. The governor, who is appointed by the president, has practically the same duties as the governor of any other territory of the United States. The present officers are: Governor, Arthur Yager; secretary, (vacancy); treasurer, Allan H. Richardson; commissioner of education, E. G. Dainter; attorney-general, Wolcott H. Pitkin, Jr.; auditor, J. W. Bonner; commissioner of interior, J. A. Wilson; director of labor, charities and correction, Manuel Camunas; United States district judge, Peter J. Hamilton; resident commissioner in the United States, Luis Munoz Rivera.

AREA AND POPULATION—The area of Porto Rico is 3,435 square miles and the population in 1910 was 1,118,012, of which 65.5 per cent was white, 30 per cent mulatto and 4.5 per cent black. The cities having more than 5,000 inhabitants in 1910 were: San Juan, 48,716; Ponce, 35,005; Mayaguez, 16,563; Arecibo, 9,612; Aguadilla, 6,125; Yauco, 6,589; Caguas, 10,354; Guayama, 8,321.

COMMERCE—For the year ended June 30, 1913, the total domestic exports from Porto Rico to foreign countries were $8,549,451, and to the United States, $40,529,665. Foreign imports amounted to $3,745,057, and imports from the United States amounted to $32,323,191. Of the exports Spain took $1,650,310; Cuba, $3,793,632; France, $1,258,810; Germany, $111,553; Austria-Hungary, $808,292.

The leading articles of export are coffee, oranges, brown sugar and tobacco.

TERRITORY OF HAWAII.

Annexed to the United States July 7, 1898.
Created a territory June 14, 1900.
Governor—L. E. Pinkham.
Secretary—Henry E. Cooper.
POPULATION—According to the federal census of 1910 the total population of the territory is 191,909,

In 1912 it was estimated at 200,065. The only large city is Honolulu, which in 1910 had a population of 52,183.

COMMERCE WITH THE UNITED STATES—The total value of the shipments of merchandise from Hawaii to the United States for the twelve months ended June 30, 1913, was $42,652,462. Brown sugar was the principal item, amounting to 1,056,244,887 pounds, valued at $35,235,170. The other articles of importance were: Coffee, $352,965; fruits, $3,779,572; rice, $185,943. The total value of the shipments of merchandise from the United States to Hawaii was $30,411,899. The principal articles were: Iron, steel and machinery, $6,269,813; leather and manufactures of, $751,260; oils, $1,963,792; provisions, $1,342,769; tobacco, $697.995; lumber and manufactures of wood, $2,139,023; wines and liquors, $825,856.

PANAMA CANAL ZONE.

Acquired by the United States, Feb. 26, 1904.
Area, 474 square miles.
Population (1911), 61,279.
Civil Governor—Richard L. Metcalfe.

TUTUILA.

Acquired by the United States January, 1900.
Area, including Manua and several other small islands, 77 square miles.
Population, about 7,200.
Merchandise shipped from United States (1912), $12,621; to the United States, $21,885.
Pango-Pango harbor acquired by United States in 1872.

GUAM.

Ceded to United States by Spain Dec. 10, 1898.
Area, 210 square miles.
Population, about 12,250.
Merchandise shipped from United States (1912), $55,634.
First American Governor—Capt. R. P. Leary, U. S. N.
Governor (1913)—Capt. Robert E. Coontz, U. S. N.

TERRITORY OF ALASKA.

Purchased from Russia in March, 1867.
Organized as noncontiguous possession July 27, 1868.
Made a civil and judicial district June 6, 1900.
Organized as territory of Alaska by act of Aug. 24, 1912.
Capital—Juneau.
Governor—J. E. A. Strong.
Secretary—William L. Distin.
Treasurer—W. G. Smith.

AREA AND POPULATION—Area, 590,884 square miles (land and water); population in 1910, 64,356, of which 25,331 were Indians.

LEGISLATURE—Senate has eight members, or two from each judicial district; house has sixteen members, or four from each judicial district; term of senators, four years; term of representatives, two years; compensation paid by government, $15 a day to each member during attendance at sessions and mileage at the rate of 15 cents a mile; sessions, biennial, beginning on first Monday in March of odd numbered years; limit of regular sessions, sixty days, and of special sessions, fifteen days; delegate to congress elected on Tuesday following first Monday of November every second year, beginning with 1914.

COMMERCE—The total value of the shipments of domestic merchandise from the mainland of the United States to Alaska in the year ended June 30, 1913, was $20,179,547. The principal articles were: Breadstuffs, $759,069; manufactures of cotton, $812,469; eggs, $436,165; fruits and nuts, $529,138; manufactures of iron and steel, $4,278,584; leather manufactures, $384,517; meat and dairy products, $2,357,590; wines and liquors, $721,593; tobacco, $636,363; vegetables, $508,507; wood and manufactures of, $1,003,912. Total value of shipments of domestic merchandise from Alaska to the mainland, $24,014,556. The main articles were: Copper ore, $3,579,474; canned salmon, $16,085,813; other fish, $969,813; furs, $751,345.

GOLD SHIPMENTS (1912)—From Alaska to the mainland, $14,707,027; from the mainland to Alaska, $1,239,045 in coin. The total gold and silver shipments, including foreign, to the United States were $18,997,273.

LOSS OF THE STEAMSHIP VOLTURNO.

Date—Oct. 9-10, 1913.
Place—Atlantic ocean, latitude 49:12 north, longitude 34:51 west.
Persons aboard—659.
Lives lost—134.
Lives saved—525.
Cause of disaster—Explosion of chemicals and fire.

The Volturno, a steamship of 3,396 tons belonging to the Uranium line, sailed from Rotterdam Oct. 2, 1913, for New York via Halifax with 22 cabin passengers, 538 steerage passengers and a crew of 99 officers and men. Most of those aboard were Russian, Dalmatian and Polish emigrants bound for Canada. Capt. Francis Inch was in command of the vessel. At 6:50 a. m. Oct. 9 fire was reported in hold No. 1, in the forward part of the ship, and in a few minutes the flames burst through to the deck. So rapidly did the fire gain headway that the watch below was imprisoned and burned to death. A series of explosions followed, wrecking the saloon and hospital amidship and damaging the compass and steering gear. Calls for help were sent out by the wireless operators and an attempt was made to launch lifeboats, though the ship was rolling heavily. Two were smashed, but two others got away from the vessel. Both were lost in the heavy sea with all their occupants.

At 11 a. m. the Carmania arrived in response to the wireless appeal for aid, and other steamers put

in an appearance from time to time until eleven in all were on the scene. They were, in addition to the Carmania, the Seydlitz, Kroonland, Grosser Kurfuerst, La Touraine, Narragansett, Devonian, Czar, Minneapolis, Rappahannock and New York (a tank steamer). On account of the rough sea boats could not be successfully launched until late in the evening and then they were not able to get close to the burning vessel. Some of the passengers equipped with life preservers jumped into the sea and were picked up. Toward daybreak of the 10th the wind moderated and the captain of the Narragansett had fifty barrels of oil pumped out near the stern of the Volturno. This had the effect of calming the stormy waters and enabling small boats to approach the burning ship's side and receive the passengers lowered to them with ropes. The captain was the last to leave the ship. The survivors were divided among the rescuing ships, some being brought back to Europe and others being taken to America, according to the destinations of the various vessels.

The cause of the fire, according to the statement of Waldron Diselman, third officer of the Volturno, was the explosion of a drum containing chemicals. He asserted that of those who perished more than eighty were burned to death, while the others lost their lives through the smashing or sinking of the lifeboats.

GETTYSBURG SEMI-CENTENNIAL.

The fiftieth anniversary of the battle of Gettysburg was observed on the historic battle field July 1-4, 1913. To meet the expenses of the occasion Pennsylvania contributed $435,000 and the United States government $150,000 together with the use of camp equipage and the services of officers and troops. Some 55,000 veterans, of whom 9,000 were former confederate soldiers, took part in the encampment and exercises. Addresses were made by President Woodrow Wilson, Alfred B. Beers, commander-in-chief of the Grand Army of the Republic; Bennett H. Young, commander-in-chief of the United Confederate Veterans, and by many others. The tents occupied by the veterans were pitched on part of the ground over which Gen. Pickett's famous charge was made.

MINNESOTA RATE CASE DECISION.

The following brief chronology will give the successive steps taken in the adjudication of the Minnesota railroad rate case, involving the right of a state to control the railroads within its borders:

April 4, 1907—Minnesota legislature passes act reducing railroad rates 33½ per cent.

April 18, 1907—Legislature enacts law reducing commodity rates 7.377 per cent.

May 31, 1907—Stockholders of the Great Northern, Northern Pacific and Minneapolis & St. Louis railroads sue for injunction to prevent enforcing of new rates.

July 8, 1907—Judge Lochren grants temporary injunction against the state, but the new rates, except as to commodities, are put in force pending court decision.

October, 1907—Attorney-General Young seeks mandamus to enforce commodity rates; he is arrested and fined $100 for contempt of court.

March 23, 1908—United States Supreme court holds rate law unconstitutional, but later grants a rehearing of the case.

April 22, 1908—C. F. Otis is appointed master in chancery to take testimony in rate case, appointment being made by Judge W. H. Sanborn.

Sept. 21, 1910—Otis reports in favor of railroads on all points.

April 8, 1910—Judge Sanborn files his decision sustaining the findings of Otis.

May 15, 1911—State appeals to United States Supreme court.

June 9, 1913—Supreme court upholds state.

Following is the text of the decision of the Supreme court as announced by Justice Hughes:

1. The constitution gives congress an authority at all times adequate to secure the freedom of interstate commercial intercourse from state control and to provide effective regulation of that intercourse as the national interests may demand.

2. The commerce that is confined within one state and does not affect other states is reserved to the state. This reservation is only of that power which is consistent with the grant to congress. The authority of congress extends to every part of interstate commerce and to every instrumentality or agency by which it is carried on, and the full control by congress over the subjects committed to its regulation is not to be denied or thwarted by the commingling of interstate and intrastate operations.

3. Even without action by congress, the commerce clause of the constitution necessarily excludes the states from direct control of subjects embraced within the clause which are of such nature that, if regulated at all, their regulation should be prescribed by a single authority. There is thus secured the essential immunity of interstate intercourse from the imposition by the states of direct burdens and restraints.

4. But there remains to the states the exercise of the power appropriate to their territorial jurisdiction in making suitable provision for local needs. The state may provide local improvements, create and regulate local facilities and adopt protective measures of a reasonable character in the interest of the health, safety, morals and welfare of its people, although interstate commerce may incidentally or indirectly be involved.

Where matters falling within the state power, as above described, are also by reason of their relation to interstate commerce within the reach of the federal power, congress must be the judge of the necessity of federal action, and until congress acts the state may act.

The paramount authority of congress enables it to intervene at its discretion for the complete and effective government of that which has been committed to its care, and for this purpose and to this extent in response to a conviction of national need to displace local laws by substituting laws of its own.

State regulation of railroad rates began with railroad transportation. The authority of the state to prescribe what shall be reasonable charges for intrastate transportation is statewide, unless it be limited by the exertion of the constitutional power of congress with respect to interstate commerce and its instruments,

As a power appropriate to the territorial jurisdiction of the state it is not confined to a part of the state, but extends throughout the state—to its cities adjacent to its boundaries as well as to those in the interior of the state. If this authority of the state be restricted it must be by virtue of the actual exercise of federal control and not by reason merely of a dormant federal power—that is, one which has not been exerted.

6. Congress, in the act to regulate commerce, expressly provided that the provisions of the act should not extend to transportation "wholly within one state."

Having regard to the terms of the federal statute, the familiar range of state action at the time it was enacted, exercise of state authority in the same manner and to the same extent after its enactment and the decisions of this court recognizing and upholding this authority, the court finds no foundation for the proposition that the act to regulate commerce contemplated interference with the authority of the state to prescribe reasonable rates for the exclusive internal traffic throughout the extent of its territory.

Neither by the original act nor by its amendment has congress sought to establish a unified control over interstate and intrastate rates; it has not set up a standard for intrastate rates or prescribed or authorized the federal commission to prescribe either maximum or minimum rates for intrastate traffic. The fixing of reasonable rates for intrastate transportation was left by the act where it had been found—that is, with the states and the agencies created by the states to deal with the subject.

7. Under the established principles governing state action, Minnesota did not transcend the limits of its authority in prescribing the rates here involved, assuming them to be reasonable intrastate rates. It exercised an authority appropriate to its territorial jurisdiction and not opposed to any action thus far taken by congress.

8. The interblending of operations in the conduct of interstate and local business by interstate carriers, and the exigencies that are said to arise with respect to the maintenance of interstate rates by reason of their relation to intrastate rates, are considerations for the practical judgment of congress. If the situation has become such that adequate regulation of interstate rates cannot be maintained without imposing requirements with respect to such intrastate rates of interstate carriers as substantially affect interstate rates it is for congress to determine, within the limits of its constitutional authority over interstate commerce and its instruments, the measure of the regulation it should supply.

It is the function of the court to interpret and apply the law already enacted, but not, under the guise of construction, to provide a more comprehensive scheme of regulation than congress has decided on. Nor in the absence of federal action may effect be denied to the laws of the state enacted within the field which it is entitled to occupy until its authority is limited through the exertion by congress of its paramount constitutional power.

On the issue of confiscation: The rate making power is a legislative power and necessarily implies a range of legislative discretion. The court does not sit as a board of review to substitute its judgment for that of the legislature or of the commission lawfully constituted by it as to matters within the province of either.

The question is whether in prescribing a general schedule of rates involving the profitableness of the intrastate operations of the carrier, taken as a whole, the state has superseded the constitutional limit by making the rates confiscatory. The property of the railroad corporation has been devoted to a public use. But the state has not seen fit to undertake the service itself and the private property embarked in it is not placed at the mercy of legislative caprices. It rests secure under the constitutional protection which extends not merely to the title but to the right to receive just compensation for the services given to the public.

10. In the cases of Northern Pacific and Great Northern companies, on the examination of estimates of value and methods of apportionment, it

is concluded that the proof is insufficient to justify a finding that the rates were confiscatory, and the decrees are reversed with instructions to dismiss the bill in each case without prejudice.

11. In the case of the Minneapolis & St. Louis Railroad company it is found, in view of the special facts appearing, that the margin of error in the estimates and calculations was not sufficient to affect the result.

The decree in that case, adjudging the rates to be confiscatory, is therefore affirmed with the modification that the members of the railroad and warehouse commission and the attorney-general of the state may apply to the court by bill or otherwise as they may be advised to a further order or decree whenever it shall appear that by reason of a change in circumstances the rates fixed by the state's acts and orders are sufficient to yield to this company reasonable compensation for the service rendered.

THE SHERMAN ANTITRUST LAW.

Passed by the 51st congress and approved July 2, 1890.

Section 1. Every contract, combination in the form of trust or otherwise or conspiracy in restraint of trade or commerce among the several states or with foreign nations is hereby declared to be illegal. Every person who shall make any such contract or engage in any such combination or conspiracy shall be deemed guilty of a misdemeanor, and, on conviction thereof, shall be punished by fine not exceeding $5,000 or by imprisonment not exceeding one year, or by both said punishments, in the discretion of the court.

Sec. 2. Every person who shall monopolize or attempt to monopolize or combine or conspire with any person or persons to monopolize any part of the trade or commerce among the several states or with foreign nations shall be deemed guilty of a misdemeanor, and on conviction thereof shall be punished by fine not exceeding $5,000 or by imprisonment not exceeding one year, or by both said punishments, in the discretion of the court.

Sec. 3. Every contract, combination in form of trust or otherwise or conspiracy in restraint of trade or commerce in any territory of the United States or of the District of Columbia, or in restraint of trade or commerce between any such territory and another, or between any such territory or territories and any state or states or the District of Columbia or with foreign nations, or between the District of Columbia and any state or states or foreign nations, is hereby declared illegal. Every person who shall make any such contract or engage in any such combination or conspiracy shall be deemed guilty of a misdemeanor, and on conviction thereof shall be punished by fine not exceeding $5,000 or by imprisonment not exceeding one year, or by both said punishments, in the discretion of the court.

Sec. 4. The several Circuit courts of the United States are hereby invested with jurisdiction to prevent or restrain violations of this act; and it shall be the duty of the several district attorneys of the United States, in their respective districts, under the direction of the attorney-general, to institute proceedings in equity to prevent and restrain such violations. Such proceedings may be by way of petition setting forth the case and praying that such violation shall be enjoined or otherwise prohibited. When the parties complained of shall have been duly notified of such petition the court shall proceed, as soon as may be, to the hearing and determination of the case; and pending such petition and before final decree the court may at any time make such temporary restraining order or prohibition as shall be deemed just in the premises.

Sec. 5. Whenever it shall appear to the court before which any proceeding under section 4 of this act may be pending that the ends of justice require that other parties should be brought before the court the court may cause them to be summoned, whether they reside in the district in which the court is held or not; and subpœnas to that end may be served in any district by the marshal thereof.

Sec. 6. Any property owned under any contract or by any combination or pursuant to any conspiracy (and being the subject thereof) mentioned in section 1 of this act and being in the course of transportation from one state to another or to a foreign country shall be forfeited to the United States and may be seized and condemned by like proceedings as those provided by law for the forfeiture, seizure and condemnation of property imported into the United States contrary to law.

Sec. 7. Any person who shall be injured in his business or property by any other person or corporation by reason of anything forbidden or declared unlawful by this act may sue therefor in any Circuit court of the United States in the district in which the defendant resides or is found, without respect to the amount in controversy, and shall recover threefold the damages by him sustained and the cost of suit, including a reasonable attorney's fee.

Sec. 8. That the word "person" or "persons" wherever used in this act be deemed to include corporations and associations existing under or authorized by the laws of either the United States, the laws of any of the territories, the laws of any state or the laws of any foreign country.

FOUNDATION FOR THE PROMOTION OF INDUSTRIAL PEACE.

Established in 1907.

In 1906 President Theodore Roosevelt was awarded the Alfred B. Nobel peace prize and at his suggestion an act was passed by congress March 2, 1907, establishing the Foundation for the Promotion of Industrial Peace. To this organization he turned over the money received from the Nobel committee to be used as the nucleus of a fund the income of which is to be used in promoting an annual conference in Washington between representatives of capital and of labor with a view to bringing about a better understanding between employers and employes, thus promoting industrial peace. The chief justice of the United States Supreme court, the secretary of agriculture and the secretary of commerce and labor, and their successors in office, and four persons appointed by the president of the United States to represent capital, labor and the general public, are the trustees. The trustees are authorized to pay over the funds from time to time to a committee of nine members, known as "the industrial peace committee," whose duty it is to make arrangements for the conferences.

THE SAGE FOUNDATION.

March 12, 1907, Mrs. Russell Sage of New York announced that she had set aside the sum of $10,-000,000 to be known as the Sage Foundation and to be devoted to the improvement of the social and living conditions in the United States. As trustees she appointed Robert W. DeForest, Cleveland H. Dodge, Daniel C. Gilman, John M. Glenn, Miss Helen Gould, Mrs. William B. Rice and Miss Louise L. Schuyler.

Following is a part of the statement given out by Mrs. Sage as to the object of the gift: "I have set aside $10,000,000 for the endowment of this foundation. Its object is the improvement of social and living conditions in the United States. The means to that end will include research, publication, education, the establishment and maintenance of charitable and beneficial activities, agencies and institutions and the aid of any such activities, agencies and institutions already established."

IMPEACHMENT OF GOV. WILLIAM SULZER OF NEW YORK.

Aug. 13, 1913, William Sulzer, governor of New York, was impeached by the lower house of the state legislature by a vote of 79 to 45. Stripped of legal verbiage, the articles of impeachment were as follows:

1. That Gov. Sulzer, in filing his statement of campaign expenses in 1912, set forth that his entire receipts were $5,460 and his expenditures $7,724; that this statement "was false and was intended by him to be false"; that his list of receipts failed to include eleven specific contributions, ranging in amount from $100 to $2,500.

2. That Gov. Sulzer attached to his statement of campaign expenses an affidavit declaring that the statement was "a full and detailed statement of all moneys received or contributed or expended by him directly or indirectly." That this affidavit "was false and was corruptly made by him," and that he was "guilty of willful and corrupt perjury."

3. That Gov. Sulzer "was guilty of mal and corrupt conduct in his office as governor and was guilty of bribing witnesses." The specific charge was that while the Frawley committee was investigating the governor's campaign accounts he "fraudulently induced" three witnesses (his campaign manager, a personal friend and a stock broker) "to withhold their testimony from said committee."

4. That the governor was guilty of "suppressing evidence" in violation of the state penal law. The specific charge is that he "practiced deceit and fraud and used threats and menaces with intent to prevent the Frawley committee from procuring the attendance and testimony of certain witnesses."

5. That the governor was guilty of "preventing and dissuading a witness from attending under a subpoena" the sessions of the Frawley committee. The witness referred to was Frederick L. Colwell, alleged to have acted as Sulzer's agent in certain stock transactions.

6. That prior to his election the governor appropriated campaign contributions to his own use, "and used the same, or a large part thereof, in speculating in stocks * * * and thereby stole such checks and was guilty of larceny."

7. That Gov. Sulzer promised and threatened to use the authority and influence of his office for the purpose of affecting the vote or political action of certain public officers, including two assemblymen.

8. That he "corruptly used his authority as governor to affect the prices of securities on the New York stock exchange, in some of which he was speculating."

The case was called for trial Sept. 18 at the bar of the court of impeachment, consisting in New York of the state senate (forty-eight members) and the nine judges of the Court of Appeals. A two-thirds vote was necessary to convict. Chief Judge Edgar M. Cullen of the Court of Appeals presided. D. Cady Herrick of Albany was chief counsel for the governor and Alton B. Parker for the managers on the part of the assembly. Efforts to exclude certain senators from sitting as members of the court and to declare the proceedings void on the ground of unconstitutionality failed and the case went to trial. Gov. Sulzer refused to appear personally and did not testify. While the trial was in progress Justice Hasbrouck of the Supreme court of New York decided that the governor was impeached in regular form and until a verdict was reached was divested of the right to exercise executive functions.

Oct. 16 Gov. Sulzer was found guilty of the offenses charged in four of the articles of impeachment. These articles and the votes upon them were:

Article 1—Charging the governor with making a false statement of campaign receipts and payments. Guilty, 39; not guilty, 18.

Article 2—Charging him with perjury in swearing that the statement was true. Guilty, 39; not guilty, 18.

Article 3—Charging him with bribing witnesses to withhold testimony from the Frawley committee. Not guilty by unanimous vote.

Article 4—Charging him with "practicing deceit and fraud and using threats and menaces" to suppress testimony desired by the Frawley committee. Guilty, 43; not guilty, 14.

The court voted not guilty as to the charges in the other four articles Oct. 17, and then by a vote of 43 to 12 ordered the removal of William Sulzer from the office of governor of New York. It was decided unanimously that he should not be disqualified from holding further office. As a result of the impeachment of Mr. Sulzer, Martin H. Glynn, lieutenant-governor, became governor of New York.

FORMER IMPEACHMENTS.

Seven other governors in the United States have faced impeachment proceedings. These men and the results that followed were:

Charles Robinson, Kansas, 1862; acquitted.
Harrison Reed, Florida, 1868; charges dropped.
William W. Holden, North Carolina, 1870; removed.
Powell Clayton, Arkansas, 1871; charges dropped.
David Butler, Nebraska, 1871; removed.
Henry C. Warmoth, Louisiana, 1872; term expired and proceedings dropped.
Adelbert Ames, Mississippi, 1876; resigned.

CIRCUIT JUDGE ROBERT W. ARCHBALD IMPEACHED.

Robert W. Archbald, Circuit judge of the United States from the 3d judicial circuit and designated to serve as a member of the Commerce court, was removed from office by the United States senate, sitting as a court of impeachment, Jan. 13, 1913. Proceedings against the judge were begun in the house of representatives in Washington, D. C., July 11, 1912, when a resolution that he be impeached for misbehavior and for high crimes and misdemeanors was passed. Thirteen articles of impeachment were presented to the senate July 15 and the trial of the case was begun Dec. 2, Judge Archbald being represented by A. S. Worthington and R. W. Archbald, Jr. Voting on the charges took place in the senate Jan. 13, the respondent being found guilty on five of the counts and not guilty as to the other eight.

The first article of impeachment charged Judge Archbald with having, while holding the office of United States Circuit judge and being a member of the Commerce court, unlawfully entered into a partnership for the purchase of the Katydid culm dump in Pennsylvania and with having used his influence to force corporations involved in litigation before the tribunal of which he was a member to sell their property. Sixty-eight senators said "guilty" and five said "not guilty." The five voting "not guilty" were Burnham of New Hampshire, Catron of New Mexico, Oliver and Penrose of Pennsylvania, Mr. Archbald's state, and Paynter of Kentucky.

On the second article, also charging high crime and misdemeanor in connection with seeking to settle favorably to certain corporations litigation before the interstate commerce commission, the verdict was "not guilty." Forty-six senators voted "guilty," but twenty-five voted "not guilty," the two-thirds necessary to convict not being shown. On the third article, charging Judge Archbald with corrupt use of his official position and influence to obtain an agreement with the Lehigh Valley Coal company, the vote was 60 to 11 for conviction. The fourth charge, involving an improper request upon an attorney for a railroad company on Judge Archbald's part, was sustained by a vote of 52 to 20.

On the fifth article, charging a wrongful attempt on the part of Judge Archbald to insist on obtaining an operating lease on a coal dump owned by the Philadelphia and Reading Coal and Iron company, only six senators voted "not guilty." These included the five who voted in Judge Archbald's favor on the initial roll call and Senator Clark of Wyoming.

Twenty-four senators voted "guilty" and forty-five "not guilty" on article 6, which charged Judge Archbald with a corrupt attempt to influence the Lehigh Valley Coal company and the Lehigh Val-

ley Railway company to purchase a certain interest in a tract of coal land.

The seventh to twelfth articles of impeachment, inclusive, involved acts alleged to have been committed by the respondent while he was a judge of the District court of Pennsylvania. The vote was "not guilty" by 65 to 1.

The thirteenth article was a sort of summary of the charges embraced in the preceding twelve articles and some dozen or more senators demanded that they be excused from voting on it. They declared they would be embarrassed in voting "guilty" or "not guilty" on a group of charges that would make some of their previous votes inconsistent.

All these senators had voted "guilty" on some of the preceding counts and "not guilty" on the others. When the roll call was finally taken forty-two senators voted "guilty" and twenty "not guilty,"

At the conclusion of the roll call on the thirteenth charge, Senator O'Gorman of New York offered a resolution as follows:

"Ordered, That the respondent, Robert W. Archbald, Circuit judge of the United States for the 3d circuit, and designated to serve as a member of the Commerce court, be and he is hereby removed from office and that he be forever disqualified from holding and enjoying any office of honor, trust or profit under the United States."

Then, in the moments leading to the climax of the trial, the roll was called on the question of disqualifying the impeached jurist from holding office in the future.

Those who voted "yea" on this proposition were:

Ashurst.
Borah.
Bourne.
Bristow.
Brown.
Bryan.
Chamberlain.
Clapp.
Clarke (Ark.).
Crawford.
Culberson.
Cummins.
Dixon.
Fletcher.
Gore.
Gronna.
Hitchcock.
Johnson.
Kenyon.
Kern.
LaFollette.
Martin.
Martine.
Newlands.
O'Gorman.
Owen.
Page.
Poindexter.
Perky.
Pomerene.
Reed.
Shively.
Simmons.
Smith (Ark.)
Smith (Md.)
Stone.
Swanson.
Tillman.
Williams.
Total, 39.

Those who voted "nay" were:

Bacon.
Bankhead.
Brandegee.
Burnham.
Burton.
Catron.
Clark (Wyo.).
Crane.
Cullom.
Curtis.
Du Pont.
Foster.
Gallinger.
Jones.
Lippett.
Lodge.
McCumber.
McLean.
Nelson.
Oliver.
Paynter.
Penrose.
Perkins.
Richardson.
Root.
Sanders.
Smith (Ga.).
Smoot.
Stephenson.
Sutherland.
Thornton.
Townsend.
Warren.
Wetmore.
Works.
Total, 35.

It required merely a majority vote to adopt the resolution removing Mr. Archbald from office and to disqualify him for future official preferment, whereas on all the charges involving the question of guilt a two-thirds vote was necessary to convict.

RECORD OF IMPEACHMENTS.

The senate has sat as a court of impeachment in the cases of the following accused officials, with the result stated:

William Blount, senator from Tennessee, in 1793; charges dismissed for want of jurisdiction, Blount having resigned previously.

John Pickering, judge of the United States District court for New Hampshire; removed from office in 1804.

Samuel Chase, associate justice of the Supreme court of the United States; acquitted 1805.

James H. Peck, judge of the United States District court for Missouri; acquitted 1831.

West H. Humphreys, judge of the United States District court for Tennessee; removed from office, 1862.

Andrew Johnson, president of the United States; acquitted 1868.

William W. Belknap, secretary of war; acquitted 1876.

Charles Swayne, judge of the United States District court for the northern district of Florida; acquitted 1905.

Robert W. Archbald, associate judge of the United States Commerce court; convicted 1913.

NATIONAL HYMNS OF VARIOUS COUNTRIES.

Following is a list of songs used as national hymns or anthems in various countries of the world:

United States—"The Star Spangled Banner."* "America" and "Hail, Columbia" are also used as national songs.

Great Britain—"God Save the King."

Germany—"Die Wacht am Rhein" (The Watch on the Rhine).

France—"La Marseillaise."

Austria—"Gott Erhalte Unsern Kaiser" (God Preserve Our Emperor).

Hungary—"Isten Aid Meg a Magyart" (Lord, Bless the Hungarian).

Belgium—"La Brabanconne" (Song of the Brabantines).

Denmark—"Kong Kristian Stod Ved Holen Mast" (King Christian Stood Beside the Lofty Mast).

Norway—"Ja, Vi Elsker Dette Landet" (Yes, We Love This Land).

Sweden—"Fosterjorden" (Land of My Birth).

Finland—"Vaart Land" (Our Land).

Russia—"God Preserve the Czar."

Italy—"Marcia Reale Italiana" (Royal Italian March).

Mexico—"Mexicanos, al Grito de Guerra" (Mexicans, at the Cry of War).

Wales—"Land of My Fathers."

*Official in navy.

THE UNITED STATES CENSUS BUREAU.

The bureau of the census in the department of commerce and labor, Washington, D. C., is charged with the duty of taking the periodical censuses of the United States and of collecting such special statistics as are required by congress, including statistics of births and deaths in registration areas, statistics of the cotton production of the country as returned by the ginners, the consumption of cotton and statistics of cities having 30,000 or more inhabitants.

The act passed at the extra session of the 61st

congress and approved July 2, 1909, for the taking of the thirteenth and subsequent censuses provided that a census should be taken of the population, agriculture, manufactures and mines and quarries of the United States in 1910 and every ten years thereafter, and that it should include each state and territory on the mainland, the District of Columbia, Alaska, Hawaii and Porto Rico. An assistant director, a geographer, a chief statistician and other officers and clerks in addition to the regular force in the census office were provided for.

HEIGHT OF SOME FAMOUS STRUCTURES.

Structure.	Feet.	Structure.	Feet.	Structure.	Feet.	Structure.	Feet.
Amiens cathedral	383	Cologne cathedral	512	Milan cathedral	360	St. Peter's, Rome	433
Bunker Hill mon't	221	Eiffel tower	984	Pyramid, Great	451	Strassburg cathedral	465
Capitol, Washington	288	Florence cathedral	387	Rouen cathedral	464	St. Stephen's, Vienna	470
City hall, Phila	535	Fribourg cathedral	386	St. Paul's, London	404	Washington mon'm't	556

PRESIDENTIAL VOTE (1828-1912).

YR.	Candidate.	Party.	Popular vote.	Per cent.	Electoral vote.	YR.	Candidate.	Party.	Popular vote.	Per cent.	Electoral vote.
1828	Jackson	Democrat.	647,231	55.97	178	1884	Blaine	Republican	4,848,334	48.27	182
1828	Adams	Federal	509,097	44.03	83	1884	Butler	Greenback.	133,825	1.33	....
1832	Jackson	Democrat.	687,502	54.96	219	1884	St. John	Prohibition	151,809	1.51	....
1832	Clay	Whig.	530,189	42.39	49	1888	Cleveland	Democrat..	5,540,050	48.66	168
1832	Floyd	Whig.			11	1888	Harrison	Republican	5,444,337	47.82	233
1832	Wirt	Anti-M	} 33,108	2.65	7	1888	Streeter	Union Lab.	146,897	1.29	....
1836	Van Buren	Democrat.	761,549	50.83	170	1888	Fisk	Prohibition	250,125	2.20	....
1836	Harrison	Whig			73	1888	Cowdrey	United Lab	2,808	.03	....
1836	White	Whig			26	1892	Cleveland	Democrat.	5,554,414	46.04	277
1836	Webster	Whig	} 736,656	49.17	14	1892	Harrison	Republican	5,190,802	43.02	145
1836	Mangum	Whig.			11	1892	Bidwell	Prohibition	271,058	2.24	....
1840	Van Buren	Democrat.	1,128,702	46.82	60	1892	Weaver	People's.	1,027,329	8.51	22
1840	Harrison	Whig.	1,275,017	52.89	234	1892	Wing	Socialist..	21,164	.19	....
1840	Birney	Liberty.	7,059	.39	....	1896	McKinley	Republican	7,035,638	50.88	271
1844	Polk	Democrat.	1,337,243	49.55	170	1896	Bryan	Democrat..	6,467,946	46.77	176
1844	Clay	Whig.	1,299,068	48.14	105	1896	Levering	Prohibition	141,676	1.03	....
1844	Birney	Liberty.	62,300	2.31	....	1896	Bentley	National	13,969	.10	....
1848	Taylor	Whig.	1,360,101	47.36	163	1896	Matchett	Soc. Labor.	36,454	.27	....
1848	Cass	Democrat.	1,220,544	42.50	107	1896	Palmer	Nat. Dem..	131,529	.95	....
1848	Van Buren	Free Soil.	291,263	10.14	....	1900	McKinley	Republican.	7,219,530	51.69	292
1852	Pierce	Democrat.	1,601,474	51.03	254	1900	Bryan	Democrat..	6,358,071	45.51	155
1852	Scott	Whig.	1,380,578	43.99	42	1900	Woolley	Prohibition	209,166	1.49	....
1852	Hale	Free Soil.	156,149	4.98	....	1900	Barker	People's..	50,232	.37	....
1856	Buchanan	Democrat.	1,838,169	45.34	174	1900	Debs	Soc. Dem.	94,768	.67	....
1856	Fremont	Republican	1,341,264	33.09	114	1900	Malloney	Soc. Lab..	32,751	.23	....
1856	Fillmore	American.	874,534	21.57	8	1900	Leonard	United Chr.	518	.00	....
1860	Douglas	Democrat.	1,375,157	29.40	12	1900	Ellis	Union R...	5,098	.04	....
1860	Breckinridge	Democrat.	845,763	18.08	72	1904	Roosevelt	Republican	7,628,834	56.41	336
1860	Lincoln	Republican	1,866,352	39.91	180	1904	Parker	Democrat.	5,084,491	37.60	140
1860	Bell	Union	589,581	12.61	39	1904	Swallow	Prohibition	259,257	1.91	....
1864	McClellan	Democrat.	1,808,725	55.06	21	1904	Debs	Socialist..	402,460	2.98	....
1864	Lincoln	Republican	2,216,067	41.94	216	1904	Watson	People's..	114,753	.85	....
1868	Seymour	Democrat.	2,709,013	47.33	80	1904	Corregan	Soc. Lab..	33,724	.25	....
1868	Grant	Republican	3,015,071	52.67	214	1904	Holcomb	Continental	830	.00	....
1872	Greeley	Democrat.	2,834,079	43.83	*66	1908	Taft	Republican	7,679,006	51.58	321
1872	O'Conor	Ind. Dem.	29,408	.45	....	1908	Bryan	Democrat..	6,409,106	43.05	162
1872	Grant	Republican	3,597,070	55.63	292	1908	Chafin	Prohibition	252,683	1.69	....
1872	Black	T'mpera'ce	5,608	.09	....	1908	Debs	Socialist...	420,820	2.83	....
1876	Tilden	Democrat.	4,284,885	50.94	184	1908	Watson	People's...	28,131	.19	....
1876	Hayes	Republican	4,033,950	47.95	185	1908	Hisgen	Ind'p'nd'ec	83,562	.56	....
1876	Cooper	Greenback.	81,740	.97	....	1908	Gillhaus	Soc. Lab...	13,825	.10	....
1876	Smith	Prohibition	9,522	.11	....	1908	Turney	Untd. Chr..	461	.00	....
1876	Walker	American.	2,636	.03	....	1912	Wilson	Democrat..	6,286,214	41.82	435
1880	Hancock	Democrat.	4,442,035	48.23	155	1912	Roosevelt	Progressive	4,126,020	27.45	88
1880	Garfield	Republican	4,449,053	48.31	214	1912	Taft	Republican	3,483,922	23.17	8
1880	Weaver	Greenback.	307,306	3.34	....	1912	Debs	Socialist...	897,011	5.97	....
1880	Dow	Prohibition	10,487	.11	....	1912	Chafin	Prohibition	208,923	1.39	....
1880	Phelps	American.	707	.01	....	1912	Reimer	Soc. Lab...	29,079	.20	....
1884	Cleveland	Democrat.	4,911,017	48.89	219						

*Owing to the death of Mr. Greeley, the 66 electoral votes were variously cast. Thomas A. Hendricks received 42, B. Gratz Brown 18, Horace Greeley 3, Charles J. Jenkins 2, David Davis 1.

PARTY PLURALITIES AND TOTAL VOTE.

Year.	Plurality.— Republican.	Democratic.	Total vote.	Year.	Plurality.— Republican.	Democratic.	Total vote.
1828	....	138,134	1,156,328	1872	762,991	....	6,466,165
1832	....	157,313	1,250,789	1876	....	250,935	8,412,733
1836	....	24,893	1,498,205	1880	7,018	......	9,209,588
1840	146,315*	....	2,410,778	1884	......	62,683	10,044,985
1844	....	38,175	3,695,611	1888	....	95,713	11,384,216
1848	139,557*	......	2,871,928	1892	......	363,612	12,064,767
1852	....	220,796	3,133,301	1896	567,692	......	13,827,212
1856	....	496,905	4,053,967	1900	861,459	......	13,970,134
1860	491,195	......	4,676,863	1904	2,544,343	......	13,524,349
1864	407,342	......	4,024,792	1908	1,269,900	......	†14,887,594
1868	305,458	......	5,724,684	1912	......	2,160,194	15,031,169

*Whig. †Includes 461 votes cast for united Christian party.

THE ELECTORAL COLLEGE.

Following is the electoral vote of the states, based upon the apportionment of representatives made by congress under the census of 1910:

State.	Vote.	State.	Vote.	State.	Vote.	State.	Vote.
Alabama	12	Indiana	15	Missouri	18	Rhode Island	5
Arizona	3	Iowa	13	Montana	4	South Carolina	9
Arkansas	9	Kansas	10	Nebraska	8	South Dakota	5
California	13	Kentucky	13	Nevada	3	Tennessee	12
Colorado	6	Louisiana	10	New Hampshire	4	Texas	20
Connecticut	7	Maine	6	New Jersey	14	Utah	4
Delaware	3	Maryland	8	New Mexico	3	Vermont	4
Florida	6	Massachusetts	18	New York	45	Virginia	12
Georgia	14	Michigan	15	North Carolina	12	Washington	7
Idaho	4	Minnesota	12	North Dakota	5	West Virginia	8
Illinois	29	Mississippi	10	Ohio	24	Wisconsin	13
				Oklahoma	10	Wyoming	3
				Oregon	5	Total	531
				Pennsylvania	38	Necessary to choice	266

PRESIDENTS AND THEIR CABINETS.

PRESIDENT AND VICE-PRESIDENT.	Secretary of state.	Secy. of treasury.	Secretary of war.
*George Washington...........1789 *John Adams...................1789	T. Jefferson......1789 E. Randolph......1794 T. Pickering.....1795	Alex. Hamilton..1789 Oliver Wolcott.. 1795	Henry Knox...1789 T. Pickering...1795 Jas. McHenry..1796
John Adams...................1797 Thomas Jefferson.............1797	T. Pickering......1797 John Marshall..1800	Oliver Wolcott..1797 Samuel Dexter ..1801	Jas. McHenry. 1797 John Marshall.1800 Sam'l Dexter..1800 R. Griswold....1801
*Thomas Jefferson ....1801 Aaron Burr...................1801 *George Clinton...............1805	James Madison..1801	Samuel Dexter..1801 Albert Gallatin..1801	H. Dearborn.. 1801
*James Madison................1809 †George Clinton...............1809 Elbridge Gerry...............1813	Robert Smith....1809 James Monroe...1811	Albert Gallatin..1809 G. W. Campbell..1814 A. J. Dallas .....1814 W. H. Crawford.1816	Wm. Eustis.....1809 J. Armstrong..1813 James Monroe.1814 W.H.Crawford 1815
*James Monroe................1817 *Daniel D. Tompkins..........1817	J. Q. Adams..... 1817	W. H. Crawford.1817	Isaac Shelby...1817 Geo. Graham..1817 J. C. Calhoun..1817
John Q. Adams...............1825 *John C. Calhoun..............1825	Henry Clay..... 1825	Richard Rush....1825	Jas. Barbour ..1825 Peter B.Porter.1828
*Andrew Jackson..............1829 †John C. Calhoun..............1829 Martin Van Buren............1833	M. Van Buren...1829 E. Livingston....1831 Louis McLane...1833 John Forsyth...1834	Sam. D. Ingham.1829 Louis McLane...1831 W. J. Duane....1833 Roger B. Taney..1833 Levi Woodbury..1834	John H. Eaton.1829 Lewis Cass....1831 B. F. Butler....1837
Martin Van Buren............1837 Richard M. Johnson..........1837	John Forsyth....1837	Levi Woodbury..1837	Joel R.Poinsett1837
†William H. Harrison.........1841 John Tyler...................1841	Daniel Webster..1841	Thos. Ewing.....1841	John Bell.......1841
John Tyler...................1841	Daniel Webster..1841 Hugh S. Legare..1843 Abel P. Upshur..1843 John C. Calhoun.1844	Thos. Ewing.....1841 Walter Forward.1841 John C. Spencer..1843 Geo. M. Bibb....1844	John Bell.......1841 John McLean..1841 J. C. Spencer.. 1841 Jas. M. Porter..1843 Wm. Wilkins.1844
James K. Polk...............1845 George M. Dallas. 1845	James Buchanan1845	Robt. J. Walker.1845	Wm. L. Marcy.1845
†Zachary Taylor..............1849 Millard Fillmore.............1849	John M. Clayton.1849	Wm.M.Meredith1849	G.W. Crawford.1849
Millard Fillmore.............1850	Daniel Webster..1850 Edward Everett..1852	Thomas Corwin..1850	C. M. Conrad...1850
Franklin Pierce..............1853 †William R. King.............1853	W. L. Marcy......1853	James Guthrie...1853	Jefferson Davis1853
James Buchanan..............1857 John C. Breckinridge........1857	Lewis Cass......1857 J. S. Black.....1860	Howell Cobb....1857 Philip F.Thomas.1860 John A. Dix....1861	John B. Floyd..1857 Joseph Holt.. .1861
†Abraham Lincoln............1861 Hannibal Hamlin.............1861 Andrew Johnson.............1865	W. H. Seward...1861	Salmon P. Chase.1861 W. P. Fessenden.1864 Hugh McCulloch.1865	S. Cameron....1861 E. M. Stanton..1862
Andrew Johnson............. 1865	W. H. Seward...1865	Hugh McCulloch.1865	E. M. Stanton..1865 U. S. Grant.....1867 L. Thomas....1868 J. M. Schofield.1868
*Ulysses S. Grant............1869 Schuyler Colfax.............1869 †Henry Wilson ,..............1873	E. B.Washburne.1869 Hamilton Fish..1869	Geo. S. Boutwell 1869 W.A.Richardson.1873 Benj. H. Bristow.1874 Lot M. Morrill..1876	J. A. Rawlins..1869 W. T. Sherman.1869 W. W. Belknap.1869 Alphonso Taft.1876 J. D. Cameron.1876
Rutherford B. Hayes.........1877 William A. Wheeler..........1877	W. M. Evarts....1877	John Sherman...1877	G. W. McCrary.1877 Alex. Ramsey..1879
†James A. Garfield...........1881 Chester A. Arthur...........1881	James G. Blaine.1881	Wm. Windom....1881	R. T. Lincoln..1881
Chester A. Arthur...........1881	F. T. Frelinghuy- sen...........1881	Chas. J. Folger..1881 W. Q. Gresham ..1884 Hugh McCulloch.1884	R. T. Lincoln...1881
Grover Cleveland............1885 †Thos. A. Hendricks.........1885	Thos. F. Bayard.1885	Daniel Manning.1885 Chas.S.Fairchild.1887	W. C. Endicott.1885
Benjamin Harrison..........1889 Levi P. Morton..............1889	James G. Blaine.1889 John W. Foster..1892	Wm. Windom....1889 Charles Foster..1891	R. Proctor.....1889 S. B. Elkins...1891
Grover Cleveland............1893 Adlai E. Stevenson..........1893	W. Q. Gresham .1893 Richard Olney...1895	John G. Carlisle..1893	D. S. Lamont..1893
†William McKinley...........1897 †Garret A. Hobart...........1897 Theodore Roosevelt..........1901	John Sherman...1897 Wm. R. Day.....1897 John Hay.......1898	Lyman J. Gage..1897	R. A. Alger....1897 Elihu Root.....1899
Theodore Roosevelt..........1901 Charles W. Fairbanks........1905	John Hay†......1901 Elihu Root.....1905 Robert Bacon...1909	Lyman J. Gage..1901 Leslie M. Shaw..1902 G. B. Cortelyou..1907	Elihu Root.... 1901 Wm. H. Taft....1904 Luke E.Wright1908
William H. Taft.............1909 †James S. Sherman...........1909	P. C. Knox......1909	F. MacVeagh....1909	J.M.Dickinson.1909 H. L. Stimson..1911
Woodrow Wilson.............1913 Thomas R. Marshall..........1913	Wm. J. Bryan....1913	W. G. McAdoo...1913	L. M. Garrison.1913

*Elected two consecutive terms.   †Died while in office.   ‡Resigned.

PRESIDENTS AND THEIR CABINETS.—Continued.

Secretary of navy.	Secretary of interior.*	Postmaster-general.†	Attorney-general.	Sec. agriculture.‡
		Samuel Osgood....1789	E. Randolph.....1789	
		Timothy Pickering1791	Wm. Bradford...1794	
		Jos. Habersham....1795	Charles Lee......1795	
Benjamin Stoddert...1798		Jos. Habersham...1797	Charles Lec......1797	
			Theo. Parsons...1801	
Benjamin Stoddert...1801		Jos. Habersham...1801	Levi Lincoln.....1801	
Robert Smith........1801		Gideon Granger...1801	Robt. Smith.....1805	
Jacob Crowninshield..1805			John Breck-	
			inridge.........1805	
			C. A. Rodney 1807	
Paul Hamilton 1809		Gideon Granger...1809	C. A. Rodney.....1809	
William Jones........1813		R. J. Meigs, Jr....1814	Wm. Pinckney...1811	
B. W. Crowninshield..1814			William Rush....1814	
B. W. Crowninshield..1817		R. J. Meigs, Jr....1817	William Rush....1817	
Smith Thompson......1818		John McLean......1823	William Wirt...1817	
S. L. Southard........1823				
S. L. Southard........1825		John McLean......1825	William Wirt...1825	
John Branch.........1829		Wm. T. Barry.....1829	John M. Berrien..1829	
Levi Woodbury......1831		Amos Kendall....1835	Roger B. Taney..1831	
Mahlon Dickerson....1834			B. F. Butler......1833	
Mahlon Dickerson....1837		Amos Kendall....1837	B. F. Butler......1837	
		John M. Niles....1840	Felix Grundy....1838	
			H. D. Gilpin.....1840	
George E. Badger.....1841		Francis Granger...1841	J. J. Crittenden.1841	
George E. Badger....1841		Francis Granger...1841	J. J. Crittenden.1841	
Abel P. Upshur......1841		C. A. Wickliffe...1841	Hugh S. Legare..1841	
David Henshaw......1843			John Nelson.....1843	
Thomas W. Gilmer...1844				
John Y. Mason......1844				
George Bancroft......1845		Cave Johnson 1845	John Y. Mason...1845	
John Y. Mason......1846			Nathan Clifford..1846	
			Isaac Toucey.....1848	
William B. Preston ...1849	Thomas Ewing.....1849	Jacob Collamer....1849	Reverdy Johnson1849	
William A. Graham...1850	Thomas A. Pearce..1850	Nathan K. Hall....1850	J. J. Crittenden..1850	
John P. Kennedy.....1852	T. M. T. McKernon1850	Sam D. Hubbard...1852		
	A. H. H. Stuart....1850			
James C. Dobbin.......1853	Robt. McClelland..1853	James Campbell...1853	Caleb Cushing...1853	
Isaac Toucey 1857	Jacob Thompson...1857	Aaron V. Brown...1857	J. S. Black........1857	
		Joseph Holt.......1859	Edw. M. Stanton.1860	
Gideon Welles........1861	Caleb B. Smith....1861	Montgomery Blair.1861	Edward Bates....1861	
	John P. Usher......1863	William Dennison.1864	Titian J. Coffey..1863	
			James Speed......1864	
Gideon Welles........1865	John P. Usher......1865	William Dennison.1865	James Speed......1865	
	James Harlan......1865	A. W. Randall.....1866	Henry Stanbery..1866	
	O. H. Browning....1866		Wm. M. Evarts...1868	
Adolph E. Borie......1869	Jacob D. Cox......1869	J. A. J. Creswell...1869	E. R. Hoar.......1869	
George M. Robeson...1869	Columbus Delano..1870	Jas. W. Marshall...1874	A. T. Ackerman..1870	
	Zach Chandler.....1875	Marshall Jewell...1874	Geo. H. Williams.1871	
		James N. Tyner...1876	Edw. Pierrepont..1875	
			Alphonso Taft...1876	
R. W. Thompson......1877	Carl Schurz........1877	David M. Key.....1877	Chas. Devens....1877	
Nathan Goff. Jr.......1881		Horace Maynard...1880		
W. H. Hunt........1881	S. J. Kirkwood....1881	T. L. James........1881	W. MacVeagh....1881	
W. E. Chandler.......1881	Henry M. Teller...1881	T. O. Howe........1881	B. H. Brewster...1881	
		W. Q. Gresham....1883		
		Frank Hatton.....1884		
W. C. Whitney........1885	L. Q. C. Lamar.....1885	Wm. F. Vilas.,....1885	A. H. Garland....1885	N. J. Colman.1889
	Wm. F. Vilas......1888	D.M.Dickinson....1888		
Benj. F. Tracy........1889	John W. Noble.....1889	J. Wanamaker....1889	W. H. H. Miller..1889	J. M. Rusk ..1889
Hilary A. Herbert....1893	Hoke Smith........1893	W. S. Bissell......1893	R. Olney.........1893	J. S. Morton.1893
	D. R. Francis......1896	W. L. Wilson......1895	J. Harmon.......1895	
John D. Long.........1897	C. N. Bliss.......1897	James A. Gary.....1897	J. McKenna......1897	J. Wilson.....1897
	E.A.Hitchcock....1899	Chas. E. Smith....1898	J. W. Griggs......1897	
			P. C. Knox.......1901	
John D. Long.........1901	E.A.Hitchcock....1901	Chas. E. Smith....1901	P. C. Knox.......1901	J. Wilson.....1901
Wm. H. Moody......1902	J. R. Garfield......1907	Henry C. Payne....1902	W. H. Moody.....1904	
Paul Morton........1904		Robt. J. Wynne....1904	C. J. Bonaparte..1907	
C. J. Bonaparte......1905		G.B.Cortelyou....1905		
Victor H. Metcalf....1907		G. v. L. Meyer....1907		
Truman H. Newberry1908				
G. von L. Meyer.....1909	R. A. Ballinger....1909	F. H. Hitchcock...1909	G. W. Wickersh'm1909	J. Wilson.....1909
	W. L. Fisher........1911			
Josephus Daniels....1913	F. K. Lane.........1913	A. S. Burleson 1913	J.C.McReynolds.1913	D.F.Houston.1913

Secretary of commerce and labor (department established Feb. 14, 1903)—George B. Cortelyou, 1903; Victor H. Metcalf, 1904-1906; Oscar S. Straus, 1907-1909; Charles Nagel, 1909; (Secretary of Commerce) Wm. C. Redfield, 1913. Secretary of labor (dept. established March 4, 1913)—William B. Wilson, 1913.
*This department was established by an act of congress March 3, 1849. †Not a cabinet officer until 1829. ‡ Established Feb. 11, 1889.

APPORTIONMENT OF REPRESENTATIVES.

[From census bureau report.]

The apportionment of representatives in congress, under the first six censuses—1790 to 1840, inclusive—was made by congress, each by a separate act. The law for taking the census of 1850, which was intended to be permanent, presented a rule of apportionment, fixed the number of members of the house at 233 and directed the secretary of the interior thereafter to make the apportionment. The apportionment of 1860 was also made under this law, but congress, on March 4, 1862, fixed the total number of representatives at 241, and the secretary of the interior apportioned the new quotas to the states. The apportionments from and after the census of 1870 were made by congress, each by a separate act, hence it may be assumed that the power conferred on the secretary of the interior by the act of May 23, 1850, was repealed by implication. The following shows the dates of the apportionment acts and the ratio of population to each representative:

Census.	Date.	Ratio.
1910—Aug. 8, 1911		211,877
1900—Jan. 16, 1901		194,182
1890—Feb. 7, 1891		173,901
1880—Feb. 25, 1882		151,911
1870—Feb. 2, 1872		131,425
1860—May 23, 1850		127,381
1850—May 23. 1850		93,423
1840—June 25, 1842		70,680
1830—May 22, 1832		47,700
1820—May 7, 1822		40,000
1810—Dec. 21, 1811		35,000
1800—Jan. 14, 1802		33,000
1790—April 14, 1792		33,000
....—Constitution, 1789		30,000

REPRESENTATIVES UNDER EACH APPORTIONMENT.

STATE.	1910.	1900.	1890.	1880.	1870.	1860.	1850.	1840.	1830.	1820.	1810.	1800.	1790.	1789.
Alabama	10	9	9	8	8	6	7	7	5	3	*1			
Arizona	*1													
Arkansas	7	7	6	5	4	3	2	1	*1					
California	11	8	7	6	4	3	2	*2						
Colorado	4	3	2	1	*1									
Connecticut	5	5	4	4	4	4	4	4	6	6	7	7	7	5
Delaware	1	1	1	1	1	1	1	1	1	1	2	1	1	1
Florida	4	3	2	2	*2	1	1	*1						
Georgia	12	11	11	10	9	7	8	8	9	7	6	4	2	3
Idaho	2	1	1	*1										
Illinois	27	25	22	20	19	14	9	7	3	1				
Indiana	13	13	13	13	13	11	11	10	7	3	*1			
Iowa	11	11	11	11	9	6	2	*2						
Kansas	8	8	8	7	3	1								
Kentucky	11	11	11	11	10	9	10	10	13	12	10	6	2	
Louisiana	8	7	6	6	6	5	4	3	3	3	*1			
Maine	4	4	4	4	*5	5	6	7	8	7	7			
Maryland	6	6	6	6	5	5	6	6	8	9	9	9	8	6
Massachusetts	16	14	13	12	11	10	11	10	12	13	13	17	14	8
Michigan	13	12	12	11	9	6	4	3	*1					
Minnesota	10	9	7	5	3	2	*2							
Mississippi	8	8	7	7	6	5	5	4	2	1	*1			
Missouri	16	16	15	14	13	9	7	5	2	1				
Montana	2	1	1	*1										
Nebraska	6	6	6	3	1	*1								
Nevada	1	1	1	1	1	*1								
New Hampshire	2	2	2	2	3	3	3	4	5	6	6	5	4	3
New Jersey	12	10	8	7	7	5	5	5	6	6	6	6	5	4
New Mexico	*1													
New York	43	37	34	34	33	31	33	34	40	34	27	17	10	6
North Carolina	10	10	9	9	8	7	8	9	13	13	13	12	10	5
North Dakota	3	2	1	*1										
Ohio	22	21	21	21	20	19	21	21	19	14	6	*1		
Oklahoma	8	*5												
Oregon	3	2	2	1	1	1	*1							
Pennsylvania	36	32	30	28	27	24	25	24	28	26	23	18	13	8
Rhode Island	3	2	2	2	2	2	2	2	2	2	2	2	2	1
South Carolina	7	7	7	7	5	4	6	7	9	9	9	8	6	5
South Dakota	3	2	2	*2										
Tennessee	10	10	10	10	10	8	10	11	13	9	6	3	*1	
Texas	18	16	13	11	6	4	2	*2						
Utah	2	1	*1											
Vermont	2	2	2	2	3	3	3	4	5	5	6	4	2	
Virginia	10	10	10	10	9	11	13	15	21	22	23	22	19	10
Washington	5	3	2	*1										
West Virginia	6	5	4	4	3									
Wisconsin	11	11	10	*9	8	6	3	*2						
Wyoming	1	1	1	*1										
Total	433	386	356	325	292	241	234	223	240	213	181	141	105	65
Added*	2	5	1	7	1	2	3	9	2		5	1	1	

*Assigned to new states after apportionment. Included in table, but not in total under apportionment.

HIGHEST MOUNTAINS IN THE WORLD.

Mountain.	Feet.	Mountain.	Feet.	Mountain.	Feet.	Mountain.	Feet.
Asia—Mt. Everest	29,002	Nanda Devi	25,660	Huascaran	22,188	Chimborazo	20,498
Godwin-Austen	28,280	Mustaghata	24,406	Aneohuma	21,430	Tupungato	20,286
Kunchinginga	28,156	Chumalari	23,946	Illampu	21,192	Haina	20,171
Gusherbrum	26,378	South America—		Huandoy	20,847	San Jose	20,020
Dhawalgiri	26,826	Aconcagua	23,080	Illimani	21,020	North America—	
Kutha Kangir	24,740	Mercedario	22,315	Pamiri	20,735	McKinley	20,300

PAST POLITICAL COMPLEXION OF THE STATES.

R., republican; W., whig; D., democratic; U., union; A., American; A. M., anti-Masonic; N. R., national republican; P., populist; Pr., Progressive.

STATE.	1828	1832	1836	1840	1844	1848	1852	1856	1860	1864	1868	1872	1876	1880	1884	1888	1892	1896	1900	1904	1908	1912
Alabama	D.	D.	D.	D.	D.	D.	D.	D.	D.	....	R.	R.	D.	D.	D.	D.	D.	D.	D.	D.	D.	D.
Arizona																						D.
Arkansas			D.	D.	D.	D.	D.	D.	D.		R.	R.	D.	D.	D.	D.	D.	D.	D.	D.	D.	D.
California						D.	D.	R.	R.	R.	R.	R.	D.	R.	R.	D.	R.	R.	R.	R.	R.	Pr.
Colorado													R.	R.	R.	R.	P.	D.	R.	D.	D.	D.
Connecticut	R.	N. R.	D.	W.	W.	W.	W.	D.	R.	R.	R.	R.	D.	R.	D.	R.	D.	R.	R.	R.	R.	D.
Delaware	R.	N. R.	W.	W.	W.	W.	D.	D.	D.	D.	R.	R.	D.	D.	D.	R.	D.	R.	R.	R.	R.	D.
Florida							W.	D.	D.		R.	R.	D.	D.	D.	D.	D.	D.	D.	D.	D.	D.
Georgia	D.	D.	W.	W.	W.	D.	D.	D.	D.		D.	D.	D.	D.	D.	D.	D.	D.	D.	D.	D.	D.
Idaho																	P.	D.	R.	R.	R.	D.
Illinois	D.	D.	D.	D.	D.	D.	D.	R.	R.	R.	R.	R.	R.	R.	R.	R.	D.	R.	R.	R.	R.	D.
Indiana	D.	D.	W.	W.	D.	D.	D.	D.	R.	R.	R.	R.	D.	R.	D.	R.	D.	R.	R.	R.	R.	D.
Iowa					D.	D.	R.	R.	R.	R.	R.	R.	R.	R.	R.	R.	R.	R.	R.	R.	R.	D.
Kansas								R.	R.	R.	R.	R.	R.	R.	R.	R.	P.	D.	R.	R.	R.	D.
Kentucky	D.	N. R.	W.	W.	W.	W.	W.	D.	U.	D.	D.	D.	D.	D.	D.	D.	D.	R.	D.	D.	D.	D.
Louisiana	D.	D.	D.	W.	D.	D.	D.	R.	R.		R.	R.	R.	D.	D.	D.	D.	D.	D.	D.	D.	D.
Maine	R.	D.	D.	W.	W.	D.	D.	R.	R.	R.	R.	R.	R.	R.	R.	R.	R.	R.	R.	R.	R.	D.
Maryland	R.	N. R.	W.	W.	W.	W.	W.	A.	R.	R.	D.	R.	D.	D.	D.	D.	D.	R.	R.	D.	D.	D.
Massachusetts	R.	N. R.	W.	W.	W.	W.	W.	R.	R.	R.	R.	R.	R.	R.	R.	R.	R.	R.	R.	R.	R.	D.
Michigan				D.	D.	D.	D.	R.	R.	R.	R.	R.	R.	R.	R.	R.	R.	R.	R.	R.	R.	Pr.
Minnesota									R.	R.	R.	R.	R.	R.	R.	R.	R.	R.	R.	R.	R.	Pr.
Mississippi	D.	D.	D.	W.	D.	D.	D.	D.	D.		R.	R.	D.	D.	D	D.	D.	D.	D.	D.	D.	D.
Missouri	D.	D.	D.	D.	D.	D.	D.	D.	R.	R.	D.	D.	D.	D.	D.	D.	D.	R.	D.	R.	D.	D.
Montana																R.	D.	D.	R.	R.	R.	D.
Nebraska										R.	R.	R.	R.	R.	R.	R.	D.	D.	R.	R.	D.	D.
Nevada									R.	R.	R.	R.	R.	R.	R.	R.	D.	D.	R.	R.	D.	D.
New Hampshire	R.	D.	D.	W.	D.	D.	D.	R.	R.	R.	R.	R.	R.	R.	R.	R.	R.	R.	R.	R.	R.	D.
New Jersey	R.	D.	W.	W.	W.	W.	D.	D.	D.	R.	D.	R.	D.	R.	D.	R.	D.	R.	R.	R.	R.	D.
New Mexico																						D.
New York	D.	D.	D.	W.	D.	W.	D.	R.	R.	R.	D.	R.	D.	R.	D.	R.	D.	R.	R.	R.	R.	D.
North Carolina	D.	D.	W.	W.	D.	W.	D.	D.	D.		R.	R.	D.	D.	D.	D.	D.	D.	D.	D.	D.	D.
North Dakota																	P.	R.	R.	R.	R.	D.
Ohio	D.	D.	W.	W.	W.	D.	D.	R.	R.	R.	R.	R.	R.	R.	R.	R.	R.	R.	R.	R.	R.	D.
Oklahoma																					D.	D.
Oregon					D.	D.	D.	W.	D.	R.	R.	R.	R.	R.	R.	R.	R.	R.	R.	R.	R.	Pr.
Pennsylvania	D.	D.	W.	W.	D.	W.	D.	R.	R.	R.	R.	R.	R.	R.	R.	R.	R.	R.	R.	R.	R.	Pr.
Rhode Island	D.	N. R.	D.	W.	W.	W.	W.	R.	R.	R.	R.	R.	R.	R.	R.	R.	R.	R.	R.	R.	R.	D.
South Carolina	D.	W.	W.	D.	D.	D.	D.	D.		R.	R.	R.	D.	D.	D.	D.	D.	D.	D.	D.	D.	D.
South Dakota																R.	R.	D.	R.	R.	R.	Pr.
Tennessee	D.	D.	W.	W.	W.	W.	W.	D.		R.	D.	D.	D.	D.	D.	D.	D.	D.	R.	D.	D.	D.
Texas						D.	D.	D.	D.		D.	D.	D.	D.	D.	D.	D.	D.	D.	D.	D.	D.
Utah																		D.	R.	R.	R.	R.
Vermont	R.	A. M.	W.	W.	W.	W.	W.	R.	R.	R.	R.	R.	R.	R.	R.	R.	R.	R.	R.	R.	R.	R.
Virginia	D.	D.	D.	D.	D.	D.	D.	D.	U.		R.	R.	D.	D.	D.	D.	D.	D.	D.	D.	D.	D.
Washington																R.	R.	D.	R.	R.	R.	Pr.
West Virginia									R.	R.	R.	R.	D.	D.	D.	R.	D.	R.	R.	R.	R.	D.
Wisconsin					D.	D.	R.	R.	R.	R.	R.	R.	R.	R.	D.	R.	R.	R.	R.	D.
Wyoming																	R.	D.	R.	R.	R.	D.

In five states in 1892 the electoral vote was divided: California gave 8 electoral votes for Cleveland and 1 for Harrison and Ohio gave 1 for Cleveland and 22 for Harrison; in Michigan, by act of the legislature, each congressional district voted separately for an elector; in Oregon 1 of the 4 candidates for electors on the people's party ticket was also on the democratic ticket; in North Dakota 1 of the 2 people's party electors cast his vote for Cleveland, this causing the electoral vote of the state to be equally divided among Cleveland, Harrison and Weaver. In 1896 California gave 8 electoral votes to McKinley and 1 to Bryan; Kentucky gave 12 to McKinley and 1 to Bryan. In Maryland in 1904 7 of the presidential electors chosen were democrats and 1 republican. In 1908 Maryland elected 6 democratic and 2 republican electors. In 1912 California elected 11 progressive and 2 democratic electors.

PARTY LINES IN CONGRESS SINCE 1881.

CONGRESS.	Years.	SENATE.			HOUSE.			CONGRESS.	Years.	SENATE.			HOUSE.		
		Rep.	Dem.	Ind.	Rep.	Dem.	Ind.			Rep.	Dem.	Ind.	Rep.	Dem.	Ind.
47th	1881-1883	37	38	1	148	138	10	56th	1899-1901	53	26	11	185	163	9
48th	1883-1885	40	36	....	124	198	1	57th	1901-1903	56	29	3	198	153	5
49th	1885-1887	42	34	....	120	204	1	58th	1903-1905	58	32	...	206	174	2
50th	1887-1889	39	37	....	153	168	4	59th	1905-1907	58	32	...	250	136	...
51st	1889-1891	39	37	....	166	159	...	60th	1907-1909	61	31	...	222	164	...
52d	1891-1893	47	39	2	88	236	8	61st	1909-1911	60	32	...	219	172	...
53d	1893-1895	38	44	3	126	220	8	62d	1911-1913	51	41	...	162	228	*1
54th	1895-1897	42	39	5	246	104	7	63d	1913-1915	51	44	†1	127	290	‡18
55th	1897-1899	46	34	10	206	134	16								

*Socialist. †Progressive. ‡Includes 9 progressives, 7 progressive republicans, 1 independent and 1 vacancy. Figures in table are for beginning of each congress.

QUALIFICATIONS FOR SUFFRAGE.

REQUIREMENTS FOR VOTERS IN THE VARIOUS STATES AND IN ALASKA.	PREVIOUS RESIDENCE REQUIRED.				Registration.	Ballot reform?	Excluded from voting.
	State.	County.	Town.	Precinct.			
ALABAMA—Citizens of good character and understanding, or aliens who have declared intention: must show poll-tax receipt.	2 y.	1 y.	3 m	3 m	Yes.	Yes.	If convicted of treason, embezzlement of public funds, malfeasance in office or other penitentiary offenses, idiots or insane.
ALASKA—Citizens, male or female.	1 y.			30 d			
ARIZONA—Male and female citizens of the United States.	1 y.	30 d	30 d	30 d	Yes.	Yes.	Persons under guardianship, non compos mentis, insane or convicted of treason or felony.
ARKANSAS—Like Alabama, except as to "good character."	1 y.	6 m	30 d	30 d	No.	Yes.	Idiots, insane, convicts until pardoned, nonpayment of poll tax.
CALIFORNIA—Citizens, male or female; naturalized for 90 days, or treaty of Queretaro.	1 y.	90 d		30 d	Yes.	Yes.	Chinese, insane, embezzlers of public moneys, convicts.
COLORADO—Citizens, male or female; aliens who declared intention 4 months before election.	1 y.	90 d	30 d	10 d	Yes.	Yes.	Persons under guardianship, insane, idiots, prisoners convicted of bribery.
CONNECTICUT — Citizens who can read English.	1 y.		6 m		Yes.	Yes.	Convicted of felony or other infamous crime unless pardoned.
DELAWARE—Citizens paying $1 registration fee.	1 y.	3 m		30 d	No.	Yes.	Insane, idiots, felons, paupers.
FLORIDA—Citizens of the U. S.	1 y.	6 m		30 d	Yes.	Yes.	Persons not registered, insane, convicts.
GEORGIA—Citizens who can read and have paid all taxes since 1877.	1 y.	6 m			(a)	No.	Persons convicted of crimes punishable by imprisonment, insane, delinquent taxpayers.
IDAHO — Citizens, male or female.	6 m	30 d	3 m	10 d	Yes.	Yes.	Chinese, Indians, insane, felons, polygamists, bigamists, traitors, bribers.
ILLINOIS—Citizens, male and female (restricted), of the U. S.	1 y.	90 d	30 d	30 d	Yes.	Yes.	Convicts of penitentiary until pardoned.
INDIANA—Citizens, or aliens who have declared intention and resided 1 year in United States.	6 m	60 d	60 d	30 d	No..	Yes.	Convicts and persons disqualified by judgment of a court, United States soldiers, marines and sailors.
IOWA—Citizens of United States.	6 m	60 d	10 d	10 d	(b)	Yes.	Idiots, insane, convicts.
KANSAS — Citizens; aliens who have declared intention; women vote at general as well as school elections.	6 m	30 d	30 d	10 d	(b)	Yes.	Insane, persons under guardianship, convicts, bribers, defrauders of the government and persons dishonorably discharged from service of United States.
KENTUCKY—Citizens of the U. S.	1 y.	6 m	60 d	60 d	(c)	No..	Treason, felony, bribery, idiots, insane.
LOUISIANA — Citizens who are able to read and write, who own $300 worth of property or whose father or grandfather was entitled to vote Jan. 1, 1867.	2 y.	1 y.		6 m	Yes.	No..	Idiots, insane, all crimes punishable by imprisonment, embezzling public funds unless pardoned.
MAINE—Citizens of the U. S.	3 m	3 m	3 m	3 m	Yes.	Yes.	Paupers, persons under guardianship, Indians not taxed.
MARYLAND—Citizens of United States who can read.	1 y.	6 m	6 m	1 d.	Yes.	Yes.	Persons convicted of larceny or other infamous crime, persons under guardianship, insane, idiots.
MASSACHUSETTS—Citizens who can read and write English.	1 y.	6 m	6 m	6 m	Yes.	Yes.	Paupers (except United States soldiers), persons under guardianship.
MICHIGAN—Citizens; aliens who declared intention prior to May 8, 1892.	6 m	20 d	20 d	20 d	Yes.	Yes.	Indians holding tribal relations, duelists and their abettors.
MINNESOTA — Citizens of the United States.	6 m	30 d	30 d	30 d	(d)	Yes.	Treason, felony unless pardoned, insane, persons under guardianship, uncivilized Indians.
MISSISSIPPI — Citizens who can read or understand the constitution.	2 y.	1 y.	1 y.	1 y.	Yes.	Yes.	Insane, idiots, felons, delinquent taxpayers.
MISSOURI—Citizens, or aliens who have declared intention not less than 1 nor more than 5 years before offering to vote.	1 y.	60 d	60 d	60 d	(e)	Yes.	Paupers, persons convicted of felony or other infamous crime or misdemeanor or violating rights of suffrage, unless pardoned; second conviction disfranchises.
MONTANA—Citizens of U. S.	1 y.	30 d	30 d	30 d	Yes.	Yes.	Idiots, felons, idiots, insane.
NEBRASKA — Citizens, or aliens who have declared intention 30 days before election.	6 m	40 d	10 d	10 d	(b)	Yes.	Lunatics, persons convicted of treason or felony unless pardoned, United States soldiers and sailors.
NEVADA — Citizens of United States.	6 m	30 d	30 d	30 d	Yes.	Yes.	Insane, idiots, convicted of treason or felony, unamnestied confederates against the United States, Indians and Chinese.
NEW HAMPSHIRE—Citizens of United States.	6 m	6 m	6 m	6 m	Yes.	Yes.	Paupers (except honorably discharged soldiers), persons excused from paying taxes at own request.
NEW JERSEY—Citizens of United States.	1 y.	5 m			Yes.	Yes.	Paupers, insane, idiots and persons convicted of crimes which exclude them from being witnesses unless pardoned.
NEW MEXICO—Male citizens U.S.	1 y.	90 d	30 d	30 d	Yes.	Yes.	Insane, idiots, convicts and Indians not taxed.
NEW YORK—Citizens who have been such for 90 days.	1 y.	4 m	30 d	30 d	Yes.	Yes.	Convicted of bribery or any infamous crime unless pardoned, bettors on result of election, bribers for votes and the bribed.
NORTH CAROLINA—Citizens of United States who can read.	2 y.	6 m		4 m	Yes.	No..	Idiots, lunatics, convicted of felony or other infamous crimes, atheists.
NORTH DAKOTA — Citizens, or aliens who have declared intention, and civilized Indians.	1 y.	6 m		90 d	(a)	Yes.	Felons, idiots, convicts unless pardoned, United States soldiers and sailors.
OHIO—Citizens of the U. S.	1 y.	30 d	20 d	20 d	(b)	Yes.	Idiots, insane, United States soldiers and sailors, felons unless restored to citizenship.

(a) Registration required in some counties. (b) In all cities. (c) In the cities of first, second and third class. (d) Required in cities of 1,200 inhabitants or over (e) In cities of 100,000 population or over.

QUALIFICATIONS FOR SUFFRAGE—CONTINUED.

REQUIREMENTS FOR VOTERS IN THE VARIOUS STATES.	PREVIOUS RESIDENCE REQUIRED.				Registration.	Ballot reform.	Excluded from voting.
	State.	County.	Town.	Precinct.			
OKLAHOMA — Citizens of the United States and native Indians	1 y.	6 m	30 d	30 d	.....	Yes.	Felons, paupers, idiots and lunatics.
OREGON — White male and female citizens, or aliens who have declared intention 1 year before election.	6 m	...	...	...	No.	Yes.	Idiots, insane, convicted felons, Chinese, United States soldiers and sailors.
PENNSYLVANIA — Citizens at least 1 month, and if 22 years old must have paid tax within 2 yrs.	1 y.	...	...	2 m	Yes.	Yes.	Persons convicted of some offense forfeiting right of suffrage, nontaxpayers.
RHODE ISLAND — Citizens of United States.	2 y	...	6 m	...	(c)	Yes.	Paupers, lunatics, idiots. convicted of bribery or infamous crime until restored.
SOUTH CAROLINA—Citizens of United States who can read.	2 y.	1 y.	4 m	4 m	Yes.	No.	Paupers, insane, idiots, convicted of treason, dueling or other infamous crime.
SOUTH DAKOTA — Citizens, or aliens who have declared intention.	6 m	30 d	10 d	10 d	(d)	Yes.	Persons under guardian, idiots, insane, convicted of treason or felony unless pardoned.
TENNESSEE—Citizens who have paid poll tax preceding year.	1 y.	6 m	...	...	(e)	Yes.	Convicted of bribery or other infamous crime, failure to pay poll tax.
TEXAS — Citizens, or aliens who have declared intention 6 months before election.	1 y.	6 m	6 m	...	(f)	Yes.	Idiots, lunatics, paupers, convicts, United States soldiers and sailors.
UTAH—Citizens of United States, male or female.	1 y.	4 m	...	60 d	.....	.....	Idiots, insane, convicted of treason or violation of election laws.
VERMONT — Citizens of United States.	1 y.	3 m	3 m	3 m	Yes.	Yes.	Unpardoned convicts, deserters from United States service during the war, ex-confederates.
VIRGINIA — Citizens of United States of good understanding who have paid poll tax for three years and all ex-soldiers.	2 y.	1 y.	1 y.	30 d	Yes.	No.	Idiots, lunatics, convicts unless pardoned by the legislature.
WASHINGTON—Citizens of United States, male or female.	1 y.	90 d	60 d	30 d	.....	Yes.	Indians not taxed.
WEST VIRGINIA — Citizens of the state.	1 y.	60 d	10 d	...	No.	Yes.	Paupers, idiots, lunatics, convicts, bribers, United States soldiers and sailors.
WISCONSIN — Citizens, or aliens who have declared intention.	1 y.	10 d	10 d	10 d	(a)	Yes.	Insane, under guardian, convicts unless pardoned.
WYOMING—Citizens, male or female.	1 y.	60 d	10 d	10 d	Yes.	Yes.	Idiots, insane, felons, unable to read the state constitution.

(a) In cities of 3,000 population or over. (b) In cities of not less than 9,000 inhabitants. (c) Nontaxpayers must register yearly before Dec. 31. (d) In towns having 1,000 voters and counties where registration has been adopted by popular vote. (e) All counties having 50,000 inhabitants or over. (f) In cities of 10,000 or over.

NOTE—The word "citizen" as used in above table means citizen of the United States in all cases.

As shown in the above table women have full suffrage in Colorado, Idaho, Utah, California, Washington, Wyoming, Arizona, Kansas and Oregon. In Illinois they can vote for all officials except those specified in the state constitution. In a more or less limited form, relating to taxation and school matters, woman suffrage exists in Delaware, Idaho, Indiana, Iowa, Kentucky, Louisiana, Massachusetts, Minnesota, Montana, Nebraska, Nevada, New Hampshire, New Jersey, North Dakota, Oklahoma, South Dakota, Texas, Vermont and Wisconsin.

CITIZENSHIP IN THE UNITED STATES.

All persons born or naturalized in the United States and subject to the jurisdiction thereof are citizens of the United States and of the state wherein they reside. (Fourteenth amendment to the constitution.)

All persons born in the United States and not subject to any foreign power, excluding Indians not taxed, are declared to be citizens of the United States. (Sec. 1992, U. S. Revised Statutes.)

All children heretofore born or hereafter born out of the limits and jurisdiction of the United States, whose fathers were or may be, at the time of their birth, citizens thereof, are declared to be citizens of the United States: but the rights of citizenship shall not descend to children whose fathers never resided in the United States. (Sec. 1993, U. S. Revised Statutes.)

Any woman who is now or may hereafter be married to a citizen of the United States and who might herself be lawfully naturalized shall be deemed a citizen. (Sec. 1995, U. S. Revised Statutes.)

Children born in the United States of alien parents are citizens of the United States.

When any alien who has formally declared his intention of becoming a citizen of the United States dies before he is actually naturalized the widow and children of such alien are citizens.

Children of Chinese parents who are themselves aliens and incapable of becoming naturalized are citizens of the United States.

Children born in the United States of persons engaged in the diplomatic service of foreign governments are not citizens of the United States.

Children born of alien parents on a vessel of a foreign country while within the waters of the United States are not citizens of the United States, but of the country to which the vessel belongs.

Children born of alien parents in the United States have the right to make an election of nationality when they reach their majority.

Minors and children are citizens within the meaning of the term as used in the constitution.

Deserters from the military or naval service of the United States are liable to loss of citizenship.

Any alien being a free white person, an alien of African nativity or of African descent may become an American citizen by complying with the naturalization laws.

"Hereafter no state court or court of the United States shall admit Chinese to citizenship; and all laws in conflict with this act are repealed." (Sec. 14, act of May 6, 1882.)

The courts have held that neither Chinese, Japanese, Hawaiians, Burmese nor Indians can be naturalized.

The naturalization laws apply to women as well as men. An alien woman who marries a citizen, native or naturalized, becomes a naturalized citizen of the United States.

Aliens may become citizens of the United States by treaties with foreign powers, by conquest or by special acts of congress.

In an act approved March 2, 1907, it is provided that any American citizen shall have expatriated himself when he has been naturalized in any foreign state in conformity with its laws, or when he has taken an oath of allegiance to any foreign state.

When any naturalized citizen shall have resided for two years in the foreign state from which he came, or five years in any other foreign state, it shall be presumed that he has ceased to be an American citizen, and the place of his general abode shall be deemed his place of residence during said years; provided, however, that such presumption may be overcome on the presentation of satisfactory evidence to a diplomatic or consular officer of the United States, under such rules and regulations as the department of state may prescribe; and, provided also, that no American citizen shall be allowed to expatriate himself when this country is at war.

Any American woman who marries a foreigner shall take the nationality of her husband. At the termination of the marital relation she may resume her American citizenship, if abroad, by registering as an American citizen within one year with a consul of the United States, or by returning to reside in the United States, or, if residing in the United States at the termination of the marital relation, by continuing to reside therein.

Any foreign woman who acquires American citizenship by marriage to an American citizen shall be assumed to retain the same after the termination of the marital relation if she continue to reside in the United States, unless she makes formal renunciation thereof before a court having jurisdiction to naturalize aliens, or, if she resides abroad, she may retain her citizenship by registering as such before a United States consul within one year after the termination of such marital relation.

A child born without the United States, of alien parents, shall be deemed a citizen of the United States by virtue of the naturalization of or resumption of American citizenship of the parent; provided that such naturalization or resumption takes place during the minority of such child; and, provided further, that the citizenship of such minor child shall begin at the time such minor child begins to reside permanently in the United States.

All children born outside the limits of the United States, who are citizens thereof in accordance with the provisions of section 1993 of the Revised Statutes of the United States (see above), and who continue to reside outside of the United States, shall, in order to receive the protection of the government, be required, upon reaching the age of 18 years, to record at an American consulate their intention to become residents and remain citizens of the United States and shall further be required to take the oath of allegiance to the United States upon attaining their majority.

NATURALIZATION LAWS.
Approved June 29, 1906.

Exclusive jurisdiction to naturalize aliens resident in their districts is conferred upon the United States Circuit and District courts and all courts of record having a seal, a clerk and jurisdiction in actions in law or equity or both in which the amount in controversy is unlimited.

An alien may be admitted to citizenship in the following manner and not otherwise:

1. He shall declare on oath before the clerk of the proper court at least two years before his admission, and after he has reached the age of 18 years, that it is bona fide his intention to become a citizen of the United States and to renounce allegiance to any foreign state or sovereignty.

Such declaration shall set forth the same facts as are registered at the time of his arrival.

2. Not less than two years nor more than seven after he has made such declaration he shall file a petition, signed by himself and verified, in which he shall state his name, place of residence, occupation, date and place of birth, place from which he emigrated, name of the vessel on which he arrived; the time when and the place and name of the court where he declared his intention of becoming a citizen; if he is married, he shall state the name of his wife, the country of her nativity and her place of residence at the time the petition is filed, and if he has children, the name, date and place of birth and place of residence of each child living. The petition shall also set forth that he is not a disbeliever in or opposed to organized government or a member of any body of persons opposed to organized government, and that he is not a polygamist or a believer in polygamy; that he intends to become a citizen of and to live permanently in the United States, and every other fact material to his naturalization and required to be proved upon the final hearing of his application. The petition shall be verified by the affidavits of at least two credible witnesses who are citizens. At the time of the filing of the petition there shall be also filed a certificate from the department of commerce and labor stating the date, place and manner of his arrival in the United States and the declaration of intention of such petitioner, which certificate and declaration shall be attached to and be a part of his petition.

3. He shall, before he is admitted to citizenship, declare on oath in open court that he will support the constitution of the United States, and that he absolutely renounces all allegiance to any foreign prince, potentate, state or sovereignty.

4. It shall be made apparent to the satisfaction of the court admitting any alien to citizenship that immediately preceding the date of his application he has resided continuously within the United States five years at least, and within the state or territory where such court is at the time held one year at least, and that during that time he has behaved as a man of good moral character, attached to the principles of the constitution. In addition to the oath of the applicant, the testimony of at least two witnesses, citizens of the United States, as to the facts of residence, moral character and attachment to the principles of the constitution shall be required.

5. He must renounce any hereditary title or order of nobility which he may possess.

6. When any alien, who has declared his intention, dies before he is actually naturalized the widow and minor children may, by complying with the other provisions of the act, be naturalized without making any declaration of intention.

Immediately after the filing of the petition the clerk of the court shall give notice thereof by posting in a public place the name, nativity and residence of the alien, the date and place of his arrival in the United States and the date for the final hearing of his petition and the names of the witnesses whom the applicant expects to summon in his behalf. Petitions for naturalization may be filed at any time, but final action thereon shall be had only on stated days and in no case until at least ninety days have elapsed after the filing of the petition. No person shall be naturalized within thirty days preceding a general election within the territorial jurisdiction of the court.

No person who disbelieves in or who is opposed to organized government, or who is a member of or affiliated with any organization entertaining and teaching such disbelief in or opposition to organized government, or who advocates or teaches the duty, necessity or propriety of the unlawful assaulting or killing of any officer or officers of the government of the United States, or of any other organized government, because of his or their official character, or who is a polygamist, shall be naturalized.

No alien shall hereafter be naturalized or admitted as a citizen of the United States who cannot speak the English language. This requirement does not apply to those physically unable to comply with it; or to those making homestead entries upon the public lands of the United States.

NATIONAL NOMINATING CONVENTIONS SINCE 1880.

Place and date of each and names of nominees for president and vice-president in the order named:

1880—Democratic: Cincinnati, O., June 22-24; Winfield S. Hancock and William H. English.
Republican: Chicago, Ill., June 2-8; James A. Garfield and Chester A. Arthur.
Greenback: Chicago, Ill., June 9-11; James B. Weaver and B. J. Chambers.
Prohibition: Cleveland, O., June 17; Neal Dow and A. M. Thompson.

1884—Democratic: Chicago, Ill., July 8-11; Grover Cleveland and Thomas A. Hendricks.
Republican: Chicago, Ill., June 3-6; James G. Blaine and John A. Logan.
Greenback: Indianapolis, Ind., May 28-29; Benjamin F. Butler and Alanson M. West.
American Prohibition: Chicago, Ill., June 19; Samuel C. Pomeroy and John A. Conant.
National Prohibition: Pittsburgh, Pa., July 23; John P. St. John and William Daniel.
Anti-Monopoly: Chicago, Ill., May 14; Benjamin F. Butler and Alanson M. West.
Equal Rights: San Francisco, Cal., Sept. 20; Mrs. Belva A. Lockwood and Mrs. Marietta L. Stow.

1888—Democratic: St. Louis, Mo., June 5; Grover Cleveland and Allen G. Thurman.
Republican: Chicago, Ill., June 19; Benjamin Harrison and Levi P. Morton.
Prohibition: Indianapolis, Ind., May 20; Clinton B. Fisk and John A. Brooks.
Union Labor: Cincinnati, O., May 15; Alson J. Streeter and Samuel Evans.
United Labor: Cincinnati, O., May 15; Robert H. Cowdrey and W. H. T. Wakefield.
American: Washington, D. C., Aug. 14; James L. Curtis and James R. Greer.
Equal Rights: Des Moines, Iowa, May 15; Mrs. Belva A. Lockwood and Alfred H. Love.

1892—Democratic: Chicago, Ill., June 21; Grover Cleveland and Adlai E. Stevenson.
Republican: Minneapolis, Minn., June 7-10; Benjamin Harrison and Whitelaw Reid.
Prohibition: Cincinnati, O., June 29; John Bidwell and J. B. Cranfill.
National People's: Omaha, Neb., July 2-5; James B. Weaver and James G. Field.
Socialist-Labor: New York, N. Y., Aug. 28; Simon Wing and Charles H. Matchett.

1896—Democratic: Chicago, Ill., July 7; William J. Bryan and Arthur Sewall.
Republican: St. Louis, Mo., June 16; William McKinley and Garret A. Hobart.
People's Party: St. Louis, Mo., July 22; William J. Bryan and Thomas E. Watson.
Silver Party: St. Louis, Mo., July 22; William J. Bryan and Arthur Sewall.
National Democratic: Indianapolis, Ind., Sept. 2; John M. Palmer and Simon B. Buckner.
Prohibition: Pittsburgh, Pa., May 27; Joshua Levering and Hale Johnson.
National Party: Pittsburgh, Pa., May 28; Charles E. Bentley and James H. Southgate.
Socialist-Labor: New York, N. Y., July 6; Charles H. Matchett and Matthew Maguire.

1900—Democratic: Kansas City, Mo., July 4-6; William J. Bryan and Adlai E. Stevenson.
Republican: Philadelphia, Pa., June 19-21; William McKinley and Theodore Roosevelt.
People's Party: Sioux Falls, S. D., May 9-10; William J. Bryan and Adlai E. Stevenson.
People's Party (Middle-of-the-Road): Cincinnati, O., May 9-10; Wharton Barker and Ignatius Donnelly.
Silver Republican: Kansas City, Mo., July 4-6; William J. Bryan and Adlai E. Stevenson.
Prohibition: Chicago, Ill., June 27-28; John G. Woolley and Henry B. Metcalf.
Socialist-Labor: New York, N. Y., June 2-8; Joseph F. Malloney and Valentine Remmel.
Social Democratic Party of the United States: Rochester, N. Y., Jan 27; Job Harriman and Max S. Hayes.
Social Democratic Party of America: Indianapolis, Ind., March 6; Eugene V. Debs and Job Harriman.
Union Reform: Baltimore, Md., Sept. 3; Seth W. Ellis and Samuel T. Nicholson.

1904—Democratic: St. Louis, Mo., July 6-9; Alton B. Parker and Henry G. Davis.
Republican: Chicago, Ill., June 21-23; Theodore Roosevelt and Charles W. Fairbanks.
People's party: Springfield, Ill., July 4-6; Thomas E. Watson and Thomas H. Tibbles.
Prohibition: Indianapolis, Ind., June 29-July 1; Silas C. Swallow and George W. Carroll.
Socialist-Labor: New York, N. Y., July 3-9; Charles H. Corregan and William W. Cox.
Socialist-Democratic Party of America: Chicago, Ill., May 1-6; Eugene V. Debs and Benjamin Hanford.
Continental: Chicago, Ill., Aug. 31; Charles H. Howard and George H. Shibley. (Nominees declined and Austin Holcomb and A. King were substituted by the national committee.)

1908—Republican: Chicago, June 16-19; William H. Taft and James S. Sherman.
Democratic: Denver, July 7-10; William J. Bryan and John W. Kern.
Socialist: Chicago, May 10-18; Eugene V. Debs and Benjamin Hanford.
Prohibition: Columbus, O., July 15-16; Eugene W. Chafin and Aaron S. Watkins.
Independence: Chicago, July 27-28; Thomas L. Hisgen and John Temple Graves.
People's: St. Louis, April 2-3; Thomas E. Watson and Samuel W. Williams.
United Christian: Rock Island, Ill., May 1; Daniel Braxton Turney and S. P. Carter.
Socialist-Labor: New York, July 2-5; Martin R. Preston and Donald L. Munro. (Preston declined and August Gillhaus was named in his place.)

1912—Democratic: Baltimore, June 25-July 3; Woodrow Wilson and Thomas Riley Marshall.
Republican: Chicago, June 18-22; William Howard Taft and James Schoolcraft Sherman.
Progressive: Chicago, Aug. 5-7; Theodore Roosevelt and Hiram W. Johnson.
Socialist: Indianapolis, May 12-18; Eugene V. Debs and Emil Seidel.
Prohibition: Atlantic City, July 10-12; Eugene W. Chafin and Aaron S. Watkins.
Socialist-Labor: New York, April 7-10; Arthur Reimer and August Gillhaus.
Populist: St. Louis, Aug. 13; no nominations made.

DECLARATION OF LONDON ON LAWS OF NAVAL WAR.

What is popularly known as the "Declaration of London" is the agreement entered into Feb. 26, 1909, at a naval conference closing on that date in London, England, between representatives of the following powers: Germany, United States, Austria-Hungary, Spain, France, Great Britain, Italy, Japan, the Netherlands and Russia. The conference was held at the invitation of Great Britain in order to arrive at an agreement as to what are the generally recognized rules of international law within the meaning of article 7 of the convention of Oct. 18, 1907 (at The Hague), relative to the establishment of an international prize court. The agreement contains nine chapters and seventy-one articles, embodying what the signatory powers declare to correspond in substance with the generally recognized principles of international law. The subjects of the chapters are as follows: Chapter I., blockade in time of war; chapter II., contraband of war; chapter III., unneutral service; chapter IV., destruction of neutral prizes; chapter V., transfer to a neutral flag; chapter VI., enemy character; chapter VII., convoy; chapter VIII., resistance to search; chapter IX., compensation.

The signatory powers undertake to insure the mutual observance of the rules contained in the present declaration in any war in which all the belligerents are parties thereto. Ratifications are to be deposited in London. Powers not represented at the naval conference were requested to accede to the declaration of London, those doing so being placed on the same footing as the signatory powers.

ELECTION CALENDAR.

PRESIDENTIAL.

Every fourth year. Next election Nov. 7, 1916.

STATE.

(Gubernatorial if not otherwise specified.)

Alabama—Every fourth year. Next election Nov. 3, 1914.

Arizona—Biennially; first Tuesday after first Monday in November; next election Nov. 3, 1914.

Arkansas—Biennially; second Monday in September. Next election Sept. 14, 1914.

California—Every fourth year. Next election Nov. 3, 1914.

Colorado—Biennially. Next election Nov. 3, 1914.

Connecticut—State officers except attorney-general, biennially; attorney-general quadreunially. Next election Nov. 3, 1914.

Delaware—Every fourth year. Next election Nov. 7, 1916.

Florida—Every fourth year. Next election Nov. 7, 1916.

Georgia—Biennially. Next election Nov. 3, 1914.

Idaho—Biennially. Next election Nov. 3, 1914.

Illinois—Governor, lieutenant-governor, secretary of state, auditor and attorney-general every fourth year. Next election Nov. 7, 1916. State treasurer biennially. Next election Nov. 3, 1914.

Indiana—Governor, every fourth year. Next election Nov. 7, 1916. Other state officers biennially. Next election Nov. 3, 1914.

Iowa—Governor, lieutenant-governor, superintendent of instruction, one justice of the Supreme court and one railroad commissioner biennially. Next election Nov. 3, 1914.

Kansas—Biennially. Next election Nov. 3, 1914.

Kentucky—Every fourth year. Next election Nov. 2, 1915.

Louisiana—Every fourth year; third Tuesday in April. Next election April 18, 1916.

Maine—Biennially; second Monday in September. Next election Sept. 14, 1914.

Maryland—Every fourth year. Next election Nov. 2, 1915.

Massachusetts—Annually. Next election Nov. 3, 1914.

Michigan—Biennially. Next election Nov. 3, 1914.

Minnesota—Biennially. Next election Nov. 3, 1914.

Mississippi—Every fourth year. Next election Nov. 2, 1915.

Missouri—Principal state officers every fourth year. Next election of governor, lieutenant-governor,

secretary of state, auditor, treasurer and attorney-general Nov. 7, 1916.

Montana—Every fourth year. Next election Nov. 7, 1916.

Nebraska—Biennially. Next election Nov. 3, 1914.

Nevada—Every fourth year. Next election Nov. 3, 1914.

New Hampshire—Biennially. Next election Nov. 3, 1914.

New Jersey—Governor every third year, other officers appointed. Next election Nov. 7, 1916.

New Mexico—Biennially; on Tuesday after the first Monday in November. Next election Nov. 3, 1914.

New York—Biennially. Next election Nov. 3, 1914.

North Carolina—Every fourth year. Next election Nov. 7, 1916.

North Dakota—Biennially. Next election Nov. 3, 1914.

Ohio—Governor, lieutenant-governor, state treasurer and attorney-general biennially. Next election Nov. 2, 1915. Secretary of state and dairy and food commissioner biennially. Next election Nov. 3, 1914. Auditor every fourth year. Next election Nov. 2, 1915.

Oklahoma—Every three years. Next election Nov. 7, 1916.

Oregon—Every fourth year; first Monday in June. Next election June 1, 1914.

Pennsylvania—Governor, lieutenant-governor and secretary of internal affairs every fourth year. Next election Nov. 3, 1914. State treasurer biennially. Next election Nov. 2, 1915. Other officials appointed.

Rhode Island—Biennially. Next election Nov. 3, 1914.

South Carolina—Biennially. Next election Nov. 3, 1914.

South Dakota—Biennially. Next election Nov. 3, 1914.

Tennessee—Biennially. Next election Nov. 3, 1914.

Texas—Biennially. Next election Nov. 3, 1914.

Utah—Every fourth year. Next election Nov. 7, 1916.

Vermont—Biennially; first Tuesday in September. Next election Sept. 1, 1914.

Virginia—Every fourth year. Next election Nov. 6, 1917.

Washington—Every fourth year. Next election Nov. 7, 1916.

West Virginia—Every fourth year. Next election Nov. 7, 1916.

Wisconsin—Biennially. Next election Nov. 3, 1914.

Wyoming—Every fourth year. Next election Nov. 3, 1914.

STUDENTS IN LEADING FOREIGN UNIVERSITIES.

[From "Minerva" for 1913.]

Paris	17,512	Kiev	3,009	Geneva	2,005	Coimbra	1,352
Berlin	14,351	Kasan	2,955	Bologna	2,009	Innsbruck	1,346
Moscow	9,666	Toulouse	2,876	Tubingen	1,994	Lausanne	1,331
Cairo	9,531	Dorpat	2,868	Marburg	1,983	Genoa	1,325
Vienna	8,746	Lüttich	2,861	Prague (German)	1,965	Aberdeen	1,300
St. Petersburg	8,400	Athens	2,890	Sendai	1,915	Tomsk	1,300
Budapest	7,667	Glasgow	2,890	Jena	1,885	Poitiers	1,278
Munich	7,579	Breslau	2,641	Durham	1,823	Erlangen	1,251
Naples	6,660	Louvain	2,630	Lille	1,806	Brussels	1,250
Leipzig	6,695	Freiburg	2,614	Bern	1,762	Melbourne	1,248
Madrid	5,675	Strassburg	2,569	Konigsberg	1,706	Lund	1,233
Tokyo (Imperial)	5,242	Bordeaux	2,528	Kiel	1,701	Czernowitz	1,232
Lemberg	5,177	Gottingen	2,525	Valencia	1,700	Liverpool	1,229
Buenos Aires	4,659	McGill (Montreal)	2,481	Manchester	1,691	Ghent	1,228
Valladolid	4,600	Barcelona	2,431	Wales, Univ. of	1,620	Greifswald	1,201
Prague (Bohemian)	4,414	Heidelberg	2,418	Padua	1,613	Salamanca	1,200
Bonn	4,269	Klausenburg	2,466	Pavia	1,600	Leiden	1,196
Rome	3,999	Odessa	2,293	Palermo	1,598	Leeds	1,163
London	3,669	Munster (Germany)	2,265	Rennes	1,573	Pisa	1,150
Cambridge	3,781	Sofia	2,260	Wurzburg	1,512	Amsterdam	1,130
Toronto	3,412	Warsaw	2,247	Kingston (Canada)	1,507	Seville	1,100
Cracow	3,090	Upsala	2,217	Christiania	1,500	Utrecht	1,096
Edinburgh	3,586	Turin	2,204	Algiers	1,442	Havana	1,070
Helsingfors	3,350	Nancy	2,190	Giessen	1,428	Belgrade	1,025
Kharkov	3,515	Graz	2,134	Grenoble	1,427	Dijon	1,000
Bucharest	3,147	Copenhagen	2,100	Zurich	1,421	Dublin	1,000
Lyons	3,661	Manila (SantoTomas)	2,100	Gothenburg	1,408	Granada	1,000
Halle	3,021	Oxford	2,961	Sydney	1,387		

ROMAN AND ARABIC NUMERALS.

I	1	V	5	IX	9	D	500
II	2	VI	6	X	10	M	1000
III	3	VII	7	L	50	MCMX	1910
IV	4	VIII	8	C	100	MCMXIV	1914

STATISTICS OF EDUCATION IN THE UNITED STATES.

[From bureau of education reports.]

COMMON SCHOOLS (1910-1911).

State.	Number.*	Children.—Enrolled.	Attendance.†	School days.‡	Teachers.—Male.	Female.	Total.	Salaries.	Total Exp'nditure.
Alabama.........	681,601	434,748	268,768	115.2	3,413	6,166	9,579	$2,952,261	$3,747,885
Arizona..........	52,312	31,312	20,094	135.6	142	709	851	695,106	1,090,628
Arkansas.........	504,478	404,760	255,405	113.9	4,453	5,291	9,834	2,966,177	3,510,122
California.......	489,891	386,911	208,637	173.6	1,766	10,390	12,156	11,281,662	20,070,928
Colorado.........	196,058	173,229	118,245	156.0	823	4,642	5,465	3,519,676	5,824,200
Connecticut......	263,341	193,055	149,019	184.9	366	5,097	5,463	3,499,958	5,426,533
Delaware........	50,914	35,950	22,559	172.5	136	857	993	411,520	604,796
District Columbia.	68,170	56,784	45,496	186.5	204	1,490	1,694	1,650,402	3,112,241
Florida..........	225,431	149,651	103,956	136.2	974	3,122	4,096	1,190,124	1,931,279
Georgia..........	847,642	565,678	352,059	151.4	3,006	10,018	13,024	2,873,028	4,990,162
Idaho............	91,940	79,126	57,359	140.0	582	1,923	2,505	1,387,403	2,797,091
Illinois.........1,	423,165	1,007,894	789,975	171.0	5,519	24,444	29,963	18,195,918	30,737,991
Indiana.........	683,584	531,459	420,780	147.0	6,156	11,111	17,267	9,024,559	14,910,500
Iowa............	587,778	492,778	361,161	172.0	2,560	24,589	27,149	8,754,560	12,591,340
Kansas..........	468,968	398,749	295,776	156.0	2,417	11,326	13,743	6,212,959	10,209,954
Kentucky........	676,068	503,022	275,060	131.8	4,239	7,301	11,540	3,889,980	6,165,719
Louisiana.......	528,973	278,355	179,299	135.2	1,441	5,065	6,506	2,616,457	4,064,820
Maine...........	172,094	144,552	108,299	162.8	824	6,673	7,497	1,943,826	3,073,603
Maryland........	344,129	237,119	145,349	185.0	915	4,734	5,649	2,935,158	4,010,289
Massachusetts....	776,326	538,845	446,603	185.0	1,516	14,463	15,979	12,991,737	22,502,934
Michigan........	705,875	545,279	408,959	170.0	2,561	15,641	18,202	9,327,930	15,292,552
Minnesota.......	575,387	443,792	326,505	161.3	1,605	13,979	15,584	7,797,963	15,006,133
Mississippi......	593,839	469,137	261,384	120.0	3,162	7,004	10,166	2,136,126	2,726,248
Missouri........	872,155	696,893	488,619	155.4	4,767	13,779	18,546	9,153,657	14,328,394
Montana.........	85,520	63,255	45,576	156.9	337	2,203	2,540	1,696,627	3,162,072
Nebraska........	329,681	282,753	197,990	168.6	1,306	9,662	10,968	4,834,178	8,045,023
Nevada..........	14,655	10,200	7,400	145.3	52	437	489	230,000	619,268
New Hampshire..	96,536	62,394	48,844	168.5	208	2,749	2,957	984,868	1,693,800
New Jersey......	633,346	442,958	339,353	183.0	1,312	10,623	11,934	9,266,170	18,076,256
New Mexico......	99,945	57,436	37,013	115.0	507	1,041	1,548	571,212	972,559
New York.......2,	148,048	1,436,580	1,134,323	186.9	5,086	40,280	45,366	36,109,811	52,328,926
North Carolina..	720,492	526,413	344,421	104.7	2,839	8,612	11,451	3,240,753	3,340,697
North Dakota....	172,846	136,668	91,835	151.0	1,304	6,351	7,655	2,753,746	5,184,936
Ohio............1,	152,327	892,875	651,746	165.5	8,368	19,655	28,023	15,243,563	28,057,151
Oklahoma........	540,407	443,227	260,018	130.0	3,142	6,878	10,028	3,449,094	6,759,413
Oregon..........	156,396	118,412	103,553	138.0	956	4,013	4,969	2,659,927	5,837,676
Pennsylvania......1,	965,804	1,286,273	1,028,290	179.4	8,044	28,136	36,180	20,244,716	42,137,647
Rhode Island....	130,236	84,037	63,026	194.0	210	2,206	2,416	1,503,559	2,360,109
South Carolina...	513,299	354,270	205,028	92.8	1,643	5,364	7,007	1,715,884	2,168,513
South Dakota.....	168,522	130,297	83,390	152.0	1,059	4,716	5,775	2,201,942	3,400,038
Tennessee........	661,463	529,669	360,205	133.0	3,597	6,362	9,959	2,795,790	5,083,469
Texas...........1,	256,089	824,686	546,832	135.1	6,396	15,026	21,422	9,050,047	11,841,818
Utah............	112,085	91,532	75,766	159.0	668	1,841	2,509	1,558,123	3,576,045
Vermont.........	83,289	68,831	53,574	160.0	265	3,021	3,286	946,303	1,647,579
Virginia........	634,446	409,397	263,241	131.5	1,925	8,759	10,684	2,935,014	4,623,240
Washington......	269,251	220,461	168,021	172.3	1,478	6,111	7,589	5,578,807	10,860,995
West Virginia....	363,433	275,252	189,169	135.0	4,133	4,937	9,070	3,001,679	4,522,573
Wisconsin.......	648,356	460,794	329,577	179.6	1,721	13,442	15,163	7,001,946	11,306,852
Wyoming........	32,178	26,040	19,453	140.9	135	1,040	1,175	536,555	1,120,839
Total.........24,	862,726	18,035,118	12,871,980	156.8	110,328	423,278	533,606	266,676,471	446,726,929
Division—									
North Atlantic.. 6,	269,020	4,257,455	3,371,331	179.8	17,831	113,247	131,078	87,550,948	149,247,686
South Atlantic.. 3,	767,956	2,611,914	1,701,228	130.6	15,775	47,893	63,668	18,963,572	23,666,669
South Central.. 5,	448,918	3,887,604	2,406,971	127.8	29,233	59,093	89,026	29,855,932	43,899,504
North Central.. 7,	775,977	6,020,231	4,446,313	164.3	3,343	168,695	208,038	100,502,921	169,070,869
Western........ 1,	600,855	1,257,914	946,137	159.3	7,446	34,350	41,796	29,815,098	55,842,301

*School year, 1911; children 5 to 18 years of age. †Average daily attendance ‡Average duration of school in days.

EXPENDITURES FOR COMMON SCHOOLS.

School year.	Build-ings, etc.	Salaries.	Other.	Total.	Per capita.	Per pupil.
1901-1902........................	$29,362,863	$151,448,681	$48,855,755	$238,262,299	$3.03	$21.53
1902-3........................	46,289,074	157,110,108	48,058,442	251,457,625	3.15	22.75
1903-4........................	49,453,269	167,824,753	55,938,205	273,216,227	3.26	24.14
1904-5........................	56,416,168	177,462,981	57,737,511	291,616,660	3.52	25.40
1905-6........................	60,608,352	186,482,464	60,673,843	307,765,659	3.66	26.27
1906-7........................	65,333,340	202,047,814	69,517,179	336,898,333	3.90	28.25
1907-8........................	73,640,408	219,780,123	77,923,879	371,344,410	4.27	30.55
1908-9........................	81,878,591	237,013,913	82,505,243	401,397,747	4.45	31.65
1909-10........................	69,978,370	253,915,170	102,356,894	426,250,434	4.64	33.33
1910-11........................	75,555,615	266,676,471	104,492,843	446,726,029	4.76	34.71

PUPILS ENROLLED IN SCHOOLS AND COLLEGES (1911).

Grades.	Public.	Private.	Total.	Grades.	Public.	Private.	Total.
Elementary	17,050,441	1,470,581	18,521,022	Universit's and colleges	68,187	115,995	184,182
Secondary (high schools and academies)........	984,677	130,649	1,115,326	Professional schools....	11,529	53,729	65,258
Secondary (preparatory dept. higher instit'ns)	17,327	66,816	84,143	Normal schools.........	75,642	8,453	84,095
				Total	18,207,803	1,846,223	20,054,026

Grades.	Public.	Private.	Total.
City evening schools....	375,000	....	375,000
Business schools.......	....	155,244	155,244
Reform schools.........	40,642	....	40,642
Schools for the deaf....	12,347	693	13,040
Schools for the blind...	4,670	....	4,670
Schools for the feeble minded	6,956	592	7,548
Gvmt. Indian schools...	39,397	....	39,397
Schools in Alaska supported by government	3,841	....	3,841
Schools in Alaska supported by incorporated municipalities (est.)..	4,500	....	4,500
Orphan asyl'ms,etc.(est.)	....	17,000	17,000
Private kinderg'ns (est.)	....	110,000	110,000

Grades.	Public.	Private.	Total.
Miscellaneous (art, music, etc.—est.)........	....	55,000	55,000
Total special schools.	487,353	338,529	825,882
Total for all schools.	18,695,156	2,184,752	20,879,908

AVERAGE MONTHLY AND ANNUAL SALARIES OF TEACHERS (1911).

Division.	Monthly.			Annual.
	Men.	Women.	All.	All.
North Atlantic....	$79.75	$49.97	$67.19	$604.04
North Central......	73.64	55.46	58.43	480.29
South Atlantic.....	60.72	42.63	46.54	303.91
South Central.....	63.26	52.60	52.05	332.60
Western	102.69	71.55	76.24	607.63
United States.....	73.86	54.98	59.49	466.40

PUBLIC HIGH SCHOOLS (1912).

Schools	11,221
Teachers—Men	22,923
Teachers—Women	28,930
Students—Boys	489,048
Students—Girls	616,312

PRIVATE HIGH SCHOOLS(1912).

Schools	2,044
Teachers—Men	5,307
Teachers—Women	7,076
Students—Boys	66,742
Students—Girls	74,725

NORMAL SCHOOLS (1912).
PUBLIC.

Schools	222
Teachers—Men	1,487
Teachers—Women	2,577
Students—Men	15,725
Students—Women	66,749

PRIVATE.

Schools	55
Teachers—Men	144
Teachers—Women	257
Students—Men	2,135
Students—Women	4,375

UNIVERSITIES, COLLEGES AND TECHNOLOGICAL SCHOOLS (1912).

Institutions	594
Instructors—Men	24,476
Instructors—Women	5,494
Preparatory students—Men.	40,154
Prepar'y students—Women..	23,197
Collegiate students—Men..	117,856
Collegiate stud'nts—Women	68,779
Colleges for Men—Number..	144
Undergraduate students...	37,633
Colleges for women—No....	109
Undergraduate students...	21,423
Coeducational colleges—No.	341
Undergr. students—Men	80,215
Undergrad. stud'ts—Wom.	47,353
Total students............	127,935

PROFESSIONAL SCHOOLS(1912).

Theology—Schools	182
Students	11,242
Law—Schools	118
Students	20,769
Medicine—Schools	115
Students	18,451
Dentistry—Schools	52
Students	7,190
Pharmacy—Schools	76
Students	6,158

Veterinary—Schools	21
Students	2,283

SCHOOLS FOR BLIND, DEAF, FEEBLE MINDED (1912).

State schools for blind—No.	60
Pupils	4,992
State schools for deaf—No.	58
Pupils	11,244
Public schools for deaf—No.	58
Pupils	1,928
Priv. schools for deaf—No.	19
Pupils	518
Schools for feeble minded:	
State—Number	33
Inmates	21,357
Private—Number	20
Inmates	749

OTHER SCHOOLS (1912).

Training nurses—Number...	1,051
Students	32,346
Commercial—Number	519
Students	137,790
Manual training—Number..	295
Students	61,453
Reform—Number	117
Inmates	51,967

COLLEGE COLORS.

Amherst—Purple and white.
Atlanta—Gray and crimson.
Baldwin—Old gold and seal brown.
Barnard—Light blue and white.
Beloit—Old gold.
Boston—Scarlet and white.
Bowdoin—White.
Brown—Brown and white.
Bryn Mawr—Yellow and white.
Bucknell—Orange and blue.
Carnegie—Plaid.
College City of New York—Lavender and black.
Columbia—Light blue and white.
Cornell—Carnelian and white.
Creighton—Blue and white.
Dartmouth—Green.
De Pauw—Old gold.
Earlham—Yellow and green.
Fordham—Maroon.
Georgetown—Blue and gray.
George Washington—Buff and blue.
Harvard—Crimson.
Indiana—Crimson and green.
Iowa State—Cardinal and gold.
Iowa—Scarlet and black.
Johns Hopkins—Black and blue.
Lafayette—Maroon and white.
Lake Forest—Red and black.
Lawrence—White and blue.
Lehigh—Seal brown and white.
Leland Stanford, Jr.—Cardinal.
Manhattan—Green and white.

Marquette—Blue and gold.
Mount Holyoke—Blue.
New Orleans—Tan and blue.
New York—Violet.
Northwestern—Purple.
Oberlin—Crimson and gold.
Ohio State—Scarlet and gray.
Ohio—Olive green and white.
Pratt—Yellow.
Princeton—Orange and black.
Purdue—Old gold and black.
Radcliffe—Crimson and white.
Rutgers—Scarlet.
Smith—White and gold.
Stevens—Silver gray and cardinal.
St. Louis—Blue and white.
Swarthmore—Garnet.
Syracuse—Orange.
Temple—Cherry and white.
Throop—Orange and white.
Tufts—Brown and blue.
Tulane—Olive and blue.
Union—Garnet.
University of California—Blue and gold.
University of Chicago—Maroon.
University of Illinois—Orange and blue.
University of Kansas—Crimson and blue.
University of Maine—Light blue.
University of Michigan—Maize and blue.

University of Minnesota—Gold and maroon.
University of Missouri—Black and old gold.
University of Notre Dame—Gold and blue.
University of Pennsylvania—Red and blue.
University ofPittsburgh—Blue and gold.
University of Rochester—Yellow.
University of Vermont—Green and gold.
University of Virginia—Orange and blue.
University of Washington—Purple and gold.
University of Wisconsin—Cardinal.
United States Military Academy—Black, gold and gray.
United States Naval Academy—Blue and gold.
Valparaiso—Old gold and brown.
Vanderbilt—Black and gold.
Vassar—Rose and gray.
Washington and Lee—Blue and white.
Washington (Mo.)—Red and green.
Wellesley—Deep blue.
Western Reserve—Crimson and white.
Williams—Royal purple.
Yale—Blue.

AMERICAN UNIVERSITIES AND COLLEGES,
Nonsectarian and undenominational schools marked with *

School, location and date of founding	President	Instructors	Students
Adelphi college,* Brooklyn, N. Y (1896) ...	S P, Cadman, D. D (acting)..	33	1,167
Adrian college, Adrian, Mich. (1859) ...	B W Anthony, D D., LL D ...	23	200
Agnes Scott college, Decatur, Ga	F H. Gaines, D. D ..	30	209
Ag. and Mech. Col of Tex ,* Col S , Tex (1876)	R. T. Milner, LL. D	39	1,130
Alabama Polytechnic Inst.,* Auburn, Ala (1872) .	C. C. Thach, M A, LL. D	65	806
Albany college, Albany, Ore (1866) ..	H M Crooks	14	140
Albion college, Albion, Mich. (1861)	Hon. Samuel Dickie, LL D	26	516
Alfred university,* Alfred, N Y (1836)	Boothe C Davis, Ph D., D. D..	58	435
Allegheny college, Meadville, Pa (1815) ..	W H. Crawford, D D., LL. D	23	406
Alma college, Alma, Mich (1887)	Thomas C Blaisdell, Ph D	25	310
American Inter. col ,* Springfield, Mass. (1885).. .	C Stowe McGowan (chancellor)	14	114
American university, Washington, D. C. (1913)	Franklin E. E. Hamilton, Ph D		
Amer Univ of Harriman, Harriman, Tenn (1893)..	W T. Robinson, M. A	12	265
Amherst college,* Amherst, Mass (1825)	Alexander Meikeljohn, A M , Ph D	44	425
Amity college,* College Springs, Iowa (1855).... ./.	Rev. R A McConagha, D D.	11	200
Andover Theological sem , Cambridge, Mass (1808).	Albert P Fitch, D. D	8	53
Antioch college,* Yellow Springs, O (1852).	S D Fess, LL D..	15	168
Arkansas college, Bateville, Ark (1872)	J P. Robinson, A. M , D D .	11	122
Armour Inst. of Technology,* Chicago, Ill (1893)	F. W Gunsaulus, D. D , LL D	60	1,488
Atlanta university,* Atlanta, Ga. (1869)	Edward T. Ware, A. B , D D	32	404
Auburn Theological sem., Auburn, N. Y (1819)	G B Stewart, D.D , LL D	12	57
Augsburg seminary, Minneapolis, Minn (1869)	George Sverdrup, Jr., D D	17	171
Augustana college, Rock Island, Ill. (1860)	Gustav Andreen, Ph D ..	33	629
Baker university, Baldwin, Kas (1858)	Wilbur N Mason, A. M , D. D	35	515
Baldwin university, Berea, O (1856)	Glezen A Reeder, D. D	30	341
Barnard college,* New York, N Y. (1859) ..	N M. Butler, LL D , Litt D..	72	818
Bates college,* Lewiston, Me (1864).....	George C Chase, A M, D D , LL. D	23	483
Baylor university, Waco, Tex. (1845)	Samuel P. Brooks, A. M., LL D	45	1,531
Bellevue college, Bellevue, Neb (1880)	Stephen W Stookey, D. D	20	200
Beloit college,* Beloit, Wis (1846)	E. D Eaton, D D , LL. D.	33	387
Berea college,* Berea, Ky. (1855) .	W Godell Frost, Ph D, D D , LL D	86	1,736
Bethany college, Bethany, W. Va. (1840).. ..	T E Cramblet, A M , LL. D.	28	354
Bethany college, Lindsborg, Kas. (1881) . .	Ernest P. Pihlblad, A M..	45	893
Bethel college, Russellville, Ky .	F. D Perkins, M A.	10	100
Bissell College of Photo-Engraving, Effingham, Ill .	L. H Bissell	3	80
Blackburn college, Carlinville, Ill (1857)	William M. Hudson, Ph. D , D D .	11	120
Boston college, Boston, Mass (1863) ...	Thomas J. Gasson, S J	50	1,230
Boston university, Boston, Mass. (1869)	Samuel H. Murlin, D D., LL D	145	1,508
Bowdoin college, Brunswick, Me. (1794)	William DeWitt Hyde, D. D , LL D	28	337
Bradley Polytechnic institute, Peoria, Ill	Theodore C Burgess, Ph D —т.	45	1,086
Brigham Young college, Logan, Utah (1877)	C N. Jensen, Ph. D..	28	700
Brown university,* Providence, R I (1764)	William H P Faunce, D D , LL D -	78	941
Bryn Mawr college,* Bryn Mawr, Pa. (1885) ..	Miss M C Thomas, Ph D , LL D	60	459
Buchtel college, Akron, O (1870) .	Parke K Kolbe, Ph D ..	19	176
Bucknell university, Lewisburg, Pa (1846). .	John Howard Harris, LL D ..	47	700
Butler college,* Indianapolis, Ind. (1850) .	Thomas C Howe, LL. D	20	611
Canisius college, Buffalo, N Y. (1870) . .	Rev. George J Krim, S J	27	451
Carleton college,* Northfield, Minn (1866)	Donald G. Cowling, D D , Ph D	34	395
Carroll college, Waukesha, Wis. (1846) .. .	Wilbur O Carrier, M A, D D. .	20	270
Carson & Neman col , Jefferson City, Tenn. (1851) .	J M Burnett, D D ..	17	417
Carthage college, Carthage, Ill. (1870). .	Henry D. Hoover, A M , B D , Ph D	20	184
Case Sc Applied Science,* Cleveland, O (1881)	Charles S Howe, Ph. D. Sc... ..	43	50o
Cath. Univ of Am , Washington, D. C. (1889)	Thomas J Shahan, D D	72	550
Cedarville college, Cedarville, O. (1887)	David McKinney, D D LL D	12	100
Central college, Fayette, Mo. (1857)	William A. Webb, D. D , Litt.-D	13	205
Central Univ. of Kentucky, Danville, Ky (1819)...	F. W Hinitt, Ph. D , D D .	20	150
Central Wesleyan college, Warrenton, Mo (1864) .	Otto E Kriege, D. D., A B .	21	320
Charles City college, Charles City, Iowa (1891)....	W F Finke, A. M., Litt D (acting)	12	175
Christian university, Canton, Mo (1853)	Carl Johns, A. M., LL. D	12	127
Claflin university, Orangeburg, S C. (1869)	Lewis M Dunton, A. M , D. D .	41	550
Clark college,* Worcester, Mass. (1902) .	Edmund C. Sanford, Ph D..	31	156
Clark university, South Atlanta Station, Ga. (1870)	W W. Foster, D D , LL. D	18	448
Clark university,* Worcester, Mass (1889)	G. Stanley Hall, Ph. D., LL. D	25	108
Clarkson School Tech ,* Potsdam, N. Y (1896)	John P. Brooks, M S	9	70
Clemson Ag. col ,* Clemson college, S C (1896) . .	W M. Riggs, E. M E., LL. D	55	—834
Coe college, Cedar Rapids, Iowa (1881)..... .	John A. Marquis, D D , LL. D	34	516
Colby college, Waterville, Me (1820)	Arthur J, Roberts, A M.	24	410
Colgate university,* Hamilton, N. Y (1819) ...	Elmer B Bryan, LL D.	50	449
College City of New York,* New York (1847) ..	(Vacancy) .	250	3,900
College of Emporia, Emporia, Kas (1882)...	Henry C. Culbertson, D. D	25	286
College of Pacific, San Jose, Cal (1851) .	William W. Guth, Ph. D. .	32	401
College of St. Elizabeth, Convent Station, N J....	Sister Mary Pauline	32	400
Colorado college,* Colorado Springs, Col (1874)	William F Slocum, D D., LL D	48	587
Columbia university,* New York, N. Y. (1754)	Nicholas M Butler, Ph D , LL. D., Litt. D	595	6,073
Concordia college, Brinxville, N Y..... .	Il! Feth, D. D	6	105
Concordia college, Fort Wayne Ind (1839)	Rev Martin Luecke	12	284
Concordia college, Milwaukee, Wis	M J F Albrecht, D D	9	236
Concordia college, New Orleans, La	Charles Niermann, D D	2	18
Concordia college, St Paul, Minn	Theodore Buenger	9	161
Converse college,* Spartanburg, S C (1890)	Robert P. Pell, Litt D	25	289
Cooper college, Sterling Kas (1887)	R. T. Campbell, D D	17	188
Cornell college, Mount Vernon, Iowa (1853).... .	James F. Harlan, LL D	37	702
Cornell university,* Ithaca, N Y. (1868)..... ..	Jacob G. Schurman, D. Sc , LL D .	696	5,000
Creighton university, Omaha, Neb (1879).........	Eugene A Magerney, S J.......	155	1,060
Cumberland university, Lebanon, Tenn,.............	Winstead P, Bone, D. D.,............	22	360

School, location and date of founding	President	Instruct-ors	Stu-dents.
Dakota Wesleyan univ , Mitchell, S D (1883) . .	William G. Seaman	33	407
Dartmouth college,* Hanover, N H (1769)	Ernest Fox Nichols, D. Sc , LL D .	133	1,294
Davidson college, Davidson, N C. (1837) . .	William J. Martin, M A., M D , Ph D	41	354
Decatur college, Decatur, Ill. (1901).	George E Fellows, Ph. D , LL. D .	69	1,128
Defiance college, Defiance, O. (1902) . . .	P. W. McReynolds, A M .	26	564
Delaware college,* Newark, Del (1833) . . .	George A. Harter, M. A , Ph D	25	169
Denison university, Granville, O (1831) .	Clark W. Chamberlain, Ph D	40	600
De Paul university, Chicago, Ill	Very Rev F X McCabe, C M , LL D	75	915
De Pauw university, Greencastle, Ind. (1837). _ . .	- George R Grose . .	43	1,000
Des Moines college, Des Moines, Iowa (1865). ¯ . .	John A Earl, D. D . .	18	400
Dickinson college, Carlisle, Pa. (1783)	Eugene A Noble, D. D .	17	300
Doane college, Crete, Neb. (1872)	(Vacancy) . .	22	193
Drake university, Des Moines, Iowa (1881) . .	Hill M Bell, A. M	160	1,591
Drew Theological seminary, Madison, N J (1866) .	Ezra S Tipple, D D , LL D .	15	170
Drury college, Springfield, Mo (1873) .	Joseph H George, M A , D D , Ph D	26	550
Earlham college, Richmond, Ind. (1847) . .	Robert L Kelly, LL D	30	500
Elmira college, Elmira, N. Y. (1855)	A. C. Mackenzie, D D , LL D .	18	210
Elon college, Elon College, N C (1890)	L. A. Harper, M A , Litt D	21	358
Emory and Henry college, Emory, Va. (1838). . . .	Charles C. Weaver, A. M , Ph. D	13	210
Emory college, Oxford, Ga. (1836)	James E Dickey, D. D	17	267
Erskine college, Due West, S C. (1839)	James S Moffat, D D . . .	9	142
Ewing college, Ewing, Ill (1867) . .	E L. Carr . . .	10	150
Fairmount college, Wichita, Kas (1895)	Henry E. Thayer . . .	24	259
Fargo college, Fargo, N D. (1888)	Charles E. Creegan, D, D	24	467
Fisk university, Nashville, Tenn (1866) . . .	Prof H H. Wright (dean)	45	494
Fordham university, New York, N. Y. (1841).	Rev. Thomas J McCluskey, D D , S J	131	1,412
Frank Hughes college, Clifton, Tenn (1906) . .	W E Johnston	8	175
Franklin & Marshall college, Lancaster, Pa (1887) .	Henry H Apple, D. D . .	16	293
Franklin college, Franklin (1834) .	Elijah A Hanley, D D	13	206
Franklin college,* New Athens, O (1825)	E M Baxter, A M	12	102
Furman university, Greenville, S C (1851)	Edwin McNeil Poteat, LL D .	16	347
General Theological sem , New York, N Y (1817)	Wilford U Robbins, D D , LL D	15	133
Georgetown university, Washington, D C (1789)	Rev. Alphonsus J Donlon, S J	200	1,501
German Wallace college, Berea, O . . . _ . .	A L. Breslich, D D , Ph D . ?	30	300
Goucher college, Baltimore, Md. (1888) . , . .	A B. Van Meter (acting)	30	368
Greer college,* Hoopeston, Ill. (1891)	E L. Bailey, B S , M S . .	15	75
Grinnell college, Grinnell, Iowa (1847)	J. H T Main, Ph D , LL D	43	634
Grove City college,* Grove City, Pa (1876) . . .	I. C Ketler, D D , LL. D , Ph D ,	30	774
Guilford college, Guilford College, N. C (1888)	Lewis L Hobbs, LL D .	15	251
Gustavus Adolphus college, St. Peter, Minn (1862)	O J Johnson, D. D . .	21	350
Hamilton college,* Clinton, N. Y. (1812) . .	M. Woolsey Stryker, D. D , LL D .	20	185
Hamline university, St Paul, Minn (1854) , ...	Samuel F. Kerfoot, D. D .	17	374
Hampden-Sidney col , Hampden-Sidney, Va (1776)	Harry T Graham, D D .	9	122
Hampton Institute,* Hampton, Va (1868).	Hollis B Frissell, D. D , LL. D	135	1,637
Hanover college, Hanover, Ind (1832) . .	William A Millis, LL D .	16	248
Harvard university,* Cambridge, Mass (1636). . . .	Abbott L Lowell, M A , LL D.	774	5,224
Hastings college, Hastings, Neb (1882)	R B. Crone . . .	13	122
Haverford college, Haverford, Pa (1833) . .	Isaac Sharpless, Sc D , LL. D	21	167
Hedding college, Abingdon, Ill (1856) . . .	Walter D Agnew, D. D	15	172
Heidelberg university, Tiffin, O (1850)	Charles E. Miller, D D , LL. D . . .	29	390
Hendrix college, Conway, Ark (1884)	A C Millar, A. M., D D	12	200
Henry Kendall college, Tulsa, Okla (1895)	F. W Hawley, A. M., D D . .	14	170
Hillsdale college, Hillsdale, Mich. (1855)	Joseph W Mauck, A. M., LL. D	23	497
Hiram college, Hiram, O (1850) . .	Miner Lee Bates, A M	25	273
Hiwassee college,* Sweetwater, Tenn (1849) . . .	Eugene-Blake, A. M., D D . ¯	7	120
Hobart college,* Geneva, N Y (1822)	Prof William P. Durfee (acting)	22	92
Holy Cross college, Worcester, Mass (1843) . .	Rev Joseph N. Dinand, S. J	31	560
Hope college, Holland, Mich (1866) . .	Ame Vennema, D D . .	20	407
Howard college, Birmingham, Ala. (1889)	James M Shelburne . .	12	175
Howard university,* Washington, D C (1867) . .	Stephen M Newman, D. D	125	1,500
Huron college, Huron, S D (1883) . .	Calvin H. French, A M., D D.. . .	23	388
Illinois college, Jacksonville, Ill. (1829)	C H Rammelkamp, Ph D	24	374
Illinois College of Photography, Effingham, Ill. . . .	L H Bissell	7	180
Illinois Wesleyan univ , Bloomington, Ill (1850) .	Theodore Kemp, D. D , LL D .	45	615
Indiana university,* Bloomington, Ind (1820)	William Lowe Bryan, Ph. D , LL. D	90	2,448
Iowa State college,* Ames, Iowa (1869) .	Raymond A Pearson, LL D	264	2,510
Iowa Wesleyan college, Mt Pleasant, Iowa (1842)	Edwin A Schell, D D , Ph. D .	25	314
Jacob Tome institute,* Port Deposit, Md	Thomas S Baker, Ph D (director)	25	227
John B Stetson university,* DeLand, Fla (1883).	Lincoln Hulley, Ph. D , Litt D., LL D .	40	462
Johns Hopkins university,* Baltimore, Md, (1876).	(Vacancy)	239	1,087
Kansas City university, Kansas City, Mo (1886) . .	D. S. Stephens, D D , LL D	71	348
Kansas Wesleyan university, Salina, Kas. (1886) . .	Robert P Smith, A. M , D. D. .	43	954
Kemper Hall, Kenosha, Wis (1871)	Mother superior . .	21	125
Kenyon college Gambier, O (1824) .	William F. Pierce, L. H D , D D	14	98
Keuka college,* Keuka Park, N Y (1892)	Joseph A Serena . .	14	100
Knox college Galesburg, Ill (1837)	Thomas McClelland, D D., LL D	32	584
Knoxville college, Knoxville, Tenn (1875)	- R W. McGranahan, D. D	35	450
Lafayette college, Easton, Pa (1832)	E D. Warfield, D D , LL D .	55	567
LaGrange college, LaGrange, Mo . . .	Ransom Harvey, A. B , D D	10	140
Lake Erie college,* Painesville, O (1857) . .	Miss Vivian Small, M A , Litt D	30	103
Lake Forest college,* Lake Forest, Ill (1876) . .	John S. Nollen, Ph. D , LL D .	19	211
Lander college, Greenwood, S C (1872) . .	John O Willson, D D . . .	20	270
LaSalle college, Philadelphia, Pa (1867)	Rev. Brother D Edward, F S. C	16	178
Lawrence university,* Appleton Wis (1847)	Samuel Plantz, Ph D , LL D .	43	630
Lebanon Valley college, Annville Pa (1866) . . .	G, O Gossard . . .	13	122
Lehigh university,* South Bethlehem, Pa (1866) .	- Henry S Drinker, E M , LL D ..	72	672
Leland Stanford, Jr , U ,* Stanford U , Cal (1891)	John Caspar Branner, LL D	201	1,803
Leland university, New Orleans, La. (1869)	Alfred E. Earle, LL. D	49	1,700

School, location and date of founding.	President.	Instructors.	Students.
Lenox college, Hopkinton, Iowa (1856)	E. E. Reed, M. A., D. D.	13	131
Lewis Institute, Chicago, Ill. (1865)	George N. Carman (director)	100	3,500
Liberty college, Glasgow, Ky. (1874)	Robert E. Hatton, A. M., Ph. D.	12	149
Lincoln college, Lincoln, Ill. (1865)	James H. McMurray, Ph. D.	15	278
Livingstone college, Salisbury, N. C.	W. H. Goler, A. M., D. D.	16	256
Lombard college,* Galesburg, Ill. (1851)	Huber W. Hurt.	14	.....
Louisiana State university,* Baton Rouge, La. (1860)	Thomas D. Boyd, A. M., LL. D.	76	761
Loyola university, Chicago, Ill. (1909)	Rev. A. J. Burrows, S. J.	127	1,272
Luther college, Decorah, Iowa (1861)	Rev. C. K. Preus.	15	213
Macalester college, St. Paul, Minn. (1884)	T. Morey Hodgman, M. A., LL. D.	27	320
Manhattan college, New York, N. Y. (1863)	Rev. Brother Edward, F. S. C.	25	290
Marietta college,* Marietta, O. (1835)	Joseph Manley (dean).	14	152
Marquette university, Milwaukee, Wis. (1864)	Rev. Joseph Grimmelsman, S. J.	310	1,606
Maryville college, Maryville, Tenn. (1819)	Samuel T. Wilson, D. D.	39	702
Massachusetts Agr. col.,* Amherst, Mass. (1863)	Kenyon L. Butterfield, A. M., LL. D.	60	500
Mass. Inst. of Technology, Boston, Mass. (1861)	R. C. Maclaurin, A. M., LL. D., D. Sc.	258	1,611
Methodist Univ. of Oklahoma, Guthrie, Okla. (1881)	William Felder (acting)	17	237
Miami university, Oxford, O. (1809)	R. M. Hughes.	47	883
Michigan Agr. college, East Lansing, Mich. (1857)	J. L. Snyder, M. A., Ph. D.	140	1,700
Michigan College of Mines,* Houghton, Mich. (1884)	F. W. McNair, B. S., D. Sc.	23	150
Middlebury college,* Middlebury, Vt. (1800)	John M. Thomas, D. D.	28	330
Midland college, Atchison, Kas. (1887)	Rev. Rufus B. Peery, D. D.	16	203
Milligan college, Milligan College, Tenn. (1882)	F. D. Kershner, M. A.	12	275
Mills college,* Oakland, Cal. (1885)	Miss L. C. Carson, Litt. D., LL. D.	34	138
Milton college, Milton, Wis. (1867)	Rev. W. C. Daland, M. A., D. D.	15	163
Milwaukee-Downer college, Milwaukee, Wis.	Miss Ellen C. Sabin, M. A.	32	321
Milwaukee-Downer seminary, Milwaukee, Wis.	Miss Mary D. Rodman.	13	205
Miss. A. & M. college, Agricultural College, Miss.	George R. Hightower.	63	1,151
Mississippi college, Clinton, Miss. (1826)	J. W. Provine, D. D., LL. D.	17	421
Missouri Valley college, Marshall, Mo. (1889)	W. H. Black, D. D., LL. D.	14	222
Monmouth college, Monmouth, Ill. (1857)	T. H. McMichael, D. D.	27	428
Moores Hill college, Moores Hill, Ind. (1807)	Henry A. King, D. D.	15	256
Morningside college, Sioux City, Iowa (1894)	Alfred E. Craig.	35	504
Morris Brown university, Atlanta, Ga. (1885)	W. A. Fountain, D. D., Ph. D.	28	898
Mount Angel college, Mount Angel, Ore. (1887)	Rev. P. A. Walsh, O. S. B.	22	140
Mount Holyoke college,* South Hadley, Mass. (1837)	Miss M. E. Wooley, M. A., Litt. D., L. H. D.	87	755
Mount St. Mary's college, Emmitsburg, Md. (1808)	Very Rev. B. J. Bradley, A. M., LL. D.	30	385
Mount Union college, Alliance, O. (1858)	W. H. McMaster, A. M.	30	572
Muhlenburg college, Allentown, Pa. (1867)	John A. W. Haas, D. D.	14	168
Muskingum college, New Concord, O. (1837)	J. K. Montgomery, D. D.	30	606
McCormick Theological seminary, Chicago, Ill. (1829)	James G. K. McClure, D. D., LL. D.	12	159
McKendree college, Lebanon, Ill. (1828)	John F. Harmon, M. A., D. D.	17	345
McMinville college, McMinville, Ore. (1857)	Leonard W. Riley, D. D.	16	195
Nebraska Wesleyan univ., Univ. Place, Neb. (1888)	Clark A. Fulmer (chancellor).	39	1,251
New Orleans university, New Orleans, La. (1873)	Charles M. Melden, D. D., Ph. D.	32	557
New Rochelle college, New Rochelle, N. Y.	M. C. O'Farrell, D. D.	32	105
Newton Theo. inst., Newton Center, Mass. (1825)	George E. Horr, D. D.	11	80
New York university,* New York, N. Y. (1830)	Elmer E. Brown, Ph. D., LL. D.	328	4,597
Niagara university, Niagara Falls, N. Y. (1856)	Very Rev. Edward J. Walsh, C. M.	31	350
Norwich university, Northfield, Vt. (1819)	Charles H. Spooner, A. M., LL. D.	15	149
N. C. Col. of Ag. & Me. Arts,* W. Raleigh, N. C. (1889)	D. H. Hill, LL. D., Litt. D.	55	669
Northwestern college, Naperville, Ill. (1861)	L. H. Saeger, D. D.	22	356
Northwestern Mil. and Nav. acad., Lake Geneva, Wis.	Col. R. P. Davidson, A. M.	14	100
Northwestern university, Evanston, Ill. (1865)	Abram W. Harris, Sc. D., LL. D.	450	4,876
Oberlin college,* Oberlin, O. (1833)	Henry C. King, D. D., LL. D.	150	1,809
Occidental college, Los Angeles, Cal. (1887)	John Willis Baer, LL. D.	25	256
Ohio Northern university, Ada, O. (1871)	Albert E. Smith, D. D., Ph. D.	40	1,764
Ohio State university,* Columbus, O. (1870)	William O. Thompson, D. D., LL. D.	233	3,988
Ohio university,* Athens, O. (1804)	Alston Ellis, Ph. D., LL. D.	85	2,037
Ohio Wesleyan university,* Delaware, O. (1842)	Herbert Welch, D. D., LL. D.	65	1,166
Olivet college,* Olivet, Mich. (1859)	E. G. Lancaster, Ph. D., LL. D.	24	237
Oregon Agricultural college,* Corvallis, Ore. (1885)	William J. Kerr, Sc. D.	150	2,316
Ottawa university, Ottawa, Kas. (1865)	Silas Eber Price, D. D.	20	350
Otterbein university, Westerville, O. (1847)	W. G. Clippinger, A. B., B. D.	30	466
Ouachita college, Arkadelphia, Ark. (1886)	R. G. Bowers, A. B., D. D.	30	354
Pacific university, Forest Grove, Ore. (1849)	William M. Ferrin, LL. D.	21	198
Park college,* Parkville, Mo. (1875)	Lowell M. McAfee, LL. D.	24	373
Parker college, Winnebago, Minn. (1889)†	Benjamin Longley, D. D.	..	.....
Parsons college, Fairfield, Iowa (1875)	Willis E. Parsons, D. D.	22	250
Peabody college, Nashville, Tenn.†	Bruce R. Payne, A. M., Ph. D.	..	.....
Penn college, Oskaloosa, Iowa (1873)	David M. Edwards, Ph. D.	39	506
Pennsylvania college, Gettysburg, Pa. (1832)	W. A. Granville, Ph. D., LL. D.	25	359
Pennsylvania Col. for Women,* Pittsburgh, Pa. (1869)	H. D. Lindsay, D. D.	24	256
Pennsylvania Military college,* Chester, Pa. (1858)	Col. C. E. Hyatt, C. E.	16	110
Philander Smith college, Little Rock, Ark. (1887)	Rev. James M. Cox.	24	478
Polytechnic institute,* Brooklyn, N. Y. (1854)	Fred W. Atkinson, Ph. D.	40	670
Pomona college,* Claremont, Cal. (1887)	James A. Blaisdell, D. D.	45	420
Pratt institute,* Brooklyn, N. Y. (1887)	Charles M. Pratt, A. M.	153	3,473
Presbyterian college, Clinton, S. C. (1905)	Davison McD. Douglas, M. A., D. D.	12	133
Princeton Theological sem., Princeton, N. J. (1812)	Francis L. Patton, D. D., LL. D.	16	185
Princeton university,* Princeton, N. J. (1746)	John Grier Hibben, Ph. D., LL. D.	192	1,568
Pritchett college,* Glasgow, Mo. (1868)	U. S. Hall, A. B.	10	135
Proseminar college, Elmhurst, Ill. (1871)	Rev. D. Irion, D. D.	8	168
Purdue university,* Lafayette, Ind. (1874)	W. E. Stone, Ph. D., LL. D.	180	2,000
Radcliffe college,* Cambridge, Mass. (1879)	LeBaron R. Briggs, A. M., LL. D.	134	584
Randolph-Macon college, Ashland, Va. (1830)	Robert E. Blackwell, A. M., LL. D.	16	150
Randolph-Macon Woman's col., Lynchburg, Va. (1893)	William A. Webb, LL. D.	46	576
Rensselaer Polytechnic institute,* Troy, N. Y. (1824)	Palmer C. Ricketts, C. E., E. D., LL. D.	64	620

School, location and date of founding	President	Instructors	Students
Rice institute, Houston, Tex. (1912)	Dr. Edgar O. Lovett, Ph. D , LL D		
Richmond college, Richmond, Va. (1832)	F W. Boatright, M. A , LL D... .	23	393
Rio Grande college, Rio Grande, O. (1876)	Simeon H. Bing	8	209
Ripon college,* Ripon, Wis. (1850)	Silas Evans, D D, ...	21	231
Roanoke college, Salem, Va. (1853). .	J A Morehead, D. D	19	167
Rochester Mechanics institute, Rochester, N Y (1885).	Carleton B. Gibson.	76	1,955
Rochester Theological sem., Rochester, N Y (1850)	J W. A. Stewart (acting) . .	15	150
Rockford college for women,* Rockford, Ill. (1847) .	Julia H Gulliver, Ph D., LL D .	32	249
Rock Hill college, Ellicott City, Md (1857) ..	Rev. Brother Maurice, F. S. C	18	182
Rose Polytechnic institute,* Terre Haute, Ind (1883).	Leo O. Mees, Ph. D,.	21	208
Rutgers college, New Brunswick, N. J. (1766)	W. H S Demarest, D. D , LL. D.. .	60	560
St. Anselm's college, Manchester, N. H (1889)	E. Helmsetter, D. D , O S. B.	18	174
St Bede college, Peru, Ill. (1891).....	Rt.-Rev Vincent Huber, O S B	15	140
St. Benedict's college, Atchison, Kas (1858)	Rt-Rev Innocent Wolf, O S B	22	250
St Charles college, Ellicott City, Md (1848)	Rev. F X McKonney, A. M., LL D ...	17	190
St. John's college, Annapolis, Md. (1784)....... ..	Thomas Fell, Ph D., LL D , D C. L ..	15	206
St John's college, Washington, D. C. (1866)... .. .	Brother Flamian, F S. C .. .	13	150
St. John's college, Winfield, Kas...	A W Meyer	9	99
St. John's Military academy, Delafield, Wis	Sidney T. Smythe, Ph D . .	14	225
St John's university, Collegeville, Minn (1857).	Rt.-Rev Peter Engel, O. S. B., Ph. D .	40	416
St Lawrence university, Canton, N Y (1858) .	Almon Gunnison, LL D	82	646
St. Louis university, St Louis, Mo (1818)	Very Rev.-Bernard J. Otting, S. J.	210	1,895
St. Mary's college, St. Mary's, Kas (1848) . .	A A. Breen, S. J	30	430
St Mary's college, St Mary's, Ky (1821)	Rev M Jaglowicz, C R..	10	110
St. Olaf college, Northfield, Minn. (1874) ...	John N Kildahl, D. D	32	541
St. Paul's college, Concordia, Mo...	J H C. Kaeppel	8	178
St Stephen's college, Annandale, N Y (1860)	Rev. W. C Rodgers, M. A , S. T D	10	75
St Vincent's college, Los Angeles, Cal (1885)	Joseph S Glass, C. M , D. D .	20	362
Scotia seminary, Concord, N. C (1870)	A W. Verner, D. D . .	18	270
Seton Hall college, South Orange, N J (1856)	James F. Mooney, D. D., LL D .	14	250
Shaw university, Raleigh, N. C (1865)...... ..	Charles F Meserve, LL. D . .	26	485
Shorter college, Rome, Ga. (1877)	A W. Van Hoose, A. M , LL D .	24	280
Shurtleff college, Alton, Ill. (1827)	George M. Potter, A. M.. . ..	15	150
Simmons college,* Boston, Mass (1899)...	Henry Lefavour, Ph. D , LL. D .	96	944
Simpson college, Indianola, Iowa (1860).. . .	F. L. Strickland, Ph. D, D .	32	535
Sioux Falls college, Sioux Falls, S. D..........	Edward F. Jorden, Ph D , D D .	18	185
Smith college,* Northampton, Mass (1872) ...	Marion Le Roy Burton. Ph D , LL. D .	116	1,529
Southern Baptist Theolog. sem , Louisville, Ky. (1859).	Edgar Y. Mullins, D D , LL D .	10	229
Southern university, Greensboro, Ala (1856).. .	Andrew Sledd, Ph D , D D , LL D .	10	129
Southwestern college, Winfield, Kas. (1885) . .	Frank E. Mossman, A. M .	30	460
Southwestern Pres. univ., Clarksville, Tenn. (1875)..	William Dinwiddie, LL D, (chancellor) .	10	86
Spelman seminary, Atlanta, Ga..	Miss Lucy Hale Tapley . .	49	652
Springhill college, Mobile, Ala. (1830)	E Cumming, S J .....\..	25	213
State College of Washington,* Pullman, Wash. (1892) .	E A. Bryan, LL D 120		1,837
State Normal and Industrial col.,* Greensboro, N C	J. I. Foust.	68	1,031
State University of Iowa,* Iowa City, Iowa (1847)	John G. Bowman, LL D...	226	2,255
State University of Kentucky, Lexington, Ky (1865)	Henry S. Barker, LL D . .	98	1,229
State university, Louisville, Ky ...	William T. Amiger, A. M , D D., LL D	16	225
Stevens Institute of Technology,* Hoboken, N J ..	A C. Humphreys, M E, Sc D , LL. D	33	341
Susquehanna university, Sellinsgrove, Pa (1869)	Charles T. Aikens, D D... . .	22	345
Swarthmore college, Swarthmore, Pa (1869)	Joseph Swain, B L , M. S , LL. D ..	42	409
Syracuse university,* Syracuse, N. Y (1870)	James R Day, LL. D (chancellor)	270	3,500
Tabor college, Tabor, Iowa (1866).. ...	Rev George E Wood	10	157
Talladega college,* Talladega, Ala. (1867)	J M P. Metcalf, M A.. . ..	45	768
Tarkio college, Tarkio, Mo. (1883) . . .	Joseph A. Thompson, D D .	22	280
Taylor university, Upland, Ind. (1848) . . .	Monroe Vayhinger, D D .	22	294
Temple university,* Philadelphia, Pa (1884)	Russell H. Conwell, D D , LL D .	240	3,124
Texas Christian university, Fort Worth, Tex, (1873)	Frederick D Kershner . .	31	565
The Geo Washington univ.,* Washington, D C (1821)	Charles H. Stockton LL D . .	192	1,347
The Pennsylvania State col.,* State College, Pa (1855).	Edwin Erle Sparks, M A , Ph D	172	1,808
Throop Col. of Technology,* Pasadena, Cal (1891) .	James A B. Scherer, Ph. D , LL D. ... 17		51
Transylvania university,* Lexington, Ky. (1798) .	R H Crossfield, Ph D	36	600
Trinity college, Durham, N. C (1838)	William P. Few, A. B , A. M , Ph D. .	32	431
Trinity college,* Hartford, (1823) .	Flavel S. Luther, LL. D... ...	22	260
Trinity university, Waxahachie, Tex. (1869). .	S L. Hornbeak, LL D . .	25	393
Tufts college, Tufts College, Mass (1852) .	Wm. L Hooper, A. M , Ph. D (acting) .223		1,062
Tusculum college, Tusculum, Tenn (1794) ...	C. O. Gray, D D	16	192
Tulane university,* New Orleans, La (1834) ...	Robert Sharp, Ph D . .	313	2,398
Tuskegee institute,* Tuskegee, Ala. (1881).........	Booker T. Washington, A. M , LL. D...	190	1,618
Union Christian college, Merom, Ind (1860) ...	Daniel A Long, D D . .	12	130
Union college, Barbourville, Ky	Percy L Ports, B. S	16	290
Union college, College View, Neb (1891) .	Frederick Griggs	24	309
Union college,* Schenectady, N. Y (1795) .	Charles A Richmond, D D., LL D ..	30	368
Union Theological seminary, New York, N Y (1836) .	Francis Brown, Ph. D , D D., LL, D .	23	252
Union university, Jackson, Tenn (1848) . .	R A Kimbrough . . .	9	202
U S. Military academy,* West Point, N Y (1802)	Col. O P Townsley, U. S A (supt) ...123		530
United States Naval academy,* Annapolis, Md (1845)	Capt. J H Gibbons, U. S. N. (supt)	110	850
University of Alabama,* Tuscaloosa (1831)	John H Denny, LL D 105		1,167
University of Arizona,* Tucson (1891) . .	Arthur H Wilde, Ph. D	40	254
University of Arkansas,* Fayetteville (1871) . .	G H Reynolds	80	625
University of California,* Berkeley (1860)	Benjamin Ide Wheeler, LL. D... . .	459	7,255 .
University of Chicago,* Chicago, Ill (1892)	Harry Pratt Judson, LL. D... .	337	6,802
University of Cincinnati,* Cincinnati O (1870) ..	Charles M Dabney, Ph D., LL. D	217	1,973
University of Colorado,* Boulder (1877). .	James H. Baker, M A , LL D .	170	1,300
University of Denver, University Park, Col (1864) ..	Henry A. Buchtel, D D , LL. D .	130	1,075
University of Florida, Gainesville (1905) . .	A H Murphree, LL. D . .	51	302
University of Georgia,* Athens (1785)	David C Barrow (chancellor). ...	80	682
University of Idaho,* Moscow (1892)	W. L. Carlyle (acting)	77	763

School, location and date of founding	President	Instructors	Students
University of Illinois,* Urbana (1867).	Edmund J. James, Ph D , LL. D	550	5,98o
University of Kansas,* Lawrence (1866)	Frank Strong, Ph. D., LL D. (chancellor)	169	2,545
University of Maine,* Orono (1865)	Robert J. Aley, Ph D , LL D	118	1,011
University of Michigan,* Ann Arbor (1837)	H. B Hutchins, LL. D..	479	5,805
University of Minnesota,* Minneapolis (1868)	George E Vincent, LL D	.450	4,067
University of Mississippi,* University (1848)	A A Kincannon, LL D. (chancellor)	33	408
University of Missouri,* Columbia (1839)	Albert Ross Hill, LL D	252	3,297.
University of Montana,* Missoula (1895)	Edwin R Craighead, LL D	35	280
University of Nebraska,* Lincoln (1869).	Samuel Avery, Ph. D., LL D (chancel or)	383	3,812
University of Nevada, Reno (1886)	Joseph E. Stubbs, D. D , LL D....	40	315
University of New Mexico, Albuquerque (1892)	David Ross Boyd, Ph. D	17	99
University of Notre Dame Notre Dame, Ind (1849).	John Cavanaugh, C. S. C , D D	86	1,026
University of North Carolina,* Chapel Hill (1789)	Francis P. Venable, Ph D , LL D	85	837
University of North Dakota, Grand Forks (1883)	Frank L McVey, Ph. D., LL D	84	1,052
University of Oklahoma,* Norman (1892)	Stratton D Brooks, Ph D , LL D	112	876
University of Oregon,* Eugene (1876)	Prince L. Campbell, A. B , LL. D	108	1,257
University of Pennsylvania, Philadelphia (1740)	Edgar F. Smith, Ph. D., LL. D (provost)	553	5,323
University of Pittsburgh, Pittsburgh, Pa (1787)	S B McCormick, LL. D. (chancellor)	283	2,516
University of Rochester, Rochester, N Y (1850)	Rush Rhees, D. D , LL D	37	445
University of Southern California, Los Angeles (1879)	George F. Bovard, A M, D, LL D	192	2,500
University of South Carolina,* Columbia (1805)	S C Mitchell, Ph. D. .	35	347
University of South Dakota,* Vermilion (1882)	Franklin P Gault, Ph. D	60	424
University of the South, Sewanee, Tenn (1868)	W. B. Hall, M A., D. D. (chancellor)	27	257
University of Tennessee,* Knoxville (1794)	Brown Ayres, Ph D , LL. D	175	4,489
University of Texas,* Austin (1883)	Sidney E Mezes, Ph. D ...	180	2,391
University of Utah,* Salt Lake City (1850) .	J T Kingsbury, Ph D	70	1,244
University of Vermont,* Burlington (1791)	Guy P Benton, D D , Ph. D , LL D .	110	559
University of Virginia,* Charlottesville (1819)	Edwin A Alderman, D C. L , LL D ..	93	845
University of Washington,* Seattle (1862)	Thomas F Kane, Ph D , LL D	155	2,825
University of Wisconsin,* Madison (1848)	Charles R Van Hise, Ph D	624	5,970
University of Wooster, Wooster, O. (1868)..	Louis E. Holden, D D , LL D	34	650
University of Wyoming,* Laramie (1886)	C A Duniway, LL D	64	327
Upper Iowa university, Fayette, Iowa (1858).	William A. Shanklin, D D , LL D	21	364
Upsala college, Kenilworth, N. J. (1893)	Rev. Peter Froeberg, B D	16	144
Urbana U. schools, Urbana, O. (1850)	Rev. Russell Eaton (head master)	6	40
Ursinus college, Collegeville, Pa. (1869).	George L. Omwake, Ph. D	15	203
Utah Agricultural college,* Logan, Utah (1890)	John A Widtsoe, A. M , Ph D.	65	1,500
Valparaiso university, Valparaiso, Ind (1873)	Henry P. Brown, A. M	195	5,625
Vanderbilt university, Nashville, Tenn (1873)	J H Kirkland, LL D. (chancellor)	125	1,129
Vassar college,* Poughkeepsie, N Y. (1861)	James M Taylor, D, D, LL D	110	1,045
Villanova college, Villanova, Pa...	Edward G Dohan, A. M., O S A	39	395
Vincennes university,* Vincennes, Ind (1806)..	Horace Ellis, A. M., Ph D	15	311
Virginia Christian college, Lynchburg, Va. (1903)	G O Davis (acting) ...	12	130
Virginia Military institute,* Lexington, Va (1839).	Gen. E W. Nichols (superintendent)	22	350
Wabash college,* Crawfordsville, Ind (1832)	George L Mackintosh, D. D., LL. D	19	312
Wake Forest college, Wake Forest, N C (1834)	G W Hubbard (acting).	70	459
Walden university, Nashville, Tenn. (1866)	John A Kumler, A. M., D. D	68	700
Washburn college, Topeka, Kas (1865)	Frank K. Sanders, D. D., Ph. D	100	800
Washington & Jefferson col ,* Washington, Pa (1802).	James D. Moffat, D. D , LL D	17	311
Washington and Lee univ ,* Lexington, Va (1749)	Henry Louis Smith, M A., Ph. D , LL D	27	495
Washington college, Chestertown, Md (1782)	James W. Cain, LL. D	10	122
Washington university, St Louis, Mo (1853)	David F. Houston, A M ,LL D (chancellor)	178	1,543
Waynesburg college,* Waynesburg, Pa. (1850)	William M. Hudson, D. D	12	300
Wellesley college,* Wellesley, Mass (1875)	Ellen F Pendleton, M. A , Litt. D	126	1,424
Wells college,* Aurora, N Y. (1868)	Kerr D Macmillan, A. B , B D .	30	168
Wesleyan university, Middletown, Conn (1831)	William A. Shanklin, D. D., LL D	40	412
Western College for Women,* Oxford, O (1854)	Mary A Sawyer (acting)....	26	232
Western Reserve university,* Cleveland, O (1826)	Charles F Thwing, D D LL. D .	278	1,304
Western Theological seminary, Pittsburgh, Pa (1825)	James A Kelso, Ph. D , D. D..	10	69
Westfield college, Westfield, Ill (1865)....	H M Tipsword... ..	9	124
West Lafayette college,West Lafayette, O (1909).	Aubrey F Hess, D. D	12	200
Westminster college, Fulton, Mo (1849).	Charles B Boving, D D .	12	161
Westminster college, New Wilmington, Pa (1852)	Robert McW. Russell, D D , LL D	24	274
West Virginia university, Morgantown (1867)	Thomas E. Hodges, LL D	75	1,271
Wheaton college, Wheaton. Ill (1860)	Charles A. Blanchard, D D	20	241
Whitman college,* Walla Walla, Wash (1882)	S B L. Penrose, D D	31	400
Whitworth college, Tacoma, Wash. (1883)	Donald D McKay, A M , D D	17	150
Wilberforce university, Wilberforce, O (1856)	William S Scarborough, Ph D , LL D	33	460
Wiley university, Marshall, Tex (1873)	M W. Dogan, A M Ph. D	34	582
Willamette university, Salem, Ore (1844)	Fletcher Homan, D. D	46	450
William and Mary col * Williamsburg, Va (1693)	L. G. Tyler, M A , LL D ..	20	184
William Jewell college, Liberty, Mo (1849)	John P, Greene, D D , LL D .	28	407
Williams college * Williamstown, Mass (1793)	Harry A. Garfield, LL. D. ..	53	521
Wilson college, Chambersburg, Pa. (1870) . . . . :	Anna Jane McKeag, Ph D.. .	27	216
Wittenberg college, Springfield, O (1845).	Charles G Heckert, D D ...	45	826
Wofford college, Spartanburg, S. C. (1854)	Henry N. Snyder, M. A.....	13	303
Worcester Polytechnic inst ,* Worcester,Mass (1865)	Levi L Conant (acting)....	53	555
Xenia Theological seminary, Xenia, O . ..	Joseph Kyle, D D , LL. D	5	27
Yale university,* New Haven, Conn (1701) .	Arthur Twining Hadley, LL D .	433	3,282
Yankton college, Yankton, S. D (1881)	Henry K Warren, M. A., LL. D.	22	418

PASSENGERS DEPARTED FROM AMERICAN SEAPORTS.

Fiscal years ended June 30.

Year.	Male.	Female.	Under 12.	12 and over.	Cabin	Steerage	Total
1910	481,846	241,172	80,789	642,229	396,040	326,978	723,018
1911	611,939	255,748	96,892	770,795	436,071	431,616	867,687
1912	689,398	279,784	102,710	866,472	463,699	505,483	969,182

DATES OF RECENT HISTORICAL EVENTS.

Aguinaldo captured, March 23, 1901.
Alaska boundary award made, Oct. 17, 1903.
Albert I. ascended throne of Belgium, Dec. 17, 1909.
Alfonso XIII. ascended throne of Spain May 17, 1902; attempted assassination of, in Paris, June 1, 1906; shot at by anarchist in Madrid April 13, 1913.
Amundsen, Roald, completes northwest passage, 1906; reaches south pole, Dec. 16, 1911.
Anarchists, Chicago, hanged, Nov. 11, 1887.
Anarchists pardoned by Altgeld, June 26, 1893.
Andree began arctic balloon trip, July 11, 1897.
Anglo-American arbitration treaty signed, Jan. 11, 1897.
Anglo-Boer war began, Oct. 10, 1899; ended May 31, 1902.
Anglo-Japanese treaty signed, Jan. 30, 1902.
Arizona admitted as a state, Feb. 14, 1912.
Armenian massacres began in 1890; culminated in 1895, 1896 and 1897.
Atlanta, Ga. (Cotton States and Industrial), exposition, Sept. 15 to Dec. 31, 1895.
Australian commonwealth inaugurated, Jan. 1, 1901.
Balkan-Turkish war began, Oct. 8, 1912.
Baltimore fire, Feb. 7, 1904.
Battle ship cruise, American, Dec. 16, 1907, to Feb. 22, 1909.
Bennington gunboat disaster, July 21, 1905.
Bering sea seal treaty signed, Nov. 8, 1897.
Bismarck resigned chancellorship, March 18, 1890; died, July 30, 1898.
Borda, president, assassinated, Aug. 25, 1897.
Bosnia and Herzegovina annexed by Austria, Oct. 6, 1908.
Boxer outbreak in China began, May, 1900.
Boyertown (Pa.) theater fire and panic, Jan. 13, 1908.
Brazil proclaimed a republic, Nov. 15, 1889.
Buffalo (Pan-American) exposition, May 1 to Nov. 2, 1901.
Bulgaria proclaims independence, Oct. 5, 1908.
Cable, Pacific, laying of begun at San Francisco, Dec. 14, 1902.
California Mid-Winter exposition, Jan. 1 to July 4, 1894.
Campanile in Venice fell, July 14, 1902.
Canadian reciprocity bill passed by congress and signed by President Taft, July 26, 1911; rejected by Canada, Sept. 21.
Carlos I., king of Portugal, assassinated, Feb. 1, 1908.
Carnot, president, assassinated, June 24, 1894.
Caroline islands bought by Germany, Oct. 1, 1899.
Cartago, Costa Rica, destroyed by earthquake, May 5, 1910.
Charleston, S. C. (Interstate and West Indian), exposition, Dec. 1, 1901, to May 20, 1902.
Chelsea (Mass.) fire, April 12, 1908.
Cherry (Ill.) mine disaster, Nov. 13, 1909.
China, revolution begins Sept. 7, 1911; republic proclaimed Dec. 29, 1911; Manchu dynasty abdicates Feb. 12, 1912.
Cholera epidemic in Hamburg, Germany, August, 1892; in Russia and Italy, summer of 1910.
Christian IX., king of Denmark, died Jan. 29, 1906.
Christian X. proclaimed king of Denmark, May 15, 1912.
Coal (anthracite) strike began, May 12, 1902; ended, Oct. 21, 1902.
Corinth ship canal open, Aug. 6, 1893.
Courriere mine disaster March 10, 1906.
Crib disaster, Chicago, Jan. 20, 1909.
Cronin murder, May 4, 1889.
Cuba under sovereignty of United States, Jan. 1, 1899.
Cuban constitution signed, Feb. 21, 1901.
Cuban-United States reciprocity treaty ratified March 19, 1903; bill to carry treaty into effect passed by congress Dec. 16, 1903.
Cuban republic inaugurated, May 20, 1902; President Palma and cabinet resigned and American control established Sept. 29, 1906; (Gen. Jose Miguel Gomez elected president, Nov. 14, 1908; American control relinquished, Jan. 28, 1909.
Cuban revolt began, Feb. 24, 1895.
Czolgosz, McKinley's assassin, tried and sentenced, Sept. 24, 1901; executed, Oct. 29, 1901.
De Lesseps, Ferdinand, convicted of Panama fraud, Feb. 9, 1893.
Delyannis, Grecian premier, assassinated, June 13, 1905.

Delhi coronation durbar began, Dec. 29, 1902.
Dewey's victory at Manila, May 1, 1898.
Diaz, Porfirio, forced by revolutionists to resign presidency of Mexico, May 25, 1911.
Dingley tariff bill signed, July 24, 1897.
Dom Pedro exiled from Brazil, Nov. 16, 1889.
Dreyfus, Capt., degraded and sent to Devil's Island, Jan. 4, 1895; brought back to France, July 3, 1899; new trial begun, Aug. 7; found guilty, Sept. 9; pardoned, Sept. 19, 1899; restored to rank in army, July 12, 1906, by decision of Supreme court of France; decorated with cross of Legion of Honor, July 21, 1906.
Earthquake in India, April 4, 1905; in Calabria, Italy, Sept. 8, 1905, and Dec. 28, 1908. (See also San Francisco, Valparaiso, Kingston, Messina and Cartago.)
Edward VII. proclaimed king, Jan. 24, 1901; crowned, Aug. 9, 1902; died, May 6, 1910.
Elizabeth, empress of Austria, assassinated, Sept. 10, 1898.
Fallieres, C. A., elected president of France, Jan. 17, 1906.
Ferreo, Francisco, executed in Spain, Oct. 13, 1909.
Field, Marshall, died, Jan. 16, 1906.
Fisheries (Atlantic) dispute settled by Hague court, June 1, 1910.
Floods in Ohio and Indiana, March 25-27, 1913.
Formosa transferred to Japan, June 4, 1895.
Frederick VIII. succeeded to throne of Denmark, Jan. 29, 1906; died, May 14, 1912.
Galveston tornado, Sept. 8, 1900.
General Slocum disaster, June 15, 1904.
George I., king of Greece, assassinated in Saloniki, Macedonia, March 18, 1913.
George V. succeeded to British throne, May 6, 1910; crowned, June 22, 1911.
Gladstone resigned premiership, March 2, 1894; died, May 19, 1898.
Goebel, Gov. William, shot, Jan. 30, 1900; died, Feb. 3.
Greco-Turkish war began, April 16, 1897; ended, May 11, 1897; peace treaty signed, Sept. 18, 1897.
Haiti, President Leconte of, and 400 persons killed by explosion in palace, Aug. 8, 1912.
Harriman, E. H., died, Sept. 9, 1909.
Harrison, Benjamin, died, March 13, 1901.
Harrison, Carter, Sr., assassinated, Oct. 28, 1893.
Hawaii made a republic, July 4, 1894; annexed to United States, Aug. 12, 1896; made a territory, June 14, 1900.
Hay-Pauncefote isthmian canal treaty signed, Nov. 18, 1901.
Homestead (Pa.) labor riot, July 6, 1892.
Hugo, Victor, centenary celebration begun in Paris, Feb. 26, 1902.
Humbert, King, assassinated, July 29, 1900.
Idaho admitted as a state, July 3, 1890.
Income tax amendment to constitution of the United States proclaimed, Feb. 25, 1913.
Irish land purchase law in force, Nov. 1, 1903.
Iroquois theater fire, Dec. 30, 1903; lives lost, 575.
Italian army routed in Abyssinia, March 1, 1896.
Italian prisoners lynched in New Orleans, March 14, 1891.
Italy declares war on Turkey over Tripoli dispute, Sept. 29, 1911; formally annexes Tripoli, Feb. 23, 1912; war ended, Oct. 18, 1912.
Ito, Prince, assassinated, Oct. 26, 1909.
Jameson raiders in Transvaal routed, Jan. 2, 1896.
Jamestown (Va.) tercentennial exposition, April 26 to Nov. 30, 1907.
Japan, battle of Sea of, May 27-28, 1905.
Japan declared war on China, Aug. 1, 1894; war ended, April 17, 1895.
Japan-Russia war began, Feb. 7, 1904; ended, Sept. 5, 1905.
Johnstown flood, May 31, 1889.
Ketteler, Baron von, killed in Pekin, June 30, 1900.
Kingston (Jamaica) earthquake and fire, Jan. 14, 1907.
Kishineff massacre, April 20, 1903.
Koch's lymph cure announced, Nov. 17, 1890.
Kongo Free State annexed by Belgium, Aug. 20, 1908.
Korea annexed by Japan, Aug. 29, 1910.
Kossuth, Louis, died, March 20, 1894.
Lawton, Gen. H. W., killed, Dec. 19, 1899.
Leiter wheat deal collapsed, June 13, 1898.

Leopold II., king of Belgium, died, Dec. 17, 1909.
Liliuokalani, queen of Hawaii, deposed, Jan. 16, 1893.
Louisville tornado, March 27, 1890.
Luiz Philippe, crown prince of Portugal, assassinated, Feb. 1, 1908.
Madagascar annexed to France, Jan. 23, 1896.
Maine blown up, Feb. 15, 1898; raised in 1911-1912 and sunk in the open sea off Havana, March 16, 1912.
Manuel II., king of Portugal, deposed, Oct. 3-4, 1910.
Marconi signals letter "S" across Atlantic, Dec. 11, 1901.
Messina destroyed by earthquake, Dec. 28, 1908.
Mexican revolution, Nov. 18, 1910, to May 25, 1911; President Diaz forced to resign, May 25, 1911.
Mexico City, revolution in, Feb. 9, 1913.
Meyerbeer centenary celebrated in Berlin, Sept. 5, 1891.
Morocco conference began, Jan. 16, 1906.
Mukden, battle of, Feb. 24-March 12, 1905.
McKinley, President, shot by anarchist, Sept. 6, 1901; died, Sept. 14, 1901.
Nansen arctic expedition started, July 21, 1893; returned, Aug. 13, 1896.
Nashville, Tenn. (Tennessee Centennial), exposition, May 1 to Oct. 31, 1897.
New Mexico admitted as a state, Jan. 6, 1912.
Nicholas II. proclaimed czar of Russia, Nov. 2, 1894; crowned, May 26, 1896; attempted assassination of, Jan. 19, 1905.
North Collinwood (O.) school disaster, March 4, 1908.
Norge disaster, June 28, 1904.
North pole reached by Commander Robert E. Peary, April 6, 1909.
Norway dissolved union with Sweden, June 7, 1905.
Oklahoma and Indian Territory admitted to union as state of Oklahoma, Nov. 16, 1907.
Omaha tornado, March 23, 1913.
Omaha, Neb. (Trans-Mississippi), exposition, June 1 to Nov. 1, 1898.
Oordurman, battle of, Sept. 4, 1898.
Oscar II., king of Sweden, died, Dec. 8, 1907.
Panama canal property bought by the United States, Feb. 16, 1903.
Panama fraud trials in Paris, Jan. 10 to March 21, 1893.
Panama revolution, Nov. 3, 1903.
Pan-American congress, first, began, Oct. 2, 1889; second, Oct. 23, 1902.
Parcel post established in United States, Jan. 1, 1913.
Paris expositions, 1878, 1889, 1900.
Paris flood, Jan. 20-Feb. 1, 1910.
Peace conference called by czar, Aug. 24, 1898; opened at The Hague, May 18, 1899; closed, July 29, 1899; second peace conference, June 15-Oct. 18, 1907.
Peace palace at The Hague dedicated, Aug. 28, 1913.
Pekin captured by the allies, Aug. 15, 1900.
Philippine-American war began, Feb. 4, 1899; ended, April 30, 1902.
Philippines ceded to the United States, Dec. 10, 1898.
Pope Leo XIII. died, July 20, 1903.
Pope Pius X. elected, Aug. 4, 1903.
Portland, Ore. (Lewis and Clark), exposition, June 1 to Oct. 14, 1905.
Port Arthur captured by the Japanese from Chinese, Nov. 21, 1894; from Russians, Jan. 1, 1905.
Porto Rico ceded to the United States, Dec. 10, 1898.
Porto Rico hurricane, Aug. 8, 1899.
Portugal, King Carlos and Crown Prince Luiz of, assassinated, Feb. 1, 1908; Manuel II. deposed and republic declared, Oct. 3-4, 1910.
Postage between United States and Britain reduced to 2 cents, Oct. 1, 1908.
Postal banks established in United States, Jan. 3, 1911.
Pretoria captured by the British, June 4, 1900.
Pullman strike began, May 11, 1894; boycott began, June 26; rioting in Chicago and vicinity, June and July; strike and boycott ended, August.

Reciprocity (with Canada) bill passed by congress and signed by President Taft, July 26, 1911; rejected by Canada, Sept. 21, 1911.
Rhodes, Cecil, died, March 26, 1902.
Roentgen ray discovery made public, Feb. 1, 1896.
Roosevelt, Theodore, became president of the United States, on death of McKinley, Sept. 14, 1901; elected to same office, Nov. 8, 1904; attempted assassination of, Oct. 14, 1912.
Russia-Japan war began, Feb. 7, 1904; ended, Sept. 5, 1905.
Salisbury, Premier, resigned, July 13, 1902; died Aug. 22, 1903.
St. Louis cyclone, May 27, 1896.
St. Louis (Louisiana Purchase) exposition, April 30 to Dec. 1, 1904.
St. Petersburg riots, Jan. 22, 1905.
St. Pierre, Martinique, destroyed, May 8, 1902.
San Francisco earthquake and fire, April 18-20, 1906.
San Juan and El Caney, battles of, July 1, 1898.
Santiago de Cuba, naval battle of, July 3, 1898.
Santiago de Cuba surrendered, July 17, 1898.
Schley inquiry ordered, July 26, 1901; began, Sept. 20; ended, Nov. 7; verdict announced, Dec. 13.
Schurz, Carl, died, May 14, 1906.
Scott, Robert F., explorer, perished in blizzard after reaching south pole.
Seattle, Wash. (Alaska-Yukon), exposition, June 1 to Oct. 16, 1909.
Senators, U. S., direct election amendment proclaimed, May 31, 1913.
Sergius, Grand Duke, assassinated, Feb. 17, 1905.
Servia, king and queen of, assassinated, June 11, 1903.
Shah of Persia assassinated, May 1, 1896.
Simplon tunnel completed, Feb. 25, 1905.
South pole reached, by Capt. Roald Amundsen, Dec. 16, 1911; reached by Capt. Robert F. Scott, Jan. 17, 1912.
Spanish-American war began, April 25, 1898; peace protocol signed, Aug. 12, 1898; Paris peace treaty signed, Dec. 12; peace treaty ratified, Feb. 6, 1899.
Springfield (Ill.) riots and lynchings, Aug. 14-15, 1908.
Standard Oil decision by United States Supreme court, May 15, 1911.
Stolypin, premier of Russia, shot by assassin, Sept. 14, 1911; died, Sept. 18.
Stone, Ellen M., captured by brigands, Sept. 3, 1901; released, Feb. 23, 1902.
Taft, William H., elected president of the United States, Nov. 3, 1908.
Titanic steamship sunk, April 15, 1912.
Tobacco trust decision, May 29, 1911.
Transvaal republic annexed to Great Britain, Sept. 1, 1900.
Turkey, sultan of, proclaimed constitution, July 24, 1908; Sultan Abdul Hamid deposed, April 27, 1909.
Turkey, war with Italy over Tripoli began, Sept. 29, 1911; ended Oct. 18, 1912.
Turkey, war with Balkan states began, Oct. 8, 1912; Nazim Pasha assassinated, Jan. 23, 1913.
Union of South Africa proclaimed, May 31, 1910.
Utah admitted as a state, Feb. 4, 1896.
Valparaiso earthquake, Aug. 16, 1906.
Venezuelan blockade by England, Germany and Italy began in first part of December, 1902; ended, Feb. 13, 1903.
Vesuvius, great eruption of, April 1-10, 1906.
Victor Emmanuel III., king of Italy, crowned, Aug. 11, 1902; attempt to assassinate, March 14, 1912.
Victoria, queen of England, died, Jan. 22, 1901.
Voiturno disaster, Oct. 9, 1913.
Wilhelmina proclaimed queen of Holland, Aug. 31, 1898.
Wilson, Woodrow, elected president of the United States, Nov. 5, 1912.
Windsor hotel, New York, burned, March 17, 1899.
World's Fair in Chicago opened, May 1, 1893; ended, Oct. 30, 1893.
Wyoming admitted as a state, July 10, 1890.
Yalu, battle of, Sept. 17, 1894.

CRUDE STEEL PRODUCTION OF THE UNITED STATES.

Calendar year.	*Tons.	Calendar year.	*Tons.	Calendar year.	*Tons.	Calendar year.	*Tons.
1870	68,750	1902	14,947,250	1905	20,023,947	1908	14,023,247
1880	1,247,335	1903	14,534,978	1906	23,398,136	1909	23,955,021
1890	4,277,071	1904	13,859,887	1907	23,362,594	1910	26,094,919
1900	10,188,329			*Tons of 2,240 pounds.		1911	23,676,106

DEATHS OF NOTED MEN AND WOMEN (1890-1913).

Abbey, Edwin A., Aug. 1, 1911.
Aehrenthal, A. L., Feb. 17, 1912.
Aldrich, T. B., March 19, 1907.
Alexander Ill., Nov. 1, 1894.
Alexis, Nord, May 1, 1910.
Allen, Grant, Oct. 25, 1895.
Allison, W. B., Aug. 4, 1908.
Alma-Tadema, L., June 24, 1912.
Altgeld, John P., March 12, 1902.
Andrassy, Count, Jan. 30, 1900.
Anthony, Susan B., March 13, 1906.
Arabi Pasha, Sept. 21, 1911.
Armour, Philip D., Jan. 6, 1901.
Arnold, Edwin, March 25, 1904.
Astor, John Jacob, Feb. 22, 1890.
Audran, Edmond, Aug. 15, 1901.
Austin, Alfred, June 1, 1913.
Avebury, Lord, May 28, 1913.
Barnum, P. T., April 7, 1891.
Barr, Robert, Oct. 22, 1912.
Bartholdi, F. A., Oct. 4, 1904
Barton, Clara, April 12, 1912.
Bascom, John, Oct. 2, 1911.
Bebel, August F., Aug. 13, 1913.
Becquerel, A. H., Aug. 25, 1908.
Beit, Alfred, July 16, 1906.
Bellamy, Edward, May 22, 1898.
Bellew, Kyrle, Nov. 2, 1911.
Belmont, August, Nov. 24, 1890.
Belmont, O. H. P., June 10, 1908.
Besant, Sir Walter, June 9, 1901.
Bigelow, John, Dec. 19, 1911.
Bismarck, Prince, July 30, 1898.
Bjornson, Bjornstjerne, April 26, 1910.
Black, William, Dec. 10, 1898.
Blackie, J. S., March 3, 1895.
Blackwood, W., Nov. 11, 1912.
Blaine, James G., Jan. 27, 1893.
Blavatsky, Mme., May 9, 1891.
Bliss, Cornelius N., Oct. 9, 1911.
Blouet, Paul, May 24, 1903.
Bonheur, Rosa, May 25, 1899.
Booth, Edwin, June 7, 1893.
Booth, William, Aug. 20, 1912.
Boucicault, Aubrey, July 10, 1913
Bragg, Edward S., June 20, 1912.
Brahms, Johannes, April 2, 1897.
Breton, Jules A., July 5, 1906.
Brewer, David J., March 28, 1910.
Brisson, Henry, April 14, 1912.
Bristow, Benj. H., June 22, 1896.
Brooks, Phillips, Jan. 23, 1893.
Brough, Lionel, Nov. 8, 1909.
Buck, Dudley, Oct. 6, 1909.
Bulow, Hans von, Feb. 13, 1894.
Burdett-Coutts, Baroness, Dec. 30, 1906.
Burnham, D. H., June 1, 1912.
Butler, Gen. B. F., Jan. 11, 1893.
Campbell-Bannerman, H., April 22, 1908.
Canalejas, J., Nov. 12, 1912.
Carle on, H. G., Dec. 10, 1910.
Carleton, Will, Dec. 18, 1912.
Carlisle, John G., July 31, 1910.
Carlos I., Feb. 1, 1908.
Carnot, President, June 24, 1894.
Carte, D'Oyly, April 3, 1901.
Casimir-Perier, March 12, 1907.
Cervera, P., April 3, 1909.
Chanute, Octave, Nov. 23, 1910.
Childs, George W., Feb. 3, 1894.
Christian IX., Jan. 29, 1906.
Chulalongkorn I., Oct. 23, 1910.
Clemens, Samuel L., April 21, 1910.
Clement, Clay, Feb. 21, 1910.
Cleveland, Grover, June 24, 1908.
Coleridge-Taylor, S., Sept. 1, 1912.
Collyer, Robert, Nov. 30, 1912.
Colonne, Edouard, March 28, 1910.
Constant, Benjamin, May 26, 1902.
Cooke, Jay, Feb. 16, 1905.
Coppee, Francois, May 23, 1908.
Coquelin, B. C., Jan. 26, 1909.
Coquelin, E. A. H., Feb. 8, 1909.
Corbin, Austin, June 4, 1896.

Corning, Erastus, Aug. 30, 1896.
Crane, Richard T., Jan. 8, 1912.
Crawford, F. M., April 9, 1909.
Croke, Archbishop, July 22, 1902.
Cronje, Piet, Feb. 4, 1911.
Crook, George, March 19, 1890.
Cummings, Amos J., May 2, 1902.
Curie, Pierre, April 19, 1906.
Curtin, Jeremiah, Dec. 14, 1906.
Curtis, George W., Aug. 31, 1892.
Curtis, William E., Oct. 5, 1911.
Curzon, Lady, July 18, 1906.
Cuyler, T. L., Feb. 26, 1909.
Dahn, Felix S., Jan. 3, 1912.
Daly, Augustin, July 7, 1899.
Dana, Charles A., Oct. 17, 1897.
Daniel, John W., June 29, 1910.
Davenport, Homer, May 2, 1912.
Davis, George R., Nov. 25, 1899.
Davis, Mrs. Jefferson, Oct. 16, 1906.
Davis, Winnie, Sept. 18, 1898.
Davitt, Michael, May 31, 1906.
De Martens, F., June 20, 1909.
Detaille, Edouard, Dec. 24, 1912.
Dilke, Charles W., Jan. 26, 1911.
Dingley, Nelson, Jan. 13, 1899.
Dolliver, J. P., Oct. 15, 1910.
Donnelly, Ignatius, Jan. 2, 1901.
Douglass, Frederick, Feb. 20, 1895.
Drachman, Holger, Jan. 15, 1908.
Draper, Andrew S., April 27, 1913.
Drexel, Anthony J., June 30, 1893.
Drummond, Henry, March 11, 1897.
Du Maurier, George, Oct. 8, 1896.
Dumas, Alexandre, Nov. 27, 1895.
Dunbar, Paul L., Feb. 9, 1906.
Dvorak, Antonin, May 1, 1904.
East, Sir Edward, Sept. 28, 1913.
Eddy, Mary Baker, Dec. 3, 1910.
Edward VII., May 6, 1910.
Edwards, Amelia B., April 15, 1892.
Eggleston, Edward, Sept. 3, 1902.
Eggleston, Geo. Cary, April 14, 1911.
Elizabeth, Empress, Sept. 10, 1898.
Elkins, Stephen B., Jan. 4, 1911.
Emmett, "Fritz," June 15, 1891.
English, William H., Feb. 7, 1896.
Evans, Robley D., Jan. 3, 1912.
Evarts, William M., Feb. 28, 1901.
Fair, James G., Dec. 28, 1894.
Fairchild, Lucius, May 23, 1896.
Faithfull, Emily, June 1, 1895.
Farjeon, B. L., July 23, 1903.
Faure, Felix, Feb. 16, 1899.
Feun, G. M., Aug. 27, 1909.
Ferrer, Francisco, Oct. 13, 1909.
Field, Cyrus W., July 12, 1892.
Field, Eugene, Nov. 4, 1895.
Field, Kate, May 18, 1896.
Field, Marshall, Jan. 16, 1906.
Field, Richard M., Nov. 11, 1902.
Field, Stephen J., April 9, 1899.
Fisk, Clinton B., July 9, 1890.
Flagler, Henry M., May 20, 1913.
Florence, Wm. J., Nov. 19, 1891.
Flower, Roswell P., May 12, 1899.
Forbes, Archibald, March 30, 1900.
Ford, Patrick, Sept. 23, 1913.
Foss, Cyrus D., Jan. 29, 1910.
Fox, Della, June 16, 1913.
Frederick VIII., May 14, 1912.
Frederick, ex-Empress, Aug. 5, 1901.
Fremont, John C., July 13, 1890.
Froude, James A., Oct. 20, 1894.
Frye, William P., Aug. 8, 1911.
Fuller, Melville W., July 4, 1910.
Furness, H. H., Aug. 13, 1912.
Gary, Joseph E., Oct. 31, 1906.
Gates, John W., Aug. 9, 1911.
Gaynor, Wm. J., Sept. 10, 1913.
George, Henry, Oct. 29, 1896.
George I., king of Greece, March 18, 1913.
Gilbert, William S., May 2, 1911.
Gilder, R. W., Nov. 18, 1909.
Gilmore, Patrick S., Sept. 24, 1892.
Gladstone, Wm. E., May 19, 1898.

Gladstone, Mrs. W. E., June 13, 1900.
Goode, George B., Sept. 6, 1896.
Goodsell, D. A., Dec. 5, 1909.
Goodwin, J. Cheever, Dec. 18, 1912.
Gould, Jay, Dec. 2, 1892.
Gounod, Charles F., Oct. 18, 1893.
Grant, F. D., April 11, 1912.
Grau, H., Oct. 27, 1912.
Gray, Elisha, Jan. 21, 1901.
Gresham, Walter Q., May 28, 1895.
Grieg, Edvard, Sept. 4, 1907.
Guilmant, F. A., March 30, 1911.
Hagenbeck, Carl, April 14, 1913.
Hale, Edward E., June 10, 1909.
Halevy, Ludovic, May 8, 1908.
Halstead, Murat, July 2, 1908.
Hamilton, Gail, Aug. 17, 1896.
Hampton, Wade, April 11, 1902.
Hanlon, Edward, Jan. 4, 1908.
Hanna, Marcus A., Feb. 15, 1904.
Harahan, J. T., Jan. 22, 1912.
Harlan, John M., Oct. 14, 1911.
Harper, William R., Jan. 10, 1906.
Harriman, E. H., Sept. 9, 1909.
Harris, Joel Chandler, July 3, 1908.
Harris, William T., Nov. 5, 1909.
Harrison, Benj., March 13, 1901.
Harrison, Carter, Sr., Oct. 28, 1893.
Hatch, Rufus, Feb. 23, 1893.
Hay, John, July 1, 1905.
Hayes, Rutherford B., Jan. 17, 1893.
Hearn, Lafcadio, Sept. 26, 1904.
Hellprin, Angelo, July 17, 1907.
Heilprin, Louis, Feb. 13, 1912.
Henderson, David B., Feb. 25, 1906.
Henry, O., June 5, 1910.
Herne, James A., June 2, 1901.
Hewitt, Abram S., Jan. 18, 1903.
Hilkoff, M., March 21, 1909.
Hill, David B., Oct. 20, 1910.
Hitchcock, E. A., April 9, 1909.
Hitt, John, April 29, 1911.
Hitt, Robert R., Sept. 20, 1906.
Hoar, George F., Sept. 30, 1904.
Hobart, Garret A., Nov. 21, 1899.
Hoe, Robert, Sept. 22, 1909.
Holleben, T. von, Feb. 1, 1913.
Holman, W. S., April 22, 1897.
Holmes, Mary Jane, Oct. 6, 1907.
Holmes, Oliver W., Oct. 7, 1894.
Howard, O. O., Oct. 26, 1909.
Howe, Julia Ward, Oct. 17, 1910.
Humbert, King, July 29, 1900.
Hunt, William H., Sept. 7, 1910.
Huntington, C. P., Aug. 14, 1900.
Hutchins, Stilson, April 22, 1912.
Huxley, Thomas H., June 29, 1894.
Hyacinthe, Pere, Feb. 9, 1912.
Ibsen, Henrik, May 23, 1906.
Ignatieff, N. P., July 4, 1908.
Ingalls, John J., Aug. 16, 1900.
Ingersoll, Robert G., July 21, 1899.
Irving, Henry, Oct. 13, 1905.
Israels, Joseph, Aug. 12, 1911.
Ito, Prince, Oct. 26, 1909.
Jefferson, Joseph, April 23, 1905.
Jewett, Sarah O., June 24, 1909.
Joachim, Joseph, Aug. 15, 1907.
Jokai, Maurus, May 5, 1904.
Johnson, Eastman, April 5, 1906.
Johnson, J. A., Sept. 21, 1909.
Jones, Fernando, Nov. 8, 1911.
Joubert, Gen., March 27, 1900.
Judd, Orange, Dec. 27, 1892.
Judge, Wm. Q., March 22, 1896.
Judith, Mme., Oct. 27, 1912.
Katsura, Taro, Oct. 10, 1913.
Keene, James R., Jan. 3, 1913.
Kelly, Myra, March 31, 1910.
Kelvin, Lord, Dec. 17, 1907.
Kiderlen-Waechter, A. von, Dec. 30, 1912.
Kjelland, Alexander, April 6, 1906.
Knott, J. Proctor, June 8, 1911.

DEATH OF J. PIERPONT MORGAN.

J. Pierpont Morgan, for many years the leading financier of America, died in Rome, Italy, a few minutes after noon Monday, March 31, 1913. His illness began soon after he had appeared before a congressional committee in Washington, D. C., as a witness in the "money trust" investigation. When he testified Dec. 18, 1912, he seemed to be cool and collected, but Dr. M. Allen Starr, one of his physicians, afterward declared that the ordeal had been a severe one and resulted in an attack of nervous prostration. Mr. Morgan sailed for Egypt Jan. 7, 1912, and spent several weeks in Cairo and in making a trip up the Nile. Reports were then circulated that he was seriously ill, but his family and physicians said that he was merely suffering from a severe cold and an attack of acute indigestion and that all he required was complete rest. March 13 he was brought to Naples, Italy, and taken to Rome by special train. He was then emaciated and weak and could walk only a short distance without assistance. His physicians, Dr. Giuseppe Bastianelli and Dr. George A. Dixon, still insisted that what he needed chiefly was rest. Mr. Morgan himself had always enjoyed good health in Rome and hoped for a speedy recovery.

For a time he did very well, resting and sleeping without the aid of drugs and taking a satisfactory amount of nourishment. Wednesday afternoon, March 26, he began to refuse food and after that it was impossible to nourish him. March 30 the two doctors named and M. Allen Starr, who arrived in Rome from Naples the previous day, issued a bulletin giving the foregoing facts and announcing that while Mr. Morgan had not developed any organic trouble he was so exceedingly weak that his condition must be considered most critical. The patient lapsed into a comatose condition and passed away at 12:05 p. m., March 31, without having regained consciousness. His daughter, Mrs. Herbert L. Satterlee, and her husband were at Mr. Morgan's bedside when he breathed his last. The end came without suffering.

April 2 Drs. Giuseppe Bastianelli, M. Allen Starr and George A. Dixon issued the following official statement:

"When Mr. Morgan left New York he was a very tired man, physically and mentally. Digestion and nutrition were impaired. It was hoped his usual trip to Egypt would be of great benefit, giving him rest and building up the nervous force, especially as he had no organic disease. His appetite, however, failed and consequently his strength and weight did not improve.

"Mr. Morgan contracted a severe cold while in Egypt, which further weakened him. A state of mental depression and feebleness developed. He arrived at Cairo in a very rundown condition, but during three weeks in Cairo he improved mentally and physically, his powers of concentration and memory showing no impairment. The trip to Rome did not fatigue him and he continued to gain slowly for ten days.

"A week before his death his strength began to fail. He was put to bed Wednesday afternoon, March 26. He became delirious and extreme exhaustion followed. This continued until Sunday evening when he passed into a state of coma. He died at 12:05 p. m., Monday."

Mr. Morgan's body was taken from Rome April 2 to Havre, France, whence it was conveyed to New York on the steamship La France. Funeral services were held in St. George's church, New York city, April 14, and on the same day the body was laid at rest in Cedar Hill cemetery at Hartford, Conn.

The financial markets of the world were little affected by the death of Mr. Morgan, that event having been discounted for some time. Prices on the stock exchanges in Europe and America declined slightly on the day when he passed away, but they quickly recovered. The prevailing view seemed to be that Mr. Morgan's leadership might be missed later on, but not immediately.

The last will and testament of the financier was filed for probate April 21, but it did not disclose the total value of his estate. Following is a summary of the bequests made in the document:

To the widow—In trust, $1,000,000; trust fund from his father (amount not given); other funds sufficient to make her annual income $100,000; his country place, Cragston, and all its contents; his Madison avenue home and contents, except wines, and family portraits.

To J. P. Morgan, Jr.—Outright gift, $3,000,000; all his wines; his rights and titles in the Metropolitan museum and similar institutions; his private art gallery and its contents; all the residue of his estate without conditions.

To his daughters, Mrs. H. L. Satterlee, Mrs. W. P. Hamilton and Miss Anne T. Morgan—In trust, $3,000,000 each.

To his sons-in-law, W. P. Hamilton and H. L. Satterlee—Gifts of $1,000,000 each.

To St. George's Episcopal church in New York city—In trust, $500,000.

To archdeaconry of Orange, N. J.—In trust, $100,000.

To House of Rest for Consumptives—Gift of $100,000.

To friends, employes and domestics—Sums ranging from $1,000 to $250,000 each. Each employe of the firm in New York and London received a year's salary.

The official valuation of the Morgan art collections in New York was $50,000,000. The Morgan estate in the British isles amounted to $5,899,155.

LORIMER ELECTION CASE CHRONOLOGY.

William Lorimer chosen United States senator by Illinois legislature May 26, 1909.

Validity of election challenged in United States senate, Jan. 9, 1911.

Beveridge resolution declaring Lorimer not legally elected defeated in senate by a vote of 46 to 40 March 1, 1911.

Senate committee in Illinois legislature reports, after investigation, that in its opinion the election of Lorimer would not have occurred but for bribery and corruption and that a new investigation by the United States senate is demanded. Report made May 17, 1911.

United States senate by a vote of 48 to 20 decides, June 1, 1911, to reopen Lorimer investigation.

Senate investigation ended Feb. 9, 1912.

Majority and minority reports submitted by investigating committee to senate May 20, 1912: majority report finds that the election was not brought about by corrupt means; minority report declares that at least ten of the Lorimer votes were corruptly cast.

Resolution offered by Senator Luke Lea of Tennessee (May 20) declaring that corrupt methods and practices were employed in the election of William Lorimer to the senate of the United States from the state of Illinois, and that his election therefore was invalid.

Lea resolution adopted by United States senate by a vote of 55 to 28, July 14, 1912.

WEIGHTS OF DIAMONDS AND FINENESS OF GOLD.

The weight of diamonds and other precious stones is expressed in carats, grains and quarter-grains. The grains are pearl grains, one of which is equal to four-fifths of a troy grain. Four quarter-grains make one grain and four grains make one carat. A carat is therefore equal to four-fifths of four troy grains, or 3.2.

The fineness of gold is also expressed in carats. Pure gold is said to be twenty-four carats fine. If it contains eight parts of a baser metal or alloy it is only sixteen carats fine. The carats therefore indicate the proportion of pure gold to alloy. Most of the gold used by jewelers is about fourteen carats fine, having ten parts of alloy.

THE BALKAN WARS.

ALLIES AGAINST TURKEY.

The war begun by Bulgaria, Servia, Greece and Montenegro against Turkey in October, 1912, came to an end May 30, 1913, when a preliminary treaty of peace was signed in London. The first peace congress, held in London from Dec. 16, 1912, to Jan. 29, 1913, was fruitless owing to the delay of Turkey in meeting all the demands of the allies. It insisted on retaining Adrianople, while Bulgaria was equally insistent on the surrender of the fortress. The powers sent a collective note to the Ottoman government asking it to yield on this point, but the request was not complied with. The negotiations continued and the Turkish officials were apparently ready to come to terms with the allies when the war party in Constantinople obtained the ascendency, made a hostile demonstration before the sublime porte Jan. 23 and compelled the grand vizier, Kiamil Pasha, and his cabinet to resign. The leader of the revolt was Enver Bey, who, with others of the young Turk party, caused Mahmoud Shefket Pasha to be made grand vizier. An incident of the demonstration was the killing of Nazim Pasha, the former war minister and commander of the Turkish army. It was claimed that orders had been given to refrain from bloodshed and that the shooting of Nazim Pasha was not intended by the leaders of the revolt.

The coup d'etat in Constantinople practically ended the peace negotiations, both Turkey and the allies recalling their delegates from London in the latter part of January. Feb. 3, after an armistice lasting two months, the war was actively resumed with the bombardment of Adrianople and an attack on the lines at Tchatalja. The Bulgarians at once began a campaign against the Turkish positions on the Gallipoli peninsula with the object of getting possession of the Dardanelles. It was found that the defenses at Tchatalja were too strong to be taken by assault and that Constantinople could only be taken by being approached from some other direction. The Bulgarians won battles at Bulair and other places in the vicinity of the city of Gallipoli and obtained possession of a long stretch of the coast of the Sea of Marmora.

In the meantime the Servians and Montenegrins laid siege to Scutari in northern Albania and captured some of the forts in its vicinity. The Turks met with reverses everywhere and the authorities in Constantinople were forced Feb. 12 to ask for the intervention of the powers. These were in no hurry to act and the war went on. March 6, after a bombardment lasting forty-eight hours, the Turkish fortress of Janina, key to the province of Epirus, surrendered to the Greek army, which made prisoners of war of Gen. Essad Pasha and 32,000 men.

The siege of Scutari was objectionable to Austria-Hungary, which did not want Albania to fall into the hands of the Montenegrins or Servians contrary to the decision of the powers, which was that Albania should be an autonomous state. Austrian warships were sent March 20 to the Montenegrin and Albanian coasts and troops were massed at convenient points to be used if necessary in land operations against Montenegro. King Nicholas of Montenegro was defiant and announced that he would return to his capital the conqueror of Scutari or not at all. The Servians were not anxious to come into conflict with the powers and withdrew from the siege. The Austro-Hungarian demands were reiterated March 22, Austria insisting particularly that the Montenegrin military operations around Scutari should be suspended until the entire civil population had left the city. Italy took similar action and Russia advised King Nicholas to comply. March 25. Montenegro consented to permit the civil population to leave Scutari, but protested to the powers that Austria had been guilty of a breach of neutrality.

FALL OF ADRIANOPLE.

Adrianople was captured by Bulgarian and Servian troops March 27, after a long bombardment and a series of desperate assaults, in which the losses were heavy on both sides. For three days and nights, beginning on the 23d, the fighting around the city was almost continuous. The inner forts were carried at the point of the bayonet in hand to hand struggles. Shukri Pasha finally surrendered with 52,000 men, including 1,220 officers. The war material, consisting in part of 54,000 rifles and 600 cannon, was estimated to be worth $35,000,000. The fall of Adrianople practically ended the war so far as Turkey was concerned. April 1 the Ottoman government accepted without reserve the terms of peace suggested by the powers March 22, which were in substance that the European frontier of Turkey should follow a line drawn from Enos to Midia, that the question of the Ægean islands should be settled by the powers, that Turkey should abandon all claim to Crete and that the matter of indemnity and other financial questions be decided by an international commission with the participation of the allies.

In spite of the hostile attitude of Austria-Hungary and the opposition of Italy and the powers generally, King Nicholas and the Montenegrins continued the siege of Scutari. April 5 the Montenegrin seaport of Antivari was blockaded by three Austrian warships, two Italian, one British, one German and one French. On the following day Vice-Admiral Cecil Burney of the British navy, who was in command of the international force, sent the following message to the Montenegrin premier, Dr. L. Tomanovlos:

"I have the honor to inform you that the international fleet is assembled in Montenegrin waters as a protest against the nonfulfillment of the wishes of the great powers. I desire to call your excellency's attention to the presence of the fleet as a proof that the great powers are acting in concert, and request that their wishes be fulfilled without further delay. Please inform me immediately that your government is ready to carry out the wishes of the great powers."

MONTENEGRO DEFIES POWERS.

To this the Montenegrin premier replied in a note expressing regret at the presence of the fleet, which he considered a violation of the neutrality proclaimed by the powers at the beginning of the war, and to the detriment of Montenegro. The premier continued:

"Despite the pressure which the presence of the fleet implies, there will be no departure from an attitude which conforms to the necessities of the state of war existing between the allies and Turkey."

Notwithstanding the blockade which was established by the powers and the anxiety of the other Balkan nations to conclude peace with Turkey, Montenegro maintained its defiant attitude and pressed the attack on Scutari until April 23, when the city and its defenses were taken by Crown Prince Danilo, commander of the Montenegrin forces. The city had been besieged for six months, the condition of the people was pitiable and the first work of the victors was to send in supplies to the starving. The garrison, consisting of about 31,000 men under the command of Essad Pasha, was allowed to march out of the fortress with full honors of war.

On learning of the fall of Scutari Austria notified the powers that they must drive the Montenegrins out or the Austrian army would do so. The powers asked Montenegro to bow to their will as the other Balkan nations had done and to evacuate the city. For the next few days the situation became more and more critical owing to the military preparations of Austria-Hungary and the possibility that if that government actually made war on Montenegro other powers would be drawn into the quarrel. In that case it was feared that a general European conflict would be almost certain to follow. Great relief was felt, therefore, when King Nicholas announced May 5 that he had decided to surrender Scutari to the powers and leave its fate in their hands. May 14 an international naval force, commanded by Vice-Admiral Burney, landed and took possession of the fortress.

TREATY OF LONDON.

May 12 the Balkan allies agreed to a peace conference to be held in London. Delegates of the allies and of Turkey met and, after a series of

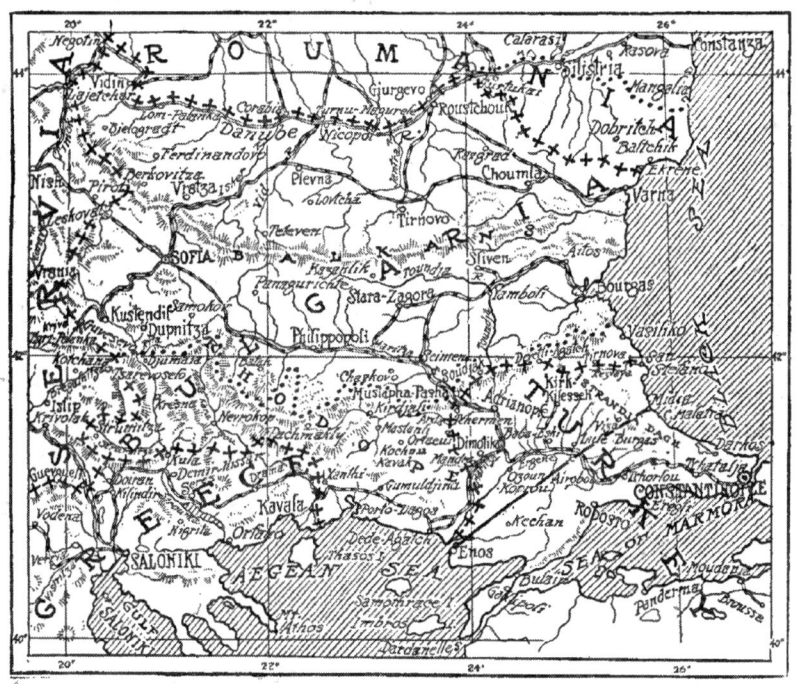

BOUNDARIES OF BULGARIA AT CONCLUSION OF BALKAN WARS.

Line of crosses shows the new frontiers and line of dots the old frontiers. Straight line between Enos and Midia shows Bulgarian-Turkish boundary as proposed by the treaty of London.

conferences, in which it was explained to them by Sir Edward Grey that the draft which he had drawn up on behalf of the powers at the request of the belligerents was a treaty between the allies and Turkey and not between the allies and the powers, an agreement was finally reached and May 30 the document was signed. The treaty provided:

1. That after the formal ratification of the treaty there should be perpetual peace and amity between the contracting parties.

2. That Turkey should cede to the allies all Turkish territory on the mainland of Europe situated west of a line to be drawn from Enos to Midia and that this boundary should be delimited by an international commission.

3. That the delimitation of Albania and all other questions relating to Albania should be left to the powers.

4. That Turkey should cede to the allies the island of Crete and renounce in their favor all its sovereignty and other rights in the island.

5. That the contracting parties should leave the powers to decide the fate of all the Turkish islands situated in the Ægean sea, with the exception of Crete and the peninsula of Mount Athos.

6. That the contracting parties should leave to the international commission, which was to meet in Paris, the settlement of the financial questions arising out of the recent war and the consequent redistribution of territory.

7. That questions relating to prisoners of war, jurisdiction, nationality and commerce should be settled by special conventions.

8. That the treaty should be ratified as soon as possible.

At the final meeting of the delegates June 9 a protocol was adopted providing that all points left unsettled should be determined by direct conventions, supplementing the treaty.

WAR BETWEEN BALKAN ALLIES.

VICTORS FIGHT OVER SPOILS.

Long before the close of the war with Turkey it had become apparent that the relations of the allies with each other were not what they should be. The existence of ill feeling, if not hatred, between Servia and Bulgaria and between Greece and Bulgaria was made plain as soon as it became evident that Turkey was whipped and that there would be a large amount of territory and a number of important cities to be apportioned among the conquerors. This was due chiefly to the conditions under which the Balkan league of alliance was formed. In April, 1911, M. Venezelos proposed an entente between Greece and Bulgaria with a view to common action in defense of the Christians in Macedonia and to provide for an eventual alliance in case of hostilities with Turkey. Bulgaria was willing, but Servian support was considered indispensable by King Ferdinand before the alliance could be effected. The war between Italy and Turkey in Tripoli hastened matters and early in 1912 the basis of a Serbo-Bulgarian alliance was agreed upon. On May 29, 1912, a treaty of alliance between Greece and Bulgaria was signed at Sofia. It was of a purely defensive character and the two

states pledged themselves to abstain from assailing Turkey. The treaty between Servia and Bulgaria was signed March 13, 1912, and it resembled the Bulgarian-Grecian alliance, which it antedated, in that it purported to be of a purely defensive character and contained an explicit agreement to avoid aggression against Turkey. At the same time it contained a feature not found in the Bulgarian-Grecian document, namely, provision for the allotment of conquered territory.

It had been Bulgaria's aim to make Macedonia an autonomous territory, but this plan had to be modified to secure Servian adhesion to the Balkan alliance. It was agreed that all the territory north of the Shar range—Old Servia and the sanjak of Novipazar—should go to Servia and all the region south and east of the Rhodope range and the Struma river to Bulgaria. The intermediate territory would form the autonomous Macedonia desired by Bulgaria, but in case autonomy should not prove feasible a line was drawn from the point where the Servian, Bulgarian and Turkish frontiers meet, a little northwest of Kustendil, to Struga, at the northernmost extremity of Lake Ochrida, leaving Kratovo, Velos, Monastir and Ochrida to Bulgaria, while the ultimate disposal of certain districts lying mainly north of this line and south of the Shar range—namely, the Kazas of Kumanovo, Uskub, Krshevo and Dibra, and the Nahie of Struga—was reserved for the arbitration of the czar of Russia.

The adhesion of Montenegro to the league was easily secured, King Nicholas having long been an advocate of a combination of Christian states against Turkey. Besides, the enlargement of Montenegrin territory had become an economic necessity.

It thus appears that Bulgaria had a definite understanding with Servia as to the partition of spoils of war, but had made no arrangements with Greece or Montenegro. Developments unforeseen when the several treaties were made changed conditions entirely and caused the alliance to become not only defensive but offensive. The allies after their victories over Turkey became ambitious and each nation sought to gain as much as possible in the way of territorial and trade expansion. Their interests conflicted and instead of resorting to arbitration they drifted into war to settle their differences. This result, it was claimed by some observers, was not displeasing to one or two of the great powers, notably Austria-Hungary, which did not want to see a strong Balkan confederation formed.

DRIFTED INTO WAR.

Bulgaria and Greece first clashed over the possession of Saloniki, which was claimed by Bulgaria, but strongly occupied by Greek troops. This was in the early part of April. A little later came reports that Bulgaria and Servia were preparing to fight for the possession of Monastir, which was held by Servian troops. By the end of April reports of armed encounters between Bulgarian troops on the one side and Greek and Servian on the other began to appear in the newspapers, although efforts to keep the affairs quiet were made by the combatants. The encounters were not serious, but they revealed to the world the severity of the tension existing between the allies. This tension continued throughout May and long into June in spite of efforts made by the premiers of the Balkan nations to come to an understanding, and offers on the part of Russia to arbitrate the differences. June 30 fighting began all along the line and the war between the allies was in full progress. July 1 all the Bulgarians in Saloniki had either been expelled or made prisoners of war.

Newspaper correspondents were excluded from the war zone and such news as came to the world was more or less unreliable. Reports of battles were meager, conflicting and generally unsatisfactory. From Athens and Belgrade came glowing accounts of victories; Sofia admitted no Bulgarian defeats. It soon became evident, however, that the Bulgarians, who had won such notable victories at Kirk Kilesseh, Bunarhissar, Lule Burgas, Tchataljia, Bulair and Adrianople, were not making an effective resistance. The Greek troops, after a fierce battle, compelled them to retire from Kilkish July 4 and

by July 9 had driven them from Kavala and Seres. A few days later a battle was fought at Demirhissar, in which the Greeks were again the victors. July 8 Servia, with Montenegro as its ally, issued a formal declaration of war against Bulgaria. Fighting of severe character occurred at Istip, Kotchana, Kustendil and other points, the general outcome being favorable to the Servians.

At this time the combatants began to charge each other with committing all kinds of atrocities on the inhabitants of the villages and towns in the districts occupied by the troops. The Bulgarians were accused of barbarous conduct at Seres, Demirhissar and elsewhere. King Ferdinand, on the other hand, asserted that the accusation was false and was made by his country's enemies for the purpose of creating a bad impression. He declared that, as a matter of fact, Bulgarians were the victims of cruel persecution at the hands of the Greeks and Servians at many places. It was further claimed that the stories of Bulgarian atrocities were circulated at a time when Sofia and the rest of Bulgaria were cut off from the world and when denials could not be sent out to counteract the charges. The accusations, whether true or false, served to intensify the bitterness existing between the nations which but a short time before had been fighting side by side against the Turks.

What the outcome of the conflict between Bulgaria and the other three Balkan states would have been had they been left to fight it out alone is a matter of opinion. The Bulgarians made the claim that they would have won, as their plan of campaign had been carefully worked out and was bound to be successful. The Servians and Greeks maintained that the Bulgarians were whipped and that they were in no condition to carry on a war after their heavy losses in the Turkish struggle. But Bulgaria had to face new foes and defeat was inevitable.

ROUMANIA ATTACKS BULGARIA.

Roumania at the opening of the war against Turkey was inclined to side with the Ottoman government, but finally consented to remain neutral, with the understanding, expressed or implied, that it should receive some compensation. As early as Jan. 10, while the peace negotiations were in progress in London, Roumania demanded of Bulgaria the cession of Silistria and the territory to the north of a line stretching from there to Kavarna on the Black sea. Bulgaria refused to comply and matters remained in abeyance until July 4, when Roumania mobilized its army. A week later it declared war and ordered its troops to invade Bulgarian territory. Silistria was occupied July 11 without resistance on the part of the garrison, and King Charles with his army began advancing toward Sofia. The Bulgarians made no opposition to the invasion.

Simultaneously with Roumania's movements the Turks left their lines near Constantinople and, disregarding the terms of the London treaty of May 30, proceeded by forced marches to retake the territory from which they had been driven by the Bulgarians. By July 16 they had occupied Lule Burgas and Bunarhissar. Then they took Kirk Kilesseh, and July 21 entered Adrianople after a brief conflict with the Bulgarian garrison.

TREATY OF BUCHAREST.

With his capital and country isolated from the world and surrounded by enemies, King Ferdinand was compelled to sue for peace and accept the terms imposed by Roumania, Servia and Greece. Austria-Hungary, with which Bulgaria was said to have a secret understanding, made a demand July 25 at Athens and Belgrade that hostilities cease, warning Greece and Servia that it would not allow Bulgaria to be too greatly humiliated. July 30 delegates representing Servia, Greece, Montenegro and Bulgaria met in Bucharest and agreed upon a five days' armistice. A peace conference was then held and an understanding was reached Aug. 6. Four days later, the terms of peace having been reduced to writing, a formal treaty of peace was signed, terminating the war between the allies and delimiting their frontiers. Bulgaria agreed to demobilize at once. The treaty was ratified Aug. 25.

The treaty fixed the meeting point of the new Servian, Bulgarian and Greek frontiers on the spur

M. MAJORESCU,
Roumania.

M. VENEZELOS,
Greece.

M. RADOSLAFOF,
Bulgaria.

M. PASHITCH,
Servia.

LEADING STATESMEN WHO ARRANGED BALKAN PEACE TREATY.

of the Belashitza range northeast of Lake Doiran. The Serbo-Bulgarian frontier follows the watershed between the Struma and Vardar rivers, being slightly to the west so as to leave Strumnitza in Bulgarian territory. Kotchana and Radovishte are on the Servian side of the line. The Serbo-Greek frontier runs southwest from Lake Doiran, past Gyevgeli (Servian), to a point due north of Vodena, where it turns west to the south end or near the south end of Lake Prespa. Vodena and Florina are on Greek territory. From Lake Doiran the Bulgar-Greek frontier runs east along the Belashitza range to a point where the Saloniki-Monastir railway line reaches the Mesta river. On the Ægean shore the Mesta river separates the Greek and Bulgarian territory. Drama, Seres and the port of Kavala are on the Grecian side. Montenegro, by the terms of the treaty, was to receive an extension of territory east and south commensurate with the aid given Servia in the war against Bulgaria.

As the net result of the war with Turkey and the war between the allies Greece, it was estimated, gained 20,000 square miles of territory and 1,000,-000 inhabitants; Servia, 19,000 square miles and 1,100,000 inhabitants; Bulgaria, 12,500 square miles and 500,000 inhabitants, and Roumania, 2,500 square miles and 250,000 inhabitants. Montenegro, it was thought, would gain about 2,000 square miles and possibly 200,000 inhabitants. The frontiers not having been exactly delimited in places, these estimates are subject to revision. It was calculated that the total population of the enlarged states in southeastern Europe would be approximately as follows: Roumania, 7,690,000; Bulgaria, 5,000,000; Greece, 4,500,000; Servia, 4,000,000; Albania, 2,000,-000; Montenegro, 500,000.

Bulgaria was compelled to surrender a large part of its share of the territory assigned to it by the treaty of Bucharest. Soon after the conclusion of that convention negotiations were begun between representatives of Bulgaria and Turkey to fix a new frontier between the two states, and Sept. 18 the protocol of a treaty was signed. According to this the boundary line was established as follows: Beginning on the Black sea at the mouth of the Pasova river, immediately north of San Stefano, it runs to the old frontier near Devotly-Agatch, follows it as far as Soudjak, turns in a southerly direction, passing one and two-tenths miles south of Mustapha Pasha and the same distance east of Orlakol, joins the Maritza river at Mandra and follows the course of that stream as far as the Ægean sea. This left Adrianople in the possession of Turkey, together with the other great battle fields on which the Bulgarians won their greatest victories. The powers made no effort to enforce the treaty of Bucharest, so far as concerned the Enos-Midia frontier.

Turkey having regained much of the territory lost to the Bulgarians turned toward Greece with the object of recovering Kavala and other towns and lands along the Ægean sea. and warlike preparations were made on both sides. The Albanians recaptured Ochrida, Dibra and other small places from the Servians. The latter hastened to retake them and was met by an ultimatum from Austria that they must surrender all the Albanian towns occupied by them.

CHRONOLOGY OF BALKAN WARS.

1912.

Oct. 9—Montenegro begins war on Turkey.

Oct. 18—Bulgaria and Greece declare war on Turkey.

Oct. 24—Turks defeated by Bulgarians at Kirk Kelisseh.

Oct. 29-31—Bulgarians win another big battle at Lule Burgas.

Nov. 1-2—Turks driven to forts at Tchatalja, near Constantinople.

Nov. 8—Greek army captures Saloniki.

Nov. 18—Servians capture Monastir.

Dec. 3—Protocol signed for peace conference in London.

Dec. 16—Peace conference begun.

1913.

Jan. 1—Turks accede to most of demands made by allies.

Jan. 6—Turkey gives up island of Crete.

Jan. 10—Roumania demands the cession of Silistria from Bulgaria.

Jan. 14—Allies threaten to resume war owing to Turkey's delay in accepting peace terms in full.

Jan. 18—Powers in collective note ask Turkey to give up Adrianople.

Jan. 23—Enver Bey and young Turks forced cabinet to resign; Nazim Pasha slain in Constantinople.

Jan. 24—New Turkish cabinet announced with Mahmoud Shefket Pasha as grand vizier and minister of war.

Jan. 29—Peace negotiations in London broken off by allies.

Feb. 5—War resumed; bombardment of Adrianople continued.

Feb. 7—Turks defeated by Bulgarians near the River Kavak on the Gallipoli peninsula.

Feb. 8—Servians and Montenegrins attack Scutari; Turks defeated by Bulgarians in battle at Bulair, losing 6,000 men.

Feb. 12—Turkish government requests powers to intervene.

March 6—Greeks capture Janina.

March 20—Austria objects to bombardment of Scutari; King Nicholas of Montenegro refuses to discontinue siege.

March 22—Powers suggest terms of peace.

March 23—Austria presents ultimatum to Montenegro demanding suspension of military operations around Scutari.

March 25—Montenegro consents to permit civilian population of Scutari to leave the city; first line of defenses around Adrianople captured.

March 27—Adrianople surrendered to the allies by Shukri Pasha, the Turkish commander.

April 1—Turkey accepts terms of peace offered by the powers.

April 2—Tarabosch forts defending Scutari captured by Montenegrins.

April 4—Five European powers establish blockade of Montenegrin coast.
April 11—Bulgaria and Greece clash over possession of Saloniki; Servians withdraw from siege of Scutari.
April 23—Montenegrin troops capture Scutari; Austria demands its evacuation.
April 24—Austria notifies powers that they must turn Montenegrins out of Scutari.
April 29—Austrian troops massed on Montenegrin frontier.
May 5—King Nicholas of Montenegro decides to evacuate Scutari at the demand of the powers.
May 12—Allies agree to a second peace conference in London.
May 14—International naval force takes possession of Scutari forts.
May 23—Clashes between Greek and Bulgarian forces near Saloniki.
May 28—Acute tension in relations of Bulgaria with Servia and Greece develops.
May 30—Treaty of peace signed in London by delegates of allies and of Turkey.
June 10—Battle between Servians and Bulgarians at Makres.
June 11—Mahmoud Shefket Pasha assassinated in Constantinople.
June 30—Bulgarians fight Servians and Greeks all along the line.
July 4—Roumania mobilizes its army; Greeks capture Kilkish from Bulgarians.
July 9—Seres captured by Greeks from Bulgarians; Kavala evacuated by latter.
July 11—Roumania declares war on Bulgaria; Roumanian troops occupy city of Silistria without opposition.
July 12—Turkish armies resume war on Bulgaria and march to Adrianople is begun.

July 14—King Ferdinand denies stories of Bulgarian atrocities.
July 17—King Constantine of Greece tells of Bulgarian outrages; King Ferdinand again denies them.
July 21—Turks recapture Adrianople.
July 22—Bulgarian capital isolated from world by surrounding states.
July 23—King Ferdinand proposes immediate cessation of hostilities.
July 24—King Ferdinand protests to powers against Turkish invasion.
July 25—Austria demands immediate cessation of hostilities by Greece and Servia.
July 30—Five days' armistice agreed to by delegates of Servia, Greece, Montenegro and Bulgaria at conference in Bucharest.
Aug. 6—Terms of peace agreed to by delegates in Bucharest.
Aug. 7—Powers demand evacuation of Adrianople by Turks.
Aug. 10—Peace treaty signed in Bucharest.
Aug. 25—Balkan peace treaty ratified.
Sept. 18—Bulgaria and Turkey sign protocol of treaty defining new frontier; Adrianople remains in possession of Turks.
Sept. 22—Greeks seize American mission school at Koritsa, Albania.
Sept. 26—Greece prepares for war with Turkey; Ottomans wish to recover port of Kavala.
Sept. 18—Albanians take Kitchevo, Jakovo, Oehrida and other towns from Servia.
Sept. 29—Treaty of peace between Turkey and Bulgaria formally signed.
Oct. 2—Servians reoccupy Ochrida, Dibra and other towns taken by Albanians.
Oct. 18—Austria sends ultimatum to Servia to evacuate points in Albania occupied by Servian troops.

VALUES OF RARE AMERICAN COINS.

The prices given are those quoted for the rarest of each denomination by dealers in New York and Chicago:

GOLD COINS.

TEN DOLLARS—EAGLE.

Date.	Value.
1797(small eagle)	$20 to $22
1798	20 to 25

FIVE DOLLARS—HALF-EAGLE.

Date.	Value.
1795(small eagle)	$6 to $8
1795(large eagle)	15 to 18
1796	7 to 10
1797(small eagle)	12 to 15
1797(large eagle)	15 to 20
1798(small eagle)	20 to 30
1815	75 to 100
1819	10 to 15
1820	8 to 10
1821	10 to 15
1822	100 to 150
1823	8 to 10
1824	16 to 32
1825	9 to 14
1826	10 to 15
1827	9 to 14

Date.	Value.
1828	$15 to $20
1829	15 to 18
1829 (new type).	17 to 20
1830	8 to 12
1831	8 to 12
1832	9 to 14
1833	7 to 10

FOUR DOLLARS.

1879	$12 to $15
1880	20 to 25

THREE DOLLARS.

1875	$20 to $30
Any date	3.55

QUARTER-EAGLE ($2.50).

1796 (with stars)	$12 to $18
1797	10 to 15
1826	15 to 20

ONE DOLLAR.

1864	$5 to $8
1875	8 to 12
Any date	1.60

SILVER COINS.

DOLLARS.

1794	$20 to $40
1804	650 to 3,600
1838(flying eagle)	30 to 50
1839(flying eagle)	25 to 35
1851	$20 to $30
1852	20 to 30
1858	15 to 20

HALF-DOLLARS.

Date.	Value.
1796	$20 to $35
1797	15 to 25
1838 (mint mark "O" bet. date and bust).	15 to 30
1853 (without arrow heads at date)	20 to 30

QUARTER-DOLLARS.

Date.	Value.
1823	$20 to $30
1827	30 to 50
1893 Col. (Isabella)	40c

TWENTY-CENT PIECES.

1874	$2 to $4
1877	1 to 2

DIMES.

1797	$2.00 to $4.00
1800	2.00 to 3.50

Date.	
1802	$2.00 to $4.00
1804	5.00 to 10.00

THREE-CENT PIECES.

1864	$1.00 to $1.50

HALF-DIMES.

1794	$1.50 to $3.00
1796	1.50 to 2.50
1802	20.00 to 40.00
1805	2.00 to 3.00

NICKEL COINS.

FIVE-CENT PIECES.

1877	.75 to $1.00

THREE-CENT PIECES.

1877	.50 to $1.00

COPPER COINS.

TWO-CENT PIECES.

1873	$1 to $2

CENTS.

1793	$1 to $5
1799	4 to 35
1804	3 to 10

HALF-CENTS.

1793	.50 to $3
1796	5.00 to 25
1802	.50 to 2
1831	3.00 to 10

1826	$4.00 to $8
1840	2.00 to 7
1841	2.00 to 7
1842	3.00 to 10
1843	2.00 to 7
1844	2.00 to 7
1845	2.00 to 7
1846	2.00 to 10
1847	4.00 to 12
1848	3.00 to 10
1849 (small date)	2.50 to 8
1852	2.00 to 6

THE PAN-AMERICAN UNION.

The Pan-American union was established upon the recommendation of the first international American conference in 1890 for the purpose of maintaining closer relations between the republics of the western hemisphere. Its duties have been broadened since then and it is now a general clearing house of information concerning the nations of North, South and Central America. It publishes a monthly bulletin in which are given the latest official data concerning the resources, commerce and other features of the republics. The officers of the union occupy a fine building at the corner of 17th street and Potomac park in Washington, D. C. The structure, which was built with money given by Andrew Carnegie, was dedicated April 26, 1910. Following are the officers:

Director-General—John Barrett.
Assistant Director—Francisco J. Yanes.
Chief Statistician—William C. Wells.
Chief Clerk—Franklin Adams.
Chief Translator—Emilio M. Amores.
Librarian—Charles E. Babcock.
Special Compilers—Albert Hale, O. E. Albes.

THE CARNEGIE HERO FUND.

April 15, 1904, Andrew Carnegie placed in the hands of a commission the sum of $5,000,000 to be known as "the hero fund." Its purpose is to reward with medals and money the men and women who perform heroic deeds, or, in case they lose their lives, to care for those dependent upon them. Widows are given support until they remarry and children are given allowances until they are 16 years of age. Only such as follow peaceful vocations on sea or land in the United States and Canada are eligible to become beneficiaries of the fund. The first awards of medals and money were made in May and others in October, 1905.

Up to Jan. 1, 1913, the commission had awarded $1,013,668.96 in cash to persons showing great bravery in the face of danger and to the nearest relatives of heroes who died in rescuing or attempting to rescue persons in danger. There had also been awarded 31 gold medals, 186 silver medals and 228 bronze medals. The pensions in force Jan. 15, 1913, amounted to $58,380 a year.

AWARDS MADE NOV. 1, 1912.

James Feeney, laborer, died in attempting to save John H. McGee from electric shock in Pittsburgh, Pa., April 13, 1912; silver medal and $25 a month pension to widow with $5 a month for each of five children.

Leo J. Lockard, schoolboy, aged 12, died trying to save John A. Roberts from drowning at Altoona, Pa., Dec. 10, 1911; silver medal and $250 to father.

Joseph K. Isenberg, contractor, saved Arabella V. and Paul K. Crist from a runaway in Altoona, Pa., Dec. 25, 1910; silver medal and $1,000.

Fred L. Manevel, brakeman, saved Elna Newburg from being run over by train at Ridgway, Pa., July 19, 1907; bronze medal and $1,000.

Biddle Hiles, bank cashier, aged 56, saved man from enraged bull at Salem, N. J., June 11, 1910; bronze medal.

John L. LaMarche, street car conductor, saved L. L. Stipp from drowning at Watertown, Mass., Oct. 8, 1908; bronze medal.

Samuel N. Parks, physician, attempted to save T. E. Meley, well digger, from suffocation at De Soto, Tex., April 27, 1909; bronze medal.

James J. Doyle, lineman, saved Abbie T. Danforth, aged 83, from being run over by train at Royalton, Vt., Aug. 30, 1910; bronze medal.

William B. Hutton, foreman, helped to save William Porter, stockman, from suffocation in Los Angeles, Cal., Aug. 19, 1911; bronze medal and $1,000.

John W. Freeman, salesman, rescued Johnnie Porter, aged 13, from runaway at Fort Smith, Ark., Dec. 25, 1908; bronze medal and $1,000.

Thomas W. Erwin, foreman, saved Jetta W. Caudill from being run over by a train at Clyffeside, Ky., Sept. 5, 1910; bronze medal and $1,000.

Roy T. Hughes, farmer, saved ten children from drowning at Letot, Tex., May 24, 1908; bronze medal and $1,000.

L. Newton Law, ranchman, helped to save four children from drowning at Letot, Tex., May 24, 1908; bronze medal and $1,000.

Nathan Record, negro farmer, helped to save three children from drowning at Letot, Tex., May 24, 1908; bronze medal and $1,000.

James A. Bales, farmer, saved W. B. Fowler from suffocation at McKinney, Tex., Nov. 14, 1910; bronze medal and $1,000.

Elijah A. Walker, laborer, tried to save John R. Northcutt from suffocation at Palopinto, Tex., Aug. 19, 1910; bronze medal and $1,000.

George A. Blitch, laborer, saved John R. Northcutt from suffocation at Palopinto, Tex., Aug. 19, 1909; bronze medal and $1,000.

George H. Paul, aged 52, farm hand, attempted to save William Hamilton from being run over by a train at California, Ky., Oct. 2, 1911; bronze medal and $1,000.

E. Thompson Benbow, farmer, helped to save Pearl Drummond, aged 15, from drowning at Bryan, Tex., Aug. 18, 1911; bronze medal and $1,000.

J. Archie Robinson, farmer, helped to save Pearl Drummond from drowning at Bryan, Tex., Aug. 18, 1911; bronze medal and $1,000.

Miss Marion P. Greiner, aged 17, a factory hand, saved Lora Madon from drowning at Plattsburg, N. Y., May 1, 1911; bronze medal and $1,000.

Charles A. W. Hansen, deck hand, helped to save J. A. Jones from drowning at Galveston, Tex., July 21, 1909; bronze medal and $1,000.

Klaus L. Larsen, deck hand, helped to save Joe A. Jones and others from drowning at Galveston, Tex., July 21, 1909; bronze medal and $1,000.

S. A. Anderson, farm hand, saved Robert B. Walker from suffocating at Collinsville, Tex., July 4, 1911; bronze medal and $1,000.

William H. McDaniel, farmer, saved Alonzo A. Smith, well-digger, from suffocation at Kosse, Tex., Sept. 22, 1909; bronze medal and $1,000.

Henry J. Schanewerk, switchman, saved man from a runaway locomotive at Fort Worth, Tex., July 9, 1909; bronze medal and $1,000.

Thomas J. Gibbons, pit motorman, saved two men from suffocation at Cokedale, Col., Feb. 10, 1911; bronze medal and $1,000.

Arvey N. Florence, painter, helped in attempt to save W. H. Arrasmith from electric shock in Cincinnati, O., Aug. 7, 1911; bronze medal and $1,000.

Benjamin F. Langsdale, painter, assisted in foregoing case; bronze medal and $1,000.

Challen A. West, express agent, assisted in Arrasmith case; bronze medal and $1,000.

Edward W. Hargett, Sr., restaurant proprietor, tried to rescue Nora A. Higdon and Anna E. Wendelbor from a runaway at Globe, Ariz., March 6, 1909; bronze medal and $1,000.

Robert McD. Logan, Jr., schoolboy, saved William B. Schell, aged 12, from drowning at Fort Worth, Tex., July 25, 1911; bronze medal and $2,000. Logan, who could not swim, mounted a pony and swam it into the stream toward Schell. When the pony came up near by, unconscious, Logan grasped him by the hair and guided the pony to the bank, drawing Schell with him. Schell was revived.

W. Sterrett Parkinson, aged 17, student, saved Charles L. Graham, aged 8, from drowning at Carlisle, Pa., July 15, 1911; bronze medal and $2,000.

John G. Wolfe died in attempting to save A. R. Eltringham from drowning at Fairview, Pa., July 4, 1907; bronze medal and $1,000.

C. Bert Raymond, office boy, died saving Hershel F. Shelby, aged 12, from drowning at Indianapolis, Ind., June 10, 1911; bronze medal and $30 a month to mother for five years.

Walter A. Smith, died in trying to save Frederick H. Voorhis, aged 4, from drowning at Middletown, O., July 11, 1912; bronze medal, $500 and $50 a month to widow with $5 a month for daughter.

Louis G. Burkhalter, machinist, died in an attempt to save Ruth E. Mastellar and Veda G. Hemstock from drowning at Bradley, Ill., July 28, 1912; bronze medal and $55 a month to widow and $5 a month for each of two children.

T. William Hutchins, clerk, died as a result of trying to save Leila de Llorens from drowning at Ship Island, Miss., July 17, 1910; bronze medal and $40 a month to widow with $5 a month for each of two children.

Michael O'Loughlin, aged 68, laborer, died attempting to save Patrick McMahon from suffocation at Stoneham, Mass., Oct. 11, 1909; bronze medal to widow and $20 a month for five years, or $1,200 otherwise as needed.

James Higgins, laborer, aged 63, saved Patrick McMahon from suffocation at Stoneham, Mass., Oct. 11, 1909; bronze medal.

Francis E. Park, physician, helped to save Patrick McMahon from suffocation at Stoneham, Mass., Oct. 11, 1909; bronze medal.

J. Louis Little, fisherman, helped to save four men from drowning at Bonavista, N. F., Sept. 19, 1907; silver medal and $1,500.

Robert Brown, collector, helped in Bonavista rescue; bronze medal and $1,000.

James C. Little, fisherman, assisted in Bonavista rescue; bronze medal and $1,000.

William Ford, fisherman, assisted in Bonavista rescue; bronze medal and $1,000.

James Ford, fisherman, assisted in Bonavista rescue; bronze medal and $1,000.

Eli Paul, fisherman, assisted in Bonavista rescue; bronze medal and $1,000.

Richard S. Stokes, aged 74, saved three persons from drowning at Lometa, Tex., July 19, 1911; silver medal and $1,000.

Lance H. Mardiss, farm hand, tried to save Charles A. Hill from suffocation at Naco, Ariz., June 17, 1908; silver medal and $1,000.

H. Frank Fizer, motorman, saved Thomas Bowen, foreman, and seven other men from a cave-in in a tunnel at Santa Barbara, Cal., April 7, 1912. Fizer discovered that a cave-in, which would cause water to back to the face of the workings, was imminent two miles from the entrance. In order to warn the other men he waded back in the tunnel a distance of over 4,400 feet, through water from 12 to 20 inches deep; all escaped; silver medal and $1,000.

Lafayette L. Davis, blacksmith, saved Alonzo M. Barnett from suffocation at Bangs, Tex., May 14, 1907; silver medal and $1,000.

Dennis P. Morgan, farm hand, saved Armanda L. Briscoe, aged 60, from drowning at Gustine, Tex., Sept. 6, 1910; silver medal and $1,000.

Henry W. Burge, farm hand, saved Walter C. Bailey from suffocation at Delba, Tex., March 6, 1911; silver medal and $1,000.

William T. Howard, farm hand, saved Thos. R. Lewis and J. E. Rogers from suffocation at Parker, Tex., July 5, 1911; silver medal and $1,000.

Alvin J. Miller, laborer, saved Hugh and Henry Cooper from suffocation at Rising Star, Tex., April 5, 1910; silver medal and $1,000.

Robert A. Atkinson, driver, died in attempting to save one or more of three persons from suffocation in Cincinnati, O., June 4, 1912; silver medal and $25 a month pension to mother.

Joseph Schlageter, Jr., driver, attempted to save Anna Espelage from suffocation in Cincinnati, O., June 4, 1912; bronze medal and $1,000.

Percy Walker, hotel proprietor, died in trying to save A. P. Henrickson from drowning at Keen Camp, Cal., Feb. 29, 1912; silver medal and $50 a month to widow with $5 a month for each of two children.

George W. T. Snare, attempted to save Percy Walker from drowning at Keen Camp, Cal., Feb. 29, 1912; bronze medal.

AWARDS MADE JAN. 15, 1913.

W. Roy Stokes, schoolboy, aged 12, died in attempting to save three children from drowning at Coral, Pa., Jan. 18, 1908; silver medal and $1,000 to father.

Frank Beaumont, aged 36, farmer, died in attempting to save his nephew, aged 9, from drowning at Beaumaris, Ont., July 27, 1912; silver medal to father.

Louis C. Scholl, carpenter, saved Raymond C. Lanfear from drowning at Santa Cruz, Cal., July 9, 1911; bronze medal and $1,000.

Clarence Van Nostrand, aged 16, attempted to save three children from drowning at Glen Cove, N. Y., Jan. 8, 1911; bronze medal and $1,000.

John McBride, laborer, saved Cyrus L. Nall from drowning at Tarpon, Tex., March 9, 1910; bronze medal and $1,000.

William H. Prather, deck hand, saved F. W. Pheasant from drowning at Knights Landing, Cal., May 27, 1911; bronze medal and $1,000.

John V. Hagemann, laborer, rescued David C. Schlueter and Minnie L. Schlueter from a runaway in Elgin, Ill., June 22, 1906; bronze medal and $1,000.

Ernest E. Boggess, machinist, attempted to save Ray S. Utter from burning at Hood River, Ore., May 18, 1910; bronze medal, $425 disablement benefits and $1,000.

Rodney A. Perry, aged 13, schoolboy, saved Albert B. Collins from drowning at Alton, Me., Dec. 1, 1909; bronze medal and $2,000.

Walter B. Wallace, aged 36, chief clerk, died in attempting to save Cathleen B. Suggs, Sallie C. McLean and Mary B. Wolfe from drowning at Santa Rosa island, Fla., June 22, 1911; bronze medal and $50 a month to widow.

Adam A. Oberst, stationary fireman, died in attempting to save Charles A. Carr from suffocation at Carpentersville, Ill., Feb. 6, 1911; bronze medal and $25 a month to mother.

Cecil R. Karberg, aged 19, reporter, died in attempting to save Dorothy McGrew, aged 13, from drowning at La Jolla, Cal., Aug. 6, 1911; bronze medal and $500 to mother.

Charles L. Clovell, superintendent of public works, saved four women from drowning at Wellington, Kas., June 29, 1908; silver medal.

Austin M. Morgan, real estate dealer, saved William E. Mason, minister, from assassination at Cleburne, Tex., Dec. 7, 1907; silver medal.

Lorenzo Ortiz, track laborer, saved A. S. Townes from drowning at Oklahoma City, Okla., Jan. 27, 1912; silver medal and $500.

Magdaleno Bargas, track laborer, saved S. B. Townes, Jr., from drowning at Oklahoma City, Okla., Jan. 27, 1912; silver medal and $500.

Sydney Metzler, dentist, saved Annie Newton, aged 12, from drowning at Whycocomagh, N. S., Oct. 25, 1909; silver medal and $1,000.

James A. Miller, foreman, tried to save two men from a cave-in at Liberal, Kas., Oct. 14, 1911; silver medal and $1,000.

Allen W. McDowell, tool dresser, saved Jessie P. and James R. Bateson from drowning at Delaware, Okla., Jan. 22, 1910; silver medal and $1,545 disablement benefits.

William P. Murley, farmer, attempted to save J. Austin Lott from a runaway at Capron, Okla., Feb. 8, 1911; silver medal, $1,000 disablement benefits and $1,000 toward liquidating indebtedness.

Miss Doris E. Lewis, aged 14, school girl, saved Benjamin W. Draper, aged 7, from drowning at Coxansville, Que., Nov. 26, 1911; silver medal and $2,000.

Albert C. Zeiner, roofer and slater, died in attempting to save Chas. P. Sullivan, aged 7, from a live electric wire at Burlington, Vt., Sept. 7, 1912; silver medal, $800 to liquidate mortgage and $45 a month to widow with $5 a month for a son.

Edwin S. Newlin, farmer, died in attempting to save two girls from drowning at Emporia, Kas., July 17, 1912; silver medal to son and $20 a month to each of three children.

Carl B. Warren, farmer and blacksmith, died in attempting to save Rupert E. Tobey, aged 5, from drowning at Vassalboro, Me., May 19, 1912; bronze medal to father, pension of $25 a month to father or mother for life and $750 to liquidate their indebtedness.

C. Henry Carr, aged 15, schoolboy, died in attempting to save George H. Crouin, aged 17, from drowning at Lynn, Mass., July 2, 1912; bronze medal and $1,000 to mother.

AWARDS MADE APRIL 25, 1913.

Thomas P. Cahill saved Isabella Mandel, aged 3, from being run down by street car in Pittsburgh, Pa., April 27, 1912; bronze medal and $1,000.

William J. Reidy, carpenter, saved Abraham Hildebrand from suffocation at Gresham, Ore., Nov. 8, 1904; bronze medal.

Alexander Johnston died in trying to save two men from suffocation at Etna, Pa., June 11, 1912; silver medal and pension of $75 a month to widow with $5 a month to her young son.

Oswald G. Beck died in trying to save Alexander Johnston from suffocation at Etna, Pa., June 11, 1912; silver medal to widow with pension of $65 a month and $5 a month for her young daughter.

Lawrence E. Riddle, superintendent, tried to save Johnston, Beck and Meyer from suffocation at Etna, Pa., June 11, 1912; silver medal.

Charles R. Lilly, station master, saved M. Frances Gooding, aged 4, from being run over by a train at Grafton, W. Va., May 4, 1912; bronze medal and $900.

Edgar H. Sherman, grocer, rescued Mabel McCalley from a runaway at Marion, Iowa, March 3, 1911; bronze medal and $1,000.

Miss Lillanne Formby, aged 22, school teacher, saved Ethel R. Y'Blood, aged 19, from being run over by a train at Waldo, Ark., Aug. 2, 1912; bronze medal and $1,000.

Ralph E. Mazey, baggage master, saved Harriett E. Malcolm and Lottie Hollenberg from being run over by a train at Monmouth, Ill., May 12, 1908; bronze medal and $1,000.

Samuel Nasser, weaver, saved Edward S. Whelan, aged 4, from burning at Elmira, N. Y., April 12, 1912; bronze medal and $1,000.

David Phillips, mine fore boss, saved Martin A. Wright, aged 79, from being run over by a train at Snowden, Pa., June 11, 1912; bronze medal and $1,000.

William J. Arthur, salesman, saved Benjamin J.

Vetrone from drowning at Erie, Pa., Aug. 25, 1912; bronze medal and $1,000.

Bernard C. King, clerk, saved Ralph C. Brown, a boy, from drowning at Warren, Pa., Dec. 28, 1912; bronze medal and $1,000.

Alexander E. Shearer, lamp tender, saved two children from burning at Dingville, W. Va., Sept. 26, 1912; bronze medal and $1,000.

Alvin M. Crafton, farmer, saved another farmer and a schoolboy from drowning at Sidney, Ark., July 4, 1912; bronze medal and $1,000.

Elliott D. Nichols, Jr., schoolboy, saved F. B. Fleck from drowning at Watts Falls, N. Y., July 29, 1906; bronze medal and $1,000.

William M. Orr, sawmill operator, saved W. McDonald Morriss, aged 10, from drowning at Glade Spring, Va., March 16, 1912; bronze medal and $1,000.

James Reynolds, foreman of linemen, saved John C. Jackson, lineman, from electric shock at New Haven, Conn., Sept. 1, 1908; bronze medal and $1,300.

Joseph T. Holland, clerk, attempted to save Hazel M. Murray from drowning at Erie, Pa., Aug. 21, 1912; bronze medal and $2,000.

Sheldon V. Clarke, student, saved J. B. Duke from drowning at Williamsport, Pa., June 3, 1912; bronze medal and $2,000.

J. Floyd Fraser, schoolboy, saved W. K. Williams from drowning at Delaney, Tex., May 28, 1911; bronze medal and $2,000.

R. Kenneth Oliver, schoolboy, saved little girl from being run over by a train at Tampico, Ill., March 15, 1912; bronze medal and $2,000.

James O. London, foreman, died in attempting to save a boy from drowning at Mahoning, Pa., June 30, 1912; bronze medal and pension of $55 a month to widow with $5 a month for each of four children.

E. Gertrude Semon saved Elizabeth G. King from burning at Galesburg, Ill., Dec. 14, 1910; silver medal and $1,000.

Iram Kevorkian, laborer, saved Henry J. Lutz, candy maker, from drowning at Niagara Falls, N. Y., May 19, 1912; silver medal and $1,000.

Martin D. Wade, flagman, tried to save a schoolboy from being run over by a train at Mount Alton, Pa., March 2, 1912; silver medal and $1,000.

Joseph M. Friel, brakeman, saved Agnes E. Walsh from being run over by a train at Riverton, Pa., Oct. 25, 1912; silver medal and $1,000.

Patrick J. Reidy, conductor, saved Thomas Hayes,

aged 6, from being run over by a train at Buffalo, N. Y., June 28, 1906; silver medal and $1,000.

Stanislaus Griemanski, crossing watchman, tried to save unidentified man from being run over by a train at Erie, Pa., July 24, 1912; silver medal and $1,000.

Charles G. Davis, laborer, saved W. F. Gorman, well digger, from suffocation at Charlotte, N. C., Sept. 19, 1911; silver medal and $2,000.

Alvah H. Gibson, aged 14, of Milwaukee, Wis., helped save H. C. Warren, aged 15, from fall following electric shock at Kalamazoo, Mich., April 16, 1912; silver medal and $2,000.

Roy W. Carney, detective, helped in preceding rescue; silver medal and $1,000.

William W. Webster, merchant, died in attempting rescue of H. C. Warren (see above); silver medal and pension of $70 a month to widow with $5 a month for each of two children.

Herbert R. Cornell, schoolboy, died in trying to save Carl O. Henry, aged 12, from drowning at Athens, O., June 28, 1912; silver medal and $600 to father.

John T. Brooke, teacher, died attempting to save student and teacher from drowning at San Mateo, Cal., Aug. 15, 1907; silver medal and $1,000 to father.

George W. Smith, teacher, died in same rescue attempt that cost the life of John T. Brooke; bronze medal and $1,000 to mother.

Peter W. H. Flipney, farmer, died attempting to save John Thomas, well digger, from suffocation at Snake Creek, Va., May 26, 1911; silver medal and monthly pension of $25 to sister.

Charles Thomas, laborer, died attempting to save Joseph E. Murphy, contractor, from suffocation at Circleville, O., Sept. 16, 1912; silver medal, $100 cash and monthly pension of $30 to widow with $5 a month for each of four children.

Elias B. Adams, crossing watchman, died attempting to save Olivia R. Schmidt from being run over by a train at Dayton, O., Nov. 14, 1912; silver medal and pension of $25 a month to widow.

HERO FUND COMMISSION, 1913.

President—Charles L. Taylor.
Vice-president—W. J. Holland.
Treasurer—J. H. Reed.
Secretary and manager—F. M. Wilmot.
Office in Carnegie building, Pittsburgh, Pa.

CARNEGIE INSTITUTION OF WASHINGTON.

The Carnegie Institution was endowed by Andrew Carnegie with $10,000,000 and incorporated under the laws of the District of Columbia Jan. 4, 1902. Incorporation by act of congress was effected April 28, 1904, section 2 of such act of incorporation specifying that the objects of the corporation shall be to encourage, in the broadest and most liberal manner, investigation, research and discovery and the application of knowledge to the improvement of mankind. Three principal agencies to forward these objects have been developed, namely:

First, large projects or departments of work whose execution requires continuous research by a corps of investigators during a series of years.

Secondly, minor projects, which may be carried out by individual experts in a limited period of time.

Thirdly, publication of the results of investigations made under the auspices of the institution, and for certain works which would not otherwise be readily printed. These publications are not distributed gratis except to a limited list of the greater libraries of the world.

Dec. 4, 1907, Mr. Carnegie added $2,000,000 to the endowment of the institution, and Jan. 20, 1911, he gave $10,000,000 more, making the total endowment $22,000,000.

The larger projects now under way and the names of the department directors or investigators are as follows:

Botanical research—D. T. MacDougal.
Economics and sociology—Henry W. Farnam.
Experimental evolution—Charles B. Davenport.

Geophysics—Arthur L. Day.
Historical research—J. F. Jameson.
Marine biology—A. G. Mayer.
Meridian astrometry—Benjamin Boss.
Nutrition—F. G. Benedict.
Solar physics—George E. Hale.
Terrestrial magnetism—A. L. Bauer.
The officers are as follows:
President of the institution—Robert S. Woodward.

Officers of the board of trustees—Elihu Root, vice-chairman; C. H. Dodge, secretary.

Executive committee—William H. Welch, chairman; S. Weir Mitchell, Elihu Root, Robert S. Woodward, C. H. Dodge, C. D. Walcott, William Barclay Parsons.

Trustees—Robert S. Brookings, John L. Cadwalader, Cleveland H. Dodge, Simon Flexner, W. N. Frew, Henry L. Higginson, Charles L. Hutchinson, Seth Low, S. Weir Mitchell, Andrew J. Montague, William W. Morrow, Elihu Root, William Barclay Parsons, Henry S. Pritchett, Martin A. Ryerson, Charles D. Walcott, Henry P. Walcott, Andrew D. White, Robert S. Woodward, William H. Taft, William H. Welch, George W. Wickersham.

The administration building of the institution is located on the southeast corner of 16th and P streets, N. W., Washington, D. C. The institution, however, is neither a branch of nor subject to any special regulations of the United States government. Neither is it a college or a university, nor does it maintain a library or museum. A prospectus of work and a list of publications may be obtained upon application to the president.

WORK OF 62D CONGRESS—THIRD SESSION.

Session began Dec. 2, 1912; ended March 4, 1913. Total appropriations (1913-1914), $1,098,647,969.21.

Act to create a department of labor; passed by house July 10, 1912; by senate Feb. 26, 1913; approved March 4, 1913.

Act to amend the act to regulate commerce by providing for a valuation of the several classes of property of carriers subject thereto; passed by house Dec. 5, 1912; by senate Feb. 24, 1913; approved March 1, 1913.

Act divesting intoxicating liquors of their interstate character in certain cases; passed by senate Feb. 10, 1913; by house Feb. 11; vetoed by president Feb. 28; passed by senate over veto Feb. 28; passed by house over veto March 1, 1913.

Act restricting the issuance of interlocutory injunctions to suspend the enforcement of the statute of a state or of an order made by an administrative board or commission created by aud acting under the statute of a state; passed by senate Feb. 25; by house March 3; approved March 4, 1913.

Act relating to the limitation of the hours of daily service of laborers and mechanics employed upon a public work of the United States, etc.; passed by house July 31, 1912; by senate Jan. 20, 1913; approved March 2, 1913.

Act to authorize the collection of the military and naval records of the revolutionary war with a view to their publication; passed by the senate Jan. 22, 1912; by the house Feb. 28, 1913; approved March 2, 1913.

Act providing for publicity in taking evidence in trust cases; passed by senate Feb. 11, 1913; by house March 2; approved March 3, 1913.

Act making appropriations for the naval service and providing for the increase of the navy; passed by the house Feb. 26, 1913; by senate Feb. 28; approved March 4, 1913.

Act incorporating the National Institute of Arts and Letters; passed by house June 17, 1912; by senate Jan 23, 1913; approved Feb. 4, 1913.

Act making Shelby M. Cullom special resident commissioner to represent Lincoln memorial commission in erection of memorial in Washington, D. C.; passed by senate Feb. 28, 1913; by house March 2; approved March 3, 1912. (See Abraham Lincoln memorial in Washington, D. C., this volume.)

Joint resolution approving plan and location for a Lincoln memorial; passed by senate Jan. 24, 1913; by house Jan. 29; approved Feb. 3. (See Abraham Lincoln memorial, this volume.)

Act extending power of the commissioner-general of immigration to the supervision of immigrants to their destination and to establish immigrant stations; passed by house Dec. 16, 1912; by senate Jan. 18, 1913; approved Feb. 25, 1913.

Act to amend an act to parole United States prisoners; passed by house March 21, 1912; by senate Jan. 18, 1913; approved Jan. 23, 1913.

MEASURES THAT FAILED.

Bill making appropriations for the sundry civil expenses of the government; passed by house Feb. 21, 1912; by the senate Feb. 28; vetoed by president March 4, 1913.

Bill to regulate the immigration of aliens to and residence of aliens in the United States; passed by senate April 20, 1912; by house Dec. 18, 1912; vetoed by president Feb. 14, 1913; passed over veto by senate Feb. 18; house refused to pass bill over veto Feb. 19.

Joint resolution proposing an amendment to the constitution of the United States making the presidential term six years without re-election; passed senate Feb. 1, 1913; no action taken in house.

DEPARTMENT OF LABOR.

There is hereby created an executive department of the government to be called the department of labor, with a secretary of labor, who shall be the head thereof, to be appointed by the president with the consent of the senate, and who shall receive a salary of $12,000 per annum, and whose tenure of office shall be like that of the heads of the other executive departments. The department of commerce and labor shall hereafter be called the department of commerce, and the secretary thereof shall be called the secretary of commerce. The purpose of the department of labor shall be to foster, promote and develop the welfare of the wage earners of the United States, to improve their working conditions and to advance their opportunities for profitable employment.

There shall be in the department an assistant secretary of labor, to be appointed by the president, who shall receive a salary of $5,000 a year. He shall perform such duties as shall be prescribed by the secretary or required by law. There shall also be one chief clerk and a disbursing clerk and such other assistants, inspectors and special agents as may from time to time be provided for by congress.

The following named offices, bureaus, divisions and branches of the public service now and heretofore under the jurisdiction of the department of commerce and labor, known as the commissioner-general of immigration, the commissioners of immigration, the bureau of immigration and naturalization, the division of information, the division of naturalization, the immigration service at large, the bureau of labor, the children's bureau and the commissioner of labor, are hereby transferred from the department of commerce and labor to the department of labor, and the same shall hereafter remain under the jurisdiction and supervision of the last-named department. The bureau of immigration and naturalization is hereby divided into two bureaus, to be known hereafter as the bureau of immigration and the bureau of naturalization, and the titles chief division of naturalization and assistant chief shall be commissioner of naturalization and deputy commissioner of naturalization. The commissioner of naturalization, or, in his absence, the deputy commissioner of naturalization, shall be the administrative officer in charge of the bureau of naturalization and of the administration of the naturalization laws under the immediate direction of the secretary of labor, to whom he shall report directly upon all naturalization matters annually and as otherwise required, and the appointments of these two officers shall be made in the same manner as appointments to competitive classified civil service positions. The bureau of labor shall hereafter be known as the bureau of labor statistics, and the commissioner of the bureau of labor shall hereafter be known as the commissioner of labor statistics, and all the powers and duties heretofore possessed by the commissioner of labor shall be retained and exercised by the commissioner of labor statistics, and the administration of the act of May 30, 1908, granting to certain employes of the United States the right to receive from it compensation for injuries sustained in the course of their employment.

The bureau of labor statistics, under the direction of the secretary of labor, shall collect, collate and report at least once each year, or oftener if necessary, full and complete statistics of the conditions of labor and the products and distribution of the products of the same, and to this end the secretary shall have power to employ any or either of the bureaus provided for his department and to rearrange such statistical work and to distribute or consolidate the same as may be deemed desirable in the public interests, and the secretary shall also have authority to call upon other departments of the government for statistical data and results obtained by them, and the secretary of labor may collate, arrange and publish such statistical information so obtained in such manner as to him may seem wise.

The secretary of labor shall have charge, in the buildings or premises occupied by or appropriated to the department of labor, of the library, furniture, fixtures, records and other property pertaining to it or hereafter acquired for use in its business; he shall be allowed to expend for periodicals and the purposes of the library and for rental of appropriate quarters for the accommodation of the

department of labor within the District of Columbia, and for all other incidental expenses, such sums as congress may provide from time to time. All officers, clerks and employes now employed in any of the bureaus, offices, departments or branches of the public service in this act transferred to the department of labor are each and all transferred to said department at their present grades and salaries, except where otherwise provided in this act. All laws prescribing the work and defining the duties of the several bureaus, offices, departments or branches of the public service by this act transferred to and made a part of the department of labor shall, so far as the same are not in conflict with the provisions of this act, remain in full force and effect, to be executed under the direction of the secretary of labor.

There shall be a solicitor of the department of justice for the department of labor, whose salary shall be $5,000 per annum.

The secretary of labor shall have power to act as mediator and to appoint commissioners of conciliation in labor disputes whenever in his judgment the interests of industrial peace may require it to be done; and all duties performed and all power and authority now possessed or exercised by the head of any executive department in and over any bureau, office, officer, board, branch or division of the public service by this act transferred to the department of labor, or any business arising therefrom or pertaining thereto, or in relation to the duties performed by and authority conferred by law upon such bureau, officer, office, board, branch or division of the public service, whether of an appellate or revisory character or otherwise, shall hereafter be vested in and exercised by the head of the department of labor.

The secretary of labor shall annually, at the close of each fiscal year, make a report in writing to congress, giving an account of all moneys received and disbursed by him and his department and describing the work done by the department. He shall also, from time to time, make such special investigations and reports as he may be required to do by the president or by congress, or which he himself may deem necessary.

The secretary of labor shall investigate and report to congress a plan of co-ordination of the activities, duties and powers of the office of the secretary of labor with the activities, duties and powers of the present bureaus, commissions and departments, so far as they relate to labor and its conditions, in order to harmonize and unify such activities, duties and powers, with a view to further legislation to further define the duties and powers of such department of labor.

This act shall take effect March 4, 1913, and all acts or parts of acts inconsistent with this act are hereby repealed. (Approved March 4, 1913.)

PHYSICAL VALUATION OF RAILROADS.

Following is the full text of the act amending the interstate commerce law by providing for the physical valuation of railroads:

Be it enacted, etc., That the act entitled "An act to regulate commerce," approved Feb. 4, 1887, as amended, be further amended by adding thereto a new section to be known as section 19a, and to read as follows:

"Sec. 19a. That the commission shall, as hereinafter provided, investigate, ascertain and report the value of all the property owned or used by every common carrier subject to the provisions of this act. To enable the commission to make such investigation and report, it is authorized to employ such experts and other assistants as may be necessary. The commission may appoint examiners who shall have power to administer oaths, examine witnesses and take testimony. The commission shall make an inventory which shall list the property of every common carrier subject to the provisions of this act in detail and show the value thereof as hereinafter provided, and shall classify the physical property, as nearly as practicable, in conformity with the classification of expenditures for road and equipment, as prescribed by the interstate commerce commission.

"1. In such investigation said commission shall ascertain and report in detail as to each piece of property owned or used by said common carrier for its purposes as a common carrier, the original cost to date, the cost or reproduction new, the cost of reproduction less depreciation and an analysis of the methods by which these several costs are obtained and the reason for their differences, if any. The commission shall in like manner ascertain and report separately other values and elements of value, if any, of the property of such common carrier, and an analysis of the methods of valuation employed, and of the reasons for any differences between any such value and each of the foregoing cost values.

"2. Such investigation and report shall state in detail and separately from improvements the original cost of all lands, rights of way and terminals owned or used for the purposes of a common carrier and ascertained as of the time of dedication to public use and the present value of the same, and separately the original and present cost of condemnation and damages or of purchases in excess of such original cost or present value.

"3. Such investigation and report shall show separately the property held for other purposes than those of a common carrier and the original and present value of the same, together with an analysis of the methods of valuation employed.

"4. In ascertaining the original cost to date of the property of such common carrier the commission, in addition to such other elements as it may deem necessary, shall investigate and report upon the history and organization of the present and of any previous corporation operating such property; upon any increases or decreases of stocks, bonds or other securities, in any reorganization; upon moneys received by any such corporation by reason of any issues of stocks, bonds or other securities; upon the syndicating, banking and other financial arrangements under which such issues were made and the expense thereof, and upon the net and gross earnings of such corporations; and shall also ascertain and report in such detail as may be determined by the commission upon the expenditure of all moneys and the purposes for which the same were expended.

"5. The commission shall ascertain and report the amount and value of any aid, gift, grant of right of way or donation made to any such common carrier, or to any previous corporation operating such property, by the government of the United States or by any state, county or municipal government, or by individuals, associations or corporations; and it shall also ascertain and report the grants of land to any such common carrier, or any previous corporation operating such property, by the government of the United States, or by any state, county or municipal government, and the amount of money derived from the sale of any portion of such grants and the value of the unsold portion thereof at the time acquired and at the present time, also the amount and value of any concession and allowance made by such common carrier to the government of the United States or to any state, county or municipal government in consideration of such aid, gift, grant or donation.

"Except as herein otherwise provided, the commission shall have power to prescribe the method of procedure to be followed in the conduct of the investigation, the form in which the results of the valuation shall be submitted and the classification of the elements that constitute the ascertained value, and such investigation shall show the value of the property of every common carrier as a whole and separately the value of its property in each of the several states and territories and the District of Columbia, classified and in detail as herein required.

"Such investigation shall be commenced within sixty days after the approval of this act and shall be prosecuted with diligence and thoroughness, and the result thereof reported to congress at the beginning of each regular session thereafter until completed.

"Every common carrier subject to the provisions of this act shall furnish to the commission or its

agents from time to time and as the commission may require maps, profiles, contracts, reports of engineers and any other documents, records and papers or copies of any or all of the same, in aid of such investigation and determination of the value of the property of said common carrier, and shall grant to all agents of the commission free access to its right of way, its property and its accounts, records and memoranda whenever and wherever requested by any such duly authorized agent, and every common carrier is hereby directed and required to co-operate with and aid the commission in the work of the valuation of its property in such further particulars and to such extent as the commission may require and direct, and all rules and regulations made by the commission for the purpose of administering the provisions of this section and section 20 of this act shall have the full force and effect of law. Unless otherwise ordered by the commission, with the reasons therefor, the records and data of the commission shall be open to the inspection and examination of the public.

"Upon the completion of the valuation herein provided for, the commission shall thereafter in like manner keep itself informed of all extensions and improvements or other changes in the condition and value of the property of all common carriers, and shall ascertain the value thereof, and shall from time to time revise and correct its valuations, showing such revision and correction classified and as a whole and separately in each of the several states and territories and the District of Columbia, which valuations, both original and corrected, shall be tentative valuations and shall be reported to congress at the beginning of each regular session.

"To enable the commission to make such changes and corrections in its valuations of each class of property, every common carrier subject to the provisions of this act shall make such reports and furnish such information as the commission may require.

"Whenever the commission shall have completed the tentative valuation of the property of any common carrier, as herein directed, and before such valuation shall become final, the commission shall give notice by registered letter to the said carrier, the attorney-general of the United States, the governor of any state in which the property so valued is located, and to such additional parties as the commission may prescribe, stating the valuation placed upon the several classes of property of said carrier, and shall allow thirty days in which to file a protest of the same with the commission. If no protest is filed within thirty days, said valuation shall become final as of the date thereof.

"If notice of protest is filed the commission shall fix a time for hearing the same and shall proceed as promptly as may be to hear and consider any matter relative and material thereto which may be presented in support of any such protest so filed as aforesaid. If after hearing any protest of such tentative valuation under the provisions of this act the commission shall be of the opinion that its valuation should not become final, it shall make such changes as may be necessary, and shall issue an order making such corrected tentative valuation final as of the date thereof. All final valuations by the commission and the classification thereof shall be published and shall be prima facie evidence of the value of the property in all proceedings under the act to regulate commerce as of the date of the fixing thereof, and in all judicial proceedings for enforcement of the act approved Feb. 4, 1887, commonly known as 'The act to regulate commerce,' and the various acts amendatory thereof, and in all judicial proceedings brought to enjoin, set aside, annul or suspend, in whole or in part, any order of the interstate commerce commission.

"If, upon the trial of any action involving a final value fixed by the commission, evidence shall be introduced regarding such value which is found by the court to be different from that offered upon the hearing before the commission, or additional thereto and substantially affecting said value, the court, before proceeding to render judgment, shall transmit a copy of such evidence to the commission and shall stay further proceedings in said action for

such time as the court shall determine from the date of such transmission. Upon the receipt of such evidence the commission shall consider the same and may fix a final value different from the one fixed in the first instance, and may alter, modify, amend or rescind any order which it has made involving said final value, and shall report its final action thereon to said court within the time fixed by the court. If the commission shall alter, modify or amend its order, such altered, modified or amended order shall take the place of the original order complained of and judgment shall be rendered thereon as though made by the commission in the first instance. If the original order shall not be rescinded or changed by the commission, judgment shall be rendered upon such original order.

"The provisions of this act shall apply to receivers of carriers and operating trustees. In case of failure or refusal on the part of any carrier, receiver or trustee to comply with all the requirements of the section and in the manner prescribed by the commission such carrier, receiver or trustee shall forfeit to the United States the sum of $500 for each such offense and for each and every day of the continuance of such offense, such forfeitures to be recoverable in the same manner as other forfeitures provided for in section 16 of the act to regulate commerce.

"That the District courts of the United States shall have jurisdiction, upon the application of the attorney-general of the United States at the request of the commission, alleging a failure to comply with or a violation of any of the provisions of this section by any common carrier, to issue a writ or writs of mandamus commanding such common carrier to comply with the provisions of this section." (Approved March 1, 1913.)

INTERSTATE SHIPMENT OF LIQUORS.

Be it enacted, etc., that the shipment or transportation, in any manner or by any means whatsoever, of any spirituous, vinous, malted, fermented or other intoxicating liquor of any kind from one state, territory or district of the United States or place noncontiguous to but subject to the jurisdiction thereof into any other state, territory or district of the United States or place noncontiguous to but subject to the jurisdiction thereof, or from any foreign country into any state, territory or district of the United States, or place noncontiguous to but subject to the jurisdiction thereof, which said spirituous, vinous, malted, fermented or other intoxicating liquor is intended, by any person interested therein, to be received, possessed, sold or in any manner used, either in the original package or otherwise, in violation of any law of such state, territory or district of the United States, or place noncontiguous to but subject to the jurisdiction thereof, is hereby prohibited.

PASSED OVER VETO.

The foregoing act was vetoed by President Taft, but was passed over his veto by a two-thirds vote of both houses of congress and thus became law. In his veto message the president said in part:

"After giving this proposed enactment full consideration I believe it to be a violation of the interstate commerce clause of the constitution, in that it is in substance and effect a delegation by congress to the states of the power of regulating interstate commerce in liquors, which is vested exclusively in congress.

"One of the main purposes of the union of the states under the constitution was to relieve the commerce between the states of the burdens which local state jealousies and purposes had in the past imposed upon it; and the interstate commerce clause in the constitution was one of the chief reasons for its adoption. The power was there conferred upon congress. Now, if to the discretion of congress is committed the question whether in interstate commerce we shall return to the old methods prevailing before the constitution or not, it would seem to be conferring upon congress the power to amend the constitution by ignoring or striking out one of its most important provisions. It was certainly intended by that clause to secure uniformity in the

regulation of commerce between the states. To suspend that purpose and to permit the states to exercise their old authority before they became states, to interfere with commerce between them and their neighbors, is to defeat the constitutional purpose. * * * I cannot think that the framers of the constitution, or that the people who adopted it, had in mind for a moment that congress could thus nullify the operation of a clause whose useful effect was deemed so important and which in fact has contributed so much to the solidarity of the nation and the prosperity that has followed unhampered, nationwide trade.

"But it is said that this is a question with which the executive or members of congress should not burden themselves to consider or decide. It is said that it should be left to the Supreme court to say whether this proposed act violates the constitution. I dissent utterly from this proposition. The oath which the chief executive takes, and which each member of congress takes, does not bind him any less sacredly to observe the constitution than the oaths which the justices of the Supreme court take. It is questionable whether the doubtful constitutionality of a bill ought not to furnish a greater reason for voting against the bill or vetoing it than for the court to hold it to be invalid. The court will only declare a law invalid where its unconstitutionality is clear, while the lawmaker may very well hesitate to vote for a bill if of doubtful constitutionality because of the wisdom of keeping clearly within the fundamental law. The custom of legislators and executives having any legislative function to remit to the courts entire and ultimate responsibility as to the constitutionality of the measures which they take part in passing is an abuse which tends to put the court constantly in opposition to the legislature and executive, and, indeed, to the popular supporters of unconstitutional laws. If, however, the legislators and the executives had attempted to do their duty this burden of popular disapproval would have been lifted from the courts, or at least considerably lessened.

"For these reasons, and in spite of the popular approval of this bill, I have not felt justified in signing it, because I feel that under principles of proper constitutional construction it violates the interstate commerce clause of our fundamental law."

EIGHT HOUR LABOR LAW.

Sections 1, 2 and 3 of the act relating to the limitation of the hours of daily service of laborers and mechanics employed upon the public works of the United States are amended so as to read:

"Section 1. That the service and employment of all laborers and mechanics who are now, or may hereafter be, employed by the government of the United States or of the District of Columbia, or by any contractor or subcontractor, upon a public work of the United States or of the District of Columbia, and of all persons who are now, or may hereafter be, employed by the government of the United States or the District of Columbia, or any contractor or subcontractor, to perform services similar to those of laborers and mechanics in connection with the dredging or rock excavation in any river or harbor of the United States or of the District of Columbia, is hereby limited and restricted to eight hours in one calendar day; and it shall be unlawful for any officer of the United States government or of the District of Columbia, or any such contractor or subcontractor whose duty it shall be to employ, direct or control the services of such laborers or mechanics or of such persons employed to perform services similar to those of laborers and mechanics in connection with dredging or rock excavation in any river or harbor of the United States or of the District of Columbia, to require or permit any such laborer or mechanic or any such person employed to perform services similar to those of laborers and mechanics in connection with dredging or rock excavation in any river or harbor of the United States or of the District of Columbia, to work more than eight hours in any calendar day, except in case of extraordinary emergency: Provided, That nothing in this act shall apply or be construed to apply to persons employed

in connection with dredging or rock excavation in any river or harbor of the United States or of the District of Columbia while not directly operating dredging or rock excavating machinery or tools, nor to persons engaged in construction or repair of levees or revetments necessary for protection against floods or overflows on the navigable rivers of the United States.

"Sec. 2. That any officer or agent of the government of the United States or of the District of Columbia, or any contractor or subcontractor whose duty it shall be to employ, direct or control any laborer or mechanic employed upon a public work of the United States or of the District of Columbia, or any person employed to perform services similar to those of laborers and mechanics in connection with dredging or rock excavation in any river or harbor of the United States or of the District of Columbia, who shall intentionally violate any provision of this act, shall be deemed guilty of a misdemeanor, and for each and every such offense shall, upon conviction, be punished by a fine not to exceed $1,000, or by imprisonment for not more than six months, or by both such fine and imprisonment, in the discretion of the court having jurisdiction thereof.

"Sec. 3. That the provisions of this act shall not be so construed as to in any manner apply to or affect contractors or subcontractors, or to limit the hours of daily service of laborers or mechanics engaged upon a public work of the United States or of the District of Columbia, or persons employed to perform services similar to those of laborers and mechanics in connection with dredging or rock excavation in any river or harbor of the United States or of the District of Columbia, for which contracts have been entered into prior to the passing of this act or may be entered into under the provisions of appropriation acts approved prior to the passage of this act.

"Sec. 4. That this act shall become effective and be in force on and after March 1, 1913." (Approved March 3, 1913.)

REGISTRATION OF TRADE MARKS.

The act of Feb. 20, 1905, as amended, is further amended so that section 5 reads as follows:

"Sec. 5. That no mark by which the goods of the owner of the mark may be distinguished from other goods of the same class shall be refused registration as a trade mark on account of the nature of such mark unless such mark—

"(a) Consists of or comprises immoral or scandalous matter.

"(b) Consists of or comprises the flag or coat of arms or other insignia of the United States or any simulation thereof, or of any state or municipality or of any foreign nation, or of any design or picture that has been or may hereafter be adopted by any fraternal society as its emblem, or of any name, distinguishing mark, character, emblem, colors, flag or banner adopted by any institution, organization, club or society which was incorporated in any state in the United States prior to the date of the adoption and use by the applicant: Provided, That said name, distinguishing mark, character, emblem, colors, flag or banner was adopted and publicly used by said institution, organization, club or society prior to the date of adoption and use by the applicant: Provided, That trade marks which are identical with a registered or known trade mark owned and in use by another and appropriated to merchandise of the same descriptive properties, or which so nearly resemble a registered or known trade mark owned and in use by another and appropriated to merchandise of the same descriptive properties as to be likely to cause confusion or mistake in the mind of the public or to deceive purchasers shall not be registered: Provided, That no mark which consists merely in the name of an individual, firm, corporation or association not written, printed, impressed or woven in some particular or distinctive manner, or in association with a portrait of the individual, or merely in words or devices which are descriptive of the goods with which they are used, or of the character or quality of such goods, or merely a geographical name or term, shall be registered under the terms of this

act: Provided further, That no portrait of a living individual may be registered as a trade mark except by the consent of such individual, evidenced by an instrument in writing: And provided further, That nothing herein shall prevent the registration of any mark used by the applicant or his predecessors, or by those from whom title to the mark is derived, in commerce with foreign nations or among the several states or with Indian tribes which was in actual and exclusive use as a trade mark of the applicant, or his predecessors from whom he derived title, for ten years next preceding Feb. 20, 1905: Provided further, That nothing herein shall prevent the registration of a trade mark otherwise registrable because of its being the name of the applicant or a portion thereof." (Approved Jan. 8, 1913.)

INTERLOCUTORY INJUNCTIONS.

Section 266 of the act to codify, revise and amend the laws relating to the judiciary, approved March 3, 1911, is amended so as to read as follows:

"Sec. 266. No interlocutory injunctions suspending or restraining the enforcement, operation or execution of any statute of a state by restraining the action of any officer of such state in the enforcement or execution of such statute, or in the enforcement or execution of an order made by an administrative board or commission acting under and pursuant to the statutes of such state, shall be issued or granted by any justice of the Supreme court, or by any District court of the United States, or by any judge thereof, or by any circuit judge acting as district judge, upon the ground of the unconstitutionality of such statute, unless the application for the same shall be presented to a justice of the Supreme court of the United States, or to a circuit or district judge, and shall be heard and determined by three judges, of whom at least one shall be a justice of the Supreme court or a circuit judge, and the other two may be either circuit or district judges, and unless a majority of said three judges shall concur in granting such application. Whenever such application as aforesaid is presented to a justice of the Supreme court, or to a judge, he shall immediately call to his assistance to hear and determine the application two other judges: Provided, however, That one of such three judges shall be a justice of the Supreme court or a circuit judge. Said application shall not be heard or determined before at least five days' notice of the hearing has been given to the governor and to the attorney-general of the state and to such other persons as may be defendants to the suit: Provided, That if of opinion that irreparable loss or damage would result to the complainant unless a temporary restraining order is granted, any justice of the Supreme court, or any circuit or district judge, may grant such temporary restraining order at any time before such hearing and determination of the application for an interlocutory injunction, but such temporary restraining order shall remain in force only until the hearing and determination of the application for an interlocutory injunction upon notice as aforesaid. The hearing upon such application for an interlocutory injunction shall be given precedence and shall be in every way expedited and be assigned for a hearing at the earliest practicable day after the expiration of the notice hereinbefore provided for. An appeal may be taken direct to the Supreme court of the United States from the order granting or denying, after notice and hearing, an interlocutory injunction in such case. It is further provided that if before the final hearing of such application a suit shall have been brought in a court of the state having jurisdiction thereof under the laws of such state, to enforce such statute or order, accompanied by a stay in such state court of proceedings under such statute or order pending the determination of such suit by such state court, all proceedings in any court of the United States to restrain the execution of such statute or order shall be stayed pending the final determination of such suit in the courts of the state. Such stay may be vacated upon proof made after hearing and notice of ten days served upon the attorney-general of the state that the suit in the state courts is not being prosecuted with diligence and good faith." (Approved March 4, 1913.)

REVOLUTIONARY WAR RECORDS.

Within the limits of the appropriation herein made, the secretary of war is hereby authorized and directed to collect or copy and classify, with a view to publication, the scattered military records of the revolutionary war, including all troops acting under state authority, and the secretary of the navy is hereby authorized and directed to collect or copy and classify, with a view to publication, the scattered naval records of the revolutionary war. All such records in the possession or custody of any official of the United States shall be transferred, the military records to the war department and the naval records to the navy department. There is hereby appropriated for the purposes of this act, out of any money in the treasury not otherwise appropriated, $25,000 for the war department and $7,000 for the navy department: Provided, That the aforesaid sums of money shall be expended, respectively, under the direction of the secretary of war and the secretary of the navy, and that they shall make to congress each year detailed statements showing how the money herein appropriated has been expended and to whom: Provided further, That no part of the sum hereby appropriated shall be used in the purchase of any such records that may be discovered either in the hands of private owners or in public depositories. (Approved March 2, 1913.)

IMMIGRANT STATIONS.

For the purpose of making effective the power of establishing rules and regulations for protecting the United States and aliens migrating thereto from fraud and loss, conferred upon the commissioner-general of immigration, subject to the direction and with the approval of the secretary of commerce and labor, by section 22 of an act entitled "An act to regulate the immigration of aliens into the United States," approved Feb. 20, 1907, the secretary of commerce and labor shall establish and maintain immigrant stations at such interior places as may be necessary, and, in the discretion of the said secretary, aliens in transit from ports of landing to such interior stations shall be accompanied by immigrant inspectors: Provided, That nothing in this act shall be construed as authorizing the commissioner-general of immigration to pay the cost of transportation of any arriving alien.

Sec. 2. That for the establishment and maintenance of such a station in the city of Chicago for the fiscal year ending June 30, 1914, there is hereby authorized, from moneys in the treasury not otherwise appropriated, the sum of $75,000, which shall be expended in such manner consistent with the purpose hereof as the secretary of commerce and labor may direct. (Approved Feb. 25, 1913.)

PAROLE OF UNITED STATES PRISONERS.

Section 1 of the "act to parole United States prisoners and for other purposes," approved June 25, 1910, is amended so as to read as follows, to wit:

"That every prisoner who has been or may hereafter be convicted of any offense against the United States and is confined in execution of the judgment of such conviction in any United States penitentiary or prison, for a definite term or terms of over one year, or for the term of his natural life, whose record of conduct shows that he has observed the rules of such institution, and who, if sentenced for a definite term, has served one-third of the total of such term or terms for which he was sentenced, or, if sentenced for the term of his natural life, has served not less than fifteen years, may be released on parole as hereinafter provided."

INCREASE OF THE NAVY.

Part of naval appropriation bill:

For the purpose of further increasing the naval establishment of the United States the president is hereby authorized to have constructed one first class battle ship, carrying as heavy armor and as powerful armament as any vessel of its class, to have the highest practical speed and greatest desirable radius of action, and to cost, exclusive of armor and armament, not to exceed $7,425,000: Provided, That the battle ship herein authorized shall be built in a government navy yard.

Six torpedo boat destroyers, to have the highest practical speed, to cost, exclusive of armor and armament, not to exceed $950,000 each.

Four submarine torpedo boats in an amount not exceeding in the aggregate $2,478,936; and the sum of $1,294,912 is hereby appropriated for said purpose.

One transport, to cost, exclusive of armor and armament, not to exceed $1,850,000.

One supply ship, to cost, exclusive of armor and armament, not to exceed $1,425,000. (Approved March 4, 1913.)

MEMORIAL BRIDGE.

Section 23 of the bill making appropriations for public buildings reads as follows: "That a commission is hereby created, to consist of the president of the United States, the president of the senate, the speaker of the house of representatives and the chairman of the committees on public buildings and grounds of the senate and house of representatives, for the purpose of investigating and reporting to congress a suitable design for a memorial bridge across the Potomac river, from the city of Washington to a point at or near the Arlington estate in the state of Virginia; and the said commission is hereby authorized to expend the sum of $25,000 in procuring such designs and for making such surveys and estimates of cost as they may deem advisable and report as early as may be to congress." (Approved March 4, 1913.)

PUBLICITY IN TAKING TESTIMONY.

In the taking of depositions of witnesses for use in any suit in equity brought by the United States under the act entitled "An act to protect trade and commerce against unlawful restraints and monopolies," approved July 2, 1890, and in the hearings before any examiner or special master appointed to take testimony therein, the proceedings shall be open to the public as freely as are trials in open court, and no order excluding the public from attendance on any such proceedings shall be valid or enforceable. (Approved March 3, 1913.)

VETOED BY PRESIDENT.

SUNDRY CIVIL BILL.

The regular sundry civil service appropriation was passed by the house Feb. 21 and by the senate Feb. 28, 1913, but was vetoed by President Taft March 4 because the clause appropriating $300,000 for the enforcement of the antitrust laws contained the following provisions:

"Provided, however, That no part of this money shall be spent in the prosecution of any organization or individual for entering into any combination or agreement having in view the increasing of wages, shortening of hours or bettering the condition of labor, or for any act done in furtherance thereof not in itself unlawful: Provided, further, That no part of this appropriation shall be expended for the prosecution of producers of farm products and associations of farmers who co-operate and organize in an effort to and for the purpose to obtain and maintain a fair and reasonable price for their products."

In his veto message the president said:

"This provision is class legislation of the most vicious sort. If it were enacted as substantive law and not merely as a qualification upon the use of moneys appropriated for the enforcement of the law, no one, I take it, would doubt its unconstitutionality. A similar provision in the laws of the state of Illinois was declared by the Supreme court to be an invasion of the guaranty of the equal protection of the laws contained in the fourteenth amendment of the constitution of the United States in the case of Connelly vs. Union Sewer Pipe company (184 U. S., 540), although the only exception in that instance from the illegality of organizations and combinations, etc., declared by that statute, was one which exempted agriculturists and live stock raisers in respect of their products or live stock in hand from the operation of the law, leaving them free to combine to do that which, if done by others, would be a crime against the state.

"The proviso is subtly worded, so as, in a measure, to conceal its full effect, by providing that no part of the money appropriated shall be spent in the prosecution of any organization or individual 'for entering into any combination or agreement having in view the increasing of wages, shortening of hours or bettering the condition of labor,' and so forth. So that any organization formed with the beneficent purpose described in the proviso might later engage in a conspiracy to destroy by force, violence or unfair means any employer or employe who failed to conform to its requirements; and yet, because of its originally avowed lawful purpose, it would be exempt from prosecution, so far as prosecution depended upon the moneys appropriated by this act, no matter how wicked, how cruel, how deliberate the acts of which it was guilty. So, too, by the following sentence in the act such an organization would be protected from prosecution 'for any act done in furtherance of 'the increasing of wages, shortening of hours or bettering the condition of labor' not in itself unlawful. But under the law of criminal conspiracy acts lawful in themselves may become the weapons whereby an unlawful purpose is carried out and accomplished. (Shawnee Compressed Coal company vs. Anderson, 209 U. S., '423-434; Aikens vs. Wisconsin, 195 U. S., 194-206; Swift vs. United States, 196 U. S., 375-396; United States vs. Reading company, Dec. 16, 1912.)

"The fourth proviso, that the appropriation shall not be used in the prosecution of producers of farm products and associations of farmers who co-operate and organize in an effort to obtain and maintain a fair and reasonable price for their products, is apparently designed to encourage, or at least to discourage the prosecution of, organizations having for their purpose the artificial enhancement of the prices of food products, and thus to avoid the effect of the construction given to the antitrust law in the case of United States against Patten, decided Jan. 6, 1913.

"At a time when there is widespread complaint of the high cost of living it certainly would be anomalous to put on the statute books of the United States an act, in effect, preventing the prosecution of combinations of producers of farm products for the purpose of artificially controlling prices; and the evil is not removed, although it may be masked, by referring to the purpose of the organization as 'to obtain and maintain a fair and reasonable price for their products.'

"An amendment almost in the language of this proviso, so far as it refers to organizations for the increasing of wages, etc., was introduced in the 61st congress, passed the house, was rejected in the senate and, after a very full discussion in the house, failed of enactment. Representative Madison, speaking in favor of the amendment which struck out the proviso, characterized it as an attempt to 'write into the law,' so far as this particular measure is concerned, a legalization of the secondary boycott. * * * The laws of this country,' he pointed out, 'are liberal to the·working-man. He can strike, he can agree to strike, he can act under a leader in a strike and he can apply the direct boycott, but when it comes to going further and so acting as to impede and obstruct the natural and lawful course of trade in this country then the law says he shall stop. And all in the world that this antitrust act does is to apply to him that simple and proper rule, that he, too, as well as the creators of trusts and monopolies, shall not obstruct the natural and ordinary course of trade in the United States of America. I believe,' he added, 'in the high aims, motives and patriotism of the American workingmen and do not believe that, rightly understanding this amendment, they would ask us to write it into the law of this republic.' (Congressional Record, p. 8850, 61st congress, second session.)

"It is because I am unwilling to be a party to writing such a provision into the laws of this republic that I am unable to give my assent to a bill which contains this provision."

The bill having been vetoed in the closing hours of the 62d congress, no attempt was made to pass it over the veto.

IMMIGRATION BILL.

The senate April 20, 1912, passed a bill to regulate the immigration of aliens to and residence of

aliens in the United States. The measure passed the house Dec. 18, the same year, but was vetoed by President Taft Feb. 14, 1913, because of the following provision:

"That after four months from the approval of this act, in addition to the aliens who are by law now excluded from admission into the United States, the following persons shall also be excluded from admission thereto, to-wit: All aliens over 16 years of age, physically capable of reading, who cannot read the English language, or some other language or dialect, including Hebrew or Yiddish: Provided, That any admissible alien or any alien heretofore or hereafter legally admitted, or any citizen of the United States, may bring in or send for his father or grandfather over 55 years of age, his wife, his mother, his grandmother or his unmarried or widowed daughter, if otherwise admissible, whether such relative can read or not; and such relatives shall be permitted to enter. That for the purpose of ascertaining whether aliens can read the immigrant inspectors shall be furnished with slips, of uniform size, prepared under the direction of the secretary of commerce and labor, each containing not less than thirty nor more than forty words in ordinary use, printed in plainly legible type in the various languages and dialects of immigrants. Each alien may designate the particular language or dialect in which he desires the examination to be made, and shall be required to read the words printed on the slip in such language or dialect. No two aliens coming in the same vessel or other vehicle of carriage or transportation shall be tested with the same slip. That the following classes of persons shall be exempt from the operation of the illiteracy test, to-wit: All aliens who shall prove to the satisfaction of the proper immigration officer or to the secretary of commerce and labor that they are seeking admission to the United States solely for the purpose of escaping religious persecution; all aliens in transit through the United States; all aliens who have been lawfully admitted to the United States and who later shall go in transit from one part of the United States to another through foreign contiguous territory."

The president in returning the bill without his approval said:

"I do, this with great reluctance. The bill contains many valuable amendments to the present immigration law which will insure greater certainty in excluding undesirable immigrants. The bill received strong support in both houses and was recommended by an able commission after an extended investigation and carefully drawn conclusions. But I cannot make up my mind to sign a bill which in its chief provision violates a principle that ought, in my opinion, to be upheld in dealing with our immigration. I refer to the literacy test. For the reasons stated in Secretary Nagel's letter to me, I cannot approve that test. The secretary's letter accompanies this."

Secretary Nagel in his letter to the president advised against approval of the bill not only because it would lead to delay and increased expense in the immigration service, but that it would shut out many desirable immigrants. "The measure is defended," wrote the secretary, "purely upon the ground of practical policy, the final purpose being to reduce the quantity of cheap labor in this country. I cannot accept this argument. No doubt the law would exclude a considerable percentage of immigration from southern Italy, among the Poles, the Mexicans and the Greeks. This exclusion would embrace probably in large part undesirable but also a great many desirable people, and the embarrassment, expense and distress to those who seek to enter would be out of all proportion to any good that can possibly be promised for this measure.

"My observation leads me to the conclusion that, so far as the merits of the individual immigrant are concerned, the test is altogether overestimated. The people who come from the countries named are frequently illiterate because opportunities have been denied them. The oppression with which these people have to contend in modern times is not religious, but it consists of a denial of the opportunity to acquire reading and writing. Frequently the attempt to learn to read and write the language of the particular people is discouraged by the government, and these immigrants in coming to our shores are really striving to free themselves from the conditions under which they have been compelled to live.

"So far as the industrial conditions are concerned, I think the question has been superficially considered. We need labor in this country, and the natives are unwilling to do the work which the aliens come over to do. It is perfectly true that in a few cities and localities there are congested conditions. It is equally true that in very much larger areas we are practically without help. In my judgment, no sufficiently earnest and intelligent effort has been made to bring our wants and our supply together, and so far the same forces that give the chief support to this provision of the new bill have stubbornly resisted any effort looking to an intelligent distribution of new immigration to meet the needs of our vast country. * * *

"Furthermore, there is a misapprehension as to the character of the people who come over here to remain. * * * The census will disclose that with rapid strides the foreign born citizen is acquiring the farm lands of this country. Even if the foreign born alone is considered, the percentage of his ownership is assuming a proportion that ought to attract the attention of the native citizens. If the second generation is included, it is safe to say that in the middle west and west a majority of the farms are to-day owned by foreign born people or they are descendants of the first generation. This does not embrace only the Germans and the Scandinavians, but is true in large measure, for illustration, of the Bohemians and the Poles. It is true in surprising measure of the Italians; not only of the northern Italians, but of the southern.

"Again, an examination of the aliens who come to stay is of great significance. During the last fiscal year 838,172 aliens came to our shores, although the net immigration of the year was only a trifle above 400,000. But, while we received of skilled labor 127,016, and only 35,898 returned; we received servants, 116,529, and only 13,449 returned; we received farm laborers, 184,154, and only 3,978 returned; it appears that laborers came in the number of 135,726, while 209,279 returned. These figures ought to demonstrate that we get substantially what we most need, and what we cannot ourselves supply, and that we get rid of what we least need and what seems to furnish, in the minds of many, the chief justification for the bill now under discussion. The census returns show conclusively that the importance of illiteracy among aliens is overestimated, and that these people are prompt after their arrival to avail of the opportunities which this country affords."

The senate by a vote of 78 to 18 passed the immigration bill over the president's veto Feb. 18, but in the house the effort to make the measure law notwithstanding the veto failed. The vote, which was taken Feb. 19, stood 213 for the bill and 114 against it, or five less than the requisite two-thirds to override a veto.

THE PRESIDENTIAL TERM.

By a vote of 47 to 23 the senate Feb. 1, 1913, adopted the following joint resolution:

"The executive power shall be vested in a president of the United States of America. The term of office of president shall be six years, and no person who has held the office by election or discharged its powers or duties or acted as president under the constitution and laws made in pursuance thereof, shall be eligible to again hold the office by election."

In the house a similar resolution, introduced by Mr. Clayton of Alabama, was referred to the judiciary committee, where it was put over to the next congress. It provided for a single six year term, effective in 1921, to exempt Taft, Wilson and Roosevelt from its operation. No action was taken on the senate or Works resolution.

WORK OF 63D CONGRESS—FIRST (EXTRA) SESSION.

Act to reduce tariff duties and to provide revenue for the government, and for other purposes (includes income tax law); passed by house May 28; by senate Sept. 9; approved Oct. 3.

Act providing for mediation, conciliation and arbitration in controversies between certain employers and their employes; passed by senate June 26; by house July 15; approved July 15.

Act making appropriations for sundry civil expenses of the government (with "rider" exempting labor unions and farmers' organizations from prosecution under the Sherman antitrust law); passed by house April 22; by senate May 7; approved June 23.

Act making appropriations to supply urgent deficiencies in appropriations for the fiscal year 1913 (with amendment abolishing the Commerce court); passed by house Sept. 9; by senate Oct. 3; approved Oct. 22.

Act to provide for establishment of federal reserve banks, to furnish an elastic currency, to afford means of rediscounting commercial paper, to establish a more effective supervision of banking in the United States, and for other purposes; passed by house Sept. 17.

Act authorizing the appointment of an ambassador to Spain; passed by senate June 18; by house Sept. 2; approved Sept. 16.

Joint resolution to provide for the relief and transportation of destitute American citizens in Mexico; passed by house Sept. 12; by senate Sept. 15; approved Sept. 16.

TARIFF MESSAGE.

The 63d congress, called into extra session by President Woodrow Wilson, began work April 7, 1913, when a copy of the Underwood tariff bill was laid before the members. The proposed measure included a section providing for a tax on all incomes in excess of a certain sum. On the following day the two houses met in joint session in the hall of the house of representatives to receive a special message from the president. Heretofore such documents have been sent to congress by a special messenger and read in each house by a clerk. The president determined to disregard this custom, which had prevailed for a century, and, reverting to the example set by Washington and John Adams, appear before the national legislative body in person and read his message. He announced his purpose to the house and senate, which, on the first day of the extra session, passed a resolution providing for a joint meeting and for receiving the chief executive. The new departure attracted wide attention and drew to the hall of representatives a large and distinguished audience. Four members of the cabinet had seats in the gallery. President Wilson prefaced his message as follows:

"I am very glad, indeed, to have this opportunity to address the two houses directly, and to verify for myself the impression that the president of the United States is a person—not a mere department of the government, hailing congress from some isolated island of jealous power, sending messages, not speaking naturally and with his own voice—that he is a human being, trying to cooperate with other human beings in a common service. After this pleasant experience I shall feel quite normal in all our dealings with one another."

The president then read the following message:

"To the senate and house of representatives: I have called the congress together in extraordinary session because a duty was laid upon the party now in power at the recent elections which it ought to perform promptly in order that the burden carried by the people under existing law may be lightened as soon as possible and in order, also, that the business interests of the country may not be kept too long in suspense as to what the fiscal changes are to be to which they will be required to adjust themselves.

"It is clear that the whole country expects the tariff duties to be altered. They must be changed to meet the radical alteration in the conditions of our economic life which the country has witnessed within the last generation. While the whole face and method of our industrial and commercial life were being changed beyond recognition, the tariff schedules have remained what they were before the change began, or have moved in the direction they were given when no large circumstance of our industrial development was what it is to-day. Our task is to square them with the actual facts. The sooner that is done the sooner we shall escape from suffering from the facts and the sooner our men of business will be free to thrive by the law of nature (the nature of free business), instead of by the law of legislation and artificial arrangement.

"We have seen tariff legislation wander very far afield in our day—very far, indeed, from the field in which our prosperity might have had a normal growth and stimulation. No one who looks the facts squarely in the face or knows anything that lies beneath the surface of action can fail to perceive the principles upon which the recent tariff legislation has been based. We long ago passed beyond the modest notion of 'protecting' the industries of the country and moved boldly forward to the idea that they were entitled to the direct patronage of the government.

"For a long time—a time so long that the men now active in public policy hardly remember the conditions that preceded it—we have sought in our tariff schedules to give each group of manufacturers or producers what they themselves thought that they needed in order to maintain a practically exclusive market as against the rest of the world. Consciously or unconsciously, we have built up a set of privileges and exemptions from competition behind which it was easy by any, even the crudest, forms of combination to organize monopoly, until at last nothing is normal, nothing is obliged to stand the tests of efficiency and economy, in our world of big business, but everything thrives by concerted arrangement. Only new principles of action will save us from a final hard crystallization of monopoly and a complete loss of the influences that quicken enterprise and keep independent energy alive.

"It is plain what these principles must be. We must abolish everything that bears even the semblance of privilege or of any kind of artificial advantage, and put our business men and producers under the stimulation of a constant necessity to be efficient, economical and enterprising, masters of competitive supremacy, better workers and merchants than any in the world. Aside from the duties laid upon articles which we do not, and probably cannot, produce, therefore, and the duties laid upon luxuries and merely for the sake of the revenues they yield, the object of the tariff duties henceforth laid must be effective competition, the whetting of American wits by contest with the wits of the rest of the world.

"It would be unwise to move toward this end headlong, with reckless haste, or with strokes that cut at the very roots of what has grown up among us by long process and at our own invitation. It does not alter a thing to upset it and break it and deprive it of a chance to change. It destroys it. We must make changes in our fiscal laws, in our fiscal system, whose object is development, a more free and wholesome development, not revolution or upset or confusion. We must build up trade, especially foreign trade. We need the outlet and the enlarged field of energy more than we ever did before. We must build up industry as well and must adopt freedom in the place of artificial stimulation only so far as it will build, not pull down.

"In dealing with the tariff the method by which this may be done will be a matter of judgment, exercised item by item. To some not accustomed to the excitements and responsibilities of greater freedom our methods may in some respects and at some points seem heroic, but remedies may be heroic and yet be remedies. It is our business to make sure that they are genuine remedies. Our object is clear. If our motive is above just challenge and only an occasional error of judgment is chargeable against us, we shall be fortunate.

"We are called upon to render the country a great service in more matters than one. Our re-

sponsibility should be met and our methods should be thorough, as thorough as moderate and well considered, based upon the facts as they are, and not worked out as if we were beginners. We are to deal with the facts of our own day, with the facts of no other, and to make laws which square with those facts.

"It is best, indeed it is necessary, to begin with the tariff. I will urge nothing upon you now at the opening of your session which can obscure that first object or divert our energies from that clearly defined duty. At a later time I may take the liberty of calling your attention to reforms which should press close upon the heels of the tariff changes, if not accompany them, of which the chief is the reform of our banking and currency laws; but just now I refrain. For the present I put these matters on one side and think only of this one thing—of the changes in our fiscal system which may best serve to open once more the free channels of prosperity to a great people whom we would serve to the utmost and throughout both rank and file. WOODROW WILSON. "The White House, April 8, 1913."

TARIFF BILL PASSED.

Representative Oscar W. Underwood of Alabama, chairman of the house ways and means committee, introduced the tariff bill, as approved by the democratic caucus, April 21, and it was referred to the ways and means committee, which reported it back to the house without amendment April 22. The measure was debated until May 8, when it was passed by the house by a vote of 281 to 139. Five democrats voted against the bill and two republicans for it. Four progressives supported the measure and fourteen opposed it. The democrats who voted against the bill were Broussard, Dupre, Lazaro and Morgan of Louisiana and C. B. Smith of New York. The Louisiana members objected to the free sugar provision. In the senate the bill was referred to the committee on finance and was not reported back to the senate until July 11 and the debate in that body continued until Sept. 9, when the bill was passed by a vote of 44 to 37. Senators LaFollette of Wisconsin, republican, and Senator Poindexter of Washington, progressive, voted for it, and Senators Thornton and Ransdell, democrats, of Louisiana against it. The amendments made by the senate were chiefly in the nature of reductions. An important change was the reduction of the normal exemption from the income tax from $4,000 to $3,000. The bill was sent into conference, the house adopting the report of the conferees Sept. 30 and the senate taking the same action Oct. 3. President Wilson signed the bill at 9:10 p. m. Oct. 3.

(See United States Customs Duties, page 244, for rates under the new tariff law on articles in common use or extensive importation, for principal articles on the free list, and some of the more important special provisions of the act. The income tax section of the Underwood-Simmons tariff act will be found in full under the title, Federal Income Tax Law, on page 249.)

MESSAGE ON CURRENCY.

President Wilson appeared before congress again June 24 and personally read to the two houses in joint session the following message on the currency question:

"Mr. Speaker, Mr. President, gentlemen of the congress, it is under the compulsion of what seems to me a clear and imperative duty that I have a second time this session sought the privilege of addressing you in person. I know, of course, that the heated season of the year is upon us, that work in these chambers and in the committee rooms is likely to become a burden as the season lengthens, and that every consideration of personal convenience and personal comfort, perhaps, in the cases of some of us, considerations of personal health even, dictate an early conclusion of the deliberations of the session; but there are occasions of public duty when these things which touch us privately seem very small; when the work to be done is so pressing and so fraught with big consequence that we know that we are not at liberty to weigh against it any

point of personal sacrifice. We are now in the presence of such an occasion. It is absolutely imperative that we should give the business men of this country a banking and currency system by means of which they can make use of the freedom of enterprise and of individual initiative which we are about to bestow upon them.

"We are about to set them free; we must not leave them without the tools of action when they are free. We are about to set them free by removing the trammels of the protective tariff. Ever since the civil war they have waited for this emancipation and for the free opportunities it will bring with it. It has been reserved for us to give it to them. Some fell in love, indeed, with the slothful security of their dependence upon the government; some took advantage of the shelter of the nursery to set up a mimic mastery of their own within its walls. Now both the tonic and the discipline of liberty and maturity are to ensue. There will be some readjustments of purpose and point of view. There will follow a period of expansion and new enterprise, freshly conceived. It is for us to determine now whether it shall be rapid and facile and of easy accomplishment. This it cannot be unless the resourceful business men who are to deal with the new circumstances are to have at hand and ready for use the instrumentalities and conveniences of free enterprise which independent men need when acting on their own initiative.

"It is not enough to strike the shackles from business. The duty of statesmanship is not negative merely. It is constructive also. We must show that we understand what business needs and that we know how to supply it. No man, however casual and superficial his observation of the conditions now prevailing in the country, can fail to see that one of the chief things business needs now and will need increasingly as it gains in scope and vigor in the years immediately ahead of us is the proper means by which readily to vitalize its credit, corporate and individual, and its originative brains. What will it profit us to be free if we are not to have the best and most accessible instrumentalities of commerce and enterprise? What will it profit us to be quit of one kind of monopoly if we are to remain in the grip of another and more effective kind? How are we to gain and keep the confidence of the business community unless we show that we know how both to aid and to protect it? What shall we say if we make fresh enterprise necessary and also make it very difficult by leaving all else except the tariff just as we found it? The tyrannies of business, big and little, lie within the field of credit. We know that. Shall we not act upon the knowledge? Do we not know how to act upon it? If a man cannot make his assets available at pleasure, his assets of capacity and character and resource, what satisfaction is it to him to see opportunity beckoning to him on every hand when others have the keys of credit in their pockets and treat them as all but their own private possession? It is perfectly clear that it is our duty to supply the new banking and currency system the country needs, and it will need it immediately than it has ever needed it before.

"The only question is, When shall we supply it —now or later, after the demands shall have become reproaches that we were so dull and so slow? Shall we hasten to change the tariff laws and then be laggards about making it possible and easy for the country to take advantage of the change? There can be only one answer to that question. We must act now, at whatever sacrifice to ourselves. It is a duty which the circumstances forbid us to postpone. I should be recreant to my deepest conviction of public obligation did I not press it upon you with solemn and urgent insistence.

"The principles upon which we should act are also clear. The country has sought and seen its path in this matter within the last few years—sees it more clearly now than it ever saw it before—much more clearly than when the last legislative proposals on the subject were made. We must have a currency, not rigid as now, but readily, elastically responsive to sound credit, the expanding and contracting credits of everyday transactions, the normal ebb and flow of personal and

corporate dealings. Our banking laws must mobilize reserves; must not permit the concentration anywhere in a few hands of the monetary resources of the country or their use for speculative purposes in such volume as to hinder or impede or stand in the way of other more legitimate, more fruitful uses. And the control of the system of banking and of issue which our new laws are to set up must be public, not private, must be vested in the government itself, so that the banks may be the instruments, not the masters, of business and of individual enterprise and initiative.

"The committees of the congress to which legislation of this character is referred have devoted careful and dispassionate study to the means of accomplishing these objects. They have honored me by consulting me. They are ready to suggest action. I have come to you, as the head of the government and the responsible leader of the party in power, to urge action now, while there is time to serve the country deliberately and as we should, in the clear air of common counsel. I appeal to you with a deep conviction of duty. I believe that you share this conviction. I therefore appeal to you with confidence. I am at your service without reserve to play my part in any way you may call upon me to play it in this great enterprise of exigent reform which it will dignify and distinguish us to perform and discredit us to neglect."

[Information as to the action taken by congress on the president's currency recommendations will be found on another page of this volume. Consult index.]

BOARD OF MEDIATION AND CONCILIATION.

The act provides for mediation, conciliation and arbitration in controversies between railroad companies and their employes engaged in railroad train service. The act does not apply to the employes of street railroads. Whenever a controversy concerning wages, hours of employment or conditions of employment shall arise between an employer or employers and employes subject to the act, interrupting or threatening to interrupt business to the serious detriment of the public interest, either party to such controversy may apply to the board of mediation and conciliation created by the act and invoke its services for the purpose of bringing about an amicable adjustment of the controversy; and upon the request of either party the board shall with all practicable expedition put itself in communication with the parties to such controversy and shall use its best efforts to bring them to an agreement; and if such efforts shall be unsuccessful, the board shall at once endeavor to induce the parties to submit their controversy to arbitration in accordance with the provisions of the act.

In any case in which an interruption of traffic is imminent and fraught with serious detriment to the public interest, the board of mediation and conciliation may proffer its services to the respective parties to the controversy.

In any case in which a controversy arises over the meaning or the application of any agreement reached through mediation under the provisions of this act either party to the agreement may apply to the board of mediation and conciliation for an expression of opinion from such board as to the meaning or application of such agreement.

Whenever a controversy shall arise between an employer or employers and employes subject to this act, which cannot be settled through mediation and conciliation in the manner provided in the preceding section, such controversy may be submitted to the arbitration of a board of six, or, if the parties to the controversy prefer so to stipulate, to a board of three persons, which board shall be chosen in the following manner: In the case of a board of three, the employer or employers and the employes, parties respectively to the agreement to arbitrate, shall each name one arbitrator; and the two arbitrators thus chosen shall select the third arbitrator; but in the event of their failure to name the third arbitrator within five days after their first meeting, such third arbitrator shall be named by the board of mediation and conciliation. In the case of a board of six, the employer or employers and the employes, parties respectively to the agreement to arbitrate, shall each name two arbitrators, and the four arbitrators thus chosen, shall, by a majority vote, select the remaining two arbitrators; but in the event of their failure to name the two arbitrators within fifteen days after their first meeting the two arbitrators, or as many of them as have not been named, shall be named by the board of mediation and conciliation.

In the event that the employes engaged in any given controversy are not members of a labor organization, such employes may select a committee which shall have the right to name the arbitrator, or the arbitrators, who are to be named by the employes as provided above in this section.

The agreement to arbitrate—
1. Shall be in writing;
2. Shall stipulate that the arbitration is had under the provisions of this act;
3. Shall state whether the board of arbitration is to consist of three or six members;
4. Shall be signed by duly accredited representatives of the employer or employers and of the employes;
5. Shall state specifically the questions to be submitted to the board for arbitration;
6. Shall stipulate that a majority of the board shall be competent to make a valid and binding award;
7. Shall fix a period from the date of the appointment of the arbitrator or arbitrators necessary to complete the board, as provided for in the agreement, within which the board shall begin its hearings;
8. Shall fix a period from the beginning of the hearings within which the board shall make and file its award: Provided, That this period shall be thirty days unless a different period be agreed to;
9. Shall provide for the date from which the award shall become effective and shall fix the period during which the award shall continue in force;
10. Shall provide that the respective parties to the award will each faithfully execute the same;
11. Shall provide that the award and the papers and proceedings, including the testimony relating thereto, shall be filed in the clerk's office of the district court of the United States for the district wherein the controversy arises or the arbitration is entered into, and shall be final and conclusive upon the parties to the agreement unless set aside for error of law apparent on the record;
12. May also provide that any difference as to the meaning or the application of the provisions of an award made by a board of arbitration shall be referred back to the same board or to a subcommittee of the board for a ruling, which ruling shall have the same force as the original award; and if any member of the original board is unable or unwilling to serve another arbitrator shall be named in the same manner as such original member was named.

The arbitrators shall have the power to administer oaths and affirmations, sign subpœnas, require the attendance and testimony of witnesses and the production of books, papers, contracts, agreements and documents.

Every agreement of arbitration shall be acknowledged by the parties thereto before a notary public, a clerk of the District or the Circuit Court of Appeals of the United States, or before a member of the board of mediation and conciliation, and shall then be filed in the office of the board. When the board has been furnished with the names of the arbitrators chosen by the respective parties to the controversy, the board shall cause a notice in writing to be served upon the arbitrators, notifying them of their appointment, requesting them to meet promptly to name the remaining arbitrator or arbitrators necessary to complete the board, and advising them of the period within which they are empowered to name such arbitrator or arbitrators.

When the arbitrators selected have agreed upon the remaining arbitrator or arbitrators, they shall notify the board of mediation and conciliation; and in the event of their failure to agree upon any or upon all of the necessary arbitrators they shall notify the board of mediation and conciliation of the arbitrators selected, if any, or of their failure to make or to complete such selection.

If the parties to an arbitration desire the recon-

vening of a board to pass upon any controversy arising over the meaning or application of an award, they shall jointly so notify the board of mediation and conciliation, and shall state the question or questions to be submitted. The board of mediation and conciliation shall thereupon promptly communicate with the members of the board of arbitration and arrange for the reconvening of the board or subcommittee.

The board of arbitration shall organize and select its own chairman and make all necessary rules for conducting its hearings; but in its award or awards the board shall confine itself to findings or recommendations as to the questions specifically submitted to it or matters directly bearing thereon. It shall, whenever practicable, be supplied with suitable quarters in any federal building located at its place of meeting.

The board of arbitration shall furnish a certified copy of its awards to the respective parties to the controversy, and shall transmit the original, together with the papers and proceedings and a transcript of the testimony taken at the hearings, to the clerk of the District court of the United States for the district wherein the controversy arose or the arbitration is entered into, to be filed. The board shall also furnish a certified copy of its award, and the papers and proceedings, to the board of mediation and conciliation, to be filed in its office. The award shall go into practical operation at the expiration of ten days from the date of filing unless an appeal has been taken.

Each member of the board of arbitration shall receive such compensation as may be fixed by the board of mediation and conciliation, together with traveling and other necessary expenses.

There shall be a commissioner of mediation and conciliation, who shall be appointed by the president, by and with the advice and consent of the senate, and whose salary shall be $7,500 per annum, who shall hold his office for a term of seven years and until a successor qualifies, and who shall be removable by the president only for misconduct in office. The president shall also designate not more than two other officials of the government who have been appointed by and with the advice and consent of the senate, and the officials thus designated, together with the commissioner of mediation and conciliation, shall constitute a board to be known as the United States board of mediation and conciliation.

There shall also be an assistant commissioner of mediation and conciliation, who shall be appointed by the president, by and with the advice and consent of the senate, and whose salary shall be $5,000 per annum. In the absence of the commissioner of mediation and conciliation, or when that office shall become vacant, the assistant commissioner shall exercise the functions and perform the duties of that office. Under the direction of the commissioner of mediation and conciliation the assistant commissioner shall assist in the work of mediation and conciliation and when acting alone in any case he shall have the right to take acknowledgments, receive agreements of arbitration, and cause the notices in writing to be served upon the arbitrators chosen by the respective parties to the controversy, as provided for in the act.

The act of June 1, 1898, relating to the mediation and arbitration of controversies between railway companies and certain classes of their employes is repealed. (Approved, July 15, 1913.)

[William L. Chambers of the District of Columbia was appointed commissioner of mediation and conciliation, and G. W. W. Hanger, also of the District of Columbia, assistant commissioner by President Wilson July 18, 1913. Martin A. Knapp and Louis F. Post were designated as the other members of the board.]

ABOLITION OF COMMERCE COURT.

The Commerce court, created and established by the act entitled "An act to create a Commerce court and to amend the act entitled 'An act to regulate commerce,' approved Feb. 4, 1887, as heretofore amended, and for other purposes," approved June 18, 1910, is abolished from and after Dec. 31, 1913, and the jurisdiction vested in said Commerce court by said act is transferred to and vested in the several District courts of the United States, and all acts or parts of acts in so far as they relate to the establishment of the Commerce court are repealed. Nothing herein contained shall be deemed to affect the tenure of any of the judges now acting as Circuit judges by appointment under the terms of said act, but such judges shall continue to act under assignment, as in the said act provided, as judges of the District courts and Circuit Courts of Appeals; and in the event of and on the death, resignation, or removal from office of any of such judges, his office is hereby abolished and no successor to him shall be appointed. (Amendment to urgent deficiency appropriation bill, approved Oct. 22, 1913.)

EXEMPTIONS FROM SHERMAN ANTITRUST LAW.

Enforcement of antitrust laws: For the enforcement of antitrust laws, including not exceeding $10,000 for salaries of necessary employes at the seat of government, $300,000: Provided, however, That no part of this money shall be spent in the prosecution of any organization or individual for entering into any combination or agreement having in view the increasing of wages, shortening of hours or bettering the conditions of labor, or for any act done in furtherance thereof, not in itself unlawful: Provided further, That no part of this appropriation shall be expended for the prosecution of producers of farm products and associations of farmers who co-operate and organize in an effort to and for the purpose to obtain and maintain a fair and reasonable price for their products. (Amendment to sundry civil appropriation bill approved by President Wilson, June 23, 1913.)

RELIEF OF AMERICANS IN MEXICO.

There is hereby appropriated out of any money in the treasury not otherwise appropriated, for relief of destitute American citizens in Mexico, including transportation to their homes in the United States, to be expended under the direction and within the discretion of the secretary of state, and to be immediately available, $100,000. Authority is hereby granted to the secretary of state to reimburse from this appropriation the appropriation for "Emergencies arising in the diplomatic and consular service," for such sums as shall have been expended from that appropriation for purposes of relief and transportation in and from Mexico since Jan. 1, 1913. (Approved, Sept. 16, 1913.)

AMBASSADOR TO SPAIN.

The president is hereby authorized to appoint, as the representative of the United States, an ambassador to Spain, who shall receive as his compensation the sum of $17,500 per annum. (Approved, Sept. 4, 1913.)

FAMOUS WATERFALLS OF THE WORLD.

Name and location.	Height in feet.	Name and location.	Height in feet.	Name and location.	Height in feet.
Gavarnie, France	1,385	Schaffhausen, Switzerland..	100	Yellowstone(lower),Montana	310
Grand, Labrador	2,000	Skjaeggedalsfos, Norway....	530	Ygnassu, Brazil	210
Minnehaha, Minnesota	50	Shoshone, Idaho	210	Yosemite(upper),California	1,436
Missouri, Montana	90	Staubbach, Switzerland	1,000	Yosemite(middle),California	626
Montmorenci, Quebec	265	Stirling, New Zealand	500	Yosemite(lower),California	400
Multnomah, Oregon	850	Sutherland, New Zealand..	1,904	Vettis, Norway	950
Murchison, Africa	120	Takkakaw, Brit'h Columbia.	1,200	Victoria, Africa	400
Niagara, New York-Ontario	164	Twin, Idaho	180	Voringfos, Norway	600
Rjukan, Norway	780	Yellowstone(upper),Montana	110		

UNITED STATES CUSTOMS DUTIES.

Following are the existing tariff rates placed by the Underwood-Simmons act of 1913 on articles in common use or of extensive importation. A list of the principal articles on the free list is appended. Amounts given in dollars and cents are specific and the percentages are ad valorem duties. The abbreviation "n. s. p." means "not specially provided for."

DUTIABLE LIST.

SCHEDULE A—CHEMICALS, OILS AND PAINTS.

Acids: Boracic, ⅝c lb.; citric, 5c lb.; formic, 1½c lb.; gallic, 6c lb.; lactic and oxalic, 1½c lb.; pyrogallic, 12c lb.; salycilic, 2½c lb.; tannic, 5c lb.; tartaric, 3½c lb.; acids n. s. p., 15%.
Albumen, dried egg, 3c lb.
Alkalies and compounds of, n. s. p., 15%.
Alumina and compounds, n. e. s., 15%.
Ammonia, carbonate and muriate, ¾c lb.; liquid anhydrous, 2½c lb.; ammoniacal gas liquor, 10%.
Argols, crude, and calcium tartrate, crude, 5%; with more than 90 per cent of potassium bitartrate, cream of tartar, Rochelle salts, 2½c lb.
Balsams, natural and crude, 10%; advanced in value, 15%.
Barium, chloride of, ¼c lb.; dioxide of, 1½c lb.; carbonate of, precipitated, 15%.
Blacking, all kinds, 15%.
Bleaching powder, chloride of lime, 1-10c lb.
Caffein, $1 lb.; compounds of, 25%.
Calomel, corrosive sublimate, 15%.
Chalk, manufactured, 25%.
Chemical and medicinal compounds, 10c lb. and 20% to 40c lb. and 20%.
Chemical and medicinal compounds in individual packages of 2½ lbs. or less, 20% to 25%.
Chloroform, 2c lb.
Coal tar dyes, n. s. p., 30%.
Coal tar products, not dyes, n. s. p., 5% to 15%.
Cobalt, oxide of, 10c lb.
Collodion, 15%; compounds, 25% to 40%.
Drugs, natural materials for, advanced in value, 10%.
Ergot, 10c lb.
Ethers, 4c to 5c lb.; ethers n. s. p., 20%.
Extracts for dyeing, ⅜c lb.
Formaldehyde, 1c lb.
Fusel oil, ¼c lb.
Gelatin, glue and glue size, 1c lb.; valued at above 10c lb., 15% to 25%.
Glycerin, crude, 1c lb.; refined, 2c lb.
Gums, crude, n. s. p., $1 lb.; arabic, ½c lb.; camphor, crude, 1c lb.; camphor, refined, 5c lb.
Ink and ink powders, 15%.
Iodoform, 15c lb.
Leaves and roots, ¼c to 10c lb.
Licorice, extracts of, 1c lb.
Lime, citrate of, 1c lb.
Magnesia, 1-10c to 3 1-3c lb.
Menthol, 50c lb.
Oils, fish, n. s. p., 3c gal.; whale, 5c gal.; sperm, 8c gal.; oils and greases, n. s. p., 15%.
Oils, expressed, castor, 12c gal.; flaxseed and linseed, 10c gal.; olive, 20c to 30c gal.; other expressed oils, n. s. p., 15%.
Oils, distilled and essential, 10% to 20% or 6c to 25c lb.
Opium, crude, $3 to $6 lb.; derivatives of, $2 to $3 oz.
Perfumery, cosmetics, dentifrices, if with alcohol, 40c lb. and 60%; without alcohol, 60%; perfumes, n. s. p., 20%.
Plasters, curative, 15%.
Pigments, 5% to 25%; lead, 25%; zinc oxide, 10% to 15%; varnishes, 10%; enamel paints, n. s. p., 20%.
Potash, bicarbonate and chloride of, ½c lb.; chromate or bichromate of, 1c lb.; saltpeter, refined, $7 ton.
Soaps, perfumed, toilet, 30%; medicinal, 20%; castile and unperfumed, 10%; other, n. s. p., 10%.
Soda, benzoate of, 5c lb.; alkalies and sulphites of, ¼c lb.; sal soda, ⅛c lb.
Sponges, 10%; bleached, 15%.
Talcum, 15%.
Vanillin, 10c oz.; vanilla beans, 30c lb.

SCHEDULE B—EARTHS, EARTHENWARE AND GLASSWARE.

Brick, 10%; glazed, decorated, 15%.
Cement, 10%.
Tiles, 1½c to 5c sq. ft.; 20% to 30%.
Lime, 5%.
Gypsum, 10%.
Pumice stone, unmanufactured, 5%; manufactured, ¼c lb. or 25%.
Clays or earths, unmanufactured, n. s. p., 50c ton; manufactured, $1 to $1.50 ton.
Mica, unmanufactured, 4c lb. to 25%; manufactured, 30%.
Earthenware, common, not ornamented, 15%; ornamented, 20% to 30%.
Earthenware of nonvitrified absorbent body, 35% to 40%.
China and porcelain wares, 50% to 55%.
Gas retorts, 10%.
Glass bottles, 30% to 45%.
Glass, window, ⅞c to 2c lb.; cylinder and crown, 3c to 10c sq. ft.; cast plate, 6c to 12c sq. ft. and 4% additional if ground, frosted, etc.
Spectacles, 35%.
Lenses, 25%.
Opera glasses, optical instruments, n. s. p., 35%.
Telescopes, microscopes, photographic lenses, 25%.
Mirrors, stained glass windows, manufactures of glass n. s. p., 30%.
Marble, breccia, onyx, rough, 50c cu. ft.; dressed, 75c cu. ft.; paving tiles of, 6c to 10c superficial ft.; mosaic cubes, 20% to 35%.
Marble, breccia, onyx, alabaster, jet, manufactured into monuments, vases, etc., 45%.
Stone, building, manufactured, 25%; unmanufactured, 3c cu. ft.
Grindstones, $1.50 ton.
Slates n. s. p., 10%.

SCHEDULE C—METALS AND MANUFACTURES OF.

Chrome metal and other alloys used in manufacture of steel n. s. p., 15%.
Bar and other rolled or hammered iron n. s. p., 5%.
Beams, girders and other structural iron and steel, 10%.
Boiler or other plate of iron and steel n. s. p., 12%.
Iron and steel anchors, 12%; antifriction balls, 35%.
Hoop, band or scroll iron or steel n. s. p.; barrel hoops of iron and steel, 10%.
Railway fishplates and splice bars, 10%.
Iron or steel sheets with other metals imposed thereon, tin plates, terne plates, 15%.
Steel bars, mill shafting, castings, not containing alloys, 15%.
Rivet, screw, fence, nail and other iron or steel wire rods, 10%.
Round iron or steel wire, 15%; wire rope, 30%.
Anvils, 15%.
Automobiles valued at $2,000 or more, 45%; under $2,000, 30%; parts, 30%.
Bicycles, motorcycles, and parts, 25%.
Axles of iron and steel, 10%.
Blacksmiths' hammers and other tools of iron and steel, 10%.
Nuts and washers, 5% to 30%.
Cast iron pipe, 10%.
Chains n. s. p., 20%; sprocket and machine, 25%.
Iron and steel tubing n. s. p., 20%.
Knives, razors, etc., with folding blades, 35% to 55%.
Knives, table, etc., with fixed blades, and without handles, 25%; with handles, 30%.
Files and rasps, 25%.
Muskets and rifles, muzzle loading, 15%; breech-loading guns, 35%.
Needles, 20%.
Fishhooks and fishing tackle, except lines and nets, 30%.
Steel plates for engraving, stereotype plates, electrotype plates, 15%; lithographic plates of stone, 25%.
Saws, 12%.
Screws, 25%.
Umbrella ribs, 35%.
Wheels, railway, 20%.
Aluminum, crude, 2c lb.; in plates, bars, rods, 3½c lb.

Antimony, 10% to 25%.
Argentine, German silver, unmanufactured, 15%.
Bronze, 25%.
Copper, 5%.
Gold leaf, 35%.
Silver leaf, 30%.
Tinsel wire, 6% to 40%.
Buckles, metal, 15%.
Lead-bearing ores, ¾c lb. on lead therein.
Lead dross, bullion, in pigs and bars, 25% on lead therein.
Metallic mineral substances n. s. p., 10%.
Nickel, 10%; in sheets or strips, 20%.
Pens, metallic, n. s. p., 8c gross.
Penholders, gold pens, combination penholders, 25%.
Pins, metal, not jewelry, 20%.
Type and type metal, 15%.
Watches and clocks, 30%.
Zinc-bearing ores, 10% on zinc therein; in blocks, pigs or sheets, 15%.
Steam engines, locomotives, printing presses, machine tools, 15%; lace-making machines, 25%.
Articles of gold, silver and platinum, n. s. p., 50%; of iron, steel, lead, copper, brass, nickel, pewter, zinc or aluminum, n. s. p., 20%.

SCHEDULE D—WOOD AND MANUFACTURES OF.

Brier, ivy or laurel root, unmanufactured, 10%.
Cedar, lignum-vitæ, ebony, box, mahogany, rosewood, satinwood, in boards and planks, 10%; veneers of wood, 15%.
Paving posts, railroad ties, telegraph poles, 10%.
Casks, barrels, packing boxes, 15%.
Boxes for fruit, 15%.
Chair cane or reeds, 10%; manufactures of osier or willow, 25%.
Toothpicks, 25%.
Blinds, screens of wood, bamboo, 20%; if dyed or ornamented, 25%.
Furniture of wood, manufactures of wood, n. s. p., 15%.

SCHEDULE E—SUGAR, MOLASSES, AND MANUFACTURES OF.

Sugars, sirups and concentrated molasses testing not above 75 degrees, 71-100c lb.; for every additional degree, 26-1000c lb.; molasses not above 40 degrees, 15%; testing above 40 degrees, 2¼c to 4½c gal. (Old duties prevail until March 1, 1914, and after May 1, 1916, sugar and molasses will be free.)
Maple sugar and sirup, 3c lb.; glucose or grape sugar, 1⅛c lb.; sugar cane in natural state, 15%; after May 1, 1916, these articles will be free.
Saccharin, 65c lb.
Sugar candy and confectionery n. s. p., valued at 15c lb. or less, 2c lb.; valued at more than 15c lb., 25%.

SCHEDULE F—TOBACCO AND MANUFACTURES OF.

Wrapper tobacco, leaf tobacco, unstemmed, $1.85 lb.; stemmed, $2.50 lb.
All other tobacco n. s. p., 55c lb.; scrap tobacco, 35c lb.
Snuff, 55c lb.
Cigars and cigarettes, $4.50 lb. and 25%.

SCHEDULE G—AGRICULTURAL PRODUCTS AND PROVISIONS.

Horses and mules, 10%.
Live animals n. s. p., 10%.
Barley, 15c bu.; barley malt, 25c bu.; pearled or hulled, 1c lb.
Macaroni, vermicelli, 1c lb.
Oats, 6c lb.; oatmeal, 30c 100 lbs.
Rice, cleaned, 1c lb.; uncleaned, ⅝c lb.
Biscuits and cakes containing confectionery or nuts, 25%.
Butter and butter substitutes, 2½c lb.
Cheese, 20%.
Beans and lentils n. s. p., 25c bu.
Beets, 5%.
Beans, peas, in tins, jars, etc., 1c lb.
Vegetables, prepared, 25%; in natural state, n. s. p., 15%.
Pickles n. s. p., 25%.
Cider, 2c gal.
Eggs, preserved, 2c lb.; dried, 10c lb.
Hay, $2 ton.
Honey, 10c gal.
Hops, 16c lb.
Garlic, 1c lb.
Onions, 20c bu.
Peas, green or dried, in bulk, 10c bu.; split peas, 20c bu.; peas in packages, ½c lb.
Orchids, palms, azalea indica, cut flowers, 25%; other flowers, $1 to $10 per 1,000.
Fruit plants, $1 per 1,000; rose plants, 4c each; nursery and greenhouse stock, n. s. p., 15%.
Seeds: Castor, 15c bu.; oil seeds, n. s. p., 20c bu.; poppy, 15c lb.; canary seed, ½c lb.; caraway, 1c lb.; anise, 2c lb.; carrot, parsley, parsnip, radish, turnip, rutabaga, 3c lb.; other seeds, 5c to 6c lb.
Straw, 50c ton.
Fish packed in oil, 25%; in tin packages, 15%.
Apples, peaches, quinces, cherries, plums and pears, 10c bu.; berries, edible, in natural condition, ½c qt.; cranberries, 10%; dried or prepared fruits, n. s. p., 1c lb.
Figs, 2c lb.; plums, prunes, 1c lb.; raisins, 2c lb.; dates, 1c lb.; currants, 1½c lb.; olives, 15c gal.
Grapes in barrels, 25c cu. ft.
Lemons, limes, oranges in packages of 1¼ cu. ft. or less, 18c per package; in larger packages up to 5 cu. ft., 35c to 70c per package; in packages exceeding 5 cu. ft. or in bulk, ½c lb.
Pineapples in packages, 6c cu. ft. of package; in bulk, $5 per 1,000.
Almonds, not shelled, 3c lb.; shelled, 4c lb.
Filberts, walnuts, not shelled, 2c lb.; shelled, 4c lb.
Peanuts, unshelled, ⅜c lb.; shelled, ¾c lb.
Nuts, n. s. p., 1c lb.
Venison, game, 1½c lb.; game birds, dressed, 30%.
Poultry, live, 1c lb.; dead, 2c lb.
Chicory root, unground, 1c lb.; ground, 2c lb.
Chocolate and cocoa, unsweetened, n. s. p., 8%; sweetened, n. s. p., valued at 20c lb. or less, 2c lb.; at more than 20c lb., 25%.
Cocoa butter, 3½c lb.
Dandelion root, substitutes for coffee, 2c lb.
Starch, potato, 1c lb.; other starch, ½c lb.
Spices, unground, 1c to 18c lb.; ground, 20% additional.
Vinegar, 4c gal.

SCHEDULE H—SPIRITS, WINES AND OTHER BEVERAGES.

Brandy and other distilled spirits, $2.60 proof gal.
Cordials, liqueurs, bitters, etc., containing spirits, $2.60 proof gal.
Bay rum, $1.75 gal.
Champagne in bottles of more than 1 pint to 1 quart, $9.60 doz.; of more than ½ pint to 1 pint, $4.80 doz.; ½ pint or less, $2.40 doz.; more than 1 quart, in addition to $9.60 doz. bottles, on excess quantity above 1 quart at rate of $3 gal.
Still wines, 45c to 60c gal. or $1.85 per case.
Ale, porter, stout, beer, in bottles or jugs, 45c gal.; not in bottles or jugs, 23c gal.
Malt extract, fluid, in casks, 23c gal.; in bottles or jugs, 45c gal.; solid, 45%.
Fruit juices, 70c to 80c gal. and in addition $2.07 proof gal. on alcohol.
Ginger ale or beer, lemonade, soda water, containing no alcohol, 12c to 28c doz. bottles, according to size.
Mineral waters, 10c to 20c doz. bottles, according to size; in bottles of more than 1 quart, 18c gal.; in bulk, 8c gal.

SCHEDULE I—COTTON MANUFACTURES.

Cotton thread, yarn, warps, not combed, bleached, dyed, mercerized or colored, 5% to 27½%, according to number.
Spool thread of cotton, crochet, darning and embroidery cottons, 15%.
Cotton cloth, not bleached, dyed, printed, figured or mercerized, 7½% to 30%, according to number.
Cloth of cotton and silk, 30%; waterproof cloth of cotton, 25%.
Cotton handkerchiefs, not hemmed, n. s. p., 25%; hemmed, 30%.
Cotton clothing, ready made, 30%.
Plushes, velvets, chiefly of cotton, 40%.
Curtains and other articles of cotton chenille, 35%.
Stockings, hose, of cotton, made on knitting machines, n. s. p., 20%.
Stockings, hose, of cotton, made on machines or knit by hand, valued at not more than 70c per doz. pair, 30%; valued at more than 70c and not more than $1.20, 40%; valued at more than $1.20, 50%.
Cotton gloves, 35%.

Cotton underwear, 30%.

Cotton bandings, belts, cords, suspenders, 25%.

Cotton table damask, 25%.

Cotton towels, quilts, blankets, 25%.

Cotton lace window curtains, 35% to 45%.

Cotton cloth, n. s. p., 30%.

SCHEDULE J—FLAX, HEMP AND JUTE AND MANUFAC-
TURES OF.

Single yarns of jute, 15% to 20%.

Cables of latie, manila, etc., 1c lb.

Threads of flax, hemp or ramie, 20% to 25%.

Single yarns of flax, hemp or ramie, 10% to 20%.

Gill nettings, nets and seines of flax, hemp or
ramie, 25%.

Floor mattings of straw, 2½c sq. yd.

Carpets, mats, rugs of flax, hemp, jute, 30%.

Tapes of flax, 20%.

Linoleum, 20% to 35%.

Linen shirt collars and cuffs, 30%.

Wearing apparel of flax, hemp or ramie, 40%.

Articles of flax, hemp or ramie, n. s. p., 40%.

Handkerchiefs of flax, hemp or ramie, 35% to 40%.

Plain woven fabrics of flax, hemp or ramie, n. s. p.,
30%.

Istle or tampico, dressed, dyed and combed, 20%.

SCHEDULE K—WOOL AND MANUFACTURES OF.

Combed wool or tops advanced beyond scoured condition, n. s. p., 8%.

Yarns of wool, 18%.

Woolen cloth, 35%; cloth of cattle or horse hair,
25%; plushes, velvets, etc., of wool, 40%; stockings, hose, made on knitting machines, all wool,
20%; stockings selvedged, fashioned or shaped by
machine or by hand, valued at not more than
$1.20 per doz. pairs, 30%; valued at more than
$1.20, 40%.

Blankets and flannels of wool, 25% to 30%.

Women's and children's dress goods of wool, n.
s. p., 35%.

Clothing, ready made, including shawls, of wool,
35%.

Webbings, suspenders, beltings, cords, etc., of
wool, 35%.

Aubusson, Axminster, moquette and chenille carpets, 35%.

Saxony, Wilton and Tournay velvet carpets, 30%.

Brussels carpets, 25%.

Tapestry Brussels carpets, 20%.

Treble ingrain, three-ply carpets, 20%.

Carpets and rugs woven whole for rooms, 50%.

Hair of Angora goat, alpaca, 15%; tops of, 20%;
yarns of, 25%; cloth of, 40%; plushes and velvets
of, 45%.

SCHEDULE L—SILKS AND SILK GOODS.

Carded or combed silk, 20c lb.

Spun silk or schappe silk yarn, 35%.

Velvets, plushes, chenilles of silk, 50%.

Silk handkerchiefs and mufflers, 40% to 50%.

Ribbons, etc., of silk, 45%.

Clothing of silk, 50%.

Woven fabrics of silk, n. s. p., 45%.

Artificial or imitation silk fabrics and articles,
35% to 60%.

SCHEDULE M—PAPERS AND BOOKS.

Sheathing paper, roofing felt, paper-box board, 5%.

Printing paper, japan paper, suitable for books and
newspapers but not for covers or bindings, n. s.
p., valued above 2½c lb., 12%; in the case of imports from countries charging an export duty or
export license fee on printing paper or wood
pulp an additional duty equal to the highest export duty or export charge shall be imposed.

Copying paper, tissue paper, filtering paper, 30%.

Paper with surface coated in any way, 25% to 40%.

Lithographed pictures, cards, booklets, 15c to 60c lb.

Writing paper, 25%.

Paper envelopes, 15%.

Books of all kinds, bound or unbound, including
blank books, engravings, photographs, etchings,
maps, charts, music in books or sheets, 15%.

Albums, 25%.

Playing cards, 60%.

Postcards, not including American views, printed
except by lithographic process, 25%.

SCHEDULE N—SUNDRIES.

Beads, 35%.

Braids, ramie hat, 40%.

Braids of straw, grass, willow, etc., suitable for
ornamenting hats, not trimmed, 15% to 25%;
trimmed, 40%.

Brooms, 15%; brushes and feather dusters, 35%.

Bristles, sorted, 7c lb.

Buttons, 15% to 40%.

Cork and articles of, 12c to 15c lb.; cork paper,
35%; manufactures of cork, n. s. p., 30%.

Dice, dominoes, chessmen, billiard balls, etc., of
ivory, bone or other materials, 50%.

Dolls, marbles and toys not of china, porcelain,
earthen or stone ware, 35%.

Emery, 1c lb.; emery wheels, 20%.

Firecrackers, 6c lb.; fireworks, 10c lb.

Matches, 3c per gross of 144 boxes; not in boxes,
5c per 1,000 matches; wax matches, tapers, 25%;
white phosphorus matches not admitted.

Percussion caps, cartridges, 15%; blasting caps,
$1 per 1,000; mining fuses, 15%.

Feathers, crude, 20%; dressed, 40%; suitable for
millinery, 60%; importation of aigrettes, egret
plumes, osprey plumes or feathers, heads, wings,
tails and skins of wild birds, except for scientific purposes, forbidden.

Furs dressed on the skin, 30%; manufactures of
furs, 40%.

Fans, except common palm-leaf, 50%.

Gun wads, 10%.

Hair, human, raw, 10%; drawn, 20%; manufactures
of, n. s. p., 35%.

Hair for mattresses, 10%.

Hair cloth or crinoline, 6c sq. yd.; hats of fur, 45%.

Jewelry, valued at above 20c per doz. pieces, 60%.

Diamonds and precious stones in the rough, not
set, 10%; cut but not set, 20%.

Laces, n. s. p., 60%.

Chamois skins, 15%.

Leather, manufactures of, 30%.

Gloves, leather, $1 to $2.50 doz. pairs.

Manufactures of amber, asbestos or wax, 10% to
20%.

Manufactures of India rubber, 15%; of palm leaf,
15%; of bone and horn, 20%; of grass straw and
weeds, 25%; combs of horn, 25%.

Ivory tusks in natural state, 20%; manufactures of
ivory, 35%; manufactures of shell, 25%.

Matting of cocoa fiber or rattan, 5c sq. ft.

Moss and sea grass, manufactured or dyed, 10%.

Musical instruments and parts of, 35%.

Phonographs, graphophones, 25%.

Works of art, n. s. p., 15%.

Pencils of wood, lead pencils, 36c gross; slate
pencils, 25%.

Pencil leads, 10%.

Photographic cameras and dry plates, n. s. p., 15%;
moving picture film, exposed but not developed.
2c ft.; exposed and developed, 3c ft.; film subject to censorship.

Clay pipes, 25%; other pipes and all smokers' articles, 50%; meerschaum, 20%.

Hatters' plush, 10%.

Umbrellas, 35%; sticks for umbrellas, walking
canes, 30%.

ON THE FREE LIST.

Acids: Acetic, carbolic, muriatic, nitric, phosphoric,
sulphuric.

Agricultural implements.

Alcohol, methyl or wood.

Alizarin.

Ammonia, sulphate, perchlorate, nitrate of.

Antimony ore.

Animals, pure bred, for breeding.

Antitoxins, vaccine virus, serums.

Arsenic.

Art works—See works of art.

Asbestos, unmanufactured.

Asphaltum and limestone rock asphalt.

Bagging for cotton.

Balm of Gilead.

Barks (quinine).

Beeswax.

Bibles.

Binding twine.

Bismuth.

Bitumen.

Bolting cloths for milling purposes only.

Bones, crude.

Books, printed more than twenty years.

Books in foreign languages.

Books for blind.
Boots and shoes, leather.
Borax.
Brass for remanufacture.
Bristles, crude.
Broom corn.
Buckwheat and buckwheat flour.
Bullion, gold or silver.
Cash registers.
Castor or castoreum.
Cement.
Chalk, crude.
Charcoal.
Charts, printed more than twenty years.
Chromate of iron.
Coal, coal tar.
Cobalt.
Cochineal.
Coffee.
Coins.
Coke.
Copper ore.
Coral, unmanufactured.
Cork wood or bark, unmanufactured.
Corn or maize, corn meal.
Cotton and cotton waste or flocks.
Curling stones.
Cream separators.
Curry and curry powder.
Dandelion roots, unground.
Dragon's blood.
Drugs, crude materials for and nonalcoholic, uncompounded, n. s. p.
Eggs.
Emery ore and corundum.
Engravings and etchings more than twenty years old.
Fans, palm leaf.
Fish, fresh water, fish, n. s. p.
Flax straw.
Flint, flint stones, unground.
Fossils.
Fruits or berries, green, ripe or dried, n. s. p.
Fulminates.
Furs, undressed.
Gloves, leather, of horsehide, pigskins and cattle hides, except calfskin.
Grasses and fibers, unmanufactured, n. s. p.
Grease for soap making, n. s. p.
Guano, manures.
Gunpowder for mining, blasting and artillery purposes.
Gutta percha, crude.
Hair of animals, unmanufactured, n. s. p.
Hemp.
Hide cuttings, raw.
Hide rope.
Hides of cattle.
Hones and whetstones.
Hoop iron or steel, for baling cotton.
Ice.
India rubber, crude.
Indigo, indigo dyes.
Iodine, crude.
Ipecac.
Iron ore, pig iron, spiegeleisen, wrought iron, ferro manganese; iron in slabs, blooms, n. s. p.
Jalap.
Jet, unmanufactured.
Lard.
Leather, n. s. p.
Lemon juice.
Linotype machines.
Lithographic prints more than twenty years old.
Lithographic stones.
Manuscripts.
Maps more than twenty years old.
Meats: Fresh beef, veal, mutton, lamb and pork; bacon and hams; meats of all kinds, n. s. p.
Medals.
Milk and cream.
Mineral salts from evaporation.
Minerals, crude, n. s. p.
Miners' rescue appliances.
Models of inventions.
Music more than twenty years old.
Nails, cut, of iron or steel, hobnails, all nails n. s. p.
Needles.
Newspapers and periodicals.
Nuts: Marrons, cocoanuts, palm nuts, not prepared.

Oakum.
Oil cake.
Oils: Cocoanut, cod, cod liver, cottonseed, croton, palm, nut; petroleum, crude or refined; kerosene, benzine, naphtha, gasoline, paraffin; fish oils of American fisheries.
Oleo stearin.
Ores of gold, silver, nickel, platinum.
Paper stock, crude, for paper making.
Photographs, printed more than twenty years.
Printing paper for books and newspapers, n. s. p., valued at not above 2½c lb.
Parchment and vellum.
Paris green.
Phosphates, crude.
Phosphorus.
Photographic and moving picture films, not exposed or developed.
Platinum, unmanufactured.
Plumbago.
Potatoes.
Quinia, sulphate of.
Radium and salts of.
Railway bars of iron or steel, T rails and punched iron or flat steel rails.
Rags, n. s. p.
Rye and rye flour.
Sago, crude, and sago flour.
Salt.
Seeds: Cauliflower, celery, cotton, mustard, sorghum, sugar beet; bulbs and bulbous roots, not edible; all flower and grass seeds.
Sewing machines.
Shoes and boots, leather.
Shrimps, lobsters.
Silk cocoons.
Silk, raw, in skeins but not advanced in manufacture.
Silkworm eggs.
Skins of hares, rabbits, dogs, goats and sheep, undressed.
Skins of all kinds n. s. p.
Soda.
Spikes, cut.
Stamps.
Statuary for use as models.
Steel ingots.
Stone and sand.
Sugar, after May 1, 1916.
Sulphur.
Swine.
Tallow.
Tanning materials, not containing alcohol.
Tapioca, tapioca flour.
Tar and pitch of wood.
Tea, n. e. s.; tea plants.
Teeth, natural.
Textbooks.
Tin ore, tin in bars, blocks or pigs.
Tobacco stems.
Tungsten-bearing ores.
Typewriters.
Uranium.
Wax, vegetable or mineral.
Wearing apparel, articles of personal adornment, toilet articles and similar personal effects, not for sale or for other persons than the owners. In the case of residents of the United States returning from abroad all wearing apparel, personal and household effects taken by them out of the United States to foreign countries shall be admitted free of duty, without regard to their value, upon their identity being established under appropriate rules and regulations to be prescribed by the secretary of the treasury. Up to but not exceeding $100 in value of articles acquired abroad by such residents of the United States for personal or household use or as souvenirs or curios, but not bought on commission or intended for sale, shall be admitted free of duty.
Whalebone, unmanufactured.
Wheat and wheat flour except when imported from a country imposing a duty on wheat and wheat flour exported from the United States.
Wire for fencing or baling purposes.
Wood: Logs, timber, pulp woods, kindling wood, firewood, hop poles, hoop poles, fence posts, hubs for wheels, posts, sawed boards, laths, pickets, palings, staves, shingles, ship timber, broom handles.

Woods: Cedar, lignum vitæ, lancewood, ebony, box, granadilla, mahogany, rosewood, satinwood and other cabinet woods in the log, rough or hewn only; red cedar timber, hewn, sided, squared or round; sticks of partridge hair wood, pimento, orange, myrtle and other woods n. e. s., in the rough.

Wood pulp, mechanically ground, chemical and rag pulp.

Wool of the sheep, hair of the camel and other like animals.

Wool waste.

Works of art: Original paintings, drawings, artists' proof etchings unbound, engravings unbound, printed by hand, original sculptures; works of art imported for exhibition purposes or for presentation to a public institution.

Works of art (except rugs and carpets) which shall have been produced more than 100 years prior to the date of importation.

SPECIAL PROVISIONS.
TRADE AGREEMENTS.

For the purpose of readjusting the present duties on importations into the United States and at the same time to encourage the export trade of this country, the president of the United States is authorized and empowered to negotiate trade agreements with foreign nations wherein mutual concessions are made looking toward freer trade relations and further reciprocal expansion of trade and commerce: Provided, however, That said trade agreements before becoming operative shall be submitted to the congress of the United States for ratification or rejection.

MARKING AND BRANDING.

All articles of foreign manufacture or production which are capable of being marked, stamped, branded or labeled, without injury, shall be marked, stamped, branded or labeled in legible English words, in a conspicuous place that shall not be covered or obscured by any subsequent attachments or arrangements, so as to indicate the country of origin. All packages containing imported articles shall be marked, stamped, branded or labeled so as to indicate legibly and plainly in English words the country of origin and the quantity of their contents.

DISCRIMINATING DUTIES.

A discriminating duty of 10 per centum ad valorem, in addition to the duties imposed by law, shall be levied, collected and paid on all goods, wares or merchandise which shall be imported in vessels not of the United States, or which, being the production or manufacture of any foreign country not contiguous to the United States, shall come into the United States from such contiguous country; but this discriminating duty shall not apply to goods, wares or merchandise which shall be imported in vessels not of the United States entitled at the time of such importation by treaty or convention or act of congress to be entered in the ports of the United States on payment of the same duties as shall then be payable on goods, wares and merchandise imported in vessels of the United States, nor to such foreign products or manufactures as shall be imported from such contiguous countries in the usual course of strictly retail trade.

No goods, wares or merchandise, unless in cases provided for by treaty, shall be imported into the United States from any foreign port or place, except in vessels of the United States, or in such foreign vessels as truly and wholly belong to the citizens or subjects of that country of which the goods are the growth, production or manufacture, or from which such goods, wares or merchandise can only be, or most usually are, first shipped for transportation. All goods, wares or merchandise imported contrary to this section, and the vessel wherein the same shall be imported, shall be forfeited to the United States.

The preceding subsection shall not apply to vessels or goods, wares or merchandise imported in vessels of a foreign nation which does not maintain a similar regulation against vessels of the United States.

DISCOUNT FOR AMERICAN SHIPS.

A discount of 5 per centum on all duties imposed by this act shall be allowed on such goods, wares and merchandise as shall be imported in vessels admitted to registration under the laws of the United States: Provided, That nothing in this subsection shall be so construed as to abrogate or in any manner impair or affect the provisions of any treaty concluded between the United States and any foreign nation.

SYNOPSIS OF TARIFF LEGISLATION SINCE 1884.

Morrison Bills—First bill presented to 48th congress during Chester A. Arthur's administration; proposed a horizontal reduction of 20 per cent with free iron ore, coal and lumber; defeated in house April 15, 1884, by vote of 159 to 155; house heavily democratic and senate republican. Second bill presented to 49th congress during Grover Cleveland's first administration; similar to first bill, proposing free wool, salt and lumber; defeated in house June 17, 1886, by a vote of 157 to 140; house democratic, senate republican.

Mills Bill—Presented to 50th congress during Cleveland's first administration; provided for free lumber and wool, reduction on pig iron and abolition of specific duties on cotton; passed by house July 21, 1888, by vote of 162 to 149, but failed in senate; house democratic, senate republican.

McKinley Bill—Passed by 51st congress during Benjamin Harrison's administration; became law Oct. 6, 1890; high protective measure, though remitting duties on sugar and providing for reciprocity treaties; both houses of congress republican.

Wilson Bill—Passed by 53d congress during Cleveland's second administration; became law Aug. 17, 1894, without the president's signature; both houses democratic; measure reduced duties in some cases and made additions to free list, notably wool.

Dingley Bill—Passed by 54th congress during Mc-

Kinley's administration; approved July 24, 1897; passed by house 205 yeas to 122 nays, 27 members not voting; passed by senate 38 yeas to 28 nays, 23 not voting; house contained 206 republicans and 134 democrats and senate 46 republicans and 34 democrats; measure raised rates to produce more revenue, but was similar in many respects to the McKinley act.

Payne-Aldrich bill passed at extra session of 61st congress in first year of President William H. Taft's administration; approved Aug. 5, 1909; passed the house by a vote of 217 to 161 and the senate by a vote of 45 to 34. The conference vote in the house was 195 yeas to 183 nays, twenty republicans voting in the negative and two democrats in the affirmative. In the senate the vote on the final conference report was 47 to 31, seven republicans voting against it. In general the revision of the Dingley act was in the direction of lower duties, but there were some increases. The law is given practically in full in The Daily News Almanac and Year-Book for 1910.

Underwood-Simmons bill—Passed by 63d congress at extra session called immediately after President Wilson's inauguration in 1913; house and senate democratic. The bill made many reductions in the tariff duties as fixed by the Payne-Aldrich law and placed numerous articles on the free list. It also contained a section establishing a tax on incomes of $3,000 or more.

UNITED STATES ARSENALS.

The largest of the United States arsenals are located at Rock Island, Ill., and Springfield, Mass. Others are at Pittsburgh, Pa.; Augusta, Ga.; Benicia, Cal.; Columbia, Tenn.; Fort Monroe, Va.; Philadelphia, Pa.; Indianapolis, Ind.; Governor's Island, N. Y.; Jefferson barracks, Mo.; Sandy Hook, N. J.; San Antonio, Tex.; Dover, N. J.; Watertown, Mass., and Watervliet, N. Y. Some of the above are merely powder depots, the principal manufacturing plants being at Rock Island, Springfield and Watervliet. The navy yards are also arsenals.

FEDERAL INCOME TAX LAW.

Following is the full text of the federal income law enacted by the 63d congress. It forms section 2 of the Underwood-Simmons tariff act, approved Oct. 3, 1913:

A. 1. That there shall be levied, assessed, collected and paid annually upon the entire net income arising or accruing from all sources in the preceding calendar year to every citizen of the United States, whether residing at home or abroad, and to every person residing in the United States, though not a citizen thereof, a tax of 1 per centum per annum upon such income, except as hereinafter provided, and a like tax shall be assessed, levied, collected and paid annually upon the entire net income from all property owned and of every business, trade or profession carried on in the United States by persons residing elsewhere.

2. In addition to the income tax provided under this section (herein referred to as the normal income tax) there shall be levied, assessed and collected upon the net income of every individual an additional income tax (herein referred to as the additional tax) of 1 per centum per annum upon the amount by which the total net income exceeds $20,-000 and does not exceed $50,000, and 2 per centum per annum upon the amount by which the total net income exceeds $50,000 and does not exceed $75,000, 3 per centum per annum upon the amount by which the total net income exceeds $75,000 and does not exceed $100,000, 4 per centum per annum upon the amount by which the total net income exceeds $100,-000 and does not exceed $250,000, 5 per centum per annum upon the amount by which the total net income exceeds $250,000 and does not exceed $500,000, and 6 per centum per annum upon the amount by which the total net income exceeds $500,000. All the provisions of this section relating to individuals who are to be chargeable with the normal income tax, so far as they are applicable and are not inconsistent with this subdivision of paragraph A, shall apply to the levy, assessment and collection of the additional tax imposed under this section. Every person subject to this additional tax shall, for the purpose of its assessment and collection, make a personal return of his total net income from all sources, corporate or otherwise, for the preceding calendar year, under rules and regulations to be prescribed by the commissioner of internal revenue and approved by the secretary of the treasury. For the purpose of this additional tax the taxable income of any individual shall embrace the share to which he would be entitled of the gains and profits, if divided or distributed, whether divided or distributed or not, of all corporations, joint stock companies or associations, however created or organized, formed or fraudulently availed of for the purpose of preventing the imposition of such tax through the medium of permitting such gains and profits to accumulate instead of being divided or distributed, and the fact that any such corporation, joint stock company or association is a mere holding company, or that the gains and profits are permitted to accumulate beyond the reasonable needs of the business, shall be prima facie evidence of a fraudulent purpose to escape such tax; but the fact that the gains and profits are in any case permitted to accumulate and become surplus shall not be construed as evidence of a purpose to escape the said tax in such case unless the secretary of the treasury shall certify that in his opinion such accumulation is unreasonable for the purposes of the business. When requested by the commissioner of internal revenue or any district collector of internal revenue, such corporation, joint stock company or association shall forward to him a correct statement of such profits and the names of the individuals who would be entitled to the same if distributed.

B. That, subject only to such exemptions and deductions as are hereinafter allowed, the net income of a taxable person shall include gains, profits and income derived from salaries, wages or compensation for personal service of whatever kind and in whatever form paid, or from professions, vocations, businesses, trade, commerce or sales, or dealings in property, whether real or personal, growing out of the ownership or use of or interest in real or personal property, also from in-terest, rent, dividends, securities or the transaction of any lawful business carried on for gain or profit, or gains or profits, and income derived from any source whatever, including the income from but not the value of property acquired by gift, bequest, devise or descent: Provided, That the proceeds of life insurance policies paid upon the death of the person insured or payments made by or credited to the insured on life insurance, endowment or annuity contracts, upon the return thereof to the insured at the maturity of the term mentioned in the contract, or upon surrender of contract, shall not be included as income.

That in computing net income for the purpose of the normal tax there shall be allowed as deductions: First, the necessary expenses actually paid in carrying on any business, not including personal, living or family expenses; second, all interest paid within the year by a taxable person on indebtedness; third, all national, state, county, school and municipal taxes paid within the year, not including those assessed against local benefits; fourth, losses actually sustained during the year, incurred in trade or arising from fires, storms or shipwreck, and not compensated for by insurance or otherwise; fifth, debts due to the taxpayer actually ascertained to be worthless and charged off within the year; sixth, a reasonable allowance for the exhaustion, wear and tear of property arising out of its use or employment in the business, not to exceed, in the case of mines, 5 per centum of the gross value at the mine of the output for the year for which the computation is made, but no deduction shall be made for any amount of expense of restoring property or making good the exhaustion thereof for which an allowance is or has been made: Provided, That no deduction shall be allowed for any amount paid out for new buildings, permanent improvements or betterments, made to increase the value of any property or estate; seventh, the amount received as dividends upon the stock or from the net earnings of any corporation, joint stock company, association or insurance company which is taxable upon its net income as hereinafter provided; eighth, the amount of income, the tax upon which has been paid or withheld for payment at the source of the income, under the provisions of this section, provided that whenever the tax upon the income of a person is required to be withheld and paid at the source as hereinafter required, if such annual income does not exceed the sum of $3,000 or is not fixed or certain, or is indefinite or irregular as to amount or time of accrual, the same shall not be deducted in the personal return of such person.

The net income from property owned and business carried on in the United States by persons residing elsewhere shall be computed upon the basis prescribed in this paragraph and that part of paragraph G of this section relating to the computation of the net income of corporations, joint stock and insurance companies, organized, created or existing under the laws of foreign countries, in so far as applicable.

That in computing net income under this section there shall be excluded the interest upon the obligations of a state or any political subdivision thereof, and upon the obligations of the United States or its possessions; also the compensation of the present president of the United States during the term for which he has been elected, and of the judges of the Supreme and inferior courts of the United States now in office, and the compensation of all officers and employes of a state or any political subdivision thereof except when such compensation is paid by the United States government.

C. That there shall be deducted from the amount of the net income of each of said persons, ascertained as provided herein, the sum of $3,000, plus $1,000 additional if the person making the return be a married man with a wife living with him, or plus the sum of $1,000 additional if the person making return be a married woman with a husband living with her, but in no event shall this additional exemption of $1,000 be deducted by both a husband and a wife: Provided, That only one deduction of $4,000 shall be made from the aggregate

income of both husband and wife when living together.

D. The said tax shall be computed upon the remainder of said net income of each person subject thereto, accruing during each preceding calendar year ending Dec. 31: Provided, however, That for the year ending Dec. 31, 1913, said tax shall be computed on the net income accruing from March 1 to Dec. 31, 1913, both dates inclusive, after deducting five-sixths only of the specific exemptions and deductions herein provided for. On or before the first day of March, 1914, and the first day of March in each year thereafter a true and accurate return, under oath or affirmation, shall be made by each person of lawful age, except as hereinafter provided, subject to the tax imposed by this section and having a net income of $3,000 or over for the taxable year, to the collector of internal revenue for the district in which such person resides or has his principal place of business, or, in the case of a person residing in a foreign country, in the place where his principal business is carried on within the United States, in such form as the commissioner of internal revenue, with the approval of the secretary of the treasury, shall prescribe, setting forth specifically the gross amount of income from all separate sources and from the total thereof, deducting the aggregate items or expenses and allowance herein authorized; guardians, trustees, executors, administrators, agents, receivers, conservators and all persons, corporations or associations acting in any fiduciary capacity shall make and render a return of the net income of the person for whom they act, subject to this tax, coming into their custody or control and management, and be subject to all the provisions of this section which apply to individuals: Provided, That a return made by one of two or more joint guardians, trustees, executors, administrators, agents, receivers and conservators or other persons acting in a fiduciary capacity, filed in the district where such person resides or in the district where the will or other instrument under which he acts is recorded, under such regulations as the secretary of the treasury may prescribe, shall be a sufficient compliance with the requirements of this paragraph, and also all persons, firms, companies, copartnerships, corporations, joint stock companies or associations and insurance companies, except as hereinafter provided, in whatever capacity acting, having the control, receipt, disposal or payment of fixed or determinable annual or periodical gains, profits and income of another person subject to tax, shall in behalf of such person, deduct and withhold from the payment an amount equivalent to the normal income tax upon the same and make and render a return, as aforesaid, but separate and distinct, of the portion of the income of each person from which the normal tax has been thus withheld, and containing also the name and address of such person or stating that the name and address or the address, as the case may be, are unknown: Provided, That the provision requiring the normal tax of individuals to be withheld at the source of the income shall not be construed to require any of such tax to be withheld prior to the first day of November, 1913: Provided further, That in either case above mentioned no return of income not exceeding $3,000 shall be required: Provided further, That any persons carrying on business in partnership shall be liable for the income tax only in their individual capacity, and the share of the profits of a partnership to which any taxable partner would be entitled if the same were divided, whether divided or otherwise, shall be returned for taxation and the tax paid under the provision of this section, and any such firm, when requested by the commissioner of internal revenue or any district collector, shall forward to him a correct statement of such profits and the names of the individuals who would be entitled to the same, if distributed: Provided further, That persons liable for the normal income tax only, on their own account or in behalf of another, shall not be required to make return of the income derived from dividends on the capital stock or from the net earnings of corporations, joint stock companies or associations and insurance companies taxable upon their net income as hereinafter provided. Any person for whom return has been made and the

tax paid, or to be paid as aforesaid, shall not be required to make a return unless such person has other net income, but only one deduction of $3,000 shall be made in the case of any such person. The collector or deputy collector shall require every list to be verified by the oath or affirmation of the party rendering it. If the collector or deputy collector have reason to believe that the amount of any income returned is understated, he shall give due notice to the person making the return to show cause why the amount of the return should not be increased, and upon proof of the amount understated may increase the same accordingly. If dissatisfied with the decision of the collector such person may submit the case, with all the papers, to the commissioner of internal revenue for his decision, and may furnish sworn testimony of witnesses to prove any relevant facts.

E. That all assessments shall be made by the commissioner of internal revenue and all persons shall be notified of the amount for which they are respectively liable on or before the first day of June of each successive year, and said assessments shall be paid on or before the thirtieth day of June, except in cases of refusal or neglect to make such return and in cases of false or fraudulent returns, in which cases the commissioner of internal revenue shall, upon the discovery thereof, at any time within three years after said return is due, make a return upon information obtained as provided for in this section or by existing law, and the assessment made by the commissioner of internal revenue thereon shall be paid by such person or persons immediately upon notification of the amount of such assessment, and to any sum or sums due and unpaid after the thirtieth day of June in any year, and for ten days after notice and demand thereof by the collector, there shall be added the sum of 5 per centum on the amount of tax unpaid and interest at the rate of 1 per centum per month upon said tax from the time the same became due, except from the estates of insane, deceased or insolvent persons.

All persons, firms, copartnerships, companies, corporations, joint-stock companies or associations and insurance companies, in whatever capacity acting, including lessees or mortgagors of real or personal property, trustees acting in any trust capacity, executors, administrators, agents, receivers, conservators, employers and all officers and employes of the United States having the control, receipt, custody, disposal or payment of interest, rent, salaries, wages, premiums, annuities, compensation, remuneration, emoluments or other fixed or determinable annual gains, profits and income of another person, exceeding $3,000 for any taxable year, other than dividends on capital stock or from the net earnings of corporations and joint-stock companies or associations subject to like tax, who are required to make and render a return in behalf of another, as provided herein, to the collector of his, her or its district, are hereby authorized and required to deduct and withhold such sum as will be sufficient to pay the normal tax imposed thereon by this section, and shall pay to the officer of the United States government authorized to receive the same, and they are each hereby made personally liable for such tax. In all cases where the income tax of a person is withheld and deducted and paid or to be paid at the source, as aforesaid, such person shall not receive the benefit of the deduction and exemption allowed in paragraph C of this section except by an application for refund of the tax unless he shall, not less than thirty days prior to the day on which the return of his income is due, file with the person who is required to withhold and pay tax for him, a signed notice in writing claiming the benefit for such exemption and thereupon no tax shall be withheld upon the amount of such exemption: Provided, That if any person for the purpose of obtaining any allowance or reduction by virtue of a claim for such exemption, either for himself or for any other person, knowingly makes any false statement or false or fraudulent representation, he shall be liable to a penalty of $300: nor shall any person under the foregoing conditions be allowed the benefit of any deduction provided for in subsection B of this section unless he shall,

not less than thirty days prior to the day on which the return of his income is due, either file with the person who is required to withhold and pay tax for him a true and correct return of his annual gains, profits and income from all other sources, and also the deductions asked for, and the showing thus made shall then become a part of the return to be made in his behalf by the person required to withhold and pay the tax, or likewise make application for deductions to the collector of the district in which return is made or to be made for him. Provided further, That if such person is a minor or an insane person, or is absent from the United States, or is unable owing to serious illness to make the return and application above provided for, the return and application may be made for him or her by the person required to withhold and pay the tax, he making oath under the penalties of this act that he has sufficient knowledge of the affairs and property of his beneficiary to enable him to make a full and complete return for him or her, and that the return and application made by him are full and complete. Provided further, That the amount of the normal tax hereinbefore imposed shall be deducted and withheld from fixed and determinable annual gains, profits and income derived from interest upon bonds and mortgages or deeds of trust or other similar obligations of corporations, joint-stock companies or associations and insurance companies, whether payable annually or at shorter or longer periods, although such interest does not amount to $3,000, subject to the provisions of this section requiring the tax to be withheld at the source and deducted from annual income and paid to the government, and likewise the amount of such tax shall be deducted and withheld from coupons, checks or bills of exchange for or in payment of interest upon bonds of foreign countries and upon foreign mortgages or like obligations (not payable in the United States), and also from coupons, checks or bills of exchange for or in payment of any dividends upon the stock or interest upon the obligations of foreign corporations, associations and insurance companies engaged in business in foreign countries, and the tax in each case shall be withheld and deducted for and in behalf of any person subject to the tax hereinbefore imposed, although such interest, dividends or other compensation does not exceed $3,000, by any banker or person who shall sell or otherwise realize coupons, checks or bills of exchange drawn or made in payment of any such interest or dividends (not payable in the United States), and any person who shall obtain payment (not in the United States), in behalf of another of such dividends and interest by means of coupons, checks or bills of exchange, and also any dealer in such coupons who shall purchase the same for any such dividends or interest (not payable in the United States) otherwise than from a banker or another dealer in such coupons, but in each case the benefit of the exemption and the deduction allowable under this section may be had by complying with the foregoing provisions of this paragraph.

All persons, firms or corporations undertaking as a matter of business or for profit the collection of foreign payments of such interest or dividends by means of coupons, checks or bills of exchange shall obtain a license from the commissioner of internal revenue and shall be subject to such regulations enabling the government to ascertain and verify the due withholding and payment of the income tax required to be withheld and paid as the commissioner of internal revenue, with the approval of the secretary of the treasury, shall prescribe, and any person who shall knowingly undertake to collect such payment as aforesaid without having obtained a license therefor, or without complying with such regulations, shall be deemed guilty of a misdemeanor and for each offense be fined in a sum not exceeding $5,000 or imprisoned for a term not exceeding one year, or both, in the discretion of the court.

Nothing in this section shall be construed to release a taxable person from liability for income tax, nor shall any contract entered into after this act takes effect be valid in regard to any federal income tax imposed upon a person liable to such payment.

The tax herein imposed upon annual gains, profits and income not falling under the foregoing and not returned and paid by virtue of the foregoing shall be assessed by personal return under rules and regulations to be prescribed by the commissioner of internal revenue and approved by the secretary of the treasury.

The provisions of this section relating to the deduction and payment of the tax at the source of income shall only apply to the normal tax hereinbefore imposed upon individuals.

F. That if any person, corporation, joint-stock company, association or insurance company liable to make the return or pay the tax aforesaid shall refuse or neglect to make a return at the time or times hereinbefore specified in each year, such person shall be liable to a penalty of not less than $20 nor more than $1,000. Any person or any officer of any corporation required by law to make, render, sign or verify any return who makes any false or fraudulent return or statement with intent to defeat or evade the assessment required by this section to be made shall be guilty of a misdemeanor and shall be fined not exceeding $2,000 or be imprisoned not exceeding one year, or both, at the discretion of the court, with the costs of prosecution.

G. (a) That the normal tax hereinbefore imposed upon the individuals likewise shall be levied, assessed and paid annually upon the entire net income arising or accruing from all sources during the preceding calendar year to every corporation, joint-stock company or association and every insurance company organized in the United States, no matter how created or organized, not including partnerships; but if organized, authorized or existing under the laws of any foreign country, then upon the amount of net income accruing from business transacted and capital invested within the United States during such year Provided, however, That nothing in this section shall apply to labor, agricultural or horticultural organizations or to mutual savings banks not having a capital stock represented by shares, or to fraternal beneficiary societies, orders or associations operating under the lodge system or for the exclusive benefit of the members of a fraternity itself operating under the lodge system and providing for the payment of life, sick, accident and other benefits to the members of such societies, orders or associations and dependents of such members, nor to domestic building and loan associations, nor to cemetery companies, organized and operated exclusively for the mutual benefit of their members, nor to any corporation or association organized and operated exclusively for religious, charitable, scientific or educational purposes, no part of the net income of which inures to the benefit of any private stockholder or individual, nor to business leagues, nor to chambers of commerce or boards of trade, not organized for profit or no part of the net income of which inures to the benefit of the private stockholder or individual; nor to any civic league or organization not organized for profit but operated exclusively for the promotion of social welfare Provided further, That there shall not be taxed under this section any income derived from any public utility or from the exercise of any essential governmental function accruing to any state, territory or the District of Columbia, or any political subdivision of a state, territory or the District of Columbia, nor any income accruing to the government of the Philippine islands or Porto Rico, or of any political subdivision of the Philippine islands or Porto Rico Provided That whenever any state, territory or the District of Columbia, or any political subdivision of a state or territory, has, prior to the passage of this act, entered in good faith into a contract with any person or corporation, the object and purpose of which is to acquire, construct, operate or maintain a public utility, no tax shall be levied under the provisions of this act upon the income derived from the operation of such public utility, so far as the payment thereof will impose a loss or burden upon such state, territory or the District of Columbia, or a political subdivision of a state or territory, but this provision is not intended to confer upon such person or corporation any financial gain or exemption or to relieve

such person or corporation from the payment of a tax as provided for in this section upon the part or portion of the said income to which such person or corporation shall be entitled under such contract.

(b) Such net income shall be ascertained by deducting from the gross amount of the income of such corporation, joint-stock company or association or insurance company, received within the year from all sources, (first) all the ordinary and necessary expenses paid within the year in the maintenance and operation of its business and properties, including rentals or other payments required to be made as a condition to the continued use or possession of property; (second) all losses actually sustained within the year and not compensated by insurance or otherwise, including a reasonable allowance for depreciation by use, wear and tear of property, if any, and in the case of mines a reasonable allowance for depletion of ores and all other natural deposits, not to exceed 5 per centum of the gross value at the mine of the output for the year for which the computation is made, and in case of insurance companies the net addition, if any, required by law to be made within the year to reserve funds and the sums other than dividends paid within the year on policy and annuity contracts: Provided, That mutual fire insurance companies requiring their members to make premium deposits to provide for losses and expenses shall not return as income any portion of the premium deposits returned to their policyholders, but shall return as taxable income all income received by them from all other sources plus such portions of the premium deposits as are retained by the companies for purposes other than the payment of losses and expenses and reinsurance reserves: Provided further, That mutual marine insurance companies shall include in their return of gross income gross premiums collected and received by them less amounts paid for reinsurance, but shall be entitled to include in deductions from gross income amounts repaid to policyholders on account of premiums previously paid by them and interest paid upon such amounts between the ascertainment thereof and the payment thereof and life insurance companies shall not include as income in any year such portion of any actual premium received from any individual policyholder as shall have been paid back or credited to such individual policyholder, or treated as an abatement of premium of such individual policyholder, within such year; (third) the amount of interest accrued and paid within the year on its indebtedness to an amount of such indebtedness not exceeding one-half of the sum of its interest bearing indebtedness and its paid-up capital stock outstanding at the close of the year, or if no capital stock, the amount of interest paid within the year on an amount of its indebtedness not exceeding the amount of capital employed in the business at the close of the year: Provided, That in case of indebtedness wholly secured by collateral the subject of sale in ordinary business of such corporation, joint-stock company or association, the total interest secured and paid by such company, corporation or association within the year on any such indebtedness may be deducted as a part of its expense of doing business: Provided further, That in the case of bonds or other indebtedness which have been issued with a guaranty that the interest payable thereon shall be free from taxation, no deduction for the payment of the tax herein imposed shall be allowed, and in the case of a bank, banking association, loan or trust company, interest paid within the year on deposits or on moneys received for investment and secured by interest bearing certificates of indebtedness issued by such bank, banking association, loan or trust company; (fourth) all sums paid by it within the year for taxes imposed under the authority of the United States or of any state or territory thereof, or imposed by the government of any foreign country: Provided, That in the case of a corporation, joint-stock company or association, or insurance company, organized, authorized or existing under the laws of any foreign country, such net income shall be ascertained by deducting from the gross amount of its income accrued within the year from business transacted and capital invested within the United States, (first) all the ordinary and necessary expenses actually paid within

the year out of earnings in the maintenance and operation of its business and property within the United States, including rentals or other payments required to be made as a condition to the continued use or possession of property; (second) all losses actually sustained within the year in business conducted by it within the United States and not compensated by insurance or otherwise, including a reasonable allowance for depreciation by use, wear and tear of property, if any, and in the case of mines a reasonable allowance for depletion of ores and all other natural deposits, not to exceed 5 per centum of the gross value at the mine of the output for the year for which the computation is made; and in case of insurance companies the net addition, if any, required by law to be made within the year to reserve funds and the sums other than dividends paid within the year on policy and annuity contracts: Provided further, That mutual fire insurance companies requiring their members to make premium deposits to provide for losses and expenses shall not return as income any portion of the premium deposits returned to their policyholders, but shall return as taxable income all income received by them from all other sources plus such portions of the premium deposits as are retained by the companies for purposes other than the payment of losses and expenses and reinsurance reserves: Provided further, That mutual marine insurance companies shall include in their return of gross income gross premiums collected and received by them less amounts paid for reinsurance, but shall be entitled to include in deductions from gross income amounts repaid to policyholders on account of premiums previously paid by them, and interest paid upon such amounts between the ascertainment thereof and the payment thereof and life insurance companies shall not include as income in any year such portion of any actual premium received from any individual policyholder as shall have been paid back or credited to such individual policyholder, or treated as an abatement of premium of such individual policyholder, within such year; (third) the amount of interest accrued and paid within the year on its indebtedness to an amount of such indebtedness not exceeding the proportion of one-half of the sum of its interest bearing indebtedness and its paid-up capital stock outstanding at the close of the year, or if no capital stock, the capital employed in the business at the close of the year which the gross amount of its income for the year from business transacted and capital invested within the United States bears to the gross amount of its income derived from all sources within and without the United States: Provided, That in the case of bonds or other indebtedness which have been issued with a guaranty that the interest payable thereon shall be free from taxation, no deduction for the payment of the tax herein imposed shall be allowed; (fourth) all sums paid by it within the year for taxes imposed under the authority of the United States or of any state or territory thereof or the District of Columbia. In the case of assessment insurance companies, whether domestic or foreign, the actual deposit of sums with state or territorial officers, pursuant to law, as additions to guarantee or reserve funds shall be treated as being payments required by law to reserve funds.

(c) The tax herein imposed shall be computed upon its entire net income accrued within each preceding calendar year ending Dec. 31: Provided, however, That for the year ending Dec. 31, 1913, said tax shall be imposed upon its entire net income accrued within that portion of said year from March 1 to Dec. 31, both dates inclusive, to be ascertained by taking five-sixths of its entire net income for said calendar year: Provided further, That any corporation, joint-stock company or association or insurance company subject to this tax may designate the last day of any month in the year as the day of the closing of its fiscal year and shall be entitled to have the tax payable by it computed upon the basis of the net income ascertained as herein provided for the year ending on the day so designated in the year preceding the date of assessment instead of upon the basis of the net income for the calendar year preceding the date of assessment, and it shall give notice of the day it

has thus designated as the closing of its fiscal year to the collector of the district in which its principal business office is located at any time not less than thirty days prior to the date upon which its annual return shall be filed. All corporations, joint-stock companies or associations and insurance companies subject to the tax herein imposed, computing taxes upon the income of the calendar year, shall, on or before the first day of March, 1914, and the first day of March in each year thereafter, and all corporations, joint-stock companies or associations and insurance companies, computing taxes upon the income of a fiscal year which it may designate in the manner hereinbefore provided, shall render a like return within sixty days after the close of its said fiscal year, and within sixty days after the close of its fiscal year in each year thereafter, or in the case of a corporation, joint-stock company or association, or insurance company, organized or existing under the laws of a foreign country, in the place where its principal business is located within the United States, in such form as the commissioner of internal revenue, with the approval of the secretary of the treasury, shall prescribe, shall render a true and accurate return under oath or affirmation of its president, vice-president, or other principal officer, and its treasurer or assistant treasurer, to the collector of internal revenue for the district in which it has its principal place of business, setting forth (first) the total amount of its paid-up capital stock outstanding, or if no capital stock, its capital employed in business, at the close of the year; (second) the total amount of its bonded and other indebtedness at the close of the year; (third) the gross amount of its income, received during such year from all sources, and if organized under the laws of a foreign country the gross amount of its income received within the year from business transacted and capital invested within the United States; (fourth) the total amount of all its ordinary and necessary expenses paid out of earnings in the maintenance and operation of the business and properties of such corporation, joint-stock company or association, or insurance company within the year, stating separately all rentals or other payments required to be made as a condition to the continued use or possession of property, and if organized under the laws of a foreign country the amount so paid in the maintenance and operation of its business within the United States; (fifth) the total amount of all losses actually sustained during the year and not compensated by insurance or otherwise, stating separately any amounts allowed for depreciation of property, and in case of insurance companies the net addition, if any, required by law to be made within the year to reserve funds and the sums other than dividends paid within the year on policy and annuity contracts: Provided further, That mutual fire insurance companies requiring their members to make premium deposits to provide for losses and expenses shall not return as income any portion of the premium deposits returned to their policyholders, but shall return as taxable income all income received by them from all other sources plus such portions of the premium deposits as are retained by the companies for purposes other than the payment of losses and expenses and reinsurance reserves; Provided further, That mutual marine insurance companies shall include in their return of gross income gross premiums collected and received by them less amounts paid for reinsurance, but shall be entitled to include in deductions from gross income amounts repaid to policyholders on account of premiums previously paid by them, and interest paid upon such amounts between the ascertainment thereof and the payment thereof and life insurance companies shall not include as income in any year such portion of any actual premium received from any individual policyholder as shall have been paid back or credited to such individual policyholder, or treated as an abatement of premium of such individual policyholder, within such year; and in case of a corporation, joint-stock company or association, or insurance company, organized under the laws of a foreign country, all losses actually sustained by it during the year in business conducted by it within the United States, not compensated by insurance

or otherwise, stating separately any amounts allowed for depreciation of property, and in case of insurance companies the net addition, if any, required by law to be made within the year to reserve funds and the sums other than dividends paid within the year on policy and annuity contracts: Provided further, That mutual fire insurance companies requiring their members to make premium deposits to provide for losses and expenses shall not return as income any portion of the premium deposits returned to their policyholders, but shall return as taxable income all income received by them from all other sources plus such portions of the premium deposits as are retained by the companies for purposes other than the payment of losses and expenses and reinsurance reserves; Provided further, That mutual marine insurance companies shall include in their return of gross income gross premiums collected and received by them less amounts paid for reinsurance, but shall be entitled to include in deductions from gross income amounts repaid to policyholders on account of premiums previously paid by them and interest paid upon such amounts between the ascertainment thereof and the payment thereof and life insurance companies shall not include as income in any year such portion of any actual premium received from any individual policyholder as shall have been paid back or credited to such individual policyholder, or treated as an abatement of premium of such individual policyholder, within such year; (sixth) the amount of interest accrued and paid within the year on its bonded or other indebtedness not exceeding one-half of the sum of its interest bearing indebtedness and its paid up capital stock, outstanding at the close of the year, or if no capital stock, the amount of interest paid within the year on an amount of indebtedness not exceeding the amount of capital employed in the business at the close of the year, and in the case of a bank, banking association, or trust company, stating separately all interest paid by it within the year on deposits; or in case of a corporation, joint stock company or association, or insurance company, organized under the laws of a foreign country, interest so paid on its bonded or other indebtedness to an amount of such bonded or other indebtedness not exceeding the proportion of its paid up capital stock outstanding at the close of the year, or if no capital stock, the amount of capital employed in the business at the close of the year, which the gross amount of its income for the year from business transacted and capital invested within the United States bears to the gross amount of its income derived from all sources within and without the United States; (seventh) the amount paid by it within the year for taxes imposed under the authority of the United States and separately the amount so paid by it for taxes imposed by the government of any foreign country; (eighth) the net income of such corporation, joint-stock company or association, or insurance company, after making the deductions in this subsection authorized. All such returns shall be transmitted forthwith by the collector to the commissioner of internal revenue.

All assessments shall be made and the several corporations, joint stock companies or associations, and insurance companies shall be notified of the amount for which they are respectively liable on or before the first day of June of each successive year, and said assessment shall be paid on or before the thirtieth day of June: Provided, That every corporation, joint stock company or association and insurance company, computing taxes upon the income of the fiscal year which it may designate in the manner hereinbefore provided, shall pay the taxes due under its assessment within 120 days after the date upon which it is required to file its list or return of income for assessment; except in cases of refusal or neglect to make such return, and in cases of false or fraudulent returns, in which cases the commissioner of internal revenue shall, upon the discovery thereof, at any time within three years after said return is due, make a return upon information obtained as provided for in this section or by existing law, and the assessment made by the commissioner of internal revenue thereon shall be paid by such corporation, joint-stock company or

association, or insurance company immediately upon notification of the amount of such assessment; and to any sum or sums due and unpaid after the thirtieth day of June in any year, or after 120 days from the date on which the return of income is required to be made by the taxpayer, and after ten days' notice and demand thereof by the collector, there shall be added the sum of 5 per centum on the amount of tax unpaid and interest at the rate of 1 per centum per month upon said tax from the time the same becomes due.

(d) When the assessment shall be made, as provided in this section, the returns, together with any corrections thereof which may have been made by the commissioner, shall be filed in the office of the commissioner of internal revenue and shall constitute public records and be open to inspection as such: Provided, That any and all such returns shall be open to inspection only upon the order of the president, under rules and regulations to be prescribed by the secretary of the treasury and approved by the president: Provided further, That the proper officers of any state imposing a general income tax may, upon the request of the governor thereof, have access to said returns or to an abstract thereof, showing the name and income of each such corporation, joint stock company, association or insurance company, at such times and in such manner as the secretary of the treasury may prescribe.

If any of the corporations, joint-stock companies or associations, or insurance companies aforesaid, shall refuse or neglect to make a return at the time or times hereinbefore specified in each year, or shall render a false or fraudulent return, such corporation, joint-stock company or association, or insurance company shall be liable to a penalty of not exceeding $10,000.

H. That the word "State" or "United States" when used in this section shall be construed to include any territory, Alaska, the District of Columbia, Porto Rico and the Philippine Islands, when such construction is necessary to carry out its provisions.

I. That sections 3167, 3172, 3173 and 3176 of the revised statutes of the United States as amended are hereby amended so as to read as follows:

"Sec. 3167. It shall be unlawful for any collector, deputy collector, agent, clerk or other officer or employe of the United States to divulge or to make known in any manner whatever not provided by law to any person the operations, style of work or apparatus of any manufacturer or producer visited by him in the discharge of his official duties, or the amount or source of income, profits, losses, expenditures or any particle thereof, set forth or disclosed in any income return by any person or corporation, or to permit any income return or copy thereof or any book containing any abstract or particulars thereof to be seen or examined by any person except as provided by law; and it shall be unlawful for any person to print or publish in any manner whatever not provided by law any income return or any part thereof or the amount or source of income, profits, losses or expenditures appearing in any income return; and any offense against the foregoing provision shall be a misdemeanor and be punished by a fine not exceeding $1,000 or by imprisonment not exceeding one year, or both, at the discretion of the court; and if the offender be an officer or employe of the United States he shall be dismissed from office and be incapable thereafter of holding any office under the government.

"Sec. 3172. Every collector shall, from time to time, cause his deputies to proceed through every part of his district and inquire after and concerning all persons therein who are liable to pay any internal revenue tax and all persons owning or having the care and management of any objects liable to pay any tax, and to make a list of such persons and enumerate said objects.

"Sec. 3173. It shall be the duty of any person, partnership, firm, association or corporation, made liable to any duty, special tax or other tax imposed by law, when not otherwise provided for, in case of a special tax, on or before the thirty-first day of July in each year, in case of income tax on or before the first day of March in each year, and in other cases before the day on which the taxes accrue, to make a list or return, verified by oath or affirmation, to the collector or a deputy collector of the district where located, of the articles or objects, including the amount of annual income charged with a duty or tax, the quantity of goods, wares and merchandise made or sold and charged with a tax, the several rates and aggregate amount, according to the forms and regulations to be prescribed by the commissioner of internal revenue, with the approval of the secretary of the treasury, for which such person, partnership, firm, association or corporation is liable: Provided, That if any person liable to pay any duty or tax, or owning, possessing or having the care or management of property, goods, wares and merchandise, articles or objects liable to pay any duty, tax or license, shall fail to make and exhibit a list or return required by law, but shall consent to disclose the particulars of any and all the property, goods, wares and merchandise, articles and objects liable to pay any duty or tax, or any business or occupation liable to pay any tax as aforesaid, then, and in that case, it shall be the duty of the collector or deputy collector to make such list or return, which, being distinctly read, consented to and signed and verified by oath or affirmation by the person so owning, possessing or having the care and management as aforesaid, may be received as the list of such person: Provided further, That in case no annual list or return has been rendered by such person to the collector or deputy collector as required by law, and the person shall be absent from his or her residence or place of business at the time the collector or a deputy collector shall call for the annual list or return, it shall be the duty of such collector or deputy collector to leave at such place of residence or business, with some one of suitable age and discretion, if such be present, otherwise to deposit in the nearest postoffice, a note or memorandum addressed to such person, requiring him or her to render to such collector or deputy collector the list or return required by law within ten days from the date of such note or memorandum, verified by oath or affirmation. And if any person, on being notified or required as aforesaid, shall refuse or neglect to render such list or return within the time required as aforesaid, or whenever any person who is required to deliver a monthly or other return of objects subject to tax fails to do so at the time required, or delivers any return which, in the opinion of the collector is false or fraudulent, or contains any undervaluation or understatement, it shall be lawful for the collector to summon such person, or any other person having possession, custody or care of books of account containing entries relating to the business of such person, or any other person he may deem proper, to appear before him and produce such books, at a time and place named in the summons, and to give testimony or answer interrogatories, under oath, respecting any objects liable to tax or the returns thereof. The collector may summon any person residing or found within the state in which his district lies; and when the person intended to be summoned does not reside and cannot be found within such state, he may enter any collection district where such person may be found and there make the examination herein authorized. And to this end he may there exercise all the authority which he might lawfully exercise in the district for which he was commissioned.

"Sec. 3176. When any person, corporation, company or association refuses or neglects to render any return or list required by law, or renders a false or fraudulent return or list, the collector or any deputy collector shall make, according to the best information which he can obtain, including that derived from the evidence elicited by the examination of the collector, and on his own view and information, such list or return, according to the form prescribed, of the income, property and objects liable to tax owned or possessed or under the care or management of such person or corporation, company or association, and the commissioner of internal revenue shall assess all taxes not paid by stamps, including the amount, if any, due for special tax, income or other tax, and in case of any return of a false or fraudulent list or valuation intentionally he shall add 100 per centum to such tax; and in case of a refusal or neglect, except in cases

of sickness or absence, to make a list or return, or to verify the same as aforesaid, he shall add 50 per centum to such tax. In case of neglect occasioned by sickness or absence as aforesaid the collector may allow such further time for making and delivering such list or return as he may deem necessary, not exceeding thirty days. The amount so added to the tax shall be collected at the same time and in the same manner as the tax unless the neglect or falsity is discovered after the tax has been paid, in which case the amount so added shall be collected in the same manner as the tax; and the list or return so made and subscribed by such collector or deputy collector shall be held prima facie good and sufficient for all legal purposes."

J. That it shall be the duty of every collector of internal revenue, to whom any payment of any taxes other than the tax represented by an adhesive stamp or other engraved stamp is made under the provisions of this section, to give to the person making such payment a full written or printed receipt, expressing the amount paid and the particular account for which such payment was made; and whenever such payment is made such collector shall, if required, give a separate receipt for each tax paid by any debtor, on account of payments made to or to be made by him to separate creditors in such form that such debtor can conveniently produce the same separately to his several creditors in satisfaction of their respective demands to the amounts specified in such receipts; and such receipts shall be sufficient evidence in favor of such debtor to justify him in withholding the amount therein expressed from his next payment to his creditor; but such creditor may, upon giving to his debtor a full written receipt, acknowledging the payment to him of whatever sum may be actually paid, and accepting the amount of tax paid as aforesaid (specifying the same) as a further satisfaction of the debt to that amount, require the surrender to him of such collector's receipt.

K. That jurisdiction is hereby conferred upon the district courts of the United States for the district within which any person summoned under this section to appear to testify or to produce books shall reside, to compel such attendance, production of books and testimony by appropriate process.

L. That all administrative, special and general provisions of law, including the laws in relation to the assessment, remission, collection and refund of internal revenue taxes not heretofore specifically repealed and not inconsistent with the provisions of this section, are hereby extended and made applicable to all the provisions of this section and to the tax herein imposed.

M. That the provisions of this section shall extend to Porto Rico and the Philippine Islands: Provided, That the administration of the law and the collection of the taxes imposed in Porto Rico and the Philippine Islands shall be by the appropriate internal revenue officers of those governments, and all revenues collected in Porto Rico and the Philippine Islands thereunder shall accrue intact to the general governments thereof, respectively: And provided further, That the jurisdiction in this section conferred upon the district courts of the United States shall, so far as the Philippine Islands are concerned, be vested in the courts of the first instance of said islands: And provided

further, That nothing in this section shall be held to exclude from the computation of the net income the compensation paid any official by the governments of the District of Columbia, Porto Rico and the Philippine Islands or the political subdivisions thereof.

N. That for the purpose of carrying into effect the provisions of section II of this act, and to pay the expenses of assessing and collecting the income tax therein imposed, and to pay such sums as the commissioner of internal revenue, with the approval of the secretary of the treasury, may deem necessary, for information, detection and bringing to trial and punishment persons guilty of violating the provisions of this section, or conniving at the same. In cases where such expenses are not otherwise provided for by law, there is hereby appropriated out of any money in the treasury not otherwise appropriated for the fiscal year ending June 30, 1914, the sum of $800,000, and the commissioner of internal revenue, with the approval of the secretary of the treasury, is authorized to appoint and pay from this appropriation all necessary officers, agents, inspectors, deputy collectors, clerks, messengers and janitors, and to rent such quarters, purchase such supplies, equipment, mechanical devices and other articles as may be necessary for employment or use in the District of Columbia or any collection district in the United States, or any of the territories thereof: Provided, That no agent paid from this appropriation shall receive compensation at a rate higher than that now received by travelling agents on accounts in the internal revenue service, and no inspector shall receive a compensation higher than $5 a day and $3 additional in lieu of subsistence, and no deputy collector, clerk, messenger or other employe shall be paid at a rate of compensation higher than the rate now being paid for the same or similar work in the internal revenue service.

In the office of the commissioner of internal revenue at Washington, District of Columbia, there shall be appointed by the commissioner of internal revenue, with the approval of the secretary of the treasury, one additional deputy commissioner, at a salary of $4,000 per annum; two heads of divisions, whose compensation shall not exceed $2,500 per annum; and such other clerks, messengers and employes, and to rent such quarters and to purchase such supplies as may be necessary: Provided, That for a period of two years from and after the passage of this act the force of agents, deputy collectors, inspectors and other employes not including the clerical force below the grade of chief of division employed in the bureau of internal revenue in the city of Washington, District of Columbia, authorized by this section of this act shall be appointed by the commissioner of internal revenue, with the approval of the secretary of the treasury, under such rules and regulations as may be fixed by the secretary of the treasury to insure faithful and competent service, and with such compensation as the commissioner of internal revenue may fix, with the approval of the secretary of the treasury, within the limitations herein prescribed: Provided further, That the force authorized to carry out the provisions of section II of this act, when not employed as herein provided, shall be employed on general internal revenue work.

THE SMITHSONIAN INSTITUTION IN WASHINGTON.

The Smithsonian institution was established by statute in 1846, under the terms of the will of James Smithson, who bequeathed his fortune in 1826 to the United States for the "increase and diffusion of knowledge among men." From the income of the fund a building, known as the Smithsonian building, was erected in Washington, D. C., on land given by the United States. The institution is legally an establishment having as its members the president and vice-president of the United States, the chief justice and the president's cabinet. It is governed by a board of regents consisting of the vice-president, the chief justice, three members of the United States senate, three members of the house of representatives and six citizens appointed by joint resolution of congress. It

is under the immediate direction of the secretary of the Smithsonian institution, who is the executive officer of the board and the director of the institution's activities. The institution aids investigators by making grants for research and exploration, providing for lectures, initiating scientific projects and publishing scientific papers. It has administrative charge of the national museum, the national gallery of art, the international exchange service, the national zoological park, the astrophysical observatory and the regional bureau for the international catalogue of scientific literature. The institution's original endowment of $541,000 has been increased by gifts and accumulated interest to $987,000, yielding an annual income of $58,375. The secretary of the institution is Charles D. Walcott.

MEN OF THE YEAR.

BRADY, James Henry—Born in Indiana county, Pa., June 12, 1862; educated in Olathe (Kas.) high school and state normal school at Leavenworth, Kas.; removed to Idaho; president Idaho Consolidated Power company; chairman advisory board of National Council of Woman Voters; republican; chairman state central committee, 1904-1908; governor of Idaho, 1909-1911; elected United States senator, 1913; term expires, 1915.

Copyright, Harris & Ewing, Washington

BRIDGES, Robert—Born in England Oct. 23, 1844; educated at Eton and Corpus Christi college, Oxford; after some time spent in travel studied medicine at St. Bartholomew's, London; served as physician there and in other London hospitals; retired in 1882; wrote many poems, essays and plays; author of "The Growth of Love," "Prometheus the Firegiver," "Eros and Psyche," etc.; appointed poet laureate of Britain in 1913.

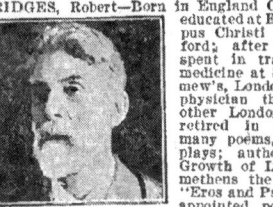

American Press assn., New York, N. Y.

BURKE, John—Born in Keokuk county, Iowa, Feb. 25, 1859; educated in public schools and in law department of the State University of Iowa, practiced for two years in Des Moines, Ia., removing to North Dakota in 1888; County judge Rolette county, 1889-1891, 1896-1898; democrat; member of assembly, 1891-1893 (house), 1893-1895 (senate); governor of North Dakota, three terms, 1907-1909, 1909-1911, 1911-1913; U. S. treasurer, March, 1913.

Copyright, Clinedinst, Washington.

BURLEIGH, Edwin C.—Born in Linneus, Me., Nov. 27, 1843; educated in common schools and Houlton academy; became publisher of Kennebec Journal, 1887; state land agent, 1876-1878; state treasurer, 1885-1888; governor, 1889-1892; republican in politics; elected to 55th, 56th, 57th, 58th, 59th, 60th and 61st congresses; primary nominee for United States senator in 1912 and elected by legislature Jan. 15, 1913; term expires in 1919.

Copyright, Harris & Ewing, Washington

CAMINETTI, Anthony—Born in Jackson, Cal., July 30, 1854; educated in schools of Jackson, Oakland and San Francisco; admitted to bar; democrat; district attorney of Amador county, Cal., 1877-1882; democrat; member of state assembly and of senate several terms; member of congress, 1891-1895; author of Caminetti mining law; student of immigration and other sociological problems; appointed United States commissioner immigration, 1913.

Bushnell Photo.

CAMPBELL, Edward K.—Born in Washington county, Virginia, April 17, 1858; attended Emory and Henry college, 1875-1876; studied law in the University of Virginia, 1882-1883; admitted to the bar in Virginia, 1883; removed to Birmingham, Ala., 1884, becoming senior member of firm of Campbell & Johnston; member democratic state executive committee; appointed chief justice United States Court of Claims May 1, 1913.

Copyright, Harris & Ewing, Washington

COLT, Le Baron Bradford—Born in Dedham, Mass., June 25, 1846; graduated from Yale university, 1868; admitted to bar, 1870; practiced law in Chicago, 1872-1874; removed to Bristol, R. I., 1875; member house of representatives, Rhode Island, 1879-1881; United States District judge, 1881-1884; United States Circuit judge, 1884-1913; republican; elected United States senator in January, 1913, to succeed George P. Wetmore.

Copyright, Clinedinst, Washington.

DAVIES, Joseph Edward—Born in Watertown, Wis., Nov. 29, 1876; educated in public schools and University of Wisconsin, graduating in 1898; admitted to bar, 1901; elected prosecuting attorney of Jefferson county, Wis., 1902; chairman democratic state central committee, 1910-1911; member democratic national committee, 1911-1913; appointed commissioner of corporations by President Woodrow Wilson in April, 1913.

Copyright, Harris & Ewing, Washington

DOCKERY, Alexander Monroe—Born in Daviess county, Missouri, Feb. 11, 1845; educated in common schools and Macon academy; studied medicine and practiced in Chillicothe, Mo., 1866-1874; removed to Gallatin, Mo., and entered banking business; mayor, 1881-1883; chairman democratic state convention, 1886, 1906; member of 48th to 55th congresses; governor of Missouri, 1901-1905; appointed third assistant postmaster-general, 1913.

Copyright, Harris & Ewing, Washington

FALL, Albert Bacon—Born in Frankfort, Ky., Nov. 26, 1861; educated in country schools; studied law and practiced law 1889-1904, making a specialty of Mexican law; engaged in farming and stock raising in New Mexico; member of territorial legislature of New Mexico several times; also associate justice Supreme court and attorney-general; republican; elected United States senator 1912 and 1913.

Copyright, Harris & Ewing, Washington

GARDNER, Washington—Born in Morrow county, Ohio, Feb. 16, 1845; served in civil war, 1861-1865; graduated from Ohio Wesleyan university, 1870, and Albany Law school, 1876; practiced in Grand Rapids, Mich.; professor in Albion college, 1889-1894; republican; secretary of state, Michigan, 1894-1899; member of congress, 3d Michigan district, 1899-1911; elected commander-in-chief Grand Army of the Republic, 1913.

American Press assn., New York, N.Y.

GERARD, James Watson—Born in Geneseo, N. Y., 1867; educated in private schools and Columbia university; studied law and began practice in New York city in 1892, becoming a partner in the firm of Bowers & Sands; associate justice of the Supreme court of New York, 1908-1911; officer in New York national guard, 1890-1900; chairman democratic campaign committee, New York county, four years; ambassador to Germany, 1913.

American Press assn., New York, N.Y.

GOFF, Nathan—Born in Clarksburg, W. Va., Feb. 9, 1843; educated at Northwestern Virginia academy, Georgetown college and University of the City of New York; served in civil war, 1861-1865; admitted to the bar, 1866; republican; member of West Virginia assembly, 1867; U. S. district attorney, 1868-1881; secretary of the navy, 1881; U. S. Circuit judge, 1892-1911; judge U. S. Court of Appeals, 1912-1913; elected U. S. senator, 1913.

Photo by Curtis M. Bell, Washington.

GUTHRIE, George Wilkins—Born in Pittsburgh, Pa., Sept. 5, 1848; educated in University of Pittsburgh; democrat; associate counsel for Tilden electors before Florida returning board, 1876; assistant secretary of democratic national convention in Chicago, 1884; delegate to democratic national convention, 1904; mayor of Pittsburgh, 1906-1909; member Pittsburgh chamber of commerce; appointed ambassador to Japan in 1913.

Copyright, Harris & Ewing, Washington

HARRISON, Francis Burton—Born in New York, N. Y., Dec. 18, 1873; graduated from Yale university, 1895, and from New York Law school, 1897; instructor in New York Law school, 1897-1899; served in Spanish-American war as a private and as assistant adjutant-general; democrat; elected to 58th congress and to the 60th, 61st, 62d and 63d congresses; appointed governor-general of the Philippines, 1913, by President Wilson.

Copyright, Harris & Ewing, Washington

HOLLIS, Henry French—Born in West Concord, N. H., Aug. 30, 1869; graduated from Harvard university, 1892; studied law in same institution and under Harry G. Sargent and William L. Foster in Concord; admitted to the bar, 1893; practiced in Concord, 1893-1913; democratic candidate for congress, 1900, and for governor, 1902 and 1904; member of democratic state central committee, 1900-1913; elected United States senator, 1913.

Copyright, Harris & Ewing, Washington

HUGHES, William—Born in Ireland, April 3, 1872; educated in public schools and business college; served in 2d New Jersey volunteers in Spanish-American war in 1898; on return home studied law and was admitted to practice in 1900; opened law office in Paterson, N. J.; active in democratic politics; elected to the 58th, 60th, 61st and 62d congresses; elected United States senator in 1913; term expires in 1919.

American Press assn., New York, N.Y.

LANE, Harry—Born in Corvallis, Benton county, Ore., Aug. 28, 1855; educated in public schools; studied medicine and was graduated in 1876; served as superintendent of the Oregon state insane asylum from July, 1887, to August, 1891; served two consecutive terms as mayor of the city of Portland, Ore., from July 1, 1905, to June 30, 1909; democrat; elected United States senator in 1913 for the term ending March 3, 1919.

American Press assn., New York, N.Y.

LEWIS, James Hamilton—Born in Danville, Va., May 18, 1866; educated in Houghton college and University of Virginia; admitted to bar in Savannah, Ga., 1884; moved to Seattle, Wash., 1886; democrat; elected to territorial senate; member of congress from Washington, 1887-1899; served on staff of F. D. Grant in Cuba, 1898; removed to Chicago, 1903; corporation counsel, 1905-1907; elected United States senator March 26, 1913.

American Press, assn., New York, N.Y.

MARBLE, John Hobart—Born in Ashland, Neb., Feb. 26, 1868; educated in public schools of Nebraska and South Dakota and University of Nebraska; admitted to the bar in 1893; practiced in San Francisco, Cal., 1903-1906; attorney for interstate commerce commission, 1906-1912; secretary of same body, 1912-1913; attorney for senate in Lorimer case, 1911-1912; appointed member interstate commerce commission, 1913.

Copyright, Harris & Ewing, Washington

MARVIN, Charles F.—Born in Putnam, O., Oct. 7, 1858; educated in public schools and in Ohio State university, graduating in 1883; instructor in mechanical drawing and physical laboratory practice, 1879-1883; appointed on civilian corps of signal or weather service, 1884; became head of instrument division in weather bureau, 1888; author of many scientific articles on meteorological subjects; appointed chief of weather bureau in 1913.

Copyright, Harris & Ewing, Washington

METCALFE, Richard Lee—Born near Upper Alton, Ill., Oct. 11, 1861; educated in public schools; learned printing business on country newspaper; reporter on Omaha World-Herald, 1888; entered actively into politics, supporting Mr. Bryan and his policies; editor Omaha World-Herald, 1896-1905; associate editor of The Commoner; appointed member of Panama canal commission by President Wilson in June, 1913.

American Press assn., New York, N.Y.

MILLER, Adolph C.—Born in San Francisco, Cal., Jan. 7, 1866; educated in University of California and Harvard university; taught history and politics in University of California, 1890-1891, and political economy and finance at Cornell, 1891-1892; professor of finance, University of Chicago, 1892-1902; professor of economics and commerce, University of California, 1902-1913; appointed assistant secretary of commerce, April 30, 1913.

Copyright, Harris & Ewing, Washington

MORGENTHAU, Henry—Born in Mannheim, Germany, April 26, 1856; came to America, 1865; educated in public schools and College of the City of New York; studied law in Columbia university, began practice in 1877 and was a member of the firm of Lachman, Morgenthau & Goldsmith, New York, N. Y., from 1879 to 1899; became interested in banking and industrial enterprises; appointed minister to Turkey, 1913.

Copyright, Harris & Ewing, Washington

M'GINTY, George Banks—Born Sept. 8, 1873, in Monroe county, Georgia; educated at Emory college, Oxford, Ga.; studied law but did not practice, preferring to enter railroad service; worked for Atlantic Coast line, Georgia railroad and Southern railroad; connected with bureau of animal industry, 1906-1908; entered service of interstate commerce commission in Washington, D. C.; made secretary of commission in 1913.

Copyright, Harris & Ewing, Washington

M'MILLIN, Benton—Born in Monroe county, Kentucky, Sept. 11, 1845; received academic education; admitted to bar and began practice at Celina, Tenn., 1871, later removing to Carthage, same state; democrat; member of house of representatives, 1874; special judge of Circuit court, 1877; member of 46th to 55th congresses; elected governor of Tennessee for two terms, 1899-1903; appointed minister to Peru, 1913.

New York Herald service.

NORRIS, George William—Born in Sandusky county, Ohio, July 11, 1861; educated in common schools, Baldwin-university and Northern Indiana Normal school; taught school; studied law; admitted to bar in 1883; removed to Nebraska, 1885; elected district attorney of 14th district, 1895 and 1899; elected to the 58th, 59th, 60th, 61st and 62d congresses as a republican; elected United States senator, 1913; term expires 1919.

American Press assn., New York, N.Y.

OSBORNE, John E.—Born in Westport, N. Y., June 19, 1864; educated in high school and University of Vermont; removed to Rawlins, Wyo., where he established a wholesale and retail drug house; member of territorial legislature; mayor of Rawlins, 1888; democrat; governor of Wyoming, 1893-1897; member 55th congress, 1897-1899; appointed first assistant secretary of state April 15, 1913, by President Wilson.

Copyright, Harris & Ewing, Washington

PAGE, Thomas Nelson—Born in Hanover county, Virginia, April 23, 1853; educated in public schools and Washington and Lee university; practiced law in Richmond, Va., 1875-1893; author of "In Ole Virginia," "Two Little Confederates," "Marse Chan," "Red Rock," "Under the Crust," "Robert E. Lee, the Southerner" and many other books; appointed ambassador to Italy, by President Wilson, June 17, 1913.

Copyright, Harris & Ewing, Washington

PAGE, Walter Hines—Born in Cary, N. C., Aug. 15, 1855; educated at Randolph-Macon college and Johns Hopkins university; editor of the Forum, 1890-1895; literary adviser of Houghton, Mifflin & Co., 1895-1899; editor of the Atlantic Monthly, 1896-1899; editor of the World's Work, 1900-1913; author; member of publishing firm of Doubleday, Page & Co., 1899-1913; appointed ambassador to Great Britain, 1913, by President Wilson.

Copyright, Harris & Ewing, Washington

PENFIELD, Frederic Courtland—Born in Connecticut, April 23, 1855; graduate of Russell Military school, New Haven; studied in Germany; served five years on editorial staff of Hartford Courant; vice consul-general in London, 1885; consul-general in Egypt, 1893-1897, with rank of minister resident; authority and writer on matters relating to diplomacy and international politics; appointed ambassador to Austria-Hungary, 1913.

American Press assn., New York, N.Y.

POINCARE, Raymond—Born in Bar-le-Duc, France, Aug. 20, 1860; educated at the Lycee de Bar-le-Duc and the Lycee de Louis le Grand; studied law and practiced in Paris; minister of public instruction, 1893 and 1895, and of finances, 1894 and 1906; chosen member of French academy, 1909, for his work in literature; prime minister of France, 1911-1913; elected president of France Jan. 17, 1913; term expires in 1920.

American Press assn., New York, N.Y.

POST, Louis Freeland—Born in Vienna, N. J., Nov. 15, 1849; admitted to New York state bar, 1870; practiced law, 1870-1874 and 1882-1890; editorial writer on New York Truth, 1874-1875; converted to Henry George single tax theory, 1881; lecturer on single tax, political and electoral reform; founded the Public in Chicago, 1898; appointed assistant secretary of department of labor, Washington, D. C., May, 1913.

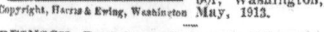
Copyright, Harris & Ewing, Washington

REINSCH, Paul Samuel—Born in Milwaukee, Wis., June 10, 1869; graduated from University of Wisconsin, 1892; studied in Berlin, Rome and Paris; assistant professor of political science in University of Wisconsin, 1899-1901, and professor in same department, 1901-1913; author of various books on historical and economic subjects; Roosevelt exchange professor in Germany, 1911-1912; appointed minister to China in July, 1913.

Copyright, Harris & Ewing, Washington

ROBINSON, John Taylor—Born in Lonoke, Ark., Aug. 26, 1872; educated in the public schools and the University of Arkansas; began practice of law, 1895; democrat, elected to general assembly of Arkansas and served in session of 1895; presidential elector for 6th congressional district, 1900; elected to the 58th, 59th, 60th, 61st and 62d congresses; elected United States senator in January, 1913; term expires March 3, 1919.

Copyright, Clinedinst, Washington.

SALTZGABER, Gaylord Miller—Born in Shelby, Richland county, Ohio, March 14, 1846; educated in common schools and Eastman college, Poughkeepsie, N. Y.; served four years with 3d Ohio cavalry in civil war; admitted to the bar in 1869; democrat; member of Ohio senate, 1876-1880; mayor of Van Wert, O.; member of Ohio democratic central committee; appointed commissioner of pensions by President Wilson in May, 1913.

Copyright, Clinedinst, Washington

SAULSBURY, Willard—Born in Georgetown, Del., April 17, 1861; educated in common schools and University of Virginia; began practice of law in Wilmington, Del., in 1882; senior member of Saulsbury, Ponder & Morris since 1888; director in Wilmington street railways, electric light companies, Equitable Trust Co. and Union National bank; prominent in democratic politics; elected United States senator in 1913.

Copyright, Harris & Ewing, Washington

SHAFROTH, John Franklin—Born in Fayette, Mo., June 9, 1854; admitted to bar in 1876 and practiced at Fayette until 1879; moved to Denver, Col., in 1879; city attorney there, 1887-1891; elected to 54th and 58th congresses as a democrat; resigned from 58th congress on ground of fraud in election; governor of Colorado two terms, 1909-1911 and 1911-1913; elected United States senator in 1913; term expires in 1919.

Copyright, Clinedinst, Washington.

SHERMAN, Lawrence Yates—Born in Miami county, Ohio, Nov. 8, 1858; removed with parents to Illinois, 1859; educated in common schools; studied law and practiced at Macomb; judge McDonough county, 1886-1890; republican; member of assembly, 1897-1903; speaker of house, 1899-1903; lieutenant-governor, 1904-1908; president board of administration of state of Illinois, 1909-1913; elected United States senator March 26, 1913.

Copyright, Harris & Ewing, Washington

SHIELDS, John K.—Born at Clinchdale, Tenn., Aug. 15, 1859; received a common school education; studied law and was admitted to bar in 1879; in partnership with father until 1890 and with R. E. L. Mounteastle until 1902; chancellor twelfth chancery division, 1892-1894; justice Supreme court of Tennessee, 1902-1910, and chief justice of same court, 1910-1913; democrat; elected United States senator, Jan. 23, 1913; term expires 1919.

Copyright, Clinedinst, Washington.

SMITH, William Alden—Born in Dowagiac, Mich., May 12, 1859; educated in common schools; moved with his parents to Grand Rapids, 1872; page in Michigan house of representatives, 1872; studied law and was admitted to bar, 1883; republican; elected to 54th, 55th, 56th, 57th, 58th, 59th and 60th congresses; elected to succeed R. A. Alger as United States senator, 1907; re-elected Jan. 16, 1913; term expires March 3, 1919.
Copyright, Harris & Ewing, Washington

SPRING-RICE, Sir Cecil Arthur—Born in England, Feb. 27, 1859; educated at Eton and Balliol college, Oxford; clerk in war and foreign offices; secretary at Brussels, Washington and other embassies; charge d'affaires, Teheran, 1900; British commissioner of public debt, Cairo, 1901; minister and consul-general, Persia, 1906-1908; minister to Sweden, 1908-1913; British ambassador to the United States, 1913, succeeding James Bryce.
American Press assn., New York, N. Y.

STERLING, Thomas—Born in Fairfield county, Ohio, Feb. 21, 1851; graduated from Illinois Wesleyan university, 1875; admitted to bar in Illinois, 1878; moved to South Dakota and practiced law; member of state constitutional convention, 1883; republican; member of first state senate of South Dakota; dean of college of law in University of South Dakota, 1901-1911; elected United States senator Jan. 22, 1913; term expires 1919.
Copyright, Harris & Ewing, Washington

STONE, John Timothy—Born near Boston, Mass., Sept. 7, 1868; graduate of Amherst college, 1891, and Auburn Theological seminary, 1894; ordained in presbyterian ministry in June, 1894; held pastorates in Utica and Cortland, N. Y., and Baltimore, Md., coming to Fourth church in Chicago, May 1, 1909; author of "Footsteps in a Parish" and "Recruiting for Christ"; moderator of presbyterian general assembly, 1913.
Ilgenport Photo, Baltimore, Md.

SWAIN, Joseph—Born in Pendleton, Ind., June 16, 1857; educated at Indiana university; instructor in mathematics and biology, 1883-1885; associate professor of mathematics and professor, 1885-1891, at Indiana university; professor of mathematics at Leland Stanford, Jr., university, 1891-1893; president Indiana university, 1893-1902; president Swarthmore college since 1902; elected president of National Education association, 1913.
New York Herald service.

SWEET, Edwin F.—Born in Dansville, N. Y., Nov. 21, 1847; graduated from Yale university, 1871, and from law department of University of Michigan, 1874; mayor of Grand Rapids, Mich., 1904-1906; democrat; member of Grand Rapids board of education, 1899-1906; elected to 62d congress, 1910; ran for same office in 1912, but was defeated by Carl E. Mapes, republican; appointed assistant secretary of commerce in March, 1913.
Copyright, Harris & Ewing, Washington

TALLMAN, Clay—Born in Ionia county, Michigan, 1874; educated in common schools, Michigan Agricultural college, University of Colorado and University of Michigan; engaged in public school work, 1895-1902; began practice of law in Rhyolite, Nev., 1905; democrat; member Nevada state senate, 1908-1912; chairman democratic state central committee, 1910-1911; appointed commissioner of general land office in June, 1913.
Copyright, Harris & Ewing, Washington

TAYLOR, Graham—Born in Schenectady, N. Y., May 2, 1851; graduated from Rutgers college, 1870, and Reformed Theological seminary, 1873; pastor in Hopewell, N. Y., 1873-1880, and in Hartford, Conn., 1880-1892; professor in Chicago Theological seminary and lecturer in University of Chicago; founder of Chicago Commons Social Settlement, 1894; president Chicago School of Civics; elected president of National Conference of Charities and Correction, 1913.

THOMAS, Charles Spalding—Born in Darien, Ga., Dec. 6, 1849; removed to Michigan in boyhood; studied law, receiving degree of LL. B. from the University of Michigan in 1871; practiced law in Denver, Col., from 1871 to 1879, in Leadville from 1879 to 1885 and since then in Denver; democrat; member of national committee of his party, 1884-1896; governor of Colorado, 1899-1901; elected United States senator in 1913.
Copyright, Harris & Ewing, Washington

TUMULTY, Joseph P.—Born in Jersey City, N. J., May 5, 1879; educated in parochial school and St. Peter's college in Jersey City, graduating in 1899; admitted to bar in 1902 and in 1904 entered into partnership with G. E. Cutley, under firm name of Tumulty & Cutley; member of New Jersey house of assembly, 1907-1910; private secretary to Gov. Woodrow Wilson, 1910-1912; appointed private secretary to President Wilson in 1913.
Copyright, Harris & Ewing, Washington

VAN DYKE, Henry—Born in Germantown, Vt., Nov. 10, 1852; of Dutch ancestry; graduate of Princeton university and Theological seminary; ordained in presbyterian ministry, 1879; pastor of churches in Newport, R. I., and New York, N. Y.; professor of English literature at Princeton university 1900 to 1913; author of many popular essays and poems; noted as lecturer; appointed minister to Netherlands, 1913.

American Press assn., New York, N. Y.

VAUGHAN, Victor Clarence—Born in Mount Airy, Mo., Oct. 27, 1851; educated at Mount Pleasant college, Missouri, and University of Michigan; connected with latter institution since 1875; dean of medical department since 1890; member of Michigan state board of health, 1883-1895 and since 1901; president American Association of Surgeons, 1908-1909; served in Spanish-American war; chosen president of American Medical association, 1913.

New York Herald service.

VOPICKA, Charles J.—Born in Bohemia, Nov. 3, 1857; educated in Prague high school and business college; emigrated to America, settling first in Racine, Wis., and then in Chicago, Ill., in 1881; engaged in real estate and banking business; established a brewery in 1891, becoming president and manager of concern; democrat; member of school board; appointed minister to Roumania, Servia and Bulgaria in September, 1913.

Copyright, Harris & Ewing, Washington

WALSH, Thomas J.—Born at Two Rivers, Wis., June 12, 1859; educated in public schools; served as principal of several high schools; graduated from law department of University of Wisconsin, 1884; practiced in Redfield, S. D., and later in Helena, Mont., to which place he moved in 1898; democrat; ran for congress in 1907, but was defeated; nominated for United States senator in 1912 and elected by legislature in 1913.

Copyright, Clinedinst, Washington, D.C.

WEEKS, John Wingate—Born in Lancaster, N. H., April 11, 1860; graduated from the United States naval academy, 1881; served in United States navy until 1883; served in Massachusetts naval brigade ten years, the last six years as commander; served in volunteer navy in war with Spain; alderman and mayor of Newton, Mass.; elected to 59th, 60th, 61st, 62d and 63d congresses as republican; elected United States senator, 1913.

Copyright, Clinedinst, Washington, D.C.

WILLARD, Joseph Edward—Born in Washington, D. C., May 1, 1865; graduate of Virginia Military Institute and in summer law course of the University of Virginia; practiced law; served as captain in Spanish-American war; representative in Virginia legislature, 1894-1902; lieutenant-governor, 1902-1906; corporation commissioner, 1906-1910; democrat; president Virginia Hotel company, Washington; appointed minister to Spain, 1913.

Copyright, Harris & Ewing, Washington

THE GENERAL EDUCATION BOARD.

Organized Feb. 27, 1902.

Chairman—Frederick T. Gates.
Secretary—Wallace Buttrick.
Assistant secretaries—E. C. Sage, Abraham Flexner.
Treasurer—L. G. Myers.
Members of Board—Frederick T. Gates, Walter H. Page, J. D. Rockefeller, Jr., Albert Shaw, Wallace Buttrick, Starr J. Murphy, Edwin A. Alderman, Hollis B. Frissell, Harry Pratt Judson, Charles W. Eliot, Andrew Carnegie, Edgar L. Marston, Wickliffe Rose, Jerome D. Greene, Anson Phelps Stokes, Jr.
Offices—17 Battery place, New York, N. Y.

The general education board was informally organized Feb. 27, 1902, at the suggestion of John D. Rockefeller's committee on benevolence and was given a charter by congress and formally organized in January, 1903. The plan was designed and adapted to assist Mr. Rockefeller in distributing his gifts to education and to afford a medium through which other men of means might contribute to the same end. The board, a few days after its initial meeting, received from Mr. Rockefeller the sum of $1,000,000, the use of which was to be confined to the study and promotion of education in the southern states.

June 30, 1905, the board was notified that Mr. Rockefeller would donate $10,000,000, the principal of which was to be held in perpetuity as a foundation for education, the income to be used for the benefit of institutions of learning in such manner as might be deemed best adapted to promote a comprehensive system of higher education in the United States. In 1907 Mr. Rockefeller gave the board $32,000,000 and in 1909 added $10,000,000 more to the fund. The board was authorized to distribute the principal of the fund, and all other endowment funds hitherto contributed by Mr. Rockefeller, whenever in the discretion of the members or their successors it should be deemed advisable to do so.

The charter of the board provides that the object of the corporation shall be "the promotion of education within the United States of America, without distinction of race, sex or creed."

AREAS OF OCEANS AND GREAT LAKES.

Oceans—	Sq. miles.		Sq. miles.		Sq. miles.		Sq. miles
Antarctic	5,731,350	Lakes—Baikal	13,000	Huron	23,800	Tanganyika	15,000
Arctic	4,781,000	Chad	50,000	Michigan	23,450	Victoria Nyan-	
Atlantic	34,801,400	Erie	9,960	Nyassa	12,000	za	26,500
Indian	17,084,000	Great Bear	10,000	Ontario	7,240	Winnipeg	9,000
Pacific	67,699,630	Great Slave	12,000	Superior	31,200		

RAILROADS OF THE UNITED STATES.

OPERATING STATISTICS OF PRINCIPAL SYSTEMS.

Fiscal year ended June 30, 1913

Railroad.	Mileage operated.	Operating revenues	Operating expenses	Taxes	Operating income
Atchison, Topeka & Santa Fe	8,238	$98,090,754	$63,830,683	$4,067,432	$30,192,639
Atlantic Coast Line.	4,616	36,123,072	24,635,532	1,451,477	10,036,063
Baltimore & Ohio	4,466	101,556,132	73,779,638	2,960,905	23,941,278
Boston & Maine	2,252	48,513,507	38,101,425	2,025,629	8,574,367
Central of New Jersey	676	28,405,757	16,404,861	1,521,495	10,413,790
Chesapeake & Ohio	2,333	35,085,278	24,451,560	1,375,863	9,303,934
Chicago & Alton	1,026	15,254,865	12,540,072	486,761	1,893,613
Chicago & Eastern Illinois	1,275	16,214,972	12,884,668	611,844	2,692,880
Chicago & Northwestern	7,976	83,035,921	58,252,780	3,597,160	21,197,277
Chicago, Burlington & Quincy	9,128	94,374,485	62,842,891	3,563,358	27,840,545
Chicago Great Western	1.496	14,000,618	10,260,142	439,419	3,303,350
Chicago, Indianapolis & Louisville	617	6,985,944	5,103,937	294,039	1,587,968
Chicago, Milwaukee & St Paul	9,592	94,084,055	62,883,968	3,823,832	27,551,003
Chicago, Rock Island & Pacific	7,573	67,968,961	50,316,578	2,857,693	14,611,279
Chicago, St. Paul, Minneapolis & Omaha	1,744	16,993,004	11,887,461	832,263	4,268,469
Cincinnati, Hamilton & Dayton	1,015	10,071,297	8,061,990	430,419	1,578,888
Cleveland, Cincinnati, Chicago & St Louis	2,014	33,963,300	26,859,000	1,243,042	5,867,591
Colorado & Southern	1,127	8,827,773	6,203,134	351,258	2,257,620
Delaware & Hudson	854	23,999,532	14,656,690	602,713	8,667,536
Delaware, Lackawanna & Western	958	40,518,044	25,283,231	1,748,340	14,068,848
Denver & Rio Grande	2,560	24,452,965	17,047,172	948,739	6,450,559
Duluth, South Shore & Atlantic	628	3,412,832	2,724,490	219,625	473,389
El Paso & Southwestern.	982	8,657,716	5,118,283	378,952	3,126,823
Elgin, Joliet & Eastern	824	13,350,782	7,511,495	404,905	5,434,382
Erie	1,988	53,971,813	35,379,385	1,768,396	16,509,733
Florida East Coast	642	5,037,056	3,554,608	214,519	1,252,673
Galveston, Harrisburg & San Antonio	1,338	12,065,517	9,571,536	368,085	2,080,269
Grand Rapids & Indiana	578	5,519,074	4,370,062	285,064	864,534
Great Northern	7,752	78,654,591	45,828,640	4 276,898	28,670,576
Gulf, Colorado & Santa-Fe	1,596	13,701,523	10,195,996	469,628	3,035,909
Hocking Valley	352	7,817,644	4,983,843	477,900	2,355,901
Houston & Texas Central	789	6,828,648	5,483,129	231,516	1,102,821
Illinois Central	4,763	64,280,903	50,048,911	2,903,551	11,250,848
International & Great Northern	1,160	11,260,565	8,627,480	340,000	2,372,073
Kansas City Southern	827	10,706,309	6,747,157	465,339	3,493,873
Lake Erie & Western	906	6,062,327	4,632,819	247,269	1,182,239
Lake Shore & Michigan Southern	1,872	58,272,052	38,543,617	1,831,098	18,069,373
Lehigh Valley	1,439	43,043,372	29,107,820	1,447,206	12 208,137
Long Island	399	11,641,883	8,358,028	717,822	3,080,900
Louisville & Nashville	4,923	59,465,699	44,810,880	1,761,626	12,913,621
Maine Central	1,206	11,321,406	8 246,998	548,621	2 495,393
Michigan Central	1,817	35,379,498	24,906,203	1,366,985	9,123,561
Minneapolis & St Louis	1,586	9,707,004	6,707,388	382,242	2,617,011
Minneapolis, St. Paul & Sault Ste Marie	3,976	31,763,787	18,891,257	1,764,124	11 236,024
Missouri, Kansas & Texas	3,817	32,346,258	22,808,412	1,287,903	8,194,318
Missouri Pacific	3,920	28,018 909	22,031,386	1,125,711	4,822,402
Mobile & Ohio	1,122	12,377,649	9,070,197	358,471	2,931,751
Nashville, Chattanooga & St Louis	1,231	13,317,162	10,438,783	304,072	2,569,078
New York Central & Hudson River	3,750	114,603,169	83,733,116	6,273 640	24,971,214
New York, New Haven & Hartford	2,090	68,613,560	47,227,339	3,714,756	18,316,855
New York, Chicago & St Louis	565	12,623,144	9,311,189	402,162	2,887,278
New York, Ontario & Western.	566	9,434,349	6,499,040	231,092	2,691,398
Norfolk & Western	2,035	43,739,921	28,565,813	1,452,000	13,714,806
Northern Central.	472	13,334,943	11,368,579	497,614	1,474,944
Northern Pacific	6,313	72,676,139	44,673,298	3,990,228	24,312,633
Northwestern Pacific	401	3,709,766	2,594,845	152,647	962,274
Oregon Short Line	1,975	22,019,856	11,429,802	1,438,893	9,150,865
Oregon, Washington Railroad and Navigation Co	1,917	18,204,220	12,253,139	1,191,098	4,697,113
Pennsylvania Company.	1,751	66,573,352	49,308,685	2,933,710	14,273,615
Pennsylvania Railroad Company	4,032	181,830,904	133,755,028	7,281,294	39 385,047
Pere Marquette	2,230	17,406,755	13,906,422	555,240	2,988,441
Philadelphia & Reading.	1,015	50,562,717	30,547,341	1,300,478	19,126,330
Philadelphia Baltimore & Washington	713	21,103,723	17 072,965	644,208	3,386,550
Pittsburgh, Cincinnati, Chicago & St Louis	1,472	44,530,900	34,981,707	1,685,955	7,833,777
Pittsburgh & Lake Erie	223	20,040,508	9,982,312	415,427	9,638 097
St. Louis & San Francisco	4,742	43,401,716	28,599,620	1,426 253	13,375 843
St. Louis, Iron Mountain & Southern	3,365	34,136,598	22,667,612	1,188,633	10 226 754
St Louis Southwestern	906	8,596,109	4,881,571	337,620	3,366 580
San Antonio & Aransas Pass	727	5,109,279	3,775,657	139,719	1,193,903
San Pedro, Los Angeles & Salt Lake	1 135	10,238,060	6,810,511	427,364	2,969,871
Seaboard	3 082	24,527,865	16,725,613	956,000	6,819 938
Southern	7,037	68,529,490	48,273,923	2,480,387	17,855,715
Southern Pacific	6,329	95,335,315	54,671 494	4,379,326	37,786 681
Texas & Pacific	1,885	18,078,783	14,772,780	499,442	2,583,394
Union Pacific	3,581	51,586,230	28,414,626	2 036,285	21,093 988
Vandalia	910	11 204,405	8,715,378	585,165	2 119,862
Wabash	2,515	31,769,296	24,693 489	905 892	6,115,222
Western Maryland	543	7,644,251	5,797 360	240,000	1,609 233
Western Pacific	937	6,173,628	4,500,489	278,096	1,383 408
Wheeling & Lake Erie	549	7,831,948	5,899,639	362,426	1 608 581
Yazoo & Mississippi Valley	1,373	10,999,673	8,624,819	466,491	1,911,253

PASSENGERS AND FREIGHT CARRIED AND EQUIPMENT (1912).

Railroad	Passengers	Freight—tons.	Locomotives.	Cars—Passenger.	Cars—Freight.
Atchison, Topeka & Santa Fe	10,996,525	17,378,033	1,803	1,386	49,476
Atlantic Coast Line	8,552,506	11,585,030	719	633	27,233
Baltimore & Ohio	22,178,298	64,704,070	2,194	1,231	87,907
Bessemer & Lake Erie	1,087,589	15,151,778	169	63	8,991
Boston & Maine	49,284,076	23,634,987	1,167	2,072	25,410
Buffalo, Rochester & Pittsburgh	1,942,226	10,698,149	290	105	16,625
Central of Georgia	5,253,945	5,375,309	322	258	10,303
Central of New Jersey	24,325,716	31,183,374	490	657	22,025
Chesapeake & Ohio	5,489,040	26,147,903	793	363	43,740
Chicago & Alton	3,823,772	10,123,710	316	207	11,756
Chicago & Eastern Illinois	4,594,737	13,781,958	396	192	24,536
Chicago & Northwestern	31,526,803	37,265,642	1,670	1,757	59,096
Chicago, Burlington & Quincy	22,404,120	30,111,513	1,672	1,254	55,726
Chicago Great Western	2,500,014	5,054,473	283	192	11,294
Chicago, Indiana & Southern	600,566	7,610,561	146	29	9,171
Chicago, Indianapolis & Louisville	2,083,373	3,858,084	136	111	6,769
Chicago, Milwaukee & Puget Sound	712,911	2,710,331	427	— 251	11,959
Chicago, Milwaukee & St Paul	14,177,026	26,575,784	1,385	1,258	47,228
Chicago, Rock Is'and & Pacific	18,789,698	18,546,732	1,498	1,052	39,759
Chicago, St Paul, Minneapolis & Omaha	4,263,640	6,946,804	364	321	11,433
Cincinnati, Hamilton & Dayton	2,916,466	10,973,591	246	201	11,068
Cleveland, Cincinnati, Chicago & St. Louis	7,500,350	23,808,027	794	498	25,068
Colorado & Southern	1,047,337	5,817,296	202	167	8,047
Delaware & Hudson	7,880,946	18,938,363	443	398	20,055
Delaware, Lackawanna & Western	25,975,909	21,220,291	732	864	28,383
Denver & R'o Grande	1,770,179	12,338,095	580	445	18,082
Duluth, South Shore & Atlantic	790,239	3,413,535	82	66	2,923
El Paso & Southwestern	285,505	3,782,320	157	57	3,217
Erie	25,640,228	35,544,620	1,379	1,170	49,764
Grand Trunk Western	2,141,757	3,654,363	229	73	4,340
Great Northern	8,661,645	17,455,975	1,189	1,020	47,640
Gulf, Colorado & Santa Fe	2,564,702	4,175,327	261	85	1,775
Hocking Valley	2,276,983	10,292,971	146	80	14,147
Houston & Texas Central	1,413,448	2,049,980	114	119	2,741
Illinois Central	27,005,956	26,339,149	1,458	926	56,108
International & Great Northern	1,933,152	3,269,554	157	89	3,979
Kansas City Southern	1,701,032	3,326,572	188	88	5,479
Lake Erie & Western	1,773,567	5,155,429	145	79	3,360
Lake Shore & Michigan Southern	9,721,314	37,177,963	988	696	53,066
Lehigh Valley	5,349,848	28,013,300	903	649	43,714
Long Island	36,146,654	4,020,438	181	974	1,526
Louisville & Nashville	12,312,662	30,425,132	962	806	44,429
Maine Central	4,640,398	6,793,519	218	309	9,119
Michigan Central	7,500,350	23,808,027	664	489	26,136
Minneapolis & St Louis	1,833,157	3,779,048	215	133	7,696
Minneapolis, St. Paul & Sault Ste Marie	3,715,268	11,345,513	498	368	23,184
Missouri, Kansas & Texas	3,046,576	5,952,359	512	382	22,642
Missouri Pacific	5,887,770	10,632,661	608	476	23,711
Mobile & Ohio	2,103,167	5,994,179	270	120	10,305
Nashville, Chattanooga & St. Louis	3,130,581	5,636,188	261	239	9,943
New York Central & Hudson River	49,519,075	48,571,491	2,339	2,532	70,745
New York, Chicago & St. Louis	804,509	8,394,769	248	99	12,780
New York, New Haven & Hartford	84,534,214	24,675,469	1,176	2,609	33,053
New York, Ontario & Western	2,159,564	5,944,499	214	314	6,409
New York, Susquehanna & Western	3,387,006	5,089,086	66	101	1,644
Norfolk & Western	5,517,563	26,147,903	1,010	394	42,065
Northern Central	4,951,043	21,776,931	234	167	9,493
Northern Pacific	8,661,645	17,455,975	1,416	1,152	43,220
Oregon Short Line	2,075,009	5,443,055	283	277	7,617
Oregon-Washington R & N	2,340,773	5,273,131	275	216	5,861
Pennsylvania Company	13,823,443	89,107,436	1,269	735	59,231
Pennsylvania Railroad Company	69,287,308	125,947,345	3,596	2,527	146,293
Pere Marquette	5,905,944	10,420,770	473	395	17,977
Philadelphia & Reading	26,987,719	48,742,960	989	861	40,210
Philadelphia, Baltimore & Washington	13,179,792	14,233,612	337	408	3,860
Pittsburgh & Lake Erie	4,449,540	29,760,419	244	135	24,835
Pittsburgh, Cincinnati, Chicago & St Louis	11,875,864	38,989,648	725	541	24,969
St Louis & San Francisco	10,238,128	15,587,233	983	679	30,979
St. Louis, Iron Mountain & Southern	6,072,353	11,740,740	552	231	20,672
St Louis Southwestern	1,291,634	2,137,650	133	123	7,079
San Pedro, Los Angeles & Salt Lake	1,504,362	2,751,063	155	118	2,796
Seaboard Air Line	4,870,104	9,406,877	471	344	15,846
Southern	18,119,253	27,214,751	1,574	1,095	51,021
Southern Pacific	34,639,576	19,619,320	1,303	1,712	28,205
Texas & Pacific	3,298,952	6,442,082	381	203	11,096
Union Pacific	4,674,184	9,262,314	759	506	16,235
Vandalia	3,159,076	9,431,487	252	166	8,726
Wabash	5,989,029	13,496,755	699	412	21,017
Western Maryland	2,271,985	10,647,841	217	154	8,035
Wheeling & Lake Erie	1,896,767	10,641,187	192	73	10,773
Yazoo & Mississippi Valley	3,549,661	4,766,471	106	74	1,517

GENERAL STATISTICS OF AMERICAN RAILWAYS.

From report of interstate commerce commission for year ended June 30, 1912.

The following abstract is based upon the annual reports of railways having gross operating revenues of $100,000 or more for the year ended June 30, 1912:

MILEAGE.

Miles operated, 240,238.81.
Aggregate mileage, 360,714.24.
Single track, 240,238.81.
Second track, 24,929.51.
Third track, 2,511.76.
Fourth, fifth and sixth track, 1,783.97.
Increase over 1911, 8,925.52 miles.

EQUIPMENT.

Passenger locomotives, 14,206.
Freight locomotives, 36,600.
Switching and other locomotives, 10,444.
Total number locomotives, 61,250.
Freight cars, 2,203,128.
Passenger cars, 50,606.
Cars in company service, 114,924.
Total number cars, 2,368,658.

EMPLOYES.

Enginemen, 63,558.
Firemen, 66,408.
Conductors, 49,051.
Other trainmen, 135,959.
Switchmen, watchmen, etc., 39,530.
Total number employes, 1,699,218.
Wages and salaries paid, $1,243,113,172.

CAPITALIZATION.

Capital outstanding, $19,533,750,802.
Common stock, $6,882,813,008.
Preferred stock, $1,586,747,679.
Mortgage bonds, $8,019,700,886.
Collateral trust bonds, $1,279,128,266.
Other bonds, notes, etc., $1,067,567,350.
Income bonds, $263,441,054.
Miscellaneous funded obligations, $116,170,300.
Equipment trust obligations, $318,182,259.

PUBLIC SERVICE.

Passengers carried, 994,158,591.
Passengers carried one mile, 33,034,995,806.
Tons of freight carried, 1,818,232,193.
Tons of freight carried one mile, 262,955,605,123.

REVENUES AND EXPENSES.

OPERATING REVENUE.

Freight	$1,956,802,927
Passenger	657,422,999
Excess baggage	7,473,128
Parlor and chair car	658,800
Mail	50,674,758
Express	72,970,758
Milk revenue (on passenger trains)	8,323,683
Other passenger revenue	5,228,969
Switching	29,331,726
Special service train	2,078,910
Miscellaneous transportation	6,174,062
Total from operations other than transportation	27,367,678
Joint facilities—Dr	918,586
Joint facilities—Cr	3,328,155
Total	2,826,917,967

OPERATING EXPENSES.

Maintenance of way and structures	$363,495,580
Maintenance of equipment	448,303,785
Traffic expenses	60,568,586
Transportation expenses	1,013,340,697
General expenses	73,254,730
Total operating expenses	1,958,963,431

INCOME AND PROFIT AND LOSS ACCOUNTS.

Following is a condensed income account and profit and loss account of operating roads, the gross operating revenues of which were $100,000 or more for the year ended June 30, 1912:

INCOME ACCOUNT.

Rail operations—Operating revenues	$2,826,917,967
Operating expenses	1,958,963,431
Net operating revenue	867,954,536
Outside operations—Revenues	63,527,073
Expenses	62,489,614
Net revenue from outside operations	1,037,459
Total net revenue	868,991,995
Taxes accrued	113,122,509
Operating income	755,869,486
Other income	255,611,495
Gross income	1,011,480,981
Rents, interest and similar deductions from gross income	609,661,490
Net corporate income	401,819,491
Disposition of net corporate income—	
Divid'ds declared from current income	246,372,011
Appropriations for additions and betterments	37,186,102
Appropriat'ns for new lines and ext'ns	77,082
Appropriations for other reserves	5,463,269
Total	289,098,464
Balance to credit of profit and loss	112,721,027

PROFIT AND LOSS ACCOUNT.

Credit balance on June 30, 1911	1,065,793,723
Credit balance for year 1912 from income account	112,721,027
Total	1,178,514,750
Dividends declared out of surplus	100,433,571
Difference	1,078,081,179
Approp'ns for additions and betterments	4,274,626
Approp'ns for new lines and extensions	106,542
Appropriations for other reserves	3,920,920
Other profit and loss items—debit bal.	16,449,742
Total	23,851,830
Balance credit June 30, 1912, carried to balance sheet	1,054,229,349

RAILROAD TRAIN SPEED.

Time 1 mile. Min. Sec.	Miles per hour.	Time 1 mile. Min. Sec.	Miles per hour.	Time 1 mile. Min. Sec.	Miles per hour.
0:36	100.00	1:11	50.70	1:46	33.96
0:37	97.30	1:12	50.00	1:47	33.64
0:38	94.74	1:13	49.31	1:48	33.33
0:39	92.31	1:14	48.65	1:49	33.03
0:40	90.00	1:15	48.00	1:50	32.73
0:41	87.80	1:16	47.37	1:51	32.43
0:42	85.71	1:17	46.74	1:52	32.14
0:43	83.72	1:18	46.15	1:53	31.86
0:44	81.82	1:19	45.57	1:54	31.58
0:45	80.00	1:20	45.00	1:55	31.30
0:46	78.26	1:21	44.44	1:56	31.03
0:47	76.59	1:22	43.90	1:57	30.77
0:48	75.00	1:23	43.37	1:58	30.51
0:49	73.47	1:24	42.86	1:59	30.25
0:50	72.00	1:25	42.35	2:00	30.00
0:51	70.59	1:26	41.86	2:01	29.75
0:52	69.23	1:27	41.38	2:02	29.52
0:53	67.92	1:28	40.91	2:03	29.27
0:54	66.66	1:29	40.45	2:04	29.03
0:55	65.45	1:30	40.00	2:05	28.80
0:56	64.29	1:31	39.56	2:06	28.57
0:57	63.16	1:32	39.13	2:07	28.34
0:58	62.07	1:33	38.71	2:08	28.12
0:59	61.02	1:34	38.29	2:09	27.91
1:00	60.00	1:35	37.89	2:10	27.69
1:01	59.02	1:36	37.50	2:11	27.48
1:02	58.06	1:37	37.11	2:12	27.27
1:03	57.14	1:38	36.73	2:13	27.09
1:04	56.25	1:39	36.36	2:14	26.87
1:05	55.39	1:40	36.00	2:15	26.67
1:06	54.55	1:41	35.64	2:16	26.47
1:07	53.73	1:42	35.29	2:17	26.28
1:08	52.94	1:43	34.95	2:18	26.06
1:09	52.17	1:44	34.61	2:19	25.90
1:10	51.43	1:45	34.29	2:20	25.72

STATISTICS OF AMERICAN EXPRESS COMPANIES.

[From interstate commerce commission report for the year ended June 30, 1912.]

MILEAGE COVERED BY OPERATIONS.

Company.	1912.	1911.
Adams	37,306.26	36.560.52
American	59,387.52	56.891.99
Canadian	7,406.31	7,243.31
Canadian Northern	5,255.49	3,391.80
Globe	2,903.63	2,903.63
Great Northern	9,050.02	8,803.54
National	1,626.89	1,640.25
Northern	7,733.55	7,685.88
Pacific*	....	16,657.98
Southern	32,948.60	32,580.60
United States	32,806.60	32,748.28
Wells, Fargo & Co	81,995.01	58,471.56
Western	4,934.69	4,859.39
Total	283,348.57	270,438.73

*Discontinued business July 31, 1911. Service taken over by Wells, Fargo & Co.

Note—The total mileage for 1912 includes 7,736.87 miles of electric lines, 26,328.31 miles of steamboat lines and 655.12 miles of stage lines.

stations, fixing the location of each such station by block number.

The publication jointly of the pick-up and delivery limits of each station.

The adoption of revised rules and regulations.

The adoption of a new form of express receipt.

Under the old method of compiling tariffs some 900,000,000 separate rates were published by the express companies. Under the block system prescribed by the commission this number was reduced to less than 650,000 rates. The United States is divided into 950 blocks, averaging 2,500 square miles each.

The order provides that between any two points rates shall be the same in both directions, and shall be the same whether one or more carriers participate in the haul.

The most important change in rates by the order was by way of modification of the graduated scale of parcel rates. The 100 pound rates for short distances were either slightly reduced or left unchanged. For long distances the 100 pound rates were somewhat reduced. By the changes in the graduated scale, however, the rates for packages

INCOME ACCOUNT (1912).

Company.	Gross receipts.	Operating revenues.	Operating expenses.	Taxes.	Gross income.	Net income.
Adams	$34,191,956	$16,357,984	$15,152,594	$224,399	$2,859,302	$1,877,429
American	43,714,874	22,633,068	20,926,047	371,606	2,976,373	2,813,260
Canadian	3,046,186	1,659,913	1,347,773	34,534	283,281	237,935
Canadian Northern	778,642	475,805	276,411	6,898	192,677	192,677
Globe	773,219	387,990	371,902	8,919	166,481	160,481
Great Northern	2,965,921	1,186,546	961,320	42,671	185,712	170,506
National	1,269,022	740,015	631,379	5,823	103,004	101,434
Northern	2,994,057	1,370,722	1,082,936	58,080	279,213	267,587
Southern	15,628,470	7,900,179	6,376,267	178,174	1,454,373	1,423,599
United States	21,131,508	11,203,731	11,130,703	134,041	258,592	233,229
Wells, Fargo & Co	32,465,971	17,026,262	14,483,415	356,764	3,453,553	3,441,674
Western	1,162,106	599,043	513,935	9,500	75,608	24,560
Total, 1912	160,121,952	81,545,658	73,676,862	1,430,809	12,182,368	10,994,371
Total, 1911	152,612,880	78,676,862	67,089,223	1,315,973	16,600,616	15,366,609

CHANGE IN EXPRESS PRACTICES AND RATES.

Reductions in express rates and changes in methods of conducting the express business in the United States were ordered by the interstate commerce commission in Washington, D. C., Aug. 4, 1913, to go into effect on or before Oct. 15, the same year. It was estimated that the reductions would cost the companies fully $26,000,000 a year, or approximately 16 per cent of their gross revenues. The order of the commission laid the following requirements upon the express companies:

The adoption and observance for two years of a schedule of rates applying between all points in the United States.

The adoption of the block system of stating rates.

The establishment of a joint directory of express

weighing fifty pounds or less were practically all reduced. For packages of more than four pounds going more than 200 miles and less than 2,000, the new rates are generally lower than the parcel post rates; for more than 3,000 miles the rates are practically the same.

The basis of the classification prescribed is that all articles of merchandise of ordinary value are to be carried at first class or ordinary merchandise rates. All articles of food and drink, with a few exceptions, are second class and are to be carried at 75 per cent of the first class rate. Articles of extraordinary value must be so declared at the time of shipment. The order provides for special rates based upon such extraordinary value.

The new form of express receipt more carefully guards the rights of shippers than did the old form employed by the express companies.

GIANT SEQUOIA TREES IN CALIFORNIA.

Within the forest districts of the Sequoia and General Grant National parks in Tulare and Fresno counties, California, are thirteen different groves of sequoia timber. The following table gives the names of the groves, approximate area, number of trees exceeding ten feet in diameter and the total number of trees of all sizes.

Groves. Sequoia National park—	Acres.	Big trees.	All sizes.
Giant forest	3,200	5,900	500,000
Muir	2,240	3,000	350,100
Garfield	1,820	2,500	300,400
Atwell	850	590	2,000
Dennison	480	500	1,175
Swanee River	320	129	1,000
Squirrel Creek	90	91	200
Redwood Creek	70	70	500
Salt Creek	60	10	50
Homer Nose	25	5	25
Lost Grove	10	9	500
Eden	10	6	50

Groves. Gen. Grant National park—	Acres.	Big trees.	All sizes.
Gen. Grant	235	190	10,000
	9,410	12,100	1,166,000

HEIGHT AND DIAMETER OF PRINCIPAL TREES.

Name.	Height in feet.	Diam'r in feet.
Gen. Sherman	264	36
Abraham Lincoln	270	31
William McKinley	291	28
Gen. Grant	264	35
George Washington	255	29
Dalton	292	27
California	260	30

The Sherman, Lincoln and McKinley trees are in the Giant Forest grove, Grant and Washington in the Gen. Grant grove, Dalton in the Muir grove and California in the Garfield grove.

PULLMAN COMPANY STATISTICS.

[From interstate commerce commission's abstract of statistics of common carriers for year ended June 30, 1912.]

Average mileage (single track) over which operations were conducted (miles) 123,060

BALANCE SHEET.

Cost of property and equipment...........	$123,362,701
Securities owned............................	9,214,884
Lands owned................................	39,871
Cash......................................	10,533,163
Bills receivable..........................	5,754
Due from agents and conductors...........	568,619
Due from companies and individuals.....	1,284,438
Materials and supplies....................	3,458,090
Sinking, insurance and other funds.......	248,660
Sundries	64,273
Total	148,780,453
Capital stock.............................	120,000,000
Audited vouchers and accounts............	2,104,359
Wages and salaries........................	608,457
Dividends not called for..................	14,591
Matured interest coupons unpaid..........	80
Miscellaneous	2,297,400
Dividends accrued on capital stock......	1,573,243
Reserve and adjustment accounts.........	19,822,087
Profit and loss...........................	2,365,236

INCOME ACCOUNT.

Car operating revenues....................	37,090,413
Car operating expenses....................	26,258,695
Net car operating revenue...............	10,831,718
Outside operations—Revenues..............	3,053,031
Expenses	1,165,197
Net revenue from outside operations....	1,887,834
Total net revenue from operation.......	12,719,552
Taxes accrued............................	931,134
Operating income.........................	11,788,418
Hire of equipment—credit balance........	$4,482
Dividends declared on stocks owned or controlled	104,793
Interest accrued on funded debt owned or controlled	93,391
Interest on other securities, loans and accounts	343,440
Total nonoperating income...............	636,106
Gross income.............................	12,424,524
Interest	81,526
Other deductions..........................	46,090
Total deductions from gross income....	127,626
Net corporate income.....................	12,296,999
Dividends on stock declared from income	9,438,655
Balance for year carried forward to credit of profit and loss.................	2,858,343

PROFIT AND LOSS ACCOUNT.

Balance for year brought forward from income	2,858,343
Miscellaneous credits during the year....	157,869
Total credits during the year..........	3,016,212
Miscellaneous charges during the year....	2,281,773
Net increase in surplus during the year	734,439
Credit balance at beginning of year......	1,630,797
Balance at end of year...................	2,365,236

OPERATING REVENUES.

Berth revenue.............................	32,346,321
Seat revenue..............................	5,846,069
Charter of cars...........................	678,654
Miscellaneous revenue.....................	124,168
Association and contract revenue—Dr....	1,904,798
Total operating revenues...............	37,090,414

OPERATING EXPENSES.

Maintenance	14,297,660
Conducting car operations.................	11,118,659
General expenses..........................	842,376
Total operating expenses...............	26,258,695

Ratio of operating expenses to operating revenues (per cent)...................... 70.80

EMPLOYES AND SALARIES.

Class—	Av. daily No.	pay.
Maintenance:		
Mechanics, electricians, seamstresses, repairmen, carpenters, etc..........	476	$2.17
Conducting car operations:		
General officers and staff (superintendence)	80	3.93
Division and district superintendents and staff............................	1,177	2.30
Conductors	2,462	2.93
Porters, maids, etc......................	6,229	1.11
Train stenographers......................	8	2.24
Car cleaners.............................	3,640	1.56
General officers.........................	23	25.50
Clerks and attendants....................	512	2.29
Commissary (superintendence)............	13	2.78
Agents and staff, conductors, waiters, cooks, etc.......................	509	1.41
Total (including general officers)......	15,129	1.75

OPERATING STATISTICS.

Total number of revenue passengers—berth	13,194,420
Total number of revenue passengers—seat.	9,720,679
Average revenue per passenger—berth.....	$2.45
Average revenue per passenger—seat.....	$0.60
Total number of car-miles................	657,816,612
Total number of car-days.................	1,661,771
Average number of revenue passengers per car per day..........................	14
Operating revenues per car-mile (cents)...	5.638
Operating revenues per car-day..........	$22.31981
Operating expenses per car-mile (cents)..	3.991
Operating expenses per car-day..........	$15.80163
Net operating revenue per car-mile (cents)	1.647
Net operating revenue per car-day.........	$6.51818
Average number of car-miles per car-day..	396

EQUIPMENT IN SERVICE.

Standard sleeping cars.....................	4,370
Tourist sleeping cars......................	695
Parlor cars...............................	861
Dining cars...............................	24
Composite cars............................	114
Private cars..............................	36
Miscellaneous cars........................	1
Total	6,101

BUILDING AND LOAN ASSOCIATIONS (JAN. 1, 1912).

State.	Number.	Membership.	Assets.
California	96	34,685	$23,340,012
Connecticut	12	3,344	2,655,758
District of Columbia....	20	31,143	16,401,243
Illinois	569	155,320	68,975,451
Indiana	351	133,381	44,060,128
Iowa	49	16,500	4,863,729
Kansas	58	41,216	13,070,170
Kentucky	104	44,500	16,816,741
Louisiana	66	38,200	18,117,329
Maine	37	10,611	4,645,137
Massachusetts	109	158,365	67,573,380
Michigan	65	44,162	20,119,823
Minnesota	62	12,110	5,364,224
Missouri	134	26,950	12,633,297
Montana	10	1,552	896,994
Nebraska	69	58,191	$24,885,285
New Hampshire..........	17	7,800	2,191,623
New Jersey..............	563	198,057	96,448,627
New York...............	245	142,292	57,634,054
North Carolina..........	113	25,174	8,375,305
North Dakota............	9	3,802	2,149,852
Ohio	643	384,257	187,434,123
Pennsylvania	1,570	443,180	197,240,000
Tennessee	14	4,602	2,831,028
West Virginia............	43	12,200	5,457,997
Wisconsin	57	20,945	7,347,683
Other states.............	978	302,527	128,788,710
Total	6,113	2,355,066	1,040,307,713

THE PUBLIC DOMAIN.

UNRESERVED LANDS (1913).

State or territory.	Surveyed. Acres.	Unsurveyed. Acres.	Total. Acres.
Alabama	77,600	....	77,600
Alaska	....	*367,963,823	367,963,823
Arizona	11,750,267	27,774,928	39,525,195
Arkansas	397,489	70,000	467,489
California	15,633,304	5,220,333	20,853,637
Colorado	17,787,548	1,565,683	19,353,231
Florida	202,886	155,531	358,417
Idaho	7,748,512	10,167,110	17,915,622
Kansas	92,568	....	92,568
Louisiana	78,014	....	78,014
Michigan	89,057	....	89,057
Minnesota	1,286,394	....	1,286,394
Mississippi	41,660	....	41,660
Missouri	713	....	713
Montana	10,977,501	10,565,352	21,542,853
Nebraska	405,469	....	405,469
Nevada	29,359,141	25,779,452	55,138,593
New Mexico	20,927,792	10,370,829	31,298,621
North Dakota	1,156,120	....	1,156,120
Oklahoma	41,636	....	41,636
Oregon	13,613,442	2,932,080	16,545,522
South Dakota	3,751,651	53,781	3,107,432
Utah	12,290,342	21,547,254	33,837,596
Washington	1,079,957	670,251	1,750,208
Wisconsin	9,880	....	9,880
Wyoming	30,405,454	1,850,225	32,255,679
Grand total	179,204,397	486,686,632	665,891,029

*The unreserved lands in Alaska are mostly unsurveyed and unappropriated.

UNITED STATES LAND OFFICES.

Alabama—Montgomery.
Alaska—Fairbanks.
  Juneau.
  Nome.
Arizona—Phœnix.
Arkansas—Camden.
  Harrison.
  Little Rock.
California—Eureka.
  Independence.
  Los Angeles.
  Sacramento.
  San Francisco.
  Susanville.
  Visalia.
Colorado—Del Norte.
  Denver.
  Durango.
  Glenwood Springs.
  Hugo.
  Lamar.
  Leadville.
  Montrose.
  Pueblo.
  Sterling.
Florida—Gainesville.
Idaho—Blackfoot.
  Boise.
  Cœur d'Alene.
  Hailey.
  Lewiston.
Kansas—Dodge City.
  Topeka.
Louisiana—Baton Rouge.
Michigan—Marquette.
Minnesota—Cass Lake.
  Crookston.
  Duluth.
Mississippi—Jackson.
Missouri—Springfield.
Montana—Billings.
  Bozeman.
  Glasgow.
  Great Falls.
  Havre.
  Helena.
  Kalispell.
  Lewistown.
  Miles City.
  Missoula.

Nebraska—Alliance.
  Broken Bow.
  Lincoln.
  North Platte.
  O'Neill.
  Valentine.
Nevada—Carson City.
New Mexico—Clayton.
  Fort Sumner.
  Las Cruces.
  Roswell.
  Santa Fe.
  Tucumcari.
North Dakota—Bismarck.
  Devils Lake.
  Dickinson.
  Fargo.
  Minot.
  Williston.
Oklahoma—Guthrie.
  Woodward.
Oregon—Burns.
  La Grande.
  Lakeview.
  Portland.
  Roseburg.
  The Dalles.
  Vale.
South Dakota—
  Bellefourche.
  Gregory.
  Lemmon.
  Pierre.
  Rapid City.
  Timber Lake.
Utah—Salt Lake City.
  Vernal.
Washington—
  North Yakima.
  Olympia.
  Seattle.
  Spokane.
  Vancouver.
  Walla Walla.
  Waterville.
Wisconsin—Wausau.
Wyoming—Buffalo.
  Cheyenne.
  Douglas.
  Evanston.
  Lander Sundance.

Persons who desire to make homestead entry should first decide where they wish to locate, then go or write to the local land office of the district in which the lands are situated and obtain from the records diagrams of vacant lands.

A personal inspection of the lands should be made to ascertain if they are suitable, and when satisfied on this point entry can be made at the local land office in the manner prescribed by law, under the direction of the local land officers, who will give the applicant full information. Should a person desire to obtain information in regard to vacant lands in any district before going there for personal inspection, he should address the register and receiver of the particular local land office, who will give such information as is available. The local land officers cannot, however, be expected to furnish extended lists of vacant lands subject to entry, except through township plats, which they are authorized to sell.

THE HOMESTEAD LAW.

Any person who is the head of a family, or who is 21 years old and is a citizen of the United States or has filed his declaration of intention to become such, and who is not the proprietor of more than 160 acres of land in any state or territory, is entitled to enter one-quarter section (160 acres) or less quantity of unappropriated public land under the homestead laws. The applicant must make affidavit that he is entitled to the privileges of the homestead act and that the entry is made for his exclusive use and for actual settlement and cultivation, and must pay the legal fee and that part of the commission required, as follows: Fee for more than eighty acres, $10; for eighty acres or less, $5; commission, $1 for each forty-acre tract entered outside the limits of a railroad grant and $2 for each forty-acre tract entered within such limits. Within six months from the date of entry the settler must take up his residence upon the land unless an extension of time is granted, and cultivate the same for three years. He may absent himself each year for one period of not exceeding five months. During the second year not less than one-sixteenth of the area entered must be actually cultivated, and during the third year and until final proof cultivation of not less than one-eighth is required. There must be actual breaking of the soil followed by planting, sowing of seed and tillage for a crop other than native grasses. Summer fallowing or grazing of cattle cannot be accepted. The homestead entryman must have a habitable house upon the land entered at the time of submitting proof. Other improvements should be of such character and amount as are sufficient to show good faith.

Either final or commutation proof may be made at any time when it can be shown that residence and cultivation have been maintained in good faith for the required length of time and to the required extent. Proof under the act of June 6, 1912, must be submitted within five years after the date of the entry, while proof submitted under the law in force before that date must be made within seven years after the date of the entry. Failure to submit proof within the proper period is ground for cancellation of the entry unless good reason for the delay appears.

ENLARGED HOMESTEADS.

The acts of February 19, 1909, June 17, 1910, and June 13, 1912 (37 Stat., 101), extending the first-named act to North Dakota and California, provide for the making of homestead entries for areas of not exceeding 320 acres of public lands in the states of Arizona, California, Colorado, Idaho, Montana, Nevada, New Mexico, North Dakota, Oregon, Utah, Washington and Wyoming, designated by the secretary of the interior as nonmineral, nontimbered, nonirrigable. As to Idaho, the act of June 17, 1910, provides that the lands must be "arid." The terms "arid" or "nonirrigable" land, as used in these acts, are construed to mean land which, as a rule, lacks sufficient rainfall to produce agricultural crops without the necessity of resorting to unusual methods of cultivation, such as the system commonly known as "dry farming," and for which there is no known source of water supply from which such land may be successfully irrigated at a reasonable cost.

CHURCHES IN THE UNITED STATES (1912).

[Compiled by Dr. H. K. Carroll for the Christian Advocate, New York, N. Y.]

Denominations.	Minis-ters.	Churches.	Communi-cants.
Adventists—1. Evangelical.	*8	*18	*481
2. Advent Christians......	*528	*550	*26,799
3. Seventh Day...........	534	1,860	65,284
4. Church of God.........	*32	*20	*611
5. Life and Advent Union	*12	*12	*509
6. Churches of God in Jesus Christ..........	58	*62	*2,124
Total Adventists......	1,172	2,522	95,808
Baptists—1. Regular (north)	8,242	9,610	1,175,923
2. Regular (south).......	14,632	23,795	2,475,609
3. Regular (colored)......	12,622	16,735	1,912,319
4. Six-Principle	10	16	731
5. Seventh Day...........	95	96	8,194
6. Free	†905	1,110	65,440
7. Freewill	‡914	834	57,231
8. General	550	545	33,600
9. Separate	*100	*76	*5,180
10. United	*260	*196	*13,698
11. Baptist Church of Christ	*99	*93	*6,416
12. Primitive	*1,500	*2,922	*102,311
13. Primitive Colored.....	*1,480	*797	*35,076
14. Old Two-Seed-in-the-Spirit Predestinarian	*35	*55	*781
15. Church of God and Saints of Christ......	*75	*48	*1,823
Total Baptists.......	41,419	56,918	5,894,232
Brethren (Dunkards)—			
1. Conservative	3,066	938	95,000
2. Old Order............:	218	72	4,000
3. Progressive	192	215	20,394
4. Seventh Day (German).	8	14	250
Total Dunk'd Breth'n	3,484	1,239	119,644
Brethren (Plymouth)—			
1. Brethren I............		*134	*2,933
2. Brethren II...........		*128	*4,752
3. Brethren III..........		*81	*1,724
4. Brethren IV...........		*69	*1,157
Total Plm. Brethren..		403	10,566
Brethren (River)—			
1. Brethren in Christ.....	178	68	3,731
2. Old Order, or Yorker...	*24	*9	*423
3. United Zion's Children.	*22	*28	*749
Total River Brethren.	224	105	4,903
Buddhists—			
1. Chinese Temples........	*1	*62	....
2. Japanese Temples......	*14	*12	*3,165
Total Buddhists.......	*15	74	3,165
Catholic Apostolic—			
1. Catholic Apostolic......	*14	*11	*2,907
2. New Apostolic..........	*19	*13	*2,020
Total Cath. Apostolic	33	24	4,927
Catholic, East'n Orthodox—			
1. Armenian Apostolic....	15	21	55,000
2. Russian Orthodox......	115	127	62,000
3. Greek Orthodox........	80	70	175,000
4. Syrian Orthodox.......	24	24	43,000
5. Servian Orthodox......	21	24	59,900
6. Roumanian Orthodox...	5	5	20,000
7. Bulgarian Orthodox.....	3	3	20,000
Total East. Catholics	263	274	434,000
Catholic, Western—			
1. Roman Catholic........	17,610	14,102	12,888,466
2. Polish Catholic........	28	*24	*15,473
3. Reformed Catholic.....	7	6	3,250
Total West. Catholics	17,645	14,132	12,907,189
Christadelphians	......	*70	*1,412
Christians	1,129	1,182	102,902
Christian Catholic (Dowie).	*35	*17	*5,865
Christian Scientists.........	2,460	1,230	85,096
Christian Union.............	295	237	13,905
Churches of God (Winebren-narian)	509	595	41,475

Denominations.	Minis-ters.	Churches.	Communi-cants.
Churches of the Living God (colored)—			
1. Christian Workers for Friendship	*51	*44	*2,676
2. Apostolic	*30	*15	*752
3. Church of Christ in God	*20	*9	*858
Total Churches of the Living God............	101	68	4,286
Churches of the New Jerusalem—			
1. General Convention....	102	127	8,500
2. General Church........	26	16	1,054
Total New Jerusalem Churches	128	143	9,554
Communistic Societies—			
1. Shakers	......	*15	*516
2. Amana	......	*7	*1,756
Total Communistic Societies		22	2,272
Congregationalists	6,125	6,070	742,350
Disciples of Christ—			
1. Disciples of Christ.....	5,954	9,818	1,340,887
2. Churches of Christ.....	*2,100	*2,649	*156,658
Total Dis. of Christ..	8,054	12,467	1,497,545
Evangelical Bodies—			
1. Evangelical Associat'n.	1,003	1,659	110,134
2. United Evang. Church.	520	968	74,732
Total Evang. Bodies..	1,523	2,627	184,866
Faith Associations—			
1. Apos. Faith Movement.	......	*6	*538
2. Peniel Missions.........	*30	*11	*703
3. Met. Church Assn.......	*29	*6	*466
4. Hepzibah Faith Assn..	*36	*19	*293
5. Mission'y Church Assn.	*35	*32	*1,256
6. Heavenly Recruit Church	*55	*27	*938
7. Apos. Christian Church	*19	*42	*4,558
8. Christian Congregation.	*26	*9	*395
9. Voluntary Missionary Society (colored)......	*11	*3	*425
Total Faith Assns...	241	146	9,572
Free Christian Zion Church	*20	*15	*1,835
Friends—1. Orthodox........	1,320	900	100,568
2. "Hicksite"	99	211	19,597
3. "Wilburite"	*47	*48	*3,880
4. Primitive	*10	*8	*171
Total Friends.........	1,476	1,167	124,216
Friends of the Temple......	3	3	*376
German Evang. Protestant.	*59	*66	*34,764
German Evangelical Synod.	1,038	1,326	258,911
Jewish Congregations......	*1,084	*1,769	143,000
Latter Day Saints—			
1. Utah Branch............	1,960	820	296,000
2. Reorganized branch.....	1,400	600	56,500
Tl. Latter Day Saints	3,360	1,420	352,500
Lutherans—			
1. General Synod.........	1,367	1,796	316,949
2. United Synod (south)..	250	468	50,669
3. General Council.......	1,530	2,347	473,295
4. Synodical Conference..	2,885	3,569	807,693
5. United Norwegian.....	574	1,538	169,710
Independent Synods—			
6. Ohio	611	857	132,316
7. Buffalo	30	42	5,600
8. Hauge's	167	362	40,000
9. Eielsen's	6	26	1,100
10. Texas	21	22	4,500
11. Iowa	530	1,000	118,322
12. Norwegian	389	1,050	92,000
13. Danish in America.....	62	109	13,500
14. Icelandic	15	37	5,112
15. Immanuel	25	21	5,027
16. Suomai (Finnish)......	31	126	14,180

17. Finnish Apostolic......	66	304	21,000
18. Finnish National.......	22	72	8,000
19. Norwegian Free.......	165	355	20,000
20. Danish United.........	129	179	11,729
21. Slovakian	21	53	13,000
22. Church of the Luther-			
an Brethren..........	13	17	1,800
23. Jehovah	9	11	1,100
Independent Cong'ns...	90	205	27,000
Total Lutherans.....	**9,038**	**14,566**	**2,353,702**
Scandinavian Ev. Bodies—			
1. Swedish Evangelical			
Mission Covenant....	394	541	48,000
2. Swed. Ev. Free Mis'n..	152	154	18,500
3. Norwegian Evang. Free	65	150	4,000
Total Scan. Evang...	**611**	**848**	**70,500**
Mennonites—1. Mennonite..	*346	*220	*18,674
2. Bruederhoef	.9	*8	*275
3. Amish	*131	*57	*7,640
4. Old Amish............	*141	*46	*5,042
5. Apostolic	2	2	209
6. Reformed	*24	*34	*2,073
7. General Conference....	*143	*90	*11,661
8. Church of God in Christ	*17	*18	*562
9. Old (Wisler).........	*18	*9	*655
10. Bundes Conference....	*36	*19	*2,533
11. Defenceless	*36	*14	*967
12. Brethren in Christ...	149	97	5,013
Separate Conferences(2)	*35	*21	*1,908
Total Mennonites....	**1,087**	**635**	**57,219**
Methodists—			
1. Methodist Episcopal...	18,714	28,433	3,293,526
2. Union American Meth-			
odist Episcopal......	138	255	18,500
3. African Meth Epis....	6,774	5,830	620,234
4. African Union Metho-			
dist Protestant	200	125	4,000
5. A f r i c a n Methodist			
Episcopal Zion......	3,488	3,298	547,216
6. Methodist Protestant..	1,371	2,288	183,318
7. Wesleyan Methodist...	613	591	13,510
8. Meth. Episcopal(south)	6,970	15,727	1,919,873
9. Congregational Meth..	337	338	15,529
10. New Cong'l Methodist.	*59	*35	*1,782
11. Zion Union Apostolic..	*33	*45	*3,059
12. Col'd Meth. Episcopal.	2,901	2,857	234,722
13. Primitive	71	94	7,114
14. Free Methodist......	1,138	1,256	32,552
15. Reformed Methodist			
Union Episcopal......	40	58	4,000
16. Independent Methodist	2	2	1,161
Total Methodists.....	**42,849**	**61,027**	**6,905,095**
Moravian Bodies—			
1. Moravians	145	122	18,970
2. Union Bohemians and			
Moravians	4	21	1,000
Tl. Moravian Bodies..	**149**	**143**	**19,970**
Nonsectarian Bible Faith			
Churches	*50	*204	*6,396
Pentecostal Bodies—			
1. Pentecostal Church.....	617	480	20,996
2. Other Pentecostal Asso-			
ciations	*115	*30	*1,420
Total Pent'l Bodies..	**732**	**510**	**22,416**
Presbyterians—1. Northern.	9,157	9,930	1,368,150
2. Cumberland	928	1,800	121,000
3. Cumberland (colored).	*375	*196	*18,066
4. Welsh Calvinistic......	93	151	13,841
5. United	1,005	1,001	139,617
6. Southern	1,734	3,392	292,845
7. Associate	*12	*22	*786
8. Associate Reformed			
(south)	113	153	14,569
9. Reformed (Synod)......	142	*111	9,213
10. Reformed (Gen. Synod)	16	18	3,400
11. Reformed (Covenanted)	......	1	40
12. Reformed in the United			
States and Canada..	1	1	422
Total Presbyterians.	**13,576**	**16,776**	**1,981,949**

Protestant Episcopal—			
1. Protestant Episcopal...	5,422	7,724	970,451
2. Reformed Episcopal....	94	80	10,400
Total Prot. Episcopal	**5,516**	**7,804**	**980,851**
Reformed—			
1. Reformed (Dutch)......	739	691	118,564
2. Reformed (German).....	1,200	1,737	300,147
3. Christian Reformed....	156	209	35,142
4. Hungarian Reformed...	*18	*16	*5,253
Total Reformed	**2,113**	**2,653**	**459,106**
Salvationists—			
1. Salvation Army........	2,935	852	26,909
2. Amer. Salvation Army.	*59	*20	*436
Total Salvationists...	**2,994**	**872**	**27,345**
Schwenkfelders	6	8	941
Social Brethren...........	*15	*17	*1,262
Society for Ethical Culture.	7	6	2,450
Spiritualists	....	2,000	200,000
Theosophical Society	.....	134	3,368
Unitarians	527	476	70,542
United Brethren—			
1. United Brethren.......	1,929	3,692	301,448
2. United Brethren (Old			
Constitution)	333	524	19,512
Tl. United Brethren..	**2,262**	**4,216**	**320,969**
Universalists	703	709	51,716
Independent Congregations.	267	879	48,673
Grand total for 1912..	**174,396**	**220,814**	**36,675,537**
Grand total for 1911..	**171,905**	**220,160**	**36,095,685**

*Federal census of 1906.

ORDER OF DENOMINATIONS.

Denominations.	Rank in 1912.	Communicants 1912.	Rank in 1890.	Communicants 1890.
Roman Catholic............	1	12,888,466	1	6,231,417
Methodist Episcopal........	2	3,293,526	2	2,240,354
Regular Baptist (south).....	3	2,475,609	4	1,280,066
Methodist Episcopal (south)	4	1,919,873	5	1,209,976
Regular Baptist, (colored)..	5	1,912,219	3	1,348,989
Presbyterian (northern)....	6	1,368,150	7	788,244
Disciples of Christ........	7	1,340,887	8	641,051
Regular Baptist (north)....	8	1,175,923	6	800,450
Protestant Episcopal.......	9	970,451	9	532,054
Luth. Synod'l Conference..10		807,693	12	367,153
Congregationalist 11		742,350	10	512,771
African Meth. Episcopal..12		620,234	11	452,725
Af'n Meth. Episcopal Zion.13		547,216	13	349,788
Lutheran Gen'l Council....14		473,295	14	324,846
Lutheran General Synod...15		316,949	20	164,640
United Brethren...........16		301,448	16	202,474
Reformed (German).......17		300,147	15	204,018
Latter Day Saints.........18		286,000	21	144,352
Presbyterian (southern)...19		282,845	18	179,721
German Evang. Synod....20		258,911	17	187,432
Col'd Meth Episcopal.....21		234,721	24	129,383
Spiritualists 22		200,000	39	45,030
Methodist Protestant......23		183,318	22	141,989
Greek Orthodox (Cath.)...24		175,000	138	100
United Norwegian Luth...25		169,710	26	119,972
United Presbyterian......26		139,617	27	94,402
Lutheran Synod of Ohio..27		132,316	33	69,505
Reformed (Dutch).........28		118,564	28	92,970
Orthodox Friends.........29		100,568	31	80,655

ORDER OF DENOMINATIONAL FAMILIES.

Denominational families.	Rank in 1912.	Communicants 1912.	Rank in 1890.	Communicants 1890.
Catholic (Roman, etc.)....	1	12,907,189	1	6,257,871
Methodist	2	6,905,095	2	4,589,284
Baptist	3	5,894,232	3	3,717,969
Lutheran	4	2,353,702	5	1,231,072
Presbyterian	5	1,981,949	4	1,278,262
Episcopal	6	980,851	6	540,509
Reformed	7	459,106	7	309,458
Latter Day Saints..........	8	352,500	9	166,125
United Brethren	9	320,969	8	225,281
Friends 10		124,216	11	107,208
Brethren (Dunkard)........11		119,644	13	73,795
Adventists 12		95,808	14	60,491

CHURCHES AND RELIGIOUS ASSOCIATIONS.

ROMAN CATHOLIC CHURCH OF THE UNITED STATES.

Apostolic Delegate—Most Rev. John Bonzano, D. D.
Cardinals—James Gibbons, Baltimore, Md.; William O'Connell, Boston, Mass.; John Farley, New York, N. Y.

Archdiocese. ARCHBISHOPS. **Name.**
Chicago, Ill...................James E. Quigley
Cincinnati, O..................Henry Moeller
Dubuque, Iowa.................James J. Keane
Manila, P. I..................Jeremiah J. Harty
Milwaukee, Wis...............Sebastian G. Messmer
New Orleans, La...............James H. Blenk
Oregon City, Oregon.............Alexander Christie
Philadelphia, Pa............Edmond F. Prendergast
St. Louis, Mo............John Joseph Glennon
St. Paul, Minn....................John Ireland
San Francisco, Cal.............Patrick W. Riordan
Santa Fe, N. M..............John Baptist Pitaval

Diocese. BISHOPS. **Name.**
Albany, N. Y.................Thomas M. A. Burke
Alexandria, La..............Cornelius Van de Ven
Alton, Ill......................James Ryan
Altoona, Pa.....................Eugene A. Garvey
Baker City, Ore..............Charles J. O'Reilly
Baltimore, Md........Owen B. Corrigan (auxiliary)
Belleville, Ill.....................(Vacancy)
Bismarck, N. D................Vincent Wehrle
Boise City, Idaho.................A. J. Glorieux
Boston, Mass........Joseph G. Anderson (auxiliary)
Brooklyn, N. Y.............Charles E. McDonnell
Buffalo, N. Y.................Charles H. Colton
Burlington, Vt.................Joseph J. Rice
Charleston, S. C.............Henry P. Northrop
Cheyenne, Wyo...............Patrick A. McGovern
Chicago, Ill............Paul P. Rhode (auxiliary)
Cleveland, O.................John P. Farrelly
Columbus, O.................James J. Hartley
Concordia, Kas............John F. Cunningham
Corpus Christi, Tex.................(Vacancy)
Covington, Ky................Camillus P. Maes
Crookston, N. D..............Timothy Corbett
Dallas, Tex..............Joseph Patrick Lynch
Davenport, Iowa................James Davis
Denver, Col...........Nicholas Chrysostom Matz
Des Moines, Iowa.................Austin Dowling
Detroit, Mich..................John S. Foley
Duluth, Minn.................James McGolrick
Erie, Pa................J. E. Fitz Maurice
Fall River, Mass.............Daniel F. Feehan
Fargo, N. D.................James O'Reilly
Fort Wayne, Ind..............Herman J. Alerding
Galveston, Tex.............Nicholas A. Gallagher
Grand Rapids, Mich............Henry J. Richter
Great Falls, Mont.............Mathias C. Lenihan
Green Bay, Wis.................Joseph J. Fox
Harrisburg, Pa...............J. W. Shanahan
Hartford, Conn..........John Joseph Nilan
Hawaiian Islands.............Libert H. Boeynaems
Helena, Mont.................John P. Carroll
Indianapolis, Ind..........Francis S. Chatard
Kansas City, Mo....................(Vacancy)
Kearney, Neb.............James Albert Duffy
LaCrosse, Wis.................J. Schwebach
Lead, S. D..................Joseph F. Busch
Leavenworth, Kas..................John Ward
Lincoln, Neb................John Henry Tihen
Little Rock, Ark..............John B. Morris
Louisville, Ky..............Denis O'Donaghue
Manchester, N. H..........George Albert Guertin
Marquette, Mich.................Frederick Eis
Mobile, Ala..................Edward P. Allen
Monterey-Los Angeles, Cal......Thomas J. Conaty
Nashville, Tenn.........Thomas Sebastian Byrne
Natchez, Miss..................John E. Gunn
Newark, N. J..................John J. O'Connor
New Orleans, La..........J. M. Laval (auxiliary)
New York, N. Y........Thomas F. Cusack (auxiliary)
Ogdensburg, N. Y...............Henry Gabriels
Oklahoma...............Theophile Meerschaert
Omaha, Neb................Richard Scannell
Peoria, Ill............Edmund Michael Dunne
Pittsburgh, Pa............J. F. Regis Canevin
Portland, Me..................Louis S. Walsh
Porto Rico...................W. A. Jones

Diocese. **Name.**
Providence, R. I...........Matthew Harkins
Richmond, Va...........Denis Joseph O'Connell
Rochester, N. Y.............Thomas F. Hickey
Rockford, Ill.............Peter James Muldoon
Sacramento, Cal................Thomas Grace
St. Augustine, Fla.................(Vacancy)
St. Cloud, Minn...............James Trobec
St. Joseph, Mo................Maurice F. Burke
Salt Lake City, Utah...........Lawrence Scanlan
San Antonio, Tex.........John William Shaw
Savannah, Ga..............Benjamin J. Keiley
Scranton, Pa............Michael John Hoban
Seattle, Wash.............Edward John O'Dea
Sioux City, Iowa.........Philip Joseph Garrigan
Sioux Falls, S. D.............Thomas O'Gorman
Springfield, Mass.............Thomas D. Beaven
Superior, Wis...........Joseph M. Koudelka
Syracuse, N. Y.................John Grimes
Toledo, O..................Joseph Schrembs
Trenton, N. J..............James A. McFaul
Tucson, Ariz.................Henry Granjon
Wheeling, W. Va.........Patrick James Donahue
Wichita, Kas..................John J. Hennessy
Wilmington, Del...............John J. Monaghan
Winona, Minn................Patrick R. Heffron

CATHOLIC CHURCH STATISTICS.

[From the Official Catholic Directory for 1912. Figures are for the United States.]

Cardinals—3.
Archbishops—14.
Bishops—100.
Secular clergy—13,273.
Religious clergy—4,672.
Total clergy—17,945.
Churches with resident priests—9,500.
Missions with churches—4,812.
Total churches—14,312.
Seminaries—85.
Students—6,169.

Colleges for boys—230.
Academies for girls—684.
Parishes with schools—5,256.
Children attending—1,360,761.
Orphan asylums—288.
Orphans—47,415.
Homes for aged—198.
Total children in catholic institutions—1,593,316.
Catholic population of U. S.—15,154,158.

COLLEGE OF CARDINALS.

Cardinal bishops— Created cardinal.
Agliardi, Anthony, b. Sept. 4, 1832..............1889
Cassetta, Francis de Paula, b. Aug. 12, 1845...1899
Oreglia, Louis di S. Stefano, b. July 9, 1828...1873
Nammtelli, Serafino, b. Nov. 26, 1834...........1873
Vannutelli, Vincent, b. Dec. 5, 1836............1889
De Lai, Cajetan, b. July 26, 1853...............1907

Cardinal priests—
Almaraz y Santos, Enriquez, b. Sept. 22, 1847..1911
Amette, Leone Adolfo, b. Sept. 6, 1850.........1911
Andrieu, Paul Pierre, b. Dec. 8, 1849..........1907
Bacilieri, Bartholomew, b. March 27, 1842......1901
Bauer, Franz, b. Jan. 26, 1841.................1911
Belmonte, Gennaro Granito di, b. April 10, 1851.1911
Boschi, Julius, b. March 2, 1838...............1901
Bourne, Francis, b. March 23, 1861.............1911
Cabrieres, Francis M. D. de, b. Aug. 30, 1830..1911
Cavalcanti, Joachim A. de A., b. Jan. 17, 1850.1905
Cavallari, Aristides, b. Feb. 8, 1849..........1907
Cos y Macho, Giuseppe, b. Aug. 6, 1838.........1911
Di Pietro, Angelo, b. May 26, 1828.............1893
Dubillard, Francis Virgilio, b. Feb. 15, 1845..1911
Falconio, Diomede, b. Sept. 20, 1842...........1911
Farley, John M., b. April 20, 1842.............1911
Ferrari, Andrew, b. Aug. 18, 1850..............1894
Ferrata, Dominic, b. March 4, 1847.............1896
Francica-Nava di Bontife, J., b. July 23, 1846.1899
Gasparri, Peter, b. May 5, 1852................1907
Gennari, Casimir, b. Dec. 27, 1839.............1901
Gibbons, James, b. July 23, 1834...............1895
Gotti, Jerome Mary, b. March 29, 1834..........1895
Herrera, Joseph M. M. b. Aug. 26, 1835.........1897
Hornig, Charles, b. Aug. 10, 1840..............1912
Katschthaler, John, b. May 20, 1832............1903
Kopp, George, b. July 27, 1837.................1893
Logue, Michael, b. Oct. 1, 1840................1893
Lorenzelli, Benedict, b. 1853..................1907
Lualdi, Alexander, b. Aug. 12, 1858............1907
Lucon, Louis Henry, b. Oct. 28, 1842...........1907
Maffi, Peter, b. Oct. 12, 1858.................1907
Martinelli, Sebastian, b. Aug. 20, 1848........1901

Cardinal priests—
Mercier, Desideratus, b. Nov. 21, 1851..........1907
Merry del Val, Raphael, b. Oct. 10, 1865.........1903
Neto, Joseph Sebastian, b. Feb. 8, 1841..........1884
O'Connell, William H., b. Dec. 8, 1859...........1911
Prisco, Joseph, b. Sept. 18, 1836................1896
Rampolla, Mariano, b. 1843.......................1887
Richelmy, Augustinus, b. Nov. 29, 1850...........1899
Rinaldini, Aristides, b. Feb. 5, 1844............1907
Skrbensky, Leo, b. June 12, 1863.................1901
Vaszary, Claudius, b. Feb. 12, 1832..............1893
Vico, Antonio, b. Jan. 9, 1847...................1911
Cardinal deacons—
Bisleti, Cajetan, b. March 20, 1856..............1911
Billot, Louis, b. Jan. 22, 1846..................1911
Cagiano de Azevedo, Ottavius, b. Nov. 7, 1845..1905
Lugari, John Baptist, b. Feb. 13, 1846...........1911
Pompili, Basilius, b. April 16, 1858.............1911
Van Rossum, William, b. Sept. 3, 1854............1911
Volpe, Francis Della, b. Dec. 24, 1814...........1899

CATHOLIC EDUCATIONAL ASSOCIATION.

Honorary President—Cardinal James Gibbons, Baltimore, Md.
President-General—The Rt.-Rev. Mgr. Thomas J. Shahan, Washington, D. C.
Vice-Presidents-General—Very Reverend James A. Burns, Washington, D. C.; Very Reverend Walter Steble, Beatty, Pa.; Rt.-Rev. Mgr. J. A. Connolly, St. Louis, Mo.
Secretary-General—The Rev. Francis W. Howard, LL. D., 1651 East Main street, Columbus, O.
Treasurer-General—The Rev. Francis T. Moran, D. D., Cleveland, O.
Office of association—1657 East Main street, Columbus, O.

AMERICAN FEDERATION OF CATHOLIC SOCIETIES.

President—Charles I. Denechaud, New Orleans, La.
Secretary—Anthony Matre, St. Louis, Mo.
Treasurer—F. W. Heckenkamp, Quincy, Ill.
Marshal—C. H. Herold, Seneca, Kas.

THE CATHOLIC CHURCH EXTENSION SOCIETY OF THE UNITED STATES OF AMERICA.

1133 McCormick building, Chicago, Ill.
Cardinal Protector—His Eminence Sebastian Cardinal Martinelli.
Chancellor Board of Governors—The Most Rev. James Edward Quigley, D. D., Chicago.
Vice-Chancellor Board of Governors—The Most Rev. S. G. Messmer, D. D., D. C. L., Milwaukee, Wis.
President—The Very Reverend Francis C. Kelley, D. D., LL. D.
First Vice-President and General Secretary—The Rev. E. B. Ledvina.
Second Vice-President and Director Women's Auxiliary—The Rev. Edward L. Roe.
Third Vice-President and Director Child Apostles—The Rev. W. D. O'Brien.
Fourth Vice-President—Leo L. Doyle.
Treasurer—John A. Lynch.
Recording Secretary Board of Governors—Mr. A. V. D. Watterson.
Superintendent Chapel Car—Mr. George C. Hennessey.
Executive Committee—The Most Reverend James Edward Quigley, D. D.; the Very Reverend Francis C. Kelley, D. D., LL. D.; the Rt.-Rev. P. J. Muldoon, D. D.; Mr. Edward Hines, Mr. Richmond Dean, Mr. Warren A. Cartier, Mr. Edward F. Carry.
Board of Auditors—The Rev. Edward A. Kelly, LL. D.; the Rev. R. F. Flynn, the Rev. F. J. O'Reilly, Mr. J. J. Fleming, Mr. S. C. Scotten.

EXTENSION MAGAZINE.

The Official Organ of the Catholic Church Extension Society of the United States of America.
Editorial Department—1133 McCormick building, Chicago.
Editor-in-Chief—The Very Reverend Francis C. Kelley, D. D., LL. D.
Managing Editor—Mr. Simon A. Baldus.

CATHOLIC TOTAL ABSTINENCE UNION.

President—The Rev. Peter O'Callaghan, Chicago.
Secretary—Thomas E. McClosky, Danbury, Conn.
Treasurer—The Rev. J. V. Moylan, Nanticoke, Pa.

PROTESTANT EPISCOPAL CHURCH.

Presiding Bishop—D. S. Tuttle, Bishop of Missouri.

Diocese.	Bishop and residence.
Alabama	C. M. Beckwith, Montgomery
Alaska	Peter Trimble Rowe, Seattle, Wash.
Albany	R. H. Nelson, Albany, N. Y.
Arizona	J. W. Atwood, Phoenix
Arkansas	James R. Winchester, Little Rock
Asheville	Junius M. Horner, Asheville, N. C.
Atlanta	C. K. Nelson, Atlanta, Ga.
Bethlehem	E. Talbot, South Bethlehem, Pa.
California	William F. Nichols, San Francisco
Central New York	Charles T. Olmsted, Utica
Chicago	C. P. Anderson, Chicago
Suffragan	William E. Toll, Chicago
Colorado	C. S. Olmsted, Denver
Connecticut	C. B. Brewster, Hartford
Dallas	A. C. Garrett, Dallas, Tex.
Delaware	F. J. Kinsman, Wilmington
Duluth	James D. Morrison, Duluth, Minn.
East Carolina	R. Strange, Wilmington, N. C.
Eastern Oklahoma	T. P. Thurston, Muskogee, Okla.
Eastern Oregon	Robert L. Paddock, Hood River, Ore.
Easton	William F. Adams, Easton, Md.
Erie	Rogers Israel, Erie, Pa.
Florida	E. G. Weed, Jacksonville
Fond du Lac	R. H. Weller, Fond du Lac, Wis.
Georgia	Frederick F. Reese, Savannah
Harrisburg	J. H. Darlington, Harrisburg, Pa.
Honolulu	H. B. Restarick, Honolulu, H. I.
Idaho	James B. Funsten, Boise, Idaho
Indianapolis	J. M. Francis, Indianapolis
Iowa	T. N. Morrison, Davenport
Suffragan	Harry S. Longley, Des Moines
Kansas	F. R. Millspaugh, Topeka
Kentucky	Charles E. Woodcock, Louisville
Lexington	L. W. Burton, Lexington, Ky.
Long Island	F. Burgess, Garden City, L. I.
Los Angeles	J. H. Johnson, Los Angeles, Cal.
Louisiana	Davis Sessums, New Orleans
Maine	Robert Codman, Portland
Marquette	G. M. Williams, Marquette, Mich.
Maryland	John G. Murray, Baltimore
Massachusetts	William Lawrence, Boston
Suffragan	Samuel G. Babcock, Boston
Michigan	Charles D. Williams, Detroit, Mich.
Michigan City	J. H. White, South Bend, Ind.
Milwaukee	William W. Webb, Milwaukee, Wis.
Minnesota	Samuel C. Edsall, Minneapolis
Suffragan	Frank A. McElwain, Faribault
Mississippi	T. Du B. Bratton, Jackson
Missouri	D. S. Tuttle, St. Louis
Coadjutor	F. F. Johnson, St. Louis
Montana	L. R. Brewer. Helena
Nebraska	Arthur L. Williams, Omaha
Nevada	Henry D. Robinson, Reno
Newark	E. S. Lines, Newark, N. J.
New Hampshire	W. W. Niles, Concord
Coadjutor	Edward M. Parker, Concord
New Jersey	John Scarborough, Trenton
New Mexico	F. B. Howden, Santa Fe
New York	David H. Greer, New York
Suffragan	Charles S. Burch, New York
North Carolina	J. B. Cheshire, Raleigh
North Dakota	J. P. Tyler, Fargo
North Texas	E. A. Temple, Amarillo, Tex.
Ohio	William A. Leonard, Cleveland
Coadjutor-elect	Frank Du Moulin, Cleveland
Oklahoma	F. K. Brooke, Oklahoma City
Olympia	F. W. Keator, Tacoma, Wash.
Oregon	Charles Scadding, Portland
Pennsylvania	Philip M. Rhinelander, Philadelphia
Suffragan	Thomas J. Garland, Philadelphia
Philippines	Charles H. Brent, Manila
Pittsburgh	C. Whitehead, Pittsburgh, Pa.
Porto Rico	W. B. Calmore, San Juan
Quincy	M. E. Fawcett, Quincy, Ill.
Rhode Island	J. De Wolfe Perry, Jr., Providence
Sacramento	W. H. Moreland, Sacramento
Salina	S. M. Griswold, Salina, Kas.
San Joaquin	L. C. Sanford, Fresno, Cal.
South Carolina	W. A. Guerry, Charleston
South Dakota	George Biller, Jr., Sioux Falls
Southern Florida	Vacant
Southern Massachusetts	T. F. Davies, Springfield
Southern Ohio	Boyd Vincent, Cincinnati
Coadjutor	Theodore I. Reese, Columbus
Southern Virginia	A. M. Randolph, Norfolk
Coadjutor	B. D. Tucker, Lynchburg

Diocese.	Bishop and residence.
Spokane	Vacant
Springfield	E. W. Osborne, Springfield, Ill.
Tennessee	Thomas F. Gallor, Memphis
Texas	G. H. Kinsolving, Austin
Utah	F. S. Spalding, Salt Lake City
Vermont	A. C. A. Hall, Burlington
Coadjutor	William F. Weeks, Rutland, Vt.
Virginia	Robert A. Gibson, Richmond
West'n Colorado	Benj. Brewster, Glenwood Spgs.
Washington, D. C	Alfred Harding, Washington
West Missouri	S. C. Partridge, Kansas City
Western Michigan	J. N. McCormick, Grand Rapids
Western Nebraska	G. A. Beecher, Hastings
Western New York	William D. Walker, Buffalo
West Texas	J. S. Johnston, San Antonio
West Virginia	G. W. Peterkin, Parkersburg
Coadjutor	William L. Gravatt, Charlestown
Wyoming	N. S. Thomas, Cheyenne

Foreign missions:

West Africa	S. D. Ferguson, Monrovia, Liberia
China (Shanghai)	F. R. Graves, Shanghai
China (Wuhu)	D. T. Huntington, Ankow
China (Haukow)	L. H. Roots, Hankow
Japan (Tokyo)	John McKim, Tokyo
Japan (Kyoto)	Henry St. G. Tucker, Kyoto
Cuba	William C. Brown, Havana
Haiti	Vacant

South'n Brazil...L. L. Kinsolving, Rio Grande do Sul
European churches—G. Mott Williams, Marquette, Mich., bishop in charge.
Mexico.................H. D. Aves, City of Mexico
Panama Canal Zone.......................Vacant
Nondiocesan—Arthur S. Lloyd, James H. Van Buren, C. C. Penick, Anson R. Graves, William M. Brown, William C. Gray, A. W. Knight, L. H. Wells.

METHODIST EPISCOPAL CHURCH.
BISHOPS.
Atlanta, Ga.—Frederick D. Leete.
Boston, Mass.—John W. Hamilton.
Buffalo, N. Y.—William Burt.
Buenos Aires, Argentina—Homer C. Stuntz.
Chattanooga, Tenn.—Theodore S. Henderson.
Chicago, Ill.—William F. McDowell.
Cincinnati, O.—William F. Anderson.
Denver, Col.—Francis J. McConnell.
Foochow, China—W. S. Lewis.
Helena, Mont.—Naphtali Luccock.
Kansas City, Kas.—William O. Shepard.
New Orleans, La.—Wilbur P. Thirkield.
New York, N. Y.—Luther B. Wilson.
Oklahoma City, Okla.—Robert McIntyre.
Omaha, Neb.—Frank M. Bristol.
Pekin, China—James W. Bashford.
Philadelphia, Pa.—Joseph F. Berry.
Portland, Ore.—Richard J. Cooke.
St. Louis, Mo.—Charles W. Smith.
St. Paul, Minn.—William A. Quayle.
San Francisco, Cal.—Edwin H. Hughes.
Washington, D. C.—Earl Cranston.
Zurich, Switzerland—John L. Nuelson.

MISSIONARY BISHOPS.
Bombay, India—John E. Robinson.
New York, N. Y.—Joseph C. Hartzell.
Lucknow, India—Frank W. Warne.
Monrovia, Liberia—Isaiah B. Scott.
Seoul, Korea—Merriam C. Harris.
Manila, P. I.—William P. Eveland.

GENERAL CONFERENCE SECRETARIES.
Board Conference Claimants—Joseph B. Hingeley.
Board of Foreign Missions—S. Earl Taylor, W. F. Oldham, Frank M. North.
Board of Home Missions and Church Extension—Ward Platt, Charles M. Boswell, Robert Forbes.
Board of Education—Thomas Nicholson.
Board of Freedmen's Aid—I. Garland Penn, P. J. Maveety.
Board of Sunday Schools—Edgar Blake.
Epworth League—Wilbur F. Sheridan.

EPWORTH LEAGUE.
Organized at Cleveland, O., May 15, 1889.
President—Bishop Frank M. Bristol, Omaha, Neb.
General Secretary—Rev. W. F. Sheridan, D. D., 1020 South Wabash avenue, Chicago, Ill.

German Assistant Secretary—Rev. A. C. Bueber, Cincinnati, O.
Assistant Secretary for Colored Conferences—Rev. W. W. Lucas, Meridian, Miss.
Editor Epworth Herald—Rev. Dan B. Brummitt, D.D., 1020 South Wabash avenue, Chicago, Ill.

METHODIST EPISCOPAL CHURCH SOUTH.
BISHOPS.
Alpheus W. Wilson, Baltimore, Md.
Eugene R. Hendrix, Kansas City, Mo.
Joseph S. Key, Sherman, Tex.
Warren A. Candler, Atlanta, Ga.
Henry C. Morrison, Leesburg, Fla.
E. Embree Hoss, Nashville, Tenn.
James Atkins, Waynesville, N. C.
Collins Denny, Richmond, Va.
John C. Kilgo, Durham, N. C.
W. B. Murrah, Jackson, Miss.
W. R. Lambuth, Nashville, Tenn.
E. D. Mouzon, San Antonio, Tex.
R. G. Waterhouse, Los Angeles, Cal.
J. H. McCoy, Birmingham, Ala.

PRESBYTERIAN CHURCH IN THE UNITED STATES OF AMERICA.
Stated Clerk—Rev. William H. Roberts, D. D., LL. D., 515 Witherspoon building, 1319 Walnut street, Philadelphia, Pa.
Permanent Clerk—Rev. William B. Noble, D. D., Coronado, Cal.
Assistant Clerk—Rev. J. M. Hubbert, D. D., room 515 Witherspoon building, Philadelphia, Pa.

TRUSTEES.
President—George Stevenson, Philadelphia, Pa.
Treasurer—The Philadelphia Trust company.
Recording Secretary—Edward R. Sterrett, 511 Witherspoon building, Philadelphia, Pa.
Office—1319 Walnut street, Philadelphia, Pa.

TRUSTEES FOR THE GENERAL ASSEMBLY OF THE CUMBERLAND PRESBYTERIAN CHURCH.
President—J. O. Carson, Bowling Green, Ky.
Secretary—W. F. Ennis, Bowling Green, Ky.

BOARD OF HOME MISSIONS.
President—Rev. D. Stuart Dodge, D. D.
Secretary—Rev. Charles L. Thompson, D. D., LL. D.
Associate Secretaries—Rev. John Dixon, D. D.; J. Ernest McAfee.
Treasurer—Harvey C. Olin.
Superintendent of School Work—Marshall C. Allaben.
Indian Department—Superintendent, Rev. Thomas C. Moffett, D. D.
Immigration Department—Superintendent, Rev. William Payne Shriver.
Department of Church and Country Life—Superintendent, Rev. Warren H. Wilson, Ph. D.
Field Secretaries—Rev. B. F. Fullerton, D. D., St. Louis, Mo.; Rev. W. S. Holt, Portland, Ore.; Rev. R. M. Donaldson, D. D., Denver, Col.; Rev. W. H. Kearns, D. D., Minneapolis, Minn.
Office—156 5th avenue, New York, N. Y.

BOARD OF FOREIGN MISSIONS.
President—Rev. George Alexander, D. D.
Corresponding Secretaries—Dr. Robert E. Speer, Rev. Arthur J. Brown, D. D.; Rev. A. Woodruff Halsey, D. D., and Rev. Stanley White, D. D.
Treasurer—Dwight H. Day.
Office—156 5th avenue, New York, N. Y.

BOARD OF EDUCATION.
President—Rev. Charles Wadsworth, Jr., D. D., Philadelphia, Pa.
Secretary—Rev. Joseph W. Cochran, D. D.
Treasurer—Edward R. Sterrett.
Office—1319 Walnut street, Philadelphia, Pa.

THE EDUCATIONAL SOCIETY.
President—W. H. Halbert, Nashville, Tenn.
Corresponding Secretary—Rev. W. J. Darby, D. D., Evansville, Ind.

BOARD OF PUBLICATION AND SABBATH SCHOOL WORK.
President—William H. Scott, Philadelphia, Pa.
Secretary—Rev. Alexander Henry, D. D.

Editorial Superintendent—(Vacancy).
Business Superintendent and Treasurer—Frank M. Braseimann.
Superintendent of Depositories—John H. Scribner.
Superintendent of Young People's Work—Rev. William Ralph Hall.
Superintendent of Sabbath School Training—Rev. James A. Worden, D. D., LL. D.
Manufacturer—Henry F. Scheetz.
Assistant Treasurer—Marshall S. Collingwood.
Office—1319 Walnut street, Philadelphia, Pa.
Chicago Office—500 South Wabash avenue.

CUMBERLAND BOARD OF PUBLICATION.
President—Hamilton Parks, Nashville, Tenn.
Secretary—John H. DeWitt, Nashville, Tenn.

BOARD OF CHURCH ERECTION.
President—Rev. William Russell Bennett.
Corresponding Secretary—(Vacancy.)
Field Secretary—Rev. Jesse C. Bruce, D. D.
Treasurer—Adam Campbell.
Office—156 5th avenue, New York, N. Y.

BOARD OF MINISTERIAL RELIEF AND SUSTENTATION.
President—Rev. John R. Davies, D. D., Philadelphia, Pa.
General Secretary—Rev. William Hiram Foulkes, D. D.
Associate Secretaries—Rev. John R. Sutherland, D. D.; Rev. William S. Holt, D. D.
Treasurer—Rev. William W. Heberton, D. D.
Office—1319 Walnut street, Philadelphia, Pa.

BOARD OF MISSIONS FOR FREEDMEN.
President—Rev. Samuel J. Fisher, D. D., Pittsburgh, Pa.
Corresponding Secretary and Treasurer—Rev. Edward P. Cowan, D. D.
Office—513 Bessemer bldg., 6th street, Pittsburgh, Pa.

COLLEGE BOARD.
President Emeritus—Rev. Herrick Johnson, D. D., LL. D., St. Louis, Mo.
President—John H. MacCracken, Ph. D.
Secretary—Robert Mackenzie, D. D., LL. D.
Assistant Secretary—Rev. James E. Clark, D. D.
Office Secretary and Assistant Treasurer—Rev. George R. Brauer.
Office—156 5th avenue, New York, N. Y.

THE BOARD OF TEMPERANCE.
President—Rev. Thomas Watters, D. D.
Corresponding Secretary and Treasurer—Rev. John F. Hill, D. D., Conestoga building, Pittsburgh, Pa.
General Secretary—Prof. Charles Scanlon.

ASSEMBLY HERALD.
Managing Committee—Rev. A. Woodruff Halsey, D. D.; chairman; Rev. John Dixon, D. D.; William H. Scott.
Manager—Horace P. Camden.
Office—1328 Chestnut street, Philadelphia, Pa.

CHRISTIAN LIFE AND WORK.
Chairman—Rev. John Timothy Stone, D. D.
Secretary—Rev. William H. Roberts, D. D., Witherspoon building, Philadelphia, Pa.

PRESBYTERIAN BROTHERHOOD.
President—(Vacancy.)
Secretaries—Rev. J. T. Henderson, D. D.; Rev. F. M. Fox, D. D.
Office—509 South Wabash avenue, Chicago, Ill.

PRESBYTERIAN HISTORICAL SOCIETY.
President—Rev. Henry Van Dyke, D. D., LL. D.
General Secretary—Rev. Joseph B. Turner, D. D.
Treasurer—DeBenneville K. Ludwig, Ph. D.
Honorary Librarian—Rev. Louis F. Benson, D. D.
Library, Museum, etc.—Witherspoon building, Philadelphia, Pa.

BAPTIST DENOMINATION.
Baptist World Alliance—President, Dr. Robert S. MacArthur, New York, N. Y.; secretaries, Rev. J. H. Shakespeare, London, England; Rev. J. N. Prestridge, Louisville, Ky.
General Convention of Baptists of North America—President, Dr. A. L. McCrimmon, Canada; secretary, Prof. W. O. Carver, Louisville, Ky.
Northern Baptist Convention—President, Henry Bond, Brattleboro, Vt.; corresponding secretary, Rev. W. C. Bitting, D. D., St. Louis, Mo.

American Baptist Publication Society—President, J. Whitcomb Brougher, D. D., Los Angeles, Cal.; secretary, A. J. Rowland, D. D., 1701 Chestnut street, Philadelphia, Pa.
American Baptist Historical Society—President, B. MacMackin, D. D., Philadelphia, Pa.
American Baptist Foreign Mission Society—President, Carter Helm Jones, D. D., Seattle, Wash.; corresponding secretaries, home department, Rev. F. P. Haggard, D. D.; foreign department, J. H. Franklin, D. D., Ford building, Boston, Mass.; treasurer, Ernest S. Butler, Boston, Mass.
American Baptist Home Mission Society—President, D. K. Edwards, Los Angeles, Cal.; treasurer, Frank T. Moulton, Yonkers, N. Y.; corresponding secretary, H. L. Morehouse, D. D., 23 East 26th street, New York city; associate corresponding secretary, Charles L. White, New York, N. Y.; field secretary, L. Call Barnes, D. D., New York, N. Y.; recording secretary, M. L. Wood, Huntington, W. Va.
Baptist Forward Movement for Missionary Education—Rev. John M. Moore, general secretary, Ford building, Boston.
Woman's Baptist Foreign Missionary Society—President, Mrs. M. Grant Edmands, Chestnut Hill, Mass.; corresponding secretary foreign department, Mrs. H. G. Safford, Ford building, Boston, Mass.; secretaries home department, Mrs. C. A. Robinson and Miss H. S. Ellis, Boston, Mass.
Women's Baptist Foreign Missionary Society of the West—President, Mrs. Andrew MacLeish, Chicago, Ill.; foreign corresponding secretary, Miss Mary E. Adkins, Chicago, Ill.; home secretary, Miss M. Jean Batty, 88 East 39th street, Chicago, Ill.; treasurer, Miss Frances K. Burr; field secretary, Miss Ella D. MacLaurin, Chicago.
Woman's American Baptist Home Mission Society—President, Mrs. Albert G. Lester, Chicago, Ill.; corresponding secretary, Mrs. Katharine S. Westfall, 2969 Vernon avenue, Chicago, Ill.; recording secretary, Mrs. F. L. Miner, Des Moines, Iowa; treasurer, Mrs. Emma C. Marshall, Chicago, Ill.
Baptist Young People's Union of America—President, Rev. C. L. Anderson, D. D., Chicago, Ill.; recording secretary, Rev. H. W. Reed, Rock Island, Ill.; general secretary, Rev. W. E. Chalmers, Philadelphia, Pa.; treasurer, H. E. Osgood, Chicago, Ill. The union is a federation of all young people's societies connected with the baptist churches in the United States and Canada.
American Baptist Education Society—President, Rev. L. A. Crandall, D. D., Minneapolis, Minn.; corresponding secretary, Prof. E. D. Burton, University of Chicago, Chicago, Ill.
Baptist Congress—President, H. W. Merrill, Atlantic City, N. J.; secretary, Rev. T. A. K. Gessler, D. D., Landing, N. J.
Chicago Baptist Executive Council—Dean, Shailer Mathews, University of Chicago; superintendent, Rev. F. L. Anderson, 107 Wabash avenue; secretary, Rev. W. P. Behan, Morgan Park, Ill.; treasurer, A. E. Wells, Monadnock block.

SOUTHERN BAPTIST CONVENTION.
Officers—President, Rev. E. C. Dargan; vice-presidents, Hon. Joseph James Darlington, Washington, D. C.; Samuel Palmer Brooks, D. D., Waco, Tex.; William Ellyson, Richmond, Va.; Hon. Lamartine Hardman, Commerce, Ga.; secretaries, Rev. Lansing Burrows, D. D., Americus, Ga.; Rev. Oliver Gregory, D. D.; Staunton, Va.; treasurer, George W. Norton, Louisville, Ky.; auditor, William P. Harvey, Louisville, Ky.
Foreign Mission Board—President, J. B. Hutson, Virginia; corresponding secretary, Rev. R. J. Willingham, D. D.; editorial secretary, W. H. Smith; educational secretary, Rev. T. B. Ray; field secretary, Rev. S. J. Porter, D. D.; recording secretary, Rev. W. S. Dorsett, D. D.; treasurer, R. R. Gwathmey; auditor, J. D. Crump.
Home Mission Board—President, Rev. John F. Purser, D. D., Georgia; corresponding secretary, Rev. B. D. Gray, D. D.; assistant corresponding secretary, Rev. J. F. Love, D. D.; treasurer, Walker Dunson; recording secretary, M. M. Welch; editorial secretary, Rev. V. I. Masters; auditor, C. A. Davis.

Sunday School Board—President, Rev. E. E. Folk, D. D., Tennessee; corresponding secretary and treasurer, Rev. J. M. Frost, D. D.; recording secretary, A. B. Hill; auditor, Roger Eastman.

THE CONGREGATIONAL CHURCHES.

AMERICAN CONGREGATIONAL ASSOCIATION.
President—Arthur S. Johnson, Boston, Mass.
Vice-President—Samuel B. Capen.
Secretary—Rev. Thomas Todd, Jr., Concord, Mass.
Treasurer—A. S. Lovett, Brookline, Mass.
Headquarters—Congregational House, Boston, Mass.

AMERICAN BOARD OF COMMISSIONERS FOR FOREIGN MISSIONS.
President—S. B. Capen, LL. D.
Treasurer—Frank H. Wiggin.
Secretaries—Rev. James J. Barton, D. D.; Rev. Cornelius H. Patton, D. D.; Rev. E. L. Smith, D. D.
Editorial Secretary—Rev. E. E. Strong, D. D., emeritus; Rev. W. E. Strong.
District Secretaries—Rev. A. N. Hitchcock, D. D., 19 South LaSalle street, Chicago, Ill.; Rev. H. M. Tenney, D. D., Mechanics' Bank building, San Francisco, Cal.
Headquarters—Congregational House, Boston, Mass.

AMERICAN MISSIONARY ASSOCIATION.
President—Cyrus Northrop, LL. D.
Treasurer—Irving C. Gaylord.
Secretaries—Rev. C. J. Ryder, D. D.; Rev. H. Paul Douglass, D. D.
Western Secretary—Rev. Lucius O. Baird, D. D., 19 South LaSalle street, Chicago, Ill.
Headquarters—287 4th avenue, New York city.

SUNDAY SCHOOL AND PUBLICATION SOCIETY.
President—Rev. Frederick H. Page, Waltham, Mass.
Treasurer—H. T. Richardson, Congregational House, Boston, Mass.
Missionary and Extension Secretary—Rev. William Ewing, Boston, Mass.
Manager Pilgrim Press—Luther H. Cary, Boston.
District Secretaries—Rev. R. W. Gammon, 19 South LaSalle street, Chicago, Ill.; Rev. M. S. Littlefield, 155 80th street, Brooklyn, N. Y.
Headquarters—Congregational House, Boston, Mass.

CHURCH BUILDING SOCIETY.
President—Lucien C. Warner, LL. D., New York city.
Secretary—Rev. C. H. Richards, D. D., New York city.
Treasurer—Charles E. Hope.
Field Secretaries—Rev. W. W. Newell, D. D., 19 South LaSalle street, Chicago, Ill.; Rev. H. H. Wikoff, San Francisco, Cal., and Rev. W. W. Leete, D. D., Boston, Mass.
Headquarters—105 East 22d street, New York city.

HOME MISSIONARY SOCIETY.
President—Rev. Watson L. Phillips.
Treasurer—M. J. Brinkerhoff.
Secretaries—Rev. Herman F. Swartz, Rev. R. L. Breed and Rev. H. C. Herring.
Headquarters—287 4th avenue, New York city.

EDUCATION SOCIETY.
President—Rev. William R. Campbell, D. D., Boston, Mass.
Secretary—Rev. Edward S. Tead, Boston, Mass.
Treasurer—S. F. Wilkins, Boston, Mass.
Headquarters—Congregational House, Boston, Mass. Chicago Office—19 South LaSalle street.

MINISTERIAL RELIEF.
Chairman—Rev. H. A. Stimson, D. D., New York city.
Secretary—Wm. A. Rice, D. D., New York city.
Treasurer—B. H. Fancher, 287 4th avenue, New York city.

NATIONAL TRIENNIAL COUNCIL.
Moderator—Rev. Charles R. Brown, Yale university, New Haven, Conn.
Secretary—Rev. Hubert O. Herring, New York, N. Y.

WOMAN'S BOARD OF MISSIONS.
Secretary—Miss Helen B. Calder, Congregational House, Boston, Mass.

WOMAN'S BOARD OF MISSIONS OF THE INTERIOR.
Secretary—Miss M. D. Wingate, Chicago, Ill.

WOMAN'S BOARD OF MISSIONS OF THE PACIFIC.
Secretary—Mrs. F. F. Barbour, Carlton hotel, Berkeley, Cal.

THE WOMAN'S HOME MISSIONARY FEDERATION.
President—Mrs. H. H. Hurt, 7 Colden avenue, White Plains, N. Y.
Secretary—Mrs. T. H. Warner, 30 Ridgeview avenue, White Plains, N. Y.
Recording Secretary—Miss Mary Brooks, 55 Essex avenue, Gloucester, Mass.
Treasurer—Mrs. H. A. Flint, 604 Willis avenue, Syracuse, N. Y.

CONGREGATIONAL BROTHERHOOD OF AMERICA.
President—H. M. Beardsley, Kansas City, Mo.
General Secretary—H. A. Atkinson, Chicago, Ill.
Treasurer—S. E. Knecht, Chicago, Ill.

CHRISTIAN SCIENCE CHURCH.

The Christian Science church was founded in 1879 by Mary Baker Eddy, the discoverer of Christian science and author of its text-book, "Science and Health, with Key to the Scriptures." The church was organized "to commemorate the word and works of our Master, which should reinstate primitive Christianity and its lost element of healing" (Church Manual). In 1892 the church was reorganized as the First Church of Christ, Scientist, known as the mother church, in Boston, Mass. The present officers of the mother church are:
President—Frederick Dixon.
Clerk—John V. Dittemore.
Treasurer—Adam H. Dickey.
Directors—Archibald McLellan, Allison V. Stewart, James A. Neal, John V. Dittemore, Adam H. Dickey.

All Christian science churches and societies, of which there are now 1,432 in the United States and 125 in foreign countries, are branches of the mother church. Lesson-sermons compiled from the bible and "Science and Health, with Key to the Scriptures" are read at the services in Christian science churches. There are about 5,300 Christian science practitioners regularly devoting their time to the practice of Christian science mind healing.

Mrs. Eddy founded the Christian Science Journal, Sentinel, Quarterly, Der Herold der Christian Science and The Christian Science Monitor (a daily newspaper), all of which are published by the Christian Science Publishing society in Boston.

There is in connection with the Christian science movement an official board of lectureship designed to furnish the public correct information concerning the fundamental teachings of Christian science. Lectures given by members of this board are free to the public.

UNITARIAN CHURCH.

AMERICAN UNITARIAN ASSOCIATION.
President—Rev. Samuel A. Eliot, D. D., Boston, Mass.
Vice-Presidents—Clarence E. Carr, Andover, N. H.; George Hutchinson, Newton, Mass.; George Soule, New Orleans, La.; Miss Emma C. Low, Brooklyn, N. Y.; Charles W. Ames, St. Paul, Minn.; Paris Gibson, Great Falls, Mont.; Horace Davis, San Francisco, Cal.; Mrs. John W. Loud, Montreal, Canada.
Secretary—Rev. Lewis G. Wilson, Boston, Mass.
Treasurer—Henry M. Williams, Cambridge, Mass.

GENERAL CONFERENCE.
President—Charles W. Eliot, LL. D., Cambridge, Mass.
Vice-Presidents—Hon. Horace Davis, San Francisco, Cal.; Hon. Adelbert Moot, Buffalo, N. Y.; Hon. Hugh McKennan Landon, Indianapolis, Ind.; Hon. Frederic A. Delano, Chicago, Ill.; Hon. Charles A. Murdoch, San Francisco, Cal.
General Secretary—Rev. Walter F. Greenman, 684 Astor street, Milwaukee, Wis.
Treasurer—Percy A. Atherton, 53 State street, Boston, Mass.

LUTHERAN DENOMINATION.

GENERAL SYNOD OF LUTHERAN CHURCH OF THE UNITED STATES.

President—Rev. H. L. Yaeger, D. D., Atchison, Kas.

Secretary—Rev. F. P. Marnhart, D. D., Selinsgrove, Pa.

Treasurer—George H. Knollenberg, Richmond, Ind.

AUGUSTANA SYNOD.

President—Rev. L. A. Johnston, D. D., 540 Olive street, St. Paul, Minn.

Vice-President—Rev. G. A. Brandelle, D. D., 2250 Court place, Denver, Col.

Secretary—Rev. Jas. A. Anderson, A. M., Boxholm, Boone county, Iowa.

Treasurer—K. T. Anderson, State bank, Rock Island, Ill.

MISSOURI SYNOD (GERMAN AND ENGLISH).

President—Rev. F. Pfotenhauer, 415 West 62d street, Chicago, Ill.

Secretary—Rev. R. D. Biedermann, 717 South New Jersey street, Indianapolis, Ind.

Secretary English District—Rev. J. F. Wenchell, 228 Morgan street, N. W., Washington, D. C.

The official title of this organization is: The German Evangelical Lutheran Synod of Missouri, Ohio and Other States.

HAUGE SYNOD.

President—Rev. M. G. Hanson, Kenyon, Minn.

Secretary—Rev. N. J. Lohre, M. A., Grand Forks, N. D.

Treasurer—O. A. Ulvin, Red Wing, Minn.

NORWEGIAN SYNOD.

President—Dr. H. G. Stub, 806 Sheldon avenue, St. Paul, Minn.

Vice-President—Prof. C. K. Preus, Decorah, Iowa.

Secretary—Rev. D. C. Jordahl, Ridgeway, Iowa.

Treasurer—Rev. H. B. Hustvedt, Decorah, Iowa.

UNITED NORWEGIAN LUTHERAN CHURCH OF AMERICA.

President—Rev. T. H. Dahl, D. D., 2117 Park avenue, Minneapolis, Minn.

Secretary—Jens C. Roseland, 515 Holly avenue, Crookston, Minn.

THE LUTHER LEAGUE.

Luther League of America—President, William C. Stoever, Philadelphia, Pa.

Secretary—Rev. Luther M. Kuhns, Omaha, Neb.

Treasurer—C. T. A. Anderson, Chicago, Ill.

Luther league is nonsynodical in organization. It has seventeen state, fifty-two district and 998 local organizations. It is also organized in Canada, Porto Rico, Japan, China and India.

CHURCH OF THE NEW JERUSALEM.

[Swedenborgian.]

THE GENERAL CONVENTION.

President—Rev. Julian K. Smyth, 230 West 59th street, New York, N. Y.

Vice-President—Hon. Job Barnard, 1306 Rhode Island avenue, N. W., Washington, D. C.

Recording Secretary—B. A. Whittemore, 134 Bowdoin street, Boston, Mass.

Treasurer—James Richard Carter, 246 Devonshire street, Boston, Mass.

UNION OF HEBREW CONGREGATIONS

EXECUTIVE COMMITTEE.

President—J. Walter Freiberg, Cincinnati, O.

Vice-President—Charles Shohl, Cincinnati, O.

Treasurer—Solomon Fox, Cincinnati, O.

Secretary—Levy Lipman, Cincinnati, O.

The next biennial council of the Union of American congregations will be held in 1915.

NATIONAL SPIRITUALISTS' ASSOCIATION.

President—Dr. George B. Warne, Chicago.

Vice-president—Joseph Whitwell, St. Paul, Minn.

Secretary—George W. Kates, Washington, D. C.

Treasurer—Cassius L. Stevens, Pittsburgh, Pa.

Trustees—G. I. Evans, Washington, D. C.; Mrs. Elizabeth Harlow-Goetz, Baltimore, Md.; Thomas Grimshaw, Long Beach, Cal.; Alonzo M. Griffin, Chicago; Dr. Otto Vierling, St. Louis, Mo.

RELIGIOUS EDUCATION ASSOCIATION.

Organized Feb. 12, 1903.

President—Dr. Charles F. Thwing, Cleveland, O.

Recording Secretary—Charles M. Stuart, Evanston, Ill.

General Secretary—Henry Frederick Cope, Chicago, Ill.

Treasurer—Charles L. Hutchinson, Chicago, Ill.

Executive Offices—332 South Michigan avenue, Chicago, Ill.

The purpose of the association is to promote the improvement and extension of moral and religious education through existing agencies in the churches, schools, etc., by serving as a center, a clearing house and a bureau of information and promotion. The association publishes a bimonthly magazine; maintains a permanent library and exhibit, superintends local guilds, holds general conventions and local conferences. It enrolls in its membership any persons interested in moral and religious education regardless of sectarian or theological lines.

AMERICAN BIBLE SOCIETY.

Bible House Astor place, New York, N. Y.

President—James Wood.

Corresponding Secretaries—Rev. John Fox, D. D., and Rev. William I. Haven, D. D., Bible House, New York, N. Y.

Recording Secretary—Rev. Henry Otis Dwight, LL. D., Bible House, New York, N. Y.

Treasurer—William Foulke, Bible House, New York, N. Y.

Agency Secretaries in the United States—Rev. S. H. Kirkbride, D. D., McCormick building, Chicago, Ill.; Rev. J. P. Wragg, D. D., 35 Gammon avenue, Atlanta, Ga.; Rev. M. B. Porter, 205 North 5th street, Richmond, Va.; Rev. G. E. Farnam, 214 Y. M. C. A. building, Denver, Col.; Rev. A. Wesley Mell, Y. M. C. A. building, San Francisco, Cal.; Rev. J. J. Morgan, 1815½ Main street, Dallas, Tex.; Rev. G. S. J. Browne, D. D., 524 Elm street, Cincinnati, O.; Rev. L. W. Eckard, D. D., 701 Walnut street, Philadelphia, Pa.; Rev. W. H. Tower, 330 Livingstone street, Brooklyn, N. Y.

AMERICAN SUNDAY SCHOOL UNION.

At headquarters, 1816 Chestnut street, Philadelphia, Pa.

President—Martin L. Finckel.

Corresponding Secretary—(Vacancy.)

Recording Secretary—William H. Hirst.

Treasurer—John E. Stevenson.

Secretary of Missions—Rev. George P. Williams, D. D.

FEDERAL COUNCIL OF THE CHURCHES OF CHRIST IN AMERICA.

Organized in December, 1908.

President—Shailer Mathews, Ph. D.

Executive Secretary—Rev. Charles S. Macfarland, D. D.

Honorary Secretary—Rev. E. B. Sanford.

Recording Secretary—Rivington D. Lord, D. D.

Treasurer—Alfred R. Kimball.

Executive Committee—Rev. Frank Mason North, D. D., chairman; Frank Mason, D. D., vice-chairman, and delegates from thirty-three denominations which are represented in the Federal council through the official action of their highest national judicatories, assemblies and conferences.

National Offices—1611 Clarendon building, 215 4th avenue, New York, N. Y.

AMERICAN TRACT SOCIETY.

Organized 1825.

President—William Phillips Hall.

General Secretary—Judson Swift, D. D.

Treasurer—Louis Tag.

Offices—150 Nassau street, New York, N. Y.

UNITED SOCIETY OF CHRISTIAN ENDEAVOR.

President—Rev. Francis E. Clark, D. D., LL. D.

General Secretary—William Shaw, Tremont Temple, Boston, Mass.

Editorial Secretary—Prof. Amos R. Wells.
Treasurer—Hiram N. Lathrop.
Publication Manager—A. K. Shartle.
Manager Western Office—Walter R. Mee, 405, 19 South LaSalle street, Chicago.

YOUNG MEN'S CHRISTIAN ASSOCIATION.

International Committee of Young Men's Christian Associations of North America—Alfred E. Marling, chairman; William Sloane, William D. Murray, vice-chairmen; B. H. Fancher, treasurer; Richard C. Morse, general secretary; John R. Mott, associate general secretary; general offices, 124 East 28th street, New York, N. Y. The annual report made in 1913 shows: Associations, 2,421; members, 597,857; value of real property, $75,049,234; total net property, $81,367,744; number of employed officers, 3,853; students in educational classes, 73,388; 628 gymnasiums; 187,539 enrolled in gymnasium classes; 290 athletic fields; 234 railroad associations with 87,397 members; 772 student associations with 69,296 members; boy membership, 120,322.

YOUNG PEOPLE'S CHRISTIAN UNION OF THE UNIVERSALIST CHURCH.

President—Rev. Stanley Manning, Minneapolis, Minn.
Secretary—Carl T. Elsner, 359 Boylston street, Boston, Mass.
Treasurer—James B. Knapp, 99 Fulton street, New York city.

THE SALVATION ARMY.

Organized in London July, 1865.
Commander in Chief—Gen. Bramwell Booth.
International Headquarters—London, England.
American National Headquarters—120 West 14th street, New York, N. Y.
Commander of United States Forces—Evangeline C. Booth.
Western Territorial Headquarters—108, 114 North Dearborn street, Chicago, Ill.
Western Territorial Commissioner—Thomas Estill. Posts in World—9,130.

THE VOLUNTEERS OF AMERICA.

Organized in March, 1896.
Commanders—Gen. Ballington and Maud B. Booth.
National Headquarters—34 West 28th street, New York, N. Y.

Northwestern Headquarters—1201-1213 Washington boulevard, Chicago, Ill.
Territorial Commander—Maj.-Gen. Edward Fielding.

BROTHERHOOD OF ANDREW AND PHILIP.

President—William M. Gordon, Philadelphia, Pa.
Vice-Presidents—Dr. D. K. Wilbur, Bryn Mawr, Pa., and Harvey C. Miller, Philadelphia, Pa.
Recording Secretary—G. Percy Fox, 2524 Girard avenue, Philadelphia, Pa.
General Secretary—The Rev. R. Howard Taylor, 704 Hale building, Philadelphia, Pa.
Treasurer—Roland M. Eavenson, 4052 Baring street, Philadelphia, Pa.

INTERNATIONAL ORDER OF THE KING'S DAUGHTERS AND SONS.

Headquarters—156 5th avenue, New York, N. Y.
President—Miss Kate Bond, New York, N. Y.
First Vice-President—(Vacancy.)
Second Vice-President—Miss Annie M. Brown, Toronto, Ont.
Third Vice-President—Miss Jennie C. Benedict, Louisville, Ky.
General Secretary-Treasurer and Editor—Mrs. Mary Lowe Dickinson, 156 5th avenue, New York, N. Y.
Corresponding Secretary—Miss Clara Morehouse, 156 5th avenue, New York, N. Y.
Recording Secretary—Mrs. A. H. Evans, 336 West 86th street, New York, N. Y.

RELIGIONS OF THE WORLD.

According to the revised (1898) edition of Mulhall's Dictionary of Statistics there are 476,100,000 Christians in the world. The same authority places the number of Roman catholics in Europe, America and Australia at 223,090,000; protestants, 157,050,000, and Greeks, 88,660,000. It has been estimated that there are in the world 256,000,000 followers of Confucius, 190,000,000 Hindus, 176,800,000 Mohammedans, 148,000,000 Buddhists, 118,000,000 polytheists, 43,000,000 Taoists, 14,000,000 Shintoists and 12,000,000 Jews. Of the Christians more than 230,000,000 are catholics, 98,000,000 orthodox Greeks, 70,000,000 Lutherans, 21,000,000 episcopalians, 17,000,000 methodists, 11,000,000 baptists, 9,000,000 presbyterians and 4,500,000 congregationalists.

CENTENARIANS IN THE UNITED STATES.

According to the census of 1910 there were then in the United States 3,555 persons 100 years of age and over. Of these, 1,380 were men and 2,175 were women. Classified according to color they were: White men, 326; white women, 438; total, 764; negro men, 1,004; negro women, 1,671; total, 2,675; Indian men, 50; Indian women, 66; total, 116. Classified as to place of birth, 439 were native white and 263 foreign-born white. The number of centenarians reported by the census of 1900 was 3,504. "It may be noted," says a census report in commenting on these figures, "that the proportion of centenarians, according to the census returns, was less in 1910 than in 1900. In fact, the proportion has steadily decreased from census to census for over half a century. The number of centenarians reported in 1910 was equal to 4 for each 100,000 of the total population, while the corresponding ratio in 1850 was 11. It is improbable that any such decrease in longevity has actually occurred. By no means have all those who report themselves as 100 years old or more, in fact, reached that age, and the apparent reduction in the proportion of centenarians is probably due to greater accuracy in the returns."

Deaths of centenarians reported from Nov. 1, 1912, to Nov. 1, 1913:
Belland, Mrs. M. A., 100, St. Paul, Minn., May 14.
Dalton, Avery, 105, Elmwood, Ill., July 15.
Dunne, John, 103, Burlington, Ia., Feb. 1.
Fisher, Eleazer, 105, Sandwich, Ill., June 16.
Haynes, Mrs. Lucy M., 100, in Girard, Ill., March 15.
Halleman, Mrs. Cornelia, 100, Raleigh, N. C., March 11.
Kennedy, Mrs. Bridget, 103, Chicago, March 2.
La Bore, Mrs. F., 104, Minneapolis, Minn., Jan. 26.
Linn, W. T., 108, Oconee, Ill., July 28.
Lugo-Leon, Mrs. Placentino, 105, Los Angeles, Cal., Feb. 26.
Neuin, Samuel, 108, Lebanon, Pa., Feb. 24.
Maugberman, Mrs. Elizabeth, 108, Bryan, O., June 14.
Metimof, Lucke, 120, Saginaw, Mich., Aug. 23.
Moran, Mrs. Bridget, 101, in Chicago, Sept. 15.
Page, Orsamus, 105, Joliet, Ill., Jan. 1.
Rheubottom, Mrs. Jane, 104, Chicago, Feb. 24.
Sloan, Jerome, 100, Princeville, Ill., April 21.
Shippiro, Peter, 108, Washington, D. C., May 29.
Trinkle, Mrs. Polly, 102, Bristol, Tenn., March 11.

KING OTTO OF BAVARIA DEPOSED.

Otto, the insane king of Bavaria, was deposed from the throne Nov. 5, 1913, and Prince Regent Ludwig proclaimed himself king in accordance with a law passed by the diet. The new ruler took the title of Ludwig III. A proclamation was posted throughout the kingdom declaring incurable the insanity which had incapacitated Otto and announcing that in consequence the regency was terminated and that Prince Ludwig had assumed the title and duties of king. Otto was born April 27, 1848, and, though insane at the time, succeeded his brother, Ludwig II., who drowned himself June 13, 1886. Otto was king for twenty-seven years without being aware of it.

FRATERNAL AND BENEVOLENT SOCIETIES.

GRAND LODGES A. F. & A. M.

NAMES AND ADDRESSES OF GRAND SECRETARIES
OCTOBER, 1913.

Alabama—George A. Beauchamp, Montgomery.
Alberta—Dr. George Macdonald, Calgary.
Arizona—George J. Roskruge, Tucson.
Arkansas—Fay Hempstead, Little Rock.
British Columbia—W. A. DeW. Smith, Westminster.
California—John Whicher, San Francisco.
Canada—Ralph L. Gunn, Hamilton, Ont.
Colorado—Charles H. Jacobson, Denver.
Connecticut—George A. Kies, Hartford.
Cuba—Carlos G. Charles, Havana.
Delaware—Virginius V. Harrison, Wilmington.
District of Columbia—A. W. Johnston, Washington.
England—Sir Edward Letchworth, London.
Florida—W. P. Webster, Jacksonville.
Georgia—W. A. Wolihin, Macon.
Idaho—Theo. W. Randall, Boise.
Illinois—Isaac Cutter, Camp Point.
Indiana—Calvin W. Prather, Indianapolis.
Iowa—Newton R. Parvin, Cedar Rapids.
Ireland—H. E. Flavelle, Dublin.
Kansas—Albert K. Wilson, Topeka.
Kentucky—Dave Jackson, Louisville.
Louisiana—Richard Lambert, New Orleans.
Maine—Stephen Berry, Portland.
Manitoba—James A. Ovas, Winnipeg.
Maryland—George Cook, Baltimore.
Massachusetts—Thomas W. Davis, Boston.
Michigan—Lou B. Winsor, Reed City.
Minnesota—John Fishel, St. Paul.
Mississippi—Frederic Speed, Vicksburg.
Missouri—John R. Parson, St. Louis.
Montana—Cornelius Hedges, Jr., Helena.
Nebraska—Francis E. White, Omaha.
Netherlands—J. Bondewinje, The Hague.
Nevada—E. D. Vanderlieth, Carson City.
New Brunswick—J. Twining Hartt, St. John.
New Hampshire—Henry M. Cheney, Concord.
New Jersey—Benjamin F. Wakefield, Trenton.
New Mexico—Alpheus A. Keen, Albuquerque.
New York—Edward M. L. Ehlers, New York.
New Zealand—Malcolm Niccol, Dunedin.
North Carolina—John C. Drewry, Raleigh.
North Dakota—Walter L. Stockwell, Fargo.
Nova Scotia—Thomas Mowbray, Halifax.
Ohio—J. H. Bromwell, Cincinnati.
Oklahoma—William M. Anderson, Tulsa.
Oregon—James F. Robinson, Portland.
Pennsylvania—John A. Perry, Philadelphia.
Philippines—Amos G. Bellis, Manila.
Prince Edward Island—W. P. Doull, Charlottetown.
Quebec—Will H. Whyte, Montreal.
Queensland—Charles H. Harley, Brisbane.
Rhode Island—S. Penrose Williams, Providence.
Saskatchewan—John M. Shaw, Regina.
Scotland—David Reid, Edinburgh.
South Australia—C. R. J. Glover, Adelaide.
South Carolina—O. Frank Hart, Columbia.
South Dakota—George A. Pettigrew, Sioux Falls.
Tasmania—John Hamilton, Hobart.
Tennessee—John B. Garrett, Nashville.
Texas—John Watson, Waco.
United Grand Lodge of Victoria—Charles J. Barrow, Melbourne.
United Grand Lodge of New South Wales—Arthur H. Bray, Sydney.
Utah—Charles B. Jack, Salt Lake City.
Vermont—Henry H. Ross, Burlington.
Virginia—Charles A. Nesbit, Richmond..
Washington—Horace W. Tyler, Tacoma.
Western Australia—J. D. Stevenson, Perth.
West Virginia—John M. Collins, Charleston.
Wisconsin—William W. Perry, Milwaukee.
Wyoming—William M. Kuykendall, Saratoga.

ROYAL ARCH MASONS.

GENERAL GRAND CHAPTER.

General Grand High Priest—Bernard G. Witt, Henderson, Ky.
General Deputy Grand High Priest—George E. Corson, Washington, D. C.
General Grand King—Frederick W. Craig, Des Moines, Iowa.
General Grand Scribe—William F. Kuhn, Kansas City, Mo.

General Grand Treasurer—John M. Carter, Baltimore, Md.
General Grand Secretary—Charles A. Conover, Coldwater, Mich.
Headquarters, Coldwater, Mich.
Number of grand chapters, 48.

ROYAL AND SELECT MASTERS.

GENERAL GRAND COUNCIL 1912-15.

General Grand Master—J. Albert Blake, Malden, Mass.
General Grand Deputy Master—Edward W. Wellington, Ellsworth, Kas.
General Grand Principal Conductor—George A. Newell, Medina, N. Y.
General Grand Treasurer—Thomas E. Shears, Denver, Col.
General Grand Recorder—Henry W. Mordhurst, Fort Wayne, Ind.
General Grand Captain of Guard—William F. Cleveland, Harlan, Iowa.
General Grand Conductor of Council—Fay Hempstead, Little Rock, Ark.
General Grand Marshal—Joseph C. Greenfield, Atlanta, Ga.
General Grand Steward—Bert S. Lee, Springfield, Mo.

KNIGHTS TEMPLAR.

OFFICERS OF THE GRAND ENCAMPMENT K. T. OF
THE UNITED STATES.

Most Eminent Grand Master—Sir Knight Arthur MacArthur, Troy, N. Y.
R. E. Deputy Grand Master—Sir Knight Lee S. Smith, Pittsburgh, Pa.
V. E. Grand Generalissimo—Sir Knight Joseph Kyle Orr, Atlanta, Ga.
V. E. Grand Captain General—Sir Knight J. W. Chamberlain, St. Paul, Minn.
V. E. Grand Senior Warden—Sir Knight Leonidas P. Newby, Knightstown, Ind.
V. E. Grand Prelate—Sir Knight Rev. John M. Walden, Cincinnati, O.
V. E. Grand Treasurer—Sir Knight Henry W. Lines, Meriden, Conn.
V. E. Grand Recorder—Sir Knight F. H. Johnson, Louisville, Ky.

ANCIENT ACCEPTED SCOTTISH RITE MASONS.

NORTHERN MASONIC JURISDICTION.

Sovereign Grand Commander—Barton Smith, Toledo, O.
Grand Lieutenant-Commander—Leon M. Abbott, Boston, Mass.
Grand Secretary-General—James H. Codding, New York, N. Y.
Grand Minister of State—Amos Pettibone, Chicago, Ill.
Grand Treasurer-General—Leroy Goddard, Chicago, Ill.

SOUTHERN MASONIC JURISDICTION.

M. P. Sovereign Grand Commander—James D. Richardson, Washington, D. C.
Secretary-General—A. B. Chamberlain, Washington, D. C.

SUPREME COUNCIL, 33D DEGREE.

Sovereign Grand Commander—M. N. Bayliss, Washington, D. C.
Lieutenant Grand Commander—Josiah H. Long, Boston, Mass.
Grand Minister of State—Charles S. Webster, Worcester, Mass.
Treasurer-General—Holden O. Hill, Providence, R. I.
Grand Secretary-General—Marcus W. Morton, Providence, R. I.
Grand Keeper of Archives—Walter Seymour, Newark, N. J.
Grand Master General of Ceremonies—Leander G. Sherman, Providence, R. I.
Grand Marshal-General—William E. Bischy, Haverhill, Mass.
Grand Standard Bearer—John H. Messenger, Syracuse, N. Y.
Grand Captain of the Guard—John W. Bean, Haverhill, Mass.
Grand Seneschal—Thomas G. Waller, Lowell, Mass.

ANCIENT ARABIC ORDER NOBLES OF THE MYSTIC SHRINE.
First temple founded Sept. 26, 1872.

IMPERIAL COUNCIL, 1913-1914.

Imperial Potentate—William W. Irwin, Wheeling, W. Va.
Imperial Deputy Potentate—Frederick R. Smith, Rochester, N. Y.
Imperial Chief Rabban—J. Putnam Stevens, Portland, Me.
Imperial Assistant Rabban—Henry F. Niedringhaus, St. Louis, Mo.
Imperial High Priest and Prophet—Charles E. Ovenshire, Minneapolis, Minn.
Imperial Oriental Guide—Elias J. Jacoby, Indianapolis, Ind.
Imperial Treasurer—W. S. Brown, Pittsburgh, Pa.
Imperial Recorder—B. W. Rowell, 206 Masonic Temple, Boston, Mass.
Imperial First Ceremonial Master—W. Freeland Kendrick, Philadelphia, Pa.
Imperial Second Ceremonial Master—Ellis L. Garretson, Tacoma, Wash.
Imperial Marshal—William J. Matthews, New York, N. Y.
Imperial Captain of Guard—Ernest A. Cutts, Savannah, Ga.
Imperial Outer Guard—James S. McCandless, Honolulu, H. I.

ORDER OF THE EASTERN STAR.
Organized Nov. 16, 1876.

OFFICERS OF GENERAL GRAND CHAPTERS 1913-1916.

Most Worthy Grand Matron—Mrs. Reta A. Mills, Duke Center, Pa.
Most Worthy Grand Patron—George A. Pettigrew, Sioux Falls, S. D.
Right Worthy Associate Grand Matron—Mrs. Emma Ocobock, Hartford, Mich.
Right Worthy Associate Grand Patron—George M. Hyland, Portland, Ore.
Right Worthy Grand Secretary—Mrs. Lorraine J. Pitkin, Chicago, Ill.
Right Worthy Grand Treasurer—Mrs. Harriette A. Ercanbrack, Anamosa, Iowa.

INDEPENDENT ORDER OF ODD FELLOWS.
SOVEREIGN GRAND LODGE.

Grand Sire—C. A. Keller, San Antonio, Tex.
Deputy Grand Sire—Robert T. Daniel, Griffin, Ga.
Grand Secretary—John B. Goodwin, Baltimore, Md.
Grand Treasurer—M. Richards Muckle, Philadelphia, Pa.
Membership Dec. 31, 1912, 2,121,921.
Total paid for relief 1830 to 1912, inclusive, $148,469,-984.87.

IMPROVED ORDER OF RED MEN.
Founded 1763-1834.

GREAT CHIEFS OF THE GREAT COUNCIL OF THE UNITED STATES.

Great Incohonce—Carl Foster, Bridgeport, Conn.
Great Senior Sagamore—Frederick O. Downes, Boston, Mass.
Great Junior Sagamore—Thomas H. Jeffries, Atlanta, Ga.
Great Prophet—George B. Griggs, Houston, Tex.
Great Chief of Records—Wilson Brooks, 230 South LaSalle street, Chicago, Ill.
Great Keeper of Wampum—William Provin, Westfield, Mass.
Number of great councils, 65.
Subordinate branches and councils, 5,291.
Number of members, 497,946.
Benefits disbursed in 1912, $1,561,289.21.
Benefits disbursed since organization, $31,343,087.08.

KNIGHTS OF PYTHIAS.
SUPREME LODGE.

Supreme Chancellor—Thomas J. Carling, Macon, Ga.
Supreme Vice-Chancellor—S. Young, Ada, O.
Supreme Prelate—Rev. Joseph H. Spearing, Columbia, Tenn.
Supreme Keeper of Records and Seal—Fred E. Wheaton, Minneapolis, Minn.
Supreme Master of Exchequer—Thomas D. Meares, Wilmington, N. C.

Supreme Master at Arms—Frank A. Godsoe, St. John, N. B.
Supreme Inner Guard—Douglas S. Wright, Vicksburg, Miss.
Supreme Outer Guard—H. M. Wadsworth, Philadelphia, Pa.
Major-General Military Department—Arthur J. Stobbart, St. Paul, Minn.
Membership, Jan. 1, 1913, 715,654.
Expended for relief in 1912, $1,686,697.41.

INDEPENDENT ORDER OF FORESTERS.
Founded 1874.

SUPREME OFFICERS.

Supreme Chief Ranger—Elliott G. Stevenson, Toronto, Ont.
Past Chief Ranger—Victor Morin, B. A., N. P., Montreal, Que.
Supreme Vice-Chief Ranger—J. D. Clark, Dayton, O.
Supreme Secretary—Fred J. Darch.
Supreme Treasurer—Robert Mathison, M. A., Temple building, Toronto, Ont.
Supreme Physician—Thomas Millman, M. D., Toronto, Ont.
Supreme Counselor—W. H. Hunter, B. A., Toronto, Ont.
Total number of members, 243,053.
Benefits disbursed since organization to Dec. 31, 1912, $38,177,063.40.

MODERN WOODMEN OF AMERICA.
Founded in 1883.

HEAD OFFICERS 1911-1914.

Head Consul—A. R. Talbot, Lincoln, Neb.
Head Adviser—Dan B. Horne, Davenport, Iowa.
Head Clerk—C. W. Hawes, Rock Island, Ill.
Assistant Head Clerk—James McNamara, Rock Island, Ill.
Head Banker—David S. Myers, Pontiac, Ill.
General Attorneys—Benjamin D. Smith, Mankato, Minn.; Truman Plantz, Warsaw, Ill.
Editor—F. O. Van Gilder, Rock Island, Ill.
Head Chaplain—Rev. Henry N. Dunning, Albany, N. Y.
Head Escort—J. G. Dickson, Spokane, Wash.
Head Watchman—J. L. Mayfield, Grausda, Col.
Head Sentry—Frank McCalip, Washington, D. C.
Board of Directors—R. R. Smith, Brookfield, Mo.; E. E. Murphy, Leavenworth, Kas.; S. S. Tanner, Minier, Ill.; F. R. Korns, Des Moines, Iowa; A. N. Bort, Beloit, Wis., chairman. These with the head consul and head clerk constitute the executive council of seven.
Supreme Medical Directors—Dr. E. L. Kerns, Rock Island, Ill.; Dr. F. A. Smith, Rock Island, Ill.; Dr. B. E. Jones, Rock Island, Ill.
Board of Auditors—Fred W. Parrott, Clay Center, Kas.; L. W. Otto, Crawfordsville, Ind.; M. R. Carrier, Lansing, Mich.; George S. Summers, Cape Girardeau, Mo.; E. B. Thomas, Columbus, O.; Martin O'Brien, Crookston, Minn., chairman; George L. Bowman, Kingfisher, Okla.
Membership Jan. 1, 1913, not including social, 962,966.
Death claims paid to Jan. 1, 1913, $118,095,249.11.
Home Office—Rock Island, Ill.
Next head camp convenes June, 1914.

ROYAL ARCANUM.
Organized June 23, 1877.

SUPREME COUNCIL.

Supreme Regent—Frank B. Wickersham, Harrisburg, Pa.
Supreme Vice-Regent—Samuel N. Hoag, Mount Vernon, N. Y.
Supreme Orator—C. Arch. Williams, Chicago, Ill.
Supreme Secretary—Alfred T. Turner, 407 Shawmut avenue, Boston, Mass.
Supreme Treasurer—A. S. Robertson, St. Louis, Mo.
Head office at 407 Shawmut avenue, Boston, Mass.
Number of subordinate councils, 1,928; state jurisdictions, 30.
Membership Oct. 1, 1913, 248,868.

NATIONAL UNION.
OFFICERS OF THE SENATE.

President—Joseph A. Wright, Third National Bank building, St. Louis, Mo.

Vice-President—Frank E. Ferguson, Washington,
D. C.
Speaker—Harry S. Anderson, 405 13th street, Oakland, Cal.
Secretary—E. A. Myers, P. O. box 563, Toledo, O.
Treasurer—C. G. Bentley, Cleveland, O.
General Counsel—George P. Kirby, Toledo, O.
Medical Director—Dr. M. R. Brown, Chicago, Ill.
Executive Committee—H. C. Smale, Joseph A.
Wright, E. A. Myers, C. G. Bentley, Leo Canman,
M. G. Jeffris, F. E. Ferguson.
Total membership, 65,000.

ANCIENT ORDER OF UNITED WORKMEN.
Founded 1868.

SUPREME LODGE OFFICERS 1911-13.
Supreme Master Workman—Will M. Narvis, Muscatine, Iowa.
Supreme Foreman—Edward J. Moore, Fargo, N. D.
Supreme Overseer—Edward E. Hohmann, Johnstown, Pa.
Supreme Recorder—M. W. Sackett, Meadville, Pa.
Supreme Receiver—E. F. Danforth, Skowhegan, Me.
Supreme Guide—F. M. Crain, M. D., Redfield, S. D.
Supreme Watchman—C. C. Rhodes, Pawtucket, R. I.
Supreme Medical Examiner—G. A. Aschman, M. D.,
Wheeling, W. Va.
Membership entire order, 400,000.

JUNIOR ORDER UNITED AMERICAN MECHANICS.
Founded 1853.
NATIONAL COUNCIL.
National Councilor—A. D. Wilkin, Pittsburgh, Pa.
National Vice-Councilor—C. B. Webb, Statesville,
N. C.
Junior Past National Councilor—John J. Weitzel,
Cincinnati, O.
National Secretary—Martin M. Woods, box 874, Philadelphia, Pa.
National Treasurer—Charles Reimer, 1832 West Saratoga street, Baltimore, Md.
National Conductor—J. H. Hambrick, Louisville,
Ky.
National Inside Sentinel—W. O. Dauchy, Savannah,
Ga.
National Outside Sentinel—J. M. Riddle, Bellingham, Wash.
National Chaplain—Rev. M. D. Lichliter, Harrisburg, Pa.
Secretary-Manager Beneficiary Degree and Funeral
Benefit Department—Stephen Collins, box 595,
Pittsburgh, Pa.
Meets at Cedar Point, O., third Tuesday in June,
1915.

WOODMEN OF THE WORLD.
Organized June 6, 1890.
Sovereign Commander—Joseph C. Root, Omaha,
Neb.
Sovereign Adviser—W. A. Fraser, Dallas, Tex.
Sovereign Clerk—John T. Yates, 211 W. O. W.
building, Omaha, Neb.
Sovereign Banker—Morris Sheppard, Texarkana,
Tex.
Sovereign Escort—H. F. Simrall, Jr., Columbus,
Miss.
Sovereign Watchman—B. W. Jewell, Omaha, Neb.
Sovereign Sentry—De E. Bradshaw, Little Rock,
Ark.
Sovereign Physicians—Dr. A. D. Cloyd and Dr. Ira
W. Porter, Omaha, Neb.
Sovereign Managers—J. E. Fitzgerald, Kansas City,
Mo., Chairman; E. R. Lewis, Kinston, N. C.;
E. D. Campbell, Port Huron, Mich.; N. B. Maxey,
Muskogee, Okla.; T. E. Patterson, Chattanooga,
Tenn.; Rainey T. Wells, Murray, Ky.; William
Ruess, Cleveland, O.
Headquarters—Omaha, Neb.
Membership Oct. 1, 1911, 864,689 (all jurisdictions and
auxiliaries).
Losses paid from organization to Oct. 1, 1911, $68,-
423,370.61.
Insurance in force, $1,181,432,400.
Emergency and surplus (total assets), $22,254,019.99.

TRIBE OF BEN-HUR.
Founded March 1, 1894.
SUPREME OFFICERS.
Supreme Chief—R. H. Gerard, Crawfordsville, Ind.
Supreme Scribe—John C. Snyder, Crawfordsville, Ind.
Supreme Keeper of Tribute—S. E. Voris, Crawfordsville, Ind.
Supreme Medical Examiner—J. F. Davidson, M. D.,
Crawfordsville, Ind.
Membership Oct. 1, 1913, 110,560.
Surplus, $1,522,851.12.
Home Office—Crawfordsville, Ind.

FRATERNAL UNION OF AMERICA.
OFFICERS OF SUPREME LODGE.
President—V. A. Young, Denver, Col.
Vice-President—H. M. Waring, Denver, Col.
Secretary—C. P. Gaylord, Denver, Col.
Treasurer—Samuel S. Raty, Denver, Col.
Physician—M. A. Hoover, Kearney, Neb.
Protector—George A. Ostrom, Portland, Ore.
Protection in force Oct. 1, 1913, $45,803,850.
Benefit members, 45,000.
Total claims paid to Oct. 1, 1913, $5,522,347.34.

KNIGHTS OF HONOR.
Organized June 30, 1873.
Supreme Dictator—Edwin C. Wood, New York, N. Y.
Supreme Vice-Dictator—Steve R. Johnston, Atlanta,
Ga.
Supreme Assistant Dictator—R. W. Finley, Austin,
Tex.
Supreme Reporter and Treasurer—Frank B. Sliger,
St. Louis, Mo.
Supreme Chaplain—Rev. A. J. Hess, Columbus, Ky.
Supreme Guide—John H. Lachmund, Jr., Westwood, N. J.
Supreme Guardian—W. W. Bosworth, New Orleans,
La.
Supreme Sentinel—Frank E. Sullivan, Dorchester,
Mass.
Supreme Trustees—D. S. Biggs, Boston, Mass.;
L. Schwartz, Mobile, Ala.; Charles Hauck, Cincinnati, O.
Supreme Medical Examiner—Dr. H. C. Dalton, St.
Louis, Mo.

INDEPENDENT ORDER FREE SONS OF ISRAEL.
Organized in 1849.
GENERAL OFFICERS.
Grand Master—M. S. Stern, New York, N. Y.
First Deputy Grand Master—I. Baer, New York,
N. Y.
Second Deputy Grand Master—H. Jacobs, New
York, N. Y.
Third Deputy Grand Master—Adolph Pike, Chicago, Ill.
Grand Secretary—Abraham Hafer, New York, N. Y.
Grand Treasurer—L. Frankenthaler, New York,
N. Y.

KNIGHTS AND LADIES OF HONOR.
Organized 1877.
SUPREME LODGE OFFICERS.
Supreme Protector—George D. Tait, Indianapolis,
Ind.
Supreme Secretary—Walter W. Connel, Indianapolis, Ind.
Supreme Treasurer—W. G. Taylor, Indianapolis,
Ind.
Supreme Medical Examiner—Dr. J. D. Nichols, Indianapolis, Ind.
Supreme Guide—W. S. Hickey, Jonesboro, Tenn.
Supreme Sentinel—M. J. P. Lacy, Dallas, Tex.
Headquarters of order in Indianapolis, Ind.
Total membership Sept. 1, 1913, 70,000.
Death claims paid since organization, $35,000,000.

MYSTIC WORKERS OF THE WORLD.
Founded 1896.
Supreme Master—J. Ross Mickey, Macomb, Ill.
Supreme Secretary—John R. Walsh, Fulton, Ill.
Supreme Banker—Al F. Schoch, Ottawa, Ill.
General Attorney—Charles E. Stutz, Kewanee, Ill.
Grand lodge, 1.
Subordinate lodges, 1,018.
Members Sept. 1, 1913, 73,898.
Benefits disbursed since organization to Sept. 1,
1913, $4,174,606.59.
Benefits disbursed last fiscal year, $554,945.33.

THE KNIGHTS OF THE MACCABEES OF THE WORLD.

Instituted 1878; reorganized 1883.

OFFICERS 1911-15.

Past Supreme Commander—D. D. Aitken, Flint, Mich.
Supreme Commander—D. P. Markey, Detroit, Mich.
Supreme Lieutenant-Commander—J. B. Sawtell, Waco, Tex.
Supreme Record Keeper—L. E. Sisler, Detroit, Mich.
Supreme Chaplain—J. A. Stackhouse, Memphis, Tenn.
Supreme Sergeant—J. A. Gordon, Chicago, Ill.
Supreme Master at Arms—J. W. Sherwood, Portland, Ore.
Supreme First Master of the Guards—J. S. Boots, New Brighton, Pa.
Supreme Second Master of the Guards—S. C. C. Ward, Augusta, Me.
Supreme Sentinel—E. L. Burns, Elkhart, Ind.
Supreme Picket—A. W. Frye, Wilmington, Del.
Membership Sept. 30, 1913, 283,231.
Benefits paid to Sept. 30, 1913, $52,826,585.83.

THE ROYAL LEAGUE.

Incorporated Oct. 26, 1883.

OFFICERS FOR 1913-1914.

Supreme Archon—W. E. Hyde, Chicago, Ill.
Supreme Vice-Archon—Thomas V. Daly, Milwaukee, Wis.
Supreme Orator—H. P. Rountree, Chicago, Ill.
Supreme Scribe—C. E. Piper, 1001 Masonic Temple, Chicago, Ill.
Supreme Treasurer—J. W. Fernald, First National bank, Chicago, Ill.
Supreme Prelate—Andrew McGarry, Chicago, Ill.
Supreme Guide—Harry M. Strawn, Cleveland, O.
Supreme Warder—Arthur J. Watling, East St. Louis, Ill.
Supreme Sentry—A. D. Marshall, Denver, Col.
Membership Dec. 31, 1912, 21,836.

FRATERNAL ORDER OF EAGLES.

OFFICERS OF THE GRAND AERIE.

Grand Worthy President—Thomas J. Cogan, Cincinnati, O.
Grand Worthy Vice-President—Conrad H. Mann, Kansas City, Mo.
Grand Worthy Chaplain—W. L. Grayson, Savannah, Ga.
Grand Secretary—John S. Parry, Kansas City, Mo.
Grand Treasurer—Frederick Hughes, Yonkers, N. Y.
Grand Worthy Conductor—Thomas P. Gleason, Minneapolis, Minn.
Grand Worthy Inside Guard—William J. Cronin, New Haven, Conn.

PATRIOTIC ORDER SONS OF AMERICA.

Organized Dec. 10, 1847.

NATIONAL CAMP OFFICERS.

President—Sam D. Symmes, Crawfordsville, Ind.
Vice-President—J. Calvin Strayer, York, Pa.
Master of Forms—William J. Heapes, Baltimore, Md.
Secretary—Charles H. Stees, 1617 North Broad street, Philadelphia, Pa.
Treasurer—O. B. Wetherhold, Reading, Pa.
Assistant Secretary—L. F. Stees, 1617 North Broad street, Philadelphia, Pa.
Chaplain—Rev. C. H. Elder, Trenton, N. J.
Conductor—Samuel Roberts, Conshocken, Pa.
Inspector—C. A. Gillespie, Pullman, Ill.
Guard—A. H. McInnes, Key West, Fla.
Medical Examiner in Chief—P. N. K. Schwenk, M. D., Philadelphia, Pa.
Place of meeting in 1915, Washington, D. C.
Membership, 240,000.

BENEVOLENT AND PROTECTIVE ORDER OF ELKS.

Grand Exalted Ruler—Edward Leach, New York, N. Y.
Grand Esteemed Leading Knight—P. H. Shields, Clarksburg, W. Va.
Grand Esteemed Loyal Knight—H. H. Jennings, Bridgeport, Conn.
Grand Esteemed Lecturing Knight—E. M. Dickerman, Tucson, Ariz.
Grand Secretary—Fred C. Robinson, Dubuque, Iowa.

Grand Treasurer—Charles A. White, Chicago, Ill.
Grand Tiler—John F. Burket, Findlay, O.
Grand Inner Guard—Edwin J. Kelley, Cheyenne, Wyo.
Membership 1913, 408,281.
Lodges 1913, 1,309.

INTERNATIONAL ORDER OF GOOD TEMPLARS

Organized in 1851

NATIONAL GRAND LODGE (U. S.).

National Chief Templar—Ben D. Wright, Lockport. N. Y.
National Secretary—Willard O. Wylie, Beverly, Mass.
National Treasurer—W. I. Sterling, Waterville, Me.
Next session of national lodge in Philadelphia, Pa., in June, 1914; of supreme lodge, in Christiania, Norway, in 1914.

SUPREME LODGE.

International Chief Templar—Edward Wavrinsky, Stockholm, Sweden.
International Secretary—Tom Honeyman, Glasgow, Scotland.
Membership (world) over 600,000.

CATHOLIC ORDER OF FORESTERS.

High Chief Ranger—Thomas H. Cannon, Chicago, Ill.
Vice-Chief Ranger—Simeon Viger, Lawrence, Mass.
High Secretary—Thomas F. McDonald, Chicago, Ill.
High Treasurer—Gustav Keller, Appleton, Wis.

UNITED ORDER OF FORESTERS.

EXECUTIVE COUNCIL.

Supreme Ranger—R. C. Sherrard, suite 660, 17 North LaSalle street, Chicago.
Supreme Vice-Ranger—J. B. McGilligan, 1316 Lincoln street, Superior, Wis.
Supreme Secretary—George W. Blann, Hathaway building, Milwaukee, Wis.
Supreme Treasurer—William A. Stolts, State Life building, Indianapolis, Ind.
Supreme Counselor—James Schoonmaker, Oppenheim building, St. Paul, Minn.
Supreme Physician—Dr. S. T. Richman, 5659 Wentworth avenue, Chicago.

KNIGHTS OF COLUMBUS.

Organized Feb. 2, 1882.

Supreme Knight—James A. Flaherty, drawer 96, New Haven, Conn.
Deputy Supreme Knight—Martin H. Carmody, Grand Rapids, Mich.
Supreme Secretary—William J. McGinley, drawer 96, New Haven, Conn.
Supreme Treasurer—D. J. Callahan, postoffice box 342, Washington, D. C.
Supreme Physician—E. W. Buckley, M. D., Young building, St. Paul, Minn.
Supreme Advocate—Joseph C. Pelletier, 18 Tremont street, Boston, Mass.
Supreme Chaplain—Rev. P. J. McGivney, Bridgeport, Conn.
Total membership as of Sept. 30, 1913, 302,365; insurance, 99,338; associate, 204,027.
Insurance in force, $104,928,900.
Assets, $4,912,685.74.
Death claims paid since beginning of organization, $6,748,482.60.

ANCIENT ORDER OF HIBERNIANS.

GENERAL OFFICERS.

President—James J. Regan, St. Paul, Minn.
Vice-President—Joseph McLaughlin, Philadelphia, Pa.
Canadian Vice-President—Charles J. Fay, Perth, Ont.
Secretary—Philip Sullivan, Thompsonville, Conn.
Treasurer—Thomas Maloney, Council Bluffs, Iowa.
Chaplain—Rev. John P. Carroll, Helena, Mont.

ORDER SONS OF ST. GEORGE.

SUPREME LODGE.

Supreme President—C. C. Meurisse, Chicago, Ill.
Supreme Secretary—W. J. Trembath, Wilkesbarre, Pa.
Number of lodges, 288.
Membership 1913, 31,566.
Benefits disbursed since organization, $3,478,839.59.

ORDER DAUGHTERS OF ST. GEORGE.
SUPREME LODGE.

Supreme President—Mrs. Sarah M. Garside, Chicago, Ill.
Supreme Vice-President—Mrs. Hattie Fox, Naugatuck, Conn.
Supreme Financial Secretary—Mrs. Matilda A. Day, Rochester, N. Y.
Supreme Recording Secretary—Mrs. Harriet A. Boyd, Joliet, Ill.
Supreme Treasurer—Mrs. Emma Baker, Cleveland, O.
Lodges (1913), 208.
Membership (1913), 7,318.

NATIONAL FRATERNAL CONGRESS OF AMERICA.

President—W. H. Powers, Boston, Mass.
Secretary—W. E. Futch, 1126 B. of L. E. building, Cleveland, O.
Treasurer—J. F. Taake, Des Moines, Ia.
Following is a list of the societies or organizations affiliated with the National Fraternal Congress of America, with name and address of secretary and membership of each:

American Insurance Union—Dr. Geo. W. Hoglan, Columbus, O.	28,900
Ancient Order of Gleaners—G. H. Slocum, Woodward avenue, Detroit, Mich.	68,000
Artisans' Order of Mutual Protection—Wm. Patton, 204 Parkway building, Philadelphia, Pa.	14,000
Ancient Order of United Workmen—M. W. Suckett, Meadville, Pa.	63,000
Brotherhood of American Yeomen—W. E. Davy, Des Moines, Ia.	165,000
Brotherhood of Locomotive Firemen and Enginemen—A. H. Hawley, Peoria, Ill.	83,000
Brotherhood of Railroad Trainmen—A. E. King, American Trust building, Cleveland, O.	118,000
Catholic Knights and Ladies of America—Henry F. Hayes, 1312 Ashland block, Chicago, Ill.	9,000
Catholic Mutual Benefit Association—Joseph Cameron, Hornell, N. Y.	61,000
Catholic Knights of America—Anthony Matre, 606 Mercantile building, St. Louis, Mo.	19,000
Catholic Order of Foresters—Thos. F. McDonald, Stock Exchange building, Chicago, Ill.	148,000
Catholic Relief and Beneficiary Association—Miss Margaret H. Graney, 120 Genesee street, Auburn, N. Y.	12,000
Catholic Women's Benevolent Legion—Mrs. Sara E. Skelly, 153 E. 44th street, New York, N. Y.	17,000
Court of Honor—W. E. Robinson, Springfield, Ill.	69,000
Degree of Honor—Mrs. Elizabeth E. Allburn, Sioux City, Ia.	42,000
Degree of Honor, A. O. U. W., Grand Lodge of Kansas—Mrs. Georgia Notestine, Winfield, Kas.	7,000
Eastern Star Benevolent Fund of America—Miss M. E. Crowe, 39 Elizabeth street W., Detroit, Mich.	2,000
Equitable Fraternal Union—Merritt L. Campbell, Neenah, Wis.	31,000
Fraternal Aid Association—L. D. Roberts, Lawrence, Kas.	48,000
Fraternal Bankers Reserve Society—R. D. Taylor, Cedar Rapids, Ia.	7,000
Fraternal Brotherhood—Chas. W. Dempster, 845 S. Figueroa street, Los Angeles, Cal.	44,000
Fraternal Mystic Circle—J. D. Myers, 1913 Arch street, Philadelphia, Pa.	19,000
Fraternal Reserve Association—C. M. Robinson, Oshkosh, Wis.	11,000
Fraternal Reserve Life Association—C. N. Carson, Jefferson building, Peoria, Ill.	6,000
Fraternal Union of America—C. P. Gaylord, 1430 Champa street, Denver, Col.	43,000
German Beneficial Union—Joseph Klaus, 1505 Carson street, Pittsburgh, Pa.	19,000
The Grand Fraternity—W. E. Gregg, 1414 Arch street, Philadelphia, Pa.	11,000

Home Guards of America—J. W. Evans, Van Wert, O.	15,000
Improved Order of Heptasophs—F. E. Pleitner, Cathedral and Preston streets, Baltimore, Md.	72,000
Independent Order of Foresters—Robert Mathison, Temple building, Toronto, Ont.	243,000
International Liberty Union—C. B. Critchlow, Covington, Ky.	12,000
Knights and Ladies of Security—J. V. Abrahams, Topeka, Kas.	123,000
Knights of Columbus—Wm. J. McGinley, drawer 96, New Haven, Conn.	93,000
Knights of Honor—Frank B. Sliger, Odd Fellows temple, St. Louis, Mo.	17,000
Knights of Pythias (Ins. Dept.)—W. O. Powers, Indiana Pythian building, Indianapolis, Ind.	71,000
Knights of the Maccabees of the World—Dr. L. E. Sisler, 1021 Woodward avenue, Detroit, Mich.	271,000
Ladies' Catholic Benevolent Association—Mrs. J. A. Royer, 443 West 11th street, Erie, Pa.	132,000
Ladies of the Maccabees of the World—Miss Frances D. Partridge, Port Huron, Mich.	147,000
Ladies of the Modern Maccabees—Emma E. Bower, Port Huron, Mich.	39,000
Locomotive Engineers M. L. & A. I. A.—W. E. Futch, Cleveland, O.	67,000
Loyal Americans of the Republic—H. D. Cowan, 1104-5 Karpen building, Chicago, Ill.	17,000
Loyal Association—Frank S. Petter, 76 Montgomery street, Jersey City, N. J.	7,000
Loyal Guard—F. H. Rankin, Flint, Mich.	4,000
Loyal Mystic Legion of America—G. O. Churchill, Hastings, Neb.	5,000
Masonic Mutual Life Association—Wm. Montgomery, New Masonic Temple, Washington, D. C.	5,000
Modern American Fraternal Order—George M. Lecrone, Effingham, Ill.	1,000
Modern Brotherhood of America—E. L. Balz, Mason City, Ia.	101,000
Modern Order of Prætorians—Geo. G. Taylor, Dallas, Tex.	17,000
Modern Woodmen of America—Chas. W. Hawes, Rock Island, Ill.	963,000
Mutual Protective League—H. W. Shafer, Decatur, Ill.	26,000
Mystic Toilers—J. F. Taake, 4th and Locust streets, Des Moines, Ia.	5,000
Mystic Workers of the World—John R. Walsh, Fulton, Ill.	73,000
National Americans—W. H. Luthy, 1020 McGee street, Kansas City, Mo.	13,000
National Croatian Society of the U. S. A.—Jos. Mahronich, 1012 Peralta street N. S., Pittsburgh, Pa.	17,000
National Protective Legion—H. C. Lockwood, Waverly, N. Y.	28,000
National Union—E. A. Myers, National Union building, Toledo, O.	63,000
New England Order of Protection—D. M. Frye, 18 Tremont street, Boston, Mass.	54,000
North American Union—G. Langhenry, Railway Exchange building, Chicago, Ill.	16,000
North Star Benefit Association—G. L. Peterson, Moline, Ill.	6,000
Order of Aztecs—V. L. Helm, Fort Worth, Tex.	5,000
Order of Columbian Knights—Edwin D. Peifer, 705 Masonic Temple, Chicago, Ill.	12,000
Order of Mutual Protection—G. Del Vecchio, 1523 Masonic Temple, Chicago, Ill.	6,000
Order of the Golden Seal—Arthur F. Bouton, Roxbury, N. Y.	15,000
Order of the Iroquois—W. A. Rice, 644-46 Ellicott square, Buffalo, N. Y.	2,000
Polish National Alliance of the U. S. A.—John K. Zawaliuski, 1406 W. Division street, Chicago, Ill.	86,000
Protected Home Circle—W. S. Palmer, Sharon, Pa.	86,000
Royal Arcanum—Alfred T. Turner, box E, station A, Boston, Mass.	250,000

Royal League—Chas. E. Piper, 1601 Masonic Temple, Chicago, Ill.......................... 32,000
Royal Neighbors of America—Mada M. Burkhart, Rock Island, Ill................. 233,900
Societe des Artisans Canadiens-Francais—Henri Roy, 20 St. Denis street, Montreal, P. Q.................................. 40,000
Sons and Daughters of Justice—W. W. Walker, Minneapolis, Kas.................. 14,000
Sons of Norway—L. Stavnheim, 310 N. Y. Life building, Minneapolis, Minn.......... 10,000
Supreme Tribe of Ben-Hur—John C. Snyder, Crawfordsville, Ind........................ 119,000
Union Fraternal League—Jas. F. Reynolds, 185 Summer street, Boston, Mass........ 3,000
United American Mechanics, Junior Order, Benevolent Degree—Stephen Collins, 741 Wabash building, Pittsburgh, Pa.......... 5,000

United Order of Foresters—G. W. Blann, Hathaway building., Milwaukee, Wis..... 14,000
United Order of the Golden Cross—W. R. Cooper, Empire building, Knoxville, Tenn. 17,000
United Order of the Pilgrim Fathers—Nathan Crary, 292 Essex street, Lawrence, Mass. 15,000
Vesta Circle—Frank H. Knapp, 1619 Masonic Temple, Chicago, Ill............... 5,000
Western Catholic Union—G. A. Hildenbrand, Quincy, Ill. 10,000
Women of Woodcraft—J. L. Wright, Portland, Ore........................... 47,000
Woodmen Circle—Miss Dora Alexander, W. O. W. building, Omaha, Neb............. 115,000
Woodmen of the World, Sovereign Camp—John T. Yates, Omaha, Neb............. 642,000

Total membership.......................5,675,000

GENERAL NATIONAL AND INTERNATIONAL ASSOCIATIONS.

American Academy of Arts and Letters—President, William Dean Howells; chancellor, William Milligan Sloane; permanent secretary, Robert Underwood Johnson, 327 Lexington avenue, New York, N. Y.

American Bankers' Association—President, Arthur Reynolds, Des Moines, Ia.; secretary, F. E. Farnsworth, New York, N. Y.

American Civic Association—President, J. Horace McFarland, Harrisburg, Pa.; treasurer, William B. Howland, New York, N. Y.; secretary, Richard B. Watrous, 913-914 Union Trust building, Washington, D. C.

American Federation of Arts—1741 New York avenue, Washington, D. C.; president, Robert W. de Forest; secretary, Leila Mechlin; treasurer, N. H. Carpenter.

American Humane Association—President, Dr. William O. Stillman, Albany, N. Y.; secretary, J. Walker, Albany, N. Y.

American National Red Cross Society—President, Woodrow Wilson, Washington, D. C.; secretary, Charles L. Magee; national director, Ernest P. Bicknell, Washington, D. C.

American Press Humorists—President, George Fitch, Peoria, Ill.; secretary-treasurer, T. Robinson, Detroit, Mich.

Drama League of America—President, Mrs. A. Starr Best, Evanston, Ill.

General Federation of Women's Clubs—President, Mrs. Percy V. Pennybacker, Texas; recording secretary, Mrs. Harry L. Keefe, Nebraska; corresponding secretary, Mrs. Eugene Reilley, North Carolina.

Indian Rights Association—General secretary, M. K. Sniffen; corresponding secretary, Herbert Welsh, 995 Drexel building, Philadelphia, Pa.

National Council of Women—President, Mrs. Kate Waller Barrett, Alexandria, Va.; corresponding secretary, Mrs. Flo Jamison Miller, Wilmington, Ill.

International Peace Forum—President, Dr. John Wesley Hill; financial secretary, Dr. Harry E. Robbins; central office, 185 Madison avenue, New York, N. Y. Object, industrial and international peace.

International Reform Bureau—206 Pennsylvania avenue, S. E., Washington, D. C.; superintendent and treasurer, Dr. Wilbur F. Crafts; devoted to suppression of intemperance, impurity, sabbath breaking, gambling and kindred evils.

International Prison Commission—Secretary, Dr. C. R. Henderson, University of Chicago, Chicago, Ill.

International Union of Criminal Law—Secretary of American group, Edwin R. Keedy, Northwestern law school, Chicago, Ill.

Investment Bankers' Association—President, George B. Caldwell, Chicago, Ill.; secretary, Frederick R. Fenton, Chicago, Ill.

Lake Mohonk Conference—Secretary, H. C. Phillips, Mohonk Lake, N. Y.

National Academy of Design—President, John W. Alexander, New York, N. Y.

National Business League—President, Philetus W. Gates, Chicago, Ill.

National Children's Home Society—President, Washington Gardner, Albion, Mich.; secretary, James L. Clark, Hearst building, Chicago, Ill.

National Civic Federation, The—President, Seth Low, 23d floor Metropolitan Tower, New York, N. Y.; chairman executive council, Ralph M. Easley, New York, N. Y.

National Commercial Teachers' Federation—President, F. M. Van Antwerp, Louisville, Ky.; secretary, Walter F. Ingersoll, Spokane, Wash.

National Conference of Charities and Correction—President, Graham Taylor, Chicago, Ill.; secretary, William T. Ross, Columbus, Mo.

National Conservation Congress—President, Charles Lathrop Pack, Cleveland, O.; executive secretary, Thomas R. Shipp, Indianapolis, Ind.

National Board of Trade—President, William S. Hurvey, Philadelphia, Pa.; secretary, John G. Dudley, Philadelphia, Pa.

National Child Labor Committee—Chairman, Felix Adler; general secretary, Owen R. Lovejoy, 105 East 22d street, New York, N. Y.

National League for Medical Freedom—President, B. O. Flower, Boston, Mass.; secretary, Joseph C. Mason, 332 South Michigan avenue, Chicago, Ill.

National League for the Protection of the Family—President, Seth Low, New York, N. Y.; corresponding secretary, Rev. Samuel W. Dike, Auburndale, Mass.

National Congress of Mothers and Parent-Teacher Associations—President, Mrs. Frederick Schoff, Philadelphia, Pa.; corresponding secretary, Mrs. Arthur A. Birney, 806 Loan and Trust building, Washington, D. C.

National German-American Alliance—President, Dr. C. J. Hexamer, Philadelphia, Pa.; secretary, Adolph Timm, Philadelphia, Pa.

National Guard Association of the United States—President, Gen. Thomas J. Stewart, Pennsylvania; secretary, Gen. Guy E. Logan, Iowa.

National Municipal League—President, William Dudley Foulke, Richmond, Ind.; secretary, Clinton Rogers Woodruff, Philadelphia, Pa. Purpose: To promote good municipal government.

American Prison Association—President, Rev. Samuel G. Smith, St. Paul, Minn.; secretary, Joseph P. Byers, State house, Trenton, N. J.

National Soil Fertility League—President, Howard H. Gross, Chicago, Ill.; office, 1328 First National Bank building, Chicago, Ill.

National Woman's Suffrage Association—President, Anna Howard Shaw, Moylan, Pa.; first vice-president, Jane Addams, Chicago, Ill.; corresponding secretary, Mrs. Mary W. Dennett, New York.

National Woman's Christian Temperance Union—President, Mrs. Lillian M. N. Stevens, Portland, Me.; corresponding secretary, Mrs. Frances P. Parks, Evanston, Ill.

Playground and Recreation Association of America—President, Joseph Lee, Boston, Mass.; secretary, H. S. Braucher, New York, N. Y.

Representative Government League—President, John E. Eastmond; secretary, W. Ward Damon, room 904, 154 Nassau street, New York, N. Y.

LEARNED SOCIETIES OF AMERICA.

American Academy of Medicine—President, John L. Heffron, M. D., Syracuse, N. Y.; secretary, Charles McIntire, M. D., 52 North 4th street, Easton, Pa.

American Academy of Political and Social Science—President, L. S. Rowe, University of Pennsylvania; secretary, J. P. Lichtenberger, University of Pennsylvania, Philadelphia, Pa.

American Asiatic Association—President, Willard Straight; secretary, John Foord, P. O. box 1500, New York, N. Y.

American Association for the Advancement of Science—President, Prof. E. B. Wilson, Columbia university, New York, N. Y.; general secretary, H. W. Springston, Western Reserve university, Cleveland, O.; permanent secretary, L. O. Howard, Smithsonian institution, Washington, D. C.

American Association of Orificial Surgeons—Presidents, Dr. E. H. Pratt, A. M., M. D., LL. D., Chicago, Ill., and Dr. B. E. Dawson, A. M., M. D., Kansas City, Mo.; secretary, Dr. W. A. Guild, M. S., M. D., Utica building, Des Moines, Iowa.

American Bar Association—President, William H. Taft, New Haven, Conn.; secretary, George Whitelock, Baltimore, Md.; assistant secretary, W. Thomas Kemp, Baltimore, Md.; treasurer, Fred E. Wadhams, Albany, N. Y.

American Chemical Society—President, A. D. Little, Boston, Mass.; secretary, Charles L. Parsons, P. O. box 505, Washington, D. C.

American Climatological Association (founded 1884) —President, Dr. James M. Anders, Philadelphia, Pa.; secretary, Dr. Guy Hinsdale, Hot Springs, Va.

American Dermatological Association—President, James M. Winfield, 47 Halsey street, Brooklyn, N. Y.; secretary, Oliver S. Ormsby, 32 North State street, Chicago, Ill.

American Dialect Society—President, Prof. W. E. Mead, Wesleyan university, Middletown, Conn.; secretary, Dr. Percy W. Long, L. 19, Harvard university, Cambridge, Mass.

American Economic Association—President, Prof. David Kinley, University of Illinois, Champaign, Ill.; secretary, Thomas Nixon Carver, Harvard university, Cambridge, Mass.

American Electro-Therapeutic Association—President, Dr. George E. Pfahler, 1321 Spruce street, Philadelphia, Pa.; secretary, Dr. J. Willard Travell, 27 East 11th street, New York, N. Y.

American Folk Lore Society—President, John A. Lomax; secretary, Dr. Charles Peabody, Cambridge, Mass.

American Forestry Association—President, Henry S. Drinker, South Bethlehem, Pa.; executive secretary, Percival S. Ridsdale, 1410 H street, N. W., Washington, D. C.

American Geographical Society—President, Archer M. Huntington; corresponding secretary, Archibald D. Russell, Broadway and 156th street. New York, N. Y.; librarian, David Randall-McIvor, M. A., D. Sc.; editor Bulletin, Cyrus C. Adams.

American Historical Association—President, Andrew C. McLaughlin, University of Chicago, Chicago, Ill.; secretary, Waldo G. Leland, Carnegie institution, Washington, D. C.

American Institute of Architects—President, Walter Cook, New York, N. Y.; secretary, Glenn Brown, the Octagon, Washington, D. C.

American Institute of Criminal Law and Criminology—President, Judge Quincy A. Myers, Indianapolis, Ind.; secretary, Henry W. Ballentine, Law school, University of Wisconsin, Madison, Wis.

American Institute of Electrical Engineers—President, C. O. Mailloux, New York, N. Y.; secretary, F. L. Hutchinson, 33 West 39th street, New York, N. Y.; membership, 7,481 (Oct. 1, 1913).

American Institute of Mining Engineers—Secretary, Bradley Stoughton, 29 West 39th street, New York, N. Y.

American Institute of Homeopathy—Secretary, Dr. J. Richey Horner, 659 Rose building, Cleveland, O.

American Library Association—President, Edwin H. Anderson, Public library, New York, N. Y.; sec-

retary and executive officer, George B. Utley, 78 East Washington street, Chicago, Ill.

American Mathematical Society—President, E. B. Van Vleck, University of Wisconsin, Madison, Wis.; secretary, F. N. Cole, Columbia university, New York, N. Y.; Chicago section, secretary, H. E. Slaught, University of Chicago; San Francisco section, secretary, W. A. Manning, Stanford university, Palo Alto, Cal.; southwestern section, secretary, O. D. Kellogg, University of Missouri, Columbia, Mo.

American Medical Association—President, Dr. Victor C. Vaughn, Ann Arbor, Mich.; general secretary, Alexander R. Craig, 535 North Dearborn street, Chicago, Ill.; editor and general manager, George H. Simmons, 535 North Dearborn street, Chicago, Ill.

American Medico-Psychological Association—President, Carlos F. MacDonald, M. D., New York, N. Y.; secretary-treasurer, Charles G. Wagner, M. D.; Binghamton, N. Y.

American Microscopical Society—President, Dr. F. Creighton Wellman, School of Tropical Medicine, Tulane university, New Orleans, La.; secretary, Prof. T. W. Galloway, Millikin university, Decatur, Ill.

American Nature Study Society—President, Anna Botsford Comstock, Ithaca, N. Y.; secretary-treasurer, Elliot R. Downing, University of Chicago, the School of Education, Chicago, Ill.

American Numismatic Society, The—Governors, Edward D. Adams, Henry R. Drowne, William B. Osgood Field, Archer M. Huntington and Daniel Parish, Jr.; secretary, Bauman Lowe Belden, Audubon Park, 156th street, west of Broadway, New York, N. Y.

American Ophthalmological Society—President, Dr. Robert Sattler, Cincinnati, O.; secretary, Dr. W. M. Sweet, Philadelphia, Pa.

American Oriental Society—President, Prof. Paul Haupt, Johns Hopkins university, Baltimore, Md.; corresponding secretary, Prof. A. V. W. Jackson, Columbia university, New York, N. Y.

American Orthopedic Association—President, Gwilym G. Davis, M. D., 1814 Spruce street, Philadelphia, Pa.; secretary, Ralph R. Fitch, M. D., 365 East avenue, Rochester, N. Y.

American Osteopathic Association—President, Dr. Percy H. Woodall, Birmingham, Ala.; secretary, H. L. Childs, Orange, N. J.

American Pediatric Society—President, Samuel McHamill, M. D., Philadelphia, Pa.; secretary, Samuel S. Adams, M. D., 1 Dupont circle, Washington, D. C.

American Philological Association—President, Prof. Harold N. Fowler, Western Reserve university, Cleveland, O.; secretary, Prof. Frank Gardner Moore, Columbia university, New York, N. Y.

American Philosophical Society—President, William W. Keen; secretaries, I. Minis Hays, Arthur W. Goodspeed, Amos P. Brown, Harry F. Keller, 104 South 5th street, Philadelphia, Pa.

American Physical Society—President, Prof. B. O. Pierce, Cambridge, Mass.; secretary, Prof. A. D. Cole, Columbus, O.

American Political Science Association—President, W. W. Willoughby, Baltimore, Md.; secretary and treasurer, W. F. Dodd, University of Illinois, Urbana, Ill.

American Public Health Association—President, Dr. W. C. Woodward, Washington, D. C.; secretary, Prof. Selskar M. Gunn, 755 Boylston street, Boston, Mass.

American Social Science Association—President, John Huston Finley, superintendent public instruction, state of New York; general secretary, Robert S. Binkerd, 55 West 44th street, New York, N. Y.

American Society of Biological Chemists—President, A. B. Macallum, University of Toronto, Toronto, Ont.; secretary, Philip A. Shaffer, Washington university, Medical school, 1806 Locust street, St. Louis, Mo.

American Society of Civil Engineers—President, George F. Swain; secretary, Charles Warren Hunt, 220 West 57th street, New York, N. Y.

American Society of Mechanical Engineers—President, W. F. M. Goss; secretary, Calvin W. Rice, 29 West 39th street, New York, N. Y.

American Society of Naturalists—President, Prof. Ross G. Harrison, Yale university, New Haven, Conn.; secretary, Prof. B. M. Davis, University of Pennsylvania, Philadelphia, Pa.

American Sociological Society—President, Albion W. Small, University of Chicago; secretary, Scott E. W. Bedford, University of Chicago, Chicago, Ill.

American Statistical Association—Secretary, Carroll W. Doten, 491 Boylston street, Boston, Mass.

American Surgical Association—President, William J. Mayo, Rochester, Minn.; secretary, Robert G. LeConte, 1530 Locust street, Philadelphia, Pa.

Archæological Institute of America (incorporated by act of congress)—President, Prof. F. W. Shipley, Ph. D., University of Michigan, Ann Arbor; general secretary, Prof. Mitchell Carroll, the Octagon, Washington. D. C.

American Association for the Study and Prevention of Infant Mortality—President, Dr. J. Whitridge Williams, Baltimore, Md.; secretary, Dr. Philip Van Inges, New York, N. Y.

American Association of Anatomists—President, Dr. Ross G. Harrison, Yale university, New Haven, Conn.; secretary-treasurer, Dr. G. Carl Huber, University of Michigan, Ann Arbor.

Association of American Physicians—President, Simon Flexner, New York, N. Y.; secretary, George M. Kober, 1819 Q street, Washington, D. C.

Astronomical and Astrophysical Society of America—President, Prof. E. C. Pickering, Cambridge, Mass.; secretary, Prof. Philip Fox, Northwestern university, Evanston, Ill.

Botanical Society of America—President, Prof. D. H. Campbell, Leland Stanford, Jr., university, Stanford, Cal.; secretary, Prof. George T. Moore, Missouri Botanical gardens, St. Louis, Mo.

Geological Society of America, The—President, George F. Becker, Washington, D. C.; secretary, Edmund Otis Hovey, American Museum of Natural History, New York, N. Y.

Mississippi Valley Medical Association—President, Dr. D'Orsay Hecht, Chicago, Ill.; secretary, Dr. Henry E. Tuley, Louisville, Ky.

National Academy of Sciences—President, Ira Remsen, Baltimore, Md.; home secretary, Arthur L. Day, Washington, D. C.; foreign secretary, George E. Hale, Pasadena, Cal.; membership, 118.

National Association for the Study and Prevention of Tuberculosis—Executive office, 105 East 22d street, New York, N. Y.; executive secretary, Dr. Livingston Farrand, New York, N. Y.; secretary, Dr. Henry Barton Jacobs, 11 Mount Vernon place, Baltimore, Md.

National Education Association—President, Joseph Swain, Swarthmore college, Swarthmore, Pa.; permanent secretary, Durand W. Springer, Detroit, Mich.

National Eclectic Medical Association—President, Dr. W. S. Glenn, State college, Pa.; corresponding secretary, Dr. William N. Mundy, Forest, O.

National Geographic Society—President, Henry Gannett, Washington, D. C.; secretary, O. P. Austin, Washington, D. C.; director and editor, Gilbert H. Grosvenor, Washington, D. C.; office, Hubbard Memorial hall, 16th and M streets, Washington, D. C.

Society of Homeopathicians—Honorary president, Dr. James T. Kent, Chicago; president, Dr. A. Eugene Austin, New York, N. Y.; secretary, Dr. Lee Norman, Louisville, Ky.

Society of Naval Architects and Marine Engineers—President, Col. Robert M. Thompson; secretary, Daniel H. Cox, 29 West 39th street, New York.

Western Economic Society—President, Shailer Mathews, Chicago, Ill.; secretary, Leon C. Marshall, University of Chicago, Chicago, Ill.

MEMBERS OF THE FRENCH ACADEMY.

Name.	Elected.	Name.	Elected.	Name.	Elected.
Ollivier, Emile. b. 1825	1870	Rostand, Edmond, b. 1868	1901	Poincare, Raymond, b. 1850	1909
Mezieres, Alfred, b. 1826	1874	Vogue, Charles de, b. 1829	1901	Duchesne, Mgr., b. 1848	1910
Haussonville, Comte de, b. 1843	1888	Bazin, Rene, b. 1853	1903	Regnier, Henri de, b. 1864	1911
Claretie, Jules. b. 1840	1888	Masson, Frederick, b. 1847	1903	Roujon Roujon	1911
Freycinet, Charles de, b. 1828	1890	Lamy, Etienne, b. 1845	1905	Cochin, Denys, b. 1851	1911
Loti-Viaud, Pierre, b. 1850	1891	Barres, Maurice, b. 1862	1906	Lyantey, Louis	1912
Lavisse, Ernest, b. 1842	1892	Ribot, Alexandre, b. 1842	1905	Boutroux, Emile	1912
Bourget, Paul, b. 1852	1894	Donnay, Maurice, b. 1866	1907		
Lemaitre, Jules, b. 1853	1895	Segur, Marquis Anatole de,		The Academie Francaise, or French academy, was instituted in 1635. It is a part of the Institute of France and its particular function is to conserve the French language, foster literature and encourage genius.	
France, Anatole, b. 1844	1896	b. 1825	1907		
Mun, Albert, Comte de, b. 1841	1897	Charmes, Francis, b. 1848	1908		
Hanotaux, Gabriel, b. 1853	1897	Richepin, Jean, b. 1849	1908		
Lavedan, Henri, b. 1859	1898	Donnic, Rene, b. 1860	1909		
Deschanel, Paul, b. 1856	1899	Prevost, Marcel, b. 1862	1909		
Hervieu, Paul, b. 1857	1899	Alcard, Jean, b. 1848	1909		
Faguet, Emile, b. 1841	1900	Brieux, Eugene, b. 1858	1909		

PANAMA-PACIFIC EXPOSITION IN SAN FRANCISCO, CAL.

The opening of the Panama canal and the 400th anniversary of the discovery of the Pacific ocean will be celebrated by an international exposition in San Francisco, Cal., in 1915. Steps with that end in view were taken in 1910, when a guaranty fund of $17,500,000 was raised. Of this amount $5,000,000 is provided by a special tax levied by the legislature upon all the property in California, an additional $5,000,000 through the issuance of bonds by the city of San Francisco and the balance of $7,500,000 by popular subscriptions. No government aid was asked.

Charles G. Moore is president of the exposition company, and Rudolph J. Taussig secretary. The executive work is in the hands of the directors of the four divisions of works, concessions and admissions, exhibits and exploitation. The site is a natural amphitheater within the residential section of San Francisco, covering 635 acres, fronting on San Francisco bay overlooking the Golden Gate. There will be fourteen main exhibit palaces, costing about $8,000,000. The entire expenditure prior to opening is estimated at $50,000,000. The exposition opens Feb. 20, 1915, and closes Dec. 4.

PANAMA-CALIFORNIA EXPOSITION IN SAN DIEGO, CAL.

To celebrate the opening of the Panama canal and to show the world what the canal will mean to commerce and the advancement of the west, San Diego, Cal., will hold an exposition during the entire year 1915, opening Jan. 1 and closing Dec. 31. The buildings, which are all to be of the Spanish-Colonial style of architecture, are being constructed on a site of 615 acres in Balboa park. Of this area 100 acres are devoted to the general exhibit and the main buildings, of which there are fifteen; 100 acres to the state and foreign section; 100 acres to open-air exhibits; 25 acres to buildings for amuse-

ment purposes ("The Isthmus"), with 5,000 feet frontage, and 250 acres to landscape gardens and park. Every building on the grounds is to be covered with vines and floriculture. The horticultural exhibit will be one of the striking features of the fair.

Following are the chief officers of the Panama-California exposition: President, D. C. Collier; first vice-president, J. D. Spreckels; director-general, H. O. Davis; director of publicity, Winfield Hogaboom; secretary, H. J. Penfold; treasurer, F. W. Jackson.

LABOR ORGANIZATIONS.

AMERICAN FEDERATION OF LABOR.

Headquarters, Washington, D. C.

President—Samuel Gompers.
Secretary—Frank Morrison.
Treasurer—John B. Lennon, Bloomington, Ill.
National and International unions, 111.
Departments, 5.
State branches, 42.
City centrals, 622.
Trade and federal labor unions, 667.
Total number of unions, 1,447.
First convention held Nov. 15-18, 1881.

AFFILIATED NATIONAL AND INTERNATIONAL ORGANIZATIONS—NAMES AND ADDRESSES OF SECRETARIES.

Asbestos Workers of America, National Association of Heat, Frost and General Insulators—Thomas J. McNamara, 2516 Slattery street, St. Louis, Mo.

Bakery and Confectionery Workers' International Union of America—Otto E. Fischer, 221 Chicago avenue, Chicago, Ill.

Barbers' International Union, Journeymen—Jacob Fischer, 222 East Michigan street, Indianapolis.

Bill Posters and Billers of America, International Alliance—William McCarthy, 1482 Broadway, New York, N. Y.

Blacksmiths, International Brotherhood of—William F. Kramer, 1270-1280 Monon building, Chicago.

Boiler Makers and Iron Ship Builders of America, Brotherhood of—W. J. Gilthorpe, Law building, Kansas City, Kas.

Bookbinders, International Brotherhood of—James W. Dougherty, 222 East Michigan street, Indianapolis, Ind.

Boot and Shoe Workers' Union—C. L. Baine, 246 Sumner street, Boston, Mass.

Brewery Workmen, International Union of the United—Louis Kemper, Vine and Hollister streets, Cincinnati, O.

Brick, Tile and Terra Cotta Workers' Alliance, International—William Van Bodegraven, 2341 West 12th street, Chicago, Ill.

Bridge and Structural Iron Workers, International Association of—Harry Jones, American Central Life building, Indianapolis, Ind.

Broom and Whisk Makers' Union, International—C. T. Dolan, 2925 Sheffield avenue, Chicago, Ill.

Brushmakers' International Union—George J. Vitzthun, 2052 Gates avenue, Brooklyn, N. Y.

Carpenters and Joiners of America, United Brotherhood of—Frank Duffy, Carpenters' building, Indianapolis, Ind.

Carriage, Wagon and Automobile Workers, International—William P. Mavell, 30 Chapin block, Buffalo, N. Y.

Carvers' Association of North America, International Wood—Thomas J. Lodge, 19 Carlisle street, Roxbury, Mass.

Cement Workers, American Brotherhood of—Henry Ullner, 705 Clunie, San Francisco, Cal.

Cigarmakers' International Union of America—George W. Perkins,* 829 Monon block, 436 South Dearborn street, Chicago, Ill.

Clerks' International Protective Association, Retail—H. J. Conway, lock drawer 248, Lafayette, Ind.

Cloth Hat and Cap Makers of North America, United—Max Zuckerman, 62 East 4th street, New York, N. Y.

Commercial Telegraphers' Union of America, The—Wesley Russell, 922-930 Monon building, Chicago.

Compressed Air and Foundation Workers' Union of the United States and Canada—Henry Kuhlmann, 238 Ten Eyke street, Brooklyn, N. Y.

Coopers' International Union of North America—William R. Deal, Suite A, Bishop building, Kansas City, Kas.

Cutting Die and Cutter Makers, International Union of—William Lalor, 642 Concord avenue, Bronx, New York, N. Y.

Diamond Workers' Protective Union of America—Andries Meyer,* 323 Washington street, Brooklyn, N. Y.

Electrical Workers of America, International Brotherhood of—Charles P. Ford, Pierick building, Springfield, Ill.

Elevator Constructors, International Union of—William Young, 418 Perry building, Philadelphia, Pa.

Engineers, International Union of Steam—James G. Hannahan, 6334 Yale avenue, Chicago, Ill.

Firemen, International Brotherhood of Stationary—C. L. Shamp, 3618 North 24th street, Omaha, Neb.

Foundry Employes, International Brotherhood of—George Bechtold, 200 South Broadway, St. Louis.

Freight Handlers and Warehousemen's Union of America, Interior—George H. Kroeger, 816-824 West Harrison street, Chicago, Ill.

Fur Workers' Union of United States and Canada—Samuel Korman, 89 East 10th street, New York, N. Y.

Garment Workers of America, United—B. A. Larger, 116-117 Bible House, New York, N. Y.

Garment Workers' Union, International Ladies'—John Alex Dyche, 32 Union square, New York.

Glass Bottle Blowers' Association of the United States and Canada—William Launer, 930-931 Witherspoon building, Juniper and Walnut streets, Philadelphia, Pa.

Glass Workers' International Association, Amalgamated—A. J. Scott, 118 East 28th street, New York, N. Y.

Glove Workers' Union of America, International—Elizabeth Christman, 506 Bush Temple of Music, Chicago, Ill.

Granite Cutters' International Association of America—James Duncan,* Hancock building, Quincy, Mass.

Grinders and Finishers' National Union, Pocket Knife Blade—F. A. Didsbury, 508 Brooks street, Bridgeport, Conn.

Hatters of North America, United—Martin Lawlor, 11 Waverly place, New York, N. Y.

Hod Carriers and Building Laborers' Union of America, International—A. Pierson, box 597, Albany, N. Y.

Horseshoers of United States and Canada, International Union of Journeymen—Hubert S. Marshall, room 605 Second National bank building, Cincinnati, O.

Hotel and Restaurant Employes' International Alliance and Bartenders', International League of America—Jere L. Sullivan, Commercial Tribune building, Cincinnati, O.

Iron, Steel and Tin Workers, Amalgamated Association of—M. F. Tighe, House building, Smithfield and Water streets, Pittsburgh, Pa.

Lace Operatives of America, the Chartered Society of Amalgamated—David L. Gould, 545 West Lehigh avenue, Philadelphia, Pa.

Lathers, International Union of Wood, Wire and Metal—Ralph V. Brant, 401 Superior building, Cleveland, O.

Laundry Workers' International Union—Harry L. Morrison, box 11, station 1, Troy, N. Y.

Leather Workers on Horse Goods, United Brotherhood of—J. J. Pfeiffer, 504-5 Postal building, Kansas City, Mo.

Lithographers, International Protective and Beneficial Association of the United States and Canada—James M. O'Connor, 309 Broadway, New York, N. Y.

Lithographic Press Feeders of United States and Canada, International Protective Association of—Harry C. Kranz, 200 East 23d street, New York.

Longshoremen's Association, International—John J. Joyce, 702 Brisbane building, Buffalo, N. Y.

Machine Printers and Color Mixers of the United States, National Association of—P. E. Lyons, 334 Trenton avenue, Buffalo, N. Y.

Machinists, International Association of—George Preston, 908-14 G street, N. W., McGill building, Washington, D. C.

Maintenance of Way Employes, International Brotherhood of—S. J. Pegg, 27 Putnam avenue, Detroit, Mich.

Marble Workers, International Association of—Stephen C. Hogan, 406 149th street, New York.

Meat Cutters and Butcher Workmen of North America, Amalgamated—Homer D. Call, 212 May avenue, Syracuse, N. Y.

Metal Polishers, Buffers, Platers and Brass Workers' Union of North America—Charles R. Atherton, Neave building, Cincinnati, O.

Metal Workers' International Alliance, Amalgamated Sheet—John E. Bray, 325 Nelson building, Kansas City, Mo.

Mine Workers of America, United—William Green, State Life building, Indianapolis, Ind.

Miners, Western Federation of—Ernest Mills, 605 Railroad building, Denver, Col.

Molders' Union of North America, International—Victor Kleiber, 530 Walnut street, Cincinnati, O.

Musicians, American Federation of—Owen Miller, 3535 Pine street, St. Louis, Mo.

Painters, Decorators and Paperhangers of America, Brotherhood of—J. C. Skemp, drawer 99, Lafayette, Ind.

Paper Makers, International Brotherhood of—J. T. Carey, 127 North Pearl street, Albany, N. Y.

Paper Makers' League of North America—J. T. Carey,* 22 Smith building, Watertown, N. Y.

Pattern Makers' League of North America—James Wilson,* 1008-1009 Second National Bank building, Cincinnati, O.

Pavers and Rammermen, International Union of—Edward I. Hannah, 223 East 59th street, New York, N. Y.

Paving Cutters' Union of the United States of America and Canada—John Sheret, lock box 27, Albion, N. Y.

Photoengravers' Union of North America, International—Louis A. Schwarz, 228 Apsley street, Philadelphia, Pa.

Piano and Organ Workers' Union of America, International—Charles Dold,* 1037 Greenwood terrace, Chicago, Ill.

Plasterers' International Association of the United States and Canada, Operative—T. A. Scully, 442 East 2d street, Middletown, O.

Plate Printers' Union of North America, International Steel and Copper—Charles T. Smith, 612 F street N. W., Washington, D. C.

Plumbers, Gas Fitters, Steam Fitters and Steam Fitters' Helpers of United States and Canada, United Association of—Thomas E. Burke, 411-416 Bush Temple of Music, Chicago, Ill.

Postoffice Clerks' National Federation—George F. Pfeiffer, 187 Burleigh street, Milwaukee, Wis.

Potters, National Brotherhood of Operative—John T. Wood, box 6, East Liverpool, O.

Powder and High Explosive Workers of America, United—Iva Sharprack, R. R. No. 3, Columbus, Kas.

Print Cutters' Association of America, National—Richard H. Scheller, 229 Hancock avenue, Jersey City, N. J.

Printing Pressmen's Union, International—Joseph C. Orr, Rogersville, Tenn.

Pulp, Sulphite and Paper Mill Workers of the United States and Canada, International Brotherhood of—John H. Malin, P. O. Drawer K, Fort Edward, N. Y.

Quarry Workers' International Union of North America—Fred W. Suitor, Scampini building, Barre, Vt.

Railroad Telegraphers, Order of—L. W. Quick, Star building, St. Louis, Mo.

Railway Carmen of America, Brotherhood—E. William Weeks, 507 Hall building, Kansas City, Mo.

Railway Clerks, Brotherhood of—R. E. Fisher, 307-310 Kansas City Life building, Kansas City, Mo.

Railway Employes of America, Amalgamated Association of Street and Electric—W. D. Mahon,* 601 Hodges block, Detroit, Mich.

Railway Express Messengers of America, Brotherhood of—William F. Morrison,* 326 Lee building, Oklahoma City, Okla.

Roofers, Composition, Damp and Waterproof Workers of the United States and Canada, International Brotherhood—D. J. Ganley, 14 North Oxford street, Brooklyn, N. Y.

Sawsmiths' National Union—F. E. Kingsley, room 42, Baldwin building, Indianapolis, Ind.

Seamen's Union, International, of America—Thomas A. Hanson, 570 West Lake street, Chicago, Ill.

Shingle Weavers' Union of America, International—W. H. Reid, 306 Maynard building, Seattle, Wash.

Slate and Tile Roofers' Union of America, International—Joseph M. Gaviak, 3643 West 47th street, Cleveland, O.

Slate Workers, International Union of—Philip Jago, Jr., Pen Argyle, Pa.

Spinners' International Union—Urban Fleming, 188 Lyman street, Holyoke, Mass.

Stage Employes' International Alliance, Theatrical—Lee M. Hart, room 607, 1547 Broadway, New York, N. Y.

Steel Plate Transferers' Association of America—J. T. Miller, 1024 Park road, N. W., Washington, D. C.

Stereotypers and Electrotypers' Union of America—George W. Williams, 29 Globe building, Boston.

Stonecutters' Association of North America, Journeymen—Walter W. Drayer, Central Life building, Indianapolis, Ind.

Stove Mounters' International Union—Frank Grimshaw, 1210 Jefferson avenue east, Detroit, Mich.

Switchmen's Union of North America—M. R. Welch, 326 Brisbane building, Buffalo, N. Y.

Tailors' Union of America, Journeymen—E. J. Brais, box 597, Bloomington, Ill.

Teamsters, Chauffeurs, Stablemen and Helpers of America, International Brotherhood of—Thomas L. Hughes, 222 East Michigan street, Indianapolis, Ind.

Textile Workers of America, United—Albert Hibbert, box 742, Fall River, Mass.

Tile Layers and Helpers' Union, International Ceramic, Mosaic and Encaustic—James P. Reynolds, 12 Federal street, N. S., Pittsburgh, Pa.

Tip Printers, International Brotherhood of—T. J. Carolan, 6 Plum street, Newark, N. J.

Tobacco Workers' International Union—E. Lewis Evans, 50-53 American National Bank building, 36th and Main streets, Louisville, Ky.

Travelers' Goods and Leather Novelty Workers' International Union of America—Murt Malone, 191 Boyd street, Oshkosh, Wis.

Tunnel and Subway Constructors' International Union—Michael Carraher, 150 East 125th street, New York, N. Y.

Typographical Union, International—J. W. Hays, Newton Claypool building, Indianapolis, Ind.

Upholsterers' International Union of North America—James H. Hatch,* 234 1st avenue, Astoria, N. Y.

Weavers' Amalgamated Association, Elastic Goring—Alfred Haughton, 50 Cherry street, Brockton, Mass.

Weavers' Protective Association, American Wire—E. E. Desmond, 27 Woodland avenue, Woodhaven, L. I.

White Rats Actors' Union of America—W. W. Waters, 227-31 West 46th street, Chicago.

DEPARTMENTS.

Building Trades Department, American Federation of Labor—William J. Spencer, rooms 412-14 Ouray building, Washington, D. C.

Metal Trades Department, American Federation of Labor—A. J. Berres, room 513 Ouray building, Washington, D. C.

Mining Department of the American Federation of Labor—Ernest Mills, 605 Railroad building, Denver, Col.

Railroad Employes' Department, American Federation of Labor—John Scott, 301 Sawyer building, St. Louis, Mo.

Union Label Trades Department, American Federation of Labor—Thomas F. Tracy, 708 Ouray building, Washington, D. C.

SECRETARIES OF STATE BRANCHES.

Alabama—Lewis Bowen, box 180, Birmingham.

Arkansas—L. H. Moore, room 9 Whipple building, Little Rock.

California—Paul Scharrenberg, 316 14th street, San Francisco.

Colorado—W. T. Hickey, 411 Exchange building, Denver.

Connecticut—R. P. Cunningham, 34 Keeler street, Danbury.

Florida—J. C. Privett, box 271, Jacksonville.

Georgia—Robert Fechner, p. o. box 288, Savannah.

Illinois—J. F. Morris, Pierick building, Springfield.

Indiana—George J. Schwab, 602 4th avenue, Evansville.

Iowa—F. A. Canfield, 208 North 20th street, Cedar Rapids.

Kansas—George B. Edgell, 315 Delaware street, Leavenworth.
Kentucky—Max Traut, 218 Louisville Trust building, Louisville.
Louisiana—V. V. Stewart, 1531 Oxford street, Shreveport.
Maine—Henry M. Donnelly, 58½ Arsenal street, Augusta.
Maryland—John R. Neal, 1023 East Baltimore street, Baltimore.
Massachusetts—Martin T. Joyce, box C, station A, Boston.
Michigan—Homer F. Waterman, 123 East Main street, Kalamazoo.
Minnesota—W. E. McEwen, Manhattan building, Duluth.
Missouri—John T. Smith, Labor Temple, Kansas City.
Montana—O. M. Parlelow, box 31, Butte.
Nebraska—W. A. Chrisman, box 25, station C, Omaha.
New Hampshire—J. J. Coyne, 202 Greene street, Manchester.
New Jersey—Henry F. Illfers, 68 South Orange avenue, Newark.
New Mexico—Arthur C. Culver, 216 Hazelden avenue, Albuquerque.
New York—Edward A. Bates, 302 Mary street, Utica.
North Carolina—O. R. Jarrett,* 18 Olive street, Asheville.
North Dakota—John Oliver, box 125, Fargo.
Ohio—Thomas J. Donnelly, 1311 Walnut street, Cleveland.
Oklahoma—Ollie S. Wilson,* 1022 State National bank building, Oklahoma City.
Oregon—Ed J. Stack, 162 2d street, Portland.
Pennsylvania—C. F. Quinn, rooms M 1-3, Commonwealth Trust building, Harrisburg.
Porto Rico—Free Federation of Workingmen—Raphael Alonso, box 807, San Juan.

Rhode Island—L. E. Hersey, 99 Weybosset street, Providence.
Tennessee—A. J. Simon, 1311 6th avenue, north, Nashville.
Texas—John R. Spencer, 209½ South 5th street, Waco.
Utah—M. C. Howard, 1175 Milton avenue, Salt Lake City.
Vermont—Alexander Ironside, 35 Ayers street, Barre.
Virginia—Howard T. Colvin, 202 Park building, Richmond.
Washington—Charles Perry Taylor, box 1285, Tacoma.
West Virginia—James L. Pauley, 610 Ohio avenue, Charleston.
Wisconsin—J. J. Handley, 401 17th avenue, Milwaukee.
Wyoming—James Morgan, room 8 Deming building, Cheyenne.
*President.

OTHER ORGANIZATIONS.

Bricklayers, Masons and Plasterers' International Union—William Dobson, University Park building, Indianapolis, Ind.
Conductors, Order of Railway—Austin B. Garretson,* Cedar Rapids, Iowa.
Engineers, Brotherhood of Locomotive—Warren S. Stone,* Society for Savings building, Cleveland, O.
Firemen and Enginemen, Brotherhood of Locomotive—A. H. Hawley, Peoria, Ill.
Knights of Labor (organized 1878)—J. Frank O'Meara, Bliss building, Washington, D. C.
Railroad Freight and Baggage Men, International Brotherhood—Robert P. Nell, 44 Broad street, Boston, Mass.
Trainmen, Brotherhood of Railroad—W. G. Lee,* American Trust building, Cleveland, O.
*President.

PROGRESS OF THE UNITED STATES SINCE 1800.

[From table prepared by O. P. Austin of bureau of statistics, department of commerce and labor Washington, D. C.]

	1800.	1850.	1860.	1870.	1880.	1900.	1913.
Area*..............sq. miles	843,255	2,996,536	3,026,789	3,026,789	3,026,789	3,026,789	3,036,789
Population...................	5,308,483	23,191,876	31,443,321	38,558,371	50,155,783	75,994,575	97,337,000
Wealth..............dols.		7,135,780,000	16,159,616,000	30,068,518,000	42,642,000,000	88,517,306,775	$107,104,212,000
Debt...............dols.	82,976,294	63,452,774	59,964,402	2,531,169,956	1,919,326,748	1,107,711,258	884,898,388
Money in circulation..dols.	26,500,000	278,761,982	435,407,252	675,212,794	973,382,228	2,055,150,998	3,371,326,007
Deposits, bank, nat'l.dols.				543,261,563	833,701,034	2,459,092,758	5,953,461,551
Deposits, savings....dols.		43,431,130	149,277,504	549,874,358	819,106,973	2,389,719,954	†4,451,555,688
Deposits, postal sav...dols.							18,061,875
Farms, value..........dols.		3,967,343,580	7,980,493,060	8,944,857,749	12,180,501,538	20,514,001,838	*40,991,449,006
Manufactures, value..dols.		1,019,106,616	1,885,861,676	4,232,325,442	5,369,579,191	13,004,400,143	*20,672,051,870
Receipts—Net ord....dols.	10,818,791	43,592,888	56,054,600	395,959,834	333,526,561	567,240,852	728,732,921
Customs.............dols.	9,080,933	39,668,686	53,187,512	194,538,374	186,522,065	233,164,871	318,142,344
Internal revenue.....dols.	809,397			184,899,756	124,009,374	295,327,927	344,426,784
Expendit's—Net ord....dols.	10,713,971	40,918,388	63,130,598	293,657,005	264,847,637	487,713,792	683,099,692
War................dols.	2,560,879	9,687,025	16,472,208	57,655,675	38,116,916	134,774,768	161,775,225
Navy...............dols.	3,448,716	7,901,725	11,514,650	21,780,230	13,536,985	55,953,078	133,154,459
Pensions............dols.	64,131	1,866,886	1,100,802	28,340,202	56,777,174	140,877,316	176,714,907
Imports, mdse........dols.	91,252,768	173,509,526	353,616,119	435,958,408	667,954,746	849,941,184	1,812,978,234
Exports, mdse........dols.	70,971,780	144,375,726	333,576,057	392,771,768	835,638,658	1,394,483,082	2,465,884,149
Production of gold...dols.		50,000,000	46,000,000	50,000,000	36,000,000	79,171,000	†91,685,168
Silver..............dols.		50,900	156,800	16,431,000	34,717,000	35,741,100	†35,670,786
Coal................tons		6,206,233	13,044,680	29,496,054	63,822,830	240,789,310	†491,071,429
Petroleum..........gallons			21,000,000	220,051,290	1,104,017,166	2,672,082,218	†9,346,621,268
Pig iron............tons		563,755	821,223	1,665,179	3,835,191	13,789,242	†29,726,937
Steel...............tons				68,750	1,247,335	10,188,329	†31,251,303
Copper.............tons		650	7,200	12,600	27,000	270,588	†557,549
Wool...............lbs.		52,516,959	60,264,913	162,000,000	232,500,000	288,636,621	†304,043,400
Wheat.............bushels		100,485,944	173,104,924	235,884,700	498,549,868	522,229,505	†730,267,000
Corn...............bushels		592,071,104	838,792,740	1,094,255,000	1,717,434,543	2,105,102,516	†3,124,746,000
Cotton.............bales	156,500	2,454,442	3,849,469	4,352,317	6,605,750	10,245,602	†14,090,863
Cane sugar..........lbs.		247,577,000	230,982,000	87,043,000	178,872,000	322,549,011	†728,840,000
Railroads...........miles		9,021	30,626	52,922	93,267	198,964	†254,732
Postoffices...........No.	903	18,417	28,498	28,492	42,989	76,688	†58,020
Postoffice receipts...dols.	280,804	5,499,984	8,518,067	19,772,221	33,315,479	102,354,579	†246,744,016
Telegrams sent........No.				9,157,646	29,215,509	79,696,227	†90,000,000
Patents issued........No.		993	4,778	13,333	13,947	26,499	†37,731
Immigrants...........No.		369,980	150,237	387,203	457,257	448,572	1,197,892

*Census of 1910. †In 1912. ‡1911. §1904.

PATRIOTIC SOCIETIES OF THE UNITED STATES.

GRAND ARMY OF THE REPUBLIC.
First post organized at Decatur, Ill., April 6, 1866.

GENERAL OFFICERS.

Commander-in-Chief—Washington Gardner, Albion, Mich.
Senior Vice-Commander-in-Chief—Thomas H. Soward, Guthrie, Okla.
Junior Vice-Commander-in-Chief—William L. Ross, Pittsfield, Mass.
Chaplain-in-Chief—Horace M. Carr, Parsons, Kas.
Surgeon-General—Dr. J. K. Weaver, Morristown, Pa.

OFFICIAL STAFF.

Adjutant-General—Oscar A. Janes, Detroit, Mich.
Quartermaster-General—Col. D. R. Stowits, 877 Ellicott square, Buffalo, N. Y.
Judge-Advocate-General—P. H. Coney, Topeka, Kas.
Inspector-General—Levi S. Warren, Albion, Mich.
National Patriotic Instructor—Levi Longfellow, Minneapolis, Minn.
Assistant Adjutant-General—George A. Newman, Des Moines, Iowa.
Assistant Quartermaster-General and Custodian of Records—J. Henry Holcomb, Independence hall, Philadelphia, Pa.
Chief of Staff—Henry A. Axline, Columbus, O.
Senior Aid de Camp—Orville J. Nave, Los Angeles, Cal.
Headquarters—Detroit, Mich.

MEMBERSHIP BY DEPARTMENTS.

Dec. 31, 1912.

Depts.	Posts.	Members.	Depts.	Posts.	Members.
Alabama	6	119	Nebraska	172	3,873
Arizona	5	128	N. Hampshire	72	1,853
Arkansas	19	366	New Jersey	106	3,479
Cal. and Nev.	106	6,227	New Mexico	10	159
Col. and Wyo.	60	2,194	New York	568	19,433
Connecticut	61	2,854	North Dakota	21	315
Delaware	18	408	Ohio	525	18,151
Florida	25	642	Oklahoma	75	1,585
Ga. & S. Car.	9	227	Oregon	63	1,983
Idaho	19	456	Pennsylvania	519	18,215
Illinois	463	14,323	Potomac	15	1,542
Indiana	232	11,537	Rhode Island	23	1,221
Iowa	330	9,057	South Dakota	46	740
Kansas	315	9,319	Tennessee	31	604
Kentucky	63	1,170	Texas	21	420
La. and Miss.	42	754	Utah	5	259
Maine	142	3,892	Vermont	87	2,131
Maryland	56	1,692	Va. & N. Car.	31	390
Massachusetts	206	11,209	Wash. & Alas.	88	3,031
Michigan	279	8,226	West Virginia	34	923
Minnesota	158	3,766	Wisconsin	202	5,703
Missouri	222	5,364			
Montana	13	352	Aggregate	5,663	190,227

MEMBERSHIP BY YEARS.

1879	44,752	1897	319,456
1880	60,521	1898	305,609
1881	85,856	1899	287,981
1882	134,701	1900	276,662
1883	215,446	1901	269,507
1884	273,168	1902	263,745
1885	294,787	1903	256,610
1886	323,571	1904	246,261
1887	355,916	1905*	232,455
1888	372,960	1905†	235,823
1889	397,774	1906	229,922
1890	409,489	1907	225,157
1891	407,781	1908	220,600
1892	399,980	1909	213,901
1893	397,223	1910	203,410
1894	369,083	1911	191,346
1895	357,639	1912	180,227
1896	340,610		

DEATH RATE BY YEARS.

	No.	Pct.		No.	Pct.
1888	4,433	1.18	1897	7,515	2.35
1889	4,696	1.18	1898	8,383	2.41
1890	5,476	1.33	1899	7,994	2.76
1891	5,965	1.46	1900	7,790	2.89
1892	6,404	1.61	1901	8,166	3.02
1893	7,002	1.73	1902	8,299	3.08
1894	7,283	2.97	1903	8,366	3.22
1895	7,368	2.06	1904	9,029	3.60
1896	7,283	2.21	1905*	9,152	3.90

	No.	Pct.		No.	Pct.
1905†	9,205	3.95	1909	11,030	5.00
1906	9,052	3.83	1910	9,151	4.49
1907	10,242	4.45	1911	11,594	5.07
1908	10,124	4.59	1912	11,338	6.28

*June 30. †Dec. 31. By a new rule the statistics were made to cover the calendar year.

NATIONAL ENCAMPMENTS AND COMMANDERS-IN-CHIEF.

1866—Indianapolis; B. F. Hurlbut, Illinois.
1868—Philadelphia; John A. Logan, Illinois.
1869—Cincinnati; John A. Logan, Illinois.
1870—Washington; John A. Logan, Illinois.
1871—Boston; A. E. Burnside, Rhode Island.
1872—Cleveland; A. E. Burnside, Rhode Island.
1873—New Haven; C. Devens, Jr., Massachusetts.
1874—Harrisburg; C. Devens, Jr., Massachusetts.
1875—Chicago; J. F. Hartranft, Pennsylvania.
1876—Philadelphia; J. F. Hartranft, Pennsylvania.
1877—Providence; J. C. Robinson, New York.
1878—Springfield; J. C. Robinson, New York.
1879—Albany; William Earnshaw, Ohio.
1880—Dayton, O.; Louis Wagner, Pennsylvania.
1881—Indianapolis; G. S. Merrill, Massachusetts.
1882—Baltimore; P. Vandervoort, Nebraska.
1883—Denver; R. B. Beath, Pennsylvania.
1884—Minneapolis; John S. Kountz, Ohio.
1885—Portland, Me.; S. S. Burdette, Washington.
1886—San Francisco; L. Fairchild, Wisconsin.
1887—St. Louis; John P. Rea, Minnesota.
1888—Columbus, O.; Wm. Warner, Missouri.
1889—Milwaukee; Russell A. Alger, Michigan.
1890—Boston; W. G. Veazy, Vermont.
1891—Detroit; John Palmer, New York.
1892—Washington; A. G. Weissert, Wisconsin.
1893—Indianapolis; J. G. B. Adams, Massachusetts.
1894—Pittsburgh; T. G. Lawler, Illinois.
1895—Louisville; I. N. Walker, Indiana.
1896—St. Paul; T. S. Clarkson, Nebraska.
1897—Buffalo; J. P. S. Gobin, Pennsylvania.
1898—Cincinnati; James A. Sexton, Illinois.
1899—Philadelphia; Albert D. Shaw, New York.
1900—Chicago; Leo Rassieur, Missouri.
1901—Cleveland; Ell Torrance, Minnesota.
1902—Washington; T. J. Stewart, Pennsylvania.
1903—San Francisco; J. C. Black, Illinois.
1904—Boston; W. W. Blackmar, Massachusetts.
1905—Denver; James Tanner, Washington, D. C.
1906—Minneapolis; Robert B. Brown, Ohio.
1907—Saratoga; Chas. G. Burton, Missouri.
1908—Toledo; Henry M. Nevius, New Jersey.
1909—Salt Lake City; S. R. Van Sant, Minnesota.
1910—Atlantic City; J. E. Gilman, Massachusetts.
1911—Rochester, N. Y.; H. M. Trimble, Illinois.
1912—Los Angeles, Cal.; A. B. Beers, Connecticut.
1913—Chattanooga, Tenn.; W. Gardner, Michigan.

MILITARY ORDER OF THE LOYAL LEGION OF THE UNITED STATES.
Instituted 1865. Membership May 1, 1913, 7,193.

GENERAL OFFICERS.

Commander-in-Chief—Bvt. Brig.-Gen. Thomas H. Hubbard, U. S. V.
Senior Vice-Commander-in-Chief — Rear-Admiral Louis Kempff, U. S. N.
Junior Vice-Commander-in-Chief—Brig.-Gen. Edward S. Godfrey, U. S. A.
Recorder-in-Chief—Bvt. Lieut.-Col. John P. Nicholson, U. S. V.
Registrar-in-Chief—First Lieut. Thomas H. McKee, U. S. V.
Treasurer-in-Chief—Brig.-Gen. Joseph W. Plume, U. S. V.
Chancellor-in-Chief—Bvt. Capt. John O. Foering, U. S. V.
Chaplain-in-Chief—Bvt. Maj. Henry S. Burrage, U. S. V.
Council-in-Chief—Capt. Urban A. Woodbury, Acting Assistant Paymaster Henry M. Rogers, Capt. William R. Hodges, Capt. Roswell H. Mason, First Lieut. Orville C. Allen.

COMMANDERS.

California—Lieut. Henry Krebs, U. S. V., commander; Bvt. Col. William C. Alberger, recorder.
Colorado—Col. Charles A. White, U. S. V., commander; Lieut. Austin W. Hogle, recorder.
District of Columbia—Brig.-Gen. Green Clay Goodloe, U. S. V., commander; First Lieut. Thomas H. McKee, recorder.

Illinois—Capt. John C. Neely, commander; Capt. Roswell H. Mason, recorder.
Indiana—Capt. Woodrow S. Marshall, commander; Lieut. Alexander M. Scott, recorder.
Iowa—Lieut.-Col. David J. Palmer, commander; Capt. E. D. Hadley, recorder.
Kansas—Lieut. Henry Bennett, commander; Capt. John T. Taylor, recorder.
Maine—Lieut. George D. Bisbee, U. S. V., commander; Lieut. Horatio Staples, U. S. V., recorder.
Maryland—Lieut. Thomas Matthews, commander; Lieut. Joseph J. Janney, recorder.
Massachusetts—Capt. Wm. W. Douglas, U. S. V., commander; Capt. Charles W. C. Rhoades, recorder.
Michigan—Capt. J. D. Dickinson, U. S. V., commander; Gen. F. W. Swift, recorder.
Minnesota—Capt. F. G. Woodward, commander; Capt. Orton S. Clark, recorder.
Missouri—Capt. Lee Rassieur, commander; Capt. W. R. Hodges, recorder.
Nebraska—Lieut. W. H. Russell, commander; Lieut. Frank B. Bryant, recorder.
New York — Paymaster-Gen. Edwin Stewart, U. S. N., commander; Bvt. Lieut.-Col. William S. Cogswell, recorder.
Ohio—Capt. Joseph W. Wilshire, U. S. V., commander; Maj. W. R. Thrall, recorder.
Oregon—Capt. Daniel Webster, commander; Maj. Cicero Newell, recorder.
Pennsylvania—Lieut.-Col. James W. Latta, commander; Bvt. Lieut.-Col. John P. Nicholson, recorder.
Vermont—Col. Herbert A. Foster, U. S. V., commander; Bvt. Capt. Henry O. Wheeler, recorder.
Washington—Lieut. Byron Phelps, U. S. V., commander; Walter B. Beals, recorder.
Wisconsin—Paymaster G. W. Meacham, commander; Lieut. Amos P. Foster, recorder.

SONS OF VETERANS, U. S. A.
NATIONAL OFFICERS, 1912-1913.
Commander-in-Chief—John E. Sautter, Pittsburgh, Pa.
Senior Vice-Commander-in-Chief—Harry L. Streib, Baltimore, Md.
Junior Vice-Commander-in-Chief—Robert W. Biese, Chattanooga, Tenn.
Council-in-Chief—Henry F. Weller, Boston, Mass.; W. B. Moynihan, Rochester, N. Y.; Charles C. Behnke, St. Louis, Mo.
Secretary (holdover)—J. H. Hammer, Reading, Pa.
Treasurer (holdover)—J. L. Rake, Reading, Pa.
Chief of Staff—E. M. Ames, Altoona, Pa.
Counselor—William Coffin, Cincinnati, O.
Patriotic Instructor—Charles F. Sherman, Mount Vernon, N. Y.
Editor The Banner—William G. Dustin, Dwight, Ill.
OBJECT.
To perpetuate the memory and history of the heroic deeds of the soldiers, sailors and marines of the civil war, the proper observance of Memorial day, to inculcate patriotism and love of country and to secure an emulation among the younger generation of the heroic loyalty of their soldier fathers. Membership is confined to lineal male descendants of honorably discharged union soldiers, sailors or marines in the civil war.

WOMAN'S RELIEF CORPS.
Organized in Denver, Col., July, 1883.
NATIONAL OFFICERS.
President—Mrs. Ida S. McBride, Indianapolis, Ind.
Senior Vice-President—Mrs. Chloe A. Warren, Plainville, Conn.
Junior Vice-President—Mrs. M. A. Archer, Chattanooga, Tenn.
Treasurer—Mrs. Abbie Lynch, Pittsburgh, Pa.
Secretary—Mrs. Sarah C. White, Rockville, Ind.
Chaplain—Mrs. Sarah J. Bradford, Livingston, Mont.

LADIES OF THE GRAND ARMY OF THE REPUBLIC.
Organized in Chicago, September, 1886.
NATIONAL OFFICERS.
President—Edith R. Brown, Pacific Grove, Cal.
Senior Vice-President—Alice D. Schneider, Chattanooga, Tenn.

Junior Vice-President—Charlotte A. Parker, Portland, Ore.
Treasurer—Nellie R. McMillan, Leavenworth, Kas.
Secretary—Eva J. French, 533 Larkin street, Monterey, Cal.
National Counselor—Ella S. Jones, Pittsburgh, Pa.

ASSOCIATION OF CIVIL WAR NURSES.
NATIONAL OFFICERS.
President—Mrs. Rebecca Price, Philadelphia, Pa.
Senior Vice-President—Mrs. Alice Carey Risley, St. Louis, Mo.
Treasurer—Mrs. Salome M. Stewart, Gettysburg, Pa.

ASSOCIATION OF PATRIOTIC INSTRUCTORS.
NATIONAL OFFICERS.
President—John B. Lewis, Boston, Mass.
First Vice-President—Mrs. Flo Jamison Miller, Wilmington, Ill.
Second Vice-President—George H. Kellogg, Newcastle, Cal.
Treasurer—Le Vant Dodge, Berea, Ky.
Secretary—Mrs. Elizabeth Robbins-Berry, Boston, Mass.

NATIONAL ASSOCIATION OF NAVAL VETERANS.
Organized in 1887.
Commodore Commanding—Sherburne C. VanTassel, Yonkers, N. Y.
Fleet Captain—William H. Comstock, Denver, Col.
Chief of Staff and Fleet Commander—Robert McWilliams, Detroit, Mich.
First Lieutenant Commander—Dr. William H. Travis, Chattanooga, Tenn.
Fleet Lieutenant—Carter C. Morgan, Syracuse, N. Y.
Fleet Chaplain—Alexander S. McWilliams, Detroit, Mich.
Fleet Surgeon—Dr. Henry F. Brewer, M. D., Brooklyn, N. Y.
Fleet Judge-Advocate—Horatio L. Wait, Chicago, Ill.
Fleet Secretary and Paymaster—Henry F. McCollum, New Haven, Conn.
Fleet Historian—Cyrus Sears, Baltimore, Md.
Fleet Boatswain—Cornelius Stringham, Jamaica, N. Y.

UNITED CONFEDERATE VETERANS.
Organized June 10, 1889.
GENERAL OFFICERS.
General Commander—Gen. Bennett H. Young, Louisville, Ky.
Adj.-Gen. and Chief of Staff—Maj.-Gen. William E. Mickle, New Orleans, La.
Honorary Commander-in-Chief—Gen. C. Irvine Walker, Charleston, S. C.
Army of Northern Virginia Dept.—Commander, Lieut.-Gen. Theodore S. Garnett, Norfolk, Va.; Adj.-Gen. and Chief of Staff, Brig.-Gen. E. V. White, Norfolk, Va.
South Carolina Div.—Commander, Maj.-Gen. B. H. Teague, Aiken, S. C.; Adj.-Gen. and Chief of Staff, Col. S. E. Welch, Charleston, S. C.
North Carolina Div.—Commander, Maj.-Gen. Julian S. Carr, Durham, N. C.; Adj.-Gen. and Chief of Staff, Col. H. A. London, Pittsboro, N. C.
Virginia Div.—Commander, Maj.-Gen. J. Thompson Brown, Richmond.
West Virginia Div.—Commander, Maj.-Gen. Charles S. Peyton, Ronceverte.
Maryland Div.—Commander, Maj.-Gen. A. C. Trippe, Baltimore, Md.; Adj.-Gen. and Chief of Staff, Col. D. S. Briscoe, Baltimore.
Army of Tennessee Dept.—Commander, Lieut.-Gen. George P. Harrison, Opelika, Ala.; Adj.-Gen. and Chief of Staff, Brig.-Gen. E. T. Sykes, Columbus, Miss.
Louisiana Div.—Commander, Maj.-Gen. Thomas J. Shaffer, Franklin; Adj.-Gen. and Chief of Staff, Col. M. L. Costley, New Orleans.
Tennessee Div.—Commander, Maj.-Gen. John P. Hickman, Nashville, Tenn.; Adj.-Gen. and Chief of Staff, Col. M. L. McKay, Nashville.
Florida Div.—Commander, Maj.-Gen. Benjamin W. Partridge, Monticello; Adj.-Gen. and Chief of Staff, Col. C. S. Bott, Monticello.

Mississippi Div.—Commander, Maj.-Gen. Patrick Henry, Brandon, Miss.; Adj.-Gen. and Chief of Staff, John A. Webb, Jackson.

Georgia Div.—Commander, Maj.-Gen. John W. Preston, Sr., Macon; Adj.-Gen. and Chief of Staff, Col. John A. Cobb, Americus.

Kentucky Div.—Commander, Maj.-Gen. W. B. Haldeman, Louisville; Adj.-Gen. and Chief of Staff, Col. W. A. Milton, Louisville.

Trans-Mississippi Dept.—Commander, Lieut.-Gen. K. M. Van Zandt, Fort Worth, Tex.; Adj.-Gen. and Chief of Staff, Brig.-Gen. W. T. Shaw, Fort Worth, Tex.

Texas Div.—Commander, Maj.-Gen. Felix Robertson, Crawford; Adj.-Gen. and Chief of Staff, Col. B. F. Weems, Houston.

Missouri Div.—Commander, Maj.-Gen. J. William Hall, Liberty; Adj.-Gen. and Chief of Staff, Col. John N. Jenkins, Liberty.

Arkansas Div.—Commander, Maj.-Gen. Charles Coffin, Batesville; Adj-Gen. and Chief of Staff, Col. James M. Stewart, Little Rock.

Oklahoma Div.—Commander, Maj.-Gen. D. M. Hailey, McAlester; Adj.-Gen. and Chief of Staff, Col. R. B. Coleman, McAlester.

Pacific Div.—Commander, Maj.-Gen. William C. Harrison, M. D., Los Angeles; Adj.-Gen. and Chief of Staff, B. L. Hoge, Los Angeles, Cal.

Membership about 60,000; camps, 1,787.
The purpose of the society is strictly social, literary, historical and benevolent.

SONS OF CONFEDERATE VETERANS.

Commander-in-Chief—W. W. Olds, Norfolk, Va.
Commander of the Army of Northern Virginia—C. O. Brealsford, North Carolina.
Commander of Army of Tennessee—P. J. Mullins, Georgia.
Commander of Army of Trans-Mississippi—W. M. Scurry, Texas.
Historian-General—Dr. Thomas M. Owen, Alabama.

ARMY AND NAVY UNION OF THE UNITED STATES OF AMERICA.

Incorporated by special act of congress.

NATIONAL CORPS.

Commander—H. Oden Lake, Philadelphia, Pa.
Senior Vice-Commander—O. H. Kurtz, St. Louis, Mo.
Junior Vice-Commander— J. P. Caugher, Fort Monroe, Va.
Adjutant-General—Thomas H. Avery, 200 Montague street, Brooklyn, N. Y.
Paymaster-General—R. C. Shepherd, New York, N. Y.
Inspector-General—A. G. Binder, Philadelphia, Pa.
Judge-Advocate-General—Lemuel Fugitt, Washington, D. C.
Surgeon-General—Dr. J. E. Hendrickson, Phoebus, Va.
Chaplain—J. M. Hinkson, Philadelphia, Pa.
Council of Administration—O. H. Kurtz, St. Louis, Mo.; W. T. Conray, Washington, D. C.; W. H. Roach, Washington, D. C.; T. J. Meadows, Brooklyn, N. Y.; J. W. Miller, St. Louis, Mo.

NAVY LEAGUE OF THE UNITED STATES.

President—Gen. Horace Porter.
Vice-President—Henry H. Ward.
Counsel—Herbert L. Satterlee.
Treasurer—Charles C. Glover.
Secretary—Arthur H. Dadmun, Southern building, Washington, D. C.
The Navy League of the United States is a nonpartisan patriotic society. Its purposes are to acquire and spread before the citizens of the country information as to the condition of the United States naval forces and ships, and to awaken public interest and activity in all matters tending to aid, improve and develop the efficiency of the navy.

NAVAL AND MILITARY ORDER OF THE SPANISH-AMERICAN WAR.

Instituted Feb. 2, 1899.

NATIONAL COMMANDERY.

Commander-in-Chief—Lieut. John S. Muckle, Pennsylvania.
Senior Vice-Commander-in-Chief—Ensign Fred D. Standish, Michigan.

Junior Vice-Commander-in-Chief—Col. Lotus Giles, Texas.
Recorder-in-Chief—Maj. Frank Keck, 29 Broadway, New York, N. Y.
Registrar-in-Chief—Lieut.-Col. E. W. M. Bailey, Massachusetts.
Deputy Registrar-in-Chief—Lieut. Chesley R. Perry, Illinois.
Treasurer-in-Chief—Lieut.-Col. George M. Cole, Connecticut.
Chaplain-in-Chief—Capt. Patrick B. Murphy, Massachusetts.
Historian-in-Chief—Capt. Cassilly Cook, New York.
Council-in-Chief—Maj. Robert Lee Longstreet, District of Columbia; Maj. Felix Rosenberg, Ohio; Capt. Charles M. Machold, Pennsylvania; Capt. W. Tyson Romaine, New York; Capt. Taylor E. Brown, Illinois.

Membership is confined to commissioned officers who served as such in the United States army, navy, marine or revenue cutter service (volunteer or regular) or as a contract surgeon during the Spanish war or the Philippine insurrection incident thereto, as well as all the sons of such officers, and such enlisted men who served in said war and insurrection and who have since become officers in the regular army, navy, marine or revenue cutter service.

UNITED SPANISH WAR VETERANS.

Organized April 18, 1904, by the amalgamation of the National Army and Navy Spanish War Veterans, National Association of Spanish-American War Veterans and the Society of the Service Men of the Spanish War, to which have been added the Legion of Spanish War Veterans and the Veteran Army of the Philippines.

NATIONAL OFFICERS.

Commander-in-Chief—John Lewis Smith, Washington, D. C.
Senior Vice-Commander-in-Chief—Edward R. Barker, Providence, R. I.
Junior Vice-Commander-in-Chief—Ben F. Atkinson, Sandusky, O.
Deputy Commander-in-Chief—George A. Seyde, Honolulu, H. I.
Deputy Commander-in-Chief—Charles E. O'Donnell, Havana, Cuba.
Deputy Commander-in-Chief—W. W. Dayton, Manila, P. I.
Adjutant-General—Gustave E. Rausch, Washington, D. C.
Surgeon-General—F. W. Veninga, St. Louis, Mo.
Chaplain-in-Chief—J. Madison Hare, Jersey City, N. J.
National Historian—William J. S. Dineen, Long Island, N. Y.
Quartermaster-General—Howard M. Peter, Washington, D. C.
Assistant Adjutant-General—James E. Maynard, Washington, D. C.
Headquarters—483 Southern building, Washington, D. C.

ARMY OF THE PHILIPPINES.

Commander-in-Chief—F. Warner Karling, Kansas City, Mo.
Vice-Commander-in-Chief—Charles F. Manahan, Chicago, Ill.
First Junior Vice-Commander—A. S. Crossfield, Manila, P. I.
Second Junior Vice-Commander—George M. Welchelt, Grand Island, Neb.
Third Junior Vice-Commander—A. V. Davidson, Denver, Col.
Fourth Junior Vice-Commander—C. T. Spear, St. Paul, Minn.
Fifth Junior Vice-Commander—Perry W. Jewett, Lincoln, Neb.
Adjutant-General—Dr. John W. Goggin, 1305 Heyworth building, Chicago, Ill.
Paymaster-General—William Nelson, Chicago, Ill.
Judge-Advocate-General—E. C. Little, Kansas City, Kas.
Surgeon-General—F. M. Rambold, St. Louis, Mo.
Assistant Adjutant-General for the Philippines—Edward F. Wilson, Manila, P. I.
Chaplain—S. J. Smith, Corregidor, P. I.
Historian—Julian E. Duvall, Norton, Kas.

SOCIETY OF THE CINCINNATI.

Organized by Gen. George Washington and his officers May 10, 1783, at the cantonments of American army on the Hudson river, New York.

GENERAL OFFICERS.

President-General—Winslow Warren, Massachusetts.
Vice-President-General—James Simons, LL. D., South Carolina.
Secretary-General—Asa Bird Gardiner, LL. D., L. H. D., Union club, New York city.
Treasurer-General—Charles Isham, Connecticut.
Assistant Secretary-General—John C. Daves, Baltimore, Md.
Assistant Treasurer-General—Henry Randall Webb, Maryland.

Only the thirteen original states have state societies. These, with the names of president and secretary of each in geographical order named, are:
New Hampshire—William Davis Sawyer, Francis Coffin Martin.
Massachusetts—Winslow Warren, David Greene Haskins.
Rhode Island—Asa Bird Gardiner, LL. D., L. H. D.; George W. Olney.
Connecticut—Henry Larcom Abbott, LL. D.; Bryce Metcalf.
New York—Talbot Olyphant, Francis Burrall Hoffman.
New Jersey—James W. S. Campbell, Louis Dunham Boggs.
Pennsylvania—Richard Dale, Grant Weidman.
Delaware—John Patten Wales, Edwin Jaquette Sellers.
Maryland—Oswald Tilghman, Thomas Edward Sears.
Virginia—William Gordon McCabe, LL. D.; Levin Joyner.
North Carolina—Wilson Gray Lamb, Marshall Delancey Haywood.
South Carolina—James Simons, LL. D.; Henry M. Tucker, Jr.
Georgia—Walter Glasco Charlton, George Francis Tamille.

The Order of the Cincinnati was organized by American and French officers who served in the war of the revolution, for the purpose of perpetuating the remembrance of that event and keeping up the friendships then formed. Membership goes to the eldest male descendant, if worthy; in case there is no direct male descendant, then to male descendants through intervening female descendants. The present membership is about 890. George Washington was the first president-general until his decease, and Alexander Hamilton the second.

GENERAL SOCIETY OF MAYFLOWER DESCENDANTS.

The Society of Mayflower Descendants was organized in the city of New York Dec. 22, 1894, by lineal descendants of the Mayflower pilgrims, "to preserve their memory, their records, their history and all facts relating to them, their ancestors and their posterity." Every lineal descendant over 18 years of age, male or female, of any passenger of the voyage of the Mayflower which terminated at Plymouth, Mass., December, 1620, including all signers of "The Compact," are eligible to membership. The General Society of Mayflower Descendants was organized at Plymouth, Mass., 1897. The triennial congress is held in September at Plymouth, Mass. Societies have been organized in New York, Connecticut, Massachusetts, Pennsylvania, Illinois, District of Columbia, Ohio, New Jersey, Wisconsin, Rhode Island, Michigan, Minnesota, Maine, Colorado, California and Washington. The officers of the general society are:
Governor-General—Thomas S. Hopkins.
Secretary-General—John Packwood Tilden, 44 East 23d street, New York city.
Treasurer-General—Henry H. Belknap.
Historian-General—Dr. George B. Stevens.
Captain-General—Miles Standish, M. D.
Surgeon-General—Dr. Abiel W. Nelson.

MILITARY ORDER OF FOREIGN WARS OF THE UNITED STATES.

Instituted Dec. 27, 1894.

OFFICERS OF THE NATIONAL COMMANDERY.

Commander-in-Chief—Maj.-Gen. Charles F. Roe, New York, N. Y.

Vice-Commanders-General—Col. William G. Bates, 43 Cedar street, New York; Brig.-Gen. James Forney, U. S. M. C., retired, Philadelphia, Pa.; Morris W. Seymour, Bridgeport, Conn.; Capt. Willis J. Wells, Chicago, Ill.; the Hon. Horace Davis, LL. D., San Francisco, Cal.; John C. Edwards, Boston, Mass.; Col. H. Ashton Ramsay, Baltimore, Md.; Gen. George H. Garretson, Cleveland, O.; Col. Harvey C. Clark, St. Louis, Mo.; Lieut. W. W. Russel, U. S. V., Vermont; Maj. William Hancock Clark, Richmond, Va.; Lieut. Charles H. Peckham, U. S. V., Providence, R. I.; Commander John W. Bostick, L. N. R., New Orleans, La.; Brig.-Gen. Edward E. Campbell, U. S. V., Newark, N. J.; Gen. Charles King, U. S. V., Milwaukee, Wis.; Rev. Francis C. Kelley, Lapeer, Mich.; Lieut. R. K. Gaston, Dallas, Tex.; Col. J. W. Pope, U. S. A., Denver, Col.; Brig.-Gen. William J. McKee, U. S. V., Indianapolis, Ind.
Secretary-General—Maj. David Banks, 23 Park place, New York, N. Y.
Deputy Secretary-General—Capt. B. H. Dailey, South Bend, Ind.
Treasurer-General—Gen. Oliver C. Bosbyshell, 4048 Chestnut street, Philadelphia, Pa.
Registrar-General—Rev. Henry N. Wayne, Tuckahoe, N. Y.
Judge-Advocate-General—H. W. Lamberton, Harrisburg, Pa.
Deputy Treasurer-General—Col. O. D. Clark, Montpelier, Vt.
Chaplain-General—Capt. Henry A. F. Hoyt, Cynwyd, Pa.
Historian-General—Capt. Edw. H. Smith, U. S. V., Oshkosh, Wis.
Recorder-General—Maj. Guy A. Boyle, Indianapolis, Ind.

Commanderies have been established in twenty-one states. Total membership about 1,400.

The order is a military organization with patriotic objects, having for its scope the period of American history since national independence. It stands for the needed and honorable principle of national defense against foreign aggression. The principal feature of the order is the perpetuating of the names, as well as the services, of commissioned officers who served in either the war of the revolution, the war with Tripoli, the war of 1812, the Mexican war or the war with Spain and all future campaigns, recognized by the United States government as war with foreign powers. Veteran companionship is conferred upon such officers and hereditary companionship upon their direct lineal descendants in the male line.

SONS OF THE REVOLUTION.

Organized 1876.

GENERAL OFFICERS 1911-1914.

General President—Hon. Edmund Wetmore, New York, N. Y.
First General Vice-President—James Mortimer Montgomery, New York, N. Y.
Second General Vice-President—Thomas Wingate Weeks, Boston, Mass.
General Secretary—Prof. William Libbey, Princeton, N. J.
Assistant General Secretary—W. Hall Harris, Jr., Baltimore, Md.
General Treasurer—Richard McCall Cadwalader, Philadelphia, Pa.
General Chaplain—Rev. Randolph H. McKim, D. D., Washington, D. C.
General Registrar—Hon. George E. Pomeroy, Toledo, O.
General Historian—Marshall De Lancey Haywood, Raleigh, N. C.
Organizations exist in thirty-two states.
Membership, 7,500.

NATIONAL SOCIETY OF THE DAUGHTERS OF THE AMERICAN REVOLUTION.

Headquarters—Memorial Continental hall, 17th and D streets, N. W., Washington, D. C.
President-General—Mrs. William C. Story, New York, N. Y.
Vice-President-General in Charge of Organization of Chapters—Mrs. Henry L. Mann, Washington, D. C.

Vice-Presidents-General—Terms expire in 1914: Mrs. Charles H. Bond, Massachusetts; Mrs. John C. Ames, Illinois; Mrs. George S. Shackleford, Virginia; Mrs. William Libbey, New Jersey; Mrs. C. F. Johnson, Maine; Mrs. A. K. Gault, Nebraska; Mrs. W. L. Peel, Georgia; Mrs. R. M. Bratton, South Carolina; Mrs. C. M. Williamson, Mississippi; Mrs. William H. Crosby, Racine, Wis. Terms expire in 1915: Mrs. John Van Landingham, North Carolina; Mrs. R. H. Cunningham, Kentucky; Mrs. Thomas Day, Tennessee; Mrs. Thomas Kite, Ohio; Mrs. Rhett Goode, Alabama; Mrs. Allen P. Perley, Pennsylvania; Mrs. Ben F. Gray, Jr., Missouri; Miss Harriet I. Lake, Iowa; Mrs. John L. Didwiddie, Indiana; Mrs. John F. Swift, California.

Chaplain-General—Mrs. Mary S. Lockwood, Washington, D. C.
Recording Secretary-General—Mrs. William C. Boyle, Washington, D. C.
Registrar-General—Mrs. Gaius M. Brumbaugh, Washington, D. C.
Historian-General—Mrs. Charles W. Bassett, Washington, D. C.
Corresponding Secretary-General—Mrs. Julius C. Burrows, Washington, D. C.
Treasurer-General—Mrs. Joseph E. Ransdell, Washington, D. C.
Assistant Historian-General—Mrs. Edward Orton, Jr., Columbus, O.
Librarian-General—Mrs. George M. Sternberg, Washington, D. C.

SOCIETY OF COLONIAL WARS.
Instituted in 1892.
OFFICERS OF THE GENERAL SOCIETY.

Governor-General—Howland Pell, New York.
Vice-Governor-General—Richard McCall Cadwalader, Philadelphia, Pa.
Secretary-General—Clarence Storm, 45 William street, New York.
Deputy Secretary-General—Henry G. Sanford, 45 William street, New York, N. Y.
Treasurer-General—William Macpherson Hornor, Philadelphia, Pa.
Deputy Treasurer-General—Francis Howard Williams, Philadelphia, Pa.
Registrar-General—George Norbury Mackenzie, Baltimore, Md.
Historian-General—T. J. Oakley Rhinelander, New York, N. Y.
Chaplain-General—Rev. Charles L. Hutchins, D. D., Concord, Mass.
Surgeon-General—Henry A. Griffin, M. D., New York, N. Y.
Chancellor-General—Hon. Henry Stockbridge, Baltimore, Md.

SECRETARIES OF STATE SOCIETIES.
California—Harrison B. Alexander, Los Angeles.
Colorado—John Wright Barrows, Denver.
Connecticut—Lucius A. Barbour, Hartford.
Delaware—Christopher L. Ward, Wilmington.
Dist. of Columbia—J. Burr Johnson, Washington.
Georgia—Harris M. King, Savannah.
Illinois—Seymour Morris, 112 West Adams street, Chicago.
Indiana—Henry R. Merritt, Indianapolis.
Iowa—Benjamin F. Swisher, Waterloo.
Kentucky—George T. Wood, Louisville.
Maine—Philip I. Jones, Portland.
Maryland—Murray P. Brush, Baltimore.
Massachusetts—Walter R. Watkins, Boston.

Michigan—Williams C. Harris, Detroit.
Minnesota—Herbert M. Temple, St. Paul.
Missouri—Hobart Brinsmade, St. Louis.
Nebraska—John P. Lord, Omaha.
New Hampshire—George B. Leighton, Monadnock.
New Jersey—J. L. Merrill, East Orange.
New York—Frederick Dwight, New York.
Ohio—Henry M. Norris, Cincinnati.
Pennsylvania—E. S. Sayres, Philadelphia.
Rhode Island—Charles E. Cannon, Providence.
Vermont—Byron N. Clark, Burlington.
Virginia—Thomas Bolling, Jr., Richmond.
Washington—H. B. Ferris, Spokane.
Wisconsin—Oliver T. Dwight, Milwaukee.

NATIONAL SOCIETY OF THE SONS OF THE AMERICAN REVOLUTION.
Organized April 30, 1889, and incorporated by act of congress June 9, 1906.

President-General—Rogers C. B. Thruston, Kentucky.
Vice-Presidents-General—W. W. Kirby, Colorado; La Verne W. Noyes, Illinois; Wallace McCamant, Oregon; Rear-Admiral George W. Baird, District of Columbia; James P. Baxter, Maine.
Secretary-General and Registrar-General—A. Howard Clark, Smithsonian Institution, Washington, D. C.
Treasurer-General—John H. Burroughs, 15 William street, New York, N. Y.
Historian-General—David L. Pierson, East Orange, N. J.
Chaplain-General—Rev. John Timothy Stone, D. D., Chicago, Ill.
Membership (1912)—14,000.

SOCIETY OF THE WAR OF 1812.
Organized Sept. 14, 1814.
GENERAL OFFICERS.
President-General—John Cadwalader (of Pennsylvania society).
Vice-Presidents-General—Reynold W. Wilcox, M. D., LL. D. (New York); James D. Iglehart, M. D. (Maryland); George Francis Pierce (Massachusetts); Walter St. George Harris (Connecticut); Hon. Charles Page Bryan (Illinois); Marcus Benjamin, Ph. D. (Washington, D. C.); Frank W. Thomas; Oscar H. Condit (New Jersey).
Secretary-General—Herbert M. Leland, Massachusetts.
Assistant Secretary-General—John Mason Dulany, 1320 Linden avenue, Baltimore, Md.
Treasurer-General—George H. Richards, M. D., 424 Main street, Orange, N. J.
Assistant Treasurer-General—James M. Henry, Washington, D. C.
Registrar-General—Henry Harmon Noble, Essex, N. Y.
Surgeon-General—George H. Burgin, M. D.
Judge-Advocate-General—Gen. A. Leo Knott, Maryland.
Chaplain-General—Henry Branch, D. D., Maryland. State societies have been formed in Pennsylvania, Maryland, Massachusetts, Connecticut, Illinois, District of Columbia, New York and New Jersey. Membership is made up of male persons above the age of 21 years who participated in or are lineal descendants of one who served during the war of 1812 in the army, navy, revenue-marine or privateer service of the United States, upon offering proof thereof satisfactory to the state society to which they may make application for membership, and who are of good moral character and reputation.

UNITED STATES PASSPORT REGULATIONS.

Passports are issued to citizens of the United States upon application to the state department in Washington. The application must be accompanied by an affidavit, attested by a notary public or other officer empowered to administer oaths, stating that the applicant is a citizen and giving the place of birth and age, and it must be accompanied by the certificate of one other citizen to whom he is personally known that the declaration made by the applicant is true. The application must also be accompanied by a description of the person, particularly as to age, height, complexion, forehead, eyes, nose, mouth, chin, hair and face.

Blank forms are furnished by the state department upon application. The fee for each passport is $1. Citizens traveling abroad may also in some cases obtain passports by applying to United States ambassadors and ministers. Where any person has made a declaration of intention to become a citizen of the United States and has resided in the United States for three years a passport valid for six months may be issued to him. This passport is not renewable and does not entitle the holder to the protection of this government in the country of which he was originally a citizen.

UNITED STATES PENSION STATISTICS.

PENSIONERS ON THE ROLL JUNE 30, 1913, AND JUNE 30, 1912.

Reg'r establishment—	1913.	1912.	Gain.	Loss.
Invalids	14,561	14,373	188	......
Widows	2,904	2,869	35	......
Minor children	175	171	4	......
Mothers	1,145	1,129	16	......
Fathers	164	159	5	......
Brothers, sisters, sons and daughters	2	4	......	2
Helpless children	7	8	......	1
Civil war—				
Act of May 11, 1912—				
Survivors	379,064	13,246	365,818	......
Act of Feb. 6, 1907—				
Survivors	16,241	333,579	......	317,338
General law—				
Invalids	61,800	103,237	......	41,437
Nurses	325	362	......	37
Widows	60,265	64,135	......	3,870
Minor children	195	351	......	156
Mothers	1,053	1,413	......	360
Fathers	137	202	......	65
Brothers, sisters, sons & daughters	403	331	72	......
Helpless children	466	515	......	49
Act of June 27, 1890—				
Invalids	5,274	47,201	......	41,927
Minor children	3,839	4,063	......	224
Helpless children	441	416	25	......
Act of April 19, 1908—				
Widows without children	228,571	227,907	664	......
Wid'ws with chil'n	4,293	5,040	......	747
War with Spain—				
Invalids	24,157	23,841	316	......

	1913.	1912.	Gain.	Loss.
Nurses	3	......	3	......
Widows	1,238	1,238	......	......
Minor children	274	304	......	30
Mothers	2,860	2,951	......	91
Fathers	473	508	......	35
Brothers, sisters, sons and daughters	6	6	......	......
Helpless children	4	2	2	......
War of 1812—				
Widows	199	238	......	39
War with Mexico—				
Survivors	1,142	1,313	......	171
Widows	5,123	5,533	......	410
Indian wars—				
Survivors	1,066	1,210	......	144
Widows	2,330	2,439	......	109
Total	820,200	860,294	367,148	407,242
Net loss				40,094

There were 497,263 survivors of the civil war on the roll at the beginning of the year and 462,379 at its close, a net loss of 34,884. The losses to this class by death during the year were 36,064—about 7¼ per cent—and the original allowances therein were 1,272. Of the 820,200 pensioners on the roll at the close of the year, 503,633 were persons who rendered service in the army or navy of the United States, including 328 army nurses, the remaining 316,567 being pensioned as widows and dependents. The number of individuals who served in the army and navy of the United States during the civil war is estimated at 2,213,365.

PENSIONS BY CLASSES AND VALUE OF PENSIONS, JUNE 30, 1913.

	General laws.		Special acts.	
Classes.	Number.	Annual value.	Number.	Annual value.
Invalids, regular establishment	14,317	$2,149,124.18	244	$60,276.00
Widows, etc., regular establishment	3,975	687,912.00	422	168,068.00
Survivors, act May 11, 1912	379,064	95,000,843.48	......	....
Survivors, act Feb. 6, 1907	16,241	2,762,340.00	......	....
Invalids, general law	46,275	14,958,678.00	15,525	5,228,322.00
Nurses	253	36,432.00	72	11,988.00
Widows, etc., general law	58,116	8,807,006.00	4,403	959,068.00
Invalids, act June 27, 1890	5,274	718,329.00	......	....
Minors, etc., act June 27, 1890	4,280	768,264.00	......	....
Widows, act April 19, 1908	232,864	33,659,278.00	......	....
Invalids, war with Spain	23,593	2,877,346.16	564	115,650.00
Nurses	......	....	3	432.00
Widows, etc., war with Spain	4,612	710,196.00	243	59,640.00
Widows, war of 1812	187	26,928.00	12	3,216.00
Survivors, war with Mexico	1,104	387,876.00	38	10,404.00
Widows, war with Mexico	4,881	702,864.00	242	39,000.00
Survivors, Indian wars	885	212,400.00	131	32,952.00
Widows, Indian wars	2,263	325,872.00	67	10,080.00
Total	798,184	164,791,688.82	22,016	6,699,096.00

Total number of pensioners	820,200
Total annual value	$171,490,786.82
Average value of each pension—	
All classes	$209.08
Regular establishment	161.69
Act May 11, 1912	250.62

Act Feb. 6, 1907	$170.09
General law, civil war	240.69
Act June 27, 1890	155.59
Act April 19, 1908	144.54
War with Spain	144.57
Survivors, civil war	256.64

PENSIONERS BY STATE OR COUNTRY IN 1913.

State or ter.	No.	Amount.	State or ter.	No.	Amount.	State or ter.	No.	Amount.
Alabama	3,230	$685,825.90	Kentucky	21,350	4,533,245.50	North Carolina	3,631	770,970.23
Alaska	80	16,986.40	Louisiana	5,373	1,140,849.09	North Dakota	2,931	632,339.23
Arizona	895	190,035.35	Maine	14,261	3,028,038.13	Ohio	77,599	16,479,146.29
Arkansas	8,808	1,870,202.64	Maryland	12,439	2,641,172.87	Oklahoma	11,397	2,419,925.01
California	28,964	6,149,926.12	Massachusetts	34,124	7,245,548.92	Oregon	7,798	1,655,749.34
Colorado	8,049	1,709,044.17	Michigan	34,298	7,282,494.34	Pennsylvania	75,618	16,058,520.56
Connecticut	10,003	2,123,936.99	Minnesota	12,703	2,697,227.99	Rhode Island	4,482	951,663.06
Delaware	2,601	552,270.33	Mississippi	4,009	851,220.97	South Carolina	1,694	359,687.02
Dist. of Col.	8,986	1,907,997.33	Missouri	39,490	8,284,911.70	South Dakota	5,392	1,144,883.28
Florida	5,085	1,079,698.06	Montana	2,364	501,948.12	Tennessee	18,954	3,599,842.82
Georgia	2,995	635,928.35	Nebraska	14,364	3,049,908.12	Texas	8,402	1,783,996.66
Idaho	2,245	476,680.85	Nevada	399	84,719.67	Utah	1,026	217,850.68
Illinois	56,482	11,992,823.06	N. Hampshire.	6,560	1,392,884.80	Vermont	6,540	1,388,638.20
Indiana	49,987	10,613,739.71	New Jersey	20,624	4,379,093.92	Virginia	8,709	1,849,181.97
Iowa	27,821	5,907,232.93	New Mexico	1,896	402,577.68	Washington	9,942	2,110,984.86
Kansas	32,399	6,879,279.67	New York	68,270	14,498,319.71	West Virginia	10,618	2,254,519.94

State or ter.	No.	Amount.	Country.	No.	Amount.	Country.	No.	Amount.
Wisconsin	19,776	4,199,038.03	Belgium	23	4,883.59	Russia	16	3,397.28
Wyoming	839	178,144.87	Canada	2,879	611,298.07	Scotland	75	15,924.75
Total	814,502	172,950,861.51	Chile	11	2,335.63	South Africa	10	2,123.30
INSULAR POSSESSIONS.			China	15	3,184.95	Sweden	69	14,650.77
	No.	Amount.	Cuba	61	12,952.13	Switzerland	66	14,013.78
Canal Zone	2	$424.66	Denmark	56	11,890.48	Wales	26	5,520.58
Guam	3	636.59	England	555	117,843.15	Other foreign		
Hawaii	84	17,835.72	France	76	16,137.08	countries or		
Philippines	70	14,863.10	Germany	520	110,411.60	possessions		
Porto Rico	44	9,342.52	Ireland	404	85,781.52	having less		
Total	203	43,102.99	Italy	58	12,315.14	than 10 pen-		
FOREIGN COUNTRIES.			Japan	33	7,006.89	sioners each		
Argentina	13	$2,760.29	Mexico	136	28,876.88	and not clas-		
Australia	101	21,445.33	New Zealand	14	2,972.62	sified	156	32,123.48
Austria-Hung'y	37	7,856.21	Norway	73	15,500.09			
			Peru	12	2,547.96	Total	5,495	1,166,753.35

SUMMARY.

		Pensioners.	Payments.
Pensioners residing in states and territories and payments to them		814,502	$172,950,861.51
Pensioners residing in insular possessions and canal zone and payments to them		203	43,102.99
Pensioners residing in foreign countries and payments to them		5,495	1,166,753.35
Total		820,200	174,160,717.85
Payments by treasury department (treasury settlements)			10,942.95
Total payments on account of army and navy pensions, 1913			174,171,660.80

CLASSIFICATION OF DISBURSEMENTS (1913)

Regular establishment—Army—Invalids	$1,927,215.98
Widows, etc	567,583.65
Navy—Invalids	633,163.29
Widows, etc	319,178.96
Civil War—Act May 11, 1912—Army	51,596,417.21
Navy	1,769,004.71
Act Feb. 6, 1907—Army	35,109,236.77
Navy	1,267,233.76
General law—Army—Invalids	25,496,691.75
Nurses	50,556.63
Widows, etc	9,863,414.34
Navy—Invalids	277,845.91
Widows, etc	154,486.47
Act June 27, 1890—Army—Invalids	4,270,632.56
Minors, etc	848,754.35
Navy—Invalids	145,315.40
Minors, etc	27,385.86
Act April 19, 1908—Army—Widows	32,753,478.19
Navy—Widows	1,226,818.57
War with Spain—Army—Invalids	3,130,866.45
Widows, etc	789,066.42
Navy—Invalids	109,978.41
Widows, etc	50,257.13
War of 1812—Widows	32,171.07
War with Mexico—Survivors	411,416.35
Widows	773,283.55
Indian War—Survivors	176,292.72
Widows	351,371.38
Total	174,160,717.85

Amount disbursed on account of regular establishment	$3,447,141.88
Amount disbursed on account of civil war	164,597,372.48
Amount disbursed on account of war with Spain	4,071,168.42
Amount disbursed on account of war of 1812	32,171.07
Amount disbursed on account of war with Mexico	1,184,699.90
Amount disbursed on account of Indian wars	527,664.10
Amount disbursed by treasury settlements	10,942.95

BOUNTY LAND WARRANTS ISSUED TO JUNE 30, 1913.

	Number.	Acres.
War of the revolution	16,663	2,666,080
War of 1812, acts prior to 1850	29,471	4,891,520
Act of 1847, Mexican war	88,274	13,213,640
Act of 1850, war of 1812, Mexican and Indian wars	189,146	13,168,560
Act of 1852, war of 1812, Mexican and Indian wars	11,992	694,400
Act of 1855, war of 1812, Mexican and Indian wars	263,148	34,158,630
Total	598,694	68,792,835

PENSIONS AND PENSIONERS BY YEARS SINCE 1866.

	Paid as pensions.	Expenses.	Total.	No. of pensioners.
1866	$15,450,549.88	$407,165.00	$15,857,714.88	126,722
1867	20,784,789.69	490,977.35	21,275,767.04	155,474
1868	23,101,509.36	553,020.34	23,654,529.70	169,643
1869	28,513,247.27	564,526.81	29,077,774.08	187,963
1870	29,351,488.78	600,397.86	29,952,486.64	198,696
1871	28,518,792.62	863,079.00	29,381,871.62	207,495
1872	29,752,746.81	951,253.00	30,703,999.81	232,229
1873	26,982,063.89	1,003,200.64	27,985,264.53	238,411
1874	30,206,778.99	966,794.13	31,173,573.12	236,241
1875	29,270,404.76	982,695.35	30,253,100.11	234,821
1876	27,936,209.53	1,015,078.81	28,951,288.34	232,137
1877	28,182,821.72	1,034,459.33	29,217,281.05	232,104
1878	26,786,009.44	1,032,500.09	27,818,509.53	223,998
1879	32,664,428.92	837,734.14	34,502,163.06	242,755
1880	56,689,229.08	935,027.28	57,624,256.36	250,802
1881	50,583,405.35	1,072,059.64	51,655,464.99	268,830
1882	54,313,172.05	1,466,236.01	55,779,408.06	285,697
1883	60,427,573.81	2,591,648.29	63,019,222.10	303,658
1884	57,912,387.47	2,835,181.00	60,747,568.47	322,756
1885	65,171,937.12	3,392,576.34	68,564,513.46	345,125
1886	64,091,142.90	3,245,016.61	67,336,159.51	365,783
1887	73,752,997.08	3,753,400.91	77,506,397.99	406,007
1888	78,950,501.81	3,515,057.27	82,465,558.94	452,557
1889	88,842,720.58	3,466,968.40	92,309,688.98	489,725
1890	106,093,850.39	3,526,382.13	109,620,232.52	537,944
1891	117,312,690.50	4,700,636.44	122,013,326.94	676,160
1892	139,394,147.11	4,898,665.80	144,292,812.91	876,068
1893	156,906,637.94	4,867,734.42	161,774,372.36	966,012
1894	139,986,726.17	3,963,976.31	143,950,702.48	969,544
1895	139,812,294.30	4,338,020.21	144,150,314.51	970,524
1896	138,220,704.46	3,991,375.61	142,212,080.07	970,678
1897	139,949,717.35	3,987,783.07	143,937,500.42	976,014
1898	144,651,879.89	4,114,091.46	148,765,971.26	993,714
1899	138,355,052.95	4,147,517.73	142,502,570.68	991,519
1900	138,462,130.65	3,841,706.74	142,303,887.39	993,529
1901	138,537,483.84	3,868,795.44	142,400,279.28	997,735
1902	137,504,267.99	3,831,378.96	141,335,646.95	999,446
1903	137,759,653.71	3,993,216.79	141,752,870.50	996,545
1904	141,093,571.49	3,849,366.25	144,942,937.74	994,762
1905	141,142,861.33	3,721,832.82	144,864,694.15	998,441
1906	139,000,288.25	3,523,269.51	142,523,557.76	985,971
1907	138,155,412.46	3,309,110.44	141,464,522.90	967,371
1908	153,093,086.27	2,800,963.36	155,894,049.63	951,687
1909	161,973,703.77	2,852,583.73	164,826,287.50	946,194
1910	159,974,056.08	2,657,673.86	162,631,729.94	921,083
1911	157,325,160.35	2,517,127.06	159,842,287.41	892,098
1912	152,986,433.72	2,448,857.81	155,435,291.03	860,294
1913	174,171,660.80	2,543,246.59	176,714,907.39	820,200
	4,461,094,380.45	125,871,965.64	4,586,966,346.09	

PENSIONS OF THE SEVERAL WARS AND OF THE PEACE ESTABLISHMENT.

The amounts that have been paid for pensions to soldiers, sailors and marines, their widows, minor children and dependent relatives, on account of military and naval service since the foundation of the government to June 30, 1913, are as follows:

War of the revolution (estimate).....	$70,000,000.00
War of 1812 (service pension).........	45,923,014.46
Indian wars (service pension)..........	12,241,273.61
War with Mexico (service pension).....	47,632,572.34
Civil war................................	4,294,596,944.47
War with Spain and insurrection in Philippine Islands.......................	42,185,230.84
Regular establishment..................	28,461,369.52
Unclassified	16,499,419.44

Total disbursements for pensions....4,557,539,824.58

SERVICE PENSIONS.

The act of May 11, 1912, grants pensions according to the length of service to persons who served ninety days or more in the military or naval service of the United States during the civil war and were honorably discharged who have reached certain ages, at rates as indicated in the following table:

Age.	90 days.	6 mos.	1 yr.	1½ yrs.	2 yrs.	2½ yrs.	3 yrs.
62....	$13.00	$13.50	$14.00	$14.50	$15.00	$15.50	$16.00
66....	15.00	15.50	16.00	16.50	17.00	18.00	19.00
70....	18.00	19.00	20.00	21.50	23.00	24.00	25.00
75....	21.00	22.50	24.00	27.00	30.00	30.00	30.00

It also grants pensions at the maximum rate, $30 per month, without regard to age or length of service, to persons who served in the military or naval service during the civil war and received honorable discharges, and who were wounded in battle or in line of duty and are now unfit for manual labor by reason thereof, or who from disease or other causes incurred in line of duty resulting in their disabilities are now unable to perform manual labor.

It also provides a rate of $30 a month for surviving soldiers and sailors of the Mexican war who served sixty days or more and were honorably discharged.

From the date of approval of this act to the close of the last fiscal year, June 30, 1913, the pension bureau received 504,938 applications for pension or increase of pension thereunder, and during that time 429,369 certificates were issued under the act. Only 894 of these, however, were original allowances, or pensions granted to persons never before on the roll under other laws.

SUMMARY OF PENSION BUREAU WORK.

To June 30, 1913.

Year.	Cases on hand.	Appli- ca- tions.	Admis- sions.	Rejec- tions.	No bene- fit cases.	Cases adjudi- cated.
1904...	285,523	1,734	254,333	151,211	108,114	8,725	268,050
1905...	220,822	1,709	217,435	182,207	81,853	4,915	268,975
1906...	182,453	1,684	201,322	138,809	82,938	4,943	226,690
1907...	356,181	1,534	440,517	238,249	60,573	3,892	302,715
1908...	123,483	1,464	185,622	325,140	59,449	3,403	387,992
1909...	66,226	1,385	152,009	123,610	52,199	1,772	177,581
1910...	47,295	1,317	132,012	97,207	38,032	1,198	136,437
1911...	36,793	1,222	120,814	92,274	20,980	1,065	124,319
1912...	42,464	1,172	508,812	91,120	24,925	623	116,668
1913...	83,581	1,169	139,565	444,558	26,576	229	471,363

PENSIONS GRANTED BY SPECIAL ACTS OF CONGRESS SINCE MARCH 4, 1861.

Congress.	Number.	Congress.	Number.
37th (1861-1863).....	13	51st (1889-1891).......	1,388
38th (1863-1865).....	27	52d (1891-1893).......	217
39th (1865-1867).....	138	53d (1893-1895).......	119
40th (1867-1869).....	275	54th (1895-1897).......	378
41st (1869-1871).....	85	55th (1897-1899).......	694
42d (1871-1873).....	167	56th (1899-1901).......	1,391
43d (1873-1875).....	182	57th (1901-1903).......	2,171
44th (1875-1877).....	98	58th (1903-1905).......	3,355
45th (1877-1879).....	230	59th (1905-1907).......	6,030
46th (1879-1881).....	96	60th (1907-1909).......	6,600
47th (1881-1883).....	216	61st (1909-1911).......	9,649
48th (1883-1885).....	598	62d (1911-1912).......	6,350
49th (1885-1887).....	856		
50th (1887-1889).....	1,015	Total	42,337

HISTORICAL.

There are now no pensioners on account of the revolutionary war on the roll. Mrs. Phœbe M. Palmeter, who was pensioned by a special act of congress as the daughter of Jonathan Wooley, who served in a New Hampshire company, died at Brookfield, N. Y., April 25, 1911, aged 90 years. The last widow pensioner of that war was Esther S. Damon of Plymouth Union, Vt., who died Nov. 11, 1906, aged 92 years. The last survivor of the revolution was Daniel F. Bakeman, who died at Freedom, Cattaraugus county, N. Y., April 5, 1869, aged 109 years 6 months and 8 days.

The last surviving pensioned soldier of the war of 1812 was Hiram Cronk of Ava, N. Y., who died May 13, 1905, aged 105 years and 16 days. The names of 199 widows of the war of 1812 remained on the pension roll June 30, 1913.

POLITICAL STRIKE IN BELGIUM.

Under the leadership of the socialist party the workers of Belgium to the number of 350,000 entered upon a general strike April 14, 1913, in support of universal suffrage on the "one man, one vote" plan. Under the system in vogue every citizen more than 25 years of age has one vote. Every citizen more than 35 years of age with one or more children and paying $1 or more in house tax has a supplementary vote, as has also a citizen of more than 25 years of age who owns at least $400 worth of real estate. Two supplementary votes are given to graduates of universities or men who hold or have held office. No person has more than three votes. In 1911 the total number of voters was 1,700,000, of whom 995,000 had one vote, 395,000 two votes and 310,000 three votes each. Workers in nearly all trades took part in the strike and the business of the country was brought almost to a standstill. Good order was maintained and little or no property was destroyed. The strike ended April 24 when a compromise offered by the liberal leader, F. Masson, was accepted by the socialist party. It was agreed that the question of equalizing the parliamentary franchise should be taken up and some plan adopted for improving upon the old suffrage scheme. Competent economists estimated the money loss caused by the general strike at $20,000,000.

CAPITAL PUNISHMENT IN THE UNITED STATES.

Capital punishment prevails in all of the states of the union except Kansas, Maine, Minnesota, Rhode Island, Washington and Wisconsin. In Michigan the only crime punishable by death is treason. The death penalty was abolished in the state of Washington in 1913. It was abolished in Iowa in 1872 and restored in 1878. It was also abolished in Colorado in 1897 but was restored in 1901. Hanging is the ordinary mode of execution, but in Indiana, New York, Nebraska, Ohio, Pennsylvania, Vermont and Virginia electrocution is the legal method. In Nevada hanging or shooting is optional with the condemned.

BATTLE EFFICIENCY, UNITED STATES NAVY.

The battle ship Idaho was awarded the pennant for battle efficiency in 1913, standing first in gunnery and second in engineering, with a final merit mark of 94.652. The Utah, which was first in engineering and second in gunnery, was second with a mark of 87.613. The Michigan was third with 83.421. The Whipple won the pennant in the torpedo class and the A2 in the submarine class.

RATES OF POSTAGE AND MONEY ORDERS.

The domestic letter rate is 2 cents an ounce or fraction thereof, and it applies to the island possessions of the United States, Cuba, Canada, Newfoundland, Labrador, united kingdom, Germany (direct), Mexico, Shanghai, the canal zone and republic of Panama. The foreign letter rate is 5 cents an ounce or fraction thereof, and it applies to all foreign countries in the universal postal union except those named above.

DOMESTIC.

FIRST CLASS—Letters and all written or partly written matter, whether sealed or unsealed, and all other matter sealed or otherwise closed against inspection, 2 cents per ounce or fraction thereof. Postal cards issued by the government sold at 1 cent each; double, or reply cards, 2 cents each. Cards must not be changed or mutilated in any way and no printing or writing other than the address is allowable on the address side. "Private mailing cards" (post cards) require 1 cent postage.

Among the articles requiring first-class postage are blank forms filled out in writing; certificates, checks and receipts filled out in writing; copy (manuscript or typewritten) unaccompanied by proof sheets; plans and drawings containing written words; letters or figures; price lists containing written figures changing individual items; old letters sent singly or in bulk; typewritten matter and manifold copies thereof, and stenographic notes.

SECOND CLASS—All regular newspapers, magazines and other periodicals issued at stated intervals not less frequently than four times a year, when mailed by publishers or news agents, 1 cent a pound or fraction thereof; when mailed by others, 1 cent for each four ounces or fractional part thereof.

THIRD CLASS—Books, circulars, pamphlets and other matter wholly in print (not included in second-class matter), 1 cent for each two ounces or fractional part thereof. The following named articles are among those subject to third-class rate of postage: Almanacs, architectural designs, blue prints, bulbs, seeds, roots, scions and plants, calendars, cards, press clippings with name and date of papers stamped or written in, engravings, samples of grain in its natural condition, imitation of hand or type written matter when mailed at postoffice window in a minimum number of twenty identical copies separately addressed; insurance applications and other blank forms mainly in print; printed labels, lithographs, maps, music books, photographs, tags, proof sheets, periodicals having the character of books, and publications which depend for their circulation upon offers of premiums.

FOURTH CLASS—All matter not in the first, second or third class which is not in its form or nature liable to destroy, deface or otherwise damage the contents of the mailbag or harm the person of any one engaged in the postal service, 1 cent an ounce or fraction thereof. Included in fourth-class mail matter are the following articles: Blank books, blank cards or paper, blotters, playing cards, celluloid, coin, crayon pictures, cut flowers, metal or wood cuts, drawings, dried fruit, dried plants, electrotype plates, framed engravings, envelopes, geological specimens, letter heads, cloth maps, samples of merchandise, metals, minerals, napkins, oil paintings, paper bags or wrapping paper, photograph albums, printed matter on other material than paper, queen bees properly packed, stationery, tintypes, wall paper and wooden rulers bearing printed advertisements.

UNMAILABLE MATTER—Includes that which is prohibited by law, regulation or treaty stipulation and that which by reason of illegible or insufficient address cannot be forwarded to destination. Among the articles prohibited are poisons, explosives or inflammable articles, articles exhaling bad odors, vinous, spirituous and malt liquors, specimens of disease germs, lottery letters and circulars, indecent and scurrilous matter.

SPECIAL DELIVERY—Any article of mailable matter bearing a 10-cent special delivery stamp in addition to the regular postage is entitled to immediate delivery on its arrival at the office of address between the hours of 7 a. m. and 11 p. m., if the office be of the free delivery class, and between the hours of 7 a. m. and 7 p. m., if the office be other than a free delivery office.

REGISTRATION—All mailable matter may be registered at the rate of 10 cents for each package in addition to the regular postage, which must be prepaid. An indemnity not to exceed $50 will be paid for the loss of first-class registered matter, and 50 francs ($10) in case of the loss of a registered article addressed to a country in the universal postal union, under certain conditions.

LIMITS OF WEIGHT—No package of third or fourth class matter weighing more than four pounds, except single books, will be received for conveyance by mail. The limit of weight does not apply to second-class matter mailed at the second-class rate of postage, or at the rate of 1 cent for each four ounces, nor is it enforced against matter fully prepaid with postage stamps affixed at the first-class or letter rate of postage.

POST CARDS—A post card must be an unfolded piece of cardboard not exceeding 3 9-16 by 5 9-16 inches, nor less than 2¾ by 4 inches in size; it must be in form and quality and weight of paper substantially like the government postal cards; it may be of any color not interfering with the legibility of the address; the face of the card may be divided by a vertical line, the right half to be used for the address only and the left for the message, etc.; very thin sheets of paper may be attached to the card, and such sheets may bear both writing and printing; advertisements may appear on the back of the card and on the left half of the face. Cards bearing particles of glass, metal, mica, sand, tinsel or similar substances are unmailable except in envelopes.

FOREIGN.

Letter postage to Germany is 2 cents an ounce or fraction (in direct German steamers only); to Newfoundland, Great Britain and Ireland, 2 cents an ounce or fraction.

The rates of postage to all foreign countries (except Canada, Mexico, Panama and Cuba, which are the same as domestic rates) are as follows:

Letters, for the first ounce or fraction......	5 cents
Letters, for each additional or fraction of an ounce...............................	3 cents
Postal cards, each...........................	2 cents
Newspapers and other printed matter, per 2 oz..	1 cent
Registration fee on letters or other articles..	10 cents
Commercial papers, packages not in excess of 10 ounces............................	5 cents
Commercial papers, packages in excess of 10 ounces, each 2 ounces or fraction......	1 cent
Samples of merchandise, packets not in excess of 4 ounces............................	2 cents
Samples of merchandise, packets in excess of 4 ounces, each 2 ounces or fraction....	1 cent

LIMIT OF WEIGHT—Packages of printed matter and commercial papers, 4 pounds 6 ounces; samples of merchandise, 12 ounces.

PREPAYMENT OF POSTAGE—Foreign mail should at all times be fully prepaid. If not fully prepaid double the deficiency will be collected upon delivery.

INTERNATIONAL REPLY COUPONS—These reply coupons, of the denomination of 6 cents each, are issued for the purpose of sending to correspondents in any of the countries named below. The foreign correspondent may exchange the coupons for postage stamps of that country equal in value to a 5 cent United States postage stamp, using the stamp for reply postage. The countries in which the reply coupon is valid are as follows:

Argentina, Austria and the Austrian postoffices in the Levant, Belgium, Bosnia-Herzegovina, Bulgaria, Chile, Korea, Costa Rica, Crete, Cuba, Denmark, Danish West Indies, Egypt, France, Germany, Great Britain, British postoffices in Morocco and Turkey, British colonies of Australia, Bahamas, Bechuanaland, Canada, Cape of Good Hope, Ceylon, Cook islands, Dominica, East Africa, Ellice, Gibraltar, Gilbert, Gold Coast, Honduras (British), Hongkong and Hongkong offices in China, India, Labuan, Malta, Natal, Newfoundland, New Guinea, New Zealand, Seychelles, Sierra Leone, Solomon, Somaliland, South Rhodesia, Straits Settlements, Tasmania, Transvaal, Trinidad, Uganda, Zululand, Greece, Haiti, Honduras (Republic of), Hungary, Italy, Japan, Liberia, Luxemburg, Mauritius and dependencies, Mexico, Netherlands, Netherlands

Guiana, the Netherlands Indies, Norway, Roumania, Salvador, Siam, Southern Nigeria, Spain, Sweden, Switzerland, Tunis, Turkey.

MONEY ORDERS.

DOMESTIC.

For domestic money orders in denominations of $100 or less the following fees are charged:

For orders for sums not exceeding $2.50 .... 3c
For over $2.50 and not exceeding $5 .... 5c
For over $5 and not exceeding $10 .... 8c
For over $10 and not exceeding $20 ....10c
For over $20 and not exceeding $30 ....12c
For over $30 and not exceeding $40 ....15c
For over $40 and not exceeding $50 ....18c
For over $50 and not exceeding $60 ....20c
For over $60 and not exceeding $75 ....25c
For over $75 and not exceeding $100 ....30c

INTERNATIONAL.

International money orders issued payable in Algeria, Apia (Samoa), Argentine Republic, Australia, Austria, Azores, Belgium, Baluchistan, Beirut, Bolivia, Borneo, Bosnia, British Bechuanaland, British Central Africa, British East Africa, Bulgaria, Cape Colony, Caroline Islands, Ceylon, Chile, China, Cook Islands, Costa Rica, Crete, Cyprus, Denmark, Dutch East Indies, Egypt, Falkland Islands, Faroe Islands, Fiji Islands, Finland, Formosa, France, Germany, Gibraltar, Great Britain and Ireland and Scotland, Greece, Helgoland, Herzegovina, Holland, Republic of Honduras, Hongkong, Hungary, Iceland, British India, Italy, Jaffa, Japan, Jask (Persia), Java, Jerusalem, Kongo Free States, Korea, Liberia, Luxemburg, Madeira Islands, Malacca, Malta, Manchuria, Mauritius, Monaco (Principality of), Montenegro, Morocco, Natal, Netherlands, New Guinea, New South Wales, New Zealand, North Borneo, Northern Nigeria, Norway, Orange River Colony, Palestine, Panama, Penrhyn Island, Persia, Peru, Pescadores Islands, Portugal, Queensland, Rhodes, Rhodesia, Roumania, Russia, St. Helena, Saghalien (Japanese), San Marino, Savage Island, Servia, Seychelle Islands, Siam, South Australia, Spice Islands, Straits Settlements, Sumatra, Sweden, Switzerland, Tasmania, Transvaal, Tripoli, Tunis, Turkey, Turks Island, Uruguay, Victoria, Wales, Western Australia, Zambesia, Zanzibar and Zululand (South Africa).

Rates of fees for money orders payable in Apia, Austria, Belgium, Bolivia, Cape Colony, Costa Rica, Denmark, Egypt, Germany, Honduras, Hongkong, Hungary, Italy, Japan, Liberia, Luxemburg, New South Wales, New Zealand, Orange River Colony, Peru, Portugal, Queensland, Russia, Salvador, Switzerland, Tasmania, Transvaal, Uruguay and Victoria.

For orders from—		For orders from—	
$0.01 to $2.50	$0.10	$30.01 to $40.00	$0.45
2.51 to 5.00	.15	40.01 to 50.00	.50
5.01 to 7.50	.20	50.01 to 60.00	.60
7.51 to 10.00	.25	60.01 to 70.00	.70
10.01 to 15.00	.30	70.01 to 80.00	.80
15.01 to 20.00	.35	80.01 to 90.00	.90
20.01 to 30.00	.40	90.01 to 100.00	1.00

When payable in Chile, France, Greece, Netherlands (Holland), Norway and Sweden:

For orders from—		For orders from—	
$0.01 to $10.00	$0.10	$50.01 to $60.00	$0.60
10.01 to 20.00	.20	60.01 to 70.00	.70
20.01 to 30.00	.30	70.01 to 80.00	.80
30.01 to 40.00	.40	80.01 to 90.00	.90
40.01 to 50.00	.50	90.01 to 100.00	1.00

The amount payable in Mexico in Mexican currency will be at the rate of 2 pesos for every dollar and 2 centavos for every cent.

The maximum amount for which a single international money order may be drawn is $100. The value of the British pound sterling in United States money is fixed by convention at $4.87; the Austrian crown at 20 4-10 cents; the German mark at 23 9-10 cents; Danish, Swedish and Norwegian kroner at 26 9-10 cents; French, Swiss or Belgian franc and Italian lire at 19 4-10 cents; Netherlands florin at 40½ cents; Portugal escudo and centavo at $1.08; Russian ruble at 51 46-100 cents, $1=1 ruble 94 33-100 kopecks.

PARCEL POST.

DOMESTIC.

Unsealed matter of the fourth class (parcel post), which embraces all mailable merchandise not exceeding in size 72 inches in length and girth combined, and not exceeding 20 pounds in weight for delivery within the first and second zones and 11 pounds within the other zones, is mailable at postoffices, branch postoffices, lettered and local named stations and such numbered stations as may be designated by the postmaster. It may also be received by rural and other carriers authorized to receive such matter. Parcels must be so prepared that their contents may easily be examined.

RATES—For packages weighing 4 ounces or less the rate is 1 cent per ounce flat. The rates on parcels weighing more than 4 ounces vary with the distance, or the zones to which the articles are addressed and are by the pound or fraction thereof. For the first zone, which includes the territory within the local delivery of any office, the rate is 5 cents for the first pound and 1 cent for each additional two pounds or fraction thereof. This rate applies also to parcels for delivery on rural routes emanating from that postoffice. For the second zone, which includes the territory embraced within 150 miles of any given postoffice, the rate is 5 cents for the first pound and 1 cent for each additional pound or fraction thereof. The limit of weight in these two zones is 20 pounds. Rates for the other zones follow:

Zone.	1st lb.	Lb.*	11 lbs.
150-300 mile zone	.07	.05	.57
300-600 mile zone	.08	.06	.68
600-1,000 mile zone	.09	.07	.79
1,000-1,400 mile zone	.10	.09	1.00
1,400-1,800 mile zone	.11	.10	1.11
Over 1,800 miles	.12	.12	1.32

*Each additional pound.

Distinctive stamps are not required; parcels may be mailed with ordinary stamps affixed.

The special delivery service includes articles sent by parcel post. The fee is the same—10 cents in special delivery or ordinary stamps.

Packages may be sent C. O. D. by parcel post. Charges, not to exceed $100 on a single package, are collected from addressees. The fee for collection is 5 cents on parcels up to a value of $25 and 10 cents on parcels up to a value of not more than $50. The fee, which is paid by the sender, insures the parcel against loss to the actual value of the contents up to $25 and $50 according to the fee paid.

FOREIGN.

Mailable merchandise in unsealed packages may be sent to the countries named in the following list subject to the conditions herewith given:

Postage—12 cents a pound or fraction thereof, fully prepaid.

Weight limit—11 pounds (except to certain postoffices in Mexico).

Dimensions—To all countries named packages are limited to 3½ feet in length, and to 6 feet in length and girth combined, except that packages for Colombia and Mexico are limited to 2 feet in length and 4 in girth.

Value limit—To Ecuador, $50; other countries, none.

Registry—Parcels may be registered on payment of a fee of 10 cents in addition to postage. Parcel post packages sent to Barbados, Curacao, Dutch Guiana, France, Great Britain and Ireland, Guadeloupe, Martinique, the Netherlands and Uruguay cannot be sent by registered mail. Packages to those countries can be registered only when sent at the letter rate of postage.

A parcel when sent as parcel post must not be posted in a letter box, but must be taken to the foreign branch, general postoffice, or any postal station, and presented to the person in charge, between the hours of 9 a. m. and 5 p. m., where a declaration of contents must be made, a record kept and a receipt given for the parcel.

Following is a list of parcel post countries:

Australia, including Tasmania.

Austria, including the Austrian offices in the Ottoman empire at Alexandretta, Beirut, Caifa, Candia, Canea, Cavalla, Chios, Dardanelles, Dedeagh,

Durazzo, Ineboli, Jaffa, Janina, Jerusalem, Kerassonda, Mersina, Mitylene, Prevesa, Ritimo, Rhodes, Saloniki, Samsoun, San Giovanni di Medua, Santi Quaranta, Scutari d'Albanie, Smyrna, Trebizond, Tripoli (Syria), Valona, Vathi (Samos).

Bermuda.   Bahamas.
Bolivia.   Barbados.
Belgium.
Brazil (cities of Rio de Janeiro, Sao Paulo, Bello Horizonte, Bahia, Pernambuco and Para only).
British Guiana.
Chile.   Costa Rica.
Colombia.
Curacao, including Aruba, Bonaire, Saba, St. Eustatius and Dutch part of St. Martins.
Danish West Indies (St. Croix, St. John, St. Thomas).
Denmark, including Iceland and Faroe Islands.
Dominican Republic.   Ecuador.
Dutch Guiana.   France.
Germany, including German postoffices in Africa and China as follows:

Cameroon (Kamerun)—Akonolinga, Bamenda, Banjo, Bihundi, Bipindihof, Bonaberi, Bonambasi, Buea, Campo, Dsehang, Duala, Dume, Ebolowo, Edea, Garua, Jabassi, Jaunce, Johann-Albrechtshohe, Joko, Kribi, Kusseri, Lobetal, Lolodori, Lomie, Longji, Marienberg, Molundu, Mundeck, Nyanga, Ossidinge, Plantation, Rio de Rey and Victoria.

Togo—Agome-Palime, Anecho, Assabun, Atakpame, Ho, Kete-Kratschi, Kpandu, Lome, Noepe, Nuatja, Porto Seguro, Sokode, Tokpli and Tsewic.

German East Africa—Amani, Aruscha, Bagamojo, Bismarckburg, Buiko, Bukoba, Daressalam, Irinza, Kilimatinde, Kilossa, Kilwa, Kondoc-Irangi, Korogwe, Lindi, Mahenge, Mikindani, Mkalama, Mkumbara, Mohoro, Mombo, Morogoro, Moschi, Mpapua, Muaja, Muansa, Huhesa, Neu-Langenburg, Ngerengere, Pangani, Ruanda, Sadani, Schirati, Ssongea, Tabora, Tanga, Tschole, Udjidpi, Usumbura, Wiedhafen and Wilhelmstal.

German Southwest Africa—Arahoab, Aris, Aus, Aus, Berseba, Bethanien, Brackwasser, Brackwater (Bz. Windhuk), Empfangnisbucht, Epukiro, Fahlgras (Bz. Windhuk), Gibeon, Gobabis, Gochas, Grootfontein, Gross-Barmen, Gross-Witvley, Guehab, Haris, Hasuur, Hatsamas, Hoachanas, Hobewarte, Jakalswater, Johann-Albrechtshohe, Kalkfeld, Kalkfontein (Sud), Kanus, Karibib, Keetmanshoop, Kahn, Koes, Kolmannskuppe, Kub, Kubas, Kulbis, Luderitzbucht, Maltahohe, Mariental, Nauchas, Neudamm, Okahandja, Okasiss, Okaukwejo, Okombahe, Omaruru, Onguati, Osona, Otawi, Otjihawera, Otjimbingwe, Otjiwarongo, Otjosonjati, Outjo, Prinzenbucht, Ramansdrift, Rehoboth, Seeheim, Seeis, Swakopmund, Tsumeb, Ukamas, Usakos, Waldau, Warmbad, Waterberg, Wilhelmstal and Windhuk.

China (through German office at Shanghai)—Chinkiang, Hangkow, Nanking, Tsinanfoo, Weihsien, Kiowchow, Litsun, Mecklinburghaus, Shatsikoo, Sifang, Tabutow, Tsangkow, Tsingtow, Tsingtow-Grosser-Hafen, Tsingtow Tapatau, Shanghai.

Great Britain and Ireland.
Guadeloupe, including Marie Galante, Deseade, Les Saints, St. Bartholomew and the French portion of St. Martins.
Guatemala.   Honduras, British.
Haiti.   Honduras, republic of.
Hongkong, including the following cities in China—Aberdeen, Amoy, Autan, Canton, Chungchow, Foochow, Hoihow (Kingchow), Hongkong, Kowloon, Liukungtau, Ningpu, Pingshan, Saikung.

Shatin, Shootowkok, Shanghai, Sheungshui, Stanley, Swatow, Taio, Taipo, Weihaiwei.
Hungary.
Italy, including Republic of San Marino, Italian colonies of Benadir and Erythrea and the Italian offices in the Ottoman empire; Bengazi (North Africa), Durazzo (Albania), Galata (Constantinople), Jerusalem (Palestine), Canea (Crete), Pera (Constantinople), Saloniki (Roumelia), Scutari (Asia Minor), Stamboul (Constantinople), Tripoli-in-Barbary, Valona (Albania).
Jamaica, including the Turks and Caicos islands.
Japan, including Formosa, Karafuto (Japanese Saghalien) and Korea; Amoy, Changsha, Chefoo, Foochow, Hangchow, Kiukiang, Newchwang, Pekin, Shanghaikwan, Shasi, Soochow, Tougku, Tientsin, Wuhu, in China; Antoken (Antung), Bujun (Fushun), Chosiun (Changchun), Dairen (Tairen, Tallen, formerly Dalny), Dalsekkio (Tashichiao), Daitoka (Tatungkou), Furanten (Puientien), Gaihei (Kaiping), Giukaton (Newchatun), Gwaboten (Wafantein), Hishiko (Pitzuwo), Honkeiko (Pengshihu), Hoten (Mukden), Howojro (Fenghuangcheng), Kaigen (Kaiyuen), Kaijo (Haimueng), Kinshu (Chinchow), Koshurei (Kungchuling), Riojun (Port Arthur), Rioyo (Liaoyang), Riujuton (Liushutun), Senkinsai (Chienchinsai), Shiheigei (Ssupingchien), Shinminfu (Shingming fu), Shoto (Changtu), Sokato (Tsaohokow), Sokaton (Suchlatun), Taikzan (Takwshan), Tetsurei (Tiebling), Yendai (Yentai), Yngakujreo (Hsiungyocheng), in Manchuria.
Leeward islands. (Antigua with Barbuda and Redonda, St. Kitts, Nevis with Anguilla, Dominica, Montserrat and the Virgin islands).
Martinique.   Mexico.
Netherlands.
Newfoundland, including Labrador. From October to June parcel post packages are not forwarded from Newfoundland to Labrador.
New Zealand, including Fanning island.
Nicaragua.
Norway.
Panama. To the following named postoffices—Aguadulce, Alange, Anton, Arraijan, Atalaya, Bastimentos, Bejuco, Bocas de Cope, Bocas del Drago, Bocas del Toro, Boqueron, Boquete, Bugaba, Cacique, Calobre, Cana, Canazas, Capira, Cermeno, Chagres, Chame, Changuinola, Chepigana, Chepo, Chiriqui Grande, Chitre, Chorrera, Cituro, Colon, David, Divala, Donoso, El Llano, El Real, Garachine, Gualaca, Guarare, Horconcitos, Isla Grande, Jaque, Jurado, La Guayra, La Mesa, La Palma, La Pintada, La Villa, Las Lajas, Las Minas, Las Palmas, Las Penas, Las Tablas, Llanosucio, Los Pozos, Los Remedios Macaracas, Miguel de la Borda, Montije, Nata, Nombre de Dios, Ocu, Ola, Otoque, Pacora Palenque, Panama, Parita, Pedasi, Penonome, Pese, Pinogana, Playa Damas, Pocri de Aguadulce, Pocri de las Tablas, Portobelo, Puerto Obaldia, Rio de Jesus, Rio Indio, Saboga, San Carlos, San Felix, San Francisco, San Lorenzo, San Miguel, San Pablo, Santa Fe, Santa Isabel, Santa Maria, Santiago, Sixaola, Sona, Taboga, Tole, Tonosi, Tocuti, Viento Frio and Yaviza.
Peru.
Salvador.   Sweden.
Trinidad, including Tobago.
Uruguay.   Venezuela.
Windward islands, including Grenada, St. Vincent, the Grenadines and St. Lucia.

COMMISSION ON INDUSTRIAL RELATIONS.

Appointed by President Wilson, June 26, 1913.
Frank P. Walsh, lawyer, Kansas City, Mo.
John R. Commons, professor of political economy at the University of Wisconsin.
Mrs. J. Borden Harriman, philanthropist, New York city.
Frederic A. Delano, president of the Wabash Railroad company, Chicago.
Harris Weinstock, merchant, Sacramento, Cal.
S. Thruston Ballard, miller, Louisville, Ky.
John B. Lennon, treasurer of the American Federation of Labor, Bloomington, Ill.

James O'Connell, vice-president of the American Federation of Labor, Washington, D. C.
Austin B. Garretson, president of the Order of Railway Conductors, Cedar Rapids, Ia.
The duty of the commission to inquire into the general condition of labor in the principal industries of the United States, including agriculture, and especially those which are carried on in corporate forms. It is to seek to discover the underlying causes of dissatisfaction in the industrial situation and report its conclusions thereon. (Act of Aug. 23, 1912.)

Election Returns.

POPULAR VOTE FOR PRESIDENT (1912).

[Compiled by the bureau of statistics from reports on file in the department of state, Washington, D. C.]

STATE.	Dem. Wilson.	Prog. Roosevelt	Rep. Taft.	Soc. Debs.	Pro. Chafin.	S. L. Reimer.	Dem. Plurality's.	Prog. Plurality's.	Rep. Plurality's.	Total vote.
Alabama	82,438	22,680	9,732	3,029			59,758			117,879
Arizona	10,324	6,949	3,021	3,163	265		3,375			23,722
Arkansas	68,838	21,673	24,467	8,153			44,371			124,029
California*	283,436	283,610	3,914	79,201	23,366			174		673,527
Colorado	114,232	72,306	58,386	16,418	5,063	475	41,926			266,840
Connecticut	74,561	34,129	68,324	10,056	2,068	1,260			6,237	190,398
Delaware	22,631	8,886	15,997	556	623				6,634	48,693
Florida	36,417	4,535	4,279	4,806	1,854		31,611			51,891
Georgia	93,076	21,980	5,191	1,026	147		71,096			121,420
Idaho	33,921	25,527	32,810	11,960	1,537		1,111			105,755
Illinois	405,048	386,478	253,593	81,278	15,710	4,066	18,579			1,146,173
Indiana	281,890	162,007	151,267	36,931	19,249	3,130	119,883			654,474
Iowa	185,325	161,819	119,805	16,967	8,440		23,506			492,356
Kansas	143,663	120,210	74,845	26,779			23,453			481,009
Kentucky	219,534	102,766	115,512	11,647	3,253	956	104,072			838,186
Louisiana	60,971	9,323	3,834	5,249			51,648			79,377
Maine	51,113	48,495	26,545	2,541	946		2,618			129,640
Maryland	112,674	57,789	54,056	3,996	2,244	322	54,885			231,981
Massachusetts	173,408	142,228	155,948	12,616	2,754	1,102	17,460			488,056
Michigan	150,751	214,584	152,244	23,211	8,984	1,252		62,340		550,975
Minnesota	106,426	125,856	64,334	27,505	7,886	2,212		19,430		334,219
Mississippi	57,227	3,645	1,595	2,061			53,582			64,528
Missouri	330,746	124,371	207,821	28,466	5,380	1,178	122,925			698,562
Montana	27,941	22,456	18,512	10,885	32		5,485			79,826
Nebraska	109,008	73,614	54,029	10,174	3,383		36,304			249,208
Nevada	7,986	5,620	3,196	3,313			2,366			20,115
New Hampshire	34,724	17,794	32,927	1,980	535		1,797			87,969
New Jersey	174,282	145,409	88,834	15,900	2,875	1,322	24,873			424,822
New Mexico	22,139	8,347	17,990	2,859			4,239			51,245
New York	655,475	390,021	455,428	63,381	19,427	4,251	200,047			1,587,983
North Carolina	144,507	69,667	29,139	117	1,025		74,840			244,455
North Dakota	29,555	25,726	23,090	6,966	1,243		3,829			86,580
Ohio	424,834	229,807	278,168	90,144	11,511	2,630	146,666			1,037,094
Oklahoma	119,156		90,786	41,674	2,185		28,370			253,801
Oregon	47,064	37,600	34,673	13,343	4,360		9,464			137,040
Pennsylvania	395,619	447,426	273,305	80,915	19,533	704		51,807		1,217,502
Rhode Island	30,412	16,878	27,703	2,049	616	236	2,709			77,894
South Carolina	48,357	1,203	536	164			47,064			50,350
South Dakota‡	48,942	58,811		4,662	3,910			9,869		116,325
Tennessee	130,335	53,725	59,444	8,492	825		70,891			247,821
Texas	219,489	28,530	26,745	24,894	1,698	430	190,959			301,788
Utah	35,579	24,174	42,100	9,023		500			6,521	112,385
Vermont	15,354	22,132	23,332	928	1,095				1,200	62,841
Virginia	90,332	21,777	23,288	820	709	50	67,044			136,976
Washington	86,840	113,698	70,445	40,134	9,810	1,872		26,858		322,799
West Virginia	113,046	78,977	56,667	15,536	4,534		34,069			268,560
Wisconsin	164,228	62,460	130,605	33,481	8,596	522	33,583			399,972
Wyoming	15,310	9,232	14,560	2,760	434		750			42,296
Total	6,286,214	4,126,020	3,483,922	897,011	208,923	29,079	1,827,099	170,478	6,721	15,031,169
Plurality	2,160,194									

*In California the electoral vote was split, the progressives getting eleven and the democrats two. The highest progressive elector received 174 more votes than the highest democratic elector †Okla- homa had no progressive ticket, though it was generally understood that the republican electors favored Roosevelt. ‡There were no republican electors on the official ballot in South Dakota.

ALABAMA (Population in 1910, 2,138 093).

COUNTIES. (67)		PRESIDENT 1912				PRES. '08		Population.		Wilson	Roosevelt	Taft	Debs	Bryan	Taft
Population in 1910.		Dem. Wilson	Prog. Roosevelt	Rep. Taft	Soc. Debs	Dem. Bryan	Rep. Taft								
20038 Autauga	622	127	42	56..	655	97	32124 Covington	1251	147	110	193..	1054	315
18678 Baldwin	623	141	37	125..	439	107	23313 Crenshaw	986	127	47	7..	1100	311
32728 Barbour	1155	88	18	17..	1303	43	28821 Cullman	1230	1374	264	27..	1239	1521
22791 Bibb	820	178	40	103..	670	139	21873 Dale	1059	443	99	3..	921	346
21456 Blount	1721	580	567	32..	1133	973	53401 Dallas	1461	18	16	16..	1420	28
30196 Bullock	736	2	4	....	782	10	28261 DeKalb	1379	623	492	31..	1305	1104
29030 Butler	903	80	86	19..	727	187	28245 Elmore	1152	167	81	10..	1063	138
39115 Calhoun	1696	425	238	32..	1438	570	18890 Escambia	820	74	52	13..	614	112
39064 Chambers	1486	113	28	9..	1025	50	39100 Etowah	1511	887	854	144..	1309	996
20228 Cherokee	814	799	88	47..	712	602	26230 Fayette	762	506	453	20..	731	678
23187 Chilton	880	1154	140	72..	656	891	16243 Franklin	849	570	309	75..	650	652
18483 Choctaw	489	66	7	4..	590	44	26230 Geneva	891	511	99	37..	854	501
36887 Clarke	1024	12	13	26..	1169	56	22717 Greene	418	4	4	—..	423	12
21006 Clay	1109	949	64	2..	863	594	27883 Hale	720	7	4	—..	714	18
13385 Cleburne	691	510	134	2..	278	344	20043 Henry	711	153	47	26..	723	79
26119 Coffee	1277	395	68	67..	1305	341	32414 Houston	1160	366	82	45..	965	242
24802 Colbert	949	242	208	79..	949	332	32918 Jackson	1597	406	229	23..	1404	469
21433 Conecuh	802	103	46	26..	851	111	226476 Jefferson	8887	2604	706	612..	7803	2182
16634 Coosa	763	317	109	17..	717	447	27487 Lamar		—	—	..	839	163
							30886 Lauderdale	1386	207	263	72..	1177	427
							21984 Lawrence	643	261	198	32..	602	344

Population.		Wilson	Roosevelt	Taft	Debs	Bryan	Taft
22887	Lee	1159	43	43	60..	1126	—
18880	Limestone	1012	83	90	34..	1188	238
31894	Lowndes	583	10	7	4..	633	36
26049	Macon	647	23	24	—..	482	38
47041	Madison	2146	357	150	91..	2168	277
39923	Marengo	1886	20	9	1..	1535	78
17495	Marion	1008	205	378	7..	1100	589
28553	Marshall	1451	1184	428	24..	1313	925
80854	Mobile	3009	445	1.0	168..	2422	447
27155	Monroe	858	21	2	3..	866	18
82178	Montgomery	3047	131	43	17..	2631	79
33781	Morgan	1686	662	241	82..	1548	494
31222	Perry	781	51	3	14..	776	12
25055	Pickens	815	73	22	16..	816	69
30815	Pike	1269	48	13	5..	1507	39
24659	Randolph	1117	356	268	—..	799	385
25087	Russell	1558	35	4	22..	516	33
26949	Shelby	1181	1253	201	42..	820	781
20715	St. Clair	787	687	260	75..	1011	1231
28699	Sumter	701	2	9	10..	719	5
37921	Talladega	1512	595	111	1..	1010	351
31034	Tallapoosa	1586	151	84	22..	1343	104
47559	Tuscaloosa	1695	158	87	49..	1729	168
37013	Walker	2005	504	881	127..	1632	1267
14454	Washington	405	18	14	12..	464	40
33810	Wilcox	878	7	5	6..	1027	2
12855	Winston	508	893	292	7..	443	949

	Total	82458	22880	9732	3029..	74374	25308
	Plurality	57758				49006	
	Per cent	69.87	19.27	8.28	2.58..	71.99	24.47
	Total vote	119832		..	103869		

For president in 1908 Debs, Soc., received 1,309 votes.

FOR REPRESENTATIVES IN CONGRESS, 1912.

At Large—John W. Abercrombie, Dem........86,662
Asa E. Stratton, Rep........................9,548
J. C. Maxwell, Soc...........................2,525

1. The counties of Choctaw, Clarke, Marengo, Mobile, Monroe and Washington.
George W. Taylor, Dem......................9,939
W. M. Doyle, Soc..............................213

2. The counties of Baldwin, Butler, Conecuh, Covington, Crenshaw, Escambia, Montgomery, Pike and Wilcox.
S. H. Dent, Jr., Dem........................11,397

3. The counties of Barbour, Bullock, Coffee, Dale, Geneva, Henry, Houston, Lee and Russell.
Henry D. Clayton, Dem.....................11,225

4. The counties of Calhoun, Chilton, Cleburne, Dallas, Shelby and Talladega.
Fred L. Blackmon, Dem......................7,740
A. P. Longshore, Prog.......................3,060
W. H. Sturdivant, Rep.........................693

5. The counties of Autauga, Chambers, Clay, Coosa, Elmore, Lowndes, Macon, Randolph and Tallapoosa.
J. Thomas Heflin, Dem......................10,210

6. The counties of Fayette, Greene, Lamar, Marion, Hale, Pickens, Sumter, Tuscaloosa and Walker.
Richmond P. Hobson, Dem...................9,156
Charles P. Lunsford, Rep...................2,174

7. The counties of Cherokee, Cullman, DeKalb, Etowah, Franklin, Marshall, St. Clair and Winston.
J. L. Burnett, Dem.........................9,770
Sumter Coggswell, Prog.....................5,462
John J. Stephens, Rep......................2,711

8. The counties of Colbert, Jackson, Lauderdale, Lawrence, Limestone, Madison and Morgan.
William Richardson, Dem...................10,752
William E. Hotchkiss, Rep..................1,160
W. L. Conner, Soc.............................245

9. The counties of Bibb, Blount, Jefferson and Perry.
O. W. Underwood, Dem......................12,584
Frederick B. Parker, Rep..................1,598

LEGISLATURE.	Senate.	House.	J.B.
Democrats	34	103	137
Republicans	1	4	5

STATE OFFICERS. (All democrats.)
Governor—Emmett O'Neal.
Lieutenant-Governor—Walter D. Seed.
Attorney-General—R. C. Brickell.
Secretary of State—Cyrus B. Brown.
State Auditor—C. Brooks Smith.
State Treasurer—John Purifoy.
Superintendent of Education—W. F. Feagin.
Commissioner of Agricult. and Industries—R. F. Kolb.

ARIZONA (Population in 1910, 204,354).

COUNTIES.	PRESIDENT 1912.					
Population (14) in 1910.		Wilson Dem.	Taft Rep.	Roosevelt Prog.	Debs Soc.	Chafin Pro.
9196	Apache	106	58	81	10	1
34591	Cochise	1947	379	1405	815	20
8130	Coconino	358	234	172	26	3
16780	Gila	774	205	531	505	9
23547	Graham	534	98	242	165	5
	Greenlee (new)	587	103	268	111	2
34488	Maricopa	2389	653	1900	406	122
3773	Mohave	319	74	220	188	4
11491	Navajo	296	161.	229	40	6
22818	Pima	686	338	620	107	23
9045	Pinal	351	77	306	61	1
6766	Santa Cruz	247	55	125	37	1
15996	Yavapai	968	452	524	355	19
7733	Yuma	422	88	358	186	5

	Total	10174	2975	6881	3169	222
	Plurality	3293				
	Per cent	43.49	12.72	29.42	13.42	.95
	Total vote	23391				

FOR REPRESENTATIVES IN CONGRESS, 1912.
Carl Hayden, Dem...........................11,389
Thomas E. Campbell, Rep.....................3,110
R. S. Fisher, Prog..........................5,819
Mr. Smith, Soc..............................3,034
Mr. Gibson, Pro...............................193

LEGISLATURE.	Senate.	House.	J.B.
Democrats	15	30	45
Republicans	4	5	9

STATE OFFICES. (All democrats.)
Governor—G. W. P. Hunt.
Secretary—S. P. Osborn.
Auditor—J. C. Callaghan.
Treasurer—D. Johnson.

ARKANSAS (Population in 1910, 1,574,449).

COUNTIES.	PRESIDENT 1912			
Population (75) in 1910.		Dem. Wilson	Rep. Taft	Prog. Soc. Roosevelt Debs
16103	Arkansas	869	319	305 49
25268	Ashley	1039	499	316 82
10389	Baxter	536	142	176 142
33389	Benton	2353	511	660 296
14318	Boone	965	290	276 81
14518	Bradley	772	137	177 101
9894	Calhoun	438	72	147 109
16629	Carroll	919	464	358 122
21987	Chicot	419	89	308 22
23286	Clark	1051	376	262 36
23690	Clay	1299	622	358 218
11903	Cleburne	517	138	118 127
18481	Cleveland	685	275	98 33
23820	Columbia	1101	340	157 42
22729	Conway	1435	527	364 53
27627	Craighead	1259	269	229 207
23942	Crawford	969	467	423 81
22447	Crittenden	423	89	285 —
11042	Cross	491	203	234 79
13921	Dallas	654	228	406 28
15274	Desha	314	52	161 13
21960	Drew	882	424	194 43
23708	Faulkner	1316	402	264 111
20638	Franklin	1113	258	194 184
12193	Fulton	590	153	235 45
22771	Garland	1046	300	533 148
9425	Grant	440	110	47 25
23852	Greene	1251	286	259 239
28285	Hempstead	1248	656	468 92
15022	Hot Springs	668	218	247 42
16998	Howard	769	321	187 66
24776	Independence	1225	412	395 168
14561	Izard	746	215	137 52
23601	Jackson	837	543	159 161
52734	Jefferson	1659	579	753 146
19698	Johnson	926	189	291 151
13741	Lafayette	498	208	165 10
20001	Lawrence	929	218	167 125
24252	Lee	948	605	194 15
15118	Lincoln	390	202	132 86
13597	Little River	615	232	87 101
26350	Logan	1319	333	765 149
27983	Lonoke	1129	254	425 71
16056	Madison	982	786	291 71
10203	Marion	587	160	145 157
19555	Miller	846	331	195 106
30468	Mississippi	787	263	183 87
19907	Monroe	537	400	201 76
12455	Montgomery	471	221	202 137
19944	Nevada	607	322	208 93

Population	Wilson	Taft	Roosevelt	Debs
10612 Newton	290	285	247	74
21774 Ouachita	913	793	181	38
9402 Perry	522	163	216	64
33535 Phillips	826	198	189	2
12565 Pike	803	331	158	32
12791 Poinsett	503	205	157	126
17216 Polk	694	162	409	197
24527 Pope	1517	334	556	134
13853 Prairie	647	377	105	60
86751 Pulaski	3369	1044	1547	288
18887 Randolph	997	264	178	130
16657 Saline	814	164	140	65
14302 Scott	640	206	225	170
14825 Searcy	438	380	180	111
52278 Sebastian	2395	514	748	445
16616 Sevier	782	173	195	183
11668 Sharp	681	114	194	71
22548 St. Francis	563	296	273	65
8946 Stone	337	113	90	70
20723 Union	1088	153	135	105
23509 Van Buren	675	254	268	90
33889 Washington	1881	565	552	159
18574 White	1448	370	481	208
30049 Woodruff	933	473	253	65
26323 Yell	1461	426	438	263
Total	68838	24467	21673	8153
Plurality	44371			
Per cent	55.50	19.73	17.48	6.58
Total vote	124029			

For president in 1912 Chafin, Pro., received 898 votes. For president in 1908 Bryan, Dem., received 87,015 votes; Taft, Rep., 56,760 and Debs, Soc., 5,842.

FOR REPRESENTATIVES IN CONGRESS, 1912.

1. Counties of Clay, Craighead, Crittenden, Cross, Greene, Lee, Mississippi, Phillips, Poinsett, St. Francis and Woodruff.
   T. H. Caraway, Dem......................15,036
2. Counties of Stone, Sharp, Randolph, Lawrence, Fulton, Izard, Independence, White, Cleburne, Jackson, Prairie and Monroe.
   W. A. Oldfield, Dem......................11,880
   G. W. Wells, Rep......................... 4,388
3. Counties of Washington, Benton, Madison, Carroll, Newton, Boone, Searcy, Baxter, Marion and Van Buren.
   John C. Floyd, Dem......................10,849
   J. F. Carlton, Rep...................... 6,524
4. Counties of Crawford, Logan, Sebastian, Scott, Polk, Sevier, Howard, Pike, Little River, Miller and Montgomery.
   Otis T. Wingo, Dem......................11,680
   J. O. Livesay, Rep...................... 5,601
5. Counties of Franklin, Johnson, Pope, Yell, Conway, Faulkner, Perry and Pulaski.
   H. M. Jacoway, Dem......................13,428
   A. C. Remmel, Rep....................... 5,680
6. Counties of Desha, Garland, Hot Springs, Saline, Dallas, Grant, Cleveland, Lincoln, Drew, Jefferson, Arkansas and Lonoke.
   Samuel M. Taylor, Dem...................15,879
7. Counties of Hempstead, Clark, Nevada, Columbia, Union, Ouachita, Calhoun, Bradley, Ashley, Chicot and Lafayette.
   W. S. Goodwin, Dem......................10,956
   Patrick McNally, Rep.................... 4,824

LEGISLATURE.	Senate.	House.	J.B.
Democrats	34	96	130
Republicans	1	4	5

STATE OFFICERS. (All democrats.)
Governor—George W. Hays.
Secretary of State—Earle W. Hodges.
Auditor—L. L. Coffman.
Treasurer—John W. Crockett.
Attorney-General—William L. Moose.
Superintendent Public Instruction—George B. Cook.

CALIFORNIA (Population in 1910, 2,377,549).

Population in 1910.	COUNTIES (58)	PRESIDENT 1912 Prog. Roosevelt	Dem. Wilson	Soc. Debs	Pro. Chafin	Rep. Taft
246131 Alameda		31542	24418	9632	1160	
309 Alpine		36	34	2	—	8
9086 Amador		684	1622	135	57	5
27301 Butte		3065	4028	930	489	10
9171 Calaveras		750	1603	309	66	5
7732 Colusa		810	1700	111	84	8
31674 Contra Costa		3569	3290	1300	181	40

Population	Roosevelt	Wilson	Debs	Chafin	Taft
2417 Del Norte	376	328	104	40	—
7492 El Dorado	776	1613	278	49	16
75657 Fresno	8839	8891	2218	590	95
7172 Glenn	906	1325	126	67	11
33857 Humboldt	3609	2887	1781	177	94
13691 Imperial	1420	1295	446	198	18
6974 Inyo	431	806	305	77	8
37715 Kern	3647	5569	1300	152	64
16230 Kings	1419	1907	406	156	—
5526 Lake	649	1118	206	123	—
4802 Lassen	559	644	148	34	26
504131 Los Angeles	75508	55110	19895	8190	1085
8368 Madera	943	1154	226	89	1
25114 Marin	2750	2849	733	68	—
3956 Mariposa	306	689	138	17	20
23929 Mendocino	2237	2507	752	141	11
15148 Merced	1571	1978	441	228	14
6191 Modoc	608	941	119	45	1
2042 Mono	106	182	67	11	3
24140 Monterey	3081	8392	557	301	1
18900 Napa	2432	2662	478	126	—
14955 Nevada	1381	1851	648	111	23
34486 Orange	5113	4106	869	852	121
18237 Placer	1913	1828	481	125	15
5259 Plumas	762	742	236	30	11
34696 Riverside	5146	2963	1066	834	122
67806 Sacramento	7534	9909	1553	213	36
8041 San Benito	1054	1238	179	74	13
56706 San Bernardino	6202	5885	1901	1238	172
61665 San Diego	7922	6731	2873	1159	65
416912 San Francisco	38610	48955	12054	1158	94
50781 San Joaquin	4314	7969	995	426	36
19383 San Luis Obispo	2373	2248	704	214	13
26585 San Mateo	2825	3246	827	80	7
27738 Santa Barbara	3395	2819	619	357	69
83539 Santa Clara	10868	9175	2068	824	175
26140 Santa Cruz	3059	2875	892	323	8
18920 Shasta	1636	3040	938	54	16
4098 Sierra	483	515	133	13	19
18901 Siskiyou	1740	2465	633	104	29
27550 Solano	3533	3650	781	109	40
48894 Sonoma	5806	6500	1494	807	32
22522 Stanislaus	3143	3127	749	864	17
6328 Sutter	846	1063	79	65	5
11101 Tehama	1218	1595	388	168	13
3301 Trinity	343	461	182	9	1
35440 Tulare	4283	4293	1238	245	73
9979 Tuolumne	755	1469	363	58	8
18347 Ventura	2055	2108	426	169	72
13026 Yolo	1332	2239	501	115	9
10042 Yuba	1132	1242	186	34	17
Total	283610	283436	79201	23366	3914
Plurality	174				
Per cent	42.18	42.15	11.78	3.47	.42
Total vote	672460				

For president in 1912 Roosevelt, Prog., received 11 electoral votes and Wilson, Dem., 2.

FOR REPRESENTATIVES IN CONGRESS, 1912.

1. Counties of Del Norte, Humboldt, Mendocino, Glenn, Butte, Lake, Colusa, Yuba, Sutter, Sonoma and Marin.
   William Kent, Prog.....................20,341
   Edward H. Hart, Rep....................10,585
   I. G. Zumwalt, Dem.....................18,756
   Joseph Bredsteen, Soc.................. 4,892
2. Counties of Modoc, Siskiyou, Trinity, Shasta, Lassen, Tehama, Plumas, Sierra, Nevada, Placer, El Dorado, Amador, Calaveras, Alpine, Tuolumne and Mariposa.
   John E. Raker, Dem.....................23,467
   Frank M. Rutherford, Rep...............10,178
   J. C. Williams, Soc.................... 3,818
3. Counties of Yolo, Napa, Sacramento, Solano, Contra Costa and San Joaquin.
   C. F. Curry, Rep.......................31,060
   Gilbert McMillan Ross, Dem.............15,197
   William I. Wilson, Soc................. 6,522
4. San Francisco (part).
   Julius Kahn, Rep.......................25,515
   Bert Schlesinger, Dem..................14,884
   N. W. Pendleton, Soc................... 6,090
5. San Francisco (part).
   John I. Nolan, Rep.....................27,902
   Stephen V. Costello, Dem...............18,516
   E. L. Reguin, Soc...................... 6,962
6. County of Alameda.
   James R. Knowland, Rep.................35,219
   Hiram A. Luttrell, Dem................. 4,135
   J. Stitt Wilson, Soc...................26,234

7. Counties of Stanislaus, Merced, Madera, Fresno, Kings, Tulare and Kern.

Denver S. Church, Dem..................23,752
James C. Needham, Rep..................22,994
J. S. Cato, Soc.........................7,171

8. Counties of San Mateo, Santa Cruz, Santa Clara, San Benito, Monterey, San Luis Obispo, Santa Barbara and Ventura.

Everis A. Hayes, Rep...................29,861
James B. Holohan, Dem..................20,620
Robert Whitaker, Soc....................8,125

9. Los Angeles (part).

Charles W. Bell, Rep...................28,845
Thomas H. Kirk, Dem....................14,571
Ralph R. Criswell, Soc.................11,123

10. Los Angeles (part).

William D. Stephens, Rep...............43,637
George Ringo, Dem......................17,890
Fred C. Wheeler, Soc...................17,126
E. D. Martindale. Pro...................2,995

11. Counties of San Bernardino, Mono, Inyo, Riverside, Orange, San Diego and Imperial.

William Kettner, Dem...................24,882
Samuel C. Evans, Rep...................21,426
Noble A. Richardson, Soc................7,059

LEGISLATURE.

	Senate.	House.	J.B.
Republicans	4	9	13
Progressives	26	45	71
Democrats	10	25	35
Socialist	..	1	1

STATE OFFICERS. (All republicans.)

Governor—Hiram W. Johnson.
Lieutenant-Governor—Albert J. Wallace.
Secretary of State—Frank C. Jordan.
Comptroller—John S. Chambers.
Treasurer—E. D. Roberts.
Adjutant-General—E. A. Forbes.
Attorney-General—U. S. Webb.
Superintendent of Education—E. C. Hyatt.

COLORADO (Population in 1910, 799,024).

COUNTIES. (59)	PRESIDENT 1912					
Population in 1910.	Dem. Wilson	Prog. Roosevelt	Rep. Taft	Soc. Debs	Pro. Chafin	S.L. Reimer
8892 Adams.......	1312	942	308	137	32	2
10263 Arapahoe....	1379	1344	705	207	40	7
3302 Archuleta....	609	234	452	36	15	1
2516 Baca........	430	241	318	111	25	1
5043 Bent........	730	680	420	38	56	6
30830 Boulder.....	4339	2069	2445	918	453	5
7622 Chaffee.....	1611	693	723	282	56	—
3637 Cheyenne....	507	414	237	148	35	1
5001 Clear Creek..	1198	243	469	65	22	3
11285 Conejos.....	2147	606	1587	225	32	22
5498 Costilla....	567	204	1072	71	83	—
Crowl'y(new)	719	556	467	60	44	1
1947 Custer......	510	109	347	19	6	1
13688 Delta......	1808	1523	803	560	194	8
215381 Denver....	20930	21657	8155	2750	555	209
642 Dolores.....	124	28	45	34	—	—
3192 Douglas.....	619	290	373	30	9	1
2085 Eagle.......	727	234	387	141	8	1
5331 Elbert......	757	630	496	121	41	3
43321 El Paso....	5559	5332	2816	928	394	17
18181 Fremont....	2823	1624	1316	476	166	10
10144 Garfield....	1806	880	834	317	76	2
4131 Gilpin.....	951	222	443	54	12	—
1862 Grand......	507	178	248	18	6	5
5897 Gunnison....	1206	357	553	156	21	8
646 Hinsdale....	137	27	136	32	—	—
13320 Huerfano...	1277	290	2814	64	26	3
1013 Jackson.....	212	34	218	10	6	—
11231 Jefferson..	2399	1650	1011	307	79	1
2999 Kiowa......	628	490	275	62	87	—
7483 Kit Carson..	719	708	569	223	49	1
10600 Lake......	1931	864	966	427	20	4
10812 La Plata...	1775	647	692	370	73	3
25270 Larimer....	2597	1631	1902	546	401	21
13643 Las Animas.	3631	1461	4318	386	79	6
5917 Lincoln.....	746	795	584	76	70	10
9549 Logan......	1338	1030	664	125	73	1
22197 Mesa.......	2733	2724	976	1131	250	11
239 Mineral.....	296	68	186	97	5	1
Moffat (new).	409	196	204	22	16	1
5029 Montezuma..	1017	352	345	120	17	3
10291 Montrose...	1428	1022	631	431	187	3
9577 Morgan.....	1005	936	855	127	109	4
20201 Otero......	2885	1592	1293	245	154	5
3514 Ouray......	710	206	273	175	9	1
2492 Park.......	529	110	296	46	3	—

Population	Wilson	Roosevelt	Taft	Debs	Chafin	Reimer
3179 Phillips......	448	393	296	46	3	—
4566 Pitkin.......	770	176	298	170	9	6
9532 Prowers.....	1042	1036	928	152	68	1
52223 Pueblo......	7643	3818	3050	722	296	44
2332 Rio Blanco..	538	185	372	17	7	—
6563 Rio Grande..	1286	625	898	118	66	1
7561 Routt......	1406	395	738	249	33	3
4160 Saguache....	859	273	790	137	7	1
3063 San Juan....	555	89	261	148	3	1
4700 San Miguel..	1029	300	639	118	17	2
3061 Sedgwick....	338	382	328	28	19	—
2003 Summit......	600	152	179	30	4	—
14351 Teller.....	3027	1405	676	674	16	11
6002 Washington..	765	719	361	71	34	18
39177 Weld........	4713	2679	3114	425	435	2
8499 Yuma........	1170	1218	466	319	59	—
Total.....	114232	72306	58386	16418	5063	475
Plurality ...	41926					
Per cent...	42.72	27.11	21.89	6.16	1.89	.18
Total vote.	266722					

For president in 1908 Taft, Rep., received 123,700 votes; Bryan, Dem., 126,644; Debs, Soc., 7,974, and Chafin, Pro., 5,559.

Popular vote for United States senators, 1912: Long term—John F. Shafroth, Dem., 118,260; Clyde C. Dawson, Rep., 66,949; Frank T. Catlin, Prog., 58,649. Short term—Charles T. Thomas, Dem., 111,633; C. W. Waterman, Rep., 66,627; I. N. Stevens, Prog., 64,405.

FOR REPRESENTATIVES IN CONGRESS, 1912.

At Large—Edward T. Taylor, Dem. (elected).
Edward Keating, Dem. (elected).
S. H. Kinsley, Rep.
J. J. Laton, Rep.
Charles E. Fisher, Prog.
Clarence P. Dodge, Prog.

1. Counties of Adams, Boulder, Denver, Jefferson, Lake, Larimer, Logan, Moffat, Morgan, Park, Phillips, Sedgwick, South Arapahoe, Washington, Weld and Yuma.

George J. Kindel, Dem. (elected).
Rice W. Means, Rep.
W. J. L. Crank, Prog.

2. Counties Archuleta, Baca, Bent, Chaffee, Cheyenne, Clear Creek, Conejos, Costilla, Crowley, Custer, Delta, Dolores, Douglas, Eagle, Elbert, El Paso, Fremont, Garfield, Gilpin, Grand, Gunnison. Hinsdale, Huerfano, Kiowa, Kit Carson, La Plata, Las Animas, Lincoln, Mesa, Mineral, Montezuma, Montrose, Otero, Ouray, Pitkin, Prowers, Pueblo, Rio Blanco, Rio Grande, Routt, Saguache, San Juan, San Miguel, Summit and Teller.

H. H. Seldomridge, Dem. (elected).
C. A. Ballreich, Rep.
Neil N. McLean, Prog.

LEGISLATURE.

	Senate.	House.	J.B.
Democrats	24	49	73
Republicans	11	16	27

STATE OFFICERS. (All democrats.)

Governor—Elias M. Ammons.
Lieutenant-Governor—
Secretary of State—James B. Pearce.
Auditor—Roady Kenehan.
Treasurer—M. A. Leddy.
Superintendent Public Instruction—M. C. C. Bradford.

CONNECTICUT (Population in 1910, 1,114,756).

COUNTIES. (8)	PRESIDENT 1912				
Population in 1910.	Dem. Wilson	Rep. Taft	Prog. Roosevelt	Pro. Chafin	Soc. Debs
245322 Fairfield.............	15608	13148	9802	416	2383
250182 Hartford............	16757	16962	6883	450	2003
70820 Litchfield..........	4661	5518	2435	140	356
43387 Middlesex...........	3102	2892	1603	62	191
337282 New Haven.........	22368	19196	9813	583	4210
91253 New London........	6912	5543	2545	223	416
26459 Tolland	1901	2027	411	66	305
48361 Windham...........	2920	3055	1113	125	116
Total...........	74561	68324	34129	2063	10056
Plurality...........	6237				
Per cent...........	39.16	35.88	17.93	1.08	5.29
Total vote...	190398				

For president in 1912 Reimer, Soc.-Lab., received 1,260 votes.

FOR REPRESENTATIVES IN CONGRESS, 1912.

1. County of Hartford.
   Augustine Lonergan, Dem.....................17,256
   Charles C. Bissell, Rep......................18,726
   Joseph W. Alsop, Prog........................6,445
2. Counties of Tolland, Windham, New London and Middlesex.
   Bryan F. Mahan, Dem.........................14,936
   William A. King, Rep.........................14,421
   G. Warren Davis, Prog........................4,742
3. County of New Haven, except twelve towns.
   Thomas Reilly, Dem..........................16,267
   John Q. Tilson, Rep..........................12,989
   Yandell Henderson, Prog......................5,480
4. County of Fairfield.
   Jeremiah Donovan, Dem.......................15,616
   Ebenezer J. Hill, Rep........................14,183
   Samuel E. Vincent, Prog......................8,263
5. County of Litchfield and twelve towns of New Haven county.
   William Kennedy, Dem........................12,073
   Thomas D. Bradstreet, Rep....................11,724
   H. G. Hoadley, Prog..........................4,807

LEGISLATURE.

	Senate.	House.	J.B.
Democrats	21	120	141
Republicans	14	132	146
Progressives	0	6	6

STATE OFFICERS.
Governor—Simeon E. Baldwin, Dem.
Secretary—Albert Phillips, Dem.
Treasurer—Edward S. Roberts, Dem.
Comptroller—Daniel P. Dunn, Dem.
Attorney-General—John H. Light, Rep.

DELAWARE (Population in 1910, 202,322).

COUNTIES. (3) Population in 1910.	PRESIDENT 1912. Dem. Wilson	Prog. Roosevelt	Rep. Taft	Soc. Debs
32721 Kent	4071	567	3132	9
12588 New Castle	13009	7091	8843	547
46413 Sussex	5551	1229	3466	—
Total	22631	8887	15000	556
Plurality	49631			
Per cent	9.53	19.45	28.46	1.21
Total vote	45093			

In 1912 Chafin, Pro., for president received 623 votes.

FOR REPRESENTATIVE IN CONGRESS, 1912.
Franklin Brockson, Dem......................22,481
George H. Hall, Rep..........................16,740
Louis A. Drexler, Prog.......................2,825
H. R. Burton, Nat. Prog........................497

LEGISLATURE.

	Senate.	Honse.	J.B.
Democrats	8	21	29
Republicans	9	14	23

STATE OFFICERS.
Governor—Charles R. Miller, Rep.
Secretary of State—Thomas W. Miller, Rep.
Lieutenant-Governor—Colen Ferguson, Dem.
Attorney-General—Josiah O. Wolcott, Dem.
Insurance Commissioner—William R. McCabe, Dem.
State Treasurer—Charles A. Hastings, Dem.
State Auditor—William P. Prettyman, Dem.

FLORIDA (Population in 1910, 751,139).

COUNTIES. (47) Population in 1910.	PRESIDENT 1912. Dem. Wilson	Rep. Taft	Soc. Debs	Pro. Chafin	Prog. Roosevelt
34305 Alachua	1304	221	56	75	75
4805 Baker	168	37	31	2	93
14000 Bradford	656	95	10	56	40
4717 Brevard	357	61	82	8	82
7465 Calhoun	352	67	192	50	59
6731 Citrus	417	11	21	10	44
6116 Clay	279	26	54	10	21
17689 Columbia	520	86	23	11	50
11933 Dade	1171	99	188	33	291
14200 DeSoto	847	110	135	89	78
75163 Duval	3514	243	350	77	485
36549 Escambia	1593	73	158	41	202
5201 Franklin	266	58	38	5	23
22198 Gadsden	609	75	31	2	54
11825 Hamilton	405	46	60	22	24
4927 Hernando	272	18	42	29	22
78374 Hillsboro	2841	159	672	164	249
11557 Holmes	411	53	79	20	110
29821 Jackson	1205	183	146	115	68
17210 Jefferson	459	47	9	2	39
6710 Lafayette	473	73	8	51	11
9509 Lake	596	92	39	21	63
6294 Lee	432	38	116	31	97
19427 Leon	546	66	15	9	46
10361 Levy	375	74	30	29	24
4700 Liberty	206	32	7	2	18
16919 Madison	480	16	19	3	30
9550 Manatee	712	55	98	63	108
26341 Marion	1165	179	124	62	117
21563 Monroe	1023	414	221	29	152
10525 Nassau	441	38	31	5	17
19107 Orange	1257	228	124	101	134
5507 Osceola	512	110	64	44	159
5557 Palm Beach	458	31	77	14	146
7502 Pasco	485	60	64	36	74
Pinellas (new)	853	87	180	39	250
24148 Polk	1520	106	291	70	141
13056 Putnam	774	229	67	51	53
14897 Santa Rosa	592	70	88	95	48
13208 St. John	636	45	116	15	132
4075 St. Lucie	352	45	64	9	86
6696 Sumter	417	22	19	29	71
18603 Suwanee	714	54	214	18	29
7103 Taylor	236	56	9	43	19
16510 Volusia	942	169	98	122	72
4802 Wakulla	215	25	23	2	15
16490 Walton	612	74	69	5	293
16403 Washington	694	82	186	48	68
Total	36417	4279	4805	1854	4535
Plurality	30537				
Per cent	69.55	8.42	9.46	3.65	8.92
Total vote	50817				

FOR REPRESENTATIVES IN CONGRESS, 1912.
At Large—Claude L'Engle, Dem...............34,324
   E. R. Gunby, Prog............................2,680
   Frances P. Coffin, Pro.........................777
   George W. Allen, Rep.........................2,942
   A. N. Jackson, Soc...........................3,636
1. Counties of Taylor, Lafayette, Levy, Marion, Citrus, Sumter, Hernando, Pasco, Pinellas, Hillsboro, Polk, Manatee, DeSoto, Lee, Monroe and Lake.
   S. M. Sparkman, Dem.........................12,400
   J. DeV. Hazzard, Prog..........................469
   George C. Kelly, Pro...........................256
   George W. Bean, Rep...........................766
   C. C. Allen, Soc.............................1,901
2. Counties of Hamilton, Suwanee, Columbia, Baker, Bradford, Nassau, Duval, Clay, Putnam, St. John, Volusia, Osceola, Orange, Brevard, Dade, Alachua and St. Lucie.
   Frank Clark, Dem............................14,635
   John W. Howell, Rep..........................1,210
   J. J. Collins, Soc...........................1,318
   C. E. Speir, Prog..............................875
3. Counties of Escambia, Santa Rosa, Walton, Holmes, Washington, Jackson, Calhoun, Franklin, Liberty, Gadsden, Leon, Wakulla, Jefferson and Madison.
   Emmett Wilson, Dem...........................9,057
   John Thomas Porter, Prog.......................280
   Thomas F. McGourin, Rep........................489
   W. N. Lamberty, Soc............................669

LEGISLATURE.
The members of the senate (32) and of the house of representatives (71) are all democrats.

STATE OFFICERS. (All democrats.)
Governor—Park Trammell.
Secretary of State—H. Clay Crawford.
Attorney-General—Thomas F. West.
Comptroller—W. V. Knott.
Treasurer—J. C. Luning.
Superintendent Public Instruction—W. N. Sheats.
Commissioner of Agriculture—W. A. McRae.

GEORGIA (Population in 1910, 2,609,121).

COUNTIES. (146) Population in 1910.	PRESIDENT 1912. Rep. Taft	Dem. Wilson	Prog. Roosevelt	Pro. Chafin	Soc. Debs
12318 Appling	94	381	150	9	4
7973 Baker	0	180	12	—	—
18554 Baldwin	24	621	47	—	—
11244 Banks	17	274	215	—	—
23348 Bartow	93	1017	561	—	—
11863 Ben Hill	34	585	263	—	—
22772 Berrien	35	709	70	—	4
56646 Bibb	122	2526	90	—	32

Population		Taft	Wilson	Roosevelt	Chafin	Debs
24832	Brooks	37	695	42	—	—
7602	Bryan	23	236	15	—	—
26494	Bulloch	17	932	44	4	—
27268	Burke	22	440	22	1	—
13624	Butts	29	490	49	2	—
11334	Calhoun	5	328	6	—	—
7690	Camden	2	219	2	—	—
10674	Campbell	6	443	104	—	—
30855	Carroll	81	1192	431	2	14
7184	Catoosa	63	286	125	—	—
4722	Charlton	23	150	48	2	—
79690	Chatham	238	3274	332	23	14
5586	Chattahoochee	1	137	11	—	—
13306	Chattooga	69	578	220	—	1
16961	Cherokee	21	603	710	8	—
23273	Clarke	66	950	81	—	2
8900	Clay	8	369	17	—	—
10453	Clayton	3	443	113	1	—
8424	Clinch	48	293	9	—	—
28397	Cobb	41	1518	442	3	—
21953	Coffee	28	895	85	—	17
19789	Colquitt	8	699	506	6	10
12328	Columbia	2	234	50	—	—
28800	Coweta	35	1044	46	—	—
8310	Crawford	1	249	3	2	—
16423	Crisp	12	644	45	—	—
4139	Dade	18	243	44	—	19
4696	Dawson	23	170	161	4	—
28045	Decatur	44	837	65	—	45
27881	DeKalb	52	1150	378	4	33
20127	Dodge	12	637	28	—	63
3564	Dooly	5	608	55	—	—
16035	Dougherty	21	731	19	—	—
8953	Douglas	18	293	307	—	—
18122	Early	7	501	27	—	36
3309	Echols	—	144	4	—	—
9971	Effingham	5	843	10	—	—
24125	Elbert	13	882	238	—	—
25140	Emanuel	22	715	129	—	8
12574	Fannin	108	451	305	—	—
10906	Fayette	13	393	95	1	1
36796	Floyd	65	1837	374	1	—
11946	Forsyth	15	235	163	—	—
17894	Franklin	26	604	331	—	—
177783	Fulton	509	7317	1696	22	111
9237	Gilmer	52	488	116	—	1
4889	Glascock	8	101	72	—	—
15720	Glynn	16	470	30	12	3
15861	Gordon	52	507	650	—	—
18457	Grady	21	453	98	—	1
18512	Greene	5	525	150	—	—
28824	Gwinnett	55	997	593	1	—
10134	Habersham	42	497	310	—	—
25730	Hall	116	1145	275	—	11
19189	Hancock	12	549	39	—	—
13514	Haralson	19	384	701	—	21
17886	Harris	4	585	28	1	—
16216	Hart	15	484	291	—	—
11189	Heard	11	326	65	—	—
19927	Henry	15	536	127	—	—
23629	Houston	24	780	16	—	—
10461	Irwin	6	423	45	—	1
20169	Jackson	45	1108	551	—	—
18552	Jasper	12	644	8	—	—
6050	Jeff Davis	19	208	52	—	—
21379	Jefferson	8	416	153	2	—
11520	Jenkins	13	279	15	—	—
12897	Johnson	23	285	92	—	—
13101	Jones	27	426	3	—	—
35501	Laurens	26	1118	106	—	—
11679	Lee	9	210	6	—	—
12924	Liberty	29	251	77	—	—
8714	Lincoln	—	253	26	—	—
24836	Lowndes	24	847	35	7	9
5444	Lumpkin	29	279	119	—	—
15016	Macon	19	411	85	—	—
16851	Madison	13	564	146	—	—
9147	Marion	17	233	51	—	—
10325	McDuffie	9	271	106	1	—
6442	McIntosh	2	118	8	—	—
25180	Meriwether	26	882	91	—	1
7986	Miller	2	200	6	2	46
7239	Milton	17	320	107	—	—
22114	Mitchell	30	917	140	—	19
20450	Monroe	9	786	93	—	—
19658	Montgomery	52	854	93	—	—
19717	Morgan	24	575	57	—	—
9763	Murray	68	366	307	—	30
36227	Muscogee	51	1817	102	1	158
18449	Newton	57	840	43	1	—
11104	Oconee	1	208	180	—	—
18680	Oglethorpe	33	508	79	—	—
14124	Paulding	32	426	684	—	—
9041	Pickens	190	324	417	—	—
10749	Pierce	83	408	97	—	—
19495	Pike	34	751	134	—	1
20203	Polk	39	706	439	—	5
22835	Pulaski	17	1080	39	—	—
13876	Putnam	6	469	10	—	—
4504	Quitman	7	112	9	—	—
5572	Rabun	12	337	119	1	—
18841	Randolph	57	559	44	—	—
58886	Richmond	177	1871	234	3	131
8916	Rockdale	11	434	61	—	—
5213	Schley	5	212	20	1	—
20202	Screven	21	400	138	2	—
19741	Spalding	26	736	45	—	—
9728	Stephens	15	409	61	—	—
18437	Stewart	17	452	7	—	—
29062	Sumter	24	1004	19	—	3
11696	Talbot	8	446	87	—	—
8766	Taliaferro	7	242	40	—	—
18569	Tattnall	18	592	254	2	1
10839	Taylor	17	342	98	—	—
13288	Telfair	20	695	19	—	—
22003	Terrell	29	608	19	—	—
23071	Thomas	47	1012	176	—	7
11487	Tift	—	427	189	1	35
11206	Toombs	20	327	75	—	1
3332	Towns	89	230	206	—	4
26228	Troup	16	1441	75	—	2
10075	Turner	25	585	75	6	28
10736	Twiggs	3	307	13	—	—
6918	Union	88	319	256	—	—
13757	Upson	7	445	138	—	—
18692	Walker	215	771	404	—	21
26393	Walton	40	885	274	—	—
22957	Ware	54	972	39	5	25
11880	Warren	11	262	67	—	1
28174	Washington	28	920	167	—	—
13069	Wayne	14	380	25	4	—
6151	Webster	2	139	1	—	—
5110	White	11	152	110	—	—
15984	Whitfield	106	761	487	1	65
18486	Wilcox	15	525	29	—	1
23341	Wilkes	5	657	68	—	7
10078	Wilkinson	10	335	17	—	—
19147	Worth	12	500	77	—	5
	Total	5191	98076	21900	147	1026
	Plurality		71096			
	Per cent	4.27	76.67	18.09	.12	.85
	Total vote		121524			

For governor John M. Slaton was elected in October to go into office in June, 1913.

FOR REPRESENTATIVES IN CONGRESS, 1912.

1. Counties of Bryan, Bulloch, Burke, Chatham, Ellingham, Jenkins, Liberty, McIntosh, Screven, Tattnall.
Charles G. Edwards, Dem....................7,944
E. J. Seymore, Rep..................................356

2. Counties of Baker, Calhoun, Colquitt, Decatur, Dougherty, Early, Grady, Miller, Mitchell, Tift, Thomas, Worth.
S. A. Roddenberry, Dem...................7,957

3. Counties of Ben Hill, Clay, Crisp, Dooly, Lee, Macon, Randolph, Quitman, Schley, Stewart, Sumter, Taylor, Terrell, Turner, Webster.
Charles R. Crisp, Dem......................7,321

4. Counties of Carroll, Chattahoochee, Coweta, Harris, Heard, Marion, Meriwether, Muscogee, Talbot, Troup.
W. C. Adamson, Dem.......................8,904

5. Counties of Campbell, DeKalb, Douglas, Fulton, Rockdale.
William Schley Howard, Dem...............12,000

6. Counties of Bibb, Butts, Clayton, Crawford, Fayette, Henry, Jasper, Jones, Monroe, Pike, Spalding, Upson.
Charles L. Bartlett, Dem....................13,171

7. Counties of Bartow, Catoosa, Chattooga, Dade, Floyd, Gordon, Haralson, Murray, Paulding, Polk, Walker, Whitfield.
Gordon Lee, Dem...........................14,099

8. Counties of Clarke, Elbert, Franklin, Greene, Hart, Madison, Morgan, Newton, Oconee, Oglethorpe, Putnam, Walton, Wilkes.
S. J. Tribble, Dem...........................10,013

9. Counties of Banks, Cherokee, Dawson, Fannin, Forsyth, Gilmer, Gwinnett, Habersham, Hall, Jackson, Lumpkin, Milton, Pickens, Rabun, Stephens, Towns, Union, White.
Thomas M. Bell, Dem.......................12,496

10. Counties of Baldwin, Columbia, Glascock, Hancock, Jefferson, Lincoln, McDuffie, Richmond, Taliaferro, Warren, Washington, Wilkinson.
Thomas W. Hardwick, Dem.................... 6,474

11. Counties of Appling, Berrien, Brooks, Camden, Charlton, Clinch, Coffee, Echols, Glynn, Irwin, Jeff Davis, Lowndes, Pierce, Wayne, Ware.
J. R. Walker, Dem............................ 7,923

12. Counties of Dodge, Emanuel, Houston, Johnson, Laurens, Montgomery, Pulaski, Telfair, Toombs, Twiggs, Wilcox.
Dudley M. Hughes, Dem........................ 7,791

The legislature consists of 44 senators and 183 representatives. All but four or five are democrats. There are no divisions along party lines.

STATE OFFICERS. (All democrats.)

Governor—John M. Slaton.
Secretary of State—Phil Cook.
Comptroller-General—W. A. Wright.
Attorney-General—Thomas S. Felder.
Treasurer—W. J. Speer.
School Superintendent—M. L. Brittain.
Commissioner of Agriculture—J. D. Price.
Prison Commission—R. E. Davison, chairman; Wiley Williams, T. E. Patterson.

IDAHO (Population in 1910, 325,594).

Population in 1910.	COUNTIES. (27)	Rep. Taft	Dem. Wilson	Prog. Roosevelt	Soc. Debs	Pro. Chafin
20088	Ada................	3198	2569	3512	599	116
	Adams (new)........	508	420	293	176	19
19242	Bannock............	2396	1486	601	412	8
7729	Bear Lake..........	1272	916	274	32	1
23306	Bingham............	1340	921	453	368	...
8387	Blaine.............	989	996	372	368	25
5250	Boise..............	652	743	504	304	16
13588	Bonner.............	744	1055	1247	1058	56
	Bonneville (new)...	1176	864	637	352	20
25323	Canyon.............	1842	2437	2846	849	311
7197	Cassia.............	1459	846	471	305	20
	Clearwater (new)...	375	549	345	284	23
3001	Custer.............	326	501	237	122	4
4785	Elmore.............	416	536	382	190	11

Taft	Wilson	Roosevelt	Debs	Chafin		
24606	Fremont............	3074	1967	1129	750	11
12384	Idaho..............	994	1679	953	686	51
22747	Kootenai...........	1693	2506	1805	1030	169
18818	Latah..............	904	1540	1943	588	278
4785	Lemhi..............	669	910	216	198	6
	Lewis (new)........	438	1131	694	259	49
12676	Lincoln............	1192	1541	1645	642	68
28460	Nez Perce..........	1013	1619	1065	406	66
15470	Oneida.............	2373	1386	—	147	24
4694	Owyhee.............	515	567	333	95	13
13903	Shoshone...........	1599	1654	1162	831	28
13543	Twin Falls.........	1074	1741	1650	181	102
11101	Washington.........	725	1065	798	227	45
	Total..............	35510	35921	25527	11990	1537
	Plurality..........		1111			
	Per cent...........	31.03	32.11	24.11	11.30	1.45
	Total vote.........			105955		

For president in 1908 Taft, Rep., received 52,657 votes; Bryan, Dem., 36,195; Debs, Dem., 6,405.

FOR REPRESENTATIVES IN CONGRESS, 1912.

Addison T. Smith, Rep.........................43,571
Burton L. French, Rep.........................53,342
Perry W. Mitchell, Dem........................30,178
Edward M. Pugmire, Dem........................30,053
P. Monroe Smock, Prog.........................12,066
G. W. Belllot, Soc............................11,393
E. L. Rigg, Soc...............................11,389
Jonathan G. Carrick, Pro......................1,169
John Tucker, Pro..............................1,176

LEGISLATURE.   Senate. House. J.B.
Republicans 21   56   77
Democrats 3   4   7

STATE OFFICERS. (All republicans.)

Governor—John M. Haines.
Lieutenant-Governor—Herman H. Taylor.
Secretary of State—Wilfred L. Gifford.
State Auditor—Fred L. Huston.
State Treasurer—O. V. Allen.
Attorney-General—Joseph H. Peterson.
Superintendent of Public Instruction—Grace M. Shepherd.
Inspector of Mines—Robert N. Bell.

ILLINOIS (Population in 1910, 5,638,591).

Population in 1910.	COUNTIES. (102)	PRESIDENT 1912 Rep. Taft	Dem. Wilson	Pro. Chafin	Soc. Debs	S.L. Reimer	Prog. Roosevelt	GOVERNOR 1912 Rep. Deneen	Dem. Dunne	Pro. Werrell	Soc. Kennedy	S.L. Francis	Prog. Funk	PRES.1908 Rep. Taft	Dem. Bryan
64588	Adams......	2733	6852	195	559	44	3780..	3087	6939	186	534	44	3498..	7283	8294
22741	Alexander..	2108	1936	28	107	10	709..	2054	1973	24	101	10	625..	3790	2027
17075	Bond.......	1152	1275	204	64	6	725..	1208	1205	212	64	4	689..	2143	1465
15481	Boone......	1361	540	38	113	6	1624..	1578	654	39	103	8	1534..	2805	687
10307	Brown......	981	1358	87	12	—	524..	523	1287	91	14	...	476..	947	1609
43975	Bureau.....	1816	2800	219	549	31	3738..	2316	2874	194	508	24	3175..	5280	2871
8610	Calhoun....	373	602	64	22	3	154..	391	606	60	20	3	126..	735	905
18055	Carroll....	1577	1098	87	84	8	1237..	1723	1115	81	72	7	1137..	2875	1129
17372	Cass.......	719	2223	53	103	11	1086..	906	2074	40	86	9	1054..	1878	2434
51829	Champaign..	3220	4454	291	172	12	4181..	4006	4227	201	148	12	3978..	7162	4880
34594	Christian..	1994	5821	213	376	14	1464..	2356	3674	192	360	11	1267..	3686	4156
23517	Clark......	1807	2517	144	49	2	943..	2682	2507	149	45	2	815..	3158	2793
14661	Clay.......	1622	1926	81	84	4	621..	1639	1884	81	79	3	620..	2250	2162
22832	Clinton....	973	2674	45	265	18	775..	957	2688	40	206	16	740..	2104	3016
34517	Coles......	2283	3453	90	170	15	2437..	2538	3492	98	162	12	2091..	4348	3567
2405233	Cook......	74951	130702	2737	52659	2302	169061..	108578	168488	3193	55520	2305	113357	239100	153980
26281	Crawford...	1293	2691	125	65	4	1525..	1409	2607	137	63	4	1459..	3090	2890
14281	Cumberland...	990	1673	51	31	3	692..	1035	1687	45	30	8	650..	1739	1810
33457	DeKalb.....	1776	1598	109	205	13	3643..	1794	1697	104	201	13	3157..	5866	1782
18906	DeWitt.....	1346	1880	64	119	10	1306..	1384	1906	58	113	9	1280..	2628	2155
19591	Douglas....	1386	1633	116	53	2	1277..	1436	1651	103	46	2	1295..	2056	1917
33432	DuPage.....	1136	2256	215	193	12	4160..	1581	2217	167	181	10	3458..	4590	1075
27336	Edgar......	2480	3479	147	91	8	1244..	2545	3432	137	89	7	1180..	3697	3433
10049	Edwards....	817	650	100	16	3	818..	917	613	80	16	+3	773..	1614	747
20055	Effingham..	1002	2575	58	46	6	622..	1138	2598	50	42	6	533..	1977	2826
29075	Fayette....	1481	2782	138	82	1	1558..	1570	2658	116	78	2	1614..	3261	3493
17006	Ford.......	882	1035	78	28	11	1720..	1004	1041	85	21	11	1338..	2 17	*1164
25943	Franklin...	2008	2435	116	407	22	731..	2122	2498	125	397	22	676..	2589	2401
49549	Fulton.....	2263	3902	230	1334	67	3384..	2543	3878	235	1321	65	3121..	6077	4906
14628	Gallatin...	1051	1697	43	107	10	203..	1106	1689	43	103	10	1.97..	1411	1845
22363	Greene.....	1064	2801	49	124	7	831..	1077	2781	59	119	7	823..	2004	3159
24162	Grundy.....	1390	1172	74	180	6	1919..	1843	1347	57	159	7	1217..	3127	1359
18827	Hamilton...	1242	1920	51	79	4	668..	1275	1860	53	79	4	604..	1409	2128
30638	Hancock....	1577	3692	186	188	6	1837..	2027	3482	150	168	5	1736..	3781	4200
7015	Hardin.....	693	644	45	47	5	158..	715	612	40	46	5	129..	813	640
9724	Henderson....	648	721	51	31	6	871..	722	691	46	31	4	821..	1547	820
41796	Henry......	1859	2219	181	376	24	4505..	2239	2304	167	352	19	4075..	6887	2499
35543	Iroquois...	1996	2474	153	52	12	2958..	2112	2613	149	48	11	2616..	4855	2906
35543	Jackson....	2780	3323	102	268	21	1378..	2918	3324	86	258	21	1324..	4016	3149
18157	Jasper.....	1227	2042	113	16	1	545..	1258	2000	113	15	1	492..	1800	2317

Population		Taft	Wilson	Chafin	Debs	Reimer	Roosevelt	Deneen	Dunne	Worrell	Kennedy	Francis	Funk		Taft	Bryan
29111	Jefferson .	1834	3237	101	142	6	1294	1948	3166	109	139	6	1234	.	3210	3377
13854	Jersey	838	1573	51	12	2	381	893	1537	45	11	2	360	.	1460	1818
22657	Jo Daviess .	1253	2226	110	139	5	1747	1526	2153	94	117	5	1539	.	3132	2810
14431	Johnson . . .	1035	952	60	66	6	809	1052	951	68	61	5	715	.	1915	1055
91862	Kane	2415	4494	219	529	15	11494	2968	4708	225	513	13	10550	.	12810	4316
40752	Kankakee .	3178	2592	77	141	8	2792	2914	3375	72	125	8	2403	.	5909	2451
10777	Kendall . .	534	551	36	21	3	1526	747	528	30	18	2	1336	.	1948	556
46159	Knox	1750	2758	152	405	16	5586	2302	2708	145	383	18	4670	.	7084	3277
55058	Lake	2183	2436	136	445	25	4888	3172	2611	130	437	23	3738	.	6892	2204
90182	LaSalle . . .	4858	7036	286	636	50	6918	5551	7978	261	593	41	5429	.	11169	7589
22661	Lawrence .	1617	2550	194	170	15	774	1673	2529	178	164	15	771	.	2197	2253
27750	Lee	1483	1995	90	115	7	2747	1575	2167	94	112	5	2510	.	4255	2144
40465	Livingston .	2444	3334	152	71	27	3240	2588	3461	127	68	23	2947	.	5458	3578
30216	Logan	1497	3279	118	163	18	1776	1781	3672	100	144	17	1546	.	3451	3546
54186	Macon . . .	3356	4445	192	293	26	3976	3977	4482	138	264	22	3421	.	1644	4615
50685	Macoupin .	2177	4902	226	806	36	2147	2684	4675	208	284	55	1880	.	4988	5775
89847	Madison . .	5462	7155	268	1703	83	3197	6233	7225	255	1668	74	2280	.	9463	7812
35094	Marion . . .	1586	3493	198	498	18	2099	1609	3480	191	486	16	2163	.	3445	4001
15679	Marshall . .	790	1685	63	42	8	1180	1027	1684	64	31	8	917	.	1893	1714
17377	Mason	948	2173	92	45	4	659	1147	2044	86	41	4	788	.	1924	2264
14200	Massac . . .	1341	599	38	21	3	788	1309	643	30	22	8	748	.	2084	652
26887	McDonough .	1876	2949	106	181	6	1785	2062	2906	152	173	7	1545	.	3733	3112
33586	McHenry . . .	2870	1913	74	39	5	3046	2504	2345	70	37	13	2575	.	5531	1887
68008	McLean . . .	4624	5356	376	562	26	4450	4519	5075	348	527	25	4861	.	8953	5892
12796	Menard . . .	620	1550	55	60	7	903	822	1393	44	50	6	774 .	1600	1748
19723	Mercer	959	1602	111	222	9	2093	1163	1532	100	203	8	1983	.	2871	1777
14508	Monroe . . .	1433	1398	4	19	2	299	1431	1409	4	16	1	250	.	1733	1512
35311	Montgomery .	2195	3705	245	469	23	1476	2412	3526	222	453	23	1444	.	3782	3909
34420	Morgan . . .	1466	3648	159	116	24	2000	2047	3254	153	158	25	1940	.	4019	3993
14630	Moultrie	747	1501	60	29	6	853	777	1478	53	25	5	857	.	1704	1695
27964	Ogle	2014	1730	200	57	4	2730	2289	1862	168	49	5	2359	.	4848	1761
100255	Peoria	2504	5364	120	1521	182	1929	5408	5125	130	1521	131	6551	.	10928	5898
22088	Perry	1341	2107	154	215	21	804	1998	2121	149	207	19	877	.	2832	2482
16376	Piatt	1064	1417	75	36	3	1150	1121	1338	62	33	2	1179	.	2319	1559
28622	Pike	1068	3371	149	253	13	1169	1801	3243	137	246	12	1162	.	2932	3850
11215	Pope	1099	. 664	25	24	—	587	. 1137	628	25	24		584	.	1706	748
15650	Pulaski	1652	978	30	78	11	454	1661	1002	25	. 80	9	421	.	2185	1080
7561	Putnam. . . .	408	. 424	23	28	2	583	466	411	18	24	2	548	.	834	413
29120	Randolph. .	1548	3217	135	308	9	1169	. 1730	2940	127	297	8	1285	.	3045	3172
15970	Richland . .	862	1800	129	114	4	811	. 1006	1645	145	110	5	755	.	1684	1952
70404	Rock Island	2334	3907	135	2128	129	6506	4185	4317	121	1921	124	4589	.	8196	4739
30204	Saline	2254	3599	98	660	32	1468	2410	2560	91	646	31	1341	.	3125	2471
91024	Sangamon .	3904	8406	245	1007	49	6196	6928	8052	189	903	46	3775	.	10422	9551
14852	Schuyler . .	853	1714	130	31	6	694	924	1704	133	29	5	619	.	1622	1876
10067	Scott	686	1341	25	25	3	379	818	1212	29	25	3	372	.	1101	1316
31693	Shelby . . .	1629	3467	231	121	10	1431	1738	3306	216	118	10	1461	.	3312	4005
10098	Stark	549	609	25	41	3	1053	731	686	27	37	4	841	.	1585	733
119870	St Clair	8156	10826	218	2498	104	4064	8649	10917	206	2435	102	3651	.	12619	11342
36821	Stephenson .	1367	3654	148	215	4	3476	1889	3796	131	202	4	3051	.	4605	4076
34027	Tazewell . . .	1054	3654	114	371	24	2500	1733	3440	98	355	25	2159	.	3767	3786
1194	Union	1194	2648	62	23	2	458	1261	2613	60	24	2	454	.	1955	2990
77596	Vermilion . .	5655	5576	564	774	40	4584	6076	5824	547	687	43	4345	.	11726	6320
14913	Wabash . . .	841	1676	131	72	4	601	1000	1628	127	69	1	492 .	1511	1914
24313	Warren	915	2080	91	237	16	2627	1042	2053	90	215	15	2494	.	3383	2327
18759	Washington .	1304	1654	67	135	16	1058	. 1395	1728	64	124	13	915	.	2355	1830
25087	Wayne	1586	2378	187	74	4	1418	1766	2292	165	72	4	1332	.	2946	2791
23052	White . .	1692	2708	114	182	11	591	1863	2645	106	180	10	492	.	2436	2984
34507	Whiteside . . .	1457	1996	276	91	7	3904	1968	2013	250	81	7	3535	.	5257	2140
84371	Will	3331	4717	140	467	20	8092	4689	5772	112	415	20	5713	.	10358	5036
45909	Williamson . .	3209	3258	230	706	79	1755	3336	3506	246	642	77	1682	.	4786	3513
63153	Winnebago .	2537	2276	210	955	53	7089	3367	2093	175	913	41	5420	.	8919	2163
20506	Woodford .	850	2051	65	83	8	1495	1241	2005	46	70	4	1161		2204	2552
	Total.	253583	405048	15710	81278	4066	386478 .	318499	443120	15231	78679	3980	303401 .	629032	450810
	Plurality .		18570						124619				179122		
	Per cent	22 12	35 64	1 38	7 09	.36	33.71 .	27.39	38 10	1.31	6.77	.34	26.09	54 53	39.02
	Total vote.				1148173					1162880					

FOR REPRESENTATIVES IN CONGRESS, 1912

At Large—William E Mason, Rep 313,608
Burnett M Chiperfield, Rep 299,945
Lawrence B Stringer, Dem 415,386
William Elza Williams, Dem 401,497
Walter H Harris, Pro 15,721
James H Shaw, Pro 15,590
Walter Huggins, Soc 84,352
D L Thomas, Soc 84,027
George Martin, Soc.-Lab 4,118
Joseph Fenyves, Soc -Lab 4,012
B. M. Maxey, Prog 304,072
Lawrence P. Boyle, Prog 311.311

1. That part of Chicago bounded as follows' From Lake Michigan west and south along river to Halsted south to 34th, east to Parnell avenue, north to 32d, east to Stewart avenue, south to 39th, east to State, south to 43d, east to the lake and north along lake shore to river.
Martin B Madden, Rep 13,608
Andrew Donovan, Dem 9,967
W H. Rogers, Pro 299
W T. Barnard, Soc 2,217

2. That part of Chicago bounded as follows. From

Lake Michigan east on 43d to State, south to 99th, west to Stewart avenue, south to 103d, west to Halsted, south to 111th, west to Peoria, south to 115th, west to Ashland, south to 123d, east to Halsted, south to Little Calumet avenue, easterly to Illinois Central tracks and Indiana avenue, south to 138th, east to state line, north along state line to the lake and along lake shore to 43d
James R Mann, Rep 21,374
John C. Vaughan, Dem 15,287
Edgar T Lee, Pro 298
John C Flora, Soc 4,637
Thomas D. Knight, Prog 15,042

3. That part of Chicago bounded as follows' From Halsted west on 51st to 48th avenue, south to 87th east to Western avenue, south to 99th, west to Ogden avenue, south to 115th east to Western, south to Lyon avenue, east to Ashland avenue, north to 115th, east to Peoria, north to 111th, east to Halsted, north to 103d, east to Stewart avenue, north to 99th, east to State, north to 51st; also the towns of Lemont, Palos, Worth, Orland, Bremen, Thornton, Rich, Bloom and Calumet, in Cook county.

George E. Gorman, Dem....................16,285
William W. Wilson, Rep...................14,132
William H. Dietz, Pro....................... 502
George H. Gibson, Soc..................... 5,123
Franklin P. Simons, Prog.................13,639

4. That part of Chicago bounded as follows: From Halsted street southwest along river to Laflin, north to 22d, west to Clifton Park avenue, south to 24th, west to Central Park avenue, south to Illinois and Michigan canal, southwest to 39th, west to 48th avenue, south to 51st, east to State, north to 39th, west to Stewart avenue, north to 32d, west to Parnell avenue, south to 34th, west to Halsted, north to river.

James T. McDermott, Dem.................14,225
Charles J. Tomklewicz, Rep................. 6,097
Carl E. Gauger, Soc......................... 4,503

5. That part of Chicago bounded as follows: From river west on 12th to Laflin, north to Taylor, west to Cypress, south to 12th, west to Homan avenue, south to Ogden avenue, southwest to Clifton Park avenue, south to 22d, east to Laflin, south to river, northeast along river to 12th.

Adolph J. Sabath, Dem....................11,150
Jacob Gartenstein, Rep..................... 4,392
Charles Toepper, Soc....................... 3,359
L. H. Clusman, Prog....................... 2,825

6. That part of Chicago bounded as follows: From Center avenue west on Madison to Ashland avenue, north to Washington boulevard, west to Homan avenue, north to Kinzie, west to Austin avenue, south to 12th, east to 46th, south to 39th, east to Illinois and Michigan canal, northeast along canal to Central Park avenue, north to 24th, east to Clifton Park avenue, north to Ogden avenue, northeast to Homan avenue, north to 12th, east to Cypress, north to Taylor, east to Loomis, north to Van Buren, east to Center avenue, north to Madison; also the towns of Proviso, Cicero, Oak Park, Berwyn, Riverside, Stickney and Lyons, in Cook county.

Arthur W. Fulton, Rep...................18,974
James McAndrews, Dem....................22,520
J. W. Troeger, Pro......................... 467
John Will, Soc............................. 7,776

7. That part of Chicago bounded as follows: From Western avenue west on Devon avenue, Fulton and Hamilton streets to 72d avenue, north to Park Ridge boulevard, west to Highland avenue, south to Devon, east to Winter, south to Everill avenue, east to 73d, south to Bryn Mawr avenue, east to 60th avenue, south to Irving Park boulevard, west to 72d avenue, south to North avenue, east to Austin avenue, south to Kinzie, east to Homan avenue, south to Washington boulevard, east to Ashland avenue, north to Chicago avenue, west to Robey, north to Fullerton, east to river, northwest along river to Belmont, east to Western avenue, north to Devon avenue; also the towns of Hanover, Schaumburg, Elk Grove, Maine, Leyden; Barrington, Palatine, Wheeling and Norwood Park, in Cook county.

Frank Buchanan, Dem....................19,452
Niels Juul, Rep...........................15,266
E. H. Parkinson, Pro....................... 427
Otto C. Christensen, Soc..................15,042
Elton C. Armitage, Prog..................18,816

8. That part of Chicago bounded as follows: From the river west on Fullerton avenue to Robey, south to Chicago avenue, east to Ashland avenue, south to Madison, east to Center avenue, south to Van Buren, west to Loomis, south to Taylor, west to Laflin, south to 12th, east to river, north and northwest along river to Fullerton avenue.

Thomas Gallagher, Dem....................19,922
William G. Herrmann, Rep................. 6,030
John Nelson, Pro........................... 206
N. F. Holm, Soc........................... 3,674

9. That part of Chicago bounded as follows: From Lake Michigan west on Irving Park boulevard to Racine avenue, south to Fullerton avenue, east to Halsted street, south to North avenue, west to river, south and east along river to lake and north along lake shore to Irving Park boulevard.

Fred A. Britten, Rep......................11,650
Lynden Evans, Dem........................10,210
Herbert V. Lyons, Pro..................... 226
Frank Schiflersmith, Soc................... 3,964
C. O. Ludlow, Prog......................... 7,566

10. That part of Chicago bounded as follows: From Lake Michigan southwest on Rogers avenue to Howard, west to Kedzie, south to Devon avenue, east to Western avenue, south to Belmont avenue, west to river, southeast along river to North avenue, east to Halsted, north to Fullerton avenue, west to Racine avenue, north to Irving Park boulevard, east to lake and north along lake shore to Rogers avenue; also Lake county and the towns of Evanston, Niles, New Trier and Northfield, in Cook county.

Charles M. Thomson, Prog.................21,028
George E. Foss, Rep......................17,325
Frank L. Fowler, Dem....................15,515
Dudley G. Hays, Pro....................... 504
Charles A. Larson, Soc..................... 5,311

11. Counties of DuPage, Kane, McHenry and Will.

Ira C. Copley, Rep........................25,750
Thomas H. Riley, Dem....................14,330
William P. Lea, Pro......................... 876
P. H. Murray, Soc......................... 1,167

12. Counties of Boone, DeKalb, Grundy, Kendall, LaSalle and Winnebago.

Charles E. Fuller, Rep....................16,905
J. W. Rausch, Dem........................12,224
C. W. Earl, Pro........................... 718
Joseph McCabe, Soc....................... 2,142
William H. Hinebaugh, Prog...............18,334

13. Counties of Carroll, Jo Daviess, Lee, Ogle, Stephenson and Whiteside.

John C. McKenzie, Rep:...................14,398
Ray Rariden, Dem........................11,704
William Beers, Pro......................... 813
C. C. Brooks, Soc......................... 616
I. F. Edwards, Prog.......................11,875

14. Counties of Hancock, Henderson, McDonough, Mercer, Rock Island and Warren.

Clyde H. Tavenner, Dem..................17,024
Charles J. Searle, Rep....................15,816
P. W. Cupler, Pro......................... 680
Charles Black, Soc......................... 2,466

15. Counties of Adams, Fulton, Henry, Knox and Schuyler.

George W. Prince, Rep....................12,008
A. S. Hoxworth, Dem....................17,156
Paul D. Ransom, Pro....................... 912
John C. Sjodin, Soc....................... 2,642
Charles F. Kincheloe, Prog................15,173

16. Counties of Bureau, Marshall, Peoria, Putnam, Stark and Tazewell.

Claude U. Stone, Dem....................20,956
F. H. Smith, Rep......................... 9,295
George W. Warner, Pro..................... 485
Rudolph Pfeiffer, Soc..................... 2,474
William E. Cadmus, Prog..................12,659

17. Counties of Ford, Livingston, Logan, McLean and Woodford.

John A. Sterling, Rep....................13,572
Louis Fitz-Henry, Dem....................14,966
Robert Means, Pro......................... 709
E. J. Brais, Soc........................... 838
George E. Stump, Prog..................... 9,266

18. Counties of Clark, Cumberland, Edgar, Iroquois, Kankakee and Vermilion.

Joseph G. Cannon, Rep....................18,707
Frank T. O'Hair, Dem....................19,485
Clay F. Gaumer, Pro....................... 1,279
John R. Walker, Soc....................... 1,132
E. F. Royse, Prog......................... 9,511

19. Counties of Champaign, Coles, DeWitt, Douglas, Macon, Moultrie, Shelby and Piatt.

William B. McKinley, Rep.................20,643
Charles M. Borchers, Dem.................22,166
Thomas C. Eiler, Pro....................... 791
C. E. Peebles, Soc......................... 834
John H. Chadwick, Prog..................10,755

20 Counties of Brown, Calhoun, Cass, Greene, Jersey, Mason, Menard, Morgan, Pike and Scott
Henry T. Rainey, Dem 21,203
E. E. Brass, Rep 9,478
Charles Corson, Pro 701
Jesse Morgan, Soc . . . , . . 785
B. O. Aylesworth, Prog 7,007
21. Counties of Christian, Macoupin, Montgomery and Sangamon.
H. Clay Wilson, Rep. . . 12,556
James M Graham, Dem . . 21,361
Lewis F Denton, Pro . . 849
Herman Rahm, Soc .. . 2,551
Robert Johns, Prog .. 7,286
22. Counties of Bond, Madison, Monroe, St Clair and Washington.
William A. Rodenberg, Rep 19,438
William N. Baltz, Dem 23,112
Andrew J. Meek, Pro 705
William C. Pierce, Soc 4,276
Utten S. Nixon, Prog 5,608
23. Counties of Clinton, Crawford, Effingham, Fayette, Jasper, Jefferson, Lawrence, Marion, Richland and Wabash
Martin D. Foster, Dem... 26,938
Robert B. Clark, Rep... 12,837
J W. Honey, Pro 1,199
John L. McKittrick, Soc 1,411
George W. Jones, Prog . . 9,116
24. Counties of Clay, Edwards, Gallatin, Hamilton, Hardin, Johnson, Massac, Pope, Saline, Wayne and White.
H. Robert Fowler, Dem 19,811
James B. Blackman, Rep................15,004

T. J. Scott, Pro. 682
T. C. Mason, Soc 933
A. J. Gibbons, Prog 5,129
25 Counties of Alexander, Franklin Jackson, Perry, Pulaski, Randolph, Union and Williamson.
N B Thistlewood, Rep . 16,706
Robert P Hill, Dem . . .19,993
Charles F. Stalker, Pro . . 859
Paul H Castle, Soc .. . 2,063
Robert T. Cook, Prog 6,545

FOR GOVERNOR.
Charles S Deneen, Rep .. 318,469
Edward F. Dunne, Dem 443,120
Edward R Worrell, Pro 15,231
John C Kennedy, Soc. .. 78,679
John M Francis, Soc -Lab 3,980
Frank H. Funk, Prog 303,401

LEGISLATURE
Senate House J B
Democrats 24 72 96
Republicans 25 52 77
Progressives 2 26 28
Socialists ... 0 3 3

STATE OFFICERS.
Governor—Edward F Dunne, Dem
Lieutenant-Governor—Barratt O'Hara, Dem
Secretary of State—Harry Woods, Dem
Auditor—James J. Brady, Dem
Treasurer—William Ryan, Jr , Dem
Attorney-General—Patrick Lucey, Dem
Superintendent of Public Instruction—Francis G. Blair, Rep
Insurance Superintendent—Rufus M Potts, Dem
The Adjutant-General—Col. F. S. Dickson

INDIANA (Population in 1910, 2,700,876).

Population in 1910	COUNTIES (92)	PRESIDENT 1912							PRESIDENT 1908						
		Dem. Wilson	Rep Taft.	Pro. Chafin	Prog Roosevelt	Soc Debs	S L Reimer		Dem. Bryan	Rep Taft	Pro S L Chafin Gillhaus	Soc Debs	Peo W'ats'n	Ind Hisgen
21840	Adams ..	2961	917	159	732	30	6		3404	1726	141	—	13	5	—
95386	Allen	8659	3423	602	4246	1512	127		12145	9468	340	14	494	11	41
24813	Bartholomew	5147	1321	233	1604	196	15		8437	3906	151	3	59	7	4
1268	Benton	1425	1040	103	796	30	2		1566	1336	104	—	15	—	—
15820	Blackford	1431	399	146	1163	356	9		2214	1835	166	1	42	—	—
24673	Boone	3280	1181	179	2014	90	11		3525	3471	166	1	11	17	7
7975	Brown	909	305	52	253	12	2		1177	663	68	—	5	3	—
11970	Carroll	2275	1467	142	926	83	—		2090	2346	152	2	68	6	1
36968	Cass ..	4421	1573	207	3094	187	29		5234	4700	349	8	38	14	2
30200	Clark ..	3415	805	50	2458	137	15		4085	3706	82	8	68	9	1
32535	Clay ...	3277	1494	174	1614	697	31		4204	3766	110	8	499	11	3
26674	Clinton	3255	2182	189	1821	219	24		3680	3826	281	1	73	13	3
12057	Crawford	1139	663	179	542	128	4		1599	1403	126	1	82	2	—
27747	Daviess	3754	2005	150	1081	827	39		3253	3424	134	9	204	53	—
21396	Dearborn ..	2997	1366	89	701	146	9		3365	2320	94	1	41	3	3
18798	Decatur	2246	1263	130	1436	88	7		2564	2838	159	1	39	6	—
25054	Dekalb	2768	1125	244	1623	447	16		3684	2991	387	2	63	5	20
51414	Delaware . \	4315	2018	637	4059	1199	52		5725	7014	475	19	316	120	7
18843	Dubois	3059	665	54	609	100	7		5344	1307	36	—	58	2	1
49008	Elkhart..	4300	1199	563	4533	856	102		5697	6245	596	8	400	3	10
11415	Fayette. ...	1455	1030	68	1214	231	21		1700	2894	114	1	81	1	2
30288	Floyd	5286	669	90	2680	341	20		4004	3431	144	4	226	4	2
20428	Fountain.	2449	1560	124	1067	140	21		2846	2894	122	2	45	8	1
15385	Franklin ...	2306	929	80	630	30	1		2816	1670	74	1	7	—	—
16879	Fulton	2022	1427	213	694	70	8..		2450	2426	125	—	13	1	2
30137	Gibson	3250	2206	226	1270	295	7		3656	3753	241	5	86	5	1
51426	Grant ..	4390	3889	1015	2185	1321	184		5819	7181	1140	32	389	11	9
30873	Greene	4373	2156	148	1563	1203	143		4172	4145	84	23	930	29	2
27026	Hamilton	2463	2247	399	1834	90	19		2947	4421	435	—	24	1	—
19030	Hancock..	2594	738	149	1375	133	9		3040	2412	146	—	22	2	1
20232	Harrison	2106	900	98	1219	118	13		2646	2419	100	2	67	3	3
20840	Hendricks	2173	1439	142	1495	48	7		2571	3241	146	2	—	2	3
29758	Henry	2087	2479	508	1550	447	56		3197	4458	332	3	61	22	5
33117	Howard ...	2824	2152	453	2181	1107	119		3497	4423	550	9	255	5	2
28982	Huntington	3119	2108	899	1680	252	12		3712	3873	405	8	211	3	2
24727	Jackson	3225	921	98	1236	175	14		3783	2631	140	3	30	1	1
13041	Jasper.	1292	1238	59	694	14	1.		1495	1939	70	—	7	1	1
24961	Jay .	2786	1282	398	1506	218	10		3370	3256	426	3	53	7	2
20483	Jefferson	2325	1563	158	943	137	5		2708	2995	176	5	97	2	—
14203	Jennings	1577	955	69	839	81	8..		1871	2100	101	2	21	4	—
20394	Johnson	2699	921	211	1408	49	13		3298	2519	193	1	9	2	—
39183	Knox	4448	2805	305	1316	892	86		5116	4217	199	17	375	27	4
27936	Kosciusko	2817	1767	307	2096	210	23		3582	4477	233	11	54	1	1
15148	Lagrange	1243	758	96	1402	22	1		1414	2357	133	—	10	2	4
82864	Lake	6136	5176	169	5659	1182	191		5502	9499	125	28	308	8	114
45797	Laporte	4847	2701	120	2749	497	48..		5690	5824	126	3	103	1	23
30625	Lawrence	2579	1633	91	2106	398	33		3118	3864	93	4	119	3	3

Population.	Wilson	Taft	Chafin	Roosevelt	Debs	Re'mer	Bryan	Taft	Chafin	Gillhaus	Debs	Wats'n	Hisgen
65,224 Madison................	6676	1771	455	4751	1947	157..	8226	7481	497	26	804	5	5
263861 Marion................	29605	12286	1241	18386	5398	418..	34078	34851	889	116	1075	75	46
24175 Marshall...............	2459	1196	192	1499	164	17..	3287	2947	189	5	55	5	6
12340 Martin..................	1440	975	27	553	23	3..	3783	1667	34	—	11	3	—
26550 Miami...................	3993	1426	253	1995	422	32..	4176	3820	233	11	187	12	1
23426 Monroe.................	2336	1388	140	1407	84	6..	2780	3031	77	—	14	4	—
29296 Montgomery...........	3821	2747	222	1246	173	7..	4727	4427	195	3	44	18	5
21182 Morgan.................	2008	1353	176	1236	185	26..	2789	3074	121	—	44	1	1
10704 Newton.................	905	892	96	683	26	2..	1190	1645	65	—	8	2	3
24009 Noble..................	2888	1443	19	1700	106	3..	3219	3507	120	1	29	3	5
4329 Ohio...................	553	406	39	120	9	—	622	619	16	—	3	—	—
17192 Orange.................	1800	1521	55	849	58	5..	1961	2483	70	2	44	2	—
14053 Owen..................	1621	711	64	784	161	12..	2025	1726	61	3	61	10	2
22214 Parke..................	2031	1891	254	684	846	11..	2707	5026	315	5	204	1	1
18078 Perry..................	1984	520	50	1190	84	5..	2356	1908	34	—	67	—	2
19384 Pike...................	1984	1515	49	488	298	4..	2360	2850	59	5	151	4	9
26540 Porter.................	3352	1519	45	1241	120	12..	1789	3940	74	5	59	3	36
21670 Posey..................	2767	1193	140	745	182	4..	3084	2444	147	3	69	5	—
13612 Pulaski................	1250	729	222	586	185	14..	1832	1561	110	2	14	11	2
20520 Putnam................	2022	1354	92	1079	91	7..	3131	2926	121	1	36	8	3
29013 Randolph..............	2153	1988	346	2471	272	20..	2900	4792	380	2	87	6	1
19452 Ripley.................	2431	1402	77	884	163	23..	2739	2660	88	5	76	2	2
19549 Rush...................	2312	1831	185	1075	77	6..	2544	3102	191	3	13	4	—
8323 Scott..................	1033	827	34	531	18	—	1243	979	51	—	8	3	—
26802 Shelby.................	3492	1254	235	1949	319	21..	4065	3329	252	2	95	9	1
22576 Spencer...............	2428	1268	117	1142	151	6..	2662	2220	61	2	18	2	—
10657 Starke.................	1208	787	49	696	64	6..	1905	1521	43	2	39	4	1
14274 Steuben................	1206	1299	477	1210	41	5..	1453	2704	182	2	13	5	2
84312 St. Joseph............	5891	3146	452	5240	1285	87..	8562	11222	272	15	705	10	27
32431 Sullivan..............	3707	1406	274	1008	1045	83..	4657	2942	58	1	14	1	3
9914 Switzerland...........	1342	882	62	822	75	5..	1537	1444	225	16	358	7	—
40063 Tippecanoe............	4442	3006	173	2838	191	3..	4384	6164	299	3	65	8	26
17459 Tipton.................	2185	1262	201	914	113	13..	2556	2395	183	1	13	7	1
6290 Union..................	705	643	65	342	58	1..	808	1066	73	—	18	—	—
77438 Vanderburg...........	7219	4830	187	2738	2572	127..	8053	9116	155	90	1084	21	14
18985 Vermillion............	1789	1821	230	680	550	21..	1844	2568	217	8	407	5	3
87840 Vigo..................	7256	3108	707	4988	1802	144..	10485	10223	257	23	690	456	8
23928 Wabash................	2871	1363	285	2432	308	50..	3116	4091	337	5	87	3	1
10899 Warren................	872	1183	64	635	46	—..	1045	2092	70	—	3	4	—
21911 Warrick...............	2218	1421	254	819	310	37..	2782	2839	138	7	101	1	1
17445 Washington...........	2253	712	63	1113	61	7..	2578	1976	74	—	12	6	—
43757 Wayne.................	3806	1851	229	4457	1032	116..	4505	6731	179	7	308	2	8
22418 Wells.................	2760	812	301	1080	132	7..	3845	2185	482	3	65	3	—
17592 White.................	2059	1913	99	822	41	5..	2826	2423	144	1	19	6	—
16822 Whitley...............	2208	1082	151	890	70	4..	2493	2302	134	1	13	—	—
Total.................	281800	151267	19248	162007	36961	3120..	338262	348963	18045	643	13476	1193	514
Plurality...........	119883							10731					
Per cent............	43.07	23.11	2.94	24.76	5.64	.48..	46.91	48.39	2.50	.10	1.87	.16	.07
Total vote..........	654473							721126					

1. The counties of Gibson, Pike, Posey, Spencer, Vanderburg and Warrick.
Charles F. Lieb, Dem.......................20,014
David H. Ortmyer, Rep.....................13,158
George F. Flannigan, Pro...................... 910
Humphrey C. Heldt, Prog................... 6,023
William H. Rainey, Soc..................... 3,737

2. The counties of Daviess, Greene, Knox, Lawrence, Martin, Monroe, Owen and Sullivan.
William H. Cullon, Dem....................22,082
Oscar E. Bland, Rep.......................15,858
Isaac C. Overman, Pro........................ 873
John N. Dyer, Prog......................... 6,001
James L. B. Shepherd, Soc................. 3,888

3. The counties of Clark, Crawford, Dubois, Floyd, Harrison, Perry, Orange, Scott and Washington.
William E. Cox, Dem.......................23,150
William D. Barnes, Rep....................10,049
H. W. White, Pro............................ 538
S. G. Wilkinson, Prog.....................10,005
John Zahnd, Soc........................... 1,192

4. The counties of Bartholomew, Brown, Dearborn, Jackson, Jefferson, Jennings, Johnson, Ohio, Ripley and Switzerland.
Lincoln Dixon, Dem........................24,256
Rollin A. Turner, Rep.....................12,436
Henry Thompson, Pro....................... 1,026
Charles Zoller, Jr., Prog................. 7,540
William F. Carmichael, Soc................ 1,000

5. The counties of Clay, Hendricks, Morgan, Parke, Putnam, Vermilion and Vigo.
Ralph W. Moss, Dem.......................20,634
F. W. Blankenbaker, Rep..................11,995
John S. L. Myers, Pro..................... 1,444
William Houston, Pro...................... 3,361
Joseph W. Amis, Soc...................... 8,268

6. The counties of Decatur, Fayette, Franklin, Hancock, Henry, Rush, Shelby, Union and Wayne.
Finly H. Gray, Dem.......................19,987

William L. Risk, Rep.....................11,242
Mercer Brown, Pro......................... 1,378
Gurllef Jensen, Prog.....................10,797
F. Foster Van Vorhis, Soc................. 2,129

7. The county of Marion.
Charles A. Korbly, Dem...................28,901
Thomas R. Shipp, Rep.....................13,320
Albert Stark, Pro......................... 1,387
J. V. Zartman, Prog......................18,402
Frank J. Hays, Soc........................ 5,501

8. The counties of Adams, Delaware, Jay, Madison, Randolph and Wells.
J. A. M. Adair, Dem......................23,530
J. P. Watts, Rep.......................... 8,298
J. Walter Gibson, Pro..................... 2,033
E. C. Toner, Prog........................13,157
Hunter McDonald, Soc...................... 3,611

9. The counties of Boone, Carroll, Clinton, Fountain, Hamilton, Howard, Montgomery and Tipton.
M. A. Morrison, Dem......................23,574
William Robinson, Rep....................15,901
A. M. Ewing, Pro.......................... 1,562
John F. Neal, Prog........................ 9,205
George N. Keller, Soc..................... 2,011

10. The counties of Benton, Jasper, Lake, Laporte, Newton, Porter, Tippecanoe, Warren and White.
John B. Peterson, Dem....................18,401
E. D. Crumpacker, Rep....................17,294
William R. Hedrich, Pro..................... 591
John E. Bowers, Prog...................... 9,793
A. K. Mark, Soc........................... 1,370

11. The counties of Blackford, Cass, Grant, Huntington, Miami and Wabash.
George W. Rauch, Dem.....................21,894
John W. G. Stewart, Rep..................12,213
Ed H. Kennedy, Pro........................ 2,232
Edgar M. Baldwin, Prog...................10,830
Ernest Malott, Soc........................ 2,813

12. The counties of Allen, Dekalb, Lagrange, Noble, Steuben and Whitley

Cyrus Cline, Dem 19,903
Charles R Lane, Rep 11,147
William F Dibble Pro . 2,022
Louis N. Litman, Prog 8,114

13. The counties of Elkhart Fulton, Kosciusko, Marshall, Pulaski, St Joseph and Starke.

Henry A. Barnhart, Dem . . . 24,968
Charles A Carlisle, Rep . 13,787
William Mamer, Pro . 1,342
R C Stephens, Prog 13,824
Erwin H Cady, Soc . 2,937

LEGISLATURE Senate House J B.
Democrats 40 95 135
Republicans 9 4 13
Progressives . . . 1 1 2

STATE OFFICERS
Governor—Samuel M Ralston, Dem
Lieutenant-Governor—William P O'Neill, Dem.
Secretary of State—L G Ellingham, Dem.
Auditor—W H O'Brien Dem.
Treasurer—William H Vollmer, Dem.
Attorney-General—Thomas Honan, Dem
Reporter Supreme Court—Philip Zoercher, Dem.
Statistician—Thomas Brollev, Dem
Superintendent Public Instruction—Charles A. Greathouse, Dem

IOWA (Population in 1910, 2,224,771).

Population in 1910	COUNTIES (99)	Dem Wilson	Prog Roosevelt	Rep Taft	Soc Debs	Pro Chafin	Rep Carroll	Dem Porter	Pro MacEachron	Soc Work	Rep Taft	Dem Bryan	Pro Chafin	Soc Debs	Peo. Watson	Ind Hisgen
14420	Adair ..	1195	890	1248	51	38	1738	1279	40	18	2185	1322	45	24	2	1
10998	Adams	1215	571	913	32	52	1374	1262	43	16	1695	1725	67	30	1	—
17328	Allamakee...	1767	1273	1269	39	16	2176	1684	35	15	2521	1725	40	7	—	4
28701	Appanoose	2058	969	2356	359	65	2886	2582	74	169	3161	2167	80	322	13	4
12671	Audubon .	983	968	692	19	33	1322	989	26	11	1701	1050	33	9	1	1
23156	Benton ...	2472	1234	1831	199	72	2393	2397	69	176	3180	2418	76	94	2	1
44865	Black Hawk .	3702	4724	1601	411	211	3746	5148	485	217	5437	3127	208	244	7	3
27626	Boone	1601	2835	802	537	105	2411	1754	171	287	4398	1959	151	850	4	5
15843	Bremer. .	1944	741	1013	24	42	1407	1934	58	19	1656	1225	56	14	1	4
19748	Buchanan........	1806	1455	1271	23	104	2112	1764	165	19	2052	1889	118	16	2	—
15981	Buena Vista	921	1802	755	61	46	1680	858	89	37	2337	1054	86	96	—	1
17119	Butler	926	1553	903	28	87	1785	968	109	14	2167	994	79	15	—	4
17890	Calhoun ..	1182	1334	963	85	65	1675	1172	127	39	2453	1152	152	64	7	5
20117	Carroll .	2526	1188	694	53	51	1259	2412	69	15	1865	2510	58	12	—	3
19047	Cass .	1510	1096	1734	103	62	2259	1589	77	42	2799	1655	47	64	6	3
17765	Cedar ..	1938	1364	1098	43	39	1973	1979	63	19	2455	1890	67	22	1	1
25011	Cerro Gordo .	1742	1813	1344	212	100	2081	1364	117	78	2990	1520	98	60	—	—
16741	Cherokee	990	1680	381	56	45	1382	1009	78	33	2400	1084	68	24	—	4
16675	Chickasaw	1891	662	1022	35	21	1431	1864	15	23	1571	1877	35	15	1	2
10738	Clarke..	910	585	882	21	81	1356	1004	46	9	1674	1134	37	8	1	1
12746	Clay	707	1347	619	50	41	1498	718	39	14	1921	778	41	16	—	—
25576	Clayton	2919	1471	1299	142	90	2162	2904	51	65	2773	3026	61	30	—	3
45894	Clinton	3633	3188	1800	403	91	3402	4642	44	154	4486	4821	80	191	2	4
20041	Crawford.	2193	1181	1169	61	61	1611	2496	61	23	2169	2322	69	29	2	3
26628	Dallas	1718	1361	1825	200	144	2526	1470	190	73	3132	1871	142	78	2	4
13315	Davis ..	1453	853	1184	44	31	1529	1527	20	21	1484	1749	40	20	2	2
16347	Decatur	1654	773	1351	90	55	1889	1672	53	44	2149	1809	56	58	17	2
17888	Delaware	1389	1145	1394	83	43	1948	1498	48	55	2396	1471	95	36	1	1
36145	Des Moines	3169	2060	2136	537	192	2761	3548	94	372	4153	3975	108	233	2	2d
8157	Dickinson..	502	850	457	38	15	1008	512	25	51	1109	508	26	25	1	1
57450	Dubuque	6237	3421	1620	415	31	2210	6616	53	400	4708	6645	51	427	1	21
9816	Emmet	486	738	602	99	18	1296	459	26	42	1401	522	24	38	—	—
27919	Fayette ..	2379	2240	1192	250	166	2725	2208	108	112	3399	2281	179	86	1	12
17119	Floyd	1244	1256	1216	142	48	1716	800	80	63	2462	1250	48	15	1	4
14780	Franklin	694	1408	776	67	129	1340	841	57	13	2154	737	50	9	—	4
15623	Fremont	1762	861	973	65	38	1680	1577	55	40	1949	1979	59	21	—	—
16023	Greene ...	980	1166	1424	29	63	1770	1011	77	13	2574	1152	84	16	—	—
18574	Grundy	1149	1465	421	12	48	1322	1276	61	2	1861	1105	45	1	—	—
17374	Guthrie	1490	1303	1258	74	72	2047	1440	101	15	2560	1632	60	11	3	1
19242	Hamilton	1041	2282	831	68	68	1584	982	148	32	2760	1145	109	34	—	3
12731	Hancock	710	899	800	8	30	1221	681	43	4	1750	804	49	3	—	—
20921	Hardin	1072	2362	732	87	201	1612	1371	213	24	3123	1187	146	19	—	2
23162	Harrison	2157	1336	1528	226	74	2409	2013	86	119	2914	2425	111	108	1	3
18640	Henry	1580	856	1664	47	105	2014	1461	81	18	2653	1606	82	11	1	3
12920	Howard......	1416	807	750	69	63	1311	1266	50	66	1530	1408	57	55	1	3
12182	Humboldt	644	1317	477	16	39	1607	613	64	20	1818	587	54	9	—	—
11236	Ida	1087	1144	543	18	13	1214	1169	9	8	1367	1130	19	13	—	—
18109	Iowa	1841	875	1237	24	45	1712	2059	69	26	2330	1907	64	19	—	—
21255	Jackson	2259	1003	1174	109	255	2082	2331	26	117	2542	2545	85	109	1	4
27034	Jasper .	2487	1581	1766	347	164	2607	2400	172	207	3543	2889	152	91	2	4
13451	Jefferson	1311	786	1378	72	115	1819	1309	136	44	2271	1430	166	17	2	1
25914	Johnson....	4327	763	1645	92	59	2300	3014	74	46	2758	3314	50	14	9	6
19050	Jones ...	2189	689	1623	84	84	2092	2025	72	31	2176	1622	52	23	2	1
21180	Keokuk	2434	1202	1361	74	119	2525	2376	166	44	2728	2459	151	40	—	2
21971	Kossuth...	1516	1880	857	21	65	1881	1715	45	14	2612	1826	35	9	—	—
36702	Lee	3891	2299	2016	285	56	3121	4227	78	150	4282	4706	73	80	6	11
60720	Linn..	5422	3038	4326	487	242	4420	4439	191	191	6938	5498	213	121	2	23
12855	Louisa ..	881	891	1070	58	43	1709	872	43	34	2025	978	46	13	4	1
13462	Lucas	908	855	959	110	52	1504	1012	119	58	1757	1267	109	55	2	1
14624	Lyon	894	1361	412	89	19	1362	1198	31	62	1655	1004	29	56	1	1
15621	Madison	1185	1121	1274	59	104	1979	1249	108	68	2425	1404	182	56	6	—
29960	Mahaska	2876	1705	1882	202	283	3249	2712	479	157	3635	3035	395	92	5	8
22996	Marion	2276	1419	1791	297	72	2929	2323	198	298	3025	2749	160	154	5	5
50279	Marshall	2192	3106	928	334	191	1917	2266	332	236	3887	1941	209	145	5	2
15811	Mills	1312	1093	850	67	33	1664	1337	58	20	1959	1422	55	17	2	3
13435	Mitchell.,...	1083	1171	590	29	30	1489	856	34	38	1932	988	36	7	—	1
16633	Monona	1358	1289	1109	86	82	1758	1490	64	25	1977	1782	85	15	1	5
25429	Monroe	2495	1495	1385	536	61	2403	1693	73	458	2486	1979	112	418	7	1
16601	Montgomery ...	1206	1713	1017	106	82	2080	1070	14	77	2543	1222	74	49	1	3
29505	Muscatine	2927	2796	780	708	85	2867	3112	56	640	3525	3098	85	475	2	8
17242	O'Brien....	1506	1659	639	53	32	1150	1512	59	40	1912	1326	36	86	—	4
8956	Osceola........	786	1609	520	29	14	853	782	16	18	1000	777	18	11	1	4

Population.	Wilson	Roosevelt	Taft	Debs	Chafin	Carroll	Porter	M'Kachron	Work	Taft	Bryan	Chafin	Debs	Watson	Hisgen
24002 Page.............	1462	2216	980	197	132..	2640	1377	154	117..	3141	1726	195	101	——	5
13845 Palo Alto......	1274	755	953	101	62..	1347	1280	43	71..	1639	1340	59	61	4	——
23129 Plymouth.......	2008	2005	825	28	46..	2008	2122	66	33..	2622	2168	99	30	1	1
14808 Pocahontas......	1176	1277	780	67	29..	1436	1177	46	55..	1857	1315	35	22	3	2
11043S Polk..........	7239	8110	4905	1695	866..	6877	7414	975	759..	12555	7924	527	604	24	9
55832 Pottawattamie...	4303	4538	1755	489	93..	4840	4755	122	246..	6137	5520	169	162	5	2
19589 Poweshiek......	1631	1492	992	107	113..	2298	1535	188	54..	2794	1661	184	33	3	3
12904 Ringgold.......	958	989	916	45	70..	1530	954	72	15..	1940	1002	83	15	1	1
16555 Sac............	1124	1819	622	58	42..	1461	998	68	22..	2066	1230	74	21	3	2
60000 Scott..........	5632	4077	1508	1444	58..	3382	6487	58	778..	6545	5845	71	667	3	58
16552 Shelby.........	1841	1073	872	38	29..	1733	1919	58	29..	1973	1935	53	33	3	2
25248 Sioux..........	1453	2596	575	55	15..	2208	1493	88	41..	2637	1891	32	22	——	——
24083 Story..........	1224	2515	1247	76	172..	2653	1686	292	54..	3790	1195	203	52	1	3
22156 Tama..........	2446	1722	1179	45	43..	2281	2574	107	19..	2774	2550	151	38	29	30
16312 Taylor.........	1372	869	1305	40	78..	2087	1539	57	58..	2480	1585	94	46	——	1
16516 Union..........	1528	1115	1076	75	78..	1774	1678	121	51..	2207	1843	124	37	4	——
15020 Van Buren......	1495	675	1538	52	63..	1875	1492	74	30..	2133	1730	77	17	2	1
37743 Wapello........	3102	1838	2755	699	76..	3608	3443	84	515..	4541	3724	124	551	3	16.
18194 Warren........	1395	1102	1386	53	114..	2229	1297	161	22..	2589	1645	163	19	2	1
19925 Washington.....	2003	1380	1267	84	116..	2197	1875	190	36..	2931	2119	122	17	——	——
16184 Wayne.........	1581	796	1193	88	113..	1810	1742	115	59..	2002	1756	119	45	1	3
34629 Webster.......	2370	1871	2123	316	147..	2900	2356	205	137..	3658	2874	241	192	4	3
11914 Winnebago.....	390	1035	582	142	132..	1190	439	84	26..	1710	489	40	9	——	——
21729 Winneshiek....	2105	2186	802	61	26..	2530	2019	39	39..	2787	2008	65	29	1	2
67616 Woodbury......	4564	5453	2441	440	155..	3724	5980	290	253..	6587	5222	256	230	9	3
9950 Worth.........	402	1147	354	42	37..	1218	381	35	12..	1433	449	30	16	——	——
17351 Wright.......	755	1856	805	54	75..	1391	776	107	20..	2498	866	77	10	——	2

Total......	185325	161819	119805	16967	8140..	205666	177287	10212	9700..	275210	200771	9837	8287	261	404
Plurality....	23506						18879			74439					
Per cent....	37.63	32.87	24.34	3.45	1.71..	49.81	45.36	2.48	2.35..	55.63	40.58	1.99	1.65	.05	.10
Total vote..			492356				412895				494770					

FOR REPRESENTATIVES IN CONGRESS, 1912.

1. Counties of Des Moines, Henry, Jefferson, Lee, Louisa, Van Buren and Washington.
Charles A. Kennedy, Rep.............14,167
Joshua F. Elder, Dem.................12,114
Joe S. Crall, Prog..................... 6,457
Frank Rubisch, Soc..................... 882

2. Counties of Clinton, Iowa, Jackson, Johnson, Muscatine and Scott.
Irven S. Pepper, Dem.................24,769
Michael T. Kennedy, Soc.............. 2,176
C. C. Bacson, Pro...................... 953

3. Counties of Black Hawk, Bremer, Buchanan, Butler, Delaware, Dubuque, Franklin, Hardin and Wright.
Maurice Connolly, Dem...............19,445
Charles E. Pickett, Rep.............18,166
R. E. Leach, Prog.................... 6,640
D. S. Cameron, Soc.................... 952
S. F. D. Kennedy, Pro................. 727

4. Counties of Allamakee, Cerro Gordo, Chickasaw, Clayton Fayette, Floyd, Howard, Mitchell, Winneshiek and Worth.
Gilbert N. Haugen, Rep...............19,829
G. A. Meyer, Dem....................16,764
James S. Mott, Soc.................... 714
Thomas McElroy, Pro................... 382

5. Counties of Benton, Cedar, Grundy, Jones, Linn, Marshall and Tama.
James W. Good, Rep..................19,034
S. C. Huber, Dem....................17,631
Fred A. Niles, Prog.................. 1,870
Louis N. Nock, Soc................... 841
F. J. Thomas, Pro.................... 522

6. Counties of Davis, Jasper, Keokuk, Mahaska, Poweshiek and Wapello.
Sant Kirkpatrick, Dem...............14,915
M. A. McCord, Rep...................13,796
John H. Patton, Pro.................. 4,350
Andrew Engle, Soc.................... 2,060

7. Counties of Dallas, Madison, Marion, Polk, Story and Warren.
Solomon F. Prouty, Rep..............17,465
Clint L. Price, Dem.................14,075
George C. White, Prog............... 5,944
Andy Swanson, Soc.................... 1,960
Ira D. Kellogg, Pro................... 1,026

8. Counties of Adams, Appanoose, Clarke, Decatur, Fremont, Lucas, Page, Ringgold, Taylor, Union and Wayne.
Horace M. Towner, Rep...............18,462
V. R. McGinnis, Dem.................15,477
Lawrence W. Laughlin, Prog.......... 2,764
S. D. Mercer, Soc..................... 871

9. Counties of Adair, Audubon, Cass, Guthrie, Harrison, Mills, Montgomery, Pottawattamie and Shelby.
William R. Green, Rep...............20,030
Orris Mosher, Dem...................16,369
Arthur C. Kelly, Soc................. 879
W. B. Crewdson, Pro................... 330

10. Counties of Boone, Calhoun, Carroll, Crawford, Emmet, Greene, Hamilton, Hancock, Humboldt, Kossuth, Palo Alto, Pocahontas, Webster and Winnebago.
Frank P. Woods, Rep................25,263
Nelson L. Rood, Dem................15,242
Sheppard B. Philpot, Prog.......... 5,251
A. E. Moxley, Soc................... 1,091

11. Counties of Buena Vista, Cherokee, Clay, Dickinson, Ida, Lyon, Monona, O'Brien, Osceola, Plymouth, Sac, Sioux and Woodbury.
George C. Scott, Rep................18,568
Anthony Van Wegenen, Dem...........16,168
Joseph W. Hallam, Prog.............10,405
John W. Bennett, Soc................. 810
A. Jamieson, Pro..................... 371

LEGISLATURE. Senate.House. J.B.
Republicans 33 66 99
Democrats 17 42 59

STATE OFFICERS. (All republicans.)
Governor—George W. Clarke.
Lieutenant-Governor—William L. Harding.
Secretary of State—William S. Allen.
Auditor of State—John L. Bleakly.
Treasurer of State—William C. Brown.
Attorney-General—George Cosson.

KANSAS (Population in 1910, 1,690,949).

		PRESIDENT 1912				PRES. 1908	
COUNTIES.	(105)	Rep.	Dem.	Soc.	Prog.	Rep.	Dem.
Population in 1910.		Taft	Wilson	Debs	Roosevelt	Taft	Bryan
27640 Allen........	1892	1739	391	1003..	3283	2579
13829 Anderson.....	618	1305	191	934..	1722	1512
28107 Atchison.....	1535	2449	91	1527..	3241	2508
9916 Barber......	205	883	113	1027..	1097	804
13876 Barton......	602	2054	185	1113..	1729	2004
24007 Bourbon.....	1448	2209	707	991..	2936	2686
21514 Brown......	1912	1774	119	1485..	2778	2044
23059 Butler......	971	2005	234	2096..	3049	2290
7527 Chase......	476	812	82	503..	1021	834
11429 Chautauqua..	818	752	277	762..	1689	958
38162 Cherokee....	1904	2641	2006	872..	3893	3819
4248 Cheyenne....	140	301	125	302..	486	329
4093 Clark......	162	485	55	412..	386	350
15251 Clay......	843	1373	249	1240..	1858	1495
18388 Cloud......	899	1658	280	1299..	2170	1923
15205 Coffey......	681	1581	184	1190..	2094	1729
3281 Comanche...	150	391	77	537..	392	245

Population in 1912	County	Taft	Wilson	Debs	Roosevelt	Taft	Bryan
31700	Cowley......	1113	2559	820	2594..	3578	2995
51178	Crawford..	2676	2781	3753	1427..	5152	4230
8975	Decatur....	256	983	121	388..	808	1250
2495?	Dickinson..	986	2183	288	1937..	2886	2282
14422	Doniphan..	1321	1017	93	945..	2307	1113
24724	Douglas....	1133	1888	129	2053..	3279	2010
7083	Edwards....	276	764	96	584..	773	704
10128	Elk.........	605	971	200	735..	1454	1187
12170	Ellis........	175	1381	38	535..	768	1421
10444	Ellsworth...	353	1045	45	860..	1213	1099
6008	Finney......	283	573	133	586..	1000	551
11306	Ford........	529	1125	165	933..	1333	1089
28884	Franklin....	872	1970	276	1871..	2958	2155
12681	Geary.......	387	800	121	918..	1257	1033
6044	Gove.......	170	355	35	356..	632	456
8700	Graham.....	327	636	169	481..	911	723
1067	Grant.......	56	80	22	111..	178	133
3121	Gray.......	112	243	80	267..	372	338
1635	Greeley.....	95	33	33	108..	206	89
16060	Greenwood..	964	1331	281	1120..	2370	1545
3360	Hamilton....	134	263	33	199..	415	275
14748	Harper......	365	1274	203	1295..	1490	1404
19200	Harvey.....	703	1499	180	1590..	2305	1475
996	Haskell.....	61	100	21	53..	172	139
2480	Hodgeman...	136	302	35	319..	411	290
16861	Jackson.....	1027	1565	45	1286..	2201	1494
15826	Jefferson....	1158	1550	74	1116..	2270	1720
18148	Jewell......	906	1871	148	1497..	2410	1932
18288	Johnson.....	834	1837	157	1562..	2313	2091
3208	Kearny......	113	236	83	232..	435	304
13386	Kingman.....	396	1421	149	1160..	1442	1479
8174	Kiowa......	276	506	72	549..	690	463
31423	Labette.....	1516	2508	1197	1746..	3397	2783
2803	Lane.......	158	237	72	155..	357	271
41207	Leavenw'h..	2562	3099	314	1778..	4846	3818
10142	Lincoln.....	381	1091	103	853..	1216	1117
14735	Linn.......	858	1282	389	1052..	1950	1657
4240	Logan.......	166	259	81	315..	524	308
24027	Lyon........	982	2363	822	1878..	2973	2602
2415	Marion......	883	1732	217	1500..	2546	1747
23380	Marshall....	1193	2278	178	1581..	3206	2614
21321	McPherson..	455	1639	147	2406..	2198	1905
5055	Meade......	204	383	110	418..	560	386
20080	Miami......	1033	1919	239	1165..	2475	2256
14089	Mitchell....	737	1441	212	951..	1765	1570
49474	Montgomery	1842	3011	1194	2924..	5166	4080
12397	Morris......	487	1144	79	1244..	1788	1273
1333	Morton.....	120	144	25	64..	154	140
19072	Nemaha.....	961	1936	40	1395..	2394	2182
23754	Neosho.....	1580	1993	472	1190..	2929	2396
5483	Ness.......	232	458	126	464..	685	461
13814	Norton.....	508	1081	141	674..	1448	1357
19305	Osage......	850	1989	417	1588..	2671	2288
12827	Osborne.....	733	970	105	915..	1665	1182
11811	Ottawa.....	517	1264	149	899..	1444	1265
8869	Pawnee.....	366	1050	77	759..	1000	961
14150	Phillips.....	594	1257	142	1181..	1762	1490
17522	Pottaw't'mie	1058	1599	55	1504..	2650	1680
1156	Pratt.......	872	947	168	984..	1193	1027
6380	Rawlins.....	220	563	181	354..	719	732
37553	Reno.......	1966	3381	480	2530..	4052	2381
7447	Republic....	895	1816	127	1278..	2156	1905
15106	Rice.......	697	1314	192	1188..	1832	1407
15783	Riley......	425	1170	173	2047..	2276	1289
11262	Rooks......	545	865	115	715..	1280	1003
7826	Rush......	210	870	92	659..	764	894
16900	Russell......	416	983	65	998..	1360	976
20838	Saline	534	2263	221	1773..	2297	2134
3047	Scott......	56	247	71	324..	324	294
7005	Sedgwick...	1416	6783	801	6546..	6756	6649
4031	Seward.....	165	394	131	359..	427	413
61874	Shawnee....	3592	5094	398	4057..	7554	6585
5451	Sheridan....	195	509	52	316..	639	631
4549	Sherman....	129	456	100	290..	439	508
15365	Smith......	970	1534	228	1022..	1843	1593
12510	Stafford.....	422	1034	160	998..	1534	1135
1034	Stanton.....	42	114	31	77..	180	107
2453	Stevens.....	117	237	37	214..	259	215
30954	Sumner.....	781	2557	445	2015..	3385	2772
5455	Thomas.....	127	432	79	259..	569	630
5389	Trego.....	100	449	90	417..	617	458
12721	Wabaunsee..	783	1128	73	936..	1349	1163
2759	Wallace.....	31	152	37	204..	350	206
20229	Washington	1326	1914	113	1314..	2711	1904
2906	Wichita.....	82	135	41	118..	283	173
19810	Wilson.....	848	1304	684	1419..	2428	1777
9460	Woodson...	694	900	180	608..	1252	1047
100068	Wyandotte..	2107	7370	1262	8100..	9684	8023
	Total....74845	143683	26779	120210..	197216	161209	
	Plurality..	..	23845	..	..	36007	
	Per cent..20.49	39.31	7.33	32.84..	52.46	42.88	
	Total vote..	..	365444	..	..	375946	

FOR REPRESENTATIVES IN CONGRESS, 1912.

1. Counties of Atchison, Brown, Doniphan, Jackson, Jefferson, Leavenworth, Nemaha and Shawnee.
   D. R. Anthony, Rep.............................22,981
   J. R. Chapman, Dem...........................20,659
   H. B. Conwell, Soc................................768

2. Counties of Allen, Anderson, Bourbon, Douglas, Franklin, Johnson, Linn, Miami and Wyandotte.
   J. L. Brady, Rep................................22,007
   Joseph Taggart, Dem..........................25,879
   R. S. Thomas, Soc..............................3,714

3. Counties of Chautauqua, Cherokee, Cowley, Crawford, Elk, Labette, Montgomery, Neosho and Wilson.
   P. P. Campbell, Rep............................20,973
   F. M. Brady, Dem..............................20,142
   George D. Brewer, Soc.........................12,724

4. Counties of Chase, Coffey, Greenwood, Lyon, Marion, Morris, Osage, Pottawatomie, Wabaunsee and Woodson.
   F. S. Jackson, Rep.............................16,481
   Dudley Doolittle, Dem.........................17,003
   S. W. Beach, Soc...............................1,534

5. Counties of Clay, Cloud, Geary, Dickinson, Marshall, Ottawa, Republic, Riley, Saline and Washington.
   R. R. Rees, Rep................................18,098
   G. T. Helvering, Dem..........................19,618
   Grant Chapin, Soc..............................1,708

6. Counties of Cheyenne, Decatur, Ellis, Ellsworth, Gove, Graham, Jewell, Lincoln, Logan, Mitchell, Norton, Osborne, Phillips, Rawlins, Rooks, Russell, Sheridan, Sherman, Smith, Thomas, Trego and Wallace.
   I. D. Young, Rep..............................19,081
   John R. Connelly, Dem........................20,057
   D. W. Stoner, Soc..............................2,102
   James K. Lane, Prog..............................564

7. Counties of Barber, Barton, Clark, Comanche, Edwards, Finney, Ford, Grant, Gray, Greeley, Hamilton, Harper, Hodgeman, Haskell, Kingman, Kiowa, Kearny, Lane, Meade, Morton, Ness, Pawnee, Pratt, Reno, Rice, Rush, Scott, Seward, Stafford, Stevens, Stanton and Wichita.
   G. L. Finley, Rep.............................21,720
   G. A. Neeley, Dem............................26,127
   M. L. Amos, Soc...............................2,864
   H. R. Ross, Prog..................................337

8. Counties of Butler, Harvey, McPherson, Sedgwick and Sumner.
   Victor Murdock, Rep..........................17,955
   John I. Saunders, Dem........................14,474
   George Burnett, Soc...........................1,292

LEGISLATURE.

	Senate.	House.	J.B.
Democrats	21	72	93
Republicans	18	51	69
Socialists	1	2	3

STATE OFFICERS

Governor—George H. Hodges, Dem.
Lieutenant-Governor—Sheffield Ingalls, Rep.
Secretary of State—Charles H. Sessions, Rep.
Treasurer—Earl Akers, Rep.
Auditor—W. E. Davis, Rep.
Attorney-General—John S. Dawson, Rep.
Superintendent Public Instruction—W. D. Ross, Rep.
Superintendent Insurance—I. S. Lewis, Rep.
Chief Justice Supreme Court—W. A. Johnston, Rep.

KENTUCKY (Population in 1910 2,289,905).

Population in 1912	COUNTIES (119)	Dem. Wilson	Rep. Taft	Prog. Roosevelt	Soc. Debs	Pro. Chafin	S.L. Reimer
16508	Adair......	1338	736	1024	9	2	
14882	Allen......	1396	1181	757	16	45	1
10146	Anderson...	1391	579	419	8	34	2
12690	Ballard.....	1706	555	119	197	137	8
25298	Barren.....	2993	1563	731	48	55	3
13368	Bath......	1477	1002	263	15	20	2
28447	Bell......	1970	1183	1705	120	22	23
17482	Bourbon....	2392	1744	429	16	39	2
23444	Boyd......	1772	1271	1236	242	26	11
14668	Boyle......	1798	701	726	22	17	—
10908	Bracken....	1415	603	278	89		
17540	Breathitt....	1882	910	896	1		

Population.	Wilson	Taft	Roosevelt	Debs	Chafin	Reimer
21064 Breckinridge	1967	1163	1292	67	57	3
9487 Bullitt	1299	209	472	15	14	3
15405 Butler	879	1070	988	53	52	9
14063 Caldwell	1231	1263	296	174	15	3
19857 Calloway	2380	628	395	258	27	19
59369 Campbell	4687	2276	2630	1307	76	97
9043 Carlisle	1409	351	126	76	27	8
8110 Carroll	1573	317	208	3	24	3
21966 Carter	1506	1174	1340	79	36	5
15479 Casey	1158	902	806	22	27	3
38845 Christian	2784	3520	717	168	36	15
17987 Clark	2321	1056	658	15	17	—
17789 Clay	625	1054	536	18	5	4
8153 Clinton	510	828	112	19	8	1
13298 Crittenden	1240	1367	371	35	18	2
9846 Cumberland	577	972	156	3	20	—
41020 Daviess	4314	1506	1839	83	92	7
10459 Edmonson	799	736	519	26	9	3
9814 Elliott	1006	306	105	3	—	—
12273 Estill	875	869	359	12	25	—
47715 Fayette	5288	4000	1337	77	52	8
16908 Fleming	1915	1400	471	21	40	6
18623 Floyd	1553	961	465	49	4	6
21135 Franklin	2940	783	694	20	13	1
14114 Fulton	1699	520	92	58	10	5
4697 Gallatin	906	174	112	2	2	—
11894 Garrard	1232	481	1055	7	19	1
10581 Grant	1592	837	171	11	27	1
33539 Graves	3868	863	939	185	39	10
19958 Grayson	1685	1075	1140	58	33	6
11871 Green	1117	687	670	9	19	2
18475 Greenup	1112	923	880	243	30	14
8512 Hancock	757	769	677	58	23	6
22936 Hardin	2956	832	1290	80	21	4
10766 Harlan	345	612	824	7	7	1
16873 Harrison	2514	1193	246	21	41	1
18173 Hart	1674	502	1314	117	21	6
29352 Henderson	3098	1157	763	302	48	29
15716 Henry	2274	805	484	12	27	1
11750 Hickman	1540	865	194	28	5	2
34291 Hopkins	3147	1357	1616	382	47	23
10754 Jackson	216	577	885	13	5	—
262920 Jefferson	24100	8519	23516	1170	210	101
12618 Jessamine	1506	845	404	12	65	—
17482 Johnson	1084	998	1264	58	12	13
70855 Kenton	7761	2512	2272	1210	87	112
10791 Knott	1114	387	129	—	7	1
22116 Knox	888	1391	1281	55	29	12
10701 Larue	1265	390	508	22	14	—
19872 Laurel	1094	1085	1020	128	15	7
20067 Lawrence	1648	1290	632	48	13	8
9551 Lee	728	570	400	19	2	2
8076 Leslie	105	606	431	2	2	1
10148 Letcher	611	978	372	8	1	2
16887 Lewis	1017	1185	1053	138	53	9
17897 Lincoln	1363	842	1001	80	85	2
10627 Livingston	1009	782	293	51	12	2
24977 Logan	2697	1632	551	95	37	9
9423 Lyon	996	568	187	25	25	1
26851 Madison	2292	2094	406	7	10	1
13654 Magoffin	891	1004	406	7	10	1
16330 Marion	1848	735	742	17	7	2
15571 Marshall	1675	554	303	85	28	8
7291 Martin	256	655	287	11	6	2
18611 Mason	2475	1558	542	30	23	6
35064 McCracken	2948	1308	1085	441	38	7
McCr'ry (new)	225	411	501	95	6	7
17341 McLean	1304	822	381	111	30	12
9783 Meade	1145	337	489	61	7	5
6153 Menifee	643	264	90	43	2	3
14093 Mercer	1792	887	606	5	27	3
10453 Metcalfe	887	642	646	9	15	1
19063 Monroe	805	1072	680	6	14	—
12868 Montgomery	1615	758	410	11	11	1
16259 Morgan	1800	876	219	31	11	—
28598 Muhlenberg	2098	1038	1689	766	48	13
16830 Nelson	2275	751	735	25	14	2
10601 Nicholas	1611	400	276	10	46	4
27642 Ohio	2363	1150	1825	361	44	25
7248 Oldham	1150	261	319	15	22	2
14248 Owen	2460	430	257	21	16	2
7979 Owsley	221	711	353	5	3	—
11985 Pendleton	1510	746	365	80	35	4
11255 Perry	560	1023	114	1	4	2
31679 Pike	2583	2777	785	47	25	8
6268 Powell	647	381	163	6	4	—
35366 Pulaski	1960	1731	1785	96	103	21
4121 Robertson	570	158	262	1	5	2
14473 Rockcastle	853	1082	556	10	16	3
9438 Rowan	737	417	458	41	6	4
10361 Russell	713	735	278	41	25	2
16956 Scott	2391	1047	480	17	17	3
18041 Shelby	2487	1120	607	25	25	2

Populat'on	Wilson	Taft	Roosevelt	Debs	Chafin	Reimer
11460 Simpson	1709	547	418	6	10	1
7557 Spencer	1052	271	256	6	8	—
11961 Taylor	1150	408	842	21	32	11
16488 Todd	1482	1435	170	79	13	5
14539 Trigg	1263	1322	101	162	10	—
4512 Trimble	1183	163	138	5	22	1
19886 Union	2108	642	303	227	13	9
30579 Warren	3447	1342	1770	55	57	5
13940 Washington	1288	723	912	10	12	6
17518 Wayne	1329	1170	312	14	28	4
20974 Webster	2168	1496	524	59	53	12
31982 Whitley	998	905	2035	136	12	10
9864 Wolfe	873	385	250	6	6	—
12571 Woodford	1561	779	446	9	13	3
Total......	219384	115512	102766	11647	3233	956

Plurality.....104072
Per cent......48.37   25.48   22.65   2.58   .71   .21
Total vote...   459698

FOR REPRESENTATIVES IN CONGRESS, 1912.

1. The counties of Ballard, Caldwell, Calloway, Carlisle, Crittenden, Fulton, Graves, Hickman, Lyon, Livingston, Marshall, McCracken and Trigg.
A. W. Barkley, Dem..................22,591
Charles Furgeson, Rep..............10,664
I. O. Ford, Soc.....................1,787

2. The counties of Christian, Daviess, Hancock, Henderson, Hopkins, McLean, Union and Webster.
A. O. Stanley, Dem.................19,739
Carr Hawkins, Soc..................1,462
L. R. Fox, Prog....................6,500

3. The counties of Allen, Barren, Butler, Edmonson, Logan, Metcalfe, Muhlenburg, Simpson, Todd and Warren.
R. Y. Thomas, Jr., Dem.............18,220
T. B. Dixon, Rep...................11,181
J. D. Duncan, Prog.................7,456
E. L. Davenport, Soc...............1,192

4. The counties of Breckinridge, Bullitt, Grayson, Green, Hardin, Hart, Larue, Marion, Meade, Nelson, Ohio, Taylor and Washington.
Ben Johnson, Dem...................22,168
John C. Thompson, Rep..............6,713
E. R. Bassett, Prog................11,907
L. A. Logsdon, Soc...................862

5. The county of Jefferson.
Swager Sherley, Dem................24,795
E. J. Ashcraft, Rep................3,823
Henry I. Fox, Prog.................23,115
Charles Dobbs, Soc.................1,493
J. H. Arnold, Soc.-Lab..............595

6. The counties of Boone, Campbell, Carroll, Gallatin, Grant, Kenton, Pendleton and Trimble.
A. B. Rouse, Dem...................20,690
D. B. Wallace, Rep.................7,265
J. G. Blackburn, Prog..............5,701
M. A. Brinkman, Soc................2,489

7. The counties of Bourbon, Clark, Estill, Fayette, Franklin, Henry, Lee, Oldham, Owen, Powell, Scott and Woodford.
J. Campbell Cantrill, Dem..........24,617
J. E. Jones, Prog..................5,841

8. The counties of Adair, Anderson, Boyle, Casey, Garrard, Jessamine, Lincoln, Madison, Mercer, Shelby, Spencer.
Harvey Helm, Dem...................18,690
J. W. Dinsmore, Prog...............7,631

9. The counties of Bracken, Bath, Boyd, Carter, Elliott, Fleming, Greenup, Harrison, Lewis, Lawrence, Mason, Menefee, Morgan, Nicholas, Robertson, Rowan, Wolfe, Montgomery, Breathitt.
W. J. Fields, Dem..................27,415
Harry Bailey, Rep..................16,608
E. S. Hutchins, Prog...............8,903
James A. Williams, Soc.............1,148

10. The counties of Floyd, Jackson, Johnson, Knott, Letcher, Martin, Magoffin, Owsley, Pike and Perry.
John W. Langley, Rep...............12,203
W. T. Stafford, Prog...............5,396

11. The counties of Bell, Clay, Clinton, Cumberland, Harlan, Knox, McCreary, Leslie, Monroe, Pulaski, Russell, Rockcastle, Wayne, Whitley and Laurel.
Ben V. Smith, Dem..................11,760
Caleb Powers, Rep..................18,531
H. H. Seavey, Prog.................9,644
M. O. Jackson, Soc...................577

LEGISLATURE. Senate.House. J.B.
Democrats 32 78 110
Republicans 6 21 27
Fusionists 0 1 1

STATE OFFICERS. (All democrats.)
Governor—James B. McCreary.
Lieutenant-Governor—Edward J. McDermott.
Secretary of State—C. F. Crecelius.
Treasurer—Thomas S. Rhea.
Auditor—Henry M. Bosworth.
Attorney-General—James Garnett.
Superintendent Public Instruction—Barksdale Hamlett.

LOUISIANA (Population in 1910, 1,656,388)

PARISHES.

Population in 1910	PARISHES. (64)	Rep. Taft	Dem. Wilson	Prog. Roosevelt	Soc. Debs
31847	Acadia....................	51	1147	164	166
23887	Ascension................	64	413	155	12
24128	Assumption..............	149	423	171	1
34102	Avoyelles................	38	949	36	116
21776	Bienville.................	8	822	34	141
21738	Bossier...................	6	427	11	43
58200	Caddo....................	34	1946	129	91
62767	Calcasieu*...............	171	2144	362	584
8593	Caldwell..................	18	366	29	106
4288	Cameron..................	13	194	9	..
10415	Catahoula................	11	275	44	42
25050	Claiborne................	10	785	20	36
14278	Concordia................	6	205	6	8
27689	De Soto..................	11	815	19	74
34580	East Baton Rouge........	46	1076	96	41
11637	East Carroll..............	4	161	19	3
20055	East Feliciana............	1	422	12	5
	Evangeline (new)........	31	457	15	43
11989	Franklin..................	8	449	39	88
15958	Grant....................	15	446	48	208
31262	Iberia....................	222	666	350	58
30854	Iberville.................	100	487	147	3
13818	Jackson..................	19	561	80	102
18247	Jefferson.................	7	607	97	27
25753	Lafayette................	244	648	53	76
33111	La Fourche...............	315	677	175	14
9402	La Salle..................	7	366	31	151
18485	Lincoln..................	3	434	42	73
10627	Livingston...............	3	579	67	24
10676	Madison..................	—	146	7	..
18786	Morehouse...............	8	411	9	83
35455	Natchitoches.............	21	759	43	188
339075	Orleans..................	904	26433	4965	732
25930	Ouachita.................	17	902	48	113
12624	Plaquemines.............	41	361	29	5
25289	Pointe Coupee...........	55	304	90	6
44545	Rapides..................	46	1334	110	182
11402	Red River................	6	357	18	..
15769	Richland.................	2	393	20	22
19854	Sabine...................	28	715	37	115
5377	St. Bernard..............	17	221	11	1
11307	St. Charles..............	28	157	9	16
9172	St. Helena...............	13	214	10	4
23009	St. James................	228	367	77	7
14339	St. John the Baptist.....	74	190	8	38
66961	St. Landry...............	101	928	150	26
23070	St. Martin...............	68	375	116	23
39368	St. Mary.................	147	652	242	17
18012	St. Tammany............	30	668	70	44
29160	Tangipahoa..............	40	1061	155	70
17060	Tensas...................	1	220	19	..
28820	Terre Bonne.............	89	455	247	31
20451	Union....................	11	696	26	61
26390	Vermilion................	124	531	119	119
17384	Vernon...................	44	754	50	434
18886	Washington..............	18	491	48	36
19186	Webster..................	9	686	13	111
12636	West Baton Rouge........	19	170	15	..
6249	West Carroll.............	1	159	14	77
13449	West Feliciana...........	3	281	50	..
18357	Winn....................	26	600	49	371
	Total.................	**3854**	**60971**	**9323**	**5249**
	Plurality................		51648		
	Per cent................	4.83	76.57	11.75	6.55
	Total vote...............		79615		

*Includes parishes of Beauregard, Allen and Jefferson Davis.

FOR REPRESENTATIVES IN CONGRESS, 1912.
1. Parishes of Orleans (half), St. Bernard and Plaquemines.
Albert Estopinal, Dem...................14,779
Richard B. Otero, Ind.......................1

2. Parishes of Orleans (half), Jefferson, St. Charles, St. James, St. John.
H. Garland Dupre, Dem...................14,406
3. Parishes of Assumption, Iberia, Lafayette, Lafourche, St. Martin, St. Mary, Terrebonne, Vermilion.
Robert F. Broussard, Dem.................. 5,035
Henri L. Gueydan, Ind.........................1
M. T. Gordy, Ind.............................1
4. Parishes of Caddo, DeSoto, Bossier, Red River, Webster, Bienville, Claiborne.
John T. Watkins, Dem...................... 5,693
Lee Norris, Soc.............................. 394
5. Parishes of Catahoula, Jackson, Caldwell, West Carroll, Concordia, East Carroll, Franklin, Madison, Morehouse, Ouachita, Richland, Tensas, Union, Lincoln.
Walter Elder, Dem......................... 5,795
6. Parishes of Ascension, Iberville, East Baton Rouge, East Feliciana, Livingston, St. Helena, St. Tammany, Tangipahoe, Washington, West Baton Rouge, West Feliciana, Pointe Coupee.
Lewis L. Morgan, Dem..................... 6,101
L. T. Dugazon, Ind............................1
7. Parishes of Acadia, Calcasieu, Cameron, Evangeline, St. Landry, Allen, Beauregard, Jefferson Davis.
Louis Lazaro, Dem......................... 4,943
Otis Putnam, Soc........................... 713
8. Parishes of Avoyelles, Grant, Rapides, Natchitoches, Winn, Sabine, LaSalle, Vernon.
J. B. Aswell, Dem.......................... 6,033
J. R. Jones, Soc........................... 1,734

LEGISLATURE.
Both branches of the legislature are democratic.
STATE OFFICERS. (All democrats.)
Governor—Luther E. Hall.
Lieutenant-Governor—Thomas C. Barret.
Secretary of State—Alvin E. Hebert.
Auditor—Paul Capdevielle.
Attorney-General—Ruffin G. Pleasant.
Register of Land Office—Fred J. Grace.
Commissioner of Agriculture and Immigration—E. O. Bruner.
Superintendent of Education—Thomas H. Harris.

MAINE (Population in 1910, 742,371).

Population in 1910.	COUNTIES. (16)	PRESIDENT 1912. Dem. Wilson	Prog. Roosevelt	Rep. Taft	Soc. Debs	PRES.1908. Rep Taft	Dem. Bryan
59822	Androscoggin..	4516	4424	850	316..	4831	3095
74664	Aroostook.....	1924	4799	898	100..	4783	1157
112014	Cumberland...	8480	6577	5154	355..	10693	5755
19119	Franklin.......	1421	1633	668	38..	2178	980
35675	Hancock.......	2655	1932	1399	186..	3169	1946
52863	Kennebec......	4397	5195	1822	175..	6153	2842
28981	Knox..........	2731	1312	1097	233..	2228	1932
18216	Lincoln........	1633	1527	457	83..	1693	1193
36256	Oxford.........	2941	3008	1234	111..	4179	2093
85285	Penobscot.....	5036	5294	3997	145..	7896	3526
19887	Piscataquis....	1210	1704	807	20..	2157	828
18574	Sagadahoc.....	1331	1129	885	108..	1778	838
36301	Somerset......	2317	2479	1235	286..	3688	1676
23383	Waldo.........	2145	1696	831	146..	2491	1335
42905	Washington....	3178	1993	1862	86..	3507	2258
68526	York..........	5121	3751	3960	183..	6700	4076
	Total......	51113	48493	26545	2541..	66987	35403
	Plurality.....	2620				31854	
	Per cent.....	39.42	37.41	20.48	1.96..	62.99	33.30
	Total vote.		129636			106385	

For president in 1912, Chafin, Pro., received 944 votes.

FOR REPRESENTATIVES IN CONGRESS, 1912.
1. Counties of Cumberland and York.
Asher H. Hinds, Rep.......................17,635
Michael T. O'Brien, Dem..................15,580
2. Counties of Androscoggin, Franklin, Knox, Lincoln, Oxford and Sagadahoc.
William B. Skelton, Rep....................16,796
D. J. McGillicuddy, Dem...................18,077
3. Counties of Hancock, Kennebec, Somerset and Waldo.
Forest Goodwin, Rep.......................17,221
Samuel Gould, Dem........................16,512

4. Counties of Aroostook, Penobscot, Piscataquis and Washington.

Frank E. Guernsey, Rep......................20,198
Charles W. Mullen, Dem......................16,725

LEGISLATURE.   Senate.House. J.B.
Republicans 21   79   100
Democrats 10   72   82

STATE OFFICERS.

Governor—William T. Haines, Rep.
Secretary—Joseph E. Alexander, Rep.
Treasurer—Joseph W. Simpson, Rep.
Auditor—T. F. Callahan, Rep.
Attorney-General—Scott Wilson, Rep.
Supt. of Public Schools—Payson Smith, Rep.

MARYLAND (Population in 1910, 1,294,450).

COUNTIES.	PRESIDENT 1912.				
Population in 1910.	(23)	Dem. Wilson	Prog. Roosevelt	Rep. Taft	Soc. Debs	Pro. Chafin
62411	Allegany.............	3382	2651	1396	1036	121
39553	Anne Arundel.......	3049	794	2222	57	105
558185	Baltimore City......	48030	33079	15597	1763	474
122399	Baltimore county...	11524	6211	4247	212	112
10325	Calvert.............	616	83	1035	10	27
19216	Caroline............	1882	196	1445	40	78
33934	Carroll.............	3616	923	2546	16	113
23759	Cecil...............	2441	646	1509	33	49
16386	Charles.............	918	113	1573	6	34
28669	Dorchester..........	2509	313	2387	51	62
52673	Frederick...........	5545	2776	2813	127	96
20105	Garrett.............	1005	1009	655	108	81
27965	Harford.............	3064	802	1737	14	87
16106	Howard..............	1523	364	1004	7	58
16457	Kent................	1816	463	1021	18	41
32089	Montgomery.........	3501	884	1675	47	119
36147	Prince George......	2424	1308	1456	47	94
16839	Queen Anne.........	1932	119	1311	32	60
17030	St. Mary............	843	144	1262	3	26
26455	Somerset...........	1617	370	1528	8	78
19620	Talbot..............	1888	190	1835	8	88
48671	Washington.........	4589	2606	1907	338	91
26815	Wicomico...........	3176	442	2038	7	95
21841	Worcester..........	1764	663	757	3	51
	Total..............	112674	57189	54956	3995	2244
	Plurality...........	54885				
	Per cent...........	43.64	24.94	23.72	1.72	.97
	Total vote.........	231659				

For president in 1912 Reimer, Soc.-Lab., received 322 votes.

FOR REPRESENTATIVES IN CONGRESS, 1912.

1. Counties of Worcester, Somerset, Wicomico, Dorchester, Talbot, Queen Anne, Caroline, Kent and Cecil.

J. Harry Covington, Dem....................17,606
Charles M. Ellerdice, Pro................... 744
R. D. Grier, Prog.......................... 2,303

2. Baltimore city, wards 15 and 16; counties of Carroll, Harford and Baltimore.

Joshua Frederick C. Talbot, Dem............22,087
Laban Sparks, Rep.........................13,732
Basil W. Bowman, Pro...................... 649
Martin O. Huttman, Soc.................... 435

3. Baltimore city, wards 1, 2, 3, 4, 5, 6, 7, 8 and 22 and the 9th, 10th, 11th and 13th precincts of the 18th ward.

George Konig, Dem.........................15,189
Albert M. Sproesser, Rep..................11,078
Edwin B. Fenby, Pro....................... 558
Charles F. Krant, Soc..................... 967

4. Baltimore city, wards 9, 10, 11, 12, 13, 14, 17, 19 and 20 and the 1st, 2d, 3d and 12th precincts of the 18th ward.

J. Charles Linthicum, Dem.................19,075
Jacob F. Murback, Rep.....................11,257
Alfred S. Day, Pro........................ 421
Charles E. Develin, Soc................... 595

5. Baltimore city, wards 21, 23 and 24 and the 4th, 5th, 6th, 7th and 8th precincts of the 18th ward, counties of St. Mary, Charles, Calvert, Prince George, Anne Arundel and Howard.

Frank O. Smith, Dem.......................13,085
Thomas Parran, Rep........................12,168
Holin D. Todd, Pro........................ 366
Mark Jackson, Soc......................... 1,113

6. Counties of Allegany, Garrett, Washington, Montgomery and Frederick.

David J. Lewis, Dem.......................20,434

Charles D. Wagaman, Rep...................14,147
William M. Purdum, Pro.................... 601
S. L. V. Young, Soc....................... 1,316

LEGISLATURE.   Senate. House. J.B.
Republicans 6   34   40
Democrats 21   67   88

STATE OFFICERS.

Governor—Phillips L. Goldsborough, Rep.
Secretary—N. Winslow Williams, Dem.
Treasurer—Murray Vandiver, Dem.
Comptroller—E. C. Harrington, Dem.
Adjutant-General—H. M. Warfield, Dem.
Attorney-General—Edgar Allan Poe, Dem.

MASSACHUSETTS (Population in 1910, 3,366,416).

COUNTIES		GOV'NOR 1913			PRESI'NT 1912		
Population in 1910.	(14)	Prog. Bird	Rep. Gardner	Dem. Walsh	Prog. Roosevelt	Rep. Taft	Dem. Wilson
27542	Barnstable.	1509	1510	840..	2315	1249	1522
105259	Berkshire..	3887	4159	5769..	3809	6507	6211
318573	Bristol....,..	9082	10732	12253..	10630	13270	12420
4504	Dukes......	241	324	157..	278	269	215
436477	Essex......	15732	23501	20094..	21066	21441	20091
43600	Franklin...	1760	2307	1799..	2298	2636	2016
231369	Hampden..	6325	6540	11828..	7099	11593	10620
63327	Hampshire	1569	2846	3262..	1606	4512	3088
669915	Middlesex..	32773	23985	37576..	33517	30511	36080
2962	Nantucket.	115	184	147..	194	123	2407
187596	Norfolk....	9552	7765	9325..	9779	9650	9344
144337	Plymouth..	8609	4679	6978..	9645	5590	6991
731388	Suffolk....	21863	14946	49775..	24977	24179	49059
399657	Worcester..	14738	13247	23694..	15013	24719	17565
	Total...	127755	116705	183267.	142238	155948	178408
	Plurality..		55512..				17460
	Per cent..	26.71	24.40	38.31..	29.15	31.95	35.53
	Total vote.	478259			488056		

For president in 1912 Chafin, Pro., received 2,754 votes, Reimer, Soc.-Lab., 1,102, and Debs, Soc., 12,616. For governor in 1913: Evans, Pro., 2,015; Foss, Ind., 20,171; Reimer, Soc-Lab., 19,321; Wrenn, Soc., 9,025.

FOR REPRESENTATIVES IN CONGRESS, 1912.

1. Counties of Berkshire, Franklin (part), Hampden (part) and Hampshire (part).

Allen T. Treadway, Rep....................12,920
Richard J. Morrissey, Dem.................12,075
Sam P. Blagden, Prog...................... 3,883
Edward A. Buckien, Soc.................... 1,308

2. Counties of Franklin (part), Hampden (part) and Hampshire (part).

Frederick H. Gillett, Rep.................12,301
William G. McKechnie, Dem.................10,940
Thomas L. Hisgen, Prog.................... 5,442

3. Counties of Franklin (part), Hampden (part), Hampshire (part) Middlesex (part) and Worcester (part).

William H. Wilder, Rep....................12,943
M. Fred O'Connell, Dem.................... 9,743
Stephen M. Marshall, Prog................. 5,287
Leon B. Stoddard, Soc..................... 813

4. Counties of Middlesex (part) and Worcester (part).

Samuel E. Winslow, Rep....................15,153
John A. Thayer, Dem.......................11,216
Burton W. Potter, Prog.................... 3,626
Thomas P. Abbott, Soc..................... 535

5. Counties of Essex (part), Middlesex (part) and Worcester .(part).

John J. Rogers, Rep.......................12,827
Humphrey O'Sullivan, Dem.................11,937
William N. Osgood, Prog................... 4,200
William J. Carroll, Soc................... 593

6. County of Essex (part).

Augustus P. Gardner, Rep..................16,918
George A. Schofield, Dem.................. 9,704
Arthur L. Nason, Prog..................... 7,326

7. County of Essex (part).

Michael F. Phelan, Dem....................12,964
Frank P. Bennett, Jr., Rep................ 8,952
Lynn M. Ranger, Prog...................... 5,086
William W. McNally, Soc................... 1,262

8. County of Middlesex (part).

Frederick S. Dietrick, Dem................12,484
Frederick W. Dallinger, Rep...............11,209
Henry C. Long, Prog....................... 6,665
Saul Beaumont, Soc........................ 445

9. Counties of Middlesex (part) and Suffolk (part)
Ernest W. Roberts, Rep 14,021
Henry C. Rowland, Dem 8,732
John Herbert, Prog 7,364
Squire E Putney, Soc 951

10. Wards 1, 2, 3, 4, 5, 6, 7, 8 9 and 11 (precincts 1 and 2) of Boston, in Suffolk county.
William F. Murray, Dem . . .. .12,031
Daniel T Callahan, Prog .. 3,711
Loyal L. Jenkins, Rep . . . 2,418
William Carpenter, Soc. . . . 634

11 Wards 10, 11 (precincts 3, 4, 5, 6, 7, 8, 9), 12, 18, 19, 21, 22, 23 of Boston, in Suffolk county
Andrew J Peters, Dem 17,875
Sherwin L. Cook, Rep 8,786
Charles F. Calus, Soc 1,253

12 Wards 13, 14, 15, 16, 17, 20 and 24 of Boston, in Suffolk county
James M Curley, Dem 14,875
James B Connolly Prog . . . 9,001
Charles H. S Robinson, Rep 5,812
Thomas G. Connolly, Soc 789

13 Counties of Middlesex (part) Norfolk (part), Suffolk (ward 25 in Boston) and Worcester (part)
John W. Weeks, Rep . . .15,394
John J. Mitchell, Dem 13,583
George A Fiel. Prog 5,853

14. Counties of Bristol (part), Norfolk (part), Plymouth (part) and Suffolk (ward 26 in Boston).

Edward Gilmore, Dem 11,930
Henry L Kincaide, Prog 11,341
Robert O. Harris, Rep 9,968
John McCarty, Soc.. 2,005

15. Counties of Bristol (part) and Plymouth (part).
William S. Greene, Rep 11,207
John W. Coughlin, Dem 8,975
Alvin G. Weeks, Prog . . . . ..— 4,172
George F. W. Wright, Soc 482

16 Counties of Barnstable, Bristol (part), Dukes, Nantucket, Norfolk (part) and Plymouth (part)
Thomas C Thacher, Dem 10,461
William J Bullock, Rep 8,186
Thomas Thompson, Prog 6,546
Joseph Palme, Soc 826

LEGISLATURE	Senate	House	J.B
Republicans	21	117	138
Democrats	17	103	120
Progressives	2	17	19
Independent	.	1	1
Socialist ...	..	1	1

STATE OFFICERS.
Governor—David I. Walsh, Dem
Lieutenant-Governor—Edward P Barry, Dem
Secretary of State—Frank J Donahue,
Treasurer and Receiver-General—Frederick W Mansfield, Dem
Auditor—Frank H. Pope, Dem
Attorney-General—Thomas J. Boynton, Dem

MICHIGAN (Population in 1910, 2,810,173).

Population in 1910	COUNTIES (83)	PRESIDENT 1912 — Rep Dem. Pro Soc S L Prog						GOVERNOR 1910 — Rep Dem Pro Soc S L						PRESIDENT 1908— Rep Dem. Pro. Soc			
		Taft	Wilson Chafin	Debs Reimer Roosevelt				Osborn Heman Corbett Warnock Richter						Taft	Bryan Chafin	Debs
5703	Alcona . . .	292	145	9	82	1	465	537	86	22	58	—	..	826	176	24	54
7675	Alger . .	294	264	18	52	—	471	485	148	27	55	4	1006	285	22	60
38819	Allegan . .	2130	1435	153	205	26	3119	2634	1981	117	100	12	5479	2211	294	135
19865	Alpena .	710	1112	24	43	4	1660	1348	690	12	52	7	2877	952	34	116
15692	Antrim .	601	455	36	181	—	1234	813	423	59	53	3 .	2032	576	101	59
9640	Arenac.. ..	423	453	43	116	3	950	729	581	32	41	4	1085	717	60	67
6127	Baraga .	297	281	17	37	—	511 .	678	239	29	8	3..	770	298	19	14
22633	Barry .	1590	1806	121	105	5	1889	2020	1947	129	43	14.	3254	2139	246	21
68238	Bay	2614	2989	238	521	83	4760	3487	3433	87	330	15.	6760	4223	180	403
10038	Benzie . . .	565	341	102	208	8	649	590	257	128	98	10	1442	555	210	77
53622	Berrien.. ..	2757	4234	179	445	—	4538	4018	4034	206	270	81..	7263	4606	275	276
25605	Branch . . .	1879	2185	126	170	8	1839	2265	2360	105	73	7 .	3721	2400	186	151
56638	Calhoun.	3469	3793	229	989	166	4472	3944	3381	111	216	53..	6850	4453	473	549
20024	Cass	1472	2081	75	344	—	1442 .	2024	2005	73	151	5..	3092	2474	148	128
19157	Charlevoix .	1300	568	46	409	6	1203 .	1830	517	66	200	30 .	2538	806	149	176
17872	Cheboygan .	900	979	31	146	15	1178 .	1658	1112	62	54	5..	2051	1217	190	84
24472	Chippewa	840	883	251	188	7	1805 .	2602	613	72	42	1..	2242	1182	130	37
9240	Clare ..	561	437	30	126	7	663 .	784	564	20	28	5..	1350	567	88	22
23129	Clinton . . .	1737	1729	91	41	3	1826 .	2172	2130	134	28	2 .	3493	2143	147	28
3934	Crawford	261	187	9	35	11	250	445	259	11	16	1	593	243	12	28
30108	Delta	1114	1061	45	246	—	1922	1759	680	33	52	17..	3257	1101	84	80
12624	Dickinson	1384	861	43	234	7	1538 .	1872	495	71	64	39..	2515	649	176	44
30499	Eaton . . .	2335	2481	112	123	19	2534	2896	3062	94	41	2.	4483	3148	268	89
18561	Emmet ..	845	925	56	420	—	1104 .	1712	746	102	201	5..	2328	1016	204	184
64555	Genesee	3447	3016	255	639	35	5048	3789	3015	378	498	27.	7268	3267	444	303
8413	Gladwin ..	639	456	26	88	5	563 .	812	345	23	22	3	1195	393	48	31
23333	Gogebic . . .	825	572	147	124	21	1168 .	1460	734	407	61	24..	2265	617	147	60
23784	Grand Traverse	910	943	58	209	19	1697	1007	673	52	228	15 .	2821	1301	184	27
28820	Gratiot . .	1810	1896	83	45	3	2135	2357	2016	155	23	4	4164	2374	178	32
29673	Hillsdale . .	1443	2248	176	60	6	2055	2303	152	20	8	37.	4517	2549	289	43
88098	Houghton	3575	2385	871	448	10	5472 .	5677	2221	499	242	17.	9381	2421	627	371
34758	Huron . . .	1821	1238	61	69	2	3188	2193	1208	94	86	5	3590	1481	104	57
53810	Ingham . . .	3519	3927	324	573	50	4810	3786	6030	364	127	35..	6725	5025	565	157
33550	Iona	2045	2766	168	173	12	2599 .	2894	3810	439	40	4..	4508	3241	461	92
9753	Iosco . . .	519	420	25	30	2	814	865	579	27	11	—	1227	670	40	9
15164	Iron .	1037	221	25	108	27	883	1356	189	136	27	11..	2060	265	40	22
23029	Isabella...	1424	1463	64	142	4	1777	1961	1888	54	40	4	3185	1646	163	53
5342b	Jackson . .	2465	4240	204	878	33	5841	3966	5427	166	154	10.	6768	5234	331	161
60127	Kalamazoo .	2659	3695	447	1448	40	4177	3861	4169	346	477	23	6571	4518	435	425
8097	Kalkaska .	419	298	44	129	4	479	438	276	42	51	—	1136	359	105	46
159145	Kent.. . . .	6548	9437	452	1900	60	13617	9229	8649	412	685	52	16663	11494	859	947
7156	Keweenaw	497	60	17	33	1	505	673	58	15	20	1.	1020	84	16	25
4939	Lake . . .	230	189	9	46	—	480	324	184	17	21	2 .	678	254	14	31
24033	Lapeer	1755	1308	104	68	4	2822	2178	1491	189	13	4	3454	1657	289	34
10608	Leelanau . .	624	349	23	86	4	687.	634	304	24	35	10..	1268	578	46	23
47907	Lenawee ..	2949	4247	158	141	—	3512 .	4020	3891	144	88	7 .	6007	4704	398	28
17736	Livingston	1107	1963	104	14	1	1457	2193	2587	115	6	—	2740	2418	219	10
4004	Luce . .	234	102	8	11	—	271	239	45	9	—	.	357	108	31	4
9240	Mackinac .	612	743	28	—	2	806 .	847	552	16	11	—	1161	773	20	—
32036	Macomb . .	2319	2858	110	81	6	1808	3193	3099	137	20	5 .	4497	3158	228	44
26688	Manistee .	1237	1804	79	240	14	1816	1848	2163	58	179	10.	2709	1805	109	149
46739	Marquette	2617	1000	110	492	22	3625 .	3841	1001	198	422	12 .	5635	1278	261	331
21832	Mason	843	1072	104	175	3	1737 .	1457	1810	70	44	11..	2390	1186	151	52
19466	Mecosta	1054	971	65	238	6	1654 .	1189	528	48	89	7...	2721	1183	151	80

Population.	Taft	Wilson	Chafin	Debs	Reimer	Roosevelt	Osborn	Lemans	Corbett	Warnock	Richter	Taft	Bryan	Chafin	Debs
25648 Menominee	1192	1109	34	195	4	1835	2085	1112	51	104	12	2863	1313	128	79
14005 Midland	906	671	43	45	1	1443	1321	755	30	25	3	2004	880	53	43
10006 Missaukee	672	346	35	83	8	903	1043	327	50	49	5	1573	446	51	19
82917 Monroe	2251	2303	89	70	9	1990	3070	3050	120	23	8	4208	3157	211	50
32069 Montcalm	1876	1381	114	290	19	2433	1971	1050	105	200	18	4585	1725	198	116
3755 Montmorency	325	163	3	16	—	237	264	95	4	10	1	588	180	3	8
40577 Muskegon	1526	1679	78	639	29	4331	2868	1554	56	202	23	5105	1803	149	273
19220 Newaygo	961	778	78	246	9	1861	1454	603	68	47	—	2082	962	148	69
49576 Oakland	4087	3676	252	217	4	3317	4448	4406	293	93	6	6287	3962	423	107
18579 Oceana	855	804	115	121	11	1847	1377	839	115	30	6	2402	903	230	58
8847 Ogemaw	539	317	42	78	6	734	731	446	34	38	2	1225	458	81	25
8650 Ontonagon	721	359	21	137	—	513	1138	265	38	42	7	1250	429	18	47
17889 Osceola	1328	612	95	103	5	1417	1696	733	58	28	3	2826	769	146	5
2027 Oscoda	110	68	1	3	1	159	221	55	3	1	1	332	114	8	3
6552 Otsego	449	195	15	12	—	381	505	179	13	5	1	866	276	34	15
45301 Ottawa	1831	2043	125	335	16	4416	3722	2056	111	74	18	5859	2441	262	165
11249 Presque Isle	732	263	12	59	1	869	966	197	9	17	4	1722	365	18	57
274 Roscommon	196	130	6	30	2	295	296	178	8	13	2	430	149	18	18
80250 Saginaw	6040	5830	175	1292	—	5679	6411	5543	88	202	41	9464	7025	244	558
33330 Sanilac	2170	1172	113	72	4	3227	3634	1240	169	94	2	4184	1484	358	43
8681 Schoolcraft	598	341	14	49	3	575	622	90	4	23	9	1364	205	42	16
33246 Shiawassee	234	1959	205	250	13	2908	2963	2270	385	37	49	4211	2050	526	171
52341 St. Clair	2974	3011	112	241	23	4428	4234	3385	145	280	53	7834	3754	382	295
25499 St. Joseph	1224	2306	90	326	10	2399	2378	2320	62	71	4	3464	2773	173	108
34913 Tuscola	2568	1257	148	58	11	3357	2750	1149	342	26	3	4448	1575	591	46
33185 Van Buren	2112	2005	88	257	—	2328	2589	1862	83	82	10	4505	2335	195	129
44714 Washtenaw	2495	4104	121	118	16	3642	3837	4620	184	51	26	5845	4441	505	88
531590 Wayne	27034	22916	583	3203	265	35170	31910	25399	680	1362	317	50618	24833	1446	2461
20709 Wexford	1076	820	127	311	17	1786	1190	837	165	69	10	2892	852	237	39
Total	153214	150751	8934	23211	1252	214584	202863	150670	9980	9662	1204	333580	175571	16974	11586
Plurality						62440	43183					158809			
Per cent	27.68	27.36	1.62	4.21	.23	38.95	52.87	41.61	2.60	2.60	.32	61.31	32.44	3.13	2.14
Total vote	550976						383718					541767			

For president in 1908 Gillhaus, Soc. Lab., received 1,096 votes, and Hisgen, Ind., 742.

FOR REPRESENTATIVES IN CONGRESS, 1912.

At Large—Patrick H. Kelly, Rep..............185,657
Edward Frensdorf, Dem..............152,188
William H. Hill, Prog..............174,451
M. F. Martin, Soc..............19,789
1. Thirteen wards city of Detroit.
Frank E. Doremus, Dem..............22,573
Ezra F. Beechler, Rep..............16,687
James H. Pound, Prog..............16,801
2. The counties of Jackson, Lenawee, Monroe, Washtenaw, ten townships in Wayne county, city of Wyandotte.
S. W. Beakes, Dem..............16,761
Hubert F. Probert, Prog..............13,660
W. W. Wedemeyer, Rep..............16,650
John P. Foster, Soc..............814
3. The counties of Branch, Calhoun, Eaton, Hillsdale and Kalamazoo.
John M. C. Smith, Rep..............14,609
Claude S. Carney, Dem..............14,482
Edward N. Dingley, Prog..............12,907
L. L. Rogers, Soc..............1,737
4. The counties of Allegan, Barry, Berrien, Cass, St. Joseph and Van Buren.
Edward L. Hamilton, Rep..............14,788
Albert E. Beebe, Dem..............14,382
George M. Valentine, Prog..............12,712
H. L. Gifford, Soc..............1,404
5. The counties of Ionia, Kent and Ottawa.
Carl E. Mapes, Rep..............16,749
Edwin F. Sweet, Dem..............16,148
Suel A. Sheldon, Prog..............11,747
E. A. Kosten, Soc..............2,203
6. The counties of Genesee, Ingham, Livingston, Oakland, six townships Wayne county, three wards city of Detroit.
Samuel W. Smith, Rep..............21,686
Alva M. Cummins, Dem..............18,412
W. S. Kellogg, Prog..............19,992
7. The counties of Huron, Lapeer, Macomb, Sanilac, St. Clair, two townships Wayne county.
Louis C. Crampton, Rep..............15,089
John J. Bell, Dem..............11,998

L. A. Sherman, Prog..............12,588
8. The counties of Clinton, Saginaw, Shiawassee and Tuscola.
Joseph W. Fordney, Rep..............13,215
Miles J. Purcell, Dem..............11,527
Albert L. Chandler, Prog..............11,593
9. The counties of Benzie, Lake, Leelanau, Manistee, Mason, Muskegon, Newaygo, Oceana and Wexford.
James C. McLaughlin, Rep..............11,966
H. R. O'Connor, Dem..............8,020
William H. Sears, Prog..............10,619
10. The counties of Alcona, Alpena, Arenac, Bay, Cheboygan, Crawford, Emmet, Gladwin, Iosco, Midland, Montmorency, Ogemaw, Otsego and Presque Isle.
Roy O. Woodruff, Prog..............12,882
George A. Loud, Rep..............12,141
Louis P. Coumans, Dem..............10,129
Miles W. Gaffney, Soc..............1,541
11. The counties of Antrim, Charlevoix, Clare, Grand Traverse, Gratiot, Isabella, Kalkaska, Mecosta, Missaukee, Montcalm, Osceola and Roscommon.
Francis O. Lindquist, Rep..............19,303
Archie McCall, Dem..............9,361
John W. Patchin, Prog..............9,231
12. The counties of Alger, Baraga, Chippewa, Delta, Dickinson, Gogebic, Houghton, Iron, Keweenaw, Luce, Mackinac, Marquette, Menominee, Ontonagon and Schoolcraft.
H. Olin Young, Rep..............18,190
John Power, Dem..............10,322
Joseph M. Rogers, Prog..............17,975

LEGISLATURE.   Senate. House. J.B.

Republicans	21	54	75
Democrats	5	35	40
Progressives	6	11	17

STATE OFFICERS.

Governor—Woodbridge N. Ferris, Dem.
Lieutenant-Governor—John Q. Ross, Rep.
Treasurer—John W. Haarer, Rep.
Secretary of State—F. C. Martindale, Rep.
Attorney-General—Grant Fellows, Rep.
Auditor—O. B. Fuller, Rep.

MINNESOTA (Population in 1910, 2,075,708).

COUNTIES.	PRESIDENT 1912						PRESIDENT 1910				PRESIDENT 1908			
Population in 1910. (86)	Rep.	Dem.	Soc.	Pro.	S.L.	Prog.	Rep.	Dem.	Pub	O.	Rep.	Dem.	Pro.	Soc.Ind.
	Taft	Wilson	Debs	Chafin	Reimer	Roosevelt	Eberhart	Gray	Barrett		Taft	Bryan	Chafin	Debs Hisgen
10371 Aitkin	362	413	378	72	16	942	807	412	168		1205	589	57	143 4
12493 Anoka	562	691	90	92	15	729	1041	690	36		1577	610	56	42 1
18840 Becker	509	737	257	165	24	1350	1648	765	187		2058	728	186	223 1
19337 Beltrami	490	790	871	30	41	794	1350	607	470		1878	648	45	884 10

Population.		Taft	Wilson	Debs	Chafin	Reimer	Roosevelt	Eberhart	Gray	Barrett	Taft	Bryan	Chafin	Debs	Hisgen
11615	Benton............	468	562	117	24	21	728	972	724	58	1001	765	26	54	4
9367	Big Stone	244	677	98	62	4	591	808	709	16	945	565	89	51	—
29837	Blue Earth	1344	2025	184	141	18	1579	3034	2248	42	3207	2191	226	149	4
20134	Brown	472	1359	348	21	18	943	1982	1195	98	1518	1536	55	246	2
17560	Carlton .. .	283	641	449	89	20	1115	914	643	206	1437	506	51	333	7
17455	Carver	742	1008	41	80	8	933	1993	755	37	1739	1101	34	21	2
11620	Cass	461	565	341	51	16	678	788	677	118	1009	461	42	197	—
13458	Chippewa	412	870	122	116	9	1153	1158	777	49	1400	799	144	32	5
13537	Chisago .	317	435	128	32	10	1649	1309	511	49	2107	408	49	71	2
19640	Clay ...	549	942	160	79	13	1300	1924	985	58	1857	1125	111	68	3
6870	Clearwater .	125	123	234	33	14	566	611	187	144	779	164	46	185	5
1336	Cook	30	65	61	15	5	172	208	54	24	255	42	11	19	—
12451	Cottonwood ...	325	611	94	99	16	1082	1127	544	34	1240	526	98	19	1
16861	Crow Wing... .	691	709	736	66	26	1079	1420	699	312	1681	661	72	410	5
25171	Dakota	609	1777	196	87	13	1608	2628	1570	65	2481	1778	131	108	7
12094	Dodge	470	543	40	59	4	897	982	410	15	1454	515	96	19	—
17609	Douglas..	435	793	161	125	19	1379	1799	1041	27	1894	979	165	70	1
19949	Faribault	393	919	77	233	11	1724	1841	786	21	2305	1039	357	28	2
25680	Fillmore .	1169	990	133	206	14	1888	2566	1057	29	3259	1153	175	77	2
22282	Freeborn... .	672	880	240	234	16	1902	2162	1055	81..	2465	976	421	167	3
31637	Goodhue.....	1051	1406	185	233	21	2844	3269	1389	61.	4484	1149	149	198	8
9114	Grant. ...	116	381	24	52	5	852	800	416	13	1089	376	69	25	—
333480	Hennepin..	14479	15530	5920	668	619	11489	20920	15226	2496	27769	16149	1016	2273	68
14297	Houston...... .	659	762	27	43	6	1278	1457	704	20	1700	745	68	11	—
9831	Hubbard.... .	359	450	285	73	23	503	881	388	92	1288	401	46	124	5
12615	Isanti.. ...	314	333	369	112	7	1095	879	679	128	1681	466	196	185	4
17208	Itasca..	446	699	578	59	27	880	1390	800	235	1883	684	44	367	5
14401	Jackson .. .	468	913	57	43	16	1234	1345	800	20	1515	1013	58	24	2
6481	Kanabec	218	270	254	29	10	498	586	284	105	803	242	42	65	2
18969	Kandiyohi....	484	855	196	98	17	1668	1883	1310	58	2412	947	222	145	8
9669	Kittson	145	362	80	46	7	770	690	526	25	969	499	84	45	2
6431	Koochiching	239	638	460	16	17	522	655	321	369	826	420	39	188	2
15435	Lac qui Parle.	343	608	68	107	7	1406	1312	666	20	1894	661	167	16	—
8011	Lake. ...	182	195	466	46	8	369	471	272	277	684	152	41	362	1
18609	Le Sueur	886	1488	133	79	16	952	1902	1699	65	1819	1699	79	199	5
9874	Lincoln......	204	548	62	62	8	666	935	715	34	891	683	63	27	1
18722	Lyon	460	1048	128	100	16	1167	1158	1061	24..	1618	1043	146	46	1
18091	McLeod	659	1225	84	69	12	891	1270	1160	27	1579	1506	73	35	4
4249	Mahnomen .	68	298	98	2	10	154	263	217	53	265	1143	5	81	—
16338	Marshall....	331	567	197	99	15	1721	1686	747	113	1148	751	186	177	6
17518	Martin	518	1141	98	140	6	1847	1684	1183	43	1922	1054	184	91	4
17022	Meeker	560	1009	67	43	8	1458	2096	1190	18	1928	1111	74	45	1
10706	Mille Lacs	492	449	329	65	19	751	699	586	117	1119	427	91	168	1
24053	Morrison...	690	1641	223	41	14	1827	1679	1523	193	1936	1513	64	118	1
22610	Mower......	1321	1228	189	82	16	1371	2259	901	46	2829	1206	124	180	4
11755	Murray...	388	775	72	57	8	958	1221	714	23	1293	762	55	82	2
14125	Nicollet .. .	525	929	70	53	24	825	1288	806	23	1392	882	72	50	3
15210	Nobles	605	994	119	62	9	1122	1291	995	24	1432	925	107	58	—
13446	Norman...	329	510	252	146	12	983	1006	546	130	1276	661	195	177	—
22497	Olmsted ...	720	1542	93	112	19	1467	2043	1702	164	2472	1621	141	16	10
46036	Otter Tail ...	755	1789	578	263	44	3168	2666	2158	241	3964	2420	329	208	5
15878	Pine	344	433	343	67	11	784	1026	712	104	1548	802	85	303	4
	Pennington (new) .	513	777	345	71	23	1281	—	—	—	—	—	—	—	—
9553	Pipestone... .	301	505	118	56	9	675	885	418	22	1057	491	49	27	—
36001	Polk	735	1602	789	199	36	2420	3048	2303	469	3311	1928	193	556	10
12746	Pope	379	443	40	126	8	1283	1450	533	10	1794	442	75	23	—
223675	Ramsey	4109	12431	2942	275	167	12436	17616	9202	842	16556	11613	400	1659	72
15940	Red Lake .	259	974	64	217	8	226	1843	1246	236	1428	856	60	342	8
18425	Redwood	542	1126	139	59	17	1291	1698	946	41	1821	1076	88	54	3
23123	Renville .. .	703	1310	99	72	6	1710	2333	1252	39	2275	1364	110	28	1
25011	Rice.......	1020	1613	78	101	20	1765	2512	1591	40	2821	1614	111	40	4
10222	Rock	463	466	72	47	5	757	902	408	18	1234	525	55	17	4
11338	Roseau .. .	278	299	426	41	15	859	878	259	274	900	414	61	361	2
163274	St. Louis. .	3881	5124	2853	420	120	8480	7908	6232	726	12076	4464	401	1305	28
14888	Scott	462	1172	25	23	4	506	856	794	17	1045	1548	52	12	3
8146	Sherburne.. .	355	360	70	64	13	676	585	477	24	1102	366	67	42	—
15340	Sibley....... .	483	890	62	43	12	1196	1996	709	21	1623	1110	61	6	2
47743	Stearns....... .	1134	1477	182	192	27	1682	3124	2297	75	2614	3855	127	159	10
16146	Steele	651	1294	59	84	7	1105	1757	1430	32	1899	1284	104	38	—
8293	Stevens...... .	286	640	33	52	6	625	749	563	17	877	582	37	16	1
12949	Swift	443	937	100	88	8	1088	1244	1006	22	1343	921	84	41	2
23407	Todd	1038	1068	404	107	24	1098	1608	1032	398	2334	1305	163	258	8
8049	Traverse	131	561	16	13	5	541	705	513	14	685	514	34	13	1
18864	Wabasha . ..	797	1422	67	50	7	1068	2066	1448	25	2150	1196	77	39	2
8662	Wadena.. .	278	336	167	28	6	515	713	359	65	991	467	29	70	2
13466	Waseca	558	1052	68	62	14	940	1305	1041	23	1455	1065	59	49	3
20013	Washington ...	581	1289	202	51	16	2078	1737	1049	60	2727	1129	68	63	4
11382	Watonwan .	254	618	33	30	4	1139	1102	572	5	1411	537	45	6	4
9063	Wilkin .	209	586	56	30	2	561	873	521	21	774	614	48	26	2
38398	Winona . .	1042	3004	338	62	178	1676	2842	2335	45	3011	3072	85	69	9
28032	Wright.....	837	1335	101	106	15	1917	2042	1530	52	2820	1396	184	87	5
15406	Yellow Medicine.. .	653	737	79	94	7	1203	1122	666	19	1745	786	130	19	2
	Total . .	64334	106426	27505	7886	2212	125950	164185	143779	11173.	19,0843	109401	11107	14527	426
	Plurality						194.30		60406			86434			
	Per cent	19 25	31 84	8 23	2 36	66	37 65 .	55.74	35 23	3 79.	59 30	33.12	3 06	4.38	13
	Total vote . . .					.834219			204607			3,0244			

For governor in 1912 Eberhart Rep., received
129,688 votes, Ringdal, Dem., 99,659, Morgan, P O ,
29,876, Collins, Prog., 33,455.

FOR REPRESENTATIVES IN CONGRESS, 1912
At Large—James Manahan, Rep 154,308
Carl J Buell, Dem................... 69,652

W G Calderwood, Pro...................... 25,863
J. S Ingalls, P. O 30,042

1 Counties of Dodge, Fillmore, Freeborn, Houston, Mower, Olmsted. Steele, Wabasha Waseca and Winona
Sydney Anderson, Rep.. 25,681

Clinton Robinson, Dem........................10,786
2. Counties of Blue Earth, Brown, Cottonwood, Faribault, Jackson, Martin, Murray, Nobles, Pipestone, Rock and Watonwan.
Franklin W. Ellsworth, Rep................13,093
W. S. Hammond, Dem........................14,718
John R. Hollister, P. O.....................1,497
3. Counties of Carver, Dakota, Goodhue, Le Sueur, McLeod, Nicollet, Rice, Scott and Sibley.
Charles R. Davis, Rep......................18,526
Frank L. Glotzbaek, Dem.....................9,763
Frank F. Matzahn, Pro.......................1,919
4. Counties of Chisago, Ramsey and Washington.
Fred C. Stevens, Rep.......................15,479
James J. Regan, Dem........................11,322
Albert Rosenquist, P. O.....................6,021
Hugh T. Halbert, Prog.......................9,220
5. County of Hennepin.
George R. Smith, Rep.......................17,861
Thomas P. Dwyer, Dem........................6,987
Thomas E. Latimer, P. O.....................6,929
Thomas D. Scholl, Prog......................8,574
6. Counties of Benton, Cass, Crow Wing, Douglas, Hubbard, Meeker, Morrison, Sherburne, Stearns, Todd, Wadena and Wright.
Charles A. Lindbergh, Rep..................21,286
Andrew J. Gilkinson, Dem....................9,920
A. W. Uhl, P. O.............................2,899
7. Counties of Big Stone, Chippewa, Grant, Kandiyohi, Lac qui Parle, Lincoln, Lyon, Pope, Redwood, Renville, Stevens, Swift, Traverse and Yellow Medicine.
Andrew J. Volstead, Rep....................25,053
No opposition.
8. Counties of Aitkin, Anoka, Carlton, Cook, Isanti, Itasca, Kanabec, Koochiching, Lake, Mille Lacs, Pine and St. Louis.
Clarence B. Miller, Rep....................20,523
John Jensvold, Jr., Dem....................12,494
Morris Kaplan, P. O.........................7,398
9. Counties of Becker, Beltrami, Clay, Clearwater, Kittson, Mahnomen, Marshall, Norman, Otter Tail, Pennington, Polk, Red Lake, Roseau and Wilkin.
Halvor Steenerson, Rep.....................22,481
M. A. Brattland, P. O......................11,190

LEGISLATURE.	Senate.	House.	J.B.
Republicans	41	99	140
Democrats	20	19	39
Prohibitionists	1	1	2
Public Ownership	..	1	1
Populist	1	..	1

STATE OFFICERS. (All republicans.)
Governor—A. O. Eberhart.
Lieutenant-Governor—J. A. A. Burnquist.
Secretary of State—Julius A. Schmahl.
Treasurer—Walter J. Smith.
Attorney-General—Lyndon A. Smith.
Auditor—S. G. Iverson.
Superintendent Public Instruction—C. G. Schulz.
Insurance Commissioner—J. A. O. Preus.

MISSISSIPPI (Population in 1910, 1,797,114).

COUNTIES. (79) Population in 1910.	PRESIDENT 1912 — Dem. Prog. Rep. Soc.			
	Wilson	Roosevelt	Taft	Debs
25305 Adams	481	282	31	9
18159 Alcorn	1010	43	40	20
22954 Amite	1666	13	5	2
2851 Attala	1060	88	49	69
10245 Benton	480	22	18	12
48905 Bolivar	624	14	10	8
17726 Calhoun	937	15	17	86
23139 Carroll	653	42	16	54
22846 Chickasaw	856	49	19	24
14357 Choctaw	609	89	24	7
17405 Claiborne	309	1	3	1
21630 Clarke	638	29	17	59
20203 Clay	396	26	4	16
34217 Coahoma	1234	31	16	27
35914 Copiah	570	44	10	8
10309 Covington	546	19	8	62
28150 DeSoto	896	10	16	10
20722 Forrest	301	59	4	112
15109 Franklin	231	88	5	21
6599 George	263	14	13	41
6050 Greene		21		9

Population.	Wilson	Roosevelt	Taft	Debs
15727 Grenada	409	21	3	2
11207 Hancock	385	56	28	3
34653 Harrison	1222	181	45	78
63726 Hinds	2065	88	40	30
30088 Holmes	936	20	5	21
10290 Issaquena	99	8	3	1
14526 Itawamba	914	67	24	18
15451 Jackson	514	64	14	21
18498 Jasper	803	51	12	39
23221 Jefferson	408	20	2	1
12860 Jefferson Davis	542	51	48	13
29985 Jones	1058	145	34	195
20348 Kemper	828	44	20	18
21885 Lafayette	913	46	28	19
11741 Lamar	399	83	16	7
40919 Lauderdale	2204	92	50	94
13080 Lawrence	332	24	9	6
18298 Leake	930	24	11	102
28894 Lee	1390	42	39	15
36290 Le Flore	616	35	12	8
28937 Lincoln	708	102	41	14
30703 Lowndes	872	15	12	11
33505 Madison	603	38	11	21
15599 Marion	438	21	12	8
26795 Marshall	779	48	9	—
35178 Monroe	1377	24	25	12
17706 Montgomery	697	23	4	18
17990 Neshoba	806	83	22	45
23005 Newton	1107	11	6	61
28503 Noxubee	646	12	5	3
19676 Oktibbeha	851	25	30	6
31274 Panola	760	68	13	11
10593 Pearl River	290	13	7	2
7685 Perry	257	22	4	31
37273 Pike	1068	79	24	58
19088 Pontotoc	1009	112	47	13
16831 Prentiss	839	141	85	33
11538 Quitman	195	15	4	5
23944 Rankin	718	15	7	25
16723 Scott	722	11	7	2
15494 Sharkey	157	8	3	—
17201 Simpson	606	32	19	25
16923 Smith	854	40	12	11
28787 Sunflower	462	23	9	6
29078 Tallahatchie	695	28	16	8
19714 Tate	612	57	23	13
14631 Tippah	1056	51	34	24
13967 Tishomingo	701	102	65	36
18846 Tunica	188	2	1	2
18997 Union	962	81	23	12
32488 Warren	1135	125	55	24
48033 Washington	731	72	20	4
14709 Wayne	549	25	15	46
14353 Webster	655	102	32	55
19075 Wilkinson	349	10	8	20
17139 Winston	743	41	8	29
21519 Yalobusha	788	29	22	24
46672 Yazoo	887	30	7	10
Total	57227	3645	1595	2061
Plurality	53582			
Per cent.	88.87	5.64	2.35	3.14
Total vote		64319		

FOR REPRESENTATIVES IN CONGRESS, 1912.

1. The counties of Alcorn, Itawamba, Lee, Lowndes, Monroe, Oktibbeha, Prentiss, Noxubee and Tishomingo.
E. S. Candler, Dem................(No opposition)
2. The counties of Benton, De Soto, Lafayette, Marshall, Panola, Tallahatchie, Tate, Tippah and Union.
H. D. Stephens, Dem................(No opposition)
3. The counties of Bolivar, Coahoma, Issaquena, Le Flore, Quitman, Sharkey, Sunflower, Tunica, Holmes and Washington.
B. G. Humphreys, Dem................(No opposition)
4. The counties of Calhoun, Carroll, Chickasaw, Choctaw, Clay, Grenada, Montgomery, Pontotoc, Webster and Attala.
T. U. Sisson, Dem................(No opposition)
5. The counties of Winston, Clarke, Jasper, Lauderdale, Leake, Neshoba, Newton, Scott, Smith and Kemper.
S. A. Witherspoon, Dem............(No opposition)
6. The counties of Covington, Greene, Hancock, Harrison, Jackson, Jones, Lawrence, Marion, Perry, Wayne, Simpson and Pearl River.
B. P. Harrison, Dem................(No opposition)
7. The counties of Claiborne, Copiah, Franklin, Jefferson, Lincoln, Adams, Pike, Amite and Wilkinson.

Percy E. Quinn, Dem..............(No opposition)
8. The counties of Warren, Yazoo, Madison, Hinds and Rankin.
J. W. Collier, Dem..................(No opposition)

LEGISLATURE.

All the members of the legislature are democrats.

STATE OFFICERS. (All democrats.)

Governor—Earl Brewer.
Lieutenant-Governor—Theodore G. Bilbo.
Secretary—J. W. Power.
Treasurer—P. S. Stovall.
Auditor—Duncan L. Thompson.
Attorney-General—Ross A. Collins.

MISSOURI (Population in 1910, 3,293,335).

Population (114) in 1910.	COUNTIES.	Dem. Wilson	Rep. Taft	Prog. Roosevelt	Pro. Chafin	Soc. Debs	S.L. Reimer
22700	Adair	1784	1428	1200	57	398	28
15282	Andrew	1750	1632	432	96	31	5
13604	Atchison	1534	1137	539	55	86	4
24087	Audrain	3532	1822	577	35	81	8
23869	Barry	2300	1397	1053	55	229	7
16747	Barton	1791	1010	689	66	280	15
25869	Bates	3057	1380	1301	117	151	19
14881	Benton	1209	1142	618	25	54	7
14576	Bollinger	1512	1101	848	25	102	3
30533	Boone	5022	1350	695	26	55	6
93020	Buchanan	8869	4412	2639	94	630	20
20624	Butler	1946	1852	408	30	407	23
14605	Caldwell	1483	1187	945	32	6	1
24400	Callaway	3544	1525	284	34	13	2
11582	Camden	667	918	246	6	29	2
27621	Cape Girardeau	2587	2202	899	45	100	10
23063	Carroll	2648	1521	1561	50	73	7
5504	Carter	458	258	116	10	78	5
22073	Cass	3247	1034	1178	51	103	4
16080	Cedar	1302	1241	628	50	134	3
23503	Chariton	3112	1528	745	43	37	4
15832	Christian	793	1204	842	33	175	5
12811	Clark	1586	1214	484	26	12	1
20302	Clay	3417	592	679	14	40	3
15297	Clinton	1968	779	679	54	10	—
21957	Cole	2447	2103	252	19	46	—
20311	Cooper	2444	2271	299	23	26	—
13576	Crawford	1037	1044	327	22	54	1
15613	Dade	1316	1195	776	38	59	1
13181	Dallas	869	1051	480	16	23	2
17605	Daviess	2284	1100	1170	63	12	6
12531	DeKalb	1652	1090	499	54	16	1
13345	Dent	1279	959	153	18	79	2
16364	Douglas	506	857	1092	21	254	9
30328	Dunklin	2723	987	494	24	1001	19
29830	Franklin	2239	2481	671	35	213	13
12847	Gasconade	518	1539	495	31	25	3
16820	Gentry	2263	1268	524	61	56	4
63831	Greene	5080	4354	2184	159	756	20
16744	Grundy	1910	1051	1484	46	24	2
20166	Harrison	1985	2051	965	70	37	2
27242	Henry	3494	1192	1600	119	128	6
8741	Hickory	421	737	375	14	63	1
14539	Holt	1519	1523	583	39	23	6
15653	Howard	2672	896	192	16	16	—
21065	Howell	1565	1470	836	47	367	13
8563	Iron	845	606	65	22	55	3
283522	Jackson-Kas.C.	37209	5594	23152	348	1691	170
89673	Jasper	6789	4571	3309	231	1673	128
27878	Jefferson	2368	2125	485	19	—	9
26297	Johnson	3468	1774	1141	72	94	11
12403	Knox	1606	1098	297	44	43	2
17903	Laclede	1634	1479	463	18	114	5
30154	Lafayette	3650	2367	1241	37	157	7
26583	Lawrence	2384	1311	1536	62	312	11
15514	Lewis	2340	1004	334	31	47	2
17033	Lincoln	2326	1258	167	32	19	—
25253	Linn	2890	1452	134	87	131	10
19453	Livingston	2314	887	1503	53	58	5
13539	McDonald	3010	1288	1830	73	171	13
30869	Macon	1126	827	171	18	53	5
11273	Madison	1056	448	128	13	49	5
10088	Maries	1326	916	442	32	157	6
30572	Marion	3471	1693	531	83	125	6
12335	Mercer	789	905	906	37	43	3
16717	Miller	1257	1240	512	27	143	2
14557	Mississippi	1388	1050	78	10	110	14
14675	Moniteau	1613	1374	215	37	67	—
18304	Monroe	3586	583	219	15	64	4
15094	Montgomery	1883	1697	219	53	24	4
15963	Morgan	1163	1239	282	20	19	2
19488	New Madrid	1945	1608	844	37	562	22
27136	Newton	2421	1489	1088	124	840	10

Population		Wilson	Taft	Roosevelt	Chafin	Debs	Reimer
28833	Nodaway	3490	2140	1307	59	49	8
14681	Oregon	1688	486	833	5	164	6
14283	Osage	1394	981	485	34	29	—
11926	Ozark	575	606	787	16	51	3
13559	Pemiscot	1617	973	248	8	259	24
14888	Perry	1564	1735	86	11	15	—
33913	Pettis	3771	2423	1512	61	210	26
15796	Phelps	1565	783	379	21	63	6
22556	Pike	2720	1901	176	19	82	8
14429	Platte	2535	510	375	14	11	—
24561	Polk	1935	1801	784	33	81	6
11488	Pulaski	1268	632	267	27	40	5
14308	Putnam	953	1861	420	54	63	7
12913	Ralls	1734	591	240	10	8	—
26182	Randolph	4186	1126	641	54	119	4
24151	Ray	3042	1191	561	49	79	6
9592	Reynolds	1030	867	169	19	78	1
13069	Ripley	1249	652	358	28	158	8
24695	St. Charles	1792	2351	525	13	105	11
16412	St. Clair	1710	1043	727	35	180	9
35758	St. Francois	2736	2307	344	40	729	14
10107	Ste.Genevieve	1148	1099	47	6	19	22
82417	St. Louis	5409	6184	2854	95	935	62
687020	St. Louis city	58815	49524	24746	434	9159	64
29148	Saline	3929	1443	1413	59	41	7
9062	Schuyler	1218	768	198	34	30	—
11803	Scotland	1525	860	879	28	65	2
22072	Scott	1945	1235	303	25	649	30
11143	Shannon	1110	385	375	17	193	14
13864	Shelby	2450	858	331	65	33	2
27807	Stoddard	2603	1901	589	39	648	15
11559	Stone	508	944	642	18	165	4
18598	Sullivan	2226	1820	576	34	48	8
9134	Taney	588	854	260	7	72	5
21458	Texas	2067	1232	553	39	130	9
28827	Vernon	3483	1657	655	94	328	17
9123	Warren	431	1008	499	7	96	4
13878	Washington	1121	1060	307	26	53	—
15181	Wayne	1433	1053	804	20	152	7
14377	Webster	649	1987	744	48	82	5
9007	Worth	973	769	183	33	6	2
18315	Wright	1356	1164	895	20	84	7

	Wilson	Taft	Roosevelt	Chafin	Debs	Reimer
Total	330746	207821	124371	5380	28466	1778
Plurality	122925					
Per cent.	44.40	27.90	16.52	3.82	7.12	.24
Total vote	744062					

FOR REPRESENTATIVES IN CONGRESS, 1912.

1. The counties of Adair, Clark, Knox, Lewis, Macon, Marion, Putnam, Schuyler, Scotland, Shelby.
James T. Lloyd, Dem............20,874
B. L. Bonfoey, Rep............12,144
Arthur B. Warner, Prog............5,666

2. The counties of Carroll, Chariton, Grundy, Linn, Livingston, Monroe, Randolph, Sullivan.
William W. Rucker, Dem............22,786
Edward F. Haley, Rep............10,132
R. H. Williams, Prog............6,776

3. The counties of Caldwell, Clay, Clinton, Daviess, DeKalb, Gentry, Harrison, Mercer, Ray, Worth.
Joshua W. Alexander, Dem............20,179
J. H. Morroway, Rep............11,192
W. S. Wightman, Prog............6,812

4. The counties of Andrew, Atchison, Buchanan, Holt, Nodaway, Platte.
C. F. Booher, Dem............20,232
C. V. Hickman, Rep............11,284
F. G. Robinson, Prog............5,347

5. Jackson county.
William P. Borland, Dem............33,397
Isaac B. Kimbrell, Rep............5,759
C. H. Summers, Prog............21,863

6. The counties of Bates, Cass, Cedar, Dade, Henry, Johnson, St. Clair.
C. C. Dickinson, Dem............17,858
Louis T. Dunnevant, Rep............9,093
G. A. Thelman, Prog............6,788

7. The counties of Benton, Green, Hickory, Howard, Lafayette, Pettus, Polk, Saline.
Courtney W. Hamlin, Dem............23,178
Theodore C. Owens, Rep............15,685
W. W. Blaine, Prog............7,905

8. The counties of Boone, Camden, Cole, Cooper, Miller, Moniteau, Morgan, Osage.
Dorsey W. Shackleford, Dem............16,219
D. W. Peters, Rep............11,965
M. W. Pemberton, Prog............2,391

9. The counties of Audrain, Callaway, Franklin, Gasconade, Lincoln, Montgomery, Pike, Ralls, St. Charles, Warren.

Champ Clark, Dem...............................21,782
W. L. Cole, Rep................................16,283

10. The county of St. Louis and the 1st, 7th, 8th, 9th, 10th, 11th, 12th, 19th, 24th, 27th (precinct 11), 28th wards of the city of St. Louis.

Maurice O'Connor, Dem.........................21,227
Richard Bartholdt, Rep........................33,242
August Siefert, Prog..........................16,417

11. The 2d, 3d, 16th, 17th, 18th, 20th, 21st, 26th, 27th (except precinct 11) wards of the city of St. Louis.

W. L. Igoe, Dem...............................19,653
Theron E. Catlin, Rep.........................12,448

12. The 4th, 5th, 6th, 7th (only precinct 12), 12th (only precincts 11 and 12), 13th, 14th, 15th (except precincts 2, 3 and 4), 20th (only precinct 1), 21st (only precincts 1 and 2), 22d, 23d, 24th, 25th (only precincts from 1 to 6, inclusive), 28th (only precincts 1 and 2) wards of the city of St. Louis.

Michael J. Gill, Dem..........................11,249
L. C. Dyer, Rep...............................11,981

13. The counties of Bollinger, Carter, Iron, Jefferson, Madison, Perry, Reynolds, St. Francois, Ste. Genevieve, Washington, Wayne.

Walter L. Hensley, Dem........................16,079
S. G. Nipper, Rep.............................13,403

14. The counties of Butler, Cape Girardeau, Christian, Douglas, Dunklin, Howell, Mississippi, New Madrid, Oregon, Ozark, Pemiscot, Ripley, Scott, Stoddard, Stone, Taney.

Joseph J. Russell, Dem........................26,031
George C. Curry, Rep. and Prog................25,066

15. The counties of Barry, Barton, Jasper, Lawrence, McDonald, Newton, Vernon.

Perl D. Decker, Dem...........................21,000
I. B. McPherson, Rep..........................12,850
H. H. Gregg, Prog.............................7,797

16. The counties of Crawford, Dallas, Dent, Laclede, Maries, Phelps, Pulaski, Shannon, Texas, Webster, Wright.

T. L. Rubey, Dem..............................15,908
J. P. O'Bannon, Rep...........................10,811
Columbus Bradford, Prog.......................3,678

LEGISLATURE.   Senate.House. J.B.
Democrats 25   113 138
Republicans   9   28   37
Progressive   1   1

STATE OFFICERS.
Governor—Elliott W. Major, Dem.
Lieutenant-Governor—William R. Painter, Dem.
Secretary of State—Cornelius Roach, Dem.
Treasurer—Edwin P. Deal, Dem.
Auditor—John P. Gordon, Dem.
Attorney-General—John F. Barker, Dem.
Superintendent Schools—W. P. Evans, Rep.

MONTANA (Population in 1910, 376,053).

COUNTIES. (31)		PRESIDENT 1912			
Population in 1910.		Dem. Wilson	Prog. Roosevelt	Rep. Taft	Soc. Debs
6466	Beaverhead............	713	320	708	110
	Blaine................	352	507	204	108
3491	Broadwater............	451	197	205	80
13462	Carbon................	796	766	646	388
28853	Cascade...............	1633	1001	1079	838
17191	Choteau...............	402	265	561	129
14125	Custer................	1068	1192	695	247
12725	Dawson................	719	1165	673	220
12383	Deer Lodge............	1197	464	1060	195
17385	Fergus................	1533	1083	745	421
8785	Flathead..............	1164	1351	493	446
14079	Gallatin..............	1407	929	683	212
2942	Granite...............	346	296	195	92
	Hill..................	624	645	536	323
6001	Jefferson.............	479	299	247	176
21853	Lewis and Clark.......	1505	1375	1062	391
3636	Lincoln...............	348	206	218	235
7329	Madison...............	822	576	601	78
4190	Meagher...............	473	327	321	75
23596	Missoula..............	1523	1773	589	773
	Musselshell...........	470	400	483	215
10731	Park..................	759	718	664	253
5904	Powell................	545	418	385	147
11666	Ravalli...............	858	896	316	282
7985	Rosebud...............	313	368	392	87
3713	Sanders...............	414	376	257	160
56848	Silver Bow............	4542	1802	2232	3320
4029	Sweet Grass...........	278	424	181	69
9546	Teton.................	646	446	612	281
13630	Valley................	696	858	663	365
32944	Yellowstone...........	1198	1386	1004	242
	Total................	27911	22456	18512	10885
	Plurality............	5455			
	Per cent.............	35.03	28.26	23.14	13.57
	Total vote...........		79826		

There was no prohibition ticket in Montana in 1912.

FOR REPRESENTATIVES IN CONGRESS, 1912.
Thomas Stout, Dem............................25,891
John M. Evans, Dem...........................24,492
Charles N. Pray, Rep.........................23,595
William R. Allen, Rep........................19,633
Thomas Everett, Prog.........................16,644
George A. Horkan, Prog.......................15,336
Henri LaBeau, Soc............................10,271
J. Frank Mabie, Soc..........................10,056

LEGISLATURE.   Senate.House. J.B.
Democrats 17   48   65
Republicans 12   20   32
Progressives   2   16   18
Socialists   1   1

STATE OFFICERS. (All democrats.)
Governor—Samuel V. Stewart.
Lieutenant-Governor—William W. McDowell.
Secretary of State—Adelbert M. Alderson.
Attorney-General—Daniel M. Kelly.
State Treasurer—William C. Rae.
State Auditor—William Keating.
Supt. Public Instruction—Henry A. Davee.
Railroad Commissioners—John H. Hall, Daniel Boyle, E. A. Morley.

NEBRASKA (Population in 1910, 1,192,214).

COUNTIES. (92)	PRESIDENT 1912					GOV. 1910			PRESIDENT 1908				GOVERNOR 1906			
Population in 1910.	Rep. Taft	Dem. Wilson	Soc. Debs	Pro. Chafin	Prog. Roosevelt	Rep. Aldrich	Dem. Dahlman	Rep. Taft	Dem. Bryan	Pro. Chafin	Soc. Debs	Rep. Sheldon	Dem. Sh'l'nb'g'r	Pro. S'tt'n	Peo. Taylor	Soc.
29900 Adams............	801	2117	188	125	948..	2124	1888..	1987	2337	119	92..	1543	1773	126	45	
14003 Antelope.........	871	1228	50	38	947..	1909	800..	1658	1455	66	29..	1314	973	68	21	
1444 Banner...........	53	57	55	3	128..	173	46..	175	74	2	17..	65	24	3	3	
1672 Blaine...........	126	165	35	7	107..	214	132..	220	160	4	8..	111	76	3	3	
13145 Boone...........	570	1390	51	40	942..	1796	1046..	1580	1583	40	12..	1407	1024	136	16	
6131 Box Butte.......	229	520	97	20	434..	698	487..	690	681	19	29..	471	404	13	19	
8826 Boyd............	241	651	57	23	653..	946	606..	954	891	34	27..	714	628	31	32	
6083 Brown...........	206	483	92	21	415..	642	384..	588	526	15	42..	458	278	14	27	
21907 Buffalo.........	1081	2061	201	57	1256..	2650	1854..	2526	2520	75	76..	2000	1647	52	86	
12726 Burt...........	865	1040	41	20	1005..	1690	1043..	1880	1215	49	14..	1640	912	42	21	
15403 Butler.........	823	1756	40	37	586..	1482	2031..	1412	2129	41	17..	1384	1508	85	11	
19786 Cass...........	967	2009	154	64	1132..	2218	1982..	2440	2587	85	55..	2365	1651	65	32	
15191 Cedar..........	722	1815	9	17	1045..	1390	1351..	1627	1732	89	5..	1170	1197	19	17	
3613 Chase...........	216	264	38	24	245..	544	179..	400	338	34	3..	211	635	9	2	
10414 Cherry.........	689	1052	229	35	631..	1149	839..	1048	1021	41	58..	654	493	80	86	
4551 Cheyenne.......	232	348	78	21	281..	473	411..	846	809	28	37..	419	293	15	23	
15729 Clay...........	557	1694	52	63	1292..	2291	1365..	1591	1939	95	31..	1582	1467	70	24	
11610 Colfax.........	620	908	80	12	300..	703	1249..	1159	1267	21	36..	845	754	18	31	
13782 Cuming.........	759	1484	30	8	476..	1023	1783..	1284	1722	29	5..	988	1340	18	9	

Population		Taft	Wilson	Debs	Chafin	Roosevelt	Aldrich	Dahlman	Taft	Bryan	Chafin	Debs	Sheldon	Sh'nb'g'r	Sh'll'n	Taylor
22498	Custer	1051	2426	353	79	1874..	3507	1783..	2788	2898	98	147..	1933	1640	117	152
6564	Dakota	409	612	50	12	357..	585	615..	720	716	22	22..	648	524	20	30
8254	Dawes	208	583	65	15	610..	872	674..	836	727	16	20..	606	384	11	31
15961	Dawson	451	1013	76	54	1207..	2118	1169..	1737	1926	87	22..	1274	1026	83	34
1786	Deuel	64	135	25	1	157..	248	134..	526	392	12	8..	236	155	7	2
11477	Dixon	582	823	24	38	955..	1276	770..	1257	1100	63	12..	906	708	70	20
22145	Dodge	1321	1987	209	74	984..	2053	2900..	2437	2964	100	49..	1948	1558	42	45
168546	Douglas	6212	12953	2154	124	7980..	9412	17141..	14096	15583	266	798..	9555	9325	74	693
4098	Dundy	148	204	72	10	347..	525	254..	483	391	17	26..	335	219	19	16
14674	Fillmore	672	1736	78	44	787..	1873	1641..	1756	1989	40	24..	1603	1469	33	39
16393	Franklin	334	1148	58	31	779..	1221	1024..	1083	1298	57	38..	909	929	40	22
8572	Frontier	293	657	120	37	582..	1008	614..	1008	847	55	54..	785	686	36	44
12083	Furnas	354	1266	83	55	815..	1653	838..	1400	1618	92	15..	1113	1145	47	15
36825	Gage	1836	2593	173	88	2159..	3050	2753..	2721	3139	131	69..	2849	1986	259	47
3338	Garden	136	282	48	18	369..	380	244..								
3417	Garfield	192	284	125	5	245..	390	250..	368	363	10	23..	322	200	12	11
4963	Gosper	129	524	10	16	283..	521	410..	499	634	32	3..	318	399	17	15
1097	Grant	82	93	7	2	52..	111	73..	95	101		1..	65	43		
8047	Greeley	371	913	65	21	376..	738	772..	691	1072	14	29..	598	732	12	20
20361	Hall	1047	2086	249	58	974..	1963	2048..	2241	2229	102	102..	1838	1508	76	90
13459	Hamilton	450	1433	87	63	1054..	1955	1141..	1633	1664	129	2..	1292	1155	161	25
9578	Harlan	325	922	142	64	618..	1236	665..	1081	1158	115	49..	726	1285	150	29
3011	Hayes	106	139	41	8	246..	319	160..	559	277	11	42..	239	183	5	36
5415	Hitchcock	128	471	60	28	371..	773	373..	633	682	17	11..	506	484	15	12
15545	Holt	778	1456	130	43	1196..	1702	1323..	1541	1777	99	64..	1327	1414	69	55
981	Hooker	103	122	19	2	57..	112	80..	100	91	3	3..	54	36	5	1
10783	Howard	481	1115	87	21	544..	1071	992..	977	1435	40	31..	857	1068	26	26
16852	Jefferson	655	1699	226	43	1208..	1552	1583..	1941	1787	77	39..	1578	908	109	54
10187	Johnson	672	890	27	21	649..	1163	1035..	1357	1150	45	8..	1235	828	51	13
9106	Kearney	398	1012	44	33	657..	1357	645..	993	1174	121	28..	836	886	189	33
3692	Keith	188	304	85	5	296..	369	318..	368	310	6	5..	189	202	2	4
3452	Keyapaha	258	321	70	11	246..	431	180..	422	354	18	49..	274	104	10	33
1942	Kimball	73	109	18	3	208..	264	72..	216	124	7	10..	77	33		2
13558	Knox	1028	1864	81	26	930..	1751	1739..	1871	2106	79	41..	1441	1257	66	65
73793	Lancaster	2566	6685	445	264	4143..	7677	5597..	7428	8540	400	85..	5754	3240	479	71
15084	Lincoln	690	1129	400	60	910..	1594	990..	1541	1382	80	179..	965	687	44	115
1521	Logan	97	153	17	6	110..	207	81..	140	155	10	8..	71	70	6	3
2188	Loup	131	114	59	7	148..	283	116..	248	170	10	32..	183	96	1	26
19101	Madison	1181	1720	56	37	1016..	1749	1763..	2137	1878	40	14..	1512	1233	37	13
2470	McPherson	114	180	45	8	232..	279	137..	234	165	11	18..	78	33	2	5
10379	Merrick	526	951	40	112	605..	1298	966..	1133	1081	186	15..	948	760	113	7
4584	Morrill	227	392	75	25	409..	508	294..								
8826	Nance	630	716	22	27	536..	1122	659..	1082	920	45	6..	807	639	27	3
13005	Nemaha	672	1374	58	45	812..	1587	1187..	1583	1674	49	41..	1408	1140	80	33
13019	Nuckolls	738	1312	78	39	852..	1656	1017..	1519	1523	35	11..	1231	964	31	6
19623	Otoe	922	1946	71	51	1054..	1870	2200..	2243	2411	71	18..	1040	1700	75	29
10582	Pawnee	500	958	53	51	711..	1334	990..	1408	1115	80	9..	1349	810	83	19
2570	Perkins	101	254	32	8	190..	357	124..	254	265	1	3..	134	156	5	1
10151	Phelps	254	974	76	33	1072..	1687	643..	1445	1238	116	29..	933	906	213	20
10122	Pierce	604	948	15	17	461..	804	1162..	1067	1035	27	9..	769	713	9	18
19000	Platte	684	2015	45	32	1227..	1622	2228..	1584	2487	67	8..	1047	2159	26	13
10521	Polk	485	936	40	140	785..	1545	798..	1171	1394	165	43..	902	930	185	28
11056	Red Willow	256	927	191	26	782..	1155	782..	1242	1317	53	78..	914	642	36	41
17448	Richardson	965	1980	107	53	1350..	2081	1854..	2123	2259	71	17..	1855	1731	76	29
3627	Rock	231	280	56	15	289..	465	171..	469	334	14	15..	390	185	13	7
17866	Saline	1185	1942	58	69	739..	1816	2217..	2048	2249	83	16..	1782	1512	80	30
9274	Sarpy	404	857	71	23	440..	761	1051..	912	1090	41	26..	722	796	26	23
21179	Saunders	864	2090	90	59	1510..	2374	2268..	2309	2679	91	32..	1850	1980	121	28
8855	Scotts Bluff	314	495	230	32	657..	915	395..	789	549	30	73..	508	232	718	61
15855	Seward	789	1575	22	27	968..	1767	1751..	1930	2029	41	3..	1616	1484	54	4
7829	Sheridan	377	630	123	31	612..	795	567..	709	733	34	43..	467	383	17	20
8778	Sherman	455	675	124	20	595..	875	693..	776	925	23	50..	620	673	19	47
5599	Sioux	151	375	63	8	396..	621	211..	516	464	24	11..	309	157	8	5
7542	Stanton	471	725	16	5	297..	671	734..	792	823	9	6..	593	641	17	3
14775	Thayer	703	1491	87	50	964..	1504	1568..	1714	1703	53	23..	1494	1177	89	30
1191	Thomas	86	172	22	3	104..	131	73..	95	130	2	7..	55	60	2	1
8704	Thurston	436	534	63	12	492..	748	677..	895	734	15	13..	403	501	9	10
9480	Valley	552	789	121	44	561..	1209	703..	1040	1045	51	10..	799	676	53	9
12788	Washington	599	1182	91	20	900..	1252	1241..	1592	1460	39	40..	1214	1087	29	45
10397	Wayne	610	808	20	9	725..	1041	917..	1007	1055	23	10..	965	739	15	12
13008	Webster	506	1163	79	71	915..	1512	1055..	1409	1364	119	17..	1107	959	193	12
2292	Wheeler	71	194	38	4	179..	225	100..	256	252	10	19..	154	111	3	12
18721	York	902	1886	86	92	1086..	2471	1421..	2209	2042	124	9..	1977	1379	154	9
	Total	54029	109008	10174	5419	72614..	120070	107780	126997	131099	5179	3524..	97858	84885	5106	2999
	Plurality	36334				15310			4102				12973			
	Per cent	21.75	43.66	4.09	1.87	29.13..	51.89	45.44..	47.60	49.13	1.97	1.20..	51.26	44.46	2.67	1.61
	Total vote		249308				237133			266799				198848		

FOR REPRESENTATIVES IN CONGRESS, 1912.

1. Counties of Cass, Johnson, Laucaster, Nemaha, Otoe, Pawnee and Richardson.

J. A. Maguire, Dem.........................17,416
P. I. Clark, Rep...........................15,706
C. R. Oyler, Soc..............................863
M. A. Carraher, Pro...........................481

2. Counties of Douglas, Sarpy and Washington.

C. O. Lobeck, Dem..........................16,069
H. H. Baldridge, Rep.......................15,662
J. N. Carter, Soc...........................2,146

3. Counties of Antelope, Boone, Burt, Cedar, Colfax, Cuming, Dakota, Dixon, Dodge, Knox, Madison, Merrick, Nance, Pierce, Platte, Stanton, Thurston and Wayne.

D. V. Stephens, Dem........................26,229
J. C. Cook, Rep............................21,637
N. H. Nye, Soc................................912
W. D. Gibson, Pro.............................537

4. Counties of Butler, Fillmore, Gage, Hamilton, Jefferson, Polk, Saline, Saunders, Seward, Thayer and York.

Charles H. Sloan, Rep......................22,293
C. M. Skiles, Dem..........................18,279
E. E. Olmsted, Soc............................950
L. A. White, Pro.............................557

5. Counties of Adams, Chase, Clay, Dundy, Franklin, Frontier, Furnas, Gosper, Hull, Harlan, Hayes, Hitchcock, Kearney, Nuckolls, Perkins, Phelps, Red Willow and Webster.

S. R. Barton, Rep.................................18,818
R. D. Sutherland, Dem.........................17,522
W. C. Elliott, Soc...............................1,421
G. W. Porter, Pro................................610

6. Counties of Banner, Blaine, Box Butte, Brown, Buffalo, Cheyenne, Cherry, Custer, Dawes, Dawson, Deuel, Garfield, Grant, Greeley, Holt, Hooper, Howard, Keith, Keyapaha, Kimball, Lincoln, Logan, Loup, McPherson, Rock, Scotts Bluff, Sheridan, Sherman, Sioux, Thomas, Valley and Wheeler.

Moses J. Kinkaid, Rep.........................24,766
W. J. Taylor, Dem.............................18,530
F. J. Warren, Soc...............................3,788
F. L. Armstrong, Prog.........................4,997

LEGISLATURE. Senate.House J.B.

Democrats 15   54   69
Republicans 18   46   64

STATE OFFICERS.

Governor—John H. Morehead, Dem.
Lieutenant-Governor—S. R. McKelvie, Rep.-Prog.
Secretary of State—Addison Wait, Rep.-Prog.
Auditor—W. B. Howard, Rep.-Prog.
Treasurer—W. A. George, Rep.-Prog.
Attorney-General—G. G. Martin, Rep.-Prog.

NEVADA (Population in 1910, 81,875).

COUNTIES. (15)	PRESIDENT 1912				GOV. 1910	
Population in 1910.	Rep. Taft	Dem. Wilson	Soc. Debs	Prog. Roosevelt	Rep. Oddie	Dem.Soc. D'k'son tiegan
2811 Churchill...	157	357	212	505..	377	332 119
3321 Clark.......	114	393	108	204..	354 4	19 53
1805 Douglas.....	80	144	22	172..	217	233 10
4133 Elko........	403	852	259	514..	854	899 77
9895 Esmeralda...	246	713	379	246..	1543	1344 154
1830 Eureka......	65	226	20	123..	282	120 8
6825 Humboldt...	208	719	339	596..	783	911 159
1786 Lander......	89	197	53	200..	344	239 49
3489 Lincoln....	100	275	28	144..	287	284 29
3558 Lyon.......	135	437	299	354..	479	352 78
Mineral.....	59	219	131	146..	..	..
7513 Nye........	346	861	714	419..	1333	607 221
3049 Ormsby......	160	294	149	65..	420 3	8 27
3045 Storey......	196	400	82	212..	457	419 30
17434 Washoe.....	646	1446	306	1149..	1953	1394 149
7441 White Pine.	259	515	302	431..	728	814 229
Total...	3126	7986	3313	5620..	10411	8796 1392
Plurality .		2396			1615	
Per cent..	16.13	40.36	16.93	26.59..	50.54	42.70 6.76
Total vote		20115		..	20599	

FOR REPRESENTATIVES IN CONGRESS. 1912.

E. E. Roberts, Rep..............................7,383
Clay Tallman, Dem.............................7,399

LEGISLATURE. Senate.House. J.B.

Republicans 8   19   27
Democrats 12   32   44
Socialists 1   1   2
Progressives 0   1   1

STATE OFFICERS.

Governor—Tasker L. Oddie, Rep.
Lieutenant-Governor—Gilbert C. Ross, Dem.
Secretary of State—George Brodigan, Dem.
Treasurer—William McMillan, Rep.
Comptroller—Jake Eggers, Rep.
Attorney-General—George B. Thatcher, Dem.

NEW HAMPSHIRE (Population in 1910, 430,572).

COUNTIES. (10)	PRESIDENT 1912				
Population in 1910.	Rep. Taft	Dem. Wilson	Prog. Roosevelt	Soc. Debs.	Pro. Chafin
21309 Belknap............	1741	1982	944	103	78
16316 Carroll	1574	1820	881	41	25
30659 Cheshire	2765	2114	1252	156	34
30753 Coos	1939	2299	1105	149	42
41652 Grafton	3520	3752	2105	93	69
2672 Hillsborough	8007	8909	4586	894	93
155335 Merrimack	4632	4741	2119	239	92
52188 Rockingham	4291	4306	2465	207	61
38861 Strafford.........	2962	3465	1265	140	31
19637 Sullivan..........	1677	1523	1014	84	19
Total	32927	34724	17794	1981	535
Plurality		1797			
Per cent.......	37.46	39.51	20.17	2.25	.61
Total vote		87961			

FOR REPRESENTATIVES IN CONGRESS, 1912.

1. The counties of Belknap, Carroll, Rockingham, Strafford, Hillsborough (part) and Merrimack (part).

Cyrus A. Sulloway, Rep......................17,363
Eugene E. Reed, Dem.........................18,888
Samuel O. Titus, Prog........................4,307
Michael B. Roth, Soc..........................856
John H. Bliss, Pro.............................207

2. The counties of Cheshire, Coos, Grafton, Sullivan, Hillsborough (part) and Merrimack (part).

Frank D. Currier, Rep........................17,961
Raymond B. Stevens, Dem....................21,794
Horace W. Spokensfield, Soc...................724
John C. Berry, Pro.............................174

LEGISLATURE. Senate.House. J.B.

Republican 10   207   217
Democrats 14   195   209

STATE OFFICERS.

Governor—Samuel D. Felker, Dem.
Secretary—E. N. Pearson.
Treasurer—George E. Farrand, Rep.
Attorney-General—James P. Tuttle, Rep.

NEW JERSEY (Population in 1910, 2,537,167).

COUNTIES. (21)	GOVERNOR 1913				PRESIDENT 1912		
Population in 1910.	Dem. Fielder.	Rep. Stokes.	Prog. Colby.	Rep. Taft.	Prog. Roosevelt.	Dem. Wilson.	
71894 Atlantic.....	3636	7496	828..	4419	4244	4881	
138002 Bergen.....	11301	8087	2999..	5078	8576	9965	
66565 Burlington..	5054	5811	1329..	3294	3931	5501	
142029 Camden....	9081	13184	2376..	7892	8706	10781	
19745 Cape May...	1745	1947	480..	907	1845	2119	
55153 Cumberland	3567	3115	1798..	1893	4091	3844	
512886 Essex.....	25310	24749	11432..	16877	33934	26242	
37308 Gloucester..	3088	3089	1199..	1853	3037	3322	
537251 Hudson.....	42041	16082	4473..	8740	24107	40419	
33569 Hunterdon..	3786	2648	373..	1908	1468	4100	
125657 Mercer.....	7211	9245	1498..	5603	6892	7764	
114436 Middlesex..	8946	6492	1220..	4730	5055	8177	
94734 Monmouth..	8069	6186	1440..	3674	6293	7849	
74704 Morris,.....	5408	4568	1773..	3822	4435	5624	
21318 Ocean......	1683	1752	907..	918	2053	1857	
215902 Passaic.....	9852	10367	2035..	5328	11658	10703	
26999 Salem.....	2508	2141	539..	1796	1862	2735	
38820 Somerset...	2925	2679	691..	2044	2952	3195	
26781 Sussex.....	2628	1392	296..	859	1505	2851	
140197 Union.....	9088	7383	3203..	5415	8418	9686	
43187 Warren.....	3941	1975	533..	1409	2036	4092	
Total ...173148	140298	41132..	88834	145409	178282		
Plurality. 32850					32873		
Per cent.. 42.83	35.53	10.42..	20.53	33.61	41.21		
Total vote. 394867			..		432522		

For governor in 1913: Butterworth, Soc. Lab., 2,460; Dwyer, Ind., 875; Reilly, Soc., 13,977; Mason, Pro.. 3,427. For president in 1912: Debs, Soc., 15,900; Chafin, Pro., 2,875.

FOR REPRESENTATIVES IN CONGRESS, 1912.

1. Counties of Camden, Gloucester and Salem.
William J. Browning, Rep....................14,472
D. Stewart Craven, Dem......................13,170
Frank B. Jess, Prog............................5,891

2. Counties of Cape May, Cumberland, Atlantic and Burlington.
J. Thompson Baker, Dem......................16,120
John J. Gardner, Rep.........................12,330
Francis D. Potter, Prog........................7,384

3. Counties of Middlesex, Monmouth and Ocean.
Thomas J. Scully, Dem........................20,596
Benjamin F. S. Brown, Prog.-Rep...............14,363

4. Counties of Hunterdon, Somerset and Mercer.
Allan B. Walsh, Dem..........................13,222
William E. Blackman, Rep......................8,607
John E. Gill, Prog..............................6,685

5. Counties of Union and Morris.
William E. Tuttle, Jr., Dem...................13,920
William N. Runyon, Rep.......................10,085
Charles W. Ennis, Prog.........................5,557

6. Counties of Bergen, Sussex, Warren and Passaic (part).
Lewis J. Martin, Dem.........................15,216
Stephen W. McClave, Rep......................8,373
Leveritt H. Sage, Prog.........................7,097

To fill vacancy in 62d congress:
Archibald C. Hart, Wilson Dem...............17,197
Albin Smith, Rep.............................15,325

Ernest A. Shay, Prog.   11,287
David J. Hanvey, Dem 3,369
7. Part of Passaic.county.
Robert G Bremner, Dem   9,990
Albin Smith, Rep   6,666
Henry Marelli, Prog   4,746
8. Essex (part) and Hudson (part).
Eugene F Kinkead, Dem   14,058
Harold Bouton, Prog ..   9,527
Robert S. Tew, Rep...... 2,269
9. Essex (part)
Walter I. McCoy, Dem. 10.196
Herman B. Walker, Prog   6,406
Richard Wayne Parker, Rep 5,813
10. Essex (part).
Edward W. Townsend, Dem   ..   10,854
William Fellowes Morgan, Prog   7,847
W. I. Lincoln Adams, Rep 7,111
11. Hudson (part).
John J. Eagan, Dem   14,208
Harlan Besson, Prog   7,018
James M Reilly, Rep....   1,429
12 Hudson (part).
James A Hamill, Dem .   . 17,980
George L Record, Rep -Prog 8,089

LEGISLATURE	Senate	House	J B
Democrats . . .	11	37	43
Republicans . . .	10	23	33

STATE OFFICERS.
Governor—James F Fielder, Dem.
Secretary of State—David V. Crater, Dem
Treasurer—Edward E Grosscup, Dem
Comptroller—Edward I Edwards, Dem

NEW MEXICO (Population in 1910, 327,396).

COUNTIES.	PRESIDENT 1912					GOV 1911
Population (2b) in 1910	Dem. Wilson	Rep. Taft	Prog Roosevelt	Soc Debs	Rep BursumMcDonald	Dem
23606 Bernalillo...	1199	1002	1394	169 . 1826	3052
16850 Chaves..	1339	465	396	347 . 645	1994
16460 Colfax.	.. 1182	1096	564	77 . 1601	1940
11443 Curry ..	. 634	123	253	194 . 839	988
12893 Dona Ana ..	. 895	912	241	16 . 1284	1394
12400 Eddy ..	. 936	145	371	166 . 880	1460

	Wilson	Taft	Roosev't	Debs	BursumMcDonald
14813 Grant. ,	. 1130	439	416	136. . 1095	1535
10327 Guadalupe .	. 781	651	154	96. . 1018	1035
7822 Lincoln	461	452	109	107. . 671	801
2914 Luna.. , ...	461	81	194	82 . 265	632
12063 McKinley ..	224	264	237	7 . 465	409
12611 Mora...	... 1002	1022	364	44 . 1449	1259
7069 Otero. . .	420	220	201	165 . 518	692
14912 Quay	884	351	358	358 . 816	1167
16719 Rio Arriba .	1004	1549	101	5 . 1941	1189
12064 Roosevelt ...	599	107	209	249 . 291	837
8579 Sandoval	. 126	211	583	— . 517	759
8504 San Juan ..	. 493	203	229	141 . 433	823
22930 San Miguel..	1740	2479	207	27 . 2919	2153
14770 Santa Fe....	. 1012	1432	590	64 . 1770	1418
5336 Sierra .	352	176	80	11 . 516	576
14761 Socorro .	1078	960	269	20 . 2085	1414
12008 Taos....	765	855	277	21 . 1289	1013
10119 Torrance .	. 890	530	232	172 . 883	844
11404 Union	1119	815	449	228 . 1288	1379
13320 Valencia ...	231	1265	111	30 . 1775	363
Total .	20477	17733	8347	2859 . 28019	31036
Plurality	2704					3017
Per cent .	41 38 35.93	16 91 5 79.	46 05 51.01
Total vote. .		49376				60842

FOR REPRESENTATIVES IN CONGRESS, 1912
H. B. Fergusson, Dem 22,139
Nathan Jaffa, Rep 17,900
Marcos C de Baca, Prog 5,883
Andrew Eggum, Soc.......... 2,644

LEGISLATURE	Senate	House.	J B.
Republicans . .	16	28	44
Progressives .	1	4	5
Democrats .	7	17	24

STATE OFFICERS.
Governor—William C. McDonald, Dem.
Lieutenant-Governor—E C. de Baca, Dem.
Secretary of State—Antonio Lucero, Dem.
Treasurer—Owen N Marron, Dem.
Attorney-General—Frank W. Clancy, Rep.
Auditor—William G Sargent, Rep
Commissioner of Public Lands—Robert P. Ervien, Rep.
Superintendent of Public Instruction—Alvan N. White, Dem.
Librarian—Mrs. Lola C. Armijo, Rep.

NEW YORK (Population in 1910, 9,113,279).

COUNTIES (61)	PRESIDENT 1912							PRESIDENT 1908				
Population in 1910.	Dem. Wilson	Rep. Taft	Soc Debs	Pro Chafin	Prog Roosevelt	S L. Reimer	Rep Taft	Dem Bryan	Ind. Hisgen	Soc Debs	Pro Chafin	S L. Gillhaus
173866 Albany......	17285	20416	625	197	4487	50	24763	18782	358	206	179	39
41412 Allegany	2777	3668	283	449	2664	23	7504	3390	51	46	597	21
78809 Broome	6530	7949	354	794	2586	31	10705	6671	102	99	824	7
65919 Cattaraugus ..	4886	4820	605	537	3487	25	9320	6096	79	281	571	24
67106 Cayuga. .	4691	5788	526	291	2428	53	9699	5789	79	545	401	61
105126 Chautauqua ..	4737	7899	1353	947	6577	112 .	15739	6158	81	983	947	72
54662 Chemung .	6308	3217	410	494	2733	23 .	7410	5906	196	80	265	35
35575 Chenango ..	3341	4042	98	360	1609	9 .	5049	3772	50	67	485	19
48230 Clinton .	3322	3903	52	214	1200	22 .	5474	3866	51	54	389	12
43658 Columbia ..	4599	3740	76	89	1318	15 .	5726	5097	122	16	138	10
29249 Cortland ..	2283	2958	69	416	1629	12 .	5090	2815	31	12	421	4
45575 Delaware..	4511	4731	327	253	1895	11 .	7342	4641	57	21	386	8
87661 Dutchess	8845	8910	292	282	2126	25 .	11162	8961	223	73	358	28
528985 Erie	35518	19182	4776	680	26353	597 .	52182	45185	249	1234	563	247
33458 Essex ..	2070	3126	68	77	1720	12 .	5167	2033	94	60	114	11
45717 Franklin ..	2706	3930	73	297	1905	17 .	5999	2935	58	21	307	35
44534 Fulton ..	2550	3741	1043	270	2173	69 .	6794	3508	188	545	408	99
37615 Genesee .	2056	3341	81	223	2061	10 .	6794	3171	93	14	222	12
30214 Greene	3647	2711	92	194	818	7 .	4191	3711	72	63	265	11
4373 Hamilton .	492	454	7	18	163	— .	632	586	2	1	4	2
56356 Herkimer ..	5120	4685	458	163	3128	42 .	8202	5918	139	156	243	24
80297 Jefferson ..	6054	6692	600	645	3603	37 .	11477	6694	171	436	974	61
1634351 Kings	107748	51239	11459	476	71173	568 .	119701	96756	10448	8422	530	625
24849 Lewis ..	2338	2064	31	139	1512	8 .	4159	2910	13	13	155	5
38037 Livingston ..	3201	3726	51	189	1786	6 .	5700	3507	29	14	224	8
39289 Madison ..	3160	3490	288	245	2709	31 .	6727	3637	46	141	410	17
283212 Monroe....	17363	16876	2043	704	14919	266 .	33250	23764	384	1521	675	115
57587 Montgomery .	4507	6040	408	121	1894	28 .	7571	5254	180	58	138	27
83930 Nassau ..	7073	4608	149	141	4563	10 .	9797	4883	613	86	135	21
2762522 New York. .	166157	53107	18124	352	98985	930 .	154958	160261	14125	15599	507	1162
92036 Niagara .	7647	5654	762	426	4256	58 .	11145	8574	52	95	455	35
154157 Oneida .	12182	11245	1266	454	8532	196 .	19346	14968	210	250	571	92
200298 Onondaga ..	15827	16202	2490	602	10094	162 .	27299	16643	175	1116	1009	143
52286 Ontario	4728	4897	165	191	2278	13 .	8245	5484	29	82	190	10
115751 Orange	9102	10360	396	291	3609	69 .	14414	9938	358	194	334	88
32000 Orleans ..	2447	2983	71	267	1865	7 .	4885	2590	64	27	281	43
71664 Oswego.... ..	5256	5906	148	622	3950	25 .	10447	6172	51	76	1176	23

Population.	Wilson	Taft	Debs	Chafin	Roosevelt	Reimer	Taft	Bryan	Hisgen	Debs	Chafin	Gillhaus
47216 Otsego..	5538	5138	125	335	1696	9..	7459	3975	57	24	442	20
14065 Putnam	1321	1267	8	20	593	2..	2275	1389	52	4	43	5
284041 Queens	28044	9201	3326	108	14967	115..	19420	20342	2284	1751	118	93
122276 Rensselaer.	11683	10853	858	262	3735	98..	17196	13163	336	224	336	57
85999 Richmond.	8438	3035	325	145	3771	34..	6831	7401	523	193	104	32
46873 Rockland.	4241	2217	177	87	2302	18..	4857	3587	203	88	129	14
80005 St. Lawrence.	5329	6403	198	643	4221	26..	14151	5808	172	61	543	24
61917 Saratoga.	5292	6508	341	362	2319	27..	8705	6518	196	155	437	24
88235 Schenectady	5345	5229	3456	244	2640	111..	9944	7129	249	1170	296	131
23855 Schoharie...	3855	2389	31	273	580	4..	3393	3841	23	5	240	2
14004 Schuyler.	1416	1649	40	155	526	2..	2417	1995	8	16	133	1
26972 Seneca.	2573	2395	83	128	1081	8..	3749	3136	26	54	131	5
83302 Steuben	7506	6983	648	813	4109	26..	12353	8966	111	237	809	23
96188 Suffolk.	7876	5390	343	318	5484	35..	10889	5877	497	283	355	29
33808 Sullivan.	3884	3057	135	78	961	11..	4593	3911	40	55	139	8
25624 Tioga.	2400	2642	125	199	1052	13..	4247	2706	29	45	224	3
33647 Tompkins.	3272	2257	122	377	2098	25..	5090	3784	25	50	324	9
91769 Ulster.	8510	7482	150	406	2951	23..	10475	8560	204	107	366	28
32228 Warren	2802	3155	235	126	1698	21..	4800	3019	70	60	229	12
47778 Washington	3855	4305	195	255	2695	14..	7933	3593	109	110	323	19
50179 Wayne.	3394	4709	82	461	2574	8..	8008	4404	46	56	257	6
283055 Westchester..	21160	15938	1345	289	15051	23..	29438	18316	1237	923	376	102
31385 Wyoming..	2540	2836	61	212	2270	7..	5308	2885	42	28	246	8
18642 Yates.	1456	1793	83	115	905	12..	3275	1927	19	30	109	11

```
Total..............655475 455428 65581 19427 390021 4251..870070 667468 35817 36451 22367  3877
Plurality......200047                                               202602
Per cent.......41.28   28.68  3.97  1.22 24.57  .28..  53.43  40.98  2.14  1.88  1.30   .20
Total vote.......1587988                                       1638350
```

FOR REPRESENTATIVES IN CONGRESS, 1912.

1. Counties of Suffolk, Nassau and Queens (part).
Lathrop Brown, Dem........................16,563
Frederick C. Hicks, Rep....................11,690
W. Bourke Cockran, Prog....................11,229
H. W. Paine, Soc................................183

2. County of Queens (part).
Denis O'Leary, Dem.........................23,090
Frank E. Hopkins, Rep.......................6,941
Felix Fritsche, Prog..........................7,175
William Danmar, Soc..........................2,918
George Traeger, Ind...........................318

3. Part of Kings county (Brooklyn).
Frank E. Wilson, Dem.......................12,658
Frank F. Schulz, Rep.........................6,633
W. Prentice, Prog.............................4,918
John H. Jennings, Soc........................1,801
David Hunter, Ind.-Lab........................225

4. Part of Kings county (Brooklyn).
Harry H. Dale, Dem...........................9,059
William Lieberman, Rep.......................3,574
Robert J. Nolan, Soc.........................1,441
Samuel Greenblatt, Prog......................5,139
C. H. Palmateer, Pro...........................33

5. Part of Kings county (Brooklyn).
James P. Maher, Dem........................12,504
John S. Gaynor, Rep..........................7,677
Charles J. Ryan, Prog........................5,794
Hugh O'Malley, Soc............................922

6. Part of Kings county (Brooklyn).
Robert H. Roy, Dem.........................13,209
William M. Calder, Rep......................21,691
R. C. Hammond, Soc............................836
Jesse Tuller, Ind.-Lab.......................9,310
John Berry, Pro...............................113

7. Part of Kings county (Brooklyn).
John J. Fitzgerald, Dem....................16,082
John E. Brady, Rep...........................5,021
M. A. Fitzgerald, Ind.-Lab...................5,513
H. Crygier, Soc...............................522
John McKee, Pro...............................67

8. Part of Kings county (Brooklyn).
Daniel J. Griffin, Dem.....................17,403
Ernest P. Seelman, Rep......................6,027
P. L. Lachemacker, Soc.......................1,078
A. H. T. Banghef, Ind.-Lab...................8,867
Frank C. Foster, Pro.........................101

9. Part of Kings county (Brooklyn).
James H. O'Brien, Dem......................15,903
Oscar W. Swift, Rep........................10,122
William Koenig, Soc.........................2,027
John F. Kennedy, Prog.......................10,372

10. Part of Kings county (Brooklyn).
Herman A. Metz, Dem..........................7,459
R. L. Haskell, Rep...........................5,174

Barnet Wolf, Soc.............................1,785
J. L. Holtzmann, Prog.......................5,889

11. County of Richmond (Staten island) and part of lower New York city.
Daniel J. Riordan, Dem.....................15,417
William G. Rose, Rep........................4,078
John H. W. Nagle, Soc.........................437
William W. Mills, Prog......................5,570

12. Part of New York city (New York county).
Henry M. Goldfogle, Dem.....................4,592
Alexander Wolf, Rep...........................839
Meyer London, Soc...........................3,646
H. Moskowitz, Prog..........................2,602

13. Part of New York city (New York county).
Timothy D. Sullivan, Dem....................5,677
John G. B. Rinehart, Rep....................1,151
Joshua Wanhope, Soc...........................799
S. S. Rotter, Prog..........................3,615

14. Part of New York city (New York county).
Jefferson M. Levy, Dem......................8,950
E. C. Kindelberger, Rep.....................3,468
Marie MacDonald, Soc..........................958
Abraham H. Goodman, Prog....................4,407

15. Part of New York city (New York county).
Michael F. Conry, Dem......................16,791
Francis A. O'Neil, Rep......................4,721
John Mullen, Soc..............................632
James H. Hickey, Prog.......................4,791
F. O. Lacey, Ind.-Lab........................232

16. Part of New York city (New York county).
Peter J. Dooling, Dem......................15,036
Francis C. Dale, Rep........................5,929
Thomas O'Byrne, Soc..........................681
Timothy Healy, Prog.........................5,019
Charles E. Manierre, Pro......................39

17. Part of New York city (New York county).
John F. Carew, Dem.........................12,350
Ogden L. Mills, Rep.........................4,891
John A. Wall, Soc...........................1,074
L. Bates, Jr., Prog.........................5,516

18. Part of New York city (New York county).
Thomas G. Patten, Dem......................13,704
S. Walter Kaufman, Rep......................4,943
A. Lee, Soc.................................2,085
Amos R. E. Pinchot, Prog....................6,644

19. Part of New York city (New York county).
Franklin Leonard, Jr., Dem.................13,584
Walter M. Chandler, Prog...................13,987
Alexander Brough, Rep.......................7,104
Jeremiah C. Trost, Soc.......................873

20. Part of New York city (New York county).
Francis B. Harrison, Dem....................5,221
Abram Goodman, Rep..........................1,596
N. Aleinikoff, Soc............................996
Julius H. Reiter, Prog......................4,694

21. Part of New York city (New York county).
Henry George, Jr., Dem...................13,189
Martin C. Ansorge, Rep................... 5,265
M. B. Bartholomew, Soc................... 1,164
Jerome F. Reilly, Prog................... 8,384

22. Part of New York city (New York county).
Henry F. Bruckner, Dem...................15,886
Rufus P. Johnston, Rep................... 6,098
Charles Gall, Soc....................... 1,835
Irving M. Crane, Prog................... 9,462

23. Part of New York city (New York county).
Joseph A. Goulden, Dem..................19,320
Peter Wynde, Rep....................... 8,779
Fred Pavlitsch, Soc..................... 2,351
E. J. L. Raldiris, Prog.................13,150

24. Part of New York city (New York and West-
chester counties).
Woodson R. Oglesby, Dem.................17,681
Barton E. Kingman, Rep................. 8,219
Allen L. Benson, Soc................... 1,767
Alfred E. Smith, Prog..................12,496

25. Counties of Rockland and Westchester (part).
Benjamin I. Taylor, Dem.................15,870
James W. Husted, Rep...................12,522
Herman Kobbe, Soc....................... 785
John C. Bucher, Prog................... 8,559

26. Counties of Orange, Putnam and Dutchess.
John K. Sague, Dem.....................20,191
Edmund Platt, Rep......................20,618
A. B. Gray, Prog....................... 4,418
H. Schefer, Soc......................... 468

27. Counties of Sullivan, Ulster, Greene, Columbia
and Schoharie.
George McLellan, Dem...................23,743
Charles B. Ward, Rep...................19,125
H. Manning, Prog....................... 4,779
Platt N. Chase, Pro.................... 1,061

28. County of Albany and part of city of Troy, in
Rensselaer county.
Peter G. Ten Eyck, Dem.................22,193
Daniel H. Prior, Rep...................27,076
J. F. McLaughlin, Prog................. 4,918
F. L. Arland, Soc....................... 787

29. Counties of Rensselaer (part), Washington, Sar-
atoga and Warren.
Milton K. Huppuch, Dem.................18,170
James S. Parker, Rep...................22,348
John Q. Reynolds, Soc.................. 1,225
F. E. Draper, Jr., Prog................ 8,163

30. Counties of Schenectady, Montgomery, Fulton
and Hamilton.
R. E. L. Reynolds, Dem.................13,881
Samuel Wallin, Rep.....................13,894
George R. Lunn, Soc.................... 9,468
E. E. Hale, Prog....................... 4,721

31. Counties of Essex, Clinton, Franklin and St.
Lawrence.
Edwin A. Merritt, Jr., Rep.............18,453
Dennis B. Lucey, Dem...................12,995
John B. Burnham, Prog.................. 7,971

32. Counties of Jefferson, Lewis, Oswego and Mad-
ison.
Robert E. Gregg, Dem...................15,830
Luther W. Mott, Rep....................20,492
Oliver Curtis, Soc..................... 1,034
William Kelley, Prog................... 8,926

33. Counties of Oneida and Herkimer.
Charles A. Talcott, Dem................17,855
Homer P. Snyder, Rep...................16,709
A. L. Byron-Curtis, Soc................ 1,679
Benjamin T. Gilbert, Prog..............10,042

34. Counties of Otsego, Delaware, Broome and
Chenango.
James J. Bayard, Jr., Dem..............20,272
George W. Fairchild, Rep...............22,972
F. DeWitt Reese, Pro................... 1,647
Jared C. Estelow, Prog................. 5,572

35. Counties of Onondaga and Cortland.
John R. Clancy, Dem....................18,009
Michael E. Driscoll, Rep...............17,874
Fred Sander, Soc....................... 2,473
G. H. Stilwell, Prog...................11,626

36. Counties of Cayuga, Wayne, Seneca, Yates and
Ontario.
Richard C. S. Drummond, Dem............17,900

Sereno E. Payne, Rep...................20,604
J. J. Tillapaugh, Pro.................. 1,127
Wilson M. Gould, Prog.................. 8,151

37. Counties of Tompkins, Tioga, Chemung, Schuy-
ler and Steuben.
Edwin S. Underhill, Dem................19,515
Thomas F. Fennell, Rep.................18,336
Martin A. Tuttle, Pro.................. 1,870
W. W. Capron, Prog..................... 7,896

38. Monroe county (part).
George P. Decker, Dem..................14,440
Thomas B. Dunn, Rep....................15,776
K. P. Shedd, Soc....................... 2,657
A. E. Babcock, Prog....................11,202

39. Counties of Monroe (part), Orleans, Genesee,
Wyoming and Livingston.
Charles Ward, Dem......................15,629
H. G. Danforth, Rep....................17,881
J. E. O'Rourke, Soc.................... 926
P. A. Carpenter, Pro................... 1,023
Silas L. Strivings, Prog............... 9,023

40. Counties of Niagara and Erie (part).
Robert H. Gittins, Dem.................16,065
James S. Simmons, Rep..................14,450
James F. Ryan, Soc..................... 1,811
Frank C. Ferguson, Prog................ 9,369

41. County of Erie (part).
Charles B. Smith, Dem..................14,866
George A. Davis, Rep................... 9,573
Edward Simons, Jr., Soc................ 2,528
Henry Kobler, Prog..................... 9,471

42. County of Erie (part).
Daniel A. Driscoll, Dem................14,851
Willard H. Ticknor, Rep................ 8,613
Samuel Leary, Soc...................... 1,613
L. Bradley Dorr, Prog.................. 7,161

43. Counties of Allegany, Cattaraugus and Chau-
tauqua.
M. M. Wywell, Dem......................12,479
Charles M. Hamilton, Rep...............17,346
Fred T. Williams, Soc.................. 2,146
Samuel A. Carlson, Prog................11,709

LEGISLATURE.	Senate.	House.	J.B.
Democrats	30	48	78
Republicans	19	79	98
Progressives	2	19	21
Independents	..	4	4

STATE OFFICERS. (All democrats.)
Governor—Martin H. Glynn.
Lieutenant-Governor—Robert F. Wagner.
Secretary of State—Mitchell May.
Comptroller—William Sohmer.
Attorney-General—Thomas Carmody.

NORTH CAROLINA (Population in 1910, 2,206,287).

Population in 1910	COUNTIES. (100)	Dem. Wilson	Rep. Taft	Prog. Roosevelt	Soc. Debs	Pro. Chafin
28712	Alamance............	2182	150	1637	10	—
11592	Alexander...........	852	523	497	—	—
7745	Alleghany...........	652	208	256	—	—
25465	Anson	1487	125	118	—	—
19074	Ashe................	1643	478	1241	1	—
217	Avery (new).........	217	138	960	2	—
30877	Beaufort............	1605	295	848	61	—
23059	Bertie..............	1571	43	61	—	—
18006	Bladen..............	1140	33	511	—	—
14432	Brunswick...........	777	280	456	—	—
49798	Buncombe............	2716	426	2385	101	—
17408	Burke...............	1365	48	1283	—	—
26240	Cabarrus............	1738	389	1584	—	—
20579	Caldwell............	1627	482	1167	11	—
5640	Camden..............	303	40	62	—	—
13776	Carteret............	1153	218	557	—	—
705	Caswell.............	705	154	45	—	—
27918	Catawba.............	2110	203	1872	—	3
22635	Chatham.............	1652	70	1346	2	—
14136	Cherokee............	905	734	477	—	—
11303	Chowan.............	963	60	77	—	—
8900	Clay................	372	17	387	—	—
29494	Cleveland...........	2851	81	945	—	—
28020	Columbus............	1938	155	892	—	—
25594	Craven..............	1819	79	190	—	—
35284	Cumberland..........	1678	235	870	10	—
7693	Currituck	622	6	8	—	—
4841	Dare................	397	238	80	—	—

Population		Wilson	Taft	Roosevelt	Debs	Chafin
29404	Davidson	2184	b1509	1143	10	12
13384	Davie	825	840	845	—	1
25442	Duplin	1757	33	1008	3	..
35276	Durham	2197	124	1204	1	..
33010	Edgecombe	1851	102	77	49	..
47311	Forsyth	3042	1689	1232	325	4
24832	Franklin	1856	71	346	1	..
37063	Gaston	2333	244	1279	46	22
10455	Gates	618	95	179	—	..
4749	Graham	416	261	223	—	..
25102	Granville	1561	192	843	—	..
13083	Greene	894	124	152	—	..
60497	Guilford	3830	460	1919	43	26
57646	Halifax	2300	42	135	—	..
22114	Harnett	1364	148	1035	5	1
21020	Haywood	2008	354	861	6	..
16262	Henderson	1092	801	380	2	..
15436	Hertford	742	61	105	—	..
	Hoke (new)	626	63	40	—	..
8840	Hyde	636	76	300	—	..
34315	Iredell	2328	392	1017	—	2
12906	Jackson	1210	315	729	5	..
41401	Johnston	2757	1335	1083	—	..
8721	Jones	655	35	125	—	..
11376	Lee	862	451	60	—	..
22763	Lenoir	1568	122	347	—	..
17182	Lincoln	1280	49	1066	3	12
12191	Macon	1020	134	841	—	..
20133	Madison	897	430	1820	—	..
17797	Martin	1251	229	34	—	..
13538	McDowell	1037	343	773	10	..
67081	Mecklenburg	3967	284	533	38	..
17245	Mitchell	386	203	718	—	..
14367	Montgomery	1012	144	845	—	..
17010	Moore	1167	252	678	17	..
33727	Nash	1802	172	576	42	..
32037	New Hanover	2021	140	107	—	..
22323	Northampton	1625	57	53	—	..
14125	Onslow	901	66	550	—	..
15004	Orange	997	172	821	4	..
9966	Pamlico	694	74	329	20	..
16693	Pasquotank	973	77	184	—	..
15471	Pender	907	19	268	—	..
11054	Perquimans	647	228	44	—	..
17558	Person	820	784	184	—	..
96340	Pitt	2303	347	433	3	..
27640	Polk	675	153	501	1	..
9191	Randolph	2955	370	1809	6	8
19673	Richmond	1319	82	174	3	..
51945	Robeson	2706	154	660	—	..
36442	Rockingham	1939	694	778	51	9
57621	Rowan	2748	280	1537	50	7
28385	Rutherford	2180	82	1553	7	..
28982	Sampson	1265	84	2520	—	..
15383	Scotland	551	9	75	—	..
19909	Stanly	1702	105	1548	—	..
20151	Stokes	1144	1450	210	22	1
29705	Surry	1919	2277	608	—	..
10403	Swain	765	230	858	—	..
37191	Transylvania	651	107	537	1	..
5219	Tyrrell	297	224	100	4	..
33277	Union	1786	92	457	19	..
19425	Vance	1204	168	234	—	..
63229	Wake	3906	282	1517	12	..
20366	Warren	987	112	46	—	..
11062	Washington	503	384	149	—	..
13556	Watauga	833	420	819	2	..
35698	Wayne	2293	95	1090	16	9
30282	Wilkes	1636	331	2571	—	..
28269	Wilson	1741	82	561	—	..
15428	Yadkin	713	791	599	—	..
12702	Yancey	1112	60	1036	—	..
	Total	144507	29139	69867	1025	117
	Plurality	75377				
	Per cent	59.24	11.94	28.35	.42	.05
	Total vote	244255				

FOR REPRESENTATIVES IN CONGRESS, 1912.

1. Counties of Beaufort, Camden, Chowan, Currituck, Dare, Gates, Hertford, Hyde, Martin, Pasquotank, Perquimans, Pitt, Tyrrell and Washington.
John H. Small, Dem 12,537
Marshall D. Leggett, Rep 202
2. Counties of Bertie, Edgecombe, Greene, Halifax, Lenoir, Northampton, Warren and Wilson.
Claude Kitchin, Dem 11,091
Thomas B. Brown, Rep 982
3. Counties of Carteret, Craven, Duplin, Jones, Onslow, Pamlico, Pender, Sampson and Wayne.
John M. Faison, Dem 11,624
James F. Kennedy, Rep 6,042

4. Counties of Chatham, Franklin, Johnston, Nash, Vance and Wake.
Edward W. Pou, Dem 13,906
John F. Mitchell, Rep 3,586
5. Counties of Alamance, Caswell, Durham, Forsyth, Granville, Guilford, Orange, Person, Rockingham, Stokes and Surry.
Charles M. Stedman, Dem 21,075
C. W. Curry, Rep 15,995
George R. Greene, Soc 469
6. Counties of Bladen, Brunswick, Columbus, Cumberland, Harnett, New Hanover and Robeson.
H. P. Godwin, Dem 13,023
Thomas A. Norment, Rep 381
7. Counties of Anson, Davidson, Davie, Hope, Lee, Montgomery, Moore, Randolph, Richmond, Scotland, Union, Wilkes and Yadkin.
Robert N. Page, Dem 17,873
R. Don Laws, Rep 12,449
8. Counties of Alexander, Alleghany, Ashe, Cabarrus, Caldwell, Iredell, Rowan, Stanly and Watauga.
Robert L. Doughton, Dem 15,180
George D. B. Reynolds, Rep 12,078
9. Counties of Avery, Burke, Catawba, Cleveland, Gaston, Lincoln, Madison, Mecklenburg, Mitchell and Yancey.
E. Y. Webb, Dem 17,072
D. B. Paul, Rep 2,228
J. A. Smith, Prog 7,969
10. Counties of Buncombe, Cherokee, Clay, Graham, Haywood, Henderson, Jackson, McDowell, Macon, Polk, Rutherford, Swain and Transylvania.
James M. Gudger, Jr., Dem 16,183
R. H. Staton, Rep 14,237

LEGISLATURE.

	Senate.	House.	J.B.
Democrats	47	104	151
Republicans	3	16	19

STATE OFFICERS. (All democrats.)

Governor—Locke Craig.
Lieutenant-Governor—E. L. Daughtridge.
Secretary—J. Bryan Grimes.
Auditor—W. P. Wood.
Treasurer—B. R. Lacy.
Attorney-General—T. W. Bickett.
Superintendent of Public Instruction—J. Y. Joyner.

NORTH DAKOTA (Population in 1910, 577,056).

COUNTIES.	PRESIDENT 1912					GOV.1910	
Population in 1910 (49)	Rep. Taft	Dem. Wilson	Prog. Roosevelt	Soc. Debs	Pro. Chafin	Rep. Johnson	Dem. Burke
5407 Adams	205	249	305	27	..	454	264
19066 Barnes	570	940	855	45	48..	1204	1432
12681 Benson	515	594	736	98	48..	846	988
10186 Billings	671	547	495	161	25..	1194	576
17295 Bottineau	700	825	625	401	47..	1313	1464
4668 Bowman	302	361	258	99	16..	393	360
Burke	264	308	207	320	21..	519	653
13087 Burleigh	720	609	552	92	16..	1282	1029
3935 Cass	1316	1814	1039	164	56..	2476	2794
15659 Cavalier	561	932	746	89	23..	1313	1043
9839 Dickey	494	723	354	69	12..	649	818
Divide(new)	404	375	459	160	15..	—	—
5302 Dunn	285	246	297	47	5..	469	328
4800 Eddy	199	376	290	34	11..	322	566
9786 Emmons	410	524	374	24	15..	789	709
5313 Foster	285	403	232	20	11..	474	567
27888 G'nd Forks	955	1492	1327	180	46..	1996	2515
6274 Griggs	144	434	314	65	58..	444	655
6557 Hettinger	442	381	248	47	14..		
5962 Kidder	522	218	210	65	19..	480	353
10724 LaMoure	436	588	419	65	15..	799	1023
6168 Logan	269	146	225	30	4..	501	260
17627 McHenry	589	959	672	246	29..	1367	1557
7251 McIntosh	262	125	607	25	4..	524	430
5720 McKenzie	285	206	228	219	10..	1367	1551
14378 McLean	505	583	526	325	31..	1085	907
4065 Mercer	147	142	389	53	6..	305	281
25389 Morton	1011	1017	1262	284	44..	1843	1346
18491 Mountrail	407	307	347	322	18..	1000	887
10140 Nelson	448	526	511	178	58..	870	727
3577 Oliver	131	139	178	116	14..	349	258
14749 Pembina	615	975	807	35	53..	1340	1638
9740 Pierce	264	453	276	159	27..	555	926
15199 Ramsey	739	917	472	150	18..	1033	1306
10345 Ransom	495	490	540	50	51..	961	678
Renville	224	420	341	212	17..	748	955
19659 Richland	1034	1389	742	34	46..	1700	1750
9558 Rolette	339	396	322	184	27..	660	1065
9202 Sargent	695	641	377	93	19..	805	770

Population.	Taft	Wilson	Roosevelt	Debs	Chafin	Johnson	Burke
12504 Stark......	387	678	597	58	8..	812	763
8103 Sheridan..	306	170	447	26	7..	752	596
7616 Steele.....	237	253	444	55	16..	617	496
18189 Stutsman..	757	1100	706	68	39..	1092	1729
8963 Towner....	352	532	517	84	28..	742	828
12545 Traill.....	365	507	755	112	21..	963	739
19491 Walsh.....	586	1206	898	185	37..	1378	1889
42185 Ward.....	686	1071	1055	613	67..	1730	1770
11814 Wells.....	356	494	611	36	13..	805	1078
20249 Williams..	549	696	402	588	45..	1093	1898

Total...23090 29555 25726 6966 1243.. 44843 47615
Plurality. 3829 2772
Per cent..26.67 34.14 29.71 8.05 1.43.. 48.50 51.50
Total vote 86580 .. 92458

FOR REPRESENTATIVES IN CONGRESS, 1912.

1. Counties of Cass, Cavalier, Grand Forks, Nelson, Pembina, Ramsey, Ransom, Richland, Sargent, Steele, Traill, Towner and Walsh.

H. T. Helgesen, Rep...........................11,156
V. R. Lovell, Dem............................ 9,699
Leon Durocher, Soc........................... 1,310

2. Counties of Barnes, Benson, Bottineau, Burleigh, Dickey, Eddy, Emmons, Foster, Griggs, Kidder, LaMoure, Logan, McHenry, McIntosh, Pierce, Rolette, Sheridan, Stutsman and Wells.
George M. Young, Rep.......................16,912
J. A. Minckler, Dem......................... 7,426

3. Counties of Adams, Billings, Bowman, Burke, Divide, Dunn, Hettinger, Mercer, Morton, Mountrail, McKenzie, McLean, Oliver, Renville, Stark, Ward and Williams.
P. D. Norton, Rep...........................12,935
Halvor Halvorsen, Dem....................... 7,596

LEGISLATURE. Senate. House. J.B.
Republicans 45   103   148
Democrats 5   8   13

STATE OFFICERS. (All republicans.)
Governor—L. B. Hanna.
Lieutenant-Governor—A. T. Kraabel.
Secretary of State—Thomas Hall.
Treasurer—Gunder Olson.
Attorney-General—Andrew Miller.

OHIO (Population in 1910, 4,767,121).

COUNTIES. (88) Population in 1940.	PRESIDENT 1912 Dem. Wilson	Rep. Taft	Soc. Debs	Pro. Chafin	S.L. B'm'n	Prog. Roosevelt	GOVERNOR 1910 Dem. Harmon	Rep. Harding	Soc. Clifford	Pro. Thom'son	S.L. Malley	PRES.1908 Rep. Taft	Dem. Bryan
24755 Adams......	2279	1863	113	54	7	563..	3243	3214	39	54	1..	5432	3048
56580 Allen.......	5696	2638	977	140	27	2337..	5837	3825	700	63	60..	5841	7195
22975 Ashland....	3364	1017	274	64	16	1559..	3322	1836	191	47	9..	2804	3627
59547 Ashtabula..	3181	2214	1552	142	30	5189..	3197	4385	738	109	38..	8213	3572
47798 Athens.....	2393	3090	1056	106	27	2811..	3151	4054	646	104	50..	6449	3654
31246 Auglaize...	3726	1401	490	56	8	1025..	3672	1802	430	34	17..	3001	4822
76856 Belmont....	6412	5267	2781	433	64	1584..	6552	5388	1459	219	—..	8193	7750
24832 Brown.....	3451	1650	125	39	2	569..	3615	2175	—	—	—..	3608	4242
70271 Butler.....	7703	3431	3500	99	83	1787..	7546	3919	2523	68	132..	7320	9678
15761 Carroll....	1298	1090	108	128	8	1039..	1521	1990	66	57	1..	2517	1500
26351 Champaign..	2763	2392	172	62	6	1423..	2992	3109	79	45	6..	4158	3100
66435 Clark......	5217	6036	1909	246	46	3239..	7661	5565	783	104	43..	8917	6529
29551 Clermont...	3610	2543	269	51	9	1115..	4138	3043	141	42	5..	4137	4150
23680 Clinton....	2010	2916	146	72	5	841..	2394	3349	53	39	5..	4207	2464
76819 Columbiana..	4816	4601	1916	915	52	3811..	5295	5215	1640	485	51..	9828	6736
30121 Coshocton..	3465	1984	687	148	22	903..	3934	2922	464	83	7..	3606	4106
34036 Crawford...	4733	1432	588	93	22	1176.;	5450	2141	315	33	17..	3061	6006
637425 Cuyahoga..	43610	14176	10096	373	545	53824..	45197	26424	5312	265	519..	56344	39954
42383 Darke.....	5027	3107	293	595	9	1175..	5511	4105	162	154	7..	4951	6391
24498 Defiance...	2784	872	331	51	7	1459..	3288	1835	159	34	13..	2531	3754
27182 Delaware...	2934	2584	128	157	8	1510..	3472	3177	131	141	3..	4007	3330
38827 Erie.......	3504	2695	961	64	30	1675..	5471	3259	188	28	13..	5366	4983
39201 Fairfield...	5101	1672	188	138	6	1774..	5023	2806	297	85	12..	4023	5821
21744 Fayette....	2261	2186	141	69	3	844..	2385	2540	31	42	5..	3343	2451
221567 Franklin ...	20937	12791	5005	398	87	11737..	18171	15590	10714	349	424..	28914	23514
22914 Fulton....	1805	929	164	55	8	2304..	1972	2512	117	34	3..	3608	2181
25745 Gallia.....	1765	1353	170	48	5	2027..	2208	2914	100	36	8..	3914	2171
14670 Geauga....	873	579	77	24	7	1618..	978	1467	30	24	4..	2596	982
29733 Greene....	2107	3342	533	151	17	963..	2508	3672	199	53	13..	4902	2582
42716 Guernsey...	2726	3426	1342	180	45	1573..	3690	4022	840	77	17..	5310	3449
460732 Hamilton...	42909	42119	7542	384	167	16828..	52531	43253	13910	197	141..	63803	45429
37860 Hancock...	4309	2241	614	104	16	1757..	4534	3621	929	76	24..	4899	5420
30407 Hardin....	3912	2775	313	93	25	1296..	4240	3879	201	49	9..	4444	4164
19076 Harrison...	1714	1950	147	76	5	704..	1899	2164	62	32	2..	3069	1961
25519 Henry.....	2994	840	204	55	11	1166..	3205	1460	129	42	11..	2425	3817
28711 Highland...	3314	2757	185	80	7	1116..	3574	3394	49	88	5..	4149	3823
23650 Hocking...	2295	1354	368	46	14	935..	2562	2039	252	58	12..	2749	2464
17909 Holmes....	2429	465	123	29	4	581..	2559	579	42	20	3..	1252	3048
34036 Huron.....	3817	1707	354	71	22	2810..	4330	3516	150	44	10..	4930	4262
30791 Jackson...	2049	1860	612	53	20	1584..	2734	3202	220	42	8..	4449	3225
65423 Jefferson..	3171	4777	1193	205	27	2042..	4083	4058	784	65	33..	7310	4882
30181 Knox.....	3632	2530	396	96	14	1226..	3967	3464	369	68	15..	4318	4233
22927 Lake.....	1429	1155	299	29	15	2115..	1397	1750	143	25	2..	3635	1605
39488 Lawrence...	2042	2650	407	45	6	1937..	2668	3315	147	25	5..	5708	2654
55590 Licking....	4438	3385	605	110	23	1268..	7163	4885	709	80	11..	6756	7685
30084 Logan.....	2727	1977	229	84	9	2278..	2816	3223	158	42	4..	4756	5196
76037 Lorain....	4591	2226	1556	67	25	5156..	5890	4560	1073	46	40..	8990	5400
192728 Lucas....	13999	5622	5173	216	158	12442..	13178	11126	6976	127	253..	18715	16208
19002 Madison...	2172	2271	66	45	1	681..	2355	2654	33	39	3..	3051	2430
116151 Mahoning..	6838	5899	2422	312	57	5226..	7383	6351	894	210	38..	10760	9312
33871 Marion....	4024	3218	439	98	15	934..	4440	3481	554	76	24..	4175	4657
23598 Medina....	2108	685	302	55	10	2514..	2102	2099	220	34	14..	3427	2378
25594 Meigs.....	1738	2120	548	63	19	1353..	2677	2504	344	34	11..	4108	2225
27596 Mercer....	3591	1324	126	67	5	570..	3487	1382	92	51	7..	2148	4456
45047 Miami.....	4310	3615	1010	111	23	2056..	4882	4713	604	54	17..	6558	5389
24244 Monroe....	3199	1055	123	77	7	380..	2977	1257	47	56	3..	1974	3961
163763 Montgomery..	15544	10841	7079	250	88	6286..	18969	14535	3855	120	60..	20079	20566
16997 Morgan...	1933	1448	141	182	5	705..	1911	1940	50	80	6..	2445	1932
16315 Morrow...	1880	1240	102	132	7	1124..	2291	2082	55	91	2..	2600	2292
57483 Muskingum..	5376	4184	1015	221	20	3397..	7003	5396	1066	206	23..	8080	6576
18601 Noble.....	1842	1804	96	76	5	681..	2007	2199	28	59	5..	2707	2154

Population.	Wilson	Taft	Debs	Chafin	Reim'r	Roosevelt	Harmon	Hard'g	Clifford	Thompson	Malley	Taft	Bryan
22950 Ottawa	2728	791	104	23	8	957..	5130	1278	25	16	2..	2202	3329
27730 Paulding	2256	1542	153	53	2	1223..	2455	2730	73	28	8..	3049	2767
35896 Perry	3147	1739	806	104	36	2220..	3656	3331	680	71	23..	4304	3485
26158 Pickaway	3311	2282	82	68	5	569..	3706	2451	59	55	2..	3119	4007
15723 Pike	1691	1184	81	34	4	443..	2146	1539	45	26	—..	1798	2085
30307 Portage	2855	1162	681	101	5	2583..	3564	2739	373	66	19..	4129	3625
23334 Preble	2859	2135	177	76	1	910..	3002	2957	58	54	3..	3519	3247
29972 Putnam	4000	1000	144	69	15	1182..	4848	1832	83	45	6..	2483	4806
47367 Richland	5201	2389	925	97	28	2658..	5790	3440	548	104	—..	5361	4702
40039 Ross	4494	3600	464	122	16	1056..	5079	4199	270	106	18..	5432	5325
35171 Sandusky	4353	1576	446	77	18	2163..	4984	2875	181	32	20..	4079	5242
48463 Scioto	3608	3009	1222	168	28	2012..	4591	4076	571	57	21..	5790	4310
42121 Seneca	6083	2362	567	147	20	2032..	5686	2434	487	77	24..	4959	6138
24663 Shelby	3305	1613	245	52	9	678..	3578	1877	75	22	1..	2668	3859
122987 Stark	9908	6083	3606	309	71	6802..	11502	10056	2246	299	153..	11412	12286
108253 Summit	7796	3502	3436	378	117	7473..	9105	5657	1606	283	88..	10356	9990
52766 Trumbull	3547	2633	1640	161	38	8556..	3756	4694	1037	88	32..	6978	4476
67035 Tuscarawas	4978	3417	2177	105	70	1749..	6375	4903	1184	57	64..	6717	6775
24871 Union	2362	2051	121	59	5	1209..	2865	2794	84	31	1..	3567	2568
29119 Van Wert	3287	2490	209	60	10	1050..	3262	3470	132	26	—..	3869	3783
13096 Vinton	1228	952	206	15	8	581..	1395	1507	78	20	—..	1916	1499
24497 Warren	2101	2788	207	61	10	1100..	2314	2880	72	34	8..	4233	2656
45422 Washington	4637	3326	618	121	17	1222..	5160	4037	378	77	22..	5648	5771
38058 Wayne	4737	1674	350	137	14	2351..	5022	3206	193	86	13..	4388	5368
25198 Williams	2575	1145	219	81	15	2081..	3352	3063	98	55	6..	3625	3329
46330 Wood	4356	2020	473	133	21	3021..	5042	4530	304	91	18..	5504	5625
20760 Wyandot	2848	1409	93	22	4	854..	3154	1792	56	18	7..	2408	3858

Total	424834	278168	90144	11511	2630	229807..	477077	376700	60637	7139	2920..	572312	502721
Plurality	146666							100577					69591
Per cent	40.94	26.87	8.70	1.11	.25	22.19..	51.61	40.75	6.55	.77	.32..	50.36	44.23
Total vote			1037094					924463					1136525

For president in 1908 Chafin, Pro., received 11,402 votes; Debs, Soc., 33,795; Watson, Peo., 162; His- gen, Ind., 475; Gillhaus, Soc-Lab., 720.

FOR REPRESENTATIVES IN CONGRESS, 1912.

At Large—Robert Crosser, Dem..................423,311
Lawrence K. Langdon, Rep..................207,355
Harry D. Thomas, Soc..................91,201
Frank W. Stanton, Pro..................11,862
Randolph P. Walton, Prog..................192,799

1. Part of Hamilton county.
Stanley E. Bowdle, Dem..................22,230
Nicholas Longworth, Rep..................22,229
Lawrence A. Zitt, Soc..................2,853
Millard F. Andrew, Prog..................5,771

2. Part of Hamilton county.
Alfred G. Allen, Dem..................26,066
Otto J. Renner, Rep..................21,113
R. S. Moore, Soc..................3,820
William B. Hay, Prog..................4,940

3. Counties of Butler, Montgomery and Preble.
Warren E. Gard, Dem..................26,711
Bert B. Buckley, Rep..................15,339
Frederick Guy Strickland, Soc..................12,774
Jasper A. Huffman, Pro..................410
Alfred G. Pease, Prog..................6,976

4. Counties of Allen, Anglaize, Darke, Mercer and Shelby.
J. Henry Goeke, Dem..................21,512
John L. Cable, Rep..................10,267
Scott Wilkins, Soc..................2,132
W. Rollo Boehringer, Pro..................1,091
William E. Rudy, Prog..................4,993

5. Counties of Defiance, Henry, Paulding, Put- nam, Van Wert and Williams.
T. T. Ansberry, Dem..................20,091
Edward Staley, Rep..................10,177
George W. Kirk, Soc..................1,121

6. Counties of Brown, Clermont, Clinton, Greene, Highland and Warren.
D. K. Hempstead, Dem..................17,300
S. D. Fess, Rep..................18,090
G. D. Vanderyort, Soc..................1,384

7. Counties of Clark, Fayette, Madison, Miami and Pickaway.
J. D. Post, Dem..................19,301
R. M. Hughey, Rep..................18,595
Winfield S. Tibbets, Soc..................3,002
Gustavus P. Raup, Pro..................438

8. Counties of Champaign, Delaware, Hancock, Hardin, Logan and Union.
W. W. Durbin, Dem..................17,965
Frank B. Willis, Rep..................19,379
Arthur G. Parthener, Soc..................1,430
Lemuel G. Herbert, Prog..................5,429

9. Counties of Fulton, Lucas, Ottawa and Wood.
Isaac R. Sherwood, Dem..................26,528
Thomas C. Devine, Soc..................5,769
Holland C. Webster, Prog..................17,490

10. Counties of Adams, Gallia, Jackson, Lawrence, Pike and Scioto.
Charles M. Caldwell, Dem..................13,424
Robert M. Switzer, Rep..................13,606
William Miller, Soc..................2,851
William E. Pricer, Prog..................7,091

11. Counties of Athens, Fairfield, Hocking, Meigs, Perry, Ross and Vinton.
Horatio C. Claypool, Dem..................21,469
Albert Douglass, Rep..................18,729
Albert Smith, Soc..................3,519

12. County of Franklin.
Clement L. Brumbaugh, Dem..................24,340
Edward L. Taylor, Jr., Rep..................14,682
Jacob L. Bachman, Soc..................7,095
John R. Schmidt, Pro..................450

13. Counties of Crawford, Erie, Marion, Sandusky, Seneca and Wyandot.
John A. Key, Dem..................26,395
Miles H. McLaughlin, Rep..................13,021
George P. Maxwell, Soc..................3,272
Benjamin F. Sheidler, Prog..................6,779

14. Counties of Ashland, Huron, Knox, Lorain, Morrow and Richland.
William G. Sharp, Dem..................25,523
W. S. Kerr, Rep..................14,142
George Storck, Soc..................3,569

15. Counties of Guernsey, Morgan, Muskingum, Noble and Washington.
George White, Dem..................18,169
James Joyce, Rep..................14,678
F. L. Martin, Soc..................605
James T. Orr, Pro..................531
Howard E. Buker, Prog..................4,968

16. Counties of Belmont, Carroll, Harrison, Jeffer- son and Monroe.
William B. Francis, Dem..................16,570
David A. Hollingsworth, Rep..................15,781
Robert Carson, Soc..................3,953

17. Counties of Coshocton, Holmes, Licking, Tus- carawas and Wayne.
William A. Ashbrook, Dem..................25,453
Dan McCarton, Soc..................3,988
Albert L. Milner, Prog..................5,985

18. Counties of Columbiana, Mahoning and Stark.
John J. Whitacre, Dem..................23,936
Roscoe C. McCullogh, Rep..................23,350
George F. Lelansky, Soc..................7,617

19. Counties of Ashtabula, Geauga, Portage, Sum- mit and Trumbull.
Ellsworth R. Bathrick, Dem..................20,251
Hiram E. Starkey, Rep..................11,574

C. E. Shepitu, Soc............................ 7,865
Nathan Johnson, Pro......................... 804
W. S. Harris, Prog......................16,035
20. Counties of Lake, Medina and part of Cuyahoga.
William Gordon, Dem....................24,385
Paul Howland, Rep.....................12,733
John G. Willert, Soc......................5,240
Frank W. Woods, Prog..................18,194
21. Part of Cuyahoga county.
Robert J. Bulkeley, Dem...................20,742
Frederick L. Taft, Rep.................... 8,811
Fred C. Rupple, Soc....................... 5,059
Augustus R. Hattou, Prog................13,760

LEGISLATURE.	Senate.	House.	J.B.
Republicans	15	49	64
Democrats	19	70	89

STATE OFFICERS. (All democrats.)
Governor—James M. Cox.
Lieutenant-Governor—Hugh L. Nichols.
Secretary of State—Charles H. Graves.
Auditor—Vic Donahey.
Treasurer—John P. Brennan.
Attorney-General—Timothy S. Hogan.

OKLAHOMA (Population in 1910, 1,657,155).

Population in 1910	Counties (75)	PRESIDENT 1912 Dem. Wilson	Rep. Taft	Soc. Debs	Pro. Chafin	PRES.1908 Dem. Bryan	Rep. Taft
10535	Adair	916	850	147	11..	826	782
18138	Alfalfa	1179	1714	395	90..	1459	1732
18908	Atoka	1100	689	567	11..	784	757
13631	Beaver	926	1070	433	74..	1212	1902
19699	Beckham	1566	648	874	21..	1807	866
17960	Blaine	744	851	349	24..	1517	1588
29854	Bryan	2278	711	842	14..	2215	1044
35685	Caddo	2614	2413	995	55..	2964	2900
25601	Canadian	2047	1794	359	42..	2124	1831
25358	Carter	1860	652	608	11..	2181	1305
16778	Cherokee	1034	982	138	9..	915	1040
21862	Choctaw	1362	692	706	20..	1088	878
4553	Cimarron	342	263	96	12..	449	371
18843	Cleveland	1471	988	427	29..	1437	1092
15817	Coal	1109	571	574	..	906	722
41489	Comanche	1931	1320	599	26..	3481	2437
	Cotton (new)..	1083	587	278	19..	—	—
17404	Craig	1772	1391	112	10..	1578	1206
26223	Creek	1681	1902	918	48..	1417	1761
23251	Custer	1774	1693	503	28..	1721	1579
11469	Delaware	983	732	174	10..	974	625
14132	Dewey	1075	1086	769	23..	1075	1210
15875	Ellis	918	1373	465	37..	1290	1379
33050	Garfield	2353	2990	398	68..	2618	2924
26545	Garvin	2114	740	1053	15..	2301	1290
30909	Grady	2677	1121	753	19..	2826	1491
18760	Grant	1559	1729	270	103..	1866	1796
16449	Greer	1334	351	385	19..	2149	708
11328	Harmon	805	197	278	12..	—	—
5189	Harper	523	679	275	23..	746	876
18875	Haskell	1388	902	672	13..	1401	1139
24040	Hughes	1769	1228	984	20..	1649	1459
23237	Jackson	1819	588	650	85..	1905	635
17430	Jefferson	1118	361	605	13..	1435	604
16734	Johnson	1289	506	732	17..	1274	658
26999	Kay	2380	2508	302	77..	2511	2754
18825	Kingfisher	1235	1527	325	36..	1541	2106
27526	Kiowa	1881	1167	221	80..	2354	1591
11321	Latimer	722	482	358	7..	720	616
29127	LeFlore	2019	1538	504	21..	1872	1771
34779	Lincoln	2132	2459	913	56..	3090	3515
31740	Logan	1700	2546	477	84..	2183	3768
10236	Love	750	199	404	5..	835	413
15348	Major	689	1200	543	51..	877	1446
11619	Marshall	958	315	682	12..	842	406
15596	Mayes	1391	1077	201	13..	1186	1021
15650	McClain	1273	553	408	61..	1234	780
20891	McCurtain	1659	701	821	17..	545	482
20061	McIntosh	1825	970	530	12..	1236	1806
12744	Murray	987	831	549	6..	1111	574
52743	Muskogee	3681	2385	526	23..	2706	3592
14945	Noble	1188	1266	266	23..	1364	1476
14223	Nowata	1012	1087	146	26..	923	1086
19995	Okfuskee	952	651	724	16..	872	1297
85232	Oklahoma	6938	5700	827	88..	4876	5401
21115	Okmulgee	1243	1140	537	27..	1105	1493
20101	Osage	1900	1713	476	29..	1584	1529
15713	Ottawa	1384	1515	163	8..	1297	1774
17332	Pawnee	1316	1332	441	31..	1500	1556
29735	Payne	1534	1699	733	71..	1980	2244
47650	Pittsburg	2707	1574	1438	35..	2898	2735
24551	Pontotoc	1842	642	919	18..	1611	860
43595	Pottawatomie	3082	2107	1013	41..	3561	2029
10118	Pushmataha	747	479	483	8..	625	484
12861	Roger Mills	902	716	548	17..	1168	839
17736	Rogers	1657	1258	426	19..	1599	1134
19964	Seminole	1172	745	741	17..	945	1188
25005	Sequoyah	1416	1115	153	12..	1648	2057
22252	Stephens	1735	598	896	19..	1761	725
14249	Texas	764	683	234	41..	1470	1315
18650	Tillman	1801	638	351	21..	1861	732
34985	Tulsa	2747	2029	523	48..	2292	2150
22086	Wagoner	888	555	261	11..	1151	2107
11484	Washington	1561	1477	822	25..	1409	1528
26034	Washita	1605	1100	731	36..	1867	1118
17557	Woods	1247	1679	499	42..	1421	1557
16592	Woodward	1083	1403	565	28..	1308	1944

Total ... 119156 90786 41674 2185.. 122593 110474
Plurality ... 28370 .. 11843
Per cent... 46.84 35.68 16.61 .86.. 47.92 43.28
Total vote... 253801 .. 255453

NOTE—Most of the electors on the republican ticket in 1912 were for Roosevelt, but as they were officially designated as republicans their vote is credited to Taft.

For president in 1908, Debs, Soc., received 21,734; Hisgen, Ind., 245; Watson, Peo., 412.

FOR REPRESENTATIVES IN CONGRESS, 1912.

1. Counties of Garfield, Grant, Kay, Kingfisher, Lincoln, Logan, Noble, Osage, Payne and Pawnee.
Bird S. McGuire, Rep..................19,035
J. J. Davis, Dem....................18,456
A. W. Renshaw, Soc.................. 4,447

2. Counties of Alfalfa, Beaver, Blaine, Caddo, Canadian, Cimarron, Custer, Dewey, Ellis, Harper, Major, Oklahoma, Roger Mills (part), Texas, Woods and Woodward.
Dick T. Morgan, Rep..................17,292
J. J. Carney, Dem...................16,513
P. D. McKenzie, Soc................. 6,603
(Vote incomplete.)

3. Counties of Adair, Cherokee, Craig, Creek, Delaware, Hughes, McIntosh, Mayes, Nowata, Okfuskee (part), Okmulgee, Sequoyah, Tulsa, Wagoner and Washington.
J. S. Davenport, Dem..................23,618
R. T. Daniel, Rep...................18,842
Lewis B. Irvin, Soc................. 6,105

4. Counties of Atoka, Bryan, Carter (part), Choctaw, Coal, Comanche (part), Grady, Haskell, Hughes, Johnston, LeFlore, Latimer, Love (part), McCurtain, McIntosh, Marshall, Murray (part), Okfuskee (part), Pittsburg, Pontotoc and Pushmataha.
E. D. Carter, Dem...................23,512
E. N. Wright, Rep...................11,309
F. W. Holt, Soc....................10,749
(Vote incomplete.)

5. Counties of Beckham, Carter (part), Cleveland (part), Comanche (part), Cotton, Garvin, Grady, Greer, Harmon, Jackson, Jefferson, Kiowa, Love (part), McClain, Murray (part), Pottawatomie, Roger Mills (part), Stephens, Tillman and Washita.
Scott Ferris, Dem...................27,474
C. O. Clark, Rep...................10,895
E. H. Stallerd, Soc................10,437
(Vote incomplete.)

LEGISLATURE.	Senate.	House.	J.B.
Republicans	6	26	32
Democrats	18	83	101

STATE OFFICERS. (All democrats.)
Governor—Lee Cruce.
Lieutenant-Governor—J. J. McAlester.
Secretary—Ben F. Harrison.
Auditor—J. C. McClelland.
Attorney-General—Charles West.
Treasurer—Robert Dunlop.
Superintendent Public Instruction—R. H. Wilson.
Examiner and Inspector—Ed Boyle.
Commissioner Labor—Charles Daugherty.
Commissioner Charities—Kate Barnard.
Corporation Commissioner—G. A. Henshaw.

OREGON (Population in 1910, 672,765).

Population in 1910.	COUNTIES. (34)	Rep. Taft	Dem. Wilson	Pro. Chafin	Soc. Debs	Prog. Roosevelt
18076	Baker	648	1305	54	459	1120
10053	Benton	715	986	195	123	588
29931	Clackamas	1503	2171	235	567	2045
16106	Clatsop	722	728	51	444	729
10580	Columbia	574	597	59	295	611
17959	Coos	701	1081	89	857	949
9315	Crook	770	1090	63	289	608
2044	Curry	102	219	4	92	192
9674	Douglas	1207	1601	116	654	1224
3701	Gilliam	348	310	16	33	150
5607	Grant	418	413	14	164	348
4059	Harney	377	538	8	141	169
8016	Hood River	395	519	54	121	491
25756	Jackson	847	2079	149	552	1620
9567	Josephine	305	702	32	604	794
8554	Klamath	433	815	30	162	502
4658	Lake	297	357	13	108	286
33783	Lane	1986	2696	343	769	1815
5587	Lincoln	410	575	42	226	245
22662	Linn	1301	2134	300	408	1229
8601	Malheur	648	656	32	165	418
39780	Marion	2523	2588	475	575	1919
4357	Morrow	447	275	20	119	187
226261	Multnomah	9213	13804	761	3489	12533
13469	Polk	1043	1301	164	211	637
4242	Sherman	244	232	57	20	106
6266	Tillamook	493	411	45	156	399
20309	Umatilla	1261	1563	182	308	1044
16191	Union	671	1090	93	332	946
8364	Wallowa	353	610	55	209	600
16336	Wasco	775	929	91	205	587
21522	Washington	1261	1429	224	286	1455
3484	Wheeler	307	222	14	15	129
18285	Yamhill	1312	1378	350	275	885
	Total	34673	47064	4360	13213	37600
	Plurality		9464			
	Per cent	25.32	34.39	3.19	9.64	27.46
	Total vote		136910			

For United States senator in 1912 Jonathan Bourne, Jr., popular government, received 25,929 votes; A. E. Clark, Prog., 11,085; Harry Lane, Dem., 40,172; L. E. Paget, Pro., 6,848; B. F. Ramp, Soc., 11,093, and Ben Selling, Rep, 38,453.

Vote on equal suffrage measure in 1912: For, 61,265; against, 57,104.

FOR REPRESENTATIVES IN CONGRESS, 1912.

1. The counties of Benton, Clackamas, Clatsop, Columbia, Coos, Curry, Douglas, Jackson, Josephine, Lane, Lincoln, Linn, Marion, Polk, Tillamook, Washington and Yamhill.

John W. Campbell, Prog.	8,679
W. C. Hawley, Rep.	26,925
W. S. Richards, Soc.	7,181
R. G. Smith, Dem.	15,410
O. A. Stillman, Pro.	4,385

2. The counties of Baker, Crook, Gilliam, Grant, Harney, Hood River, Klamath, Lake, Malheur, Morrow, Sherman, Umatilla, Union, Wallowa, Wasco and Wheeler.

C. H. Abercrombie, Soc.	3,037
George L. Cleaver, Pro.	1,800
James H. Graham, Dem.	8,322
N. J. Sinnott, Rep.	15,121

3. The county of Multnomah.

A. W. Lafferty, Rep.-Prog.	16,783
M. G. Munly, Dem.	11,553
Thomas McCusker, Ind.	6,280
Lee Campbell, Soc.	3,065
LeGrand M. Baldwin, Pro.	1,419

LEGISLATURE.	Senate.	House.	J. B.
Republicans	29	48	76
Democrats	2	5	7
Progressives	0	7	7

STATE OFFICERS.

Governor—Oswald West, Dem.
Secretary of State—Ben W. Olcott, Rep.
Treasurer—T. B. Kay, Rep.
Attorney-General—A. M. Crawford, Rep.
State Printer—R. A. Harris, Dem.
Superintendent of Public Instruction—J. A. Churchill, Rep.

PENNSYLVANIA (Population in 1910, 7,665,111).

Population in 1910.	COUNTIES. (67)	Rep. Taft	Dem. Wilson	Soc. Debs	Bull Roosevelt	M. Roosevelt	Prog. Roosevelt	Wash.
	34319 Adams	819	3052	90	1565	121	862	
1018463	Allegheny	23822	31345	19554	9598	3874	36450	
67880	Armstrong	1904	3027	643	400	427	3470	
78353	Beaver	2759	3037	1748	560	299	3658	
38879	Bedford	1140	2694	523	212	282	2477	
183222	Berks	3822	16430	3636	849	730	9715	
108858	Blair	3138	4108	1500	524	450	7205	
54526	Bradford	2034	2900	238	305	531	4543	
76530	Bucks	5452	6773	411	202	243	3775	
72689	Butler	1273	4022	450	407	202	3718	
166131	Cambria	3262	7282	805	1309	68	8119	
7644	Cameron	388	291	36	79	30	444	
52846	Carbon	1246	3652	428	307	268	5023	
43421	Center	1507	3445	227	183	291	2138	
109213	Chester	5708	6501	314	1257	412	4437	
38638	Clarion	916	3079	315	168	209	1347	
93788	Clearfield	1523	4070	1410	341	611	3950	
31545	Clinton	1214	2200	613	327	243	1356	
48467	Columbia	889	4905	242	121	157	2419	
61565	Crawford	2497	3908	1041	213	208	3658	
54479	Cumberland	2566	5023	345	210	202	3095	
136152	Dauphin	6012	7470	1363	950	290	9436	
117906	Delaware	8418	6001	374	1857	813	5502	
35871	Elk	603	2057	963	170	128	2340	
115357	Erie	4958	2653	1972	752	541	3736	
167449	Fayette	4168	7363	2462	720	453	5684	
9435	Forest	240	373	263	78	46	464	
59775	Franklin	2710	4505	414	245	183	3359	
9703	Fulton	317	1080	23	57	58	527	
28982	Greene	1150	3551	176	107	104	852	
38304	Huntingdon	903	1558	263	172	220	3101	
66210	Indiana	1720	1593	524	333	426	3210	
63000	Jefferson	1608	2510	572	341	372	2888	
15013	Juniata	374	1148	72	86	116	1282	
239570	Lackawa'na	3792	12423	959	1425	723	13653	
167029	Lancaster	12098	8574	687	10815	199	1517	
70032	Lawrence	2128	1976	1641	551	285	2502	
59685	Lebanon	2378	2972	393	141	196	4200	
118832	Lehigh	2722	10684	1059	597	407	6576	
343186	Luzerne	4915	13495	2464	2393	3640	16557	
80813	Lycoming	1631	6039	1523	515	488	4205	
47868	McKean	1345	2362	512	446	370	2674	
77629	Mercer	1873	4039	1708	383	410	3625	
27785	Mifflin	654	1400	551	145	143	1543	
22941	Monroe	539	3107	23	137	101	616	
169590	Montgom'ry	8978	11894	1129	735	577	10179	
14868	Montour	308	1492	39	49	53	835	
127497	North'mpt'n	3893	10525	639	544	606	5452	
111420	N'umberl'd	371	6802	27	247	358	6459	
24136	Perry	1140	1941	72	171	160	1339	
1549008	Philadelp'a	91944	66308	9784	6308	7527	68528	
8053	Pike	191	995	18	37	27	373	
29729	Potter	850	1445	310	208	182	1311	
207834	Schuylkill	3567	11812	2846	1699	1600	10877	
10800	Snyder	626	991	74	50	69	1504	
67717	Somerset	1428	2164	655	227	182	4617	
11293	Sullivan	547	912	43	22	44	406	
37748	Susqueh'na	1988	2588	25	154	136	2208	
42829	Tioga	1895	1901	130	405	319	3590	
16349	Union	470	1126	48	59	128	1589	
56559	Venango	1660	2507	1214	532	286	2473	
39573	Warren	1564	1680	628	187	187	2690	
143690	Washington	4297	6563	2050	550	428	6616	
29236	Wayne	650	1924	52	217	248	2132	
231304	Westmorel'd	4299	9262	4622	1127	761	8305	
15509	Wyoming	480	1505	23	95	68	1301	
136405	York	5251	14979	1503	4676	420	291	
	Total	273305	395619	83915	60064	35513	350909	
	Plurality						51907	
	Per cent	22.45	32.50	6.61	5.01	2.92	28.84	
	Total vote			1217603				

For president in 1912 Chafin, Pro., received 19,533 votes and Reimer, Soc.-Lab., 704. For president in 1908 Taft, Rep., received 745,779 votes; Bryan, Dem., 448,785; Chafin, Pro., 36,694, and Debs, Soc., 33,913.

FOR REPRESENTATIVES IN CONGRESS, 1912.

At Large—John M. Morin, Prog.-Rep.	618,537
Frederick E. Lewis, Prog.-Rep.	607,701
Anderson H. Walters, Prog.-Rep.	608,769
Arthur R. Rupley, Prog.-Rep.	606,709
George Benton Shaw, Dem.	357,562
Joseph Howley, Dem.	346,814
George R. McLean, Dem.	352,396
E. E. Greenewalt, Dem.	343,163
E. L. McKee, Pro.	21,074
Howard J. Force, Pro.	20,284

Henry S. Gill, Pro..................... 20,465
Thomas H. Hamilton, Pro................. 20,211
Charles W. Ervin, Soc................... 80,808
William Parker, Soc..................... 81,125
E. S. Musser, Soc....................... 80,247
John W. Slayton, Soc.................... 81,785
1. Philadelphia county (part).
William S. Vare, Rep...................25,305
John H. Hall, Dem.......................10,462
Harry Gantz, Soc........................ 1,006
2. Philadelphia county (part).
George S. Graham, Rep..................14,806
William Schlpf, Jr., Dem................ 7,604
Harry C. Parker, Soc.................... 938
3. Philadelphia county (part).
J. Hampton Moore, Rep..................15,491
John H. Fow, Dem........................ 6,212
George Ruby, Soc........................ 986
Harry K. Walter, Wash................... 5,920
4. Philadelphia county (part).
George W. Edmonds, Rep.................21,733
Thomas T. Nelson, Dem................... 8,482
Charles DeKyne, Soc..................... 1,410
5. Philadelphia county (part).
Henry S. Borneman, Rep.................15,181
Michael Donohoe, Dem...................21,971
John Whitehead, Soc..................... 2,604
6. Philadelphia county (part).
Harry A. Mackey, Rep...................19,291
J. Washington Logue, Dem...............22,091
Perry R. Long, Soc...................... 1,897
Frederick S. Drake, Wash...............19,642
7. Chester and Delaware counties.
Thomas S. Butler, Rep..................18,276
Eugene C. Bonniwell, Dem...............12,225
Edwin P. Sellew, Pro.................... 378
Walter N. Lodge, Soc.................... 611
Frederick A. Howard, Wash.............. 7,647
8. Bucks and Montgomery counties.
Oscar O. Bean, Rep.....................15,840
Robert E. Difenderfer, Dem.............18,230
James C. Hogan, Sr., Soc................ 1,456
Thomas K. Ober, Jr., Wash..............12,205
9. Lancaster county.
William W. Griest, Rep.................14,112
E. S. Musser, Soc....................... 667
John N. Hetric, Bull Moose............. 9,947
10. Lackawanna county.
John R. Farr, Rep......................14,939
Michael A. McGinley, Dem...............12,777
L. H. Gibbs, Soc........................ 865
11. Luzerne county.
Charles C. Bowman, Rep................. 9,864
John J. Casey, Dem.....................15,343
C. F. Quinn, Soc........................ 2,119
Clarence D. Coughlin, Wash.............10,597
12. Schuylkill county.
Alfred B. Garner, Rep..................10,463
Robert E. Lee, Dem.....................14,902
Cornelius F. Foley, Soc................. 3,464
13. Berks and Lehigh counties.
Charles T. Reno, Rep...................20,403
John H. Rothermel, Dem.................26,569
Clarence T. Wixson, Soc................ 4,938
14. Bradford, Susquehanna, Wayne and Wyoming
counties.
William D. B. Ainey, Rep...............14,747
John G. Hill, Dem...................... 8,384
W. S. H. Heermans, Pro................. 706
Charles Welch, Soc..................... 312
15. Clinton, Lycoming, Potter and Tioga counties.
Edgar R. Kiess, Rep....................14,211
William B. Wilson, Dem.................13,643
David Salmon, Pro....................... 814
Aaron Noll, Soc........................ 2,282
16. Columbia, Montour, Northumberland and Sul-
livan counties.
I. Clinton Kline, Rep..................12,783
John V. Lesher, Dem....................14,209
T. P. Jepson, Pro....................... 453
George W. Dornbach, Soc................ 2,737
17. Franklin, Fulton, Huntingdon, Juniata, Mifflin,
Perry, Snyder and Union counties.
Benjamin K. Focht, Rep.................10,978
Frank L. Dershem, Dem..................14,073
William G. Bowers, Soc.................. 1,377
Frank B. Clayton, Wash................. 9,442

18. Cumberland, Dauphin and Lebanon counties.
Aaron S. Krieder, Rep..................14,485
David L. Kaufman, Dem..................14,082
L. M. Ibach, Soc........................ 1,988
Harvey C. Demming, Wash................13,504
19. Bedford, Blair and Cambria counties.
Jesse L. Hartman, Rep..................12,633
Warren Worth Bailey, Dem...............13,626
D. W. B. Murphy, Soc................... 2,879
Lynn A. Brua, Wash.....................12,688
20. Adams and York counties.
Daniel F. Lafean, Rep..................14,283
Andrew R. Brodbeck, Dem................16,514
George W. Bacon, Soc................... 1,498
Robert C. Bair, Wash................... 3,186
21. Cameron, Center, Clearfield and McKean coun-
ties.
Charles E. Patton, Rep.................13,722
James A. Gleason, Dem..................10,588
George Fox, Soc........................ 2,041
22. Butler and Westmoreland counties.
Abraham L. Keister, Rep................15,560
Curtis H. Gregg, Dem...................14,943
Daniel K. Albright, Pro................ 2,206
Charles Cunningham, Soc................ 4,735
23. Fayette, Greene and Somerset counties.
Thomas S. Crago, Rep................... 7,836
Wooda N. Carr, Dem.....................12,211
Charles L. Gans, Soc................... 2,928
Harvey L. Berkeley, Wash............... 7,588
24. Beaver, Lawrence and Washington counties.
Charles Matthews, Rep..................10,797
S. A. Lacock, Dem...................... 8,585
James B. Peebles, Pro.................. 1,363
George C. Frethy, Soc.................. 5,082
Henry W. Temple, Wash..................11,495
25. Crawford and Erie counties.
Milton W. Shreve, Rep..................13,078
Turner W. Shacklett, Dem...............10,446
R. B. Pike, Pro........................ 1,243
Sidney A. Schwarz, Soc................. 2,727
26. Carbon, Monroe, Northampton and Pike coun-
ties.
Francis A. March, Jr., Rep.............14,451
A. Mitchell Palmer, Dem................18,201
George R. Miller, Soc.................. 1,032
27. Armstrong, Clarion, Indiana and Jefferson coun-
ties.
J. N. Langham, Rep.....................17,138
Foster D. Mohney, Dem.................. 9,472
John Houk, Pro......................... 1,743
Thomas J. Fredericks, Soc.............. 1,858
28. Elk, Forest, Mercer, Venango and Warren
counties.
Peter M. Speer, Rep.................... 7,136
John P. Hines, Dem..................... 9,471
J. W. Neilly, Pro...................... 1,692
John R. McKeown, Soc................... 4,097
Willis J. Hulings, Wash................10,363
29. Allegheny county (part).
Stephen W. Porter, Rep.................15,925
Joseph Gallagher, Dem.................. 5,509
George T. McConnell, Soc............... 8,899
30. Allegheny county (part).
M. Clyde Kelly, Rep....................17,230
D. K. Ferree, Dem...................... 6,708
Fred H. Merrick, Soc................... 7,570
31. Allegheny county (part).
James F. Burke, Rep....................19,679
Joseph F. Joyce, Dem................... 4,804
William A. Prosser, Soc................ 5,101
32. Allegheny county (part).
Andrew J. Barchfield, Rep..............23,265
Herman L. Hegner, Dem.................. 7,987
Thomas F. Kennedy, Soc................. 5,672
William McClintock Shrodes, Key........ 4,169

LEGISLATURE.
Legislature—Republicans, 161; democrats, 72;
progressives, 15; keystone, 9.
STATE OFFICERS.
Governor—John K. Tener, Rep.
Lieutenant-Governor—John M. Reynolds, Rep.
Secretary—Robert McAfee, Rep.
Treasurer—Robert K. Young, Rep.
Auditor—Archibald W. Powell, Rep.
Adjutant-General—Thomas J. Stewart, Rep.

Attorney-General—John C. Bell, Rep.
Superintendent Public Instruction—N. C. Schaeffer, Dem.

RHODE ISLAND (Population in 1910, 542,674).

COUNTIES. ——————PRESIDENT 1912——————

Population in 1910.	(5)	Rep. Taft	Dem. Wilson	Pro Chafin	Soc Debs	S. L. Reimer	Prog. Roosevelt
17603 Bristol	.	1126	1077	27	21	7	437
36378 Kent	.	2170	2030	44	40	11	1284
39.395 Newport	.	2583	2437	59	50	12	1279
124417 Providence	.	19685	23127	408	1899	195	13090
24942 Washington	.	2129	1691	83	35	11	788
	Total. ...	27703	30412	616	2049	236	16878
	Plurality ...		2709				
	Per cent	35 57	39 04	79	2 63	30	21 67
	Total vote .		77894				

For president in 1908 Taft, Rep , received, 43,942 votes, Bryan, Dem., 24,706; Debs, Soc., 1,365

FOR REPRESENTATIVES IN CONGRESS, 1912.

1. Counties of Newport, Bristol and Providence (part)
   George F O'Shaughnessy, Dem , plurality   3,583
   William P Sheffield, Rep.
   John E. Bolan, Prog
2. Counties of Kent, Washington and Providence (part).
   Peter Goelet Gerry, Dem., plurality   368
   George H Utter, Rep.
   Claude C Ball, Prog
3. County of Providence (part)
   Ambrose Kennedy, Rep , plurality. .   1,877
   F. X. L Rattey, Dem.
   Edwin F. Tuttle, Prog

LEGISLATURE.

	Senate	House.	J.B.
Republicans	32	56	88
Democrats .	7	38	45
Progressives	0	4	4

STATE OFFICERS (All republicans.)
Governor—Aram J Pothier
Lieutenant-Governor—Roswell B. Burchard.
Secretary of State—J. Fred Parker.
Treasurer—Walter A. Read
Attorney-General—Herbert A. Rice.

SOUTH CAROLINA (Population in 1910, 1,515,400).

COUNTIES.   PRESIDENT 1912 — GOV 1910

Population in 1910	(42)	Dem. Wilson	Prog Roosevelt	Rep Taft	Soc Debs	Dem Blease	Soc Thompson
34904 Abbeville	.	1095	4	9	—	394	—
41849 Aiken	.	1442	4	2	—	1028	—
60568 Anderson	.	2153	66	25	16..	802	—
18544 Bamberg	.	616	1	3	—	390	—
34209 Barnwell	..	1149	5	16	—	673	—
30355 Beaufort	.	464	62	50	—	349	—
23487 Berkeley. ...	.	323	13	5	—	253	—
16634 Calhoun	.	460	16	15	—	302	—
88594 Charleston	.	1760	100	34	54	1474	20
26179 Cherokee...	.	1259	7	16	—	630	—
29425 Chester	.	1286	20	—	—	474	—
26301 Chesterfield	.	1170	4	—	1	712	—
32188 Clarendon	.	932	32	—	—	556	—
35300 Colleton	.....	797	12	14	—	440	—
36027 Darlington	.	883	2	—	—	349	—
22615 Dillon	.	680	11	2	—	314	—
17891 Dorchester	.	576	13	18	—	836	—
28281 Edgefield	..	779	18	3	—	621	—
29442 Fairfield	.	622	8	3	2	352	—
35671 Florence	.	1496	65	6	6	508	—
22270 Georgetown	.	405	37	10	—	452	—
68377 Greenville	.	3140	—	—	—	2009	13
34225 Greenwood	.	1307	11	17	3	562	1
25126 Hampton...	.	631	—	—	—	667	—
26995 Horry	.	863	7	3	—	1434	—
	Jasper .	198	—	—	—	—	—
27094 Kershaw	.	705	25	7	—	305	—
26840 Lancaster	.	1140	5	6	—	733	—
41550 Laurens	.	1566	17	6	1	1600	—
25318 Lee	.	671	6	3	—	322	—
32040 Lexington	.	1201	30	3	31	1148	13
20596 Marion	.	710	11	3	—	449	—
31189 Marlboro	.	719	—	—	—	217	—
34586 Newberry	...	1206	12	6	6	627	—
27337 Oconee..	.	760	69	58	2 .	325	—
55894 Orangeburg .	.	1550	95	40	—	1539	4
25422 Pickens	.	815	18	15	—	455	—
55143 Richland	.	1557	161	23	25	536	8
20943 Saluda	.	850	4	—	14	716	—
83465 Spartanburg .	.	3616	185	37	6	2284	—

Population.		Wilson	Roosevelt	Taft	Debs	Blease	Thompson
38472 Sumter		910	52	31	— .	603	—
29911 Union ..		1649	56	20	— .	914	—
37635 Williamsburg	...	729	18	6	— .	500	—
47718 York	.	1641	12	12	1..	543	—
	Total	.43357	1293	536	164..	39739	70
	Plurality	.4764				3069	
	Per cent	.96 04	2 57 1	06	.33..	99.77	.23
	Total vote	..		59350		30809	

FOR REPRESENTATIVES IN CONGRESS, 1912.

1. Berkeley, Charleston, Clarendon, Colleton and Dorchester counties
   George S. Legare, Dem   4,550
   A. P Prioleau, Rep   85
   William Eberhard, Rep   48
2. Aiken, Bamberg, Beaufort, Edgefield, Hampton, Jasper and Saluda counties.
   James F Byrnes, Dem ..   6,083
3. Abbeville, Anderson, Greenwood, Newberry, Oconee and Pickens counties
   Wyatt Aiken, Dem   7,458
4. Greenville, Laurens, Spartanburg and Union counties.
   Joseph T. Johnson, Dem. .   7,244
5. Cherokee, Chester, Chesterfield, Fairfield, Kershaw, Lancaster and York counties
   D. E. Finley, Dem   7,901
6. Darlington, Dillon, Florence, Georgetown, Horry, Marion, Marlboro and Williamsburg counties
   J. W. Ragsdale, Dem   6,446
7. Calhoun, Lee, Lexington, Richland and Sumter counties.
   A. F. Lever, Dem   6,660
   A D. Dantzier, Rep .   105

LEGISLATURE
The legislature is democratic
STATE OFFICERS (All democrats.)
Governor—Cole L Blease.
Lieutenant-Governor—C. A. Smith.
Secretary of State—R M. McCown.
Attorney-General—T H. Peeples
State Treasurer—S. T. Carter
Comptroller-General—A. W. Jones.
State Superintendent of Education—J. E. Swearingen.
Adjutant and Inspector-General—W W. Moore.
Railroad Commissioner—J. G. Richards, Jr
Commissioner of Agriculture, Commerce and Industries—E J. Watson.

SOUTH DAKOTA (Population in 1910, 583,888).

COUNTIES   PRES 1912 — PRES '08

Population in 1910	(64)	Prog Roosevelt	Dem Wilson	Pro Chafin	Soc Debs	Rep Taft	Dem Bryan
6143 Aurora		652	801	68	42	686	694
15776 Beadle		1493	1464	70	166	1776	1105
	Bennett. ..	69	175	3	1	—	—
11061 Bon Homme		1223	1059	40	45	1324	1014
14178 Brookings		1388	740	208	58	1807	588
25867 Brown		1743	2479	389	385	2646	1772
6451 Brule		644	850	—	—	753	823
1589 Buffalo		83	105	3	4	105	69
4993 Butte		647	600	25	188.	1636	915
5244 Campbell	.	574	150	30	4..	627	175
14899 Charles Mix		1769	1597	—	—	1863	1391
10901 Clark .		949	658	83	36	1234	557
8711 Clay		1248	945	15	10	1291	803
14025 Codington ..		1195	1105	89	71	1618	831
2929 Corson		508	455	16	46	—	—
4438 Custer		395	419	8	90	487	428
1625 Davison		1368	1288	95	56	1276	1081
14372 Day.....		1203	780	272	118	1616	813
17778 Deuel		884	416	71	14	1022	425
1145 Dewey	.	509	411	12	42 .	—	—
6400 Douglas		757	710	14	12	839	647
7654 Edmunds		640	729	89	27	726	658
7763 Fall River		838	726	—	—	726	466
6716 Faulk		568	614	92	21 .	845	421
10393 Grant ..		639	619	80	55	1122	628
19061 Gregory		1338	1175	25	96	1550	1264
17475 Hamlin		1058	474	35	17	1095	454
7870 Hand		743	826	87	45	851	655
6287 Hanson		708	632	42	21	668	630
4228 Harding	...	587	318	72	103,	—	—
6671 Hughes		447	554	23	71	795	349
12919 Hutchinson		1454	647	29	12	1507	619
5507 Hyde		369	342	17	51 .	455	212
5120 Jerauld		545	438	155	11	582	463
12593 Kingsbury		1150	747	152	113	1337	799
10711 Lake	..	1181	657	52	81..	1415	636

Population		Roosevelt	Wilson	Chafin	Debs	Taft	Bryan
19694	Lawrence	1092	2412	40	326..	2735	1564
12712	Lincoln	1673	729	72	56..	1887	899
10848	Lyman	995	759	45	112..	1524	1183
8021	Marshall	601	548	68	45..	874	463
9589	McCook	1003	961	75	56..	1209	826
6791	McPherson	409	327	13	6..	785	157
12640	Meade	732	975	66	151..	963	792
	Mellette	261	320	7	5..	—	—
7661	Miner	848	721	48	39..	905	720
29631	Minnehaha	3051	2576	195	236..	4125	1948
8636	Moody	932	667	101	119..	1275	623
12453	Pennington	1003	1130	32	117..	1702	1160
11348	Perkins	1070	811	—	—..	—	—
4496	Potter	438	423	28	16..	614	400
14897	Roberts	1314	760	73	197..	1562	777
6307	Sanborn	880	577	78	19..	847	513
292	Schnasse	—	—	—	—..	—	—
15581	Spink	1432	1347	118	128..	1847	1121
14975	Stanley	981	1027	44	127..	2313	1308
252	Sterling	—	—	—	—..	—	—
2462	Sully	292	212	19	19..	368	154
8323	Tripp	1153	982	32	82..	—	—
13840	Turner	1605	906	82	22..	1792	793
10676	Union	1396	965	86	24..	1322	1009
6488	Walworth	589	445	24	56..	825	351
13135	Yankton	1511	1249	67	61..	1644	1118
	Ziebach	371	349	19	36..	—	—
	Total	58811	48042	3910	4662..67536	40296	
	Plurality	9869			..37200		
	Per cent	50.65	42.35	3.85	3.75..57.95	35.11	
	Total vote	116825			.. 114705		

There was no regular republican or Taft ticket in the field in election of 1912.

FOR REPRESENTATIVES IN CONGRESS, 1912.

1. Counties of Aurora, Bon Homme, Brule, Buffalo, Charles Mix, Clay, Davison, Douglas, Hanson, Hutchinson, Jerauld, Lake, Lincoln, Miner, Moody, Minnehaha, McCook, Sanborn, Turner, Union and Yankton.

Charles H. Dillon, Rep......................25,498
R. E. Dowdell, Dem.........................18,051
C. W. Templeton, Pro........................1,174
E. M. Jacobson, Soc..........................997

2. Counties of Beadle, Brookings, Brown, Campbell, Clark, Codington, Day, Deuel, Edmunds, Faulk, Grant, Hamlin, Hand, Hughes, Hyde, Kingsbury, Marshall, McPherson, Potter, Spink, Sully and Walworth.

Charles H. Burke, Rep......................23,170
C. Boyd Garrett, Dem.......................14,283
W. J. Edgar, Pro............................1,172
E. Francis Atwood, Soc.....................1,573

3. Counties of Bennett, Butte, Corson, Custer, Dewey, Fall River, Gregory, Harding, Lawrence, Lyman, Meade, Mellette, Pennington, Perkins, Shannon, Stanley, Todd, Tripp, Washabaugh, Washington and Ziebach.

Eben W. Martin, Rep.......................15,141
Harry L. Gandy, Dem.......................12,154
J. E. Ballinger, Soc........................1,564

LEGISLATURE.

	Senate.	House.	J.B.
Republicans	35	89	124
Democrats	10	11	21

STATE OFFICERS. (All republicans.)

Governor—Frank M. Byrne.
Lieutenant-Governor—E. L. Abel.
Secretary of State—Frank Glasiar.
Treasurer—A. W. Ewart.
Superintendent Instruction—C. G. Lawrence.
Attorney-General—Royal C. Johnson.
State Auditor—Henry B. Anderson.

TENNESSEE (Population in 1910, 2,184,789).

Population in 1910.	COUNTIES. (96)	PRESIDENT 1912				
		Dem. Wilson	Rep. Taft	Prog. Roosevelt	Pro. Chafin	Soc. Debs
17717	Anderson	597	589	1148	1	55
22667	Bedford	2308	1474	96	1	6
12452	Benton	1085	652	249	—	30
6329	Bledsoe	464	379	401	—	10
20609	Blount	836	870	1110	39	—
16336	Bradley	645	485	548	7	10
27887	Campbell	454	302	1193	20	52
10825	Cannon	1184	651	48	—	7
20971	Carroll	3658	1302	992	1	49
19638	Carter	478	1243	1029	3	—
10540	Cheatham	1095	317	123	—	23
9090	Chester	636	312	388	1	38

Population		Wilson	Taft	Roosevelt	Chafin	Debs
23504	Claiborne	908	549	1098	3	19
9009	Clay	718	440	83	—	12
19909	Cocke	597	757	549	14	10
15625	Coffee	1705	521	63	1	28
16976	Crockett	1297	852	509	—	27
9327	Cumberland	489	372	434	2	11
149478	Davidson	9617	1428	1330	60	206
10093	Decatur	758	405	491	—	15
15434	DeKalb	1394	1219	205	1	2
19655	Dickson	1939	448	236	20	55
27721	Dyer	1469	318	348	11	82
30257	Fayette	830	59	93	2	—
7446	Fentress	839	444	317	—	21
20491	Franklin	2172	370	164	—	32
41630	Gibson	2671	1002	518	12	55
32629	Giles	3081	1596	419	5	2
13888	Grainger	841	741	900	—	—
31083	Greene	2076	1650	1242	5	5
8322	Grundy	529	122	87	—	121
13630	Hamblen	722	427	326	9	14
39267	Hamilton	4834	1443	2454	77	291
10778	Hancock	427	659	84	—	—
23011	Hardeman	1826	320	264	3	8
17521	Hardin	728	955	592	—	32
22587	Hawkins	1026	828	690	6	18
25910	Haywood	1069	34	88	2	28
17050	Henderson	738	475	947	4	19
25434	Henry	2526	941	282	7	111
15527	Hickman	1288	868	111	1	13
6224	Houston	586	172	65	—	86
13308	Humphreys	1283	349	160	1	30
15036	Jackson	1344	743	251	—	—
5210	James	203	169	408	—	—
17755	Jefferson	514	540	940	7	9
13191	Johnson	256	933	1025	—	—
94187	Knox	4069	1984	3816	109	122
8704	Lake	497	122	31	—	13
21105	Lauderdale	1020	186	503	2	28
17569	Lawrence	1504	875	783	4	48
6058	Lewis	359	126	144	—	6
25908	Lincoln	2051	672	98	2	18
13612	Loudon	415	322	348	10	6
14559	Macon	787	1251	183	5	11
21046	McMinn	912	667	557	74	17
16356	McNairy	1155	616	1001	—	—
30757	Madison*	—	—	—	—	—
18820	Marion	810	463	442	29	79
16872	Marshall	1554	376	87	15	11
40456	Maury	2309	616	389	43	48
6131	Meigs	517	397	163	—	1
20716	Monroe	1196	721	475	11	4
43672	Montgomery	1658	514	199	27	82
4800	Moore	604	116	11	—	1
	Morgan	466	312	841	11	35
29946	Obion	2152	455	196	18	68
15834	Overton	1531	743	181	4	66
8815	Perry	604	379	94	—	42
6087	Pickett	411	365	134	—	1
14116	Polk	867	533	622	—	9
20025	Putnam	1867	923	386	2	5
15410	Rhea	692	253	552	12	9
22860	Roane	570	482	826	20	70
25466	Robertson	2287	513	142	—	125
33199	Rutherford	3406	1217	280	4	64
12947	Scott	160	123	1234	5	126
4202	Sequatchie	354	139	83	—	39
22236	Sevier	340	967	2410	3	1
191439	Shelby	6732	589	2951	41	228
16648	Smith	1803	915	184	3	—
14860	Stewart	1312	585	54	—	197
28120	Sullivan	2413	538	1205	—	12
25631	Sumner	2477	769	89	4	61
29159	Tipton	987	564	322	11	12
5874	Trousdale	544	211	35	—	—
7201	Unicoi	170	280	765	4	11
11414	Union	404	307	1192	—	10
2784	Van Buren	225	106	30	—	24
16531	Warren	1745	539	250	4	16
28968	Washington	1530	1134	1502	15	9
12043	Wayne	435	971	380	—	9
31929	Weakley	2810	1265	350	7	33
15420	White	1222	830	279	1	67
24218	Williamson	2205	979	62	1	9
25894	Wilson	2325	682	292	—	6
	*Returns stolen					
	Total	130035	59444	53725	825	3492
	Plurality	70591				
	Per cent	52.59	23.99	21.68	.33	1.41
	Total vote	247321				

For president in 1908 Bryan, Dem., received 135,608 votes; Taft, Rep., 118,834; Debs, Soc., 1,870; Watson, Peo., 1,081; Hisgen, Ind., 332, and Chafin, Pro., 330.

FOR REPRESENTATIVES IN CONGRESS, 1912.

1. The counties of Carter, Claiborne, Cocke, Grainger, Greene, Hamblen, Hancock, Hawkins, Johnson, Sullivan, Unicoi and Washington.
Sam R. Sells, Rep..............................16,660
Z. D. Massey, Rep.............................16,053
2. The counties of Anderson, Blount, Campbell, Jefferson, Knox, Loudon, Morgan, Roane, Scott, Sevier and Union.
R. W. Austin, Rep............................12,712
J. C. J. Williams, Dem........................6,681
3. The counties of Bledsoe, Bradley, Franklin, Grundy, Hamilton, James, McMinn, Marion, Meigs, Monroe, Polk, Sequatchie, Van Buren, Warren and White.
John A. Moon, Dem...........................18,240
Clarence Steward, Rep.........................6,380
J. W. Eastman, Prog...........................2,168
4. The counties of Clay, Cumberland, Fentress, Jackson, Macon, Overton, Pickett, Putnam, Rhea, Smith, Sumner, Trousdale and Wilson.
Cordell Hull, Dem............................17,077
I. J. Human, Rep.............................9,165
5. The counties of Bedford, Coffee, Cannon, De Kalb, Lincoln, Marshall, Moore and Rutherford.
W. C. Houston, Dem..........................12,055
Jesse C. Beesley, Dem.........................8,437
6. The counties of Cheatham, Davidson, Houston, Humphreys, Montgomery, Robertson and Stewart.
Joseph W. Byrns, Dem........................15,341
J. A. Althauser, Rep..........................2,860
7. The counties of Dickson, Giles, Hickman, Lawrence, Lewis, Maury, Wayne and Williamson.
L. P. Padgett, Dem...........................12,751
C. W. Turner, Dem............................9,380
8. The counties of Benton, Carroll, Chester, Decatur, Hardin, Henderson, Henry, Madison, McNairy and Perry.
W. T. Sims, Dem.............................10,162
J. W. Ross, Rep..............................7,461
Grissam, Prog................................2,035
(Madison county vote missing.)
9. The counties of Crockett, Dyer, Gibson, Haywood, Lake, Lauderdale, Obion and Weakley.
F. J. Garrett, Dem...........................13,392
R. C. Cochran, Rep...........................3,500
10. The counties of Fayette, Hardeman, Shelby and Tipton.
K. D. McKellar, Dem.........................12,916

LEGISLATURE.	Senate.	House.	J.B.
Democrats	27	75	102
Republicans	6	25	31

STATE OFFICERS.
Governor—Ben W. Hooper, Ind. Rep.
Secretary—R. R. Sneed, Dem.
Treasurer—W. P. Hickerson, Dem.
Comptroller—George P. Woollen, Dem.
Adjutant-General—Frank Maloney, Rep.
Attorney-General—F. M. Thompson, Dem.

TEXAS (Population in 1910, 3,896,542).

Counties (249) Population in 1910.	President 1912				
	Dem. Wilson	Prog. Roosevelt	Rep. Taft	Pro. Chafin	Soc. Debs
29650 Anderson	1745	104	446	6	300
975 Andrews	....	....	....	....	....
17705 Angelina	1107	25	45	8	374
2106 Aransas	189	29	7	2	7
6525 Archer	480	42	25	5	78
2682 Armstrong	274	31	32	3	8
10004 Atascosa	647	17	16	5	81
17699 Austin	1202	77	244	3	11
312 Bailey	....	....	....	....	....
4521 Bandera	414	130	158	10	78
25344 Bastrop	1086	165	216	10	55
8411 Baylor	553	48	15	5	64
12090 Bee	495	64	30	3	48
49186 Bell	3656	42	128	1	231
119976 Bexar	4300	2506	1022	32	259
4311 Blanco	419	76	127	3	14
1386 Borden	128	....	....	....	....
19013 Bosque	1225	87	65	2	84
4827 Bowie	1542	218	317	15	474
13299 Brazoria	748	342	263	32	79
18919 Brazos	708	43	142	7	8
5220 Brewster	553	40	29	3	24
2162 Briscoe	148	5	2	....	4
Brooks (new)	403	104	21	3	....
22935 Brown	1466	129	115	12	181
18687 Burleson	1000	79	228	3	19

Population.		Wilson	Roosevelt	Taft	Chafin	Debs
10755	Burnet	637	67	85	7	42
24237	Caldwell	1068	82	56	1	20
3635	Calhoun	356	61	36	7	66
12973	Callahan	785	46	45	6	127
27158	Cameron	2145	126	151	8	19
9551	Camp	492	61	155	2	25
2127	Carson	201	58	19	4	4
27587	Cass	1284	239	402	17	225
1950	Castro	177	19	18	—	8
4234	Chambers	219	30	80	—	29
29938	Cherokee	1686	61	143	8	280
9538	Childress	723	46	34	3	79
17043	Clay	1005	140	54	9	95
65	Cochran	—	—	—	—	—
6412	Coke	302	22	8	—	47
22618	Coleman	1284	59	52	7	212
49021	Collin	3197	223	342	16	312
5224	Collingsworth	414	27	15	2	55
18897	Colorado	1024	140	106	15	45
8434	Comal	602	174	157	—	30
27186	Comanche	1661	183	69	23	540
6054	Concho	345	33	16	—	88
26938	Cooke	1780	143	206	8	208
21703	Coryell	1270	67	70	1	57
4396	Cottle	311	18	8	1	109
331	Crane	—	—	—	—	—
1206	Crockett	53	3	5	—	7
1765	Crosby	247	41	1	1	64
	Culberson (new)	145	1	1	—	60
4001	Dallam	217	68	18	6	60
135748	Dallas	7925	1260	591	109	358
2320	Dawson	95	4	7	1	21
3942	Deaf Smith	221	22	21	5	5
14566	Delta	908	35	51	11	170
31258	Denton	2268	113	190	17	181
25501	DeWitt	1080	162	219	2	28
3092	Dickens	279	38	11	8	107
5430	Dimmit	292	36	184	—	9
5284	Donley	388	86	12	3	40
8964	Duval	917	31	80	—	2
23421	Eastland	1459	79	66	12	388
1178	Ector	89	4	4	—	—
3708	Edwards	133	75	114	—	52
53629	Ellis	3484	159	293	12	129
52599	El Paso	2914	799	291	32	122
32095	Erath	1549	161	156	22	355
35649	Falls	1663	190	353	4	192
44801	Fannin	2931	222	227	19	279
29736	Fayette	2016	214	461	2	95
12596	Fisher	572	21	11	7	124
4638	Floyd	383	41	21	18	81
5726	Foard	431	41	19	4	122
18168	Fort Bend	681	145	275	10	35
9331	Franklin	474	9	19	3	19
20557	Freestone	1306	29	455	1	175
6895	Frio	418	50	25	—	10
1255	Gaines	68	5	—	—	3
44479	Galveston	2601	472	459	40	130
1995	Garza	147	11	7	—	8
9447	Gillespie	307	1070	219	3	5
1143	Glasscock	53	—	—	—	8
9909	Goliad	500	76	414	5	68
28055	Gonzales	1839	98	318	4	79
3405	Gray	273	65	13	9	56
65096	Grayson	3037	444	510	59	378
14140	Gregg	605	32	126	2	33
21205	Grimes	969	51	39	8	25
24913	Guadalupe	1140	538	1072	8	15
7566	Hale	554	58	20	5	38
8279	Hall	775	46	24	2	124
15315	Hamilton	993	119	68	6	51
935	Hansford	93	35	12	8	7
11213	Hardeman	861	62	36	8	117
12947	Hardin	989	101	114	5	210
115693	Harris	6451	1124	726	61	746
37243	Harrison	1145	89	180	19	69
1298	Hartley	106	29	16	1	2
16249	Haskell	1001	53	45	1	362
15319	Hays	989	52	60	5	9
3170	Hemphill	315	116	61	5	32
20131	Henderson	1208	79	186	8	373
13728	Hidalgo	1205	94	30	11	43
46709	Hill	2680	144	129	23	114
137	Hockley	....	....	....	....	....
10003	Hood	675	59	38	4	55
31038	Hopkins	1989	80	146	19	288
1401	Houston	1401	64	342	1	250
8881	Howard	531	32	21	3	114
48116	Hunt	4040	213	225	43	309
892	Hutchinson	91	6	16	—	9
1283	Irion	132	4	—	—	11
11817	Jack	762	96	86	4	219
6471	Jackson	326	88	35	3	82

Population.	Wilson	Roosevelt	Taft	Chafin	Debs
14000 Jasper	628	44	40	4	208
1678 Jeff Davis	120	10	62	—	4
38182 Jefferson	1726	330	188	12	173
Jim Wells (new)	242	24	43	1	42
34460 Johnson	2487	109	109	5	302
24299 Jones	1391	55	63	4	196
14942 Karnes	710	49	66	—	—
35323 Kaufman	2088	75	226	7	260
4517 Kendall	223	229	178	—	9
2655 Kent	135	19	7	—	22
5505 Kerr	578	146	127	5	37
3261 Kimble	131	19	19	—	22
810 King	77	—	2	—	2
3401 Kinney	76	91	99	—	10
9625 Knox	649	54	32	2	125
46544 Lamar	2231	108	206	12	137
540 Lamb	53	18	6	7	—
9632 Lampasas	517	66	66	9	63
4747 LaSalle	339	35	21	2	16
26418 Lavaca	1498	237	267	5	195
13192 Lee	688	65	134	1	100
16583 Leon	856	57	191	1	266
10686 Liberty	548	106	80	6	74
34621 Limestone	1667	79	153	12	216
2634 Lipscomb	251	105	47	11	51
3442 Live Oak	308	42	26	—	20
6520 Llano	432	45	50	1	38
249 Loving	—	—	—	—	—
3624 Lubbock	285	27	16	3	12
1713 Lynn	122	3	6	—	12
16318 Madison	379	23	37	41	47
10472 Marion	339	36	85	1	1
1549 Martin	125	2	4	1	5
5683 Mason	473	172	152	6	82
13594 Matagorda	718	174	108	27	103
5151 Maverick	185	72	141	1	6
13405 McCulloch	593	61	41	3	144
73250 McLennan	3896	310	296	20	172
1081 McMullen	50	3	9	—	—
13415 Medina	651	263	220	5	28
2707 Menard	169	39	17	—	57
3464 Midland	216	10	11	1	8
36780 Milam	1939	110	214	6	488
9894 Mills	577	86	92	5	179
8956 Mitchell	573	32	18	4	79
25123 Montague	1534	114	151	4	341
15679 Montgomery	616	113	130	2	99
561 Moore	—	—	—	—	—
10459 Morris	608	48	89	5	13
2396 Motley	195	15	8	1	29
27406 Nacogdoches	1619	42	94	7	339
47070 Navarro	2500	128	185	8	159
10859 Newton	278	12	8	—	47
11999 Nolan	656	24	60	8	72
21855 Nueces	910	125	85	—	170
1602 Ochiltree	84	17	4	—	3
812 Oldham	92	18	22	4	4
6528 Orange	556	44	35	1	46
19506 Palo Pinto	1237	88	68	24	366
20424 Panola	1213	59	82	1	182
26531 Parker	1700	146	135	17	406
1555 Parmer	115	54	9	1	3
2071 Pecos	256	83	76	3	10
17459 Polk	615	42	41	5	77
12424 Potter	801	124	41	11	84
5218 Presidio	191	66	88	—	5
6787 Raines	441	20	67	3	237
3312 Randall	269	29	21	7	5
392 Reagan	34	—	—	—	—
28564 Red River	1497	203	255	10	140
4392 Reeves	276	43	8	5	3
2814 Refugio	207	34	118	9	35
950 Roberts	183	31	16	1	6
27454 Robertson	1053	58	153	3	62
8072 Rockwall	648	16	17	—	5
20858 Runnels	1128	73	58	9	200
26946 Rusk	1453	73	488	2	213
8582 Sabine	430	10	19	2	57
11264 San Augustine	375	18	12	11	76
9542 San Jacinto	379	46	196	1	25
7307 San Patricio	558	72	174	25	71
11345 San Saba	692	35	39	7	165
1893 Schleicher	111	13	3	1	2
10924 Scurry	665	20	30	11	90
4901 Shackelford	246	23	18	5	53
26423 Shelby	1509	20	76	2	287
97 Sherman	97	24	22	1	9
44746 Smith	1958	418	485	23	389
3981 Somervell	241	21	12	4	103
13151 Starr	674	2	252	—	2
7980 Stephens	463	4	11	1	95
1403 Sterling	165	9	4	1	1
5820 Stonewall	334	12	7	1	109

Population.	Wilson	Roosevelt	Taft	Chafin	Debs
1569 Sutton	63	17	12	—	1
4012 Swisher	280	24	8	—	3
198672 Tarrant	7219	1112	533	56	482
26293 Taylor	1536	90	59	5	188
1450 Terrell	118	39	36	—	8
1474 Terry	94	5	3	—	—
4563 Throckmorton	252	13	4	2	57
16422 Titus	943	87	70	4	151
17882 Tom Green	907	99	50	5	65
55620 Travis	2734	453	466	38	180
12768 Trinity	661	44	92	3	129
10250 Tyler	589	11	32	1	79
19960 Upshur	895	61	168	8	76
501 Upton	23	3	—	—	1
11233 Uvalde	601	73	53	2	45
8613 Val Verde	298	196	183	5	133
25651 Van Zandt	1700	194	110	13	829
14990 Victoria	698	162	199	10	55
16901 Walker	623	99	323	—	52
12158 Waller	595	98	144	2	20
2389 Ward	147	34	6	2	1
25561 Washington	1109	192	546	1	4
22503 Webb	654	31	888	—	3
21123 Wharton	794	195	109	13	129
5258 Wheeler	403	48	33	2	54
16094 Wichita	1128	131	108	7	38
12000 Wilbarger	994	71	44	5	188
Willacy (new)	105	—	4	—	—
42228 Williamson	2056	192	246	17	101
17066 Wilson	709	113	100	5	44
442 Winkler	26	—	—	—	—
26450 Wise	1842	151	156	12	148
23417 Wood	1449	74	147	15	352
602 Yoakum	41	9	1	—	—
13657 Young	923	47	35	3	182
3809 Zapata	—	—	—	—	—
1889 Zavalla	242	54	42	4	65
Total	219489	28530	26745	1698	24890
Plurality	190959				
Per cent	72.64	8.78	9.41	.57	8.45
Total vote	301788				

In 1912 for president Reimer, Soc.-Lab., received 430 votes.

FOR REPRESENTATIVES IN CONGRESS, 1912.

At Large—Hatton W. Summers, Dem..........226,319
Daniel E. Garrett, Dem.....................219,632
Z. T. White, Prog..........................52,476
F. M. Etheridge, Prog......................32,498
J. E. Elgin, Rep...........................29,172
R. B. Harrison, Rep........................29,217
D. H. Conniber, Pro........................1,736
D. D. Richardson, Soc......................14,839
J. M. Haggard, Soc.........................14,872

1. Counties of Bowie, Red River, Lamar, Delta, Hopkins, Franklin, Titus, Camp, Morris, Cass and Marion.
Horace W. Vaughan, Dem.....................11,180
J. B. Baker, Rep...........................760

2. Counties of Jefferson, Orange, Hardin, Tyler, Jasper, Newton, Sabine, San Augustine, Angelina, Cherokee, Nacogdoches, Shelby, Panola and Harrison.
Martin W. Dies, Dem........................11,120
Horace W. Smith, Rep.......................226
E. G. Christian, Pro.......................96

3. Counties of Wood, Upshur, Gregg, Rusk, Smith, Henderson, Van Zandt and Kaufman.
James Young, Dem...........................10,140

4. Counties of Grayson, Collin, Fannin, Hunt and Raines.
Sam Rayburn, Dem...........................9,872

5. Counties of Dallas, Rockwall, Ellis, Hill and Bosque.
Jack Beall, Dem............................11,220
Fred E. Johnston, Prog.....................86
S. T. Green, Soc...........................125

6. Counties of Navarro, Freestone, Limestone, Robertson, Brazos and Milam.
Rufus Hardy, Dem...........................7,930
W. H. Wilson, Soc..........................157

7. Counties of Anderson, Houston, Trinity, Polk, San Jacinto, Liberty, Chambers and Galveston.
A. W. Gregg, Dem...........................8,168

8. Counties of Harris, Fort Bend, Austin, Waller, Montgomery, Grimes, Walker, Madison and Leon.
Joe Eagle, Dem.............................11,928
J. V. Miller, Rep..........................462

9. Counties of Gonzales, Fayette, Colorado, Wharton, Matagorda, Brazoria, Jackson, Lavaca, De Witt, Victoria, Calhoun, Aransas, Refugio, Bee, Goliad and Karnes.
G. F. Burgess, Dem.....................................11,391

10. Counties of Williamson, Travis, Hays, Caldwell, Bastrop, Lee, Burleson and Washington.
A. S. Burleson, Dem.....................................12,109

11. Counties of McLennan, Falls, Bell, Coryell and Hamilton.
R. L. Henry, Dem.......................................7,623

12. Counties of Tarrant, Parker, Johnson, Hood, Somervell, Earth and Comanche.
Oscar Calloway, Dem...................................10,769

13. Counties of Cook, Denton, Wise, Montague, Clay, Jack, Young, Archer, Wichita, Wilbarger, Baylor, Throckmorton, Knox, Foard, Hardeman, Cottle, Motley, Dickens, Floyd, Hale, Lamb, Bailey, Childress, Hall, Briscoe, Swisher, Castro, Parmer, Deaf Smith, Randall, Armstrong, Donley, Collingsworth, Wheeler, Gray, Carson, Potter, Oldham, Hartley, Moore, Hutchinson, Roberts, Hemphill, Lipscomb, Ochiltree, Hansford, Sherman and Dallam.
J. H. Stephens, Dem...................................20,363
H. H. Cooper, Rep.......................................1,116

14. Counties of Bexar, Comal, Kendall, Bandera, Kerr, Gillespie, Blanco, Burnet, Llano, Mason, McCulloch, San Saba, Lampasas, Mills, Brown and Coleman.
J. L. Slayden, Dem...................................14,636

15. Counties of Cameron, Hidalgo, Starr, Zapata, Webb, Duval, Nueces, San Patricio, Live Oak, Atascosa, Wilson, Guadalupe, McMullen, LaSalle, Dimmit, Maverick, Zavalla, Frio, Medina, Uvalde, Kinney and Val Verde.
J. N. Garner, Dem...................................15,672

16. Counties of El Paso, Jeff Davis, Presidio, Brewster, Pecos, Crockett, Schleicher, Sutton, Edwards, Kimble, Menard, Concho, Tom Green, Irion, Upton, Crane, Ward, Reeves, Loving, Winkler, Ector, Midland, Glasscock, Sterling, Coke, Runnels, Eastland, Callahan, Taylor, Nolan, Mitchell, Howard, Martin, Andrews, Gaines, Dawson, Borden, Scurry, Fisher, Jones, Shackelford, Stephens, Palo Pinto, Haskell, Stonewall, King, Kent, Garza, Crosby, Lubbock, Lynn, Terry, Yoakum, Cochran and Hockley.
W. R. Smith, Dem...................................21,186

LEGISLATURE.

	Senate.	House.	J.B.
Democrats	30	142	172
Republicans	1	0	1

STATE OFFICERS. (All democrats.)
Governor—O. B. Colquitt.
Lieutenant-Governor—Will H. Mays.
Secretary of State—F. C. Weinert.
Attorney-General—B. F. Looney.
Comptroller—W. P. Lane.
Treasurer—J. M. Edwards.
Supt. of Public Instruction—W. F. Doughty.

UTAH (Population in 1910, 373,351).

COUNTIES.

Population in 1910. (27)	Rep. Taft	Dem. Wilson	Prog. Roosevelt	Soc. Debs
4717 Beaver	674	602	328	2
13894 Box Elder	1650	1402	996	
23062 Cache	2845	3388	1169	20
8624 Carbon	783	508	599	341
10191 Davis	1295	1143	458	21
6750 Emery	762	755	536	190
3660 Garfield	673	349	128	23
1595 Grand	192	215	118	45
3933 Iron	695	544	64	95
10702 Juab	1171	985	347	803
1652 Kane	429	115	20	5
6118 Millard	970	865	357	124
2467 Morgan	319	234	273	45
1734 Piute	206	110	146	87
1883 Rich	329	257	99	5
131426 Salt Lake	12091	10468	8809	3798
2377 San Juan	146	145	95	4
16704 San Pete	2489	1975	1272	171
9775 Sevier	1451	909	758	287
8200 Summit	1294	983	425	226
7924 Tooele	952	647	261	284
7050 Uintah	543	566	642	165

Population in 1910.	Taft	Wilson	Roosevelt	Debs
37942 Utah	4175	4636	2295	696
8920 Wasatch	1216	924	452	294
5123 Washington	712	845	72	6
1749 Wayne	283	183	24	53
35179 Weber	3171	2991	3608	969
Total	42100	36579	24174	9023
Plurality	5521			
Per cent	37.63	32.69	21.61	8.07
Total vote	111876			

FOR REPRESENTATIVES IN CONGRESS, 1912.

Joseph Howell, Rep.....................................43,133
Jacob Johnson, Rep.....................................42,049
T. D. Johnson, Dem.....................................36,640
Mathonihah Thomas, Dem................................37,192
S. H. Love, Prog.......................................22,358
Lewis Larson, Prog.....................................21,934
Murray E. King, Soc.....................................8,971
W. M. Knerr, Soc..8,953

LEGISLATURE.

	Senate.	House.	J.B.
Republicans	16	31	47
Democrats	2	14	16

STATE OFFICERS. (All republican.)
Governor—William Spry.
Secretary of State—David Mattson.
Attorney-General Albert R. Barnes.
Auditor—Lincoln G. Kelly.
Treasurer—Jesse D. Jewkes.
Superintendent of Public Instruction—Andrew C. Nelson.

VERMONT (Population in 1910, 355,956).

COUNTIES.

Population in 1910. (14)	PRESIDENT 1912 Rep. Taft	Dem. Wilson	Prog. Roosevelt	Soc. Debs	PRES. 1908 Rep. Taft	Dem. Bryan
20010 Addison	1335	621	1487	19..	2396	444
21378 Bennington	1464	1057	1380	105..	2458	748
26031 Caledonia	1583	1065	2049	82..	2700	764
42147 Chittenden	2368	2266	1663	42..	3806	1650
7284 Essex	463	348	353	10..	744	527
29896 Franklin	1483	1317	1437	25..	2360	1048
3761 Grand Isle	193	210	204	6..	364	188
12585 Lamoille	852	431	996	30..	1455	311
18703 Orange	1289	956	1426	32..	2262	667
23337 Orleans	1475	628	1891	17..	2535	384
48139 Rutland	2999	2079	2027	79..	5643	1542
State House	29	4	3	..		
41702 Washington	2797	1743	1730	373..	3823	1610
26933 Windham	2143	1327	2020	67..	3728	905
33681 Windsor	2409	1802	2546	91..	4683	907
Total	22132	15354	22132	928..	39552	11496
Plurality	1200				28056	
Per cent	37.13	24.44	35.22	□1.47..	75.11	21.83
Total vote	62838				52654	

For president in 1912 Chafin, Pro., received 1,092 votes.
For president in 1908 Chafin, Pro., received 802 votes and Hisgen, Ind., 804.

FOR REPRESENTATIVES IN CONGRESS, 1912.

1. Counties of Addison, Bennington, Chittenden, Franklin, Grand Isle, Lamoille and Rutland.
Frank L. Greene, Rep...................................15,469
Patrick M. Meldon, Dem.................................9,154
George L. Story, Pro.....................................797
John Spargo, Soc..454

2. Counties of Caledonia, Essex, Orange, Orleans, Washington, Windham and Windsor.
Frank Plumley, Rep....................................13,316
O. C. Sawyer, Dem.......................................8,269
Elmer E. Phillips, Pro...................................532
Charles E. Ordway, Soc..................................766

LEGISLATURE.

	Senate.	House.	J.B.
Republicans	27	146	173
Democrats	3	56	59
Progressives	..	22	22
Progressive republicans	..	7	7
Prohibitionist	..	1	1
Others	..	12	12

STATE OFFICERS. (All republicans.)
Governor—Allen M. Fletcher.
Lieutenant-Governor—Frank E. Howe.
Treasurer—Edward H. Deavitt.
Secretary of State—Guy W. Bailey.
Auditor—Horace F. Graham.
Attorney-General—Rufus E. Brown.

VIRGINIA (Population in 1910, 2,061,612).

COUNTIES.

Population in 1910	(100)	Dem. Wilson	Rep. Taft	Prog. Roosevelt	Soc. Debs	Pro. Chafin
36650	Accomac	1825	153	110	1	25
29871	Albemarle	1215	144	126	15	3
15329	Alexandria city	951	132	104	11	2
10231	Alexandria county	346	86	153	8	2
14173	Alleghany	394	125	263	10	15
8720	Amelia	325	32	60	—	2
18932	Amherst	765	64	60	8	—
8304	Appomattox	654	28	51	—	1
32445	Augusta	1556	568	272	11	78
6538	Bath	329	159	39	3	11
29549	Bedford	1219	142	343	9	20
5154	Bland	299	206	118	1	1
17727	Botetourt	889	517	191	2	9
6247	Bristol city	405	86	64	8	3
19244	Brunswick	643	67	43	5	6
12334	Buchanan	524	223	389	—	2
15304	Buckingham	603	97	110	—	—
3245	Buena Vista city	155	43	48	8	3
23043	Campbell	810	97	126	11	8
16596	Caroline	590	144	126	—	6
21116	Carroll	765	874	346	—	3
5253	Charles City	121	37	28	—	—
15785	Charlotte	609	175	123	10	1
6705	Charlottesville city	454	39	24	4	1
21209	Chesterfield	702	61	75	8	2
7468	Clarke	576	39	14	1	—
5448	Clifton Forge city	233	63	61	34	1
4711	Craig	337	62	150	1	4
13472	Culpeper	752	108	49	1	5
9195	Cumberland	362	10	31	1	—
19020	Danville city	1006	93	79	11	7
9199	Dickenson	529	398	137	5	—
15442	Dinwiddie	512	58	75	1	3
21225	Elizabeth City	347	43	56	8	1
9196	Essex	278	72	11	—	—
20536	Fairfax	932	187	150	6	3
22626	Fauquier	1187	182	87	2	3
14092	Floyd	409	232	712	5	13
8323	Fluvanna	409	53	58	5	—
20480	Franklin	1238	415	691	5	3
12787	Frederick	922	181	112	3	16
5874	Fredericksburg city	414	51	100	—	1
11628	Giles	725	267	247	4	3
13477	Gloucester	510	74	56	—	—
9237	Goochland	332	114	32	6	—
10856	Grayson	842	832	290	1	1
6837	Greene	238	141	95	—	5
11890	Greenesville	294	31	72	1	3
40044	Halifax	1260	426	127	15	8
	Hampton city	353	13	31	1	1
17200	Hanover	609	87	4	—	2
23437	Henrico	952	83	105	16	6
18450	Henry	707	216	360	8	3
5517	Highland	313	221	84	—	14
14929	Isle of Wight	708	75	101	—	—
3624	James City	128	10	15	1	2
6378	King George	236	48	103	—	—
9576	King and Queen	246	68	48	—	—
8547	King William	305	69	63	1	1
9732	Lancaster	479	82	16	1	5
23840	Lee	1023	699	677	9	10
21167	Loudoun	1386	256	87	4	35
18518	Louisa	578	91	141	6	4
13790	Lunenburg	508	66	50	4	—
29494	Lynchburg city	1487	111	218	19	5
10515	Madison	402	210	63	1	1
9715	Manchester City					
8922	Mathews	523	45	34	—	—
28956	Mecklenburg	1039	191	91	1	5
8852	Middlesex	374	128	22	—	—
17298	Montgomery	684	349	531	2	27
26886	Nansemond	544	53	63	2	9
16821	Nelson	706	163	95	5	2
4682	New Kent	160	30	46	—	1
20205	Newport News city	988	100	231	53	3
67452	Norfolk city	3539	555	451	33	10
52744	Norfolk county	1089	422	215	11	4
16672	Northampton	726	83	76	1	—
10777	Northumberland	470	102	52	—	—
13462	Nottoway	683	72	70	4	7
13486	Orange	619	87	57	—	2
14147	Page	703	340	138	10	26
17195	Patrick	698	434	550	3	4
24127	Petersburg city	1122	75	44	2	1
50709	Pittsylvania	1558	527	321	15	5
33190	Portsmouth city	1529	64	321	16	1
6099	Powhatan	230	109	51	11	3
14296	Prince Edward	584	72	46	—	1
7848	Prince George	204	42	48	1	—
11526	Princess Anne	422	40	63	—	—

Population		Wilson	Taft	Roosevelt	Debs	Chafin
12026	Prince William	814	82	93	5	6
17246	Pulaski	781	196	484	13	3
4202	Radford city	185	36	95	8	4
8041	Rappahannock	356	94	9	13	2
127628	Richmond city	5632	465	488	91	10
7415	Richmond county	342	110	40	—	—
34874	Roanoke city	1913	268	502	39	16
19323	Roanoke county	696	108	191	9	15
21171	Rockbridge	949	433	212	13	7
34903	Rockingham	1761	937	421	25	47
23474	Russell	1248	588	623	6	4
23814	Scott	1311	557	1075	12	6
20942	Shenandoah	1396	706	488	7	12
20726	Smyth	1022	609	578	6	3
26302	Southampton	861	95	49	—	8
9655	Spottsylvania	390	58	158	—	11
8650	Stafford	347	141	185	2	—
10694	Staunton city	632	65	287	—	—
	Suffolk city	480	71	83	2	17
9715	Surrey	390	57	37	6	5
13964	Sussex	435	59	55	—	14
24946	Tazewell	979	598	871	19	7
8589	Warren	571	122	39	2	0
6041	Warwick	124	17	30	1	—
32830	Washington	1731	599	936	4	4
9613	Westmoreland	341	69	43	2	—
2214	Williamsburg city	113	11	14	—	1
5864	Winchester city	447	141	85	3	22
34162	Wise	1279	851	575	34	1
20372	Wythe	1110	633	650	5	1
7757	York	211	34	26	3	3
	Total	90332	23288	21777	820	709
	Plurality	67044				
	Per cent	65.95	17.00	15.89	.59	.51
	Total vote			136976		

For president in 1912 Reimer, Soc.-Lab., received 50 votes.

FOR REPRESENTATIVES IN CONGRESS, 1912.

1. The counties of Accomac, Caroline, Essex, Gloucester, King and Queen, Lancaster, Mathews, Middlesex, Northampton, Northumberland, Richmond, Spottsylvania, Westmoreland and city of Fredericksburg.

W. A. Jones, Dem.................................10,361
T. E. Coleman, Soc.................................753

2. The counties of Charles City, Elizabeth City, Isle of Wight, James City, Nansemond, Norfolk, Princess Anne, Southampton, Surrey, Warwick, York and the cities of Newport News, Norfolk, Portsmouth and Williamsburg.

E. E. Holland, Dem.................................10,061
N. T. Green, Prog.................................1,121

3. The counties of Chesterfield, Goochland, Hanover, Henrico, King William, New Kent and the cities of Richmond and Manchester.

Andrew J. Montague, Dem.................................10,541
Charles A. Haight, Soc.................................154

4. The counties of Amelia, Brunswick, Dinwiddie, Greensville, Lunenburg, Mecklenburg, Nottoway, Powhatan, Prince Edward, Prince George, Sussex and the city of Petersburg.

Walter A. Watson, Dem.................................7,847
Fred Herzig, Soc.................................269

5. The counties of Carroll, Floyd, Franklin, Grayson, Henry, Patrick, Pittsylvania and the city of Danville.

E. W. Saunders, Dem.................................9,479
A. R. Hammer, Rep.................................5,449

6. The counties of Bedford, Campbell, Charlotte, Halifax, Montgomery, Roanoke and the cities of Lynchburg, Radford and Roanoke.

Carter Glass, Dem.................................8,194
James S. Browning, Prog.................................1,589

7. The counties of Albemarle, Clark, Frederick, Greene, Madison, Page, Rappahannock, Rockingham, Shenandoah, Warren and the cities of Charlottesville and Winchester.

James Hay, Dem.................................10,015
George N. Earman, Rep.................................3,539
E. C. Garrison, Soc.................................446

8. The counties of Alexandria, Culpeper, Fairfax, Fauquier, King George, Loudoun, Louisa, Orange, Prince William, Stafford and the city of Alexandria.

C. C. Carlin, Dem.................................9,083
F. T. Evans, Soc.................................628

9. The counties of Bland, Buchanan, Craig, Dickenson, Giles, Lee, Pulaski, Russell, Scott, Smyth,

Tazewell, Washington, Wise, Wythe and the city of Bristol.

R. A. Ayers, Dem......................................13,857
C. B. Slemp, Rep......................................14,868
Walter Graham, Prog..................................1,004

10. The counties of Alleghany, Amherst, Appomattox, Augusta, Bath, Botetourt, Buckingham, Cumberland, Fluvanna, Highland, Nelson, Rockbridge and the cities of Buena Vista and Staunton.

H. D. Flood, Dem.....................................9,615
E. J. McCulloch, Prog................................2,458
Nathan Parkins, Soc..................................842

LEGISLATURE.	Senate.	House.	J.B.
Democrats	35	92	127
Republicans	5	7	12

STATE OFFICERS. (All democrats.)
Governor—William H. Mann.
Lieutenant-Governor—J. T. Ellyson.
Attorney-General—Samuel W. Williams.
Secretary—B. O. James.
Treasurer—A. W. Harman, Jr.

WASHINGTON (Population in 1910, 1,141,990).

COUNTIES.	PRESIDENT 1912			
(39)	Rep.	Dem.	Prog.	Soc.
Population in 1910.	Taft	Wilson	Roosevelt	Debs
10920 Adams	350	551	748	154
5831 Asotin	574	549	512	133
7937 Benton	726	1234	1370	356
35590 Chehalis	3712	2479	2201	1682
15104 Chelan	1083	1350	1886	652
6755 Clallam	720	463	680	608
26115 Clarke	1867	2551	2077	995
7042 Columbia	636	845	812	172
12561 Cowlitz	1348	949	990	495
9227 Douglas	641	1352	795	318
4800 Ferry	286	619	502	269
5153 Franklin	282	607	525	308
4199 Garfield	358	426	659	86
8698 Grant	458	769	914	414
4701 Island	332	395	504	347
5337 Jefferson	656	638	740	282
284638 King	15501	20082	20602	6843
17647 Kitsap	1224	989	2321	1129
18561 Kittitas	1157	1407	1902	515
10180 Klickitat	1637	1028	795	351
32127 Lewis	3185	2482	2049	1638
17539 Lincoln	691	1829	1845	289
5156 Mason	440	531	464	337
12587 Okanogan	801	1461	1388	424
12532 Pacific	1270	971	1250	382
Pend d'Oreille (new)	274	701	637	288
120812 Pierce	6339	6604	12506	4075
3908 San Juan	341	510	346	..
20241 Skagit	2420	2528	1950	1665
2857 Skamania	247	250	221	..
59209 Snohomish	3041	3005	7844	3695
139404 Spokane	4218	10441	16687	2556
25297 Stevens	808	1979	1970	988
17581 Thurston	1930	1455	1470	1365
3285 Wahkiakum	296	185	288	75
31931 Walla Walla	1928	2505	2727	446
49511 Whatcom	4187	2776	4562	2816
32280 Whitman	1896	3601	2290	629
41709 Yakima	3271	3242	4282	1147
Total	70445	86840	113046	40134
Plurality			26853	
Per cent	22.66	27.49	35.11	12.40
Total vote			322799	

For president in 1912 Chafin, Pro., received 9,810 votes.

FOR REPRESENTATIVES IN CONGRESS, 1912.

J. A. Falconer, Prog................................92,276
J. W. Bryan, Prog..................................88,940
J. E. Frost, Rep...................................84,510
Henry B. Dewey, Rep................................85,386
E. O'Connor, Dem...................................72,089
Henry M. White, Dem................................70,033

1. Counties of King, Island, Kitsap, Snohomish and Whatcom.
William E. Humphrey, Rep...........................35,138
Charles G. Helfner, Dem............................28,290
Daniel Landon, Prog................................34,101

2. Counties of Chehalis, Clarke, Cowlitz, Jefferson, Klickitat, Lewis, Mason, Pacific, Pierce, Thurston and Wahkiakum.
Albert Johnson, Rep................................22,815
J. A. Munday, Dem..................................15,638
Stanton Warburton, Prog............................21,970

3. Counties of Asotin, Benton, Chelan, Columbia, Franklin, Garfield, Kittitas, Okanogan, Pend d'Oreille, Stevens, Walla Walla, Whitman and Yakima.
William L. LaFollette, Rep.........................19,466
Roscoe Drumheller, Dem.............................15,499
F. M. Goodwin, Prog................................12,609

LEGISLATURE.	Senate.	House.	J.B.
Republicans	27	49	76
Democrats	9	18	27
Progressives	6	29	35
Socialist	0	1	1

STATE OFFICERS.
Governor—Ernest Lister, Dem.
Lieutenant-Governor—Louis F. Hart, Rep.
Secretary of State—I. M. Howell, Rep.
State Treasurer—Edward Meath, Rep.
Auditor—C. W. Clausen, Rep.
Attorney-General—W. V. Tanner, Rep.

WEST VIRGINIA (Population in 1910, 1,222,119).

COUNTIES.	PRESIDENT 1912				
(55)	Dem.	Prog.	Rep.	Soc.	Pro.
Population in 1910.	Wilson	Roosevelt	Taft	Debs	Chafin
15858 Barbour	1564	1425	609	100	78
21999 Berkeley	2703	1203	1349	155	123
10331 Boone	1119	624	416	314	12
23023 Braxton	2611	1814	580	39	56
11098 Brooke	850	446	972	244	60
46685 Cabell	4793	3193	1798	480	170
11258 Calhoun	1349	474	573	13	9
10238 Clay	932	796	352	55	45
12672 Doddridge	866	1189	622	44	37
31905 Fayette	3757	3126	2937	1128	151
11379 Gilmer	1495	815	469	22	24
7838 Grant	356	1024	559	13	27
24833 Greenbrier	2707	1794	622	186	38
11694 Hampshire	1777	266	406	4	24
10465 Hancock	634	557	662	125	122
9163 Hardy	1209	314	344	7	15
48381 Harrison	4378	3439	1754	1077	360
20956 Jackson	1937	1855	1199	49	27
15889 Jefferson	2395	153	988	55	32
81457 Kanawha	9558	6846	1780	3671	198
18261 Lewis	1929	1153	1019	146	138
20491 Lincoln	1876	1619	631	56	26
14476 Logan	1812	601	519	245	11
42794 Marion	4535	2443	1625	826	359
32388 Marshall	2105	1832	1610	521	280
23019 Mason	1812	1686	1024	247	28
38371 Mercer	3497	2958	1507	158	66
16674 Mineral	1567	1464	448	164	30
19431 Mingo	1852	884	1563	72	12
24334 Monongalia	3678	1761	1216	580	148
13055 Monroe	1570	740	708	17	17
7848 Morgan	550	518	512	72	34
47856 McDowell	2437	2425	4341	64	90
17699 Nicholas	2018	1451	584	29	105
57572 Ohio	5771	2646	3966	1579	248
9349 Pendleton	1052	435	475	17	22
8074 Pleasants	797	364	495	22	35
14710 Pocahontas	1428	1684	589	94	114
26341 Preston	1485	2437	1461	212	153
14587 Putnam	1538	1401	581	326	20
25633 Raleigh	2343	2951	897	484	51
26028 Randolph	2563	1415	756	371	83
17875 Ritchie	1270	1262	988	91	149
21543 Roane	2045	1670	708	52	65
18420 Summers	2111	1248	791	88	32
16554 Taylor	1445	1313	791	175	81
18675 Tucker	1221	1265	548	253	81
16211 Tyler	1193	1125	704	169	94
16629 Upshur	893	1695	834	61	139
24081 Wayne	2634	700	1465	83	39
9680 Webster	1390	524	307	23	26
20855 Wetzel	2710	739	1050	163	97
9047 Wirt	958	761	214	28	19
38001 Wood	3784	1814	2509	428	101
10392 Wyoming	881	620	569	8	10
Total	113046	79977	56967	15369	4534
Plurality	34069				
Per cent	42.09	29.41	21.10	5.71	1.69
Total vote		268560			

For president in 1908 Taft, Rep., received 137,869 votes; Bryan, Dem., 111,418; Chafin, Pro., 5,139; Debs, Soc., 3,679.

FOR REPRESENTATIVES IN CONGRESS, 1912.

At Large—Howard Sutherland, Rep..................132,723
Ben H. Hiner, Dem.................................114,578
Peters, Soc.......................................15,291

1. Counties of Hancock, Brooke, Ohio, Marshall, Wetzel, Marion, Harrison and Lewis
John W. Davis, Dem 24,777
George A Laughlin, Rep.. 24,613
Holt, Soc 4,230
2 Counties of Barbour, Berkeley, Grant, Hampshire, Hardy, Jefferson, Mineral, Monongalia, Morgan, Pendleton, Preston, Randolph, Taylor, Tucker
William G Brown, Dem ... 23,469
William G. Conley, Rep ... 23,455
Smith, Soc 1,974
3 Counties of Clay Fayette, Greenbrier, Kanawha, Monroe, Nicholas, Pocahontas, Summers, Upshur, Webster
Adam C. Littlepage, Dem ... 24,573
Samuel V. Avis, Rep ... 26,041
Rogers, Soc ... 5,163
4 Counties of Braxton, Calhoun, Doddridge, Gilmer, Jackson, Pleasants, Ritchie, Roane, Tyler, Wirt, Wood

John M Hamilton, Dem ... 19,346
H. H. Moss, Jr , Rep ... 20,446
5. Counties of Boone, Cabell, Lincoln, Logan, Mason, Mercer, Mingo, McDowell, Putnam, Raleigh, Wayne, Wyoming.
James A. Hughes, Rep ... 33,128
James F. Beavers, Dem ... 27,697
Gillespie, Soc 2,468

LEGISLATURE.　　Senate.House J B.
Republicans　.　15　53　68
Democrats .. .. 15　33　48

STATE OFFICERS. (All republicans.)
Governor—Henry D. Hatfield.
Secretary—Stuart F. Reed.
Auditor—John S Darst
Treasurer—E Leslie Long.
Attorney-General—Abraham A. Lilly.
Superintendent Schools—M. P. Shawkey.

WISCONSIN (Population in 1910, 2,833,860).

Population in 1910	COUNTIES (71)	Dem Wilson	Pro Chafin	Rep. Taft	Soc Deba	S L. Reimer	Prog Roosev't	Dem. Karel	Pro Hill	Rep M'Gov'n	Soc Thompson	S L. Curtis	Rep Taft	Dem Bryan	Pro. Chafin	Soc Debs	S L Gillhaus
8604	Adams ..	462	52	689	66	22	204	326	34	991	53	3	1167	436	56	213	1
21965	Ashland	1451	109	937	315	4	677	1235	107	1797	243	11	2259	1582	110	32	3
29914	Barron .	1065	253	1414	205	5	968	920	257	2330	226	24	3247	1266	243	128	2
15987	Bayfield .	666	68	514	306	7	671	539	79	1239	275	23	1957	569	72	174	3
54098	Brown. ...	3537	141	2764	569	10	1396	3444	146	3936	510	23	4917	3353	129	516	8
16008	Buffalo .	848	40	1339	45	3	378	804	47	1525	28	17	1987	1027	56	20	—
9028	Burnett	805	50	403	172	7	570	214	54	683	158	33	1181	286	98	63	1
16701	Calumet...	1306	17	931	85	7	454	1393	25	1317	65	8	1576	1711	80	85	—
82103	Chippewa	2028	113	1736	102	6	1132	2383	90	2471	83	12	3526	2203	148	90	2
30074	Clark	1528	109	2035	145	—	648	1433	114	2650	115*	28	3491	1576	153	92	—
31129	Columbia	2473	148	2463	121	—	585	2395	132	3045	98	11	4072	2363	198	140	—
16238	Crawford	1515	64	1407	69	1	323	1634	64	1571	49	4	2041	1586	72	64	—
77435	Dane..	9017	391	5244	298	7	1292	7102	398	8358	232	41	9441	7818	489	256	5
47136	Dodge	5246	119	2569	118	—	705	5656	129	2637	98	4	4015	5883	162	63	—
18711	Door	789	135	1167	77	3	890	1156	125	1358	67	8	2405	778	53	87	1
47422	Douglas .	1181	117	790	752	60	2235	1584	149	2450	935	69	3509	1715	257	652	146
25260	Dunn	833	94	1403	235	7	1174	621	91	2571	205	22	3297	914	102	119	—
32721	Eau Claire .	1728	116	2012	239	5	895	1497	108	2947	228	17	4980	1859	173	158	—
3381	Florence	131	9	262	15	1	182	146	11	396	12	1	541	102	19	5	—
51610	Fond du Lac	4838	174	3014	349	4	1236	4824	314	3955	289	9	5872	5194	244	230	5
6782	Forest. ...	567	22	518	30	—	212	603	29	569	45	5	1023	324	31	40	3
49007	Grant	3815	221	3283	99	1	667	3496	214	3868	93	11	4980	3096	288	83	—
21641	Green	1716	201	1601	83	7	516	1707	172	2044	83	20..	2617	1856	209	122	—
15491	Green Lake	1407	74	1269	39	—	195	1526	96	1299	39	1.	2094	1608	63	42	—
22197	Iowa.... ..	2103	224	1886	82	1	438	2009	160	2413	32	1..	2684	2077	233	42	—
8806	Iron	847	84	479	72	3	254	450	81	828	65	25.	1184	314	43	42	—
17075	Jackson	606	86	1394	78	4	477	550	81	1830	68	7	2603	631	65	40	2
34306	Jefferson	4381	122	1926	100	3	490	4546	150	2075	101	8	3207	4492	161	70	3
19569	Juneau. ..	1236	59	1322	135	—	435	1179	62	1675	153	14	2454	1691	77	37	2
32929	Kenosha	2216	104	1671	492	9	1619	2722	175	2750	462	38	3409	2006	239	601	—
16784	Kewaunee	1690	19	1115	22	7	263	1635	26	1415	19	—	1590	1781	37	64	—
43206	LaCrosse ...	4264	148	2272	337	14	999	3628	153	3088	346	17	4382	4054	189	113	2
20075	Lafayette .	1852	77	1844	39	—	185	1971	62	2414	19	4	2852	2100	105	24	—
17062	Langlade .	1587	36	719	91	2	810	1446	45	1341	54	1.	2308	1313	83	99	—
19064	Lincoln .	1760	45	712	312	2	637	1421	29	1661	188	12 .	2308	1313	83	99	—
44978	Manitowoc .	3436	44	2389	890	12	919	3818	62	2951	808	8	4126	3052	61	917	5
55054	Marathon .	4043	164	5033	597	24	1274	4374	176	3865	505	32.	5258	4703	143	275	3
38812	Marinette...	1558	95	1818	276	10	1125	1764	90	2612	210	12	3454	1597	235	154	—
10741	Marquette .	923	42	881	22	2	365	925	44	1161	15	4..	1555	798	44	17	—
433187	Milwaukee .	27628	536	17877	19243	79	5889	31746	991	17771	21301	1785	26625	26000	1278	17496	57
28881	Monroe .	2084	160	1841	125	—	628	1889	185	2441	117	22.	3304	2155	136	91	—
25657	Oconto .	1523	54	1986	139	—	554	1710	46	2273	120	12	3020	1453	75	114	1
11443	Oneida .	717	20	773	175	1	431	700	22	1107	169	10	1586	688	28	354	1
49102	Outagamie .	4149	155	2984	192	10	1401	3851	157	4070	179	59	5079	4356	209	118	13
17123	Ozaukee .	1878	24	719	76	—	241	2074	22	714	55	6	1216	1856	27	60	1
7577	Pepin.. .	410	24	528	27	2	324	453	27	748	21	4	1010	447	36	5	—
22079	Pierce	985	103	986	102	5	1204	694	100	2295	81	54	2988	978	150	56	—
21387	Polk	830	99	848	270	10	1075	465	109	2045	266	41	2788	816	146	121	—
30945	Portage . .	2300	85	1932	101	2	890	2652	89	2466	99	10	3269	2362	112	50	1
13795	Price . .	662	75	708	290	8	662	682	67	1225	273	35	1738	609	79	236	1
57424	Racine. ...	3909	286	2866	616	6	1440	3918	328	3725	550	120	5490	3688	429	794	1
18809	Richland	1408	345	1623	127	3	367	1444	331	1930	107	15	2464	1689	291	54	1
55543	Rock	3632	413	4276	261	11	2002	4243	319	4717	227	74	7830	4227	391	265	12
11160	Rusk	522	54	515	204	3	344	427	50	976	181	13	1431	532	48	90	3
25910	St Croix	1806	99	1728	188	4	823	1720	121	2442	154	7	8224	1773	98	83	4
32869	Sauk	2464	302	2171	81	3	720	2348	290	2774	58	11 .	3854	2571	294	83	—
6277	Sawyer .	432	22	295	15	1	144	354	15	485	10	1.	815	299	18	19	—
31884	...wano .	1660	112	1545	99	13	1106	1386	114	2759	107	14	3349	1750	102	40	—
54888	Sheboygan	3068	109	2692	1084	11	1628	4227	138	4197	1047	16.	6948	4405	245	752	—
13641	Taylor	821	35	773	21	8	379	757	21	1195	246	6	1627	924	42	82	1
22728	Trempealeau	1236	102	1763	50	3	795	1200	34	2474	69	5	3785	1085	117	22	—
28116	Vernon ..	1263	184	2664	74	2	810	1310	172	3680	70	14	4114	1540	188	39	—
6019	Vilas	327	9	361	14	1	213	383	12	416	61	9	794	273	18	83	—
29614	Walworth ..	2125	305	2096	78	—	1247	2287	325	2535	88	21	4151	1960	487	73	2
8196	Washburn	398	43	409	148	—	488	476	40	821	193	5	1114	396	35	69	—
23784	Washington	2425	26	1790	150	—	302	2785	20	1808	138	—.	2588	2625	41	77	1

Population		Wilson	Chafin	Taft	Debs	Reimer	Roosev't	Karel	Hill	M'Gov'n	Thomps'n	Curtis	Taft	Bryan	Chafin	Debs	Gillhaus
37100	Waukesha	3594	281	2714	196	1	597..	3521	295	8235	183	13..	4758	3206	346	197	8
32782	Waupaca	1563	178	2204	131	10	1767..	1339	199	3741	141	72..	4785	1483	239	143	2
18886	Waushara	772	75	1343	92	6	741..	586	93	2142	75	31..	2821	507	114	82	14
62116	Winnebago	4631	146	1922	478	21	4008..	4396	202	5190	498	166..	6797	5511	412	288	3
30583	Wood	2523	139	1742	367	38	525..	2340	122	2422	340	16..	3018	2498	132	274	—

Total.....164228 8586 130695 35481 522 62469...167316 9433 179360 34468.8253.. 247747 166633 11572 28170 314
Plurality...... 33533 .. 12044 .. 81115
Per cent...... 41.06 2.15 32.67 8.37 .13 15.62.. 42.48 2.40 45.54 8.75 .83.. 54.52 36.66 2.55 6.20 .07
Total vote...... 399972 . 393830 . 451421

FOR REPRESENTATIVES IN CONGRESS, 1912.

1. Counties of Kenosha, Racine, Rock, Walworth and Waukesha.
Henry A. Cooper, Rep...18,914
Calvin Stewart, Dem...13,816
Marcus S. Kellogg, Pro... 1,333
Joseph Orth, Soc. Dem... 1,523

2. Counties of Columbia, Dodge, Jefferson, Ozaukee, Sheboygan and Washington.
Michael E. Burke, Dem...20,665
Will E. Mack, Pro... 538
Henry J. Grell, Rep...14,698
Edward D. Deuss, Soc. Dem... 1,512

3. Counties of Crawford, Dane, Grant, Green, Iowa, Lafayette and Richland.
John M. Nelson, Rep...22,388
Albert H. Long, Dem...18,219
Charles H. Berryman, Pro... 1,219
William E. Middleton, Soc. Dem... 496

4. The 3d, 4th, 5th, 8th, 11th, 12th, 14th, 16th, 17th, 23d and 24th wards of the city of Milwaukee; towns of Wauwatosa, Greenfield, Franklin, Oak Creek and Lake; village of West Milwaukee and cities of West Allis, South Milwaukee and Cudahy, all in Milwaukee county.
William J. Cary, Dem.-Rep...14,906
William R. Nethercut, Pro... 541
John M. Beffel, Rep... 6,946
W. R. Gaylord, Soc. Dem...10,846

5. The 1st, 2d, 6th, 7th, 9th, 10th, 13th, 15th, 18th, 19th, 20th, 21st, 22d and 25th wards of the city of Milwaukee; towns of Granville and Milwaukee and villages of North Milwaukee, East Milwaukee and Whitefish Bay, all in Milwaukee county.
William H. Stafford, Dem.-Rep...15,933
Augustin C. Forster, Pro... 406
James F. Trottman, Rep... 8,251
Victor L. Berger, Soc. Dem...14,023

6. Counties of Calumet, Fond du Lac, Green Lake, Manitowoc, Marquette and Winnebago.
Michael K. Reilly, Dem...16,742
Frank L. Smith, Pro... 605
James H. Davidson, Rep...15,505
Martin Georgeson, Soc. Dem... 1,659

7. Counties of Adams, Clark, Jackson, Juneau, La Crosse, Sauk and Vernon.
William N. Coffland, Dem...10,795
B. S. Hawley, Pro... 901
John Jacob. Esch, Rep...20,060
C. A. Noetzleman, Soc. Dem... 826

8. Counties of Marathon, Portage, Shawano, Waupaca, Waushara and Wood.
Arthur J. Plowman, Dem...12,265
Adolph B. Buckman, Pro... 687
Edward F. Browne, Rep...17,094
Curtis A. Boorman, Soc. Dem... 1,256

9. Counties of Brown, Door, Florence, Forest, Kewaunee, Langlad, Marinette, Oconto and Outagamie.
Thomas F. Konop, Dem...16,843
Jason L. Sizer, Pro... 631
Elmer A. Morse, Rep...16,129
John Oliver, Soc. Dem... 1,133

10. Counties of Barron, Buffalo, Chippewa, Dunn, Eau Claire, Pepin, Pierce, St. Croix and Trempeleau.
James A. Frear, Rep...19,915
Charles Donohue, Dem... 8,794

Beverley White, Pro... 868
Albert Slaughter, Soc. Dem... 1,031

11. Counties of Ashland, Bayfield, Burnett, Douglas, Iron, Lincoln, Oneida, Polk, Price, Rush, Sawyer, Taylor, Vilas and Washington.
Henry A. Johnson, Dem... 7,998
David W. Emerson, Pro... 726
Irvine L. Lenroot, Rep...17,885
Ellis B. Harris, Soc. Dem... 3,017

LEGISLATURE.

	Senate.	House.	J.B.
Republicans	26	60	86
Democrats	6	34	40
Social Democrats	1	6	7

STATE OFFICERS. (All republicans.)
Governor—Francis E. McGovern.
Lieutenant-Governor—Thomas Morris.
Secretary of State—John S. Donald.
Treasurer—Henry Johnson.
Attorney-General—Walter C. Owen.
Insurance Commissioner—Herman L. Ekern.
Superintendent of Schools—Charles P. Cary.

WYOMING (Population in 1910, 145,965).

COUNTIES (21)		PRESIDENT 1912				
Population in 1910	County	Rep. Taft	Dem. Wilson	Prog. Roosevelt	Soc. Debs	Pro. Chafin
11574	Albany	882	1044	831	177	59
8886	Big Horn	794	691	504	136	26
	Campbell	186	361	183	19	11
11282	Carbon	1106	957	489	258	15
6294	Converse	540	496	349	40	14
6492	Crook	505	726	461	166	14
11822	Fremont	811	933	511	131	9
	Goshen	292	318	235	23	30
	Hot Springs	275	343	298	80	12
3453	Johnson	522	524	327	21	2
26127	Laramie	1371	1923	385	131	44
	Lincoln	1430	1028	580	334	6
4796	Natrona	640	447	262	52	5
	Niobrara	500	282	142	30	59
4909	Park	534	672	470	88	28
	Platte	500	785	353	87	40
16324	Sheridan	862	1649	1305	398	34
11575	Sweetwater	838	916	390	279	10
16882	Uinta	717	535	463	207	1
	Washakie	258	221	168	23	5
4960	Weston	449	459	306	80	11
	Total	14560	15310	9232	2760	434
	Plurality		750			
	Per cent	34.42	36.20	21.83	6.52	1.03
	Total vote		42296			

For president in 1908 Taft, Rep., received 20,846 votes; Bryan, Dem., 14,918, and Debs, Soc., 1,715.

FOR REPRESENTATIVE IN CONGRESS, 1912.
Frank W. Mondell, Rep...19,130
Thomas P. Fahey, Dem...14,720
C. E. Winter, Prog... 4,828
Antony Carlson, Soc... 2,230
L. Laughlin, Pro... 296

LEGISLATURE.

	Senate.	House.	J.B.
Republicans	16	30	46
Democrats	11	27	38

STATE OFFICERS.
Governor—J. M. Carey, Prog. Rep.
Secretary—F. L. Houx, Dem.
Auditor—R. B. Forsythe, Rep.
Treasurer—J. L. Baird, Rep.
Supt. Public Instruction—Mrs. Rose A. Maley, Dem.
Attorney-General—D. A. Preston, Dem.

NATIONAL POLITICAL COMMITTEES (1912-1916).

REPUBLICAN.

Headquarters—Chicago and New York.
Chairman—Charles D. Hilles, New York.
Secretary—James B. Reynolds, Washington, D. C.
Assistant Secretary—John Eversman.
Treasurer—George R. Sheldon, New York.
Assistant Treasurer—Walter H. Wilson, Illinois.
Sergeant-at-Arms—William F. Stone, Maryland.
Director Western Headquarters—D. W. Mulvane, Illinois.
Executive Committee—John T. Adams, Iowa; Fred W. Estabrook, New Hampshire; James P. Goodrich, Indiana; Thomas A. Marlow, Montana; Alvah H. Martin, Virginia; Thomas K. Niedringhaus, Missouri; Samuel A. Perkins, Washington; Newell Sanders, Tennessee; Charles B. Warren, Michigan; Roy O. West, Illinois; Ralph E. Williams, Oregon.

Alabama—Prelate D. Barker..................Mobile
Alaska—William S. Bayliss..................Juneau
Arizona—Ralph H. Cameron........Grand Canyon
Arkansas—Powell Clayton....Washington, D. C.
California—P. A. Stanton...............Los Angeles
Colorado—Simon Guggenheim................Denver
Connecticut—William F. Henney..........Hartford
Delaware—Coleman DuPont.............Wilmington
District of Columbia—Chapin Brown....Washington
Florida—Henry S. Chubb................Gainesville
Georgia—Henry S. Jackson..................Atlanta
Hawaii—Charles A. Rice..................Honolulu
Idaho—John W. Hart..........................Menan
Illinois—Roy O. West......................Chicago
Indiana—James P. Goodrich.............Indianapolis
Iowa—John T. Adams......................Dubuque
Kansas—F. S. Stanley......................Wichita
Kentucky—John W. McCulloch..........Owensboro
Louisiana—Victor Loisel...............New Orleans
Maine—Frederick Hale......................Portland
Maryland—William P. Jackson..........Salisbury
Massachusetts—W. Murray Crane..........Dalton
Michigan—Charles B. Warren..............Detroit
Minnesota—E. B. Hawkins..................Duluth
Mississippi—L. B. Moseley..................Jackson
Missouri—Thomas K. Niedringhaus.......St. Louis
Montana—Thomas A. Marlow.................Helena
Nebraska—R. B. Howell........................Omaha
Nevada—H. B. Maxson..........................Reno
New Hampshire—Fred W. Estabrook.......Nashua
New Jersey—Franklin Murphy..............Newark
New Mexico—Charles A. Spiess.........Las Vegas
New York—William Barnes, Jr..............Albany
North Carolina—E. C. Duncan..............Raleigh
North Dakota—Thomas E. Marshall..........Oakes
Ohio—Sherman Granger..................Zanesville
Oklahoma—J. A. Harris......................Wagoner
Oregon—Ralph E. Williams..................Dallas
Pennsylvania—Henry G. Wasson.........Pittsburgh
Philippines—H. B. McCoy....................Manila
Porto Rico—S. Behn........................San Juan
Rhode Island—William P. Sheffield........Newport
South Carolina—Joseph W. Tolbert......Greenwood
South Dakota—Thomas Thorson..............Canton
Tennessee—Newell Sanders............Chattanooga
Texas—H. F. MacGregor......................Houston
Utah—Reed Smoot............................Provo
Vermont—John L. Lewis.................North Troy
Virginia—Alvah H. Martin..................Norfolk
Washington—Samuel A. Perkins............Tacoma
West Virginia—(Vacancy).
Wisconsin—Alfred T. Rogers................Madison
Wyoming—George E. Pexton................Evanston

CHAIRMEN STATE COMMITTEES (1913).

Alabama—Pope M. Long..................Birmingham
Arizona—J. L. Hubbell......................Phœnix
Arkansas—H. L. Remmel................Little Rock
California—(Vacancy).
Colorado—Jesse F. McDonald................Denver
Connecticut—Henry Roraback.............Hartford
Delaware—Edmund Mitchell.............Wilmington
Florida—Henry S. Chubb................Gainesville
Georgia—W. H. Johnson....................Atlanta
Idaho—George A. Day..........................Boise
Illinois—Roy O. West......................Chicago
Indiana—Fred A. Sims................Indianapolis
Iowa—Charles A. Rawson................Des Moines
Kansas—(Vacancy).

Kentucky—W. D. Cochran..................Louisville
Louisiana—C. S. Herbert...............New Orleans
Maine—Warren C. Philbrook.............Waterville
Maryland—John B. Hanna..................Baltimore
Massachusetts—Charles E. Hatfield........Boston
Michigan—Alex J. Groesbeck..............Detroit
Minnesota—Edward E. Smith.........Minneapolis
Mississippi—Fred W. Collins................Summit
Missouri—Politte Elvins..................St. Louis
Montana—J. E. Edwards......................Forsyth
Nebraska—Frank M. Currie............Broken Bow
Nevada—Dr. E. H. Reid......................Reno
New Hampshire—Jesse M. Barton........Concord
New Jersey—Edmund W. Blakelee..........Newark
New Mexico—Herbert W. Clark..........Santa Fe
New York—William Barnes, Jr..............Albany
North Carolina—John M. Morehead..........Spray
North Dakota—George H. Gray.............Keumore
Ohio—H. M. Daugherty....................Columbus
Oklahoma—Arthur H. Gessler........Oklahoma City
Oregon—Charles B. Moores..................Portland
Pennsylvania—H. G. Wasson.............Pittsburgh
Rhode Island—Charles A. Wilson.......Providence
South Carolina—Joseph W. Tolbert......Greenwood
South Dakota—Willis G. Cook..........Sioux Falls
Tennessee—James S. Beasley..............Nashville
Texas—C. K. McDowell......................Del Rio
Utah—Henry Gardner.............Salt Lake City
Vermont—Frank C. Williams................Newport
Virginia—C. Bascom Slemp.........Big Stone Gap
Washington—W. A. Rupp..................Aberdeen
West Virginia—James S. Lakin.........Clarksburg
Wisconsin—Henry Krumrey..............Plymouth
Wyoming—Patrick Sullivan................Cheyenne

DEMOCRATIC.

Headquarters—New York and Chicago.
Chairman—William F. McCombs, New York.
Vice-Chairman—Homer S. Cummings, Connecticut.
Secretary—Joseph E. Davies, Madison, Wis.
Treasurer—Rolla Wells, Missouri.
Sergeant-at-Arms—John I. Martin, Illinois.
Executive Committee—William F. McCombs, W. G. McAdoo, Joseph E. Davies, T. P. Gore, James A. O'Gorman, James A. Reed, A. Mitchell Palmer, A. S. Burleson, Daniel J. McGillicuddy, Josephus Daniels, R. S. Hudspeth, Willard Saulsbury, Robert Ewing, Will R. King.

Alabama—William Dorsey Jelks.........Birmingham
Arizona—Reese M. Ling......................Phœnix
Arkansas—W. M. Kavanaugh............Little Rock
California—John B. Sanford.................Ukiab
Colorado—(Vacancy).
Connecticut—Homer S. Cummings.........Stamford
Delaware—Willard Saulsbury.............Wilmington
Florida—J. T. G. Crawford.............Jacksonville
Georgia—Clark Howell......................Atlanta
Idaho—P. H. Elder.................Cœur d'Alene
Illinois—Charles Boeschenstein.......Edwardsville
Indiana—Thomas Taggart..............French Lick
Iowa—Martin J. Wade....................Iowa City
Kansas—William F. Sapp....................Galena
Kentucky—John C. C. Mayo..............Paintsville
Louisiana—Robert Ewing...............New Orleans
Maine—E. L. Jones......................Waterville
Maryland—J. Fred C. Talbott...........Lutherville
Massachusetts—J. W. Coughlin..........Fall River
Michigan—Edwin O. Wood....................Flint
Minnesota—Frederick B. Lynch...........St. Paul
Mississippi—Robert Powell................Jackson
Missouri—Edward F. Goltra...............St. Louis
Montana—J. Bruce Kremer....................Butte
Nebraska—P. L. Hall......................Lincoln
Nevada—W. J. Bell......................Winnemucca
New Hampshire—E. E. Reed.............Manchester
New Jersey—Robert S. Hudspeth........Jersey City
New Mexico—A. A. Jones................Las Vegas
New York—Norman E. Mack..................Buffalo
North Carolina—Josephus Daniels..........Raleigh
North Dakota—John Bruegger...Williston-Bottineau
Ohio—E. H. Moore......................Columbus
Oklahoma—Robert Galbraith..................Tulsa
Oregon—Will R. King......................Portland
Pennsylvania—A. Mitchell Palmer......Stroudsburg
Rhode Island—George W. Greene.......Woonsocket
South Carolina—B. R. Tillman..............Trenton
South Dakota—Thomas Taubman.......Plankington

Tennessee—(Vacancy) ....
Texas—Cato Selle.............................Cleburne
Utah—William R. Wallace.........Salt Lake City
Vermont—Thomas H. Browne.............Rutland
Virginia—J. Taylor Ellyson.................Richmond
Washington—John Pattison..................Seattle
West Virginia—John T. McGraw.............Grafton
Wisconsin—Joseph E. Davies.................Madison
Wyoming—John E. Osborne..................Juneau
Alaska—Z. R. Cheney.......................Juneau
Dist. of Columbia—John F. Costello....Washington
Hawaii—John H. Wilson....................Honolulu
Porto Rico—Henry W. Dooley.......New York city
Philippine Islands—R. E. Manly...........Manila

CHAIRMEN STATE COMMITTEES (1913).
Alabama—R. Tyler Goodwin............Montgomery
Arkansas—A. J. Walls.......................Lonoke
Arizona—A. J. Michelson....................Phoenix
California—J. O. Davis.................San Francisco
Colorado—George T. Bradley................Denver
Connecticut—Charles W. Comstock........Norwich
Delaware—Thomas F. Bayard.............Wilmington
Florida—P. J. Fearnside....................Palatka
Georgia—William J. Harris,................Atlanta
Idaho—Ben R. Gray.........................Boise
Illinois—Arthur W. Charles................Chicago
Indiana—Bernard Korbley..............Indianapolis
Iowa—N. F. Reed.........................Ottumwa
Kansas—H. S. Martin........................Topeka
Kentucky—J. N. Camden..................Louisville
Louisiana—Horace Wilkinson...........Port Allen
Maine—John S. P. Wilson....................Auburn
Maryland—Murray Vandever.......Havre de Grace
Massachusetts—Thomas P. Riley.............Boston
Michigan—Ed C. Shields....................Detroit
Minnesota—Martin O'Brien.................St. Paul
Mississippi—J. M. McBeath,...............Meridian
Missouri—D. C. McClurg.....................St. Louis
Montana—T. M. Swindlehurst...............Helena
Nebraska—W. H. Thompson..........Grand Island
Nevada—C. H. McIntosh......................Reno
New Hampshire—John B. Jameson..........Concord
New Jersey—Ed R. Grosscup................Trenton
New York—George M. Palmer..............Cobleskill
New Mexico—A. H. Hudspeth..............Santa Fe
North Carolina—Charles A. Webb...........Raleigh
North Dakota—D. H. McArthur..............Fargo
Ohio—W. L. Finley.........................Columbus
Oklahoma—Tom C. Harrill..................Wagoner
Oregon—B. E. Haney.......................Portland
Pennsylvania—Roland B. Morris........Philadelphia
Rhode Island—F. E. Fitzsimmons.......Pawtucket
South Carolina—John G. Evans.......Spartanburg
South Dakota—James Coffey................Yankton
Tennessee—J. D. G. Morton..............Nashville
Texas—Walter Collins......................Hillsboro
Utah—Sam R. Thurman.............Salt Lake City
Vermont—E. S. Harris....................Bennington
Virginia—J. Taylor Ellyson................Richmond
Washington—Hugh C. Todd..................Seattle
West Virginia—Stuart W. Walker.......Martinsburg
Wisconsin—Paul Hemmy.................Milwaukee
Wyoming—John E. Osborne..................Rawlins

PROGRESSIVE.
Headquarters—New York and Washington, D. C.
Chairman—Joseph M. Dixon, Montana.
Vice-Chairman—J. Medill McCormick, Illinois.
Secretary—Oscar King Davis, Washington, D. C.
Treasurer—Elon Huntington Hooker, New York.
Chairman Executive Committee—George W. Per-
  kins, New York.
Alabama—J. O. Thompson.............Birmingham
Arizona—J. F. Cleveland...................Phoenix
Arkansas—H. M. Trieber.................Little Rock
California—Chester R. Rowell................Fresno
Colorado—E. P. Costigan...................Denver
Connecticut—Joseph W. Alsop.............Hartford
Delaware—Lewis A. Drexler..........Bethany Beach
District of Columbia—Frank J. Hogan..Washington
Florida—F. L. Anderson...............Jacksonville
Georgia—C. W. McClure....................Atlanta
Idaho—P. Monroe Smock......................Boise
Illinois—J. Medill McCormick..............Chicago
Indiana—Rudolph G. Leeds.................Richmond
Iowa—John L. Stevens.......................Boone
Kansas—William Allen White...............Emporia

Kentucky—Leslie Combs..................Louisville
Louisiana—Pearl Wight...............New Orleans
Maine—Halbert P. Gardiner.................Portland
Maryland—Joseph R. Baldwin.............Aberdeen
Massachusetts—Mathew Hale.................Boston
Michigan—Henry M. Wallace.................Detroit
Minnesota—Milton D. Purdy..........Minneapolis
Mississippi—B. F. Fridge................Ellisville
Missouri—L. R. Kirkwood.............Kansas City
Montana—Joseph M. Dixon................Missoula
Nebraska—Nathan Merriam..................Omaha
Nevada—P. L. Flannigan.....................Reno
New Hampshire—William Sevascool....Manchester
New Jersey—Borden D. Whiting...........Newark
New Mexico—Miguel A. Otero..............Santa Fe
New York—Geo. W. Perkins.........New York city
North Carolina—Jas. F. Williamson, Jr..Burlington
North Dakota—A. Y. More.....................Fargo
Ohio—John J. Sullivan...................Cleveland
Oklahoma—George C. Priestly............Bartlesville
Oregon—Henry Waldo Coe.................Portland
Pennsylvania—William Flinn..............Pittsburgh
Rhode Island—Edwin F. Tuttle........Woonsocket
South Carolina—T. H. Wannamaker....Columbia
South Dakota—O. S. Basford..................Pierre
Tennessee—G. Tom Taylor.................Nashville
Texas—Cecil A. Lyon.......................Sherman
Utah—Moroni Heiner.............Salt Lake City
Vermont—Charles H. Thompson.........Montpelier
Virginia—Thomas L. Moore.................Roanoke
Washington—Lorenzo Dow...................Tacoma
West Virginia—William M. O. Dawson..Charleston
Wisconsin—Henry F. Cochems............Milwaukee
Wyoming—Robert D. Carey..................Cheyenne

WOMAN MEMBERS AT LARGE.
Illinois—Jane Addams......................Chicago
California—Mrs. Catherine Hooker...San Francisco
New York—Miss Frances Kellor......New York city

CHAIRMEN STATE COMMITTEES (1912).
Alabama—R. A. Perryman.............Birmingham
Arizona—J. L. B. Alexander...............Phoenix
Arkansas—J. A. Comer..................Little Rock
California—Meyer Lissner...............Los Angeles
Colorado—Clarence P. Dodge...............Denver
Connecticut—Joseph W. Alsop...........Hartford
Delaware—Robert G. Houston............Georgetown
Dist. Columbia—John C. O'Laughlin....Washington
Florida—H. L. Anderson................Jacksonville
Georgia—W. J. Tilson......................Atlanta
Idaho—J. P. Gipson..........................Boise
Illinois—Raymond Robins..................Chicago
Indiana—Edwin M. Lee..................Indianapolis
Iowa—J. H. Wyllie......................Sigourney
Kansas—U. S. Sartin...................Kansas City
Kentucky—W. S. Lawwill.................Louisville
Louisiana—Gen. W. J. Behan..........New Orleans
Maine—Irving E. Vernon...................Portland
Maryland—J. Stuart MacDonald.........Baltimore
Massachusetts—Mathew Hale................Boston
Michigan—Chas. P. O'Neil...................Detroit
Minnesota—Hugh T. Halbert...............St. Paul
Mississippi—(Vacancy)
Missouri—L. A. Ellis..................Kansas City
Montana—N. J. Bielenberg..................Helena
Nebraska—F. P. Corrick....................Lincoln
Nevada—R. B. Lind...........................Reno
New Hampshire—Geo. W. Wicker......Manchester
New Jersey—John Franklin Fort..........Newark
New Mexico—Miguel A. Otero..............Santa Fe
New York—T. D. Robinson..................New York
North Carolina—Zeb V. Walser..........Lexington
North Dakota—Dorr H. Carroll...............Fargo
Ohio—Walter F. Brown.....................Columbus
Oklahoma—Alva L. McDonald......Oklahoma City
Oregon—Thos. B. Newhausen................Portland
Pennsylvania—Thomas R. Hicks.......Philadelphia
Rhode Island—Charles E. Holmes........Providence
South Carolina—(Vacancy)
South Dakota—Herman Ellerman...........Yankton
Tennessee—H. B. Anderson................Memphis
Texas—Cecil A. Lyon.......................Sherman
Utah—Wesley K. Walton.............Salt Lake City
Vermont—M. L. Aseltine...................Montpelier
Virginia—Thomas L. Moore.................Roanoke
Washington—L. Roy Slater..................Spokane
West Virginia—William M. O. Dawson..Charleston
Wisconsin—Norman L. Baker..............Milwaukee
Wyoming—H. N. Gottlieb...................Sheridan

PROHIBITION.

Headquarters—106 North LaSalle street, Chicago, Ill.
Executive Committee—Chairman, Virgil G. Hinshaw, Chicago, Ill.; vice-chairman, J. B. Lewis, Boston, Mass.; secretary, Mrs. Frances E. Beauchamp, Lexington, Ky.; treasurer, H. P. Faris, Clinton, Mo.; Finley C. Hendrickson, Maryland; W. G. Calderwood, Minnesota; Robert H. Patton, Illinois; F. W. Emerson, Oregon; Frank J. Sibley, Arizona.

Alabama—J. B. Albritton.....................Bellwood
  W. B. Smith.................................Mobile
Arizona—Frank J. Sibley......................Tucson
  Eugene W. Chafin...........................Tucson
Arkansas—George Kimball................Little Rock
  J. M. Parker...........................Little Rock
California—F. W. Emerson.........................
  B. J. Vincent...............................Hermon
Colorado—J. H. Ketchum..........Colorado Springs
  O. A. Reinhardt............................Denver
Connecticut—Frederick G. Platt......New Britain
  J. L. Randall...............................Groton
Delaware—George W. Todd..............Wilmington
  Lewis W. Brosius......................Wilmington
District of Columbia—M. E. O'Brien....Washington
  John R. Mahoney........................Washington
Florida—John P. Coffin....................Johnstown
  C. B. Wetherell............................Orlando
Illinois—Robert H. Patton.................Springfield
  Alonzo E. Wilson...........................Wheaton
Indiana—F. W. Lough....................Indianapolis
  Charles Eckhart............................Auburn
Iowa—Capt. K. W. Brown.......................Ames
  O. D. Ellett...........................Marshalltown
Kansas—Earle R. DeLay.......................Emporia
  J. N. Woods................................Ottawa
Kentucky—T. B. Demaree.....................Filmore
  Mrs. Frances E. Beauchamp...........Lexington
Maine—N. F. Woodbury.........................Auburn
  James H. Ames.........................Bowdoinham
Maryland—F. C. Hendrickson.............Cumberland
  George R. Gorsuch........................Baltimore
Massachusetts—John B. Lewis.................Boston
  John M. Fisher...........................Attleboro
Michigan—F. W. Corbett.....................Lansing
  William A. Brubaker........................Detroit
Minnesota—W. G. Calderwood..........Minneapolis
  J. D. Engle...........................Minneapolis
Missouri—H. P. Faris.........................Clinton
  Charles E. Stokes...........................
Montana—Mrs. Kate M. Hamilton..............Butte
Nebraska—A. G. Wolfenbarger...............Lincoln
  D. B. Gilbert..............................Lincoln
New Hampshire—Alva H. Morrill...........Franklin
  George L. Thompson.........................Laconia
New Jersey—W. D. Martin.....Hasbrouck Heights
  Grafton E. Day.......................Collingswood
New York—Olin S. Bishop.......................Utica
  Dr. T. A. MacNicholl.....................New York
North Carolina—T. P. Johnston.............Salisbury
  J. M. Templeton........................Greensboro
Ohio—Aaron S. Watkins...........................Ada
  H. L. Peeke................................Sandusky
Oklahoma—Rev. Charles Brown..............Carmen
  George E. Rouch...........................Guthrie
Pennsylvania—David B. McCalmont...........Franklin
  Henry S. Gill............................Franklin
Rhode Island—L. E. Remington...............Rumford
  F. T. Jenks.........................West Barrington
South Dakota—Quincy L. Morrow..........Brookings
  W. T. Rafferty..............................Miller
Texas—J. L. Campbell........................El Paso
  P. F. Paige................................Dallas
Vermont—L. W. Hanson....................Montpelier
  Fred L. Page................................Barre
Virginia—W. F. Rife....................Waynesboro
  Rev. H. M. Hoge............................Lincoln
Washington—R. E. Dunlap.....................Seattle
  O. L. Fowler...............................Tacoma
West Virginia—Jay E. Cunningham.......Pennsboro
  U. A. Clayton.............................Fairmont
Wisconsin—J. Burritt Smith..................Madison
  B. E. Van Keuren..........................Oshkosh
Wyoming—C. J. Sawyer......................Laramie
  J. R. Cortner...............................Jireh

CHAIRMEN STATE COMMITTEES (1913).
Arizona—John Wix Thomas..................Phœnix
Arkansas—G. H. Kimball...............Little Rock

California—Chas. R. Burger................Pasadena
Colorado—Rev. J. H. Ketchum.....Colorado Springs
Connecticut—E. L. G. Hohenthal....S. Manchester
Delaware—L. W. Brosius..................Wilmington
Florida—John P. Coffin....................Johnstown
Georgia—George Gordon........................Atlanta
Idaho—Harry Hayes........................Greenleaf
Illinois—Robert H. Patton.................Springfield
Indiana—F. W. Lough....................Indianapolis
Iowa—R. H. Williams.......................Oskaloosa
Kansas—M. F. King (acting)..................Ottawa
Kentucky—Mrs. Frances E. Beauchamp..Lexington
Louisiana—E. E. Israel..................Baton Rouge
Maine—James Perrigo.......................Portland
Maryland—Charles R. Woods..............Baltimore
Massachusetts—A. J. Orem....................Boston
Michigan—William A. Brubaker.............Detroit
Minnesota—W. G. Calderwood..........Minneapolis
Missouri—W. H. Dalton.......................Joplin
Montana—R. R. Crowe........................Billings
Nebraska—D. B. Gilbert.....................Lincoln
New Hampshire—Rev. G. L. Thompson.....Laconia
New Jersey—Donald MacMillan...............Nutley
New Mexico—James M. Shimer.............Santa Fe
New York—Olin S. Bishop.......................Utica
North Dakota—F. B. Stevenson............Emerado
Ohio—R. R. Roberts.........................Columbus
Oklahoma—T. E. Sisson.......................Guthrie
Oregon—J. P. Newell.........................Portland
Pennsylvania—B. E. P. Prugh.............Harrisburg
Rhode Island—Roscoe Phillips...........Providence
South Dakota—C. V. Templeton.........Woonsocket
Texas—A. A. Everts (acting)..................Dallas
Vermont—L. W. Hanson....................Montpelier
Virginia—William A. Rife................Waynesboro
Washington—Mrs. Nettie Hallenbeck......Tacoma
West Virginia—J. W. Bedford..............Parsons
Wisconsin—J. Burritt Smith..................Madison
Wyoming—J. R. Cortner........................Jireh

SOCIALIST.

National Headquarters—111 North Market street, Chicago, Ill.
Executive Secretary—Walter Lauferslek, Chicago, Ill.
National Executive Committee—Victor L. Berger, Wisconsin; Adolph Germer, Colorado; George H. Goebel, New Jersey; James H. Maurer, Pennsylvania; J. Stitt Wilson, California.
International Bureau Delegate—Kate Richards O'Hare, St. Louis, Mo.

NATIONAL COMMITTEE.
Alabama—W. M. Doyle..........................Mobile
Arizona—W. S. Bradford......................Phoenix
Arkansas—Ida Callery.....................Fort Smith
California—N. A. Richardson......San Bernardino
  J. Stitt Wilson...........................Berkeley
Colorado—S. B. Hutchinson........Grand Junction
Connecticut—Samuel E. Beardsley............Shelton
Delaware—Frank A. Houck................Wilmington
Dist. Columbia—Charles F. Nesbit......Washington
Florida—Franklin Pimbley......................Tampa
Georgia—Al Schwartz.........................Atlanta
Idaho—S. W. Motley......................Twin Falls
Illinois—Adolph Germer..............Denver, Col.
  John C. Kennedy...........................Chicago
  Duncan McDonald.......................Springfield
Indiana—S. M. Reynolds..............Chicago, Ill.
  Wm. Houston............................Terre Haute
Iowa—M. F. Wiltse.....................Marshalltown
Kansas—S. M. Stallard...................Fort Scott
Kentucky—J. Raphaelson.....................Newport
Louisiana—W. F. Dietz.................Lake Charles
Maine—Fred E. Irish......................Woodfords
Maryland—Charles E. Develin..............Baltimore
Massachusetts—Dan A. White........Chicago, Ill.
  George E. Roewer...........................Boston
Michigan—James Hoogerhyde......Grand Rapids
  Frank Aaltonen..........................Negaunee
Minnesota—Morris Kaplan......................Duluth
  T. E. Latimer.........................Minneapolis
Mississippi—J. J. Lipscomb...................Jackson
Missouri—William H. Garver............Independence
Montana—Lewis J. Duncan.......................Butte
Nebraska—John C. Chase......................Omaha
Nevada—Justus E. Taylor........................Reno
New Hampshire—J. Foster Nichols........Franklin

New Jersey—George H. Goebel.............Newark
James M. Reilly...................West Hoboken
New Mexico—Chas. F. Goddard...........Carrizozo
New York—Gustave A. Strebel...........Syracuse
Charles J. Ball.............................Buffalo
Morris Hillquit........................New York
U. Solomon...............................New York
North Carolina—Wm. T. Bradford...Winston-Salem
North Dakota—Arthur Le Sueur...........Minot
Ohio—M. J. Beery.........................Crestline
Tom Clifford.............................Cleveland
Max S. Hayes............................Cleveland
Oklahoma—H. M. Sinclair...........Oklahoma City
P. S. Nagle............................Kingfisher
Oregon—Floyd C. Ramp.....................Brooks
Pennsylvania—Gertrude B. Fuller.......Pittsburgh
Joseph E. Cohen.......................Philadelphia
Charles A. Maurer........................Reading
Robert B. Ringler........................Reading
John W. Slayton........................Pittsburgh
Rhode Island—Fred Hurst...............Providence
South Carolina—R. B. Britton..........Charleston
South Dakota—M. G. Opsahl............Sioux City
Tennessee—W. A. Weatherall.............Memphis
Texas—T. A. Hickey..................Hallettsville
W. S. Noble.............................Rockdale
Utah—Jacob E. Gease.......................Helper
Vermont—John Spargo....................Bennington
Virginia—A. J. Hauser...............Newport News

Washington—Franz Bostrom................Everett
Kate Sadler.............................Seattle
Hortense Wahenknecht....................Everett
West Virginia—John W. Brown.........Charleston
Wisconsin—Victor L. Berger............Milwaukee
W. R. Gaylord..........................Milwaukee
Wyoming—A. Carlson......................Sheridan

WOMEN'S NATIONAL COMMITTEE.

Winnie E. Branstetter, Chicago, Ill., general correspondent.
Gertrude B. Fuller, Pittsburgh, Pa.
Alma M. Krieger, Butte, Mont.
Lena M. Lewis, San Francisco, Cal.
Bertha H. Mailly, New York, N. Y.
Anna A. Maley, New York, N. Y.
Gertrude Reilly, West Hoboken, N. J.
May Wood-Simons, Milwaukee, Wis.

POPULIST.

Chairman—Samuel S. Williams, Vincennes, Ind.
Vice-Chairman—J. A. Parker, Parma, Mo.
Secretary and Treasurer—F. J. S. Robinson, Cloverdale, Ind.

SOCIALIST LABOR PARTY.

Headquarters—28 City Hall place, New York, N. Y.
National Secretary—Paul Augustine, New York.

POLITICAL PARTY PLATFORMS OF 1912 IN BRIEF.

The following summary includes the principal planks in the platforms adopted at the national conventions in 1912:

DEMOCRATIC.

Collection of tariff duties to be limited to the necessities of the government honestly and economically administered.
Immediate downward revision of the tariff duties, especially upon necessaries of life.
Placing upon free list of articles competing with trust controlled products.
Enforcement of criminal and civil law against trusts and trust officials.
Prevention of holding companies and interlocking directorates.
Preservation of the rights of the states.
Ratification of the income tax and direct senatorial election propositions.
Prohibiting corporations from making campaign contributions.
Amendment of constitution providing for single presidential term with no re-election.
Valuation of railroads, telegraph and telephone lines, and property of express companies.
Systematic revision of the banking and currency laws.
Establishment of a system of rural credits.
Prevention of overflows of the Mississippi river.
Development of inland waterways.
Protection of labor unions from unjust court proceedings.
Employes' compensation law.
Prevention of gambling in agricultural products by organized exchanges.
Conservation of natural resources.
Fostering of merchant marine.
Exemption of American ships engaged in coasting trade from Panama canal tolls.
United and independent health service.
Extension and maintenance of the civil service.
Reform in administration of civil and criminal law.
Recognition of independence of Philippines as soon as a stable government can be established.
Protection of American citizenship abroad irrespective of race or creed.
Establishment of parcel post.
Generous pension policy.
Protection of uniform of the United States.

POPULIST.

Issuance of money by the government direct to the people.
Loans by the government to the people.
Government ownership of telegraph and telephone systems and the parcel post.

The initiative, the referendum, direct election of United States senators, direct primaries, presidential primaries and equal suffrage.
Registration of lobbyists.
Graduated income and inheritance tax.
Free schools in the lines of manual and occupational training.
Recognition of the Chinese republic.
Old age pensions.
The commission form of government for cities.
Granting of franchises to public utility corporations by popular vote.

PROGRESSIVE.

Providing for an easier method of amending the federal constitution.
Bringing under effective national jurisdiction those problems which have expanded beyond the reach of the individual states.
Equal suffrage for men and women.
Limitation and publicity of campaign contributions.
Registration of lobbyists.
"The progressive party demands such restriction of the power of the courts as shall leave to the people the ultimate authority to determine fundamental questions of social welfare and public policy. To secure this end it pledges itself to provide:
"(1) That when an act, passed under the police power of the state, is held unconstitutional under the state constitution by the courts, the people, after an ample interval for deliberation, shall have an opportunity to vote on the question whether they desire the act to become law notwithstanding such decision.
"(2) That every decision of the highest appellate court of a state declaring an act of the legislature unconstitutional on the ground of its violation of the federal constitution shall be subject to the same review by the Supreme court of the United States as is now accorded to decisions sustaining such legislation."
Reform of legal procedure and judicial methods.
Conservation of human resources.
Legislation looking to prevention of industrial accidents, occupational diseases, overwork and involuntary unemployment.
Fixing of minimum safety and health standards in the various occupations.
Prohibition of child labor.
Establishment of an eight hour day for women and young persons.
One day's rest in seven for wage workers.
Abolition of convict contract labor system.
Standards of compensation for death by industrial accident and trade disease,

Protection of home life against sickness, irregular employment and old age through a system of social insurance adapted to American use.

Establishment of continuation schools for industrial education.

Establishment of a department of labor.

Development of agricultural credit and co-operation.

Inquiry into the high cost of living.

Establishment of single national health service.

Establishment of a strong federal administrative commission, which shall maintain permanent active supervision over industrial corporations engaged in interstate commerce, or such of them as are of public importance.

Revision of patent law to prevent its abuse by monopolies.

Physical valuation of railroads.

Revision of the national currency system on the basis of soundness and elasticity.

Extension of foreign commerce through appointment of competent diplomatic and consular officers.

Conservation of the national resources.

Building of national highways and extension of good roads.

Improvement of waterways through co-operation of nation, states and cities.

"We believe in a protective tariff which shall equalize conditions of competition between the United States and foreign countries, both for the farmer and the manufacturer, and which shall maintain for labor an adequate standard of living."

"We demand tariff revision because the present tariff is unjust to the people of the United States. Fair dealing toward the people requires an immediate downward revision of those schedules wherein duties are shown to be unjust or excessive. We pledge ourselves to the establishment of a nonpartisan scientific tariff commission, reporting both to the president and to either branch of congress."

Passage of federal law for graduated inheritance tax; ratification of income tax amendment.

Settlement of international differences by judicial and other peaceful means.

Building of two battle ships a year.

Creation of a parcel post.

Extension and enforcement of civil service law.

Governmental supervision over investments.

PROHIBITION.

Prohibition of the manufacture, importation, exportation, transportation and sale of alcoholic beverages.

Suffrage for women on the same terms as for men.

Uniform marriage and divorce law. Extermination of polygamy.

Absolute protection of the rights of labor, without impairment of the rights of capital.

Settlement of international disputes by arbitration.

Abolition of child labor in mines, workshops and factories.

Election of United States senators by direct vote of the people.

Presidential term of six years and one term only.

Court review of postoffice and other departmental decisions and orders; the extension of the postal savings bank system and of rural delivery and the establishment of an efficient parcel post.

Initiative, referendum and recall.

As the tariff is a commercial question, it should be fixed on the scientific basis of accurate knowledge, secured by means of a permanent, omnipartisan tariff commission with ample powers.

Equitable graduated income and inheritance taxes.

Conservation of our forest and mineral reserves and the reclamation of waste lands.

Clearly defined laws for the regulation and control of corporations transacting an interstate business.

Efficiency and economy in governmental administration.

The protection of one day in seven as a day of rest.

REPUBLICAN.

Protection of the rights of the individual to freest possible development of his own powers.

Upholding of the authority and integrity of the courts, both state and federal.

Legislation to prevent long delays and costly appeals in civil and criminal cases.

"While we regard the recall of judges as unnecessary and unwise, we favor such action as may be necessary to simplify the process by which any judge who is found to be derelict in his duty may be removed from office."

Measures for maintaining international peace.

Enactment of legislation supplementary to the antitrust act which will define as criminal offenses those specific acts that mark attempts to restrain and monopolize trade.

Creation of a federal trade commission.

"We reaffirm our belief in a protective tariff."

"We hold that the import duties should be high enough while yielding a sufficient revenue to protect adequately American industries and wages. Some of the existing import duties are too high and should be reduced. Readjustment should be made from time to time to conform to changed conditions and to reduce excessive rates, but without injury to any American industry.

"To accomplish this correct information is indispensable. This information can best be obtained by an expert commission."

Scientific inquiry into the causes of the high cost of living.

Revision of banking and currency systems; these, however, to be safeguarded from sectional, financial or political domination.

Passage of state and federal laws for the establishment of organizations having for their purpose the loaning of funds to farmers.

Extension and enforcement of civil service law.

Publicity and further restriction of campaign contributions.

Conservation of the national resources.

Establishment of parcel post.

Protection of American citizenship abroad, regardless of race, religion or previous political allegiance.

Maintenance of an adequate navy.

Revival of the merchant marine.

Flood prevention along Mississippi river.

Reclamation of arid lands.

Improvement of rivers and harbors.

Revision of immigration laws.

Enactment of laws for the protection of seamen and requiring the use of additional safety appliances at sea.

SOCIALIST.

Absolute freedom of press, speech and assemblage.

Collective ownership of patents with royalties for inventors.

Equal suffrage for men and women.

Adoption of initiative, referendum, recall and proportional representation.

Abolition of senate and president's veto power.

Election of president and vice-president by direct vote.

Abolition of power of United States Supreme court to pass upon constitutionality of laws passed by congress.

Enactment of laws for vocational education; bureau of education to be made a department.

Abolition of federal district courts and United States Circuit Court of Appeals.

Creation of an independent bureau of health.

Revision of constitution of the United States.

Collective ownership of railroads, telegraphs, telephones, steamboat lines and large scale industries.

Acquisition by cities, states or nation of grain elevators, stockyards, storage warehouses and other distributing agencies in order to reduce the cost of living.

Inclusion of mines, oil wells, quarries, forests and water power in public domain.

Further conservation and development of natural resources for the benefit of all the people.

Collective ownership of land.

Collective ownership and democratic management of banking and currency system.

Conservation of human resources, particularly of

the lives and well-being of workers and their families.

Establishment of minimum wage scales.

Establishment of a noncontributory system of old age pensions, insurance by the state against unemployment and invalidism, and compulsory insurance by employers of their workers, without cost to the latter, against industrial diseases, accidents and death.

The platform advocates these and other similar measures as "calculated to strengthen the working class in its fight for the realization of its ultimate aim, the co-operative commonwealth."

SOCIALIST LABOR.

Substitution of industrial or socialist republic for political state.

Placing of land and all means of production, transportation and distribution in the hands of the people as a collective body.

National congress to consist of representatives of the useful occupations of the land.

ELECTORAL VOTE BY STATES (1900-1912).

STATE.	1912. Wilson, D.	1912. Roosevelt, Prog.	1912. Taft, R.	1908. Taft, R.	1908. Bryan, D.	1904. Roosevelt, R.	1904. Parker, D.	1900. McKinley, R.	1900. Bryan, D.
Alabama........	12			11		11		11	
Arizona.........	3								
Arkansas.......	9			9		9		9	
California......	2	11		10		10		9	
Colorado.......	6			5		5		4	
Connecticut....	7			7		7		6	
Delaware.......	3			3		3		3	
Florida........	6			5		5		4	
Georgia........	14			13		13		13	
Idaho..........	4		3		3			3	
Illinois........	29		27		27		24		24
Indiana........	15		15		15		15		
Iowa...........	13		13		13		13		
Kansas.........	10		10		10		10		
Kentucky.......	13			13		13		13	
Louisiana......	10			9		9		8	
Maine.........	6		6		6		6		
Maryland......	8		2	6	1	7	8		
Massachusetts..	18		16		16		15		
Michigan.......		15	14		14		14		
Minnesota......		12	11		11		9		
Mississippi.....	10			10		10		9	
Missouri.......	18		18		18			17	
Montana.......	4		3		3			3	
Nebraska.......	8			8		8		8	
Nevada.........	3				3	3			3
New Hampshire	4		4		4		4		
New Jersey....	14			12		12		10	
New Mexico....	3								
New York......	45			39		39		36	
North Carolina.	12			12		12		11	
North Dakota..	5			4		4	3		
Ohio...........	24		23		23		23		
Oklahoma......	10			7					
Oregon........	5		4		4		4		
Pennsylvania...		38	34		34		32		
Rhode Island...	5		4		4		4		
South Carolina.	9			9		9		9	9
South Dakota..		5	4		4		4		
Tennessee......	12			12		12		12	
Texas.........	20			18		18		15	
Utah..........			4	3		3		3	
Vermont.......			4	4		4		4	
Virginia.......	12			12		12		12	
Washington....		7	5		5		4		
West Virginia..	8		7		7		6		
Wisconsin......	13		13		13		12		
Wyoming.......	3			3		3		3	
Total..........	**435**	**88**	**8**	**321**	**162**	**336**	**140**	**292**	**155**

MAYORS OF LARGE CITIES (1913).

Albany, N. Y.—Joseph W. Stevens, Rep.
Baltimore, Md.—James H. Preston, Dem.
Boston, Mass.—John F. Fitzgerald, Dem.
Bridgeport, Conn.—Clifford B. Wilson, Rep.
Buffalo, N. Y.—Louis P. Fuhrmann, Dem.
Camden, N. J.—Charles H. Ellis, Rep.
Charleston, S. C.—John P. Grace, Dem.
Chicago, Ill.—Carter H. Harrison, Dem.
Cincinnati, O.—Frederick S. Spiegel, Rep.
Cleveland, O.—Newton D. Baker, Dem.
Columbus, O.—George J. Karb, Dem.
Dayton, O.—Edward Phillips, Rep.
Denver, Col.—J. M. Perkins, nonpartisan.
Detroit, Mich.—B. Marx, Rep.
Duluth, Minn.—W. J. Prince, nonpartisan.
Fall River, Mass.—James H. Kay, Rep.
Fort Wayne, Ind.—Wm. J. Hosey, Dem.
Grand Rapids, Mich.—George E. Ellis, Rep.
Hartford, Conn.—Louis R. Cheney, Rep.
Indianapolis, Ind.—Joseph E. Bell, Dem.
Jersey City, N. J.—H. O. Wittpen, Dem.
Kansas City, Mo.—Henry L. Jost, Dem.
Lincoln, Neb.—F. C. Zehring, Rep.
Los Angeles, Cal.—H. H. Rose, Ind.
Louisville, Ky.—John L. Buschemeyer, Dem.
Lowell, Mass.—James E. O'Donnell, nonpartisan.
Memphis, Tenn.—Edward H. Crump, Dem.
Milwaukee, Wis.—Gerhard A. Bading, nonpartisan.
Minneapolis, Minn.—W. G. Nye, nonpartisan.
Nashville, Tenn.—Hilary E. Howse, Dem.

Newark, N. J.—Jacob Haussling, Dem.
New Haven, Conn.—Frank J. Rice, Rep.
New Orleans, La.—Martin Behrman, Dem.
New York, N. Y.—John Purroy Mitchel, nonpartisan.
Omaha, Neb.—James C. Dahlman, Dem.
Paterson, N. J.—Robert H. Fordyce, Rep.
Peoria, Ill.—E. N. Woodruff, Rep.
Philadelphia, Pa.—Rudolph Blankenburg, Ind. Rep.
Pittsburgh, Pa.—Joseph C. Armstrong, Rep.
Portland, Ore.—Harrison R. Albee, nonpartisan.
Providence, R. I.—Joseph H. Gainer, Dem.
Reading, Pa.—Ira W. Stratton, Rep.
Richmond, Va.—George Ainslee, Dem.
Rochester, N. Y.—H. H. Edgerton, Rep.
St. Louis, Mo.—Henry W. Kiel, Rep.
St. Paul, Minn.—Herbert P. Keller, Rep.
Salt Lake City, Utah—Samuel C. Park, nonpartisan.
San Antonio, Tex.—A. H. Jones, Dem.
San Francisco, Cal.—James Rolph, Jr., nonpartisan.
Schenectady, N. Y.—J. Teller Schoolcraft, nonpartisan.
Seattle, Wash.—George F. Cotterill, nonpartisan.
Springfield, Ill.—John S. Schnepp, Dem.
Springfield, Mass.—John A. Denison, Rep.
Syracuse, N. Y.—Louis Will, Prog.
Toledo, O.—Carl Keller, Rep.
Trenton, N. J.—Frederick W. Donnelly, Dem.
Troy, N. Y.—Cornelius F. Burns, Dem.
Wilmington, Del.—Dr. Harrison W. Howell, Rep.

MINE DISASTER IN WALES.

Four hundred and twenty-three coal miners lost their lives in the Universal colliery at Senghenydd, Wales, Oct. 14, 1913. In the morning 935 men went down into the pit and just after they had gone to work an explosion occurred, followed by fire. Rescuing parties succeeded in saving 512 men, most of whom were on the east side of the mine where the ventilation was good. The others perished.

INTERNAL REVENUE RECEIPTS.

Comparative statement showing the receipts from the several objects of internal taxation in the United States during the fiscal years ended June 30, 1912 and 1913:

OBJECTS OF TAXATION	1912.	1913.	Increase.	Decrease.
SPIRITS.				
Spirits distilled from apples, peaches, grapes, pears, pineapples, oranges, apricots, berries, prunes, figs and cherries.....	$2,634,264.47	$3,081,943.66	$387,679.19	
Spirits distilled from materials other than apples peaches, grapes, pears, pineapples, oranges, apricots, berries, prunes, figs and cherries.....	146,715,203.60	154,460,118.09	7,744,914.49	
Rectifiers (special tax).....	327,210.70	296,642.28		$30,568.42
Wine made in imitation of champagne.....	52.00	66.00	14.00	
Retail liquor dealers (special tax).....	5,396,991.25	4,864,773.36		532,217.89
Wholesale liquor dealers (special tax).....	730,440.53	645,236.81		85,203.72
Manufacturers of stills (special tax).....	1,218.76	1,256.28	37.52	
Stills and worms, manufactured (special tax).....	1,920.00	2,460.00	540.00	
Stamps for distilled spirits intended for export.....	2,920.05	2,597.40		322.65
Case stamps for distilled spirits bottled in bond.....	332,274.30	376,492.30	44,218.00	
Grape brandy used in the fortification of sweet wines.....	189,292.11	148,056.36		41,235.75
Total.....	156,391,487.77	163,879,342.54	7,487,854.77	
TOBACCO.				
Cigars weighing more than 3 pounds per thousand.....	21,769,170.91	23,097,112.63	1,327,941.72	
Cigars weighing not more than 3 pounds per thousand.....	820,206.60	775,223.62		44,982.98
Cigarettes weighing more than 3 pounds per thousand.....	64,482.55	65,247.52	764.97	
Cigarettes weighing not more than 3 pounds per thousand...	14,027,031.23	17,845,963.95	3,818,932.72	
Snuff.....	2,406,858.60	2,656,757.44	250,398.84	
Tobacco, manufactured, all kinds.....	31,502,811.71	32,349,009.59	846,197.88	
Total.....	70,590,161.60	*76,789,424.75	6,199,273.15	
FERMENTED LIQUORS.				
Ale, beer, lager beer, porter and other similar fermented liquors.....	62,108,633.39	65,245,544.40	3,136,911.01	
Brewers (special tax).....	153,812.61	137,304.30		16,508.31
Retail dealers in malt liquors (special tax).....	354,206.46	311,639.66		42,656.80
Wholesale dealers in malt liquors (special tax).....	652,028.05	572,501.24		79,526.81
Total.....	63,268,770.51	66,266,989.60	2,998,219.00	
OLEOMARGARINE.				
Oleomargarine, domestic, artificially colored in imitation of butter.....	325,948.33	417,165.38	91,217.05	
Oleomargarine, free from coloration that causes it to look like butter of any shade of yellow.....	307,479.16	347,463.96	39,984.80	
Oleomargarine imported from foreign countries.....	8.40			8.40
Manufacturers of oleomargarine (special tax).....	24,925.00	16,750.00		8,175.00
Retail dealers in oleomargarine artificially colored in imitation of butter (special tax).....	23,258.50	21,048.00		2,210.50
Retail dealers in oleomargarine free from artificial coloration (special tax).....	271,145.74	291,645.08	20,499.34	
Wholesale dealers in oleomargarine artificially colored in imitation of butter (special tax).....	4,466.67	3,340.00		1,126.67
Wholesale dealers in oleomargarine free from artificial coloration (special tax).....	171,475.45	182,575.25	8,900.20	
Total.....	1,128,707.25	1,259,987.67	131,280.42	
FILLED CHEESE.				
Filled cheese, domestic.....	330.31			330.31
Manufacturers of filled cheese (special tax).....	300.00			300.00
Retail dealers in filled cheese (special tax).....				
Wholesale dealers in filled cheese (special tax).....				
Total.....	630.31			630.31
MIXED FLOUR.				
Per barrel of 196 lbs or more than 98 lbs.....	20.00	149.88	129.88	
Half barrel of 98 lbs or more than 49 lbs.....	1,034.50	1,201.60	167.10	
Quarter barrel of 49 lbs or more than 24½ lbs.....	1,889.19	1,539.10		350.09
Eighth barrel of 24¼ lbs or less.....	42.56	43.90	1.34	
Manufacturers, packers or repackers of mixed flour (special tax).....	157.00	289.50	132.50	
Total.....	3,143.25	3,223.98	80.73	
ADULTERATED BUTTER.				
Adulterated butter manufactured or sold, etc.....	9,651.60	13,980.72	4,329.12	
Manufacturers of adulterated butter (special tax).....	31,556.80	37,325.00	5,768.20	
Retail dealers in adulterated butter (special tax).....	614.00	24.00		590.00
Wholesale dealers in adulterated butter (special tax).....	4,880.00	3,460.00		1,420.00
Total.....	46,102.40	54,189.72	8,087.32	
PROCESS OR RENOVATED BUTTER.				
Process or renovated butter manufactured or sold, etc.....	117,544.50	96,854.01		20,690.49
Manufacturers of process or renovated butter (special tax).....	1,991.68	1,387.51		604.17
Total.....	119,536.18	98,241.52		21,294.66
MISCELLANEOUS.				
Excise tax on corporations.....	28,583,259.81	35,006,299.84	6,423,040.03	
Playing cards.....	616,233.60	655,283.10	39,049.50	
Penalties.....	856,407.83	401,910.26		454,497.57
Collections not otherwise herein provided for.....	11,464.18	9,560.87		1,903.31
Total.....	30,067,365.42	36,073,054.07	6,005,688.65	
Aggregate receipts.....	321,615,894.69	344,424,453.85	22,808,559.16	

*Includes $319,100.64 from sale of internal revenue stamps affixed to Philippine products, as provided for in act of Aug. 5, 1909.

RECEIPTS BY STATES AND TERRITORIES.

Alabama	$361,463.81	Nevada	92,513.17
Alaska	19,994.00	N.Hampshire	505,881.75
Arizona	156,614.56	New Jersey.	12,403,126.53
Arkansas ...	190,665.24	New Mexico.	83,723.68
California ..	9,684,145.09	New York...	46,661,853.07
Colorado ...	943,793.27	N. Carolina..	10,635,276.47
Connecticut..	1,987,074.48	N. Dakota...	61,279.83
Delaware ...	579,013.25	Ohio	25,169,957.10
D. Columbia.	913,104.23	Oklahoma ..	177,649.30
Florida	1,429,929.61	Oregon	822,730.30
Georgia	523,632.24	Pennsylvania	28,959,530.66
Hawaii	240,553.28	Porto Rico..	591,356.36
Idaho	88,282.04	Rhode Island	1,241,087.01
Illinois	58,362,601.36	S. Carolina..	192,104.14
Indiana	31,623,505.62	S. Dakota...	137,260.63
Iowa'	1,180,855.47	Tennessee ...	2,384,189.03
Kansas	732,152.46	Texas	1,584,440.94
Kentucky ...	35,200,906.44	Utah	328,130.83
Louisiana ...	4,462,094.33	Vermont ...	78,429.93
Maine	300,932.99	Virginia	8,059,986.86
Maryland ...	7,546,012.45	Washington .	1,428,013.90
Massachus'ts	7,236,312.89	West Virginia	1,898,998.78
Michigan ...	8,302,016.91	Wisconsin ..	9,564,192.13
Minnesota ..	3,274,511.22	Wyoming ..	69,483.35
Mississippi ..	80,181.10	Philippines .	319,100.64
Missouri ...	12,470,712.72		
Montana ...	445,545.87	Total 344,424,453.85	
Nebraska ...	2,697,049.76		

NOTE—Alabama and Mississippi compose the district of Alabama; Colorado and Wyoming, the district of Colorado; Connecticut and Rhode Island, the district of Connecticut; Maryland, Delaware, District of Columbia and the counties of Accomac and Northampton, Virginia, the district of Maryland; Montana, Idaho and Utah, the district of Montana; New Hampshire, Maine and Vermont, the district of New Hampshire; New Mexico and Arizona, the district of New Mexico; North Dakota and South Dakota, the district of North and South Dakota; Washington and Alaska, the district of Washington, and Nevada forms a part of the 4th district of California.

The collections credited to Porto Rico were returned from the following named districts, viz.:

1st district of New York	$81,129.40
2d district of New York	507,463.87
3d district of Massachusetts	2,763.09

Total 591,356.36

AGGREGATE COLLECTIONS BY DISTRICTS.
Fiscal year ended June 30, 1913.

Districts and collectors.	Collections.
Alabama—Joseph O. Thompson......	$32,471.72
Alabama—William E. Hooper (acting)..	18,496.04
Alabama—Sim T. Wright...............	390,877.15
Arkansas—Frank W. Tucker..........	190,665.24
1st California—August E. Muenter......	8,242,952.95
4th California—Wanton A. Shippee.....	143,721.44
5th California—Claude I. Parker.......	1,389,985.67
Colorado—Frank W. Howbert..........	1,013,276.62
Connecticut—Robert O. Eaton........	3,228,161.49
Florida—Joseph E. Lee..............	1,254,018.12
Florida—Henry Hayes Lewis........	175,911.49
Georgia—Henry S. Jackson..........	523,632.24
Hawaii—Charles A. Cottrill..........	240,553.38
1st Illinois—Samuel M. Fitch........	13,135,972.58
5th Illinois—Percival G. Rennick.....	34,000,994.53
8th Illinois—Frank L. Smith........	7,904,566.12
8th Illinois—Herbert F. Adams (acting)	2,618,464.03
13th Illinois—Walter S. Louden..........	642,604.10
6th Indiana—Elam H. Neal..........	10,902,839.17
7th Indiana—Charles G. Covert........	20,720,666.45
3d Iowa—Michael J. Tobin...........	541,356.03
4th Iowa—Harry O. Weaver.............	639,499.44
Kansas—Fremont Leidy..............	732,152.46
2d Kentucky—Lawson Reno.............	4,395,948.11
5th Kentucky—Ludlow F. Petty........	18,859,830.88
6th Kentucky—Maurice L. Galvin......	4,135,486.30
7th Kentucky—Timothy A. Field........	3,788,199.16
7th Kentucky—Harry R. McEldowie (acting)	374,137.66
7th Kentucky—Ben Marshall............	329,676.09
8th Kentucky—Winston W. Wiseman..	3,317,628.24
Louisiana—Walter Y. Kemper..........	4,462,094.33
Maryland—John B. Hanna.............	9,038,928.27

Districts and collectors.	Collections.
3d Massachusetts—James D. Gill.......	7,239,575.98
1st Michigan—Malcolm J. McLeod......	7,324,920.80
4th Michigan—George Clapperton.......	977,096.11
Minnesota—Frederick von Baumbach..	3,274,511.22
1st Missouri—Edmund R. Allen.......	10,615,889.29
6th Missouri—Charles G. Burton.....	1,854,823.43
Montana—Edward H. Callister.........	861,958.74
Nebraska—Ross L. Hammond..........	2,697,049.76
New Hampshire—Edgar O. Crossman...	885,244.67
1st New Jersey—Isaac Moffett.......	843,214.35
5th New Jersey—H. C. H. Herold....	11,559,912.18
New Mexico—Manuel B. Otero.......	240,338.24
1st New York—William J. Maxwell....	12,327,343.28
2d New York—Charles W. Anderson...	10,951,402.85
3d New York—Frederick L. Marshall...	11,508,611.70
14th New York—Cyrus Durey.........	5,617,513.95
21st New York—Charles C. Cole.......	3,564,921.74
28th New York—Archie D. Sanders.....	3,280,652.82
4th North Carolina—Wheeler Martin...	5,517,138.71
5th North Carolina—George H. Brown..	5,259,129.15
North and South Dakota—Willis C. Cook	198,540.46
1st Ohio—Bernhard Bettmann........	17,024,160.69
10th Ohio—William V. McMaken.......	3,050,528.31
11th Ohio—Willis G. Bowland.........	1,280,155.45
18th Ohio—Alfred N. Rodway.........	3,815,112.65
Oklahoma—George T. Knott...........	177,649.30
Oregon—David M. Dunne.............	822,730.30
1st Pennsylvania—William McCoach....	10,078,808.59
9th Pennsylvania—Henry L. Hershey..	5,239,219.96
12th Pennsylvania—Griffith T. Davis...	680,378.02
23d Pennsylvania—David B. Heiner....	12,961,124.09
South Carolina—Micah J. Jenkins......	51,112.75
Tennessee—William A. Dunlap........	2,384,189.03
3d Texas—Webster Flanagan............	1,509,462.57
4th Texas—Philemon B. Hunt.........	74,978.37
2d Virginia—Marion K. Lowry........	6,725,970.93
6th Virginia—Louis P. Summers........	88,087.54
6th Virginia—David F. Bailey........	1,235,129.82
Washington—Millard T. Hartson.......	1,448,007.90
West Virginia—George E. Work........	1,898,998.78
1st Wisconsin—Henry Fink...........	8,380,883.67
2d Wisconsin—Frank L. Gilbert.......	904,732.11
2d Wisconsin—Herbert H. Manson.....	278,576.35
Philippine Islands—Wm. T. Nolting*...	319,100.64

Aggregate collections..................344,424,453.85

*United States internal revenue stamp agent for the Philippine Islands, located at Manila, P. I.

UNITED STATES INTERNAL REVENUE TAXES.
SPECIAL TAXES IN FORCE.

Brewers of less than 500 barrels..............	$50.00
Brewers of 500 barrels or more..............	100.00
Rectifiers of less than 500 barrels...........	100.00
Rectifiers of 500 barrels or more...........	200.00
Dealers, retail liquor....................	25.00
Dealers, wholesale liquor..............	100.00
Dealers in malt liquors, wholesale........	50.00
Dealers in malt liquors only, retail........	20.00
Manufacturers of stills....................	50.00
And for each still manufactured...........	20.00
And for each worm manufactured...........	20.00
Manufacturers of oleomargarine............	600.00
Wholesale dealers in oleomargarine..........	480.00
Wholesale dealers in oleomargarine not artificially colored....................	200.00
Retail dealers in oleomargarine..........	48.00
Retail dealers in oleomargarine not artificially colored...............	6.00
Manufacturers of renovated butter*........	50.00
Manufacturers of adulterated butter........	600.00
Wholesale dealers in adulterated butter......	480.00
Retail dealers in adulterated butter........	48.00
Manufacturers of filled cheese..........	400.00
Wholesale dealers in filled cheese........	250.00
Retail dealers in filled cheese..........	12.00
Manufacturers and packers of mixed flour....	12.00

*No special taxes are imposed upon dealers in renovated butter.

SPIRITS, WINES AND LIQUORS.

Distilled spirits, per gallon................	$1.10
Wines, imitation, pint bottle.................	.10
Quart bottle....................	.20
Fermented liquor (beer), per brl. of 31 gals...	1.00

TOBACCO.

Tobacco, per pound............................	$0.06
Snuff, per pound............................	.06

Cigars, over 3 lbs. per 1,000........................ 3.00
  Not over 3 lbs. per 1,000......................... .54
Cigarettes, over 3 lbs. per 1,000.... .... 3.00
  Not over 3 lbs., value over $2.00............... 1.08
  Not over 3 lbs., value not over $2.00........ . .54

BUTTER AND CHEESE.

Adulterated butter, per lb........................$0.10
Renovated butter, per lb........................... ¼c
Filled cheese, per lb............................... .01
Imported .... .08

OLEOMARGARINE.

Oleomargarine, colored, per lb..................$0.10
  Not colored .... ¼c
Imported .... .15

MISCELLANEOUS.

Opium, smoking, per lb...........................$10.00
Playing cards, 54 in pack.......................... .02
Mixed flour, barrel of 196 lbs..................... .04
  Half barrel....................................... .02
  Quarter barrel.................................... .01
Corporation tax (on net income)................. 1%

THE PANAMA CANAL.

CANAL STATISTICS (OFFICIAL).

Length from deep water to deep water—50.5 miles.
Length on land—40.5 miles.
Length at summit level—31.7 miles.
Bottom width of channel—Maximum, 1,000 feet;
  minimum (in Culebra cut), 300 feet.
Depth—Minimum, 41 feet; maximum, 45 feet.
Summit level—85 feet above mean tide.
Locks in pairs—12.
Locks, usable length—1,000 feet.
Locks, usable width—110 feet.
Gatun lake, area—164 square miles.
Gatun lake, channel depth—85 to 45 feet.
Concrete required—5,000,000 cubic yards.
Time of transit through canal—10 to 12 hours.
Time of passage through locks—3 hours.
Length of relocated Panama railroad—46.2 miles.
Canal zone area—About 448 square miles.
Canal zone area owned by United States—About
  322 square miles.
French buildings acquired—2,150.
French buildings used—1,537.
Value of utilized French equipment—$1,000,000.
Canal force, average at work—About 39,000.
Estimated total cost of canal—$375,000,000.

CANAL COMMISSION.

Lieut.-Col. George W. Goethals, U. S. A., chairman
  and chief engineer.
Lieut.-Col. David Du B. Gaillard, U. S. A., corps
  of engineers.
Lieut.-Col. William L. Sibert, U. S. A., corps of
  engineers.
Col. William C. Gorgas, U. S. A., medical de-
  partment.
Harry H. Rousseau, U. S. N., civil engineer.
Col. H. F. Hodges, U. S. A.
Maurice H. Thatcher, civilian.
Headquarters of commission in Panama.
  As chairman, Lieut.-Col. Goethals receives a sal-
ary of $15,000 annually. Lieut.-Cols. Gaillard and
Sibert and Civil Engineer Rousseau $14,000 each
and Dr. Gorgas, Col. Hodges and Mr. Thatcher
$10,000 each.

CIVIL ADMINISTRATION.

Head of Department—Richard L. Metcalfe, Ancon.
Chief Clerk—G. A. Ninas, Ancon.

CANAL ZONE JUDICIARY.

Chief Justice Supreme Court—H. A. Gudger.
Associate Justices—Thomas E. Brown, Jr., and
  William H. Jackson.
  The salary of the chief justice is $6,500 a year
and of the associate justices $6,000 each.

SANITATION.

Chief—Col. W. C. Gorgas.
Assistant—Lieut.-Col. John L. Phillips.
General Inspector—Maj. Robert E. Noble.

CHRONOLOGY.

First exploration of route 1527.
Advocated by Humboldt 1803.
Panama railroad built 1850-1855.
Panama Canal company formed by De Lesseps 1879.
Work on canal begun Feb. 24, 1881.
Canal company failed Dec. 11, 1888.
De Lesseps and others sentenced to prison for
  fraud Feb. 9. 1893.
New French canal company formed October, 1894.
De Lesseps died Dec. 7, 1894.
Hay-Pauncefote treaty superseding the Clayton-
  Bulwer treaty signed Nov. 18, 1901; ratified by
  senate Dec. 16; ratified by Great Britain Jan.
  20, 1902.
Canal property offered to the United States for
  $40,000,000 Jan. 9, 1902; accepted Feb. 16, 1903.

Bill authorizing construction of canal passed by
  house of representatives Jan. 9, 1902; passed by
  senate June 19, 1902; approved June 28, 1902.
Canal treaty with Colombia signed Jan. 22, 1903;
  ratified by senate March 17, 1903; rejected by
  Colombia Aug. 12, 1903.
Revolution in Panama Nov. 3, 1903.
Canal treaty with Panama negotiated Nov. 18,
  1903; ratified by republic of Panama Dec. 2, 1903;
  ratified by United States senate Feb. 23, 1904.
Canal commissioners appointed Feb. 29, 1904.
Papers transferring canal to the United States
  signed in Paris April 22, 1904.
Bill for government of canal zone passed by the
  senate April 15, 1904; passed by the house April
  21; approved April 26.
Canal property at Panama formally turned over
  to the United States commissioners May 4, 1904.
Work begun by Americans May 4, 1904.
President outlines rules for the government of the
  canal zone and war department takes charge of
  the work May 9, 1904.
Gen. George W. Davis appointed first governor of
  canal zone May 9, 1904.
John F. Wallace appointed chief engineer May
  10, 1904; resigned June 29, 1905.
Republic of Panama paid $10,000,000 May 21, 1904.
First payment on $40,000,000 to French canal com-
  pany made May 24, 1904.
Lorin C. Collins appointed Supreme court judge
  for canal zone June 17, 1905.
New commission with Theodore P. Shonts as chair
  man named April 3, 1905; Shonts resigned March
  4, 1907.
John F. Stevens appointed chief engineer June 29,
  1905; resigned Feb. 26, 1907.
Lieut.-Col. George W. Goethals appointed chief en-
  gineer Feb. 26, 1907.
Gatun dam finished, June 14, 1913.
Dry excavation completed, Sept. 10, 1913.
First vessel lifted through Gatun locks, Sept. 26,
  1913.
Gamboa dike blown up, Oct. 10, 1913.
First vessels pass through Miraflores locks, Oct. 14,
  1913.
Official opening of canal fixed for Jan. 1, 1915.

PLAN OF THE CANAL.

The entire length of the Panama canal from
deep water in the Atlantic to deep water in the
Pacific is 50.5 miles. Its length on land is 40.5
miles. In passing through the canal from the
Atlantic to the Pacific a vessel will enter a
channel with a bottom width of 500 feet in Limon
bay and follow this for about seven miles to
Gatun, where it will enter a series of three locks
in flight and be lifted eighty-five feet to the level
of the Gatun lake. It will sail at full ocean
speed through this lake, in a channel varying from
1,000 to 500 feet in width, for a distance of about
twenty-four miles, to Bas Obispo, where it will
enter the Culebra cut. It will sail through the
cut, a distance of about nine miles, in a channel
with a bottom width of 300 feet, to Pedro Miguel.
There it will enter a lock and be lowered 30½
feet to a small lake at an elevation of 54½ feet
above sea level, and will sail through this for
about 1½ miles to Miraflores. There it will enter
two locks in series and be lowered to sea level,
passing out into the Pacific through a channel 8½
miles in length, with a bottom width of 500 feet.
The depth of the approach channel on the Atlantic side, where the tidal oscillation does not exceed 1½ feet, will be 41 feet at mean tide, and on
the Pacific side, where the maximum oscillation is
23 feet, the depth will be 45 feet at mean tide.

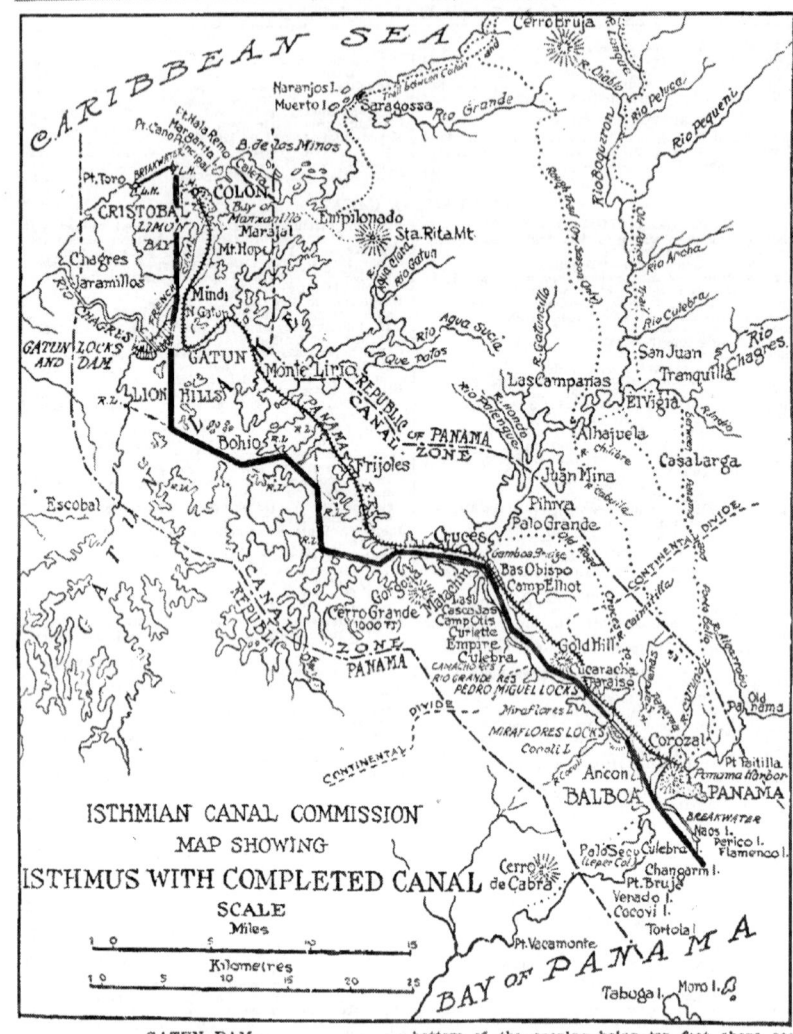

ISTHMIAN CANAL COMMISSION
MAP SHOWING
ISTHMUS WITH COMPLETED CANAL
SCALE
Miles
Kilometres

GATUN DAM.

The Gatun dam, which forms Gatun lake by impounding the waters of the Chagres river and other streams, is nearly 1½ miles long measured on its crest, nearly half a mile wide at its base, about 100 feet wide at the water surface, about 100 feet wide at the top and its crest is at an elevation of 115 feet above mean sea level, or 30 feet above the normal level of the lake. The top and upstream slope are riprapped. The spillway is a concrete lined opening 1,200 feet long and 300 feet wide, cut through a hill of rock nearly in the center of the dam, the bottom of the opening being ten feet above sea level. It is fitted with gates and machinery for regulating the water level of the lake.

The water level of Gatun lake, extending through the Culebra cut, is maintained at the south end by an earth dam connecting the locks at Pedro Miguel with the high ground to the westward, about 1,700 feet long, with its crest at an elevation of 105 feet above mean tide. A small lake between the locks at Pedro Miguel and Miraflores is formed by dams connecting the walls of Miraflores locks with the high ground on either side. The dam to the west-

ward is of earth, about 2,700 feet long, having its crest about 15 feet above the water in Miraflores lake. The east dam is of concrete, about 500 feet long, and forms a spillway for Miraflores lake, with crest gates similar to those at the spillway of the Gatun dam.

GATUN LAKE.

Gatun lake covers an area of 164 square miles, with a depth in the ship channel varying from 85 to 45 feet. Throughout the first 16 miles from Gatun the width of the channel is 1,000 feet; then for 4 miles it is 800 feet and for 4 miles more 500 feet, when the entrance to Culebra cut, at Bas Obispo, is reached. The water level in the cut is that of the lake and the bottom width of the channel is 300 feet.

CANAL ZONE.

The canal zone contains about 448 square miles. It begins at a point three marine miles from mean low-water mark in each ocean and extends for five miles on each side of the center line of the route of the canal. It includes the group of islands in the Bay of Panama named Perico, Naos, Culebra and Flamenco. The cities of Panama and Colon are excluded from the zone, but the United States has the right to enforce sanitary ordinances and maintain public order there in case the republic of Panama should not be able to do so. Of the 448 square miles in the zone the United States owns 322 and private persons 126. The private property may, however, be acquired at any time by the United States by purchase or by the exercise of the right of eminent domain.

THE LOCKS.

There are twelve locks in the canal, all in duplicate; three pairs in flight at Gatun, with a combined lift of 85 feet; one pair at Pedro Miguel, with a lift of 30½ feet, and two pairs at Miraflores, with a combined lift of 54⅔ feet at mean tide. The dimensions of all are the same—a usable length of 1,000 feet and a usable width of 110 feet. Each lock is a chamber, with walls and floors of concrete and water-tight gates at each end.

The side walls are 45 to 50 feet wide at the surface of floor, perpendicular on the face and narrow from the point 24½ feet above the floor until they are 8 feet wide at the top. The middle wall is 60 feet wide, approximately 81 feet high and each face is vertical. At a point 42½ feet above the surface of the floor and 15 feet above the top of the middle culvert this wall divides into two parts, leaving a space down the center much like the letter "U," which is 19 feet wide at the bottom. In this center space, which is 44 feet wide at the top, is a tunnel divided into three stories or galleries. The lowest gallery is for drainage; the middle for the wires that carry the electric current to operate the gate and valve machinery, which will be installed in the center wall, and the upper is a passageway for the operators. The lock chambers are filled and emptied through lateral culverts in the floors, connected with main culverts, 18 feet in diameter, in the walls, the water flowing in and out by gravity.

The lock gates are steel structures, 7 feet thick, 65 feet long and from 47 to 82 feet high. They weigh from 300 to 600 tons each. For the entire canal 92 leaves are required, the total weighing 57,000 tons. Intermediate gates are used in the locks to save water and time, if desired, in locking small vessels through, the gates being so fixed as to divide the locks into chambers 600 and 400 feet long, respectively. Of the vessels navigating the high seas 95 per cent are less than 600 feet long.

No vessel is permitted to enter or pass through the locks under its own power. Electricity is used to tow all vessels into and through the locks and to operate all gates and valves, power being generated by water turbines from the head created by Gatun lake. The time required to pass a vessel through all the locks is three hours, one hour and a half in the three locks at Gatun and about the same time in the three locks on the Pacific side. Time of the passage of a vessel through the entire canal varies from ten to twelve hours.

COMPLETION OF CANAL.

The Panama canal would have been completed early in the fall of 1913 so that small vessels could have passed through it but for delays occasioned by slides and breaks in the Culebra cut. This necessitated a large amount of additional excavation by steam shovels and dredges. Dry excavation was completed Sept. 10. The massive Gatun dam was finished June 14 and Sept. 26 the first vessel, a tug, was locked through the gates. At the Pacific end canal vessels passed through the Miraflores and Pedro Miguel locks Oct. 14 and 15. Dredges were put at work at both ends of the principal slide at Cucaracha on the east bank of the canal just south of Gold Hill, to excavate a passage which would permit water communication from the Atlantic to the Pacific. The slides and breaks numbering about thirty increased the total amount of excavation necessary to complete the canal by more than 20,000,000 cubic yards. The Gamboa dike separating the waters of Gatun lake from the Culebra cut was dynamited Oct. 10, the blast being fired by President Wilson, who depressed an electric lever in the white house in Washington.

The formal opening of the canal will take place Jan. 1, 1915.

TOLLS.

Under the Panama canal act, approved Aug. 24, 1912, the president of the United States is authorized to fix the tolls to be charged for use of the canal. He may change them by giving six months' notice. The act provides that no tolls shall be levied upon vessels engaged in the coastwise trade of the United States. Vessels owned by railroads or by any company or person doing business in violation of antitrust laws are excluded from the use of the canal.

By a proclamation issued Nov. 13, 1912, President Taft fixed the tolls to be paid by foreign shipping for passage through the Panama canal as follows:

On merchant vessels carrying passengers or cargo, $1.20 per net vessel ton—each 100 cubic feet—of actual earning capacity.

On vessels in ballast without passengers or cargo, 40 per cent less than the rate of tolls for vessels with passengers or cargo.

Upon naval vessels other than transports, colliers, hospital ships and supply ships, 50 cents per displacement ton.

Upon army and navy transports, colliers, hospital ships and supply ships, $1.20 per net ton, the vessels to be measured by the same rules as are employed in determining the net tonnage of merchant vessels.

CANAL FORCE.

The total force at work on the canal and railroad Aug. 27, 1913, was 42,885. Canal employes numbered 35,005, Panama railroad 4,957 and contractors' employes 2,943. The number of "gold" or white American employes was 4,087. The great majority of laborers were West Indian negroes.

CANAL EXCAVATION TO OCT. 1, 1913.

	Cu. yds.
By French companies	78,146,960
French excavation useful to canal	29,908,000
By Americans—	
Dry excavation	127,816,168
Dredges	83,232,130
Total	211,048,198
May 4 to Dec. 31, 1904	243,472
Jan. 1 to Dec. 31, 1905	1,799,227
Jan. 1 to Dec. 31, 1906	4,948,497
Jan. 1 to Dec. 31, 1907	15,765,290
Jan. 1 to Dec. 31, 1908	37,116,735
Jan. 1 to Dec. 31, 1909	35,096,166
Jan. 1 to Dec. 31, 1910	31,427,671
Jan. 1 to Dec. 31, 1911	31,603,899
Jan. 1 to Dec. 31, 1912	30,269,349
Jan. 1 to Oct. 1, 1913	22,767,886

The amount remaining to be excavated Oct. 1, 1913, was 21,304,802 cubic yards.

CANAL APPROPRIATIONS.

Act of Congress.	Appropriation.	Deficiency.
June 28, 1902	*$40,000,000.00	
April 28, 1904	†10,000,000.00	
June 28, 1902	10,000,000.00	
Dec. 21, 1905	11,000,000.00	
Feb. 27, 1906		$5,990,746
June 30, 1906	25,456,415.08	

Act of Congress.	Appropriation.	Deficiency.
March 4, 1907	27,161,367.50	....
Feb. 15, 1908	....	12,178,300
May 27, 1908	29,187,000.00	....
March 4, 1909	33,638,000.00	5,458,000
Feb. 25, 1910	....	76,000
June 20, 1910	37,855,000.00	....
Special acts	21,411.56	
March 4, 1911	45,560,000.00	....
Aug. 24, 1912	28,980,000.00	....
June 23, 1913	16,265,393.00	....
Total	315,124,587.14	23,703,686
Deficiency	23,703,686.00	
Grand total	338,828,273.14	

FORTIFICATIONS.

March 4, 1911	$3,000,000
Aug. 24, 1912	2,806,950
June 23, 1913	4,870,000
Total	10,676,950

*For purchase of canal rights from French. †Paid to republic of Panama for canal zone rights.

EXPENDITURES TO OCT. 1, 1913.

Civil administration	$6,454,781.54
Sanitation	16,371,652.40
Construction and engineering	187,454,636.14
Miscellaneous	88,104,427.83
Law	46,580.18
Fortifications	3,245,691.23
Total	301,677,779.32

PANAMA CANAL TOLLS CONTROVERSY.

Before the Panama canal bill became a law (Aug. 24, 1912), Great Britain had protested that the paragraph exempting American vessels in the coastwise trade from the payment of tolls was in violation of section 1, article 3, of the Hay-Pauncefote treaty of Nov. 8, 1901, providing for the neutrality of the proposed isthmian canal. This treaty was entered into to remove any objection which might arise under the Clayton-Bulwer treaty of April 19, 1850. Section 1, article 3, of the Hay-Pauncefote treaty provides:

"The canal shall be free and open to the vessels of commerce and of war of all nations observing these rules on terms of entire equality, so that there shall be no discrimination against any nation or its subjects in respect of the conditions or charges of traffic or otherwise. Such conditions and charges of traffic shall be just and reasonable."

After the passage of the Panama canal act with the paragraph exempting American coastwise vessels from paying tolls, Great Britain, through Ambassador Bryce, presented a formal protest Dec. 9, 1912, insisting that the exemption was contrary to the Hay-Pauncefote treaty as interpreted in the light of the Clayton-Bulwer treaty. Jan. 23, 1913, Secretary of State Knox replied to the British protest, declaring that the American coastwise trade would not be permitted to extend its operations into foreign competitive fields, and that increased tolls would not be laid on foreign shipping to balance the remission to American ships. He said he could not agree with the British interpretation of the canal treaties so far as they limit the freedom of action of America or infringe on British treaty rights. The secretary suggested that if the difference could not be arranged through diplomatic channels it might be submitted to a special commission of inquiry.

The matter was the subject of controversy in and out of congress during the spring and summer of 1913. The opponents of free tolls for American coastwise vessels, led by Senator Elihu Root of New York, maintained that national honor required the observance of the Hay-Pauncefote treaty as viewed by Great Britain. The defenders of the free tolls clause in the Panama canal act insisted that the hands of the United States were not tied by the treaty. They claimed that the words "all nations" did not apply to the country that built the canal but to foreign nations. Many others, including ex-President Taft, urged that the whole matter be referred to the international court at The Hague for arbitration. It was understood that the matter would be taken up by the senate committee on foreign relations at the first regular session of the 63d congress.

LIQUORS AND SPIRITS PRODUCED IN THE UNITED STATES.

Year ended June 30, 1912.

	Barrels.
Fermented liquors	62,176,694
Distilled spirits—	Gallons.
Whisky	98,209,574
Rum	2,832,516
Gin	3,577,862
Highwines	131,002
Alcohol	27,629,346
Commercial alcohol	45,869,685
Fruit brandy	9,321,823
Total spirits	187,571,808

PRODUCTION BY STATES.

State.	Spirits, gallons.	Liquors, barrels.
Alabama[1]	122,348	39,835
Arkansas	69,655	8,850
California[2]	11,926,361	1,315,017
Colorado[3]	....	404,696
Connecticut[4]	161,739	1,403,645
Florida	120,882	21,290
Georgia	....	138,955
Hawaii	11,221	20,967

State.	Spirits, gallons.	Liquors, barrels.
Illinois	38,932,758	6,263,862
Indiana	27,522,220	1,546,292
Iowa	....	447,114
Kansas	....	101
Kentucky	43,749,193	801,935
Louisiana	10,887,595	483,988
Maryland[5]	5,589,729	1,093,838
Dist. Columbia	626,863	284,576
Delaware	....	129,695
Massachusetts	5,355,847	2,386,905
Michigan	2,284,627	1,792,105
Minnesota	....	1,512,139
Missouri	495,934	4,030,390
Montana[3]	....	391,314
Nebraska	2,388,874	413,014
N. Hampshire[7]	583	267,075
New Jersey	120,743	3,397,375
New Mexico[8]	891	28,090
New York	10,179,057	13,677,850
North Carolina	727	....
Ohio	11,419,929	4,742,665
Oklahoma	....	72

State.	Spirits, gallons.	Liquors, barrels.
Oregon	1,357	245,819
Pennsylvania	10,583,503	7,449,543
South Carolina	586,329	2,688
South Dakota	....	44,808
Tennessee	....	273,850
Texas	....	673,262
Virginia	1,505,780	195,756
Washington[9]	115,492	861,564
West Virginia	294,117	270,142
Wisconsin	2,537,890	5,016,701
Total	187,571,808	62,176,694

[1] Including Mississippi. [2] Including Nevada. [3] Including Wyoming. [4] Including Rhode Island. [5] Including District of Columbia, Delaware and two counties of Virginia. [6] Including Idaho and Utah. [7] Including Maine and Vermont. [8] Including Arizona. [9] Including Alaska.

GREAT SHIP CANALS OF THE WORLD.

Canal.	Opened, year.	Length, miles.	Depth, feet.	Width,* feet.	Cost.
Corinth (Greece)	1893	4	26.25	72	$5,000,000
Kronstadt-St. Petersburg (Russia)	1890	16	20.50	220	10,000,000
Elbe and Trave (Germany)	1900	41	10	72	5,831,000
Kaiser Wilhelm (Germany)	1895	61	29.50	72	37,128,000
Manchester ship (England)	1894	35.5	26	120	75,000,000
Sault Ste. Marie (U. S.)	1855	1.6	22	100	10,000,000
Sault Ste. Marie (Canada)	1895	1.11	20.25	142	2,791,873
Suez (Egypt)	1869	90	31	108	100,000,000
Welland (Canada)	1887	26.75	14	100	25,000,000

*At the bottom.

NATIONAL INSTITUTE OF ARTS AND LETTERS.

Organized, 1898; incorporated by act of congress.

President—Brander Matthews, New York, N. Y.
Secretary—Henry D. Sedgwick, New York, N. Y.

DEPT. OF LITERATURE.

Adams, Brooks.
Adams, Charles Francis.
Adams, Henry.
Ade, George.
Alden, Henry M.
Aldrich, Richard.
Allen, James Lane.
Baldwin, Simeon E.
Bates, Arlo.
Bridges, Robert.
Brownell, W. C.
Burroughs, John.
Burton, Richard.
Butler, Nicholas M.
Cable, George W.
Carman, Bliss.
Cawein, Madison J.
Channing, Edward.
Cheney, John Vance.
Churchill, Winston.
Connolly, James B.
Cortissoz, Royal.
Cross, Wilbur L.
Crothers, Samuel McChord.
DeKay, Charles.
Dunne, Finley Peter.
Egan, Maurice Francis.
Fernald, Chester B.
Finck, Henry T.
Finley, John Huston.
Ford, Worthington C.
Fox, John, Jr.
Furness, Horace H.
Garland, Hamlin.
Gildersleeve, Basil L.
Gillette, William.
Gilman, Lawrence.
Gordon, George A.
Grant, Robert.
Greenslet, Ferris.
Griffis, William B.
Gummere, Francis B.
Hadley, A. T.
Hardy, Arthur S.
Harper, George McLean.
Herford, Oliver.
Herrick, Robert.
Hitchcock, Ripley.
Howe, M. A. De Wolfe.
Howells, W. D.
Huntington, Archer M.
James, Henry.
Johnson, Owen.
Johnson, Robert U.
Kennan, George.
Lloyd, Nelson.
Lodge, Henry Cabot.
Long, John Luther.
Lounsbury, T. R.
Lovett, Robert M.
Lowell, Abbott L.
Lummis, Charles F.
Mabie, H. W.
Mackaye, Percy.
Mahan, A. T.
Markham, Edwin.
Martin, Edward S.
Mather, Frank J.
Matthews, Brander.
McKelway, Saint Clair.
McMaster, John Bach.
Miller, Joaquin.*
Mitchell, John A.
Mitchell, Langdon E.
More, Paul Elmore.
Morris, Harrison S.
Morse, John T., Jr.
Muir, John.
Nicholson, Meredith.
Page, Thomas Nelson.

Payne, Will.
Payne, William Morton.
Peck, Harry Thurston.
Perry, Bliss.
Perry, Thomas S.
Phelps, William L.
Pier, A. S.
Rhodes, James F.
Riley, James Whitcomb.
Roberts, Charles G. D.
Robinson, Edward A.
Roosevelt, Theodore.
Royce, Josiah.
Schelling, Felix E.
Schuyler, Montgomery.
Scollard, Clinton.
Sedgwick, Henry D.
Seton, Ernest Thompson.
Sherman, Frank Dempster.
Shorey, Paul.
Sloane, William M.
Smith, F. Hopkinson.
Sullivan, Thomas R.
Tarkington, Booth.
Thayer, Abbott H.
Thayer, William R.
Thomas, Augustus.
Thorndike, Ashley H.
Tooker, Frank L.
Torrence, Ridgely.
Trent, William P.
Van Dyke, Henry.
Van Dyke, John C.
Wendell, Barrett.
West, Andrew F.
White, Andrew Dickson.
White, William Allen.
Whiting, Charles G.
Whitlock, Brand.
Williams, Jesse Lynch.
Wilson, Harry Leon.
Wilson, Woodrow.
Wister, Owen.
Woodberry, George E.

DEPT. OF ART.

Adams, Herbert.
Alexander, John W.
Babb, George F.
Bacon, Henry.
Bailin, Hugo.
Barnard, George Gray.
Bartlett, Paul W.
Beckwith, J. Carroll.
Benson, Frank W.
Bitter, Karl.
Blashfield, Edwin H.
Brooks, Richard E.
Brown, Glenn.
Bruner, Arnold W.
Brush, George Deforest.
Bunce, William G.
Burnham, Daniel H.*
Carlsen, Emil.
Chase, William M.
Cole, Timothy.
Cook, Walter.
Cox, Kenyon.
Crowninshield, Frederic.
Dannat, William T.
Day, Frank M.
De Camp, Joseph.
Dewey, Charles M.
Dewing, Thomas W.
Dielman, Frederick W.
Donaldson, John M.
Dougherty, Paul.
Duveneck, Frank.
Foster, Ben.
French, Daniel C.
Gay, Walter.
Gibson, Charles Dana.
Gilbert, Cass.

Grafly, Charles.
Guerin, Jules.
Hardenburgh, H. J.
Harrison, Alexander.
Harrison, Birge.
Hassam, Childe.
Hastings, Thomas.
Henri, Robert.
Howard, John Galen.
Howe, William Henry.
Isham, Samuel.
Jaeger, Albert.
Jones, Francis C.
Jones, H. Bolton.
Kendall, W. Sergeant.
La Farge, Bancel.
Low, Will H.
Macmonnies, Frederick.
MacNeil, H. A.
Marr, Carl.
McEwen, Walter.
Mead, William R.
Melchers, Gari.
Metcalf, Willard L.
Mowbray, H. Siddons.
Ochtman, Leonard.
Parrish, Maxfield.
Peabody, Robert S.
Pearce, Charles S.
Pennell, Joseph.
Platt, Charles A.
Post, George B.
Potter, Edward Clark.
Pratt, Bela L.
Proctor, A. Phimister.
Redfield, Edward W.
Reid, Robert.
Roth, F. G. R.
Ruckstuhl, F. W.

Ryder, Albert P.
Sargent, John S.
Schofield, W. E.
Shrady, H. M.
Simmons, Edward.
Smedley, William T.
Taft, Lorado.
Tarbell, Edmund C.
Thayer, Abbott H.
Tryon, D. W.
Vedder, Elihu.
Walden, Lionel.
Walker, Henry O.
Walker, Horatio.
Warren, Whitney.
Weinman, Adolph A.
Weir, J. Alden.
Wiles, Irving R.

DEPT. OF MUSIC.

Bird, Arthur.
Brockway, Howard.
Chadwick, G. W.
Converse, F. S.
Damrosch, Walter.
De Koven, Reginald.
Foote, Arthur.
Gilchrist, W. W.
Hadley, H. K.
Herbert, Victor.
Kelley, Edgar S.
Loeffler, Charles M.
Parker, Horatio W.
Schellings, Ernest.
Shelley, Harry Rowe.
Smith, David S.
Van der Stucken, F.
Whiting, Arthur.

*Deceased.

The purposes of the corporation are the furtherance of the interests of literature and the fine arts. The organization is limited to 250 regular members. It is authorized to receive bequests and donations and to hold the same in trust for the furtherance of the interests of literature and the fine arts.

AMERICAN ACADEMY OF ARTS AND LETTERS.

Founded in 1904.

President—William Dean Howells.
Chancellor—William Milligan Sloane.
Permanent Secretary—Robert Underwood Johnson, 327 Lexington avenue, New York, N. Y.

Members in department of literature:

Charles Francis Adams.
Henry Adams.
Henry M. Walton.
W. C. Brownell.
Nicholas Murray Butler.
George W. Cable.
Horace Howard Furness.
Basil L. Gildersleeve.
Arthur Twining Hadley.
William Dean Howells.
Henry James.
Robt. Underwood Johnson.
Henry Cabot Lodge.
Thomas R. Lounsbury.
Abbott L. Lowell.
Hamilton Wright Mabie.

Alfred T. Mahan.
John Burroughs.
Brander Matthews.
John Muir.
Thomas Nelson Page.
Bliss Perry.
James Ford Rhodes.
James Whitcomb Riley.
Theodore Roosevelt.
William M. Sloane.
F. Hopkinson Smith.
Henry Van Dyke.
Andrew Dickson White.
Woodrow Wilson.
George E. Woodberry.

Members in department of art:

John W. Alexander.
Paul W. Bartlett.
Edwin H. Blashfield.
George Deforest Brush.
William M. Chase.
Kenyon Cox.

Daniel C. French.
Thomas Hastings.
Wm. Rutherford Mead.
John S. Sargent.
Abbott Thayer.
Elihu Vedder.

Members in department of music:

Horatio W. Parker. | Geo. Whitfield Chadwick.

Membership in the academy is limited to fifty. Only those who belong to the National Institute of Arts and Letters are eligible, and they are elected by that body.

REVOLUTION IN MEXICO.

American Press assn., New York, N.Y.

Francisco I. Madero, president of Mexico since October, 1911, was deposed from office Feb. 18, 1913, after a short but sanguinary military revolution led by Gen. Felix Diaz in the City of Mexico. Feb. 22 he was killed while being taken to a prison. The events leading up to this new chapter in the history of the republic may be briefly recapitulated. When Gen. Porfirio Diaz

VICTORIANO HUERTA. was elected president of Mexico in June, 1910, his opponents, who called themselves antire-electionists, began to plan for his overthrow, and in November of that year they organized a revolution and began fighting both in the south and the north. Francisco I. Madero was one of the most active of the rebels and Nov. 23 he proclaimed himself "provisional president of Mexico." Fighting continued throughout November and December, 1910, and until May 25, 1911, when President Diaz resigned and went to Europe. Francisco de la Barra was made provisional president and he served until October, when Madero was elected to the office of chief executive.

While Madero represented the opposition to the autocracy of Porfirio Diaz, he himself had enemies who charged him with using the same methods as his predecessor. Among them were Gen. Pascual Orozco, Emilio Vasquez Gomez, Gen. Geronimo Trevino, Emiliano Zapata and Gen. Felix Diaz, a nephew of the deposed president. The country was kept in a generally disturbed condition by these men and others, though Madero appeared to be well in control of the situation. Oct. 16, 1912, Gen. Diaz with 500 men took possession of Vera Cruz, but within a week he and his men were taken without a struggle by the federal troops. Two of his officers were tried by court-martial and shot and he was condemned to meet the same fate, but sentence was suspended and he remained in prison until released by a military uprising in the City of Mexico, Feb. 9, 1913.

BEGINNING OF REVOLT.

The mutinous troops were led by students from the military school at Tlalpam, a suburb. They first took possession of a powder magazine and then early on the morning of the 9th marched to the central square in the city, where the government buildings are located. On the way they went to the prisons where Gen. Felix Diaz and Gen. Bernardo Reyes were confined and released them. Accompanied by their leaders, and followed by huge crowds shouting "Death to Madero!" the men proceeded to the Zocalo and Plaza de la Constitucion in front of the national palace. They were joined by portions of several cavalry and infantry regiments under command of Gen. Manuel Mondragon. In front of the palace about 500 loyal troops were lined up and firing began as soon as the mutineers approached. One of the first to fall was Gen. Reyes, who was instantly killed by a rifle ball through the head. Men stationed on the roof of the palace and in the windows began a fusillade, while machine guns were also brought into play.

Finding the palace strongly defended, Gen. Diaz, who had taken command of the mutinous troops, withdrew and with his men proceeded to the citadel, or arsenal, about a mile distant in a westerly direction. The place was promptly attacked and soon surrendered. Here the rebels came into possession of all the government's reserve artillery, a large number of rifles and more ammunition than they could use. The place was turned into a fortress and thereafter was used as the headquarters of Gen. Diaz. Belem prison, near the arsenal, was also seized and the prisoners turned loose. The artillery from Tacubaya came in and joined the rebels.

Gen. Lauro Villar, post commander of the capital, who remained loyal, was wounded in the fighting

at the Zocalo, and was replaced by Gen. Victoriano Huerta, who had charge of Madero's forces until Feb. 13, when he arrested his former chief and was himself made provisional president of the republic. The casualties of the first day's fighting were 506, including 170 women, 6 children and 208 noncombatant men.

AN EXTRAORDINARY SITUATION.

On the 10th but little was done on either side except to prepare for the continuation of the struggle. On the 11th fighting began again and did not cease except at short intervals until the 19th. In that time, so far as could be learned, some 3,000 persons were killed and perhaps 7,000 wounded. Several Americans, including two women, lost their lives. Most of the victims were not soldiers but noncombatants—men, women and children—who were unable to escape from the zone of danger. In fact, there was danger in nearly all parts of the city, as the projectiles from modern high-powered guns reached everywhere. The situation was an extraordinary one. The opposing forces occupied two large structures about a mile apart and fired at each other across the very heart of the city. The finest business district and also a part of the best residence district were in the direct line of fire and few structures escaped serious damage. Business houses, schools, churches, convents, public structures and private homes were pierced by shells and bullets. The American embassy building was frequently struck and its occupants, including the American ambassador, had narrow escapes from death. The same was true of the American consulate. It was even more exposed than the embassy and finally had to be abandoned.

Some of the larger buildings, like the unfinished national theater at the east end of the Alameda, the Young Men's Christian association building near the arsenal, and the Mutual Life insurance building, were conspicuous targets, as the combatants at times fought each other from them or from places near by. Many persons were killed in the Alameda, the beautiful park at the east end of the Paseo de la Reforma, one of the famous streets of the world. Porter's hotel, the principal rendezvous for Americans in the City of Mexico, was struck repeatedly and one of the guests was killed. The American club was riddled with bullets and shells and was all but demolished. The cable office was also struck frequently, but the operators remained at their places throughout the whole of the bombardment.

While most of the fighting was done from the shelter of the arsenal, the national palace and other buildings, skirmishes in the streets were frequent. The rebels commanded all the approaches to the arsenal and also had outposts in the western part of the city to prevent attacks from the rear. The federals, who at first were most aggressive, planted batteries in the Zocalo, the Alameda, the Paseo de la Reforma and at other points to the east and north. Detachments of rurales were sent against the rebels, but horses and men were swept away by a hail of bullets from machine guns. The fire of Gen. Diaz' riflemen and artillerists was accurate and deadly. They were well supplied with range finders and were amply supplied with ammunition. Though it was announced on several occasions that a general attack would be made by one side or the other, nothing of the kind was attempted. Neither side felt able to rush the other without incurring great loss of life and the risk of irretrievable disaster.

During the bombardment the people of the city remained passive. There was no rioting and no mobs appeared in the streets. Order was maintained as usual and few robberies were committed. The general sympathy was with the rebels and against Madero.

On the 14th and 15th efforts were made to have President Madero resign. He was urged to do so by Francisco de la Barra and by members of the senate, but he refused to listen to them. He said he was willing to arbitrate or do anything that a man might do honestly and properly to bring peace

to his country, but he would not act the part of a coward. De la Barra soon found himself in danger and was obliged to take refuge in the British legation. Conferences were frequently held in the American embassy between members of the diplomatic corps to consider the situation and also between Ambassador Henry Lane Wilson and representatives of the government as well as of the rebels. Mr. Wilson was, in fact, the dominating influence in the legation quarter and did much to assure the safety not only of the Americans but of all foreigners resident in the city. After the overthrow of Madero he was personally visited by Gens. Huerta and Diaz and consulted upon important matters. He was also in constant touch with Washington, where the authorities were much concerned over the situation.

NO INTERVENTION.

Intervention by the United States was urged in many quarters, but President Taft and his advisers firmly adhered to the policy followed ever since the revolution in Mexico began in 1910. The matter was discussed at several meetings of the cabinet and the position taken was explained by President Taft in a message sent in reply to a communication from President Madero protesting against possible intervention. The message, dated Feb. 16, asserted that the military and naval measures taken by the United States were merely precautionary. It concluded: "I feel it my duty to add sincerely and without reserve that the course of events during the last two years, culminating in the present most dangerous situation, creates in this country extreme pessimism and the conviction that the present paramount duty is the prompt relief of the situation."

Though declining to intervene in Mexico, the Washington administration made preparations to take that step should it become necessary. The battle ships Georgia, Vermont and Nebraska were sent to Vera Cruz, the battle ship Virginia to Tampico, the cruiser Colorado to Mazatlan and the cruiser South Dakota to Acapulco. These ships were prepared to receive and protect imperiled Americans and also to send armed men ashore should the occasion arise. Three thousand marines were ordered to Guantanamo, Cuba, to be held in readiness for immediate service.

MADERO IS DEPOSED.

On the afternoon of Feb. 18 there was another kaleidoscopic change in the situation in the City of Mexico. It was engineered by Gen. Aureliano Blanquet and Gen. Victoriano Huerta, who up to that time had apparently given President Madero loyal support. In the forenoon they fought the insurgents vigorously; at 3 o'clock in the afternoon they arrested Madero, forced him to resign the presidency and locked him up. Gen. Huerta assuming at once the powers of the chief executive. Precisely how the plot against President Madero took form was not disclosed. On the one hand it was asserted that a group of senators had urged Gen. Huerta to put an end to the long battle in the heart of the city and to remove the Madero family from public affairs in Mexico; on the other it was asserted that Gen. Blanquet, who had a son fighting under Gen. Diaz, was at heart opposed to Madero from the beginning and only waited for a favorable opportunity to overthrow him. At all events, to Gen. Blanquet was assigned the duty of placing President Madero under arrest. With this end in view he brought into the city 1,000 men from his own command and stationed them near the national palace in place of the reserves who had been loyal to Madero.

Hundreds of persons, attracted by the unusual movements about the palace, had gathered there in the afternoon and they were surprised when Gens. Blanquet and Huerta announced in brief speeches that the time had come when peace must be restored in the city, and that they proposed to bring it about. Gen. Blanquet detailed twenty men under Col. Riveroll to arrest President Madero. The first intimation the latter had of the new turn in affairs was when he entered the hall of ambassadors, which he found guarded by soldiers standing with rifles at "ready." The president engaged in

a scuffle with one of the guards and the man's rifle was discharged. This brought a number of Madero's own men hurrying to the scene. A brief encounter took place, resulting in the death of two guards and the wounding of six others. Col. Riveroll fell mortally wounded and died a short time afterward. It was officially charged that Madero himself fired the fatal shot. When the president had been overcome he was asked to make out his resignation in legal form and he did so. In the meantime other arrests were made, including those of Vice-President Jose Pino Suarez, Gov. Federico Gonzales Garza of the federal district, and Gustavo Madero, brother of the president. The last named was taken in a restaurant where he had gone to lunch with Gen. Huerta. Members of the cabinet and other government officials were also placed under arrest but were soon released on parole.

Later in the day Gen. Huerta called on the executive officers of the senate and chamber of deputies to summon a special session of congress to legalize the change of government and name a provisional president. All this was done, it was claimed, without the knowledge of Gen. Felix Diaz, and the first news he had of it was from the American embassy. The first official act of Gen. Huerta as de facto ruler was to send notice to Ambassador Wilson of what had been done, asking him to notify the other members of the diplomatic corps and to advise President Taft that the battle was ended and that the foreigners in the city were safe. At the same time he requested that the American embassy be used as a channel for communication with the insurgents. Ambassador Wilson agreed to act as an intermediary, and an exchange of notes was begun which terminated in a complete accord. An incident of the negotiations was the ovation received by the messenger of the United States minister in carrying communications between the arsenal and the palace. When his automobile bearing a white flag on one side and the American colors on the other was slowly making its way through San Francisco street, the crowd, which had learned the truth about what was going on, shouted "Viva Los Americanos!"

In the evening a large crowd assembled in the Zocalo and cheered for Diaz, Huerta, Blanquet and Mondragon. Banners bearing the words "Peace" and "Liberty" were displayed. Some lawless acts occurred at this time. The office of the Nueva Era, a Madero organ, was set on fire and burned by a mob. Marco Hernandez, a brother of the minister of the interior, was shot and killed for shouting "Viva Madero."

On the morning of the 19th Gen. Felix Diaz went to the American embassy and formally ratified an agreement with Gen. Huerta bringing the crisis to an end. Later Gen. Huerta also called and had a conference with the ambassador. A tragic occurrence of the day was the execution of Gustavo Madero, who after his arrest on the previous day had been confined in the arsenal. He was subjected to the so-called "fugitive law," by which he was free to run under the rifle fire of his guards. He fell dead before he had proceeded many paces. He was regarded as "the power behind the throne" and was cordially disliked. It was said of him that his political activities led to the unpopularity of the administration and to its final undoing.

In the evening at a special session of congress Gen. Huerta was chosen provisional president of Mexico. The first act of the congress was to accept the resignation of President Madero; then Pedro Lascurain, in his capacity as minister of foreign affairs, took the oath as president ad interim and Gen. Huerta, to make the succession legal, was appointed a cabinet minister. Then, after these formalities had been complied with, he was duly elected provisional president. Thus Mexico had three presidents within the space of about an hour.

It was at first proposed by the new government to send Madero into exile, but other counsels prevailed and he was kept as a prisoner of war by the military in the national palace until the night of Feb. 22-23, when he and the former vice-presi-

dent, Jose Pino Suarez, were ordered to be conveyed to the penitentiary, at the eastern end of the city. They were placed in an automobile, which was followed by another car, and escorted by 100 rurales under Commandant Francisco Cardenas and Col. Rafael Pimiento. According to the official account given to the press by President Huerta, the automobiles had traversed about two-thirds of the way to the penitentiary when they were attacked by an armed group, and the escort descended from the machines to offer resistance. "Suddenly the group grew larger and the prisoners tried to escape," ran the official story. "An exchange of shots then took place in which two of the attacking party were killed and two were wounded. Both prisoners were killed. The automobiles were badly damaged."

Madero, it was found, had been shot through the head, the bullet entering at the back and passing out of the forehead. The body of Suarez showed many wounds, the bullets having entered from the front. In spite of the official versions of the affair, there was considerable mystery about it and the general view taken was that it was a case of premeditated assassination, or another application of the "ley fuga" (fugitive law), to which Gustavo Madero had already fallen a victim. Some accounts of the shooting placed the time when it occurred at shortly after midnight, making the date Feb. 23; others placed it before midnight, or on Feb. 22. Francisco de la Barra was quoted as saying that he was informed of the killing at 11:30 p. m. on the 22d.

The members of the escort were placed under arrest and the government promised to have the whole matter made the subject of a rigid judicial inquiry. The investigation resulted in a verdict that no one could be held legally responsible. The members of the diplomatic corps decided not to recognize the provisional government, although in a statement issued Feb. 24 Ambassador Wilson said that in the absence of other reliable information he was disposed to accept the government version of the manner in which the ex-president and ex-vice-president lost their lives. "Certainly the violent deaths of these persons were without government approval," he declared, "and if the deaths were the result of a plot it was of restricted character and unknown to the higher officers of the government."

On the 22d of February, before the killing of Madero and Suarez had taken place, the authorities in Washington ordered the fifth brigade of the second army division to proceed to Galveston, Tex., for possible service in Mexico. When the news of the tragedy in the Mexican capital became known additional troops were ordered south from various army posts and within a few days some 10,000 men, under the command of Maj.-Gen. William H. Carter, had assembled at Galveston and other points within striking distance of the Mexican border. President Taft disclaimed any intention of intervening in Mexico but deemed it prudent to prepare for emergencies.

NEW REVOLUTION BEGUN.

The election of Gen. Huerta as provisional president did not bring peace to Mexico. Most of the followers of Madero assumed that he had been deliberately murdered and they refused to be pacified. They did not regard the election of Huerta as constitutional but saw in it a revival of the Diaz regime which they had overthrown in 1912. A leader of the discontented arose in the person of Venustiano Carranza, governor of the state of Coahuila. He with other friends of the dead president organized the Mexican constitutionalist party and carried on an active military campaign in the northern half of the republic. March 26 some of the leading members of the new organization met at Guadalupe, Coahuila, and adopted a declaration of which the following is the substance:

1. We repudiate Gen. Victoriano Huerta as president of the republic.

2. We repudiate also the legislative and judicial powers of the federation.

3. We repudiate the governments of the states which thirty days hence shall recognize the

federal authorities which form the present administration.

4. For the organization of the military forces necessary to enforce compliance with our purposes we name as first chief of the party, which shall be called the constitutionalist party, Don Venustiano Carranza, governor of Coahuila.

Francisco Escudero, one of Gov. Carranza's aids and for many years a professor of history in the University of Guadalajara, in an article published in The Independent, New York, Aug. 14, pointed out the following as the principal reforms sought by the constitutionalists:

"The weeding out of the administration personnel and the reconstruction of the judiciary; honesty in the management of the treasury; equitable distribution of taxes; legislation to better labor conditions, so as to develop better relations between capital and the working classes, especially in respect to the peasantry and the great landholders; establishment of agricultural banks; legislation providing for extensive irrigation throughout the land; passing of necessary laws to make titles to real estate respected and easy of transfer; revision of civil laws; fair distribution of communal land; the breaking up of large estates by means of proper expropriation; the betterment of the farming population; the construction of roads and turnpikes, and the imparting of public instruction on a large scale."

Not all of the Madero men joined the constitutionalists. Gen. Pascual Orozco, Sr., one of the noted leaders in the north, joined the Huerta forces, as did some of the Zapatistas in the south. Zapata himself refused to come to terms and continued his guerrilla warfare. Federals and constitutionalists were nearly evenly divided and in the fighting, which continued throughout the greater part of the year, neither side could claim any decided advantage. In the central part of the republic the Huerta forces were in control, but in the north they maintained possession of a few places, such as Laredo, Monterey, Saltillo, Juarez, Jiminez and Parral. Life and property were safe nowhere. Railroad communication was interrupted everywhere except between Mexico City and Vera Cruz, and business of all kinds was interrupted. Tales of robbery and violence, in which Americans and other foreigners were frequently the victims, came from nearly all parts of the country. Thousands had to flee to the United States for protection.

In May it was reported that President Huerta was seeking a foreign loan of $75,000,000 and that English and French bankers had promised to furnish the money provided he could secure recognition from the American government. In this he was disappointed, as the Washington authorities held that he had no constitutional or moral right to the presidency and would not recognize him or the Mexican administration until after the presidential election which, it had been announced, would take place in the latter part of October. Gen. Huerta retorted by telling Ambassador Wilson that he had no legal standing as a diplomat and that the American claims for damages would not be taken up until after recognition had been accorded.

The relations of the United States and Mexico became more and more unsatisfactory as time went on, especially in view of the fact that many clashes between Mexican and American troops were taking place on the border and in view of the further fact that foreign nations were disposed to complain of the attitude of the Washington authorities toward the Huerta regime. July 16 Ambassador Wilson was called to Washington for a conference with the president. As railroad communication was interrupted the ambassador had to make the journey by water and did not arrive in Washington until July 26. What occurred at the white house conference was not made public, but it soon became apparent that the views of the president and the ambassador were not in accord. The latter, it was reported, advised a guarded recognition to prevent chaos, but this suggestion was not favorably received. The result of the difference of opinion was the acceptance, Aug. 4, of

the resignation of Ambassador Wilson, to take
effect Oct. 14. "The part which he felt it his
duty to take in the earlier stages of the recent
revolution in Mexico," said Secretary of State
Bryan, "would make it difficult for him to represent now the views of the present administration."
The Mexican embassy was left in charge of the
secretary, Nelson O'Shaughnessy.

JOHN LIND SENT TO MEXICO.

On the same day that Ambassador Wilson's resignation was accepted, the president directed John
Lind, former governor of Minnesota, to proceed to
Mexico City as his personal representative for the
purpose of acting as adviser to the American embassy and of mediating between the warring fac-
tions. Mr. Lind left at once and arrived at his
destination Aug. 10. It had been previously announced by President Huerta that he would brook
no foreign interference in the conduct of his task
of pacifying the nation, but that Mr. Lind, like
any other foreigner, might pass through the country without fear of molestation. The following
statement was issued Aug. 8 by Manuel Garza
Adalpe, acting minister of foreign affairs:

"By order of the president of the republic I declare, as minister of foreign affairs ad interim,
that if Mr. Lind does not bring credentials in due
form, together with recognition of the government
of Mexico, his presence in this country will not be
desirable."

The administration in Washington declared that
this statement was based on misinformation as to
Mr. Lind's mission in Mexico and the president's
envoy was permitted to proceed. After his arrival
in the capital Mr. Lind was informally received
by the Mexican minister of foreign affairs, Federico Gamboa, and a number of conferences followed. No agreement could be reached on the proposals of the Washington government which were,
in brief:

1. Immediate cessation of fighting in Mexico.
2. Giving of security for an early and free election, all agreeing to take part in it.
3. Consent of Gen. Huerta to bind himself not
to be a candidate for election as president of the
republic at this election.
4. Agreement of all parties to abide loyally by
the result of the election.

It was maintained by Senor Gamboa that the
United States could best accomplish neutrality by
refusing to aid the rebels, that the suggestion that
Gen. Huerta pledge himself not to be a candidate
was strange and unwarranted and that the United
States government should recognize the Huerta administration because it was constitutional. In
reply to this Mr. Lind proposed that only two
conditions be complied with, the holding of a constitutional election and the giving of an assurance
by Gen. Huerta that he would not be a candidate
for president at that election. Mr. Lind further
declared:

"The president of the United States of America
further authorizes me to say that if the de facto
government of Mexico at once acts favorably upon
the foregoing suggestions, then in that event the
president will express to American bankers and
their associates assurances that the government of
the United States of America will look with favor
upon the extension of an immediate loan sufficient
in amount to meet the temporary requirements of
the de facto government of Mexico."

Replying to these suggestions, Secretary Gamboa
maintained that it was not necessary for Gen.
Huerta to pledge himself not to be a candidate
because under the constitution an ad interim
president could not be a candidate at the ensuing
election. The offer of a possible loan he repudi-
ated as in effect a bribe.

Mr. Lind, deeming that a further stay in the
capital would be useless, left Aug. 26 for Vera
Cruz, expecting to proceed to the United States
in a few days. Developments both in Washington
and the City of Mexico, however, caused him to
defer his departure. President Wilson in Washington had a conference Aug. 25 with the members of the foreign relations committees of the two
houses of congress and disclosed to them the pol-

icy which he had adopted and which he proposed
to make public in a message to congress on the
following day. Aug. 26 a cablegram was received
from President Huerta requesting that the message
be delayed for another twenty-four hours. This
was agreed to. Aug. 27 the senate and house met
in joint session and heard President Wilson read
his message in person. After referring to the deplorable condition of affairs in Mexico—a condition touching the United States very nearly—he
said that the peace, prosperity and contentment of
Mexico meant more than merely an enlarged field
for commerce and enterprise. "We shall yet prove
to the Mexican people," he declared, "that we
know how to serve them without first thinking
how we shall serve ourselves." The president
pointed out that things had grown worse instead
of better and that those who claimed to constitute
the legitimate government of the republic had
failed to make good their claim in fact. War and
disorder, devastation and confusion seemed to
threaten to become the settled fortune of the
country. Referring to Mr. Lind's mission to Mexico, Mr. Wilson detailed the instructions given to
the envoy. These were, as previously noted, that
he should press upon those exercising authority in
the City of Mexico the fact that the government
of the United States did not feel at liberty any
longer to stand inactively by while it became daily
more and more evident that no real progress was
being made toward the establishment of a government which the country would obey and respect;
that the situation in Mexico was incompatible with
the fulfillment of the international obligations on
the part of that country and that all America cried
out for a settlement. Mr. Lind was instructed that
such a settlement seemed to be conditioned on:

(a) An immediate cessation of fighting throughout Mexico, a definite armistice solemnly entered
into and scrupulously observed;
(b) Security given for an early and free election in which all will agree to take part;
(c) The consent of Gen. Huerta to bind himself
not to be a candidate for election as president of
the republic at this election; and
(d) The agreement of all parties to abide by the
results of the election and co-operate in the most
loyal way in organizing and supporting the new
administration.

The president said that Mr. Lind had executed
his delicate mission with singular tact, firmness
and good judgment, but the proposals he submitted
had been rejected in a note from the Mexican
minister of foreign affairs. Meanwhile it was the
duty of the United States to remain patient, to
exercise self-restraint and to wait for a further
opportunity to offer friendly counsels. "We
should," the president continued, "earnestly urge
all Americans to leave Mexico at once, and should
assist them to get away in every way possible—
not because we would mean to slacken in the least
our efforts to safeguard their lives and their interests, but because it is imperative that they
should take no unnecessary risks when it is physically possible for them to leave the country." In
concluding his message the president said:

"The steady pressure of moral force will, before
many days, break the barriers of pride and prejudice down, and we shall triumph as Mexico's
friends sooner than we could triumph as her enemies—and how much more handsomely, with how
much higher and finer satisfaction of conscience
and of honor."

The substance of Foreign Minister Gamboa's
note, referred to in the president's message, has
already been given. It amounted to a flat rejection of the suggestions made by the United States.
In accordance with the announcement made in
President Wilson's message, Americans in Mexico
were warned to leave that country and were advised that to enable them to do so money and
warships would be placed at their disposal. Steps
were also taken to prohibit the shipment of arms
to Mexico.

At the opening of the second session of the 27th
Mexican congress, Sept. 16, Gen. Huerta prom-

ised to spare no efforts to bring about the unrestricted election of a president and vice-president of the republic in October. He deplored the stand taken by the American government, intimating, however, that there was no unfriendliness between the American and Mexican peoples. French bankers, he announced, had taken $30,000,000 of the $100,000,000 loan authorized in May. The sum of $24,900,000 had been used in pacifying the country.

Throughout the remainder of September and part of October the situation continued without much change. The catholic party nominated Federico Gamboa for president and Gen. Eugenio Rascon for vice-president of the republic. Manuel Calero and Flores Magnon were nominated by the liberals. Other candidates were also announced, among them being Gen. Felix Diaz. Oct. 10 another upheaval occurred in Mexico City when by order of President Huerta 110 members of the chamber of deputies were arrested for signing resolutions of warning to him because of the sudden disappearance of Senator Belisario Dominguez of Chiapas, who had criticised the chief executive. Both branches of the Mexican national congress were declared suspended and new elections of senators and deputies were ordered for Oct. 26, the day of the presidential election. Oct. 14 President Huerta suspended constitutional guaranties and declared himself dictator of the republic.

ELECTION OF OCT. 26.

The presidential and congressional elections took place Oct. 26, but the result was unsatisfactory. The vote cast was extremely small and Huerta, who was ineligible and not a candidate, was found to have received a majority for president. Gen. Blanquet led for vice-president. Huerta had previously been notified by President Wilson that under the conditions created by the arrest of the deputies and the suspension of constitutional guaranties a fair election could not be held and that the American government would refuse to recognize the men chosen. Gen. Felix Diaz, who had arrived in Vera Cruz from Europe, deemed himself in danger and Oct. 27 took refuge in the American consulate. Later he went aboard an American warship, whence he was transferred to a vessel which took him to Havana. There on Nov. 6 he was stabbed in the neck but not seriously hurt, by Pedro Guerra, a Carranza sympathizer, whom he shot.

Under instructions from the American state department, Nelson O'Shaughnessy, charge d'affaires, notified Gen. Huerta Nov. 2 that he must resign the presidency of Mexico, and that he must not leave as his successor Gen. Aureliano Blanquet, his minister of war, or any other member of his official family. In a formal note to foreign diplomats, Gen. Huerta announced Nov. 9 that the newly elected congress would be installed in a few days and would pass upon the elections of president and vice-president. If this congress declared the election of Oct. 26 void new elections would be called. In the meantime he would continue in office and direct his efforts toward the pacification of the country.

After having received assurances of nonintervention from Great Britain and other European powers, President Wilson, through his personal representative, John Lind, notified Gen. Huerta early on Nov. 12 that unless he returned an answer that day to a demand that he must prevent the newly elected congress from being called into session and must make this action known to the diplomatic corps the United States would have no further parleying with the Mexican government. Huerta returned no reply and Mr. Lind, who had been in the capital some days, returned to Vera Cruz, announcing that he would not set foot in the City of Mexico until the new congress had been dissolved.

Dec. 1, 1913, the situation as between Mexico and the United States was practically unchanged.

CHRONOLOGY OF REVOLUTIONS.

Following is a chronology of the main events in the political history of Mexico since the overthrow of President Porfirio Diaz:

June 26, 1910—Porfirio Diaz elected president for eighth successive term.
Nov. 18, 1910—Revolution started by anti-re-electionists.
Nov. 23, 1910—Francisco I. Madero proclaims himself provisional president of Mexico.
May 25, 1911—Porfirio Diaz resigns presidency of Mexico.
May 31, 1911—Gen. Diaz and family sail from Vera Cruz for Europe.
Oct. 1, 1911—Francisco I. Madero elected president of Mexico.
Oct. 16, 1912—Gen. Felix Diaz begins new revolution.
Oct. 27, 1912—Gen. Diaz captured by federal troops.

1913.

Feb. 9—Military uprising in City of Mexico; Gen. Diaz liberated; rebels seize arsenal after sharp fighting in which 500 persons are killed, among them Gen. Reyes.
Feb. 10—President Madero remains in national palace guarded by loyal troops.
Feb. 11—Bombardment occurs in heart of City of Mexico, the rebels firing from the arsenal and the federals from the national palace; President Taft orders three warships sent to the gulf coast of Mexico.
Feb. 12—Bombardment continues; two American women killed.
Feb. 14-15—Fighting continues; Madero refuses to resign.
Feb. 17—President Taft refuses to intervene.
Feb. 19—President Madero's own troops revolt; he is arrested by Gen. Blanquet; Gen. Victoriano Huerta, commander of federal troops, proclaimed provisional president; fighting ceases.
Feb. 19—Gen. Felix Diaz formally ratifies agreement with Gen. Huerta, ending the crisis; Gustavo Madero, brother of deposed president, executed; congress in special session elects Gen. Huerta provisional president of the republic.
Feb. 20—Members of new Mexican cabinet sworn in.
Feb. 21—New revolution started in the states of Coahuila, Chihuahua, Zacatecas, San Luis Potosi, Sonora, Nuevo Leon, Sinaloa and Puebla; Venustiano Carranza, governor of Coahuila, leader of revolt.
Feb. 22—Fifth brigade of second army division ordered by war department in Washington to proceed to Galveston, Tex.
Feb. 22-23—Francisco I. Madero, president, and Jose Pino Suarez, vice-president, shot to death about midnight of Feb. 22-23; government disclaims all responsibility.
Feb. 24—Henry Lane Wilson, American ambassador to Mexico, issues statement declaring that violent deaths of Madero and Suarez were without approval of new government.
Feb. 26—Gen. Pascual Orozco, Sr., promises allegiance to Huerta government; Gov. Carranza of Coahuila denounces Huerta regime as spurious.
March 2-4—Clashes between United States cavalrymen and Mexican soldiers on border near Douglas, Ariz.
March 5—Emilio and Raoul Madero, brothers of dead president, arrive at San Antonio, Tex., after narrowly escaping death at the hands of federals in Mexico.
March 6—Ambassador Wilson accused of working against the Madero government.
March 7—Ambassador Wilson offers resignation; President Huerta makes official denial of charge that President Madero and his brother Gustavo were murdered at the instigation of the government.
March 8—Secretary of State Bryan sends message to Ambassador Wilson congratulating him in the name of the state department for the "very cool, capable and successful manner in which, throughout the recent difficult situation in the City of Mexico, the United States citizens there, the American organizations and especially the United States embassy and its staff have conducted themselves."
March 10—Reported in Washington that Secretary Bryan signed congratulatory message to Ambassador Wilson without reading it.

March 11—Announcement made that Great Britain will recognize Huerta government; Huerta troops win victory at Parral.

March 12—Gen. Ojeda, federal commander, evacuates Agua Prieta; state of Sinaloa revolts against Huerta.

March 13—Rebels capture Nogales, Sonora.

March 15—Gen. Ojeda defeats rebels at Naco, Sonora.

March 22—Gov. Martin Epinoza of territory of Tepic joins revolutionists.

March 26—Leaders of opposition to Huerta hold conference at Guadalupe, Coahuila, and adopt name of constitutionalists; severe fighting at Cananea.

March 30—Mexico protests against shipment of arms across border by Americans.

April 11—Americans in Mazatlan ask that United States cruiser be sent for their protection.

April 13—Gen. Pedro Ojeda and 300 federal soldiers at Naco, Sonora, cross the border and surrender to United States troops.

May 2—Presidential election in Mexico announced for Oct. 26.

May 8—Constitutionalists, led by Gen. Carranza, control northern part of Mexico with the exception of a few points; situation causing worry to administration in Washington.

May 9—Huerta government reported to be seeking large loan from foreign bankers; President Huerta angry because United States has withheld recognition; says Ambassador Wilson has no standing diplomatically in Mexico.

May 10—Parral captured by constitutionalists.

May 22—Constitutionalists defeat federals near Sacramento, Coahuila.

July 16—Ambassador Wilson summoned to Washington for conference with President Wilson; announcement made that foreign powers were pressing for indication of American attitude toward the disorders in Mexico.

July 26—Ambassador Wilson and president have conference in Washington; Charles B. Dixon, United States immigration inspector, shot by federal soldiers in Juarez, Mex.

Aug. 4—Resignation of Ambassador Wilson accepted to take effect Oct. 14; John Lind, former governor of Minnesota, sent to Mexico as personal representative of President Wilson.

Aug. 10—Mr. Lind arrives in City of Mexico.

Aug. 12—Japanese government refuses to accept Gen. Felix Diaz as special envoy from Mexico.

Aug. 19—President Huerta, through Foreign Secretary Gamboa, rejects all the proposals made by Mr. Lind.

Aug. 26—President Wilson personally reads message before joint session of congress on relations between Mexico and the United States; Americans in Mexico requested to leave that country.

Sept. 6—Lieut. F. Acosta fires at American officers on the Texas side of international bridge at El Paso and is killed; Customs Inspector T. F. Jonah and Immigration Inspector Thomas N. Heifron arrested for shooting.

Sept. 9—Announced at American embassy in Mexico City that negotiations may be resumed.

Sept. 11—Venustiano Carranza reported to be seeking the presidency of Mexico.

Sept. 16—President Huerta in message at opening of Mexican congress deplores stand taken by American government; says American people are friendly.

Sept. 18—Gen. Felix Diaz asked to return from Europe to Mexico.

Sept. 19—Passenger train dynamited sixty miles south of Saltillo; fifty persons killed.

Sept. 24—Federico Gamboa nominated for presidency and Gen. Eugenie Rascon for the vice-presidency by the catholic party.

Oct. 5—Battle at Santa Rosalio, Chihuahua, reported.

Oct. 7—Piedras Negras occupied by federal troops.

Oct. 10—Gen. Huerta orders arrest of 110 deputies for signing resolutions of warning against him. Both branches of congress suspended.

Oct. 14—Gen. Huerta suspends constitutional guaranties and proclaims himself dictator of republic.

Oct. 26—Presidential and congressional elections take place. Huerta and Blanquet in the lead for president and vice-president.

Oct. 27-28—Gen. Felix Diaz takes refuge on American warship at Vera Cruz; goes to Havana.

Nov. 2—Gen. Huerta notified by President Wilson that he must resign the presidency of Mexico.

Nov. 6—Gen. Felix Diaz stabbed by Carranza sympathizer.

Nov. 9—Gen. Huerta notifies diplomats that the new congress would soon be called into session to pass upon elections.

Nov. 12—President Wilson demands immediate answer to demand that new Mexican congress shall not be installed; Gen. Huerta makes no reply.

Nov. 15—The new Mexican congress begins sessions.

Nov. 25—Juarez captured by rebels.

AMERICAN CAPITAL IN MEXICO.

According to a report made by Consul Letcher at Chihuahua to the state department in 1913 the amount of money invested in Mexico by Americans is more than $1,000,000,000, classified as follows:

Railway bonds	$408,926,000
Railway stocks	235,464,000
Mines	223,000,000
National bonds	52,000,000
Smelters	26,500,000
Bank deposits	22,700,000
The oil industry	15,000,000
The rubber industry	15,000,000
Factories	10,800,000
Live stock	9,000,000
Timber lands	8,100,000
Bank stocks	7,850,000
Houses and personal property	4,500,000
Insurance	4,000,000
Ranches	3,150,000
Wholesale stores	2,700,000
Retail stores	1,680,000
Professional outfits	3,600,000
Public institutions	1,200,000
Tramways and power plants	760,000
Farms	960,000
Hotels	260,000
Breweries	600,000

Small additions of a miscellaneous character bring the total up to $1,057,770,000. American investments very largely exceed those of any other foreign country.

THE CARNEGIE FOUNDATION FOR THE ADVANCEMENT OF TEACHING.

The Carnegie Foundation for the Advancement of Teaching was founded by Andrew Carnegie in 1905 and incorporated by the congress of the United States in 1906 for the purpose of providing retiring allowances for teachers and officers of universities, colleges and technical schools in the United States, Canada and Newfoundland, and, in general, of advancing the profession of the teacher and the cause of higher education. By the eighth annual meeting of the trustees in 1913, 316 allowances were being paid to teachers and eighty-eight pensions to widows of teachers, the amount of the average allowance being $1,703.34, the total annual cost being $618,120, and the average age of retirement being about 69 years.

In the administration of its endowment, which now amounts to $15,000,000, the Foundation has restricted its allowances to professors and officers in a list of seventy-three institutions, selected for their educational standing, and has published a series of widely influential reports and bulletins concerning educational conditions. The president of the Foundation is Henry S. Pritchett; its trustees are presidents of universities and colleges and financiers. Further information may be had by addressing the secretary, Clyde Furst, 576 5th avenue, New York.

Sporting Records.

Corrected to Dec. 1, 1913.

BASEBALL SEASON OF 1913.

NATIONAL LEAGUE.

STANDING OF THE CLUBS.

Club.	New York.	Philadelphia.	Chicago.	Pittsburgh.	Boston.	Brooklyn.	Cincinnati.	St. Louis.	Won.	Percentage.
New York	—	14	14	14	14	14	17	14—101		.604
Philadelphia	8	—	9	15	13	17	17— 88			.583
Chicago	7	13	—	13	13	13	13	16— 88		.575
Pittsburgh	8	11	9	—	10	14	13	13— 78		.523
Boston	8	7	9	11	—	10	8	16— 69		.457
Brooklyn	8	8	9	8	10	—	9	13— 65		.436
Cincinnati	5	5	9	8	14	13	—	10— 64		.418
St. Louis	7	5	6	8	6	7	12	—— 51		.340
Lost	51	63	65	71	82	84	89	99		

TWENTY LEADING BATSMEN IN 1913.
(Playing in fifty games or more.)

McDonald, Cin.-Bos.	73	155	25	55	67	7	4	.355
Daubert, Brooklyn	139	508	76	178	215	17	25	.350
Miller, Phila	69	87	9	30	36	0	2	.345
Cravath, Phila	147	525	78	179	298	11	10	.341
Hyatt, Pittsburgh	63	81	8	27	49	2	0	.333
Viox, Pittsburgh	137	492	86	156	210	19	14	.317
Tinker, Cin	110	382	47	121	170	15	10	.317
Becker, Cin.-Ph.	118	414	64	131	208	7	11	.316
Zimmerman, Chi.	127	447	69	140	219	16	18	.313
Meyers, New York	120	378	37	118	155	4	7	.312
Magee, Phila	138	470	92	144	225	21	28	.306
Wheat, Brooklyn	138	535	64	161	280	11	19	.301
Lobert, Phila	150	573	92	172	243	26	41	.300
Wagner, Pittsb'h	114	413	51	124	159	10	21	.300
Fletcher, N. Y.	136	538	76	160	210	17	23	.297
Marsans, Cin	118	435	49	129	148	15	37	.297
Titus, Boston	87	269	33	80	113	6	4	.297
Smith, Brooklyn	151	540	70	160	238	22	22	.296
Oakes, St. Louis	147	539	60	158	182	26	22	.293
Snodgrass, N. Y.	141	457	65	133	175	9	27	.291

CHAMPION BATTERS SINCE 1876.

Batter and club.	Average.
1876—Barnes, Chicago	.403
1877—White, Boston	.385
1878—Dalrymple, Milwaukee	.389
1879—Anson, Chicago	.407
1880—Gore, Chicago	.365
1881—Anson, Chicago	.383
1882—Brouthers, Buffalo	.367
1883—Brouthers, Buffalo	.371
1884—O'Rourke, Buffalo	.350
1885—Connor, New York	.371
1886—Kelly, Chicago	.388
1887—Maul, Philadelphia	.343
1888—Anson, Chicago	.343
1889—Brouthers, Boston	.313
1890—Luby, Chicago	.342
1891—Hamilton, Boston	.338
1892—Brouthers, Boston	.335
1893—Stenzel, Pittsburgh	.409
1894—Duffy, Boston	.438
1895—Burkett, Cleveland	.438
1896—Burkett, Cleveland	.419
1897—Keeler, Baltimore	.417
1898—Keeler, Baltimore	.387
1899—Delehanty, Philadelphia	.408
1900—Wagner, Pittsburgh	.384
1901—Burkett, St. Louis	.382
1902—Beaumont, Pittsburgh	.357
1903—Wagner, Pittsburgh	.355
1904—Wagner, Pittsburgh	.349
1905—Seymour, Cincinnati	.377
1906—Wagner, Pittsburgh	.339
1907—Wagner, Pittsburgh	.350
1908—Wagner, Pittsburgh	.354
1909—Wagner, Pittsburgh	.341
1910—Magee, Philadelphia	.331

Batter and club.	Average.
1911—Wagner, Pittsburgh	.334
1912—Zimmerman, Chicago	.372
1913—Daubert, Brooklyn	.350

CHAMPIONSHIP RECORD.

Club.	Won.	Lost.	Pct.
1876—Chicago	52	14	.788
1877—Boston	31	17	.648
1878—Boston	41	19	.707
1879—Providence	55	22	.705
1880—Chicago	67	17	.798
1881—Chicago	56	28	.667
1882—Chicago	55	29	.655
1883—Boston	63	35	.643
1884—Providence	84	28	.750
1885—Chicago	87	25	.776
1886—Chicago	90	34	.725
1887—Detroit	79	45	.637
1888—New York	84	47	.641
1889—New York	83	43	.659
1890—Brooklyn	86	43	.667
1891—Boston	87	51	.630
1892—Boston	102	48	.680
1892—Boston	86	44	.662
1894—Baltimore	89	39	.695
1895—Baltimore	87	43	.663
1896—Baltimore	90	39	.698
1897—Boston	93	39	.795
1898—Boston	91	47	.659
1899—Brooklyn	101	47	.682
1900—Brooklyn	82	54	.603
1901—Pittsburgh	90	49	.647
1902—Pittsburgh	103	36	.741
1903—Pittsburgh	91	49	.650
1904—New York	106	47	.693
1905—New York	105	48	.686
1906—Chicago	116	36	.763
1907—Chicago	107	45	.704
1908—Chicago	99	55	.643
1909—Pittsburgh	110	42	.725
1910—Chicago	104	50	.675
1911—New York	99	54	.647
1912—New York	103	48	.682
1913—New York	101	51	.664

AMERICAN LEAGUE.

STANDING OF THE CLUBS.

Club.	Philadelphia.	Washington.	Cleveland.	Boston.	Chicago.	Detroit.	New York.	St. Louis.	Won.	Percentage.
Philadelphia	—	14	13	11	11	15	17	15—96		.627
Washington	8	—	15	16	11	10	16	14—90		.584
Cleveland	9	7	—	13	13	14	14	16—86		.566
Boston	11	6	8	—	10	13	14	17—79		.527
Chicago	11	11	9	11	—	13	11	12—78		.513
Detroit	7	12	7	9	9	—	11	11—66		.431
New York	5	6	8	6	10	11	—	11—57		.377
St. Louis	6	8	6	5	10	11	11	——57		.373
Lost	57	64	66	71	74	87	94	96		

TWENTY LEADING BATSMEN IN 1913.
(Playing in fifty games or more.)

	G.	AB.	R.	H.	TB.	SH.	SB.	Pct.
Cobb, Detroit	122	428	70	167	229	11	52	.390
Jackson, Cleveland	148	528	109	197	291	10	26	.373
Speaker, Boston	141	520	94	190	278	16	46	.366
Collins, Phila	148	534	125	184	236	20	54	.345
Baker, Phila	149	565	116	190	278	7	33	.336
Lajoie, Cleveland	137	465	66	156	188	12	17	.335
McInnis, Phila	148	543	79	177	227	25	16	.326
Schaefer, Wash	52	100	17	32	35	3	6	.320
Gandil, Wash	147	550	62	175	219	13	21	.318
Crawford, Detroit	153	610	78	193	298	11	13	.316
Strunk, Phila	93	292	30	89	124	13	14	.305
Milan, Wash	154	578	89	173	218	20	74	.299
Lewis, Boston	149	551	54	164	219	28	12	.298
Pratt, St. Louis	154	592	59	175	238	18	37	.296
Ryan, Cleveland	73	243	26	72	80	12	9	.296

	G.	AB.	R.	H.	TB.	SH.	SB.	Pct.
E. Murphy, Phila.	136	508	105	150	181	9	21	.295
O'Neill, Cleveland.	78	234	19	69	88	8	5	.295
Shotten, St. Louis.	149	556	107	163	205	7	43	.293
Fugie, Boston	143	497	75	144	191	13	27	.290
Hooper, Boston	148	585	100	169	234	14	26	.289

CHAMPION BATTERS SINCE 1900.

Batter and club.

1900—Duncan, Kansas City	.337
1901—Lajole, Philadelphia	.422
1902—Delehanty. Washington	.376
1903—Lajole, Cleveland	.355
1904—Lajole, Cleveland	.381
1905—Lajole, Cleveland	.329
1906—Stone, St. Louis	.358
1907—Cobb, Detroit	.350
1908—Criss, St. Louis	.354
1909—Cobb, Detroit	.375
1910—Cobb, Detroit	.385
1911—Cobb, Detroit	.420
1912—Cobb, Detroit	.410
1913—Cobb, Detroit	.390

CHAMPIONSHIP RECORD.

Club.	Won.	Lost.	Pct.
1900—Chicago	82	53	.607
1901—Chicago	83	53	.610
1902—Philadelphia	83	53	.610
1903—Boston	91	47	.659
1904—Boston	95	59	.617
1905—Philadelphia	92	56	.622
1906—Chicago	93	58	.616
1907—Detroit	92	58	.613
1908—Detroit	90	63	.588
1909—Detroit	98	54	.645
1910—Philadelphia	102	48	.680
1911—Philadelphia	101	50	.669
1912—Boston	105	47	.691
1913—Philadelphia	96	57	.627

CHALMERS TROPHY WINNERS.

Trophy awarded annually by vote of baseball reporters to best and most valuable player in each of the two major leagues.

1911—Frank Schulte. Chicago Nationals.
Tyrus Cobb, Detroit Americans.
1912—Tris Speaker, Boston Americans.
Larry Doyle, New York Nationals.
1913—Walter Johnson, Washington Americans.
Jake Daubert, Brooklyn Nationals.

BEST PLAYERS IN 1913.

AMERICAN LEAGUE.	Points.	Pct.
Johnson (p.), Washington	54	.844
Jackson (rf.), Cleveland	43	.672
Collins (2b.), Philadelphia	30	.469
Speaker (cf.), Boston	26	.406
Baker (3b.), Philadelphia	21	.328
Gandil (1b.), Washington	14	.219
McInnis (1b.), Philadelphia	12	.188
Schang (c.), Philadelphia	11	.172
Milan (cf.), Washington	8	.125
Barry (ss.), Philadelphia	8	.125
Lajole (2b.), Cleveland	7	.109
Bush (ss.), Detroit	6	.094
Wagner (ss.), Boston	6	.094
Russell (p.), Chicago	5	.078
Shotton (cf.), St. Louis	5	.078
McBride (ss.), Washington	5	.078
Scott (p.), Chicago	5	.078
Stovall (1b.), St. Louis	5	.078
Crawford (rf.), Detroit	5	.075
Cobb (cf.), Detroit	3	.047
Schalk (c.), Chicago	3	.047
Bender (p.), Philadelphia	2	.031
Turner (3b.), Cleveland	2	.031
O'Neill (c.), Cleveland	1	.016
Hooper (rf.), Boston	1	.016

NATIONAL LEAGUE.		
Daubert (1b.), Brooklyn	50	.781
Cravath (rf.), Philadelphia	40	.625
Maranville (ss.), Boston	23	.359
Mathewson (p.), New York	21	.328
Meyers (c.), New York	20	.312
Safer (1b.), Chicago	15	.234
Cheney (p.), Chicago	12	.188
Miller (1b.), Pittsburgh	11	.172
Wagner (ss.), Pittsburgh	11	.172
Evers (2b.), Chicago	10	.156
Seaton (p.), Philadelphia	9	.141

	Points.	Pct.
Fletcher (ss.), New York	7	.109
Archer (c.), Chicago	6	.094
Doolan (ss.), Philadelphia	6	.094
Sweeney (2b.), Boston	6	.094
Viox (ss.), Pittsburgh	6	.094
Doyle (2b.), New York	5	.078
Shafer (3b.), New York	5	.078
Murray (rf.), New York	4	.063
Zimmerman (3b.), Chicago	4	.063
Knabe (2b.), Philadelphia	4	.063
Adams (p.), Pittsburgh	3	.047
Cutshaw (2b.), Brooklyn	3	.047
Burns (lf.), New York	2	.031
Marsans (rf.), Cincinnati	2	.031
Humphries (p.), Chicago	2	.031
Brown (p.), Cincinnati	1	.016

WORLD'S CHAMPIONSHIP GAMES.

The New York National and the Philadelphia American league baseball teams, champions of their respective associations in 1913, played for the championship of the world with the following result:

IN NEW YORK, OCT. 7.

Philadelphia.	AB.	R.	H.	TB.	BR.	SH.	SB.	PO.	A.	E.
E. Murphy, rf	4	0	1	1	0	0	2	0	0	
Oldring, lf	4	0	1	1	0	0	2	0	0	
Collins, 2b	3	3	3	5	1	0	1	4	6	0
Baker, 3b	4	1	3	6	0	0	0	1	4	0
McInnis, 1b	3	0	1	2	0	1	0	10	0	0
Strunk, cf	4	1	0	0	0	0	0	3	0	0
Barry, ss	4	1	1	2	0	0	0	1	1	1
Schang, c	4	0	1	3	0	0	0	4	1	0
Bender, p	4	0	0	0	0	0	0	2	0	
Total	34	6	11	20	2	1	1	27	14	1

New York.	AB.	R.	H.	TB.	BR.	SH.	SB.	PO.	A.	E.
Shafer, cf	5	0	1	1	0	0	0	3	0	0
Doyle, 2b	4	1	2	2	0	0	0	2	2	0
Fletcher, ss	4	0	2	2	0	0	0	2	2	0
Burns, lf	4	0	1	2	0	0	0	3	0	0
Herzog, 3b	4	0	0	0	0	0	0	1	2	0
Murray, rf	4	0	2	2	0	0	0	4	0	0
Meyers, c	4	0	0	0	0	0	0	4	2	0
Merkle, 1b	4	2	2	2	0	0	0	11	0	0
Marquard, p	0	0	0	0	0	1	0	0	6	0
Crandall, p	1	0	0	0	0	0	0	0	0	0
Tesreau, p	0	0	0	0	0	0	0	0	1	0
*McCormick	1	1	1	1	0	0	0	0	0	0
†McLean	1	0	0	0	0	0	0	0	0	0
Total	36	4	11	12	0	1	0	27	15	0

*Batted for Marquard in fifth. †Batted for Tesreau in ninth.

Philadelphia .... 0 0 0 3 2 0 0 1 0—6
New York ....0 0 1 0 3 0 0 0 0—4

Two-base hits—Barry, Burns, McInnis. Three-base hits—Collins, Schang. Home run—Baker. Struck out—By Marquard (Strunk); by Crandall (Bender); by Tesreau (Strunk); by Bender (Burns, Murray, Merkle). Bases on balls—Off Marquard, 1; off Tesreau, 1. Double play—Barry-Collins-McInnis. Hits—Off Marquard, 8 in 5 innings; off Crandall, 3 in 2 innings (none out in eighth). Time—2.06. Umpires—Klem behind bat, Egan on bases, Rigler and Connolly in field.

IN PHILADELPHIA, OCT. 8.

New York.	AB.	R.	H.	TB.	BB.	SH.	SB.	PO.	A.	E.
Herzog, 3b	5	1	0	0	0	0	1	4	0	
Doyle, 2b	4	0	0	0	0	0	3	5	2	
Fletcher, ss	5	0	2	2	0	0	1	3	0	
Burns, lf	4	0	0	1	0	0	0	0	0	
Shafer, cf	5	0	0	0	0	0	0	0	0	
Murray, rf	4	0	0	0	0	0	0	0	0	
McLean, c	4	0	2	2	0	0	0	5	1	0
Wilson, c	0	0	0	0	0	0	0	1	0	0
Snodgrass, 1b	1	0	1	1	0	0	1	1	0	
Wiltse, 1b	2	0	0	0	0	0	0	13	3	0
Mathewson, p	3	1	2	2	1	0	0	1	3	0
*Grant	0	1	0	0	0	0	0	0	0	0
Total	37	3	7	2	1	0	30	20	2	

*Ran for McLean in tenth.

Philadelphia.	AB.	R.	H.	TB.	BB.	SH.	SB.	PO.	A.	E.
E. Murphy, rf	5	0	0	0	0	0	0	5	0	0
Oldring, lf	5	0	1	1	0	0	0	4	0	0
Collins, 2b	4	0	1	1	0	1	0	2	2	1

Philadelphia.	AB.	R.	H.	TB.	BB.	SH.	SB.	PO.	A.	E.
Baker, 3b	5	0	2	2	0	0	0	0	0	1
McInnis, 1b	4	0	0	0	0	0	0	6	0	0
Strunk, cf	3	0	1	1	1	0	0	4	0	0
Barry, ss	4	0	1	1	0	0	0	2	1	0
Lapp, c	4	0	1	1	0	0	0	7	1	0
Plank, p	4	0	1	1	0	0	0	0	2	0
Total	38	0	8	8	1	1	0	30	6	2
New York		0	0	0	0	0	0	0	0	3–3
Philadelphia		0	0	0	0	0	0	0	0	0–0

Struck out—By Mathewson (Baker, Collins 2, Lapp, McInnis); by Plank (Burns 3, Fletcher, Murray, Wiltse). Hit by pitcher—By Plank (Doyle). Time—2:22. Umpires—Connolly at plate, Rigler on bases, Egan and Klem in field.

IN NEW YORK, OCT. 9.

Philadelphia.	AB.	R.	H.	TB.	BB.	SH.	SB.	PO.	A.	E.
E. Murphy, rf	5	1	2	2	0	0	0	2	0	0
Oldring, lf	5	3	2	2	0	0	1	0	0	0
Collins, 2b	5	2	3	5	0	0	1	5	4	0
Baker, 3b	4	1	2	2	0	0	1	3	1	0
McInnis, 1b	4	0	0	0	0	0	0	9	0	0
Strunk, cf	4	0	0	0	0	0	1	0	0	0
Barry, ss	4	0	1	1	0	0	0	2	3	0
Schang, c	4	1	1	4	0	0	0	5	2	1
Bush, p	4	0	1	1	0	0	0	0	1	0
Total	39	8	12	17	0	0	3	27	11	1

New York.	AB.	R.	H.	TB.	BB.	SH.	SB.	PO.	A.	E.
Herzog, 3b	4	0	0	0	0	0	0	1	0	0
Doyle, 2b	4	0	1	1	0	0	5	1	0	
Fletcher, ss	2	0	1	1	1	0	1	2	2	1
Burns, lf	4	0	0	0	0	0	3	0	0	
Shafer, cf	3	1	1	2	1	0	0	2	0	0
Murray, rf	3	1	1	1	0	1	4	0	0	
McLean, c	2	0	1	1	0	0	3	1	0	
Wilson, 1b	2	0	0	0	0	0	2	0	0	
Merkle, 1b	2	0	0	1	0	0	3	0	0	
Wiltse, 1b	0	0	0	0	0	0	0	0	0	
Tesreau, p	2	0	0	0	0	0	0	0	0	
Crandall, p	1	0	0	0	0	0	0	2	0	
*Cooper	0	0	0	0	0	1	0	0	0	
Total	29	2	5	6	4	0	3	27	6	1

*Ran for McLean in fifth.

Philadelphia	3	2	0	0	0	2	1	0–8
New York	0	0	0	1	0	1	0	0–2

Two base hit—Collins. Three base hit—Shafer. Home run—Schang. Struck out—By Tesreau (McInnis, Schang 2); by Crandall (Bush); by Bush (Tesreau, Burns, Wilson). Double plays—Collins-Barry; Bush-Barry-McInnis; Doyle (unassisted); Schang-Collins. Hits—Off Tesreau, 11 in 6 1-3 innings; off Crandall, 1 in 2 2-3 innings. Hit by pitcher—By Bush (Fletcher). Time—2:11. Umpires—Rigler at plate, Connolly on bases, Klem and Egan in field.

IN PHILADELPHIA, OCT. 10.

New York.	AB.	R.	H.	TB.	BB.	SH.	SB.	PO.	A.	E.
Snodgrass, cf	2	0	0	0	0	0	0	2	0	0
Herzog, 3b	2	0	1	1	0	0	0	2	0	0
Doyle, 2b	4	0	0	0	0	0	2	4	0	
Fletcher, ss	4	1	0	0	0	0	1	0	0	
Burns, lf	4	2	2	3	0	0	1	2	0	0
Shafer, 3b, cf	4	0	1	3	0	0	0	1	0	
Murray, rf	2	1	1	1	0	1	2	0	0	
McLean, c	2	0	2	2	0	0	1	1	0	
Wilson, c	1	0	0	0	0	0	1	0	0	
Merkle, 1b	4	1	1	4	0	0	10	1	0	
Demaree, p	1	0	0	0	0	0	0	2	0	
Marquard, p	1	0	0	0	0	0	0	2	0	
*Cooper	0	0	0	0	0	0	0	0	0	
†Crandall	1	0	0	0	0	0	0	0	0	
‡McCormick	1	0	0	0	0	0	0	0	0	
§Grant	1	0	0	0	0	0	0	0	0	
Total	34	5	8	14	1	0	2	24	11	2

*Ran for McLean in fifth. †Batted for Demaree in fifth. ‡Batted for Wilson in ninth. §Batted for Marquard in ninth.

Philadelphia.	AB.	R.	H.	TB.	BB.	SH.	SB.	PO.	A.	E.
E. Murphy, rf	5	0	0	0	0	0	3	0	0	
Oldring, lf	4	0	2	4	0	0	1	0	0	
Collins, 2b	4	0	0	0	0	0	3	3	0	
Baker, 3b	4	0	0	0	0	0	0	2	0	
McInnis, 1b	4	1	1	1	0	0	7	0	0	
Strunk, cf	2	2	1	1	1	0	3	0	0	
Barry, ss	4	2	3	5	0	0	2	2	0	

IN NEW YORK, OCT. 11.

Philadelphia.	AB.	R.	H.	TB.	BB.	SH.	SB.	PO.	A.	E.
Schang, c	2	1	2	2	2	0	6	1	0	
Bender, p	4	0	0	0	0	0	0	3	0	
Total	33	6	9	13	3	1	1	27	9	0
New York		0	0	0	0	0	3	2	0	0–5
Philadelphia		0	1	0	3	2	0	0	*–6

Two base hits—Barry 2, Burns. Three base hits—Oldring, Shafer. Home run—Merkle. Struck out—By Bender (Shafer 2, Merkle, Doyle, Wilson); by Marquard (Baker, Oldring). Bases on balls—Off Demaree, 1; off Marquard, 2; off Bender, 1. Hits—Off Demaree, 7 in 4 innings; off Marquard, 2 in 4 innings. Hit by pitcher—By Bender (Murray). Passed ball—McLean. Time—2:09. Umpires—Egan at plate, Klem on bases, Connolly and Rigler in field.

IN NEW YORK, OCT. 11.

Philadelphia.	AB.	R.	H.	TB.	BB.	SH.	SB.	PO.	A.	E.
E. Murphy, rf	3	1	2	1	0	0	0	0	0	
Oldring, lf	4	2	0	0	1	0	3	0	0	
Collins, 2b	3	0	1	1	0	1	0	2	3	0
Baker, 3b	4	0	2	2	0	0	0	2	0	
McInnis, 1b	2	0	0	0	0	2	0	14	0	0
Strunk, cf	4	0	0	0	0	0	2	0	0	
Barry, ss	4	0	0	0	0	0	2	7	0	
Schang, c	4	0	1	1	0	0	1	0	0	
Plank, p	3	0	0	0	0	0	0	1	1	
Total	31	3	6	6	1	3	0	27	13	1

New York.	AB.	R.	H.	TB.	BB.	SH.	SB.	PO.	A.	E.
Herzog, 3b	4	0	0	0	0	0	1	2	0	
Doyle, 2b	4	0	0	0	0	0	1	7	1	
Fletcher, ss	3	0	0	0	0	0	2	3	0	
Burns, lf	3	0	0	0	0	0	2	0	1	
Shafer, cf	2	1	0	1	0	0	2	0	0	
Murray, rf	3	0	0	0	0	0	2	0	0	
McLean, c	3	0	1	1	0	0	3	1	0	
Merkle, 1b	3	0	0	0	0	0	14	0	0	
Mathewson, p	2	0	1	1	0	0	0	2	0	
*Crandall	1	0	0	0	0	0	0	0	0	
Total	28	1	2	2	1	0	27	15	2	
Philadelphia		1	0	2	0	0	0	0	0–3
New York		0	0	0	1	0	0	0	0–1

*Batted for Mathewson in ninth.

Struck out—By Plank (Herzog); by Mathewson (Schang 2). Double plays—Collins-McInnis; Barry-Collins-McInnis. Time—1:39. Umpires—Klem at the plate, Egan on bases, Rigler and Connolly in the field.

SUMMARY.

Games won, Philadelphia, 4; New York, 1.	
Paid attendance	150,992
Total receipts	$325,979.50
Players' share	185,163.59
Each club's share	79,108.83
Commission's share	32,597.95

Each player on the winning team received $3,244 and each player on the losing team $2,162. The winners received 60 per cent and the losers 40 per cent of the players' share of the receipts at the first four games.

ATTENDANCE AND RECEIPTS BY YEARS.

Year.	Attendance.	Receipts.	Players' pool.
1905 (5 games)	91,033	$68,405	$27,391
1906 (6 games)	99,864	106,550	33,401
1907 (5 games)	78,068	101,728	54,933
1908 (4 games)	62,232	94,975	46,173
1909 (7 games)	145,807	188,362	66,925
1910 (5 games)	124,222	179,980	79,072
1911 (6 games)	179,851	342,364	127,910
1912 (8 games)	252,237	490,833	147,572
1913 (5 games)	150,992	325,979	135,164

PREVIOUS WORLD'S SERIES.

1903—Games won, Boston Americans, 5; Pittsburgh Nationals, 3. Winning pitchers, Dineen, 3; Young 2; Phillippi, 3.

1905—Games won, New York Nationals, 4; Philadelphia Americans, 3; Winning pitchers, Mathewson, 3; McGinnity, 1; Bender, 1.

1906—Games won, Chicago Americans, 4; Chicago Nationals, 2. Winning pitchers, Walsh, 2; White, 1; Altrock, 1; Brown, 1; Reulbach, 1.

1907—Games won, Chicago Nationals, 4; Detroit Americans, 0; draw, 1. Winning pitchers, Brown, 2; Reulbach, 1; Overall, 1.

1908—Games won, Chicago Nationals, 4; Detroit Americans, 0. Winning pitchers, Brown, 2; Overall, 1; Reulbach, 1.
1909—Games won, Pittsburgh Nationals, 4; Detroit Americans, 3. Winning pitchers, Adams, 3; Willis, 1; Mullin, 2; Donovan, 1.
1910—Games won, Philadelphia Americans, 4; Chicago Nationals, 1. Winning pitchers, Bender, 1; Coombs, 3; Cole, 1.
1911—Games won, Philadelphia Americans, 4; New York Nationals, 2. Winning pitchers, Plank, 1; Coombs, 1; Bender, 2; Mathewson, 1; Crandall, 1.
1912—Games won, Boston Americans, 4; New York Nationals, 3; tied game, 1. Winning pitchers, Wood, 2; Bedient, 1; Collins, 1; Marquard, 2; Tesreau, 1.

LONG GAMES IN 1913.

National League—There were twenty-five games of ten innings each, sixteen of eleven innings, seven of twelve innings, six of thirteen innings, four of fourteen innings, one of sixteen innings and one of seventeen.
American League—There were thirty-one games of ten innings each, twelve of eleven innings, eleven of twelve innings, three of thirteen innings, one of fourteen innings and four of fifteen innings.

LONGEST GAMES IN BIG LEAGUES.

AMERICAN LEAGUE.

Twenty-Four Innings.
Sept. 1, 1906—Philadelphia, 4; Boston, 1.

Twenty Innings.
July 4, 1905—Philadelphia, 4; Boston, 2.

Nineteen Innings.
Sept. 27, 1912—Washington, 5; Philadelphia, 4.

Eighteen Innings.
June 25, 1903—Chicago, 6; New York 6 (tie).
July 19, 1909—Detroit, 0; Washington, 0 (tie).

Seventeen Innings.
Aug. 9, 1900—Milwaukee, 3; Chicago, 2.
Sept. 21, 1901—Chicago, 1; Boston, 0.
May 18, 1902—Chicago, 2; St. Louis, 2 (tie).
July 9, 1902—Philadelphia, 4; Boston, 2.
Sept. 30, 1907—Detroit, 9; Philadelphia, 9 (tie).
May 13, 1909—Chicago, 1; Washington, 1 (tie).
May 25, 1912—Chicago, 5; Detroit, 4.

NATIONAL LEAGUE.

Twenty Innings.
June 30, 1892—Chicago, 7; Cincinnati, 7 (tie).
Aug. 24, 1901—Chicago, 2; Philadelphia, 1.

Nineteen Innings.
June 22, 1902—Chicago, 3; Pittsburgh, 2.
July 31, 1912—Pittsburgh, 7; Boston, 6.

Eighteen Innings.
Aug. 17, 1882—Providence, 1; Detroit, 0.
Aug. 17, 1902—Brooklyn, 7; St. Louis, 7 (tie).
June 24, 1905—Chicago, 2; St. Louis, 1.

Seventeen Innings.
June 26, 1893—Cincinnati, 5; New York, 5 (tie).
Aug. 11, 1904—St. Louis, 4; Brooklyn, 3.
Sept. 18, 1904—Chicago, 2; Cincinnati, 1.
June 4, 1908—Chicago, 1; Boston, 1 (tie).
Aug. 22, 1908—Pittsburgh, 1; Brooklyn, 0.
Sept. 2, 1908—Philadelphia, 2; Brooklyn, 2.
July 26, 1909—New York, 3; Boston 3 (tie).
May 28, 1913—Chicago, 8; St. Louis, 7.

IN OTHER LEAGUES.

May 31, 1901—I. I. I. league: Decatur, 2; Bloomington, 1, twenty-six innings.
Sept. 10, 1911—Pacific Coast league: Portland, 1; Sacramento, 1, twenty-four innings.

RECORD OF NO-HIT GAMES.

1879—Richmond (Worcester) vs. Cleveland.
1880—Corcoran (Chicago) vs. Boston.
  Galvin (Buffalo) vs. Worcester.
1882—Corcoran (Chicago) vs. Worcester.
1883—Radbourne (Providence) vs. Cleveland.
  Daly (Cleveland) vs. Philadelphia.
1884—Corcoran (Chicago) vs. Providence.
  Galvin (Buffalo) vs. Detroit.
1885—Clarkson (Chicago) vs. Providence.
  Ferguson (Philadelphia) vs. Providence.
1887—Seward (Philadelphia) vs. Brooklyn.
  Weyhing (Philadelphia) vs. Baltimore.
1891—Lovett (Brooklyn) vs. New York.
  Rusie (New York) vs. Brooklyn.

1892—Stivetts (Boston) vs. Brooklyn.
  Jones (Pittsburgh) vs. Cincinnati.
1893—Hawke (Baltimore) vs. Washington.
1897—Young (Cleveland) vs. Cincinnati.
1898—Hughes (Baltimore) vs. Boston.
  Breitenstein (Cincinnati) vs. Pittsburgh.
  Donahue (Philadelphia) vs. Boston.
1899—Phillippe (Louisville) vs. Washington.
  Willis (Boston) vs. New York.
1900—Hahn (Cincinnati) vs. Philadelphia.
1901—Mathewson (New York) vs. St. Louis.
1902—Callahan (Chicago) vs. Detroit.
1903—Fraser (Philadelphia) vs. Chicago.
1904—Young (Boston) vs. Philadelphia.
  Tannehill (Boston) vs. Chicago.
1905—Mathewson (New York) vs. Chicago.
  Henley (Philadelphia) vs. St. Louis.
  Smith (Chicago) vs. Detroit.
  Dineen (Boston) vs. Chicago.
1906—Eason (Brooklyn) vs. St. Louis.
  Lush (Philadelphia) vs. Brooklyn.
1907—Pfeffer (Boston) vs. Cincinnati.
  Maddox (Pittsburgh) vs. Brooklyn.
1908—Young (Boston) vs. New York.
  Wiltse (New York) vs. Philadelphia.
  Rucker (Brooklyn) vs. Boston.
  Rhoades (Cleveland) vs. Boston.
  Smith (Chicago) vs. Philadelphia.
  Joss (Cleveland) vs. Chicago.
1909—None in National or American league.
1910—Joss (Cleveland) vs. Chicago.
  Bender (Philadelphia) vs. Cleveland.
1911—Wood (Boston) vs. St. Louis.
  Walsh (Chicago) vs. Boston.
1912—Mullin (Detroit) vs. St. Louis.
  Hamilton (St. Louis) vs. Detroit.
  Tesreau (New York) vs. Philadelphia.

POST SEASON SERIES (1913).

WORLD'S CHAMPIONSHIP.

	Won.	Lost.	Pct.
Philadelphia (American)	4	1	.800
New York (National)	1	4	.200

CHICAGO PENNANT.

White Sox (American)	4	2	.667
Cubs (National)	2	4	.333

INTERCITY SERIES.

Cleveland (American)	4	3	.571
Pittsburgh (National)	3	4	.429

ST. LOUIS PENNANT.

Browns (American)	3	3	.500
Cardinals (National)	3	3	.500

BASEBALL THROWING RECORD.

The world's record for the long distance throwing of a baseball was broken at Cincinnati, O., Oct. 10, 1910, when Sheldon Lejeune of the Evansville (Ind.) club, Central league, threw the sphere 426 feet 6¼ inches. The old record, made in Brooklyn, N. Y., Oct. 15, 1872, by John Hatfield, was 400 feet 7½ inches.

HIGH PRICES PAID FOR BASEBALL PLAYERS.

1913—Chappell, White Sox	$18,000
1911—Marty O'Toole, Pittsburgh	22,500
1910—"Lefty" Russell, Athletics	12,000
1910—Fred Hunter, Pittsburgh	10,000
1910—Lena Blackburne, White Sox	10,000
1908—Rube Marquard, New York	11,000
1906—Spike Shannon, New York	10,000
1859—Clarkson and Kelly, Boston	20,000

STANDING IN OTHER LEAGUES.

INTERNATIONAL LEAGUE.

	W.	L.	Pct.		W.	L.	Pct.
Newark	95	57	.625	Montreal	74	77	.490
Rochester	92	62	.597	Providence	69	80	.463
Baltimore	77	73	.513	Toronto	70	83	.458
Buffalo	78	75	.510	Jersey City	53	101	.344

AMERICAN ASSOCIATION.

	W.	L.	Pct.		W.	L.	Pct.
Milwaukee	100	67	.599	St. Paul	75	87	.463
Minneapolis	97	70	.581	Kansas City	69	98	.413
Louisville	94	72	.566	Toledo	69	98	.413
Columbus	93	74	.556	Indianapolis	68	99	.407

FEDERAL LEAGUE.

	W.	L.	Pct.		W.	L.	Pct.
Indianapolis	74	44	.627	Chicago	56	62	.475
Cleveland	64	54	.542	Kansas City	53	65	.449
St. Louis	59	60	.496	Pittsburgh	49	71	.408

NEW ENGLAND LEAGUE.

	W.	L.	Pct.		W.	L.	Pct.
Lowell	81	45	.643	Lynn	61	60	.504
Portland	71	49	.592	New Bedford.	47	75	.385
Worcester	71	54	.568	Fall River..	45	76	.372
Lawrence	67	53	.558	Brockton	44	75	.370

NEW YORK STATE LEAGUE.

	W.	L.	Pct.		W.	L.	Pct.
Binghamton	84	53	.613	Albany	72	67	.518
Wilkesbarre	82	56	.594	Syracuse	61	76	.445
Troy	76	61	.555	Elmira	56	85	.397
Utica	74	65	.532	Scranton	49	91	.350

SOUTHERN LEAGUE.

	W.	L.	Pct.		W.	L.	Pct.
Atlanta	81	56	.591	Montgomery	69	68	.504
Mobile	81	57	.587	Memphis	64	74	.463
Birmingham	74	64	.536	Nashville	62	75	.452
Chattanooga	70	64	.523	New Orleans.	45	83	.338

KITTY LEAGUE.

	W.	L.	Pct.		W.	L.	Pct.
Paducah	80	46	.635	Owensboro	69	56	.552
Clarksville	78	47	.624	Cairo	56	67	.455
Hopkinsville	74	53	.583	Harrisburg	44	85	.341
Henderson	70	56	.556	Vincennes	31	92	.252

THE I. I. I. LEAGUE.

	W.	L.	Pct.		W.	L.	Pct.
Quincy	79	60	.571	Decatur	67	68	.496
Dubuque	74	62	.544	Springfield	66	70	.485
Davenport	68	66	.507	Bloomington	64	71	.474
Danville	69	68	.504	Peoria	57	79	.419

EASTERN TRI-STATE LEAGUE.

	W.	L.	Pct.		W.	L.	Pct.
Wilmington	66	45	.595	Harrisburg	59	62	.532
Allentown	59	52	.532	Trenton	50	61	.450
York	59	52	.532	Atlantic City	42	73	.365

WESTERN TRI-STATE LEAGUE.

FIRST SEASON.	W.	L.	Pct.	SECOND SEASON.	W.	L.	Pct.
Walla Walla.	45	20	.682	Boise	32	22	.593
Boise	40	23	.635	North Yakima	27	27	.500
Pendleton	31	29	.517	Walla Walla.	26	28	.481
North Yakima	30	34	.469	Pendleton	23	31	.434

WISCONSIN-ILLINOIS LEAGUE.

	W.	L.	Pct.		W.	L.	Pct.
Oshkosh	75	46	.620	Madison	64	61	.512
Racine	71	52	.577	Fond du Lac	63	61	.508
Green Bay	69	57	.548	Wausau	45	80	.360
Rockford	65	56	.537	Appleton	43	82	.344

WESTERN LEAGUE.

	W.	L.	Pct.		W.	L.	Pct.
Denver	104	62	.627	Omaha	79	86	.478
Des Moines	94	72	.563	Sioux City..	73	92	.442
St. Joseph	89	79	.531	Topeka	73	92	.442
Lincoln	87	90	.521	Wichita	65	101	.389

CANADIAN LEAGUE.

	W.	L.	Pct.		W.	L.	Pct.
Ottawa	66	39	.629	Guelph	54	49	.524
London	64	39	.621	Hamilton	52	52	.500
St. Thomas	56	48	.538	Berlin	37	67	.356
Peterboro	55	48	.534	Brantford	31	73	.298

PENNANT WINNERS IN 1913.

American association	Milwaukee
American league	Philadelphia
Appalachian league	Johnson City
Border league	W'yandotte
California league	Stockton
Canadian league	Ottawa
Central association	Ottumwa
Central league	Grand Rapids
Connecticut league	New Haven
Cotton States league	Jackson
Eastern association	Hartford
Empire league (Georgia)	Thomasville
Federal league	Indianapolis
Illinois-Missouri league	Champaign-Lincoln
International league	Newark
Kansas State league	Great Bend
Kitty league	Paducah
Michigan State league	Manistee
Minnesota-Wisconsin league	Disbanded
Mountain States league	Disbanded
National league	New York
Nebraska league	Kearney
New England league	Lowell
New York State league	Binghamton
North Carolina State league	Winston-Salem
Northern league	Winona
Northwestern league	Vancouver
Ohio State league	Charleston
Pacific Coast league	Portland
South Atlantic league	Savannah
Southern league	Atlanta
South Michigan league	Battle Creek
Texas league	Houston
Texas-Oklahoma league	Denison
The I. I. I. league	Quincy
Tri-State league (Mass.-Vt.)	Northampton
Union association	Great Falls
Virginia league	Petersburg
Western Canada	Moose Jaw
Western league	Denver
Western Tri-State league	Boise
Wisconsin-Illinois	Oshkosh

BALL TEAMS ON WORLD'S TOUR.

The New York Giants of the National league and the White Sox of the American league started on a tour of the world, playing the first of a long series of exhibition games in Cincinnati, O., Oct. 18, 1913. Most of the regular players of both teams made the trip.

SCORES OF PRINCIPAL COLLEGE GAMES IN 1913.

YALE.

	Op.	Yale.
March 22—Holy Cross	4	7
March 24—Pennsylvania	5	4
April 5—Trinity	0	6
April 17—Fordham	3	14
April 19—Vermont	0	5
April 23—Columbia	4	6
April 25—Georgetown	0	3
April 26—Pennsylvania	5	13
April 30—Tufts	7	1
May 3—Virginia	2*	4
May 3—Brown	2	0
May 7—Amherst	1	14
May 10—Pennsylvania	2	4
May 14—Dartmouth	4	5
May 17—Holy Cross	3	4
May 21—Brown	4	6
May 24—Cornell	0	4
May 27—Williams	2	0
May 31—Princeton	3	4
June 4—Holy Cross	5	6
June 14—Cornell	0	3
June 17—Harvard	0	2
June 18—Harvard	4	3
June 21—Harvard	6	5

HARVARD.

	Op.	Har.
April 18—Columbia	4	6
April 19—Army	9	7
April 22—Bowdoin	4	8
April 26—Colby	5	2
April 29—Bates	3	11
May 1—Vermont	1	4
May 3—Amherst	0	5
May 10—Holy Cross	7	5
May 14—Syracuse	0	3
May 19—Pennsylvania	1	3
May 24—Princeton	0	7
May 30—Brown	9	4
May 31—Phillips-And	0	4
June 4—Williams	1	5
June 11—Holy Cross	7	2
June 14—Pennsylvania	4	3
June 17—Yale	2	0
June 18—Yale	3	4
June 21—Yale	5	6

PRINCETON.

	Op.	Prin.
March 19—North Carolina	3	0
March 22—Georgetown	7	1
March 24—Georgetown	4	1
April 5—New York U	1	15
April 19—Pennsylvania	12	1
April 26—Brown	8	1
April 30—Columbia	6	7
May 1—Virginia	6	1
May 3—Pennsylvania	2	0
May 7—Brown	3	1
May 10—Cornell	1	7
May 14—Williams	3	8
May 17—Cornell	4	11
May 24—Harvard	7	0
May 29—Lafayette	1	3
May 31—Yale	4	3
June 4—Amherst	6	0

BROWN.

	Op.	Br.
April 5—Tufts	0	3
April 19—Colgate	2	14
April 26—Princeton	1	8
April 30—Vermont	8	10
May 3—Yale	4	2
May 7—Princeton	1	3
May 17—Amherst	8	12
May 21—Yale	6	4
May 28—Holy Cross	2	6
May 30—Harvard	4	9
May 31—Colby	2	8
June 4—Tufts	3	1
June 14—Holy Cross	1	6

COLUMBIA.

	Op.	Col.
April 5—Rutgers	7	9
April 18—Harvard	6	4
April 23—Yale	6	4
April 26—Cornell	1	6
April 30—Princeton	7	6
May 3—Lehigh	1	2
May 7—Pennsylvania	2	1
May 9—Cornell	5	13
May 14—Wesleyan	4	3
May 17—New York U	0	15
June 4—Pennsylvania	6	0

PENNSYLVANIA.

	Op.	Pa.
March 24—Yale	4	5
March 29—Holy Cross	3	0
April 5—Swarthmore	4	5
April 14—Dartmouth	6	2
April 19—Princeton	1	12
April 26—Yale	13	5
April 30—Lehigh	5	6
May 3—Princeton	0	2
May 7—Columbia	1	2

Op. Pa

May 10—Yale	4	2
May 19—Harvard	3	1
May 21—Fordham	2	3
May 24—Michigan	0	3
May 30—Lehigh	3	5
June 4—Columbia	0	4
June 10—Swarthmore	2	5
June 13—Brown	6	1
June 14—Harvard	3	4
June 17—Cornell	7	3
June 23—Michigan	7	2
June 24—Michigan	0	1

DARTMOUTH. Op. Dar.

April 14—Pennsylvania	2	6
April 16—Army	9	5
April 23—Colby	1	11
April 28—Cornell	0	1
April 29—Syracuse	0	8
May 14—Yale	5	4
May 17—Williams	3	2
May 30—Holy Cross	8	2
May 31—Tufts	2	3
June 24—Amherst	2	3

WILLIAMS. Op. Wil.

May 7—Army	4	14
May 14—Princeton	8	3
May 17—Dartmouth	2	3
May 27—Yale	0	2
May 30—Amherst	12	2
May 31—Holy Cross	5	8
June 4—Harvard	5	1
June 12—Cornell	1	9
June 14—Wesleyan	2	3

HOLY CROSS. Op. H.C.

March 22—Yale	7	4
March 29—Pennsylvania	0	3
April 19—Cornell	4	3
April 30—Army	3	2
May 10—Harvard	5	7
May 17—Yale	4	3
May 28—Brown	6	2
May 30—Dartmouth	2	8
May 31—Williams	8	5
June 4—Yale	6	5
June 11—Harvard	2	7

CORNELL. Op.Cor.

June 14—Brown	0	5
April 5—Georgetown	8	2
April 7—Georgetown	4	3
April 9—Navy	4	0
April 17—Tufts	2	0
April 19—Holy Cross	3	4
April 26—Columbia	6	1
April 28—Dartmouth	1	0
April 30—Lafayette	8	6
May 6—Penn State	3	6
May 9—Columbia	13	9
May 10—Princeton	7	1
May 14—Michigan	6	2
May 17—Princeton	11	4
May 22—Michigan	5	3
May 24—Yale	4	0
May 31—Pennsylvania	3	4
June 12—Williams	9	1
June 13—Vermont	3	1
June 14—Yale	3	0
June 17—Pennsylvania	3	7

ARMY. Op. Ar.

April 5—Dickinson	1	2
April 9—Lafayette	5	8
April 16—Dartmouth	5	9
April 19—Harvard	7	9
April 23—Swarthmore	9	10
April 26—Penn State	13	2
April 30—Holy Cross	2	3
May 3—Virginia	3	9
May 7—Williams	14	4
May 10—Catholic U.	8	9
May 14—Lehigh	5	6
May 17—Fordham	2	0
May 24—Notre Dame	0	8
May 31—Navy	1	2
June 4—Ursinus	2	9

NAVY. Op. Nav.

April 5—Amherst	0	5
April 9—Cornell	0	4
April 19—St. John's Col.	5	0

Op.Nav.

April 23—Dickinson	4	5
April 30—Virginia	4	10
May 7—Georgetown	1	9
May 14—Mt. St. Mary's	0	12
May 21—Notre Dame	1	7
May 31—Army	2	1

NEW YORK. Op. N.Y.

April 5—Princeton	15	1
May 17—Columbia	15	0

AMHERST. Op. Am.

April 5—Navy	5	0
April 26—Wesleyan	3	5
May 3—Harvard	5	0
May 7—Yale	14	1
May 17—Brown	12	8
May 30—Williams	2	12
June 4—Princeton	0	6
June 14—Massachusetts	4	5
June 24—Dartmouth	3	2

GEORGETOWN. Op. Geo.

March 22—Princeton	1	7
March 24—Princeton	4	0
April 5—Cornell	2	8
April 7—Cornell	3	4
April 25—Yale	3	0
April 28—Virginia	8	2
May 2—Bucknell	5	10
May 7—Navy	9	1

VERMONT. Op. Ver.

April 19—Yale	5	0
April 30—Brown	10	8
May 17—Syracuse	0	2
June 13—Cornell	3	1

TUFTS. Op. Tuf.

April 5—Brown	3	0
April 17—Cornell	0	2
April 30—Yale	18	7
May 13—Syracuse	1	3
May 31—Dartmouth	3	2
June 4—Brown	4	3

CATHOLIC UNIVERSITY. Op. C.U.

May 3—Navy	0	4
May 10—Army	9	8
May 22—Notre Dame	9	5

MICHIGAN. Op.Mich.

April 5—U. of Kentucky	3	11
April 6—Georgia	3	10
April 8—Georgia	2	3
April 9—U. of South	2	8
April 11—Vanderbilt	2	14
April 12—Vanderbilt	8	7
April 16—Alma	1	4
April 19—Western Reserve	3	4
April 23—Georgia	3	4
May 1—Pittsburgh	1	6
May 3—Case	1	12
May 8—Syracuse	5	1
May 9—Syracuse	1	14
May 14—Cornell	2	6
May 17—Syracuse	1	15
May 20—Syracuse	8	10
May 21—Cornell	3	5
May 30—Michigan A. C.	4	5
May 30—Michigan A. C.	2	4
June 23—Pennsylvania	2	7

NOTRE DAME. Op. N.D.

April 19—Earlham	24	1
April 24—Arkansas	3	17
April 26—Arkansas	0	11
May 1—Ottawa	5	8
May 2—Ottawa	4	7
May 8—Wash and Jeff.	1	9
May 17—Beloit	1	2
May 19—Penn State	3	5
May 21—Navy	7	1
May 22—Catholic U.	5	9
May 23—Fordham	3	6
May 24—Army	8	0
May 28—Colgate	2	9
May 30—Wabash	0	8
May 31—Wabash	0	3
June 4—Lake Forest	7	5
June 7—St. Viator	0	16

CHICAGO. Op. Chi.

April 16—Iowa	7	12
April 19—Northwestern	1	13

Op.Chi.

April 22—Armour	3	2
April 26—Indiana	1	5
April 28—Minnesota	7	3
May 6—Armour	6	5
May 10—Northwestern	4	6
May 17—Illinois	7	8
May 24—Illinois	1	2
May 31—Wisconsin	2	6

ILLINOIS. Op. Ill.

April 16—Indiana	5	9
April 19—Iowa	1	6
April 22—Arkansas	3	5
April 26—Northwestern	4	3
April 29—Purdue	1	1
May 2—Northwestern	1	5
May 3—Iowa	3	4
May 9—Minnesota	3	12
May 10—Wisconsin	8	4
May 16—Wisconsin	0	9
May 17—Chicago	8	7
May 21—Purdue	2	7
May 24—Chicago	2	1

INDIANA. Op. Ind.

April 16—Illinois	9	5
April 18—Iowa	2	4
April 24—Wisconsin	3	9
April 25—Beloit	1	2
April 26—Chicago	5	1
May 3—Wisconsin	4	5
May 6—Rose Poly	1	5
May 10—Ohio State	5	6
May 24—Ohio State	5	6
May 28—Purdue	3	2
May 31—De Pauw	1	2

PURDUE. Op.Pur.

April 17—Rose Poly	6	4
April 29—Illinois	1	1
May 2—Wisconsin	4	7
May 9—Ohio State	3	4
May 16—Wisconsin	9	3
May 16—Northwestern	6	5
May 24—Northwestern	4	5
May 28—Indiana	2	3
June 5—Chicago	4	7

MINNESOTA. Op.Min.

April 26—Wisconsin	6	4
April 28—Chicago	3	7
April 29—Iowa	3	7
May 5—Hamline	2	3
May 9—Illinois	12	3
May 17—Iowa	9	6
May 24—Wisconsin	4	9

NORTHWESTERN. Op.Nor.

April 16—Loyola	7	9
April 19—Chicago	13	1
April 22—Lake Forest	10	10
April 26—Illinois	3	4
May 2—Illinois	5	1
May 8—Ohio State	3	5
May 16—Chicago	4	6
May 16—Purdue	5	6
May 17—Wisconsin	5	3
May 24—Purdue	5	4

WISCONSIN. Op.Wis.

April 26—Minnesota	4	6
May 2—Purdue	7	4
May 3—Indiana	5	4
May 10—Illinois	4	8
May 15—Purdue	9	9
May 16—Illinois	9	0
May 17—Northwestern	3	5
May 24—Minnesota	9	4
May 31—Chicago	6	2

IOWA. Op. Ia.

April 16—Chicago	12	7
April 17—Wabash	2	3
April 18—Indiana	4	2
April 19—Illinois	6	1
April 21—Coe	2	8
May 3—Illinois	4	3
May 6—Cornell College	1	4
May 10—Ames	2	3
May 17—Minnesota	6	9
May 22—Nebraska	3	7
May 30—Ames	5	4
May 31—Grinnell	3	11

OHIO STATE.	Op.Ohio.		LAKE FOREST.	Op. L.F.	
May 8—Northwestern.....	5	3	April 22—Northwestern...10	10
May 9—Purdue............	4	3	May 2—Knox............15	16
May 10—Indiana..........	6	5	May 6—Beloit.......... 4	3
May 24—Indiana..........	6	5	May 14—Racine........11	29
May 30—Ohio U. (a. m.)..	1	7	May 17—Knox.......... 2	7
May 30—Ohio U. (p. m.)..	0	9	May 24—Lombard........ 0	3
			May 31—Beloit.......... 1	0
WABASH.	Op.Wab.		June 4—Notre Dame...... 5	7
April 17—Iowa...........	3	2		
April 22—De Pauw.......	6	3		
April 26—Rose Poly......	5	3	BELOIT.	Op.Bel.
April 30—Butler.........	1	9	April 25—Indiana........ 2	1
May 5—De Pauw.........	1	4	May 6—Lake Forest...... 3	4
May 9—Franklin........	0	13	May 9—Monmouth...... 2	1
May 31—Notre Dame.....	3	0	May 10—Knox.......... 1	4
June 2—De Pauw........	5	6	May 17—Notre Dame..... 2	1

	Op.Bel.	
May 24—Monmouth.......	1	6
May 31—Lake Forest.....	0	1

STANDING OF CONFERENCE TEAMS (1913).

Clubs.	W.	L.	Pct.
Chicago	7	2	.778
Illinois	8	4	.667
Indiana	6	3	.667
Purdue	5	4	.555
Minnesota	3	3	.500
Northwestern	3	5	.375
Wisconsin	3	6	.333
Iowa	1	5	.167
Ohio	0	4	.000

ARCHERY.

(By Dr. Edward B. Weston, Chicago.)
NATIONAL MEETING.

The thirty-fifth annual meeting of the National Archery Association of the United States was held in Boston, Mass., Aug. 19, 20, 21 and 22, 1913. The shooting took place in Soldier's field, Harvard's athletic grounds. The men's championship, scoring by the point system, was won by Dr. J. W. Doughty of Tacoma, Wash., and the women's championship by Mrs. P. S. Fletcher of Chicago. Boston won the men's team championship, and Newton, Mass., won the women's. The leading scores:

DOUBLE YORK ROUND.	Hits.	Score.
G. P. Bryant, Melrose, Mass............176	832
Dr. J. W. Doughty, Tacoma, Wash....178	802
H. S. Taylor, Chicago, Ill............161	697
Dr. R. P. Elmer, Wayne, Pa..........150	672
W. H. Wills, New York city..........154	652
Dr. O. L. Hertig, Pittsburgh, Pa......159	643
Will H. Thompson, Seattle, Wash.....150	618
C. E. Dallin, Arlington Heights, Mass..139	597
H. B. Richardson, Boston, Mass.......139	597
F. W. Clay, Bloomfield, N. J.........130	566

DOUBLE AMERICAN ROUND.		
Dr. R. P. Elmer, Wayne, Pa..........170	1,000
C. E. Dallin, Arlington Heights, Mass..165	937
Dr. O. L. Hertig, Pittsburgh, Pa......167	923
G. P. Bryant, Melrose, Mass.........169	905
Dr. C. S. Case, Chicago, Ill.........163	883
H. B. Richardson, Boston, Mass.......160	852
Dr. J. W. Doughty, Tacoma, Wash....164	848
J. S. Jiles, Pittsburgh, Pa..........157	825
Will H. Thompson, Seattle, Wash......149	815
H. S. Taylor, Chicago, Ill...........157	807

DOUBLE NATIONAL ROUND.		
Mrs. P. S. Fletcher, Chicago, Ill..... 93	377
Mrs. L. C. Smith, Newton Centre, Mass. 90	348
Mrs. B. P. Gray, Newton Centre, Mass. 76	276
Miss M. A. Brownell, Brookline, Mass... 67	263
Mrs. G. P. Bryant, Melrose, Mass...... 54	238

DOUBLE COLUMBIA ROUND.		
Mrs. P. S. Fletcher, Chicago, Ill......114	586
Mrs. L. C. Smith, Newton Centre, Mass..116	574
Mrs. B. P. Gray, Newton Centre, Mass..102	480
Mrs. E. W. Frentz, Melrose, Mass......105	459
Miss Norma Pierce, Boston, Mass......100	464

MEN'S TEAM ROUND.		
Boston 328	1,533
Keystone Club..........................308	1,410

WOMEN'S TEAM ROUND.		
Newton, Mass..........................231	1,083
Boston, Mass..........................181	741

FLIGHT SHOOTING.		
Dr. R. P. Elmer, Wayne, Pa.........261 yds., 1 ft.
Mrs. G. P. Bryant, Melrose, Mass............251.4

The next meeting will be held on the grounds of the Merion Cricket club, Philadelphia. Officers for 1914:

President—Dr. Robert P. Elmer, Wayne, Pa.
Vice-Presidents—Dr. Edward B. Weston, Chicago, Ill.; G. B. Bryant, Melrose, Mass.; Will H. Thompson, Seattle, Wash.
Secretary-Treasurer—Allan C. Hale, Wayne, Pa.
Executive Committee—The officers, with Louis W. Maxson, Washington, D. C.; Burton P. Gray, Boston, Mass.; T. Truxton Hare, Radnor, Pa.; E. Earl Trout, Wayne, Pa.

PRE-OLYMPIC GAMES.

Chicago, July 3, 4, 5, 1913. Range in Grant park.

DOUBLE AMERICAN ROUND.	Hits.	Score.
B. J. Rendtorff, Lake Forest, Ill......179	1,169
H. S. Taylor, Chicago, Ill............171	1,009
G. L. Nichols, Chicago, Ill...........165	911
J. H. Pendry, Chicago, Ill...........147	735
H. L. Walker, Chicago, Ill...........155	731
Dr. C. S. Case, Kenilworth, Ill.......141	699

DOUBLE YORK ROUND.		
E. J. Rendtorff, Lake Forest, Ill......209	989
H. S. Taylor, Chicago, Ill...........175	699
H. L. Walker, Chicago, Ill...........122	504
G. L. Nichols, Chicago, Ill...........107	437

DOUBLE COLUMBIA ROUND.		
Mrs. P. S. Fletcher, Chicago, Ill......110	570
Mrs. Witwer-Taylor, Chicago, Ill......113	556
Priscilla Williams, Chicago, Ill...... 54	162

DOUBLE NATIONAL ROUND.		
Mrs. P. S. Fletcher, Chicago, Ill...... 71	341
Mrs. Witwer-Taylor, Chicago, Ill...... 53	185
Priscilla Williams, Chicago, Ill...... 12	56

MEN'S TEAM ROUND.		
E. J. Rendtorff.......................... 94	562
G. L. Nichols........................... 88	468
H. L. Walker............................ 85	395
H. W. Bishop............................ 69	339
	336	1,764

EASTERN ARCHERY ASSOCIATION.

Met on July 4, at Wayne, Pa., and shot a double American round.

	Hits.	Score.
R. P. Elmer, Wayne, Pa...............174	1,032
A. C. Hale, Wayne, Pa...............166	896
O. L. Hertig, Pittsburgh, Pa.........165	837
J. S. Jiles, Pittsburgh, Pa..........157	829
B. P. Gray, Newton Centre, Mass.....160	798
J. Duff, Jersey City, N. J...........146	783
C. E. Dallin, Arlington Heights, Mass..144	736
J. M. Manser, Laury's Station, Pa.....150	720
F. U. Clay, Bloomfield, N. J.........138	603

PEDESTRIANISM.

EDWARD P. WESTON'S LONG WALKS.

Starting from New York, N. Y., June 2, 1913, Edward Payson Weston, 75 years old, walked to Minneapolis, Minn., arriving there Aug. 2. His route took him through New Jersey, Pennsylvania, New York, Ohio, Indiana, Illinois, Wisconsin and Minnesota. The distance covered was 1,546 miles. He did not walk on Sundays.

Weston in 1867 walked from Portland, Me., to Chicago, Ill., in 25 days 22 hours. In 1907 he covered the same distance of 1,230 miles in 24 days 19 hours. In 1909 he walked from New York to San Francisco, starting March 15 and arriving at his destination July 14. The distance covered was 3,975 miles. His route was by way of Chicago, St. Louis, Kansas City, Denver, Ogden and Reno. In 1910 he walked from Los Angeles, Cal., to New York, N. Y., in seventy-seven days, following the Santa Fe road to Chicago and the New York Central from there to New York. The total distance was 3,483 miles.

SAMUEL A. DEBS' WALK.

Samuel A. Debs left New York, N. Y., June 9, 1913, and walked to Minneapolis, Minn., arriving there July 21. His route was about 1,600 miles long.

FOOTBALL RESULTS IN 1913.

HARVARD. Op. Har.
Sept. 27—Maine 0   24
Oct. 4—Bates 0   14
Oct. 11—Williams 3   23
Oct. 18—Holy Cross....... 7   47
Oct. 25—Penn State....... 0   29
Nov. 1—Cornell 0   23
Nov. 8—Princeton 0   3
Nov. 15—Brown 0   37
Nov. 22—Yale 5   15

YALE. Op. Yale.
Sept. 24—Wesleyan 0   21
Sept. 27—Holy Cross...... 0   10
Oct. 4—Maine 0   0
Oct. 11—Lafayette 0   27
Oct. 18—Lehigh 0   37
Oct. 25—Wash.-Jeff. 0   0
Nov. 1—Colgate 16   6
Nov. 8—Brown 0   17
Nov. 15—Princeton 3   3
Nov. 22—Harvard 15   5

PRINCETON. Op. Pr.
Sept. 27—Rutgers 3   14
Oct. 4—Fordham 0   69
Oct. 11—Bucknell 6   28
Oct. 18—Syracuse 0   13
Oct. 25—Dartmouth 6   0
Nov. 1—Holy Cross....... 0   54
Nov. 8—Harvard 3   0
Nov. 15—Yale 3   3

CORNELL. Op. Cor.
Sept. 24—Ursinus 0   41
Sept. 27—Colgate 0   0
Oct. 4—Oberlin 12   37
Oct. 11—Carlisle 7   0
Oct. 18—Bucknell 7   10
Oct. 25—Pittsburgh 20   7
Nov. 1—Harvard 23   6
Nov. 8—Michigan 17   0
Nov. 15—Lafayette 3   10
Nov. 26—Pennsylvania 0   21

PENNSYLVANIA. Op. Pa.
Sept. 27—Gettysburg 0   53
Oct. 4—Lafayette 0   10
Oct. 11—Swarthmore 0   20
Oct. 18—Brown 0   28
Oct. 25—Carlisle 7   7
Nov. 1—Penn State....... 0   17
Nov. 8—Dartmouth 34   21
Nov. 15—Michigan 13   0

CARLISLE. Op. Car.
Sept. 27—W. Va. Wesleyan 0   35
Oct. 4—Lehigh 7   21
Oct. 11—Cornell 7   7
Oct. 18—Bucknell 7   10
Oct. 25—Pittsburgh 20   7
Nov. 1—Georgetown 0   34
Nov. 8—Johns Hopkins.... 0   61
Nov. 15—Dartmouth 10   35
Nov. 22—Syracuse 27   35
Nov. 26—Brown 0   13

BROWN. Op. Br.
Oct. 11—Ursinus 0   6
Oct. 18—Pennsylvania ...28   0
Oct. 25—Springfield 6   26
Nov. 1—Vermont 0   19
Nov. 8—Yale 17   0
Nov. 15—Harvard 37   0
Nov. 36—Carlisle 13   0

WILLIAMS. Op. Wil.
Sept. 27—Rensselaer 0   7
Oct. 4—Vermont 0   20
Oct. 11—Harvard 23   3
Oct. 18—Dartmouth 48   6
Oct. 25—New York U. 0   23
Nov. 1—Spgfi'ld Y.M.C.A. 6   0
Nov. 8—Wesleyan 0   0
Nov. 15—Amherst 13   0

DARTMOUTH. Op. Dar.
Sept. 27—Mass. Aggies..... 3   13
Oct. 4—Colby 0   53
Oct. 11—Vermont 7   33
Oct. 18—Williams 6   48
Oct. 25—Princeton 0   6
Nov. 1—Amherst 7   21
Nov. 8—Pennsylvania ...21   34
Nov. 15—Carlisle 35   10

ARMY. Op. Army.
Oct. 4—Stevens Inst..... 0   34
Oct. 11—Rutgers 0   29
Oct. 18—Colgate 6   7
Oct. 25—Tufts 0   2
Nov. 1—Notre Dame......35   13
Nov. 8—Albright 0   77
Nov. 15—Villa Nova...... 0   55
Nov. 22—Springfield 7   14
Nov. 29—Navy 9   22

NAVY. Op. Navy.
Oct. 4—Pittsburgh 0   0
Oct. 11—Georgetown 0   23
Oct. 18—Dickinson 0   29
Oct. 25—Maryland Aggies. 0   76
Nov. 1—Lehigh 0   39
Nov. 8—Bucknell 7   70
Nov. 15—Penn State...... 0   10
Nov. 22—New York........ 0   48
Nov. 29—Army 22   9

AMHERST. Op. Am.
Sept. 27—R. Island State.. 0   10
Oct. 4—Colgate 21   0
Oct. 11—Springfield T. S..20   6
Oct. 18—Trinity 14   0
Oct. 25—Wesleyan 9   0
Nov. 1—Dartmouth 21   7
Nov. 8—Worcester 0   38
Nov. 15—Williams 0   13

SYRACUSE. Op. Syr.
Oct. 4—Hamilton 0   18
Oct. 11—Rochester 0   6
Oct. 18—Princeton 13   0
Oct. 25—Western Reserve 0   36
Nov. 1—Michigan 43   7
Nov. 8—New York........ 0   48
Nov. 15—Colgate 35   13
Nov. 22—Carlisle 35   27
Nov. 26—St. Louis........ 0   74

CHICAGO. Op. Chi.
Oct. 4—Indiana 7   21
Oct. 18—Iowa 6   23
Oct. 25—Purdue 0   6
Nov. 1—Illinois 7   28
Nov. 8—Northwestern ... 0   14
Nov. 15—Minnesota 7   13
Nov. 22—Wisconsin 0   19

WISCONSIN. Op. Wis.
Oct. 4—Lawrence 7   58
Oct. 11—Marquette 0   13
Oct. 18—Purdue 7   7
Oct. 25—Mich. Aggies....12   7
Nov. 1—Minnesota 21   3
Nov. 8—Ohio State...... 0   12
Nov. 22—Chicago 19   0

MINNESOTA. Op. Min.
Sept. 27—S. Dakota....... 0   14
Oct. 4—Ames 0   25
Oct. 18—Nebraska 7   0
Oct. 25—N. Dakota 0   30
Nov. 1—Wisconsin 3   21
Nov. 15—Chicago 13   7
Nov. 22—Illinois 9   19

ILLINOIS. Op. Ill.
Oct. 4—Kentucky 0   21
Oct. 11—Missouri 7   24
Oct. 18—Northwestern ... 0   37
Oct. 25—Indiana 0   10
Nov. 1—Chicago 28   0
Nov. 15—Purdue 0   0
Nov. 22—Minnesota 19   9

NORTHWESTERN. Op. Nor.
Oct. 4—Lake Forest..... 0   10
Oct. 11—Purdue 24   0
Oct. 18—Illinois 37   0
Oct. 25—Iowa 78   6
Nov. 8—Chicago 14   0
Nov. 22—Ohio 58   0

NEBRASKA. Op. Neb.
Oct. 4—Washburn 0   19
Oct. 11—Kansas A. C..... 6   24
Oct. 18—Minnesota 0   7
Oct. 25—Haskell Indians.. 6   7
Nov. 1—Ames 9   18
Nov. 8—Neb. Wesleyan... 7   42
Nov. 15—Kansas 0   9
Nov. 22—Iowa 0   12

PURDUE. Op. Pur.
Oct. 4—Wabash 0   26
Oct. 11—Northwestern ... 0   34
Oct. 18—Wisconsin 7   7
Oct. 25—Chicago 6   0
Nov. 8—Rose Poly 0   62
Nov. 15—Illinois 0   0
Nov. 22—Indiana 7   42

IOWA. Op. Ia.
Oct. 4—Normal 3   45
Oct. 11—Cornell Col..... 0   73
Oct. 18—Chicago 23   6
Oct. 25—Northwestern ... 6   78
Nov. 8—Indiana 0   60
Nov. 15—Ames 7   45
Nov. 22—Nebraska 12   0

INDIANA. Op. Ind.
Sept. 27—De Pauw......... 3   48
Oct. 4—Chicago 21   7
Oct. 25—Illinois 0   0
Nov. 1—Ohio State...... 6   7
Nov. 8—Iowa 60   0
Nov. 15—Northwestern ...20   21
Nov. 22—Purdue 42   7

OHIO STATE. Op. Ohio
Oct. 4—O. Wesleyan..... 0   58
Oct. 11—Western Reserve. 8   14
Oct. 18—Oberlin 0   0
Nov. 1—Indiana 7   6
Nov. 8—Miami 44   6
Nov. 15—Case 0   18
Nov. 22—Wooster 7   6

MICHIGAN. Op. Mich.
Oct. 4—Case 0   48
Oct. 11—Mount Union..... 0   14
Oct. 18—Mich. Aggies....12   7
Oct. 25—Vanderbilt 2   33
Nov. 1—Syracuse 7   43
Nov. 8—Cornell 0   17
Nov. 15—Pennsylvania ... 0   13

NOTRE DAME. Op. N.D.
Oct. 4—Ohio Northern... 0   87
Oct. 18—South Dakota... 7   20
Nov. 1—Army 13   35
Nov. 8—Penn State..... 7   14
Nov. 22—Christian 7   20
Nov. 26—Texas 7   29

MICHIGAN AGGIES.
Op. M.A.
Oct. 4—Olivet 0   26
Oct. 18—Michigan U..... 7   12
Oct. 25—Wisconsin 7   12
Nov. 8—Mt. Union...... 7   13
Nov. 15—S. Dakota...... 7   19

FOOTBALL ACCIDENTS.
[Compiled by the Chicago Record-
Herald.]

	In-			In-
	Dead.jured.			Dead.jured.
1902	15 106	1908	11 304
1903	14 63	1909	30 216
1904	14 276	1910	22 499
1905	24 200	1911	11 178
1906	14 160	1912	13 183
1907	15 165	1913	14 175

MOTORING.

[Compiled by C. G. Sinsabaugh.]

Outside of road racing there wasn't much to motor competitions in this country in 1913, and there were even fewer road races than in 1912. American makers have found that it costs a pretty penny to pay the racing piper, and wherever possible they have dodged the issue, leaving to a few sportsmen, who like to see their cars in the classics, and to free lance drivers the responsibility of maintaining the honor of motor sport in this country. It isn't that the great American public does not care for road races and the like—far from it, as was shown when 80,000 spectators watched the running of the last 500 mile race on the Indianapolis speedway and returned the promoters a profit which has been estimated at around $200,000. And Indianapolis was no exception to the rule either; speed events elsewhere were supported on a liberal scale. But it is the maker who feels the pinch and in consequence the sport lacks his support because of the cost.

The 500 mile speedway race, run May 30, again was the feature event of the season. It was made remarkable by the competition for the first time of the foreigners and it was a European car, driven by a French driver, who pulled down the long end of the purse, Jules Goux in a Peugeot writing his name on the roll of honor on which had been previously inscribed the names of Ray Harroun and the Marmon in 1911 and Joe Dawson and the National in 1912. There was some satisfaction, however, in the fact that the invaders failed to break Dawson's 500 mile record, made the year before.

As for road racing, the Elgin meet of the Chicago Automobile club was the bright light, made all the more prominent through the failure of the Savannah Automobile club to put on the Vanderbilt and Grand Prix as the Georgians had contracted to do. Their excuse for failure to stage the classics was that road racing no longer was sport—it was that road racing no longer was sport—it was commercialized, and when the racing men refused to pay the Georgians big entry fees Savannah called off the meet. But the road speed carnivals at Elgin, San Diego, Santa Monica and Tacoma all made money and led the critics to take Savannah's excuse with a grain of salt.

Despite the fact that the speed in the 1913 road races was faster on the average than ever before, no one was able to disturb the world's mark of 78.7 miles an hour, made in 1911 by Teddy Tetzlaff in a Fiat on the Santa Monica course. The fastest American road race was at Corona, where Earl Cooper in a Stutz won at 74.63 miles an hour. This was not as fast as the foreign best, Bablot in a Delage doing 77 miles per hour at Le Mans, France. This was one of the minor European races, the feature being the French Grand Prix at Amiens, where Boillot in a Peugeot won, with Goux, his team mate and the Indianapolis winner, a good second.

Many world's records were broken on the two and three-quarter mile speedway at Brooklands,

England. Probably the sensation of the year was the feat of actually driving 100 miles in the hour, which was accomplished by Percy Lambert, an Englishman, driving the earl of Shrewsbury's Talbot. Lambert did 103 miles 114 yards in the hour, only to lose the record two months later to Goux and the Peugeot, the record being raised to 106 miles 387 yards. In October even this remarkable record was beaten, Coatalen's twelve cylinder Sunbeam doing 107 miles 1,672 yards. Lambert tried to regain his laurels late in October, but met his death in doing it. He had smashed the world's fifty mile record, traveling at the rate of 111 miles an hour, and two days later he tackled the hour record. He was traveling at 114 miles per hour when a burst tire sent him over the bank, death resulting. Besides the one-hour record, the Englishmen were most persistent in their attacks on the twelve-hour record. May 28, at Brooklands, Scott and Hornsted in an Argyll drove 914 miles 640 yards in the journey once around the clock. Oct. 10, Guinness, Resta and Chassaigne, in the twelve-cylinder Sunbeam, broke even this, going to 1,078 miles 460 yards.

No attempts were made on the world's straightaway mile record, held by Bob Burman and made at Daytona, Fla. The 1 mile dirt track record, though, was dropped by Barney Oldfield in his front driving Christie, the veteran turning the distance in .46⅔ at Bakersfield, Cal., April 28.

In picking champions the critics give the American honors to Earl Cooper of Los Angeles, driver of a Stutz, who started in six road races, winning five of them and finishing second in the other. On the other side of the Atlantic there is no disputing the claims of Georges Boillot, who won the championship in 1912. Boillot captured the 1913 Grand Prix at Amiens and again came to the front in the three liter or small car race at Boulogne, Goux running second both times.

In comparison with previous years there were few reliability runs in this country and even fewer hill climbs. The historic Glidden was repeated, but it was far from being the classic it used to be. The Glidden ran from Minneapolis to Glacier Park, Mont., the rules being so elastic that all that was required of the cars was that they make the various controls on time to preserve their perfect scores. The Glidden trophy itself went to the Metz team; a Hupmobile won the Anderson trophy and the A. A. A. trophy was captured by Dr. J. D. Park in a 1907 Locomobile.

A feature of the year in a record breaking way was the feat of S. G. Averill driving an air cooled Franklin, who astonished the world by covering 83.5 miles on one gallon of gasoline. When one remembers that the average motorist is delighted with sixteen or seventeen miles to the gallon, Averill's work is all the more astounding. The drive was made on Long Island and the car was built with this record breaking in view. It is said, in the way of light weight, absence of friction, etc.

AMERICAN ROAD RACES IN 1913.

Race.	Distance.	Driver and car.	Average M. P. H.
Elgin National, Elgin, Ill.	301.68	G. Anderson, Stutz	71.5
Chicago Automobile club cup, Elgin, Ill.	301.68	R. De Palma, Mercer	66.8
Corona free for all, Corona, Cal.	301.81	E. Cooper, Stutz	74.63
Corona medium car, Corona, Cal.	251.97	E. Cooper, Stutz	75.03
Corona light car, Corona, Cal.	102.45	C. Waterman, Buick	63.15
San Diego free for all, San Diego, Cal.	190	W. Hill, Fiat	47.69
San Diego free for all, San Diego, Cal.	200	C. Carlson, Benz	59.11
San Diego 231-300 class, San Diego, Cal.	100	Campbell, Buick	51.02
Santa Monica free for all, Santa Monica, Cal.	445.2	E. Cooper, Stutz	73.77
Albuquerque free for all, Albuquerque, N. M.	130	Sperry, Overland	30.1
Potlach trophy, Tacoma, Wash.	200	E. Cooper, Stutz	71.07
Intercity cup, Tacoma, Wash.	200	Parsons, Stutz	71.07
Montamarathon cup, Tacoma, Wash.	250	E. Cooper, Stutz	70.71
Los Angeles-Phœnix desert race	564	O. Davis, Locomobile	34.94
El Paso-Phœnix desert race	517	J. Newkirk, Simplex	34.98
Los Angeles-Sacramento	443.6	Verbeck, Fiat	39.39

FOREIGN ROAD RACES IN 1913.

French Grand Prix, Amiens	569	Boillot, Peugeot	72.03
French Grand Prix, Le Mans	335	Bablot, Delage	77
Targa Florio, Sicily	620	Nazzaro, Nazzaro	31.83
Coupe de l'Auto, Boulogne, France	388	Boillot, Peugeot	63.25

AMERICAN SPEEDWAY RECORDS, REGARDLESS OF CLASS.

Distance.	Time.	Driver.	Car.	Place.	Date.
¼ mile	8.16	Burman	Blitzen-Benz	Indianapolis	May 29, 1911
½ mile	16.80	Burman	Blitzen-Benz	Indianapolis	May 29, 1911
1 kilo	21.40	Burman	Blitzen-Benz	Indianapolis	May 29, 1911
1 mile	35.35	Burman	Blitzen-Benz	Indianapolis	May 29, 1911
2 miles	1:15.96	Bragg	Fiat	Los Angeles	April 13, 1910
3 miles	1:54.83	Bragg	Fiat	Los Angeles	May 5, 1912
4 miles	2:33.37	Bragg	Fiat	Los Angeles	May 5, 1912
5 miles	3:11.75	Bragg	Fiat	Los Angeles	May 5, 1912
10 miles	6:35.62	Robertson	Simplex	Los Angeles	April 9, 1910
15 miles	10:25.17	Hearne	Benz	Indianapolis	July 4, 1910
20 miles	14:06.72	Hearne	Benz	Indianapolis	July 4, 1910
25 miles	18:22.60	Tetzlaff	Lozier	Los Angeles	Mar. 19, 1911
50 miles	36:35.80	Tetzlaff	Lozier	Los Angeles	Mar. 19, 1911
75 miles	54:50.20	Tetzlaff	Lozier	Los Angeles	Mar. 19, 1911
100 miles	1:13:37.25	Tetzlaff	Fiat	Indianapolis	May 30, 1912
150 miles	1:49:52.84	Tetzlaff	Fiat	Indianapolis	May 30, 1912
200 miles	2:25:59.52	Tetzlaff	Fiat	Indianapolis	May 30, 1912
250 miles	3:07:13.94	Tetzlaff	Fiat	Indianapolis	May 30, 1912
300 miles	3:48:49.30	Dawson	National	Indianapolis	May 30, 1912
350 miles	4:25:15.27	Dawson	National	Indianapolis	May 30, 1912
400 miles	5:04:14.23	Dawson	National	Indianapolis	May 30, 1912
450 miles	5:44:04.54	Dawson	National	Indianapolis	May 30, 1912
500 miles	6:21:06.03	Dawson	National	Indianapolis	May 30, 1912
(Hour records.)					
74 miles	1:00:00	Harroun	Marmon	Los Angeles	April 16, 1910
148 miles	2:00:00	Harroun	Marmon	Los Angeles	April 16, 1910

ONE MILE CIRCULAR DIRT TRACK RECORDS.

Distance.	Time.	Driver.	Car.	Place.	Date.
1 mile	:46.40	Oldfield	Christie	Bakersfield, Cal	April 28, 1913
2 miles	1:32.60	Burman	Jumbo Benz	St. Louis, Mo	Sept. 30, 1912
3 miles	2:30.55	De Palma	Fiat	Syracuse	Sept. 17, 1910
4 miles	3:22.27	De Palma	Fiat	Syracuse	Sept. 17, 1910
5 miles	4:11.90	De Palma	Fiat	Syracuse	Sept. 17, 1910
10 miles	8:31.20	De Palma	Fiat	Narbeth, Pa	Sept. 24, 1910
15 miles	13:30.00	Disbrow	Simplex	San Jose, Cal	April 14, 1912
20 miles	17:57.40	Disbrow	Simplex	San Jose, Cal	April 14, 1912
25 miles	22:26.60	Disbrow	Simplex	San Jose, Cal	April 14, 1912
50 miles	47:21.65	De Palma	Simplex	Syracuse	Sept. 16, 1911
75 miles	1:19:39	Strang	Buick	Columbus, O	July 3, 1909
100 miles	1:41:00.40	Burman	Buick	Columbus, O	July 3, 1909

ANNUAL 500 MILE SPEEDWAY RACE, INDIANAPOLIS.

Year. Winner and car.	No. starters.	No. finishers.	Time.	Miles per hour.
1911—Harroun, Marmon	40	12	6:42:08	74.59
1912—Dawson, National	24	10	6:21:06	78.7
1913—Goux, Peugeot	27	10	6:35:05	75.92

HOUR RECORDS.

The world's record for twenty-four hours is 1,581 miles 1,310 yards, an average pace of 65.9 miles an hour, made June 28-29, 1907, by S. F. Edge in a six-cylinder Napier on the three and one-quarter mile cement track at Weybridge, England.

The circular track twenty-four hour record was raised to 1,253 miles by Patschke and Poole in a Stearns at Brighton Beach track, New York, Aug. 19-20, 1910. The former record was 1,196 miles, made by Patschke and Mulford in a Lozier in 1909.

An American competitive speedway twenty-four hour record was created at Los Angeles, where a Fiat covered 1,491 miles.

The one-hour record was put at 107 miles 1,672 yards by a twelve-cylinder Sunbeam on the English Brooklands track Oct. 11, 1913.

The twelve hour record was put at 1,078 miles 400 yards by the same car and on the same track on Oct. 11, 1913.

TRANSCONTINENTAL RECORD.

A record of 10 days 18 hours 12 minutes from New York to San Francisco was made Aug. 8-18, 1910, by L. L. Whitman, driving a four-cylinder Reo, the fastest trip ever made across the continent in a motor car. The record from San Francisco to New York is 15 days 12 hours, made in a Franklin in 1906 by Whitman.

CHICAGO-NEW YORK RECORD.

The record by automobile between Chicago and New York is 39:53:00. It was made by a Franklin twenty-eight horse power runabout Aug. 21-22, 1907. The route followed was via Elkhart, Cleveland, Erie, Buffalo, Rochester, Syracuse, Utica, Newburgh and along the east side of the Hudson to New York. The distance was 1,050 miles. The previous record was 56:58:00, also made by a Franklin, a six-cylinder car.

ROAD RACING CLASSICS.

VANDERBILT CUP.

Year. Winner and car.	Miles.	H.M.S.
1904—George Heath, France, Panhard	284.40	5:26:45
1905—Hemery, France, Darracq	283	4:36:08
1906—Louis Wagner, France, Darracq	297.10	4:50:10⅗
1907—(No race)		
1908—George Robertson, America, Locomobile	258.60	4:00:48⅕
1909—H. F. Grant, America, Alco	278.08	4:25:42
1910—H. F. Grant, America, Alco	278.08	4:15:58
1911—R. K. Mulford, America, Lozier	291.38	3:56:00⅗
1912—R. De Palma, Germany, Mercedes	300.00	4:20:31
1913—(No race)		

BENNETT CUP.

Year. Winner.	Miles.	H.M.S.
1900—M. Charron, France	351	9:09:39
1901—M. Girardot, France	327	8:50:30
1902—S. F. Edge, England	383	10:42:00
1903—M. Jenatzy, Germany	386	8:36:00
1904—R. B. Thery, France	350	5:40:03
1905—R. B. Thery, France	342	7:02:42⅗

FRENCH GRAND PRIX.

Year. Winner.	Miles.	H.M.S.
1906—F. Szisz, France	474	12:14:05⅗
1907—Nazzaro, Italy	478.30	6:46:33
1908—Lautenschlager, Germany	478	6:55:43
1912—Boillot, France	956	13:58:02
1913—Boillot, France	300	6:07:00

AMERICAN STRAIGHTAWAY FREE-FOR-ALL RECORDS, REGARDLESS OF CLASS.

Distance.	Time.	Driver.	Car.	Place.	Date.
1 kilometer	15.88	Burman	Blitzen-Benz	Daytona	April 23, 1911
1 mile	25.40	Burman	Blitzen-Benz	Daytona	April 23, 1911
2 miles	51.28	Burman	Blitzen-Benz	Daytona	April 23, 1911
5 miles	2:34	Hemery	Darracq	Daytona	Jan. 24, 1906
10 miles	5:14.40	Bruce-Brown	Benz	Daytona	Mar. 24, 1909
15 miles	10:00	Lancia	Fiat	Daytona	Jan. 29, 1906
20 miles	13:11.92	Burman	Buick Bug	Jacksonville	Mar. 30, 1911
50 miles	35:52.31	Burman	Buick Bug	Jacksonville	Mar. 28, 1911
100 miles	1:12:45.20	Bernin	Renault	Daytona	Mar. 6, 1908
150 miles	1:55:18	Disbrow	Special	Jacksonville	Mar. 31, 1911
200 miles	2:34:12	Disbrow	Special	Jacksonville	Mar. 31, 1911
250 miles	3:14:55	Disbrow	Special	Jacksonville	Mar. 31, 1911
300 miles	3:53:33.50	Disbrow	Special	Jacksonville	Mar. 31, 1911
81.65 miles	1:00:00	Disbrow	Special	Jacksonville	Mar. 28, 1911

(Standing start.)

| 1 mile | 40.53 | Oldfield | Benz | Daytona | Mar. 16, 1910 |

GOLF.

NATIONAL OPEN CHAMPIONSHIP.

The national open golf championship tournament of 1913 took place on the links of the Country club at Brookline, Mass., Sept. 16-20, and resulted in a victory for Francis Ouimet of the Woodland club of Brookline. The final round resulted in a triple tie between Ouimet, Harry Vardon and Edward Ray, English professionals, each having a score of 304 for seventy-two holes. In the eighteen-hole playoff Ouimet had a score of 72, while Vardon's was 77 and Ray's 78. Record of the event:

1894—Willie Dunn (New York), St. Andrew's links, won by 2 up.
1895—H. Rawlins (Newport), Newport links, 173.
1896—James Foulis (Chicago), Shinnecock Hills, 152.
1897—Joe Floyd (Essex), Wheaton links, 162.
1898—Fred Herd (Washington Park), Myopia links, 328.
1899—W. Smith (Midlothian), Baltimore links, 315.
1900—H. Vardon (Ganton, England), Wheaton links, 313.
1901—Willie Anderson (Pittsfield, Mass.), Myopia links, 321.
1902—Lawrence Auchterlonie (Glen View), Garden City links, 307.
1903—Willie Anderson (Apawamis), Baltusrol links, 307.
1904—Willie Anderson (Apawamis), Glen View, 303.
1905—Willie Anderson (Apawamis), Myopia links, 314.
1906—Alexander Smith (Nassau), Onwentsia links, 295.
1907—Alec Ross (Brae Burn), Philadelphia Cricket club, 302.
1908—Fred McLeod (Midlothian), Myopia Hunt club, 322.
1909—George Sargent (Hyde Manor), Englewood (N. J.) links, 290.
1910—Alexander Smith (Wykagyl), Philadelphia Cricket club, 298.
1911—J. J. McDermott (Atlantic City), Chicago Golf club, 308.
1912—J. J. McDermott (Atlantic City), Buffalo Country club, 294.
1913—Francis Ouimet (Woodland), Brookline Country club, 304.

AMERICAN AMATEUR CHAMPIONSHIP.

Jerome D. Travers of the Upper Mont Clair (N. J.) Country club won the American Amateur golf championship for the fourth time at the annual championship tournament of the United States Golf association at Garden City, N. Y., Sept. 1-6, 1913. His opponent in the final thirty-six holes was John G. Anderson of Brae Burn, Mass., whom he defeated 5 up and 4 to play. Record of event to date:
1894—At Newport, R. I.—W. G. Lawrence, Newport, medal play, 188.
1895—At Newport Golf club—C. B. Macdonald, Chicago Golf club, won.
1896—At Shinnecock Hills Golf club—H. J. Whigham, Onwentsia, won. Low score in qualifying round, H. J. Whigham, 163.
1897—At Chicago Golf club—H. J. Whigham, Onwentsia, won. Low score in qualifying round, H. J. Whigham, 177.
1898—At Morris County, N. J.—F. S. Douglas, Fair-

field, won. Low score in qualifying round, J. H. Choate, Jr., Stockbridge, 175.
1899—At Onwentsia—H. M. Harriman, Meadowbrook, won. Low score in qualifying round, C. B. Macdonald, Chicago, 168.
1900—At Garden City—W. J. Travis, Garden City, won. Low score in qualifying round, W. J. Travis, 166.
1901—At Atlantic City—W. J. Travis won. Low score in qualifying round, W. J. Travis, 157.
1902—At Glen View, Ill.—L. N. James, Glen View, won. Low score in qualifying round, G. A. Ormiston, Pittsburgh, and W. J. Travis tied at 79, the latter winning the playoff.
1903—At Nassau, L. I.—W. J. Travis, Garden City, won. All match play.
1904—At Short Hills, N. J.—H. Chandler Egan, Exmoor Country club, won. Low score in qualifying round, H. C. Egan, 242 for 54 holes.
1905—At Wheaton, Ill.—H. Chandler Egan, Exmoor, won. Low score in qualifying round, Dr. D. P. Fredericks, 155 for 36 holes.
1906—At Englewood, N. J.,—Eben M. Byers of Pittsburgh won. Low score in qualifying round, W. J. Travis, 152 for 36 holes.
1907—At Cleveland, O.—Jerome D. Travers of Mont Clair, N. J., won. Low score in qualifying round, W. J. Travis, 146 for 36 holes.
1908—At Garden City, N. Y.—Jerome D. Travers of Mont Clair, N. J., won. Low score in qualifying round, Walter J. Travis, 153 for 36 holes.
1909—At Chicago Golf club—Robert A. Gardner, Hinsdale, won. Low score in qualifying round, Charles Evans, Jr., Thomas M. Sherman and Robert E. Gardner tied with 151 for 36 holes. Evans won the playoff.
1910—At Brookline, Mass.—W. C. Fownes, Pittsburgh, won. Low score in qualifying round, Fred Herreshoff, Ekwanok, 152 for 36 holes.
1911—At Rye, N. Y.—Harold H. Hilton, England, won. Low score in qualifying round, Harold H. Hilton, 150 for 36 holes.
1912—At Chicago Golf club—Jerome D. Travers of Mont Clair, N. J., won. Low score in qualifying round, Harold Hilton and Charles Evans, Jr., 152; in playoff, eighteen holes, Evans won, 72 to 75.
1913—At Garden City, N. Y.—Jerome D. Travers of Mont Clair, N. J., won. Low score in qualifying round, Charles Evans, Jr., 148 for 36 holes.

WOMEN'S NATIONAL CHAMPIONSHIP.

Miss Gladys Ravenscroft, representing the Bromborough club, England. won the women's national golf championship of the United States Oct. 13-18, 1913, on the links of the Wilmington (Del.) Country club. Her opponent in the final round was Miss Marion Hollis of Westbrook, whom she defeated 2 up. Record of event to date:
1895—Beatrix Hoyt, on Meadowbrook Country club links.
1896—Beatrix Hoyt, Morris Country club, 2 up, 1 to play.
1897—Beatrix Hoyt, Essex County Country club, 5 up, 4 to play.
1898—Beatrix Hoyt, Ardsley club, 5 up, 3 to play.
1899—Ruth Underhill, Philadelphia Country club, 2 up, 1 to play.

1900—Frances Griscom, Shinnecock Hills, 6 up, 4 to play.
1901—Genevieve Hecker, Baltusrol Golf club, 5 up, 3 to play.
1902—Genevieve Hecker, Brookline, 4 up, 3 to play.
1903—Bessie Anthony, Chicago Golf club, 7 up, 6 to play.
1904—Georgeanna Bishop, Philadelphia, 5 up, 3 to play.
1905—Pauline Mackay, Oakley Country club, 1 up.
1906—Harriet S. Curtis, Brae Burn Country club, 2 up, 1 to play.
1907—Margaret Curtis, Midlothian, 7 up, 6 to play.
1908—Catherine C. Harley, Fall River, 6 up, 5 to play.
1909—Dorothy Campbell (North Berwick, Scotland), Merion Cricket club, 3 up, 1 to play.
1910—Dorothy Campbell (Hamilton, Ont.), Homewood Country club, 2 up, 1 to play.
1911—Margaret Curtis (Boston), Baltusrol Golf club, 5 up, 3 to play.
1912—Maragaret Curtis (Boston), Essex Country club, 3 up, 2 to play.
1913—Miss Gladys Ravenscroft (Bromborough club, England), Wilmington (Del.) Country club, 2 up.

BRITISH AMATEUR CHAMPIONSHIP.

Year.	Winner.	Runner up.	
1886	H. Hutchinson	Henry Lamb	7 and 6
1887	H. Hutchinson	John Ball, Jr.	1 hole
1888	J. Ball, Jr.	J. E. Laidlay	5 and 4
1889	J. E. Laidlay	L. W. Balfour	2 and 1
1890	J. Ball, Jr.	J. E. Laidlay	4 and 3
1891	J. E. Laidlay	H. H. Hilton	1 hole
1892	J. Ball, Jr.	H. H. Hilton	3 and 1
1893	Peter Anderson	J. E. Laidlay	1 hole
1894	J. Ball, Jr.	S. M. Ferguson	1 hole
1895	L. B. Melville	J. Ball, Jr.	*1 hole
1896	F. G. Tait	H. H. Hilton	8 and 7
1897	A. J. T. Allan	J. Robb	4 and 2
1898	F. G. Tait	S. M. Ferguson	7 and 5
1899	J. Ball, Jr.	F. G. Tait	*1 hole
1900	H. H. Hilton	J. Robb	8 and 7
1901	H. H. Hilton	J. L. Low	1 hole
1902	C. Hutchings	S. H. Fry	1 up
1903	R. Maxwell	H. Hutchinson	6 and 5
1904	W. J. Travis	E. Blackwell	4 and 3
1905	A. G. Barry	Hon. O. Scott	3 and 2
1906	James Robb	C. C. Lengen	4 and 3
1907	J. Ball, Jr.	A. Palmer	6 and 4
1908	E. A. Lassen	H. F. Taylor	7 and 6
1909	R. Maxwell	C. K. Hutchinson	1 hole
1910	John Ball	C. Aylmer	10 and 9
1911	H. H. Hilton	E. A. Lassen	4 and 3
1912	John Ball	H. A. Mitchell	1 hole
1913	H. H. Hilton	R. Harris	6 and 5

*After a tie.

BRITISH OPEN CHAMPIONSHIP.

1890—*John Ball, Jr. (R. L. G. C.), Prestwick, 164.
1891—H. Kirkcaldy (St. Andrew's), St. Andrew's, 166.
1892—*H. H. Hilton (R. L. G. C.), Muirfield, †305.
1893—W. Auchterlonie (St. Andrew's), Prestwick.322.
1894—J. H. Taylor (Winchester), Sandwich, 325.
1895—J. H. Taylor (Winchester), St. Andrew's, 322.
1896—H. Vardon (Scarborough), Muirfield, 316.
1897—*H. H. Hilton (R. L. G. C.), Muirfield, 305.
1898—H. Vardon (Scarborough), Prestwick, 307.
1899—H. Vardon (Ganton), Sandwich, 310.
1900—J. H. Taylor (Richmond), St. Andrew's, 309.
1901—James Braid (Romford), Muirfield, 309.
1902—Alex. Herd (Huddersfield), Hoylake, 307.
1903—Alex. Herd (Huddersfield).
1904—J. White (Sunningdale), Sandwich, 296.
1905—Jas. Braid (Walton Heath), St. Andrew's, 318.
1906—James Braid (Walton Heath), Muirfield, 300.
1907—Arnaud Massey (France), Hoylake, 317.
1908—James Braid (Walton Heath), Prestwick. 291.
1909—J. H. Taylor (Mid-Surrey), Sandwich. 295.
1910—Jas. Braid (Walton Heath), St. Andrew's, 299.
1911—H. Vardon (South Herts), Sandwich, 303.
1912—Edw. Ray (Ganton), Muirfield, 294.
1913—J. H. Taylor (Mid-Surrey), Hoylake, 304.

*Amateur. †Changed to 72 holes.

OTHER TOURNAMENT WINNERS (1913).

Advertisers (midwinter)—Marshall Whitlash.
Advertisers (summer)—Joseph J. Hazen.
Canada (open)—Albert Murray.

Canada (women)—Miss Muriel Dodd.
Eastern Intercollegiate (team)—Yale.
Eastern Intercollegiate (individual) — Nathaniel Wheeler (Yale).
Eastern (women)—Mrs. Ronald G. Barlow.
France (amateur)—Lord Charles Hope.
Metropolitan (amateur)—Jerome D. Travers.
Metropolitan (open)—Alex Smith.*
Metropolitan (women)—Miss Marion Hollins.
Middle Atlantic—William G. Ballantyne.
Southern—Nelson M. Whitney.
Southern (women)—Mrs. Edwin W. Daley.
Tom Morris Memorial Trophy—Los Angeles Country club.
Trans-Mississippi—Stuart Stickney.
Western (indoor)—Charles Evans, Jr.
Western (amateur)—Warren K. Wood.
Western (open)—John J. McDermott.*
Western (women)—Miss Myra Helmer.
Western Intercollegiate (team)—Chicago.
Western Intercollegiate (individual)—Charles F. Grimes (Chicago).
United North and South (amateur)—Harold J. Topping.
*Professional.

STATE CHAMPIONS (1913).

California—Jack Neville.
California (women)—Miss Alice Warner.
Carolinas—W. M. Paul.
Connecticut—Robert Abbott.
Florida (open)—Charlie Thom.*
Florida (amateur)—Walter Fairbanks.
Indiana—Robert L. Resener.
Iowa—Roland G. Harrison.
Kansas—Lawrence W. Kinnear.
Massachusetts (open)—T. L. McNamara.*
Massachusetts (amateur)—Francis J. Ouimet.
Michigan—Philip Stanton.
Minnesota—Harry G. Legg.
Missouri—Raymond C. Thorne.
Nebraska—John W. Hughes.
New Hampshire—J. P. Gulliford.
New Jersey—Jerome D. Travers.
Olympic Cup—Western Golf association team.
Oregon—Russell Smith.
Oregon (women)—Mrs. James Gillison.
Ohio—DeWitt Balch.
Pennsylvania—W. C. Fownes, Jr.
Rhode Island—Roger H. Hovey.
Texas—George V. Rotan.
Wisconsin—Richard P. Cavanaugh.
*Professional.

POLO.

ENGLAND VS. AMERICA.

Teams representing England and the United States contested for the polo championship emblem, the Meadowbrook cup, at New York, N. Y., June 10 and 14, 1913, the Americans winning both games by net scores of 5½ to 3 and 4½ to 4¼. The Americans taking part were L. E. Stoddard, Larry and J. M. Waterbury, Harry P. Whitney and D. Milburn. The English players were Capt. L. St. George Cheape, F. M. Freake, Capt. R. G. Ritson, Capt. Vivian Lockett and Capt. A. N. Edwards.

MIDWESTERN CHAMPIONSHIP.

The Onwentsia Polo club of Lake Forest, Ill., won the polo championship of the middle west on its own grounds June 24-28, 1913. The other teams taking part in the contest represented the Cincinnati Polo club, the Kansas City Country club and the St. Louis Country club. The deciding game was between Onwentsia and Cincinnati, the former winning by a score of 11 to 2¾.

TENNIS.

NATIONAL CHAMPIONSHIPS.

The tournament to decide the national tennis championships of the United States took place on the Casino courts at Newport, R. I., Aug. 18-26, 1913. In the finals of the singles Maurice E. McLoughlin of San Francisco, holder of the title, successfully defended it by defeating R. Norris Williams II. of Philadelphia. Score: 6-4, 5-7, 6-3, 6-1.
The preliminary matches for the national championship in doubles were played on the Onwentsia

club courts at Lake Forest, Ill., Aug. 5-6. On the first day Gustave F. Touchard and M. W. Washburne, eastern champions, defeated Heath Byford and Ralph H. Burdick, western title holders, 6-4, 5-7, 6-3, 9-7. Clarence Griffin and John Strachan, Pacific coast champions, defeated Robert Shelton and J. B. Adoue, southern champions, 6-1, 6-4, 9-7. On the second day Griffin and Strachan defeated Touchard and Washburne by the score of 6-1, 8-6, 6-4, giving them the right to meet M. E. McLoughlin and T. C. Bundy, holders of the national title, at Newport. The latter team retained the honor by defeating the Pacific coast men, Aug. 20, in straight sets, 6-4, 7-5, 6-1.

NATIONAL TENNIS CHAMPIONS IN SINGLES.

1881—R. D. Sears.	1898—M. D. Whitman.
1882—R. D. Sears.	1899—M. D. Whitman.
1883—R. D. Sears.	1900—M. D. Whitman.
1884—R. D. Sears.	1901—W. A. Larned.
1885—R. D. Sears.	1902—W. A. Larned.
1886—R. D. Sears.	1903—H. L. Doherty.
1887—H. W. Slocum.	1904—H. Ward.
1888—H. W. Slocum.	1905—B. C. Wright.
1889—H. W. Slocum.	1906—W. J. Clothier.
1890—O. S. Campbell.	1907—W. A. Larned.
1891—O. S. Campbell.	1908—W. A. Larned.
1892—O. S. Campbell.	1909—W. A. Larned.
1893—R. D. Wrenn.	1910—W. A. Larned.
1894—R. D. Wrenn.	1911—W. A. Larned.
1895—F. H. Hovey.	1912—M. E. McLoughlin.
1896—R. D. Wrenn.	1913—M. E. McLoughlin.
1897—R. D. Wrenn.	

DAVIS CHALLENGE CUP.

The Davis international tennis challenge cup was won by the United States in 1913. The deciding matches for the trophy were played at Wimbledon, England, July 25, 26 and 28, 1913. In the singles, played July 25, J. C. Parke, representing England, defeated M. E. McLoughlin, representing the United States, 8-10, 7-5, 6-4, 1-6, 7-5, while R. N. Williams, American, defeated C. P. Dixon, English, 8-6, 3-6, 6-2, 1-6, 7-5. In the doubles, played July 26, Maurice E. McLoughlin and Harold H. Hackett, Americans, defeated H. Roper Barrett and C. P. Dixon, Englishmen, 5-7, 6-1, 2-6, 7-5, 6-4. In the singles, played July 28, McLoughlin defeated Dixon in straight sets, 8-6, 6-3, 6-2, giving the cup to America. R. N. Williams was defeated by J. S. Parke, 8-2, 5-7, 5-7, 6-4, 6-2, but this did not affect the result.

Seven teams, representing the United States, Canada, Australasia, South Africa, Germany, France and Belgium, competed in the elimination matches for the honor of challenging the English holders of the trophy. The American and Canadian teams met in the final round of the preliminary and the former won, taking two single matches and the doubles.

The Davis cup preliminary matches between America and Australia were played in New York. N. Y., June 6, 7 and 9, 1913, the American team winning the right to go to England to contest with other teams for the right to meet the English team. June 6 M. E. McLoughlin defeated H. M. Rice, Australian, 6-1, 6-3, 6-3, and R. Norris Williams, American, defeated Stanley N. Doust, Australian, 6-4, 6-4, 1-6, 7-5. In the doubles, June 7, Doust and A. B. Jones defeated McLoughlin and H. H. Hackett, 2-6, 6-2, 5-7, 6-2, 9-7. June 9 McLoughlin defeated Doust, 6-4, 6-4, 6-3, and Williams defeated Rice, 1-6, 4-6, 6-1, 9-7, 6-2.

RECORD OF DAVIS CHALLENGE CUP CONTESTS.

Year. Played at.	Holder.	Challenger.	Winner.	Score.
1900—Longwood C. C., Boston	America	British Isles	America	3-0
1902—Crescent A. C., New York	America	British Isles	America	3-2
1903—Longwood C. C., Boston	America	British Isles	British Isles	4-1
1904—Wimbledon, England	British Isles	Belgium	British Isles	5-0
1905—Wimbledon, England	British Isles	America	British Isles	5-0
1906—Wimbledon, England	British Isles	America	British Isles	5-0
1907—Wimbledon, England	British Isles	Australasia	Australasia	3-2
1908—Melbourne, Australia	Australasia	America	Australasia	3-2
1909—Sydney, Australia	Australasia	America	Australasia	5-0
1911—Christchurch, New Zealand	Australasia	America	Australasia	5-0
1912—Melbourne, Australia	Australasia	British Isles	British Isles	3-2
1913—Wimbledon, England	England	America	America	3-2

EASTERN CHAMPIONSHIPS.

The eastern tennis championships in singles and doubles were decided at the twenty-third annual tournament of the Longwood Cricket club, Boston, July 20-29, 1913. In the finals of the singles William Johnston, champion of the Pacific coast, defeated G. P. Gardner, Jr., of Boston, 6-2, 6-4, 6-4. M. E. McLoughlin, winner in 1912, was absent in Europe and did not defend his title. In the doubles G. F. Touchard and M. W. Washburne of New York defeated N. W. Niles and A. S. Dabney of Boston, 6-2, 7-5, 3-6, 14-12.

WESTERN CHAMPIONSHIPS.

The twenty-sixth annual western championship tennis tournament was held on the courts of the Onwentsia club at Lake Forest, Ill., July 26-Aug. 2, 1913. In the final of the singles Clarence Griffin of San Francisco, Cal., defeated Joseph Armstrong of St. Paul, Minn., 6-4, 6-0, 4-6, 6-1. Owing to the absence in Europe of Maurice McLoughlin, holder of the title, no challenge round was played. In the final round of the men's doubles Heath Byford and R. H. Burdick of Chicago defeated Walter T. Hayes and J. H. Winston, 6-1, 6-2, 6-4. In the consolation doubles Green and Forstall of Chicago defeated Adams and Armstrong of St. Paul, 6-2, 4-6, 8-6. In the women's singles, final round, Miss Gwendolyn Rees of Dallas, Tex., defeated Miss Carrie B. Neely of Chicago, 6-4, 6-4. In the women's doubles Miss Rees and Miss Neely defeated Miss Edith Hoyt and Miss Miriam Steever, 4-6, 6-2, 6-1.

WESTERN INTERCOLLEGIATE.

In the western intercollegiate tennis championship tournament held in Chicago and ending May 31, 1913, Albert Green of the University of Chicago won in the finals of the singles, defeating his teammate, Alexander Squair, 2-6, 3-6, 6-4, 7-5, 6-1. In the doubles Green and Squair defeated Stellwagen and McGee of the University of Minnesota, 6-3, 5-7, 6-2, 6-3.

EASTERN INTERCOLLEGIATE.

In the eastern intercollegiate tennis championship tournament held in Haverford, Pa., Sept. 3-6, 1913, on the grounds of the Merion Cricket club, the winner in singles was R. Norris Williams II. of Harvard, who defeated M. W. Washburne, also of Harvard, in the finals, 6-4, 3-6, 6-4, 6-1. J. J. Armstrong and M. W. Washburne won the doubles championship by defeating R. Norris Williams and T. H. Whitney of the same university, 4-6, 4-6, 7-5, 8-6, 6-2.

INTERNATIONAL TOURNAMENT.

In the international tennis tournament at Niagara on the Lake, Ont., Aug. 26-30, 1913, the winner in singles was Clarence Griffin of San Francisco, Cal., who defeated E. H. Whitney of Boston, 8-6, 1-6, 6-4, 8-6. In the doubles William Johnston and Clarence Griffin of San Francisco defeated E. H. Whitney and R. C. Seaver of Boston, 6-3, 6-3, 6-2. The winner in women's singles was Mrs. Robert Williams of Philadelphia, whose opponent in the finals was Miss May Browne of Los Angeles. The score was 8-6, 3-6, 6-4.

NORTH CENTRAL STATES TOURNAMENT.

In the north central states tennis tournament in Chicago Aug. 23-30, 1913, the winner in singles was Heath T. Byford of Chicago, who defeated Walter T. Hayes, 7-5, 7-5, 7-5. In the doubles the winners

were Heath Byford and Ralph Burdick, who defeated Walter T. Hayes and Harold Gifford, 6-4, 7-5, 2-6, 4-6, 6-1. Miss Carrie B. Neely won in the women's singles, defeating Miss Margaret Manson, 6-0, 6-2. Miss Neely and Miss Mabel Lee won the doubles championship by defeating Miss Edith Hiuz and Mrs. Malcolm McNeill, 6-2, 2-6, 6-3.

NORTHWESTERN CHAMPIONSHIPS.

The twenty-fourth annual tournament of the Northwestern Lawn Tennis association took place at Minneapolis, Minn., Aug. 4-11, 1913. In the finals of the singles Harry Waidner of Chicago was defeated by J. J. Armstrong of St. Paul, 6-2, 8-6, 5-7, 6-4. In the challenge round Armstrong defeated the title holder, Selford Stellwagen, 6-2, 6-3, 6-4. In the finals of the doubles Armstrong and John Adams of St. Paul defeated Harry Belden and Ward Burton of Minneapolis, 6-4, 6-3, 6-2, but in the challenge match Stellwagen and T. N. Jayne of Minneapolis defeated Adams and Armstrong, 5-7, 7-5, 6-4, 6-2. Miss Gwendolyn Rees of Dallas, Tex., won the women's championship in singles by defeating Miss Margaret Davis of St. Paul, 8-6, 4-6, 6-4.

MEADOW CLUB TOURNAMENT.

In the Meadow club tournament at Southampton, N. Y., Aug. 16, 1913, W. J. Clothier won in the singles by defeating G. F. Touchard, 6-2, 6-1, 6-3. In the doubles J. S. Strachan and C. J. Griffin defeated W. A. Larned and W. J. Clothier, 3-6, 6-4, 2-6, 6-3, 6-2.

MISSOURI VALLEY TOURNAMENT.

In the Missouri Valley tennis tournament ending July 19, 1913, the championship in singles was won by Roland Hoerr of St. Louis, Mo., who defeated Jack Cannon of Kansas City, Mo., in the finals, 3-6, 6-4, 9-7, 6-1. Jack Cannon and Dix Teachenor won the doubles championship by defeating Hubert Allen and Howard Robertson, 6-1, 6-4, 6-2. The tournament was held on the courts of the Kansas City Athletic club.

ALL-ENGLAND CHAMPIONSHIPS.

In the all-England lawn tennis championship tournament at Wimbledon, England, ending July 4, 1913. A. F. Wilding of New Zealand, holder of the title in singles, retained the honor by defeating M. E. McLoughlin of the United States in three straight sets, 8-6, 6-3, 10-8. The doubles championship was won by H. Roper Barrett and C. P. Dixon of Great Britain, the title holders, who defeated Friedrich W. Rabe and H. Kleinschroth of Germany, the challengers, 6-2, 6-4, 4-6, 6-2.

CHAMPIONSHIP OF LONDON.

Wallace F. Johnson of Philadelphia was defeated in the final round of the London lawn tennis championship tournament in London, England, June 21, 1913, by F. G. Lowe. Score: 7-5, 6-4, 4-6, 4-6, 6-4.

STATE CHAMPIONSHIPS.

ILLINOIS.

The annual championship tennis tournament of Illinois was held on the courts of the Wanderers' club, Chicago, July 12-20, 1913. In the finals of the men's singles Walter Hayes defeated Heath Byford, 7-5, 6-4, 2-6, 7-5. In the men's doubles Heath Byford and Ralph Burdick defeated Walter Hayes and John Winston, 5-7, 6-1, 3-6, 6-2, 7-5. In the women's singles Miss Carrie B. Neely defeated Mrs. Harold F. Colson, 6-3, 6-3, while in the women's doubles Miss Neely and Miss Miriam Steever defeated Mrs. Malcolm McNeil and Miss Edith Paradise, 6-3, 6-3.

NEW YORK.

In the New York state tennis tournament played on the courts of the Crescent Athletic club in New York city and ending Aug. 9, 1913, William Johnston of San Francisco, Cal., won the championship in singles by defeating S. H. Voshell of the Borough Park club, New York, 6-4, 6-4, 4-6, 6-2. The championship in doubles was won by Frederick C. Inman and R. D. Little, who defeated S. H. Voshell and F. C. Baggs, 6-1, 6-0, 7-5.

RHODE ISLAND.

E. H. Whitney of Harvard university won the Rhode Island tennis championship in singles at East Providence, R. I., Aug. 7, 1913, by defeating H. A. MacKinney of Providence, R. I., 6-3, 7-5, 6-1.

MINNESOTA.

Joe Armstrong won the tennis championship of Minnesota in singles by defeating Stellwagen of Minneapolis in the finals at the state tournament at Duluth, ending July 19, and by winning the challenge match with John Adams by a score of 6-1, 6-2, 6-5. In the men's doubles Armstrong and Adams defeated Wheeler and Burton, 4-6, 6-3, 6-3, 6-1. Miss Gwendolyn Rees won the championship in singles by defeating Miss Wetherby in the finals, 6-2, 6-1, and Miss Marguerite Davis in the challenge round, 6-2, 6-0. In the women's doubles Miss Wetherby and Miss Davis defeated Mrs. Gardiner and Miss Marie Merrill, 6-3, 6-4.

WISCONSIN.

In the Wisconsin state tennis tournament ending Aug. 16, 1913, Heath Byford of Chicago won the championship in singles by defeating Reginald Hamilton of Milwaukee, 6-1, 6-1, 6-8, 6-2. In the doubles Forstall and Larned won from Byford and Weber, 6-4, 3-6, 6-4, 6-4.

WOMEN'S CHAMPIONSHIPS.

NATIONAL.

The women's national tennis championship tournament of 1913 was held on the grounds of the Philadelphia Cricket club at Philadelphia, June 9-14. In the finals of the singles Miss Dorothy Green of Philadelphia defeated Miss Edna Wildey of Plainfield, N. J., 6-2, 6-4. In the challenge round, Miss Mary Browne of California, holder of the title, defeated Miss Green, 6-8, 7-5. In the doubles, Miss Browne and Mrs. Robert Williams defeated Miss Green and Miss Wildey, 12-10, 3-6, 6-2.

LONGWOOD CUP.

Mrs. G. W. Wightman of Brookline, Mass., who as Hazel Hotchkiss was national tennis champion, defeated Miss Evelyn Sears of Boston, also a former title holder, in the finals for the Longwood cup at Boston, Mass., Sept. 27, 1913, by a score of 6-4, 6-2. In the challenge match, played Sept. 29, Mrs. Wightman defeated Miss Mary Browne, the national champion, 6-0, 6-2.

PENNSYLVANIA AND EASTERN STATES.

Miss Mary Browne of Los Angeles, Cal., defeated Miss Edna Wildey of Plainfield, N. J., in the final round of the singles in the women's tennis championship of Pennsylvania and eastern states at the Merion Cricket club, Haverford, Pa., May 31, 1913, by 6-2, 6-4. In the final round of the doubles Miss Dorothy Greene and Miss Edna Wildey defeated Mrs. Robert Williams and Miss Mary Browne, 6-3, 8-6.

CLAY COURT CHAMPIONSHIPS.

The clay court championship tournament for the championship of the United States took place on the grounds of the Omaha (Neb.) Field club July 21-26, 1913. In the singles John Strachan of San Francisco, Cal., defeated Merrill Hall of New York in the final match, 6-0, 6-4, 4-6, 6-4. In the doubles the championship was forfeited to John Strachan and Clarence Griffin by Fred Harris and Merrill Hall.

COURT TENNIS.

For the eighth consecutive year Jay Gould of Lakewood, N. J., successfully defended his title of national amateur court tennis champion by defeating Joshua Crane of Boston in Boston, Mass., April 12, 1913. The scores were 6-4, 6-0, 6-2. Jay Gould and W. H. T. Huhn of Philadelphia won the court tennis championship in doubles in New York, N. Y., April 19, 1913, by defeating Payne Whitney and Milton S. Barger of New York, 6-4, 6-0.

INDOOR TENNIS.

Gustave F. Touchard won the national indoor tennis championship in New York, N. Y., Feb. 20, defeating George C. Shafer, 6-4, 3-6, 6-3, 6-4.

TENNIS CHAMPIONS IN 1913.

National (singles)—M. E. McLoughlin.
National (doubles)—M. E. McLoughlin and T. C. Bundy.
Davis Challenge Cup—America.
Eastern (singles)—William Johnston.
Eastern (doubles)—G. F. Touchard-M. W. Washburne.

Western (singles)—Clarence Griffin.
Western (doubles)—Heath Byford-R. H. Burdick.
Pacific Coast (singles)—William Johnston.
Pacific Coast (doubles)—Clarence Griffin-John Strachan.
Southern (singles)—Nat Thornton.
Southern (doubles)—R. Shelton-J. B. Adoue.
New England (singles)—Alrie H. Man, Jr.
North Central States (singles)—Heath Byford.
North Central States (doubles)—Heath Byford-Ralph Burdick.
South Central States (singles)—C. Drummond Jones.
Tristate at Cincinnati (singles)—W. S. McElroy.
Northwestern (singles)—J. Armstrong.
Northwestern (doubles)—S. Stellwagen-T. N. Jayne.
Cotton States (singles)—Carleton Smith.
Meadow Club (singles)—W. J. Clothier.
Meadow Club (doubles)—J. Strachan-C. J. Griffin.
Metropolitan (doubles)—C. M. Bull, Jr.-M. W. Washburne.
International at Niagara-on-the-Lake (singles)—Clarence Griffin.
International at Niagara-on-the-Lake (doubles)—Wm. Johnston-C. Griffin.
London, England (singles)—Wallace F. Johnson.
All-England (singles)—A. F. Wilding.
All England (doubles)—H. R. Barrett-C. P. Dixon.
Missouri Valley (singles)—Roland Hoerr.
Missouri Valley (doubles)—J. Cannon-D. Teachenor.
Eastern Intercollegiate (singles)—R. N. Williams, Jr.
Eastern Intercollegiate (doubles)—J. Armstrong-M. W. Washburne.
Western Intercollegiate (singles)—Albert Green.
Western Intercollegiate (doubles)—Albert Green-Alexander Squair.
New York State (singles)—William Johnston.
New York State (doubles)—Frederick C. Inman-F. C. Baggs.
Illinois State (singles)—Walter Hayes.
Illinois State (doubles)—Heath Byford-Ralph Burdick.
Rhode Island (singles)—E. H. Whitney.
Ohio (singles)—Charles O. Benton.
Michigan (singles)—Charles O. Benton.
Michigan (doubles)—A. L. Green-J. Lindauer.
Minnesota (singles)—J. Armstrong.
Minnesota (doubles)—J. Armstrong-J. W. Adams.
Nebraska (singles)—Harry Koch.
Wisconsin (singles)—Heath Byford.
Wisconsin (doubles)—J. J. Forstall-B. Larned.

WOMEN.

National (singles)—Miss Mary Browne.
National (doubles)—Miss Mary Browne-Mrs. Robert Williams.
Eastern (singles)—Miss Mary Browne.
Eastern (doubles)—Miss Dorothy Greene-Miss Edna Wildey.
Longwood cup—Mrs. G. W. Wightman (Hazel Hotchkiss).
Western (singles)—Miss Gwendolyn Rees.
Western (doubles)—Miss Gwendolyn Rees-Miss Carrie B. Neely.
International—Mrs. Robert Williams.

BOWLING.

AMERICAN BOWLING CONGRESS.

Leading winners in the thirteenth annual tournament of the American Bowling congress, held in Cleveland, O., Feb. 22-March 13, 1912:

FIVE-MAN TEAMS.

Team and City.	Score.	Prize.
Flor de Knispels, St. Paul	3,006	$600
Overlands, Toledo	2,992	525
Hudson Stars, Newark, N. J	2,946	450
Sir Cliftons, Chicago	2,943	400
Cadillacs, Detroit	2,934	350
Gambrinus, Columbus	2,902	300
Colonnas, Chicago	2,909	275
Ducators, Chicago	2,896	250
Morgenroths, Milwaukee	2,894	225
Lexington No. 1, Lexington, Ky	2,890	200

TWO-MAN TEAMS.

Schultz-Koster, Newark, N. J	1,291	$350
Mountain-Carlson, Chicago	1,277	300
Seibert-Ad Root, Toledo	1,268	260
Mauser-Welsh, Youngstown, O	1,266	220

	Score.	Prize.
Fischer-Bruck, Chicago	1,259	195
Smith-O. Riddell, New York	1,258	170
Wilson-Christy, Excelsior Springs, Mo	1,253	150
Haley-O'Connell, Detroit	1,251	135
Hoyer-Ashley, Sioux City	1,247	60
Haas-Carr, Fort Wayne	1,247	60

SINGLES.

F. Peterson, Columbus, O	693	$225.00
W. King, Cleveland, O	680	200.00
*J. Genahl, Oshkosh, Wis	672	162.50
*W. Knox, Philadelphia	672	162.50
M. Matser, Youngstown, O	662	125.00
L. Huebner, Chicago	662	110.00
*J. Higgins, Detroit	661	90.00
*E. Hilker, St. Louis	661	90.00
*W. Heins, Newark, N. J	661	90.00
W. A. Spencer, Chicago	658	70.00
*Tied, prizes split.		

ALL EVENTS.

Hermann, Cleveland	1,972	$150
Haas, Fort Wayne	1,894	125
Heins, Newark, N. J	1,891	100
Schultz, Newark, N. J	1,870	90
L. Higgins, Detroit	1,866	80
Smith, New York	1,865	70
Scully, Chicago	1,860	60
Sallander, Chicago	1,857	50
Haley, Detroit	1,855	40
Erickson, Oshkosh, Wis	1,854	35

CHAMPIONSHIP RECORD.
Five-Man Teams.

Year. Team and city.	Score.
1901—Standards, Chicago	2,720
1902—Fidellas, New York	2,792
1903—O'Learys, Chicago	2,819
1904—Ansons, Chicago	2,737
1905—Gunthers No. 2, Chicago	2,795
1906—Centurys No. 1, Chicago	2,794
1907—Furniture Citys, Grand Rapids	2,775
1908—Bonds, Columbus, O	2,927
1909—Lipmans, Chicago	2,962
1910—Cosmos, Chicago	2,880
1911—Flenners, Chicago	2,924
1912—Brunswick All Stars, New York	2,904
1913—Flor de Knispels, St. Paul	3,006

TWO-MAN TEAMS.

1901—Voorhees-Starr, New York	1,203
1902—McLean-Steers, Chicago	1,237
1903—Collins-Selbach, Columbus	1,227
1904—Kraus-Spies, Washington	1,184
1905—Stretch-Rolfe, Chicago	1,213
1906—Hamilton-Husey, Philadelphia	1,268
1907—Richter-Bigley, Louisville	1,164
1908—Klene-Chalmers, Chicago	1,254
1909—Schwoegler brothers, Madison, Wis	1,304
1910—Dalker-Wetterman, Cincinnati	1,231
1911—Hartley-Seiler, East Liverpool, O	1,246
1912—Owen-Sutton, Louisville, Ky	1,259
1913—Schultz-Koster, Newark, N. J	1,291

SINGLES.

1901—Frank Brill, Chicago	648
1902—Fred Strong, Chicago	649
1903—David A. Jones, Milwaukee	683
1904—Martin Kern, St. Louis	647
1905—C. Anderson, St. Paul	651
1906—Frank T. Favour, Oshkosh	669
1907—M. Levey, Indianapolis	624
1908—A. Wengler, Chicago	699
1909—Larry Sutton, Rochester, N. Y	691
1910—Thomas Haley, Detroit	705
1911—J. Blouin, Chicago	681
1912—Larry Sutton, Rochester, N. Y	679
1913—F. Peterson, Columbus, O	693

American Bowling Congress Officials (1913-1914)—President, George B. Howard, Chicago; secretary, A. L. Langtry, Milwaukee, Wis.; treasurer, F. L. Pasdeloup, Chicago.

NATIONAL BOWLING ASSOCIATION.

In the seventh annual tournament of the National Bowling association, held in Rochester, N. Y., April 5-22, 1913, the Bronx Centrals of New York, N. Y., won the five-man team event with a score of 2,938. The doubles event was won by Smith and Riddell of New York, N. Y., with a score of 1,259, and the individual event by George Kumpf of Buffalo, N. Y., with the record score of 712.

Winners to date:

FIVE-MAN TEAMS.	Score.
1907—Corinthians, New York	2,814
1908—Brunswicks, New York	2,893
1909—Corinthians No. 8, New York	2,899
1910—Chalmers, Detroit	2,917
1911—Bonds, Cleveland	2,969
1912—Grand Centrals, Rochester	2,997
1913—Bronx Centrals, New York	2,938

TWO-MAN TEAMS.

1907—Tuthill-Nelson, Brooklyn	1,220
1908—McGuirk-Grady, Paterson	1,318
1909—Satterthwaite Rodgers, Philadelphia	1,293
1910—Burvine-Eckstein, Washington, D. C.	1,305
1911—Kelsey-Johnson, New Haven, Conn.	1,355
1912—Johnson-Lindsey, New Haven, Conn.	1,301
1913—Smith-Riddell, New York	1,259

INDIVIDUALS.

1907—Frank Sauer, New York	657
1908—Fred Schwartje, Brooklyn	697
1909—E. Thompson, Brooklyn	699
1910—Tony Prio, Brooklyn	705
1911—Joseph West, London, Ont.	694
1912—Leo Lucke, Brooklyn	699
1913—George Kumpf, Buffalo	712

National Bowling Association Officials (1913-1914)—President, E. E. Dungan, Philadelphia, Pa.; permanent secretary, Major Gage, Rochester, N. Y.; treasurer, William Cordes, New York, N. Y.

INTERNATIONAL BOWLING ASSOCIATION.

In the International bowling association tournament in Minneapolis, Minn., ending March 24, 1913, the Biatz team of Chicago was the winner in the five-man event with a score of 2,916, which is a record for the organization. In the doubles, J. and M. Klaes, father and son, were the winners with a score of 1,221. In the individuals, Harry Steers of Chicago won first place with 654. The tournament of 1914 will also be held in Minneapolis. Summary of winners to date:

FIVE-MAN TEAMS.

1903—Acmes, St. Paul	2,726
1904—Capitols, St. Paul	2,694
1905—Courts, St. Paul	2,820
1906—Capitols, St. Paul	2,746
1907—Pfisters, St. Paul	2,781
1908—Anheuser-Busch, St. Paul	2,789
1909—Doris, St. Paul	2,653
1910—Chalmers-Detroit, Chicago	2,760
1911—Capitols, St. Paul	2,849
1912—Americans, St. Paul	2,905
1913—Blatz, Chicago	2,916

TWO-MAN TEAMS.

1903—Olness-Wooley, Minneapolis	1,213
1904—Hansen-Parker, Minneapolis	1,174
1905—Wooley-Garland, Minneapolis	1,277
1906—Gosewich-Muggley, St. Paul	1,160
1907—Listy-Ferguson, Duluth	1,196
1908—Moshofsky-Hinderer, St. Paul	1,246
1909—Yost-Miller, St. Paul	1,195
1910—Martin-Vandertunk, St. Paul	1,243
1911—Martin-Vandertunk, St. Paul	1,308
1912—Lee-De Vos, Milwaukee	1,222
1913—Klaes-Klaes, Duluth	1,221

INDIVIDUALS.

1903—Skorish, St. Paul	674
1904—Alness, Minneapolis	658
1905—Kampman, St. Paul	636
1906—Werner, Winona	539
1906—G. Olson, Duluth	589
1907—Wooley, Minneapolis	617
1908—Campbell, Duluth	622
1909—Dolan, Minneapolis	636
1910—Johnson, Minneapolis	618
1911—Con Sandblom, St. Paul	693
1912—F. L. Trainer, Sioux City	642
1913—Harry Steers, Chicago	654

International Bowling Association Officials (1913-1914)—President, Frank R. Mahone, St. Paul, Minn.; secretary, Theodore Grouewald, St. Paul, Minn.; treasurer, Walter Ryberg, Minneapolis, Minn.

BILLIARDS.

AMATEUR 18-2 CHAMPIONSHIP.

NATIONAL.

The annual class A championship tournament of the National Amateur Billiard Players of America took place in Philadelphia, Pa., March 23-April 4,

1913. Joseph Mayer of Brooklyn was the winner. Final standing:

	W.	L.	Pct.	H. R.	H. A.	G. A.
Mayer	6	0	1,000	130	22 4-18	14 132-162
Conklin	5	1	.833	100	17 9-23	11 155-200
Gardner	4	2	.667	89	15 10-26	11 100-187
Collins	2	4	.333	93	14 8-28	8 113-262
Morton	2	4	.333	72	11 11-22	7 147-253
Duniway	1	5	.167	81	11 11-33	7 214-217
Uffenheimer	1	5	.167	61	10 0-40	7 205-234

Until 1908 the amateur billiard championship was decided at the 14-2 balkline game of 300 points. In that year it was changed to the 18-2 game of 400 points now played. Following is the championship record since the tournaments were started:

1901—A. R. Townsend, New York.
1902—Edward W. Gardner, Montclair, N. J.
1903—W. P. Foss, Haverstraw, N. Y.
1904—J. F. Poggenburg, New York.
1905—C. F. Conklin, Chicago.
1906—Edward W. Gardner, Montclair.
1907—Calvin Demarest, Chicago.
1908—Calvin Demarest, Chicago.
1909—H. A. Wright, San Francisco.
1910—Edward W. Gardner, Montclair.
1911—J. F. Poggenburg, New York.
1912—Morris Brown, Brooklyn.
1913—Joseph Mayer, Brooklyn.

PROFESSIONAL 18-1 CHAMPIONSHIP.

In a game for the professional 18-1 balkline billiard championship, played in Pittsburgh, Pa., Jan. 9, 1913, Ora C. Morningstar of that city retained the title by defeating George Sutton of Chicago, 500 to 478. Score in detail:

Morningstar—0, 13, 24, 3, 1, 8, 47, 1, 4, 13, 0, 0, 2, 31, 15, 13, 0, 65, 12, 0, 8, 29, 16, 3, 0, 34, 17, 38, 0, 59, 43, 1—500. Average, 15 20-32.

Sutton—6, 0, 13, 0, 1, 32, 29, 30, 1, 2, 2, 42, 4, 16, 22, 3, 0, 14, 45, 1, 58, 15, 26, 3, 40, 0, 44, 6, 14, 8, 1—478—Average, 15 13-31.

In another game for the 18-1 championship, played in Pittsburgh, Pa., March 19, 1913, Willie Hoppe of New York defeated Ora C. Morningstar by a score of 500 to 211. Scores:

Hoppe—1, 25, 2, 26, 0, 56, 0, 2, 2, 8, 0, 2, 96, 10, 26, 29, 0, 1, 24, 1, 2, 3, 19, 7, 26, 3, 11, 3, 0, 1, 24, 80—500. High run, 96. Average, 15 20-32.

Morningstar—0, 0, 0, 2, 0, 26, 10, 0, 10, 10, 0, 2, 0, 0, 4, 1, 0, 1, 5, 0, 24, 8, 15, 0, 0, 2, 73, 13, 5, 0, 0—211—High run, 73. Average, 6 25-31.

PROFESSIONAL 18-2 CHAMPIONSHIP.

Willie Hoppe defeated George Sutton in a match game for the 18-2 balkline billiard championship in New York, N. Y., Feb. 5, 1913, by the following score:

Hoppe—12, 1, 1, 117, 19, 2, 45, 18, 3, 53, 16, 19, 34, 9, 48, 12, 0, 22, 5, 0, 17—500.

Sutton—5, 22, 5, 2, 12, 1, 0, 13, 21, 99, 9, 9, 11, 7, 22, 39, 8, 0, 0, 16, 0—301.

Willie Hoppe defeated Koji Yamada of Japan in a challenge game of 18-2 balkline billiards in New York, N. Y., May 27, 1913, by the following score:

Hoppe—0, 115, 67, 39, 8, 0, 0, 50, 35, 29, 66, 91—500. Average, 41 8-12.

Yamada—15, 2, 10, 0, 4, 0, 0, 0, 1, 0, 1—33. Average, 3.

THREE CUSHION BILLIARDS.

NATIONAL LEAGUE SERIES.

The National Billiard league's three cushion championship season, ending April 9, 1913, resulted in a tie between Chicago and Pittsburgh, each having won 26 and lost 16 games. The standing of the clubs was:

	W.	L.	Pct.		W.	L.	Pct.
Chicago	26	16	.619	New York	21	21	.500
Pittsburgh	26	16	.619	Philadelphia	19	22	.488
St. Louis	24	18	.571	Kansas City	19	23	.452
Brooklyn	24	18	.571	Boston	9	33	.281

In the play-off Chicago and Pittsburgh each won three games, but the former scored 288 points to 273 for the latter, and Chicago was consequently declared winner. The last game in the series of six was played in Pittsburgh, April 30.

THREE CUSHION CHAMPIONSHIP.

Alfred De Oro of New York regained the three cushion billiard championship of the world by defeating John Horgan of St. Louis in a match contest of 150 points in San Francisco, Cal., May 29, 1913. The final score was: De Oro, 150; Horgan, 120. The match was played in blocks of 50 points each.

POCKET BILLIARDS.

In a match, the last block of which was played Feb. 27, 1913, in New York city, for the pocket billiard championship of the world, Alfred De Oro defeated Thomas Hueston by a total score of 600 to 386.

Benny Allen of Kansas City, Mo., won the pocket billiard championship from Alfred De Oro in a match, the last block of which was played in New York city Oct. 3, 1913. The total score was: Allen, 800; De Oro, 516.

YACHTING.

THE AMERICA'S CUP.

The New York Yacht club and the Royal Ulster Yacht club, representing Sir Thomas Lipton, reached an agreement in July, 1913, to contest for the historic America's cup in September, 1914. Owing chiefly to a disagreement as to the size of the competing boats no races for the trophy have been sailed since 1903. Sir Thomas Lipton proposed that the yachts be limited to seventy-five feet on the water line. According to the deed of gift, the defending club has the right to select a vessel of such size as it pleases, provided it be not less than sixty-five nor more than ninety feet on the water line, and the New York Yacht club was therefore unwilling to meet the condition proposed. July 20, 1913, the Ulster Yacht club of Belfast cabled that the conditions prescribed by the New York Yacht club had been accepted and signed and that Sir Thomas Lipton would send his Shamrock IV. to contest with an American defender. The conditions and rules, announced Aug. 28, do not differ materially from those under which the last races for the America's cup were sailed.

Starting on Thursday, Sept. 10, 1914, the races will be sailed on Thursdays, Saturdays and Tuesdays, until a winner of the cup is determined. Should Shamrock IV., the challenger, be detained by weather or other cause from reaching here in time it will be given time for fitting out after its arrival, but the first race must, under the rules, be started not later than Sept. 17.

The first race will be thirty miles to windward, the second over an equilateral triangle, and the third similar to the first. If fourth and fifth races are necessary they are to be sailed respectively as the second and first. The races are to be started from the Sandy Hook lightship. The time limit of the races, it is agreed, is to be six hours instead of five and one-half as hitherto. The Shamrock IV. is a seventy-five foot cutter.

The challenger shall be informed at least one week before the first race what vessel is to defend the cup. The system of measurement, time allowance and racing rules of the New York Yacht club, as they exist, shall govern the races, unless inconsistent with the provisions of the agreement between the clubs. It was announced Sept. 5 that a seventy-five foot all steel sloop of keel type would be built at the Herreshoff yards at Bristol, R. I., as a candidate to defend the America's cup.

RECORD OF RACES TO DATE.

1851—Aug. 22. In this the year of the great exhibition in London the Royal Yacht Club of England offered a cup to the winner of a yacht race around the Isle of Wight. The course was 60 miles in length and was won by the schooner yacht America, designed by George Steers for John C. Stevens of the New York Yacht club. The America was 94 feet over all, 88 feet on the water line, 22½ feet beam and 11½ feet draft. There was no time allowance and the competing yachts ranged in size from a three-masted 392-ton schooner, the Brilliant, to the 47-ton cutter, the Aurora, which came in second in the race. The time of the America was 10 hours* and

34 minutes; that of the Aurora was 24 minutes slower. The cup after that became known as the America's cup and has now been successfully defended for sixty-two years.

1870—Aug. 8, New York Yacht club course: Magic, 3:58:21; Cambria, 4:37:38.

1871—Oct. 16, New York Yacht club course: Columbia, 6:19:41; Livonia, 6:46:45. Oct. 18, 20 miles to windward off Sandy Hook and return: Columbia, 3:07:41¾; Livonia, 3:18:15½. Columbia disabled in third race Oct. 19. Oct. 21, 20 miles to windward off Sandy Hook and return: Sappho, 5:39:02; Livonia, 6:09:23. Oct. 23, New York Yacht club course: Sappho, 4:16:17; Livonia, 5:11:55.

1876—Aug. 11, New York Yacht club course: Madeleine, 5:23:54; Countess of Dufferin, 5:34:53. Aug. 12, 20 miles to windward off Sandy Hook and return: Madeleine, 7:18:46; Countess of Dufferin, 7:46:00.

1881—Nov. 9, New York Yacht club course: Mischief, 4:17:00; Atalanta, 4:45:39¼. Nov. 10, 16 miles to leeward off Sandy Hook and return: Mischief, 4:54:53; Atalanta, 5:33:47.

1885—Sept. 14, New York Yacht club course: Puritan, 6:06:05; Genesta, 6:22:24. Sept. 16, 20 miles to leeward off Sandy Hook light and return: Puritan, 5:03:14; Genesta, 5:04:52.

1886—Sept. 9, New York Yacht club course: Mayflower, 5:26:41; Galatea, 5:38:43. Sept. 11, 20 miles to leeward off Sandy Hook light and return: Mayflower, 6:49:10; Galatea, 7:18:09.

1887—Sept. 27, New York Yacht club course: Volunteer, 4:53:18; Thistle, 5:12:41¾. Sept. 30, 20 miles to windward off Scotland light and return: Volunteer, 5:42:56¼; Thistle, 5:54:45.

1893—Oct. 7, 15 miles to windward off Sandy Hook light and return: Vigilant, 4:05:47; Valkyrie, 4:11:35. Oct. 9, triangular 30-mile course, first leg to windward: Vigilant, 3:25:01; Valkyrie, 3:35:36. Oct. 13, 15 miles to windward off Sandy Hook light and return: Vigilant, 3:24:39; Valkyrie, 3:25:19.

1895—Sept. 7, 15 miles to windward and return, east by south off Point Seabright, N. J.; Defender, 4:57:55; Valkyrie III., 5:08:44. Sept. 10, triangular course, 10 miles in each leg; Valkyrie III., 3:55:09; Defender, 3:55:56; won by Defender on a foul. Sept. 13, Defender sailed over course and claimed cup and race; claim allowed.

1899—Oct. 16, 15 miles to windward and return, off Sandy Hook: Columbia, 4:53:53; Shamrock, 5:04:07. Oct. 17, triangular course, 10 miles to a leg: Columbia, 3:37:00; Shamrock snapped its topmast. Oct. 20, 15 miles to leeward and return: Columbia, 3:38:09; Shamrock, 3:43:26.

1901—Sept. 28, 15 miles to windward and return, off Sandy Hook: Columbia, 4:30:24; Shamrock II., 4:31:44. Oct. 3, triangular course: Columbia, 3:12:35; Shamrock II., 3:16:10. Oct. 4, 15 miles to leeward and return: Columbia, 4:32:57; Shamrock II., 4:33:38.

1903—Aug. 22, 15 miles to leeward and return, off Sandy Hook: Reliance, 3:31:17; Shamrock III., 3:41:17. Aug. 25, triangular course, 10 miles to leg: Reliance, 3:14:54; Shamrock III., 3:18:10. Sept. 3, 15 miles to windward and return: Reliance, 4:28:04; Shamrock III. did not finish.

THE EMPEROR'S CUP.

The first international ocean yacht race for a cup offered by the emperor of Germany was sailed in 1905. The course was from Sandy Hook, N. J., to the Lizard, England, a distance of approximately 3,000 miles. The Atlantic, which was sailed by Capt. Charles Barr, won the race, arriving at the Lizard at 9:16 p. m., May 29, and beating the best previous record, made by the Endymion, by one day and sixteen hours. The actual elapsed time was twelve days and four hours, and the best day's run was 341 miles. The Hamburg came in second May 30 and the Valhalla third May 31.

MANHASSET CUP.

Michicago, representing the Chicago Yacht club, which won the Manhasset cup at Greenwich, Conn., in 1912, successfully defended the trophy in a series of races sailed on Lake Michigan off Chicago Sept. 22-25, 1913. It won the first two races but was beaten in the third by South Shore, which had

been second in the other contests. Michicago was third in the third race and consequently was tied in points with South Shore, each having thirteen. In the sail-off of the tie Michicago won. The only eastern yacht competing was Stranger, owned by R. P. Jencks of the Rhode Island Yacht club of Providence. It was third in the first and second races and fourth in the third.

SONDER YACHT RACING.

In a series of five races between three German and three American boats of the sonder class, off Marblehead, Mass., Sept. 1-9, 1913, the American yachts were easily victorious, their rivals being eliminated in the first three contests. In the final race the Ellen, owned by C. P. Curtis of Boston, was the winner, the victory carrying with it the President Wilson cup. The German boats were Angela IV., Serum and Wittelsbach X. The American boats, in addition to Ellen, were Cima, which won second place, and Sprig. Most of the races were sailed in light winds.

CAMERON CUP.

Nomad of the White Bear Yacht club, St. Paul, Minn., representing the United States, won the Cameron cup given by Lieut.-Gov. D. G. Cameron of Manitoba, Canada, by defeating Verve of the Lake of the Woods Yacht club, Manitoba, on White Bear lake, Minnesota, July 21 and 22, 1913. The races were over a twelve-mile course.

OCEAN CHALLENGE CUP.

The Ocean Challenge cup of the Brooklyn Yacht club was won by the 31-foot sloop Ediana of the Harlem Yacht club, July 4-6, 1913. The course was from Echo bay to and around Vineyard Sound lightship, thence outside of Block island and Long island to Gravesend bay, a distance of 280 miles. Amada was second and Hyperion third.

LONG ISLAND SOUND CHAMPIONS.

Winners of championship honors in the races sailed under the auspices of the Long Island Sound Yacht Racing association in 1913:

Class P—Josephine.
N. Y. Y. C. 30-footers—Nepsi.
Stamford schooners—Hopewell.
Sound schooners—Vandalia.
Manhasset Bay 20-footers—Mdle. Boss.
Larchmont Inter-Club—Wild Thyme.
Jewell class—Jade.
Bayside Birds—Dodo.
American dories—Tautog.
Star class—Star Faraway.

PUT-IN-BAY REGATTA.

Winners of the principal events at the regatta of the Interlake Yachting association at Put-in-Bay, O., July 22-23, 1913:

Class P—Michicago, Chicago.
Class R—Psammiad II., Cleveland.
Class F, 21-footers—Camille, Detroit.
Class A, modern cruisers—Cardenia, Toronto.
Class H, 18-footers—Dorchen II., Boston.
Class Y, yawls—Nahma, Detroit.
Class J, 16-footers—Sella II., Toledo.
Class D, veteran cruisers—Enright, Toledo.
Class L, 14-footers—Tyro, Toledo.
Class K, catboats—Old Sam, Toledo.

MIDDLE STATES REGATTA.

The twenty-fourth annual rowing regatta of the Middle States Regatta association took place on the Harlem river, New York city, Sept. 1, 1913. Winners and time:

Junior double sculls—Columbia Boat club, Pittsburgh; 5:56.
Senior double sculls, 140-pound class—Lone Star Boat club; no time taken.
Intermediate single shells—F. Miller, New York Athletic club; no time taken.
Junior four oared gig—Malta Boat club, Philadelphia; 5:05.
Intermediate quadruple sculls—Nassau Boat club; 4:40⅘.
Senior quadruple sculls—Riverside Boat club; 4:37⅘.
Intermediate four oared gig—Potomac Boat club, Washington; 5:30⅘.
Senior four oared barge—Ariel Rowing club, Baltimore; 5:44⅗.
Senior four oared shell—Wahnetah Boat club; no time taken.
Senior double sculls—Union Boat club, Boston; 5:31.
Intermediate double scull—Potomac Boat club, Washington; 5:31⅘.
Junior eight oared shells—Arundel Boat club, Baltimore; 4:50.
Intermediate eight oared shells—Metropolitan Rowing club; 4:55⅘.
Junior quadruple shells—Bayonne Rowing club; 5:08⅘.
Senior single sculls—Thomas J. Rooney, Ravenswood Boat club, 5:25.
Senior eight oared shells—New York Athletic club, 4:29⅖.
Senior four oared shells, 140-pound class—Ariel Boat club, Baltimore; no time taken.

CENTRAL STATES ROWING REGATTA.

The seventh annual regatta of the Central States Amateur Rowing association took place at Peoria, Ill., July 16 and 17, 1913. Winners and time in principal events:

JUNIOR DAY.

Six oared barges, ¾ mile dash—St. Louis Rowing club; 5:02.
Single scull shells, 1½ miles—E. Schopps, Grand Rapids Boat and Canoe club; 11:51⅕.
Pair oared shells, 1½ miles—Vogler and Bartsch, St. Louis Rowing club; 11:54⅖.
Single scull shells, ¼ mile dash—E. Schopps, Grand Rapids Boat and Canoe club; 1:41.
Four oared scull shells, 1½ miles—Central Rowing club, No. 1, St. Louis; 9:57.
Double scull shells, 1½ miles—Grand Rapids Boat and Canoe club; 11:10½.
Eight oared shells, 1¼ miles straightaway—St. Louis Rowing club; 7:09⅗.

SENIOR DAY.

Six oared barges, ¾ mile straightaway—Mound City Rowing club, St. Louis; 3:59.
Single scull shells, 1½ miles—J. Kortlander, Grand Rapids Boat and Canoe club; 9:56⅖.
Four oared shells, 1½ miles—Mound City Rowing club, St. Louis; 9:10⅗.
Pair oared shells, 1½ miles—Oestreicher and Goessling, Century Boat club, St. Louis; 11:00.
Four oared scull shells, ½ mile open—Mound City Rowing club, St. Louis; 2:32.
Double scull shells, 1½ miles—Ewert and Gordon, Lincoln Park Boat club, Chicago; 12:24.
Eight oared shells, 1¼ miles straightaway—St. Louis Rowing club; 6:36.

SOUTHWESTERN REGATTA.

The regatta of the Southwestern Amateur Rowing association took place at Peoria, Ill., July 18-19, 1913. Winners and time in principal events:

JUNIOR DAY.

Six oared barges, ¾ mile straightaway—Western Rowing club, St. Louis, Mo.; 4:03.
Single scull shells, 1½ miles—Greene, Lincoln Park Boating club, Chicago, Ill.; 11:50¾.
Pair oared scull shells, 1½ miles—Buder and Luth, Century Boat club, St. Louis; 10:56.
Single scull shells, open, ¼ mile dash—Floerke, Central Rowing club, St. Louis; 1:19⅘.
Four oared scull shells, 1½ miles—South Side Boat club, Quincy, Ill.; 9:37.
Double scull shells, 1½ miles—Korf and Rehberger, Lincoln Park Boat club; 10:35.
Eight oared shells, 1½ miles straightaway—Peoria Canoe club; 7:08.

SENIOR DAY.

Six oared barges, ¾ mile straightaway—Mound City Rowing club, St. Louis; 4:13⅗.
Single scull shells, 1½ miles—E. Schopps, Grand Rapids Boat and Canoe club; 10:46⅘.
Pair oared shells, 1½ miles—A. Bechestobill and A. Goessling, Century Boat club, St. Louis; 11:00.
Four oared shells, ½ mile dash—Western Rowing club, St. Louis; 2:39.
Double sculls, 1½ miles—J. Kortlander and E. Schopps, Grand Rapids Boat and Canoe club; 9:39.
Eight oared shells, 1¼ miles—Mound City Rowing club; 6:44¼.

Four oared shells, 1½ miles—Western Rowing club, St. Louis; 9:15½.
Junior four oared shells, 1½ miles—Grand Rapids Boat and Canoe club; 10:15⅝.

HENLEY REGATTA (ENGLAND).

The annual royal regatta took place July 2-5, 1913, at Henley-on-Thames, England, over the course of 1 mile 550 yards. Winners and time in principal events:
Grand challenge cup—Leander; 7:11.
Diamond challenge sculls—C. McVilly, Tasmania; 8:49.
Thames challenge cup—Oriel college; 7:30.
Stewards' challenge cup—New college (no competition in final).
Silver goblets and Nickalls' challenge cup—Trinity Hall; 8:39.
Visitors' challenge cup—Pembroke college; 8:13.
Ladies' challenge cup—First Trinity; 7:24.
Wyfold challenge cup—Lady Margaret; 8:01.

NORTHWESTERN INTERNATIONAL REGATTA.

The northwestern international regatta took place at St. Paul, Minn., July 18-19, 1913, on the Mississippi river, over a course of 1½ miles. Winners and time in principal events:
Junior singles—D. Connelly, Minnesota; 8:25.
Bantam fours—Duluth; 7:03.
Senior fours (1 mile)—Winnipeg; 4:37½.
Junior doubles—D. Connelly and T. Ellerbee, Minnesota; 7:46.
Junior eights—Duluth; 6:46½.
Senior singles—D. Connelly, Minnesota; 8:09.
Junior fours—Duluth; 7:19.
Lapstreak fours (1 mile)—Duluth; 4:37⅝.
Senior fours—Connelly and Ellerbee, Minnesota; 7:37⅜.
Senior eights—Duluth No. 1; 6:45.

CANADIAN HENLEY.

The annual regatta of the Canadian Association of Amateur Oarsmen took place on the Henley course, Lake Ontario, at Port Dalhousie, Ont., Aug. 1 and 2, 1913. Winners and time in principal events:
Intermediate fours—Argonaut Rowing club, Toronto; 8:57.
Junior eights—Detroit (Mich.) Boating club; 7:01.
Junior doubles—Don Rowing club, Toronto, Ont.; 9:11.
140 pound fours—Argonauts; 9:28.
Senior eights—Winnipeg (Man.) Rowing club; 6:48.
Senior singles—R. J. Dibble, Don R. C.; no time taken.
Intermediate doubles—Don R. C.; no competition.
Senior doubles—Don R. C.; no competition.
Senior fours—Winnipeg R. C.; no time announced.
Junior fours—Britannia R. C., Ottawa; 9:16.
Junior singles—T. Finley, Don R. C.; 10:22.
Intermediate singles—T. Finley, Don R. C.; 10:00.

SCULLING.

Ernest Barry of London, England, champion professional sculler of the world, successfully defended his title July 21, 1913, by defeating Harry Pearce, champion of Australia, by two lengths over the Putney-Mortlake course on the Thames, England. Stakes of $2,000 accompanied the title.

ROWING RECORDS.

¼ mile—*:57, single scull, straightaway, Edwin Henley, Newark, N. J., July 11, 1901.
½ mile—*2:03⅝, single scull, straightaway, Edwin Henley, Newark, N. J., July 11, 1893.
1 mile—4:28, single scull, straightaway, James Stansbury, with tide, Thames river, England, July 11, 1896; *4:46, single scull, straightaway, Rupert Guiness, Thames river, England, 1893.
2 miles—*9:18, eight oars, straightaway, Cornell freshmen, Poughkeepsie, N. Y., June 26, 1902.
3 miles—*14:27½, eight oars, straightaway, Cornell varsity, New London, Conn., June 25, 1891.
4 miles—*18:53½, straightaway, eight oars, Cornell university, Poughkeepsie, N. Y., July 2, 1901.
*Performance by amateurs.

POWER-BOAT RACING.

HARMSWORTH CUP.

Maple Leaf IV., owned by E. Mackay Edgar and representing the Royal Motor Yacht Club of England, retained the Harmsworth international motor boat trophy in 1913 by winning two out of three races in Osborne bay, Isle of Wight, Sept. 10-12. A French boat, Despujols II., won the first race, covering the course of 42.4 miles in 41:34. Maple Leaf IV. was second and Ankle Deep, one of the American entries, was third. Disturber III., the other American boat, did not finish, owing to a slight accident. The second race was won by Maple Leaf IV., in 39:29⅝. Despujols I. was second, Ankle Deep third and Disturber III. fourth. Despujols II. was disabled. The third and last race was won by Maple Leaf IV., in 40:10⅝. Ankle Deep was second in 43:25. Despujols I. and Disturber III. were third and fourth respectively, but their time was not taken.
The Harmsworth cup has now been won five times by Great Britain, four times by the United States and once by France.

WRIGLEY CUP.

James A. Pugh's Disturber III. won the Wrigley cup and the American free-for-all championship at the water carnival held at Chicago in August, 1913, in connection with the Perry centennial celebration. The course of 30 miles was covered by Disturber III. in 42:37, or at the rate of 42.3 miles per hour. J. Stuart Blackton's Baby Reliance, winner in 1912, was second.
The thirty-two foot hydroplane championship was won by Milton Smith's Oregon Kid and the twenty-six foot championship by J. Stuart Blackton's Baby Speed Demon. The twenty-foot championship was taken by Oregon Kid.

PHILADELPHIA TO BERMUDA.

The power boat Dream won the annual race for craft of its kind from Philadelphia to Hamilton, Bermuda, June 7-11, 1913. The Barbara II. was the first to cross the finishing line at 3:25:20 a. m., June 11, the Dream not arriving until 4:55 p. m. The latter, however, had a time allowance of 16:44:42 and was declared the winner by 3:14:56. The time occupied by the Barbara II. in making the trip of 734 nautical miles was 85 hours 14 minutes 20 seconds.
In a return race from Bermuda to Brooklyn, June 17-21, the Tocsam was the winner on a time allowance of eleven hours, reaching the goal 6 hours 39 minutes after Barbara II. Dream did not compete.

AROUND MANHATTAN ISLAND.

June 15, 1913, in a motor boat race around Manhattan island, New York, a distance of 25.25 miles, the Valiant was the winner in the open boat class on time allowance, defeating Bunk III. by 2 minutes 47 seconds. Bunk III. made the distance in 2:38:26.

PHILADELPHIA-OVERFALLS RACE.

Caliph, owned by M. E. Brigham, won the Philadelphia-Overfalls lightship motor boat race of 154 nautical miles in 14 hours 54 minutes 31 seconds May 30-31, 1913. It had a time allowance of 3:29:16. C. L. Lagen's Dream was second.

GOLD CHALLENGE CUP.

In the races for the gold challenge cup of the American Power Boat association at Alexandria Bay, N. Y., July 31, Aug. 1 and 2, 1913, Ankle Deep was the winner, with P. D. Q. III. second.

NEW YORK TO ALBANY AND RETURN.

Ten motor boats took part in the race of 235 nautical miles from New York to Albany and back June 28-29, 1913. Blue Peter, owned by A. Nachman, was the winner, its elapsed time being 23 hours 55 minutes 21 seconds. This is the best record for the course. Respite was second, Excelsior third and Thistle fourth. The race was under the auspices of the New York Motor Boat club.

THOMAS TROPHY.

J. Stuart Blackton's Baby Reliance III. won the Thomas trophy and the international championship of America in the power boat races on Niagara river at Buffalo, N. Y., Sept. 4-6, 1913. Halda Papoose was second.
The Blackton $5,000 trophy was taken by Halda Papoose, owned by Max C. Fleischmann of Cincinnati.

REGATTA AT KEOKUK, IOWA.

In the power boat regatta on the Mississippi river at Keokuk, Iowa, Aug. 27-29, 1913, Oregon Kid was the winner in the principal event, the class E races. It covered twenty miles in 26:50⅖ and ten miles in 15:07⅗.

REGATTA AT KANSAS CITY, MO.

Baby Reliance won the national motor boat speed contest over a seven-mile course on the Missouri river at Kansas City, Mo., Sept. 27, 1913, in 11:09. Oregon Kid was second.

ROWING.

INTERUNIVERSITY RACES.

UNIVERSITY EIGHT OARED.

In 1898 the race took place on Saratoga lake over a three-mile course; the other contests were on the four-mile course at Poughkeepsie, N. Y.

June 26, 1896—(1) Cornell, 19:59; (2) Harvard, 20:08; (3) Pennsylvania, 20:18; (4) Columbia, 21:25.
June 25, 1897—(1) Cornell, 20:34; (2) Yale, 20:44; (3) Harvard, 21:00.
July 2, 1897—(1) Cornell, 20:47⅘; (2) Columbia, 21:20⅖; (3) Pennsylvania, swamped.
July 2, 1898—(1) Pennsylvania, 15:51½; (2) Cornell, 16:06; (3) Wisconsin, 16:10; (4) Columbia, 16:21.
June 27, 1899—(1) Pennsylvania, 20:04; (2) Wisconsin, 20:05½; (3) Cornell, 20:13; (4) Columbia, 20:20.
June 30, 1900—(1) Pennsylvania, 19:44⅗; (2) Wisconsin, 19:46⅖; (3) Cornell, 20:04⅕; (4) Columbia, 20:08⅕; (5) Georgetown, 20:19⅕.
July 2, 1901—(1) Cornell, 18:53⅕; (2) Columbia, 18:58; (3) Wisconsin, 19:06⅘; (4) Georgetown, 19:21; (5) Syracuse, distanced; (6) Pennsylvania, distanced.
June 21, 1902—(1) Cornell, 19:05⅗; (2) Wisconsin, 19:13⅗; (3) Columbia, 19:18⅗; (4) Pennsylvania, 19:26; (5) Syracuse, 19:31⅗; (6) Georgetown, 19:32.
June 26, 1903—(1) Cornell, 18:57; (2) Georgetown, 19:27; (3) Wisconsin, 19:29⅗; (4) Pennsylvania, 19:30⅖; (5) Syracuse, 19:36⅕; (6) Columbia, 19:54.
June 28, 1904—(1) Syracuse, 20:22⅗; (2) Cornell, 20:31⅕; (3) Pennsylvania, 20:32⅘; (4) Columbia, 20:45⅖; (5) Georgetown, 20:52⅗; (6) Wisconsin, 21:01⅕.
June 28, 1905—(1) Cornell, 20:29⅖; (2) Syracuse, 21:47⅗; (3) Georgetown, 21:49; (4) Columbia, 21:53⅘; (5) Pennsylvania, 21:59⅘; (6) Wisconsin, 22:06⅕.
June 23, 1906—(1) Cornell, 19:36⅘; (2) Pennsylvania, 19:43⅘; (3) Syracuse, 19:45⅕; (4) Wisconsin, 20:13⅘; (5) Columbia, 20:18⅗; (6) Georgetown, 20:35.
June 26, 1907—(1) Cornell, 20:02⅗; (2) Columbia, 20:04; (3) Navy, 20:13⅘; (4) Pennsylvania, 20:33⅖; (5) Wisconsin (no time); (6) Georgetown (no time); (7) Syracuse (shell sunk).
June 27, 1908—(1) Syracuse, 19:34⅕; (2) Columbia, 19:35⅕; (3) Cornell, 19:39; (4) Pennsylvania, 19:52⅗; (5) Wisconsin, 20:00⅘.
July 2, 1909—(1) Cornell, 19:02; (2) Columbia, 19:04⅖; (3) Syracuse, 19:15⅕; (4) Wisconsin, 19:24⅕; (5) Pennsylvania, 19:32⅕.
June 26, 1910—(1) Cornell, 20:42⅕; (2) Pennsylvania, 20:44⅕; (3) Columbia, 20:54⅕; (4) Syracuse, 21:13; (5) Wisconsin, 21:15⅗.
June 27, 1911—(1) Cornell, 20:10⅘; (2) Columbia, 20:16⅘; (3) Pennsylvania, 20:33; (4) Wisconsin, 20:34; (5) Syracuse, 21:03⅖.
June 29, 1912—(1) Cornell, 19:21⅗; (2) Wisconsin, 19:25; (3) Columbia, 19:41⅖; (4) Syracuse, 19:47; (5) Pennsylvania, 19:55; (6) Stanford, 20:25.
June 21, 1913—(1) Syracuse, 19:28⅗; (2) Cornell, 19:31; (3) Washington, 19:33; (4) Wisconsin, 19:36; (5) Columbia, 19:38⅕; (6) Pennsylvania, 20:11⅕.

FOUR OARED RACES.

Poughkeepsie course, two miles.

July 2, 1901—(1) Cornell, 11:39⅘; (2) Pennsylvania, 11:45⅖; (3) Columbia, 11:51⅗.
June 21, 1902—(1) Cornell, 10:43⅗; (2) Pennsylvania, 10:54⅘; (3) Columbia, 11:08.
June 26, 1903—(1) Cornell, 10:34; (2) Pennsylvania, 10:35⅘; (3) Wisconsin, 10:55⅘; (4) Columbia, 11:14.
June 28, 1904—(1) Cornell, 10:53⅗; (2) Columbia, 11:12⅘; (3) Pennsylvania, 11:15⅗; (4) Wisconsin, 11:18⅗; (5) Georgetown, 11:34⅖.
June 28, 1905—(1) Syracuse, 10:16⅗; (2) Cornell, 10:17⅗; (3) Pennsylvania, 10:33⅗; (4) Columbia, 10:45; (5) Wisconsin, 10:52.
June 28, 1906—(1) Cornell, 10:34; (2) Syracuse, 10:48⅘; (3) Columbia, 10:55⅗; (4) Pennsylvania, 11:06⅘.
June 26, 1907—(1) Syracuse, 10:37⅕; (2) Cornell, 10:40; (3) Pennsylvania, 10:49; (4) Columbia, 10:59⅘.
June 27, 1908—(1) Syracuse, 10:52⅘; (2) Columbia, 11:06⅗; (3) Pennsylvania (disqualified for foul), 10:57⅘. (Cornell did not finish.)
July 2, 1909—(1) Cornell, 10:01; (2) Syracuse, 10:10; (3) Columbia, 10:12; (4) Pennsylvania, 10:27.
June 26, 1910—(1) Cornell, 11:37⅘; (2) Syracuse, 11:43⅖; (3) Columbia, 11:48⅕; (4) Pennsylvania, 12:22.
June 27, 1910—(1) Cornell; (2) Syracuse; (3) Columbia; (4) Pennsylvania. No official time taken.
June 29, 1912—(1) Cornell, 10:34⅕; (2) Columbia, 10:41⅕; (3) Syracuse, 10:58⅗; (4) Pennsylvania, 11:23⅗.
June 21, 1913—(1) Cornell, 10:47⅖; (2) Pennsylvania, 10:52⅕; (3) Columbia, 10:54⅘; (4) Wisconsin, 10:58⅘; (5) Washington, 12:08⅗; (6) Syracuse (no time taken).

UNIVERSITY FRESHMAN EIGHTS.

Poughkeepsie course, two miles.

June 30, 1900—(1) Wisconsin, 9:45⅗; (2) Pennsylvania, 9:54⅗; (3) Cornell, 9:55⅕; (4) Columbia, 10:08.
July 2, 1901—(1) Pennsylvania, 10:20⅕; (2) Cornell, 10:23; (3) Columbia, 10:36⅕; (4) Syracuse, 10:44.
June 21, 1902—(1) Cornell, 9:34⅘; (2) Wisconsin, 9:42⅘; (3) Columbia, 9:49; (4) Syracuse, 9:53; (5) Pennsylvania, 10:05.
June 26, 1903—(1) Cornell, 9:18; (2) Syracuse, 9:22⅕; (3) Wisconsin, 9:32; (4) Columbia, 9:41; (5) Pennsylvania, 9:45.
June 28, 1904—(1) Syracuse, 10:01; (2) Cornell, 10:12⅖; (3) Pennsylvania, 10:18⅘; (4) Columbia, 10:28½.
June 28, 1905—(1) Cornell, 9:35⅖; (2) Syracuse, 9:49; (3) Columbia, 9:53; (4) Pennsylvania, 9:58⅘.
June 23, 1906—(1) Syracuse, 9:51⅗; (2) Cornell, 9:55; (3) Wisconsin, 9:55⅗; (4) Columbia, 10:07⅕; (5) Pennsylvania, 10:13⅕.
June 26, 1907—(1) Wisconsin, 9:58; (2) Syracuse, 10:03; (3) Pennsylvania, 10:04; (4) Columbia, 10:05⅖; (5) Cornell, 10:07⅘.
June 27, 1908—(1) Cornell, 9:29⅗; (2) Syracuse, 9:38⅗; (3) Columbia, 9:43; (4) Wisconsin, 9:55⅕; (5) Pennsylvania, 10:42.
July 2, 1909—(1) Cornell, 9:07⅗; (2) Syracuse, 9:14⅘; (3) Pennsylvania, 9:21; (4) Wisconsin, 9:22⅘; (5) Columbia, 9:26.
June 26, 1910—(1) Cornell, 10:40⅕; (2) Columbia, 10:53⅖; (3) Syracuse, 10:53⅘; (4) Pennsylvania, 11:09⅕; (5) Wisconsin, 11:15⅕.
June 27, 1911—(1) Columbia, 10:13⅕; (2) Cornell; 10:20⅖; (3) Syracuse, 10:23⅕; (4) Pennsylvania, 10:24⅘; (5) Wisconsin, 10:38.
June 29, 1912—(1) Cornell, 9:31⅗; (2) Wisconsin, 9:35⅖; (3) Syracuse, 9:42⅗; (4) Pennsylvania, 9:46⅖; (5) Columbia, 9:47.
June 21, 1913—(1) Cornell, 10:04⅘; (2) Wisconsin, 10:07⅘; (3) Syracuse, 10:14⅘; (4) Pennsylvania, 10:25⅗; (5) Columbia, 10:29.

HARVARD-YALE RACES.

UNIVERSITY EIGHTS.

Year. Winner.	Time.	Loser's time.
1876—Yale	22:02	22:33
1877—Harvard	24:36	24:44
1878—Harvard	20:44¾	21:29
1879—Harvard	22:15	23:58
1880—Yale	24:27	25:09
1881—Yale	22:13	22:19
1882—Harvard	20:47	20:50½
1883—Harvard	24:26	25:59
1884—Yale	20:31	20:46
1885—Harvard	25:15½	26:30
1886—Yale	20:41½	21:05¾
1887—Yale	22:56	23:14½
1888—Yale	20:10	21:24
1889—Yale	21:30	21:55
1890—Yale	21:29	21:40
1891—Harvard	21:23	21:57
1892—Yale	20:48	21:40
1893—Yale	25:01½	25:15
1894—Yale	22:47	24:40
1895—Yale	21:30	25:15

Year. Winner.	Time.	Loser's time.
899—Harvard	20:52½	21:13
900—Yale	21:12⅘	21:37⅗
901—Yale	23:37	23:45
902—Yale	20:20	20:33
903—Yale	20:19⅘	20:29⅖
904—Yale	21:40½	22:10
905—Yale	22:33½	22:36
906—Harvard	23:02	23:11
907—Yale	21:10	21:13
908—Harvard	24:10	*
909—Harvard	21:50	22:10
910—Harvard	20:46½	21:04
911—Harvard	22:44	23:40
912—Harvard	21:43½	22:04
913—Harvard	21:42	22:20

*Time not taken. Yale stroke oar collapsed at end of 2½ miles.

Of the above races the first two were rowed on the Springfield (Mass.) course and the remainder on the New London course, which is four miles straightaway. There were no dual races in 1896, 897 and 1898. The Harvard-Yale freshmen and four-oared races are rowed at the same time and place as the eight-oared races.

HARVARD-YALE FRESHMAN EIGHTS.

Two miles.

Year. Winner.	Time.	Loser's time.
901—Yale	10:37⅘	10:58
902—Dead heat	10:13	10:13
1903—Yale	9:43⅕	9:48⅗
904—Yale	10:20	10:20½
905—Harvard	9:59	10:04
906—Yale	10:39⅘	10:41
907—Harvard	11:15	11:19
1908—Harvard	9:38⅕	9:47⅕
909—Harvard	'1:32	12:09
910—Harvard	11:54½	12:02
911—Yale	11:58	11:59⅕
912—Harvard	10:52	10:54½
913—Harvard	10:41	10:45

HARVARD-YALE FOUR-OARED RACE.

Year. Winner.	Time.	Loser's time.
901—Harvard	11:49⅕	12:02⅕
902—Harvard	11:19½	11:25⅕
903—Yale	10:59⅘	11:10⅘
904—Harvard	12:12	12:15
905—Harvard	11:22	11:27
1906—Yale	12:15	12:21
907—Yale	12:33	13:15
908—Yale	10:33½	10:43
909—Harvard	13:14	13:23
910—Harvard	13:02½	13:18
911—Harvard	13:37½	13:52
912—Harvard	11:24	11:55
913—Harvard	11:52	12:11

PRINCETON-HARVARD-PENNSYLVANIA.

Crews representing Princeton, Harvard and the University of Pennsylvania met in a race on the Charles river course of 1⅞ miles at Cambridge, Mass., May 12, 1913. Princeton won by a length in 10:18. Harvard was second in 10:22 and Pennsylvania third in 10:34.

COLUMBIA-ANNAPOLIS-PRINCETON.

Columbia university defeated Annapolis academy and Princeton university in an eight-oared race over a course of 1 5-16 miles on Lake Carnegie at Princeton, N. J., May 17, by half a length in 3:45⅘. Annapolis was second in 6:48⅘ and Princeton third in 6:49⅘.

CORNELL-HARVARD.

Cornell university defeated Harvard in an eight-oared race on Cayuga lake in 10:06, May 24, 1913. In a race between freshman eights Harvard defeated Cornell in 10:48. The races were over a two-mile course.

ANNAPOLIS-PENNSYLVANIA.

In a race between Annapolis (navy) and Pennsylvania eights at Annapolis, Md., May 24, the navy crew won by four lengths in 6:36⅘. The Pennsylvania freshmen defeated the navy "plebes" by one length in 6:56. The races were over the inside or Henley course on the Severn river.

WISCONSIN-MINNESOTA.

The University of Wisconsin eight-oared crew defeated the Minnesota Boat club in a 1½ mile race on Lake Mendota, at Madison, Wis., May 24. No time taken, Minnesota not finishing.

OXFORD-CAMBRIDGE RECORD.

Course from Putney to Mortlake, London.

Year.	Winner.	Time.
1880	Oxford	21:23
1881	Oxford	21:51
1882	Oxford	20:12
1883	Oxford	21:08
1884	Cambridge	21:39
1885	Oxford	21:36
1886	Cambridge	22:29½
1887	Cambridge	20:52
1888	Cambridge	20:48
1889	Cambridge	20:14
1890	Oxford	22:03
1891	Oxford	21:48
1892	Oxford	19:21
1893	Oxford	18:47
1894	Oxford	21:39
1895	Oxford	20:50
1896	Oxford	20:01
1897	Oxford	19:12
1898	Oxford	22:15
1899	Cambridge	21:04
1900	Cambridge	18:47
1901	Oxford	22:31
1902 (March 22)	Cambridge	19:09
1903 (April 1)	Cambridge	19:32½
1904 (March 25)	Cambridge	21:36
1905 (April 1)	Oxford	20:35
1906 (April 7)	Cambridge	19:25
1907 (March 16)	Cambridge	20:26
1908 (April 4)	Cambridge	19:19
1909 (April 3)	Oxford	19:50
1910 (March 23)	Oxford	20:14
1911 (April 1)	Oxford	18:29
1912 (April 1)	Oxford	22:05
1913 (March 13)	Oxford	20:53

NOTE—The race of 1913 was the seventieth in the history of the event. The first contest took place in 1845.

PRINCETON VS. YALE.

In a race over a course of 1⅝ miles on Lake Carnegie at Princeton, N. J., Oct. 25, 1913, the Princeton eight oared crew defeated Yale by two lengths in 9:39⅕. Yale's time was 9:46⅗.

NATIONAL ROWING REGATTA.

The forty-first annual regatta of the National Association of Amateur Oarsmen was held on the Charles river course at Boston, Mass., Aug. 8-9, 1913. Winners and time:

Intermediate four oared shells, 1¼ miles—Duluth Boat club; 7:59.

Senior ¼ mile dash, single scull shells—Robert Dibble, Don Rowing club, Toronto; 1:34.

Intermediate double sculls, 1¼ miles—Union Boat club, Boston; 8:21.

International four oared shells, 1¼ miles—Argonaut Rowing club, Toronto; 7:55.

Senior quadruple sculls, 1¼ miles—Riverside Boat club, Cambridge, Mass.; 7:07⅗.

Intermediate eight oared shells, 1¼ miles—Duluth Boat club; 6:57.

Championship senior singles, 1¼ miles—Robert Dibble, Don R. C., Toronto; 8:09.

Association senior singles, 1¼ miles—Robert Dibble, Don R. C., Toronto; 8:21.

Intermediate singles, 1¼ miles—W. T. Gardiner. Union B. C., Boston; 8:35⅗.

Senior four oared shells, 1¼ miles—Duluth B. C.; 7:34.

Senior double sculls, 1¼ miles—Don R. C., Toronto; 7:45⅗.

Senior eight oared shells, 1¼ miles—Duluth B. C. Intermediate crew; 6:58.

Intercity octuple sculls, 1¼ miles—Boston-Cambridge; 6:48.

AMERICAN ROWING REGATTA.

The eleventh annual regatta of the American Rowing association took place May 31, 1913, over the Henley distance, 1 mile 550 yards, on the Schuylkill river, Philadelphia, Pa. Winners and

WESTY HOGAN TOURNAMENT.

The annual Westy Hogan tournament took place at Atlantic City, N. J., Sept. 16-20. 1913. The handicap was won by Louis Colquitt of Orange, N. J., with a score of 93 made from the 19-yard mark. The Westy Hogan championship at singles was won by Jay Clark, Jr., with a score of 99. Allen Heil won the championship in doubles with a score of 91 out of 100. The state team contest was won by Pennsylvania with a total score of 479.

STATE CHAMPIONS (1913).

Alabama—John Livingston.
Connecticut—W. R. Newsome.
Delaware—W. S. Colfax, Jr.
Idaho—A. G. Adelman.
Illinois—Lon Hall.
Indiana—C. A. Edmonson.
Iowa—William Hoon.
Kentucky—J. D. Gay.
Maine—E. Randall.
Maryland—Dwight E. Mallory.
Montana—J. C. Norris.
Nebraska—L. S. German.
New Jersey—E. D. Springer.
New York—Jay D. Green.
North Carolina—J. B. Pennington.
Ohio—J. A. Smith.
Tennessee—W. M. Griffith.
Texas—H. R. Bosley.
Vermont—F. E. Adams.
Virginia—P. Gallagher.
Wisconsin—William J. Raup.

RIFLE SHOOTING.

CAMP PERRY TOURNAMENT.

NATIONAL RIFLE ASSOCIATION MATCHES.

The annual shooting matches of the National Rifle Association of America took place at Camp Perry, O., Aug. 15-23, 1913. Winners of principal events:
Wimbledon cup match, 20 shots at 1,000 yards—Won by Corporal Thomas E. Vereer, 14th U. S. infantry; score, 99.
Hale match, 600 yards—Won by B. F. Cole, 1st West Virginia; score, 50-10.
Catrow match, 800, 900 and 1,000 yards—Won by Quartermaster Sergeant S. Pearson of Oregon; score, 103 out of 105 points.
Governor's cup match, skirmish, 200 yards surprise fire, 600 and 1,000 yards—Won by Lieut. Hawley, U. S. A.; score 244 out of a possible 250.
Adjutant-general's match, 1,000 yards—Won by Lieut. Col. C. B. Winder of Ohio; score, 100.
Enlisted men's team match, 600 and 1,000 yards—Won by United States cavalry team; score, 96.
Surprise fire match, 200 yards—Won by 2d Lieut. R. Sears, U. S. infantry; score, 50.
Members' match, 600 yards—Won by Capt. W. Dabney, U. S. infantry; score, 50 and 1.
Championship company team match, 200 and 600 yards—Won by Co. A, 1st infantry, West Virginia; score, 389.
Marine corps match, 600 and 1,000 yards—Won by J. W. Hessian, National Rifle association; score, 195.
Leech cup match, 800, 900 and 1,000 yards—Won by G. W. Chesley; score, 105.
Herrick trophy match, teams of eight men, 800, 900 and 1,000 yards—Won by Iowa team; score, 1,727.
President's match, skirmish, 200 yards surprise fire, 600 and 1,000 yards—Won by Capt. W. H. Clopton, Jr., U. S. cavalry; score, 266.
National individual match, skirmish, 200 yards surprise fire, 600 and 1,000 yards—Won by Artificer E. W. Sweeting, 16th Pennsylvania infantry; score, 238.
Company team match, 600 yards—Won by West Virginia; score, 389.

NATIONAL TEAM MATCHES.

The national matches took place at Camp Perry, O., Aug. 25-30, 1913. In the principal event, the national team match, the conditions called for surprise fire at 200 yards, slow fire at 600 and 1,000 yards and skirmish fire. The winning teams and scores in each class were:
Class A—United States cavalry, 2,675.

Class B—Alabama, 2,547.
Class C—Utah, 2,423.
The United States navy was second in Class A, Texas in Class B, and Rhode Island in Class C.
The United service match, open to teams of twenty men, 200 yards surprise fire, 600 and 1,000 yards slow fire and skirmish fire, was won by the United States army team with a score of 4,414. The United States marine corps was second with 4,409 and the United States navy third with 4,358.

PALMA TROPHY AND OTHER INTERNATIONAL MATCHES.

Several important international matches in rifle shooting were decided at Camp Perry, O., Sept. 1-9, 1913. The main event, the Palma trophy match at 800, 900 and 1,000 yards, was won by the United States team with a score of 1,714. Argentine Republic was second with 1,684, Canada third with 1,675, Sweden fourth with 1,484 and Peru fifth with 1,465. The record of this event now stands:

Year.	Country.	Score.	Year.	Country.	Score.
1876—United States		....	1903—United States	..	1,570
1877—United States	..3,334		1907—United States	..	1,712
1880—United States	..1,292		1912—United States	..	1,720
1901—Canada	..1,522		1913—United States	..	1,714
1902—Britain	..1,447				

The individual Palma match at 800, 900 and 1,000 yards was won by Maj. E. Hart McHarg of Canada with a score of 220 out of a possible 225. Capt. Neil Smith and Lieut. Mortimer, both of Canada, were second and third respectively with scores of 220 each. McHarg made 74 at 1,000 yards, Smith 72 and Mortimer 71, which determined their relative standing.
The international team match for teams of five men, any rifle, 120 shots per man at 300 meters, was won by Switzerland with a score of 4,956. France was second with 4,767, and the United States third with 4,578. Casper Widmer won the world's championship at the standing position at 300 meters with 334 points. Conrad Stahell of Switzerland was first in the kneeling position with 352, and Lieut. A. Paroche of France first in the prone position with 358.
The international team match for countries in the Pan-American union was won by Argentina with a score of 4,662. The United States was second with 4,553 and Peru third with 4,130. The match was open to teams of five, each man firing with military rifle forty shots at 300 meters, standing, kneeling and prone.
In the individual match, army rifle, Mauritz Ericson of Sweden won with a score of 485.
The grand international individual match was won by Conrad Stahell of Switzerland with a score of 426.
The Argentine-American naval trophy, in which the shooting was at 300 meters, 600 yards and 1,000 yards, was won by the Argentine team with a score of 1,612. The American team scored 1,499 points.

SEAGIRT TOURNAMENT.

The twenty-third annual shooting tournament of the New Jersey State Rifle association and the New York State Rifle association took place at Seagirt, N. J., Sept. 12-20, 1913. Results in principal events:
North American match, 200, 600, 900 and 1,200 yards—Won by United States rifle team with a total score of 2,259 points; Argentine team second with 2,244 points.
Columbia trophy match—Won by 2d infantry, New Jersey national guard; score, 829.
Gould individual rapid fire match—Won by Capt. A. J. McNab, 14th U. S. infantry; score, 149.
Company team match—Won by Co. K, 1st District of Columbia; score, 232.
Interstate regimental team match—Won by 1st District of Columbia; score, 858.
New York company team match—Won by 1st District of Columbia; score, 387.
Expert match—Won by Corp. Moore, U. S. M. C.; score, 74.
Company team match—Won by Co. C, 4th New Jersey; score, 145.
Cruikshank trophy match—Won by 1st District of Columbia; score, 569.
Cavalry team match—Won by 3d New Jersey; score, 453.

McAlpin trophy match—Won by U. S. Marine corps; score, 1,050.

Libbey trophy match—Won by Sergt. Nordstrom, U. S. M. C.; score, 93.

Nevada trophy match—Won by Capt. George H. Emerson, Ohio; score, 143.

Spencer match—Won by Capt. W. H. Richard, Ohio; score, 74 out of possible 75. (World's record on 1,200-yard range.)

Dryden trophy match—Won by Massachusetts national guard team; score, 1,143.

Officers and inspectors' match—Won by Capt. K, K. V. Casey, Pennsylvania; score, 99 out of possible 100.

Hayes medal match—Won by Sergt. Robinson, U. S. cavalry; score, 16 continuous bull's-eyes.

Seagirt championship—Won by Corp. F. Lueders, U. S. cavalry; score, 194.

Meany match—Won by Capt. W. H. Richard, Ohio; score, 23 continuous bull's eyes. (World's record on 500-yard range with 16-inch targets.)

Sadler trophy match—Won by Massachusetts team; score, 1,721.

Veterans' match—Won by Co. C, 4th New Jersey infantry; score, 285.

NEW YORK NATIONAL GUARD TOURNAMENT.

The rifle contests of the New York national guard took place at Peekskill, Sept. 22-24, 1913. Winners in chief events:

Headquarters match—Won by 1st cavalry team; score, 1,490.

First brigade match—Won by 7th regiment; score, 1,558.

Second brigade match—Won by 23d regiment; score, 1,486.

Third brigade match—Won by 1st regiment; score, 1,547.

Fourth brigade match—Won by 74th infantry; score, 1,575.

Governor's match—Won by Ord. Sergt. G. H. Doyle, 71st infantry; score, 87.

State match—Won by 74th infantry; score, 2,694.

Adjutant-General's match—Won by headquarters team of 74th infantry; score, 314.

INTERCOLLEGIATE COMPETITION.

Massachusetts Agricultural college won the ninth annual competition on outdoor ranges for the intercollegiate rifle championship of the United States in June, 1913, with a score of 825 out of a possible 900. Harvard was second with 791 and George Washington university third with 747.

RECORD ON 800-YARD RANGE.

In the Palma match elimination rifle shoot at Camp Perry, O., Aug. 30, 1913, George W. Chesley of New Haven, Conn., made a score of 224 out of a possible 225 on the 800-yard range. This is a world's record.

INTERSCHOLASTIC CHAMPIONSHIP.

Following is the interscholastic rifle shooting championship record in the annual competition for the Astor cup:

Year.	Winner.	Score.
1909—Morris high school, New York, N. Y..		*485
1910—Morris high school, New York, N. Y..		941
1911—Iowa City high school, Iowa City, Ia..		952
1912—Iowa City high school, Iowa City, Ia..		980
1913—Iowa City high school, Iowa City, Ia..		984

*Military count.

INDOOR CHAMPIONSHIP.

The United States championship of the National Rifle Association Indoor league was won by the Warren (Pa.) Rifle club, April 25, 1913. It shot at Warren while its opponent, the Engineers' Rifle and Revolver club of Cleveland, shot in that city. The score was: Warren, 994; Cleveland, 986.

NEW ENGLAND TOURNAMENT.

The ninth annual tournament of the New England Rifle association was held at Wakefield, Mass., July 21-26, 1913. On the first day of the meeting Capt. Stuart W. Wise of the Massachusetts militia broke the world's record for consecutive bull's-eyes, making 103 at 800 yards; his 104th shot was a center. The best previous record was 57, made by J. W. Hessian of Connecticut in 1912. The United

States Marine corps, first team, in the service match broke another world's record by making 558 points at 1,000 yards. The winners and scores in the principal matches follow:

McGregor match, two-men teams, 600 and 1,000 yards—Won by Sergts. P. S. Schofield and C. B. Long, 5th Massachusetts; score, 191.

Hayden trophy match, teams of eight men, 200, 600, 800 and 1,000 yards—Won by Massachusetts Y team; total score, 1,484.

New England interstate match, teams of twelve men, 200, 600 and 1,000 yards and skirmish—Won by Massachusetts; total score, 2,603.

Service match, teams of twelve men, 200. 600 and 1,000 yards and skirmish—Won by United States navy, first team; total score, 2,681; the United States Marine corps, first team, was second with 2,662 points.

Sergt. C. B. Long of Massachusetts made the best general aggregate at the meet with a total score of 372 in seven matches.

BRITISH COMPETITION.

At Bisley Camp, England, July 12, 1913, the empire rifle match was won by the team representing Great Britain with a score of 2,210. Australia was second with 2,120, Canada third with 2,073 and India fourth with 1,958.

At the annual Bisley meeting ending July 26 the king's prize was won by Private W. Hawkins of the 48th highlanders of Canada with a total score of 330. The St. George's challenge vase match was won by Private A. G. Fulton of the Queen's Westminsters with a score of 119. The challenge cup and gold jewel match was taken by Sergt. Ommundsen, the challenge trophy and gold cross medal by Sergt. G. McHaffie and the challenge cup and gold medal match by Private A. T. Rowland.

REVOLVER SHOOTING.

AT CAMP PERRY TOURNAMENTS.

Championship revolver team match, 15 shots deliberate fire at 50 yards, rapid fire 3 strings, 8 seconds—Won by 1st cavalry team, New York; score 916.

National revolver match—Won by J. H. Snook, Columbus, O.; score, 393.

Pan-American revolver match—Won by United States team with score of 2,315; Argentine team second, 2,005; Peru team third, 1,605. P. Hanford of the United States teams made the highest individual score—488.

ICE SKATING.

CHAMPIONSHIP MEETINGS IN 1913.

NATIONAL (INDOOR).

Place and date—Boston, Mass., Feb. 3 and 4.

220 yards—Won by Robert McLean, Chicago; R. L. Wheeler, Montreal, second; A. J. O'Sickey, Cleveland, third. Time, :21½.

440 yards—Won by McLean; W. Gunderson, Chicago, second; O'Sickey, third. Time, :41½.

2 miles—Won by Wheeler; O'Sickey, second; Joseph Hoerning, Cleveland, third. Time, 6:04½.

1 mile—Won by McLean; Wheeler, second; Gunderson, third. Time, 2.55.

½ mile—Won by McLean; Wheeler, second; Gunderson, third. Time, 1:23.

1 mile handicap—Won by McLean; Gunderson, second; O'Sickey, third. Time, 2:49.

440 yards backwards—Won by Hoerning; G. Thompson, Halifax, second; R. Gordon, Montreal, third. Time, :51½.

WESTERN (INDOOR).

Place and date—St. Paul, Minn., Jan. 17, 18 and 19.

¼ mile—Won by Robert McLean, Chicago. Time, :38½.

½ mile—Won by McLean. Time, 1:19.

¾ mile—Won by H. Kaad, Chicago. Time, 2:12½.

1 mile—Won by McLean. Time, 3:06½.

2 miles—Won by McLean. Time, 6:22½.

3 miles—Won by McLean. Time, 9:30.

INTERNATIONAL (INDOOR).

Place and date—Cleveland, O., Jan. 22-23.

1-6 mile—Won by R. Wheeler, Montreal; W. E. Gunderson, Chicago, second; F. J. Robson, Toronto, third. Time, :26½.

½ mile—Won by Robert McLean, Chicago; Wheeler, second; A. J. O'Sickey, Cleveland, third. Time, 1:19⅘.

1 mile—Won by McLean; Jack Walker, Saranac, second; O'Sickey, third. Time, 2:55.

¼ mile—Won by McLean; Robson, second; Gunderson, third. Time, :37⅗.

⅓ mile—Won by Wheeler; Gunderson, second; O'Sickey, third. Time, 1:16.

¾ mile—Won by McLean; Wheeler, second; O'Sickey, third. Time, 2:06.

INTERNATIONAL (OUTDOOR).

Place and date—Saranac Lake, N. Y., Jan. 29-30.

220 yards—Won by R. T. Logan, Montreal; Robert McLean, Chicago, second; John Hoerning, Cleveland, third. Time, :21.

½ mile—Won by McLean; W. Gunderson, Chicago, second; A. J. O'Sickey, Cleveland, third. Time, 1:25.

3 miles—Won by R. L. Wheeler, Montreal; O'Sickey, Cleveland, second; McLean, third. Time, 10:37⅕.

¼ mile—Won by Wheeler; Gunderson, second; Edmund Horton, Saranac Lake, third. Time, :41⅗.

1 mile—Won by McLean; Gunderson, second; O'Sickey, third. Time, 3:03.

220 yard hurdles—Won by Horton; Thompson, second; Gunderson, third. Time, :23⅘.

2 miles—Won by McLean; O'Sickey, second; Gunderson, third. Time, 6:50.

CANADIAN CHAMPIONSHIPS (OUTDOOR).

Place and date—Montreal Feb. 1.

220 yards—Won by H. Jackson, Montreal; McLean, second; O'Sickey, third. Time, :22⅗.

440 yards—Won by R. T. Logan, Montreal; McLean, second; Gunderson, third. Time, :40⅕.

880 yards—Won by McLean; Gunderson, second; O'Sickey, third. Time, 1:27.

1 mile—Won by McLean; O'Sickey, second; Wheeler, third. Time, 3:06⅗.

2 miles—Won by Wheeler; O'Sickey, second; D. Drew, Montreal, third. Time, 7:03.

WESTERN (OUTDOOR).

Place and date—Chicago, Ill., Feb. 9.

⅛ mile—Won by Harry Kaad, Chicago. Time, :22.

¼ mile—Won by Kaad. Time, :44⅘.

1 mile—Won by Leon Greib, Milwaukee. Time, 3:19⅕.

2 miles—Won by Kaad. Time not taken.

INTERNATIONAL (EUROPEAN).

Place and date—Christiania, Norway, Feb. 1-2.

1,500 meters—Won by Oscar Mathiesen, Norway. Time, 2:22.1.

5,000 meters—Won by M. Ippolitow, Russia. Time, 8:43.4.

10,000 meters—Won by Mathiesen; Ippolitow, second. Time, 17:22.6.

STANDING IN SPEED CHAMPIONSHIPS.

Following is the standing by points of the amateur skaters in the international speed contests of 1913:

Skater.	Points.
Robert G. McLean, I. A. C., Chicago	520
R. L. Wheeler, M. A. C., Montreal, Que.	490
Anton J. O'Sickey, Cleveland, O.	260
Walter E. Gunderson, I. A. C., Chicago	200
Fred Logan, Montreal, Que.	60
John Hoerning, Cleveland, O.	30
Fred Robson, Toronto, Ont.	30
W. L. Jackson, Montreal, Que.	30
Edmund Horton, Saranac Lake, N. Y.	10
Lot Roe, Toronto, Ont.	10
R. L. Brunet, Cleveland, O.	10
B. O'Sickey, Cleveland, O.	10
Jack Walker, Saranac Lake, N. Y.	10

International Skating Union of America—President, Allen I. Blanchard, Chicago; first vice-president, James W. Taylor, Montreal, Que.; second vice-president, Cornelius Fellowes, New York, N. Y. Board of control: David J. Slayback, Verona, N. Y.; J. W. Norfalk, Boston, Mass.; Dr. Geo. K. Herman, Chicago; Louis Rubenstein, Montreal, Que.

HORSE RACING.

METROPOLITAN HANDICAP.

Belmont park, New York; distance, 1 mile.

1903—Gunfire, 1:38½; $11,080.
1904—Irish Lad, 1:40; $10,880.
1905—Sysonby and Race King, 1:41⅗ (dead heat); $9,230.
1906—Grapple, 1:39; $10,850.
1907—Glorifier, 1:40⅘; $10,570.
1908—Jack Atkin, 1:38⅘; $9,620.
1909—King James, 1:40; $3,875.
1910—Fashion Plate, 1:37⅘; $5,000.
1911-1912—No race.
1913—Whisk Broom, 1:39; $3,475.

KENTUCKY DERBY.

For 3-year-olds, Louisville, Ky. Distance changed in 1896 from 1½ to 1¼ miles.

1890—Riley, 118lbs, 2:45; $5,460.
1891—Kingman, 122lbs, 2:52½; $4,680.
1892—Azra, 122lbs, 2:41½; $4,230.
1893—Lookout, 122lbs, 2:39¼; $4,090.
1894—Chant, 122lbs, 2:41; $4,000.
1895—Halma, 122lbs, 2:37½.
1896—Ben Brush, 117lbs, 2:07¾.
1897—Typhoon II., 117lbs, 2:12½.
1898—Plaudit, 117lbs, 2:09.
1899—Manuel, 117lbs, 2:12.
1900—Lieut. Gibson, 117lbs, 2:06¼.
1901—His Eminence, 117lbs, 2:07¾.
1902—Alan-a-Dale, 117lbs, 2:08¾; $6,000.
1903—Judge Himes, 117lbs, 2:09; $6,000.
1904—Elwood, 117lbs, 2:08½; $5,000.
1905—Agile, 122lbs, 2:10¾; $6,000.
1906—Sir Huon, 117lbs, 2:08⅘; $5,000.
1907—Pink Star, 117lbs, 2:12⅗; $5,000.
1908—Stone Street, 117lbs, 2:15⅕; $6,000.
1909—Wintergreen, 117lbs, 2:08⅕; $5,000.
1910—Donau, 112lbs, 2:06⅖; $6,000.
1911—Meridian, 117lbs, 2:05⅗; $6,000.
1912—Worth, 117lbs, 2:09⅖; $6,000.
1913—Donerail, 117lbs, 2:04⅘; $6,000.

ENGLISH DERBY.

First race run at Epsom May 4, 1780. In 1784 distance was increased from 1 mile to 1½ miles.

1890—Sain Foin, by Springfield, 2:49¼.
1891—Common, by Isonomy, 2:56⅘.
1892—Sir Hugo, by Wisdom, 2:44.
1893—Isinglass, by Isonomy, 2:43.
1894—Ladas, by Hampton, 2:45⅘.
1895—Sir Visto, by Barcaldine, 2:43⅘.
1896—Persimmon, by St. Simon, 2:42.
1897—Galtee Moore, by Kendal, 2:47.
1898—Jeddah, by Janissary, 2:37.
1899—Flying Fox, by Orme, 2:38⅘.
1900—Diamond Jubilee, by St. Simon, 2:42.
1901—Volodyovski, by Florizel, 2:40⅘.
1902—Ard Patrick, by St. Florian, 2:42⅘.
1903—Rock Sand, by Sain Foin-Roquebrune.
1904—St. Armant, by Frusquin-Loverule, 2:45⅘.
1905—Cicero, by Cyllene, 3:11.
1906—Spearmint, by Carbine, 2:36⅘.
1907—Orby, by Orme, 2:44.
1908—Signorinetta, by Chalereux-Signorina, 2:39⅘.
1909—Minoru, by Cyllene-Mother Siegel, 2:42⅘.
1910—Lemberg, by Cyllene-Galicia, 2:35⅕.
1911—Sunstar, by Sundridge-Norris, 2:36⅘.
1912—Tagalie, by Cyllene-Tagale, 2:38⅘.
1913—Aboyeur, by Desmond-Pawky, 2:37⅗.

GRAND PRIX DE PARIS.

First race run in 1863. Distance about 1 mile 7 furlongs, for 3-year olds. Stake, $40,000.

1901—Cheri, by St. Damien.
1902—Kizil-Kourgan.
1903—Quo Vadis.
1904—Ajax, by Flying Fox-Amie.
1905—Finasseur.
1906—Spearmint.
1907—Sans Souci II.
1908—Northeast (value of race, $72,000).
1909—Verdun, $74,155.
1910—Nuage, $60,000.
1911—As d'Atout, $70,200.
1912—Houli, $73,000.
1913—Bruleur, $72,000.

BEST RUNNING RECORDS.

¼ mile—:21¼. Bob Wade, 4yrs, Butte, Mont., Aug. 20, 1890.

2½ furlongs—:31½, Best Boy, 2yrs, Clifton, N. J., March 12, 1890.

⅜ mile—:34, Red S., aged, 122lbs, Butte, Mont., July 22, 1896.

½ mile—:46, Geraldine, 4yrs, 122lbs, straight course, Morris Park, Aug. 30, 1889.

3½ furlongs—:39⅗, Calisse, 2yrs, Juarez, Mex., Jan. 17, 1911.

4 furlongs—:46⅘, Miss Nett, 2yrs, Belmont park, May 14, 1910.

4½ furlongs—:51⅗, Tanya, 2yrs, 107lbs, Morris Park, straight course, May 12, 1904.

5 furlongs—:56¾, Maid Marian, 4yrs, 111lbs, Morris park, straight course, Oct. 9, 1894.

5½ furlongs—1:02⅘, Plater, 2yrs, 107lbs, Morris park, straight course, Oct. 21, 1902.

6 furlongs, less 170 feet (Futurity course)—1:08, Kingston, aged, 139lbs, Sheepshead Bay, L. I., June 22, 1891.

6 furlongs—1:08, Artful, 2yrs, 130lbs, Morris Park, straight course, Oct. 15, 1904; 1:10⅘, Iron Mask, 5yrs., 127lbs., Louisville, Ky., Sept. 23, 1913.

6½ furlongs—1:16⅗, Lady Vera, 2yrs, 90lbs, Belmont Park, straight track, Oct. 19, 1906.

⅞ mile—1:22, Roseben, 5yrs, 126lbs, Belmont Park, New York, Oct. 16, 1906.

7½ furlongs—1:31⅓, Restigouche, 3yrs, 106lbs, Belmont Park, May 29, 1908.

1 mile—1:35½, against time, Salvator, 4yrs, 110lbs, Monmouth Park, straight course, Aug. 28, 1890; 1:37¼, in race, Kildeer, 4yrs, 91lbs, Monmouth Park, straight course, Aug. 13, 1892; 1:37½, Centre Shot, 3yrs., 105lbs, Los Angeles, Cal., Dec. 22, 1908; 1:37⅘, Dick Welles, 3yrs, 112lbs, Harlem, Aug. 14, 1903; Kiamesha, 3yrs, 104lbs, Belmont Park, Oct. 9, 1905, and Fern L., 3yrs, 80lbs, Seattle, Aug. 15, 1908.

1 mile and 20 yds—1:39, Froglegs, 4yrs., 107lbs., Churchill Downs, Ky., May 13, 1913.

1 mile and 25 yds—1:45½, Ruperta, 3yrs, 107lbs, Latonia, Ky., July 4, 1890.

1 mile and 50 yds.—1:41⅕, Haviland, 6yrs, 98lbs, Washington Park, July 7, 1903.

1 mile and 70 yds.—1:42⅘, Jiminez, 101lbs, Harlem, Sept. 5, 1901; Dalvay, 3yrs, 96lbs, same course, Aug. 31, 1904, and Convent Belle, 4yrs, 94lbs, Seattle, Aug. 24, 1908.

1 mile and 100 yds.—1:44⅘, Grand Opera, 4yrs, 77 lbs, Harlem, Aug. 12, 1903.

1 1-16 miles—1:43⅗, Gretna Green, Fort Erie, Ont., Aug. 28, 1909.

1⅛ miles—1:50, Vox Populi, 3yrs, 110lbs, Los Angeles, Cal., Dec. 19, 1908.

1 3-16 miles—1:57⅘, Scintillant II., 4yrs, 109lbs, Harlem, Sept. 1, 1902.

1¼ miles—2:00, Whisk Broom II., 6yrs., 139lbs., Belmont Park, N. Y., June 28, 1913.

1 mile and 500 yds.—2:10½, Bend Or, 4yrs, 115lbs, Saratoga, July 25, 1892.

1 5-16 miles—2:09⅘, Ballot, 4yrs, 126lbs, Sheepshead Bay, July 1, 1908.

1⅜ miles—2:17⅘, Irish Lad, 4yrs, 126lbs, Sheepshead Bay, June 25, 1904.

1½ miles—2:30¼, Goodrich, 3yrs, 102lbs, Washington Park, July 16, 1898.

1⅝ miles—2:45, Fitz Herbert, 3yrs, 122lbs, Sheepshead Bay, July 13, 1909; 2:45⅘, Africander, 3yrs, 126lbs, Sheepshead Bay, July 7, 1903.

1¾ miles—2:57, Major Daingerfield, 4yrs, 120lbs, Morris Park, Oct. 3, 1903.

1⅞ miles—3:17⅗, Orcagna, Oakland, Cal., March 2, 1909.

2 miles—3:25⅘, Fitz Herbert, 3yrs, 105lbs, Baltimore, Md., Nov. 8, 1909.

2⅛ miles—3:42, Joe Murphy, 4yrs, 99lbs, Harlem, Aug. 30, 1894.

2¼ miles—3:49, Ethelbert, 4yrs, 124lbs, Brighton Beach, Aug. 4, 1900.

2½ miles—4:24½, Kyrat, 3yrs, 88lbs, Newport, Ky., Nov. 8, 1899.

2⅝ miles—4:58½, Ten Broeck, 4yrs, 110lbs, Lexington, Ky., Sept. 16, 1876.

2¾ miles—4:58¾, Hubbard, 4yrs, 107lbs, Saratoga, Aug. 9, 1873.

3 miles—5:19, Mamie Algol, 5yrs, 105lbs, City Park, New Orleans, Feb. 16, 1907.

4 miles—7:10⅘, Sotemia, 119lbs, Louisville, Ky., Oct. 7, 1912.

10 miles—26:18, Mr. Brown, 6yrs, 160lbs, Rancocas, N. J., March 2, 1880.

HEAT RACING.

¼ mile—:21½, :22¼, Sleepy Dick, aged, Kiowa, Kas., Nov. 24, 1888.

½ mile—:47½, :47½, Quirt, 3yrs, 122lbs, Vallejo, Cal., Oct. 5, 1894; :48, :48, :48, Eclipse, Jr., 4yrs, Dallas, Tex., Nov. 1, 1890.

⅝ mile—1:00, 1:00, Kittie Pease, 4yrs, Dallas, Tex., Nov. 2, 1887.

5½ furlongs—1:09, 1:08¼, 1:09, Dock Wick, 4yrs, 100lbs, St. Paul, Minn., Aug. 5, 1891.

¾ mile—1:10½, 1:12¾, Tom Hayes, 4yrs, 107lbs, Morris Park, straight course, June 17, 1892; 1:13¼, 1:13¼, Lizzie S., 5yrs, 118lbs, Louisville, Ky., Sept. 28, 1883.

1 mile—1:41½, 1:41, Guido, 4yrs, 117lbs, Washington Park, July 11, 1891; 1:43, 1:44, 1:47¾, L'Argentine, 6yrs, 115lbs, St. Louis, Mo., June, 1879.

1 1-16 miles—1:50½, 1:48, Slipalong, 5yrs, 115lbs, Washington Park, Sept. 25, 1885.

1⅛ miles—1:56, 1:54¾, What-Er-Lou, 5yrs, 119lbs, San Francisco, Feb. 18, 1899.

1¼ miles—2:10, 2:14, Glenmore, 5yrs, 144lbs, Sheepshead Bay, Sept. 25, 1880.

1½ miles—2:41¾, 2:41, Patsy Duffy, aged, 115lbs, Sacramento, Cal., Sept. 17, 1884.

2 miles—3:33, 3:31¼, Miss Woodford, 4yrs, 107½lbs, Sheepshead Bay, Sept. 20, 1884.

3 miles—5:27½, 5:29½, Norfolk, 4yrs, 100lbs, Sacramento, Cal., Sept. 23, 1865.

4 miles—7:23½, 7:41, Ferida, 4yrs, 105lbs, Sheepshead Bay, Sept. 18, 1880.

LONG-DISTANCE RIDING.

10 miles—20:02, Miss Belle Cook, 5 horses, changing five times, Minneapolis, Minn., Sept. 10, 1882.

20 miles—40:59, Little Cricket, changing horses at will, Minneapolis, Minn., Sept. 7, 1882.

50 miles—1:50:03½, Carl Pugh, ten horses, changing at will, match race, San Bernardino, Cal., July 7, 1883. Woman: 2:27:00, Miss Nellie Burke, Galveston, Tex., Feb. 24, 1884.

60 miles—2:33:00, George Osbaldiston, 11 horses, Newmarket, England, Nov. 5, 1831.

100 miles—4:19:40, George Osbaldiston, 16 horses, as above.

BEST TROTTING RECORDS.

¼ mile—:27, Uhlan, Lexington, Ky., Oct. 2, 1913.

½ mile—:57½, Uhlan (paced by runner), at Cleveland, July 13, 1911; :58¾, Lou Dillon, at Cleveland, Sept. 17, 1904; in race, 1:01, Major Delmar, Memphis, Oct. 23, 1903.

1 mile—1:54½, Uhlan, Lexington, Ky., Oct. 9, 1913 (with running mate); 1:58, Uhlan, Lexington, Ky., Oct. 8, 1912 (without wind shield); 1:58½, Lou Dillon, Memphis, Tenn., Oct. 24, 1903 (with wind shield).

1 mile, yearlings—Best mile by a filly, 2:19¼, Miss Stokes, Lexington, Ky., Sept. 17, 1909. Best mile by a colt, 2:15¾, Airdale, Lexington, Ky., Oct. 2, 1912; race record, 2:26, Adbell, Woodland, Cal., Aug. 27, 1894.

1 mile, 2-year-olds—2:04½, Peter Volo, Lexington, Ky., Oct. 3, 1913. Best mile by a gelding, 2:12¾, Judge Jones, Lexington, Ky., Oct. 3, 1913.

1 mile, 3-year-olds—2:04¾, Colorado E., Lexington, Ky., Oct. 15, 1910.

1 mile, 4-year-olds—2:04¾, Joan, Lexington, Ky., Oct. 13, 1910.

1 mile, 5-year-olds—1:58½, Lou Dillon, Memphis, Tenn., Oct. 24, 1903.

1 mile, fastest two-heat race—2:01¼, 2:01¾, Hamburg Belle, North Randall, O., Aug. 25, 1909. By a stallion, 2:04¼, 2:03¼, The Harvester, at Cleveland, O., Aug. 13, 1910.

1 mile, fastest three heat race—2:04¼, Anvil, and 2:04¼, 2:04¼, Dudie Archdale, Detroit, Mich., Aug. 15, 1913.

1 mile—fastest four heat race—2:03¼ (Billy Burke), 2:06¼, 2:04½, 2:06¾, Dudie Archdale, Columbus, O., Oct. 1, 1912.

1 mile, fastest five-heat race—2:05¾, 2:04½, 2:05, 2:08½, 2:09, Sweet Marie, Lexington, Ky., Oct. 6, 1904 (Tiverton won the first and second heats).

1 mile, fastest six-heat race—2:07¾, 2:08, 2:08½, 2:08¼, 2:09¾, 2:07¼, Manrico, Lexington, Ky., Oct. 8, 1912. (First heat won by Baldy McGregor and second and third by Rythmell.)

1 mile, over half-mile track—2:02¾, Uhlan, Goshen, N. Y., Aug. 24, 1911.

TROTTING TO WAGON.

½ mile—:56¼, Uhlan (paced by runner), Cleveland, O., Aug. 11, 1911.

1 mile—2:00, Lou Dillon, Memphis, Tenn., Oct. 28, 1903, and Uhlan, Cleveland, O., Aug. 8, 1911.

TEAMS TO POLE.

1 mile—2:03¼, Uhlan and Lewis Torrent, Lexington, Ky., Oct. 11, 1912.

TROTTING TO HIGH SULKY.

1 mile—2:05, Lou Dillon, Cleveland, O., Sept. 11, 1903; 2:07, Major Delmar, Memphis, Tenn., Oct. 26, 1904 (nonball-bearing sulky); 2:08¾, Maud S., Glenville, 1885.

BEST PACING RECORDS.

¼ mile—:27½, Dan Patch, Memphis, Tenn., Oct. 27, 1903; :28, Star Pointer, Sept. 28, 1897 (against time, accompanied by a running horse).

½ mile—:56, Dan Patch, Memphis, Tenn., Oct. 27 1903 (against time).

¾ mile—1:26¼, Prince Alert (with wind shield), Empire track, New York, Sept. 23, 1903.

1 mile—1:55, Dan Patch, St. Paul, Sept. 8, 1906 (with dust shield, a runner in front and at one side). 1:58½, Minor Heir (without wind shield), Indianapolis, Ind., Sept. 16, 1910; fastest in competition, 1:59, by Minor Heir, at Indianapolis, Ind., Sept. 12, 1910.

1 mile, yearlings—2:20¾, Belle Acton, Lyons, Neb., Oct. 14, 1892.

1 mile, 2-year-olds—2:07¾, Directly, Galesburg, Ill., Sept. 20, 1894.

1 mile, 3-year-olds—2:05, William, Peoria, Ill., Aug. 16, 1913.

1 mile, 4 year olds—2:02¾, Braden Direct, Lexington, Ky., Oct. 8, 1912; race record, 2:04½, Searchlight, Dubuque, Iowa, Aug. 23, 1898; Be Sure, Terre Haute, Ind., Aug. 9, 1895, and Ananias, Terre Haute, Ind., Sept. 29, 1897.

1 mile, 5-year-olds—2:02¼, Braden Direct, Hartford, Conn., Sept. 1, 1913.

1 mile, fastest two-heat race—2:01½, 2:01, Minor Heir, Terre Haute, Ind., July 17, 1908.

1 mile, fastest three-heat race—2:00¾, 2:02¼, 2:03½, Bolivar, Readville, Mass., Aug. 25, 1906.

1 mile fastest four-heat race—2:03, 2:03, 2:03½, 2:02¼ (second heat won by Earl, Jr.), Evelyn W., Columbus, O., Aug. 22, 1911; fastest fourth heat in a race, 2:02¼, as above.

1 mile fastest five-heat race—2:01½, 2:03½, 2:01½, 2:03½, 2:04¾, Evelyn W. and Earl, Jr., Columbus, O., Oct. 3, 1912. (Evelyn W. won the first, third and fourth heats.)

1 mile, fastest six-heat race—2:06¼, 2:05¾, 2:04¼, 2:05¾, 2:08, 2:04¼, Babe and Ty Cobb, Columbus, O., Oct. 4, 1912. (Babe won third, fifth and sixth heats.)

1 mile, fastest seven-heat race—2:00½, 2:02, 2:05¾, 2:08½, 2:06½, 2:06¼, 2:07½ (first two by Minor Heir, third by The Eel, fourth by Copa de Oro and last three by Jersey B.), Lexington, Ky., Oct. 6, 1908.

1 mile, half-mile track—2:04¼, Joe Patchen, Boston, Mass., Oct. 28, 1896.

PACING TO WAGON.

1 mile—1:57¼, Dan Patch, Memphis, Tenn., Oct. 27, 1903; best three heats in race, 2:06¼, 2:04½, 2:06¼. Angus Pointer, Memphis, Tenn., Oct. 20, 1904 (Baron Grattan won first heat).

TEAMS TO POLE.

¼ mile—:29¾, Hontas Crooke and Prince Direct, Cleveland, O., July 22, 1905.

½ mile—1:00¾, Prince Direct and Morning Star, Memphis, Tenn., Oct. 21, 1904.

1 mile—2:02, Minor Heir and George Gano, Columbus, O., Oct. 1, 1912.

WRESTLING.

ZBYSZKO VS. CUTLER.

Stanislaus Zbyszko defeated Charley Cutler in a match for the heavy weight championship of the world at the Globe theater, Chicago, Jan. 13, 1913, in straight falls. He won the first fall in 33:00 with a crotch hold and bar arm, and the second in 20:15 with a body scissors and arm lock.

GOTCH VS. LURICH.

Frank Gotch, champion wrestler of the world, won a match with George Lurich of Russia in Kansas City, Mo., April 1, 1913, in straight falls. He took the first fall in 18:10 with an arm and toe hold and the second with a double nelson in 5:35. The match took place in Convention hall and was witnessed by 17,000 persons.

ZBYSZKO VS. LE MARIN.

Stanislaus Zbyszko, Pole, defeated Le Marin, Belgian, in a wrestling match at the Coliseum, Chicago, April 23, 1913, in straight falls, by the use of the toe hold and the crotch and toe hold. The time was 53:00 for the first fall and 39:30 for the second. All bets were declared off before the contest began.

COLLEGE WRESTLING.

Cornell university won the intercollegiate wrestling championship in the finals at Ithaca, N. Y., March 22, with a total of 27 points. Princeton was second with 19, Lehigh third with 14, Columbia fourth with 10 and Pennsylvania fifth with 7 points. Gile of Princeton won in the heavy weight class, defeating Hellman of Pennsylvania with bar and body hold in 5:34.

NATIONAL AMATEUR CHAMPIONSHIPS.

The national amateur wrestling championships were decided in New York city May 5, 1913. In the heavy weight class Jack Gunderson of the Norwegian-American Athletic club, New York, N. Y., won over Karl Langer of the German-American Athletic club of the same city. The winners in other classes were:

175-pound class—Joseph Varga.
158-pound class—J. Waldo Smith.
145-pound class—Carl Johnson.
135-pound class—A. Z. Anderson.
125-pound class—V. V. Vosen.

SKI JUMPING.

NATIONAL TOURNAMENT.

The ninth annual national tournament of the American Ski association took place at Ironwood, Mich., Feb. 15 and 16, 1913. In the professional class Ragnar Omtvedt of the Norge Ski club, Chicago, was the winner, making 345⅔ points with jumps of 158 and 154 feet, both exceeding the American record of 152 feet held by Anders Haugen and Sigurd Hansen. He also made a standing jump without a fall of 169 feet, making a new world's record. The best previous mark was 156 feet made by Harold Smith of Norway. It is to be noted that form counts in the championship competition while it does not figure in the long standing jump, the only thing required being that the jumper shall keep his feet. John Jobe of Ironwood was the winner in the amateur class. In the cross country run Einar Lund won by making the eight-mile distance in 1 hour 13 minutes.

SCORE OF PROFESSIONALS.

	1st.	2d.	Points.
Ragnar Omtvedt, Chicago	158	154	345⅔
A. Haugen, Chippewa Falls, Wis.	144	149	325
Axel Hendrickson, Virginia, Minn.	152	145	325
John Evenson, Duluth, Minn.	148	140	316⅔
Ben Lodgard, Ironwood, Mich.	141	142	315
Tollef Hemestvedt, Arcadia	134	144	309⅓
Sigurd Hansen, Fergus Falls, Minn.	132	145	308⅔
Ottar Landwick, Stoughton, Wis.	138	137	306
Einar Lund, Chippewa Falls, Wis.	134	142	305
August Norby, Superior, Wis.	140	135	305
Carl E. Eck, Redwing, Minn.	138	134	303
John Bratlund, Ironwood, Mich.	135	133	295

SCORE OF AMATEURS.

John Jobe, Ironwood, Mich.	307⅔
Ingolf Sands, Stoughton, Wis.	296
John Fieldseth, Ironwood, Mich.	278⅓
Sigurd Gustafson, Ironwood, Mich.	278⅔
John Guttormsen, Beloit, Wis.	277⅔
Albert Fortl, Virginia, Minn.	276⅔
Ludwig Holby, Glenwood, Minn.	274
Alf Ern, Ironwood, Mich.	273
Arne Sletner, Chicago	272
Einar Bakke, Beloit, Wis.	271
Evar Gustafson, Ironwood, Mich.	269⅔
Henry Fieldseth, Ironwood, Mich.	268

PUGILISM.

Following is a list of the most noteworthy ring battles in the United States since 1882, the heavy weight championship contests being the first given.

Date.	Winner	Loser.	Place.	Rounds
Feb. 7, 1882	John L. Sullivan	Paddy Ryan	Mississippi City	9
July 8, 1889	John L Sullivan	Jake Kilrain	Richburg, Miss.	75
Jan. 14, 1891	Bob Fitzsimmons	Jack Dempsey	New Orleans, La	13
Sept. 7, 1892	James J Corbett	John L. Sullivan	New Orleans, La	21
Jan. 25, 1896	James J. Corbett	Charles Mitchell	Jacksonville, Fla	3
Feb. 21, 1896	Bob Fitzsimmons	Peter Maher	Mexico	1
March 17, 1897	Bob Fitzsimmons	James J Corbett	Carson City, Nev	14
June 9, 1899	James J. Jeffries	Bob Fitzsimmons	Coney Island, N. Y.	11
Nov. 3, 1899	James J. Jeffries	Thomas J Sharkey	Coney Island, N. Y.	25
Nov. 16, 1901	James J. Jeffries	Gus Ruhlin	San Francisco, Cal	5
July 25, 1902	James J. Jeffries	Bob Fitzsimmons	San Francisco, Cal	8
Aug. 14, 1903	James J. Jeffries	James J. Corbett	San Francisco, Cal	10
Aug. 26, 1904	James J. Jeffries	Jack Monroe	San Francisco, Cal	2
July 4, 1907	Tommy Burns	Bill Squires	San Francisco, Cal	1
July 17, 1907	Jack Johnson	Bob Fitzsimmons	Philadelphia, Pa	2
Feb. 10, 1908	Tommy Burns	Jack Palmer	London, England	4
Dec 26, 1908	Jack Johnson	Tommy Burns	Sydney, N S W.	14
March 26, 1909	Stanley Ketchel	Jack O'Brien	New York, N Y	10
July 5, 1909	Stanley Ketchel	Billy Papke	San Francisco, Cal	20
Sept. 9, 1909	Jack Johnson	Al Kaufman	San Francisco, Cal	10
Oct. 16, 1909	Jack Johnson	Stanley Ketchel	San Francisco, Cal	12
July 4 1910	Jack Johnson	James J. Jeffries	Reno, Nev	15
Sept. 5, 1910	Al Kaufman	Bill Lang	Philadelphia, Pa	6
Feb. 21, 1911	Sam Langford	Bill Lang	London, England	6
Aug 9, 1911	Bill Lang	Bill Squires	Sydney, N S. W	5
Sept 15, 1911	Jim Flynn	Carl Morris	New York, N. Y	10
April 8, 1912	Sam Langford	Sam McVey	Sydney, N S W	20
July4, 1912	Jack Johnson	Jim Flynn	Las Vegas, N. M	9
Jan. 1, 1913	Luther McCarty	Al Palzer	Los Angeles, Cal	18
April 16, 1913	Luther McCarty	Jim Flynn	Philadelphia, Pa.	6
May 24, 1913	Arthur Pelkey	*Luther McCarty	Calgary, Man	1
April 30, 1901	Terry McGovern	Oscar Gardner	San Francisco, Cal.	4
May 31, 1901	Terry McGovern	Aurelio Herrera	San Francisco, Cal	5
Nov. 28, 1901	Young Corbett	Terry McGovern	Hartford, Conn.	2
Feb. 22, 1902	Terry McGovern	Dave Sullivan	Louisville, Ky.	15
May 23, 1902	Young Corbett	Kid Broad	Denver, Col	10
March 31, 1903	Young Corbett	Terry McGovern	San Francisco, Cal	11
July 4, 1903	George Gardner	Jack Root	Buffalo, N. Y.	12
Nov. 25, 1903	Bob Fitzsimmons	George Gardner	San Francisco, Cal	20
Feb. 29, 1904	Young Corbett	Dave Sullivan	San Francisco, Cal	11
March 25, 1904	Jimmy Britt	Young Corbett	San Francisco, Cal	20
July 29, 1904	Battling Nelson	Eddie Hanlon	San Francisco, Cal	19
Feb. 28, 1905	Battling Nelson	Young Corbett	San Francisco, Cal	9
Sept. 9, 1905	Battling Nelson	Jimmy Britt	Colma, Cal	18
Sept. 3, 1906	Joe Gans	Battling Nelson	Goldfield, Nev.	42
Jan. 1, 1907	Joe Gans	Kid Herman	Tononah, Nev	8
July 31, 1907	Jimmy Britt	Battling Nelson	San Francisco, Cal	20
Sept. 9, 1907	Joe Gans	Jimmy Britt	San Francisco, Cal	5
Feb 4, 1908	Rudolph Unholz	Battling Nelson	Los Angeles, Cal	10
April 11, 1908	Packey McFarland	Jimmy Britt	San Francisco, Cal	6
June 4, 1908	Stanley Ketchel	Billy Papke	Milwaukee, Wis	10
July 4, 1908	Battling Nelson	Joe Gans	San Francisco Cal	17
Sept. 7, 1908	Billy Papke	Stanley Ketchel	Los Angeles, Cal	12
Sept. 9, 1908	Battling Nelson	Joe Gans	San Francisco, Cal.	21
Jan. 15, 1909	Packey McFarland	Dick Hyland	San Francisco, Cal	10
Feb. 19, 1909	Jem Driscoll	Abe Attell	New York N Y	10
Feb 22, 1909	Johnny Summers	Jimmy Britt	London, England	20
May 29, 1909	Battling Nelson	Dick Hyland	San Francisco, Cal	23
Feb. 22, 1910	Adolph Wolgast	Battling Nelson	San Francisco Cal	40
Feb. 26, 1911	Johnny Coulon	Frankie Conley	New Orleans, La	20
July 4, 1911	Ad Wolgast	Owen Moran	San Francisco, Cal	13
Sept 20, 1911	Matt Wells	Abe Attell	New York, N Y	10
Jan 11, 1912	Johnny Coulon	George Kitson	South Bend, Ind	3
Jan. 22, 1912	Johnny Coulon	Harry Forbes	Kenosha, Wis	3
Feb. 3, 1912	Johnny Coulon	Frank Conley	Los Angeles, Cal	20
Feb. 14, 1912	Packey McFarland	Eddie Murphy	South Bend, Ind	10
Feb. 18, 1912	Johnny Coulon	Frankie Burns	New Orleans, La	20
Feb 22 1912	Johnny Kilbane	Abe Attell	Los Angeles, Cal	20
March 15, 1912	Packey McFarland	Kid Burns	Kenosha, Wis	8
April 26 1912	Packey McFarland	Matt Wells	New York, N Y	10
July 4 1912	Ad Wolgast	Joe Rivers	Los Angeles, Cal	13
Oct. 23, 1913	Billy Papke	G. Carpentier	Paris, France	17
March 7, 1913	Packey McFarland	Jack Britton	New York, N Y	10
April 19, 1913	T Murphy	Ad Wolgast	San Francisco, Cal	20
July 4, 1913	Willie Ritchie	Joe Rivers	San Francisco, Cal	11

*Luther McCarty died in the ring from dislocation of the neck caused by a blow on the jaw

SKAT.

George Palmer of Detroit, Mich, won the championship and a prize of $500 at the annual tournament of the North American Skat league held at Cedar Point, O, June 21 22, 1913 He took 29 out of 32 games The 1914 tournament will be held in Milwaukee, Wis.

BASKET BALL.

The Cornell team of Armour Square, Chicago, won the national basket ball championship at th international games in Grant park, Chicago, July 4, 1913, by defeating the Quincy Athletic association team of Boston in the final game by the score of 27 to 2.

RACQUETS.

NATIONAL TOURNAMENT.

Lawrence Waterbury of New York won the national racquet tournament in New York city Feb. 18-22, 1913, by defeating Harold F. McCormick of Chicago in the final match by scores of 7-15, 15-12, 15-8, 15-11. Championship record:

1901—Quincy A. Shaw, Boston.
1902—C. H. Mackay, New York.
1903—Payne Whitney, New York.
1904—George A. Brooke, Philadelphia.
1905—Lawrence Waterbury, New York.
1906—Percy D. Haughton, Boston.
1907—Reginald R. Fincke, New York.
1908—Quincy A. Shaw, Boston.
1909—Harold F. McCormick, Chicago.
1910—Quincy A. Shaw, Boston.
1911—Reginald R. Fincke, New York.
1912—Reginald R. Fincke, New York.
1913—Lawrence Waterbury, New York.

GOLD RACQUET CHAMPIONSHIP.

Harold F. McCormick of the University club, Chicago, won the gold racquet championship of the United States at Tuxedo Park, N. Y., Feb. 9-12, 1913, defeating Ernest Greenshields, Jr., of the Tennis and Racquet club of Montreal, three games to one in the final round. J. Gordon Douglas was the winner in 1912.

DOUBLES CHAMPIONSHIP.

The national amateur racquet doubles championship was won by Percy D. Haughton and H. D. Scott of Boston, Jan. 26, 1913, in the final match of the annual tournament. They defeated the title holders, Quincy A. Shaw and George R. Fearing, Jr., also of Boston, by a score of 15-11, 8-15, 15-9, 18-13, 15-12.

PROFESSIONAL CHAMPIONSHIP.

"Jock" Soutar of Philadelphia won the professional racquets championship of the world and a stake of $2,500 in Philadelphia, Pa., May 3, 1913, by defeating Charles Williams of England, the title holder. The score was 15-2, 15-8, 15-4 and 15-3. It was the second half of the match, the first having been played in London, April 5, when Williams won four games to two, but had an advantage of only ten aces. To win the championship Soutar had to take four straight games and score more aces than were made by his rival. This he succeeded in doing.

CHESS.

AMERICAN MASTERS' TOURNAMENT.

The second American National Chess Masters' tournament was held in the rooms of the Manhattan Chess club, New York, N. Y., Jan. 19-Feb. 5, 1913. Jose R. Capablanca of Havana, Cuba, won the championship with a score of eleven games won and two lost. The complete score follows:

Players.	Won.	Lost.	Players.	Won.	Lost.
Capablanca	11	2	Tenenwurzel	5½	7½
Marshall	10½	2½	Whitaker	5½	7½
Jaffe	9½	3½	Rubinstein	4½	8½
Janowski	9	4	Kline	4½	8½
Chajes	8	5	Morrison	4	9
Stapfer	8	5	Liebenstein	2½	10½
Kupchik	6½	6½	Zapoleon	2	11

QUADRANGULAR TOURNAMENT.

Frank J. Marshall won a quadrangular masters' chess tournament held in Newark, N. J., and ending Sept. 13, 1913. Final standing:

Players.	Won.	Lost.	Players.	Won.	Lost.
Frank J. Marshall	5	1	Oscar Chajes	2½	3½
Oldrich Duras	4	2	Charles Jaffe	½	5½

OTHER TOURNAMENTS IN 1913.

F. J. Marshall of Brooklyn took first place in a chess tournament held in Havana, Cuba, Feb. 15-March 6.

Jose R. Capablanca won first place in a second masters' tournament held in New York, N. Y., in July.

In an international chess tournament held at Scheveningen, Holland, in August, the first prize was won by A. A. Alechine of Moscow, Russia.

B. J. Jefferson of Memphis, Tenn., won the championship of the Western Chess association in Chicago, Ill., Aug. 24. E. P. Elliott of Minneapolis was second.

The intercollegiate chess championship of the west was won by the University of Chicago team in January.

WHIST.

TROPHY WINNERS SINCE 1901.

(In American Whist league.)

Trophy.	Winning club.
1901—A. W. L. Challenge	Minneapolis
Hamilton	Chicago
Minneapolis	Ypsilanti
1902—A. W. L. Challenge	Philadelphia
Hamilton	Cleveland
Minneapolis	Milwaukee
Brooklyn	New York
1903—A. W. L. Challenge	Baltimore
Hamilton	Cleveland
Minneapolis	Grand Rapids
Brooklyn	Michigan
1904—A. W. L. Challenge	Minneapolis and St. Paul
Hamilton	Racine, Wis.
Minneapolis	Scranton, Pa.
Brooklyn	Minnesota
1905—Hamilton	Chicago
Minneapolis	Chicago
Brooklyn	Chicago
1906—Hamilton	Brookline, Mass.
Minneapolis	Providence, R. I.
Brooklyn	New England Whist league
1907—Hamilton	Grand Rapids
Minneapolis	Chicago
Brooklyn	New England
1908—Hamilton	Boston
Minneapolis	Albany
Brooklyn	New England Whist league
1909—Hamilton	Boston
Minneapolis	Boston
Brooklyn	New England Whist league
1910—Hamilton	Chicago Whist club
Minneapolis	Knickerbocker club, New York
Brooklyn	New England Whist league
1911—Hamilton	Scranton
Minneapolis	Detroit
Brooklyn	Atlantic Whist association.
A. W. L. Challenge	Grand Rapids
1912—Hamilton	New York Bridge Whist club
Minneapolis	Huguenot Whist club, New York
Associate Members	Cincinnati
1913—Hamilton	Chicago Whist club
Minneapolis	Knickerbocker club, New York
Associate members	Mrs. E. E. Davidson and J. C. Beardslee
Manhattan	Mrs. C. M. Stewart and J. W. Weston

Officers of American Whist League—President, C. L. Patton, New York, N. Y.; vice-president, A. J. Mouatt, Chicago, Ill.; recording secretary, J. C. Beardslee, Cleveland, O.; corresponding secretary, M. P. Kaiser, St. Louis, Mo.; treasurer, E. G. Comstock, Milwaukee, Wis.

BICYCLING.

The bicycle race around France, a distance of 3,367 miles, run in fifteen stages June 29 to July 27, 1913, was won by M. Theiss. He made the whole distance in 197 hours 54 minutes.

Joe Fogler of Brooklyn and Goullet of Australia won a six-day bicycle race in Paris, France, ending Jan. 19, 1913, with a record of 4,467½ kilometers (approximately 2,680 miles) in 144 hours.

ROLLER SKATING.

AMERICAN RECORDS.

100 yards—:10, Henry Becker, Chicago, 1910.
¼ mile—:36, Fred Tyrrell, Chicago, 1909.
½ mile—1:15, Ollie Moore, Chicago, 1908.
1 mile—2:28, Clarence Hamilton, Chicago, 1912.
2 miles—5:04⅘, John Flannery, Chicago, 1908.
3 miles—7:55⅗, Ollie Moore, Chicago, 1908.
10 miles—33:20, L. Bierwirth, San Francisco, 1909.

ATHLETICS.

NATIONAL A. A. U. CHAMPIONSHIPS.

The annual championship contests of the Amateur Athletic Union of the United States took place in Chicago, Ill., July 4-5, 1913. The junior championships were taken by the Chicago Athletic association with a total of 42 points. The Irish-American Athletic club of New York was second with 22 points and the New York Athletic club third with 19 points. The only new junior A. A. U. record established was made by Arthur Kohler of the University of Michigan track team, who threw the discus 129 feet 3 inches. The senior championships were taken by the Irish-American Athletic club of New York with a total of 44 points. Three senior records fell, as will appear from the appended summary. Table of points:

N. Y. Irish-A. A. C.	44	Univ. of S. Cal.	8
Chgo. Ath. Ass'n.	27	Mohawk A. C.	5
Boston A. A.	21	Kansas City A. C.	2
New York A. C.	18	Long Island A. C.	1
Illinois A. C.	13	Paterson (N. J.) A. C.	1
Missouri A. C.	11	Unattached	1
Springfield H. S.	10		

Summary of senior contests:

100-yard dash—Won by Howard Drew, Springfield (Mass.) H. S.; C. A. Reller, Missouri A. C., second; Alva T. Meyers, Irish-American A. C., third. Time, :10⅗.

220-yard dash—Won by Howard Drew, Springfield H. S.; C. C. Cooke, Chicago A. A., second; J. M. Rosenberger, Irish-American A. C., third. Time, :22⅘.

440-yard run—Won by C. B. Haff, Chicago A. A.; T. J. Halpin, Boston A. C., second; C. B. Cortis, Chicago A. A., third. Time, :51⅗.

880-yard run—Won by H. Barker, New York A. C.; C. De Ernchy, New York A. C., second; Melvin Sheppard, Irish-American A. C., third. Time, 2:00⅖.

1-mile run—Won by N. S. Taber, Boston A. C.; J. A. Powers, Boston A. C., second; A. R. Kiviat, New York A. C., third. Time, 4:26⅗.

3-mile walk—Won by Edward Kenz, Mohawk (N. Y.) A. C.; T. Neundorfer, New York A. C., second; F. Plant, Long Island A. C., third. Time, 23:19⅕.

5-mile run—Won by Hannes Kolehmainen, New York A. C.; Joe Ray, Illinois A. C., second; Gaston Strobino, Paterson, N. J., third. Time, 26:10⅗.

120-yard high hurdles—Won by F. Kelly, Southern California; J. P. Nicholson, Missouri A. C., second; E. Reidel, Chicago A. A., third. Time, :16⅗.

220-yard low hurdles—Won by Charles Cory, Chicago A. A.; F. Kelly, Southern California, second; J. A. High, Boston A. C., third. Time, :25⅗.

Running broad jump—Won by Phil Stiles, Chicago A. A.; J. Whitney, New York A. C., second; Platt Adams, New York A. C., third. Distance made by Stiles, 22 feet ¾ inch.

Running high jump—Won by Alva Richards, Illinois A. C.; H. Barwise, Boston A. C., second; E. Ericson, unattached, third. Height made by Richards, 6 feet 1⅝ inches.

Running hop, step and jump—Won by Dan Ahearn, Illinois A. C.; Tim Ahearn, Irish-American A. C., second; M. Fahey, Irish-American A. C., third. Distance made by D. Ahearn, 50 feet (new A. A. U. record).

Pole vault—Won by S. B. Waggoner, Missouri A. C.; F. Murphy, Chicago A. A., second; J. Gold, Chicago A. A., third. Height made by Waggoner, 13 feet (new A. A. U. record).

Hammer throw—Won by F. Ryan, Irish-American A. C.; Matt McGrath, Irish-American A. C. second; Lee Talbot, Kansas City A. C., third. Distance thrown by Ryan, 177 feet 7¾ inches (new A. A. U. record).

Discus throw—Won by E. Millar, Irish-American A. C.; A. W. Mucks, Chicago A. A., second; L. A. Whitney, Boston A. C., third. Distance thrown by Millar, 132 feet 7⅛ inches.

Javelin throw—Won by E. Brodd, Irish-American A. C.; Platt Adams, New York A. C., second; F. Lund, Irish-American A. C., third. Distance thrown by Brodd, 161 feet 3 inches.

Shot put—Won by L. A. Whitney, Boston A. C.; Pat McDonald, Irish-American A. C., second; Lee Talbot, Kansas City A. C., third. Distance put by Whitney, 46 feet 2⅝ inches.

Throwing 56-lb. weight—Won by Matt McGrath, New York A. C.; Pat McDonald, Irish-American A. C., second; P. Ryan, Irish-American A. C., third. Distance thrown by McGrath, 38 feet 5½ inches.

INDOOR CHAMPIONSHIPS.

NATIONAL.

The Amateur Athletic union's senior indoor championship tournament took place in Madison Square garden, New York, N. Y., March 6, 1913. Summary:

70-yard hurdle—Won by James I. Wendell, Wesleyan university. Time, :09⅗.

75-yard dash—Won by Howard P. Drew, Springfield (Mass.) high school. Time, :07⅗.

300-yard run—Won by Fred Burns, Boston Athletic association. Time, :33⅕.

600-yard run—Won by Abel R. Kiviat, Irish-American Athletic club, New York, N. Y. Time, 1:15⅕.

1,000-yard run—Won by Abel R. Kiviat, I.-A. A. C., New York, N. Y. Time, 2:15⅗.

2-mile run—Won by William J. Kramer, Long Island Athletic club. Time, 9:19⅕.

2-mile walk—Won by R. B. Gifford, McCaddin Lyceum. Time, 14:32⅗.

Running high jump—Won by J. O. Johnstone, Harvard; 6 feet 1 inch.

Standing broad jump—Won by Platt Adams, New York Athletic club; 10 feet 9 inches.

Standing high jump—Won by Platt Adams, New York Athletic club; 5 feet 2 inches.

Pole vault for distance—Won by Platt Adams, N. Y. A. C.; 27 feet 9⅝ inches.

24-pound shot put—Won by Patrick J. McDonald, Irish-American Athletic club, New York, N. Y.; 39 feet 3¼ inches (new world's record).

Throwing 56 pound weight for height—Won by P. J. McDonald, I.-A. A. C., New York, N. Y.; 15 feet 7 inches.

ALL AROUND CHAMPIONSHIP.

Fred C. Thompson of Los Angeles won the all around athletic championship of America at the meet held in Los Angeles, Cal., July 12, 1913, under the auspices of the National Amateur Athletic union, making a total of 7,411½ points. Charles Morris of the Olympic Athletic club of San Francisco, Cal., was second with 6,082 and E. T. Campbell of the Leland Stanford, Jr., university was third with 5,921 points. Record of champions and points:

1884—W. R. Thompson, Montreal	5,304
1885—M. W. Ford, New York	5,045
1886—M. W. Ford, New York	5,899
1887—A. A. Jordan, New York	5,236
1888—M. W. Ford, New York	5,161
1889—A. A. Jordan, New York	5,520
1890—A. A. Jordan, New York	5,358
1891—A. A. Jordan, New York	6,189
1892—E. W. Goff, New York	5,232
1893—E. W. Goff, New York	4,860
1894—E. W. Goff, New York	5,748
1895—J. Cosgrave, Albany	4,406½
1896—L. P. Sheldon, Yale	5,380
1897—E. H. Clark, Boston	6,244½
1898—E. C. White, New York	5,243
1899—J. F. Powers, Worcester	6,203
1900—Harry Gill, Toronto	6,360½
1901—A. B. Gunn, Buffalo	5,739
1902—A. B. Gunn, Buffalo	6,260⅛
1903—E. H. Clark, Boston	6,318¼
1904—Thomas F. Kieley, Ireland	6,086
1905—M. J. Sheridan, New York	6,820½
1906—Thomas F. Kieley, Ireland	6,274
1907—Martin J. Sheridan, New York	7,130½
1908—J. L. Bredemus, Princeton	5,809
1909—Martin J. Sheridan, New York	7,385
1910—F. C. Thompson, Los Angeles	6,991
1911—F. C. Thompson, Los Angeles	6,709
1912—James Thorpe, Carlisle	7,476
1913—F. C. Thompson, Los Angeles	7,411½

Mr. Thompson, then a student in the Princeton theological seminary, made a record of 7,499 points in the all around championships at Princeton, N. J., June 5, 1913, making a world's record.

FRANKLIN FIELD RELAY RACES.

The national championship relay races for colleges were run on Franklin field, Philadelphia, April 26, 1913, with the following results:

1-mile college championship of America—Won by Illinois (Henderson, Hunter, Sanders, Cortis); Pennsylvania, second; Dartmouth, third; Chicago, fourth. Time, 3:22⅘.

2-mile college championship—Won by Michigan (Brown, Jansen, Haimbaugh, Hoff); Dartmouth, second; Pennsylvania, third; Virginia, fourth. Time, 8:00 (new record).

4-mile college championship—Won by Pennsylvania (Gutherz, Laugner, McCurdy, Madeira); Princeton, second; Ohio State, third; Pennsylvania State, fourth; Northwestern, fifth. Time, 18:08⅗.

The 1-mile freshman relay race was won by Pennsylvania in 3:25⅘, the mile preparatory school relay race by Phillips Exeter in 3:26⅕, and the mile high school relay race by Franklin and Marshall in 3:32.

EASTERN INTERCOLLEGIATE CHAMPIONSHIPS.

(Harvard stadium, May 30-31, 1913.)

100-yard dash—Patterson, Pennsylvania; :09⅘.
220-yard dash—Lippincott, Pennsylvania; :21⅕.
440-yard run—Haff, Michigan; :48⅘.
880-yard run—Brown, Yale; 1:55⅕.
1-mile run—Jones, Cornell; 4:14⅘.
2-mile run—McCurdy, Pennsylvania; 9:45⅗.
120-yard hurdles—Wendell, Wesleyan; :15⅗.
220-yard hurdles—Wendell, Wesleyan; :28⅗.
High jump—Beeson, California, and Camp, Harvard; 6 ft. ⅛ in.
Broad jump—Mercer, Pennsylvania; 23 ft. 3⅞ in.
Pole vault—Fiske, Princeton; 12 ft. 4 in.
16-lb. hammer—Cable, Harvard; 156 ft.
16-lb. shot—Whitnet, Dartmouth; 47 ft. 2⅝ in.

Summary of points—Pennsylvania, 24; Harvard, 21½; Michigan, 19; Cornell, 17½; Dartmouth, 14½; Yale, 10; California, 10; Wesleyan, 10; Princeton, 6; Columbia, 4; Brown, 3; Penn State, 1; Syracuse, 1.

EASTERN INTERCOLLEGIATE RECORDS.

(Made in annual championship meets.)

100-yard dash—:09⅘, B. J. Wefers, Georgetown, 1896; R. C. Craig, Michigan, 1911, and J. E. Patterson, Pennsylvania, 1913.
220-yard dash—:21⅕, R. C. Craig, Michigan, 1910 and 1911, and Don Lippincott, Pennsylvania, 1913.
440-yard run—:48, C. D. Reidpath, Syracuse, 1912.
880-yard run—1:53⅘, J. P. Jones, Cornell, 1912.
1-mile run—4:14⅘, J. P. Jones, Cornell, 1913 (world's amateur record).
2-mile run—9:24⅗, P. R. Withington, Harvard, 1912.
120-yard hurdles—:15⅕, Garrels, Michigan, 1907, and Shaw, Dartmouth, 1908.
220-yard hurdles—:23⅗, A. C. Kraenzlein, Pennsylvania, 1898, and J. Wendell, Wesleyan, 1913.
High jump—6 ft. 3 in., J. D. Winsor, Jr., Pennsylvania, 1897.
Broad jump—24 ft. 4½ in., A. C. Kraenzlein, Pennsylvania, 1899.
Pole vault—13 ft. 1 in., Robert Gardner, Yale, 1912 (world's record).
16-lb. hammer—173 ft. 6 in., Lee J. Talbot, Penn State, 1910.
16-lb. shot—48 ft. 10¾ in., R. L. Beatty, Columbia, 1912.
1-mile walk—6:45⅗, W. B. Fetterman, Jr., Pennsylvania, 1898.

WESTERN INTERCOLLEGIATE CHAMPIONSHIPS.

Madison, Wis., June 7, 1913.

100-yard dash—Hammitt, Illinois; :10⅕.
220-yard dash—Parker, Chicago; :22⅗.
440-yard run—Hunter, Illinois; :51.
880-yard run—East, Purdue; 2:03⅗.
1-mile run—Wood, California; 4:34⅗.
2-mile run—Kraft, Northwestern; 9:58⅗.
120-yard high hurdles—Case, Illinois; :15⅗.
220-yard low hurdles—Kuh, Chicago; :25⅗.
Running high jump—Wahl, Wisconsin, and Ellis, Wabash; 5 ft. 8½ in.
Running broad jump—Lambert, Minnesota; 22 ft. 3 in.
Pole vault—Gold, Wisconsin; 12 ft. 8¼ in.
Discus throw—Butt, Illinois; 127 ft. 9 in.
Shot put—Thatcher, Missouri; 41 ft. 8 in.
Hammer throw—Shattuck, California; 160 ft. 4 in.
1-mile relay—Illinois; 3:27⅕.

Summary of points: Illinois, 47½; Wisconsin, 28½; Chicago, 17½; California, 15; Missouri, 14½; Northwestern, 9½; Minnesota, 8; Purdue, 8; Ohio State, 4; Wabash, 4; Iowa, 3½; Kansas, 3; Notre Dame, 2.

WESTERN INTERCOLLEGIATE RECORDS.

(Made in annual championship meets.)

100-yard dash—:09⅘, Blair, Chicago, 1903, and W. W. May, Illinois, 1907 and 1908.
220-yard dash—:21⅗, Hahn, Michigan, 1903.
440-yard run—:48⅘, Davenport, Chicago, 1910.
880-yard run—1:56⅗, Davenport, Chicago, 1910-1911.
1-mile run—4:20⅘, Baker, Oberlin, 1910.
2-mile run—9:42⅘, T. V. Metcalf, Oberlin, 1912.
120-yard hurdles—:15⅕, J. P. Nicholson, Missouri, 1912.
220-yard hurdles—:24⅘, Fletcher, Notre Dame, 1910.
High jump—6 ft. ⅝ in., French, Kansas, 1910.
Broad jump—23 ft. 1 in., F. H. Allen, California, 1911.
Pole vault—12 ft. 8¼ in., J. Gold, Wisconsin, 1913.
16-lb. hammer—160 ft. 4 in., K. Shattuck, California, 1913.
16-lb. shot—47 ft. ¼ in., Rose, Michigan, 1904.
Discus—140 ft. 2⅜ in., Garrels, Michigan, 1905.

LONG DISTANCE RUNNING AND WALKING.

Following were the results in the more important Marathon (26 miles 385 yards) and other long distance foot races in 1913. Date, place, distance, winner and time are given in order:

Jan. 18—New York, N. Y.; 10 miles; Hannes Kolehmainen; 51:25.
Feb. 12—New York, N. Y.; 5 miles; H. Kolehmainen; 24:29⅘.
April 19—Boston, Mass.; 25 miles; Fritz Carlson; 2:25:14⅘.
April 19—St. Louis, Mo.; Marathon; William J. Kennedy; 3:02:11.
May 17—St. Louis, Mo.; 11.6 miles; William J. Kennedy; 1:08:12.
May 31—Chicago, Ill.; 9 miles; William J. Kennedy; 50:10.
June 22—Chicago, Ill.; 15 miles; Fritz Carlson; 1:29:05.
July 4—Chicago, Ill.; 15 miles; William J. Kennedy; 1:39:54.
Aug. 2—Minneapolis, Minn.; Marathon; Fritz Carlson; 4:11:00.
Aug. 2—Manchester, Eng.; 10 miles; Hans Holmer; 54:11⅘.
Sept. 1—Chicago, Ill.; 15 miles; Sidney Hatch; 1:44:00.
Sept. 28—Chicago, Ill.; 15 miles; C. Christenson; 1:30:10.
Oct. 3—Brockton, Mass.; 25 miles; J. M. Lordan; 2:36:30.
Nov. 1—New York, N. Y.; 10 miles; H. Kolehmainen; 51:03⅗.
Nov. 1—New York, N. Y.; 7 mile walk; Fred Kaiser; 55:09⅘.

NOTABLE RECORDS MADE IN 1913.

Feb. 6—5-mile run indoor—24:18, Hannes Kolehmainen, New York, N. Y.
Feb. 6—Putting 56-lb. shot with follow—25 ft., Patrick Ryan, New York, N. Y.
Feb. 8—Three standing jumps—34 ft. 9½ in., Platt Adams, Boston, Mass.
Feb. 15—Throwing 24-lb. shot—39 ft. ¼ in., Ralph Rose, San Francisco, Cal.
Feb. 22—Throwing 18-lb. shot—45 ft. 5¾ in., Ralph Rose, San Francisco, Cal.
Feb. 22—Throwing 56-lb. weight—16 ft. 7 in., Pat Donovan, San Francisco, Cal.
Feb. 23—Indoor pole vault—12 ft. 6 in., John Gold, Madison, Wis.
March 15—¾-mile run—3:07, J. Driscoll, Buffalo, N. Y.

March 15—120-yard high hurdles—:15, Fred Kelly, Los Angeles, Cal.
April 4—Pole vault—12 ft. 6 1-16 in., Bergstrom, San Francisco, Cal.
April 11—600-yard run—1:13⅘, Jas. E. Meredith, Brooklyn, N. Y.
April 19—Throwing 16-lb. hammer—175 ft. 10 in., Karl Shattuck, Berkeley, Cal.
May 2—100-yard dash—:09⅗, Arthur Robinson, Philadelphia, Pa.
May 2—220-yard dash—:20⅘, Arthur Robinson, Philadelphia, Pa.
May 10—Broad jump—23 ft. 7½ in., P. Stiles, Lake Forest, Ill.
June 14—Standing jump—5 ft. 5¾ in., Lee Goehring, Travers Island, N. Y.
June 28—150-yard dash—:14⅘, W. F. Applegarth, Cardiff, Wales.
June 28—100-yard dash—:09⅘, W. F. Applegarth, Cardiff, Wales.
July 6—1-hour run—11 miles 1,443 yards, Jean Bouin, Stockholm, Sweden.
Aug. 4—300-yard run—:29¾, Jack Donaldson, Manchester, England.
Aug. 4—1-mile walk—6:23; C. Cummings, Manchester, England.
Aug. 17—Throwing 16-lb. hammer—189 ft. 6½ in., Patrick Ryan, New York, N. Y.
Sept. 1—100-yard dash—:09⅗, Howard P. Drew, Hartford, Conn.
Sept. 2—Throwing 16-lb. hammer—189 ft. 3 in., Patrick Ryan, New York, N. Y.
Sept. 2—Putting 14-lb. shot—52 ft. 4 in., Pat McDonald, New York, N. Y.
Nov. 1—10-mile run—51:03⅗, H. Kolehmainen, New York, N. Y.

INTERNATIONAL AMATEUR ATHLETIC FEDERATION.

The International Amateur Athletic federation was formally organized in Berlin, Germany, Aug. 21, 1913. Its object is to draft rules for international athletic competitions, register world, Olympic and national records and arrive at a common definition of an amateur. J. S. Edstrom of Sweden is president of the executive council and Kristian Hellstroem, also of Sweden, secretary. James E. Sullivan, secretary of the Amateur Athletic Union of the United States, is a member of the council.

WORLD'S ATHLETIC RECORDS.

100-yard dash—:09⅗, R. E. Walker.*
150-yard dash—:14, Jack Donaldson.
180-yard dash—:17⅘, R. E. Walker.*
220-yard dash—:20⅘, Arthur Robinson.*
300-yard run—:29¾, Jack Donaldson.
440-yard run—:47, M. W. Long.*
880-yard run—1:53½, F. S. Hewitt.*
1-mile run—4:12¾, W. G. George.
2-mile run—9:09⅗, A. Shrubb.
4-mile run—19:23⅗, A. Shrubb.
5-mile run—24:18, H. Kolehmainen.*
Marathon—2:29:39⅕, W. Kolehmainen.
50-mile run—6:13:58, E. W. Lloyd.
100-mile run—13:26:30, C. Rowell.
120-yard hurdles—:15, Arthur B. Shaw* and Fred Kelly.*
220-yard hurdles—:23⅗, A. C. Kraenzlein.*
High jump—6 ft. 5⅝ in., M. F. Sweeney.
Broad jump—24 ft. 11¾ in., P. O'Connor.
Standing broad jump—11 ft. 6 in., Ray C. Ewry.*
Pole vault—13 ft. 2¼ in., Marc S. Wright.*
Throwing 16-lb. hammer—189 ft. 3 in., Pat Ryan.
Putting 8-lb. shot—67 ft. 7 in., Ralph Rose.*
Putting 12-lb. shot—55 ft. 11¾ in., Ralph Rose.*
Putting 14-lb. shot—53 ft. 4 in., Ralph Rose.*
Putting 16-lb. shot—54 ft. 4 in., Ralph Rose.*
Putting 18-lb. shot—45 ft. 5⅝ in., Ralph Rose.*
Putting 21-lb. shot—40 ft. 3⅝ in., Ralph Rose.*
Putting 24-lb. shot—39 ft. ¼ in., Ralph Rose.*
Throwing discus—148 ft. 1½ in., A. R. Taipale.
*Amateur.

PRINCIPAL OLYMPIAN RECORDS.

Olympian records to date are as follows:
60 meter run—:04, A. C. Kraenzlein, Archie Hahn (1904), W. Hogenson (1904).
100 meter run—:10⅗, S. F. Lippincott (1912).
200 meter run—:21⅗, Archie Hahn, (1904).
400 meter run—:48, James E. Meredith (1912).
1,500 meter run—3:56⅘, A. S. Jackson (1912).
800 meter run—1:51 9-10, James E. Meredith (1912).
2,500 meter steeplechase—7:34, G. W. Orton.
4,000 meter steeplechase—12:58⅘, C. Reimmer, England.
Marathon race, 25 miles—2:36:54⅘, K. K. McArthur (1912).
1,600 meter relay—3:16⅗, America (1912).
110 meter hurdle race—:15, F. C. Smithson (1908).
200 meter hurdle race—:24⅗, H. Hillman (1904).
400 meter hurdle race—:55, C. J. Bacon (1908).
Running high jump—6 feet 4 inches, Alma W. Richards (1912).
Running broad jump—24 feet 11¼ inches, L. Gutterson (1912).
Standing high jump—5 feet 5 inches, Ray C. Ewry.
Standing broad jump—11 feet 4⅞ inches, Ray C. Ewry (1904).
Standing triple jump—36 feet 1 inch, Peter O'Connor (1906).
Pole vault—12 feet 11 inches, Harry S. Babcock (1912).
Running hop, skip and jump—48 feet 11¼ inches, Ahearne, England (1908).
Putting 16 pound shot—50 feet 4 inches, P. J. McDonald (1912).
Throwing 16 pound hammer—180 feet 5 inches, M. J. McGrath (1912).
Throwing discus (Greek style)—148 feet 1½ inches. A. R. Taipale (1912).
Throwing javelin (free style)—199 feet 11⅝ inches, E. V. Lemming (1912).
Throwing javelin (middle)—179 feet 10½ inches, E. V. Lemming (1908).

CURLING.

NORTHWESTERN BONSPIEL.

The twentieth annual bonspiel of the Northwestern Curling association took place at St. Paul, Minn., Jan. 20-28, 1913. The American rinks won the international trophy, a fine silver cup, from the Canadian rinks, with an aggregate score of 254 to 27. The Duluth trophy was won by R. H. Dunbar's rink of St. Paul, which defeated Dr. G. V. Williams' rink of Winnipeg by a score of 11 to 9. The St. Paul trophy was won by Dr. Williams, who defeated A. M. Hastings of Minneapolis, 10 to 7.

INTERNATIONAL BONSPIEL.

The Gordon medal, emblematic of the curling championship of the United States and Canada, was won for the fourteenth time in the closing games of the international bonspiel in the Boston arena, Feb. 8, 1913. The Canadian teams scored a total of 176 points to 137 for the United States players.

FENCING.

In a tournament held in New York, N. Y., April 18, 1913, the national championships of the Amateur Fencers' league were decided. The dueling sword title was won by A. E. Sauer of the Illinois Athletic club, Chicago. The men's championship with foils was won by Paul Meylan of the Fencers' club of New York, while the women's championship with foils was won by Mrs. William H. Dewar of Philadelphia, Pa. A. G. Anderson of the New York Athletic club won the sabers championship.

GYMNASTIC CHAMPIONSHIP.

The Pilzen Sokol turners with 515 points won the seventh annual International Gymnastic union championship Jan. 26, 1913, in Chicago. The events embraced horizontal bars, parallel bars, sidehorse and flying rings. F. Paul of the winning team made a score of 95¼, giving him the individual championship.

CHECKERS.

M. E. Pomeroy of Binghamton, N. Y., won the world's checker championship by defeating Alfred E. Jordan of England, holder of the title, at Binghamton, Sept. 25, 1913.

AERONAUTICAL PROGRESS IN 1913.

Experimenting with aeroplanes, hydroaeroplanes and dirigible balloons continued throughout 1913, but without the announcement of any radical improvements being made. The appended list of casualties shows that aviation is still one of the most perilous of vocations, not only as regards the use of the heavier-than-air machines, but of dirigibles. Greater speed was acquired and it became possible to cover greater distances. Some remarkable feats were recorded, such as that of M. Pegoud, a French aviator, who on numerous occasions flew with his head to the earth, the element of safety was lacking. It was announced early in the year that a Frenchman named Moreau had discovered a practicable airship "balancer," consisting of a freely swinging pendulum with an arrangement making capsizing almost impossible. Tests made seemed to prove that the invention possessed merit and Moreau was awarded the Bonnot prize, Sept. 24, for his device.

In spite of the many fatalities occurring to aviators in all parts of the world, the great nations continued to add to their aerial fleets and to make aviation an important part of their military preparations. The leaders in the movement were France, Germany, Great Britain and Italy.

According to the annual bulletin of the International Aeronautical association there were in 1913 2,490 certified aviators in the world. They were distributed as follows: France, 968; Great Britain, 376; Germany, 335; United States, 193; Italy, 189; Russia, 162; Austria, 84; Belgium, 68; Switzerland, 27; Holland, 26; Spain, 16; Argentina, 15; Sweden, 10; Denmark, 8; Norway, 5, and Egypt, 1.

JAMES GORDON BENNETT CUP.

Maurice Prevost, French, won the fifth annual contest for the James Gordon Bennett cup, emblematic of the world's aeroplane championship, at Rheims, France, Sept. 29, 1913. His time for the course of 124.28 miles was 59 minutes 45⅘ seconds, making his average speed 125 miles an hour. In 1912 Jules Vedrines, in winning the cup at Clearing, near Chicago, covered the same distance in 70 minutes 56.8 seconds, or at the rate of nearly 105.5 miles an hour. Belgium was the only other country besides France represented at the Rheims contest. Winners of cup to date:

1909—Glenn H. Curtiss, America.
1910—Claude Grahame-White, England.
1911—Charles T. Weymann, America.
1912—Jules Vedrines, France.
1913—Maurice Prevost, France.

FLYING WITH HEAD TO EARTH.

M. Pegoud performed the extraordinary feat of flying in an aeroplane upside down for the first time at Juvisy, France, Sept. 1, 1913. Ascending 3,000 feet in the air, he caused the forward part of his monoplane to point toward the earth until the machine was in a perpendicular position. It descended swiftly and for several seconds the aviator flew in a straight line with his head downward. Then the monoplane was righted and descended to the earth in a series of spirals. Briefly, the aviator caused his monoplane to describe a gigantic letter S in the sky and made a flight of a quarter of a mile upside down. Experts declared that the experiment indicated progress toward the attainment of safety in aeroplane flying. The feat was repeated frequently by M. Pegoud and other aviators.

LONG DISTANCE FLIGHTS IN 1913.

FROM DOVER TO COLOGNE.

Gustave Hamel, a British aviator, accompanied by Frank Dupre, American, made a monoplane non-stop flight from Dover, England, to Cologne, Germany, Thursday afternoon, April 17, 1913, in 4 hours 5 minutes. The distance covered was something over 250 miles.

ACROSS ISTHMUS OF PANAMA.

Robert G. Fowler, American aviator, made a flight across the Isthmus of Panama April 27, 1913, in an aeroplane with a passenger. He started from Panama beach, circled over the city of Panama for half an hour and then crossed the isthmus, follow-

ing the line of the canal to Gatun and Colon, landing at Cristobal. He met strong wind currents over the Culebra cut.

FROM BIARRITZ TO KOLLUM.

Ernest F. Guillaux, a French aviator, left Biarritz, France, at 4:22 a. m., Sunday, April 27, 1913, and arrived at Kollum, Holland, a little before daybreak Monday morning, having covered the distance of more than 1,000 miles in his aeroplane in a little over 24 hours. He descended twice to replenish his fuel.

KEY WEST TO HAVANA.

Domingo Rosillo, a Cuban aviator, started from the Florida East Coast railroad terminal at Key West, Fla., at 5:35 a. m., May 17, 1913, in a Moisant aeroplane, and arrived at Havana, Cuba, at 7:30 a. m. The distance covered was between ninety-five and 100 miles. The aviator, who was followed across the gulf stream by a cruiser and gunboat, received a prize of $10,000 for his performance.

Augustine Parla, another Cuban aviator, made a flight from Key West to Mariel, forty miles west of Havana, Monday afternoon, May 19, 1913. He had no escort of war ships.

FLIGHTS OVER THE ALPS.

Jean Bielovucci, a Peruvian aviator, made a flight across the Alps from Switzerland to Italy Jan. 25, 1913. Using a monoplane, he ascended at Brig on the Swiss side at noon and exactly 25 minutes later landed at Domodossola on the Italian side. Bielovucci followed the same course over the Simplon pass that was taken by his compatriot, Chavez, in September, 1910. Chavez accomplished the flight but in landing met with an accident, resulting in his death a few days later.

Oscar Bider, French, flew from Barni, Switzerland, over the Alps to Milan, Italy, July 13, 1913, a distance of 130 miles, in two and a half hours. July 26 he flew from Milan to Basel, Switzerland, in 3 hours 45 minutes; distance, 360 miles.

MILAN TO ROME.

The Italian aviators, DeRoy and Cevasco, made a monoplane flight from Milan to Rome, a distance of 410 miles, in 6 hours 7 minutes, Tuesday, May 27, 1913.

PARIS TO PORTUGAL.

Eugene Gilbert made a flight from Paris, France, to Pejabo, a town on the Portuguese frontier, Aug. 2, 1913. The distance was 1,030 miles and the flight was made in competition for the Pommery cup, which is awarded the airman who makes the longest cross-country trip in one day between sunrise and sunset. Gilbert bettered the record made by Brindejonc des Moulinais, June 10, when he flew from Paris to Warsaw, a distance of 906 miles.

SPEEDY PARIS-LONDON FLIGHT.

Marcel G. Brindejonc des Moulinais, a French aviator, left Paris in his monoplane at 9 a. m., Feb. 25, 1913, landed at Calais at 10:50 a. m., resumed his flight at noon and descended in London at 1:30 p. m. The crossing of the channel was made in a fog. The distance was 287 miles and the actual flying time 185 minutes, making the speed ninety-four miles an hour, or more than a mile and a half a minute.

LONG EUROPEAN FLIGHT.

The airman Brindejonc des Moulinais returned July 2, 1913, to Villacoublay, France, after a most remarkable series of flights. In eight days of actual flying the airman covered practically 5,000 kilometers (3,125 miles), traversed northern Europe, visiting five capitals and seven different countries, and all was accomplished with no accident, save the breaking of a wheel when landing on rough ground at Dvinsk. The following are details of the distances covered:

Date.	Flight.	Miles.
June 10—Paris to Warsaw (via Berlin)		906
June 15—Warsaw to Dvinsk		344
June 16—Dvinsk to St. Petersburg		281
June 22—St. Petersburg to Reval		248
June 25—Reval to Stockholm		250

Date. Flight. Miles.
June 29—Stockholm to Copenhagen.............344
July 1—Copenhagen to The Hague.............450
July 2—The Hague to Villacoublay.............281
For his flight from Paris to Warsaw in thirteen hours Brindejonc was awarded the Pommery cup.

FROM PARIS TO BERLIN.

Pierre Daucourt, a French aviator, won an aeroplane race from Paris, France, to Berlin, Germany, April 16, 1913, defeating Edmond Audemars and winning the $1,500 Pommery cup. Daucourt left Paris at about 5 o'clock in the morning and arrived at the Johannisthal aerodrome near Berlin at 6:39 o'clock in the evening. The distance covered was 535 miles. The weather during part of the flight was stormy. Audemars stopped when he reached Wanne, Germany.

Edmond Audemars made a flight from Berlin to Paris July 13, making one stop for petrol at Hanover. He left at 4:10 a. m. and reached Paris at 7:15 p. m. Aviator Setort left Paris at 4:10 a. m. and flew to Berlin without making a stop, arriving there at 1:10 p. m. The distance covered was about 575 miles.

FLIGHT ACROSS MEDITERRANEAN.

Roland G. Garros, the French aviator, flew across the Mediterranean sea from St. Raphael, France, to Bizerta, Tunis, Sept. 23, 1913. The distance was 558 miles and the flight was the longest oversea journey ever made in an aeroplane. The time was 7 hours 53 minutes. No floats were attached to the machine and no torpedo boats were stationed along the route from France to Tunis.

FIRST ACROSS LAKE MICHIGAN.

Jack Vilas, with William Bastar as passenger, made an aeroplane flight from St. Joseph, Mich., to Grant park, Chicago, July 1, 1913, covering the sixty-four miles in 1 hour and 34 minutes. It was the first aeroplane flight across Lake Michigan.

CHICAGO-DETROIT FLYING BOAT CRUISE.

Beckwith Havens of Hammondsport, N. Y., in a Curtiss hydroaeroplane and accompanied by J. B. Verplanck, owner of the craft, completed an aerial cruise from Chicago to Detroit, July 18, 1913. The distance covered was about 900 miles. The cruise was originally intended to be a race between a number of aero yachts. Five were entered and four started, but three of the craft were disabled by accidents resulting from gales and heavy seas and were forced to give up the contest. Walter E. Johnson of Bath, N. Y., stopped at Robertsdale, Ind.; Glenn L. Martin at Muskegon, Mich., and Roy M. Francis at Pentwater, Mich. Havens, who began his flight July 8, also experienced many delays on account of the weather, but managed to reach Charlevoix July 14, Point Lookout, Mich., July 16, and Detroit two days later.

LONG FLIGHT IN GERMANY.

Victor Stoeffler in a 100 horse power biplane started from Johannisthal, Germany, Oct. 14, 1913, and landed the next morning at Muelhausen after having covered 1,376 miles in 22 hours 47 minutes actual flying time.

RECORD FOR ALTITUDE.

Georges Legagneux, Pau, France, Dec. 9, 1910, 10,499 feet.
Arch Hoxsey, Los Angeles, Cal., Dec. 26, 1910, 11,474 feet (unofficial).
Capt. Felix, Etampes, France, Aug. 5, 1911, 11,339 feet.
Lincoln Beachey, Chicago, Ill., Aug. 20, 1911, 11,642 feet.
Roland G. Garros, Parame, France, Nov. 7, 1911, 13,943 feet.
Lieut. Blaschke, Vienna, June 29, 1912, 14,300 feet.
Roland G. Garros, Houlgate, Sept. 6, 1912, 16,076 feet.
Georges Legagneux, Villacoublay, Sept. 17, 1912, 17,881 feet.
Edmond Perreyon, Buc aerodrome, France, March 11, 1913, 19,650 feet.

RECORD FOR WEIGHT CARRIED.

Aviator Noel flew in an "aerobus" for seventeen minutes with seven passengers at Hendon, Eng-

land, Sept. 22, 1913. The weight of pilot and passengers was 1,134 pounds. Oct. 2, at the same place, Noel took up nine passengers to a height of 600 feet and remained in the air 20 minutes.

RECORD FOR SPEED.

The record for speed is held by Maurice Prevost of France, who in the James Gordon Bennett cup race at Rheims, France, covered 124.28 miles at an average speed of 125 miles an hour. He had previously made records of 111, 111½ and 117 miles an hour. Emile Vedrines made a record of 118 miles an hour at Rheims Sept. 27.

MAX LILLIE KILLED.

Maximilian Liljenstrand, better known in the aviation world as Max Lillie, was killed at Galesburg, Ill., Sept. 15, 1913, while giving an exhibition flight at the fair grounds in the presence of 5,000 spectators. As he was making a turn at a height of between 150 and 200 feet the wind caught the right wing with considerable force, causing it to snap and break. The aeroplane turned turtle and fell to the ground. The aviator was pinned underneath the machine and was instantly killed.

AVIATION FATALITIES.

Nov. 21, 1912, to Nov. 24, 1913.
Nov. 21, 1912—Andre Frey, Rheims, France.
Dec. 24, 1912—Edward Petre, Redcar, England.
Jan. 3, 1913—M. Mallot, Fecamp, France.
Jan. 13—L. F. Macdonald and passenger England, Dartford, England.
Jan. 19—Lieut. Origone, Brandzen, Argentina.
Jan. 23—Lieut. Otto Schlegel, near Burg, Germany.
Jan. 23—Frank Boland, Port of Spain, Trinidad.
Jan. 24—Charles Nieuport and mechanic, Etampes, France.
Jan. 26—Senor Enserione, near Buenos Aires, Argentina.
Jan. 27—Herr Huell, Aix-la-Chapelle, Germany.
Feb. 3—Giuseppe Nosari, Turin, Italy.
Feb. 8—Lieut.-Com. Walter Janetzky and Machinist Dieckmann, Danzig, Germany.
Feb. 15—Herr Lenk, Leipsic, Germany.
Feb. 17—Lieut. Mittner, Vienna, Austria.
Feb. 26—Sergt. Helfersnider, Muelhausen, Germany.
March 5—Geoffrey England, Salisbury Plain, England.
March 13—Two sergeants fatally injured, Rheims, France.
March 16—M. Mercier, Amberieu, France.
March 19—M. Primaves, Lugano, Switzerland.
March 28—Lieuts. Tokuda and Kimura, Kakinoda, Japan.
March 30—Lieut. Periokski, Warsaw, Russia (suicide).
April 8—George Veroinck, near Mitho, French Cochin China.
April 8—Lieut. Rex Chandler, San Diego, Cal.
April 9—Herr Lichte, Gelsenkirchen, Germany.
April 11—Perez Arzemo, Buenos Aires, Argentina.
April 15—Louis Gaudart, Monte Carlo, France (hydroaeroplane).
April 17—Lieut. Arghiropoulos and Constantinos Manos, Saloniki.
April 19—Otto W. Brodie, Chicago, Ill.
April 19—Sig. Gallo, Turin, Italy.
April 21—Lieut. De Blamont, Villacoublay, France.
April 23—Lieut. von Germersheim, Munich, Germany (died April 28).
April 24—Herr Dunetz, Johannisthal, Germany.
April 24—V. Abramovitch, Johannisthal, Germany.
April 28—Lieut. Roger Harrison, Farnborough, England.
April 30—Lieuts. Von Mirbach and Von Brunn, Darmstadt, Germany.
May 2—Herman E. Jansen, Oakland, Cal.
May 3—M. Bellini, Versailles, France.
May 4—Koba Takeishi, Kyoto, Japan.
May 5—Charles Carlson, Akron, O.
May 9—Lieut. J. D. Park, Olive, Cal.
May 14—Capt. Zucher, Johannisthal, Germany.
May 27—Lieut. Desmond L. Arthur, Montrose, Scotland.
May 28—A. Horn, Hanover, Germany.
May 30—Lieut. Jean F. Kroyder, Bourges, France.
May 31—James Colovan, Chicago, Ill.

May 31—Lieut. Ralabichken, Peterhof, Russia.
June 5—M. Bernard and passenger, Paris, France.
June 12—Andrew Drew, Lima, O.
June 13—Naval Lieut. Jas. R. B. Kennedy, London, England.
June 14—Senor Manlo, Lisbon, Portugal.
June 18—Sapper Dewever, Etampes, France.
June 19—Aviator Kraftet and Herr Gerbitz, Johannisthal, Germany.
June 20—Eusign W. D. Billingsley, Annapolis, Md.
June 23—Mr. Fairbairns, Shoeburyness, England.
June 23—Fred F. Gardiner, Bath, N. Y.
June 29—M. Parisot and passenger, Liege, France.
June 29—Mr. Wight, Bristol, England.
July 8—Lieut. Loren H. Call, Houston, Tex.
July 8—Herr Leudner and passenger, Wurzburg, Germany.
July 14—M. Bertin and son, near Paris, France.
July 14—Herr Dietrichs, Muelhausen, Germany.
July 16—Lieut. Stoll, Juterbog, Germany.
July 17—Maj. A. W. Hewetson, Salisbury, Eng.
July 18—Herr Westphelly, Frankfort-on-Main, Germany.
July 22—Lieut. Gabriel, Chalons, France.
July 26—Herr Stengel, Frankfort-on-Main, Germany.
July 27—M. Chambeners, Hauterive, France.
July 29—Military aviator, Gatchina, Russia.
Aug. 4—Herr Broks, Johannisthal, Germany.
Aug. 5—Lieut. Polikarpoff and mechanic, Krasnoye Selo, Russia.
Aug. 6—John Bryant, Victoria, B. C.
Aug. 7—Col. S. F. Cody and passenger, Aldershot, England.
Aug. 10—Fritz Roessler and pupil, Brueck, Germany.
Aug. 22—Lieut. Schmidt, Halberstadt, Germany.
Aug. 25—Lieut. Sansever and Sapper Laforgue, Villaconblay, France.
Sept. 2—George Schmidt, Rutland, Vt.
Sept. 2—Louis Ollivier and passenger, Melun, France.
Sept. 3—Herr Kahl, Strassburg, Germany.
Sept. 4—Lieut. Von Eckenbrecher and Lieut. Prinz, Brieg, Germany.
Sept. 4—Lieut. Moss L. Love, San Diego, Cal.
Sept. 5—Perry C. Davis, Mauston, Wis. (died Sept. 16).
Sept. 8—Herr Senge, Grevenbroich, Germany.
Sept. 9—Dr. Ringer, Johannisthal, Germany.
Sept. 9—M. Dr.schinin, Sebastopol, Russia.
Sept. 9—M. Chomirnie, Lyons, France.
Sept. 12—Hans Lorenz, Munster, Germany.
Sept. 14—M. Vlalou, Bucharest, Roumania.
Sept. 15—Max Lillie, Galesburg, Ill.
Sept. 23—French aviator, Mogador, Morocco.
Sept. 24—Lieut. A. Soulelllan, Oujda, Morocco.
Sept. 26—Lieut. Schulz, Johannisthal, Germany.
Oct. 3—Maj. George C. Merrick, Salisbury, England.
Oct. 5—M. Sivol, Marmande, France.
Oct. 13—Lieut. Koenig, Neundorf, Germany.
Oct. 13—Albert J. Jewel, Hempstead, N. Y.
Oct. 17—Capt. Haeseler, near Breslau, Germany.
Oct. 17—Lieut. Koch and Sergt. Mante, near Wuerzburg, Germany.
Oct. 20—Lieut. Garnier and Sapper Jenrot, Epinal, France.
Oct. 20—Corporal Dautroche, Epinal, France.
Oct. 28—Sergt. Canal, Rheims, France.
Nov. 12—Capt. de la Garde, Villacoublay, France.
Nov. 14—Lieut. O. Perry Rich, Manila, P. I.
Nov. 24—Lieuts. Fric L. Ellington and Hugh M. Kelly, San Diego, Cal.

BALLOONING.

CONTEST FOR BENNETT CUP.

The ninth international balloon race for the James Gordon Bennett cup was won in 1913 by the Goodyear of Akron, O., piloted by Ralph H. Upson. The start was made from Paris, France, Sunday morning, Oct. 12, eighteen balloons, representing eight nations, taking part in the race. Wind conditions were unfavorable and the flights were comparatively short. The Goodyear landed at Bridlington, England, at noon Tuesday, Oct. 14, after having covered a little over 400 miles airline distance.

BENNETT CUP RECORD.

Year.	Winner.	Distance.
1906—America (American)		402 miles
1907—Pommern (German)		880 miles
1908—Helvetia (Swiss)		620 miles
1909—America II. (American)		695 miles
1910—America II. (American)		1,171 miles
1911—Berlin II. (German)		471 miles
1912—Picardie (French)		1,354 miles
1913—Goodyear (American)		400 miles

AMERICAN ELIMINATION RACE.

Four balloons started from Kansas City, Mo., July 4, 1913, in the American elimination race for the selection of entries for the James Gordon Bennett race. First place was won by the Goodyear balloon of Akron, O., piloted by R. H. Upson. It landed at West Branch, Mich., with a mileage of 685. Kansas City II., John Watts, pilot, was second, landing at Goodrich, Mich., 673 miles. Kansas City Post, H. E. Honeywell, pilot, was third, with 658 miles, landing at Rockwood, Mich., and the Million Population Club of St. Louis was fourth with 590 miles, at Manchester, Mich. All the balloons came to earth July 5.

RECORD FOR DISTANCE.

The record for distance traveled in a balloon in continuous flight is held by Maurice Benalms of France, who made 1,354 miles in contesting for the James Gordon Bennett cup Oct. 27-29, 1912. In 1900 Count de la Vaulx made a journey of 1,193 miles and in 1910 Alan R. Hawley and Augustus Post covered 1,171 miles.

The record for distance traveled over water in a dirigible balloon is held by Walter Wellman, who on Oct. 15-18, 1910, made approximately 1,000 miles in an attempt to cross the Atlantic in the America.

RECORD FOR HEIGHT.

The record for height made in an ordinary gas balloon is 28,750 feet. It was made by Prof. Berson of Berlin Dec. 4, 1894. A record of nearly 33,000 feet was claimed for the French balloon Icare in 1913.

The world's dirigible balloon record for altitude is 9,514 feet. It was made by the French dirigible Clement-Bayard III. May 20, 1912. It carried six passengers.

BALLOON DISASTER IN FRANCE.

The military balloon Zodiac, carrying five men, collapsed and fell to the ground at Noisy-le-Grand, near Paris, France, April 17, 1913. All the occupants of the car were killed. The balloon, which was of the spherical type, was inflated with ordinary gas, and left the Aero club park at St. Cloud with the military aeronauts Capt. Clavenad, Capt. De Noue, Lieut. de Vaisselot and Artilleryman Rechy, and the civilian pilot Aumont Thieville aboard. The craft was carried over Paris by a strong wind and was passing over Noisy-le-Grand at a height of about 650 feet when laborers working in a field below saw the balloon shrivel up and fall. Three of the aeronauts were killed outright, one died on the way to a hospital and the other died after reaching there. The collapse of the balloon was due to a tear in the cover, supposed to have been made intentionally when something went wrong with the valve.

ZEPPELIN AIRSHIP DISASTERS.

Two disasters to Zeppelin dirigible airships occurred in Germany in 1913. The first was near Helgoland Sept. 9, when the naval dirigible L-1 was wrecked in the North sea while on a voyage from the mainland, thirteen of the crew of twenty men losing their lives. The craft, which was a new one of the latest Zeppelin model, had been ordered to take part in the maneuvers of the battle ship fleet. It started out in bad weather and when eighteen miles from its destination ran into a gale accompanied by cold rain, which caused the gas sustaining the airship to condense. The weight of the crew was too great under the circumstances and the craft sank into the sea. Wireless appeals for aid had been sent out and these were responded to quickly by torpedo boats, which, however, were able to save only seven of the crew.

LOSS OF THE L-2.

The second disaster took place Oct. 17 when the L-2, the largest and finest of the Zeppelin type of airships, was destroyed by the explosion of a gasoline tank, which occurred as the ship was making a trial trip above the city of Johannisthal, near Berlin. All except one of the twenty-seven military men on board, including the entire admiralty trial board, were killed. Thousands, who had been watching the evolutions of the L-2, which, if accepted, was to have been the flagship of Germany's new aerial fleet, heard a heavy detonation and saw the craft suddenly become enveloped in flames and drop to the ground from a height of 900 feet. On reaching the spot in the highway where the airship fell the spectators found nothing but a mass of crumpled aluminum and twisted wreckage. The only man found alive was Lieut. Baron von Bleul, a guest on the trip, who was fatally injured. Many of the bodies of the others were so burned as to be unrecognizable. The inmates of the center gondola were blown through the sides of the car by the explosion and their bodies fell a quarter of a mile away from the wreck of the dirigible. The pilot of the airship was Capt. Gluth, who had been in Count Zeppelin's employ for a long time. The admiralty trial board consisted of seven officers, including Lieutenant-Commander Behnish and Lieut. Freyer, both personal friends of Emperor William. Naval Constructors Neumann and Pietzler, Naval Engineer Busch, Lieut. Trenk and Chief Engineer Haussmann were among the others killed.

WOMAN SUFFRAGE.

FREE STATES.

Alaska (territory).
Arizona.
California.
Colorado.
Idaho.
Illinois.
Kansas.
Oregon.
Utah.
Washington.
Wyoming.

AMENDMENT PENDING.

Montana.
Nevada.
North Dakota.
South Dakota.

In the four states last named amendments granting the suffrage to women will be voted on by the people in 1914.

In Michigan an amendment giving women the right to vote was defeated at the election of April 7, 1913, by a vote of 264,882 nays to 168,738 yeas.

In Wisconsin a woman suffrage bill passed both houses of the legislature in 1913 but was vetoed by the governor.

Woman suffrage amendments were defeated in the Florida, Nebraska, Maine, Massachusetts, West Virginia, Missouri and Delaware legislatures. The subject was considered in the legislatures of Iowa, New York and Pennsylvania but final action was not taken.

THE PANKHURST CASE.

Mrs. Emmeline Pankhurst, leader of the British militant suffragettes, arrived at New York, N. Y., Oct. 18, 1913, to begin a lecture tour in America. She was detained at Ellis Island by an immigration inspector and a board of special inquiry ordered her exclusion from the country on the ground that she had been convicted abroad of "acts involving moral turpitude," making her an undesirable. The case was appealed to Washington and Commissioner of Immigration Caminetti recommended that she be admitted on her own recognizance to depart from the country at the termination of her engagements. The recommendation was concurred in by the secretary of labor, William B. Wilson, and President Wilson, and Mrs. Pankhurst was thereupon permitted to land.

MILITANCY IN ENGLAND.

The Willoughby Dickinson suffrage bill, giving the franchise to every woman who, if she were a man, would be registered as a parliamentary elector in respect of a household qualification, or who was the wife of a man so qualified, was defeated in the house of commons May 6, 1913, by a vote of 266 to 219. More than fifty Irish nationalists voted against the measure. The cabinet was divided on the question.

Miss Emily Wilding Davison, a militant, ran in front of the king's horse at the Derby at Epsom, England, June 4, 1913, and received injuries from which she died four days later.

In furtherance of the militant movement a number of country houses, for the most part unoccupied, and other structures were burned by suffragettes. As early as May 8, 1913, it was estimated that the damage from fires of this kind in the British Isles amounted to $5,000,000.

Mrs. Emmeline Pankhurst was sentenced April 3 to three years' penal servitude for inciting persons to commit damage. She resorted to the "hunger strike" and was released, enabling her to make her trip to America.

PROGRESS IN OTHER LANDS.

In Norway the storthing by unanimous vote June 11, 1913, agreed to extend the suffrage so as to give all women the right to vote at parliamentary elections without regard to the amount of their income tax.

In the Netherlands states general Sept. 16, 1913, it was announced in the speech from the throne that the vote would be given to women.

IRISH HOME RULE BILL.

The Irish home rule bill was first introduced in the house of commons April 11, 1912. It passed its first reading April 16 and its second reading May 9, 1912. It passed its third reading Thursday night, Jan. 16, 1913, by a majority of 110 votes. The division was 367 for and 250 against the measure. Immediately after its passage in the house the measure was sent to the house of lords, which held a special session to receive it. It came to a vote Jan. 30 and was rejected, 326 to 69, the result being a foregone conclusion.

Parliament was prorogued March 7 but met again March 10. The home rule bill was reintroduced and passed by the house of commons July 8 by a vote of 352 to 243. The measure was rejected by the house of lords July 15 by a vote of 302 to 64. The session ended Aug. 15. In accordance with the act of Aug. 10, 1911, if a bill is passed by the house of commons in three successive sessions and is rejected by the house of lords on each occasion, that bill will on being signed by the king become an act of parliament notwithstanding that the house of lords has rejected it. Two years must, however, elapse between the first introduction of the bill and the time of its passage in the house of commons for the first time.

Preparations for armed resistance to Irish home rule were made by the unionists of Ulster, led by Sir Edward Carson. Delegates met in Belfast Sept. 24, 1913, and created the machinery of a provisional government to take over the administration of Ulster in case the home rule bill became a law. Drilling of volunteers for war was actively engaged in by large numbers of men in Belfast and vicinity.

NOTABLE NEW YORK BUILDINGS.
Height in stories and feet.

American Surety—23; 306.
American Tract—23; 306.
Bankers' Trust—39; 529.
Bank of Com'erce—20; 270.
Broad Exchange—20; 276.

Com'ercial Cable—21; 255.
Empire—20; 293.
Evening Post—32; 385.
Flatiron—20; 286.
Germania Life—20; 281.

Heidelberg—30; 410.
Metropolitan Life—50; 700.
Municipal—24; 560.
Park Row—29; 382.
Pulitzer—22; 375.

Singer—41; 612.
St. Paul—26; 308.
Times—28; 419.
Woolworth—51; 785.

HISTORICAL DATA AS TO STATES AND TERRITORIES.

STATE OR TERRITORY.	Admitted to the union.	Population, 1910.	Area. Sq. M.	Settled at	Date	By whom.	Rep. in cong.	Electoral vote.
Alabama	Dec. 14, 1819	2,138,093	51,998	Mobile	1702	French	10	12
Alaska Territory	†July 27, 1868	64,356	590,884	Sitka	1801	Russians	††	....
Arizona	June 20, 1910	204,354	113,956	Tucson	1580	Spaniards	1	3
Arkansas	June 15, 1836	1,574,449	53,335	Ark'nsas Post	1685	French	7	9
California	Sept. 9, 1850	2,377,549	158,297	San Diego	1769	Spaniards	11	13
Colorado	Aug. 1, 1876	799,024	103,948	Near Denver	1858	Americans	4	6
Connecticut	*Jan. 9, 1788	1,114,756	4,965	Windsor	1635	Puritans	5	7
Delaware	*Dec. 7, 1787	202,322	2,370	Cape Henlopen	1627	Swedes	1	3
District of Columbia	†July 16, 1790	331,069	70		1660	English	....	....
Florida	March 3, 1845	752,619	58,666	St. Augustine	1565	Spaniards	4	6
Georgia	*Jan. 2, 1788	2,609,121	59,265	Savannah	1733	English	12	14
Guam Colony	‡Aug. 12, 1898	9,000	150	Agana		Spaniards	....	....
Hawaii Territory	*April 30, 1900	191,909	6,449				††	....
Idaho	July 3, 1890	325,594	83,888	Cœur d'Alene	1842	Americans	2	4
Illinois	Dec. 3, 1818	5,638,591	56,655	Kaskaskia	1720	French	27	29
Indiana	Dec. 11, 1816	2,700,876	36,354	Vincennes	1730		13	15
Iowa	March 3, 1845	2,224,771	56,147	Burlington	1788	French	11	13
Kansas	Jan. 29, 1861	1,690,949	82,158		1831	Americans	8	10
Kentucky	Feb. 4, 1792	2,289,905	40,598	Lexington	1765	From Va	11	13
Louisiana	April 8, 1812	1,656,388	48,506	Iberville	1699	French	8	10
Maine	March 3, 1820	742,371	33,040	Bristol	1624	English	4	6
Maryland	*April 28, 1788	1,295,346	12,327	St. Mary's	1634	English	6	8
Massachusetts	*Feb. 6, 1788	3,366,416	8,266	Plymouth	1620	Puritans	16	18
Michigan	Jan. 26, 1837	2,810,173	57,980	Near Detroit	1650	French	13	15
Minnesota	May 11, 1858	2,075,708	84,682	St. Peter's R.	1805	Americans	10	12
Mississippi	Dec. 10, 1817	1,797,114	46,865	Natchez	1716	From S. C.	8	10
Missouri	March 2, 1821	3,293,335	69,420	St. Louis	1764	French	16	18
Montana	Nov. 8, 1889	376,053	146,997		1809	Americans	2	4
Nebraska	March 1, 1867	1,192,214	77,520	Bellevue	1847	Americans	6	8
Nevada	*Oct. 13, 1864	81,875	110,690	Genoa	1850	Americans	1	3
New Hampshire	*June 21, 1788	430,572	9,341	Dover and Portsmouth	1623	Puritans	2	4
New Jersey	*Dec. 18, 1787	2,537,167	8,224	Bergen	1620	Swedes	12	14
New Mexico	June 20, 1910	327,301	122,634	Santa Fe	1580	Spaniards	1	3
New York	*July 26, 1788	9,113,614	49,204	Manhattan Id	1614	Dutch	43	45
North Carolina	*Nov. 21, 1789	2,206,287	52,426	Albemarle	1650	English	10	12
North Dakota	Nov. 2, 1889	577,056	70,837	Pembina	1780	French	3	5
Ohio	Nov. 29, 1802	4,767,121	41,040	Marietta	1788	Americans	22	24
Oklahoma	Nov. 16, 1907	1,657,155	70,057		1889	Americans	8	10
Oregon	Feb. 14, 1859	672,765	95,609	Astoria	1810	Americans	3	5
Pennsylvania	*Dec. 12, 1787	7,665,111	45,126	Delaware R.	1682	English	36	38
Philippines	*Nov. 28, 1898	7,635,426	114,000	Manila	1570	Spaniards	....	....
Porto Rico	*Aug. 12, 1898	1,118,012	3,455	Caparra	1510	Spaniards	†††	....
Rhode Island	*May 29, 1790	542,610	1,248	Providence	1638	English	3	5
South Carolina	*May 23, 1788	1,515,400	30,989	Port Royal	1670	Huguenots	7	9
South Dakota	Nov. 2, 1889	583,888	77,615	Sioux Falls	1856	Americans	3	5
Tennessee	June 1, 1796	2,184,789	42,022	Ft. Louden	1757	English	10	12
Texas	Dec. 29, 1845	3,896,542	265,896	Matagorda B.	1686	French	18	20
Utah	Jan. 4, 1896	373,351	84,990	Salt Lake City	1847	Americans	2	4
Vermont	Feb. 18, 1791	355,956	9,564	Ft. Dummer	1764	English	2	4
Virginia	*June 26, 1788	2,061,612	42,627	Jamestown	1607	English	10	12
Washington	Nov. 11, 1889	1,141,990	69,127	Astoria	1811	Americans	5	7
West Virginia	Dec. 31, 1862	1,221,119	24,170	Wheeling	1774	English	6	8
Wisconsin	May 29, 1848	2,333,860	56,066	Green Bay	1670	French	11	13
Wyoming	July 11, 1890	145,531	97,914	Ft. Laramie	1834	Americans	1	3

*Ratified the constitution. †Organized as territory. ‡Delegate. §Signing of protocol relinquishing sovereignty. **Yielding sovereignty. Population in 1903. ††Commissioner.

Historians do not all agree as to some of the dates in the above table. The dates given are from the statistical abstract of the United States published by the government and are well supported in all disputed cases.

TRUST PROSECUTION.

NATIONAL CASH REGISTER COMPANY.

Twenty-nine officials of the National Cash Register company of Dayton, O., were declared guilty of having violated the criminal provisions of the Sherman antitrust law, by a jury in the United States District court, Cincinnati, O., Feb. 13, 1913. The indictments were returned Feb. 22, 1912, and the trial began before Judge H. C. Hollister in Cincinnati Nov. 13, the same year. There were three counts. The first charged that nearly all the competitors of the concern had been bought or driven out of business through bribery and other illegal methods. The second and third counts charged the defendants with monopolizing the cash register business by the same means. The verdict of the jury was "guilty as charged in all three counts." John H. Patterson, president of the company, was sentenced by Judge Hollister Feb. 17 to one year in jail and the payment of a fine of $5,000. Most of the other officials were sentenced to one year in jail, only two or three escaping with shorter terms.

BATHTUB TRUST.

Thirteen corporations and fourteen individuals, forming what had become known as the "bathtub trust," were convicted Feb. 14, 1913, by a jury in the United States District court in Detroit of criminal conspiracy in restraint of trade. On the following day Judge Clarence W. Sessions imposed on them fines ranging from $1 to $10,000 each.

SUIT AGAINST CORN PRODUCTS REFINING COMPANY.

In a bill filed by United States Attorney Henry A. Wise in New York, N. Y., March 1, 1913, the government asked the dissolution of the Corn Products Refining company on the ground that it had violated the Sherman antitrust law by entering into contracts and conspiracies to destroy competition.

STATES, CAPITALS, GOVERNORS AND LEGISLATURES.

STATE OR TERRITORY.	Capital.	Governor.	T'rm Yrs.	Sal- ary.	Term expires.	Next ses. sion leg- islature.	Limit of ses- sion.
Alabama	Montgomery	E. O'Neal, D.	4	$5,000	Jan. 1915	‡Jan. 1915	50 days
Alaska Territory	Juneau	‡J. E. A. Strong, D.	4	7,000	Oct. 1915	*Mar. 1915	60 days
Arizona	Phoenix	G. W. P. Hunt, D.	2	4,000	Feb. 1914	*Nov. 1915	None.
Arkansas	Little Rock	Geo. W. Hays, D.	2	4,000	Jan. 1915	*Jan. 1915	60 days
California	Sacramento	H. W. Johnson, Pr.	4	10,000	Jan. 1915	*Jan. 1915	60 days
Colorado	Denver	E. M. Ammons, D.	2	5,000	Jan. 1915	*Jan. 1915	90 days
Connecticut	Hartford	S. E. Baldwin, D.	2	5,000	Jan. 1915	*Jan. 1915	None.
Delaware	Dover	Chas. R. Miller, R.	4	4,000	Jan. 1917	*Jan. 1915	None.
District of Columbia	Washington						
Florida	Tallahassee	P. M. Trammell, D.	4	5,000	Jan. 1917	*Jan. 1915	60 days
Georgia	Atlanta	J. M. Slaton, D.	2	5,000	June 1915	June 1914	50 days
Hawaii	Honolulu	L. E. Pinkham, D.	4	7,000	Aug. 1917	*Jan. 1915	
Idaho	Boise City	J. M. Haines, R.	2	5,000	Jan. 1915	*Jan. 1915	60 days
Illinois	Springfield	E. F. Dunne, D.	4	12,000	Jan. 1917	*Jan. 1915	None.
Indiana	Indianapolis	S. M. Ralston, D.	4	8,000	Jan. 1917	*Jan. 1915	60 days
Iowa	Des Moines	G. W. Clarke, R.	2	5,000	Jan. 1915	*Jan. 1915	None.
Kansas	Topeka	G. H. Hodges, D.	2	5,000	Jan. 1915	*Jan. 1915	50 days
Kentucky	Frankfort	J. B. McCreary, D.	4	6,500	Dec. 1915	*Jan. 1914	60 days
Louisiana	Baton Rouge	L. E. Hall, D.	4	5,000	May 1916	*May 1914	60 days
Maine	Augusta	Wm. T. Haines, R.	2	3,000	Jan. 1915	*Jan 1915	None.
Maryland	Annapolis	P. L. Goldsborough, R	4	4,500	Jan. 1916	*Jan. 1914	90 days
Massachusetts	Boston	D. I. Walsh, D.	1	8,000	Jan. 1915	*Jan. 1914	None.
Michigan	Lansing	W. N. Ferris, D.	2	5,000	Jan. 1915	*Jan. 1915	None.
Minnesota	St. Paul	A. O. Eberhart, R.	2	7,000	Jan. 1915	*Jan. 1915	90 days
Mississippi	Jackson	Earl Brewer, D	4	5,000	Jan. 1916	*Jan. 1914	60 days
Missouri	Jefferson City	E. W. Major, D.	4	5,000	Jan. 1917	*Jan. 1915	70 days
Montana	Helena	S. V. Stewart, D.	4	5,000	Jan. 1917	*Jan. 1915	60 days
Nebraska	Lincoln	J. H. Morehead, D.	2	2,500	Jan. 1915	*Jan. 1915	60 days
Nevada	Carson City	T. L. Oddie, R.	4	4,000	Jan. 1915	*Jan. 1915	60 days
New Hampshire	Concord	S. D. Felker, D.	2	3,000	Jan. 1915	*Jan. 1915	None.
New Jersey	Trenton	J. E. Fielder	3	10,000	Jan. 1917	Jan. 1914	None.
New Mexico	Santa Fe	W. C. McDonald, D.	4	5,000	Jan. 1917	*Jan. 1914	60 days
New York	Albany	M. A. Glynn, D.	2	10,000	Jan. 1915	*Jan. 1914	None.
North Carolina	Raleigh	Locke Craig, D	4	6,000	Jan. 1917	*Jan. 1915	60 days
North Dakota	Bismarck	L. B. Hanna, R.	2	5,000	Jan. 1915	*Jan. 1915	60 days
Ohio	Columbus	Jas. M. Cox, D	2	10,000	Jan. 1915	*Jan. 1914	None.
Oklahoma	Oklahoma City	Lee Cruce, D.	4	4,500	Jan. 1915	*Jan. 1915	None.
Oregon	Salem	Oswald West, D.	4	5,000	Jan. 1915	*Jan. 1915	40 days
Pennsylvania	Harrisburg	John K. Tener, R.	4	10,000	Jan. 1915	*Jan. 1915	None.
Philippines	Manila	F. B. Harrison, D.		15,000			
Porto Rico	San Juan	Arthur Yager, D.	4	8,000	Dec. 1917		
Rhode Island	Providence	A. J. Pothier, R.	2	3,000	Jan. 1915	Jan. 1914	None.
South Carolina	Columbia	C. L. Blease, D.	2	3,000	Jan. 1915	*Jan. 1914	None.
South Dakota	Pierre	F. M. Byrne, R	2	3,000	Jan. 1915	*Jan. 1915	60 days
Tennessee	Nashville	B. W. Hooper, R.	2	4,000	Jan. 1915	*Jan. 1915	75 days
Texas	Austin	O. B. Colquitt, D.	2	4,000	Jan 1915	*Jan. 1915	90 days
Utah	Salt Lake City	William Spry, R.	4	6,000	Jan. 1917	*Jan. 1915	60 days
Vermont	Montpelier	A. M. Fletcher, R.	2	2,500	Oct. 1914	*Oct. 1914	None.
Virginia	Richmond	H. C. Stuart, D.	4	5,000	Feb. 1918	*Jan. 1914	90 days
Washington	Olympia	E. Lister, D.	4	6,000	Jan. 1917	*Jan. 1915	60 days
West Virginia	Charleston	H. D. Hatfield, R.	4	5,000	Mar. 1917	*Jan. 1915	45 days
Wisconsin	Madison	F. E. McGovern, R.	2	5,000	Jan. 1915	*Jan. 1915	None.
Wyoming	Cheyenne	J. M. Carey, R.	4	4,000	Jan. 1915	*Jan. 1915	40 days

*Biennial sessions. †Appointed by the president. ‡Quadrennial sessions.

SALARIES OF THE PRESIDENTS OF THE REPUBLICS OF LATIN AMERICA.

[Table furnished by International Bureau of American Republics, Washington, D. C.]

Republic.	Amount per year, national currency.	Approximate gold equivalent.	Republic.	Amount per year, national currency.	Approximate gold equivalent.
Argentina	72,000 pesos	$31,500	Dominican Rep.	$7,200	$7,200
Bolivia	18,000 bolivianos	7,200	Haiti	$24,000	24,000
Brazil	120,000 milreis (papel)	40,000	Costa Rica	18,000 colones	8,350
Chile	18,000 pesos	6,570	Guatemala	30,000 pesos	12,000
Colombia	£3,600	18,000	Honduras	24,000 pesos	9,600
Ecuador	12,000 sucres	6,000	Nicaragua	24,000 pesos	9,600
Paraguay	7,000 pesos (oro)	7,000	Salvador	22,500 pesos	9,000
Peru	£3,000	15,000			
Uruguay	$36,000	36,000	NOTE—In addition to the sums given above as personal salaries, each government appropriates an additional sum, varying with the country, for what are termed the expenses of the office of president. This in most cases adds a substantial amount to the regular salary.		
Venezuela	60,000 bolivars	12,000			
Panama	18,000 Moneda de Curso nacional	18,000			
Mexico	137 pesos a day	25,000			
Cuba	25,000 pesos	15,000			

CALIFORNIA LAND LAW AND JAPAN.

May 19, 1913, Gov. Hiram Johnson of California signed an act passed by the legislature excluding aliens from possessing land in the state except on short term leases. The government of Japan protested vigorously against the action, claiming that it was in direct violation of the treaty of Feb. 21, 1911, article 1 of which provides that the citizens or subjects of the two countries have the right to enter, travel or reside in the territories of the other, to carry on trade and lease houses and shops and residences. Though President Wilson and Secretary Bryan had urged California to take less drastic action, they upheld the state and in the exchange of diplomatic notes with Japan denied that the land law complained of was contrary to the treaty. Much popular resentment was shown in Japan and meetings were held at which some of the speakers urged the government to make war on the United States.

IMMIGRATION INTO THE UNITED STATES.
Fiscal years ended June 30.

Country.	Male.	—1913.— Female.	Total.	Male.	—1912.— Female.	Total.
Austria	82,939	54,306	137,245	48,366	37,488	85,854
Hungary	71,828	45,752	117,580	57,695	35,333	93,028
Belgium	4,971	2,434	7,405	2,580	1,589	4,169
Bulgaria, Servia, Montenegro	1,537	216	1,753	4,145	302	4,447
Denmark	4,163	2,315	6,478	4,356	1,835	6,191
France, including Corsica	5,649	4,026	9,675	4,949	3,679	8,628
German empire	19,992	14,337	34,329	15,921	11,867	27,788
Greece	20,421	2,396	22,817	19,118	2,331	21,449
Italy, including Sicily and Sardinia	201,502	64,040	265,542	105,613	51,521	157,134
Netherlands	4,196	2,706	6,902	4,276	2,343	6,619
Norway	5,092	3,495	8,587	5,058	3,617	8,675
Portugal, including Cape Verde and Azore Islands	9,217	4,954	14,171	6,648	3,582	10,230
Roumania	1,290	865	2,155	1,183	814	1,997
Russian empire and Finland	200,815	90,225	291,040	99,707	62,688	162,395
Spain, including Canary and Balearic islands	4,805	1,362	6,167	4,854	1,473	6,327
Sweden	10,548	6,654	17,202	7,735	4,953	12,688
Switzerland	2,563	1,541	4,104	2,254	1,251	3,505
Turkey in Europe	12,557	1,271	14,128	13,448	1,033	14,481
United Kingdom—England	23,929	19,434	43,363	21,043	19,365	40,408
Ireland	13,619	14,257	27,876	13,046	12,833	25,879
Scotland	7,422	6,798	14,220	7,519	7,059	11,578
Wales	1,667	1,078	2,745	1,394	768	2,162
Europe, not specified	298	73	371	183	60	243
Total Europe	711,320	344,535	1,055,855	451,091	267,784	718,875
China	1,732	373	2,105	1,495	270	1,765
Japan	3,126	5,155	8,281	2,107	4,007	6,114
India	149	30	179	148	27	175
Turkey in Asia	18,755	5,200	23,955	9,967	2,821	12,788
Other Asia	696	142	838	475	132	607
Total Asia	24,458	10,900	35,358	14,192	7,257	21,449
Africa	995	414	1,409	707	302	1,009
Australia, Tasmania, New Zealand	824	405	1,229	570	224	794
Pacific islands, not specified	83	28	111	93	11	104
British North America	51,304	22,498	73,802	36,107	19,883	55,990
Central America	1,113	360	1,473	947	295	1,242
Mexico	7,066	4,860	11,926	16,080	7,158	23,238
South America	3,224	1,024	4,248	2,230	759	2,989
West Indies	7,738	4,720	12,458	7,905	4,562	12,467
Other countries	19	4	23	9	6	15
Grand total	808,144	389,748	1,197,892	529,931	308,241	838,172

IMMIGRATION BY MONTHS.
Fiscal year ended June 30, 1913.

July	78,101	February	59,156
August	82,377	March	96,958
September	105,611	April	136,371
October	108,300	May	137,262
November	94,739	June	176,261
December	76,315		
January	46,441	Total	1,197,893

DEPORTATION OF ALIENS.

The following table shows the deportation of aliens from the United States after entry by fiscal years:

1893	577	1898	199	1903	547	1908	2,069
1894	417	1899	263	1904	779	1909	2,124
1895	177	1900	356	1905	845	1910	2,695
1896	238	1901	363	1906	676	1911	2,788
1897	263	1902	465	1907	995	1912	2,450

IMMIGRATION SINCE 1873.
Years ended June 30.

1874	313,339	1884	518,592	1894	285,631	1904	813,361
1875	227,498	1885	395,346	1895	258,536	1905	1,026,499
1876	169,986	1886	334,203	1896	343,267	1906	1,100,735
1877	141,857	1887	490,109	1897	230,832	1907	1,285,349
1878	138,469	1888	546,889	1898	229,299	1908	782,870
1879	177,826	1889	444,427	1899	311,715	1909	751,786
1880	457,257	1890	455,302	1900	448,572	1910	1,041,570
1881	669,431	1891	560,319	1901	487,918	1911	878,587
1882	788,992	1892	623,084	1902	648,743	1912	838,172
1883	603,322	1893	502,917	1903	857,046	1913	1,197,892

The total recorded immigration into the United States since the organization of the government is 30,808,944 persons.

IMMIGRATION LAW OF THE UNITED STATES.

The immigration law provides for a poll tax of $4 for every alien entering the United States. This tax is not levied upon aliens who shall enter the United States after an uninterrupted residence of at least one year immediately preceding such entrance in Canada, Newfoundland, Cuba or Mexico, nor upon aliens in transit through the United States, nor upon aliens arriving in Guam, Porto Rico or Hawaii.

Whenever the president shall be satisfied that passports issued by any foreign government to its citizens to go to any country other than the United States or to any insular possession of the United States or to the canal zone are being used for the purpose of enabling the holders to come to the continental territory of the United States to the detriment of labor conditions therein, the president may refuse to permit such citi-zens of the country issuing such passports to enter the continental territory of the United States from such other country or from such insular possessions or from the canal zone.

The following classes are excluded from admission into the United States: All idiots, imbeciles, feeble-minded persons, epileptics, insane persons and persons who have been insane within five years; persons who have had two or more attacks of insanity at any time previously; paupers; persons likely to become a public charge; professional beggars; persons afflicted with tuberculosis or with a loathsome or dangerous contagious disease; persons who have committed a felony or other crime involving moral turpitude; polygamists or persons who believe in the practice of polygamy; anarchists or persons who believe in or advocate the overthrow by force or violence of

the government of the United States, or of all governments, or of all forms of law, or the assassination of public officials; prostitutes, or women and girls coming into the United States for any immoral purpose; contract laborers who have been induced to migrate to this country by offers of employment or in consequence of agreements of any kind, verbal or written, express or implied, to perform labor in this country of any kind, skilled or unskilled; any person whose ticket or passage is paid for with the money of another, or who is assisted by others to come, unless it is satisfactorily shown that such person does not belong to one of the foregoing excluded classes and that said ticket or passage was not paid for by any corporation, society, municipality or foreign government, directly or indirectly; all children under 16 years of age unaccompanied by one or both of their parents, at the discretion of the secretary of commerce and labor. Nothing in the act shall exclude, if otherwise admissible, persons convicted of an offense purely political, not involving moral turpitude. Skilled labor may be imported if labor of like kind unemployed cannot be found in this country. The provisions of the law applicable to contract labor shall not be held to exclude professional actors, artists, lecturers, singers, clergymen, professors for colleges or seminaries, persons belonging to any recognized learned profession or persons employed strictly as personal or domestic servants.

It is unlawful to assist or encourage the importation or migration of any alien by promise of employment through advertisements printed in any foreign country. This, however, does not apply to states or territories advertising the inducements they offer to immigration thereto.

All aliens brought to this country in violation of law shall be immediately sent back by the owners of the vessels bringing them. Any alien entering the United States in violation of law and such as become public charges from causes existing prior to their landing shall be deported at any time within three years after their arrival.

No person who disbelieves in or who is opposed to all organized government, or who is a member of or affiliated with any organization entertaining and teaching such belief in or opposition to all organized government, or who advocates or teaches the duty, necessity or propriety of the unlawful assaulting or killing of any officer or officers, either of specific individuals or of officers generally, of the government of the United States, or of any other organized government, because of his or their official character, shall be permitted to enter the United States.

PROGRESS OF THE CHINESE REPUBLIC.

The first national assembly of the Chinese republic began work April 8, 1913, but it soon developed that party feeling was stronger than patriotism, and but little real progress was made in the framing of a constitution or the enactment of laws. It was not until late in the year that so much of the fundamental law was passed as to permit the election of a president and vice-president. This occurred Oct. 6, when Yuan Shih-kai, the provisional executive, was elected by the assembly to serve as the first regular president of the republic for a term of five years. Oct. 7 Gen. Li Yuen Heng was chosen vice-president, also for a term of five years.

In April the government secured a loan of $125,000,000 from Great Britain, France, Germany, Russia and Japan. The United States group of bankers withdrew from participation in the transaction. Possession of ample funds enabled Yuan Shih-kai to strengthen the army, and when a rebellion broke out in the southern provinces in July he had little difficulty in crushing it. He was accused of autocratic methods in administering the affairs of the republic. His plans were bitterly opposed by the members of the kuomintang or democratic party in and out of the national assembly, until finally he took the drastic action of causing the arrest of 300 assemblymen and ordering the dissolution of the party. The progress of events in the Chinese republic in 1913 may be gathered from the following chronological summary:

January and February—Members of assembly elected; Chinese in America represented by two senators.

Feb. 21—Lung Yu, former empress, dies.

March 19—American group of bankers withdraw from Chinese loan, President Wilson refusing to back them.

April 8—First national assembly of republic opens.

April 27—Contract for five-nation $125,000,000 loan signed in Pekin.

May 2—Chinese republic formally recognized by the United States.

May 14—Kuomintang, or democratic party, opposed to quintuple loan.

May 22—Signs of unrest in southern provinces appear.

July 3—Many members of house of representatives censure government and demand cabinet's resignation.

July 14—Rebellion breaks out in Kiangsi and other southern provinces.

July 23—Sun Yat Sen, first provisional president, backs the rebellion.

July 24—Rebels repulsed in Shanghai.

July 30—Rebel flag hauled down in Nanking.

Aug. 6—Dr. Sun Yat Sen flees from China to Japan.

Aug. 13—Rebels surrender Woosung forts near Canton.

Sept. 1—Government forces drive rebels from Nauking; several Japanese killed.

Sept. 9—Chinese cabinet reorganized.

Sept. 11—Japan demands apology for insult to Japanese flag and the killing of Japanese in Nanking by government troops.

Sept. 28—China apologizes to Japan.

Oct. 2—National assembly decides that presidential and vice-presidential terms shall be five years, with only one re-election.

Oct. 6—Yuan Shih-kai elected president at joint session of upper and lower houses of national assembly.

Oct. 7—Li Yuen Heng elected vice-president.

Oct. 10—President Yuan Shih-kai inaugurated.

Nov. 5—Three hundred assemblymen, members of the kuomintang party, expelled by President Yuan Shih-kai; dissolution of party ordered.

Nov. 10—China borrows $20,000,000 from Chino-French bank.

Nov. 13—Session of assembly suspended.

PROHIBITION STATES.

Arkansas (Jan. 1, 1914).
Georgia.
Kansas.
Maine.
Mississippi.
North Carolina.

North Dakota.
South Carolina.
Tennessee.
West Virginia (July 1, 1914).

Anti-Saloon League of America—President, Bishop Luther B. Wilson, New York, N. Y.; secretary, S. E. Nicholson, Richmond, Ind.; treasurer, Foster Copeland, Columbus, O.; superintendent, Rev. Dr. Purley A. Baker, Westerville, O.

BANK CLEARINGS IN THE UNITED STATES.

Year.	Clearings.	Year.	Clearings.	Year.	Clearings.	Year.	Clearings.
1903	$113,963,298,912	1906	157,681,259,999	1909	158,877,192,100	1911	159,373,450,000
1904	102,356,435,047	1907	154,476,830,537	1910	163,986,664,000	1912	163,506,362,000
1905	140,501,341,957	1908	126,238,694,398				

WEATHER FORECASTS AND SIGNALS.

The operations of the weather bureau of the department of agriculture are based on observations of the weather taken at about 200 observatories throughout the United States at the same moment of time and telegraphed daily to Washington, D. C., and to other important cities. These observations, comprising barometric pressure, temperature, precipitation, winds and clouds, are entered in the United States to whom the weather forecasts are available is more than 4,000,000.

When No. 4 is placed above No. 1, 2 or 3 it indicates warmer; when below, colder; when not displayed, the temperature is expected to remain about stationary. During the late spring and early fall the cold-wave flag is used to indicate anticipated frosts.

No. 1. White flag.	No. 2. Blue flag.	No. 3 White and blue flag.	No. 4. Black triangular flag.	No. 5. White flag with black square in center.

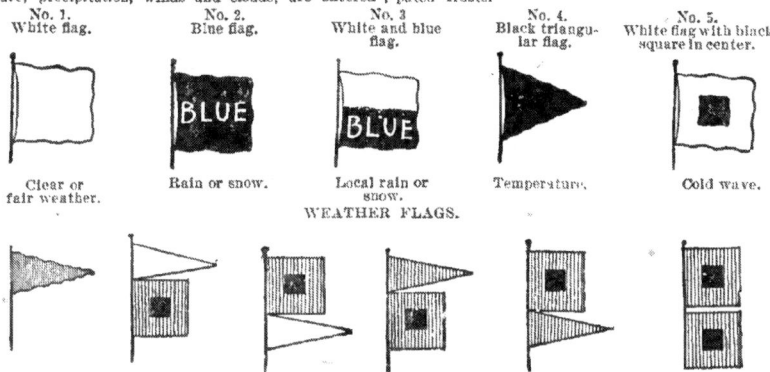

Clear or fair weather.	Rain or snow.	Local rain or snow.	Temperature.	Cold wave.

WEATHER FLAGS.

Small craft.   Northwest winds. Southwest winds. Northeast winds, Southeast winds. "Hurricane" signal.

STORM-WARNING FLAGS.

upon outline charts of the United States by means of symbols, forming the "daily weather map," from which the forecasts are made. These forecasts are issued every day for every state in the union, and whenever necessary special warnings are sent out of storms, frosts, cold waves, heavy snows and floods. In addition to the main office in Washington, there are subordinate forecast centers in Chicago, New Orleans, Denver, San Francisco and Portland, Ore. Weather forecasts for a week in advance are now sent out from Washington and published each Monday.

The forecasts are first telegraphed to about 2,300 principal distributing points, whence they are further disseminated by telegraph, telephone and through the mail by means of forecast cards, rural free delivery slips and newspapers.

It is estimated that the total number of persons

Small craft warning—A red pennant indicates that moderately strong winds are expected.

Storm warnings—A red flag with a black center indicates that a storm of marked violence is expected. The pennants displayed with the flags indicate the direction of the wind: Red, easterly; white, westerly (from southwest to north). The pennant above the flag indicates that the wind is expected to blow from the northerly quadrants; below, from southerly quadrants.

By night a red light indicates easterly winds and a white light above a red light westerly winds.

Two red flags, with black centers, displayed one above the other, indicate the expected approach of tropical hurricanes, and also of those extremely severe and dangerous storms which occasionally move across the lakes and northern Atlantic coast. Hurricane warnings are not displayed at night.

DESTRUCTIVE TORNADOES IN CENTRAL WEST AND SOUTH.

OMAHA SWEPT BY FATAL GALE.

Omaha and many other places in Nebraska, Iowa, Illinois, Indiana and Wisconsin were visited by a series of tornadoes or violent gales of wind accompanied by heavy rains Sunday afternoon and evening, March 23, and early Monday morning, March 24, 1913. Approximately 225 persons were killed and 800 injured. The exact number could not be ascertained owing to the wide extent of the storm and the havoc wrought in remote rural communities. The greatest disaster occurred in Omaha, Neb., where 140 persons were killed and 402 injured. Many were also killed or hurt in Yutan and Berlin, Neb.; Council Bluffs, Glenwood, Bartlett, Weston and Neola, Iowa, and Terre Haute and Lafayette, Ind.

Sunday morning a general storm area of low barometer was central over Colorado and conditions were so threatening that the United States weather bureau deemed it necessary to cause warnings to be sent out of shifting gales Sunday afternoon and night over the plains states and the upper Mississippi valley. In the vicinity of Omaha the day was one of fitful sunshine and windy. About 5 o'clock in the afternoon there was a violent downpour of rain and then it began to grow darker and darker until just before 6 o'clock, when the storm broke in earnest. It came upon Omaha from the southwest and cut a pathway twenty-four blocks long and from three to seven blocks wide through the residence part of the city. From 54th and Center streets it traveled north and east to Leavenworth street and then it took a northeasterly course to 40th and Farnam streets. Still traveling a little east of north, it covered a course from 40th street east to 34th street, a distance of six blocks. Striking Bemis park, the storm turned sharply to the east and passed along Parker and Blondo streets to 24th street, where its path was six blocks wide. Finally at 14th and Spencer streets it swept over the bluffs along the Missouri river and after demolishing a number of buildings on the outskirts of the city disappeared to the northeast.

The Commercial Club of Omaha, after a careful investigation of the situation, announced that the number of houses destroyed or made uninhabitable was 642 and that 1,027 houses had been partly destroyed. The people made homeless numbered 2,179, while those made entirely destitute were 263. Most of the latter were cared for at the homes of friends and comparatively few made use of the public kitchen established at the Auditorium. Eleven churches and eight schools were wrecked.

Various estimates of the total loss on property in

Omaha were made, but the figure generally agreed upon as approximately correct was $5,000,000.

Scenes similar to those in Omaha, but on a smaller scale, were witnessed in Council Bluffs, Iowa, on the other side of the Missouri river. The dead there numbered twelve and the injured thirteen. Yutan, Neb., west of Omaha and near the Platte river, reported sixteen killed and twenty injured. The village of Berlin, Neb., fifty miles south of Omaha, had ten killed and seventeen injured. Neola, Iowa, twenty-one miles northeast of Council Bluffs, suffered severely, as did Glenwood, Bartlett and Weston in the same state.

TORNADO AT TERRE HAUTE, IND.

The storm center, which was over Colorado Sunday morning, crossed Nebraska and Iowa Sunday afternoon and evening and passed over into Illinois, Indiana and Wisconsin, where most of the damage was done after midnight Monday morning. It developed into tornadoes at several points, the most destructive sweeping over Terre Haute and vicinity in Indiana. Here twenty-one persons were killed, 275 homes wrecked and property valued at about $1,000,000 destroyed. Hundreds of persons were cared for at charitable institutions and citizens and the wrecked district was patrolled by a company of the 1st Indiana national guard, which had been ordered out by Gov. Ralston.

GALE IN CHICAGO.

In Chicago six persons were killed and some fifty more or less seriously injured. The gale, accompanied by thunder and lightning, rain and sleet struck the city shortly after midnight Monday morning. It traveled at the rate of fifty-six miles an hour, uprooting trees, tearing down telegraph and telephone lines, toppling over chimneys and wrecking houses. Most of the damage was done in the northwestern part of the city and suburbs in that direction.

Heavy rains, gales and floods caused serious losses in Milwaukee, Racine, Fond du Lac and other places in Wisconsin early Monday morning. A great number of towns and farming communities in that state as well as in Illinois reported heavy damage to buildings, stock and other property.

SUMMARY OF STORM CASUALTIES.

	Dead.	Injured.
Omaha, Neb.	140	402
Terre Haute, Ind.	21	250
Chicago, Ill.	6	40
Yutan, Neb.	16	20
Berlin, Neb.	7	17
Council Bluffs, Iowa	12	13
Bartlett, Iowa	3	10
Weston, Iowa	2	2
Neola, Iowa	2	2
Danville Crossing, Iowa	1	..
Glenwood, Iowa	5	2
Lafayette, Ind.	2	..
Walton, Ill.	1	3
Sterling, Ill.	1	..
Erie, Ill.	1	..
Traverse City, Mich.	1	..
Total	221	761

STORM IN SOUTHERN STATES.

Scores of people were killed and millions of dollars' worth of property was destroyed by a widespread storm of wind and rain which passed over some of the central southern states Thursday afternoon and night, March 13, 1913. The greatest havoc was wrought in Georgia, Tennessee, Alabama and Louisiana. Among the towns and cities reporting losses of life were the following:

Tucker, Ga.	9
Eaglesville, Ga.	4
Clarkston, Ga.	3
Rosedale, Ga.	14
Columbus, Ga.	2
South Berlin, Tenn.	3
Near Provincal, La.	2

Louisville, Ky.	2
Near Huntsville, Ala.	5
Near Middleton, Tenn.	14
Calera, Ala.	3
Hokes Bluff, Ala.	2
Gayesville, Ala.	2
Duke, Ala.	2

The total number of deaths caused by the storm could not be definitely ascertained but careful estimates placed it at about 100. The weather both in the south and the north before the gale had been warm and springlike. In the northwestern states the mild weather was succeeded by blizzards, March 14 and 15, which stopped traffic on the railroads and did much damage to property.

HEAVY GALES ON GREAT LAKES.

Sunday and Monday, Nov. 9 and 10, 1913, a storm of unusual violence raged on all of the great lakes, causing the loss of many lives and much damage to property. More than a dozen vessels were wrecked and a score driven ashore but released afterward. The number of casualties so far as could be ascertained exceeded 200. Among the vessels reported wrecked were the steamers Charles S. Price, J. P. Hutchinson, John McGean, Regina, Wexford, James Carruthers, Northern Queen, Leafield, F. G. Hartwell, Lafayette, M. H. Hanna, Jr., William Nottingham, Matoa, L. C. Waldo and Turret Chief. The loss on vessel property was estimated at nearly $3,000,000.

The gale did much damage to shore park property in Chicago, the loss there amounting to $600,000. In Cleveland, O., the gale was accompanied by a heavy fall of snow, which almost paralyzed traffic for three days and caused damages estimated at $5,000,000.

PERRY CENTENNIAL CELEBRATIONS.

The centennial anniversary of the victory of Commodore Oliver Hazard Perry at the battle of Lake Erie Sept. 10, 1813, was observed by a series of celebrations beginning at Put-in-Bay, O., July 4, 1913, and ending at the same place Sept. 10 and 11. The other celebrations occurred at Erie, Pa., Fairport, O., Lorain, O., Monroe, Mich., Toledo, O., Detroit, Mich., Green Bay, Wis., Milwaukee, Wis., Chicago, Ill., Buffalo, N. Y., and Sandusky, O. Commodore Perry's restored flagship, Niagara, made a cruise of the great lakes and was exhibited at the cities named. The corner stone of the Perry victory monument was laid at Put-in-Bay, O., July 4.

FIRST ELECTIONS UNDER 17TH AMENDMENT.

Augustus O. Bacon (dem.) was elected to the United States senate by the direct vote of the people July 15, 1913. It was the first election held under the new amendment to the constitution of the United States providing that voters shall cast direct ballots for members of the national senate.

The second senatorial election by the new method was in Maryland, where Blair Lee (dem.) was chosen Nov. 4, 1913, to fill the unexpired term of Senator Isidor Rayner, deceased.

CLIMATOLOGY OF THE UNITED STATES.

The following table of average rainfall, highest and lowest temperatures, based upon observations of forty-two or fewer years at selected stations in the several states and territories of the United States, was compiled from the records of the weather bureau for The Chicago Daily News Almanac by the United States weather bureau, Washington, D. C.:

State. Stations.	Barometer No. above sea level (ft.)	yrs	Temperature.* Max.	Year.	Min.	Year.	Av pre-cipita-tion.
Alabama—Mobile	84	42	102	1901	—1	1899	62.0
Montgomery	240	40	107	1881	—5	1889	51.2
Arizona—Yuma	141	37	120	1910	22	1911	3.1
Arkansas—Little Rock..	398	33	106	1901	—12	1899	49.9
California—S. Francisco	207	42	101	1904	29	1888	22.3
San Diego	59	41	101	1883	32	1894	10.0
Colorado—Denver	5,272	41	105	1878	—29	1875	14.0
Pueblo	4,685	24	104	1902	—27	1899	12.0
Connecticut—New Haven	120	40	100	1881	—14	1873	47.2
Dist. Col.—Washington	111	42	104	1881	—15	1899	43.5
Florida—Jacksonville	74	31	104	1879	10	1899	53.2
Key West	14	42	100	1886	41	1886	38.7
Georgia—Atlanta	1,218	44	100	1887	—8	1899	49.4
Savannah	154	42	105	1879	8	1899	50.3
Idaho—Boise	2,770	28	111	1898	—28	1888	12.7
Lewiston	756	20	108	1905	—18	1884	13.5
Pocatello	4,483	14	102	1901	—20	1905	12.9
Illinois—Cairo	356	41	106	1901	—16	1884	41.7
Chicago	816	42	103	1901	—23	1872	33.3
Springfield	614	33	107	1901	—24	1905	37.0
Indiana—Indianapolis	822	39	106	1901	—25	1884	41.5
Iowa—Des Moines	861	34	109	1901	—30	1884	32.4
Kansas—Dodge City	2,533	38	108	1876	—26	1899	20.8
Kentucky—Louisville	654	40	107	1901	—20	1884	44.3
Louisiana—New Orleans	51	42	102	1901	7	1899	57.4
Shreveport	238	40	110	1909	—5	1899	45.7
Maine—Eastport	76	40	93	1901	—21	1884	43.3
Portland	103	41	103	1911	—17	1872	42.5
Maryland—Baltimore	78	40	104	1898	—7	1899	43.2
Massachusetts—Boston..	125	42	104	1911	—13	1882	43.4
Michigan—Alpena	616	40	101	1913	—27	1882	33.2
Detroit	782	42	101	1887	—24	1872	32.2
Marquette	709	38	198	1901	—27	1875	32.6
Minnesota—St. Paul	940	40	104	1901	—41	1888	28.7
Moorhead	913	32	102	1894	—48	1887	24.9
Mississippi—Vicksburg..	247	40	101	1881	—1	1899	52.7
Missouri—St. Louis	633	42	107	1901	—1	1899	37.2
Montana—Helena	4,121	33	103	1886	—42	1893	12.8
Havre	2,422	32	108	1900	—55	1887	13.7
Nebraska—North Platte	2,809	28	107	1877	—35	1899	18.9
Omaha	1,105	40	107	1911	—32	1884	30.7
Nevada—Winnemucca	4,291	34	104	1877	—28	1888	8.4
N.Jersey—Atlantic City	16	37	99	1880	—7	1899	40.8
New York—Albany	97	39	104	1911	—24	1904	36.4
Rochester	523	41	101	1911	—14	1904	34.3
New Mexico—Santa Fe.	7,018	39	97	1878	—13	1883	14.5
N. Carolina—Charlotte..	773	34	102	1887	—5	1899	49.2
Wilmington	78	42	103	1879	5	1899	51.0
N. Dakota—Bismarck..	1,674	38	107	1910	—44	1887	17.6
Fort Buford, Williston	1,896	40	107	1883	—49	1888	13.1
Ohio—Cincinnati	628	42	105	1901	—17	1899	38.3
Cleveland	762	41	99	1881	—17	1873	35.0
Oklahoma—Okla. City..	1,262	21	108	1909	—17	1899	31.7
Oregon—Portland	58	40	102	1891	—2	1888	45.1
Roseburg	510	35	106	1905	—6	1888	34.4
Pennsylvania—Philadelphia	117	42	103	1901	—6	1899	41.2
Pittsburgh	1,070	40	103	1881	—20	1899	36.4
Rhode Isl'd—Block Isl'd	43	32	92	1911	—4	1896	44.4
S. Carolina—Charleston	48	40	104	1879	7	1899	52.1
S. Dakota—Rapid City	3,234	27	106	1900	—34	1899	18.7
Yankton	1,231	38	107	1894	—36	1912	25.4
Tennessee—Knoxville	1,007	42	100	1887	—16	1884	49.4
Memphis	316	40	104	1901	—9	1899	50.3
Texas—Abilene	1,735	27	110	1886	—6	1899	24.7
Galveston	69	41	98	1901	8	1899	47.1
Utah—Salt Lake City	4,408	39	102	1889	—20	1883	16.0
Vermont—Northfield	848	26	98	1911	—35	1908	33.6
Virginia—Norfolk	149	42	102	1887	2	1895	49.5
Washington—Spokane	1,955	32	104	1898	—30	1888	18.8
West Virginia—Parkersburg	638	24	102	1901	—27	1899	40.2
Wisconsin—Milwaukee..	681	42	100	1901	—25	1875	31.4
Wyoming—Cheyenne	6,110	40	100	1881	—38	1875	13.6

*Corrected to Dec. 31, 1912, inclusive. †Precipitation normals adopted in 1907.

NOTABLE GIFTS AND BEQUESTS IN 1913.

Altman, Benjamin, New York, N. Y., by will to Metropolitan Museum of Art, art collection valued at $5,000,000 to $15,000,000; to National Academy of Design, $100,000.

Anderson, Mrs. Elizabeth M., New York, N. Y., to New York Association for Improving the Condition of the Poor, $650,000.

Borden, William W., Chicago, Ill., by will to churches and missions, $900,000.

Butterfield, Mrs. Julia L., New York, N. Y., to Young Men's Christian association, $2,000,000.

Carnegie, Andrew, New York, N. Y., to Carnegie Foundation for Endowment of a "division of educational inquiry and study," $1,250,000; to Carnegie technical schools, Pittsburgh, $1,000,000; to Vanderbilt university medical department, $1,000,000.

Culver, Mrs. Mary F., St. Louis, Mo., to Christian university, Canton, Mo., $160,000.

Doremus, Robert P., New York, N. Y., by will to Washington and Lee university, Lexington, Va., $1,000,000.

Drummond, Edward A., Chicago, Ill., by will to Bowdoin college, $85,000.

Harris, Norman W., Chicago, Ill., to Northwestern university, $250,000.

Higginson, Henry L., Boston, Mass., by will to Boston Symphony orchestra, $1,000,000.

Hill, Martha E., Chicago, Ill., by will to charitable and philanthropic institutions, $75,000.

Hooper, Mrs. George W., San Francisco, Cal., to University of California, $1,000,000 for medical research.

Milliken, Mrs. Anna B., Decatur, Ill., by will to educational and charitable projects, $1,000,000.

Morgan, J. Pierpont, New York, N. Y., by will to St. George's Episcopal church, $500,000; to archdeaconry of Orange, $100,000; to House of Rest for Consumptives, $100,000.

Morris, Edward, Chicago, Ill., by will to charities, $315,000.

McKnight, Mrs. Mary D., Galesburg, Ill., by will, $435,000 to churches and charity.

McPherson, Mrs. Ella J., Jersey City, N. J., by will to Yale university, $218,000.

Noyes, LaVerne W., Chicago, Ill., to University of Chicago, $300,000.

Payne, Oliver H., New York, N. Y., $4,350,000 to Cornell university medical school in New York city.

Pell, Mrs. Mary B., New York, N. Y., by will to Rutgers college, $1,000,000; to Columbia university, $1,000,000; to Reformed Church in America, $1,000,000.

Rockefeller, John D., New York, N. Y., to American Baptist Home Mission society, $100,000; to Johns Hopkins Medical school, $1,500,000; to Barnard college, $200,000; to Wellesley college, $200,000; to Ripon (Wis.) college, $50,000.

Rosenwald, Julius, Chicago, Ill., to Hebrew Union college, $25,000; to colored Y. M. C. A. in Cincinnati, O., $25,000; to Hebrew Institute, Chicago, $50,000.

Rutherford, Henry, Grand Isle, Vt., by will to Rockefeller Institute for Medical Research, $200,000.

Schiff, Jacob, New York, N. Y., to Hebrew Union college, $30,000.

Selz, Morris, Chicago, Ill., by will to charity, $150,000.

Taylor, Charles L., Pittsburgh, Pa., to Lehigh university for gymnasium, $200,000.

Thompson, Ferris S., New York, N. Y., by will to Princeton university, $2,000,000; to Mercy hospital, Chicago, $300,000; to Salvation army, $100,000.

WINNERS OF THE NOBEL PRIZES.

PHYSICS.

1901—William Conrad Roentgen, professor of physics at the University of Munich.

1902—Divided equally between Henrik Anton Lorentz, professor of physics at the University of Leyden, and Peter Zeeman, professor of physics at the University of Amsterdam.

1903—Half to Antoine Henri Becquerel, professor of physics at the Ecole Polytechnique and at the Museum d'Histoire Naturelle, Paris, France, member Institut Francaise, and half to Pierre Curie, professor of physics at the University of Paris (Sorbonne) and teacher in physics at the Paris Municipal School of Industrial Physics and Chemistry, and his wife, Marie Sklodovska Curie, preceptress at the Higher Normal School for Young Girls at Sevres.

1904—Lord Rayleigh, professor of natural philosophy, Royal Institution of Great Britain, London.

1905—Philippe Lenard, professor of physics at the Physical Institute of Kiel.

1906—J. J. Thomson, professor of experimental physics at the University of Cambridge.

1907—Albert A. Michelsen, professor of physics at the University of Chicago.

1908—Prof. Gabriel Lippman of the University of Paris.

1909—G. Marconi, Italy, and Prof. Ferdinand Braun of Strassburg.

1910—Johannes Diderik van der Waals, professor of experimental physics in the University of Amsterdam, Holland.

1911—Prof. Wilhelm Wien, University of Wuerzburg.

1912—Gustaf Dalen, Swedish engineer.

1913—Prof. H. Kamerlingh Onnes, University of Leyden.

MEDICINE.

1901—Emil Adolf von Behring, professor of hygiene and medical history at the University of Marburg, Prussia.

1902—Donald Ross, professor of tropical medicine at the University college of Liverpool.

1903—Niels Ryberg Finsen, professor of medicine, Copenhagen, Denmark.

1904—Ivan Petrovic Pawlow, professor of physiology in the Military Academy of Medicine, St. Petersburg.

1905—Robert Koch, member of the Royal Academy of Science, Berlin.

1906—Profs. Ramon y Cajal and Camillo Golgi of the Pavia university, Italy.

1907—Charles L. A. Laveran of the Pasteur institute in Paris.

1908—Dr. Paul Ehrlich of Berlin and Prof. Elie Metchnikoff of the Pasteur institute, Paris.

1909—Prof. E. T. Kocher, Switzerland.

1910—Dr. Albrecht Kossel, professor of physiology, Heidelberg university, Germany.

1911—Alivar Gullstrand, professor of diseases of the eye, Upsala university, Sweden.

1912—Dr. Alexis Carrel of the Rockefeller Institute for Medical Research, New York, N. Y.

1913—Prof. Charles Richet, University of Paris.

CHEMISTRY.

1901—Jakob Hendrik van't Hoff, professor of chemistry in the University of Berlin.

1902—Emil Fischer, professor of chemistry in the University of Berlin.

1903—Svante August Arrhenius, professor at the University of Stockholm.

1904—Sir William Ramsay, professor of chemistry in the University college, London.

1905—Adolf von Baeyer, professor of chemistry at Munich.

1906—H. Moissan, professor of chemistry at the Sorbonne, Paris.

1907—Eduard Buchner, professor of chemistry in the agricultural high school of Berlin.

1908—Prof. Ernest Rutherford of the University of Manchester, England.

1909—Prof. W. Ostwald of Leipsic.

1910—Otto Wallach, professor of chemistry in the University of Gottingen.

1911—Mme. Marie S. Curie, professor of sciences, University of Paris.

1912—Prof. Grignard, Nancy university, and Prof. Paul Sabatier, Toulouse university.

1913—Prof. Alfred Werner, University of Zurich.

LITERATURE.

1901—Rene Francois Armand Sully-Prudhomme, member of the French academy.

1902—Theodor Mommsen, a professor of history at the University of Berlin.

1903—Bjornstjerne Bjornson, author, Norway.

1904—Half to Frederic Mistral of France and half to Jose Echegaray of Spain.

1905—Henryk Sienkiewicz, author of "Quo Vadis?"

1906—Prof. Giosue Carducci of Bologna, Italy.

1907—Rudyard Kipling of England.

1908—Prof. Rudolf Eucken, University of Java.

1909—Selma Lagerlof, Sweden.

1910—Paul Johann Ludwig Heyse, Germany.

1911—Maurice Maeterlinck, Belgium.

1912—Gerhart Hauptmann, German author and dramatist.

1913—Rabindranath Tagore, Hindu poet.

PEACE.

1901—Divided equally between Henri Dunant, founder of the International Red Cross Society of Geneva, and Frederic Passay, founder of the first French peace association, the "Societe Francaise pour l'Arbitrage Entre Nations."

1902—Divided equally between Elie Ducommum, secretary of the international peace bureau at Bern, and Albert Gobat, chief of the interparliamentary peace bureau at Bern.

1903—William Randal Cremer, M. P., secretary of the International Arbitration league, London.

1904—The Institute of International Right, a scientific association founded in 1873 in Ghent, Belgium.

1905—Baroness Bertha von Suttner for her literary work written in the interest of the world's peace movement.

1906—Theodore Roosevelt, president of the United States, for the part he took in bringing the Russo-Japanese war to an end. Money set apart by the president for the establishment of a permanent industrial peace commission.

1907—Divided equally between Ernesto T. Moneta, president of the Lombardy Peace union, and Louis Renault, professor of international law at the University of Paris.

1908—K. P. Arnoldsen of Sweden and M. F. Bajer of Denmark.

1909—Baron d'Estournelles de Constant, Paris, and M. Beernaert, Holland.

1910—International Permanent Peace Bureau, Bern.

1911—Prof. T. C. M. Asser, Holland, and Alfred Fried, Austria.

1912—Elihu Root of New York.

1913—Henri La Fontaine of Belgium.

The prizes are awarded on the 10th of December of each year. They amount to about $38,000 each.

LYNCHINGS IN THE UNITED STATES.

1894	190	1899	107	1904	90	1909	36
1895	171	1900	116	1905	64	1910	45
1896	131	1901	135	1906	68	1911	39
1897	166	1902	96	1907	33	1912	33
1898	127	1903	106	1908	68	1913	23

CLINICAL CONGRESS OF SURGEONS.

President—Dr. John B. Murphy, Chicago, Ill.
Vice-President—Dr. George E. Armstrong, Montreal, Que.

Secretary—Dr. Franklin H. Martin, Chicago, Ill.
Treasurer—Allen B. Kanavel, Chicago, Ill.

EVENTS OF THE YEAR 1913.

FIRE LOSSES AND CASUALTIES.

Aikens, S. C., Feb. 2—Park-in-the-Pines hotel burned; loss, $250,000.

Akron, O., Aug. 17—Loewenthal Rubber company plant burned; loss, $250,000.

Bangor, Pa., July 31—8. Flory Manufacturing company's plant burned; loss, $1,000,000.

Battle Creek, Mich., Jan. 16—Eldred block and other buildings burned; loss, $250,000.

Bay Point, Cal., Aug. 27—C. A. Smith lumber yards burned; loss, $1,000,000.

Binghamton, N. Y., July 22—Sixty-five women employes burned to death in factory.

Buffalo, N. Y., May 15—Erie grain elevator; loss, $1,000,000.

Buffalo, N. Y., Sept. 13—Milling company's plant burned; loss, $200,000.

Calgary, Alberta, Jan. 12—P. Burns & Co.'s packing plant burned; loss, $2,000,000.

Calgary, Alberta, April 18—Morning Albertan office burned; loss, $300,000.

Chicago, Ill., Jan. 3—Kimball building burned; loss, $250,000.

Chicago, Jan. 21—One killed and six injured in fire at 2010 West Kinzie street.

Chicago, Jan. 30—Iowa hotel, 330 North Clark street, burned; four lives lost—many injured.

Chicago, Feb. 11—Ingraham and Kall apartments burned; seven firemen injured; loss, $300,000.

Chicago, Feb. 13—Brunswick-Balke-Collender building, 324-28 South Wabash avenue, burned; loss, $300,000.

Chicago, Feb. 26—Building at 215-223 West Congress street burned; loss, $100,000.

Chicago, March 9—Grain elevator at East 121st street and South Park avenue burned; loss, $125,000.

Chicago, March 18—Manufacturing plants at 428 West Ohio street burned; loss, $250,000.

Chicago, April 7—Fire in Armour & Co.'s plant at the stock yards causes loss of $500,000; four firemen hurt.

Chicago, May 2—Building at 80-82 East South Water street burned; loss, $100,000.

Chicago, May 9—Garage at 416 East 47th street burned; loss, $175,000.

Chicago, May 11—Four buildings at Stewart avenue and West 63d street burned; loss, $100,000.

Chicago, May 24—Fire at 409 South Green street causes loss of $150,000.

Chicago, June 4—Tannery at Warde street and Elston avenue burned; loss, $200,000.

Chicago, June 19—At 2231-51 South Western avenue; loss, $175,000.

Chicago, July 24—Globe laundry burned; loss, $100,000.

Chicago, Aug. 11—American Cocoanut Butter company's plant burned; loss, $125,000.

Chicago, Sept. 2-3—Fire at 440 South State street causes loss of one life; many firemen hurt.

Chicago, Sept. 10—Railroad machine shops at South Chicago burned; loss, $500,000.

Chicago, Sept. 27—Miller, Hall & Son's bedstead factory, 2535-2553 West Taylor street, burned; loss, $250,000.

Cincinnati, O., Jan. 2.—Carlisle building burned; loss, $250,000.

Clifton, Ariz., April 7—Five persons killed and property loss of $200,000 caused by fire.

Dubuque, Ia., April 8—Julien hotel and other buildings burned; loss, $400,000.

East St. Louis, Oct. 19-20—Grain elevator and other buildings burned; loss, $1,000,000.

Ebenezer, Pa., Feb. 9—Seven children burned to death in absence of parents from home.

Fort Worth, Tex., Feb. 15—Hotel Seibold burned; loss, $150,000.

Gretna, Man., April 29—Business section burned; loss, $600,000.

Hot Springs, Ark., Sept. 5—Fifty city blocks swept by fire; 2,500 made homeless; property loss, $6,-000,000.

Janesville, Wis., April 1—Business buildings burned; loss, $300,000.

Jersey City, N. J., Aug. 20—Forty dwellings and factories burned; loss, $800,000.

Malone, N. Y., April 17—DeWilson hotel burned; seven persons killed and fifteen injured.

Manchester, England, Sept. 3—Bonded warehouse burned; loss, $1,250,000.

Michigan City, Ind., July 12—Haskell & Barker Car company's plant burned; loss, $700,000.

Milwaukee, Wis., Oct. 26—Seven firemen killed and a score hurt in burning of Goodyear Rubber company building; property loss, $500,000.

Monteville, N. J., Feb. 17—Columbia paint works burned; loss, $750,000.

New York, N. Y., Feb. 2—Two women killed and a dozen other persons badly injured in a Houston street theater panic.

New York, N. Y., April 21—Shooters' Island shipyard burned; loss, $1,000,000.

Omaha, Neb., Feb. 28—Many persons lose their lives by burning of hotel.

Omaha, Neb., Aug. 17—Business buildings burned; loss, $500,000.

Orangeburg, S. C., Jan. 9—Main building of Claflin university burned; loss, $75,000.

Peotone, Ill., May 8—Business part of village burned; loss, $200,000.

Pueblo, Col., April 11—Swift block burned; loss, $300,000.

Quincy, Ill., Feb. 17—Dayton Tablet works burned; loss, $500,000.

Richland, Iowa, Jan. 31—Family of five burned to death in farm house.

Sacramento, Cal., Feb. 2—Apartment house fire results in death of four persons and injury to eleven others.

St. Paul, Minn., Oct. 3—Union railroad station burned; loss, $150,000.

Savannah, Ga., Feb. 2—Wharves and warehouses burned; loss, $1,500,000.

Springfield, Ill., Oct. 12—Mendenhall and other buildings burned; loss, $500,000.

Springfield, Mo., June 9—Business buildings burn; loss, $500,000.

Tokyo, Japan, Feb. 19—Fire in Kanda district destroys 3,300 buildings and makes 15,000 persons homeless.

Vandalia, Ill., March 16—Ford Manufacturing plant burned; loss, $150,000.

White Plains, N. Y., March 4—Eleven buildings in business section burned; loss, 700,000.

Winnipeg, Man., Feb. 11—Hotel Sutherland burned; loss, $100,000.

Yokohama, Japan, March 6-7—Loss of $7,500,000 caused by fire in business quarter.

MISCELLANEOUS CASUALTIES.

Boston, Mass., July 13—Eight men drowned by capsizing of sloop.

Buffalo, N. Y., July 24—Eighteen persons killed and sixty-two injured by explosion in Hested mill.

Cambridge, Mass., May 3—Six school children drowned by sinking of pleasure boat.

Carrollton, Mo., Aug. 16—Six persons killed when train strikes automobile.

Chicago, March 20—Five persons killed by escaping gas at 2635 North Lawndale avenue.

Chicago, June 19—Four persons lose lives in river when launch sinks.

Cincinnati, O., July 30—Seven persons burned to death and a score injured in motordrome accident.

Collinsville, Okla., May 12—Five men killed by a stroke of lightning.

Dublin, Ireland, Sept. 2—Forty persons killed by collapse of four houses.

Duluth, Minn., July 31—Six men killed and fourteen injured in train collision on ore dock.

Duluth, Minn., Aug. 13—Seven lives lost in launch accident.

East Freetown, Mass., Aug. 9—Six persons drowned by sinking of motor boat.

Greencastle, Ind., Nov. 1—Bleachers fall at football game; 100 persons hurt.

Hartford, Conn., Nov. 3—Seven persons killed by explosion in warehouse.

Ithaca, N. Y., May 17—Four Cornell students drowned by overturning of canoe in Cayuga lake.

Lawrence, Mass., June 30—Collapse of wooden bathhouse walk causes death of twelve boys in Merrimac river.

Lemberg, Austria-Hungary, Oct. 11—Sixteen women killed in synagogue panic.

Long Beach, Cal., May 24—Thirty-six persons killed and 100 injured by collapse of a pier.

Los Angeles, Cal., July 13—Twelve persons killed and 200 injured by collision of interurban car at Vineyard station.

Mexico City, Mex., Aug. 19—Nearly 100 persons killed by dynamite explosion in Tacubaya.

Mount Morrison park, Colorado, May 30—Thirty persons injured by fall of tallyho over high embankment.

New Madrid, Mo., June 22—Nine men drowned by capsizing of boat.

New York, N. Y., Oct. 24—Five lives lost in fire at 206 Canal street.

Oakley Farm, Miss., July 22—Thirty-five negro convicts burned to death in cage.

Quebec, Can., Sept. 26—Eight children burned to death.

Racine, Wis., June 11—Five men killed and seven injured by boiler explosion on the barge E. M. Peck.

Riverside, Cal., April 23—Eleven men killed by dynamite explosion at cement plant.

Riverton, Ill., June 10—Four business men killed by automobile colliding with train.

St. John, Ind., Aug. 24—Family of five killed by train striking automobile.

St. Louis, Mo., June 15—Twenty-four persons injured in collision on Creve Cœur trolley line.

San Diego, Cal., May 23—Two men killed by explosion of cylinders on torpedo boat destroyer Stewart.

Swinemunde, Germany, Aug. 7—Seventeen persons drowned by capsizing of sailing boat.

Tompkinsville, N. Y., June 27—Five men killed by explosion of fuel oil on steamer Mohawk.

Vallejo, Cal., June 19—Eleven persons killed in collision on interurban line.

Wausau, Wis., May 11—Six lives lost by overturning of motor boat.

Windmill Point, Lake Erie, July 6—Five young men drowned by upsetting of canoe.

MARINE DISASTERS.

Agada, bark, foundered off mouth of Humber, England, Jan. 21—Twelve men drowned.

Alum Chive, British steamer, destroyed by dynamite explosion in Baltimore (Md.) harbor, March 7—Fifty lives lost.

Balmes, Spanish steamer, burned at sea Nov. 15—No lives lost.

Bridgeport, steam collier, wrecked in St. Lawrence river, about Nov. 9—Forty-two lives lost.

Burgmeister Hackman, oil steamer, burned with cargo at New York, N. Y., Aug. 29—Loss, $200,000.

Calvados, British steamer, foundered in Sea of Marmora, March 1—200 lives lost.

Christiania, steamer, sunk in collision off Borkum, Germany, Feb. 14—Five lives lost.

Concordia, steamer, sunk in Mississippi river at Clayton, La., May 2—Thirteen lives lost.

Craven, U. S. torpedo boat, damaged by boiler explosion at sea—Two men killed and three injured.

El Dorado, steamer, lost in storm Jan. 2 or 3 on Atlantic coast—Thirty-nine lives lost.

Ferryboat sunk in Tcheptca river, Russia, June 5—Fifty persons drowned.

Gardenia, British steamer, sunk in collision in North sea—Eighteen lives lost.

Henry Bosse, steamer, capsized in Mississippi river at Keokuk, Ia., Aug. 19—Seven lives lost.

Imperator, steamship, damaged by fire in hold while at Hoboken, N. J., Aug. 28—One life lost.

Iowa, steamer, sunk in collision in Chicago harbor, July 17—No lives lost.

James T. Staples, steamer, sunk in Tombigbee river, Alabama, Jan. 9—Eighteen persons killed; ten injured.

John A. McGean, steamer, lost on Lake Erie, Nov. 9—Twenty-nine lives lost.

Julia Luckenbach, steamer, sunk in collision in Chesapeake bay, Jan. 3—Twenty-two lives lost.

Launch founders in River Rangoon, India, Jan. 28—Seventy lives lost.

Massena, French battle ship, Jan. 6—Eight men killed by explosion of steam pipe.

Mimi, German bark, wrecked on Oregon coast April 6—Eighteen men drowned.

Nebraska, battle ship, loses launch in hurricane at Newport News, Va., Sept. 3—Eight lives lost.

Nevada, steamer, sunk by mine in Gulf of Smyrna May 24—Forty lives lost.

O'Brien, Thomas F., tugboat, sunk in East river at New York, N. Y., April 1—Five lives lost.

Pangani, German bark, sunk in collision in British channel, Jan. 28—Twenty-six lives lost.

Patrie, French bark, burned on Atlantic ocean, Oct. 31—Three lives lost.

Penn, steamship, burned at Philadelphia, Pa., Sept. 6—Loss, $100,000.

Pilot, river tow boat, wrecked by boiler explosion near Pittsburgh, Pa., Aug. 30—Eight lives lost.

Rosecrans, oil steamer, wrecked on Oregon coast Jan. 7—Thirty-one lives lost.

S178, German torpedo boat destroyer, sunk in collision in North sea March 5—Seventy-one lives lost.

Senegal, French liner, wrecked at Smyrna, by explosion of mine, May 21—Five persons killed and six fatally injured.

State of California, steamer, wrecked near Juneau, Alaska, Aug. 17—Forty lives lost.

Uranium, steamer, ran on reef near Halifax, N. S., Jan. 12—No lives lost.

Urd, Swedish gunboat, sunk in collision near Malmo, Sweden, Aug. 22—No lives lost.

Veronese, British steamer, wrecked near Oporto, Portugal, Jan. 16—Sixteen lives lost.

Volturno, steamship, wrecked by explosion and fire in mid-Atlantic, Oct. 9—134 lives lost.

Westkuesten, Finnish steamer, wrecked in Gulf of Bothnia, Oct. 22—44 lives lost.

STORMS AND FLOODS.

Alabama, Mississippi and other states swept by destructive storm, March 21—Scores of lives lost.

Africa, Jan. 22—Three hundred and fifty pilgrims to Mecca drowned by flood near Medina, Arabia.

Berlin, Neb., March 23—Seven persons killed and seventeen injured by tornado.

California, Jan. 5-7—Loss of $30,000,000 caused by frost damaging fruit crops in southern California.

Cerbere, France, Sept. 30—Fourteen persons killed and thirty injured in heavy thunderstorm.

Chicago, March 24—Six persons killed and fifty or more injured in heavy wind and rain storm; fifty houses blown down.

Cleveland, O., Nov. 9-11—City traffic paralyzed by blizzard; damage, $5,000,000.

Constantinople, Turkey, Sept. 30—Cloudburst causes loss of 260 lives.

Council Bluffs, Iowa, March 23—Twelve persons killed and thirteen injured by tornado.

Dayton, O.—See "Ohio and Indiana Floods."

Decatur, Ala., March 21—Seven persons killed in storm.

Fulton, Ala., March 21—Twenty-nine persons killed in storm; fifty injured.

Georgia, Tennessee, Louisiana and other southern states visited by severe storm, March 13—Nearly 100 persons killed.

Gijon, Spain, Feb. 25—Nearly 200 persons killed or wounded by powder explosion.

Glenwood, Iowa, March 23—Five persons killed and three injured by tornado.

Great lakes swept by heavy gale Nov. 9-11—Many lives lost in wrecks; property loss, $2,500,000.

Hoxie, Ark., March 21—One killed and twenty-five injured.

India, June 14—Loss of 300 lives caused by floods in the Palitana district north of Bombay.

Indiana—See "Ohio and Indiana Floods."

Irvine, Scotland, March 10—Seven persons killed and ten seriously injured by dynamite explosion; many houses damaged.

Italy, July 11—Heavy storm of rain and wind sweeps over country, doing great damage.

Japan, Aug. 26-28—Typhoon causes loss of 1,000 lives and much property.

McKinney, Tex., Jan. 23—Eight persons killed and fifteen injured by collapse of building.

Nome, Alaska, Oct. 6—City partly destroyed by tidal storm; 500 persons made homeless; property loss, $1,000,000.

North Carolina, Sept. 3-4—Heavy storm sweeps the coast; loss, $2,500,000.

Ohio—See "Ohio and Indiana Floods."

Omaha, Neb., March 23—Cyclonic storm causes death of 152 persons, the injury of 350 others, and a property loss of $5,000,000.

Peach Tree, Ala., March 21—Twenty-seven persons killed in storm; thirty-two injured.

Philippine islands, May 11—About sixty lives lost in typhoon.

Seward, Neb., May 15—Eleven persons killed and thirty injured by tornado; property loss, $100,000.

Solomon, Alaska, Oct. 6—Town wiped out by gale; no lives lost.

San Salvador, Oct. 27-28—Many lives lost in floods caused by heavy rains throughout republic.

Terre Haute, Ind., March 23.—Tornado causes death of twenty persons, the injury of 250 others, and a property loss of $1,000,000.

Thomasville, Ala., March 21—Twenty-eight persons killed in storm.

Tiffin, O., March 21—Seven persons killed in storm.

Verins, France, March 9—Ten persons fatally injured and forty-six seriously in theater panic.

Washington, D. C., July 30—Storm of wind, rain and hail causes three deaths and much damage.

Yutan, Neb., March 23—Sixteen persons killed and twenty injured by tornado.

RAILROAD WRECKS.

Baltimore & Ohio road, at Hoytville, O., April 5—Two killed and nine injured in wreck.

Big Four road, at Stockwell, Ind., Jan. 7—One man killed; thirty-six persons injured.

Canadian Pacific line, near Ottawa, Ont., June 25—Eight persons killed and a score injured.

Central of Georgia line, near Eufaula, Ala., Nov. 13—Twelve persons killed and more than 100 hurt.

Central Vermont road, near St. Lambert, Que., April 13—Seven killed, fifteen hurt in wreck.

Chesapeake & Ohio, at Fulton, Ind., June 28—Twenty-five persons injured.

Chicago & Northwestern line at Baldwin, Wis., April 27—Two killed, a dozen injured.

Great Northern road, near Moorhead, Minn., June 1—One killed, six hurt.

Great Northern, near Crary, N. D., Aug. 19—Two killed and twenty-one injured in wreck.

Illinois Central line, near Melvin, Ill., Jan. 24—Twenty-four persons injured.

Kongo (Africa) railroad, April 5—Twenty-three lives lost by train plunging through bridge.

Michigan Central, near Cayuga, Ont., March 3—Eight persons injured.

Mobile & Ohio road, near Buckatunne, Miss., Oct. 19—Twenty-three soldiers killed and eighty-five injured in wreck.

Midland road, near Hawes Junction, England, Sept. 2—Fifteen persons killed and thirty injured in collision.

New Haven road, near Wallingford, Conn., Sept. 2—Twenty-one persons killed and fifty injured in collision.

New Haven road, near Westerley, R. I., Oct. 25—Fifteen persons hurt in wreck caused by spreading of rails.

Paris-Marseilles road, near Melun, France, Nov. 4—Thirty-nine persons killed in collision.

Pennsylvania road, near Wooster, O., Nov. 12—Three persons killed and a dozen injured.

Pennsylvania road, near Wylie's station, O., Sept. 9—Thirty-five persons hurt by train leaving rails.

Rock Island road, near Maynard, Iowa, Sept. 1—Three persons killed by train leaving track.

Union Pacific, near Gothenburg, Neb., March 14—Four persons killed and thirty injured in collision.

New York, New Haven & Hartford, near Stamford, Conn., June 12—Five killed and a dozen injured.

MINE DISASTERS.

Bangalore, India, Aug. 22—Fifty men killed by fall of cage in Mysore gold mine.

Belle Valley, O., May 17—Fifteen men killed by fire damp explosion in Imperial mine.

Clifton, Ariz., Aug. 13—Nine men killed by snapping of a cable in Coronado mine.

Dawson, N. M., Oct. 22—261 men killed by explosion in Stag Canon coal mine.

Finleyville, Pa., April 23—One hundred men killed in Cincinnati coal mine.

Gellenkirchen, Germany, July 22—Fourteen men killed by cave-in in coal mine.

Glasgow, Scotland, Aug. 3—Twenty-three men entombed in Navis valley mine near Glasgow.

Peoria, Ill., Jan. 15—Three men killed by explosion in Crescent coal mine.

Senghenydd, Wales, Oct. 14—423 lives lost by fire and afterdamp in Universal coal mine.

Tower, Pa., Aug. 2—Eighteen men killed by explosion in East Brookside coal mine.

Yale, B. C., Feb. 20—Seventy-two men killed in coal mine explosion.

BLUE SKY LEGISLATION.

Laws having for their object the regulation and supervision of investment companies are now generally termed "blue sky" laws. The name originated in Kansas, where an act was passed by the legislature in 1911 to give investors protection from fraudulent concerns selling stocks, bonds and other "securities" based on nothing more substantial than the blue sky. It was intended to put a stop to the operations especially of fake mining, oil, gas and land companies which swindled the people out of thousands of dollars annually by means of alluring promises of easily acquired wealth.

The Kansas "blue sky" law, which has been taken as a model for similar legislation, in force or proposed, in many other states and also in some foreign governments, such as New South Wales and Manitoba, compels all companies or persons wishing to sell stocks, bonds or other securities to submit information to the state banking department, enabling it to determine whether they have a genuine proposition to submit to investors. They must produce a detailed statement of the scheme, a copy of all contracts, bonds or instruments to be made or sold, an itemized account of its true financial condition and the amount of its actual properties and liabilities. If the bank commissioner is satisfied that the company intends to do a legitimate business he issues a statement that it has complied with the provisions of the law and is entitled to do business in the state. Agents of companies attempting to do business without such official recognition are subject to fines of from $100 to $5,000 or imprisonment of not less than ninety days, or both fine and imprisonment.

Among the states which have passed "blue sky" laws are Kansas, Arizona, Connecticut, West Virginia, Vermont, Indiana and Wisconsin.

FOURTH OF JULY CASUALTIES.

[From the Journal of the American Medical Association.]

	1908.	1909.	1910.	1911.	1912.	1913.
Deaths—Tetanus	55	125	67	10	6	3
Other causes	108	90	64	47	35	29
Total	163	215	131	57	41	32
Injuries—Sight lost	11	16	7	8	8	2
One eye lost	93	36	33	26	21	22
Loss of legs, arms and hands	57	41	26	30	13	10

	1908.	1909.	1910.	1911.	1912.	1913.
Loss of fingers	184	176	114	83	43	46
Other injuries	5,115	4,823	2,612	1,339	862	1,051
Total injured	5,460	5,093	2,792	1,546	947	1,121
Total casualties	5,623	5.307	2.923	1.603	988	1.163

Total casualties in 1903, 4,449; in 1904, 4,769; in 1905, 5,176; in 1906, 5,466; in 1907, 4,413.

DEATH ROLL OF THE YEAR 1913.
From Dec. 1, 1912, to Dec. 1, 1913.

UNITED STATES.

Abe, Chris Von Der (1852), baseball magnate, in St. Louis, Mo., June 5.

Allen, Oscar Dana, scientist, in Ashford, Wash., March 6.

Altman, Benjamin (1840), dry·goods merchant, in New York, N. Y., Oct. 7.

Amen, Harlan Page (1850), educator, in Exeter, N. H., Nov. 9.

Arlington, Billy (1835), minstrel, in Los Angeles, Cal., May 24.

Atkins, Gen. Smith D. (1835), civil war veteran and editor, in Freeport, Ill., March 27.

Bacon, John M. (1853), brigadier-general, U. S. A., retired, in Portland, Ore., March 19.

Bergh, Louis de Coppet (1856), architect, in Washington, D. C., Jan. 28.

Ball, Samuel (1841), physician, in Beloit, Wis., April 18.

Berry, James H. (1840), ex-United States senator, in Bentonville, Ark., Jan. 30.

Bischoff, Henry (1852), judge, in New York, N. Y., March 28.

Black, Frank S. (1853), former governor of New York, in Troy, N. Y., March 21.

Blinn, E. D. (1853), lawyer, in Lincoln, Ill., Jan. 23.

Bogardus, Capt. A. H. (1833), champion wing shot, in Lincoln, Ill., March 23.

Boradnax, Francis (1853), electrical engineer, in Utica, N. Y., March 14.

Boucicault, Aubrey (1868), actor, in New York, N. Y., July 10.

Boulware, Jefferson R. (1870), politician, in Springfield, Ill., April 8.

Bowman, Edward M. (1842), musician, in Brooklyn, N. Y., Sept. 3.

Brady, Anthony N. (1843), capitalist, in London, Eng., July 22.

Briggs, Charles A. (1841), theologian, in New York, N. Y., June 8.

Briggs, Frank O. (1851), ex-United States senator, in Trenton, N. J., May 8.

Brown, George (1835), rear-admiral, U. S. N., in Indianapolis, Ind., June 29.

Brown, Henry B. (1836), jurist, in Bronxville, N. Y., Sept. 4.

Brown, John G. (1841), artist, in New York, N. Y., Feb. 8.

Bryan, Mrs. Mary E. (1844), editor, in Atlanta, Ga., June 16.

Bull, Stephen (1822), manufacturer, in Racine, Wis., Nov. 15.

Burns, T. H., jockey, in Brooklyn, N. Y., Nov. 14.

Burt, Horace G. (1849), railroad official, in Chicago, May 19.

Busch, Adolphus (1829), St. Louis, brewer, at Langenschwalbach, Germany, Oct. 10.

Carleton, Will (1845), poet, in New York, N. Y., Dec. 18, 1912.

Carter, Joseph N. (1843), judge, in Quincy, Ill., Feb. 6.

Casey, Silas (1841), rear-admiral, U. S. N., retired, at Warm Springs, Va., Aug. 14.

Caswell, Thomas T. (1840), rear-admiral U. S. N., in Weekapaugh, R. I., July 9.

Ceballos, Juan M. (1859), banker, in New York, N. Y., Feb. 1.

Chapman, Henry L. (1845), educator, in Brunswick, Me., Feb. 24.

Chariton, James (1832), railroad official, in Chicago, Ill., Nov. 19.

Cochrane, Henry C. (1843), brigadier-general, U. S. A., in Chester, Pa., April 27.

Collier, Price (1860), author, in Copenhagen, Denmark, Nov. 3.

Collyer, Robert (1823), clergyman, in New York, N. Y., Nov. 30.

Cramp, Charles H. (1828), shipbuilder, in Philadelphia, Pa., June 6.

Cramp, Edwin S., shipbuilder, in New York, N. Y., June 20.

Crawford, Samuel J. (1835), former governor and soldier, in Topeka, Kas., Oct. 21.

Creighton, J. B. (1819), financier, in Wichita, Kas., Aug. 21.

Crocker, Charles W. (1842), insurance man, Sept. 26.

Daniels, Fred H. (1853), engineer, in Worcester, Mass., Aug. 31.

Davidson, Harlan Page (1838), military educator, in Avon Park, Fla., Jan. 20.

Davis, Jeff (1862), United States senator, in Little Rock, Ark., Jan. 3.

Deere, Mrs. Mary M. (1845), philanthropist, in Moline, Ill., April 28.

De Haven, John J. (1845), jurist, at Napa, Cal., Jan. 26.

Didier, Eugene L. (1838), author, in Baltimore, Md., Sept. 8.

Doane, William C. (1832), episcopal bishop, in New York, N. Y., May 17.

Dodd, Amzi (1823), insurance official, in Bloomfield, N. J., Jan. 22.

Donahue, Frank (1872), ball player, in Philadelphia, Pa., Aug. 25.

Donahue, "Jiggs," baseball player, in Columbus, O., July 19.

Draper, Andrew Sloan (1848), educator, in Albany, N. Y., April 27.

Ducat, Arthur C. (1856), colonel, U. S. A., in New York, N. Y., March 8.

Eastman, John Robie (1836), astronomer, in Franklin, N. H., Sept. 26.

Eaton, Homer (1832), book publisher, in Madison, N. J., Feb. 9.

Eaton, Joseph Giles (1847), rear-admiral, U. S. N., in Norwell, Mass., March 8.

Egan, Dr. James A. (1859), secretary Illinois state board of health, in Springfield, Ill., March 30.

Emerson, T. M. (1851), railroad president, in Wilmington, N. C., Nov. 25.

Endicott, Harry (1881), motor car racer, in Jackson, Mich., Sept. 5.

Evarts, Maxwell (1862), lawyer, in Windsor, Vt., Oct. 7.

Faber, Ludewig B. (1856), portrait painter, in Philadelphia, Pa., May 18.

Fairbanks, Mrs. Charles W., in Indianapolis, Ind., Oct. 24.

Farley, James (1873), strike breaker, in Pittsburgh, Pa., Sept. 10.

Field, Stephen Dudley (1845), inventor, in Stockbridge, Mass., May 18.

Finley, W. W. (1853), railroad official, in Washington, D. C., Nov. 26.

Flagler, Henry M. (1830), capitalist and railroad official, at West Palm Beach, Fla., May 20.

Fletcher, C. L., Indianapolis physician, in Glacier National park, Montana, Aug. 19.

Ford, Patrick (1837), editor, in Brooklyn, N. Y., Sept. 23.

Fox, Della (Mrs. J. D. Levy) (1871), actress, in New York, N. Y., June 16.

French, Mrs. Anne W. (1869), American novelist, in England, Feb. 1.

Gates, Charles G. (1880), capitalist, at Cody, Wyo., Oct. 28.

Gaynor, William J. (1851), mayor of New York city, at sea, Sept. 10.

Goodwin, J. Cheever (1852), librettist, in New York, N. Y., Dec. 18, 1912.

Grubb, Edward B. (1841), soldier and diplomat, in Newark, N. J., June 7.

Guenther, Richard W. (1846), former consul-general, in Oshkosh, Wis., April 5.

Hall, James (1868), pugilist, in Stevens Point, Wis., March 15.

Hammond, James B. (1839), typewriter inventor, in St. Augustine, Fla., Jan. 27.

Havemeyer, William F. (1850), sugar refiner, in New York, Sept. 7.

Henderson, John B. (1827), former U. S. senator, in Washington, D. C., April 12.

Hitchcock, George (1850), painter, at Marken, Holland, Aug. 2.

Hogan, John J. (1829), Roman catholic bishop, in Kansas City, Mo., Feb. 21.

Holland, E. M. (1848), actor, in Cleveland, O., Nov. 24.

Howland, Henry E. (1835), attorney, in New York, N. Y., Nov. 8.

Janssen, John (1835), bishop, in Belleville, Ill., July 2.

Johnson, H. (1832), clergyman, in Philadelphia, Pa., Nov. 20.

Johnston, Joseph H. (1843), U. S. senator, in Washington, D. C., Aug. 8.

Johnston, J. Stoddard (1833), editor, in St. Louis, Mo., Oct. 4.

Jones, Charles H. (1848), editor and soldier, in Ospededaletti, Italy, Jan. 27.

Jones, Edward F. (1828), officer in civil war, in Binghamton, N. Y., Aug. 14.

Keene, James R. (1838), financier, in New York, N. Y., Jan. 3.

Kenny, William J. (1844), bishop, in Baltimore, Md., Oct. 23.

Kidd, J. H. (1840), civil war veteran and Indian fighter, in Ionia, Mich., March 19.

Kittredge, Abbott E. (1834), clergyman, in New York, N. Y., Dec. 17, 1912.

Koelling, Adolph (1840), pianist, in Los Angeles, Cal., May 2.

Konig, George (1856), congressman, in Baltimore, Md., May 31.

Lacey, John F. (1841), former congressman, in Oskaloosa, Ia., Sept. 29.

Larned, Francis M. (1862), journalist, in Seattle, Wash., Sept. 6.

Lathbury, Mary E. (1841), hymn writer, in East Orange, N. J., Oct. 21.

Ledaum, Henry (1872), educator, in Grand Forks, N. D., March 11.

Legare, George S. (1870), congressman, in Charleston, S. C., Jan. 30.

Locke, William (1869), baseball official, in Ventnor, N. J., Aug. 14.

Luders, Gustav Carl (1865), composer, in New York, N. Y., Jan. 24.

Lyman, Joseph (1848), landscape artist, in Wallingford, Conn., March 7.

Lyon, William P. (1822), Wisconsin jurist, in San Jose, Cal., April 4.

Maggioli, Frank (1853), billiard player, in New Orleans, La., Feb. 22.

Major, Charles (1853), author, in Shelbyville, Ind., Feb. 13.

MacCameron, Robert L. (1866), artist, in New York, N. Y., Dec. 29, 1912.

Magill, Samuel E. (1861), consul, in Hot Springs, Ark., Jan. 30.

Marble, J. H. (1869), member interstate commerce commission, in Washington, D. C., Nov. 21.

Marion, Henri, educator, in Culver, Ind., Aug. 14.

Martin, Bradley (1841), New York lawyer, in London, Eng., Feb. 5.

Martin, John (1833), ex-United States senator, in Topeka, Kas., Sept. 3.

Martin, Lewis J. (1844), New Jersey congressman, in Washington, D. C., May 5.

Maxwell, W. J. (1859), labor official, in Cedar Rapids, Iowa, July 14.

Maynard, Washburn (1844), rear-admiral, U. S. N., retired, in Newton, Mass., Oct. 25.

Mead, Albert E. (1861), ex-governor, in Bellingham, Wash., March 19.

Millar, Addison T. (1860), artist, at Norwalk, Conn., Sept. 8.

Miller, Joaquin (1841), poet, near San Francisco, Cal., Feb. 17.

Miller, Mrs. Emily Huntington (1833), former dean of women at Northwestern university, in Northfield, Minn., Nov. 1.

Miller, Roswell (1843), railroad official, in New York, N. Y., Jan. 3.

Millington, Charles C. (1855), former congressman, in Herkimer, N. Y., Oct. 25.

Moffett, James A. (1851), capitalist, at Palm Beach, Fla., Feb. 26.

Morgan, J. Pierpont (1837), financier, in Rome, Italy, March 31.

Morris, Edward (1866), packer, in Chicago, Nov. 3.

Morris, Edward L. (1870), scientist, in New York, N. Y., Sept. 15.

Mounteastle, R. E. L. (1865), democratic national committeeman, in Knoxville, Tenn., June 4.

Murphy, Michael C. (1860), trainer of athletes, in Philadelphia, Pa., June 4.

Murray, Robert (1822), former surgeon-general, in Baltimore, Md., Jan. 1.

McBurney, Charles (1845), surgeon, in Brookline, Mass., Nov. 7.

McCarty, Luther (1892), pugilist, in Calgary, Ont., May 24.

McCrea, James (1848), railroad president, in Haverford, Pa., March 28.

McDowell, Alexander (1831), former clerk of national house of representatives, in Sharon, Pa., Sept. 30.

Nebeker, Enos H. (1837), ex-treasurer of the United States, in Covington, Ind., Jan. 6.

Nindemann, William F. C., arctic explorer, in Hollis, N. Y., May 6.

Ober, Frederick A. (1849), author and ornithologist, in Hackensack, N. J., June 1.

Ockenden, Mrs. Ina M. P., novelist, in Galveston, Tex., March 15.

Ogden, Robert C. (1836), philanthropist, in Kennebunkport, Me., Aug. 6.

Oldberg, Oscar (1847), scientist, in Pasadena, Cal., Feb. 27.

Palmer, Thomas W. (1840), former U. S. senator, in Detroit, Mich., June 1.

Peavey, George W., capitalist, in Minneapolis, Minn., June 8.

Pell, S. Osgood, capitalist, Long Beach, N. Y., Aug. 3.

Platt, James P. (1831), jurist, in Meriden, Conn., Jan. 26.

Post, Geo. B. (1838), architect, in New York, N. Y., Nov. 28.

Potts, Robert (1835), rear-admiral, U. S. N., in Washington, D. C., June 24.

Richardson, Charles F. (1851), educator, in Lisbon, N. H., Oct. 8.

Roddenbery, Seaborn A. (1870), congressman, in Thomasville, Ga., Sept. 25.

Rose, Ralph (1885), athlete, in San Francisco, Cal., Oct. 16.

Ross, Mrs. Ida H. (1832), philanthropist, in Los Angeles, Cal., March 15.

Sabine, William T. (1837), bishop, in New York, Aug. 11.

St. Gaudens, Louis (1854), sculptor, in Cornish, N. H., March 8.

Salomon, Edward S., general in civil war, in San Francisco, Cal., July 19.

Sawtelle, Charles G. (1834), brigadier-general, U. S. A., retired, in Washington, D. C., Jan. 4.

Seabrooke, Thomas Q. (1860), actor, in Chicago, April 3.

Seeger, R. W. (1831), composer, in Los Angeles, Cal., Jan. 8.

Selz, Morris (1826), shoe manufacturer, in Chicago, June 3.

Seward, Janet W. (1839), in Auburn, N. Y., Nov. 9.

Shields, Ben (1868), song writer, in Massapequa, N. Y., Oct. 25.

Smith, Benjamin Eli (1857), editor, Century dictionary, in Rochelle Park, N. Y., Feb. 24.

Smith, Sylvester C. (1858), congressman, in Los Angeles, Cal., Jan. 26.

Snyder, Simon (1838), brigadier-general, U. S. A., retired, in Reading, Pa., April 14.

Sperry, Thomas A., capitalist, in New York, N. Y., Sept. 1.

Stocking, Charles H. W., clergyman, in Bowling Green, Ky., Jan. 27.

Stokes, Anson Phelps (1838), banker, in New York, N. Y., June 28.

Strong, James W. (1833), educator, in Northfield, Minn., Feb. 24.

Sullivan, Timothy D. (1862), congressman, in New York, N. Y., Aug. 31.

Swift, Lewis (1820), astronomer, in Marathon, N. Y., Jan. 5.

Taylor, Aaron H. (1831), horse breeder, in Central Valley, N. Y., Jan. 28.

Templeton, James W. (1839), former state senator, in Princeton, Ill., March 28.

Thatcher, George (1851), minstrel, in Orange, N. J., June 25.

Thompson, John O. (1850), assistant U. S. attorney-general, in Chicago, Feb. 26.

Thwaites, Reuben G. (1853), historian, in Madison, Wis., Oct. 22.

Tucker, Charles Henry (1839), clergyman, in Atlantic City, N. J., March 10.

Upham Mrs. E. C. (1834), newspaper correspondent, in Washington, D. C., Feb. 18.

Wait, Lucien A. (1846), educator, at Clifton Springs, N. Y., Sept. 6.

Waterman, Theodore H. (1859), grain commission merchant, in Albany, N. Y., Sept. 11.

Wedemeyer, Wm. W. (1873), congressman, at Colon, Panama, Jan. 2.

Weeks, Alice M., author, in Philadelphia, Pa., Aug. 26.

West, "Billy" (William West Cox) (1837), actor, at Actors' home, Staten Island, N. Y., April 2.

Wheeler, Eben S. (1839), engineer, in Detroit, Mich., Jan. 4.

White, Stephen V. C. (1831), broker, in New York, N. Y., Jan. 18.

Wilder, William H. (1855), congressman, in Washington, D. C., Sept. 11.

Williams, Samuel W. (1851), political leader, in Vincennes, Ind., Aug. 5.

Wilson, Charles. I. (1837), brigadier-general, U. S. A., retired, in New York, N. Y., Sept. 22.

Wilson, Harry L. (1867), educator, in Pittsburgh, Pa., Feb. 23.

Wise, John S. (1849), former congressman, at Prince Anne, Md., May 12.

Woodruff, Carle A. (1841), brigadier-general, U. S. A., in Raleigh, N. C., July 29.

Woodford, Stewart L. (1835), diplomat, in New York, N. Y., Feb. 14.

Woodruff, Timothy L. (1858), former lieutenant-governor of New York, in New York, N. Y., Oct. 12.

Young, Chanler De (1881), publisher, in San Francisco, Cal., Sept. 17.

FOREIGN.

Aiguirre y Garcia (1835), cardinal, in Toledo, Spain, Oct. 9.

Araujo, Manuel E., president of Salvador, in San Salvador, Feb. 9.

Arroll, Sir William (1839), engineer, in London, England, Feb. 20.

Ashbourne, Baron (1838), in London, England, May 22.

Ashburnham, Lord (1841), in Paris, France, Jan. 15.

Asser, Tobias M. C. (1838), statesman, in The Hague, Holland, July 29.

Austin, Alfred (1835), British poet laureate, in Ashford, England, June 2.

Avebury, Lord (Sir John Lubbock) (1834), scientist, in London, England, May 28.

Ball, R. S. (1840), astronomer, in London, Nov. 25.

Bebel, August F. (1840), socialist leader, in Zurich, Switzerland, Aug. 13.

Becke, George Louis (1848), novelist, in Sydney, N. S. W., Feb. 18.

Bonilla, Don Manuel, president of Honduras, in Tegucigalpa, March 21.

Callletet, Louis Paul (1832), physicist, in Paris, Jan. 5.

Carrington, Sir Frederick (1834), soldier, at Collesbourne, England, March 22.

Cantacuzene, George, statesman, in Bucharest, Roumania, April 5.

Coats, Sir James (1834), manufacturer, in London, Jan. 20.

Constans, Jean A. E. (1833), diplomat, in Paris, France, April 7.

Detaille, Edouard (1848), artist, in Paris, France, Dec. 24.

East, Sir Alfred (1849), artist, in London, England, Sept. 28.

Fava, Saverio (1832), diplomat, in Rome, Italy, Oct. 3.

Freyne, Baron de (1855), in County Roscommon, Ireland, Sept. 22.

George I. (1845), king of Greece, in Saloniki, Macedonia, March 18.

Hagenbeck, Carl (1844), animal trainer, near Hamburg, Germany, April 14.

Hayashi, Tadasu (1850), statesman, in Tokyo, Japan, July 10.

Hollebon, Theodor von (1838), diplomat, in Berlin, Germany, Feb. 1.

Katsura, Prince Taro (1847), statesman, in Tokyo, Japan, Oct. 10.

Kiderlen-Waechter, Alfred von (1852), foreign secretary, in Stuttgart, Germany, Dec. 30.

Korbay, Francis A. (1846), singer and composer, in London, March 10.

Krag, Thomas P. (1868), author, in Christiania, Norway, March 14.

Law, William A. (1844), dramatist, at Parkstone, Dorset, England.

Lawless, Emily, writer, in London, England, Oct. 22.

Lemonnier, Camille (1847), author, in Brussels, Belgium, June 13.

Lindsay, Sir Coutts (1824), artist, in London, May 8.

Lindsay, James L., earl of Crawford (1847), in London, Jan. 31.

Lockroy, E. (1838), statesman, in Paris, France, Nov. 22.

Lucas-Championniere Just (1843), surgeon, in Paris, France, Oct. 22.

Lung Yu, former empress of China, in Pekin, Feb. 21.

Lyne, William John (1844), former premier, in Sydney, N. S. W., Aug. 3.

Marchesi, Mme. Mathilde de Castrone (1826), vocal teacher, in London, England, Nov. 18.

Milne, John (1850), seismologist, Newport, England, July 31.

Monvel, Louis Maurice Boutet de (1850), artist, in Paris, France, March 16.

Morot, Aime (1850), artist, in Dinard, France, Aug. 12.

Naeyer, Count de Smet de, statesman, in Brussels, Belgium, Sept. 10.

Nagl, Franz X. (1855), cardinal, in Vienna, Feb. 4.

Nazim Pasha (1843), soldier and statesman, killed in Constantinople, Turkey, Jan. 23.

Neville, Lady Dorothy (1826), author, in London, March 24.

Ollivier, Emile (1825), statesman, in Annecy, France, Aug. 20.

Pelissier, Harry G. (1874), entertainer and composer, in London, England, Sept. 26.

Popper, David (1846), cellist, in Vienna, Aug. 8.

Preece, Sir William H. (1833), inventor, in London, England, Nov. 6.

Respighi, Peter (1843), cardinal, in Rome, Italy, March 22.

Reyes, Bernardo (1851), soldier, shot in Mexico City, Mex., Feb. 9.

Rochefort, Henri (1830), journalist and politician, in Aix-les-Bains, France, July 1.

Rospigliosi, Prince Joseph (1848), in Stresa, Italy, Sept. 23.

Ross, James (1848), railroad builder, in Montreal, Que., Sept. 20.

Rumbold, Sir Horace (1829), diplomat, in London, England, Nov. 3.

Sarto, Rosa (1836), sister of Pope Pius X., in Rome, Italy, Feb. 11.

Schefket Pasha, Mahmoud, grand vizier, in Constantinople, Turkey, June 11.

Scott, Robert F. (1868), antarctic explorer, near south pole, March 29, 1912.

Solomon, Sir Richard (1850), capitalist, in London, England, Nov. 10.

Sophia, Princess of Saxe-Weimar-Eisenach, in Heidelberg, Germany, Sept. 17.

Sutherland, Duke of (1851), in London, England, June 26.

Takehito, Prince (1862), near Kobe, Japan, July 6.

Auguste, Tancrede, president of Haiti, in Port au Prince, May 2

Thureau-Dangan, Paul (1837), member of French academy, in Paris, Feb. 24.

Tredegar, Viscount (1831), survivor of light brigade charge at Balaklava, in London, March 11.

Trieber, Conrad (1847), historian, in Frankfort-on-the-Main, Germany, Sept. 11.

Vambery, Arminius (1831), traveler and orientalist, in Budapest, Hungary, Sept. 15.

Vives y Tuto (1854), cardinal, in Rome, Italy, Sept. 7.

Wallace, Alfred Russel (1822), scientist, in London, England, Nov. 7.

White, Sir William Henry (1845), naval constructor, in London, England, Feb. 27.

Wolff, Gustav W. (1834), Belfast shipbuilder, in London, England, April 17.

Wolseley, Field Marshal Viscount (1833), British soldier, in Mentone, France, March 25.

The National Government.

Corrected to Dec. 20, 1913.

EXECUTIVE DEPARTMENT.

President—Woodrow Wilson (N. J.)..........$75,000
Secretary to the President—Joseph P. Tumulty (N. J.).......................... 7,500
Vice-President—Thomas R. Marshall (Ind.)... 12,000
Executive Clerk—Rudolph Forster (Va.)...... 5,000
Chief Clerk—T. W. Brahany (Wis.)........... 4,000
United States District Marshal—Aulick Palmer (D. C.).................................. 6,000

DEPARTMENT OF STATE.

Secretary—William J. Bryan (Neb.)..........$12,000
Assistant Secretary—John E. Osborne (Wyo.) 5,000
Second Asst. Secretary—Alvey A. Adee (D. C.) 4,500
Third Asst. Secretary—(Vacancy)............ 4,500
Director Consular Service—Wilbur J. Carr (N. Y.)..................................... 4,500
Chief Clerk—Ben G. Davis (Neb.)............ 3,000
Counselor for Department—John Bassett Moore (N. Y.).............................. 7,500
Solicitor—Joseph W. Folk (Mo.).............. 5,000
Assistant Solicitors—Frederick Van Dyne (N. Y.); Lester H. Woolsey (N. Y.) and Edwin M. Borchard (Ill.).................. 3,000
Law Clerks—Henry Y. Bryan (D. C.) and L. H. Woolsey (N. Y.)....................... 2,500
Chief of Diplomatic Bureau—Sydney Y. Smith (D. C.).............................. 2,250
Chief of Consular Bureau—Herbert C. Hengstler (O.)................................. 2,250
Chief of Bureau of Indexes and Archives—John R. Buck (Me.)....................... 2,100
Chief of Bureau of Accounts and Disbursing Clerk—William McNair (Mich.)............ 2,300
Chief of Bureau of Rolls and Library—John A. Tonner (O.)............................ 2,500
Chief of Bureau of Appointment—Miles M. Shand (N. J.)............................ 2,100
Chief of Bureau of Citizenship—Richard W. Flournoy, Jr. (Md.)..................... 2,100
Translators—John S. Martin Jr. (Pa.) and Wilfred Stevens (Minn.)................. 2,100
Private Secretary to Secretary of State—Manton M. Wyvell (N. Y.)................ 2,500
Chief of Division of Latin-American Affairs—Boaz V. Long (N. M.).................... 4,500
Chief of Division of Far Eastern Affairs—Ransford S. Miller, Jr. (N. J.)........... 4,500
Chief of Division of Near Eastern Affairs—Albert H. Putney (Ill.)................. 4,500
Chief of Division of Information—John H. James (Ohio)............................ 4,500
Foreign Trade Advisers—Robert F. Rose (Mont.) and William B. Fleming (Ky.).... 4,500

TREASURY DEPARTMENT.

Secretary—William G. McAdoo (N. Y.)......$12,000
Secretary to the Secretary—George R. Cooksey (D. C.).............................. 2,500
Assistant Secretary—Charles S. Hamlin (Mass.)................................. 5,000
Assistant Secretary—John S. Williams (Va.) 5,000
Assistant Secretary—Byron R. Newton (N. Y.) 5,000
Chief Clerk—James L. Wilmeth (Ark.)....... 4,000
Chief of Appointment Division—James F. Harper (S. C.)............................ 3,000
Chief of Warrants Division—Charles H. Miller (Mass.)............................... 3,500
Chief of Public Moneys Division—Eugene B. Daskam (Conn.)........................ 3,000
Chief of Customs Division—Frank M. Halstead (Ore.)............................ 4,000
Chief of Revenue Cutter Division—F. P. Bertholf (N. J.)............................ 5,000
Chief of Stationery, Printing and Blanks Division—Frederick F. Weston (Iowa)........ 2,500
Chief of Loans and Currency Division—Andrew T. Huntington (Mass.)............. 3,500
SUPERVISING ARCHITECT'S OFFICE.
Supervising Architect—Oscar Wenderoth(N.Y.) 6,000
BUREAU OF ENGRAVING AND PRINTING.
Director—Joseph E. Ralph (Ill.)............. 6,000

Assistant Director—Frank E. Ferguson (Md.) 3,500
Superintendent Engraving Division—Geo. U. Rose, Jr. (D. C.)........................ 4,800
LIFE SAVING SERVICE.
General Superintendent—S. I. Kimball (Me.) 4,500
Assistant—Oliver M. Maxam (Ind.)........... 2,500
REGISTER OF THE TREASURY.
Register—Gabe E. Parker (Okla.)............ 4,000
Assistant—(Vacancy) 2,500
COMPTROLLER OF THE TREASURY.
Comptroller—George E. Downey (Ind.)....... 6,000
Assistant—Walter W. Warwick (Ohio)....... 4,500
Chief Clerk—C. M. Force (Ky.).............. 2,500
Chief Law Clerk—Jared D. Terrell (Mich.)....2,500
AUDITORS.
Auditor for the Treasury Department—William E. Andrews (Neb.)................... 4,000
Chief Clerk—Albion B. Jameson (Pa.)........ 2,250
Auditor for War Department—James L. Baity (Mo.)............................. 4,000
Chief Clerk—James E. Maulding (Ill.)........ 2,250
Auditor for the Interior Department—Robert W. Woolley (Va.)....................... 4,000
Chief Clerk—Preston E. Northup (Pa.)....... 2,250
Auditor for the Navy Department—Edward Luckow (Wis.)............................ 4,000
Chief Clerk—Byron J. Price (Wis.).......... 2,250
Auditor for the State and Other Departments—Edward D. Hearne (Del.)............ 4,000
Chief Clerk—W. W. Scott (N. C.)........... 2,250
Auditor for Post Office Department—Charles A. Kram (Pa.)........................... 5,000
Chief Clerk—Charles H. Keating (O.)........ 3,000
TREASURER OF THE UNITED STATES.
Treasurer—John Burke (N. D.).............. 8,000
Assistant Treasurer—(Vacancy)............. 3,600
Deputy Assistant Treasurer—George Fort (Ga.) 3,200
Supt. Nat. Bank Red. Div.—E. W. Wilson (Md.).................................... 3,500
COMPTROLLER OF THE CURRENCY.
Comptroller—(Vacancy) 5,000
Deputy—Thomas P. Kane (D. C.)............ 3,500
COMMISSIONER OF INTERNAL REVENUE.
Commissioner—William H. Osborn (N. C.)... 6,000
Deputy—Robert Williams, Jr. (N. Y.)....... 4,000
Deputy—George E. Fletcher (La.)........... 3,600
DIRECTOR OF THE MINT.
Director—George E. Roberts (Iowa).......... 5,000
PUBLIC HEALTH SERVICE.
Surgeon-General—Rupert Blue (S. C.)........ 6,000

WAR DEPARTMENT.

Secretary—Lindley M. Garrison (N. J.)......$12,000
Assistant Secretary—Henry S. Breckinridge (Ky.)................................... 5,000
Assistant and Chief Clerk—John C. Scofield. 4,000
Chief of Staff—Maj.-Gen. Leonard Wood..... 8,000
Chief Clerk—N. Hershler (Ill.).............. 2,000
THE ADJUTANT-GENERAL'S OFFICE.
The Adjutant-General—Brig.-Gen. George Andrews.
Assistants—Cols. H. O. S. Heistand, William A. Simpson, H. P. McCain, James T. Kerr, Alexander O. Brodie.
Chief Clerk—Jacob Frech.
INSPECTOR-GENERAL'S DEPARTMENT.
Inspector-General—Brig.-Gen. E. A. Garlington.
Assistants—Cols. S. C. Mills, J. L. Chamberlain, H. P. Kingsbury.
Chief Clerk—John D. Parker.
JUDGE-ADVOCATE GENERAL'S OFFICE.
Judge-Advocate General—Brig.-Gen. E. H. Crowder.
Assistants—Cols. John A. Hull, George M. Dunn.
Chief Clerk and Solicitor—Lewis W. Call.
QUARTERMASTER'S CORPS.
Chief of Quartermaster's Corps—Brig.-Gen. James B. Aleshire.
Assistants—Brig.-Gens. H. G. Sharpe, C. A. Devol.
Chief Clerk—Charles P. Daly.
MEDICAL DEPARTMENT.
Surgeon-General—Brig.-Gen. George H. Torney.

Assistants—Cols. W. C. Gorgas, L. M. Maus, D. M.
Appell, L. Brechemin, Charles Richard, R. G.
Ebert, W. H. Arthur, G. E. Bushnell, H. P.
Birmingham, W. Stephenson, J. L. Phillips, G. L.
Edie, Wm. D. Crosby, C. M. Gandy, W. D.
McCaw.
Chief Clerk—John Wilson.

SIGNAL OFFICE.
Chief Signal Officer—Brig.-Gen. Geo. P. Scriven.
Chief Clerk—Herbert S. Flynn.

CORPS OF ENGINEERS.
Chief of Engineers—Brig.-Gen. Dan C. Kingman.
Chief Clerk—P. J. Dempsey.

PUBLIC BUILDINGS AND GROUNDS.
Officer in Charge—Col. Spencer Cosby.

ORDNANCE DEPARTMENT.
Chief of Ordnance—Brig.-Gen. William Crozier.
Chief Clerk—John J. Cook.

BUREAU OF INSULAR AFFAIRS.
Chief of Bureau—Brig.-Gen. Frank McIntyre.
Chief Clerk—Adolphus D. Wilcox.

NAVY DEPARTMENT.
Secretary—Josephus Daniels (N. C.)..........$12,000
Assistant Secretary—Franklin D. Roosevelt
(N. Y.)................................ 5,000
Aid to Secretary of Navy—Lieutenant-Commander
Needham L. Jones.
Aids—Rear-Admirals Bradley A. Fiske and Henry
T. Mayo, Capts. William F. Fullam and Albert
J. Winterhalter.
Chief Clerk—F. S. Curtis.

OFFICE OF ADMIRAL OF NAVY.
Admiral of the Navy—George Dewey.
Aid—Lieutenant-Commander Leonard R. Sargent.
Secretary—Lieut. Leonard G. Hoffman.

OFFICE OF NAVAL INTELLIGENCE.
Director, Capt. Thomas S. Rodgers; Commanders
Henry F. Ryan and Andrew T. Long; Lieutenant-
Commanders Austin Kautz, Adolphus E. Watson,
William F. Bricker; Lieuts. George M. Baum,
Thomas Withers; Major of Marines John H.
Russell.

BUREAU OF YARDS AND DOCKS.
Chief Civil Engineer—Homer R. Stanford.
Civil Engineers—E. R. Gayler, Paul L. Reed, Arch-
ibald L. Parsons, Carl A. Carlson, J. V. Rock-
well.
Chief Clerk—William M. Smith.

BUREAU OF NAVIGATION.
Chief, Rear-Admiral Victor Blue; Commanders
Carlo B. Brittain, John R. Y. Blakely, Martin
E. Trench, Lieutenant-Commanders, Joseph K.
Taussig, Lieut. Ralph A. Koch.
Chief Clerk—G. Earle Yancey.

HYDROGRAPHIC OFFICE.
Hydrographer—Commander George F. Cooper.
Assistant — Lieutenant-Commander Frank E.
Ridgely.
Clerk—H. L. Ballentine.

NAVAL OBSERVATORY.
Superintendent—Capt. Joseph L. Jayne.
Professors—Milton Updegraff, William S. Eichel-
berger, Frank B. Littell, Asaph Hall.
Librarian—W. D. Horigan.

BUREAU OF ORDNANCE.
Chief, Rear-Admiral Joseph Strauss.
Chief Clerk—E. S. Brandt.

BUREAU OF CONSTRUCTION AND REPAIR.
Chief, Chief Constructor Richard M. Watt; Naval
Constructors David W. Taylor, William P. Rob-
ert, William G. DuBose, John A. Spilman, Lewis
B. McBride, George S. Radford, James L. Acker-
son, Emory S. Land.
Chief Clerk—Michael D. Schaefer.

BUREAU OF STEAM ENGINEERING.
Chief, Engineer-in-Chief Robert S. Griffin.
Chief Clerk—Augustus C. Wrenn.

BUREAU OF SUPPLIES AND ACCOUNTS.
Chief—Paymaster-General Thomas J. Cowle.
Assistant—Pay Inspector Joseph J. Cheatham.

BUREAU OF MEDICINE AND SURGERY.
Chief—Surgeon-General Charles F. Stokes.
Assistant to Bureau—Surgeon Theodore W. Rich-
ards.
Chief Clerk—Dr. W. S. Gibson.

NAVAL MEDICAL SCHOOL.
Medical Director—James D. Gatewood, in command.
Medical Inspectors—Edward R. Stitt, Edward S.
Bogert.

NAVAL DISPENSARY.
Medical Inspector—Robert M. Kennedy.

OFFICE OF THE JUDGE-ADVOCATE GENERAL.
Judge-Advocate General, Capt. Robert L. Russell;
Lieutenants Frank B. Freyer, W. B. Woodson,
C. M. Austin, Leslie E. Bratton, Captain of
Marines Arthur E. Harding, First Lieutenant of
Marines E. N. McLellan.

NAVAL EXAMINING BOARD.
President, Rear-Admiral Thomas B. Howard;
Capts. Wythe M. Parks, Clifford J. Boush, Wal-
ter McLean.

NAVAL RETIRING BOARD.
President, Rear-Admiral Thomas B. Howard;
Capt. Walter McLean, Medical Directors Ed-
ward H. Green, William R. DuBose, Frank S.
Nash.

BOARD OF INSPECTION AND SURVEY FOR SHIPS.
President—Capt. Augustus F. Fechteler.
Members—Capts. Emil Theiss, A. S. Halsted,
Naval Constructor George H. Rock.
Recorder—Commander Thomas J. Senn.

BOARD OF INSPECTION FOR SHORE STATIONS.
President—Rear-Admiral John R. Edwards.
Member—Capt. George R. Evans.

GENERAL INSPECTOR OF THE PAY CORPS.
Pay Inspector—Thomas S. Jewett.
Pay Inspector—Joseph J. Cheatham.

GENERAL BOARD.
President, Admiral of the Navy George Dewey;
Rear-Admirals W. H. H. Southerland, Bradley
A. Fiske, Charles E. Vreeland, Capts. Albert G.
Winterhalter, Thomas S. Rodgers, William L.
Rodgers, Harry S. Knapp, John Hood, Wm. R.
Shoemaker, Commander E. H. Campbell, secre-
tary.

JOINT BOARD.
President, Admiral of the Navy George Dewey;
Rear-Admirals Charles E. Vreeland, Bradley A.
Fiske, Capt. Harry S. Knapp.

HEADQUARTERS MARINE CORPS.
Commandant—Maj.-Gen. William P. Biddle.
Assistant Adjutants and Inspectors—Col. Charles
H. Lauchleimer, Maj. Albert S. McLemore.
Assistant Quartermaster—Lieut.-Col. Charles L. Mc-
Cawley.
Assistant Quartermaster—Lieut. Col. William B.
Lemly, Capt. Percy F. Archer, Capt. Russell H.
Davis.
Paymaster—Col. George Richards.

DEPARTMENT OF COMMERCE.
Secretary—Wm. C. Redfield (N. Y.)..........$12,000
Assistant Secretary—Edwin F. Sweet (Mich.) 5,000
Chief Clerk and Superintendent—George C.
Havener (D. C.)............................ 3,000

BUREAU OF CORPORATIONS.
Commissioner—Joseph E. Davies (Wis.)...... 5,000
Deputy Commissioner—Francis Walker (Mass.) 3,500

BUREAU OF LIGHTHOUSES.
Commissioner—G. R. Putnam (Iowa).......... 5,000
Deputy Commissioner—John S. Conway (Mont.) 4,000

BUREAU OF CENSUS.
Director—William J. Harris (Ga.)............ 6,000
Chief Clerk—William L. Austin (Miss.)...... 2,500

COAST AND GEODETIC SURVEY.
Superintendent—O. H. Tittmann (Mo.)........ 6,000
Assistant—F. W. Perkins (N. J.)............ 4,000

STEAMBOAT INSPECTION SERVICE.
Supervising Inspector-General—George Uhler
(Pa.) 4,000
Chief Clerk—Dickerson N. Hoover, Jr. (D. C.) 2,000

BUREAU OF FISHERIES.

Commissioner—Hugh M. Smith (D. C.)..... 6,000
Deputy Commissioner—Ernest Lester Jones (Va.) 3,500

BUREAU OF NAVIGATION.

Commissioner—E. T. Chamberlain (N. Y.).... 4,000
Deputy Commissioner—Arthur J. Tyrer (Wash.) 2,400

BUREAU OF STANDARDS.

Director—S. W. Stratton (Ill.).............. 6,000
Secretary—H. D. Hubbard (Ill.).............. 2,200

BUREAU OF FOREIGN AND DOMESTIC COMMERCE.

Chief—Albertus H. Baldwin (Conn.).......... 4,000
Assistant Chief—Oscar P. Austin (D. C.).... 3,000
Assistant Chief—E. A. Brand (Va.).......... 2,750

DEPARTMENT OF LABOR.

Secretary—William B. Wilson (Pa.)..........$12,000
Assistant Secretary—Louis F. Post (Ill.).... 5,000
Chief Clerk—Robert Watson (Mass.).......... 3,000
Solicitor—John B. Densmore (Mont.)......... 5,000
Disbursing Clerk—George G. Box (N. Y.)..... 3,000
Private Secretary to Secretary—Hugh L. Kerwin (Pa.).............................. 2,500
Private Secretary to Assistant Secretary— Herbert A. Stevens (Mass.).............. 2,100

BUREAU OF IMMIGRATION AND NATURALIZATION.

Commissioner-General of Immigration—A. Caminetti (Cal.)........................ 5,000
Assistant Commissioner-General—F. H. Larned (Md.)............................... 3,500
Commissioner of Naturalization—Richard K. Campbell (Va.)......................... 3,500
Deputy Commissioner of Naturalization—Raymond F. Crist (D. C.).................. 3,000

BUREAU OF LABOR STATISTICS.

Commissioner of Labor Statistics—Royal Meeker (N. J.)............................ 5,000
Chief Statistician and Chief Clerk—Ethelbert Stewart (Ill.)..................... 3,000

CHILDREN'S BUREAU.

Chief of Bureau—Julia C. Lathrop (Ill.)..... 5,000
Assistant Chief—Lewis Meriam (Mass.)...... 2,400

POSTOFFICE DEPARTMENT.

Postmaster-Gen'l—Albert S. Burleson (Tex.)..$12,000
Chief Clerk and Superintendent—Merritt O. Chance (Ill.)........................... 4,000
Private Secretary to Postmaster-General— Ruskin McArdle (Tex.).................. 2,500
Assistant to Chief Clerk — Malcolm Kerlin (N. J.)............................... 2,000
Assistant Attorney-General for the P. O. D. —William H. Lamar (Md.)................ 5,000
Assistant Attorney—DeLeon Carlton (N. C.).. 2,750
Purchasing Agent—James A. Edgerton (N. J.) 4,000
Chief Clerk to Purchasing Agent—William L. K. Barrett (Md.)....................... 2,000
Chief Postoffice Inspector—Joe P. Johnston (Mo.)................................. 4,000
Chief Clerk, Division Postoffice Inspectors— John W. Johnston (N. Y.)................ 2,000
Appointment Clerk—George S. Pauli (O.)..... 2,000
Disbursing Clerk—William M. Mooney (O.).. 2,250

OFFICE FIRST ASSISTANT POSTMASTER-GENERAL.

First Assistant Postmaster-General—Daniel C. Roper (S. C.)....................... 5,000
Chief Clerk—Charles F. Trotter (W. Va.).... 2,500
Superintendent of Salaries and Allowances— John C. Koons (Md.).................... 4,000
Assistant Superintendent of Salaries and Allowances—David W. Duncan (Pa.)....... 2,250
Superintendent Division Appointments—Goodwin D. Ellsworth (N. C.).............. 3,000
Assistants Division Appointments—Simon E. Sullivan (Md.), Lorel N. Morgan (W. Va.).. 2,000
Superintendent City Free Delivery Service— W. R. Spilman (Kas.)................... 3,000
Assistant Superintendent City Free Delivery Service—Charles R. Hodges (Tex.)....... 2,000

OFFICE SECOND ASSISTANT POSTMASTER-GENERAL.

Second Assistant Postmaster-General—Joseph Stewart (Mo.)......................... 5,000
Chief Clerk—Aleyne A. Fisher (Vt.)......... 2,500
Superintendent of Railway Adjustments— Charles H. McBride (N. Y.)............. 3,000
Assistant Superintendent of Railway Adjustments—George E. Bandel (Md.)........... 2,250

Superintendent Division Miscellaneous Transportation—John McNitt, Jr. (Mich.)....... 2,000
Superintendent Division Mail Equipment— Thomas P. Graham (N. Y.).............. 2,000
General Superintendent Railway Mail Service —Alexander H. Stephens (Cal.)......... 4,000
Assistant General Superintendent Railway Mail Service—George F. Stone (N. Y.)... 3,500
Chief Clerk Railway Mail Service—Edward W. Chatterton (N. Y.).................. 2,000
Superintendent Foreign Mails — Robert L. Maddox (Ky.).......................... 3,000
Assistant Superintendent Foreign Mails—Edwin Sands (N. Y.)..................... 2,500

OFFICE THIRD ASSISTANT POSTMASTER-GENERAL.

Third Assistant Postmaster-General—Alexander M. Dockery (Mo.)................. 5,000
Superintendent Foreign Mails—Basil Miles (Pa.) 3,000
Chief Clerk—William J. Barrows (Mo.)...... 2,500
Superintendent of Money Order Division— Charles E. Matthews (Okla.)............ 3,500
Chief Clerk of Money Order Division—Frank H. Rainey (D. C.)..................... 2,250
Superintendent Registry System—Clarence H. Buckler (Md.).......................... 2,500
Superintendent Division of Finance—William E. Buffington (Pa.)................... 2,250
Superintendent Division of Stamps—William C. Fitch (N. Y.)....................... 2,750
Superintendent Classification Division—William C. Wood (Kas.).................. 2,750
Chief Redemption Division—Edward McCauley (D. C.)............................. 2,000
Stamped Envelope Agent—William W. Barre (Neb.)................................. 2,500

OFFICE FOURTH ASSISTANT POSTMASTER-GENERAL.

Fourth Assistant Postmaster-General—James I. Blakslee (Pa.)..................... 5,000
Chief Clerk—William J. Satterfield (W. Va.) 2,500
Superintendent Rural Mails—George L. Wood (Md.)................................. 3,000
Assistant Superintendent Div. Rural Mails— Edgar R. Ryan (Pa.).................... 2,000
Chief Clerk Div. Rural Mails—Robert H. Prender (D. C.)....................... 2,000
Superintendent of Postoffice Supplies—James B. Cook (Md.)......................... 2,750
Superintendent Dead Letter Office—Marvin M. McLean (Tex.)..................... 2,750
Chief Clerk Dead Letter Office—Charles N. Dalzell (N. Y.)........................ 1,800
Topographer—David M. Hildreth (N. H.).... 2,750

POSTAL SAVINGS SYSTEM.

Director—Carter B. Keene (Me.)............. 5,000
Assistant Director—Charles H. Fullaway (Pa.) 2,500

OFFICE OF AUDITOR FOR POSTOFFICE DEPARTMENT.

Auditor—Charles A. Kram (Pa.)............. 5,000
Assistant and Chief Clerk—Charles H. Keating (O.).............................. 3,000
Law Clerk—Faber Stevenson (O.)........... 3,000
Expert Accountant—Lewis M. Bartlett (Mass.) 3,000
Chief Division of Postmasters' Accounts— T. H. Sweeney (Minn.).................. 2,250
Division of Electrical Tabulation — Louis Brehm (Ill.), acting chief.............. 2,000
Division of Warrant Payments—D. N. Burbank (N. Y.), chief..................... 2,250
Division No. 1, Mechanical Tabulation—M. O. Accounts, Wm. H. Wanamaker (Minn.), chief 2,250
Division No. 2, Mechanical Tabulation—M. O. Accounts, J. H. Clark (Md.), chief...... 2,250
Division of Mails and Files—Chas. F. Cummins (Va.), chief...................... 2,250

DEPARTMENT OF JUSTICE.

Attorney-General — James C. McReynolds (Tenn.)................................$12,000
Secretary to Attorney-General—John T. Suter (D. C.)............................... 3,000
Solicitor-General—John William Davis (W. Va.)................................... 10,000
Assistant Attorney-General—George C. Todd (N. Y.)................................ 7,000
Assistant Attorney-General—Winfred T. Denison (N. Y.)............................ 5,000

Assistant Attorney-General—Ernest Knaebel
(Col.) 5,000
Assistant Attorney-General—Jesse C. Adkins 5,000
Assistant Attorney-General — Samuel H.
Thompson, Jr. (Col.)........................... 5,000
Assistant Attorney-General — Samuel J.
Graham (Pa.).................................... 5,000
Assistant Attorney-General—William Wal-
lace, Jr. (Mont.)............................... 5,000
Assistant Attorney-General (Department of
Interior)—Preston C. West (Okla.).......... 5,000
Assistant Attorney-General—William H. Lewis
(Mass.) 5,000
Solicitor for Department of State—Joseph W.
Folk (Mo.)....................................... 5,000
Attorney in Charge of Titles—Henry L. Gil-
bert (Mich.)..................................... 3,500
Chief Clerk and Superintendent of Building
—Orin J. Field (Kas.).......................... 3,500
Disbursing Clerk—James H. Mackey (Col.)... 2,750
Appointment Clerk—Chas. B. Sornborger (Vt.) 2,000
Attorney in Charge of Pardons—James A.
Finch (N. Y.)................................... 3,000
Solicitor of Treasury (Treasury Department)
—William T. Thompson (Neb.)................ 5,000
Assistant Solicitor—Felix A. Reeve (Tenn.).. 3,000
Chief Clerk Solicitor's Office (Treasury De-
partment)—Charles E. Vrooman (Iowa)..... 2,000
Solicitor (Department Commerce)—Albert Lee
Thurman (O.).................................... 5,000
Solicitor (Department of Labor)—William H.
Lamar (Md.)..................................... 5,000
Assistant Solicitor (Department of Commerce)
—Edward T. Quigley............................ 3,000
Assistant Attorney-General (Postoffice Depart-
ment)—Russell P. Goodwin (Ill.)............ 5,000
Solicitor Internal Revenue—Ellis C. Johnson
(Wash.) 5,000
Superintendent of Prisons and Prisoners—
Robert V. LaDow (N. Y.)..................... 4,000
Chief Division of Investigation—Alexander B.
Bielaski (Md.).................................. 3,500
Chief of Division of Accounts—John J. Glov-
er (O.).. 2,500

INTERIOR DEPARTMENT.

Secretary—Franklin K. Lane (Cal.)..........$12,000
First Assistant Secretary—Andrieus A. Jones
(N. M.)... 5,000
Assistant Secretary—Lewis C. Laylin (O.)... 4,500
Chief Clerk—James I. Parker (Ind.).......... 4,000
Assistant Attorney-General—Preston C. West
(Okla.) 5,000

GENERAL LAND OFFICE.
Commissioner—Clay Tallman (Nev.)............ 5,000
Asst. Commissioner—Charles M. Bruce (Va.) 3,500
Chief Clerk—Frank Bond (Wyo.).............. 2,750

OFFICE OF INDIAN AFFAIRS.
Commissioner—Cato Sells (Tex.).............. 5,000
Asst. Commissioner—Edgar B. Merritt (Ark.) 3,500
Second Assistant Commissioner—Charles F.
Hauke (Wash.).................................. 2,750

PENSION OFFICE.
Commissioner—Gaylord M. Saltzgaber (Ohio) 5,000
Deputy Com'r—Edward C. Tieman (Mo.)..... 3,600
Chief Clerk—Frank D. Byington (Md.)...... 2,500
Medical Referee—Thomas Featherstonbaugh
(N. Y.).. 3,000

PATENT OFFICE.
Commissioner—Thomas Ewing (N. Y.)......... 5,000
First Assistant Commissioner—Robert T.
Frazier (Tenn.)................................. 4,500
Assistant Commissioner—James T. Newton
(Ga.) 3,500
Chief Clerk—William F. Woolard (Ill.)...... 3,000

BUREAU OF EDUCATION.
Commissioner—Philander P. Claxton (Tenn.).. 5,000
Chief Clerk—Lewis A. Kalbach (Pa.)......... 2,000

GEOLOGICAL SURVEY.
Director—George Otis Smith (Me.)............ 6,000
Chief Clerk—Henry C. Rizer (Kas.).......... 2,500

RECLAMATION SERVICE.
Director—Frederick H. Newell (Pa.).......... 7,500
Chief Engineer—Arthur P. Davis (Kas.)...... 6,000
Chief Clerk—Edwin G. Paul (Pa.)........... 2,400

BUREAU OF MINES.
Director—Joseph A. Holmes (N. C.).......... 6,000
Asst. and Chief Clerk—Van H. Manning (Miss.) 3,600

DEPARTMENT OF AGRICULTURE.

Secretary—David Franklin Houston (Mo.)....$12,000
Asst. Secretary—Beverly T. Galloway (Mo.) 5,000
Chief Clerk—Robert M. Reese (D. C.)........ 3,500
Private Secretary to the Secretary of Agri-
culture—Wm. F. Callander (Ill.)............ 2,500
Private Secretary to the Assistant Secretary
of Agriculture—Floyd R. Harrison (Va.)... 2,250
Appointment Clerk—Richard W. Roberts (Ill.) 2,000
Solicitor—Francis G. Caffey (N. Y.)......... 5,000
Chief, Forest Service—Henry S. Graves
(Conn.) 5,000
Chief, Weather Bureau—Charles F. Marvin
(Ohio) 6,000
Chief, Bureau of Animal Industry—A. D.
Melvin (Ill.).................................... 5,000
Chief, Bureau of Plant Industry—William A.
Taylor (Mich.).................................. 5,000
Chief, Bureau of Chemistry—Carl L. Als-
berg (Mass.).................................... 5,000
Chief, Bureau of Soils—Milton Whitney (Md.) 4,000
Chief, Bureau of Entomology—L. O. Howard
(N. Y.).. 4,500
Chief, Bureau of Biological Survey—Henry
W. Henshaw (Mass.)........................... 3,500
Chief, Bureau of Statistics—Leon M. Esta-
brook (Texas).................................. 4,000
Chief, Division of Accounts and Disburse-
ments—A. Zappone (D. C.).................... 4,000
Chief, Division of Publications—Joseph A.
Arnold (Ind.)................................... 3,250
Chief, Office of Markets—Charles J. Brand
(Ill.) 3,600
Chief, Office of Information—George W.
Wharton (N. Y.)................................ 2,500
Director, Office of Experiment Stations—A.
C. True (Conn.)................................. 4,500
Director, Office of Public Roads—L. W. Page
(Mass.) 4,000
Chairman, Insecticide and Fungicide Board—
John K. Hayward (N. Y.)...................... 3,800
Chairman, Federal Horticultural Board—
Charles L. Marlatt (Kas.)..................... 4,000

INDEPENDENT BUREAUS.

INTERSTATE COMMERCE COMMISSION.

Chairman—Edgar E. Clark (Iowa)............$10,000
Judson C. Clements (Ga.)..................... 10,000
Charles A. Prouty (Vt.)....................... 10,000
James S. Harlan (Ill.)......................... 10,000
Chas. C. McChord (Ky.)....................... 10,000
Balthasar H. Meyer (Wis.).................... 10,000
(Vacancy) 10,000
Secretary—George B. McGinty................ 5,000
Assistant Secretary—Alfred Holmead......... 3,000
Chief Clerk—Lester Sisler.................... 2,500

GOVERNMENT PRINTING OFFICE.

Public Printer—Cornelius Ford (N. J.)....... 5,500
Deputy Public Printer—Henry T. Brian (Md.) 4,500
Chief Clerk—William J. Dow (Mo.).......... 2,500
Private Secretary—Joseph P. O'Lone (N. J.) 2,500
Superintendent of Work—Daniel V. Chis-
holm (S. C.).................................... 3,600
Superintendent of Documents—Frank C. Wal-
lace (Pa.)....................................... 3,500
Purchasing Agent—Edward S. Moores (Wis.) 3,600

UNITED STATES CIVIL SERVICE COMMISSION.

Commissioners—John A. McIlhenny (La.),
president ($4,500); Charles M. Galloway,
(S. C.), Hermon W. Craven (Wash.)........ $4,000
Chief Examiner—George R. Wales (Vt.)..... 3,000
Secretary—John T. Doyle (N. Y.)............ 2,500

MINIMUM WAGE LAWS FOR WOMEN.

The following states enacted minimum wage laws
for women during the legislative sessions of 1912
and 1913:

California, May 26, 1913. | Oregon, Feb. 17, 1913.
Colorado, May 14, 1913. | Utah, March 18, 1913.
Massachusetts, June 4, | Washington, March 24,
1912. | 1913.
Minnesota, April 26, 1913. | Wisconsin, Aug., 1913.
Nebraska, April 21, 1913.

The Federal Judiciary.

SUPREME COURT.

Salaries: Chief justice, $13,000; justices, $12,000; clerk, $6,000; marshal, $3,500; reporter, $4,500.
Chief Justice—Edward D. White, Louisiana...*1910
Associate Justices—Joseph R. Lamar, Georgia...1910
Joseph McKenna, California...........................1898
Oliver W. Holmes, Massachusetts..............1902
William R. Day, Ohio...........................1903
Horace H. Lurton, Tennessee...................1909
Charles E. Hughes, New York..................1910
Willis Van Devanter, Wyoming................1910
Mahlon Pitney, New Jersey....................1912
Clerk—J. H. McKenney, District of Columbia.1880
Marshal—J. M. Wright, Kentucky..............1888
Reporter—C. H. Butler, New York..............1902
*Appointed associate justice, 1894.

COURT OF CLAIMS.

Salaries of judges, $6,000 each; chief justice, $6,500.
Chief Justice—Edward K. Campbell, Alabama..1913
Judges—Fenton W. Booth, Illinois.............1905
Samuel S. Barney, Wisconsin..................1906
C. B. Howry, Mississippi......................1897
George W. Atkinson, West Virginia............1906

COURT OF CUSTOMS APPEALS.

(Acts of Aug. 5, 1909, and Feb. 25, 1910.)
Salaries: Judges, $7,000 each; marshal, $3,000; clerk, $2,500.
Presiding Judge—Robert M. Montgomery, Mich..1910
Associate Judges—James F. Smith, California..1910
Orion M. Barber, Vermont....................1910
Marion De Vries, California..................1910
George E. Martin, Ohio.......................1911
Marshal—Frank H. Briggs, Maine..............1911
Clerk—Arthur B. Shelton, Dist. of Columbia..1910

COMMERCE COURT.

(Act of June 18, 1910.)
Salaries: Judges of the Commerce court received $7,000 a year each as Circuit court judges and $1,500 additional for expenses in Washington, where the court sat. The clerk got $4,000 and the marshal $3,000 a year. (The Court of Commerce was discontinued Dec. 31, 1913. See page 243.)
Judges—Martin A. Knapp, New York............1910
Robert W. Archbald, Pennsylvania............1911
William H. Hunt, Montana.....................1911
John Emmett Carland, South Dakota...........1911
Julian W. Mack, Illinois.....................1911
Marshal—Frank J. Starek, Ohio...............1911
Clerk—G. F. Snyder, West Virginia...........1911

CIRCUIT COURTS OF APPEALS.

FIRST CIRCUIT—Judges: Mr. Justice Oliver W. Holmes; circuit judges, W. L. Putnam, Frederick Dodge, George H. Bingham; district judges, Clarence Hale, Arthur L. Brown, Edgar Aldrich, James M. Morton, Jr.
SECOND CIRCUIT—Judges: Mr. Justice Charles E. Hughes; circuit judges, E. H. Lacombe, Henry G. Ward, Alfred C. Coxe, Martin A. Knapp; district judges, Julius M. Mayer, George C. Holt, George W. Ray, John R. Hazel, Charles M. Hough, Thomas I. Chatfield, Learned Hand, Van V. Veeder, James L. Martin.
THIRD CIRCUIT—Judges: Mr. Justice Mahlon Pitney; circuit judges, George Gray, Joseph Buffington, John B. McPherson; district judges, Edward G. Bradford, Joseph Cross, James B. Holland, J. W. Thompson, James S. Young, John Rellstab, Charles P. Orr, Charles B. Witmer.
FOURTH CIRCUIT—Judges: Mr. Chief Justice Edward D. White; circuit judges, Jeter C. Pritchard, Charles A. Woods; district judges, Benjamin F. Keller, Henry G. Connor, James E. Boyd, Edmund Waddill, Jr., H. Clay McDowell, Alston G. Dayton, John C. Rose, Henry A. M. Smith.
FIFTH CIRCUIT—Judges: Mr. Justice Joseph R. Lamar; circuit judges, D. A. Pardee, A. P. McCormick, David D. Shelby; district judges, W. T. Newman, Emory Speer, Thomas G. Jones, H. T. Toulmin, H. C. Niles, Aleck Boarman, Edward R. Meek, T. S. Maxey, Waller T. Burns, William

I. Grubb, Rufus E. Foster, William B. Sheppard, Gordon Russell, Rhydon M. Call.
SIXTH CIRCUIT—Judges: Mr. Justice William R. Day; circuit judges, Arthur C. Denison, Loyal E. Knappen, John W. Warrington; district judges, Walter Evans, A. M. J. Cochran, John E. McCall, John E. Sater, Edward T. Sanford, Clarence W. Sessions, J. M Killits, H. C. Hollister, Arthur J. Tuttle, William L. Day.
SEVENTH CIRCUIT—Judges: Mr. Justice Horace H. Lurton; circuit judges, Francis E. Baker, William H. Seaman, C. C. Kohlsaat, Julian W. Mack; district judges, Albert B. Anderson, J. Otis Humphrey, K. M. Landis, A. L. Sanborn, Francis M. Wright, George A. Carpenter, Ferdinand A. Geiger.
EIGHTH CIRCUIT—Judges: Mr. Justice Willis Van Devanter; circuit judges, W. H. Sanborn, William C. Hook, Elmer B. Adams, Walter I. Smith, John E. Carland; district judges, William H. Munger, Smith McPherson, Page Morris, Jacob Trieber, J. A. Riner, Charles F. Amidon, John A. Marshall, Henry T. Reed, J. C. Pollock, W. H. Pope, D. P. Dyer, T. C. Munger, R. E Campbell, J. H. Cotteral, Robert E. Lewis, Charles A. Willard, A. S. Van Valkenburgh, Frank A. Youmans, James D. Elliott.
NINTH CIRCUIT—Judges: Mr. Justice Joseph McKenna; circuit judges, E. M. Ross, William B. Gilbert, W. W. Morrow, William H. Hunt; district judges, O. Wellborn, Sanford B. Dole, John T. De Bolt, W. J. Robinson, J. A. Matthewman, C. F. Parsons, C. E. Wolverton, William C. Van Fleet, E. S. Farrington, F. S. Dietrich, R. S. Bean, E. E. Cushman, A. Perry, W. L. Whitney, S. B. Kingsbury, C. D. Murane, Henry E. Cooper, A. G. M. Robertson, Charles F. Clemons, Frank H. Rudkin, George M. Bourquin, F. E. Fuller, Lyle A. Dickey, Jeremiah Neterer, Robert W. Jennings, Frederick M. Brown.

CIRCUIT COURT JUDGES.

Salaries of circuit judges, $7,000 each.
FIRST JUDICIAL CIRCUIT—Districts of Maine, New Hampshire, Massachusetts, Rhode Island. Circuit judges, W. L. Putnam, Portland, Me., March 17, 1892; Frederic Dodge, Boston, Mass., July 23, 1912; George H. Bingham, Concord, N. H., June 5, 1913.
SECOND JUDICIAL CIRCUIT—Districts of Vermont, Connecticut, New York. Circuit judges, E. H. Lacombe, New York, N. Y., May 26, 1887; Alfred C. Coxe, New York, N. Y., June 3, 1902; Henry G. Ward, New York, N. Y., Dec. 17, 1907; Martin A. Knapp, Washington, D. C., Dec. 20, 1910; Henry Wade Rogers, 1913.
THIRD JUDICIAL CIRCUIT—Districts of New Jersey, Pennsylvania, Delaware. Circuit judges, Joseph Buffington, Pittsburgh, Pa., Sept. 25, 1906; George Gray, Wilmington, Del., Dec. 18, 1899; John B. McPherson, Philadelphia, Pa., April 3, 1912.
FOURTH JUDICIAL CIRCUIT—Districts of Maryland, Virginia, West Virginia, North Carolina, South Carolina. Circuit judges, Jeter C. Pritchard, Asheville, N. C., April 27, 1904; Charles A. Woods, Marion, S. C., June 5, 1913.
FIFTH JUDICIAL CIRCUIT—Districts of Georgia, Florida, Alabama, Mississippi, Louisiana, Texas. Circuit judges, Don A. Pardee, Atlanta, Ga., May 13, 1881; A. P. McCormick, Dallas, Tex., March 17, 1892; D. D. Shelby, Huntsville, Ala., March 2, 1899.
SIXTH JUDICIAL CIRCUIT—Districts of Ohio, Michigan, Kentucky, Tennessee. Circuit judges, Arthur C. Denison, Grand Rapids, Mich., Oct. 3, 1911; John W. Warrington, Cincinnati, O., March 16, 1909; Loyal E. Knappen, Grand Rapids, Mich., Jan. 31, 1910.
SEVENTH JUDICIAL CIRCUIT—Districts of Indiana, Illinois, Wisconsin. Circuit judges, Francis E. Baker, Indianapolis, Ind., Jan. 21, 1902; William H. Seaman, Milwaukee, Wis., March 1, 1905; Christian C. Kohlsaat, Chicago, Ill., March 18, 1905; Julian W. Mack, Washington, D. C., Jan. 31, 1911.
EIGHTH JUDICIAL CIRCUIT—Districts of Minnesota, North Dakota, South Dakota, Wyoming, Iowa, Missouri, Kansas, Arkansas, Nebraska, Colorado,

Utah, New Mexico, Oklahoma Circuit Judges, W. H Sanborn, St Paul, Minn, March 17, 1892, William C. Hook, Leavenworth, Kas, Nov. 17, 1903, Elmer B. Adams, St Louis, Mo, Dec. 12, 1905; John E Carland, Washington, D C., Jan. 31, 1911, Walter I Smith, Council Bluffs, Iowa, Jan. 31, 1911.

NINTH JUDICIAL CIRCUIT—Districts of California, Montana, Washington, Idaho, Oregon, Nevada, Alaska, Arizona, Hawaii Circuit Judges, E M. Ross, Los Angeles, Cal, Feb. 22, 1895, W. B. Gilbert, Portland, Ore, March 18, 1892, William W. Morrow, San Francisco, Cal, May 20. 1897; William H Hunt, Washington, D. C., Jan. 31, 1911.

JUDGES OF THE UNITED STATES DISTRICT COURTS.

With date of commission. Salaries, $6,000 each.

ALABAMA—Northern and Middle Districts	Thomas Goode Jones	Montgomery	Dec 17, 1901
Southern District	H T Toulmin	Mobile.	Jan 13, 1887
Northern District	William I. Grubb	Birmingham	May 30, 1908
ALASKA—First District	Robert W Jennings	Juneau	May 6, 1913
Second District	C. D. Murane	Nome	July 5, 1910
Third District	Frederick M Brown	Valdez	June 17, 1913
Fourth District	Frederick E Fuller	Fairbanks.	Aug. 16, 1912
ARIZONA	William H. Sawtelle	Phœnix	1913
ARKANSAS—Eastern District	Jacob Trieber	Little Rock	Jan. 9, 1901
Western District	Frank A. Youmans	Fort Smith	June 20 1911
CALIFORNIA—Northern District	Maurice T. Dooling	San Francisco	1913
Southern District	Olin Wellborn	Los Angeles	Mar. 1, 1895
COLORADO	Robert E Lewis	Denver	Apr. 10, 1906
CONNECTICUT	(Vacancy)		
DELAWARE	Edward G. Bradford	Wilmington	May 11, 1897
DISTRICT OF COLUMBIA	Seth Shepard, Ch J	Washington	Jan. 5, 1905
FLORIDA—Northern District	Wm B Sheppard.	Pensacola	May 20, 1908
Southern District	Rhydon M Call	Jacksonville	Apr. 24, 1913
GEORGIA—Northern District	William T Newman	Atlanta.	Aug. 13, 1886
Southern District.	Emory Speer	Macon	Feb 18, 1885
HAWAII	A G M Robertson, Ch J.	Honolulu	May 15. 1911
IDAHO	Frank S. Dietrich	Boise	Dec. 17, 1907
ILLINOIS—Northern District	Kenesaw M. Landis	Chicago	Mar 18, 1905
	Geo A Carpenter	Chicago	Jan. 11, 1910
Eastern District	Francis M. Wright.	Urbana	Mar 11, 1905
Southern District	J. Otis Humphrey	Springfield	Mar. 8, 1901
INDIANA	A. B. Anderson	Indianapolis.	Dec. 8, 1902
IOWA—Northern District	Henry T Reed	Cresco.	Mar. 7, 1904
Southern District	Smith McPherson	Red Oak	May 7, 1900
KANSAS	John C. Pollock	Kansas City	Dec. 1, 1901
KENTUCKY—Eastern District	A M J. Cochran.	Maysville	Dec 17, 1901
Western District	Walter Evans	Louisville	Mar. 3, 1899
LOUISIANA—Eastern District.	Rufus E Foster	New Orleans	Feb. 2, 1909
Western District.	Aleck Boarman	Shreveport.	May 18, 1881
MAINE	Clarence Hale	Portland	July 1, 1902
MARYLAND	John C. Rose	Baltimore.	Apr. 4, 1910
MASSACHUSETTS	James M. Morton, Jr.	Boston	Aug. 12, 1912
MICHIGAN—Eastern District	Arthur J. Tuttle.	Detroit.	Aug. 6, 1912
Western District	C W Sessions	Grand Rapids.	Oct. 3, 1911
MINNESOTA	Charles A. Willard	Minneapolis	May 18, 1905
	Page Morris	Duluth	July 1, 1903
MISSISSIPPI—Two Districts	Henry C. Niles	Kosciusko	Jan. 11, 1902
MISSOURI—Eastern District	David P. Dyer	St Louis	Mar. 1, 1907
Western District	A. S. Van Valkenburg	Kansas City	June 25, 1910
MONTANA	Geo M. Bourquin	Butte	Mar. 9, 1912
NEBRASKA	William H Munger	Omaha	Feb 18, 1897
	T C Munger	Lincoln	Mar. 1, 1907
NEVADA	E S. Farrington	Carson	Jan 10, 1907
NEW HAMPSHIRE	Edgar Aldrich	Littleton	Feb. 20, 1891
NEW JERSEY	John Rellstab	Trenton	May 18. 1909
	Joseph Cross	Elizabeth.	Mar. 17, 1905
NEW MEXICO	William H Pope.	Roswell.	Feb. 20, 1912
NEW YORK—Northern District	George W. Ray	Norwich	Dec. 8, 1902
Southern District	Julius M. Mayer	New York city	Feb. 26, 1912
	George C Holt	New York city	1901
	Charles M Hough	New York city	June 27, 1906
	Learned Hand.	New York city	Apr. 26, 1909
Eastern District	Thos I Chatfield	Brooklyn	Jan. 9, 1907
	Van V Veeder.	Brooklyn	Jan 26, 1911
Western District	John R Hazel	Buffalo	June 5, 1900
NORTH CAROLINA—Eastern District	Henry G. Connor	Wilson	May 25, 1909
Western District	James E Boyd	Greensboro	Jan. 9 1901
NORTH DAKOTA	Charles F Amidon.	Fargo	Feb. 18, 1897
OHIO—Northern District	William L Day.	Cleveland	May 9, 1911
	John M Killits	Toledo	June 24, 1910
Southern District	H C Hollister	Cincinnati	Mar. 7, 1910
	John E Sater	Columbus	May 30, 1908
OKLAHOMA—Eastern District	Ralph E Campbell.	Muskogee	Jan 13, 1908
Western District	John H. Cotteral	Guthrie	Jan. 13, 1908
OREGON	C E Wolverton.	Portland	Jan. 10, 1906
	Robert S. Bean	Portland	Apr. 23, 1909
PENNSYLVANIA—Eastern District.	Jas B Holland	Philadelphia.	Apr. 19, 1904
	J Whitaker Thompson	Philadelphia.	July 16, 1912
Middle District	Charles B Witmer.	Sunbury	May 2, 1911
Western District	James S Young.	Pittsburgh.	Feb. 1, 1908
	Charles P. Orr.	Pittsburgh.	Apr. 8, 1909
PORTO RICO	Jose C. Hernandez, Ch J.	San Juan	Apr 9, 1909
RHODE ISLAND	Arthur L Brown	Providence	Oct 15, 1896
SOUTH CAROLINA.	Henry A. M Smith.	Charleston	June 7, 1911
SOUTH DAKOTA	James D Elliott	Sioux Falls	June 7, 1911
TENNESSEE—Eastern and Middle Districts	Edward T Sanford.	Knoxville.	May 18, 1908
Western District	John E. McCall	Memphis.	Jan. 17, 1905

TEXAS—Eastern District	Gordon Russell	Tyler	June 6, 1910
Western District	Thomas S. Maxey	Austin	June 25, 1888
Northern District	Edw. R. Meek	Dallas	Feb. 15, 1899
Southern District	Walter T Burns	Houston	July 1, 1902
UTAH	John A. Marshall	Salt Lake City	Feb. 4, 1896
VERMONT	Jas. L. Martin	Brattleboro	Mar. 16, 1906
VIRGINIA—Eastern District	Edmund Waddill, Jr.	Richmond	Mar. 22, 1898
Western District	H. Clay McDowell	Bigstone Gap	Dec. 18, 1901
WASHINGTON—Western District	Edward E. Cushman	Tacoma	May 1, 1912
	Jeremiah Neterer	Seattle	July 21, 1913
Eastern District	Frank H. Rudkin	Spokane	Jan. 31, 1911
WEST VIRGINIA—Northern District	Alston G. Dayton	Philippi	Mar. 14, 1905
Southern District	Benjamin F. Keller	Bramwell	July 1, 1901
WISCONSIN—Eastern District	Ferdinand A. Geiger	Milwaukee	Mar. 20, 1912
Western District	A. L. Sanborn	Madison	Jan. 9, 1905
WYOMING	John A. Riner	Cheyenne	Sept. 22, 1890

UNITED STATES DISTRICT ATTORNEYS.

Alabama—Northern district, O. D. Street, Birmingham; middle district, Warren S. Reese, Montgomery; southern district, James B. Sloan, Mobile.

Alaska—First division, John Rustgard, Juneau; second division, F. M. Saxton, Nome; third division, Geo. R. Walker, Valdez; fourth division, Jas. J. Crossley, Fairbanks.

Arizona—Joseph E. Morrison, Tucson.

Arkansas—Eastern district, William G. Whipple, Little Rock; western district, J. V. Bourland, Fort Smith.

California—Northern district, Benjamin L. McKinley, San Francisco; southern district, Albert Schoonover, Los Angeles.

Colorado—Harry E. Kelly, Denver.

Connecticut—Frederick A. Scott, Hartford.

Delaware—John P. Nields, Wilmington.

District of Columbia—Clarence R. Wilson, Washington.

Florida—Northern district, Edward C. Love, Pensacola; southern district, Herbert S. Phillips, Jacksonville.

Georgia—Northern district, Alexander Hooper, Atlanta; southern district, Alexander Akerman, Macon.

Hawaii—Robert W. Breckons, Honolulu.

Idaho—C. H. Lingenfelter, Boise.

Illinois—Northern district, James H. Wilkerson, Chicago; eastern district, William E. Trautmann, Danville; southern district, William A. Northcott, Springfield.

Indiana—Charles W. Miller, Indianapolis.

Iowa—Northern district, Anthony Van Wagenen, Sioux City; southern district, Marcellus L. Temple, Des Moines.

Kansas—Fred Robertson, Topeka.

Kentucky—Western district, George Du Relle, Louisville; eastern district, Edwin P. Morrow, Covington.

Louisiana—Eastern district; Walter Guion, New Orleans; western district, George W. Jack, Shreveport.

Maine—R. T. Whitehouse, Portland.

Maryland—John P. Hill, Baltimore.

Massachusetts—Asa P. French, Boston.

Michigan—Eastern district, Clyde I. Webster, Detroit; western district, Fred C. Wetmore, Grand Rapids.

Minnesota—Charles C. Houpt, St. Paul.

Mississippi—Northern district, Lester G. Fant, Oxford; southern district, Robert C. Lee, Vicksburg.

Missouri—Eastern district, Charles A. Houts, St. Louis; western district, Francis M. Wilson, Kansas City.

Montana—Burton K. Wheeler, Helena.

Nebraska—Francis S. Howell, Omaha.

Nevada—Samuel Platt, Carson City.

New Hampshire—Charles W. Hoitt, Nashua.

New Jersey—J. Warren Davis, Trenton.

New Mexico—(Vacancy).

New York—Northern district, John H. Gleason, Binghamton; southern district, H. Snowden Marshall, New York city; eastern district, William J. Youngs, Brooklyn; western district, John Lord O'Brian, Buffalo.

North Carolina—Eastern district, Herbert F. Seawell, Raleigh; western district, Alfred E. Holton, Winston.

North Dakota—Edward Engerud, Fargo.

Ohio—Northern district, Ulysses G. Denman, Cleveland; southern district, Sherman T. McPherson, Cincinnati.

Oklahoma—Eastern district, D. Hayden Linebaugh, Muskogee; western district, Homer N. Boardman, Guthrie.

Oregon—Clarence L. Reames, Portland.

Pennsylvania—Eastern district, Francis F. Kane, Philadelphia; middle district, Andrew B. Dunsmore, Scranton; western district, Edwin L. Humes, Pittsburgh.

Porto Rico—William N. Landers, San Juan.

Rhode Island—Walter R. Stiness, Providence.

South Carolina—Ernest F. Cochran, Charleston.

South Dakota—Robert P. Stewart, Sioux Falls.

Tennessee—Eastern district, Lewis M. Coleman, Knoxville; middle district, Abram M. Tillman, Nashville; western district, Casey Todd, Memphis.

Texas—Eastern district, James W. Ownby, Paris; northern district, James C. Wilson, Dallas; western district, J. L. Camp, San Antonio; southern district, Lock McDaniel, Houston.

Utah—Hiram E. Booth, Salt Lake City.

Vermont—Alex. Dunnett, Burlington.

Virginia—Eastern district, D. L. Groner, Richmond; western district, Barnes Gillespie, Roanoke.

Washington—Western district, Clay Allen, Seattle; eastern district, Oscar Cain, Spokane.

West Virginia—Northern district, H. Roy Waugh, Parkersburg; southern district, William G. Barnhart, Huntington.

Wisconsin—Eastern district, Guy D. Goff, Milwaukee; western district, John A. Aylward, Madison.

Wyoming—H. S. Ridgely, Cheyenne.

UNITED STATES MARSHALS.

Alabama—Northern district, Pope M. Long, Birmingham; middle district, Benjamin E. Walker, Montgomery; southern district, Gilbert B. Deans, Mobile.

Alaska—First division, Herbert L. Faulkner, Juneau; second division, Emmet R. Jordan, Nome; third division, F. R. Brenneman, Valdez; fourth division, Lewis T. Erwin, Fairbanks.

Arizona—Charles A. Overlock, Tucson.

Arkansas—Eastern district, H. L. Remmel, Little Rock; western district, John F. Mayes, Fort Smith.

California—Northern district, Charles T. Elliott, San Francisco; southern district, L. V. Youngworth, Los Angeles.

Colorado—Dewey C. Bailey, Denver.

Connecticut—Sidney E. Hawley, Hartford.

Delaware—George L. Townsend, Wilmington.

District of Columbia—Aulick Palmer, Washington.

Florida—Northern district, James B. Perkins, Pensacola; southern district, J. C. Brown, Tampa.

Georgia—Northern district, Howard Thompson, Atlanta; southern district, Joseph F. Davis, Macon.

Hawaii—E. R. Hendry, Honolulu.

Idaho—S. L. Hodgkin, Boise.

Illinois—Northern district, Luman T. Hoy, Chicago; eastern district, Charles P. Hitch, Danville; southern district, William H. Behrens, Springfield.

Indiana—Edward H. Schmidt, Indianapolis.
Iowa—Northern district, Edward Knott, Dubuque; southern district, Frank B. Clark, Des Moines.
Kansas—John R. Harrison, Topeka.
Kentucky—Western district, George W. Long, Louisville; eastern district, Asbury B. Patrick, Covington.
Louisiana—Eastern district, Victor Loisel, New Orleans; western district, Ben Ingouf, Shreveport.
Maine—Henry W. Mayo, Portland.
Maryland—George W. Padgett, Baltimore.
Massachusetts—Guy Murchie, Boston.
Michigan—Eastern district, M. D. Campbell, Detroit; western district, Nicholas J. Whelan, Grand Rapids.
Minnesota—William H. Grimshaw, St. Paul.
Mississippi—Northern district, Aaron M. Storer, Oxford; southern district, William O. Ligon, Jackson.
Missouri—Eastern district, Edward F. Regenhardt, St. Louis; western district, Albert J. Martin, Kansas City.
Montana—William Lindsay, Helena.
Nebraska—William P. Warner, Omaha.
Nevada—A. B. Gray, Carson City.
New Hampshire—Eugene P. Nute, Concord.
New Jersey—Thomas J. Alcott, Trenton.
New Mexico—Andrew H. Hudspeth, Santa Fe.
New York—Northern district, D. F. Breitenstein, Utica; southern district, William Henkel, New York city; eastern district, Charles J. Haubert, Brooklyn; western district, Henry L. Fassett, Elmira.
North Carolina—Eastern district, Claudius Dockery, Raleigh; western district, William E. Logan, Greensboro.
North Dakota—James F. Shea, Fargo.
Ohio—Northern district, Charles W. Lapp, Cleve-

land; southern district, Eugene L. Lewis, Cincinnati.
Oklahoma—Western district, William S. Cade, Guthrie; eastern district, A. B. Enlee, Jr., Muskogee.
Oregon—John Montag, Portland.
Pennsylvania—Eastern district, Frank J. Noonan, Philadelphia; middle district, James M. Yeager, Scranton; western district, Henry H. Wilson, Pittsburgh.
Porto Rico—Harry S. Hubbard, San Juan.
Rhode Island—Daniel R. Ballou, Providence.
South Carolina—J. Duncan Adams, Charleston.
South Dakota—Seth Bullock, Sioux Falls.
Tennessee—Eastern district, James G. Crumbliss, Knoxville; middle district, John W. Overall, Nashville; western district, J. Sam Johnson, Memphis.
Texas—Eastern district, Benjamin F. Sherrill, Sherman; northern district, William J. McDonald, Dallas; western district, John H. Rogers, San Antonio; southern district, Jacob A. Herring, Galveston.
Utah—James H. Anderson, Salt Lake City.
Vermont—Horace W. Bailey, Rutland.
Virginia—Eastern district, Clarence G. Smithers, Norfolk; western district, Robert A. Fulwiler, Staunton.
Washington—Eastern district, W. A. Halteman, Spokane; western district, Joseph R. H. Jacoby, Tacoma.
West Virginia—Northern district, James E. Doyle, Parkersburg; southern district, Frank H. Tyree, Huntington.
Wisconsin—Eastern district, H. A. Weil, Milwaukee; western district, Rockwell J. Flint, Madison.
Wyoming—Hugh L. Patton, Cheyenne.

SPEAKERS OF THE HOUSE.

CONGRESS.	Years.	Name.	State.	Born	Died	CONGRESS.	Years.	Name.	State.	Born	Died
1....	1789-91	F. A. Muhlenberg	Pa.	1750	1801	29....	1845-47	J. W. Davis	Ind.	1799	1859
2....	1791-93	J. Trumbull	Conn.	1740	1809	30....	1847-49	R. C. Winthrop	Mass.	1809	1894
3....	1793-95	F. A. Muhlenberg	Pa.	1750	1801	31....	1849-51	Howell Cobb	Ga.	1815	1868
4-5....	1795-99	Jonathan Dayton	N. J.	1760	1824	32-33..	1851-55	Linn Boyd	Ky.	1800	1859
6....	1799-01	Theodore Sedgwick	Mass.	1746	1813	34....	1855-57	N. P. Banks	Mass.	1816	1894
7-9....	1801-07	Nathaniel Macon	N. C.	1757	1837	35....	1857-59	James L. Orr	S. C.	1822	1873
10-11..	1807-11	J. B. Varnum	Mass.	1750	1821	36....	1860-61	W. Pennington	N. J.	1796	1862
12-13..	1811-14	Henry Clay	Ky.	1777	1852	37....	1861-63	G. A. Grow	Pa.	1823	1907
13....	1814-15	Langdon Cheves	S. C.	1776	1857	38-40..	1863-69	S. Colfax	Ind.	1823	1885
14-16..	1815-20	Henry Clay	Ky.	1777	1852	41-43..	1869-75	J. G. Blaine	Me.	1830	1893
16....	1820-21	J. W. Taylor	N. Y.	1784	1854	44....	1875-76	M. C. Kerr	Ind.	1827	1876
17....	1821-23	P. P. Barbour	Va.	1783	1841	44-46..	1876-81	S. J. Randall	Pa.	1828	1890
18....	1823-25	Henry Clay	Ky.	1777	1852	47....	1881-83	J. W. Keifer	O.	1836	....
19....	1825-27	J. W. Taylor	N. Y.	1784	1854	48-50..	1883-89	J. G. Carlisle	Ky.	1835	1910
20-23..	1827-34	A. Stevenson	Va.	1784	1857	51....	1889-91	Thomas B. Reed	Me.	1839	1902
23....	1834-35	John Bell	Tenn.	1797	1869	52-53..	1891-95	C. F. Crisp	Ga.	1845	1896
24-25..	1835-39	James K. Polk	Tenn.	1795	1849	54-55..	1895-99	Thomas B. Reed	Me.	1839	1902
26....	1839-41	R. M. T. Hunter	Va.	1809	1887	56-57..	1899-03	D. B. Henderson	Iowa	1840	1906
27....	1841-43	John White	Ky.	1805	1845	58-61..	1903-11	J. G. Cannon	Ill.	1836	....
28....	1843-45	J. W. Jones	Va.	1805	1848	62....	1911-14	Champ Clark	Mo.	1850	....

ANNUAL PAY OF EUROPEAN SOVEREIGNS AND PRESIDENTS.

Austria-Hungary—$4,250,000.
Belgium—$710,000; large income from various sources.
Bulgaria—$390,000.
Denmark—$270,000.
France—$120,000; expenses, $120,000.
Germany: Prussia—$3,772,631.
 Bavaria—$1,296,664.
 Saxony—$852,000.
 Wurttemberg—$485,975.
Great Britain—$2,350,000; annuities to members of royal family, $530,000.

Greece—$260,000.
Italy—$3,010,000.
Netherlands—$260,000; large income from royal domains.
Norway—$189,000.
Roumania—$240,000.
Russia—$8,497,000 (estimated).
Servia—$240,000.
Spain—$1,400,000, exclusive of allowances to royal family.
Turkey—$4,500,000.

BEILISS RITUAL MURDER TRIAL.

Mendel Beiliss, a Jew, was arrested in Kiev, Russia, in 1911, on the charge of having taken the life of Andrew Yushinsky, a boy, in the performance of a religious ceremony or ritual. The victim's body was found March 25, that year, in a mutilated condition in a cave near Kiev. The trial began Oct. 8, 1913, and attracted widespread atten-

tion because of the unusual nature of the charge, which was attributed generally to the anti-Jewish agitation in Russia. The prosecution made strong efforts to convict the defendant, but there was practically no evidence against him and he was acquitted by the jury Nov. 10.

Sixty-Third Congress.

From March 4, 1913, to March 3, 1915.

SENATE.

President, Thomas R. Marshall, vice-president of the United States; compensation, $12,000 a year. Democrats, 52; republicans, 43; progressive, 1. Compensation of senators, $7,500 a year.

ALABAMA.
Frank D. Glass, Dem..............Birmingham..1915
John H. Bankhead, Dem...................Jasper..1919

ARIZONA.
Henry F. Ashurst, Dem..............Prescott..1917
Marcus A. Smith, Dem................Tucson..1915

ARKANSAS.
James P. Clarke, Dem............Little Rock..1915
Joseph T. Robinson, Dem.............Lonoke..1919

CALIFORNIA.
George C. Perkins, Rep..............Oakland..1915
John D. Works, Rep.............Los Angeles..1917

COLORADO.
John F. Shafroth, Dem................Denver..1919
Charles S. Thomas, Dem..............Denver..1915

CONNECTICUT.
Frank B. Brandegee, Rep.........New London..1915
George P. McLean, Rep............Simsbury..1917

DELAWARE.
Henry A. du Pont, Rep...........Winterthur..1917
Willard Saulsbury, Dem..........Wilmington..1919

FLORIDA.
Duncan U. Fletcher, Dem.........Jacksonville..1915
Nathan P. Bryan, Dem...........Jacksonville..1917

GEORGIA.
Hoke Smith, Dem....................Atlanta..1915
Augustus O. Bacon, Dem...............Macon..1919

IDAHO.
James H. Brady, Rep..............Pocatello..1915
William E. Borah, Rep................Boise..1919

ILLINOIS.
J. Hamilton Lewis, Dem.............Chicago..1919
Lawrence Y. Sherman, Rep.........Springfield..1915

INDIANA.
Benjamin F. Shively, Dem........South Bend..1915
John W. Kern, Dem.............Indianapolis..1917

IOWA.
Albert B. Cummins, Rep...........Des Moines..1915
William S. Kenyon, Rep..........Fort Dodge..1919

KANSAS.
Joseph L. Bristow, Rep..............Salina..1915
William H. Thompson, Dem.......Garden City..1919

KENTUCKY.
William O. Bradley, Rep...........Louisville..1915
Ollie M. James, Dem.................Marion..1919

LOUISIANA.
John R. Thornton, Dem............Alexandria..1915
Joseph E. Ransdell, Dem.....Lake Providence..1919

MAINE.
Charles F. Johnson, Dem...........Waterville..1917
Edwin C. Burleigh, Rep.............Augusta..1919

MARYLAND.
John Walter Smith, Dem..........Snow Hill..1915
Blair Lee, Dem...............Silver Springs..1917

MASSACHUSETTS.
Henry Cabot Lodge, Rep...............Nahant..1917
John W. Weeks, Rep..........West Newton..1919

MICHIGAN.
Charles E. Townsend, Rep............Jackson..1917
William A. Smith, Rep.........Grand Rapids..1919

MINNESOTA.
Moses E. Clapp, Rep................St. Paul..1917
Knute Nelson, Rep...............Alexandria..1919

MISSISSIPPI.
John Sharp Williams, Dem...........Benton..1917
James K. Vardaman, Dem.............Jackson..1919

MISSOURI.
William J. Stone, Dem..............St. Louis..1915
James A. Reed, Dem.............Kansas City..1917

MONTANA.
Henry L. Myers, Dem...............Hamilton..1917
Thomas J. Walsh, Dem................Helena..1919

NEBRASKA.
Gilbert M. Hitchcock, Dem...............Omaha..1917
Norris Brown, Rep....................McCook..1919

NEVADA.
Francis G. Newlands, Dem................Reno..1915
Key Pittman, Dem....................Tonopah..1917

NEW HAMPSHIRE.
Jacob H. Gallinger, Rep.............Concord..1915
Henry F. Hollis, Dem...............Concord..1919

NEW JERSEY.
James E. Martine, Dem.............Plainfield..1917
William Hughes, Dem...............Paterson..1919

NEW MEXICO.
Thomas B. Catron, Rep..............Santa Fe..1917
Albert B. Fall, Rep............Three Rivers..1919

NEW YORK.
Elihu Root, Rep..................New York..1915
James A. O'Gorman, Dem..........New York..1917

NORTH CAROLINA.
Lee S. Overman, Dem................Salisbury..1915
F. M. Simmons, Dem.................Newbern..1919

NORTH DAKOTA.
Porter J. McCumber, Rep..........Wahpeton..1917
Asle J. Gronna, Rep.................Lakota..1915

OHIO.
Theodore E. Burton, Rep..........Cleveland..1915
Atlee Pomerene, Dem................Canton..1917

OKLAHOMA.
Thomas P. Gore, Dem................Lawton..1915
Robert L. Owen, Dem..............Muskogee..1919

OREGON.
George E. Chamberlain, Dem.........Portland..1915
Henry Lane, Dem....................Portland..1919

PENNSYLVANIA.
Boies Penrose, Rep..............Philadelphia..1915
George T. Oliver, Rep.............Pittsburgh..1917

RHODE ISLAND.
Henry F. Lippitt, Rep.............Providence..1917
Le Baron B. Colt, Rep...............Bristol..1919

SOUTH CAROLINA.
Ellison D. Smith, Dem...............Florence..1915
Benjamin R. Tillman, Dem...........Trenton..1919

SOUTH DAKOTA.
Coe I. Crawford, Rep.................Huron..1915
Thomas Sterling, Rep..............Vermilion..1919

TENNESSEE.
Luke Lea, Dem.....................Nashville..1917
John K. Shields, Dem..............Knoxville..1919

TEXAS.
Charles S. Culberson, Dem...........Dallas..1917
Morris Sheppard, Dem.............Texarkana..1919

UTAH.
Reed Smoot, Rep.................Provo City..1915
George Sutherland, Rep.......Salt Lake City..1917

VERMONT.
William P. Dillingham, Rep.......Montpelier..1915
Carroll S. Page, Rep.............Hyde Park..1917

VIRGINIA.
Claude A. Swanson, Dem.............Chatham..1917
Thomas S. Martin, Dem.......Charlottesville..1919

WASHINGTON.
Wesley L. Jones, Rep............North Yakima..1915
Miles Poindexter, Prog............Spokane..1917

WEST VIRGINIA.
William E. Chilton, Dem...........Charleston..1917
Nathan Goff, Rep................Clarksburg..1919

WISCONSIN.
Isaac Stephenson, Rep.............Marinette..1915
Robert M. LaFollette, Rep..........Madison..1917

WYOMING.
Clarence D. Clark, Rep.............Evanston..1917
Francis E. Warren, Rep.............Cheyenne..1919

OFFICERS OF SENATE.
President..............Thomas R. Marshall, Indiana
President Pro Tempore..James P. Clarke, Arkansas
Secretary.....James Marion Baker, South Carolina
Sergeant at Arms......Charles P. Higgins, Missouri

HOUSE OF REPRESENTATIVES.

Democrats, 291; republicans, 128; progressives, 15; independent, 1; total, 435. Asterisk (*) after name indicates that member served in 62d congress. †At large. Speaker, Champ Clark of Missouri; compensation of speaker, $12,000; of other members of house, $7,500 a year.

ALABAMA.
John W. Abercrombie,† Dem.........Tuscaloosa
1. George W. Taylor,* Dem..............Demopolis
2. S. H. Dent,* Dem......................Montgomery
3. Henry D. Clayton,* Dem...............Eufaula
4. Frederick L. Blackmon,* Dem ....Anniston
5. James Thomas Heflin,* Dem...........Lafayette
6. Richmond P. Hobson,* Dem...........Greensboro
7. John L. Burnett,* Dem.................Gadsden
8. William Richardson,* Dem............Huntsville
9. Oscar W. Underwood,* Dem........Birmingham

ARIZONA.
Carl Hayden,*† Dem....................Phœnix

ARKANSAS.
1. T. H. Caraway, Dem..................Jonesboro
2. W. A. Oldfield,* Dem.................Batesville
3. John C. Floyd,* Dem..................Harrison
4. Otis T. Wingo, Dem..................DeQueen
5. H. M. Jacoway,* Dem................Dardanelle
6. Samuel M. Taylor, Dem..............Pine Bluff
7. William S. Goodwin,* Dem............Warren

CALIFORNIA.
1. William Kent, Ind....................Kentland
2. John E. Baker, Dem..................Alturas
3. Charles F. Curry, Rep...............Sacramento
4. Julius Kahn,* Rep................San Francisco
5. John I. Nolan, Prog. Rep........San Francisco
6. Joseph R. Knowland,* Rep...........Alameda
7. Denver S. Church, Dem...............Fresno
8. Everis A. Hayes,* Rep...............San Jose
9. Charles W. Bell, Prog. Rep.........Pasadena
10. William D. Stephens,* Prog. Rep...Los Angeles
11. William Kettner, Dem...............San Diego

COLORADO.
Edward E. Taylor,*† Dem.....Glenwood Springs
Edward Keating,† Dem..................Pueblo
1. George J. Kindel, Dem...............Denver
2. H. H. Seidomridge, Dem.......Colorado Springs

CONNECTICUT.
1. Augustine Lonergan, Dem............Hartford
2. Bryan F. Mahan, Dem.............New London
3. Thomas L. Reilly,* Dem.............Meriden
4. Jeremiah Donovan, Dem..........South Norwalk
5. William Kennedy, Dem.............Naugatuck

DELAWARE.
Franklin Brockson,† Dem................Clayton

FLORIDA.
Claude L'Engle,† Dem...............Jacksonville
1. Stephen M. Sparkman,* Dem...........Tampa
2. Frank Clark,* Dem..................Gainesville
3. Emmett Wilson, Dem.................Pensacola

GEORGIA.
1. Charles C. Edwards,* Dem...........Savannah
2. Frank Park, Dem....................Sylvester
3. Charles R. Crisp, Dem..............Americus
4. W. C. Adamson,* Dem...............Carrollton
5. William Schley Howard,* Dem........Decatur
6. Charles L. Bartlett,* Dem...........Macon
7. Gordon Lee,* Dem................Chickamauga
8. Samuel J. Tribble,* Dem............Athens
9. Thomas M. Bell,* Dem..............Gainesville
10. Thomas W. Hardwick,* Dem........Sandersville
11. John H. Walker, Dem...............Valdosta
12. Dudley M. Hughes,* Dem............Danville

IDAHO.
Addison T. Smith,† Rep..............Twin Falls
Burton L. French,*† Rep...............Moscow

ILLINOIS.
Lawrence B. Stringer,† Dem............Lincoln
William Elza Williams,† Dem.........Pittsfield
1. Martin B. Madden,* Rep.............Chicago
2. James R. Mann,* Rep...............Chicago
3. George E. Gorman, Dem..............Chicago
4. James T. McDermott,* Dem..........Chicago
5. Adolph J. Sabath,* Dem.............Chicago
6. James McAndrews,* Dem.............Chicago
7. Frank Buchanan,* Dem..............Chicago
8. Thomas Gallagher,* Dem............Chicago
9. Fred A. Britten, Rep...............Chicago
10. Charles M. Thomson, Prog...........Chicago
11. Ira C. Copley,* Rep................Aurora
12. William H. Hinebaugh, Prog.........Ottawa
13. John C. McKenzie,* Rep............Elizabeth
14. Clyde H. Tavenner, Dem............Cordova
15. Stephen A. Hoxworth, Dem..........Rapatee
16. Claude U. Stone,* Dem..............Peoria
17. Louis FitzHenry, Dem............Bloomington
18. Frank T. O'Hair, Dem...............Paris
19. Charles M. Borchers, Dem............Decatur
20. Henry T. Rainey,* Dem.............Carrollton
21. James M. Graham,* Dem...........Springfield
22. William N. Baltz, Dem.............Millstadt
23. Martin D. Foster,* Dem..............Olney
24. H. Robert Fowler,* Dem.........Elizabethtown
25. Robert P. Hill, Dem................Marion

INDIANA.
1. Charles Lieb, Dem..................Rockport
2. William A. Cullop,* Dem............Vincennes
3. William E. Cox,* Dem...............Jasper
4. Lincoln Dixon,* Dem............North Vernon
5. Ralph W. Moss,* Dem................Brazil
6. Finley H. Gray,* Dem............Connersville
7. Charles A. Korbly,* Dem.........Indianapolis
8. John A. M. Adair,* Dem.............Portland
9. Martin A. Morrison,* Dem..........Frankfort
10. John B. Peterson, Dem...........Crown Point
11. George W. Rauch,* Dem.............Marion
12. Cyrus Cline,* Dem..................Angola
13. Henry A. Barnhart.* Dem..........Rochester

IOWA.
1. Charles A. Kennedy,* Rep...........Montrose
2. Irvin S. Pepper,* Dem.............Muscatine
3. Maurice Connolly, Dem..............Dubuque
4. Gilbert N. Haugen,* Rep...........Northwood
5. James W. Good,* Rep...........Cedar Rapids
6. S. Kirkpatrick, Dem................Ottumwa
7. Solomon F. Prouty,* Rep.........Des Moines
8. Horace M. Towner,* Rep.............Corning
9. William R. Green,* Rep............Audubon
10. Frank P. Woods,* Rep.............Estherville
11. George O. Scott, Rep.............Sioux City

KANSAS.
1. Daniel R. Anthony, Jr.,* Rep.....Leavenworth
2. Joseph Taggart,* Dem...........Kansas City
3. P. P. Campbell,* Rep..............Pittsburg
4. Dudley Doolittle, Dem............Strong City
5. Guy T. Helvering, Dem............Marysville
6. John R. Connelly, Dem..............Colby
7. George A. Neeley, Dem............Hutchinson
8. Victor Murdock,* Prog.............Wichita

KENTUCKY.
1. Alben W. Barkley, Dem..............Paducah
2. Augustus O. Stanley,* Dem.........Henderson
3. Robert Y. Thomas,* Dem.........Central City
4. Ben Johnson,* Dem................Bardstown
5. Swager Sherley,* Dem.............Louisville
6. Arthur B. Rouse,* Dem............Burlington
7. J. Campbell Cantrill,* Dem.......Georgetown
8. Harvey Helm,* Dem.................Stanford
9. W. J. Fields,* Dem...............Olive Hill
10. John W. Langley,* Rep............Pikeville
11. Caleb Powers,* Rep..............Barbourville

LOUISIANA.
1. Albert Estopinal,* Dem...........Estopinal
2. H. Garland Dupre,* Dem..........New Orleans
3. Robert F. Broussard,* Dem........New Iberia
4. John T. Watkins.* Dem.............Minden
5. Walter Elder, Dem.................Monroe
6. Louis L. Morgan, Dem.............Covington
7. Ladislas Lazaro, Dem.............Opelousas
8. James B. Aswell, Dem...........Natchitoches

MAINE.
1. Asher C. Hinds,* Rep..............Portland
2. Daniel J. McGillicuddy,* Dem......Lewiston
3. John A. Peters, Rep...............Ellsworth
4. Frank E. Guernsey,* Rep..............Dover

MARYLAND.
1. J. Harry Covington,* Dem...........Easton
2. Joshua F. C. Talbott,* Dem........Lutherville

3. Charles T. Coady, Dem....................Baltimore
4. J. Charles Linthicum,* Dem............Baltimore
5. Frank O. Smith, Dem.......................Dunkirk
6. David J. Lewis,* Dem...................Cumberland

MASSACHUSETTS.

1. Allen T. Treadway, Rep..............Stockbridge
2. Frederick H. Gillett,* Rep............Springfield
3. Calvin D. Paige, Rep..................Southbridge
4. Samuel E. Winslow, Rep................Worcester
5. John J. Rogers, Rep..........................Lowell
6. Augustus P. Gardner,* Rep..............Hamilton
7. Michael F. Phelan, Dem........................Lynn
8. Frederick S. Deitrick, Dem..............Cambridge
9. Ernest W. Roberts,* Rep...................Chelsea
10. William F. Murray,* Dem..................Boston
11. Andrew J. Peters,* Dem....................Boston
12. James M. Curley, Dem......................Boston
13. John J. Mitchell, Dem....................Marlboro
14. Edward Gilmore, Dem......................Brockton
15. William S. Greene,* Rep................Fall River
16. Thomas C. Thacher, Dem..................Yarmouth

MICHIGAN.

Patrick H. Kelley,† Rep....................Lansing
1. Frank E. Doremus,* Dem....................Detroit
2. Samuel W. Beakes, Dem....................Ann Arbor
3. J. M. C. Smith,* Rep....................Charlotte
4. Edward L. Hamilton,* Rep....................Niles
5. Carl E. Mapes, Rep..................Grand Rapids
6. Samuel W. Smith,* Rep.....................Pontiac
7. Louis C. Crampton, Dem.....................Lapeer
8. Joseph W. Fordney,* Rep..................Saginaw
9. James C. McLaughlin,* Rep..............Muskegon
10. Roy O. Woodruff, Prog...................Bay City
11. Francis O. Lindquist, Rep.........Mount Pleasant
12. William J. Macdonald, Prog..................

MINNESOTA.

James Manahan,† Rep......................St. Paul
1. Sydney Anderson,* Rep...................Lanesboro
2. W. S. Hammond,* Dem.....................St. James
3. Charles R. Davis,* Rep..................St. Peter
4. Frederick C. Stevens,* Rep..............St. Paul
5. George R. Smith, Dem..................Minneapolis
6. Charles A. Lindbergh,* Rep..........Little Falls
7. Andrew J. Volstead,* Rep............Granite Falls
8. Clarence B. Miller,* Rep...................Duluth
9. Halvor Steenerson,* Rep..................Crookston

MISSISSIPPI.

1. Ezekiel S. Candler, Jr.,* Dem............Corinth
2. Hubert D. Stephens,* Dem.............New Albany
3. Benjamin G. Humphreys,* Dem.......Greenville
4. Thomas U. Sisson,* Dem.....................Winona
5. Samuel A. Witherspoon,* Dem..........Meridian
6. Byron P. Harrison,* Dem..................Gulfport
7. Percy E. Quin, Dem..................McComb City
8. James W. Collier,* Dem..................Vicksburg

MISSOURI.

1. James T. Lloyd,* Dem..................Shelbyville
2. William W. Rucker,* Dem..............Keytesville
3. Joshua W. Alexander,* Dem.............Gallatin
4. Charles F. Booher,* Dem................Savannah
5. William P. Borland,* Dem..........Kansas City
6. Clement C. Dickinson,* Dem..............Clinton
7. Courtney W. Hamlin,* Dem............Springfield
8. Dorsey W. Shackleford,* Dem.....Jefferson City
9. Champ Clark,* Dem..................Bowling Green
10. Richard Bartholdt,* Rep................St. Louis
11. William L. Igoe, Dem....................St. Louis
12. Leonidas C. Dyer,* Rep................St. Louis
13. Walter L. Hensley,* Dem..............Farmington
14. Joseph J. Russell,* Dem..............Charleston
15. Perl D. Decker, Dem........................Joplin
16. Thomas L. Rubey,* Dem..................Lebanon

MONTANA.

Thomas Stout,† Dem....................Lewistown
John M. Evans,† Dem......................Missoula

NEBRASKA.

1. John A. Maguire,* Dem....................Lincoln
2. C. O. Lobeck, Dem............................Omaha
3. Dan V. Stephens,* Dem....................Fremont
4. Charles H. Sloan,* Rep......................Geneva
5. Silas R. Barton, Rep..................Grand Island
6. Moses P. Kinkaid,* Rep.....................O'Neill

NEVADA.

E. E. Roberts,*† Rep................Carson City

NEW HAMPSHIRE.

1. Eugene E. Reed, Dem..................Manchester
2. Raymond B. Stevens, Dem.................Landall

NEW JERSEY.

1. William J. Browning,* Rep,..............Camden
2. J. Thompson Baker, Dem..................Wildwood
3. Thomas J. Scully,* Dem............South Amboy
4. Allan B. Walsh, Dem.......................Trenton
5. William E. Tuttle, Jr.,* Dem..........Westfield
6. Alexander C. Hart, Dem...............Hackensack
7. Robert G. Bremner, Dem..................Paterson
8. Eugene F. Kinkead,* Dem..........Jersey City
9. Walter I. McCoy,* Dem...........East Orange
10. Edward W. Townsend,* Dem..........Montclair
11. John J. Eagan, Dem...................Jersey City
12. James A. Hamill, Dem.................Weehawken

NEW MEXICO.

Harvey B. Fergusson,† Dem........Albuquerque

NEW YORK.

1. Lathrop Brown, Dem.......................St. James
2. Dennis J. O'Leary, Dem.................Douglaston
3. Frank E. Wilson,* Dem....................Brooklyn
4. Harry H. Dale, Dem.......................Brooklyn
5. James P. Maher,* Dem....................Brooklyn
6. William M. Calder,* Rep..................Brooklyn
7. John J. Fitzgerald,* Dem................Brooklyn
8. Daniel J. Griffin, Dem...................Brooklyn
9. James H. O'Brien, Dem..................New York
10. Herman A. Metz, Dem....................Brooklyn
11. Daniel J. Riordan,* Dem...............New York
12. Henry M. Goldfogle,* Dem...........New York
13. George W. Loft, Dem....................New York
14. Jefferson M. Levy,* Dem...............New York
15. Michael F. Conry,* Dem...............New York
16. Peter J. Dooling, Dem..................New York
17. John F. Carew, Dem......................New York
18. Thomas G. Patten,* Dem...............New York
19. Walter M. Chandler, Prog.............New York
20. Jacob H. Cantor, Dem...................New York
21. Henry George, Jr.,* Dem...............New York
22. Henry Bruckner, Dem....................New York
23. Joseph A. Goulden, Dem...............New York
24. Woodson R. Oglesby, Dem.........Mohegan Park
25. Benjamin I. Taylor, Dem................Harrison
26. Edmund Platt, Rep....................Poughkeepsie
27. George McClellan, Dem................Kinderhook
28. Peter G. Ten Eyck, Dem..................Albany
29. James S. Parker, Rep........................Salem
30. Samuel Wallin, Rep....................Amsterdam
31. Edward A. Merritt, Jr., Rep...........Potsdam
32. Luther Mott,* Rep...........................Oswego
33. Charles A. Talcott,* Dem....................Utica
34. George W. Fairchild,* Rep..............Oneonta
35. John R. Clancy, Dem....................Syracuse
36. Sereno E. Payne,* Rep....................Auburn
37. Edwin S. Underhill,* Dem..................Bath
38. Thomas B. Dunn, Rep..................Rochester
39. Henry G. Danforth,* Rep..............Rochester
40. Robert H. Gittins, Dem.............Niagara Falls
41. Charles B. Smith,* Dem..................Buffalo
42. Daniel A. Driscoll,* Dem................Buffalo
43. Charles M. Hamilton, Rep..................Ripley

NORTH CAROLINA.

1. John H. Small,* Dem..................Washington
2. Claude Kitchin,* Dem.............Scotland Neck
3. John M. Faison,* Dem........................Faison
4. Edward W. Pou,* Dem..................Smithfield
5. Charles M. Stedman,* Dem...........Greensboro
6. H. L. Godwin,* Dem..........................Dunn
7. Robert N. Page,* Dem........................Bisco
8. R. L. Doughton,* Dem...........Laurel Springs
9. Edwin Y. Webb,* Dem.......................Shelby
10. James M. Gudger, Jr.,* Dem...........Asheville

NORTH DAKOTA.

1. Henry T. Helgesen,* Rep....................Milton
2. George M. Young, Rep..................Valley City
3. P. D. Norton, Rep.........................Nottinger

OHIO.

Robert Crosser,† Dem..................Cleveland
1. Stanley E. Bowdle, Dem................Cincinnati
2. Alfred G. Allen,* Dem..................Cincinnati
3. Warren Gard, Dem...........................Hamilton

4. J. Henry Goeke,* Dem...............Wapakoneta
5. Timothy T. Ansberry,* Dem............Defiance
6. Simeon D. Fess, Rep.........Yellow Springs
7. James D. Post,* Dem.........Washington C. H.
8. Frank B. Willis,* Rep......................Ada
9. Isaac R. Sherwood,* Dem...................Toledo
10. Robert M. Switzer,* Rep.................Waverly
11. Horatio C. Claypool,* Dem...........Chillicothe
12. Clement Brumbaugh, Dem..............Columbus
13. John A. Key, Dem.......................Marion
14. William G. Sharp,* Dem..................Elyria
15. George White,* Dem....................Marietta
16. William B. Francis,* Dem........Martins Ferry
17. William A. Ashbrook,* Dem..........Johnstown
18. J. J. Whitacre,* Dem.....................Canton
19. E. R. Bathrick,* Dem......................Akron
20. William Gordon, Dem...................Cleveland
21. Robert J. Bulkeley,* Dem..............Cleveland

OKLAHOMA.

W. H. Murray,† Dem................Tishomingo
Claude Weaver,† Dem...........Oklahoma City
J. B. Thompson,† Dem...........Pauls Valley
1. Bird S. McGuire,* Rep....................Pawnee
2. Dick T. Morgan,* Rep..................Woodward
3. James S. Davenport,* Dem................Vinita
4. Charles D. Carter,* Dem................Ardmore
5. Scott Ferris,* Dem........................Lawton

OREGON.

1. Willis C. Hawley,* Rep....................Salem
2. Nicholas J. Sinnott, Rep..............The Dalles
3. A. Walter Lafferty,* Prog. Rep.........Portland

PENNSYLVANIA.

John M. Morin,† Rep..................Pittsburgh
Frederick E. Lewis,† Rep...............Allentown
Anderson H. Walters.† Rep.............Johnstown
Arthur R. Rupley,† Prog. Rep...........Carlisle
1. William S. Vare, Rep...............Philadelphia
2. George S. Graham, Rep.............Philadelphia
3. J. Hampton Moore,* Rep...........Philadelphia
4. George W. Edmonds, Rep...........Philadelphia
5. Michael Donohoe,* Dem...........Philadelphia
6. J. Washington Logue, Dem.........Philadelphia
7. Thomas S. Butler,* Rep...........West Chester
8. Robert E. Difenderfer,* Dem........Jenkintown
9. William W. Griest,* Rep.............Lancaster
10. John R. Farr,* Rep.....................Scranton
11. John J. Casey, Dem..................Wilkesbarre
12. Robert E. Lee,* Dem...................Pottsville
13. John H. Rothermel,* Dem...............Reading
14. William D. B. Ainey,* Rep.............Montrose
15. Edgar R. Kiess, Rep...............Williamsport
16. John V. Lesher, Dem....................Sunbury
17. Frank L. Dershem, Dem................Lewisburg
18. Aaron S. Kreider, Rep...................Annville
19. Warren Worth Bailey, Dem...........Johnstown
20. Andrew R. Brodbeck, Dem...............Hanover
21. Charles E. Patton,* Rep...........Curwensville
22. Abraham L. Keister, Rep...............Scottdale
23. Wooda N. Carr, Dem...................Uniontown
24. Henry W. Temple,* Prog...........Washington
25. Milton W. Shreve, Rep......................Erie
26. A. Mitchell Palmer,* Dem...........Stroudsburg
27. J. N. Langham,* Rep......................Indiana
28. Willis J. Hulings, Prog..................Oil City
29. Stephen G. Porter,* Rep...............Pittsburgh
30. M. Klyde Kelly, Rep.............North Braddock
31. James F. Burke,* Rep..................Pittsburgh
32. Andrew J. Barchfeld,* Rep.............Pittsburgh

RHODE ISLAND.

1. George F. O'Shaughnessy,* Dem......Providence
2. Peter Goelet Gerry, Dem................Newport
3. Ambrose Kennedy, Rep................Woonsocket

SOUTH CAROLINA.

1. Richard S. Whaley, Dem...............Charleston
2. James F. Byrnes,* Dem....................Aiken
3. Wyatt Aiken,* Dem.....................Abbeville
4. Joseph T. Johnson,* Dem.............Spartanburg
5. D. E. Finley,* Dem.....................Yorkville
6. J. W. Ragsdale, Dem....................Florence
7. A. F. Lever,* Dem.....................Lexington

SOUTH DAKOTA.

1. Charles H. Dillon, Rep..................Yankton
2. Charles H. Burke,* Rep...................Pierre
3. Eben W. Martin,* Rep..................Deadwood

TENNESSEE.

1. Sam R. Sells,* Rep................Johnson City
2. Richard W. Austin,* Rep.............Knoxville
3. John A. Moon,* Dem...............Chattanooga
4. Cordell Hull,* Dem.....................Carthage
5. William C. Houston,* Dem..............Woodbury
6. Joseph W. Byrns,* Dem..................Nashville
7. Lemuel P. Padgett,* Dem................Columbia
8. Thetus W. Sims,* Dem....................Linden
9. Finis J. Garrett,* Dem...................Dresden
10. Kenneth D. McKellar,* Dem..............Memphis

TEXAS.

Hatton W. Summers,† Dem.................Dallas
Daniel E. Garrett,† Dem..................Houston
1. Horace W. Vaughan,* Dem.............Texarkana
2. Martien Dies,* Dem...................Woodville
3. James Young,* Dem.....................Kaufman
4. Sam Rayburn, Dem.......................Bonham
5. Jack Beall,* Dem.....................Waxahachie
6. Rufus Hardy,* Dem...................Corsicana
7. Alexander W. Gregg,* Dem...............Palestine
8. Joe H. Eagle, Dem.......................Houston
9. George F. Burgess,* Dem...............Gonzales
10. John P. Buchanan, Dem.................Brenham
11. Robert L. Henry,* Dem......................Waco
12. Oscar Callaway,* Dem...................Comanche
13. John H. Stephens, Dem....................Vernon
14. James L. Slayden,* Dem............San Antonio
15. John N. Garner,* Dem....................Uvalde
16. William R. Smith,* Dem...............Colorado

UTAH.

Joseph Howell,*† Rep......................Logan
Jacob Johnson,† Rep................Spring City

VERMONT.

1. Frank L. Green, Rep.....................St. Albans
2. Frank Plumley,* Rep...................Northfield

VIRGINIA.

1. William A. Jones,* Dem....................Warsaw
2. Edward E. Holland,* Dem..................Suffolk
3. Andrew J. Montague, Dem...............Richmond
4. Walter A. Watson, Dem......Jenning's Ordinary
5. Edward W. Saunders,* Dem........Rocky Mount
6. Carter Glass,* Dem....................Lynchburg
7. James Hay,* Dem........................Madison
8. Charles C. Carlin,* Dem...............Alexandria
9. C. Bascomb Slemp,* Rep........Big Stone Gap
10. Henry D. Flood,* Dem..................Appomattox

WASHINGTON.

A. J. Falconer,† Prog.....................Everett
J. W. Bryan,† Prog.....................Bremerton
1. W. E. Humphrey,* Rep....................Seattle
2. Albert Johnson, Rep......................Hoquiam
3. W. L. LaFollette,* Rep....................Pullman

WEST VIRGINIA.

Howard Sutherland,† Rep....................Elkins
1. Matthew M. Neely, Dem..................Fairmont
2. William G. Brown, Jr.,* Dem.............Kingwood
3. Samuel V. Avis, Rep...................Charleston
4. Hunter H. Moss, Jr., Rep.............Parkersburg
5. James A. Hughes,* Rep..................Huntington

WISCONSIN.

1. Henry A. Cooper,* Rep.....................Racine
2. Michael E. Burke,* Dem.............Beaver Dam
3. John M. Nelson,* Rep......................Madison
4. William J. Cary,* Rep..................Milwaukee
5. William H. Stafford,* Rep.............Milwaukee
6. Michael R. Reilly, Dem............Fond du Lac
7. John J. Esch,* Rep....................LaCrosse
8. Edward E. Browne,* Rep................Waupaca
9. Thomas F. Konop,* Dem................Kewaunee
10. James A. Frear, Rep......................Hudson
11. Irvine L. Lenroot,* Rep..................Superior

WYOMING.

Frank W. Mondell,*† Rep................Newcastle

DELEGATES.

Alaska—James Wickersham,* Prog.......Fairbanks
Hawaii—J. K. Kalanole, Rep..............Honolulu

COMMISSIONERS.

Philippines—Manuel Quezon and Manuel Earnshaw
Porto Rico—Luis Munoz Rivera*..........San Juan

OFFICERS OF HOUSE.

Speaker.....................Champ Clark, Missouri
Clerk.................South Trimble, Kentucky
Sergeant at Arms..........Robert B. Gordon, Ohio
Doorkeeper..Joseph J. Sinnott, District of Columbia

United States Diplomatic and Consular Service.

DIPLOMATIC SERVICE—DEC. 1, 1913.

Explanation—A. E. and P., ambassador extraordinary and plenipotentiary; E. E. and M. P., envoy extraordinary and minister plenipotentiary; M. R., | minister resident; M. R. and C.-G., minister resident and consul-general. Appointed by the president and confirmed by the senate.

Country.	Representative.	Location.	Appointed from.	Salary.
Argentine Republic	John W. Garrett, E. E. & M. P.	Buenos Aires	Maryland.	$12,000
	G. L. Lorillard, Sec. of Leg.	Buenos Aires	Rhode Island.	2,625
Austria-Hungary	Frederic C. Penfield, A. E. & P.	Vienna	Pennsylvania.	17,500
	U. Grant-Smith, Sec. of Emb.	Vienna	Pennsylvania.	3,000
	Arthur H. Frazier, 2d Sec. of Emb.	Vienna	Pennsylvania.	2,000
	Lieut.-Com. R. D. White, Nav. Att.	Vienna	Navy.	
	Capt. A. L. Briggs, Mil. Att.	Vienna	Army.	
Belgium	Theodore Marburg, E. E. & M. P.	Brussels	Maryland.	12,000
	Fred M. Dearing, Sec. of Leg.	Brussels	Missouri.	2,625
Bolivia	John D. O'Rear, E. E. & M. P.	LaPaz	Missouri.	10,000
	C. E. Staugeland, Sec. of Leg.	LaPaz	Washington.	2,000
Brazil	Edwin V. Morgan, A. E. & P.	Rio de Janeiro	New York.	17,500
	J. Butler Wright, Sec. of Leg.	Rio de Janeiro	Wyoming.	3,000
Bulgaria	Charles J. Vopicka, E. E. & M. P.	Bucharest	Illinois.	10,000
	Charles Campbell, Jr., Sec. of Leg.	Bucharest	Virginia.	2,000
Chile	Henry P. Fletcher, E. E. & M. P.	Santiago	Pennsylvania.	12,000
	R. B. Harvey, Sec. of Leg.	Santiago	Maryland.	2,625
China	Paul S. Reinsch, E. E. & M. P.	Pekin	Wisconsin.	12,000
	John Van A. Macmurray, Sec. of Leg.	Pekin	District of Columbia.	2,625
	George T. Summerlin, 2d Sec. of Leg.	Pekin	Louisiana.	1,800
	Lieut.-Com. L. A. Cotton, Nav. Att.	Pekin	Navy.	
	Maj. A. J. Bowley, Mil. Att.	Pekin	Army.	
Colombia	Thaddeus A. Thomson, E. E. & M. P.	Bogota	Texas.	10,000
	Leland Harrison, Sec. of Leg.	Bogota	Illinois.	2,000
Costa Rica and Nicaragua	Edward J. Hale, E. E. & M. P.	San Jose	North Carolina.	10,000
	M. M. Langhorne, Sec. of Leg.	San Jose	Virginia.	2,000
Cuba	William E. Gonzales, E. E. & M. P.	Havana	South Carolina.	12,000
	Hugh S. Gibson, Sec. of Leg.	Havana	California.	2,625
	F. T. Coxe, 2d Sec. of Leg.	Havana	Pennsylvania.	1,800
Denmark	Maurice F. Egan, E. E. & M. P.	Copenhagen	Dist. of Columbia.	10,000
	Alexander R. Magruder, Sec. of Leg.	Copenhagen	Maryland.	2,000
Dominican Republic	James M. Sullivan, M. R. & C.-G.	Santo Domingo	New York.	10,000
Ecuador	Charles S. Hartman, E. E. & M. P.	Quito	Montana.	10,000
	W. P. Cresson, Sec. of Leg.	Quito	Nevada.	2,000
France	Myron T. Herrick, A. E. & P.	Paris	Ohio.	17,500
	A. W. Bliss, Sec. of Emb.	Paris	New York.	3,000
	S. Whitehouse, 2d Sec. of Emb.	Paris	New York.	2,000
	W. D. Robbins, 3d Sec. of Emb.	Paris	Massachusetts.	1,200
	Com. H. H. Hough, Nav. Att.	Paris	Navy.	
	Maj. Spencer Cosby, Mil. Att.	Paris	Army.	
Germany	James W. Gerard, A. E. & P.	Berlin	New York.	17,500
	Joseph C. Grew, Sec. of Emb.	Berlin	Massachusetts.	3,000
	W. Spencer, 2d Sec. of Emb.	Berlin	Pennsylvania.	2,000
	A. B. Ruddock, 3d Sec. of Emb.	Berlin	Illinois.	1,200
	Lieut.-Com. W. R. Gherardi, Nav. Att.	Berlin	Navy.	
	Maj. George T. Langhorne, Mil. Att.	Berlin	Army.	
Great Britain	Walter Hines Page, A. E. & P.	London	New York.	17,500
	I. B. Laughlin, Sec. of Emb.	London	Pennsylvania.	3,000
	Edward Bell, 2d Sec. of Emb.	London	Nevada.	2,000
	H. Johnson, 3d Sec. of Emb.	London	New Jersey.	1,200
	Com. P. Symington, Nav. Att.	London	Navy.	
	Lieut.-Col. George O. Squier, Mil. Att.	London	Army.	
Greece	(Vacancy), E. E. & M. P.	Athens		10,000
	F. O. de Billier, Sec. of Emb.	Athens	District of Columbia.	2,000
Guatemala	William H. Leavell, E. E. & M. P.	Guatemala	Mississippi.	10,000
	H. R. Wilson, Sec. of Leg.	Guatemala	Illinois.	2,000
Haiti	Madison R. Smith, E. E. & M. P.	Port au Prince	Missouri.	10,000
Honduras	John Ewing, E. E. & M. P.	Tegucigalpa	Louisiana.	10,000
Italy	Thomas Nelson Page, A. E. & P.	Rome	Virginia.	17,500
	Post Wheeler, Sec. of Emb.	Rome	Washington.	3,000
	A. Benson, 2d Sec. of Emb.	Rome	Pennsylvania.	2,000
	Lieut.-Com. R. D. White, Nav. Att.	Rome	Navy.	
	Lieut.-Com. George M. Dunn, Mil. Att.	Rome	Army.	
Japan	George W. Guthrie, E. E. & P.	Tokyo	Pennsylvania.	17,500
	A. Bailly-Blanchard, Sec. of Emb.	Tokyo	Louisiana.	3,000
	R. B. Strassburger, 2d Sec. of Emb.	Tokyo	New York.	2,000
	Frank D. Arnold, 3d Sec. of Emb.	Tokyo	Pennsylvania.	1,200
	Lieut.-Com. L. A. Cotton, Nav. Att.	Tokyo	Navy.	
	Col. James A. Irons, Mil. Att.	Tokyo	Army.	
	Charles J. Arnell, Int.	Tokyo	Washington.	3,600
Liberia	George W. Buckner, M. R. & C.-G.	Monrovia	Indiana.	5,000
	Richard C. Bundy, Sec. of Leg.	Monrovia	Ohio.	2,000
Luxemburg	Henry Van Dyke, E. E. & M. P.	The Hague	New Jersey.	12,000
Mexico	(Vacancy), A. E. & P.	Mexico		17,500
	N. O'Shaughnessy, Sec. of Emb.	Mexico	New York.	3,000
Montenegro	(Vacancy), E. E. & M. P.	Athens		10,000
Morocco	(Vacancy), E. E. & M. P.	Tangier		10,000

Country.	Representative.	Location.	Appointed from.	Salary.
Netherlands	Henry Van Dyke, E. E. & M. P.	The Hague	New Jersey	$12,000
	James G. Bailey, Sec. of Leg.	The Hague	Kentucky	2,625
Nicaragua	Benjamin L. Jefferson, E. E. & M. P.	Managua	Colorado	10,000
Norway	Albert G. Schmedeman, E. E. & M. P.	Christiania	Wisconsin	10,000
	F. M. Endicott, Sec. of Leg.	Christiania	Massachusetts	2,000
Panama	William J. Price, E. E. & M. P.	Panama	Kentucky	10,000
	Cyrus F. Wicker, Sec. of Leg.	Panama	New York	2,000
Paraguay and Uruguay	Nicolay A. Grevstad, E. E. & M. P.	Montevideo	Illinois	10,000
Persia	Charles W. Russell, E. E. & M. P.	Teheran	District of Columbia	10,000
	C. W. Wadsworth, Sec. of Leg.	Teheran	New York	2,000
Peru	Benton McMillin, E. E. & M. P.	Lima	Tennessee	10,000
	R. E. Pennoyer, Sec. of Leg.	Lima	California	2,000
Portugal	Thomas H. Birch, E. E. & M. P.	Lisbon	New Jersey	10,000
	W. W. Andrews, Sec. of Leg.	Lisbon	Ohio	2,000
Roumania and Servia	Charles J. Vopicka, E. E. & M. P.	Bucharest	Illinois	10,000
	Chas. Campbell, Jr., Sec. of Leg.& C.-G.	Bucharest	New York	2,000
Russia	(Vacancy), A. E. & P.	St. Petersburg		17,500
	Charles S. Wilson, Sec. of Emb.	St. Petersburg	Maine	3,000
	F. A. Sterling, 2d Sec. of Emb.	St. Petersburg	Pennsylvania	2,000
	F. R. Furness, 3d Sec. of Emb.	St. Petersburg	Pennsylvania	1,200
	Com. H. H. Hough, Nav. Att.	Paris	Navy	
Salvador	William Heimke, E. E. & M. P.	San Salvador	Kansas	10,000
	Thomas Hinckley, Sec. of Leg. & C.-G.	San Salvador	Dist. of Columbia	2,000
Servia (see Roumania)				
Siam	Fred W. Carpenter, E. E. & M. P.	Bangkok	California	10,000
	S. L. Crosby, Sec. of Leg. & C.-G.	Bangkok	New York	2,000
	Leng Hui, Int.	Bangkok		500
Spain	Joseph E. Willard, A. E. & P.	Madrid	Virginia	17,500
	Gustave Scholle, Sec. of Leg.	Madrid	Minnesota	2,000
Sweden	Charles H. Graves, E. E. & M. P.	Stockholm	Minnesota	10,000
	J. Caffery, Sec. of Leg.	Stockholm	Louisiana	2,000
Switzerland	Pleasant A. Stovall, E. E. & M. P.	Bern	Georgia	10,000
Turkey	Henry Morganthau, A. E. & P.	Constantinople	New York	17,500
	Hoffman Philip, Sec. of Leg.	Constantinople	New York	2,625
Uruguay and Paraguay	Nicolay A. Grevstad, E. E. & M. P.	Montevideo	Illinois	10,000
Venezuela	Preston McGoodwin, E. E. & M. P.	Caracas	Oklahoma	10,000

UNITED STATES CONSULAR SERVICE.

Abbreviations: C.-G., consul-general; C., consul; V.-C., vice-consul; C. A., commercial agent.

CONSULS-GENERAL AT LARGE.
George H. Murphy, N. C. $5,000
Alfred L. M. Gottschalk, N. Y. 5,000
Charles C. Eberhart, Kansas 5,000
James E. Dunning, Me. 5,000

ABYSSINIA.
Adis Ababa—(Vacancy), O., V. and D. C.-G. ....

ARGENTINE REPUBLIC.
Buenos Aires—R. M. Bartleman, Mass., C.-G.. 4,500
Rosario—T. B. Van Horne, O., V. and D. C.. 2,500

AUSTRIA-HUNGARY.
Budapest—William Coffin, Ky. 3,500
Carlsbad—Charles L. Hoover, Mo., C. 3,000
Fiume—Samuel H. Shank, Ind., C. 3,500
Prague—Frank Deedmeyer, Ala., C. 3,500
Reichenberg—William J. Pike, Pa., C. 4,000
Trieste—C. Busser, Pa., C. 3,000
Vienna—Charles Denby, Ind., C.-G. 6,000

BELGIUM.
Antwerp—Henry W. Diederich, D. C., C.-G.. 5,500
Brussels—Ethelbert Watts, Pa., C.-G. 5,500
Ghent—Henry A. Johnson, D. C., C. 3,000
Liege—Alexander Heingartner, O., C. 3,000

BRAZIL.
Bahia—David R. Birch, Pa., C. 4,000
Para—George H. Pickerell, O., C. 4,000
Pernambuco—P. M. Griffith, O., C. 4,000
Rio de Janeiro—Julius G. Lay, D. C., C.-G.. 8,000
Santos—Jay White, Mich., C. 4,000

CHILE.
Iquique—Percival Gassett, D. C., C. 3,000
Punta Arenas—Charles L. Lathain, N. C. C.. 3,000
Valparaiso—Alfred A. Winslow, Ind., C. ... 4,500

CHINA.
Amoy—Lester Maynard, Cal., C. 4,500
Antung—E. L. Neville, O., D. C., C. 2,500
Canton—Fleming D. Cheshire, N. Y., C.-G.. 5,500
Chefoo—J. H. Arnold, Cal., C. 4,500
Chungking—E. C. Baker, Cal., C. 3,500
Fuchau—John Fowler, N. Y., C. 4,500
Hankow—Roger S. Greene, Mass., C.-G. 4,500
Harbin—Southard P. Warner, D. C., C. 4,000
Mukden—F. D. Fisher, Ore., C.-G. 4,500
Nanking—(Vacancy), C. 4,000
Newchwang—William P. Kent, Va., C.-G. 4,500

Shanghai—Amos P. Wilder, Wis., C.-G. $8,000
Swatow—Charles L. L. Williams, O., C. 2,500
Tientsin—S. S. Knabenshue, O., C.-G. 5,500

COLOMBIA.
Barranquilla—Isaac A. Manning, Ore., C. .. 3,500
Bogota—(Vacancy), C.-G. 3,500
Cartagena—Henry P. Starrett, Fla., C. 2,000

COSTA RICA.
Port Limon—Chester Donaldson, N. Y., C. .. 2,500
San Jose—Samuel T. Lee, Mich., C. 3,000

CUBA.
Cienfuegos—Max J. Baehr, Neb., C. 4,500
Havana—James L. Rodgers, O., C.-G. 8,000
Santiago—R. E. Holaday, O., C. 4,500

DENMARK AND DOMINIONS.
Copenhagen—E. D. Winslow, Ill., C.-G. 3,000
St. Thomas—C. H. Payne, W. Va., C. 3,000

DOMINICAN REPUBLIC.
Puerto Plata—C. M. Hathaway, Pa., C. 2,000
Santo Domingo—William W. Smith, O., C.-G. ..

ECUADOR.
Guayaquil—Frederic W. Goding, Ill., C.-G.. 4,500

FRANCE AND DOMINIONS.
Algiers—Dean B. Mason, O., C. 2,500
Bordeaux—Alfred K. Moe, N. Y., C. 4,000
Calais—James B. Milner, Ind., C. 3,000
Cognac—George H. Jackson, Conn., C. 2,500
Goree-Dakar—(Vacancy), C. 2,000
Grenoble—(Vacancy), C. 2,000
Guadeloupe—Frank A. Henry, N. Y., C. 2,000
Havre—John O. Osborne, Pa., C. 5,000
Limoges—Eugene I. Belisle, Mass., C. 2,500
Lyons—Carl B. Hurst, D. C., C. 5,000
Marseilles—Alphonse Gaulin, R. I., C.-G.. 5,500
Martinique—Thomas R. Wallace, Iowa, C. ... 2,500
Nantes—Walter H. Schultz, Okla., C. 3,000
Nice—W. D. Hunter, Minn., C. 2,500
Paris—A. M. Thackera, Pa., C.-G. 12,000
Rheims—William Bardel, N. Y., C. 2,500
Ronbaix—Joseph E. Haven, Ill., C. 2,500
Rouen—Lucien Memminger, S. C., C. 2,000
Saigon—(Vacancy), C. 2,000
St. Etienne—William H. Hunt, N. Y., C. ... 2,500
St. Pierre, St. P.—John K. Baxter, Tenn., C. 2,000
Tahiti—James H. Goodier, N. Y., C. 2,000

Tamatave—James G. Carter, Ga., C...........$2,500

GERMAN EMPIRE.

Aix la Chapelle—(Vacancy), C..................3,000
Apia—Mason Mitchell, N. Y., C................3,500
Barmen—George E. Eager, Ill., C..............3,500
Berlin—(Vacancy), C.-G.......................8,000
Bremen—William T. Fee, O., C.................5,900
Breslau—Herman L. Spahr, S. C., C...........2,500
Brunswick—T. J. Albert, Md., C...............2,500
Chemnitz—Thomas H. Norton, O., C............3,500
Coburg—Joseph I. Brittain, O., C.-G..........4,500
Cologne—(Vacancy), C.........................3,500
Dresden—Leo A. Bergholz, N. Y., C.-G........4,500
Erfurt—Graham H. Kemper, Ky., C.............2,500
Frankfort-on-Main—Heaton W. Harris, O., C.-G.5,500
Hamburg—Robert P. Skinner, O., C.-G.........8,000
Hanover—Albert H. Michelson, Mass., C.......3,000
Kehl—Milo A. Jewett, Mass., C................3,000
Leipzig—Nicholas R. Snyder, Pa., C...........4,000
Magdeburg—A. W. Donegan, Ala., C............2,500
Mannheim—William C. Teichmann, Mo., C.......3,500
Munich—T. St. John Gaffney, N. Y., C.-G......4,500
Nuremburg—George N. Ifft, Idaho, C...........4,000
Plauen—Robert B. Mosher, D. C., C...........4,000
Stettin—H. C. A. Damm, Tenn., C..............2,500
Stuttgart—Edward Higgins, Mass., C...........4,000
Tsingtau, China—James C. McNally, Pa., C.....4,000

GREAT BRITAIN.

Aden—Felix W. Smith, N. Y., C................2,500
Auckland—William A. Prickitt, N. J., C.-G....4,500
Barbados—Chester W. Martin, Mich., C.........3,000
Belfast—Hunter Sharp, N. C., O...............5,000
Belize—William L. Avery, Mont., C............2,500
Birmingham—Albert Halstead, D. C., C.........4,500
Bombay—(Vacancy), C..........................4,000
Bradford—A. E. Ingram, Cal., C...............3,500
Bristol—Roger C. Tredwell, Ind., C...........2,000
Burslem—Robert S. S. Bergh, N. D., C.........2,000
Calcutta—James A. Smith, Vt., C.-G...........6,000
Calgary—Samuel G. Reat, Ill., C..............3,000
Campbellton—T. Botkin, Utah, C...............2,000
Cape Town—(Vacancy), C.-G....................6,000
Cardiff—Lorin A. Lathrop, Cal., C............2,500
Charlottetown—Wesley Frost, Ky., C...........2,000
Colombo—Charles K. Moser, Va., C.............3,000
Cork—George E. Chamberlin, N. Y., C..........2,500
Cornwall—Giles R. Taggart, N. J., C..........2,000
Dawson—George C. Cole, W. Va., C.............5,000
Dublin—Edward L. Adams, N. Y., C.............4,000
Dundee—E. H. Dennison, O., C.................4,000
Dunfermline—Howard D. Van Sant, N. J., C.....3,500
Durban—Stuart J. Fuller, C...................3,500
Edinburgh—Rufus Fleming, O., C...............3,500
Fernie—Frank C. Denison, C...................2,000
Fort Erie—H J. Harvey, N. Y., C..............2,000
Georgetown—Rea Hanna, N. Y., C...............3,500
Gibraltar—R. L. Sprague, Mass., C............2,500
Glasgow—John N. McCunn, Wis., C..............4,500
Halifax—Evan E. Young, D. C., C.-G...........4,500
Hamilton, Ber.—W. M. Greene, R. I., C........2,500
Hamilton, Ont.—James M. Shepard, Mich., C....3,000
Hobart—George M. Hanson, Utah, C.............2,000
Hongkong—George E. Anderson, Ill., C.-G......8,000
Huddersfield—Franklin D. Hale, Vt., C........3,000
Hull—Lewis W. Haskell, S. C., C..............2,500
Johannesburg—Edwin N. Gunsaulus, O., C.......5,000
Karachi—Stuart K. Lupton, Tenn., C...........4,500
Kingston, Jamaica—Thos. W. Peters, D. C., C..4,500
Kingston, Ont.—Felix S. S. Johnson, N. J., C.2,500
Leeds—H. M. Byington, Conn., C...............2,500
Liverpool—H. L. Washington, D. C., C.........8,000
London—John L. Griffiths, Ind., C.-G........12,000
Madras—Jose de Olivares, N. Y., C............3,000
Malta—James O. Laing, Mo., C.................2,500
Manchester—William H. Robertson, Va., C......6,000
Melbourne—W. C. Magelssen, Minn., C.-G.......3,000
Moncton—M. J. Hendrick, N. Y., C.............2,000
Montreal—William H. Bradley, Ill., C.-G......6,000
Nassau—Henry D. Baker, Ill., C...............3,000
Newcastle, N. S. W.—G. B. Killmaster, Mich., C.3,000
Newcastle-on-Tyne—Walter C. Hamm, Pa., C.....3,000
Niagara Falls—E. W. Trimmer, N. Y., C........2,000
Nottingham—Samuel M. Taylor, O., C...........4,500
Orilla—Harry P. Dill, Me., C.................2,500
Ottawa—John G. Foster, Vt., C................6,000
Owen Sound—North Winship, Ga., C.............2,500
Plymouth—J. G. Stephens, Ind., C.............2,500
Port Antonio—Julius D. Dreher, S. C., C......3,000
Port Elizabeth—E. A. Wakefield, Me., C.......3,500

Port Louis—(Vacancy), C......................$2,000
Prescott—Martin R. Sackett, N. Y., C.........2,500
Quebec—Gebhard Willrich, Wis., C.............3,500
Rangoon—M. K. Moorhead, Pa., C...............3,500
Rimouski—F. M. Ryder, Conn., C...............3,500
St. John, N. B.—Henry S. Culver, O., C.......3,000
St. John's, N. F.—Jas. S. Benedict, N. Y., C.2,500
St. John's, Que.—(Vacancy), C................2,500
St. Stephen—C. A. McCullough, Me., C.........2,000
Sandakan—(Vacancy), C........................3,000
Sarnia—Fred C. Slater, Kas., C...............2,500
Sault Ste. Marie—Geo. W. Shotts, Mich., C....2,500
Sheffield—Robert J. Thompson, Ill., C........3,000
Sherbrooke—Charles N. Daniels, Conn., C......3,500
Sierra Leone—William J. Yerby, Tenn., C......2,000
Singapore—E. S. Cunningham, Tenn., C.-G......4,500
Southampton—Albert W. Swalm, Iowa, C.........4,500
Suva—(Vacancy), C............................2,000
Swansea—C. L. Livingston, Pa., C.............3,000
Sydney, N. S.—Charles M. Freeman, N. H., C...3,000
Sydney, N. S. W.—John P. Bray, N. D., C.-G...5,500
Toronto—(Vacancy), C.........................4,000
Trinidad—Andrew J. McConnico, Miss., C.......3,000
Turks Island—Charles Forman, La., C..........2,000
Vancouver—Robert E. Mansfield, Ind., C.-G....4,500
Victoria—A. E. Smith, Ill., C................4,000
Windsor, Ont.—H. A. Conant, Mich., C.........2,500
Winnipeg—Frank Dillingham, Cal., C.-G........4,500
Yarmouth—A. J. Fleming, Mo., C...............2,500

GREECE.

Athens—William H. Gale, Va., C.-G............3,000
Patras—Arthur B. Cooke, S. C., C.............2,000

GUATEMALA.

Guatemala—George A. Bucklin, Jr., Okla., C.-G.3,500

HAITI.

Cape Haitien—L. W. Livingston, Fla., C.......2,000
Port au Prince—John B. Terres, N. Y., C......3,000

HONDURAS.

Ceiba—Harold D. Clum, N. Y., C...............2,000
Puerto Cortes—David J. D. Myers, Ga., C......2,500
Tegucigalpa—A. T. Haeberle, Mo., C...........2,500

ITALY.

Catania—Alexander W. Weddell, Va., C.........3,000
Florence—Leo J. Keena, Mich., C..............3,000
Genoa—John E. Jones, D. C., C.-G.............4,500
Leghorn—Benjamin F. Chase, Pa., C............3,000
Milan—N. B. Stewart, Ga., C..................4,000
Naples—William W. Handley, N. Y., C..........4,000
Palermo—Hernando de Soto, Cal., C............3,500
Rome—Chapman Coleman, Ky., C.................3,500
Tripoli—John Q. Wood, Hawaii, C..............2,500
Turin—Charles B. Perry, Neb., C..............2,000
Venice—James V. Long, Pa., C.................2,000

JAPAN.

Dalny—Albert H. Pontius, Minn., C............3,500
Kobe—George N. West, D. C., C................5,000
Nagasaki—Carl F. Deichman, Mo., C............3,500
Seoul—G. H. Scidmore, Wis., C.-G.............5,500
Tamsui—A. A. Williamson, C...................3,000
Yokohama—Thomas Sammons, Wash., C.-G.........6,000

KONGO.

Boma—(Vacancy), C.-G.........................4,500

LIBERIA.

Monrovia—Geo. W. Buckner, Ind., C.-G.........5,000

MEXICO.

Acapulco—C. S. Edwards, Minn., C.............2,500
Aguascalientes—Gaston Schmutz, La., C........2,000
Chihuahua—Marion Letcher, Ga., C.............2,500
Ciudad Juarez—T. D. Edwards, S. D., C........2,500
Ciudad Porfirio Diaz—(Vacancy), C............2,500
Durango—Theodore C. Hamm, Va., C.............2,000
Ensenada—(Vacancy), C........................2,000
Frontera—A. J. Lespinasse, N. Y., C..........3,000
Guadalajara—(Vacancy), C.....................3,500
Hermosillo—Louis Hostetter, Neb., C..........2,000
LaPaz—L. N. Sullivan, Pa., C.................2,000
Manzanillo—Milton B. Kirk, Ill., C...........2,000
Matamoros—J. H. Johnson, Tex., C.............2,500
Mazatlan—William E. Alger, Mass., C..........2,500
Mexico—Arnold Shanklin, Mo., C.-G............6,000
Monterey—P. C. Hanna, Iowa, C.-G.............3,500
Nogales—(Vacancy), C.........................2,500
Nuevo Laredo—A. B. Garrett, W. Va., C........2,500
Progreso—Wilbur T. Gracey, Mass., C..........3,000
Salina Cruz—(Vacancy), C.....................2,000
Saltillo—(Vacancy), C........................2,000
San Luis Potosi—W. L. Bonney, Ill., C........2,500

Tampico—Clarence A. Miller, Mo., C..........$3,000
Tapachula—(Vacancy), C...................... 2,000
Vera Cruz—William W. Canada, Ind., C...... 4,500

MOROCCO.
Tangier—Maxwell Blake, Mo., C.-G........... 3,500

NETHERLANDS.
Amsterdam—Frank W. Mahin, Iowa, C....... 5,000
Batavia—B. S. Rairden, Me., C............... 3,000
Curacao—Elias H. Cheney, N. H., C......... 2,500
Rotterdam—Soren Listoe, Minn.. C.-G........ 5,500

NICARAGUA.
Bluefields—Arthur J. Clare, D. C., C......... 3,500
Cape Gracias a Dios—(Vacancy), C.......... 2,000
Corinto—(Vacancy), C...................... 3,000
Managua—(Vacancy), C...................... 3,000

NORWAY.
Bergen—B. M. Rasmussen, Iowa, C......... 2,500
Christiania—Charles A. Holder, Col., C.-G... 3,000
Stavanger—Walter A. Leonard, Ill., C....... 2,000

OMAN.
Maskat—(Vacancy), C...................... 2,000

PANAMA.
Colon—James C. Kellogg, La., C............ 4,000
Panama—A. G. Snyder, W. Va., C.-G....... 5,500

PARAGUAY.
Asuncion—Cornelius Ferris, Jr., Cal., C...... 2,000

PERSIA.
Tabriz—Gordon Paddock, N. Y., C.......... 3,000
Teheran—C. W. Wadsworth, N. Y., C.-G.... 2,000

PERU.
Callao—(Vacancy), C...................... 4,500
Iquitos—(Vacancy), C...................... 3,000

PORTUGAL.
Lisbon—Will L. Lowrie, Ill., C.-G.......... 3,500
Lonrenco Marquez—G. A. Chamberlain, N. M., C. 5,000
St. Michels—Edward A. Creevey, N. J., C... 3,000

ROUMANIA.
Bucharest—Charles Campbell, Jr., Va., C.-G.. 2,000

RUSSIA.
Batum—Leslie A. Davis, N. Y., C.......... 2,500
Moscow—J. H. Snodgrass, W. Va., C.-G.... 5,500
Odessa—John H. Grout, Mass., C............ 3,500
Riga—William F. Doty, N. J., C............ 3,000
St. Petersburg—Jacob E. Conner, Iowa, C... 5,500
Vladivostok—John F. Jewell, Ill., C......... 3,500

Warsaw—Thomas E. Heenan, Minn., C....... $4,000

SALVADOR.
San Salvador—Thomas Hinckley, D. C., C.-G.. 3,500

SERVIA.
Belgrade—Maddin Summers, Tenn., C........ 2,000

SIAM.
Bangkok—Sheldon L. Crosby, N. Y., C.-G.... 2,000

SPAIN.
Barcelona—Henry H. Morgan, La., C.-G...... 5,500
Jeres de la Frontera—W. R. Dorsey, Md., C.. 2,500
Madrid—F. T. F. Dumont, Pa., C........... 2,500
Malaga—Robert Frazer, Jr., Pa., C.......... 3,000
Seville—Charles S. Winans, Mich., C........ 3,000
Tenerife—Homer Brett, Miss., C............ 2,500
Valencia—Claude I. Dawson, S. C., C....... 2,500

SWEDEN.
Gothenburg—Douglas Jenkins, S. C., C...... 2,500
Stockholm—Ernest L. Harris, Ill., C.-G..... 3,500

SWITZERLAND.
Basel—Philip Holland, Tenn., C............ 3,500
Bern—George Heimrod, Neb., C............ 3,500
Geneva—Francis B. Keene, Wis., C......... 3,500
St. Gall—D. I. Murphy, D. C., C........... 4,500
Zurich—David F. Wilber, N. Y., C.-G....... 4,500

TURKEY.
Aleppo—J. B. Jackson, O., C............... 3,000
Alexandria—Arthur Garels, Mo., C......... 3,500
Bagdad—Emil Sauer, Tex., C.............. 3,500
Beirut—W. S. Hollis, Mass., C.-G.......... 4,500
Cairo—Olney Arnold, R. I., C.-G.......... 6,500
Constantinople—G. B. Ravndal, S. D., C.-G.. 6,000
Harput—W. W. Masterson, Ky., C......... 3,000
Jerusalem—(Vacancy), C.................... 3,000
Mersina—Edward I. Nathan, Pa., C........ 2,500
Saloniki—John E. Kehl, O., C............. 3,500
Sivas—(Vacancy), C...................... 2,000
Smyrna—George Horton, Ill., C............ 3,500
Trebizond—Alfred S. Northrup, Ill., C...... 2,500

URUGUAY.
Montevideo—Ralph J. Totten, Tenn., C..... 3,500

VENEZUELA.
La Guaira—Thomas W. Voelter, N. M., C.... 3,000
Maracaibo—John A. Ray, Tex., C.......... 2,500
Puerto Cabello—Herbert R. Wright, Iowa, C.. 2,000

ZANZIBAR.
Zanzibar—Perry C. Hays, Mont., C.......... 2,500

FOREIGN LEGATIONS IN THE UNITED STATES.

Argentine Republic—Senor Don Romulo S. Naon, E. E. and M. P.
  Dr. Edouardo Lebougle, secretary of legation.
Austria-Hungary—Dr. Constantin T. Dumba, A. E. and P.
  Baron Erich Zwiedinek von Sudenhorst, connselor of legation.
  Konstantin von Masirevich, secretary.
Belgium—Mr. E. Havenith, E. E. and M. P.
  Mr. Charles Symon, secretary of legation.
Bolivia—Senor Don Ignacio Calderon, E. E. & M. P.
Brazil—Mr. Domicio da Gama, A. E. and M. P.
  Mr. E. L. Clermont, counselor.
Chile—Senor Don Eduardo Suarez, E. E. and M. P.
  Senor Don Felipe Aninat, first secretary.
China—Mr. Chang Yin Tang, E. E. and M. P.
  Mr. Chang Kang-jen, first secretary.
Colombia—Senor Don Julio Betancourt, E. E. and M. P.
Costa Rica—Senor Don Joaquin B. Calvo, F. E. and M. P.
Cuba—Dr. Pablo Desvetnine, E. E. and M. P.
  Senor Don Manuel de la Vega-Calderon, first secretary.
Denmark—Mr. Constantin Brun, E. E. and M. P.
Dominican Republic—Senor Don Francisco J. Peynado, E. E. and M. P.
Ecuador—Senor Dr. Don Gonzalo S. Cordova, E. E. and M. P.
France—Mr. J. J. Jusserand, A. E. and P.
  Mr. de Peretti de la Rocca, counselor.
  Capt. de Bertier de Sanvigny, military attache.
  Lieut.-Com. B. d'Azy, naval attache.
Germany—Count Johann Heinrich von Bernstorff, A. E. and P.
  Mr. H. von Haimhausen, counselor and first secretary.

Maj. von Herwarth, military attache.
  Commander Boy-Ed, naval attache.
Great Britain—Sir Cecil Arthur Spring-Rice, A. E. and P.
  Mr. Colville Barclay, counselor of embassy.
  Lieut.-Col. Moreton F. Gage, military attache.
  Capt. Heathcoat S. Grant, naval attache.
Greece—Mr. L. A. Coromilas, M. R.
Guatemala—Senor Don Joaquin Mendez, E. E. and M. P.
Haiti—Mr. Ulrich Duvivier, E. E. and M. P.
Honduras—Dr. Alberto Membreno, E. E. and M. P.
Italy—Marchese Cusani Confalonieri, A. E. and P.
  Mr. Giuseppe Catalani, counselor.
Japan—Viscount Sutemi Chinda, A. E. and P.
  Mr. K. Shidehara, counselor.
Mexico—Senor Don Manuel Calero, A. E. and P.
  Senor Don A. Alzara R. de Terreros, first secretary.
Netherlands—Jonkheer J. Loudon, E. E. and M. P.
  Mr. F. M. Schmolck, secretary.
Nicaragua—Senor Gen. Don Emiliano Chamorro, E. E. and M. P.
Norway—Mr. H. H. Bryn, E. E. and M. P.
  Mr. William M. Johannessen, secretary.
Panama—Senor Don Eusebio A. Morales, E. E. and M. P.
Paraguay—Mr. Hector Velasquez.
Persia—Mirza Ali Kuli Khan, E. E. and M. P.
Peru—Mr. Fredrico Alfonso Pezet, E. E. and M. P.
Portugal—Viscount de Alte, E. E. and M. P.
Russia—Mr. George Bakhmetieff, A. E. and P.
  Mr. A. Stcherbatsky, counselor.
  M. A. Lyssakovsky, first secretary.
  Col. Nicolai Golejevski, military attache.
  Capt. Vassilieff, naval attache.

Salvador—Senor Don Francisco Duenas, E. E. and M. P.
Siam—Prince Traidos Prabandh, E. E. and M. P.
Spain—Senor Hontorio, A. E. and P.
Senor Don Manuel Walls y Merino, first secretary.
Lieut.-Col. Nicolas Urcullo y Cercijo, military attache.
Sweden—Mr. W. A. F. Ekengren, E. E. and M. P.

Count Claes Boude, counselor of legation.
Switzerland—Dr. Paul Ritter, E. E. and M. P.
Dr. Ernest Baumann, secretary of legation.
Turkey—Youssouf Zia Pasha, E. E. and M. P.
Djevad Bey, counselor.
Uruguay—Dr. Carlos Maria de Pena, E. E. and M. P.
Venezuela—Don P. Ezequiel Rojas, E. E. and M. P.

RAILROAD ACCIDENTS.

For years ended June 30. Reported by Interstate-commerce commission.

DERAILMENTS AND COLLISIONS.

	1912			1911		
	No.	Killed.	Injured.	No.	Killed.	Injured.
Collisions, rear	1,142	117	2,019	1,099	109	1,526
Collisions, butting	704	157	3,136	609	187	2,610
Collisions, train separating	353	4	138	370	7	163
Collisions, miscellaneous	3,284	100	2,656	3,527	133	2,695
Total collisions	5,483	378	7,949	5,605	436	6,994
Derailments due to:						
Defects of roadway, etc	1,877	102	2,766	1,225	57	1,560
Defects of equipment	3,847	68	1,197	2,824	64	689
Negligence of trainmen, signal men, etc	423	18	548	397	36	508
Unforeseen obstructions of track, etc	412	61	595	309	66	492
Malicious obstruction of track, etc	75	16	378	84	16	176
Miscellaneous causes	1,581	129	1,663	1,421	110	1,374
Total derailments	8,215	394	7,147	6,260	349	4,799
Total collisions and derailments	13,698	772	15,096	11,865	785	11,793
Damage to cars, engines, roadway	$11,527,453			$9,851,780		

	1912.		1911.		1910.		1909.	
	Killed.	Injured.	Killed.	Injured.	Killed.	Injured.	Killed.	Injured.
Passengers—In train accidents	139	9,391	142	6,722	217	7,516	131	5,865
Other causes	179	6,995	214	6,711	204	6,240	204	6,251
Total passengers	318	16,386	356	13,433	421	13,756	335	12,116
Employes*—In train accidents	596	7,098	683	6,775	715	6,791	520	4,877
In coupling accidents	192	3,234	209	2,966	206	2,985	161	2,353
Overhead obstructions, etc	77	1,523	78	1,523	96	1,377	76	1,229
Falling from cars, etc	573	13,874	588	12,346	586	13,196	481	10,259
Other causes	1,482	23,391	1,655	22,192	1,780	44,269	1,218	33,086
Total employes	2,920	49,120	3,163	46,802	3,383	68,618	2,456	51,804
Grand total	3,238	65,506	3,519	60,235	3,804	82,374	2,791	63,920

*On duty.

MAYORALTY ELECTION IN NEW YORK CITY.

Nov. 4, 1913.

Copyright, Underwood & Underwood, N.Y.
JOHN PURROY MITCHEL.

John Purroy Mitchel, fusion candidate, was elected mayor of New York city Nov. 4, 1913, by a plurality of 124,296 votes over Edward Mc-Call, the Tammany candidate. Mr. Mitchel was supported by republicans, progressives and independents of various shades of political opinion. Personally he is an independent democrat. He was appointed collector of customs at New York by President Wilson and was confirmed May 20, but resigned the position later to assume the leadership of the anti-Tammany forces in the municipal campaign. The total vote for each candidate was:

John P. Mitchel, Ind. 358,215
Edward E. McCall, Tam. Dem. 223,919
Charles E. Russell, Soc. 32,133
William H. Raymond, Pro. 1,213
William A. Walters, Soc. Lab. 1,647

VOTE BY COUNTIES.

	Kings.	Queens.	New York.	Richm'd.
Mitchel	137,074	34,277	178,224	8,640
McCall	77,826	20,097	129,113	6,883
Russell	11,636	2,865	17,383	249
Raymond	587	118	412	96
Walters	538	129	952	28
Total	227,661	57,486	326,084	15,896

VOTE FOR UNITED STATES SENATOR IN MARYLAND.

Nov. 4, 1913.

Blair Lee, Dem. 112,485
Thomas Parran, Rep. 73,306
C. H. Wellington, Prog. 7,033

F. C. Hendrickson, Pro. 2,405
R. J. Fields, Soc. 2,982

DEATH OF DAVID D. GAILLARD.

Lieut.-Col. David Du Bose Gaillard, member of the Panama canal commission and engineer in charge of the excavation of the Culebra section of the canal, died in the Johns Hopkins hospital, Baltimore, Md., Dec. 5, 1913. A nervous breakdown caused by his seven years of hard work on the isthmus and the burden of responsibility placed upon him compelled him to leave the canal zone and seek medical treatment at the Baltimore institution. He was admitted to the hospital Aug. 16, but failed to rally. He was born Sept. 4, 1859.

The Navy of the United States.

Corrected to Nov. 1, 1913.

ACTIVE LIST.

ADMIRAL.

George Dewey, president general board.

REAR-ADMIRALS.

Charles E. Vreeland, general and joint board.
William H. H. Sutherland, general board.
Vincendon L. Cottman, commanding navy yard, Puget sound.
Thomas B. Howard, president examining and retiring boards.
Walter C. Cowles, commanding Pacific fleet.
Austin M. Knight, commandant naval station, Newport, and superintendent 2d naval district.
Charles J. Badger, commanding Atlantic fleet.
Reginald F. Nicholson,* commanding U. S. Asiatic fleet.
Charles B. T. Moore, commandant naval station, Hawaii.
Alfred Reynolds, naval examining and retiring boards.
Bradley A. Fiske, aid for operations and joint board.
John R. Edwards, president board of inspection for shore stations.
James H. Helm, commandant navy yard, Charleston, and superintendent 6th naval district.
Cameron McR. Winslow, commanding 1st division U. S. Atlantic fleet.
Nathaniel R. Usher, commandant navy yard, Norfolk.
Frank F. Fletcher, commanding 3d division U. S. Atlantic fleet.
Frank E. Beatty, commanding 4th division Atlantic fleet.
Wythe M. Parks, general inspector of machinery for navy.
William B. Caperton, commanding Atlantic reserve fleet.
George S. Willits, inspection duty (bureau of steam engineering).
Walter F. Worthington, inspection duty (bureau of steam engineering and ordnance).
William N. Little, inspection duty (bureau of steam engineering and ordnance).
Clifford J. Boush, commanding 2d division, Atlantic fleet.
Henry T. Mayo, special duty, navy department.
Robert M. Doyle, commanding Pacific reserve fleet.

CAPTAINS.

Charles C. Rogers, commandant navy yard, Portsmouth, and superintendent 1st naval district.
Benjamin Tappan, commandant naval stations, Olongapo and Cavite.
Charles F. Pond, commandant 12th naval district, and president naval examining and retiring boards, Mare Island.
Walter McLean, member examining and retiring boards.
Charles A. Gove, commandant naval training station, San Francisco, and senior member board survey, Pacific coast.
DeWitt Coffman, commandant navy yard, Boston.
Reynold T. Hall, inspection duty (bureau of steam engineering).
William F. Fullam, aid for personnel.
Albert G. Winterhalter, aid for material.
Augustus F. Fechteler, aid for inspection.
Albert Gleaves, commandant navy yard, New York.
Herbert O. Dunn, supervisor of New York harbor.
Albert W. Grant, commanding Texas.
William S. Benson, commandant navy yard, Philadelphia, and superintendent 3d, 4th and 5th naval districts.
Thomas S. Rogers, director of naval intelligence.
James H. Glennon, president board of naval ordnance.
William R. Rush, commanding Washington and the receiving ship at New York.
Harry S. Knapp, general and joint boards.
William L. Rodgers, commanding North Dakota.
Harry McL. P. Huse, naval war college.
Ray C. Smith, commanding Arkansas.
George W. McElroy, inspection duty.

Robert S. Griffin, engineer-in-chief and chief bureau steam engineering with rank of rear-admiral.
Frank W. Bartlett, engineer officer navy yard, Portsmouth.
George R. Clark, commandant naval training station great lakes, and superintendent 9th, 10th and 11th naval districts.
George E. Burd, engineer officer navy yard, New York.
James H. Oliver, commanding New Hampshire.
John J. Knapp, commanding Connecticut.
John Hood, general board.
Edward E. Hayden, commandant naval station, Key West, and superintendent 7th naval district.
Benjamin C. Bryan, director of navy yards.
Clarence A. Carr, inspection duty (bureau steam engineering).
William A. Gill, supervisor of naval auxiliaries.
Harold P. Norton, naval examining board.
Frank M. Bennett, commandant navy yard, Mare Island.
John H. Gibbons, superintendent naval academy.
Thomas Snowden, naval war college.
Frank W. Kellogg, commanding North Carolina.
Albert P. Niblack, naval war college.
Edward Simpson, commanding Minnesota.
Thomas W. Kinkaid, naval academy.
William S. Sims, commanding torpedo flotilla, Atlantic fleet.
Louis S. Van Duzer, commanding Utah.
William J. Maxwell, commanding Florida.
William S. Smith, engineer officer navy yard, Philadelphia.
Hugh Rodman, commanding Delaware.
John A. Hoogewerff, naval war college.
Edward E. Capehart, commanding Michigan.
Henry B. Wilson, president board inspection and survey for ships.
Gustav Kaemmerlin, bureau of steam engineering.
Kenneth McAlpine, inspection duty (bureau steam engineering).
Emil Thiess, board of inspection and survey.
Spencer S. Wood, commanding Nebraska.
William B. Fletcher, commanding Kansas.
Marbury Johnston, naval war college.
Edward A. Anderson, commanding New Hampshire.
Joseph L. Jayne, superintendent navy observatory.
William L. Howard, captain navy yard, New York.
Robert B. Higgins, inspector of machinery.
John C. Leonard, commanding Virginia.
Charles W. Dyson, bureau of steam engineering.
Frederick L. Chapin, commanding Wyoming.
Alexander S. Halsted, board inspection and survey for ships.
Harry A. Field, commanding Louisiana.
Clarence S. Williams, commanding Rhode Island.
Frank K. Hill, commanding New Jersey.
Roger Welles, commanding training station, Newport and Constellation.
John D. McDonald, commanding Virginia.
Hillary P. Jones, commandant navy yard, Washington, and superintendent gun factory.
William R. Shoemaker, member general board.
Charles P. Plunkett, commanding South Dakota.
Volney O. Chase, naval war college (staff).
George W. Kline, commanding Vermont.
Joseph Strauss, chief of bureau of ordnance, with rank of rear-admiral.
Robert L. Russell, commanding South Carolina.
Harrison A. Bispham, captain navy yard, Philadelphia.
George R. Evans, board of inspection for shore stations.
Edward W. Eberle, naval war college.
William W. Gilmer, commanding Pittsburgh.
Robert E. Coontz, commanding Georgia.
William H. G. Bullard, superintendent naval radio service.
Joseph W. Oman, captain navy yard, Boston.
Philip Andrews,* commanding Maryland.
George F. Cooper, hydrographer.
Josiah S. McKean, commanding Ohio.
Benton C. Decker, naval war college (staff).

Mark L. Bristol, waiting orders.
Newton A. McCully, commanding California.
George W. Logan, naval academy.
Henry F. Bryan, office naval intelligence.

James G. Field, naval training station, great lakes.
George Pickrell, hospital, Norfolk.
Albert M. D. McCormick, naval academy.
George B. Wilson, naval hospital, Boston.

MEDICAL CORPS.

MEDICAL DIRECTORS.
Rank of captain.

Edward H. Green, retiring board.
Frank Anderson, president examining board.
William R. Du Bose, examining board.
James D. Catewood, president examining board.
Oliver Diehl, recruiting duty, Philadelphia.
Philip Leach, naval hospital, New York.
Lloyd W. Curtis, hospital, Newport, R. I.
Francis S. Nash, recruiting duty, Philadelphia.
Francis W. F. Wieber, navy yard, Boston.
Andrew R. Wentworth, recruiting duty, New York.
T. A. Berryhill, medical supply depot, New York.
Eugene P. Stone, sick leave.

PAY CORPS.

PAY DIRECTORS.
With rank of captain.

John N. Speel, special duty, navy department.
Reah Frazier, navy pay office, New York, N. Y.
William W. Galt, navy pay office, Norfolk.
John R. Martin, navy pay office, Baltimore.
Charles M. Ray, navy yard, Mare island.
Mitchell C. McDonald, hospital, Yokohama, Japan.
Leeds C. Kerr, leave.
Charles S. Williams, navy pay office, Washington.
Thomas J. Cowie, paymaster-general of the navy.
John S. Carpenter, navy yard, Boston.
Livingston Hunt, navy pay office, Newport, R. I.
Samuel L. Heap, navy pay office, Washington.

GREAT OCEAN STEAMSHIPS.

Name.	Reg. ton'ge.	L'th. Ft.	B'th Ft.	Name.	Reg. ton'ge.	L'th. Ft.	B'th Ft.	Name.	Reg. ton'ge.	L'th. Ft.	B'th Ft.
Imperator	52,000	898	97	Empress of Britain	14,189	549	65	Duca d'Aosta	12,000	476	54
Europa	50,000	911	96	Ivernia	14,068	582	65	Duca di Genova	12,000	476	54
Aquitania	47,000	901	92	Canada	14,000	500	60	Camerenian	12,000	540	60
Olympic	45,000	890	92	Æona	14,000	485	60	Frederick VIII	12,000	540	62
Mauretania	32,000	790	83	Verona	14,000	485	60	Kristianiafjord	12,000	530	61
Lusitania	32,000	790	88	Taormina	14,000	485	60	Bergensfjord	12,000	530	61
George Washington	27,000	722	78	Sant Anna	14,000	500	60	Medic	11,985	550	63
K. Aug. Victoria	24,581	677	77	Mongolia	13,639	600	65	Persic	11,973	550	63
Adriatic	24,541	726	75	Carpathia	13,603	540	63	Zeeland	11,905	561	60
Rotterdam	24,170	668	77	Cretic	13,507	520	60	Haverford	11,635	531	59
Baltic	23,876	726	75	Patricia	13,424	560	62	St. Louis	11,629	535	63
France	23,666	720	75	Minneapolis	13,401	600	66	St. Paul	11,629	535	63
Amerika	22,622	687	74	Minnewaska	13,401	600	66	Merion	11,621	530	59
Cedric	21,035	680	75	Minnetonka	13,398	600	66	Bremen	11,570	550	60
Celtic	20,904	680	75	Pennsylvania	13,333	559	62	Batavia	11,490	501	62
Minnesota	20,718	622	75	Andania	13,300	540	64	Corsican	11,436	500	61
Caronia	19,594	650	72	Alaunia	13,300	540	64	Romanic	11,394	550	69
Carmania	19,524	650	72	Pretoria	13,234	561	62	La Savoie	11,168	562	69
Kronp. Cecile	19,500	706	72	Graf Waldersee	13,193	561	62	La Lorraine	11,146	563	60
Æneas	19,500	600	60	Grosser Kurfurst	13,182	560	62	Chicago	11,103	326	57
Kaiser Wilhelm II.	19,361	684	72	Cymric	13,096	585	64	Barbarossa	10,915	526	60
Lapland	18,694	620	70	Oceania	13,000	477	56	New York	10,798	517	63
President Lincoln	18,074	616	68	Kenilworth Castle	12,975	570	64	Philadelphia	10,786	527	63
President Grant	18,072	616	68	Lucania	12,952	601	65	Virginian	10,754	520	60
Franconia	18,000	625	72	Campania	12,950	650	72	Scotian	10,750	540	60
Berlin	17,324	612	70	Finland	12,760	578	60	Konigin Luise	10,711	523	60
Oceanic	17,274	685	68	Kroonland	12,760	560	60	Friedrich der Grosse	10,695	523	60
Pr. Fr. Wilhelm	17,084	613	68	Walmer Castle	12,546	570	64	Konig Albert	10,643	499	60
Cleveland	17,000	608	65	Noordam	12,534	550	62	Victorian	10,629	520	60
Cincinnati	17,000	608	65	Ryndam	12,527	550	62	Slavonia	10,606	510	59
New Amsterdam	16,697	600	69	Potsdam	12,522	550	62	Tunesian	10,576	500	59
Deutschland	16,502	661	67	Suevic	12,500	550	63	Hamburg	10,531	499	60
Megantic	15,877	565	67	Runic	12,482	550	63	Marmora	10,509	530	60
Arabic	15,801	616	65	Saxon	12,385	570	64	Statendam	10,491	515	60
Republic	15,378	570	68	Moltke	12,335	525	62	Devonian	10,418	552	59
Kronprinz Wilhelm	14,908	637	66	Bluecher	12,334	525	62	Winnifredian	10,405	552	59
Laurentic	14,892	565	67	Ionic	12,232	500	63	Ultonia	10,405	500	57
La Provence	14,744	602	65	Corinthic	12,231	500	63	Bavarian	10,387	501	59
Empress of Ireland	14,500	549	66	Canopic	12,097	594	59	Majestic	10,147	565	58
Nestor	14,500	560	60	Vaderland	12,018	600	60	Amazon	10,100	513	60
Kaiser Wm.d.Grosse	14,349	626	66	America	12,000	506	56	United States	10,091	515	58
Saxonia	14,281	580	64	Duca degli Abruzzi	12,000	476	54	Hellig Olav	10,085	500	58

FASTEST VOYAGES ACROSS THE ATLANTIC.

Queenstown to New York, 4 days and 15 hours, by the Lusitania, Aug. 15-20, 1908; Raunt's Rock to Ambrose channel lightship (short course), 4 days 10 hours 48 minutes, Mauretania, Sept. 11-15, 1910; long course (2,891 miles), 4 days 17 hours 6 minutes, Mauretania, Feb. 13-18, 1909.

New York to Queenstown, 4 days 13 hours 41 minutes, by the Mauretania, Sept. 15-20, 1909.

Hamburg to New York, 5 days 11 hours 54 minutes, by the Deutschland, Sept. 2-8, 1903.

Cherbourg to New York, 5 days 11 hours 9 minutes, by the Kronprinzessin Cecilie, Aug. 19-25, 1908.

New York to Cherbourg, 5 days 16 hours, by the Kaiser Wilhelm der Grosse, Jan. 4-10, 1900.

Southampton to New York, 5 days 20 hours, by the Kaiser Wilhelm der Grosse, March 30-April 5, 1898.

Havre to New York, 6 days 1 hour 12 minutes, by La Provence, Sept. 6-13, 1907.

New York to Southampton, 5 days 17 hours 8 minutes, by the Kaiser Wilhelm der Grosse, Nov. 23-29, 1897.

New York to Havre, 6 days 2 hours 48 minutes, by La Provence, May 31-June 6, 1906.

New York to Plymouth, short course, 2,962 miles, 5 days 7 hours 28 minutes, by the Deutschland, Sept. 5-10, 1900; long course, 3,080 miles, 5 days 9 hours 55 minutes, Kaiser Wilhelm II., Aug. 18-24, 1908.

Plymouth to New York, 5 days 15 hours 46 minutes, by the Deutschland, July 7-12, 1900.

Moville, Ireland, to Cape Race, N. F., 4 days 10 hours, by the Virginian (turbine), June 9-13, 1905.

The best day's run by any steamer was 671 miles, made by the Mauretania, February, 1909.

Distances: New York to Southampton, 3,100 miles; to Plymouth, 2,962 miles; to Queenstown, 2,800 miles; to Cherbourg, 3,047 miles; to Havre, 3,170 miles; to Hamburg, 3,820 miles.

LIST OF SHIPS OF THE UNITED STATES NAVY.

Note—Abbreviations: T. S. twin screw; Tr. S. triple screw; S., screw. Where size of guns is expressed in inches, only main battery is given. Where size is expressed in pounds and under four inches, vessels have only a secondary battery.

THE FLEET.

FIRST CLASS BATTLE SHIPS.	Displacement. Tons	Length. Ft. In.	Beam. Ft. In.	Maximum draft. Ft. In.	Speed (trial). Knots	Propulsion.	Maximum coal supply. Tons	Steaming radius at 10 knots. Knots	Battery, guns.
Alabama	11,552	368 0	72 2	23 6	17.01	T.S.	1,275	4,591	4 13-in., 14 6-in.
Arkansas	26,000	554 0	93 2	28 6	21.05	Turb.	1,924		12 12-in., 21 5-in., 4 3-pdr
Connecticut	16,000	450 0	76 10	24 6	18.78	T.S.	2,275	5,000	4 12-in., 8 8-in., 12 7-in.
Delaware	20,000	510 0	85 2	26 11	21.56	T.S.	2,500		10 12-in., 14 5-in.
Florida	21,825	510 0	88 2	28 6	22.08	Turb.	2,500		10 12-in., 16 5-in.
Georgia	14,948	435 0	76 2	23 9	19.26	T.S.	1,925	3,800	4 12-in., 8 8-in., 12 6-in.
Idaho	13,000	375 0	77 0	24 8	17.12	T.S.	1,750		4 12-in., 8 8-in., 8 7-in.
Illinois	11,552	368 0	72 2	23 6	17.42	T.S.	1,275	4,250	4 13-in., 14 6-in.
Indiana	10,288	348 0	69 3	24 0	15.55	T.S.	1,500	4,000	4 13-in., 8 8-in., 4 6-in.
Iowa	11,346	360 0	72 2	24 0	17.09	T.S.	1,650	4,500	4 12-in., 8 8-in., 4 4-in.
Kansas	16,000	450 0	76 10	24 6	18.00	T.S.	2,350		4 12-in., 8 8-in., 12 7-in.
Kearsarge	11,520	368 0	72 2	23 6	16.82	T.S.	1,600	5,316	4 13-in., 4 8-in., 14 5-in.
Kentucky	11,520	368 0	72 2	23 6	16.90	T.S.	1,600	5,360	4 13-in., 4 8-in., 14 5-in.
Louisiana	16,000	450 0	76 10	24 6	18.82	T.S.	2,400	5,000	4 12-in., 8 8-in., 12 7-in.
Maine	12,500	388 0	72 2	23 10	18.00	T.S.	1,875	4,925	4 12-in., 16 6-in.
Massachusetts	10,288	348 0	69 3	24 0	16.21	T.S.	1,475	4,500	4 13-in., 8 8-in
Michigan	16,000	450 0	80 2	24 6	18.78	T.S.	2,200		8 12-in., 22 3-in.
Minnesota	16,000	450 0	76 10	24 6	18.85	T.S.	2,400		4 12-in., 8 8-in., 12 7-in.
Mississippi	13,000	375 0	77 0	24 8	17.11	T.S.	1,750		4 12-in., 8 8-in., 8 7-in.
Missouri	12,500	388 0	72 0	23 11	18.15	T.S.	1,825	4,900	4 12-in., 16 6-in.
Nebraska	14,948	435 0	76 2	23 9	19.06	T.S.	1,775		4 12-in., 8 8-in., 12 6-in.
New Hampshire	16,000	450 0	76 12	24 6	18.16	T.S.	2,325		4 12-in., 8 8-in., 12 7-in.
New Jersey	14,948	435 0	76 0	23 9	19.18	T.S.	2,000		4 12-in., 8 8-in., 12 6-in.
North Dakota	20,000	510 0	85 2	26 11	21.01	T.S.	2,500		10 12-in., 14 5-in.
Ohio	12,500	388 0	72 2	23 7	17.82	T.S.	2,150	4,900	4 12-in., 16 6-in.
Oregon	10,288	348 0	69 3	24 0	16.79	T.S.	1,450	5,500	4 13-in., 8 8-in.
Rhode Island	14,948	435 0	76 2	23 9	19.01	T.S.	2,000		4 12-in., 8 8-in., 12 6-in.
South Carolina	16,500	450 0	80 2	24 6	18.86	T.S.	2,200		8 12-in., 22 3-in.
Utah	21,825	510 0	88 2	28 6	21.04	Turb.	2,500		10 12-in., 16 5-in.
Vermont	16,000	450 0	76 10	24 6	18.35	T.S.	2,425		4 12-in., 8 8-in., 12 7-in.
Virginia	14,948	435 0	76 2	23 9	19.01	T.S.	1,900		4 12-in., 8 8-in., 12 6-in.
Wisconsin	11,552	368 0	72 2	23 6	17.17	T.S.	1,600	4,260	4 13-in., 14 6-in.
Wyoming	26,000	554 0	93 2	28 6	21.22	Turb.	1,924		12 12-in., 21 5-in., 4 3-pdr
ARMORED CRUISERS.									
Brooklyn	9,215	400 6	64 8	24 0	21.91	T.S.	1,350	5,000	8 8-inch, 12 5-inch.
California	13,680	502 0	69 6	24 1	22.20	T.S.	2,075		4 8-inch, 14 6-inch.
Colorado	13,680	502 0	69 6	24 1	22.24	T.S.	1,925	5,000	4 8-inch, 14 6-inch.
Maryland	13,680	502 0	69 6	24 1	22.41	T.S.	1,950		4 8-inch, 14 6-inch.
Montana	14,500	502 0	72 10	25 0	22.26	T.S.	1,950		4 10-inch, 16 6-inch.
North Carolina	14,500	502 0	72 10	25 0	22.48	T.S.	1,950		4 10-inch, 16 6-inch.
Pittsburgh	13,680	502 0	69 6	24 1	22.44	T.S.	1,825	5,000	4 8-inch, 14 6-inch.
Saratoga	8,150	380 6	64 10	23 3	21.00	T.S.	1,325	4,800	4 8-inch, 10 5-inch.
South Dakota	13,680	502 0	69 6	24 1	22.24	T.S.	2,075	5,000	4 8-inch, 14 6-inch.
Tennessee	14,500	502 0	72 10	25 0	22.16	T.S.	1,975		4 10-inch, 16 6-inch.
Washington	14,500	502 0	72 10	25 0	22.27	T.S.	1,950		4 10-inch, 16 6-inch.
West Virginia	13,680	502 0	69 6	24 1	22.15	T.S.	1,950	5,000	4 8-inch, 14 6-inch.
PROTECTED CRUISERS.									
Albany	3,430	346 0	43 9	16 10	20.52	T.S.	750	4,372	10 5-inch.
Baltimore	4,413	327 6	48 7	19 6	20.10	T.S.	1,075	5,300	12 6-inch.
Boston	3,000	277 0	42 2	16 10	15.60	T.S.	42		2 8-inch, 6 6-inch.
Charleston	9,700	424 0	66 0	22 6	22.04	T.S.	1,700		14 6-inch.
Chattanooga	3,200	292 0	44 0	15 9	16.65	T.S.	675	6,925	10 5-inch.
Chicago	4,500	325 0	48 2	19 0	18.00	T.S.	850	8,806	4 8-inch, 14 5-inch.
Cincinnati	3,183	300 0	42 0	18 0	19.91	T.S.	575	4,500	11 5-inch.
Cleveland	3,200	292 0	44 0	15 9	16.45	T.S.	675	6,925	10 5-inch.
Columbia	7,350	411 7	58 2	22 6	22.80	Tr. S.	1,525	6,800	1 8-inch, 2 6-in., 8 4-in.
Denver	3,200	292 0	44 0	15 9	16.75	T.S.	675	6,925	10 5-inch.
Des Moines	3,200	292 0	44 0	15 9	16.65	T.S.	700	6,925	10 5-inch.
Galveston	3,200	292 0	44 0	15 9	16.41	T.S.	700	6,925	10 5-inch.
Milwaukee	9,700	424 0	66 0	22 6	22.22	T.S.	1,650		14 6-inch.
Minneapolis	7,350	411 7	58 2	22 6	23.07	Tr. S.	1,400	6,500	1 8-inch, 2 6-in., 8 4-in.
New Orleans	3,430	346 0	43 9	18 9	20.00	T.S.	750	4,582	10 5-inch.
Olympia	5,865	340 0	53 0	16 10	21.69	T.S.	1,075	4,200	4 8-inch, 10 5-in.
Raleigh	3,183	300 0	42 0	21 6	21.12	T.S.	575	4,500	11 5-inch
San Francisco	4,088	310 0	49 2	18 0	19.52	T.S.	625	4,000	12 6-inch.
St. Louis	9,700	424 0	66 0	22 6	22.13	T.S.	1,650		14 6-inch.
Tacoma	3,200	292 0	44 0	15 9	16.58	T.S.	675	5,000	10 5-inch.
Topeka	2,255	251 0	35 0	17 8	16.00	T.S.	394	3,800	
UNPROTECTED SCOUT CRUISERS.									
Birmingham	3,750	420 0	47 1	16 9	24.33	T.S.	1,250		2 5-inch, 6 3-inch.
Chester	3,750	420 0	47 1	16 9	26.52	Turb.	1,250		2 5-inch, 6 3-inch.
Salem	3,750	420 0	47 1	16 9	25.95	Turb.	1,250		2 5-inch, 6 3-inch.
UNPROTECTED CRUISERS.									
Marblehead	2,072	257 0	37 0	14 6	18.44	T.S.	346	3,126	10 5-inch.
Montgomery	2,072	257 0	37 0	14 6	19.05	T.S.	289	3,126	
TORPEDO BOAT DESTROYERS.									Tor. tubes.　Guns.
Bainbridge	420	245 0	23 1	6 6	28.45	T.S.	102		2 18-in., 2 3-in., 5 6-pdr.
Barry	420	245 0	23 1	6 6	28.13	T.S.	169		2 18-in., 2 3-in., 2 6-pdr.
Cassin	1,020	305 3	30 5	9 4	29.00				4 18-in.,　　4 4-in.
Cummings	1,139	305 3	30 5	9 4	29.00				4 18-in.,　　4 4-in.

LIST OF SHIPS OF THE UNITED STATES NAVY.—CONTINUED.

TORPEDO BOAT DESTROYERS.	Displacement.	Length.	Beam.	Maximum draft.	Speed (trial).	Propulsion.	Maximum coal supply.	Steaming radius at 10 knots.	Battery, guns.	
	Tons.	Ft. In.	Ft. In.	Ft. In.	Knots.		Tons.	Knots	Tor. tubes.	Guns.
Henley	742	293 10	26 1½	8 4	29.50				3 18-in.	5 3-in.
Jarvis	743	293 10	26 1½	8 4	30.01				3 18-in.	5 3-in.
Maynart	742	293 10	26 1½	8 4	30.22				3 18-in.	5 3-in.
Ammen	742	289 0	26 2	8 4	30.48	T.S.	210		5 3-in.	
Beale	742	289 0	26 2	8 4	29.65	Turb.	*65974		3 18-in., 5 3-in., 5 6-pdr.	
Burrows	742	289 0	26 2	8 4	29.50	T.S.	210		5 3-in.	
Chauncey	420	245 0	23 1	6 6	28.04	T.S.	169	3,024	2 18-in., 2 3-in., 5 6-pdr.	
Dale	420	245 0	23 1	6 6	28.00	T.S.	174	1,044	2 18-in., 2 3-in., 5 6-pdr.	
Decatur	420	245 0	23 1	6 6	28.10	T.S.	174	1,044	2 18-in., 2 3-in., 5 6-pdr.	
Drayton	742	289 0	26 2	8 4	30.53	T.S.	210		5 3-in.	
Fanning	742	289 0	26 2	8 4	29.99	Turb.	*65074		3 18-in., 5 3-in., 5 6-pdr.	
Flusser	700	289 0	26 0	8 0	30.41	T.S.	295		3 18-in., 5 3-in.	
Hopkins	408	258 9	23 1	6 0	29.02	T.S.	143		2 18-in., 2 3-in., 5 6-pdr.	
Hull	408	258 9	23 1	6 0	28.04	T.S.	143		2 18-in., 2 3-in., 5 6-pdr.	
Jenkins	742	289 0	26 2	8 4	31.27	Turb.	*65074		3 18-in., 5 3-in., 5 6-pdr.	
Jouett	742	289A 0	26 2	8 4	32.27	Turb.	*65074		3 18-in., 5 3-in., 5 6-pdr.	
Lamson	700	289 0	26 0	6 2	28.61	T.S.	285		3 18-in., 5 3-in.	
Lawrence	400	240 7	22 3	6 2	28.41	T.S.	108		2 18-in.	7 6-pdr.
Macdonough	400	240 7	22 3	6 2	28.03	T.S.	108	1,920	2 18-in.	
McCall	742	289 0	26 2	8 4	30.66	Turb.	*70575		3 18-in., 5 3-in., 5 6-pdr.	
Monaghan	742	289 0	26 2	8 4	29.50	Turb.	*70074		3 18-in., 5 3-in., 5 6-pdr.	
Patterson	742	289 0	26 2	8 4	29.69	Turb.	*71457		3 18-in., 5 3-in., 5 6-pdr.	
Paulding	742	289 0	26 1	8 4	32.80	T.S.	298		3 18-in., 5 3-in.	
Paul Jones	420	245 0	23 1	6 6	28.91	T.S.	168	1,500	2 18-in., 2 3-in., 5 6-pdr.	
Perkins	742	289 0	26 2	8 9	29.76	T.S.	210		5 3-in.	
Perry	420	245 0	23 1	6 6	28.32	T.S.	168	1,500	2 18-in., 2 3-in., 5 6-pdr.	
Preble	420	245 0	23 1	6 6	28.05	T.S.	172	1,500	2 18-in., 2 3-in., 5 6-pdr.	
Preston	700	289 0	26 0	8 0	29.18	T.S.	298		3 18-in., 5 3-in.	
Reid	700	289 0	26 0	8 0	31.82	T.S.	298		3 18-in., 5 3-in.	
Roe	742	289 0	26 1	8 9	29.60	T.S.	298		3 18-in., 5 3-in.	
Smith	700	289 0	26 0	8 0	28.55	T.S.	298		3 18-in., 5 3-in.	
Sterett	742	289 0	26 2	8 9	30.57	T.S.	210		5 3-in.	
Stewart	420	245 0	23 1	6 6	29.62	T.S.	172		2 18-in., 2 3-in., 5 6-pdr.	
Terry	742	289 0	26 2	8 9	30.24	T.S.	210		5 3-in.	
Trippe	742	289 0	26 2	8 9	30.89	T.S.	210		5 3-in.	
Truxtun	433	248 0	22 3	6 0	29.58	T.S.	166		2 18-in., 2 3-in., 6 6-pdr.	
Walke	742	289 0	26 2	8 9	29.78	T.S.	210		5 3-in.	
Warrington	742	289 0	26 2	8 9	30.12	T.S.	210		5 3-in.	
Whipple	433	248 0	22 3	6 0	28.24	T.S.	166		2 18-in., 2 3-in., 6 6-pdr.	
Worden	433	248 0	22 3	6 0	29.86	T.S.	166		2 18-in., 2 3-in., 6 6-pdr	

*Gallons of oil fuel.

COAST DEFENSE VESSELS.

MONITORS.										
Amphitrite	3,990	259 3	55 4	14 6	10.50	T.S.	271	1,570	4 10-inch,	2 4-inch.
Cheyenne	3,225	252 0	50 0	12 6	11.80	T.S.	*129	1,680	2 12-inch,	4 4-inch.
Miantonomoh	3,990	260 3	55 4	14 6	10.50	T.S.	250	1,378	4 10-inch.	
Monadnock	3,990	258 6	55 5	14 6	11.63	T.S.	386	2,179	4 10-inch,	2 4-inch.
Monterey	4,084	256 0	59 0	14 10	13.60	T.S.	206	1,430	2 12-inch,	2 10-inch.
Ozark	3,225	252 0	50 0	12 6	12.03	T.S.	341	1,680	2 12-inch,	4 4-inch.
Tallahassee	3,225	252 0	50 0	12 6	12.40	T.S.	355	1,080	2 12-inch,	4 4-inch.
Terror	3,990	268 8	55 6	14 6	10.50	T.S.	276	1,300	4 10-inch.	
Tonopah	3,225	252 0	50 0	12 6	13.04	T.S.	338	1,680	2 12-inch,	4 4-inch.

TORPEDO BOATS.								14knots	Torpedo tubes.	
Bagley	175	157 0	17 7	4 11	29.15	T.S.	43	3,000	3 18-inch	Whitehead.
Bailey	280	205 0	19 3	6 10	30.20	T.S.	99		3 18-inch	Whitehead.
Barney	175	157 0	17 7	4 11	29.04	T.S.	43	3,000	3 18-inch	Whitehead.
Biddle	175	157 0	17 7	4 11	28.57	T.S.	43		3 18-inch	Whitehead.
Blakely	196	175 1	17 9	5 11	25.58	T.S.	72		3 18-inch	Whitehead.
Craven	146	147 0	16 4	4 7	30.00	T.S.	32		2 18-inch	Whitehead.
Davis	154	146 0	15 4	5 10	23.41	T.S.	40		3 18-inch	Whitehead.
Dahlgren	146	147 0	16 4	4 7	30.00	T.S.	32		2 18-inch	Whitehead.
DeLong	196	175 1	17 9	5 11	25.52	T.S.	72		3 18-inch	Whitehead.
DuPont	165	175 0	17 8	4 8	28.58	T.S.	76		3 18-inch	Whitehead.
Farragut	279	213 6	20 8	6 0	30.13	T.S.	95		3 18-inch	Whitehead.
Foote	142	160 0	16 1	5 0	24.53	T.S.	44	1,355	3 18-inch	Whitehead.
Fox	154	146 0	15 4	5 10	24.18	T.S.	40		3 18-inch	Whitehead.
Goldsborough	255	198 0	20 7	6 10	27.40	T.S.	89		2 18-inch	Whitehead.
Gwin	46	99 6	12 6	3 3	20.88	S.	9		2 18-inch	Whitehead.
Mackenzie	65	99 3	12 9	4 3	20.11	S.	15		2 18-inch	Whitehead.
Manley	30	60 8	9 5	2 11	17.00	S.	76			
Morris	105	138 3	15 9	4 1	24.00	T.S.	26		3 18-inch	Whitehead.
Rodgers	142	160 0	16 1	5 0	24.49	T.S.	44	1,200	3 18-inch	Whitehead.
Shubrick	200	175 0	17 6	5 2	26.07	T.S.	82	1,755	3 18-inch	Whitehead.
Somers	150	149 4	17 6	5 10	17.50	T.S.	37		2 18-inch	Whitehead.
Stockton	200	175 0	17 6	5 2	25.79	T.S.	79	1,756	3 18-inch	Whitehead.
Stringham	340	225 0	22 0	6 6	25.23	T.S.	95		2 18-inch	Whitehead.
Thornton	200	175 0	17 6	5 2	24.88	T.S.	86	1,755	3 18-inch	Whitehead.
Tingey	165	175 0	17 6	4 8	24.94	T.S.	73		3 18-inch	Whitehead.
Wilkes	165	175 0	17 7	4 8	25.99	T.S.	86	2,400	3 18-inch	Whitehead.

*Also 60,816 gallons of oil fuel.

LIST OF SHIPS OF THE UNITED STATES NAVY.—Continued.

GUNBOATS.	Displacement.	Length.	Beam.	Maximum draft.	Speed (trial).	Propulsion.	Maximum coal supply.	Steaming radius at 10 knots.	Battery, guns.
	Tons.	Ft. In.	Ft. In.	Ft. In.	Knots.		Tons.		
Alert	1,110	177 4	32 0	13 0	10.00	S.	197	3,742	6 4-inch.
Annapolis	1,010	168 0	36 0	12 0	13.17	S.	240	5,245	6 under 4-inch.
Callao	243	115 3	17 10	6 6	10.00	T.S.	33	......	7 under 4-inch.
Castine	1,177	204 0	32 1	12 0	16.03	T.S.	210	3,480	8 4-inch.
Concord	1,710	244 5	36 0	14 0	16.80		......	......	6 4-inch.
Don Juan de Austria	1,130	210 0	32 0	12 6	12.30		204	2,250	8 under 4-inch.
Dubuque	1,085	174 0	35 0	12 3	12.90	T.S.	246	......	6 4-inch.
Elcano	620	157 11	26 0	10 0	11.00	T.S.	94	......	7 under 4-inch.
Helena	1,392	250 9	39 8	9 0	15.50	T.S.	300	2,370	8 4-inch.
Isla de Luzon	1,030	192 10	31 0	11 6	11.23	T.S.	159	2,000	4 4-in.. 8 under 4-in.
Machias	1,177	204 0	32 1	12 0	15.46	T.S.	261	3,480	8 4-in.. 8 under 4-in.
Marietta	990	174 0	34 0	12 0	13.02	T.S.	229	3,529	6 4-inch.
Nashville	1,371	220 0	38 1	11 0	16.30	T.S.	363	3,315	8 4-inch.
Newport	1,010	168 0	36 0	12 2	12.30	S.	224	4,904	6 4-inch.
Paducah	1,085	174 0	35 0	12 3	12.85	T.S.	246	......	6 4-inch.
Pampanga	243	115 3	17 10	6 6	10.00	T.S.	33	......	8 under 4-inch.
Panay	170	94 10	17 3	7 1	8.00	T.S.	20	......	5 under 4-inch.
Peoria	487	131 0	25 0	10 6	9.00	S.	68	......	7 under 4-inch.
Petrel	890	181 4	31 0	11 6	11.40	S.	193	3,254	4 6-inch.
Princeton	1,010	168 0	36 0	12 0	10.64	S.	228	4,904	6 4-inch.
Quiros	350	157 9	22 9	7 9	11.00	S.	78	......	8 under 4-inch.
Ranger	1,261	177 4	32 0	13 0	10.00	S.	178	......	6 under 4-inch.
Samar	243	115 3	17 10	6 6	10.50	T.S.	33	1,000	8 under 4-inch.
Sandoval	100	110 0	15 6	5 4	8.0	S.	16	......	4 under 4-inch.
Vicksburg	1,010	168 0	36 0	12 1	12.71	S.	243	4,904	6 4-inch.
Villalobos	370	148 0	23 0	7 6	11.00	S.	65	......	8 under 4-inch.
Wheeling	990	174 0	34 0	12 0	12.88	T.S.	236	3,874	6 4-inch.
Wilmington	1,392	250 9	39 8	9 0	15.08	T.S.	300	2,370	8 4-inch.
Wolverine	685	164 11	27 0	9 0	10.50	S.	115	2,240	
Yorktown	1,710	250 0	36 0	14 0	16.14		• 341	3,445	6 6-inch.

WOODEN CRUISERS.

Hartford	2,790	226 0	44 0	18 2	12.00	S.	262	......	9 5-inch.
Mohican	1,900	216 0	37 0	16 6	10.65	S.	108	......	6 4-inch.

ARMED TRANSPORTS.

Buffalo	6,000	391 6	48 3	19 5	14.50	S.	1,375	7,800	2 5-in., 4 4-inch.
Dixie	6,114	391 6	48 3	19 11	14.50	S.	1,075	7,000	10 3-inch.
Panther	3,380	312 1	40 8	15 9	13.50	S.	675	4,800	2 6-pdr.
Prairie	6,620	391 6	48 3	20 9	14.50	S.	1,800	8,200	10 3-inch.

TRANSPORT.

General Alava	1,115	212 6	29 9	11 0	10.50	S.	240	2,200	......
Hancock	8,500	......	43 4	24 3	......		......	......	2 6-pounder.

SUPPLY SHIPS.

Arethusa	6,159	352 0	42 2	20 11	......		......	6,400	1 6-pounder.
Celtic	6,750	371 4	44 7	24 9	10.50	S.	739	6,503	2 6-pounder.
Culgoa	6,000	384 4	43 0	21 9	13.25	S.	957	8,880	4 1-pounder.
Glacier	8,325	353 0	45 1	25 4	12.30	S.	917	5,760	......
Iris	6,100	310 6	39 0	24 0	10.00	S.	800	8,300	......
Rainbow	4,360	326 0	41 0	17 2	12.00	S.	1,139	4,872	6 6-pounder, 6 1-pdr.
Supply	4,525	342 7	43 0	19 5	9.95	S.	1,029	8,160	6 6-pounder, 4 1-pdr.

HOSPITAL SHIPS.

Relief	3,360	299 2	46 0	15 20	......	S.	607	......	......
Solace	5,700	361 2	44 0	22 0	15.00	S.	1,000	7,000	3 6-pounder.

CONVERTED YACHTS.

Aileen	192	190 0	20 0	8 0	14.00	S.	45	......	......
Dorothea	594	182 4	23 5	11 5	14.00	S.	78	......	8 under 4-inch.
Eagle	434	155 6	24 0	11 6	12.50	S.	65	......	4 under 4-inch.
Elfrida	164	101 6	18 0	7 9	10.50	S.	23	......	......
Gloucester	786	204 0	27 2	12 0	17.00	S.	120	......	10 under 4-inch.
Hawk	375	145 0	22 0	11 6	14.50	S.	70	......	......
Huntress	92	97 0	16 9	7 3	14.00	S.	17	......	......
Mayflower	2,690	273 0	36 0	17 4	16.80	T.S.	525	......	14 under 4-inch.
Oneida	150	110 11	18 6	7 6	12.00	S.	20	......	3 under 4-inch.
Restless	158	115 0	16 0	6 0	12.00	S.	12	......	3 under 4-inch.
Scorpion	775	212 9	28 1	11 0	17.85	T.S.	155	......	10 under 4-inch.
Stranger	329	173 0	23 9	10 6	14.00	S.	50	......	......
Sylph	152	123 8	20 0	7 6	15.00	S.	47	......	1 under 4-inch.
Sylvia	302	130 0	18 6	10 0	9.00	S.	60	......	......
Vixen	806	182 3	28 0	12 8	16.00	S.	190	......	8 under 4-inch.
Wasp	630	180 0	23 0	12 0	16.50	S.	79	......	6 under 4-inch.
Yankton	975	185 0	27 6	13 10	14.00	S.	170	......	4 under 4-inch.

SPECIAL CLASS.

Dolphin	1,486	240 0	32 0	14 3	15.50	S.	265	3,180	2 4-inch.
Manila	1,750	209 3	31 2	13 0	10.00	S.	186	2,696	2 4.7-inch.
Vesuvius	930	252 4	26 6	10 7	21.65	T.S.	132	1,800	For torpedo training

LIST OF SHIPS OF THE UNITED STATES NAVY.—CONTINUED.

COLLIERS.	Displace-ment.	Length over all.	Beam.	Extreme draft.	Speed, loaded.	Speed, light.	Bunker capacity	Cargo capacity	Battery, guns.
	Tons.	Ft. In.	Ft. In.	Ft. In.	Knots.	Knots.	Tons.	Tons.	
Abarenda	6,705	325 6	42 0	26 6	9.00	9.50	813	3,400	4 3-pounder. 4 Colts
Ajax	9,250	387 6	46 6	25 3	10.00	11.00	500	5,000	1 6-pounder.
Alexander	6,181	348 3	43 0	28 0	8.75	10.00	800	4,200	1 6-pounder.
Brutus	6,600	332 0	41 6	26 0	10.00		547	4,000	1 6-pounder.
Cæsar	5,920	322 1	44 0	21 6	10.00	11.00	761	3,156	1 6-pounder.
Cyclops	19,360	542 0	65 0	27 8	14.61		2,043	10,457	
Hannibal	4,000	275 0	39 3	19 0	9.00	10.00	480	2,500	1 6-pounder.
Hector	11,230	403 0	53 0	24 8	12.87		818	7,200	
Jason	19,132	536 0	65 0	27 8	14.00		2,000	10,500	
Jupiter	19,360	542 0	65 0	27 8	14.00		2,043	10,457	
Justin	3,300	287 6	39 0	21 6	9.98	10.90	167	2,900	1 6-pounder.
Lebanon	3,285	258 0	37 6	19 0	10.00	12.50	188	1,800	
Leonidas	4,242	273 11	39 3	19 7	8.50	9.50	200	2,200	1 6-pounder.
Mars	11,200	403 0	53 0	24 6	12.65		977	8,017	
Nanshan	4,950	300 0	39 0	21 3	10.50	11.00	400	2,300	1 6-pounder.
Neptune	19,360	542 0	65 0	27 8	12.98		2,043	10,457	
Nereus	19,000	522 0	62 0	27 8	14.00		2,000	10,500	
Nero	6,360	320 0	41 0	22 11	9.00		800	3,500	1 6-pounder.
Orion	19,132	536 0	65 0	27 8	14.00		2,000	10,500	
Pompey	3,085	245 0	33 6	16 10	10.50	13.00	200	1,400	
Prometheus	12,585	465 9	60 1	26 0	16.00		1,576	6,410	4 3-inch.
Proteus	19,000	522 0	62 0	27 8	14.00		2,000	10,500	
Saturn	4,342	297 1	40 0	22 8	11.00		335	2,400	1 6-pounder.
Sterling	5,663	284 0	37 0	23 8	11.00	11.00	469	2,672	1 6-pounder.
Vestal	12,585	465 9	60 1	26 0	16.00		1,576	6,410	4 3-inch.
Vulcan	11,200	403 0	53 0	24 6	12.82		877	8,017	

SAILING SHIPS.

NAME.	Displace-ment.	Length.	Beam.	Draft.	Speed.	Propul-sion.	Description.	Battery, guns
	Tons	Ft. In.	Ft. In.	Ft. In.	Knots			
Boxer	316	108 0	29 9	9 2		Sl.	Brig	
Constellation	1,970	176 0	42 0	20 0		Sl.	Ship	14 under 4-inch.
Cumberland	1,800	176 5	45 8	16 6		Sl.	Bark	6 4-in., 8 under 4-in.
Intrepid	1,800	176 5	45 8	16 6		Sl.	Bark	6 4-in., 8 under 4-in.
Severn	1,175	175 0	37 0	16 6		Sl.	Ship	6 4-in., 8 under 4-in.

UNDER CONSTRUCTION AND AUTHORIZED.

Nevada	27,500	575 0	95 2	28 6	20.05	Turb	1st-class battleship	10 14-inch, 21 5-inch.
New York	27,000	565 0	95 3	28 6	21.00	Turb	1st-class battleship	10 14-inch, 21 5-inch.
Oklahoma	27,500	575 0	95 2	28 6	20.05	Turb	1st-class battleship	10 14-inch, 21 5-inch.
Pennsylvania	31,000	600 0	97 0	28 6		Turb	1st-class battleship	12 14-inch, 20 5-inch.
Texas	27,000	565 0	95 3	28 6	21.00	Turb	1st-class battleship	10 14-inch, 21 5-inch.
No. 39	31,000	600 0	97 0	28 6		Turb	1st-class battleship	10 14-inch, 21 5-inch.

In addition to the above there are 17 torpedo boat destroyers, 26 submarines, 3 gunboats, 2 colliers, 3 tenders to torpedo vessels, 1 transport and 1 supply ship under construction.

TUGS.

There are attached to the different navy yards and stations 45 tugs, ranging from 100 to 854 tons displacement and from 70 to 2,000 horse power.

UNSERVICEABLE FOR WAR PURPOSES.

The Philadelphia, Reina Mercedes, Richmond, Southey, Franklin, Hancock, Independence, Pensacola, Adams, Topeka, Constitution. Essex, Gopher, Granite State, Lancaster, Omaha, Portsmouth and Yantic are no longer fit for sea service. Some are loaned to the naval militia of different states as practice ships.

NAVY AND MARINE CORPS PAY TABLE.

Navy (line).	Pay per annum.*
Admiral of the navy	$13,500
Rear-admirals—First nine	8,000
Second nine	6,000
Chiefs of bureaus	6,000
Captains	4,000
Judge-advocate general	4,000
Commanders	3,500
Lieutenant-commanders	3,000
Lieutenants	2,400
Lieutenants (junior grade)	2,000
Ensigns	1,700
Chief boatswains, gunners, carpenters, sailmakers	1,700
Midshipmen at sea	1,400
Midshipmen at academy	600
Marine corps.	
Major-general	8,000
Colonels	4,000
Lieutenant-colonels	3,500
Majors	3,000
Captains (line)	2,400

Marine corps.	Pay per annum.*
Captains (staff)	$2,600
First lieutenants	2,000
Second lieutenants	1,700

*On sea duty, or on shore duty beyond sea, 10 per cent increase.

Chaplains of or above the rank of lieutenant-commander get the pay and allowance of a lieutenant-commander, those who have rank of lieutenant, appointed prior to July 1, 1906, $2,800; others according to rank in above table; naval constructors, $3,200 to $4,200; assistant naval constructors, $2,000; or pay of rank according to above table; warrant officers, $1,125 to $2,250.

Petty officers and chief petty officers get a salary ranging from $33 to $77 per month.

First-class seamen get $26 a month; seamen gunners, $28; firemen, first-class, $38; ordinary seamen, $21; firemen, second-class, $33; shipwrights, $27; apprentice seamen, $18; coal passers, $24.

The term of enlistment in the United States navy is four years.

Army of the United States.
Corrected to Oct. 20, 1913.

GENERAL OFFICERS AND OFFICERS OF STAFF CORPS AND DEPARTMENTS.

GENERAL OFFICERS.

MAJOR-GENERALS.

Leonard Wood.
J. Franklin Bell.
Thomas H. Barry.
William H. Carter.
Arthur Murray.
Wm. W. Wotherspoon.

BRIGADIER-GENERALS.

Frederick Funston.
Tasker H. Bliss.
Albert L. Mills.
John J. Pershing.
Ramsay D. Potts.
Ralph W. Hoyt.
Montgomery M. Macomb.
Robert K. Evans.
Clarence R. Edwards.
James Parker.
Hunter Liggett.
Hugh L. Scott.

GENERAL STAFF CORPS.

Maj.-Gen. Leonard Wood, chief of staff
Maj.-Gen. William W. Wotherspoon.

BRIGADIER-GENERALS.

Albert L. Mills.
Erasmus M. Weaver.

COLONELS.

John Biddle, engineers.
William A. Mann, infantry.
Edwin St. J. Greble, field artillery.
William A. Nichols, infantry.

LIEUTENANT-COLONELS.

John E. McMahon.
Henry C. Hodges, Jr.
Henry C. Benson.
William G. Haan.
Frederick S. Fotz.
Henry T. Allen.

MAJORS.

Daniel B. Devore.
Daniel W. Ketcham.
Benjamin A. Poore.
Frank E. Harris.
Edward N. Jones, Jr.
William D. Connor.
Robert A. Brown.
Harry R. Lee.
Charles Crawford.
Joseph D. Leitch.
Arthur S. Conklin.
Samuel G. Jones.

CAPTAINS.

Howard L. Laubach.
Thomas L. Smith.
S. J. B. Shindel.
Powell Clayton, Jr.
Berkeley Enochs.
William Mitchell.
Henry C. Smither.
Frank R. McCoy.
Robert O. Van Horn.
William T. Merry.
William H. Raymond.
James P. Robinson.

DEPARTMENTS, DIVISIONS AND BRIGADES.

THE EASTERN DEPARTMENT—Embracing the New England states, New York, New Jersey, Pennsylvania, Delaware, Maryland, District of Columbia, Virginia, West Virginia, North Carolina, South Carolina, Kentucky, Tennessee, Georgia, Florida, Alabama, Mississippi, the post of Fort Logan H. Roots, Arkansas, the coast defenses of New Orleans and Galveston, the Panama canal zone, and the island of Porto Rico with the islands and keys adjacent thereto; headquarters, Governor's island, New York; commander, Maj.-Gen. T. H. Barry.

FIRST DIVISION—Headquarters, Governor's island, New York; commander, Maj.-Gen. T. H. Barry.
First brigade; headquarters, Albany, N. Y.
Second brigade; headquarters, Atlanta, Ga.

THE CENTRAL DEPARTMENT—Embracing the states of Ohio, Michigan, Indiana, Illinois, Wisconsin, Minnesota, North Dakota, South Dakota, Iowa, Missouri, Kansas, Nebraska, Wyoming (except Yellowstone park), Colorado and the post at Fort Missoula, Montana; headquarters, Chicago, Ill.; commander, Col. William A. Shunk.
Third cavalry brigade; headquarters, Fort Riley, Kansas.

SECOND DIVISION—Headquarters, Texas City, Tex.; commander, Maj.-Gen. W. H. Carter.
Fourth brigade; headquarters, Texas City, Tex.
Fifth brigade; headquarters, Galveston, Tex.
Sixth brigade; headquarters, Texas City, Tex.

THE SOUTHERN DEPARTMENT—Embracing the states of Texas (except the coast defenses of Galveston), Louisiana (except the coast defenses of New Orleans), Arkansas (except the post of Fort Logan H. Roots), Oklahoma, New Mexico and Arizona; headquarters, Fort Sam Houston, Texas; commander, Brig.-Gen. Tasker H. Bliss.
First cavalry brigade; headquarters, Fort Sam Houston, Texas.
Second cavalry brigade; headquarters, El Paso, Tex.

THE WESTERN DEPARTMENT—Embracing the states of Washington, Oregon, Idaho, Montana (except the post of Fort Missoula), so much of Wyoming as includes Yellowstone park, California, Nevada, Utah and Alaska; headquarters, San Francisco, Cal.; commander, Maj.-Gen. A. Murray.

THIRD DIVISION—Headquarters, San Francisco, Cal.; commander, Maj.-Gen. A. Murray.
Seventh brigade; headquarters, Vancouver barracks, Washington.
Eighth brigade; headquarters, Presidio of San Francisco, Cal.

THE PHILIPPINE DEPARTMENT—Embracing all the islands of the Philippine archipelago, subdivided into districts of Luzon and Mindanao; headquarters, Manila, P. I.; commander, Maj.-Gen. J. F. Bell.

THE HAWAIIAN DEPARTMENT—Embracing the Hawaiian islands and their dependencies; headquarters, Honolulu; commander, Brig.-Gen. F. Funston.

DEPARTMENT OFFICERS.

THE ADJUTANT-GENERAL—With rank of brigadier-general: George Andrews.

ADJUTANT-GENERALS—With rank of colonel: Henry O. S. Heistand, William A. Simpson, Henry P. McCain, James T. Kerr, Alexander O. Brodie.
With rank of lieutenant-colonel: Benjamin Alvord, Eugene F. Ladd, Charles H. Barth, Peyton C. March, Archibald Campbell, John W. Heard, Leon S. Roudiez.
With rank of major: William M. Wright, David J. Baker, Harry H. Whitney, James T. Dean, Frank L. Winn, F. D. Evans, William R. Sample, George T. Patterson, A. S. Fleming, Francis J. Koester.

INSPECTOR-GENERAL—With rank of brigadier-general: Ernest A. Garlington.

INSPECTORS-GENERAL—With rank of colonel: Stephen C. Mills, John L. Chamberlain, Henry P. Kingsbury.
With rank of lieutenant-colonel: James B. Erwin, David C. Shanks, Alfred M. Hunter, Frederick R. Day.
With rank of major: Andre W. Brewster, Frank G. Mauldin, James H. Frier, E. A. Helmick, Leroy S. Lyon, John M. Jenkins, Alonzo Gray, A. L. Dade, William P. Jackson.

JUDGE-ADVOCATE GENERAL—With rank of brigadier-general: Enoch H. Crowder.

JUDGE-ADVOCATES—With rank of colonel: John A. Hull, George M. Dunn.
With rank of lieutenant-colonel: Frank L. Dodds, John B. Porter, Lewis E. Goodier.
With rank of major: Henry M. Morrow, Walter A. Bethel, B. Winship, Beverly A. Read, Edward A. Kreger, Samuel T. Ansell, Herbert A. White.

QUARTERMASTER CORPS—Chief of corps, with rank of major-general: James B. Aleshire.

BRIGADIER-GENERALS—Henry G. Sharpe, Carroll A. Devol.

COLONELS—John L. Clem, Abiel L. Smith, Harry L. Rogers, F. Von Schrader, Frederick G. Hodgson, John B. Bellinger, Isaac W. Littell, Gonzales S. Bingham, Webster Vinson, Wallace S. Hamilton, David L. Brainard, Thomas Cruse, Daniel E. McCarthy, George B. Davis.

SURGEON-GENERAL—With rank of brigadier-general: George H. Torney.

ASSISTANT SURGEONS-GENERAL—With rank of colonel: W. C. Gorgas, Marvin L. Maus, Daniel M. Appel, Louis Brechemin, Charles Richard, R. G. Ebert, W. H. Arthur, George E. Bushnell, H. P. Birmingham, William Stephenson, John L. Phillips, Guy L. Edie, William D. Crosby, Charles M. Gaudy, Walter D. McCaw.

CHIEF OF ENGINEERS—With rank of brigadier-general: William T. Rossell.
Colonels: Dan C. Kingman, William M. Black, S. W. Roessler, F. V. Abbot, Curtis McD. Townsend, George W. Goethals, John Millis, John Biddle, Harry F. Hodges, James G. Warren, Edward Burr, Lansing H. Beach.
Lieutenant-colonels: George A. Zinn, William C. Langfitt, James C. Sanford, David DuB. Gall-

lard, Harry Taylor, William L. Sibert, Joseph E. Kuhn, William E. Craighill, Henry C. Newcomer, Patrick M. Mason, Charles H. Riche, Thomas H. Rees, Charles L. Potter, Francis R. Shunk, Henry Jervey, Charles H. McKinstry, William V. Judson, E. E. Winslow, Clement A. F. Flagler, Chester Harding.

CHIEF OF ORDNANCE—With rank of brigadier-general: William Crozier.
Colonels: Rogers Birnie, Frank Baker, Orin B. Mitcham, J. W. Benet, William W. Gibson, Edwin B. Babbitt.

CHIEF SIGNAL OFFICER—With rank of brigadier-general: George P. Scriven.

SIGNAL OFFICER—With rank of colonel: William A. Glassford.

CHIEF OF BUREAU OF INSULAR AFFAIRS—With rank of brigadier-general: Frank McIntyre.
Colonel: Charles C. Walcutt, Jr.
Major; Irvin L. Hunt.

REGIMENTAL OFFICERS.

CAVALRY.

1. Colonel, Walter L. Finley; lieutenant-colonel, L. M. Brett; majors, James B. Hughes, E. S. Wright, William T. Littebrant.
2. Colonel, Frank West; lieutenant-colonel (vacancy); majors, John S. Winn, Francis C. Marshall, William F. Clark.
3. Colonel, Augustus P. Blacksom; lieutenant-colonel, Guy Carleton; majors, Sedgwick Rice, Arthur Thayer.
4. Colonel, William D. Beach; lieutenant-colonel, John B. McDonald; majors, L. Hardeman, Guy H. Preston, Ralph Harrison.
5. Colonel, Wilbur E. Wilder; lieutenant-colonel, Daniel L. Tate; majors, N. F. McClure, George T. Langhorne, Lawrence J. Fleming.
6. Colonel, Charles M. O'Connor; lieutenant-colonel, Thomas B. Dugan; majors, John P. Ryan, M. C. Butler, Jr., James J. Hornbrook.
7. Colonel, George K. Hunter; lieutenant-colonel, George H. Sands; majors, S. R. H. Tomkins, Peter E. Traub, Francis H. Beach.
8. Colonel, Eben Swift; lieutenant-colonel, Daniel H. Boughton; majors, Robert D. Walsh, George O. Cress, Thomas O. Donaldson.
9. Colonel, John F. Guilfoyle; lieutenant-colonel, Augustus C. Macomb; majors, George W. Read, Malvern-Hill Barnum, Charles Young.
10. Colonel, John C. Gresham; lieutenant-colonel, (vacancy); majors, W. A. Holbrook, George L. Byram, W. H. Hay.
11. Colonel, James Lockett; lieutenant-colonel, George H. Morgan; majors, DeRosey C. Cabell, Robert L. Howze, Melvin W. Rowell.
12. Colonel, Murray H. Cunliffe; lieutenant-colonel, Joseph T. Dickman; majors, S. H. Elliott, Edw. Anderson.
13. Colonel, Charles A. P. Hatfield; lieutenant-colonel, Tyree R. Rivers; majors, G. H. MacDonald, Robert E. L. Michie, P. D. Lochridge.
14. Colonel, Frederick W. Sibley; lieutenant-colonel, Franklin O. Johnson; majors, George H. Cameron, Frank M. Caldwell, Oren B. Meyer.
15. Colonel, Joseph Garrard; lieutenant-colonel (vacancy); majors, Charles A. Hedekin, M. M. McNamee, Charles D. Rhodes.

INFANTRY.

1. Colonel, G. K. McGunnegle; lieutenant-colonel, Robert L. Hirst; majors, Julius A. Penn, Charles E. Tayman, Joseph Frazier.
2. Colonel, Francis H. French; lieutenant-colonel, Benjamin W. Atkinson; majors, E. V. Smith, Michael J. Lenihan, Herbert O. Williams.
3. Colonel, Henry Kirby; lieutenant-colonel (vacancy); majors, Walter H. Gordon, William H. Bertsch, Lutz Wahl.
4. Colonel, John H. Bascom; lieutenant-colonel, Elmore F. Taggart; majors, Paul A. Wolf, Charles G. French, John S. Switzer.
5. Colonel, Charles G. Morton; lieutenant-colonel, S. L. Faison; majors, William F. Martin, James H. McRae, A. I. Lasseigne.
6. Colonel, Lea Febiger; lieutenant-colonel, James M. Arrasmith; majors, Edson A. Lewis, John I. Hines, M. Crowley.

7. Colonel, Daniel Cornman; lieutenant-colonel (vacancy); majors, Tredwell W. Moore, Charles Miller, Hanson E. Ely.
8. Colonel, Frank B. Jones; lieutenant-colonel, William H. Allaire; majors, Thomas G. Hanson, W. O. Johnson, Harry J. Hirsch.
9. Colonel, Charles J. Crane; lieutenant-colonel (vacancy); majors, E. V. Bookmiller, George B. Duncan.
10. Colonel, Henry A. Greene; lieutenant-colonel, W. F. Blauvelt; majors, Charles Gerhardt, Samuel Seay, LaRoy S. Upton.
11. Colonel, Abner Pickering; lieutenant-colonel, Omar Bundy; majors, William F. Grote, William M. Morrow.
12. Colonel, William H. C. Bowen; lieutenant-colonel, Walter K. Wright; majors, Herman Hall, Robert W. Rose, Lewis S. Sorley.
13. Colonel, R. H. R. Loughborough; lieutenant-colonel, George W. McIver; majors, Beaumont B. Buck, U. G. McAlexander, Peter C. Hains.
14. Colonel, Richard H. Wilson; lieutenant-colonel, Maury Nichols; majors, F. H. Albright, H. G. Learnard, John W. Heavey.
15. Colonel, John C. F. Tilson; lieutenant-colonel, Edwin A. Root; majors, A. B. Shattuck, Charles C. Clark, Palmer E. Pierce.
16. Colonel, George Bell, Jr.; lieutenant-colonel, Chase W. Kennedy; majors, William C. Bennett, George D. Guyer.
17. Colonel, John T. Van Orsdale; lieutenant-colonel, Henry D. Styer; majors, George W. Martin, George C. Saffarans, Benjamin F. Hardaway.
18. Colonel, Thomas F. Davis; lieutenant-colonel, Alfred Hasbrouck; majors, Mark L. Hersey, Francis E. Lacey, Jr., George D. Moore.
19. Colonel, Millard F. Waltz; lieutenant-colonel, Daniel L. Howell; majors, Edward M. Lewis, Samuel Burkhardt, Jr., Truman O. Murphy.
20. Colonel, James A. Irons; lieutenant-colonel, Frederick Perkins; majors, Charles Crawford, William S. Graves, Frank D. Webster.
21. Colonel, George S. Young; lieutenant-colonel, John F. Morrison; majors, A. P. Buffington, Samuel E. Smiley, Wilson Chase.
22. Colonel, Daniel A. Frederick; lieutenant-colonel, Harris L. Roberts; majors, Tredwell W. Moore, William T. Wilder, Peter Murray.
23. Colonel, Edwin F. Glenn; lieutenant-colonel, Benjamin C. Morse; majors, Charles B. Hagadorn, William Weigal, Henry J. Hunt.
24. Colonel, William C. Butler; lieutenant-colonel, Clarence E. Dentler; majors, Charles C. Ballou, Marcus D. Cronin, M. S. Jarvis.
25. Colonel, L. W. V. Kennon; lieutenant-colonel, Carl Reichmann; majors, Ernest B. Gose, Vernon L. Caldwell, Edmund L. Butts.
26. Colonel, Robert L. Bullard; lieutenant-colonel, William H. Johnston; majors, Lucius L. Durfee, Ross L. Bush, Thomas F. Schley.
27. Colonel, Robert N. Getty; lieutenant-colonel, Walter H. Chatfield; majors, Edmund Wittenmyer, William R. Dashiell, John B. Bennett.
28. Colonel, Edward H. Plummer; lieutenant-colonel (vacancy); majors, Joseph D. Leitch, James R. Lindsay, Harry A. Smith.
29. Colonel, John S. Mallory; lieutenant-colonel (vacancy); majors, Edward R. Chrisman, M. McFarland, Douglas Settle.
30. Colonel, Charles McClure; lieutenant-colonel, Joseph P. O'Neil; major, John J. Bradley.

Porto Rico Regiment—Lieutenant-colonel, Lewis M. Koehler; majors, Alvan C. Read, Howard C. Price.

Philippine Scouts—Major, Evan H. Humphrey.

FIELD ARTILLERY.

1. Colonel, Samuel D. Sturgis; lieutenant-colonel, Charles T. Menoher.
2. Colonel, Eli D. Hoyle; lieutenant-colonel, Edward F. McGlachlin.
3. Colonel, Charles G. Treat; lieutenant-colonel, T. Bentley Mott.
4. Colonel, Lucien G. Berry; lieutenant-colonel, William Lassiter.
5. Colonel, Granger Adams; lieutenant-colonel, Ernest Hinds.
6. Colonel, Edward A. Miller; lieutenant-colonel, William L. Kenly.

TABLE OF ARMY PAY.

OFFICERS IN ACTIVE SERVICE—ACT MAY 11, 1908.

Grade.	Yearly.	Pay of grade. M'hly.	After 5 yrs. M'hly.	After 10 yrs. M'hly.	After 15 yrs. M'hly.	After 20 yrs. M'hly.
Lieut.-gen.	$11,000	$916.67	......	......	......	......
Maj.-gen..	8,000	666.67	......	......	......	......
Brig.-gen..	6,000	500.00	......	......	......	......
Colonel ...	4,000	333.33	$366.67	$400.00	$416.67	$416.67
Lieut.-col..	3,500	291.67	320.83	350.00	375.00	375.00
Major	3,000	250.00	275.00	300.00	325.00	333.33
Captain ...	2,400	200.00	220.00	240.00	260.00	280.00
1st lieut...	2,000	166.67	183.33	200.00	216.67	233.33
2d lieut...	1,700	141.67	155.83	170.00	184.17	198.33

In case any officer below the grade of major required to be mounted provides himself with suitable mounts at his own expense, he shall receive an addition to his pay of $150 per annum if he provides one mount and $200 per annum if he provides two mounts.

RETIRED OFFICERS—ACT MAY 11, 1908.

Grade.	Yearly.	Pay of grade. M'hly.	After 5 yrs. M'hly.	After 10 yrs. M'hly.	After 15 yrs. M'hly.	After 20 yrs. M'hly.
Lieut.-gen..	$8,250	$687.50	......	......	......	......
Maj.-gen...	6,000	500.00	......	......	......	......
Brig.-gen...	4,500	375.00	......	......	......	......
Colonel ...	3,000	250.00	$275.00	$300.00	$312.50	$312.50
Lieut.-col..	2,625	218.75	240.62	262.50	281.25	281.25
Major	2,250	187.50	206.25	225.00	243.75	250.00
Captain ...	1,800	150.00	165.00	180.00	195.00	210.00
1st lieut...	1,500	125.00	137.50	150.00	162.50	175.00
2d lieut...	1,275	106.25	116.87	127.50	138.12	148.75

MONTHLY PAY OF ENLISTED MEN—ACT MAY 11, 1908.

Grade.			Enlistment				
	1st.	2d.	3d.	4th.	5th.	6th.	7th.
Master electrician, signal corps, coast artillery; chief musician	$75	$79	$83	$87	$91	$95	99
Engineer, coast artillery	65	69	77	77	81	85	89
Sergeant, first class, hospital corps	50	54	58	62	66	70	74
First sergeant, all arms	45	49	53	57	61	65	69
Battalion sergeant-major, field artillery, infantry; squadron sergeant major, cavalry; junior sergeant-major, coast artillery; battalion quartermaster sergeant, field artillery; master gunner, coast artillery; principal musician, bands	40	44	48	52	56	60	64
Electrician sergeant, second class, coast artillery; sergeant engineers, ordnance, signal corps; sergeant, bands; quartermaster sergeant, engineers; drum major, bands; color sergeant, cavalry, field artillery, infantry	36	40	44	48	52	56	60
Sergeant, cavalry, field artillery, coast artillery, infantry; sergeant, hospital corps; corporal, bands; quartermaster sergeant, cavalry, field artillery, coast artillery, infantry; stable sergeant, field artillery; cook, all arms	30	33	36	39	42	45	48
Corporal, engineers, ordnance, signal corps, hospital corps; chief mechanic, field artillery; mechanic, coast artillery; private, bands	24	27	30	33	36	39	42
Corporal, cavalry, field artillery, coast artillery, infantry; mechanic, field artillery; farrier, blacksmith, saddler, wagoner, cavalry; artificer, infantry	21	24	27	30	33	36	39
Private, first class, engineers, ordnance, signal corps, hospital corps	18	21	24	27	30	33	36
Private, hospital corps	16	19	22	23	24	25	26
Trumpeter, cavalry; musician, infantry, field artillery, coast artillery, infantry, signal corps; private, second class, engineers, ordnance	15	18	21	22	23	24	25

The rates of pay to retired enlisted men are based upon length of service and their pay at the time of retirement. Thus a private of the first class gets $15.75 a month if he is retired after his second enlistment and $27 a month after his seventh enlistment. A retired master signal electrician, the highest paid of enlisted men, gets from $59.25 to $74.25 a month.

AUTHORIZED STRENGTH OF THE ARMY.

	Major-generals.	Brigadier-generals.	Colonels.	Lieutenant-colonels.	Majors.	Captains.	First lieutenants.	Second lieutenants.	Chaplains.	Total commissioned officers.	Enlisted men.
General officers	6	15								21	......
Adjutant-general's department	..	1	5	7	10					23	......
Inspector-general's department	..	1	3	4	9					17	......
Judge-advocate general's department	1	2	2	3	7					13	......
Quartermaster corps	..	1	2	12	18	49	102			183	*403
Medical department	..	1	15	24	105	171	†274			†590	†
Corps of engineers	..	1	13	20	43	54	50	43	1	225	1,942
Ordnance department	..	1	6	9	19	25	25			85	735
Signal corps	..	1	1	2	6	18	18			46	1,212
Bureau of insular affairs	..	1	1		1					3	......
Fifteen regiments of cavalry	..		15	15	45	225	225	225	15	765	14,144
Six regiments of field artillery	..		6	6	12	66	78	78	6	252	5,457
Coast artillery corps	..	1	14	14	42	210	210	210	14	715	18,607
Thirty regiments of infantry	..		30	30	90	450	450	450	30	1,530	33,107
Porto Rico regiment of infantry	..					11	10	10	1	32	591
Military academy	..		2	5						7	630
Detached officers	..		8	9	27	77	79			200	......
Additional officers	..		30	7						37	......
Recruiting parties, recruit depots and unassigned recruits											7,000
Service school detachments											587
United States military prison guards											320
Indian scouts											75
Total regular army	7	26	163	173	464	1,409	1,419	1,016	67	4,744	84,810
Additional force: Philippine scouts						52	64	64		180	5,732
Grand total	7	26	163	173	464	1,461	1,483	1,080	67	4,924	90,542

*Under the act of congress approved Aug. 24, 1912, the 5,000 authorized enlisted men of the quartermaster corps are not to be counted as part of the strength of the army. †Includes 85 first lieutenants of the medical reserve corps on active duty and 60 dental surgeons. ‡Under the act of congress approved March 1, 1887 (24 Stat. L., 435), the enlisted men of the medical department (hospital corps) are not to be counted as part of the strength of the army. The authorized strength of the hospital corps is 3,500 enlisted men.

ARMIES AND NAVIES OF THE WORLD.

[Data chiefly from the Statesman's Year-Book and Brassey's Naval Annual for 1913.]

COUNTRY.	ARMY.		NAVY.		Total of armed forces.	Annual cost of army and navy.¶
	Peace footing.	War footing.	Ships.§	Men.		
Abyssinia	150,000				150,000	
Afghanistan	60,000				60,000	
Argentine Republic	215,000	365,000	38	5,000	220,000	$24,494,949
Australian Commonwealth	168,048			5,009	173,057	27,191,900
Austria-Hungary	402,388	2,000,000	122	16,311	418,699	80,884,775
Belgium	46,574	180,000			46,574	16,299,453
Bolivia	3,153				3,153	1,331,565
Brazil	32,000		32	8,800	40,800	20,000,000
Bulgaria	59,900	235,000			59,900	8,100,000
Canada*	71,712				71,712	9,482,094
Chile	21,597		31	6,084	27,181	8,100,000
China	500,000		6		500,000	61,240,000
Colombia	6,000		11		6,000	
Costa Rica	1,000	50,000	2		1,000	
Cuba	4,523		11		4,523	
Denmark	13,720	50,000	33		13,720	7,312,250
Ecuador	6,000	100,000	3	200	6,200	
Egypt	17,274				17,274	3,579,085
France	645,844	1,300,000	407	25,500	671,144	268,755,912
Germany	656,144	3,320,000	296	33,500	689,644	217,526,950
Great Britain	809,403		637	136,461	945,864	359,727,000
Greece	28,888	80,000	24	4,900	33,788	6,066,457
Guatemala	55,535	126,110			55,535	2,253,996
Haiti	5,000		4		5,000	
Honduras	2,000	54,000			2,000	
Italy	302,252	2,000,000	225	28,957	331,209	110,520,232
Japan	225,000	800,000	186	48,049	273,049	58,803,074
Mexico	55,675	84,509	5	1,163	56,858	14,090,892
Montenegro	30,000				30,000	52,000
Nepal	30,000				30,000	
Netherlands	24,244	125,000	77	9,182	33,396	20,279,468
Nicaragua	4,000	40,000	10		4,000	
Norway†	80,000	110,000	37	1,280	81,280	5,420,150
Panama	300		2	50	300	
Paraguay	2,600		3		2,600	
Persia	60,000	110,000	8		60,000	
Peru	6,500		6		6,500	2,000,000
Portugal	30,000	300,000	29	6,107	30,107	14,800,654
Roumania	98,139	220,000	23		98,139	14,885,605
Russia	1,850,000	4,000,000	242	60,000	1,260,000	326,039,698
Salvador	16,144	55,870	1		16,144	
Santo Domingo	1,300		6		1,300	
Servia	361,747				361,747	6,032,000
Siam	26,200		21	5,000	31,200	
Spain	128,073	220,000	42		128,073	46,092,340
Sweden	81,654	485,000	94	4,960	86,614	29,292,875
Switzerland	214,022				214,022	8,859,225
Turkey	230,000	905,000	39	30,929	269,929	40,000,000
United States‡	95,468		323	59,651	155,119	‖214,183,721
Uruguay	4,000	36,000	3		4,000	4,710,491
Venezuela	9,400	60,000	3		9,800	

*Active militia. †Troops of the line. ‡In 1913. §Warships of all kinds except those absolutely worthless, including torpedo boats, submarines, guard boats, etc. ¶Figures are chiefly for 1912-1913. A few are estimates. ‖Appropriations for 1913.

TROOPS ENGAGED IN UNITED STATES WARS.

Military and naval forces employed by the government since 1775.

War.	Date.	Total.	War.	Date.	Total.
Revolution	1775-83	309,791	Utah Indian	1851-53	540
Northwestern Indian	1790-95	8,983	Oregon, Washington Indian	1851-56	5,145
France	1798-1800	4,593	Comanche	1854	593
Tripoli	1801-05	3,330	Seminole	1855-58	2,687
Indian (Harrison)	1811-12	910	Civil war	1861-66	2,778,304
War of 1812	1812-15	576,622	Spanish-American	1898-99	312,523
Creek Indian	1813-14	13,781	Philippine	1899-1902	140,038
Seminole	1817-18	6,911	Pekin (China) expedition	1900-01	6,913
Winnebago (Wis.)	1827	1,416			
Sac and Fox (Ill.)	1831	......	Total		4,371,839
Black Hawk	1832	6,465			
Cherokee removal	1833-39	9,494			
Seminole (Fla.)	1835-42	41,122			
Sabine Indian	1836-37	4,429			
Creek (Ala.)	1836-37	13,413			
"Patriot" (frontier)	1838-39	1,500			
Seminole (Fla.)	1842-58	112,230			
Mexico	1846-48	1,118			
Cayuse Indian (Ore.)	1848	4,243			
Texas Indian	1849-56	2,561			
Apache (Utah)	1849-55	265			
California Indian	1849-55				

The total in this table includes re-enlistments. The total number of individuals is estimated at 3,304,992, of whom 2,213,363 served in the civil war.

AMERICAN LOSSES IN SPANISH AND PHILIPPINE WARS.

From wounds or disease.

	Officers.	En. men.
May 1, 1898, to June 30, 1899	224	6,395
June 30, 1899, to July 1, 1900	74	1,930
July 1, 1900, to June 30, 1901	57	1,993

REGULAR ARMY AND MILITIA.

Organized strength, 1908-1912. [From reports of the war department.]

STATE OR TER.	1908.		1909.		1910.		1911.		1912.	
	Officers.	Privates	Officers.	Privates	Officers.	Privates	Officers.	Privates	Officers.	Privates
Regular army	3,850	67,184	4,048	74,615	4,273	70,823	4,281	73,454	4,470	81,331
Phil. scouts	116	5,278	160	5,586	166	5,386	179	5,401	180	5,480
MILITIA.										
Alabama	216	3,010	221	3,093	216	3,011	206	2,914	213	3,212
Arizona	33	340	43	588	56	692	59	631	51	491
Arkansas	122	1,174	129	1,327	139	1,426	127	1,258	139	1,328
California	193	2,082	192	2,348	205	2,789	219	3,000	234	3,191
Colorado	69	644	71	774	97	1,053	109	1,234	110	1,498
Connecticut	181	2,536	186	2,677	184	2,308	191	2,482	188	2,535
Delaware	39	349	40	361	42	337	40	337	34	339
Dist. of Columbia	132	1,203	196	1,329	120	1,525	123	1,314	134	1,396
Florida	94	1,160	101	1,242	97	1,125	102	1,007	100	1,145
Georgia	212	2,806	239	2,794	222	2,695	222	2,396	237	2,676
Hawaii	40	452	49	557	47	561	46	507	47	569
Idaho	61	469	59	592	62	642	62	627	57	709
Illinois	500	5,813	530	6,165	507	5,828	521	5,774	521	5,586
Indiana	186	2,121	198	2,293	179	2,061	193	2,198	192	2,200
Iowa	202	2,455	216	2,523	218	2,964	221	2,880	215	2,825
Kansas	128	1,275	129	1,383	134	1,539	139	1,666	138	1,741
Kentucky	150	1,590	159	1,941	161	1,956	143	1,768	145	1,680
Louisiana	106	1,142	111	1,248	125	1,670	122	1,869	119	1,869
Maine	108	1,174	107	1,221	108	1,253	108	1,252	106	1,356
Maryland	163	1,741	157	1,911	160	1,878	152	1,662	160	1,706
Massachusetts	424	5,102	443	5,538	444	5,404	446	5,413	443	5,421
Michigan	213	2,648	204	2,578	206	2,510	207	2,499	215	2,696
Minnesota	196	2,612	201	2,747	204	2,545	199	2,406	210	2,655
Mississippi	119	1,063	197	1,325	135	1,372	125	1,316	106	1,188
Missouri	208	2,811	223	3,217	258	2,675	248	2,462	262	2,995
Montana	36	386	40	501	54	694	64	698	61	728
Nebraska	108	1,299	102	990	126	1,021	122	1,208	118	1,171
New Hampshire	125	1,443	131	1,545	92	1,184	92	1,182	92	1,171
New Jersey	351	3,982	309	4,116	362	3,783	367	3,716	345	3,934
New Mexico	31	243	27	181	57	887	56	793	64	700
New York	945	13,800	981	14,503	992	14,344	963	13,688	990	14,477
North Carolina	204	1,835	215	1,903	237	2,043	238	1,965	230	2,308
North Dakota	64	639	54	693	65	683	57	599	53	614
Ohio	446	5,099	495	5,511	505	5,095	513	5,466	518	5,462
Oklahoma	53	660	56	988	59	901	60	955	59	939
Oregon	101	1,343	112	1,457	104	1,415	107	1,291	102	1,362
Pennsylvania	703	9,345	732	9,776	738	9,683	755	9,862	743	9,705
Rhode Island	116	961	110	1,041	107	1,027	109	1,199	100	1,257
South Carolina	175	1,714	190	1,751	184	1,772	192	1,710	177	1,792
South Dakota	64	562	73	707	80	714	84	802	83	787
Tennessee	111	1,430	122	1,401	126	1,515	127	1,396	128	1,785
Texas	202	2,032	216	2,378	216	2,513	215	1,396	171	2,678
Utah	37	330	47	359	40	330	39	328	34	339
Vermont	63	781	63	767	62	769	67	702	71	810
Virginia	163	1,903	170	2,222	189	2,231	180	2,017	190	2,237
Washington	56	639	54	969	88	1,242	86	1,178	87	1,905
West Virginia	98	998	116	1,194	98	1,346	103	1,238	100	1,918
Wisconsin	194	2,825	198	2,898	197	2,836	198	2,809	197	2,992
Wyoming	41	439	41	408	52	598	49	592	53	591
Total	8,583	102,358	8,975	109,951	9,155	110,595	9,172	108,816	9,142	113,710

NAVY AND NAVAL MILITIA.

STATE OR TER.	1908.		1909.		1910.		1911.		1912.	
	Officers.	Privates	Officers.	Privates	Officers.	Privates	Officers.	Privates	Officers.	Privates
Navy	2,703	39,346	2,823	44,129	2,921	45,076	3,099	46,759	3,114	46,651
Marine corps	209	8,811	334	9,360	334	9,152	330	9,454	319	9,567
NAVAL MILITIA.										
California	49	509	49	552	50	575	58	600	58	606
Connecticut	22	220	22	202	22	253	23	230	21	221
Dist. of Columbia	14	187	14	132	14	143	13	147	12	131
Florida	....	....	....	....	....	....	16	134	14	134
Georgia	10	107	3	44	3	60	3	60	Disbanded.	
Illinois	50	669	51	587	49	235	44	526	50	587
Indiana	....	....	....	....	21	186	14	184	14	216
Louisiana	48	577	52	583	49	553	51	508	46	544
Maine	4	60	4	65	7	125	7	108	9	104
Maryland	21	272	23	271	21	272	21	183	16	141
Massachusetts	43	406	41	481	44	409	41	523	42	541
Michigan	49	356	46	295	41	289	37	291	41	434
Minnesota	13	162	11	123	11	123	14	201	12	195
Missouri	11	120	10	96	18	196	17	231	16	210
New Jersey	27	301	29	321	25	325	33	293	29	377
New York	52	741	53	767	52	768	62	789	72	1,095
North Carolina	44	343	47	317	46	300	44	320	44	265
Ohio	19	183	18	247	16	234	17	23"	23	319
Oregon	....	....	....	....	....	....	25	208	21	214
Pennsylvania	8	57	7	118	8	112"	11	178	13	213
Rhode Island	19	212	17	209	15	185	16	178	18	162
South Carolina	21	185	21	185	20	187	20	187	21	179
Washington	....	....	....	....	....	....	12	112	13	193
Wisconsin	....	....	8	44	8	61	9	74	10	112
Total nav. militia	515	5,787	535	5,639	540	5,951	602	6,592	615	7,185

COMPARATIVE STRENGTH OF NAVIES.

[Based on tables published in Brassey's Naval Annual for 1913.]

COUNTRY.	Modern battle ships. No.	Displacement, Tons.	Battle cruisers. No.	Displacement, Tons.	Older battle ships. No.	Displacement, Tons.	First-class cruisers. No.	Displacement, Tons.	Light cruisers. No.	Displacement, Tons.
Great Britain	29	643,850	10	215,800	38	556,200	42	484,800	90	397,515
Germany	19	440,350	7	177,900	20	243,270	9	94,135	46	180,000
Austria-Hungary	4	80,000			9	98,601	1	7,185	9	32,277
Italy	8	181,900			8	95,418	7	61,458	14	46,545
France	17	270,568			15	183,838	18	191,761	13	69,469
Russia	9	193,000	4	120,000	5	96,954	6	63,396	15	87,267
United States	13	308,050			25	333,847	15	186,565	10	45,270

EFFECTIVE FIGHTING SHIPS.

CLASS.	Great Britain. Built	Building	Total	Germany. Built	Building	Total	Austria-Hungary. Built	Building	Total	Italy. Built	Building	Total	France. Built	Building	Total	Russia. Built	Building	Total	United States. Built	Building	Total
BATTLE SHIPS.																					
Modern	18	11	29	10	9	19	1	3	4	1	7	8	6	11	17	2	7	9	8	5	13
Cruiser	7	3	10	3	4	7											4	4			
Older	38		38	20		20	9		9	8		8	15		15	8		8	25		25
Total	63	14	77	33	13	46	10	3	13	9	7	16	21	11	32	10	11	21	33	5	38
CRUISERS.																					
First class	42		42	9		9	1		1	7		7	18		18	6		6	15		15
Light	76	14	90	40	6	46	6	3	9	9	5	14	13		13	6	14	10	10		10
Total	118	14	132	49	6	55	7	3	10	16	5	21	31		31	14	6	20	25		25

TORPEDO BOATS AND SUBMARINES.

	Built	Building	Total	Built	Building	Total	Built	Building	Total	Built	Building	Total	Built	Building	Total	Built	Building	Total	Built	Building	Total
Destroyers	193	34	227	127	14	141	14	4	18	27	8	35	75	12	87	96	9	105	41	14	55
Torpedo boats	58		58	47		47	41	12	53	57	16	73	173		173	23		23	24		24
Submarines	66	19	85	18	12	30	8	7	15	17	3	20	76	14	90	30	18	48	28	16	44

Japan, which is omitted from the Brassey tables, had in 1913 2 dreadnoughts, 16 pre-dreadnoughts, 13 armored cruisers, 20 protected cruisers, 61 destroyers, 50 torpedo boats and 12 submarines.

NAVAL EXPENDITURES OF CHIEF POWERS.

TOTAL EXPENDITURES.	1900.	1910.	1913.
Great Britain...	£29,998,529	£40,603,700	£46,309,300
Germany	7,648,781	21,247,588	22,887,870
United States...	13,385,574	26,515,468	28,932,530
France	12,511,053	13,659,820	18,826,755
Russia	8,662,801	10,219,766	24,477,487
Italy	4,903,129	6,960,987	10,269,460
Austria-Hungary		3,545,727	5,985,715

VOTED FOR NEW CONSTRUCTION.	1900.	1910.	1913.
Great Britain....	£9,788,146	£13,279,830	£13,276,400
Germany	3,401,907	11,921,195	11,176,407
United States....	4,344,127	6,222,100	4,430,000
France	4,718,566	5,918,292	7,595,010
Russia	3,149,014	1,424,013	10,653,616
Italy	1,156,921	2,662,406	2,800,000
Austria-Hungary		1,583,333	3,280,473

FAILURES IN THE UNITED STATES.

[From Dun's Review, New York.]

CALENDAR YEAR.	1st Quar. No. failures.	Amt. of liabilities.	2d Quar. No. failures.	Amt. of liabilities.	3d Quar. No. failures.	Amt. of liabilities.	4th Quar. No. failures.	Amt. of liabilities.	Total for Year. No. failures.	Amt. of liabilities.	Average liabilities.
1897	3982	$48,007,911	2889	$43,684,876	3881	$25,601,188	3649	$37,038,095	13,351	$154,332,071	$11,559
1898	3087	32,946,565	3081	44,498,074	2540	25,104,778	2508	38,113,482	12,186	130,662,869	10,722
1899	2772	27,152,031	2081	14,910,902	2001	17,640,972	2483	31,175,984	9,397	90,879,889	9,733
1900	2894	33,022,573	2438	41,724,879	2519	27,119,996	2923	36,628,225	10,774	138,495,673	12,854
1901	3385	31,703,486	2424	24,101,204	2324	24,756,172	2919	32,581,514	11,145	113,092,376	10,279
1902	3418	33,731,758	2747	26,645,098	2511	25,082,634	2860	32,005,279	11,615	117,476,769	10,114
1903	3605	34,344,433	2248	32,452,827	2548	34,858,595	3395	53,785,830	12,009	155,444,185	12,879
1904	3644	48,006,721	2870	31,434,188	2969	32,168,296	3016	32,543,106	12,199	144,202,311	11,820
1905	3443	30,162,505	2767	25,712,080	2596	20,339,443	2774	26,442,144	11,520	102,676,172	8,913
1906	3102	33,761,107	2510	28,902,987	2400	21,996,488	2770	34,541,278	10,682	119,201,515	11,159
1907	3130	32,075,591	2481	38,411,880	2453	46,467,686	3635	81,348,877	11,725	197,385,225	16,834
1908	4900	75,706,191	3860	58,797,264	3457	55,302,690	3524	42,638,161	15,690	222,515,684	14,169
1909	3850	44,460,950	2981	41,080,426	2936	27,504,498	3257	36,967,594	12,924	154,606,465	11,954
1910	3515	73,079,154	2963	39,180,152	3011	42,177,998	3253	47,339,796	12,652	201,757,097	15,947
1911	3985	59,651,761	3078	44,046,590	2880	35,167,269	3500	52,196,045	13,441	191,061,665	14,215
1912	4828	68,012,823	3849	44,999,900	3499	45,532,137	3636	49,573,031	15,452	208,117,391	13,115
1913	4458	76,882,277	3705	56,076,784	3559	88,734,153					

THE PRESIDENT'S MESSAGE TO CONGRESS.

President Woodrow Wilson read the following message at a joint session of the house and senate Dec. 2, 1913:

Gentlemen of the Congress: In pursuance of my constitutional duty to "give to the congress information of the state of the union," I take the liberty of addressing you on several matters which ought, it seems to me, particularly to engage the attention of your honorable bodies, as of all who study the welfare and progress of the nation.

I shall ask your indulgence if I venture to depart in some degree from the usual custom of setting before you in formal review the many matters which have engaged the attention and called for the action of the several departments of the government or which look to them for early treatment in the future, because the list is long—very long—and would suffer in the abbreviation to which I should have to subject it. I shall submit to you the reports of the heads of the several departments, in which these subjects are set forth in careful detail, and beg that they may receive the thoughtful attention of your committees and of all members of the congress who may have the leisure to study them. Their obvious importance, as constituting the very substance of the business of the government, makes comment and emphasis on my part unnecessary.

The country, I am thankful to say, is at peace with all the world, and many happy manifestations multiply about us of a growing cordiality and sense of community of interest among the nations, foreshadowing an age of settled peace and good will. More and more readily each decade do the nations manifest their willingness to bind themselves by solemn treaty to the processes of peace, the processes of frankness and fair concession. So far the United States has stood at the front of such negotiations. She will, I earnestly hope and confidently believe, give fresh proof of her sincere adherence to the cause of international friendship by ratifying the several treaties of arbitration awaiting renewal by the senate. In addition to these, it has been the privilege of the department of state to gain the assent, in principle, of no less than thirty-one nations, representing four-fifths of the population of the world, to the negotiation of treaties by which it shall be agreed that whenever differences of interest or of policy arise which cannot be resolved by the ordinary processes of diplomacy they shall be publicly analyzed, discussed and reported upon by a tribunal chosen by the parties before either nation determines its course of action.

There is only one possible standard by which to determine controversies between the United States and other nations, and that is compounded of these two elements: Our own honor and our obligations to the peace of the world. A test so compounded ought easily to be made to govern both the establishment of new treaty obligations and the interpretation of those already assumed.

MEXICAN SITUATION.

There is but one cloud upon our horizon. That has shown itself to the south of us and hangs over Mexico. There can be no certain prospect of peace in America until Gen. Huerta has surrendered his usurped authority in Mexico; until it is understood on all hands, indeed, that such pretended government will not be countenanced or dealt with by the government of the United States. We are the friends of constitutional government in America; we are more than its friends, we are its champions, because in no other way can our neighbors, to whom we would wish in every way to make proof of our friendship, work out their own development in peace and liberty.

Mexico has no government. The attempt to maintain one at the City of Mexico has broken down, and a mere military despotism has been set up which has hardly more than the semblance of national authority. It originated in the usurpation of Victoriano Huerta, who, after a brief attempt to play the part of constitutional president, has at last cast aside even the pretense of legal right and declared himself dictator. As a consequence a condition of affairs now exists in Mexico which has made it doubtful whether even the most elementary and fundamental rights either of her own people or of the citizens of other countries resident within her territory can long be successfully safeguarded, and which threatens, if long continued, to imperil the interests of peace, order and tolerable life in the lands immediately to the south of us.

Even if the usurper had succeeded in his purposes, in despite of the constitution of the republic and the rights of its people, he would have set up nothing but a precarious and hateful power, which could have lasted but a little while, and whose eventual downfall would have left the country in a more deplorable condition than ever. But he has not succeeded. He has forfeited the respect and the moral support even of those who were at one time willing to see him succeed. Little by little he has been completely isolated. By a little every day his power and prestige are crumbling and the collapse is not far away.

We shall not, I believe, be obliged to alter our policy of watchful waiting. And then, when the end comes, we shall hope to see constitutional order restored in distressed Mexico by the concert and energy of such of her leaders as prefer the liberty of their people to their own ambitions.

PLEA FOR CURRENCY BILL.

I turn to matters of domestic concern. You already have under consideration a bill for the reform of our system of banking and currency, for which the country waits with impatience, as for something fundamental to its whole business life and necessary to set credit free from arbitrary and artificial restraints. I need not say how earnestly I hope for its early enactment into law. I take leave to beg that the whole energy and attention of the senate be concentrated upon it till the matter is successfully disposed of. And yet I feel that the request is not needed—that the members of the great house need no urging in this service to the country.

I present to you, in addition, the urgent necessity that special provision be made also for facilitating the credits needed by the farmers of the country. The pending currency bill does the farmers a great service. It puts them upon an equal footing with other business men and masters of enterprise, as it should; and upon its passage they will find themselves quit of many of the difficulties which now hamper them in the field of credit. The farmers, of course, ask and should be given no special privilege, such as extending to them the credit of the government itself. What they need and should obtain is legislation which will make their own abundant and substantial credit resources available as a foundation for joint, concerted local action in their own behalf in getting the capital they must use. It is to this we should now address ourselves.

It has, singularly enough, come to pass that we have allowed the industry of our farms to lag behind the other activities of the country in its development. I need not stop to tell you how fundamental to the life of the nation is the production of its food. Our thoughts may ordinarily be concentrated upon the cities and the hives of industry, upon the cries of the crowded market place and the clangor of the factory, but it is from the quiet interspaces of the open valleys and the free hillside that we draw the sources of life and of prosperity—from the farm and the ranch, from the forest and the mine. Without these every street would be silent, every office deserted, every factory fallen into disrepair.

And yet the farmer does not stand upon the same footing with the forester and the miner in the market of credit. He is the servant of the seasons. Nature determines how long he must wait for his crops and will not be hurried in her processes. He may give his note, but the season of its maturity depends upon the season when his crop matures, lies at the gates of the market where his products are sold. And the security he gives is of a character not known in the broker's office or as familiarly as it might be on the counter of the banker.

RURAL CREDIT SYSTEM.

The agricultural department of the government is seeking to assist as never before to make farming an efficient business, of wide co-operative effort, in quick touch with the markets for foodstuffs. The farmers and the government will henceforth work together as real partners in this field, where we now begin to see our way very clearly and where many intelligent plans are already being put into execution. The treasury of the United States has, by a timely and well considered distribution of its deposits, facilitated the moving of the crops in the present season and prevented the scarcity of available funds too often experienced at such times. But we must not allow ourselves to depend upon extraordinary expedients. We must add the means by which the farmer may make his credit constantly and easily available and command when he will the capital by which to support and expand his business. We lag behind many other great countries of the modern world in attempting to do this. Systems of rural credit have been studied and developed on the other side of the water while we left our farmers to shift for themselves in the ordinary money market. You have but to look about you in any rural district to see the result—the handicap and embarrassment which have been put upon those who produce our food.

Conscious of this backwardness and neglect on our part, the congress recently authorized the creation of a special commission to study the various systems of rural credit which have been put into operation in Europe, and this commission is already prepared to report. Its report ought to make it easier for us to determine what methods will be best suited to our own farmers. I hope and believe that the committees of the senate and house will address themselves to this matter with the most fruitful results, and I believe that the studies and recently formed plans of the department of agriculture may be made to serve them very greatly in their work of framing appropriate and adequate legislation. It would be indiscreet and presumptuous in any one to dogmatize upon so great and many sided a question, but I feel confident that common counsel will produce the results we must all desire.

TRUST LEGISLATION ADVOCATED.

Turn from the farm to the world of business, which centers in the city and in the factory, and I think that all thoughtful observers will agree that the immediate service we owe the business communities of the country is to prevent private monopoly more effectually than it has yet been prevented. I think it will be easily agreed that we should let the Sherman antitrust law stand, unaltered, as it is, with its debatable ground about it, but that we should as much as possible reduce the area of that debatable ground by further and more explicit legislation, and should also supplement that great act by legislation which will not only clarify it but also facilitate its administration and make it fairer to all concerned.

No doubt we shall all wish, and the country will expect, this to be the central subject of our deliberations during the present session; but it is a subject so many sided and so deserving of careful and discriminating discussion that I shall take the liberty of addressing you upon it in a special message at a later date than this. It is of capital importance that the business men of this country should be relieved of all uncertainties of law with regard to their enterprises and investments and a clear path indicated which they can travel without anxiety. It is as important that they should be relieved of embarrassment and set free to prosper as that private monopoly should be destroyed. The ways of action should be thrown wide open.

PRESIDENTIAL PRIMARIES FAVORED.

I turn to a subject which I hope can be handled promptly and without serious controversy of any kind. I mean the method of selecting nominees for the presidency of the United States. I feel confident that I do not misinterpret the wishes or the expectations of the country when I urge the prompt enactment of legislation which will provide for primary elections throughout the country at which the voters of the several parties may choose their nominees for the presidency without the intervention of nominating conventions.

I venture the suggestion that this legislation should provide for the retention of party conventions, but only for the purpose of declaring and accepting the verdict of the primaries and formulating the platforms of the parties; and I suggest that these conventions should consist not of delegates chosen for this single purpose but of the nominees for congress, the nominees for vacant seats in the senate of the United States, the senators whose terms have not yet closed, the national committees and the candidates for the presidency themselves, in order that platforms may be framed by those responsible to the people for carrying them into effect.

PROBLEM IN THE PHILIPPINES.

These are all matters of vital domestic concern, and besides them, outside the charmed circle of our own national life in which our affections command us, as well as our consciences, there stand out our obligations toward our territories over sea. Here we are trustees. Porto Rico, Hawaii, the Philippines, are ours, indeed, but not ours to do what we please with. Such territories, once regarded as mere possessions, are no longer to be selfishly exploited; they are part of the domain of public conscience and of serviceable and enlightened statesmanship. We must administer them for the people who live in them and with the same sense of responsibility to them as toward our own people in our domestic affairs.

No doubt we shall successfully enough bind Porto Rico and the Hawaiian islands to ourselves by ties of justice and interest and affection, but the performance of our duty toward the Philippines is a more difficult and debatable matter. We can satisfy the obligations of generous justice toward the people of Porto Rico by giving them the ample and familiar rights and privileges accorded our own citizens in our own territories and our obligations toward the people of Hawaii by perfecting the provisions for self-government already granted them, but in the Philippines we must go further. We must hold steadily in view their ultimate independence, and we must move toward the time of that independence as steadily as the way can be cleared and the foundations thoughtfully and permanently laid.

Acting under the authority conferred upon the president by congress, I have already accorded the people of the islands a majority in both houses of their legislative body by appointing five instead of four native citizens to the membership of the commission. I believe that in this way we shall make proof of their capacity in counsel and their sense of responsibility in the exercise of political power, and that the success of this step will be sure to clear our view for the steps which are to follow.

Step by step we should extend and perfect the system of self-government in the islands, making test of them and modifying them as experience discloses their successes and their failures; that we should more and more put under the control of the native citizens of the archipelago the essential instruments of their life, their local instrumentalities of government, their schools, all the common interests of their communities, and so by counsel and experience set up a government which all the world will see to be suitable to a people whose affairs are under their own control. At last I hope and believe we are beginning to gain the confidence of the Filipino peoples. By their counsel and experience, rather than by our own, we shall learn how best to serve them and how soon it will be possible and wise to withdraw our supervision. Let us once find the path and set out with firm and confident tread upon it and we shall not wander from it or linger upon it.

RAILWAYS NEEDED IN ALASKA.

A duty faces us with regard to Alaska which seems to me very pressing and very imperative; perhaps I should say a double duty, for it concerns both the political and the material development of the territory. The people of Alaska should be given the full territorial form of government, and Alaska,

as a storehouse, should be unlocked. One key to it is a system of railways. These the government should itself build and administer, and the ports and terminals it should itself control in the interest of all who wish to use them for the service and development of the country and its people.

But the construction of railways is only the first step; is only thrusting in the key to the storehouse and throwing back the lock and opening the door. How the tempting resources of the country are to be exploited is another matter, to which I shall take the liberty of from time to time calling your attention, for it is a policy which must be worked out by well considered stages, not upon theory, but upon lines of practical expediency. It is part of our general problem of conservation. We have a freer hand in working out the problem in Alaska than in the states of the union; and yet the principle and object are the same, wherever we touch it. We must use the resources of the country, not lock them up. There need be no conflict or jealousy as between state and federal authorities, for there can be no essential difference of purpose between them. The resources in question must be used, but not destroyed or wasted; used, but not monopolized upon any narrow idea of individual rights as against the abiding interests of communities. That a policy can be worked out by conference and concession which will release these resources and yet not jeopard or dissipate them, I for one have no doubt, and it can be done on lines of regulation which need be no less acceptable to the people and governments of the states concerned than to the people and government of the nation at large, whose heritage these resources are. We must bend our counsels to this end. A common purpose ought to make agreement easy.

JUSTICE TO RAILWAY EMPLOYES.

Three or four matters of special importance and significance I beg that you will permit me to mention in closing.

Our bureau of mines ought to be equipped and empowered to render even more effectual service than it renders now in improving the conditions of mine labor and making the mines more economically productive, as well as more safe. This is an all important part of the work of conservation, and the conservation of human life and energy lies even nearer to our interest than the preservation from waste of our material resources.

We owe it, in mere justice to the railway employes of the country, to provide for them a fair and effective employers' liability act, and a law that we can stand by in this matter will be no less to the advantage of those who administer the railroads of the country than to the advantage of those whom they employ. The experience of a large number of the states abundantly proves that.

We ought to devote ourselves to meeting pressing demands of plain justice like this as earnestly as to the accomplishment of political and economic reforms. Social justice comes first. Law is the machinery for its realization and is vital only as it expresses and embodies it.

An international congress for the discussion of all questions that affect safety at sea is now sitting in London at the suggestion of our own government. So soon as the conclusions of that congress can be learned and considered we ought to address ourselves, among other things, to the prompt alleviation of the very unsafe, unjust and burdensome conditions which now surround the employment of sailors and render it extremely difficult to obtain the services of spirited and competent men such as every ship needs if it is to be safely handled and brought to port.

PRAISE FOR CONGRESS.

May I not express the very real pleasure I have experienced in co-operating with this congress and sharing with it the labors of common service to which it has devoted itself so unreservedly during the past seven months of uncomplaining concentration upon the business of legislation? Surely it is a proper and pertinent part of my report on "the state of the union" to express my admiration for the diligence, the good temper and the full comprehension of public duty which has already been manifested by both the houses; and I hope that it may not be deemed an impertinent intrusion of myself into the picture if I say with how much and how constant satisfaction I have availed myself of the privilege of putting my time and energy at their disposal alike in counsel and in action.

CURRENCY BILL IN CONGRESS.

President Woodrow Wilson made a strong effort to have a currency law enacted at the first or extra session of the 63d congress, but succeeded only in having a bill passed by the house. It was delayed in the senate finance committee until the special session merged into the regular session in December. The president appeared in person before congress and urged the members to give the country a new banking and currency system. (See page 241.) The administration currency bill was introduced in the house Aug. 29 by Carter Glass of Virginia, and was referred to the committee on banking and currency, of which he was chairman. It was reported back to the house Sept. 9, debated and passed Sept. 18 by a vote of 286 to 84. Three democrats voted against it, while twenty-four republicans and eleven progressives voted for it. The gold standard was reaffirmed by the adoption by a vote of 298 to 69 of the following amendment:

"Provided, That nothing in this act contained shall be considered to repeal the parity provision or provisions contained in an act approved March 14, 1900, entitled 'An act to define and fix the standard of value, to maintain the parity of all forms of money issued or coined by the United States, to refund the public debt, and for other purposes.'"

By a vote of 266 to 100 the house refused to pass an amendment forbidding interlocking directorates. The bill, after passing the house in substantially the same form as reported, was sent to the senate, where it was referred to the finance committee, where it remained until the regular session began.

The formal title of the Glass currency bill was "A bill to provide for the establishment of federal reserve banks, to furnish an elastic currency, to afford means of rediscounting commercial paper, to establish more effective supervision of banking in the United States, and for other purposes." The first section in the act itself provided that its short title should be "Federal reserve act." The main features of the measure were:

The designation by the secretary of the treasury, the secretary of agriculture and the comptroller of the currency from among the reserve and central reserve cities now authorized by law of a number of such cities to be known as federal reserve cities, and the division of continental United States into districts, each district to contain one such federal reserve city; the districts thus constituted to be known as reserve districts.

The organization in each of the federal reserve cities of a federal reserve bank.

Total number of reserve cities to be not less than twelve.

Every national bank within a given district to subscribe to the capital stock of the federal reserve bank of that district a sum equal to 20 per cent of the capital stock of such national bank.

No federal reserve bank to be organized with a capital of less than $5,000,000.

Every federal reserve bank to be under the control of a board of nine directors, three representing the stockholding banks, three representing the general public interests of the district and three to be designated by the federal reserve board.

Federal reserve board to consist of seven members, including the secretary of the treasury, the secretary of agriculture and the comptroller of the currency, members ex officio, and four members chosen by the president of the United States, each to receive an annual salary of $10,000 and traveling expenses.

Such federal reserve board to be empowered to examine the accounts of each federal reserve bank and make weekly reports of the condition of each

reserve bank; to permit or require in time of emergency federal reserve banks to rediscount the discounted prime paper of other federal reserve banks; to suspend for thirty days every reserve requirement specified in the act; to supervise and regulate the issue and retirement of federal reserve notes; to add to the number of reserve and central reserve cities; or to reclassify existing reserve and central reserve cities; to suspend the operations of any federal reserve bank and appoint a receiver therefor.

Creation of a federal advisory council to consist of as many members as there are federal reserve districts; such council to have the power to confer with the federal reserve board on general business conditions; to make representations concerning matters within the jurisdiction of the board, and to call for complete information respecting discount rates, rediscount business, note issues, reserve conditions in the various districts, the purchase and sale of gold or securities by reserve banks and the general affairs of the reserve banking system.

All moneys held in the general fund of the treasury to be deposited in federal reserve banks, such banks to act as the fiscal agents of the United States.

Federal reserve notes to be issued at the discretion of the federal reserve board for the purpose of making advances to federal reserve banks, such notes to be receivable for all taxes, customs and other public dues and to be redeemed in gold or lawful money on demand.

Any federal reserve bank to be at liberty to make application for such amount of treasury notes as it may deem best and to tender as collateral security notes and bills accepted for rediscount under the provisions of the act.

POPULATION BY NATIVE LANGUAGE.

Table prepared by the bureau of the census showing the mother tongue or native language or "foreign white stock" in the United States in 1910:

Mother Tongue.	Foreign stock.	Foreign born.
English*	10,037,420	3,363,792
Germanic:		
German	3,817,271	2,759,032
Dutch and Frisian	324,930	126,045
Flemish	44,896	25,780
Scandinavian:		
Swedish	1,445,869	683,218
Norwegian	1,009,854	402,587
Danish	446,473	186,345
Latin and Greek:		
Italian	2,151,422	1,365,110
French	1,357,169	528,842
Spanish	448,198	258,131
Portuguese	141,282	73,649
Roumanian	51,124	42,277
Greek	130,379	118,379
Slavic and Lettic:		
Polish	1,707,640	943,781
Bohemian and Moravian	539,392	228,738
Slovak	284,444	166,474
Russian	95,137	57,926
Ruthenian	35,359	25,131
Slovenian	183,431	123,631
Sebro-Croatian—		
Croatian	92,936	74,036
Dalmatian	5,505	4,344
Servian	26,732	23,403
Montenegrin	3,961	3,886
Bulgarian	19,380	18,341
Slavic, not specified	35,195	21,012
Lithuanian and Lettish	211,235	140,963
Miscellaneous:		
Yiddish and Hebrew	1,676,762	1,051,767
Magyar	320,893	229,094
Finnish	200,688	120,086
Armenian	30,021	23,938
Syrian and Arabic	46,727	32,868
Turkish	5,441	4,709
Albanian	2,366	2,312
All other	790	646
Unknown	313,044	116,272
All mother tongues	32,243,382	13,345,545

*Includes persons reporting Irish, Scotch or Welsh.
Note—See also page 73.

IRON WORKERS' DYNAMITE CASES.

Forty-six men, chiefly union labor officials and agents, were placed on trial before Federal Judge A. B. Anderson in Indianapolis, Ind., Oct. 1, 1912, on the charge of complicity in nearly 100 dynamite explosions growing out of the strike against the American Bridge company declared by the International Association of Bridge and Structural Iron Workers. These explosions occurred between August, 1905, and April, 1911, and one of them, that in the Los Angeles Times building, Oct. 1, 1910, resulted in the loss of twenty-five lives. For this last crime James Boyd McNamara was sentenced Dec. 5, 1911, to life imprisonment in San Quentin prison, California, his brother, John J. McNamara, getting a sentence of fifteen years in the same prison for another explosion. Both had pleaded guilty.

The men brought before Judge Anderson were tried on counts charging conspiracy and violation of the law against carrying explosives. Edward S. Clark of Cincinnati, business agent and president of a local union of the bridge workers' organization, pleaded guilty and was given a suspended sentence. The trial ended Dec. 28, 1912, in a verdict of guilty as to thirty-three of the defendants and Dec. 30 Judge Anderson sentenced them to serve terms ranging from one year and one day to seven years in the federal prison at Leavenworth, Kas. Among those receiving the heaviest sentences were Frank M. Ryan, Chicago; John T. Butler, Buffalo; Herbert S. Hockin, Detroit; Olaf A. Tveitmoe, San Francisco; Eugene A. Clancy, San Francisco; Philip A. Cooley, New Orleans, and Michael J. Young, Boston.

Jan. 3, 1913, the defendants were admitted to bail by the United States Circuit Court of Appeals in Chicago, the bonds being fixed at $10,000 for each year of imprisonment imposed.

BUCK'S STOVE COMPANY BOYCOTT CASE.

Proceedings were brought in the Supreme court of the District of Columbia in August, 1907, against the officers of the American Federation of Labor to enjoin them from conducting a boycott against the Buck's Stove and Range company of St. Louis, Mo., by advertising that the concern was on the "unfair" and "we don't patronize" lists of the federation's official organ. The injunction was issued by Judge Gould Dec. 23, 1907. On the plea that the injunction was being violated proceedings for contempt of court were brought against Samuel Gompers, president; John Mitchell, vice-president, and Frank Morrison, secretary of the federation. They were declared guilty by Justice Wright of the Supreme court of the District of Columbia Dec. 23, 1908. Mr. Gompers was sentenced to one year's imprisonment. Mr. Mitchell to nine months' and Mr. Morrison to six months' imprisonment. They were admitted to bail and the case was taken to the Court of Appeals of the District of Columbia, which tribunal decided Nov. 2, 1909, that the decree against them was valid.

An appeal was taken to the United States Supreme court, which on May 15, 1911, reversed the judgments of the lower courts and remanded the case. May 5, 1913, the Court of Appeals of the District of Columbia again affirmed the original findings in the contempt case, but reduced Mr. Gompers' sentence to thirty days in jail and held that Mitchell and Morrison should be exempt from prison sentences, but should each pay a fine of $500. June 19, 1913, Chief Justice White of the United States Supreme court granted an appeal by the defendants that the case be heard again by the highest tribunal.

PROTECTION OF BIRDS AND GAME.

FEDERAL LAW.

By an act of congress approved March 4, 1913, all wild geese, wild swan, brant, wild ducks, snipe, plover, woodcock, rail, wild pigeons and all other migratory game and insectivorous birds which in their northern and southern migrations pass through or do not remain permanently the entire year within the borders of any state were placed under the protection of the government of the United States. The department of agriculture was authorized to adopt suitable regulations to give effect to the law by prescribing fixed closed seasons within which such birds are not to be taken or killed. Such regulations were made by the department and proclaimed by President Wilson Oct. 1, 1913. Migratory game birds under the rules include the following: Waterfowl, including brant, wild ducks, geese and swans; cranes, including little brown, sandhill and whooping cranes; rails, including coots, gallinules, sora and other rails; shore birds, including avocets, curlew, dowitchers, godwits, knots, oyster catchers, phalaropes, plover, sandpipers, snipe, stilts, surf birds, turnstones, willet, woodcock and yellow legs; pigeons, including doves and wild pigeons.

Migratory insectivorous birds include bobolinks, catbirds, chickadees, cuckoos, flickers, flycatchers, grosbeaks, humming birds, kinglets, martens, meadowlarks, nighthawks or bull bats, nuthatches, orioles, robins, shrikes, swallows, swifts, tanagers, titmice, thrushes, vireos, warblers, waxwings, whippoorwills, woodpeckers and wrens, and all other perching birds which feed entirely or chiefly on insects.

None of the above named birds may be taken or shot between sunset and sunrise at any time.

The closed season on migratory insectivorous birds is from Jan. 1 to Dec. 31, or the entire year. The closed season continues to Sept. 1, 1918, on the following migratory game birds: Bandtailed pigeons, little brown, sandhill and whooping cranes, swans, curlew, and all shorebirds except the blackbreasted and golden plover, Wilson or jacksnipe, woodcock and the greater and lesser yellowlegs.

There is a closed season also until Sept. 1, 1918, on wood ducks in Maine, New Hampshire, Vermont, Massachusetts, Rhode Island, Connecticut, New York, New Jersey, Pennsylvania, West Virginia, Ohio, Indiana, Illinois, Michigan, Wisconsin, Minnesota, Iowa, Kansas, California, Oregon and Washington; on rails in California and Vermont; and on woodcock in Illinois and Missouri.

On migratory birds passing over or at rest on the waters of the Mississippi river between New Orleans and Minneapolis, the Ohio river between its mouth and Pittsburgh and the Missouri river between its mouth and Bismarck, N. D., there is a closed season between Jan. 1 and Oct. 1, both dates inclusive, of each year.

ZONES.

The following zones for the protection of migratory game and insectivorous birds are established:

Zone No. 1, the breeding zone, comprising states lying wholly or in part north of latitude 40 degrees and the Ohio river, and including Maine, New Hampshire, Vermont, Massachusetts, Rhode Island, Connecticut, New York, New Jersey, Pennsylvania, Ohio, Indiana, Illinois, Michigan, Wisconsin, Minnesota, Iowa, North Dakota, South Dakota, Nebraska, Colorado, Wyoming, Montana, Idaho, Oregon and Washington.

Zone No. 2, the wintering zone, comprising states lying wholly or in part south of latitude 40 degrees and the Ohio river, and including Delaware, Maryland, the District of Columbia, West Virginia, Virginia, North Carolina, South Carolina, Georgia, Florida, Alabama, Mississippi, Tennessee, Kentucky, Missouri, Arkansas, Louisiana, Texas, Oklahoma, Kansas, New Mexico, Arizona, California, Nevada and Utah.

OPEN SEASONS IN ZONE NO. 1.

Waterfowl—Sept. 1 to Dec. 15. Exceptions: Massachusetts and Rhode Island, Sept. 15 to Dec. 31; Minnesota and North Dakota, Sept. 7 to Dec. 15; New York (other than Long Island) and Oregon, Sept. 16 to Dec. 15; New Hampshire, Long Island, New Jersey and Washington, Oct. 1 to Jan. 15; South Dakota, Sept. 10 to Dec. 15.

Rails, coots, gallinules—Sept. 1 to Nov. 30. Exceptions: Massachusetts and Rhode Island, Aug. 1 to Nov. 30; New York (including Long Island), Sept. 16 to Nov. 30; Vermont and California, rails protected until Sept. 1, 1918.

Woodcock—Oct. 1 to Nov. 30. Exceptions: Maine and Vermont, Sept. 15 to Nov. 30; Massachusetts, Connecticut and New Jersey, Oct. 10 to Nov. 30; Rhode Island, Pennsylvania and Long Island, Oct. 15 to Nov. 30; Illinois and Missouri, protected until Sept. 1, 1918.

Shore birds (including black-breasted and golden plover, jacksnipe or Wilson snipe, greater or lesser yellowlegs)—Sept. 1 to Dec. 15. Exceptions: Maine, Massachusetts and Long Island, Aug. 1 to Dec. 15; Minnesota and North Dakota, Sept. 17 to Dec. 15; South Dakota, Sept. 10 to Dec. 15; New York (except Long Island) and Oregon, Sept. 16 to Dec. 15; New Hampshire and Washington, Oct. 1 to Dec. 15.

OPEN SEASONS IN ZONE NO. 2.

Waterfowl—Oct. 1 to Jan. 15. Exceptions: Kansas, Oklahoma, New Mexico and Arizona, Sept. 1 to Dec. 15; Maryland, Virginia, North Carolina and South Carolina, Nov. 1 to Jan. 31.

Rails, coots and gallinules—Sept. 1 to Nov. 30. Exceptions: Tennessee and Louisiana, Oct. 1 to Nov. 30; Arizona, Oct. 15 to Nov. 30.

Woodcock—Nov. 1 to Dec. 31. Exceptions: Louisiana, Nov. 15 to Dec. 31; Georgia, Dec. 1 to Dec. 31.

Shore birds (including black-breasted and golden plover, jacksnipe or Wilson snipe and greater and lesser yellowlegs)—Sept. 1 to Dec. 15. Exceptions: Alabama, Nov. 1 to Dec. 15; Louisiana and Tennessee, Oct. 1 to Dec. 15; Arizona, Oct. 15 to Dec. 15; Utah, Oct. 1 to Dec. 15 on snipe; plover and yellowlegs protected until Sept. 1, 1918.

STATE GAME AND FISH LAWS.

Each state in the United States and each province in Canada has its own game and fish laws, the enforcement of which is intrusted to game commissioners, wardens or other officials. In most cases a printed synopsis of the laws will be furnished by these officials upon application. It is advisable for those desiring to hunt or fish in any particular state or province to get information as to open and closed seasons and licenses from the game department, which in nearly all cases is located in the capital of the state or province. The agricultural department in Washington publishes a pamphlet which may be obtained upon application, giving the addresses of the game commissions, wardens, etc.

The open season on deer hunting in the states where deer are chiefly found are: Maine, Oct. 1 to Dec. 16 in certain counties and Nov. 1 to Dec. 1 in others; New York, Oct. 1 to Nov. 16 (in Adirondacks only); Michigan, Nov. 10 to Dec. 1; Wisconsin, Nov. 11 to Dec. 1; Minnesota, Nov. 10 to Nov. 30. In Colorado deer are protected until Oct. 1, 1918.

RAILWAY SPEED IN AMERICA.

FAST REGULAR RUNS.

New York Central—Between Chicago and New York, 960 miles, in 18 hours; average speed, including stops, 53.3 miles an hour. (Summer schedule.)

Pennsylvania—Between Chicago and New York, 908 miles, in 18 hours; average speed, including stops, 50.4 miles an hour. (Summer schedule.)

FAST SPECIAL RUNS—SHORT DISTANCES.

May, 1823—New York Central, 1 mile at rate of 112.5 miles an hour.

August, 1895—Pennsylvania, 5.1 miles at rate of 102 miles an hour.

January, 1899—Burlington, 2.1 miles at rate of 108 miles an hour.

March, 1901—Plant system, 5 miles at rate of 120 miles an hour.
January, 1903—New York Central, 7.29 miles at rate of 139.35 miles an hour.
April, 1904—Michigan Central, 3.73 miles at rate of 111.30 miles an hour.
July, 1904—Philadelphia & Reading, 4.8 miles at rate of 115.20 miles an hour.

FAST SPECIAL RUNS—LONG DISTANCES.
June 13, 1905—Lake Shore road, Chicago to Buffalo, 526 miles, in 453 minutes; average speed, deducting time for stops, 70.9 miles an hour.
July 9-11, 1905—"Death Valley" Scott's special, Los Angeles, Cal., to Chicago, Ill., 2,415 miles, in 44 hours and 54 minutes; average speed, deducting stops, 51 miles an hour.
October, 1905—Harriman special, Oakland, Cal., to

Jersey City, N. J., 3,389 miles, in 73 hours 12 minutes; average speed, 44.30 miles an hour.
Oct. 24 1905—Pennsylvania road, 257 miles, from Crestline, O., to Clark Junction, Ind., in 3 hours 27 minutes; average speed, 74.55 miles an hour.
May, 1906—Harriman special, Oakland, Cal., to New York, N. Y., in 71 hours and 27 minutes; average speed, 45.30 miles an hour.
March 27-28, 1909—Frank Vanderlip special on New York Central lines, New York to Chicago, 965 miles, in 15 hours 43 minutes; average, excluding stops, 62.45 miles an hour; some stretches made at rate of 75 miles an hour.
February, 1911—Charles G. Gates special, Yuma, Ariz., to New York, N. Y., 2,787 miles, in 74 hours 19 minutes; average speed, including all stops, 40.41 miles an hour.

POSTMASTERS OF LARGE CITIES (1913).

Albany, N. Y.—Henry F. Snyder.
Atlanta, Ga.—Bolling H. Jones.
Baltimore, Md.—Sherlock Swann.
Boston, Mass.—E. C. Mansfield.
Buffalo, N. Y.—Fred Greiner.
Camden, N. J.—Harry M. Knight.
Charleston, S. C.—Joseph M. Poulnot.
Chicago, Ill.—Daniel A. Campbell.
Cincinnati, O.—E. R. Monfort.
Cleveland, O.—Raymond G. Floyd.
Columbus, O.—H. W. Krumm.
Dayton, O.—Forrest L. May.
Denver, Col.—Joseph H. Harrison.
Des Moines, Iowa—Louis C. Kurtz.
Detroit, Mich.—William J. Nagel.
Duluth, Minn.—Arthur P. Cook.
Fall River, Mass.—George T. Durfee.
Fort Wayne, Ind.—Robert B. Hanna.
Galveston, Tex.—Harry A. Griffin.
Grand Rapids, Mich.—W. M. Palmer.
Hartford, Conn.—Frank A. Hagarty.
Indianapolis, Ind.—Robert E. Springsteen.
Jersey City, N. J.—Peter F. Wanser.
Kansas City, Mo.—Joseph H. Harris.
Lincoln, Neb.—E. R. Sizer.
Los Angeles, Cal.—W. H. Harrison.
Louisville, Ky.—E. T. Schmitt.
Lowell, Mass.—Robert J. Crowley.
Memphis, Tenn.—J. C. French.
Milwaukee, Wis.—David C. Owen.

Minneapolis, Minn.—W. D. Hale.
Nashville, Tenn.—A. W. Wills.
Newark, N. J.—Frank J. Bock.
New Haven, Conn.—J. A. Howarth.
New Orleans, La.—A. F. Leonhardt.
New York, N. Y.—Edward M. Morgan.
Omaha, Neb.—John C. Wharton.
Paterson, N. J.—James P. McNair.
Peoria, Ill.—L. F. Meek.
Philadelphia, Pa.—John A. Thornton.
Pittsburgh, Pa.—William H. Davis.
Portland, Me.—Oscar R. Wish.
Portland, Ore.—Frank S. Myers.
Providence, R. I.—Walter A. Kilton.
Reading, Pa.—Charles N. Seitzinger.
Richmond, Va.—Edgar Allen, Jr.
Rochester, N. Y.—Joseph A. Crane.
St. Joseph, Mo.—Laurence G. Weakley.
St. Louis, Mo.—Colin M. Selph.
St. Paul, Minn.—Edward Yanish.
Salt Lake City, Utah—A. L. Thomas.
San Antonio, Tex.—John J. Stevens.
San Francisco, Cal.—Charles W. Fay.
Seattle, Wash.—Edgar Battle.
Springfield, Ill.—L. E. Wheeler.
Springfield, Mass.—Louis C. Hyde.
Toledo, O.—W. H. Tucker.
Trenton, N. J.—A. C. Yard.
Troy, N. Y.—A. E. Bonesteel.
Washington, D. C.—Norman A. Merritt.

CONGRESSMEN ELECTED IN 1913.

MAINE, THIRD DISTRICT, SEPT. 8.
John A. Peters, Rep. 15,081
William A. Pattengall, Dem. 14,556
Edward M. Lawrence, Prog. 6,558
William W. Wyer, Soc. 475

MARYLAND, THIRD DISTRICT, NOV. 4.
Charles T. Coady, democrat, was elected to fill vacancy in third district.

MASSACHUSETTS, THIRD DISTRICT, NOV. 4.
Calvin D. Paige, Rep. 11,173
M. Fred O'Connell, Dem. 10,831
Stephen M. Marshall, Prog. 5,284
John J. Mitchell, democrat, was elected April 15, to represent the thirteenth Massachusetts district. His plurality over Alfred H. Cutting was 4,148, while Cutting's plurality over Norman H. White, progressive, was 3,200.

NEW JERSEY, SIXTH DISTRICT, JULY 22.
Archibald C. Hart, Dem. 8,722
Steven W. McClave, Rep. 2,993
Herbert M. Bailey, Prog. 2,420
Henry M. Dutt, Nat. Pro. 259
Frederick Krafft, Soc. 85

NEW YORK, THIRTEENTH DISTRICT, NOV. 4.
George W. Loft, Dem.-Ind. 5,945
Samuel M. Hyman, Rep. 2,409
Victor Tozzi, Prog. 2,132
Joshua Wanhope, Soc. 828
Harry M. Applebaum, Home Rule. 303

NEW YORK, TWENTIETH DISTRICT, NOV. 4.
Jacob A. Cantor, Dem.-Ind. 5,337
Louis A. Guterman, Rep. 2,991
Isaac A. Hourwich, Prog. 3,206
Edwin F. Cassidy, Soc. 1,210

FLAG OF THE UNITED STATES.

The national flag of the United States now consists of thirteen alternate red and white stripes, representing the original thirteen states, and a blue field on which are forty-eight white stars arranged in six rows of eight stars each, representing the forty-eight states now constituting the union. The last two stars were added in 1912 when New Mexico and Arizona were officially admitted as states. June 14 is generally observed as flag display day.

Laws are in force in some of the states forbidding the desecration or mutilation of the flag or its use in any way for advertising purposes. A federal law forbids the use of the national flag on trade marks.

FATAL HOTEL FIRE IN BOSTON.

Twenty-eight men lost their lives in a fire which occurred in the upper floors of the Arcadia hotel, a lodging house in Boston, Mass., early on the morning of Dec. 3, 1913. Many others were seriously injured in making their escape from the building.

HUNTING ACCIDENTS.

In the big game hunting season ending Nov. 30, 1913, 125 men were killed and 125 injured. The states having the largest number of fatalities were: Wisconsin, 29; Michigan, 28; New York, 19, and Maine, 12.

OHIO AND INDIANA FLOODS.

Time—March 22-27, 1913.
Lives lost—In Ohio, 452; in Indiana, 54.
Houses destroyed—3,000.
Damage to property, $163,000,000.

Torrential rains falling over the greater part of Ohio and Indiana March 22-27, 1913, resulted in one of the most disastrous floods in the history of the United States. More than 500 lives were lost, while the damage to property, as carefully estimated by the weather bureau, amounted to the enormous total of $163,000,000. Two distinct storms from the west and southwest caused the excessive precipitation. The first was the tornadic disturbance which wrought havoc in Omaha, Neb., Terre Haute, Ind., and intermediate places; the second came directly after the first so that the rainfall blended. The heaviest precipitation reported for the two storms of five days' duration was at Bellefontaine, O., where a total of 11.16 inches was recorded, 5.61 inches falling on the 25th alone. Marion, O., reported 10.60 inches and Bangerville, O., Madison, Ind., and Shoals, Ind., each had more than eight inches. The precipitation at Cincinnati for a period of 72 hours—March 24-27, inclusive—was greater than during any previous like period in the history of the city, and the same statement, according to the weather officials, was probably true of all other places in Ohio and Indiana in the region of greatest rainfall between March 23 and March 27.

This unprecedented amount of water falling on ground already saturated from previous rains caused all the rivers and streams to overflow their banks even where the latter were protected by levees. The flood-plains were inundated and everything situated on low ground was submerged. Houses, railway bridges and structures of all kinds were either swept away or almost irreparably damaged. Though in most cases warning had been given of the coming flood many persons remained in their dwellings until it was too late to escape.

The cities in which the greatest loss of life occurred were Dayton, Hamilton and Columbus, O. Drownings occurred in twenty-three cities in Ohio and in fourteen places in Indiana. In Dayton, O., according to the records of the American National Red Cross, there were 108 fatalities, in Hamilton, O., 98, and in Columbus, 92. The remainder of the 452 deaths in the state occurred at Chillicothe, Miamisburg, Piqua, Zanesville, Delaware, Tiffin, Mount Vernon, Middletown, Fremont, Harrison, Massillon, Troy, Coshocton and smaller towns. In Brookville, Ind., 16 deaths were reported, while there were 11 in Peru, 7 in Fort Wayne and 4 each in Washington and Terre Haute. Other Indiana cities in which drownings occurred were West Indianapolis, Frankfort, Logansport, Lafayette, Rushville, Skelton, New Castle and East Mount Carmel. Probably there never will be an agreement as to the exact number of fatalities in the places named. In Ohio, for example, only 444 bodies were recovered, but it was known that at least eight more were drowned.

The experience of Dayton was typical of that of other cities. The town is situated on the Miami river, which receives two tributary streams within the city limits, the Mad river and the Stillwater river. One-half of Dayton stands on a flood-plain which is protected by levees built to withstand a stage of twenty-three feet. The main river flows in a narrower channel below the confluences than it does above, and this channel was also further obstructed by bridges. The water rose above the levees, broke them in places and suddenly submerged the lower part of the city to a depth of ten feet. The lighter structures were swept away by the rush of the flood and those who had not sought higher ground were drowned. For a time the city was without communication with the outside world and rumors were circulated that several thousand lives had been lost. These, happily, were far from being true, grave as the calamity was in reality. More than 10,000 homes were invaded by water to a depth ranging from a few inches to fifteen feet. It was estimated by Ernest P. Bicknell, national director of the American Red Cross, that in the Ohio river valley, including the flooded sections of Ohio, West Virginia, Indiana, Illinois and Kentucky, more than 50,000 homes were inundated and about 3,000 destroyed. The rivers that caused the greatest amount of damage were the Great Miami, Scioto, Muskingum, Mahoning, Maumee, Sandusky, Wabash, White and Ohio. The cities in Illinois that were chiefly affected were Cairo, Shawneetown and Golconda. On the Kentucky side of the Ohio the towns of Birdsville, Smithland, Columbus and Wickliffe were inundated.

While the floods were in progress the national guard, naval reserves and members of the life saving service were used for rescue work, guard duty, distribution of supplies and various other purposes. To the Red Cross organization, however, fell the bulk of the arduous work of providing emergency relief to thousands of persons in the flooded regions. In this its officers were assisted by the state and federal authorities, the headquarters for most of the operations being established in Columbus, O. Contributions came in rapidly both in the shape of money and supplies. The total amount so contributed cannot be given, as much was sent direct by individuals or was distributed by the neighbors and friends of the destitute. The Red Cross Magazine for July, 1913, published the following statement of contributions received by the national treasurer of the Red Cross for the storm and relief fund of 1913. It does not include money remitted direct to Red Cross and other relief agents in the flood district:

Alabama	$2,064.69	Nevada	392.50
Arizona	811.95	New Jersey..	15,106.40
Arkansas	2,905.98	New Mexico..	2,176.08
California ...	148,386.76	New York....	652,773.78
Canal Zone...	50.00	N. Carolina..	7,664.40
Colorado	28,677.70	N. Dakota....	4,626.95
Connecticut..	50,397.15	Ohio	24,266.48
Delaware ...	3,065.00	Oklahoma ...	723.59
Dist. Columbia	44,197.89	Oregon	852.15
Florida	5,325.65	Pennsylvania.	61,099.09
Georgia	6,035.62	Porto Rico...	1,045.85
Idaho	1,688.35	Rhode Island.	10,667.33
Illinois	177,716.80	S. Carolina..	9,022.82
Indiana	1,699.55	S. Dakota....	2,045.21
Iowa	22,825.88	Tennessee ...	2,170.93
Kansas	9,517.97	Texas	15,658.79
Kentucky ...	915.57	Utah	663.80
Louisiana ...	2,772.30	Vermont	2,703.14
Maine	4,398.37	Virginia	16,270.47
Maryland ...	28,129.49	Washington..	20,756.28
Massachusetts	219,777.86	W. Virginia..	7,535.62
Michigan ...	108,304.46	Wisconsin ...	20,273.85
Minnesota ...	77,335.77	Wyoming	187.50
Mississippi ..	1,509.57	Foreign	24,805.19
Missouri	88,521.19	Unclassified..	201.42
Montana	14,390.85		
Nebraska	196.67	Total........$1,961,198.79	
N. Hampshire	5,890.50		

Among the heaviest losers in the flooded districts were the railroads. Scores of bridges were carried away, miles of roadbed were washed out and the service was suspended or disorganized for weeks. Their total loss was estimated at between $10,000,000 and $15,000,000. The Pennsylvania, Baltimore & Ohio, Big Four and Monon roads suffered the most severely.

FLOODS IN TEXAS.

Heavy rains caused the Brazos and Colorado rivers and tributary streams in central and southern Texas to overflow their banks during the first two weeks of December, 1913. The loss of nearly 200 lives was reported, most of the victims being colored, while the damage to property was estimated at about $5,000,000. Hundreds of homes in Waco were submerged by the waters of the Brazos river. Drownings occurred at Belton, Bryan, Brownwood, Marlin, Temple, Sunnyside and other places.

UNITED STATES POSTAL SERVICE.

GROWTH OF SERVICE SINCE 1850.

Year.	Revenue.	Expenditures.	Deficit.	Total offices.	Presidential offices.
1850	$5,499,984.86	$5,212,953.43		18,417	....
1860	8,518,067.40	19,170,609.89	$19,652,542.49	28,498	433
1870	19,772,220.65	23,998,837.63	4,226,616.98	28,492	1,093
1880	33,315,479.34	36,542,805.65	3,227,324.34	42,989	1,760
1890	60,882,097.92	66,259,547.84	5,377,449.93	52,401	2,748
1895	76,983,128.19	87,179,551.28	10,196,423.09	70,064	3,506
1900	102,354,579.29	107,740,267.99	5,385,688.70	76,691	4,237
1910	224,128,657.62	229,977,224.50	5,881,481.95	59,580	7,592
1911	237,879,823.60	237,648,926.68	*219,118.12	59,237	7,977
1912	246,744,015.88	248,525,450.08	1,785,523.10	58,729	8,228
1913	266,619,525.65	262,067,540.33	*4,510,650.91	58,020	8,406

*Surplus.

NOTE—July 1, 1863, first-class postage, 3 cents per one-half ounce, any distance; Oct. 1, 1883, first-class postage, 2 cents per one-half ounce, any distance; July 1, 1885, first-class postage, 2 cents per ounce, any distance.

RAILWAY MAIL SERVICE.

Year	Clerks.	Cost.	Year.	Clerks.	Cost.
1868 (est.)	64	....*....	1905	12,284	$13,285,242.94
1870	1,157	....*....	1906	13,401	14,177,969.99
1880	2,946	$1,367,463.35	1907	14,184	16,175,687.76
1890	5,836	5,562,844.26	1908	15,295	17,373,336.92
1895	6,481	7,103,025.30	1909	15,866	18,356,800.13
1900	8,695	8,838,993.92	1910	16,579	19,389,414.44
1901	9,105	9,675,436.52	1911	16,792	20,106,909.40
1902	9,627	10,264,588.38	1912	16,636	20,711,675.12
1903	10,418	11,228,845.75	1913	17,547	22,925,614.11
1904	11,437	12,105,549.77			

*Cost of service included with "Transportation of mails" prior to 1876.

CITY FREE-DELIVERY SERVICE.

Year.	Carriers.	Cost.	Year.	Carriers.	Cost.
1863 (est.)	685	$204,477.77	1905	21,778	$20,919,078.13
1870	1,362	1,231,340.68	1906	22,965	22,057,176.70
1880	2,628	2,363,717.71	1907	24,577	23,248,535.90
1890	9,066	7,977,514.26	1908	26,352	26,343,201.19
1895	12,714	12,145,408.77	1909	27,620	29,770,650.36
1900	15,322	14,512,190.04	1910	28,715	31,737,673.64
1901	16,389	15,752,600.00	1911	29,168	33,087,478.80
1902	17,785	17,123,310.90	1912	29,962	34,162,562.83
1903	19,542	18,337,986.00	1913	30,920	36,317,196.99
1904	20,761	20,561,209.01			

RURAL FREE-DELIVERY SERVICE.

1897	44	....*....	1906	35,866	$24,738,980.79
1898	148	$49,999.71	1907	37,582	26,653,304.36
1899	391	149,979.69	1908	39,143	34,355,209.04
1900	1,276	420,433.17	1909	40,499	35,549,260.34
1901	4,301	1,749,525.06	1910	40,997	37,041,156.09
1902	8,466	3,993,708.51	1911	41,560	37,122,264.02
1903	15,119	8,011,635.48	1912	42,169	41,840,910.94
1904	24,465	12,640,070.35	1913	42,685	45,663,071.62
1905	32,055	20,819,944.69			

*Cost included in "City free-delivery" service.

RECEIPTS AND EXPENDITURES.

Fiscal year ended June 30, 1913.

RECEIPTS.

Sales of stamps, cards, etc.	$239,749,038.55
Second class postage, paid in money	9,975,348.92
3d and 4th class postage, paid in money	6,044,760.25
Box rents	4,780,762.77
Miscellaneous receipts	155,380.31
Letter postage, paid in money	207,309.65
Fines and penalties	93,650.46
Dead letters	31,143.01
Revenue from money-order business	5,188,740.97
Unpaid money orders more than one year old	393,390.76
Total	266,619,525.65

EXPENDITURES.

Advertising	$4,278.69
Rent of buildings, postoffice department	34,400.00
Electric power, light, etc.	4,633.75
Postoffice inspectors	1,190,320.47

Payment of rewards	17,741.15
Mis. expenses, postmaster-general	184.70
Compensation to postmasters	29,146,662.47
Assistant postmasters and clerks	45,785,826.34
Rent, light and fuel	4,421,136.00
Mis. items, 1st and 2d class offices	620,217.59
Canceling machines, etc.	307,033.57
Mechanical and labor-saving devices	45,949.32
City delivery service	36,317,196.99
Special delivery service	1,675,653.57
Miscellaneous expenses first assistant postmaster-general	328.46
Mail transportation in Alaska, star	231,283.16
Mail transportation, boat	835,965.26
Mail-messenger service	1,647,202.26
Pneumatic tube service	959,765.87
Wagon service	1,721,016.90
Mail bags, etc.	283,219.43
Laborers, mail-bag repair shops	97,567.11
Mail equipment shop, Chicago, Ill.	2,204.87
Mail locks and keys, etc.	13,111.07
Laborers, mail-lock repair shop	24,607.37
Mail transportation, railroad	47,393,266.39
Freight on mail bags, postal cards, etc.	443,770.24
Railway postoffice car service	4,566,121.27
Railway mail service	22,925,614.11
Electric and cable car service	693,862.25
Transportation of foreign mails	3,457,222.11
Assistant supt., division foreign mails	2,708.34
Balance due foreign countries	690,762.38
Miscellaneous expenses, second assistant postmaster-general	335.22
Manufacture of postage stamps	687,381.02
Manufacture of stamped envelope and newspaper wrappers	1,417,525.71
Distribution of stamped and official envelopes, etc.	20,949.50
Manufacture of postal cards	271,926.40
Ship, steamboat and way letters	67.95
Indemnities, domestic registered mail	42,338.88
Indemnities, internat'l registered mail	7,326.25
Miscellaneous expenses, third assistant postmaster-general	508.61
Unpaid money orders more than one year old	391,892.22
Stationery	195,179.00
Official and registry envelopes	71,051.51
Blanks, etc., money order service	132,543.81
Miscellaneous items, registry system	5,874.56
Supplies, city delivery service	82,412.09
Postmarking, rating and money order stamps	43,422.75
Letter balances and scales	5,743.75
Wrapping paper	9,770.95
Wrapping twine and tying devices	207,291.09
Facing slips, etc.	75,801.71
Typewriters, etc.	53,191.44
Supplies, rural delivery service	29,341.58
Shipment of supplies	93,558.01
Intaglio seals, foreign mail service	7,989.65
Mail transportation, star	6,851,276.32
Rural delivery service	45,663,071.32
Miscellaneous expenses, fourth assistant postmaster-general	416.80
Parcel post	87,104.82
Labor saving device Chicago postoffice	5,644.21
Village delivery	23,948.98
Inspection agency, Cincinnati, O.	5,010.54
Net audited expenditures	262,067,541.33

ILLINOIS STATE OFFICIALS.

ILLINOIS CIVIL LIST.
Corrected to Dec. 1, 1913.

EXECUTIVE DEPARTMENT. Salary.
Governor—Edward F. Dunne, D., Cook county.$12,000
Lieutenant-Governor—Barratt O'Hara, D., Cook
county 2,500
Secretary of State—Harry Woods, D., Cook
county 7,500
Auditor—James J. Brady, D., Cook county... 7,500
Treasurer—William Ryan, Jr., D., Vermilion
county 10,000
Superintendent of Public Instruction—Francis
G. Blair, R., Coles county................. 7,500
Attorney-General—Patrick J. Lucey, D., La-
Salle county............................... 10,000
Insurance Superintendent—Rufus M. Potts... 5,000
The Adjutant-General—Col. F. S. Dickson.... 5,000

THE SUPREME COURT.
The Supreme court consists of seven judges, elected for a term of nine years, one from each of the
seven districts into which the state is divided.
The election is held in June of the year in which
any term expires.

JUSTICES.
Dist.   Salary $10,000.   Term expires.
1. Alonzo K. Vickers, East St. Louis....June, 1915
2. William M. Farmer, Vandalia.........June, 1915
3. Frank K. Dunn, Charleston...........June, 1915
4. George A. Cooke, chief justice, Aledo..June, 1921
5. Charles C. Craig, Galesburg.........June, 1918
6. James H. Cartwright, Oregon.........June, 1915
7. Orrin N. Carter, Chicago............June, 1915
Reporter—Samuel P. Irwin, Bloomington; salary,
$6,000.
Clerk—J. McCan Davis.
Deputy Clerk—Robert L. Conn.
Librarian—Ralph H. Wilkin; salary, $2,400.
Terms of court are held in Springfield, commencing on the first Tuesday in February, April,
June, October and December.

BOARD OF LAW EXAMINERS.
George W. Wall, president...............DuQuoin
Wm. B. Wright, secretary and treasurer..Effingham
Charles L. Bartlett.....................Quincy
Russell Whitman.........................Chicago
D. B. Snow..............................Ottawa

COURT OF CLAIMS.
Office in Springfield. Salary, $1,500.
Martin A. Brennan, presiding judge...Bloomington
Benjamin P. Alschuler...................Aurora
Geo. W. Dowell..........................DuQuoin
Secretary—James J. Brady, ex officio.

UNIVERSITY OF ILLINOIS.
Located at Champaign and Urbana.
BOARD OF TRUSTEES.
Ex Officio Members—The governor, the president
of the state board of agriculture, the state super-
intendent of public instruction.
Mary E. Busey, Urbana...................1917
Otis W. Holt, Geneseo...................1917
William L. Abbott, Chicago..............1917
Arthur Meeker, Chicago..................1915
John R. Trevett, Champaign..............1919
Ellen M. Henrotin, Chicago..............1919
Laura B. Evans, Taylorville.............1915
Florence E. Watson, Effingham...........1919
Allen F. Moore, Monticello..............1915
(Ex officio members as above.)
President of University—Dr. Edmund J. James.
Secretary and Registrar—Charles Maxwell McConn,
Urbana.
Comptroller—George E. Frazer, Urbana.

STATE NORMAL UNIVERSITY.
Located at Normal.
THE STATE BOARD OF EDUCATION.
Charles L. Capen, president............Bloomington
F. G. Blair, secretary.................Springfield
E. R. E. Kimbrough.....................Danville
J. Stanley Brown.......................Joliet
F. R. Stitt............................El Paso
C. W. Mundell..........................Benton
William P. Wall........................Staunton

A. R. Smith............................Quincy
Silas Echols...........................Mount Vernon
Adrian M. Doolin.......................Chicago
John J. Amsler.........................East Peoria
Henry Hoff.............................Germantown
John L. Brummerstedt...................Altamont
George W. Hughes.......................Hume
Henry Oakes............................Bluffs
President of University—David Felmly.

TRUSTEES EASTERN STATE NORMAL SCHOOL.
Located at Charleston.
J. M. Hicks............................Newton
R. W. Briscoe..........................Kansas
Edward B. Rogers.......................Champaign
E. E. Elstun...........................Greenup
C. C. Lee..............................Charleston
Francis G. Blair, ex officio...........Springfield
President—L. C. Lord.

TRUSTEES WESTERN STATE NORMAL SCHOOL.
Located at Macomb.
C. W. Flack, president.................Macomb
H. E. McLaren, secretary...............Rushville
D. P. Hollis...........................Pittsfield
Joab Green.............................Carthage
S. S. Hallam...........................Monmouth
Albert Eads............................Macomb
Francis G. Blair, ex officio...........Springfield
President—W. P. Morgan.................Macomb

TRUSTEES SOUTHERN NORMAL UNIVERSITY.
Located at Carbondale.
J. M. Burkhart.........................Marion
Hugh Lauder............................Carbondale
William F. Bundy.......................Centralia
H. T. Goddard..........................Mount Carmel
William M. Grissom, Jr.................Vienna
Francis G. Blair, ex officio...........Springfield
President—D. B. Parkinson.

TRUSTEES NORTHERN STATE NORMAL
SCHOOL.
Located at DeKalb.
A. C. Metzel, secretary................Elgin
Leroy A. Goddard.......................Chicago
Frank E. Richey........................LaSalle
R. L. Russell..........................Princeton
E. W. Vaile............................Dixon
Francis G. Blair, ex officio...........Springfield
President—John W. Cook.

TRUSTEES OF STATE HISTORICAL LIBRARY.
Located at Springfield. Salary of librarian, $2,000.
Evarts B. Greene.......................Urbana
Otto L. Schmidt........................Chicago
C. H. Rammelkamp.......................Jacksonville
Librarian—Mrs. Jessie Palmer Weber.

STATE BOARD OF AGRICULTURE 1913-1914.
President—Dr. J. T. Montgomery, Charleston.
Vice-President at Large—George A. Anthony, Kewanee.
Secretary—J. K. Dickirson, Springfield. Salary, $2,000.
Treasurer—J. F. Prather, Williamsville.
Dist.   VICE-PRESIDENTS.
1. Martin Conrad.......................Chicago
2. B. H. Heide.........................Chicago
3. George H. Cooper....................Mokena
4. Albert Mares........................Chicago
5. August W. Miller....................Chicago
6. Dr. John D. Robertson...............Chicago
7. J. J. McComb........................Chicago
8. Louis F. Wilk.......................Chicago
9. J. F. Rehm..........................Chicago
10. W. E. Davis........................Libertyville
11. C. F. Dike.........................North Crystal Lake
12. George H. Madden...................Mendota
13. J. E. Taggart......................Freeport
14. Frank Thornber.....................Carthage
15. W. F. Aten.........................Ray
16. James K. Hopkins...................Princeton
17. Hiett B. Taylor....................Fairbury
18. R. M. Davison......................Marshall
19. A. M. Burk.........................Champaign
20. L. O. Skiles.......................Virginia

21. Charles M. Woods......................Springfield
22. John S. Culp.........................Bethalto
23. Thomas S. Marshall..................Carbondale
24. John W. Shaw........................Harrisburg
25. Joab Goodall............................Marion

BOARD OF COMMISSIONERS OF LABOR.
Salary $5 per day for thirty days.
Salary of secretary, $2,500.
J. T. Patterson............................Chicago
J. D. Peters............................Carbondale
Frank B. Mott..........................Galesburg
M. H. Madden...............................Chicago
Secretary—Patrick H. Hart................Springfield

ILLINOIS FARMERS' INSTITUTE.
Created by act of June 24, 1895. Term, two years.
Salary of secretary, $2,000.
President—A. N. Abbott...................Morrison
Vice-President—H. E. Young...............Chicago
Secretary—H. A. McKeene................Springfield
Treasurer—J. P. Mason.......................Elgin
Auditor—Frank I. Mason.....................Gilman

BOARD OF DIRECTORS.
Ex Officio—Superintendent of public instruction, dean of the college of agriculture, president of state board of agriculture, president State Horticultural society, president State Dairymen's association.
Elected by congressional districts:
1. H. E. Young...........................Chicago
2. August Geweke......................Des Plaines
3. M. K. Sweet..........................Glenwood
4. John M. Clark.........................Chicago
5. O. V. Gregory.........................Chicago
6. P. R. Barnes.......................Forest Glen
7. Henry H. Schwinge...............Norwood Park
8. James B. Clark........................Chicago
9. O. C. Pickett.........................Chicago
10. R. W. Chittenden.......................Gurnee
11. J. P. Mason.............................Elgin
12. George F. Tullock....................Rockford
13. A. N. Abbott........................Morrison
14. William H. Ashdown................Port Byron
15. Frank S. Haynes......................Geneseo
16. Ralph Allen...........................Delavan
17. S. B. Mason.......................Bloomington
18. F. I. Mann............................Gilman
19. J. B. Burrows.........................Decatur
20. A. P. Grout.........................Winchester
21. Edward Grimes........................Raymond
22. E. W. Burroughs..................Edwardsville
23. Joseph Oldfield......................Vandalia
24. D. M. Marlin.......................Norris City
25. W. E. Braden..........................Sparta

INSPECTORS OF GRAIN.
John D. Gibbons, chief (salary, $6,000)....Chicago
J. B. Stevenson (salary, $2,400).......East St. Louis

LIVE STOCK COMMISSIONERS.
Salary $10 a day and expenses; of secretary, $2,000; of veterinarian, $10 a day.
Office at Springfield.
R. J. Shanley, chairman....................Ottawa
L. F. Brown...........................Galesburg
Secretary—C. A. Lowery, Springfield.
State Veterinarian—Dr. O. E. Dyson, Record building, Union stock yards, Chicago.
BOARD OF VETERINARY EXAMINERS, PER DIEM, $5.
C. H. Merrick, M. D. C.................Okawville
John Scott, V. S..........................Peoria
Albert C. Worms, M. D. C................Chicago

STATE BOARD OF EQUALIZATION.
Salary, $1,000.
Elected Nov. 5, 1912. Term of office four years.
1. James J. Murphy, D..3233 Wentworth-av., Chicago
2. Charles W. Secord, P.*..437 W. 117th-st., Chicago
3. Frank McGovern, D......5517 Center-av., Chicago
4. Dennis F. Sullivan, D..1524 W. 51st-st., Chicago
5. J. J. Viterna, D........2157 Hastings-st., Chicago
6. Frank P. Duffy, D..20 N. Hermitage-av., Chicago
7. W. H. Malone, P.*....................Park Ridge
8. Jos. Rushkewicz, D..3536 W. Chicago-av., Chicago
9. Arthur Donoghue, D....820 Sheridan-rd.. Chicago
10. H. T. Nightingale, P.*................Evanston
11. F. H. Ackerman, P.*......................Elgin

12. G. C. Tallerday, P.*................Belvidere
13. Isaac N. Evans, P.*...............Milledgeville
14. John Day, D.............................Moline
15. James R. Albright, D...................Quincy
16. Charles J. Skaggs, D....................Pekin
17. W. E. Baker, D.........................Pontiac
18. Frank P. Martin, R....................Watseka
19. Marion Watson, D........................Arthur
20. Louis D. Hirsheimer, D...............Pittsfield
21. A. W. Crawford, D....................Hillsboro
22. Charles Becker, D.....................Freeburg
23. H. Gregory Weber, D...................Carlyle
24. Louis W. Goetzman, D.............Shawneetown
25. Albert L. Cline, D......................Marion
*Progressive.

STATE ENTOMOLOGIST.
Prof. Stephen A. Forbes.....................Urbana

STATE FOOD COMMISSIONER.
Office, Manhattan building, Chicago. Salary, $3,600.
W. Scott Matthews......................Carbondale

FOOD STANDARD COMMISSION
Created by act of May, 14, 1907. Term, indefinite. Per diem, $15. Office at 431 South Dearborn street, Chicago.
W. Scott Matthews, state food commissioner,
   ex officio.........................Carbondale
Dr. Walter S. Haines.....................Chicago
Thomas P. Sullivan.......................Chicago

BOARD OF HEALTH.
Office at Springfield. Salary of secretary, $3,600.
G. W. Webster. M. D., president..........Chicago
A. Szwajkart, M. D........................Chicago
R. D. Luster, M. D....................Granite City
Walter R. Schussler, M. D.................Orland
T. B. Lewis, M. D........................Hammond
John A. Robinson, M. D...................Chicago

FACTORY INSPECTORS.
Office, 1543 Transportation building, Chicago.
                                          Salary.
Oscar F. Nelson, chief, Chicago............$3,000
Barney Cohen, assistant, Chicago........... 2,250

STATE MINING BOARD.
Office at Springfield. Salary $5 per day and expenses while in service; of secretary, $2,000.
John Bohlander, president...................Pekin
James Forester......................Hallidayboro
Thomas L. Jones.............................Ladd
James Shaw, secretary.....................Virden
J. B. McKiernan, H. E.....................Peoria
Chief Clerk—Martin Bolt.

INSPECTORS OF MINES.
Dist.   Salary, $1,800 per annum.
1. Hector McAllister.....................Streator
2. Thomas Hudson............................Galva
3. John Dunlop............................Peoria
4. James Taylor...........................Peoria
5. J. W. Starks........................Georgetown
6. Thomas P. Back......................Springfield
7. W. W. Williams.......................Litchfield
8. W. L. Morgan...........R. R. 2, East St. Louis
9. Walton Rutledge.........................Alton
10. Thomas Little.....................Murphysboro
11. Frank Rosbottom.......................Benton
12. J. W. Fairbairn.......................Marion

BOARD OF PHARMACY.
Office at Springfield. Salary, $8 a day. Secretary's salary, $3,000.
James P. Crowley, president..............Chicago
J. B. Michela, vice-president.............El Paso
H. C. Christensen........................Chicago
Frederic T. Provost......................Chicago
Lee L. Hrazek............................Chicago
Secretary—Fred C. Dodds.

DENTAL EXAMINERS.
Salary, $5 a day.
Dr. O. H. Seyfert......................Springfield
Dr. Charles F. O'Connor...............Springfield
Dr. N. W. Cox.........................Springfield
Dr. B. A. Smith..........................Chicago
Dr. P. T. Diamond........................Chicago

STATE BOARD OF ADMINISTRATION.
Created by act of June 15, 1909. Term, six years.
Salary, $6,000.

Fred J. Kern, president....................Belleville
James Hyland, secretary.5536 LaSalle street, Chicago
Frank D. Whipp, fiscal supervisor.......Springfield
(Vacancy), alienist...
Thomas O'Connor...............................Peoria

STATE CHARITABLE INSTITUTIONS.
Elgin State hospital—Ralph T. Hinton, M. D.,
superintendent.
Kankakee State hospital—P. M. Kelly, M. D.,
superintendent.
Jacksonville State hospital—H. B. Carriel, M. D.,
superintendent.
Anna State hospital—R. A. Goodner, M. D., super-
intendent.
Watertown State hospital—J. A. Campbell, M. D.,
superintendent.
Peoria State hospital—G. A. Zeller, M. D., super-
intendent.
Chester State hospital—George K. Ferris, M. D.,
superintendent.
Chicago State hospital (Dunning)—George Leining-
er, M. D., superintendent.
Alton State hospital—Frank R. Dinges, business
manager.
The Illinois School for the Deaf at Jacksonville—
C. P. Gillett, superintendent.
Lincoln State School and Colony at Lincoln—T. H.
Leonard, M. D., superintendent.
The Illinois School for the Blind at Jacksonville—
R. W. Woolston, superintendent.
Illinois Industrial Home for the Blind at Chicago—
Wm. F. Schultz, superintendent.
Illinois Soldiers and Sailors' home at Quincy—
Col. J. E. Andrews, superintendent.
The Soldiers' Widows' Home of Illinois at Wil-
mington—Mrs. Flo Jamison Miller, superintendent.
The Illinois Soldiers' Orphans' home at Normal—
Maj. C. E. Bassett, superintendent.
The Illinois Eye and Ear Infirmary at Chicago—
Maj. C. T. Garrard, superintendent.
The State Training School for Girls at Geneva—
Margaret M. Elliott, superintendent.
The St. Charles School for Boys at St. Charles—
Col. C. B. Adams, superintendent.

DEPARTMENTS.
Visitation and Instruction of Adult Blind—Charles
Comstock, 5456 Lexington avenue, Chicago.
Visitation of Dependent, Neglected and Delinquent
Children—Rev. Charles Virden, Springfield.
Support of Inmates—E. R. Amick, Springfield.
Supervising Engineer—James Shea, 818 South
Adams street, Peoria.
Deportation Agent—J. V. Callahan, care of Chi-
cago State hospital, Dunning.
State Psychopathic Institute—H. D. Singer, M. D.,
director, Kankakee.

CHARITIES COMMISSION.
Created by act of June 15, 1909. Term, four years.
No compensation. Secretary's salary, $3,600.
Dr. Edward H. Ochsner......................Chicago
Emil G. Hirsch.............................Chicago
Dr. Anna Dwyer.............................Chicago
Frank Trutter.............................Springfield
John B. Harris............................Champaign
Secretary—A. L. Bowen.

STATE REFORMATORY.
Managers.   Located at Pontiac.
Albert H. Gravenhorst, president.........Effingham
Frank R. Robinson, vice-president..........Oregon
Charles H. May..............................Peoria
John A. Califf...............................Bowen
Dan D. Roughton............................Sullivan
Superintendent—W. C. Graves.

PENITENTIARY COMMISSION.
Created by act of June 5, 1907.
James A. Patten............................Chicago
Ira C. Copley...............................Aurora
John Lambert................................Joliet

COMMISSIONERS OF STATE PENITENTIARY.
Prison located at Joliet. Salary, $1,500.
Warden's salary, $5,000.
James D. McGrath............................Ottawa
Ralph R. Tilton.............................Danville
Charles M. Faltz...........................Somonauk
Warden—Edmund M. Allen.

COMMISSIONERS SOUTHERN PENITENTIARY.
Prison located at Chester. Salary, $1,500.
Frank Orr..............................Mount Sterling
C. F. Colema..............................Vandalia
Omar S. Pace..........................Mount Vernon
Warden—W. V. Cloisser.

BOARD OF PARDONS.
Office at Springfield. Secretary's salary, $2,000.
Lewis G. Stevenson, chairman.........Bloomington
C. E. Jennings..............................Salem
William Colvin............................Springfield
Clerk—Thos. M. Kilbride.

BOARD OF ARBITRATION.
Office at Springfield. Salary, $1,500. Secretary's
salary, $2,500.
D. J. Normoyle.............................Chicago
Harry M. Powell.............................Peoria
R. F. Shadley.............................Galesburg
Secretary—Fred E. Sterling................Rockford

STATE SUPERVISING ARCHITECT.
Salary, $5,000.
James B. Dibelka...........................Chicago

EXAMINERS OF ARCHITECTS.
Office, 1113 Chamber of Commerce, Chicago.
N. Clifford Ricker, president..............Urbana
Peter B. Wight, secretary-treasurer.......Chicago
Francis M. Barton..........................Chicago
Leonard F. W. Stoebe.......................Danville
Michael B. Kane.........................Edwardsville
Salary of secretary, $1,800; of members, $10 a
day for actual service. Fee charged for examina-
tion, $15; fee for issuing license, $25.

RAILROAD AND WAREHOUSE COMMISSION-
ERS.
Office at Springfield. Salary, $4,000; of chairman,
$6,000; of secretary, $3,500.
O. F. Berry, chairman......................Carthage
Richard Yates.............................Springfield
James A. Willoughby.......................Belleville
Secretary—William Kilpatrick.
Note—The commission ceased to exist Dec. 31,
1913, and was succeeded by the public utilities
commission.

VOTING-MACHINE COMMISSIONERS.
Term, four years. Compensation not to exceed
$1,500 a year and expenses.
Morris Emmerson...........................Lincoln
Amos Miller...............................Hillsboro
Secretary of state.......................Springfield

CANAL COMMISSIONERS.
Office at Lockport. Salary, $5 a day.
Sherman L. Marshall.........................Ipava
H. P. Dwyer................................Minooka
Edward S. Monahan..........................Sheridan

STATE VETERINARIAN.
Salary, $10 a day.
Dr. O. E. Dyson, Union stock yards........Chicago

STATE CIVIL SERVICE COMMISSION.
Office at Springfield.
Created by act of May 11, 1905. Salary of presi-
dent, $4,000; of two members, $3,000 each;
of secretary, $3,500.
James H. Burdett, president................Chicago
A. B. Culhane.............................Rockford
William B. Moulton.........................Chicago
Secretary—Ward R. Robinson.

BOARD OF EXAMINERS OF PUBLIC ACCOUNTANTS.
Office at University of Illinois, Urbana.
S. H. Strawn..................................Chicago
W. A. Chase..................................Chicago
J. A. Cooper.................................Chicago
Secretary—M. H. Robinson, Urbana.

STATE HIGHWAY COMMISSION.
Created by act of June 27, 1913. Term, six years.
Office in Springfield.
A. D. Gash, president........................Chicago
S. E. Bradt, secretary.......................DeKalb
James P. Wilson.................................Polo
State Highway Engineer—A. N. Johnson.
Assistant State Highway Engineer—R. C. McArdle.

COMMISSIONERS OF UNIFORM LAWS.
Created by act of June 3, 1909. Term, four years.
John C. Richberg.............................Chicago
O. A. Harker..................................Urbana
John H. Wigmore..............................Chicago
Ernest Freund................................Chicago
Nathan W. McChesney..........................Chicago

STATE AGENTS TO ENFORCE THE LAW IN RELATION TO CRUELTY TO ANIMALS.
Created by act of May 25, 1877. Term, two years.
Salary, $1,200.
Bernard Shine................................Chicago
Thomas C. Johnson..............................Peoria
Philip D. Liehner.......................East St. Louis
Charles Ahrens..........................East St. Louis

ILLINOIS FREE EMPLOYMENT OFFICES.
Created by act of April 11, 1899. Term, two years.
Salary, $1,500.
Chicago Offices—South side, 732 South Wabash avenue; John Rowland, superintendent. North side, 826 North Clark street; August A. Berkes, superintendent. West side, corner Canal and Randolph streets; William Mazurek, superintendent.
Peoria Office—John W. Kimsey, superintendent.
East St. Louis Office—William Roach, superintendent.
Springfield Office—Charles H. Kay, superintendent.
Rockford Office—John A. Croon, superintendent.
Rock Island and Moline Office—Cornelius Donovan, superintendent.

STATE ART COMMISSION.
Created by act of June 4, 1909. Term, four years.
No compensation.
Lorado Taft..................................Chicago
Ralph Clarkson...............................Chicago
W. Carbys Zimmerman..........................Chicago
Karl Bell....................................Chicago
Frederic Clay Bartlett.......................Chicago
William Holabird.............................Chicago
J. C. Vaughan................................Chicago

ILLINOIS PARK COMMISSION.
Created by act of June 10, 1911. Term, three years.
No compensation.
J. A. James.................................Evanston
Alexander Richards...........................Ottawa

CHIEF INSPECTOR OF PRIVATE EMPLOYMENT AGENCIES.
Created by act of June 15, 1909. Term, indefinite.
Salary, $3,600.
R. J. Knight, 732 South Wabash avenue....Chicago

ILLINOIS LIBRARY EXTENSION BOARD.
Created by act of June 14, 1909. Term, two years.
Joseph H. Freeman............................Aurora
Eugenie M. Bacon.............................Decatur
Secretary of state, ex officio.

BARBERS' EXAMINING BOARD.
Created by act of June 10, 1909. Term, two years.
Compensation, $4 per day each and expenses.
James Ahern, president.......................Chicago
Thomas Casey, treasurer..................Rock Island
Thomas T. Notter, secretary, 2824 Lee-av., Chicago

RIVERS AND LAKES COMMISSION.
Created by act of June 10, 1911. Term, three years.
Salary, $5,000.
Thomas J. Healy..............................Chicago
Arthur W. Charles..............................Carmi
Walter A. Shaw...............................Chicago

BOARD OF EXAMINERS OF REGISTERED NURSES.
Created by act of May 2, 1907. Term, three years.
Anna L. Tittman, Springfield....................1914
Julia E. Pubbick, Rockford......................1915
Mary A. Walsh, Chicago..........................1915
Bena Henderson, Chicago.........................1911
Anna Hanrahan, Chicago..........................1910

STATE FIRE MARSHAL.
Created by act of June 15, 1909. Term, four years.
Salary, $3,000.
R. F. Mogaridge (acting)..................Springfield

STATE INSPECTOR OF APIARIES.
Created by act of June 7, 1911. Term, two years.
Salary, $2,000.
Abraham L. Kildow........................Putnam

COMMISSION TO REVISE AND CODIFY BUILDING LAWS.
Created by act of May 25, 1911.
N. C. Ricker, architect, chairman............Urbana
Richard E. Schmidt, architect...............Chicago
W. C. Armstrong, engineer...................Chicago
I. O. Baker, engineer........................Urbana
W. H. Merrill, fireproofing.................Chicago
George J. Jobst, contractor...................Peoria
William Sherman Stahl, attorney, secretary.Chicago

STATE GAME AND FISH CONSERVATION COMMISSION.
Office in Springfield. Salary of president, $4,000; of other two members, $3,000 each.
C. J. Dittmer, president...................Freeport
Henry Von Meeteren..........................Chicago
John B. Vaughn...........................Carlinville

STATE BOARDS EX OFFICIO.
BOARD OF PRISON INDUSTRIES.
Created by act of May 11, 1903. Salary of sales manager, $3,600.
Commissioners of Illinois state penitentiary.
Commissioners of southern Illinois penitentiary.
Board of managers of Illinois state reformatory.
H. Dollarhide, sales manager, Springfield.
COMMISSIONERS OF STATE CONTRACTS.
Created by act of March 31, 1874.
Secretary of state, auditor of public accounts, state treasurer, attorney-general.
COMMISSIONERS OF THE STATE LIBRARY.
Created by act of March 6, 1867.
Governor, secretary of state, superintendent of public instruction; secretary of state, librarian, Springfield.
TRUSTEES OF THE LINCOLN MONUMENT.
Created by act of May 18, 1895. Salary of custodian, $1,200.
Governor, superintendent of public instruction, state treasurer; E. S. Johnson, custodian, Springfield.
TRUSTEES OF THE NATURAL HISTORY MUSEUM.
Created by act of May 25, 1877. Salary of curator, $3,000.
Governor, secretary of state, superintendent of public instruction; A. R. Crook, curator, Springfield.
STATE CANVASSING BOARD.
Created by act of April 3, 1872.
Governor, secretary of state, auditor, state treasurer, attorney-general.
TRUSTEES OF THE LINCOLN HOMESTEAD.
Created by act of June 16, 1887. Salary of custodian, $1,500.
Governor, secretary of state, auditor of public accounts, state treasurer, superintendent of public instruction; Albert S. Edwards, custodian, Springfield.
FORT MASSAC TRUSTEES.
Created by act of May 15, 1903. Salary of custodian, $600.
Governor, secretary of state, auditor of public accounts, state regent Illinois Daughters of Amer-

ican Revolution. two Illinois Daughters of American Revolution, D. E. Bailey, custodian, Metropolis.

STATE GEOLOGICAL COMMISSION.
Created by act of May 12, 1905
Governor, president of the University of Illinois; T. C. Chamberlin, Chicago; Frank W. De Wolf, director, Urbana

STALLION REGISTRATION BOARD.
Created by act of June 10, 1909
Secretary state board of agriculture
State veterinarian
President Illinois Horse Breeders' association.
Secretary Illinois Horse Breeders' association.
President Illinois Farmers' institute.

ILLINOIS COUNTY OFFICERS.

County. County seat	County and Probate judges.	County clerk.	Circuit clerk and recorder.
Adams—Quincy	Lyman McCarl	John A Connery	Erde W. Beatty
			J M Buffinton, R
Alexander—Cairo	Wm S Dewey	Jesse E. Miller	C O Foster
Bond—Greenville	Wm. H Dawdy	W. E. McCaslin	J. F. Johnston
Boone—Belvidere	Wm. C. DeWolf	William Bowley	A. O. Fassett
Brown—Mount Sterling	W. Y. Baker	William C. Perry	E B Glaze
Bureau—Princeton	J. R. Pritchard	James Fletcher	Henry Fuller
Calhoun—Hardin	O. E Cooke	John Day, Jr	W. D. Godar
Carroll—Mount Carroll	J D Turnbaugh	A B. Adams.	V. Boerner
Cass—Virginia	Charles A E Martin	Louis O. Skiles	L. D. Springer
Champaign—Urbana	William G. Spurgin	Fred Hess	Boyd S. Blaine
Christian—Taylorville	Charles A Prater	Henry J. Burke	J. A. Foll
Clark—Marshall	H R Snaveley	W. F. Martin, Jr	Jay Swern
Clay—Louisville	A. N. Tolliver	Samuel A. Stanford	W H Burns
Clinton—Carlyle	James Allen	Adam Junker	H H Schlarmann
Coles—Charleston	John P. Harragh	George S. Boulware	Bert E. Cole
Cook—Chicago	John E. Owens	R. M. Sweitzer	John W. Rainey
	Daniel H. Gregg, P.	J. A. Cervenka, P	Joseph F. Connery, R.
Crawford—Robinson	J. C. Maxwell	Charles V. Coulter	Charles A. Montgomery
Cumberland—Toledo	S B. Rariden	Philip Meyer	Charles Cox
DeKalb—Sycamore	W L Pond	S M. Henderson	Walter M Hay
DeWitt—Clinton	Fred C. Hill	E. F. Campbell	Elmer Metz
Douglas—Tuscola	W J. Dolson	Charles A. Hawkins	H. B Morgan
DuPage—Wheaton	Charles D. Clark	H. F. Lawrence	George W. Thoma
Edgar—Paris	D V. Dayton	Charles Crum	T. J. Brewer
Edwards—Albion	Peter C. Walters	Arch O. Smith	Earl S. Bunting
Effingham—Effingham	Barney Overbeck	Calvin O. Loy	J. G. Habing
Fayette—Vandalia		George A. Brown	M L. Staff
Ford—Paxton	M L. McQuiston	L. B. Jackson	Carl E. Bengtson
Franklin—Benton	Thomas J. Layman	William D seeber	J J Hill
Fulton—Lewistown	Hobart S. Bayd	Austin Onion.	Eugene Whiting
Gallatin—Shawneetown	H P. Bogarth	Henry G. Sanks.	James G Gregg
Greene—Carrollton	Thos Henshaw	Thomas D. Doyle	J. W. Farrelly
Grundy—Morris.	George Bedford	George W. Anderson	F. S Johnson
Hamilton—McLeansboro	Isaac H Webb	L E Lambert	Frank Porter
Hancock—Carthage	J. Arthur Baird	Frank Thornber.	E O. Reaugh
Hardin—Elizabethtown	E N Hall	L. T. Rash.	Charles L. Hess
Henderson—Oquawka.	R F. Robinson	J. J. Barnes.	W. P Martin
Henry—Cambridge	L E. Telleen	Elmer E Fitch	J. A. Horberg
Iroquois—Watseka	John H Gillan	Clarence South.	Fred Benjamin
Jackson—Murphysboro	W. F. Ellis	James W. Browne	Reynold Gardner
Jasper—Newton	H M. Kasserman	H K Powell	W E Trainor
Jefferson—Mount Vernon.	A D Webb	John G. Young	Burrell Hawkins
Jersey—Jerseyville	H W Pogue	John C. McGrath.	A H. Quinn
Jo Daviess—Galena	John C. Boevers	E J Menzemer.	H. L. Heer
Johnson—Vienna	F. H. Hight	E F Throgmorton	Grant McFatridge
Kane—Geneva	F. G. Plain	William F Lynch	J. L. Johnson
	John H Williams, P.	B. D. Galbraith, P	Frank E. George. R.
Kankakee—Kankakee	A W Deselm	J B. Flageole.	Luther B Brattou
Kendall—Yorkville	C. S. Williams	Edward Budd, Jr	Avery N. Beebe
Knox—Galesburg.	R. C Rice	Frank L. Adams.	C. H Westerberg
Lake—Waukegan	Perry L Persons	A L Hendee	L O. Brockway
LaSalle—Ottawa	W. H Hinebaugh	A. E Back	J. L Witzeman
	A T Lardin P.	J. N. St Clair P	J F. Buchner, R.
Lawrence—Lawrenceville	J. A Benson	George A Brookhart	O H. Hedden
Lee—Dixon	Robert H Scott	W. C Thompson	W B McMahan
Livingston—Pontiac	W. C Graves	William W Kenny.	J G Whitson
Logan—Lincoln	Charles J. Gelbach	J W. Corwine	Lynn R. Parker
Macon—Decatur	O W. Smith	M F Pentwell.	John Allen
Macoupin—Carlinville	Truman A Snell	W. C Seehausen	Thomas Cain
Madison—Edwardsville	J E Hilliskotter	Harry J. Mackinaw	Simon Kellerman
	J P. Streuber, P.	J. B Coppinger.	John Berner, R.
Marion—Salem.	Charles E Jennings	Robert J Bransou	John M. Shultz
Marshall—Lacon	Dan H. Gregg	Thomas A Connell	William L Wescott
Mason—Havana.	Jas. A. McComas	A F Terrell.	C F. Walsh
Massac—Metropolis	W F Smith	George C. Schneeman.	Arthur H. Finley
McDonough—Macomb	C. G. Gumbart	J H Foster	A Warren Ford
McHenry—Woodstock	D. T. Smiley	Guy E. Still	Theodore Hamer
McLean—Bloomington	Homer W. Hall	P. A. Guthrie	John C. Allen
			N B Carson, R
Menard—Petersburg.	G. E. Nelson	A W. Hartley	Ross A. Nance
Mercer—Aledo	H E. Burgess	F A Gibson	S. A Nelson
Monroe—Waterloo	Frank Durfee	Henry Eisenbart.	Louis A. Wiebl
Montgomery—Hillsboro.	J L Dryer	A N Banes	Hugh Hall
Morgan—Jacksonville	Edward P Brockhouse	C. A. Boruff	Eugene D Pyatt
Moultrie—Sullivan	Isaac Hudson	Cash W. Green	Fred O Gaddis
Ogle—Oregon	Frank E. Reed	R. F. Adams	John D. Mead

County. County seat.	County and Probate judges.	County clerk	Circuit clerk and recorder
Peoria—Peoria	C. E. Stone	O. Heinrich	George F. Thade
	Walter L. Clinch, P.	C. A. Roberts, P	John J. Gallagher, R.
Perry—Pinckneyville.	M. C Cook	H R Sims	Charles H. S. Ross
Piatt—Monticello..	E. J. Hawbaker	Harvey Fay	B G. Duncan
Pike—Pittsfield	Paul F. Grote	W S Binns	Henry Bowers
Pope—Golconda..	W. A. Whiteside	Charles A. Werner	T. Roy Vaughn
Pulaski—Mound City.	W. A. Wall	Roy N. Adams	E P. Easterday
Putnam—Hennepin	W. H. Westcott	Charles C. Grelner	H. B. Ramage
Randolph—Chester	W M. Schuwerk	William R. Karstetel	Charles J. Kilbu
Richland—Olney	Stephen C Lewis	I. C. Head	Charles Goudy
Rock Island—Rock Island	Robert W. Olmsted	Henry B, Hubbard, P	Sam Ryerson, R.
	B. S. Bell, P.		G. W. Gamble
Saline—Harrisburg	K. C. Ronalds	John Rinck, P	
Sangamon—Springfield	J. B. Weaver	Charles W. Byres	Joseph H. Drennan
	C. H Jenkins, P.		Herbert Woods, R
Schuyler—Rushville	John C. Work	Isaac Lewis	E. Ross Chitwood
Scott—Winchester..	F. C. Funk	John R King	J W Kellem
Shelby—Shelbyville	J. K P Gridel	J. T Zimmer.	E E Herron
Stark—Toulon	B F Thompson	William E. Nixon..:	Walter F. Young
St. Clair—Belleville	John B Hay	E. F. Winkler	John F O'Flaherty
	Frank Perrin, P	L. P. Mellon, P..	C. A. Summers, R.
Stephenson—Freeport	A. J Clarity	W. L. Boeke	Conrad D Cramer
Tazewell—Pekin	James M. Rahn	George Behrens.	C. O. Myers
Union—Jonesboro	M C. Crawford	C L. Kimmel	H. C. Sifford
Vermilion—Danville.	Lawrence T Allen	Thomas J. Dale..	Ben G Seibert
	Clinton O. Abernethy, P.		W. H. Carter, R.
Wabash—Mount Carmel..	Milburn J White	James H. McClain	G. L. Hockgeiger
Warren—Monmouth	L E Murphy	F. W. Bateman	Arthur S Gibson
Washington—Nashville.	W. P Green	H. F. Heckert.	Oscar H Rinne
White—Carmi.	J C Kern	Matthew Martin	William Poynton
Wayne—Fairfield	Virgil W. Mills	Charles C Johnson	William L Grubb
Whiteside—Morrison.	W. A. Blodgett	W. C. Stilson	Albert T. Skelly
Will—Joliet	G. J Cowing	Edward G. Young	L. H Piepenbrink
	J. B. Fithian, P		
Williamson—Marion	W F Slater	John M Dodd	Leslie O. Caplinger
Winnebago—Rockford	L. M Reckhow	M. A. Norton	L. F Lake
Woodford—Eureka	Arthur O. Furt	Joseph Hertschuh	D. C. Belsley
	P —Probate	R.—Recorder.	

County. Treasurer.	Sheriff	State's attorney	Sup't schools.
Adams—Joseph L. Thomas	Joseph H Lipps	Fred G. Wolffe.	John H. Steiner
Alexander—William D. Pippitt.	A. S. Fisher	Alex Wilson	Fanny P. Hacker
Bond—Joseph M Brown	Shelby W Robinson	John D. Biggs.	H. A. Meyer
Boone—C. W. Watson	William E Gorman	P H O'Donnell.	Elizabeth B. Harvey
Brown—John D. Northern	David W. Shankland	Warren McNeff	C. W. Sellars
Bureau—H C Smith	Charles Beyer	C. N. Holerick	George O. Smith
Calhoun—William Fulkerson	Peter A. Gotway	Thomas J. Selby	S. J. Sibley
Carroll—William H Stitcley	David B Doty	F. J. Stransky.	John Hay
Cass—James R. Sligh	E P. Widmayer	A T. Lucas	Henry Jacobs
Champaign—L N Beal	George W Davis	Louis A Busch	C. H. Watts
Christian—Joseph Brockamp	G. W Brents	Harry Hershey	Henry L Fowkes
Clark—A. M. Tarman	Jesse Gellatin	E. D. Jones	H. W. Drake
Clay—W J Holaday	W H. Thrash	Thomas S Williams	G. O Lewis
Clinton—J. M. Krebs	William Ragen	Hugh V Murray	William Johnston
Coles—Frank F Freeman	Vincent Aye	R G Hammond	W. Ed Miller
Cook—W. L. O'Connell	M Zimmer	Maclay Hoyne	E. J. Tobin
Crawford—E. G. Stifle.	H E. Highsmith	Joseph B. Crowley.	H. E. Green
Cumberland—Jacob C Lyons	Col S. Young	W. O Greathouse	J. W Castelo
DeKalb—Edward Johnson	Frank C Poust	Lowell B. Smith	W W Coultas
DeWitt—William M Price	William H Armstrong	Louis O Williams	John L Costley
Douglas—G R. Duncan	C G Stovall	W. T. Coleman..	E. E. Gere
DuPage—Frank J. Knight	A A Kuhn	O. W. Hadley	R T. Morgan
Edgar—A E. Woods	J. I. Blackman	Wilber H. Hickman	George W. Brown
Edwards—Nathan E. Smith	W. S Rothrock	Edward A Schroeder	W. H Slefferman
Effingham—John Shea	Matt Faber	Byron Piper	J W. Davis
Fayette—Charles E. Yakel	L J. Browning	J. O Burnside..	Frank C. Crawford
Ford—J. H Nelson	M Bristle	O H Wylie	H. M Rudolph
Franklin—J. A McClintock	John A. Vaughn	G. A Hickman	C W. Mundell
Fulton—Butler Fouts	W. H Roy	M. P Rice..	M M. Cook
Gallatin—E. A Harrell	W P Clayton	R. M. McGhee	J. B Boswell
Greene—F. B Dawson	John B. Morrow	Norman L Jones.	G. B. McClelland
Grundy—A H Gleghorn	J H Francis	Frank H Hayes..	C. H Root
Hamilton—G W Mason.	A S Crouse	J. H. Lane.	W W. Dally
Hancock—Charles S. Tyler	Elmer E. McAdams	Clyde P. Johnson.	Stephen D. Faris
Hardin—J. T. Kibler	Edward Ferrell	James E. Denton.	John H. Oxford
Henderson—James E Amerman	R T. McDill	Albert F. Fawley.	Mrs. Della Yeomans
Henry—Charles A. Kellogg	Samuel Wilson	Nels F. Anderson.	A. L. Odenweller
Iroquois—George P. Helkes	James F Ireland	J. W. Kern	E. A. Gilbreath
Jackson—H D Lee	Charles T Edwards	W. A. Schwartz	A. J. Rendelman
Jasper—Taylor Randolph	William Pippin	Charles D Fithian	Milo D. Yelvington
Jefferson—D. C. Youngblood	W. S Payne	Joel F Watson.	A E. Summers
Jersey—Richard Kiely	A R Chappell	Walter J. Chapman	J W. Roberts
Jo Daviess—J A Blughum	Robert Irwin	Frank T. Sheean	Benjamin L. Birkbeck
Johnson—Harry V Carter	John L. Veach	H A Spann	Emma Rebman
Kane—John Evaus.	O. T McBrlarty	William J Tyers	Edw Ellis
Kankakee—Robert A Hewett	Daniel G. Lee	Wayne Dyer	S. D Saltsgiver
Kendall—A. P. Hill	J. R. Henderson	Oliver A Burkhart	A D Curran
Knox—George J Eastes.	Frank F. Seaman	A. J. Boutelle	W. F. Boyes

ILLINOIS COUNTY OFFICERS—CONTINUED

County Treasurer	Sheriff	State's attorney.	Sup't schools.
Lake—Carl P Westerfield	..Elmer J. Green	.. Ralph J Dady.	...T. A Simpson
LaSalle—Edward G. Zilm	J. G. Mischke	George S. Wiley	W R. Foster
Lawrence—John P. Marlin.	W. A. Cochran	..Rolla Shaw...	...R. R. Kimmell
Lee—Frank C. Vaughan..	C. E Reid	... Harry Edwards	. L W Miller
Livingston—L S Henderson ...	W. A. Patterson	. F. A. Ortman ...	. W. E. Herbert
Logan—C. Quisentcrry.	William Schaffenacker	...Everett Smith	D P Nichols
Macon—James T. Lebo	J P Nicholson	..Jesse L Deck	. Mary W. Moore
Macoupin—S. T. Carmody	Elmo Etter	. James H Murphy .	.R C Moore
Madison—Fred A. Elsele)	H. Simon Henry	. James M Baudy.	,J U Uzzel
Marion—J T Arnold ..	...Charles W. Vursell	...Samuel N. Finn ..	... J. F. Hickman
Marshall—Charles R Scoon. ..	Charles F. Motter	H E Jacobs ...	. E F. Perry
Mason—Adolph Schill	..A A Brookes	E P Nischwitz..	.Fannie S Merwin
Massac—Elmer Brown.. . ..	Oscar Miller	... Fred R. Young . .	...W. A. Spence
McDonough—John E. Lane ..	A. P. McKee	⸱.George A. Falder	B. E. Decker
McHenry—Arthur R Crisse).	A H Henderson	. David R. Joslyn..	.A. M. Shelton
McLean—P. M. Stubblefield.	James Reeder	Miles K. Young	B. C. Moore
Menard—E W Boeker... .	T E Courtwright	.. H. E. Pond .	...Eva B. Batterton
Mercer—Samuel S Johnston. .	... C. A. Hickok	. John M Wilson ...	.........C. L. Gregory
Monroe—Andrew Lutz	A C Rexroth	.. Henry Reichenback ..	. J W. Jackson
Montgomery—C. E. Landers ...	M T Kiggins	. J Earl Major	...John W. Harp
Morgan—Jerry Cox..	W. B Rogers	Robert Tilton	... H. C. Montgomery
Moultrie—G A. Daugherty	. Warren M Fleming	J K Martin	Van D. Roughton
Ogle—C. M Myers . ..	...W. B. Delaney	.. W. J. Emerson.. . ..	. John E. Cross
Peoria—Lewis M. Hines	..... F. G Minor	. C. E. McNemar...	John A. Hayes
Perry—William Brey .	. S T. Duncan	.. S. A Warden..	. Elmo W. Lee
Piatt—O. L. Cline ..	. F D Duvall	. Thomas Kastel . .	. C McIntosh
Pike—Hayes Colvin. .	David F Allen	...George O Weaver .	. D. P. Hollis
Pope—Thomas Phelps ..	...H. G McCormick	..John W Browning	R. R. Randolph
Pulaski—R J. Caster	C E Wehrenberg	.C S Miller	Miss May S. Hawkins
Putnam—W. M. Durley	.. O. C Cofoid	....Harry K. Ward .	...... W. A. Paxon
Randolph—Robert M Boyd	. H S Burbes	.. Alfred D. Riess .	William F. Stine
Richland—F. W Schilt	... E. W Houser	. H G. Morris . .	. E. Van Arsdal
Rock Island—W. H. Whiteside....	. O L. Bruner	.. F E Thompson .	S. J. Ferguson
Saline—J Lusk	. J Mooneyham	. Sam Thomson ...	.....R. E. Rhine
Sangamon—Charles H Edmands, Jr..	...Henry Mester	. Edmund Burke	. E C Pruitt
Schuyler—A. C Edgar..	... Harry Pratt	... George B. Steele	.. George R. Hermetel
Scott—N. J. Moore..	John E Coultas	R M. Riggs	...J..C. Moore
Shelby—William Klauser ..	F D Crook	. W. E Lowe	Lee W. Frazer
Stark—E. G Williamson	Thomas J. Malone	John W. Fling, Jr.	..... George C. Baker
St Clair—Paul W Abt	.W Mulconnery	Charles Webb	... W. A Hough
Stephenson—John Bruce .	.R J. Stewart	.Albert H. Manus ...	...Cyrus S. Grove
Tazewell—W. E Schurman	Chris Flueget	.W. J Reardon	. B. L. Smith
Union—Thomas O. Urv............	G. H. Huggins	...W. D. Lyerle......	...William O Brown
Vermilion—O. B. Wyson.....	John T. Shpard	J H. Lewman . .	O P. Haworth
Wabash—George C Harvey .	William A. Milburn	Harry M. Phipps	. S. A. Mayne
Warren—W. E Stevenson	..W. T Fitzpatrick	Joseph N. Thomas ...	....J. D. Regan
Washington—H. W Finke	. H F Vogelpohl	J. P Carter	Robert Pence
Wayne—William M Daubs	George H Anderson	H S. Burgess	...W G. Clsne
White—Jess Grisson	.... C. W. Frazler	W. L Martin ...	. V W. Smith
Whiteside—A E. Parmenter ..	. J F Wahl	J. J. Ludens	B F. Hendricks
Will—W. W Gifford. . .	Thomas Stevenson	Robert W Martin ..	.William H. Nevins
Williamson—W T Harris... ..	..M L. Duncan	D T Hartwell ..	.. R. O. Clarlda
Winnebago—Frank A Carson	H W. Young	G E Johnson ...	... O. J Kern
Woodford—D. H. Bendinger	John E. Woltzen	...Thomas Kennedy . .	Roy L. Moore

---

ILLINOIS STATE ASSOCIATIONS.

Anti-Saloon League—President, Alfred Capps, Jacksonville, secretary, W B Millard, Morgan Park, headquarters, 1200 Security building, 189 West Madison street, Chicago

Bankers' Association—President, S. B. Montgomery, Quincy; secretary, R L Crampton, Chicago

Bar Association—President, Robert McCurdy, Chicago, secretary, John F Voight, Mattoon

Civil Service Association—President Charles L Capen, Bloomington, secretary, E R. Blackwood, 951, 140 South Dearborn street, Chicago

Equal Suffrage Association—President, Mrs. George W Trout, Oak Park, corresponding secretary, Mrs. Edward L Stewart, Chicago

Federation of Women's Clubs—President, Mrs. Frederick A Dow, corresponding secretary, Mrs. Charles E Hull, Salem.

Humane Society—President, John L Shortall; secretary, George A. H. Scott; office, 1145 South Wabash avenue, Chicago

Illinois Music Teachers' Association—President, Edgar A Nelson, Chicago, secretary-treasurer, Herbert O Merry, Lincoln

Illinois Osteopathic Association—President, Dr. E. C.Thaaley, Peoria; secretary-treasurer, Dr A. P. Kottler, Chicago

Illinois State Dental Society—President, Dr William H G Logan, Chicago; secretary, Dr. Henry L Whipple, Quincy

Illinois State Good Roads Association—President, Arthur C. Jackson; secretary, Miss Maude E Jones.

Illinois Woman's Press Association—President, Miss Ethel M. Colson; corresponding secretary, Miss Ruth Herrick

National Civic Federation (Illinois branch)—President, Dr Abram W Harris, Evanston, corresponding secretary, Donald R Richberg, Chicago

Postmasters' Association—President, D A Campbell, Chicago; secretary, T J Cunningham, Taylorville.

Press Association—President, George W Hughes, Clinton, secretary, J. M. Page, Jerseyville

State Historical Society—President, Otto L Schmidt, Chicago, secretary-treasurer, Mrs. Jessie Palmer Weber, Springfield

State Medical Association—Secretary, Dr E W. Weiss, Ottawa.

Woman's Christian Temperance Union—President, Miss Helen L Hood, Chicago; corresponding secretary, Mrs. Epha Marshall, Chicago

MEMBERS OF THE 48TH GENERAL ASSEMBLY OF ILLINOIS (1913-1914).

Senators and representatives are paid $1,000 each per year. Senators are elected for four years and representatives for two.

SENATE.

Democrats, 24; republicans, 26; progressives, 1.

Dist.		Residence.
1.	Francis P. Brady, Rep	Chicago
2.	Francis A. Hurley, Dem	Chicago
3.	Samuel A. Ettelson, Rep	Chicago
4.	Al F. Gorman, Dem	Chicago
5.	Walter Clyde Jones, Rep. (Prog.)	Chicago
6.	George W. Harris, Prog	Chicago
7.	William H. Maclean, Rep	Wilmette
8.	Albert J. Olson, Rep	Woodstock
9.	Patrick J. Carroll, Dem	Chicago
10.	Henry Andrus, Rep	Rockford
11.	Carl Lundberg, Rep	Chicago
12.	Michael H. Cleary, Dem	Galena
13.	Albert C. Clark, Rep	Chicago
14.	Thomas B. Stewart, Rep. (Prog.)	Aurora
15.	Edward J. Forst, Dem	Chicago
16.	Christian Haase, Dem	Washburn
17.	Edward J. Glackin, Dem	Chicago
18.	John Dailey, Rep	Peoria
19.	John T. Denvir, Dem	Chicago
20.	Edward C. Curtis, Rep	Grant Park
21.	John E. Madigan, Dem	Chicago
22.	Martin B. Bailey, Rep	Danville
23.	Niels Juul, Rep	Chicago
24.	Raymond D. Meeker, Dem	Sullivan
25.	Johann Waage, Dem	Chicago
26.	Noah Elmo Franklin, Rep	Lexington
27.	John Broderick, Dem	Chicago
28.	Willis R. Shaw, Rep	Decatur
29.	John M. O'Connor, Dem	Chicago
30.	Walter I. Manny, Dem	Mount Sterling
31.	Willett H. Cornwell, Rep	Chicago
32.	William A. Compton, Dem	Macomb
33.	Frank A. Landee, Rep	Moline
34.	John R. Hamilton, Rep	Mattoon
35.	John H. Gray, Rep	Morrison
36.	Campbell S. Hearn, Dem	Quincy
37.	H. S. Magill, Jr., Rep	Princeton
38.	Stephen D. Canaday, Dem	Hillsboro
39.	Henry W. Johnson, Rep	Ottawa
40.	F. Jeff Tossey, Dem	Toledo
41.	Richard J. Barr, Rep	Joliet
42.	F. C. Campbell, Dem	Xenia
43.	Charles F. Hurburgh, Rep	Galesburg
44.	Kent E. Keller, Dem	Ava
45.	Logan Hay, Rep	Springfield
46.	D. Duff Piercy, Dem	Mount Vernon
47.	Edmond Beall, Rep	Alton
48.	J. A. Womack, Dem	Equality
49.	J. M. Chamberlain, Jr., Rep	East St. Louis
50.	D. T. Woodard, Dem	Benton
51.	Douglas W. Helm, Rep	Metropolis

HOUSE OF REPRESENTATIVES.

Democrats, 73; republicans, 52; progressives, 25; socialists, 3.

Dist.		Residence.
1.	Maurice J. Clarke, Rep	Chicago
	John Griffin, Dem	Chicago
	John H. Taylor, Prog	Chicago
2.	Frank J. McNichols, Rep	Chicago
	John F. McCarty, Dem	Chicago
	Frank J. Snite, Prog	Chicago
3.	John P. Walsh, Dem	Chicago
	Robert R. Jackson, Rep	Chicago
	F. E. J. Lloyd, Prog	Chicago
4.	Thomas A. Boyer, Rep	Chicago
	George C. Hilton, Dem	Chicago
	Hubert Kilens, Dem	Chicago
5.	Isaac S. Rothschild, Rep	Chicago
	Morton D. Hull, Rep	Chicago
	M. L. Igoe, Dem	Chicago
6.	Robert E. Wilson, Dem	Chicago
	Joseph A. Weber, Dem	Chicago
	Charles S. Graves, Prog	Evanston
7.	Frederick B. Roos, Rep	Forest Park
	J. J. O'Rourke, Dem	Harvey
	John M. Curran, Prog	Winnetka
8.	E. D. Shurtleff, Rep	Marengo
	Thomas E. Graham, Dem	Ingleside
	Fayette S. Munro, Prog	Highland Park
9.	David E. Shanahan, Rep	Chicago

Dist.		Residence.
	Robert J. Mulcahy, Dem	Chicago
	Rudolph Stokiasa, Dem	Chicago
10.	John A. Atwood, Rep	Stillman Valley
	Andrew J. Lovejoy, Rep	Roscoe
	John Coleman, Dem	Rochelle
11.	Frank J. Ryan, Dem	Chicago
	Henry F. Schuberth, Dem	Chicago
	Robson Barron, Prog	Chicago
12.	Martin J. Dillon, Dem	Galena
	R. R. Thompson, Dem	Kent
	T. H. Hollister, Prog	Freeport
13.	Benton F. Kleeman, Rep	Chicago
	Seymour Stedman, Soc	Chicago
	Elmer J. Schnackenberg, Prog	Chicago
14.	Frank W. Shepherd, Rep	Elgin
	Charles F. Clyne, Dem	Aurora
	Henry B. Fargo, Prog	Geneva
15.	Thomas Curran, Rep	Chicago
	Peter F. Smith, Dem	Chicago
	Joseph O. Hruby, Dem	Chicago
16.	Michael Faby, Dem	Toluca
	Henry A. Foster, Dem	Fairbury
	Charles H. Carmon, Prog	Forrest
17.	Edward J. Smejkal, Rep	Chicago
	Tony Teimarco, Dem	Chicago
	John S. Burns, Dem	Chicago
18.	Lucas I. Butts, Rep	Peoria
	Thomas N. Gorman, Dem	Peoria
	George Fitch, Prog	Peoria
19.	Joseph C. Blaha, Rep	Chicago
	John J. McLaughlin, Dem	Chicago
	R. E. Sherman, Prog	Chicago
20.	Israel Dudgeon, Rep	Morris
	Daniel O'Connell, Dem	Kinsman
	William H. Dunn, Prog	Essex
21.	Benjamin M. Mitchell, Dem	Chicago
	Edward T. Farrar, Rep	Chicago
	John Grunau, Prog	Chicago
22.	William P. Holaday, Rep	Georgetown
	George W. Myers, Dem	Paris
	Charles W. Fleming, Prog	Danville
23.	George A. Miller, Rep	Oak Park
	Christian M. Madsen, Soc	Chicago
	Emil M. Zolla, Prog	Chicago
24.	William F. Burres, Rep	Urbana
	Francis E. Williamson, Dem	Urbana
	Joseph Carter, Prog	Champaign
25.	Charles G. Hutchinson, Rep	Chicago
	Edward J. Costello, Dem	Chicago
	Joseph M. Mason, Soc	Chicago
26.	William Rowe, Rep	Saybrook
	Frank Gillespie, Dem	Bloomington
	Abraham C. Thompson, Prog	Piper City
27.	Albert Rostenkowski, Rep	Chicago
	Joseph Pitlock, Dem	Chicago
	James M. Donlan, Dem	Chicago
28.	William McGinley, Rep	Decatur
	William W. McCormick, Dem	Emden
	Cyrus J. Tucker, Dem	Decatur
29.	Patrick J. Sullivan, Dem	Chicago
	James H. Farrell, Dem	Chicago
	Medill McCormick, Prog	Chicago
30.	Homer J. Tice, Rep	Greenview
	A. M. Foster, Dem	Rushville
	William M. Groves, Dem	Petersburg
31.	Franklin S. Catlin, Rep	Chicago
	Harry L. Shaver, Rep	Chicago
	William McKinley, Dem	Chicago
32.	John Huston, Dem	Blandinsville
	Robert A. Elliott, Dem	Monmouth
	J. H. Jayne, Prog	Monmouth
33.	Thomas Campbell, Rep	Rock Island
	Everett L. Werts, Dem	Ogoawka
	William Hartquist, Prog	Stronghurst
34.	William T. Hollenbeck, Rep	Marshall
	Polk B. Briscoe, Dem	Westfield
	Edward F. Poorman, Dem	Mattoon
35.	Alfred N. Abbott, Rep	Morrison
	John P. Devine, Dem	Dixon
	Roy D. Hunt, Prog	DeKalb
36.	George H. Wilson, Rep	Quincy
	William H. Hoffman, Dem	Quincy
	Edwin T. Strubinger, Dem	El Dara

Dist.	Residence.
37. Randolph Boyd, Rep	Galva
Clayton C. Pervier, Rep	Sheffield
Frank W. Morrasy, Dem	Sheffield
38. S. Elmer Simpson, Rep	Carrollton
William A. Hubbard, Dem	Carrollton
Henry A. Shephard, Dem	Jerseyville
39. O. E. Benson, Rep	Ottawa
William M. Scanlan, Rep	Peru
Lee O'Neil Browne, Dem	Ottawa
40. Walter M. Provine, Rep	Taylorville
Arthur Roe, Dem	Vandalia
John C. Richardson, Dem	Edinburg
41. M. F. Henneberry, Dem	Wilmington
William R. McCabe, Rep	Lockport
Ezra E. Miller, Prog	Naperville
42. Robert S. Jones, Rep	Flora
Walter E. Rinehart, Dem	Effingham
Fred J. Koch, Dem	New Baden
43. Edward J. King, Rep	Galesburg
E. W. Duvall, Dem	Lewistown
W. B. Elliott, Prog	Williamsfield
44. Judson E. Harriss, Rep	Duquoin
James M. Etherton, Dem	Carbondale
A. H. Cohlmeyer, Dem	Nashville
45. Thomas E. Lyon, Rep	Springfield
James F. Morris, Dem	Springfield
James M. Bell, Dem	Rochester
46. Charles L. Wood, Rep	Keens

Dist.	Residence.
John M. Rapp, Dem	Fairfield
R. J. Kasserman, Dem	Newton
47. Norman G. Flagg, Rep	Moro
Ferdinand A. Garesche, Dem	Madison
William Dickman, Dem	Edwardsville
48. James A. Watson, Rep	Elizabethtown
Charles L. Scott, Dem	Grayville
William E. Finley, Dem	Bridgeport
49. Fred Keck, Rep	Belleville
Charles A. Karch, Dem	Belleville
Lewis S. McWilliams, Dem	East St. Louis
50. Charles Curren, Rep	Mound City
George W. Crawford, Dem	Anna
R. D. Kirkpatrick, Rep	Benton
51. George B. Baker, Rep	Golconda
Elwood Barker, Rep	McLeansboro
W. C. Kane, Dem	Harrisburg

SUMMARY.

	Senate.	House.	J. B.
Democrats	24	73	97
Republicans	26	51	77
Progressives	1	25	26
Socialists	0	3	3

NOTE—Senators are classified politically according to tickets on which they were elected. There was no progressive ticket in the field when the holdovers were chosen.

SENATORIAL ELECTION IN ILLINOIS.

After a deadlock continuing from Feb. 11 to March 26, 1913, James Hamilton Lewis, democrat, of Chicago, and Lawrence Y. Sherman, republican, of Macomb, were elected United States senators by the legislature of Illinois. Mr. Lewis was given the long term, expiring March 4, 1919, in succession to Shelby M. Cullom, and Mr. Sherman was chosen to fill out the unexpired term, ending March 4, 1915, of William Lorimer, who was declared by the senate July 14, 1912, not to have been duly elected May 26, 1909, and therefore not entitled to a seat in the United States senate. Both Mr. Lewis and Mr. Sherman were indorsed for the senatorship at the primary election of April 9, 1912, the former receiving 228,872 democratic votes in the state and the latter 178,063 republican votes. Lewis had no opposition in the primary, while the republican vote was divided between Shelby M. Cullom, W. Grant Webster, Hugh S. Magill (Prog.) and L. Y. Sherman.

The legislature, as the result of the election of Nov. 5, 1912, was composed of 97 democrats, 76 republicans, 27 progressives and 4 socialists, no one party being sufficiently strong to elect on joint ballot. Factional differences developed among the democrats, republicans and progressives and efforts to form a winning combination between them were for a long time fruitless. Some of the democrats insisted on electing two democrats to the United States senate. Gov. Edward F. Dunne, seeing that this was impossible, favored the election of Lewis to the long term and Sherman to the short term. The republicans, however, wished to give Sherman the six year term and it was not until after it became evident that it was the short term or nothing that they agreed to the Dunne programme.

Fifteen ballots were taken on the long term and fourteen on the short term.

Summary of long term ballot:

	Senate.	House.	Total.
Lewis, Dem	46	118	164
Sherman, Rep	..	9	9
Funk, Prog	2	20	22
Berlyn, Soc	..	4	4

Necessary to a choice, 103.

Summary of short term ballot:

	Senate.	House.	Total.
Sherman, Rep	38	105	143
Boeschenstein, Dem	8	17	25
Funk, Prog	3	19	22
McDonald, Soc	..	4	4

Necessary to a choice 103.

ILLINOIS WEIGHTS AND MEASURES.

Established by act of June 27, 1913.

Bushel of—	Pounds.	Bushel of—	Pounds.	Bushel of—	Pounds.	Bushel of—	Pounds.
Alfalfa seed	60	Cranberries	33	Orchard grass seed	14	Rough rice	45
Apples, green	50	Cucumbers	48	Osage orange seed	33	Rutabagas	50
Apples, dried	24	Emmer	40	Parsnips	50	Rye meal	50
Barley	48	Flax seed	56	Peaches	48	Rye	56
Beans, green or string	24	Flour, wheat, barrel	196	Peaches, dried	33	Salt, coarse	55
Beans, wax	24	Half barrel	98	Peanuts, green	22	Salt, fine	50
Beans, white	60	Quarter barrel sack	49	Peanuts, roasted	20	Shorts	20
Beans, castor	46	Eighth barrel sack	24½	Pears	58	Sorghum seed	50
Beets	60	Gooseberries	40	Peas, dried	60	Spelt	40
Blue grass seed	14	Hair, plastering, unwashed	8	Peas, green, in pod	32	Spinach	12
Bran	20	Washed	4	Popcorn, in ear	70	Sweet clover seed, unhulled	33
Buckwheat	52	Hemp seed	44	Popcorn, shelled	56	Timothy seed	45
Carrots	50	Hickory nuts	50	Potatoes, Irish	60	Tomatoes	56
Charcoal	20	Hungarian grass seed	50	Potatoes, sweet	50	Turnips	55
Clover seed	60	Indian corn or maize	56	Quinces	48	Walnuts	50
Coal	80	Lime	80	Rape seed	50	Wheat	60
Coke	40	Malt	38	Red top seed	14		
Corn seed, broom	48	Millet	50				
Corn meal, unbolted	48	Millet, Japanese	35				
Corn in ear	70	Oats	32				
Corn, kaffir	56	Onions	57				
Corn, shelled	56	Onion sets, top	30				
Cotton seed	32	Onion sets, bottom	32				

Whenever any of the following articles are sold by the cubic yard and the same are weighed, the following weights shall govern:
Crushed stone, 2,500 pounds, 1 cubic yard.
Bank sand, 2,500 pounds, 1 cubic yard.
Torpedo sand, 3,000 pounds, 1 cubic yard.
Gravel, 3,000 pounds, 1 cubic yard.

ILLINOIS ELECTORAL DISTRICTS.

COUNTY.	County seat.	Sena-torial.	Congres-sional.	Judicial circuit.	JUDICIAL DIS. Appel-late.	Su-preme.
Adams	Quincy	36	15	8	3	4
Alexander	Cairo	50	25	1	4	1
Bond	Greenville	47	22	3	4	2
Boone	Belvidere	8	12	17	2	6
Brown	Mount Sterling	30	20	8	3	4
Bureau	Princeton	37	16	13	2	5
Calhoun	Hardin	36	20	8	3	2
Carroll	Mount Carroll	12	13	15	2	6
Cass	Virginia	30	20	8	3	4
Champaign	Urbana	24	19	6	3	3
Christian	Taylorville	40	21	4	3	2
Clark	Marshall	34	18	5	3	2
Clay	Louisville	42	24	4	4	2
Clinton	Carlyle	42	23	4	4	1
Coles	Charleston	34	19	5	3	3
Cook	Chicago	1,2,3,4,5,6 7,9,11,13,15 17,19,21,23 25,27,29,31	1,2,3,4,5 6,7,8,9,10	Not num-bered	1	7
Crawford	Robinson	48	23	2	4	2
Cumberland	Toledo	40	18	5	3	2
DeKalb	Sycamore	35	12	16	2	6
DeWitt	Clinton	28	19	6	3	3
Douglas	Tuscola	34	19	6	3	3
DuPage	Wheaton	41	11	16	2	7
Edgar	Paris	32	18	5	3	3
Edwards	Albion	48	24	2	4	1
Effingham	Effingham	42	23	4	4	2
Fayette	Vandalia	40	23	4	4	2
Ford	Paxton	26	17	11	3	3
Franklin	Benton	50	25	2	4	1
Fulton	Lewistown	43	15	9	8	4
Gallatin	Shawneetown	48	24	2	4	1
Greene	Carrollton	33	20	7	3	2
Grundy	Morris	20	12	13	2	5
Hamilton	McLeansboro	51	24	2	4	1
Hancock	Carthage	32	14	9	3	4
Hardin	Elizabethtown	48	24	2	4	1
Henderson	Oquawka	83	14	9	2	4
Henry	Cambridge	37	15	14	2	5
Iroquois	Watseka	20	18	12	2	3
Jackson	Murphysboro	44	25	1	4	1
Jasper	Newton	48	23	4	4	2
Jefferson	Mount Vernon	46	23	2	4	1
Jersey	Jerseyville	38	20	7	3	2
Jo Daviess	Galena	12	13	15	2	6
Johnson	Vienna	51	24	1	4	1
Kane	Geneva	14	11	16	2	6
Kankakee	Kankakee	20	18	12	2	7
Kendall	Yorkville	14	12	16	2	6
Knox	Galesburg	43	15	9	2	5
Lake	Waukegan	8	10	17	2	7
LaSalle	Ottawa	30	12	13	2	5
Lawrence	Lawrenceville	48	23	2	4	2
Lee	Dixon	35	13	15	2	6
Livingston	Pontiac	16	17	11	2	3
Logan	Lincoln	28	17	11	3	3
Macon	Decatur	28	19	6	3	3
Macoupin	Carlinville	38	21	7	3	2
Madison	Edwardsville	47	22	3	4	2
Marion	Salem	42	23	4	4	2
Marshall	Lacon	16	16	10	2	5
Mason	Havana	30	20	8	3	4
Massac	Metropolis	51	24	1	4	1
McDonough	Macomb	32	14	9	3	4
McHenry	Woodstock	8	11	17	2	6
McLean	Bloomington	26	17	11	3	3
Menard	Petersburg	30	20	4	3	4
Mercer	Aledo	33	14	14	2	4
Monroe	Waterloo	44	22	3	4	1
Montgomery	Hillsboro	38	21	4	5	2
Morgan	Jacksonville	45	20	7	3	2
Moultrie	Sullivan	24	19	6	3	3
Ogle	Oregon	10	13	15	2	6
Peoria	Peoria	18	16	10	2	5
Perry	Pinckneyville	44	25	3	4	1
Platt	Monticello	24	19	6	3	3
Pike	Pittsfield	36	20	8	3	4
Pope	Goleonda	51	24	1	4	1
Pulaski	Mound City	50	25	1	4	1
Putnam	Hennepin	16	16	10	2	5
Randolph	Chester	44	25	3	4	1
Richland	Olney	46	23	2	4	2
Rock Island	Rock Island	33	14	14	2	4
Saline	Harrisburg	51	24	1	4	1
Sangamon	Springfield	45	21	7	3	3
Schuyler	Rushville	30	15	8	3	4

ILLINOIS ELECTORAL DISTRICTS—CONTINUED.

COUNTY.	County seat.	Sena-torial.	Congres-sional.	Judicial circuit.	JUDICIAL DIS.	
					Appel-late.	Su-preme.
Scott	Winchester	56	20	7	3	2
Shelby	Shelbyville	40	19	4	3	2
Stark	Toulon	37	16	10	2	5
St. Clair	Belleville	49	22	3	4	1
Stephenson	Freeport	12	13	15	2	6
Tazewell	Pekin	30	16	10	3	3
Union	Jonesboro	50	25	1	4	1
Vermilion	Danville	22	18	5	3	3
Wabash	Mount Carmel	48	23	2	4	1
Warren	Monmouth	22	14	9	2	4
Washington	Nashville	44	22	3	4	1
Wayne	Fairfield	46	24	2	4	1
White	Carmi	48	24	2	4	1
Whiteside	Morrison	35	13	14	2	6
Will	Joliet	41	11	12	2	7
Williamson	Marion	50	25	1	4	1
Winnebago	Rockford	10	12	17	2	6
Woodford	Eureka	16	17	11	2	5

GOVERNMENT OF ILLINOIS.

Legislative power is vested in a general assembly, consisting of a senate and house of representatives, both elected by the people. The state is divided into fifty-one senatorial districts, each of which elects a senator and three representatives. The general assembly makes laws and appropriates money for the government of the state and in general stands in the same relation to the state as congress does to all the states as a whole. The powers and duties of the chief executive officers are as follows:

Governor—The governor is vested with the chief executive power of the state. He is the commander in chief of the military and naval forces and may call out the militia to maintain the peace. He is required to inform the general assembly, by message, of the condition of affairs of the state and to recommend needed legislation. He may, by proclamation, call a special session of the assembly or adjourn it in case of disagreement between the two houses. He has the power to appoint certain officers and during a recess of the senate may fill vacancies or remove certain officers and may call special elections to fill vacancies in certain offices. He may make requisitions upon the governors of other states for the return of fugitives from justice or other rewards for the arrest of offenders against the laws of the state. He exercises a general supervision over the penitentiaries and may grant reprieves, commutations and pardons and may restore the rights of citizenship to ex-convicts. He may approve acts of the legislature and exercise the veto power.

Lieutenant-Governor—This officer is ex-officio president of the senate and has the power to cast the deciding vote in case of a tie. In case of the death, conviction on impeachment, failure to qualify, resignation, absence from the state or other disability on the part of the governor, the lieutenant-governor succeeds to the office to the close of the term.

Secretary of State—The secretary of state is charged with the safekeeping of the original laws and resolutions of the general assembly; with all books, bills and documents deposited with him by either house, and with all bonds, records and papers filed in his office. He keeps a record of the official acts of the governor, furnishes certified copies of the same to the assembly on request and certified copies of any of the records of his office on the payment of the statutory fees. He countersigns and affixes the seal of the state to all proclamations and commissions issued by the governor; issues licenses for incorporations and certificates of organization to cities and villages and incorporated towns. He has charge of most of the buildings and grounds belonging to the state in Springfield, furnishes supplies for the general assembly and supervises the printing and distribution of all the public documents of the state. He calls the house of representatives to order at the beginning of each general assembly and presides over the same until the election of a speaker. He is the keeper of the great seal of the state and is the custodian and sealer of weights and measures.

Auditor—The auditor is required to keep all the accounts of the state; to audit the accounts of all officers or other persons authorized to receive moneys from the state treasury; to personally sign all warrants drawn on the treasury; to institute suits wherein the state is a plaintiff, and to make a biennial report of the business of his office to the governor. With the governor and treasurer he determines the state tax rate. He exercises a general supervision over state banks, building, loan and homestead associations.

State Treasurer—The state treasurer is custodian of the revenues and public moneys of the state. He must make monthly settlements with the auditor and a biennial report to the governor.

Superintendent of Public Instruction—The superintendent exercises a general supervision over all the public schools of the state. He is the general and legal adviser of the county superintendents and must report biennially to the governor the general condition of all the schools of the state, the amount raised by taxation for school purposes and the manner of its expenditure and the general condition of all the school funds. He may grant state certificates to teachers or cause them to be withheld and must visit charitable institutions which are educational in character.

Attorney-General—It is the duty of the attorney-general to represent the state in the Supreme court in all cases in which the state is interested; to act as counsel for all state officials; to be the legal adviser of the governor and other state officers in matters relating to their official duties, and, on request, to furnish them, as well as either branch of the general assembly, with written opinions upon constitutional or legal questions.

CENTRAL DIVISION OF UNITED STATES ARMY.

Headquarters, fifth floor Federal building, Chicago.
Commander—Col. Edward A. Millar.
Chief of Staff—Col. William A. Mann.
Adjutant—Lieut.-Col. Benjamin Alvord.
Inspector—Col. Henry P. Kingsbury.
Judge Advocate—Capt. M. W. Howze.
Quartermaster—Col. Daniel E. McCarthy.

Surgeon—Col. William Stephenson.
Engineer—Maj. Harley B. Ferguson.
Ordnance Officer—Lieut.-Col. George W. Burr.
Signal Officer—Maj. Carl F. Hartmann.
Officer in Charge of Militia Affairs—Col. William A. Shunk.

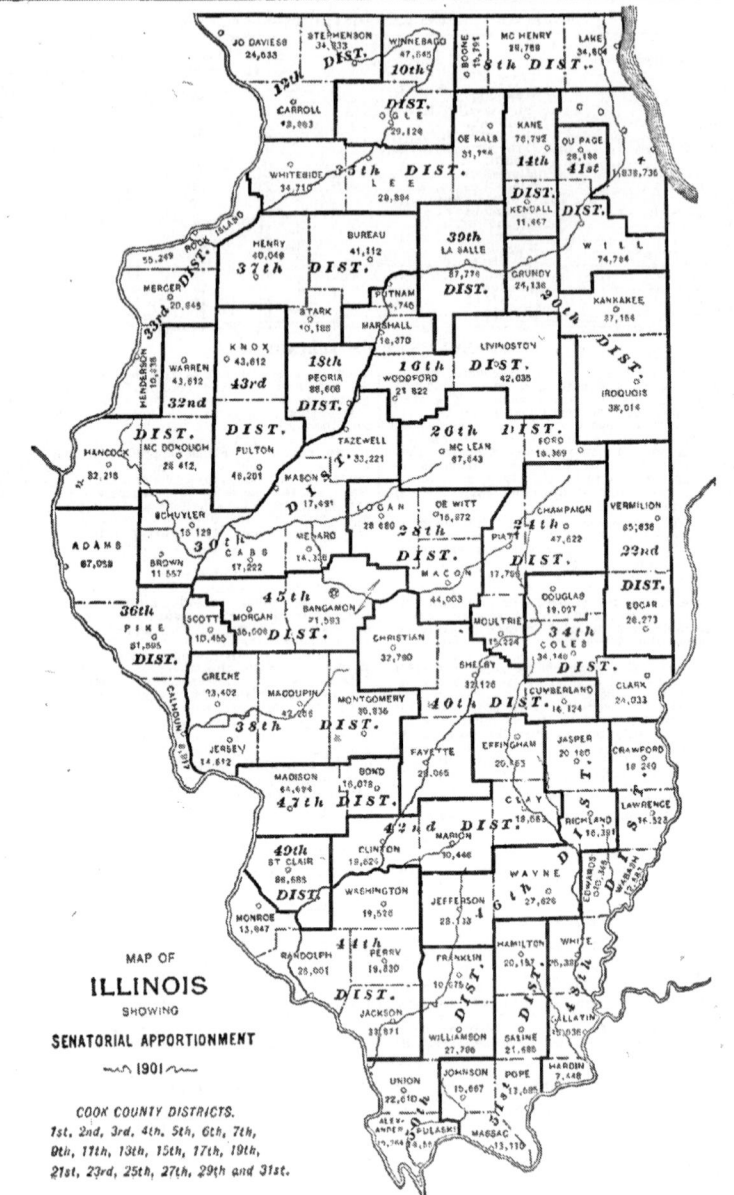

MAP OF

ILLINOIS

SHOWING

SENATORIAL APPORTIONMENT

~~⊷ 1901 ~~

COOK COUNTY DISTRICTS.
1st, 2nd, 3rd, 4th, 5th, 6th, 7th,
9th, 11th, 13th, 15th, 17th, 19th,
21st, 23rd, 25th, 27th, 29th and 31st.

ILLINOIS SENATORIAL DISTRICTS.

Established May 10, 1901.

The establishment of new ward lines by the ordinance of Dec. 4, 1911, having made the terms of the state senatorial apportionment act of 1901 inapplicable or misleading so far as concerns Chicago, the districts lying within or partly within the city are herewith described in accordance with their street boundaries.

Dist.

1. From Lake Michigan west and south along the Chicago river to 22d street, east to Clark, south to 26th, west to Princeton avenue, south to 32d, east to South Park avenue, south to 33d, east to the lake, northward along lake shore to river. (South side.)

2. From South Racine avenue west on Madison to North Ashland boulevard, north to Washington boulevard, west to Western avenue, south to 12th, west to California avenue, south to 16th, east to Laflin, north to Taylor, east to Loomis, north to Van Buren, east to South Racine avenue, north to Madison. (West side.)

3. From Clark street west on 22d to river, southwest along river to Halsted, south to 34th, east to Union avenue, south to 35th, east to Parnell avenue, south to 39th, east to State, south to 43d, east to Lake Michigan, northwest along lake shore to 33d, west to South Park avenue, north to 32d, west to Princeton avenue, north to 26th, east to Clark, north to 22d. (South side.)

4. From State street west on 39th to South Cicero avenue, south to 55th, east to Rock Island tracks, south to 57th place, east to State, north to 39th. (Southwest side.)

5. From Lake Michigan west on 43d to State, south to 71st, east to Cottage Grove avenue, north to 63d, east to the lake, northwest along lake shore to 43d. (South side.)

6. From Lake Michigan west on Devon avenue to Clark, south to Irving Park boulevard, east to Racine avenue, south to Fullerton avenue, east to Halsted, south to North avenue, west to river, along river northwest to Belmont avenue, east to Western avenue, north to Devon avenue, west to Kedzie, north to Howard; also all that part of the town of Evanston lying outside the city of Chicago, and those parts of the towns of Niles and New Trier lying within the city of Evanston. (North side.)

7. Towns of Thornton, Bloom, Rich, Bremen, Orland, Lemont, Palos, Worth, Lyons, Stickney, Proviso, Leyden, Elk Grove, Schaumburg, Hanover, Barrington, Palatine, Wheeling, Northfield; that part of Niles outside the city of Chicago and outside the city of Evanston; that part of New Trier outside the city of Evanston, and those parts of the towns of Norwood Park and Maine outside of Chicago, all in Cook county.

8. Lake, McHenry and Boone counties.

9. From Halsted street southwest along river to Hoyne avenue, north to 16th, west to California avenue, south and southwest along C., B. & Q. tracks to Clifton Park avenue, west to Central Park avenue, south to Illinois and Michigan canal, southwest to 39th, east to Parnell avenue, north to 35th, west to Union avenue, north to 34th, west to Halsted, north to river. (Southwest side.)

10. Ogle and Winnebago counties.

11. From State street west on 57th place to Rock Island tracks, north to Garfield boulevard (55th street), west to South Cicero avenue, south to 87th, east to Western avenue, south to 107th, east to Halsted, north to 103d, east to Stewart avenue, north to 99th, east to State, north to 57th place. (Southwest side.)

12. Stephenson, Jo Daviess and Carroll counties.

13. From Indiana avenue east on 138th to Illinois and Indiana state line, north to Lake Michigan, northwest along lake shore to 63d, west to Cottage Grove avenue, south to 71st, west to State, south to 99th, west to Stewart avenue, south to 103d, west to Halsted, south to 107th; and all that part of the town of Calumet lying outside the city of Chicago. (South side.)

14. Kane and Kendall counties.

15. From the river west on Maxwell to Johnson, south to 14th, west to Throop, south to 16th, west to Hoyne avenue, south to Illinois and Michigan canal, northeast along canal and river to Maxwell. (West side.)

16. Marshall, Putnam, Livingston and Woodford counties.

17. From the river west on Van Buren to Loomis, south to Taylor, west to Laflin, south to 16th, east to Throop, north to 14th, east to Johnson, north to Maxwell, east to river, along river northwest to Van Buren. (West side.)

18. Peoria county.

19. From South Cicero avenue east on 39th to Illinois and Michigan canal, northeast along canal to Central Park avenue, north to 24th, east to Clifton Park avenue, north to C., B. & Q. tracks, northeast along tracks to California avenue, north to 12th, east to Western avenue, north to Washington boulevard, west to Homan avenue, north to Kinzie, west to South Cicero avenue, south to 12th, west to Austin avenue; also the village of Berwyn and the town of Riverside. (West side.)

20. Kankakee, Grundy and Iroquois counties.

21. From Ashland avenue west on Chicago avenue to Park avenue, south to Lake, west to Austin avenue, south to 12th, east to South Kenton avenue, north to Kinzie, east to Homan, south to Washington boulevard, east to Ashland avenue, north to Kinzie, east to Green, north to Milwaukee avenue, northwest to Cornell, west to Holt, north to Augusta, west to Ashland avenue, south to Chicago avenue. (West side.)

22. Vermilion and Edgar counties.

23. From Austin avenue east on Lake to Park avenue, north to Chicago avenue, east to Ashland avenue, north to North avenue, west to Harlem avenue; and village of Oak Park. (West side.)

24. Champaign, Piatt and Moultrie counties.

25. From Western avenue west on Devon avenue, Fulton and Hamilton to city limits, south on Winter to Everell avenue, east to 73d avenue, south to Bryn Mawr avenue, east to North Maynard avenue, south to Irving Park boulevard, west to Harlem avenue, south to North avenue, east to Robey, north to Fullerton avenue, east to river, northwest along river to Belmont avenue, east to Western avenue, north to Devon avenue. (Northwest side.)

27. From the river west on Fullerton avenue to Robey, south to North avenue, east to Ashland avenue, south to Augusta, east to Holt, south to Cornell, east to Milwaukee avenue, southeast to Green, south to Kinzie, west to Ashland avenue, south to Madison, east to South Racine avenue, south to Van Buren, east to river and northwest along river to Fullerton avenue. (West side.)

28. Logan, DeWitt and Macon counties.

29. From Lake Michigan west on Schiller to State, south to Goethe, west to Sedgwick, north to Sigel, west to Cleveland avenue, south to Clybourn avenue, northwest to Larrabee, south to Division, west to Halsted, south to river, thence along river southeast and east to Lake Michigan, north along lake shore to Schiller. (North side.)

30. Tazewell, Mason, Menard, Cass, Brown and Schuyler counties.

31. From Lake Michigan west on Devon avenue to Clark street, south and southeast to Irving Park boulevard, east to Racine avenue, south to Fullerton avenue, east to Halsted, south to North avenue, west to river, southeast along river to Halsted, north to Division, east to Larrabee, north to Clybourn avenue, southeast to Cleveland avenue, north to Sigel, east to Sedgwick, south to Goethe, east to State, north to Schiller, east to Lake Michigan, north and northwest along lake shore to Devon avenue. (North side.)

32. McDonough, Hancock and Warren counties.

33. Rock Island, Mercer and Henderson counties.

34. Douglas, Coles and Clark counties.

35. Whiteside, Lee and DeKalb counties.

36. Scott, Calhoun, Pike and Adams counties.

37. Henry, Bureau and Stark counties.

38. Greene, Montgomery, Jersey and Macoupin counties.
39. LaSalle county.
40. Christian, Shelby, Fayette and Cumberland counties.
41. DuPage and Will counties.
42. Clinton, Marion, Clay and Effingham counties.
43. Knox and Fulton counties.
44. Washington, Randolph, Perry, Monroe and Jackson counties.
45. Morgan and Sangamon counties.
46. Jefferson, Wayne, Richland and Jasper counties.
47. Madison and Bond counties.
48. Hardin, Gallatin, White, Edwards, Wabash, Lawrence and Crawford counties.
49. St. Clair county.
50. Franklin, Williamson, Union, Alexander and Pulaski counties.
51. Hamilton, Saline, Pope, Johnson and Massac counties.

ILLINOIS NATIONAL GUARD AND NAVAL RESERVE.
Commissioned officers, 565; enlisted men, 6,300.

Commander in Chief—Gov. Edward F. Dunne.
The Adjutant-General—Brig.-Gen. Frank S. Dickson.
Adjutant-General—Col. Richings J. Shand.
Assistant Quartermaster-General—Col. S. O. Tripp.
The Division (headquarters Chicago)—Maj.-Gen. Edward C. Young commanding.
First Brigade (headquarters Chicago)—Brig.-Gen. D. Jack Foster commanding.
Second Brigade (headquarters Decatur)—Brig.-Gen. Frank P. Wells commanding.
Third Brigade (headquarters Rock Island)—Brig.-Gen. Edward Kittilsen commanding.
First Infantry (headquarters Chicago)—Col. J. B. Sanborn commanding.
Second Infantry (headquarters Chicago)—Col. John J. Garrity commanding.
Third Infantry (headquarters Chicago)—Col. Charles H. Greene commanding.
Fourth Infantry (headquarters Murphysboro)—Col. Edward J. Lang commanding.
Fifth Infantry (headquarters Quincy)—Col. Frank S. Wood commanding.
Sixth Infantry (headquarters Chicago)—Col. W. F. Lawrie commanding.
Seventh Infantry (headquarters Chicago)—Col. Daniel Moriarty commanding.
Eighth Infantry (colored, headquarters Chicago)—Col. John R. Marshall commanding.
First Cavalry (nine troops, Chicago)—Col. Milton J. Foreman commanding.
Battalion, Field Artillery (headquarters Waukegan)—Maj. A. V. Smith commanding.
Signal Corps (Chicago)—Capt. Alvin H. McNeal commanding.
Medical Department (attached to the various commands)—Col. S. C. Stanton, Chicago, surgeon-general, commanding.
Inspector-General—Col. Henry Barrett Chamberlin, Chicago.
Assistant Chief of Ordnance—Col. Gordon Strong, Chicago.
Judge-Advocate-General—Col. Nathan W. MacChesney, Chicago.

ARMORIES IN CHICAGO.
First Regiment Infantry—1542 Michigan avenue.
Second Regiment Infantry—Washington boulevard and North Curtis street.
Seventh Regiment Infantry—Wentworth avenue, between 33d and 34th streets.
Eighth Regiment Infantry—1442 Forest avenue.
First Regiment Cavalry Headquarters—1330 North Clark street.
First Brigade Headquarters—Room 410 Harris Trust building, 111 West Monroe street.
Signal Corps Headquarters—In 2d regiment armory.

ILLINOIS NAVAL RESERVE.
COMMISSIONED AND WARRANT OFFICERS.
1. Official designation—Illinois Naval Reserve.
2. Plan of organization—Ship's company (ten deck divisions, three engineer divisions).
3. Address of Headquarters—S. S. Commodore, State street bridge.
4. Vessels loaned to state, where located and by which portion of command used—U. S. S. Dubuque, Chicago, by entire command at different times; Nashville returned to U. S. navy, U. S. S. Dubuque loaned instead.
5. Number of commissioned officers...............44
   Number of petty officers and enlisted men..526
   Total 570
6. Location of divisions—
   First, Chicago, mustered in May 15, 1900.
   Second, Chicago, mustered in May 15, 1900.
   Third, Chicago, mustered in May 15, 1900.
   Fourth, Chicago, mustered in May 15, 1900.
   Fifth (engineer), Chicago, mustered in July 1, 1903.
   Sixth (engineer), Chicago, mustered in July 1, 1903.
   Seventh, Moline, mustered in Sept. 30, 1893.
   Eighth, Alton, mustered in Feb. 18, 1896.
   Ninth, Quincy, mustered in May 21, 1897.
   Tenth, Peoria, mustered in Jan. 24, 1912.

ILLINOIS STATE APPROPRIATIONS.

Assembly.	Amount.	Assembly.	Amount.	Assembly.	Amount.
29th—1875-1876	$6,475,207.09	36th—1889-1890	$7,396,737.30	43d—1903-1904	$15,467,316.00
30th—1877-1878	6,562,653.47	37th—1891-1892	8,757,901.15	44th—1905-1906	15,889,363.50
31st—1879-1880	6,584,364.55	38th—1893-1894	9,032,514.49	45th—1907-1908	20,208,146.00
32d—1881-1882	6,605,399.61	39th—1895-1896	10,055,800.41	46th—1909-1910	20,330,042.29
33d—1883-1884	7,342,742.03	40th—1897-1898	11,178,902.00	47th—1911-1912	27,682,077.00
34th—1885-1886	7,776,458.54	41st—1899-1900	12,499,655.57	48th—1913-1914	37,915,457.00
35th—1887-1888	7,940,413.69	42d—1901-1902	13,273,586.12		

ILLINOIS RECEIPTS AND EXPENDITURES.
[From biennial reports of state treasurers.]

Year.	Balance.	Receipts.	Disbursements.	Year.	Balance.	Receipts.	Disbursements.
1820	....	$62,226.00	$47,145.00	1890	$4,445,467.99	$10,586,743.28	$10,682,659.89
1830	....	106,898.00	119,370.00	1900	2,617,955.88	16,382,020.34	15,621,652.19
1840	....	305,284.00	374,401.00	1902	3,278,324.03	16,491,486.11	16,422,576.33
1850	$230,095.27	937,394.67	709,371.74	1904	3,447,233.76	19,763,176.57	17,661,017.36
1860	919,231.68	7,407,363.36	7,279,051.97	1906	5,549,226.65	19,558,842.06	21,278,895.27
1870	4,502,970.58	10,749,084.54	13,261,279.14	1908	3,859,263.44	21,611,919.46	21,046,572.46
1880	2,468,606.89	10,049,206.97	8,727,811.87	1910	4,424,610.44	26,957,187.79	25,882,587.93

STATE'S ATTORNEYS OF COOK COUNTY (1864-1914).

1864-1876—Charles H. Reed, Rep.
1876-1884—Luther Laflin Mills, Rep.
1884-1888—Julius S. Grinnell, Dem.
1888-1892—Joel M. Longenecker, Rep.
1892-1896—Jacob J. Kern, Dem.

1896-1904—Charles S. Deneen, Rep.
1904-1908—John J. Healy, Rep.
1908-1912—John E. W. Wayman, Rep.
1912-1916—Maclay Hoyne, Dem.

ILLINOIS STATE CENTRAL COMMITTEES.
Elected April 9, 1912.

REPUBLICAN.
Headquarters—Springfield and Chicago.
Chairman—Roy O. West, Chicago.
Secretary—C. J. Doyle, Springfield.
Treasurer—B. A. Eckhart, Chicago.
Dist.
1. Francis P. Brady........119 E. 20th-st., Chicago
2. Roy O. West.........5633 Woodlawn-av., Chicago
3. Charles W. Vail........7159 Normal-bd., Chicago
4. Thomas J. Healy......4621 Emerald-av., Chicago
5. Max Levitan............1006 Ashland-bd., Chicago
6. George E. Nye.........3442 Jackson-bd., Chicago
7. Kai P. Hammer..1101 N. Spaulding-av., Chicago
8. John F. Devine.........1929 Fowler-st., Chicago
9. Francis A. Becker....148 W. Huron-st., Chicago
10. Henry D. Capitain..1544 Kenilworth-av., Chicago
11. R. J. Barr.................................Joliet
12. Charles E. Hook.........................Ottawa
13. Delos W. Baxter.......................Rochelle
14. Walter A. Rosenfield.................Rock Island
15. Charles H. Williamson..................Quincy
16. Garret DeF. Kinney.....................Peoria
17. Col. Frank L. Smith.....................Dwight
18. John H. Harrison.......................Danville
19. Charles G. Eckhart....................Tuscola
20. Homer J. Tice.........................Greenview
21. Lewis H. Miner.......................Springfield
22. W. C. Hadley........................Collinsville
23. Alfred H. Jones.......................Robinson
24. W. S. Phillips.........................Ridgeway
25. James A. White......................Murphysboro

DEMOCRATIC.
Headquarters—Hotel Sherman, Chicago.
Chairman—Arthur W. Charles, Carmi.
First Vice-Chairman—H. N. Wheeler, Quincy.
Second Vice-Chairman—John W. Williams, Carthage.
Third Vice-Chairman—Edward F. Brennan, Chicago.
Secretary—Robert M. Sweitzer, Chicago.
Treasurer—Ernest Hoover, Taylorville.
Sergeant-at-Arms—John A. Logan, Elgin.
Dist.
1. George Noonan...........2915 Butler-st., Chicago
2. Edw'd F. Brennan..6430 Greenwood-av., Chicago
3. Frank J. Walsh..........542 W. 65th-st., Chicago
4. Jas. J. McCormick..3462 S. Halsted-st., Chicago
5. Michael Zimmer........2256 W. 21st-pl., Chicago
6. Robt. M. Sweitzer..2968 W. Jackson-bd., Chicago
7. James Furlong.........3229 Park-av., Chicago
8. Michael F. Sullivan..21 N. Ashland-bd., Chicago
9. (Vacancy)...
10. Peter Reinberg........5440 N. Robey-st., Chicago
11. John A. Logan.............................Elgin
12. Fred LeRoy.............................Streator
13. C. J. Dittmar..........................Freeport
14. John W. Williams.......................Carthage
15. H. N. Wheeler...........................Quincy
16. Joseph A. Weil..........................Peoria
17. Martin A. Brennan...................Bloomington
18. Clint C. Tilton........................Danville
19. (Vacancy)..
20. James McNabb.........................Carrollton
21. Ernest Hoover........................Taylorville
22. Jerry K. Kane.......................East St. Louis
23. Thomas J. Newlin......................Robinson
24. Arthur W. Charles.......................Carmi
25. William S. Cantrell......................Benton

PROGRESSIVE.
(Not elected at primary.)
Headquarters—1205 City Hall Square building, Chicago.
Chairman—Raymond Robins.
Vice-Chairman—Fred S. Wilbur, East St. Louis.
Secretary—Harold L. Ickes, Evanston.
Treasurer—H. L. Fordham, Dixon.
Dist.
1. Joel F. Longenecker......................Chicago
2. Charles Ringer.........7716 Saginaw-av., Chicago
3. James H. Gilmore....6954 Princeton-av., Chicago
4. S. J. Napieralski.....2222 Marshall-bd., Chicago
5. John Siman............2959 Parnell-av., Chicago
6. L. M. Jones...........2137 Lawndale-av., Chicago

7. Clifton R. Bechtel......324t N. Troy-st., Chicago
8. Emil N. Zolla.........139 N. Clark-st., Chicago
9. John F. Bass......743 Lincoln Park-bd., Chicago
10. Harold L. Ickes......................Evanston
11. A. M. Hirsch..........................Evanston
12. J. G. Fillmore.........................Rockfor
13. H. L. Fordham...........................Dixon
14. H. W. Cooper...........................Moline
15. Robert A. Chandler...................Galesburg
16. W. M. Allen............................Peoria
17. Frank H. Funk.......................Bloomington
18. Dr. W. H. Stephens....................Danville
19. B. F. Harris.........................Champaign
20. George B. Weimer......................San Jose
21. A. R. Stansifer......................Litchfield
22. Fred S. Wilbur.....................East St. Louis
23. Robert Hunt, Jr........................Ramsey
24. I. A. Sturgis.........................Metropolis
25. George W. Dowell.......................DuQuoin

WOMAN MEMBERS AT LARGE.
Mrs. Raymond Robins......................Chicago
Mrs. H. D. Bentley.......................Freeport

PROHIBITION.
Headquarters—508 Myers building, Springfield.
Chairman—Robert H. Patton, Springfield.
Vice-Chairman—Alonzo E. Wilson, Wheaton.
Secretary—Louis F. Gumbart, Macomb.
Executive Committee—The above officers and John H. Shup, Newton; Charles R. Jones, Evanston; George W. Woolsey, Danville; L. J. Kendall, LaMoille.
Dist.
7. John E. Larson......2713 N. Whipple-st., Chicago
10. Charles R. Jones.......................Evanston
11. Alonzo E. Wilson......................Wheaton
12. Frank Hook..........................Grand Ridge
13. Fremont D. Lehman..................Franklin Grove
14. Louis F. Gumbart.......................Macomb
15. H. O. Munson..........................Rushville
16. Lorenzo J. Kendall.....................LaMoille
17. Marion Gallup..........................Pontiac
18. George W. Woolsey......................Danville
19. Alexander M. Caldwell.................Champaign
20. John E. Vertrees.....................Pittsfield
21. Robert H. Patton.....................Springfield
22. Eldon G. Burritt......................Greenville
23. John H. Shup...........................Newton
24. Wilber A. Morgan......................Bone Gap
25. H. A. Dubois............................Cobden

SOCIALIST.
Headquarters—184 W. Washington street, Chicago.
Chairman—J. D. Dobleman, Chicago.
Secretary—Guy Underwood, Aurora.
Executive Committee — Chas. W. Kuen, J. A. Gajeski, J. D. Dobleman, John McGill, Dan Donohue, W. G. Hammond, Guy Underwood and Rudolph Pusch.
Dist.
1. Chas. W. Kuen...........3101 State-st., Chicago
2. J. A. Gajeski..........11826 State-st., Chicago
3. J. D. Dobleman........6343 Halsted-st., Chicago
4. John Lewin............3058 Lyman-st., Chicago
5. Rudolph Pusch........1727 W. 20th-st., Chicago
6. John McGill........2231 Springfield-av., Chicago
7. Dan N. Donohue.4448 W. Van Buren-st., Chicago
8. E. A. Hannenberg..616 W. Madison-st., Chicago
11. Guy Underwood..........325 Fulton-st., Chicago
12. W. G. Hammond......815 Chicago-st., Belvidere
13. Leroy Lattig...........339 Homer-st., Freeport
14. John T. Krone...........1432 25th-st., Moline
15. A. P. Gillett...........................Canton
16. John W. Ryner........107 Abingdon-st., Peoria
17. John A. Bruell.........323 Elm-st., Lincoln
18. John F. Demlow......48 Bismarck-st., Danville
19. W. R. Sinclair......707 N. Morgan-st., Chicago
20. L. P. Hoffman.......................Jacksonville
21. W. H. Penrod...........................Pawnee
22. A. F. Murphy............................Alton
25. W. J. Allen............................Sparta
Vacancies in 9th, 10th, 23d and 24th districts (Dec. 1, 1913).

COOK COUNTY COMMITTEES.

COOK COUNTY REPUBLICAN EXECUTIVE COMMITTEE.

Headquarters—801 Otis building.
Chairman—John F. Devine.
Vice-Chairman—Isaac J. Bryan.
Secretary—William H. Weber.
Assistant Secretary—Emil J. Wentzlaff.
Treasurer—Isaac N. Powell.
Ward.

1. Francis P. Brady................2030 Indiana-av.
2. Martin B. Madden.............3829 Michigan-av.
3. Robert R. Levy................4639 Prairie-av.
4. Charles L. Strook.............509 W. 28th-st.
5. Edward R. Litzinger..........3359 S. Western-bd.
6. Roy O. West...................5633 Woodlawn-av.
7. Isaac N. Powell...............6826 Bennett-av.
8. John J. Hanberg...............9120 Erie-av.
9. Edward E. Erstman............11300 Morse-av.
10. Joseph E. Bidwill, Sr........1113 Ashland-bd.
11. Charles V. Barrett...........1942 22d-st.
12. A. W. Miller..................3135 Carlisle-pl.
13. David W. Clark................3125 Warren-av.
14. D. A. Campbell................2852 Washington-bd.
15. George Mugler.................1351 N. California-av.
16. John F. Devine................1929 Fowler-st.
17. L. D. Sitts...................1471 Grand-av.
18. Homer K. Galpin..............2237 Jackson-bd.
19. Christopher Mamer.............501 Throop-st.
20. William J. Cooke.............1920 S. Halsted-st.
21. Frank A. Vogler..............1364 N. LaSalle-st.
22. Bernard F. Clettenberg.......1136 Orleans-st.
23. John J. Healy.................503 Barry-av.
24. Leonard A. Brundage..........2210 Clifton-av.
25. Isaac J. Bryan...............5422 Lakewood-av.
26. John C. Cannon...............1811 Larchmont-av.
27. Victor P. Arnold.............5945 E. Circle-av.
28. Joseph F. Haas...............2712 W. Fullerton-av.
29. Matt A. Mueller..............5617 S. Wood-st.
30. Thomas J. Healy..............4621 Emerald-av.
31. Charles S. Deneen............497 W. 61st-pl.
32. Charles W. Vail..............7159 Normal-bd.
33. George Hitzman...............3554 Dickens-av.
34. Charles Vavrik...............1452 S. Kaskaskia-av.
35. J. F. Gainty.................4217 Jackson-bd.

COUNTRY DISTRICTS.

1. A. Van Steenberg......................Lansing
2. W. H. Weber........................Blue Island
3. Peter M. Hoffman...................Des Plaines
4. Allen S. Ray.........................Oak Park
5. William Busse...................Mount Prospect
6. Frank H. Anderson.....................Evanston

CENTRAL COMMITTEE OF THE DEMOCRATIC PARTY OF COOK COUNTY.

Headquarters—Suite 216, 217, 218 Hotel LaSalle.
Chairman—John McGillen.
Secretary—George L. McConnell.
Treasurer—William Legner.
Vice-Presidents—B. F. Weber, Stanley S. Walkowiak, Frank McDermott.
Sergeant-at-Arms—Michael F. Maber.
Ward.

1. Michael Kenna.................397 S. Clark-st.
   John J. Coughlin...............17 N. LaSalle-st.
2. Daniel J. Harris..............3631 LaSalle-st.
   Clem Kuehne..................3854 Cottage Grove-av.
3. William L. O'Connell..........4322 Drexel-bd.
   Peter J. Angsten..............4321 Michigan-av.
4. Henry Stuckart................2517 Archer-av.
   James M. Dailey...............549 W. 31st-st.
5. Patrick J. Carr..............3521 S. Western-av.
   Charles Martin...............3635 Emerald-av.
6. John P. Gibbons..............5007 Wabash-av.
   Peter Foy....................5231 Calumet-av.
7. Edw. F. Brennan...........6310 Cottage Grove-av.
8. John H. Mack..................732 Sherman-st.
   William Powers...............9123 Superior-av.
9. Sheldon Govler...............10547 Corliss-av.
   D. E. Wittenberg.............10736 Stephenson-av.
10. Fred Rohde...................114 N. LaSalle-st.
    Edw. J. Novak..1524 First National Bank bldg.
11. John Lagodny................1735 W. 18th-st.
    Leo V. Roeder...............139 N. Clark-st.
13. M. H. Rogers................1009 S. Fairfield-av.
    W. R. Skidmore..............115 N. Clark-st.
14. Patrick A. Nash............2946 Washington-bd.
    M. F. Maher................2159 W. Huron-st.

15. Joseph Strauss..............1559 Milwaukee-av.
    John P. Tansey..............1506 N. Fairfield-av.
16. William Mazurek..............3329 Robey-st.
    Joseph F. Trandel............1332 Fox-pl.
17. Stanley S. Walkowiak.........139 N. Clark-st.
    Thomas J. O'Brien............600 County building
18. George L. McConnell..........218 S. Seeley-av.
    William Gaynor...............506 W. Adams-st.
19. John Powers.................1284 Macalister-pl.
    Peter O'Brien................744 S. Racine-av.
20. Mose Ginsberg...............1366 Waller-st.
    Dennis J. Egan...............654 W. 18th-st.
21. Albert J. Flynn.............409 N. Clark-st.
    John M. O'Conner..1610 Title and Trust building
22. Thomas Sturch...............1132 Chatham-ct.
    John Ciskowski...............1860 Maud-av.
23. Henry H. Gibbons............2434 Orchard-st.
    Dennis W. Sullivan...........Temple building
24. Fred Esau...............1720 Diversey parkway
    James Fitzgerald............2240 Clifton-av.
25. William F. Quinlan...........1115 Devon-av.
    John T. Conery...............5228 Sheridan-rd.
26. Thomas J. Dawson.........1518 Ashland block
    N. J. Dalciden...............2016 Leland-av.
27. Neil Murley.................3553 Elston-av.
    William McRae................5346 Leland-av.
28. Francis D. Connery.......2702 N. Washtenaw-av.
    Ben M. Sharvy..............1656 N. Campbell-av.
29. Frank McDermott...........1552 W. 55th-st.
    Joseph Callahan..............4843 Ashland-av.
30. Dennis D. McCarthy...........5305 S. Halsted-st.
    Joseph T. Mahoney............217 W. 43d-st.
31. James A. Long................237 W. 60th-st.
    M. J. Flynn..................6532 LaSalle-st.
32. Richard J. Knight............7308 Peoria-st.
    Frank J. Walsh...............542 W. 65th-st.
33. T. J. Crowe.................2448 Spaulding-av.
    Matt L. Cullem..............2554 Milwaukee-av.
34. J. J. Cullerton.............3300 Ogden-av.
    K. M. Rads..................3615 W. 26th-st.
35. William J. Clark............4209 W. North-av.
    William P. Fecacy............17 N. LaSalle-st.

COMMITTEE AT LARGE.

John McGillen...................105 S. Halsted-st.
Hans Blase...................4167 Milwaukee-av.
Frank S. Ryan................4707 Washington-bd.
Salvatore Romano..............916 W. Ohio-st.
John J. Brennan...............716 W. Madison-st.
Chilton P. Wilson............140 S. Dearborn-st.
John J. McLaughlin............7 S. LaSalle-st.
Thomas Little................2248 W. Lake-st.
Stanley H. Kunz..............1349 Noble-st.
John P. Hayes...............1645 W. Jackson-bd.
George E. Brennan............134 S. LaSalle-st.
William Legner...............916 N. Paulina-st.
Joseph Kacena................1458 S. 41st-ct.
John F. O'Malley.............47 E. Superior-st.
William Graham...............3717 Indiana-av.
E. F. Silha.................3350 Douglas-pl.
B. F. Weber.................4423 N. Ashland-av.

COUNTRY TOWNS.

E. H. Poehlsen...................Blue Island
I. M. Kuebser....................Palatine
W. E. Hess.......................Wilmette
George McNamee...................Cicero
August Koelling............Arlington Heights
H. L. M. McCullen...............Glen View
James Turnock....................Evanston
A. A. McKinley...................Evanston
W. H. Stolte...............Chicago Heights
L. N. Richter.................Melrose Park
Francis M. Keogh..................Lemont
W. B. McAuliffe.............Franklin Park
W. A. Lantz.....................LaGrange
J. L. Butler.................North Berwyn
A. L. Tompkins...................Oak Park
J. J. O'Rourke....................Harvey
Ross C. Hall.....................Oak Park

MANAGING COMMITTEE OF THE COUNTY CENTRAL COMMITTEE OF THE DEMOCRATIC PARTY OF COOK COUNTY.

Headquarters—Briggs house.
Chairman—A. J. Sabath.
Vice-Chairman—John J. Coughlin.
Vice-Chairman—M. S. Furman.
Vice-Chairman—Otto Spankuch.
Recording Secretary—James S. McInerney.

Financial Secretary—Harry Goldstine.
Assistant Secretary—John Downey.
Treasurer—James F. Bowers.
Sergeant-at-Arms—Daniel Ryan.

THE PROHIBITION CENTRAL COMMITTEE OF COOK COUNTY.

Headquarters—Room 16, 106 North LaSalle street.
Chairman—Edward E. Blake.
Vice-Chairman—Orange F. Sorber.
Secretary—John E. Larsen.
Treasurer—John Harper.
County Organizer—Leo F. Jeanmene.
Executive Committee—Edward E. Blake, O. F. Sorber, John E. Larsen, John Harper, Carl T. E. Schultze, Edwin R. Worrell, Dr. Axel Gustafson, O. A. Harding, David B. Decker.

Ward.	Chairman.	Address.
1.	Frank F. Hoble	243 W. 25th-st.
2.	George W. Doolittle	3441 Vernon-av.
3.	Esdros B. Trubey	4152 Berkeley-av.
4.	Joseph F. Styles	3020 Lloyd-av.
5.	Stewart McDonald	3252 S. Irving-av.
6.	R. A. Doubt	731 E. 50th-st.
7.	Harry C. Harman	6557 Woodlawn-av.
8.	A. Gustafson	9818 Ewing-av.
9.	Chas. J. Malmsten	11045 Michigan-av.
10.	Henry Jacobsma	1446 S. Ashland-av.
11.	Andrew Johnson	2250 W. 22d-st.
12.	A. J. Terwell	3452 W. 23d-st.
13.	O. F. Garner	2514 Wilcox-av.
14.	Dr. J. S. Sageser	2220 Park-av.
15.	Otto Seidelwitz	822 N. Rockwell-st.
16.	Dr. F. H. Booth	1627 W. North-av.
17.	Mrs. O. L. Stangeland	1208 W. Erie-st.
18.	Victor Behrens	2252 W. Jackson-bd.
19.	Henry Lindvall	508 S. Paulina-st.
20.	Amos H. Leaman	639 W. 18th-st.
21.	Albert P. Ford	606 St. Clair-st.
22.	J. M. Hestenes	709 Vedder-st.
23.	E. Lincoln Walker	1037 Lill-av.
24.	Jos. B. Seiler	1519 Melrose-st.
25.	W. R. Van Sant	1649 Greenleaf-av.
26.	Dr. John H. Gill	1725 Wilson-av.
27.	George L. Chindahl	4642 N. Kenton-av.
28.	Marcus I. Underwood	2500 Artesian-av.
29.	Alfred Browne	6953 S. Lincoln-st.
30.	Berthel Johnson	313 W. 52d-st.
31.	George S. Hicks	520 W. 60th-st.
32.	Frank W. Stafford	6855 S. Halsted-st.
33.	Ernest T. Thorsen	604 N. Central-av.
34.	Harry G. Rowe	2318 S. Central Park-av.
35.	Dr. O. Eugene Larkin	4249 W. Jackson-bd.

Town.	Chairman.	Address.
Thornton—Paul Graybill	14614 Jefferson-av., Harvey

Bloom—
Gus Ankarberg..114 Grant-av., Chicago Heights
Cicero—
Edward C. Parkhurst..2824 S.Lavergne-av., Clyde
Proviso—S. E. M. Allen..110 15th-av., Melrose Park
Palos—Lloyd G. Spencer....................Palos Park
Hanover—S. C. Spaulding.................Spaulding
Palatine—C. J. Nason.....................Palatine
Riverside—G. A. Schwitzer, Jr.............Riverside
Berwyn—Shelby Mays......................Berwyn
Wheeling—Wm. M. Guild.........Arlington Heights
Lyons—J. W. Troeger..112 N. Spring-av., LaGrange
New Trier—W. R. Wilson..................Kenilworth
Lemont—Fred J. Shattuck.................Lemont
Rich—Vandyke Fort.....................Flossmoor
Maine—J. Harry Schulkins............Park Ridge
Worth—O. W. King...........90 York-st., Blue Island
Northfield—Thos. Heslington..............Glenview
Orland—A. C. Loebe......................Orland
Barrington—J. F. Gieske.................Barrington
Leyden—E. H. Mabler..............Franklin Park
Calumet—
Geo. A. Cressey..2304 Morgan-av., Morgan Park
Evanston—
Malcolm C. Harper..2115 Sherman-av., Evanston
Oak Park—
Geo. W. Hoover, 711 N. Kenilworth-av., Oak Park

COOK COUNTY DELEGATE COMMITTEE OF THE SOCIALIST PARTY.

Headquarters—536 Wells street, second floor.
Chairman—Andrew Lafin, 724 Langdon street.
Secretary—Jas. P. Larsen, 536 Wells street.

Frederick Pischel..........1440 Warner-av., Chicago
Robt. H. Howe.................Unity bldg., Chicago
Ernest A. Hoerich...........950 Willow-st., Chicago
Emil Kuhne............4126 N. Richmond-st., Chicago
Otto Christensen......Y. M. C. A. building, Chicago
Wilbur C. Benton......154 W. Randolph-st., Chicago
S. A. Koppnagel..........4424 Armitage-av., Chicago
E. Richter...................4841 Prairie-av., Chicago
D. J. Bentall.............5432 Ingleside-av., Chicago

PROGRESSIVE.

Headquarters—1205 City Hall Square building.
Chairman—Harold L. Ickes.
Vice-Chairman—Walter Clyde Jones.
Secretary—Charles Ringer.
Treasurer—Mrs. Frederic C. Bartlett.

Ward.		
1.	John H. Taylor	2446 Prairie-av.
2.	Charles Slobig	3032 S. Michigan-av.
3.	Charles H. Sergel	4578 Oakenwald-av.
4.	Felix J. Wengierski	3137 S. Morgan-st.
5.	Philip Gollner	33d-st. and Archer-av.
6.	Walter Clyde Jones	5541 Woodlawn-av.
7.	Charles E. Merriam	6041 Lexington-av.
8.	Charles Ringer	7716 Saginaw-av.
9.	Fred C. Bendle	11108 S. Michigan-av.
10.	John Siman	710 Washington-bd.
11.	W. W. Haupt	1893 Hastings-st.
12.	Dr. Fred Formaneck	1333 S. California-av.
13.	L. G. Ross	3809 Polk-st.
14.	Elton C. Armitage	Fort Dearborn bldg.
15.	Charles F. Thoms	2205 W. Walton-st.
16.	William Gieldzinski	1238 Noble-st.
17.	Charles J. Ryberg	715 N. Ashland-av.
18.	John R. Swift	25 Honore-st.
19.	Guy C. Crapple	849 Taylor-st.
20.	Samuel Heller	1212 Blue Island-av.
21.	Thomas J. Graydon	159 N. State-st.
22.	Wm. A. Burmeister	1424 Larrabee-st.
23.	Jacob A. Hey	2050 N. Halsted-st.
24.	Fred C. Evers	213 N. Morgan-st.
25.	C. M. Moderwell	5944 Winthrop-av.
26.	A. F. Nusser	4703 Winchester-av.
27.	C. R. Bechtel	3240 N. Troy-st.
28.	J. M. Dempsey	2500 N. Mozart-st.
29.	William LaBatt	6215 Wabash-av.
30.	J. T. Simpson	728 W. 61st-st.
31.	H. L. Du Charu	5653 Normal-bd.
32.	Willis E. Thorne	7400 Harvey-av.
33.	Henry Nelson	154 W. Randolph-st.
34.	Robert F. Kolb	2120 Millard-av.

COUNTRY DISTRICTS.

1.	Frank J. Grattan	Harvey
2.	Charles L. Anderson	Morgan Park
3.	Sherman M. Booth	Glencoe
	George E. Fernald	Wilmette
4.	B. F. Hales	Oak Park
5.	C. DeWitt Taylor	Palatine
6.	Harold L. Ickes	Evanston

WOMAN MEMBERS AT LARGE.

Mrs. Raymond Robins.........1437 W. Ohio-st.
Mrs. Frederic C. Bartlett.........2901 Prairie-av.
Mrs. Thomas W. Allinson........701 W. 14th-pl.
Mrs. John F. Bass.........743 Lincoln Park-bd.
Mrs. Kellogg Fairbank..........1225 N. State-st.
Miss Anna Nicholes...............6710 May-st.
Miss Jane Addams...Hull House, 800 S. Halsted-st.
Mrs. Harold L. Ickes...........Evanston, Ill.
Miss Mary E. McDowell.........
................University of Chicago Settlement
Mrs. Charles E. Merriam.........6041 University-av.

POLITICAL ASSOCIATIONS IN CHICAGO.

Chicago Equal Suffrage Association—President, Mrs. Joseph T. Bowen.
Chicago Civil Service League, room 711, 169 West Madison street—President, Daniel P. Riordan; secretary, Cora F. Rohde.
Chicago Political Equality League, 410 South Michigan avenue—President, Mrs. Harriet T. Treadwell; corresponding secretary, Mrs. Stella S. Jaunetta.
Chicago Progressive Club—19 West Jackson boulevard; president, Thomas D. Knight; secretary, William R. Mcdaris.
Chicago Single Tax Club, 508 Schiller building—Secretary, H. H. Hardinge.

Citizens' Association of Chicago (nonpartisan), room 33, 106 North LaSalle street—President, George E. Cole; secretary, Shelby M. Singleton.

City Club, 315 Plymouth court—President, Alfred L. Baker; secretary, Laird Bell; civic secretary, George E. Hooker.

Civic Federation (nonpartisan), room 416, 108 South LaSalle street—President, Henry M. Byllesby; secretary, Douglas Sutherland.

Civil Service Reform Association of Chicago, 951 Marquette building—President, Russell Whitman; secretary, R. E. Blackwood.

Cook County Suffrage Alliance—President, Miss Marion Drake; secretary, Mrs. James Morrison.

County Democracy Club, 167 West Randolph street, second floor—Chairman, Miles Devine; secretary, Charles C. Fitzmorris.

County Democracy Club—President, Daniel H. McMahon; corresponding secretary, Robert E. Burke.

Illinois Jewish Republican Club—President, Joseph W. Schulman; secretary, Paul W. Rothenburg.

Illinois Equal Suffrage Association—President, Mrs.

Grace Wilbur Trout; secretary, Mrs. Helen Stewart.

Illinois Woman's Democratic League—President, Mrs. Joanna E. Downes; corresponding secretary, Miss Dora Furlong.

Legislative Voters' League of Illinois (nonpartisan), 1634, 7 South Dearborn street—President, Clifford W. Barnes; secretary, Ralph Ellis.

Municipal Voters' League (nonpartisan)—President, Lessing Rosenthal; secretary, Kellogg Fairbank, 556 Monadnock building.

No Vote No Tax League—President, Miss Belle Squire.

United Societies for Self-Government, 202, 153 North Dearborn street—President, George Landau; secretary, A. J. Cermak.

Woman's Party of Cook County—President, Mrs. Charles Rhodus; corresponding secretary, Mrs. Jane R. Snell.

Locations and secretaries of semipolitical social clubs like the Hamilton (rep.) and the Iroquois (dem.) will be found under "Chicago Clubs and Clubhouses."

REGISTRATION OF VOTERS IN CHICAGO.
REVISED FIGURES (FALL).

Ward.	1904.	1906.	1908.	1910.	*1912.	Ward.	1904.	1906.	1908.	1910.	*1912.
1	10,952	9,574	9,525	7,335	12,366	20	14,190	11,319	13,282	11,117	5,158
2	12,640	10,659	11,984	10,176	15,420	21	13,615	10,615	12,666	10,038	15,239
3	11,863	9,692	11,858	9,217	16,113	22	10,233	8,952	8,284	8,760	8,652
4	9,518	7,752	8,396	7,286	8,847	23	10,233	8,252	9,509	8,294	15,520
5	9,751	7,952	9,859	8,423	9,601	24	9,829	8,323	9,850	8,983	11,426
6	16,890	14,597	18,122	15,342	17,606	25	17,007	16,642	21,316	22,012	18,995
7	17,804	15,885	20,923	19,259	17,479	26	11,545	10,871	14,836	15,360	15,946
8	9,648	8,390	9,914	9,201	10,228	27	12,752	12,815	18,358	19,115	15,541
9	7,945	5,899	5,298	4,320	10,638	28	12,191	10,516	12,667	11,972	12,178
10	8,158	6,226	5,995	4,873	6,776	29	9,819	8,057	10,121	9,645	10,610
11	10,019	7,914	8,555	6,695	8,227	30	11,881	9,668	10,794	9,555	10,908
12	12,577	10,802	13,296	12,474	9,888	31	13,014	11,462	15,016	14,503	14,374
13	12,791	11,537	13,472	12,872	16,016	32	12,660	11,384	14,953	14,244	18,069
14	12,290	10,178	11,278	9,893	12,727	33	11,171	9,562	11,498	11,081	16,775
15	10,844	9,090	10,981	9,889	12,949	34	8,330	8,887	12,439	13,504	14,140
16	10,117	7,984	8,784	7,028	7,530	35	8,771	8,554	11,590	11,777	15,705
17	11,644	8,710	8,262	6,248	6,150	Cicero	1,159	1,090	1,789	1,835	2,147
18	9,658	8,393	8,340	7,952	15,733						
19	10,391	8,144	7,842	5,894	7,235	Total	404,130	345,544	411,120	375,146	448,062

*Ward boundaries changed Dec. 4, 1911.

REVISED FIGURES (SPRING).

Ward.	1913.	*1912.	1911.	1910.	Ward.	1913.	*1912.	1911.	1910.	Ward.	1913.	*1912.	1911.	1910.
1	12,789	15,789	9,614	10,995	15	12,863	12,773	11,014	11,220	29	19,864	10,936	10,976	11,816
2	15,051	17,113	11,314	12,696	16	7,533	8,150	8,001	8,870	30	10,974	12,033	10,432	11,432
3	15,577	16,026	11,317	11,737	17	5,993	6,956	6,899	8,107	31	14,337	14,327	16,592	16,229
4	9,116	10,115	7,948	9,022	18	15,113	17,685	9,180	9,362	32	17,804	17,128	16,021	15,579
5	9,683	10,665	9,477	10,148	19	7,238	8,534	6,599	7,686	33	16,744	15,382	12,211	12,403
6	17,095	15,675	17,721	17,582	20	5,452	6,317	12,626	13,544	34	14,388	13,539	15,405	14,378
7	17,105	15,341	23,192	20,959	21	14,076	15,039	11,457	11,923	35	15,798	15,194	14,015	12,978
8	10,088	10,211	10,162	10,336	22	8,607	9,591	7,427	8,566					
9	10,545	10,446	4,737	5,273	23	14,956	14,938	9,181	9,766	Total.	437,346	444,910	423,529	430,809
10	6,702	7,253	5,338	5,785	24	11,414	11,831	9,766	10,354					
11	8,128	8,791	7,741	8,513	25	18,709	16,165	24,551	22,795	*First registration after passage
12	9,910	9,772	14,000	13,970	26	15,820	15,043	16,979	18,007	of redistricting ordinance Dec. 4,
13	16,031	16,351	14,568	13,879	27	15,832	14,300	22,750	21,436	1911.
14	12,583	13,197	10,983	11,575	28	12,338	12,292	13,250	13,516					

FLAG DISPLAY DAYS IN CHICAGO.

In accordance with instructions issued by Mayor Carter H. Harrison Feb. 9, 1912, the American flag is to be displayed on the city buildings of Chicago on the following anniversaries:

Feb. 12—Lincoln's birthday.
Feb. 15—Anniversary of the sinking of the Maine.
Feb. 22—Washington's birthday.
April 19—Anniversary of the battle of Lexington.
May 30—Memorial day.
June 14—Flag day.
June 17—Anniversary of the battle of Bunker Hill.

July 4—Independence day.
Oct. 12—Columbus day.
Oct. 17—Anniversary of the battle of Saratoga.
Oct. 19—Anniversary of the surrender at Yorktown.
Nov. 25—Anniversary of the evacuation of Yorktown.

On all the above dates the flag should be hoisted at full mast, with the exception of Memorial day and the anniversary of the sinking of the Maine, when it should be at half mast. The hours of displaying the flag are from sunrise to sunset.

CHICAGO SUBWAY AND HARBOR COMMISSION.
City Hall Square building, 139 North Clark street, 20th floor.

Members. Salaries.
E. C. Shankland, chairman.................$12,000
John Ericson..................................*12,000
James J. Reynolds.............................12,000
Secretary, William J. Shanks.
*$8,000 as city engineer.
The above named commissioners were appointed

by Mayor Harrison July 27, 1911, to make the necessary investigations preliminary to the preparation of plans for a municipally owned subway in the downtown district of Chicago and for the proposed outer harbor. Mr. Ericson is the city engineer, Mr. Shankland a designing engineer and Mr. Reynolds an operating engineer.

POPULAR VOTE OF ILLINOIS (1880-1912).

Year. Office.	Prog.	Rep.	Dem.	Pro.	Peo.	Soc.	Total.
1880—President	......	318,037	277,321	440	26,338	......	622,306
1882—Treasurer	......	250,722	244,585	11,130	15,511	......	521,948
1884—President	......	337,469	312,351	12,074	10,776	......	672,670
1886—Treasurer	......	276,680	240,664	19,766	34,821	......	572,986
1888—President	......	370,475	348,371	21,703	7,134	......	747,683
1890—Treasurer	......	321,991	331,929	22,236	......	......	677,133
1892—President	......	399,288	426,281	25,871	22,207	......	873,647
1894—Treasurer	......	455,788	321,551	19,460	60,067	......	858,551
1896—President	......	607,130	464,523	9,796	1,090	1,147	1,090,766
1898—Treasurer	......	448,940	405,490	11,753	7,886	4,517	878,577
1900—President	......	597,985	503,061	17,626	1,141	11,060	1,131,897
1902—Treasurer	......	450,695	360,925	18,434	1,521	28,399	859,975
1904—President	......	632,645	327,606	34,770	6,725	73,923	1,076,499
1906—Treasurer	......	417,544	271,984	89,293	......	45,862	824,583
1908—President	......	629,932	450,810	29,364	683	34,711	1,155,254
1910—Treasurer	......	436,484	376,046	20,013	......	49,687	882,230
1912—President	386,478	253,593	405,048	15,710	......	85,344	1,146,173

NOTE—In the above table the total vote includes the scattering vote for minor party candidates. The vote in the people's party column prior to 1890 is that cast for the greenback party and in 1888 for the labor party. The socialist vote as given includes that of the social labor and social democratic parties.

VOTE FOR ILLINOIS GOVERNORS, 1880-1912.

1880.
Shelby M. Cullom, Rep...314,565
Lyman Trumbull, Dem.....277,532
A. J. Streeter, Greenback.. 28,899

1884.
Richard J. Oglesby, Rep...334,234
Carter H. Harrison, Sr., D.319,635
Jesse Harper, Peo.......... 8,605
James B. Hobbs, Pro........ 10,905

1888.
Joseph W. Fifer, Rep.....367,860
John M. Palmer, Dem.....355,313
David H. Harts, Pro....... 18,874
Willis W. Jones, U. L..... 6,394

1892.
John P. Altgeld, Dem.....425,558
Joseph W. Fifer, Rep.....402,686
Robert R. Link, Pro....... 24,908
Nathan Barnett, Peo....... 20,108

1896.
John R. Tanner, Rep.....587,637
John P. Altgeld, Dem.....474,256
George W. Gere, Pro...... 14,559
Wm. S. Formau, Gold D''. 8,102
C. A. Banstin, Soc. Lab.... 985
J. W. Higgs, Nat.......... 723

1900.
Richard Yates, Rep.......580,199
Samuel Alschuler, Dem...518,966
V. V. Barnes, Pro........ 16,643
Herman C. Perry, Soc. D.. 8,611
L. P. Hoffman, Soc. Lab... 1,319
A. C. Van Tine, Peo...... 1,106
L. G. Spencer, U. R....... 650
John Cordingly, U. C...... 534

1904.
Charles S. Deneen, Rep...634,029
Laurence B. Stringer, D...334,880
John Collins, Soc........ 59,062
Robert H. Patton, Pro.... 35,440
Philip Veal, Soc. Lab..... 4,379
James Hogan, Peo......... 4,364
A. G. Specht, Continental. 730

1908.
Charles S. Deneen, Rep...550,076
Adlai E. Stevenson, Dem..526,912
Daniel R. Sheen, Pro..... 33,922
James H. Brower, Soc..... 31,293
Gustav A. Jennings, Soc. L.. 1,526
George W. McCaskrin, Ind. 10,883

1912.
Charles S. Deneen, Rep....318,469
Edward F. Dunne, Dem...443,120
Edward R. Worrell, Pro... 15,231
John C. Kennedy, Soc..... 78,679
John M. Francis, Soc.-Lab.. 3,950
Frank H. Funk, Prog.......303,401

VOTE FOR STATE TREASURERS, 1880-1912.

(Minor candidates omitted.)

1880.
Edward Rutz, Rep.........317,872
Thos. Butterworth, Dem..276,679
J. W. Evans, Greenback.. 26,658

1882.
John C. Smith, Rep.......250,722
Alfred Orendorff, Dem....244,585
Daniel McLaughlin, Gbk.. 15,511
John G. Irwin, Pro....... 11,130

1884.
Jacob Gross, Rep.........338,171
Alfred Orendorff, Dem....313,400
B. W. Goodhue, Peo...... 10,451
Uriah Copp, Pro.......... 11,119

1886.
John R. Tanner, Rep.....276,680
Henry F. J. Ricker, Dem..240,864
H. W. Austin, Pro....... 19,766
John Budlong, Un. Lab.... 34,701

1888.
Charles Becker, Rep......369,981
Francis A. Hoffman, Jr., D.348,834
John W. Hart, Pro....... 21,174
Nathan Barnett, Un. Lab.. 7,491

1890.
Edwin S. Wilson, Dem.....331,837
Franz Amberg, Rep........321,990
R. R. Link, Pro.......... 22,306

1892.
Rufus N. Ramsay, Dem.....425,855
Henry L. Hertz, Rep......396,318
Thos. S. Marshall, Pro... 26,426
John W. McElroy, Peo..... 21,579

1894.
Henry Wulff, Rep.........455,888
B. J. Claggett, Dem......322,459
John Randolph, Peo....... 59,793
H. J. Puterbaugh, Pro.... 19,487

1896.
Henry L. Hertz, Rep......589,816
Edw. C. Pace, Dem.-Peo..473,043
E. K. Hayes, Pro......... 11,849
Edward Ridgeley, Gold. D. 8,411

1898.
Floyd K. Whittemore, Rep.448,940
Millard F. Dunlap, Dem...405,490
John W. Hess, Pop........ 7,893
Wm. H. Boles, Pro........ 11,732

1900.
Moses O. Williamson, Rep.582,002
Millard F. Dunlap, Dem...508,720
Henry C. Tunison, Pro.... 16,613
Jacob Winnen, Soc. Dem.. 8,881

1902.
Fred A. Busse, Rep.......450,655
George Duddleston, Dem..360,925
Chas. H. Tuesburg, Pro... 18,434
A. W. Nelson, Soc........ 20,157
Gottlieb Renner, Soc. Lab. 8,235

1904.
Len Small, Rep...........610,300
Chas. E. Thomas, Dem....353,232
J. Ross Hanna, Pro....... 35,664
E. S. Tebbetts, Soc...... 62,848

1906.
John F. Smulski, Rep.....417,544
Nicholas L. Piotrowski, D.271,984
William P. Allin, Pro.... 89,293
Wilson E. McDermut, Soc. 42,005

1908.
Andrew Russel, Rep.......619,698
John B. Mount, Dem......449,978
Albert S. Spalding, Pro... 31,037
William Bross Lloyd, Soc.. 32,707

1910.
Edward E. Mitchell, Rep..436,484
Alpheus K. Hartley, Dem..376,046
Lorenzo J. Kendall, Pro... 20,012
O. T. Fraenkel, Soc...... 49,687

1912.
Andrew Russel, Rep.......321,577
William Ryan, Jr., Dem...402,292
Philip Decker, Prog......310,265
L. F. Haemer, Soc........ 84,031
Frank B. Vennum, Pro.... 15,385

COOK COUNTY VOTE FOR SHERIFF AND STATE'S ATTORNEY (1900-1910).

1900—FOR STATE'S ATTORNEY.
Charles S. Deneen, Rep..205,709
Julius Goldzier, Dem.....179,696
Walter Hawk, Pro......... 5,236
O. H. Becker, Peo......... 153
Thos. J. Morgan, Soc. Dem. 6,227

1902—FOR SHERIFF.
Daniel D. Healy, Rep......135,036
Thomas E. Barrett, Dem..141,822
Joseph P. Tracy, Pro..... 4,840
Henry Sale, Soc. Lab..... 5,973
James P. Larsen, Soc..... 13,134
Thos. Donegan, Single Tax. 908

1904—FOR STATE'S ATTORNEY.
John J. Healy, Rep.......206,487
George A. Trude, Dem 132,811
M. C. Harper, Pro........ 5,630
Seymour Stedman, Soc.... 39,736
Henry Sale, Soc. Lab..... 2,547
L. A. Shaw, Peo.......... 1,468

1906—FOR SHERIFF.
Christopher Strassheim, R.131,608
Harry R. Gibbons, Dem... 93,836
S. A. Wilson, Pro.......... 3,745
James P. Larsen, Soc..... 26,055
Jas. J. Gray, Ind. League. 49,296
John Fitzpatrick, Prog. Al. 1,400
1908—FOR STATE'S ATTORNEY.
John E. W. Wayman, Rep..197,805

Jacob J. Kern, Dem.......146,133
William Street, Pro........ 45,528
Seymour Stedman, Soc..... 17,471
Charles H. Mitchell, Ind... 9,279
  See "Election Returns" for 1912
  vote.

1910—FOR SHERIFF.
Michael Zimmer, Dem......165,445
Frank A. Vogler, Rep.....146,598

O. F. Sorber, Pro........... 5,038
Wm. Van Bodegraven, Soc. 27,583
1912—FOR STATE'S ATTORNEY.
Maclay Hoyne, Dem.......122,419
Lewis Rinaker, Rep.......113,181
Xm. A. Cunnea, Soc......107,647
Geo. I. Haight, Prog....... 93,495
John H. Hill, Pro......... 2,896

PRESIDENTIAL VOTE FROM 1884 TO 1912 IN CHICAGO AND COOK COUNTY.

1884.	Chicago.	Cook Co.
James G. Blaine, Rep.	51,420	69,251
Grover Cleveland, Dem.	48,530	60,609
B. F. Butler, Greenback.	540	810
John P. St. John, Pro.	484	997

1888.		
Benjamin Harrison, Rep.	60,102	85,307
Grover Cleveland, Dem.	63,706	84,491
Clinton B. Fisk, Pro.	1,308	2,577
Alson J. Streeter, Union Labor.	255	303
R. H. Cowdrey, United Labor.	126	140

1892.		
Grover Cleveland, Dem.	136,474	144,604
Benjamin Harrison, Rep.	100,849	111,254
James B. Weaver, Peo.	1,506	1,614
John Bidwell, Pro.	3,029	3,858

1896.		
William McKinley, Rep.	200,747	221,823
William J. Bryan, Dem.	144,736	151,910
Joshua Levering, Pro.	1,849	2,149
Charles E. Bentley, Nat.	141	163
Charles H. Matchett, Soc. Lab.	712	727
John M. Palmer, Gold Dem.	2,300	2,600

1900.		
William McKinley, Rep.	184,786	203,760
William J. Bryan, Dem.	177,165	186,193
John G. Woolley, Pro.	2,977	3,490
Wharton Barker, Peo.	185	211
Eugene V. Debs, Soc. Dem.	6,553	6,752

	Chicago.	Cook Co.
Joseph P. Malloney, Soc. Lab.	410	434
Seth W. Ellis, Union Reform.	145	160
J. F. R. Leonard, United Chr.	130	134

1904.		
Theodore Roosevelt, Rep.	208,689	229,878
Alton B. Parker, Dem.	98,765	103,762
Silas C. Swallow, Pro.	4,652	5,290
Eugene V. Debs, Soc.	45,929	47,743
C. H. Corregan, Soc. Lab.	2,656	2,660
Thomas E. Watson, Peo.	3,155	3,323
Austin Holcomb, Cont.	288	319

1908.		
William H. Taft, Rep.	205,830	230,400
William J. Bryan, Dem.	143,544	152,990
Eugene Chafin, Pro.	4,982	5,965
Eugene V. Debs, Soc.	17,712	18,842
Thomas L. Hisgen, Ind.	5,633	5,994
Daniel B. Turney, U. Chr.	169	178
August Gillhaus, Soc. Lab.	616	649
Thomas E. Watson, Peo.	49	73

1912.		
William H. Taft, Rep.	67,859	74,851
Woodrow Wilson, Dem.	120,209	130,702
Theodore Roosevelt, Prog.	144,392	166,061
Eugene V. Debs, Soc.	49,959	52,650
Eugene Chafin, Pro.	2,403	2,737
Arthur E. Reimer, Soc. Lab.	2,171	2,300

PATRIOTIC SOCIETIES IN ILLINOIS.

GRAND ARMY OF THE REPUBLIC.
DEPARTMENT OF ILLINOIS.
Commander—J. H. Crowder, Bethany.
Senior Vice-Commander—O. R. McKinney, Chicago.
Junior Vice-Commander—James M. Brown, Quincy.
Chaplain—Samuel T. Maxey, Mount Vernon.
Medical Director—W. M. Hanna, Aurora.
Assistant Adjutant and Quartermaster-General—
  Henry C. C. Cooke, Chicago.
Inspector—M. H. Peters.
Judge Advocate—William E. Church.
Chief Mustering Officer—George Knapp.
Patriotic Instructor—H. J. Yarnell.
Chief of Staff—P. F. Cox.
Headquarters—Memorial Hall, Chicago.

SONS OF VETERANS.
DIVISION OF ILLINOIS.
Commander—George B. Holmes, Chicago.
Treasurer—William G. Dustin, Dwight.
Secretary—A. D. Rhinesmith, Peoria.
ILLINOIS STATE CAMP NO. 100.
Officers, 1913-1914.
Commander—Charles J. O'Connor, Chicago.
Secretary-Treasurer—William G. Dustin, Dwight.

UNITED SPANISH WAR VETERANS.
DEPARTMENT OF ILLINOIS.
Commander—Carl McKee, Joliet.
Senior Vice-Commander—Charles L. Daniels, Chicago.
Junior Vice-Commander—M. J. Donahue, Streator.

Adjutant—Martin Sipple, Joliet.
Quartermaster—Philo A. Hoyt, Joliet.
Inspector—Leslie J. Snyder, Bloomington.
Judge Advocate—R. E. Hickman, Benton.
Surgeon—Dr. C. H. Blankenmeyer, Springfield.
Chaplain-Rev. H. W. Jameson, D. D., Decatur.
Marshal—J. L. Sweeney, East St. Louis.
Membership of Department—3,000.
Headquarters—106 Liberty street, Elgin.

SONS OF THE REVOLUTION.
ILLINOIS SOCIETY (1914).
President—Thomas E. Green, Chicago.
Secretary—Frederick Dickinson, 562 Bryant avenue, Chicago.
Treasurer—Nelson J. Ludington.
Registrar—John R. Dickinson.
Chaplain—Rev. George D. Wright.
Historian—Harrison Kelley.

SOCIETY OF THE WAR OF 1812.
ILLINOIS SOCIETY.
President—Col. Nathan W. MacChesney.
First Vice-President—James Edgar Brown.
Second Vice-President—William Porter Adams.
Third Vice-President—Gen. C. C. Carr.
Treasurer—Charles Cromwell.
Registrar—John William Lowe.
Chaplain—Jared Wilson Young.
Historian—James Edward Slocum.
Secretary—Ernest F. Manrose, 3045 North Western avenue, Chicago.

WILD FLOWER PRESERVATION SOCIETY OF AMERICA.
COOK COUNTY BRANCH.
President—Mrs. Lyman A. Walton, 5737 Woodlawn avenue.
Secretary-Treasurer—Huron H. Smith, Field Museum of Natural History.
Field Marshal—Mrs. Paul R. Wright, 2320 Greenleaf avenue.

Executive Committee—Above officers and Mrs. C. B. Cory and Dr. H. C. Cowles.
Purpose—The preservation of the wild flowers of Cook county by educating the public to refrain from gathering them and preventing the scattering of seed.

CHICAGO ELECTION CALENDAR FOR 1914.

Issued by board of election commissioners.

Jan. 26—First day to file petitions with city clerk or town clerk of Cicero for February primary.

Feb. 3—Registration for February primary.

Feb. 4—Last day to file petitions with city clerk or town clerk for February primary.

Feb. 4 and 5—Canvass of precincts by clerks of election.

Feb. 6—Last day to file petitions under public policy act for April election.

Feb. 7—Revision of primary registration.

Feb. 24—Primary for nomination of aldermen in Chicago and town officers in Cicero.

March 13—Last day to file independent petitions for April election with city clerk.

March 17—Registration for April election.

March 18 and 19—Canvass of precincts by clerks of election.

March 21—Revision of the registry.

March 23—Last day to file independent petitions with town clerk of Cicero for April election.

April 7—April election—Aldermen in Chicago and town officers in Cicero.

July 11—First day to file petitions with secretary of state and county clerk for September primary.

July 31—Last day to file petitions with secretary of state and county clerk for September primary.

Aug. 5—Last day to file withdrawals with the secretary of state, account of September primary.

Aug. 10—First day to file petitions with city clerk for September primary.

Aug. 19—Registration for September primary.

Aug. 20—Canvass of precincts by clerks of election.

Aug. 20—Last day to file petitions with city clerk for September primary.

Aug. 20—Last day to file withdrawals with city clerk for September primary.

Aug. 22—Revision of registry for September primary.

Sept. 4—Last day to file petitions under public policy act for November election.

Sept. 9—Primary for election of Nov. 3.

Oct. 3—Last day to file independent petitions with the secretary of state or county clerk for election of Nov. 3.

Oct. 3—First day of registration for election of Nov. 3.

Oct. 13—Second day of registration for election of Nov. 3.

Oct. 14 and 15—Canvass of precincts by clerks of election.

Oct. 17—Revision of registry.

Nov. 3—Election for state, county and city offices.

OFFICERS TO BE ELECTED APRIL 7, 1914.

One alderman* in each of 35 wards in Chicago.

One alderman* to fill vacancy in 20th ward, Chicago.

Assessor,* collector,* supervisor,* town clerk* and one trustee* in town of Cicero.

OFFICERS TO BE ELECTED NOV. 3, 1914.

(In territory wholly or in part within the jurisdiction of the board of election commissioners.)

State treasurer.

Superintendent of public instruction.

Clerk of Supreme court.

Three trustees* of University of Illinois.

United States senator.

Representatives in congress at large—two to be elected.

Representatives in congress—1st, 2d, 3d, 4th, 5th, 6th, 7th, 8th, 9th and 10th districts.

State senators—1st, 3d, 5th, 7th, 9th, 11th, 13th, 15th, 17th, 19th, 21st, 23d, 25th, 27th, 29th, 31st districts.

Representatives in general assembly—three from each of following districts: 1st, 2d, 3d, 4th, 5th, 6th, 7th, 9th, 11th, 13th, 15th, 17th, 19th, 21st, 23d, 25th, 27th, 29th, 31st.

Sheriff.

County treasurer.

County clerk.

Judge of County court.

Judge of Probate court.

Clerk of Probate court.

Clerk of Criminal court.

Clerk of Appellate court.*

County superintendent of schools.

Two members board of assessors.*

One member board of review.*

Three sanitary district trustees.*

President board of county commissioners.

Ten county commissioners from Chicago.

Five county commissioners from country districts.

Ten associate judges of the Municipal court of Chicago.*

*Women may vote for these officers.

GENERAL ELECTION CALENDAR.

(For Chicago, Cook county and Illinois.)

FIRST TUESDAY IN APRIL.

Aldermen in Chicago (one from each ward) annually.

Mayor quadrennially, treasurer and city clerk biennially. Next election of mayor April 6, 1915.

Town officers, officers in cities containing one or more towns and officers in villages whose boundaries coincide with the boundaries of a town, annually.

THIRD TUESDAY IN APRIL.

Officers of cities organized under the general law (except such as contain within their limits one or more townships) annually.

Officers of villages organized under the general law (except where territorial limits coincide with the territorial limits of a township) annually.

FIRST MONDAY IN JUNE.

Judges of the Circuit court (fourteen in Cook county) every sixth year, counting from 1873. Next election in 1915.

One judge of the Superior court of Cook county every sixth year, counting from 1897. Next election in 1915.

Judges of the Supreme court of the state; 5th district, every ninth year, counting from 1873 (next election in 1918): from the 4th district every ninth year, counting from 1876 (next election in 1921); from the 1st, 2d, 3d, 6th and 7th districts every ninth year, counting from 1879 (next election in 1915).

FIRST TUESDAY AFTER FIRST MONDAY IN NOVEMBER.

Presidential electors, governor, lieutenant-governor, secretary of state, auditor, attorney-general, state senators in even-numbered districts, members of the state board of equalization, clerk of the Superior court and recorder of deeds in Cook county, clerks of the Circuit courts, state's attorneys, county surveyors and county coroners every fourth year, counting from 1872. Next election Nov. 7, 1916.

State treasurer, representatives in congress, representatives in the general assembly and three trustees of the University of Illinois every second year, counting from 1872.

Clerk of the state Supreme court every sixth year, counting from 1902.

Clerks of the Appellate courts every sixth year, counting from 1878.

Clerk of Criminal court every fourth year, counting from 1886.

Superintendent of public instruction, state senators in odd-numbered districts, clerk of the Criminal court in Cook county, county clerks, county judges, county treasurers, county superintendents of schools and sheriffs every fourth year, counting from 1886.

President and fifteen members of the Cook county board biennially.

Members of the board of assessors in Cook county every second year as terms (six years) expire.

Members of the board of review in Cook county every second year as terms (six years) expire.

Judges of the Superior court of Cook county as terms (six years) expire.

Sanitary district trustees in Cook county as terms expire. Three are elected every other year. Next president to be elected in 1916.

Judges, one chief justice, one clerk and one bailiff of the Municipal court as terms expire. Next election of chief justice, clerk and bailiff in 1918.

CHICAGO AND COOK COUNTY ELECTION RETURNS.

VOTE FOR CITY CLERK BY PRECINCTS.

Election April 1, 1913.

Nominees: Francis D. Connery, democrat; William F. Peters, republican; Joel F. Longenecker, progressive; Robert H. Howe, socialist.

	Longenecker.	Connery.	Peters.	Howe
I.				
1....	25	116	13	7
2....	13	71	24	4
3....	18	202	4	7
4....	9	176	10	7
5....	9	201	16	3
6....	7	186	8	5
7....	7	154	5	4
8....	5	130	7	14
9....	..	184	11	4
10....	6	182	8	5
11....	7	122	16	8
12....	6	66	22	5
13....	21	103	21	3
14....	14	99	15	4
15....	6	142	29	7
16....	8	182	7	2
17....	18	55	14	5
18....	22	118	28	2
19....	4	186	4	1
20....	4	166	19	2
21....	13	90	16	11
22....	18	129	18	11
23....	18	116	26	16
24....	18	64	13	8
25....	15	67	32	10
26....	10	34	22	4
27....	10	50	21	..
28....	8	80	22	1
29....	17	102	27	4
30....	6	144	8	2
31....	20	104	20	6
32....	17	86	10	4
33....	20	61	19	6
34....	19	65	21	8
35....	7	112	17	9
36....	23	84	34	8
37....	20	63	14	13
T'l.	468	4292	621	220
II.				
1....	29	84	44	16
2....	18	58	71	6
3....	14	56	93	..
4....	6	12	72	3
5....	4	12	69	3
6....	8	23	77	2
7....	20	13	92	2
8....	13	41	65	5
9....	9	16	65	..
10....	9	43	64	4
11....	31	97	39	7
12....	14	54	36	11
13....	13	57	70	8
14....	28	33	40	3
15....	24	56	47	1
16....	30	63	57	11
17....	35	37	53	3
18....	9	45	38	6
19....	19	62	62	3
20....	25	34	45	1
21....	18	33	43	8
22....	22	42	54	10
23....	19	81	51	5
24....	24	61	59	8
25....	22	40	55	4
26....	13	40	55	4
27....	17	15	66	2
28....	20	22	67	2
29....	20	47	74	9
30....	14	42	69	8
31....	18	87	96	15
32....	16	67	44	6
33....	12	70	69	5
34....	10	19	90	3
35....	14	5	57	..
36....	15	7	68	1
37....	24	15	72	4
38....	36	74	73	6
39....	11	40	126	2
40....	27	43	76	3
41....	29	35	81	7
42....	12	36	111	5
43....	23	70	64	4
44....	31	78	91	4
45....	28	69	72	5
46....	29	50	38	5
47....	28	77	39	3
48....	28	54	56	2
49....	28	103	78	13
50....	41	102	49	10
51....	20	56	36	5
52....	44	56	57	5
T'l.	1071	2532	3335	267
III.				
1....	59	51	36	5
2....	37	35	37	3
3....	41	40	19	1
4....	52	58	20	3
5....	54	43	30	4
6....	61	62	29	7
7....	49	69	24	8
8....	114	85	10	5
9....	39	58	27	11
10....	27	50	20	5
11....	41	70	25	2
12....	60	102	15	..
13....	77	69	27	6
14....	52	99	27	2
15....	58	109	35	6
16....	45	74	27	8
17....	26	121	37	3
18....	11	111	23	8
19....	54	117	31	4
20....	41	117	33	6
21....	38	99	37	4
22....	57	56	38	2
23....	55	66	45	3
24....	37	82	21	4
25....	79	80	38	4
26....	71	61	29	5
27....	57	87	36	5
28....	77	80	29	10
29....	66	62	36	2
30....	58	66	34	1
31....	106	68	34	..
32....	65	66	44	3
33....	58	64	57	..
34....	31	59	39	4
35....	62	51	27	4
36....	23	79	42	12
37....	40	55	38	1
38....	48	50	23	4
39....	42	71	36	6
40....	47	72	19	1
41....	32	83	62	2
42....	66	79	43	10
43....	40	67	39	3
44....	72	94	39	2
45....	22	54	39	4
46....	22	55	22	3
47....	29	177	15	3
48....	10	107	13	6
49....	46	46	27	3
T'l.	2444	3676	1533	203
IV.				
1....	27	161	31	20
2....	4	120	9	11
3....	7	55	20	5
4....	24	134	42	12
5....	16	83	33	15
6....	7	136	33	12
7....	7	119	31	12
8....	6	108	23	10
9....	12	170	22	13
10....	8	165	33	14
11....	13	176	41	6
12....	15	190	30	17
13....	21	154	18	10
14....	11	141	28	10
15....	12	170	34	12
16....	12	182	28	15
17....	7	177	20	11
18....	39	68	29	10
19....	10	141	22	7
20....	16	101	16	10
21....	19	112	9	10
22....	12	134	21	8
23....	12	149	21	11
24....	11	167	17	6
25....	17	125	9	5
26....	9	145	22	11
27....	21	118	22	16
28....	8	171	15	4
T'l.	383	3872	679	303
V.				
1....	13	188	30	11
2....	4	137	12	12
3....	7	161	11	8
4....	1	190	9	8
5....	9	170	9	9
6....	8	199	10	10
7....	6	123	23	22
8....	15	101	10	14
9....	16	131	22	4
10....	25	112	34	23
11....	13	142	35	22
12....	38	106	59	13
13....	24	106	54	17
14....	40	130	23	16
15....	5	161	22	13
16....	6	130	23	4
17....	17	149	39	5
18....	17	160	46	1
19....	23	145	52	24
20....	10	190	26	13
21....	22	141	32	13
22....	17	140	33	10
23....	15	113	19	13
24....	12	126	46	27
25....	17	82	34	20
26....	13	156	28	17
27....	10	113	18	9
28....	2	126	21	5
29....	2	210	9	5
30....	8	167	11	5
T'l.	414	4305	800	372
VI.				
1....	56	42	47	1
2....	46	45	65	..
3....	47	39	65	..
4....	36	25	40	2
5....	46	47	62	2
6....	47	80	81	2
7....	55	65	39	4
8....	40	85	44	4
9....	37	91	43	4
10....	37	78	61	5
11....	48	72	55	5
12....	31	65	49	2
13....	27	96	43	7
14....	19	100	40	3
15....	37	86	58	4
16....	33	103	43	2
17....	53	84	44	3
18....	43	77	41	4
19....	46	117	81	4
20....	38	79	53	2
21....	39	99	37	3
22....	30	78	51	7
23....	84	125	67	8
24....	43	106	49	3
25....	57	85	61	3
26....	51	90	63	4
27....	38	48	41	3
28....	31	89	62	3
29....	61	70	50	2
30....	43	33	49	1
31....	29	62	38	0
32....	40	59	39	5
33....	69	45	45	5
34....	55	47	42	2
35....	29	77	32	5
36....	51	83	70	8
37....	45	52	20	12
38....	37	108	70	17
39....	51	81	69	8
40....	50	81	63	6
41....	31	79	60	2
42....	33	69	38	6
43....	46	97	56	7
44....	39	104	49	6
45....	62	66	66	3
46....	41	92	40	9
T'l.	2007	3501	2331	207
VII.				
1....	44	97	36	7
2....	42	93	69	3
3....	77	119	61	8
4....	58	62	65	7
5....	118	99	84	15
6....	65	61	61	5
7....	79	50	41	4
8....	89	70	66	6
9....	49	57	47	9
10....	39	59	50	7
11....	77	69	54	3
12....	59	71	68	4
13....	43	68	40	19
14....	48	69	74	9
15....	30	61	50	16
16....	60	71	62	5
17....	63	78	71	6
18....	68	75	98	6
19....	68	61	54	4
20....	86	111	89	2
21....	81	114	67	7
22....	63	67	66	12
23....	32	165	102	10
24....	46	118	66	10
25....	40	122	37	11
26....	33	160	84	14
27....	27	133	45	13
28....	34	128	75	26
29....	24	100	103	16
30....	33	95	78	24
31....	39	96	62	24
32....	28	70	67	11
33....	58	135	109	17
34....	76	91	83	16
35....	36	89	71	20
36....	52	122	81	31
37....	40	147	71	19
38....	60	93	51	7
39....	40	88	37	14
40....	54	98	66	29
41....	33	68	51	19
42....	32	116	47	19
43....	46	94	66	21
44....	75	57	73	16
45....	38	58	81	14
46....	61	133	80	13
47....	55	76	70	4
48....	65	81	51	2
T'l.	2548	4415	3160	583
VIII.				
1....	120	109	96	16
2....	71	81	63	12
3....	60	63	45	11
4....	62	64	55	46
5....	126	73	68	31
6....	31	34	21	17
7....	126	148	47	18
8....	13	128	27	11
9....	6	96	49	9
10....	19	257	9	12
11....	10	53	91	14
12....	12	99	27	11
13....	17	79	29	13

	Longenecker	Connery	Peters	Howe
14...	22	114	28	21
15...	21	59	25	11
16...	32	72	52	10
17...	28	69	39	21
18...	38	106	47	12
19...	13	125	19	7
20...	12	132	19	14
21...	21	146	25	10
22...	41	71	73	20
23...	36	85	49	11
24...	18	76	33	12
25...	45	99	34	32
26...	59	61	80	33
27...	51	97	80	39
28...	59	60	71	52
29...	34	65	45	43
30...	24	47	30	25
31...	57	90	23	8
32...	29	62	43	10
33...	20	42	28	3
T'l.	1333	2952	1470	615

IX.

	Longenecker	Connery	Peters	Howe
1...	40	92	33	15
2...	57	92	55	39
3...	30	104	18	50
4...	37	84	24	26
5...	67	150	49	22
6...	22	85	41	16
7...	59	149	29	23
8...	102	66	17	53
9...	31	89	28	10
10...	135	58	24	32
11...	170	56	17	52
12...	109	61	32	35
13...	103	74	20	38
14...	45	91	18	51
15...	70	83	24	53
16...	63	52	38	113
17...	113	107	33	25
18...	91	83	18	47
19...	38	94	30	22
20...	59	101	27	24
21...	46	73	9	6
22...	73	96	15	46
23...	138	84	30	31
24...	100	115	16	7
25...	33	75	12	12
26...	93	149	18	27
27...	75	88	17	53
28...	52	117	14	41
29...	116	64	23	61
30...	152	38	17	38
T'l.	2319	2670	746	1068

X.

	Longenecker	Connery	Peters	Howe
1...	8	61	19	25
2...	21	144	35	54
3...	15	98	27	43
4...	25	105	36	20
5...	43	114	52	31
6...	20	125	52	37
7...	36	86	35	21
8...	29	84	47	40
9...	51	94	26	32
10...	20	149	31	29
11...	16	130	54	51
12...	21	128	40	41
13...	19	149	46	32
14...	6	107	39	28
15...	11	102	125	19
16...	12	152	42	30
17...	15	120	16	16
18...	11	137	39	29
19...	22	152	28	24
20...	8	122	25	29
T'l.	409	2359	784	634

XI.

	Longenecker	Connery	Peters	Howe
1...	16	138	38	33
2...	21	76	38	41
3...	9	140	21	18
4...	10	134	26	25
5...	19	175	31	22
6...	17	131	38	22
7...	26	143	44	26
8...	17	157	84	10

	Longenecker	Connery	Peters	Howe
9...	50	118	65	15
10...	54	147	35	17
11...	21	139	42	16
12...	49	141	45	16
13...	29	114	58	26
14...	34	118	85	25
15...	4	104	84	14
16...	35	132	54	27
17...	20	101	53	25
18...	42	119	43	18
19...	14	142	50	27
20...	33	134	34	14
21...	17	104	48	43
22...	18	134	50	22
23...	22	159	47	16
24...	7	133	57	12
T'l.	584	3139	1170	530

XII.

	Longenecker	Connery	Peters	Howe
1...	6	185	52	54
2...	13	120	77	54
3...	16	153	74	45
4...	6	181	61	43
5...	16	202	67	26
6...	10	145	66	55
7...	15	116	93	48
8...	15	152	74	24
9...	21	146	56	22
10...	20	144	100	37
11...	31	120	91	39
12...	28	129	65	33
13...	19	130	70	43
14...	9	112	89	55
15...	22	156	50	28
16...	22	127	102	31
17...	12	95	61	35
18...	12	89	51	23
19...	22	145	60	33
20...	21	113	71	25
21...	33	107	36	18
22...	31	153	49	13
23...	33	147	75	39
24...	21	139	34	21
25...	17	104	55	28
26...	8	93	28	15
27...	18	120	42	18
T'l.	497	3622	1749	915

XIII.

	Longenecker	Connery	Peters	Howe
1...	32	105	35	18
2...	38	99	28	11
3...	35	57	54	18
4...	23	82	24	11
5...	18	104	18	17
6...	29	71	42	7
7...	41	79	39	3
8...	33	79	45	17
9...	43	103	42	6
10...	32	154	26	8
11...	28	122	39	5
12...	48	90	31	14
13...	39	88	42	5
14...	40	70	40	1
15...	30	101	41	9
16...	36	137	32	8
17...	55	72	32	5
18...	47	215	72	9
19...	74	213	55	7
20...	70	129	34	6
21...	43	156	36	13
22...	13	154	18	6
23...	22	150	26	13
24...	22	123	29	15
25...	32	113	38	5
26...	20	82	34	6
27...	29	81	32	14
28...	35	101	25	4
29...	27	73	23	15
30...	48	100	28	6
31...	24	80	26	9
32...	37	87	24	17
33...	28	154	31	19
34...	22	134	34	17
35...	27	126	29	15
36...	22	182	23	9
37...	36	197	25	12
38...	22	132	22	9
39...	41	107	23	29

	Longenecker	Connery	Peters	Howe
40...	30	134	21	17
41...	33	178	11	13
42...	43	217	26	11
43...	64	224	45	5
44...	45	180	31	11
45...	30	243	23	6
46...	41	316	31	9
T'l.	1620	5894	1495	497

XIV.

	Longenecker	Connery	Peters	Howe
1...	33	114	77	13
2...	17	98	67	34
3...	9	76	34	24
4...	18	143	34	6
5...	13	110	55	12
6...	21	115	56	16
7...	17	111	65	28
8...	26	155	55	17
9...	24	161	62	21
10...	13	163	45	21
11...	16	120	59	23
12...	14	150	57	20
13...	5	98	92	20
14...	44	165	79	45
15...	43	89	78	21
16...	64	170	107	34
17...	42	109	49	38
18...	17	93	49	15
19...	32	133	53	28
20...	27	142	112	6
21...	33	88	68	6
22...	37	110	75	14
23...	26	90	61	13
24...	30	132	62	20
25...	21	99	48	7
26...	20	120	51	17
27...	49	86	38	12
28...	20	74	48	12
29...	16	134	72	19
30...	20	127	78	21
31...	33	77	63	28
32...	32	70	44	15
33...	27	88	52	10
34...	33	63	71	7
35...	29	43	58	5
36...	43	66	65	22
37...	20	85	46	20
T'l.	977	4072	2276	684

XV.

	Longenecker	Connery	Peters	Howe
1...	45	65	50	32
2...	20	47	67	34
3...	26	98	66	52
4...	30	48	40	64
5...	31	144	45	24
6...	31	78	40	65
7...	33	92	22	38
8...	26	133	29	45
9...	50	77	32	55
10...	67	62	23	67
11...	46	70	44	52
12...	47	55	45	47
13...	62	52	23	50
14...	55	65	42	47
15...	95	96	46	54
16...	80	97	52	65
17...	66	104	29	87
18...	84	98	20	60
19...	61	90	24	59
20...	47	95	32	72
21...	64	122	42	50
22...	42	129	19	58
23...	65	136	65	48
24...	163	135	57	45
25...	111	71	32	35
26...	78	56	18	30
27...	59	81	16	47
28...	68	64	29	40
29...	57	114	15	42
30...	45	95	29	41
31...	49	58	23	28
32...	48	77	49	37
33...	53	85	48	32
34...	32	97	12	29
35...	72	76	42	59
36...	44	68	37	57
37...	49	70	26	62

	Longenecker	Connery	Peters	Howe
38...	81	58	44	72
39...	45	130	38	64
T'l.	2217	3291	1422	1926

XVI.

	Longenecker	Connery	Peters	Howe
1...	6	146	41	13
2...	11	113	29	13
3...	12	149	43	13
4...	19	127	62	12
5...	17	110	41	26
6...	12	133	39	27
7...	8	160	17	18
8...	7	161	16	11
9...	6	161	17	1
10...	5	125	26	7
11...	11	153	12	5
12...	8	261	23	8
13...	9	170	12	3
14...	16	192	14	9
15...	15	162	11	10
16...	6	171	15	11
17...	19	142	45	10
18...	21	134	21	12
19...	16	108	41	44
20...	18	143	43	11
21...	17	75	76	25
22...	24	70	33	35
T'l.	283	3157	677	324

XVII.

	Longenecker	Connery	Peters	Howe
1...	11	92	60	19
2...	13	129	41	19
3...	21	83	51	20
4...	14	116	55	17
5...	8	98	50	10
6...	21	91	50	15
7...	13	164	40	8
8...	37	82	40	21
9...	14	83	83	17
10...	19	72	73	7
11...	12	105	71	16
12...	6	52	129	12
13...	16	52	129	12
14...	17	68	58	14
15...	13	57	105	21
16...	21	131	47	22
17...	15	78	63	23
18...	14	69	83	16
19...	10	91	121	18
T'l.	300	1712	1331	302

XVIII.

	Longenecker	Connery	Peters	Howe
1...	13	111	35	15
2...	10	105	31	11
3...	7	77	46	6
4...	7	87	34	9
5...	6	93	39	32
6...	13	96	37	28
7...	6	74	33	28
8...	6	70	24	12
9...	13	79	46	12
10...	9	181	23	11
11...	1	297	5	2
12...	12	123	14	10
13...	12	50	13	12
14...	8	215	24	13
15...	13	85	34	17
16...	10	91	25	7
17...	5	102	34	16
18...	7	137	27	12
19...	9	133	35	7
20...	10	49	25	18
21...	9	65	48	15
22...	13	61	41	22
23...	16	100	44	19
24...	18	97	28	14
25...	22	73	76	55
26...	12	87	42	24
27...	16	78	40	12
28...	16	74	23	20
29...	25	63	43	13
30...	19	73	49	16
31...	24	58	43	12
32...	23	83	42	12
33...	21	99	56	21
34...	28	57	34	7
35...	18	90	64	19

	Longenecker.	Connery.	Peters.	Howe
36....	17	66	64	13
37....	22	91	[illegible]	12
38....	17	[illegible]	[illegible]	8
39....	16	[illegible]	[illegible]	18
40....	8	[illegible]	25	18
41....	13	60	68	14
42....	21	78	41	30
43....	4	56	46	19
44....	4	76	42	20
45....	8	76	84	31
46....	21	46	41	19
47....	16	69	66	14
48....	21	72	38	17
T'l.	650	4284	1840	745
XIX.				
1....	7	130	8	13
2....	24	128	15	16
3....	19	128	11	8
4....	17	186	9	16
5....	17	106	8	13
6....	14	135	2	4
7....	14	178	6	6
8....	9	141	11	19
9....	13	126	10	20
10....	10	181	16	12
11....	11	113	7	12
12....	12	141	7	9
13....	12	141	7	24
14....	6	224	13	35
15....	9	167	6	17
16....	14	94	16	26
17....	12	92	16	17
18....	10	105	4	29
19....	19	107	14	22
20....	18	78	8	13
21....	18	75	26	16
22....	7	98	10	24
T'l.	293	2874	230	371
XX.				
1....	33	174	17	15
2....	14	149	14	19
3....	30	118	16	17
4....	21	115	14	26
5....	40	149	16	28
6....	13	201	8	14
7....	17	200	18	25
8....	17	214	14	13
9....	22	164	24	15
10....	27	135	15	19
11....	25	184	32	10
12....	19	147	38	12
13....	25	165	26	29
14....	22	159	21	13
15....	30	149	26	27
T'l.	365	2423	299	287
XXI.				
1....	35	68	40	11
2....	41	72	31	12
3....	17	58	39	18
4....	34	57	22	16
5....	36	124	35	18
6....	24	81	18	14
7....	20	75	31	11
8....	15	81	22	12
9....	23	86	24	12
10....	18	68	24	14
11....	32	92	35	10
12....	56	67	31	6
13....	56	62	48	2
14....	21	63	18	5
15....	31	70	19	8
16....	21	55	17	7
17....	25	69	30	13
18....	30	87	15	7
19....	15	98	26	14
20....	29	82	16	9
21....	28	69	20	9
22....	29	61	17	14
23....	28	61	41	6
24....	44	92	36	2
25....	37	97	34	10
26....	25	80	36	14
27....	23	107	22	14
28....	18	66	24	12
29....	27	77	30	7
30....	20	68	17	15
31....	32	60	24	11
32....	12	97	33	16
33....	9	62	24	12
34....	16	68	19	11
35....	8	97	16	7
36....	20	138	13	13
37....	31	61	20	7
38....	23	104	33	23
39....	16	102	18	6
40....	27	89	42	6
41....	37	84	35	8
42....	50	91	35	10
43....	16	77	24	9
44....	10	166	21	13
45....	13	79	26	4
46....	..	157	9	13
47....	16	104	16	9
48....	8	107	20	11
49....	7	113	28	11
T'l.	1199	4102	1274	621
XXII.				
1....	19	120	25	27
2....	39	133	38	43
3....	19	111	21	38
4....	22	111	17	45
5....	36	118	30	40
6....	18	118	25	62
7....	26	91	20	62
8....	26	106	25	46
9....	29	112	15	32
10....	28	157	16	30
11....	23	165	28	14
12....	22	102	34	24
13....	25	110	31	16
14....	31	118	41	27
15....	34	126	31	25
16....	51	99	24	66
17....	39	133	23	59
18....	26	112	99	52
19....	23	130	42	25
20....	48	120	31	10
21....	16	113	24	19
22....	25	85	34	19
23....	28	91	32	27
24....	20	90	54	24
25....	17	130	12	20
T'l.	690	2896	772	852
XXIII.				
1....	68	93	42	8
2....	70	94	67	6
3....	56	95	42	19
4....	66	114	30	16
5....	74	74	53	8
6....	54	84	56	16
7....	74	93	56	17
8....	52	107	60	18
9....	67	74	31	12
10....	49	85	38	17
11....	46	61	29	20
12....	38	73	35	15
13....	51	60	42	28
14....	64	65	32	9
15....	100	127	67	12
16....	72	93	48	12
17....	31	63	38	4
18....	65	79	85	10
19....	64	92	67	3
20....	76	116	69	7
21....	71	102	52	9
22....	57	72	46	18
23....	59	65	75	26
24....	61	43	67	17
25....	76	39	55	38
26....	50	42	33	36
27....	44	70	39	12
28....	76	81	42	7
29....	43	39	50	18
30....	57	43	50	21
31....	54	68	37	10
32....	47	58	36	27
33....	45	64	27	6
34....	41	100	36	19
35....	60	98	27	12
36....	57	93	29	10
37....	44	96	32	17
38....	44	112	33	9
39....	50	114	22	20
40....	88	94	36	14
41....	66	61	29	21
42....	56	93	45	18
43....	45	62	36	8
44....	36	100	46	4
45....	35	101	20	11
46....	73	83	48	11
47....	69	64	26	23
T'l.	2731	3789	2050	690
XXIV.				
1....	18	93	25	37
2....	26	74	32	13
3....	.29	144	20	22
4....	17	120	20	33
6....	18	84	16	27
6....	36	103	20	31
7....	37	118	55	43
8....	23	120	28	48
9....	33	105	48	58
10....	21	97	15	76
11....	34	129	22	39
12....	38	121	34	33
13....	30	63	32	36
14....	73	78	25	26
15....	62	131	22	18
16....	37	121	13	10
17....	25	168	20	23
18....	11	114	22	17
19....	24	117	16	14
20....	15	109	13	8
21....	49	77	34	7
22....	28	129	25	7
23....	33	100	26	16
24....	36	145	33	27
25....	29	85	29	23
26....	23	84	32	27
27....	22	65	40	40
28....	32	77	35	37
29....	35	55	23	48
30....	26	59	28	33
31....	34	92	34	24
32....	30	77	21	32
33....	21	57	16	24
34....	34	64	48	28
35....	24	76	30	28
T'l.	1062	3450	952	1013
XXV.				
1....	46	65	60	23
2....	92	101	69	17
3....	40	68	62	17
4....	84	79	63	10
5....	36	73	44	8
6....	37	73	48	23
7....	58	68	63	10
8....	59	86	60	9
9....	49	92	54	6
10....	55	95	54	13
11....	47	103	67	9
12....	70	100	60	4
13....	70	84	53	3
14....	73	110	87	5
15....	47	63	39	5
16....	66	104	87	2
17....	44	67	36	6
18....	67	51	47	1
19....	72	72	65	5
20....	108	76	93	1
21....	69	76	61	6
22....	61	84	83	6
23....	65	91	101	14
24....	53	89	63	4
25....	71	91	84	7
26....	69	85	78	2
27....	99	88	72	2
28....	103	102	101	11
29....	90	101	74	3
30....	58	136	96	1
31....	115	142	90	11
32....	51	90	42	8
33....	102	116	114	16
34....	103	99	61	1
35....	50	98	54	3
36....	63	129	70	12
37....	87	193	72	4
38....	69	118	75	4
39....	63	96	62	12
40....	56	51	75	5
41....	128	114	152	2
42....	63	67	66	5
43....	54	67	53	10
44....	48	96	88	3
T'l.	3010	4049	3086	328
XXVI.				
1....	26	76	60	43
2....	35	58	52	45
3....	48	69	67	29
4....	45	108	54	24
5....	40	93	64	16
6....	42	87	49	29
7....	48	69	48	41
8....	52	89	49	26
9....	54	109	52	33
10....	42	71	59	11
11....	42	69	66	21
12....	48	59	42	10
13....	87	98	73	39
14....	39	187	80	45
15....	53	123	95	31
16....	47	104	91	28
17....	85	73	75	35
18....	93	65	79	6
19....	78	98	63	7
20....	95	81	64	5
21....	89	93	114	31
22....	33	75	66	34
23....	72	104	111	26
24....	83	86	92	11
25....	60	94	78	15
26....	68	76	77	8
27....	78	88	53	6
28....	54	72	77	4
29....	81	104	84	27
30....	90	87	65	37
31....	71	129	92	32
32....	61	107	77	52
33....	61	97	65	29
34....	44	56	86	18
35....	48	166	93	16
36....	72	128	63	14
37....	31	112	46	8
38....	31	110	34	25
39....	39	69	70	25
40....	43	134	51	51
T'l.	2370	3773	2756	972
XXVII.				
1....	101	132	87	27
2....	31	47	81	14
3....	61	98	30	17
4....	74	115	45	37
5....	44	132	32	83
6....	26	93	23	71
7....	35	146	52	69
8....	75	72	66	20
9....	35	89	45	52
10....	58	84	30	18
11....	24	106	18	64
12....	64	117	45	65
13....	85	90	37	66
14....	56	131	65	92
15....	69	132	70	55
16....	46	120	50	94
17....	45	94	35	97
18....	86	67	35	21
19....	80	77	57	25
20....	36	139	64	66
21....	128	148	66	26
22....	26	90	31	53
23....	17	118	35	59
24....	28	146	49	69
25....	23	126	32	48
26....	24	126	27	63
27....	25	155	46	51
28....	38	182	30	51
29....	27	174	19	43
30....	36	96	39	37
31....	47	134	45	32
32....	22	107	37	67
33....	21	149	42	36

	Longenecker	Connery	Peters	Howe
34	10	141	32	40
35	21	168	36	58
36	38	124	81	66
37	33	81	83	41
T'l.	1594	4364	1637	1883

XXVIII.

	Longenecker	Connery	Peters	Howe
1	14	105	40	21
2	34	128	37	30
3	34	80	31	37
4	29	110	45	43
5	24	134	39	44
6	35	62	51	36
7	41	78	44	37
8	64	89	53	34
9	22	65	38	32
10	48	139	30	59
11	36	84	38	52
12	29	79	35	32
13	24	49	35	29
14	16	136	43	21
15	28	112	33	42
16	52	109	32	22
17	13	136	101	29
18	13	127	47	8
19	6	109	16	11
20	11	149	59	11
21	19	146	93	26
22	21	136	37	25
23	50	118	85	36
24	52	106	77	57
25	35	197	52	31
26	34	79	49	31
27	40	63	45	32
28	30	98	51	26
29	42	95	61	30
30	47	104	57	18
31	51	108	45	14
32	38	122	51	21
33	28	116	114	20
34	41	107	83	32
35	42	129	60	27
36	21	105	42	37
37	46	103	48	32
38	22	94	64	37
T'l.	1232	4016	1961	1162

XXIX.

	Longenecker	Connery	Peters	Howe
1	16	88	20	14
2	28	98	17	12
3	22	99	42	10
4	23	128	27	10
5	17	144	27	13
6	36	72	26	16
7	15	114	28	29
8	16	108	47	25
9	21	182	69	17
10	12	224	30	29
11	56	101	29	19
12	17	111	33	11
13	9	110	30	8
14	22	171	28	9
15	11	138	46	10
16	14	145	57	21
17	15	120	50	28
18	19	142	32	22
19	15	183	35	42
20	29	130	63	37
21	20	52	54	19
22	32	141	97	41
23	37	80	138	21
24	18	140	52	31
25	36	206	88	39
26	64	93	69	28
27	23	125	78	22
28	25	139	63	27
29	24	111	54	18
30	26	160	53	24
T'l.	718	3855	1482	645

XXX.

	Longenecker	Connery	Peters	Howe
1	23	73	37	7
2	15	91	47	21
3	14	46	19	7
4	13	87	8	13
5	21	139	40	14
6	6	191	7	2
7	10	219	15	4
8	15	161	8	7
9	9	178	8	5
10	8	158	22	3
11	18	125	22	7
12	11	135	9	10
13	13	92	22	12
14	8	111	24	28
15	16	145	28	10
16	10	170	16	4
17	14	115	40	15
18	17	137	26	14
19	9	15	32	3
20	13	39	27	2
21	16	19	44	2
22	14	28	23	5
23	21	109	39	13
24	24	114	32	18
25	12	104	31	15
26	13	133	26	14
27	16	128	24	8
28	12	137	16	4
29	22	166	20	3
30	17	158	33	18
31	19	146	18	10
32	13	128	14	7
33	14	168	24	5
T'l.	476	3965	807	306

XXXI.

	Longenecker	Connery	Peters	Howe
1	24	111	50	7
2	24	117	41	9
3	38	112	26	2
4	31	161	69	9
5	42	128	73	17
6	18	138	53	5
7	32	108	58	7
8	59	96	54	4
9	48	92	47	11
10	55	63	49	8
11	29	58	52	3
12	52	70	54	3
13	39	100	48	15
14	35	112	44	4
15	65	101	42	14
16	25	94	49	14
17	32	104	31	13
18	53	140	48	12
19	34	186	36	7
20	52	240	59	6
21	77	151	92	15
22	46	104	64	18
23	35	114	48	25
24	25	67	62	33
25	30	46	67	26
26	39	64	39	18
27	45	40	79	36
28	42	200	78	13
29	43	208	47	14
30	34	202	48	18
31	45	96	80	20
32	30	62	79	16
33	35	129	36	13
34	48	149	36	13
35	56	115	77	33
36	57	117	46	26
37	35	75	63	6
38	29	113	52	16
39	29	125	39	24
40	43	143	64	6
T'l.	1610	4651	2178	566

XXXII.

	Longenecker	Connery	Peters	Howe
1	53	59	70	2
2	41	71	65	4
3	49	31	66	2
4	67	53	64	6
5	58	59	66	7
6	35	46	38	12
7	48	68	52	12
8	37	72	65	11
9	50	73	72	21
10	22	147	81	19
11	22	126	75	6
12	38	101	52	8
13	30	89	70	8
14	43	57	48	5
15	53	84	77	5
16	57	68	57	6
17	33	50	91	10
18	43	85	96	7
19	54	58	72	9
20	59	67	66	6
21	55	61	116	6
22	62	68	77	5
23	61	67	87	7
24	50	94	67	12
25	33	133	70	20
26	49	124	65	16
27	25	146	61	12
28	25	171	69	22
29	41	141	71	37
30	41	122	65	25
31	58	89	82	19
32	48	86	55	7
33	50	134	59	10
34	53	91	52	13
35	83	80	100	8
36	52	97	69	16
37	25	67	53	8
38	22	102	55	21
39	32	125	33	4
40	31	71	51	14
41	37	69	75	24
42	43	54	52	16
43	28	63	73	22
44	48	77	73	16
45	89	77	100	8
46	79	82	117	11
47	36	75	75	16
48	20	93	49	7
49	33	77	56	6
T'l.	2221	4200	3370	577

XXXIII.

	Longenecker	Connery	Peters	Howe
1	33	76	35	10
2	44	70	72	15
3	41	82	41	27
4	43	74	68	10
5	51	56	83	16
6	49	70	65	23
7	26	84	77	23
8	50	60	74	33
9	63	105	85	43
10	37	83	42	16
11	31	58	67	33
12	55	74	99	55
13	30	72	92	51
14	88	66	86	60
15	46	84	79	69
16	31	114	39	55
17	31	91	57	56
18	28	107	53	51
19	28	66	60	52
20	21	85	70	51
21	31	94	54	84
22	32	80	70	58
23	7	91	65	21
24	17	63	57	52
25	30	75	83	62
26	46	64	99	31
27	58	46	104	8
28	70	91	102	25
29	123	100	94	21
30	41	120	93	40
31	24	73	86	26
32	33	61	64	18
33	17	112	80	9
34	47	145	32	15
35	33	91	86	33
36	31	90	47	14
37	17	171	45	8
38	40	205	53	12
39	46	188	69	27
40	15	103	23	42
T'l.	2046	3458	3191	1320

XXXIV.

	Longenecker	Connery	Peters	Howe
1	32	150	49	36
2	20	127	63	24
3	19	113	71	25
4	20	109	61	19
5	30	159	46	19
6	24	189	62	27
7	47	142	57	24
8	48	140	36	20
9	59	123	39	36
10	38	135	42	30
11	36	93	49	..
12	10	109	28	16
13	37	88	37	23
14	57	113	30	22
15	32	103	34	14
16	39	119	38	15
17	48	140	64	20
18	47	145	42	14
19	38	162	51	18
20	44	149	57	5
21	28	158	60	14
22	25	212	62	39
23	49	210	85	41
24	25	255	41	19
25	34	128	47	40
26	55	170	53	38
27	18	179	70	42
28	26	122	43	33
29	65	115	73	26
30	40	161	76	59
31	24	156	92	59
32	41	170	63	57
33	24	164	79	7
T'l.	1212	5054	1832	994

XXXV.

	Longenecker	Connery	Peters	Howe
1	24	77	49	16
2	26	96	48	28
3	30	90	62	21
4	44	15	47	47
5	25	47	42	54
6	24	85	76	37
7	35	118	43	42
8	23	74	35	66
9	34	104	53	43
10	20	107	73	58
11	24	112	48	41
12	22	89	29	55
13	49	120	29	50
14	25	104	44	42
15	28	153	46	43
16	41	123	34	63
17	43	87	23	51
18	30	83	35	65
19	22	148	30	63
20	14	105	18	12
21	19	127	24	17
22	18	135	13	13
23	22	132	41	24
24	44	188	33	15
25	30	220	46	9
26	49	188	12	9
27	32	182	44	19
28	29	124	31	13
29	25	168	29	15
30	22	166	27	16
31	22	123	25	23
32	31	166	40	9
33	17	112	30	9
34	47	145	32	15
35	33	143	50	33
36	31	90	47	14
37	37	171	45	8
38	40	205	53	12
39	46	188	69	27
40	15	103	23	42
T'l.	1202	5124	1538	1199

SUMMARY.

Longenecker 44,554
Connery 129,588
Peters 56,834
Howe 24,081

Connery's plurality 73,054

CITY TREASURER.

Nominees: Charles W. Moderwell, progressive; Michael J. Flynn, democrat; Arthur W. Peterson, republican; T. J Vind, socialist.

Ward.	Moderwell.	Flynn.	Peterson.	Vind.	Ward.	Moderwell.	Flynn.	Peterson.	Vind.	Ward.	Moderwell.	Flynn.	Peterson.	Vind.
1	528	4193	661	218	13	1640	5768	1610	471	25	3643	3215	3242	316
2	1168	2431	3370	258	14	1019	4003	2369	671	26	2626	3292	2906	963
3	2238	3723	1725	202	15	2279	3095	1646	1913	27	1853	3849	1875	1886
4	314	4023	736	292	16	289	3193	690	312	28	1348	3330	2331	1181
5	427	4382	839	358	17	264	1760	1400	289	29	520	4083	1536	643
6	2395	2991	2477	209	18	752	4246	1897	741	30	453	4103	862	291
7	2835	3876	3462	566	19	302	2896	242	367	31	1478	4952	2288	522
8	1224	2914	1529	692	20	335	2531	282	287	32	2382	3910	3558	550
9	2349	2601	836	1049	21	1384	3869	1345	527	33	2380	2878	3537	1290
10	427	2383	782	630	22	710	2918	684	836	34	1296	4946	1921	1015
11	449	3301	1164	522	23	2953	3404	2267	648	35	1334	4860	1690	1193
12	554	3580	1777	916	24	1017	3477	989	1021	Total	47119	124976	60525	23845

SUPERIOR COURT JUDGE.

Nominees: Henry W. Leman, progressive; John M. O'Connor, democrat; Homer E. Tinsman, republican; Wilbur C. Benton, socialist.

Ward.	Leman.	O'Connor.	Tinsman.	Benton.	Ward.	Leman.	O'Connor.	Tinsman.	Benton.	Ward.	Leman.	O'Connor.	Tinsman.	Benton.
1	448	4191	815	231	14	834	3974	2645	718	27	1579	3872	2219	1956
2	908	2304	3809	289	15	2110	3088	1915	2006	28	1227	3317	2570	1224
3	1785	3486	2442	228	16	289	3173	775	336	29	478	3961	1756	681
4	334	3848	820	337	17	268	1709	1459	329	30	433	3978	992	311
5	396	4335	924	387	18	572	4158	2207	803	31	1241	4351	3009	576
6	1540	2924	3477	225	19	304	2892	314	387	32	1452	3660	4859	571
7	2081	3823	4303	602	20	322	2387	460	320	33	1771	2869	4138	1365
8	1156	2940	1663	619	21	1085	4022	1638	551	34	1126	4880	2278	1057
9	2145	2668	1080	1106	22	644	2894	813	872	35	1096	4841	2014	1241
10	400	2352	889	666	23	2486	3325	2870	711	Cicero	115	419	865	416
11	411	3145	1392	551	24	1027	3371	1171	1026	Total	38478	122923	74559	25575
12	487	3544	1951	947	25	2501	3212	4515	357	Towns	3860	6590	11467	2095
13	1318	5675	2085	516	26	2111	3335	3427	1027	Gd.total.	42338	129513	86026	27670

VOTE FOR ALDERMEN.
April 1, 1913.

Ward.
1. Andrew Donovan, Prog... 713
Michael Kenna, Dem....4,458
Rice Wasbrough, Soc.... 203
2. Alfred Tanser, Prog.... 440
Thomas F. Ennis, Dem...1,808
George F. Harding,Jr.,Rep.5,193
Samuel Block, Soc....... 261
3. W. W. Mitchell, Prog....2,338
Thomas D. Nash, Dem....4,613
Sanford K. Huston, Rep..1,625
Michael J. DeMuth, Soc.. 163
4. Joseph F. Ryan, Dem....1,133
Arthur W. Sullivan, Rep.1,091
Carl J. Wegener, Soc.... 230
5. John E. Jones, Prog..... 310
Patrick J. Carr, Dem....4,686
Joseph Pavelchik, Rep... 966
Henry P. Turner, Soc.... 323
6. Henry F. Porter, Prog...1,299
William A. Harrison, Dem.2,953
Theodore K. Long, Rep..3,904
J. Clifford Cox, Soc..... 176
7. Edward J. Hess, Prog... 256
Oscar W. Eckland, Dem..8,626
Bernard W. Snow, Rep..3,465
John F. Caulfield, Soc... 341
Charles E. Merriam, Ind..3,766
8. Thomas H.McKinney,Prog.1,221
John R. Emerson, Dem...3,215
John E. Tyden, Rep.....1,714
John Morrison, Soc...... 533
9. Hiram Vanderbilt, Prog..2,848
John Prystalski, Dem....2,701
William C. Hunt, Rep... 693
Henry J. Le Cren, Soc... 988
10. Wm. Schimelpfenig, Prog. 453
Frank Klaus, Dem......2,352
James McClorey, Rep...1,671
Joseph J. Thomas, Jr., Soc. 567
11. William E. Downey, Prog. 244
Edward F. Cullerton, Dem.3,256
John A. Pelka, Rep.....2,123
Frank Raisl, Soc....... 403
12. StephenJ.Napieralski,Prog. 392
Otto Kerner, Dem......3,474
Rudolph Mulac, Rep....2,911
Marcel Kulcynski, Soc... 638
SHORT TERM.
12. Alexander Jasinski, Prog. 359

Ward.
Joseph I. Novak, Dem....3,746
Otto Besserer, Rep......2,499
Charles Beranek, Soc.... 803
13. Samuel P. Reese, Prog...1,489
Thomas J. Abern, Dem...5,820
Ninian H. Welch, Rep....1,738
Joseph I. Granger, Soc... 405
John Edward Scully, Ind. 661
14. James N. Cowder, Prog... 574
Michael F. Maher, Dem..3,630
James H. Lawley, Rep...3,759
Charles Larney, Soc..... 564
15. Henry Utpatel, Prog....3,076
M. D. Grace, Dem......2,679
Max Loster, Rep.......1,650
William E. Rodriguez, Soc.2,302
16. Stanley Henry Kunz, Dem.3,435
Henry Schuleuburg, Rep..1,087
M. Sahud, Soc......... 322
17. Charles J. Ryberg, Prog.. 184
Theodore Lein, Dem.....1,189
Lewis D. Sitts, Rep.....2,697
N. F. Holm, Soc........ 188
18. F. H. Scheuermann, Prog. 394
Frank F. Gazzolo, Dem..3,176
Andrew J. O'Donnell, Rep.2,456
George W. Perry, Soc.... 790
John J. Cassidy, Ind....1,837
19. John Duff, Prog........ 238
John Powers, Dem......3,154
Robert Orlando, Soc..... 46
Joseph Edelson, Soc..... 546
20. Samuel Heller, Prog.....1,298
Emanuel Abrahams, Dem.2,378
Sam Golden, Soc........ 298
21. George P. Braun, Prog...1,722
Ellis Geiger, Dem......4,048
R. R. Baldwin, Rep.....1,242
Charles Roux, Soc...... 492
22. Patrick H. Regan, Prog... 693
Victor J. Schaeffer, Dem.3,478
Fred W. Forsberg, Rep... 599
Andrew Lafin, Soc....... 785
23. Jacob A. Hey, Prog.....3,617
Harry H. Lampert, Dem..3,563
Alfred O. Erickson, Rep..2,178
C. B. Robel, Soc....... 499
24. L. O. Hensel, Prog.....1,342
August Krumbolz, Dem...3,563

Ward.
Jos. L. Cunningham, Rep. 972
John E. Noesen, Soc....1,107
25. Harper E. Osborn, Prog..2,206
Burrell D. Jones, Dem...3,103
Henry D. Capitain, Rep..5,194
Charles W. Greene, Soc.. 300
SHORT TERM.
25. L. D. Wallace, Jr., Dem.3,208
Jacob Albert Freund, Rep.3,768
Paul Pause, Soc....... 312
C. I. Backus, Ind......2,941
26. A. W. Stanmeyer, Prog..2,027
Albert J. W. Appell, Dem.2,883
William F. Lipps, Rep...4,594
Charles F. Hohman, Soc.. 886
27. G. Ed Trebing, Dem.....4,624
John G. Buerkle, Rep...1,329
William F. Gubbins, Soc.1,755
Frank P. Mies, Ind.....2,431
28. M. J. Dempsey, Prog....1,736
Edward J. Green, Dem...2,681
Harry E. Littler, Rep...3,513
A. A. Wigsness, Soc....1,007
29. Felix B. Janovsky, Dem..4,297
George M. Tobey, Rep...2,624
J. H. Carbray, Soc..... 565
30. George P. Latchford,Dem.4,346
John W. Courtney, Rep.. 959
Aaron Henry, Soc...... 354
31. Anson H. Brown, Prog...1,852
John H. Dorsey, Dem....3,365
James A. Kearns, Rep...3,798
William Henning, Soc.... 498
32. Robert C. Thorne, Prog..1,402
Thomas M. Crane, Dem..3,977
Albert J. Fisher, Rep...4,922
John W. Deal, Soc...... 423
33. Amandus E. Hostier,Prog.1,267
Charles A. Reading, Dem.3,122
Irwin R. Hazen, Rep....4,872
Benjamin N. Olin, Soc...1,259
34. Leon Edelman, Prog.....1,326
Winfield J. Held, Dem...4,892
Frank Zeman, Rep......2,925
Steve Skala, Soc....... 821
35. Everett S. Hughes, Prog..1,108
Martin J. Healy, Dem...5,142
Harry W. Skallerup, Rep.2,074
Rudolph Borkenhgen, Soc.1,134

VOTE ON PROPOSITIONS.
April 1, 1913.

Ward.	*Bond issue. For.	Against.	†Cicero annex. For.	Against.	Ward.	*Bond issue. For.	Against.	†Cicero annex. For.	Against.	Ward.	*Bond issue. For.	Against.	†Cicero annex. For.	Against.
1.....	3,537	479	2,124	622	15.....	3,602	4,861	4,081	2,673	29.....	3,161	3,091	2,481	1,293
2.....	4,573	2,309	2,726	1,105	16.....	1,472	2,463	1,146	1,053	30.....	2,970	2,280	2,350	1,225
3.....	4,612	2,955	4,563	1,308	17.....	1,834	1,565	1,279	586	31.....	3,891	4,577	4,583	1,759
4.....	2,939	2,057	1,737	997	18.....	1,892	971	2,141	636	32.....	4,576	5,353	5,710	1,980
5.....	3,275	2,269	2,209	1,084	19.....	2,869	864	1,753	606	33.....	3,756	5,999	5,937	1,974
6.....	4,765	3,132	5,219	1,243	20.....	2,080	1,250	1,373	883	34.....	4,958	4,100	4,767	1,647
7.....	3,596	5,161	6,486	1,717	21.....	2,448	1,322	2,546	911	35.....	4,359	4,568	5,136	1,749
8.....	2,856	2,752	2,367	1,229	22.....	2,463	2,330	1,625	1,637					
9.....	2,699	3,465	2,713	1,442	23.....	4,256	4,846	4,888	2,259	Total.	120,512	115,627	121,260	50,186
10.....	2,002	2,264	1,475	861	24.....	2,618	3,670	2,383	1,943	*Issuing bonds to the amount of				
11.....	2,610	2,522	2,001	1,085	25.....	5,282	5,001	6,502	2,285	$2,880,000 for corporate purposes.				
12.....	3,083	3,274	2,944	1,287	26.....	3,644	5,897	4,988	2,705	†Cicero voted against annexation,				
13.....	5,206	4,235	5,730	1,532	27.....	3,561	5,749	4,714	2,392	1,655 to 995, and so the proposition				
14.....	3,893	3,547	4,020	1,293	28.....	3,174	4,457	3,470	1,875	failed.				

PRIMARY ELECTION, FEB. 25, 1913.
VOTE FOR CITY CLERK.

Candidates—Republican: William F. Peters, William E. Stevens, Alexander F. Wolf. Democratic: Francis D. Connery, Joseph M. Coffey, Frank H. Landmesser, Fred L. Yeager, John C. Guenther, Randall E. Marshall, Vincent S. Zwiefka. Socialist: Robert H. Howe. Progressive: Joel F. Longenecker.

Ward.	Republican. Peters.	Stevens.	Wolf.	Democratic. Connery.	Coffey.	Landmesser.	Yeager.	Guenther.	Marshall.	Zwiefka.	Soc. Howe.	Prog. Long'ecke
1..................	111	57	105	954	528	48	163	19	27	15	15	31
2..................	340	204	509	651	579	15	62	25	30	10	17	77
3..................	304	266	582	1063	1222	58	72	34	80	15	12	170
4..................	158	94	121	1869	1532	190	243	45	47	385	10	5
5..................	114	71	71	1454	766	55	80	36	32	43	14	15
6..................	583	324	678	854	736	37	51	29	65	9	15	120
7..................	759	519	784	884	1091	27	38	27	52	7	41	193
8..................	136	93	162	490	774	80	67	17	29	371	38	53
9..................	117	77	70	590	983	80	70	30	56	51	40	77
10..................	50	39	87	865	1046	77	69	32	40	142	23	18
11..................	88	36	76	674	1063	72	84	28	26	108	32	46
12..................	129	72	216	737	1307	100	155	49	60	265	38	44
13..................	272	220	211	2905	1629	93	137	53	131	25	26	74
14..................	230	145	254	2143	653	56	62	62	71	48	38	84
15..................	289	131	333	1429	827	139	124	79	68	177	69	273
16..................	64	33	153	402	606	174	29	19	28	1509	11	6
17..................	92	66	271	340	389	25	15	4	13	247	12	7
18..................	182	134	305	1175	1087	52	93	18	402	22	33	81
19..................	27	21	65	735	787	29	20	17	31	8	8	30
20..................	91	41	85	958	1068	93	135	40	39	52	3	4
21..................	249	171	403	1744	1083	109	121	55	95	32	40	114
22..................	72	37	83	1121	1735	150	175	99	48	39	40	31
23..................	513	291	445	1190	642	82	72	59	50	20	27	136
24..................	137	64	148	1083	1094	254	182	138	66	144	46	21
25..................	1128	643	798	986	650	40	40	28	58	12	20	343
26..................	693	282	454	1121	772	162	137	117	84	23	27	152
27..................	255	142	192	1457	784	381	123	91	105	511	76	35
28..................	243	99	272	1228	827	183	44	24	20	146	55	57
29..................	394	265	437	1162	1452	177	216	56	79	242	46	3
30..................	133	81	95	2004	1668	135	186	53	79	62	17	24
31..................	562	358	365	1836	1080	85	135	44	65	18	39	106
32..................	546	352	405	1188	1086	54	71	27	54	14	29	133
33..................	684	326	512	930	568	77	55	39	49	44	38	90
34..................	246	144	267	1638	1465	189	237	82	150	184	47	21
35..................	357	204	286	2327	1239	116	129	58	120	44	57	50
Total	10348	6102	10152	42187	34929	3704	3692	1633	2439	5063	1104	2748

VOTE FOR CITY TREASURER.

Candidates—Republican: Arthur W. Peterson, Byron L. Kanaley. Democratic: Michael J. Flynn, John A. Richert, Patrick J. Byrne, Francis J. McKeon, Otto Heickien, Ernst Jentzsch, Michael C. Buckley, Cornelius E. Sullivan, William T. Mahoney, Michael H. Zuber, Joseph Mitchell. Socialist: T. J. Vind. Progressive: Charles M. Moderwell.

Ward.	Republican. Peterson.	Kanaley.	Democratic. Flynn.	Richert.	Byrne.	McKeon.	Heickien.	Jentzsch.	Buckley.	Sullivan.	Mahoney.	Zuber.	Mitchell.	Soc. Vind.	Prog. Moderwell.
1..............	144	126	964	747	27	25	25	7	41	19	9	22	33	15	30
2..............	573	478	605	548	40	18	8	2	56	12	53	7	25	17	76
3..............	545	566	1149	1110	63	27	8	9	137	16	17	11	50	12	168
4..............	204	154	1446	2912	39	24	28	19	53	15	19	37	21	10	5
5..............	162	90	1542	626	47	29	17	8	121	20	24	22	40	14	15
6..............	818	615	992	621	43	16	9	10	48	12	11	11	39	15	130
7..............	1170	892	1194	691	54	29	18	3	51	26	13	13	38	41	201
8..............	235	152	801	703	58	20	22	26	32	39	12	41	52	38	52
9..............	197	63	576	861	85	36	31	25	69	21	34	36	70	39	77
10..............	80	105	808	1062	82	46	33	28	41	32	28	37	87	23	18
11..............	97	113	637	1121	57	20	27	22	48	24	17	36	47	33	46
12..............	190	222	595	1490	76	50	48	58	91	32	38	94	146	38	43
13..............	422	274	2809	1282	253	60	27	23	224	89	49	42	145	26	73
14..............	384	235	1855	636	79	43	20	14	73	63	36	36	221	39	81
15..............	462	266	948	1234	65	65	78	38	93	32	43	68	132	68	276
16..............	88	165	1059	949	55	50	24	83	40	48	50	64	71	11	6

Ward.	Peterson.	Kanaley.	Flynn.	Richert.	Byrne.	McKeon.	Heleklen	Jentasch	Buckley.	Sullivan.	Mahoney.	Zuber.	Mitchell.	Vind.	Moderwell
17	147	283	361	462	13	18	6	31	10	14	17	20	42	12	7
18	309	317	1128	1108	241	41	30	9	58	79	42	29	78	33	82
19	58	62	698	698	127	29	15	9	40	21	10	8	25	8	29
20	105	99	912	1220	56	29	27	51	46	31	23	27	69	8	5
21	423	398	1529	1139	85	152	42	20	64	48	52	66	86	41	114
22	128	72	920	942	42	57	39	20	40	28	34	319	49	40	31
23	857	422	968	763	51	23	24	21	50	27	21	93	65	27	137
24	205	145	663	1304	63	46	57	28	72	28	40	696	70	46	21
25	1720	878	559	731	68	24	12	6	28	15	17	26	43	20	351
26	966	445	755	1097	49*	29	46	28	76	35	38	205	74	27	349
27	423	172	1000	1255	79	135	53	414	105	43	55	127	142	76	35
28	385	228	781	1202	43	45	28	33	70	30	33	43	72	55	57
29	650	442	1217	1545	211	44	41	48	98	29	40	66	78	46	3
30	215	97	2656	936	88	40	43	29	405	34	93	30	45	17	23
31	903	396	2081	546	33	11	15	10	56	13	13	9	27	39	107
32	981	417	1464	828	36	14	19	10	95	16	8	9	43	29	134
33	1029	490	693	768	55	31	40	17	34	22	27	35	66	38	98
34	393	251	1570	1603	127	51	62	78	120	52	58	103	177	47	21
35	575	268	1970	1196	177	58	72	50	167	77	93	54	136	60	50
Total	16193	10397	40865	35886	2767	1438	1095	1297	2852	1132	1147	2543	2604	1108	2750

VOTE FOR SUPERIOR COURT JUDGE.

Candidates—Republican: Homer E. Tinsman, William H. Fish, Julius A. Johnson. Democratic: John M. O'Connor, James Maher, Elijah A. Zolline, John Coburn. Socialist: Wilbur C. Benton. Progressive: Henry W. Leman.

	Republican.			Democratic.				Pro.	Soc.
Ward.	Tinsman	Fish	Johnson	O'Connor	Maher	Zolline	Coburn	Benton	Leman
1	221	30	59	903	570	319	169	16	31
2	739	150	221	599	495	161	148	18	77
3	779	151	199	929	952	437	276	12	168
4	224	82	93	1425	1821	496	629	10	...
5	144	52	71	1364	645	165	416	14	15
6	1005	192	248	686	591	369	162	15	132
7	1418	245	439	762	827	353	189	41	193
8	219	62	135	684	813	194	143	38	52
9	170	46	72	634	951	157	166	42	77
10	135	43	29	746	1029	389	221	28	18
11	155	36	36	641	1072	161	222	34	46
12	261	78	94	632	1506	257	391	39	42
13	416	134	167	2328	1689	359	667	26	73
14	371	111	167	1870	862	208	240	39	84
15	283	142	243	1086	816	736	272	71	279
16	214	32	39	1175	749	475	170	11	6
17	327	50	80	413	429	128	84	12	7
18	467	76	108	1250	1110	274	259	34	83
19	70	33	24	534	765	321	194	9	24
20	160	47	38	722	858	907	192	9	5
21	584	112	164	2032	809	226	236	41	114
22	129	30	60	1216	795	273	214	40	32
23	745	145	426	1073	644	203	214	27	137
24	226	78	67	1074	1319	320	318	46	21
25	1600	318	724	804	708	168	175	20	353
26	840	223	398	897	908	269	355	27	151
27	310	85	219	1373	1095	448	486	76	35
28	397	70	162	1091	894	403	154	55	57

Ward.	Tinsman	Fish	Johnson	O'Connor	Maher	Zolline	Coburn	Benton	Leman
29	682	229	243	1133	1410	352	525	47	3
30	184	59	70	2300	1044	372	538	16	23
31	741	108	474	1689	884	281	439	39	107
32	1019	121	289	923	910	412	307	29	N46
33	867	126	496	713	637	149	295	29	29
34	393	124	166	1119	1524	760	657	47	21
35	440	155	267	1758	1385	372	691	60	51
Cicero	109	52	66	52	27	14	33	16	10
Total	17144	3895	6785	38635	33450	11898	10758	1141	2776
Towns	1360	333	350	744	342	163	281	100	237
Gd. t'l	18504	4228	7135	39379	33792	12061	11039	1241	3013

VOTE FOR ILLINOIS SUPREME COURT JUDGE.

In 5th judicial district Oct. 20, 1913.
Candidates—Charles C. Craig, democrat; A. H. Shay, progressive; L. D. Puterbaugh, republican; Dan R. Shean, prohibition.

	Dem.	Prog.	Rep.	Proh.
	Craig.	Shay.	Puterbaugh.	Shean
Knox	2763	1336	1577	44
Henry	1454	1835	1133	70
Stark	303	224	495	4
Peoria	3830	1271	5240	102
Marshall	1086	158	645	7
Putnam	266	177	205	3
Bureau	1558	686	1094	32
LaSalle	4970	2656	2114	80
Grundy	507	412	1058	46
Woodford	1034	333	709	27
Total	17721	9088	14270	415

SOCIAL SETTLEMENTS IN CHICAGO.

Abraham Lincoln—Oakwood boulevard and Langley avenue; secretary, James P. Hall.

Archer Road Settlement—239 West 24th street; Charles W. Espey.

Association House—2150 West North avenue; Miss Carrie B. Wilson.

Chicago Commons—North Morgan street and Grand avenue; Graham Taylor.

Chicago Hebrew Institute—West Taylor and Lytle streets; superintendent, Dr. J. Pedott.

Christopher House—1618 Fullerton avenue; Miss Marjorie Howe.

Eli Bates House—621 West Elm street; Mrs. C. Franklin Leavitt.

Emerson—1802 Emerson avenue; Mrs. Rhoda A. Leach.

Esther Falkenstein Settlement House—1915 North Humboldt street; Miss Myrtle Falkenstein.

Fellowship House—831 West 33d place; Mrs. Amelia H. Jerome.

Forward Movement—1356 West Monroe street; Rev. George W. Gray.

Frederick Douglass—3032 Wabash avenue; Mrs. Celia P. Woolley.

Gads Hill—1959 West 20th street; Frank P. Blessing.

Graeme Stewart—Graeme Stewart school; secretary, Winfield W. Dudley.

Halsted Street Institutional Church Settlement—1935 South Halsted street; Rev. J. B. Martin.

St. Mary's—44th street and Union avenue; Mrs. Katherine M. Farren.

South Deering Neighborhood Center—10441 Hoxie avenue; W. C. Miller.

South End—3212 East 91st street; Miss Edna Hudlee.

Union Home—2932 Groveland avenue; Mrs. Hilda N. Johnson-Haskins.

University of Chicago—4630 Gross avenue; Miss Mary E. McDowell.

Wendell Phillips—2009 Walnut street; Birdye H. Haynes.

Henry Booth House—707 West 14th place; T. W. Allison.

Hull House—800 South Halsted street; Miss Jane Addams.

Institutional Church—3825 Dearborn street; Rev. A. J. Carey.

Marcy Center—1335 Newberry avenue; Mrs. Helen G. Wagoner.

Maxwell Settlement—1214 South Clinton street; Miss Ernestine Haller.

Neighborhood House—6710 South May street; Mrs. H. M. Van Der Vaart and Anne E. Nichols.
Northwestern University—Augusta and Noble streets; Miss Harriet E. Vittum.

Oakley—646 North Oakley avenue; Mrs. Josephine Judkins.
Olivet Institute—701 Vedder street; Rev. Norman E. Barr.

CHICAGO MORTALITY STATISTICS.

[From reports of health department.]

POPULATION, DEATHS AND DEATH RATES BY YEARS.

Year.	Population.	Deaths.	Deaths in 1,000 of population.	Year.	Population.	Deaths.	Deaths in 1,000 of population.	Year.	Population.	Deaths.	Deaths in 1,000 of population.
1844	10,170	336	33.04	1868	252,054	5,984	23.74	1892	1,199,730	26,219	21.85
1845	12,088	344	28.46	1869	280,000	6,448	23.77	1893	1,253,022	27,083	21.61
1846	14,169	394	27.51	1870	306,605	7,323	23.88	1894	1,308,682	23,892	18.26
1847	16,859	572	33.93	1871	324,270	6,976	20.97	1895	1,366,813	24,219	17.72
1848	20,023	638	31.86	1872	367,396	10,156	27.64	1896	1,427,527	23,257	16.29
1849	23,047	1,701	73.80	1873	380,000	9,557	25.15	1897	1,490,937	21,809	14.64
1850	29,963	1,467	48.96	1874	395,408	8,025	20.30	1898	1,557,164	22,793	14.64
1851	34,000	927	27.96	1875	400,500	7,899	19.73	1899	1,626,333	25,503	15.68
1852	38,734	1,809	46.70	1876	407,661	8,573	21.03	1900	1,698,575	24,941	14.68
1853	59,130	1,325	22.41	1877	430,000	8,026	18.67	1901	1,751,968	24,406	13.93
1854	65,872	4,217	64.02	1878	436,731	7,422	16.99	1902	1,801,255	26,455	14.69
1855	80,023	2,181	27.26	1879	491,516	8,614	17.53	1903	1,850,542	28,914	15.62
1856	84,113	2,086	24.80	1880	503,185	10,462	20.79	1904	1,899,829	26,311	13.85
1857	87,600	2,414	27.56	1881	540,000	14,101	26.11	1905	1,949,116	27,212	13.96
1858	90,000	2,255	25.06	1882	560,693	13,234	23.60	1906	1,998,403	29,048	14.54
1859	93,000	2,008	21.59	1883	580,000	11,555	19.92	1907	2,047,690	32,198	15.72
1860	109,206	2,264	20.73	1884	629,985	12,471	19.79	1908	2,096,977	30,388	14.49
1861	120,000	2,279	18.99	1885	665,000	12,474	18.76	1909	2,146,264	31,296	14.58
1862	138,186	2,835	20.52	1886	703,715	13,699	19.47	1910	2,195,551	33,241	15.14
1863	150,000	3,875	25.83	1887	760,000	15,409	20.27	1911	2,244,835	32,672	14.55
1864	169,353	4,448	26.26	1888	802,651	15,772	19.65	1912	2,294,120	33,998	14.68
1865	178,492	4,029	22.57	1889	935,000	16,946	18.13	1913	*2,344,018	29,936	15.30
1866	200,418	6,524	32.55	1890	1,099,850	21,856	19.87				
1867	225,000	4,773	21.21	1891	1,148,795	27,754	24.16				

NOTE—The population is for midyear. *First ten months.

STATISTICS FOR 1912.
DEATHS BY AGES.

Under 1 year	6,709
1 to 5 years	3,299
5 to 10 years	1,030
10 to 20 years	1,292
20 to 30 years	2,884
30 to 40 years	3,438
40 to 50 years	3,891
50 to 60 years	4,002
60 to 70 years	3,479
70 to 80 years	2,662
Over 80 years	1,312

BY IMPORTANT CAUSES.

Disease.	Cases.
Typhoid fever	173
Smallpox	7
Measles	119
Scarlet fever	602
Whooping cough	140
Diphtheria and croup	950
Influenza	64
Rabies	8
Tetanus	28
Pellagra	7
Cerebrospinal fever	40
Anterior poliomyelitis	18
Tuberculosis (all forms)	3,750
Pneumonia (all forms)	5,056
Diarrhea and enteritis (under 2 years of age)	3,073
Congenital debility and malformations	1,757
Sunstroke	27
All other causes	18,179

STATISTICS FOR 1913.
(First ten months.)
DEATHS BY AGES.

Under 1 year	6,034
1 to 5 years	3,223
5 to 10 years	1,050
10 to 20 years	1,170
20 to 30 years	2,489
30 to 40 years	2,840
40 to 50 years	3,385
50 to 60 years	3,491
60 to 70 years	3,018
70 to 80 years	2,209
Over 80 years	1,027

BY IMPORTANT CAUSES.

Disease.	Cases.
Typhoid fever	175
Smallpox	1
Measles	282
Scarlet fever	852
Whooping cough	89
Diphtheria and croup	801
Influenza	73
Rabies	2
Tetanus	20
Pellagra	3
Tuberculosis (all forms)	3,272
Pneumonia (all forms)	4,164
Cerebrospinal fever	51
Anterior poliomyelitis	3
Diarrheal diseases (under 2 years of age)	2,918
Congenital defects and accidents	1,704
Sunstroke	75
Streptococcus sore throat	21

CONTAGIOUS DISEASES (1912).

Disease.	Cases.
Typhoid fever	1,051
Smallpox	68
Chickenpox	2,027
Measles	6,784
German measles	136
Scarlet fever	8,703
Whooping cough	2,462
Diphtheria, cases	7,285
Diphtheria, carriers	722
Cerebrospinal fever	49
Anterior poliomyelitis	135
Ophthalmia neonatorum	21
Streptococcus sore throat	15
Erysipelas	547
Mumps	1,679
Puerperal fever	21
Tuberculosis (all forms)	7,512
Pneumonia	1,512
Diarrhea and enteritis	28
All others	100

THE CHICAGO ACADEMY OF SCIENCES.

In Lincoln park, opposite Center street.

President—Dr. Thomas C. Chamberlin.
Secretary—Dr. Wallace W. Atwood.
Curator—Frank C. Baker.
Trustees—La Verne W. Noyes, president; Charles F. Gunther, Charles A. Heath, Louis E. Laflin, Henry J. Furber, Charles Dickinson, Ira J. Geer, Charles S. Raddin, Henry S. Henschen, F. L. Wilk, Frances Dickinson, Carroll H. Sudler, Eugene Garnett, T. C. Chamberlin (ex officio), Timothy J. O'Byrne (ex officio).
The museum is open from 9 a. m. to 5 p. m. on weekdays and from 1 to 5 p. m. on Sundays. There is no charge for admission. The academy is in co-operation with the public and private schools of the city in the promotion of nature study and scientific courses of instruction. Lecture courses, classroom instruction and laboratory work are given at the academy for the benefit of teachers, children and members. Field excursions are conducted during the fall and spring months and museum material is loaned to the schools.

POPULATION OF ILLINOIS BY COUNTIES.

[From federal census reports]

Counties	1820	1830	1840	1850	1860	1870	1880	1890.	1900	1910.
Adams .	.	2,186	14,476	26,508	41,323	56,362	59,148	61,188	67,058	64,588
Alexander ..	626	1,390	3,313	2,484	4 707	10,564	14,809	16,563	19,384	22,741
Bond	2,931	3,124	5,060	6,144	9,815	13,152	14,873	14,550	16,708	17,075
Boone .	.	.....	1,705	7,624	11,678	12,942	11,527	12,203	15,791	15,481
Brown	.. .	...	4,183	7,198	9,938	12,205	13,044	11,951	11,557	10,397
Bureau .	. .		3,067	8,841	2o,426	34,415	33,189	35,014	41,112	43,975
Calhoun .	. ..	1,090	1,741	3,231	5,144	6,562	7,471	7,652	8,917	8,610
Carroll	.. ..	....	1,023	4,586	11,733	16,705	16,985	18,320	18,963	18,035
Cass	.		2,981	7,253	11,325	11,580	14,494	15,963	17,222	17,372
Champaign ..	.	.	1,475	2,649	14,629	22,737	40,869	42,159	47,622	51,829
Christian ..	.	.	1,878	3,203	10,492	10,363	28,232	30,531	32,790	34,594
Clark	. 931	3,940	7,453	9,522	14,987	18,719	21,900	21,899	24,033	23,517
Clay	. 755	3,228	4,289	9,336	16,875	16,195	16,772	19,553	18,661
Clinton .	.	2,330	3,718	5,139	10,941	16,285	18,718	17,411	19,324	22,832
Coles ..	...	.	9,616	9,335	14,203	25,535	27,055	30,093	34,146	34,517
Cook	.		10,201	43,385	144,954	349,966	607,719	1,191,922	1,838,735	2,405,233
Crawford	2,999	3,117	4,422	7,133	11,551	13,889	16,190	17,283	19,240	26,281
Cumberland ..	.	.	...	3,718	8,311	12,223	13,762	15,443	16,124	14 281
DeKalb	. . . .	1,697	7,540	19,086	23,265	26,774	27,066	31,756	33,457
DeWitt	.	. ..	3,247	5,002	10,820	14,768	17,014	17,011	18,927	18,906
Douglas	.	.	...	...	7,140	13,484	15,857	17,669	19,097	19,591
DuPage	.	.	8,535	9,290	14,701	16,685	19,187	22,551	28,196	33,432
Edgar .	..	4,071	8,225	10,692	16,925	21,450	25,504	26,787	28,273	27,336
Edwards	3,444	1,649	3,070	3,524	7,454	7,565	8,600	9,444	10,345	10,049
Effingham	.	.	1,675	3,799	7,816	15,653	18,924	19,358	20,465	20,055
Fayette .	.	2,704	6,238	8,075	11,189	19,629	23,243	23,367	28,065	23,075
Ford .	.	.	.	.	1,979	9,103	15,105	17,035	18,359	17,096
Franklin .	.. 1,763	4,083	3,682	5,681	9,393	12,652	16,129	17,138	19,675	26,943
Fulton	.	1,841	13,142	22,508	33,338	38,291	41,249	43,110	46,201	49,549
Gallatin	3,155	7,405	10,760	5,418	8,055	11,134	12,862	14,935	15,836	14,628
Greene .	.	7,674	11,951	12,429	16,093	20,277	23,014	23,791	23,402	22,363
Grundy .	.	.		3,023	10,379	14,928	16,738	21,024	24,136	24,162
Hamilton	.	2,616	3,945	6,362	9,915	13,014	16,712	17,800	20,197	18,227
Hancock ...	.	483	9,946	14,652	29,061	35,935	35,352	31,907	32,215	30,638
Hardin ..	.	.	1,378	2,887	3,759	5,113	6,024	7,234	7,448	7,015
Henderson ..	.	.	... ...	4,612	9,501	12,582	10,755	9,876	10,836	9,724
Henry	.	41	1,260	3,809	20,660	35,506	36,609	33,338	40,049	41,736
Iroquois ...	.	.	1,695	4,149	12,325	25,782	35,457	35,167	38,014	35,543
Jackson ..	 1,542	1,828	3,566	5,862	9,589	19,634	22,508	27,809	33,871	35,143
Jasper ...	..	.	1,472	3,220	8,364	11,238	14,615	18,188	20,160	18,157
Jefferson	691	2,555	5,762	8,109	12,965	17,864	20,686	22,590	28,133	29,111
Jersey	.	.	4,536	7,354	12,051	16,054	15,546	14,810	14,612	13,954
Jo Daviess	.	2,111	6,180	18,604	27,325	27,820	27,534	25,101	24,533	22,657
Johnson	843	1,596	3,626	4,114	3,342	11,248	13,079	15 013	15,667	14,331
Kane	.	.	6,501	16,703	30,062	39,091	44,956	65,061	78,792	91,862
Kankakee ..	..	.	... .	...	15,412	24,352 .	24,961	28,732	37,154	40,752
Kendall .	.	.		7,730	13,074	12,399	13,084	12,106	11,467	10,777
Knox ..	.	274	7,060	13,278	28,663	39,522	38,360	38,752	43,612	46,159
Lake ..	.	. ....	7,654	14,226	18,257	21,914	21,299	24,235	34,504	55,058
LaSalle ..	.	.	9,348	17,815	48,332	69,792	70,420	80,798	87,776	90,132
Lawrence	.	3,668	7,092	8,121	9,214	12,533	13,633	14,693	16,523	22,661
Lee .	...	. ..	2,035	5,292	17,691	27,171	27,494	26,187	29,894	27,750
Livingston .	.	.	759	1,552	11,637	31,471	38,450	38,455	42,035	40,465
Logan ..	.	.	2,333	6,128	14,272	23,053	25,041	25,489	28,680	30,216
Macon ...	.	1,122	3,039	3,988	13,738	26,463	30,671	30,083	44,003	54,186
Macoupin	.. ..	1 990	7,826	12,355	24,602	32,726	37,705	40,380	42,256	50,685
Madison ...	13,550	6,221	14,433	20,441	31,351	44,131	50,141	61,535	64,694	89,847
Marion .	.. .	2,125	4,752	6,720	12,739	20,622	23,691	24,341	30,446	35,094
Marshall ..	.	.	1,849	5,180	13,437	16,506	15,036	13,653	16,370	15,679
Mason ..	4. ..	.	..	5,021	10,931	16,184	16,244	16,067	17,491	17,377
Massac ..	.	.	.	4,092	6,213	9 581	10,443	11,314	13,110	14,200
McDonough	.	..	5,308	7,616	20,069	26,509	27,984	27,467	28,312	26,887
McHenry .	.	.	2,578	14,918	22,089	23,762	24,914	26,114	29,759	32,509
McLean .	.	.	6,665	10,163	28,772	53,988	60,115	63,036	67,843	68,008
Menard .	. ./	.	4,431	6,349	9,584	11,735	13,028	13,120	14,336	12,796
Mercer .	.	26	2 352	5,246	15,042	18,769	19,501	18,545	20,944	19,723
Monroe .	1,516	2,000	4,481	7,679	12,532	12,982	13,682	12,948	13,847	13,508
Montgomery .	.	2 953	4,490	6,277	13,979	25,314	28,086	30,003	30,836	35,311
Morgan .	.	12,714	19,547	16,064	22,112	28,463	31,519	32,636	35,006	34,420
Moultrie ..	.	.	.	2,234	6,385	10,385	13,705	14,481	15,224	14,630
Ogle	.	.	3,479	10,020	22,888	27,492	29,946	28,710	29,129	27,864
Peoria	.	.	6,153	17,547	36,601	47,540	55,419	70,378	88,608	100,255
Perry	.	1,215	3,222	5,278	9,552	13,723	16,008	17,529	19,830	22,088
Platt ..	....		... ..	1,696	6,127	10,953	15,583	17,062	17,706	16,376
Pike	.	2 396	11,728	18,819	27,249	30,768	33,761	31,000	31,595	28,622
Pope .	. 2,610	3,216	4,094	3,975	6,742	11,437	13,256	14,017	13,585	11,215
Pulaski .	.	.	.	2,264	3,943	8,752	9,507	11 355	14,554	15,650
Putnam . .	.	1,310	2,131	3,924	5,587	6,280	6,555	4,730	4,746	7,561
Randolph .	3,492	4,425	7,944	11,079	17,205	20,859	25,691	25,049	28,901	29,120
Richland ..	. .	.	.	3,012	9,711	12,803	15,546	15,019	16,391	15,970
Rock Island	.	.	2,610	6,938	21,005	29,783	38,314	41,917	55,249	70,404
Saline ..	. .	.	.	5,688	9,331	12,714	15,940	19,342	21,686	30,204
Sangamon	.	12,960	14,716	19,228	32,274	46,252	52,902	61,195	71,593	91,029
Schuyler	. .	3,569	6 972	10,573	14,684	17 419	16,249	16,013	16,129	14,852
Scott .	. .	....	6,215	7,914	9,069	10,530	10,743	10,304	10,455	10,067
Shelby ..	. . ..	2,972	6,659	7,807	14,613	25,476	30,282	31,191	32,126	31,693

Counties.	1820.	1830.	1840.	1850.	1860.	1870.	1880.	1890.	1900.	1910.
Stark	.....	.....	1,573	3,710	9,004	10,751	11,209	9,982	10,186	10,098
St. Clair	5,248	7,078	13,631	20,180	37,694	51,068	61,850	66,571	86,685	119,870
Stephenson	.....	.....	2,800	11,667	25,112	39,608	31,970	31,338	34,933	36,821
Tazewell	.....	4,716	7,221	12,052	21,470	27,903	29,679	29,556	33,221	34,027
Union	2,362	3,239	5,524	7,615	11,181	17,513	18,100	21,549	22,610	21,856
Vermilion	.....	5,836	9,303	11,402	19,800	20,388	41,600	49,905	65,635	77,996
Wabash	.....	2,710	4,240	4,690	7,313	8,841	9,945	11,866	12,583	14,913
Warren	.....	308	6,739	8,176	18,336	23,174	22,940	21,281	23,163	23,313
Washington	1,547	1,675	4,810	6,953	13,731	17,599	21,117	19,262	19,526	18,759
Wayne	1,114	2,653	5,123	6,825	12,223	10,758	21,297	23,806	27,626	25,697
White	4,828	6,091	7,919	8,925	12,403	16,846	23,089	25,005	25,386	23,052
Whiteside	.....	.....	2,514	5,361	18,737	27,503	30,888	30,854	34,710	34,507
Will	.....	.....	10,167	16,703	29,389	43,013	53,424	62,007	74,764	84,371
Williamson	.....	.....	2,457	7,216	12,241	17,329	19,326	22,226	27,796	45,098
Winnebago	.....	.....	4,609	11,773	24,491	29,301	30,518	39,938	47,845	63,153
Woodford	.....	.....	.....	4,415	13,282	18,956	21,630	21,429	21,822	20,506
Aggregate	**55,162**	**157,445**	**476,183**	**851,470**	**1,711,951**	**2,539,891**	**3,077,871**	**3,826,351**	**4,821,550**	**5,638,591**

NOTE—In 1800 and 1810 the territory of Illinois contained but two organized counties, Randolph and St. Clair. In 1800 the population of Randolph county was 1,103 and of St. Clair, 1,255, total 2,358; in 1810 Randolph 7,275 and St. Clair 5,007, total 12,282.

COLOR, NATIVITY, PARENT-AGE (1910).

Color.

White	5,526,962
Negro	109,049
Indian	188
Chinese	2,103
Japanese	285
Filipino	3
Hindu	1

Nativity.

Total native	4,433,277
Total foreign born	1,205,314
Native white	4,324,402
Foreign born white	1,203,560

Parentage.

Native	2,600,555
Foreign	1,232,155
Mixed	491,692

SEX (1910).

Class.	Male.	Female.
White	2,852,386	2,674,576
Negro	56,909	52,140
Other	2,379	201
Native white	2,178,791	2,145,611
Native par'ge.	1,324,922	1,275,633
For. parentage.	611,275	620,880
Mixed par'tage	242,594	249,098
For'n born white	673,595	528,965
Urban	1,779,839	1,697,090
Rural	1,131,835	1,029,827

STATE OR DIVISION OF BIRTH (1910).

Illinois	3,406,638

Other states ... 1,026,639

Indiana	143,188
Ohio	122,391
New York	92,300
Missouri	85,161
Pennsylvania	78,116
Kentucky	74,543
Wisconsin	67,296
Iowa	57,948
Michigan	46,419
Tennessee	36,939
Kansas	19,008
Virginia	17,360
Massachusetts	16,280
Minnesota	12,753
Nebraska	11,968
New Jersey	10,434
All other*	134,535

Division.

New England	37,533
Middle Atlantic	180,850
East north central	3,785,932
West north central	190,546
South Atlantic	51,057
East south central	125,716
West south central	18,108
Mountain	7,728
Pacific	6,357
Other*	29,450

*Includes persons born in the United States, state not specified; persons born in outlying possessions or at sea under United States flag, and American citizens born abroad.

FOREIGN WHITE STOCK BY NATIONALITY (1910).

Includes all white persons in Illinois of foreign birth or having one or both parents foreign born.

Country.	Number.
Austria	286,844
Belgium	14,858
Canada—French	23,577
Canada—Other	86,092
Denmark	33,519
England	168,396
Finland	3,182
France	21,757
Germany	1,014,408
Greece	11,178
Holland	32,494
Hungary	52,764
Ireland	336,434
Italy	116,685
Norway	68,438
Roumania	5,352
Russia	227,960
Scotland	53,609
Sweden	230,131
Switzerland	21,658
Turkey (Asia)	3,382
Turkey (Europe)	2,672
Wales	11,637
All other	111,640
Total	**2,926,407**

POPULATION OF ILLINOIS CITIES (1910).

Color, nativity, sex and other details as to inhabitants of places having a population of 25,000 or more, excepting Chicago, which is treated separately.

AURORA.

Population	29,807
White	29,511
Negro	293
Chinese	2
Japanese	1
Native white—Native par.	12,232
Foreign or mixed par.	10,577
Foreign-born white	6,702
Male population	15,118
Female population	14,689
Males of voting age	9,711
Naturalized	1,795
First papers	171
Alien	1,150
Illiterate	494
Attending school	4,517
Dwellings	6,235
Families	6,864

BLOOMINGTON.

Population	25,768
White	24,953
Negro	809
Indian	1
Chinese	5
Native white—Native par.	14,642
Foreign or mixed par.	6,904
Foreign-born white	3,407
Male population	12,321
Female population	13,447
Males of voting age	8,009
Naturalized	1,152
First papers	53
Alien	137
Illiterate	260
Attending school	4,269
Dwellings	6,082
Families	6,455

DANVILLE.

Population	27,871
White	26,393
Negro	1,465
Indian	1
Chinese	12
Native white—Native par.	19,951
Foreign or mixed par.	4,874
Foreign-born white	1,998
Male population	13,721
Female population	14,150

Males of voting age	8,514
Naturalized	727
First papers	46
Alien	60
Illiterate	544
Attending school	4,983
Dwellings	6,793
Families	7,167

DECATUR.

Population	31,140
White	30,354
Negro	775
Chinese	7
Japanese	3
Native white—native par.	22,566
Foreign or mixed par.	5,366
Foreign-born white	2,422
Male population	15,443
Female population	15,697
Males of voting age	9,703
Naturalized	694
First papers	58
Alien	270
Illiterate	336
Attending school	5,199
Dwellings	7,131
Families	7,588

EAST ST. LOUIS.

Population 58,547
White 52,646
Negro 5,882
Chinese 19
Native white—Native par....30,447
Foreign or mixed par.....12,799
Foreign-born white..........9,400
Male population..............32,363
Female population............26,184
Males of voting age..........21,005
Naturalized 1,613
First papers.................374
Alien 2,701
Illiterate 2,614
Attending school.............8,519
Dwellings 11,628
Families 12,888

ELGIN.

Population 25,976
White 25,794
Negro 171
Chinese 10
Japanese 1
Native white—Native par....10,346
Foreign or mixed par.....9,787
Foreign-born white..........5,661
Male population..............12,290
Female population............13,686
Males of voting age..........7,910
Naturalized 1,608
First papers.................127
Alien 280
Illiterate 615
Attending school.............4,274
Dwellings 5,383
Families 6,024

JOLIET.

Population 34,670
White 34,161
Negro 497
Chinese 12
Native white—Native par....9,753
Foreign or mixed par.....13,967

Note—In the above tables those classed as illiterate are persons 10 years of age or over. The

Foreign-born white..........10,441
Male population..............18,417
Female population............16,253
Males of voting age..........11,477
Naturalized 2,483
First papers.................284
Alien 2,671
Illiterate 1,619
Attending school.............5,363
Dwellings 6,005
Families 7,199

PEORIA.

Population 66,950
White 65,361
Negro 1,569
Indian 1
Chinese 17
Japanese 1
Native white—Native par....36,615
Foreign or mixed par.....19,936
Male population..............8,810
Female population............32,588
Males of voting age..........23,054
Naturalized 2,598
First papers.................191
Alien 1,020
Illiterate 724
Attending school.............10,124
Dwellings 14,111
Families 15,225

QUINCY.

Population 36,587
White 34,978
Negro 1,696
Chinese 12
Japanese 1
Native white—Native par....19,103
Foreign or mixed par.....12,234
Foreign-born white..........3,641
Male population..............17,879
Female population............18,708
Males of voting age..........11,388
Naturalized 1,342

figures for school attendance include persons 6 to 20 years inclusive.

First papers.................21
Alien 51
Illiterate 553
Attending school.............5,729
Dwellings 7,685
Families 8,792

ROCKFORD.

Population 45,401
White *45,196
Negro 197
Chinese 7
Japanese 1
Native white—Native par....15,395
Foreign or mixed par.....15,973
Foreign-born white 13,828
Male population 23,302
Female population 22,099
Males of voting age..........15,014
Naturalized 4,094
First papers.................625
Alien 1,822
Illiterate 761
Attending school.............7,020
Dwellings 8,802
Families 10,437

SPRINGFIELD.

Population 51,678
White 48,699
Negro 2,961
Indian 7
Chinese 11
Native white—Native par....27,944
Foreign or mixed par.....13,865
Foreign-born white 25,483
Male population..............25,488
Female population 26,190
Males of voting age..........16,090
Naturalized 1,940
First papers.................242
Alien 454
Illiterate 1,981
Attending school.............8,064
Dwellings 11,214
Families 11,905

POPULATION OF CHICAGO.

Federal census, 1910..........................2,185,283
School census estimate, 1912..................2,381,700
City directory, estimate, 1913................2,388,500

POPULATION BY CENSUS YEARS.

1840............	4,479	1880............	503,298
1850............	28,269	1890............	1,099,850
1860............	109,206	1900............	1,698,575
1870............	298,977	1910............	2,185,283

POPULATION BY DIVISIONS.

[School census reports.]

Year.	South.	West.	North.	Total.
Dec., 1853...........	26,592	14,679	17,859	50,130
Aug., 1856...........	30,339	28,260	25,524	84,113
Oct., 1862...........	45,470	67,193	35,525	138,186
Oct., 1864...........	56,955	73,475	38,923	169,353
Oct., 1866...........	58,755	90,739	50,924	200,418
Oct., 1868...........	71,073	118,435	62,546	252,054
Aug., 1870...........	87,461	149,780	70,354	306,605
Oct., 1872...........	88,946	214,344	64,556	367,396

Year.	South.	West.	North.	Total.
Oct., 1874...........	96,771	220,874	77,763	395,408
Oct., 1876...........	104,768	222,545	80,348	407,661
Oct., 1878...........	111,116	237,696	88,009	436,731
June, 1880...........	122,032	269,971	99,513	491,516
June, 1882...........	135,648	312,687	112,258	660,636
May, 1884...........	149,564	351,931	128,490	629,935
May, 1886...........	172,379	392,905	138,533	703,817
May, 1888...........	194,164	454,287	154,220	802,961
May, 1890...........	413,922	555,983	238,764	1,208,669
May, 1892...........	515,736	645,428	279,846	1,438,010
May, 1894...........	582,980	696,525	307,212	1,567,727
Apr., 1896...........	585,298	734,245	286,870	*1,690,413
May, 1898...........	680,527	844,244	326,817	1,851,588
May, 1900...........	725,691	938,883	343,121	2,007,695
July, 1904...........	652,093	764,621	297,430	1,714,144
May, 1908...........	724,018	872,056	327,986	1,924,060
Apr., 1910†........	813,406	1,003,261	372,853	2,289,520

*Exclusive of 16,222 unclassified. †United States census.

Note—No census of adults was taken by the school board enumerators in 1906, 1910 or 1912.

FOREIGN NATIONALITIES (1910).

[From federal census report.]

The following table includes all white persons in Chicago in 1910 of foreign birth or parentage, classified by nationalities:

Country.	Total.	*Per cent.	Country.	Total.	*Per cent.	Country.	Total.	*Per cent.
Austria	227,958	13.5	Greece	7,454	0.4	Sweden	116,740	6.9
Belgium	3,931	0.2	Holland	26,456	1.3	Switzerland	7,192	0.4
Canada, French.....	12,873	0.8	Hungary	37,990	2.2	Turkey (Asia)......	1,486	0.1
Canada, other......	53,680	3.2	Ireland	204,821	12.1	Turkey (Europe)....	758	‡
Denmark	20,772	1.2	Italy	74,943	4.4	Wales	4,696	0.3
England	63,054	3.7	Norway	47,235	2.8	All other...........	†65,531	3.9
Finland	1,569	0.1	Roumania	4,322	0.3			
France	7,138	0.4	Russia	184,757	10.9	Total	1,693,918	100.0
Germany	501,833	29.6	Scotland	22,840	1.3			

*Of white population of foreign birth or parentage. †Native whites whose parents were born in different foreign countries. ‡Less than one-tenth of 1 per cent.

NATIVITY AND PARENTAGE.

Country.	Foreign born.	Native. *Parents foreign.	Native. †One parent foreign.	Country.	Foreign born.	Native. *Parents foreign.	Native. †One parent foreign.
Austria	132,059	85,208	10,691	Roumania	3,344	931	17
Belgium	2,665	904	362	Russia	121,786	58,417	4,554
Canada, French	4,633	4,507	3,733	Scotland	10,303	6,279	6,258
Canada, other	26,313	7,202	20,965	Sweden	63,035	46,321	7,384
Denmark	11,484	7,020	2,278	Switzerland	3,493	2,033	1,666
England	27,890	14,860	20,304	Turkey (Asia)	1,175	284	27
Finland	1,191	339	39	Turkey (Europe)	711	36	11
France	3,030	1,845	2,263	Wales	1,818	1,467	1,401
Germany	182,281	244,185	75,366	All other	3,554	‡60,889	1,083
Greece	6,564	697	193				
Holland	9,633	8,070	2,754	Total	781,217	705,019	207,682
Hungary	28,938	8,286	786				
Ireland	65,963	99,346	39,512				
Italy	45,169	27,737	2,037				
Norway	24,186	18,156	4,893				

*Both parents born in same foreign country. †One parent foreign born, the other native born. ‡Parents born in different foreign countries.

COLOR AND NATIVITY.

White	2,139,057
Negro	44,103
Black	25,760
Mulatto	18,343
Indian	108
Chinese	1,778
Japanese	233
All other	4
Native white—	
Native parentage	445,139
Foreign or mixed par.	912,701
Foreign-born white	781,217

SEX.

Total—Male	1,125,764
Female	1,069,519
White—Male	1,101,110
Female	1,037,947
Negro—Male	22,685
Female	21,418

MALES OF VOTING AGE.

Total number	700,590
Native white—Native par.	125,703
Native white—For. par.	175,397
Foreign-born white	379,850
Negro	17,845
Chinese, etc.	1,795

CITIZENSHIP.
FOREIGN-BORN WHITE.

Naturalized	190,693
First papers	31,585
Alien	124,553
Unknown	33,019

ILLITERACY.
ILLITERATE MALES OF VOTING AGE.

Total number	35,636
Per cent	5.1
Native white	717
Foreign-born white	34,145

Negro	546

PERSONS 10 YEARS OLD AND OVER.

Total number	1,770,222
Number illiterate	79,911

PERSONS 10 TO 20 YEARS, INCLUSIVE.

Total number	443,003
Number illiterate	6,541

SCHOOL AGE AND ATTENDANCE.

Number 6 to 20 years old	594,012
Attending school	349,037
Per cent at school	58.8
Number 6 to 14 years old	336,808
Attending school	296,766
Per cent at school	88.1

DWELLINGS AND FAMILIES.

Dwellings	246,744
Families	473,141

POPULATION OF COOK COUNTY (1910).

BY TOWNSHIPS.

Barrington	1,953
Berwyn	5,841
Bloom	18,339
Bremen	1,898
Calumet	8,881
Cicero	14,557
Elk Grove	1,302
Evanston	690
Hanover	1,649
Lemont	4,296
Leyden	2,813
Lyons	11,289
Maine	7,193
New Trier	12,632
Niles	4,203
Northfield	2,675
Norwood Park	5,251
Oak Park	19,444
Orland	1,230
Palatine	2,147
Palos	1,405
Proviso	26,921
Rich	1,301
Ridgeville	24,978
Riverside	1,980
Schaumburg	964
Stickney	962
Thornton	22,067
Wheeling	3,845
Worth	7,354
Total population, includg. Chicago.	2,405,233

BY CITIES AND VILLAGES.

Arlington Hghts.	1,943	Franklin Park	683	Park Ridge	2,009
Barrington*	1,144	Glen View	652	Phoenix	679
Bartlett	408	Glencoe	1,899	Posen	343
Bellwood	943	Glenwood	581	Riverdale	917
Berwyn	5,841	Gross Point	1,008	River Forest	2,456
Blue Island	8,043	Harvey	7,227	River Grove	418
Brookfield	2,186	Hillside	328	Riverside	1,702
Burnham	328	Hodgkins	480	Riverview	312
Chicago	2,185,283	Homewood	713	Shermerville	441
Chicago Heights.	14,525	Kenilworth	881	S. Chi. Heights.	552
Cicero	14,557	LaGrange	5,282	South Holland	1,065
Des Plaines	2,348	LaGrange Park.	1,131	Spring Forest	334
Dolton	1,869	Lansing	1,060	Steger‡	2,161
Edison Park	543	Lemont	2,284	Summit	949
Elgin†	25,976	Lyons	1,483	Tessville	258
Evanston¶	24,978	Matteson	461	Thornton	1,030
Evergreen Park.	424	Maywood	8,033	Tinley Park	309
Forest Park	6,594	Melrose Park	4,806	West Hammond.	4,948
		Morgan Park	3,694	Western Springs.	905
		Morton Grove	836	Wheeling	260
		Mt. Greenwood	276	Wilmette	4,943
		Niles	569	Winnetka	3,168
		Niles Center	568		
		Oak Lawn	287		
		Oak Park	19,444		
		Orland Park	369		
		Palatine	1,144		

*Partly in Lake county. †Partly in Kane county. ‡Partly in Will county. ¶Population in 1912, 26,253.

FOREIGN NATIONALITIES.

FOREIGN-BORN WHITE. Born in—				NATIVE WHITE—BOTH PARENTS FOREIGN. Parents born in—	
Austria	138,513	Hungary	30,091	Austria	89,036
Belgium	2,761	Ireland	68,688	Canada, French	4,900
Canada, French	5,027	Italy	49,747	Canada, other	7,970
Canada, other	28,714	Norway	25,731	Denmark	7,464
Denmark	12,223	Roumania	3,283	England	17,022
England	31,257	Russia	128,269	France	1,995
France	3,279	Scotland	11,415	Germany	275,178
Germany	203,315	Sweden	68,775	Holland	10,047
Greece	6,947	Switzerland	3,829	Negro	18,694
Holland	11,414	Turkey	1,972		
		Wales	1,965		
		Other countries	5,236		

Chinese, Japanese, etc....	1,862
Hungary	8,563
Ireland	102,884
Italy	30,101
Norway	19,073
Russia	61,125
Scotland	7,006
Sweden	50,281
Switzerland	2,335
All others	71,256

COLOR AND NATIVITY.

White	2,356,379
Negro	46,627
Black	27,511
Mulatto	19,116
Chinese, Japanese, etc...	2,227
Native white—	
Native parentage..	515,223
Foreign or mixed par...	998,505
Foreign-born white	842,651

SEX.

Total—Male	1,239,892
Female	1,165,341
White—Male	1,213,922
Female	1,142,457
Negro—Male	23,915
Female	22,712

MALES OF VOTING AGE.

Total number	767,537
Native white—Native par.	142,182
Native white—For. par...	193,479
Foreign-born white	411,340

CITIZENSHIP.
FOREIGN-BORN WHITE.

Naturalized	207,262
First papers	33,281
Alien	133,230
Unknown	37,447

ILLITERACY.
ILLITERATE MALES OF VOTING AGE.

Total number	40,045
Per cent	5.2
Native white	891
Foreign-born white	38,324
Negro	586

PERSONS 10 TO 20 YEARS, INCLUSIVE.

Total number	489,073
Number illiterate	7,164
Per cent illiterate	1.5

SCHOOL AGE AND ATTENDANCE.

Number 6 to 20 years old	667,732
Attending school	389,321
Per cent at school	59.2
Number 6 to 14 years old	375,840
Attending school	330,229
Per cent at school	87.9

FARMS AND FARM PROPERTY IN ILLINOIS.
[From census bureau report.]

SUMMARY FOR STATE.

	1910.	1900.
Population	5,638,591	4,821,550
Number farms	251,872	264,151
Average acres per farm..	129.1	124.2
Average value per acre....	$95.02	$46.17
Value land	3,090,411,148	1,514,113,970
Value buildings	432,381,422	251,467,680
Value machinery	73,724,074	44,977,310
Value stock	308,804,431	193,758,037
Total value property....	3,905,321,075	2,004,316,897

The average value of an Illinois farm, including its equipment, rose from $7,588 in 1900 to $15,505 in 1910. The counties showing the highest average value of farm land per acre—$125 and over—were Cook, Iroquois, Vermilion, Edgar, LaSalle, Livingston, Ford, Champaign, Douglas, Coles, Woodford, McLean, Dewitt, Piatt, Macon, Moultrie, Tazewell, Logan and Sangamon. The next highest—$100 to $125 per acre—were De Kalb, Lee, Kendall, Will, Kankakee, Grundy, Bureau, Henry, Rock Island, Mercer, Warren, Knox, Stark, Peoria, McDonough, Marshall, Putnam, Morgan and Christian. Of the farms in Illinois in 1910, 58.6 per cent were operated by owners and managers and 41.4 by tenants. Of the farms 60.8 per cent were free from mortgages and 39.2 were mortgaged.

DOMESTIC ANIMALS ON ILLINOIS FARMS.

	Number.	Value.
Cattle	2,440,577	$73,454,745
Horses	1,452,887	163,263,400
Mules	147,833	18,140,335
Asses and burros	2,863	568,194
Swine	4,686,862	36,210,179
Sheep	1,059,846	4,843,736
Goats	12,485	35,564

POULTRY.

Chickens	21,409,835	$11,696,850
Turkeys	20,563,850	10,941,491
Ducks	189,411	374,544
Geese	201,350	109,124
Guinea fowls	84,057	25,547
Pigeons	144,268	27,445

DAIRY PRODUCTS (1909).

	Amounts.	Value.
Milk, gallons	320,240,399	
Butter, made, pounds	46,609,592	$10,493,217
Cheese, made, pounds	81,918	8,396
Milk sold, gallons	158,031,333	18,314,172
Cream sold, gallons	2,104,352	1,515,676
Butter fat sold, pounds	4,637,745	1,210,745
Butter sold, pounds	24,442,251	5,674,830
Cheese sold, pounds	54,502	5,422

SMALL FRUITS (1909).

	Quarts.	Value.
Strawberries	8,031,824	$613,917
Blackberries	2,915,473	237,058
Raspberries	1,834,337	191,401
Currants	265,858	21,863
Gooseberries	541,498	44,238
Cranberries	13,418	1,248
Other berries	268	22
Total	13,602,676	1,109,747

ORCHARD FRUITS (1909).

	Amount.	Value.
Apples, bushels	3,093,321	$2,111,866
Peaches, nectarines, bushels...	1,222,570	999,516
Pears, bushels	249,365	262,965
Plums, prunes, bushels	78,566	80,384
Cherries, bushels	287,376	453,474
Apricots, bushels	1,250	1,457
Quinces, bushels	6,723	8,037
Mulberries, bushels	40	44
Total	4,939,211	3,857,743
Grapes, pounds	16,582,785	426,468

NUTS (1909).

	Pounds.	Value.
Walnuts, English, Persian	3,497	$331
Pecans	107,069	10,301
Black walnuts	530,730	7,411
Butternuts	2,515	76
Chestnuts	4,833	321
Hickory nuts	60,124	1,954
Total	714,478	20,550

Note—Total includes almonds, hazelnuts, Japanese walnuts and other nuts.

SUGAR CROPS (1909).

	Amount.	Value.
Maple sugar made, pounds	5,366	$1,113
Maple sirup made, gallons	18,492	22,389
Sugar beets produced, tons	14,981	77,732
Sorghum cane grown, tons	90,287	....
Sorghum cane sold, tons	240	360
Sorghum sirup made, gallons..	977,238	490,569

VALUE OF CROPS BY COUNTIES (1909).
[From report of bureau of the census.]

County.	All crops.*	Cereals.	Vegetables.	Fruits & nuts.
Adams	$5,102,564	$3,788,357	$279,733	$154,333
Alexander	619,027	425,471	30,479	14,545
Bond	1,567,839	1,141,581	76,819	17,872
Boone	1,759,344	1,222,271	84,874	11,335
Brown	1,578,005	1,228,566	52,550	23,525
Bureau	7,165,497	6,008,965	175,702	43,218
Calhoun	1,016,754	724,427	49,424	130,564
Carroll	2,796,898	1,990,327	111,305	18,057
Cass	2,574,318	2,330,705	73,340	29,503
Champaign	9,991,658	9,194,789	178,107	114,753
Christian	5,463,041	4,722,435	122,928	55,529
Clark	1,863,009	1,203,773	102,112	39,476
Clay	1,652,385	1,093,024	97,123	45,362
Clinton	2,488,129	2,117,627	83,965	28,712
Coles	4,463,738	3,279,962	112,437	62,643
Cook	8,941,836	2,166,113	2,845,926	44,485
Crawford	1,624,673	1,168,718	98,744	32,729
Cumberland	1,371,699	714,715	60,937	47,669
DeKalb	5,457,231	4,436,283	113,801	22,230
DeWitt	3,693,839	3,378,497	70,375	44,163
Douglas	4,200,444	3,745,992	68,680	24,594
DuPage	2,170,616	1,273,117	99,173	17,434
Edgar	5,315,601	4,839,697	104,547	36,587
Edwards	1,107,364	814,623	43,082	17,666
Effingham	1,724,101	1,211,587	86,720	31,855
Fayette	2,724,967	2,013,765	143,616	51,251

County.	All crops.*	Cereals.	Vege-tables.	Fruits & nuts.	County.	All crops.*	Cereals.	Vege-tables.	Fruits & nuts.
Ford	6,272,957	4,901,850	86,821	21,181	Montgomery ..	4,144,905	3,286,261	128,369	71,585
Franklin	1,301,461	829,940	147,219	25,843	Morgan	4,695,526	4,161,828	130,393	58,209
Fulton	5,690,830	4,522,392	159,737	140,832	Moultrie	2,788,818	2,319,852	65,084	27,645
Gallatin	1,550,741	1,313,805	67,191	21,817	Ogle	5,327,453	4,269,777	208,969	24,825
Greene	2,206,145	2,587,907	100,625	117,998	Peoria	4,480,392	3,422,396	192,361	106,637
Grundy	3,774,569	3,488,722	63,351	5,328	Perry	1,200,385	826,677	102,332	25,843
Hamilton...	1,359,868	864,692	97,230	37,120	Piatt	4,366,082	3,976,758	68,442	26,588
Hancock ...	4,926,365	3,823,112	139,810	129,835	Pike	4,569,131	3,576,055	135,527	125,374
Hardin	471,629	316,658	31,274	24,186	Pope	912,613	577,756	74,677	44,766
Henderson ...	2,124,501	1,815,909	43,473	30,546	Pulaski	1,076,587	562,224	146,682	186,116
Henry	6,236,444	5,096,109	140,053	58,202	Putnam	1,083,398	917,319	32,319	10,870
Iroquois	10,607,811	9,795,841	211,061	68,135	Randolph	2,433,694	1,899,959	118,380	34,770
Jackson	2,185,086	1,488,649	240,313	79,747	Richland	1,406,436	804,303	82,976	60,862
Jasper	1,801,961	1,076,740	112,717	36,740	Rock Island...	2,447,691	1,628,115	186,690	80,548
Jefferson ...	1,807,737	1,175,155	182,047	40,245	Saline	1,363,656	890,071	97,821	66,134
Jersey	2,009,284	1,656,781	76,391	28,752	St. Clair......	4,761,122	3,488,491	689,389	67,776
Jo Daviess...	2,764,066	1,680,056	137,798	23,075	Sangamon ...	7,458,942	6,419,931	232,361	104,982
Johnson	1,129,554	653,627	95,187	84,922	Schuyler	2,579,011	2,092,579	82,464	40,602
Kane	3,928,086	2,682,250	165,871	33,485	Scott	1,782,674	1,560,993	51,891	29,090
Kankakee ...	6,032,515	4,298,265	156,379	27,667	Shelby	4,380,769	3,325,398	126,042	64,454
Kendall	2,723,457	2,407,369	42,626	8,210	Stark	2,417,177	2,092,760	43,401	22,472
Knox	5,146,135	4,190,537	128,341	86,448	Stephenson ...	3,643,588	2,547,340	186,061	28,014
LaSalle	10,222,235	9,044,498	247,674	44,460	Tazewell	5,673,605	4,827,583	128,610	110,540
Lake	2,393,597	1,122,242	170,335	35,256	Union	2,917,613	865,030	490,294	279,967
Lawrence ...	1,701,015	1,360,872	89,415	13,393	Vermilion ...	7,416,946	6,561,752	254,085	90,875
Lee	5,378,794	4,397,607	158,355	30,531	Wabash	1,399,965	1,181,333	43,209	8,884
Livingston ...	11,377,297	10,678,861	165,435	48,032	Warren	4,239,718	3,636,464	73,653	44,899
Logan........	6,411,272	5,842,373	125,140	66,521	Washington ..	2,326,226	1,981,154	89,601	28,652
McDonough ...	4,385,419	3,780,900	94,321	75,672	Wayne	2,414,287	1,415,708	160,943	48,825
McHenry	3,432,771	2,290,113	182,459	22,458	White	2,627,360	2,182,817	135,996	24,900
McLean	12,811,506	11,480,655	270,661	121,962	Whiteside ...	4,616,745	3,550,012	243,761	38,465
Macon	5,986,350	5,341,789	155,624	86,968	Will	6,426,239	5,273,693	207,014	39,147
Macoupin ...	4,866,433	3,939,451	144,805	55,569	Williamson ...	1,317,585	778,964	143,232	71,139
Madison	4,857,487	3,614,917	514,136	61,912	Winnebago ...	3,107,191	2,026,776	182,449	35,497
Marion	1,946,201	1,296,929	132,955	68,797	Woodford ...	4,525,319	4,030,029	128,338	54,470
Marshall	3,087,730	2,748,028	52,578	22,172					
Mason	3,586,196	3,267,410	55,527	39,428	Total 372,270,470	297,523,098	16,300,654	5,411,054	
Massac	903,054	579,452	67,750	50,052					
Menard	2,555,316	2,271,130	61,827	43,842	*The total of all crops includes grains and seeds				
Mercer	3,525,524	2,844,867	76,393	36,494	other than cereals, hay and forage and miscella-				
Monroe	2,072,504	1,693,413	155,923	18,432	neous crops.				

FACTS ABOUT ILLINOIS COUNTIES.

Date of organization, area in square miles and origin of names.

Adams—Jan. 13, 1825—830—John Quincy Adams.
Alexander—March 4, 1819—220—Wm. M. Alexander.
Bond—Jan. 4, 1817—380—Gov. Shadrach Bond.
Boone—March 4, 1837—288—Daniel Boone.
Brown—Feb. 1, 1839—306—Gen. Jacob Brown.
Bureau—Feb. 28, 1837—846—Pierre de Buero (Indian trader).
Calhoun—Jan. 10, 1825—251—John C. Calhoun.
Carroll—Feb. 22, 1839—450—Charles Carroll of Carrollton.
Cass—March 3, 1837—460—Gen. Lewis Cass.
Champaign—Feb. 20, 1833—1,008—County in Ohio.
Christian—Feb. 15, 1839—702—County in Kentucky.
Clark—March 22, 1819—513—George Rogers Clark.
Clay—Dec. 23, 1824—466—Henry Clay.
Clinton—Dec. 27, 1824—487—DeWitt Clinton.
Coles—Dec. 25, 1830—520—Gov. Edward Coles.
Cook—Jan. 15, 1831—993—Daniel P. Cook.*
Crawford—Dec. 31, 1816—470—Wm. H. Crawford of Georgia.
Cumberland—March 2, 1843—350—Cumberland road.
DeKalb—March 4, 1837—650—Baron DeKalb.
DeWitt—March 1, 1839—440—DeWitt Clinton.
Douglas—Feb. 8, 1859—410—Stephen A. Douglas.
DuPage—Feb. 9, 1839—317—DuPage river.
Edgar—Jan. 3, 1823—640—John Edgar (merchant).
Edwards—Nov. 28, 1814—220—Gov. Ninian Edwards.
Effingham—Feb. 15, 1831—486—Gov. Edw. Effingham.
Fayette—Feb. 14, 1821—720—Marquis de Lafayette.
Ford—Feb. 17, 1859—580—Gov. Thomas Ford.
Franklin—Jan. 2, 1818—430—Benjamin Franklin.
Fulton—Jan. 28, 1823—864—Robert Fulton.
Gallatin—Sept. 14, 1812—340—Albert Gallatin.
Greene—Jan. 20, 1821—540—Gen. Nathaniel Greene.
Grundy—Feb. 17, 1841—432—Felix Grundy of Tennessee.
Hamilton—Feb. 8, 1821—440—Alexander Hamilton.
Hancock—Jan. 13, 1825—780—John Hancock.
Hardin—March 2, 1839—180—County in Kentucky.
Henderson—Jan. 30, 1841—380—Henderson river.
Henry—Jan. 13, 1825—825—Patrick Henry.
Iroquois—Feb. 26, 1833—1,100—Indian name.

Jackson—Jan. 10, 1816—580—Andrew Jackson.
Jasper—Feb. 15, 1831—484—Sergt. Wm. Jasper.
Jefferson—March 26, 1819—466—Thomas Jefferson.
Jersey—Feb. 28, 1839—360—New Jersey.
Jo Daviess—Feb. 17, 1827—650—Col. Jo Daviess of Kentucky.
Johnson—Sept. 14, 1812—340—Col. Richard M. Johnson.
Kane—Jan. 16, 1836—540—Senator Elias K. Kane.
Kankakee—Feb. 11, 1853—692—Indian name.
Kendall—Feb. 19, 1841—321—Amos Kendall (postmaster-general).
Knox—Jan. 13, 1825—720—Gen. Henry Knox.
Lake—March 1, 1839—463—Lake Michigan.
LaSalle—Jan. 15, 1831—1,152—Explorer LaSalle.
Lawrence—Jan. 16, 1821—382—Com. Jas. Lawrence.
Lee—Feb. 27, 1839—728—Richard Henry Lee.
Livingston—Feb. 27, 1837—1,026—Edward Livingston.
Logan—Feb. 15, 1839—620—Dr. John Logan.†
Macon—Jan. 19, 1829—580—Nathaniel Macon of North Carolina.
Macoupin—Jan. 17, 1829—864—Indian name.
Madison—Sept. 14, 1812—740—James Madison.
Marion—Jan. 24, 1823—576—Gen. Francis Marion.
Marshall—Jan. 19, 1839—350—John Marshall.
Mason—Jan. 20, 1841—518—County in Kentucky.
Massac—Feb. 8, 1843—240—Fort Massac.
McDonough—Jan. 25, 1826—576—Gen. Thomas McDonough.
McHenry—Jan. 16, 1836—609—Gen. Wm. McHenry.
McLean—Dec. 25, 1830—1,161—John McLean (congressman).
Menard—Feb. 15, 1839—311—Lieut.-Gov. Pierre Menard.
Mercer—Jan. 13, 1825—560—Gen. Hugh Mercer.
Monroe—Jan. 6, 1816—380—James Monroe.
Montgomery—Feb. 12, 1821—740—Gen. R. Montgomery.
Morgan—Jan. 31, 1823—563—Gen. Daniel Morgan.
Moultrie—Feb. 16, 1843—340—Gen. Wm. Moultrie.
Ogle—Jan. 16, 1836—773—Lieut. Joseph Ogle.
Peoria—Jan. 13, 1825—630—Indian name.

Perry—Jan. **29**, 1827—432—Com. Oliver H. Perry.
Platt—Jan. 27, 1841—440—Benj. Platt (atty.-gen.).
Pike—Jan. 31, 1821—756—Zebulon M. Pike.
Pope—Jan. 10, 1816—360—Nathaniel Pope.
Pulaski—March 3, 1843—190—Count Casimir Pulaski.
Putnam—Jan. 13. 1825—170—Gen. Israel Putnam.
Randolph—Oct. 5, 1795—560—Edmund Randolph.
Richland—Feb. 24, 1841—380—County in Ohio.
Rock Island—Feb. 9, 1839—420—Island same name.
Saline—Feb. 25, 1847—396—Saline creek.
Sangamon—Jan. 30, 1821—875—Indian name.
Schuyler—Jan. 13, 1825—414—Gen. Philip Schuyler.
Scott—Feb. 16, 1839—252—County in Kentucky.
Shelby—Jan. 23, 1827—760—Gov. Isaac Shelby.
Stark—May 2, 1839—290—Gen. John Stark.
St. Clair—April 27, 1790—Gen. Arthur St. Clair.
Stephenson—March 4,1837—573—Col.Benj.Stephenson.

Tazewell—Jan. 31, 1827—650—Gov. L. W. Tazewell.
Union—Jan. 2, 1818—400—Union of states.
Vermilion—Jan. 18, 1826—882—Vermilion river.
Wabash—Dec. 27, 1824—220—Indian name.
Warren—Jan. 13, 1825—540—Gen. Joseph Warren.
Washington—Jan. 2, 1818—557—George Washington.
Wayne—March 26, 1819—720—Gen. Anthony Wayne.
White—Dec. 9, 1815—500—Capt. Leonard White.
Whiteside—Jan. 16, 1836—676—Col. Sam Whiteside.
Will—Jan. 12, 1836—850—Conrad Will.‡
Williamson—Feb. 28, 1839—440—County in Tennessee.
Winnebago—Jan. 16, 1836—540—Indian name.
Woodford—Feb. 27, 1841—556—County in Kentucky.
*Lawyer and first attorney-general of Illinois.
†Father of Gen. John A. Logan. ‡Member of constitutional convention of 1818.

CHICAGO OUTER HARBOR PLANS.

Four outer harbor sites along Chicago's lake front were established by the city council Nov. 20, 1911. The ordinances provided for the following districts:

No. 1.—From the mouth of the Chicago river north to Chicago avenue and extending one mile into Lake Michigan.

No. 2.—From the mouth of the Chicago river south to Randolph street and extending one mile into the lake.

No. 3—From the south end of Grant park south to 31st street and extending one mile into the lake.

No. 4—All of the Calumet river within the city and all of Lake Calumet.

Feb. 7, 1913, the harbor and subway commission submitted to the council committee on harbors, wharves and bridges preliminary plans and drawings for the initial development of "outer harbor district No. 1." In this report the commission stated that it had proceeded on the theory that joint and parallel action by the federal government would be taken to protect the initial piers recommended by the construction of an adequate outer breakwater. The plan proposed by the commission provided for the construction of five piers extending eastward from the shore line between the mouth of the Chicago river and Chicago avenue, with a uniform length for four piers of 2,500 feet and one pier of 3,000 feet. The detailed plans were for the construction of two piers only—one for freight and one for passenger purposes. The water slips between the piers were to be 300 feet wide. The piers were to be 292 feet wide with an eighty foot roadway in the center. The outer 645 feet of the passenger pier, which was to be 3,000 feet long, was to be reserved for boats with an exclusively passenger traffic. Part of the pier was to be used for recreation purposes. The estimated cost of these two piers was $4,400,000. The plan made provision for adequate street car service.

At the election of April 3, 1912, a proposition to issue $5,000,000 in bonds for harbor construction was approved by popular vote. Congress in the river and harbor appropriation act, approved July 25, included the following paragraph:

"Improving harbor at Chicago, Ill., by the construction of a breakwater to form an outer harbor, in accordance with the report submitted in house

document numbered 710, 62d congress, second session, $350,000: Provided, that the work hereby contemplated shall not be commenced until assurances satisfactory to the secretary of war shall have been received that the work contemplated by the city of Chicago as a part of said improvement will be actually undertaken and completed by said city."

With plans prepared, the consent of the government secured and financial means provided, it seemed as if an actual beginning would be made in the construction of an outer harbor, but July 25 it was announced by Mayor Harrison and Corporation Counsel Sexton that the legislative act known as the O'Connor harbor law contained a "joker" in the shape of a provision prohibiting the city from purchasing or acquiring any title to property along the lake shore line where it has been filled in or where riparian or littoral rights are in dispute. Certain property which it was desired to use for harbor purposes is claimed by the Chicago Canal and Dock company, which has leased its holdings to the Pugh Terminal Warehouse company. The Pugh company was willing to treat with the city, but the corporation counsel held that the provision referred to would have to be eliminated from the act by legislative action before anything further could be done. The subway and harbor commission also sent the city authorities the following statement:

"The commission respectfully submits that in view of legal entanglements in the matter of shore titles it is inadvisable to proceed with actual construction work until the method of quieting titles along the shore line has assumed a more definite form."

The work of harbor construction was therefore halted to await further legislative action. The harbor law was re-enacted by the legislature in June, 1913, in amended form, and Aug. 21 a deal was closed by the city with the Chicago Canal and Dock company for land along the lake shore between Indiana and Ohio streets on which to construct a recreation pier and wharf. The price paid was $300,000. Bids on the construction work were opened in December and it was then expected that the building of the pier and wharf would be actively pushed in 1914.

TERMS OF ILLINOIS, COOK COUNTY AND CHICAGO ELECTIVE OFFICIALS.

Office.	Years.	Office.	Years.	Office.	Years.
State—Representatives	2	Treasurer	4	Aldermen	2
Senators	4	Coroner	4	City clerk	2
Governor	4	State's attorney	4	City treasurer	2
Lieutenant-governor	4	Superintendent of schools	4	Municipal court judges	6
Secretary of state	4	County clerk	4	Chief justice Municipal court	6
Treasurer	4	Recorder	4	Clerk Municipal court	6
Auditor	4	County judge	4	Bailiff Municipal court	6
Attorney-general	4	Probate judge	4	Sanitary district trustees	6
Supt. public instruction	4	Clerk Probate court	4	President sanitary board	6
University trustees	4	Circuit court judges	6	County officers throughout the	
Members board equalization	4	Clerk Circuit court	4	state are elected for four years.	
Judges Supreme court	9	Judges Superior court	6	Township officers, such as supervisors, assessors, collectors and	
Clerk Supreme court	6	Clerk Superior court	6		
Appellate court clerks	4	Clerk Criminal court	4	town clerks, are elected for one-year terms. Highway commissioners are elected for three years.	
Cook County—Commissioners	2	Assessors	6		
Pres. county commissioners	2	Members board of review	6		
Sheriff	4	Chicago—Mayor	4		

MANUFACTURES IN ILLINOIS.

[From reports of the bureau of the census.]

SUMMARY FOR 1909 AND 1899.

	1909	1899		1909	1899.
Establishments	18,026	14,374	Capital $1,548,171,000		$732,830,000
Persons in industry ...	561,044	....	Salaries	91,449,000	40,549,000
Firm members.	17,357	....	Wages	273,319,000	159,104,000
Salaried employes	77,923	40 964	Cost of materials 1,160,927,000		681,450,000
Wage earners (average)...	485,764	332,871	Value of products . .. ,... 1,919,277,000		1,120,868,000
Primary horse power......	1,013,071	559,347	Value added 758,350,000		439,418,000

LEADING INDUSTRIES OF ILLINOIS (1909).

(Abbreviations "n. e s " mean "not elsewhere specified.")

Industry.	Establish-ments	Persons.**	Wage earn-ers †	Capital.	Wages	Total expenses.	Value products.
Agricultural implements.....	79	21,511	19,241	$110,605,187	$11,718,384	$44,148,098	$57,268,325
Artificial flowers, etc	25	338	284	174,548	85,975	332,502	406,030
Artificial stone ..	366	1,312	785	1,236,408	438,214	1,123,179	1,488,299
Automobiles and parts.......	65	2,804	2,382	4,083,973	1,653,186	6,774,357	7,153,818
Babbitt metal, solder.......	19	291	183	1,469,799	108,517	3,817,757	4,145,789
Bags, other than paper......	6	213	189	575,574	175,042	895,618	965,442
Bags, paper	4	231	194	1,690,925	98,899	1,028,829	1,123,610
Baking powders, yeast..	24	1,133	657	6,115,498	346,259	6,017,782	7,632,063
Belting, leather	11	403	233	1,279,476	164,536	2,051,612	2,187,555
Bicycles, motorcycles	14	1,005	910	1,276,356	600,233	1,755,516	1,177,464
Billiard tables, materials ..	8	204	167	381,023	87,690	359,957	403,163
Blacking, etc...	58	407	236	516,683	122,922	997,542	1,229,961
Bluing	10	28	18	15,271	7,862	52,649	66,949
Boots and shoes	53	6,392	792	7,569,620	3,142,912	15,485,947	16,754,704
Boxes, cigar.	18	463	404	358,050	158,099	581,630	684,469
Boxes, fancy and paper	61	4,509	4,035	3,813,498	1,501,273	5,650,611	6,349,621
Brass and bronze products. .	79	2,652	1,688	4,055,823	1,136,179	6,180,929	6,841,735
Bread and baker products ..	2,099	12,566	8,611	24,224,216	5,494,607	30,899,184	36,117,986
Brick and tile	340	7,347	6,574	18,495,247	4,386,001	8,285,610	9,765,051
Brooms	87	682	494	722,783	235,069	1,248,615	1,464,896
Brushes	32	392	326	497,181	180,370	874,123	984,850
Butter, cheese, condensed milk	295	3,000	1,732	7,819,996	942,206	16,485,553	17,798,278
Buttons	28	623	548	262,004	246,892	557,542	675,981
Calcium lights ..	3	12	7	29,265	5,292	32,385	26,729
Canning and preserving ..	113	2,800	2,333	5,623,637	903,632	6,704,951	7,619,586
Carpets, rag . ..	67	366	266	173,701	115,229	249,365	340,799
Carriages and wagons	325	6,746	6,852	17,856,786	3,588,016	14,810,098	16,831,283
Cars by steam roads	73	24,406	23,131	18,722,338	15,287,571	32,226,134	32,229,243
Cars, street railroads	30	2,364	2,240	3,885,611	1,395,029	3,439,334	3,430,643
Cars, for steam roads	28	11,782	10,945	37,934,778	7,823,919	25,685,563	27,001,092
Cement	6	1,526	1,395	6,686,567	854,797	3,197,433	4,087,507
Chemicals .	19	972	836	4,639,170	531,315	3,927,458	4,656,274
Clocks and watches	19	5,883	5,665	12,411,573	3,217,149	5,819,648	7,045,275
Cloth, sponging, etc. . .	6	106	91	30,806	51,824	93,072	119,290
Clothing, men's .. .	715	41,122	36,152	38,762,929	16,580,002	80,393,385	89,472,755
Clothing, women's .	221	7,279	6,151	5,567,194	3,151,998	14,992,614	16,635,236
Coffee and spice roasting, etc.	35	1,792	1,018	8,751,861	524,869	18,352,146	19,751,188
Coffins, etc .	21	924	732	2,088,863	405,910	2,042,393	2,259,783
Confectionery ..	140	4,622	3,799	6,094,450	1,428,645	11,214,390	12,798,077
Cooperage, wooden goods	80	2,617	2,388	4,452,842	1,126,580	6,137,357	6,610,969
Copper, tin, sheet iron products	483	8,897	7,473	31,018,411	4,314,684	20,300,274	22,822,810
Cordage ..	7	1,884	1,799	13,014,494	669,584	6,888,306	8,237,165
Cork, cutting	4	112	102	180,918	44,071	207,433	238,468
Corsets	16	1,663	1,502	1,306,114	524,530	2,280,612	2,711,212
Cotton goods . ..	5	1,397	1,319	1,979,075	522,073	1,896,952	2,111,208
Cutlery and tools, n e s .	80	1,661	1,322	2,455,288	760,385	2,363,064	2,757,762
Dairymen's supplies, etc.	29	427	323	859,129	178,333	978,164	1,180,898
Dentists' materials	10	85	* 48	71,764	36,043	201,740	231,884
Electrical machinery	143	11,854	9,641	24,201,532	6,412,671	24,937,852	26,826,177
Electroplating .. .	43	457	375	289,762	245,432	562,107	696,572
Emery wheels, etc	4	67	41	84,866	19,784	119,180	155,313
Enameling and japanning	5	35	29	14,066	14,745	40,230	45,065
Explosives	8	327	290	1,561,612	189,558	1,250,894	1,469,469
Fancy articles, n e s .	44	613	444	659,251	221,757	1,119,375	1,319,861
Files	4	85	76	84,200	49,081	86,973	99,522
Fire extinguishers, chemical	5	54	28	109,771	14,596	142,098	164,437
Fireworks	6	114	98	180,844	38,548	142,939	142,973
Flags, regalia, etc .	24	376	293	383,331	111,923	576,368	675,845
Flour mill products..........	461	3,634	2,464	18,453,727	1,271,182	48,852,744	51,110,681
Foundry products.	1,178	61,303	52,266	143,276,987	33,156,824	123,396,892	138,578,993
Fur goods	63	473	319	971,515	229,532	1,584,835	1,929,470
Furnishing goods, men's	61	3,116	2,688	2,881,103	1,014,719	6,726,981	7 213 487
Furniture	267	15,240	13,575	22,383,174	8,099,683	25,169,458	27,900,262
Gas and electric fixtures ...	78	2,619	2 090	3,657,369	1,184,283	5,102,485	5,797 373
Gas, illuminating, heating .	78	8,020	6,301	131,789,940	2,967 342	13,938,452	21,052,100
Glass	11	3,686	3,507	7,738,236	2,181,683	4,664,447	5,047,333
Gloves, leather . . .	29	1,463	1,309	1,093,490	518 862	2,331,900	2,522,963
Gold and silver, leaf and foil	7	159	143	65,747	61,153	209,833	225,806
Grease and tallow.	36	959	778	2,852,246	531,365	5,076,472	5,589,617
Hand stamps, stencils	33	284	175	295,106	102,930	396,973	478,911
Hats, caps, other than felt .	88	574	463	279,637	266 879	902,607	1 046 485

Industry.	Establish-ments.	Persons.*	Wage earn-ers.†	Capital.	Wages.	Total expenses.	Value products.
Hosiery, knit goods..........	43	3,141	2,913	5,115,992	1,116,476	4,938,859	5,946,737
Ice, manufactured...........	83	1,013	804	5,574,739	534,166	1,424,435	1,928,323
Ink, printing................	7	86	38	254,387	25,508	316,498	415,025
Iron and steel, blast furnaces	6	2,927	2,493	52,389,822	1,792,965	34,196,011	38,299,897
Iron and steel, rolling mills.	24	19,437	17,584	69,682,495	12,962,087	75,221,710	86,608,137
Jewelry	67	1,280	980	1,622,666	650,223	2,358,271	2,779,962
Kaolin, ground earths........	7	122	76	687,177	37,195	368,440	431,352
Lapidary work...............	3	18	14	34,067	12,974	70,525	87,883
Leather goods................	168	3,569	2,949	5,359,975	1,633,407	7,985,071	8,948,324
Leather, tanned, etc..........	29	3,194	3,001	15,971,532	1,582,030	14,736,180	14,911,782
Lime	16	572	511	1,258,141	282,967	591,605	687,976
Liquors, distilled............	9	851	750	7,500,230	478,685	53,219,662	55,199,874
Liquors, malt................	106	5,361	4,398	56,141,185	3,473,300	23,618,940	28,449,148
Liquors, vinous..............	12	17	3	34,150	1,989	15,846	28,711
Lumber products.............	814	19,025	16,567	29,777,623	9,109,584	41,125,559	44,951,804
Marble and stone work.......	278	2,821	2,226	4,689,083	1,766,107	5,567,371	6,770,996
Mattresses, spring beds......	86	1,036	831	1,150,945	447,591	2,503,832	2,860,042
Millinery and lace goods.....	103	3,987	3,328	2,188,576	1,383,832	6,444,318	7,281,914
Mirrors	10	396	353	447,280	231,681	992,144	1,106,480
Models, patterns, not paper..	81	585	426	520,759	308,255	701,416	889,437
Musical instruments, n. e. s.	30	425	336	511,662	200,606	502,478	629,163
Pianos, organs...............	68	9,628	8,777	27,718,851	5,009,042	16,686,065	19,176,328
Paint and varnish............	74	2,906	1,792	15,725,376	1,114,298	17,926,283	20,434,291
Paper and wood pulp.........	19	1,542	1,397	8,400,333	727,420	4,567,670	4,983,075
Paper goods, n. e. s.........	49	1,659	1,517	2,260,405	546,165	5,435,708	2,775,297
Patent medicines, etc........	359	3,902	1,869	7,988,944	804,761	10,742,989	13,114,307
Pens, fountain, gold.........	7	65	35	117,164	23,224	141,815	170,467
Photographic apparatus......	13	356	284	708,269	156,562	642,709	739,557
Photo engraving.............	27	1,561	1,114	1,300,855	949,109	2,268,578	2,673,304
Pottery, terra cotta, etc.....	39	3,474	3,157	14,900,981	1,884,879	3,946,183	4,614,728
Printing and publishing......	2,608	43,074	28,644	60,084,133	18,436,924	73,964,422	87,247,090
Pumps, not steam............	14	348	282	664,286	179,136	641,106	658,554
Rubber goods, n. e. s........	13	145	104	251,977	62,875	323,529	381,363
Scales and balances..........	13	306	248	515,477	151,166	528,831	574,420
Sewing machines, etc........	7	2,073	1,713	4,430,468	1,113,885	3,306,683	3,621,554
Ship and boat building.......	23	470	413	2,069,884	251,594	532,277	583,783
Show cases	16	442	386	539,256	247,809	691,413	829,472
Signs	51	1,835	1,290	2,693,629	750,349	2,915,025	3,271,331
Slaughtering, packing........	109	32,642	26,705	131,026,247	14,601,961	378,189,429	389,594,996
Smelting, zinc...............	5	2,034	1,922	7,596,278	1,275,162	8,409,661	9,003,624
Smelting, not from ore.......	11	423	363	1,603,060	206,679	3,638,984	3,929,155
Soap	34	3,408	2,188	11,693,653	1,052,608	18,835,398	20,130,799
Steam packing...............	15	160	108	156,862	61,942	355,569	407,890
Stereotyping, electrotyping..	21	747	592	777,366	472,476	1,156,678	1,282,292
Stoves and furnaces.........	71	5,223	4,499	9,862,626	2,957,046	9,025,626	10,287,335
Surgical appliances..........	29	820	536	1,673,702	284,512	1,855,796	2,098,942
Tobacco manufactures.......	1,944	10,707	8,034	12,794,293	4,215,848	18,230,593	21,870,252
Typefounding, etc...........	19	589	438	1,852,184	302,566	1,288,288	1,247,937
Wall paper..................	5	389	290	1,139,847	173,127	1,168,877	1,366,763
Wall plaster................	6	92	80	261,035	33,361	177,930	203,312
Woolen goods...............	9	543	499	1,063,075	236,760	1,190,230	1,314,100
All other industries..........	1,397	44,544	35,794	169,900,392	20,944,403	181,930,730	205,467,461
Total	18,026	561,044	465,764	1,548,170,701	273,318,005	1,733,327,352	1,919,276,594

*Persons engaged in industry; includes proprietors, firm members, salaried employes and wage earn-ers. †Average number employes.

MANUFACTURES IN CHICAGO.
[From reports of bureau of the census.]
SUMMARY FOR 1909 AND 1899.

	1909.	1899.		1909.	1899.
Establishments	9,656	7,668	Capital	$971,841,000	$511,249,000
Persons engaged............	356,954	......	Salaries	65,925,000	32,068,000
Firm members...............	8,156	......	Wages........................	174,112,000	108,727,000
Salaried employes...........	54,821	32,406	Cost of materials.............	793,470,000	502,222,000
Wage earners (average)......	293,977	221,191	Value of products............	1,281,171,000	797,879,000
Primary horse power.........	525,236	......	Value added..................	487,701,000	295,657,000

LEADING INDUSTRIES OF CHICAGO (1909).
(Abbreviations "n. e. s." mean "not elsewhere specified.")

Industry.	Establish-ments.	Persons.	Wage earn-ers.	Capital.	Wages.	Cost of materials.	Value of products.
Artificial stone...............	19	192	150	$240,000	$104,000	$146,000	$356,000
Automobiles	41	1,725	1,460	2,094,000	1,131,000	1,707,000	3,940,000
Bags, other than paper......	6	213	189	576,000	175,000	685,000	965,000
Baking powders, yeast.......	16	940	522	5,873,000	304,000	2,888,000	7,009,000
Baskets, willow ware........	10	52	41	29,000	26,000	34,000	81,000
Belting, leather.............	11	403	233	1,279,000	165,000	1,385,000	2,188,000
Boots and shoes.............	31	3,326	3,027	3,881,000	1,920,000	6,045,000	9,855,000
Boxes, cigar.................	9	348	304	292,000	125,000	258,000	541,000
Boxes, fancy and paper......	48	3,984	3,609	3,118,000	1,311,000	2,232,000	5,044,000
Brass and bronze products...	56	1,430	1,167	2,492,000	810,000	3,266,000	5,131,000
Bread and bakery products..	1,177	8,842	6,437	20,800,000	4,146,000	16,280,000	26,903,000
Brick and tile...............	7	657	612	2,210,000	559,000	210,000	1,172,000
Brooms and brushes.........	56	616	497	690,000	281,000	918,000	1,560,000

Industry.	Establish-ments.	Persons	Wage earn-ers.	Capital.	Wages	Cost of materials.	Value of, products
Buttons	13	231	190	151,000	72,000	139,000	335,000
Calcium lghts	3	12	7	29,000	5,000	18,000	27,000
Canning and preserving ...	47	1,107	904	2,058,000	395,000	2,533,000	3,827,000
Carpets, rag . . .	25	205	163	87,000	68,000	43,000	206,000
Carriages and wagons . .	126	2,263	1,965	7,616,000	-1,253,000	2,602,000	5,203,000
Cars, by steam roads .	22	11,562	11,059	9,558,000	7,305,000	7,310,000	15,359,000
Cars, by street railways	7	1,721	1,164	3,061,000	1,069,000	1,520,000	2,758,000
Cars for steam roads	18	9,226	8,553	29,730,000	6,387,000	11,620,000	20,892,000
Chemicals .	10	218	143	887,000	92,000	598,000	1,149,000
Clocks and watches. ..	5	145	109	421,000	60,000	282,000	445,000
Cloth, sponging, etc	6	106	91	21,000	52,000	1,000	119,000
Clothing, men's, shirts	678	38,370	33,615	36,521,000	15,777,000	42,768,000	85,296,000
Clothing, women's ..	204	6,666	5,615	5,193,000	2,997,000	8,658,000	15,677,000
Coffee and spice, roasting, etc.	32	1,775	1,006	8,696,000	521,000	14,969,000	19,593,000
Coffins,- etc. . . .	13	733	576	1,721,000	339,000	764,000	1,838,000
Confectionery, .	87	3,365	3,241	5,275,000	1,250,000	6,703,000	11,222,000
Cooperage goods, n. e. s .	37	1,269	1,166	1,860,000	601,000	2,188,000	3,368,000
Copper, tin, sheet iron products	263	4,610	3,859	12,216,000	2,472,000	6,463,000	12,242,000
Corsets	10	1,124	1,005	925,000	340,000	705,000	1,779,000
Cutlery and tools, n e. s ...	53	1,167	982	1,796,000	554,000	680,000	1,895,000
Dairymen's supplies	7	70	49	179,000	37,000	147,000	340,000
Dentists' materials	10	85	48	72,000	38,000	115,000	232,000
Electrical machinery	123	7,333	6,096	16,624,000	3,360,000	11,405,000	20,669,000
Electroplating	34	374	310	181,000	214,000	107,000	484,000
Fancy articles, n e. s	40	603	438	641,000	218,000	568,000	1,289,000
Fire extinguishers, chemical.	5	54	28	110,000	15,000	62,000	164,000
Foundry products	669	36,368	31,055	90,050,000	20,490,000	40,755,000	89,669,000
Fur goods	59	455	308	959,000	225,000	1,060,000	1,903,000
Furnishing goods, men's. ...	38	2,273	1,905	2,340,000	829,000	3,877,000	6,122,000
Furniture	202	11,097	9,376	16,373,000	6,026,000	9,096,000	20,512,000
Gas and electric fixtures.....	63	2,068	1,602	2,706,000	914,000	2,124,000	4,683,000
Gloves, leather.	25	1,223	1,109	900,000	441,000	1,308,000	2,181,000
Gold and silver, leaf and foil	7	159	143	66,000	61,000	128,000	226,000
Grease and tallow	10	773	649	2,181,000	452,000	3,781,000	4,948,000
Hand stamps, stencils	27	273	172	287,000	101,000	167,000	467,000
Hats and caps, not felt.. .	38	574	463	280,000	267,000	479,000	1,046,000
Hosiery, knit goods	29	837	743	908,000	289,000	783,000	1,477,000
Ice, manufactured	6	229	206	1,136,000	153,000	126,000	569,000
Ink, printers .. .	7	86	38	254,000	26,000	164,000	415,000
Iron and steel, mills	6	7,689	6,983	32,577,000	5,603,000	29,023,000	45,984,000
Jewelry	55	1,169	910	1,574,000	606,000	1,218,000	2,635,000
Lapidary work	3	18	14	34,000	18,000	53,000	83,000
Leather goods.	99	2,581	2,178	2,877,000	1,174,000	3,280,000	5,861,000
Leather, tanned, etc	24	2,841	2,674	14,486,000	1,418,000	10,788,000	13,244,000
Liquors, malt .. .	45	3,450	2,867	29,385,000	2,378,000	4,850,000	19,512,000
Lumber products .	195	11,680	10,462	17,695,000	6,149,000	20,768,000	32,709,000
Marble and stone work ...	107	1,640	1,388	2,557,000	1,137,000	1,714,000	3,930,000
Mattresses, spring beds	58	835	683	837,000	271,000	1,349,000	2,377,000
Models and patterns, not paper	56	435	322	362,000	227,000	161,000	687,000
Musical instruments, n e s	27	418	232	502,000	199,000	172,000	614,000
Pianos and organs ..	37	5,792	5,209	17,335,000	3,034,000	4,848,000	11,487,000
Paint and varnish ..	61	2,667	1,606	13,830,000	996,000	11,845,000	18,942,000
Paper goods, n. e s	41	1,255	957	7,367,000	410,000	1,393,000	2,831,000
Patent medicines, etc .	273	3,011	1,361	5,377,000	632,000	3,216,000	10,360,000
Photographic goods ...	13	356	284	708,000	157,000	318,000	740,000
Photo engraving	21	1,186	878	902,000	848,000	422,000	2,156,000
Printing and publishing.	1,395	33,439	22,326	47,982,000	15,077,000	21,256,000	74,211,000
Pumps, not steam ..	6	74	52	94,000	38,000	72,000	179,000
Rubber goods, n. e s . .	13	145	104	252,000	53,000	200,000	381,000
Ship and boat building	8	308	282	1,858,000	174,000	108,000	359,000
Slaughtering	67	27,147	22,064	115,312,000	11,985,000	285,250,000	325,062,000
Smelting, not ore	7	127	91	816,000	63,000	2,237,000	2,574,000
Soap	27	3,329	2,189	11,474,000	1,035,000	13,787,000	19,989,000
Steam packing	15	160	108	157,000	62,000	194,000	408,000
Stereotyping, electrotyping. .	21	747	592	777,000	472,000	316,000	1,282,000
Stoves and furnaces	28	1,263	1,048	2,546,000	726,000	1,157,000	3,183,000
Surgical appliances....	24	807	529	1,658,000	279,000	917,000	2,075,000
Tobacco manufactures	1,050	6,758	5,220	10,331,000	2,735,000	6,722,000	16,633,000
Typefounding, etc	19	588	438	1,852,000	308,000	375,000	1,248,000
All other industries..........	1,305	60,504	50,477	326,874,000	28,397,000	142,590,000	234,104,000
Total	9,656	356,954	293,977	971,841,000	174,112,000	793,470,000	1,281,171,000

EAST ST. LOUIS INDUSTRIES (1909).

Industry	Establish-ments	Persons.	Wage earn-ers.	Capital	Wages	Cost of materials.	Value of products
Bread, bakery products .	20	121	71	$128,000	$53,000	$177,000	$336,000
Carriages, wagons .	5	35	28	55,000	15,000	24,000	56,000
Copper, tin, sheet iron products	14	92	73	53,000	66,000	82,000	183,000
Foundry products	11	925	857	2,081,000	513,000	1,053,000	1,872,000
Lumber products	7	147	102	405,000	62,000	250,000	328,000
Printing and publishing ...	8	77	50	148,000	38,000	27,000	105,000
Tobacco manufactures ...	12	23	11	19,000	9,000	12,000	40,000
All other industries	62	4,585	4,060	28,459,000	2,494,000	9,854,000	15,308,000
Total	139	6,005	5,252	31,298,000	3,250,000	11,479,000	18,228,000

PEORIA INDUSTRIES (1909).

Industry.	Establish-ments.	Wage earn-Persons.	ers.	Capital.	Wages.	Cost of materials.	Value of products.
Bread, bakery products.......	39	274	194	$289,000	$104,000	$482,000	$764,000
Carriages, wagons............	8	78	63	105,000	41,000	69,000	141,000
Cooperage goods..............	5	643	514	935,000	172,000	840,000	1,153,000
Copper, tin, sheet iron products	9	283	239	415,000	130,000	453,000	684,000
Flour mill products..........	4	54	54	199,000	22,000	640,000	759,000
Foundry products.............	20	438	420	915,000	315,000	515,000	1,082,000
Leather goods................	4	55	37	30,000	24,000	21,000	72,000
Liquors, distilled...........	4	652	582	5,959,000	380,000	7,478,000	44,570,000
Liquors, malt................	3	228	197	2,211,000	143,000	199,000	1,101,000
Lumber products..............	6	190	166	366,000	120,000	184,000	398,000
Models and patterns..........	4	16	11	15,000	9,000	2,000	21,000
Printing and publishing......	32	513	325	606,000	209,000	221,000	881,000
Tobacco manufactures........	36	369	308	273,000	204,000	240,000	647,000
All other industries.........	109	3,580	2,891	12,626,000	1,679,000	6,429,000	10,788,000
Total	283	7,323	5,981	24,945,000	3,552,000	17,773,000	63,061,000

SPRINGFIELD INDUSTRIES (1909).

Industry.	Establish-ments.	Wage earn-Persons.	ers.	Capital.	Wages.	Cost of materials.	Value of products.
Bread, bakery products.......	16	88	55	$124,000	$43,000	$182,000	$310,000
Carriages and wagons.........	7	70	54	100,000	35,000	41,000	98,000
Copper, tin, sheet iron products	10	77	60	79,000	39,000	90,000	178,000
Foundry products.............	19	270	221	647,000	135,000	255,000	482,000
Lumber products..............	7	176	147	220,000	82,000	110,000	242,000
Marble and stone work........	5	36	26	96,000	20,000	52,000	119,000
Printing and publishing......	27	549	208	584,000	203,000	163,000	739,000
Tobacco manufactures........	30	157	122	54,000	61,000	73,000	206,000
All other industries.........	59	2,932	2,646	5,270,000	1,471,000	3,238,000	6,123,000
Total	171	4,355	3,652	7,174,000	2,096,000	4,304,000	8,497,000

INDUSTRIES OF OTHER ILLINOIS CITIES (1909)

City.	Establish-ments.	Wage earn-Persons.	ers.	Capital.	Wages.	Cost of materials.	Value of products.
Alton	69	2,729	2,429	$5,585,000	$1,528,000	$7,262,000	$10,096,000
Aurora	165	5,884	5,095	11,427,000	2,936,000	5,580,000	10,954,000
Belleville	119	2,248	1,878	5,541,000	1,062,000	2,324,000	4,615,000
Bloomington	107	2,495	2,077	4,762,000	1,186,000	2,527,000	4,868,000
Cairo	56	1,444	1,237	4,854,000	628,000	2,957,000	4,440,000
Canton City	33	1,421	1,262	3,189,000	692,000	1,183,000	2,942,000
Champaign	42	381	273	895,000	174,000	419,000	846,000
Chicago Heights	79	4,444	3,953	10,421,000	2,471,000	5,611,000	10,830,000
Cicero	7	735	658	2,496,000	406,000	733,000	1,461,000
Danville	76	2,044	1,744	2,656,000	1,077,000	1,430,000	3,351,000
Decatur	157	3,447	2,699	6,579,000	1,420,000	5,918,000	9,768,000
Elgin	115	6,583	6,094	16,079,000	3,379,000	4,638,000	11,120,000
Evanston	60	1,040	827	4,241,000	590,000	2,350,000	3,778,000
Freeport	69	3,225	2,853	6,403,000	1,570,000	4,417,000	7,811,000
Galesburg	62	1,738	1,465	2,454,000	887,000	1,416,000	2,919,000
Jacksonville	57	1,096	947	1,503,000	487,000	1,307,000	2,299,000
Joliet	137	7,266	6,383	25,586,000	4,435,000	27,758,000	38,817,000
Kankakee	55	1,552	1,349	2,593,000	622,000	1,493,000	2,723,000
LaSalle	29	1,439	1,293	4,393,000	856,000	2,928,000	5,870,000
Lincoln	40	308	220	611,000	115,000	290,000	570,000
Mattoon	35	1,102	948	832,000	561,000	668,000	1,424,000
Moline	66	6,106	5,449	26,334,000	3,523,000	11,189,000	20,892,000
Oak Park	23	362	282	6,061,000	197,000	591,000	1,118,000
Quincy	235	5,056	4,032	11,906,000	2,083,000	5,792,000	11,436,000
Rock Island	74	2,179	1,754	9,287,000	1,026,000	2,813,000	5,387,000
Rockford	205	10,523	9,309	22,412,000	5,213,000	10,582,000	22,266,000
Streator	45	1,409	1,275	4,588,000	644,000	817,000	2,137,000
Waukegan	59	3,773	3,096	17,092,000	2,103,000	14,164,000	19,934,000

UNITED STATES SENATORS FROM ILLINOIS.

Name.	Term.	Name.	Term.	Name.	Term.
Ninian Edwards, Dem	1818-1819	Stephen A. Douglas, Dem	1847-1853	Chas. B. Farwell, Rep	1887-1891
Jesse B. Thomas, Dem	1818-1823	James Shields, Dem	1849-1855	Shelby M. Cullom, Rep	1889-1895
Ninian Edwards, Dem	1819-1824	Stephen A. Douglas, Dem	1853-1859	John M. Palmer, Dem	1891-1897
Jesse B. Thomas, Dem	1823-1829	Lyman Trumbull,† Dem	1855-1861	Shelby M. Cullom, Rep	1895-1901
John McLean, Dem	1824-1825	Stephen A. Douglas, Dem	1859-1861	William E. Mason, Rep	1897-1903
Elias K. Kane, Dem	1825-1831	Lyman Trumbull, Rep	1861-1867	Shelby M. Cullom, Rep	1901-1907
John McLean, Dem	1829-1830	O. H. Browning, Rep	1861-1863	Albert J. Hopkins, Rep	1903-1909
David J. Baker,* Dem	1830-1830	Wm. A. Richardson, Dem	1863-1865	Shelby M. Cullom, Rep	1907-1913
John M. Robinson, Dem	1830-1835	Richard Yates, Rep	1865-1871	William Lorimer,‡ Rep	1909-1912
Elias K. Kane, Dem	1831-1835	Lyman Trumbull, Rep	1867-1873	Lawrence Y. Sherman, Rep	1913-1915
John M. Robinson, Dem	1835-1841	John A. Logan, Rep	1871-1877	J. Hamilton Lewis, Dem	1913-1919
Wm. L. D. Ewing, Dem	1835-1837	R. J. Oglesby, Rep	1873-1879		
Richard M. Young, Dem	1837-1843	David Davis, Ind. Rep	1877-1883	*Appointed to serve unexpired	
Samuel McRoberts, Dem	1841-1843	John A. Logan, Rep	1879-1885	term of McLean—one month.	
Sidney Breese, Dem	1843-1849	Shelby M. Cullom, Rep	1883-1889	†Anti-Nebraska democrat. ‡Elec-	
James Semple, Dem	1843-1847	John A. Logan, Rep	1885-1886	tion declared void.	

ILLINOIS LEGISLATION IN 1913.

The regular biennial session of the 48th general assembly of Illinois began Jan. 8 and ended June 30, 1913. Among the more important laws enacted were these: Providing for a public utilities commission, granting the right of suffrage to women, reorganizing the road building system of the state and amending primary and election acts so as to permit the direct election of United States senators. Summaries of these and other acts and resolutions of the legislature follow.

PUBLIC UTILITY LAW.

There is created a state public utilities commission of five members to be appointed by the governor and to serve six years each except that of the first commission two members will serve until March 1, 1915, two until March 1, 1916, and one until March 1, 1917. Not more than three members shall be affiliated with the same political party. The commission shall appoint a secretary, a counsel and such additional officers and employes as may be necessary. No person connected with any corporation financially or officially may be appointed to the commission. The annual salary of each commissioner shall be $10,000, of the secretary $5,000, and of the counsel $6,000. The office of the commission shall be in Springfield.

The commission shall have general supervision of all public utilities, shall inquire into the management of the business thereof and shall keep itself informed as to the manner and method in which the business is conducted. It shall examine such public utilities and keep informed as to their general condition, their franchises, capitalization, rates and other charges, and the manner in which their plants, equipments and other property owned, leased, controlled or operated are managed, not only with respect to the adequacy, security and accommodation afforded by their service but also with respect to their compliance with the provisions of this act and any other law, with the orders of the commission and with the charter and franchise requirements. In case any public utility is engaged in carrying on any business other than that of a public utility, which other business is not otherwise subject to the jurisdiction of the commission, such public utility in respect of such other business shall be subject to inquiry, examination and inspection by the commission in the same manner as the public utility business in so far as such inquiry, examination and inspection may be necessary to enforce any provision of this act.

Every public utility shall furnish to the commission all the information required and shall obey and comply with every order, decision or rule made by it. The term public utility as used in the act embraces every company or individual, except municipalities, owning, controlling or operating, directly or indirectly, for the public use, any plant, equipment or property used in connection with the transportation of persons or property or the transmission of telegraph and telephone messages; or for the furnishing of heat, cold, light, power, electricity or water; or for the conveyance of oil or gas by pipe line; or for the storage or warehousing of goods; or for the conduct of the business of a wharfinger.

The commission shall have the power to establish a uniform system of accounts to be kept by public utilities or to classify such utilities and establish a uniform system of accounts for each class, but such accounts shall not be inconsistent with those established by the interstate commerce commission. The power of public utilities to issue stocks, stock certificates, bonds, notes and other evidences of indebtedness and to create liens on their property is a special privilege, the right of supervision, regulation, restriction and control of which is vested in the state, and such power shall be exercised by the commission according to the provisions of this act and under such rules and regulations as the commission may prescribe. No two or more public utilities may enter into contracts with each other that will enable such public utilities to operate their lines or plants in connection with each other. No public utility may purchase, lease, or in any other manner acquire con-

trol, direct or indirect, over the franchises, plants, business or other property of any other public utility.

All rates or other charges made by any public utility for any product or commodity furnished or for any service rendered shall be just and reasonable. Every unjust or unreasonable charge made is prohibited.

Every public utility shall furnish and maintain such service, instrumentalities, equipment and facilities as shall promote the safety, health, comfort and convenience of its patrons, employes and the public. All rules and regulations made by a public utility affecting or pertaining to its charges or service to the public shall be just and reasonable.

Every public utility shall file with the commission and shall print and keep open to public inspection schedules showing all rates and other charges and classifications which are in force at the time for any product or commodity furnished by it, or for any service performed by it. Unless the commission otherwise orders no change shall be made by any public utility in any rate or other charge or classification, or in any rule, regulation, practice or contract relating to or affecting any rate or other charge, classification or service, or in any privilege or facility, except after thirty days' notice to the commission and to the public.

No public utility shall, as to rates or other charges, services, facilities or in any other respect, make or grant any preference or advantage to any corporation or person or subject any corporation or person to any prejudice or disadvantage. No public utility, or any officer or agent thereof, shall, directly or indirectly, permit any corporation or person to obtain any service, commodity or product at less than the rate or other charge then in force as shown by the schedules filed and in effect at the time.

No common carrier subject to the provisions of this act shall charge or receive any greater compensation in the aggregate for the transportation of persons or of a like kind of property for a shorter than for a longer distance over the same line or route in the same direction within this state, the shorter being included within the longer distance, or charge any greater compensation as a through rate than the aggregate of the intermediate rates. Upon application to the commission, any common carrier may, in special cases, after investigation, be authorized by the commission to charge less for a longer than for a shorter distance for the transportation of persons or property. The same rule applies to telephone and telegraph companies. Whenever the commission, after a hearing had upon its own motion or upon complaint, shall find that the rates or other charges or classifications charged by any public utility are unjust, unreasonable, discriminatory or preferential, the commission shall determine the just, reasonable or sufficient rates, classifications, rules or practices to be thereafter observed and shall fix the same by order.

Common carriers, telephone and telegraph companies are required by the act to afford proper facilities for the interchange of traffic or service, to provide track or wire connections, to provide adequate service and to make joint use of certain facilities when necessary.

Public utilities are to report accidents and the commission to investigate them when an investigation seems necessary.

No highway shall hereafter be constructed at grade across any railroad track nor shall the track of any railroad be constructed at grade over any highway.

The commission, or any commissioner, or officer of the commission designated by the commission, shall have power to hold investigations, inquiries and hearings concerning any matters covered by the provisions of this act, or by any other acts relating to public utilities, subject to such rules and regulations as the commission may establish. In the conduct of any investigation, inquiry or hearing, neither the commission nor any commissioner or officer of the commission shall be bound

by the technical rules of evidence, and no informality in any proceeding or in the manner of taking testimony before the commission, any commissioner or an officer of the commission shall invalidate any order, decision, rule or regulation made, approved or confirmed by the commission. All hearings conducted by the commission shall be open to the public.

Within thirty days after the service of any order or decision of the commission made after a final hearing, or within thirty days after a hearing or refusal of a hearing upon any rule, regulation, order or decision which the commission is authorized to issue without a hearing and has so issued, any person or corporation affected by such rule, regulation, order or decision may appeal to the Circuit court of Sangamon county for the purpose of having the reasonableness or lawfulness of the rule, regulation, order or decision inquired into and determined. Appeals from all final orders and judgments entered by the Circuit court in review of rules, regulations, orders or decisions of the commission, may be taken directly to the Supreme court by either party to the action within sixty days after service of a copy of the order or judgment of the Circuit court.

Any proceeding in any court directly affecting a rule, regulation, order or decision of the commission, or to which the commission is a party, shall have priority in hearing and determination over all other civil proceedings pending in such court, excepting election contests.

An act entitled "An act to establish a board of railroad and warehouse commissioners and prescribe their powers and duties," approved April 13, 1871, in force July 1, 1871, together with the amendments thereto; and an act entitled "An act defining and regulating express companies and carriers by express operating within the state of Illinois, declaring them to be common carriers and placing them under the jurisdiction and control of the Illinois railroad and warehouse commission," approved June 9, 1911, in force July 1, 1911, are repealed from and after the appointment of the state public utilities commission herein created. (Approved June 30, 1913.)

WOMAN SUFFRAGE.

All women, citizens of the United States, above the age of 21 years, having resided in the state one year, in the county ninety days and in the election district thirty days next preceding any election therein, shall be allowed to vote at such election for presidential electors, member of the state board of equalization, clerk of the appellate court, county collector, county surveyor, members of board of assessors, members of board of review, sanitary district trustees, and for all officers of cities, villages and towns (except police magistrates), and upon all questions or propositions submitted to a vote of the electors of such municipalities or other political divisions of this state.

All such women may also vote for the following township officers: Supervisor, town clerk, assessor, collector and highway commissioner, and may also participate and vote in all annual and special town meetings in the township in which such election district shall be.

Separate ballot boxes and ballots shall be provided for women, which ballots shall contain the names of the candidates for such offices which are to be voted for and the special questions submitted as aforesaid, and the ballots cast by women shall be canvassed with the other ballots cast for such officers and on such questions. At any such election where registration is required, women shall register in the same manner as male voters. (Approved June 26, 1913.)

STATE HIGHWAYS.

The laws of the state relating to roads and bridges are codified, revised and amended. A state highway department is created to consist of the state highway commission, the chief state highway engineer, the assistant state highway engineer and various subordinate officers. The office is to be in the capitol building in Springfield. The state highway commission shall consist of three persons appointed by the governor for terms of six years. One of the first appointees is to serve for two

years and one for four. They are to receive $3,500 a year each and are to devote their whole time to the duties of their position.

The commission shall have general supervision of highways and bridges which are constructed, improved or maintained in whole or in part by the aid of state moneys; prescribe rules and regulations, fixing the duties of all persons employed in the state highway department and the various county superintendents of highways; aid county superintendents of highways and town and district commissioners of highways in establishing grades, preparing suitable systems of drainage and advise them as to the construction, improvement and maintenance of highways and bridges; cause plans, specifications and estimates to be prepared for the repair and improvement of highways and the construction and repair of bridges when requested so to do by a county superintendent of highways or by a highway commissioner of any town or road district therein; investigate and determine upon the various methods of road and bridge construction adapted to different sections of the state and as to the best methods of construction and maintenance of highways and bridges; compile statistics relating to public highways throughout the state and collect such information in regard thereto as they shall deem expedient; aid at all times in promoting highway improvement throughout the state and perform such other duties and have such other powers in respect to highways and bridges as may be imposed or conferred upon them by law; approve and determine the final plans, specifications and estimates for all state aid roads upon the receipt of the report of the plans, specifications and estimates of the state highway engineer as provided herein; let all contracts for the construction or improvement of state aid roads.

The governor shall appoint a chief state highway engineer (salary, $4,000 a year) and an assistant state highway engineer (salary, $2,500), each of whom shall be a competent civil engineer. They are to be the administrative and technical agents of the state highway commission.

In each county of the state there shall be a county superintendent of highways to be appointed by the county board after a competitive examination conducted by the state highway commission. He shall, subject to the rules of the state highway commission, act for the county in all matters relating to construction and maintenance of roads and bridges built at the expense of the county and supervise the repair and maintenance of all state aid roads in his county.

STATE AID ROADS.

Public highways or sections thereof, including bridges therein, may be laid out, improved or constructed at the joint expense of the state and any county within the state. In such case the state shall contribute one-half the expense and the county or counties through which the highway passes shall contribute the remaining one-half. No road or part thereof lying within the corporate limits of any city or village shall be improved or constructed with state aid. It shall be the duty of the supervisors in counties under township organization, or the board of county commissioners in counties not under township organization, to designate those public highways within their respective counties that shall come under the provisions of this act. The highways to be designated by the county boards shall be as nearly as possible those highways connecting the principal cities and trading points in each county with each other, and also with the principal cities and trading points in other counties.

The improvement of the system of state highways shall be carried on as follows: From such appropriations as the general assembly may from time to time make for the purpose of carrying out the provisions of this act there shall be allotted by the state highway commission each year for each county an amount that shall bear the same ratio to the total appropriation for that year that the total amount levied in each county for roads and bridges bears to the total amount levied in the state for roads and bridges, as determined from the published reports of the auditor of public ac-

counts from the last year so reported: Provided, That to counties in which more than 40 per cent of the total amount appropriated by the general assembly for building roads is collected, including any amount collected for automobile and kindred licenses and devoted to road building by such appropriation, there shall be allotted an amount equal to 25 per cent of the amount collected in such county. The sum so allotted to each county shall be used to defray the cost of constructing state aid roads when such work is carried on in conformity with the provisions of the act: Provided, That the allotment made by the state shall not be used to defray more than one-half the cost of any improvement done under the provisions of the act. (Approved June 27, 1913.)

ELECTION OF U. S. SENATORS.

The election law of 1872 is amended by adding sections providing for the election of a United States senator on the Tuesday next after the first Monday in November preceding the expiration of the term of office of each senator in congress from the state. If congress shall fix a different day then the election shall take place on the day so fixed by congress. When a vacancy shall occur in the office of senator the governor shall make a temporary appointment to fill such vacancy until the next election of representatives in congress. The act of 1885 is amended so as to include in the canvass of votes those cast for United States senator. Section 29 of the primary law of 1910 is amended so as to permit any candidate for United States senator to have his name printed upon the primary ballot of his political party by filing in the office of the secretary of state a petition signed by not less than 1,000 nor more than 2,000 primary electors of his party. (Approved June 27, 1913.)

INDUSTRIAL BOARD.

The workmen's compensation act of June 10, 1911, was repealed and a revised law enacted. It provides for a more definite award to injured employes and for a commission to be known as the industrial board, which is to consist of three members to be appointed by the governor for terms of six years each. One of the members shall be a representative of the employing class, one of the employe class and one not identified with either class. The salary of each member of the board shall be $4,000 a year. The board shall have jurisdiction over the operation and administration of the compensation act. (Approved June 28, 1913.)

GAME AND FISH COMMISSION.

The governor shall appoint three persons to be called the state game and fish conservation commission. One member of the commission shall be designated by the governor as the president of the commission, who shall be the executive officer of the commission. It shall be the duty of the commission to conserve the game, wild fowl, birds and fish of the state, to secure the enforcement of all the statutes of the state for the preservation of game, wild fowl, birds and fish and bring, or cause to be brought, actions and proceedings to recover any and all fines and penalties provided for in such laws relating to game, wild fowl, birds and fish, and to prosecute all violators of the statutes. The commission shall have the power to appoint six wardens and sixty deputy wardens, who shall serve continuously, and may appoint in addition thereto not to exceed sixty deputy wardens for temporary service during such seasons as in the judgment of the commission such extra service is required. The president of the commission shall receive $4,000 a year, the other two members $3,000 each, the six wardens $1,500 each and the deputy wardens $1,200 each. (Approved June 23, 1913.)

PROPERTY EXEMPT FROM TAXATION.

Section 2 of the act for the assessment of property and for the levy and collection of taxes is amended so as to read as follows:

All property described in this section, to the extent herein limited, shall be exempt from taxation, that is to say:

1. All lands donated by the United States for school purposes, not sold or leased; all property of schools, including the real estate on which the schools are located, not leased by such schools or otherwise used with a view to profit.

2. All property used exclusively for religious purposes, or used exclusively for school and religious purposes and not leased or otherwise used with a view to profit.

3. All lands used exclusively as graveyards or grounds for burying the dead.

4. All unentered government lands; all public buildings or structures of whatsoever kind, and the contents thereof, and the land on which the same are located belonging to the United States.

5. All property of every kind belonging to the state of Illinois.

6. All property belonging to any county, town, village or city used exclusively for the maintenance of the poor; all swamp or overflowed lands belonging to any county, so long as the same remain unsold by such county; all public buildings belonging to any county, township, city or incorporated town, with the ground on which such buildings are erected, not exceeding in any case ten acres.

7. All property of institutions of public charity, when actually and exclusively used for such charitable purposes, not leased or otherwise used with a view to profit; and all free public libraries.

8. All fire engines or other implements used for the extinguishment of fires, with the buildings used exclusively for the safe keeping thereof, and the lot of reasonable size on which the building is located, when belonging to any city, village or town.

9. All market houses, public squares or other public grounds used exclusively for public purposes; all works, machinery and fixtures belonging exclusively to any town, village or city, used exclusively for conveying water to such town, village or city; all works, machinery and fixtures of drainage districts, when used exclusively for pumping water from the ditches and drains of such district for drainage purposes.

10. All property which may be used exclusively by societies for agricultural, horticultural, mechanical and philosophical purposes, and not for pecuniary profit.

SHERIDAN ROAD.

The commissioners of Lincoln park in Chicago are authorized to take charge of, improve and maintain the boulevard or driveway known as Sheridan road as far as the northern boundary of Illinois, provided that the consent of the various local authorities and of the owners of a majority of the frontage of the lots and lands abutting on the driveway is first obtained. (Approved June 28, 1913.)

ARMORY BUILDINGS AND SITES.

The act creates a commission consisting of the adjutant-general, division commander and the regimental commanders of the organizations for which armories are to be erected, to select and procure suitable sites for the construction of armories for the use of the 1st cavalry, Chicago; 3d infantry, Ottawa; 6th infantry, Galesburg; 6th infantry, Moline, and 3d infantry, Kankakee. To carry out the provisions of the act there is appropriated $225,000 for 1st cavalry armory, $30,000 for the 3d infantry armory, and $50,000 for the 6th infantry (Galesburg) armory. [The sums appropriated for the other armories were vetoed by the governor.] (Approved June 28, 1913.)

EPILEPTIC COLONY.

There is created and established a state colony for epileptics to be under control of the board of administration. The board is authorized to secure a site of not less than 1,000 acres of land and to provide for an institution on the cottage system sufficient for the care and comfort of not less than 1,500 inmates. The object of the colony shall be to secure for the resident epileptics of Illinois a place of employment, instruction, treatment and custody. It shall maintain a staff of physicians, educated and trained in the care and treatment of nervous and mental diseases. (Approved May 27, 1913.)

TERMS OF ALDERMEN, CITY CLERK AND CITY TREASURER.

The act provides that, if the voters of Chicago approve the measure, the terms of aldermen, city clerk and city treasurer shall be four years instead

of two as at present. Those now holding such positions shall continue to hold them until their terms expire. (Approved June 27, 1913.)

DRAINAGE DISTRICT ENLARGED.

The corporate limits of the sanitary district of Chicago are enlarged so as to include the villages of Franklin Park, River Grove, Melrose Park, Maywood, River Forest, Forest Park, Riverside and Bellwood. (Approved June 27, 1913.)

HOURS OF FIREMEN.

In all cities and villages which shall adopt the act on referendum no employe of the fire department shall be on duty more than ten consecutive hours during the day nor more than fourteen during the night time. (Approved June 26, 1913.)

FIRE ESCAPES ON HOTELS.

Every hotel more than three stories high shall be provided with an iron stairway fire escape. (Approved June 26, 1913.)

EQUALIZED ASSESSMENT OF ILLINOIS PROPERTY.

YEAR.	Real estate.	Personal property.	Railroad property.	Total valuation.*	Tax rate per $100.
1840				$58,752,168	$0.20
1850	$96,532,237	$33,335,799		119,868,396	.58
1860	266,258,155	88,854,115	$12,085,472	367,227,742	.67
1870	347,876,690	113,545,227	19,242,141	480,664,058	.65
1880	575,404,141	155,846,994	47,365,259	786,616,394	.36
1890	587,045,386	149,158,000	72,688,396	808,892,782	.36
1900	509,619,469	162,285,264	77,878,672	803,783,405	.50
1901	689,210,143	223,736,346	86,285,340	999,231,829	.50
1902	710,571,904	231,350,427	88,270,104	1,030,292,435	.40
1903	758,249,645	234,133,427	90,669,907	1,083,050,979	.52
1904	763,280,719	226,356,632	90,854,641	1,082,744,063	.55
1905	771,040,262	213,970,049	93,634,247	1,035,881,557	.50
1906	783,081,075	228,171,948	95,131,416	1,126,663,187	.50
1907	891,802,748	246,819,650	100,161,503	1,251,974,306	.50
1908	884,231,942	245,087,647	104,742,848	1,263,500,487	.50
1909	1,508,984,520	435,610,615	175,683,593	2,158,698,480	.35
1910	1,532,525,070	467,482,556	177,217,518	2,199,701,976	.90
1911	1,630,014,052	462,719,174	178,195,461	2,318,314,614	.35
1912	1,648,500,546	470,904,243	178,082,000	2,343,879,691	.38
1913	1,658,541,334	509,623,714	210,907,669	2,420,880,841	.70

*Includes assessment on capital stock of railroads, property of interurban lines and capital stock of franchise corporations.

Note—The assessed value is one-third of actual value. Prior to 1909 it was one-fifth. Property in Illinois in 1913 was $7,261,169,523 as against $7,031,639,073 in 1912.

INHERITANCE TAX IN ILLINOIS.

The Illinois law taxing gifts, legacies and inheritances was passed by the legislature in 1895 and amended in 1901. Its constitutionality was contested, but the United States Supreme court in a decision rendered Jan. 19, 1903, held it to be valid.

Under the provisions of this law all property, real, personal and mixed, which shall pass by will or by the intestate laws of the state from any resident of the state or any one whose property is in this state to any person or persons is subject to a tax at the following rates: When the beneficial interests to any property or income therefrom shall pass to any father, mother, husband, wife, child, brother, sister, wife or widow of the son or the husband of the daughter, or any adopted child or children, or to any lineal descendant born in lawful wedlock, the rate of tax shall be $1 on every $100 of the clear market value of such property received by each person and at the same rate

for any less amount, provided that any estate which may be valued at less than $20,000 shall not be subject to any such tax; and the tax is to be levied in the above cases only upon the excess of $20,000 received by each person.

When the property passes to any uncle, aunt, niece, nephew or any lineal descendant of the same rate the rate shall be $2 on every $100 in excess of $2,000.

In all other cases the rate shall be as follows: On each and every $100 of the clear market value of all property and at the same rate for any less amount; on all estates of $10,000 and less, $3; on all estates of over $10,000 and not exceeding $20,000, $4; on all estates over $20,000 and not exceeding $50,000, $5, and all estates over $50,000, $6; provided, that an estate in the above case which may be valued at a less sum than $500 shall not be subject to any tax.

INAUGURATION OF GOV. DUNNE.

Edward F. Dunne was inaugurated as governor of Illinois at noon Feb. 3, 1913. The ceremony should have taken place Jan. 13, but the assembly was deadlocked on the selection of a speaker until Jan. 29, when William McKinley, democrat, was chosen by a combination of republican and democratic votes. It was held by Attorney-General Stead that the new state officials could not be sworn in until the vote at the election of Nov. 5, 1912, had been formally canvassed by the two houses of the legislature in joint session and the result officially declared by the speaker. This occurred Thursday, Jan. 30. Gov. Dunne was sworn in by Chief Justice Frank K. Dunn of the Illinois Supreme court. In his inaugural address the new state executive recommended that immediate steps be taken to amend the constitution so as to pro-

vide for the initiative and referendum. He also favored the creation of a state commission with plenary powers over all public service companies and suggested the giving of power to cities of more than 100,000 inhabitants to establish local utilities commissions. The abolition of the state board of equalization was asked and the creation of a permanent state tax court recommended.

Other reforms urged were the direct election of United States senators, the short ballot, an effective corrupt practices act, penal punishment for the violation of political pledges, reduction of the expenses of the administration of the charitable institutions, establishment of a state epileptic colony, good roads, and amendment of the jury law so that "hung juries" will be prevented in civil cases.

DEATH OF CARDINAL OREGLIA.

Cardinal Luigi Oreglia, dean of the Sacred college, died in Rome, Italy, Dec. 5, 1913, of pneumonia. He was born July 9, 1828, and was the only surviving cardinal created by Pope Pius IX.

ILLINOIS PRIMARY ELECTIONS.

(For full outline of the Illinois primary law of March 9, 1910, see The Daily News Almanac and Year-Book for 1911, page 47.)

DATES OF PRIMARIES.

A primary shall be held on the second Tuesday in April in every year in which officers are to be voted for on the first Tuesday after the first Monday in November of such year, for the nomination of candidates for such offices as are to be voted for at such November election, and shall be known as the April primary. This includes the nomination of candidates for members of the general assembly.

A primary shall be held on the second Tuesday in April in any year in which the judges of the Supreme court, judges of the Circuit court and judges of the Superior court of Cook county are to be elected on the first Monday in June of such year for the nomination of candidates for such offices, respectively.

A primary shall be held on the last Tuesday in February in each year for the nomination of such officers as are to be voted for on the first Tuesday in April of such year.

A primary shall be held on the second Tuesday in March in each year for the nomination of such officers as are to be voted for on the third Tuesday in April of such year.

A primary shall be held on the first Wednesday after the second Tuesday in September, 1914, and every two years thereafter, for the nomination of candidates for senatorial officers and for the election of senatorial committeemen.

A primary for the nomination of all other officers, nominations for which are required to be made under the provisions of the act, shall be held three weeks preceding the date of the general election for such offices, respectively.

The polls shall be open from 6 o'clock a. m. to 5 o'clock p. m.

Any person entitled to vote at such primary shall be entitled to absent himself from his work for two hours between the opening and closing of the polls without incurring loss of wages or salary, providing application shall have been made on the preceding day. The employer may specify the hours.

PETITIONS.

Petitions for nomination shall be signed:

For a state office, by not less than 1,000 nor more than 2,000 primary electors of his party.

For state senator or assemblyman, by at least one-half of 1 per cent of the qualified primary electors of his district.

For a congressional office, by at least one-half of 1 per cent of the qualified primary electors of his party in his congressional district.

For a judicial office, by at least one-half of 1 per cent of the qualified electors in the district.

For a county office, by at least one-half of 1 per cent of the qualified primary electors of his party cast at the last preceding general election in his county; if for the nomination for county commissioner of Cook county, then by at least one-half of 1 per cent of the qualified primary electors of his party in his county in the division in which such person is a candidate for nomination.

For a city or village office, to be filed by the electors of the entire village, by at least one-half of 1 per cent of the qualified primary electors of his party in his city or village; if for alderman, by at least one-half of 1 per cent of the voters of his party in his ward.

For state central committeeman, by at least 100 of the primary electors of his party of his congressional district.

For a candidate for trustee of a sanitary district, by at least one-half of 1 per cent of the primary electors of his party from such sanitary district.

For a candidate for clerk of the Appellate court, by at least one-half of 1 per cent of the primary electors of his party of the district.

For any other office, by at least ten primary electors of his party of the district or division for which nomination is made.

Any candidate for president of the United States or for United States senator may have his name printed upon the primary ballot of his party by filing with the secretary of state not more than sixty nor less than thirty days prior to the April primary a petition signed by not less than 1,000 primary electors nor more than 2,000 members of the party of which he is a candidate.

CONVENTIONS.

On the first Monday after the April primary the county central committee of each political party shall meet at the county seat and organize, such meeting to be called the county convention. The county convention of each political party shall choose delegates to the congressional and state conventions of its party. Only precinct committeemen residing within a congressional district shall take part in the selection of delegates to a congressional convention. Each delegate to the county convention shall have one vote and one additional vote for each fifty or major fraction thereof of his party as cast in his precinct at the last general election.

All congressional conventions shall be held on the first Wednesday after the first Monday next succeeding the April primary. The congressional convention of each political party shall have power to select delegates to national nominating conventions and to recommend to the state convention of its party the nomination of candidate or candidates from such congressional district for elector or electors of president and vice-president of the United States.

All state conventions shall be held on the first Friday after the first Monday next succeeding the April primary. The state convention of each political party shall have power to make nominations of candidates for the electors of president and vice-president of the United States, and for trustees of the University of Illinois, to adopt any party platform and to select delegates and alternates to the national nominating conventions.

NEW CABINET IN FRANCE.

Formed Dec. 8, 1913.

Premier and Minister of Foreign Affairs—Gaston Doumergue.
Interior—Rene Renoult.
Justice—Bienvenu Martin.
War—Joseph J. B, E. Noulens.
Marine—Ernest Monis.
Finance—Joseph Caillaux.

Public Instruction—Rene Viviani.
Public Works—Ferdinaud David.
Commerce—Louis J. Malvy.
Colonies—Albert F. Lebrun.
Agriculture—Maurice Raynaud.
Labor—Albert Metin.

NATIONAL DEMOCRATIC LEAGUE OF CLUBS.

President—Frank S. Clark, Indianapolis, Ind.
First Vice-President—John E. Raker, Alturas, Cal.
Secretary and General Organizer—William C. Liller, Indianapolis, Ind.

General Treasurer—C. A. Haulenbeck, Jr., Manhattan, Kas.
Sergeant-at-Arms—Col. John I. Martin. St. Louis, Mo.
Headquarters—Indianapolis, Ind.

CONGRESSIONAL CAMPAIGN COMMITTEES.

The chairman of the democratic congressional campaign committee is James T. Lloyd of the 1st Missouri district. The chairman of the republican congressional campaign committee is Frank P. Woods of the 10th Iowa district.

COOK COUNTY OFFICIALS.

Koehne Photo.
ALEX. A. M'CORMICK,
President County Board.

Morrison Photo.
W. L. O'CONNELL,
Treasurer.

Wallacer Photo.
R. M. SWEITZER,
County Clerk.

Hussagh Photo.
MICHAEL ZIMMER,
Sheriff.

Root Studios.
MACLAY HOYNE,
State's Attorney.

Gehrig Studio, Chicago.
JOSEPH F. CONNERY,
Recorder.

Morrison Photo.
JOHN E. OWENS,
County Judge.

Morrison Photo.
E. J. TOBIN,
County Supt. Schools.

Wallacer Photo.
FRANK J. WALSH,
Clerk Criminal Court.

Nemecek Photo.
J. A. CERVENKA,
Clerk Probate Court.

Gibson Photo.
THOMAS A. SMYTH,
Pres. Sanitary District.

Coover Photo.
P. M. HOFFMAN,
Coroner.

Monfort Photo.
THOMAS J. WEBB,
Board of Review.

Koehns Photo.
ROY O. WEST,
Board of Review.

Stevens & Son Photo.
F. W. BLOCKI,
Board of Review.

WM. H. WEBER,
Board of Assessors.

Halton Photo.
W. K. SHERIDAN,
Board of Assessors.

Wallacer Photo.
F. W. KORALESKI,
Board of Assessors.

Photo by Young, N.Y.
D. M. PFAELZER,
Board of Assessors.

Coover Photo.
ADAM WOLF,
Board of Assessors.

COOK COUNTY OFFICIALS.
Hours 9 a. m. to 5 p. m.

BOARD OF COMMISSIONERS.
Room 537 courthouse.

President—Alex. A. McCormick, R., 523 courthouse.
Clerk of County Board—Robert M. Sweitzer, D., 600 courthouse.

Commissioners—Alexander A. McCormick, R.; Peter Bartzen, D.; Frank Ragen, D.; Joseph M. Fitzgerald, D.; Bartley Burg, D.; Daniel J. Harris, D.; Stanley Kuflewski, D.; Daniel Moriarty, D.; John E. Maloney, D.; Albert Nowak, D., city districts. Avery Coonley, Prog.; Harley B. Mitchell, Prog.; Ellsworth M. Board, Prog.; John J. Gard, Prog.; A. N. Anderson, Prog., country districts. Room 537 courthouse.

Committee Clerk—Peter Ellert, 527 courthouse.

Meetings—The regular meetings of the board of commissioners are held on the first Monday of December, January, February, March, June and September of each year.

Duties—The commissioners are charged with the management of the county affairs of Cook county, as provided by law, having the same powers as the boards of supervisors in other counties. They make all appropriations and contracts and authorize all expenditures. The president appoints, with the approval of the board, the superintendent of public service and other officers and employes whose election or appointment is not otherwise provided for by law.

COUNTY CLERK'S OFFICE.
Courthouse, 2d floor, south end.

County Clerk—Robert M. Sweitzer, D.
Chief Deputy—John H. Mack.
Chief Clerk—Al F. Gorman.
Chief Election Department—Daniel Herlihy.

Duties—The county clerk is clerk of the county board and ex officio comptroller of county financial affairs. As such he has charge of all deeds, mortgages, contracts, bonds, notes and similar papers belonging to the county, settles all accounts, keeps books showing appropriations and expenditures, makes out report for fiscal year and submits estimates for the expenses of all the departments of the county organization.

COUNTY TREASURER'S OFFICE.
Courthouse, 1st and 2d floors, north end.

County Treasurer—William L. O'Connell, D.
Assistant Treasurer—Marcus Jacobowsky.
Chief Clerk—D. J. Egan.

Duties—The county treasurer receives and disburses, pursuant to law, all the revenues and other public moneys belonging to the county. He personally countersigns county orders and renders accounts to the board of commissioners.

COMPTROLLER'S OFFICE.
Room 511 courthouse.

Comptroller—Robert M. Sweitzer, D.
Deputy Comptroller—Frank S. Ryan, D.
Chief Clerk—Michael J. O'Connor.
Duties—See County Clerk.

SUPERINTENDENT OF PUBLIC SERVICE.
Room 519 courthouse.

Superintendent—Robert E. Kenyon.

Duties—Purchases all supplies for the county institutions, advertising for bids at specified times and entering into yearly or quarterly contracts and making tests from time to time of the articles furnished to determine if they are up to contract requirements. Has supervision of all maintenance and rehabilitation of county buildings. Represents owners on all new construction work; advertises for bids and handles all plans and specifications.

RECORDER'S OFFICE.
Courthouse, 1st floor, south end.

Recorder of Deeds—Joseph F. Connery, D.
Chief Deputy—John P. Dougherty.
Chief Clerk—Florence F. Moran.

Duties—The recorder is the keeper of the records and upon the filing of any instrument in writing in his office entitled to be recorded he must spread the same on the record books provided for that purpose, in the order of the time of filing. He is also the official abstract maker for Cook county.

REGISTRAR OF TITLES.
Courthouse, 1st floor, south end.

Registrar—Joseph F. Connery, D.
Examiners—Albert H. Tyrrell, Edgar H. Parnell, James F. Fardy.
Advisory Examiners—Nathaniel C. Sears, John S. Hummer, A. F. Reichmann, Charles T. Farson.

Duties—The registrar of titles under the Torrens system of land registration directs the procedure by which title is confirmed by decree of court, which does away with the need of an abstract, and the certificate of title which is issued is guaranteed by the county.

CIVIL SERVICE COMMISSION.
Room 547 courthouse.

Commissioners—Robert H. Catherwood, chairman; Anna E. Nicholes, secretary; W. Francis Corby.

Duties—The commissioners examine applicants for positions in the county service. Before an examination is held fourteen days' notice is given by advertisement. The rules are practically the same as those governing other bodies of the kind.

JURY COMMISSION.
Room 824 courthouse.

Commissioners—Richard J. Finnegan, president; William A. Amberg, secretary; Joseph H. Barnett.
Clerk—Roswell H. Mason.

Duties—The commissioners are required to prepare a list of electors qualified to act as jurors, to select names from such list and place them in a jury box and a grand jury box, and to be present when the names of jurors needed at each term of court are drawn.

BOARD OF ASSESSORS.
Courthouse, 3d floor, north end.

Members of the Board—William H. Weber, R., chairman; Frank W. Koraleski, D., secretary; David M. Pfaelzer, D.; Adam Wolf, R.; Michael K. Sheridan.
Chief Clerk—James A. Long.

Duties—Fix the amount of assessment on all real and personal property according to the rate required by law.

BOARD OF REVIEW.
Courthouse, third floor, south end.

Members of Board—Roy O. West, R., president; T. J. Webb, D.; Fred W. Blocki, D.
Chief Clerk—Stephen D. Griffin.

Duties—The board of review takes the place of the old town board in revising and correcting the findings of the assessors and in hearing and adjusting complaints of property owners. The decisions of the board of review are final.

COUNTY INSTITUTIONS.
AT OAK FOREST.

Superintendent—James Mullenbach, Prog.

Duties—Has general management of infirmary or poor house, poor farm and tuberculosis hospital.

COUNTY ARCHITECT.
Room 1303, 64 West Randolph street.

County Architect—Richard E. Schmidt.

Duties—The county architect makes designs for new buildings, alterations in old ones, etc., as required by the county board. (Paid in fees.)

SUPERINTENDENT OF SCHOOLS.
Room 546 courthouse.

Superintendent—Edward J. Tobin, D.
Assistant Superintendent—James W. Calley.

Duties—He is required to visit each school in his district at least once a year, to see that the teachers are qualified for the performance of their duties and to do all in his power to increase the efficiency and elevate the standards of the schools.

COUNTY HOSPITAL.
Harrison and Honore streets.

Warden—William O. Chapman.

Duties—Exercises general supervision over the county hospital.

COUNTY SURVEYOR.
Room 1020 courthouse.

County Surveyor—George C. Waterman, D.

Duties—The surveyor is required to make all official surveys in the county. (Paid in fees.)

COUNTY PHYSICIAN.
Office in detention hospital.
County Physician—Dr. Haine I. Davis.
Duties—The county physician resides at the detention hospital and gives medical attention to the patients in that institution.

COUNTY AGENT'S OFFICE.
213-215 South Peoria street; branch offices, 1054 North Ashland avenue, 837 West 47th street, 6330 Madison avenue.
County Agent—Joseph Meyer.
Duties—The county agent is responsible to the president and board of county commissioners in the carrying out of the plans for the relief of the poor in the city of Chicago. He undertakes the return of all nonresident and alien paupers to their legal place of residence; is the medium whereby all defective children are sent to the Lincoln State School and Colony and the blind and deaf and dumb children to the state schools at Jacksonville, Ill.; keeps a record of and closely scrutinizes all cases passed upon at the detention hospital; passes on all applications for institutional care or infirmary cases; interests himself in any wrong existing or being perpetrated on any family to which his attention may be called.

CORONER'S OFFICE.
Room 500 courthouse.
Coroner—Peter M. Hoffman. R.
Chief Physician—Dr. H. G. W. Reinhardt.
Chief Deputy—David R. Jones.
Deputies—Matt Conrad, David J. Gillespie, Michael P. Hartney, Adolph Herrmann, George Hitzman, George A. Webster, Charles F. Kennedy, William Ostrom, Michael G. Walsh, Henry Spears, Samuel L. Davis.
Physicians—E. R, LeCount, Wm. H. Burmeister, Joseph Springer.
Duties—The coroner is required to take charge of bodies of all persons in the county supposed to have come to their deaths through other than natural causes, to summon a jury of six men and to inquire into the cause of death. If any person is implicated by the inquest as the slayer of the deceased, or as an accessory, the coroner shall cause his arrest if not already in custody.

SHERIFF'S OFFICE.
Courthouse, 4th floor, center.
Sheriff—Michael Zimmer, D.
Assistant Sheriff—William H. Ehemann, D.
Chief Deputy—Charles W. Peters.
Jailer—William T. Davies, D.
Duties—The sheriff serves and returns all writs, warrants, processes, orders and decrees legally directed to him. He is the conservator of peace in his county and may arrest offenders on view. He is the keeper of the jail and has the custody of prisoners. It is also his duty to attend the courts of record of the county and obey their orders.

STATE'S ATTORNEY'S OFFICE.
Criminal court building, 2d floor.
State's Attorney—Maclay Hoyne, D.
Chief Assistant—Frank Johnston, Jr.
Secretary—Edward J. Fleming.
Assistants—Michael F. Sullivan, Everett Jennings, Edwin J. Raber, John T. Fleming, R. J. Mahony, Marvin E. Barnhart, Charles C. Case, Henry A. Berger, Stephen Malato, Hayden N. Bell, William W. Witty, Dwight McKay, Francis W. Hinckley, P. J. Murphy, J. K. Murphy, Ernest Langtry, John Prystalski, Thomas J. Finn, George C. Bliss, Eugene C. O'Reilly, Malcolm B. Sterrett, Irwin N. Walker, John R. Herren, Robert E. Hogan, James A. Smejkal, Abel B. Kretske, James C. Dooley, William H. Duval, John A. Fahy, E. E. Wilson, Eliott H. Evans.
Duties—The state's attorney begins and prosecutes all actions, civil and criminal, in any court of record in the county, in which the people of the state or county may be interested, prosecutes forfeited bonds and actions for the recovery of debts due the state or county and acts as adviser to county officers.

COUNTY ATTORNEY'S OFFICE.
Room 507 courthouse.
County Attorney—Carl R. Chindblom.
Assistant County Attorneys—William F. Struckman, John P. Barnes, Charles J. Jones, Louis B. Anderson, Paul T. Barnes, Walter E. Moss.
Manager Tax Department—P. H. Schmitz.
Duties—The county attorney is the legal adviser of the county board and has charge of all suits for or against the county and of all suits for the collection of delinquent taxes and to compel the support of poor persons by relatives of sufficient ability.

PUBLIC ADMINISTRATOR.
Appointed by governor.
Room 1008 City Hall Square building.
James F. Bishop, D.
Duties—The public administrator is appointed by the governor to administer the estates of deceased persons under certain contingencies regulated by the statutes of the state of Illinois.

CUSTODIAN COUNTY BUILDING.
Room 325 courthouse.
Robert E. Burke, D.

DIRECTORY OF COUNTY DEPARTMENTS AND COURTS.

LOCATION OF COUNTY BUILDINGS.
Courthouse—Clark street, between Washington and Randolph; south side.
County Jail—Dearborn avenue and Illinois street; north side.
Criminal Court building—Michigan street and Dearborn avenue; north side.
Children's Hospital—Wood street, near Polk; west side.
County Hospital—Harrison and Honore streets; west side.
County Infirmary—Oak Forest; reached by the Rock Island railroad.
County Morgue—Wood and Polk streets; west side.
Detention Hospital—Wood and Polk-sts.; west side.
County Agent—213 South Peoria street, west side.
Juvenile Court—771 Ewing street, west side.
Home for Delinquent and Dependent Children—771 Ewing street.

IN COURTHOUSE.
Board of Assessors—Third floor, north end.
Board of Review—Third floor, south end.
County Commissioners—Room 531.
Committee Clerk—Room 527.
County Treasurer—First and second floors, north end.
County Clerk—Second floor, south end.

County Court—Room 602.
County Court Clerk—Room 600.
County Comptroller—Room 511.
County Attorney—Room 507.
County Superintendent of Schools—Room 546.
County Surveyor—Room 426.
Custodian—Room 325.
Coroner—Room 500.
Civil-Service Commissioners—Room 547.
Circuit Court—Seventh floor.
Circuit Court Clerk—Fourth floor, north end.
Jury Commissioners—Room 824.
President County Board—Room 523.
Probate Court—Sixth floor.
Probate Court Clerk—Sixth floor.
Sheriff—Fourth floor, center.
Superior Court—Eighth floor.
Superior Court Clerk—Fourth floor, south end.
Superintendent of Public Service—Room 519.

CRIMINAL COURT BUILDING.
Criminal Court Clerk—First floor.
Criminal Courts—Third, fourth and fifth floors.
Sheriff (Bailiffs) in Charge of Criminal Court—First floor.
Grand Jury Assembly Room—Second floor.
State's Attorney—Second floor.

EMPLOYES ON THE CHICAGO CITY PAY ROLLS.
Average number in 1912.

General government	9,787	Waterworks	3,027	Public library ... 389
Public works	5,113	Board of education	8,011	Total ... 26,327

SALARIES OF COOK COUNTY OFFICIALS AND EMPLOYES (1913).
Yearly except where otherwise specified.

COUNTY BOARD.
President $7,000
Commissioners, 14 at......... 3,600
Secretary to president....... 2,500
Committee clerk.............. 2,500
Assistant committee clerk... 1,500
Stenographer 1,200

COMPTROLLER.
Comptroller (see county clerk).
Deputy comptroller...........$4,800
Chief clerk................... 2,500
Auditor 2,200
Auditor 1,800
Cashiers, 2 at................ 1,800
Bookkeeper 1,800
Clerks, $1,200 to............. 1,800
Stenographer 1,260

SUPERINTENDENT PUBLIC SERVICE.
Superintendent $5,000
Head clerk.................... 2,000
Senior clerk.................. 1,800
Inspector purchases.......... 2,400
Principal bookkeeper......... 1,980
Buyer 1,200
Storekeeper 1,200
Stenographers, 2 at.......... 1,200
Superintendent mechanics... 3,000
Note—Mechanics are paid prevailing union wages.

SHERIFF.
Sheriff $9,960
Assistant sheriff............ 3,000
Chief deputy................. 4,000
Chief bailiffs, 2 at.......... 2,100
Assistant bailiffs, 2 at...... 1,650
Real estate clerk............ 1,980
Cashier 1,800
Summons clerk................ 1,800
Execution clerk.............. 1,800
Clerk 1,500
Clerks, 4 at.................. 1,200
Deputy sheriffs, 24 at....... 1,800
Bailiffs, 109 at.............. 1,380

CRIMINAL COURT BUILDING.
Custodian $1,680
Elevator men, 4 at........... 900
Watchmen, 8 at............... 840
Janitors, 10 at.............. 750
Janitresses, 15 at........... 510
Chief engineer............... 1,800
Engineers, 3 at.............. 1,440
Electrician 1,800
Plumber 1,800
Steamfitter 1,800

COUNTY JAIL.
Jailer........................$2,500
Assistant jailers, 3 at...... 1,680
Clerk 1,380
Clerk 1,080
Physicians, 2 at............. 1,000
Matrons, 3 at................ 900
Engineer 1,440
Instructor 1,000
Jail guards, 53 at........... 1,000
Chief cook................... 1,200
Baker 1,080
Storekeeper 1,200

COUNTY BUILDING.
Custodian $3,000
Assistant custodian.......... 1,200
Chief engineer............... 2,500
Steamfitter 1,800
Plumber 1,800
Electrician 1,800
Elevator starters, 2 at...... 1,080
Window washers, 14 at....... 720
Elevator men, 18 at.......... 900
Watchmen, 8 at............... 840
Chief janitors, 2 at......... 900
Janitors, 40 at.............. 750
Janitresses, 96 at........... 510
Marble caretaker............. 1,545

CIVIL SERVICE COMMISSION.
Commissioner, 1 at...........$4,000
Commissioners, 2 at.......... 3,000
Chief examiner............... 2,400
Chief efficiency division..... 3,000
Examiner 1,200
Senior clerk................. 2,000

COUNTY ATTORNEY.
County attorney..............$5,200
Assistant county attorney... 4,200
Assistant county attorney... 4,000
Assistant attorneys, 2 at.... 2,700
Tax expert................... 2,700
Senior clerk................. 1,650
Senior stenographer......... 1,260
Clerk, 1 at.................. 1,380

BOARD OF ASSESSORS.
Assessors, 5 at..............$5,000
Chief clerk.................. 3,600
Head clerks, 2 at............ 2,500
Valuation expert............. 2,200
Chief draftsman.............. 1,500
Real estate expert........... 2,400
Clerks, $1,200 to............ 2,200

BOARD OF REVIEW.
Members, 3 at................$7,000
Clerk of board............... 3,600
Assistant clerk of board..... 3,000
Secretary to board........... 3,000
Principal clerk.............. 2,000
Clerks, $1,100 to............ 1,800

COUNTY TREASURER.
Treasurer* $14,500
Assistant treasurer.......... 4,000
Chief clerk.................. 3,600
Principal clerk.............. 3,600
Auditor 3,000
Head bookkeeper.............. 3,000
Head cashier................. 2,700
Clerk 2,500
Clerks, 2 at................. 2,400
Assistant cashier............ 2,100
Bookkeepers, 3 at............ 1,800
Clerks, $780 to.............. 1,800
*Allowed by board, $4,000; as ex officio town collector of each of seven towns ($1,500 each), $10,500.

COUNTY CLERK.
County clerk.................$9,000
Private secretary............ 1,500
Chief deputy................. 3,300
Chief clerk.................. 3,000
Cashier 2,520
Chief tax extension.......... 3,300
Head clerk................... 2,400
Head bookkeeper.............. 2,520
Clerks, $840 to.............. 2,100

RECORDER.
Recorder $9,000
Chief deputy................. 3,300
Chief clerk.................. 2,400
Clerks, each, $720 to........ 1,800

ABSTRACT DEPARTMENT.
Superintendent $2,200
Clerks, $800 to.............. 1,800

TORRENS DEPARTMENT.
Attorney and examiner......$4,000
Attorney and examiner....... 2,500
Chief clerk.................. 2,500
Clerks, $1,200 to............ 1,800

CIRCUIT COURT CLERK.
Clerk of court...............$9,000
Chief clerk.................. 3,000
Cashier 1,800
Execution clerk.............. 2,000
Clerks, $1,000 to............ 2,000

SUPERIOR COURT CLERK.
Clerk of court...............$9,000
Chief clerk.................. 3,000

Principal clerk.............. 2,000
Cashier 1,800
Clerks, $1,000 to............ 1,800

CLERK COUNTY COURT.
Chief clerk..................$3,000
Cashier 1,800
Clerks, $1,000 to............ 1,800

PROBATE COURT CLERK.
Clerk Probate court..........$9,000
Assistants to judge, 3 at... 3,300
Chief clerk.................. 2,250
Clerks, $1,000 to............ 2,000

CRIMINAL COURT CLERK.
Clerk Criminal court.........$9,000
Chief clerk.................. 3,000
Cashier 1,800
Clerks, $900 to.............. 1,800

STATE'S ATTORNEY.
State's attorney.............$9,600
Assistants, 2 at............. 6,000
Assistant, 1 at.............. 5,000
Assistants, 3 at............. 4,500
Assistants, 5 at............. 4,000
Assistants, 2 at............. 3,600
Assistants, 8 at............. 3,000
Assistants, 9 at............. 2,400
Assistants, 3 at............. 1,800
Clerks, 3 at................. 1,200
Secretary 2,200
Investigators, 3 at.......... 1,200
Investigator, 1 at........... 1,800
Chief court reporter......... 3,000
Court reporters, 3 at........ 1,620

COUNTY INSTITUTIONS.
AT OAK FOREST.
Superintendent $3,600
Assistant superintendent.... 2,100
Senior physician............. 1,800
Assistant physicians, 2 at... 1,200
Druggist 1,020
Chief engineer............... 1,920
Wages of minor employes run from $20 to $90 a month. Nurses get from $30 to $50 a month. Nearly all are provided with board and lodging and laundry service free.

AT COUNTY HOSPITAL.
Warden $3,600
County physician............. 3,500
Assistant warden............. 2,700
Assistant warden, 1 at....... 2,500
Interpreter 1,200
Druggist 1,200
Pathologist 1,800
Head clerk................... 1,800
Chief engineer............... 1,800
Other employes, $240 to..... 1,080
Board, etc., is in some cases free.

DUNNING TUBERCULOSIS HOSPITAL.
Business manager.............$2,000
Physician 1,800
Physician, 9 months.......... 900

COUNTY AGENT.
County agent.................$3,600
Assistant agent, 1 at........ 2,500
Deporting agents............. 1,650
Investigators, $1,200 to..... 1,800
Clerks, $600 to.............. 1,200

G. A. R. RELIEF.
Superintendent $1,200
Secretary 900
Visitor 900
Stenographer 600

DELINQUENT HOME.
Superintendent $1,500
Physician 1,200
Graduate nurse............... 960
Other employes, $360 to..... 960

JUVENILE COURT.		JURY COMMISSION.		Physicians, 3 at	2,100

JUVENILE COURT.
Chief probation officer......$3,000
Assistants, $1,050 to...... 1,200
SUP'T OF SCHOOLS.
Superintendent *$7,500
Assistants, 2 at............. 3,000
Stenographer 1,200
Stenographer 1,000
*Paid by state.
ADULT PROBATION.
Chief probation officer......$1,500
Stenographer 1,080
Probation officers, 4 at..... 1,320

JURY COMMISSION.
Commissioners, 3 at.........$1,500
Principal clerk................ 1,800
Clerks, 7 at.................. 1,200
Clerks, 4 at.................. 1,100
ELECTION COMMISSION.
Commissioners, 3 at........$4,000
Chief clerk................... 5,000
Assistant chief clerk........ 3,000
CORONER.
Coroner $9,000
Chief deputy................. 3,300
Chief physician.............. 2,500

Physicians, 3 at.............. 2,100
Deputies, 11 at............... 2,000
Shorthand reporters, 4 at.... 1,800
JUDGES.
Circuit judges, 14 at......*$10,000
Superior judges, 17 at.. *10,000
Superior judge, 1 at...... †11,500
County court judge......... 10,000
Probate court judge........ 10,000

*$5,000 from county and $5,000 from state. †$6,500 from county and $5,000 from state.

COOK COUNTY APPROPRIATIONS FOR 1913.

GENERAL.
Bonds and interest...$1,180,013.75
New infirmary......... 69,345.37
New county hospital.. 2,693,937.58
Dunning fire insurance 3,749.70
New detention hospital 500,000.00
Oak Forest infirmary.. 1,000,000.00
Liabilities outstanding 211,519.52
Light, heat and power 164,845.00
Furniture and repair.. 88,750.00
Claims and refunds.... 79,095.00
Dieting, bridewell..... 30,000.00
State institutions..... 35,000.00
Industrial school..... 180,000.00
Telephone fund........ 14,000.00
Deporting indigents... 2,500.00
Inspection fund....... 4,000.00
President's fund...... 2,000.00
Hospital nursing...... 165,000.00
Roads and bridges.... 90,000.00
Transportation 6,250.00
Postage 12,500.00
Coroner's expense..... 5,000.00
Assessment lists...... 23,000.00
Soldiers' widows' home 500.00
Charity board visits... 3,000.00
Outdoor relief......... 23,075.00
Jurors' fund........... 340,000.00
Birth record fund..... 5,000.00
Election purposes..... 52,500.00
Judges' fund.......... 206,500.00
Social service........ 9,960.00
Finance committee.... 3,500.00
Interest on loans..... 60,000.00
Printing 6,000.00
Insurance 12,000.00
Parents' pensions..... 165,000.00
No fee-cases fund.... 30,000.00
Building fund......... 30,000.00
Miscellaneous 25,088.35
Rebate gen. tax fund. 3,241,223.42
Tax error and rebate.. 325,000.00

Total general........11,295,152.27

SALARIES AND WAGES.
County board.......... $68,430.00
Comptroller 34,756.66
Supt. public service... 34,139.98
Mechanics 146,778.19

Sheriff—County bldg... 157,667.20
Civil service commis'n 33,615.00
County attorney....... 26,022.26

Total administration. 501,409.29

Board of assessors..... $155,776.29
Country towns....... 16,890.00
Board of review...... 77,579.98
County treasurer..... 357,120.00
County clerk......... 228,448.00

Total tax division... 835,814.27

Recorder $165,994.25
Abstract dept....... 74,640.00
Torrens dept........ 22,620.00
Circuit court clerk... 89,268.65
Superior court clerk.. 73,316.95
County court clerk... 83,171.00
Probate court clerk... 88,024.19
Sheriff—General office. 252,157.40
Jury commission..... 19,100.00
Election commissioners 20,000.00
Coroner 63,714.51

Total civil courts.... 902,006.95

Clerk Criminal court.. $57,424.54
State's attorney....... 148,740.00
Sheriff—Crim. ct. bldg. 51,028.00
Sheriff—Jail 89,060.00

Total criminal cts... 346,252.54

Oak Forest institut'ns $93,244.52
County hospital...... 263,761.26
Tuberculosis hospital.. 20,916.00
County agent........ 94,269.35
Physicians 25,600.00
G. A. R. relief....... 3,600.00
Home for delinquents. 31,830.00
Juv. court probat'n of. 95,527.50
Supt. schools......... 10,200.00
Adult probation office.. 9,810.00

Total charitable, etc. 648,158.73
Total salaries, etc.. 3,233,641.78

OFFICE SUPPLIES.
Administration division $15,100.00
Taxation division..... 32,000.00
Civil courts division... 28,125.00

Crim. courts division.. 4,450.00
Charitable division.... 16,535.00

Total office supplies. 96,210.00

GENERAL SUPPLIES.
Oak Forest institut'ns $201,917.50
Tuberculosis hospital.. 29,160.00
County hospital...... 247,500.00
County agent........ 229,540.00
Home for delinquents. 17,000.00
Sheriff—County bldg... 11,424.00
Sheriff—Crim. ct. bldg. 4,186.00
Sheriff—Jail 5,720.00
Dieting prisoners..... 25,000.00
Supt. public service... 15,000.00

Total gen. supplies.. 786,447.50
T'l appropriations...15,295,152.27
Total in 1912....13,952,899.19

ESTIMATED RESOURCES.
General taxes......$8,750,517.10
FEE OFFICES.
County treasurer....... $606,941.00
County clerk......... 251,456.00
Recorder 253,510.00
Abstract department. 19,795.00
Torrens department.. 32,916.00
Circuit court clerk... 116,035.00
Superior court clerk.. 102,182.00
County court clerk... 70,493.00
Probate court clerk... 146,586.00
Sheriff 59,350.00
Coroner 3,577.00
Criminal court clerk. 1,723.00
State's attorney..... 5,647.00

Total fee offices..... 1,670,191.00
OTHER SOURCES.
Miscellaneous $29,693.00
County clerk's fees.. 20,901.57
Cash available....... 441,523.86
Cash in fee offices.. 176,203.65
Accounts receivable.. 170,292.79
New hospital fund.... 2,693,937.88
New infirmary fund.. 69,345.37
Fire insurance fund... 3,749.70
Bond issues.......... 1,500,000.00

Total 5,105,647.83
Grand total........15,526,355.92

COOK COUNTY FINANCES.

[From Comptroller Robert M. Sweitzer's annual report for the fiscal year ended Dec. 2, 1912, and brought down to Jan. 4, 1913.]

GENERAL BALANCE SHEET.
ASSETS.
Capital assets—
Remunerative real estate................ $25,171.76
Buildings and equipment................ 40,727.50
Unremunerative real estate............... 3,729,167.16
Buildings and equipment................ 8,881,297.77
Dunning cottages....................... 17,561.90
Hospital building bonds................. 1,900,000.00
Cash in hands of treasurer.............. 867,632.95

Total capital assets......................15,460,959.04
Current assets—
Cash in hands of treasurer.............. 633,942.59
Taxes 4,366,966.48
Uncollected fees........................ 930,794.72

Accounts receivable..................... 164,720.44
Supply department....................... 1,322.87

Total current assets.................... 6,097,747.10
Contingent assets—
Cash in hands of treasurer.............. 15,721.64
Trust fund securities................... 17,488.50

Total contingent assets................. 33,210.14
Grand total............................21,591,916.28
LIABILITIES.
Capital liabilities—
Funded debt............................$9,710,000.00
Capital surplus......................... 5,750,959.04

Total capital liabilities................15,460,959.04

Current liabilities—
Warrants outstanding...................... 193,733.69
Audited vouchers.......................... 297,685.52
Uncompleted contracts..................... 13,834.04
Bond and interest accounts................ 166,815.49
Tax error and rebate fund................. 319,000.90
Delinquent taxes.......................... 652,426.81
Uncollected fees.......................... 690,794.46
Revenue surplus........................... 3,763,457.18

Total current liabilities............ 6,097,747.10
Contingent liabilities.................... 33,210.14

Grand total.........................21,591,916.28

CORPORATE SURPLUS ACCOUNT.
Dec. 2, 1912.
REVENUE.

1912 taxes extended....................$5,506,539.67
Interest on delinquent taxes.............. 132,938.86
Interest on tax forfeitures............... 366.75
Fee offices............................... 1,706,058.68
Tavern licenses........................... 11,666.69
Miscellaneous 19,429.89

Total gross revenue.................. 7,377,000.54
Deductions—Tax error and rebate fund.. 319,000.00
Reserve for uncollected fees............ 29,813.15
Torrens indemnity fund.................. 3,326.00
Abstract guaranty fund.................. 1,094.52
Expenses of fee offices, etc............ 8,033.18

Total deductions.................... 360,666.85
Total net revenue................... 7,016,333.69

EXPENSES.

Administration $642,606.80
Taxation and collection................... 1,029,954.70
Civil courts.............................. 1,630,952.37
Criminal courts........................... 683,886.70
Charitable and educational................ 2,273,561.53
General 574,555.83
Uncompleted contracts..................... 13,834.04

Total operating expenses............. 6,849,351.97
Bonds matured............................. 775,000.00
Additions to property..................... 35,126.64

Total expenses...................... 7,659,478.61
Excess of expense......................... 643,144.92
Surplus as of Dec. 4, 1911................ 4,406,602.10
Surplus as of Dec. 2, 1912................ 3,763,457.18

EXPENSES BY DIVISION.
To Jan. 4, 1913.

Administration $639,808.19
Taxation and collection................... 1,029,459.73
Civil courts.............................. 1,631,167.16
Criminal courts........................... 600,359.47
Charitable and educational................ 2,273,923.24
General 489,975.50

Total operating.................... 6,664,683.99
Liquidation deferred liabilities.......... 723,773.45
Tuberculosis hospital, Oak Forest......... 10,753.91
Building construction..................... 35,781.98
Storeroom fund............................ 589.11

Total other corporate.............. 770,898.45
New infirmary building.................... 20,604.51
New county hospital....................... 150,645.53

Total special appropriations....... 171,250.04

Total by division.................. 7,606,832.48

EXPENSES BY FUNDS.
To Jan. 4, 1913.

Salaries $3,365,326.58
Office supplies, etc...................... 132,040.75
General supplies.......................... 908,264.08
Light, heat and power..................... 195,939.78
Furniture and repairs..................... 126,716.07
Services or benefits...................... 38,239.96
Judges' salary fund....................... 181,585.98
Extra judges' fund........................ 36,372.75
Bonds 622,500.00
Interest 390,751.99
New infirmary............................. 20,604.51

County hospital........................... 150,645.53
Tuberculosis building..................... 10,753.91
Construction and betterments.............. 35,781.98
Miscellaneous 1,391,307.66

Total by funds..................... 7,606,832.08

RECEIPTS IN DETAIL.
General fund account Dec. 2, 1912.
FROM FEE OFFICES.

County treasurer.......................... $656,941.68
County clerk.............................. 235,341.62
Recorder 253,510.50
Abstract department.................... 20,795.98
Torrens department..................... 32,916.19
Clerk Circuit court....................... 116,035.03
Clerk Superior court...................... 110,821.34
Clerk County court........................ 66,019.45
Clerk Probate court....................... 146,161.65
Sheriff 60,560.40
Coroner 3,435.40
Clerk Criminal court...................... 1,723.20

Total fee offices.................. 1,824,262.35

FROM TAXES.

General taxes 1911.....................$5,315,411.81
Delinquent taxes.......................... 12,549.39
Interest on delinquent taxes.............. 132,938.86
Interest on tax forfeitures............... 366.75
Tax levy loans 1911 taxes................. 700,000.00
Tax levy loans 1912 taxes................. 1,817,000.00

Total taxes........................ 7,978,266.81

MISCELLANEOUS.

Superintendent public service............. $1,680.24
Oak Forest institutions................... 644.27
County hospital........................... 4,498.92
Dunning institutions...................... 500.00
County agent.............................. 5,984.47
Canceled warrants, refunds................ 45,251.88
Tavern licenses........................... 2,246.69
Sale of building.......................... 826.00
Forfeited deposits........................ 100.00
Sundries 3,831.10
Criminal court judgments.................. 795.75

Total miscellaneous................ 66,359.32
Cash balance Dec. 21, 1911................ 343,889.39
Total receipts.....................10,212,777.87
Total disbursements................ 9,832,281.89

Balance 280,495.98

EXPENDITURES IN DETAIL.
To Jan. 4, 1913.
ADMINISTRATION DIVISION.

Salaries—Commissioners $71,017.62
Comptroller 23,187.63
Superintendent public service, regular... 34,244.24
Superintendent pub. service, mechanics... 100,941.08
Sheriff, county building.................. 153,354.20
Civil service commission.................. 25,892.06
County attorney........................... 32,833.26

Total salaries..................... 451,470.09
Light, heat and power..................... 46,659.05
Supplies—Commissioners 754.09
Comptroller 2,914.91
Superintendent public service........... 2,827.76
Civil service commission................ 2,206.97
County attorney......................... 2,224.27
County surveyor......................... 326.93

Total supplies..................... 11,264.93
Supplies, sheriff, county building........ 9,844.09
Furniture and repairs..................... 33,152.65
Services or benefits...................... 7,952.09
President's fund.......................... 3,500.00
Board proceedings......................... 6,899.23
Special audit............................. 26,023.25
Telephones 15,031.56
Inspection 4,312.35
Postage 14,422.70
Insurance 1,108.75
County attorney........................... 8,167.45

Total administration............... 639,808.19

TAXATION AND COLLECTION DIVISION.

Salaries—Board of assessors.............	$128,738.36
Board of assessors, extra.............	74,620.00
Assessors, country towns.............	16,600.00
Board of review, regular.............	66,379.42
Board of review, extra.............	43,915.00
County treasurer, regular.............	174,439.42
County treasurer, extra.............	220,644.25
County clerk, regular.............	99,582.77
County clerk, extra.............	147,188.18
Total salaries.............	972,057.41
Supplies—Board of assessors.............	5,323.74
Board of review.............	1,203.42
County treasurer.............	19,881.12
County clerk.............	8,107.79
Total supplies.............	34,616.07
Printing assessment lists.............	23,786.25
Total taxation division.............	1,029,459.73

GENERAL DIVISION.

Bond interest.............	$291,286.25
Interest tax levy loans.............	59,179.49
Miscellaneous purposes.............	63,927.67
Roads and bridges.............	66,161.79
Tavern license.............	9,420.00
Total current expenses.............	489,975.20
Liquidation deferred liabilities.............	622,500.00
Liabilities outstanding.............	60,175.45
Bond interest reappropriated.............	40,286.25
Judgments.............	811.75
Total deferred liabilities.............	723,773.45
Tuberculosis hospital.............	10,753.91
Building construction.............	35,781.98
Storeroom fund.............	589.11
New infirmary building.............	20,604.51
New county hospital.............	150,645.53
Total general division.............	1,432,123.69

CIVIL COURTS DIVISION.

Salaries—Recorder, regular.............	$93,710.35
Recorder, folio writers.............	82,978.65
Recorder, abstract department.............	43,624.26
Recorder, Torrens department.............	30,441.48
Clerk Circuit court.............	95,936.14
Clerk Superior court.............	85,746.80
Clerk County court, regular.............	27,300.00
Clerk County court, extra.............	13,244.00
Clerk Probate court.............	93,004.43
Sheriff, general office.............	266,539.10
Jury commissioners.............	18,841.42
Election commissioners.............	19,999.80
Coroner.............	57,031.58
Total.............	934,398.01
Supplies—Recorder.............	11,631.30
Clerk Circuit court.............	4,311.64
Clerk Superior court.............	2,521.65
Clerk County court.............	1,704.65
Clerk Probate court.............	4,327.90
Sheriff, general office.............	1,730.39
Jury commissioners.............	1,185.24
Coroner.............	1,947.39
Total.............	29,369.29
Judges—Salaries.............	181,585.98
Extra judges Circuit court.............	10,850.00
Extra judges Superior court.............	450.00
Extra judges County court.............	10,883.75
Extra judges Appellate court.............	14,190.00
Total.............	217,959.73
Less judges Criminal court.............	21,249.66
Total judges civil courts.............	196,710.07
Birth record.............	4,553.25
Coroner's incidental expenses.............	3,057.49
Election purposes.............	234,476.51
Jurors (less Criminal court).............	228,602.55
Total.............	470,689.80
Total civil courts division.............	1,631,167.16

CRIMINAL COURTS DIVISION.

Salaries—Clerk Criminal court.............	$66,714.76
State's attorney, regular.............	122,211.54
State's attorney, extra.............	14,309.27
Sheriff, Criminal court building.............	49,966.59

Sheriff, jail.............	86,915.94
Total salaries.............	340,118.16
Supplies (gen'l)—Sheriff, Crim. ct. bldg..	4,015.02
Sheriff, jail.............	5,395.94
Sheriff, dieting prisoners.............	23,933.24
Total supplies.............	33,254.20
Supplies (office)—Clerk Criminal court....	1,559.43
State's attorney.............	38,982.08
Sheriff.............	733.27
Total office supplies.............	41,275.78
Light, heat and power.............	14,233.78
Furniture and repairs.............	27,989.01
Services or benefits.............	5,882.20
Transportation.............	4,843.70
Judges.............	21,249.66
Jurors.............	111,539.70
Total Criminal courts division.............	600,250.47

CHARITABLE AND EDUCATIONAL DIVISION.

Salaries—Oak Forest institutions.............	$73,540.47
County hospital.............	240,460.94
Dunning institutions.............	120,668.96
County agent, regular.............	110,328.94
County agent, physicians.............	22,856.45
County agent, G. A. R.............	3,600.00
Home for delinquents.............	21,516.11
Probation officers (juvenile).............	59,305.46
Probation officers (adult).............	7,057.67
Superintendent of schools.............	7,948.97
Total salaries.............	667,282.97
General supplies—Oak Forest institutions	194,067.43
Dunning institutions.............	142,012.63
County hospital.............	250,664.73
County agent.............	262,117.51
Home for delinquents.............	15,714.33
Total general supplies.............	864,576.63
Light, heat and power.............	135,046.95
Furniture and repairs.............	65,610.16
Services or benefits.............	24,405.67
Office supplies—Oak Forest institutions.	1,396.59
County hospital.............	5,675.04
Dunning institutions.............	789.87
Home for delinquents.............	515.19
County agent.............	3,249.15
Juvenile court.............	2,684.32
Superintendent of schools.............	751.78
Adult probation office.............	439.75
Total office supplies.............	15,514.69
Parents' pensions.............	78,836.77
Outdoor relief.............	26,796.67
Deporting indigents.............	3,494.01
Hospital nursing.............	135,000.00
Insane, etc.............	25,265.00
Industrial schools.............	182,957.47
State institutions.............	51,436.25
Total charitable division.............	2,273,923.24

INTERNAL REVENUE COLLECTIONS IN CHICAGO.

For 1st district of Illinois, calendar year 1912.

Corporation tax.............	$2,812,958.96
Fermented liquor.............	5,396,314.59
Distilled spirits.............	452,482.76
Cigars and cigarettes.............	706,354.92
Snuff.............	431,669.80
Tobacco.............	1,564,889.45
Special tax.............	479,993.30
Oleomargarine (¼c lb.).............	} 457,870.13
Oleomargarine (10c lb.).............	
Process butter.............	43,794.35
Playing cards.............	32,231.08
Penalties, costs, etc.............	106,905.72
Filled cheese.............	330.33
Total, 1912.............	12,485,795.59
Total, 1911.............	12,152,064.72

COURTS IN COOK COUNTY.

APPELLATE COURT, FIRST DIST., ILLINOIS.
Ashland block, 7th floor.

A—Frank Baker, presiding justice; Edward O. Brown, William H. McSurely.

B (Branch)—Frederick A. Smith, presiding justice; Albert C. Barnes, Thomas C. Clark.

C (Branch)—Emery C. Graves, presiding justice; James S. Baume, Warren W. Duncan.

D (Branch)—Joseph H. Fitch, presiding justice; Martin M. Gridley, Kickham Scanlan.

Clerk—Alfred R. Porter, R.; chief deputy, Roy S. Gaskill.

Jurisdiction—The Appellate court has jurisdiction of all matters of appeal or writs of error from the Superior, Circuit and County courts, and from the Municipal court of Chicago, except in criminal cases and those affecting a franchise or freehold or the validity of a statute. Decisions are final except that an appeal may be granted on a certificate of importance, or a review may be allowed on a writ of certiorari from the Supreme court.

Terms of Court—First Tuesdays in March and October of each year.

SUPERIOR COURT.
Courthouse, 4th floor.

Judges—W. H. McSurely, R.; term expires 1917; Theodore Brentano, R., 1915; Marcus A. Kavanagh, R., 1917; Joseph H. Fitch, D., 1917; William E. Dever, D., 1916; Richard E. Burke, D., 1916; Martin M. Gridley, D., 1916; Thomas C. Clark, D., 1916; Charles A. McDonald, D., 1916; W. F. Cooper, D., 1916; Henry V. Freeman, R., 1917; Albert C. Barnes, R., 1917; Hugo Pam, R., 1917; M. L. McKinley, D., 1917; Clarence N. Goodwin, D., 1917; Charles M. Foell, R., 1917; Denis E. Sullivan, D., 1917; John M. O'Connor, D., 1919.

Clerk—Richard J. McGrath, D.; courthouse, fourth floor, south end. Chief deputy, Silas F. Leachman.

Jurisdiction—The Superior court has concurrent jurisdiction with the Circuit court in all cases of law and equity and in appeals from inferior courts.

Terms of Court—Begin on the first Monday of every month.

CIRCUIT COURT.
Courthouse, 4th floor.

Terms of judges all expire in June, 1915, except those of Judges McGoorty and Brown, which expire in 1917.

Judges—Edward O. Brown, D.; Thomas G. Windes, D.; Merritt W. Pinckney, R.; R. S. Tuthill, R.; Frank Baker, D.; John Gibbons, R.; C. M. Walker, D.; Lockwood Honore, D.; John P. McGoorty, D.; George Kersten, D.; Frederick A. Smith, R.; Adelor J. Petit, R.; Kickham Scanlan, D.; Jesse A. Baldwin, R.

Clerk—John W. Rainey, D.; chief deputy, William J. Graham, D.; assistant chief deputy, Arthur P. O'Brien, D.; fourth floor, north end.

Jurisdiction—Same as that of the Superior court.

Terms of Court—Begin on the third Monday of every month.

COUNTY COURT.
Courthouse, 6th floor.

Judge—John E. Owens, D.; term expires in December, 1914.

Clerk—R. M. Sweitzer, D.; 600 courthouse.

Jurisdiction—The County court has concurrent jurisdiction with the Circuit courts in all cases of appeal from justices of the peace and police magistrates and in all common-law matters where the value of property does not exceed $1,000; concurrent jurisdiction with courts of record in condemnation and special assessment proceedings; exclusive jurisdiction in voluntary assignments, release of insolvent debtors, trials of the right of property, commitment of insane and the support of paupers by their relatives; objections to the sale of real estate for nonpayment of general or special taxes are heard in the County court and all inheritance taxes are levied and collected under its direction; the official bonds of most county and township officers and the yearly reports of clerks, justices of the peace and state's attorneys and other officers of fees

collected are subject to the approval of that court; the County court in Cook county has entire management and control of all elections in Chicago.

CRIMINAL COURT.
Criminal court building, West Austin avenue and North Dearborn street.

Judges—Judges of the Superior and Circuit courts alternate in presiding over the Criminal court.

Clerk—Frank J. Walsh, D.; office in Criminal court building.

Jurisdiction—The Criminal court of Cook county has original jurisdiction of all criminal offenses except such as is conferred upon justices of the peace, and appellate jurisdiction from justices of the peace.

Terms of Court—Begin on the first Monday of every month.

PROBATE COURT.
Courthouse, 6th floor.

Judge—Daniel H. Gregg, D.; term expires in 1914.

Assistants—Philip P. Bregstone, Harry G. Keats and I. T. Dankowski.

Clerk—John A. Cervenka, D.

Public Administrator—James F. Bishop, D.

Public Guardian—Mary Carlin.

Jurisdiction—The Probate court has original jurisdiction in all matters of probate, the settlement of estates of deceased persons, the appointment of guardians and conservators and settlement of their accounts, and in all matters relating to apprentices, and in cases of sales of real estate of deceased persons for the payment of debts.

Terms of Court—Begin on the first Monday of every month.

JUVENILE COURT.
771 Ewing street.

Judge—Merritt W. Pinckney.

Jurisdiction—The Juvenile court hears and disposes of cases brought before it under the act to regulate the treatment and control of dependent, neglected and delinquent children.

CIRCUIT COURT OF APPEALS.
Federal building, 7th floor.

Associate Justice—Horace H. Lurton.

Judges—Francis E. Baker, William H. Seaman, Christian C. Kohlsaat.

Clerk—Edward M. Holloway.

Salary of judges, $7,000 a year.

Jurisdiction—The Circuit Courts of Appeal have appellate jurisdiction to review final decisions in district courts of Indiana, Illinois and Wisconsin in all cases other than those which may be taken direct to the United States Supreme court.

UNITED STATES DISTRICT COURT.
Federal building, 6th floor.

Judges—Kenesaw M. Landis, George A. Carpenter.

Clerk—Thomas C. Mac Millan.

Marshal—Luman T. Hoy.

Salary of judges, $6,000 a year.

Jurisdiction—United States District courts have jurisdiction of cases where the United States is plaintiff or defendant; of crimes and offenses cognizable under the authority of the United States; of suits relating to debts by or to the United States; of admiralty and maritime cases; of suits arising under the postal, patent, trade-mark, copyright, immigration, contract labor, national banking, antitrust laws, etc.

MASTERS IN CHANCERY.
Circuit Court—William F. Cooper, M. H. Guerin, Fred Sass, Albert W. Brickwood, Granville W. Browning, Stillman B. Jamieson, Roswell B. Mason, Dennis W. Sullivan, George Mills Rogers, Farlin Q. Ball, Horatio L. Wait, Sigmund Zeisler, William A. Doyle, Ralph W. Condee, John W. Ellis, Richard S. Folsom.

Superior Court—Wirt E. Humphrey, Charles P. Abbey, David F. Matchett, James V. O'Donnell, C. Arch Williams, Joseph E. Weissenbach, Charles T. Mason, Martin J. Isaacs, Charles C. Stilwell, James Turnock, Frank Hamlin, Charles J. Trainor, James I. Ennis, Leo J. Doyle, John H. Hummer, Michael E. Maher, Sidney S. Pollock, Edward F. Dunne, Jr.

TOWN OFFICERS IN COOK COUNTY.

Supervisors, town clerks, assessors and collectors.

Barrington—Supervisor, Charles P. Hawley, Barrington, 1913-1914; clerk, J. F. Gieske, Barrington, 1912-1914; assessor, John C. Plagge, Barrington, 1913-1914; collector, L. H. Bennett, Barrington, 1912-1914.

Berwyn—Supervisor, Harry J. Falthorn, Berwyn, 1913-1914; clerk, John Jaros, Berwyn, 1911-1914; assessor, Joseph H. Macauley, Berwyn, 1913-1914; collector, George W. Dolan, Berwyn, 1912-1914.

Bloom—Supervisor, Joseph Bergin, Chicago Heights, 1913-1914; clerk, Joseph J. Knagge, Chicago Heights, 1912-1914; assessor, Harry Green, Chicago Heights, 1913-1914; collector, Ernest H. Wells, Chicago Heights, 1912-1914.

Bremen—Supervisor, Samuel L. Fulton, Tinley Park, 1913-1914; clerk, William Funk, Tinley Park, 1912-1914; assessor, William Malhoff, Tinley Park, 1913-1914; collector, Herman Siemsen, Tinley Park, 1912-1914.

Calumet—Supervisor, William Becker, Jr., Blue Island, 1913-1914; clerk, Emil J. Wanek, 10183 South Elizabeth street, 1912-1914; assessor, Jacob Hoekstra, 310 West 111th place, 1913-1914; collector, Walter G. Davis, 11959 Harvard avenue, 1912-1914.

Cicero—President, Christ Jepson, 3441 South 52d avenue; supervisor, Walenty J. Kasperski, 3029 South 49th avenue, 1913-1914; clerk, Charles Stoffel, 5102 29th place, 1912-1914; assessor, Edwin E. Lovejoy, 2720 South 60th avenue, 1913-1914; collector, David T. Brennan, 1232 South 50th court, 1912-1914.

Elk Grove—Supervisor, J. F. Everding, Arlington Heights, 1913-1914; clerk, A. B. Scharringhausen, Arlington Heights, 1912-1914; assessor, George Meier, Mount Prospect, 1913-1914; collector, Louis C. Busse, Mount Prospect, 1912-1914.

Evanston—Supervisor, Harry S. Gilbert, 2116 Lunt avenue, 1913-1914; clerk, Norman Copeland, 6902 North Clark street, 1912-1914; assessor, H. C. W. Laubenheimer, 1628 Morse avenue; collector, Peter Phillip, 1812 Lunt avenue, 1912-1914.

Hanover—Supervisor, A. C. Schick, Bartlett, 1913-1914; clerk, Ben Schultz, Bartlett, 1912-1914; assessor, H. L. Ottendorf, Bartlett, 1913-1914; collector, Albert Piegorsch, Bartlett, 1912-1914.

Lemont—Supervisor, Patrick Hennehry, Lemont, 1913-1914; clerk, Vincent S. Buszkiewicz, 1912-1914; assessor, John Gerbarz, Lemont, 1913-1914; collector, Julius Ott, Lemont, 1912-1914.

Leyden—Supervisor, Frederick Joss, Bensenville, 1913-1914; clerk, Henry Buckman, River Grove, 1912-1914; assessor, Edgar H. Boesenberg, Manheim, 1913-1914; collector, Albert H. Dunteman, Bensenville, 1912-1914.

Lyons—Supervisor, George O. Pratt, 222 South Spring avenue, LaGrange, 1913-1914; clerk, Henry R. Gauger, 27 Harris avenue, LaGrange, 1912-1914; assessor, James G. Wolcott, 117 South 6th avenue, LaGrange, 1913-1914; collector, Charles W. Northrup, 231 South Waiola avenue. LaGrange, 1912-1914.

Maine—Supervisor, Adam H. Imig, Des Plaines, 1913-1914; clerk, M. H. Brown, Des Plaines, 1912-1914; assessor, August Jarnecke, Des Plaines, 1913-1914; collector, M. Schiessle, Park Ridge, 1912-1914.

New Trier—Supervisor, Harry K. Snider, 500 Lake avenue, Wilmette, 1913-1914; clerk, G. Sesterhenn, Gross Point, 1912-1914; assessor, Joseph H. Long, 611 Lake avenue, Wilmette, 1913-1914; collector, Carlton Prouty, Wilmette, 1912-1914.

Niles—Supervisor, David Fielweber, Morton Grove, 1913-1914; clerk, Robert F. Hoffman, Niles Center, 1912-1914; assessor, John H. Ruesch, Norwood Park, 1913-1914; collector, Ferdinand Bauman, Morton Grove, 1912-1914.

Northfield—Supervisor, Peter Bellert, Shermerville, 1913-1914; clerk, A. C. Clavey, Glen View, 1912-1914; assessor, William R. Lanwehr, Shermerville, 1913-1914; collector, Fred Rugen, Glen View, 1912-1914.

Norwood Park—Supervisor, Robert Horton, Norwood Park, 1913-1914; clerk, Roy G. Harris, Norwood Park, 1912-1914; assessor, Edwin D. Smith, 5831 Circle avenue, Norwood Park, 1913-1914; collector, Frank J. Phillips, Norwood Park, 1912-1914.

Oak Park—Supervisor, George Walker, 350 Forest avenue, Oak Park, 1913-1914; clerk, James E. Tristram, 319 Maple avenue, Oak Park, 1912-1914; assessor, James P. Willing, 433 North boulevard, Oak Park, 1913-1914; collector, G. Whittier Gale, 124 North Kenilworth avenue, Oak Park, 1912-1914.

Orland—Supervisor, John Humphrey, Orland, 1913-1914; clerk, B. F. Sippel, Tinley Park, 1912-1914; assessor, Martin Smith, Orland, 1913-1914; collector, F. H. Arnold, Tinley Park, 1912-1914.

Palatine—Supervisor, J. G. Horstman, Palatine, 1913-1914; clerk, Harry H. Schoppe, Palatine, 1912-1914; assessor, J. H. Schierding, Palatine, 1913-1914; collector, Henry Roper, Palatine, 1912-1914.

Palos—Supervisor, Peter Lucas, Worth, 1913-1914; clerk, P. J. O'Connell, Worth, 1912-1914; assessor, John McCord, Orland, 1912-1914; collector, Henry Elliott, Oak Lawn, 1912-1914.

Proviso—Supervisor, L. W. Richter, Melrose Park, 1913-1914; clerk, Fred Samuels, Forest Park, 1912-1914; assessor, John Wolf, Hillside, 1913-1914; collector, Charles W. Strook, Maywood, 1912-1914.

Rich—Supervisor, John Scheidt, Matteson, 1913-1914; clerk, Albert Reese, Matteson, 1912-1914; assessor, Louis Mahler, Matteson, 1913-1914; collector, Henry Thies, Homewood, 1912-1914.

Ridgeville (city of Evanston)—City and town clerk, John F. Hahn, Evanston, 1912-1914; assessor, Charles H. Rose, Evanston, 1913-1914; city treasurer and town collector, George P. Mill, Evanston, 1912-1914.

Riverside—Supervisor, Frank Frederick, Riverside, 1913-1914; clerk, Charles H. Glanz, Riverside, 1912-1914; assessor, Charles D. Sherman, Riverside, 1913-1914; collector, Fred K. Crowe, Riverside, 1912-1914.

Schaumburg—Supervisor, Albert Sporleder, Palatine, 1913-1914; clerk, August Sunderlage, Palatine, 1912-1914; collector, Henry E. Quindel, Palatine, 1913-1914; collector, Henry C. Winkelhake, Palatine, 1912-1914.

Stickney—Supervisor, Charles Kluck, Clearing, 1913-1914; clerk, William J. Wangerow, Clearing, 1912-1914; assessor, John Brower, Summit, 1913-1914; collector, Charles Jacobs, Oak Lawn, 1912-1914.

Thornton—Supervisor, Henry I. Heckler, Harvey, 1913-1914; clerk, George Koenig, Harvey, 1912-1914; assessor, J. J. O'Rourke, Harvey, 1913-1914; collector, John Shilling, South Holland, 1912-1914.

Wheeling—Supervisor, F. W. Mueller, Arlington Heights, 1913-1914; clerk, Julius Fleutie, Arlington Heights, 1912-1914; assessor, Jacob Schwingel, Wheeling, 1913-1914; collector, F. H. Lorenzon, Arlington Heights, 1912-1914.

Worth—Supervisor, Ernest Knott, Blue Island, 1913-1914; clerk, Adolph Helquist, Blue Island, 1912-1914; assessor, John H. Kruse, Blue Island, 1913-1914; collector, William H. Harnew, Oak Lawn, 1912-1914.

The towns of Hyde Park, Jefferson, Lake, Lake View, North Chicago, South Chicago and West Chicago lie wholly within the city of Chicago. The ex officio supervisor and collector for all is William L. O'Connell, the county treasurer, and the ex officio assessor and town clerk is Robert M. Sweitzer, the county clerk.

Terms of supervisors, town clerks and collectors expire in April, 1914; terms of assessors expire Dec. 31, 1914.

MUNICIPAL COURT OF CHICAGO.

City hall, 8th and 9th floors.

Chief Justice—Harry Olson, room 915.
Chief Clerk—Frank P. Danisch.
Chief Bailiff—Anton J. Cermak.
Judges—Terms expire in 1914; Henry C. Beitler, Charles N. Goodnow, Joseph Z. Uhlir, Hosea W. Wells, Oscar M. Torrison, Frederick L. Fake, Jr., Sheridan E. Fry, Hugh R. Stewart, Frank H. Graham, Joseph E. Ryan. Terms expire in 1916: John R. Caverly, John J. Rooney, Thomas F. Scully, Jacob H. Hopkins, James C. Martin, Harry P. Dolan, Joseph Sabath, John R. Newcomer, Charles A. Williams, David Sullivan. Terms expire in 1918: Harry Olson, chief justice; William N. Gemmill, John K. Prindiville, Harry M. Fisher, John A. Mahoney, John Courtney, Edward T. Wade, Joseph P. Rafferty, Joseph S. LaBuy, John J. Sullivan, Hugh J. Kearns.
Salaries—Chief justice, $10,000 a year; associate justices, $6,000; clerk, $6,000; chief deputy clerk, $4,000; two assistant chief deputy clerks and one auditor, $3,000; other clerks, $1,800 to $2,500; bailiff, $6,000; chief deputy bailiff, $4,000; two assistant chief deputy bailiffs, $2,500; other bailiffs, $1,500 to $2,000.
Civil Courts—First district, city hall; second district, 8855 and 8857 Exchange avenue, South Chicago.
Criminal Courts—First district: Branches 1 and 2, Criminal court building; South Clark street branches 1 and 2, 625 South Clark street; Desplaines street branch, 119 North Desplaines street; Maxwell street branch, Maxwell and Morgan streets; Hyde Park branch, 5223 Lake avenue;

West Chicago avenue branch, 1125 West Chicago avenue; Shakespeare avenue branch, Shakespeare and California avenues; East Chicago avenue branch, 115 East Chicago avenue; Sheffield avenue branch, Sheffield avenue and Diversey boulevard; Englewood branch, 6347 Wentworth avenue; 35th street branch, 728 West 35th street. Second district; 8855-8857 Exchange avenue, South Chicago.

JURISDICTION.

1. All actions on contracts when the amount claimed by the plaintiff exceeds $1,000; all actions for the recovery of personal property the value of which exceeds $1,000; all actions for the recovery of damages for the conversion of personal property when the amount sought to be recovered exceeds $1,000.
2. Criminal cases of the grade of felony, except treason and murder, and cases of habeas corpus.
3. Criminal cases below the grade of felony, except habeas corpus cases.
4. Civil actions for the recovery of money only when the amount does not exceed $1,000; actions for recovery of personal property valued at less than $1,000; actions of forcible detainer; actions and proceedings over which justices of the peace have jurisdiction and actions not otherwise provided for by the act.
5. Quasi criminal actions.
6. Proceedings for the prevention of crime; for the arrest, examination and commitment of persons charged with criminal offenses; proceedings involving use of search warrants.

CHICAGO THEATERS.

Seating capacity given in parentheses.

Academy (1,467)—16 South Halsted street.
Alhambra (1,461)—State street and Archer avenue.
American (1,200)—Wabash avenue and Peck court.
Archer (800)—3510 Archer avenue.
Auditorium (3,747)—Congress-st. and Wabash-av.
Avenue (1,140)—3108 Indiana avenue.
Bijou (1,238)—300 South Halsted street.
Blackstone (1,200)—Hubbard-ct., near Michigan-av.
Bryn Mawr (1,200)—1125 Bryn Mawr avenue.
Bush Temple (845)—110 West Chicago avenue.
Calumet (895)—9206 South Chicago avenue.
Casino (1,217)—493 North Clark street.
Clark (670)—4553 North Clark street.
Cohan's Grand (1,379)—121 North Clark street.
Coliseum (15,000)—Wabash avenue, near 16th street.
College (1,325)—Webster and Sheffield avenues.
Colonial (1,447)—26 West Randolph street.
Columbia (1,193)—North Clark, near Madison street.
Columbus (1,324)—1840 Wabash avenue.
Cort (962)—Dearborn street, near Randolph.
Criterion (1,233)—1226 Sedgwick street.
Crown (1,458)—Ashland avenue and Division street.
Empire (1,332)—673 West Madison street.
Empress (1,500)—6226 South Halsted street.
Englewood (1,400)—726 West 63d street.
Folly (976)—531 South State street.
Garrick (1,257)—60 West Randolph street.
Globe (1,390)—700 South Wabash avenue.
Hamlin (1,215)—3826 West Madison street.
Harrison (617)—501 South Kedzie avenue.
Haymarket (1,800)—723 West Madison street.
Howard (708)—66 East Van Buren street.
Hyde Park (634)—5500 Lake Park avenue.
Illinois (1,282)—75 East Jackson boulevard.
Imperial (1,300)—2329 West Madison street.
Indiana (759)—228 East 43d street.
Julian (799)—920 Belmont avenue.
Kedzie (1,461)—West Madison-st. and Kedzie-av.
LaSalle (767)—110 West Madison street.
Lincoln (1,500)—3160 Lincoln avenue.
Logan Square (1,400)—2538 Milwaukee avenue.
Lyceum (476)—3851 Cottage Grove avenue.

Lyda (543)—317 North 48th avenue.
Lyric (1,350)—26 West Jackson boulevard.
Lyric (560)—115th street and Michigan avenue.
Majestic (1,986)—18 West Monroe street.
Marlowe (1,139)—Stewart avenue and W. 63d street.
Marshfield (1,077)—3305-11 North Marshfield avenue.
McVicker's (1,868)—23 West Madison street.
National (1,460)—6235 South Halsted street.
New American (1,400)—1600 West Madison street.
New Apollo (965)—1540 North Crawford avenue.
New Windsor (1,290)—1225 North Clark street.
North Avenue (1,300)—316 West North avenue.
Oak (1,054)—2000 North Western avenue.
Olympic (1,760)—165 North Clark street.
Orchestra Hall (2,556)—216 South Michigan avenue.
Orpheum (670)—110 South State street.
Palace (1,303)—North Clark street, near Randolph.
Palace (1,433)—1135 Blue Island avenue.
Parkway (757)—2636-2638 North Clark avenue.
Pekin (739)—2700 State street.
Powers' (1,106)—124 West Randolph street.
President (700)—55th street, near Calumet avenue.
Princess (934)—319 South Clark street.
Roseland (496)—11307 Michigan avenue.
St. Alphonsus (1,004)—Southport and Lincoln avenues.
Star (1,500)—1455 Milwaukee avenue.
Star and Garter (1,897)—815-817 West Madison street.
Studebaker (1,330)—418 South Michigan avenue.
Swanson (500)—3863 Cottage Grove avenue.
Thalia (800)—1215 West 18th street.
Thirty-First Street (737)—77 31st street.
Trevett (900)—Cottage Grove-av. and 63d street.
Unnamed (750)—4856 South Ashland avenue.
Unnamed (1,200)—5234 Rosalie avenue.
Victoria (1,800)—Belmont and Sheffield avenues.
Virginia (800)—Halsted and West Madison streets.
Whitney (708)—66 East Van Buren street.
Willard (1,177)—340 East 51st street.
Wilson (1,000)—Wilson and Evanston avenues.

Dec. 6, 1913, there were 649 theaters of all kinds in Chicago in operation, not including those under construction.

EVANSTON HISTORICAL SOCIETY.

Incorporated November, 1898.

President—J. Seymour Currey.
Vice-President—Frank R. Grover.
Treasurer—John F. Hahn.
Secretary—William C. Levere.

The Evanston Historical society has rooms in the Public Library building there. It has a library of 1,000 volumes, 1,000 pamphlets and a large amount of historical data.

CHICAGO AT A GLANCE.

Fort Dearborn established....................1803
Fort Dearborn massacre..................Aug. 15, 1812
Chicago surveyed and platted.....................1830
Cook county organized.........................1831
Town of Chicago incorporated...........August, 1833
City of Chicago incorporated..........March 4, 1837
First election held......................March 31, 1837
First railroad opened.........................1848
Cholera epidemic.............................1854
Serious money panic..........................1857
Great fire (loss $200,000,000)............Oct. 8-9, 1871
Second financial panic........................1873
City incorporated under general law....April 23, 1875
Savings bank crash...........................1877
World's Fair held............................1893
Centennial celebrated................Sept. 26-30, 1903
Iroquois theater fire.................Dec. 30, 1903

Population Jan. 1, 1914 (estimated)—2,393,325.
Appropriations, all purposes (1913)—$65,378,511.68.
Area in square miles—191.325.
Assessed value real estate and personal property (1913)—$936,911,332 (one-third actual value).
Asylums—98.
Banks, national, state and private—131.
Boulevards, mileage of—48.
Building permits issued (1912)—11,325.
Buildings erected (1912)—$88,786,960.
Cemeteries, number of—53.
Churches, chapels and missions—1,114.
Clearings by associated banks (1912)—$15,380,795,541.
Convents and monasteries—37.
Debt (1913)—$25,784,586.90.
Dispensaries—25.
Duties collected on imported merchandise (1912)—$10,698,891.11.
Elevation—Above sea level, 582 feet; above lake Michigan, 25 feet.
Employes on city pay rolls (1912)—26,327.
Firemen, number of, including officers—1,938.
Fire alarm boxes—1,979.
Fireboats—6.

Fire engine companies—119.
Fire hydrants, number—25,542.
Fire cisterns—117.
Fire hook and ladder companies—34.
Halls (except theaters)—473.
Hospitals—86.
Imports of merchandise (1912)—$30,278,600.
Internal revenue collected in Chicago district (1912)—$12,485,795.50.
Latitude—N. 41 deg. 53 min. 6 sec.
Length of city, north to south, miles—25½.
Libraries—22.
Lights, electric, in service—15,841.
Lights, gas, in service—15,740.
Lights, gasoline, in service—8,678.
Longitude—87 deg. 38 min. 1 sec. west.
Mail carriers (1913)—2,039.
Mail, pieces of, handled, fiscal year 1913—1,827,289,126.
Manufactures in 1909, value of product—$1,281,313,000.
Medical schools—32.
Newspapers and periodicals—760.
Parks, area of, in acres—4,611.
Policemen, number of, including officers—4,955.
Postal receipts, year ended June 30,1913—$23,597,878.03.
Pupils enrolled in public schools (1913)—315,737.
Railroads (divisions not included) entering Chicago—27.
Saloons, number of (Dec. 1, 1913)—7,152.
Schools, public, number of (not including branches)—294.
Street, longest (Western avenue), miles—23½.
Street railway mileage—1,350.
Streets, paved, mileage—1,863.36.
Streets and alleys, total mileage—4,446.
Teachers in public schools, number of—7,013.
Theaters, all kinds, in operation Dec. 1, 1913—640.
Tonnage of vessels cleared in 1912—10,086,209.
Value (actual) of real estate and personal property, 1913—$2,810,733,996.
Water used in a year (1912), gallons—170,294,738,000.
Width of city, east to west, miles—9.

CHICAGO AND CALUMET HARBOR LIGHTS AND FOG SIGNALS.

CHICAGO HARBOR—LIGHTS.

On the southerly end of the northerly inner breakwater, a fixed red light in gray conical metal tower 31½ feet high; light visible 9¾ miles.

On the northerly end of the inner breakwater, a fixed white light from lens lantern shown from top of white post 19 feet high.

On the easterly end of the north pier at the entrance of Chicago river, a fixed red light shown from lens lantern on post 22 feet high; with the next light it forms a range showing the direction of the piers and course for entering the harbor.

On the north pier, near its easterly end, at the entrance to Chicago river, a fixed white light, in gray framework tower 27 feet high; light visible 13 miles.

In 30 feet of water, inside of and near the southeasterly end of the outer breakwater; flashing alternately red and white; interval between flashes, 10 seconds; red conical tower on rock-faced masonry tower, 59½ feet high; light 67½ feet above lake level and visible 16 miles.

On the northwesterly end of the outer breakwater, a fixed red light, shown from lens lantern in gray skeleton metal tower 19 feet high; height of lantern above lake level 55 feet.

CHICAGO HARBOR—FOG SIGNALS.

On the north pier in front of and attached to the light tower, a bell, struck by machinery, a double and single blow alternately with intervals of 20 seconds.

At the light tower near the southeasterly end of the outer breakwater, a 10-inch steam whistle; blasts 5 seconds, silent intervals 25 seconds.

CALUMET HARBOR—LIGHTS.

Calumet bar gas buoy, moored in 21 feet of water, on the northerly end of the Calumet bar; fixed white light with 10-second eclipse, shown from lens lantern.

On the southeasterly end of the new breakwater, a fixed white light, shown from buff metal tower 34 feet high; light visible 13½ miles.

On the outer end of the north pier, entrance to the mouth of the Calumet river and South Chicago harbor and about 11 miles southeasterly from the Chicago breakwater, a fixed red light, shown from gray cylindrical tower 30 feet high; light visible 13 miles.

CALUMET HARBOR—FOG SIGNALS.

At the breakwater tower, a first-class compressed-air siren which sounds thus: Blast, 3 seconds; silent interval, 12 seconds; blast, 3 seconds; silent interval, 42 seconds.

At the north pier light, a bell struck by machinery every 20 seconds.

STREET LIGHTING IN CHICAGO.

Number of lights of specified kinds used:

Light.	1909.	1910.	1911.	1912.
Gas	18,313	17,416	17,385	15,740
Gasoline	6,806	7,319	7,977	8,678
Elect. (by city)	11,592	12,366	12,449	14,854
Elect. (rented)	810	893	897	987
Tot. operated	37,521	37,994	38,708	40,259
Total cost....	$1,034,822	$1,043,401	$1,013,041	$1,038,699

In 1912 the cost of operating the various kinds of light was as follows: Gas, $293,459.43; gasoline, $238,573.64; rented electric lights, $70,361.10; municipal electric lights, $436,305.20. The cost of maintaining each arc light operated from a municipal plant was $34.26; cost per light for rented arc lights, $75.

POINTS OF INTEREST IN AND ABOUT CHICAGO.

NORTH SIDE.

Academy of Sciences museum in Lincoln park.
Cemeteries—Graceland, Rosehill, Calvary.
Fort Sheridan, near Highwood.
Grant, Lincoln, Schiller, Goethe and other monuments in Lincoln park.
Historical society library and collection, Dearborn avenue and Ontario street.
Indian trail tree, near Glencoe.
Lake Shore drive.
Lincoln park conservatories and zoo.
Newberry library, Clark street and Walton place.
Northwestern university in Evanston.
Waterworks, Chicago avenue, near Lake.

SOUTH SIDE.

Armour Institute of Technology, 3300 Armour avenue.
Art institute galleries of paintings, sculptures and art collections; on the lake front, foot of Adams street.
Auditorium tower, Wabash avenue and Congress street; view of city.
Blackstone branch library, Lake avenue and 49th street.
Board of trade, LaSalle street and Jackson boulevard; admission to gallery.
Cahokia courthouse on Wooded island in Jackson park.
Central Trust Company building, interior mural decorations, 125 West Monroe street.
Chamber of Commerce building (interior), LaSalle and Washington streets.
Chicago Normal school, 68th street and Stewart avenue.
City hall, Washington, LaSalle and Randolph streets.
Confederate monument in Oakwoods cemetery.
County building, Clark, Randolph and Washington streets.
Crerar library, 106 North Wabash avenue, 6th floor.
Douglas monument, 35th street and Ellis avenue.
Drexel, Grand and 55th Street boulevards.
Field museum in Jackson park.
Fire tablet (1871), 137 DeKoven street.
Fort Dearborn site tablet, River street, opposite Rush street bridge.
Grand Army hall in public library building, Randolph street and Michigan avenue.
Iroquois theater fire, scene of, 28-30 West Randolph street; memorial tablet by Lorado Taft in Iroquois Memorial hospital, 28 North Market street.

Jackson park, site of World's Fair in 1893.
Life saving station at mouth of Chicago river.
Lincoln wigwam tablet, Market and Lake streets.
Logan statue in Grant park (lake front).
Marquette building sculpture panels, Dearborn and Adams streets.
Marquette-Joliet cross, Robey street and drainage canal.
Masonic Temple; view of city from roof.
Massacre monument in 18th street near the lake.
Midway plaisance.
Montgomery Ward tower, Michigan avenue and Madison street; view of city.
McKinley statue in McKinley park.
Orchestra hall, 216-220 South Michigan avenue.
Postoffice, on square bounded by Adams, Clark and Dearborn streets and Jackson boulevard.
Public library, Michigan avenue and Washington street.
Pullman, suburb and manufactory.
South Water street; commission house district.
State street department stores; shopping district.
Stockyards, Halsted and Root streets.
University of Chicago quadrangles, Ellis avenue and 58th street.
Washington statue, Grand boulevard and 51st street.
Wendell Phillips high school, Prairie avenue and 39th street.
Wooded island in Jackson park.

WEST SIDE.

Ashland, Humboldt, Washington and Garfield boulevards.
Northwestern railway passenger station, Canal and West Madison streets.
Douglas park.
Drainage canal.
Garfield park.
Ghetto district on South Canal, Jefferson and Maxwell streets; fish market on Jefferson street from 12th to Maxwell.
Haymarket square, Randolph and Desplaines streets; scene of anarchist riot.
Hull House, 800 South Halsted street.
Humboldt park.
Humboldt, Leif Ericson, Reuter and Kosciusko monuments in Humboldt park.
Parental school, St. Louis and Berwyn avenues.
Police monument (Haymarket), in Union park.

DISTANCES IN CHICAGO.

FROM MADISON STREET SOUTH.

Twelfth street, 1 mile.
Twenty-Second street, 2 miles.
Thirty-First street, 3 miles.
Thirty-Ninth street, 4 miles.
Forty-Seventh street, 5 miles.
Fifty-Fifth street, 6 miles.
Sixty-Third street, 7 miles.
Seventy-First street, 8 miles.
Seventy-Ninth street, 9 miles.
Eighty-Seventh street, 10 miles.
Ninety-Fifth street, 11 miles.
One Hundred and Third street, 12 miles.
One Hundred and Eleventh street, 13 miles.
One Hundred and Nineteenth street, 14 miles.
One Hundred and Twenty-Seventh street, 15 miles.
City limits, 16½ miles.

FROM MADISON STREET NORTH.

Chicago avenue, 1 mile.
North avenue, 2 miles.
Fullerton avenue, 3 miles.
Belmont avenue, 4 miles.
Graceland avenue, 5 miles.

Lawrence avenue, 6 miles.
Bryn Mawr avenue, 7 miles.
Devon avenue, 8 miles.
Touhy avenue, 9 miles.
City limits, 9½ miles.

FROM STATE STREET WEST.

Halsted street, 1 mile.
Ashland boulevard, 2 miles.
Western avenue, 3 miles.
Kedzie avenue, 4 miles.
Crawford avenue, 5 miles.
Cicero avenue, 6 miles.
Central avenue, 7 miles.
Ridgeland avenue, 8 miles.
City limits (west on North avenue), 9 miles.

FROM STATE STREET EAST.

To lake on 22d street, 2-3 mile.
To Cottage Grove avenue on 31st street, 2-3 mile.
To Cottage Grove avenue south of 39th street, 1 mile.
To Stony Island avenue on 55th, 2 miles.
To Yates avenue, south of 71st street, 3 miles.

SHERIFFS OF COOK COUNTY (1871-1914).

1871-1874—Timothy M. Bradley, Rep.
1874-1876—Francis Agnew, Pen.
1876-1878—Charles Kern, Dem.
1878-1880—John Hoffman, Rep.
1880-1882—O. L. Mann, Rep.
1882-1886*—Seth F. Hanchett, Rep.
1886-1890—Canute R. Matson, Rep.
1890-1894—James H. Gilbert, Rep.

1894-1898—James Pease,† Rep.
1898-1902—Ernest J. Magerstadt, Rep.
1902-1906—Thomas E. Barrett, Dem.
1906-1910—Christopher Strassheim, Rep.
1910-1914—Michael Zimmer, Dem.
*Term changed from two to four years. †Also appointed to serve unexpired term of Thomas E. Barrett, who died in March, 1906.

CHICAGO CITY OFFICIALS.

Daily News Photo
WILLIAM H. SEXTON,
Corporation Counsel.

Matzene Photo
JOHN E. ERICSON,
City Engineer.

Matzene Photo
FRANCIS D. CONNERY,
City Clerk.

Brand Photo
LAWRENCE E. M'GANN,
Public Works Commiss'r.

Daily News Photo
JOHN E. TRAEGER,
Comptroller.

Matzene Photo
CARTER H. HARRISON,
Mayor.

Walinger Photo
M. J. FLYNN,
City Treasurer.

HARRY OLSON,
C. J. Municipal Court.

Stein Photo
RAY PALMER,
City Electrician.

Koehne Photo
JAMES A. QUINN,
Oil Inspector.

Daily News Photo
WILLIAM J. M'COURT,
Supt. Water Bureau.

J. L. WHITMAN,
Supt. House of Correct'n.

Daily News Photo
DR. GEO. B. YOUNG,
Commissioner of Health.

Daily News Photo
JAMES GLEASON,
Chief of Police.

Daily News Photo
CHAS. F. SEYFERLICH,
Fire Marshal.

Coovar Photo
N. L. PIOTROWSKI,
City Attorney.

Gibson Photo
HENRY ERICSSON,
Building Commissioner.

CHICAGO CITY OFFICIALS.

Heads of departments, assistants, chief clerks and other employes. Their offices unless otherwise specified are open from 9 a. m. to 5 p. m.

MAYOR'S OFFICE.

Room 507 city hall. Hours 9:30 a. m. to 1 p. m.
Mayor—Carter H. Harrison, D.
Private Secretary—Charles C. Fitzmorris, D.
Duties—The mayor presides over meetings of the city council, approves or vetoes the acts of that body, appoints all nonelective city officials, sees that all the laws and ordinances are faithfully executed, issues and revokes licenses and exercises a general supervision over all the various subordinate departments of the city government.

THE CITY COUNCIL (1913-1914).

Presiding Officer—Mayor Carter H. Harrison.
City Clerk—Francis D. Connery.
Chief Clerk—Edward J. Padden.
Sergeant-at-Arms—William H. Brown.
Total membership of council, 70; democrats, 45; republicans, 21; progressives, 3; independent, 1.

Ward.　　　　ALDERMEN.
1. Michael Kenna, D.......307 South Clark street
　　John J. Coughlin, D......17 North LaSalle street
2. George F. Harding, Jr., R..504, 117 N. Dearborn
　　Hugh Norris, R............3638 South 5th avenue
3. SI Mayer, D.........4603 South Michigan avenue
　　Thomas D. Nash, D..........1617 Ashland block
4. Joseph F. Ryan, D..........524 West 25th place
　　John A. Richert, D...2603 South Halsted street
5. Patrick J. Carr, D...3508 South Western avenue
　　Charles Martin, D.........3635 Emerald avenue
6. Theodore K. Long, R......4823 Kimbark avenue
　　Willis O. Nance, R..........5213 Hibbard avenue
7. John H. Helwig, R..........418 East 63d street
　　Charles E. Merriam, Ind...1410, 139 North Clark
8. John R. Emerson, D....2665 East 77th street
　　Ernest M. Cross, R...............10209 Avenue L
9. Hiram Vanderbilt, Prog...11232 South Michigan
　　Eugene Block, D............9311 Evans avenue
10. Frank Klaus, D........1726 South Center avenue
　　Frank J. Vavricek, D........1720 Loomis street
11. E. F. Cullerton, D.............519 Reaper block
　　Frank W. Bewersdorf, D....2103 S. Western-av.
12. Joseph I. Novak, D..2401 South Trumbull avenue
　　Otto Kerner, D............402 Rector building
13. Thomas J. Ahern, D....214 South Kedzie avenue
　　Frank McDonald, D..2851 West Congress street
14. James H. Lawley, R..1925 West Chicago avenue
　　J. Edward Clancy, D........1104 Ashland block
15. Henry Utpatel, Prog..408 Chamber of Com. bldg.
　　Albert W. Bellfuss, R........2258 Cornelia street
16. Stanley H. Kunz, D..........1349 Noble street
　　John Czekala, D.........1837 Evergreen avenue
17. Lewis D. Sitts, R............1471 Grand avenue
　　Stanley S. Walkowiak, D...1317, 139 N. Clark-st.
18. Frank F. Gazzolo, D.....12 North Leavitt street
　　William J. Healy, R...11, 716 W. Madison street
19. John Powers, D....162 West Washington street
　　James B. Bowler, D............1223 Taylor street
20. Hugo L. Pitte, D..404, 25 North Dearborn street
21. Ellis Geiger, D......366, 7 West Madison street
　　James F. Burns, R.....Title and Trust building
22. V. J. Schaeffer, D......1841 North Halsted street
　　John H. Bauler, D.......515 West North avenue
23. Jacob A. Hey, Prog..2050 North Halsted street
　　John Kjellander, R......3033 North Clark street
24. August Krumholz, D.......1662 Fullerton avenue
　　John Haderlein, D..........3150 Southport avenue
25. Henry D. Capitain, R...171 N. Wabash avenue
　　Jacob A. Freund, R.......5447 Winthrop avenue
26. William F. Lipps, R.......2180 Wilson avenue
　　George Pretzel, R.......3830 North Hoyne avenue
27. G. Ed Trebing, D.......3244 North Troy street
　　Frank J. Wilson, D......5153 Montrose avenue
28. Harry E. Littler, R...............113 Ann street
　　Charles Twigg, D............2518 Lyndale street
29. Felix B. Janovsky, D....1824 West 47th street
　　Frank McDermott, D....1552 West 55th street
30. George P. Latchford, D.....721 West 47th street
　　Joseph A. Swift, D...5428 South Halsted street
31. James A. Kearns, R........5510 Lafayette avenue
　　Henry F. Bergen, D.......1633 West 63d street
32. Albert J. Fisher, R.........219 West 72d street
　　Melville G. Holding, D....127 N. Dearborn street

33. Irwin R. Hazen, R..508 Title and Trust building
　　Geo. H. Bradshaw, R..659 Washington boulevard
34. Winfield J. Held, D........4125 West 26th street
　　John Toman, D..............4141 West 21st place
35. James Donahoe, D............1606 Ashland block
　　Martin J. Healy, D....1958 Humboldt boulevard

STANDING COMMITTEES (1913-1914).

Finance—Richert, Harding, Long, Emerson, Lawley, Bellfuss, Sitts, Pitte, Geiger, Krumholz, Lipps, Wilson, Twigg, Kearns, Holding. Meets Fridays, 2 p. m.

Local Transportation—Block, Mayer, Richert, Carr, Long, McDonald, Clancy, William J. Healy, Capitain, Lipps, Wilson, Twigg, Bergen, Fisher, Hazen, Toman, Donahoe. Meets Wednesdays, 10:30 a. m.

Gas, Oil and Electric Light—Sitts, Ryan, Long, Merriam, Block, Vavricek, Bellfuss, Walkowiak, Bowler, Burns, Hey, Haderlein, Twigg, Janovsky, Kearns, Bradshaw, M. J. Healy. Meets Thursdays, 2 p. m.

Harbors, Wharves and Bridges—Littler, Kenna, Norris, Nance, Emerson, Kerner, Czekala, Gazzolo, Geiger, Bauler, Hey, Freund, Trebing, McDermott, Swift. Meets Mondays, 2 p. m.

Local Industries—Fisher, Mayer, Carr, Klaus, Cullerton, Novak, Lawley, Czekala, Sitts, Schaeffer, Krumholz, Pretzel, Wilson, McDermott, Bergen. Meets Tuesdays, 2 p. m.

Judiciary, State Legislation, Elections and Rules—Donahoe, Coughlin, Helwig, Bewersdorf, Kerner, Ahern, Clancy, Utpatel, Walkowiak, Powers, Bauler, Kjellander, Capitain, Swift, Holding, Hazen, Held. Meets Tuesdays, 2 p. m.

Streets and Alleys, Taxation and Street Nomenclature—Wm. J. Healy, Coughlin, Norris, Cross, Klaus, McDonald, Utpatel, Kunz, Burns, Kjellander, Haderlein, McDermott, Swift, Toman. Meets Mondays, 2 p. m.

License—Pitte, Norris, Ryan, Merriam, Cross, Vavricek, Novak, Ahern, Utpatel, Bowler, Hey, Haderlein, Janovsky, Bradshaw, Held. Meets Thursdays, 2 p. m.

Buildings and City Hall—Clancy, Nash, Carr, Cross, Vanderbilt, Klaus, Bewersdorf, Walkowiak, Powers, Schaeffer, Pretzel, Trebing, Littler, Latchford, M. J. Healy. Meets Fridays, 2 p. m.

Schools, Fire, Police and Civil Service—Ryan, Harding, Mayer, Richert, Martin, Helwig, Block, Vavricek, Bewersdorf, Geiger, Kjellander, Bergen, Bradshaw, Held, M. J. Healy. Meets Tuesdays, 11:30 a. m.

Health—Nance, Nash, Martin, Merriam, Vanderbilt, Cullerton, Ahern, Lawley, Kunz, Gazzolo, Freund, Pretzel, Littler, Latchford. Meets Wednesdays, 2 p. m.

Water—Toman, Kenna, Ryan, Martin, Helwig, Vanderbilt, Kerner, Kunz, Gazzolo, Powers, Schaeffer, Freund, Latchford, Hazen. Meets Fridays, 10:30 a. m.

Railway Terminals—Geiger, Kenna, Harding, Richert, Helwig, Bewersdorf, McDonald, Utpatel, Wm. J. Healy, Bowler, Schaeffer, Capitain, Littler, Fisher, Donahoe. Meets Mondays, 10:30 a. m.

SELECT COMMITTEES (1913-1914).

Track Elevation—Janovsky, Fisher, Emerson, Kearns, Bauler, Nance, Czekala, Trebing, Nash. Meets Wednesdays, 3:30 p. m.

Compensation—Harding, Bellfuss, Lipps, Krumholz, Holding, Pitte. Meets Fridays, 1 p. m.

Bathing Beaches and Recreation Piers—Norris, Bowler, Novak, Cross, Burns. Meets Fridays, 3:30 p. m.

Special Park Commission—Aldermen Bellfuss, Capitain, Coughlin, Cullerton and McDonald, and Messrs. Oscar F. Mayer, Jens Jensen, Cyrial Fiala, Paul Drzymalski, Peter S. Goodman, George Landau, Charles E. Bock, F. A. Lindstrand, Samuel J. Rosenblatt and Rev. Julius Rappaport. Meets Wednesdays, 10:30 a. m.

MEETINGS OF COUNCIL.

Regular meetings of the council are held every Monday at 7:30 p. m., except when otherwise ordered at a regular meeting.

Duties—In a general way the duties of the board of aldermen are to enact ordinances for the government of the city, levy and collect taxes, make appropriations, regulate licenses, etc. The matters coming under the jurisdiction of the council are indicated by the names of the committees given above.

CITY CLERK'S OFFICE.

City hall, first floor, south end.

City Clerk—Francis D. Connery, D.
Chief Clerk to City Clerk—E. J. Padden, D.
Duties—The city clerk keeps the corporate seal and all papers belonging to the council and keeps a record of the proceedings. All city licenses are issued through his office.

CITY TREASURER'S OFFICE.

City hall, second floor.

Hours—10 a. m. to 3 p. m.

City Treasurer—M. J. Flynn, D.
Assistant—Albert J. Keefe.
Chief Clerk—Joseph Friedman.
Duties—The treasurer receives all moneys belonging to the corporation, deposits the funds in bank, keeps separate accounts of each fund or appropriation, pays warrants, receives fines and renders monthly accounts of the condition of the treasury to the council. The city treasurer is also treasurer of the following pension funds: Firemen's, public school teachers', public library employes', public school employes', house of correction and municipal employes'.

CITY COMPTROLLER'S OFFICE.

Room 501 city hall.

Comptroller—John E. Traeger, D.
Deputy Comptroller—Louis E. Gosselin, D.
Chief Clerk—C. J. O'Connor.
Duties—The comptroller is at the head of the department of finance, of which the treasurer and collector are also members. He is charged with a general supervision over all the officers of the city who take in or pay out city money. He is the fiscal agent of the city and as such has charge of deeds, mortgages, contracts, etc. He audits and settles claims, keeps a record of persons committed to the house of correction, with fines, etc.; keeps books relating to appropriations, makes the annual estimates, signs warrants upon the city treasury, etc.

PAYMASTER'S BUREAU.

Room 503 city hall.

Paymaster—John L. Healy.
Duties—The city paymaster has immediate charge of paying the salaries of city employes, including school teachers and library employes.

CITY COLLECTOR'S OFFICE.

City hall, first floor.

City Collector—Edward Cohen, D.
Deputy City Collector—J. F. McCarty.
Duties—The city collector collects all license fees, fees for inspections and permits, compensation for franchises and vehicle tax; collects on special assessment warrants; transmits such payments to city treasurer daily, receipts for which are filed with the city comptroller.

CORPORATION COUNSEL'S OFFICE.

Room 511 city hall.

Corporation Counsel—William H. Sexton, D.
Assistants—Bryan Y. Craig, Lee D. Mathias, John W. Beckwith, William Dillon, Nicholas Michels, Charles M. Haft, Patrick W. Sullivan, James G. Skinner, Leon Hornstein, S. Crawford Ross, A. L. Gettys, John F. Power, J. J. Viterna, Max M. Korshak, George L. Reker, S. A. T. Watkins, Otto C. Bruhlman, Harry J. Ganey, J. F. Grossman, James J. St. Lawrence, Loring R. Hoover, William Naughton, George B. O'Reilly.
Assistant Corporation Counsel and Attorney Board Local Improvements—Philip J. McKenna.
Assistant Corporation Counsels and Assistant Attorneys Board Local Improvements—George P. Foster, Eugene H. Dupee, E. C. Frank Meier, Alexander Arkin.

Assistant Corporation Counsel and Attorney Fire Department—Joseph F. Murray.
Secretary to the Corporation Counsel—A. J. Callaghan.
Duties—The corporation counsel superintends and, with the assistance of the prosecuting and city attorneys, conducts all the law business of the city; draws the leases, deeds and other papers connected with the finance department and all contracts for any of the other departments of the corporation; drafts such ordinances as may be required of him by the city council or its committees and furnishes written legal opinions upon subjects submitted to him by the mayor or the city council or any department of the city government.

CITY ENGINEER'S OFFICE.

City hall, fourth floor.

City Engineer—John Ericson, C. E.
Assistant City Engineer—H. S. Baker.
Chief Clerk—W. J. Roach.
Duties—The city engineer has charge of the construction, maintenance and operation of bridges, viaducts and waterworks and performs all such services for the commissioner of public works as require the skill and experience of a civil engineer.

IN CHARGE OF DIVISIONS.

Construction—Henry W. Clausen.
Operation—Henry A. Allen.
Water Pipe Extension—H. L. Lucas.
Repairs and Shop—F. Miller.
Designing—Myron B. Reynolds.
Inspection and Testing—L. S. Marsh.
Bridges and Viaducts—Thomas G. Pihlfeldt.
Harbor Master—Thomas Moynihan.
Water Meter Shops—F. D. Anderson.

BOARD OF SUPERVISING ENGINEERS—CHICAGO TRACTION.

105 South LaSalle street.

Secretary—Lucius H. Davidson.

BOARD NO. 1.

Chairman—Bion J. Arnold.
Representing City of Chicago and Engineer for Board—George Weston.
Representing Chicago City Railway Company and Southern Street Railway Company—Harvey B. Fleming.
Representing Chicago Railways company—John Z. Murphy.

BOARD NO. 2.

Chairman—Bion J. Arnold.
Representing City of Chicago and Engineer for Board—George Weston.
Representing Calumet & South Chicago Railway Company—A. L. Drum.

BUREAU OF WATER.

City hall, first floor.

Superintendent—William J. McCourt.
Accountant—James J. Dunn.
Chief Clerk—John C. Schubert.
Cashier—Otto A. Dieier.
Chief Water Assessor—Thomas H. Byrne.
Field Assessor in Charge—J. J. Ward.
Duties—The superintendent of water has special charge of the assessment and collection of water rates.

BUREAU OF STREETS.

Room 408 city hall.

Superintendent—Walter G. Leininger.
First Assistant Superintendent—Patrick McCarthy.
Second Assistant Superintendent—W. J. Galligan.
Third Assistant Superintendent—(Vacancy).
Duties—The superintendent of streets performs such duties as are required of him by the commissioner of public works or the ordinances of the city. He has special charge of the streets, sidewalks and public ways of the city and of the improvement and repair thereof, except where such repair or improvement is to be paid for by special assessment. The first assistant superintendent performs such duties as may be required of him by the commissioner of public works, the superintendent of streets or the city ordinances, and acts as superintendent in the latter's absence.

The second assistant superintendent has charge of the cleaning of the streets and alleys of the city, including the removal and disposition of garbage, litter, dirt, ashes, offal and other materials. He also sees that the ordinances relating to garbage, etc., are enforced and that violations thereof are reported for prosecution. The third assistant has charge of the improvement and repairs of the streets and alleys, except where such repairs or improvements are to be paid for by special assessment.

BUREAU OF SEWERS.
Room 409 city hall.

Superintendent (acting)—George E. McGrath.
Engineer—William R. Mathews.
Engineer in Charge of Benches and Grades—W. H. Hedges.
Inspector in Charge—Edward J. Hayes.
Principal Clerk—Ed Cullerton, Jr.
Duties—The superintendent has special charge of the maintenance of sewers, including cleaning and repairing, and also of the issuance of permits for all connections.

BUREAU OF MAPS.
Room 410 city hall.

Superintendent—John D. Riley, D.
Duties—Has special charge of city maps and plats and all matters pertaining to street numbering, and is examiner of subdivisions.

BUREAU OF COMPENSATION.
Room V-15 city hall.

Superintendent—Henry V. McGurren.
Duties—Shall, under the direction of the commissioner of public works, have charge of and receive all applications for permits to use streets and alleys, or public grounds, or any space beneath the same; shall attend to all matters connected with the issuance of such permits; also act in an advisory capacity to the committee on compensation of the city council.

BOARD OF LOCAL IMPROVEMENTS.
City hall, second floor, south end.

Members—George A. Schilling, president; Edward J. Glackin, secretary; Frank Sima, Frank X. Rydzewski, Clayton F. Smith, Fred Burkhard.
Superintendent of Special Assessments and Secretary—Edward J. Glackin.
Engineer Board of Local Improvements—Cicero D. Hill.
Chief Engineer of Streets—John B. Hittell.
Superintendent of Sidewalks—N. E. Murray.
Chief Clerk Special Assessments—T. Sullivan.
Duties—The board of local improvements is that part of the city of Chicago government created by law for the purpose of making local improvements, the cost of which is paid by special assessments or direct taxation on the property directly and indirectly benefited. Among such local public improvements are sewers, house drains, water mains, water service pipes, sidewalks, street and alley paving and the taking of private property by condemnation proceedings for the purpose of opening, extending or widening public highways.

CITY ATTORNEY'S OFFICE.
Room 602 city hall.

City Attorney—Nicholas L. Piotrowski.
Chief Assistant City Attorney—Morton A. Mergentheim.
Trial Attorneys—Myer Emrich, Edward A. Prindiville, James R. Considine, George McMahon, Matthew J. O'Brien. Assistant Trial Attorneys—Matthew E. Clark, Michael C. Zacharias, John B. Brenza, Justin F. McCarthy, James J. O'Toole, Walter J. LaBuy and Michael B. Morris.
Appellate Court Attorney—David R. Levy.
Chief Investigator—George Self.
Supervisor of Investigations—Frank C. Sebring.
Chief Clerk—Claude Dyckman.
Docket Clerk—Joseph M. Coffey.
Judgment and Waiver Clerk—Alfred Ebenstein.
Duties—The city attorney keeps a register of all actions in courts of record, prosecuted or defended, in which the city may be a party, and defends all damage suits against the city. His chief duty is the defense or settlement of per-

sonal injury cases against the corporation. He may be called upon to draft ordinances for the city council or for heads of departments. He is the attorney for the fire pension board.

PROSECUTING ATTORNEY'S OFFICE.
Room 604 city hall.

Prosecuting Attorney—James S. McInerney, D.
Chief Assistant—Albert J. W. Appell.
Chief Clerk—Edward V. Peterson.
Assistants—Morris Barnett, George A. Basta, Frank J. Calupny, George Emmicke, Henry Eckhardt, LeRoy Hackett, Arthur Haggenjos, Frank T. Huening, Julius Jaffe, J. Henry Kraft, Z. H. Kadow, Ota P. Lightfoot, Roman G. Lewis, William Navigato, Walter Rooney, Frank C. Soubrada, U. S. Schwartz, Marshall Solberg, W. J. Vavra.

DEPARTMENT OF HEALTH.
City hall, seventh floor.

Commissioner of Health—George B. Young, M. D.
Assistant Commissioner—Gottfried Koehler, M. D.
Secretary—E. R. Pritchard.
Assistant Secretary—S. F. Manning.
Chief Bureau of Vital Statistics—M. O. Heckard, M. D.
Assistant Chief Bureau of Vital Statistics—C. St. Clair Drake, M. D.
Chief Bureau of Medical Inspection—Heman Spalding, M. D.
Assistant Chief Bureau of Medical Inspection—I. D. Rawlings, M. D.
Assistant Chief Bureau of Medical Inspection—H. O. Jones, M. D.
Chief Bureau of Sanitation—Charles B. Ball.
Assistant Chief Bureau of Sanitation—Thomas J. Claffy.
Chief Bureau of Food Inspection—B. E. Sherman.
Assistant Chief Bureau of Food Inspection—Henry Weisberg.
Chief Bureau of Hospitals, Public Baths and Lodging House—W. K. Murray, M. D.
Director of Laboratory—F. O. Tonney, M. D.
City Physician—Dr. John McGregor.
Duties—The commissioner of health and his assistants enforce state laws and city ordinances relating to sanitation and cause all nuisances to be promptly abated. They keep records of deaths and other vital statistics, investigate all cases of contagious diseases and take all necessary steps to prevent their spread, such as providing for vaccination, disinfection, etc.
The city physician attends to all cases in the police stations requiring medical attention.

DEPARTMENT OF PUBLIC WORKS.
Room 406 city hall.

Commissioner—Lawrence E. McGann, D.
Deputy Commissioner—J. O. Kostner, D.
Duties—The commissioner of public works is the head of the department of public works, which embraces the bureaus of engineering, streets, sewers, water, maps and plats, compensation, architecture and city hall. The commissioner of public works has special charge and superintendence, subject to the ordinances of the city, of all streets, alleys, highways, walks, bridges, viaducts, docks, wharves, public places, public landings, public grounds, markets and market places and public buildings belonging to the city; of all works for the deepening and widening or dredging of the Chicago river and its branches, and of the harbor of said city; of all sewers and works pertaining thereto; and of the waterworks and collection of water rates and fees for the use of water or for permits issued in connection with the waterworks system, and of all sewerage permits and licenses; the awarding and execution of all contracts for any work or public improvement not done by special assessment, and the letting of all contracts for coal for use of any department of the city.

BOARDS OF EXAMINERS.
Suite 1002 city hall.

BOARD OF EXAMINERS OF STATIONARY ENGINEERS.
President—Henry A. Zender.
First Vice-President—Adolph Jenczewsky.
Second Vice-President—W. F. Mellean.
Chief License Inspector—Henry G. McMahon.

Duties—The board of examiners of stationary engineers is appointed by the mayor. It consists of three members, all of them practical engineers and competent judges of the construction of steam boilers and engines and experienced in their operation. The board examines applicants for licenses as engineers and boiler or water tenders and issues to such applicants as are found qualified proper certificates; each certificate issued expires by limitation one year from date. An application for an engineer's license must be accompanied by a fee of $2.00 and for a boiler tender or water tender's license by a fee of $1.00. Applicants are required to pass by a percentage of 70 or more.

BOARD OF EXAMINERS OF PLUMBERS.
Chairman (ex officio)—Dr. George B. Young, commissioner of health.
Master Plumber—Charles J. Herbert.
Journeyman Plumber—William W. Petrie.
BOARD OF EXAMINERS OF MOVING PICTURE OPERATORS.
Chairman—Ray Palmer, city electrician.
Examiner—William H. Havill.
Secretary Boards of Examiners—William H. Luthardt.
Duties—The secretary of the boards of examiners is by law secretary of all the three boards enumerated above. The duties of the two boards last mentioned are sufficiently indicated by their titles. They are similar, within their scope, to those of the board of examiners of stationary engineers.

TRACK ELEVATION DEPARTMENT.
Room 1003 city hall.
Track Elevation Commissioner—Francis J. Owens, D.
Duties—Frames ordinances for the elevation of steam surface roads in Chicago and has supervision of track elevation.

DEPARTMENT OF BUILDINGS.
Room 702 city hall.
Commissioner—Henry Ericsson, D.
Deputy Commissioner—Robert Knight.
Secretary—Peter C. Hoey.
Duties—The building commissioner sees that new buildings are put up in accordance with the city ordinances, that fire escapes are provided wherever needed, that unsafe structures are demolished or repaired, that safe exits are provided in halls, theaters, etc.

DEPARTMENT OF ELECTRICITY.
Room 814 city hall.
City Electrician—Ray Palmer, D.
Chief Operator—Frank W. Swenie.
Superintendent of Construction—Harry Leser.
Chief Clerk—John E. Bradley.
Chief Electrical Inspector—Victor H. Tousley.
Chief Gas Inspector—William D. Wilcox.
Duties—The city electrician has charge of construction and operation of the city's street lighting and substations, and the police and fire alarm telegraph systems, and the inspection of all electrical installation within the city limits.

DEPARTMENT OF SUPPLIES.
City hall, floor 3½.
Business Agent—Richard J. Reynolds, D.
Duties—The business agent buys all supplies for city departments which involve an expenditure of less than $500. He has nothing to do with supplies used by contractors employed by the city.

BUREAU OF STATISTICS.
Room 1006 city hall.
City Statistician—Francis A. Eastman.
Stenographer and Recorder—Margaret E. Lynch.
Duties—The bureau of statistics being in the department of the mayor, the city statistician does whatever work may be assigned him from the mayor's office, and he supplies data on municipal subjects to the aldermen and heads of departments whenever such are required of him. And he renders like service to the general public upon call, or letter received, from any person residing in Chicago or elsewhere.

MUNICIPAL REFERENCE LIBRARY.
Room 1005 city hall.
Municipal Reference Librarian—Frederick Rex.
Stenographer—Margaret E. Lynch.
Library Assistant—Adele Bergmann.

Duties—The Municipal Reference library is the city hall branch of the Chicago Public library. Its function is to provide, arrange and index information on all matters pertaining to municipal administration and legislation. There is on file in the library one of the most complete collections of the charters and ordinances of domestic and foreign cities extant in the United States, as well as of municipal reports and documents. An index is made of all ordinances pending before the city councils of Chicago and other cities. If any information desired is not on file, an effort is always made to secure it as promptly as possible.

HOUSE OF CORRECTION.
California avenue, near 26th street.
Superintendent—John L. Whitman, R.
Deputy Superintendent—P. J. O'Connell.
House of Correction Inspectors—Mathias Aller, chairman; A. A. Burgar, secretary; Dr. M. A. Weiskopf.
Duties—The superintendent has charge of the house of correction under the supervision and direction of the board of inspectors, enforces order and discipline, receives prisoners and discharges them on order or on expiration of sentence.

POLICE DEPARTMENT.
Headquarters—5th floor city hall, north end.
General Superintendent—James Gleason.
Secretary to General Superintendent—Vernon L. Bean.
First Deputy Superintendent—H. F. Schuettler (3d floor).
Second Deputy Superintendent—M. L. C. Funkhouser (10th floor, north end).
Secretary Police Department—Edward M. Cummings (10th floor, north end).
Chief Clerk—Phil McKenna (10th floor, north end).
Drillmaster—John Bauder (5th floor).
Custodian—DeWitt C. Cregier (3d floor, north end).
Captains—John J. Halpin, P. J. Gibbons, Charles C. Healy (mounted squadron), P. D. O'Brien, Michael Ryan, Max Nootbaar, James O'D. Storen, P. J. Lavin, John A. Alcock, Morgan A. Collins, John S. Ryan, Thomas J. Coughlin, John D. McCarthy, John E. Ptacek, Bernard P. Baer, Thomas F. Meagher, Joseph Smith, Stephen K. Healy, Henry E. Gorman, Stephen B. Wood, John Rehm, Max Danner, James Madden, William W. Cudmore.
Duties—The police department is charged with preserving order, peace and quiet and enforcing the laws and ordinances throughout the city. Police officers have the power to make arrests and to serve warrants. They are required to assist firemen in saving property, in giving alarms of fire and in keeping the streets in the vicinity of burning buildings clear. They are also required to take notice of all obstructions and defects in the streets, nuisances, etc.

FIRE DEPARTMENT.
Headquarters—Room 105 city hall.
Fire Marshal—Charles F. Seyferlich.
First Assistant Fire Marshal—Thomas O'Connor.
Second Assistant Fire Marshal—P. J. Donohue.
Third Assistant and Department Inspector—E. J. Buckley.
Fifth Assistant Fire Marshal—A. R. Seyferlich.
Sixth Assistant—J. McAuliffe.
Department Attorney—Joseph Murray.
Secretary—William C. Gamble.
Battalion Chiefs—1st, P. J. Egan; 2d, Benjamin O'Connor; 3d, Jacob Grauer; 4th, Charles N. Heaney; 5th, John Evans; 6th, Thomas J. Reynolds; 7th, Michael Kerwin; 8th, Thomas Hackett; 9th, Walter Powers; 10th, David J. Mahoney; 11th, Martin Lacey; 12th, Joseph L. Kenyon; 13th, Frank Conway; 14th, Michael R. Driscoll; 15th, James Ward; 16th, John F. Smith; 17th, George H. McAllister; 18th, Eugene Sweeney; 19th, James Costin; 20th, Thomas P. Kenney; 21st, Edward F. McGurn; 22d, Michael Corrigan.
Superintendent Insurance Patrol—E. T. Shepherd, 163 West Monroe street.
Duties—The fire marshal has sole and absolute control over all persons connected with the fire department and has the custody of the equipment

and other property of the department. The fire inspector investigates the causes of fires and keeps a record of the same. The secretary keeps all books and papers of the department and delivers to the city council and other departments the written communications of the fire marshal.

BUREAU OF FIRE PREVENTION AND PUBLIC SAFETY.

Headquarters—Room 604 city hall.
Chief of Bureau and Fourth Assistant Fire Marshal—John C. McDonnell.
Fire Prevention Engineer—Elisha A. Case.
Fire Prevention Inspector in Charge—Charles W. Hejda.
Chief Clerk—T. J. Sullivan.
Duties—The chief of fire prevention and public safety shall have the power and it shall be his duty to enforce the provisions of all ordinances of the city of Chicago which may tend to prevent the starting or spreading of fires or disastrous results in case of fires.

CIVIL-SERVICE COMMISSIONERS.
Room 610 city hall.

Commissioners—H. M. Campbell, D., president; Elton Lower, R.; J. J. Flynn, D.
Secretary and Chief Examiner—R. A. Widdowson.
Attorney—Herbert J. Friedman.
Duties—The commissioners classify offices and places in the city service, examine applicants for employment in such offices and places, certify to the heads of departments as required the names of those standing highest on the list of eligibles, investigate charges against employes in the classified service and remove employes for cause. Two weeks' notice by advertisement of the time and place of holding examinations is given.

ELECTION COMMISSIONERS.
City hall, third floor, south end.

Commissioners—Charles H. Kellerman, chairman; Anthony Czarnecki, secretary; Howard S. Taylor.
Chief Clerk—William H. Stuart.
Attorney—Charles H. Mitchell.
Duties—The commissioners fix the election precincts, provide ballot boxes, tally sheets, pollbooks and all other blanks and stationery necessary in an election, select judges and clerks of elections, canvass the returns of votes and, in brief, have charge of everything pertaining to the registration of voters and the holding of all regular, special and primary elections.

DEPARTMENT OF SMOKE INSPECTION.
Room 608 city hall.

Chief Smoke Inspector—O. Monnett.
Chief Assistant Smoke Inspector—S. H. Viall.
Deputy in Charge—F. A. Chambers.
Chief Clerk—Edward R. Laub.

DEPARTMENT FOR THE INSPECTION OF STEAM BOILERS, STEAM AND COOLING PLANTS.
Room 613 city hall.

Chief Inspector—M. J. Ryan.
Supervising Engineer—R. B. Wilcox.

CITY ARCHITECT.
Room 1012 city hall.

Charles W. Kallal.

DEPARTMENT OF WEIGHTS AND MEASURES.
Vault floor, city hall.

Inspector Weights and Measures—Peter Zimmer, D.
Chief Deputy—William F. Cluett.

OIL INSPECTOR'S OFFICE.
Room 1013 city hall.

Oil Inspector—James A. Quinn, D.

MUNICIPAL LODGING HOUSE.
162 North Union avenue.

Superintendent—Charles F. Rogers.

IMPORTS OF MERCHANDISE INTO CHICAGO.

Value of imported merchandise entered for consumption and withdrawn from warehouse, with amounts of duty collected thereon, for the year 1912, at the port of Chicago:

Articles free of duty.	Value.	Duty.
American whisky returned....	$5,832	$6,422.31
Art works over 20 years old...	160,835	....
Antiquities over 100 years old.	257,515	....
Tea	1,856,302	....
Other free articles..............	4,819,191	....

Articles subject to duty.		
Ale, beer and porter...........	69,882	41,564.54
Art works......................	54,735	8,210.32
Automobiles and parts of......	23,164	10,423.73
Books, music, etc..............	95,525	23,881.23
Breadstuffs	478,675	153,871.99
Brushes	69,028	27,719.28
Cheese	618,054	193,209.11
Chemicals, drugs, etc.........	1,187,595	261,556.69
China and glassware...........	1,002,805	585,616.55
Cigars and cigarettes.........	151,968	129,310.53
Clocks, watches and parts of..	307,268	71,541.68
Cocoa and chocolate...........	103,519	18,147.25
Cutlery	36,505	23,608.80
Diamonds, precious stones.....	502,596	51,419.90
Dry goods......................	6,089,517	3,563,053.42
Fish, all kinds................	857,037	179,579.70
Fruits and nuts................	1,295,120	398,284.27
Furs and manufactures of.....	111,529	42,479.94
Gold and silver, manufactures	80,598	44,518.86
Guns and firearms.............	17,999	7,690.84
Hops	45,140	16,757.14
Iron and steel, manufactures..	459,173	163,411.95

Articles free of duty.	Value.	Duty.
Jewelry	70,127	49,073.73
Lead ore.......................	59,800	66,376.84
Leather, mfrs. of, gloves......	953,975	428,408.58
Leather, mfrs. of, all other...	111,057	30,316.70
Maple sugar....................	62,378	30,693.99
Matches	81,375	24,497.29
Matting of straw, etc..........	27,757	16,272.95
Metals and manufactures of...	114,359	52,737.50
Millinery goods................	602,771	250,672.33
Musical instruments...........	366,286	164,828.84
Oilcloth and linoleum.........	133,647	60,993.56
Oils	419,642	150,184.80
Paints and varnish............	71,137	25,147.26
Paper, manufactures of.......	311,686	90,594.76
Pickles, sauces, etc..........	218,051	66,995.34
Plate and window glass.......	25,490	12,544.26
Salt	37,330	10,475.88
Seeds, plants, bulbs..........	777,003	121,498.46
Soap	70,501	47,881.60
Smokers' articles.............	58,037	34,540.45
Spirits, distilled.............	660,297	865,193.84
Tobacco, leaf.................	1,409,240	841,662.63
Toys and dolls................	488,616	171,014.00
Wines, champagne.............	316,571	181,158.86
Wines, still..................	256,020	130,444.64
Wood, lumber.................	324,723	26,297.58
Wood, mfrs. of, all other....	104,975	31,252.20
Miscellaneous	1,598,927	694,912.13
Totals, 1912.................	30,278,600	10,698,891.11
Totals, 1911.................	28,089,068	10,131,150.12
Totals, 1910.................	28,281,331	10,102,062.56
Totals, 1906.................	24,141,004	10,005,952.35

DISTRIBUTION OF NATIONALITIES IN CHICAGO.

According to the school census of May 2, 1912, the different nationalities of Chicago are chiefly distributed throughout the wards (as now constituted) of the city as follows:

Americans*—25th, 26th, 23d, 7th, 32d and 33d.
Germans—24th, 26th, 25th, 27th, 15th, 16th, 28th and 5th.
Poles—16th, 27th, 17th, 28th, 29th, 4th and 5th.
Italians—19th, 22d and 17th.
Irish—30th, 31st, 32d, 35th, 19th and 5th.

Russians—20th, 19th, 10th, 12th, 34th and 3d.
Bohemians—12th, 11th, 34th, 10th and 29th.
Hollanders—9th.
Austrians—20th, 17th and 29th.
Swedes—25th, 23d, 26th, 27th, 31st, 33d, 8th and 9th.
Norwegians—28th, 27th, 15th, 33d and 35th.
Lithuanians—29th, 4th and 5th.
Scotch and French—Scattered throughout city.
Negroes—30th, 14th, 2d and 3d.
*Born in America of American born parents.

CHICAGO CITY OFFICES AND POSITIONS.

[From charts prepared by the efficiency division of the city civil service commission.]

City offices and places of employment are divided by the civil service commission into eleven classes, according to the general character of the duties performed. Offices and places filled by election or appointment are designated as "exempt." Under the civil service act of March 20, 1895, the following are excepted from the classified service: Officers who are elected by the people or by the city council pursuant to the city charter, or whose appointment is subject to confirmation by the city council; judges and clerks of election, members of any board of education, the superintendent and teachers of schools, heads of any principal department and one private secretary to the mayor. Following are the titles of the exempt positions, including the yearly salary attached to each as fixed by the appropriation bill for 1913:

ELECTED BY THE PEOPLE.

Associate judge*....$6,000 | Clerk* 6,000
Bailiff* .... 6,000 | Mayor 18,000
Chief justice..........10,000 | Members city coun-
City clerk........... 5,000 | cil, each........... 3,000
City treasurer.......12,000 | *Municipal court.

ELECTED BY CITY COUNCIL.

Sergeant-at-arms $1,000

APPOINTED BY THE MAYOR.

Assistant harbor master.........................$1,200
Assistant vessel dispatcher.................... 1,080
Board of education............................No comp.
Board of examiners (engineers).......$2,000 to 2,220
Board of local improvements...........$4,000 to 5,000
Business agent............................... 6,000
City collector............................... 6,500
City electrician............................. 6,500
City physician............................... 4,000
Civil service commission.............$3,000 to 5,000
Commissioner of buildings.................... 6,000
Commissioner of health...................... 8,000
Commissioner of public works.................10,000
Commissioner of track elevation.............. 5,000
Comptroller 10,000
Corporation counsel.........................10,000
Deputy commissioner of public works.......... 5,000
Fire marshal................................. 8,000
General superintendent of police............. 8,000
Harbor master............................... 1,800
Inspector gas and sewer meters............... 3,600
Inspector of oils............................ 4,890
Inspector boilers, steam plants.............. 3,600
Inspector weights and measures............... 3,600
Inspectors house of correction............No comp.
Library directors.........................No comp.
Market master............................... 945
Master plumber.............................. 1,716
Municipal tuberculosis sanitary directors..No comp.
Prosecuting attorney......................... 6,000
Secretary harbor and subway commission...... 4,000
Secretary to the mayor....................... 5,000
Smoke inspector............................. 4,000
Subway commissioner.........................12,000
Superintendent house of correction........... 3,600
Traction expert............................. 3,000
Vessel dispatcher........................... 1,200

SCHOOL SUPERINTENDENTS AND TEACHERS.
(See board of education.)

EXCEPTED BY OTHER SECTIONS OF CIVIL SERVICE ACT.

Civil service examiner and secretary.........$3,000

SPECIFICALLY EXCEPTED UNDER SECTION 2 OF CIVIL SERVICE ACT.

Members of law department and Municipal courts:
Appellate court attorney.....................$3,000
Assistant chief deputy bailiff............... 2,500
Assistant chief investigator................. 1,800
Assistant city attorney...................... 1,800
Assistant corporation counsel........$1,500- 7,500
Asst. atty. board local improvements..$2,800- 5,000
Attorney board local improvements........... 6,000
Attorney fire department.................... 3,000
Attorney civil service commission........... 3,000
Attorney for bureau of water................ 2,500

Assistant prosecuting attorney..........$2,000- 2,400
Assistant trial attorney.................$1,500- 2,150
Assistant to chief justice...............$1,800- 4,000
Attorney $3,000- 7,500
Auditor 2,500
Chief assistant city attorney............... 3,800
Chief assistant prosecuting attorney........ 3,000
Chief deputy bailiff........................ 4,000
Chief deputy clerk.......................... 4,000
Chief investigator......................... 2,400
Chief law clerk............................ 2,100
Chief law clerk and secretary to corp. counsel 2,500
Chief probation officer..................... 3,000
City attorney.............................. 6,000
Deputy bailiff.......................$1,000- 3,000
Deputy clerk..........................$300- 3,000
Docket and law clerk.................$1,500- 1,800
Executive to chief justice.................. 4,000
General counsel, board of education......... 7,500
Investigator Circuit court cases............ 1,500
Investigator Municipal court cases.......... 1,300
Investigator Superior court cases........... 1,500
Investigator (preliminary).................. 1,090
Investigator (trial)....................... 1,200
Law and docket clerk....................... 1,200
Law and filing clerk....................... 1,200
Law and notice clerk....................... 1,000
Law and voucher clerk...................... 1,200
Law claim investigator..................... 2,000
Law clerk and copyist.................$720- 900
Law clerk and messenger...............$600- 1,000
Law clerk and preliminary investigator...... 1,000
Law clerk and stenographer............$900- 1,200
To board local improvements................ 1,000
To attorney fire department................ 1,200
To attorney bureau of water................ 900
Law clerk and telephone operator........... 1,020
Law clerk and trial investigator........... 1,200
Law clerk, board local improvements..$1,000- 2,400
Probation officer.......................... 1,200
Special assessment examiner................ 2,040
Supervisor of investigations............... 1,800
Trial attorney.......................$2,500- 3,600
Trial attorney action over................. 3,000
*Elected.

CLASSIFIED SERVICE.

The nonexempt classes of service with the letter designating each are:

A—Medical. F—Fire.
B—Engineering. G—Library.
C—Clerical. H—Inspection.
D—Police. I—Supervising.
E—Operating engineer- K—Skilled labor.
ing.* L—Labor.

*The operating engineering service is divided into branches A and B. Branch B includes only positions under the board of education.

GRADES AND GROUPS.

All classes of service except unskilled labor are divided into grades according to the authority, responsibility and importance of the duties performed. There are from three to eight grades in each class, the first grade being the lowest. In some of the services the grades are subdivided into groups, group A being the highest.

DEPARTMENTS AND BUREAUS.

City offices and places of employment are distributed among departments and bureaus, in each of which one or more classes of service are represented. In the building department, for example, the engineering, clerical and inspection services are represented. The clerical service is represented in all the departments. On the civil service chart the departments are arranged alphabetically according to the code letter designating each, as follows:

B—Department of buildings.
C-F—City council finance committee.
C-G—Committee on gas, oil and electric light.
C-T—Committee on local transportation.
C-L—Lake shore reclamation commission.
CC—City clerk.
CT—City physician.
CS—Civil service commission.

E—Board of education.
EC—Board of election commissioners.
EL—Department of electricity.
EE—Board of examiners (engineers).
F-C—Department of finance—city collector's office.
F-M—City markets.
F-T—City treasurer's office.
F-O—Comptroller's office.
FI—Fire department.
H—Department of health.
HC—House of correction.
L—Department of law.
LP—Chicago public library.
LI—Board of local improvements.
M—Mayor's office.
MC—Municipal courts.
OI—Office of inspector of oils.
PO—Department of police.
P-A—Dept. of public works—bureau of architecture.
P-O—Bureau of city hall.
P-E—Bureau of engineering.
P-I—Commissioner's office.
P-P—Bureau of compensation.
P-M—Bureau of maps and plats.
P-S—Bureau of sewers.
P-T—Bureau of streets.
P-W—Bureau of water.
S—Special park commission.
SI—Department of smoke inspection.
SP—Department of inspection of steam boilers and steam plants.
ST—Bureau of statistics.
SU—Department of supplies.
T—Department of track elevation.
TR—Department of transportation.
TS—Municipal tuberculosis sanitarium.
W—Department of weights and measures.

TITLES OF POSITIONS—NUMBER.

Service and grade.	I.	II.	III.	IV.	V.	VI.	VII.	VIII.	Total
Medical	3	11	10	12	5	1	..	..	42
Engineering	6	14	16	30	7	..	..	..	63
Clerical	2	3	10	9	13	9	9	9	64
Police	4	3	3	2	..	..	..	..	12
Operat. Eng. (A)	4	4	2	2	..	1	..	..	17
Operat. Eng. (B)	1	1	1	..	..	1	..	..	3
Fire	6	4	1	1	6	..	..	..	18
Library	2	4	3	4	3	2	..	..	18
Inspection	5	24	29	18	5	..	..	..	82
Supervising	12	25	16	6	6	..	..	..	65
Skilled labor	47	80	36	..	..	..	..	..	163
Labor, not graded	..	..	..	..	..	..	..	..	12

Total classified...92 173 127 84 49 13 9 9 560
Exempt 131

Total titles..691

NUMBERS OF POSITIONS—AVERAGE.

Service and grade.	I.	II.	III.	IV.	V.	VI.	VII.	VIII.	Total
Medical	22	227	23	19	5	1	..	..	347
Engineering	111	103	90	40	7	..	..	..	352
Clerical	82	28	709	216	58	18	26	9	1146
Police	3593	728	136	24	1	..	..	..	4482
Operat.Eng.(A)	170	27	24	12	36	..	..	..	289
Operat.Eng.(B)	278	8	1	..	..	..	..	..	287
Fire	1400	307	158	22	6	..	..	..	1893
Library	51	65	18	9	14	2	..	..	149
Inspection	33	398	242	49	4	..	..	..	723
Supervising	147	109	52	5	6	..	..	..	320
Skilled labor	972	1210	85	..	..	..	..	..	2267
Labor	..	..	..	..	..	..	..	..	2674
Exempt	..	..	..	..	..	..	..	..	7891

Total positions in city service...............22,825

SALARIES OF CHICAGO CITY OFFICIALS AND EMPLOYES (1913).

BY SERVICES.

Service.	Total.	Yearly average.
Medical	$347,925	$1,003
Engineering	647,819	1,843
Clerical	1,400,365	1,222
Police	5,921,935	1,323
Operating engineering (A)	360,612	1,274
Operating engineering (B)	922,672	*
Fire	2,718,641	1,436
Library	141,350	954
Inspection	945,705	1,401
Supervising	398,558	1,383
Skilled labor	2,594,960	*
Labor	1,902,881	*
Exempt—Educational	8,360,865	*
Law and courts	989,560	*
All other	456,371	*

†28,782,699

*Average salaries omitted because of special nature of service. †Includes $662,660 blanket salary appropriations for services of a noncontinuous or emergency character.

BY GRADES.

MEDICAL SERVICE.
Grade.	Yearly salary.
I	$240- $960
II	800-1,500
III	900-1,800
IV	1,200-2,640
V	2,040-3,780
VI	4,020

ENGINEERING SERVICE.
Grade.	Yearly salary.
I	$1,080-$1,320
II	1,500- 1,740
III	1,920- 2,400
IV	3,000 and up
V	4,020 and up

CLERICAL SERVICE.
Grade.	Yearly salary.
I	$300- $480
II	540- 720
III	840- 1,200
IV	1,320- 1,680
V	1,800- 2,160
VI	2,340- 2,700
VII	3,000 and up
VIII	4,020 and up

POLICE SERVICE.
Grade.	Yearly salary.
I	$900-$1,320
II	1,500- 1,700
III	1,800- 2,000
IV	2,500- 2,750
V	5,000

OPERATING ENGINEERING (A).
I	$1,080
II	1,200
III	1,460
IV	1,560
V	2,000
VI	2,500

OPERATING ENGINEERING (B).
I	*
II	$2,040- $2,520
III	4,020 and up

*Fixed by school group.

FIRE SERVICE.
Grade.	Yearly salary.
I	$900-$1,392
II	1,518- 1,815
III	1,815
IV	2,750
V	3,500- 5,000

LIBRARY SERVICE.
I	$480- $660
II	720- 960
III	1,020- 1,200
IV	1,260- 1,440
V	1,500- 2,400
VI	3,000 and up

INSPECTION SERVICE.
I	$960-$1,200
II	960- 1,800
III	1,200- 2,100

Grade.	Yearly salary.
IV	1,740- 2,520
V	2,100- 3,600

SUPERVISING SERVICE.
I	$660-$1,080
II	780- 1,800
III	1,800- 3,000
IV	2,400- 3,800
V	3,600- 5,000

LABOR SERVICE.
Rates not to exceed the union scale are paid by the city for skilled labor. Ordinary labor is paid for at the rate of $2 to $3 a day.

SALARIES BY CERTAIN POSITIONS.

Title.	Salary.
Accountants	$1,200-$2,160
Accountants—Head	2,340- 2,700
Accountants—Expert	3,000 and up
Assessors	3,000 and up
Attendants—Office	340- 480
Auditors—Chief	3,000 and up
Bacteriologists	1,200- 1,800
Bookkeepers—Junior	840- 1,200
Bookkeepers—Senior	1,320- 1,680
Cashiers	2,340- 2,700
Cashiers—Chief	3,000 and up
Clerks—Chief	3,000 and up
Clerks—Head	2,340- 2,700
Clerks—Junior	840- 1,200
Clerks—Principal	1,800- 2,160
Clerks—Senior	1,320- 1,680
Clerical assistants	540- 720
Collectors	1,320- 1,680
Draftsmen	1,080- 1,740
Engineers—Junior	1,500- 1,740
Examiners—Junior	840- 1,200
Examiners—Principal	1,800- 2,160
Examiners—Senior	1,320- 1,680
Firemen—Stationary	900- 1,080
Guards	1,080- 1,200
Health officers	800
Internes	240- 300

Title.	Salary.	Title.	Salary.
Investigators	1,320- 1,680	Scrubwomen	540
Janitors	600- 1,200	Stenographers—Junior	840- 1,200
Janitresses	600- 720	Stenographers—Principal	1,800- 2,160
Labor—Skilled	Union rates	Stenographers—Senior	1,320- 1,688
Matrons	780- 900	Storekeepers	1,800- 2,160
Messengers	540- 900	Surgeons—Ambulance	1,080- 1,320
Nurses—Field	1,000- 1,200	Teamsters	750- 960
Nurses—Hospital	780- 808	Telephone operators	840- 1,200
Orderlies	720- 900	Tellers	1,800- 2,160
Pages	300- 480	Vaccinators, per day	5.00
Rate takers	840- 1,200	Window washers	750- 780

DEPARTMENTS AND BUREAUS.

The following list includes the more important offices and positions in the exempt and classified service except those in the educational department, which will be found elsewhere. The salaries are those fixed by the appropriation bill of 1913 and are yearly if not otherwise specified,

MAYOR'S OFFICE.
Mayor $18,000
Secretary 5,000

BUREAU OF STATISTICS.
City statistician $3,000
Assistant statistician........ 1,320

TRANSPORTATION DEPT.
Traction expert...............$3,000
Inspectors, each.............. 1,200

CITY COUNCIL.
Aldermen, each...............$3,000

FINANCE COMMITTEE.
Chairman $3,000
Secretary 3,600

TRANSPORTATION COMMITTEE.
Secretary and engineer.....$3,600

COMMITTEE ON GAS, OIL AND ELECTRIC LIGHT.
Expert, per day, not over...$50.00
Accountant, per day, not over 25.00

LAKE SHORE RECLAMATION COMMISSION.
Title searcher.................$1,800

CITY CLERK.
City clerk....................$5,000
Chief clerk................... 4,000
Reading clerk................ 2,500
Council secretary............ 2,340
Sergeant-at-arms 1,000

LAW DEPARTMENT.
CORPORATION COUNSEL.
Corporation counsel.........$10,000
Assistant, 1 at............... 7,500
Assistants, 2 at.............. 6,000
Assistants, 2 at.............. 5,000
Assistants, 5 at.............. 4,000
Assistant, 1 at............... 3,600
Assistants, 7 at.............. 3,000
Assistants, 2 at.............. 2,500
Assistants, 5 at.............. 2,000
Assistant, 1 at............... 1,500
Fire dept. attorney.......... 3,000
Secretary corp. counsel...... 2,500
Atty. board local imprvts... 6,000
Assistant 5,000
Assistants, 2 at.............. 2,860
Law clerk.................... 2,400
Atty. civil service commis.. 3,000
Attorney water dept......... 2,500

PROSECUTING ATTORNEY.
Prosecuting attorney........$6,000
Chief assistant.............. 3,000
Assistants, 3 at.............. 2,400
Assistants, 16 at............. 2,000

CITY ATTORNEY.
City attorney................$6,000
Chief assistant.............. 3,800
Trial attorney, 3 at......... 3,600
Trial attorney, 1 at......... 2,500
Assist. trial attorneys, 2 at. 2,150
Assist. trial attorney, 1 at.. 2,100
Assist. trial attorneys, 2 at. 1,800
Assist. trial attorney, 1 at.. 1,500
Trial attorney, action over.. 3,000
Investigators, 2 at........... 1,500
Appellate court attorney..... 3,000
Assist. city attorneys, 2 at.. 1,800
Chief law clerk.............. 2,100

Chief investigator........... 2,400
Assist. chief investigator.... 1,800
Investigators, 2 at........... 1,500
Investigator, 1 at............ 1,300
Investigators, 25 at.......... 1,200
Investigators, 23 at.......... 1,000
Docket and law clerk........ 1,800

DEPARTMENT OF FINANCE.
COMPTROLLER'S OFFICE.
Comptroller $10,000
Deputy and city auditor.... 4,500
Chief clerk.................. 3,600

ACCOUNTING DIVISION.
Expert accountant...........$3,600
Real estate agent............ 2,040
Teller 1,680

AUDIT DIVISION.
Chief auditor................$3,000
Senior bookkeeper........... 1,440

PAYMASTER'S DIVISION.
Paymaster $3,300
Tellers, 2 at................. 1,680

SPECIAL ASSESSMENT DIVISION.
Principal clerk..............$2,160

CITY TREASURER.
City treasurer...............$12,000
Assistant treasurer.......... 5,000
Chief clerk.................. 3,600
Chief cashier................ 3,000
Cashiers, 2 at................ 2,520

CITY COLLECTOR.
City collector...............$6,000
Deputy city collector........ 4,000
Cashier 2,700
Head clerk.................. 2,340

ELECTION COMMISSIONERS.*
Attorney for board...........$5,000
Chief investigator........... 2,500
Investigators, 5 at........... 1,200
Chief auditor................ 2,500
*Paid by county. See county salaries.

CIVIL SERVICE COMMISSION.
President $5,000
Commissioners, 2 at.......... 3,000
Chief examiner............... 3,000
Examiner in charge.......... 2,040
Principal examiner........... 1,680

EFFICIENCY DIVISION.
Examiner in charge..........$4,020
Experts on system, 2 at..... 3,000
Examiner efficiency, general. 2,400
Examiner clerical efficiency. 2,340

DEPARTMENT OF SUPPLIES.
Business agent...............$6,000
Head buyer.................. 2,400
Storekeeper 2,040

DEPARTMENT OF POLICE.
General superintendent......$8,000
First deputy superintendent. 6,000
Second deputy superintend't 5,000
Secy. to gen. superintendent 3,000
Secretary 3,600
Department inspector........ 3,600
Inspector moral conditions.. 2,400
Private sec. to assist. supt.. 1,320

SUBORDINATE OFFICERS.
Captains, 27 at...............$2,250
Drillmaster 1,800

Lieutenants 1,800
Sergeants 1,500

PATROLMEN.
First year, 3d grade..........$900
Second year, 2d grade....... 1,000
After 2d year, 1st grade..... 1,320

DETECTIVE BUREAU.
Chief $3,000
Lieutenants, 3 at............ 2,000
Head clerk.................. 2,500
Detective sergts., 1st class.. 1,600
Detective sergts., 2d class... 1,450

BUREAU OF IDENTIFICATION.
Identification expert.........$2,250
Finger print operator........ 1,200
Photographers, 2 at.......... 1,100

DEPARTMENT STABLES.
Foreman of horses...........$2,400
Veterinary surgeon........... 2,100
Feed inspector............... 1,500
Foremen, 2 at................ 1,200
Hostlers, 32 at............... 960

TELEGRAPH BUREAU.
Chief operator...............$2,000
Assistant chief operator..... 1,620
Police operators, 157 at..... 1,100
Telephone inspector......... 1,500

REPAIR SHOP.
Foreman $1,800
Assistant 1,200

MISCELLANEOUS.
Custodian lost property.....$1,800
Electrical mechanic.......... 1,980
Sergeant bureau of records.. 1,700

AMBULANCE BUREAU.
Chief surgeon................$2,500
Surgeons, 24 at.............. 1,200

MOTOR VEHICLE DIVISION.
Examiner of operators.......$1,500

MUNICIPAL COURT.
CHIEF JUSTICE.
Chief justice................$7,500
Associate judges, 30 at...... 6,000
Executive to chief justice... 4,000
Assistant to chief justice.... 4,000
Assistants, 2 at.............. 1,800
Auditor 2,500

PROBATION OFFICERS.
Chief probation officer.......$3,000
Probation officers, 10 at.... 1,500

OFFICE OF THE CLERK.
Clerk $6,000
Chief deputy clerk........... 4,000
Attorney 3,000
Deputy clerks $300 to....... 2,800

OFFICE OF THE BAILIFF.
Bailiff $6,000
Chief deputy bailiff......... 4,000
Assistant deputy bailiff..... 2,500
Attorney 3,000
Deputy bailiffs, $1,000 to.... 1,500

HOUSE OF CORRECTION.
Superintendent $3,600
Assistant superintendent.... 2,100
Medical superintendent...... 2,700

DOG POUND.
Superintendent $1,700
Kennelmen, 2 at.............. 1,200
Dog catchers, 12 at.......... 1,200

FIRE DEPARTMENT.

Fire marshal....................$8,000
First assistant................. 5,600
Second assistant............... 4,000
Third assistant................ 3,500
Fifth assistant................ 3,500
Secretary 3,000
Office secretary............... 2,340
Storekeeper 1,815
Feed inspector................. 1,500
Veterinary surgeon............. 2,500
Battalion chiefs, 22 at........ 2,750
Captains, 158 at............... 1,815
Lieutenants, 161 at............ 1,529
Engineers, 118 at.............. 1,518
Marine engineers, 13 at....... 1,680
Assistant engineers, 116 at... 1,392
Stokers, 20 at................. 1,392
Firemen, 1st class............ 1,371
Firemen, 2d class............. 1,155
Firemen, 3d class............. 1,056
Firemen, probationary......... 900

REPAIR SHOP.

Supt. of machinery............$2,000
Foreman machinists........... 1,800

FIRE ALARM TELEGRAPH.

Chief operator................$2,600
Superintendent construction.. 2,500
Chief electrical repairs...... 2,620
Operators, $1,200 to.......... 2,000

FIRE PROTECTION AND PUBLIC SAFETY.

Fourth asst. marshal, chief.$3,500
Fire prevention engineer..... 3,000
Deputy engineer 2,400
Engineers, 3 at.............. 1,500

BUILDING DEPARTMENT.

Building commissioner........$6,000
Deputy commissioner.......... 4,000
Building inspector in charge 2,500
Office secretary............. 2,400
Senior clerk................. 1,680
Architectural engineers, 2 at 2,400
Architectural engineer....... 1,920
Asst. bldg. inspectors, 5 at.. 1,890
Elevator inspector in charge 1,920
Plan examiner, 1 at.......... 1,920
Plan examiner, 1 at.......... 1,740
Estimator 1,500
Fire escape inspector........ 1,400
Building inspectors, 50 at... 1,400
Structural iron inspector.... 1,400

HEALTH DEPARTMENT.

COMMISSIONER'S OFFICE.

Commissioner of health......$8,000
Assistant commissioner...... 4,020
Secretary 3,000
Office secretary............. 1,800

BUREAU MEDICAL INSPECTION.

Bureau chief.................$3,780

DIVISION OF CONTAGIOUS DISEASES.

Assistant bureau chief.......$2,640
Health officers, 3 at........ 1,200
Health officers, 30 at....... 800

DIVISION OF CHILD HYGIENE.

Assistant bureau chief.......$2,040
Superintendent of nurses.... 1,500
Field nurses, $900 to....... 1,000
Supervising dentist.......... 1,200
Vaccinators, per day......... 5

BUREAU OF HOSPITALS, BATHS AND LODGING HOUSES.

Bureau chief. $2,040
Medical inspectors, 2 at..... 1,800

CONTAGIOUS DISEASES HOSPITAL.

Medical superintendent......$1,980
Assistant superintendent.... 1,500
Ambulance surgeon........... 1,320

ISOLATION HOSPITAL.

Medical superintendent......$1,800

EMERGENCY HOSPITAL.

Medical superintendent......$1,500

MUNICIPAL LODGING HOUSE.

Superintendent $1,400
Assistant superintendent.... 1,080

PUBLIC BATHS.

Superintendents, 14 at.......$1,200
Quarantine officer........... 1,000

Bath attendants, 16 at...... 720

BUREAU OF VITAL STATISTICS.

Bureau chief.................$2,800
Assistant bureau chief....... 2,040

BUREAU OF FOOD INSPECTION.

Bureau chief.................$2,100
Assistant bureau chief....... 1,980
Supervising inspectors, 3 at 1,500
Veterinarian 1,500
Food inspectors, 11 at....... 1,320
Food inspectors, 15 at....... 1,200
Food inspectors, 40 at....... 1,080

BUREAU OF SANITARY INSPECTION.

Bureau chief.................$3,600
Assistant bureau chief....... 2,520
Supervising inspectors, 5 at. 1,740
Plumbing plan examiner..... 1,740
Plumbing inspectors, 24 at... 1,716
Sanitary inspectors, 5 at.... 1,320
Sanitary inspectors, 33 at... 1,200
Sanitary inspectors, 5 at.... 1,080
Ventilating inspec. in charge 2,400
Ventilating inspectors, 4 at 1,200

BOARD OF EXAMINERS OF PLUMBERS.

Secretary $3,600
Master plumber............... 1,716
Journeyman plumber.......... 1,716

LABORATORY.

Director $2,520
Assistant director........... 2,000
Bacteriologist, $1,200 to.... 1,800
Chemists, $1,200 to......... 1,600

CITY PHYSICIAN.

City physician...............$4,000
Assistant, 1 at.............. 2,000
Assistant, 1 at.............. 1,500

DEPARTMENT OF TRACK ELEVATION.

Commissioner $5,000
Engineer 4,200

DEPARTMENT OF INSPECTION OF STEAM BOILERS AND STEAM PLANTS.

Chief inspector..............$3,600
Engineer and dep. inspector 3,000
Inspectors, $960 to......... 1,800

DEPARTMENT OF WEIGHTS AND MEASURES.

Inspector $3,600
Chief deputy................. 2,100
Deputy inspectors $960 to.. 1,200
Taximeter inspector.......... 1,320

SMOKE INSPECTION.

Smoke inspector..............$4,000
Chief deputy................. 3,000
Deputy in charge............. 1,800
Mech. eng. draftsmen, 11 at 1,500
Deputy smoke inspecs., 14 at 1,900

OFFICE OF INSPECTOR OF OILS.

Inspector of oils............$4,800
Chief deputy................. 2,400
Deputy, 1 at................. 1,500
Deputies, 4 at............... 1,200

BOARD OF EXAMINERS (ENGINEERS).

President and member........$2,200
Members, 2 at................ 2,000
Chief license inspector...... 1,800
License inspectors, 3 at..... 1,200

BOARD OF LOCAL IMPROVEMENTS.

President $5,000
Members, 4 at................ 4,000
Supt. special assessments... 4,020
Chief clerk.................. 3,000
Principal clerk.............. 2,040
Prin. spcl. assessment clerk 2,400
Head accountant............. 2,340
Engineer of board........... 3,600
Chief street engineer........ 3,600
Assistant chief street eng... 2,700
Assistant chief sewer eng... 2,700

Gen. street repair inspector. 2,340
Superintendent of sidewalks 3,000
Assistant supt. sidewalks.... 1,500
Assistant engineers, $1,500 to 2,160
Rodmen, 20 at................ 1,080
Inspectors, $1,320 to........ 2,400
Draftsmen 1,320
Expert asphalt chemist....... 2,400
Assistant eng. chemist....... 1,500
Paving brick tester.......... 1,500

CITY MARKETS.

Market master (Haymarket)...$945
Market master (Maxwell)...... 900

SPECIAL PARK COMMISSION.

ADMINISTRATION.

Office secretary.............$1,800

PARKS, FARM AND NURSERY.

Superintendent $2,500
Gardeners, per day, $2.25 to. 3.00
Attendants, per day.......... 1.35
Laborers, per day............ 2.00

PLAYGROUNDS.

Superintendent $2,000
Directors, $1,020 to......... 1,200
Assistant directors, per mo.. 60
Physical instructors, per mo. 60

CITY FORESTRY.

City forester................$2,000
Foremen 840

BATHING BEACHES.

Directors, per month..........$90

DEPARTMENT OF ELECTRICITY.

City electrician.............$6,500
Assistant electrician........ 4,000
Head clerk................... 2,340

FIRE ALARM AND POLICE TELEGRAPH—REPAIRS.

General foreman..............$1,800
Foremen linemen, 4 at....... 1,680
Tel. repairers, 12 at........ 1,200
Telegraph repairers, 20 at.. 1,680
Batteryman 1,200

ELECTRICAL INSPECTION.

Inspector in charge..........$2,200
Inspectors, 44 at............ 1,900

BUREAU OF ELECTRIC LIGHTS.

General foreman..............$1,800
Lamp repairers, 8 at........ 1,320
Lamp trimmers, 6 at......... 1,100

OPERATION.

Foreman lamp trimmers.......$1,800
Trimmers, 105 at............ 1,100

GAS LIGHTING SYSTEM.

Gas and meter inspector.....$3,600
Gas lamp inspector.......... 1,740
Supervisors, 3 at............ 1,416
Gas meter testers, 5 at...... 1,200
Lamp checker................ 1,200

GAS TESTING.

Chief gas tester.............$2,500
Gas testers, 3 at............ 1,200

MAINTAINING GAS LAMPS.

Lamplighters, 1c per light per day. 10c per lamp per month for mantle lamps.

STREET LAMP REPAIR SHOP.

Superintendent $1,680

BOARD OF EXAMINERS OF MOVING PICTURE OPERATORS.

Examiner of moving picture operators $1,200

BUREAU OF ELECTRIC ENGINEERING.

Electrical engineer..........$1,620
Draftsmen, $1,080 to........ 1,500

DEPARTMENT OF PUBLIC WORKS.

COMMISSIONER'S OFFICE.

Commissioner $10,000
Deputy commissioner........ 5,000

Chief clerk................... 3,600
Principal clerk.............. 2,000
Head accountant............ 2,250
   BUREAU OF COMPENSATION.
Supt. of compensation......$3,600
Investigator 1,500
   BUREAU OF MAPS AND PLATS.
Superintendent of maps....$4,000
Chief draftsman.............. 1,740
Draftsman, $1,080 to........ 1,500
Title searcher................ 1,800
   BUREAU OF ARCHITECTURE.
City architect................$4,500
   BUREAU OF CITY HALL.
Chief janitor.................$1,800
Elevator starters, 2 at...... 1,200
Elevator operators, per mo.. 80
Chief engineer............... 2,500
City hall electrician.......... 1,980

BUREAU OF STREETS.
   SUPERINTENDENT'S OFFICE.
Superintendent $5,000
First assist. superintendent. 3,000
Principal clerk................ 2,040
Assistant engineer........... 1,920
Housemoving inspector 1,680
   PERMIT DIVISION.
Senior clerk.................$1,200
Inspectors, 7 at.............. 1,000
STREET AND ALLEY CLEANING DI-
VISION.
Second assist. supt. streets.$3,840
Principal clerk................ 1,800
   WARD SUPERVISION.
Superintendents, 36 at......$2,200
   PUBLIC UTILITY INSPECTION.
Inspector in charge..........$3,000
Inspectors, 16 at............. 2,100
Inspectors, 2 at.............. 1,800
   OPERATION OF DUMPS.
Superintendent $2,200
Foremen, 5 at................ 1,080
   GARBAGE LOADING STATIONS.
Superintendent $2,200
STREET OR ALLEY IMPROVEMENT.
Third assist. supt. streets..$3,600
Engineering chemist........ 2,000
   BUREAU OF SEWERS.
   SUPERINTENDENT'S OFFICE.
Superintendent $4,000
Assistant superintendent.... 2,400
Assistant engineer (benches) 2,500
   PUMPING STATIONS (SEWER).
Engineers in charge, $1,560-$2,000
Firemen 1,080
Oilers 1,080
   REPAIRING SEWERS.
Foreman bricklayer..........$2,200
Foreman sewer pipe yards.. 2,160
Foreman carpenter........... 1,800

BUREAU OF ENGINEERING.
City engineer................$8,000
Assistant city engineer..... 5,000
Chief clerk................... 3,000
   TESTING DIVISION.
Engineer of tests............$3,000
Engineering chemists, 5 at.. 1,500
   RIVER AND HARBOR.
Dredge inspectors, 6 at.....$1,200
Harbor police, 6 at.......... 1,080
   SUPERINTENDENCE.
Mechanical engineer.........$7,500
Engineer water surveys..... 3,000
Supt. waterworks shops.... 2,500
   PUMPING STATIONS (WATER).
Chief engineers, 9 at.......$2,500
Assistant engineers, 27 at.. 2,000
Conveyor engineers, 5 at... 1,460
Firemen and oilers.......... 1,080
   LAKE CRIBS AND TUNNELS.
Diver $2,400
Diver's helpers, 2 at........ 1,200
Crib keepers, 5 at........... 1,200
Junior crib keepers, 11 at... 1,000
   WATER PIPE EXTENSION.
Superintendent $4,500
Assistant superintendent... 2,400
Assistant engineer.......... 2,160
Principal clerk............... 2,160
Plumbing inspector......... 2,160
   PIPE YARDS.
General foreman.............$1,800
Foremen, 5 at............... 1,500
   WATER WASTE SURVEYS.
Engineer $3,000
Junior engineers, 2 at....... 1,500
   REPAIRS AND REPLACEMENTS.
Foremen, construction, 9 at.$2,100
Assistant foremen, 23 at.... 1,680
WATERWORKS SHOPS AND REPAIR.
Assistant superintendent...$1,800
Chief steamfitter............ 2,112
Foremen, 3 at............... 1,800
   WATER METER SHOPS.
Foreman meter shop........$1,540
**DIVISION OF BRIDGES AND
HARBORS.**
   SUPERINTENDENCE.
Engineer in charge..........$5,000
Engineer designs............ 2,600
Assistant engineer.......... 2,160
   REPAIRS AND REPLACEMENTS.
Engineer $3,000
Foreman 2,520
Foremen, $1,680 to.......... 2,000
   BRIDGE OPERATION.
Superintendent bridges.....$3,000
Bridgetenders, $960 to...... 1,200
DIVISION OF RIVERS AND HARBORS.
Assistant engineer..........$2,100
Junior engineer.............. 1,500
   HARBOR MASTER'S OFFICE.
Harbor master...............$1,800
Launch operator............. 1,500
Vessel dispatcher........... 1,200
Assist. harbor masters, 5 at 1,200

   NEW BRIDGES.
Engineer in charge..........$3,000
Assistant engineer.......... 2,100
Designing engineers, $1,500 to 1,800

BUREAU OF WATER.
   SUPERINTENDENT'S OFFICE.
Superintendent $4,500
Senior stenographer 1,500
   COLLECTION DIVISION.
Chief clerk...................$2,800
Principal clerk............... 1,800
Cashier 2,500
Teller 2,040
   ASSESSED RATES SUBDIVISION.
Senior clerks, 6 at..........$1,500
Junior clerks, 24 at.......... 1,200
   METER RATES SUBDIVISION.
Senior clerk.................$1,440
Rate takers, per month..... 100
   ASSESSOR'S DIVISION.
Assessor $3,600
Field assessor............... 2,040
Principal clerk............... 1,500
Field assessors, per month.. 100
   SHUT-OFF SUBDIVISION.
Foreman laborers...........$1,200
Shut-off men, per month.... 75
PERMIT AND MAP SUBDIVISION.
Senior clerk.................$1,680
Draftsman 1,620
Draftsmen, 6 at.............. 1,080
   AUDITING DIVISION.
Accountant $2,040
Senior clerk.................. 1,680
Junior clerks, 7 at........... 1,200

**HARBOR AND SUBWAY COM-
MISSION.**
   SUBWAYS.
Commissioners, 2 at........$12,000
Commissioner, 1 at......... 4,000
Secretary 4,000
Assistant chief engineer.... 6,000
Subway engineers, 4 at..... 3,000
Subway engineers, 5 at..... 1,920
   HARBOR.
Harbor engineer.............$3,000
Designing engineer......... 2,000

PUBLIC LIBRARY.
Librarian $7,500
Secretary 4,500
Assistant librarian.......... 3,500
Director training class....... 1,500
Supervisor of branches..... 2,100
Class 4—Department heads: Grade
A, $1,500; grade B, $1,620; grade
C, $1,800; grade D, $2,040.
Class 3—Senior assistants: Grade
A, $960 to $1,140; grade B, $1,200
to $1,500.
Class 2—Junior assistants: Grade
A, $420 to $600; grade B, $660 to
$900.
Class 1—Pages, $300, $360 and $420.

FINANCES OF THE CITY OF CHICAGO (1912).

[From annual report of Comptroller John E. Traeger.]

CORPORATE PURPOSES.
   REVENUE.

Taxes $8,670,601.88
Miscellaneous 12,272,055.27
Proceeds of bonds.......... 1,194,870.78

Total, 1912................ 22,137,527.93
Total, 1911................ 23,053,282.22

   EXPENSE.

Operating $19,430,338.64
Repairs and renewals....... 1,876,604.46
Interest 1,323,228.05
Construction and betterments. 955,565.82
Loss collecting taxes....... 413,798.08
Judgments paid............. 723,269.09

Total, 1912................ 24,725,804.14
Total, 1911................ 28,030,628.33

VEHICLE TAX FUND.
   REVENUE.

Balance, Dec. 31, 1911...... $84,847.29
Vehicle tax licenses........ 598,004.48
Interest on funds........... 5,278.22

Total, 1912................ 688,129.99
Total, 1911................ 661,042.83

   EXPENSE.

Repair—Macadam pavements. $276,241.62
  Asphalt pavements....... 109,775.60
  Brick pavements......... 54,290.35
  Cedar block pavements... 4,041.04
  Granite block pavements.. 42,481.87
Cost of collection.......... 14,389.42
Superintendence 61,176.65

Total, 1912................ 562,358.85
Total, 1911................ 576,195.54

WATERWORKS.

REVENUE.

Ordinary	$6,527,926.73
Rebates	2,131.50

Total, 1912.............................	6,530,057.23
Total, 1911.............................	5,993,771.32

EXPENSE.

Operating	$2,143,713.38
Repairs and renewals................	1,270,778.83
Interest	193,686.37
Construction and betterments.........	2,456,841.57
Redemption certificates (pipe extension)	64,366.11
Judgments	44,377.58
Investments in special funds.........	215,000.00
Redemption water certificates.........	500,000.00

Total, 1912.............................	6,888,763.84
Total, 1911.............................	5,126,101.61

SCHOOLS.

REVENUE.

Taxes	$13,072,257.37
Miscellaneous	2,627,841.45

Total, 1912.............................	15,700,098.82
Total, 1911.............................	14,350,963.80

EXPENSE.

Operating	$10,552,846.63
Repairs and renewals................	645,303.87
Interest	17,272.32
Bonds and investments................	16,825.00
Construction and betterments.........	3,582,950.08
Collecting taxes.........................	522,890.29

Total, 1912.............................	15,318,088.19
Total, 1911.............................	14,059,645.87

PUBLIC LIBRARY.

REVENUE.

Taxes	$376,180.06
Miscellaneous	4,384.54

Total, 1912.............................	380,564.60
Total, 1911.............................	374,455.09

EXPENSE.

Operating	$285,620.43
Repairs and renewals................	8,665.62
Increase of library.....................	35,492.75
Collecting taxes.........................	15,047.20

Total, 1912.............................	344,826.00
Total, 1911.............................	341,089.09

SINKING FUND.

REVENUE.

Taxes	$1,674,350.00
Interest	59,855.50
Refunding bonds.........................	223,380.00

Total, 1912.............................	1,958,695.50
Total, 1911.............................	1,644,700.00

EXPENSE.

Redemption of bonds...................	$2,743,771.25

Total, 1911.............................	1,227,210.00

TUBERCULOSIS SANITARIUM.

REVENUE.

Taxes	$940,450.17
Miscellaneous	6,227.50

Total, 1912.............................	946,677.67
Total, 1911.............................	373,178.17

EXPENSE.

Operation	$56,906.40
Construction and betterments.........	297,977.03
Loss collection of taxes................	37,618.00

Total, 1912.............................	392,501.43
Total, 1911.............................	228,379.50

TOTAL REVENUE (1912).

Corporate purposes....................	$22,137,527.93
Sinking funds.........................	1,958,085.50
Schools	15,700,998.82
Public library.........................	380,564.60
Tuberculosis sanitarium................	946,677.67
Water fund.........................	6,530,057.23

Special assessment fund................	6,596,134.57

Total, 1912.............................	54,248,546.33
Total, 1911.............................	52,177,591.24

TOTAL EXPENSE (1912).

Corporate purposes....................	$24,725,804.14
Sinking funds.........................	2,743,771.25
Schools	15,318,088.19
Public library.........................	344,826.00
Tuberculosis sanitarium................	392,501.43
Water fund.........................	6,888,763.84
Special assessment fund................	5,925,979.37

Total, 1912.............................	56,339,734.22
Total, 1911.............................	49,941,462.97

SOURCES OF ORDINARY REVENUE (NET).

	1912.	1911.
Licenses, saloon............	$6,828,600.00	$6,831,360.00
Licenses, other................	911,173.33	933,335.33
Municipal courts............	530,275.23	492,825.27
House of correction.........	152,300.10	153,841.35
Police department...........	19,392.16	6,127.54
Fire department.............	7,132.52	5,470.88
Health department..........	64,517.13	63,143.64
Department of inspection....	146,279.57	126,092.03
Department of public works	714,505.84	476,185.76
Department of buildings....	181,722.08	156,394.66
Department of electricity...	215,859.16	148,827.57
Public pounds...............	910.50	2,224.50
Real estate and buildings...	43,376.68	45,565.64
Markets	6,426.35	4,300.35
Franchise compensations...	1,616,955.64	1,205,350.14
Insurance tax	110,586.11	108,805.04
Vehicle tax..................	562,358.65	576,195.54
Interest on city deposits...	44,968.83	135,613.37
Traction deposits*..........	66,201.81	....
Miscellaneous sources.......	49,788.68	40,879.92

Total.	12,271,336.27	11,506,548.53

*Amount expended.

CORPORATE EXPENSES BY DEPARTMENTS.

Department.	1912.	1911.
Mayor's office................	$27,967.57	$30,225.75
Bureau of compensation.....	5,985.76	6,132.81
Departm't of transportation	8,501.18	4,032.36
City council..................	208,674.47	207,957.43
Committee on finance........	7,159.92	7,400.00
Com. on local transportation	15,647.44	29,633.52
Com. on gas, oil, elec. light	27,469.38	20,810.24
Lake shore reclamation......	3,905.77	2,746.36
Harbor commission..........	410.00	4,448.92
Com. harbors, wharves, bridges	7,124.63	933.00
Chicago plan commission...	10,867.85	4,598.94
Com. on city expenditures..	....	942.44
City vice commission........	....	4,993.86
City clerk....................	63,984.78	67,847.42
Corporation counsel.........	134,359.66	191,383.52
Prosecuting attorney........	53,203.40	51,956.17
City attorney................	95,309.74	88,837.33
City comptroller.............	103,747.82	136,798.33
Finance—interest	1,323,228.95	1,358,091.23
Finance—miscellaneous	612,704.18	694,566.05
City treasurer................	45,269.94	49,157.41
City collector................	106,393.52	113,045.65
Election commissioners......	678,381.98	428,173.18
Civil service commission....	93,372.94	87,356.92
Department of supplies......	15,684.82	20,576.18
Department of police........	6,643,121.98	6,050,201.68
Municipal courts.............	761,637.92	766,063.29
House of correction..........	316,061.01	300,083.98
Dog pound...................	22,489.94	20,458.98
Department of fire...........	3,332,175.74	3,028,659.89
Department of buildings.....	160,776.05	133,584.83
Department of health........	659,597.00	643,389.10
City physician...............	7,942.77	7,481.85
Dept. of track elevation....	10,835.86	12,105.97
Inspect. stm. boilers, plants	46,205.89	46,179.54
Dept. weights and measures	35,257.47	34,607.90
Dept. of smoke inspection..	44,854.30	46,500.73
Board examiners (engineers)	12,834.32	12,925.92
Hospitals	18,000.00	18,000.00
Board of local improvements	804,106.34	802,677.13
City real estate and bldgs..	21,627.55	24,649.95
City markets.................	945.00	945.00
Special park commission....	114,860.42	118,259.37
Department of electricity...	1,274,454.84	1,203,778.18

Dept. of public works—	1912	1911
Commissioner's office........	4,633.05	4,221.28
Bureau of compensation.....	6,439.03	6,946.39
Bureau of maps and plats..	10,371.66	10,037.02
Bureau of architecture.....	6,783.55	6,411.87
Bureau of city hall........	141,064.76	199,798.70
Bureau of streets..........	3,800,392.66	3,556,801.21
Bureau of sewers..........	469,575.17	497,270.46
Bureau of engineering......	599,377.27	537,264.39
Harbor and subway com....	7,104.46	
Total ordinary............	22,973,820.81	21,686,380.63
Total extraordinary........	503,036.83	1,344,247.70
From tributary sources.....	1,248,946.50	....
Grand total...............	24,725,804.14	23,030,628.33

NET RECEIPTS FROM LICENSES (1912).

Description.	1912.	1911.
Acetylene gas—Sales.........	$134.40	$350.40
Acetylene gas—Collection....	144.00	
Amusements	138,916.87	126,014.74
Auctioneers	6,480.00	8,064.00
Auto hacks..................	....	19.20
Bakers	6,278.40	5,969.76
Bar permits.................	17,902.08	17,069.76
Bathing beaches.............	86.40	115.20
Billiards and pool..........	23,995.20	20,793.60
Bill posters................	96.00	96.00
Bill posters without wagons..	24.00	....
Boats	24.56	48.00
Bottlers carbonated waters...	2,264.02	2,169.60
Bowling alleys..............	2,390.40	2,788.80
Brewers and distillers.......	26,160.00	25,840.00
Brokers	47,088.00	45,528.00
Butchers	59,227.20	57,052.80
Cartridges and shells.......	734.40	681.60
Certif. of fitness—Explosives.	412.80	388.80
Cigarettes	153,792.00	128,064.00
Deadly weapons.............	984.00	1,296.00
Delicatessen	5,654.40	6,105.60
Detective agencies..........	2,688.00	3,592.00
Dog licenses...............	27,635.04	29,175.36
Drivers	133.44	134.40
Druggists	5,995.20	5,846.40
Dry cleaners...............	1,548.00	201.60
Fireworks	9.60	4,819.20
Fishmongers	1,929.60	1,569.60
Fish peddlers...............	172.80	273.60
Garages	5,868.00	4,548.00
Gasoline launches..........	....	....
Gunpowder	1,608.00	1,560.00
Hacks, cabs and coupes......	379.20	504.00
Hospitals	4,728.00	2,880.00
House movers...............	220.80	....
Ice dealers................	11,035.20	10,401.60
Junk dealers...............	4,023.00	4,107.00
Liquors—Malt	9,096.31	8,740.04
Liquors—Spirituous	23,568.02	21,592.08
Liquors—Vinous	13,996.98	13,256.25
Livery stables.............	2,894.40	3,369.60
Lumber yards...............	11,432.01	11,984.01
Medical dispensaries........	268.80	134.40
Milk dealers...............	31,761.55	28,387.20
Milk wagons...............	28,809.65	27,284.80
Moving picture operators.....	2,199.36	7,008.00
Renewals	894.72	....
Natatoriums	....	43.20
Nurseries	38.40	19.20
Omnibus	460.80	513.60
Pawnbrokers	17,760.00	17,094.00
Peddlers—Oil	2,121.60	1,977.60
Peddlers—Wagon	92,112.00	93,171.23
Peddlers—Wood	422.40	556.80
Peddlers—Hand cart.........	5,466.00	7,404.00
Peddlers—Pack or solicitors..	2,538.81	1,688.40
Peddlers—Basket	318.44	421.13
Peddlers—Coal	249.60	273.60
Poulterers	432.00	388.80
Public horse drawn vehicles..	823.20	327.36
Public motor vehicle operators	2,570.82	2,092.80
Renewals	1,952.64	1,767.36
Public carts...............	4,299.84	5,347.20
Public passenger automobiles.	4,308.01	3,165.60
Not on stands.............	148.80	....
Public express automobiles...	432.00	288.00
Rendering tanks............	5,990.40	5,606.40
Restaurants	28,798.80	28,146.00

Description.	1912.	1911.
Roofers	1,027.20	969.60
Runners	898.08	912.04
Saloons	6,823,600.00	6,831,360.00
Scales—Public	720.00	662.40
Scavengers—Offal	1,248.00	1,152.00
Scavengers—Night	96.00	96.00
Scavengers—Private	1,041.60	1,003.20
Second hand dealers.........	9,675.50	9,398.00
Sewer cleaners.............	9.60	....
Shooting galleries..........	624.00	672.00
Slaughtering and rendering..	11,232.00	11,232.00
Soap factories.............	2,304.00	2,160.00
Stables—Boarding	547.20	676.80
Stables—Sales	1,752.00	1,824.00
Storage—Moving picture films	614.02	648.00
Street cars.................	69,150.00	69,200.00
Tanneries	1,200.00	1,296.00
Tickers	484.80	428.16
Undertakers	4,238.40	4,152.00
Wagons—Junk	9,475.20	9,187.20
Workshops	7,336.32	6,387.84
Total, net*................	7,808,923.33	7,762,534.53
Total, gross...............	8,302,905.29	8,201,520.17

*After deductions for police and firemen's pension
funds—$411,644.42 and $82,337.53, respectively, in 1912.

FIXED ASSETS OF CHICAGO (1912).

CORPORATE PURPOSES.

Real estate.................	$1,581,499.77
Buildings	9,422,627.92
Equipments	7,876,954.10
Bridges, viaducts, etc.......	2,705,786.54
Miscellaneous	572,668.49
Wharfing	25,247.04
Total	22,184,783.86

SCHOOLS.

Real estate.................	$8,389,436.96
Buildings and equipment.....	45,415,565.93
Total	53,805,002.89

PUBLIC LIBRARY.

Real estate.................	$14,750.00
Buildings	2,090,200.55
Equipment	660,767.75
Total	2,765,713.30

WATERWORKS.

Real estate.................	$882,034.00
Buildings	1,873,720.77
Equipment	5,605,573.66
Miscellaneous	48,434,357.26
Total	56,795,685.69

TUBERCULOSIS SANITARIUM.

Real estate.................	$192,702.11
Buildings	278,448.28
Total	471,150.39

SUMMARY.

Corporate purposes.........	$22,184,783.86
Schools	53,805,002.89
Public library..............	2,765,713.30
Waterworks	56,795,685.69
Tuberculosis sanitarium.....	471,150.39
Total	136,022,336.13

STATEMENT OF CHICAGO'S DEBT (1912).

Bonds—General	$23,724,000.00
Water	2,447,400.00
Judgments	384,335.57
Accrued interest—Corporate.	114,753.97
Water fund debt,..........	1,016,214.65
Total	27,686,704.22
Less cash in sinking funds...	1,902,117.32
Total debt.................	25,784,586.90
Assessed valuation.........	940,450,171.00
Authorized indebtedness (5%)	47,022,508.55
Debt. Dec. 31, 1912........	25,784,586.90
Unexercised borrowing power.	21,237,921.65

CHICAGO APPROPRIATIONS FOR 1913.

FROM CORPORATE PURPOSES FUND.

Mayor's office	$28,375.00
Bureau of statistics	6,242.00
Department of transportation	6,832.50
City council	168,600.00
Committee on finance	5,516.00
Committee on local transportation	6,835.00
Committee on gas, oil and electric light	15,000.00
Lake shore reclamation committee	3,540.00
Committee on wharves, harbors, bridges	1,500.00
Chicago plan commission	9,700.00
City clerk	51,968.00
Corporation counsel	158,014.50
Prosecuting attorney	54,169.40
City attorney	98,687.00
Department of finance	118,832.00
Interest	1,627,085.00
Miscellaneous	608,283.00
City treasurer	50,473.71
City collector	107,820.00
Election commissioners	386,954.86
Civil service commission	56,829.50
Department of supplies	15,759.37
Department of police	6,898,898.64
Municipal court	866,786.69
House of correction	39,200.00
Dog pound	22,295.00
Fire department	3,359,313.50
Department of buildings	146,890.00
Department of health	1,098,211.20
City physician	7,985.00
Department of track elevation	11,085.00
Department of boiler inspection	47,065.00
Department of weights and measures	36,990.00
Department of smoke inspection	37,590.00
Board of examiners (engineers)	13,345.00
Hospitals	18,000.00
Inspector of oils	15,370.00
Board of local improvements	841,957.58
City real estate and buildings	25,850.00
City markets	1,860.00
Special park commission	382,170.58
Department of electricity	1,730,253.47
Commissioner of public works	4,430.50
Completion of city hall	230,075.35
Bureau of compensation	7,660.00

Bureau of maps and plats	32,691.50
Bureau of architecture	6,825.00
Bureau of city hall	169,291.50
Bureau of streets	4,119,209.85
Bureau of sewers	531,181.87
Bureau of engineering (bridges, harbors)	4,825,781.22
Harbor and subway commission	1,198,470.00
Total	30,383,700.42
Less reimbursements from bond issues	5,972,934.00
Total	24,410,766.42

FROM WATER FUND.

Corporation counsel	$42,150.00
City attorney	42,273.00
Comptroller's office	50,928.00
Finance department—interest	106,146.66
Finance department—miscellaneous	676,400.00
City treasurer	21,631.59
Civil service commission	24,355.50
Department of supplies	14,259.38
City clerk	12,992.00
Board of local improvements	70,029.16
Special park commission	4,500.00
Health department	4,640.00
Commissioner's office, public works	46,739.50
Bureau of maps and plats	30,574.50
Bureau of city hall	72,553.50
Bureau of engineering	6,648,810.41
Bureau of water	836,979.00
Total	8,276,046.70

RECAPITULATION.

Corporate purposes fund	$24,410,766.42
Water fund	8,276,046.70
From bond fund	5,780,934.00
Contingent on bond issues	211,303.31
From traction deposits	192,000.00
Sinking fund	2,287,821.25
Public library	851,640.09
Public library contingent	500,000.00
Municipal tuberculosis sanitarium	945,000.00
School purposes	18,941,250.00
Total all purposes	66,378,511.68
Total appropriations 1912	71,640,408.78

GOVERNMENT OFFICES IN CHICAGO.

The postoffice and all other United States department offices, except where otherwise noted, are in the federal building, which stands on the square bounded by Clark, Adams and Dearborn streets and Jackson boulevard. Postmaster, Daniel A. Campbell.

Appraiser's Office—Harrison and Sherman streets; appraiser, Thomas O'Shaughnessy.

Bureau of Labor—Room 851; special agent, Lucian W. Chancy; radio inspector, W. O. Hensgen.

Custom House—South wing, fourth floor; collector, John C. Ames; special deputy collector, John R. Ford; deputy collector at barge office, 376 River street, James M. Nash.

Hydrographic Office—Room 528; Lieut. A. J. James in charge.

Immigration Bureau—522, 115 Adams street; inspector in charge, Dr. P. L. Prentis.

Inspectors of Steam Vessels—Room 529; inspector of hulls, Ira B. Mansfield; inspector of boilers, William Nicholas.

Internal Revenue Department—East wing, fourth floor; collector, S. M. Fitch; chief deputy, Frank E. Hemstreet; cashier, Frederick W. Rech.

Life-Saving Service—Room 500; inspector, A. J. Henderson.

Lighthouse Department—Room 504; inspector, Lewis M. Stoddard.

Marine Hospital—Clarendon and Graceland ave-

nues; surgeon in command, Dr. J. O. Cobb.

Naval Office—Room 451; naval officer, William Brown; special deputy, Edgar C. Hawley; deputy, Thomas Carr.

United States District Attorney—Rooms 825 to 833; James H. Wilkerson; chief clerk, Wm. A. Small.

United States Engineer—Room 508; Lieut.-Col. George A. Zinn.

United States Marshal—Rooms 804 and 806; marshal, Luman T. Hoy; chief deputy, John P. Wolf.

United States Secret Service—Room 881; Thomas I. Porter, chief operator.

United States Subtreasury—First floor, northwest section; assistant treasurer, Irving Shuman; cashier, Frank C. Russell.

Weather Bureau—Fourteenth floor; professor in charge, Henry J. Cox.

SALARIES OF PRINCIPAL OFFICIALS.

District attorney	$10,000
Postmaster	8,000
Collector of customs	7,000
Treasurer	5,000
Marshal	5,000
Naval officer	5,000
Internal-revenue collector	4,500
United States engineer	3,500
Appraiser	3,000
Professor of meteorology (weather)	3,500

HOUSE OF CORRECTION.

South California avenue, near 26th street. Statistics for calendar years.

	1911.			1912.		
	Male.	Female.	Total.	Male.	Female.	Total.
Prisoners received	11,924	1,271	13,195	10,276	1,181	11,453
Prisoners discharged	11,658	1,246	12,904	10,569	1,204	11,773
From juvenile court	396	.....	396	175	.....	175
Discharged by juvenile court	371	.....	371	293	.....	293
Prisoners receiving medical treatment	9,693	899	10,592	10,310	590	10,900

CHICAGO WARD BOUNDARIES.

As fixed by the redistricting ordinance of Dec. 4, 1911.

Ward.

1. Chicago river west and south of Wallace, south to W. 25th, east to Princeton, south to W. 29th-pl., cast to S. 5th-av., south to W. 30th, east to Wentworth-av., south to W. 31st. east to Lake Shore right of way, north to W. 26th, east to S. Michigan-av., north to E. 25th, east to Indiana-av., south to E. 26th, east to South Park-av., south to E. 31st, east to Lake Michigan, north to river.

2. Lake Michigan and 31st-st., west to South Park-av., north to E. 26th, west to Indiana-av., north to E. 25th, west to S. Michigan-av., south to E. 26th, west to Lake Shore right of way, south to W. 31st, west to Wentworth-av., north to W. 30th, west to S. 5th-av., south to W. 33d, west to Stewart-av., south to W. 39th, east to Cottage Grove-av., north to 38th, east to Lake Michigan, north to 31st.

3. Lake Michigan and 47th, west to St. Lawrence-av., south to E. 49th, west to S. State, north to W. 43d, west to Princeton-av., north to W. 39th, east to Cottage Grove-av., north to E. 38th, east to Lake Michigan, southeast to 47th.

4. Wallace and river west and south to W. 34th-pl., east to S. Halsted, north to W. 34th, east to Union-av., south to W. 35th, east to Wallace, north to W. 33d, east to S. 5th-av., north to W. 28th-pl., west to Princeton-av., north to W. 25th, west to Wallace, north to river.

5. From intersection of river and south fork southwest along canal to W. 39th, west to S. 48th-av., south to W. 45th, east to S. Ashland-av., north to W. 43d, east to Princeton-av., north to W. 39th, west to Stewart-av., north to W. 33d, west to Wallace, south to W. 35th, west to Union-av., north to W. 34th, west to S. Halsted, south to W. 35th, west to south fork of river and northwesterly to river.

6. Lake Michigan and E. 47th-st. west to St. Lawrence-av., south to E. 49th, west to S. State, south to E. 63d, east to South Park-av., north to E. 60th, east to Lake Michigan, northwest to 47th.

7. Lake Michigan and E. 60th-st., west to South Park-av., south to E. 63d, west to Stewart-av., south to W. 66th, east to Harvard-av., south to W. 67th, east to Wentworth-av., south to W. 71st, east to S. State, south to E. 75th, east to Stony Island-av., north to E. 73d, east to lake, northwest to E. 60th.

8. Lake Michigan and E. 73d-st. west to Stony Island-av., south through Lake Calumet to city limits, east to Indiana state line, north to lake and northwest to E. 73d.

9. Stony Island-av. and E. 75th, west to S. State, south to W. 79th, west to Wallace, south to W. 84th, east to Stewart-av., south to W. 103d, west to S. Halsted, south to W. 111th, west to S. Peoria, south to W. 115th, west to Vincennes-av., southwest to Lyon-av., east to S. Ashland-av., south to W. 123d, east to S. Halsted, south to city limits, east to Stony Island-av., projected, and north to E. 75th.

10. S. Racine-av. and W. 12th, west to Loomis, north to Taylor, west to S. Wood, south to W. 16th, east to S. Ashland-av., south to river, northeast to S. Morgan, north to W. 18th, east to S. Morgan, north to W. 16th, west to S. Racine-av., north to W. 12th.

11. S. Wood and Taylor, west to S. Oakley-bd., south to W. 12th, west to P., C., C. & St. L. R. R., south to canal, northeast to S. Ashland-av., north to W. 16th, west to S. Wood, north to Taylor.

12. W. 12th and P., C., C. & St. L. R. R., west to S. Kedzie-av., south to W. 19th, west to S. Homan-av., north to Ogden-av., southwest to Clifton Park-av., south to W. 24th, west to S. Central Park-av., south to canal, northeast to P., C., C. & St. L. R. R., north to W. 12th.

13. W. Washington-bd. and N. Oakley-bd., west to N. 40th-av., south to W. 12th, east to S. Oakley-bd., north to W. Washington-bd.

14. W. Chicago-av. and N. Ashland-av., west to N. 40th-av., south to W. Washington-bd., east to N. Ashland-bd., north to W. Chicago-av.

15. W. North-av., and N. Robey, west to N. St. Louis-av., south to W. Chicago-av., east to N. Ashland-av., north to W. Division, west to N. Robey, north to W. North-av.

16. River and Fullerton-av., west to N. Robey, south to W. Division, east to river, northwest to Fullerton-av.

17. River and W. Division, west to N. Ashland-av., south to W. Kinzie, east to river, northwest to W. Division.

18. River and W. Kinzie, west to N. Ashland-av., south to W. Washington-bd., west to N. Oakley-bd., south to Taylor, east to S. Hermitage-av., north to W. Van Buren, east to river, north to W. Kinzie.

19. River and W. Van Buren, west to S. Hermitage-av., south to Taylor, east to Loomis, south to W. 12th, east to S. Halsted, north to Taylor, east to S. Desplaines, south to DeKoven, east to S. Jefferson, south to Bunker, east to river, north to W. Van Buren.

20. River and Bunker, west to S. Jefferson, north to DeKoven, west to S. Desplaines, north to Taylor, west to S. Halsted, south to W. 12th, west to S. Racine-av., south to W. 16th, east to S. Morgan, south to W. 18th, west to S. Morgan, south to W. 18th, west to S. Morgan, south to river, northeast to Bunker.

21. Lake Michigan and Fullerton-av., west to N. Clark, southeast to Sedgwick, south to W. Division, east to Orleans, south to river, east to lake and north to Fullerton-av.

22. Menomonee and Sedgwick, west to Larrabee, north to Center, west to Racine-av., south to Clybourn-pl., west to river, south and southeast to Orleans, north to W. Division, west to Sedgwick, north to Menomonee.

23. Cornelia-av. and Lake Michigan, west to Southport-av., south to Roscoe, east to Racine-av., south to Fullerton-av., east to Sheffield-av., south to Center, east to Larrabee, south to Menomonee, east to Sedgwick, north to N. Clark, northwest to Fullerton-av., east to Lake Michigan.

24. Roscoe and Racine-avs., west to N. Western-av., south to Belmont-av., west to river, southeast to Clybourn-pl., east to Racine-av., north to Center, east to Sheffield-av., north to Fullerton-av., west to Racine-av., north to Roscoe.

25. Lake Michigan and Rogers-av., southwest to Howard, west to Ridge-rd., southeast to Devon-av., east to N. Clark, southeast to Southport-av., south to Cornelia-av., east to Lake Michigan, northwest to Rogers-av.

26. Ridge-rd. and Howard, west to N. Kedzie-av., south to Devon-av., west to north shore channel, south along channel and river to Belmont-av., east to N. Western-av., north to Roscoe, east to Southport-av., north to N. Clark, northwest to Devon, west to Ridge-rd., northwest to Howard.

27. North shore channel and Devon-av., west to N. Narragansett-av., thence along city limits as established by annexation of Norwood Park to Park Ridge-bd. on north and Highland-av. on west, east and south to Bryn Mawr-av., east to N. Maynard-av., south to Irving Park-bd., west to N. Harlem-av., south to Belmont-av., east to N. Crawford-av., south to Fullerton-av., east to N. Central Park-av., north to Diversey-av., east to N. Francisco, north to Belmont-av., east to river, northwest along river and channel to Devon-av.

28. River and Belmont-av., west to N. Francisco, south to Diversey-av., west to N. Sacramento-av., south to W. North-av., east to N. Robey, north to Fullerton-av., east to river, northwest to Belmont-av.

29. S. Racine-av. and W. 43d, west to S. Ashland-av., south to W. 45th, west to S. Cicero-av., south to W. 69th, east to S. Robey, south to W. 71st, east to Loomis, north to W. 66th, west to S. Wood, north to W. Garfield-bd., east to Loomis, north to W. 47th, east to S. Racine-av., north to W. 43d.

30. S. State and W. 43d, west to S. Racine-av., south to W. 47th, west to Loomis, south to W. Garfield-bd., east to S. State, north to W. 43d.

Ward.
31. S. State and W. Garfield-bd., west to S. Wood, south to W. 66th, east to Loomis, north to W. 63d, east to S. State, north to W. Garfield-bd.
32. Stewart-av. and W. 63d, west to Loomis, south to W. 71st, west to S. Robey, north to W. 68th, west to S. Cicero-av., south to W. 87th, east to S. Western-av., south to W. 99th, west to Ogden-av. (Morgan Park), south to W. 115th, east to S. Western-av., south to Lyon-av., east to Vincennes-av., northeast to Raymond, east to S. Morgan, north to W. 111th, east to S. Racine-av., north to W. 107th, east to S. Halsted, North to W. 103d, east to Stewart-av., north to W. 84th, west to Wallace, north to W. 79th, east to S. State, north to W 71st, west to Wentworth-av., north to W. 67th, west to Harvard-av., north to W. 66th, west to Stewart-av., north to W. 63d.
33. Diversey and N. Sacramento-avs., west to N. Central Park-av., south to Fullerton-av., west to N. Crawford-av., north to Belmont-av., west to N.

Ward.
Harlem-av., south to North-av., east to S. Austin-av., south to Madison, east to N. Laramie-av., north to W. Kinzie, east to N. Kenton-av., north to North-av., east to N. Crawford-av., north to Armitage-av., east to Sacramento-av., north to Diversey-av.
34. S. Kedzie-av. and W. 12th, west to S. Kenton-av., south to W. 39th, east to canal, northeast to S. Central Park-av., north to W. 24th, east to Clifton Park-av., north to Ogden-av., northeast to S. Homan-av., south to W. 19th, east to S. Kedzie-av., north to W. 12th.
35. N. Sacramento and Armitage-avs., west to N. Crawford-av., south to W. North-av., west to N. Kenton-av., south to W. Kinzie, west to N. Laramie-av., south to Madison, west to S. Austin-av., south to W. 12th, east to S. Crawford-av., north to W. Chicago-av., east to St. Louis-av., north to W. North-av., east to Sacramento-av., north to Armitage-av.

CHICAGO'S LAKE TRADE.

ARRIVALS AND CLEARANCES OF VESSELS.*

Year.	Arrivals. No.	Tons.	Clearances. No.	Tons.
1870	12,739	3,049,265	12,433	2,983,942
1871	12,320	3,096,101	12,312	3,052,235
1872	12,824	3,059,752	12,531	3,017,790
1873	11,858	3,225,911	11,876	3,338,803
1874	10,827	3,195,633	10,720	3,134,078
1875	10,488	3,122,004	10,607	3,157,061
1876	9,621	3,089,072	9,628	3,078,264
1877	10,233	5,274,332	10,284	3,311,683
1878	10,490	3,608,534	10,494	3,631,139
1879	11,859	3,887,095	12,104	3,870,300
1880	13,218	4,616,969	13,392	4,537,382
1881	13,048	4,533,558	12,957	4,228,689
1882	13,861	4,849,950	13,626	4,904,999
1883	11,967	3,812,464	12,015	3,980,873
1884	11,354	3,756,973	11,472	3,751,723
1885	10,744	3,653,936	10,798	3,652,285
1886	11,157	3,926,318	11,215	3,950,762
1887	11,950	4,326,292	12,023	4,421,560
1888	10,989	4,393,768	11,106	4,496,893
1889	10,804	5,102,790	10,984	5,155,041
1890	10,507	5,138,253	10,547	5,150,665
1891	10,224	5,524,852	10,294	5,506,700
1892	10,556	5,966,626	10,567	5,698,337
1893	8,754	5,456,637	8,789	5,449,470
1894	8,259	5,181,260	8,329	5,211,160
1895	9,212	6,329,702	9,363	6,392,497
1896	8,683	6,481,153	8,773	6,591,203

Year.	Arrivals. No.	Tons.	Clearances. No.	Tons.
1897	9,156	7,209,442	9,201	7,185,324
1898	9,428	7,557,215	9,562	7,686,448
1899	8,346	6,353,715	8,429	6,390,260
1900	8,714	7,044,995	8,839	7,141,105
1901	8,430	6,900,999	8,471	6,930,883
1902	8,083	7,179,063	8,164	7,229,342
1903	7,650	7,587,410	7,721	7,720,225
1904	6,631	6,430,088	6,671	6,514,934
1905	7,236	7,364,193	7,268	7,375,963
1906	7,017	7,969,621	7,055	7,665,709
1907	6,745	8,067,062	6,736	7,995,211
1908	5,787	7,241,845	5,805	7,296,745
1909	6,390	8,772,667	6,390	8,785,841
1910	6,523	9,430,074	6,551	9,470,572
1911	6,252	8,787,586	6,284	8,859,007
1912	6,240	9,971,738	6,243	10,086,209

*Comprises Chicago, Michigan City, Waukegan, Gary and Indiana Harbor.

TONNAGE OF THE CHICAGO DISTRICT (1912).

Port.	Arrivals. No.	Tonnage.	Clearances. No.	Tonnage.
Chicago	5,751	8,471,023	5,749	8,594,518
Michigan City	68	21,019	70	21,308
Waukegan	70	96,270	68	97,747
Gary	282	1,146,317	282	1,130,039
Indiana Harbor	69	237,109	74	242,597
Total	6,240	9,971,738	6,243	10,086,209

RECEIPTS BY LAKE IN 1912.

Coal, hard, tons.	881,380
Coal, soft, tons.	831,579
Salt, tons	166,696
Iron ore, tons*.	5,558,000
Iron, manufactured, tons...	47,097
Cement, tons...	6,449
Lumber, M	284,596
Shingles, M	1,660
Lath, M	11,967
Posts, pieces...	63,340
Railroad ties, pieces	320,315
Telegraph poles, pieces	2,115
Wood, cords	2,970
Copper, tons...	1,245
Hides and leather, bales	12,135
Sugar, tons	88,874
Green fruits, tons	48,717
Wheat, bushels..	3,660,712
Barley, bushels..	11,116
Corn, bushels....	13,941
Flaxseed, bushels	852,287

*Exclusive of 2,973,219 tons received at Gary, Ind., and 287,914 tons received at Indiana Harbor.

SHIPMENTS BY LAKE IN 1912.

Flour, barrels..	2,762,291
Wheat, bushels..17,523,384	
Corn, bushels....24,599,769	
Oats, bushels...	5,345,172
Grass seed, tons	548
Millstuffs, tons.	214,347
Oil cake, tons..	9,373
Corn and oat meal, barrels..	4,280
Wool and hair, sacks	4,522
Oil, barrels*....	899,033
Iron, manufactured, tons...	146,135
Mdse, unclassified, tons....	442,222
*Exclusive of 415,329 barrels shipped from Indiana Harbor, Ind.	

CITY CLERKS SINCE 1837.

I. N. Arnold	1837	H. Kreisman	1857-1859	D. W. Nickerson	1887-1889
George Davis	1837-1838	Abraham Kohn	1860	Franz Amberg	1889-1891
William H. Brackett	1839	A. J. Marble	1861-1862	James R. B. Van Cleave	
Thomas Hoyne	1840-1841	Albert H. Bodman	1865-1869		1891-1893, 1895-1897
James M. Lowe	1843	Charles T. Hotchkiss	1869-1873	Charles D. Gastfield	1893-1895
E. A. Rucker	1844-1845	Joseph K. C. Forrest	1873-1875	William Loeffler	1897-1903
William S. Brown	1845	Caspar Butz	1876-1878	Fred C. Bender	1903-1905
Henry B. Clarke	1846-1847	P. J. Howard	1879-1883	A. C. Anson	1905-1907
Sidney Abell	1848-1850	J. G. Neumeister	1883-1895	John R. McCabe	1907-1909
H. W. Zimmerman	1851-56, 1863-64	C. Herman Plautz	1885-1887	F. D. Connery	1909-1915

CHICAGO FIRE DEPARTMENT CHIEFS.

Alex. Lloyd	1837-1838	C. E. Peck	1847-1848	S. McBride	1855-1857	D. J. Swenie	1879-1901
A. Calhoun	1839	A. Gilbert	1849	D. J. Swenie	1858-1901	Wm. H. Musham	1901-1904
L. Nicholl	1840	C. P. Bradley	1850-1851	U. P. Harris	1859-1867	John Campion	1904-1906
A. Sherman	1841-1843	U. P. Harris	1852-1853	R. A. Williams	1867-1873	James Horan	1906-1910
S. F. Gale	1844-1846	J. M. Donnelly	1854	Matt. Benner	1873-1879	C. F. Seyferlich	1910

FIRE DEPARTMENT STATIONS.
FIRE ENGINE COMPANIES.
General headquarters, city hall.

No. Location.	No. Location.	No. Location.	No. Location.
1. 333 S. 5th avenue.	41. Sampson's slip,Throop and Lumber-sts.	82. 761 East 95th street.	101. 1533 West 69th-st.
2. 2421 Lowe avenue.		83. 1219 South place.	102. 7077 N. Clark street.
3. 855 West Erie street.	42. 236 West Illinois-st.	84. 5721 S. Halsted-st.	103. 1459 W. Harrison-st.
4. 1244 N. Halsted-st.	43. 2183 Stave street.	85. 3700 West Huron-st.	104. 1401 Michigan-av.
5. 323 S. Jefferson-st.	44. 3138 W. Lake street.	86. 2414 Cuyler avenue.	105. 2337 W. Erie street.
6. 514 Maxwell street.	45. 4602 Cottage Grove-av.	87. 8701 Escanaba-av.	106. 2754 N. Fairfield-av.
7. 636 Blue Island-av.	46. 9321-23 So. Chicago-av.	88. 3500 W. 60th street.	107. 2258 W. 13th street.
8. 1931 Archer avenue.	47. 7531 Dobson avenue.	89. 4456 N. Knox avenue.	108. 4835 Lipps avenue.
9. 2627 Cottage Grove-av.	48. 4005 Dearborn street.	90. 1016 W. Division-st.	109. 2358 S. Whipple-st.
10. 214 Lomax place.	49. 1642 W. 47th street.	91. 3000 Elbridge avenue	110. 2641 Foster avenue.
11. 10 E. Austin avenue.	50. 4659 Wentworth-av.	92. Center Deering yard.	111. 1701 N.Washtenaw-av
12. 1641 West Lake-st.	51. 6345 Wentworth-av.	93. 331 South 5th avenue.	112. 1732 Byron street.
13. 209 N. Dearborn-st.	52. 4714 Elizabeth street.	94. 326 S. Jefferson-st.	113. 4658 Lexington-st.
14. 509 W. Chicago-av.	53. 40th and Packers-av.	95. 4000 Wilcox avenue.	114. 3542 W. Fullerton-av.
15. 1154 W. 22d street.	54. 8023 Vincennes road.	96. 439 North Waller-av	115. 11940 S. Peoria-st.
16. 23 W. 31st street.	55. 2740 Sheffield avenue.	97. 13359 Superior-av.	116. 5929 Wood street.
17. 558 West Lake street.	56. 2214 Harry avenue.	98. 202 East Chicago-av.	117. 816 N. Laramie-av.
18. 1123 West 12th street.	57. 2412 Haddon avenue.	99. 3042 S. Kedvale-av.	118. 13401 Indiana-av.
19. 3444 Rhodes avenue.	58. 92d street bridge.	100. 6843 Jefferson-av.	119. 6030 Avondale-av.
20. 1318 Rawson street.	59. 826 Exchange avenue.		
21. 14 W. Taylor street.	60. 1315 E. 55th street.	**HOOK AND LADDER COMPANIES.**	
22. 520 Webster avenue.	61. 5300 Wentworth-av.		
23. 1702 West 21st place.	62. 34 East 114th street.	1. 218 Lomax place.	18. 4738 Halsted street.
24. 2447 Warren avenue.	63. 6328-30 Rosalie-av.	2. 540 W. Washington-st.	19. 1129 W. Chicago-av.
25. 1975 Canalport-av.	64. 6244 Laflin street.	3. 158 W. Erie street.	20. 446 West 69th street.
26. 457 N. Pulaski-av.	65. 2714 West 39th street.	4. 214 W. 22d street	21. 1529 Belmont avenue.
27. 1244 Wells street.	66. 2856 Fillmore street.	5. 1125 West 12th street.	22. 1620 Winnemac-av.
28. 2867 Loomis street.	67. 4666 Fulton street.	6. 117 North Franklin-st.	23. 4837 Lipps avenue.
29. 744 West 35th street.	68. 1642 N. Kostner-av.	7. 455 N. Pulaski-av.	24. 10400 Vincennes road.
30. 1125 N. Ashland-av.	69. 4017 N. Kenosha-av.	8. 2865 Loomis street.	25. 1545 Rosemont-av.
31. 2012 W. Congress-st.	70. 2100 Eastwood avenue.	9. 61 E. South Water-st.	26. 4002 Wilcox avenue.
32. 59 E. South Water-st.	71. Deering yards (fire-	10. 1613 Hudson avenue.	27. 30 East 114th street.
33. 2208 Clybourn avenue	boat Chicago).	11. 9 East 36th place.	28. 1621 N. Robey street.
34. 114 N. Curtis street.	72. 7914 Sherman avenue.	12. -2256 W. 13th street	29. 441 N. Waller-av.
35. 1625 N. Robey street.	73. 8630 Emerald avenue.	13. 2756 N. Fairfield av.	30. 6017 S. State street.
36. 2946 West 25th street.	74. 10615 Ewing avenue.	14. 918 West 19th street.	31. 1401 Michigan avenue.
37. Foot of Franklin-st.	75. 12054-56 Wallace-av.	15. 4600 Cottage Grove-av.	32. 2360 S. Whipple-st.
(fireboat Graeme Stewart).	76. 3519 Cortland street.	16. 1405 East 62d place.	33. 4457 Marshfield-av.
	77. 1224 S. Kedvale-av.	17. 9323 South Chicago-av.	34. 1024 East 73d street.
	78. 1052 Waveland-av.		
38. 2246 S. Ridgeway-av.	79. 5358 N. Ashland-av.	**FIRE-INSURANCE PATROLS.**	
39. 1618 West 33d place.	80. 623 East 108th street.		
40. 119 N. Franklin-st.	81. 10458 Hoxie avenue.	1. 163 West Monroe-st.	5. 221 Whiting street.
		2. 427 S. Sangamon-st.	6. 334 S. Hoyne avenue.
		3. 15 West 23d street.	7. 1628 West Division-st.
		4. Union stockyards.	8. 324 North Michigan-av.

CHARITY ORGANIZATIONS IN CHICAGO.

American National Red Cross Society (Illinois branch)—Secretary, James Whittaker. Springfield, Ill.; treasurer, Orson Smith, 112 West Adams street.

Associated Jewish Charities of Chicago—916, 30 North LaSalle street; president, Julius Rosenwald; secretary, Joseph Weissenbach.

Austro-Hungarian Benevolent Association—Secretary, Gustave F. Fischer, 1418, 110 South LaSalle street.

Chicago Daily News Fresh-Air Fund—Manager, H. L. Rogers, Sanitarium, Lincoln park, foot of Fullerton avenue.

Children's Benefit League—President, Mrs. Edward Tilden; corresponding secretary, Mrs. Charles Salmon.

Children's Day Association—President, Mrs. L. L. Funk; corresponding secretary, Miss Pauline Kelly.

Christian Industrial League—President, Arthur Meeker; superintendent, George A. Kilby.

Elizabeth McCormick Memorial Fund—City Club building, 315 Plymouth court, sixth floor; director, Sherman C. Kingsley.

Frances Juvenile Aid Association—President, Dr. Clara P. Seippel; corresponding secretary, Mrs. Fred G. Harris.

German Society of Chicago—153 North LaSalle street; president, Michael P. Girten; secretary, Rudolf Seifert; manager, F. von W. Wysow.

Hungarian Charity Society of Chicago—President, Samuel Kohn; secretary, Leo Newman, 2603 Evergreen avenue.

Illinois Charitable Relief Corps—President, John McShane; secretary, Miss Bessie Crowley, 3440 North Marshfield avenue.

Illinois Children's Home and Aid Society—President, R. J. Bennett; secretary and superintendent, Wilford S. Reynolds, 1816, 209 South State street.

Infant Welfare Society—President, Lucius Teter; secretary, Dr. Frank S. Churchill.

Italian Ladies' Charitable Association—President, Mrs. M. Mastroglovanni; secretary, Miss I. Libonati.

Jewish Aid Society—1336 South Morgan street; president, Solomon L. Sulzberger; secretary, Morton D. Cahn.

Legal Aid Society of Chicago—230, 31 West Lake street; president, Rudolph Matz; corresponding secretary, Mrs. Albert F. Holden.

Mothers' Relief Association—President, Mrs. D. Harry Hammer; corresponding secretary, Mrs. Edward S. Smith.

Ruth Club—6001 Indiana avenue; president, Mrs. Joseph Myers; recording secretary, Mrs. Morris Rosenbaum.

Societe Francaise de Bienfaisance de l'Illinois—President, Z. P. Brosseau; secretary, J. S. Townsend, 1554 Wabash avenue.

Societe Francaise de Secours Mutuels—President, A. Campion; secretary, Gaston Bloch, 32 South Clark street.

United Charities of Chicago—President, Dr. Charles R. Henderson; secretary, Walter S. Brewster; office, sixth floor, 168 North Michigan avenue; superintendent, Eugene T. Lies.

Visiting Nurse Association of Chicago—829, 104 South Michigan avenue; president, Mrs. Arthur Aldis; secretary, Mrs. Robert McGann, 120 East Pearson street.

Young Men's Jewish Charities Association—President, Isaac Rothschild; secretary, Monte H. Sadler.

Young Men's Federated Jewish Charities—3322 Douglas boulevard; president, A. H. Rosenberg; secretary, Lewis F. Jacobson.

FIRE LIMITS OF CHICAGO.

The fire limits of Chicago, within which wooden buildings shall not be erected, as fixed by the ordinance of July 25, 1912, are as follows:

(a) Beginning at Lake Michigan and Devon avenue west to North Clark street, south to Lawrence avenue, west to North Western avenue, south to Addison street, west to North Whipple street, south to Elston avenue, southeast to Roscoe street, east to north branch of river, southeast along river to Belmont avenue, west to North Kedzie avenue, south to Diversey avenue, west to North Central Park avenue, south to Fullerton avenue, west to North Kostner avenue, south to West Chicago avenue, west to North Austin avenue, south to Baltimore & Ohio Chicago Terminal railroad, easterly to South Kenton avenue, south to West 22d street, east to South Kostner avenue, south to West 33d street, east to South Crawford avenue, south to Illinois and Michigan canal, northeasterly to South Western avenue, south to West 39th street, east to South Robey street, south to West 43d street, east to a line 125 feet west of South Ashland avenue, north to West 41st street, east to South Ashland avenue, north to West 40th street, east to within 125 feet of South Ashland avenue, south to West 43d street, west to South Ashland avenue, south to West 47th street, east to within 125 feet of South Halsted street, south to West 51st street, east to a line 125 feet east of Halsted street, north to West 43d street, east to Wallace street, south to West 40th street, east to Butler street, south to West 43d street, east to within 125 feet of Wentworth avenue, south to West Garfield boulevard, east to within 125 feet of Wentworth avenue, north to West 43d street, east to within 125 feet of South State street, south to West Garfield boulevard, west to Union avenue, north to West 51st street, west to South Racine avenue, south to within 125 feet of West 63d street, west to South Ashland avenue, south to a line 125 feet south of West 63d street, east to South Racine avenue, south to West 75th street, east to South Shore avenue, southeasterly to East 79th street, east to Ontario avenue, south to East 83d street, east to Superior avenue, south to East 89th street, west to Manistee avenue, south to Lake Shore railroad tracks, southeasterly to East 95th street, west to South Chicago branch of the Fort Wayne railroad, along said branch to East 106th street, east to within 200 feet of the Calumet river, northerly to East 95th street, east to Lake Michigan and thence northerly and northwesterly along the lake shore to the place of beginning.

(b) Also beginning at the shore of Lake Calumet and Stony Island avenue, north to East 95th street, west to South Park avenue, south to East 103d street, east to Corliss avenue, south to East 106th street, west to Cottage Grove avenue, southwesterly to East 109th street, east to South Park avenue, south to East 115th street, east to Michigan Central tracks, southeasterly to East 127th street, east to Lake Calumet, thence northerly along shore of lake to place of beginning at Stony Island avenue.

(c) Excepting the district bounded as follows: Beginning at Belmont avenue and the north branch of the river, east to Southport avenue, south to Fullerton avenue, east to north branch of river, northwesterly along river to Belmont avenue, the place of beginning.

(d) Excepting also so much of the land from which clay has been removed and in which filling has been placed in the district bounded as follows: Beginning at Addison street and North Western avenue, south to Belmont avenue, west to the north branch of the river, northwesterly along river to Addison street and east to North Western avenue, the place of beginning.

(e) Excepting also the following territory, which shall be known as a provisional fire limit: Beginning at Lake Michigan and East 79th street, west to South Shore avenue, northwesterly to East 75th street, west to South State street, north to Lake Shore tracks, southeasterly to East 67th street, east to South Park avenue, north to East 63d street, east to Cottage Grove avenue, south to East 67th street, east to Lake Michigan, southeasterly along the shore to the place of beginning.

(f) The following district outside of the above described fire limits is hereby established as a provisional fire limit: Beginning at Stony Island avenue and East 75th street, south to East 79th street, east to Jeffery avenue, north to east 75th street, east to Stony Island avenue, the place of beginning.

(g) Any person desiring to erect a frame or wooden building, to be used for residence or mercantile purposes, within the provisional fire limits above described shall have a right to do so upon presenting a petition to the commissioner of buildings, together with a plat, plans and specifications showing where the building is to be erected. Such petition shall be verified by the affidavit of the applicant and shall contain the written consent of the owners of a majority of the frontage upon both sides of streets surrounding the square in which the building is to be erected.

(h) No frame or wooden building shall be erected within the provisional fire limits exceeding forty feet in height.

LOCATION OF RAILWAY AND PASSENGER STATIONS.

CENTRAL STATION—Park row and 12th street; south side.
 Chicago, Cincinnati & Louisville.
 Cleveland, Cincinnati, Chicago & St. Louis (Big Four).
 Illinois Central.
 Michigan Central.
 Minneapolis, St. Paul & Sault Ste. Marie (Soo line; formerly Wisconsin Central).
 West Michigan.
CHICAGO & NORTHWESTERN—West Madison and Canal streets, west side.
 All divisions.
DEARBORN STATION—Dearborn and Polk streets; south side.
 Atchison, Topeka & Santa Fe.
 Chesapeake & Ohio.
 Chicago & Eastern Illinois.
 Chicago & Western Indiana.
 Chicago, Indianapolis & Louisville (Monon).
 Erie.
 Grand Trunk.
 Wabash.

GRAND CENTRAL STATION—Fifth avenue and Harrison street; south side.
 Baltimore & Ohio.
 Chicago Great Western.
 Chicago Terminal Transfer.
 Pere Marquette.
LASALLE STREET STATION—Van Buren and LaSalle streets; south side.
 Chicago, Rock Island & Pacific.
 Lackawanna.
 Lake Shore & Michigan Southern.
 New York, Chicago & St. Louis (Nickel Plate).
UNION STATION—Canal street, between Adams and Madison; west side.
 Chicago & Alton.
 Chicago, Burlington & Quincy.
 Chicago, Milwaukee & St. Paul.
 Pittsburgh, Fort Wayne & Chicago.
 Pittsburgh, Cincinnati, Chicago & St. Louis (Pan Handle).

BEEF AND PORK PACKING IN CHICAGO.

Year ended March 1.

Years.	No. cattle.	No. hogs.	Years.	No. cattle.	No. hogs.	Years.	No. cattle.	No. hogs.
1897-8	1,732,286	6,747,265	1902-3	2,017,553	6,911,947	1907-8	1,817,737	6,342,717
1898-9	1,603,380	8,016,675	1903-4	2,163,976	6,763,685	1908-9	1,637,295	6,298,205
1899-1900	1,784,776	7,544,219	1904-5	1,918,665	6,044,753	1909-10	1,638,921	5,161,552
1900-1	1,814,921	7,364,859	1905-6	1,988,955	6,170,341	1910-11	1,735,189	4,812,916
1901-2	2,047,489	7,691,513	1906-7	1,988,504	6,079,641	1911-12	1,733,188	6,275,463

CHICAGO FIRE STATISTICS SINCE 1863.

[From reports of fire marshals]

Years.	Fires	Property involved.	Loss	Insurance.	Average loss per fire.	Percentage of loss on property involved.	Population	Population to each fire	Loss per ea.cita
1863-4	186		$355,600	$212,500	$1,912	....	153,796	827	$2.31
1864-5	193		651,798	685,300	3,377	...	169,353	877	3.85
1865-6	243		1,216,466	941,602	5,003	...	178,492	735	6 82
1866 7	315	No record.	2,487,973	1,643,445	7,898	.....	200,413	636	12 41
1867-8	515		4,315,332	3,417,288	8,193	.....	226,236	439	19 07
1868-9	405		560,169	632,248	1,383	.....	252,054	622	2 22
1869-70	605		871,905	600,061	1 453	.....	279,330	466	3 12
1870-1	669		2,447,845	2,183,498	3,653	....	306,605	458	7 98
1871-2*	489		672,800	745,000	1,989	....	337,000	685	2 89
1872-3	441		680,099	3,763,275	1,543	....	367,398	833	1 85
1873-4	466	$7,041,700	1,013,246	3,641,735	2,175	14.39	381,403	818	2.66†
1874-5†	473	11,063,616	2,345,684	6,789,300	1,959	21.22	395,408	836	5.93
1875‡	3.2	4,601,770	127,014	2,328,150	386	2.76	401,535	1,209	.43
1876	477	9,173,004	387,951	3,780,060	813	4 23	407,661	855	.95
1877	445	10,868,921	1,044,997	6,173,575	2,348	9.62	442,196	949	2 48
1878	478	6,751,234	306,317	3,327,348	641	4.54	436,731	914	.70
1879	638	11,501,473	573,082	5,112,631	897	4.97	469,515	736	1 22
1880	804	14,752,066	1,135,816	5,409,480	1,413	7 70	503,298	626	2 26
1881	895	19,788 508	921,495	9,662,326	1,030	4 67	531,996	594	1.73
1882	981	26,435,705	569,865	12,587,090	581	2 16	560,493	572	1.02
1883	1,153	42,383,215	1,379,736	21,790,767	1,197	3 26	595,339	517	2.32
1884	1,278	22,655,601	968,229	12,048,663	758	4 27	629,985	492	1 54
1885	1,209	48,055,541	2 225,184	22 404,225	1,700	4 06	661,923	506	3 36
1886	1,543	43,646,453	1,492,084	22,676,518	967	3 42	693,861	450	2.15
1887	1,853	62,241,191	1,839,058	22,695,202	992	2 95	748,256	404	2.46
1888	1,871	76,618,085	1,363,427	33,610,407	729	1 78	802,651	429	1 70
1889	2,075	66,409,323	2,154,340	34,440,627	1,033	3 24	1,000,000	482	2.15
1890	2,755	108,650,005	2,092,071	47,937,840	759	1.93	1,099,133	397	1.91
1891	3,353	124,003,193	3,053 874	59,703,511	911	2 46	1,147,000	342	2.66
1892	3,649	123,482,011	1 521,445	65,535,291	429	1 23	1,197,000	337	1 27
1893	5,224	330,028,212	3,149,590	180,937,590	603	.95	1,250,000	239	2 52
1894	5,174	129,046,541	3,254,140	72,185,581	629	2 52	1,305,000	252	2 49
1895	5,416	120,794,760	2,974,760	73,443,646	560	2 37	1,362,000	256	2 19
1896	4,414	97,061 640	1,979,355	59,970,130	448	2 04	1,427,000	323	1 39
1897	5,326	98,882,270	2,272,990	65,233,596	425	2.30	1,485,000	279	1.53
1898	5,048	91,922,210	2,651,735	56,550,470	525	2.88	1,558,000	309	1.70
1899	6,031	128,304,413	4,534,065	70,851,165	752	3 53	1,626,000	270	2.79
1900	5 503	112,599 125	2,213,699	72,893,463	402	1.98	1,698,575	309	1.30
1901	6,136	133,195,220	4,296 433	83,079,743	700	3.22	1,747,286	285	2.46
1902	5,125	112,998,325	4,118,933	71,615,759	803	3.64	1,795,897	350	2.29
1903	6,054	111,743,441	3,062 931	65,748 203	489	2 73	1,844,566	305	1 66
1904	6,661	122,075,301	2,950,254	77,224,240	443	2.40	1,893,219	284	1 56
1905	6,622	117,497,315	3,303 929	76,553,530	507	2.81	1,941,880	298	1 70
1906	6,187	119,974,033	4,179,235	75,358 085	654	3.49	1,990,541	312	2 01
1907	6,257	142,900,863	3,937,105	92,575 189	629	2.76	2,039,202	326	1 93
1908	7,793	114,527,300	3,873,444	72,048,810	497	3 38	2,087,862	268	1 86
1909	7,414	135,730,618	3,046,797	90,950,970	411	2 24	2,136,525	288	1 43
1910	9,083	129,674,681	4,884,793	83,808,768	538	3,77	2,185,283	241	2.24
1911	9,151	121 156,470	3,864,123	80,653,116	422	3 19	2,262,756	247	1.71
1912	9,410	125,860,590	4,352,470	88,656,020	463	3.47	2,307,538	245	1.89

*The great fire not included. †The large fire included ‡Nine months, ending Dec. 31, 1875,

MAYORS OF CHICAGO.

Their politics and order and year of election.

No. Name.	Party.	Elected.	Died.
1. William B. Ogden	Democratic	1837	1877
2. Buckner S Morris	Whig	1838	1879
3. Benjamin W. Raymond.	Whig	1839	1883
4. Alexander Lloyd	Democratic	1840	1872
5. Francis C. Sherman.	Democratic	1841	1870
6. Benjamin W. Raymond	Democratic	1842	1883
7. Augustus Garrett	Democratic	1843	1848
8 Alson S Sherman	Democratic	1844	1903
9. Augustus Garrett	Democratic	1845	1848
10 John P Chapin	Whig	1846	1864
11 James Curtiss	Democratic	1847	1860
12 James H. Woodworth	Dem -Whig.	1848	1869
13 James H. Woodworth	Dem -Whig	1849	1869
14. James Curtiss	Democratic	1850	1860
15. Walter S Gurnee	Democratic	1851	1903
16. Walter S Gurnee	Democratic	1852	1903
17. Charles M Gray	Democratic	1853	1885
18. Isaac L. Milliken	Democratic	1854	1889
19 Levi D Boone	Knownothing	1855	1882
20 Thomas Dyer	Democratic	1856	1862
21 John Wentworth	Rep -Fusion	1857	1888
22 John C Haines	Republican	1858	1896
23. John C Haines	Republican	1859	1896
24. John Wentworth	Republican	1860	1888
25. Julian S Rumsey	Republican	1861	1886
26 Francis C. Sherman.	Democratic	1862	1870
27 Francis C Sherman*..	Democratic	1863	1870
28. John B Rice.	Republican	1865	1874

No. Name.	Party	Elected.	Died.
29. John B. Rice	Republican	1867	1874
30 Roswell B. Mason	People's	1869	1892
31 Joseph Medill	Citizens'†	1871	1899
32. Harvey D Colvin	People's	1873	1892
33. Thomas Hoyne	Republican	1875	1894
34. Monroe Heath	Republican	1876	1894
35. Monroe Heath	Republican	1877	1894
36. Carter H. Harrison, Sr.	Democratic.	1879	1893
37. Carter H Harrison, Sr	Democratic	1881	1893
38. Carter H. Harrison, Sr	Democratic	1883	1893
39. Carter H Harrison, Sr	Democratic	1885	1893
40. John A. Roche	Republican	1887	1904
41. DeWitt C. Cregier	Democratic	1889	1898
42. Hempstead Washburne	Republican	1891	
43. Carter H Harrison, Sr	Democratic	1893	1893
44 John P. Hopkins	Democratic	1893	
45. George B. Swift	Republican	1895	1912
46. Carter H Harrison, Jr	Democratic	1897	
47. Carter H Harrison, Jr	Democratic	1899	
48. Carter H. Harrison, Jr	Democratic	1901	
49. Carter H Harrison, Jr	Democratic	1903	
50 Edward F Dunne	Democratic	1905	
51. Fred A Busse	Republican	1907	
52. Carter H Harrison, Jr	Democratic	1911	

*Two-year terms for mayor began in 1863 †"Fire-proof" ticket. ‡Four-year term for mayor began in 1907.

CHICAGO POSTOFFICE.

Entrances on Adams, Clark and Dearborn streets; telephone Harrison 4700; private exchange, all departments.

Postmaster—Daniel A. Campbell; room 358, south wing.

Secretary to Postmaster—John T. McGrath, room 358, south wing.

Assistant Postmaster—John M. Hubbard; room 357, south wing.

Auditor—John Matter; room 362, south wing.

Superintendent of Mails—Frank H. Galbraith; room 350, south wing.

Superintendent of Delivery—L. T. Steward; room 379, west wing.

Superintendent of Registry Division—Perry H. Smith, Jr.; room 102, Adams street lobby.

Superintendent of Money-Order Division—Joseph B. Schlossman; room 403, north wing.

Superintendent of Inquiry Division—D. J. Foster, room 706.

Superintendent Second-Class Matter—Michael J. O'Malley, room 703.

Superintendent of Bureau of Printing and Supplies —James N. Brady; 712 West Monroe street.

Cashier—Theron W. Bean; room 125, Dearborn street lobby.

Draftsman—M. L. Kirchman; room 379, west wing.

Secretary Civil-Service Board—Peter Newton, 13th floor.

Inspector in Charge—James E. Stuart; room 334, east wing.

Superintendent 6th Division, Railway Mail Service —E. L. West; room 308, north wing.

CARRIER STATIONS AND SUPERINTENDENTS.

Armour—3017 Indiana avenue; Henry Welch, Jr.

Auburn Park—612 West 79th street; David Herriott.

Austin—5658-5660 West Lake street; Howard Robertson.

C—1247-1249 West Madison street; George Berz.

Canal—Washington street, between Clinton and Canal; Robert T. Howard.

Carpenter Street—741 and 745 North Carpenter street; Frank A. Kwasigroch.

Chicago Lawn—3510 West 63d street; Martin McVeagh.

Cragin—4207 Armitage avenue; Peter J. O'Connor.

D—2108-2110 West Madison street; John Davy.

Danphin Park—9033 Cottage Grove avenue; George B. Grunau.

Douglas Park—1205-1207 South Western avenue; Albert P. Treleaven.

Dunning—6443 West Irving Park boulevard; Milton M. Potter.

Eastside—9909 Ewing avenue; Walter G. Seborg.

Edgewater—5501-5503 Evanston avenue; Michael J. Keigher.

Elsdon—3435 West 51st street; Leonard Withall.

Englewood—449 West 63d street; John E. Vreeland.

Fifty-First Street—5052 and 5054 Halsted street; Frederick A. Bosworth.

Garfield Park—3907-3909 West Madison street; David J. Geary.

Grand Crossing—7462 South Chicago avenue; Eben J. Beach.

Hawthorne Station—3647-3649 Ogden avenue; Edward O'Connell.

Hegewisch—13305 Erie avenue; Frank Lonn.

Hyde Park—1448-1450 East 55th street; Wilbur E. Crumbacker.

Irving Park—4218 West Irving Park boulevard; John T. McCormick.

Jackson Park—1113-1115 East 63d street; William Arens.

Jefferson—4841 Milwaukee avenue; Ernest Willman.

Chicago Avenue station—210 West Chicago avenue; William S. Snorf.

Lake View—929-931 Belmont avenue; W. S. Hussander.

Lincoln Park—1546-1548 North Clark street; William R. Rennacker.

Logan Square—2311-2313 Milwaukee avenue; James Stott.

M—40th street and Cottage Grove avenue; James N. McArthur.

McKinley Park—3475 and 3477 Archer avenue; Henry Blattner.

Mont Clare—2314-2316 North 70th avenue (vacancy).

Morgan Park—Frederick W. Dayton.

North Halsted—2454-2458 North Halsted street; William J. Beeslenberg.

Norwood Park—6040 Avondale avenue; Stanley C. de Long.

Ogden Park Station—1714 and 1716 West 63d street; Albert L. Anderson.

Pilsen—1507-1509 West 18th street; Joseph H. Richak.

Pullman—4 Arcade building; Gustav A. Ernst.

Ravenswood—4202 West Ravenswood Park; Redmond P. Hogan.

Riverdale—13565 Indiana avenue; Jeremiah F. Collins.

Rogers Park—7001 North Clark street; George Bartlett.

South Chicago—9210 Commercial avenue; Patrick T. O'Sullivan.

Stockyards—4193 Halsted street; Henry C. Smale.

Twentieth Street Station—1927 Indiana avenue; Thomas A. Kenny.

Washington Heights—1260 West 103d street; William D. Giesman.

West Pullman—12005 Halsted street; Frank M. Turner.

Wicker Park—1633-1645 Milwaukee avenue; C. W. Worthington.

STATIONS WITHOUT CARRIERS.

Masonic Temple—159 North State street; Laurence J. P. White.

South Water—207 North LaSalle street; H. H. Henshaw.

Stock Exchange—30 North LaSalle street; Cassius C. Roberts.

Sheridan Park—William L. Blood.

In addition to the above there are 286 numbered stations served from the carrier stations and each with a clerk in charge.

There are 3,921 clerks in the general postoffice and stations and 2,039 carriers, including collectors.

COLLECTIONS AND DELIVERIES.

In the downtown district there are twenty-six collections of mail matter between 7 a. m. and 11 p. m.; in the outlying districts there are from four to twelve collections. Mail is delivered six times a day in the business district and three times in the outlying districts.

Special delivery letters are delivered in the central postoffice district between 7 a. m. and 11 p. m. and from stations within their respective districts between 7 a. m. and 6 p. m. Special delivery mail received in special delivery section which can reach the point of delivery up to approximately 11 p. m. daily will be given service throughout the city.

In the district bounded by the Chicago river on the north and west, and on the south by 12th street, hotels, clubs, newspapers, telegraph offices and undertakers have all-night service.

POSTAL RECEIPTS.

Fiscal year 1913.

Stamps	$19,556,623.56
Postal cards	935,670.09
Envelopes	1,298,595.34
Second-class postage	933,672.59
Third and fourth class postage	830,233.99
Postage due	111,603.65
Box rent, waste paper, etc.	21,478.81

Total $23,597,878.03

Increase over 1912, $2,971,282.26 or 13 41-100 per cent.

REGISTERED MAIL.

Fiscal year 1913.

Letters registered with fee prepaid	1,406,359
Parcels registered with fee prepaid	526,285
Registered letters received for delivery	2,471,776
Registered parcels received for delivery	401,475
Official registered fee prepaid	23,960
Distribution, foreign mail re-registered free, forwarded, returned, missent and dead letters	329,846
Exchange office articles received in transit	58,253

Registered jackets and sack jackets received
and opened.................................... 123,455
Registered jackets and sack jackets made
up and dispatched............................ 23,085
Through registered pouches and inner sacks
received..................................... 95,982
Through registered pouches and inner sacks
made up and dispatched...................... 95,766
Official letters and parcels registered free... 209,683

Total number of registered articles handled.5,766,030

MONEY-ORDER BUSINESS (MAIN OFFICE).
Fiscal year 1913.

Domestic orders paid (20,009,204), $111,665,709.61.
International orders paid (43,835), $1,096,566.91.
Domestic orders issued (164,564), $1,953,498.87.
International orders issued (38,417), $818,910.61.
Total fees (domestic), $12,277.78.
Total fees (international), $12,059.60.
Certificates of deposit issued (156,930), $125,858,575.62.
Transferred to credit postmaster-general, $22,820,000.
Transferred to stations account, $359,250.
Auditor's circulars, $2,680.73.
P. M. drafts on New York, $350,000.

STATIONS, 1913.

Number of domestic orders issued, 1,208,136.
Amount received for domestic orders issued (including fees), $10,369,323.88.
Increase in transactions (domestic), 6.93 per cent.
Increase in amount (domestic), 5.51 per cent.
Number of international orders issued, 206,917.
Amount received for international orders issued (including fees), $4,355,076.50.
Increase in transactions (international), 1.58 per cent.
Decrease in amount (international), 0.39 per cent.

DELIVERY DIVISION.

Amount of mail matter of all classes received for delivery during the fiscal year ended June 30, 1913:
Mail letters, 287,171,762.
Local letters, 234,958,715.
Mail letters received at stations, 123,073,612.
Local letters received at stations, 100,696,592.
Total number of letters, 745,900,681.
Newspapers, circulars, etc., 152,363,639.
Grand total of all classes of matter received for delivery, 898,264,320.

MAILING DIVISION.

Mails handled in the mailing division during the fiscal year ended June 30, 1913:

	Pounds.	Pieces.
Letters	23,623,411	1,110,300,320
Specials	32,595	814,891
Nixies*	524,143	13,103,599
Second class	93,367,259	373,469,036
Third and fourth class	82,400,320	329,691,280
Total	199,947,728	1,827,289,126
Increase	11,704,879	133,353,854

Percentage increase in weight, 6.22.
Percentage increase in pieces, 7.87.
Proportion of errors in handling mail, .006.
*Mail received with insufficient postage or misdirected.

POSTAL SAVINGS BANK.

The postal savings bank was opened at the main postoffice, Chicago, Aug. 1, 1911. Any one 10 years old or over may open an account. No account may be opened for less than $1, nor will fractions of a dollar be accepted for deposit. No person is permitted to deposit more than $100 in any one calendar month, nor to have a total balance to his credit at one time of more than $500, exclusive of accumulated interest.

Deposits are evidenced by postal savings certificates issued in denominations of $1, $2, $5, $10, $20, $50 and $100.

Depositors of the postal savings system by applying therefor thirty days in advance may exchange the whole or a part of their deposits on Jan. 1 or July 1 of each year for United States registered or coupon bonds in denominations of $20, $100 and $500, bearing interest at the rate of 2½ per cent per annum, payable semiannually, and redeemable at the pleasure of the United States after one year from the date of issue, both principal and interest payable twenty years from that date in United States gold coin.

Postal savings banks have also been established at the following postal stations: Armour, Auburn Park, Austin, C. Carpenter street, Chicago Lawn, Cragin, D, Dauphin Park, Douglas park, Eastside, Edgewater, Elsdon, Englewood, 51st street, Garfield park, Grand Crossing, Hawthorne, Hegewisch, Hyde Park, Irving Park, Jackson park, Jefferson, Lake View, Lincoln park, Logan square, M, McKinley park, North Halsted, Norwood Park, Ogden park, Pilsen, Pullman, Ravenswood, Riverdale, Rogers Park, South Chicago, Stockyards, 20th street, Washington Heights, West Pullman, Wicker Park and at Morgan Park, branch postoffice.

MAIL TIME FROM CHICAGO TO PRINCIPAL CITIES.

Cities.	Hours.	Cities.	Hours.	Cities.	Hours.
Atlanta, Ga.	22	Little Rock, Ark.	24	Portland, Me.	33
Baltimore, Md.	23	Los Angeles, Cal.	66	Portland, Ore.	75
Boston, Mass.	27	Louisville, Ky.	10	Providence, R. I.	28
Buffalo, N. Y.	12	Memphis, Tenn.	16	Quebec, Can.	47
Charleston, S. C.	33	Mexico City, Mexico.	120	Richmond, Va.	26
Chihuahua, Mexico.	72	Milwaukee, Wis.	2	St. Louis, Mo.	8
Cincinnati, O.	10	Minneapolis, Minn.	17	St. Paul, Minn.	11
Cleveland, O.	9	Mobile, Ala.	27	Salt Lake City, Utah.	46
Denver, Col.	28	Monterey, Mexico.	98	San Antonio, Tex.	50
Des Moines, Iowa.	9	Montreal, Can.	27	San Francisco, Cal.	75
Detroit, Mich.	7	Newark, N. J.	25	Seattle, Wash.	75
Guadalajara, Mexico.	120	New Haven, Conn.	30	Toronto, Ont.	18
Halifax, N. S.	60	New Orleans, La.	28	Vancouver, B. C.	92
Houston, Tex.	40	New York, N. Y.	24	Washington, D. C.	24
Indianapolis, Ind.	5	Omaha, Neb.	12	Wheeling, W. Va.	15
Jacksonville, Fla.	37	Philadelphia, Pa.	22	Winnipeg, Man.	29
Kansas City, Mo.	11	Pittsburgh, Pa.	13		

Note—Certain limited trains make the time to New York, 18; Philadelphia, 17; Pittsburgh, 9, and Baltimore, 21 hours; Boston, 24; Newark, N. J., 18; Washington, D. C., 22.

MAIL TIME FROM NEW YORK TO FOREIGN CITIES.

Distances via postal routes in statute miles. Time given makes liberal allowance for delays. To get time and distance from Chicago add one day and 912 miles if via London and subtract one day and 912 miles if via San Francisco; via New Orleans the time is about one day less from Chicago to points in Central America. From table prepared by postoffice department.

Place.	Days.	Miles.	Place.	Days.	Miles.	Place.	Days.	Miles.
Adelaide, via San Francisco	34	12,845	Auckland, N. Z., via San Francisco	19	10,120	Barcelona, via London.	10	4,790
Alexandria, Egypt, via London	13	6,150	Basel, via London.	9	4,420	Batavia, via London.	34	12,830
Amsterdam, via London.	9	3,995	Bangkok, via London.	41	13,125	Berlin, via London.	9	4,385
Antwerp, via London.	9	4,000	Bangkok, via San Francisco	43	12,990	Bern, via London.	9	4,490
Athens, via London.	12	5,655	Barbados, W. I.	8	2,145	Bombay, via London.	24	9,765
						Bremen, via London.	8	4,235
						Brindisi, via London.	10	5,205

Place.	Days.	Miles.	Place.	Days.	Miles.	Place.	Days.	Miles.
Brussels, via London....	9	3,975	Gibraltar, via London...	11	5,150	Iceland, via London.....	18	5,350
Budapest, via London...	10	4,910	Glasgow	10	3,370	Kingston, Jamaica.......	5	1,820
Buenos Aires............	26	8,045	Gothenburg, via London.	9	4,755	Lisbon, via London......	10	5,335
Cadiz, via London......	10	5,375	Guatemala City, via New			Liverpool	8	3,540
Cairo, Egypt, via London.	12	6,280	Orleans	7	2,645	London	8	3,740
Calcutta, via London....	26	11,120	Hague, The, via London	9	3,950	Lyons, via London......	9	4,340
Callao, via Panama.....	22	4,145	Hamburg, direct.........	9	4,820	Madrid, via London.....	9	4,925
Cape Town, via London..	27	11,245	Hamilton, Bermuda......	2	780	Marseilles, via London..	9	4,560
Christiania, via London.	10	4,650	Havana	3	1,368	Melbourne, via San Fran-		
Colon, Panama..........	6	2,281	Havre, direct...........	8	3,340	cisco	26	12,265
Constantinople, via Lon-			Hongkong, via San Fran-			Montevideo	25	7,165
don	11	5,810	cisco	25	10,590	Moscow, via London.....	10	5,535
Dresden, via London....	9	4,555	Honolulu, via San Fran-			Munich, via London.....	9	4,610
Genoa, via London......	9	4,615	cisco	13	5,645			

PROGRESS OF CHICAGO SINCE 1850.

(For corresponding data for 1913 consult index.)

	1850.	1860.	1870.	1880.	1890.	1900.	1910.
Area ....sq.miles	14.0	17.9	35.6	35.6	179.1	190.6	191.3
Population	28,269	109,206	298,977	503,298	1,099,850	1,698,679	2,185,283
Valuation ......dols.	7,220,249	37,053,512	275,986,550	117,133,726	219,354,388	276,565,880	*848,994,536
Tax levy........dols.	25,271	373,315	4,139,799	3,899,127	9,558,335	18,384,195	23,485,533
Bonded debt....dols.	93,395	2,336,000	11,041,000	12,752,000	13,545,400	16,328,400	26,229,642
Receipts—Flour brls.	....	713,348	1,766,037	3,215,389	4,338,058	9,513,591	8,006,283
Wheat ....bu.	1,687,465	14,927,083	17,394,409	23,541,607	14,248,770	48,048,298	27,540,100
Corn ....bu.	2,869,329	15,862,394	20,189,175	97,272,844	91,387,754	134,663,456	102,592,850
Total grain.....bu.	6,928,459	37,235,027	60,432,574	165,855,370	219,052,518	349,637,295	294,858,724
Cattle ....No.	....	....	532,964	1,382,477	3,484,280	3,039,206	3,062,958
Shipments—							
Flour ....brls.	100,871	698,132	1,705,977	2,862,737	4,134,586	7,396,697	7,038,351
Wheat ....bu.	883,644	12,402,197	16,422,585	22,796,288	11,975,276	36,649,956	18,679,100
Corn ....bu.	262,013	13,700,113	17,777,377	93,572,934	90,674,379	111,039,653	78,623,100
Total grain.....bu.	1,830,968	31,108,759	54,745,903	154,377,115	204,674,918	265,552,246	214,901,980
Hogs packed.....No.	20,000	151,339	688,149	4,680,637	4,473,467	7,119,440	3,161,552
Imports, value..dols.	....	....	....	6,955,234	15,406,786	15,441,320	28,281,331
Vessel arrivals..tons	....	....	3,043,265	4,616,969	5,138,253	7,044,995	9,439,074
Clearances ....tons	....	....	2,983,942	4,627,382	5,189,665	7,141,105	9,470,572
Manufactures, value							
................dols.	....	20,000,000	92,518,742	249,022,948	664,567,927	888,945,311	†1,281,313,000
Bank clearings..dols.	....	....	810,676,026	1,725,684,894	4,093,145,904	6,799,535,598	13,939,689,984.43
Internal revenue col-							
lections ......dols.	....	....	8,395,132	8,936,615	13,518,996	13,391,410	11,652,567.87
National bank depos-							
its ....dols.	....	....	16,774,514	{ 64,764,000 }	105,785,470	231,386,146	403,941,474
State bank deposits							
................dols.	....	....	....		41,679,296	158,238,138	430,468,495
Postoffice repts..dols.	....	....	1,071,342	1,446,014	3,318,989	7,063,704	18,502,954
Water used per day							
................gals.	590,000	4,703,525	21,766,260	57,384,376	152,372,288	322,599,630	517,117,000
Pipe ....miles	30.0	91.0	272.4	455.4	1,205.0	1,872.0	2,272
Revenue ....dols.	....	131,162	539,180	865,618	2,109,508	3,250,481	5,685,005
Policemen ....No.	9	100	274	473	1,900	2,800	4,260
Schools ....No.	7	14	59	73	238	329	280
Teachers ......No.	35	123	572	898	2,711	5,321	6,383
Pupils ....No.	3,000	14,199	40,832	59,562	135,541	255,861	300,893

*One-third of full value. †In 1909.

CHICAGO JUVENILE COURT PROCEEDINGS.

	1910.	1911.	1912.
Delinquent boys in court...........	1,161	1,320	1,105
Delinquent girls in court...........	475	483	537
Dependent boys in court...........	961	1,076	1,363
Dependent girls in court...........	699	920	1,235
Delinquents put on probation.......	709	715	818
Dependents put on probation.......	452	779	599
Delinquents sent to institutions.....	741	847	611
Dependents sent to institutions.....	1,075	1,068	1,422
Delinquents dismissed...............	171	203	178
Dependents dismissed...............	68	107	107
Boys held to grand jury.............		2	2

	Dec.1, 1907.	Dec.1, 1908.	Dec.1, 1909.	Dec.1, 1910.	Dec.1, 1911.	Dec.1, 1912.
Delinquent boys..	2,540	1,779	1,283	1,081	892	707
Delinquent girls..	396	236	325	294	351	392
Total	2,936	2,115	1,608	1,375	1,243	1,199
Total boys.......	3,294	2,758	1,802	1,585	1,556	1,437
Total girls.......	1,201	987	955	938	1,206	1,194
Total	4,495	3,345	2,757	2,523	2,762	2,631

JUVENILE DETENTION HOME.
Year ended Nov. 30, 1912.

Delinquent boys received......................	2,658
Delinquent girls received.....................	566
Dependent boys received......................	455
Dependent girls received.....................	354
Total number received........................	4,033
Daily average population..,..................	86
Total meals for children......................	87,936

TOTAL CHILDREN ON PROBATION.

	Dec.1, 1907.	Dec.1, 1908.	Dec.1, 1909.	Dec.1, 1910.	Dec.1, 1911.	Dec.1, 1912.
Dependent boys..	754	579	549	504	644	640
Dependent girls..	805	651	630	644	855	802
Total	1,559	1,230	1,179	1,148	1,519	1,442

RULER OF ALBANIA CHOSEN.

Prince Albert of Wied was selected by the powers in December, 1913, to be king of Albania, the new autonomous state created as a result of the war of the Balkan states against Turkey. The new king is 41 years old, is a nephew of Carmen Sylva, queen of Roumania, and was married in 1898 to Princess Pauline of Wurttemberg.

POLICE DISTRICTS, PRECINCTS AND STATIONS.

General headquarters in city hall.

Chicago is divided for police purposes into twenty-two districts and forty-four precincts, as follows:

Dist. Prec.   Station.
1...... 1....*180 North LaSalle street.
2...... 2....*625 South Clark street.
3...... 3....*210 West 22d street.
     4...... 2523 Cottage Grove avenue.
4...... 5.... 454 East 35th street.
     6....*740 West 35th street.
5...... 7.... 2913 Loomis street.
     8....*3900 South California avenue.
6....10....*5233 Lake avenue.
    11.... 5001 South State street.
7....12....*6346 Jefferson avenue.
    13.... 834 East 75th street.
    14.... 200 East 115th street.
8....15....*2938 East 89th street.
    16.... 3525 East 106th street.
9....17....*6347 Wentworth avenue.
    18.... 8501 South Green street.
10....19....*4736 South Halsted street.
    20.... 1760 West 47th street.
11....21....*943 Maxwell street.
    22.... 2075 Canalport avenue.

Dist. Prec.   Station.
12....23....*1700 West 21st place.
    25.... 2656 South Lawndale avenue.
13....24.... 2250 West 13th street.
    26....*4001 Filmore street.
14....27....*120 North Desplaines street.
    28.... 1637 West Lake street.
15....29....*2433 Warren avenue.
    30.... 4250 West Lake street.
    31.... 5619 West Lake street.
16....32....*1123 West Chicago avenue.
    33.... 1312 West North avenue.
17....34.... 2256 West North avenue.
    35....*2138 North California avenue.
18....36....*3973 Milwaukee avenue.
    37.... 4905 Grand avenue.
19....38....*113 West Chicago avenue.
    39.... 1501 Hudson avenue.
20....40.... 2126 North Halsted street.
    41....*2742 Sheffield avenue.
21....42....*3600 North Halsted street.
    43.... 3801 North Robey street.
22....44....*1940 Foster avenue.
    45.... 7075 North Clark street.

*District headquarters.

WORK OF THE POLICE DEPARTMENT (1912).

PERSONS ARRAIGNED IN COURT.

	Male.	Female.	Total.
Total number..........	74,292	9,561	83,852
Married	24,822	3,129	27,951
Single	49,470	6,432	55,902
Under 16..............	59	10	69
From 16 to 20........	10,200	717	10,917
From 20 to 25........	17,826	2,705	20,531
From 25 to 30........	14,593	2,145	16,738
From 30 to 40........	18,069	2,585	20,654
From 40 to 50........	9,039	993	10,032
From 50 to 60........	3,439	276	3,715
Over 60..............	1,069	130	1,197

OCCUPATION OF PRISONERS.

Actors	177	Machinists	1,510
Agents	776	Masons	325
Artists	14	Merchants	962
Attorneys	102	Midwives	13
Bakers	359	Milkmen	88
Barbers	529	Miners	20
Barkeepers	822	Molders	254
Billposters	25	Musicians	227
Blacksmiths	223	No occupation......10,195
Boilermakers	138	Painters	1,246
Brokers	109	Patternmakers	7
Butchers	556	Peddlers	2,376
Carpenters	1,162	Physicians	318
Chauffeurs	4,079	Plasterers	173
Cigarmakers	192	Plumbers	391
Clergymen	19	Policemen	26
Clerks	4,199	Porters	1,131
Confectioners	46	Printers	718
Cooks	606	Prostitutes	648
Dentists	62	Roofers	107
Detectives	20	Sailors	187
Draftsmen	70	Salesmen	1,686
Druggists	98	Saloonkeepers	838
Electricians	584	Servants	413
Engineers	401	Shoemakers	211
Farmers	173	Soldiers	23
Firemen	305	Steamfitters	353
Florists	44	Stock dealers......	7
Grocers	219	Stonecutters	22
Harnessmakers	37	Street car employes	201
Horseshoers	107	Students	269
Housekeepers	3,774	Tailors	923
Janitors	555	Teamsters	6,693
Jewelers	87	Tinsmiths	127
Junk dealers.......	119	Undertakers	43
Laborers 18,257		Upholsterers	40
Lathers	68	Wagonmakers	17
Letter carriers....	23	Watchmen	212
Liverymen	40	Other occupations..11,685

NATIVITY OF PRISONERS.

	1912.	1911.	1910.	1909.	1908.	1907.
American ..46,773	42,729	40,395	36,174	33,627	31,084
Colored 6,603	5,049	5,434	4,852	3,871	4,653

	1912.	1911.	1910.	1909.	1908.	1907.
Austrian ...	1,040	1,817	1,808	1,486	998	896
Bohemian ..	909	1,050	1,320	1,051	1,044	1,067
Canadian ...	504	537	552	493	435	473
Chinese ...	456	245	83	134	168	187
Danish	350	356	280	293	258	223
English	566	667	655	593	517	485
French	223	236	189	220	205	199
German	4,975	4,645	4,071	4,214	4,370	4,001
Greek	1,889	1,793	1,391	997	1,069	899
Hollander ..	85	128	144	149	103	110
Italian	2,632	2,768	2,805	1,831	1,761	1,416
Irish	2,687	2,479	2,666	2,334	2,147	2,303
Norwegian..	530	598	657	550	568	506
Polish	5,430	6,728	6,527	5,180	5,459	4,572
Russian ...	3,411	3,655	3,326	2,557	2,319	1,937
Scotch	377	335	354	300	251	215
Swedish ...	1,541	1,460	1,589	1,368	1,164	1,223
Swiss	74	63	65	69	64	61
Others	2,987	2,411	2,320	1,79:	2,987	1,492

DISPOSITION OF CASES IN MUNICIPAL COURTS.

Held to grand jury........................	2,725
Held to Juvenile court....................	24
Sentenced to county jail..................	128
Sentenced to house of correction.........	1,209
Sentenced to other institutions..........	3
Fined 27,448	
Paroled	701
Released on peace bonds...................	88
Ordered to make weekly payments...........	910
Discharged 48,563	
Stricken from docket......................	3,415
Otherwise disposed of.....................	167
Total 85,381	

CLASSIFICATION OF CHARGES.

FELONIES.

	1912.	1911.	1910.	1909.	1908.
Abandonment of child	11	1	2	6	2
Abduction	36	22	23	18	26
Abortion	25	17	10	17	16
Arson or attempt to commit arson........	73	100	45	13	21
Bigamy	35	21	26	26	20
Burglary	1,012	1,183	1,124	1,229	1,634
Burglary, attempt to commit	81	87	58	73	83
Children, crime against	169	80	78	77	.....
Children, contributing to delinquency of....	821	666	692	523	.....
Confidence game......	740	641	599	621	647
Conspiracy	29	53	38	45	.....
Counterfeiting	3	7	.....	5	8
Embezzlement	167	272	234	230	137
Forgery	89	87	59	74	89
Having burglars' tools	23	5	3	8	.....

	1912.	1911.	1910.	1909.	1908.
Kidnaping	9	18	27	14	9
Larceny and larceny as bailee	4,138	3,977	4,007	4,369	5,224
Larceny, accessory to.	41	35	23	40	19
Larceny, attempt to commit	19	18	11	13	....
Malicious mischief....	227	212	219	264	231
Manslaughter	31	33	20	22	18
Mayhem	16	25	20	18	27
Murder	170	88	61	73	53
Murder, accessory to..	13	15	22	13	10
Murder, assault to commit	238	391	312	261	328
Perjury	53	16	9	19	19
Receiv'g stolen prop'y	240	389	413	465	429
Robbery	866	852	679	507	709
Robbery, accessory to.	16	18	23	9	17
Robbery, assault to commit	224	138	105	165	142

MISDEMEANOR.

Abandonment of wife or children	1,017	1,104	1,076	932	965
Assault	1,241	875	714	682	730

	1912.	1911.	1910.	1909.	1908.
Assault with deadly weapon	1,128	1,193	1,080	993	1,036
Carrying concealed weapon	1,129	1,203	970	836	948
Compounding a felony.	1	4	3	29	....
Cruelty to animals....	212	100	368	289	350
Cruelty to children....	1	12	14	11	26
Disorderly conduct....	43,635	49,384	51,791	43,398	40,875
Gaming devices, hav'g	3	29	35	94	112
Gaming house, inn. of	2,112	2,579	1,230	1,531	1,671
Gaming house, kprs. of	2,318	330	386	505	454
Intimidation	10	24	5	5	4
Imperson't'g an officer	53	43	54	65	60
Opium den, inmts. of..	358	34	37	102	176
Resisting an officer....	133	350	359	348	372
Riot	10	18	16	5	32
Selling liquor to minors or drunkards...	20	32	79	158	160
Vagrancy	850	795	1,572	1,040	1,196
Total*	86,950	84,838	81,269	70,575	68,220

*Including crimes not specified in above list.

SUMMARY OF POLICE WORK BY YEARS.

Year.	No. officers and men.	Arrests.*	Fines imposed.	Property recovered.	Salaries.	Miscellaneous expenditures.	Total expenditures.
1886	1,032	44,261	$202,036.00	$149,988.52	$1,084,259.25	$108,510.31	$1,192,769.56
1887	1,145	46,505	259,249.00	168,023.03	1,199,022.28	106,539.79	1,305,562.07
1888	1,255	50,432	305,176.00	193,141.67	1,297,379.20	177,756.12	1,475,135.32
1889	1,624	48,119	275,925.00	206,822.12	1,432,189.25	170,405.35	1,602,594.60
1890	1,900	62,230	363,938.00	228,885.73	2,066,308.92	133,818.04	2,200,126.96
1891	2,306	70,550	464,850.92	309,585.45	2,485,981.24	136,067.21	2,622,048.45
1892	2,726	82,832	615,822.10	319,305.00	2,822,220.27	212,823.65	3,035,043.92
1893	3,189	96,676	523,359.00	294,129.83	3,287,530.84	263,026.86	3,550,557.70
1894	3,188	88,323	452,340.00	392,032.14	3,433,129.30	210,806.87	3,643,936.17
1895	2,850	83,464	301,555.00	360,268.82	3,253,195.20	166,619.60	3,419,814.80
1896	3,033	96,847	300,319.00	429,882.00	3,150,569.19	153,839.58	3,304,408.77
1897	3,551	83,680	216,284.00	390,628.89	3,290,419.66	167,163.69	3,457,583.35
1898	3,594	77,441	212,056.00	372,934.73	3,281,092.08	160,777.77	3,441,869.85
1899	3,267	71,349	203,687.00	339,914.59	3,257,256.17	181,318.28	3,438,574.45
1900	3,314	70,438	219,902.00	414,181.37	3,230,627.63	154,532.41	3,385,160.04
1901	2,782	69,440	258,060.00	381,654.45	3,260,608.80	148,398.15	3,409,006.95
1902	2,732	70,314	245,440.00	436,792.73	3,179,948.96	158,833.67	3,338,782.63
1903	2,773	77,763	330,026.00	392,181.63	3,420,079.92	149,397.85	3,569,477.77
1904	2,676	79,026	393,003.00	298,696.07	3,363,059.47	182,882.36	3,545,941.83
1905	2,590	82,572	440,021.00	382,159.61	3,551,447.60	409,826.87	3,961,274.47
1906	3,578	91,471	527,450.00	545,043.35	3,796,430.94	274,771.42	4,071,202.36
1907	4,110	63,132	477,969.00	498,571.63	4,822,509.36	565,600.65	5,388,110.01
1908	4,293	68,220	384,518.00	668,286.17	5,407,117.87	296,799.46	5,703,917.33
1909	4,706	70,575	364,509.00	735,957.76	5,544,545.68	266,072.89	5,810,618.57
1910	4,360	81,269	445,292.00	1,145,451.00	5,611,840.47	213,614.40	5,825,454.87
1911	4,437	84,838	531,316.00	1,634,148.46	5,846,167.53	295,464.80	6,141,632.32
1912	4,436	86,950	539,615.00	1,762,599.26	6,343,897.35	293,554.63	6,687,451.98

*Charges brought.

EXECUTIONS IN COOK COUNTY.

John Stone............July 10, 1840	George H. Painter....Jan. 26, 1894	George Dolinski.......Oct. 11, 1901
William Jackson....June 19, 1857	Thomas ("Buff") Higgins....	Louis G. Toombs....Aug. 8, 1902
Albert Staub.........April 20, 1858	...................March 23, 1894	Louis Pesant........April 15, 1904
Michael McNamee...May 6, 1859	Patrick E. J. Prendergast....	Peter Niedemeyer...April 22, 1904
Walter Fleming....Dec. 15, 1865	...................July 13, 1894	Gustav Marx.........April 22, 1904
Jerry Corbett.......Dec. 15, 1865	Harry ("Butch") Lyons....	Harvey Van Dine....April 22, 1904
George Driver.......March 14, 1873	...................Oct. 11, 1895	Frank Lewandowski.Sept. 30, 1904
Chris Rafferty......Feb. 27, 1874	Henry Foster (col.)..Jan. 24, 1896	John Johnson........Jan. 20, 1905
George Sherry......June 21, 1878	Alfred C. Fields (col.).May 15, 1896	Robert E. Newcomb..Feb. 16, 1906
Jeremiah Connolly...June 21, 1878	Joseph Windrath.....June 5, 1896	John Miller.........Feb. 16, 1906
James Tracey.......Sept. 15, 1882	Julius Manow........Oct. 30, 1896	Johann Hoch........Feb. 16, 1906
Isaac Jacobsen......Sept. 19, 1884	Daniel McCarthy.....Feb. 19, 1897	Richard G. Ivens....June 22, 1906
Ignazio Sylvestri....Nov. 14, 1885	John Lattimore (col.).May 28, 1897	Daniel Francis (col.).Oct. 12, 1906
Agostino Gilardo....Nov. 14, 1885	Wm. T. Powers (col.).May 28, 1897	Richard Walton (col.).Dec. 13, 1907
Giovanni Azzaro....Nov. 14, 1885	Chris Merry.........April 22, 1898	William Johnson (col.).Oct. 22, 1909
Frank Mulkowski...March 26, 1886	John Druggan........Oct. 14, 1898	Ewald Shiblawski....Feb. 16, 1912
Albert Parsons......Nov. 11, 1887	George H. Jacks......Oct. 14, 1898	Frank Shiblawski....Feb. 16, 1912
August Spies........Nov. 11, 1887	Robert Howard (col.).Feb. 17, 1899	Philip Sommerling...Feb. 16, 1912
George Engel........Nov. 11, 1887	August A. Becker.....Nov. 10, 1899	Thomas Schultz......Feb. 16, 1912
Zephyr Davis (col.)...May 12, 1888	Michael E. Rollinger.Nov. 17, 1899	Thos. Jennings (col.)..Feb. 16, 1912

John Stone was executed publicly on the prairie on the south side. William Jackson and Albert Staub were also executed publicly, but on the west side. After that executions were private and took place in the courthouse until 1878, since which time they have taken place in the county jail on the north side. Rafferty was hanged in Waukegan for murder in Chicago. All the executions have been on Fridays except those of Sylvestri, Gilardo, Azzaro and Zephyr Davis, which occurred on Saturdays.

COST OF ELECTIONS IN CHICAGO AND COOK COUNTY.

[From a report prepared by the Chicago Bureau of Public Efficiency.]

Election costs for Chicago and Cook county almost reached the $1,000,000 mark in 1912. In 1896 expenditures for election purposes in the city of Chicago and town of Cicero amounted to $288,281.96. In 1912 the corresponding figures were $904,139.89. The election expenses paid by Cook county for 1912 for the portion of the county outside Chicago and Cicero aggregated $31,080.25, making the total of direct expenditures for the territory comprising the entire county, $935,220.14.

COST OF A CITY PRIMARY.

Pay of judges and clerks.......................	$33,225
Rental of polling places.......................	9,503
Printing ballots...............................	4,000
Cartage.......................................	2,000
Legal advertising.............................	1,000
Total direct expenditure...................	49,728

Note—The pay of judges and clerks is based upon a total of 1,329 precincts at $25 for each precinct. The number of precincts now is 1,266. The number of polling places is correspondingly reduced.

The cost of a judicial primary is about $55,728. The cost of a judicial election is practically the same.

COST OF A CITY ELECTION.

The pay of judges and clerks in a city election is for each precinct:

Election day..................................	$25
Registration day..............................	25
Canvass (two clerks)..........................	10
Revision night................................	25
Total..	85
Total 1,329 precincts.........................	112,965
Rental polling places.........................	20,135
Printing ballots..............................	4,000
Cartage.......................................	2,000
Legal advertising.............................	1,000
Total direct.................................	140,100

A biennial November election is more expensive than a city election because it involves two registration days instead of one, and larger bills for printing.

EXPENSES IN ELECTIONS SINCE 1895.

For territory under jurisdiction of the board of election commissioners—the city of Chicago and town of Cicero.

	Administration.	Election.	Primary.	Total.
1895......	$76,799.24	$174,241.62	....	$251,040.86
1896......	100,458.77	187,822.59	....	288,281.36
1897......	103,426.48	164,261.77	....	267,688.25
1898......	129,432.50	390,576.52	$42,700.71	472,709.73
1899......	114,470.30	139,320.12	18,977.89	272,768.31
1900......	151,442.72	300,924.77	44,617.29	496,984.78
1901......	98,048.74	156,385.68	23,926.51	278,360.93
1902......	111,687.64	327,726.95	56,492.99	495,907.58
1903......	105,348.47	193,536.36	26,216.06	325,100.89
1904......	129,600.77	337,399.65	48,951.69	515,842.11
1905......	127,418.92	295,914.90	57,963.46	481,297.28
1906......	148,522.65	378,063.54	92,858.37	619,444.56
1907......	134,715.89	288,502.33	30,684.38	453,903.60
1908......	180,506.10	348,082.40	76,643.27	605,232.77
1909......	165,286.69	219,409.50	91,221.79	475,918.07
1910......	181,967.91	358,988.82	77,493.73	618,450.46
1911......	207,455.84	368,503.20	98,096.26	674,055.30
1912......	224,346.00	384,736.34	106,357.55	*904,139.89

*188,500.00 for voting machines.

DISTRIBUTION OF EXPENSES.

The cost of maintaining the election machinery for the territory under the jurisdiction of the board of election commissioners—Chicago and Cicero—is apportioned among the governing authorities affected—Cook county, city of Chicago and town of Cicero. The county pays the salaries of the three election commissioners and their chief clerk and assistant chief clerk. Chicago and Cicero pay the other expenses of administering the office of the board of election commissioners. Chicago meets the expenses of the actual holding of elections which are directly chargeable to it. Cicero does likewise.

The county, besides paying its share of the cost of holding elections within the territory subject to the jurisdiction of the board of election commissioners, pays the expense of general elections and primaries for the portion of Cook county outside the jurisdiction of the election commissioners.

For municipal elections in Chicago, the city pays for the printing and delivery of ballots and cards of instructions. For other elections these expenses are borne by the county. For city elections, the salaries of judges and clerks are paid by the city; for other elections, the county pays these bills. The city pays the rent of the polling places within the city in all cases. Cicero pays like expenses for precincts within the town.

ELECTION CALENDAR UP TO 1919.

1914—City primaries in February.
Registration, canvass and revision days in March.
City election in April.
General primaries in April.
Two registration days and canvass and revision days in October.
General election in November.

1915—City primaries in February.
Registration, canvass and revision days in March.
City election in April.
Judicial primaries in April.
Judicial election in June.

1916—City primaries in February.
Registration, canvass and revision days in March.
City election in April.
General primaries in April.
Two registration days and canvass and revision days in October.
General election in November.

1917—City primaries in February.
Registration, canvass and revision days in March.
City election in April.
Judicial primaries in April.
Judicial election in November.

1918—City primaries in February.
Registration, canvass and revision days in March.
City election in April.
General primaries in April.
Two registration days and canvass and revision days in October.
General election in November.

1919—City primaries in February.
Registration, canvass and revision days in March.
City election in April.

CONCLUSIONS OF THE BUREAU.

The enormous expenditures for election purposes are due chiefly to the large number of primaries and elections. City and judicial primaries should be abolished. Nominations for city and judicial offices should be made by petition only and party columns and party designations should be eliminated from the election ballot. An average annual saving of $68,304 could be effected by the elimination of city and judicial primaries. The number of judicial and city elections should also be reduced. The legislature ought to remove from the existing statutes the provision making all primary and election days legal holidays.

"CLOSED" HOURS ON BRIDGES OF CHICAGO.

Following are the hours when the bridges of Chicago are closed to river traffic: Bridges on the main river, on the south branch as far south as 12th street, inclusive, and on the north branch to Kinzie street, inclusive, 6:30 to 9 a. m. and 4:30 to 6:30 p. m.; on the north branch from Kinzie, exclusive, to Halsted street, inclusive, and on the south branch from 12th street, exclusive, to Halsted street, inclusive, 6 to 7 a. m. and 5:30 to 6:30 p. m.; all other bridges from 6 to 7 a. m. and 6 to 7 p. m. Rush street bridge may be opened half an hour earlier in evening to admit passage of passenger boats.

BANKS AND BANK STATISTICS OF CHICAGO.

American State—1825 Blue Island avenue; capital, $200,000; president, John Karel; cashier, James F. Stepina.

Ashland State—1610 West 63d street; capital, $200,-000; president, John Bain; cashier, Edward T. Barry.

Austin State—South Park and South boulevard, Austin; capital, $100,000; president, Charles S. Castle; cashier, Perley D. Castle.

Bank of Montreal—108 South LaSalle; capital, $14,-400,000; manager Chicago branch, J. M. Greata.

Calumet National—9117 Commercial avenue; capital, $100,000; president, John Cunnea; cashier, John J. Cunnea.

Capital State Savings—5400 North Clark street; capital, $200,000; president, W. J. Klingenberg; cashier, E. F. Turnbloom.

Calumet Trust and Savings—2115 Morgan avenue; capital, $25,000; president, Frank Nay; cashier, F. Bateman.

Central Manufacturing District Bank—1112 West 35th street; capital, $250,000; president, Edward E. Payne; cashier, M. A. Graettinger.

Central Trust Company of Illinois—125 West Monroe street; capital, $4,500,000; president, Charles G. Dawes; cashier, William R. Dawes.

Chicago City Bank and Trust—6225 Halsted; capital, $500,000; president, Louis Rathje; cashier, E. H. Holtorff.

Chicago Savings and Trust—Chicago Savings Bank building, State and Madison; capital, $1,000,000; president, Lucius Teter; cashier, Henry C. Burnett.

Citizens' Trust and Savings—Garfield boulevard and State street; capital, $50,000; president, Oliver F. Smith; cashier, A. H. Luken.

Colonial Trust and Savings—137 South LaSalle; capital, $600,000; president, L. C. Rose; cashier, R. C. Keller.

Continental and Commercial National—72 West Adams street; capital, $21,500,000; president, George M. Reynolds; cashier, N. R. Losch.

Continental and Commercial Trust and Savings—Monroe and Clark; capital, $3,000,000; president, George M. Reynolds; cashier, Charles C. Willson.

Cook County State Savings—608 Blue Island avenue; capital, $50,000; president, Raymond Cardona.

Corn Exchange—LaSalle and Adams; capital, $3,-000,000; president, Ernest A. Hamill; cashier, J. Edward Maass.

Drexel State—3846 Cottage Grove avenue; capital, $300,000; president, Myron B. Cottrell; cashier, R. J. Neal.

Drovers' National—4201 Halsted; capital, $750,000; president, Edward Tilden; cashier, George M. Benedict.

Drovers' Trust and Savings—Union stockyards; capital, $250,000; president, William O. Cummings; cashier, Murray M. Otstott.

Edgewater—5545 Evanston avenue; capital, $25,000; president, W. H. Paisley; cashier, O. S. Paisley.

Englewood State—237 West 63d; capital, $200,000; president, John R. Burges; cashier, E. W. Stansbury.

First National—Dearborn and Monroe; capital, $10,-000,000; president, James B. Forgan; cashier, H. A. Howland.

First National of Englewood—349 West 63d; capital, $150,000; president, J. J. Nichols; cashier, V. E. Nichols.

First Trust and Savings—Dearborn and Monroe; capital, $5,000,000; president, J. B. Forgan; cashier, Burt O. Hardenbrook.

Foreman Bros. Banking Company—30 North LaSalle; capital, $1,000,000; president, Edwin G. Foreman; cashier, John Terborgh.

Fort Dearborn National—76 West Monroe; capital, $2,000,000; president, William A. Tilden; cashier, George H. Wilson.

Fort Dearborn Trust and Savings—76 West Monroe; capital, $250,000; president, William A. Tilden; cashier, John E. Shea.

Franklin Trust and Savings—Michigan avenue and 35th street; capital, $300,000; president, S. W. Straus; cashier, Edgar F. Olson.

Garfield Park State Savings—4004 West Madison street; capital, $200,000; president, J. E. Decker; cashier, A. A. Marquart.

Greenebaum Sons Bank and Trust Company—Clark and Randolph streets; capital, $1,500,000; president, Moses E. Greenebaum; cashier, Walter J. Greenebaum.

Guarantee Trust and Savings—835 West 63d; capital, $200,000; president, William H. C. Stege; cashier, C. H. Dehning.

Harris Trust and Savings—115 West Monroe; capital, $1,500,000; president, Albert W. Harris; cashier, John S. Brocksmit.

*Hibernian Banking Association—Clark and Monroe; capital, $2,000,000; president, George M. Reynolds; cashier, John W. MacGeagh.

Home Bank and Trust Company—Ashland and Milwaukee avenues; capital, $300,000; president, R. I. Terwilliger; cashier, L. H. Prybylski.

Hyde Park State—Lake avenue and 53d street; capital, $200,000; president, John A. Carroll; cashier, Thomas Jansen.

Illinois State Bank of Chicago—Clark and Kinzie streets; capital, $200,000; president, Louis Mayer; cashier, William H. Tholen.

Illinois Trust and Savings—LaSalle and Jackson; capital, $5,000,000; president, John J. Mitchell; cashier, Joseph I. Cooper.

Interstate National—13304 Erie avenue (Hegewisch); capital, $25,000; president, Lawrence Cox; cashier, William Sippel.

Jefferson Park National—4815 Milwaukee avenue; capital, $50,000; president, George M. Hayes; cashier, Fred H. Esdohr.

Kaspar State—1900 Blue Island avenue; capital, $400,000; president, William Kaspar; cashier, Joseph Sikyta.

Kenwood Trust and Savings—Grand boulevard and 47th; capital, $200,000; president, A. K. Brown; cashier, R. C. Kent.

Lake View State—3160 North Clark; capital, $200,-000; president, George W. McCabe; cashier, Joseph E. Olson.

Lake View Trust and Savings—3211 North Ashland avenue; capital, $200,000; president, Charles Johnson; cashier, J. H. Hahn.

LaSalle Street Trust and Savings—209 South LaSalle; capital, $1,000,000; president, William Lorimer; cashier, Charles G. Fox.

Lawndale National—3341 West 26th street; capital, $50,000; president, J. Salat; cashier, Rudolph Hajicek.

Lawndale State—3113 West 22d; capital, $200,000; president, Frank G. Hajicek; cashier, Joseph Kopecky.

Liberty Trust and Savings—Kedzie avenue and 12th street; capital, $250,000; president, C. Hollenbach; cashier, J. Louis Kohn.

Live Stock Exchange National—Union stockyards; capital, $1,250,000; president, W. A. Heath; cashier, G. F. Emery.

Market Trust and Savings—127 North Halsted street; capital, $200,000; president, William Bruckner; cashier, Fred S. Fulton.

Mechanics and Traders' State—Washington boulevard and Desplaines street; capital, $200,000; president, Calvin F. Craig; cashier, Norton F. Stone.

Mercantile Trust and Savings—547 West Jackson boulevard; capital, $250,000; president, Frederick H. Rawson; cashier, Harry V. Grut.

Merchants' Loan and Trust—112 West Adams; capital, $3,000,000; president, Orson Smith; cashier, Paul O. Peterson.

Michigan Avenue Trust—2218 Michigan avenue; capital, $200,000; president, Landon C. Rose; cashier, T. A. Fitz Simmons.

Mid-City Trust and Savings—Halsted and Madison; capital, $500,000; president, William J. Rathje; cashier, D. B. Kennedy.

National Bank of the Republic—LaSalle and Monroe; capital, $2,000,000; president, John A. Lynch; cashier, R. M. McKinney.

National City—Dearborn and Monroe; capital, $2,-000,000; president, David R. Forgan; cashier, Walker G. McLaury.

National Produce—196 North Clark; capital, $250,000; president, Edwin L. Wagner; cashier, R. N. Ballou.

North Avenue State—North avenue and Larrabee; capital, $200,000; president, L. C. Rose; cashier, C. E. Schick.

North Side State Savings—808 North Clark street; capital, $200,000; president, William R. Dawes; cashier, P. H. Wellbrenner.

Northern Trust—LaSalle and Monroe; capital, $1,-500,000; president, Byron L. Smith; cashier, Thomas C. King.

Northwest State—Milwaukee and North avenues; capital, $200,000; president, Joseph R. Noel; cashier, Albert S. Boos.

Northwestern Trust and Savings—1152 Milwaukee avenue; capital, $250,000; president, J. F. Smulski; cashier, T. M. Helinski.

Ogden Avenue State—3644 Ogden avenue; capital, $200,000; president, Benjamin J. Glaser; cashier, Arthur C. Amsler.

Old Colony Trust and Savings—37 West Van Buren street; capital, $200,000; president, Thad H. Howe; cashier, Hugo Meyer.

Pearsons-Taft Land Credit—181 LaSalle street; capital, $200,000; president, Oren B. Taft; cashier, H. N. Mellin.

People's Stockyards State—Ashland and 47th; capital, $500,000; president, R. J. Schlesinger; cashier, H. C. Laycock.

People's Trust and Savings—Michigan avenue and Adams; capital, $500,000; president, Charles H. Bosworth; cashier, E. H. Reynolds.

Pullman Trust and Savings—Pullman, Ill.; capital, $300,000; president, Edward F. Bryant; cashier, Marcus A. Aurelius.

Ravenswood National—4600 West Ravenswood park; capital, $50,000; president, Walter D. Rathje; cashier, George T. Keeler.

Roseland State Savings—11500 Michigan avenue; capital, $200,000; president, John S. Runnells; cashier, David J. Harris.

Second Security Bank of Chicago—Milwaukee and Western avenues; capital, $200,000; president, Charles H. Meyer; cashier, James B. Forgan, Jr.

Security Bank of Chicago—Milwaukee avenue and Carpenter; capital, $400,000; president, Charles H. Meyer; cashier, R. L. Redheffer.

Sheridan Trust and Savings—4611 Evanston avenue; capital, $200,000; president, W. J. Klingenberg; cashier, Edwin L. Read.

South Chicago Savings—3017 East 92d; capital, $200,-000; president, Ralph Van Vechten; cashier, Warren W. Smith.

South Side State—4259 Cottage Grove avenue; capital, $200,000; president, H. W. Mahan; cashier, D. W. Cahill.

South-West Trust and Savings—35th street, Archer and Hoyne avenues; capital, $200,000; president, Thomas J. Healy; cashier, August J. Schoenecke.

Standard Trust and Savings—29 South LaSalle; capital, $1,000,000; president, Charles S. Castle; cashier, F. T. Joyner.

State Bank of Chicago—LaSalle and Washington; capital, $1,500,000; president, L. A. Goddard; cashier, Henry S. Henschen.

State Bank of Italy—Halsted and Taylor; capital, $200,000; president, P. Schiavone; cashier, E. C. Dapples.

State Bank of West Pullman—120th and Lowe; capital, $25,000; president, C. D. Rounds; cashier. Harry Paul.

Stockmen's Trust and Savings—5425 South Halsted; capital, $200,000; president, P. J. Harmon; cashier, E. J. A. Gold.

Stockyards Savings—4162 South Halsted; capital, $250,000; president, C. N. Stanton; cashier, H. I. Tiffany.

Union Bank of Chicago—25 North Dearborn street; capital, $500,000; president, Charles E. Schlytern; cashier, G. Hallbom.

Union Trust—Dearborn and Madison; capital, $1,-200,000; president, F. H. Rawson; cashier, F. P. Schreiber.

Washington Park National—730 East 63d street; capital, $100,000; president, H. W. Mahan; cashier, A. E. Olson.

Wendell State—Madison street and Ashland boulevard; capital, $50,000; president, J. A. Wendell.

West Englewood Ashland State—1610 West 63d street; capital, $250,000; president, John Bain; cashier, Edward C. Barry.

West Side Trust and Savings—Halsted and 12th; capital, $400,000; president, B. S. Mayer; cashier, Charles O. Fetscher.

West Town State—2325 West Madison street; capital, $200,000; president, Robert Forgan; cashier, Scott Ransom.

Woodlawn Trust and Savings—1204 East 63d; capital, $200,000; president, Charles M. Poague; cashier, John W. Watson.

Chicago Clearing House Association—Northern Trust building, LaSalle and Monroe streets; president, F. H. Rawson; manager, W. D. C. Street.

*Stock of Hibernian Banking association owned by stockholders of the Continental and Commercial National bank.

CHICAGO BANK STATISTICS.

Oct. 21, 1913.

	Deposits.	Loans.	Surplus and undivided profits
Cont'l & Com. Nat.	$180,380,678	$124,862,527	*$18,941,378
First National.....	115,448,333	88,662,295	†21,386,356
Illinois Trust......	91,705,491	58,496,247	10,607,231
Corn Exchange...	61,654,261	41,399,115	6,558,717
Merchants' Loan...	58,009,504	32,459,345	7,281,744
First Trust.........	54,067,994	33,391,526	3,441,710
Central Trust....'	39,292,963	28,958,022	2,211,063
Fort Dearborn Nat'l	32,843,167	24,381,059	‡1,242,244
Northern Trust...	31,488,011	19,584,607	2,960,642
Hibernian Banking.	27,462,503	17,664,806	1,197,444
National City......	26,495,709	17,309,046	743,099
State Bank of Chi.	24,911,678	19,756,279	2,709,291
Nat. Bank of Rep.	23,852,482	16,305,187	1,515,367
Cont'l-Com'l Trust.	20,826,054	11,081,370	1,972,864
Union Trust......	20,521,999	13,143,937	1,657,272
Harris Trust......	19,865,872	11,393,843	2,456,310
Foreman Bros.....	12,153,913	9,362,695	568,837
Live Stock Exch...	10,990,640	8,116,808	719,738
Drovers' National..	9,551,152	7,563,405	407,547
People's Trust.....	7,426,523	6,765,122	243,234
Chicago Savings...	7,395,324	5,052,154	262,970
Colonial Trust.....	6,987,209	6,574,392	491,610
Kaspar State......	5,351,900	4,303,061	248,484
West Side Trust...	5,180,166	4,518,728	178,408
LaSalle Street Trust	5,058,586	4,363,398	300,659
Northwestern Trust	4,597,801	2,843,465	180,206
Standard Trust....	4,604,846	3,265,741	424,555
People's Stocky'ds.	4,539,406	4,097,203	173,429
Pullman Trust.....	4,296,989	2,865,501	278,844
Drovers' Trust....	3,856,678	3,245,117	187,566
First of Englewood	3,793,867	2,093,874	243,057
Chicago City......	3,718,433	3,132,434	408,529
Greenebaum Sons..	3,572,646	2,767,576	295,820
Security	3,447,265	2,405,712	*411,798
Stockyards Savings	3,415,055	2,796,528	284,662
Ft. Dearb'n Trust.	2,115,675	1,842,423	27,414
Drexel State......	2,924,591	2,364,539	125,426
Mid-City Trust....	2,694,266	2,105,529	131,879
So. Chicago Sav'gs.	2,687,104	1,638,866	143,000
North Ave. State..	2,615,457	2,215,288	104,884
National Produce..	2,245,907	1,583,537	117,175
Lake View Trust...	2,195,484	2,073,313	109,344
Union Bank........	2,154,058	1,850,029	180,320
Austin State.......	2,123,582	1,071,850	60,204
Kenwood Trust....	2,097,679	1,796,734	107,496
Northwest State...	1,863,250	1,453,696	63,608
South Side State..	1,830,803	1,564,456	31,142
Woodlawn Trust...	1,748,236	1,637,244	114,059
Washington Park..	1,532,728	1,204,305	25,308
American State....	1,501,828	1,468,754	209,146
Mich. Ave. Trust..	1,444,263	1,132,931	72,829
Home Bk. & Trust.	1,408,786	1,168,832	99,466
Englewood State...	1,346,807	1,009,969	60,151
North Side State..	1,286,520	1,186,358	19,622
Lawndale State....	1,276,649	1,138,953	‡132,466
Sheridan Trust.....	1,275,240	900,379	49,817
Calumet National..	1,189,051	984,618	77,523
Wendell State.....	1,159,355	448,510	40,132
Mercantile Trust..	1,150,450	1,131,221	53,426
Franklin Trust.....	1,103,962	802,799	129,510
Stockmen's Trust..	1,091,186	901,599	56,698
Lawndale Nat'l....	1,046,530	759,786	22,343
W. Englew'd-Ash'd	1,016,719	865,555	31,938

*Includes capital, surplus and undivided profits of Continental-Commercial Trust and Savings Bank and Hibernian Banking association. †Includes capital, surplus and undivided profits of First Trust and Savings bank. ‡Includes capital, surplus and undivided profits of Fort Dearborn Trust and Savings bank. §Includes capital, surplus and undivided

profits of Second Security bank. ¶Includes capital, surplus and undivided profits of Lawndale National bank.

Banks with less than $1,000,000 reported the following amounts held Oct. 21: Austin National, $129,-999; Bowmanville National, $158,740; Illinois State, $176,499; Calumet Trust, $254,984; Capital State, $137,088; Interstate National, $180,602; Irving Park National, $260,731; Jefferson Park National, $276,584; Ravenswood National, $264,312; Rogers Park National, $94,816; Central Manufacturing District, $953,002; Citizens' Trust and Savings, $552,975; Garfield Park State Savings, $323,009; Guarantee Trust and Savings, $683,635; Halsted Street State, $461,338; Hyde Park State, $669,047; Illinois State, $177,589; Lake View State, $622,491; Lake and State, $99,507; Liberty Trust and Savings, $739,702; Lincoln State, $263,449; Market Trust and Savings, $241,798; Mechanics and Traders', $884,694; Ogden Avenue State, $285,095; Old Colony Trust and Savings, $591,490; Pioneer State, $248,532; Roseland State Savings, $828,768; Second Security, $976,939; Southwest Trust and Savings, $653,881; State Bank of Italy, $728,692; State Bank of West Pullman, $400,322; West Town State, $276,781.

CHICAGO BANK CLEARINGS.

Year.	Clearings.	Year.	Clearings.
1900	$6,799,535,598.36	1907	12,087,647,870.08
1901	7,756,372,455.31	1908	11,853,814,943.56
1902	8,394,872,351.59	1909	13,781,843,612.86
1903	8,755,553,649.93	1910	13,939,689,984.43
1904	8,989,983,764.40	1911	13,925,709,802.70
1905	10,191,765,732.59	1912	15,380,795,541.00
1906	11,047,311,894.50		

CLEARINGS OF 1912 AND 1913 BY MONTHS.

	1912.	1913.
January	$1,252,985,283	$1,412,245,475
February	1,152,969,770	1,240,420,411
March	1,302,396,484	1,384,006,707
April	1,309,363,131	1,329,181,104
May	1,322,685,932	1,334,337,837
June	1,190,331,820	1,290,839,722
July	1,271,131,184	1,343,100,451
August	1,232,885,831	1,245,128,185
September	1,206,651,833	1,308,471,747
October	1,156,179,036	1,454,186,257
November	1,313,851,484	....
December	1,360,413,732	....
Total	15,380,795,541	....

CHICAGO RECEIPTS AND SHIPMENTS (1905-1912).
[From board of trade reports.]
RECEIPTS.

ARTICLE.	1905.	1906.	1907.	1908.	1909.	1910.	1911.	1912.
Pork, brls	12,320	5,034	13,072	9,260	24,953	5,306	9,050	9,737
Other meats, lbs	274,012,012	204,641,412	208,872,674	235,477,303	207,405,026	180,881,600	228,741,800	153,990,300
Lard, lbs	84,653,195	80,597,434	70,361,665	77,301,152	70,852,783	44,735,400	42,171,800	61,228,100
Butter, lbs	271,914,805	248,648,088	263,711,642	316,694,782	284,546,835	318,985,500	334,932,400	287,798,800
Wool, lbs	43,521,005	57,312,218	58,805,470	66,018,883	91,085,097	53,407,700	71,810,900	55,778,600
Hides, lbs	155,346,035	132,878,718	120,642,541	136,729,644	150,036,892	155,993,000	166,136,500	149,058,500
Flaxseed, bu	2,900,241	2,086,385	1,861,442	2,119,335	1,198,119	1,388,300	959,500	2,298,500
Other seeds, lbs	78,589,913	62,729,180	51,141,500	83,583,558	91,132,313	66,143,600	37,844,100	44,120,000
Salt, brls	1,984,190	1,811,380	1,908,886	1,820,030	1,728,395	1,725,825	1,656,799	2,008,694
Lumber, 1,000 ft	2,193,540	2,362,856	2,479,458	2,053,639	2,584,518	2,519,357	2,194,567	2,393,305
Flour, brls	7,944,955	9,069,329	9,435,311	9,496,037	8,526,200	8,006,289	5,859,395	7,070,898
Wheat, bu	26,899,012	28,249,475	24,943,690	21,168,442	26,985,118	27,540,100	37,118,100	35,914,000
Corn, bu	110,823,444	98,895,563	125,159,932	91,169,147	90,894,922	102,592,850	108,550,500	112,690,000
Oats, bu	92,486,761	89,912,881	83,906,779	52,529,017	87,884,238	101,859,000	94,099,800	118,491,300

SHIPMENTS.

Pork, brls	144,909	182,906	111,840	168,265	182,222	126,178	105,913	138,752
Other meats, lbs	754,942,985	804,642,049	753,239,255	730,804,686	720,032,586	562,203,800	550,849,300	566,827,100
Lard, lbs	405,629,825	421,914,539	388,629,530	402,779,488	255,652,422	268,702,900	202,499,300	253,176,100
Butter, lbs	254,130,889	262,397,516	252,005,932	269,178,313	235,648,837	268,398,900	285,688,400	271,109,500
Wool, lbs	46,757,734	60,346,206	63,907,814	83,267,708	118,156,696	94,226,200	139,088,600	98,491,000
Hides, lbs	173,406,223	175,170,520	166,736,304	199,176,623	180,677,234	185,626,000	194,764,900	162,800,300
Flaxseed, bu	238,652	435,171	98,292	213,984	150,834	244,000	165,800	403,100
Other seeds, lbs	54,210,439	61,683,329	75,130,500	83,337,110	76,043,562	56,227,200	36,964,200	59,513,500
Salt, brls	362,920	244,462	409,089	415,121	403,509	402,966	523,653	671,830
Lumber, 1,000 ft	956,377	1,041,491	977,746	771,539	961,822	962,775	803,926	1,002,378
Flour, brls	7,361,867	8,100,628	9,231,696	9,180,855	8,316,943	7,038,351	5,781,092	6,268,876
Wheat, bu	13,922,744	16,788,573	24,314,822	22,579,044	23,484,171	18,679,100	23,839,500	35,726,100
Corn, bu	91,155,342	78,974,686	95,770,979	69,692,749	78,835,859	78,623,100	87,900,000	73,799,100
Oats, bu	66,131,725	73,718,199	88,897,313	79,857,557	77,298,653	77,890,100	77,428,500	102,077,000

CHICAGO PUBLIC SERVICE LEAGUE.
Organized Jan. 18, 1913.

President—W. L. Bodine, superintendent of compulsory education.
First Vice-President—Judge M. W. Pinckney of the Juvenile court.
Second Vice-President—Joseph Meyer, county agent.
Secretary—Robert M. Sweitzer, county clerk.
Treasurer—Dr. George B. Young, commissioner of health.
Executive Committee—Edgar T. Davies, chairman;

County Judge John E. Owens; Mrs. Ella Flagg Young, superintendent of schools; Judge William Gemmill of the Court of Domestic Relations; John L. Whitman, superintendent of the house of correction, and the officers of the league.
The principal object of the league is to improve the condition of children in Chicago and throughout the state, through more co-operation between public officials.

CHICAGO BOARD OF TRADE.
Jackson boulevard and LaSalle street.

President—Edward Andrew.
Vice-President—Albert E. Cross.
Secretary—J. C. F. Merrill.
Treasurer—Ernest A. Hamill.
Directors—Terms expire 1914: Charles B. Pierce, Theodore E. Cunningham, David S. Lasier, Caleb H. Canby, Leslie F. Gates. Terms expire 1915: Robert McDougall, Joseph Simons, Adolph Gers-

tenberg, Benjamin S. Wilson, L. Harry Freeman. Terms expire 1916: George B. Quinn, John R. Mauff, John A. Rodgers, William L. Gregson.

A gallery is set apart for the use of visitors, but admission is by card only. The trading hours are from 9:30 a. m. to 1:15 p. m., except on Saturday, when the closing hour is 12 o'clock noon.

CHICAGO WATERWORKS SYSTEM.

The following table shows the growth of Chicago's waterworks system by decades since 1854, when the first large pumping station at Chicago avenue and the lake was built, and by years since 1900:

Year.	*Population using city water.	Gallons pumped per day.	Gallons per capita.	Total revenue.
1854........	65,000	591,000	9.1	$58,106.00
1860........	109,000	4,704,000	43.1	131,162.00
1870........	307,000	21,766,000	70.9	539,180.00
1880........	503,000	57,384,000	114.1	865,618.35
1890........	1,107,000	152,372,000	137.6	2,109,508.00
1900........	1,727,566	322,683,000	189.0	3,250,481.85
1901........	1,776,236	342,961,000	195.6	3,370,600.88
1902........	1,824,906	358,179,000	199.2	2,611,558.81
1903........	1,873,576	376,090,000	204.1	3,689,625.80
1904........	1,922,266	393,045,000	211.2	3,834,543.30
1905........	1,970,936	410,936,000	212.4	4,013,205.88
1906........	2,019,606	437,059,000	218.5	4,281,065.50
1907........	2,068,276	455,194,000	223.0	4,450,349.61
1908........	2,116,946	469,282,000	223.4	4,648,299.54
1909........	2,165,616	480,905,000	222.3	5,022,008.48
1910........	2,214,236	518,579,000	232.5	5,448,257.55
1911........	2,262,956	507,332,000	190.0	5,993,771.32
1912........	2,345,315	551,324,000	203.0	6,263,234.75

*Estimated from United States government census.

In 1912 the total amount of water pumped was 170,294,738,000 gallons.

The pumping stations, with the year of construction of each, follow:

Chicago avenue.......1854		Washington Heights.1892
Twenty-second street.1875		Norwood Park........1897
Harrison street.......1889		Central Park.........1900
Lake View............1892		Springfield avenue...1901
Fourteenth street....1892		Rogers Park..........1899
Sixty-eighth street...1892		Roseland 1910

The total daily capacity of the waterworks in gallons is 728,226,000.

Other statistics: Number of taps, 270,932; meters in use, 16,052; mileage of water pipe, 2,425.

LAKE TUNNELS.

One 5-foot tunnel from two-mile crib to Chicago avenue pumping station; built 1867; cost $464,-866.06.

One 7-foot tunnel from two-mile crib to Chicago avenue pumping station; built 1874; cost $415,-709.36.

One 7-foot tunnel from two-mile crib to Chicago avenue pumping station; built 1887-1895; cost $242,786.64.

One 14-foot tunnel lake extension of Chicago avenue and Blue Island avenue system; begun 1911; cost $7,530.28.

One 8-foot tunnel from four-mile crib to 14th street pumping station; built 1892; cost $1,104,744.12.

One 10-foot tunnel from Carter H. Harrison crib to foot of Oak street; built 1898; cost $677,577.55.

One 7-foot tunnel from Lake View crib to Lake View pumping station; built 1896; cost $701,792.45.

One 7-foot tunnel from Hyde Park crib to 68th street pumping station; built 1898; cost $771,556.07.

One 14-foot tunnel from Hyde Park to 73d street and Railroad avenue; built 1912; cost $1,592,953.51.

LAND TUNNELS.

One 7-foot tunnel from Chicago avenue pumping station to 22d street pumping station; built 1874; cost $542,912.63.

One 7-foot tunnel from Polk row shaft to foot of Peck place and thence to Harrison street pumping station; built 1891; cost $279,848.78.

One 6-foot connecting tunnel in Jefferson street from Van Buren to Harrison; built 1891; cost $15,968.17.

One 10-foot tunnel foot of Oak street to Green street and Grand avenue, and two 8-foot tunnels from that point to Central Park avenue and Springfield avenue pumping stations respectively; built 1900; cost $2,121,525.02.

One 7-foot tunnel connecting above 10-foot tunnel with Chicago avenue pumping station (remodeled); built 1898; cost $42,436.45.

One 9-foot tunnel from 104th street and Stewart avenue to 73d and State streets; one 12-foot tunnel in 73d street from State street to Yates avenue, and one 14-foot tunnel from Yates avenue to Railroad avenue; in course of construction; estimated cost, $3,000,000.

One 7-foot tunnel in Polk street connecting Peck place shaft and Jefferson street shaft.

One 8-foot tunnel from Chicago avenue to 22d street and Ashland avenue; built, 1911; cost, $855,267.77.

WATER-PIPE TUNNELS UNDER CHICAGO RIVER.

Dimen'ns in ft.	Length in ft.	Year built.	Cost.	Location.
5..........	280	1871	$7,550.00	Adams-st.
6..........	249	1871	7,633.00	Archer-av.
7½x10½...	225	1891	17,453.56	Ashland-av.
6..........	306	1871	7,750.00	Chicago-av.
5..........	227	1880	6,875.00	Clybourn-pl.
6..........	468	1903	13,324.00	Division-st.*
7x8½...	330	1871	11,220.00	Division-st.
8..........	297	1880	14,620.00	18th-st.
6½x8...	214	1880	7,883.00	Harrison-st.
5..........	272	1889	8,390.00	95th-st.
6x7.......1,548		1899	35,561.75	Drainage canal.
5..........	403	1895	29,614.58	N. Western-av.
5..........	485	1880	11,250.00	Rush-st.
7x10......	241	1892	17,495.20	35th-st.
6..........	311	1876	7,550.00	Throop-st.
7x8......	345	1905	28,584.54	Montrose-bd.
7½.......1,680		1907	61,307.10	Ashland-av.
7x8½...	335	1907	24,831.30	Grand-av.
7x8½...	450	1907	21,603.48	Diversey-bd.
7x8......	326	1908	11,962.36	Western-av.
7x8......	289	1908	16,013.60	Western-av.*
7x8......	225	1908	8,387.77	Western-av.*

*Under canal.

WATERWORKS CRIBS.

Name.	Built.	Cost.
Two-mile	1867	$106,679.63
Four-mile	1891	472,890.93
Lake View	1896	164,085.82
Hyde Park	1896	137,624.77
C. H. Harrison...................	1900	232,738.10

VALUE OF WATERWORKS PROPERTY.

The total appraised value of the Chicago waterworks property Dec. 31, 1912, was $49,608,184.21, divided as follows: Real estate, $4,246,160.05; buildings, $2,647,654.94; equipment, $2,939,099.09; cribs, tunnels, mains, etc., $39,775,270.13.

CHICAGO'S BRIDGE SYSTEM.

The first ferry across the river was established in 1829, where the Lake street bridge now is. In 1833 a floating bridge of logs was in operation just north of the present Randolph street bridge. A foot bridge over the north branch was built in 1832 at Kinzie street. The first drawbridge over the main branch of the river was placed at Dearborn street in 1834. In 1854 a pivot bridge was built at Clark street. These and other bridges of that time were built by the persons most directly benefited by them. It was not until 1857 that a bridge was built entirely at the city's expense. This was the structure over the south branch at Madison street. It cost $30,000. Until 1872 the swing bridges were turned by hand, but in the year named steam power was installed on the Dearborn street structure and later on most of the other bridges in the downtown section were similarly equipped. In 1895 the Rush, Lake and Van Buren street bridges were operated by electric motors. The last named structure, which was opened for traffic in that year, was the first of the Scherzer rolling type. The Halsted street lift bridge, the first and only one of its kind, was opened in 1894 and was operated by steam. It cost the city $242,880.

Of the bridges operated by the city thirty-eight are operated by electricity and eight by hand power. Twelve are bascule bridges of various types, one is a vertical lift bridge and the others are swing bridges.

SANITARY DISTRICT OF CHICAGO.

Offices in Karpen building.
President—Thomas A. Smyth, D.
Clerk—John McGillen.
Treasurer—John A. McCormick.
Chief Engineer—George M. Wisner.
Electrical Engineer—Edward B. Ellicott.
Consulting Engineer—Lyman E. Cooley.
Attorney—Edmund D. Adcock.
Board of Trustees—Terms expire in 1914: Wallace G. Clark, R.; George W. Paullin, R.; Paul A. Hazard, R. Terms expire in 1916: Thomas A. Smyth, D.; Thomas M. Sullivan, D.; Edward Kane, D. Terms expire in 1918: James M. Dailey D.; Fred D. Brett, D.; Charles E. Reading, D.

CHRONOLOGY.

First investigation made in 1885.
Sanitary bill signed May 29, 1889.
Sanitary district organized Jan. 18, 1890.
Earth broken ("shovel day") Sept. 3, 1892.
Lake water turned into canal Jan. 2, 1900.
Formal opening of canal Jan. 17, 1900.

DIMENSIONS OF CANAL.

Length of main and water power channel, 39.16 miles.
Length of river, lake to Robey street, 6 miles.
Length river diversion channel, 13 miles.
Width main channel, Robey street to Summit: Bottom, 110 feet; top, 198.
Width main channel, Summit to Willow Springs: Bottom, 202 feet; top, 290.
Width main channel, Willow Springs to Lockport (rock section): Bottom, 160 feet; top, 162.
Width river diversion channel: Bottom, 200 feet.
Minimum depth of water in main channel, 22 feet.
Current in earth sections, 1¼ miles per hour.
Current in rock sections, 1.9 miles per hour.
Present capacity of canal, 300,000 cubic feet per minute.
Total amount of excavation, 42,229,695 cubic yards.
The north shore channel, extending from Lawrence avenue to Lake Michigan, in the village of Wilmette, is about 8 miles long with a water depth of 13.6 feet.
The construction of the Sag canal to drain the Calumet region was begun in the summer of 1911. When completed it will be 16 miles long. Its estimated cost is $6,762,000.

REVENUES AND EXPENDITURES.

From organization to Dec. 31, 1912.

REVENUES.

Taxation	$55,170,841.52
Bonds outstanding	17,599,000.00
Interest and premiums on bonds	367,043.98
Interest on deposits	465,418.04
Land revenues	563,732.34
From electrical plant	2,506,391.48
Miscellaneous	15,845.28
Total	76,688,272.64

FIXED CHARGES.

Interest on bonds	$12,759,698.50
Interest on tax warrants	468,453.69

Interest on loans	$27,168.19
Taxes paid	216,782.30
Total	13,472,102.68
Available for disbursement	63,216,169.96

EXPENDITURES.

Administration	$7,455,025.16
Construction—River improvement	10,640,739.52
Main channel work	24,136,762.98
River diversion	1,462,545.13
Joliet project	2,285,158.48
Channel extension, water power	6,180,375.08
Pumping stations	557,565.61
North branch	370,905.99
North shore channel	3,254,815.28
Calumet-Sag channel	655,961.29
Sewers	224,584.59
Warehouses	22,337.19
Total construction	49,692,251.34
Maintenance and operation	2,104,211.60
City of Chicago contract	1,688,053.62
Fixed charges	13,472,102.68
Total expenditures	74,411,644.40
Emergency funds	56,800.00
Bonds and securities	41,733.13
Bank deposit in Joliet	3,056.11
Cash in hands of treasurer	2,175,039.00
Total income	76,688,272.64

PETITION DENIED.

In a decision announced Jan. 12, 1913, Henry L. Stimson, then secretary of war, denied the petition of the Chicago sanitary district for a permit to divert 10,000 cubic feet of water per second from Lake Michigan, or 4,167 cubic feet more than the amount allowed under prior permits. Mr. Stimson said that he had reached the conclusions that the diversion of 10,000 cubic feet per second from Lake Michigan would substantially interfere with the navigable capacity of the great lakes and their connecting rivers. This being so, it would not be appropriate for him, without express congressional sanction, to permit such a diversion. The provisions of the Canadian treaty for a settlement by joint commission of "questions or matters of difference" between the United States and Canada offered a further reason why no administrative officer should authorize a further diversion of water, manifestly so injurious to Canada, against Canadian protest.

SANITARY DISTRICT ENLARGED.

By an act of the legislature approved June 27, 1913, the sanitary district of Chicago was enlarged so as to include the territory embracing the villages of Franklin Park, River Grove, Melrose Park, Maywood, River Forest, Forest Park, Riverside and Bellwood.

POSTMASTERS OF CHICAGO.

No.	Name	Appointed.	Died.	No.	Name	Appointed.	Died.	No.	Name	Appointed.	Died.
1.	Jonathan N. Bailey	1831	1850	10.	Isaac Cook	1858	1886	19.	Solomon C. Judd	1885	1895
2.	John S. C. Coates	1832	1868	11.	John L. Scripps	1861	1866	20.	Walter C. Newberry	1888	1912
3.	Sydney Abell	1837	1863	12.	Samuel Hoard	1865	1881	21.	James A. Sexton	1889	1899
4.	William Stuart	1841	1878	13.	Thomas O. Osborne	1866	....	22.	Washington Hesing	1893	1897
5.	Hart L. Stewart	1845	1883	14.	Robert A. Gillmore	1866	1867	23.	Charles U. Gordon	1897	....
6.	Richard L. Wilson	1849	1856	15.	Francis T. Sherman	1867	1905	24.	F. E. Coyne	1901	....
7.	George W. Dole	1850	1860	16.	Francis A. Eastman	1869	....	25.	Fred A. Busse	1905	....
8.	Isaac Cook	1853	1886	17.	John McArthur	1872	1906	26.	Daniel A. Campbell	1907	....
9.	William Price	1857	1885	18.	Francis W. Palmer	1877	1907				

CHICAGO PEACE SOCIETY.

President—Leroy A. Goddard.
Vice-President—Edward M. Skinner.
Director Central West Department—Charles E. Beals, 30 North LaSalle street.
Treasurer—Charles L. Hutchinson.
Auditor—Maurice S. Kuhns.
Executive committee—Leroy A. Goddard, Edward M. Skinner, Charles E. Beals, Charles L. Hutch-

inson, Maurice S. Kuhns, Miss Jane Addams, Edward P. Bailey, Clifford W. Barnes, Edward O. Brown, Walter L. Fisher, Richard C. Hall. Harlow N. Higinbotham, Charles Cheney Hyde, John C. Kennedy, S. W. Lamson, Benjamin F. Methven, Henry C. Morris, John S. Nollen, Julius Rosenwald, Albert H. Scherzer.

CHICAGO STREET RAILWAY CHRONOLOGY.

Omnibuses—First regular omnibus line started by Frank Parmelee May 9, 1853.

Horse Cars—South side: First line on State street, between Randolph and 12th streets, open April 25, 1859. West side: Madison street line, Halsted to State, opened May 20, 1859; Randolph street line opened July 15, 1859. North side: Wells street line, river to Chicago avenue, opened late in spring of 1859; Clark street line opened in August, 1859.

Cable Cars—South side: First cable line in Chicago operated on State to 39th street; began business Jan. 28, 1882; Cottage Grove avenue line built same year. North side: Clark street line opened March 27, 1888; Wells street line opened same year; Lincoln avenue line opened Jan. 22, 1889; Clybourn avenue line opened May 2, 1891. West side: Madison street line opened July 16, 1890; Milwaukee avenue line opened at same time; Blue Island avenue line opened July 28, 1893.

Electric Cars—South side: First electric line in city began operating Oct. 2, 1890, from 95th street and Stony Island avenue to South Chicago; trolley substituted for horse cars on most of the lines (except cable) in 1893 and 1894 in all divisions of the city and in the suburbs; trolley substituted for cable cars on State street July 22, 1906, and on Cottage Grove avenue Oct. 21, 1906. West side: Trolley cars substituted for cable on Blue Island avenue July 22, 1906, and on Madison street and Milwaukee avenue Aug. 19, 1906. North side: All cables changed to trolley lines Oct. 21, 1906.

Elevated Railways—South side: South Side elevated railroad began regular operation on line between Congress street and 39th street, June 6, 1892, with steam as motive power; extended to Stony Island avenue in May, 1893; extended to Englewood in 1906 and to Kenwood in 1907; trains began running around loop Oct. 19, 1897; motive power changed to electricity July 27, 1898. West side: Lake street line (Chicago & Oak Park) began running Nov. 6, 1893, with steam as motive power; electricity substituted June 14, 1896; Metropolitan road opened May 20, 1895, with electricity as motive power; began running over loop Oct. 10, 1897; extension of Garfield park and Douglas park lines completed in 1902. North side: Northwestern line opened for business May 31, 1900, with electricity as motive power; Ravenswood branch opened May 10, 1907; through routing of trains between north and south sides and giving of transfers on all elevated roads begun Nov. 3, 1913.

STREET-RAILWAY FRANCHISE.

Ordinances passed by city council Feb. 4, 1907; vetoed by mayor and passed over veto Feb. 11, 1907; approved by people on referendum vote April 2, 1907.

Systems to be reconstructed and rehabilitated within three years.

City to supervise rehabilitation through board of three engineers.

Life of grant not to extend in any event beyond Feb. 1, 1927.

City to receive 55 per cent and companies 45 per cent of the net profits from the operation of the roads.

Twenty-one through routes specified and provision made for others.

Fares for adults to be 5 cents for continuous trips in one general direction within the present or future city limits.

Transfers to be given at all connecting points on and to all lines except in section on south side between 12th street and the river.

Motive power of cars to be electricity applied by the overhead or underground trolley systems.

Cars to be of the latest and most approved pattern and to be kept clean and warm and well lighted.

Cars to be operated singly after one year.

Companies to pay $5,000,000 toward the construction of subways in the downtown section at the city's option.

City given the right to purchase the property of both the present great systems at any time upon giving six months' notice.

STREET-RAILWAY EARNINGS.

	GROSS EARNINGS.*		CITY'S SHARE (55 PCT.).†
1908	$18,823,094.31	1908	$1,564,618.47
1909	19,580,351.74	1909	1,386,877.96
1910	22,832,882.64	1910	1,276,252.65
1911	25,155,629.89	1911	1,705,550.30
1912	28,898,887.93	1912	1,870,908.00
1913	30,299,172.55	1913	2,529,992.26

*Year ending Feb. 1. †Of net receipts.
NOTE—The total capitalization of all companies Feb. 1, 1913, was $133,770,390.51.

LEARNED SOCIETIES IN CHICAGO.

American Library Association—Public library building; secretary, George B. Utley.

Chicago Academy of Sciences, The—Lincoln park; president, Thomas C. Chamberlin; secretary, Wallace W. Atwood.

Chicago Architectural Club—Art Institute; president, George A. Awsumb; secretary, Harry C. Bentley.

Chicago Astronomical Society—President, Elias Colbert; secretary, Charles H. Taylor, 4402 Greenwood avenue.

Chicago Bar Association—Library rooms, 105 Monroe street; president, Silas H. Strawn; secretary, Richard S. Folsom.

Chicago Historical Society—Dearborn avenue and Ontario street; president, Clarence A. Burley; secretary, Seymour Morris; librarian, Caroline M. McIlvaine.

Chicago Library Club—President, Charles J. Barr; secretary, Agnes J. Petersen. Newberry library.

Chicago Literary Club—410 South Michigan avenue; president, Walter L. Fisher; secretary and treasurer, Frederick W. Gookin.

Chicago Medical Society—President, Charles P. Caldwell, M. D.; secretary, Charles H. Parkes, M. D.

Chicago Numismatic Society—1622 Masonic Temple;

president, F. Elmo Simpson; secretary, Ben G. Green, 1535 Masonic Temple.

Chicago Opthalmological Society—President, Dr. Willis O. Nance; secretary and treasurer, Dr. W. H. Peck.

Chicago Philatelic Society — President, Fred Michael; secretary, Thomas C. Hunter, 202, 116 South Michigan avenue.

Council for Library and Museum Extension—President, Newton H. Carpenter, Art Institute; secretary, Wallace W. Atwood, Chicago Academy of Sciences.

Geographic Society of Chicago—President, Dr. Henry C. Cowles; secretary, Dr. Otis W. Caldwell.

National League for Medical Freedom (Illinois branch)—1237 McCormick building; secretary, Joseph C. Mason.

State Microscopical Society of Illinois—President, Albert McCalla, Ph. D.; secretary, V. A. Latham, M. D., D. D. S., 1844 Morse avenue.

The Fortnightly Club of Chicago—President, Mrs. Henry Spencer Robbins, 1100 Lake Shore drive; corresponding secretary, Mrs. Ralph Clarkson, 410 South Michigan avenue.

Western Society of Engineers—1735 Monadnock block; president, Albert Reichmann; secretary, J. H. Warder.

SOCIETIES OF PIONEERS.

Chicago Pioneers' Sons and Daughters—President, Frank W. Smith; corresponding secretary, John S. Zimmerman.

Englewood Old Settlers' Association—President, E. R. Lewis; secretary, S. B. Maynard, 340 West 64th street.

Old Time Printers' Association—President, Samuel

K. Parker; secretary, William Mill, 1346 North Hoyne avenue.

Old Time Printing Pressmen's Association—President, Garrett Burns; secretary, James H. Bowman.

Western Association of California Pioneers—Secretary, George W. Hotchkiss, 1509, 431 South Dearborn street.

CHICAGO BOARD OF EDUCATION.

Offices on the sixth, seventh and eighth floors of the Tribune building.
President—Peter Reinberg.
Vice-President—Henry W. Huttmann.
Secretary—Lewis E. Larson.
Assistant Secretary—C. N. Fessenden.

MEMBERS.	Terms expire.
Daniel R. Cameron	1916
Peter Reinberg	1916
Dean Walter T. Sumner	1915
Julius F. Smietanka	1915
John C. Harding	1914
Charles O. Sethness	1914
Harry A. Lipsky	1914
Mrs. John McMahon	1914
Jacob M. Loeb	1914
James B. Dibelka	1914
Henry W. Huttmann	1914
John J. Sonsteby	1915
Thomas Kelly	1915
William Rothmann	1915
Dr. Otto F. Warning	1916
Robert J. Roulston	1915
Michael J. Collins	1916
Charles S. Peterson	1915
Mrs. Florence Vosbrink	1916
Mrs. Gertrude Howe Britton	1916
Dr. Peter C. Clemensen	1916

STANDING COMMITTEES (1913-1914).

School Management—Dean Sumner, chairman; Messrs. Cameron, Smietanka, Lipsky, Loeb, Peterson, Dr. Clemensen, Mrs. McMahon, Mrs. Vosbrink, Mrs. Britton. Member ex officio, the president.

Committee on Buildings and Grounds—Mr. Sethness, chairman; Messrs. Harding, Huttmann, Dibelka, Kelly, Rothmann, Sonsteby, Warning, Collins, Roulston. Member ex officio, the president.

Committee on Finance—Mr. Rothmann, chairman; Messrs. Kelly, Sonsteby, Roulston and chairmen of two preceding committees. Member ex officio, the president.

Meetings of Board—On alternate Wednesday afternoons at 4 o'clock.

SUPERINTENDENTS.

Superintendent—John D. Shoop.
Assistant Superintendent—Elizabeth W. Murphy.
Bureau of Compulsory Education—W. L. Bodine.
Superintendent of Parental School—Peter A. Mortenson.

DISTRICT SUPERINTENDENTS.

1. Ella C. Sullivan.	6. Kate S. Kellogg.
2. William C. Dodge.	7. Edward C. Rosseter.
3. Charles D. Lowry.	8. Gertrude E. English.
4. Rufus M. Hitch.	9. Orville T. Bright.
5. Henry C. Cox.	10. Minnie R. Cowan.

Wm. M. Roberts, in charge of evening and vocational schools.
Samuel B. Allison, district superintendent in charge of special divisions.

SUPERVISORS.

Physical Education—Henry Suder.
Technical Work in High Schools—Robert M. Smith.
Household Arts and Science—Ida M. Cook.
Schools for Blind—John B. Curtis.
German—Martin Schmidhofer.
Elementary Manual Training and Construction Work —Edward F. Worst.
Director of Child Study—Daniel P. MacMillan.
Director of School Grounds—Carl A. Meltzer.

OFFICE HOURS.

General offices open from 9 a. m. to 5 p. m.; Saturday to 12 m.
Business manager, 4 p. m. to 5 p. m.; Saturday, 9 a. m. to 12 m.
Superintendent, Tuesday, Wednesday and Thursday, 2 p. m. to 4 p. m.; Saturday, 9 a. m. to 12 m.
District superintendents, Saturdays, 9 a. m. to 10:15 a. m. and 4 p. m. to 5 p. m. on stated days.

SCHOOLS OF CHICAGO.

With the location and principal of each.

Chicago Teachers' College—68th street and Stewart avenue; William Bishop Owen.
Parker Practice School—68th street and Stewart avenue; Charles W. French.
Haines Practice School—23d place and Wentworth avenue; Elizabeth R. Daly.
Carter Practice—58th street and Michigan avenue; Abby E. Lane.
Chicago Parental School—West Foster and North Central Park avenues; Peter A. Mortenson, superintendent.

HIGH SCHOOLS.

Austin—Frink street and Walnut avenue; George H. Rockwood.
Bowen—89th street and Manistee avenue; Charles I. Parker.
Calumet—Normal avenue, near 81st street; Grant Beebe.
Crane Technical—West Van Buren street and Oakley boulevard; William J. Bartholf.
Curtis (high school department)—114th and State streets; Thomas C. Hill.
Englewood—Stewart avenue and 62d street; James E. Armstrong.
Harrison Technical—Marshall boulevard and West 24th street; Frank L. Morse.
Flower Technical—26th street and Wabash avenue; Dora Wells.
Hyde Park—62d street and Stony Island avenue; Hiram B. Loomis.
Lake—Union avenue and West 47th place; Edward F. Stearns.
Lake View—Ashland avenue and Irving Park boulevard; B. Frank Brown.
Lane Technical—Division and Sedgwick streets; William J. Bogan.
Marshall—Adams street, near Kedzie avenue; Louis J. Block.
McKinley—Adams street and Hoyne avenue; George M. Clayberg.

Medill—14th place, near Throop street; Avon S. Hall.
Parker—68th street and Stewart avenue; William B. Owen.
Phillips—39th street and Prairie avenue; Spencer R. Smith.
Schurz—Milwaukee avenue, Addison street and West Waveland avenue; Walter F. Slocum.
Senn—Ridge and Francis avenues; Benjamin F. Buck.
Tuley—North Claremont and Potomac avenues; Franklin P. Fisk.
Waller—Orchard and Center streets; Oliver S. Westcott.

ELEMENTARY SCHOOLS.

Adams—Townsend street, between Chicago avenue and Locust street; Inger M. Schjoldager.
Agassiz—Seminary avenue, near Wolfram street; Lina E. Troendle.
Albany Avenue—Albany avenue and 16th street; Annette M. Chapin.
Alcott—Wrightwood avenue and Orchard street; A. Esther Camfield.
Altgeld—71st and Loomis streets; James W. Brooks.
Andersen—Lincoln and Division streets; Francis M. McKay.
Armour—33d place and Auburn avenue; Martin E. Hurney.
Armstrong—Greenleaf avenue and Pingree street; Azile B. Reynolds.
Arnold—Burling and Center streets; John E. Adams.
Auburn Park—Normal avenue, near 81st street; A. S. Hall.
Audubon—Cornelia and Hoyne avenues; Mary E. Vaughan.
Avondale—North Sawyer avenue and Wellington street; John H. Stehman.

Bancroft—Maplewood avenue, near North avenue; Carrie F. Patterson.
Barnard—Charles and 104th streets; Elizabeth H. Sutherland.
Bass—66th and May streets; Fulton B. Ormsby.
Beale—Sangamon and 61st streets; John W. May.
Beaubien—North Laramie and Winnemac avenues; Sarah J. O'Keefe.
Beethoven (site)—North Humboldt street and Berteau avenue.
Beidler—Walnut street and Kedzie avenue; Jay C. Edwards.
Belding—Tripp and West Cullom avenues; Delos Buzzell.
Bismarck—McLean and North Central Park avenues; Cora E. Lewis.
Blaine—Grace street and Janssen avenue; Mary J. Zollman.
Bradwell—Sherman avenue, near 77th street; Georgia A. Seaman.
Brainard—Washburne avenue and Leavitt street; Mina P. Scheurer.
Brennan—Lime street, near Archer avenue; Helen C. Maine.
Brentano—North Fairfield avenue and Schubert street; Washington D. Smyser.
Brown—Warren avenue and Wood street; Matilda M. Niehaus.
Brownell—Perry avenue, near 65th street; Alma M. Willard.
Bryant—South Karlov avenue, near 14th street; Ida Mighell.
Bryn Mawr—74th street and Jeffery avenue; Margaret J. McKee.
Burke—South Park avenue and 54th street; J. Clara Breese.
Burley—Barry avenue, near Ashland avenue; Mary F. Willard.
Burns—Central Park avenue and 25th street; Robert Nightingale.
Burnside—91st place and Langley avenue; Frank W. Rieder.
Burr—Ashland and Wabansia avenues; John H. Stube.
Burroughs—36th street and Washtenaw avenue; Elizabeth B. Letzkuss.
Byford (Austin)—Iowa street and Central avenue; Novella M. Close.
Calhoun—Jackson boulevard and Francisco avenue; Luella V. Little.
Cameron—Monticello and Potomac avenues; Herbert L. Merrill.
Carpenter—North Racine avenue and Huron street; Volney Underhill.
Chalmers—14th street and Fairfield avenue; J. Katherine Cutler.
Chase—Cornelia court and Point place; Solon S. Dodge.
Chicago Lawn—Homan avenue and 66th street; Helen N. Blanchard.
Chopin (site)—Iowa street and Campbell avenue.
Clarke—Ashland avenue and West 13th street; Henry G. Clark.
Clay—133d street and Superior avenue; Flora V. Renaud.
Cleveland—Albany avenue and Byron street; Lewis W. Colwell.
Colman—Dearborn street, near 47th; Lillas M. Williamson.
Columbus—Augusta street, between Hoyne avenue and Leavitt street; Kate A. Reedy.
Cooney—Leavitt street and Belle Plaine avenue; Elizabeth A. McGillen.
Cooper—West 19th street, near Ashland avenue; Ida A. Shaver.
Copernicus—Throop and 60th streets; Cora Caverno.
Corkery—West 25th street and South Kildare avenue; Daniel F. O'Hearn.
Cornell—Drexel avenue, near 75th street; Flora J. Joslyn.
Cregar—Campbell avenue, between Taylor and Fillmore streets; Henry F. Kling.
Curtis—114th street, near State; Thomas C. Hill.
Dante—Desplaines, Ewing and Forquer streets; Harriet F. Hayward.
Darwin—Edgewood avenue and Catalpa court; Ernest E. Cole.

Davis—Sacramento avenue and 39th street; Jaroslav J. Zmrhal.
Delano—West Adams street and Springfield avenue; Gerbrandles A. Osinga.
Dewey—54th street and Union avenue; Edward McLoughlin.
Doolittle—35th street, near Cottage Grove avenue; Frederick M. Sisson.
Dore—Harrison street, near Halsted; Fred J. Watson.
Douglas—32d street and Forest avenue; Lucia Johnston.
Drake—Calumet avenue, between 26th and 28th streets; Helen W. McLaughlin.
Drummond—Clybourn place and North Lincoln street; Horace N. Herrick.
Dunning—Addison street and Nagle avenue; Mary E. Marnell.
Earle—61st street and Hermitage avenue; Ira C. Baker.
Emerson—Walnut and Paulina streets; June H. MacConkey.
Emmet (Austin)—Corner Madison street and Pine avenue; Helen B. Eastman.
Ericsson—West Harrison street, near Sacramento avenue; John M. Duggan.
Everett—Irving avenue and 34th street; Patrick F. Haley.
Fallon—Wallace and 42d streets; James E. McDade.
Farragut—Spaulding avenue and 24th street; Frank L. Morse.
Farren—Wabash avenue, near 51st street; Rose A. Pesta.
Felsenthal—Calumet avenue and 41st street; Walter J. Harrower.
Field—Greenleaf and North Ashland avenues; Charles A. Kent.
Fiske—62d street and Ingleside avenue; Harry T. Baker.
Forrestville—45th street and St. Lawrence avenue; Florence Holbrook.
Foster—Union avenue and O'Brien street; Mary B. Catelain.
Franklin—Goethe street, near Wells; Etta Q. Gee.
Froebel—21st and Robey streets; Harry S. Vaile.
Fuller—42d street and St. Lawrence avenue; Louise K. Stone.
Fulton—Hermitage avenue and 53d street; Clara H. McFarlin.
Gage Park—55th and Rockwell streets; Martha V. Bishop.
Gallistel—104th street and Ewing avenue; James H. Henry.
Garfield—Newberry avenue and 14th place; James E. Welsh.
Gary—30th street and Lawndale avenue; Frank W. Stahl.
Gladstone—Robey street and Washburne avenue; Daniel A. Tear.
Goethe—Rockwell street, near Fullerton avenue; Charles S. Bartholf.
Goodrich—Taylor and Sangamon streets; Charles J. Lunak.
Goudy—Foster and Winthrop avenues; Harriet A. Eckhardt.
Graham—45th street and Union avenue; Mary T. Maroney.
Grant—Wilcox avenue, near Western avenue; Marguerite L. O'Brien.
Gray—North Laramie avenue and Grace street; Ella R. Connell.
Greeley—Grace street and Sheffield avenue; Abigail Cannon Ellings.
Greene—Paulina and 36th streets; Edward Wildeman.
Gresham—85th and Green streets; Robert H. Rennie.
Hamilton—Cornelia street and North Marshfield avenue; M. Elizabeth Farson.
Hamline—48th and Bishop streets; Eleanor Reese Dunn.
Hammond—21st place, near California avenue; John A. Long.
Hancock—Princeton avenue and 46th place; Nora F. Doran.
Hanson Park (Mont Clare)—North Linder and Grand avenues; Fannie L. Marble.

Harper—65th, Wood and Honore streets; Morgan G. Hogge.

Harvard—Harvard avenue, between 75th and 76th streets; Mary S. L. Hartigan.

Haugan—Hamlin, Avers and Sunnyside avenues; Thomas C. Johnson.

Haven—Wabash avenue and 15th street; Margaret Madden.

Hawthorne—School street and Seminary avenue; George W. Davis.

Hayes—Leavitt and Fulton streets; Simeon V. Robbins.

Hayt—Granville and Greenview avenues; Elmer L. Kletzing.

Headley—Lewis street and Garfield avenue; Caroline J. Utter.

Healy—Wallace street, near 31st; William C. Payne.

Hedges—48th street and Winchester avenue; Marcella R. Hanlon.

Hendricks—43d street and Shields avenue; Elizabeth Haines.

Henry—West Cullom and Eberly avenues; Mary E. C. Lyons.

Herzl (site)—Lawndale avenue and 15th street.

Holden—Loomis and 31st streets; Lincoln P. Goodhue.

Holmes—56th and Morgan streets; James W. McGinnis.

Howe (Austin)—Laurel avenue and Superior street; Mary E. Vance.

Howland—Spaulding avenue and 16th street; Amelia D. Hookway.

Irving—Lexington street and Hoyne avenue; John W. Troeger.

Irving Park—North Kedvale avenue and Grace street; Mary McMahon.

Jackson—Sholto and Better streets; William Hedges.

Jahn—North Lincoln street and Belmont avenue; Cephas H. Leach.

Jefferson—Elburn avenue and Laflin street; Catharine M. Delanty.

Jenner—Oak street and Milton avenue; Frederick J. Lane.

Jirka—17th and Laflin streets; Mary F. Rodgers.

Jones—Plymouth court and Harrison street; Thomas C. M. Jamieson.

Jungman—Nutt and West 18th streets; Sarah A. Fleming.

Keeler avenue—North Keeler avenue and Hirsh street; Katherine Riordan.

Keith—Dearborn and 34th streets; Louise Schroll.

Kenwood—Washington avenue and 50th street; Abigail M. Hunt.

Kershaw—Union avenue, near 64th street; William Radebaugh.

Key (Austin)—Ohio street and Park avenue; Lillian H. Wright.

King—Harrison street, near Western avenue; Ellen J. Hardick.

Kinzie—Ohio street and LaSalle avenue; J. Edward Huber.

Knickerbocker—Clifton and Belden avenues; Mary G. Guthrie.

Kohn—104th and State streets; Charles C. Cobb.

Komensky—Throop and 20th streets; Clara H. Mahony.

Kosciuszko—Holt and Cleaver streets; Harriet P. Johnston.

Kozminski—54th street and Ingleside avenue; Leslie Lewis.

Lafayette—Washtenaw avenue and Augusta street; Mary I. Purer.

Langland—Cortland street, near Leavitt; Effie C. Then.

LaSalle—Hammond and Eugenie streets; Dora W. Zollman.

Lawson—Homan avenue and 13th street; Charles C. Krauskopf.

Lewis-Champlin—62d street and Princeton avenue; Henry S. Crane.

Libby—53d and Loomis streets; Florence U. Colt.

Lincoln—Hamilton court and Kemper place; Albert L. Stevenson.

Linne—Sacramento avenue and School street; Charles A. Cook.

Lloyd—Dickens and North Lamon avenues; Jacob H. Hauch.

Logan—Oakley avenue and Rhine street; James B. Farnsworth.

Longfellow—35th street, near South Lincoln street. Mary E. Gilbert.

Lowell—North Spaulding avenue and Hirsch street; Clarence E. De Butts.

Madison—Dorchester avenue, near 75th street; Sarah A. Milner.

Manierre—Hudson avenue, near Blackhawk street; Luman Hewes.

Mann—37th street and Princeton avenue; Jeannette I. Robinson.

Marquette—Harrison and Wood streets; Mary E. Tobin.

Marsh—98th street and Exchange avenue; Elliott A. Hamilton.

Marshall—Adams street, near Kedzie avenue; Louis J. Block.

May—South LaVergne avenue and West Harrison street; Thomas J. Plant.

Mayfair—West Wilson and North Kenton avenues; Annie S. Newman.

Medill—14th place, near Throop street; Avon S. Hall.

Mitchell—North Oakley avenue and Ohio street; Chester C. Dodge.

Monroe—Schubert and Monticello avenues; Ada B. Sempill.

Montefiore—Sangamon street and Grand avenue; G. Ovedia Jacobs.

Moos—California and Wabansia avenues; Esther J. W. Barker.

Morris—Barry avenue and Blucher street; Luella Heinroth.

Morse—Sawyer avenue and Ohio street; George L. Voorhees.

Moseley—Michigan avenue and 24th street; Leone L. Thorne.

Motley—North Ada street, near West Chicago avenue; Frank H. Chase.

Mozart—North Hamlin and Humboldt avenues; Harriet B. Davis.

Mulligan—Sheffield avenue, near Willow street; Hanna Schill.

McAllister—36th and Gage streets; Esther R. Perry.

McClellan—Wallace and 35th streets; Miriam Del Banco.

McCormick—Sawyer avenue and 27th street; William H. Chamberlin.

McCosh — Champlain avenue, near 66th street; Ida M. Pahlman.

McLaren—York and Laflin streets; Carolyn G. Adams.

McPherson—North Lincoln street, near Lawrence; Adelaide E. Jordan.

Nash—North Lamon avenue and West Erie street; Margaret S. Gill.

Nettelhorst—Evanston and Aldine avenues; Robert L. Hughes.

Newberry—Willow and Orchard streets; Albert A. Evans.

Nixon—Dickens and North Keeler avenues; Charles H. Ostrander.

Nobel—North Karlov avenue and Hirsch street; Marie A. Dunne.

Norwood Park—Walnut street and Cheney avenue; Charles A. Myall.

Oakland—40th street and Cottage Grove avenue; Louise M. Ripple.

Ogden—Chestnut and North State streets; Martha M. Ruggles.

Oglesby—Green and 77th streets; Daniel J. Beeby.

Otis—Armour street, near Ohio; G. Charles Griffiths.

Parkman—51st street and Princeton avenue; John B. McGinty.

Park Manor—71st street and Rhodes avenue; Genevieve Melody.

Parkside—70th street and East End avenue; Edmund B. Smith.

Peabody—Augusta and Noble streets; Mary H. Smyth.

Peirce (site)—Southport and Bryn Mawr avenues.

Penn—Avers avenue and 16th street; Bertha Benson.

Pickard—21st place and Oakley avenue; Mary Ryan.

Plamondon—15th place and Washtenaw avenue; William W. Reed.

Poe—106th and Fulton streets; Grace R. Barbour.

Prescott—Wrightwood and Marshfield avenues; Margaret S. Fitch.

Pulaski—Leavitt street, between Lubeck and Coblentz streets; Anna C. Goggin.

Pullman—Morse avenue and 113th street; Daniel R. Martin.

Raster—Wood and 70th streets; David L. Murray.

Ravenswood—Paulina street and Montrose avenue; Josiah F. Kletzing.

Ray—57th street and Monroe avenue; Arthur O. Rape.

Raymond—Wabash avenue and 36th place; John L. Lewis.

Reilly (site)—Monticello and Lawndale avenues.

Revere—Ellis avenue and 72d street; Frank Mayo.

Rogers—West 13th street, near Throop; Alice A. Hogan.

Ryder—89th street and Lowe avenue; Minnie M. Wrisley.

Ryerson—Lawndale avenue and Huron street; John T. Ray.

Sabin (site)—Hirsch street, Irving avenue and North Leavitt street.

Sawyer Avenue—Sawyer avenue and 53d street; Robert G. Jeffrey.

Scammon—Morgan and Monroe streets; Cecelia B. Schmek.

Scanlan—Perry avenue, near 117th street; Alfred Harvey.

Schiller—Vedder and Halsted streets; Belle B. Murphy.

Schley—North Oakley avenue, near Potomac avenue; Minra S. Heuermann.

Schneider—Hoyne avenue, near Wellington street; Elizabeth E. Fisk.

Scott—64th street and Washington avenue; John W. Akers.

Seward—46th street and Hermitage avenue; Mary A. Perkin.

Sexton, Austin O. (site)—60th street, Langley and Champlain avenues.

Sexton, James A.—Wells and Wendell streets; Visa McLaughlin.

Shakespeare—Greenwood avenue and 46th street; Walter H. Comstock.

Sheldon—State and Elm streets; Jane S. Atwater.

Shepard (site)—Mozart and Fillmore streets.

Sheridan, Mark—27th and Wallace streets; John A. Johnson.

Sheridan, Phil—90th street and Escanaba avenue; Edward L. C. Morse.

Sherman—Morgan street and 51st place; Levi T. Regan.

Sherwood—57th street and Princeton avenue; Sarah A. Kirkley.

Shields—43d and Rockwell streets; Walter R. Hatfield.

Sixty-Second Place—62d place and Hamlin avenue; Mary Taylor.

Skinner—Jackson boulevard and Aberdeen street; William L. Smyser.

Smyth—13th street, near Blue Island avenue; William R. Hornbaker.

South Deering—Calhoun and 107th streets; Myra C. Billings.

Spalding—Park avenue, between Ashland avenue and Paulina street; Lucy I. Laing.

Spencer—Park and Lavergne avenues; Otto M. Becker.

Springfield Avenue—Springfield avenue and Roscoe street; Helen H. Robinson.

Spry—Marshall boulevard and West 24th street; William J. Fraser.

Stewart—Kenmore avenue, between Wilson and Sunnyside avenues; Archibald O. Coddington.

Stowe—Wabansia avenue and Ballou street; Frank A. Larck.

Sullivan—83d street and Houston avenue; Anna F. Mullay.

Sumner—South Kildare and Colorado avenues; Orris J. Milliken.

Swift (not open)—Winthrop avenue, between Ardmore and Thorndale avenues.

Swing—String street, between 16th and 17th; Margaret C. Adams.

Talcott—Ohio and North Lincoln streets; Ambrose B. Wight.

Taylor—Avenue J, near 100th street; Annie K. Sullivan.

Tennyson—California avenue and Fulton street; Mary E. Fellows.

Thomas—Belden avenue and High street; M. Therese Norton.

Thorp, J. N.—89th street and Superior avenue; Henry D. Hatch.

Thorp, Ole A.—Foster and Lincoln avenues; Minnie M. Jamieson.

Throop—Throop street, near 18th; Mary W. O'Keefe.

Tilden—Lake and Elizabeth streets; Harriet N. Winchell.

Tilton—West Randolph street and 44th avenue; Bertha S. Armbruster.

Trumbull—North Ashland, Foster and Farragut avenues; Helen R. Ryan.

University Avenue—University avenue and East 91st street; Jessie B. Black.

Vanderpoel—95th street and Prospect avenue; Catherine A. Burke.

Van Vlissingen—108th place, near Wentworth avenue; George A. Brennan.

Von Humboldt — Rockwell and Hirsch streets; Mary J. W. Boughan.

Wadsworth—Lexington avenue, near 64th street; Isabel J. Burke.

Walsh—20th and Johnson streets; Alfred E. Logie.

Ward—Shields avenue and 27th street; Augustus R. Dillon.

Warren—92d street and Central avenue; Edith P. Shepherd.

Washburne—West 14th street, near Union; Charles W. Thompson.

Washington—North Morgan street and Grand avenue; Samuel R. Meck.

Waters—Wilson and Campbell avenues; Esther E. Morgan.

Webster—Wentworth avenue and 33d street; Adrian M. Doolin.

Wells—Ashland avenue and Augusta street; George B. Massillch.

Wentworth—70th and Sangamon streets; Humphrey J. Moynihan.

West Pullman—120th street and Parnell avenue; Harriette T. Treadwell.

Whitney—28th street and South Kaskaskia avenue; Ella R. Coles.

Whittier—South Lincoln and 23d streets; Mary Greene.

Wicker Park—Evergreen avenue, near Robey street; Fred E. Smith.

Willard—49th street and St. Lawrence avenue; Grace Reed.

Worthy—California avenue and 26th street; Edgar W. Trout.

Yale—70th and Yale streets; William Schoch.

Yates—Cortland and Humboldt streets; Blanca R. Daigger.

SALARIES IN CHICAGO SCHOOLS (1913).

(Per year unless otherwise specified.)

Superintendent	$10,000
First assistant superintendent	6,000
Assistant superintendent	4,000
Dist. superintendents, first and second years	3,500
Third and subsequent years	4,000
Examiner	4,000
Supervisor physical education	4,000
Supervisor manual training	4,000
Supervisor household arts	3,500
Supervisor German	2,500
Supervisor school for blind	2,000
Head special teacher of music	2,200

DRAWING AND SINGING TEACHERS (ELEMENTARY).

First year	$1,500	Sixth year	$2,000
Second year	1,600	Seventh year	2,100
Third year	1,700	Eighth and subse-	
Fourth year	1,800	quent years	2,200
Fifth year	1,900		

HOUSEHOLD ARTS TEACHERS (ELEMENTARY).

LOWER GROUP.		UPPER GROUP.	
First year	$850	First year	$1,150
Second year	900	Second year	1,225
Third year	950	Third and subse-	
Fourth year	1,000	quent years	1,300
Fifth and subsequent years	1,075		

MANUAL TRAINING AND PHYSICAL EDUCATION TEACHERS (ELEMENTARY).

LOWER GROUP.		UPPER GROUP.	
First year	$850	First year	$1,200
Second year	925	Second year	1,300
Third year	1,000	Third year	1,400
Fourth and subsequent years	1,100	Fourth and subsequent years	1,500

CHICAGO TEACHERS' COLLEGE.

Principal normal school	$5,000
Assistant to principal	3,200

HEADS OF DEPARTMENTS.			
First year	$2,300	Fourth year	$1,500
Second year	2,400	Fifth year	1,600
Third year	2,500	Sixth and subsequent years	1,700
Fourth year	2,600		
Fifth year	2,700	INSTRUCTORS—UPPER GROUP.	
Sixth and subsequent years	2,800	First year	$1,800
INSTRUCTORS—LOWER GROUP.		Second year	1,900
		Third year	2,000
First year	$1,200	Fourth year	2,100
Second year	1,300	Fifth year	2,200
Third year	1,400	Sixth and subsequent years	2,300

CHILD STUDY DEPARTMENT.

Director	$3,000	Assistant director	$2,800

HIGH SCHOOL PRINCIPALS.

LOWER GROUP.		Fourth year	$3,000
First year	$2,290	Fifth year	3,100
Second year	2,300	Sixth year	3,200
Third year	2,400	Seventh year	3,300
Fourth year	2,500	Eighth year	3,400
Fifth year	2,600	Ninth year	3,500
Sixth and subsequent years	2,700	Tenth year	3,600
		Eleventh year	3,700
UPPER GROUP.		Twelfth year	3,800
First year	$2,790	Thirteenth year	3,900
Second year	2,800	Fourteenth and subsequent years	4,000
Third year	2,900		

HIGH SCHOOL TEACHERS.

LOWER GROUP.		UPPER GROUP.	
First year	$1,000	First year	$1,700
Second year	1,100	Second year	1,800
Third year	1,200	Third year	1,900
Fourth year	1,300	Fourth year	2,000
Fifth year	1,400	Fifth year	2,100
Sixth and subsequent years	1,500	Sixth year	2,200
Seventh and subsequent years	1,600	Seventh year	2,300
		Eighth year	2,400
		Ninth year	2,500
		Tenth and subsequent years	2,600

PHYSICAL EDUCATION TEACHERS (HIGH SCHOOLS).

LOWER GROUP.

Flat $1,300

Teachers in high schools holding limited certificates as teachers of drawing, French, German, commercial subjects, manual training or household arts:

LOWER GROUP.

First year	$1,000	Fifth year	$1,200
Second year	1,050	Sixth year	1,250
Third year	1,100	Seventh and subsequent years	1,300
Fourth year	1,150		

Teachers of physical education, music, art and manual training in high schools, holding limited certificates:

UPPER GROUP.

First year	$1,400	Sixth year	$1,900
Second year	1,500	Seventh year	2,000
Third year	1,600	Eighth year	2,100
Fourth year	1,700	Ninth and subsequent years	2,200
Fifth year	1,800		

Teachers in high schools holding limited certificates as teachers of modern languages, commercial subjects or household arts:

UPPER GROUP.

First year	$1,350	Fifth year	$1,550
Second year	1,400	Sixth year	1,600
Third year	1,450	Seventh and subsequent years	1,700
Fourth year	1,500		

SUBSTITUTES (HIGH SCHOOL).

Substitutes in high schools receive $5 or $6 per day for days of actual service; rate is determined by superintendent.

PRINCIPALS OF ELEMENTARY SCHOOLS.

LOWER GROUP.		Second year	$2,800
First year	$1,800	Third year	2,900
Second year	1,900	Fourth year	3,000
Third year	2,000	Fifth year	3,050
Fourth year	2,100	Sixth year	3,100
Fifth year	2,200	Seventh year	3,150
Sixth year	2,300	Eighth year	3,200
Seventh year	2,400	Ninth year	3,250
Eighth year	2,500	Tenth year	3,300
Ninth and subsequent years	2,600	Eleventh year	3,350
		Twelfth year	3,400
UPPER GROUP.		Thirteenth year	3,450
First year	$2,700	Fourteenth and subsequent years	3,500

HEAD ASSISTANTS.

LOWER GROUP.

First and subsequent years $1,175

UPPER GROUP.			
First year	$1,025	Fourth and subsequent years	$1,225
Second year	1,075		
Third year	1,125		

EIGHTH GRADE TEACHERS.

LOWER GROUP.

First and subsequent years $975

UPPER GROUP.			
First year	$1,250	Fourth year	$1,400
Second year	1,300	Fifth and subsequent years	1,500
Third year	1,350		

ELEMENTARY TEACHERS (PRIMARY).

LOWER GROUP.		UPPER GROUP.	
First year	$650	First year	$975
Second year	675	Second year	1,025
Third year	725	Third year	1,075
Fourth year	775	Fourth and subsequent years	1,175
Fifth year	825		
Sixth year	875		
Seventh and subsequent years	925		

GRAMMAR.

LOWER GROUP.		UPPER GROUP.	
First year	$650	First year	$1,000
Second year	700	Second year	1,050
Third year	750	Third year	1,100
Fourth year	800	Fourth and subsequent years	1,200
Fifth year	850		
Sixth year	900		
Seventh and subsequent years	950		

MISCELLANEOUS.

Teachers of the deaf and of crippled children get from $750 to $1,300 a year, according to group and length of service. Teachers in schools for blind get same salaries as teachers in elementary schools. Teachers in John Worthy school get $25 per school month in excess of schedule for elementary schools.

Each elementary school having twenty-five or more divisions is allowed one extra teacher, who is paid according to the elementary school schedule, lower group.

Teachers in charge of branch schools receive extra compensation of $75 per annum.

Teachers in charge of classes in German receive extra compensation of $50 per annum.

Teachers in charge of industrial rooms and of rooms for subnormal children receive $50 per annum in advance of grammar grade schedule.

Substitutes in elementary schools receive $3 per day for days of actual service.

Teachers in practice schools receive $200 a year in excess of grammar grade teachers.

Principals in evening schools receive from $3 to $5 per evening, according to length of service and size of school. Teachers get from $2 to $3.50 per evening.

Principals in vacation schools get $100 for term of six weeks; teachers get $75 per term; cadets get $30 per term.

CHICAGO PUBLIC SCHOOL STATISTICS.

Year.	Enrollment.	Teachers.	Year.	Enrollment.	Teachers.	Year.	Enrollment.	Teachers.	Year.	Enrollment.	Teachers.
1841	410	5	1860	14,199	123	1879	56,587	851	1897	225,718	4,914
1842	531	7	1861	16,441	160	1880	59,862	898	1898	236,239	5,268
1843	808	7	1862	17,521	187	1881	63,141	958	1899	242,807	5,535
1844	915	8	1863	21,188	212	1882	68,614	1,019	1900	255,861	5,806
1845	1,051	9	1864-5	29,080	240	1883	72,509	1,107	1901	262,738	5,951
1846	1,107	13	1866	24,851	265	1884	76,044	1,195	1902	268,392	5,775
1847	1,317	18	1867	27,360	319	1885	79,278	1,296	1903	268,968	5,444
1848	1,517	18	1868	29,954	401	1886	83,022	1,440	1904	264,397	5,670
1849	1,794	18	1869	34,740	481	1887	84,902	1,574	1905	267,837	5,695
1850	1,919	21	1870	38,939	557	1888	89,575	1,663	1906	272,086	5,809
1851	2,287	25	1871	40,832	572	1889	93,737	1,801	1907	273,050	5,981
1852	2,404	29	1872	38,035	476	1890	135,541	2,711	1908	292,581	6,106
1853	3,086	34	1873	44,091	654	1891	146,751	3,000	1909	296,427	6,296
1854	3,500	35	1874	47,963	679	1892	157,743	3,300	1910	300,893	6,383
1855	6,826	42	1875	49,121	700	1893	166,895	3,520	1911	304,146	6,584
1856-7	8,577	61	1876	51,128	762	1894	185,368	3,812	1912	307,281	6,740
1858	10,786	81	1877	53,529	736	1895	201,380	4,326	1913	315,737	7,013
1859	12,873	101	1878	55,109	797	1896	213,835	4,668			

MAYORALTY ELECTIONS IN CHICAGO SINCE 1871.

Nov. 7, 1871.
Joseph Medill, Rep......... 16,125
Chas. C. P. Holden, Dem.. 5,988
Nov. 4, 1873.
H. D. Colvin, Peo. Party...28,791
L. L. Bond, Law and Order. 18,540
July 12, 1876.
Monroe Heath, Rep....... 19,248
Mark Kimball, Dem....... 7,509
J. J. McGrath, Ind....... 3,362
April 3, 1877.
Monroe Heath, Rep....... 30,881
Perry H. Smith, Dem..... 19,449
April 1, 1879.
C. H. Harrison, Sr., Dem. 25,685
Abner M. Wright, Rep.... 20,496
Ernst Schmidt, Soc....... 11,829
April 5, 1881.
C. H. Harrison, Sr., Dem. 35,668
John M. Clark, Rep....... 27,925
Timothy O'Mara, Ind..... 764
George Schilling, Soc...... 240
April 3, 1883.
C. H. Harrison, Sr., Dem. 41,225
Eugene Cary, Rep........ 30,963
April 7, 1885.
C. H. Harrison, Sr., Dem. 43,352
Sidney Smith, Rep....... 42,977
William H. Bush, Pro.... 221
April 5, 1887.
John A. Roche, Rep....... 51,249
Robert L. Nelson, Lab.... 23,490
Joseph L. Whitlock, Pro.. 372
April 2, 1889.
John A. Roche, Rep....... 45,328
Ira J. Mason, Pro........ 410
DeWitt C. Cregier, Dem.. 57,340
Charles Orchardson, Soc... 303

April 7, 1891.
Hempst'd Washburne, Rep. 46,957
DeWitt C. Cregier, Dem.. 46,588
Elmer Washburn, Citizens'. 24,027
C. H. Harrison, Sr., Ind. D. 42,931
Thomas Morgan, Soc...... 2,376
April 4, 1893.
C. H. Harrison, Sr., Dem..114,237
S. W. Allerton, Rep....... 93,148
DeW. C. Cregier, Un. Cit. 3,033
J. Ehrenpreis, Soc. Lab... 1,000
Dec. 19, 1893.
Special election to fill vacancy caused by assassination of Carter H. Harrison, Sr.
John P. Hopkins, Dem....112,959
George B. Swift, Rep......111,660
Michael Britzius, Soc..... 2,064
Ebenezer Wakeley, Pop... 535
April 2, 1895.
George B. Swift, Rep......143,884
Frank Wenter, Dem........103,725
Bayard Holmes, Peo...... 12,882
Arthur J. Bassett, Pro.... 994
Ebenezer Wakeley, Peo. Sil. 302
April 6, 1897.
C. H. Harrison, Sr., Dem..148,880
John M. Harlan, Ind. Rep. 69,730
Nathaniel C. Sears, Rep... 59,512
Wash. Hesing, Ind. Dem.. 15,427
John Glambock, Soc. Lab.. 1,230
H. L. Parmelee, Pro...... 910
J. Irving Pearce, Jr., Ind.. 561
Frank H. Collier, Ind. Dem. 110

April 4, 1899.
C. H. Harrison, Jr., Dem..148,496
Zina R. Carter, Rep.......107,437
John P. Altgeld, M. O... 47,169
John A. Wadhams, Pro... 1,023
August Klenkie, Soc. Lab.. 1,175
T. G. Kerwin, Soc. Dem... 367
April 2, 1901.
C. H. Harrison, Jr., Dem..156,756
Elbridge Hanecy, Rep.....128,413
Avery E. Hoyt, Pro........ 3,329
Gus Hoyt, Soc. Dem....... 2,043
John R. Pepin, Soc. Lab... 679
Thomas Rhodes, Sin. Tax.. 1,028
John Collins, Soc.......... 5,384
April 7, 1903.
C. H. Harrison, Jr., Dem..146,208
Graeme Stewart, Rep......138,648
Thomas L. Haines, Pro... 2,674
Charles L. Breckon, Soc... 11,124
Daniel L. Cruice, Ind. Lab. 9,947
Henry Sale, Soc. Lab...... 1,014
April 4, 1905.
Edward F. Dunne, Dem...163,189
John M. Harlan, Rep......138,548
Oliver W. Stewart, Pro.... 3,294
John Collins, Soc.......... 23,034
April 2, 1907.
Fred A. Busse, Rep........164,702
Edward F. Dunne, Dem...151,779
W. A. Brubaker, Pro...... 6,020
George Koop, Soc......... 13,429
April 4, 1911.
Carter H. Harrison, Dem..177,997
Charles E. Merriam, Rep..160,672
W. A. Brubaker, Pro...... 2,239
W. E. Rodriguez, Soc..... 24,825
Anthony Prince, Soc. Lab.. 1,059

MUNICIAL ART LEAGUE.

Incorporated Jan. 30, 1901. Secretary's office at the Art Institute.

President—Ralph Clarkson.
Vice-President—Lorado Taft.
Second Vice-President—Eames MacVeagh.
Secretary—Everett L. Millard.
Assistant Secretary—Louis A. Damon.
Treasurer—Charles L. Hutchinson.
Directors—Ralph Clarkson, Lorado Taft, O. C. Simonds, William H. Bush, Mrs. William Frederick Grower, Eames MacVeagh, Mrs. C. S. Downs, Kenneth Sawyer Goodman, Myron H. West.
Exhibition Committee—Mrs. William Frederick Grower, chairman; Mrs. H. H. Kingsley, vice-chairman; Mrs. William F. Young, secretary.

The objects of the association are to promote the beautifying of the streets, public buildings and places of Chicago; to bring to the attention of the officials and people of the city the best methods for instituting artistic municipal improvements and to stimulate civic pride in the care and improvement of private property. The board of directors of the league is composed of one sculptor, one architect, one painter, one landscape architect, four laymen and the chairman of the exhibition committee.

WIDTH OF TIRES REQUIRED IN CHICAGO.

The wide-tire ordinance passed by the Chicago city council Feb. 4, 1908, requires that all four-wheeled vehicles shall have tires proportionate to the load they carry, as follows:

Load.	Tires, inches.
3,000 pounds or under	1½
Between 3,000 and 4,000 pounds	2
Between 4,000 and 6,000 pounds	2½
Between 6,000 and 8,000 pounds	3¼
Between 8,000 and 10,000 pounds	3¾
Between 10,000 and 14,000 pounds	4¼
Between 14,000 and 18,000 pounds	6
Over 18,000 pounds	8

The width for two-wheeled trucks is double.

CHICAGO CLUBS AND CLUBHOUSES.

Arche—President, Mrs. Charles B. Caldwell; corresponding secretary, Mrs. A. M. Fogg.

Bankers'—President, Nelson N. Lampert; secretary and treasurer, W. D. C. Street.

Builders'—412-418 Chamber of Commerce building; president, Harry C. Knisely; secretary, Thomas J. Maney.

Calumet—Michigan avenue and 20th street; president, Lawrence Heyworth; secretary, Walter E. Falthorn.

Caxton—Tenth floor Fine Arts building; president, James W. Thompson; secretary, Thomas W. Swan.

Chicago Athletic Association—12 South Michigan avenue; president, David B. Gann;. secretary, Louis Wolff.

Chicago Architectural—39 West Adams street; president, George A. Awsumb; secretary, Harry C. Bentley.

Chicago Automobile—321 Plymouth court; president, Allan S. Ray; secretary, C. G. Sinsabaugh.

Chicago Club—Michigan avenue and Van Buren street; president, John S. Runnells; secretary, W. R. Odell.

Chicago Polo—President, Jarvis Hunt; secretary and treasurer, Wilson Nixon.

Chicago Woman's—410 South Michigan avenue; president, Mrs. George Bass; corresponding secretary, Mrs. Otis L. Beardsley.

Chicago Woman's Aid—Indiana avenue and 21st street; president, Mrs. Moses L. Purvin; corresponding secretary, Mrs. Maurice L. Ash, 5210 South Park avenue.

Chicago Yacht—Foot of Monroe street, outer harbor; commodore, William A. Lydon; secretary, George L. Weed.

City Club—315 Plymouth court; president, Alfred L. Baker; secretary, Henry P. Chandler; civics secretary, George E. Hooker.

Cliff Dwellers—216 South Michigan avenue; president, Hamlin Garland; secretary, W. N. C. Carlton.

Colonial Club of Chicago—4445 Grand boulevard; president, A.K.Brown; secretary, Thomas J. Finn.

Columbia Yacht—Lake front, foot of Randolph street; commodore, James B. Pugh; secretary, Arthur G. Fox.

Commercial—President, Benjamin Carpenter; secretary, Walter B. Smith.

Edgewater Country—5658 Winthrop avenue; president, J. A. McLean; secretary, Lee H. Stiles.

Englewood—6323 Harvard avenue; president, Frank M. Fulton; secretary, Harold Dickey.

Englewood Woman's Club—6732 Wentworth avenue; president, Mrs. F. T. Avery; secretary, Mrs. F. B. Ormsby.

Evanston Woman's—President, Mrs. Rufus C. Dawes; corresponding secretary, Mrs. Perkins B. Bass.

Farragut Yacht Club—Lake shore, foot of 33d street; commodore, F. W. Weston; secretary, H. L. Rich.

Fortnightly—Fine Arts building; president, Mrs. Henry S. Robbins; corresponding secretary, Mrs. Ralph Clarkson.

Forty Club—President, Wilbur D. Nesbit; secretary, Charles H. Burras.

German Club of Chicago—President, Oscar A. Kropf; secretary, Charles Wurster.

Germania Mænnerchor—106 Germania place; president, H. O. Lange; secretary, E. A. Stebel.

Hamilton—20 South Dearborn street; president, Guy Guernsey; secretary, Richard Y. Hoffman.

Illinois Athletic—112 South Michigan avenue; president, W. Y. Perry; secretary, Albert MacRae.

Illinois—113 South Ashland boulevard; president, Harry McCormack; secretary, P. J. V. McKian.

Industrial—President, Marvin B. Pool; secretary, W. R. Abbott.

Irish Fellowship—President, Charles Ffrench; secretary, George E. Warren.

Iroquois—21 North LaSalle street; president, A. F. Reichmann; corresponding secretary, William Rathmann.

Kenwood—Lake avenue and 47th street; president, George R. Jenkins; secretary, G. E. Bliss.

Kenwood Country—Drexel boulevard and 48th street; president, Charles S. Winston; secretary, D. W. Westervelt.

Kilo—26 South Wabash avenue; president, Mrs. John S. McClelland; corresponding secretary, Mrs. Charles D. Campbell.

Lincoln Park Yacht—Commodore, A. M. Andrews; secretary, O. P. Sundell.

Mid-Day—First National Bank building, 17th floor; president, Silas H. Strawn; secretary, J. L. Cochran.

Nike—700 Oakwood boulevard; president, Mrs. Anna M. Mullin; secretary, Miss Cecilia Hefter.

Oak Park—President, A. S. Ray; secretary, R. B. Flitcraft.

Oaks—Lake street and Waller avenue; president, George H. Grounds; secretary, A. G. Seaholm.

Press Club—26 North Dearborn street; president, Walter A. Washburne; recording secretary, J. H. Ashley.

Quadrangle—Lexington avenue and 58th street; president, Gordon J. Laing; secretary, Gilbert A. Bliss.

Rotary—33 South Dearborn street; president, George L. Wilson; secretary, Alfred A. Packer.

Saddle and Cycle—Sheridan road and Foster avenue; president, B. M. Winston; secretary, J. A. Stevenson.

Social Service—President, Frank E. Wing; secretary, Arthur J. Strawson.

South End Woman's—President, Mrs. E. Cohen; recording secretary, Mrs. Frank Clute, 8918 Exchange avenue.

South Shore Country—Lake shore and 67th street; president, Frederick Bode; secretary, J. W. Carey.

Southern—116 South Michigan avenue; president, Dixon C. Williams; secretary, Y. B. Jones.

Southern Woman's—President, Mrs. Thomas White; secretary, Miss Mary L. Behan.

Standard—Michigan avenue and 24th street; president, Samuel Deutsch; secretary, Joseph Weisenbach.

Swedish Club of Chicago—1258 LaSalle avenue; president, C. S. Peterson; secretary, Axel Hulten.

Tavern—President, James T. Clyde; secretary, J. C. Hutchins.

Three Arts—1614 LaSalle avenue; president, Miss Gwethalyn Jones; secretary, Mrs. George A. Seavens, Jr.

Town and Country—2841 Washington boulevard; president, Dr. C. St. Clair; secretary, Harry G. Dengel.

Twentieth Century—President, Franklin H. Head; secretary, William M. Payne, 2246 Michigan avenue.

Union League—Jackson boulevard and Federal street; president, Judge W. H. McSurely; secretary, A. F. Allen.

Union Printers'—28 North 5th avenue; president, Charles G. Stevens; secretary, Joseph Larson.

United Irish Societies of Chicago—President, James T. Clarke; corresponding secretary, Charles McGready.

University—Michigan avenue and Monroe street; president, Walter L. Fisher; secretary, William F. Anderson.

West End Catholic Woman's—President, Mrs. D. R. McAuley; corresponding secretary, Mrs. Joseph P. Kampp.

West End Woman's—35 South Ashland boulevard; president, Mrs. J. Hobart Beers; corresponding secretary, Mrs. Gilman W. Smith.

Woman's Athletic—606 South Michigan avenue; president, Mrs. Will H. Lyford; secretary, Mrs. George W. Dixon.

Woman's City—President, Mrs. Mary H. Wilmarth; secretary, Mrs. W. B. Owen.

Woman's Club of Austin—President, Mrs. Charles J. Gibson; corresponding secretary, Mrs. E. G. Snodgrass.

Woman's New Century—President, Mrs. W. J. Austin; corresponding secretary, Mrs. C. E. Hodge.

Woodlawn Park—64th street and Woodlawn avenue; president, S. A. Kennedy; secretary, H. B. Taylor.

Woodlawn Woman's—President, Mrs. Anna F. Johns; corresponding secretary, Mrs. Victoria K. Waite.

Young Fortnightly—925, 410 South Michigan avenue; president, Mrs. Lillian R. Montgomery; corresponding secretary, Mrs. Mary T. Lord.

MUSIC IN CHICAGO.

CHICAGO SYMPHONY ORCHESTRA.
Founded by Theodore Thomas.

The Theodore Thomas orchestra was organized in Chicago in 1890-1891 by a number of men interested in promoting the highest class of instrumental music. The Orchestral association was incorporated Dec. 16, 1890, and Theodore Thomas, famous for many years as a conductor, was engaged to lead the new organization, which was then named the Chicago orchestra. The preparations were completed in 1891 and the first public rehearsal was given at the Auditorium Friday afternoon, Oct. 16, of that year. Financially the result of the first season was discouraging, the fifty or more gentlemen guaranteeing the expenses being compelled to meet a deficit of about $53,000. Receipts, however, continued to increase from year to year until the orchestra was finally placed on a permanent basis. This was accomplished when Orchestra Hall, erected by subscriptions from more than 8,000 persons, was erected at 220 South Michigan avenue, and the organization was provided with a home of its own. The first concert there was given Wednesday evening, Dec. 14, 1904. Theodore Thomas died Jan. 4, 1905, and the orchestra, which until then had been called the Chicago orchestra, was named the Theodore Thomas orchestra. Feb. 24, 1913, the title was changed to The Chicago Symphony orchestra (founded by Theodore Thomas). Frederick Stock, after the death of Mr. Thomas, was made conductor, a position he still holds. The plan of giving two performances a week—a public rehearsal on Friday afternoon and a concert on Saturday evening—has been followed from the beginning. The season consists of twenty-eight weeks, beginning in October and ending in April.

The first officers of the Orchestral association were: N. K. Fairbank, president; C. Norman Fay, vice-president; P. A. McEwan, treasurer and secretary; Milward Adams, manager.

OFFICERS IN 1913.

President—Bryan Lathrop.
Vice-President—Clyde M. Carr.
Secretary—Philo A. Otis.
Treasurer and Manager—Frederick J. Wessells.
Assistant Manager—Henry E. Voegeli.
Trustees—George E. Adams, Joseph Adams, Max Baird, William L. Brown, Clyde M. Carr, Frederic A. Delano, J. J. Glessner, C. H. Hamill, Chauncey Keep, Bryan Lathrop, Harold F. McCormick, Philo A. Otis, Clarence M. Woolley.
Office—$50 Orchestra building.

CHICAGO GRAND OPERA COMPANY.

The Chicago Grand Opera company was established in 1910 by a number of citizens of Chicago and New York, who organized with a capital of $500,000, of which $300,000 was subscribed in Chicago and the remainder in the east. The Auditorium was leased, important alterations made and the first performance by the new company was given there in November, 1910. The officers were: President—Harold F. McCormick.
Vice-Presidents—Charles G. Dawes and Otto H. Kahn.
Treasurer—Charles L. Hutchinson.
Secretary—Philip M. Lydig.
Chairman Executive Committee—Clarence H. Mackay.
Vice-Chairman Executive Committee—John C. Shaffer.
Directors—The above named officers and Robert Goelet, Frederick T. Haskell, John J. Mitchell, Ira N. Morris, LaVerne W. Noyes, Max Pam, Julius Rosenwald, John G. Shedd, Charles A. Stevens, Harry Payne Whitney, H. Rogers Winthrop.
General Manager—Andreas Dippel.
General Musical Director—Cleofonte Campanini.
Business Manager—Bernhard Ulrich.

FIRST SEASON (1910-1911).
First performance ("Aida") given Nov. 3, 1910.
First season ended Jan. 18, 1911.
Receipts $400,407.50.
Operas produced for the first time in Chicago:
Debussy's "Pelleas et Melisande" (Nov. 5, 1910).

Charpentier's "Louise" (Nov. 9, 1910).
Richard Strauss' "Salome" (Nov. 25, 1910).
Massenet's "Thais" (Dec. 6, 1910).
Puccini's "The Girl of the Golden West" (Dec. 27, 1910).

Principal singers:

Mary Garden.	Jeanne Korolewicz.
Nellie Melba.	Enrico Caruso.
Geraldine Farrar.	Amedeo Bassi.
Lillian Grenville.	Charles Dalmores.
Carolina White.	Mario Sammarco.
Marguerita Sylva.	Antonio Scotti.
Suzanne Dumesnil.	Mario Guardabassi.
Jane Osborn-Hannah.	John McCormack.
Eleonora de Cisneros.	Hector Dufranne.
Johanna Gadski.	

SECOND SEASON (1911-1912).
First performance ("Samson et Dalila") Nov. 22.
Second season ended Jan. 27, 1912.
Receipts, $471,600.98.
Operas produced for first time in Chicago:
Massenet's "Cendrillon" (Nov. 27, 1911).
Wolf-Ferrari's "Il Segreto di Susanna" (Dec. 7).*
Massenet's "Le Jongleur de Notre Dame" (Dec. 7).
Victor Herbert's "Natoma" (Dec. 15).
Jean Nougues' "Quo Vadis" (Dec. 20).
Wolf-Ferrari's "The Jewels of the Madonna" (Jan. 16, 1912).*
*First time in America.

Principal singers:

Mary Garden.	Jenny Dufau.
Luisa Tetrazzini.	Alice Zeppilli.
Mme. Schumann-Heink.	Rosina Galli.
Olive Fremstad.	Henri Scott.
Maggie Teyte.	Hector Dufranne.
Jane Osborn-Hannah.	Mario Sammarco.
Jeanne Gerville-Reach.	Armand Crabbe.
Minnie Saltzman-Stevens.	Charles Dalmores.
Carolina White.	Amedeo Bassi.
Marta Wittkowska.	Edmond Warnery.
Eleonora de Cisneros.	George Hamlin.
Agnes Berry.	Mario Guardabassi.
Mabel Riegelman.	Clarence Whitehill.
Marie Cavan.	John McCormack.

THIRD SEASON (1912-1913).
First performance ("Manon Lescaut") Nov. 26.
Third season ended Feb. 1, 1913.
Receipts for ten weeks, $508,000.
Operas produced for the first time in Chicago:
Erlanger's "Noel" (Jan. 8, 1913).*
Zandonai's "Conchita" (Jan. 30, 1913).
*First time in the United States.
Principal singers:

	Ernestine Schumann-Heink.*
Mary Garden.	Jane Osborn-Hannah.
Luisa Tetrazzini.	Minnie Saltzman-Stevens.
Maggie Teyte.	Louise Berat.
Tarquinia Tarquini.	Titta Ruffo.
Jennie Dufau.	Mario Sammarco.
Mabel Riegelman.	Charles Dalmores.
Minnie Egener.	Aristodemo Giorgini.
Carolina White.	Constantin Nicolay.
Eleonora de Cisneros.	Nicolo Fossetta.
Ruby Heyl.	Henri Scott.
Alice Zeppilli.	Emilio Venturini.
Marie Cavan.	*Guest artists.
Lillian Nordica.*	

MANAGEMENT (1913-1914).
President—Harold McCormick.
Vice-Presidents—Charles G. Dawes, Otto H. Kahn.
Treasurer—Charles L. Hutchinson.
Board of directors—John C. Shaffer, vice-chairman; R. T. Crane, Charles G. Dawes, Harold F. McCormick, La Verne W. Noyes, Max Pam, John G. Shedd.
Board of Directors—Frederick Bode, H. M. Byllesby, R. T. Crane, Charles G. Dawes, Frederick T. Haskell, Charles L. Hutchinson, Otto H. Kahn, Harold F. McCormick, John J. Mitchell, Ira N. Morris, La Verne W. Noyes, Max Pam, George F. Porter, Julius Rosenwald, John C. Shaffer, John G. Shedd, Charles A. Stevens, F. D. Stout.
General Director—Cleofonte Campanini.
Business Manager—Bernhard Ullrich.

PROPOSED PASSENGER SUBWAY SYSTEM FOR CHICAGO.

The harbor and subway commission and the sub-committee of the council committee on local transportation submitted a joint report Sept. 10, 1912, on a "comprehensive scheme of subways which shall extend into the outlying districts and which shall be designed to remedy the existing traction evils of the city of Chicago." The general plan recommended was a high level subway as close as possible to the surface of the streets and avoiding all grade crossings. The power system contemplated comprised alternating current generation and distribution and direct current operation of motors. The estimates were based on a third rail direct current system of conductors. The capacity of the subways outlined in the report was estimated at 180,000 seats per hour.

PROPOSED ROUTES.

Following were the routes recommended:
North to South Side—Beginning at Lawrence and Evanston avenues, a two track subway in Evanston avenue to Irving Park boulevard and Halsted street; south in Halsted street to Fullerton avenue.

Beginning at Lawrence and Lincoln avenues, a two track subway in Lincoln avenue to Halsted street and Fullerton avenue.

The two subways from the north joining at Halsted street and Fullerton avenue are continued as a four track subway southeast in Lincoln avenue to Clark street; south in Clark street to some point just north of the river (subject to further engineering investigation). Thence a two track subway for express trains south in Clark street to Polk street or some street farther south; east in Polk street or some other street to State street; south in State street in a four track subway to 55th street. A two track subway east in 55th street to Cottage Grove avenue; south in Cottage Grove avenue to 79th street. Transfers can be made from this subway at Fullerton avenue to the Halsted street subway; at Clark and Madison streets to the Madison street subway; at Harrison and Clark streets to the southwest subway.

North Side to Southwest Side—Two of the four tracks from the North Clark street subway continue in a two track subway east from Clark street to State street; thence south in State street to Harrison street; west in a two track subway in Harrison street to Halsted street and Blue Island avenue; thence continuing southwest in Blue Island avenue to 22d street and Ashland avenue; west in 22d street to Marshall boulevard; south in Marshall boulevard to 26th street; west in 26th street to South 40th avenue. Transfers can be made from the subway at Fullerton avenue to the Halsted street subway, at State street to the "Northwest Side to South Side" subways, at Halsted and Harrison streets to Halsted street subway.

Northwest Side to South Side—Beginning at Elston and Kedzie avenues, a two track subway in Elston avenue southeast to Belmont and California avenues; south in California avenue to Milwaukee avenue; southeast in Milwaukee avenue to Desplaines or Canal street. Continuing south in Desplaines or Canal street to Randolph street; east in Randolph street to State street; south in State street in the four track subway to 55th street and State street; thence west in 55th street in a two track subway to Western avenue. Transfers can be made from the subway at Milwaukee avenue and Halsted street to the Halsted street subway; at State street to the "North Side to Southwest Side" subway; at 55th street and Halsted street to Halsted street subway.

A two track subway in Armitage avenue from North 40th avenue to Milwaukee avenue, connecting with the Elston-Milwaukee avenue line.

Halsted Street—Beginning at the junction of the Lincoln and Evanston avenue lines at Fullerton avenue, a two track subway in Halsted street to 79th street. Transfers can be made from this subway at Fullerton avenue to the "North Side to South Side" and the "North Side to Southwest Side" subways; at Milwaukee avenue to the "Northwest Side to South Side" subway; at Harrison street to the "North Side to Southwest Side" subway; at 55th street to the "Northwest Side to South Side" subway.

Madison Street—Beginning at South Clark street, a two track subway in Madison street to 40th ave nue. Transfers can be made from the subway at Halsted street to the Halsted street subway; at Clark and Madison streets to the "North Side to South Side" subway. This subway may eventually be extended south in Clark street and other streets to serve the southwestern part of the city.

ESTIMATED COST OF SUBWAYS.

North side to Lawrence avenue............$20,123,000
South side to 79th street.................. 25,778,000
West side to 40th avenue.................. 31,049,000
Halsted street........................... 19,307,000

Total 96,257,000
Estimated cost of equipment.............. 34,844,000

Total 131,101,000
The equipment will be furnished by the operating company.

Two plans for financing the project were suggested. One was to have the city build the subways out of the proceeds of legalized Mueller certificates and the other to have them built by private capital under such conditions as would insure absolute municipal control. It was subsequently ascertained that the scheme could not be financed by the issuance of Mueller certificates.

The joint report was signed by John Ericson, James J. Reynolds and E. C. Shankland of the harbor and subway commission and by Aldermen Eugene Block (chairman), John A. Richert, Patrick J. Carr, William F. Schultz, William J. Healy, Henry D. Capitain and Charles Twigg, subcommittee of the council committee on local transportation.

ARNOLD SUBWAY PLAN.

Little or no progress was made with the subway project, but the matter was taken up by the council transportation committee in the fall and expert advice was sought. A plan submitted by Bion J. Arnold received favorable consideration from the committee. He recommended that the city proceed to the construction of two initial subways for the use of the surface lines. The north and south route, he said, should be under Clark street from North avenue to 22d street. For the east and west bores he outlined a "loop back" in the downtown section, entering it by way of the Washington street tunnel, proceeding east to Michigan avenue, and leaving the loop by the Van Buren street tunnel, and vice versa.

He estimated the first of these routes to cost $9,600,000 and the second $4,900,000, a total of $14,500,000. This figure, he pointed out, is well within the amount held available under the subway provisions of the traction ordinances. The city had $11,000,000 in its subway fund, it would receive another $2,000,000 next April, and it could compel the companies to contribute $5,000,000, making the total $18,000,000.

TUNNELS UNDER THE CHICAGO RIVER.

Washington Street—Built 1867-1869; length, 1,605 feet; cost $517,000; rebuilt 1909-1911.
LaSalle Street—Built 1869-1871; length, 1,890 feet; cost $566,000; rebuilt 1909-1912; length, 2,000 feet; cost $1,200,000.
Van Buren Street—Built 1891-1892; length, 1,514 feet; cost $1,000,000; rebuilt 1909-1912.
All used for street railway purposes.

CHICAGO STREET GRADES.

The grade of the streets in the central portion of Chicago has been raised three times. In 1855 it was raised from 2½ to 3 feet above the then existing surface, and it was again raised by about the same amount in 1857 and 1872, making the present level fourteen feet above "city datum," which is the low-water mark of the lake in 1847.

HOSPITALS AND DISPENSARIES OF CHICAGO.

Abraham Lincoln—2941 Calumet avenue.
Alexian Brothers'—1200 Belden avenue.
Augustana—2043 Cleveland avenue.
Beulah—2148 North Clark street.
Bohemian—1333 South California avenue.
Chicago Baptist—Rhodes avenue and 34th street.
Chicago Charity—2407 Dearborn street.
Chicago City Infant—721 LaSalle avenue.
Chicago Fresh Air—2450 Howard avenue.
Chicago Homeopathic—711 South Wood street.
Chicago Hospital—811 East 49th street.
Chicago Lying-In—515 South Ashland boulevard.
Chicago Maternity—2314 North Clark street.
Chicago Policlinic—221 West Chicago avenue.
Chicago Union—830 Wellington street.
Children's—Wood street, near Polk.
Children's Memorial—735 Fullerton avenue.
Columbia—4607 Champlain avenue.
Columbus—2540 Lake View avenue.
Columbus Extension—West Polk and Lytle streets.
Cook County—West Harrison and Wood streets.
Detention—Wood and West Polk streets.
Durand, Annie W.—Wood and York streets.
Emergency (city)—1065 West Monroe street, 540
   West Van Buren street, 1260 West Madison street
   and 621 Orleans street.
Englewood—West 60th and South Green streets.
Evangelical Deaconesses'—408 Wisconsin street.
Fort Dearborn—3830 Rhodes avenue.
Frances E. Willard National Temperance—710
   South Lincoln street.
Garfield Park—3815 Washington boulevard.
George Smith Memorial—See St. Luke's.
German-American—741 Diversey boulevard.
German Hospital—549-559 Grant place.
Grace—398 South Sangamon street.
Hahnemann—2814 Groveland avenue.
Henrotin Memorial—939 LaSalle avenue.
Illinois Charitable Eye and Ear Infirmary—904
   West Adams street.
Iroquois Memorial Emergency—23 North Market-st.
Isolation—S. Lawndale-av. and W. 36th-st.
Jefferson Park—1402 West Monroe street.
Lakeside—4147 Lake avenue.
Lake View—4420 Clarendon avenue.
Lincoln—2943 Calumet avenue.
Littlejohn—1410 West Monroe street.
Lynde—1957 West 20th street.
Maimonides—1519 South California avenue.
Mary Thompson—West Adams and Paulina streets.
Memorial Institute for Infectious Diseases—South
   Wood and York streets.
Mercy—Calumet avenue and 26th street.
Michael-Reese—Groveland avenue and 29th street.
Monroe Street—2501 West Monroe street.
North Chicago—2551 North Clark street.
Northwest Side—1627 West North avenue.
Norwegian Lutheran—1138 North Leavitt street.
Norwegian Lutheran Tabitha—1044 N. Francisco-av.
Park Avenue—1940 Park avenue.
Passavant Memorial—147 West Superior street.
People's—2184 Archer avenue.
Post-Graduate—Dearborn and 24th streets.
Presbyterian—West Congress and Wood streets.
Provident—Dearborn and 36th streets.
Pullman—11217 Watt avenue.
Ravenswood—1917 Wilson avenue.
Rhodes Avenue—Rhodes avenue and 32d street.
Robert Burns—3807 Washington boulevard.
St. Ann's—4900 Thomas street.
St. Anthony de Padua—West 19th street and Mar-
   shall boulevard.

St. Bernard's Hotel Dieu—6337 Harvard avenue.
St. Elizabeth's—North Claremont avenue and Le-
   moyne street.
St. Joseph's—Garfield avenue and Burling street.
St. Luke's—1433 Michigan avenue.
St. Mary of Nazareth—North Leavitt and Thomas
   streets.
Sarah Morris Hospital for Children—Groveland ave-
   nue and East 29th street.
South Chicago—2323 East 92d place.
Streeter—2646 Calumet avenue.
Swedish Covenant—2745 Foster avenue.
United States Marine—4141 Clarendon avenue.
University—432 South Lincoln street.
Washington Park—60th street and Vernon avenue.
Wesley—2449 Dearborn street.
West Side—1844 West Harrison street.

DISPENSARIES.

Alexian Brothers' Hospital—Belden and Racine
   avenues.
American Medical Missionary—828 West 35th place;
   open 1 to 5 and 7 to 8 p. m.
Bennett Free—300 North Ada; open 9 a. m. to
   5 p. m.
Bureau of Personal Service—720 West 12th street;
   10 a. m. to 2 p. m.
Central Free—West Harrison and Wood: 9 a. m.
   to 5 p. m., except Sundays.
Chicago Lying-In—Maxwell and Newberry.
Chicago Policlinic—219 West Chicago avenue; 8:30
   a. m. to 6 p. m. daily.
Chicago Public—Dearborn and 24th: all day.
German Hospital—Hamilton court and Grant place;
   9 a. m. to 5 p. m., except Sundays.
Hahnemann College Free—2811 Cottage Grove ave-
   nue; all day.
Hahnemann College Free Clinic for Tuberculosis—
   2817 Cottage Grove avenue.
Hering College Free—703 South Wood; 8 a. m. to
   5 p. m., except Sundays.
Illinois Charitable Eye and Ear—124 South Peoria;
   1:30 to 3 p. m., except Sundays and holidays.
Jewish Aid Society and Emanuel Mandel, West
   Side, Free—1012 Maxwell; daily except Sunday.
Littlejohn College—1422 West Monroe street.
Marcy Center—1335 Newberry avenue; 2 to 4 p. m.,
   except Fridays and Sundays; Saturday, 11 a. m.
   to 4 p. m.
Mary Thompson—West Adams and Paulina; 2 to 4
   p. m., except Sundays.
Mercy Free—2526 Calumet avenue.
North Star—157 West Superior; 1 to 2 p. m., except
   Sundays and holidays.
Olivet—717 Vedder street.
Provident—Dearborn and 36th.
St. Anthony's Free—2033 Frankfort; daily.
South Side—2431 Dearborn; 10 a. m. to 12 m. and
   2 to 4 p. m. daily.
Volunteers of America, Free—1201 Washington boule-
   vard.
West Side Free—Congress and Honore (College of
   Physicians and Surgeons); daily, except Sun-
   days, 1 to 4 p. m.

CHICAGO TUBERCULOSIS INSTITUTE.
1012 Otis building.

President—Theodore B. Sachs, M. D.
Superintendent—James Minnick.
Assistant Superintendent—Arthur J. Strawson.

CHICAGO BUREAU OF PUBLIC EFFICIENCY.
Organized in 1910.

The purposes of the organization are:
   (1) To scrutinize the systems of accounting in
the eight local governments of Chicago.
   (2) To examine the methods of purchasing materials and supplies and letting and executing construction contracts in these bodies.
   (3) To examine the pay rolls of these local governing bodies with a view of determining the efficiency of such expenditures.
   (4) To make constructive suggestions for improvements in the directions indicated under 1, 2
and 3, and to co-operate with public officials in the
installation of these improved methods.
   (5) To furnish the public with exact information
regarding public revenues and expenditures, and
thereby promote efficiency and economy in the public service.

NEW STREET NAMES IN CHICAGO.

[Established by ordinances of city council effective Aug. 15, 1913.]

Old name and district.	New name.
"A"-st. (N. D.)	Hamburg-st.
Adams-av. (H. P.)	Dante-av.
Adeptus-ct. (J.)	Llano-av.
Aldine-st. (S. D.)	Eden-av.
Alexander-st. (L. V.)	Crescent-pl.
Alma-av. (Aus.)	Latrobe-av.
Alton-av. (N. P.)	Nordica-av.
Anderson-st. (J.)	Larned-av.
Archer-pl. (L.)	W. 40th st.
Arlington-av. (Aus.)	S. Mayfield-av.
Armour-av. (S. D., L.)	Federal-st.
Ash-st. (J.)	Neenah-av.
Ashland-pl. (W. D.)	Emerson-av.
Atlantic-av. (N. P.)	Oketo-av.
Baird-av. (Aus.)	Lorel-av.
Baldwin-st. (W. D.)	N. Winchester-av.
Batavia-av. (J.)	Magnet-av.
Bates-av. (J.)	Lieb-av.
Beach-ct. (L. V.)	Frontier-av.
Belden-ct. (N. D.)	Cambridge-av.
Bellevue-av. (N. P.)	Sayre-av.
Berry-st. (J.)	Farragut-av.
Bishop-ct. (W. D.)	N. Bishop-st.
Blaine-av. (J.)	Miltimore-st.
Blaine-pl. (W. D.)	Quincy-st.
Bloomingdale-rd. (W. D.)	Blomingdale-av.
Blucher-st. (L. V.)	Wilton-av.
Bowmanville-rd. (L. V.)	Bowmanville-av.
Bowen-st. (J.)	Berwyn-av.
Bowen-st. (J.)	Lynch-av.
Bowen-av. (H. P.)	E. 41st-pl.
Bradley-av. (N. P.)	Ignatius-st.
Brantwood-av. (J.)	Kercheval-av.
Brock-av. (J.)	Le Mai-av.
Bross-ct. (S. D.)	Hoyt-av.
Bryan-av. (R. P.)	Juniata-st.
Buena Vista-pl. (S. D.)	W. 25th-st.
Buena Vista-ter. (N. D.)	Vista-ter.
Burhans-av. (N. P.)	Oconto-av.
Butler-st. (S. D., L., Cal.)	Normal-av.
"C"-st. (N. D.)	McLean-av.
Caldwell-av. (J.)	Miami-av.
Calland-ct. (J.)	Kongee-av.
Calumet-av. (H. P.)	Forest-av.
Calumet-av. (E. P.)	Oliphant-av.
Campbell-av., S. (L.)	S. Artesian-av.
Campbell-st. (S. D.)	Heald-av.
Canal-pl. (W. D.)	McLean-av.
Canal-st., S. (Cal.)	Eggleston-av.
Candis-av. (J.)	Lacey-av.
Carpenter-rd. (J.)	Lillard-av.
Carpenter-ct. (J.)	Lovejoy-av.
Catalpa-pl. (W. D.)	N. Albany-av.
Catalpa-ct. (W. D.)	N. Albany-av.
Cedar-st. (Aus.)	W. Superior-st.
Central-st. (R. P.)	N. Hilldale-av.
Central-av. (J.)	Narragansett-av.
Central-av. (H. P.)	Chappel-av.
Center-st. (E. P.)	Touhy-av.
Center-av., N. (W. D.)	N. Racine-av.
Center-av., S. (S. D., L., Cal.)	S. Racine-av.
Ceylon-av. (N. P.)	Nina-av.
Charles-ct. (H. P.)	Booth-av.
Chase-st. (W. D.)	N. Elizabeth-st.
Cheney-st. (J.)	Ludlam-av.
Cheney-av. (N. P.)	New Hampshire-av.
Cherry-pl. (W. D.)	Shakespeare-av.
Chestnut-st. (E. P.)	Olcott-av.
Chestnut-pl. (N. D.)	Ernst-ct.
Chicago-av. (E. P.)	Avondale-av.
Chicago-ter. (W. D.)	W. Erie-st.
Choctaw-av. (J.)	Kasson-av.
Church-ct. (S. D.)	Grady-ct.
Church-pl. (W. D.)	Arcade-pl.
Cicero-ct. (W. D.)	S. Maplewood-av.
Clare-av. (J.)	Markham-av.
Claremont-st. (N. P.)	Palatine-av.
Clarendon-st. (N. P.)	Newcastle-av.
Clark-av. (Aus.)	Latrobe-av.
Clarke-pl. (N. P.)	Isham-av.
Clark-st., S. (L.)	Federal-st.
Clybourn-pl. (N. D., W. D.)	Cortland-st.
Colfax-pl. (N. P.)	Peterson-av.
Columbia-st. (W. D.)	Caton-st.

Old name and district.	New name.
Columbia-st. (W. D.)	Concord-pl.
Congress-pk. (W. D.)	S. Talman-av.
College-av. (N. P.)	Naper-av.
Cornelia-st. (W. D.)	W. Walton-st.
Cottage Grove-av. (H. P.)	Corliss-av.
Crescent-av. (N. P.)	Ardmore-av.
Crescent-av. (N. P.)	Nickerson-av.
Crescent-rd. (J.)	Hennepin-st.
Crescent-rd. (J.)	McClellan-av.
Curtis-av. (H. P.)	Edurooke-av.
Davis-av. (J.)	Moreland-av.
Dearborn-av. (E. P.)	Greenleaf-av.
Dearborn-av. (N. D.)	N. Dearborn-st.
Dearborn-st., S. (L.)	Lafayette-av.
Depot-st. (W. D.)	S. Rockwell-st.
Diversey-ct. (L. V.)	Magnolia-av.
Division-av. (J.)	Marietta-av.
Dixon-av. (J.)	Livermore-av.
Douglas-pl. (S. D.)	E. 34th-pl.
Drexel-bd. (E. P.)	Olmsted-av.
Drexel-ct. (H. P.)	Maryland-av.
East-ct. (L. V.)	Hudson-av.
East River-st. (H. P.)	Boyd-av.
East Wharf (J.)	Libby-av.
Eberly-av. (J.)	N. St. Louis-av.
Edgewater-pl. (L. V.)	Hecker-av.
Edgewater-ter. (L. V.)	Gregory-st.
Edison-st. (N. P.)	Olcott-av.
Edwards-st. (J.)	Gale-st.
Eldredge-pl. (S. D.)	E. 9th st.
Elizabeth-av. (H. P.)	Cahokia-av.
Ellerton-av. (J.)	Loyd-av.
Ellis-av. (E. P.)	Iroquois-av.
Elmer-av. (J.)	Manton-av.
Elston-av. (J.)	Indian-rd.
Elston-ct. (J.)	Argyle-st.
Emerald-st. (Aus.)	Kamerling-av.
Emerson-rd. (J.)	Lehigh-av.
Enfield-av. (J.)	Lundy-av.
Erie-av. (H. P.)	Baltimore-av.
Euclid-st. (N. P.)	Newcastle-av.
Euclid-av. (E. P.)	Avondale-av.
Euclid-av. (E. P.)	Imperial-st.
Eugenie-ct. (N. D.)	Fern-ct.
Evanston-st. (L. V.)	Broadway.
Evanston-av. (R. P.)	Sheridan-rd.
Evergreen-st. (N. P.)	Newark-av.
Evergreen-ct. (W. D.)	Holly-av.
Ewing-st. (W. D.)	Gilpin-pl.
Ewing-pl. (W. D.)	Pierce-av.
Fairview-av. (J.)	Las Casas-av.
Faraday-av. (J.)	Kewanee-av.
Farragut-av. (J.)	Buffalo-av.
Fiftieth-av., N. (J., W. D.)	N. Lavergne-av.
Fiftieth-av., S. (Aus.)	S. Lavergne-av.
Fiftieth-ct., N. (J., W. D.)	Lawler-av.
Fifty-first-av., N. (J., W. D.)	Leclaire-av.
Fifty-first-av., S. (Aus.)	S. Leamington-av.
Fifty-first-ct., N. (J., W. D.)	N. Leamington-av.
Fifty-second-av., N. (J., Aus.)	N. Laramie-av.
Fifty-second-av., S. (Aus.)	S. Laramie-av.
Fifty-second-ct., N. (J., Aus.)	Latrobe-av.
Fifty-third-av., N. (J., Aus.)	N. Lockwood-av.
Fifty-third-av., S. (Aus.)	S. Lockwood-av.
Fifty-third-ct., N. (J., Aus.)	Lorel-av.
Fifty-fourth-ct., N. (J., Aus.)	Long-av.
Fifty-fourth-ct., N. (J., Aus.)	N. Lotus-av.
Fifty-fourth-ct., N. (J.)	Lind-av.
Fifty-fifth-ct., N. (J., W. D.)	Linder-av.
Fifty-fourth-ct., N. (J.)	Linder-av.
Fifty-fifth-ct., N. (J., Aus.)	Luna-av.
Fifty-sixth-av., N. (J.)	N. Central-av.
Fifty-sixth-ct., N. (J.)	N. Parkside-av.
Fifty-seventh-ct., N. (J.)	N. Major-av.
Fifty-seventh-ct., N. (J.)	Mango-av.
Fifty-eighth-av., N. (J.)	N. Menard-av.
Fifty-eighth-ct., N. (J.)	Mascouten-av.
Fifty-ninth-av., N. (J.)	N. Marmora-av.
Fifty-ninth-ct., N. (J.)	N. Mason-av.
Fontenoy-pl. (W. D.)	Girard-st.
Forest-st. (R. P.)	N. Paulina-st.
Fortieth-av., N. (J., W. D.)	N. Crawford-av.
Fortieth-av., S. (W. D., L.)	S. Crawford-av.
Fortieth-ct., N. (J., W. D.)	N. Kaskaskia-av.

Old name and district.	New name.
Fortieth-ct., S. (W. D., L.)	S. Kaskaskia-av.
Forty-first-av., N. (J.)	N. Kaskaskia-av.
Forty-first-av., N. (J., W. D.)	N. Karlov-av.
Forty-first-av., S. (W. D., L.)	S. Karlov-av.
Forty-first-ct., N. (J.)	N. Karlov-av.
Forty-first-ct., N. (J., W. D.)	N. Kedvale-av.
Forty-first-ct., S. (W. D., L.)	S. Kedvale-av.
Forty-second-av., N. (J.)	N. Kedvale-av.
Forty-second-av.,N. (J.,W.D.)	N. Keeler-av.
Forty-second-av.,S. (W.D.,L.)	S. Keeler-av.
Forty-second-ct., N. (J.)	Kenosha-av.
Forty-second-ct.,N. (J.,W.D.)	N. Tripp-av.
Forty-second-ct.,S. (W.D.,L.)	S. Tripp-av.
Forty-second-pl., N. (J.)	N. Tripp-av.
Forty-third-av., N. (J., W. D.)	N. Kildare-av.
Forty-third-av., S. (W. D., L.)	S. Kildare-av.
Forty-third-ct., N. (W. D.)	N. Kolin-av.
Forty-third-ct., S. (W.D.,L.)	S. Kolin-av.
Forty-fourth-av., N. (J.,W.D.)	N. Kostner-av.
Forty-fourth-av., S. (W.D.,L.)	S. Kostner-av.
Forty-fourth-ct.,N. (J.,W.D.)	Kenneth-av.
Forty-fourth-ct.,S. (W.D.,L.)	Komensky-av.
Forty-fifth-av., N. (J.,W.D.)	N. Kral-av.
Forty-fifth-av.,S. (W.D.,L.)	S. Kral-av.
Forty-fifth-ct., N. (J.,W.D.)	N. Kolmar-av.
Forty-fifth-ct., S. (W.D.,L.)	S. Kolmar-av.
Forty-sixth-av.,N. (J.,W.D.)	N. Kenton-av.
Forty-sixth-av., S. (W. D.)	S. Kenton-av.
Forty-sixth-ct., N. (J.)	N. Knox-av.
Forty-sixth-ct., S. (L.)	S. Knox-av.
Forty-seventh-av.,N. (J.,W.D.)	N. Kilpatrick-av.
Forty-seventh-av., S. (L.)	S. Kilpatrick-av.
Forty-seventh-av., S. (W. D.)	S. Kromberg-av.
Forty-seventh-ct.,N. (J.,W.D.)	N. Keating-av.
Forty-seventh-ct., S. (L.)	S. Keating-av.
Forty-eighth-av.,N. (J.,W.D.)	N. Cicero-av.
Forty-eighth-av.,S. (W.D.,L.)	S. Cicero-av.
Forty-eighth-ct.,N. (J.,W.D.)	La Crosse-av.
Forty-ninth-av.,N. (J.,W.D.)	N. Lamon-av.
Forty-ninth-ct.,N. (J.,W.D.)	Laporte-av.
Fountain-av. (J.)	Meredith-av.
Fourteenth-pl., W. (W. D.)	W. 15th-st.
Fox-ct. (N. P.)	Nordica-av.
Fox-pl. (W. D.)	Julian-st.
Francis-st. (L. V.)	Ardmore-av.
Francisco-st., N. (J.)	N. Francisco-av.
Francisco-st., N. (W. D.)	N. Francisco-av.
Francisco-st., S. (W. D.)	S. Francisco-av.
Francisco-st., S. (L.)	S. Francisco-av.
Frank-ct. (N. P.)	Napoleon-av.
Franklin-av. (Aus.)	N. Mayfield-av.
Frink-st. (Aus.)	Fulton-st.
Front-st. (W. D.)	Fry-st.
Follerton-ct. (N. D.)	Cambridge-av.
Fulton-av. (N. P.)	Albion-av.
Fulton-av. (N. P.)	Hayes-av.
Fulton-av. (H. P.)	Langley-av.
Gage-pl. (L.)	S. Artesian-av.
Gage-ct. (L.)	W. 56th-st.
Gage Park-av. (L.)	S. Claremont-av.
Garfield-ct. (N. D.)	Garfield-av.
Gault-ct. (N. D.)	Cambridge-av.
George-ct. (W. D.)	N. Seeley-av.
Grace-st. (N. D.)	Burling-st.
Graceland-av. (L. V.)	Irving Park-bd.
Grand-av. (E. P.)	Oshkosh-av.
Grand-av. (E. P.)	Pratt-av.
Grant-st. (N. P.)	Hood-av.
Grassmere-rd. (J.)	Massac-av.
Greenwood-ter. (L. V.)	Da Tamble-st.
Griffin-st. (J.)	Manila-av.
Gross-st. (J.)	Lester-av.
Gross-ter. (W. D.)	S. Whipple-st.
Grove-pl. (N. D.)	Hamburg-st.
Groveland-ct. (L.)	Lowe-av.
Groveland-ter. (Cal.)	Harper-av.
Guernsey-av. (J.)	N. Kenton-av.
Guernsey-av. (J.)	Kimberly-av.
Hamilton-st. (N. P.)	Albion-av.
Hamilton-ct. (L. V.)	Larrabee-st.
Hamilton-ct. (N. D.)	Larrabee-st.
Harlem-av. bd. (E. P.)	Harlem-av.
Harmon-pl. (S. D.)	E. 11th st.
Harvard-st. (W. D.)	Arthington-st.
Hawley-av. (W. D.)	Kirkland-av.
Hawthorne-av. (L.)	Fergus-av.
Hawthorne-st. (W. D.)	Kingsbury-st.
Hayes-st. (J.)	Drummond-pl.

Old name and district.	New name.
Hayes-av. (R. P.)	Loyola-av.
Hayes-av. (R. P.)	Arthur-av.
Henry-st. (Aus.)	W. Walton-st.
Hibbard-av. (H. P.)	Kenwood-av.
Highland-av. (E. P.)	Ozanam-av.
Hills-ct. (L. V.)	Giddings-st.
Hobart-av. (N. P.)	Neva-av.
Holden-st. (W. D.)	Ellsworth-st.
Howard-av. (H. P.)	Brainard-av.
Howard-av., N. (Aus.)	N. Mason-av.
Howard-av., S. (Aus.)	S. Mason-av.
Howard-ct. (Cal.)	Vanderpoel-av.
Hubbard-pl. (S. D.)	E. 7th-st.
Hubbard-st. (J.)	Long-av.
Humboldt-st. (W. D.)	N. Richmond-st.
Humboldt-st. (W. D.)	S. Richmond-st.
Humboldt-st. (J.)	Palmer-st.
Hunter-av. (J.)	N. Menard-av.
Hutchinson-av. (J.)	Windsor-av.
Hyde Park-ter. (H. P.)	Berkeley-av.
Ingomar-av. (N. P.)	Nassau-av.
Illinois-av. (H. P.)	Laker-av.
Illinois-ct. (S. D.)	Lime-st.
Independence-pl. (W. D.)	Wayman-st.
India-st. (J.)	Kelso-av.
Indiana-st. (W. D., Aus.)	Ferdinand-st.
Indiana-av. (E. P.)	Osceola-st.
Indiana-st. (E. P.)	Grand-av.
Jackson-av. (H. P.)	Maryland-av.
Jackson Park-ter. (H. P.)	E. 65th-st.
Jackson-pl. (W. D.)	Gladys-av.
Jefferson-av. (H. P.)	Rosalie-av.
Jefferson-ct. (J.)	Kennison-av.
Johnson-st. (W. D.)	S. Peoria-st.
Johnston-av. (W. D.)	Lyndale-st.
Josephine-av. (N. P.)	Normandy-av.
Karnatz-av. (J.)	Lansing-av.
Kenwood-ter. (H. P.)	E. 72d-pl.
Kingston-st. (N. P.)	Neola-av.
Kingston-st. (N. P.)	Natoma-av.
Kosciuszko-av. (J.)	Medina-av.
Kosciusko-st. (W. D.)	Lyndale-st.
Lafayette-ct. (N. D.)	Seneca-st.
Lafayette-pkwy. (L. V.)	Lafayette-st.
Lake-av. (S. D., H. P.)	Lake Park-av.
Lakeside-av. (H. P.)	Chippewa-av.
Lakeside-ter. (R. P.)	Garrison-av.
LaSalle-av. (N. D.)	N. LaSalle-st.
LaSalle-av. (E. P.)	Ottawa-av.
Laurel-av. (Aus.)	Lorel-av.
Lawrence-st. (N. D.)	Center-st.
Lee-av. (W. D.)	Fletcher-st.
Leland-st. (N. P.)	Schreiber-av.
Le Moyne-av. (J.)	Mercer-av.
Leo-pl. (J.)	Ainslie-st.
Lewis-st. (Aus.)	Massasoit-av.
Lexington-av. (H. P.)	University-av.
Lily-av. (N. P.)	Naples-av.
Lincoln-pl. (N. D.)	Hudson-av.
Lincoln-pl. (N. P.)	Niagara-av.
Linden-av. (J.)	Keokuk-av.
Linden-av. (E. P.)	Onarga-av.
Linden-ct. (L. V.)	Cambridge-av.
Linne-av. (N. P.)	Nixon-av.
Logan-st. (N. P.)	Newell-av.
Logan-av. (Cal.)	Genoa-av.
Lorraine-pl. (J.)	Mandell-ay.
Lowell-av. (J.)	N. Kirby-av.
Lydia-pl. (J.)	Gettysburg-pl.
Lyman-av. (L. V.)	N. Seeley-av.
Madison-av. (H. P.)	Dorchester-av.
Maple-av. (J.)	Kiona-av.
Maple-av. (E. P.)	Olympia-av.
Marguerite-av. (J.)	Lambert-av.
Market-st. (H. P.)	E. 134th-pl.
Market-sq. (S. D.)	Robinson-st.
Marquette-ter. (L. V.)	Pensacola-av.
McGrane-ct. (J.)	Kentucky-av.
Meridian-st., E. (Cal.)	Hale-av.
Michigan-st., E. (N. D.)	E. Austin-av.
Michigan-st., W. (N. D.)	W. Austin-av.
Michigan-av. (E. P.)	Ivy-st.
Michigan-av. (E. P.)	Ozark-av.
Michigan-ter. (H. P.)	Oakenwald-av.
Miller-av. (J.)	Wilson-av.
Miller-ct. (L. V.)	Horan-av.
Milton-st. (N. P.)	Neva-av.
Milton-pl. (J.)	Patterson-av.

Old name and district.	New name.
Monitor-av. (N. P.)	Navarre-av.
Monroe-av. (H. P.)	Kenwood-av.
Morgan-pl. (W. D.)	Quincy-st.
Morse-av. (H. P.)	Forrestville-av.
Morton-st. (J.)	N. Parkside-av.
Mulberry-av. (N. P.)	Nicolet-av.
Myrtle-st. (W. D.)	S. Seeley-av.
Myrtie-av. (N. P.)	Ninnewa-av.
New W.North Water-st.(N.D.)..	Carroll-av.
Noble-av. (J.)	Barry-av.
Noble-ct. (H. P.)	De Soto-av.
Normal-pkwy., N. (L.)	Normal-pkwy.
Normal-pkwy., S. (L.)	Normal-pkwy.
North-pl. (W. D.)	Holly-av.
Norwood-av. (J.)	Mohican-av.
Norwood-pl. (N. P.)	Heyden-st.
Nutt-st. (W. D.)	Loeffler-ct.
Oak-av. (Cal.)	Beverly-av.
Oak-av. (E. P.)	Ogallah-av.
Oak-pl. (L. V.)	Wilton-av.
O'Brien-av. (J.)	N. Keating-av.
Ogden-pl. (W. D.)	Arcade-pl.
Ohio-st., W. (Aus.)	Race-av.
Olive-st. (E. P.)	Oriole-av.
Olive-st. (W. D.)	S. Hamilton-av.
Ontario-st., W. (W. D., Aus.).	W. Ohio-st.
Ontario-av. (H. P.)	Brandon-av.
Orchard-av. (E. P.)	Lunt-av.
Ormonde-av. (J.)	Larcom-av.
Our-st. (J.)	Lipps-av.
Palmer-av. (H. P.)	Crandon-av.
Panama-st. (N. P.)	Niagara-av.
Park-st. (W. D.)	Wicker Park-av.
Park-av., N. (Aus.)	N. Parkside-av.
Park-av., S. (Aus.)	S. Parkside-av.
Park-ct. (S. D.)	Irwin-av.
Park-pl. (H. P.)	E. 47th-pl.
Park row (S. D.)	E. 11th-pl.
Paulina-pl. (W. D.)	Hobson-av.
Pearce-st. (W. D.)	Tilden-st.
Pease-av. (J.)	Newcastle-av.
Peck-pl. (S. D.)	E. 8th-st.
Penn-pl. (W. D.)	Walnut-st.
Pennsylvania-av. (E. P.)	Osage-av.
Perry-st. (N. D., L. V.)	Greenview-av.
Peterson-av. (L. V.)	Elmdale-av.
Peterson-av. (J.)	Rogers-av.
Peterson-st. (W. D.)	Willow-st.
Phillip-av. (R. P.)	Chase-av.
Phillips-st. (W. D.)	Bismarck-st.
Pleasant-st. (N. D.)	Frontier-av.
Pleasant-pl. (W. D.)	Lyndale-st.
Poplar-av. (Aus.)	N. Lotus-av.
Potomac-st. (Aus.)	Potomac-av.
Powell Park (W. D.)	McLean-av.
Prairie-av., N. (Aus.)	N. Menard-av.
Prairie-av., S. (Aus.)	S. Menard-av.
Prairie-av. (E. P.)	Onondaga-av.
Pratt-st. (W. D.)	W. Huron-st.
Prospect-av. (E. P.)	Otsego-av.
Racine-ct. (L. V.)	Draper-st.
Railroad-ct. (W. D.)	Forsyth-av.
Railroad-pl. (W. D.)	S. Marshfield-av.
Ravenswood-av. (L. V.)	N. Honore-st.
Ravenswood Park, E. (L. V.).	Ravenswood-av.
Ravenswood Park, W. (L. V.).	Ravenswood-av.
Ravenswood Park, W. (L. V.).	Sarak-av.
Reed-pl. (L. V.)	Pensacola-av.
River-st. (H. P.)	E. 134th-pl.
Roberts-av. (J.)	London-av.
Roberts-av. (J.)	Giddings-st.
Roberts-ct. (J.)	Giddings-st.
Robinson-av. (J.)	Moultrie-av.
Rosalie-ct. (H. P.)	Rosalie-av.
Sacramento-ct. (W. D.)	N. Whipple-st.
School-pl. (W. D.)	Arcade-pl.
School-st. (J.)	Otto-st.
Scott-av. (J.)	Neva-av.
Sedgwick-ct. (N. D.)	Felton-ct.
Selby-ter. (J.)	McCormick-av.
Selwyn-av. (J.)	Kennicott-av.
Seminary-pl. (L. V.)	Drummond-pl.
Seventieth-av., N. (N. P.)	Nicolet-av.
Seventieth-av., N. (J.)	Sayre-av.

Old name and district.	New name.
Seventieth-ct., N. (J., N. P.).	Nordica-av.
Seventieth-ct., N. (J.)	Nora-av.
Seventy-first-av., N. (J.)	Nottingham-av.
Seventy-first-av., N. (J.)	Nordica-av.
Seventy-first-ct., N. (N. P.)..	Neva-av.
Seventy-first-ct., N. (J.)	Neva-av.
Seventy-first-ct., N. (J.)	Nottingham-av.
Seventy-second-av.,N.(N.P.,J.).	Harlem-av.
Sheridan-av. (N. P.)	Nettleton-av.
Sheridan-av. (N. P.)	Oak Park-av.
Sherman-av. (H. P.)	Burnham-av.
Sherman-pl. (L. V.)	Dole-av.
Sherman-pl. (N. P.)	Armstrong-st.
Short-pl. (J.)	Grimm-av.
Simpson-av. (J.)	Midas-av.
Sixtieth-av., N. (J., N. P.).....	N. Maynard-av.
Sixtieth-ct., N. (J.)	McVicker-av.
Sixty-first-av., N. (J.)	Meade-av.
Sixty-first-av., N. (J.)	Moody-av.
Sixty-first-ct., N. (J.)	Moody-av.
Sixty-second-av., N. (J.)	Melvina-av.
Sixty-second-ct., N. (J.)	Merrimac-av.
Sixty-third-av., N. (J.)	Mobile-av.
Sixty-third-ct., N. (J.)	Mulligan-av.
Sixty-fourth-av., N. (J.)	Narragansett-av.
Sixty-fourth-av., N. (N. P.)..	Nagle-av.
Sixty-fourth-ct., N. (J.)	Nagle-av.
Sixty-fifth-av., N. (J.)	Natchez-av.
Sixty-fifth-ct., N. (J.)	Neenah-av.
Sixty-fifth-st., N. (J.)	Ardmore-av.
Sixty-sixth-av., N. (J.)	Nashville-av.
Sixty-sixth-ct., N. (J.)	Natoma-av.
Sixty-seventh-av., N. (J.)	Normandy-av.
Sixty-seventh-ct., N. (J.)	Ronan-av.
Sixty-eighth-av., N. (J.)	Oak Park-av.
Sixty-eighth-ct., N. (J.)	Newcastle-av.
Sixty-eighth-ct., N. (J.)	New England-av.
Sixty-ninth-av., N. (J.)	New England-av.
Sixty-ninth-av., N. (J.)	Newland-av.
Sixty-ninth-ct., N. (J.)	Newland-av.
Somerset-ter. (Cal.)	Hunt-av.
Sophia-st. (Aus.)	Rice-st.
Soult-st. (L. V.)	Florence-av.
South-pl. (L. V.)	Lafayette-st.
Southport-av. (L. V., R. P.)..	Glenwood-av.
Star-av. (H. P.)	Dante-av.
State-st. (N. P.)	Talcott-av.
State-ct. (L. V.)	Abbott-ct.
St. Charles-ct. (J.)	Lawson-av.
Steiner-rd. (J.)	Leader-av.
Sullivan-ct. (S. D.)	Gratten-av.
Summit-st. (S. D.)	S. Irving-av.
Superior-st., W. (Aus.)	W. Huron-st.
Superior-st. (E. P.)	Oneida-av.
Superior-av. (H. P.)	Burley-av.
Syracuse-av. (J.)	N. Harding-av.
Tell-st. (N. D.)	Willow-st.
Third-av., N. (Aus.)	Mascouten-av.
Town-st. (N. D.)	Frontier-av.
Tremont-av. (Cal.)	Horicon-av.
Union-ct. (W. D.)	Inanda-av.
Union-st., N. (W. D.)	N. Union-av.
Union-st., S. (W. D.)	S. Union-av.
Union-pl. (W. D.)	Ford-av.
Van Buren-pl. (W. D.)	Tilden-st.
Vernon-av. (E. P.)	Owen-av.
Vernon-av. (E. P.)	Ibsen-st.
Vincennes-rd. (L.)	Vincennes-av.
Vincennes-av. (H. P.)	Eberhart-av.
Wabansia-av. (N. D.)	Clifton-av.
Wabash-av. (E. P.)	Estes-av.
Waite-av. (J.)	Muriel-av.
Waldemar-av. (J.)	Manassas-av.
Waller-st. (W. D.)	Miller-st.
Walnut-av. (N. P.)	Hurlbut-st.
Walnut-av., N. (Aus.)	N. Lotus-av.
Walnut-av., S. (Aus.)	S. Lotus-av.
Warner-st. (L.)	S. Leavitt-st.
Warren-st. (N. P.)	Imlay-st.
Warwick-av. (N. P.)	Newburg-av.
Washburne-st. (N. P.)	Nashotah-av.
Washburne-st. (J.)	Hodge-st.
Washington-av. (H. P.)	Blackstone-av.
Washington-st. (W. D.)	Altgeld-st.
Washington-bd. (E. P.)	Overhill-av.

Old name and district.	New name.
Washington-pl. (N. D.)	Brenan-st.
Waterville-st. (S. D.)	Benson-st.
Waveland-ct. (L. V.)	Clifton-av.
Wellingtou-st. (L. V., J.)	Wellington-av.
Wellington-ct. (H. P.)	Dever-av.
Wells-pl. (N. P.)	Devon-av.
West-st. (J.)	N. Central-av.
Western-av. (E. P.)	Harlem-av.
Whipple-ct. (W. D.)	Garden-st.
Wilcox-av. (W. D.)	Wilcox-st.
Willis-ct. (W. D.)	Heath-av.
Willow-av. (N. P.)	Natoma-av.
Willow-av. (Aus.)	Long-av.

Old name and district.	New name.
Wilson-av. (N. P.)	Odell-av.
Winchester-av. (J.)	Matson-av.
Winter-st. (N. P.)	Oriole-av.
Winthrop-ct. (W. D.)	S. Bishop-st.
Wisconsin-av. (J.)	Kruger-av.
Wright-ct. (W. D.)	N. Talman-av.
York-st. (W. D.)	Flournoy-st.

Abbreviations: Aus., Austin; Cal., Calumet; E. P., Edison Park; H. P., Hyde Park; J., Jefferson; L. V., Lake View; N. D., North Division; N. P., Norwood Park; R. P., Rogers Park; S. D., South Division; W. D., West Division.

GREAT LAKES NAVAL TRAINING STATION,
North Chicago, Ill.

The great lakes naval training station at North Chicago, Ill., was placed in commission July 1, 1911, and the work of fitting young men for service in the enlisted force of the United States navy was at once begun. By Aug. 15 389 recruits had been enrolled as apprentice seamen, most of them coming from the central west and south. The total amount expended for buildings and grounds before the station opened was $3,475,000 and for maintenance $406,648.

Enlistment—The term of enlistment is four years, except minors under 18 years of age, who are enlisted for the period of minority. Only such persons are enlisted as can be reasonably expected to remain in the service, and when enlisted they must serve out the term specified. The age limit is 17 to 35 years.

Physical Requirements—For a minor enlisting as an apprentice seaman the following minimum heights (barefooted), and weights (without clothes) are required:

Age.	Height.	Weight.
17	62 inches	110 pounds
18	64 inches	115 pounds
19	64 inches	120 pounds
20	64 inches	125 pounds

Any one of the following conditions will be sufficient to cause the rejection of an applicant: Feeble constitution, general poor physique or impaired general health; any disease or deformity, either congenital or acquired, that would impair efficiency; any acute disease.

Mental Requirements—Applicants for enlistment must be able to read and write English.

Other Requirements—Applicants for enlistment must be American citizens, native or naturalized. A minor must present a certificate of birth or verified written statement by his parents, or either of them, or in case of their death a similar statement by his legal guardian, showing the applicant to be of the age required by the navy regulations.

Pay—The pay of apprentice seamen is $17.60 per month. Each enlisted man is furnished with a free outfit of clothing, amounting to $69, on first enlistment.

How to Enlist—Any one who wishes to enlist in the navy should write to the bureau of navigation, navy department, Washington, D. C., stating such desire, and the bureau will immediately reply, giving the address of the nearest recruiting station, where applicants are examined physically and either accepted or rejected. The government pays the expenses from the point of enlistment to the training station, but not to the recruiting station.

There are similar training stations at Narragansett Bay, R. I., and San Francisco, Cal.

OFFICERS AT GREAT LAKES STATION.
Commandant—Capt. George R. Clark.
Lieutenant-Commander—W. Smith.
Lieutenant—Earle F. Johnson.
Lieutenant—John B. Earle.
Surgeon—James S. Taylor.
Paymaster—Reginald Spear.
Chaplain—Frank Thompson.
Chief Boatswain—Gerald Oliff.
Boatswain—James E. Quirk.
Boatswain—George R. Reed.
Machinist—Edwin W. Abel.
Carpenter—Tony L. Hannah.

THE CHICAGO ASSOCIATION OF COMMERCE.
Headquarters, 10 South LaSalle street.

President—Joseph H. Defrees.
Vice-President Interstate Division—Edward E. Gore.
Vice-President Civic-Industrial Division—Charles D. Richards.
Vice-President Local Division—John F. Smulski.
Vice-President Foreign Trade Division—John J. Arnold.
General Treasurer—Joseph R. Noel.
General Secretary—James W. Morrisson.
Board of directors for 1914—James S. Agar, J. J. Arnold, W. W. Baird, Joseph Belfeld, Edward C. Brown, W. W. Buchanan, Richmond Dean, Joseph H. Defrees, Charles L. Dering, Howard Elting, E. C. Ferguson, F. E. French, W. A. Gardner, Edward E. Gore, John P. Hovland,

E. U. Kimbark, Frank R. McMullin, James W. Morrisson, J. F. Nickerson, Joseph R. Noel, William Reiss, Charles D. Richards, B. J. Rosenthal, Henry Paulman, Frank L. Shepard, John F. Smulski.

OFFICIAL STAFF.
Business Manager—Hubert F. Miller.
Assistant Business Manager—Robert B. Beach.
Editor Chicago Commerce—William Hudson Harper.
Traffic Director—H. C. Barlow.
Industrial Commissioner—W. R. Humphrey.
Manager Convention Bureau—George M. Spangler, Jr.
Representative—F. C. Enright, Casilla de Correo 1779, Buenos Aires, Argentina.

CHICAGO RAILROAD PASSENGER TRAFFIC.

Total daily train, car and passenger movements at Chicago railway stations in 1913. From Bion J. Arnold's report on steam railroad terminals.

Stations.	Through			Suburban			Total		
	Trains.	Cars.	Pass.	Trains.	Cars.	Pass.	Trains.	Cars.	Pass.
Union	167	1,097	19,145	112	450	16,323	279	1,547	35,468
Grand Central	34	206	3,175	4	13	470	38	219	3,645
C. & N. W.	121	785	16,811	189	845	32,583	310	1,630	49,394
LaSalle street	80	531	10,384	111	517	24,718	191	1,048	35,102
Dearborn	104	617	9,968	42	138	8,337	146	755	18,305
Illinois Central	85	582	10,140	288	1,245	40,757	373	1,827	50,897
Grand total	591	3,818	69,623	746	3,208	123,188	1,337	7,026	192,811

FIRST AID IN ACCIDENTS OR ILLNESS.

Apoplexy—Take patient to cool room, loosen clothes, apply cold to head and use mustard foot baths.

Bleeding—Make patient lie down in horizontal position, generally on his back. If the wound is in a limb raise the limb above the body. Put pressure on the bleeding points with fingers covered with gauze. Keep the patient warm with clothing, artificial heat and hot water bags. Where the blood spurts, as from an artery, pressure must be applied directly to the wound; if it is large, push gauze into it and press down. A tight bandage should also be placed a short distance above, between the heart and the wound. Tight bandages should not be left on too long. Bleeding in the scalp may be stopped by pressing down upon it near the edge of the wound on the side from which the blood comes. Alcoholic stimulants should not be used.

Bleeding from Internal Wounds—Have the head of the patient a little lower than the rest of the body; apply ice cold cloths to the stomach.

Bleeding from Lungs—Put ice or cold cloths on the chest; the body should be in a sitting position. The patient may also be given small doses of vinegar mixed with salt.

Bleeding from the Nose—Slight cases may be controlled by the application of ice or cold water. In more serious cases place the patient on his back, raise the arms above the head and let him draw salt water or vinegar and water into his nostrils.

Bleeding from Varicose Veins—Raise the limb above the level of the body, bandage the vein where ruptured and place a tight bandage below the wound.

Bites—In the case of poisonous bites, as from snakes, bandage tightly above the wound, cut out edges of wound with knife or cauterize with nitrate of silver; wash the wound with whisky or with a solution of bichloride of mercury. The important thing is to keep a tight bandage above the wound for several hours. Dog bites, if hydrophobia is feared, should be treated in the same way. In the case of ordinary bites half melted tallow rubbed vigorously into the wound is efficacious in removing poisonous substances.

Burns and Scalds—Cut away clothing, if necessary; do not pull it off; put loose cotton on burned part, exposing the skin to the air as little as possible. Dress with a warm solution of baking soda or use olive oil, vaseline, sweet oil, the white of an egg or a mixture of linseed oil and lime water. Wet earth or clay, starch or toilet powder may also be used in emergencies. Burns from acids should first have water poured over them and should then be washed with a solution of baking soda or lime water. In burns from drinking acids, take a dose of baking soda diluted so as to be quite weak. Oil and the whites of eggs are good for burns in the mouth caused by chemicals or fluids.

Choking—Bend the body forward and face downward and slap vigorously on the back.

Concussion or Stunning—Treat like apoplexy. Lay the patient flat on his back with the head slightly raised; cool applications to the head and warm to the body are sometimes advisable.

Dislocation of Fingers—Pull the bones into place and apply cold wet cloths.

Drowning—Loosen clothing, if any. Empty lungs of water by laying body face downward and lifting by the middle so that the head hangs down; jerk the body a few times; pull the tongue forward, using handkerchief or pin with string if necessary; imitate motion of respiration by alternately compressing and expanding the lower ribs about twenty times a minute; stimulate the action of the lungs by alternately raising and lowering the arms from the sides up above the head, doing it gently; apply warmth and friction to extremities.

Ear, Foreign Substance in—Great care must be used in attempting to remove anything from the ear. To get out live insects, put glycerin in ear and syringe with tepid water; must be done gently.

Emetics—The most quickly obtainable emetic is mustard flour and plenty of warm water, followed by copious drafts of warm water.

Eye, Foreign Substances in—Relief is often obtained by closing the eye affected and rapidly winking the other eye. A grain or two of whole flaxseed may also be tried. Another method is to pull the upper lid out and down over the lower lid and blow the nearest nostril; the resulting free flow of tears will usually wash away the disturbing particles.

Fainting—Place flat on back, allow fresh air and sprinkle with cold water.

Fits—Apply mustard plasters to the feet or wrists in case of hysterics; in ordinary cases treat like fainting.

Fracture—Place the limb on a pillow in a restful and natural position and call a surgeon.

Freezing—Keep away from the fire, rub the frozen parts with snow or ice, or give cold bath with rubbing. Stimulate with tea or coffee.

Gas, Asphyxiation from—Get into fresh air and administer ammonia, twenty drops in a tumbler of water, at frequent intervals.

Poisoning of Blood—This may be caused by scratches from rusty nails, cuts, bruises and lacerations. The simplest and quickest way to prevent the spread of the poison into the system is to rub an ounce of warm, half melted tallow into the wound by means of a clean, smooth linen rag, keeping up the rubbing patiently until the swelling subsides. In serious cases use tight ligatures or bandages. Butter, oil or fat may be used as antiseptics, but ammonia and carbolic acid, the latter diluted with 95 per cent of water, are the best.

Poisoning from Arsenic (paris green, rat poison, etc.)—Use peroxide of iron, freshly prepared; if not within reach, make the patient drink a pint of cream or milk or take bacon fat and lard oil, but get an emetic for expelling the poison as soon as possible.

Poisoning from Ivy—Paint the affected part with common white lead, allowing the color to dry and after a few hours removing it with a soft rag soaked in turpentine.

Poisoning from Opiates—Sponge the patient's head and neck with ice water at half minute intervals, rub briskly with coarse towels and keep him on his feet and in motion in a draft or before an open window.

Poisons, Antidotes for Other—For corrosive sublimate, white of egg, milk, gluten of wheat; for creosote, emetics, ammonia, mucilage; for iodine, emetics; for lead, sulphuric acid diluted with aerated water, mucilage; for mushroom poison, emetics and stimulants; for nitrate of silver, copious drafts of salt water; for phosphorous, emetics and magnesia; for potash, vinegar, lemon juice, oils, emetics.

Sprains of Wrists or Ankles—Hot or cold bandages frequently applied will lessen the pain. The "cold water cure" is to let the wrist or ankle remain under a running faucet as long as the pain can be endured and repeating the operation every few minutes. Arnica is a common remedy.

Suffocation—Get into fresh air, throw cold water over face and chest, put mustard plasters on soles of feet and wrists and apply hot bottles to the body.

Sunstroke—Get the sufferer into as cool and shady a place as possible, loosen clothing, dash cold water over the head and face and rub body with ice. In ordinary heat prostration, as distinguished from sunstroke, lay the sufferer flat on his back and apply heat to the body and limbs, bathing the face with warm water. Avoid giving alcoholic stimulants; give tea, coffee or warm milk instead.

Tests of death—Hold mirror to mouth; if living moisture will gather. Place fingers in front of strong light; if living they will appear red, if dead dark or black. Push pin into flesh; if alive hole will close, if dead it will remain open.

CHICAGO SCHOOL CENSUS OF MAY, 1912.

Taken under the supervision of W. L. Bodine for the board of education.

ADULT POPULATION.

The school census of May 2, 1912, did not include inhabitants of Chicago 21 years of age and over, but W. L. Bodine, director of the count, estimated the total population of the city on the date named at 2,381,700. In 1900 he estimated it at 2,100,000 and the figure was practically verified by the federal census, which gave 2,185,283.

AGE AND SEX OF MINORS.

Age.	Male.	Female.	Total.
Under 4	97,076	90,899	187,975
Between 4 and 5	31,275	30,765	62,040
Between 5 and 6	30,110	29,846	59,956
Between 6 and 7	25,749	26,063	51,812
Between 7 and 14	129,425	129,025	258,450
Between 14 and 16	41,885	42,616	84,501
Over 16 and under 21	88,334	89,448	177,782
Total	443,854	438,662	882,516

The net increase of minors over the school census of 1910 was 68,401. In 1906 the increase was 25,958; in 1908 it was 40,797 and in 1910 it was 66,768.

TOTAL MINOR POPULATION BY WARDS.

School census, May 2, 1912.

Ward.	Male.	Female.	Tot'l.	Ward.	Male.	Female.	Tot'l.
1	4,919	4,643	9,562	20	12,548	12,320	24,868
2	6,310	6,437	12,747	21	6,462	6,528	12,999
3	6,390	7,457	14,447	22	12,764	11,920	24,684
4	12,924	12,674	25,598	23	10,515	10,624	21,139
5	13,277	13,464	26,741	24	12,758	12,553	25,311
6	8,354	9,144	17,498	25	11,868	11,903	23,771
7	9,579	9,945	19,524	26	14,304	13,832	28,136
8	14,932	14,736	29,668	27	18,335	17,592	35,927
9	15,664	15,026	30,690	28	15,664	15,370	31,034
10	14,905	14,672	29,577	29	16,894	16,137	33,031
11	14,777	15,230	30,007	30	13,025	13,223	26,248
12	14,776	14,175	28,951	31	11,978	12,214	24,192
13	9,717	9,886	19,603	32	15,411	15,053	30,464
14	11,482	11,541	23,023	33	15,716	15,708	31,424
15	14,598	13,999	28,597	34	13,678	13,330	27,008
16	17,286	16,813	34,099	35	13,713	13,091	26,804
17	15,064	14,986	30,050				
18	7,827	7,896	15,723	Tt'l.	443,854	438,662	882,516
19	14,840	14,540	29,380				

NATIVITY OF MINORS.

	American born. Father American.	Foreign born.	American born. Father foreign.	Total.
American	267,270			267,270
Negro	11,191			11,191
Austrian		2,954	19,893	22,847
Belgian		301	788	1,089
Bohemian		3,666	42,745	46,411
Bulgarian		41	382	423
Canadian		725	9,955	10,680
Chinese		11	99	110
Croatian		273	1,490	1,763
Danish		388	5,714	6,102
English		1,282	10,984	12,266
Finnish		78	349	427
French		72	1,156	1,228
German		4,913	135,232	140,145
Greek		295	1,153	1,448
Hollander		901	7,617	8,518
Hungarian		2,335	6,630	8,965
Irish		822	49,700	50,522
Italian		5,447	37,833	43,280
Japanese		4	26	30
Lithuanian		319	8,250	8,569
Mexican		8	33	4,
Norwegian		966	14,318	15,284
Polish		6,589	91,388	97,977
Roumanian		673	1,256	1,929
Russian*		15,378	53,534	68,912
Scotch		574	4,570	5,144
Servian		20	84	104
Spanish		11	148	159
Swedish		1,413	44,673	46,086
Swiss		79	1,470	1,549
Welsh		60	557	617
Other countries		203	1,227	1,430
Total	278,461	50,791	553,264	882,516

*Includes Jewish children born in Russia and American born Jewish children whose fathers were born in Russia.

NATIVITY STATISTICS OF MINORS BY WARDS.

In the following tables the abbreviations "For." and "Amer." signify "foreign born" and "American born, father foreign," respectively.

Ward.	Ameri-can.	Ne-gro.	Austrian. For.	Amer.	Belgian. For.	Amer.	Bohemian. For.	Amer.
1	2,568	902	83	233	4	4	3	78
2	5,735	2,981	3	83	...	9	.....	5
3	8,024	1,016	21	156	6	4	7	52
4	7,865	.....	17	273	6	6	25	549
5	9,145	.....	37	258	1	8	18	213
6	11,247	181	14	154	2	15	2	26
7	12,131	111	8	119	...	18	3	21
8	6,542	14	209	1,897	9	8	10	92
9	7,958	27	176	1,061	...	23	32	232
10	1,899	.....	159	1,000	63	78	1,352	10,451
11	3,998	.....	169	1,013	3	17	120	5,045
12	6,141	3	...	387	...	3	993	12,063
13	11,246	26	6	147	2	16	4	49
14	10,289	1,536	92	658	7	36	3	70
15	6,066	9	166	1,146	11	61	52	330
16	2,822	.....	117	431	8	23	17	38
17	2,554	11	331	2,521	...	9	20	82
18	7,037	127	17	115	7	9	3	25
19	7,354	.....	76	239	1	3	9	58
20	3,233	2	454	2,656	10	14	45	460
21	6,405	92	18	115	2	4	3	8
22	5,145	65	118	476	13	13	4	47
23	10,025	33	35	150	4	21	8	38
24	8,521	4	96	235	68	143	9	86
25	12,852	8	8	78	4	5	4	27
26	11,210	10	21	175	3	15	.....	50
27	7,278	2	69	452	9	16	55	447
28	7,362	1	20	266	31	98	8	134
29	6,814	1	115	1,246	1	13	269	3,174
30	8,320	3,321	42	267	9	14	34	309
31	9,622	545	26	137	7	9	2	125
32	14,712	139	13	144	...	7	2	169
33	11,921	20	87	276	6	43	16	182
34	7,968	4	81	869	...	4	508	7,763
35	10,251	.....	50	460	4	21	26	258
Tt'l.	267,270	11,191	2,954	19,893	301	788	3,666	42,745

	Bulgarian. For.	Amer.	Canadian. For.	Amer.	Chinese. For.	Amer.	Croatian. For.	Amer.
1	...	...	22	96	10	50	...	5
2	1	4	16	215	...	1	...	7
3	...	3	37	255	...	11	...	...
4	...	19	3	202	...	...	...	...
5	...	...	9	517	...	...	...	8
6	...	3	2	49	387	...	4	3
7	...	...	3	29	513	...	2	...
8	...	...	6	15	293	...	...	27
9	...	...	12	46	578	...	3	1	31
10	...	27	265	...	37	...	1	115	403
11	...	...	8	151	...	...	6	60
12	...	...	18	10	83	...	6	42	105
13	...	2	5	55	633	1	11	...	...
14	...	...	43	393	...	...	3	5
15	...	...	12	8	126	...	...	7
16	...	...	...	28	...	...	...	2
17	...	...	5	60	...	...	3	31
18	...	2	3	35	163	...	...	1	9
19	...	...	30	302	...	...	...	...
20	...	1	9	3	25	...	...	1	9
21	...	...	42	150	...	...	...	...
22	...	...	5	83	...	...	...	...
23	...	1	...	23	262	...	...	...	...
24	...	...	6	158	...	...	1	4
25	...	...	30	342	...	...	2	2
26	...	...	33	277	...	...	1	9
27	...	5	21	368	...	...	...	8
28	...	4	2	10	171	...	2	...	...
29	...	1	19	367	...	...	89	717
30	...	15	408	...	...	1	7
31	...	...	17	500	...	3	6	20
32	...	...	25	647	...	4	...	...
33	...	1	21	395	...	...	...	...
34	...	...	12	309	...	1	1	12
35	...	1	6	23	471	...	...	...	...
Tt'l.	41	382	725	9,955	11	99	273	1,496

	Danish. For.	Amer.	English. For.	Amer.	Finnish. For.	Amer.	French. For.	Amer.
1	1	27	6	114	...	1	...	36
2	15	109	36	314	...	4	3	47
3	21	165	27	356	...	...	...	29
4	...	26	23	188	...	8	4	22

Ward.	Danish For.	Amer.	English For.	Amer.	Finnish For.	Amer.	French For.	Amer.
5....	7	36	33	288	..	8	..	40
6....	4	86	42	422	..	10	5	49
7....	21	249	71	548	..	1	..	39
8....	5	194	49	452	..	2	1	28
9....	9	216	71	558	4	23	1	46
10....	...	2	20	139	1	2	..	26
11....	...	23	38	121	..	3	3	29
12....	1	22	13	121	..	11	..	7
13....	3	72	62	485	2	5	..	38
14....	2	164	64	469	..	1	3	30
15....	56	524	36	180	..	4	..	26
16....	...	23	9	31	..	..	..	15
17....	2	68	2	51	2	5	..	26
18....	9	40	68	257	..	5	4	34
19....	1	9	26	126	..	..	2	28
20....	...	6	18	50	..	..	2	13
21....	1	22	40	280	7	10	1	40
22....	2	33	7	132	12	27	5	29
23....	4	70	43	268	11	57	2	30
24....	1	70	21	131	4	8	5	34
25....	3	81	26	375	..	24	4	26
26....	1	161	71	438	7	48	6	67
27....	25	516	54	485	8	14	5	30
28....	93	907	26	265	..	2	..	45
29....	6	140	30	357	1	3	1	44
30....	2	69	38	334	..	7	..	38
31....	8	177	54	498	6	12	2	22
32....	9	158	53	674	..	5	2	36
33....	41	705	44	598	13	26	6	42
34....	...	24	34	262	..	8	3	31
35....	35	521	55	616	..	5	..	35
Ttl..	388	5,741	1,282	10,984	78	349	72	1,156

Ward.	Irish For.	Amer.	Italian For.	Amer.	Japanese For.	Amer.	Lithuanian For.	Amer.
16...	3	212	16	112	...	...	40	163
17...	4	225	604	5,105	...	...	...	7
18...	21	1,032	74	388	...	2	...	8
19...	28	1,524	1,943	11,472	...	...	...	...
20...	5	308	170	1,039	...	...	...	18
21...	27	1,246	94	647	...	1	...	...
22...	21	800	1,144	7,087	...	3	...	...
23...	10	651	15	127	...	4	...	1
24...	9	1,102	25	165	...	3	...	...
25...	17	487	3	93	...	1	...	...
26...	33	514	6	122	...	...	...	1
27...	13	536	17	214	...	1	...	2
28...	2	412	8	129	...	...	2	...
29...	50	1,996	82	611	...	...	140	3,865
30...	49	6,336	53	391	...	2	2	166
31...	27	4,371	4	62	...	...	...	5
32...	59	4,162	4	169	...	4	...	6
33...	11	586	26	273	...	...	...	3
34...	20	1,085	3	68	...	...	...	5
35...	27	4,117	9	217	...	...	...	2
Ttl.	822	49,700	5,447	37,853	4	26	319	8,250

	Mexican For.	Amer.	Norwegian For.	Amer.	Polish For.	Amer.	Roumanian For.	Amer.
1...	...	2	...	18	2	14	...	...
2...	...	...	...	25	2	53	6	27
3...	1	6	...	36	5	31	6	15
4...	...	...	4	29	125	4,861	...	1
5...	...	...	...	47	219	2,553	...	15
6...	...	...	6	47	2	86	18	3
7...	...	...	12	108	...	11	...	5
8...	...	...	3	103	739	8,676	1	...
9...	...	1	36	240	108	1,233	5	12
10...	...	...	19	91	903	...	80	167
11...	...	...	25	551	6,543	...	16	40
12...	...	1	1	63	301	3,506	12	22
13...	...	...	6	74	8	40	5	17
14...	...	...	30	344	75	666	2	...
15...	1	2	176	1,311	163	1,529	26	73
16...	...	...	2	42	1,621	21,772	32	27
17...	...	4	22	401	1,359	12,702	1	1
18...	...	...	2	53	...	30	3	25
19...	...	7	...	15	45	359	141	198
20...	...	...	...	7	76	1,264	294	444
21...	6	1	3	28	7	35	...	...
22...	...	1	3	55	43	236	...	6
23...	...	...	12	95	2	19	5	6
24...	...	...	1	97	46	815	...	...
25...	...	1	1	110	10	29	...	...
26...	...	...	16	137	8	105	...	1
27...	...	3	81	1,436	127	9,444	1	17
28...	...	3	237	2,568	222	7,733	8	24
29...	...	...	...	38	304	3,287	...	...
30...	...	...	4	65	234	1,208	1	6
31...	138	416	46	295	...	...	...	...
32...	...	...	2	93	4	66	1	3
33...	...	...	153	3,909	38	948	...	6
34...	...	...	4	32	17	433	6	75
35...	...	...	141	2,547	16	182	1	3
Ttl.	8	33	966	14,318	6,589	91,388	673	1,256

	German For.	Amer.	Greek For.	Amer.	Hollander For.	Amer.	Hungarian For.	Amer.
1...	63	616	16	30	2	8	21	35
2...	36	915	3	39	..	19	9	38
3...	61	1,148	4	2	3	17	28	129
4...	151	4,978	4	24	3	28	7	67
5...	86	5,988	...	9	10	21	18	75
6...	57	2,175	1	17	5	36	26	195
7...	22	1,554	2	27	2	52	9	40
8...	111	3,426	5	6	1	26	34	265
9...	158	2,757	18	62	251	4,165	331	879
10...	73	1,132	11	47	193	549	39	280
11...	218	3,911	3	11	12	133	60	148
12...	63	2,185	13	25	5	65	24	68
13...	37	2,488	6	14	15	75	6	47
14...	105	2,836	6	33	17	92	65	279
15...	173	7,296	3	18	...	51	170	786
16...	144	3,862	2	6	...	10	109	231
17...	133	1,816	3	45	...	15	104	416
18...	59	1,097	28	99	1	44	37	55
19...	45	883	86	185	1	14	26	85
20...	60	1,373	3	22	...	11	51	156
21...	156	1,762	10	90	1	6	35	47
22...	599	5,055	6	43	4	25	467	591
23...	213	5,733	3	22	2	13	69	107
24...	412	11,052	9	32	7	23	125	255
25...	76	4,724	1	23	4	29	13	36
26...	193	8,467	1	15	12	29	45	84
27...	316	9,185	5	14	14	55	55	150
28...	218	6,593	6	20	19	43	23	121
29...	314	6,390	8	33	47	180	59	287
30...	129	2,518	...	30	2	30	88	257
31...	45	2,810	13	29	44	235	4	47
32...	70	5,558	7	33	142	994	17	47
33...	128	5,843	4	10	28	156	26	102
34...	86	2,860	2	11	27	196	30	69
35...	92	4,246	3	26	27	167	45	205
Ttl.	4,913	135,232	295	1,153	901	7,617	2,335	6,630

	Russian For.	Amer.	Scotch For.	Amer.	Servian For.	Amer.	Spanish For.	Amer.
1..	52	243	3	22	1	4	1	...
2..	68	724	19	106	...	...	2	16
3..	56	655	13	90	...	1	1	2
4..	147	1,253	15	108	...	...	...	...
5..	106	424	6	141	...	1	...	...
6..	119	472	19	152	...	...	...	6
7..	41	264	35	333	...	...	...	6
8..	154	934	44	176	...	3	...	4
9..	183	924	46	185	...	...	...	...
10..	2,951	6,439	1	8	...	...	...	7
11..	601	4,674	10	40	1	13	...	11
12..	169	1,148	2	40	...	...	...	...
13..	169	746	23	314	...	...	...	8
14..	103	351	37	186	...	...	...	6
15..	1,924	4,617	13	65	...	4	...	8
16..	683	1,355	...	1	...	...	...	...
17..	194	790	5	24	...	...	...	6
18..	657	3,776	20	93	...	...	...	4
19..	1,794	6,033	10	55	...	6	...	6
20..	3,649	9,799	1	14	...	...	...	4
21..	27	219	4	59	...	1	...	9
22..	50	351	7	28	...	3	...	10
23..	43	219	4	80	...	...	...	...
24..	63	188	1	60	11	31	...	2
25..	57	3,853	...	39	...	6	2	30
26..	9	63	21	112	...	7	4	...

Ward.	Irish For.	Amer.	Italian For.	Amer.	Japanese For.	Amer.	Lithuanian For.	Amer.
1....	11	353	417	3,177	...	...	...	...
2....	22	526	20	173	...	2	...	...
3....	11	1,403	2	64	...	1	...	...
4....	25	2,141	85	606	...	...	10	1,136
5....	47	3,624	14	93	...	...	23	2,176
6....	32	704	1	48	...	...	...	5
7....	31	1,619	11	50	3	3	...	...
8....	17	1,257	72	389	1	1	...	16
9....	23	1,028	232	2,004	...	...	61	354
10....	2	308	...	26	...	...	3	10
11....	28	896	68	398	...	...	31	283
12....	7	388	21	42	...	...	3	12
13....	62	2,966	33	248	...	...	...	1
14....	44	1,452	152	1,171	...	...	...	4
15....	1	323	18	153	...	...	1	...

Ward.	Russian. For. Amer.		Scotch. For. Amer.		Servian. For. Amer.		Spanish. For. Amer.	
27..	176	365	19	168	2	3	2	10
28..	167	696	8	131	...	...	...	3
29..	143	850	16	164	...	4	...	...
30..	85	551	16	161	...	...	...	...
31..	136	416	46	295	...	...	...	...
32..	62	275	22	427	...	7	...	5
33..	27	230	32	188	1	...	...	2
34..	478	3,148	5	82	...	...	...	11
35..	35	256	42	367	...	...	...	d
Tl.	15,378	53,534	574	4,570	20	84	11	148

Ward.	Swedish. For. Amer.		Swiss. For. Amer.		Welsh. For. Amer.		Others. For. Amer.	
1...	6	106	1	10	...	2	15	68
2...	13	259	5	22	...	7	8	26
3...	12	354	...	28	...	2	5	41
4...	24	447	3	34	...	4	...	43
5...	3	350	3	20	...	21	...	9
6...	21	460	1	21	...	18	6	32
7...	37	1,243	5	37	2	32	7	35
8...	84	3,116	...	48	1	74	2	28
9...	121	3,953	1	58	1	34	31	97
10...	...	27	...	...	4	...	6	101
11...	15	363	...	7	...	4	6	80
12...	37	484	...	9	...	1	15	95
13...	...	87	...	14	24	78	...	28
14...	12	337	...	39	...	17	3	51
15...	32	798	...	30	...	7	1	14
16...	...	46	...	18	...	...	6	6
17...	2	232	...	10	...	5	6	37
18...	3	90	...	16	3	8	3	20
19...	3	33	...	12	...	3	25	70
20...	3	18	2	...	...	...	5	16
21...	18	1,090	4	50	...	7	17	40
22...	55	1,697	10	61	...	14	2	10
23...	141	2,377	26	103	2	10	6	26
24...	53	1,012	2	83	...	...	3	19
25...	57	3,853	...	39	...	6	2	30
26...	114	5,224	1	133	...	16	14	27
27...	93	3,384	1	97	...	2	5	40
28...	49	2,037	2	80	...	3	1	19
29...	22	604	...	94	5	14	...	11
30...	33	529	...	20	...	31	...	18
31...	144	3,420	3	44	...	26	...	20
32...	31	1,300	...	68	1	28	...	14
33...	119	4,100	1	57	...	7	...	16
34...	5	301	...	35	...	4	1	27
35...	50	942	1	73	7	82	2	13
Tl.	1,413	44,673	79	1,470	50	567	203	1,227

MINORS BETWEEN 14 AND 16 AT WORK.

Ward.	Store and office. Male. Fem. T'l.			Factory Male. Fem. T'l.			Miscellaneous. Male. Fem. T'l.		
1.....	30	23	53	23	25	48	31	44	75
2.....	26	20	46	5	2	7	29	23	52
3.....	35	15	50	6	2	8	24	34	58
4.....	125	98	223	91	123	214	88	124	212
5.....	200	114	314	48	78	126	99	139	238
6.....	14	15	29	...	...	...	3	6	9
7.....	22	12	34	1	2	3	18	20	38
8.....	25	29	54	52	102	154	82	176	258
9.....	57	27	84	35	19	54	86	192	278
10.....	184	107	291	216	228	444	71	121	192
11.....	122	90	212	113	146	259	146	162	308
12.....	160	114	274	125	133	258	158	262	420
13.....	61	30	91	8	9	17	36	48	84
14.....	83	64	147	51	50	101	102	105	207
15.....	138	92	230	73	89	162	77	196	273
16.....	104	97	201	412	450	862	78	157	235
17.....	91	64	155	135	169	304	102	146	248
18.....	43	26	69	18	15	33	54	32	86
19.....	91	44	135	116	117	233	99	129	228
20.....	110	95	205	78	106	184	68	79	147
21.....	42	24	66	12	17	29	21	28	49
22.....	108	60	188	103	100	203	75	163	238
23.....	51	35	86	7	18	25	61	86	147
24.....	175	74	249	93	105	198	125	236	361
25.....	11	8	19	3	5	8	13	20	33
26.....	102	53	155	19	22	41	69	151	220
27.....	193	107	300	89	121	210	123	233	356
28.....	144	96	240	159	179	338	136	196	332
29.....	215	125	340	81	110	191	152	275	427
30.....	90	43	133	24	28	52	108	105	213
31.....	71	46	117	10	12	22	39	64	103
32.....	72	35	107	11	1	12	76	115	191
33.....	107	78	185	29	38	67	64	101	165
34.....	87	70	157	41	38	79	58	89	147
35.....	91	65	156	28	21	44	53	91	144
Tl.	3,280	2,095	5,375	2,310	2,680	4,990	2,624	4,148	6,772

PRIVATE SCHOOLS IN CHICAGO.

(Not including parochial.)

	Teachers. Male. Female. Total.			Pupils. Male. Female. Total.		
High schools.	149	106	255	2,780	1,202	3,982
Elementary ..	27	93	120	979	889	1,868
Kindergartens.	3	31	34	110	268	378
Business coll's	57	41	98	1,839	2,183	4,022
Law schools...	145	2	147	1,396	38	1,434
Medic'l schools	98	...	98	878	21	899
Other	435	160	595	8,612	5,093	13,705
Total........	914	433	1,347	16,594	9,694	26,288

NUMBER OF TEACHERS.

May 2, 1912, there were 6,740 teachers in the public school system, 1,588 in the parochial schools and 1,347 in private schools (not parochial), business colleges, etc.

EPILEPTIC CHILDREN.

The school census enumerators found 291 epileptic children of school age, though the canvass was handicapped to some extent by the sensitiveness of parents who attempted to conceal the facts. The greater number of epileptics was found in the 33d, 17th, 22d, 16th and 29th wards.

BLIND, DEAF AND DUMB.

The enumerators found 259 blind children in the city, the greatest number being reported from the 8th, 3d and 26th wards. Deaf minors numbered 651, most of them being in the 32d ward. There were 210 mutes.

CRIPPLED CHILDREN.

The count showed 676 crippled children in the city. Of this number the 9th, 10th, 11th, 8th, 19th, 22d, 26th, 27th, 30th, 15th, 28th and 35th wards contributed the greater number.

ILLITERATES.

The census enumerators found only 157 children over 12 and under 21 years of age who were unable to read or write in any language. There were many who could not read or write in English, but who were able to read or write in some other language. In 1910 there were 401 illiterate minors.

CHICAGO REAL ESTATE TRANSFERS.

Year.	No. sales.	Consideration.	Year.	No. sales.	Consideration.
1895....	15,802	$114,597,724	1904....	24,459	$102,870,570
1896....	14,022	91,022,602	1905....	28,940	139,601,896
1897....	13,924	101,195,313	1906....	31,562	141,342,020
1898....	13,558	93,100,276	1907....	26,390	131,982,811
1899....	14,356	108,210,111	1908....	29,821	133,326,639
1900....	14,356	87,917,968	1909....	32,821	140,909,512
1901....	15,871	100,664,279	1910....	30,058	155,464,768
1902....	18,063	111,441,112	1911....	37,615	154,320,911
1903....	19,880	107,680,304	1912....	45,743	113,693,768

TORRENS SYSTEM.

TRANSFERS.

Year.	Number.	Consideration.	Year.	Number.	Consideration.
1912........	2,786	$4,434,250	1906.......	998	$1,607,189
1911........	2,014	3,295,198	1905.......	748	1,254,049
1910........	1,789	3,295,850	1904.......	445	1,142,410
1909........	1,253	2,186,587	1903.......	309	741,030
1908........	1,006	1,683,337	1902.......	165	384,850
1907........	976	1,287,406	1901.......	55	198,170

STREETS, ALLEYS AND PAVEMENTS.

The combined length of the streets and alleys of Chicago is 4,445.71 miles. The street mileage is 2,948.15 and the alley mileage 1,497.56. Of the streets 1,863.36 miles are paved. The total of each kind of pavement in use Jan. 1, 1913, was:

Pavement.	Miles.	Pavement.	Miles.
Asphalt	623.87	Granite	106.52
Asphalt concrete..	3.41	Macadam	580.28
Asphalt macadam.	9.68	Medina stone......	1.19
Bituminated concrete	2.09	Slag	7.48
		Novaculite	2.00
Block asphalt.....	1.74	Rock asphalt......	0.67
Brick	204.34	Tar macadam	4.96
Cedar	272.92	Wood asphalt.....	0.05
Concrete	7.35		
Creosoted block...	35.00	Total............	1,863.36

SOUTH SHORE LAKE FRONT DEVELOPMENT AND FIELD MUSEUM SITE.

March 30, 1912, a contract was entered into between the Illinois Central Railroad company and the south park commissioners in order to enable the park commissioners to carry out the development of the shore of Lake Michigan between Grant and Jackson parks, as proposed in the plan of Chicago, which plan was originated by the Commercial club of Chicago and committed by the city council to the Chicago plan commission for development.

The south shore plan enables the new Field Museum of Natural History to be located downtown, where it will be easily accessible to all, facing north on the new widened 12th street at its intersection with South Park avenue extended and overlooking Grant park. The necessary authority having been granted by the United States government, on Oct. 19, 1912, work was begun on the breakwaters and the filling in of land east of the Illinois Central station for the early erection of the Field museum.

The park plan provides for the creation of approximately 1,500 acres of park space along Chicago's lake front, beginning at Grant park in the center of the city, by the filling in, first, of a strip of shore land approximately 300 feet wide, facing the open lake, this strip to extend solidly to connect with Jackson park on the south. The strip is to be planted with trees and given informal landscape treatment with flowers and shrubs growing throughout its extent. Along this shore will run a watercourse, approximately 500 feet wide, for small craft, for sailboats, motor boats, canoes and racing shells. Beyond the watercourse, built to protect it and provide safety and shelter to pleasure craft, will be an island, approximately 700 feet wide, and extending from Grant to Jackson parks, planted with trees, having a shore driveway and winding walks, and, under the proposed plan, providing frequent bathing beaches for the city's summer multitudes, as well as athletic grounds, baseball fields, running tracks, tennis courts, football fields, a stadium and a public gymnasium.

This agreement, made March 30, 1912, between the south park commissioners and the Illinois Central Railroad company, provides for the acquiring by the park commissioners of the riparian rights attaching to the land lying between Grant and Jackson parks; for the establishment of a specified permanent boundary line dividing the railroad property from the submerged lands to be acquired by the park commissioners; for the construction of specified viaducts over the railroad tracks; for the extension of South Park avenue north over the railroad tracks to connect with Grant park at 12th street; for the removal of the 12th street station to land south of the new widened 12th street extended to the lake shore; for the transfer of all land east of Michigan avenue and north of 12th street, as far as the present southern boundary of Grant park, to the park commissioners for park purposes; for the transfer to the railroad company of certain specified lands for right of way, and for various other minor agreed changes in present conditions. This agreement was ratified, in accordance with law, by Judge Lockwood Honore of the Circuit court July 20, 1912.

The contract was modified by a supplemental agreement, signed June 26, 1912, which provides for a reduction in the land granted the railroad for right of way; for depression of roadbed; for prohibition of buildings (except switch towers and platform passenger stations) upon the right of way between 29th and 51st streets, in order to permit an unobstructed view of the lake; for a prohibition upon the use of the additional right of way until the railroad company arranges for the operating of four tracks by motive power other than steam (which is designed to encourage the electrification of the road); for specified viaducts over right of way; for widening and relocation of Indiana avenue and for specified widening of Michigan avenue between 12th and 13th streets.

Objections were made by army engineers to the building of a city park from Grant park to Jackson park on the ground that it would interfere with the development of harbor facilities, and but little progress was made in 1913. In November, however, a delegation of citizens visited the war department and obtained the consent of Secretary Garrison to proceed with the improvement, subject to certain conditions. These were that there should be no further filling in from Randolph to 12th streets until an outer breakwater inclosing a new harbor has been provided for by congress and built; that from 12th street to 16th street there should be no further filling in other than that under way for the Field museum and that as to the stretch between 16th and 50th streets legal steps should be taken to reserve to the proper authorities the right to construct harbor facilities if such should be demanded.

CHICAGO BUILDING STATISTICS.

Number of buildings erected since 1894, with estimated cost.

Year.	Buildings.	Cost.	Year.	Buildings.	Cost.	Year.	Buildings.	Cost.
1894	9,755	$33,863,465	1901	6,053	$34,962,075	1908	10,771	$68,203,920
1895	8,633	25,010,043	1902	6,074	48,070,399	1909	11,241	90,559,590
1896	6,444	22,730,615	1903	6,221	37,447,175	1910	11,409	96,982,700
1897	5,294	21,777,230	1904	7,151	44,724,790	1911	11,106	105,269,700
1898	4,067	21,294,325	1905	8,442	63,970,950	1912	11,325	88,786,960
1899	3,794	29,856,750	1906	10,629	64,822,030	1913*	10,139	83,733,977
1900	3,554	19,100,050	1907	9,353	59,093,080	*Jan. 1 to Dec. 1.		

CHICAGOANS OF ADVANCED YEARS.

The following list contains the names of residents of Chicago who are more than 90 years of age:

Austin, Alvin (100), 747 Komensky avenue.
Broderick, Michael (96), 1927 Belle Plaine avenue.
Childs, Mrs. Henrietta (92), 4439 Berkeley avenue.
Foglestad, Mrs. Bertha (92), 539 West 103d street.
Kuznierz, Anton (100), 1239 North Ashland boulevard.
Kuznierz, Mrs. Madeline (98), 1239 North Ashland-bd.

Reynolds, John F. (93), 67 Washington place.
Savage, Rev. George S. F. (96), 1857 Washington-bd.
Schoellickopf, Henry (97), 19 West Chicago avenue.
Todd, William G. (92), 4714 North Robey street.
Warner, Archelœus (96), 302 West 65th street.
Wheeler, Mrs. Eleanor (101), 6062 South State-st.
Williams, M. de La F. (97), King home.
Wright, Andrew J. (97), 4619 North Ashland avenue.

CHICAGO HIGH SCHOOL COLORS.

Austin—Red and white.
Bowen, James H.—Purple and gold.
Calumet—Maroon and light blue.
Carl Schurz—Purple and gold.
Crane, Richard T.—Crimson and royal blue.
Curtis, George W.—Red and green.

Englewood—Purple and white.
Farragut—Red and white.
Hyde Park—Blue and white.
Jefferson—Purple and gold.
Lake—Old blue and gold.
Lake View—Red and white.
Lane Technical—Myrtle green and old gold.

Marshall—Maroon and old gold.
McKinley—Orange and black.
Medill—Maroon and white.
Phillips, Wendell—Red and black.
South Chicago—Purple and gold.
Tuley—Old gold and blue.
Waller, Robert A.—Royal blue and yellow.

CHARITY AND OTHER SERVICES OF COOK COUNTY.

Extracts from President A. A. McCormick's annual report made to the board of commissioners Dec. 1, 1913:

The government of Cook county was last year required by law to house, feed and supply medical aid and treatment to about 34,000 sick people, 3,000 irresponsible, incurable or infirm paupers, and 1,000 tuberculous patients; to give food, clothing and coal to about 200,000 persons; to care for 10,587 delinquent and dependent children; to investigate 5,274 cases of death from violence or sudden and unknown causes and bury at public expense 978 friendless and pauper dead. It investigated crimes of all kinds committed within the boundaries of the county; maintained the Circuit court with 10,000 suits and 25,000 litigants; the Superior court with 5,770 cases and 12,000 litigants; the Criminal court with 2,500 prosecutions; the Probate court with 4,412 cases, and the County court with 5,925 cases. It compelled about 5,500 defendants to support their wives, children and near relations; gathered in and cared for 2,334 insane patients, of whom 569 were discharged, 89 died, and 1,766 were committed to state institutions, and gave $165,000 in pensions to 350 indigent mothers for the support of 1,128 children. It levied, assessed, collected and allotted to the state, county and municipal governments an annual revenue of $47,000,000; served legal processes and enforced court orders upon 191,460 persons; maintained public order in riot cases; recorded all deeds affecting the title of real estate; held national, state, county and municipal elections and primaries; issued marriage licenses to 36,000 couples; issued saloon licenses outside Chicago; recorded documents affecting the title of personal property; housed, fed and cared for about 11,000 prisoners in the county jail, of whom 473 were charged with murder or assault with intent to kill, 758 with burglary, 1,448 with larceny, 539 with robbery, 2,386 with violation of the city code, 202 with assault and 282 with confidence games. About 10,000 of these prisoners required medical attention. It housed, fed and cared for 4,000 boys and girls in the juvenile detention home and 2,400 insane in the detention hospital; maintained the courthouse, a ten-story office building occupying one-half of a city block; repaired and constructed roads and bridges throughout the county and supervised the common school education of 40,000 children outside Chicago and provided 1,000 teachers.

To perform these duties, it takes all of the time of about 3,000 employes and part of the time of about 10,000 other persons. It costs in money to maintain the county government approximately what it costs to maintain the government of the state of Illinois. The county's bill for groceries alone in the first six months of 1912 was $65,000; and in the first six months of 1913 it was $50,000.

In November, 1910, the voters of Cook county approved a bond issue of $3,000,000 for the construction of a new county hospital, which was sadly needed. After two years, not a brick of the superstructure had been laid. * * * The board has made every effort to complete the building for use this winter but for lack of funds has been unable to do so. Before the hospital can be used it will be necessary for the taxpayers of Cook county to vote another bond issue of $1,000,000 to $2,000,000 to finish and equip it for use.

NEW PSYCHOPATHIC HOSPITAL.

The new psychopathic hospital, now in course of construction, is considered one of the best designed, and, when completed, will be the best equipped psychopathic hospital in the country. It provides for 220 beds, divided among private chambers for disturbed patients, small rooms containing two or three beds for restless sufferers and wards containing a maximum of twenty-four beds. The building will have three entrances—the court, witness and administration rooms being independent of the rest of the building. Patients will be housed on the second, third and fourth floors of the wings. The fifth floor, which covers only the main part of the building, will be provided with hydriatic rooms, continuously flowing bath rooms and other equipment for the treatment of patients suffering from mental abnormalities. A kitchen, with dumb waiters direct to the dining room and equipped with the most modern facilities, will occupy an independent wing of the building.

One of the inner courts provides space for outdoor exercise, in addition to which is a large screened balcony on each floor and a roof garden over the kitchen wing. Bars on windows have been entirely eliminated by the use of steel window frames, dividing the lights of glass into small sections, the frames having sufficient strength to prevent the escape of the patients. The receiving department has rooms for bathing patients, proper examinations, and special rooms for observation before assigning patients to wards or private rooms in which their conditions indicate they should be kept. The building provides facilities that permit patients to be classified and assigned to rooms or wards according to their condition, so that patients suffering from nervous breakdown are not confined with others who are violently insane.

CONDITIONS AT OAK FOREST.

The daily average of the population has been about 2,100 inmates in the infirmary and about 250 tuberculosis patients in the hospital. Besides the service to these two groups about 5,000 children were given a week's outing at the summer camp. Of the infirmary population, nearly 500 are irresponsible, idiots, imbeciles and feeble minded. There are eighty-three children, of whom a dozen are normal and the rest under par mentally. Of the tuberculosis patients, 100 are bed patients.

An investigation carried on by County Agent Meyer disclosed the fact that a number of inmates were not entitled to the care of the institution. Inmates were found who had been in the institution for years—one for twenty years—who had relatives legally responsible for their care. A number were forced to leave the institution because they were able to earn their own living or had relatives capable of taking care of them. The legal responsibility of these relatives was brought home to them and they were compelled to pay for the care of their indigent kin.

Desertion of wives and children by husbands and fathers is a constantly growing evil. More cases have been prosecuted in the County court than heretofore, but the desertions continue to increase. The county agent has on his books the names of nearly 1,800 families with 6,683 children made dependent by absconding husbands. These dependents are costing Cook county $100,000 a year. It is estimated that 25 per cent of the deserters are in Chicago and within the jurisdiction of the county courts. The others are outside the jurisdiction of the local courts, but under the law may be brought back when located elsewhere and prosecuted. A number have been returned to their families and are now supporting them.

FINANCES OF THE COUNTY.

The financial situation of Cook county, in my judgment, cannot be bettered or solved without a constitutional convention or some relief by which the situation can be more readily changed than at present. It is hard to conceive a situation that is more complicated and more archaic than that which confronts the board of county commissioners. The legislature at almost every session will pass laws imposing additional burdens upon the county but does not provide any means by which the income can be increased to meet them. Two years ago the amount expended by the county for industrial schools was $72,000 a year. The legislature changed the law in such a way that any industrial school by application to the state board of charities could secure a charter and all children in their care be chargeable to the county at $10 for each boy and $15 for each girl. The consequence is this year the county has been compelled to pay $280,000, an increase over expenditures under the old law of $208,000.

The mothers' pension law passed by the legislature placed an additional expenditure of approximately $150,000 a year upon the county. The juror's pay was increased from $2 to $3, with the result that the expense to the county is increased to $160,000, making a total expenditure of $360,000 this year.

CHICAGO STREET GUIDE.
GUIDE TO NUMBERS.

Numbers on the north and south streets where they are intersected by the principal east and west streets and numbers on the east and west streets where they are intersected by the principal north and south streets are given herewith. Numbered streets are omitted, as their location is indicated by their names.

NORTH FROM MADISON.		
1	Madison.	
100	Washington.	
150	Randolph.	
200	Lake.	
300	S. Water.	
400	Kinzie.	
430	Michigan.	
590	Illinois.	
530	Grand-av.	
600	Ohio.	
630	Ontario.	
660	Erie.	
700	Huron.	
720	Superior.	
800	Chicago-av.	
848	Chestnut.	
867	Brenan-st.	
920	Locust.	
940	Walton-pl.	
1000	Oak.	
1100	Maple.	
1149	Elm.	
1200	Division.	
1300	Goethe.	
1400	Schiller.	
1500	Burton-pl.	
1536	Germania-pl.	
1600	North-av.	
1700	Eugenie.	
1800	Menomonee.	
1900	Wisconsin.	
2000	Center.	
2100	Garfield-av.	
2200	Webster-av.	
2300	Belden-av.	
2400	Fullerton-pky.	
2460	Arlington-pl.	
2473	Roslyn-pl.	
2501	St. James-pl.	
2530	Deming-pl.	
2600	Wrightwood-av.	
2761	Sherman-pl.	
2800	Diversey-pky.	
2901	York-pl.	
2932	Oakdale-av.	
3000	Wellington-av.	
3100	Barry-av.	
3200	Belmont-av.	
3300	School.	
3400	Roscoe.	
3500	Cornelia.	
3538	Eddy.	
3600	Addison.	
3700	Waveland.	
3800	Grace.	
3900	Byron.	
4000	Irving Park-bd.	

4100	Belle Plaine-av.
4200	Berteau-av.
4300	Cullom-av.
4400	Montrose-av.
4500	Sunnyside-av.
4600	Wilson-av.
4700	Leland-av.
4800	Lawrence-av.
4900	Ainslie.
5000	Argyle.
5100	Carmen-av.
5200	Foster-av.
5300	Berwyn-av.
5400	Balmoral-av.
5500	Catalpa-av.
5600	Bryn Mawr-av.
5700	Hollywood-av.
5730	Edgewater-av.
5800	Victoria.
5900	Thorndale-av.
5956	Ridge-av.
6000	Peterson-av.
6100	Norwood-av.
6200	Granville-av.
6300	Rosemont-av.
6400	Devon-av.
6700	North Shore-av.
6800	Pratt-av.
6900	Farwell-av.
6944	Morse-av.
7000	Lunt-av.
7100	Estes-av.
7200	Kenilworth-av.
7390	Chase-av.
7400	Juniata-st.
7500	Birchwood-av.
7548	Howard.
7548	City limits.

SOUTH FROM MADISON.	
1	Madison.
100	Monroe.
200	Adams.
232	Quincy.
300	Jackson-bd.
400	Van Buren.
500	Congress.
600	Harrison.
700	East 7th-st.
800	Polk.
900	East 9th-st.
1000	Taylor.
1100	East 11th-st.

EAST FROM STATE.	
(North of river.)	
1	State.
40	Cass.
100	Rush.

112	Tower-ct.
140	Lincoln Park-bd.
201	St. Clair.
300	Fairbanks-ct.
326	*Lake Shore drive
	*At Chicago-av.

EAST FROM STATE.	
(South of river.)	
1	State.
46	Wabash.
100	Michigan-av.
200	Indiana-av.
300	Prairie-av.
347	Calumet-av.
400	South Park-av.
435	Vernon-av.
500	Vincennes-av.
533	Rhodes-av.
600	St. Lawrence-av.
634	Champlain-av.
700	Langley-av.
734	Evans-av.
834	Maryland-av.
900	Drexel-av.
934	Ingleside-av.
1000	Ellis-av.
1100	Greenwood-av.
1152	Woodlawn-av.
1300	Kimbark-av.
1334	Kenwood-av.
1400	Dorchester-av.
1434	Dante-av.
1500	Blackstone-av.
1690	Stony Island-av.
1631	Cornell-av.
1700	East End-av.
1735	Ridgeland-av.
1800	Cregier-av.
1900	Baldwin-av.
1934	Euclid-av.
2000	Jeffery-av.
2100	Cahokia-av.
2200	Paxton-av.
2300	Crandon-av.
2400	Yates-av.
2500	Essex-av.
2600	Colfax-av.
2700	Marquette-av.
2800	Burnham-av.
2900	Escanaba-av.
3000	Commercial-av.
3100	Baltimore-av.
3200	Brandon-av.
3300	Buffalo-av.
3400	Green Bay-av.

WEST FROM STATE.	
1	State.
50	Dearborn-st.
100	Clark.
150	LaSalle.
200	5th-av.
200	*Wells.
300	Franklin.
300	*Franklin.

340	*Orleans.
350	Market.
400	*Sedgwick.
412	The river.
434	*Townsend.
460	*Milton-av.
500	Canal.
530	*Larrabee.
540	Clinton.
600	Jefferson.
640	Desplaines.
700	Union.
700	*Orchard.
800	Halsted.
829	Green.
900	Peoria.
932	Sangamon.
1000	Morgan.
1000	*Sheffield-av.
1032	Carpenter.
1034	*Osgood.
1100	Curtis.
1100	*Seminary-av.
1111	Aberdeen.
1132	May.
1134	*Clifton-av.
1164	Ann.
1200	Racine-av.
1248	Elizabeth.
1300	Throop.
1400	*Southport-av.
1401	Loomis.
1408	Sheldon.
1448	Bishop-st.
1501	Laflin.
1600	Ashland-bd.
1700	Paulina.
1734	Hermitage-av.
1800	Wood.
1835	Honore.
1900	Lincoln.
1935	Winchester-av.
2000	Robey.
2035	Seeley-av.
2100	Hoyne-av.
2200	Leavitt.
2300	Oakley-bd.
2400	Western-av.
2500	Campbell-av.
2600	Rockwell.
2700	Washtenaw-av.
2800	California-av.
2900	Francisco-av.
3000	Sacramento-av.
3100	Albany-av.
3200	Kedzie-av.
3300	Spaulding-av.
3356	Homan-av.
3501	St. Louis-av.
3553	Central Park-av.
3800	Hamlin-av.
3900	Springfield-av.
4000	Crawford-av.

*North side only.

CHANGES IN PARCEL POST RATES.

The following changes in parcel post rates and weights, going into effect Jan. 1, 1914, were announced Dec. 6, 1913:

Increasing weight limits of parcels in the first and second zone from 20 to 50 pounds.

Increasing maximum weight of parcels to all zones beyond the second from 11 to 20 pounds.

Reducing the rates for the third zone from 7 cents for the first pound and 5 cents for each additional pound to 6 cents for the first pound and 2 cents for each additional pound.

Reducing the rates for the fourth zone from 8 cents for the first pound and 6 cents for each additional pound to 7 cents for the first pound and 4 cents for each additional pound.

Reducing the rates for the fifth zone from 9 cents for the first pound and 7 cents for each additional pound to 8 cents for the first pound and 6 cents for each additional pound.

Reducing the rates for the sixth zone from 10 cents for the first pound and 9 cents for each additional pound to 9 cents for the first pound and 8 cents for each additional pound.

The rate of postage on parcels containing books weighing eight ounces or less shall be 1 cent for each two ounces or fractional part thereof, and on those weighing in excess of eight ounces, the zone parcel post rates shall apply. This is to be effective March 16, 1914.

ILLINOIS INDUSTRIAL BOARD.
Appointed by the governor. Salary of members, $4,000.
H. S. Tanner (chairman), Paris. | Peter Angsten, Chicago.

SURFACE LINE. THROUGH ROUTES IN CHICAGO.

In operation Dec. 1, 1913.

Route No. 1—Beginning at 56th street and Lake Park avenue, north on Lake Park avenue to 55th street, west on 55th street to Cottage Grove avenue, north on Cottage Grove avenue to Indiana avenue, north to 18th street, west to Wabash avenue, north to Lake, west to State, north to Division, west to Clark, north to Broadway, north to Devon, west to Clark—returning the same route. Cars 8 minutes apart.

Route No. 2—Beginning at 80th street and Vincennes avenue loop; north on Vincennes avenue to Wentworth, north to 22d, east to Clark, north to Division, west to Clybourn, north to Belmont—returning by the same route. Cars 8 minutes apart.

Route No. 3—Beginning at 51st street and South Park avenue, west on 51st street to Indiana avenue, north to Lake street, west to State, north to Kinzie, west to Clark, north to Center street, west to Lincoln avenue, northwest to Foster avenue—returning same route. Cars 8 minutes apart.

Route No. 4—Beginning at 119th and Morgan streets loop, east on 120th to Halsted, north to 119th, east to Michigan avenue, north to 95th, east to Cottage Grove, north to 22d and Indiana, north to 18th, west to Wabash avenue, north to Washington, east to Garland court, north to Randolph street, west to Wabash avenue—returning same route. Cars every 12 minutes.

Route No. 5—Beginning at 92d and South Chicago avenue loop, north on Baltimore avenue to 91st, west to South Chicago avenue, northwest to Cottage Grove, north to 22d and Indiana avenue, north to 18th, west to Wabash avenue, north to Washington street, east to Garland court, north to Randolph street, west to Wabash avenue—returning same route. Cars every 6 minutes.

Route No. 6—Beginning at 63d and State streets, north on State to Lake, west to Milwaukee avenue, northwest to C. & N. W. R. R.'s right of way north of Lawrence avenue—returning by the same route. Cars 12 minutes apart.

Route No. 7—Beginning at State street and 63d street, north on State street to Madison, west to North Maynard avenue—returning by the same route. Cars 12 minutes apart.

Route No. 8—Beginning at Halsted street and 79th street, north on Halsted to Grace—returning by the same route. Cars 5-8 minutes apart.

Route No. 9—Beginning at 71st street and Ashland avenue, north on Ashland to 12th, west to Paulina, north to Lake, east to Ashland, north to Courtland street, east to Southport, north to Clark

—returning by the same route. Cars 3-5 minutes apart.

Route No. 10—Beginning at 71st street and Western avenue, north on Western avenue to Lincoln avenue—returning by the same route. Cars 5-10 minutes apart.

Route No. 11—Beginning at South Kenton and Ogden avenues, northeast on Ogden to Madison street, east to Clark, north to Diversey boulevard loop—returning by the same route. Cars 27 minutes apart.

Route No. 12—Beginning at 26th street and South Kenton avenue, east on 26th to Blue Island avenue, northeast to the intersection of Halsted street and Blue Island avenue, east on Harrison street to Clinton, north to Adams, east to 5th avenue, north on 5th avenue and Wells street to Clark street, north to Diversey boulevard—returning by the same route. Cars 32 minutes apart.

Route No. 13—Beginning at 63d and Halsted, north on Halsted to North Clark—returning by the same route. Cars 5-8 minutes apart.

Route No. 14—Beginning at North Cicero avenue and 12th street, east on 12th to 5th avenue, north on 5th avenue and Wells street to Clark; north to Diversey—returning by the same route. Cars 20 minutes apart.

Route No. 17—Beginning at 63d street and Kedzie avenue, north on Kedzie to Chicago, east to California, north to Elston avenue, northwest to Kedzie avenue, north to Lawrence avenue—returning by the same route. Cars 6-12 minutes apart.

Route No. 18—Beginning at Broadway and Grace street, south on Halsted to 26th—returning by the same route. Cars 1 minute apart (rush only).

Route No. 20—Beginning at Madison street and Maynard avenue, east on Madison to and around the State street loop—returning by the same route. Cars 2-4 minutes apart.

Route No. 22—Beginning at 80th street and Vincennes avenue loop, north on Vincennes avenue to Wentworth avenue, north to 22d, east to Clark, north to Howard avenue—returning by same route. Cars 8 minutes apart.

Route No. 23—Beginning at Morgan and 39th streets, north on Morgan to private right of way at 51st street, thence along private right of way to Throop street, north on Throop to 21st, east to South Racine avenue, north to Adams street, east to Sangamon, north to Austin avenue, west to North Racine, north to Erie street, west to Ashland avenue—returning by the same route. Cars 15 minutes apart.

THE DANBURY HATTERS' CASE.

In the United States District court in Hartford, Conn., Oct. 11, 1912, a jury returned a verdict for $80,000 and costs against the United Hatters of North America in the suit brought by D. E. Loewe & Co., hat manufacturers in Danbury, Conn., charging the defendants with conducting a boycott against hats made by the firm. Under the Sherman antitrust law the damages are trebled, making the award in this instance equivalent to $240,000.

The suit was originally brought in the Circuit court in 1903, when Loewe & Co. filed a bill alleging that the labor organization had undertaken to unionize the company's hat factory in Danbury, and, failing to do so, had gone on a strike. This act was followed by the declaration of a boycott against the firm's hats wherever they were found, and as it controlled an extensive trade throughout many states the boycott, in the language of the bill, constituted a combination to limit and restrain

interstate commerce. On a demurrer by the hatters' union, the Circuit court decided that the Sherman law was inapplicable and dismissed the case. The Court of Appeals, however, certified the suit to the United States Supreme court, and that tribunal, Feb. 3, 1908, reversed the decision of the Circuit court, deciding, without a dissenting voice, that boycotting, where it affected interstate commerce, was in violation of the Sherman antitrust act.

The case then went back to the Circuit court, and after a trial lasting eleven weeks resulted Feb. 4, 1910, in a verdict for $74,000 damages for the plaintiff. An appeal was taken and the case was sent to the United States District court with the result stated above. The plaintiffs were backed by the Antiboycott society and the defendants by the American Federation of Labor.

COLLEGE FRATERNITY HOUSES IN CHICAGO.

Alpha Delta Phi—975 East 60th street.
Alpha Tau Omega—923 East 60th street.
Beta Theta Pi—5555 Woodlawn avenue.
Chi Psi—5344 Ellis avenue
Delta Kappa Epsilon—5754 Woodlawn avenue.
Delta Sigma Phi—5604 Maryland avenue.
Delta Tau Delta—5607 University avenue.
Delta Upsilon—5400 Ellis avenue.
Gamma Alpha—5731 Kenwood avenue.

Kappa Sigma—6032 Kimbark avenue.
Phi Delta Theta—6111 Woodlawn avenue.
Phi Gamma Delta—935 East 60th street.
Phi Kappa Psi—5635 University avenue.
Phi Kappa Sigma—5824 Woodlawn avenue.
Psi Upsilon—5845 Dorchester avenue.
Sigma Alpha Epsilon—1364 East 56th street.
Sigma Chi—5557 Blackstone avenue.
Sigma Nu—5725 Kenwood avenue.

CENTENNIAL OF ADMISSION OF ILLINOIS.

The following resolution was adopted by the Illinois state senate Feb. 12 and concurred in by the house Feb. 18, 1913:

"Whereas, Illinois was admitted to the union of states Dec. 3, 1818, the centennial anniversary thereof being rapidly approaching, and it being meet and fit that the state which has given of its sons so liberally to the progress of the nation and the world during the period of its statehood should fittingly observe its hundredth anniversary by a celebration which shall do honor to itself and to the nation;

"Resolved, by the senate, the house of representatives concurring, That a commission, consisting of five members of the senate and five members of the house of representatives of the forty-eighth general assembly shall be appointed to have charge of the preliminary arrangements of such celebration to be held in Springfield, the state capital, on such centennial date, and to determine, as may be, the character and necessities of such celebration, and to report the result of its findings to the forty-ninth general assembly; such joint commission to hold its meetings in the city of Springfield at such time or times as may be necessary to successfully inaugurate such movement."

Subsequently by another joint resolution E. J. James, E. B. Greene and J. W. Garner of the University of Illinois and Mrs. Jessie Palmer Webber and Dr. Otto L. Schmidt of the Illinois Historical society were appointed as additional members of the committee. The sum of $10,000 was appropriated to defray the expenses of the commission.

At a meeting held in Springfield July 22 Senator Campbell S. Hearn was elected chairman and Mrs. Jessie Palmer Webber secretary. The following proposals were adopted:

1. Promotion of local celebrations throughout the state.

2. Holding of a state celebration at the capital, consisting of an exposition and a pageant illustrative of the social, economic and educational development of the state.

3. Preparation of a series of publications putting into permanent form the record of the state's progress in all lines of development.

4. Erection of a permanent memorial building for the use of the historical and educational departments of the state, where shall be preserved the historical relics of the state; containing a memorial hall where shall be placed statues of Illinois' illustrious men.

5. Erecting and unveiling of bronze statues of Lincoln and Douglas on the capitol-grounds as provided for in bills enacted at the session of the legislature in 1913.

A comprehensive and elaborate plan was presented to the state commission by President Edmund J. James of the University of Illinois. His suggestion, similar to that of the commission's, was to have chief celebrations in Springfield, at the University of Illinois, which completes its fiftieth year of organization in 1918, and in Chicago. Lesser celebrations are suggested for the county seats.

WIND-BAROMETER TABLE FOR THE GREAT LAKES.

[Prepared by United States weather bureau.]

Height of barometer (lake level).	Direction of wind.	Character of weather and wind indicated.
29.40 to 29.60, and steady	West	Fair, slight changes in temperature, gentle to fresh winds.
29.40 to 29.60, rising	West	Fair, cooler, fresh west to northwest winds.
29.40 to 29.60, falling	South	Warmer, increasing southerly winds.
29.60, or above, falling rapidly	East to south	Warmer, rain or snow within 36 hours, increasing east to southeast winds.
29.60, or above, rising rapidly	West to north	Cool and clear, quickly followed by warmer, variable winds.
29.60, or above, steady	Variable	No immediate change, but winds will go to south inside of 36 hours.
29.40, or below, falling slowly	South to east	Rain or snow, increasing easterly winds.
29.40, or below, falling rapidly	South to east	Rain or snow, high easterly winds, followed within 48 hours by clearing, cooler, west to northwest winds.
29.40, or below, rising slowly	South to west	Clearing, colder, fresh to brisk west to northwest winds.
29.20, or below, falling rapidly	South to east	Severe storm of wind and rain, and wind shifting to northwest within 36 hours.
29.20, or below, falling rapidly	East to north	Severe northeaster, with heavy rain or snow, and winds backing to northwest.
29.20, or below, rising rapidly	Going to west	Clearing and cooler, probably cold wave in winter.

THE BOY SCOUT MOVEMENT.

The boy scout movement was started in England by Lieut.-Gen. Sir Robert S. S. Baden-Powell in 1908. Boys were enrolled in a uniform corps, properly officered, for the purpose of training them in patriotism, chivalry, self-reliance, woodcraft, tracking, healthful exercises and good citizenship. The plan was successful from the start and thousands of boys in all parts of the British empire belong to the organization. Similar corps have been started in the United States, Germany, Argentina, Chile, Smyrna, China, Japan and other countries. The movement is nonmilitary. The president of the National Council of Boy Scouts of America is Colin Livingstone of Washington, D. C., and the treasurer is George D. Pratt of Brooklyn, N. Y.

ELECTRIC RAILROADS IN THE UNITED STATES.

[Compiled by the Electric Railroad Journal from the McGraw Electric Railway Manual for 1911.]

Year.	Companies.	Mileage.	Cars.	Capital stock.*	Funded debt.	Capitalization.†
1910	1,279	40,083	89,601	$2,386,011,921	$2,302,094,296	$4,682,102,217
1909	1,253	40,490	91,153	2,427,935,397	2,224,500,236	4,652,735,633
1908	1,252	40,247	89,216	2,444,892,057	2,112,244,086	4,557,136,143
1907	1,238	38,812	86,204	2,251,425,882	1,872,408,516	4,123,834,598

*Outstanding. †Total outstanding.

DEATH OF WILLIAM DEERING.

William Deering, widely known throughout the United States as a manufacturer of harvesting machinery and other agricultural implements, died at his country home near Miami, Fla., Dec. 9, 1913, after an illness of several months from the effects of a paralytic stroke. He was born in South Paris, Me., April 25, 1826. He established his manufacturing business in Chicago in 1870 and made a great success of it. Mr. Deering made many generous gifts to charitable and educational institutions.

LAKES-TO-GULF DEEP-WATERWAY PROJECT.

Oct. 16, 1907, the legislature of Illinois passed a joint resolution providing for the submission to the electors of the state of an amendment to the constitution permitting the general assembly to provide for the construction of a deep waterway from Lockport to Utica and to authorize the issue of bonds to the amount of $20,000,000 for this purpose. At the election of Nov. 3, 1908, the people approved the proposed amendment by a vote of 692,523 for to 195,177 against. At the regular session of the legislature in 1909 the waterway project was considered, but no agreement could be reached as to the question of going ahead immediately with the work or waiting for federal aid and no bill was passed. The matter was included in the list of subjects to be considered at the extra session of the legislature in the winter and spring of 1909-1910, but no action was taken.

At the regular session in 1911 a waterway bill was passed by the senate, but in the house Speaker Charles Adkins prevented any action being taken. Gov. Deneen called an extra session of the legislature, which began June 14, but adjourned without taking final action.

WATERWAY ASSOCIATION.

The Lakes-to-Gulf Deep-Waterway association is an organization formed to aid in every way possible the realization of the deep-waterway project. It is made up chiefly of men representing the states most directly interested in the plan and annual meetings are held, the seventh gathering taking place in Little Rock, Ark., in September, 1912. The chief officers are:

President—William K. Kavanaugh, St. Louis, Mo.
Secretary—Thomas H. Lovelace, 914 New Bank of Commerce building, St. Louis, Mo.
Treasurer—Edwin S. Monroe, Joliet, Ill.

THE HENNEPIN CANAL.

Preliminary surveys begun—1871.
Excavation begun—1892.
Work completed—1907.
Canal formally opened—Oct. 24, 1907.
Length of main channel—75 miles.
Length of feeder—29.3 miles.
Total length—104 miles.
Depth—7 feet.
Width at bottom—52 feet.
Width at water line—80 feet.
Locks on main canal—32.
Locks on feeder—1.
Total cost—$7,500,000.

The Hennepin, or, more comprehensively, the Illinois and Mississippi canal, extends from the Illinois river near Hennepin to the Mississippi three miles below Rock Island. The navigable feeder extends from Rock river at Sterling and Rock Falls to the main line near Sheffield and is of the same size and just as navigable as the main line. Water is forced into it by a dam a quarter of a mile long at Sterling.

SAULT STE. MARIE CANAL TRAFFIC (1912).

Summary of traffic through both American and Canadian canals.

Freight carried, tons	72,472,676
Total tons net register	56,736,807
Total mile-tons	60,242,833,014
Valuation placed on freight carried	$791,357,837
Amount paid for freight carried	$40,578,225
Registered vessels using canals	853
Valuation registered vessels	$138,546,300
Passengers transported	66,877
Cost per ton freight transportation	$0.56
Freight carried by—	
Registered vessels, tons	72,300,591
Unregistered vessels, tons	172,085
American vessels, per cent	94
Canadian vessels, per cent	6
Passengers carried by—	
American vessels, per cent	32
Canadian vessels, per cent	68
Average number of vessels passing per day—	
Through Poe lock	39
Weitzel lock	27
Canadian lock	33
Poe, Weitzel and Canadian locks	99

SUMMARY BY YEARS.

		Freight.	
Year.	Tons.	Value.	Charges.
1887	5,494,649	$79,031,757	$10,075,153
1888	6,411,423	82,156,019	7,883,677
1889	7,516,022	82,732,527	8,634,246
1890	9,041,213	102,214,948	9,472,214
1891	8,888,759	128,178,208	9,849,022
1892	11,214,333	135,117,267	12,072,850
1893	10,796,572	145,436,957	9,957,483
1894	13,195,860	143,114,502	10,798,319
1895	15,062,580	159,675,129	14,238,758
1896	16,239,061	195,146,842	13,511,615
1897	18,982,755	218,235,927	13,220,099
1898	21,234,664	233,069,740	14,125,896
1899	25,255,810	281,364,750	23,959,707
1900	28,543,072	267,041,959	24,953,314
1901	28,403,065	289,906,865	23,217,974
1902	35,961,146	358,396,300	26,566,189
1903	34,674,437	349,405,014	26,727,735
1904	31,546,106	334,502,686	31,552,894
1905	44,270,680	416,965,484	31,420,585
1906	51,751,080	537,463,454	36,686,889
1907	58,217,214	569,830,188	38,457,245
1908	41,390,557	470,141,318	23,903,244
1909	57,895,149	626,104,173	36,291,948
1910	62,363,218	654,010,844	38,710,904
1911	53,477,216	595,019,844	29,492,196
1912	72,472,676	791,357,837	40,578,225

STATISTICS OF UNEMPLOYMENT.

Four censuses of the United States have considered the question of unemployment, namely, those of 1880, 1890, 1900 and 1910. The first was never made up for lack of funds; and the last one is not yet at hand, for the same reason. According to the census of 1890, out of 23,318,730 persons gainfully occupied 3,523,730, or 15 per cent, had reported being unemployed during some time of the year. The aim of the census of 1900 was "to find out the number of months or parts of months during which persons ordinarily engaged in gainful labor were not employed at all." That census shows that out of 29,073,233 persons ordinarily employed 6,468,964, or 22.3 per cent, were reported unemployed at some period during the preceding year. The figures are as follows:

		Per cent	
		Per cent	total work-
Unemployed.	Cases.	unemployed.	ing force.
1 to 3 months	3,177,753	49.1	10.0
4 to 6 months	2,554,923	39.5	8.8
7 to 12 months	736,286	11.4	2.5

Generally speaking, one out of five of the workers was unemployed during the census year from one to twelve months. Frank B. Sargent, special agent of the bureau of labor, in his report on unemployment and employment offices, Oct. 1, 1912, shows from the census compiled by the manufacturers that in one year unemployment varied from 67,000 persons in October to 415,000 in January; and that in both New York and Massachusetts the unemployed organized workers are two and three times as numerous at the end of March as at the end of September each year. The quarterly reports of the New York bureau of labor, which deal with the working conditions in the New York trade unions, show that between the end of September and the end of March, from 1899 to 1908, unemployment fluctuated between 4.7 per cent and 22 per cent. In March, 1908, it reached its maximum of 35.7 per cent.

NATIONAL BUSINESS LEAGUE OF AMERICA

President—Philetus W. Gates, Chicago.
Vice-President—Benjamin J. Rosenthal, Chicago.
Treasurer—George W. Dixon, Chicago.
General Secretary—Austin A. Burnham, Chicago.
General Counsel—E. Allen Frost, Chicago.
Headquarters—Chicago Stock Exchange building.

The league was organized Jan. 26, 1897, and was incorporated June 15, 1907. It is an alliance of leading diversified business interests of the United States for the promotion of federal legislation for the advancement of American commerce and industry.

INCREASE IN PRICE OF EGGS SINCE 1907.

Highest and lowest quotations on fresh eggs on Nov. 15 of each year from 1907 to 1913, inclusive, as shown by reports furnished to the bureau of labor statistics by retail merchants in thirty-two of the principal industrial cities of the United States:

	Nov. 15, 1907		Nov. 15, 1908		Nov. 15, 1909		Nov. 15, 1910		Nov. 15, 1911		Nov. 15, 1912		Nov. 15, 1913	
	High.	Low.	High.	Low.	High.	Low.	High.	Low.	High.	Low.	High.	Low.	High.	Low.
Atlanta	30	25	35	30	35	29	40	30	40	35	40	35	45	40
Baltimore	36	34	36	35	36	30	44	35	40	35	45	35	50	42
Boston	50	28	55	32	48	45	56	32	60	40	65	48	67	55
Buffalo	34	32	36	32	36	33	45	32	50	35	55	32	60	42
Chicago	35	29	35	28	40	27	38	30	40	32	40	30	46	35
Cincinnati	28	27	36	30	36	35	38	32	28	35	40	35	48	40
Cleveland	38	34	45	30	45	30	48	30	50	35	48	40	55	45
Dallas	30	30	35	35	40	35	40	35	35	30	40	30	45	35
Denver	30	30	40	30	35	30	35	30	45	35	40	35	50	40
Detroit	32	31	22	30	36	32	38	32	40	32	38	34	45	38
Indianapolis	34	50	38	30	35	28	38	30	40	35	42	36	45	42
Jacksonville, Fla.	35	30	35	30	35	25	40	30	40	35	45	38	50	40
Kansas City	28	27½	35	35	32	30	38	20	40	30	35	30	42	30
Los Angeles	45	35	50	40	45	35	60	40	65	50	60	45	65	55
Louisville	25	25	30	30	30	30	35	28	40	30	35	27½	45	37½
Memphis	30	25	35	34	35	28	35	26	35	26	35	32	50	35
Milwaukee	..	..	36	36	36	30	38	35	..	..	50	30	45	45
Minneapolis	30	25	40	30	40	30	38	35	36	33	40	34	45	38
New Haven	50	45	50	48	50	45	60	45	60	50	65	55	65	58
New Orleans	30	25	35	25	35	30	35	30	35	30	45	36	55	38
New York	46	33	53	33	50	32	53	40	60	37	60	41	75	49
Omaha	30	28	35	25	35	24	35	24	40	28	35	33	45	40
Philadelphia	42	28	42	34	40	32	45	35	50	36	60	35	60	40
Pittsburgh	35	25	35	30	36	30	40	30	40	33	45	34	50	42
Providence	55	35	55	42	53	45	60	45	60	55	65	58	65	60
Richmond	30	28	35	32	34	32	35	30	40	30	49	35	55	40
St. Louis	38	22	38	28	38	30	40	32	40	28	35	30	42½	35
Salt Lake City	40	30	40	35	40	40	40	35	50	40	50	40	55	45
San Francisco	60	45	60	50	60	60	65	55	60	57½	60	50	65	60
Scranton	40	32	45	30	40	35	45	30	45	30	60	44	55	50
Seattle	55	50	65	50	70	50	70	45	60	50	65	55	60	60
Washington	36	36	36	30	40	35	40	35	40	45	35	48	35	60

FRAUDS IN ELECTION OF NOV. 5, 1912.

The vote for state's attorney at the election of Nov. 5, 1912, was recounted by the board of election commissioners in 1913 with the following result:

FOR MACLAY HOYNE, DEM.

	Official count.	Recount.
City	112,291	107,120
Country towns	10,172	9,924
Total	122,463	117,044

FOR LEWIS RINAKER, REP.

City	99,643	98,460
Country towns	13,560	13,395
Total	113,203	111,855

FOR WILLIAM A. CUNNEA, SOC.

City	102,686	106,527
Country towns	4,846	4,914
Total	107,532	111,441

FOR GEORGE I. HAIGHT, PROG.

City	78,021	76,418
Country towns	15,576	15,438
Total	93,597	91,856

The gross irregularities disclosed by the recount resulted in an investigation by a special grand jury. This body returned indictments July 18 against four men on the charge of tampering with the ballots. Seven men were indicted Aug. 7 on similar charges. Aug. 14 indictments were returned against seventeen judges and clerks of election in the 12th and 19th wards on charges of altering ballots in favor of Maclay Hoyne, Peter Bartzen and Anton J. Cermak at the November election in 1912. Sept. 19 ten more true bills were returned, the men charged with falsifying ballots and returns including a number of city and county employes.

RAILROAD TRACK ELEVATION.

The elevation of steam railroad tracks in Chicago is carried on in accordance with ordinances prepared by the department of track elevation and passed by the city council, and accepted by the railroad companies. The first track elevation ordinance was passed May 23, 1892.

The track elevation work done to Dec. 31, 1913, is approximately as follows:

Miles of roadbed elevated	141
Miles of additional roadbed required by ordinance to be elevated	48
Miles of track elevated	874
Miles of additional track required by ordinance to be elevated	272
Estimated cost of work completed to Dec. 31, 1913	$72,000,000.00

"FOUNTAIN OF TIME" ON MIDWAY.

Lorado Taft, the sculptor, was authorized Feb. 19, 1913, to place his "Fountain of Time" on a space 130 by 70 feet at the west end of the Midway, near Cottage Grove avenue. The fountain will be 110 feet long, 20 feet high and 10 feet wide. It is to be chiseled out of Georgia marble and will depict Father Time, a rugged, solitary figure, reviewing a throng of hurrying people of all ages and conditions in life. The cost of the fountain will be paid by the trustees of the Art institute out of the income from the $1,000,000 fund left by Benjamin F. Ferguson as a legacy to beautify Chicago.

GARNISHMENT LAW OF ILLINOIS.

Section 14 of the act of 1872 as amended in 1897 and 1901 declares: "The wages for services of a wage earner who is the head of a family and residing with the same, to the amount of fifteen ($15) dollars per week, shall be exempt from garnishment. All above the sum of fifteen ($15) dollars per week shall be liable to garnishment."

Employers are obliged to pay wages amounting to $15 or less, notwithstanding the service of a writ of garnishment, providing the person to whom wages are due makes affidavit that he is the head of a family and is living with the same.

LABOR UNIONS IN CHICAGO.

Organizations affiliated with the Chicago Federation of Labor, with names of secretaries. List corrected to Dec. 1, 1913.

Amalgamated Association Street Railway Employes No. 241—C. W. Mills, room 55, 138 North La-Salle street.
No. 260—Edward S. Bechtloff, 7032 Emerald avenue.
No. 273—William Rock, 8664 Vincennes road.
No. 308—W. S. McClenathan, room 1211 Unity building.

Asphalt and Pavers and Helpers No. 25—J. H. Wilson, 316 North Irving avenue.

Actors (White Rats)—Abner All, 28 North 5th avenue.

Asbestos Workers No. 17—James P. Fauls, 3719 Irving Park boulevard.

Baggage and Mail Handlers' Union No. 175—William Fenton, 649 East 42d street.

Bakers and Confectioners No. 2—Tony Weth, 540 Wells street.
No. 62—A. Anderholm, 1082 North Paulina street.

Bakers' Union No. 237—W. Krausz, 1253 South Kedzie avenue.

Barbers (Journeymen) No. 548—P. A. Holzer, 184 West Washington street, room 606.

Bartenders No. 401—George C. Barden, 6656 South Halsted street.
No. 456—George J. Schober, 232 North Clark street.
No. 507—E. G. Reynolds, 2117 Pensacola avenue.
No. 649—C. J. Boyle, 808 South California avenue.

Beer Bottlers No. 248—William Vorsatz, 215 Blue Island avenue.

Bill Posters and Billers—Roger B. Pearson, 37 West Garfield boulevard.

Bindery Women No. 30—431 South Dearborn street, room 422.

Blacksmiths and Helpers No. 14—William Zickgraff, 1134 North Franklin street.
No. 80—George Peacock, 4054 Carroll avenue.
No. 122—P. W. Moeller, 4462 Princeton avenue.
No. 325—M. D. Murphy, 1428 West 15th street.
No. 326—Edward King, 9321 Burnside avenue.

Boot and Shoe Workers No. 93—W. Eichelberger, 873 Wells street.
No. 94—Mary Anderson, 166 West Washington street.
No. 133—John Roach, 1924 School street.
No. 298—G. R. Sundvahl, 3831 Herndon street.

Book Binders No. 8—Otto F. Wasem, 59 East Van Buren street.

Bottlers' Protective Union No. 8434—Charles Schmidt, 1848 North Washtenaw avenue.

Brewers and Maltsters No. 18—Charles Gaude, 2135 Blue Island avenue.
No. 121—Frank Z. Leilvelt, 2135 Blue Island avenue.

Brewery Teamsters (Keg Beer) No. 342—George G. Hottinger, 184 West Washington street, room 504.

Brewery Teamsters (Bottle Beer) No. 344—184 West Washington street, room 503.

Brickmakers No. 2—A. H. Koselke, Lansing, Ill., postoffice box 1.
No. 3—Martin Hannauer, 615 Greenwood avenue, Blue Island, Ill.
No. 4—C. Gibson, 146 East 114th place.
No. 5—A. C. Kasten, 15 West 138th street, Riverdale, Ill.
No. 14—Edwin E. Clapper, Deerfield, Ill.
No. 34—William E. Klostir, Grant Park, Ill.
No. 49—W. Johnston, 7451 North California avenue, Rogers Park, Ill.
No. 188—Carl J. Bunge, Glen View, Ill.
No. 205—R. A. W. Manrke, Chicago Heights, Ill., R. R. No. 2, box 94.
No. 253—John J. Moriarity, 2337 North Maynard avenue.

Bridge Tenders' Association—William L. Devereux, 3617 West Congress street.

Broom and Whisk Makers No. 29—W. E. Harvey, 152 West Chestnut street.

Brushmakers No. 1—Henry C. Peters, 1058 North Lincoln street.

Butcher Workmen (Casing Workers) No. 158—John Mischka, 3894 Honore street.

Butcher Workmen (Cattle) No. 87—W. Patrick Sullivan, 5800 Bishop street.

Calumet Joint Labor Council—John H. DeYoung, 11311 Edbrooke avenue.

Carpenters and Joiners No. 1—James McKinnon, 1841 Nebraska avenue.

No. 10—D. J. Ryan, 4222 Prairie avenue.
No. 13—P. F. Hayes, 3147 Carlisle place.
No. 21—Joseph Julien, 1631 Hastings street.
No. 58—Henry Keuth, 1541 Addison street.
No. 62—W. Shogren, 6622 Sangamon street.
No. 70—Wilfred Huden, 2835 38th place.
No. 141—Mark D. Taylor, 6636 Sangamon street.
No. 181—K. G. Torkelson, 4508 Nevada street.
No. 242—George Wahl, 5142 Ada street.
No. 272—Frank C. Bauch, 12 East 16th street, Chicago Heights, Ill.
No. 419—B. Dornbrowski, 1837 North Hermitage avenue.
No. 504—Sam Sivin, 736 South Hoyne avenue.
No. 521—A. L. Yost, 501 South Oakley boulevard.
No. 643—T. M. Swanson, 2226 North Kimball avenue.
No. 1307—F. L. Deatherage, 1408 Elmwood avenue, Evanston, Ill.
No. 1693—C. M. Chase, 2466 Linden place.
No. 1784—H. Febling, 1928 Otto street.
No. 1786—James Smith, 1127 West 17th street.
No. 1922—Paul J. Berndgen, 652 West 59th street.

Carriage, Wagon and Automobile Workers No. 174—B. Sangman, 2434 Belle Plaine avenue.

Calkers' Union No. 1—Thomas H. Meagher, 2241 Taylor street.

Cement Finishers No. 2—Elgrin C. Hawkins, 3456 Narragansett avenue.

Cement and Construction No. 4—William Carroll, 363 West Madison street.

Cement Workers No. 29—Anton Jacobson, 4923 West Ohio street.

Chicago Trades Union Label League—Philip Jorneaux, 5634 Laflin street.

Cigar Makers No. 14—N. F. Lentz, 211 West Madison street.
No. 15—August Geissler, southeast corner Market and Randolph streets, second floor.

Cigar Packers No. 227—Nic. Medinger, 2931 North Halsted street.

Clerks (Retail)—William Coyle, 1250 Columbia avenue.

Cloth Hat and Cap Makers—J. Rosen, 1817 West Washington boulevard.

Cooks' Union No. 865—71 West Monroe street, 4th floor.

Coopers' Union No. 15—Henry Smith, 3733 Union avenue.
No. 39—J. Maurer, 6752 Bishop street.
No. 94—August Boering, 2932 Princeton avenue.
(Tank) No. 193—Julius G. Brown, 1118 Center street.

Cutting Die and Cutter Makers No. 305—Edward Bedore, 518 West 63d street.

Dredgeworkers' Protective Association No. 1—Martin Andrews, 406 North Clark street.

Egg Inspectors—P. F. Donlan, 76 West South Water street.

Electrical Workers No. 9—A. M. Parish, 1046 South Leamington avenue.
No. 49—William M. Hickey, 2225 Seminary avenue.
No. 134—500 South State street.
No. 282—William J. O'Leary, 5532 South Loomis street.
No. 713—A. Lang, 1433 South Marmora avenue.

Elevator Conductors and Starters' Union—175 West Washington street, room 305.

Elevator Constructors' Union No. 2—184 West Washington street, room 303.

Embroiderers' Union (United)—Kuno Hungartuer, 2630 Magnolia avenue.

Federal Labor Union of Burnside No. 10829—William Hyman, 1134 East 81st place.

Firemen's Association (City)—Masonic Temple building, room 1631.

Firemen (Stationary)—William Fisher, 156 West Washington street, third floor.

Franklin Union No. 4—L. S. Mills, 409 South Halsted street.

Freight Handlers No. 1—814 West Harrison street.

Gardeners and Florists No. 10615—Louis Heldtman, 3610 North Richmond street.

Garment Workers (Custom Cutters) No. 21—George H. Alexander, 175 West Washington street, 4th floor.
No. 23—Gus Olson, 4233 North St. Louis avenue.
No. 39—Sidney Hillman, 818 West Harrison street.
No. 61 (Clothing Cutters)—361 West Madison street.

No. 96—Harry Hultgren, 1725 Fletcher street.
No. 152—Morris Goldenstein, 1228 North Wood street.
No. 193—Sam Sax, 826 Lowell place.
No. 194 (Exam. and B.)—John Luepke, 319 South LaSalle street, room 660.
No. 197—A. Gradman, 3443 West 13th street.
No. 236 (S. O. C.)—Erik Johnson, 5322 North Clark street.
Gas and Electric Fixture Hangers No. 381—590 South State street.
Gas Fitters No. 250—Frank Culleeney, 3302 West Harrison street.
Glass Workers (Amalgamated) No. 4—Harry Stift, 4100 Cornelia street.
Glaziers' Union No. 27—M. Hahn, 544 West 20th street.
Glove Workers No. 4—Ernest Trogg, 1744 North Hermitage avenue.
No. 18—Mayme Butler, 1202 Webster avenue.
Hair Spinners No. 10399—John Hannemann, 3053 Lock street.
Hat Finishers' Association No. 9—James Loughbridge, 2827 West Fullerton avenue.
Hod Carriers and Building Laborers No. 4—J. Moresch, 814 West Harrison street.
Hoisting (Portable) Engineers—Oliver Stingley, 3361 South Park avenue.
Horse Nail Makers No. 7180—Kitty Murphy, 1623 West 20th street.
Horseshoers No. 4—Thomas Downs, 2930 Emerald avenue.
Iron Molders No 233—M. T. Mulchay, 201 South Halsted street.
(Bench) No. 239—Thomas Nelson, 1362 Milwaukee avenue.
(Core Makers) No. 448—Harry G. Ray, 2415 Fillmore street.
Ironworkers (Bridge and Structural) No. 1—814 West Harrison street.
Ironworkers (Bridge and Structural) No. 132—Roy Taylor, 2438 West Chicago avenue.
Janitors (Flat) No. 12361—C. R. Rowens, 5753 Grove avenue.
Laborers (Municipal)—P. J. Flannery, 816-824 West Harrison street.
Ladies' Cloaks and Suit Cutters' No. 81—Julia A. Brady, 2039 Kendall street.
Ladies' Garment Workers No. 44 (Cloak)—H. Schoolman, 1392 Milwaukee avenue.
No. 54—Peter Ostiller, 1125 Blue Island avenue.
No. 71—M. Schuchter, 1125 Blue Island avenue.
Ladies' Straw and Felt Hat Workers—Helen Phillips, 127 East 51st street.
No. 12675—T. Wollenburg, 1741 North Kimball avenue.
Laundry Workers' Union No. 46—Marie Curry, 1736 West 14th street.
Leather Workers (on Travelers' Goods and Novelties) No. 12—F. A. Lohn, 522 South Halsted street.
Leather Workers No. 17—Sam Polinsky, 1008 Olive street.
Lithograph Apprentices and Press Feeders No. 2—Henry A. Schenk, 1250 North Springfield avenue.
Lithographers' Union No. 4—Charles H. Scharien, Elmhurst, Ill.
Machinists—Progressive No. 126—F. B. Johnson, 4033 Armitage avenue.
Prosperity No. 128—F. A. Lampert, 6541 Drexel avenue.
Unity No. 134—F. R. Stahlik, 1446 South Harding avenue.
Maywood No. 185—J. Williamson, 217 South 13th avenue, Maywood, Ill.
Bethany No. 208—F. L. Lee, 6529 Laflin street.
Liberty No. 229—L. Rickert, 2947 Warsaw avenue.
Reliable No. 253—James Carmichael, 507 North 7th avenue, Maywood. Ill.
Grand Crossing Lodge No. 265—R. J. Weber, 6231 University place.
Freiheit No. 337—H. Thielberg, 2832 Palmer avenue.
LaSalle No. 338—C. Bade, 2981 Wisner avenue.
Gleichheit No. 366—F. H. Voelker, 254 West 23d place.
Lake View No. 390—J. A. Weydert, 1245 Webster avenue.
Garfield Park No. 478—F. C. Abel, 945 North Ridgeway avenue.
Tool and Diemakers No. 510—Clarence Gate, 2318 Park avenue.

Brass Workers No. 766—E. C. Langman, 841 North Mozart street.
Mailers' Union No. 2—James P. McNichols, 442 Garfield avenue.
Marble Workers' Union No. 21—John O'Connell, 625 West 48th street.
No. 67—Joseph P. Hauger, 204 North Lamon avenue.
Meat, Food and Sanitary Inspectors—Frank Crosby, 7422 Emerald avenue.
Metal Polishers No. 6—38 South Peoria street, rooms 1 and 2.
Musicians' Union No. 10—George H. Riley, 175 West Washington street.
Musical Instrument Makers No. 100—John L. Ward, 3917 North Drake avenue.
Painters and Decorators No. 54—John Roy, postoffice box 104, Evanston, Ill.
No. 180—H. A. Sommers, 7556 Brown avenue, Forest Park, Ill.
No. 194—A. A. Wigsness, 1774 Kimball avenue.
No. 396—Sam Leaper, 1124 West 62d street.
No. 430—William La Vassar, 1906 Jackson boulevard.
No. 637—Mathias Marte, 3649 North Ashland avenue.
Paper Hangers No. 584—E. L. Maxwell, 1418 Orleans street.
Park Employes No. 14388—P. A. Knudson, 1717 North Ridgeway avenue.
Painters (Sign and Pictorial) No. 830—J. F. Irwin, 7706 Normal avenue.
Pattern Makers—J. S. Forrest, 738 West Madison street, room 829.
Photo Engravers No. 5—431 South Dearborn street.
Piano Workers No. 1—Theo Schlicht, 1620 North Irving avenue.
No. 2—E. E. Findeisen, 4013 Fillmore street.
Pile Drivers' Union No. 365—James E. Fello, 9508 Commercial avenue.
Plumbers' Association—John Bushnell, 167 West Washington street, room 700.
Postoffice Clerks No. 1—Carl F. Wagner, 626 Belden avenue.
Pressmen No. 3—E. H. Heine, 319 South LaSalle street, room 332.
Pressmen (Web) No. 7—L. A. Waltman, 1644 North Kedzie avenue.
Printers' Roller Makers No. 10638—James Burke, 1221 North Tripp avenue.
Sail and Tent Makers' Union No. 12757—Nels Nelson, 2839 North Maplewood avenue.
Seamen's Union—Victor Olander, 570 West Lake street.
Sewer Cleaners and Repairers—John Boyle, 5923 5th avenue.
Sheet Metal Workers No. 51—M. Karczewski, 1135 North Winchester avenue.
No. 73—365 West Madison street.
No. 115—Aug. Fick, 2718 Cortez street.
Sprinkler Fitters No. 281—A. Baish, 11 North May street.
South Chicago Trades and Labor Assembly—A. W. Smith, 2913 East 97th street.
Steam Engineers No. 23—William Roll, R. F. D. No. 2, box 21, Blue Island, Ill.
No. 85—F. H. Mowry, 11946 Butler street.
No. 143—James J. Spain, 4721 Washington boulevard.
No. 395—James Lyons, 2847 Congress street.
No. 399—Fred Bartell, 6640 South Green street.
No. 400—Stephen Clay, 4317 St. Lawrence avenue.
No. 401—Charles Graff, 2159 West 12th street.
No. 402—Andrew S. Martin, 2214 Racine avenue.
No. 464 (Paving)—J. B. Evans, 2656 Warren avenue.
Steamfitters' Union No. 597—Room 37, 112 North LaSalle street.
Steam Shovel and Dredge Men—T. J. Dolan, 105 West Monroe street.
Stenographers and Typists No. 12755—Gladys Taylor, 165 North LaSalle street.
Stenographers (Court Reporters) No. 14171—T. G. Vance, 167 West Washington street, room 710.
Stone Planer Men No. 13093—W. A. Fanning, 2539 Frankfort street.
Sub-Paving Inspectors—Raymond F. Stanton, 2150 Grace street.
Suspender Workers—Mae Nihil, 849 Sherman place.
Switchmen's Union No. 19—H. E. Ensworth, 4817 Jackson boulevard.
No. 58—W. J. Sweeney, 2522 Lexington street.

No. 79—J. H. Landers, 708 West 50th street.
No. 199—J. W. Heinen, 3319 South Lowe avenue.
Tailors No. 5—W. S. Nylen, 232 North Clark street.
Teachers' Federation—127 North Dearborn street.
Teachers' Federation (Men)—F. G. Stecker, 3310 Adams street.
Teamsters—Commission No. 703—F. H. Ray, 222 North State street.
 Truck Drivers No. 705—Harry Hanson, 145 North Market street.
 Newspaper No. 706—John Lee, 3530 South 5th avenue.
 Packing House No. 710—George Golden, 4201 South Halsted street.
 Laundry No. 712—Frank Theis, 1053 North Park avenue.
 Livery No. 720—John Butler, 6420 Langley avenue.
 Furniture and Department Store No. 722—A. J. Reed, 20 West Randolph street.
 Auto Livery Chauffeurs No. 727—T. Neary, 175 West Washington street.
 Park B. and D. No. 733—J. C. Hourihan, 925 East 55th street.
 Bakery No. 734—Louis Larson, 175 West Washington street, third floor.
 Grease and Tallow No. 735—John Mulconrey, 3322 South Hamilton avenue.
 No. 738—Mat Cox, 3538 5th avenue.
 Milk Drivers No. 753—175 W. Washington street, third floor.
 Tea and Coffee No. 772—F. A. Mondschein, 175 West Washington street, third floor.
Technical League (Chicago)—Louis A. Heyn, 524 Grant place.
Telegraphers—Commercial No. 1—Wesley Russell, 440 South Dearborn street.
 Railroad Division No. 91—W. E. Carter, 5443 Broadway.

Theatrical Employes—Clarence B. Savage, 39 West Adams street, room 403.
Theatrical Moving Picture Operators—39 West Adams street, room 403.
Tuck Pointers and Front Cleaners—W. G. Blount, 3812 North Leavitt street.
Tugmen Protective Association (Licensed) No. 2—Louis Hohmann, 405 North Clark street.
Typographical Union No. 9—Anton Chonarzewski, 2913 North Oakley avenue.
 No. 16—John C. Harding, 324 South LaSalle street, second floor.
United Association Steamfitters and Helpers No. 520—365 West Madison street.
Upholsterers No. 24—Otto Luedtke, 2047 Cortez street.
 No. 111—R. J. Hull, 2561 Washington boulevard.
 Carriage and Automobile No. 131—John Spamer, 3352 Emerald avenue.
Wall Paper and Color Mixers No. 8—Emil Ziman, 2445 South Harding avenue.
Waiters No. 336—176 North Franklin street.
Waitresses' Union No. 484—Elizabeth Maloney, 35 South Dearborn street, room 41.
Waiters' Progressive League No. 530—71 West Monroe street.
Well Drillers and Levermen's Union—F. Rudolph, 6603 South May street.
Window Washers' Union No. 12065—Frank Sieg, 156 West Washington street.
Women's Union Label League—Mrs. J. F. O'Neil, 2230 North Kildare avenue.
Women's Trade Union League—Emma Steghagen, 166 West Washington street, room 609.
Wood Block and Brick Pavers' Union—Fred Scully, 1026 South May street.
Wood and Wire Lathers No. 74—Harry A. Quanstrom, 857 North Robey street.

PRINCIPAL HOTELS IN CHICAGO.

Arlington..................839 N. Dearborn street
Auditorium..............430 South Michigan avenue
Bismarck..................177 West Randolph street
Blackstone................636 South Michigan avenue
Briggs house.............188 West Randolph street
Chicago Beach.......51st street and Cornell avenue
Congress hotel............520 South Michigan avenue
Commercial hotel..........533 South Wabash avenue
Continental................5 South Wabash avenue
De Jongho's................12 East Monroe street
Drexel Arms.......29th street and Drexel boulevard
Grand Pacific.............232 South Clark street
Great Northern...........237 South Dearborn street
Hotel Brevoort...........120 West Madison street
Hotel Del Prado..59th street and Dorchester avenue
Hotel Grace..............75 West Jackson boulevard
Hotel Grant..............6 North Dearborn avenue
Hotel Mayer.............1154 South Wabash avenue
Hotel Luzerne..North Clark street and Touhy avenue
Hotel Metropole....23d street and Michigan avenue
Hotel Morrison............83 West Madison street
Hotel Warner..33d street and Cottage Grove avenue

Hotel Windermere...56th street and Cornell avenue
Hyde Park.........51st street and Lake Park avenue
Jackson.......Halsted street and Jackson boulevard
Kaiserhof.................324 South Clark street
Lakota............30th street and Michigan avenue
LaSalle..................10 North LaSalle street
Lexington.........Michigan avenue and 22d street
Majestic..................29 Quincy street
Palmer house............115 South State street
Planters.................17 North Clark street
Plaza.........North Clark street and North avenue
Revere house..N. Clark street and W. Austin avenue
Saratoga.................29 South Dearborn street
Sherman house...........106 West Randolph street
Stratford...............75 East Jackson boulevard
Union hotel..............72 West Randolph street
Vendome.......63d street and Kenwood avenue
Victoria.................332 South Clark street
Virginia...............Ohio and Rush streets
Wellington...........241 South Wabash avenue
Windsor-Clifton..............28 East Monroe street

BOARD OF EDUCATION CHANGES.

At a meeting of the Chicago board of education Dec. 11, 1913, Mrs. Ella Flagg Young was forced out as superintendent of schools and the first assistant superintendent, John D. Shoop, was elected to fill her place. The vote by which the change was made was a secret one and the action, it was claimed, was against the expressed wish of Mayor Carter H. Harrison, who subsequently accepted the resignations of the following members of the board: Harry A. Lipsky, Henry W. Huttmann, James B. Dibelka, John C. Harding and Charles O. Sethness, all of whom voted against Mrs. Young. Their resignations were dated from the time of their appointment. No such documents were held by the mayor in the cases of other members who opposed the retention of Mrs. Young. Peter Reinberg, who opposed the action of the board, resigned his position as president but not his membership on the board. Dean Sumner resigned as chairman of the school management committee. He was one of Mrs. Young's leading champions. The action of the board aroused much popular resentment.

DEATH OF A. MONTGOMERY WARD.

A. Montgomery Ward, founder of the first mail order business and known in Chicago as the "watchdog of the lake front," died at his home in Highland Park, Ill., Dec. 7, 1913, from pneumonia largely induced by a fall about six weeks previously in which he fractured a hip. He had also been a sufferer from Bright's disease. He left a fortune estimated at about $15,000,000. For more than twenty years he fought successfully to keep buildings of all kinds from the Grant park lake front.

CHICAGO STOCK EXCHANGE.

President—Frederick C. Aldrich.
Secretary—Charles T. Atkinson, 2d floor The Rookery.
Location—The Rookery, 209 South LaSalle street.
Hours—"Calls" at 11 a. m. on stocks and bonds.

CHICAGO'S DEATH ROLL.
Dec. 1, 1912, to Dec. 1, 1913.

Abrahams, Emanuel M. (1866), alderman, July 1.
Allen, Geo. Q., civil war veteran, Nov. 9.
Allen, J. Frank (1856), journalist, Nov. 3.
Amberg, John (1823), contractor, March 31.
Anable, Samuel L. (1821), civil war veteran, July 29.
Arter, Francis G. (1838), physician, Jan. 22.
Augarde, Adrienne (1882), actress, March 17.
Augur, Colon (1848), soldier, Feb. 13.
Austin, Henry L., claim agent, July 16.
Bacon, Thomas R. (1850), educator, in Berkeley, Cal., March 26.
Badoilet, Mrs. Isadora (1830), Jan. 8.
Badt, Francis B. (1849), electrical engineer, April 12.
Baker, Newell C. (1846), printer, Aug. 19.
Barnard, Mrs. Mariana B. (1830), April 5.
Ballentine, Robert M. (1850), broker, Oct. 21.
Barnhart, Arthur M. (1844), typefounder, May 13.
Barrett, Samuel E. (1833), manufacturer, in Baltimore, Md., Dec. 29, 1912.
Bauer, Solomon H. (1861), rabbi, Aug. 9.
Beck, Rudolph (1869), dentist, March 15.
Bell, Kossuth H. (1853), packer, July 12.
Bierbower, Austin, lawyer and author, April 12.
Billings, Mrs. Augusta S. F. (1821), March 30.
Billings, Henry F. (1839), manufacturer, Sept. 18.
Bishop, Henry Walker, lawyer, in Pittsfield, Mass.
Blackman, Chester S., grain dealer, in Hinsdale, Oct. 22.
Blocki, William F. (1842), druggist, Aug. 23.
Bolter, Edward (1862), manufacturer, Jan. 27.
Borden, William W. (1888), missionary, in Cairo, Egypt, April 9.
Boyd, Robert D. (1848), physician, Jan. 9.
Brennan, John J. (1849), alderman, Feb. 16.
Brennock, James (1831), labor leader, March 25.
Brittan, Arthur (1832), merchant, March 4.
Browne, Francis F. (1843), author, in Santa Barbara, Cal., May 11.
Browning, T. Walter (1866), broker, in Glencoe, June 2.
Brush, Homer J. (1858), commission merchant, March 25.
Buckingham, Clarence (1855), capitalist, Aug. 29.
Burnes, Mrs. Frances B., in Paris, France, Feb. 20.
Burridge, Walter W., artist, in Albuquerque, N. M., June 25.
Burroughs, Geo. T. (1833), manufacturer, Feb. 15.
Burt, Horace G. (1849), railroad official, May 19.
Butzow, R. C. (1858), real estate, in Evanston, Nov. 30.
Cairns, John J. (1857), soldier, Feb. 18.
Canfield, Gertrude (1856), actress, March 6.
Chapin, Charles A. (1845), manufacturer, Oct. 22.
Charlton, Jas. (1832), railroad official, Nov. 19.
Charlton, Mrs. Mary D. (1836), Oct. 28.
Chase, Horace G. (1827), real estate dealer, in New York, N. Y., Feb. 4.
Christin, Ferrier V. (1842), civil war veteran, July 8.
Cleland, Jonas M. (1852), business man, Jan. 22.
Coon, Mrs. Sarah B. (1823), in Oak Park, June 12.
Collins, Jr., Ben (1871), lumberman, Sept. 29.
Conkey, Willard F. (1881), lawyer, May 13.
Conner, Edward D. (1853), labor leader, April 3.
Cooke, Mrs. Homer (1839), in Lausanne, Switzerland, Oct. 30.
Corbin, Calvin Rich (1831), wholesale grocer, May 2.
Crane, Jonathan M. (1856), journalist, June 18.
Cushman, John Clark, manufacturer, June 4.
Cratty, Thomas (1833), lawyer, Sept. 19.
Darnell, Riley (1837), haberdasher, in Westgate, Cal., March 24.
Darrow, William H. (1854), police official, Sept. 3.
Davis, A. B. (1832), naval veteran, Oct. 1.
De Souchet, Osman C. (1826), lumberman, March 5.
Devlin, Patrick J., journalist and politician, Jan. 8.
Dickason, Livingston T. (1843), civil war veteran, in Naples, Italy, March 22.
Dickson, Maxwell E. (1848), newspaper man, April 1.
Dillon, John (1832), actor, April 21.
Dunn, J. Austin (1841), dentist, April 9.
Dupee, Mrs. F. W. (1822), in Glencoe, June 6.
Dyrenforth, J. W. (1860), lawyer, Nov. 24.
Eastman, Royal A. (1855), manufacturer, Feb. 10.
Eckels, George M. (1863), attorney, Oct. 7.
Ede, Elphick R. (1871), attorney, Jan. 12.
Eden, William S. (1843), hotel owner, June 29.

Egbert, Jerome W. (1873), physician, May 21.
Eggert, Frederick C. (1875), surgeon, March 6.
Ennis, Robert B. (1838), banker, in Evanston, Sept. 9.
Erikson, Charles F. (1866), publisher, March 15.
Ernst, Otto (1846), brewer, Nov. 15.
Evans, Bernard (1845), civil war veteran, Jan. 30.
Farwell, John Albro (1833), jeweler, in Evanston, March 31.
Faye, Charles M. (1851), editor, in Aurora, Ill., June 8.
Feely, J. B. (1856), priest, June 29.
Fewer, Michael S., politician, March 23.
Fisher, Daniel W. (1838), clergyman, in Washington, D. C., Jan. 28.
Fitch, Amza L. (1839), civil war veteran, July 13.
Fitzgerald, William (1842), former alderman and county commissioner, April 7.
Forrester, George (1836), confederate veteran, Nov. 10.
Friese, Carl P. (1833), physician, Aug. 28.
Frith, A. J. (1852), educator, Nov. 10.
Furness, William E. (1839), lawyer, at Great Spruce Head Island, Maine, July 19.
Gage, Eliphalet B. (1839), business man, in San Francisco, Cal., March 12.
Gage, Henry H. (1835), real estate dealer, in Evanston, Ill., Jan. 3.
Gallion, Charles H. (1868), editor, Aug. 9.
Gauer, John H. (1896), merchant, at Riverton, Ill., June 10.
Geeting, Henry C. (1844), attorney, Sept. 3.
Geeting, John F. (1851), attorney, in Washington, D. C., Feb. 28.
Gerts, John (1844), piano manufacturer, May 14.
Geudtner, Francis (1834), banker, Feb. 1.
Gilbert, E. E. (1842), ex-collector of internal revenue, Feb. 8.
Gleason, Edward (1874), secretary Cook County Democracy, May 17.
Gleeson, Rev. Edward J. (1861), educator, Oct. 22.
Gordon, Cliff (Morris Saltpetre), actor, April 21.
Gott, John R. (1852), commission merchant, May 13.
Greene, John E. (1841), civil war veteran, March 3.
Greensfelder, Isaac (1827), philanthropist, Nov. 14.
Gross, Samuel E. (1843), real estate dealer, in Battle Creek, Mich., Oct. 24.
Guerin, John (1839), physician, member board of education, in Memphis, Tenn., Jan. 2.
Haley, Augustus F. (1852), educator, April 29.
Hamburg, Ephraim (1815), war veteran, May 31.
Hanlon, Jas. H. (1867), printer, Nov. 23.
Hammond, Lyman D. (1844), insurance man, in Magnolia Springs, Ala., Feb. 14.
Hanton, Tom (1862), sportsman, May 26.
Harkness, Latham J. (1851), clergyman, Oct. 29.
Hartley, Frank (1856), surgeon, in New York, N. Y., June 19.
Hartt, Charles F. (1859), dentist, June 17.
Hatch, George (1839), salesman, Nov. 3.
Haynie, Mrs. Abner F. (1826), educator, Feb. 8.
Heinemann, Arnold H. (1831), journalist, April 21.
Herrick, Eugene K. (1844), commission merchant, March 3.
Hess, John M., clergyman and educator, July 22.
Higgie, Francis B. (1839), lake captain, Feb. 11.
Hill, Miss Martha S., Aug. 4.
Hill, Matson (1843), real estate dealer, May 17.
Hinkle, John F. (1847), hotelkeeper, July 11.
Hoffman, Jonas (1843), manufacturer, Aug. 15.
Holmes, William P, (1870), business man, May 10.
Honore, Benjamin (1827), retired business man, at Sarasota, Fla., Nov. 9.
Hopkins, Edward O. (1858), railroad man, April 3.
Horner, Isaac (1854), merchant, May 21.
Humphrey, Mrs. Elizabeth E. (1836), Feb. 14.
Hunter, Mary C. (1832), civil war nurse, May 7.
Hyde, Edward Everett (1875), physician and editor, July 4.
Isham, Mrs. Katherine Snow (1832), Feb. 23.
Iverson, Emil (1861), merchant, at Riverton, Ill., June 10.
Jacobs, William B. (1840), Sunday school worker, July 16.
Jackson, Rachel (1852), charity worker, Feb. 2.

Jannotta, Alfredo (1837), composer, in Los Angeles, Cal., April 12.
John, James, Masonic official, April 12.
Johnson, James Whiting (1862), manager, Jan. 14.
Jones, Cyrus M. (1854), merchant, Sept. 12.
Kalas, Luke (1864), ex-police inspector. May 27.
Kean, Samuel A. (1847), banker, July 10.
Kelley, Paul D. (1875), Chicago club man, at Berry-ville, Va., May 6.
Kersten, Mrs. Sophia (1829), June 10.
Kienappel, Miss Carrie, charity worker, Feb. 7.
Kimbell, Mrs. Annie C. (1845), May 16.
King, John A. (1856), manufacturer, May 21.
Kirchberg, Edward (1844), jeweler, Sept. 9.
Kirk, Alfred (1832), teacher, June 30.
Kittridge, Mrs. Rosalia B., Nov. 15.
Kline, James D., lumber merchant, May 28.
Kretzinger, Geo. W. (1846), attorney, Nov. 17.
Lane, Mrs. Charles Bowman (1818), club woman, June 9.
Leake, Joseph B. (1828), lawyer, June 1.
Lee, William H. (1847), publisher, July 1.
Lefens, Thies J. (1846), real estate dealer. April 14.
Legnard, John B. (1835), brick manufacturer, in Waukegan, Ill., Aug. 10.
Leiter, Mrs. Levi Z., in Washington, D. C., March 6.
Lensman, Frederick A. (1853), surgeon, Aug. 3.
Litt, Solomon, theater manager, Oct. 24.
Loughlin, William M. (1824), veteran of civil war, Aug. 20.
Lyon, George R. (1846), civil war veteran, in Wau-kegan, Ill., Aug. 7.
MacGeagh, John W. (1841), banker, Nov. 12.
Marble, Earl (1840), writer, March 8.
Mauch, Carl (1850), artist, June 18.
Merchant, George F. (1835), real estate dealer, June 13.
Meyer, Martin (1838), merchant, July 32.
Mills, Harry I. (1859), merchant, in Rochester, Minn., Feb. 25.
Meyer, John B. (1841), banker, June 7.
Mix, Mrs. James (1832), Jan. 16.
Monett, Mrs. Minnie R., Aug. 2.
Moore, William S. (1835), Illinois pioneer, in Evans-ton, June 10.
Morin, Denis (1841), physician, Nov. 14.
Morris, Edward (1866), packer, Nov. 3.
Moss, William L. (1835), lawyer, in Kenosha, Wis., May 13.
Munn, Daniel W. (1834), attorney, in La Grange, Ill., Sept. 17.
Munroe, James E. (1846), attorney, June 3.
McDermott, John (1823), civil war veteran, Jan. 14.
McDougall, Alexander (1835), commission merchant, in Highland Park, July 8.
McKenna, William J., former alderman, in San Antonio, Tex., Jan. 5.
McLoughlin, Patrick A. (1853), clergyman, March 21.
McMahon, Charles (1856), superintendent. May 1.
McNiff, Margaret S. (1850), physician, Aug. 21.
Nestor, Timothy (1846), capitalist, Nov. 3.
Neville, James A. (1834), physician, Feb. 20.
Nicholson, George T. (1856), railroad official, in Los Angeles, Cal., March 30.
Nourse, John A. (1845), merchant, in Wilmette, Ill., June 16.
Noyes, Mrs. LaVerne W., Dec. 5, 1912.
O'Donnell, Mary E. (1882), editor, in Council Bluffs, Iowa, Aug. 11.
Otis, Ephraim (1834), attorney, Sept. 6.
Perce, Mrs. Sarah M. (1842), Aug. 2.
Petrie, William J. (1843), clergyman, in San An-tonio, Tex., Feb. 1.
Phillips, James M. (1834), veteran of civil war. July 24.
Piric, John O. (1827), merchant, April 24.
Prins, Raphael J. (1843), shoe merchant, Feb. 4.
Rappleye, Nicholas B. (1834), retired business man, Aug. 25.
Ratcliffe, James L., contractor, in Evanston, Oct. 21.
Ray, Mrs. Julia, in New Haven, Conn., Oct. 6.
Reed, Benjamin H. (1859), police official, Aug. 10.
Rietz, Frederick (1834), lumber dealer, Feb. 19.
Rishel, Austin C. (1859), educator, Oct. 24.
Ritter, Henry F. (1857), attorney, Feb. 1.
Robinson, Mrs. Martha B. (1827), Jan. 20.
Rockwood, Fred S. (1840), merchant, in Elmhurst, Ill., May 22.

Rodgers, John W. (1860), broker, in Evanston, Sept. 7.
Root, Mrs. John W. (1857), May 27.
Rowley, Frank, editor, Nov. 27.
Rubel, Benjamin F. (1866), merchant, April 18.
Runyan, Mrs. Flora R. (1833), Feb. 2.
Sabin, Albert R. (1837), educator, Jan. 29.
Salmonsen, Morris (1843), insurance agent, May 1.
Sargent, Geo. M. (1830), manufacturer, in Atlantic City, N. J., Jan. 16.
Sayler, Harry L. (1863), journalist, in Indianapolis, Ind., May 30.
Schacks, Henry (1836), railroad official, May 16.
Schmidt, Mrs. Therese (1829), Aug. 8.
Schultz, Frederick (1848), manufacturer, July 22.
Scott, William (1834), real estate dealer, May 21.
Seabrooke, Thomas Q. (1860), actor, April 3.
Sebree, James K. (1846), hotel owner, Nov. 17.
Seidnadel, Charles W., linguist, Aug. 9.
Selby, Paul (1824), veteran editor, March 13.
Seiz, Morris (1826), shoe manufacturer, June 3.
Sempill, Walter M. (1851), druggist, July 18.
Sercomb, Albert L. (1847), jeweler, May 12.
Shaw, Mrs. Ralph M., July 8.
Sheldon, George (1847), customs broker, near Lon-don, England, July 13.
Sherwood, Nehemiah (1833), wholesale grocer, Aug. 11.
Shippy, George M. (1854), ex-chief of police, April 13.
Shirer, Seward S. (1871), attorney, Feb. 18.
Sicard, Ernest (1851), teacher. May 8.
Sidley, William K. (1838), merchant, at Coronado Beach, Cal., Feb. 9.
Sidwell, George H. (1831), grain broker, June 4.
Silsbee, Joseph (1849), architect, Jan. 31.
Simonds, Gilbert (1816), pioneer, Oct. 10.
Sloan, Henry H. (1836), physician, Oct. 9.
Smalley, Edmund H. (1852), attorney, Aug. 20.
Smith, Hayden K. (1834), writer, March 26.
Snider, Alonzo (1822), insurance man, in Waukegan, June 11.
Spengler, John H. (1866), engineer, Jan. 11.
Stiles, Josiah, packer, March 26.
Steely, Guy, journalist and dramatist, in Cleve-land, O., April 22.
Stone, Mrs. H. O. (1840), at Beach Bluff, Mass., July 5.
Stow, Nelson L. (1833), ex-member of school board. in Evanston, Ill., March 30.
Strelitz, Victor B. (1871), jeweler, in New York, N. Y., March 12.
Stromberg, Alfred (1861), inventor, March 8.
Sullivan, Alexander, attorney, Aug. 21.
Sullivan, Mrs. Rose A. (1846), March 16.
Sutcliffe, John (1853), church architect, Oct. 23.
Swanson, S. A. (1856), tailor, Aug. 8.
Tabor, Merritt E. (1858), mining engineer, Aug. 29.
Thenrer, Joseph, brewer, May 14.
Thompson, Thomas O., journalist, April 24.
Thurber, W. Scott (1848), art dealer. Sept. 24.
Tobey, Frank B. (1833), merchant, in Lincoln, Neb., Oct. 15.
Tolman, Judson A. (1850), hardware merchant, Aug. 18.
Townsend, James J. (1862), broker, Aug. 29.
Tracy, Frank D. (1842), tax agent, April 18.
Treider, Christian (1844), clergyman, April 15.
Tremain, Charles W. (1830), inventor, Jan. 22.
Troy, Rev. Thos. F., priest, July 4.
Trude, Frederick H. (1851), lawyer, Nov. 11.
Van Buren, William (1842), lawyer, April 24.
Virden, Frederick B. (1869), educator, Aug. 16.
Wadhams, Frederick E. (1853), physician, Nov. 1.
Walte, Catherine V. V., author and editor, Nov. 16.
Walbridge, Mrs. Ann Eliza L. (1828), Illinois pio-neer, March 29.
Walser, Jacob G., manufacturer, Oct. 16.
Ward, Frank E., railway official, June 6.
Warner, Archelaus G. (1817), pioneer, July 30.
Warner, George L. (1851), real estate dealer, June 14.
Waterloo, Stanley (1846), journalist and author, Oct. 11.
Watson, Mrs. Regina (1847), pianist, July 31.
Watson, William W. (1846), lecturer, March 11.
Wayman, John E. W. (1872), former state's attor-ney, April 18.
Wells, Robert M. (1848), banker, Sept. 8.

Whipple, Enoch A. (1851), hotel manager, Jan. 12.
White, Hamilton (1834), educator, June 3.
White, Henry W. (1852), insurance adjuster, June 20.
White, John M. (1826), real estate investor, May 3.
White, William F. (1842), real estate dealer, Jan. 9.
Whitfield, Thomas (1839), druggist, Jan. 23.
Wilde, Reuben M. (1845), veteran of civil war, Aug. 25.

Wilkinson, Dudley P. (1833), iron monger, Nov. 17.
Willard, Samuel (1821), educator, Feb. 9.
Williams, Fitzallen B. (1828), merchant, March 10.
Wing, Miss Anna E., bible class teacher, March 12.
Wolf, Bernhard (1841), packer, March 30.
Woolfolk, Clinton S., capitalist, March 26.
Wright, Joseph (1840), lawyer, Jan. 6.

ALUMNI ASSOCIATIONS IN CHICAGO.
University and college.

Amherst—Henry H. Tittsworth; secretary-treasurer, Bowles King.
Association of Alumni Secretaries of Chicago—President, Carroll Shaffer; secretary, Marcus D. Richards, 5729 Woodlawn avenue.
Beloit—President, Ira J. Couch; secretary and treasurer, John W. Wilder, 5737 Kenmore avenue.
Brown University—Secretary and treasurer, F. L. Morse, 6432 Monroe avenue.
Cornell—President, P. P. Bird; secretary, R. Warren Sailor, 1415 Michigan avenue.
Harvard Club of Chicago—President, Redmond D. Stephens; secretary and treasurer, Theodore Sheldon.
Illini Club of Chicago—314 Federal street; president, George R. Carr; secretary, J. T. Hanley.
Illinois College—President, Arthur D. Black; secretary, Charles C. Clement.
Illinois Woman's College—President, Mrs. E. O. Frady; secretary, Miss Clara Allen.
Iowa State—President, W. M. Wilson; secretary-treasurer, J. C. Horning.
Knox—President, Sherman C. Kingsley; secretary-treasurer, Robert Szold.
Michigan—President, Frank P. Graves; secretary, Beverly B. Vedder.

Northwestern—President, Ben M. Smith; secretary and treasurer, Francis Adams, Jr., 209 South LaSalle street.
Notre Dame—President, John B. Kanaley; secretary, John C. Tully.
Princeton Club of Chicago—President, J. D. Hulburd; secretary, Robert C. McNamara, 623 South Wabash avenue.
Purdue—President, Edward C. DeWolfe; secretary, F. G. Winslow.
Swarthmore—Secretary, Francis E. Broomell, 74 West Washington street.
University of Chicago—President, Agnes Wayman; secretary, Frank W. Dignan.
University of Chicago Alumnae—President, Mrs. Ethel R. McDowell; secretary, Florence G. Fanning.
University of Wisconsin—President, Fred S. White; secretary and treasurer, J. G. Wray, 212 West Washington street, 19th floor.
Washington and Jefferson—President, Rev. D. C. Milner; secretary and treasurer, C. C. Meloy, 6342 Winthrop avenue.
Yale Club of Chicago—President, Wallace C. Winter; secretary and treasurer, Carroll Shaffer, 234 South LaSalle street.

CHICAGO'S FREE PUBLIC BATHS.

Operated by the health department; G. B. Young, M. D., commissioner; W. K. Murray, M. D., chief of bureau of hospitals, public baths and lodging house. Names and location of baths:
Carter H. Harrison—759 Mather street.
Martin B. Madden—3825 Wentworth avenue.
William Mavor—4647 Gross avenue.
Robert A. Waller—19 South Peoria street.
Kosciuszko—1444 Holt street.
DeWitt C. Cregier—1153 Gault court.
John Wentworth—2839 South Halsted street.
Theodore T. Gurney—1141 West Chicago avenue.
William B. Ogden—3346 Emerald avenue.
Joseph Medill—2138 Grand avenue.
Thomas Gahan—4226 Wallace street.
Pilsen—1849 Throop street.
Fernand Henrotin—2415 North Marshfield avenue.
William Loeffler—1217 South Union street.
Simon Baruch—1911 West 20th street.
Lake Shore—Chicago avenue and East Pearson.
Seward—Sedgwick and Elm streets.

Free baths are given at the 14th street and 22d street pumping stations and at several lake beaches, such as at Jackson park, foot of Ohio street, etc. The Carter H. Harrison bath, opened in January, 1904, is said to have been the first free public bath in the United States. Similar baths in Vienna charged a fee of 2 cents and those in New York 5 cents. The Madden bath was opened in April, 1897; the Mavor bath in May, 1900; the Waller bath in February, 1901; the Kosciuszko bath in April, 1904; the Cregier bath in October, 1905; the Wentworth bath in December, 1905; the Gurney bath in May, 1906; the Ogden bath in July, 1906; the Medill bath in September, 1906; the Gahan bath in November, 1907; the Pilsen bath in March, 1908; the Henrotin bath in September, 1908; the Loeffler bath in February, 1909, and the Baruch bath in April, 1910. The average cost of each plant has been between $15,000 and $20,000, and the average annual cost of maintenance, $4,000.

CHICAGO ACADEMY OF FINE ARTS.
81 East Madison street.

President—Carl N. Werntz.
Vice-President—M. M. Newman.
Secretary—E. M. Ashcraft, Jr.

The Chicago Academy of Fine Arts was founded in October, 1902. Its object is to popularize art and art education through the more practical channels of illustration, cartooning, commercial illustration, design, normal art training, crafts, miniature, etc. It was the first school to teach commercial art, craftswork, miniature and cartooning

in exclusive classes. The average attendance is 700 pupils per year, with twenty instructors, the faculty including well-known local artists. There are day and evening classes and the rates of tuition are as follows: Afternoons only, $26 for three months; mornings only, $31 for three months; all day classes, $150 per season of ten months; evening classes, $23 for ten months, three nights weekly; Sunday class, $23 for ten months; Saturday classes, for school teachers, high school students and children, $6.00 for three months; all classes limited.

CHICAGO AND COOK COUNTY REAL ESTATE BOARDS.

THE CHICAGO REAL ESTATE BOARD.
26 North Dearborn street, second floor.
OFFICERS FOR 1913.
President—Edward M. Willoughby.
Vice-President—Ayres Boal.
Secretary—Francis E. Manierre.

COOK COUNTY REAL ESTATE BOARD.
35 North Dearborn street.
OFFICERS FOR 1913.
President—Henry T. Davis.
Vice-President—A. J. Brockman.
Secretary—H. W. Harpold.
Treasurer—Frank L. Dean.

FOREIGN ORDERS CONFERRED ON CHICAGOANS.

Abrahamson, Rev. L. G.—Royal North Star, Sweden.

Adams, Milward—Legion of Honor, France; Leopold, Belgium; Crown, Italy; White Elephant (officer), Siam; Savior (officer), Greece; Nichan Iftikhar (commander), Tunis; Merit Agricole (commander), Portugal.

Anderson, John—St. Olaf, Norway.

Andreen, Rev. Gustav—Royal North Star, Sweden.

Antonsen, Carl—Danebrog, Denmark.

Birkhoff, George, Jr.—Orange-Nassau (officer), Holland.

Bjorn, Emil—St. Olaf, Norway.

Brosseau, Z. P.—Legion of Honor, France.

Bryan, Charles Page—Order of Rising Sun (highest grand cordon), Japan.

Barry, William—Legion of Honor, France.

Burton, Le Grand S.—Legion of Honor (chevalier), France.

Chatfield-Taylor, Hobart C.—Isabella the Catholic, Spain; Garter, Spain; St. James, Portugal; Legion of Honor, France; Crown of Italy, Italy.

Cooley, Edwin G.—Francis Joseph, Austria.

Cuneo, Frank—Crown (chevalier), Italy.

Cutting, Starr W.—Crown (class III.), Prussia.

Dan, Rev. Adam—Danebrog, Denmark.

Daae, Dr. A.—St. Olaf, Norway.

Deering, Charles—Legion of Honor, France; Crown (class III.), Prussia.

D'Urso, Luigi—Crown (chevalier), Italy.

Eddy, Arthur J.—Red Eagle (class III.), Prussia.

Enander, John A.—Gold medal, Litteris et Artibus, Sweden.

Ericson, John E.—Vasa, Sweden.

Fischer, Gustave F.—Red Eagle (class IV.), Prussia.

Furber, Harry J.—Legion of Honor, France.

Gauzel, Louis—Crown (class IV.), Prussia.

Gass, Martin—Lion of Zaeringen, Baden.

Gauss, E. F. L.—Crown (class IV.), Prussia.

Grevstad, Nicolay—St. Olaf. Norway.

Hachmeister, Henry—Red Eagle (class IV.), Prussia.

Halle, Edward G.—Crown (class II.), Prussia.

Hanson, Christian H.—Danebrog, Denmark.

Henius, Dr. Max—Danebrog, Denmark.

Heurotin, Charles—Legion of Honor, France; Leopold (chevalier, officer and civic cross of first class), Belgium; commander of Medjidie, Turkey; Osmanie, Turkey.

Henrotin, Mrs. Ellen M.—Leopold, Belgium; Palmes Academiques, France; Officer of Public Instruction, France; Chefakat (Order of Mercy), Turkey.

Hertz, Henry—Danebrog, Denmark.

Hutchinson, Charles L.—Redeemer, Greece.

Judson, Prof. Harry Pratt—Red Eagle (class III.), Prussia; Legion of Honor (officer), France.

Klein, Dr. S. R.—"Goldenes Verdienst Kreuz mit der Krone," "Militær Kreuz" and "Jubilæum's Medaille," Austria; Takova Orden IV. Klasse, Servia.

Klenze, Prof. Camillo von—Red Eagle (class IV.), Prussia.

Kozminski, Maurice W.—Legion of Honor, France.

Kraus, Adolf—Francis Joseph, Austria.

Lagorio, Dr. Antonio—Crown (knight), Italy.

Lindgren, John R.—Royal Order of Vasa, Sweden.

Laverde, Giuseppe—Crown (chevalier), Italy.

Mair, Charles A.—Chamberlain of the Sword and Mantle, pope.

Mareschalchi, Arturo—Crown (chevalier), Italy.

Merou, Henri—Legion of Honor, France.

Miller, Harry I.—Order of the Sacred Treasure, Japan.

McCormick, R. S.—Order of St. Alexander of Nevsky, Russia.

McCormick, Mrs. R. S.—Chefakat (Order of Mercy), Turkey.

McEwen, Walter—Legion of Honor, France.

Nelson, H. P.—St. Olaf, Norway.

Onahan, William J.—Chamberlain of the Sword and Mantle, pope.

Ortengren, John R.—Vasa, Sweden.

Palmer, Mrs. Potter—Legion of Honor, France; Leopold, Belgium.

Peterson, William A.—Vasa, Sweden.

Quales, Niles T.—St. Olaf, Norway.

Reichle, C.—Crown (class IV.), Prussia.

Revell, Alexander H.—Legion of Honor (chevalier), France.

Rubens, Harry—Crown (class III.), Prussia.

Schinkel, C.—Crown (class IV.), Prussia.

Schlenker, Joseph—Frederick (class II.), Wurttemberg; Crown (class IV.), Prussia.

Schmidt, William—Crown (class IV.), Prussia.

Skiff, Frederick J. V.—Sanctified Treasure (class II.), Japan; Legion of Honor (commander), France; Crown, Italy; Leopold, Belgium.

Smulski, John F.—Cross of Knightly Order of Francis Joseph, Austria.

Starr, Prof. Frederick—Leopold II. (commander), Belgium.

Tree, Lambert—Leopold (commander), Belgium.

Urbano, Salvatore—Crown (chevalier), Italy.

Urgos, Francesco—Crown (chevalier), Italy.

Volini, Dr. Camillo—Crown (knight), Italy.

Wever, Dr. Walther—Crown (class III.), Prussia; Red Eagle (class IV.), Prussia; Ernestine House Order (class I.), Saxe-Weimar.

Ziegfeld, Carl—Officer of French Academy of Public Instruction and Fine Arts, France.

Ziegfeld, Dr. F.—Chevalier of the Legion of Honor, France.

Zimmerman, Dr. Gustav—Red Eagle (class III.), Prussia.

COAL INDUSTRY OF ILLINOIS.
Summary for year ended June 30, 1912.

Counties producing coal	52	Total number employes	79,411
Mines of all kinds	879	Persons at work underground	71,842
New mines open or mines reopened	176	Persons at work on surface	7,049
Mines closed or abandoned	142	Av. price paid gross ton—For hand mining	$0.636
Total output (tons of 2,000 lbs.)	57,514,240	For machine mining	$0.496
Shipping or commercial mines	380	Kegs of powder used	1,316,488
Output of shipping mines, tons	56,096,695	Men accidentally killed	150
Mines in local trade	499	Men injured	800
Output of local mines, tons	1,417,545	Gross tons mined to each life lost	319,524
Total tons of mine run coal	13,366,509	Number employes to each life lost	441
Total tons of lump coal	21,795,527	Deaths per 1,000 men employed	2.26
Total tons of egg coal	4,940,431	Tons mined to each man hurt	71,893
Total tons of nut coal	3,193,956	Number employes to each man hurt	99
Total tons of pea coal	11,109,191	Total coal output since 1833, tons	889,716,576
Total tons of slack coal	3,108,636	Total fatalities since 1883	3,563
Total tons shipped	51,502,382		
Tons supplied locomotives at mines	924,854		
Tons sold to local trade	2,815,678		
Tons consumed at plant	2,471,326		
Average days active operation	172		
Mines using mining machinery	133		
Mining machines in use	1,581		
Tons undercut by machines	25,550,019		
Tons mined by hand	31,964,221		
Miners employed during year	39,149		
Other employes underground	31,689		
Boys employed underground	1,526		

MAIN PRODUCING COUNTIES (1912).

County.	Tons.	County.	Tons.
Williamson	7,058,621	Montgomery	2,280,341
St. Clair	4,409,341	Bureau	1,664,092
Sangamon	5,402,065	LaSalle	1,404,599
Macoupin	4,890,622	Perry	1,394,940
Saline	4,076,756	Christian	1,340,503
Franklin	4,026,815	Marion	1,203,947
Madison	3,400,930	Peoria	1,026,151
Vermilion	3,221,314	Clinton	1,012,982
Fulton	2,333,758		

CHICAGO PARKS AND BOULEVARDS.

LINCOLN PARK SYSTEM.

Commissioners (appointed by governor with consent of senate)—Timothy J. O'Byrne, Leo Austrian, Bernard Jung, Daniel F. Rice, William Rehm, Bertram M. Winston, Amos Pettibone.

Officers—President, Timothy J. O'Byrne; vice-president, Leo Austrian; auditor, Bernard Jung; secretary, George D. Crowley; superintendent, William C. Niesen; attorney, Francis O'Shaughnessy; treasurer, Frederick H. Rawson.

Office—In Lincoln park near Clark and Center streets.

The Lincoln park district consists of the towns of North Chicago and Lake View, with Fullerton avenue as the dividing line, and is bounded on the north by Devon avenue, on the south by the Chicago river and extends from Lake Michigan on the east to the north branch of the river and North Western avenue on the west.

The area of the Lincoln park district is 12.64 square miles. The total area of the parks and boulevards is 699.94 acres, with 9.33 miles of boulevards.

Lincoln Park—Lincoln park, previously known as Lake park, began its history under its present name by resolution passed by the common council of Chicago under date of June 5, 1865. The park proper is 317 acres in extent and extends from Diversey boulevard to Oak street along the lake front. To this 235 acres of land is being added by filling in Lake Michigan north of Diversey boulevard. This extension will contain a seventy-acre yacht harbor and will have bathing facilities.

The park contains a large floral department, also an extensive zoological garden containing about 1,700 animals. Boating and bathing facilities are furnished and the park lagoon—one mile in length—gives an admirable course for racing. The Academy of Sciences is located in the park at the foot of Center street. This building was erected in 1893 and contains about 250,000 specimens. It is noted for its collection of local natural history specimens and for its complete collection of mollusks.

The park has provided facilities for outdoor games during both the winter and summer seasons.

Stanton Park—At Vedder, Vine and Rees streets; area 5 acres.

Lake Shore Playground—Area 9.160 acres; is situated between Pearson street and Chicago avenue, extending from the Chicago avenue pumping works to the lake. This park is fitted up as a playground, containing a shelter house and refectory, with outdoor gymnasium apparatus.

Seward Park—Contains 1.73 acres; is fitted with outdoor and indoor gymnasium and has a field-house which contains reading rooms, assembly hall, clubrooms, restaurant, a branch of the public library and facilities for gymnastic work and aquatic sports.

Hamlin Park—Wellington and Robey streets; area 10 acres; is fully equipped with fieldhouse and out-of-door gymnasium facilities.

Welles Park—Western avenue and Montrose boulevard; area 10 acres.

LENGTH OF NORTH SIDE BOULEVARDS.

In miles and fractions of miles.

Dearborn parkway, .123.	North avenue, .450.
Diversey parkway, 2.356.	Lincoln park, west, .450.
Fullerton parkway, .510.	North Shore, .886.
Garfield avenue, .030.	Ohio, .682.
Lake Shore drive, .745.	Sheridan road, 2.148.
Lake View, .490.	North State parkway,
Lincoln parkway, .539.	.123.

SOUTH PARKS.

Commissioners (appointed by Circuit court judges)—Albert Mohr, Charles L. Hutchinson, Joseph Donnersberger, Edward Tilden, John Barton Payne.

Officers—John Barton Payne, president; Joseph Donnersberger, auditor; George M. Reynolds, treasurer; John F. Neil, secretary; Robert Redfield, attorney; J. F. Foster, general superintendent; H. C. Carbaugh, superintendent of employment.

Offices—In Washington park, 57th street and Cottage Grove avenue.

The south park district is bounded on the north by the Chicago river and the Illinois and Michigan canal, east by Lake Michigan and the state of Indiana, south by 87th street and 138th street and west by South Cicero avenue and State street.

The area of the south park district is 92.6 square miles; population is in excess of 600,000. The total area of parks is 2,043.98 acres and of parks and boulevards 2,494.59 acres, consisting of twenty-four parks and 32.98 miles of boulevards. The following is a list of the parks and boulevards:

Jackson Park—Area 542.89 acres; bounded on the north by 56th street, east by Lake Michigan, south by 67th street and west by Stony Island avenue; this park is provided with facilities for boating, rowboats and launches, has two golf courses, one of nine holes and the other of eighteen holes, with golf shelter, lockers and showers for both men and women; it has baseball and football fields, tennis courts, refectory, beach bathing, music court, the Field museum of natural history occupying the World's Fair art building located in the northern part of the park, and in the winter skating is provided.

Washington Park—Area 371 acres; bounded on the north by 51st street, east by Cottage Grove avenue, south by 60th street, west by South Park avenue; has the same accommodations for the public as Jackson park except the golf facilities and the museum and in addition has croquet courts, archery range, horse speedway, accommodations for fly casting, wading pool and sand court for children and a house for the game of curling.

Marquette Park—Area 322.68 acres; bounded on the north by 67th street, east by California avenue, south by 71st street and west by the Grand Trunk Western railroad. The east 80 acres have been improved. It has ball fields and tennis courts and skating in the winter.

Grant Park—Area 205.14 acres; bounded on the north by Randolph street, east by Lake Michigan, south by Park row, west by Michigan avenue. This park is under construction. Temporary provision is made for athletic work in the northern part of the park. The Logan monument and the Art institute are located in this park.

Midway Plaisance—The connecting way between Washington and Jackson parks; bounded on the north by 59th street, east by Stony Island avenue, south by 60th street, west by Cottage Grove avenue. Has tennis courts and in the winter skating and hockey.

McKinley Park—Area 74.88 acres; bounded on the north by 37th street and Archer avenue, east by Robey street, south by 39th street, west by Western Avenue boulevard. Has swimming pool, outdoor gymnasiums for men and women, tennis courts, ball field, children's playground, wading pool and skating in the winter.

Gage Park—Area 20 acres; situated at the intersection of Western avenue and 55th street. Has wading pool, ball field and tennis court.

Sherman Park—Area 60.60 acres; bounded on the north by 52d street, east by South Racine avenue, south by Garfield boulevard, west by Loomis street. Has recreation buildings which include an assembly hall used by the people free of charge for various entertainments, clubrooms for meetings of the various clubs of the community, reading room supplied with periodicals by the park commissioners, luncheon, gymnasiums for men and for women, shower and plunge baths and locker rooms. There are also outdoor gymnasiums for men and women, playground for children, wading pool and swimming pool with the necessary dressing booths. Provision is made for baseball, football, tennis and boating. There is also a band stand under which concerts are given during the summer every Sunday evening. Also skating in the winter.

Ogden Park—Area 60.56 acres; bounded on the north by 64th street, east by South Racine avenue, south by 67th street, west by Loomis street. The

same facilities for recreation and pleasure are provided as in Sherman park, except lunch counter.

Palmer Park—Area 40.48 acres; bounded on the north by 111th street, east by South Park avenue, south by 113th street, west by Indiana avenue. The same facilities for recreation and pleasure are provided as in Sherman park, except boating and lunch counter.

Hamilton Park—Area 29.95 acres; bounded on the north by 72d street, east by C., R. I. & P. railway, south by 74th street, west by C. & W. I. railway. The same facilities for recreation and pleasure are provided as in Sherman park, except swimming pool and boating.

Bessemer Park—Area 22.88 acres; bounded on the north by 89th street, east by Muskegon avenue, south by 91st street, west by South Chicago avenue. The same facilities as Sherman park except lunch counter and boating.

Mark White Square—Area 10 acres; bounded on the north by 29th street, east by Halsted street, south by 30th street, west by Poplar avenue. The same facilities as Sherman park except boating and lunch counter.

Armour Square—Area 10 acres; bounded on the north by 33d street, east by 5th avenue, south by 34th street, west by Shields avenue. The same facilities as Sherman park except boating.

Cornell Square—Area 10 acres; bounded on the north by 50th street, west by South Lincoln street, south by 51st street, east by Wood street. The same facilities as Sherman park except boating and lunch counter.

Davis Square—Area 10 acres; bounded on the north by 44th street, east by Marshfield avenue, south by 45th street, west by Hermitage avenue. The same facilities as Sherman park except boating.

Russell Square—Area 11.47 acres; bounded on the north by 83d street, east by Bond avenue, south by Baker avenue, west by Houston avenue. The same facilities as Sherman park except boating and lunch counter.

Calumet Park—Area 66.19 acres; bounded on the north by 95th street, east by Lake Michigan, south by 102d street, west by Avenue G and a line about 50 feet east of C., L. S. & E. railway.

Hardin Square—Area 7.41 acres; bounded on the north by 25th street, east by the Rock Island right of way, south by 26th street, west by Wentworth avenue.

Fuller Park—Area 10 acres; bounded on the north by 45th street, east by Princeton avenue, south by 46th place, west by Stewart avenue. Improved with same facilities as Sherman park in a more extensive form.

No. 15 Park—Area 19.16 acres; bounded on the north by 76th street, east by Dobson avenue, south by 78th street, west by Ingleside avenue.

No. 16 Park—Area 18.52 acres; bounded on the north by 103d street, east by Bensley avenue, south by 105th street, west by Oglesby avenue.

No. 17 Park—Area 20 acres; bounded on the north by 130th street, east by Carondolet avenue, south by 132d street, west by Exchange avenue.

No. 18 Park—Area 20.19 acres; bounded on the north by 90th street, east by St. Lawrence avenue, south by 91st street, west by South Park avenue.

Michigan Avenue Boulevard—80 to 100 feet wide: from Garfield boulevard to Randolph street.

Garfield Boulevard—200 feet wide: from South Park avenue to Western Avenue boulevard on the line of 55th street.

Western Avenue Boulevard—200 feet wide; a strip of land east of and adjoining the center line of Western avenue from the Illinois and Michigan canal to 55th street (Garfield boulevard).

Grand Boulevard—198 feet wide: on the line of South Park avenue from 35th to 51st street.

Drexel Boulevard—200 feet wide: first street east of Cottage Grove avenue and extending from Oakwood boulevard to 51st street.

Prairie Avenue—66 feet wide; the street of that name from 16th to 29th street.

South Park Avenue—66 feet wide; being the street of that name between 35th and 29th streets.

Jackson Street—66 feet wide; being the street of that name extending from Michigan avenue to the south branch of the Chicago river.

Oakwood Boulevard—100 feet wide; the first street south of 39th street between Grand boulevard and Cottage Grove avenue.

Thirty-Third Street—66 feet wide; being the street of that name between Michigan avenue and South Park avenue.

Sixteenth Street—50 feet wide; being the street of that name between Michigan avenue and Prairie avenue.

Twenty-Ninth Street—66 feet wide; being the street of that name between Prairie avenue and South Park avenue.

Fifty-Seventh Street—100 feet wide; being the street of that name between the I. C. railroad right of way and the west line of Jackson park.

Sixty-Sixth Street—66 feet wide; being the street of that name from Jackson park to Vincennes avenue.

Vincennes Avenue—66 feet wide; from 66th street to 67th street.

Sixty-Seventh Street—66 feet wide; being the street of that name from Vincennes avenue to California avenue.

Normal Avenue—66 feet wide; from Garfield boulevard to 72d street.

Loomis Street—66 feet wide; being the street of that name from Garfield boulevard to 67th street.

Hyde Park Boulevard—100 feet wide; being that part of 51st street between Drexel avenue and East End avenue.

East End Avenue—85 feet wide; being the street of that name from 51st street to Jackson park.

Yates Avenue—100 feet wide; being the street of that name from Jackson park to 71st street.

Seventy-First Street—100 feet wide, being the street of that name from Yates avenue to Bond avenue.

Bond Avenue—66 feet wide; being the street of that name from 71st street to 83d place.

WEST CHICAGO PARKS.

Commissioners (appointed by governor with consent of senate)—John Anda, James C. Denvir, William F. Grower, Michael Kolassa, Edward Mullen, Peter J. O'Brien, Camillo Volini, M. D.

Officers—William F. Grower, president; James C. Denvir, auditor; Edward Mullen, treasurer; Timothy Cruise, secretary; Frederick Papenbrook, assistant secretary and chief accountant; Jens Jensen, consulting landscape architect; Alfred C. Schrader, superintendent and engineer; Jacob C. LeBosky, attorney; Arthur J. Stiles, captain of police.

Offices—Union park, Lake street and Ashland boulevard.

The west park district comprises all that part of the town of West Chicago lying between the Illinois and Michigan canal and the Chicago river and the following described lines: Beginning at the north branch of the Chicago river at Belmont avenue, thence west to North Kedzie avenue, thence south along Kedzie avenue to North avenue, thence west along North avenue to North Maynard avenue, thence south along Maynard avenue to 12th street, thence east along 12th street to South Kenton avenue, thence south along South Kenton avenue to West 39th street, thence east along 39th street to the Illinois and Michigan canal.

The area of the west park district is 35.5 square miles. The total area of parks and boulevards is 1,035.43 acres, consisting of thirteen parks and twenty-five miles of boulevard. Area of parks, 629.28 acres. The following is a list of the parks and boulevards.

Humboldt Park—Area 205.86 acres; bounded on the north by West North avenue, east by California and Sacramento avenues, south by Division and Augusta streets and west by Kedzie avenue; has rose garden with pergola and garden hall and fountains; refectory building, also a pavilion and boat landing, music court, a wading pool and shelter building for children; is provided with facilities for boating, has baseball diamonds and tennis courts and in winter skating and tobogganing are provided.

Garfield Park—Area 187.53 acres; bounded on the north by Kinzie and Lake streets, east by Central Park avenue and Homan avenue, south by Madi-

son street and Colorado avenue and west by Hamlin avenue. Has a conservatory, the largest in the country; refectory building, boat landing and pavilion, music court and band stand, water courts with fountain, basin and extensive flower gardens. Has a golf course with fieldhouse containing lockers for men and women; also has tennis courts and facilities for fly casting, and in winter skating, tobogganing and curling facilities are provided.

Douglas Park—Area 181.99 acres; bounded on the north by West 12th street, east by California avenue, south by 19th street and west by Albany avenue. Has refectory building, boat landing and pavilion, music court, flower gardens, outdoor gymnasium and natatorium with swimming pools, shower baths and dressing rooms for men and women. Facilities are provided for baseball, boating and lawn tennis, and in winter skating and tobogganing.

Union Park—Area 17.37 acres; bounded on the north by Lake street, east by Ogden avenue and Bryant place, south by Warren avenue and west by Ashland boulevard. In this park the offices of the West Chicago park commissioners are located. In winter facilities for skating are provided.

Jefferson Park—Area 7.02 acres; bounded on the north by Monroe street, east by Throop street, south by Adams street and west by Loomis street.

Vernon Park—Area 6.14 acres; bounded on the north by Macalister place, east by South Racine avenue, south by Gilpin place and west by Loomis street.

Wicker Park—Area 4.03 acres; bounded on the north and east by Wicker Park avenue, south by Fowler street and west by Robey street.

Holstein Park—Area 1.94 acres; bounded on the north by Elm street, south by Hamburg street and located one block east of Western avenue. Has an outdoor gymnasium and play field and shelter building, and in winter skating is provided.

Campbell Park—Area 1.38 acres; a strip of land 100 feet wide lying between Oakley boulevard and Leavitt street and one block north of Polk street.

Shedd's Park—Area 1.13 acres; located at 23d street and Millard avenue, opposite Lawndale station of the Chicago, Burlington & Quincy Railway company.

Bernard A. Eckhart Park—Area, 8.125 acres; bounded on the north by Cornell street, east by Chase street, south by Chicago avenue and west by Noble street. A fieldhouse has been provided containing gymnasium and shower baths for men and women, lunchrooms, library and reading room and assembly hall; also an outdoor swimming pool with shower baths and dressing rooms for men and women. An outdoor gymnasium for men and women, play field with wading pool and sand courts for children and tennis courts and ball grounds have been provided; also skating in the winter.

Stanford Park—Area, 2.89 acres; bounded on the north by Barber street, east by Jefferson street, south by 14th place and west by South Union avenue. In this park the same facilities for recreation and pleasure are provided as in the small parks and playgrounds mentioned above.

Dvorak Park—Area, 3.85 acres; bounded on the north by 20th street, east by Fisk street, south by 21st street and west by May street. The same facilities for recreation and pleasure are provided as in the Bernard A. Eckhart park.

Franklin Park—Area, 8.26 acres; bounded by West 14th street, West 15th street, South Keeler avenue and South Kolin avenue. Baseball and skating facilities provided.

Pulaski Park—Area, 3.2 acres; bounded by Noble, Blackhawk, Cleaver and Bradley streets; contains elaborate field house, swimming pool and other facilities for recreation.

Harrison Park—Area, 8.24 acres; bounded by West 18th street, West 19th street, South Wood street and South Lincoln street.

Sheridan Park—Area, 3.44 acres; bounded by Polk, May and Aberdeen streets and first east and west 16-foot alley north of Taylor street.

New Park in Austin ("Warren's Woods")—Area, approximately 160 acres; bounded by Adams street, Central avenue, Austin avenue and the Metropolitan elevated railroad; unimproved.

Humboldt boulevard, 2.94 miles long, 100 feet to 400 feet wide, from Diversey boulevard bridge to Humboldt park, connecting the west park system with the Lincoln park system on the north, is named for house-numbering purposes as follows:
Logan Boulevard—From the Diversey boulevard bridge to North Kedzie boulevard.
North Kedzie Boulevard—From Logan boulevard to Palmer square.
Palmer Square—From North Kedzie boulevard to Humboldt boulevard.
Humboldt Boulevard—From Palmer square to Humboldt park.

Franklin boulevard, 1.5 miles long, 250 to 400 feet wide, connecting Humboldt and Garfield parks, is named for house-numbering purposes as follows:
North Sacramento Boulevard—From Humboldt park south to Franklin boulevard.
Franklin Boulevard—West from North Sacramento boulevard to North Central Park boulevard.
North Central Park Boulevard—South from Franklin boulevard to Garfield park.

Douglas boulevard, 1.68 miles long, 250 feet wide, connecting Garfield and Douglas parks, is named for house-numbering purposes as follows:
Independence Boulevard—South from Garfield park to Douglas boulevard.
Douglas Boulevard—East from Independence boulevard to Douglas park.

Marshall boulevard, 2.17 miles long, 250 feet wide, from Douglas park to the Illinois and Michigan canal, connecting the west park system on the south with the south park system at Western avenue, is named for house-numbering purposes as follows:
Marshall Boulevard—From Douglas park south to West 24th boulevard.
West 24th Boulevard—East from Marshall boulevard to South California boulevard.
South California boulevard—From West 24th boulevard south to West 31st boulevard.
West 31st Boulevard—From South California boulevard east to South Western Avenue boulevard.
South Western Avenue Boulevard—South from West 31st boulevard to the Illinois and Michigan canal.

West Washington boulevard, 6.31 miles long, from 66 to 100 feet wide, from Canal street west to the city limits through Union park and Garfield park, a continuation of Washington street on the south side.

Jackson boulevard, 3.94 miles long, from 66 to 80 feet wide, from river west to Garfield park.

Ashland boulevard, 1.26 miles long, 100 feet wide, from Lake street south to 12th street, is named for house-numbering purposes as follows:
North Ashland Boulevard—From West Lake street south to West Madison street.
South Ashland Boulevard—South from West Madison street to West 12th boulevard.

West Twelfth Street boulevard, 0.98 mile long, 70 feet wide, from Ashland boulevard to the intersection of Oakley and Ogden boulevards, a continuation of West 12th street.

Ogden boulevard, 0.74 mile long, from 70 to 112 feet wide, from the intersection of Oakley boulevard and West 12th boulevard through Douglas park.

South Central Park boulevard, 0.33 mile long, 80 feet wide, from West Madison street to Colorado avenue, along the east side of Garfield park.

Oakley boulevard, 1.10 miles long, from Washington boulevard to the intersection of West 12th boulevard and Ogden boulevard, is named for house-numbering purposes as follows:
North Oakley Boulevard—South from West Washington boulevard to West Madison street.
South Oakley Boulevard—South from West Madison street to West 12th boulevard.

North Homan boulevard, 0.25 mile long, from West Lake street to West Madison street, along the east side of Garfield park.

Sacramento avenue, 1.59 miles long, from Franklin boulevard to Douglas park, is named for house-numbering purposes as follows:

North Sacramento Boulevard—From Franklin boulevard south to West Madison street.

South Sacramento Boulevard—From West Madison street south to Douglas park.

SMALL PARKS AND PLAYGROUNDS.

Special Park Commission (appointed by the mayor) —Aldermen A. W. Beilfus (chairman), Henry D. Capitain, John J. Coughlin, Edward F. Cullerton and Frank McDonald, and Messrs. Oscar F. Mayer, Jens Jensen, Cyril Fiala, Paul Drzymalski, Peter S. Goodman, George Landau, Charles E. Bock, F. A. Lindstrand, Samuel J. Rosenblatt, Rev. Julius Rappaport.

Secretary—Walter Wright.

Superintendent of Parks and Acting Forester—J. H. Prost.

Superintendent of Playgrounds and Bathing Beaches —Theodore A. Gross.

Office of Commission—1004 city hall.

The special park commission is appointed by the mayor by authority of the city council. It has charge of a number of small parks and squares which are under the immediate jurisdiction of the city, and it also conducts several bathing beaches on the lake shore and a number of municipal playgrounds. The parks are provided with ornamental and drinking fountains, wherever it is practicable, lagoons, swings, tennis courts and landscape and other features according to circumstances. The playgrounds are provided with play apparatus, athletic fields, baseball diamonds, basket-ball courts, skating ponds, drinking fountains, running tracks, gymnastic apparatus and buildings containing toilet rooms, offices, sand courts and roofed platforms. The bathing beaches are provided with bathhouses containing dressing rooms, lockers, checkrooms, washrooms, toilets and office.

In 1912 the total appropriation was $150,382.54. The expenditures amounted to $119,287.05, distributed as follows: Parks, $49,318.59; playgrounds, $52,517.27; forestry, $8,094.18; beaches, $5,568.97, and office, $3,788.04.

Following is a list of the small parks, playgrounds and bathing beaches in charge of the special park commission, with the area of the parks in acres. Two parks maintained privately are included in the list and are so described:

Adams Park—75th place, 76th street and Dobson avenue; 1½.

Aldine Square—Vincennes avenue, 37th place and alley north of 38th place; 1½.

Amy L. Barnard Park—105th street, between Longwood boulevard and Walden parkway; 1¼.

Arbor Rest—Chestnut, Rush and Cass streets; ⅛.

Arcade Park—111th place, 112th street, Morse avenue and Watt avenue; ⅞.

Archer Point—Archer avenue, 20th street and Dearborn street; ⅛.

Auburn Park—Normal, Stewart and Hawthorne avenues.

Austin Park—Waller avenue, Northwestern railway, Austin avenue and Lake street; 4½.

Belden Avenue Triangle—North Clark street, Sedgwick street and Belden avenue; ⅛.

Bickerdike Square—Ohio street, Bickerdike street, Emerson avenue and Armour place; 1¾.

Blackstone Point—Lake Park avenue, Blackstone avenue and 49th street; ⅛.

Buena Circle—Buena avenue and Kenmore avenue; ½.

Buena Terrace—Sheridan road, Broadway and Buena terrace.

Chamberlin Triangle—Greenwood avenue, 43d street and Lake Park avenue; 27-100.

Colorado Point—Colorado avenue, Monroe street and Francisco avenue; ⅓.

Columbus Circle—Exchange avenue, South Chicago avenue and 92d street.

Congress Park—Van Buren street, Rockwell street, Harrison street and Washtenaw avenue; ¾.

DeKalb Square—Lexington street, Hoyne avenue, Flournoy street and DeKalb street; ¾.

Dickinson Park—North Lavergne avenue, Dickinson avenue and Belle Plaine avenue; 1⅛.

Douglas Monument Park—Woodland park, Illinois Central, 35th street and alley west of railroad; 3.

East End Park—East End avenue, 51st street, 53d street and the lake; 10.

Eldred Grove—Long avenue, Norwood Park avenue, North Lockwood and Northwestern railway; 1.

Ellis Park—36th street, Langley avenue, 37th street and Elmwood court; 4.

Eugenie Triangle—Eugenie street, North Clark street and North LaSalle street; ⅛.

Fernwood Park—103d street, 95th street, Stewart avenue and Canal street; 8.

Gage Farm and Nursery—22d street, 26th street, west of Oak Park avenue; 240 acres.

Green Bay Triangle—North State street, Rush street and Bellevue place; ⅓.

Gross Park—Otto street, North Paulina street, School street, Ravenswood avenue; ½.

Groveland (private)—Cottage Grove avenue, 34th street and Illinois Central railway; 3⅛.

Harding Avenue Parkway—West Byron and West Addison streets and Springfield and North Crawford avenues.

Holden Park—Lake street, West Grand avenue, Central avenue and Park avenue; 4.

Irving Park—Irving Park boulevard, Northwestern railway, near North Keeler avenue; ⅛.

Kedzie Park—Kedzie avenue, between Palmer place and North avenue; 2.

Kinzie Parkway—Kinzie street, between North Laramie avenue and Willow avenue; 1¼.

Lakewood Point—Greenwood avenue, Lake Park avenue and 43d street; .27.

Lily Gardens, The—Lowe avenue, Chicago and Western Indiana railroad, 71st and 73d streets; 3.

Merrick Park—Pine avenue, Willow avenue, East Grand avenue and Kinzie street; 6½.

Midway, The—Midway, between Waller and Austin avenues; 1⅛.

Montrose Point—Montrose avenue, Sheridan road and Broadway.

Mulberry Point—Nickerson avenue, Ceylon avenue and Mulberry avenue; ⅖.

McKenna Triangle—38th street, Archer avenue and Campbell avenue.

Normal Park—67th street, 69th street, Lowe avenue and Western Indiana railroad; 2½.

Norwood Circle—Hobart avenue, Colfax place and Circle avenue; 2½.

Oak Park—Oak, Rush and State streets; ⅛.

Oakland Park—Lake Park avenue, 39th street and Illinois Central road; ¾.

Ogden Arrow—North Clark street, Wells street and Ogden front; ⅖.

Patterson Park—Leavitt, Boone and DeKalb streets; ¾.

Pullman Park—111th street and place, Cottage Grove avenue and Morse avenue; ⅝.

Rice Triangle—Grand avenue and Western avenue; ⅓.

Rocky Ledge—Lake Michigan and 79th street; 3¼.

Railway Gardens—Avondale and Ceylon avenues, south of Northwestern railroad; also on Norwood Park avenue, north of Northwestern railroad; 2½.

Roberts Square—Winnemac avenue, North Laramie avenue, Argyle avenue and North Lockwood avenue; 5.

Rutherford Park—Humboldt, North New England and North Oak Park avenues; 4⅛.

Sacramento Avenue Parking—Sacramento avenue, 26th street and House of Correction; ⅛.

Sayre Park—New England avenue, West Belden avenue, Newcastle avenue and Humboldt avenue; 3½.

Schoenhofen Place—Canal street, Canalport avenue and 18th street; ¾.

Washington Square—North Clark street, Walton place, North Dearborn street and Brenan street. 3.

Winnemac Avenue Park—Robey street, Winnemac avenue, Foster avenue and Clay street; 40.

Woodland Park (private)—Cottage Grove avenue, Illinois Central road, between 34th and 35th streets; 2¾.

UNIMPROVED.

Crescent Park—Hennepin street, Prescott avenue, Ormonde avenue and Grassmere road; 8.

Dauphin Park—87th street, Illinois Central line, 91st street and Dauphin avenue; 5⅓.

Governor's Parkway—North St. Louis avenue, North Homan avenue and West Kinzie street.

Higgins Road Triangle—Milwaukee avenue and Higgins road.

Kosciusko Triangle—Kosciusko avenue, between Milwaukee avenue and Melvina avenue; ⅓.

Parkway—In center of Canal street, between West 43d street and West 44th street.

Parkway—In North Avers avenue, bounded by North Springfield avenue, Northwestern railroad, North Hamlin avenue and West Addison street.

Triangle at West Belmont avenue, Elston avenue and California avenue.

Triangle at West 69th street, Vincennes avenue and Lafayette avenue.

Triangle at Blue Island avenue, 16th street and Throop street.

MUNICIPAL PLAYGROUNDS.

Names, location and dimensions of the municipal playgrounds in Chicago:

Corkery—South Kildare avenue and 25th street; 157 by 266.

George E. Adams—Seminary avenue, south of Center street; 102 by 288 feet.

Audubon—Hoyne avenue, Cornelia avenue and Hamilton avenue; 125 by 165 feet.

Holden—Bonfield street, near West 35th; 696 by 116 feet.

Commercial Club—West Chicago avenue, near North Lincoln street, main ground, 200 by 125 feet; annex, 120 by 123 feet.

John B. Drake—Calumet avenue, between 26th and 28th streets; 194 by 181 feet.

Mosely—Wabash avenue and 24th street; 200 by 200 feet.

McLaren—West Polk street, near Laflin; 175 by 185 feet.

Northwestern Elevated—Alaska and Larrabee streets; 90 by 350 feet.

Sampson—15th street, near Loomis; 215 by 125 feet.

Hamlin Avenue—Springfield avenue, Hamlin avenue, 16th street, north to Avers avenue; 309 by 593 feet.

Orleans—Institute place and Orleans street; 136 by 126 feet.

Max Beutner—Wentworth avenue and 33d and La Salle street; 113 by 200 and 346 by 258 feet.

Wrightwood Avenue—Corner Greenview and Wrightwood avenues; 454 by 361 feet.

McCormick—Sawyer avenue and 28th street; 275 by 125 feet.

Walter Christopher—22d street, west of Robey; 325 by 125 feet.

Dante—Forquer and Ewing streets, west of Desplaines; 90 by 235 feet.

Washington—Carpenter street and Grand avenue; 128 by 174 feet.

Fiske—Ingleside avenue and 62d street; 400 by 300.

MUNICIPAL BATHING BEACHES.

Walker—Lake Michigan, foot of 25th street.

Rocky Ledge—Lake Michigan, foot of 79th street.

Swimming Pool—Washington Heights; 104th street, Vincennes road and Charles street.

SUMMARY OF PARK AREAS.

South park system (acres)	2,494.59
West park system	1,218.57
Lincoln park system	699.94
Other parks and squares	143.56
Unimproved	54.83
Total	4,611.49

CHICAGO TELEPHONE RATES.

Under ordinance passed by city council May 26, 1913.

Following are the maximum rates which may be charged by the Chicago Telephone company for a period of five years or until May, 1918:

MEASURED RATE SERVICE.

BUSINESS.

For single party line, including 960 outgoing conversations, messages or calls, $48 a year; next 240 outgoing messages, 5 cents each; next 1,200 messages, 3 cents each; next 1,200 messages, 2½ cents each; for all messages in excess of 3,600, 2 cents each.

For single party line, including 1,200 outgoing messages, $60 a year; next 1,200 messages, 3 cents each; next 1,200 messages, 2½ cents each; all messages in excess of 3,600, 2 cents each.

RESIDENCE.

For single party line, including 800 outgoing messages, $40 a year; next 400 messages, 4 cents each; next 1,200 messages, 3 cents each; next 1,200 messages, 2½ cents each; all messages in excess of 3,600, 2 cents each.

FLAT RATE SERVICE.

BUSINESS.

For single party line, including not to exceed 500 outgoing messages, in any one month, $10.42 per month; all messages in excess of 500 in any one month, 2 cents each. Present subscribers to single party business line, with right to unlimited use of same at $125 a year, have the right to a continuance of the same service at the same rate.

RESIDENCE.

For a single party line, including all messages, $18 per quarter.

For a two-party line, including all messages, $14 per quarter.

NICKEL COIN BOX SERVICE.

NICKEL FIRST.

One-party line, at a guarantee of 20 cents a day, including four messages.

Two-party line, at a guarantee of 12½ cents a day, including two and one-half messages.

Two party line (for residences only), at a guarantee of 10 cents a day, including two messages.

Four-party line (for residences only), at a guarantee of 5 cents a day, including one message.

Additional messages in excess of the guaranteed number per day in each of foregoing cases, 4 cents each.

At the time of making collection the company shall allow subscribers 1 cent for each message in excess of the total guaranteed number of messages since the last preceding collection.

NICKEL LAST.

Nickel last rates are the same as nickel first rates except that all messages in excess of guaranteed number are 5 cents each.

DEFICIENCY PAYMENTS.

Subscribers making deficiency payments shall be given receipts therefor and if at any succeeding collection within sixty days there is an excess amount in the box it shall be applied to the repayment of the deficiency collected.

GOVERNORS OF ILLINOIS.

Shadrach Bond, Dem	1818-1822	John Wood. Rep	1860-1861	John R. Tanner, Rep	1897-1901
Edward Coles, Dem	1822-1826	Richard Yates. Rep	1861-1865	Richard Yates, Jr., Rep	1901-1905
Ninian Edwards, Dem	1826-1820	Richard J. Oglesby, Rep	1865-1869	Charles S. Deneen, Rep	1905-1909
John Reynolds, Dem	1830-1834	John M. Palmer,‡ Rep	1869-1873	Charles S. Deneen, Rep	1909-1913
Wm. L. D. Ewing,* Dem	1834-1834	Richard J. Oglesby, Rep	1873-1873	Edward F. Dunne, Dem	1913-
Joseph Duncan, Whig	1834-1838	John L. Beveridge, Rep	1873-1877	*Served only fifteen days, completing Reynolds' term. †Died in office; succeeded by John Wood. ‡Democrat after 1872. §Elected United States senator; succeeded by John M. Hamilton.	
Thomas Carlin, Dem	1838-1842	Shelby M. Cullom, Rep§	1877-1883		
Thomas Ford, Dem	1842-1846	John M. Hamilton, Rep	1883-1885		
Augustus C. French, Dem	1846-1853	Richard J. Oglesby, Rep	1885-1889		
Joel A. Matteson, Dem	1853-1857	Joseph W. Fifer, Rep	1889-1893		
Wm. H. Bissell.† Rep	1857-1860	John P. Altgeld, Dem	1893-1897		

LICENSE RATES IN CHICAGO DEC. 1, 1913.

Per year unless otherwise specified.

AMUSEMENTS.

	Rate.
Theaters—	
(a) Highest admission fee, except for box seats, $1.00 or more..........................	$1,000.00
(b) Highest admission fee, except for box seats, exceeds 50c but is less than $1.00...	400.00
(c) Highest admission fee, except for box seats, exceeds 30c but does not exceed 50c	300.00
(d) Highest admission fee, except for box seats, exceeds 20c, but does not exceed 30c	250.00
(e) Highest admission fee, except for box seats, does not exceed 20c.................	200.00
Lectures, art exhibits, etc..................	200.00
Concerts	100.00
Penny arcades, etc............................	200.00
Halls for Dances, Bazaars, etc.—	
(a) Seating capacity not exceeding 300 persons	25.00
(b) Seating capacity more than 300 persons but not exceeding 500 persons........	50.00
(c) Seating capacity more than 500 persons but not exceeding 800 persons........	75.00
(d) Seating capacity exceeding 800 persons	100.00
Summer gardens, per week..................	20.00
Amusement parks, per week..................	40.00
Picnic grounds..............................	10.00
Roller or ice skating rinks..................	200.00
Baseball, Football, Etc., Fields—	
(a) Seating capacity 15,000 persons or more	1,000.00
(b) Seating capacity less than 15,000 persons but not less than 10,000 persons....	700.00
(c) Seating capacity less than 10,000 persons but more than 4,000 persons........	300.00
(d) Seating capacity not exceeding 4,000 persons	75.00
Wrestling Matches—	
(a) Seating capacity 500 persons or less, per day.................................	5.00
(b) Seating capacity more than 500 persons but not more than 1,000 persons, per day	10.00
(c) Seating capacity more than 1,000 persons but not more than 2,000 persons, per day.................................	20.00
(d) Seating capacity more than 2,000 persons but not more than 3,000 persons, per day.................................	30.00
(e) Seating capacity more than 3,000 persons but not more than 4,000 persons, per day.................................	40.00

	Rate.
Wrestling matches—	
(f) Seating capacity more than 4,000 persons but less than 5,000 persons, per day	$50.00
(g) Seating capacity 5,000 persons or more, per day..............................	60.00
Poultry, Horse, Stock, Dog, Etc., Shows—	
(a) Highest admission fee exceeds 75c, per day.................................	25.00
(b) Highest admission fee exceeds 50c, but does not exceed 75c, per day............	15.00
(c) Highest admission fee exceeds 10c, but does not exceed 50c, per day............	10.00
(d) Highest admission fee does not exceed 10c, per day.............................	1.00
Circuses, Menageries, etc.—	
(a) Seating capacity more than 6,000 persons, per day..........................	150.00
(b) Seating capacity more than 3,000 persons but not more than 6,000 persons, per day.................................	50.00
(c) Seating capacity more than 1,500 persons but not more than 3,000 persons, per day.................................	35.00
(d) Seating capacity more than 750 persons but not more than 1,500 persons, per day	25.00
(e) Seating capacity more than 400 persons but not more than 750 persons, per day	10.00
(f) Seating capacity not more than 400 persons, per month.........................	10.00
Air domes, sideshows, etc., per day.....	10.00
Swimming and diving shows, per week.....	2.00
Platform, walk-around, etc., shows, per week	2.00
Skill and strength testing devices, per week	.50
Merry-Go-Rounds, Coasters, etc.—	
(a) Highest fee or fare for one ride does not exceed 5c, per week...............	2.00
(b) Highest fee or fare for one ride exceeds 5c but does not exceed 10c, per week	5.00
(c) Highest fee or fare for one ride exceeds 10c, per week.......................	10.00
Pony or animal rides, etc., per week.......	.50
Fireworks exhibitions, per day.............	50.00
Entertainments not included in the foregoing, per day.............................	5.00

NOTE—Where a license fee is fixed at so much per week, no license to issue for a less period than ten weeks.

MISCELLANEOUS.

	Rate.
Acetylene gas, collection or compression of.............	$150.00
Acetylene gas, sale or distribution of................	5.00
Auctioneers	300.00
Auctioneers, special sales, per day.....................	10.00
Automobiles, public passenger (on stands), seating three persons or less.....	2.50
Automobiles, public passenger (on stands), seating four to eight persons......	5.00
Automobiles, public passenger (on stands), seating nine to twenty persons...	10.00
Automobiles, public passenger (on stands), seating more than twenty persons	25.00
Automobiles, public passenger (not on stands)........	5.00
Automobiles, passenger, 35 horse power or less (wheel tax)	10.00
Automobiles, passenger, more than 35 horse power (wheel tax).................	20.00
Automobile delivery wagons, capacity less than one ton (wheel tax)..............	15.00
Automobile trucks (wheel tax)	30.00
Automobiles, demonstrating or testing (wheel tax).....	1.00

	Rate.
Automobiles (state fee)—	
25 horse power or less....	4.00
35 horse power and more than 25 horse power....	6.00
50 horse power and more than 35 horse power....	8.00
More than 50 horse power	10.00
Electric vehicles............	5.00
Manufacturers of and dealers in....................	15.00
Bakeries	5.00
Bathing beaches, etc.......	15.00
Billiard and pool tables, each	5.00
Bill posting, with wagons.	100.00
Bill posting, without wagons	25.00
Boarding stables..........	10.00
Boats, launches, etc., $2.00, 10.00 and............	25.00
Bowling alleys, each........	5.00
Brewers	500.00
Brokers	25.00
Cabs, public...............	1.00
Carbonated waters, etc.....	20.00
Cars, elevated railway, each	50.00
Cartridges and shells, $10.00 and	25.00
Catch basins and sewers, cleaners of, per wagon..	10.00
Chauffeurs (state fee)—Original	5.00
Chauffeurs (state fee)—Renewal	3.00
Cigarette dealers...........	100.00

	Rate.
Coupes, public.............	1.00
Deadly weapons, dealers in	25.00
Delicatessen stores.........	5.00
Detective agencies.........	100.00
Distillers	500.00
Dispensaries, medical......	20.00
*Dogs	2.00
Drain layers...............	5.00
Drivers of public passenger horse-drawn vehicles....	1.00
Drug stores................	5.00
Dry cleaners...............	15.00
Electrical contractor, certificate of registration (renewal $10.00)............	25.00
Engineers, stationary......	2.00
Fireworks, sale of..........	10.00
Fireworks, permit to discharge	10.00
Fitness, certificates of (for handling high explosives)	5.00
Fishmongers	15.00
Garages	25.00
Gunpowder and explosives, sale or use of.........	25.00
Hacks, public..............	2.50
Hospitals	100.00
Hotels	15.00
Housemovers	15.00
Ice dealers, retail, per wagon	10.00
Junk dealers...............	50.00
Junk wagons, each.........	10.00
Liquors, malt, wholesale (one to six gallons)............	50.00

	Rate.		Rate.		Rate.
Liquors, malt, wholesale (more than six gallons at a time)	500.00	Omnibuses, public	5.00	Sale stable	25.00
		Operators of public motor vehicles (original)	3.00	Saloons	1,000.00
Liquors, spirituous, wholesale	100.00	Operators of public motor vehicles (renewal)	2.00	Scavengers, night	50.00
Liquors, vinous, wholesale..	50.00	Pawnbrokers	300.00	Scavengers, offal	100.00
Liquors, malt and vinous, in amusement places (by special permit), per day..	6.00	Peddlers—Basket	10.00	Scavengers, private, per wagon	5.00
		Coal, charcoal and coke..	5.00	Second-hand dealers	50.00
Livery stables	10.00	Fish (Thursdays and Fridays only)	15.00	Shooting galleries	25.00
Lumber dealers	100.00	Hand cart	25.00	Slaughtering, rendering, etc.	300.00
Marriage (county)	1.50	Oil, per wagon	10.00	Soap factories	150.00
Meat markets	15.00	Pack	15.00	Tanneries	50.00
Milk dealers	10.00	Wagon, each	50.00	Tenders, boiler or water	1.00
Milk peddlers, per wagon..	10.00	Wood, per wagon	10.00	Tickers	1.00
Motor bicycles and motor tricycles (wheel tax)	3.00	Plumbers, master or employing (renewal $10.00)...	50.00	Undertakers	10.00
Motor bicycles (state fee)..	2.00	Plumbers, journeymen	1.00	Undertakers' assist. (permit)	5.00
Moving picture films, storage of	25.00	Poulterers	15.00	Vehicles (wheel tax)—	
		Public cart, horse-drawn ("express"), each	1.00	One-horse	5.00
Moving picture operators (original)	3.00	Public cart, automobiles ("express")	15.00	Two-horse	10.00
				Three-horse	15.00
Moving picture operators (renewal)	2.00	Public passenger horse-drawn vehicles (not on stands)..	5.00	Four-horse	25.00
Moving picture operators (assistant)	1.00	Rendering tanks, each	20.00	Six (or more) horse	35.00
Natatoriums and swimming pools	15.00	Restaurants	15.00	Weighers, public	10.00
Nurseries, public	10.00	Roofers, composition	10.00	Workshops	2.00
		Runners	25.00	*On and after May 1, 1914, the registration fee for each male or spayed female dog will be $2.00, and $3.00 for each unspayed female dog.	

HOUSE NUMBER SYSTEM IN CHICAGO.

[From report of John D. Riley, superintendent of maps.]

Sept. 20, 1910, the city council passed an amendment to the house number ordinance (of Sept. 1, 1909), the effect of which was to include the downtown district in the new system of numbers, making the same complete for the entire city, the change becoming effective, so far as the downtown district was concerned, April 1, 1911.

The system is laid out on two base lines, State street dividing the east and west streets and Madison street dividing the north and south streets, the numbers being assigned on the basis of 800 numbers to each mile or 100 numbers to the prevailing city block of 660 feet or one eighth of a mile. An exception to this assignment, however, is made on the north and south streets between Madison street and 31st street, in which territory 1,200 numbers are assigned between Madison and 12th streets, 1,000 between 12th and 22d streets and 900 between 22d and 31st streets. This was necessitated by reason of the fact that it was not deemed expedient or advisable to interfere with the system of numbered streets on the south side.

The system further provides for the use of the prefixes "North," "South," "East" and "West" on all streets which either cross or are open on either side of the base lines and on all streets of numerical nomenclature, whether open on either side of the base line or not. Names of streets open only on one side of either of the base lines do not carry the prefix, the result of this being that all of the east and west streets north of North avenue, at about which point the line of State street runs into Lake Michigan, do not require the use of the prefix "West." This, of course, also applies to such streets as Plymouth court, Polk street and all other named streets open on only one side of either of the base lines.

In the assignment of numbers in the downtown district it was not possible to have 100 numbers to each block by reason of the fact that the blocks, instead of being laid out on the basis of one-eighth of a mile or 660 feet long, are approximately only 400 feet. The assignment, however, was made in as systematic a manner as possible. On the east and west streets downtown, commencing at State street and running west, we get numbers 1 and 2 at State, 50 Dearborn, 100 Clark, 150 LaSalle, 200 5th avenue, 300 Franklin, 350 Market, the terminating numbers at the river picking up those heretofore assigned on the same streets west of the river. On the east and west streets running east of State street we get numbers 1 and 2 at State, 50 at Wabash, the terminating numbers at the west side of Michigan avenue being something less than 100. On the north and south streets, going north from Madison street, we get 1 and 2 at Madison, 100 Washington, 150 Randolph, 200 Lake and 300 South Water street, the terminating numbers at the river picking up with those heretofore assigned to the same streets north of the river. Going south from Madison street on the north and south streets we commence with 1 and 2 at Madison street, 100 Monroe, 200 Adams, 300 Jackson, 400 Van Buren, 500 Congress, 800 Polk, 1000 Taylor and 1200 12th street, all of those numbers being in conformity with those for the same streets as heretofore assigned west of the river. In the business district downtown an individual number is assigned to each entrance on the street level.

GROWTH OF CHICAGO IN AREA.

Date.	Added. Sq. mi.	Total. Sq. mi.	Date.	Added. Sq. mi.	Total. Sq. mi.	Date.	Added. Sq. mi.	Total. Sq. mi.
Feb. 11, 1835 (original town)		2.550	Feb. 27, 1869	11.380	35.662	April 7, 1891	.981	180.138
March 4, 1837 (city incorporated)	8.085	10.635	May 16, 1887	1.000	36.662	April 4, 1893	3.875	184.013
			April 29, 1889	7.150	43.812	Nov. 7, 1893	2.125	186.138
Feb. 16, 1847	3.375	14.010	June 29, 1889	126.070	169.882	Feb. 25, 1895	1.000	187.138
Feb. 12, 1853	3.988	17.998	April 1, 1890	1.773	171.655	April 4, 1899	3.500	190.638
Feb. 13, 1863	6.284	24.282	May 12, 1890	2.899	174.564	Nov. 8, 1910	.687	191.325
			Nov. 4, 1890	4.603	179.157			

The original town of Chicago in 1835 extended from Chicago avenue on the north to 12th street on the south and from Halsted street on the west to Lake Michigan on the east. When the city was incorporated in 1837 the city limits were as follows: From Lake Michigan west along Center street to North Clark street, south to North avenue, west to Wood street, south to 22d street and east to the lake. The largest addition to the area of the city was made in 1889, when Lake View, Jefferson, Hyde Park and Lake were annexed. Edison Park was annexed Nov. 8, 1910. The annexation of Morgan Park in 1911 was declared illegal by the State Supreme court in 1912.

CHICAGO BASEBALL CHAMPIONSHIP.

The Cubs of the National league and the White Sox of the American league played for the 1913 baseball championship of Chicago with the following result:

WEST SIDE, OCT. 8.

Cubs.	AB.	R.	H.	TB.	BB.	SH.	SB.	PO.	A.	E.
Leach, cf	5	0	3	4	0	0	0	1	0	
Evers, 2b	5	0	1	1	0	0	0	5	3	0
Schulte, lf	4	0	0	0	0	0	0	0	0	
Zimmerman, 3b	5	0	1	1	0	0	0	2	3	0
Saier, 1b	5	2	2	5	0	0	0	12	2	0
Good, rf	4	2	2	5	0	0	0	1	0	0
Bridwell, ss	3	0	1	2	1	0	0	1	5	3
Archer, c	3	0	2	3	0	1	0	6	4	0
Cheney, p	3	0	0	0	0	0	0	0	2	0
*Williams	1	0	0	0	0	0	0	0	0	0
Lavender, p	0	0	0	0	0	0	0	0	0	0
Total	38	4	12	21	1	1	0	27	20	3

*Batted for Cheney in the eighth inning.

White Sox.	AB.	R.	H.	TB.	BB.	SH.	SB.	PO.	A.	E.
Weaver, ss	5	0	2	3	0	0	0	4	1	
Lord, 3b	4	1	1	2	1	0	0	0	0	
Chase, 1b	2	1	0	1	1	0	0	10	0	1
Bodie, cf	3	1	1	2	1	0	0	2	0	0
Collins, rf	4	1	2	2	0	0	0	1	0	0
Chappell, lf	3	0	1	2	2	0	1	3	0	0
Schalk, c	4	2	2	3	0	0	0	9	0	0
Berger, 2b	3	0	1	1	1	0	0	3	3	0
Russell, p	4	0	1	1	0	0	0	1	2	0
Scott, p	0	0	0	0	0	0	0	0	1	0
Total	32	6	11	19	4	2	0	27	10	2

Cubs ....9 0 0 1 0 2 0 1 0—4
White Sox ....2 0 0 1 0 2 1 0—6

Two base hits—Weaver, Chappell, Schalk, Bridwell, Collins, Lord, Bodie, Archer, Leach. Three base hit—Collins. Home runs—Good, Saier. Struck out—By Cheney, Weaver, Collins, Chappell; by Lavender, Lord; by Russell, Schulte (2), Zimmerman, Good, Cheney, Archer; by Scott, Williams. Bases on balls—Off Cheney, 4; off Russell, 1. Double plays—Berger-Chase; Russell-Chase. Hits—Off Cheney, 11 in 8 innings; off Russell, 11 in 7⅔ innings. Hit by pitcher—By Russell, Chase. Wild pitch—Russell. Time—2:08. Umpires—O'Day at plate, Sheridan on bases, Orth and O'Loughlin in outfield.

SOUTH SIDE, OCT. 9.

White Sox.	AB.	R.	H.	TB.	BB.	SH.	SB.	PO.	A.	E.
Weaver, ss	6	0	1	1	0	0	0	6	7	1
Lord, 3b	4	1	1	1	0	0	3	4	0	
Chase, 1b	6	1	1	1	0	0	0	17	2	0
Bodie, cf	4	2	2	2	0	1	0	2	0	
Fournier, rf	1	0	0	0	0	0	0	0	0	
Collins, rf-cf	6	1	2	2	0	0	0	3	0	0
Chappell, lf	6	0	2	2	0	0	0	3	1	0
Schalk, c	6	0	0	0	0	0	0	5	1	1
Berger, 2b	5	0	1	1	0	0	0	3	1	
Cicotte, p	3	0	1	1	0	0	0	2	0	
Benz, p	3	0	0	0	0	0	0	6	0	
Total	49	5	11	11	2	1	0	39	26	3

Cubs.	AB.	R.	H.	TB.	BB.	SH.	SB.	PO.	A.	E.
Leach, cf	5	1	1	1	0	0	2	0	0	
Evers, 2b	4	1	2	2	1	0	1	6	1	
Schulte, lf	6	1	2	2	0	0	1	1	0	
Zimmerman, 3b	6	2	2	2	0	0	0	1	1	
Saier, 1b	4	0	0	0	1	0	0	21	0	
Good, rf	6	1	1	1	0	0	0	3	0	
Bridwell, ss	3	0	0	0	3	0	0	3	5	1
Archer, c	4	0	2	3	1	1	0	8	1	0
Vaughn, p	5	0	0	0	0	0	0	0	3	0
Total	44	6	10	11	7	2	0	39	18	3

White Sox......0 0 0 3 0 1 0 1 0 0 0 0—5
Cubs ....0 0 0 4 1 0 0 0 0 0 0 1—6

Two base hit—Archer. Struck out—by Cicotte, Evers, Vaughn; by Benz, Zimmerman, Saier; by Vaughn, Benz (2), Chappell, Fournier, Collins, Schalk. Bases on balls—Off Cicotte, 3; off Vaughn, 2; off Benz, 4. Double play—Lord (unassisted). Hits—Off Cicotte, 6 in 4 innings and 3 men at bat in fifth. Wild pitches—Vaughn, Benz. Time—2:55. Umpires—O'Loughlin at plate, Orth on bases, Sheridan and O'Day in outfield.

WEST SIDE, OCT. 10.

Cubs.	AB.	R.	H.	TB.	BB.	SH.	SB.	PO.	A.	E.
Leach, cf	5	1	1	2	0	0	0	2	0	0
Evers, 2b	3	2	1	1	2	0	0	1	2	0
Schulte, lf	4	2	3	3	0	0	0	5	0	0
Zimmerman, 3b	4	1	1	1	0	0	0	0	1	0
Saier, 1b	3	1	1	1	1	0	0	8	0	0
Good, rf	4	1	2	2	0	0	1	0	0	
Bridwell, ss	4	0	1	1	0	0	0	2	3	0
Archer, c	4	0	0	0	0	0	0	8	0	0
Humphries, p	3	0	0	0	0	0	0	0	1	0
Total	34	8	10	11	3	0	0	27	7	0

White Sox.	AB.	R.	H.	TB.	BB.	SH.	SB.	PO.	A.	E.
Weaver, ss	4	0	0	0	0	0	0	3	1	2
Lord, 3b	4	0	1	2	0	0	1	0	0	
Chase, 1b	4	0	1	2	0	0	0	6	0	0
Bodie, cf	4	0	0	0	0	0	0	1	0	1
Collins, rf	3	0	1	1	0	0	0	3	0	1
Fournier, lf	2	0	0	0	0	1	0	1	0	0
Schalk, c	3	0	0	0	0	0	0	5	3	0
Berger, 2b	2	0	0	0	0	0	0	3	2	1
*Easterly	1	0	0	0	0	0	0	0	0	0
Breton, 2b	0	0	0	0	0	0	0	1	0	0
Scott, p	2	0	0	0	0	0	0	0	1	0
†Chappell	1	0	1	1	0	0	0	0	0	0
Lathrop, p	0	0	0	0	0	0	0	0	0	0
Total	30	0	4	6	0	1	0	24	7	5

*Batted for Berger in eighth. †Batted for Scott in eighth.

Cubs ....0 0 0 0 0 3 5 0 *—8
White Sox ....0 0 0 0 0 0 0 0 0—0

Two base hits—Chase, Lord, Leach. Struck out—By Humphries, Schalk (2), Berger, Scott, Bodie (2), Chase; by Scott, Bridwell, Zimmerman, Saier. Bases on balls—Off Scott, 3. Double play—Schalk-Lord. Hits—Off Scott, 10 in 7 innings. Hit by pitcher—By Scott, Humphries. Time—1:53. Umpires—O'Day at plate, Sheridan on bases, Orth and O'Loughlin in outfield.

SOUTH SIDE, OCT. 11.

White Sox.	AB.	R.	H.	TB.	BB.	SH.	SB.	PO.	A.	E.
Weaver, ss	5	2	3	5	0	0	2	2	1	
Lord, 3b	4	1	1	1	0	0	4	1	
Chase, 1b	4	0	1	1	0	0	8	0	0
Bodie, cf	4	0	1	1	0	0	0	0	0
Collins, rf-cf	4	0	0	0	0	0	0	0	0
Fournier, lf	3	0	2	2	1	0	4	0	0
Schalk, c	4	0	1	1	0	0	12	0	0
Berger, 2b	4	0	0	0	0	0	0	2	1
Cicotte, p	4	2	3	5	0	0	0	1	0
Total	36	5	13	17	3	0	0	27	9	3

Cubs.	AB.	R.	H.	TB.	BB.	SH.	SB.	PO.	A.	E.
Leach, cf	5	0	0	0	0	0	1	1	6	
Evers, 2b	4	0	0	1	0	2	2	0	
Schulte, lf	4	0	0	1	0	1	1	0	
Zimmerman, 3b	5	1	1	2	0	0	2	1	0
Saier, 1b	3	0	1	3	1	0	9	0	0
Good, rf	4	0	2	2	0	0	0	0	0
Bridwell, ss	3	0	1	1	0	1	0	5	2	0
Archer, c	3	1	2	2	1	0	3	0	0
Pierce, p	3	0	0	0	0	0	0	5	0
Lavender, p	0	0	0	0	0	0	0	0	1
*Williams	1	0	0	0	0	0	0	0	0
Smith, p	0	0	0	0	0	0	0	0	0
Total	35	2	7	10	4	1	0	24	12	1

*Batted for Lavender in eighth.

White Sox ....0 0 0 0 1 0 3 1 *—5
Cubs ....0 1 1 0 0 0 0 0—2

Two base hits—Zimmerman, Cicotte (2), Weaver (2). Three base hit—Saier. Struck out—By Cicotte, Saier, Good, Pierce (2), Evers, Schulte (2), Zimmerman, Williams; by Pierce, Weaver, Collins. Bases on balls—Off Cicotte, 4; off Pierce, 3. Hits—Off Pierce, 10 in 6 innings and 4 men at bat; off Lavender, 1 in 1 inning. Time—2:20. Umpires—O'Loughlin at plate, Orth on bases, Sheridan and O'Day in outfield.

WEST SIDE, OCT. 12.

Cubs.	AB.	R.	H.	TB.	BB.	SH.	SB.	PO.	A.	E.
Leach, cf	4	0	1	1	0	0	0	8	0	0
Evers, 2b	4	0	1	2	0	0	0	3	1	0
Schulte, lf	4	0	0	0	0	0	0	1	0	

Cubs.	AB.	R.	H.	TB.	BB.	SH.	SB.	PO.	A.	E.
Zimmerman, 3b...	4	0	0	0	0	0	0	1	2	0
Saier, 1b.......	4	0	0	0	0	0	0	13	1	0
Good, rf....,...	4	0	0	0	0	0	0	0	0	0
Bridwell, ss....	4	0	0	0	0	0	0	1	6	0
Archer, c........	4	0	1	1	0	0	0	6	3	1
Cheney, p.......	3	0	1	1	0	0	0	3	0	0
*Miller	1	0	0	0	0	0	0	0	0	0
Total	36	0	3	4	0	0	0	33	16	1

*Batted for Cheney in eleventh.

White Sox.	AB.	R.	H.	TB.	BB.	SH.	SB.	PO.	A.	E.
Weaver, ss.......	5	0	1	1	0	0	1	3	0
Lord, 3b..........	4	1	2	5	1	0	0	1	0	0
Chase, 1b.........	4	0	0	0	0	1	0	15	0	0
Bodie, cf.........	5	0	1	1	0	0	0	1	0	0
Collins, rf........	5	1	4	6	0	0	1	3	0	0
Fournier, lf.......	5	0	1	1	0	0	1	2	0	0
Schalk, c.........	4	0	0	0	0	0	0	9	0	0
Berger, 2b........	4	0	1	2	0	0	0	1	9	0
Benz, p...........	4	0	0	0	0	0	0	0	2	0
Total	40	2	10	16	1	1	2	33	14	0

Cubs ....0 0 0 0 0 0 0 0 0 0 0—0
White Sox.........0 0 0 0 0 0 0 0 0 2—2

Two base hits—Collins (2), Evers, Berger, Lord.
Three base hit—Lord. Struck out—By Cheney, 8
(Weaver 2, Benz 3, Chase, Berger, Bodie); by Benz,
9 (Schulte 2, Zimmerman, Saier 2, Archer 2, Cheney,
Good). Bases on balls—Off Cheney, 1. Time—2:02.
Umpires—O'Day at plate, Sheridan on bases, Orth
and O'Loughlin in outfield.

SOUTH SIDE, OCT. 13.

Cubs.	AB.	R.	H.	TB.	BB.	SH.	SB.	PO.	A.	E.
Leach, cf........	3	0	1	2	1	0	0	1	1	0
Evers, 2b........	4	1	1	1	0	0	1	1	2	0
Schulte, lf.......	4	0	0	0	0	0	0	1	0	0
Zimmerman, 3b...	4	0	0	0	0	0	2	0	0
Saier, 1b........	3	1	2	2	1	0	0	11	1	0
Good, rf.........	4	0	0	0	0	0	0	4	0	0
Bridwell, ss......	4	0	2	3	0	0	0	1	3	0
Archer, c........	4	0	3	3	0	0	0	3	1	1
Humphries, p.....	1	0	0	0	0	0	0	0	2	0
*Miller	1	0	0	0	0	0	0	0	0	0
Lavender, p......	1	0	0	0	0	0	0	0	3	0
†Williams	1	0	0	0	0	0	0	0	0	0
Total	34	2	9	10	2	0	1	24	13	1

*Batted for Humphries in the fifth.
†Batted for Lavender in the ninth.

White Sox.	AB.	R.	H.	TB.	BB.	SH.	SB.	PO.	A.	E.
Weaver, ss.......	4	0	1	1	0	0	0	6	1	1
Lord, 3b.........	3	1	1	2	1	0	0	3	1	0
Chase, 1b........	4	2	2	2	0	0	0	7	1	0
Bodie, rf-cf......	4	1	2	3	0	0	2	0	0
Collins, cf-rf.....	4	1	2	3	0	0	0	0	0
Fournier, lf.......	4	0	3	4	0	0	0	3	0	0
Schalk, c.........	4	0	0	0	0	0	0	5	0	0
Berger, 2b........	4	0	0	0	0	0	0	1	5	0
Scott, p..........	3	0	0	0	0	0	0	0	2	0
Total	34	5	11	15	1	0	0	27	10	1

White Sox...............0 0 0 3 2 0 0 0 *—5
Cubs ....0 0 0 1 0 0 0 0 1—2

Two base hits—Collins, Fournier, Lord, Bodie,
Leach. Struck out—By Scott, Humphries, Zimmer-
man, Miller, Good, Lavender; by Humphries, Scott;
by Lavender, Collins. Bases on balls—Off Scott, 2;
off Humphries, 1. Double play—Weaver-Berger.
Hits—Off Humphries, 4 in 4 innings. Time—1:53.
Umpires—O'Loughlin at plate, Orth on bases,
Sheridan and O'Day in outfield.

SUMMARY.

Games won: White Sox, 4; Cubs, 2.
Paid attendance............................. 153,819
Total receipts...................$105,815.50
Players' share............................. 36,325.12
Each club's share............................. 29,454.41
National commission......................... 10,581.55
Each player on the winning team received $807.22
and each player on the losing team received $538.15. The
division of the players' pool was 60 per cent to the
winners and 40 per cent to the losers.

PREVIOUS CITY SERIES.
(Games won.)

1903—White Sox, 7; Cubs, 7.
1905—Cubs, 4; White Sox, 1.

1906—White Sox, 4; Cubs, 2.
1909—Cubs, 4; White Sox, 1.
1911—White Sox, 4; Cubs, 0.
1912—White Sox, 4; Cubs, 3.

GOLF.

WESTERN OPEN CHAMPIONSHIP.

John J. McDermott, professional, of Atlantic
City won the western open golf championship on
the links of the Memphis Country club Oct. 16-17,
1913, with a score of 295. Michael J. Brady of the
Wollaston club, Boston, was second with 302.
Championship record to date:

1899—Will Smith (Midlothian), Glen View.
1900—No championship meet held.
1901—Lawrence Auchterlonie (Glen View), Midlothian, 160.
1902—Willie Anderson (Pittsfield), Euclid, 299.
1903—Alexander Smith (Nassau), Milwaukee, 318 (72
holes).
1904—Willie Anderson (Apawamis), Kent Country
(Grand Rapids, Mich.), 304.
1905—Arthur Smith (Columbus, O.), Cincinnati, 278.
1906—Alexander Smith (Nassau), Homewood, 306.
1907—Robert Simpson (Omaha), Hinsdale, Ill., 307.
1908—Willie Anderson (Onwentsia), St. Louis, 299.
1909—Willie Anderson (St. Louis), Chicago, 288.
1910—Charles Evans, Jr. (Edgewater), Chicago, 151
(36 holes).
1911—Robert Simpson (Kenosha), Grand Rapids, 146
(36 holes).
1912—Macdonald Smith (Del Monte, Cal.), Idlewild,
Chicago, 299.
1913—John J. McDermott (Atlantic City), Memphis,
295.

WESTERN AMATEUR CHAMPIONSHIP.

Warren K. Wood of the Homewood Country club,
Chicago, won the championship in the fifteenth annual tournament of the Western Golf association
on the links of the Homewood Country club July
19-26, 1913. His opponent in the thirty-six hole
final was Ned Allis of Milwaukee, Wis., whom he
defeated 4 up, 3 to play. Championship record to
date:

1899—David R. Forgan (Onwentsia); Glen View, 6 up.
1900—Wm. Waller (Onwentsia), Lake Forest, 1 up.
1901—Phelps B. Hoyt (Glen View), Midlothian, 6 up.
1902—H. C. Egan (Exmoor), Wheaton, 1 up.
1903—Walter E. Egan (Exmoor), Cleveland, 1 up.
1904—H. C. Egan (Exmoor), Highland Park, 6 up,
5 to play.
1905—H. C. Egan (Exmoor), Glen View, 3 up, 2 to
play.
1906—D. E. Sawyer (Wheaton), Glen Echo, 5 up,
4 to play.
1907—H. C. Egan (Exmoor), Wheaton, 5 up, 4 to
play.
1908—Mason Phelps (Midlothian), Rock Island, 6 up,
5 to play.
1909—Charles Evans, Jr. (Edgewater), Flossmoor,
1 up.
1910—Mason Phelps (Midlothian), Minikahda, 2 up,
1 to play.
1911—Albert Seckel (Riverside), Detroit, 8 up, 7 to
play.
1912—Charles Evans, Jr. (Edgewater), Denver, 1 up.
1913—Warren K. Wood (Homewood), Homewood, 4
up, 3 to play.

WESTERN WOMEN'S CHAMPIONSHIP.

Miss Myra Helmer of the Midlothian club, Chicago, won the eleventh annual championship tournament of the Women's Western Golf association,
held on the links of the Memphis Country club at
Memphis, Tenn., Sept. 23-27, 1913. Her opponent in
the final round was Miss Ruth Chisholm of Cleveland, O., whom she defeated 5 up and 3 to play.
Record of event:

1901—Miss Bessie Anthony (Glen View), Onwentsia,
3 up, 1 to play.
1902—Miss Bessie Anthony (Glen View), Onwentsia,
1 up.
1903—Miss Bessie Anthony (Glen View), Exmoor,
3 up, 2 to play.
1904—Miss Frances Everett (Exmoor), Glen View,
1 up.
1905—Mrs. Charles L. Dering (Midlothian), Homewood, 4 up, 2 to play.

1906—Mrs. Charles L. Dering (Midlothian), Exmoor, 1 up.
1907—Miss Lillian French (Windsor), Midlothian, 1 up.
1908—Mrs. W. Frances Anderson (Hinsdale), St. Louis Country club, 3 up, 2 to play.
1909—Miss Vida Llewellyn (LaGrange), Homewood, 6 up, 5 to play.
1910—Mrs. Thurston Harris (Westward Ho), Skokie, 3 up, 2 to play.
1911—Miss Caroline Painter (Midlothian), Midlothian, 3 up, 2 to play.
1912—Miss Caroline Painter (Midlothian), Hinsdale, 1 up.
1913—Miss Myra Helmer (Midlothian), Memphis, 5 up, 3 to play.

OLYMPIC CUP.

The Western Golf association team, consisting of Charles Evans, K. P. Edwards, Warren K. Wood and W. I. Howland, won the Olympic cup on the links of the Homewood Country club, July 19, 1913, with a score of 628. The Intercollegiate Golf association team was second with 669 and the Wisconsin Golf. association team third with 680. Winners of event to date:
1905—At Chicago, Western Pa. A., 655.
1906—At St. Louis, Western G. A., 635.
1907—At Cleveland, Metropolitan G. A., 641.
1908—At Rock Island, Western G. A., 632.
1909—At Chicago, Western G. A., 623.
1910—At Minneapolis, Western G. A., 615.
1911—At Detroit, Western G. A., 606.
1912—At Chicago, Western G. A., 622.
1913—At Chicago, Western G. A., 628.

HOLE OF 306 YARDS IN ONE STROKE.

What was claimed to be a world's record was made by Ned Allis of Milwaukee, Wis., when with one stroke he put the ball into the first hole 306 yards away. This feat was accomplished July 22, 1913, on the course of the Homewood Country club, Chicago, during the qualifying race for the western amateur golf championship. His drive had a slight hook and the ball rolled over the green and into the cup, the flag being out.
The amateur record was afterward claimed for John G. Anderson of Newton, Mass., who on Sept. 23, 1908, ran down a 328-yard drive from the tee to the sixteenth green on the course of the Brae Burn Country club.

BOWLING.

ILLINOIS STATE CHAMPIONSHIP.

The sixteenth annual Illinois State Bowling association tournament was held in Chicago April 19-May 6, 1913. The five-man event was won by the Concordia Reds with a score of 2,878. The two-man event was won by James Stevens and John Rosendal with a score of 1,243. The individual event went to A. Lutz, who made 721 points, while Al Toemmel won the all-events medal with a score of 1,877. Record in each event to date:

FIVE-MAN TEAMS.
	Score
1898—Interclub league, Chicago	2,425
1899—Interclub league, Chicago	2,581
1900—Chicago league, Chicago	2,574
1901—Chicago league, Chicago	2,944
1902—Chicago league, Chicago	2,900
1903—South Chicago league, Chicago	2,875
1904—Chicago league, Chicago	2,853
1905—West Side Business Men's league, Chicago	2,855
1906—Bensingers, Chicago	2,882
1907—Lake View league, Chicago	2,920
1908—Howard Majors, Chicago	2,857
1909—Lincolns No. 1, Chicago	2,960
1910—Lipmans, Chicago	2,977
1911—Chalmers-Detroits	2,865
1912—Bruck's league, Chicago	2,884
1913—Concordia Reds	2,878

TWO-MAN TEAMS.
1904—O. W. Schmidt-H. Steers	1,269
1905—P. Ward-D. McGuire	1,216
1906—C. H. Wood-F. Bartsch	1,270
1907—F. Bomer-G. Bomer	1,223
1908—Jack Hoffenkamp-H. Glassner	1,339
1909—J. J. Zust-W. P. Gomph	1,249
1910—Phil Wolf-Jack Reilly	1,213

1911—Louis Levine-Fred Bliss	1,269
1912—Harry Ruth-Fred Collins	1,256
1913—James Stevens-John Rosendal	1,243

INDIVIDUALS.
1898—W. B. Hanna, Chicago	*172 5-6
1899—H. E. Shepard, Chicago	*190
1900—W. V. Thompson, Interclub	*197 11-12
1901—Fred Worden, Anson	*201 7-9
1902—J. E. Berlin, Sheridan	*201 7-9
1903—Fred Worden, Star	643
1904—Andrew Hall, Chicago	630
1905—R. Wienold, Monroe	711
1906—James Foley, Union	662
1907—C. Heitschmidt, Lake View	649
1908—Dan Ward, Tosettis	687
1909—Otto A. Kupfer, Southwest	678
1910—Andrew Hall, Chicago	725
1911—Arthur Anderson, Lake View	665
1912—George Haug, Chicago	671
1913—Arthur Lutz, Berghoffs	721

ALL EVENTS.
1904—H. Steers, Chicago	1,803
1905—Al Toemmel, Chicago	1,769
1906—D. Woodbury, Chicago	1,826
1907—August Trapp, Chicago	1,851
1908—Eddie Meyer, Indianapolis	1,854
1909—Sylvester A. Murray, Chicago	1,841
1910—Phil Wolf, Chicago	1,836
1911—W. V. Thompson, Chicago	1,882
1912—Fred Collins, Chicago	1,826
1913—Al Toemmel, Chicago	1,877

*Averages.

Illinois Bowling Association Officials (1913)—President, Oscar W. Schmidt, Chicago; first vice-president, David Luby, Chicago; secretary, J. C. Mueller, Chicago; treasurer, Gus Burkhardt, Chicago.

CHICAGO CHAMPIONSHIP RECORD.

FIVE-MAN TEAMS.
1904-5—Hoffmanns	2,885
1905-6—Kloempkens	2,874
1906-7—Quirk No. 1	2,890
1907-8—Eclipse	2,827
1908-9—Lederers	2,865
1909-10—Boller Pianos	2,961
1910-11—Seng's Springs	2,899
1911 (December)—Goodfriends	2,990
1912—El Utilas	2,960

TWO-MAN TEAMS.
1904-5—Meyer-Peterson	1,283
1905-6—Faetz-Schneider	1,221
1906-7—Woodbury-Stolke	1,246
1907-8—Ehlman-Weeks	1,240
1908-9—Pelfer-Steers	1,250
1909-10—Flenner-Collier	1,298
1910-11—Nelson-Metcalfe	1,303
1911 (December)—Blouin-Rolfe	1,312
1912—Toemmel-Kelly	1,310

INDIVIDUALS.
1904-5—George A. Rost	671
1905-6—Robert Wienold	659
1906-7—James Hartwell	678
1907-8—Charles Nelson	684
1908-9—E. D. Pelfer	659
1909-10—H. A. Walker	697
1910-11—R. Kirch	676
1911 (December)—Ned Nelson	711
1912—Joe Shaw	674

ALL EVENTS.
1905—Eddie Meyer	1,845
1906—Matt Faetz	1,876
1907—D. Woodbury	1,957
1908—James Blouin	1,912
1909—Charles Langmeyer	1,892
1910—H. A. Walker	1,942
1911—A. Toemmel	1,902
1911 (December)—Ned Nelson	1,870
1912—Al Toemmel	1,843

ATHLETICS.

CENTRAL A. A. U. CHAMPIONSHIPS.

The Chicago Athletic association won the Central Amateur Athletic union contests June 21, 1913, on Northwestern field, Evanston, Ill., scoring a total of 88 points. The University of Michigan was second with 15 points, while the University of Chicago and the Illinois Athletic club were tied for third

place with 11 each. Five Central A. A. U. records were bettered. George Waage of the Illinois A. C. ran a mile in 4:32⅗; J. Mucks of the Chicago A. A. threw the discus 140 feet 7 inches; Garnett Wykoff ran two miles in 9:53⅗; A. W. Kohler of the University of Michigan heaved the shot 44 feet 9¼ inches, and Charles Cory of the C. A. A. got a mark of :24⅘ in the 220-yard low hurdle race. C. B. Haff of the University of Michigan equaled the quarter-mile record of :50⅘.

WESTERN A. A. U. CHAMPIONSHIPS.

The Kansas City Athletic club won the Western A. A. U. track meet at St. Louis June 21, 1913, with 78 points. The Missouri A. C. was second with 53 points and the Hibernian A. C. third with 10 points. In the 880-yard run Porter Craig of the Kansas City team made a record of 1:58⅘, bettering the old western mark by :01⅕.

CENTRAL AMATEUR ATHLETIC UNION.

The Chicago Athletic association team won the Central Amateur Athletic union indoor track and field championships at a tournament held in the 1st regiment armory, Chicago, March 1, 1913, with a total of 51 points. The Illinois Athletic club was second with 22 points, Notre Dame third with 14, Oak Park high school fourth with 5, Illinois university fifth with 5 points and the First Regiment Athletic association sixth with 1 point. Ira Davenport, running under the I. A. C. colors, made a record of 1:58⅘ for the half mile, and the C. A. A. team established a new mark of 3:28⅕ for the mile open relay.

INTERNATIONAL GAMES IN CHICAGO.

International athletic games and exhibitions, similar to those at the quadrennial Olympic meets, took place in a stadium in Grant park, Chicago, June 28-July 6, 1913. One of the features was the Marathon race of 25 miles 50 yards, which was won by William J. Kennedy of the Illinois Athletic club in 3:05:20. The national interscholastic track and field meet was won by the Oak Park (Ill.) high school team with 44 points. The national intercollegiate track and field meet was won by the University of Michigan with 16 points. Southern California was second with 15 points and the University of Chicago was third with 13 points. The track was soft and no records were broken. The decathlon prize was won by Harry Goelitz of the Oak Park (Ill.) high school and the pentathlon by Charles Cooke of the Chicago Athletic association. In the archery competition E. J. Rendtorff of Lake Forest, Ill., scored 179 hits and 1,169 points in the double American round, beating all previous records. Mrs. S. P. Fletcher was the victor in the women's archery events.

Bart Lewis of Chicago took the international target championship with a score of 98 out of 100. The international professional title at 300 targets from 18 yards was won by Fred Bills of Chicago with a score of 291. In addition to the field and track events there were exhibition drills of various kinds, calisthenics, dancing and singing. The results of the National A. A. U. championships, the boy scouts' relay run, basket ball contest and the national amateur wrestling matches are given elsewhere.

UNIVERSITY OF CHICAGO INTERSCHOLASTIC.

The twelfth annual interscholastic athletic meet of the University of Chicago took place on Marshall field June 7, 1913. The Oak Park (Ill.) high school won with 26 points; University High of Chicago was second with 19½ and Ukiah of California was third with 15. C. Hoyt of Greenfield, Iowa, ran 100 yards in :09⅘, equaling the American record. Winners and records:

100-yard dash—C. Hoyt, Greenfield, Iowa; :09⅘.
220-yard dash—C. Hoyt, Greenfield, Iowa; :21⅘.
440-yard run (A)—Shiverick, Chicago (University High); :53⅗.
440-yard run (B)—F. Stager, Lake Forest, Ill.; :53⅗.
880-yard run (A)—W. Cummings, Hector, Iowa; 2:08⅘.
880-yard run (B)—J. Allenby, Ukiah, Cal.; 2:09⅗.
1-mile run—G. Tenney, Des Moines, Iowa; 4:46⅗.
2-mile run—C. Kraft, Oak Park, Ill.; 10:29⅗.
120-yard high hurdles—H. Goelitz, Oak Park, Ill.; :15⅘.
220-yard low hurdles—C. Cory, Chicago (University high); :24⅗.
Running high jump—Shepard, Chicago (Hyde Park); 5 ft. 8 in.
Running broad jump—J. Irish, Oak Park, Ill.; 24 ft. 4 in.
Discus throw—H. Goelitz, Oak Park, Ill.; 107 ft.
12-lb. shot-put—E. Caughey, Ukiah, Cal.; 48 ft. 3 in.
12-lb. hammer—F. Bedell, Iowa City, Iowa; 158 ft. 1½ in.
Pole vault—F. Foss, Chicago (University high); 11 ft. 9 in.
440-yard relay—Evanston (Ill.) academy; :45.

OTHER INTERSCHOLASTIC MEETS.

University of Michigan, May 24—Won by University high school, Chicago with 25½ points; Lewis institute, second, 18½; Evanston academy, third, 16½.
Northwestern university, May 31—Won by West Division high school, Milwaukee, with 27 points; Castle Heights, Lebanon, Tenn., second, 17; New Trier, third, 13.

CONFERENCE INDOOR MEET.

Wisconsin won the third annual indoor track and field meet of the Western Intercollegiate Athletic association, held in Patten gymnasium, Evanston, Ill., March 29, 1913, with 33¼ points. Illinois was second with 33, Chicago third with 18¾, Northwestern fourth with 16¾, Iowa fifth with 6 and Purdue sixth with 1¼ points. Capt. Gold of Wisconsin set a new world's indoor pole vault mark of 12 feet 8 inches. Record of conference indoor championship:

Year. University.	Points.
1911—Chicago	36
1912—Illinois	31
1913—Wisconsin	33¼

YACHTING.

THE LIPTON CUP.

The twelfth contest for the silver cup donated by Sir Thomas Lipton to the Columbia Yacht club of Chicago, to be competed for annually by 21-foot cabin class yachts, took place Aug. 14, 15 and 24, 1913, on Lake Michigan at Chicago. The first race was over a triangular course of eighteen miles; the second over a windward and leeward course of twelve miles and the fourth over a quadrangular course of twelve miles. Edith II. of the Jackson Park Yacht club won the first race; the second race was a tie between Susan II. of the Chicago Yacht club and Cherry of the Jackson Park Yacht club; Susan II. won the third and deciding race and with it the Lipton cup.

RECORD OF WINNERS.

1902—La Rita, Chicago.
1903—La Rita, Chicago.
1904—Ste. Claire, Detroit.
1905—Ste. Claire, Detroit.
1906—Cherry Circle, Chicago.
1907—Cherry Circle, Chicago.
1908—Chicago, Chicago.
1909—Spray, Chicago.
1910—Spray, Chicago.
1911—Columbia, Chicago.
1912—Susan II., Chicago.
1913—Susan II., Chicago.

THE LIPTON TROPHY.

The fourth race for the special trophy donated by Sir Thomas Lipton was sailed over a triangular course of fifteen miles on Lake Michigan, off Chicago, July 5, 1913. The winner was James O. Heyworth's Polaris, which covered the distance in 1:45:50 corrected time. Record of event:

Winner.	Time.	Winner.	Time.
1910—Valmore	3:24:10	1912—Michicago	2:45:05
1911—Valmore	2:35:28	1913—Polaris	1:45:50

SIR JOHN NUTTING CUP.

RECORD OF WINNERS.

1906—Pequod.	1910—Invader.
1907—Pequod.	1911—Invader.
1908—No race.	1912—Invader.
1909—Sand Dab.	1913—No race.

MICHIGAN CITY RACE.

Distance, 32.1 nautical miles.

The Columbia Yacht club's annual race from Chicago to Michigan City was sailed June 14, 1913. The time prize was won by W. W. Shaw's schooner Valmore in 3:31:54 corrected time. Its elapsed time was 3:32:10. The Polaris was second in 3:40:40. The class winners with time of each follow:

20-foot sloops—Rascal, J. P. Y. C., 3:54:44.
25-foot sloops—Wenonah II., Col. Y. C., 3:56:42.
30-foot (B) sloops—Kayoshk, Col. Y. C., 4:34:03.
30-foot (A) sloops—Chloris, J. P. Y. C., 3:37:11.
21-foot raceabouts—Invader, Col. Y. C., 3:51:34.
21-foot cabin class—Edith II., Col. Y. C., 3:50:28.
35-foot sloops—Michicago, Col. Y. C., 4:04:11.
65-foot schooners—Valmore, Col. Y. C., 3:31:54.
Small schooners—Natant, Col. Y. C., 4:39:53.

HARBOR SPRINGS CUP.

The Chicago Yacht club's tenth annual long distance race was sailed July 13-17, 1913, the goal being Petoskey, Mich. The first leg was from Chicago to Milwaukee, the second Milwaukee to Onekampa, Mich., and the third from Onekampa to Petoskey. The proposed fourth leg from Petoskey to Mackinac was called off. The Harbor Springs cup, the principal prize of the race, was won by James O. Heyworth's class P sloop Olympian on time allowance, though the Polaris finished first on the final leg. The winning boat led by a margin of 18:15 corrected time for the whole race. The goal until 1911 was Mackinac island and in 1912 it was Harbor Springs, Mich. Winners of the event to date:

1904—Vencedor.	1909—Valmore.
1905—Mistral.	1910—Valmore.
1906—Vanadis.	1911—Mavourneen.
1907—Vencedor.	1912—Polaris.
1908—Valmore.	1913—Olympian.

The best record to Mackinac island, 28:21:51 for the 331 miles, was made by the Mavourneen in 1911.

INLAND LAKES REGATTA.

In the Inland Lakes Yachting association regatta on Lake Winnebago at Oshkosh, Wis., Aug. 18-21, 1913, Dr. O. L. Schmidt's Senta won the championship. Kathryn II. was second. In class C Edith of the Butte des Morts club was the winner. Natomah took the class B championship.

Dr. O. L. Schmidt of Chicago was elected president of the association.

FELKER CHALLENGE CUP.

The annual race for the Felker challenge cup was sailed on Lake Winnebago, Wis., Aug. 16, 1913, and was won by Troubadour II. Kathryn II. was the winner in 1912.

POWER-BOAT RACING.

CHICAGO-MICHIGAN CITY.

June 14, 1913. Distance, 32.1 nautical miles.

Boat.	Start.	Corrected time.
Wee Wee	12:15:00	6:01:15
Francesca	1:36:17	6:06:10
J. V. Clarke	2:49:17	6:07:05
Avis	2:08:09	6:15:20
Fennwood	1:41:17	6:16:10
Fearnaught	2:15:00	6:25:50
Fleur de Lis	2:08:09	6:51:55

SWIMMING.

CHICAGO CHAMPIONSHIPS.

The first annual Chicago swimming championships were held in connection with the water carnival on Lake Michigan Aug. 24, 1913. The swimmers representing the Illinois Athletic club scored 57 points, the Chicago Athletic association 30 and the University of Chicago 2. The races were held inside of the breakwater at the foot of Harrison street. No official time was announced, as the distances were made somewhat uncertain by the instability of the markers in the rough water. The winners of the chief events were:

50 yards—K. Huszagh, C. A. A.
100 yards—K. Huszagh, C. A. A.
150 yards, back stroke—H. J. Hebner, I. A. C.
200 yards, breast stroke—Smith Taylor, C. A. A.
220 yards—Perry McGillivray, I. A. C.
1 mile—M. McDermott, I. A. C.
440 yards—H. J. Hebner, I. A. C.
880 yards—A. C. Raithel, I. A. C.
400-yard relay—I. A. C. team.

CENTRAL A. A. U. CHAMPIONSHIPS.

INDOOR.

The Central Amateur Athletic union's championship swimming contests in 1913 resulted as follows:

50-yard swim—Won by A. C. Raithel, I. A. C., in the I. A. C. tank, Chicago, Jan. 9. Time, :25.
150-yard back stroke—Won by H. J. Hebner, I. A. C., in I. A. C. tank, Jan. 9. Time, 1:50⅘ (world's record).
1-mile swim—Won by Perry McGillivray, I. A. C., in I. A. C. tank, Jan. 9. Time, 24:54⅗.
100-yard swim—Won by A. C. Raithel, I. A. C., in I. A. C. tank, Feb. 6. Time, :55.
440-yard swim—Won by Perry McGillivray, I. A. C., in I. A. C. tank, Feb. 6. Time, 5:31⅗.
200-yard breast stroke—Won by Michael McDermott, unattached, in I. A. C. tank, Feb. 6. Time, 2:47⅗.
160-yard relay—Won by I. A. C. team (W. C. Woodward, Perry McGillivray, A. C. Raithel, E. E. McGillivray), in I. A. C. tank, Feb. 6. Time, 1:17⅗ (world's record).
½-mile swim—Won by Perry McGillivray, I. A. C., in I. A. C. tank, March 6. Time, 11:45⅗.
220-yard swim—Won by A. C. Raithel, I. A. C., in I. A. C. tank, March 6. Time, 2:31⅗.
Fancy diving—Won by Charles Wohfeld, I. A. C., in I. A. C. tank, March 6, with 177½ points.

OUTDOOR.

The Central A. A. U. championship outdoor swimming events were contested at Put-in-Bay, O., Aug. 27, 28, 1913, with the following results:

100 yards—Won by A. C. Raithel, I. A. C., Chicago, Ill.
100 yards, juniors—Won by E. J. O'Connor, Cleveland, O.
200 yards, breast stroke—Won by Michael McDermott, I. A. C., Chicago, Ill.
880 yards—Won by Michael McDermott, I. A. C., Chicago, Ill.
Fancy diving, men—Won by Charles Wohfeld, I. A. C., Chicago, Ill.
Fancy diving, women—Won by Miss Elsie M. Hanneman, Bath Beach, N. Y.

CHICAGO RIVER SWIM.

The sixth annual Chicago river swim took place Aug. 16, 1913, over a course approximately 2 miles long, beginning at a point in Lake Michigan off Harrison street to the Wells street bridge. The contest was under the auspices of the Illinois Athletic club. Perry McGillivray of the I. A. C. was first in 46:54⅗; M. McDermott, I. A. C., second in 48:32⅘, and A. C. Raithel, I. A. C., third in 49:42. Record of event:

Year and winner.	Time.
1908—S. C. Jensen, I. A. C.	44:41⅘
1909—H. J. Handy, I. A. C.	38:12⅘
1910—Perry McGillivray, I. A. C.	38:03
1911—Joseph Stener, unattached	43:21
1912—W. R. Vosburgh, Univ. of Illinois	1:03:22
1913—Perry McGillivray, I. A. C.	46:54⅗

NOTE—Prior to 1912 the course used was about 1½ miles in length; in 1912 it was 2¾ miles and in 1913 2 miles.

WILSON BEACH RACE.

Perry McGillivray of the Illinois Athletic club won the ninth annual swim from the Lake View crib to Wilson beach, Chicago, Aug. 2, 1913, covering the distance of approximately 2 miles in 54:20. A. C. Raithel and M. McDermott of the same club were second and third respectively in 55:02 and 55:20. Winners of event to date:

Year and winner.	Time.
1906—H. J. Handy, I. A. C.	1:09:00
1907—L. Chiville, Y. M. C. A.	1:17:00
1908—H. J. Handy, I. A. C.	1:12:00
1909—W. S. Merriam, M. C., Indianapolis	:52:25
1910—M. McDermott, C. Y. M. C. A.	1:06:25
1911—M. McDermott, C. A. A.	1:04:27
1912—L. Chiville, I. A. C.	1:00:46⅘
1913—Perry McGillivray, I. A. C.	:54:20

MILWAUKEE RIVER SWIM.

Perry McGillivray of the Illinois Athletic club, Chicago, won the annual Milwaukee river swim of 1½ miles, Aug. 9, 1913, making the distance in 43:17. A. C. Raithel and M. McDermott, also of the I. A. C., were second and third respectively.

CENTRAL A. A. U. RECORDS.

40 yards—:19, A. C. Raithel, I. A. C.
100 yards—:56⅗, K. Huszagh, C. A. A.
220 yards—2:31, P. McGillivray, I. A. C.
440 yards—5:50, H. J. Handy, I. A. C.
500 yards—6:15⅘, Perry McGillivray, I. A. C.
880 yards—12:04⅗, H. J. Handy, I. A. C.
1 mile—24:43⅗, H. J. Handy, I. A. C.
100 yards, back stroke—1:11⅗, H. J. Hebner, I. A. C.
150 yards, back stroke—1:50⅘, H. J. Hebner, I. A. C.
100 yards, breast stroke—1:17⅗, H. J. Handy, I. A. C.
Plunge for distance—65 feet 10 inches, C. L. Brown, I. A. C.
Under water swim—320 feet, E. P. Swatek, I. A. C.
160 yards, relay—1:18⅗, I. A. C. team (H. J. Hebner, P. McGillivray, A. C. Raithel, T. Winans).
100 yard medley swim—1:10⅘, H. J. Hebner, I. A. C.
Fancy diving—F. A. Bornamann, C. A. A., and G. Gaidzik, C. A. A.

SKATING.

ILLINOIS CHAMPIONSHIPS.

In the Illinois state championship events at Humboldt park, Chicago, Jan. 12, 1913, Robert McLean carried off the honors, W. E. Gunderson taking second place. Summary:

1 mile—Won by McLean; Gunderson, second, W. O. Simonson, third. Time, 2:50 (new state record).
½ mile—Won by McLean; Gunderson, second; Simonson, third. Time, 1:15⅗.
2 miles—Won by McLean; Gunderson, second; Thomas Norman, third. Time, 6:15⅗.

CHICAGO CHAMPIONSHIP.

Robert McLean, international ice skating champion, won the mile and half-mile Chicago city championships Feb. 16, 1913, in 3:36⅗ and 1:30⅗. Harry Kaad won the two-mile championship in 6:48⅗.

In the Sleipner A. C. skating Derby at Humboldt park Jan. 5, 1913, Robert McLean won the 1-mile race for the Nestor Johnson trophy in 3:05, giving him permanent possession of the prize.

Western Skating Association—Honorary president, Allen I. Blanchard; president, Dr. Harold H. Hayes, Illinois Athletic club, Chicago; first vice-president, Henry H. Erland, Illinois Athletic club, Chicago; second vice-president, P. J. Sjolie, Sleipner Athletic club, Chicago; secretary-treasurer, Julian T. Fitzgerald, 2858 West Madison street, Chicago. Board of control: Otto J. Krejci, Carl Carlson, Dr. G. K. Herman, Nestor Johnson, Roy E. Davis, William Hackett, S. Huseby, George Anson, Nicholas Halvorsen, Dr. M. J. Latimer, Hugh Baker, Dr. Harold H. Hayes, Henry H. Erland, P. J. Sjolie, Julian T. Fitzgerald.

SHOOTING.

GRAND CHICAGO HANDICAP.

The fourth annual Grand Chicago handicap shoot took place on the grounds of the Chicago Gun club June 14-15, 1913. J. F. Caldwell of Concordia, Kas., was the victor, with a score of 98 out of 100. He shot from the 21-yard mark. Harris Kenniscott, C. Clark and Schook divided second place honors with 96 hits each. Kenniscott shot from the 20-yard mark, Clark from 22 yards and Schook from 17 yards.

Grand Chicago handicap winners to date:

1910—Albert Southard, Pecatonica, Ill.	94
1911—W. F. Riley, Chicago, Ill.	93
1912—Henry Carstens, Lowell, Ind.	93
1913—J. F. Caldwell, Concordia, Kas.	98

ILLINOIS STATE SHOOT.

The thirty-seventh annual state shoot of the Illinois State Sportsmen's association took place at Peoria May 26-29, 1913. In the preliminary practice event at 100 yards, J. Graham, professional, was high with 98 hits. Mark Airle and Lon Hall led the amateurs with 96 out of 100. J. P. Graham of Chicago won the Chicago Board of Trade diamond badge and the state championship title in a shoot-off with T. Hall and Voorhees, following a tie score of 96. Ditto won the Jefferson trophy with a score of 49 out of 50, defeating Stannard, who had the same score, in the shoot-off. The special professional championship was won by Cadwallader and the amateur by Hall. The high guns of the tournament as a whole were George Crosby and Bart Lewis with 388 each.

PRE-OLYMPIC SHOOT.

In the shooting tournament held in connection with the international or "Olympic" games in Chicago, July 3-5, 1913, the winner of the amateur championship was Bart Lewis of Auburn, Ill. He was tied at 94 with H. H. Logan of Chicago, but won the shoot-off at 22 targets with a score of 22 to his opponent's 19. The international team championship, teams of five men, was won by the Chicago Gun club's team No. 1. The professional championship was won by Fred Bills of Chicago with a total score of 291 out of a possible 300.

INTERSTATE TOURNAMENT.

At the interstate tournament held at Chicago May 18, the amateur individual championship was won by J. Kammermann of Grant Park, Ill., with a score of 98 out of 100 targets from the 16-yard mark. The professional championship was won by Jay Graham of Long Lake, Ill., with a score of 96. The teams championship was won by the Lowell (Ind.) Gun club with a score of 455.

MOTORING.

By C. G. Sinsabaugh.

CHICAGO COMPETITIONS.

Formerly Chicago used to have a very busy summer in a contest way, but 1913 was an exception. The Chicago Motor club was forced to abandon all its classics because of the inability to secure entries—the Algonquin hill climb, the fuel tests and the annual reliability. The Algonquin defection was to be regretted, for the Chicago hill climb had been run for seven consecutive years. The Chicago Motor club ran off only two events—both of them team matches—but neither was a success. In May the C. M. C. and the Illinois Athletic club participated in a team match to Indianapolis and return, but half the two teams scratched on the home journey, so the results were hard to compile, although the decision was given to the C. M. C. The Banta trophy trade vs. amateur match in the fall also fizzled because threatening weather scared out all but three cars—two on the amateur side and one on the trade. The match went to the amateurs.

The Chicago Automobile club repeated its Elgin success, staging only two road races, instead of five. The meet was held in August, the first day's race, the Chicago Automobile club cup, formerly the Cobe trophy, being won by Ralph De Palma in a Mercer. The Elgin National trophy was won by Gil Anderson in a Stutz, who broke the course record by averaging 71.5 miles per hour for 305 miles. A larger crowd than ever before attended and as a result the Elgin Automobile Road Race association was able to declare a 10 per cent dividend.

The Chicago Automobile club and the Chicago Athletic association again clashed in two team matches. The summer run, or the "regular interclub," went to Waukesha, Wis., and return, the Cherry Circle again winning. In the fall, however, when the two clubs went to Hudson lake, Indiana, and return, a one-day event, the Chicago Automobile club captured both cups—the Allen Ray trophy for having the fewest penalties and the Carleton White for the greater number of perfect scores. Mayor Carter H. Harrison of Chicago participated as a guest.

BASKET BALL.

Wisconsin won the basket ball championship of the conference universities in 1913.

Lake Forest won the "little five" championship.

WRESTLING.

CENTRAL A. A. U. CHAMPIONSHIPS.

The wrestling championships of the Central Amateur Athletic union were decided at the Illinois Athletic club, Chicago, Jan. 18. Winners:
105-pound class—Harry Churan, Sleipner A. C.
115-pound class—Hans Torp, Sleipner A. C.
125-pound class—Richard Crotty, North Side A. C.
135-pound class—August Putkonen, Elmira A. C.
145-pound class—Ben Reuben, Chicago Hebrew institute.
158-pound class—Glenn R. Browne, Irving Park Country club.
Heavy weight class—Jack Pavish, Cornell Square Athletic association.

BOY SCOUTS LONG RELAY RUN.

More than 1,500 boy scouts of America took part in a relay run from Washington, D. C., to Chicago, Ill., in connection with the international games in the Grant park stadium. The start was made June 24 from in front of the north portico of the white house, when President Wilson delivered a message to Fred Reed, the first runner, to be carried by him and his fellow scouts to Mayor Harrison and Lawrence Heyworth, president of the international games. The message expressed the interest taken by the chief executive in athletics and field sports for the development of the country's youth. The route of the runners was through Frederick, Md., Gettysburg, Chambersburg, Greensburg and Pittsburgh, Pa., Youngstown, Cleveland and Toledo, O., and South Bend, Laporte and Valparaiso, Ind., to Chicago. The boys were closely followed by reporters of The Chicago Daily News in an automobile and by a number of officials. Bad roads were encountered in places, causing some delay, but in general it was difficult to restrain the lads from getting ahead of the schedule.

The relay run ended at 2:50 p. m., June 28, when Lauron Chenowith dashed up to Mayor Harrison's stand in the stadium and handed him President Wilson's message. The elapsed time from start to finish was 4 days 3 hours 57 minutes.

CHICAGO WEATHER.
Compiled in Chicago office of the weather bureau.

MONTH.	TEMPERATURE.						PRECIPITATION.				
	Highest, degrees.	Date.	Lowest, degrees.	Date.	Mean for month, degrees.	Normal, degrees.	Inches per month.	Normal, Inches.	Clear days.	Partly cloudy days.	Cloudy days.
1912—November	70	11	25	28	42.8	39.2	1.45	2.50	12	10	8
December	57	5	3	12	33.4	29.3	1.08	2.07	11	7	13
1913—January	55	17	0	12	29.3	23.7	1.33	2.00	4	10	17
February	62	19	—2	5	24.8	25.4	1.97	2.16	10	9	9
March	65	24	—4	2	35.2	34.4	3.44	2.55	4	12	15
April	80	23	32	7	48.8	45.9	1.91	2.88	13	5	12
May	85	2	38	10	57.6	56.5	4.68	3.87	11	9	11
June	99	30	44	7	70.5	66.3	1.08	3.66	17	8	5
July	99	29	59	21	74.9	72.4	3.30	3.64	19	6	6
August	97	9	60	30	74.3	71.2	4.06	2.88	12	13	6
September	97	2	38	22	65.4	64.6	1.49	3.02	12	10	8
October	83	10	27	21	53.3	53.2	2.23	2.55	12	6	13

COLDEST DAYS IN CHICAGO.

The cold spell ending Jan. 7, 1912, established a record for duration of below zero weather in Chicago—72 hours. The minimum reached was 16 degrees below zero. The longest previous below zero stretch was 71 hours, Jan. 21, 22 and 23, 1883, when the minimum reached was 17 degrees below zero. Following are the coldest days officially recorded in Chicago:

Dec. 24, 1872	—23	Jan. 15, 1893	—16
Jan. 29, 1873	—16	Jan. 25, 1897	—20
Jan. 9, 1875	—20	Feb. 9, 1899	—21
Jan. 3, 1879	—18	Jan. 25, 1904	—15
Jan. 22, 1883	—17	Feb. 13, 1905	—18
Jan. 5, 1884	—18	Jan. 7, 1912	—16
Feb. 9, 1888	—13		

HOTTEST DAYS IN CHICAGO.

July 21, 1901, when the temperature rose to 103 degrees above zero, was the hottest day in the history of Chicago so far as the weather bureau records go. The next hottest was July 5, 1911, when 102 degrees was recorded. The hottest days in each year since 1899 were:

Sept. 5, 1899	98	Aug. 11-Sept. 1, 1907	92
Aug. 5, 1900	94	July 11-Aug. 3, 1908	96
July 21, 1901	103	Aug. 8, 1909	93
June 12, 1902	91	June 24, 1910	97
July 1-Aug. 24, 1903	92	July 5, 1911	102
July 17, 1904	94	Aug. 31, 1912	95
July 18, 1905	95	June 30-July 29, 1913	99
June 28, 1906	93		

CHIEFS OF POLICE OF CHICAGO.

Names and dates of appointment:
W. W. Kennedy, April, 1871.
Elmer Washburn, April, 1872.
Jacob Rehm, December, 1873.
Michael C. Hickey, Oct. 7, 1875.
Valerius A. Seavey, July 30, 1878.
Simon O'Donnell, Dec. 15, 1879.
William J. McGarigle, Dec. 13, 1880.
Austin J. Doyle, Nov. 13, 1882.
Frederick Ebersold, Oct. 26, 1885.
George W. Hubbard, April 17, 1888.

Frederick H. Marsh, Jan. 1, 1890.
Robert W. McClaughry, May 18, 1891.
Michael Brennan, Sept. 11, 1893.
John J. Badenoch, April 11, 1895.
Joseph Kipley, April 16, 1897, and April, 1899.
Francis O'Neill, April 30, 1901, and June 26, 1903.
John M. Collins, July 26, 1905.
George M. Shippy, April 15, 1907.
LeRoy T. Steward, Aug. 14, 1909.
John McWeeny, May 1, 1911.
James Gleason, Nov. 3, 1913.

CHICAGO WARDS AND ALDERMEN.
Number of, since 1837.

Year.	Wards.	Aldermen.	Year.	Wards.	Aldermen.	Year.	Wards.	Aldermen.	Year.	Wards.	Aldermen.
1837-1838	6	10	1857-1862	10	20	1876*-1888	18	36	1889-1901	34	68
1839-1846	6	12	1863-1869	16	32	1888-1889	24	48	1901-1912	85	70
1847-1856	9	18	1869-1875	20	40						

*Under the general incorporation act of 1875 Chicago was divided into eighteen wards.

CHICAGO TELEPHONE COMPANY.

The Chicago Telephone Company was incorporated Jan. 14, 1881, under the laws of the State of Illinois. Its charter is for a period of ninety-nine years.

Prior to the incorporation of the Company an agreement had been reached providing for the merging of the American District Telegraph Company and the Bell Telephone Company. This action was taken June 15, 1880, and early in 1881 this merger was effected and resulted in the formation of the Chicago Telephone Company.

The original authorized stock issue of the Company under its original Articles of Association was $500,000. This has been increased from time to time as the business grew until there is at present an authorized stock capital of $30,000,000, of which $27,000,000 has been issued.

Nearly a year after the organization of the Chicago Telephone Company, on Dec. 23, 1881, the American Bell Telephone Company issued to it a license covering the use of the Bell apparatus in the counties of McHenry, Lake, Kane, DuPage, Cook, Kendall, Grundy and Will in the State of Illinois and Lake and Porter in the State of Indiana.

Men prominent in the business life of Chicago have occupied the executive chair of the Telephone Company from its incorporation down to the present time. The list is as follows:

Norman Williams.
Anson Stager.
Geo. L. Phillips.
Henry B. Stone.
Robert T. Lincoln.
John M. Clark.
John I. Sabin.
Arthur D. Wheeler.
B. E. Sunny.

Henry B. Stone's tenure was the longest, covering the period from 1890 to 1897. The next in length of service is the present incumbent, B. E. Sunny, who was elected in May, 1908, and who is therefore rounding out his sixth year.

By reason of the license granted by the American Bell Telephone Company the Chicago Telephone Company is one of the Associated Companies of the Bell System and over its wires connections may be had with the long distance lines of the American Telephone and Telegraph Company and other Associated and Connecting Companies throughout the United States and Canada.

The Company owns and occupies thirty-eight buildings which are used for exchange purposes and supply stations in Chicago. It also owns its exchange building in Evanston, Waukegan, Elgin, Aurora, Joliet, Chicago Heights, Ill., Hammond, Ind., and in several other smaller exchange areas.

The Company's underground cable and conduit system is the largest and most complete in the world, embracing 700 miles of conduit, which contain 3,200 miles of duct, carrying 700,000 miles of underground wire.

The aerial plant contains 65,000 miles of wire strung on poles and 90,000 miles of aerial cable.

The Telephone Company's expenditures run to enormous proportions in a year. As the money is almost entirely paid to Chicago concerns for materials and supplies, to Chicago workmen, skilled and otherwise, and to Chicago men who compose the engineering, operating and clerical forces, it can readily be seen what an important factor the Company occupies as a distributor of money throughout the community. The sum of $8,000,000 was paid out for material and services during the year ended Dec. 31, 1913. The number of men now employed in the Company's service is 6,000, while there are 7,800 women employed as clerks and operators.

The Telephone Directory has become a factor in business and social circles in Chicago and its suburbs, where it is consulted more frequently than any other book of reference. It is used not only as a telephone directory, but as a city directory as well, as a street guide, as a mailing list, as a check for the proper initials of persons whose name and location you know, but whose initials have for the moment slipped you. From a pamphlet containing less than 500 names, back in the early days, to the June issue of 1913, in which 450,000 listings appear, one may gain some idea of the vast growth of the telephone business and the increasing importance of the telephone directory.

The new Administration Building of the Chicago Telephone Company was completed in the fall of 1912, having been about a year in course of construction. It is an imposing structure with a frontage of 140 feet on West Washington Street; it rises to a height of twenty stories and adjoins the old building formerly used for general office purposes.

The site of the first Chicago Telephone Building, at the corner of Washington and Franklin Streets, was occupied in early days by a blacksmith shop, owned by a Mr. Haas. This shop was destroyed in the great fire of 1871. The building erected by the Telephone Company in 1887 was seven stories in height and was occupied as an exchange and warehouse. It was regarded as a monster structure and wonder was freely expressed as to how the Company could make use of so much space.

To the east of this building was the old Forbes Building, erected just after "The Fire." The razing of this structure to make way for the new twenty-story Telephone Building began in May, 1911, and October, 1912, the officials and employes of the company began moving in.

Lack of space will not permit of a description of the building, which has the distinction of being the largest telephone building in the world. It was planned and constructed to

meet the special needs of the great business that plays such an important part in Chicago's life, touching it intimately in every quarter. There are several buildings in the city that, for ornate architectural design, surpass the Bell Telephone Building, but for quiet dignity and impressiveness it is distinctive, and there are few whose utilitarian features can compare with it. It is estimated that the Telephone Building will meet the Company's requirements for office space for about twelve years.

THE FRANCHISE: In November, 1907, an ordinance was passed extending the franchise of the Company in Chicago to Jan. 8, 1929. This ordinance was accepted by the Company and became effective Dec. 2, 1907. It provides that within sixty days after the first days of January and July of each year the Company shall file with the comptroller of the city a statement of all gross receipts from business done within the City of Chicago during the six months ending on the first days of said months and that the Company shall pay the city three per cent of such gross receipts. The Company is required to keep at its office a separate record showing receipts from Chicago business, and in addition such records and accounts as shall be prescribed by the comptroller. The council is given power to change the schedule of rates prescribed in the ordinance thirty months after the ordinance became effective, and at five-year intervals thereafter during the life of the ordinance. The right of purchase by the city is described in section 16 as follows:

The City of Chicago shall have the right on the first day of January, 1919, or on the first day of January, 1924, or within thirty days after either of said dates, if it shall so elect, to terminate the grant of privileges of said Chicago Telephone Company, conferred hereby, and on either of said dates, or at the expiration of the term hereof, or within thirty days after either of the times mentioned, to take over for municipal, state or federal operation, the plant and system of the grantee, or its successor or successors, including the property hereinafter mentioned; provided that twelve months' previous notice in writing shall have been given of the intention of the city to take over the telephone plant and system of the grantee, or its successor or successors, within the City of Chicago, including all appurtenances, appliances, equipment, lines, leaseholds, buildings, stores, furniture, and fixtures, suitable to and used by it for the purposes of this grant, taking into consideration the then condition of the art, and in the event that the city council shall so terminate this grant, or that said grant shall have expired and the city council shall take over the property of said company above mentioned, then the city shall pay therefor in cash the then cost of the duplication, taking into consideration the then condition of the art, less depreciation, of said telephone plant and system and other property aforesaid, together with, if the said grant shall not then have expired, 5 per cent thereon in addition as compensation for the compulsory sale, but there shall be no allowance for earning power or for the value of the rights and privileges hereby granted, or for any franchise or license value.

B. E. Sunny, president, early in 1913, speaking of the examination of the Company's business in connection with a revision of the rates said: "Previous examinations were made somewhat difficult by the absence of an inventory of the property, and to provide against this and to prevent further attempts to reduce its value by questioning the accuracy of the books, the Company employed H. M. Byllesby & Co. and The Arnold Company to make an inventory. The work was completed several months ago and shows a value in excess of the books of more than $6,000,000, indicating that the charges to plant account have been conservative and that the real estate and other items have increased in value over their cost."

Rates for Telephone Service Within the Chicago City Limits.

Application for new service, changes in or additions to existing service, or equipment, may be made by telephone (Official 100, Commercial Department), by mail, or in person, at the Company's headquarters, 212 West Washington street, between Fifth avenue and Franklin street.

The new schedule of rates as fixed by the City Council was accepted by the Company June 23, 1913.

RATES FOR BUSINESS SERVICE.

MEASURED RATE SERVICE—For use of subscribers and their employes in their business.

CLASS M12—Single line, $60 per year, including 1,200 outgoing messages. Next 1,200 messages, 3c each; next 1,200 2½c each; excess messages above 3,600 per year, 2c each.

CLASS M—Single line, $48 per year, including 960 outgoing messages. Next 240 messages, 5c each; next 1,200, 3c each; next 1,200, 2½c each; excess messages above 3,600 per year, 2c each.

CLASS M72—Two single lines, $198 per year, including 7,200 outgoing messages. Excess messages, 2c each.

CLASS M60—Single line, $120 per year, including 6,000 outgoing messages. Auxiliary to M72 only.

CLASS ML—Single line, $24 per year, including no messages; outgoing messages used over said lines to be accounted and paid for as part of total messages. Auxiliary to any of the above classes.

Any line of the above classes may be used wholly for incoming service, or outgoing, or both, as subscriber may request.

Outgoing conversations or messages from more than one Measured Service line on same

premises shall be computed at the same rates as though transmitted over one single line.

Subscribers contracting for two or more Measured Service single lines at same premises shall be furnished if they desire, without additional charge. Private Branch Exchange switching apparatus, appliances and equipment, including an operator's telephone.

COMMUTED TRUNK lines in connection with a Private Branch Exchange, at $1 per day each for the transmission of outgoing messages or conversations without limit, were abolished by the ordinance of May 26, 1913, with the exception that present subscribers to that class of service shall have the right to a continuance thereof at their present or any future location within the city at the rate and upon the conditions prescribed and fixed therefor in the ordinance passed by the City Council, November 6, 1907.

TERMINAL TELEPHONES connected with and located in the same premises with a Private Branch Exchange switchboard, $6 per year each.

METHOD OF BILLING MEASURED SERVICE CALLS—For the convenience of the subscriber a bill is rendered each month in advance for one-twelfth of the yearly contract quantity and each month in arrears for any excess messages used to the 20th of the preceding month. If a subscriber is charged excess messages and, in a subsequent month or months of that contract year, uses less than one-twelfth of the yearly contract quantity, he will be credited at the excess call rate with all calls so saved, up to the number of excess calls previously paid for within the current contract year.

METERS ON MEASURED SERVICE LINES—At the request of any subscriber to a single party measured service line not connected with a Private Branch Exchange the Company will install upon the premises of such subscriber a meter or meters for recording the number of outgoing messages or conversations over said line at a charge of $3 for each meter. A refund of $1 will be allowed the subscriber in the event the meter is at his request removed by the Company.

NICKEL COIN BOX SERVICE—NICKEL FIRST—Nickel Prepayment or Nickel First Service, where nickel must be deposited to call the operator.

CLASS N—Single line, guarantee 20c per day, including four outgoing messages. Additional messages in excess of the guarantee per day, 4c each.

CLASS 2N—Two party line, guarantee 12½c per day, including 2½ outgoing messages. Additional messages, in excess of the guarantee per day, 4c each.

NICKEL LAST—Nickel Last Service, where the nickel must be deposited immediately upon the request of the operator.

CLASS NL—Single line, guarantee 20c per day, including four outgoing messages, additional messages 5c each.

CLASS 2NL—Two party line, guarantee

12½c per day, including 2½ outgoing messages, additional messages 5c each.

COLLECTIONS—On both Nickel First and Nickel Last Service, when the amount in the coin box at a regular collection is less than the guaranteed amount and the deficit is paid to the collector at that time, and, at a succeeding collection or collections within 60 days, the coin box contains more than the guarantee between collections, the excess shall be applied to the repayment of deficit previously paid—or—when the amount in the coin box exceeds the guaranteed amount and a complete settlement is made with the collector, the portion of such excess not allowed on a previous deficit (or allowed to a Nickel First subscriber to reduce his excess message rate to 4c) will be applied on any deficit at a succeeding collection within 60 days.

LIMITED FLAT RATE SERVICE—For use of subscribers and their employes only in their business.

CLASS L—Single line limited service, $10.42 per month, payable in advance, including not to exceed five hundred (500) outgoing messages in any one month; excess messages above 500 in any one month, 2c each.

METHOD OF BILLING—$10.42 is billed in advance for each calendar month. Messages are counted from the 21st of one month to the 20th of the next month, inclusive, and all messages over 500 billed at 2c each.

CLASS F—Service with unlimited outgoing messages was abolished by the ordinance of May 26, 1913, with the exception that present subscribers to that class of service shall have the right to a continuance thereof at their present or any future location within the city at the rate and upon the conditions prescribed and fixed therefor in the ordinance passed by the City Council, November 6, 1907.

NEIGHBORHOOD EXCHANGE SERVICE—For the unlimited use within the area of the neighborhood exchange by subscribers and their employes only in their business.

CLASS B—Single line, $48 per year, payable monthly in advance.

CLASS 2B—Two party line, $36 per year, payable monthly in advance.

CLASS 4B—Four party line, $24 per year, payable monthly in advance.

For a message to any telephone in Chicago outside the limits of the neighborhood exchange with which the subscriber is connected, 5c for each five minutes or fraction.

RATES FOR RESIDENCE SERVICE

MEASURED RATE SERVICE—For use of subscribers and their families only at their residences.

CLASS RM—Single line, $40 per year, including 800 outgoing messages. Next 400 messages, 4c each; next 1,200, 3c each; next 1,200, 2½c each; excess messages above 3,600 per year, 2c each.

METHOD OF BILLING MEASURED SERVICE CALLS—For the convenience of the subscriber a bill is rendered each month in advance for

one-twelfth of the yearly contract quantity and each month in arrears for any excess messages used to the 20th of the preceding month. If a subscriber is charged for excess messages and, in a subsequent month or months of that contract year, uses less than one-twelfth of the yearly contract quantity, he will be credited at the excess call rate with all calls so saved, up to the number of excess calls previously paid for within the current contract year.

METERS ON MEASURED SERVICE LINES—At the request of any subscriber to a single party measured service line the Company will install upon the premises of such subscriber a meter or meters for recording the number of outgoing messages or conversations over said line at a charge of $3 for each meter. A refund of $1 will be allowed the subscriber in the event the meter is at his request removed by the Company.

NICKEL COIN BOX SERVICE—NICKEL FIRST—Nickel Prepayment or Nickel First Service, where nickel must be deposited to call the operator.

CLASS 2RN—Two party line, guarantee 10c per day, including two outgoing messages. Additional messages in excess of the guarantee per day, 4c each.

CLASS 4N—Four party line, guarantee 5c per day, including one outgoing message. Additional messages in excess of the guarantee per day, 4c each.

NICKEL LAST—Nickel Last Service, where the nickel must be deposited immediately upon request of the operator.

CLASS 2RNL—Two party line, guarantee 10c per day, including two outgoing messages, additional messages 5c each.

CLASS 4NL—Four party line, guarantee 5c per day, including one outgoing message, additional messages 5c each.

COLLECTIONS—On both Nickel First and Nickel Last Service, when the amount in the coin box at a regular collection is less than the guaranteed amount and the deficit is paid to the collector at that time, and, at a succeeding collection or collections within 60 days, the coin box contains more than the guarantee between collections, the excess shall be applied to the repayment of deficit previously paid—or—when the amount in the coin box exceeds the guaranteed amount and a complete settlement is made with the collector, the portion of such excess not allowed on a previous deficit (or allowed to a Nickel First subscriber to reduce his excess message rate to 4c) will be applied on any deficit at a succeeding collection within 60 days.

FLAT RATE SERVICE—For use of subscribers and their families only at their residences.

CLASS RF—Single line, unlimited service, $72 per year, payable monthly in advance.

CLASS 2RF—Two party line, unlimited service, $56 per year, payable monthly in advance.

NEIGHBORHOOD SERVICE EXCHANGE—For unlimited use within the area of the neighborhood exchange by the subscribers and their families only.

CLASS R—Single line, $36 per year, payable monthly in advance.

CLASS 2R—Two party line, $24 per year, payable monthly in advance.

CLASS 4R—Four party line, $18 per year, payable monthly in advance.

For a message to any telephone in Chicago outside the limits of the neighborhood exchange with which the subscriber is connected, 5c for each five minutes or fraction.

Financial Statistics.

BALANCE SHEET—DEC. 31.

ASSETS.

	1908	1909	1910	1911	1912
Plant	$26,115,867	$27,840,341	$30,207,132	$33,776,612	$36,522,784
Real estate	2,551,488	2,749,986	2,795,372	3,946,960	4,913,178
Material, furniture, fixtures, etc.	861,675	932,276	1,114,752	1,314,366	1,597,864
Other investments	82,933	72,588	....	....	....
Accounts receivable	613,475	760,731	950,994	865,233	11,230,892
Cash	455,364	3,758,692	1,820,503	874,948	935,663
Total assets	$30,680,802	$36,114,614	$37,888,753	$40,778,119	$55,200,381

LIABILITIES.

	1908	1909	1910	1911	1912
Capital stock	$27,000,000	$27,000,000	$27,000,000	$27,000,000	$27,000,000
Bonds	....	5,000,000	5,000,000	‡5,000,000	19,014,000
Bills and accounts payable	377,247	411,005	1,545,998	2,948,696	1,777,111
Reserved for taxes	....	....	....	....	....
Deferred maintenance	1,838,840	1,925,149	....	....	....
Miscellaneous reserves	780,037	1,033,075	134,038	134,023	†599,523
§Replacements reserves	....	....	4,113,644	5,497,787	6,614,689
Surplus	684,678	745,385	95,073	197,613	105,058
Total liabilities	$30,680,802	$36,114,614	$37,888,753	$40,778,119	$55,200,381

*Included in "real estate and buildings."
†Includes $65,500 premium on first mortgage bonds and $400,000 "Employes Benefit Fund."
§New account opened in 1910. It includes reserve for depreciation, surplus as of Dec. 31,

1909, that portion of 1910 net earnings charged to depreciation, and several items transferred from miscellaneous reserves. These amounts are invested in the plant.
‡In April, 1912, the Company sold $14,000,-000 additional first mortgage bonds.

LEGAL FARES FOR CABS, CARRIAGES AND TAXICABS.

ONE-HORSE VEHICLES.

1. For one or two passengers, not exceeding one mile...$0.50
2. For each additional passenger, 25 cents for the first mile or part thereof only.............. .25
3. For one or more passengers for the second mile and subsequent miles or part thereof, 25 cents for all for each such mile or part thereof .... .25
4. For children between 5 and 14 years of age, when accompanied by an adult, not more than half of the above rates shall be charged for like distances. For children under 5 years of age, when accompanied by an adult, no charge shall be made.
5. For the use of any vehicle mentioned in this section conveying one or more passengers, when hired by the hour with the privilege of going from place to place and stopping as often as may be required, as follows:
For the first hour................................. 1.00
For each additional hour or part thereof at the rate of $1 an hour.
6. In the case of any vehicle described in this section being engaged by the hour and discharged at a distance from the place where it was engaged, the driver shall have the right to charge for the time necessary to return to such place.

TWO-HORSE VEHICLE.

1. For one or two passengers not exceeding one mile $1.00
2. For each additional passenger, 50 cents each for the first mile or part thereof only......... .50
3. For one or more passengers for the second mile and subsequent miles or part thereof, 50 cents for all for each mile or part thereof .50
4. Children between 5 and 14 years of age, when accompanied by an adult, not more than half of the above rates shall be charged for like distances. For children under 5 years of age, when accompanied by an adult, no charge shall be made.
5. For the use of any vehicle mentioned in this section conveying one or more passengers, when hired by the hour with the privilege of going from place to place and stopping as often as may be required, as follows:
For the first hour................................. 2.00
For each additional hour or part thereof, at the rate of $1.50 an hour.
6. In the case of any vehicle described in this section being engaged by the hour and discharged at a distance from the place where it was engaged, the driver shall have the right to charge for the time necessary to return to such place.

Hiring by the Hour—Must be so specified at the time of hiring. In all cases where the hiring of any vehicle licensed under the provisions of this article is not at the time of such hiring specified by the person hiring same to be by the hour, it shall be deemed to be by the mile, and for any detention exceeding a total period of fifteen minutes during the whole period of such hiring, when so working by the mile, the driver may demand pay for such period of detention at the rate of $1.50 per hour in addition to the rate per mile.
Baggage—Every passenger upon any vehicle licensed under the provisions of this article shall be allowed to have conveyed with him upon such vehicle without charge therefor his ordinary light traveling baggage in an amount not to exceed in weight seventy-five pounds.
Lost Baggage—Whenever any package, article of baggage or goods of any kind shall be left in or upon any vehicle licensed under the provisions of this article, the driver of such vehicle shall upon the discovery of such package, baggage or goods forthwith deliver the same to the board of inspectors of passenger vehicles.

TAXICABS.

No person, firm or corporation owning, operating or controlling any taxicab shall let the same for hire or reward for a fee or charge to be fixed and determined by the hour or fraction thereof, but the fare demanded and received shall (excepting for waiting time as herein provided for) be computed by the distance traveled and shall not exceed the following rates:
For the first one-half mile or fraction thereof, for one person.................................$0.50
For each one-fourth mile thereafter............. .10
For each additional person for whole journey. .20
For each four minutes of waiting............... .10
Waiting Time—Waiting time shall include the time during which the taxicab is not in motion, beginning with its arrival at the place to which it has been called, or the time consumed while standing at the direction of a passenger, but no charge shall be made for time lost for inefficiency of the taxicab or its operator or for time consumed by a premature arrival in response to a call; provided, however, that no operator or driver of any taxicab which has responded to the call of a prospective passenger shall throw down or place in a recording position the flag attached to the taximeter until at least eight minutes' waiting time has elapsed or been consumed.
Operator to Announce Charge Before Changing Position of Flagpost—It shall be the duty of the operator or driver of every taxicab at the termination of his services to throw the flag to the nonrecording position on the taximeter and call the passenger's attention to the amount registered. The taximeter shall not be changed until after the fare is paid or a charge ticket therefor made out and delivered to the person hiring such taxicab.
Baggage—Every passenger upon any taxicab shall be allowed to have conveyed with him upon such vehicle, without charge therefor, his ordinary light traveling baggage in an amount not to exceed in weight fifty pounds. A fee of 20 cents may be charged for conveying a trunk.
Lost Baggage—Whenever any package, article of baggage or goods of any kind shall be left in or upon any vehicle licensed under the provisions of this article, operator of such vehicle shall, upon discovery of such package, baggage or goods, forthwith deliver the same to the board of inspectors of passenger vehicles.

AUTOMOBILES (OTHER THAN TAXICABS).

Rates of Fare—The rate of fare to be asked or demanded by the operator or person in charge or control of any automobile, autocar or other similar vehicle operated for the conveyance of passengers, for hire or reward, within the city, shall not exceed the following prescribed rates:
Seating Capacity Not Exceeding Two Passengers —For the use of any such vehicle the seating capacity of which shall not exceed two persons, at the rate of $3 per hour; provided, however, that no operator of such vehicle shall be compelled to rent the same for a fee of less than $1.
Seating Capacity from Three to Five Passengers —For the use of any such vehicle the seating capacity of which shall be more than two persons, and not exceeding five persons, at the rate of $4 per hour; provided, however, that no operator of such vehicle shall be compelled to rent the same for a fee of less than $1.50.
Seating Capacity More than Five Passengers— For the use of any such vehicle the seating capacity of which is more than five persons, at the rate of $5 per hour; provided, however, that no operator of such vehicle shall be compelled to rent the same for a fee of less than $2.
Rate to Be Based on Time Vehicle Is in Use— The rate of fare to be asked or demanded by such vehicles not equipped with taximeters shall be determined in accordance with the time in which the vehicle is in use by the passenger or passengers engaging the same.
Operator's Seat Not to Be Counted—In determining the seating capacity of any such vehicle, neither the operator's seat nor any portion thereof shall be computed, but the seating capacity shall be determined by the number of persons which can be accommodated in the interior or tonneau of such vehicle.
No Charge for Answering Call or for Return from Call—No charge shall be made for the time con-

sumed in responding to a call or in returning to the place from which such vehicle is called.

"Hour" Rates to Be Charged Only When Passenger So Elects—The foregoing rates shall apply only in cases where the passenger at the time of the hiring of any vehicle referred to in this section expressly elects to pay therefor at the rate herein provided, and if such passenger so elects, the operator in charge of such vehicle shall hand to such passenger at the time of such hiring a card upon which shall appear: First, the name of the owner; second, the name of the operator of such vehicle; third, the exact time of such hiring; and in the absence of an express agreement as to the rate of fare to be charged for any vehicle referred to in this section, the rate of fare charged shall be the same as now is or hereafter may be provided by ordinance to be charged for the hire of taxicabs.

No Charge in Case of Breakdown—In case any automobile, autocar or other similar vehicle shall, while conveying for hire or reward any passenger or passengers, become disabled or shall break down so as to be unable to convey such passenger or passengers to his or their destination, and such disablement or breaking down cannot be remedied so that such vehicle shall be enabled to proceed within fifteen minutes from the time such vehicle shall have become disabled, or shall have stopped, no fare shall be charged or collected for any service rendered or distance traveled up to the time of such stoppage, disablement or breakdown. Provided, however, that if any such passenger or passengers elect to remain in such vehicle and desire to be conveyed to their destination thereby, after such breakdown or disablement shall have been remedied, in such event full rates for the distance traveled shall be charged as if no breakdown or stoppage had occurred, or if such vehicle was employed by the hour, the time of stoppage shall be deducted from the time charged for.

Baggage—Every passenger upon any public automobile, autocar or other similar vehicle shall be allowed to have conveyed with him upon such vehicle, without charge therefor, his ordinary light traveling baggage in an amount not to exceed in weight fifty pounds. A fee of 25 cents may be charged for conveying a trunk.

Lost Baggage—Whenever any package, article of baggage or goods of any kind shall be left in or upon any vehicle licensed under the provisions of this article, the operator of such vehicle shall, upon discovery of such package, baggage or goods, forthwith deliver the same to the board of inspectors of public vehicles.

MONUMENTS IN CHICAGO.
Name, location and date of dedication or completion of each.

Alarm, The—Lincoln park; May 17, 1884.

Anarchists'—Waldheim cemetery; June 25, 1893.

Andersen, Hans Christian—Lincoln park; Sept. 26, 1896.

Armstrong, George B.—Postoffice, north entrance; May 19, 1881.

Beethoven—Lincoln park; June 19, 1897.

Bohemian Soldiers and Sailors—Bohemian National cemetery; May 29, 1892.

Burns, Robert—Garfield park; Aug. 25, 1906.

Columbia Post No. 706, G. A. R.—Forest Home cemetery; June 8, 1913.

Confederate Soldiers—Oakwoods cemetery; July 23, 1893.

Douglas—Foot of 35th street; corner stone laid Sept. 6, 1866; dedication June 3, 1868.

Drake Fountain—Exchange avenue and 92d street, South Chicago; dedicated Oct. 11, 1908; presented to city Dec. 28, 1892, and first stood on Washington street in front of courthouse.

Drexel Fountain and Statue—Drexel boulevard and 51st street; completed in June, 1883; no formal dedication.

Ericson, Leif—Humboldt park; Oct. 12, 1901.

Ferguson Fountain of the Great Lakes—On south terrace of Art institute; Sept. 9, 1913.

Fire (1371) Tablet—137 DeKoven street; 1881.

Fort Dearborn Massacre—Calumet avenue and 18th street; June 22, 1893.

Fort Dearborn Tablet—River street and Michigan avenue; unveiled May 21, 1881.

Franklin—Lincoln park; June 6, 1896.

Garibaldi—Lincoln park; Oct. 12, 1901.

Grant—Lincoln park; Oct. 7, 1891.

Grant Post No. 28, G. A. R.—Elmwood cemetery; June 28, 1903.

Harrison, Carter H.—Union park; June 29, 1907.

Havlicek, Karel—Douglas park; July 30, 1911.

Haymarket—Union park; May 30, 1889.

Humboldt—Humboldt park; Oct. 16, 1892.

Indian Trail Tree Tablet—Glencoe; Nov. 7, 1911.

Iroquois Theater Fire Tablet—In hospital, 28 North Market street; Dec. 30, 1911.

Kennison—Lincoln park; Dec. 19, 1903.

Kinzie Tablet—Pine and Kinzie streets; July 11, 1913.

Kosciusko—Humboldt park; Sept. 11, 1904.

LaSalle—Lincoln park; Oct. 12, 1889.

Lincoln—Lincoln park; Oct. 22, 1887.

Lincoln Post No. 91, G. A. R.—Oakwoods cemetery; June 14, 1905.

Lincoln Wigwam Tablet—Market and Lake streets; unveiled May 11, 1910.

Linne—Lincoln park; May 23, 1891.

Logan—Lake Front park; July 22, 1897.

Logan Post No. 540, G. A. R.—Rosehill cemetery; June 1, 1900.

Marquette-Joliet—South Robey street and river; cross dedicated Sept. 23, 1907; tablet, May 6, 1909.

Mulligan—Calvary cemetery; May 30, 1895.

McKinley—McKinley park; July 4, 1905.

Press Club—Mount Hope cemetery; Nov. 12, 1893.

Reese, Michael—29th street and Groveland avenue; completed spring of 1884.

Reuter—Humboldt park; May 14; 1893.

Rosenberg Fountain—Park row and Michigan avenue; accepted by city Oct. 16, 1893.

Schiller—Lincoln park; May 15, 1886.

Shakespeare—Lincoln park; April 23, 1894.

Signal of Peace, The—Lincoln park; June 9, 1894.

Sweeney Post No. 275, G. A. R.—Evergreen cemetery, Barrington; Sept. 9, 1906.

Thomas Post No. 5, G. A. R.—Rosehill cemetery; Feb. 22, 1895.

Victoria—Garfield park; Oct. 16, 1893.

Washington—Grand boulevard and 51st street; completed June 6, 1904; no formal unveiling.

Washington Post No. 94, G. A. R.—Elmwood cemetery; Aug. 22, 1909.

Willich Post No. 780, G. A. R.—Town of Maine cemetery; Oct. 13, 1901.

REVENUE FROM THE ILLINOIS CENTRAL.

Since March 24, 1855, the Illinois Central Railroad company, in accordance with the terms of its charter, accepted March 15, 1851, has been paying into the Illinois state treasury semiannually a certain percentage of the gross receipts from its charter lines. This percentage up to 1857 was 5 and since then has been 7. The total amount paid by the road to the state up to April 30, 1912, was $31,502,713.29. The gross receipts and the semiannual payments to the state since April 30, 1905, have been:

Time.	Receipts.	Payments.
April 30, 1905	$7,635,116.74	$534,458.17
Oct. 31, 1905	7,868,214.35	550,775.00
April 30, 1906	8,461,749.42	592,322.46
Oct. 31, 1906	$8,572,893.57	$600,102.55
April 30, 1907	8,517,289.72	596,210.28
Oct. 31, 1907	9,176,082.43	642,325.84
April 30, 1908	7,619,184.14	533,342.89
Oct. 31, 1908	7,986,765.05	559,773.55
April 30, 1909	8,047,250.33	563,207.52
Oct. 31, 1909	8,419,454.63	589,361.82
April 30, 1910	8,684,545.71	607,918.20
Oct. 31, 1910	8,714,423.43	610,009.61
April 30, 1911	8,844,230.28	619,096.12
Oct. 31, 1911	8,862,687.42	620,388.12
April 30, 1912	8,006,149.85	560,430.49
Oct. 31, 1912	9,410,429.28	658,730.05
April 30, 1913	9,199,924.00	643,995.38

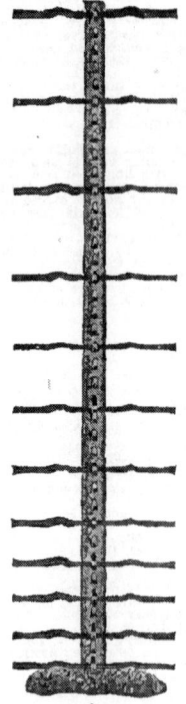

Brooks, 630, 440 South Dearborn street.
Church Club of Chicago (Episcopal)—1705, 29 East Madison street; secretary, Rev. J. H. Emerson.
Congregational Ministers' Union—Secretary, Rev. George W. Colman; meets on Monday forenoons at 913 Masonic Temple.
Cook County Sunday School Association—1415, 5 South Wabash avenue; chairman executive committee, H. W. Allen; general secretary, Elbert Beeman.
Epworth League—Central office, 1020 South Wabash avenue; general secretary, Rev. Wilbur F. Sheridan.
Illinois Christian Endeavor Union—405, 19 South LaSalle street; secretary, Estella Jorgenson.
Illinois Sunday School Association—1418, 5 South Wabash avenue; secretary, Hugh Cork.
Laymen's Evangelistic Council of Chicago—1007, 19 South LaSalle street; secretary, George C. Lazear.

Luther League of Chicago—Secretary, Miss Carrie Anderson, 2035 North Sawyer avenue.
Lutheran Ministers' Association—President, Rev. L. Harrisville, 1406 Washtenaw avenue.
National Christian Association—850 West Madison street; secretary, William I. Phillips.
Presbyterian Brotherhood of Chicago—President, Robert E. Ross, 924, 140 South Dearborn street.
Presbyterian Ministerial Association—Secretary, Rev. R. D. Kearns; meets Monday forenoons at 509 South Wabash avenue.
Presbyterian Social Union—Secretary, Thomas G. McCulloh, 5130 Hibbard avenue.
Young Men's Christian Association—19 South LaSalle street; general secretary, L. Wilbur Messer.
Young Women's Christian Association—830 South Michigan boulevard; corresponding secretary, Mrs. William W. Abbott.

INFORMATION FOR TAXPAYERS.
By Robert M. Sweitzer, county clerk.

Errors in Assessment.—The board of review holds its first meeting of the summer session for the purpose of revising the assessment of property on the third Monday of June, annually, and remains in session until Sept. 7, or until all complaints have been disposed of. New assessment of real estate and buildings is made every four years. The last quadrennial assessment was in 1911 and the next will be in 1915. The board has the power to revise assessment where an overvaluation exists, but it will not reduce the land value on single lots, where overassessment is found on lots the entire block or street will have to be reduced so that land values remain uniform. Complaints of errors in assessments must be filed on blanks provided by the board before Aug. 1 to affect the taxes for the current year. The board holds sessions in November, December, February and March to hear complaints, but action taken in any of these months cannot affect the taxes for the current year.

Payment of Taxes—The county clerk delivers on Jan. 2, annually, the tax books for the previous year's taxes to the county and various town collectors, after which date general taxes are due and payable up to March 10 as follows: On property inside the city of Chicago to the county collector; on property outside the city to the proper town collector at his town office. Special assessments may become due at any time during the year and should be paid to the city or village collector at his office.

After March 10 each year all bills for taxes and special assessments must be obtained from and paid to the county collector in the county building. On and after April 1 of each year he advertises all unpaid taxes as delinquent. He also gives notice of his intention to apply for judgment and an order for the sale of all property upon which taxes remain unpaid.

May 1 of each year all unpaid taxes on real estate are delinquent and a charge at the rate of 1 per cent per month on general taxes must be added by the county collector. The county collector applies shortly after the June term (usually in July) for judgment against all delinquent property in the county and at the same time a court order for the sale of all unpaid general taxes and special assessments is obtained. Objections to such judgment and sale must be made in writing and be filed in the office of the clerk of the County court at or before 10 a. m. of Wednesday, July 16 (in 1913), as that is the time usually set for filing the same.

On or shortly after Aug. 1 the collector and clerk begin the annual tax sale and sell all real estate upon which judgment has been given. The penalty for the redemption of real estate sold for taxes may be as high as 25 per cent, which penalty is added to the amount of taxes sold each six months after the date of sale.

Redemption of real estate sold for taxes must be made at the office of the county clerk before the expiration of two years. Penalties increase each six months after date of sale and two years is the limit allowed for redemption. A penalty of 7 per cent must be included in redemptions, the same being charged on account of any and all taxes or assessments which may have accrued subsequent to the date of sale, unless such assessments or taxes have been paid by the person making the redemption.

Tax deeds on unredeemed tax sales will necessarily be issued by the county clerk upon proper application after the time for redemption (two years) expires. After the tax deed is issued the former owner cannot redeem through the county clerk, as he has no such power. The release must be obtained by private arrangement with the tax purchaser or his assignee.

MUNICIPAL LODGING HOUSE.

162 North Union avenue. Operated by health department; G. B. Young, M. D., commissioner; W. R. Murray, M. D., chief of bureau of hospitals, public baths and lodging house.

The municipal lodging house is for the benefit of all homeless and indigent men and boys in the city. Lodging, a bath and food are provided free for every applicant for one night, and longer if he is honestly seeking employment. The crippled, old or infirm are sent each morning to hospitals, dispensaries or homes. Employment is found for the able-bodied and industrious. Statistics for the calendar years 1910, 1911 and 1912 are as follows:

	1910.	1911.	1912.
Lodgings given	36,710	71,410	71,459
Meals served	73,420	142,820	142,397
Situations supplied	1,727	1,457	1,707
Cripples received	193	185	206
Skilled laborers received	4,015	4,870	3,876
Unskilled laborers received	8,089	12,195	9,195
Sent to county agent	350	472	299
Sent to county hospital	263	180	73
Sent to charitable organizat's	223	277	210
Sent to dispensary	441	441	1,387

STATE SOCIETIES IN CHICAGO.

California Society of Illinois—President, Peter T. Mather; secretary, Edward P. Critcher, 402, 337 West Madison street.
Empire State Society of Chicago—President, John F. C. Merrill; secretary, F. J. Benbow.
Indiana Society of Chicago—President, William B. Austin; secretary, Edward M. Holloway, 725 Federal building.
Kansas Society of Chicago—President, George S. Wood; secretary, Miss Rena Stillwell, Chicago Beach hotel.
Michigan Society of Chicago—President, William L. Park; secretary, William R. Moss.
New England Society of Chicago—President, Seymour Morris; secretary, B. F. Paine, 415 West 61st street.
New York Society of Chicago—President, Dr. Alfred L. Cole; secretary, Ira Fogel, 1100, 8 South Dearborn street.
Ohio Society of Chicago—President, Orva G. Williams; secretary, Dr. Liston H. Montgomery.
Wisconsin Society of Chicago—President, Frederick W. Upham; secretary, Arba B. Marvin, 1020 Marquette building.

ASSESSMENT OF TAXABLE PROPERTY IN CHICAGO.

The following is a statement of the valuation of taxable real estate and personal property and the amount of taxes levied each year, from 1838 to 1913, inclusive:

YEAR.	Real estate.	Personal property.	Total valuation.	Tax levy.	YEAR.	Real estate.	Personal property.	Total valuation.	Tax levy.
1838......	$235,996	....	$235,996	$8,849.86	1876......	$128,822,403	$49,165,754	$167,908,157	$4,046,805.80
1839......	94,803	....	94,803	4,664.55	1877......	116,082,553	32,317,615	148,400,148	4,013,410.44
1840......	94,437	....	94,437	4,721.85	1878......	104,420,053	27,563,386	131,983,439	3,777,757.23
1841......	127,024	$39,720	166,744	10,004.67	1879......	91,152,229	26,517,806	117,970,035	3,776,450.79
1842......	108,757	42,585	151,342	9,181.27	1880......	89,032,039	28,101,688	117,133,729	3,899,126.98
1843......	962,221	479,093	1,441,314	8,647.89	1881......	90,099,045	29,053,743	119,152,288	4,198,008.38
1844......	1,992,085	771,196	2,763,281	17,168.24	1883......	95,881,714	29,479,022	125,360,736	4,227,402.98
1845......	2,273,171	791,851	3,065,022	11,077.58	1883......	101,595,705	31,618,893	153,213,598	4,540,506.13
1846......	3,664,425	857,231	4,521,656	15,825.86	1884......	105,606,743	31,720,237	137,326,980	4,872,456.00
1847......	4,995,466	853,704	5,849,170	18,159.01	1885......	107,146,881	32,811,411	139,958,292	5,152,366.03
1848......	4,998,266	1,302,174	6,300,440	22,051.54	1886......	122,960,123	35,516,009	158,456,132	5,368,469.76
1849......	5,181,637	1,495,047	6,676,684	30,045.09	1887......	123,169,455	38,055,080	161,204,535	5,602,712.56
1850......	5,685,965	1,534,284	7,220,249	25,270.87	1888......	123,292,358	37,349,385	160,641,723	5,723,087.25
1851......	6,804,262	1,758,455	8,562,717	63,385.87	1889......	127,372,618	40,763,213	168,135,831	6,326,561.21
1852......	8,190,769	2,272,645	10,463,414	76,948.96	1890......	170,553,854	48,800,514	219,354,368	9,558,335.00
1853......	13,130,677	3,711,154	16,841,831	135,062.68	1891......	203,353,791	53,245,783	256,599,574	10,453,270.41
1854......	18,990,744	5,401,495	24,392,239	199,051.64	1892......	190,614,636	53,117,502	243,732,138	12,142,448.75
1855......	21,637,500	5,355,393	26,992,893	208,209.05	1893......	189,259,120	56,491,251	245,750,351	11,810,969.69
1856......	25,892,308	5,843,776	31,736,084	396,652.39	1894......	190,960,897	56,461,825	247,422,722	12,297,643.82
1857......	29,807,628	7,027,653	36,835,281	572,046.00	1895......	192,498,842	50,977,983	243,476,825	14,239,685.13
1858......	30,175,825	5,816,407	35,991,732	430,190.00	1896......	195,684,875	48,672,411	244,357,286	12,250,145.21
1859......	30,732,313	5,821,067	36,553,380	513,164.00	1897......	184,632,905	47,393,755	232,026,660	12,959,333.10
1860......	31,198,135	5,855,377	37,053,512	373,315.29	1898......	178,801,172	42,165,275	220,966,447	12,207,906.82
1861......	31,314,749	5,037,631	36,352,380	559,968.00	1899......	260,265,058	84,931,361	345,196,419	13,359,270.53
1862......	31,587,545	5,552,300	37,139,845	564,103.06	1900......	202,884,012	73,681,568	276,565,580	17,086,408.86
1863......	35,143,252	7,524,072	42,667,324	853,346.00	1901......	259,354,598	115,325,842	374,580,440	14,245,294.12
1864......	37,148,023	11,584,759	48,732,782	971,655.61	1902......	276,508,730	125,985,401	402,495,131	14,039,030.16
1865......	44,065,499	20,644,678	64,710,177	1,291,183.50	1903......	289,377,249	122,053,031	411,424,280	14,815,388.81
1866......	65,495,116	29,458,134	85,953,250	1,719,054.05	1904......	291,820,703	111,951,487	408,281,190	15,294,410.89
1867......	141,445,920	53,580,924	195,026,844	2,518,472.00	1905......	295,514,443	112,477,182	407,991,625	16,845,974.19
1868......	174,490,660	55,756,340	230,247,000	3,223,457.80	1906......	305,033,228	123,230,068	426,263,296	17,454,168.80
1869......	211,371,240	54,653,640	266,024,890	3,990,873.20	1907......	346,843,590	131,078,886	477,921,976	22,605,709.45
1870......	223,643,600	52,342,950	275,986,550	4,139,798.70	1908......	344,499,927	132,690,473	477,190,599	22,666,543.94
1871......	236,898,650	52,847,820	289,746,470	2,897,464.70	1909......	586,253,555	212,574,401	833,150,997	24,078,030.96
1872......	239,154,880	45,042,540	284,197,420	4,462,961.46	1910......	603,022,875	245,971,661	848,994,536	23,485,538.22
1873......	262,969,820	49,103,175	312,072,995	5,817,313.91	1911......	663,376,027	235,578,274	927,747,492	27,811,841.58
1874......	258,549,310	45,155,830	303,705,140	4,466,692.54	1912......	670,552,219	195,473,058	940,450,171	24,733,839.48
1875......	125,468,605	48,295,641	173,764,246	5,108,987.40	1913......	688,389,520	248,523,812	981,788,078	....

The valuation since 1875 is the equalized valuation fixed by the state board of equalization. From 1867 to 1875 the valuation was made by the city for the city tax. From 1898 to 1908, inclusive, the assessed value was one-fifth of the actual value. In 1909 the rate was fixed at one-third. The total valuation includes capital stock and railroads.

ASSESSMENT OF TAXABLE PROPERTY IN COOK COUNTY.

Includes equalized valuation of railroads and capital stock of corporations.

1900..........	$306,957,900	1907..........	$514,757,122
1901..........	408,189,960	1908..........	514,730,532
1902..........	433,489,922	1909..........	897,212,850
1903..........	445,028,259	1910..........	915,895,947
1904..........	437,850,426	1911..........	997,787,837
1905..........	441,990,246	1912..........	1,012,882,262
1906..........	461,812,707	1913..........	1,056,673,878

The above figures are one-fifth of the actual valuation down to and including 1908. The rate was changed to one-third in 1909.

CHICAGO TAX RATES FOR 1913.

Town	State	County	City	School	Sanit'y	Park	Town	Total
West Chicago..	.70	.54	1.66	1.51	.52	...	...	$5.67
South Chicago.	.70	.54	1.66	1.51	.52	.39	...	5.32
North Chicago.	.70	.54	1.66	1.51	.52	.12	*5.64	
Hyde Park...	.70	.54	1.66	1.51	.52	.39	...	5.33
Lake	.70	.54	1.66	1.51	.52	.39	...	5.32
Lake View....	.70	.54	1.66	1.51	.52	.55	.10	†5.64
Jefferson	.70	.54	1.66	1.51	.52	...	...	4.93

*Includes .06 for Lincoln park bonds and .01 for lake shore protection. †Includes .06 for park bonds.

RATES FOR 1912.

	State	County	City	School	Sanit'y	Park	Town	Total
West Chicago..	.38	.52	1.24	1.69	.49	.69	...	$4.71
South Chicago.	.38	.52	1.24	1.39	.49	.38	...	4.40
North Chicago.	.38	.52	1.24	1.39	.49	.41	.12	*4.63
Hyde Park....	.38	.52	1.24	1.39	.49	.38	...	4.40
Lake	.38	.52	1.24	1.39	.49	.38	...	4.40
Lake View.....	.38	.52	1.24	1.39	.49	.49	.11	†4.69
Jefferson	.38	.52	1.24	1.39	.49	...	...	4.93

*Includes .01 for lake shore protection and .07 for Lincoln park bonds. †Includes .07 for Lincoln park bonds.

TAXING BODIES IN CHICAGO.

1. STATE TAX—For state purposes. The governor, auditor and treasurer constitute the board which ascertains the rate per cent required to produce the amount of taxes levied by the general assembly. The "state school tax" is levied in the same manner.

2. COUNTY TAX—The county board levies the taxes for all county purposes.

3. CITY TAX—The city council, acting with the mayor, levies the taxes for all city purposes.

4. SCHOOL TAX—The city council and the mayor make a separate levy for this purpose.

5. LIBRARY TAX—The city council and the mayor make a separate levy for this purpose.

6. SANITARY DISTRICT—The tax is levied by the board of trustees.

7. SOUTH PARK SYSTEM—The south park commissioners levy for park purposes in the towns of South Chicago, Hyde Park and Lake.

8. WEST PARK SYSTEM—The West Chicago park commissioners levy for park purposes in the town of West Chicago.

9. LINCOLN PARK—The Lincoln park commissioners are not "corporate authorities," the Lincoln park act not having been adopted by popular vote. The levy for Lincoln park is made by the county treasurer, acting as ex officio supervisor.

10. RIDGE PARK—A small park district in Rogers Park, organized under the law providing for local park districts by popular vote. The board of five commissioners levies for the district.

11. THE NORTH SHORE PARK DISTRICT—Organized the same as Ridge Park.

There are in addition a number of minor taxing bodies, such as the Calumet, Irving, Northwest and Fernwood park boards.

By an act of the legislature approved May 11, 1901, and by the vote of the people at the spring election in 1902 the townships lying within the limits of Chicago were consolidated and the powers of the town boards transferred to the city council.

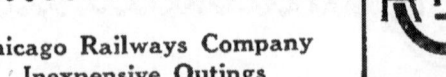

Chicago Railways Company
Inexpensive Outings

Trip No. 1—TO LINCOLN PARK AND THE "ZOO": Time one way, twenty-five minutes. Take Clark-Devon, Broadway or Bowmanville car at Dearborn and Monroe; ride to park entrance at Center street, passing on the way through the company's tunnel under the Chicago River, and also within one block of the Chicago Historical Society's library and museum on Dearborn and Ontario streets, and also past the Newberry Library (famous collection of books) at Walton place.

Trip No. 2—TO GARFIELD PARK: Time one way, thirty minutes. Take Madison street car at State and Madison to park entrance at Central Park avenue, passing on the way the new $20,000,000 Northwestern railroad station at Canal street, and through the great west side shopping district.

Trip No. 3—TO DOUGLAS PARK: Time one way, thirty minutes. Take Ogden avenue car at State and Washington to park entrance near 16th street, passing on the way through the famous Haymarket Square, where anarchists and police met in deadly combat, many years ago. This location (on Randolph street from Desplaines to Halsted) is now a great wholesale market, where farmers bring their products.

Trip No. 4—TO HUMBOLDT PARK: Time one way, thirty-five minutes. Take Division street car at State and Randolph, direct to park entrance at California avenue, passing on the way through the lower section of Milwaukee avenue's great center of trade for the cosmopolitan west side.

Trip No. 5—TO THE GHETTO DISTRICT: Time one way, twenty minutes. Take 12th street car at Dearborn and Adams to Jefferson street. Walk south through the crowded tenement district, where a large section of Chicago's foreign population transact their business. An interesting sight.

Trip No. 6—TO DUNNING INSTITUTION: Time one way, sixty minutes. Take Milwaukee avenue car from State and Madison streets to Irving Park boulevard. Transfer west to Chicago State Hospital entrance near end of line. Here are confined many unfortunate charges of the state, insane and others.

Trip No. 7—TO BOWMANVILLE: Time one way, fifty minutes. Take Bowmanville (Clark-Lincoln) car at Dearborn and Monroe to end of line. This is Bowmanville, a great truck gardening center. On the way the passenger sees all the points of interest of Trip 1, and continues northwest through Lincoln avenue's retail store district.

Trip No. 8—TO EVANSTON (10c): Time one way, eighty minutes. Take Broadway-Howard car at Monroe and Dearborn to end of line (city limits), passing through the same territory as Trip 1, beyond through the old town of Lake View, through Buena Park and Sheridan Park residence districts, through Edgewater (always within a few blocks of Lake Michigan and aristocratic Sheridan road), to city limits. Pay another 5c on a connecting car to Evanston, a wealthy suburb, home of Northwestern University. Here one may take a Chicago & Milwaukee electric car for a long ride to Milwaukee, Wis.

Trip No. 9—TO RIVER FOREST (10c). Time one way, seventy minutes. Take Lake street car at Lake and State streets, through the old west side factory district to end of the line at 60th avenue. Pay another fare on a connecting car, riding through Oak Park, Melrose Park and over the Des Plaines River to River Forest, a beautiful scenic trip.

THE ART INSTITUTE OF CHICAGO.

A museum of fine arts and school of drawing, painting, etc.

Michigan avenue and Adams street.

OFFICERS.

President—Charles L. Hutchinson.
Vice-Presidents—Martin A. Ryerson, Frank G. Logan.
Secretary—Newton H. Carpenter.
Assistant Secretary—William F. Tuttle.
Treasurer—Ernest A. Hamill.
Auditor—William A. Angell.
Director—W. M. R. French.
Librarian—Miss Mary Van Horne.
School Registrar—Theodore J. Keane.
Trustees, 1913-1914—Edward E. Ayer, Adolphus C. Bartlett, John C. Black, Chauncey J. Blair, Edward B. Butler, Clyde M. Carr, Wallace S. DeWolf, Henry H. Getty, John J. Glessner, William O. Goodman, Frank W. Gunsaulus, Charles L. Hutchinson, Bryan Lathrop, Frank G. Logan, R. Hall McCormick, John J. Mitchell, Samuel M. Nickerson, Honore Palmer, Martin A. Ryerson, Howard Shaw, Albert A. Sprague. Ex officio: Carter H. Harrison, mayor; John E. Traeger, city comptroller; John Barton Payne, president south park commissioners; Joseph Donnersberger, auditor south park commissioners.

The Art Institute of Chicago was incorporated May 24, 1879, for the "founding and maintenance of schools of art and design, the formation and exhibition of collections of objects of art and the cultivation and extension of the arts of design by any appropriate means." The museum building upon the lake front, first occupied in 1893, has never been closed for a day. It is open to the public every week day from 9 to 6, Sundays from 12:15 to 10 p. m. Admission is free to members and their families at all times, and free to all upon Wednesdays, Saturdays, Sundays and legal holidays. Upon other days the entrance fee is 25 cents.

All friends of art are invited to become members. Annual members pay a fee of $10 a year. Life members pay $100 and are thenceforth exempt from dues. Governing members pay $100 upon election and $25 a year thereafter. Upon the payment of $400 governing members become governing life members and are thenceforth exempt from dues. All receipts from life memberships are invested and the income only expended. All members are entitled, with their families and visiting friends, to admission to all exhibitions, receptions, public lectures and entertainments given by the Art Institute and to the use of the Ryerson reference library upon art. Visitors desiring to see the collections under guidance may make appointments with the museum instructors at the office of the director.

MUSEUM.

The Art museum now ranks among the first three or four in the country. It contains excellent examples of the old masters and of the modern painters. There is also a large and comprehensive collection of sculptures, including reproductions of the work of the greatest sculptors, ancient and modern. There is an extensive collection of architectural casts. Other fields of art are represented by collections of etchings, engravings, textiles, oriental art, Egyptian and classical antiquities, etc.

There is a constant succession of passing exhibitions, thirty or more in a year. All students enjoy the full use of the collections and the library. The number of visitors to the museum during the year ended June 1, 1913, was 925,697.

SCHOOL.

The school of instruction in the practice and theory of art includes departments of painting, sculpture, decorative designing, illustration, architecture and normal instruction. There are day and evening classes for beginners and for advanced pupils and special classes on Saturdays. The instructors number about 80 and the pupils average about 3,000 a year. The principle upon which the school is founded is to maintain in the highest efficiency the severe practice of academic drawing and painting, from life, from the antique and from objects, and around this practice, as a living stem, to group the various departments of art education.

The school is conducted upon the most modern methods and has grown to be the most comprehensive and probably the largest fine arts school in the United States. Constant communication and interchange are kept up with European art centers and distinguished teachers from a distance are called in from time to time. Students may enter at any time. The tuition rates are as follows:

Day School—Full time for full term of twelve weeks, $30; four weeks, $12; four days a week, full term, $27; four weeks, $11; three days a week, full term, $24; four weeks, $9; two days a week, full term, $18; four weeks, $7; one day a week, full term, $12; four weeks, $5.

Half-Day Courses—Five half days a week, $24 a term; four weeks, $10; four half days a week, $21 a term; four weeks, $9; three half days a week, $17 a term; four weeks, $7; two half days a week, $13 a term; four weeks, $5; one half day a week, $8 a term; four weeks, $4.

Evening Rates—Three nights a week, $7 for twelve weeks or $3 for four weeks; two nights a week, $5.50 a term or $2.50 for four weeks; one night a week, $4 a term or $2 for four weeks.

Saturday Rates for Juvenile Class—Twelve half days for $5.

Special Classes—

Pottery—Twelve half days	$8.00
Leather—Twelve half days	6.00
Metal—Twelve half days	6.00
Bookbinding—Twelve half days	6.00
Drawing—Twelve half days	5.00
Design—Twelve half days	5.00
Ceramic Painting—Twelve half days	8.00
Ceramic Design—Twelve half days	6.00

The attendance of students for the year ended June 1, 1913, was as follows:

Day school	1,024
Saturday school	735
Evening school	888
Summer school	235
Total	3,116
Students belonging to two schools	230
Grand total	2,886

SOCIETIES OF ARTISTS AND ART CLUBS.

Art Students' League—Art institute; president, Henry Kiefer; secretary, Beatrice Levy.
Artists' Guild—602, 410 South Michigan avenue; president, Charles T. Brown; secretary, Edward M. Ericson.
Chicago Arts and Crafts Society—Secretary, R. R. Jarvie, 842 Exchange avenue.
Chicago Camera Club—329 Plymouth court; president, George C. McKee; secretary, Thomas E. Kiely.
Chicago Ceramic Art Association—Art institute; president, Mrs. Isabella C. Kissinger; corresponding secretary, Miss Marie Bohman, 1161 West Madison street.

Chicago Public School Art Society—President, Mrs. John H. Buckingham; corresponding secretary, Mrs. Alfred M Walter, 2729 Prairie avenue.
Chicago Socie.. of Artists (organized 1902)—President, Charles E. Bontwood; secretary, George F. Schultz, 818 Schiller building; meets in Art institute.
Chicago Water Color Club (organized 1907)—President, George F. Schultz; secretary, Dudley Crafts Watson.
Municipal Art League of Chicago—President, Ralph Clarkson; secretary, Everett L. Millard.
Palette and Chisel Club — President, Fred S. Bertsch; secretary, Gordon St. Clair.

PRINCIPAL LIBRARIES OF CHICAGO AND EVANSTON.

THE CHICAGO PUBLIC LIBRARY.

Michigan avenue and Washington street.

Board of Directors—Antonio Lagorio, president; Max Henius, vice-president; Philip M. Ksycki, Samuel Despres, Charles C. Breyer, Malcolm McDowell, James J. Healy, Frank J. Pokorney, T. Frank O'Connell.

Standing Committees (1913-1914)—Library: Despres, Henius, Healy. Administration: Henius, McDowell, Pokorney. Branches: McDowell, Henius, O'Connell. Delivery stations: Ksycki, Breyer, Despres, O'Connell. Finance: Healy, McDowell, Breyer. By-Laws: O'Connell, Despres, Ksycki. Meetings—Regular meetings of the board are held at 5 p. m. on the second and fourth Mondays of each month.

Librarian—Henry E. Legler.
Assistant Librarian—Carl B. Roden.
Secretary—Harry G. Wilson.

DEPARTMENTS AND HOURS.

Circulating, open shelf and registry departments, third floor; open 9 a. m. to 8:30 p. m.; closed on Sunday.

Reference room and public card catalogue, fourth floor; open 9 a. m. to 10 p. m.; Sundays and holidays, 9 a. m. to 6 p. m.

Thomas Hughes room for young people, fourth floor; open 9 a. m. to 6:30 p. m.; closed on Sunday.

Art room, fifth floor; open 9 a. m. to 5:30 p. m.; closed on Sunday.

Patents, documents and bound newspapers room, first floor, Randolph street entrance; open 9 a. m. to 5:30 p. m.; closed on Sunday.

Civics room, first floor, Randolph street entrance; open 9 a. m. to 10 p. m.; closed on Sunday.

Reading room for current magazines and newspapers, fourth floor, Randolph street entrance; open 9 a. m. to 10 p. m.; Sundays and holidays, 9 a. m. to 6 p. m.

GENERAL INFORMATION.

The Chicago public library is a free public institution, established under the Illinois library law of 1872. It derives its revenue from an annual library tax of approximately four-tenths of a mill. A board of directors of nine members is appointed by the mayor, three annually for terms of three years. The library occupies the site formerly known as Dearborn park, bounded by Michigan avenue, Washington street, Garland court and Randolph street. The cost of the building was about $2,000,000, including the furniture, book stacks and machinery. There are twenty-six branches and 118 delivery stations.

The right of drawing books from the public library belongs to all who reside in the city of Chicago, and also to those who make their homes in the suburbs within the limits of Cook county and are regularly employed in the city. In order to become a book borrower it is necessary only to file an application giving the name and residence of the applicant and bearing the signature of a second person, who must be an actual resident of the city, appearing as such in the latest city directory. This person becomes the guarantor to the library for the proper observance of the library regulations on the part of the applicant. These regulations merely provide that books drawn for home use must be returned within the stated period and must not be defaced or injured.

At the close of May 31, 1913, the public library contained 514,259 volumes. The aggregate circulation for the year ending May 31, 1913, was 3,037,035 volumes, which does not include the use of books kept on the open shelves at the main library or its branches or the periodicals or newspapers used in the reading rooms. This use would bring the total book issue to 3,665,796.

BRANCHES.

Open from 1 to 9 p. m. Blackstone, Lewis Institute and Lincoln Center open forenoons also.

Blackstone.......................49th-st. and Lake-av.
Lewis Institute...................1943 W. Madison-st.
Austin..5642 Lake-st.
Burr school...............Ashland and Wabansia-avs.
Lincoln Center.........Oakwood-bd. and Langley-av.

Lawndale......................Millard-av. and 23d-st
Twenty-sixth street...................2347 W. 26th-st
West Park 1..............Chicago-av. and Noble-st
West Park 2..................14th-pl. and Union-st
West Park 3.....................20th and Fisk-sts.
Sherman....................Loomis and W. 53d-sts.
Cornell.......................Wood and W. 51st-sts.
Mark White..................Halsted and 30th-sts.
Hebrew Institute................Taylor and Lytle-sts.

DELIVERY STATIONS.

North.
1. Elm and Orleans-sts.
2. 2004 Larrabee-st.
3. 2544 Lincoln-av.
4. 4356 N. Hermitage-av.
5. 4016 Lincoln-av.
6. 651 North-av.
7. 7013 N. Clark-st.
8. 3175 Lincoln-av.
9. 6708 Ridge-av.
10. 3230 N. Clark-st.
11. 3701 N. Halsted-st.
12. 1126 Argyle-st.
13. 1133 Wilson-av.
14. 6175 Broadway.
15. 5942 N. Clark-st.

South.
1. 52 E. 22d-st.
2. 804 E. 31st-st.
3. Oakwood-bd. and Langley-av.
4. 563 W. 43d-st.
5. 49th-st. and Lake-av.
6. 443 W. 63d-st.
7. 2876 Archer-av.
8. 89th-st. and Muskegon-av.
9. 9901 Ewing-av.
10. 72d-st. and Normal-av.
11. 956 E. 55th-st.
12. 336 E. 39th-st.
13. 541 E. 47th-st.
14. 657 W. 120th-st.
15. 11100 Michigan-av.
16. 146 W. 69th-st.
17. 1304 E. 63d-st.
18. 1246 E. 75th-st.
19. 45th-st. and Marshfield-av.
20. 8671 Vincennes-av.
21. 5523 S. Halsted-st.
22. 64th-st. and S. Racine-av.
23. 33d-st. and Shields-av.
24. 7502 Saginaw-av.
25. 5005 State-st.
26. 6603 Cottage Grove-av.
27. 3584 63d-st.
28. 5902 Wentworth-av.
29. 629 92d-pl.
30. 313 E. 58th-st.
31. 553 E. 71st-st.

32. 94th-st. and Winchester-av.
33. 3805 Washtenaw-av.
34. 68th-st. and Stewart-av.

West.
1. 14th-pl. and Union-av.
2. 1722 Grand-av.
3. 1943 W. Madison-st.
4. 1813 S. Ashland-av.
5. 1500 Milwaukee-av.
6. 728 S. Western-av.
7. 1625 N. California-av.
8. 3555 Ogden-av.
9. 1011 W. Harrison-st.
10. 4035 W. Madison-st.
11. 4200 Irving Park-bd.
12. 2822 W. Madison-st.
13. 3249 W. Belmont-av.
14. 2639 N. Rockwell-st.
15. 4431 N. Kilpatrick-av.
16. 4055 W. 26th-st.
17. 3306 W. 12th-st.
18. 2286 Milwaukee-av.
19. 3605 Armitage-av.
20. 6013 Ceylon-av.
21. Taylor and Lytle-sts.
22. 636 N. Lawndale-av.
23. 4056 W. North-av.
24. Grand-av. and Sangamon-st.
25. 5642 Lake-st.
26. 2248 W. Ohio-st.
27. 4209 Armitage-av.
28. 426 N. Harrison-st.
29. 426 N. Kedzie-av.
30. 1959 W. 20th-st.
31. 3123-3125 W. 22d-st.
32. 3347 W. 26th-st.
33. 4822 Milwaukee-av.
34. 5124 W. Chicago-av.
35. 20th and Fisk-sts.
36. Chicago-av. and Noble-st.
37. 2659 Monticello-av.
38. 3406 W. North-av.
39. 610 N. Cicero-av.
40. Ashland and Wabansia-avs.
41. 2063 W. 12th-st.
42. 1105 N. California-av.
43. Millard-av. and 23d-st.
44. 628 S. Cicero-av.

THE JOHN CRERAR LIBRARY.

110 North Wabash avenue, 6th floor.

President—Hon. Peter S. Grosscup.
Vice-Presidents—Thomas D. Jones and Robert Forsyth.
Secretary—Leonard A. Busby.
Treasurer—William J. Louderback.
Librarian—Clement W. Andrews.
Board of Directors—E. W. Blatchford, Robert T. Lincoln, John M. Clark, Frank S. Johnson, Peter S. Grosscup, Marvin Hughitt, Thomas D. Jones, John J. Mitchell, Leonard A. Busby, Robert Forsyth, Chauncey Keep, Frederick H. Rawson and the mayor and the comptroller of the city of Chicago, ex officio.
Hours—The library is open daily, except Sunday, from 9 a. m. to 10 p. m.

The John Crerar library contained in October, 1913, 319,000 volumes and 100,000 pamphlets on the social, physical, natural and medical sciences and

their applications. They cannot be taken from the library, but may be freely consulted by all who wish to do so. The department of medical science, formerly housed in the Newberry library building, has now been moved to the main library, where the Senn reading room is open to physicians and students.

THE NEWBERRY LIBRARY.
North Clark street and Walton place.

President—E. W. Blatchford.
Librarian—William N. C. Carlton.
Secretary—Jesse L. Moss.
Trustees—George E. Adams, Eliphalet W. Blatchford, Frederick I. Carpenter, Franklin H. Head, David B. Jones, Bryan Lathrop, George Manierre, Horace H. Martin, Edward L. Ryerson, John A. Spoor, John P. Wilson, John P. Wilson, Jr., Moses J. Wentworth.
Hours—From 9 a. m. to 10 p. m. every day except Sundays and the following holidays: Jan. 1, May 30, July 4, Thanksgiving and Christmas.
The Newberry library, Nov. 1, 1913, contained 350,955 books and pamphlets. These are not circulated, but are kept for reference purposes. The library is free to the public.

EVANSTON PUBLIC LIBRARY.
Orrington avenue and Church street.

Free to residents of Evanston and open to others on payment of an annual fee of $2.50, or 25 cents a month. Reference department free to all. Library open from 9 a. m. to 9 p. m. week days. Reading room open from 2 to 6 p. m. Sundays, except during July and August, and holidays, except Jan. 1, July 4, Thanksgiving day and Dec. 25. The Coe music collection, which contains more than 1,400 books, 388 pieces of sheet music and 560 pianola rolls, is open to all. The medical science room, containing over 600 medical books and periodicals, is open to resident physicians and nurses and to others by special arrangement. Total number of volumes June 1, 1913, 49,638. Librarian, Mary B. Lindsay.

LEWIS INSTITUTE LIBRARY.
West Madison and Robey streets.

The Lewis institute library contains about 21,000 volumes and 6,000 pamphlets. The public is invited to use the library for reference, but books are loaned only to instructors and students of the institute. Throughout the school year the library is open from 8 a. m. to 5 p. m. daily except on Saturday, when it closes at 3 p. m.; during the session of the night school the library is also open from 8 a. m. to 9:30 p. m. Librarian, Miss Frances S. Talcott.

UNIVERSITY OF CHICAGO LIBRARY.
At the university, 59th street and Ellis avenue.

This library contained July 1, 1913, 403,503 bound volumes and 195,000 pamphlets. It is primarily for the use of the faculty and students at the university, but others may have the privilege of drawing books available for circulation upon the payment of a fee. Properly accredited scholars visiting Chicago will receive complimentary cards for a term of four weeks or less upon application. The reading room is open to all. The director of the library is Ernest D. Burton; the associate director is J. C. M. Hanson.

CHICAGO HISTORICAL SOCIETY LIBRARY.
Dearborn avenue and West Ontario street.

President—Clarence A. Burley.
First Vice-President—Charles H. Conover.
Second Vice-President—Dr. Otto L. Schmidt.
Secretary—Seymour Morris.
Treasurer—Orson Smith.
Librarian—Caroline M. McIlvaine.
Executive Committee—Clarence A. Burley, Seymour Morris, Edward L. Ryerson, William A. Fuller, Charles F. Gunther, Edward F. Swift, Joy Morton, John A. Spoor.
The library, museum and portrait gallery are open free to the public from 9 a. m. to 5 p. m. on week days. It is a repository of matter relating to the history and archæology of the northwest, particularly of Chicago, comprising some 40,000 volumes and 75,000 pamphlets and a large collection of MSS., maps, views, etc., illustrative of the development of Illinois and the central west.

ST. IGNATIUS' COLLEGE LIBRARY.
1076 West 12th street.

The library of the college of arts of Loyola university. It contains about 45,000 volumes for the use of the faculty and students, but may be consulted by others on application to the librarian. Open from 8 a. m. to 4 p. m. Librarian, A. J. Garvy, S. J.

WESTERN SOCIETY OF ENGINEERS.
1735 Monadnock block.

The library of this society contains over 9,2[..] volumes, almost altogether engineering, scientific and technical works, and is maintained at the cost of the society. It is a free public reference library, open for use during business hours of business day. Secretary and librarian, J. H. Warder.

CHICAGO LAW INSTITUTE LIBRARY.
1025 County building.

President—Frederick A. Smith.
Secretary—Alfred E. Barr.
Treasurer—Frederic S. Hebard.
Librarian—William H. Holden.
The library contains about 58,000 volumes.

GARRETT BIBLICAL INSTITUTE LIBRARY.
Evanston, Ill.

This is a reference library of theology for the use of the faculty and students of the institute, but open to the public October to June from 8 a. m. to 6 p. m. and from 7 to 10 p. m. Nov. 1, 1913, the library contained 37,835 volumes. Librarian, Doremus A. Hayes; assistant librarian in charge, Samuel G. Ayres.

NORTHWESTERN UNIVERSITY LIBRARY.
Evanston, Ill.

The Northwestern university library contains 145,000 bound volumes and 87,000 pamphlets July 1, 1913. The library is open during the college year from 8 a. m. to 10 p. m. daily, except Sunday, and during the summer vacation from 8 a. m. to 12 m. and from 1:30 to 5 p. m. Librarian, Walter Lichtenstein.

PULLMAN PUBLIC LIBRARY.
73 to 77 Arcade building, Pullman, Ill.

Contains 10,000 volumes. Library open from 1 a. m. to 5:30 p. m. and in the evenings from 6:45 to 9 o'clock; also Sundays and holidays, 2 to 6 p. m. Librarian, Bertha S. Ludlam; assistants, Caroline H. Mott and Rhoda Hiestand.

FIELD MUSEUM OF NATURAL HISTORY LIBRARY.
Jackson park.

The museum library occupies three rooms in the north end of the building and is open to the public every week day from 9 a. m. to 4:30 p. m. It is a scientific reference library. Visitors can consult books by making application to the office of the library. The magazines in the reading room are accessible to the public. Sept. 30, 1913, the library contained approximately 60,000 books and pamphlets. Librarian, Elsie Lippincott.

RYERSON LIBRARY.
Art institute, Michigan avenue and Adams street

The Ryerson library of the Art institute is devoted to works on fine art and travel. It contains more than 8,500 bound volumes and collections of 29,500 photographs and 11,000 lantern slides. Open every day from 8:30 a. m. to 5:30 p. m. The library is primarily for the students of the institute, but is practically a free reference library on fine art. Librarian, Mary Van Horne.

HAMMOND LIBRARY.
1610 Warren avenue.

The Hammond library of the Chicago Theological seminary contains 32,000 volumes. It is intended for the use of the faculty and students of the Chicago Theological seminary, but may be used by clergymen and others. The library is open on week days from Sept. 29 to May 5 from 8:30 a. m. to 12 m. and from 1 to 10 p. m., except Saturdays, when it is closed at 5 p. m.; May 6 to Sept. 23 from 8:30 a. m. to 12 m. and 1 to 5 p. m.; Saturdays 8:30 a. m. to 12 m.; closed Sundays. Assistant librarian, Edith M. Morgan.

CHILDREN'S SCIENCE LIBRARY.

The Chicago Academy of Sciences, Lincoln park, contains over 600 volumes for children on natural history, including plants, animals, astronomy, geography and industries. The reading room is open from 9 a. m. to 4:30 p. m. each week day. Individual guidance in the proper use of nature study books is given by the librarian.

ELBERT H. GARY LAW LIBRARY.
Northwestern University building, North Dearborn and West Lake streets, Chicago.

The Gary Library of Law, one of the largest of the kind in existence, was the gift of Elbert H. Gary of New York, N. Y., to the Northwestern University Law school. It is open, without charge, to nonresident lawyers presenting satisfactory credentials. Resident lawyers who are graduates of the Northwestern University Law school are charged a registration fee of $1 per year for the privilege of using the library; all other resident lawyers are charged a registration fee of $4 a year. The library in 1913 contained about 43,000 volumes. Librarian, F. B. Crossley.

FIELD MUSEUM OF NATURAL HISTORY.

President—Stanley Field.
Vice-Presidents—Martin A. Ryerson, Watson F. Blair.
Director of the Museum and Secretary—Frederick J. V. Skiff.
Treasurer—Byron L. Smith.
Assistant Secretary and Recorder—D. C. Davies.

The Field Museum of Natural History, established in 1894 at the close of the World's Columbian exposition of 1893, occupies the temporary building erected for fine arts in Jackson park, the exposition site. The founding of a scientific institution of this character in Chicago was made possible by the gift of $1,000,000 by Marshall Field, who on his death (Jan. 16, 1906) bequeathed the institution a further $8,000,000, $4,000,000 for the erection of a permanent building and $4,000,000 for endowment. In addition $800,000 has been donated by other individuals and there is an annual income from other sources than endowment of about $25,000. The citizens of Chicago have confirmed legislative provision for the levy of a tax for the maintenance of the museum when a new building shall have been erected, which it is estimated will eventually produce approximately $100,000 per annum.

The nucleus of the exhibition material was gathered by gift and purchase at the World's Columbian exposition. Most of this material, however, has since been rearranged, readapted or discarded. Several departments created at the organization have been abandoned, until, after the lapse of eleven years and the expenditure of over $4,000,000, the museum is now divided into four departments—namely, anthropology, botany, geology and zoology. Many expeditions for the purpose of obtaining study, exhibition and exchange material and data have been dispatched to all parts of North America and to different countries. The results of these expeditions, investigations and researches have been published by the museum from time to time, which publications have been distributed to kindred societies and institutions both at home and abroad. Two courses of free lectures are given annually. An important contribution of $250,000 by Norman W. Harris was announced in December, 1911, for the extension of the work of the museum into the public schools of Chicago. The plans for carrying out Mr. Harris' wishes were placed in operation in the spring of 1913. The museum has a working library of about 52,000 titles, an extensive exchange system, fully equipped departmental laboratories, a herbarium of 280,000 sheets, study collections in mammals and birds reaching many thousand specimens, a large two-story taxidermy section, a well equipped printing shop, illustration studios and assaying and lapidary rooms. In North American ethnology, in the world's mineralogy, in economic botany the museum is particularly prominent, while its series of mounted mammals furnish examples of advanced museum methods. The present main building covers nine acres and is open to the public on all days except Christmas and Thanksgiving. An admission fee of 25 cents is charged except on Saturdays and Sundays, when admission is free to all. Students, scholars and teachers are admitted free on all days between 9 a. m. and 4 p. m.

The museum is incorporated under state law and the administrative control rests in a board of trustees with president, secretary, etc. The executive of the museum is the director, under whom there are four head curators with divisional assistant curators, preparators, etc. The entire museum records, the accessions system, the historical files, publications and supplies are in charge of a recorder.

CHICAGO CITY ATTORNEYS SINCE 1837.

N. B. Judd	1837-1839	John C. Miller	1857	George F. Sugg	1889-1891
Samuel L. Smith	1839	Elliott Anthony	1858	Jacob J. Kern	1891-1893
Mark Skinner	1840	George F. Crocker	1859	George A. Trude	1893-1895
George Manierre	1841, 1843	John Lyle King	1860	Roy O. West	1895-1897
Henry Brown	1842	Ira W. Buell	1861	Miles J. Devine	1897-1899
Henry W. Clarke	1844-1845	George A. Meech	1862	Andrew J. Ryan	1899-1902
Charles H. Larrabee	1846	Francis Adams	1863-1864	John E. Owens	1902-1903
Patrick Ballingall	1847, 1854	Daniel D. Driscoll	1865-1866	John F. Smulski	1903-1905
Giles Spring	1848	Hasbrouck Davis	1867-1869	Frank D. Ayers	1905-1907
O. R. W. Lull	1849	Israel N. Stiles	1869-1873	John R. Caverly	1908-1910
Henry H. Clark	1850-1851	Egbert Jamieson	1873-1876	Clyde L. Day	1910-1911
Arno Voss	1852-1853	R. S. Tuthill	1876-1878	Nicholas L. Piotrowsky	1911
J. A. Thompson	1855	Julius S. Grinnell	1879-1885	The city attorneyship became an appointive office in 1905.	
J. L. Marsh	1856	Hempstead Washburne	1885-1889		

WAGES OF CHICAGO STREET RAILWAY EMPLOYES.

In August, 1912, the employes of the Chicago street railway companies voted to strike unless given an advance in wages. The matter was referred to an arbitration board consisting of Justice Orrin N. Carter of the State Supreme court, representing the public; Herbert E. Fleming, representing the companies, and Judge Kickham Scanlan, representing the employes. The board after a long and careful examination made its award March 29, 1913, announcing the following scale to date back to Aug. 1, 1912:

First 3 months	$0.23	Third year	.29
Second 3 months	.25	Fourth year	.30
Second 6 months	.26	Fifth year	.31
Third 6 months	.27	Sixth year	.32
Fourth 6 months	.28		

This was practically an advance of 2 cents an hour over the old scale. Judge Scanlan made a minority report advocating a higher scale.

MAP OF THE CHICAGO CITY RAILWAY COMPANY

(Including the Calumet and Southern Companies)

SHOWING ELECTRIC INTERURBAN CONNECTIONS

(Dotted line indicates Chicago Railways Company)

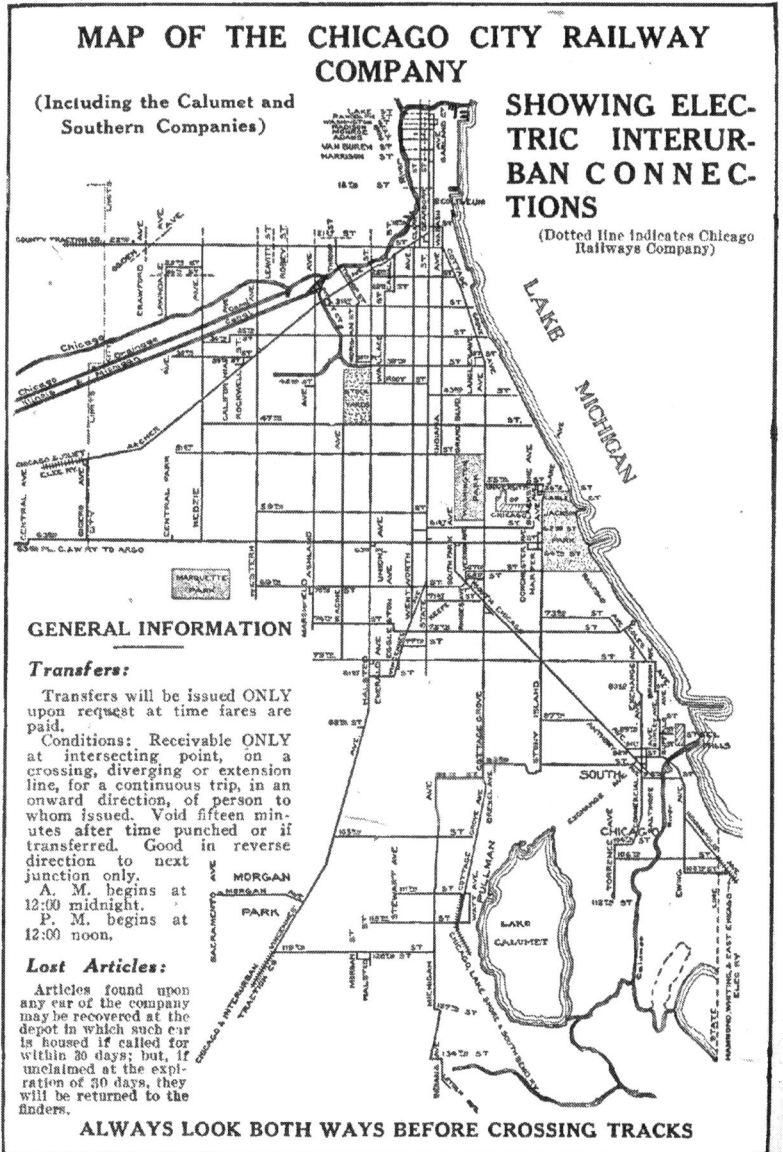

GENERAL INFORMATION

Transfers:

Transfers will be issued ONLY upon request at time fares are paid.

Conditions: Receivable ONLY at intersecting point, on a crossing, diverging or extension line, for a continuous trip, in an onward direction, of person to whom issued. Void fifteen minutes after time punched or if transferred. Good in reverse direction to next junction only.

A. M. begins at 12:00 midnight.

P. M. begins at 12:00 noon.

Lost Articles:

Articles found upon any car of the company may be recovered at the depot in which such car is housed if called for within 30 days; but, if unclaimed at the expiration of 30 days, they will be returned to the finders.

ALWAYS LOOK BOTH WAYS BEFORE CROSSING TRACKS

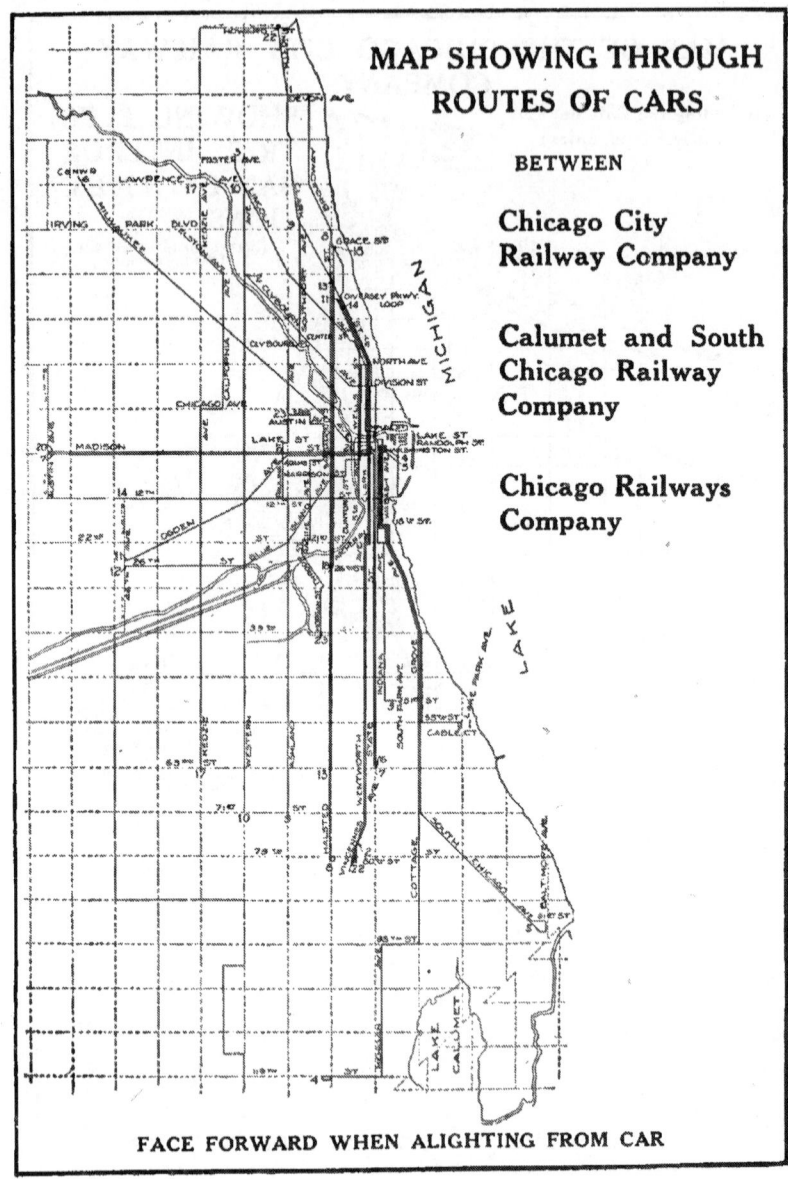

MAP SHOWING THROUGH
ROUTES OF CARS

BETWEEN

Chicago City
Railway Company

Calumet and South
Chicago Railway
Company

Chicago Railways
Company

FACE FORWARD WHEN ALIGHTING FROM CAR

CONDENSED TIME TABLE—OWL CAR SERVICE
NORTH AND SOUTH LINES

So. Chgo. No. 5 Interval 45 min.	Cottage Grove				Indiana 51st Interv'l 15 min.		State 73d Interv'l 15 min.		Went-worth 79th Interv'l 15 min.		TIME POINTS Intersecting Lines	Halsted 79th Interv'l 15 min.		Wall'ce and Racine Interv'l 30 min.		Ashl'nd No. 9 Interv'l 15 min.		West'rn No. 10 Interv'l 30 min.		Kedzie 22d-63d Interv'l 1 hour	
	Grand Cross'g Interv'l 15 min.		55th Interv'l 15 min.																			
	1st owl	last owl	1st owl	last owl	1st owl	last owl	1st owl	last owl	1st owl	last owl	**NORTHBOUND**	1st owl	last owl	1st owl	last owl	1st owl	last owl	1st owl	last owl	1st owl	last owl
Lv. 93d & Baltimore	12.48	5.08	1.47	5.02	12.55	4.55	1.00	4.15	12.15	4.00	Lv..Terminal..Lv.	12.08	4.38	12.01	4.31	12.00	6.15	12.00	5.00	11.55	4.53
	12.53	5.08					1.02	4.17	12.24	4.09	Lv..67th-69th..Lv.	12.14	4.44	12.04	4.34	12.01	4.16				
	12.56	5.11					1.06	4.21	12.28	4.13	Lv.....63d.....Lv.	12.20	4.50	12.08	4.38	12.05	4.20	12.05	5.05	11.58	4.53
	12.57	5.12					1.07	4.22	12.30	4.15	Lv..59th-61st..Lv.	12.22	4.52	12.10	4.40	12.07	4.22				
	1.01	5.16	1.58	5.13							Ar.55th&C.G.Ar.										
	1.03	5.18			12.56	4.56	1.13	4.28	12.35	4.20	Lv.....51st.....Lv.	12.27	4.57	12.15	4.45	12.12	4.27				
	1.05	5.21			12.58	4.58	1.16	4.31	12.38	4.23	Lv.....47th.....Lv.	12.30	5.00	12.18	4.48	12.15	4.30	12.15	5.15	12.08	5.03
12.30	1.08	5.23			1.00	5.00	1.19	4.34	12.41	4.26	Lv..Root-43d..Lv.	12.33	5.03	12.24	4.54						
1.15	1.11	4.56			1.03	5.03	1.21	4.36	12.43	4.28	Lv.....39th.....Lv.	12.35	5.05	12.27	4.57						
2.00	1.13	4.58			1.05	5.05	1.23	4.38	12.45	4.30	Lv.....35th.....Lv.	12.37	5.07	12.29	4.59	12.23	4.27				
2.45	1.16	5.01			1.08	5.08	1.26	4.41	12.48	4.33	Lv.....31st.....Lv.	12.40	5.10	12.32	5.02	12.25	4.30				
3.30							1.33	4.48	12.55	4.40	Lv....Archer....Lv.	12.44	5.14	12.37	5.07	12.25	4.40	12.19	5.19	12.05	6.05
4.15	1.31	5.06			1.13	5.13	1.31	4.46	12.53	4.38	Lv.....22d.....Lv.	12.48	5.18	12.38	5.08	12.30	4.45	12.28	5.28	12.20	5.20
5.02	1.34	5.19			1.26	5.26	1.45	5.00	1.06	4.51	Ar..Terminal..Ar.	1.01	5.31	12.53	5.23	1.00	5.15	1.10	6.10	12.20	5.20
											SOUTHBOUND										
Lv. 71st & Cottage	1.40	5.25			1.32	5.32	1.50	5.05	1.12	4.57	Lv..Terminal..Lv.	1.07	5.57	12.55	5.25	12.00	4.15	11.45	5.15	12.22	5.22
	1.53	5.38			1.45	5.45	2.04	5.19	1.25	5.10	Lv.....22d.....Lv.	1.20	5.50	1.10	5.40	12.30	4.45	12.27	5.57	12.22	5.22
							2.02	5.17	1.24	5.09	Lv....Archer....Lv.	1.24	5.54	1.11	5.41	12.35	4.50	12.36	6.06	12.36	5.36
	1.56	5.43			1.50	5.50	2.09	5.24	1.30	5.15	Lv.....31st.....Lv.	1.28	5.58	1.16	5.46	12.35	4.60				
	2.00	5.45			1.52	5.52	2.11	5.26	1.32	5.17	Lv.....35th.....Lv.	1.30	6.00	1.18	5.48	12.38	4.53				
	2.03	4.33			1.55	4.40	2.14	5.29	1.35	5.20	Lv.....39th.....Lv.	1.33	6.03	1.21	5.51						
	2.05	4.35			1.57	4.42	2.16	5.31	1.36	5.21	Lv..Root-43d..Lv.	1.34	6.04	1.24	5.54						
12.54	2.08	4.38			2.00	4.45	2.19	5.34	1.40	5.25	Lv.....47th.....Lv.	1.38	6.08	1.30	6.00	12.45	5.00	12.40	6.10	12.39	5.39
1.39	2.10	4.40			2.02	4.47	2.21	5.36	1.42	5.27	Lv.....51st.....Lv.	1.40	6.10	1.32	6.02	12.48	5.03				
2.24	2.13	4.43	2.01	5.01							Lv.55th&C.G.Lv.										
3.09	2.16	4.46					2.26	5.41	1.47	5.32	Lv..59th-61st..Lv.	1.45	6.15	1.37	6.07	12.53	5.08				
3.54	2.18	4.48					2.29	5.44	1.50	5.35	Lv......63......Lv.	1.48	6.18	1.40	6.10	12.55	5.10	12.50	6.20	12.49	5.49
4.59	2.21	4.51					2.33	5.48	1.54	5.39	Lv.67th-69th..Lv.	1.52	6.23	1.44	6.14	12.59	5.14				
4 50	2.26	4.56	2.12	5.12	2.03	4.48	2.35	5.50	2.01		Ar..Terminal..Ar.	1.58	6.29	1.47		1.00	5.15	12.55	6.25	12.49	5.49

FIRST AND LAST DAY CARS

	Leaving Time						Leaving Time			
	Week Days		Sundays				Week Days		Sundays	
	1st car	last car	1st car	last car			1st car	last car	1st car	last car
Through Route 1 56th-st. and Lake Park-av........ Clark-st. and Devon-av........	5.28 am 4.52 am	12.08 am 12.00 mdt	5.44 am 5.40 am	12.00 mdt 11.56 am		**Through Route 13** 63d and Halsted-sts........... Clark and Halsted-sts........	5.10 am 4.52 am	11.50 pm 11.42 pm	5.05 am 5.00 am	12.08 am 11.50 pm
Through Route 2 77th-st. and Vincennes-av ...... 80th-st. and Vincennes-av........ Belmont and Clybourn-avs......	4.34 am 4.52 am	12.08 am 12.29 am	4.34 am 4.42 am	12.14 am 12.23 am		**Through Route 22** 77th-st. and Vincennes-av...... 80th-st. and Vincennes-av........ Howard & Clark-sts...........	4.26 am 4.22 am	12.11 am 12.17 am	4.47 am 4.42 am	12.11 am 12.16 am
Through Route 3 51st-st and Grand boulevard...... Foster and Lincoln-avs.......	5.28 am 5.00 am	12.15 am 12.10 am	6.00 am 6.06 am	11.46 pm 11.26 pm		**Through Route 23** 39th and Morgan-sts........... Ashland-av. and Erie-st..........	5.55 am 5.10 am	9.40 pm 9.25 pm	5.50 am 5.30 am	10.00 pm 9.55 pm
Through Route 4 119th and Halsted-sts....... Randolph-st. and Wabash-av......	6.02 am 7.24 am	9.05 pm 9.33 pm	7.34 am 8.56 am	9.50 pm 9.38 pm		**26th Street** Halsted-st......... Cottage Grove-av.	5.15 am 5.25 am	12.15 am 12.25 am	5.15 am 5.25 am	12.15 am 12.25 am
						71st Street State-st.......... Cottage Grove-av.	5.52 am 6.00 am	11.54 pm 12.00 mdt	5.52 am 6.00 am	11.54 pm 12.00 mdt
Through Route 6 63d-st. and State-st......... Milwaukee-av. & C. & N. W. Ry...	6.02 m 5.50 am	11.26 pm 11.18 pm	6.23 am 6.14 am	10.14 pm 10.02 pm		**79th Street** Ashland-av......... State-st...........	5.38 am 5.50 am	12.18 am 12.06 am	5.38 am 5.50 am	12.10 am 11.58 pm
Through Route 7 63d and State-sts.. Austin-av. and Madison-st......	5.56 am 5.50 am	11.45 pm 11.38 pm	6.17 am 6.20 am	10.56 pm 10.56 pm		**63d St.—Clearing** Chicago Lawn (CentralPk.-av.) Clearing (Central-av.).........	4.58 am 5.13 am	12.13 am 12.28 am	5.28 am 5.43 am	12.13 am 12.28 am
Through Route 8 79th and Halsted-sts............ Grace and Halsted-sts..........	4.44 am 4.30 am	12.14 am 12.20 am	4.46 am 5.00 am	12.30 am 12.25 am		**Argo—Limits** Archer and Cicero-avs........ Argo (63d and Archer-av.).....	5.30 am 6.00 am	11.45 pm 12.15 am	5.30 am 6.00 am	11.45 pm 12.15 am

ENTER AND LEAVE CAR ONLY WHEN IT STOPS.

CONDENSED TIME TABLE—OWL CAR SERVICE

EAST AND WEST LINES

Limits Interval 30 min.		Archer 38th Interval 30 min.		22d Interval 15 min.		31st Interval 15 min.		35th Interval 30 min.		39th Interval 30 min.		TIME POINTS Intersecting Lines	43d and Root Interval 15 min.		47th Interval 15 min.		51st Interval 20 min.		58th and 61st Interval 15 min.		63d Robey Interval 15 min.		C. Lawn Interval 30 min.		67th and 69th Interval 15 min.	
1st Owl	Last Owl	1st Owl	Last Owl	1st Owl	Last Owl	1st Owl	Last Owl	1st Owl	Last Owl	1st Owl	Last Owl		1st Owl	Last Owl	1st Owl	Last Owl	1st Owl	Last Owl	1st Owl	Last Owl	1st Owl	Last Owl	1st Owl	Last Owl	1st Owl	Last Owl
												EASTBOUND														
11.51	4.51	12.15	4.45	12.10	4.55	12.57	5.00	12.28	4.56	12.50	4.50	Lv. Terminal..Lv	12.06	5.05	12.03	5.03	12.20	5.20	12.05	5.05	12.45	5.00	12.33	4.35	12.10	4.55
12.07	5.07	12.22	4.52	12.33	5.08	12.15	5.00	12.28	5.03			Lv. Western..Lv			12.08	5.08							12.43	4.43	12.14	4.59
12.15	5.15	12.30	5.00	12.28	5.14	12.15	5.00	12.33	5.03			Lv. Ashland..Lv			12.13	5.13	12.25	5.25	12.09	5.09	12.43	5.03	12.45	4.48	12.16	5.01
												Lv. Racine..Lv			12.18	5.18	12.25	5.25	12.14	5.14	12.50	5.06	12.50	4.50	12.19	5.04
12.23	5.22	12.37	5.07	12.35	5.20	12.21	5.06	12.39	5.09			Lv. Halsted..Lv	12.06	5.06	12.18	5.18	12.28	5.28			12.53	5.06	12.53	4.53		
12.24	5.24	12.39	5.09			12.26	5.08	12.41	5.14	12.53	4.53	Ar. Wallace..Ar	12.08	5.08												
									12.44	5.11	12.56	4.56	Lv. Wallace..Lv	12.11	5.11	12.23	5.23			12.18	5.18					12.24	5.09
						12.29	5.14	12.45	5.16			Ar. Wentworth..Ar			12.25	5.25	12.32	5.32	12.20	2.20	12.56	5.13	12.56	4.56	12.24	5.09
				12.39	5.24	12.29	5.11	12.45	5.17	12.56	4.59	Lv. Wentworth..Lv	12.12	5.12	12.25	5.25	12.32	5.33			12.59	5.14	12.59	4.59	12.25	5.10
12.28	5.28	12.43	5.13	12.40	5.25	12.30	5.15	12.47	5.17	12.59	4.59	Lv. State..Lv	12.15	5.15	12.28	5.28	12.35	5.35							12.25	5.10
								12.49	5.19	1.01	5.01	Ar. Indiana..Ar			12.28	5.28	12.36	5.36	12.28	5.26	1.04	5.19	1.04	5.04	12.31	5.16
						12.32	5.17	12.52	5.22	1.03	5.03	Lv. Indiana..Lv	12.19	5.19	12.30	5.30	12.36	5.34	12.31	5.31					12.37	5.22
						12.35	5.20	12.52	5.22	1.03	5.05	Lv. C. Grove..Lv	12.22	5.22	12.34	5.34					1.11	5.26	1.11	5.11	12.37	5.22
12.40	5.40	12.55	5.26	12.41	5.26	12.36	5.21	12.52	5.22	1.05	5.05	Ar. Terminal..Ar	12.22	5.22	12.37	5.37	12.36	5.36	12.31	5.31						
												WESTBOUND														
12.42	5.42	12.57	5.27	12.43	5.28	12.57	5.22	12.55	5.25	1.05	4.35	Lv. Terminal..Lv	12.23	5.23	12.38	5.38	12.36	5.36	12.38	5.38	1.13	5.28	4.13	4.13	12.40	5.25
						12.58	5.28	12.55	5.28	1.05	4.35	Lv. C. Grove..Lv	12.26	5.26	12.41	5.41	12.37	5.37	12.38	5.38	1.19	5.34	4.19	4.19	12.45	5.30
12.54	5.54	1.09	5.39	12.44	5.29	12.41	5.26	1.01	5.30	1.08	4.38	Lv. Indiana..Lv	12.30	5.30	12.45	5.45	12.37	5.37	12.44	5.44	1.24	5.39	4.24	4.24	12.51	5.36
				12.45	5.30	12.44	5.29	1.01	5.31	1.10	4.40	Lv. State..Lv	12.31	5.31	12.46	5.46	12.39	5.39	12.46	5.46	1.26	5.41	4.26	4.26	12.53	5.38
								1.04	5.34	1.11	4.41	Ar. Wentworth..Ar	12.34	5.34	12.48	5.48	12.40	5.40	12.46	5.46	1.28	5.43	4.28	4.28	12.54	5.39
12.56	5.56	1.13	5.43	12.46	5.32	12.47	5.32	1.04	5.34	1.14	4.44	Lv. Wentworth..Lv	12.38	5.38	12.53	5.53	12.44	5.44	12.50	5.50	1.33	5.48	4.33	4.33	12.59	5.44
1.00	6.00	1.15	5.45	12.49	5.34	12.49	5.34	1.06	5.38	1.16	4.46	Lv. Wallace..Lv	12.39	5.39	12.55	5.55	12.44	5.44	12.52	5.52	1.35	5.50	4.37	4.37	1.03	5.46
								1.08	5.38			Ar. Halsted..Ar	12.40	5.40			12.44	5.44	12.55	5.55	1.37	5.53	4.40	4.40	1.04	5.49
1.10	6.10	1.25	5.55	12.55	5.40	12.55	5.40					Lv. Racine..Lv			12.55	5.55	12.46	5.46			1.40	5.55	4.43	4.43		
1.17	6.17	1.32	6.02	1.01	5.46			1.14	5.44			Lv. Ashland..Lv			12.58	5.58	12.49	5.49	12.52	5.52	1.43	5.56	4.45	4.45		
1.33	6.33	1.39	6.09	1.15	6.00	12.55	6.40	1.19	5.49	1.18	4.48	Lv. Western..Lv	12.41	5.41	1.05	6.05							4.53	4.53	1.08	
						12.55	6.40	1.21	5.51	1.18	4.48	Ar. Terminal..Ar	12.41	5.41	1.08	6.08	12.52	5.52	12.59	5.59						

ARM SHOULD NOT BE PUT OUT OF WINDOW OF CAR.

NOTABLE BUILDINGS IN CHICAGO.

Name, location, height in stories, height in feet and approximate cost given in order.

Adams Express—115 South Dearborn street; 10; 140; $450,000.

Advertisers'—123 West Madison street; 16; 209; $350,000.

American Trust and Savings Bank—Clark and Monroe streets; 18; 272; $1,000,000.

Art Institute—Michigan avenue and Adams street; 3; 75; $600,000.

Ashland—Clark and Randolph streets; 16; 200; $1,500,000.

Auditorium—Michigan avenue and Congress street; 11; 145 (to top of tower, 270); $3,200,000.

Auditorium Annex—Michigan avenue and Congress street; 11; 152; $1,000,000.

Auditorium Annex No. 2—528 South Michigan avenue; 13; 180; $750,000.

Barnheisel—616-622 Michigan avenue; 10; 150; $350,000.

Bedford—Adams and Dearborn streets; 14; 188; $475,000.

Blackstone Hotel—Michigan avenue and Hubbard court; 20; 220; $1,500,000.

Board of Trade—Jackson boulevard and LaSalle street; 9; 135; $1,800,000.

Borland—Monroe and LaSalle streets; 17; 239; $630,000.

Born—342-344 5th avenue; 12; 165; $300,000.

Born—533 South Franklin street; 10; 185; $500,000.

Boston Store—State street and Calhoun place; 12; 195; $1,500,000; addition, 17; 260; $1,000,000.

Boyce—30 North Dearborn street; 12; 155; $250,000.

Breda—105 North Dearborn street; 13; 160; $325,000.

Brevoort House—120 West Madison street; 12; 175; $500,000.

Brooks—315 Franklin street; 10; 142; $330,000.

Burlington-Brothers—Jackson boulevard and Clinton street; 21; 260; $1,500,000.

Butler Brothers—Randolph and Canal streets; 14; 200; $1,750,000.

Cable—307 South Wabash avenue; 10; 140; $350,000.

Carson, Pirie, Scott & Co.—State and Madison streets; 12; 168; $1,350,000.

Caxton—506 South Dearborn street; 12; 150; $270,000.

Central Trust Bank—117 West Monroe street; 3; 75; $250,000.

Chamber of Commerce—LaSalle and Washington streets; 13; 190; $1,000,000.

Champlain—State and Madison streets; 15; 197; $800,000.

Chicago Athletic Association—12 South Michigan avenue; 10; 165; $600,000.

Chicago Athletic Association Addition—71 East Madison street; 13; 214; $500,000.

Chicago Opera House—Clark and Washington streets; 10; 130; $600,000.

Chicago Savings Bank—State and Madison streets; 14; 196; $750,000.

Chicago Title and Trust—69 West Washington street; 16; 210; $600,000.

Church—32 South Wabash avenue; 12; 150; $300,000.

City Hall—LaSalle street, between Randolph and Washington streets; 12; 247; $5,000,000.

City Hall Square—119-121 North Clark street; 20; 250; $1,500,000.

Columbia—Clark, near Madison; 11; 125; $500,000.

Columbia Memorial—State and Washington streets; 14; 251; $600,000.

Commercial National Bank—Clark and Adams streets; 18; 274; $2,800,000.

Congress Hotel—See Auditorium annex.

Consumers'—State and Quincy streets; 21; 260; $1,500,000.

Continental—South 5th avenue and Quincy street; 10; 140; $250,000.

Continental and Commercial National Bank—5th avenue and Adams street; 20; 260; $4,500,000.

Conway—Washington near Clark street; 21; 260; $2,000,000.

Cook County Courthouse—Clark street, between Randolph and Washington streets; 12; 247; $5,000,000.

Corn Exchange National Bank—LaSalle and Adams streets; 16; 189; $1,000,000.

Counselman—LaSalle street and Jackson boulevard; 9; 145; $325,000.

Dexter—35 West Adams street; 8; 140; $150,000.

Federal Life—166 North Michigan avenue; 12; 175; $400,000.

Dry Goods Reporter—Market and Quincy streets; 12; 150; $130,000.

Ellsworth—537 South Dearborn street; 14; 170; $300,000.

Fair—State and Adams streets; 11; 165; $1,500,000.

Farwell Trust—226 South LaSalle street; 12; 165; $275,000.

Federal Building—See postoffice.

Field, Marshall (retail)—State street, between Randolph and Washington streets; 12; 225; $6,000,000; addition, Wabash avenue and Randolph street; 12; $2,000,000.

Field, Marshall (men's store)—Wabash avenue and Washington street; 20; 260; $2,500,000.

Field, Marshall (wholesale)—Adams street and 5th avenue; 8; 130; $2,000,000.

Field Warehouse—West Polk and Ellsworth streets; 13; 160; $500,000.

Fine Arts—410 South Michigan avenue; 10; 150; $750,000.

First National Bank—Dearborn and Monroe streets; 17; 257; $3,000,000.

Fisher—Dearborn and Van Buren streets; 20; 274; $965,000.

Fisk—Wabash avenue and South Water street; 13; 150; $390,000.

Fort Dearborn—Clark and Monroe streets; 12; 150; $400,000.

Fort Dearborn Hotel—Van Buren and LaSalle streets; 17; 256; $1,100,000.

Gaff—230 South LaSalle street; 9; 145; $275,000.

Gage—18 South Michigan avenue; 12; 168; $500,000.

Gibbons—49 W. Jackson boulevard; 16; 200; $398,000.

Goddard—Wabash avenue and Monroe street; 13; 160; $300,000.

Grand Central Station—Harrison street and 5th avenue; 7; 212½ (to top of tower); $1,000,000.

Great Northern Hotel—Dearborn street and Jackson boulevard; 17; 176; $900,000.

Harris Trust and Savings Bank—111 West Monroe street; 21; 260; $2,500,000.

Hamilton Club—10 South Dearborn street; 10; 150; $250,000.

Hart, Schaffner & Marx—Franklin and Monroe streets; 12; 190; $1,000,000.

Hartford—Madison and Dearborn streets; 14; 165; $1,000,000.

Harvester—Michigan avenue and Harrison street; 15; 212; $1,000,000.

Heyworth—Madison street and Wabash avenue; 18; 286; $1,500,000.

Hibbard, Spencer, Bartlett & Co.—South Water and State streets; 10; 135; $1,000,000.

Hirsh, Wickwire & Co.—337 South Franklin street; 10; 114; $500,000.

Home Insurance—LaSalle and Adams streets; 12; 156; $800,000.

Hotel LaSalle—LaSalle and Madison streets; 23; 260; $3,500,000.

Hunter—Madison and Market streets; 12; 148; $500,000.

Illinois Athletic Club—112 South Michigan avenue; 12; 200; $500,000.

Illinois Central Station—Park row, near Michigan avenue; 13; 225 (to top of tower); $1,000,000.

Illinois Trust and Savings Bank—LaSalle street and Jackson boulevard; 2; 58; $300,000.

Insurance Exchange—Jackson boulevard and 5th avenue; 22; 260; $4,000,000.

Isabella—21 East Van Buren street; 10; 166; $200,000.

Kaiserhof Hotel—324 South Clark street; 9; 110; $200,000.

Karpen—Michigan avenue and Eldredge place; 12; 200; $1,400,000.

Kent—Franklin and Congress streets; 10; 140; $500,000.

Kesner—Madison street and Wabash avenue; 17; 226; $850,000.

Kling Bros. & Co.—411 South 5th avenue; 10; 150; $250,000.

Kohn—425 South Franklin street; 10; 150; $300,000.

Kuppenheimer—415 South Franklin street; 10; 150; $350,000.

Lake View—116 South Michigan avenue; 12; 200; $250,000.

Lakota—Michigan avenue and 30th street; 10; 140; $750,000.
LaSalle Street Station—Van Buren and LaSalle streets; 14; 192; $2,500,000.
Lees—19 South 5th avenue; 14; 165; $400,000.
Lexington Hotel—Michigan avenue and 22d street; 10; 130; $750,000.
Lombard—Fifth avenue and Quincy street; 11; 175; $500,000.
Ludington—1104 S. Wabash avenue; 8; 112; $275,000.
Lytton—State street and Jackson boulevard; 18; 260; $2,250,000.
Majestic Theater—22 West Monroe street; 20; 240; $1,000,000.
Mallers—Wabash avenue and Madison street; 21; 260; $1,500,000.
Mallers—226 South LaSalle street; 12; 175; $275,000.
Mallers—Market and Quincy streets; 10; 150; $200,000.
Maudel—Wabash avenue and Madison street; 15; 226; $2,000,000.
Manhattan—431 S. Dearborn street; 16; 208; $700,000.
Marquette—Dearborn and Adams streets; 16; 229; $1,000,000.
Masonic Temple—State and Randolph streets; 21; 354 (to observation platform); $3,000,000.
Medinah Temple—5th avenue and Jackson boulevard; 12; 190; $500,000.
Mentor—State and Monroe streets; 16; 192; $500,000.
Merchants' Loan and Trust Bank—Clark and Adams streets; 13; 157; $1,000,000.
Michigan Avenue—Michigan boulevard and Washington street; 15; 200; $1,500,000.
Monadnock—Dearborn and Van Buren streets; 16; 194; $2,000,000.
Monon—440 South Dearborn street; 12; 180; $285,000.
Monroe—Michigan avenue and Monroe street; 14; 200; $1,500,000.
McClurg—218 South Wabash avenue; 9; 125; $200,000.
McCormick—Michigan avenue and Van Buren street; 20; 260; $1,000,000; addition, 20; 260; $1,500,000.
McNeill—321 W. Jackson boulevard; 10; 140; $250,000.
National Life—29 South LaSalle street; 12; 160; $1,200,000.
Newberry Library—Clark street and Walton place; 5; 70; $850,000.
New York Life—LaSalle and Monroe streets; 14; 166; $1,000,000.
North American—State and Monroe streets; 20; 260; $1,800,000.
Northern Trust Bank—LaSalle and Monroe streets; 4; 74; $500,000.
Northwestern Railway (office)—226 West Jackson boulevard; 14; 212; $2,000,000.
Northwestern Railway (terminal station)—West Madison and Canal streets; 3; 116; $20,000,000 (including site).
Old Colony—Dearborn and Van Buren streets; 17; 203; $900,000.
Orchestra Hall—216 South Michigan avenue; 8; 110; $900,000.
Otis—Madison and LaSalle streets; 18; 250; $1,500,000.
Palmer—367 West Adams street; 10; 140; $450,000.
Palmer House—State and Monroe streets; 9; 100; $3,500,000.
Patten—Harrison and Sherman streets; 12; 168; $450,000.
Peoples Gas—Michigan avenue and Adams street; 20; 260; $3,000,000.
Pontiac—Dearborn and Harrison streets; 14; 170; $350,000.
Pope—633 Plymouth court; 12; 160; $290,000.
Post—167 Washington street; 11; 154; $225,000.
Postal Telegraph—137-153 Van Buren street; 11; 150; $800,000.
Postoffice—Adams and Clark streets; 8; 300 (to top of dome); $4,000,000.
Powers—Wabash avenue and Monroe street; 13; 160; $400,000.
Printers—Polk and Sherman streets; 8; 120; $400,000.
Public Library—Michigan avenue, between Randolph and Washington streets; 3; 95; $1,200,000.
Pullman—Adams street and Michigan avenue; 9; 125; $800,000.

Railway Exchange—Michigan avenue and Jackson boulevard; 17; 220; $1,600,000.
Record-Herald—163 West Washington street; 7; 124; $500,000.
Rector—Clark and Monroe streets; 13; 175; $700,000.
Reid, Murdoch & Co.—North side of river between Clark and LaSalle streets; 9; 175; $1,000,000.
Reliance—State and Washington streets; 16; 200; $500,000.
Republic—State and Adams streets; 19; 260; $1,100,000.
Rialto—140 West Van Buren street; 9; 144; $700,000.
Rookery—LaSalle and Adams streets; 11; 165; $1,500,000.
Rothschild—304 South State street; 8; 138; $250,000.
Royal Insurance—160 West Jackson boulevard; 13; 185; $800,000.
Schiller—64 West Randolph street; 16; 211; $750,000.
Security—Madison street and 5th avenue; 14; 147; $450,000.
Sherman House—Clark and Randolph streets; 14; 200; $2,500,000.
Siegel, Cooper & Co.—State and Van Buren streets; 8; 123; $1,250,000.
Silversmiths—10 S. Wabash avenue; 10; 135; $250,000.
Society Brand—Franklin and Congress streets; 13; 160; $450,000.
Spitz & Schoenberg—529 South Franklin street; 10; 150; $250,000.
Star—538 South Dearborn street; 12; 150; $250,000.
Steger—Wabash avenue and Jackson boulevard; 20; 250; $800,000.
Steinway—64 E. Van Buren street; 11; 188; $280,000.
Stevens—Wabash avenue near Washington; 19; 250; $1,000,000.
Stewart—State and Washington streets; 12; 145; $800,000.
Stock Exchange—LaSalle and Washington streets; 13; 173; $1,250,000.
Straus—Clark and Madison streets; 10; 141; $250,000.
Studebaker—629 S. Wabash avenue; 10; 135; $350,000.
Tacoma—Madison and LaSalle streets; 13; 165; $500,000.
Telephone—Washington, between 5th avenue and Market street; 20; 260; $2,500,000.
Temple—LaSalle and Monroe streets; 12; 185; $1,000,000.
Temple Court—219 South Dearborn street; 9; 100; $300,000.
Teutonic—Washington street and 5th avenue; 10; 130; $500,000.
Theodore Thomas Hall—See Orchestra hall.
Tower (old Montgomery Ward)—Michigan avenue and Madison street; 25; 394 (to top of tower); $1,500,000.
Transportation (Heisen)—Dearborn and Harrison streets; 22; 260; $2,000,000.
Tribune—Dearborn and Madison streets; 17; 244; $1,500,000.
Trude—Wabash avenue and Randolph street; 14; 190; $500,000.
Unity—127 North Dearborn street; 16; 208; $800,000.
University Club—Michigan avenue and Monroe street; 9; 130; $1,150,000.
Van Buren—Van Buren street and 5th avenue; 10; 130; $250,000.
Venetian—15 E. Washington street; 13; 181; $350,000.
Virginia—Ohio and Rush streets; 10; 150; $500,000.
Vogue—286-290 South 5th avenue; 10; 150; $200,000.
Webster—127 South Market street; 10; 150; $150,000.
Western Methodist Book Concern—14 West Washington street; 11; 133½; $250,000.
Western Union—111 West Jackson boulevard; 13; 176; $700,000.
Westminster—Monroe and Dearborn streets; 16; 200; $1,200,000.
Williams—205 West Monroe street; 10; 140; $200,000.
Wilson—528 South 5th avenue; 10; 150; $500,000.
Y. M. C. A.—19 South LaSalle street; 17; 269; $1,000,000.

The limit of height under a building ordinance passed Feb. 6, 1911, is 200 feet.

CHICAGO FEDERATION OF LABOR.

President—John J. Fitzpatrick.
Vice-President—Oscar F. Nelson.
Secretary—E. N. Nockels.

Financial Secretary—Fred G. Hopp.
Treasurer—Thomas F. Kennedy.
Headquarters—166 West Washington street.

ASYLUMS AND HOMES IN CHICAGO AND VICINITY.

Agard Deaconess Rest Home—Lake Bluff.
Altenheim—(See German Old People's Home).
Augustana Central Home—1346 LaSalle avenue.
Augustana Nursery—1346 LaSalle avenue.
Augustana Nurses' Home—351 Garfield avenue.
Baptist Deaconesses and Girls' Home—1346 West Superior street.
Bethany Home for the Aged—5015 N. Paulina street.
Beulah Home—2144 North Clark street.
Bohemian Old People's Home—5061 North Crawford avenue.
Chicago Baptist Old People's Home—Maywood.
Chicago Baptist Orphanage—Maywood.
Chicago Deaconesses' Home—22 West Erie street.
Chicago Home for Boys—1500 West Adams street.
Chicago Home for Convalescent Women and Children—1516 West Adams street.
Chicago Home for Incurables—5535 Ellis avenue.
Chicago Home for Jewish Orphans—Drexel avenue and 62d street.
Chicago Industrial Home for Children—Office 1132 West Washington boulevard.
Chicago Municipal Lodging House—162 North Union avenue.
Chicago Nursery and Half Orphan—1932 Burling-st.
Chicago Orphan—5120 South Park avenue.
Chicago Refuge for Girls—5024 Indiana avenue.
Chicago State Home—Dunning.
Church Home for Aged Persons—4325 Ellis avenue.
Cook County Home (for Poor)—Oak Forest.
Cook County Kinderheim—1356 North Rockwell-st.
Danish High School Home—3925 Michigan avenue.
Danish Lutheran Orphan—3320 Evergreen avenue.
Danish Old People's Home—6909 Walnut avenue.
Danish Young People's Home—706 East 56th street.
Evangelical Deaconesses' Home—408 Wisconsin-st.
Faith Missionary Home—300 West 74th street.
Florence Crittenton Anchorage—2615 Indiana-av.
Foundlings' Home—15 South Wood street.
Frances Juvenile Home—3929 Indiana avenue.
German Baptist Old People's Home—1843 North Spaulding avenue.
German Deaconesses' Home—2048 Dayton street.
German Hospital Nurses' Home—2329 Belden court.
German Old People's Home—Forest Park, Ill.
Guardian Angel, German Orphan—2001 Devon-av.
Helen Day Nursery—702 Barber street.
Home for the Aged—West Harrison and Throop.
Home for Aged Jews—Drexel avenue and 62d street.
Home for Aged and Infirm Colored People—510 West Garfield boulevard.
Home for Destitute Crippled Children—1653 Park avenue.
Home for the Friendless—Vincennes avenue and 51st street.
Home for Jewish Friendless and Working Girls—Ellis avenue and 53d street.
Home for Missionaries' Children—Morgan Park.
Hope Hall—6036 West Ravenswood park.
House of the Good Shepherd—1126 Grace street.
Illinois Industrial Home for the Blind—1900-1932 Marshall boulevard.
Illinois Industrial School for Girls—Park Ridge, Ill.
Illinois Masonic Orphans' Home—LaGrange, Ill.
Illinois Manual Training School Farm—Glenwood, Ill. Office 608, 160 West Jackson boulevard.

Illinois St. Andrew Society Old People's Home—Riverside, Ill.
Immanuel Women's Home—1505 LaSalle avenue.
Jackson Park Sanitarium—64th street and the lake.
King (James C.) Home for the Aged—Garfield boulevard and South Park avenue.
Lutheran Children's Home—Rockwell and Hirsch.
Lutheran Mission Home for Young Women—1307 East 64th street.
Lutheran Orphans' Home—Addison, Ill.
Margaret Etter Creche—2421 Wabash avenue.
Marks Nathan Jewish Orphan—1550 S. Albany-av.
Martha Washington Home—North Western avenue and Irving Park boulevard.
Mercy Home—2824 Wabash avenue.
Methodist Deaconess Orphanage—Lake Bluff.
Methodist Episcopal Old People's Home—1417 Foster avenue.
Miriam Club, Homes for Jewish Working Girls—434 Bowen avenue and 4501 Forrestville avenue.
Mission of Our Lady of Mercy—1138 Jackson-bd.
Norwegian-Danish Deaconess Home—1925 N. Sawyer avenue.
Norwegian Lutheran Bethesda Home—2244 Haddon avenue.
Norwegian Lutheran Deaconess Home—1138 North Leavitt street.
Norwegian Old People's Home—6054 Avondale-av.
Old People's Home—4720 Vincennes avenue.
Olivet Girls' Home—668 Gardner street.
Olivet Old Ladies' Home—668 Gardner street.
Orthodox Jewish Home for the Aged—Albany and Ogden avenues.
Park Ridge School for Girls—Park Ridge.
Paulist Day Nursery—919 South Wabash avenue.
Phyllis Wheatley Home—3530 Forest avenue.
Ruth Club Home for Jewish Working Girls—6001 Indiana avenue.
St. Anthony's Orphanage—2033 Frankfort street.
St. Charles School for Boys—St. Charles, Ill.
St. Joseph's Home for Aged and Crippled—2649 North Hamlin avenue.
St. Joseph's Home for the Friendless—Lake avenue and 35th street.
St. Joseph's Orphan Asylum—Lake-av. and 35th-st.
St. Mary's Home for Children—2822 W. Jackson-bd.
St. Mary's Mission House—850 Washington-bd.
St. Mary's Nursery—2822 West Jackson boulevard.
St. Mary's Training School for Boys—Des Plaines.
St. Vincent's Infant Asylum—721 LaSalle avenue.
St. Vincent's Orphan Asylum—2649 North Hamlin avenue.
Sarah Hackett Stevenson Memorial Lodging House for Women—2412 Prairie avenue.
Susanna Wesley Home—3330 Indiana avenue.
Swedish Baptist Old People's Home—Morgan Park.
Uhlich Evangelical Lutheran Orphan Asylum—2014 Burling street.
Volunteers of America Children's Home—Evanston.
Volunteers of America Day Nursery—1201 Washington boulevard.
Washingtonian Home—1529 West Madison street.
Western German Baptist Old People's Home—1843 North Spaulding avenue.
Young Woman's Christian Association Home—830 South Michigan avenue.
Young Woman's Christian Home—501 S. Ashland-bd.

CHICAGO INTERURBAN TROLLEY LINES.

Following are the principal electric interurban lines with terminals in or near Chicago, with the names of the principal points reached by them:

Chicago & Milwaukee—Terminal in Evanston; makes connection with Northwestern elevated and surface lines to Chicago; runs north to Waukegan, Kenosha, Racine and Milwaukee; branch from Lake Bluff to Libertyville and Rockefeller. Electric lines run from Milwaukee to Burlington, to East Troy, to Waukesha, Pewaukee, Oconomowoc and Watertown and to Sheboygan and Elkhart lake.

Chicago & Joliet—Terminal at 48th street and Archer avenue; runs southwest to Lockport and Joliet; connects at Joliet with line for Aurora, Chicago Heights and other cities.

Aurora, Elgin & Chicago—Terminal at 256 5th avenue, runs in a westerly direction to Wheaton, where one branch runs northwest to Elgin and one southwest to Aurora; at Eola Junction on the latter branch a line runs to Batavia. Aurora and Elgin are connected by a line which runs as far south as Yorkville and as far north as Carpentersville. At Elgin connection is made with a line running to Belvidere and Rockford and from the latter place a line runs west to Freeport and another north to Beloit and Janesville. At Aurora a line runs northwest to DeKalb. The Aurora, Elgin & Chicago road is operated on the third-rail system.

Chicago & Southern Traction—Terminal at 79th and Halsted streets; runs in a southeasterly direction to Chicago Heights and Kankakee.

Chicago, Lake Shore & South Bend—Terminal at Pullman; runs in an easterly direction to Michigan City and South Bend; connects at South Bend with interurban lines reaching various points in Michigan and Indiana.

ELEVATED RAILROAD STATIONS.

ON THE "LOOP."

Wabash and Adams, Wabash and Madison, Wabash and Randolph, Lake and State, Lake and Clark, 5th avenue and Randolph, 5th avenue and Madison, 5th avenue and Quincy, Van Buren and LaSalle, Van Buren and Dearborn and Van Buren and State.

CHICAGO & OAK PARK LINE.

Route: West on Lake street to Central avenue and west on South boulevard to Forest Park.

Stations: Clinton, Halsted, Morgan, Ann, Sheldon, Ashland, Wood, Robey, Oakley, Campbell, California, Sacramento, Kedzie, Garfield Park, Hamlin, Crawford avenue, Kostner avenue, Cicero avenue, Laramie avenue, Central, North Menard avenue, Austin avenue, Lombard avenue, Ridgeland avenue, Oak Park avenue, Wisconsin avenue, to Forest Park.

METROPOLITAN ROAD.

GARFIELD PARK LINE.

Route: West from Franklin and Van Buren streets to Desplaines avenue.

Stations: Franklin, Canal, Halsted, Racine, Ladlin, Marshfield, Ogden, Hoyne, Western, California, Sacramento, Kedzie, St. Louis, Garfield, Crawford avenue, Tripp avenue, Kral avenue, Cicero avenue, Laramie avenue, Central avenue, Austin avenue, Lombard avenue, Gunderson avenue, Oak Park avenue, Home avenue, Harlem avenue, Hannah street, Des Plaines avenue.

DOUGLAS PARK LINE.

Route: South from Marshfield avenue station to West 21st street and west to South Laramie avenue.

Stations: Polk, 12th street, 14th place, 18th street, Wood, Hoyne, Western, California, Douglas Park, Kedzie, Homan, Clifton Park, Lawndale, South Crawford avenue, South Kildare avenue, South 46th avenue, South 50th avenue, South 52d avenue, South 54th avenue, South 56th avenue.

HUMBOLDT PARK LINE.

Route: Northwest from Marshfield avenue station to Robey street, thence west to Lawndale avenue.

Stations: Madison, Lake, Grand, Chicago, Division, Robey, Western, California, Humboldt, Kedzie, Ballou, Lawndale.

LOGAN SQUARE LINE.

Route: Same as Humboldt park line to Robey street and North avenue; thence northwest to Logan square.

Stations beyond Robey: Western, California, Sacramento, Logan square.

Note—Trains on all the Metropolitan elevated lines run around the "loop" and stop at the stations between Franklin and Marshfield except that during the rush hours in the morning and evening some of them run through from Halsted to Marshfield without stopping at the intermediate stations. Trains also run west from terminal station in 5th avenue near Van Buren street.

NORTHWESTERN LINE.

Route: North from 5th avenue and Lake street to North avenue, west to Sheffield and north to Wilmette.

Stations: Kinzie, Chicago, Oak, Division, Schiller, Sedgwick and North avenue, Larrabee, Halsted, Willow, Center, Webster, Fullerton, Wrightwood, Diversey, Wellington, Belmont, Clark and Roscoe, Addison, Grace, Sheridan and Graceland, Buena Park, Wilson, Argyle, Edgewater (Bryn Mawr), North Edgewater, Hayes avenue, Rogers Park (Farwell), Birchwood, Howard avenue, Calvary, Main street (Evanston), Dempster street, Davis street, Noyes street, Central avenue and Wilmette. Trains also arrive at and depart from station at North Clark and Kinzie streets.

Express trains stop at Kinzie, Chicago, Fullerton, Belmont, Sheridan road and Wilson avenue.

RAVENSWOOD BRANCH.

Route: West from Clark and Roscoe streets to west side of Chicago & Northwestern tracks, north to Leland avenue and west to Kimball avenue.

Stations: Southport, Paulina, Addison, Irving Park boulevard, Montrose, Wilson, Robey, Western, Rockwell, Francisco, Kedzie.

SOUTH SIDE (ALLEY L) LINE.

Route: South from Van Buren street and Wabash avenue to 40th street, east to alley between Prairie avenue and Grand boulevard, south to 63d street and east to Stony Island avenue.

Stations: Congress, old Congress, 12th street, 18th street, 22d street, 26th street, 29th street, 31st street, 33d street, 35th street, 39th street, Indiana avenue, 43d street, 47th street, 51st street, 55th street, 58th street, 61st street, South Park, Cottage Grove, University avenue, Dorchester avenue, Stony Island.

ENGLEWOOD BRANCH.

Route: West from Prairie avenue and 58th street to Wentworth avenue, south to 63d street and west to Loomis street.

Stations: State and 59th, Wentworth and 59th, Princeton and 61st, Harvard and 63d, Parnell and 63d, Halsted and 63d, Racine and 63d, Loomis and 63d.

NORMAL PARK BRANCH.

Route: South from 63d street and Stewart avenue to 67th street, west to Normal avenue and south to 69th street.

Stations: 65th street and Stewart avenue, 67th and Stewart, 69th and Normal avenue.

KENWOOD BRANCH.

Route: East from 40th street and Calumet avenue to Oakenwald avenue and 42d street.

Stations: Grand boulevard and 40th street, Vincennes avenue and 40th, Cottage Grove avenue and 41st, Drexel boulevard and 41st, Ellis avenue and 41st, Lake Park and 41st street, 42d street and Oakenwald avenue.

STOCKYARDS BRANCH.

Route: West from Indiana avenue and 40th street to the stockyards.

Stations: Indiana avenue, Wallace street, Halsted street, Exchange station, Morris station, Swift station, Packers' station, Armour station.

TRANSFERS AND TRANSFER STATIONS.

Transfers from one line to another are given by the elevated roads at four stations on the loop—Randolph street and 5th avenue, Clark and Lake streets, State and Van Buren streets and Adams street and Wabash avenue. Passengers on the Northwestern may transfer to the Metropolitan at Randolph and 5th avenue, to the Oak Park line at State and Van Buren and to the South Side line at Randolph and 5th avenue. On the South Side line the best transfer point during the morning is at Clark and Lake streets and during the evening at Adams and Wabash. On the Metropolitan the best transfer points in the morning are: To the South Side, State and Van Buren, and to the Northwestern or Oak Park at Clark and Lake; in the evening the best transfer points are at State and Van Buren for the South Side or Oak Park, and at Adams and Wabash for the Northwestern. On the Oak Park line the best transfer points in the morning are: To the Metropolitan, West Lake near Paulina; to the South Side, State and Van Buren; to the Northwestern, Adams and Wabash; in the evening the best transfer points are: To the Metropolitan or South Side, Randolph and 5th avenue; to the Northwestern, Adams and Wabash.

THROUGH ROUTES NORTH AND SOUTH.

Through trains are run between the north and south sides on the Northwestern and South Side lines. The through routes designated by their terminals are: Evanston and Jackson park (express); Wilson avenue and Englewood (express); Wilson avenue and South park (local). North bound through trains use Wabash avenue and Lake street; south bound through trains use 5th avenue and Van Buren street.

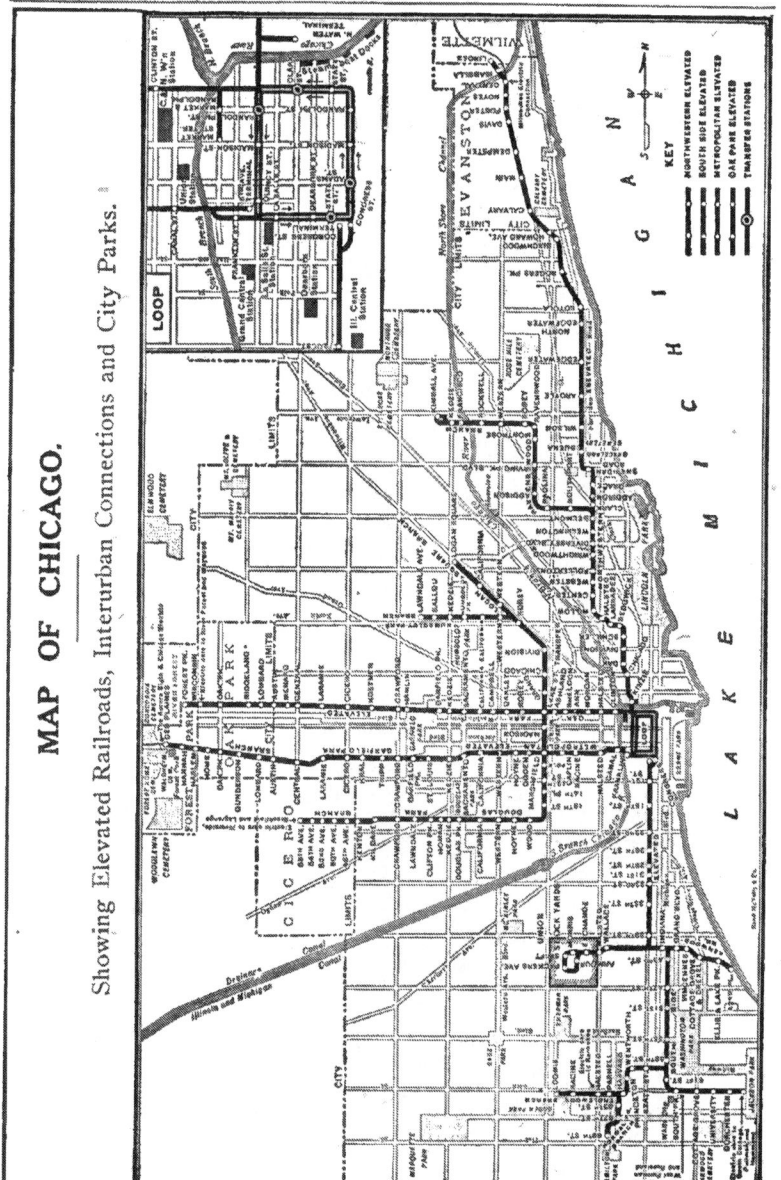

MAP OF CHICAGO.

Showing Elevated Railroads, Interurban Connections and City Parks.

PUBLIC BUILDINGS

Name.	Location.		Nearest Elevated Railroad and Station.
Coliseum	Wabash-av. and 16th-st.	South Side	12th-st. or 18th-st.
Postoffice	Clark and Jackson	All Roads	Dearborn and Van Buren.
Board of Trade	Jackson and LaSalle	All Roads	LaSalle and Van Buren.
Cook County Building	Clark and Washington	All Roads	Clark and Lake-sts.
City Hall	LaSalle and Washington	All Roads	Clark and Lake-sts.
Field Museum	Jackson Park	South Side	Jackson Park-av.
Art Institute	Michigan and Adams	All Roads	Adams and Wabash.
Public Library	Randolph and Michigan	All Roads	Randolph and Wabash.

HOTELS (IN LOOP DISTRICT)

Auditorium	Michigan and Congress	South Side	Congress and Wabash.
Bismarck	175 Randolph-st	All Roads	Randolph and 5th-av.
Blackstone	Michigan and Hubbard	South Side	Congress and Wabash.
Brevoort House	143 Madison-st	All Roads	Madison and 5th-av.
Briggs House	Randolph and 5th-av	All Roads	Randolph and 5th-av.
Congress Hotel	Michigan and Congress	South Side	Congress and Wabash.
Fort Dearborn	LaSalle and Van Buren	All Roads	LaSalle and Van Buren.
Grand Pacific	Jackson and Clark	All Roads	LaSalle and Van Buren.
Great Northern	Jackson and Dearborn	All Roads	Dearborn and Van Buren.
Grace Hotel	Clark and Jackson	All Roads	LaSalle and Van Buren.
Kaiserhof Hotel	Clark, near Jackson	All Roads	LaSalle and Van Buren.
LaSalle Hotel	Madison and LaSalle	All Roads	Madison and 5th-av.
Majestic Hotel	22 Quincy-st	All Roads	Dearborn & Van Buren.
Morrison Hotel	Madison and Clark-sts	All Roads	Madison and 5th-av.
Palmer House	State and Monroe-sts	All Roads	Adams and Wabash.
Planters Hotel	Clark and Madison-sts	All Roads	Clark and Lake.
Saratoga Hotel	29 S. Dearborn-st	All Roads	Madison and Wabash.
Sherman House	Clark and Randolph-sts	All Roads	Clark and Lake-sts.
Stratford Hotel	Michigan and Jackson	All Roads	Adams and Wabash.
Victoria Hotel	Clark and Van Buren	All Roads	LaSalle and Van Buren.
Wellington	Jackson and Wabash	All Roads	Adams and Wabash.
Windsor-Clifton	Monroe and Wabash	All Roads	Adams and Wabash.

OUTLYING HOTELS

Lexington	22d and Michigan	South Side	22d-st.
Vendome	6200 Kenwood-av	South Side	Dorchester-av.
Park Gate	63d and Jackson Park	South Side	Jackson Park.
Lakota	30th and Michigan	South Side	31st-st.
Hayes Hotel	64th and University-av	South Side	University-av.
Colonial	63d and Kenwood-av	South Side	Dorchester-av.
Del Prado	59th and Blackstone-av	South Side	Dorchester-av.
Metropole	23d and Michigan-av	South Side	22d-st.

HOSPITALS

Alexian Brothers	Belden and Racine-avs	Northwestern	Fullerton-av.
Cook County	Wood and Harrison-sts	Metropolitan	Ogden-av.
Mercy Hospital	26th and Calumet	South Side	26th-st.
Presbyterian	Congress and Wood-sts	Metropolitan	Marshfield-av.
St. Anthony de Padua	W. 19th & Marshall-bd	Metropolitan	Douglas Park.
St. Bernard's	Harvard and 63d	South Side	63d-st.
St. Luke's	1416 Indiana-av	South Side	12th-st.
U. S. Marine	4141 Clarendon-av	Northwestern	Buena Park.
Wesley Hospital	2449 Dearborn-st	South Side	26th-st.

CEMETERIES

Forest Home	Desplaines-av.	Metropolitan	Desplaines-av.
Concordia	Desplaines-av.	Metropolitan	Desplaines-av.
Waldheim	Desplaines-av.	Metropolitan	Desplaines-av.
Calvary	Evanston, Ill.	Northwestern	Calvary Station.
Graceland	Buena Park	Northwestern	Buena Station.
Mount Carmel	A. E. & C. R. R.	Metropolitan	To Desplaines-av.
Oak Ridge	A. E. & C. R. R.	Metropolitan	To Desplaines-av.
Oakwoods	71st and Cottage Grove	South Side	63d and Cottage Grove.

UNIVERSITIES AND COLLEGES

University of Chicago	Ellis-av. and Midway	South Side	University-av.
Armour Institute	32d-st. and Armour-av.	South Side	33d-st.
Bennett Medical College	Fulton and Ada-sts	Oak Park	Sheldon-st.
Chicago Clinic School	819 W. Harrison-st	Metropolitan	Marshfield-av.
Chicago Homeo. Med. School	Wood and Flournoy-sts	Metropolitan	Polk-st.
Chicago Veterinary College	2537 State-st	South Side	26th-st.
De La Salle Institute	35th-st. and Wabash-av	South Side	35th-st.
McCormick Theo. Seminary	2330 N. Halsted-st	Northwestern	Fullerton-av.
Moody Bible Institute	LaSalle and Chicago-avs	Northwestern	Chicago-av.
Northwestern University	Evanston, Ill.	Northwestern	Noyes-st.
Rush Medical College	Harrison and Wood-sts	Metropolitan	Marshfield-av.
Cook Co. Normal School	68th-st. and Stewart-av.	South Side	69th-st., Norm. P. Branch.

RELIGIOUS ORGANIZATIONS IN CHICAGO.

THE CONGREGATIONAL CHURCHES.

CONGREGATIONAL CONFERENCE OF ILLINOIS.

Moderator—Rev. J. M. Lewis, Ph.D.
Superintendent—Rev. George T. McCollum, D. D.
Treasurer—John W. Iliff.
Office—Room 1324, 19 South LaSalle street, Chicago.

MINISTERIAL RELIEF ASSOCIATION OF ILLINOIS.

President—William Spooner, Oak Park.
Treasurer—R. R. Baldwin, 35 North Dearborn street, Chicago, Ill.

ILLINOIS HOME MISSIONARY SOCIETY.

Chairman Executive Committee—Dr. W. T. McElveen.
Superintendent and Corresponding Secretary—Rev. George T. McCollum, D. D.
Treasurer—John W. Iliff.
Office—19 South LaSalle street, Chicago, Ill.

CHICAGO CITY MISSIONARY SOCIETY.

President—Frank Kimball.
Secretary—William Spooner, Otis building.
Treasurer—Willis S. Herrick.
Superintendent—Rev. J. C. Armstrong, D. D., 19 South LaSalle street.
Assistant Superintendent—Rev. Philip W. Yarrow, 19 South LaSalle street.

EPISCOPAL CHURCH.

DIOCESE OF CHICAGO.

Bishop—Rev. Charles P. Anderson, D. D.; office 1705, 29 East Madison street.
Secretary—Rev. Luther Pardee, 5001 Washington avenue.

METHODIST EPISCOPAL CHURCH.

Bishop—Rev. William F. McDowell; office, 324, 1920 South Michigan avenue.

ROMAN CATHOLIC CHURCH.

ARCHDIOCESE OF CHICAGO.

The Roman catholic archdiocese of Chicago comprises the counties of Cook, Lake, DuPage, Kankakee, Will and Grundy. The archbishop is the Most Reverend James Edward Quigley, D. D., and the auxiliary bishop is the Rt.-Rev. Paul P. Rhode. The following statistics are from the Official Catholic Directory for 1913:

Archbishop—1.	Parishes with schools—
Bishops—2.	227.
Clergy—781.	Children attending—105,-
Churches with resident	898.
priests—310.	Orphan asylums—6.
Missions with churches—	Orphans—1,700.
22.	Homes for aged—5.
Total churches—332.	Total children in catho-
Seminaries—2.	lic institutions—120,276.
Students—352.	Catholic population—
Colleges for boys—12.	About 1,150,000.
Academies for girls—21.	

CHRISTIAN SCIENCE CHURCH.

There are in Chicago twelve Christian science churches having an average total attendance of about 13,000. Each of these churches maintains a free reading room in addition to joint reading rooms at 104 South Michigan avenue and 108 South LaSalle street, where the public may have free access to all authorized publications on the subject of Christian science.

The offices of the Christian science committee on publication and the Christian science committee for the distribution of literature in Chicago are in the Orchestra building, 220 South Michigan avenue.

The office of the western representative of the Christian Science Monitor is at 750 Peoples Gas building.

CHURCH OF THE NEW JERUSALEM.

ILLINOIS ASSOCIATION OF THE NEW JERUSALEM.

Presiding Minister—Rev. John S. Saul, 510 Steinway building, Chicago, Ill.
Secretary—Rev. L. G. Landenberger, St. Louis, Mo.
Treasurer—A. H. Cline, 510 Steinway building, Chicago, Ill.
Executive Committee—Robert Matheson, 824 Dakin street, Chicago, Ill.; Dr. J. P. Cobb, 4649 Wood-

lawn avenue, Chicago, Ill.; Mrs. E. A. Munger, Chicago, Ill.; Joel B. Waddell, Union City, Tenn.; William C. Dickman, St. Louis, Mo.; William Niles, Laporte, Ind.; George Copeland, Jefferson, Wis.

CHICAGO SOCIETY OF THE NEW JERUSALEM.

President—Dr. J. P. Cobb, 4649 Woodlawn avenue.
Secretary—Edwin A. Munger, 1907, 105 West Monroe street.
Treasurer—L. Brackett Bishop, Harris Trust building.
Executive Committee—Dr. J. P. Cobb, F. A. Smith, Allan Owen, Mrs. E. A. Munger, C. Jasper Cobb, A. H. Cline, J. G. Gustafson, C. L. Moulton, Albert Curry, R. O. Barier and officers ex officio.

WESTERN NEW CHURCH BOOKROOMS.

510 Steinway building.
President—C. L. Moulton.
Secretary—Rev. L. G. Landenberger.
Treasurer—J. W. Saul.

UNITARIAN CHURCH.

WESTERN CONFERENCE.

President—Morton D. Hull, Chicago.
Secretary—Rev. Ernest C. Smith, Chicago.
Treasurer—C. K. Pittman, Evanston, Ill.
Directors—Morton D. Hull, F. A. Delano, Mrs. E. A. Delano, J. W. Hosmer, C. K. Pittman, Mrs. S. F. Lynn, Rev. Fred V. Hawley, Rev. W. H. Pulsford and Rev. Ernest C. Smith, all of Chicago, Ill.; Dana Slade, Jr., Hinsdale, Ill.; Rev. Eugene R. Shippen, Detroit, Mich.; Rev. Walter F. Greenman, Milwaukee, Wis.; Rev. F. A. Gilmore, Madison, Wis.; Rev. W. M. Backus, Minneapolis, Minn.; Rev. George R. Gebauer, Duluth, Minn.; Rev. Everett D. Martin, Des Moines, Iowa; Mrs. C. V. Mersereau, St. Louis, Mo.; C. S. Udell, Grand Rapids, Mich.; Rev. M. O. Simons, Cleveland, O.
Headquarters—105 S. Dearborn street, Chicago, Ill.

ILLINOIS CONFERENCE.

President—Mrs. J. E. Williams, Streator.
Secretary—Rev. A. R. Vail, Urbana.
Treasurer—Geo. L. Parker, Bloomington.

ILLINOIS CHRISTIAN ENDEAVOR UNION.

President—Walter R. Mee, 19 South LaSalle street.
Vice-Presidents—A. G. Fegert, Chicago; Charles Randolph, Springfield.
Secretary—Estella Jorgensen, 4302 Lowell avenue, Chicago.
Treasurer—William V. Martin, 1326 North 6th street, Quincy.

MISCELLANEOUS SOCIETIES.

American Bible Society—332 South Michigan avenue; secretary, Rev. S. H. Kirkbridge.
American Federation of Catholic Societies (Cook County Branch)—President, Michael F. Girten, 5827 Princeton avenue.
American Sunday School Union—1310, 19 South LaSalle street; superintendent, Rev. William W. Johnstone.
Baptist Ministers' Conference—901 Masonic Temple; meetings, Monday forenoons.
Baptist Young People's Union (Chicago)—Secretary, Rev. William E. Chalmers, 107 South Wabash avenue.
Chicago Bible Society—332 South Michigan avenue; secretary, Rev. S. H. Kirkbridge.
Chicago Christian Endeavor Union—Secretary, Jean Behrens, 405, 19 South LaSalle street.
Chicago Congregational Club—Secretary, William C. Miller.
Chicago Congregational Sunday School Association—President, A. F. Allen.
Chicago Methodist Preachers' Meeting—Secretary, Rev. H. C. Godden; meetings on Monday forenoons at 1020 South Wabash avenue.
Chicago Methodist Social Union—Corresponding secretary, Edwin H. Forkel.
Chicago Sunday Evening Club—President, Clifford W. Barnes; secretary, Ezra J. Warner, Jr., 1340, 8 South LaSalle street.
Chicago Tract Society—Secretary, Rev. Jesse W.

OLD RESIDENTS OF CHICAGO.

Nov. 15, 1913.

In the following list of men and women who have lived in the city or its suburbs for sixty-three years or more there are doubtless many omissions, though an effort has been made to make it as complete as possible. Additions to, changes of residence and other corrections of this list, which will be continued in future editions of this publication, will be gladly received. Names marked with an * are those of persons born in Chicago or Cook county. Ages when known are given in parentheses:

1832—Allison, John, Northfield.
Heartt, Adaline N. (82), 3219 Prairie avenue.
Keenon, Mrs. Eleanor H.* (81), 2145 W. Adams-st.
Outhet, Miss Elizabeth (82), 522 Pleasant street, Oak Park.
1833—Brooks, F. T. (87), 5224 Ainslie street.
Foote, George C.* (80), 1123 W. Van Buren street.
Vanatta, Charles (81), 2336 Grand avenue.
1834—Ludwig, Catherine, 1465 West Superior street.
1835—Dewey, Mrs. Mary R. (81), 5700 Jackson-av.
Gordon, Nelly Kinzie* (78), Savannah, Ga.
Harman, William (79), 3840 West End avenue.
Healy, Daniel E. (79), 2700 Lime street.
Hubbard, Elijah K.* (78), Middletown, Conn.
Sinclair, George (79), 4327 Berkeley avenue.
Thies, Mrs. A. C., 1157 West Van Buren street.
Whitehead, William H. (78), 1808 Chicago avenue, Evanston, Ill.
Young, Mrs. George H. (80), 327 Warren avenue.
1836—Brooks, Mrs. E. C. (81), 1072 Sheridan road.
Goeden, Susan (79), 1900 Estes avenue.
Hampton, Mrs. S. A. (88), 651 Warren avenue.
Lewis, Mrs. Jane (91), 5004 Blackstone avenue.
Morrison, E. W. (77), 4145 Kenmore avenue.
McNulty, Mary (78), 1751 West Erie street.
1837—Ashman, Thomas (95), 106 N. Washtenaw-av.
Bohlander, John* (76), Hinsdale.
Calhoun, William A.* (76), 1043 Wilcox avenue.
Colby, Mary A. (76), 2839 Indiana avenue.
Collins, Miss Elizabeth (94), 2700 South Park-av.
Doty, Harvey C. (80), 1104 Grand avenue.
Fraser, Mrs. D. R. (78), 1245 Washington-bd.
Goodrich, H. A.* (76), 522 Deming place.
Howland, Mrs. Jane E. (79), 5405 Woodlawn-av.
Kimbark, Mrs. Seneca D.,* Chicago Beach hotel.
Pratt, Charles O.* (76), 2119 Wilcox avenue.
Satterlee, Emily T. (93), 2704 Michigan avenue.
Startup, Jane D. (77), 1414 Garfield court.
1838—Blair, Claudius* (75), 5741 South Peoria street.
Clark, Catherine C.* (75), 7628 South Sangamon-st.
Collins, W. M. (77), 5604 Princeton avenue.
Edbrooke, W. S.* (75), 1646 North Oakley avenue.
Flagg, Emma J. T.* (75), 14 Woodland park.
Hubbard, Gurdon S.* (75), Windsor-Clifton house.
Hughes, Edward (75), 54 Lewis street.
Irwin, Mrs. Caroline F. (78), 668 Roscoe boulevard.
Mattes, Peter (77), 613 Belden avenue.
Mitchell, Phœbe Le Beau (81), 363 West Eddy-av.
O'Neil, John J. (76), 230 West Illinois street.
Russer, Henry, 216 Rush street.
Sinclair, Mrs. J. E.* (75), Maywood.
1839—Beaubien, Mrs. A. (75), 431 South Willow-av.
Chase, Mrs. Benjamin F. (79), 3353 Forest avenue.
Cherry, Mrs. C. H.* (74), 6550 Kenwood avenue.
Clark, Dena G. (74), 210 Foster avenue.
Gray, Allen W.* (74), 3213 Washington boulevard.
Harpel, Eliza* (74), 51 East Oak street.
Height, Margaret A. (76), 310 West 60th place.
Lewis, Charles J. (75), 1900 Carroll avenue.
Lewis John (81), 2414 Gladys avenue.
Periolat, Clemens F. (74), 710 Masonic Temple.
Pitkin, Mary J., 224 Schiller street.
Russell, Isaac (74), 2135 Carroll avenue.
Smith, Mrs. Joshua,* 4648 S. Marshfield avenue.
Speer, Charles W. (74), 246 S. Sangamon street.
Tron, Mrs. Anna, 1239 North Halsted street.
1840—Bishop, Orris A.* (73), 3721 Forest avenue.
Farrar, Mrs. S. D. (73), 3130 Dearborn street.
Fishbeck, Mary* (73), 6938 Wentworth avenue.
Fuller, Mrs. Ann C. (74), 810 Oakwood avenue, Wilmette.
George, John B. (77), 3119 South Wabash avenue.
Gray, Mrs. Sarah H.* (73), 1410 Washington-bd.
Hamilton, Henry E.* (73), 817 Dearborn avenue.
Jackson, Abram V. (78), 3267 N. Western avenue,

Kent, Benjamin A. (94), 110 Lake-st., Oak Park,Ill.
Lewis, Mrs. W. F.* (73), 615 West Congress street.
Link, Marie (80), 57 East Walton place.
Miller, Mathilde C. (74), 3515 64th street.
Murphy, Mrs. Hiram P. (74), 4402 Greenwood-av.
Ray, James* (73), 1439 West 12th place.
Rehm, Jacob (85), 1517 Dearborn avenue.
Robinson, Robert W.* (73), 1879 N. Sacramento-av.
Seamens, Mrs. Amelia (73), 868 Carroll avenue.
1841—Blake, Mrs. Adeline Jones (76), 3344 Prairie-av.
Bohlander, Peter* (72), Hinsdale, Ill.
Breit, Adam (75), 1302 Wolfram street.
Ebert, Albert E. (73), 276 Michigan avenue.
Foster, Orrington C. (72), 1401 Dearborn avenue.
Lammers, Maria (80), 2 Catalpa court.
Lewis, Eli R.* (72), 7453 Normal avenue.
Loring, Stella Dyer* (72), 4600 Ellis avenue.
Merriell, George H. (74), 150 South Leavitt street.
Peck, Clarence I.* (72), 2254 Michigan avenue.
Sauter, John* (72), 5946 Normal avenue.
Smith, Graeme Lisle* (72), 1238 Eddy street.
Smith, Orson* (72), 50 Bellevue place.
Wheeler, E. B.* (72), Arlington Heights, Ill.
Williams, Edward M.* (72), Oak Park, Ill.
1842—Armstrong, John M.* (71), 628 Briar place.
Brettmann, Henry (71), 2836 Armitage avenue.
Burton, Mrs. Stiles (93), Congress hotel.
Cleveland, Henry H.* (71), 1210 Milwaukee-av.
Clybourn, Henry C.*(71), 1390 Humboldt boulevard.
Cowper, John H. (72), 1918 Warren avenue.
Culferton, Edward F.* (71), 4242 West Harrison-st.
Curtis, DeWitt H. (74), 1302 Washington boulevard.
Dickerman, Mrs. Martha R.* (71), 5946 Normal-av.
Ertinger, Katherine (75), 3257 Wentworth avenue.
Fries, William (71), 4054 North Paulina street.
Hall, Mrs. J. S. (71), 3701 Sheridan road.
Hamilton, David G.* (71), 2929 Michigan avenue.
Jax, Nicholas (77), 2310 Seminary avenue.
Johnson, George B.* (71), 532 West Adams street.
Kellogg, J. H. (83), 2238 Michigan avenue.
Law, Mrs. Ellen (81), 1944 Warren avenue.
Leibunguth, Caroline* (71), Downers Grove, Ill.
Meyer, Mary (74), 125 West 16th street.
Parsons, Mrs. Julia W. K. (71), 1192 Garfield-bd.
Rooney, Henrietta B. (71), 2080 Jackson boulevard.
Russell, Ellen I.* (71), 888 Carroll avenue.
Schnur, Peter* (71), 783 North Winchester avenue.
Simon, Peter (84), 484 Sedgwick street.
Tebbetts, Mrs. W. G.* (71), 2977 North Paulina-st.
Ward, Mrs. E. J. Watson (88), 339 East 62d-st.
Watson, N. W. (82), 4100 Lake avenue.
Watson, Silas B. (74), 3317 Park avenue.
Weller, George W.* (71), 7008 Normal avenue.
1843—Allmendinger, Peter (71), 438 Arlington place.
Bernard, Mrs. Gwinthellyn* (70), 46 Best avenue.
Dunne, Mrs. William (87), 865 S. Central Park-av.
Follansbee, George A. (70), 2342 Indiana avenue.
Ford, Elisha M. (77), 1000 Warren avenue.
Garraghan, Bedelia K.* (70), 3424 Prairie avenue.
Getzler, W. H., 217 Frankfort street.
Gaffney, James (72), 1210 Morse-av., Rogers Park.
Gavin, Rev. E. W.* (70), Waukegan, Ill.
Grimme, Louis (86), 3253 Herndon street.
Holden, William H.*(70), 1145 Forest-av.,Evanston.
Knorst, Mathias (72), 198 Vine street.
Ludwig, Katherine (89), 215 West Goethe street.
Magee, Henry W. (72), 5626 Dorchester avenue.
McDonald, Mrs. P. S.* (70), 2839 Indiana avenue.
McNamara, James* (70), 1892 Fillmore street.
Neebes, William J. (78), 3823 Forest avenue.
Perkins, Mrs. Marion Heald (74), 2319 Lincoln street, Evanston.
Perry, Mrs. Silas O.* (70), 343 East 53d street.
Remond, Mrs. E. Pelletier (92), 3223 Archer-av.
Rohmer, A. (86), Hinsdale, Ill.
Schaefer, M. (80), Gross Point.
Sherman, Charles D.* (70), Riverside, Ill.
Simons, Edward* (70), 1652 Armitage avenue.
Spahn, Joseph M. (70), 10307 Indianapolis avenue.
Stannard, Helen F., 871 Jackson boulevard.
Tron, Mrs. Anna Maria (80), 523 North Halsted-st.
Turner, Mrs. Mary (70), 502 Addison street.
Weber, Herman (71), 812 Junior terrace.
Weckler, Adam J. (71), 3448 Broadway.
Wolcott, Mrs. Mary A. (87), Niles, Ill,

THE A. T. WILLETT COMPANY began in 1868 with twenty horses. The one horse two wheel dray was the popular wagon of that time. Some of our first customers whom early settlers will recall were McKinley-Gilchrist, C. T. Reynolds & Co., Davis Bros., H. A. & H. D. Bogardus, Mauran Wright & Co., and R. B. Boak & Co. Of this old bunch only R. B. Boak & Co. and the Willett Co. still survive.

To-day we operate three hundred teams and motor trucks. A few of our customers are Steele-Wedeles Co., Montgomery Ward & Co., International Paper Co., The Tribune, James S. Kirk & Co., Procter & Gamble Co., W. F. McLaughlin & Co. and The Daily News.

One reason for our success is the personal loyalty we feel for our customers. Our customers are part of our gang and in labor troubles we stick with them to the finish.

The service of the Willett Company has never failed to any customer for a single hour since 1868.

Williamson, Mrs. Emma B. (71), 959 South Spaulding avenue.
1844—Arnold, Miss Katherine D.* (69), 674 Lincoln Park boulevard.
Bailey, George W.* (69), 513 West 60th street.
Bailey, Mrs. J.* (69), 355 Jackson boulevard.
Bartlett, Mrs. Mary J. (74), 2705 N. Hermitage-av.
Bennett, Robert J. (74), 4250 North Paulina street.
Bowes, George H.* (69), 182 West 23d street.
Bradshaw, Hugh (73), 1919 Fulton street.
Butts, Milton D. (75), 4414 North Paulina street.
Cherry, Charles H. (79), 6530 Kenwood avenue.
Crocker, Madeline (89), 3651 Wentworth avenue.
Einhorn, Joseph (89), 172 South Sangamon street.
Fergus, John B.* (69), 837 Windsor avenue.
Fergus, John Q. (72), 3114 Vernon avenue.
Flanders, Isabel W. (84), 4911 Christiana avenue.
Green, Mrs. Bessie (72), 1803 Melrose street.
Hall, Eugene* (69), 2106 South State street.
Horne, Mrs. Hannah R. (90), Old People's home, Indiana avenue and 39th street.
Hoyne, Thomas M. (69), 3369 Calumet avenue.
Josenhans, Mary M.* (69), 842 West 61st place.
Kastens, Katherine (88), 935 Perry street.
Kay, Joseph A.* (69), Elston and Linder-avs.
Knopp, Bernard* (69), 599 Mildred avenue.
Lawrence, Susan L. (37), 16 St. John's court.
Macdonald, Ada Lane, 6347 Blackstone avenue.
Mann, Mathias* (69), 3793 North Clark street.
Marshall, James F.* (69), 2978 Vernon avenue.
Mason, George (73), 511 West Monroe street.
Mattes, Frank* (69), 1606 North Ashland avenue.
Morgan, George C. (80), 6112 Stony Island avenue.
Nicholson, John G.* (69), 1509 Montrose avenue.
Peck, Helen M.* (69), 2726 North Robey street.
Reed, Florence S.* (69), 1028 Diversey boulevard.
Rehm, William (69), 123 Grand avenue.
Reid, Mrs. Elizabeth G.* (69), 1023 N. Halsted-st.
Runge, Henry (77), 436 West Chicago avenue.
Russer, Mrs. Caroline (69), 44 Pearson street.
Sauter, Charles J.* (69), 2142 Cleveland avenue.
Schram, C. B. (79), 51 South Halsted street.
Seavert, E. G. (75), 34 North Grove place.
Skinner, Miss Elizabeth (69), 100 Rush street.
Smith, Frederick A.* (69), 609 Rush street.
Snowden, Orpha (88), 1552 Lill avenue.
Tibbetts, Elizabeth* (69), 2763 North Paulina-st.
Van Horn, Mrs. A. G. Sinclair (69), 4510 Perry-st.
Van Zandt, George* (69), Oak Park, Ill.
Walsh, John F.* (69), 2813 North Ashland avenue.
Walshe, Mrs. Robert J. (69), 2339 Calumet avenue.
Weihe, John C. (73), 3017 N. Winchester avenue.
1845—Bacon, Rebecca S. (71), 2243 Cleveland avenue.
Barrett, John P. (77), 4400 Michigan avenue.
Best, Jacob (68), 1443 Berteau avenue.
Bradley, J. Harley (69), 607 Rush street.
Breese, A. K. (68), 9711 Parnell avenue.
Breese, Mrs. A. K. (68), 9711 Parnell avenue.
Breyer, Mrs. Sophia (73), 680 Fulton street.
Casey, Mrs. Helen M. (78), 161 South Leavitt-st.
Catlin, Charles (69), 451 Belden avenue.
Catlin, George (70), 5111 Hibbard avenue.
Clancy, Sylvester T. (70), 4008 Dearborn street.
Clark, Mrs. David W.* (68), 3125 Warren avenue.
Crowe, Mrs. Marie B.* (68), 433 Grand avenue.
Cushing, Edward T.* (68), 4820 Greenwood avenue.
Dalton, Mrs. Mary A. B.* (68), 758 S. Kedzie-av.
Davis, Mrs. Kate E.* (68), 135 Wells street.
Feldman, Mary (75), 1440 Wrightwood avenue.
Ford, John W.* (68), 3950 Lexington avenue.
Gilmore, William (68), 217 Central Park avenue.
Hatch, J. M. (81), 128 South Waller avenue.
Heyder, Mrs. Mary (72), 1829 Fremont street.
Jackson, Oliver* (68), 4460 Oakenwald avenue.
Jerrain, Mrs. Julie Pelletier (95), 3222 Archer-av.
Knickerbocker, A. V.* (68), 3541 Douglas Park-bd.
Martin, Patrick (91), 4537 Wabash avenue.
O'Brien, Timothy M., 2234 Campbell park.
Robinson, William R.* (68), 75 West Adams street.
Rutherford, T. A. (75), North 68th and Grand-avs.
Satterlee, George A.* (68), 2704 Michigan avenue.
Schimmels, Christian* (68), 1410 South Halsted-st.
Semmler, Mrs. Catherine* (68), 10337 Throop-st.
Sickinger, John* (68), 2847 North Hermitage-av.
Trauscht, Anna M.* (68), 2481 Archer avenue.
1846—Berger, Louis A. (81), 231 Cuyler avenue.
Block, Mrs. Mary (69), 2037 Edgewood avenue.
Bournique, Mrs. A. E.* (67), 315 East 23d street.
Boyd, Mrs. Charles L.* (67), 5009 Wabash avenue.

Brachtendorf, Anton (69), 348 Mohawk street.
Brinkman, Henry (72), 32d-st. and Vincennes-av.
Brinkworth, Mrs. Emma A.* (67), 884 Irving place.
Brown, Edward C. (68), 6056 Kenwood avenue.
Burkhart, Mrs. A. E. (81), Austin, Ill.*
Clark, John M. (77), 2000 Prairie avenue.
Dayton, Mrs. Martha S.* (67), 6950 Lowe avenue.
Dunn, Mrs. Evaline (90), 2016 West Adams street.
Fishback, Mrs. Mary (73), 6938 Wentworth avenue.
Ganshow, Mrs. Anna M. (67), 617 South Kedzie-av.
Gray, George L. (67), 2644 Indiana avenue.
Griffin, Mrs. F. A. (77), 907 West Monroe street.
Gross, George M. (67), 3826 Rhodes avenue.
Halifax, Mrs. Martha A. (69), 424 South Oakley-bd.
Hayes, Michael (68), 4546 West Adams street.
Healy, James T. (67), 3220 Indiana avenue.
Hitz, Louis J. (79), 95th street and Western-av.
Hough, Albert J.* (67), 4828 Kenwood avenue.
Husted, Frank T. (67), 2231 South Morgan avenue, Morgan Park.
Jacobs, Mrs. Amelia (77), 88 Cleveland avenue.
Klassen, Jacob (78), 3123 South Park avenue.
Klossman, Charlotte (73), 695 North Maplewood-av.
Knight, Jennie H.* (67), 3336 Rhodes avenue.
Lawrence, Theodore F.* (66), 1955 N. Halsted-st.
Lemmon, Vina (66), 1552 Lill avenue.
Mackway, Mrs. Marian (77), 16 Kendall street.
Mahler, J. Martin (76), 1530 Lill avenue.
McCarthy, John Thomas, 1339 Jackson boulevard.
McHenry, Abbie Colby* (67), 1815 Indiana avenue.
Mendsen, J. F. (88), 251 Washington boulevard.
Monheimer, Conrad (80), 4033 Prairie avenue.
Monroe, Benjamin F. (73), 135 East 71st place.
Muenzenberg, Charles (82), 16 Orchard street.
Munch, Peter (77), 4850 Bishop street.
Nelson, Andrew G. (87), 4635 Langley avenue.
Niehoff, Katherine (72), 1108 Wellington street.
Norton, F. F., 1178 Fillmore street.
Polkey, Margaret* (66), 3564 Vernon avenue.
Rock, Daniel J. (78), 1141 Lill avenue.
Schade, Henry (74), 6332 Evergreen avenue.
Sears, Joseph (70), Kenilworth, Ill.
Sickinger, Jacob* (67), 902 Devon avenue.
Sinclair, Mrs. A. E. A. (77), 6542 Lafayette-av.
Smalley, Mrs. Angeline K.* (67), 2544 Kimball-av.
Smele, Mrs. James (100), 7301 Langley avenue.
Smith, James H. (69), 418 Oak street.
Stratton, Helen A., 914 West Monroe street.
Tyler, Albert S.* (66), 5461 East End avenue.
Vernon, John M. (72), Wilmette.
Volmuth, Mrs. Maria (84), 139 East Division-st.
Weir, Robert (73), 6323 Yale avenue.
Yoe, Lucien G.* (67), Highland Park.
1847—Amberg, Mrs. William A.* (66), 1301 North State street.
Barnard, Frederick (77), Oak Park.
Barrell, James (79), 4717 Kenwood avenue.
Barts, John (67), 5135 Dearborn street.
Bender, George A. (79), 3250 Humboldt avenue.
Beers, Cyrenius (67), 3417 South Paulina street.
Beers, George T. (76), 3416 South Paulina street.
Berry, Mrs. John J.* (66), 258 Bissell street.
Bishop, Joseph H. (74), 600 York place.
Brethauer, Mrs. Fredericke (70), 1506 Oakdale-av.
Brettmann, Mrs. Louisa (66), 2836 Armitage-av.
Brinkman, Mrs. Henry (73), 92d street and Vincennes road.
Chamberlain, Thomas S. (66), 1668 W. Chicago-av.
Charlette, Mrs. Mary L. S.* (66), 1463 Fulton-st.
Chatterton, Martha S.* (66), 2024 Washington-bd.
Clausen, Mrs. Lizzie* (66), 359 East North avenue.
Condon, Caroline (80), 321 West 63d street.
Cosgrove, Matthew J.* (66), 1582 Harvard street.
Crosby, Benjamin F. (87), Oak Park.
Curtis, Charles C.* (66), 110 Astor street.
Dony, John F.* (66), 171 Hill street.
Haggard, John D.* (66), 154 North Pine avenue.
Hart, John E. (86), 32 Beethoven place.
Henderson, Robert* (66), 1462 West Polk street.
Hespen, John R. (82), 2244 Lumber street.
Higgins, Mrs. L. A. R. (66), 383 Orchard street.
Horn, Martin (78), 546 Wells street.
Hotchkiss, Gen. C. T. (81), 1906 West Monroe-st.
Hough, Charles H.* (66), 4828 Kenwood avenue.
Hoxie, Mary H.* (66), 4440 Michigan avenue.
Hunt, Mrs. Ellen L. (84), 3224 Forest avenue.
Klein, Catherine (69), Rogers Park.
Kosh, Magdalena (87), 363 Carroll avenue.
Lauer, Maria (83), 616 East Belmont avenue.

Lunn, Harvey W.* (66), 2184 West 24th place.
Manierre, William R.* (66), 1507 N. Dearborn-st.
Markus, Fritz (74), 661 Milwaukee avenue.
Meech, George A. (88), Morgan Park, Ill.
Morgan, William R.* (66), 231 South Central-av.
Morris, Timothy E. (69), 3151 Prairie avenue.
Murphy, James C.* (66), 2340 West Polk street.
McAuliffe, John (93), 648 South Racine avenue.
Noll, Mrs. Louisa (83), 4927 St. Lawrence avenue.
Redden, John, 5 Edgemont avenue.
Schmidt, Mrs. Dorothea (74), 5335 Princeton-av.
Schubert, Mrs. Margaret (72), 5635 Princeton-av.
Sherman, Frederick J. (66), 3670 Milwaukee-av.
Simon, William (75), 3221 North Clark street.
Stumpf, Sierna (82), 872 Armitage avenue.
Taylor, Mrs. Agnes M.* (66), 32 Best avenue.
Thiele, Heinrich (84), 522 Cleveland avenue.
Thiele, Maria (85), 522 Cleveland avenue.
Thilo, Mrs. Elizabeth (78), 807 North Halsted-st.
Turner, John W.* (66), 1854 Addison street.
Vernon, Sarah A., 432 Claremont avenue.
Wayman, James B.* (66), 4858 Kenmore avenue.
Webber, Mrs. Mary A.* (66), 431½ Belden avenue.
Whitehead, Edward J. (74), 5465 Blackstone-av.
Williamson, Elizabeth V., 432 Claremont avenue.
Winchell, Juliet A. (71), 2223 North Tripp avenue.
Waltz, Fred (76), 1279 North Clark street.
1848—Apfel, Mrs. Anna (93), 76 Hammond street.
Batterman, John Otto (83), 1015 Ashland boulevard.
Belden, William* (65), 71 South Colin avenue.
Bremner, David F. (74), 5009 Greenwood avenue.
Broderick, Michael (96), 1921 Belle Plaine avenue.
Bryan, Frederick W.* (65), 1423 Kenilworth-av.
Caldwell, Peter (91), 4424 Wallace street.
Cleveland, Silas E. (75), 929 West Monroe street.
Creet, Catherine (94), 30 Spruce street.
De Wolf, Edward P.* (85), Waukegan, Ill.
Dimond, Philippine S. (76), 45 Bryant avenue.
Docter, Margaretha* (65), 6333 South Racine-av.
Douaire, Sarah S. (73), 4022 Perry street.
Dougall, John T. (65), 1079 West Grace street.
Doyle, James M. (74), 719 S. Ashland boulevard.
Eberlein, George P.* (65), 647 Sheffield avenue.
Fenster, Maria (65), 1103 South Harlem avenue.
Flanders, John J.* (65), Glencoe, Ill.
Frauenberger, Gustav* (65), 2620 Mildred avenue.
Fredericks, Mrs. Anna (72), 2021 Michigan avenue.
Gray, P. W. (65), 2563 North Winchester avenue.
Greenebaum, Elias (91), 4510 Grand boulevard.
Greenebaum, Henry (80), 4556 Ellis avenue.
Grimme, Louis E. (86), 99 Diversey court.
Gunderson, Martin A. (78), 2531 N. Francisco-av.
Hector, Jacob S. (65), 3011 Archer avenue.
Henrotin, Charles (70), 745 Lincoln parkway.
Hoge, Holmes (71), Evanston, Ill.
Huchsold, Mrs. Annie (69), 49 Canalport avenue.
Joyce, Thomas (79), 3440 Prairie avenue.
Joyce, Mrs. Thomas (75), 3440 Prairie avenue.
Kappelman, Fred P. (70), 2207 Colfax street, Evanston.
Kernan, George P.* (65), 1203 West Adams street.
Kistner, Valentine (94), 10324 Prospect avenue.
Koehsel, John E.* (65), 935 Winona street.
Kramer, M. (78), 83 East 34th street.
Langguth, J. F. (71), 2706 Byron street.
Miller, Thomas E. (80), 1449 LaSalle avenue.
Monheimer, Leonard (80), 4419 Prairie avenue.
Murphy, Joseph (90), 5648 Michigan avenue.
McConnell, John* (65), 546 Hawthorne street.
Olson, Oliver (66), 610 West Melrose street.
Page, Charles L.* (64), 40 Scott street.
Parker, John D. (73), 31 Aldine square.
Pease, O. A. (78), 875 Austin avenue.
Peck, Ferdinand W.* (65), 1826 Michigan avenue.
Price, Mrs. Laura J.* (65), 888 Warren avenue.
Pringle, Mrs. Isabelle M. (94), 5746 Jackson-av.
Pringle, Margaret* (65), 5446 Jackson avenue.
Pringle, Thomas A. (67), Brainard, Ill.
Randall, Mrs. T. D. (74), 2624 Calumet avenue.
Redell, Richard F. (70), 1215 Dearborn avenue.
Reid, William G.* (65), 5214 Cornell avenue.
Renich, Mrs. Helen (66), 432 School street.
Riley, John P. (68), 338 Hudson avenue.
Rofinot, Victor F. (65), 6354 Langley avenue.
Rogan, John J. (67), 4253 South State street.
Rudolph, Joseph (88), 527 Briar place.
Sampson, John C.* (65), 1243 East 44th place.
Schimmels, Capt. N. C., 1410 South Halsted street.
Schlecht, Mrs. Catherine (70), 6803 Ohio street.

Schlossman, Joseph B. (65), 5341 Calumet avenue.
Schmidt, Mrs. Sophie (78), Oak Park, Ill.
Scouton, T. B.* (65), 521 West Madison street.
Scudder, Mrs. Mary A.* (65), 102 Bellevue place.
Seaton, Isabel D.* (65), 1016 West Monroe street.
Sedgwick, Mrs. A. G. (76), 603 Park avenue.
Sheppard, Robert D.* (65), Evanston, Ill.
Sinclair, J. E. (76), Maywood, Ill.
Smyth, Thomas A.* (65), 2022 West Jackson-bd.
Spikings, William H.* (65), 5031 N. Crawford-av.
Starkweather, Charles H.* (65), 4901 Woodlawn-av.
Stewart, Bridget (79), 646 West 12th street.
Varges, Edward E. (65), 712 Summerdale avenue.
Vial, Jennie* (65), LaGrange, Ill.
Walsh, James J. (79), 4839 Washington boulevard.
Walter, Lorns (89), 1717 Roscoe street.
Wempic, Leonard C. (77), 662 North Curtis street.
Zimmerman, John S. (72), 1847 Park avenue.
Zimmerman, Mrs. Minna (70), 1279 Perry street.
1849—Balken, Peter M. (76), 71 Keystone avenue, River Forest.
Boyd, Charles L. (65), 5009 Wabash avenue.
Boyd, Mrs. Charles L.* (64), 5009 Wabash avenue.
Boyd, Robert (72), Hinsdale, Ill.
Brennan, Matthew J. (78), 4018 Vincennes avenue.
Brown, Mrs. Sophia (84), 3847 Dearborn street.
Buggle, James (65), 2701 West Jackson boulevard.
Clowry, James, 4200 Ellis avenue.
Clowry, John K., 437 Blue Island avenue.
Clowry, Thomas, 2859 North Robey street.
Clowry, Mrs. Bridget (81), 463 West 14th street.
Cobb, Weldon J.* (64), 6455 Wheaton, Ill.
Cullen, Mrs. M. (64), 604 East 46th street.
Culver, John (67), 2201 Dewey avenue, Evanston.
Curtis, Rev. Edward H. (70), 6455 Kenwood-av.
Curtis, Henry M. (72), 4943 Blackstone avenue.
Donoghue, Daniel R.* (64), 6325 Kenwood avenue.
Doty, Virginia E.* (64), 5547 Blackstone avenue.
Doyle, A. J.* (64), Orland, Ill.
Elsey, Mrs. Anna (72), 1532 West Adams street.
Erskine, Cecilia D. W.* (64), 50 East Schiller-st.
Foley, Mrs. Ellen (77), 656 West 20th street.
Franzen, Alexander (84), 17 Artesian avenue.
Furst, Conrad (84), 1400 Astor street.
Glasebrook, George (88), 2230 Flournoy street.
Glasebrook, Mrs. Mary Ann (84), 2230 Flournoy-st.
Goodwillie, Mrs. Cecilia (84), 450 Roslyn place.
Goold, John E.* (64), 2216 Prairie avenue.
Grupe, Conrad (80), 1189 North Maplewood avenue.
Guenther, Rebecca E. (72), 3020 Lake Park avenue.
Hatch, Wm. H. (64), 211 Park-av., River Forest.
Jaeger, Julius F.* (64), 1126 George street.
Jaworski, Stephen D.* (64), 1337 West Jackson-bd.
Joslyn, Walter S. (70), 1610 Garfield boulevard.
Kehoe, Miles, 639 South Ashland avenue.
Keller, George (95), 164 Newton street.
Kindberg, N. A. (73), 1496 West Foster avenue.
Kinzie, Mrs. Arthur E.* (64), Riverside, Ill.
Laiger, Fred G. (67), 1136 Orleans street.
Larson, Iver (83), 691 North Hoyne avenue.
Lay, A. Tracy (89), 321 Michigan avenue.
Leopold, Mrs. C.* (64), 1295 North Halsted street.
Loughlin, William M. (89), 4650 North Robey-st.
Mahler, H. F. (71), 14 DeKalb street.
Melvin, Thomas H.* (64), 2508 North Artesian-av.
Miller, Brice A. (75), 46 Roslyn place.
Moore, William J. (68), 66 Osgood street.
Nelson, Sarah Earl* (64), 4204 Greenwood avenue.
Norton, Mrs. Louise C.* (64), 150 Lincoln Park-bd.
O'Byrne, Mrs. Elizabeth (69), 2545 Washington-bd.
Olberts, Mrs. Catherina (64), 3302 Archer avenue.
Oliver, Lucy Hicks (69), 1541 West Monroe street.
Peckler, Katharine A. (65), 4038 Archer avenue.
Peeble, Cassius M. (69), 296 West Monroe street.
Prindiville, William H.* (64), 1212 Fullerton-av.
Ritchie, Hugh (89), 28 West Chestnut street.
Rogers, Edward K.* (64), 159 East Ontario street.
Rooks, Mrs. Mary S., 964 Jackson boulevard.
Rumsey, George D.* (64), 62 East Division street.
Scott, George M. (71), Riverside, Ill.
Shepard, D. A.* (64), 2030 West Harrison street.
Smith, Frank Waldo* (64), 5539 Cornell avenue.
Sutter, John D. (67), 745 Evanston avenue.
Talbot, H. Plumer, 241 Michigan avenue.
Theis, Theodore (68), 2729 Pine Grove avenue.
Thomas, Mrs. John W.* (64), 515 Jackson-bd.
Ulrich, Mrs. Maria (77), 833 Lill avenue.
Weber, Mrs. Barbara M. (78), 1728 Wilmot avenue.
Weber, Mary (67), 1634 Barry avenue.

Wood, Seth* (64), 361 West Harrison street.
1850—Baumann, Frederick (87), 43 Pine Grove-av.
Becker, Fred (79), 331 North LaSalle street.
Boddeker, B. (75), 1541 West Chicago avenue.
Bomhake, William* (63), 5442 Leland avenue.
Brown, Canute (68), 1912 Winona street.
Butterfield, Caroline S. (63), 1322 N. LaSalle-st.
Carpenter, George B. (79), 107 Lincoln Park-bd.
Catlin, Mrs. Mary E.* (63), 451 Belden avenue.
Clingman, Charles W.* (63), 4748 Kenwood avenue.
Coleman, Edward* (63), 2829 Archer avenue.
Conroyd, James, 26 South Curtis street.
Dennis, John (70), 34 St. John's court.
Dunne, Michael J. (73), 4901 Dorchester avenue.
Erickson, Mrs. Martha (91), 3424 South Park-av.
Finke, Mrs. Anna M. (84), 2098 Grenshaw street.
Gerts, George E. (86), Oak Park, Ill.
Goodwillie, Robert* (63), 5038 Washington Park-ct.
Gordon, Elizabeth C. (73), 1850 Fulton street.
Groble, Mrs. Mary* (63), 959 Sawyer avenue.
Haake, George* (63), 2508 Sheffield avenue.
Haines, Walter S.* (63), 1401 West Adams street.
Hawes, Robert (78), 2935 Bonfield street.
Heald, James H.* (63), Oak Park, Ill.
Houlihan, Robert D.* (63), 865 Osgood street.
Howe, Miss Frances* (63), Porter, Ind.
Husted, Julia Hoyt* (63), 429 East 55th street.
Jiroch, Joseph (67), 1837 Mohawk street.
Johnson, Peter (71), 1506 North Robey street.
Kent, Mrs. L. B.* (63), 4024 Prairie avenue.
Koehler, B. (85), 1808 West Jackson boulevard.
Kotz, Charles E.* (68), 1543 Devon avenue.
Langheinrich, Edward* (63), 2929 Sheffield avenue.
Lawson, Victor F.* (63), 1500 Lake Shore drive.
Loebr, Justus P. C. (72), 2824 Burling street.
Martin, Mrs. Mary (65), 6418 Langley avenue.
Miller, Ed M. (63), 664 South Halsted street.
Moore, John M. (92), 3907 Michigan avenue.
Moore, William J. (76), 1910 Fremont street.
Morris, William (70), 499 Woodlawn avenue.
Moser, George W.* (63), 400 Maple-av., Oak Park.
Munson, John (74), West Foster and North Kilpatrick avenues.
McDermott, Michael (67), 3528 Wabash avenue.
Newton, Hanna Reimers, 1815 Melrose street.
Norton, Mrs. Lucy, 231 East 54th street.
Nurnberger, Mrs. Emilie (75), 2968 South State-st.
Ohlerking, John H. (71), 832 West Adams street.
Pfeifer, Charles* (63), Hinsdale, Ill.
Pinkerton, William A. (67), 217 South Ashland-bd.
Pomy, Mrs. Anna (68), 431 Webster avenue.
Poole, Manning S. (81), 3834 Langley avenue.
Powell, John, 1852 West Congress street.
Redell, Mrs. J.* (63), 547 Berenice avenue.
Reinhart, John (65), 1033 Wellington street.
Retsin, John (96), 2325 North Rockwell street.
Sammons, E. Hudson* (67), 3149 Rhodes avenue.
Schaffer, Ferdinand (64), Blue Island, Ill.
Senf, Sophia (65), River Grove, Ill.
Seelye, Henry E. (86), 1134 Chicago-av., Evanston.
Shackelford, Collins (71), 1622 Greenleaf avenue.
Smith, Mrs. Mary Ann* (63), 1242 W. Madison-st.
Spies, Mary (82), 1918 Montrose avenue.
Stender, C. F. G., 308 South Hamlin avenue.
Spry, Ellen (75), 481 West Monroe street.
Uchtmann, John D. (81), 824 South Halsted street.
Weigelsbaum, Joseph* (63), 1826 Spaulding avenue.
Weihe, Mrs. Caroline (72), 919 Roscoe street.
Wells, Edwin S. (84), Lake Forest, Ill.
Werkmeister, John* (63), 3308 Calumet avenue.
White, John M. (86), 5211 Cornell avenue.
Winsauer, Mrs. Louise* (63), 120 E. Walton place.

DIED IN 1913.

Allison, Benjamin F. (83), 2454 West Huron street; arrived 1839; died May 11.
Barbe, Martin (84); arrived 1846; died Oct. 29.
Bermm, Mrs. Antje (82), 62 North Waller avenue; arrived 1842; died Jan. 4.
Barnum, William E. (78), 6400 Normal boulevard; born in Chicago 1835; died July 7.
Barrell, James, Evanston; arrived 1846; died June 28.
Beers, Samuel (80), 3646 Wabash avenue; arrived 1847; died Jan. 13.
Benedict, Amzi (87), 933 Galt avenue; arrived 1849; died April 20.
Best, Mrs. Minnie (64), 4402 South Michigan avenue; born in Chicago 1849; died Feb. 13.

Blackmer, O. C. (85), 311 North Grove avenue; born in Chicago 1828; died Jan. 5.
Blocki, William F. (71), 6403 Kimbark avenue; arrived 1850; died Aug. 22.
Brooks, Frederick W. (86), Morgan Park; arrived 1833; died June 22.
Brown, Mrs. Eliza H. (99), Berwyn; arrived 1850; died April 25.
Bruker, John H. (95), 520 West 20th street; arrived 1849; died March 21.
Burns, Mrs. Ellen W. (70), 35 East Oak street; arrived 1849; died June 17.
Cobb, Mrs. Ella Parsons, Greenwood Inn, Evanston; arrived 1845; died Jan. 17.
Cochran, Timothy F. (82), 4336 Sheridan road; born in Cook county 1831; died Aug. 4.
Commons, William H. (72), 223 North Ada street; born in Chicago 1841; died March 17.
Cosgrove, Mrs. Hannah M. (78), 4804 Champlain avenue; arrived 1848; died Sept. 2.
Crain, Mrs. Sarah Burroughs (84), 1031 Asbury avenue, Evanston; arrived 1841; died Oct. 29.
Crocroft, Joseph E. (92), Lyons, Wis.; arrived in Chicago, 1842; died Sept. 2.
Dennis, Mrs. Mary (94), 424 South Kenilworth avenue, Oak Park; arrived 1841; died Jan. 14.
Dolese, John (76), Morton Park; arrived in Chicago 1837; died Sept. 23.
Doyle, Edward (92), 2820 Harvard street; arrived 1835; died Jan. 22.
Dupee, Mrs. Elizabeth R., Kenwood; arrived 1850; died Sept. 7.
Dutch, James B. (73), 6637 Parnell avenue; arrived 1848; died Dec. 30, 1912.
Ebersold, Mrs. Julia S. (69), 4401 Lake avenue; arrived 1850; died July 24.
Farnsworth, George (87), 1421 Astor street; arrived 1840; died Jan. 26.
Foley, Mrs. Catherine (76), 1012 East 47th street; born in Chicago 1837; died Feb. 9.
Foster, Mrs. Mary C. (68), 1404 North Dearborn street; born in Chicago 1844; died Dec. 5, 1912.
Gale, Edward F. (67), Exeter, N. H.; born in Chicago 1846; died Sept. 18.
Gale, Edwin O. (81), Oak Park; arrived 1835; died Jan. 2.
Gerber, Barbara (85), 6154 South Halsted street; arrived 1834; died July 12.
Giezen, Mrs. Barbara (75), 1310 Norwood street; arrived 1848; died June 13.
Gilbert, Henry S. (76), 1325 Iowa street; arrived 1836; died Jan. 11.
Gleeson, Mrs. Ellen (85), 5428 Winthrop avenue; arrived 1853; died Jan. 18.
Gordon, Mrs. Emma (60), 225 North Howard avenue, Austin; born in Chicago, 1853; died March 20.
Green, Mrs. Caroline E. (88), Oak Park; arrived in Chicago 1828; died Dec. 27, 1912.
Grusendorf, Henry (83), 1520 North Hoyne avenue; arrived 1850; died July 30.
Howe, Charles M. (68), 1800 Asbury avenue, Evanston; arrived in Chicago, 1845; died Oct. 18.
Huehn, Mrs. Anna (77), 1230 Wells street; arrived 1836; died Feb. 19.
Isham, Mrs. Katherine Snow (81), 945 Dearborn avenue; born in Chicago, 1832; died Feb. 23.
Johnston, Richard M., Philadelphia, Pa.; arrived in Chicago, 1848; died May 23.
Kearns, Michael (76), 3617 Colorado avenue; arrived 1847; died Sept. 26.
Kedzie, Mrs. Mary E. (75), Evanston; arrived 1849; died June 25.
Kelly, Joseph (90), Marshalltown, Iowa; arrived in Chicago, 1850; died Feb. 2.
Kennicott, Mrs. J. Asa (92), Largo, Fla.; arrived in Chicago, 1849; died May 30.
Kimbell, Mrs. Almora Hazel (81), Hinsdale, Ill.; born in Chicago, 1832; died March 6.
Langbenry, Mrs. Catherine (92), 1049 Chestnut street; arrived 1847; died April 4.
Lloyd, Alexander T. (65), 2318 West Washington boulevard; born in Chicago, 1848; died Oct. 27.
Loeb, Moses (83); arrived 1848; died June 6.
Logeman, John (73), 733 Robbins terrace; arrived 1848; died Nov. 5.
Marshall, John (72), 1070 North Marshfield avenue; arrived 1845; died March 6.

Mitchell, Mrs. Fanny Clark, 440 North Normal
  parkway; arrived 1848; died Dec. 25, 1912.
McEvoy, William (81), 2019 Racine avenue; arrived
  1848; died Nov. 16.
McGurn, Christopher (71), 2918 Fulton street; ar-
  rived 1848; died Oct. 1.
North, Isaac (95); arrived 1837; died July 12.
Phelan, Mrs. Patrick (69), 748 Belden avenue; arrived 1845; died June 5.
Prindville, Mary T. (65), 5116 Sheridan road; born
  in Maple Park, 1848; died May 31.
Prindville, Redmond (88), 1212 Fullerton avenue;
  arrived 1836; died Oct. 31.
Reilly, Michael H. (64), 3707 Colorado avenue; born
  in Chicago, 1849; died June 6.
Rice, Albert E. (86), 221 North Baird avenue, Aus-
  tin; arrived 1847; died Oct. 16.
Richey, Alexander M. (87), 9437 Langley avenue;
  arrived 1840; died Sept. 8.
Robinson, Mrs. Elizabeth (89), 4912 West Grand
  avenue; arrived 1844; died Sept. 21.
Sargent, Walter A. (72), 2827 West Van Buren
  street; born in Chicago, 1840; died Dec. 23, 1912.
Sayre, Harriet E. (92), Mont Clare; arrived 1835;
  died Nov. 16.
Schneider, Mrs. Marina (81), Aurora, Ill.; arrived
  as 3-day old infant, 1832; died March 22.
Schroeder, William, 2817 Logan boulevard; arrived
  1842; died July 31.

Shaughnessy, Mrs. Thomas (72), 1716 Sedgwick
  street; arrived 1849; died March 31.
Snow, Miss Helen E. (76), 945 Dearborn avenue;
  born in Chicago, 1836; died in St. Augustine,
  Fla., Feb. 7.
Sollitt, Mrs. Mary (89), 4020 Prairie avenue; ar-
  rived 1845; died Aug. 21.
Soule, Mrs. Ursula T. (81), West Palm Beach, Fla.;
  arrived 1832; died March 22.
Stebbins, Mrs. Julia A., 1551 Morgan Park avenue;
  arrived 1848; died Oct. 6.
Steinhaus, George (81), Oak Park; arrived 1844;
  died June 10.
Todd, William G. (91), 4714 North Robey street;
  arrived 1837; died Aug. 7.
Ton, Mrs. Anna (78), Roseland; arrived 1839; died
  Aug. 5.
Wall, Thomas F. (74), 224 Latrobe avenue, Austin;
  arrived in Chicago, 1840; died April 16.
Wesencraft, Mrs. Jane (90), Riverside, Ill.; arrived
  1838; died Aug. 17.
Walsh, Michael (64), 2016 Leland avenue; arrived
  1852; died Oct. 12.
Wheaton, Mrs. Sarah M. (66), Wheaton; born near
  Wheaton, 1846; died April 8.
White, Mrs. Jennie McLaren (73), 5464 University
  avenue; arrived 1850; died March 4.
Yoe, Mrs. Mary W. (69), Highland Park; arrived
  1847; died Nov. 12, 1912.

CEMETERIES IN CHICAGO AND VICINITY.

Arlington—West thirteen miles, near Elmhurst.
Bethany—Archer avenue and 79th street.
Bohemian National—North Crawford and Foster
  avenues.
D'nai Abraham—South of Waldheim.
B'nai Sholom—North Clark street, near Irving Park
  boulevard.
B'rith Abraham—Desplaines avenue and 14th street,
  Forest Park.
Brookside—West sixteen miles, near South Elm-
  hurst.
Calvary—North ten miles, near South Evanston.
Chebra Gemilath Chasadim Ublkur Cholim—North
  Clark street, near Irving Park boulevard.
Chebra Kadisha Ublkur Cholim—North Clark street,
  near Irving Park boulevard.
Chevra Shomer Hadas—Nine miles west on Des-
  plaines avenue, north of West 12th street.
Concordia—Nine miles west on Madison street.
Crown Hill—Fourteen miles west on Aurora, Elgin
  & Joliet railway.
Eden—Irving Park boulevard, near Franklin Park.
Elm Lawn—West thirteen miles on Lake street,
  near Elmhurst.
Elmwood—Grand and Beach avenues.
Evergreen—South Kedzie avenue and 87th street.
Forest Home—West ten miles on 12th street.
Free Sons of Israel—Waldheim.
German Lutheran—North Clark street and Irving
  Park boulevard.
Graceland—North five miles on Clark street.
Hebrew Benevolent Society—North Clark street,
  near Irving Park boulevard.
Highland—West Chicago.
Montrose—Bryn Mawr and Crawford avenues.
Moses Montefiore—South of Forest Home.
Mount Auburn—Southwest nine and one-half miles,
  at 39th street and Oak Park avenue.
Mount Carmel—Hillside Station.
Mount Forest—Thornton, Ill.
Mount Glenwood—Thornton, Ill.

Mount Greenwood—Near Morgan Park; south.
Mount Hope—Near Morgan Park.
Mount Israel—Dunning.
Mount Maariv—Dunning; northwest.
Mount Olive—North Narragansett avenue, near
  West Irving Park boulevard.
Mount Olivet—South sixteen miles, near Morgan
  Park.
New Light—East Prairie road, near Lincoln ave-
  nue, Morton Grove; northwest.
North Chicago Hebrew Congregation—At Roschill;
  north.
Norwood Park—Sanford avenue and Higgins road.
Oak Hill—West 119th street and Kedzie avenue.
Oakland—Proviso; west twelve miles.
Oak Lawn—South Halsted and 180th streets.
Oakridge—Oakridge avenue and West 12th street;
  west twelve miles.
Oakwoods—Greenwood avenue and 67th street;
  south.
Oesterelch-Ungarischer Kranken Unterstuetzungs-
  Verein—At Waldheim.
Ohavo Amuno—South of Forest Home.
Ohavo Sholom—At Oakwoods.
Polish—Milwaukee avenue, near Norwood Park.
Ridgelawn—North Crawford and Peterson avenues.
Roschill—North seven miles.
St. Adalbert—Norwood Park.
St. Boniface—North Clark street and Lawrence
  avenue.
St. Henry—Ridge and Devon avenues.
St. Joseph's—River Grove.
St. Lukas—5232 North Crawford avenue.
St. Maria—Grand Trunk railway and 87th street;
  south.
Sinai Congregation—At Roschill.
Society of Benevolence and Relief of the Sick—
  North Clark street and Irving Park boulevard.
Union Ridge—Higgins avenue, near Norwood Park.
Waldheim—West ten miles on Harrison street.
Zion Congregation—At Roschill.

LAW AND ORDER LEAGUES AND PROTECTIVE ASSOCIATIONS.

Anti-Cruelty Society—President, George L. Douglass;
  secretary, Hugo Krause, 155 West Grand avenue.
Anti-Saloon League of Illinois—1200, 189 West Madison street; superintendent, F. Scott McBride.
Chicago Law and Order League—President, Arthur
  B. Farwell; secretary, Wm. F. Mulvihill, 1305,
  19 South LaSalle street.
Citizens' Association—33, 106 North LaSalle street;
  secretary, S. M. Singleton.
Citizens' League of Chicago for the Suppression of
  the Sale of Liquor to Minors—1405, 155 North
  Clark street; secretary, W. R. Ceperly; superin-
  tendent, Henry King Grose.

Englewood Law and Order League—6305 Yale ave-
  nue; secretary, J. H. Lyle.
Garfield Park Protective Association—President, E.
  Worthing; secretary, William Watters, 4147 West
  Congress street.
Hyde Park Protective Association—Secretary, Ar-
  thur B. Farwell, 501, 19 South LaSalle street.
Society for Prevention of Crime—1118, 8 South Dear-
  born street; secretary, George E. Girling.
Vice Commission of the City of Chicago (appointed
  by the mayor)—President, Dean W. T. Sumner;
  secretary, Edwin W. Sims.

THE WORLD'S GREATEST BASEBALL PALACE

Comiskey Park, home of the "White Sox," 35th street between Wentworth and Shields avenues, containing fourteen acres, the largest field devoted to baseball in the United States and with a seating capacity of 35,000 persons, grandstand and bleachers. Twelve hundred tons of steel were used in the construction of the plant, which is re-enforced with concrete.

PRICES OF MESS PORK AND LARD FOR FORTY YEARS.

The following table shows the lowest and highest cash prices for mess pork and prime steamed lard in the Chicago market for the past forty years and the months in which extreme prices were reached:

YEAR.	MESS PORK.			LARD.		
	Lowest in	Range.	Highest in	Lowest in	Range.	Highest in
1874	Jan., Feb., Mar.	$13.75 @24.75	Aug	Jan	$8.20 @15.50	Oct
1875	Jan	17.70 @23.50	Oct	Nov	11.80 @15.75	Apr. and May
1876	Oct	15.20 @22.75	Apr	Sept	9.55 @13.85	Mar. and Apr
1877	Dec	11.40 @17.95	Jan	Dec	7.55 @11.55	Jan
1878	Dec	8.02½@11.35	Jan	Dec	5.32½@ 7.80	Aug
1879	Jan	7.27½@13.75	Dec	Aug	5.30 @ 7.75	Dec
1880	Apr	9.37½@19.00	Oct	June	6.85 @ 7.85	Nov
1881	Jan	12.40 @20.00	Sept	Feb	9.20 @13.00	July
1882	Mar	16.00 @24.75	Oct	Mar	10.05 @13.10	Oct
1883	Sept. and Oct	10.20 @20.15	May	Oct	7.15 @12.10	May
1884	Dec	19.55 @19.50	May, June, July	Dec	6.45 @10.00	Feb
1885	Oct. and Nov	8.00 @13.25	Feb	Oct	5.82½@ 7.10	Feb. and Apr
1886	May	8.20 @12.20	Dec	May	5.82½@ 7.50	Sept
1887	Jan	11.60 @24.00	May	June and Oct	6.20 @ 7.92½	Dec
1888	Dec	12.90 @16.00	Oct	Jan	7.25 @11.20	Oct
1889	Dec	8.35 @13.37½	Jan	Dec	5.55 @ 7.55	Jan
1890	Dec	7.50 @13.62½	Apr	Dec	5.50 @ 6.52½	Apr
1891	Dec	7.45 @13.00	May	Feb	5.47½@ 7.05	Sept
1892	Apr	9.25 @15.05	Dec	Jan	8.05 @10.60	Dec
1893	Aug	10.25 @21.90	May	Aug	6.00 @13.20	Mar
1894	Mar	10.67½@14.57½	Sept	Mar	6.45 @ 9.05	Sept
1895	Dec	7.50 @12.87½	May	Dec	5.15 @ 7.17½	Mar
1896	Aug	5.50 @10.85	Jan	July	3.05 @ 5.85	Jan
1897	Dec	7.15 @ 9.00	Sept	June	3.42½@ 4.90	Sept
1898	Oct	7.65 @12.30	May	Jan. and Oct	4.52½@ 6.82½	May
1899	May and Oct	7.85 @10.45	Jan	May	4.93 @ 5.77½	Jan
1900	Nov	10.37½@16.00	Oct	Feb	5.65 @ 7.40	Oct
1901	Jan	12.60 @16.80	Mar	Jan	6.90 @10.25	Sept
1902	Feb. and Mar	15.00 @18.70	July	Feb	9.07½@11.60	Sept
1903	Oct	10.95 @18.37½	Mar	Oct	6.20 @11.00	Sept
1904	Sept	10.60 @16.50	Feb	May	6.15 @ 7.92½	Feb
1905	Apr	11.70 @16.50	Oct	Jan	6.55 @ 8.10	Aug
1906	Dec	13.45 @20.00	July	Jan	7.82½@ 9.85	Nov
1907	Sept. and Oct	13.75 @17.75	Feb	Oct	8.42½@ 9.97½	Feb
1908	Feb	10.75 @16.60	July	Feb	8.97½@10.45	Oct
1909	Jan	18.25 @25.20	Sept	Jan	9.40 @12.65	Sept. and Oct
1910	Oct	17.25 @27.00	July	Aug	11.50 @14.65	Mar
1911	Oct	14.50 @21.50	Feb	Apr	7.70 @10.67½	Jan
1912	Jan	15.00 @19.62½	Apr	Feb	8.65 @11.97½	Oct
1913*	Jan	17.50 @22.75	July and Sept	Jan	9.47½@11.87½	July

*Jan. 1 to Nov. 20.

FOREIGN CONSULS AND CONSULATES IN CHICAGO.

Argentine Republic—Albert W. Brickwood, Jr., 1201. 79 West Monroe street.
Austria-Hungary—Hugo Silvestri (consul-general), 817, 108 South LaSalle street.
Belgium—Charles Henrotin, 1166, 209 S. LaSalle-st.
Bolivia—F. W. Harnwell, 1502, 105 S. LaSalle-st.
Brazil—S. R. Alexander, 10, 183 N. Wabash avenue.
Chile—M. H. Ehlert, 616, 29 South LaSalle street.
Costa Rica—B. Singer, 616, 29 South LaSalle street.
Cuba—T. Estrada Palma, 601 Security building.
Denmark—Georg Bech, 79, 154 W. Randolph street.
Dominican Republic—Frederick W. Job, 832, 140 South Dearborn street.
Ecuador—F. Plaza, 914 Lakeside place.
France—Baron de St. Laurent, 652, 175 West Jackson boulevard.
Germany—Alfred Geissler (consul-general), 916, 122 South Michigan avenue.
Great Britain—Horace D. Nugent (consul-general), 805 Pullman building.
Greece—N. Salopoulos, 24, 143 N. Dearborn street.
Guatemala—Jule F. Brower, 1331. 38 S. Dearborn-st.
Italy—Count Ziulio Bolognesi, 432, 72 W. Adams-st.
Japan—Kabachi Abe, 929, 122 S. Michigan avenue.

Mexico—Augustin Pina, 602, 332 South Dearborn-st.
Netherlands—George Birkhoff, Jr. (consul-general), 58 West Washington street.
Nicaragua—Berthold Singer, 616, 29 S. LaSalle-st.
Norway—Oscar H. Haugan, 210, 133 West Washington street.
Panama—Gustave de Obaldia, 1125 Masonic Temple.
Paraguay—D. T. Hunt, 704, 140 S. Dearborn street.
Persia—(Vacancy).
Peru—W. M. L. Fiske, 234 South LaSalle street.
Portugal—S. C. Simms (vice-consul), 1960 Kenwood terrace.
Russia—Victor Chichkine, 1108, 10 South LaSalle-st.
Siam—Milward Adams, 404 South Michigan avenue.
Spain—B. Singer, 616, 29 South LaSalle street.
Sweden—Henry S. Henschen (acting), 135 West Washington street.
Switzerland—A. Holinger, 201, 179 West Washington street.
Turkey—Charles Henrotin, 1166, 209 S. LaSalle-st.
Uruguay—Juan Moffit, 1614, 127 N. Dearborn street.
Venezuela—Alberto W. Brickwood, Jr., 1201, 79 West Monroe street.

SOCIETIES OF TEACHERS.

Cook County Teachers' Association—Fullerton hall, Art institute; president, L. A. Pringle; superintendent, E. J. Tobin, 512 County building.
Chicago Principals' Club—1808, 5 South Wabash avenue; president, Morgan G. Hogge; secretary, Miss Etta Q. Gee.
Chicago Teachers' Federation—Room 844, 127 North Dearborn street; president, Mrs. Ida L. Fursman;

corresponding secretary, Frances E. Harden; financial secretary, Catherine Goggin; business representative, Margaret A. Haley.
Chicago Teachers' Relief Society—President, Ella Flagg Young; secretary, Miss Marion H. Dyer, Gladstone school.
Head Assistants' Association—President, Miss Myra C. Billings; secretary, Miss Anna Strauss, 4415 Drexel boulevard.

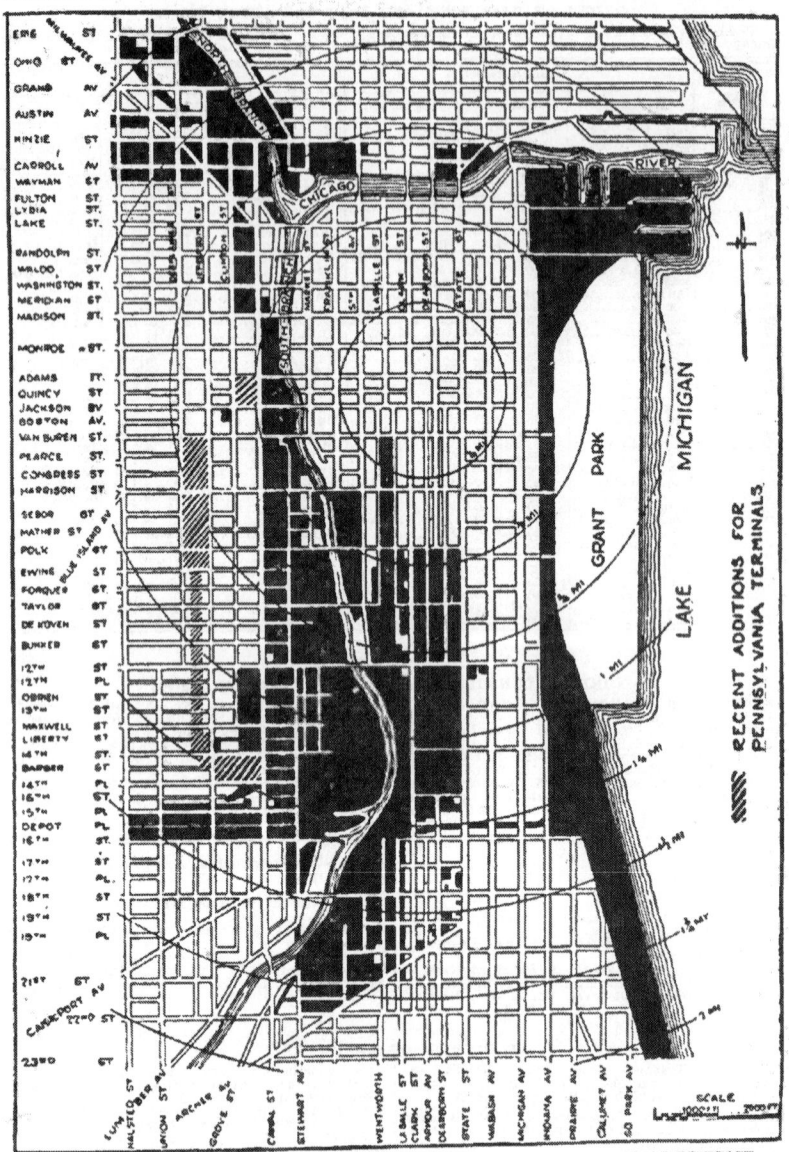

AREA IN BLACK SHOWS RAILROAD POSSESSIONS IN CHICAGO'S BUSINESS DISTRICT.

CHICAGO GRAIN STATISTICS.

The following tables show the extreme prices in each year for forty years for cash wheat, corn and oats, indicating the month in which such prices were obtained:

Year.	Wheat. Lowest in	Wheat. Range.	Wheat. Highest in	Year.	Wheat. Lowest in	Wheat. Range.	Wheat. Highest in
1874	Oct.	$0.81½@1.28	Apr.	1894	July	$0.50⅜@ .63¾	Apr.
1875	Feb	.83¾@1.30½	Aug.	1895	Jan	.48⅞@ .81⅛	May.
1876	July	.83 @1.26¾	Dec.	1896	Aug	.53 @ .94⅜	Nov.
1877	Aug	1.01½@1.76½	May.	1897	Apr	.66½@1.06	Dec.
1878	Oct	.77 @1.14	Apr.	1898	Oct	.62 @1.85	May.
1879	Jan	.81⅝@1.33½	Dec.	1899	Dec	.64 @ .79⅛	May.
1880	Aug	.86½@1.32	Jan.	1900	Jan	.61⅛@ .87⅛	June.
1881	Jan	.95⅜@1.43¼	Oct.	1901	July	.63⅛@ .77¼	June.
1882	Dec	.91⅛@1.40	Apr. and May.	1902	Oct	.67½@ .95	Sept.
1883	Oct	.90 @1.13½	June.	1903	Jan	.70¾@ .93	Sept.
1884	Dec	.69 @ .96	Feb.	1904	Jan	.81¼@1.22	Sept., Oct., Dec
1885	Mar	.73⅜@ .91¾	Apr.	1905	Aug	.77⅛@1.24	Feb.
1886	Oct	.69⅜@ .84¾	Jan.	1906	Aug	.69⅛@ .94¾	May.
1887	Aug	.66⅝@ .94¾	June.	1907	Jan	.71 @1.22	Oct.
1888	Apr	.71⅛@2.00	Sept.	1908	July	.84½@1.24	Aug.
1889	June	.75⅛@1.08¾	Feb.	1909	Oct	1.03 @1.60	June.
1890	Feb	.74¼@1.08¼	Aug.	1910	Oct	.91¼@1.29½	July.
1891	July	.84¾@1.16	Apr.	1911	Apr	.83¼@1.17	Oct.
1892	Oct	.69¼@ .91¾	Feb.	1912	Nov	.85 @1.22	Apr. and May
1893	July	.54¼@ .85	Apr.	1913*	July-Aug.	.84 @1.15⅝	Jan.

Year.	Corn. Lowest in	Corn. Range.	Corn. Highest in	Oats. Lowest in	Oats. Range.	Oats. Highest in
1874	Jan	$0.49 @ .86	Sept.	Aug	$0.37¼@ .71	July.
1875	Dec	.45½@ .76⅛	May and July	Dec	.29½@ .64⅛	May.
1876	Feb	.38⅜@ .49	May	July	.27 @ .35	Sept.
1877	Mar	.37⅝@ .58	Apr	Aug	.22 @ .45¾	May.
1878	Dec	.29⅛@ .43⅝	Mar	Oct	.18 @ .72½	July.
1879	Jan	.29⅜@ .49	Oct.	Jan	.19½@ .36¾	Dec.
1880	Apr	.31⅛@ .43¾	Nov	Aug	.22½@ .35	Jan. and May
1881	Feb	.35¾@ .76⅜	Oct.	Feb	.29½@ .47¾	Oct.
1882	Dec	.79¼@ .81⅛	July	Sept.	.30⅛@ .62	July.
1883	Oct.	.46 @ .70	Jan.	Sept.	.25 @ .43½	Mar.
1884	Dec.	.34½@ .87	Sept.	Dec.	.23 @ .34¼	Apr.
1885	Jan.	.34¼@ .49	Apr. and May	Sept.	.24¼@ .36½	Apr.
1886	Oct.	.33⅛@ .45	July	Oct.	.22⅞@ .35	Jan.
1887	Feb	.33 @ .51⅛	Dec	Mar. and April	.23½@ .31⅛	Dec.
1888	Dec.	.33½@ .60	May	Sept.	.23⅛@ .38	May.
1889	Dec.	.29¼@ .60	Nov	Oct.	.17¾@ .26⅛	Feb.
1890	Feb.	.27¼@ .54¼	Nov	Feb	.19¼@ .45	Nov.
1891	Dec.	.39⅛@ .80	Nov	Oct.	.26 @ .56⅛	Apr.
1892	Jan.	.37½@1.00	May	Jan.	.28 @ .34⅝	Aug.
1893	Dec	.34⅛@ .44⅞	May	July	.21⅜@ .32¼	May.
1894	Feb	.33¾@ .59⅛	Aug	Jan.	.26 @ .50	June.
1895	Dec.	.24⅞@ .54¾	May	Dec	.16⅝@ .31⅛	June.
1896	Sept.	.19½@ .30⅝	Apr.	Sept.	.14¾@ .20¼	Feb. and Mar
1897	Jan. and Feb.	.21¾@ .32⅝	Aug.	Feb	.15⅝@ .23⅞	Dec.
1898	Jan.	.26 @ .38	Dec.	Aug. and Sept.	.20¼@ .32	May.
1899	Dec	.30 @ .38¼	Jan.	Aug.	.19¼@ .28¼	Feb.
1900	Jan.	.30½@ .49⅛	Nov	Aug.	.21 @ .26¼	June.
1901	Jan.	.36 @ .62⅜	Nov.	Jan	.23¼@ .42⅛	Nov.
1902	Oct	.55 @ .88	July.	Aug.	.25 @ .56	July.
1903	Mar.	.41⅜@ .53	July and Aug.	Mar	.31¼@ .45	July.
1904	Jan.	.42¾@ .58⅛	Nov.	Oct.	.28¼@ .46	Feb.
1905	Jan.	.42 @ .64⅛	May.	Sept.	.25 @ .34¾	July.
1906	Feb. and March	.39 @ .54¾	June.	Mar.	.28⅞@ .42¾	June.
1907	Jan.	.39¾@ .66½	Oct.	Jan.	.33½@ .56⅛	Sept.
1908	Feb.	.56⅛@ .82	May and Sept.	Aug.	.46 @ .60⅛	July.
1909	Jan.	.58¼@ .77	June.	Oct.	.38⅛@ .62⅛	May.
1910	Oct.	.47½@ .68	Jan.	Oct.	.29¾@ .49	Feb.
1911	Jan., Feb., Mar.	.45½@ .75	Oct.	Mar.	.28⅞@ .47¼	Oct.
1912	Nov	.53 @ .83	Aug.	Nov.	.30¼@ .58⅛	Apr.
1913*	Jan.	.46½@ .78¼	Aug. and Sept.	March	.31⅝@ .43⅜	Sept.

*Jan. 1 to Nov. 20.

CITY TREASURERS SINCE 1837.

Hiram Pearsons....1837-1838
George W. Dole.... 1839
Walter S. Gurnee...1840, 1843-1844
N. H. Bolles....1840-1841
Wm. L. Church.1845-1846, 1848-1849
Andrew Getzler.... 1847
Edward Manierre....1850-1853
Uriah P. Harris.... 1854
William F. DeWolf.... 1855
O. J. Rose.... 1856
C. N. Holden.... 1857
Alonzo Harvey....1858-1860
Charles H. Hunt.... 1860
W. H. Rice....1861-1862
David A. Gage..1863-1864, 1869-1873
A. G. Throop....1865-1866
Willard F. Wentworth....1867-1869
Daniel O'Hara....1873-1875
Clinton Briggs.... 1876
Charles R. Larrabee....1877-1878
William C. Seipp....1879-1881
Rudolph Brand....1881-1883
John M. Dunphy....1883-1885
William M. Devine....1885-1887
C. Herman Plautz....1887-1889
Bernard Roesing....1889-1891
Peter Kiolbassa....1891-1893
M. J. Bransfield....1893-1895
Adam Wolf....1895-1897
Ernst Hummel....1897-1899
Adam Ortseifen.1899-1901, 1903-1905
Charles F. Gunther....1901-1903
Frederick W. Blocki....1905-1907
John E. Traeger....1907-1909
Isaac N. Powell....1909-1911
Henry Stuckart....1911-1913
Michael J. Flynn....1913-1915

CIRCULATION OF THE CHICAGO DAILY NEWS FOR 1913.

DATE.	Jan.	Feb.	March.	April.	May.	June.	July.	Aug.	Sept.	Oct.	Nov.	Dec.
1.......	Holid'y	389,696	345,045	410,159	358,558	Sunday	339,970	336,595	243,812	352,079	328,364	
2.......	354,077	Sunday	372,559	355,996	358,304	358,304	339,848	303,797	342,689	343,610	Sunday	
3.......	358,457	368,968	374,389	368,991	332,773	355,474	335,254	Sunday	346,590	347,958	364,878	
4.......	335,805	368,276	385,057	367,456	Sunday	356,563	Holid'y	341,749	344,189	322,136	371,300	
5.......	Sunday	362,824	372,665	345,255	357,350	352,126	266,051	341,457	345,834	Sunday	356,961	
6.......	357,369	363,852	309,768	Sunday	359,950	349,452	Sunday	338,221	309,336	364,084	358,518	
7.......	359,205	363,094	370,832	371,958	359,584	321,061	344,069	338,285	Sunday	373,525	359,459	
8.......	360,646	345,242	358,270	369,450	356,457	Sunday	329,922	335,735	349,029	377,846	355,420	
9.......	359,852	Sunday	Sunday	364,192	355,223	356,562	339,772	301,500	348,501	370,451	Sunday	
10.......	358,621	371,925	372,691	369,701	331,158	353,081	340,551	Sunday	357,081	361,171	365,697	
11.......	341,807	370,278	372,696	369,429	Sunday	351,394	358,864	342,707	349,503	353,780	361,585	
12.......	Sunday	367,461	371,547	349,937	358,372	350,302	305,419	343,232	345,262	Sunday	368,388	
13.......	362,360	367,490	369,612	Sunday	333,851	345,736	Sunday	343,376	314,398	366,616	359,516	
14.......	363,037	389,330	368,360	377,708	355,437	315,433	342,952	337,941	Sunday	353,893	367,223	
15.......	365,729	359,770	347,345	370,898	355,377	Sunday	342,698	336,319	355,907	356,170	353,236	
16.......	363,761	Sunday	Sunday	371,226	354,467	348,154	339,572	300,246	350,024	355,636	Sunday	
17.......	365,239	372,471	372,902	372,845	328,006	347,312	339,485	Sunday	356,159	356,061	365,124	
18.......	342,815	375,814	376,530	385,800	Sunday	349,719	338,310	344,882	352,747	329,833	363,592	
19.......	Sunday	374,855	368,543	343,465	357,844	344,253	305,652	Sunday	351,846	Sunday	362,355	
20.......	3,3,143	374,050	365,708	Sunday	354,342	342,293	Sunday	346,525	318,180	361,039	363,611	
21.......	364,807	364,305	361,680	369,313	355,806	316,402	343,096	342,601	Sunday	355,908	362,851	
22.......	366,819	388,308	343,218	367,134	358,884	Sunday	344,255	341,557	356,820	353,846	335,700	
23.......	366,766	Sunday	Sunday	367,428	353,540	349,830	358,833	506,888	353,291	356,989	Sunday	
24.......	365,146	375,690	397,825	361,222	337,507	345,349	358,986	Sunday	351,324	355,381	364,308	
25.......	347,939	406,883	389,588	357,378	Sunday	343,509	339,401	Sunday	348,914	329,859	362,716	
26.......	Sunday	357,560	417,523	338,671	351,697	340,384	303,862	341,963	348,329	Sunday	357,925	
27.......	368,091	365,096	402,701	Sunday	357,704	337,593	Sunday	344,580	319,366	360,414	Holid'y	
28.......	367,610	375,235	392,003	363,396	355,616	509,234	349,466	340,515	Sunday	359,767	361,925	
29.......	369,755	....	363,344	362,293	354,364	Sunday	349,703	347,553	355,550	358,878	355,473	
30	369,298	....	Sunday	382,725	359,431	359,356	358,642	307,124	352,141	354,766	Sunday	
31.......	367,354	....	382,029	....	318,686	....	336,361	Sunday	....	359,021	....	
Total....	9,355,624	8,797,806	9,704,941	9,485,844	9,362,102	8,569,652	8,650,575	8,692,261	8,855,971	9,559,199	8,846,120	
Average	359,831	366,575	373,262	364,840	346,744	342,786	332,706	334,317	340,614	354,044	356,088	

Unsold copies are deducted in the totals.

TOTAL FOR THE YEAR 1912 (excluding December)...................................... 99,579,897 COPIES
DAILY AVERAGE FOR THE YEAR 1912 (excluding December) .... 351,872 COPIES

AVERAGE DAILY ISSUE OF THE CHICAGO DAILY NEWS FOR EACH MONTH FROM THE SECOND YEAR OF ITS PUBLICATION.

YEAR.	Jan.	Feb.	Mar.	April.	May.	June.	July.	Aug.	Sept.	Oct.	Nov.	Dec.	Av'ge.
1877......	11,429	14,841	16,414	18,408	20,715	22,789	35,320	25,396	25,204	23,312	24,439	26,715	22,087
1878......	25,406	37,019	37,736	37,997	38,348	43,743	49,844	40,911	39,371	38,777	39,380	36,817	38,814
1879......	58,067	41,346	46,299	46,608	47,105	49,428	47,560	46,500	44,571	44,310	44,292	44,760	45,194
1880......	48,991	49,425	49,874	49,445	53,834	58,776	56,049	60,623	57,958	58,506	59,672	54,473	54,801
1881......	57,795	62,935	67,959	69,305	65,067	63,832	71,309	70,397	68,551	62,097	58,100	60,305	64,870
1882......	61,679	66,941	66,058	65,208	65,199	70,409	73,078	70,456	67,808	64,819	64,399	66,680	66,690
1883......	67,278	71,379	77,158	78,094	77,467	78,603	78,177	79,423	73,185	71,953	74,527	74,919	75,115
1884......	76,877	83,598	86,878	87,852	88,645	93,292	91,231	88,455	86,221	89,896	107,429	92,465	89,306
1885......	84,119	89,550	98,029	104,513	100,802	100,238	108,823	101,329	97,900	96,817	102,705	102,497	99,005
1886......	104,197	110,325	116,021	117,959	125,294	113,471	112,438	117,677	109,728	110,460	115,103	110,148	113,815
1887......	114,022	119,148	123,010	124,912	118,743	122,714	126,925	132,178	121,958	122,659	154,006	122,419	125,225
1888......	120,057	126,991	137,123	136,490	135,921	140,525	128,897	123,852	113,894	127,724	131,777	159,098	128,676
1889......	120,947	126,446	130,828	132,348	131,378	148,516	142,653	134,238	130,016	128,470	135,527	147,786	134,059
1890......	136,365	141,885	142,655	143,683	136,928	130,414	125,196	125,190	124,437	120,304	139,020	130,850	132,957
1891......	136,926	139,769	144,467	156,196	141,953	141,733	141,868	139,707	138,025	137,294	140,524	145,707	142,022
1892......	148,232	155,402	150,849	162,963	161,804	169,006	170,493	168,259	171,053	164,626	173,070	168,430	164,175
1893......	171,519	180,013	185,567	191,393	194,219	202,367	201,591	202,216	190,491	188,963	192,575	200,389	192,495
1894......	206,388	204,471	207,500	201,285	198,495	195,885	232,022	194,071	185,585	196,070	198,017	197,380	200,886
1895......	198,947	207,246	211,378	212,992	205,732	202,605	201,378	195,907	193,311	195,502	202,555	202,762	202,496
1896......	208,781	213,032	216,542	212,104	209,945	210,205	206,272	199,853	189,106	190,700	200,669	201,649	204,724
1897......	201,540	208,779	226,892	231,388	222,960	217,707	212,111	219,557	229,763	238,605	228,113	232,997	222,595
1898......	239,065	249,951	240,222	295,313	358,695	310,820	288,526	279,243	267,839	267,339	269,085	254,947	275,514
1899......	269,995	266,761	267,597	296,677	253,148	252,405	249,243	240,698	250,564	255,681	271,733	269,975	259,662
1900......	279,219	287,116	288,389	286,657	275,427	272,508	262,081	261,109	268,278	276,969	290,789	271,584	275,788
1901......	281,609	287,113	292,285	295,874	283,207	283,686	275,916	271,783	304,780	292,919	295,635	296,526	288,156
1902......	304,466	300,198	310,825	305,825	300,007	307,406	301,915	305,153	308,607	301,732	312,165	319,518	304,216
1903......	304,870	310,033	311,771	311,574	302,644	304,305	297,500	294,617	295,351	301,590	305,211	305,534	305,634
1904......	331,808	338,466	338,784	333,524	330,867	319,054	310,249	310,677	308,491	309,212	314,616	307,765	319,539
1905......	315,800	317,894	325,024	322,697	325,374	318,204	308,335	302,624	301,714	301,500	305,211	306,805	312,432
1906......	318,373	325,877	328,589	336,797	320,372	318,865	313,428	311,351	309,372	311,166	313,521	313,344	318,185
1907......	322,586	336,876	337,125	336,366	324,524	320,081	312,069	308,511	310,822	330,136	323,614	324,845	323,079
1908......	334,006	338,955	343,811	336,485	324,474	324,572	314,509	311,147	313,850	318,928	326,050	322,278	325,674
1909......	329,925	334,398	337,599	334,429	325,881	325,791	315,633	311,883	316,844	321,928	320,251	324,682	325,098
1910......	332,574	336,242	338,469	342,346	331,309	328,932	316,901	316,553	316,844	321,346	315,828	334,301	326,023
1911......	317,628	321,475	321,645	322,159	320,962	320,862	312,409	318,406	321,362	329,042	328,226	330,999	322,858
1912 *....	334,364	343,173	348,445	359,538	*127,306	*183,945	*187,248	*203,950	*229,159	*276,338	*323,551	347,536	*271,314
1913......	359,831	366,575	373,262	364,840	346,744	342,786	332,706	334,317	340,614	354,044	356,088	....	....

*A strike in the mechanical and distributing departments of all Chicago newspapers began May 2, 1912, affecting circulation until Nov. 18. The records for May and the first part of June of that year are incomplete because of the demoralization of the machinery of distribution.

TABLE OF CONTENTS

OF FIRST TWENTY-NINE VOLUMES (1885 TO 1913 INCLUSIVE) OF THE CHICAGO DAILY NEWS ALMANAC AND YEAR-BOOK.

NOTE—The figures following the year are the page numbers of that volume.

Complete sets of THE DAILY NEWS ALMANAC AND YEAR-BOOK from the year 1885 to 1914 inclusive can be supplied for $15.00, transportation prepaid. The first five issues for the years 1885, 1886, 1887, 1888 and 1889 are bound in one volume, half morocco, library style. This volume is sold only to purchasers of complete sets. A complete set embraces the library volume and a cloth bound issue for each succeeding year.

Single cloth bound copies can be bought only for the years 1890, 1893, 1894, 1895, 1896, 1898, 1899, 1900, 1903, 1909, 1911 and 1914. These are supplied at the rate of 50 cents each, transportation prepaid. Single paper covered copies can be supplied for each year from 1886 to 1903, except 1897 and 1899, for 25 cents each at the office of publication, or 25 cents by mail.

Orders should be addressed to THE DAILY NEWS office, 15 North 5th avenue, Chicago, Ill.

FOR INDEX OF THE CURRENT VOLUME SEE PAGES 3-12.

FOR INDEX OF THE CURRENT VOLUME SEE PAGES 3-12.

FOR INDEX OF THE CURRENT VOLUME SEE PAGES 3-12.

FOR INDEX OF THE CURRENT VOLUME SEE PAGES 3-12.

FOR INDEX OF THE CURRENT VOLUME SEE PAGES 3-12.

FOR INDEX OF THE CURRENT VOLUME SEE PAGES 3-12.

FOR INDEX OF THE CURRENT VOLUME SEE PAGES 3-12.

FOR INDEX OF THE CURRENT VOLUME SEE PAGES 3-12.

FOR INDEX OF THE CURRENT VOLUME SEE PAGES 3-12.

FOR INDEX OF THE CURRENT VOLUME SEE PAGES 3-12.

FOR INDEX OF THE CURRENT VOLUME SEE PAGES 3-12.

FOR INDEX OF THE CURRENT VOLUME SEE PAGES 3-12.

FOR INDEX OF THE CURRENT VOLUME SEE PAGES 3-12.

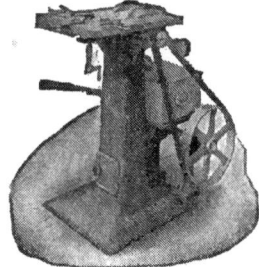

Marlakis

September W Crokerland — 184